The Dictionary of Art · volume two

The Dictionary of Art

EDITOR Jane Turner

2

Ancona
TO
Azzolino

GROVE

The Dictionary of Art

edited by JANE TURNER, in thirty-four volumes, 1996

Reprinted with minor corrections, 1998, 2002

This edition is distributed within the United Kingdom and Europe by Macmillan Publishers Limited, London, and within the United States and Canada by Grove's Dictionaries Inc., New York.

Text keyboarded by Wearset Limited, Sunderland, England
Database management by Pindar plc, York, England
Imagesetting by William Clowes Limited, Suffolk, England
Printed and bound by China Translation and Printing Services Ltd, Hong Kong

British Library Cataloguing in Publication Data

The dictionary of art
1. Art - Dictionaries 2. Art - History - Dictionaries
I. Turner, Jane
703

ISBN 1-884446-00-0

Library of Congress Cataloging in Publication Data

The dictionary of art / editor, Jane Turner.
p. cm.
Includes bibliographical references and index.
Contents: 1. A to Anckerman
ISBN 1-884446-00-0 (alk. paper)
1. Art—Encyclopedias.
I. Turner, Jane, 1956–
N31.D5 1996 96–13628
703—dc20 CIP

Contents

General Abbreviations

The abbreviations employed throughout this dictionary, most of which are listed below, do not vary, except for capitalization, regardless of the context in which they are used, including bibliographical citations and for locations of works of art. The principle used to arrive at these abbreviations is that their full form should be easily deducible, and for this reason acronyms have generally been avoided (e.g. Los Angeles Co. Mus. A. instead of LACMA). The same abbreviation is adopted for cognate forms in foreign languages and in most cases for plural and adjectival forms (e.g. A.= Art, Arts, Arte, Arti etc). Not all related forms are listed below. Occasionally, if a name, for instance of an artists' group or exhibiting society, is repeated within the text of one article, it is cited in an abbreviated form after its first mention in full (e.g. The Pre-Raphaelite Brotherhood (PRB) was founded...); the same is true of archaeological periods and eras, which are abbreviated to initial letters in small capitals (e.g. In the Early Minoan (EM) period...). Such abbreviations do not appear in this list. For the reader's convenience, separate full lists of abbreviations for locations, periodical titles and standard reference books and series are included as Appendices A–C in vol. 33.

A. Art, Arts
A.C. Arts Council
Acad. Academy
AD Anno Domini
Add. Additional, Addendum
addn addition
Admin. Administration
Adv. Advances, Advanced
Aesth. Aesthetic(s)
Afr. African
Afrik. Afrikaans, Afrikaner
A.G. Art Gallery
Agrar. Agrarian
Agric. Agriculture
Agron. Agronomy
Agy Agency
AH Anno Hegirae
A. Inst. Art Institute
AK Alaska (USA)
AL Alabama (USA)
Alb. Albanian
Alg. Algerian
Alta Alberta (Canada)
Altern. Alternative
a.m. ante meridiem [before noon]
Amat. Amateur
Amer. American
An. Annals
Anatol. Anatolian
Anc. Ancient
Annu. Annual
Anon. Anonymous(ly)
Ant. Antique
Anthol. Anthology
Anthropol. Anthropology
Antiqua. Antiquarian, Antiquaries
app. appendix
approx. approximately
AR Arkansas (USA)
ARA Associate of the Royal Academy
Arab. Arabic
Archaeol. Archaeology
Archit. Architecture, Architectural
Archv, Archvs Archive(s)
Arg. Argentine
ARHA Associate of the Royal Hibernian Academy
ARIBA Associate of the Royal Institute of British Architects
Armen. Armenian
ARSA Associate of the Royal Scottish Academy
Asiat. Asiatic
Assist. Assistance
Assoc. Association
Astron. Astronomy
AT&T American Telephone & Telegraph Company
attrib. attribution, attributed to
Aug August
Aust. Austrian
Austral. Australian
Auth. Author(s)
Auton. Autonomous
Aux. Auxiliary
Ave. Avenue
AZ Arizona (USA)
Azerbaij. Azerbaijani
B. Bartsch [catalogue of Old Master prints]
b born
BA Bachelor of Arts
Balt. Baltic
bapt baptized
BArch Bachelor of Architecture
Bart Baronet
Bask. Basketry
BBC British Broadcasting Corporation
BC Before Christ
BC British Columbia (Canada)
BE Buddhist era
Beds Bedfordshire (GB)
Behav. Behavioural
Belarus. Belarusian
Belg. Belgian
Berks Berkshire (GB)
Berwicks Berwickshire (GB; old)
BFA Bachelor of Fine Arts
Bibl. Bible, Biblical
Bibliog. Bibliography, Bibliographical
Biblioph. Bibliophile
Biog. Biography, Biographical
Biol. Biology, Biological
bk, bks book(s)
Bkbinder Bookbinder
Bklore Booklore
Bkshop Bookshop
BL British Library
Bld Build
Bldg Building

Bldr	Builder
BLitt	Bachelor of Letters/Literature
BM	British Museum
Boh.	Bohemian
Boliv.	Bolivian
Botan.	Botany, Botanical
BP	Before present (1950)
Braz.	Brazilian
BRD	Bundesrepublik Deutschland [Federal Republic of Germany (West Germany)]
Brecons	Breconshire (GB; old)
Brez.	Brezonek [lang. of Brittany]
Brit.	British
Bros	Brothers
BSc	Bachelor of Science
Bucks	Buckinghamshire (GB)
Bulg.	Bulgarian
Bull.	Bulletin
bur	buried
Burm.	Burmese
Byz.	Byzantine
C	Celsius
C.	Century
c.	*circa* [about]
CA	California
Cab.	Cabinet
Caerns	Caernarvonshire (GB; old)
C.A.G.	City Art Gallery
Cal.	Calendar
Callig.	Calligraphy
Cam.	Camera
Cambs	Cambridgeshire (GB)
can	canonized
Can.	Canadian
Cant.	Canton(s), Cantonal
Capt.	Captain
Cards	Cardiganshire (GB; old)
Carib.	Caribbean
Carms	Carmarthenshire (GB; old)
Cartog.	Cartography
Cat.	Catalan
cat.	catalogue
Cath.	Catholic
CBE	Commander of the Order of the British Empire
Celeb.	Celebration
Celt.	Celtic
Cent.	Centre, Central
Centen.	Centennial
Cer.	Ceramic
cf.	confer [compare]
Chap., Chaps	Chapter(s)
Chem.	Chemistry
Ches	Cheshire (GB)
Chil.	Chilean
Chin.	Chinese
Christ.	Christian, Christianity
Chron.	Chronicle
Cie	Compagnie [French]
Cinema.	Cinematography
Circ.	Circle
Civ.	Civil, Civic
Civiliz.	Civilization(s)
Class.	Classic, Classical
Clin.	Clinical
CO	Colorado (USA)
Co.	Company; County
Cod.	Codex, Codices
Col., Cols	Collection(s); Column(s)
Coll.	College
collab.	in collaboration with, collaborated, collaborative
Collct.	Collecting
Colloq.	Colloquies
Colomb.	Colombian
Colon.	Colonies, Colonial
Colr	Collector
Comm.	Commission; Community
Commerc.	Commercial
Communic.	Communications
Comp.	Comparative; compiled by, compiler
Concent.	Concentration
Concr.	Concrete
Confed.	Confederation
Confer.	Conference
Congol.	Congolese
Congr.	Congress
Conserv.	Conservation; Conservatory
Constr.	Construction(al)
cont.	continued
Contemp.	Contemporary
Contrib.	Contributions, Contributor(s)
Convalesc.	Convalescence
Convent.	Convention
Coop.	Cooperation
Coord.	Coordination
Copt.	Coptic
Corp.	Corporation, Corpus
Corr.	Correspondence
Cors.	Corsican
Cost.	Costume
Cret.	Cretan
Crim.	Criminal
Crit.	Critical, Criticism
Croat.	Croatian
CT	Connecticut (USA)
Cttee	Committee
Cub.	Cuban
Cult.	Cultural, Culture
Cumb.	Cumberland (GB; old)
Cur.	Curator, Curatorial, Curatorship
Curr.	Current(s)
CVO	Commander of the [Royal] Victorian Order
Cyclad.	Cycladic
Cyp.	Cypriot
Czech.	Czechoslovak
$	dollars
d	died
d.	denarius, denarii [penny, pence]
Dalmat.	Dalmatian
Dan.	Danish
DBE	Dame Commander of the Order of the British Empire
DC	District of Columbia (USA)
DDR	Deutsche Demokratische Republik [German Democratic Republic (East Germany)]
DE	Delaware (USA)
Dec	December
Dec.	Decorative
ded.	dedication, dedicated to
Democ.	Democracy, Democratic
Demog.	Demography, Demographic
Denbs	Denbighshire (GB; old)
dep.	deposited at
Dept	Department
Dept.	Departmental, Departments
Derbys	Derbyshire (GB)
Des.	Design
destr.	destroyed
Dev.	Development
Devon	Devonshire (GB)
Dial.	Dialogue
diam.	diameter
Diff.	Diffusion
Dig.	Digest
Dip. Eng.	Diploma in Engineering
Dir.	Direction, Directed
Directrt	Directorate
Disc.	Discussion
diss.	dissertation
Distr.	District
Div.	Division
DLitt	Doctor of Letters/Literature
DM	Deutsche Mark
Doc.	Document(s)
Doss.	Dossier
DPhil	Doctor of Philosophy
Dr	Doctor
Drg, Drgs	Drawing(s)
DSc	Doctor of Science/Historical Sciences
Dut.	Dutch
Dwell.	Dwelling
E.	East(ern)

EC	European (Economic) Community
Eccles.	Ecclesiastical
Econ.	Economic, Economies
Ecuad.	Ecuadorean
ed.	editor, edited (by)
edn	edition
eds	editors
Educ.	Education
e.g.	*exempli gratia* [for example]
Egyp.	Egyptian
Elem.	Element(s), Elementary
Emp.	Empirical
Emul.	Emulation
Enc.	Encyclopedia
Encour.	Encouragement
Eng.	English
Engin.	Engineer, Engineering
Engr., Engrs	Engraving(s)
Envmt	Environment
Epig.	Epigraphy
Episc.	Episcopal
Esp.	Especially
Ess.	Essays
est	established
etc	*etcetera* [and so on]
Ethnog.	Ethnography
Ethnol.	Ethnology
Etrus.	Etruscan
Eur.	European
Evangel.	Evangelical
Exam.	Examination
Excav.	Excavation, Excavated
Exch.	Exchange
Excurs.	Excursion
exh.	exhibition
Exp.	Exposition
Expermntl	Experimental
Explor.	Exploration
Expn	Expansion
Ext.	External
Extn	Extension
f, ff	following page, following pages
F.A.	Fine Art(s)
Fac.	Faculty
facs.	facsimile
Fam.	Family
fasc.	fascicle
fd	feastday (of a saint)
Feb	February
Fed.	Federation, Federal
Fem.	Feminist
Fest.	Festival
fig.	figure (illustration)
Fig.	Figurative
figs	figures
Filip.	Filipina(s), Filipino(s)
Fin.	Finnish
FL	Florida (USA)
fl	*floruit* [he/she flourished]
Flem.	Flemish
Flints	Flintshire (GB; old)
Flk	Folk
Flklore	Folklore
fol., fols	folio(s)
Found.	Foundation
Fr.	French
frag.	fragment
Fri.	Friday
FRIBA	Fellow of the Royal Institute of British Architects
FRS	Fellow of the Royal Society, London
ft	foot, feet
Furn.	Furniture
Futur.	Futurist, Futurism
g	gram(s)
GA	Georgia (USA)
Gael.	Gaelic
Gal., Gals	Gallery, Galleries
Gaz.	Gazette
GB	Great Britain
Gdn, Gdns	Garden(s)
Gdnr(s)	Gardener(s)
Gen.	General
Geneal.	Genealogy, Genealogist
Gent.	Gentleman, Gentlemen
Geog.	Geography
Geol.	Geology
Geom.	Geometry
Georg.	Georgian
Geosci.	Geoscience
Ger.	German, Germanic
G.I.	Government/General Issue (USA)
Glams	Glamorganshire (GB; old)
Glos	Gloucestershire (GB)
Govt	Government
Gr.	Greek
Grad.	Graduate
Graph.	Graphic
Green.	Greenlandic
Gr.-Roman	Greco-Roman
Gt	Great
Gtr	Greater
Guat.	Guatemalan
Gym.	Gymnasium
h.	height
ha	hectare
Hait.	Haitian
Hants	Hampshire (GB)
Hb.	Handbook
Heb.	Hebrew
Hell.	Hellenic
Her.	Heritage
Herald.	Heraldry, Heraldic
Hereford & Worcs	Hereford & Worcester (GB)
Herts	Hertfordshire (GB)
HI	Hawaii (USA)
Hib.	Hibernia
Hisp.	Hispanic
Hist.	History, Historical
HMS	His/Her Majesty's Ship
Hon.	Honorary, Honourable
Horiz.	Horizon
Hort.	Horticulture
Hosp.	Hospital(s)
HRH	His/Her Royal Highness
Human.	Humanities, Humanism
Hung.	Hungarian
Hunts	Huntingdonshire (GB; old)
IA	Iowa
ibid.	*ibidem* [in the same place]
ICA	Institute of Contemporary Arts
Ice.	Icelandic
Iconog.	Iconography
Iconol.	Iconology
ID	Idaho (USA)
i.e.	*id est* [that is]
IL	Illinois (USA)
Illum.	Illumination
illus.	illustrated, illustration
Imp.	Imperial
IN	Indiana (USA)
in., ins	inch(es)
Inc.	Incorporated
inc.	incomplete
incl.	includes, including, inclusive
Incorp.	Incorporation
Ind.	Indian
Indep.	Independent
Indig.	Indigenous
Indol.	Indology
Indon.	Indonesian
Indust.	Industrial
Inf.	Information
Inq.	Inquiry
Inscr.	Inscribed, Inscription
Inst.	Institute(s)
Inst. A.	Institute of Art
Instr.	Instrument, Instrumental
Int.	International
Intell.	Intelligence
Inter.	Interior(s), Internal
Interdiscip.	Interdisciplinary
intro.	introduced by, introduction
inv.	inventory

Inven.	Invention
Invest.	Investigation(s)
Iran.	Iranian
irreg.	irregular(ly)
Islam.	Islamic
Isr.	Israeli
It.	Italian
J.	Journal
Jam.	Jamaican
Jan	January
Jap.	Japanese
Jav.	Javanese
Jew.	Jewish
Jewel.	Jewellery
Jord.	Jordanian
jr	junior
Juris.	Jurisdiction
KBE	Knight Commander of the Order of the British Empire
KCVO	Knight Commander of the Royal Victorian Order
kg	kilogram(s)
kHz	kilohertz
km	kilometre(s)
Knowl.	Knowledge
Kor.	Korean
KS	Kansas (USA)
KY	Kentucky (USA)
Kyrgyz.	Kyrgyzstani
£	libra, librae [pound, pounds sterling]
l.	length
LA	Louisiana (USA)
Lab.	Laboratory
Lancs	Lancashire (GB)
Lang.	Language(s)
Lat.	Latin
Latv.	Latvian
lb, lbs	pound(s) weight
Leb.	Lebanese
Lect.	Lecture
Legis.	Legislative
Leics	Leicestershire (GB)
Lex.	Lexicon
Lg.	Large
Lib., Libs	Library, Libraries
Liber.	Liberian
Libsp	Librarianship
Lincs	Lincolnshire (GB)
Lit.	Literature
Lith.	Lithuanian
Liturg.	Liturgical
LLB	Bachelor of Laws
LLD	Doctor of Laws
Lt	Lieutenant
Lt-Col.	Lieutenant-Colonel
Ltd	Limited
m	metre(s)
m.	married
M.	Monsieur
MA	Master of Arts; Massachusetts (USA)
Mag.	Magazine
Maint.	Maintenance
Malay.	Malaysian
Man.	Manitoba (Canada); Manual
Manuf.	Manufactures
Mar.	Marine, Maritime
Mason.	Masonic
Mat.	Material(s)
Math.	Mathematic
MBE	Member of the Order of the British Empire
MD	Doctor of Medicine; Maryland (USA)
ME	Maine (USA)
Mech.	Mechanical
Med.	Medieval; Medium, Media
Medic.	Medical, Medicine
Medit.	Mediterranean
Mem.	Memorial(s); Memoir(s)
Merions	Merionethshire (GB; old)
Meso-Amer.	Meso-American
Mesop.	Mesopotamian
Met.	Metropolitan
Metal.	Metallurgy
Mex.	Mexican
MFA	Master of Fine Arts
mg	milligram(s)
Mgmt	Management
Mgr	Monsignor
MI	Michigan
Micrones.	Micronesian
Mid. Amer.	Middle American
Middx	Middlesex (GB; old)
Mid. E.	Middle Eastern
Mid. Eng.	Middle English
Mid Glam.	Mid Glamorgan (GB)
Mil.	Military
Mill.	Millennium
Min.	Ministry; Minutes
Misc.	Miscellaneous
Miss.	Mission(s)
Mlle	Mademoiselle
mm	millimetre(s)
Mme	Madame
MN	Minnesota
Mnmt, Mnmts	Monument(s)
Mnmtl	Monumental
MO	Missouri (USA)
Mod.	Modern, Modernist
Moldav.	Moldavian
Moldov.	Moldovan
MOMA	Museum of Modern Art
Mon.	Monday
Mongol.	Mongolian
Mons	Monmouthshire (GB; old)
Montgoms	Montgomeryshire (GB; old)
Mor.	Moral
Morav.	Moravian
Moroc.	Moroccan
Movt	Movement
MP	Member of Parliament
MPhil	Master of Philosophy
MS	Mississippi (USA)
MS., MSS	manuscript(s)
MSc	Master of Science
MT	Montana (USA)
Mt	Mount
Mthly	Monthly
Mun.	Municipal
Mus.	Museum(s)
Mus. A.	Museum of Art
Mus. F.A.	Museum of Fine Art(s)
Music.	Musicology
N.	North(ern); National
n	refractive index of a medium
n.	note
N.A.G.	National Art Gallery
Nat.	Natural, Nature
Naut.	Nautical
NB	New Brunswick (Canada)
NC	North Carolina (USA)
ND	North Dakota (USA)
n.d.	no date
NE	Nebraska; Northeast(ern)
Neth.	Netherlandish
Newslett.	Newsletter
Nfld	Newfoundland (Canada)
N.G.	National Gallery
N.G.A.	National Gallery of Art
NH	New Hampshire (USA)
Niger.	Nigerian
NJ	New Jersey (USA)
NM	New Mexico (USA)
nm	nanometre (10^{-9} metre)
nn.	notes
no., nos	number(s)
Nord.	Nordic
Norm.	Normal
Northants	Northamptonshire (GB)
Northumb.	Northumberland (GB)
Norw.	Norwegian
Notts	Nottinghamshire (GB)
Nov	November
n.p.	no place (of publication)
N.P.G.	National Portrait Gallery
nr	near

Nr E.	Near Eastern
NS	New Style; Nova Scotia (Canada)
n. s.	new series
NSW	New South Wales (Australia)
NT	National Trust
Ntbk	Notebook
Numi.	Numismatic(s)
NV	Nevada (USA)
NW	Northwest(ern)
NWT	Northwest Territories (Canada)
NY	New York (USA)
NZ	New Zealand
OBE	Officer of the Order of the British Empire
Obj.	Object(s), Objective
Occas.	Occasional
Occident.	Occidental
Ocean.	Oceania
Oct	October
8vo	octavo
OFM	Order of Friars Minor
OH	Ohio (USA)
OK	Oklahoma (USA)
Olymp.	Olympic
OM	Order of Merit
Ont.	Ontario (Canada)
op.	opus
opp.	opposite; opera [pl. of opus]
OR	Oregon (USA)
Org.	Organization
Orient.	Oriental
Orthdx	Orthodox
OSB	Order of St Benedict
Ott.	Ottoman
Oxon	Oxfordshire (GB)
oz.	ounce(s)
p	pence
p., pp.	page(s)
PA	Pennsylvania (USA)
p.a.	per annum
Pak.	Pakistani
Palaeontol.	Palaeontology, Palaeontological
Palest.	Palestinian
Pap.	Paper(s)
para.	paragraph
Parag.	Paraguayan
Parl.	Parliament
Paroch.	Parochial
Patriarch.	Patriarchate
Patriot.	Patriotic
Patrm.	Patrimony
Pav.	Pavilion
PEI	Prince Edward Island (Canada)
Pembs	Pembrokeshire (GB; old)
Per.	Period
Percep.	Perceptions
Perf.	Performance, Performing, Performed
Period.	Periodical(s)
Pers.	Persian
Persp.	Perspectives
Peru.	Peruvian
PhD	Doctor of Philosophy
Philol.	Philology
Philos.	Philosophy
Phoen.	Phoenician
Phot.	Photograph, Photography, Photographic
Phys.	Physician(s), Physics, Physique, Physical
Physiog.	Physiognomy
Physiol.	Physiology
Pict.	Picture(s), Pictorial
pl.	plate; plural
Plan.	Planning
Planet.	Planetarium
Plast.	Plastic
pls	plates
p.m.	post meridiem [after noon]
Polit.	Political
Poly.	Polytechnic
Polynes.	Polynesian
Pop.	Popular
Port.	Portuguese
Port.	Portfolio
Posth.	Posthumous(ly)
Pott.	Pottery
POW	prisoner of war
PRA	President of the Royal Academy
Pract.	Practical
Prefect.	Prefecture, Prefectural
Preserv.	Preservation
prev.	previous(ly)
priv.	private
PRO	Public Record Office
Prob.	Problem(s)
Proc.	Proceedings
Prod.	Production
Prog.	Progress
Proj.	Project(s)
Promot.	Promotion
Prop.	Property, Properties
Prov.	Province(s), Provincial
Proven.	Provenance
Prt, Prts	Print(s)
Prtg	Printing
pseud.	pseudonym
Psych.	Psychiatry, Psychiatric
Psychol.	Psychology, Psychological
pt	part
Ptg(s)	Painting(s)
Pub.	Public
pubd	published
Publ.	Publicity
pubn(s)	publication(s)
PVA	Polyvinyl acetate
PVC	polyvinyl chloride
Q.	quarterly
4to	quarto
Qué.	Québec (Canada)
R	reprint
r	*recto*
RA	Royal Academician
Radnors	Radnorshire (GB; old)
RAF	Royal Air Force
Rec.	Record(s)
red.	reduction, reduced for
Ref.	Reference
Refurb.	Refurbishment
reg	*regit* [ruled]
Reg.	Regional
Relig.	Religion, Religious
remod.	remodelled
Ren.	Renaissance
Rep.	Report(s)
repr.	reprint(ed); reproduced, reproduction
Represent.	Representation, Representative
Res.	Research
rest.	restored, restoration
Retro.	Retrospective
rev.	revision, revised (by/for)
Rev.	Reverend; Review
RHA	Royal Hibernian Academician
RI	Rhode Island (USA)
RIBA	Royal Institute of British Architects
RJ	Rio de Janeiro State
Rlwy	Railway
RSA	Royal Scottish Academy
RSFSR	Russian Soviet Federated Socialist Republic
Rt Hon.	Right Honourable
Rur.	Rural
Rus.	Russian
S	San, Santa, Santo, Sant', São [Saint]
S.	South(ern)
s.	solidus, solidi [shilling(s)]
Sask.	Saskatchewan (Canada)
Sat.	Saturday
SC	South Carolina (USA)
Scand.	Scandinavian
Sch.	School
Sci.	Science(s), Scientific
Scot.	Scottish
Sculp.	Sculpture

SD	South Dakota (USA)
SE	Southeast(ern)
Sect.	Section
Sel.	Selected
Semin.	Seminar(s), Seminary
Semiot.	Semiotic
Semit.	Semitic
Sept	September
Ser.	Series
Serb.	Serbian
Serv.	Service(s)
Sess.	Session, Sessional
Settmt(s)	Settlement(s)
S. Glam.	South Glamorgan (GB)
Siber.	Siberian
Sig.	Signature
Sil.	Silesian
Sin.	Singhala
sing.	singular
SJ	Societas Jesu [Society of Jesus]
Skt	Sanskrit
Slav.	Slavic, Slavonic
Slov.	Slovene, Slovenian
Soc.	Society
Social.	Socialism, Socialist
Sociol.	Sociology
Sov.	Soviet
SP	São Paulo State
Sp.	Spanish
sq.	square
sr	senior
Sri L.	Sri Lankan
SS	Saints, Santi, Santissima, Santissimo, Santissimi; Steam ship
SSR	Soviet Socialist Republic
St	Saint, Sankt, Sint, Szent
Staffs	Staffordshire (GB)
Ste	Sainte
Stud.	Study, Studies
Subalp.	Subalpine
Sum.	Sumerian
Sun.	Sunday
Sup.	Superior
suppl., suppls	supplement(s), supplementary
Surv.	Survey
SW	Southwest(ern)
Swed.	Swedish
Swi.	Swiss
Symp.	Symposium
Syr.	Syrian
Tap.	Tapestry
Tas.	Tasmanian
Tech.	Technical, Technique
Technol.	Technology
Territ.	Territory
Theat.	Theatre
Theol.	Theology, Theological
Theor.	Theory, Theoretical
Thurs.	Thursday
Tib.	Tibetan
TN	Tennessee (USA)
Top.	Topography
Trad.	Tradition(s), Traditional
trans.	translation, translated by; transactions
Transafr.	Transafrican
Transatlant.	Transatlantic
Transcarpath.	Transcarpathian
transcr.	transcribed by/for
Triq.	Triquarterly
Tropic.	Tropical
Tues.	Tuesday
Turk.	Turkish
Turkmen.	Turkmenistani
TV	Television
TX	Texas (USA)
U.	University
UK	United Kingdom of Great Britain and Northern Ireland
Ukrain.	Ukrainian
Un.	Union
Underwtr	Underwater
UNESCO	United Nations Educational, Scientific and Cultural Organization
Univl	Universal
unpubd	unpublished
Urb.	Urban
Urug.	Uruguayan
US	United States
USA	United States of America
USSR	Union of Soviet Socialist Republics
UT	Utah
v	*verso*
VA	Virginia (USA)
V&A	Victoria and Albert Museum
Var.	Various
Venez.	Venezuelan
Vern.	Vernacular
Vict.	Victorian
Vid.	Video
Viet.	Vietnamese
viz.	*videlicet* [namely]
vol., vols	volume(s)
vs.	versus
VT	Vermont (USA)
Vulg.	Vulgarisation
W.	West(ern)
w.	width
WA	Washington (USA)
Warwicks	Warwickshire (GB)
Wed.	Wednesday
W. Glam.	West Glamorgan (GB)
WI	Wisconsin (USA)
Wilts	Wiltshire (GB)
Wkly	Weekly
W. Midlands	West Midlands (GB)
Worcs	Worcestershire (GB; old)
Wtrcol.	Watercolour
WV	West Virginia (USA)
WY	Wyoming (USA)
Yb., Y.-b.	Yearbook, Year-book
Yem.	Yemeni
Yorks	Yorkshire (GB; old)
Yug.	Yugoslavian
Zamb.	Zambian
Zimb.	Zimbabwean

A Note on the Use of the Dictionary

This note is intended as a short guide to the basic editorial conventions adopted in this dictionary. For a fuller explanation, please refer to the Introduction, vol. 1, pp. xiii–xx.

Abbreviations in general use in the dictionary are listed on pp. vii–xii; those used in bibliographies and for locations of works of art or exhibition venues are listed in the Appendices in vol. 33.

Alphabetization of headings, which are distinguished in bold typeface, is letter by letter up to the first comma (ignoring spaces, hyphens, accents and any parenthesized or bracketed matter); the same principle applies thereafter. Abbreviations of 'Saint' and its foreign equivalents are alphabetized as if spelt out, and headings with the prefix 'Mc' appear under 'Mac'.

Authors' signatures appear at the end of the article or sequence of articles that the authors have contributed; in multipartite articles, any section that is unsigned is by the author of the next signed section. Where the article was compiled by the editors or in the few cases where an author has wished to remain anonymous, this is indicated by a square box (□) instead of a signature.

Bibliographies are arranged chronologically (within section, where divided) by order of year of first publication and, within years, alphabetically by authors' names. Abbreviations have been used for some standard reference books; these are cited in full in Appendix C in vol. 33, as are abbreviations of periodical titles (Appendix B). Abbreviated references to alphabetically arranged dictionaries and encyclopedias appear at the beginning of the bibliography (or section).

Biographical dates when cited in parentheses in running text at the first mention of a personal name indicate that the individual does not have an entry in the dictionary. The presence of parenthesized regnal dates for rulers and popes, however, does not necessarily indicate the lack of a biography of that person. Where no dates are provided for an artist or patron, the reader may assume that there is a biography of that individual in the dictionary (or, more rarely, that the person is so obscure that dates are not readily available).

Cross-references are distinguished by the use of small capital letters, with a large capital to indicate the initial letter of the entry to which the reader is directed; for example, 'He commissioned LEONARDO DA VINCI . . .' means that the entry is alphabetized under 'L'.

A

[continued]

Ancona. Italian city on the Adriatic coast. It stands on a promontory that comprises the easternmost spur of Mt Conero, in a natural amphitheatre that forms the only major harbour between Venice and Bari. The principal city of the Marches, it has a population of *c.* 110,000. According to legend, Ancona was founded as a Greek colony by Dionysus of Syracuse *c.* 390 BC, on the site of an earlier and well-protected settlement on the northern slopes of the promontory. To the south were the Picene people and to the north the Gauls. The colonists built an acropolis and a temple dedicated to Venus Euplea, the remains of which have been found beneath the cathedral of S Ciriaco. In 268 BC Ancona was conquered by the Romans and became a municipal town. It doubled in size, and because of its proximity to the Via Salaria and the Via Flaminia its trade with the hinterland increased. In 49 BC it was fortified by Julius Caesar, and it continued to flourish as a port under the Roman emperors. It was favoured by Trajan, who commissioned Apollodoros of Damascus to renovate the port so as to improve links between Italy and the eastern Mediterranean. The triumphal arch (after AD 115) that concluded the work on the port is also attributed to Apollodoros.

Despite the city's declining prosperity after the 3rd century AD, several Early Christian monuments were built, including the three-aisled basilican church of S Lorenzo (5th century). By the 6th century AD, however, Ancona had become no more than a fortress, subject to the nearby town of Osimo. In the late 6th century Ancona passed from the Goths to the Byzantine empire and became a member of the Exarchate. A period of recovery ensued, and the city developed along traditional mercantile lines. Between the 11th and 12th centuries the basilica of S Lorenzo was transformed into the present centrally planned domed cathedral of S Ciriaco; its plan and decoration were derived from Byzantine ecclesiastical architecture. In the late 12th century and early 13th, the city became an independent maritime republic; the fortifications were strengthened, and several important buildings were erected, including the churches of S Stefano and S Maria della Piazza, which also reflect Byzantine influence. The latter has a façade of Dalmatian marble (1210) built by Master Filippo with blind arcaded galleries similar to those of the cathedral (13th century) at Zadar, Croatia. He also built the Porta della Farina (1221), known as the Porta di S Pietro. Other 13th-century buildings include the Bishop's Palace next to the cathedral, and the Palazzo del Senato; the Palazzo della Farina was enlarged to house the new municipal authority.

In the 15th century the Piazza Nuova (now the Piazza Plebiscito) with the Hospital (destr.) dedicated to St Thomas Becket was laid out. At a slightly higher level the Palazzo degli Anziani (Palace of the Elders) was begun by Pietro Amoroso in 1493, perhaps after designs by Francesco di Giorgio Martini. Lower down, in the Piazza di S Nicola, was the Palazzo del Podestà, which housed the law courts and the prison. The palaces of the most prominent families overlooked the sea. The churches of S Francesco alle Scale (1323) and S Agostino (1338; destr.) were embellished in 1454–9 and 1460–?70 respectively with portals in late Venetian Gothic style by GIORGIO DA SEBENICO, who also designed the façade of the Loggia dei Mercanti (1451–4; see fig.).

In 1532 Ancona was absorbed into the Papal states. The fortifications were modernized, and the Capodimonte fortress was built (1532–43) after designs by Antonio da Sangallo (ii). The city lost its independence, but its commercial importance increased and the population rose to 23,000. Many foreign merchants established themselves there and were thus able to circumvent the Venetian monopoly of the trade route between northern Europe and the East. Between 1558 and 1561 Pellegrino Tibaldi (*see* TIBALDI, (1)) resided in Ancona and painted the frescoes in the Loggia dei Mercanti (destr.), perhaps the frescoes (now Mus. Archeol. N. Marche) that once decorated the hall on the first floor of the Palazzo Ferretti and a panel of the *Baptism* in S Francesco delle Scale. This church also contains an altarpiece of the *Assumption of the Virgin* (1550) by Lorenzo Lotto.

By the late 17th century the importance of the port had been greatly reduced as a result of the drastic decline throughout the Mediterranean in trade with the East. In the 18th century the fortunes of the city revived, and the port was renovated by Pope Clement XII to designs by LUIGI VANVITELLI, who built the pentagonal Lazzaretto (1733–8) and the Arco Clementino (1737) and extended the Molo di Traiano (Trajan's Wharf; 1735–8). Vanvitelli was also responsible for devising a concave façade (1743) for the church of Il Gesù (1605) that anticipated the design he later employed for SS Annunziata (1760–82) at

Ancona, Loggia dei Mercanti, façade by Giorgio da Sebenico, 1451–4

Naples. Between 1763 and 1788 the Gothic church of S Domenico was completely transformed by CARLO MARCHIONNI. The coastal road was constructed in 1783, as well as an access route to the town through the Porta Pia (façade of 1789 by Filippo Marchionni). During the French occupation of Ancona (1797–1815) the city's defences and the port were further improved. A noteworthy building of the 19th century is the Teatro delle Muse (1821–6), designed by Pietro Ghinelli (*d* 1834) in the Neo-classical style. The appearance of the city has altered significantly since the late 19th century, particularly as a result of the rebuilding that followed the devastation of World War II.

The Museo Archeologico Nazionale delle Marche houses antique objects and artefacts from the Marches, including the particularly rich items of Gallic goldwork from the necropolis of Montefortino di Arcevia. The Pinacoteca Comunale displays paintings by Carlo Crivelli, Lotto, Titian, Andrea Lilli and Guercino. Objects of interest in the cathedral include an antependium (15th century) in red velvet and gold with six scenes from the *Life of St Lawrence* and the monument to the *Blessed Girolamo Giannelli* (1509) by the sculptor Giovanni da Trau.

BIBLIOGRAPHY

A. Ricci: *Memorie storiche delle arti e degli artisti della Marca di Ancona*, 2 vols (Macerata, 1834)

M. Marinelli: *L'architettura romanica in Ancona* (Recanati, 1921, rev. Ancona, 2/1961)

L. Serra: 'Ancona: Monumenti', *Enc. It.*, iii (1929), pp. 152–5

——: *L'arte nelle Marche: Il periodo del rinascimento* (Rome, 1934)

M. Moretti: *Ancona* (Rome, 1945)

G. Marchini: *La Pinacoteca Comunale di Ancona* (Ancona, 1960)

M. Natalucci: *Ancona attraverso i secoli*, 3 vols (Città di Castello, 1960–61)

F. Farinelli: 'Ancona', *Atlante* (1976), vi of *Storia d'Italia* (Turin, 1972–6), pp. 398–404

R. Paci, M. Pasquali and E. Sori, eds: *Ancona e le Marche nel cinquecento* (Ancona, 1982)

R. Pavia and E. Sori: *Ancona* (Rome, 1990)

ADRIANO GHISETTI GIAVARINA

Ancona, Andrea d'. *See* LILLI, ANDREA.

Ancona, Cyriac of. *See* CYRIAC OF ANCONA.

Ancyra. *See* ANKARA.

Andachtsbild [Ger.: 'devotional image']. Type of religious image intended for devotional contemplation and the stimulation of affective piety that evolved in the late Middle Ages. Many of these images were developed in the 14th century in response to the writings of the Cistercians and Benedictines, in particular, but also of the Franciscans and Dominicans. Many of the authors encouraged self-identification with the joys and sufferings of the Virgin and Christ, and the images served as a means of meditating on the events described in the texts. They were frequently painted on small panels or illustrated in Books of Hours and were available to a wider audience through woodcuts and engravings. Larger carved representations and altarpieces were also common in churches.

Many of these devotional images were extracted from a narrative and in some cases preserve its essential elements, for example such close-up emotive groups as Christ and St John the Evangelist from the Last Supper, or the Pietà from the Lamentation at the foot of the Cross (see below). Other *Andachtsbilder*, however, have images designed to present an emotionally expressive or symbolic theme without a narrative context, for example the Madonna of Mercy, in which a standing figure of the Virgin holds out her cloak to shelter a group of figures, symbolizing the protection she gives to her devotees. Some *Andachtsbilder* originated from images believed to have been created by divine intervention, notably the Veronica, the face of Christ miraculously imprinted on St Veronica's veil after she had wiped his face on the way to Calvary. Such images were produced as icons in the Byzantine Church and became widespread in western Europe following their import into Italy and occasionally also Germany and France. *Andachtsbilder* are frequent in such formats as the diptych, with the Virgin juxtaposed with the Man of Sorrows or, very rarely, the Trinity (see fig.), or with a donor on one side facing a devotional image on the other.

The imagery of a great number of *Andachtsbilder* is based on both biblical and apocryphal Passion narratives. One of the most important representations is that of the Man of Sorrows showing his wounds, either as a half- or full-length figure. Others are extracted from narrative scenes by isolating the single image of Christ, for example from the Flagellation, Christ carrying the Cross, Ecce homo or Christ seated before he is put on the Cross. These are most frequently wood sculptures, above all from Germany where many of them originated during the 14th century. *Andachtsbilder* also include abstracted isolated images of the wounds in the hands, feet, side and heart of Christ, as well as the *Arma Christi*, which functioned as mnemonic signs for meditation on the whole Passion narrative, each episode of which was given a symbolic representation. A rare instance of an allegorical subject as an *Andachtsbild* is the Mystic Wine-press in which the wounded Christ is shown with the Blood of Redemption issuing from the press and being collected in a chalice. Giovanni Bellini's *Blood of the Redeemer* (*c.* 1465; London, NG), showing the standing Man of Sorrows with blood from his side being collected in a chalice, is a related image. The Mass of St Gregory, in which the Man of Sorrows appears on the altar to St Gregory during the celebration of mass, became a popular image in the 15th century; the figure was often surrounded by the *Arma Christi.* The devotional image of Christ as a standing naked baby developed in the 14th century, probably owing to the increasing popularity of the Christmas crib in Franciscan 13th-century practice. In the late Middle Ages the naked Christ child was often associated with such Passion imagery as the wounds and the heart, and these representations are particularly common in woodcuts.

The second major group of *Andachtsbilder* is focused on the Virgin. By far the most common among these are

Andachtsbild by the Master of Flémalle: the *Trinity* (left wing of a diptych), panel, 345×245 mm, 1430s (St Petersburg, Hermitage Museum)

the innumerable and diverse representations of the Virgin and Child. Other references to the Virgin's motherhood include the *Madonna del Parto*, in which she is shown pregnant, the *Wochenbett Mariens*, where she is isolated on the bed holding the Child after birth, or holding the Child and seated in the lap of her mother St Anne, *Anna Selbdritt.* The Virgin's role as intercessor is signified by the image of her holding her breast to appeal to God the Father or Christ the Judge; her freedom from sin is conveyed by images that signify her immaculate conception, and her compassion is symbolized by the image of the sword of sorrow penetrating her breast. The best known of all *Andachtsbilder* is the PIETÀ, a devotional image that expresses equally devotion to Christ and to the Virgin. The subject, isolated from the narrative of the Descent from the Cross and the Lamentation, shows the dead body of Christ held by the Virgin. This iconography originated *c.* 1300 in south German wood sculpture and spread throughout Europe in both sculpture and painting. Other forms of Pietà developed in which the body of Christ is held by angels or by God the Father, the latter group usually presented as an image of the Holy Trinity. In the later Middle Ages devotion to the Holy Trinity was expressed in visual images. The most popular forms are the *Gnadenstuhl* (Throne of Grace) Trinity, in which God the Father holds the Son on the Crucifix with the Holy Ghost in between, and the *Not Gottes* (Trinity Pietà), in which God the Father holds the body of the Son with the Holy Ghost between them. These images carry the theological message of the acceptance by God the Father of the Son as victim of the redemptive sacrifice. An essential feature in the various forms of *Andachtsbilder* is the significance of the visual presentation for the stimulation of an empathic response. Most of these images were intended to make a strong emotional impact, and some of the most powerfully expressive works of Christian art have originated from this imagery.

BIBLIOGRAPHY

LCI: 'Ährenkleidmaria', 'Anna Selbdritt', 'Arma Christi', 'Blut, Heiliges', 'Christus, Christusbild', 'Christus-Johannes-Gruppe', 'Dreifaltigkeit', 'Ecce homo', 'Geisselsäule, Christus an der', 'Gregoriusmesse', 'Herz Jesu', 'Immaculata Conceptio', 'Interzessio, Mariae und Christi vor Gottvater', 'Jesuskind', 'Kelter, Mystische', 'Kreuztragung Jesu', 'Lauretanische Litanei', 'Madonna del Parto', 'Maria, Marienbild', 'Pest, Pestbilder', 'Rast Christi, Letze', 'Schmerzen Mariens', 'Schmerzensmann', 'Schutzmantelschaft', 'Sippe, Heilige', 'Sudarium', 'Vesperbild', 'Weinrebenmadonna', 'Wochenbett Mariens', 'Wunden Christi', 'Veronika'; *LM*; *RDK*: 'Andachtsbild', 'Antlitz, heiliges', 'Hl. Blut', 'Christkind', 'Christus im Elend', 'Christus–Johannes Gruppe', 'Christus in der Kelter', 'Devotionsbild', 'Dreifaltigkeit', 'Ecce homo', 'Engelpietà', 'Feiertagschristus'

E. Panofsky: 'Imago Pietatio', *Festschrift M. J. Friedländer* (Leipzig, 1927), pp. 261–308

G. von der Osten: *Der Schmerzensmann* (Berlin, 1935)

R. Berliner: 'Arma Christi', *Münchn. Jb. Bild. Kst*, vi (1955), pp. 33–152

C. Feudale: 'The Iconography of the Madonna del Parto', *Marsyas*, vii (1957), pp. 8–24

S. Ringbom: *Icon to Narrative* (Åbo, 1965/R Doornspijk, 1984)

U. Ulbert-Schede: *Das Andachtsbild des kreuztragenden Christus in der deutschen Kunst* (Munich, 1968)

S. Ringbom: 'Devotional Images and Imaginative Devotions', *Gaz. B.-A.*, lxxiii (1969), pp. 159–70

U. Schlegel: 'The Christ Child as a Devotional Image in Medieval Italian Sculpture', *A. Bull.*, lii (1970), pp. 1–10

R. Suckale: 'Arma Christi', *Städel-Jb.*, vi (1977), pp. 177–208

L. M. La Favia: *The Man of Sorrows: Its Origin and Development in Trecento Florentine Painting* (Rome, 1980)

F. O. Büttner: *Imitatio Pietatis* (Berlin, 1983)

J. Hamburger: 'The Visual and the Visionary: The Image in Late Medieval Monastic Devotions', *Viator*, xx (1989), pp. 163–82

H. Belting: *The Image and its Public in the Middle Ages: Form and Function of Early Paintings of the Passion* (New York, 1990)

NIGEL J. MORGAN

Andelys, les. *See* CHÂTEAU-GAILLARD.

Anderle, Jiří (*b* Pavlíkov, nr Rakovník, 14 Sept 1936). Czech draughtsman, painter and printmaker. From 1955 to 1961 he studied painting and graphic art at the Academy of Fine Arts in Prague. From 1961 to 1968 he worked at the Black Theatre of Jiří Srnec, a centre of the Prague avant-garde. He was assistant to Professors Jiří Trnka and Zdeněk Sklenář at the Faculty of Applied Art in Prague from 1969 to 1973, and in 1982–4 his work was shown at the central exhibition of the Biennale in Venice. His primary means of expression is drawing. His work forms closed complexes that capture moments of human existence, either in connection with ancient myths and legends or as aspects of contemporary life, for example the cycles of paintings, drawings and graphics *Village Dancing Girl* (1960–62), *Illusion and Reality* (1980–83; 1981, Ljubljana, Grand Prix BIB; 1982, Venice Biennale) and *Apocalyptic Genetics* (1982–3) and the cycle of paintings *Space and Time* (1983). The phenomenon of time is an important expressive element in his work, whether as a metaphor or in the form of a phased record of change, for instance aging. His whole work is based on the contrast of the real and the fantastic, logic and absurdity, beauty and ugliness, good and evil. These contrasts are already evident in his early complex drawings of figural scenes from dreams that are connected with the later apocalyptic visions. In his cycle of paintings, drawings and graphics *Commedia dell'arte* (1985), scenes of atrocities are merged with fantastic drawings of human figures and heads. In the cycle of paintings, drawings and graphics *Appassionata humana* (1989) he re-evaluated Surrealist imagery and formlessness.

BIBLIOGRAPHY

Jiří Anderle (exh. cat. by J. Mašín, Prague, Czech. A. Cent., 1968)

G. Köhrmann and others: *Jiří Anderle* (Ljubljana, 1983)

Jiří Anderle: Kresby a grafika [Jiří Anderle: drawings and graphic art] (exh. cat. by J. Mašín, Prague, Czech A. Fund, 1987)

Jiří Anderle (exh. cat. by J. Mašín, Rakovník, Rabas Gal., 1991)

HANA LARVOVÁ

Andersen, Gunnar Aagaard. *See* AAGAARD ANDERSEN, GUNNAR.

Anderson, Alexander (*b* New York, 21 April 1775; *d* Jersey City, NJ, 17 Jan 1870). American wood-engraver. He was the first important American wood-engraver. He was self-taught and made woodcuts for newspapers at the age of 12. Between *c.* 1792 and 1798, when he studied and practised medicine, he engraved wood as a secondary occupation, but, following the death of his family in the yellow fever epidemic of 1798, he abandoned medicine and worked as a graphic artist. He was an early follower of Thomas Bewick's white line style. He usually engraved the designs of others, such as Benjamin West, but he was a skilful and original draughtsman as can be seen in his illustrations for Durell's edition of Homer's *Iliad* (New York, 1808). He exhibited frequently at the American Academy and was a founder member of the National Academy of Design (1825). Anderson spent his long and prolific career in New York, engraving mainly for book publishers and magazines, but also producing pictorial matter for printed ephemera. He worked steadily until the late 1850s, cut his last blocks in 1868 and was described by Linton as 'the father of American wood engraving'. His reputation rests on his solid craftsmanship rather than his artistic abilities. A large collection of his proofs is in the New York Public Library and his tools and some of his blocks are kept by the New York Historical Society.

BIBLIOGRAPHY

W. J. Linton: *History of Wood Engraving in America* (Boston, 1882), pp. 1–9

F. M. Burr: *Life and Works of Alexander Anderson, M.D., the First American Wood Engraver* (New York, 1893)

H. Knubel: 'Alexander Anderson and Early American Book Illustration', *Princeton U. Lib. Chron.*, i (April, 1940), pp. 8–18

A. Gardner: 'Doctor Alexander Anderson', *Bull. Met.*, ix/x (1950–52), pp. 218–24

J. R. Pomeroy: 'Alexander Anderson's Life and Engravings before 1800', *Amer. Antiqua. Soc. Proc.*, c (1990), pp. 137–230

DAVID TATHAM

Anderson, James [Atkinson, Isaac; Dunbar, William Nugent] (*b* Blencarn, Cumb. [now Cumbria], 11 March

1813; *d* Rome, 27 Feb 1877). English photographer, active in Italy. Born Isaac Atkinson, he went to Paris as a young man to study painting, and in 1838 he went to Rome, where he adopted the names William Nugent Dunbar and later James Anderson, and where he participated in the annual exhibition of the Società degli Amatori e Cultori delle Belle Arti. By 1849 he was established as a photographer of ancient Greek and Roman sculpture and views of Rome, all for the tourist market. In 1859 he published his first album of photographic prints. Later he turned more exclusively to reproducing famous works of art. The business was continued into the 20th century by his eldest son, Domenico Anderson, and into the 1950s by the third generation of the family. In the 1960s Anderson's prints and negatives became part of the great art-historical archive in Florence.

BIBLIOGRAPHY

Catalogue des photographies de Rome de James Anderson (Paris, 1859)
H. Gernsheim: *Creative Photography: Aesthetic Trends, 1839–1960* (New York, 1962)
P. Becchetti: *Fotografi e fotografia in Italia, 1839–1880* (Rome, 1978)
M. Bugli, C. Gardioni and H. Gernsheim: *Fotografia italiana dell'ottocento* (Milan, 1979)

MARY CHRISTIAN

Anderson, Laurie (*b* Chicago, 5 June 1947). American performance artist, sculptor, draughtsman and writer. She completed her BA in art history at Barnard College, New York, in 1969 and had her first one-woman show there in 1970, exhibiting sculptures and drawings among other works. She then trained as a sculptor at Columbia University, New York, receiving her MFA in 1972. Her first performance, in which 'music' was played on car horns, took place in 1972 at Town Green in Rochester, NY. She continued to work primarily as a performance artist, using photographs, films, projected texts and, above all, music to create sophisticated and precisely staged events. The most complex and spectacular of these, *United States*, first performed in full at the Brooklyn Academy of Music in New York in 1983, was a four-part compendium of spoken texts and songs in which she addressed themes that she continued to explore in her later work, notably the use and abuse of language and of political power in its many forms.

BIBLIOGRAPHY

Laurie Anderson: Works from 1969 to 1983 (exh. cat. by J. Kardon, Philadelphia, U. PA, Inst. Contemp. A., 1983)

□

Anderson, Peirce. *See under* GRAHAM, ANDERSON, PROBST & WHITE.

Anderson, Sir **(Robert) Rowand** (*b* Edinburgh, 5 April 1834; *d* Edinburgh, 1 June 1921). Scottish architect. He was the dominant figure in Scottish architecture during the late Victorian and Edwardian periods. The son of a solicitor, he abandoned legal training in 1852 to begin an architectural career in the office of John Lessels, a leading practitioner in Edinburgh. He studied at the Trustees' Academy and was influenced by Alexander Christie, director of its School of Design. In 1857 Anderson joined George Gilbert Scott's staff in London, leaving for a continental tour in 1859 and returning to Edinburgh in 1860 as a civilian architect with the Royal Engineers. While attached to the Engineers, he designed a number of small Episcopal churches that show his mastery of the archaeologically accurate Gothic style popularized in England by the Ecclesiological Society, for example All Saints, Edinburgh (1866–78).

He began independent practice in 1868 and shortly afterwards published a book of measured drawings from his foreign tour. In 1871–2 he carried out a tasteful and scholarly restoration at the 13th-century church of St Vigean, Arbroath. By this time his reputation was established and his theoretical position had emerged. Believing that architectural beauty derived from functional efficiency, he criticized the revived Scottish Baronial style, in which, he felt, visual considerations had ousted sound building and planning. His views may have contributed to the dissolution of a brief partnership with David Bryce in 1873. During the 1870s Anderson won competitions for the Catholic Apostolic Church, Edinburgh (1872; built 1873–94), the Edinburgh School Board (1874) and Edinburgh University Medical School (1875–97); his designs, in various styles, combine elegance and restraint with sound planning. In 1878 the 3rd Marquess of Bute commissioned him to rebuild Mount Stuart, near Rothesay, confirming his pre-eminent position in Scotland.

Anderson next completed a number of large and influential works that included the Conservative Club, Edinburgh (1884; now Debenhams plc), Glasgow Central Station Hotel (1884) and the National Portrait Gallery and Museum of Antiquities, Edinburgh (1889). His ecclesiastical work during these years set new standards: Govan Old Parish Church, near Glasgow (1888), influenced Protestant church architecture in the direction of greater archaeological accuracy, and his restoration of Dunblane Cathedral (1893) was widely recognized as the finest Scottish work of its kind. Having resigned his associateship of the Royal Scottish Academy in 1883, he organized a vigorous campaign in 1889–90 to protest at its neglect of architecture. In due course, the Academy substantially increased its architectural membership.

In 1893 Anderson founded the School of Applied Art to provide much needed training for architects and craftsmen in Edinburgh. Shortly afterwards he inaugurated the National Art Survey, involving bursars from the School in recording details of historical Scottish architecture. He had meanwhile been designing buildings in the Scots 17th-century style, beginning with his own house, Allermuir, Colinton, Lothian (1879), and including Glencoe House, Glencoe (1896), Pollokshaws Burgh Buildings, Glasgow (1897), and the Pearce Institute, Govan (1900–06). These examples and periodic exhibitions of the survey helped to inspire a widespread revival of the style, which was much more restrained and practical in character than the Baronial revival earlier in the 19th century.

He was knighted in 1902 and received the Gold Medal of the RIBA in 1916. His final achievement was the creation of a central professional body for Scottish architects, which survives as the Royal Incorporation of Architects in Scotland, and to which he left when he died his Edinburgh town house as its headquarters (where it remains) and the residue of his estate. Among Anderson's most distinguished pupils were Robert Stodart Lorimer, Robert Weir Schultz and Arthur George Sydney Mitchell.

WRITINGS

Examples of the Municipal, Commercial and Street Architecture of France and Italy from the 12th to the 15th Centuries (London, 1868)

'Presidential Address: Section of Architecture', *Transactions of the National Association for the Advancement of Art and its Application to Industry: Edinburgh, 1889*, pp. 141–54

'The Royal Gold Medal Presentation', *RIBA J.*, n. s. 3, xxiii (1916), pp. 265–73

BIBLIOGRAPHY

A. N. Paterson: 'Sir Robert Rowand Anderson: An Appreciation', *RIBA J.*, n. s. 3, xxviii (1921), pp. 511–13

P. Savage: 'Edinburgh University's Extension Scheme of 1874', *Bk Old Edinburgh Club*, xxxiv/2 (1979), pp. 95–104

I. Gow: 'Sir Rowand Anderson's National Art Survey of Scotland', *Archit. Hist.*, xxvii (1984), pp. 543–54

S. McKinstry: *The Life and Work of Sir Robert Rowand Anderson, 1834–1921* (diss., U. St Andrews, 1987)

SAM McKINSTRY

Andiparos. *See* ANTIPAROS.

Andiron. *See under* FIREPLACE FURNISHINGS.

Andjar. *See* ANJAR.

Andlau, abbey church. Former Benedictine convent of nuns, dedicated to St Saviour, in Alsace, France. Founded in the 9th century, it was suppressed at the Revolution in 1789. The west tower and the nave with tribunes were rebuilt in the 17th century, but the crypt and western block survive and contain important Romanesque remains. The sculptural decoration, executed in sandstone from the Vosges, is concentrated on the façade block.

The finest work is found on the portal, which is abundantly decorated with low-relief sculpture. The doorframe belongs to the 11th-century church, but the sculptures are contemporary with the construction of the westwork in 1140. Their iconography is linked to the theme of paradise, a term used in medieval times to denote both the parvis in front of a church and the entrance porch. Standing out in the centre of the tympanum, Christ confers a key on St Peter and a book on St Paul. The scene takes place in a celestial garden, reminiscent of Early Christian decorative backgrounds, but here the trees are emphasized and the traditional scheme is combined with other allegorical subjects: the climbing of a heavenly tree and bird-hunting. On the lintel is the story of Adam and Eve, from the Creation of Eve to the Expulsion. The Lamentation of Adam and Eve, represented on the extreme right, is exceptional in the region and is derived from Byzantine iconography. Each of the pilasters flanking the jambs bears five superimposed niches, sheltering Abbey benefactors and their spouses, designated by name. The lowest niches are supported by atlas figures. Over the porch arch are three groups in high relief: the keystone bears Christ treading a dragon under his feet, flanked by Samson opening the lion's mouth (right) and David victorious over Goliath (left).

The historiated frieze crowning the façade block is 29.5 m long, composed of panels 600 mm high. On the north side, and up to the middle of the façade, are representations of animals and monsters, fighting and hunting, many of which (e.g. the elephant and castle and the centaur shooting at interlaced dragons) are widespread motifs. The sculptor was more inventive in the depiction of a peasant pursuing a fox who has stolen a goose. His narrative ability, humour and acute sense of observation are especially evident in the scene drawn from the epic of Theodoric of Ravenna and in the bear hunt, the latter possibly inspired by a Norse saga. There are also two moralizing scenes: an imp lies in wait for a vine grower who surrenders to its intrigues in a cellar, while another ensnares an avaricious banker seated on his strong-box. The frieze ends with the representation of preparations for a feast, an episode from the story of Samson.

Although the sculptors employed the same techniques as the workshop at Eschau (the use of surface incisions for folds and drilled pupils outlined by heavy, incised lines), they attempted to work in deeper relief, with crude results. Their use of model books seems undeniable, as does their knowledge of contemporary works in northern Italy (e.g. the frieze of S Michele, Pavia, and the portal of S Fedele, Como).

BIBLIOGRAPHY

R. Forrer: 'Les Frises historiées de l'église romane d'Andlau', *Cah. Archéol. & Hist. Alsace* (1931–2), pp. 57–67

R. Jullian: *L'Eveil de la sculpture italienne: La Sculpture romane dans l'Italie du Nord* (Paris, 1945)

R. Will: *Alsace romane*, Nuit Temps (La Pierre-qui-vire, 1965, 3/1982), pp. 260–63

——: 'Die epischen Themen der romanischen Bauplastik des Elsass', *Festschrift H. E. Kubach: Baukunst des Mittelalters in Europa* (Stuttgart, 1988), pp. 323–6

ROBERT WILL

Andlau, Peter Hemmel von. *See* HEMMEL VON ANDLAU, PETER.

Ando. *See* KAIGETSUDŌ, (1).

Andō, Tadao (*b* Osaka, 13 Sept 1941). Japanese architect. Between 1962 and 1969 he travelled extensively, studying first-hand the architecture of Japan, Europe, America and Africa. In 1969 he founded his own practice in Osaka. An inheritor of the Japanese anti-seismic reinforced-concrete tradition, Andō became one of the leading practitioners in this genre. Capable of using fair-faced, precision-cast reinforced-concrete walls to maximum effect, he created a uniquely minimalist modern expression, yielding an architecture of very firmly bounded domains. He spoke of using 'walls to defeat walls', by which he meant deploying the orthogonal, strictly geometric volumes of his earlier work as a way of resisting the empirical, not to say random, chaos of the average Japanese megalopolis. To this end most of his early houses are highly introspective; notable examples include two houses in Sumiyoshi, Osaka: the award-winning, diminutive terraced Azuma House (1976) and the Glass Block Wall House (1979), built for the Horiuchi family. The latter is a courtyard house that gains light and views solely from its small internal atrium. The Koshino House (1981), built in the pine-wooded, upper-class suburbs of Ashiya (Hyōgo Prefecture), takes a more open courtyard form, but again, as in all of Andō's subsequent work, its subtle beauty stems from the ever-changing impact of natural light on its concrete surfaces. As in the in-situ concrete Sōseikan tea house added to the Yamaguchi House, Takarazuka (Hyōgo Prefecture), in 1982, Andō never alluded to the Japanese tradition directly but always instead to the qualities of both

Tadao Andō: Mt Rokko Chapel, Kobe, 1986 (this, like all his Kobe buildings, surivived the 1995 earthquake unscathed)

half-muted and sharply contrasting light in which this tradition is steeped.

Andō's later work opened up towards the surrounding landscape, particularly where he worked on sites graced with spectacular views over mountainous escarpments and the ocean. This more expansive spirit runs as a continuous theme in his architecture after 1983, the year in which he completed his stepped Rokko Housing, Kobe, reminiscent of Le Corbusier's Roy et Rob project of 1946. This new-found topographic poetic is patently evident in his Mt Rokko Chapel (1986, see fig.), Kobe, and in the later Chapel-on-the-Water and Chapel of Light (both completed between 1988 and 1990), Ibaraki; in the latter a huge cruciform shape was cut out of the concrete wall behind the altar so that the morning sun creates a cross of light. After completing more than 50 buildings in 15 years, Andō began to adopt a more public caste in his work, as is evident from his Children's Museum (1990), Hyōgo. At this juncture his strict geometry opened up a little, admitting cylindrical forms and diagonal episodes in conjunction with the highly contoured sites on which he worked. Like many other Japanese architects, Andō sought a synthesis between archaic values and modern technology. To this end, eschewing fashionable form and ironic comment, he aspired to an architecture that would be as symbolic and laconic as the traditional Japanese *haiku* form in poetry.

WRITINGS

Tadao Andō (Tokyo, 1981)

Tadao Andō: Buildings, Projects, Writings (New York, 1984)

BIBLIOGRAPHY

A New Wave of Japanese Architecture (exh. cat., ed. K. Frampton; New York, Inst. Archit. & Urb. Stud., 1978)

C. Fawcett: *The New Japanese House* (New York, 1980)

F. Chaslin, A. Isozaki, V. Gregotti and others: *Tadao Andō: Minimalisme* (Paris, 1982)

'Tadao Andō', *Japan Architect*, 301 (1982) [whole issue]

B. Bognar: *The New Japanese Architecture* (New York, 1990)

Tadao Andō (exh. cat., ed. K. Frampton; New York, MOMA, 1991)

KENNETH FRAMPTON

Andō Hiroshige [Utagawa Hiroshige; Ichiryūsai; Ichiyūsai; Ryūsai] (*b* Edo [now Tokyo], 1797; *d* Edo, 1858). Japanese painter and printmaker. He was one of the greatest and most prolific masters of the full colour landscape print and one of the last great *ukiyoe* ('pictures of the floating world') print designers (*see* JAPAN, §IX, 3(iii)). A master of colour and composition, Hiroshige won popularity and lasting fame for his sensitive and atmospheric designs.

1. EARLY DEVELOPMENT, BEFORE 1818. Hiroshige was the eldest son of a samurai, a minor official associated with the shogunal fire department. As a child Hiroshige showed skill in drawing and seems to have aspired to become an artist. He was first apprenticed to Ōkajima Rinsai, a minor member of the KANŌ SCHOOL, from whom he learnt the elements of brushwork and composition. His brushwork became freer and more spontaneous when he studied under Ōoka Unpō (1765–1848), a painter in the Chinese style, who also taught him the importance of atmosphere. Independently, Hiroshige experimented with the naturalistic and Western-influenced styles of the Nagasaki and Shijō schools (*see* JAPAN, §VI, 4(vi)(c) and (viii)). By the age of 14 or 15, Hiroshige had decided that the *ukiyoe* genre held the most appeal for him, and he

applied to become a pupil of Utagawa Toyokuni (*see* UTAGAWA, (2)), a master of the largest and most powerful school of *ukiyoe*. Toyokuni being overstretched, Hiroshige was assigned instead to Toyohiro (*see* UTAGAWA, (4)), whose work was characterized by the lyrical charm for which Hiroshige later became famous. In 1812, after only a year's apprenticeship, Hiroshige graduated from Toyohiro's studio. He took the name Utagawa Hiroshige as token of his affiliation with the school, although within a few years he had broken his ties with it, and in 1818 he made his debut as a serious print designer.

2. 1818–48. Hiroshige did not immediately begin to produce landscape prints. From about 1818 to 1830 his main output consisted of inimitably individualistic prints of beautiful women (*bijinga*) and actors (*yakushae*), a speciality of the Utagawa masters. At the same time he tried his hand at *surimono* ('printed things'; deluxe prints) and book illustrations, of which many examples exist. These were executed in the plain, uniform style he had inherited from Toyohiro and proved over time less popular than the figurative subjects depicted by Hiroshige's rivals Kunisada and Kuniyoshi (*see* UTAGAWA, (5) and (6)).

It was a time of discontent for Hiroshige, who, by constant trial and error, was seeking his own artistic style. It was also a time when both *ukiyoe* and the print movement were flagging: new ideas and subjects were rare and execution lacklustre. Landscape, which had been out of favour for some years, being regarded as too traditional and, perhaps, too highbrow for the print-buying public, was returning to popularity and in so doing giving print production a new lease of life. This process received a boost from the publication of KATSUSHIKA HOKUSAI's *Fūgaku sanjūrokkei* ('Thirty-six views of Mount Fuji'). Hiroshige too became aware of the possibilities of the landscape print, and *c.* 1826 he released the series *Tōto meisho* ('Famous views of the eastern capital'; e.g. Amsterdam, Rijksmus.), a simple landscape series which illustrated the various sites in Edo. It met with very favourable criticism. This series was unusually coloured, successfully employing the pink pigment derived from safflower and indigo blue. It was apparently issued to rival Hokusai's work but was wholly different in character. Hiroshige's were frank and refreshingly true-to-life sketches as seen through the eyes of an inhabitant of Edo, not vain displays of personal eccentricity.

Sent on a shogunal delegation to Kyoto in 1830, Hiroshige travelled along the Tokaido, the eastern sea road. The activity on the road and the surrounding scenery made a deep impression on him, and in 1833–4 he published the sequential series of 55 single sheet prints, the *Tōkaidō gojūsantsugi no uchi* ('Fifty-three stages on the Tokaido', Tokyo, N. Mus.), supervising the production personally. The images were based on his own sketches of views that touched him, but in technique also hinted at the compositions in an earlier published collection of famous views of the Tokaido. Using such elements as the wind, rain or snow, the moon and flowers, the pictures achieved a subtlety that struck a chord with the innermost sentiments of the Japanese. The compositions overflow with beautiful and sensitive observations. Earlier periods in Japanese history had yielded many examples of *sansuiga* ('mountain-and-water pictures'; landscapes) and *fūkeiga* (natural scenes), but Hiroshige's series was without doubt a work of outstanding novelty and enduring merit. The series was a resounding success, and Hiroshige became the Japanese landscape artist *par excellence*, socially on an equal footing with other famous print designers of the period. The success of the Tokaido series encouraged Hiroshige to become increasingly a true landscapist. He executed such print series as the *Kisōkaidō rokujūkyūtsugi* ('Sixty-nine stations on the Kisokaido', *c.* 1839; e.g. Amsterdam, Rijksmus.) and the better-known environs of the provinces or of large cities such as Edo and Kyoto, for example *Ōmi hakkei no uchi* ('Eight views of Lake Biwa in Ōmi Province'; *c.* 1834; see fig.) and the *Kyoto meisho* ('Famous views of Kyoto'; 1834; e.g. Amsterdam, Rijksmus.). A huge number of landscape prints were constantly being released by different publishers; prolific though he was, Hiroshige designed only a small proportion. At the same time, he was trying his hand at prints of birds and flowers and in this field too he competed with Hokusai. For these works he used principally an adapted long compositional format such as that of *tanzaku(ban)* (poem cards, narrow strips of paper, *c.* 300 mm long). Unlike Hokusai, he did not intend to include text. The lyricism, intimacy and harmony of his landscape prints are also manifest in these bird-and-flower works, in which the brushwork seeks to represent both the rich splendour and the tranquillity of nature. He also experimented with such new devices as the combination of beautiful women and landscapes.

3. 1849 AND AFTER. In 1849 Hokusai died, leaving the field of landscape prints principally to Hiroshige, Kunisada and Kuniyoshi. For the next four or five years, however, Hiroshige's enormous productivity (his total output is estimated at 5000 designs) took its toll of artistic quality and inspiration. His works became mediocre and repetitive, partly as a result of a decline in demand from publishers for pure landscape designs. It was not until about 1853 that he began again to produce works of note and quality. From the period 1853–8 date compilations of intimate landscape prints in vertical format, such as the *Rokujū yoshū meisho zue* ('Famous places of the sixty provinces'; 1853; e.g. Amsterdam, Rijksmus.) and the *Meisho Edo hyakkei* ('One hundred famous views of Edo'; 1856–8; e.g. New York, Brooklyn Mus.). In two or three works he defied the conventional large triptych format.

The later works lack the sensitivity and easy grace of those produced at the peak of his output in the 1830s and early 1840s. On the other hand, Hiroshige also produced a number of *nikuhitsuga* (*ukiyoe* paintings) in his later years. These were notable for their elegant simplicity and their capacity to reveal the artist's inner character. The light brushwork was adept and skilful, producing compositions full of charming artistic effects. In this genre the enormously talented Hiroshige towered above his rivals.

From the Bakumatsu ('end of the shogunate') period (1853–68) date many great works by Hiroshige, most of them *ukiyoe* prints rather than paintings. Hiroshige's abilities unfolded *pari passu* with the development of the polychrome print (*nishikie*), which was a collaborative art involving the print designer, carver and printer. While the

Andō Hiroshige: *Night Rain at Karasaki* from the series *Ōmi hakkei no uchi* ('Eight views of Lake Biwa in Ōmi Province'), 229×330 mm, *c.* 1834 (London, Victoria and Albert Museum)

craftsmen served the print master in the interpretation and rendition of his designs, he in turn knew how to take optimum advantage of the techniques of cutting and printing, incorporating great strength of expression into his exquisite designs. Of particular use to him was the *bokashi* ('gradation or shading') technique, one of many technical innovations that permitted the full splendour of his *meishoe* ('pictures of famous places') to be revealed. Indeed, it is no exaggeration to say that Hiroshige owed his greatness and success to the development of the *nishikie*.

Hiroshige died two years after his retirement, and is buried in a Zen temple in Asakusa, Tokyo. His work is imbued with candour, genuineness, humility, a deep love of the landscape and sensitivity, all reflections of his gentle and genial character. Some of its special traits—the turbid, deep background plane, for example—are a function of his identity as a resident of Edo, influenced by its artistic traditions and responding to the requirements of its publishers and markets. While some artists, such as those of the Maruyama–Shijō school (*see* JAPAN, §VI, 4(viii)) associated with each other and developed a broader outlook, Hiroshige stood apart. Yet, paradoxically, it was he who captured in his work a universality of experience and sentiment. He had few pupils, and they proved relatively undistinguished; the last was Hirokage (*fl* 1851–66). Nevertheless, Hiroshige significantly influenced European, especially French, artists from the 1870s onwards: his shadowless drawing, mastery of telling detail, starkly geometric compositions, and above all the overall 'arrangement' of form were emulated by van Gogh, Degas, Toulouse Lautrec, Monet and Manet, among others. The American painter Whistler also borrowed elements of Hiroshige's style.

BIBLIOGRAPHY

Y. Noguchi: *Hiroshige* (London, New York and Tokyo, 1935)
J. Michener: *The Floating World* (New York, 1954)
S. Takahashi and C. S. Terry: *Andō Hiroshige* (Tokyo, 1956)
R. Lane: *Masters of the Japanese Print* (London and New York, 1962)
J. Suzuki: *Hiroshige* (Tokyo, 1970)
D. B. Waterhouse: *Images of Eighteenth-century Japan* (Toronto, 1975)
A. G. Poster and H. D. Smith: *Hiroshige: One Hundred Famous Views of Edo* (London, 1986)

MASATO NAITŌ

Andokides Painter. *See* VASE PAINTERS, §II.

Andorra. Principality in the Pyrenees between Spain and France. It is divided into three mountainous areas by deep rivers, principally the River Valira. The official language is Catalan. The earliest documentary evidence dates from the early Middle Ages, when Andorra was part of the Hispanic March. From the 11th century it belonged to the Counts of Urgel, who presented it to the Bishop of Urgel in 1133. Its later ownership was fought over, and it became part of the Kingdom of Navarre. Emperor Charles V did not incorporate it into the Spanish crown but left it as an independent state, technically under the joint rule of the Spanish Bishop of Urgel and the French Comte de Foix.

Andorra's artistic importance rests on its many 11th- and 12th-century Romanesque structures. The single-cell churches, which are fine examples of the earliest Iberian Romanesque, have a semicircular apse and a façade decorated with Lombard blind arcading. Many have a slender, multi-storey tower, sometimes round, as at S Coloma (12th century). These churches, including Ars, S Vincenç, S Romá de Auvinyá, S Romá dels Vicars and S Jaume dels Cortals, correspond stylistically to early medieval Hispanic tradition. Most are decorated with Romanesque frescoes, for example at S Cerní de Nagol, S Coloma, S Martín at La Cortinada, S Miquel d'Engolasters and S Joan de Caselles (examples now in Barcelona, Mus. A. Catalunya). Medieval secular buildings include bridges at Aixovall, La Margineda and San Clemente de Pal and the castle of St Vicens, built by Roger Bernat III, Comte de Foix. The 14th-century Casa de la Vall in Andorra la Vella, the capital, is a large rectangular mansion with a tower and battlements; it now houses the Museo de Arte e Historia de Andorra.

BIBLIOGRAPHY

J. Ainaud de Lasarte: 'Andorra y la pintura románica', *Andorra* (Andorra la Vella, 1956)
M. Palau Marti: *Andorra* (Barcelona, 1967)
J. Puigoriol: *Andorra románica: Pintura* (Barcelona, 1969)
E. Carbonell: *L'art romanic a Catalunya (segle XII)* (Barcelona, 1974)
A. Puigoriol and J. Puigoriol: *Andorra: Monuments et paysages* (Barcelona, 1974)

CONCEPCIÓN ABAD CASTRO

Andrade [D'Andrade]**, Alfredo (Cesare Reis Freire) de** (*b* Lisbon, 26 Aug 1839; *d* Genoa, 30 Nov 1915). Portuguese painter, architect and restorer, active in Italy. He came from a middle-class family with trading interests in Italy. In 1854 Andrade went to Genoa, and friendships there with such artists as Tammar Luxoro (1824–99) led him to study painting with Alexandre Calame and later to study architecture at the Accademia Ligustica di Belle Arti. He travelled widely, and in Italy he came into contact with ANTONIO FONTANESI and Carlo Pittura (1835/6–91), with whom he became one of the most active painters of the SCUOLA DI RIVARA. According to Telamaro Signorini, Andrade was among the painters who frequented the Caffè Michelangiolo in Florence. The influence of the *macchiaioli* painters is also evident from 1863 in his paintings, especially in *Return from the Woods at Dusk* (1869; Genoa, Mus. Accad. Ligustica B.A.).

1. PAINTING. Andrade's work represents a transition from the Romantic school of Calame to the Naturalism of the Barbizon school. His landscapes show careful observation of nature. The locations in northern Italy seem to have been chosen for their melancholy and serenity, as in the landscapes of Fontanesi. Andrade's pastoral scenes at dawn or dusk are seen through morning mists or against sunsets, or they depict uninhabited countryside. Most of these works, for example *Slope near Rivara* (*c*. 1869), are in the Galleria Civica d'Arte Moderna, Turin. The *Pond* (*c*. 1863; Lisbon, Mus. N.A. Contemp.), painted by morning light, shows the romantic quality and the luminosity of Andrade's work. Although he exhibited in Portugal between 1862 and 1865, it was in Italy, where he exhibited in 1868 and 1870, that his reputation as a landscape painter was established. At the Exposition Universelle of 1867 in Paris, his *Passage from Bormida to Carcare* (*c*. 1865; Genoa, Mus. Accad. Ligustica B.A.) was considered representative of Italian landscape painting.

LUCÍLIA VERDELHO DA COSTA

2. ARCHITECTURE. From the late 1860s Andrade turned his attentions to the study of medieval Piedmontese monuments, although he continued to paint and occasionally exhibited in Genoa, Parma and elsewhere; he also maintained close links with such artists as Pittara, Federico Pastoris (1837–84), Carlo Felice Biscarra (1824–94) and Vittorio Avondo (1836–1910), later Director of the Museo Civico, Turin. All were important figures in Piedmontese antiquarian circles, and at the recommendation of Pittara, Andrade was put in charge of the restoration of the Castello di Rivara Canavese (1873–7). In 1882 he was appointed superintendent of the building of the *Borgo medievale*, built in the Parco del Valentino, Turin, for the Esposizione Nazionale of 1884. The success of this project led in 1886 to his appointment as Director of the Conservazione dei Monumenti del Piemonte e Liguria, a post he held until his death. His work, which is extensively documented by the drawings in the Galleria Civica d'Arte Moderna in Turin, was deeply influenced by the theories of Viollet-le-Duc: rebuilding always took precedence over the conservation of historical stratifications, a typical example being the restoration of the 12th-century church of S Donato in Genoa. Although his practice was regarded as outdated even by his contemporaries, his influence was felt among Piedmontese restorers for almost half a century.

SANDRO CALLERIO

WRITINGS

Relazione dell'Ufficio regionale per la conservazione dei monumenti del Piemonte e della valle d'Aosta (Turin, 1891)

BIBLIOGRAPHY

Catalogo officiale della sezione di storia dell'arte dell'Esposizione nazionale italiana (Turin, 1884/*R* Turin, 1981)
J. da Costa Lima: *O artista Alfredo de Andrade* (Lisbon, 1937)
R. D'Andrade: *Quadros de Alfredo D'Andrade* (Lisbon, 1955)
M. Bernardi and V. Viale: 'Alfredo de Andrade', *Atti Soc. Piemont. Archaeol. & B.A.*, n. s., iii (1957) [whole issue ded. to Andrade]
V. Viale and M. Bernardi: *Alfredo de Andrade: La vita, l'opera e l'arte* (Turin, 1957)
R. D'Andrade: *Alfredo d'Andrade: Sua actividade artistica: Desenhos de paisagem* (Lisbon, 1959)
Alfredo de Andrade: Tutela e restauro (exh. cat., Turin, Pal. Reale, 1981)
G. Bruno, ed.: *L'alba del vero: Pitture del secondo '800 in Liguria* (Genoa, Mus. Accad. Ligustica B.A., 1993)

SANDRO CALLERIO, LUCÍLIA VERDELHO DA COSTA

Andrade (Moscoso), Jaime (*b* Quito, 10 Sept 1913; *d* Quito, 11 April 1990). Ecuadorean sculptor, painter and engraver. He studied sculpture at the Escuela de Bellas Artes in Quito, graduating in 1932. He was a pupil of Luigi Cassadio (*fl* 1915–33), an Italian sculptor who stimulated sculptural activity in the school and whom Andrade succeeded as professor. With his *Mother Earth* (Quito, Mus. Mun. Alberto Mena Caomaño) Andrade won the Mariano Aguilera national prize in 1940. His early work was realist and academic but in 1941 he studied mural decoration with the Ecuadorean artist Camilo Egas at the New School for Social Research in New York. His previous low reliefs in stone were transformed into vast murals depicting stylized and geometric human scenes (e.g. the untitled mural, 18×9 m, at the Universidad Central del Ecuador in Quito, 1949–54). In the late 1960s he used hammered steel sheeting in his sculptures, and in the

1970s he executed what he called his 'flying sculptures' (e.g. *Flight*, 1979; Quito, priv. col.), in which expanses of spiralling pebbles wrapped in brightly coloured sheets produced sounds generated by the wind. He continued also to execute large-format public murals, in which he experimented continually with materials, creating for example a mosaic landscape in 1976–7 for the Municipio de Quito building. In 1982 the Banco Central del Ecuador held a large retrospective of Andrade's work, affirming his reputation as the greatest Ecuadorean sculptor of the 20th century.

BIBLIOGRAPHY

Jaime Andrade: Obra escultórica y gráfica (Quito, 1977)

Retrospectiva de Jaime Andrade (exh. cat., Quito, Banco Cent. del Ecuador, 1982)

El siglo XX de las artes visuales en Ecuador (exh. cat. by H. R. Castello, Goayoquil, Mus. Antropol. & Mus. A. Banco Cent., 1988), pp. 39–40

L. Oña: Obituary, *Rev. Diners*, 100 (1990), pp. 56–61

ALEXANDRA KENNEDY TROYA

Andrade, Manuel Costa. *See* COSTA ANDRADE, MANUEL.

Andras, Catherine (*b* Bristol, *c.* 1775; *d* London, 1860). English wax modeller. She taught herself the techniques of wax modelling; being orphaned, she was adopted by the miniature painter Robert Bowyer and his wife. Andras worked at the Historical Gallery in London and also produced wax models for James Tassie. Through the Bowyers, Andras was introduced to various celebrities, of whom she made wax portrait models in relief or in the round; and she exhibited at the Royal Academy from 1799 to 1824. In 1802 she was appointed Modeller in Wax to Queen Charlotte (1744–1818), producing wax portraits, such as that of the Queen's granddaughter *Princess Charlotte of Wales* (1802; London; V&A). The same year Andras was awarded the Larger Silver Pallet by the Society for the Encouragement of the Arts, Manufactures and Commerce. After the death of Lord Nelson in 1805 Andras, who had earlier modelled him from life, was commissioned to provide a life-size effigy for Westminster Abbey in London (*in situ*). Except for this, her work was all small-scale; her models often had real hair or fur for eyebrows and lashes. She continued to work until 1855.

BIBLIOGRAPHY

A. Graves: *The Royal Academy of Arts*, i (1905), p. 34

E. J. Pyke: *A Biographical Dictionary of Wax Modellers* (Oxford, 1973), pp. 5–6

□

Andrault and Parat. French architectural partnership formed in 1957 by Michel Andrault (*b* Montrouge, 17 Dec 1926) and Pierre Parat (*b* Versailles, 16 April 1928). Both Andrault and Parat studied architecture at the Ecole des Beaux-Arts, Paris, graduating in 1955, and they formed their partnership after winning an international competition for the Basilica of Syracuse (1957; completed 1994). In the 1960s, following on the housing work of Candilis-Josic-Woods, Andrault and Parat built a very large number of housing complexes in various French towns, including Bordeaux, Marseille, Montpellier and Nanterre, culminating in the construction of a group of terraced units (1972–80) in the new town of Evry. For its commercial and public commissions the partnership's trademark became the bold contrast between a core of 'brutalist' concrete, expressing vertical circulation, and adjoining cubes of reflective glass. This formula was well adapted to suburban office buildings such as the Caisse Régionale de Crédit Agricole (1969–70) in Auxerre; it was less successful when blown out of proportion at the educational facility for the Faculté des Lettres et des Sciences Humaines Tolbiac (1971–3) in Paris, but another building based on similar principles, the faceted Tour Totem (1975–8), Paris, is one of the most original skyscrapers in the Front de Seine development. The bold design of the headquarters of the Agence Havas (1970–73), Neuilly-sur-Seine, with a cylindrical foyer and a main building expressed by horizontal metal beams, conveys an impression of dynamism close in spirit to Erich Mendelsohn's department stores in Germany of the late 1920s. In 1985 Andrault and Parat were awarded the Grand Prix National d'Architecture by the French government for their monumental and mechanistic sports arena, the Palais Omnisports de Bercy (1979–84) near the Gare de Lyon, Paris, in which four concrete shafts, surrounded by sloping grass-covered mounds, support huge metal beams.

BIBLIOGRAPHY

M. Gaillard: *Andrault Parat: Architectes* (Paris, *c.* 1980)

'Un Colisée moderne dans la capitale: Palais Omnisports de Bercy', *Tech. & Archit.*, 353 (1984), pp. 103–9

'Un Grand Prix pour les architectes de Bercy', *Archit. Intérieure Créée*, 209 (1985–6), pp. 7–12

ISABELLE GOURNAY

Andravida [Fr. Andreville]. Town in Elis, Greece, 55 km south-west of Patras. As Andreville it was the unfortified capital of the Frankish principality of the Morea from the 13th to the 15th century. Andravida, the strongly fortified port of Clarence (modern Killini) and CHLEMOUTSI CASTLE formed a triangle at the north-western tip of the Peloponnese, designed to control the hinterland and the sea lanes. The only physical evidence of the Franks at Andravida are the remains of the Roman Catholic Cathedral of Hagia Sophia, in which Prince Geoffrey Villehardouin I and his barons met to determine policy and justice.

The cathedral is the only surviving example of a rib-vaulted Gothic church in Greece. The extant remains consist of three square-ended eastern chapels and the foundations of a nave of at least ten bays. There was no transept. The building was of sandstone, with re-used ancient granite columns in the nave. The first building campaign was during the reign of Prince Geoffrey Villehardouin I, from 1210 to *c.* 1226, when the east end was probably unvaulted. The unbuttressed nave, with its tall, narrow windows, had a strongly fortified appearance. In a second campaign, probably before 1259, rib vaults were inserted in the eastern chapels, those of the sanctuary on corner colonnettes. The arches and windows were pointed and the windows enlarged. The cathedral was abandoned during the 15th century and later re-used as an Orthodox sanctuary. In the early 20th century it was severely restored with a flat roof. It went out of ecclesiastical use in 1964. The remains were investigated by the Minnesota (USA)–Andravida Project in 1984 and 1985.

BIBLIOGRAPHY

Chronique de la Morée (1204–1305): Livre de la conqueste de la Princée de l'Amorée, ed. J. Lognon (Paris, 1911)

A. Bon: *La Morée franque* (Paris, 1969)

C. Sheppard: 'Excavations at the Cathedral of Hagia Sophia, Andravida, Greece', *Gesta*, xxv/1 (1986), pp. 139–44

CARL D. SHEPPARD

André, Albert (*b* Lyon, 24 May 1869; *d* Laudun, Gard, 11 July 1954). French painter, writer and museum curator. He received his initial art training in Lyon and began his career designing patterns for silk, the city's principal industry. After moving to Paris in 1889, he attended the Académie Julian and subsequently met Louis Valtat, Paul Ranson, Georges D'Espagnat and Henri Bataille (1872–1922). Perhaps the most important influence on his work was Auguste Renoir, who first saw André's paintings in 1894 at the Salon des Indépendants and was so favourably impressed that he recommended André to the dealer Paul Durand-Ruel. The two artists struck up a close relationship, which lasted until Renoir's death in 1919. André's monograph *Renoir* (1919) is one of the most accurate contemporary accounts of the artist's work.

By 1900 André had met the writers and artists associated with the *Revue blanche*, and in 1902 he helped to organize the journal's exhibition of the Lyonese painter François Vernay (1821–96). In 1918 he became Curator of the Fondation Léon Alègre, the museum at Bagnols-sur-Cèze. There he amassed a valuable collection of works by 19th-century Lyonese artists and, with generous donations from such artists as Pierre Bonnard and Henri Matisse, acquired important 20th-century paintings as well. Thereafter he divided his time between curatorial duties, painting and writing.

In his painted work André's choice of themes and compositional arrangements shows a strong allegiance to the ideals of Impressionism and Post-Impressionism. His brushwork might reveal the soft, feathery quality of Renoir's Impressionist works or the geometric substructure of a work by Paul Cézanne. Such paintings as *Autumn Morning* (1913; Chicago, IL, A. Inst.) exemplify his balanced, muted palette and soft modelling of forms, which retain a masterful sense of structure and mass.

WRITINGS

Renoir (Paris, 1919)

BIBLIOGRAPHY

M. Mermillon: *Albert André* (Paris, 1927)
Hommage-souvenir à Albert André, 1869–1954 (exh. cat., Cagnes-sur-Mer, Château-Mus., 1958)
Albert André, 1869–1954: Paintings and Watercolours (exh. cat., ed. G. Besson; London, Wildenstein's, 1970)

LYNN BOYER FERRILLO

André, Carl (*b* Quincy, MA, 16 Sept 1935). American sculptor. He attended the Phillips Academy, Andover, MA, from 1951 to 1953, and in 1954 he visited England, where he was greatly impressed by Stonehenge. From 1955 to 1956 he served in the US Army; in 1957 he moved to New York, where he began to write poetry. He also made drawings and sculpture in perspex and wood. He met Frank Stella in 1958 and in 1959 he shared his studio where he made large sculptures, such as *Last Ladder* (wood, 2.14×1.55×1.55 m; 1959; London, Tate). The *Black Paintings* on which Stella was working had a considerable influence on André both for their non-referentiality and for their symmetrical and non-hierarchic compositions, in which no part was given more emphasis than any other. André's totemic wooden sculptures, such as *Ladder No. 2* (wood, 2.1×0.15×0.15 m, 1959; London, Tate), are indebted to Constantin Brancusi but were cut rather than carved. Many of them were constructed according to what André called structural building principles, in which elements were stacked and interlocked.

In 1965, however, after spending four years working as a freight brakeman and then a conductor on the railway, André abandoned this manner of working and began to look for new materials. 'The railway completely tore me away from the pretensions of art, even my own, and I was back on the horizontal lines of steel and rust and great masses of coal and material, timber, with all kinds of hides and glue and the burdens and weights of the cars themselves' (exh. cat. 1978). André's sculpture after 1965, central to the movement labelled MINIMALISM, consisted of series of similar units placed together in a manner reminiscent of coupled railway trucks. As each unit is replaceable by another, all units are equally important, thereby obeying the principle of what André called 'axial symmetry', where the whole is the same on each side of a central axis.

After 1965 André's sculptures were made to be placed directly on the floor and were constructed out of common building materials. These included aluminium, lead and magnesium plates, as well as common building bricks, each sculpture comprising one material only, as in *144 Aluminium Squares* (1967; Pasadena, CA, Norton Simon Mus.; see fig.). These floor pieces were intended not only to be looked at but also to be walked on, so that the material difference between the floor and the sculpture could be physically experienced. In terms of structure these works were composed simply by placing the elements alongside each other in shapes that were suggested by the elements themselves. Thus the configuration of a work was to a great extent self-determined and logical. The structure of the sculpture would be immediately apparent. In this sense André was concerned to retain the identity of each of his building materials in a way that he had not been earlier by his action of cutting into wood. The artist's hand would not be visibly apparent.

Carl André: *144 Aluminium Squares*, aluminium, 0.01×3.6×3.6 m, 1967 (Pasadena, CA, Norton Simon Museum)

Such sculptures were often meant to be seen not in isolation but in the context of an entire installation that articulated the architecture of the gallery. The titles of individual works such as *Equivalent VIII*, made of building bricks (1966, destr.; remade 1969; London, Tate), drew attention to the fact that the work was part of a whole just as each work was composed of standard elements. Another characteristic of André's sculpture after 1965 was its sense of weight and mass, another product of the artist's experience on the railway. He experimented with sculpture in wood but rejected it as an unsuitably light material for the floor pieces, as he felt that they were likely to move, and that the shape of the sculpture would therefore be difficult to maintain.

In the early 1970s André made some major wood sculptures, such as *Henge on Threshold (Meditation of the Year 1960)* (1971; Otterlo, Kröller-Müller). After 1975 he again began to use wood, but this time as unaltered blocks reminiscent of the sleepers on the railway, as in *The Way North, East, South, West (Uncarved Blocks)* (western red cedar, 0.91×1.5×1.5 m, 1975; New York, Agnes Gind priv. col.; see 1987 exh. cat., pl. 66).

For André a sculpture had no meaning outside of its existence, and for this reason he did not consider himself in any way to be a conceptual artist. The idea cannot be divorced from the object for it must be physically experienced. Its creation arises out of a desire 'to make something to be in the world', and its importance lies in the effect it has on its environment and on the viewer's perception of space.

BIBLIOGRAPHY

P. Tuchman: 'An Interview with Carl André', *Artforum*, viii/10 (1970), pp. 55–61
D. Waldman: *Carl André* (New York, 1970)
Carl André: Sculpture, 1959–1978 (exh. cat., ed. N. Serota; London, Whitechapel A.G., 1978)
Carl Andre: *12 Dialogues 1962–1963 with Hollis Frampton* (Halifax, NS, and New York, 1980)
Carl André (exh. cat., ed. P. de Jonge; The Hague, Gemeentemus.; Eindhoven, Stedel. Van Abbemus.; 1987) [includes catalogue raisonné]

JEREMY LEWISON

André, Edouard. *See under* JACQUEMART-ANDRÉ.

André, Emile (*b* Nancy, 22 Aug 1871; *d* Nancy, 10 March 1933). French architect. His grandfather, François André (1811–1904), was a developer and his father, Charles André (1841–1928), became a county architect and was one of the organizers of the Exposition des Arts Décoratifs et Industriels Lorrains of 1894, which proved to be a prelude to the formation of the Ecole de Nancy seven years later. Emile André studied architecture with Victor Laloux at the Ecole des Beaux-Arts in Paris. In 1896 he travelled to the Nile with Gaston Munier (1871–1918), his friend and fellow student. On the advice of the French archaeologist Jacques de Morgan, they excavated the temple of Kom Ombo (154 BC–AD 14) to the north of Aswan and under his direction they also took part in an archaeological mission to Persia (now Iran). André made drawings and watercolours on his travels and he went to India with the aid of a travel grant awarded to him for his contribution on Kom Ombo to the Salon of 1897.

In 1902 André returned to Nancy and joined the Art Nouveau circle founded a decade earlier by Emile Gallé and established as the Ecole de Nancy in 1901. With Henri Gutton (1873–1963) he planned a new suburban development of 28 villas, the Parc de Saurupt. He himself designed the concierge's hut and two houses, Les Roches, for his own use and another, Les Glycines, for Fernbach, an industrialist from Lorraine. Although the former is built in rusticated stonework, while the latter is precisely dressed, the placing of openings in both is informally and asymmetrically arranged according to the location of the internal spaces. The variety of the openings also conveys a picturesque quality by the use of verandahs, porches, bow-windows and balconies. One of his most famous works is the double house (1903) built between arch abutments on the Strasbourg–Paris railway line. As at Les Glycines there are an exaggerated broken arch and curious figural ventilation openings. Here, too, is the carved decoration of natural forms imparting an Art Nouveau modernism and a graphic quality seen previously in his botanical designs on the wood frames of the shopfronts of the Vaxelaire and Pignot stores (1901), a project in which his father and Eugène Vallin had participated. Similar surface decoration appears on the tower of the Renauld Bank (1910), Nancy.

In Nancy, however, as elsewhere, exuberant Art Nouveau was shortlived. Even in André's two buildings of 1902 and 1904 on the Avenue Foch there are signs of ambivalence. In the first of these houses only one of four rows of symmetrically arranged windows is interrupted by balconies, and the second has only two asymmetrical projections. His design for the Ecole des Beaux-Arts competition in 1909 shows a classical symmetry, while that for the Pavillon Solvay at the Exposition Internationale de l'Est de la France in Nancy of the same year makes use of Ionic columns. Although the later house, Les Pins (1912), 2 Rue Albin-Haller, has one of the most picturesque of André's broken façades—with an imposing pinnacle on the gable and a door framed in floral decoration—the six windows are symmetrically arranged and the Art Nouveau panels placed between them resemble a giant order, evidence of André's attempts to fulfil both functional and picturesque requirements.

BIBLIOGRAPHY

E. Nicolas: 'Une Maison moderne de M. Emile André', *Lorraine Artiste* (1 April 1904), pp. 97–105
E. Badel: *Le Parc de Saurupt à Nancy: Hier, aujourd'hui, demain* (Nancy, 1907)
W. D. Strauchs: *Emile André und die Architektur des Ecoles de Nancy* (n.p.) [*c.* 1976]
F. Loyer: 'Viollet-le-Duc to Tony Garnier: The Passion for Rationalism', *Art Nouveau Architecture*, ed. F. Russel (London, 1979), pp. 102–35
F. T. Charpentier and others: *Art Nouveau: L'Ecole de Nancy* (Paris 1987)
J.-C. Vigato: 'L'Architecture', *Nancy 1900: Rayonnement de l'Art Nouveau*, H. Claude and others (Thionville, 1989), pp. 120–55

JEAN-CLAUDE VIGATO

André, Frère **Jean** (*b* Paris, 1662; *d* Paris, 14 April 1753). French ecclesiastic and painter. He entered the Dominican Order at the age of 17. He may have begun his artistic training only in 1687, when he was given leave to travel to Rome; he seems to have spent several years there. According to tradition, it was Carlo Maratti's painting that most influenced him; however, the classical stylistic elements in André's paintings would seem to reflect the general influence of contemporary Roman and French art, rather than that of any particular artist. Apart from a few portraits, such as his *Self-portrait with Rosary* (after 1731; Paris, Louvre), André painted works with an exclusively religious content. Many of his surviving monumental paintings may be seen in churches in Lyon and Bordeaux, as well as in several in Paris, for instance the *Supper at Emmaus* (1741) in St Nicolas du Chardonnet, *St Dominic Expounding the Rules of the Order* (1738) in St Thomas d'Aquin and *St Vincent de Paul Preaching* (1734) in Ste Marguerite.

The last work, part of a cycle by several artists depicting the saint's life, was moved to Ste Marguerite after the French Revolution (1789–95). With its deep landscape setting and its emphasis on diagonal axes, it reveals a Baroque influence; but with its muted colours, it otherwise fits into the context of contemporary French history painting. The precisely captured facial features, hands and gestures in this work reveal André as a realistic observer. This painting, like André's work generally, shows also the influence of Jean Jouvenet, who dominated Parisian history painting around 1700.

BIBLIOGRAPHY

DBF; Thieme–Becker

C. Marionneau: *Frère André: Artiste peintre de l'Ordre des Frères prêcheurs, 1662–1753* (Bordeaux, 1878)

G. Janneau: *La Peinture française au XVIIe siècle* (Paris, 1963), p. 270

A. Schnapper: *Jean Jouvenet, 1644–1717, et la peinture d'histoire à Paris* (Paris, 1974), pp. 76–7, 87, 180

J. Fritsch: 'Une Oeuvre du frère André', *Paris & Ile-de-France: Mem.*, xxx (1988), pp. 299–306

CATHRIN KLINGSÖHR

André, Louis-Jules (*b* Paris, 24 June 1819; *d* Paris, 20 Jan 1890). French architect. Born into a petty bourgeois family and orphaned at an early age, he entered the Ecole des Beaux-Arts, Paris, in 1836. He first studied under Jean-Nicolas Huyot, an outstanding teacher of composition, and then under Louis Hippolyte Lebas. In 1847 André won the Grand Prix de Rome with his project for a Palace for the Chamber of Deputies. In Rome and in Athens he concentrated on the graphic work required for submission to the Académie; his last project while abroad was for a building for the Banque de France. In 1852 he constructed a military monument in the church of S Luigi dei Francesi, Rome.

On his return to Paris in 1852 André was appointed Deputy Inspector, and soon after Inspector, of work on the Musée d'Histoire Naturelle, under the supervision of Charles Rohault de Fleury. The following year he became Inspector of building work on the Bibliothèque Nationale under Henri Labrouste. That same year he was appointed diocesan architect in Ajaccio (Corsica); he designed a bishop's palace and a cathedral for Ajaccio, but neither was built. In 1855 he married the daughter of the architect P.-J. Garrez. In 1861 he took part in a competition for the new Paris Opéra, and his plan was praised for its simplicity and for the skill with which he adapted for a modern theatre the designs of Classical amphitheatres. In 1867 he succeeded Rohault de Fleury as chief architect of the Musée d'Histoire Naturelle. In this capacity André produced his major works. He first built the reptile gallery (1870–74), a light, well-ventilated building with carefully planned air and water supplies. It consists of glazed bays centrally divided by delicately designed small cast-iron columns. He then built the laboratories and completed the large greenhouses, but his main work was rebuilding the zoology galleries (1877–89), a severe and impressive long building linked by porticos to the greenhouses and to the mineralogy and botany galleries. The large central hall is a masterpiece of cast-iron architecture, with three tiers of galleries and a glass roof.

André was also an active and influential teacher. He took over Labrouste's atelier in 1855, and in 1867 he succeeded to the highly regarded atelier of Alexis Paccard (1813–67). André's teaching laid great stress on the architecture of Antiquity and the Renaissance, but he always taught his pupils to seek out the simplest option when designing any plan or ensemble. An academic and a rationalist, he had numerous pupils including Julien Azais Guadet, Victor Laloux and Henri-Adolphe-Auguste Deglane. Among his official positions, André was a member of the jury for the rebuilding of the Hôtel de Ville, Paris (1870s), and in 1880 was made Inspecteur Général des Bâtiments Civils.

BIBLIOGRAPHY

Thieme–Becker

J. Guadet: *J. André: Notice sur sa vie et ses oeuvres* (Paris, 1890)

J.-L. Pascal: *Notice sur L.-J. André* (Paris, 1891)

VINCENT BOUVET

André, Piètre (*fl* 1456–91). ?Italian painter, active in France. His work is known only through documents. He is first recorded at the court of Charles, Duke of Orléans, in Blois in January 1456, when he was paid for painting two chariots with the motto *Rien ne m'est plus* and for including gilt red and blue curtains, for the use of the Duke's wife, Mary of Cleves (1426–86). In 1457 André coloured and gilded sculptures of *SS Hadrian and Sebastian* by Jean Hervieu, which the Duchess gave to a chapel dedicated to St Catherine at Champbourdon (Loiret). In 1471 he provided at a cost of 110 livres a large altarpiece of the *Birth of the Virgin* installed in the chapel of the château of Montils-les-Tours. In 1472 André sold to the Duchess for 100 écus a gilt and polychrome altarpiece ('à ymages enlevez') of the *Passion*, which she intended for the chapel at Coucy-le-Château. According to Durrieu, André also supplied a panel of the *Virgin and Child with Adoring Seraphim* for the chapel of the château of Amboise. In 1483–4 the artist was paid for the gilding and painting of various jousting gear for the future king Louis XII and for painting large silk banners on which figured a pelican in piety and St Barbara. André also held the post of 'huissier de salle', organized receptions and ceremonies, including the funerals of Duke Charles in 1465 and of Jean de Dunois in 1469, and repeatedly travelled on confidential missions. On the death of Mary of Cleves, the artist probably resettled in Paris since an André (Pietre) is listed among painters and booksellers resident in the capital in 1491.

BIBLIOGRAPHY

L. de Laborde: *Les Ducs de Bourgogne*, II/iii (Paris, 1852)

A. Leroux de Lincy and L.-M. Tisserand: *Paris et ses historiens aux XIVe et XVe siècles* (Paris, 1867)

U. Chevalier: *Répertoire des sources historiques du moyen âge: Bio-Bibliographie* (Paris, 1877, 2/1905)

U. Robert: 'Piètre André, peintre des ducs d'Orléans (1456–1491)', *Nouv. Archvs A. Fr.*, v (1877), pp. 120–35
P. Champion: *Vie de Charles d'Orléans* (Paris, 1911)
P. Durrieu: 'La Peinture en France depuis l'avènement de Charles VII jusqu'à la fin des Valois (1422–1589)', *Histoire de l'art*, ed. A. Michel, IV/ii (Paris, 1925), pp. 701–71

PATRICK M. DE WINTER

André, Yves-Marie de l'Isle [Père André] (*b* Châteaulin, Finistère, 22 May 1675; *d* Caen, 26 Feb 1764). French priest, philosopher and writer. He entered the Society of Jesus in 1693, studied theology in Paris, then philosophy at the Collège de Clermont, and he was ordained a priest in 1706. He was a great scholar, who knew Greek, Latin and Hebrew; he devoted himself to philosophical research and poetry, at the same time teaching for the Society of Jesus in numerous institutions of learning in France. A staunch Cartesian, Père André inevitably incurred the hostility of the Society, which was wedded to Scholastic doctrines and Aristotelian philosophy. His innovative philosophical opinions and his suspect theology caused him to suffer various penalties, including imprisonment (1721). Under duress, he made a submission and in 1726 was appointed Royal Professor of Mathematics at Caen, where he remained for the rest of his life.

Père André is best known for his *Essai sur le beau* (1741), one of the earliest treatises on aesthetics published in French (preceded by Abbé Jean-Baptiste Dubos's *Réflexions critiques sur la poésie et la peinture*, 1719). André was the first to propose a complete system of the beautiful, based not on feeling but on reason, in which he distinguished three levels of beauty—absolute, natural and artificial—corresponding to Descartes's three categories of ideas—the innate, the adventitious and the invented. His work is divided into discourses on such topics as beauty in general and visible beauty; beauty in relation to morality; musical beauty; the Modes; decorum; the three Classical Graces; the graces of mind and body; the love of beauty; and disinterested love. Père André was also the author of a series of philosophical discourses assembled under the title *Traité de l'homme* (1766). His works were collected and published in 1766 by his friend Abbé Guillaume-Germain Guyot (1724–*c.* 1800).

WRITINGS

Essai sur le beau, où l'on examine en quoi consiste précisément le beau dans le physique, dans le moral, dans les ouvrages d'esprit et dans la musique (Paris, 1741)

BIBLIOGRAPHY

Rouxelin: 'Eloge du Père André', *Acad. B.-Lett. Caen* (1764)
G.-G. Guyot: 'Eloge historique du R.P. André', *Oeuvres du feu Père André, Professeur Royal de Mathématiques de la Société des Belles-Lettres de Caen, contenant un traité de l'homme selon les différentes merveilles qui le composent*, i (Paris, 1766), pp. 1–67
V. Cousin: *Oeuvres philosophiques du P. André de la Compagnie de Jésus: Avec une introduction sur sa vie et ses ouvrages* (Paris, 1843)
A. Charma and G. Mancel: *Le Père André: Documents inédits pour servir à l'histoire philosophique, religieuse et littéraire du XVIIIe siècle, contenant la correspondance de ce père avec Malebranche, Fontenelle*, 2 vols (Caen, 1844–56)
T. M. Mustoxidi: *Histoire de l'esthétique française* (Paris, 1920), pp. 34–9

ALEXANDRA SKLIAR-PIGUET

Andrea, Salvi d'. *See* SALVI D'ANDREA.

Andrea Cordeliaghi. *See* PREVITALI, ANDREA.

Andrea (di Guido) da Fiesole [de Fesulis] (*fl c.* 1393; *d* 1427). Italian sculptor and architect. The only work that can definitely be attributed to him is the tomb of *Bartolomeo da Saliceto* (1412; ex-S Domenico, Bologna; Bologna, Mus. Civ. Med.), which is dated and signed *opus Andreae de Fesulis.* Saliceto was a reader in law at Bologna University, and the tomb sculpture represents him among his pupils. Motifs and facial types are borrowed directly from the tombs in the Bolognese tradition of *Giovanni di Legnano* (1383) by Pierpaolo dalle Masegne and of *Carlo, Roberto and Riccardo Saliceto* (1403; both Bologna, Mus. Civ. Med.), a work indebted to Masegne, but despite this Andrea's Tuscan origins remain apparent. Gnudi was of the opinion that Andrea da Fiesole was in Florence until *c.* 1410. However, Andrea subsequently moved away from the Tuscan Renaissance tradition towards a northern Gothic style, following his contact with Venetian–Emilian sculpture. This can be seen in the tomb of *Bernardino Zambeccari* (1424; ex-S Martino, Bologna; Bologna, Mus. Civ. Med.) attributed to him (Gnudi). As for Andrea's work as an architect, it is known that he built the chapel of S Domenico in the church of that name in Bologna, of which only two tall, pointed-arched windows survive. In 1416 he was working on the construction of the Palazzo di Notai. He has in the past been confused with Andrea di Piero Ferrucci (da Fiesole) and also—in work done before 1398—with Guido da Firenze (*fl* 1393–1424).

BIBLIOGRAPHY

DBI; Thieme–Becker
S. Bettini: 'Un'opera sconosciuta di A. da Fiesole', *L'Arte*, xxxiv (1931), pp. 506–12
G. Gnudi: 'Intorno ad A. da Fiesole', *Crit. A.*, iii (1938), pp. 23–39

MARIA CRISTINA CHIUSA

Andrea da Firenze (i) [Andrea di Bonaiuto] (*fl* 1346; *d* ?Florence, after 16 May 1379). Italian painter. From January 1346 Andrea was registered in the Arte dei Medici e Speziali in Florence. The earliest paintings that can be attributed to him suggest that he must have formed a close association with the workshop of Andrea di Cione. The small portable triptych of the *Virgin and Child with Saints and Angels* (centre panel, Copenhagen, Stat. Mus. Kst; side panels of the *Nativity* and the *Crucifixion*, Houston, TX, Mus. F.A.) shows the influence of Maso di Banco and of the painter of the Strozzi Chapel frescoes in the Chiostrino dei Morti, S Maria Novella, Florence (Boskovits).

Andrea's fame rests chiefly on the frescoes in the chapter house of S Maria Novella, also known as the Spanish Chapel. The contract of 30 December 1365 specified that the painter and his wife were to live in a house opposite the church owned by the friars, and the rent was to be paid by his carrying out work over the subsequent two years. The fresco decoration was paid for by a bequest on 2 August 1355 from a Florentine merchant, Buonamico di Lapo Guidalotti, a close friend of the prior Fra Jacopo Passavanti (*c.* 1300–57), the Dominican writer and preacher. Fra Jacopo is usually credited with being chiefly responsible for the iconographic programme of the frescoes, but the commission was actually assigned eight years after the death of Passavanti by a later prior, Zanobi Guasconi. The programme was probably worked out in the theological school attached to the convent. The central theme is the glorification of the Dominican Order. On the entrance wall are scenes from the *Life of St Peter Martyr*, with the *Road to Calvary*, the *Crucifixion* and the *Descent into Limbo* opposite. The main scenes are on the side walls, on the left the *Triumph of St Thomas Aquinas* (see fig.) and on the right the *Church Militant* and the *Church Triumphant*. Scenes of the *Pentecost*, the *Navicella*, the *Resurrection* and the *Ascension* decorate the vault. Discussion has concentrated on the iconography of the cycle (Romano), while the artistic qualities of the frescoes have been neglected. This is probably due to the fact that Andrea is usually ranked as a secondary figure among Florentine painters of the second half of the 14th century. Nevertheless, he showed considerable skill in organizing large compositions on a wall that is not divided by the usual decorative bands, and he displayed imagination in individualizing the numerous characters depicted in the scenes. In the chapel the artist must have had collaborators, including probably Antonio Veneziano, since the vault scenes of the *Navicella* and the *Pentecost* contain figures in the latter's style. According to Boskovits, Andrea, having escaped from Andrea di Cione's influence, progressively moved towards a greater refinement of design and colour, reaching, in the small panels of *St Agnes* and *St Domitilla* (both *c.* 1370; Florence, Accad.), a formal elegance that foreshadows the work of both Lorenzo Monaco and the Master of the Straus Madonna.

Between 13 July 1366 and 31 May 1367 Andrea was among the artists who advised on the construction of Florence Cathedral. Probably as a result of the fame of the Spanish Chapel frescoes, he was commissioned to paint the *Legend of St Raniero*, patron saint of Pisa, in the Camposanto there, for which he received a payment on 13 October 1377. He worked on the Camposanto frescoes until his death; thereafter the frescoes were completed by Barnaba da Modena. The three scenes executed by Andrea, the *Temptations and Miracles of St Raniero*, the *Conversion of St Raniero* and *St Raniero in the Holy Land* and the related *sinopie* show that the artist sought to emulate the early 14th-century concentration on narrative, perhaps as a result of studying frescoes in the Camposanto by some of Giotto's greatest followers, notably Stefano Fiorentino's *Assumption* and Taddeo Gaddi's *Story of Job* (Caleca). On 2 November 1377 Andrea made his will but did not die until shortly after 16 May 1379, when his name last appears in the tax register for the inhabitants of the S Maria Novella quarter.

Although Andrea da Firenze followed traditional models, he was innovative in the way he softened details and contours with soft, blended shadows and emphasized the two-dimensional quality of the picture surface with painted and punched decorative effects. The formal elegance of works such as *St Agnes* and *St Domitilla* and the inventiveness of his frescoes in the Spanish Chapel introduce some aspects of the emerging Late Gothic style.

Andrea da Firenze (i): *Triumph of St Thomas Aquinas* (*c.* 1365), fresco, S Maria Novella, Florence

BIBLIOGRAPHY
Colnaghi; *DBI*; Meissner: 'Andrea di Bonaiuto'; Thieme–Becker
I. Taurisano: 'Il capitolo di Santa Maria Novella in Firenze: Memorie domenicane', *Il Rosario*, iii (1916), pp. 217–30
P. Toesca: *Il trecento* (Turin, 1951), pp. 639–42
M. Boskovits: *Pittura fiorentina alla vigilia del rinascimento* (Florence, 1975), pp. 31–3, 276–9, pls 26–8, figs 38–47
R. Fremantle: *Florentine Gothic Painters* (London, 1975), pp. 203–12
S. Romano: 'Due affreschi del Cappellone degli Spagnoli: Problemi iconologici', *Stor. A.*, xxviii (1976), pp. 181–213
A. Caleca: 'Le *Storie di S Ranieri* di Andrea di Bonaiuto', *Pisa: Museo delle Sinopie del Camposanto Monumentale* (Pisa, 1979), pp. 76–9
R. Offner and K. Steinweg: *Corpus*, IV/vi (1979) [good plates]

ANGELO TARTUFERI

Andrea da Firenze (ii) (*b* Florence, 1388; *d* Florence *c.* 1455). Italian sculptor. He is probably identical with Andrea di Onofrio, also called Andrea Nofri. In Neapolitan documents he is also called Andrea Ciccione. In 1419 he was documented as executing a coat of arms over the door of the lodgings of Pope Martin V in the cloister of S Maria Novella, Florence. In 1420 he sculpted statues and ornamentation for the chapel of St Lawrence in S Lucia de' Bardi, Florence. Five years later he assessed one of Donatello's statues for the Campanile (probably the *Jeremiah*). Later he worked in the cloister of S Francesco at Prato and in November 1428 in Florence as a 'lastrajuolo' (stonecutter) for Michelozzo and Donatello.

By 1428 Andrea was in Naples working on the funeral monument of *King Ladislas of Durazzo* (*reg* 1386–1414) in S Giovanni a Carbonara, commissioned by Queen Joanna II, which had probably been started after 1427. This is documented by an inscription formerly on the tomb of *Simone Vigilante, Bishop of Senigallia* (*d* 1428), originally in S Francesco alle Scale, Ancona, and dismembered in the 18th century, which read: 'the work of Andrea of Florence who also executed the tomb of King Ladislas'. There is no critical accord on whether Andrea worked on the tomb or for which part he might have been responsible.

The tomb of *Ruggero Sanseverino* (*d* 1433) in the chapel of St Monica of the oratory of SS Filippo e Giacomo attached to S Giovanni a Carbonara is signed by Andrea. The tomb is a compromise of Late Gothic and early Renaissance forms, some iconographic motifs deriving from the Bertini brothers' tomb of *Robert of Anjou* (Naples, S Chiara), others from Donatello's and Michelozzo's *Brancacci* monument (Naples, S Angelo a Nilo). Slightly earlier, Andrea had also carved the portal of the chapel of St Monica. The tomb of *Simone Vigilante* must date from after Andrea's sojourn in Naples. The tomb of *Ser Gianni Caracciolo* (Naples, S Giovanni a Carbonara) attributed to Andrea Ciccione by de Dominici and others, however, does not seem to be his work, both on stylistic grounds and because it was not started before 1441, by which time Andrea had probably returned to Florence.

In 1441–2 Andrea is documented working on the gallery of the cupola of Florence Cathedral. In 1453 Andrea Nofri was recorded in Florence as a 'lastrajuolo'; by 1459 he had been dead for some years. His style is known only from the works in Naples; it can be interpreted as a tentative up-dating of a Late Gothic style derived from Michelozzo's early work. However, the identification of Andrea da Firenze, documented in Naples in the 1420s and 1430s, with Andrea di Onofrio is not universally accepted: it has been variously suggested that the sculptor working in Naples was Andrea Ferrucci (Filangieri), Andrea Guardi (Abbate), a follower of Nanni di Banco (Venturi) or a follower of Jacopo della Quercia and brother of a Marco da Firenze, both brothers having been active in Padua in 1424 (Causa).

BIBLIOGRAPHY
DBI: 'Andrea di Onofrio'; Thieme–Becker
B. de Dominici: *Vite* (1742–5), i, pp. 187–200
M. Buglioni: *Istoria del Convento di San Francesco d'Ancona* (Ancona, 1795)
G. A. Galante: *Guida sacra della città di Napoli* (Naples, 1872); ed. N. Spinosa (Naples, 1985), pp. 29–32, 40–43
N. F. Faraglia: 'Il sepolcro di re Ladislao', *Archv Stor. Prov. Napolet.*, vii (1882), 169–71
C. von Fabriczy: 'Zur Biographie des Bildhauers Andrea de Florentia', *Repert. Kstwiss.*, ii (1888), p. 96
A. Venturi: *Storia* (1901–40), vi, p. 839
A. Munoz: 'Studi sulla scultura napoletana del rinascimento', *Boll. A.*, iii (1909), pp. 55–73, 83–101
R. Filangieri: 'La scultura a Napoli nei primi albori del rinascimento', *Napoli Nob.*, i (1920), p. 89
A. Filangieri di Candida: *La chiesa e il monastero di San Giovanni a Carbonara* (Naples, 1924)
C. Gnudi: 'Intorno ad Andrea da Fiesole', *Crit. A.*, iii (1938), pp. 23–39
R. Causa: 'Contributi alla conoscenza della scultura del '400 a Napoli', *Sculture lignee della Campania* (exh. cat., Naples, Pal. Reale, 1950), pp. 105–9
F. Abbate: 'Problemi della scultura napoletana del '400', *Storia di Napoli* (Naples, 1967–78), iv, pp. 449–94 (451–6)
G. L. Hersey: *The Aragonese Arch at Naples, 1443–1475* (New Haven and London, 1973), pp. 18, 30
R. Pane: *Il rinascimento nell'Italia meridionale* (Milan, 1975–7), i, pp. 107–11

GIOVANNA CASSESE

Andrea dal Monte Sansovino. *See* SANSOVINO, ANDREA.

Andrea da Murano (*fl* 1463; *d* 25 Feb 1512). Italian painter. He is first recorded working as a gilder at S Zaccaria, Venice, in 1463–5. He was one of a number of artists from the island of Murano. Among these he is closest to Bartolomeo Vivarini, whose pupil he may have been. The two collaborated in 1468 on a narrative canvas (destr.) for the Scuola di S Marco, Venice, which probably depicted scenes from the *Life of Abraham*. The rather harsh sculptural quality of his forms owes much to the influence of Mantegna and Donatello in Padua, and his work has often been associated (and sometimes confused) with that of Andrea del Castagno. He did not, however, ignore the more recent developments of Giovanni Bellini. His triptych depicting *SS Vincent Ferrer, Roch, Sebastian and Peter Martyr*, with a lunette of the *Madonna of Mercy and Four Saints* (Venice, Accad.), probably painted in the late 1470s, shows a real concern with light and colour. By the mid-1480s Andrea had settled in Castelfranco on the mainland, chiefly painting altarpieces in the (by then well established) Venetian *sacra conversazione* form. The altarpiece (1484–1502) in the parish church at Trebaseleghe, nr Padua, is a variation on the form, with Christ embracing the plague saints Sebastian and Roch above and other saints and musicians below, all showing the high degree of expression characteristic of his works. It is one of his finest paintings and also perhaps the most expensive Venetian altarpiece of its day. The altarpiece depicting the *Virgin Enthroned with SS Peter, Nicholas of Bari, John the Baptist and Paul* (1502; Mussolente, Santuario della Madonna dell' Acqua) is typical of Andrea's work and shows both the strengths and limitations of his art: firm draughtsmanship and expressive qualities combined with a rather conservative composition and somewhat ungainly figures.

BIBLIOGRAPHY

F. Zeri: 'A Note on Andrea da Murano', *A. Q.* [Detroit], xxxi (1968), pp. 76–82

A. De Nicolò Salmazo: 'Per una ricostruzione della prima attività di Andrea da Murano', *Saggi & Mem. Stor. A.*, x (1976), pp. 7–29

——: 'Andrea Murano', *La pittura in Italia: Il quattrocento*, ed. F. Zeri (Milan, 1987), pp. 555–6

JOHN G. BERNASCONI

Andrea d'Ancona. *See* LILLI, ANDREA.

Andrea da Pontedera. *See* PISANO (ii), (1).

Andrea de' Bartoli (*fl c.* 1349–69). Italian painter and illuminator. In 1359 he was paid for buying pigments by the Collegio di Spagna, Bologna, which was founded by Cardinal Egidio Albornoz (*reg* 1350–67), papal legate in charge of the Papal States. In the same accounts Andrea's brother Bartolomeo, the leading Bolognese scribe of the later 14th century, was paid for writing manuscripts. In 1365, on the instructions of Albornoz's successor, Cardinal Androine de Rocha, Andrea painted for two months in the palace of Galeazzo Visconti at Pavia, assisted by Jacopino Bavosi (*fl* 1360–83) and his son Pietro Bavosi (*fl* 1365–83). In 1368 'Andreas pictor de Bononia' was paid the large sum of 450 florins for painting the surviving frescoes in Albornoz's chapel dedicated to St Catherine of Alexandria in the Lower Church of S Francesco, Assisi, and 10 florins for painting Albornoz's tomb in the chapel (*see* ASSISI, §II, 2(vii)). It is reasonable to attribute the frescoes to Albornoz's 'court artist', Andrea de' Bartoli rather than to ANDREA DA BOLOGNA, the other recorded mid-14th-century Bolognese artist called Andrea. These paintings, and the frescoes in the chapel of S Lorenzo also attributed to him, have elaborate but rather confused architectural settings, landscapes with fine details of woods, hedgerows, birds and hunting animals and illusionistic architectural borders. The figures, though often clumsy, show a great range of character and type and unusual attention to realistic detail. The frescoes provide a stylistic basis for attributing to Andrea illuminations and drawings in two manuscripts written by his brother Bartolomeo.

A Book of Hours written by Bartolomeo in 1349 (Kremsmünster, Stiftskirche, Schatzkammer, MS. 4) was illuminated throughout by Niccolò di Giacomo da Bologna except for the border of fol. 11*r*, signed ANDREAS ME PINSIT. The gold-lettered signature and kufic ornament on a red frame is also found in the Missal of Cardinal Bertrand de Deux (Rome, Vatican, Bib. Apostolica, MS. Cap. 63B), on which he may have worked. The choir of blue angels and various facial types in the border of fol. 11*r* recur in the Assisi frescoes. The luminous modelling of the figures, the cool peach flesh-tones and the painterly treatment of the rocky landscape, sheep and birds are quite distinct from the work of the ILLUSTRATORE MASTER (*see* MASTERS, ANONYMOUS, AND MONOGRAMMISTS, §I), with whom Cassee has identified Andrea. A poem on the virtues, arts and sciences, composed and written by Bartolomeo for Bruzio Visconti (Chantilly, Mus. Condé, MS. 1426), has drawings by Andrea coloured with washes, showing tall figures with short torsos and very angular draperies within emphatically closed contours.

Andrea's politically powerful patrons, his association with Bartolomeo and with illumination as well as painting, his observation and varied if inelegant technique make him one of the major artists of the 14th century.

BIBLIOGRAPHY

DBI

F. Filippini: 'Andrea da Bologna, miniatore e pittore del secolo XIV', *Boll. A.*, v (1911), pp. 50–62

G. Schmidt: '"*Andreas me pinsit*": Frühe Miniaturen von Niccolò di Giacomo und Andrea de' Bartoli in dem Bologneser Offiziolo der Stiftsbibliothek Kremsmünster', *Wien. Jb. Kstgesch.*, xxvi (1973), pp. 57–73

F. Arcangeli: *Pittura bolognese del '300* (Bologna, 1978), pp. 164–77 [notes by M. Ferretti]

C. Volpe: 'Andrea de' Bartoli e la svolta antigotica nella seconda metà del trecento', *Paragone*, xxxii/373 (1981), pp. 3–16

F. Avril, ed.: *Dix siècles d'enluminure italienne* (Paris, 1984), pp. 85–6

R. Gibbs: *Tomaso da Modena: Painting in Emilia and the March of Treviso 1340–1380* (Cambridge, 1988)

D. Benati: *Jacopo Avanzi* (Bologna, 1992), pp. 56–63

ROBERT GIBBS

Andrea dei Bruni [Andrea da Bologna] (*fl c.* 1355–77). Italian painter. Two mid-14th-century Bolognese artists called Andrea are recorded: Andrea dei Bruni, living in Ancona in 1377, and ANDREA DE' BARTOLI. Arcangeli suggested that Bruni was the author of a group of works including the polyptych (Fermo, Pin. Com.), signed and dated *1369 de Bononia natus Andreas* and the *Madonna of Humility* (Corridonia, S Agostino), signed and dated 1372. Longhi had already distinguished these from the work of Andrea de' Bartoli. Bruni was a modest follower of Vitale da Bologna; his figures are naive in expression and usually stilted in drawing, although, disconcertingly, some of those in the Fermo polyptych reflect the sophisticated style of Andrea de' Bartoli. The architectural settings show an interest in space perhaps inspired by the frescoes in the church of S Francesco in nearby Assisi. Some of the frescoes in the nave of the abbey church, Pomposa, may be early works (*c.* 1355). Modest frescoes in S Maria della Rocca, Offida, and a more sophisticated *Coronation of the Virgin and Musician Angels* recently removed from S Niccolò, Osimo, suggest that Andrea's pleasant version of Vitale's expressive style found widespread favour in the Marches, and he may have been in the service of Giovanni da Oleggio, who exchanged the Signoria of Bologna for the position of papal vicar of Fermo in 1360.

BIBLIOGRAPHY

B. Berenson: *Central and North Italian Schools* (London, 1968), i, p. 9; ii, pls 252–6

R. Longhi: *La pittura del trecento nell'Italia settentrionale* (Bologna, 1934–5); repr. in R. Longhi: 'Lavori in Valpadana', *Opera completa*, vi (Florence, 1973), pp. 52–6

F. Arcangeli: *Pittura bolognese del '300* (Bologna, 1978), pp. 150–63 [notes by M. Ferretti]

P. Zampetti: *Pittura nelle Marche*, i (Florence, 1990)

ROBERT GIBBS

Andrea del Castagno. *See* CASTAGNO, ANDREA DEL.

Andrea di Ardito. *See* ARDITI, ANDREA.

Andrea di Bartolo. *See* CINI, (2).

Andrea di Cione. *See* CIONE, (1).

Andrea di Cosimo. *See* FELTRINI, ANDREA.

Andrea di Giusto (Manzini) (*b* Florence, *c.* 1400; *d* Florence, 2 Sept 1450). Italian painter. He was an eclectic minor Florentine master who was influenced by, and at different times imitated, the styles of Masaccio, Masolino, Lorenzo Monaco, Fra Angelico and Domenico Veneziano. In 1426 he was an assistant of Masaccio in the execution of the altarpiece for the Carmine church in Pisa (London N.G.; Naples, Capodimonte; Berlin, Gemäldegal.; Malibu, CA, Getty Mus.; Pisa, Mus. N. & Civ. S Matteo) and painted its predella panels of the *Legend of St Julian* and the *Charity of St Nicholas* (Berlin, Gemäldegal.). His name appears in the tax registers of the Florentine Archivio delle Decime from 1427 to 1447 and in the protocols of the Arte della Calimala in 1436, the same year in which he received 60 florins for an altarpiece (destr.) for S Lucia dei Magnoli. In 1437 he signed and dated the *Assumption of the Virgin with SS Catherine and Francis* (Florence, Accad.). His other dated works are a *Virgin and Child with Four Saints* (1435; Prato, Mus. Com.), which is a copy of Lorenzo Monaco's Monte Oliveto Altarpiece of 1410 (Florence, Pal. Davanzati); a *Virgin and Child* (1435; Florence, Villa I Tatti), a rustic interpretation of a *Virgin and Child* by Fra Angelico (Turin, Gal. Sabauda); and an altarpiece with the *Adoration of the Magi with Four Saints* (1436; Figline, S Andrea a Ripalta) commissioned by Bernardo Serristori. Towards the end of his life, Andrea painted three frescoes, the *Martyrdom of St Stephen*, the *Burial of St Stephen* and the *Marriage of the Virgin* (probably completed 1447) in the Cappella dell'Assunta in Prato Cathedral. He was the father of GIUSTO D'ANDREA.

BIBLIOGRAPHY

Thieme–Becker

G. Vasari: *Vite* (1550, rev. 2/1568); ed. G. Milanesi (1878–85), iii, pp. 54–5

A. Sanesi: 'Gli affreschi della Cappella Boccherini nel Duomo di Prato', *Prato*, i/1 (1960), pp. 45–50

G. Marchini: *Due secoli di pittura murale a Prato* (Prato, 1969), pp. 51–133

R. Fremantle: *Florentine Gothic Painters* (London, 1975), pp. 513–22 [with full bibliog.]

J. Beck: *Masaccio: The Documents* (Locust Valley, 1978), p. 22

H. Wohl: *The Paintings of Domenico Veneziano* (New York, 1980), passim

Andrea di Giusto: Trittico di San Valdarno a Mormiano (exh. cat., Incisa Valdarno, Sala Consiliare and S Allessandro, 1984)

HELLMUT WOHL

Andrea di Jacopo d'Ognabene (*fl* 1286–*c.* 1317). Italian goldsmith. His earliest documented work dates from 1286, when together with his brother Tallino he made a chalice, identified by Gai (1988) with the chalice of S Atto (Pistoia, Mus. Dioc.), for the Opera di S Jacopo; he was paid 48 lire for this work on 29 April 1286. The following year the Opera di S Jacopo commissioned a silver retable, decorated with high reliefs of the *Virgin and Child Enthroned* and the *Twelve Apostles*, for the altar of S Jacopo in Pistoia Cathedral. This retable was restored in March–April 1293 and again in 1314. In 1316 it was enlarged, and the added silver antependium was signed ANDREA DI JACOPO D'OGNABENE, although it is unclear whether Andrea was the author of both the antependium and the earlier retable. Most scholars consider the two parts to be stylistically distinct and thus by two different artists. Ragghianti, however, gave the authorship of both parts to another goldsmith, whom he identified as the Master of Convalle, named after the processional cross from SS Simone e Guida at Convalle, near Lucca (see below). He believed that Andrea di Jacopo merely assembled the work executed by others. Gai (1984), on the other hand, proposed that Andrea was responsible for both the retable of 1287 and the antependium of 1316, also suggesting that Andrea's work on the altar included the fifteen large circular and four quadrilobed enamels decorating the antependium, and the restoration in 1314 of two *Apostles* on the retable. A number of other works have been attributed to Andrea, although none is unanimously accepted as autograph. Five silver-gilt and enamel plaques from the reliquary of the Holy Girdle (*c.* 1290s; Pisa, Mus. N. S Matteo) have been associated with him. The cross of Convalle (Lucca, Mus. & Pin. N.), datable *c.* 1317, is usually considered a product of Andrea's artistic maturity. The cross of Lucchio (Lucca, S Pietro) is also attributed to him, as is the cross of S Maria Albiano (Lucca, S Maria). Gai (1988) also identified Andrea as the author of the chalice of the Umiliati (Pistoia, Mus. Civ.).

BIBLIOGRAPHY

C. L. Ragghianti: 'Aenigmata pistoriensia, 2', *Crit. A.*, xxviii/8 (March 1955), pp. 102–29

A. R. Calderoni Masetti: 'L'altare di S Jacopo a Pistoia e altre opere di Andrea di Jacopo d'Ognabene', *Atti del convegno: Le Rayonnement de l'art siennois du Trecento en Europe: Avignon, 1983*

L. Gai: *L'altare argenteo di San Jacopo nel Duomo di Pistoia* (Turin, 1984)

A. R. Calderoni Masetti: 'Le croci di Retignano, Farnocchia, La Cune, S Quirico di Valleriana, S Maria Albiano', *Oreficerie e smalti traslucidi nell'antica diocesi di Lucca* (Florence, 1986)

L. Gai: 'Un "inedito" di Andrea di Jacopo d'Ognabene orefice pistoiese', *An. Scu. Norm. Sup. U. Pisa*, n. s. 2, xviii/1 (1988), pp. 67–100

Andrea di Nerio (*fl c.* 1350s; *d* before 1387). Italian painter. Long known only through meagre documents, this founder of the 14th-century Aretine school of painting was identified (1974–5 exh. cat.) through the discovery of his signature on an *Annunciation* panel (Arezzo, Mus. Dioc.) probably painted for the Compagnia di SS Annunziata, Arezzo, in the 1350s. His authorship can now be established for a group of stylistically similar works formerly attributed to several hands, including the Master of the Vescovado and Spinello Aretino, who was doubtless Andrea's pupil (and whose sculptor brother, Niccolò, married Andrea's daughter, Rebecca). Andrea's most distinguished works, combining the influence of Pietro Lorenzetti, Maso di Banco and Buffalmacco, include the poetic pair of predella panels with scenes from the *Life of St John the Baptist* (both Berne, Kstmus.) and the narrative frescoes in S Bartolomeo, Arezzo. His compositional clarity, incisive figure style and refined technique place him in the first rank of 14th-century Tuscan painters.

BIBLIOGRAPHY

P. P. Donati: 'Per la pittura aretina del trecento', *Paragone*, xix/215 (1968), pp. 22–39; xix/221 (1968), pp. 10–21; xxi/247 (1970), pp. 3–11

Arte nell'Aretino: Recuperi e restauri dal 1968 al 1974 (exh. cat., ed. L. G. Boccia and others; Arezzo, S Francesco, 1974–5), pp. 53–8

M. Boskovits: *The Martello Collection: Paintings, Drawings and Miniatures from the XIVth to the XVIIIth Centuries* (Florence, 1985), pp. 17–22

S. Pieri: 'Due famiglie di artisti aretini', *Boll. Inf. Brigata Aretina Amici Mnmt.*, 49 (Dec 1989), pp. 22–6

'Manifestatori delle cose miracolose': Arte italiana del '300 e '400 da collezioni in Svizzera e nel Liechtenstein (exh. cat. by G. Freuler, Lugano, Col. Thyssen-Bornemisza, 1991), pp. 189–91

FRANK DABELL

Andrea di Niccolò (di Giacomo) (*b c.* 1445; *d c.* 1525). Italian painter. Most scholars since Berenson have considered this minor Sienese painter to have been a pupil of il Vecchietta. The influence of such Sienese painters as Neroccio de' Landi, il Vecchietta and Matteo di Giovanni can be seen in his earliest signed and dated painting, the *Virgin and Child with Saints* (1498; Casole d'Elsa, Collegiata). In the early years of the 16th century Andrea's work began to show the influence of the foreign artists then working in Siena, including Pinturicchio, Perugino, Sodoma and Signorelli. This is especially evident in the landscape of the *Crucifixion with Saints* (1502; Siena, Pin. N.). Other works include a signed *Virgin and Child with Saints* (1500; Siena, Pin. N.); a signed *Virgin and Child with Angels and Saints* (1504; Cincinnati, OH, A. Mus.); and another *Virgin and Child with Saints* (1510; Siena, S Mustiola delle Rose).

BIBLIOGRAPHY

DBI; Thieme–Becker

E. Romagnoli: *Biografia cronologica de' bell'artisti senesi del secolo XII a tutto il XVIII*, v (MS., *c.* 1835; Siena, Bib. Com. Intronati); facs. edn (Florence, 1976)

G. L. McCann: 'A Sienese Altarpiece in the Museum Collection', *Cincinnati A. Mus. Bull.*, ix (1934), pp. 22–9

L. Vertova: 'On Pacchiarotto's Dismembered *Assumption* and a Cut-up Altarpiece by Andrea di Niccolò', *Gaz. B.-A.*, 6th ser., lxix (1967), pp. 154–68

B. Berenson: *Central and North Italian Schools* (1968), i, p. 10

E. Carli: *Sienese Painting* (New York, 1983)

L. Vertova: 'Cicli senesi di virtù: Inediti di Andrea di Niccolò e del Maestro di Griselda', *Scritti. . .di storia dell'arte in onore di Federico Zeri*, i (Milan, 1984), pp. 200–12

B. Cole: *Sienese Painting in the Age of the Renaissance* (Bloomington, 1985)

D. Vatne: *Andrea di Niccolò, c. 1445–c. 1525: Sienese Painter of the Renaissance* (diss., Bloomington, IN U., 1989)

LINDA CARON

Andrea di Niccolò da Durazzo. *See* ALESSI, ANDREA.

Andreani, Andrea (*b* Mantua, 1558–9; *d* 1629). Italian woodcutter and printer. He was the only printmaker to produce a significant number of chiaroscuro woodcuts in Italy in the second half of the 16th century; he also reprinted chiaroscuro woodblocks originally cut 60 or 70 years earlier. He made at least 35 prints in both black and white and colour (many multiple-sheet), using a sophisticated style of cutting characterized by thin, closed contours. Based in Florence in 1584–5 and from 1586 in Siena, by 1590 he was also finding work in his native Mantua, where he is documented as establishing a workshop. He reproduced the designs of artists in diverse media with great fidelity: for example he made several prints (1586–90) after Domenico Beccafumi's intarsia pavement designs in Siena Cathedral, three prints (1584) from different angles of Giambologna's marble sculpture of the *Rape of the Sabines* (Florence, Loggia Lanzi), as well as of the bas-relief on the base of the same group and of Giambologna's relief of *Christ before Pilate* (Florence, SS Annunziata), both in 1585; in the same year he also made prints after paintings and wash drawings by Jacopo Ligozzi and in 1591–2 others after Alessandro Casolani (1552–1608). His admiration for the woodcuts of Titian's workshop is evident in his copies of the *Triumph of Faith* (his only work published in Rome, ?*c.* 1600) and *Pharaoh Crossing the Red Sea* (Siena, 1589) and in his practice of making very large prints composed of many joined sheets. Usually he used four overlapping chiaroscuro blocks per sheet; his most ambitious projects could call for 40 to 52 blocks each, as in the *Sacrifice of Isaac* (1586) after Beccafumi's pavement, the *Deposition* (1595) after Casolani's painting in S Quirico, Siena, and the *Triumph of Caesar* (1598–9) based on drawings by Bernardo Malpizzi after Andrea Mantegna's cartoons (London, Hampton Court, Royal Col.). The fact that Andreani dedicated prints to so many different people, as the inscriptions on his prints show, suggests he had difficulty in finding patrons, though he briefly enjoyed assistance from the Gonzagas. This scarcity of patronage doubtless led to his reprinting, and, where wear or damage required, recutting earlier blocks, probably acquired from Niccolò Vicentino. In the period 1608 to 1610 the quality of Andreani's printing seriously declined.

BIBLIOGRAPHY

DBI; Thieme–Becker

A. von Bartsch: *Le Peintre-graveur* (1803–21), xii

C. d'Arco: *Di cinque valenti incisori mantovani* (Mantua, 1840)

H. T. Goldfarb: 'Chiaroscuro Woodcut Techniques and Andrea Andreani', *Bull. Cleveland Mus. A.*, (1981)

C. Karpinski: *Italian Chiaroscuro Woodcuts*, 48 [XII] of *The Illustrated Bartsch*, ed. W. Strauss (New York, 1983)

JAN JOHNSON

Andreasi, Ippolito (*b* Mantua, 1548; *d* Mantua, 4–5 June 1608). Italian painter and draughtsman. A leading exponent of late Mannerism at the Gonzaga court in Mantua, he probably trained there with an associate of Giulio Romano. About 80 drawings of the Palazzo del Te (*see* GIULIO ROMANO, fig. 3) and the Palazzo Ducale, Mantua (Düsseldorf, Kstmus.), were commissioned from Andreasi *c.* 1568 by Jacopo Strada. In 1574 Andreasi collaborated on the design of a series of tapestries of the *Acts of Moses* for Milan Cathedral. He is documented in 1579–80 collaborating on decorations in the Palazzo Ducale for Guglielmo Gonzaga, 3rd Duke of Mantua, where he painted the ceiling of the Duke's *studiolo*, the vault of the Sala Nuova and, *c.* 1581, the ceiling frescoes in the Sala del Falconi (preparatory study; London, BM). Documents indicate that in 1586–7 Andreasi collaborated on the decoration of the castle of Goito (destr.). As early as August 1590 he was Prefetto delle Fabbriche (Head of Works) for the Gonzaga family. He also executed book illustrations (e.g. for the second canto of Torquato Tasso's *Gerusalemme liberata*, 1581) and stage sets (e.g. for Battista Guarini's *Pastor Fido*, 1592). In 1592 Andreasi restored the theatre of Giovanni Battista Bertani in the Palazzo Ducale, after a fire. Also in this period he painted a series of *Twelve Famous Dramatists* in gouache. With Teodoro Ghisi, he designed a tapestry series, presented by Bishop Francesco Gonzaga to Mantua Cathedral in 1599. He collaborated with Ghisi on frescoes (*Pentecost*, the *Death of the Virgin* and the *Assumption of the Virgin*) in the Cappella dell'Incoronata in Mantua Cathedral, as well as those in the transept, depicting the *Feast Days of the Mantuan Church*. The altarpiece of the *Annunciation* in S Maria Assunta del Castello, Viadana, is signed and dated

1602. The date 1605 inscribed on one of the arches in the transept of Mantua Cathedral refers to Andreasi's decoration of the cupola, pendentives and barrel-vaults. Andreasi was murdered by his wife's lover.

BIBLIOGRAPHY

DBI; Thieme–Becker

C. Tellini Perina: 'Ippolito Andreasi', *Mantova: Le arti*, iii (Mantua, 1965), pp. 367–77, 389–93, pls 230–63

R. Harprath: 'Ippolito Andreasi as a Draughtsman', *Master Drgs*, xxii (1984), pp. 3–28, pls 1–26

G. Briganti, ed.: *La pittura in Italia: Il cinquecento* (Milan, 1987, rev. 1988), ii, p. 625

RICHARD HARPRATH

Andreas Martini. *See under* ÖRJAN THE PAINTER.

Andrea (di) Vanni (d'Andrea Salvani) (*b c.* 1330; *d* 2 Oct 1413). Italian painter and illuminator. He was one of the foremost members of the political faction that ruled Siena from 1368 to 1385; his career of painting fresco cycles and altarpieces for the city's cathedral and churches is also well documented. His art, however, was less noteworthy. Although he travelled to Avignon and Naples on behalf of the Sienese Comune, his style remained true to the ever popular though increasingly unimaginatively interpreted idioms he had assimilated as a young man from Simone Martini's artistic heirs. His small-scale early works of the *Virgin and Child* (Oxford, Ashmolean; Berlin, Gemäldegal.), which draw on the figure types of the Master of the Palazzo Venezia Madonna (*fl c.* 1350), display soft contours, fairly light skin tones and light brushwork. The Child in particular possesses a degree of appealing spontaneity and a sense of arrested movement that is totally lacking in the later series of large panels, such as those to be found in the churches of S Donato, S Francesco and S Stefano, all in Siena.

Andrea's most successful surviving work is the signed portable triptych (ex-Naples; Washington, DC, Corcoran Gal. A.) of the *Crucifixion*, the *Agony in the Garden* and the *Descent into Limbo*. The panels are packed with a wealth of narrative detail within a carefully orchestrated composition; they are technically accomplished, and great care was taken to achieve a variety of colouristic and textural effects. In the *Crucifixion* the crucified figures are lithe and compact, their tortured limbs contrasted against the gold ground. The other figures are set against a grey rocky landscape, the luminous colours of some of their garments dramatically emphasizing gesture and movement. Although usually dated to the mid-1380s, this triptych may well be a product of Andrea's early maturity.

Andrea belonged to the Confraternità di S Maria Vergine, the principal religious confraternity of Siena, and he painted a fresco in their oratory (now the hospital of S Maria della Scala) of the Sibyl's revelation of the Virgin and Child to the emperor Augustus, an unusual subject. A small nucleus of the confraternity's members, including Andrea, were devotees of St Catherine, and her portrait in the church of S Domenico is usually attributed to him. The sole surviving example of Andrea's work as an illuminator is perhaps to be seen in a copy of St Bridget's *Revelations* (Siena, Bib. Com. Intronati, MS.IV 25/26; attributed by Dini to Andrea di Bartolo Cini), commissioned in 1399 for the confraternity; the saint is shown divinely inspired, in the act of writing. Its realism depends on the accuracy of carefully observed and rendered details, the way the saint holds knife and pen, the texture of the wooden furniture and even the ink spots on the desk.

BIBLIOGRAPHY

Meissner

A. Cornice: 'Andrea Vanni', *Il gotico a Siena: Miniature, pitture, oreficerie, oggetti d'arte* (exh. cat., Siena, Pal. Pub., 1982), pp. 286–9 [see also entry by G. C. Dini, pp. 315–26]

VALERIE WAINWRIGHT

Andree, A(dolphus) W(illiam) (*b* Jaffna, Ceylon [now Sri Lanka], 26 Sept 1869; *d* Colombo, 2 July 1910). Ceylonese photographer. His family had practised photography for three generations. His grandfather, Adolphus Wilhelmus Andree (*b* 1799), was one of the early pioneers of daguerreotypy in Ceylon, and his father, Adolphus William Andree, had a flourishing photographic business between the 1860s and 1880s with studios in the capital Colombo and the provincial towns of Jaffna, Galle and Matara. At 18, he was already working as an apprentice in the studio of an American photographer at Chatham Street, Colombo, using the ferrotype process (*see* PHOTOGRAPHY, §I). By 1893 he had established the Hopetown Studio, Slave Island, Colombo, which within a decade was one of the most fashionable and best-equipped in the country. Andree earned several awards at the Exposition Universelle, Paris, in 1900 and at the World's Fair in St Louis, MO, in 1904. In 1901 the government appointed him as one of its official photographers to cover the visit to Ceylon of the Duke and Duchess of York.

Andree was one of the first to introduce to Ceylon cinematographic and other new photographic processes prevalent in Europe, including those techniques popularized by the Lumière brothers, Auguste (1865–1954) and Louis (1864–1948). Although Andree's firm had a great turnover from commercial work, he is best recognized for his innovative portraiture. His death was a setback to the growth of photography in Ceylon: his studio had been a haven for younger artists and photographers in the process of establishing their reputations, including Lionel Wendt, who received his first lessons in photography in Andree's studio.

PHOTOGRAPHIC PUBLICATIONS

Ceylon: A Handbook for the Residents and the Traveller (London, 1907)

BIBLIOGRAPHY

A. Wright, ed.: *Twentieth Century Impressions of Ceylon and its History, People, Commerce, Industries and Resources* (London, 1907), pp. 645ff

ISMETH RAHEEM

Andreescu, Ioan (*b*?Bucharest, 27 Feb 1850; *d* Bucharest, 13 Nov 1882). Romanian painter. He studied from 1869 to 1872 at the Academy of Fine Arts in Bucharest, where he attended Theodor Aman's drawing classes and learnt calligraphy. After graduating he was appointed teacher of drawing and calligraphy at the Episcopal Seminary in Buzau. From 1873 he was also a teacher at the local grammar school. He made his début in December 1874 with the painting *Gooseberries* (1874; Bucharest, N. Mus. A.), which was shown at the *Exhibition of Living Artists*, held in the Academy Halls, Bucharest University. Other paintings of this period, such as *Pot with Wild Flowers* (*c.* 1873; Aurel Stroe priv. col., see Bogdan, p. 61) and *Poplars at the Outskirts of a Village* (*c.* 1876; Bucharest,

Mus. A.), were overlooked by art critics but were noticed by Nicolae Grigorescu and by some important collectors.

Andreescu shared Grigorescu's taste for *plein-air* painting. He was attracted by images of rural life and painted many pictures in the 1870s and early 1880s representing village outskirts, houses, country roads, fairs, fields at dusk and landscapes (e.g. *Landscape with Houses and Trees*, 1881; Bucharest, N. Mus. A.), although he also painted still-lifes, nude studies and portraits (e.g. *Peasant Woman with Green Headscarf*, 1881–2; Bucharest, N. Mus. A.). He tried to avoid any suggestion of the picturesque or idyllic, attempting instead to describe reality and deeper meanings. A face or a country view was evidence of a way of life and an atmosphere. These were conveyed by purely pictorial means, without rhetorical accents and exaggerated effects. The light is soft and even, and the colouring is sober.

Through Grigorescu's assistance, Andreescu obtained a year's grant to study in France. He arrived in January 1879 in Paris, where he studied at the Académie Julian. At Grigorescu's suggestion he also painted at Barbizon and Fontainebleau. In 1879 his exhibits at the Paris Salon included the *Fair at Dragaică Festival* (1877–8; Bucharest, N. Mus. A.). After a short stay in Paris Andreescu returned to Barbizon, remaining there until spring 1880. He exhibited two paintings, *Beech Forest* (Dumitru Dumitrescu priv. col., see Bogdan, p. 127) and *The Main Road* (Bucharest, Mus. A.), at the Paris Salon of 1880, but, having exhausted his study grant, he had to return to Romania. The experience of French art, particularly the work of the Barbizon school and the Impressionists, led Andreescu to refine his use of colour, gave a confidence and spontaneity to his brushstrokes and enriched the range of his subject-matter. From this period his work showed a particular affinity to that of Courbet, Camille Pissarro and Sisley (the last two especially before their Impressionist period), and in terms of subject-matter there are some similarities to Jean-François Millet, especially in *Ploughing* (1880; Bucharest, Mus. A.). Although Andreescu gained from these associations, his work tended to be more luminous and colourful than that of the Barbizon school and more direct in transmitting *plein-air* sensations; he was also less willing than the Impressionists to sacrifice form for effects of atmosphere and light.

Andreescu's abandonment of his studies in France attracted sympathetic comment in the Romanian press, as he was seen as a leading representative of the modern Realist school. As a result of this publicity he succeeded in selling a few canvases, and at the end of 1881 he left for Paris, where at the Salon he showed one of his finest paintings, *Winter at Barbizon* (1881; Bucharest, Mus. A. Col.). It was received with indifference, and Andreescu, impoverished and suffering from tuberculosis, returned at the end of October 1881 to Romania. Knowing that he did not have long to live, he feverishly prepared his only one-man exhibition, which opened during April in Bucharest at the Sala Stavropoleos (destr.). He had some success and sold a number of paintings. Eventually the state bought *Old Man with Long Hair* (1881–2; Iaşi, Mus. A.), but Andreescu died without enjoying the prestige that he was beginning to acquire. His last canvases, painted in 1882, *Bucharest Seen at Dawn from the Spirei Hill* (Aristide Pandele priv. col., see Bogdan, p. 254) and *Self-portrait* (Bucharest, Mus. A.), remained unfinished.

BIBLIOGRAPHY

A. Busuioceanu: *Andreescu* (Bucharest, 1936); rev. in *Scrieri despre arta* [Writings on art] (Bucharest, 1980)
G. Oprescu: *Trei maeştri ai picturei româneşti în secolul XIX* [Three masters of Romanian painting in the 19th century] (Bucharest, 1947), pp. 25–45
R. Bogdan: *Andreescu*, 3 vols (Bucharest, 1969–70)
V. Varga and E. Costescu: *Andreescu* (Bucharest, 1978)
Expoziţia comemorativă Ioan Andreescu, anii de creaţie în ţară [Commemorative exhibition of Ioan Andreescu, the creative years in Romania] (exh. cat. by R. Bogdan, Bucharest, Mus. A., 1983)

RADU BOGDAN

Andreini, Pietro Andrea (*b* Florence, 1650; *d* Florence, 1729). Italian abbot, writer and collector. The son of Girolamo Andreini and Maria Bussini, in 1670 he married Isabella Marsuppini, who bore him two daughters. Widowed at an early age, he devoted his time to his studies, becoming a connoisseur of antique *objets d'art*. He was frequently consulted by famous collectors and erudites, including Cardinal Leopoldo de' Medici, who often approached him for valuations of coins and gemstones. From 1674 to 1687 he lived in Naples as the Consul to the Florentine Nation. Subsequently he moved to Venice and then to Rome, returning eventually to Florence. He was a friend to such important figures as Queen Christina of Sweden, Filippo Buonarroti, Antonio Francesco Gori and Antonimo Magliabechiano. He was also interested in matters of chivalry, which forms the subject-matter of many of his surviving writings. A dedicated collector, he gathered Etruscan and Roman archaeological finds, including ancient funerary inscriptions, bronzes, coins, gems and sculptures, enjoying to the full the contemporary fashion for the study of antiquity. Alongside such artefacts, he also acquired several paintings by Luca Giordano, of which the only one now known is *Apollo and Marsyas* (Florence, Mus. Bardini). The most famous objects in his collection, however, were his cameos, mostly antique and signed. This collection of gemstones, which numbered *c*. 300, was acquired in 1731 by Gian Gastone Medici and is now in the Museo Archeologico in Florence. One of the most notable pieces is the cameo by Protarcos depicting *Cupid Riding on a Lion's Back, Playing the Lyre*.

BIBLIOGRAPHY

R. Tommasi: *Delle lodi dell'abate Pier Andrea Andreini nobil fiorentino, accademico etrusco: Orazione funebre detta nell'Accademia Etrusca in Cortona il dì primo dicembre 1729 da Ranieri Tommasi, nobil cortonese ed accademico etrusco* (Florence, 1730)
F. Scalia and C. de Benedictis: *Il Museo Bardini a Firenze* (Florence, 1984), pp. 249–50
L'Accademia Etrusca (exh. cat., ed. P. Barocchi and D. Gallo; Milan, 1985), pp. 109–12, 176–80
A. Giuliano: *I cammei della collezione medicea nel Museo Archeologico di Firenze* (Rome and Milan, 1989), pp. 118–21, 158–9
L. Battista: 'Le collezioni di gemme dell'abate Andreini', *Ant. Viva*, xxxii (1993), pp. 53–60

LUCIA BATTISTA

Andreoli, Giorgio [Giorgio da Gubbio] (*b* Intra, *c*. 1465–70; *d* Gubbio, 1553). Italian potter. He probably learnt the rudiments of pottery at Pavia and seems to have moved to Gubbio *c*. 1490, together with his brothers Giovanni Andreoli (*d c*. 1535) and Salimbene Andreoli (*d c*. 1522). He became a citizen of Gubbio in 1498. He is particularly well known for his lustrewares, and other potters, especially from the Metauro Valley, sent their work to be lustred in his workshop. His wares made in 1518–19 were frequently signed and dated. His *istoriato* (narrative) wares (e.g. plate decorated with *Hercules and the Hydra*, *c.* 1520; Oxford, Ashmolean) can be dated until at least 1537. In 1536 the workshop seems to have been taken over by his sons Vincenzo Andreoli (Mastro Cencio) and Ubaldo Andreoli.

BIBLIOGRAPHY

G. Mazzatinti: 'Mastro Giorgio', *Il Vasari*, iv (1931), pp. 1–16, 105–22
F. Filippini: 'Nuovi documenti interno a Mastro Giorgio e alla sua bottega (1515–1517)', *Faenza*, xxx (1942), pp. 76ff
G. Polidori: 'Errori e pregiudizi su Mastro Giorgio', *Stud. A. Urbin.*, ii (1953), pp. 13–29

CARMEN RAVANELLI GUIDOTTI

Andrés de Nájera [Andrés de San Juan] (*b* ?Nájera, Rioja; *fl* 1504–33). Spanish woodcarver. In 1504 he was described by Simón de Colonia as 'a clever and expert man in the said crafts of carving and figure-making'. It is possible that he received his early training in Italy. He was much admired by his contemporaries, including Alonso Berruguete, who in 1532 regretted that he did not know him personally.

Nájera's output is not easily identified because he always worked in collaboration, although he may be considered as one of those responsible for introducing Italian decorative ornament into the early Spanish Renaissance. His work is documented between 1504 and 1533 in Burgos, Santo Domingo de la Calzada, Valladolid, Burgo de Osma and Covarrubias. In 1505 he began work on the choir-stalls in Burgos Cathedral, in collaboration with Felipe Vigarny, where he was responsible for the most Italianate forms of decoration. Also in Burgos he collaborated with Nicolás Vergara (i) on a retable (untraced) for the Convent of S Dorotea. During the 1520s he lived in Covarrubias, but no work by him is known there. In 1521 he contracted to execute the choir-stalls for the Cathedral of S Domingo de la Calzada, Logroño, where Guillén de Holanda and others worked under his direction. He probably designed the choir-stalls in the Monastery of S Benito el Real, Valladolid, and directed their construction (1523–8), the main contributor being Guillén de Holanda, with work by other artists including a relief of *St John* by Diego de Siloé.

BIBLIOGRAPHY

J. M. Azcárate Ristori: *Escultura del siglo XVI*, A. Hisp., xiii (Madrid, 1958)

SALVADOR ANDRÉS ORDAX

Andresen, Andreas (*b* Loit, Schleswig-Holstein, 14 Nov 1828; *d* Leipzig, 1 May 1871). German art historian and critic. After studying in Kiel, Berlin, Bonn and Munich, he obtained in 1857 a post at the Germanisches Museum, Nuremberg. From 1862 he was in charge of preparing the catalogues of the Weigel art auction house, becoming its director in 1870. His works included the continuation of G. K. Nagler's *Monogrammisten*, on the fourth volume of which he collaborated, but his most important publications were in the field of graphic art. In *Der deutsche Peintre-Graveur* Andresen traced the history of German engraving from the end of the 16th century to the 18th. This was followed from 1866 by *Die deutschen Maler-Radirer*, a study of German graphic art in the 19th century. Finally, in the *Handbuch für Kupferstichsammler oder Lexicon der Kupferstecher* (from 1870), Andresen widened the scope of his research to include 'all countries and schools'.

WRITINGS

Der deutsche Peintre-Graveur oder Die deutschen Maler als Kupferstecher (nach ihren Leben und ihren Werken) von dem letzten Drittel des 16. Jahrhunderts bis zum Schluss des 18. Jahrhunderts, 5 vols (Leipzig, 1864–78))
Die deutschen Maler-Radirer 'peintres-graveurs' des neunzehnten Jahrhunderts nach ihren Leben und Werken, 4 vols (Leipzig, 1866–70)
Handbuch für Kupferstichsammler oder Lexicon der Kupferstecher, Maler-Radirer und Formenschneider aller Länder und Schulen nach Massgabe ihrer geschätztesten Blätter und Werke, 2 vols (Leipzig, 1870–73)

BIBLIOGRAPHY

Meyers Konversationslexikon, Bibliographisches Institut, i (Leipzig and Vienna, 6/1902), p. 504

ELISABETH GUROCK

Andrews, John (Hamilton) (*b* Sydney, 29 Oct 1933). Australian architect. He graduated from the University of Sydney in 1956 and from the Graduate School of Design, Harvard, in 1958. He established his practice in Toronto in 1962 and received early acclaim for the design of Scarborough College (1963), University of Toronto. This was followed by major commissions throughout North America, including Gund Hall (1968), Harvard, Cambridge, MA. Andrews's North American buildings are characterized by heroic forms, usually in reinforced concrete, determined by the functional programme. Circulation patterns and geometry are the primary ordering devices in complexes of bold articulated units such as Scarborough College, University Student Residences (1965), Guelph, Ont., and the Port Passenger Terminal (1967), Miami.

These interests dominate the buildings he designed after his return to Sydney in 1969. The Cameron Offices (1976), Canberra, demonstrates his concern for the user and his belief that buildings are not independent entities but parts of the larger whole that is the city. However, the very containment of the urban enclave constituted by the Merlin Hotel (1984), Perth, suggests disillusionment with the ability of others to accept and build upon the invitations his earlier urban offerings represented. Response to place became increasingly evident in his Australian buildings such as the Andrews farmhouse (1980), Eugowra, NSW, which, with its use of passive energy systems, displays the sense and symbolism of the Australian rural vernacular tradition. Andrews's Australian buildings are less well known than his North American works, but his greatest contribution has been in his own country where, by example, he has provided leadership and raised confidence and aspiration.

WRITINGS

with J. Taylor: *John Andrews: Architecture, a Performing Art* (Melbourne, 1982)

BIBLIOGRAPHY

C. Moore, ed.: *Canadian Architecture, 1960–70* (Toronto, 1971)
A + U (May, 1974) [supernumerary issue]
Archit. Australia (Feb, 1981) [supernumerary issue]
J. Taylor: *Australian Architecture since 1960* (Sydney, 1986)

JENNIFER TAYLOR

Andrews, Michael (*b* Norwich, 30 Oct 1928; *d* London, 19 July 1995). English painter. He studied from 1949 to 1953 under William Coldstream at the Slade School of

Fine Art, London. *August for the People* (1951; London, U. Coll., Slade Sch. F.A.) was typical of his early work, which respected systematic drawing and factual notations associated with Coldstream and the Euston Road School. Andrews's work was, however, imbued with an instinct for capturing the mood and social behaviour of a familiar milieu: on this occasion, family holidays on the coast of his native Norfolk. In the 1960s Andrews was occupied with large party scenes that came to epitomize the decade's pleasure-seeking. Images appropriated from the media, fashion, pop music, literature and the cinema were all incorporated into paintings of people he knew. The *Deer-park* (1962; London, Tate), an extraordinary vision of a sophisticated gathering, borrowed the composition of Velázquez's *Philip IV Hunting Wild Boar* (*'La tela real'*, *c.* 1630–35; London, N.G.). In the triptych *Good and Bad at Games* (1964–8; Canberra, N.G.) the use of templates and silkscreen printing allowed discrete images to be fused.

Anonymity of touch and a thin surface of spray-painted acrylic paint were fully exploited in the *Lights* series of paintings: scenes of a skyscraper, ocean liner, pier and so forth, seen from the aerial perspective of a gas balloon. In *Lights II: The Ship Engulfed* (1972; AC Eng) the balloon passes through the city, a backdrop of skyscrapers. Its progress referred to the individual's desire for enlightenment and an ego-less state of being. Between 1976 and 1986 Andrews made 25 pictures of an estate in Scotland where he participated in deerstalking. Panoramic vistas and a sensual response to the light and forms of hills and valleys also characterized the paintings and watercolours, begun in 1983 after a trip to Australia, of Ayers Rock and the area around it; these works, such as the *Cathedral, North-east Face* (acrylic on canvas, 1985; priv. col., see 1986 exh. cat., no. 2), explored the common ground between Aboriginal sacred sites and Western religious and ethical beliefs. In 1992 Andrews moved back to London, and in 1994 completed *The Thames at Low Tide* (London, priv. col.). His last works, set in London and Scotland, continued to explore the idea of belonging and spiritual release through the experience of nature.

BIBLIOGRAPHY

Michael Andrews (exh. cat., intro. L. Gowing; London, Hayward Gal.; Edinburgh, Fruitmarket Gal.; U. Manchester, Whitworth A.G.; 1981)

Rock of Ages Cleft for Me. Recent Paintings by Michael Andrews (exh. cat. by M. Andrews and W. Feaver, London, Anthony d'Offay Gal., 1986)

Michael Andrews: The Delectable Mountain: The Ayers Rock Series and Other Landscape Paintings (exh. cat., intro. B. Bernard and J. Raban; London, Whitechapel A. G.; Paris, Hôtel des Arts; New York, Grey Gal. & Stud. Cent., 1991)

Michael Andrews: The Scottish Paintings (exh. cat., intro. R. Calvocoressi; Edinburgh, N. G. Mod. A. 1991)

CATHERINE LAMPERT

Andreyev, Nikolay (Andreyevich) (i) (*b* Moscow, 14 Oct 1873; *d* Moscow, 24 Dec 1932). Russian sculptor, graphic artist and stage designer. He trained at the Stroganov School in Moscow (1883–91) before entering the Moscow School of Painting, Sculpture and Architecture, where he studied under the sculptor Sergey Volnukhin (1859–1921). He graduated in 1900 before joining the Wanderers in 1902.

Andreyev was well aware of contemporary European trends in sculpture, especially the work of Emile-Antoine Bourdelle and Auguste Rodin, which he saw during a stay in Paris in 1900. However, he remained strongly attached to the 19th-century academic tradition, an allegiance that perhaps facilitated his acceptance of many official commissions both before and after the October Revolution of 1917. For example, he was responsible for the figure and pedestal of the monument to *Nikolay Gogol'* on the Boulevard Ring in Moscow (1909; now at Suvorovsky Boulevard, 7) and for the bronze and granite monument to *Aleksandr Ostrovsky* (1929) in front of the Maly Theatre, Moscow. Andreyev was a principal contributor to Lenin's Monumental Propaganda Plan from 1918 onwards, producing busts (e.g. *Danton*; destr., formerly on Revolution Square, Moscow), bas-reliefs (e.g. *Vissarion Belinsky*) and also metaphorical subjects such as his concrete statue *Freedom* (1918–19; destr., head only in Moscow, Tret'yakov Gal.) for the obelisk on Soviet Square commemorating the Soviet Constitution. During the 1920s Andreyev produced numerous bronze and plaster renderings of *Lenin* (e.g. bronze, 1920; Moscow, Tret'yakov Gal.), some of the early ones made directly from life.

Andreyev was a competent draughtsman in sanguine and pastel, which he used in portraits of political and cultural figures in the 1920s, such as *Mikhail Kalinin* and *Anatoly Lunacharsky* (both early 1920s; Moscow, Tret'yakov Gal.). Andreyev also executed stage designs both for intimate productions such as Nikita Baliyev's Chauve Souris cabaret in Moscow in 1913 and for the Moscow Arts Theatre (Mkhat) in the 1920s.

BIBLIOGRAPHY

A. V. Bakushinsky: *N. A. Andreyev* (Moscow, 1939)

L. P. Trifonova: *Skul'ptor Andreyev i ego 'Leniniana'* [The sculptor Andreyev and his 'Leniniana'] (Moscow, 1969)

N. N. Dubovitskaya: *N. Andreyev* (Moscow, 1970)

JOHN E. BOWLT

Andreyev, Nikolay (Platonovich) (ii) (*b* Serpukhov, Moscow district, 1 Oct 1882; *d* Serpukhov, 29 April 1947). Russian photographer. He was the son of a hairdresser. In 1901 Andreyev studied painting and, at the same time, 'art' photography. In his later works he successfully combined the qualities of easel painting and photography, and he experimented widely with printing techniques involving oil pigment, bromoil and gum arabic. He was a master of delicate, lyrical landscapes, striving for the broadest tonal generalization of forms in his depictions of the countryside of middle Russia. Among his most famous landscape photographs are the coarse-grained *Crimean Landscape* (1929; see Morozov, no. 140) and *Into the Blizzard* (1930; see Morozov, no. 141). The same rich tonality and picturesque quality are also present in his genre photographs. From 1906 he successfully exhibited at national and international photographic exhibitions, where he was awarded many diplomas and gold medals.

BIBLIOGRAPHY

S. Morozov: *Tvorcheskaya fotografiya* [Creative photography] (Moscow, 1986)

L. Ukhtomskaya and A. Fomin: *Antologia soveskoy fotografii, 1917–70*, 3 vols (Moscow, 1987)

A. N. LAVRENTIEV

Andries [di Savino]**, Guido** (*b* ?Castel Durante, *fl* 1512; *d* Antwerp, 1541). South Netherlandish potter of Italian birth. He probably worked in Venice before settling in

Antwerp at the beginning of the 16th century (*see* ANTWERP, §III, 2). In 1512 he purchased a house called De Groote Aren in the Oude Veemerct and in 1520 established the Den Salm workshop in the Kammenstraat, which became the most important in Antwerp. His five sons also worked as potters in Antwerp and abroad: Guido Andries the younger (1535/41–*c.* 1587) in Antwerp; Frans Andries (*b* before 1535; *d* after 1565) in Seville; Joris Andries (*c.* 1535–*c.* 1579) in Middelburg; Jaspar Andries (1535/41–*c.* 1580) in Norwich and London; while Lucas Andries (*b* before 1535; *d c.* 1573), the eldest son, eventually inherited his father's workshop in Antwerp. Guido Andries the elder produced faience pots and paving-tiles, the most remarkable of which are those from the abbey of Herkenrode, which are influenced by Venetian maiolica (1532–3; Brussels, Musées Royaux & Hist.), and the paving-tiles in The Vyne (*c.* 1525; The Vyne, Hants). After Andries's death, his widow married Franchois Frans, who managed the workshop from 1543 to 1561–2.

BIBLIOGRAPHY

M. Laurent: 'Guido di Savino and the Earthenware of Antwerp', *Burl. Mag.*, xli (1922), pp. 288–97
——: 'A Jug of 16th-century Antwerp Majolica', *Burl. Mag.*, xlvii (1925), pp. 319–24
H. Nicaise: 'Les Origines italiennes des faïenceries d'Anvers et des Pays-Bas au XVIe siècle', *Bull. Inst. Hist. Belge Rome*, xiv (1934), pp. 109–29
——: 'Notes sur les faïenciers italiens établis à Anvers dans le premier tiers du XVIe siècle', *Rev. Belge Philol. & Hist.*, xvi (1937), pp. 189–202

CLAIRE DUMORTIER

Andriessen. Dutch family of painters and draughtsmen. Although they came from a non-artistic background, the brothers (1) Jurriaan Andriessen and (2) Anthonie Andriessen became successful painters, specializing in supplying painted wallpapers, which they made at their factory in Amsterdam. Jurriaan also produced work for the theatre. Both brothers were active in the Amsterdam Tekenacademie; their pupils included some of the best-known 19th-century Dutch artists, such as Wouter Johannes van Troostwijk, Hendrik Voogd and Jean Grandjean, as well as Jurriaan's son Christiaan Andriessen and granddaughter Cornelia Aletta van Hulst.

(1) Jurriaan [Jurriaen] **Andriessen** (*b* Amsterdam, 12 July 1742; *d* Amsterdam, 31 July 1819). From 1754 to 1758 he was apprenticed to Antoni Elliger and from 1759 to 1760 to Jan Maurits Quinkhard. Although he produced a few allegorical history paintings, his most important work was for the Amsterdam wallpaper factories, making painted wallcoverings for manufacture, mainly for private residences. He began as an assistant to Johannes van Dregt (1737–1807) but later worked with his brother Anthonie and Izaak Schmidt (1740–1818) in his own factory. He also attended classes two evenings a week at the Amsterdam Tekenacademie, where in 1766 he won first prize and became a teacher himself. The same year he joined the Guild of St Luke; by 1794 he had become co-director with Cornelis Buys of the Tekenacademie.

Andriessen's wallpaper factory received its first major decorative commission in 1767, from David van Lennep; from then until around 1800 Jurriaan and his colleagues decorated a large number of residential rooms. The factory's production was far greater than the quantity of work that has been preserved, as is known from surviving albums of designs (Amsterdam, Rijksmus. and Gemeente Archf). Andriessen's wallpaper designs followed the prevailing 18th-century taste for arcadian and native Dutch landscapes with small figures, and especially for decorative architecture. The décor of the room was rounded off with a number of small painted overdoors, mainly representing imitation reliefs (e.g. *Six Putti with Flowers and Fruit and Attributes of the Art of Drawing*, 1782; Amsterdam, Rijksmus.), similar to the painted grisailles of Gerard de Lairesse and Jacob de Wit.

In his later years Andriessen designed theatrical scenery and properties, but none of these has been preserved. Aside from his wallpaper designs, his many surviving drawings (large collection in Amsterdam, Rijksmus.) include academic studies, nude and clothed figures, portraits, landscapes and sketches of events, several in pastel. His art collection was auctioned in Amsterdam on 16 February 1903.

BIBLIOGRAPHY

J. Knoef: *Tusschen Rococo en Romantiek* (The Hague, 1943), pp. 1–20, 277
T. H. Lunsingh Scheurleer: 'Een Amsterdamse zaal met wandschilderingen van Jurriaan Andriessen', *Bull. Rijksmus.*, i (1953), pp. 18–24
——: 'Jurriaan Andriessen', *Bull. Rijksmus.*, ii (1954), p. 47
I. H. van Eeghen: *'In mijn journal gezet', Amsterdam 1805–1808: Het getekende dagboek van Christiaan Andriessen* (Alphen aan den Rijn, 1983)

MICHIEL JONKER

(2) Anthonie Andriessen (*b* Amsterdam, 23 Jan 1747; *d* Amsterdam, 19 Nov 1813). Brother of (1) Jurriaan Andriessen. In 1767 he became a practising member of the Amsterdam Tekenacademie, where he was awarded three prizes. He assisted his brother, who was his teacher, in painting wallpaper decorations with landscape subjects. He is known mainly for his drawings and watercolours, mostly landscapes, but he also produced a few portraits.

BIBLIOGRAPHY

Thieme–Becker

FRANS GRIJZENHOUT

Andrieu, Bertrand (*b* Bordeaux, 4 Nov 1761; *d* Paris, 10 Dec 1822). French medallist, engraver and illustrator. He was first apprenticed to the medallist André Lavau (*d* 1808) and then attended the Académie de Peinture et de Sculpture in Bordeaux. In 1786 he travelled to Paris and entered the workshop of Nicolas-Marie Gatteaux. His first great success was a large, realistic and highly detailed medal representing the *Fall of the Bastille* (1789); because it would have been difficult and risky to strike, he produced it in the form of single-sided lead impressions or clichés, coloured to resemble bronze. The following year he used this novel technique again, to produce an equally successful companion piece illustrating the *Arrival of Louis XVI in Paris*. Andrieu lay low during the latter part of the French Revolution, engraving vignettes and illustrating an edition of Virgil by Firmin Didot (1764–1836). He reappeared in 1800, with medals of the *Passage of the Great St Bernard* and the *Battle of Marengo*. His elegant *Peace of Lunéville* (1801) was much admired: from then on, Andrieu flourished, receiving numerous commissions from Vivant Denon, such as those for medals commemorating the *Battle of Austerlitz*, the *Battle of Jena*, the *Marriage of Jérôme Bonaparte*, and the *Marriage of Napoleon and Maria Louisa*. His medallic portraits of Napoleon, which were used for the majority of the pieces in Vivant Denon's series commemorating Napoleon's reign, were among the most beautiful and widely circulated images of the Emperor. Andrieu likewise found favour under the Bourbon Restoration, particularly with his medal of 1818 commemorating the *Erection of a Statue to Henry IV* and another in 1820–21 celebrating the *Birth of the Duc de Bordeaux*, which brought him 15,000 francs from the Municipality of Paris and the Order of St Michel from Louis XVIII.

BIBLIOGRAPHY

DBF
C. Gabet: *Dictionnaire des artistes de l'Ecole française au XIXe siècle* (Paris, 1831), pp. 9–10
A. Evard de Fayolle: *Recherches sur Bertrand Andrieu* (Paris, 1902)
D. Nony: 'Bertrand Andrieu', *Bull. Club. Fr. Médaille*, xxiii (1969), pp. 12–14

MARK JONES

Andriolo de' Santi. *See* SANTI, ANDRIOLO DE'.

Andronicos, Manolis (*b* Bursa, 1919; *d* Salonika, 30 March 1992). Greek archaeologist. He is best known for the discovery in November 1977 of a royal tomb, presumed to be that of PHILIP II of Macedon, at VERGINA (anc. Aigai), although this sensational event was in fact the culmination of some 40 years of excavating in and around the area. Though he was born in Asia Minor, Andronicos's family fled to Thessaloniki in 1921. He studied at the university there with Constantinos Romeos, who found the first evidence of the site of the Macedonian capital and royal necropolis of Aigai, later firmly identified and fully excavated by Andronicos. During World War II he took part in the Greek resistance movement. After 1945 his attention was devoted to the excavation of the huge tumulus at Vergina, where his discoveries included the theatre where Philip II was assassinated in 336 BC and another unlooted royal tomb, possibly that of Alexander IV (*d* 310 BC), son of Alexander the Great. The Vergina tombs yielded extraordinarily rich materials. An ivory portrait head of *Philip II* (*see* GREECE, ANCIENT, fig. 166c) and other objects are striking both artistically and as personal records of the Macedonian dynasty, and the precious-metal artefacts among the grave goods and the wall paintings on the tombs themselves (for illustration *see* VERGINA) provide examples of types of art that are seldom preserved in ancient Greek contexts. Andronicos's fame after the Vergina discoveries ensured ample funding for his work from the Greek government, and he received numerous public honours.

WRITINGS

To nekrotapheion ton tymvon [The cemetery of tombs] (1969), i of *Vergina* (Athens, 1969–)
Vergina: The Royal Tombs and the Ancient City (Athens, 1984)

BIBLIOGRAPHY

J. Crossland: Obituary, *The Guardian* (2 April 1992)
Obituary, *The Times* (6 April 1992)

□

Andronikos of Kyrrhos (*fl* late 2nd century BC–mid-1st). Greek architect and astronomer. He is associated with a single building, the Tower of the Winds (Horologion) on the edge of the Roman agora in Athens, of which he was named the architect by Vitruvius (*On Architecture* I.vi.4). This elegant and ingenious small marble octagonal building was designed externally as a monumental sundial and weather-vane, with a representation of each of the eight winds carved on the sides of the octagon; at the apex of the roof was a bronze Triton that acted as a weathercock. The interior of the building contained a complicated waterclock; apart from the Triton and the clock, the building is well preserved. Andronikos' home town of Kyrrhos appears to be that in Macedonia, rather than the town of the same name in Syria, because a sundial from the island of Tenos carries an epigram in honour of its maker, who is named as Andronikos of Kyrrhos in Macedonia, son of Hermias, and compares him with the famous Hellenistic astronomer Aratos of Soli in Cilicia (*fl c.* 315–*c.* 240 BC; *Inscr. Gr./1*, XII/v, 891). The date of the Tower of the Winds, and hence of Andronikos, is uncertain. The tower has usually been dated to the mid-1st century BC, connecting its construction with that of the Roman agora and relying on the fact that the tower was mentioned by Varro (*On Agriculture* III.v.17) and Vitruvius, writing just after the middle of the century: certainly the building cannot be later than 37 BC, the date of Varro's treatise. It has also been plausibly argued, however, that the monument dates to the late 2nd century BC. An upper limit for the date of Andronikos is given by the Tenos epigram's comparison of him with Aratos, who flourished *c.* 315–240 BC.

BIBLIOGRAPHY

J. Stuart and N. Revett: *Antiquities of Athens*, i (London, 1762), ch. 3
A. W. Lawrence: *Greek Architecture*, Pelican Hist. A. (Harmondsworth, 1957), p. 237
J. von Freeden: *Oikia Kyrrestou: Studien zum sogenannten Turm der Winde in Athen* (Rome, 1983)
R. R. R. Smith: Review of J. von Freeden: *Oikia Kyrrestou*, *J. Hell. Stud.*, cv (1985), pp. 230–31

MARGARET LYTTELTON

Anegondi. *See under* HAMPI, 4.

Anemospilia. *See under* ARCHANES.

Anesi, Paolo (*b* Rome, 9 July 1697; *d* Rome, 1773). Italian painter, draughtsman and engraver. He was the son of Pietro Anesi, a silk weaver from Venice. Paolo studied figure painting with Giuseppe Chiari and, in 1715, landscape painting with Bernardino Fergioni (1674–?1738), who was also teaching Andrea Locatelli at that time. Sebastiano Conca was another of Anesi's teachers. In 1723 Anesi married the daughter of the architect Giuseppe Sardi. His earliest known work is a drawing (1719; Florence, Uffizi), but he made his reputation with the only known example of his engraved work: *Varie vedute inventate ed intagliate*, dedicated to Cardinal Giuseppe Renato Imperiali and published in Rome in 1725.

Anesi visited Florence at least twice and made drawings of the local countryside. After his first journey at the beginning of 1729, four of his drawings (Florence, Uffizi), belonging to Francesco Maria Niccolò Gabburri, were exhibited at SS Annunziata, Florence. During another visit, in 1737, after Anesi had been there for six months, several admirers of his art, including the Marchese Carlo Rinuccini, submitted eleven of his works to the Accademia, of which he duly became a member. He also had a few lines devoted to him by Gabburri in the *Vite degli artisti* (Florence, Bib. N. Cent., MS. Palatino E.B. 9.5). These circumstances, and the fact that Francesco Zuccarelli was a pupil of his, gave rise to a belief that Anesi was a

Florentine, but his time in Florence was in fact no more than a successful interlude in a career otherwise based in Rome, where, on 8 January 1747, his achievements won him entry to the assembly of Virtuosi al Pantheon.

Anesi's clientele was prestigious; Charles-Emanuel III, King of Sardinia, bought six landscapes from him in 1731 through the painter Claudio Francesco Beaumont and went on to buy four more the following year. Foreign art lovers—British and French, both visitors to and residents in Italy—sought him out, including Henry Hoare (i) for Stourhead, Wilts, and Cardinal François-Joachim de Pierres Bernis, two of whose acquisitions can still be traced, the *Landscape in the Roman Campagna* and *Ruins of the Temple of Bacchus* (both Toulouse, Mus. Augustins). Anesi's work was best represented, however, in the collections of the Roman aristocracy, including the Colonna, Pallavicini, Valenti Gonzaga, Pamphili and Rondinini collections (six paintings in the 1809 inventory). His works were also in the collections of well-known contemporary artists, such as Piranesi.

Anesi owed part of his reputation to his wall decorations painted in gouache, which continued the tradition of the 17th-century masters. Many of his wall paintings have been destroyed, but he is known to have worked at the Roman priory of the Knights of Malta in 1732 and to have decorated the Villa Pamphili, Janicule, in 1749, and to have executed four overdoor paintings there; he also collaborated with Marco Benefial, his friend in later life, at the Palazzo Massimo d'Arsoli. Towards 1760 Anesi was one of the team that decorated Cardinal Alessandro Albani's villa in the Via Salaria, but the extent of his contribution is not known. He was certainly responsible for eight panels, celebrating ancient Rome in a happy, arcadian light, in the Zeus room. He also painted landscape panels (1767; figures by Paolo Monaldi) for the Villa Chigi, 11 of which survive (Milan, Alemagna priv. col.), including the *View of Ariccia* and the *Rustic Scene in Latium with a Country Dance* (see Busiri-Vici, pp. 114–15). In 1767–8 Anesi decorated two rooms in the Palazzo Borghese with architectural *capricci* and *vedute* exalting Rome's ideal beauty in monumental and rustic style. The style of these decorations, graceful and a shade melancholic, anticipates the Romantic movement.

BIBLIOGRAPHY

G. Michel and O. Michel: 'Recherches biographiques sur Paolo Anesi', *Misc. Soc. Romana Stor. Patria*, xxiii (1973), pp. 323–36

F. Borroni Salvadori: 'Le esposizioni d'arte a Firenze del 1674 al 1767', *Mitt. Ksthist. Inst. Florenz*, xviii (1974), p. 61

A. Busiri-Vici: *Trittico paesistico romano del '700: Paolo Anesi, Paolo Monaldi, Alessio de Marchi* (Rome, 1975)

C. Benocci: 'Francesco Nicoletti e Paolo Anesi a Villa Doria-Pamphili, 1748–1758', *Carlo Marchionni, architettura, decorazione e scenografia contemporanea*, ed. E. Debenedetti, Studi sul Settecento Romano, iv (Rome, 1988), pp. 209–78

OLIVIER MICHEL

Anet, château of. French 16th-century château *c.* 75 km west of Paris, in the département of Eure-et-Loire. In 1546 DIANE DE POITIERS, widow of Louis de Brézé (*d* 1531), began to build a modest house in the village of Anet; it underwent considerable and magnificent enlargement (after 1547, until 1553) when her lover Henry II became King of France and placed Philibert de L'Orme and virtually unlimited resources at her disposal. The château is built on a moated site (see fig.) around three courtyards with gardens to the north. Around the middle court, the Cour du Seigneur, were three residential wings and the entrance gate set in a screen wall. To the east lay the estate farm buildings around the Basse Cour, while to the west was the Cour de la Fontaine and beyond it the tennis-court, the stables and Diane de Poitiers' burial chapel. Largely demolished (1798–1811) after the French

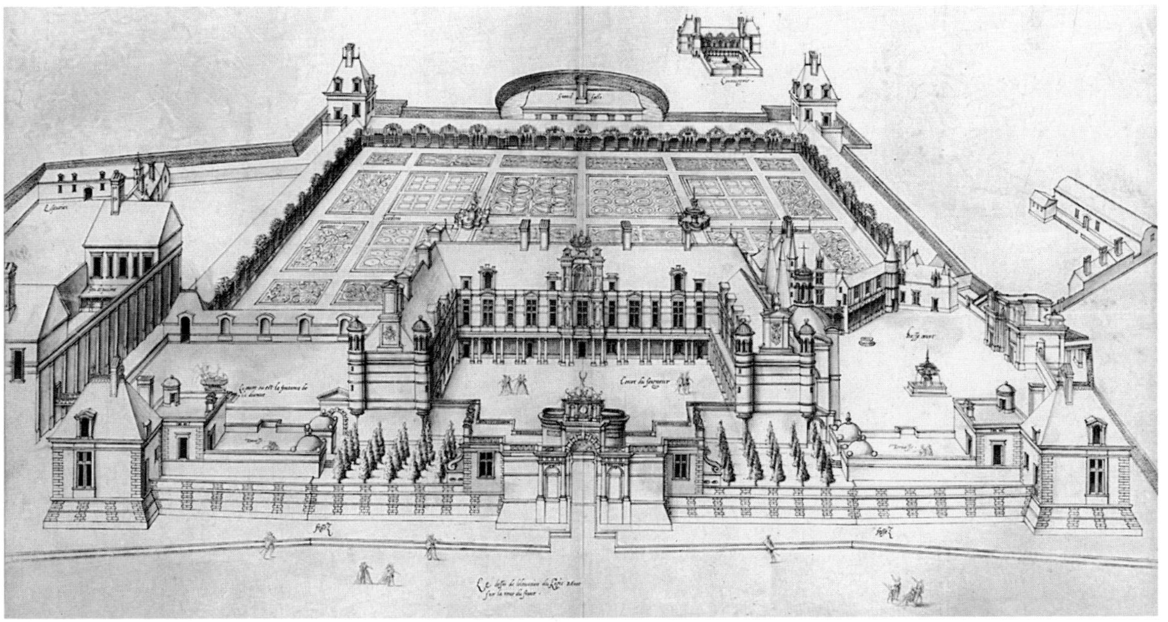

Anet, château and garden, begun *c.* 1547; from a drawing by Jacques Androuet Du Cerceau (i), pen, ink and wash on vellum, 514×752 mm, *c.* 1575 (London, British Museum)

Revolution, all that remains of this complex are the entrance gate and screen wall, a section of the west wing, the frontispiece of the north wing (now Paris, Ecole B.-A.; for illustration *see* DUBAN, FÉLIX) and parts of the cryptoporticus, the chapel in the east wing and the Basse Cour gateway.

The entrance gateway is a Doric triumphal arch of very unclassical type, derived from the west portal of the Romanesque abbey of Saint-Gilles-du-Gard in Provence. In the tympanum above the lintel, which bears a Latin inscription alluding to Henry II and Diane de Poitiers, was a bronze relief (Paris, Louvre) by Benvenuto Cellini (*see* CELLINI, BENVENUTO, §4) depicting the *Nymph of Fontainebleau*, now replaced by a plaster copy. On top of the gateway stands a bronze group; a deer surrounded by four hunting dogs, formerly set in motion by a clockwork mechanism, alluding to Diana the huntress. The chimneys flanking the entrance screen resemble sarcophagi, symbolizing the eternal grief of Louis de Brézé's widow. The cypresses on either side of the gateway represent the grove where Diana hunted. The north wing of the main courtyard, already begun before de L'Orme was engaged, was refaced (completed 1549), with a three-storey frontispiece articulated by the Doric, Ionic and Corinthian orders in its centre. The top storey was conceived as a triumphal arch containing a statue of de Brézé. In an angle of the garden front the Cabinet du Roi was erected, supported on the famously complicated squinch, the construction of which de L'Orme described and illustrated in Book VI of his *Premier Tome de l'architecture* (1567). The long gallery was on the first floor of the east wing, and was lavishly decorated with panelling and a coffered ceiling by Francisco Scibec de Carpi, grisaille windows, landscape and mythological paintings, and realistic portraits of Diane de Poitiers. At one end was an equestrian portrait of *Henry II* surrounded by portraits of numerous kings and queens of France. The chapel (completed 1553) was built on to the eastern side of this wing so that Mass could be watched from the gallery. It is one of de L'Orme's most ingenious designs, inspired by the Tepidarium of the Baths of Diocletian in Rome and an unexecuted design by Antonio da Sangallo (ii) for the Medici Chapel at Montecassino, Italy (*see* L'ORME, PHILIBERT DE, fig. 2). It has a Greek-cross plan with a central domed rotunda with spiral coffering and barrel-vaulted subsidiary chapels. The innermost arches of these vaults conform to the curve of the rotunda, producing curved arcades, of a type later widely used in Baroque architecture. Anet was not only de L'Orme's most important work, it was one of the finest buildings of its date in France, combining elements of Classical and Italian architecture with French building traditions to produce highly original and novel forms. It is also the first French château where the extremely rich decoration was subjected to a coherent iconographic programme, honouring Diana and Apollo as its central theme.

The garden to the north was surrounded on three sides by single-storey vaulted arcades enclosing a parterre divided into 24 compartments of plants forming geometric patterns and depicting the initials and emblems of Diane de Poitiers. Beyond the moat were further gardens containing an orangery, a heronry, an aviary, arbours, topiary and mazes. The arcades, orangery and many other buildings were swept away when the park and garden were remodelled by André Le Nôtre in 1685, and what survived was destroyed in 1854, when the park was turned over to agricultural use.

BIBLIOGRAPHY

P. de L'Orme: *Le Premier Tome de l'architecture* (Paris, 1567)

J. Du Cerceau: *Les Plus Excellents Bastiments de France*, 2 vols (Paris, 1576–9)

W. H. Ward: *French Châteaux and Gardens in the XVIth Century: A Series of Reproductions of Contemporary Drawings Hitherto Unpublished by Jacques Androuet Du Cerceau* (London, 1909)

F. Gebelin: *Les Châteaux de la Renaissance* (Paris, 1927)

E. Grasshoff: 'Die Schlosskapelle von Anet und die deutsche Barockarchitektur', *Z. Dt. Ver. Kstwiss.* (1940), pp. 123ff

P. Héliot: 'Documents inédits sur le château d'Anet', *Mém. Soc. N. Antiqua. France* (1951), pp. 257ff

M. Mayer: *Le Château d'Anet* (Paris, 1952)

F. Bardon: *Diane de Poitiers et le mythe de Diane* (Paris, 1963)

A. Blunt: *Art and Architecture in France, 1500 to 1700*, Pelican Hist. A. (Harmondsworth, 1970)

V. Hoffmann: 'Philibert Delorme und das Schloss Anet', *Architecture* ([Paris], 1973)

——: 'Artisti francesi a Roma: Philibert Delorme e Jean Bullant', *Colloq. Sodalizio* (1973–4), pp. 55ff

——: 'DONEC TOTUM IMPLEAT ORBEM: Symbolisme impérial au temps de Henri II', *Bull. Soc. Hist. A. Fr.* (1978), pp. 29ff

W. Prinz and R. Kecks: *Das französische Schloss der Renaissance: Form und Bedeutung der Architektur, ihre geschichtlichen und gesellschaftlichen Grundlagen* (Berlin, 1985)

V. HOFFMANN

Ange Etienne Martel. *See* MARTELLANGE, ETIENNE.

Angel(o), Pedro (*fl* 1588–1617). Spanish engraver and etcher. Although he lived in Oropesa until 1598, completing woodcuts for Alonso Villegas's *Flos sanctorum* . . . (Madrid, 1588), Angel had already established contacts in Toledo. There he joined the Cofradía del Santísimo Sacramento in 1590 and finally settled in the city in 1598. In Toledo he gained a reputation among the humanist circles; in addition to Villegas, such writers as Juan de Narbona and Jerónimo Ceballos commissioned engraved portraits to accompany their books. The accomplished strength and presence he achieved is evident in such works as the oval portrait of *Cardinal Tavera*, which appeared in Pedro Salazar de Mendoza's *Chronica del Cardenal Juan de Tavera* (Toledo, 1603). Angel's last known engraving is dated 1617.

BIBLIOGRAPHY

A. M. de Barcia: *Catálogo de los retratos de personajes españoles que se conservan en la Sección de Estampas de Bellas Artes de la Biblioteca Nacional* (Madrid, 1901)

J. Ainaud de Lasarte: *Grabado*, Ars Hispaniae, xviii (Madrid, 1962)

E. Paez Rios: *Iconografía Hispana* (Madrid, 1966)

A. M. Roteta: 'El retrato-grabado español en Pedro Angel', *Goya*, cxxx (1976), pp. 220–27

E. Paez Rios: *Repertorio de grabados españoles en la Biblioteca Nacional*, i (Madrid, 1981), pp. 53–5

B. García Vega: *El grabado del libro español: Siglos XV–XVI–XVII* (Valladolid, 1984)

A. M. Roteta: *La illustración del libro en la España de la Contrarreforma: Grabados de Pedro Angel y Diego de Astor, 1588–1637* (Toledo, 1985)

BLANCA GARCÍA VEGA

Angel, Philips (i) (*b* Middelburg, *bapt* 14 Sept 1616; *d* after 22 Oct 1683). Dutch painter. His life and works were only brought to light comparatively recently. Bol convincingly distinguished him from his famous namesake from Leiden who was probably his cousin (*see* ANGEL, PHILIPS (ii)). Angel joined the Guild of St Luke in Haarlem in 1639 and was appointed its secretary in 1643. He later returned to Middelburg, where he worked from 1662 to 1683. At present some 30 paintings are attributed to him, some with dates between 1642 and 1664 or 1668 (Segal). His works are divided into three main groups: barn interiors with emphasis on the still-life element; still-lifes with food, dishes and kitchen-objects sometimes known as *ontbijtjes* (Dut.: breakfast-pieces); and still-lifes with dead fowl. The former two groups bear close resemblance to the works of François Rijkhals (1600–47), who may have been Angel's teacher in Middelburg. As regards his modest breakfast-pieces, however, the influence of the still-lifes of Haarlem painters such as Floris van Dyck can also be detected in his tendency to build compositions from individually studied components and in the rendering of various details. Angel's best works belong to the third category (e.g. *Still-life with Dead Birds*, Middelburg, Stadhuis) and are similar to the game-pieces popularized in Flanders by Jan Fyt. In these works, and in his rare pictures of living fowl, Angel demonstrated his talent for painting fur and feathers.

BIBLIOGRAPHY

L. Bol: 'Philips Angel van Middelburg en Philips Angel van Leiden', *Oud-Holland*, lxiv (1949), pp. 2–19

L. Bol: 'Goede Onbekenden 3, François Rijkhals, een Middelburgse schilder die zijn naam verduisterde, zijn invloed op tijdgenoten' [Good unknown masters 3: François Rijkhals, a Middelburg painter who obscured his name, his influence on his contemporaries'], *Tableau*, ii (1980), pp. 304–11

S. A. Sullivan: *The Dutch Game-piece* (Totowa, NJ, 1984)

S. Segal: 'Still-lifes by Middelburg painters', in *Masters of Middelburg* (exh. cat., ed. N. Bekker and others; Amsterdam, Waterman Gal., 1984), pp. 84–6

Angel, Philips (ii) (*b* Leiden, *c.* 1618; *d* ?Batavia [Jakarta] after 11 July 1664). Dutch writer, painter and etcher. He is now known chiefly as the author of *Lof der schilder konst* (Dut.: Praise of painting). Originally a lecture given to Leiden artists on 18 October 1641, St Luke's Day, it was published the following year. At present virtually no works of art are attributed to this Philips Angel except the etching *Head of an Old Man* (1637), a rather coarse imitation of Rembrandt. Although nothing is known about his training, this etching and certain ideas within *Lof der schilder-konst* suggest that Angel had been in contact with Rembrandt shortly before becoming a master painter in Leiden in 1638. The first half of this small book enumerates the most famous painters from antiquity to Angel's contemporaries and makes the traditional comparisons between painting, sculpture and poetry. The second half discusses the skills necessary for a good painter. The latter section is more original as the author occasionally refers to such new genres as seascapes, battle scenes and guard-room scenes. His interest in the exact depiction of appearances has a close relation to the extremely minute renderings for which Gerrit Dou and other Leiden painters became famous.

The largest section of Angel's book, however, is devoted to history painting, with full accounts of several contemporary Old Testament paintings including Rembrandt's *Samson's Wedding Feast* (1638; Dresden, Gemäldegal. Alte Meister). Angel asserted that character and circumstance should be consistent with the essence of the story, an idea which corresponded to contemporary anti-Mannerist trends in the history paintings of the so-called 'Pre-Rembrandtists', such as Peter Lastman, and Rembrandt. After resigning as Dean of the guild in 1645 Angel joined the Dutch East India Company. He went to Batavia (now Jakarta) in 1646 and accompanied a trade mission to Persia in 1651, arriving in Isfahan the next year. When Angel was dismissed from the company in 1653 for mismanagement he returned to painting, serving Shāh 'Abbās II as court painter. Sometime thereafter he returned to Batavia, where he lived from 1656 to 1664.

WRITINGS

Lof der schilder-konst (Leiden, 1642, *R*/Utrecht, 1969, facs. ed. Amsterdam, 1972)

BIBLIOGRAPHY

Hollstein: *Dut. & Flem.*

L. Bol: 'Philips Angel van Middelburg en Philips Angel van Leiden', *Oud-Holland*, lxiv (1949), pp. 2–19

H. Miedema: 'Philips Angels *Lof der schilder konst*', *Proef*, iii (1973), pp. 27–32

——: *De terminologie van Philips Angels 'Lof der schilder-konst'* (Amsterdam, 1975)

T. Takahashi: 'Reflections on the Description of Wheels in Motion: Philips Angel's *Lof der schilder-konst* and Contemporary Dutch Painting', *Bijutsushi*, xxxi (1982), pp. 76–94 [in Jap., with Eng. summary]

——: 'Philips Angel's *Lof der schilder-konst* and Dutch History Painting during the First Half of the 17th Century', *Nichiran–Gakkai kaishi/Bull. Jap.-Neth. Inst.*, vii/1 (1982), pp. 63–113 [in Jap., with Eng. summary on pp. 103–5]

L. Slatkes: *Rembrandt and Persia* (New York, 1983)

TATSUSHI TAKAHASHI

Angel Card, Abraham (*b* El Oro, nr Acambaro, 7 March 1905; *d* Mexico City, 27 Oct 1924). Mexican painter and teacher of Scottish descent. He studied briefly at the Escuela Nacional de Bellas Artes, Mexico City, where in 1921 he met the painter Manuel Rodríguez Lozano, who introduced him to Mexican avant-garde artists. Under Rodríguez Lozano's tutelage he joined the 'brigade' of teachers who trained primary and secondary school students using Adolfo Best Maugard's method of teaching drawing based on the motifs of popular art. Angel developed a pictorial style characterized by a deliberately naive drawing technique and vivid, unnaturalistic colours; he typically made portraits of friends and relatives superimposed on backdrops of village scenes or simplified rural landscapes. A commemorative book published shortly after his death featured texts by major artistic and literary figures of the period, including Rodríguez Lozano, Diego Rivera, José Juan Tablada and Xavier Villaurrutia and revealed the process of romantic mythification of Angel, characterizing him as a 'pure popular painter' and even inventing for him exotic Argentinian origins.

BIBLIOGRAPHY

M. Rodríguez Lozano and others: *Abraham Angel* (Mexico City, 1924)

M. Moreno Sánchez: *Notas desde Abraham Angel*, Monografías de arte (Toluca, 1976)

Abraham Angel y su tiempo (exh. cat. by O. Debroise, Coahuila, Mus. Bib. Pape, 1984)

KAREN CORDERO REIMAN

Angeles Ortiz, Manuel (*b* Jaén, 13 Jan 1895; *d* Paris, 4 April 1984). Spanish painter. He moved to Granada as a young man and studied painting in the studio of José Larrocha. After studying briefly in Madrid in the studio of the painter Cecilio Plá (1860–1934) in 1912 he returned to Granada, where he befriended the Spanish poet Federico García Lorca, who for many years was his greatest champion and with whom he collaborated in 1933 on the popular travelling theatre La Barraca. He worked intensely while living again in Madrid from 1919 to 1922, and it was during this period that the Cubist tendencies already evident in his work became predominant. At the end of this period he produced a poster for the *Primer Concurso de Cante Jondo* (1922), the competition for Andalusian gypsy singing, expressing his great love for this popular culture in a novel surrealistic language—a bleeding heart pierced by a sadly watching eye; it was a controversial work, regarded by some as too modern for its context.

On the death of his wife in 1922 Angeles Ortiz moved to Paris armed with a letter of introduction to Picasso from the Spanish composer Manuel de Falla. In Paris he attended the Académie de la Grande Chaumière, where he met Alberto Giacometti, and met with other artists at La Rotonde café; he became particularly friendly with other Spanish artists working in Paris, including Salvador Dalí, Joan Miró and Francisco Borès. He acted in Luis Buñuel's film *L'Age d'or* (1930) and designed the costumes for Manuel de Falla's *El retablo de maese Pedro*, staged in 1923 in Paris at the home of Princess Edmond de Polignac. Until his departure from Paris in 1936 he worked in a fully Cubist style in works such as *Still-life with Mandolin* (1926; V. de Olivares priv. col., see 1980 exh. cat., p. 21) and *Fruit in a Dish on the Table* (1926; Venezuela, V. Lis priv. col., see 1980 exh. cat., p. 50). He also painted portraits, for example of *Marcelino Domingo* (1936; Madrid, Mus. A. Contemp.). During the Spanish Civil War (1936–9) he lived in Madrid, joining the Alianza de Intelectuales Antifascistas, and at the end of the war he was interned in a concentration camp, though Picasso arranged his release soon afterwards. He left in 1940 for Buenos Aires, where he continued to paint, returning only in 1949 to Paris; he visited Picasso in Vallauris and produced his first ceramics. Although he had not seen his native Granada since leaving it in 1922, his memories of the city had continued to inspire his work; he made the first of his return visits there in 1955, although he remained based in Paris. His later paintings, such as *Polymorph Heads* (1975; Madrid, Mus. A. Contemp.), remained rooted in figurative subject-matter and continued to bear traces of post-Cubist formal concerns, but were virtually abstract, with a great emphasis on surface textures and colour relationships.

BIBLIOGRAPHY

A. Caffarena: *Manuel Angeles Ortiz, pintor-poeta* (Malaga, 1972)
A. Bonet Correa: *Manuel Angeles Ortiz* (Granada, 1980)
Homenaje a Manuel Angeles Ortiz (exh. cat., Madrid, Min. Cult., 1980)
F. Rivas: *Recuerdos de Granada* (Granada, 1981)
Manuel Angeles Ortiz: Premio Nacional de Artes Plásticas, 1981 (exh. cat., intro. M. F. Prieto Barral; Madrid, Mus. A. Contemp., 1982)

PILAR BENITO

Angeli [Angelo], **Filippo d'.** *See* NAPOLETANO, FILIPPO.

Angeli, Heinrich (Anton) von (*b* Ödenburg [now Sopron, Hungary], 8 July 1840; *d* Vienna, 21 Oct 1925). Austrian painter. In 1853 he moved to Vienna to live with his uncle, who was a collector and a friend of the painters Friedrich von Amerling and Mathias Ranftl (1805–54). Angeli's early *Self-portrait* reflects the precocious maturity of his style, and in 1854 he enrolled at the Akademie der Bildenden Künste in Vienna. In 1856, on the advice of Amerling, he went to study under Emanuel Gottlieb Leutze in Düsseldorf, where he executed one of his most significant history paintings, *Mary Stuart Reading her Death Warrant* (1857). In 1859 he moved to Munich, where he worked independently and was encouraged by Karl Theodor von Piloty, producing the history paintings *Ludwig XI and Franz de Paula* (1859) and *Antony and Cleopatra* for Ludwig I of Bavaria. In 1862 he again settled in Vienna, where he enjoyed increasing success. The life-size portrait of *Baronin Seidler* and the genre painting *Avengers of Honour* (1869), both exhibited at the Weltausstellung in Vienna in 1873, secured his reputation. After brief stays in Paris and Berlin (*c.* 1866), he went in 1871 to Italy, where he painted numerous portraits and the genre work *Absolution Denied.* His final genre paintings, *Youthful Love* (sold London, Sotheby's, 3 Oct 1980) and *Calabrian Shepherd Couple*, also date from this year. Henceforth he devoted himself entirely to portrait painting, receiving important commissions from such aristocratic circles as the Kinsky and Auersperg families (e.g. *Graf Anton Alexander Auersperg*, 1876; Vienna, Präsidium des Nationalrates). Whereas his early portraits were influenced by Amerling, Anton Einsle and 17th-century Dutch art, from the 1870s he developed his own elegant and restrained style. This helped him to obtain commissions at the courts of Vienna, St Petersburg and London (e.g. *Queen Victoria on the Throne*, 1885; Windsor Castle, Berks, Royal Col.). As well as these imposing portraits, he created such portrait studies as that of *Franz Grillparzer*, the Austrian dramatist (1791–1872). In 1876 he was appointed professor of a Spezialschule at the Akademie in Vienna and was President of the Künstlerhaus, Vienna, until 1910.

BIBLIOGRAPHY

Thieme–Becker
A. T. Leitich: *Verklungenes Wien* (Vienna, 1942), pp. 117–19
H. Fuchs: *Die österreichischen Maler des 19. Jahrhunderts*, i (Vienna, 1972)
H. Schöny: *Wiener Künstler-Ahnen*, ii (Vienna, 1975)
R. Schmidt: *Österreichisches Künstlerlexikon*, i (Vienna, 1980)

REGINE SCHMIDT

Angelico, Fra [Fra Giovanni da Fiesole; Guido di Piero da Mugello] (*b* nr Vicchio, *c.* 1395–1400; *d* Rome, 18 Feb 1455). Italian painter, illuminator and Dominican friar. He rose from obscure beginnings as a journeyman illuminator to the renown of an artist whose last major commissions were monumental fresco cycles in St Peter's and the Vatican Palace, Rome. He reached maturity in the early 1430s, a watershed in the history of Florentine art. None of the masters who had broken new ground with naturalistic painting in the 1420s was still in Florence by the end of that decade. The way was open for a new generation of painters, and Fra Angelico was the dominant figure among several who became prominent at that time, including Paolo Uccello, Fra Filippo Lippi and Andrea del Castagno. By the early 1430s Fra Angelico was operating the largest and most prestigious workshop in Florence. His paintings offered alternatives to the traditional polyptych altarpiece type and projected the new naturalism of panel painting on to a monumental scale. In fresco projects of the 1440s and 1450s, both for S Marco in Florence and for S Peter's and the Vatican Palace in Rome, Fra Angelico softened the typically astringent and declamatory style of Tuscan mural decoration with the colouristic and luminescent nuances that characterize his panel paintings. His legacy passed directly to the second half of the 15th century through the work of his close follower Benozzo Gozzoli and indirectly through the production of Domenico Veneziano and Piero della Francesca. Fra Angelico was undoubtedly the leading master in Rome at mid-century, and had the survival rate of 15th-century Roman painting been greater, his significance for such later artists as Melozzo da Forlì and Antoniazzo Romano might be clearer than it is.

I. Life and work. II. Working methods and technique.

I. Life and work.

1. Early career, to 1433. 2. *c.* 1433–9. 3. S Marco, *c.* 1440–45. 4. *c.* 1446–55.

1. EARLY CAREER, TO 1433. Fra Angelico's baptismal name was Guido di Piero. At an unknown date he and his brother Benedetto (*d* 1448) moved to Florence, where they were trained in the manuscript industry then flourishing in the parish of S Michele Visdomini. The identity of their master has never been established, but it is clear that Benedetto was trained as a scribe and Guido as an illuminator. By 1417 Guido had begun to receive commissions for small panel paintings, and by 1425 he was sufficiently well known to be indicated as the author of an altarpiece, apparently never executed, for the Medici family's parish church of S Lorenzo, Florence. The document refers to the artist as a friar of St Dominic, which means that at some date between 1417 and 1425 he had entered the Order of Preachers at the recently founded reformed, or Observant, convent of S Domenico, Fiesole, where he took the name Fra Giovanni. The name Angelico is first documented 14 years after the artist's death.

The 16th-century chronicle of S Domenico, Fiesole, states that three altarpieces were in place when the church was consecrated in 1435, but scholars disagree as to both the reliability of this account and the relative chronology of the altarpieces and other works from these years. Similarly, considerable disagreement makes it impossible to establish a firm canon for Fra Angelico's early period, although his authorship of the three altarpieces for S Domenico is now generally accepted. The triptych depicting the *Virgin and Child Enthroned, with Eight Angels, SS Barnabas, Dominic, Peter Martyr and Thomas Aquinas* (Fiesole, S Domenico) was probably painted around 1426 (but greatly modified in 1500). The *Annunciation* (Madrid, Prado) is probably datable to shortly before 1430 and the *Coronation of the Virgin* (Paris, Louvre) to soon thereafter.

The S Domenico Triptych executed for the high altar follows the conventional Tuscan format showing the Virgin and Child surrounded by angels and flanked in the wings by pairs of saints appropriate to the Order and to the convent's benefactor, Barnaba degli Agli (*d* 1418). The predella (London, N.G.) depicts the *Risen Christ Adored by Angels, Saints and Blessed Persons of the Dominican Order*. The figures in the main panels testify to Fra Angelico's close study of both Masolino and, more importantly, Gentile da Fabriano, whose *Virgin and Child with Angels and Four Saints* (the Quaratesi Altarpiece; 1425) was then in S Niccolò sopr'Arno, Florence (now dispersed). The two later altarpieces for Fiesole reflect Fra Angelico's knowledge of Masaccio's painting, particularly the *Virgin and Child Enthroned* (1426; London, N.G.; *see* MASACCIO, fig. 1) from the polyptych (now largely destr.) for S Maria del Carmine, Pisa, and the collaborative work with Masolino, the *Virgin and Child with St Anne* (1423–5; Florence, Uffizi), while acknowledging a continuing debt to Gentile, whose sophisticated handling of light and colour seems to have held even more attraction for Fra Angelico than the chiaroscuro of Masolino and Masaccio. The two later altarpieces for Fiesole required a descriptive ambience for the action, and Fra Angelico may have derived the setting for the *Annunciation* from Masaccio's untraced painting of the same subject for S Niccolò sopr'Arno, Florence. The perspectival space of the *Coronation* is an elaboration of the system of geometric perspective based on the vanishing-point construction invented by Brunelleschi *c.* 1413 but employed with consistent success before Fra Angelico's attempts only by Masaccio. In the latter's work the space is controlled by a single point rather than by the complex of superimposed projections that Fra Angelico designed for the *Coronation*.

The scriptorium at S Domenico was headed by Fra Angelico's brother, the scribe Fra Benedetto, who had also joined the Order and who, like the painter, continued to practise his trade. Illuminations by Fra Angelico and assistants in a Missal (Florence, Mus. S Marco, MS. 558) produced in the early 1430s at the scriptorium display the narrative liveliness and vivid coloration characteristic of Florentine illumination of the period, features that the artist extended with great effect to predella panels. Taken as a group, these early works show that Fra Angelico entered the mainstream of Florentine painting far more skilled as an illuminator than as a panel painter.

Apart from the Missal and the three altarpieces for S Domenico, Fiesole, the most important surviving works from Fra Angelico's early period are the altarpiece depicting the *Virgin and Child with SS Dominic, John the Baptist, Peter Martyr and Thomas Aquinas* executed for the Dominican nuns at the Florentine convent church of S Pietro Martire and the *Annunciation* for S Domenico, Cortona (*c.* 1432; Cortona, Mus. Dioc.; *see* NARRATIVE ART, fig. 8). The S Pietro Martire Altarpiece was installed by March 1429. Of main interest is its curved pediment with scenes in the spandrels depicting the *Preaching and Death of St Peter Martyr*. The close relationship between Fra Angelico's evident pleasure in designing historiated predellas or, as here, filling the spandrels and his early training as an illuminator is most evident in a comparison of these spandrel scenes with the historiated initial depicting the *Death of St Peter Martyr* in the Missal (fol. 41*v*). They share the robust action, chromatic brilliance and sure but suggestive brushwork associated with late medieval manuscript illumination. The altarpiece's curved pediment does not derive from Florentine tradition but is a prominent feature in contemporary works by the Sienese painters Sassetta and the Master of the Osservanza. The nuns at S Pietro Martire were closely associated with the Observant reform promulgated by Sienese friars, and the unusual altarpiece type possibly reflects the regional loyalties of

1. Fra Angelico: *St James the Great Freeing Hermogenes*, tempera on panel, 260×240 mm, *c.* 1431 (Fort Worth, TX, Kimbell Art Museum)

particular Dominican communities. At any rate, Fra Angelico's interest in Sienese painting steadily increased over the next four or five years.

Fra Angelico's skill in working on a small scale is fully evident in a group of four reliquaries (Florence, Mus. S Marco) painted in the early 1430s for Fra Giovanni Masi (*d* 1434), sacristan of S Maria Novella, the major Dominican house in Florence. The reliquaries and a *Coronation of the Virgin* painted for the nuns of S Maria Nuova (*c.* 1431–5; Florence, Uffizi) confirm the painter's determination to expand the preciosity of manuscript illumination on to larger formats. Two predella panels from an untraced altarpiece datable to *c.* 1431 depicting the *Naming of St John the Baptist* (Florence, Mus. S Marco) and *St James the Great Freeing Hermogenes* (Fort Worth, TX, Kimbell A. Mus.; see fig. 1) — an episode from Voragine's *Golden Legend* — epitomize Fra Angelico's achievements in the period. The planimetric composition of the *St James* panel and the sheets of light falling behind the figures in the second rank reveal Fra Angelico's scrutiny of Masaccio's *Adoration of the Magi* (1426; Berlin, Gemäldegal.) from the predella of the Pisa Polyptych.

2. *c.* 1433–9. The sumptuous winged triptych depicting the *Virgin and Child Enthroned with SS John the Evangelist, John the Baptist, Mark and Peter* (1433–6; Florence, Mus. S Marco), commissioned by the Florentine Arte de' Linaiuoli and thus known as the Linaiuoli Tabernacle (see fig. 2), is Fra Angelico's earliest surviving painting of unambiguous date. It epitomizes the artist's early maturity and the processes by which he reached it. In the autumn of 1432 the officers of the linenworkers guild commissioned Lorenzo Ghiberti to design for the interior of their guildhall a marble frame to house an image of the Virgin that would be even larger and more sumptuous than the panel by Bernardo Daddi of 1347, standing over the altar of the miraculous Virgin at nearby Orsanmichele. The frame was ready by the summer of 1433, and on 11 July Fra Angelico agreed to paint the triptych for 190 florins, a staggering sum by comparison with what is known of his income before that date. The choice of Fra Angelico for the commission has been explained by the fact that in 1430 the treasurer of the Arte de' Linaiuoli was Filippo de' Lapaccini, whose son Giuliano entered the Dominican Observance at S Domenico, Fiesole, in 1433 (Orlandi). The painting is the largest single-panel image of the Virgin and Child executed in the 15th century. The central panel

2. Fra Angelico: Linaiuoli Tabernacle, tempera on panel, 2.66×1.32 m (central panel), 1433–6 (Florence, Museo San Marco)

depicts the Virgin seated in a richly draped, barrel-vaulted chamber with Christ, shown as a child, not an infant, standing on her left thigh. The Dove of the Holy Spirit hovers just above them and God the Father is sculpted in the pediment of the marble frame. Thus all three persons of the Trinity are represented on the tabernacle. On the curved inner frame, surrounding the main panel and standing on clouds, are 12 musicmaking angels. When open, the shutters show *St John the Baptist* on the left and the patron saint of the guild, *St Mark*, usually wrongly identified as St John the Evangelist, on the right. When closed, *St Mark* appears again on the left and *St Peter* on the right. The predella consists of three independent, framed scenes. On the left is *St Peter Preaching* (see fig. 3), a scene that shows St Mark writing down the sermon on a tablet, an illustration of the ancient tradition that St Mark's gospel is essentially St Peter's eye-witness account. On the right is the *Martyrdom of St Mark*, which shows the dead body of the saint being dragged through the streets of Alexandria in a hailstorm. The central scene depicts the *Adoration of the Magi.*

The pose and psychological bearing of the Virgin and Child are much more stable and solemn than in their counterparts by Daddi. Fra Angelico's Virgin accommodates the mass and weight of the frontally posed Child with only the slightest shift backwards and to the left of her centre of gravity, her head and gaze only barely turning off the main axis of her body. The Child, unlike Daddi's gurgling infant, stands calm and expressionless, regally dressed in a belted tunic, both arms extended to hold an orb in the left hand and to raise the right in blessing. This young Christ's royal status has already deprived him of the innocence and vulnerability of childhood. In the Linaiuoli Tabernacle Fra Angelico has eschewed reflective gold surfaces and at the same time chosen to enhance the plasticity of the Virgin and Child. Although figures and ground participate in the same representational discourse, Fra Angelico's painting has little to do with the feelings of real human mothers and babies for each other. Even more than highly idealized representations of a young woman and a little boy, these are theophanic figures and, as such, vehicles of dogma. Icons of majesty, they exist fixed and motionless within a draped chamber, the curtains of which have been pulled back to reveal divinity. Once the subject-matter and the requirements of the commission are thus understood, Fra Angelico's formal solution becomes perfectly intelligible, if not predictable. The general form of the Linaiuoli Tabernacle recalls Giotto's Ognissanti *Madonna* (*c.* 1310; Florence, Uffizi; *see* GIOTTO, fig. 6) and late 13th-century panels such as Duccio's Rucellai *Madonna* (begun 1285; Florence, Uffizi; *see* DUCCIO, fig. 1).

Like Masaccio, Fra Angelico looked to sculpture rather than to painted images to achieve an effect of monumentality in large-scale standing figures, and Ghiberti's work provided the model for the four saints in the wings (Middeldorf). Fra Angelico had the intellectual capacity to understand the recent innovations in Florentine art, and these greatly interested him, but only to the degree that they served expressive ends. His stylistic decisions were motivated by notions of decorum and were always

3. Fra Angelico: *St Peter Preaching*, tempera on panel, predella panel from the Linaiuoli Tabernacle, 1433–6 (Florence, Museo San Marco)

in the service of the function and subject-matter of the work. The Linaiuoli Tabernacle reveals an artist of faultless technical accomplishment who fully understood and exploited the typological symbolism inherent in, for example, the large Virgin and Child panels of the 13th century. He not only respected but even celebrated the chromatic brilliance and dazzling patterning of 14th-century Sienese panel painting. He was wary of full-scale capitulation to chiaroscuro modelling as it was shortly to be developed by Fra Filippo Lippi, because of his unwillingness to forgo the brilliant palette that he had inherited from the 14th century.

The commission for the Linaiuoli Tabernacle caught the attention of a wider circle of rich and powerful citizens. Among these were Cosimo de' Medici and Palla Strozzi, rivals both in politics and business. Within a year or so of beginning work for the Arte de' Linaiuoli, Fra Angelico was working for both men, perhaps at the same time. Palla Strozzi is known to have commissioned Fra Angelico to paint the *Deposition* (Florence, Mus. S Marco), to hang in the sacristy of Santa Trìnita, Florence, with Gentile da Fabriano's *Adoration of the Magi* (1423; Florence, Uffizi; *see* GENTILE DA FABRIANO, fig. 3). The *Deposition*, which was not an altarpiece, had been left unfinished at Lorenzo Monaco's death, *c.* 1425. The frame dates to that period and the three scenes in the gables are by Lorenzo. Fra Angelico's shop executed the 12 standing figures on the pilasters and the *Deposition*, with its sublime landscape, in the main panel, but there is no consensus among scholars as to when the work was undertaken. In Fra Angelico's surviving large-scale work nothing resembles the vast landscape, whose vistas extend into distant invisibility and beyond the lateral edges of the painted field, though the *tour de force* views of hills and valleys in the Cortona *Annunciation* predella seem to have prepared the way. The exactitude of his sympathetic penetration of human psychology in the central group around the dead Christ is incomparable, except perhaps in the tremulous exchange between the Virgin and the Angel Gabriel in, again, the Cortona painting. The groups of women to the left of centre and men to the right were undoubtedly designed by Fra Angelico, although probably executed by others. The painter of the left-hand group has been identified as present in Fra Angelico's shop from an early period. He stayed for a number of years and is recognizable as part of the team that later worked at S Marco. Highly trusted, this painter was largely responsible for the execution of the *Lamentation* (1436; Florence, Mus. S Marco), painted for the Florentine Confraternità di S Maria della Croce al Tempio. The master responsible for the right-hand group appeared briefly in Fra Angelico's shop from *c.* 1432 to *c.* 1437. Among his first assignments was extensive work on the *Coronation of the Virgin* (*c.* 1430–35; Paris, Louvre) executed for S Domenico, Fiesole. Around 1434–5 Fra Angelico entrusted to him most of the execution of the *Virgin and Child Enthroned with SS Peter Martyr, Cosmas, Damian, John the Evangelist, Lawrence and Francis* (ex-S Vincenzo d'Annalena, Florence; Florence, Mus. S Marco), a work most probably commissioned by the Medici family. Prestigious commissions such as the Annalena Altarpiece, the Strozzi *Deposition* and the Linaiuoli Tabernacle make it plain that Fra Angelico had emerged as the dominant painter in Florence by the mid-1430s.

Ordered less than eight months earlier, the Croce al Tempio *Lamentation* was finished by 2 December 1436. This is the last documented notice of Fra Angelico until March 1438, when he was in Cortona and it is possible that he was already in Umbria by the autumn of 1437. The *Virgin and Child Enthroned with Angels between SS Dominic, Nicholas of Bari, John the Baptist and Catherine of Alexandria* (Perugia, G. N. Umbria), executed for the chapel of S Niccolò dei Guidalotti, S Domenico, Perugia, belongs to this period and was Fra Angelico's last essay in the polyptych format, which was soon to be superseded by the rectangular, single-field *pala* commonly associated with Florentine Renaissance altarpieces. The Guidalotti altarpiece may have been painted in Cortona and can be compared with the altarpiece depicting the *Virgin and Child Enthroned between SS (?)Mark, John the Baptist, John the Evangelist and Mary Magdalene* made for S Domenico, Cortona, earlier in the decade (Cortona, Mus. Dioc.), where Fra Angelico had responded deeply to the Sienese style of Sassetta, whose own triptych of the same date formed a pendant to Fra Angelico's. Just as the congress of natural and pictorial light and the brilliance of saturated hues are found in the Linaiuoli tabernacle of 1433–6, so the presence of these qualities locate the Perugia panel in the mid- to late 1430s. Moreover, the searching but tender exploration of human feeling registered in facial expressions, carried to such heights in the Strozzi *Deposition*, here enlivens the standing figures of saints and angels, whose psychological presence on altarpieces such as this is usually unmotivated.

3. S MARCO, *c.* 1440–45. In 1436 Pope Eugenius IV ceded the Sylvestrine monastery of S Marco, Florence, to the Dominicans of Fiesole, who thus expanded the Observant presence into the city. Cosimo de' Medici and his brother Lorenzo (1395–1440) guaranteed the financial resources necessary to renovate the dilapidated fabric of S Marco, which stood at the north-east boundary of the neighbourhood dominated by the Medici family. Until his death in 1464 Cosimo was S Marco's only real patron, spending, in the five years between 1441 and 1455, approximately 36,000 ducats on the convent, where he also established and largely furnished the first public library since antiquity. His favourite architect, Michelozzo di Bartolommeo, was entrusted with the design and construction of the new church and adjacent buildings, and the complex was consecrated on 6 January 1443 in ceremonies attended by the Pope himself. Fra Angelico was entrusted with a programme of decoration that included an altarpiece for the church and over 50 frescoes for the convent itself, the largest group of related works to survive almost intact from the workshop of a single Renaissance painter. The payment records for the refurbishment and decoration of S Marco seem to have perished and neither the chronological sequence of the works nor the number and names of Fra Angelico's assistants has ever met with universal consensus, although it is likely that Fra Angelico himself was heavily involved with the project until he left for Rome, probably in 1445. The altarpiece was almost certainly the first work executed, probably in 1440–41.

Work in the conventual buildings seems to have proceeded intermittently, some parts remaining unpainted until the early 1450s.

(i) The altarpiece. The central panel (Florence, Mus. S Marco) shows the *Virgin and Child Enthroned* against an extensive landscape that is glimpsed through a luxuriant screen of trees. They are surrounded by angels and six standing saints (Lawrence, John the Evangelist, Mark, Dominic, Francis and Peter Martyr), with SS Cosmas and Damian kneeling in the foreground. In the predella, scenes from the *Lives of SS Cosmas and Damian* flank the central panel of the *Entombment* (Dublin, N.G.; Florence, Mus. S Marco; Munich, Alte Pin.; Paris, Louvre; Washington, DC, N.G.A.). A small, rectangular, framed *Crucifixion* rises directly above the centre of the predella and cuts into the space of the ornately patterned foreground. Disastrously cleaned in the 19th century, the S Marco Altarpiece has lost almost all of its surface refinement, but here and there its original brilliance and sharpness of focus are discernible.

Fra Angelico began work on the painting just as Fra Filippo Lippi was completing his earliest documented altarpiece, the *Virgin and Child with SS Fredianus and Augustine* (Paris, Louvre; *see* LIPPI, (1), fig. 1), begun in 1437 for the Barbadori Chapel, Santo Spirito, Florence. The placing of two kneeling figures well into the foreground in both works suggests that Fra Angelico may have studied the younger painter's design before he began to plan his altarpiece, although Sassetta had preceded both Florentine painters with this invention in his *Madonna of the Snow* (Florence, Pitti; *see* SASSETTA, fig. 1), commissioned in 1430. The iconography of the S Marco Altarpiece is a subtle fusion of Dominican and Medicean interests. All but the central scene of the predella depict scenes from the *Lives of SS Cosmas and Damian*, major patron saints of the Medici family in general and of Cosimo in particular. In the main panel the two kneeling figures of these saints in the foreground serve to introduce the Medici as patrons into the scene. The patron saints of Cosimo's closest male relations are also represented in the main field: SS Francis, Peter Martyr, Lawrence and John the Evangelist. Fra Angelico wrapped these Medicean interests in a cloak of Dominican iconographical conventions. The Infant Christ holding the orb that symbolizes the world is a motif traceable in Dominican art at least to the mid-14th century. The verses on the borders that embellish the Virgin's cloak and the specific varieties of trees in the landscape background derive from Dominican liturgical usage. The central panel of the predella refers to the adoration of the Eucharist, and other features fall into a long tradition of Dominican altarpieces as far back as Simone Martini's S Caterina Altarpiece (1319–20; Pisa, Mus. N. S Matteo).

(ii) Frescoes. In accordance with custom, frescoes embellished the public spaces of S Marco. Half-length saints appear in pointed lunettes over each doorway in the cloister, and on the north wall Fra Angelico painted a large representation of *Christ on the Cross Adored by St Dominic* (after 1442) on an axis with the main entrance from the Piazza S Marco. The entire north wall of the chapter room was reserved for a huge, semicircular *Crucifixion with Saints* (1441–2). The south wall of the refectory, opposite the entrance, was covered by a painting of unknown subject (destr. 1554) but probably either a Crucifixion or a miraculous episode from the life of St Dominic, or possibly both. Upstairs in the dormitory, each of the 43 original cells received a frescoed composition and three others were painted in the corridors. There is no precedent in known schemes of conventual decoration for such an extensive suite of frescoes in a dormitory, Dominican or otherwise.

(a) Ground-floor. Although the extent and location of the ground-floor decoration is conventional, Fra Angelico's choice of subject for the most public painting of all, *Christ on the Cross Adored by St Dominic*, is without precedent. In the 15th century, cloisters and their adjacent rooms—the sacristy, chapter room, refectory and guest quarters—were generally accessible to all men, both lay and clerical, though not to women. The social function of these spaces was to mediate between the private monastic enclosure of the monks or friars and the public sphere that surrounded it. In the second quarter of the 15th century a number of Florentine religious communities adopted a local and short-lived Sienese practice of the early 14th century by commissioning extensive cycles of fresco decoration for their cloisters. Most commonly, cloister decoration, in Florence as elsewhere, lacked any chronological, stylistic or iconographical cohesiveness. The formal and ideological integrity of carefully planned programmes, such as those in Florence at S Maria Novella, the Badia, S Miniato and others, was new in this period. These pictorial cycles were forms of institutional propaganda orientated towards the public and thus different in both kind and effect from the private self-representations of religious institutions that were preserved in the texts and other instruction directed towards their members only. Unexceptionally, these programmes stressed the relevant order's history and mission in the Church. By contrast, Fra Angelico stressed St Dominic's inner or mystical life and thus by association the mystical lives of the friars at S Marco.

The *Crucifixion* in the chapter room pairs and even opposes sacred history and its interiorization by means of disciplined contemplation. To the left of the figure of Christ, Fra Angelico included the biblical figures traditionally represented at the scene of the Crucifixion with SS Mark, Lawrence, Cosmas and Damian. On the right, however, he arranged a group of 11 standing and kneeling figures representing Dominican saints and renowned monastic reformers. All of them are shown in attitudes of prayer and meditation and can therefore be understood as models for the contemplation of Christ's saving death, serving as examples for the friars who gathered daily in the chapter room to examine and expose their faults. Such joining of two levels of representation, the narrative and contemplative, within the same field also characterizes some of the cell frescoes in the dormitory.

(b) Dormitory. As early as the 13th century the Constitution of the Order of Preachers stipulated that dormitories were to be decorated with an image of the Virgin in the corridor and that the cells were to contain images of Christ or the Virgin. It is thought that the Dominicans

were the first order to specify the use of images in this context, though apart from those at S Marco no other such suites are known. A number of small panels with secure Dominican provenances showing St Dominic or some other Dominican figure kneeling before Christ on the Cross may be relics of this practice, and Fra Angelico's *Crucifixion with the Virgin, St John the Evangelist and Cardinal Juan de Torquemada* (*c.* 1450–55; Cambridge, MA, Fogg) is probably one of these. S Marco must therefore be understood as a special case of a broad phenomenon, its extraordinary survival accountable in part to the medium of fresco. Fra Angelico certainly executed at least one fresco (Paris, Louvre) for the dormitory corridor at S Domenico, Fiesole, and he may also have painted the dormitory at S Domenico, Cortona, in 1438–9, although that structure was destroyed and no description survives.

The dormitory corridor at S Marco contains three frescoes, one of which is entirely by Fra Angelico. The composition and iconography of the *Virgin and Child Enthroned with Eight Saints* (the *Madonna of the Shadows*; see fig. 4) in the east corridor, designed but probably not entirely executed by Fra Angelico, recalls the S Marco Altarpiece and suggests that this was the spot where the community gathered to sing the Night Office of the Virgin, which the Constitutions specify was to be sung in the dormitory. *Christ on the Cross Adored by St Dominic*, on an axis with the east corridor, is a variation of the cloister fresco and may be a late 15th-century addition in the style of Fra Angelico. The autograph *Annunciation* opposite the head of the staircase leading from the ground-floor is the first image to greet the visitor on entering the most private area of the complex. In the 15th century only Dominican and Franciscan friars were permitted to enter the Order's dormitories. A Dominican would have been singularly well equipped to read the messages of the *Annunciation* fresco because the traditional theme is embedded in the Order's ethos. For example, the inscription across the bottom reads, 'When you come before the figure of the intact Virgin, do not fail to say a Hail Mary'. It was the custom for Dominicans to greet the Virgin with the angelic salutation on entering the dormitory, and as this was done while genuflecting—just as the Angel Gabriel does in the *Annunciation*—Fra Angelico's painting forged an indissoluble link between the image and its beholder. Exactly the same purpose informs the frescoes in the cells.

The attribution and chronology of the 43 frescoes in the cells is an enormous and probably insoluble problem. The overall conception and the design of most of the individual scenes are undoubtedly Fra Angelico's. The frescoes wholly or almost wholly painted by the master are those in cells 3, 6, 7, 9 and 10, depicting, respectively, the *Annunciation*, the *Transfiguration* (see fig. 5), the *Mocking of Christ*, the *Coronation of the Virgin* and the *Presentation in the Temple.* Others show signs of his intervention

4. Fra Angelico: *Virgin and Child Enthroned with Eight Saints* (*c.* 1440–45), fresco (detail), east corridor, monastery of S Marco, Florence

5. Fra Angelico: *Transfiguration* (*c.* 1440–45), fresco, Cell 6, monastery of S Marco, Florence

alongside an assistant, and still others were executed on his designs but wholly independently. Iconographically, with the exception of two scenes, the cell frescoes fall into three groups, each corresponding to the section of the community assigned to live there. Novices were housed in the seven cells along the south corridor, clerics in the twenty on the east corridor, and lay brothers and guest friars probably in the north corridor, where cells 38 and 39 were reserved for the private use of Cosimo de' Medici. These two were decorated, appropriately, with a *Crucifixion with Patron Saints of the Medici Family* in Cell 38 and the *Adoration of the Magi*, a subject with strong Medicean associations, in Cell 39.

The frescoes in the novitiate are the most uniform group. They are white-ground vertical rectangles in which St Dominic kneels before the Cross, the only variation from fresco to fresco being in the gestures employed by the saint. These are derived from the gestures both described and illustrated in *De modo orandi*, a Dominican textbook for prayer based on eye-witness observations of the founder's attitudes during personal prayer. Compiled in the 13th century, the text fell largely out of use but was revived by the Dominican Observance in its houses all over Europe in the 15th century.

The cells in the east corridor continue the theme of *De modo orandi* in compositions signifying feasts of Christ or the Virgin. The symbol of the Cross used in the novitiate is replaced with more historiated references that include ancillary figures and descriptive settings rather than the reduced *dramatis personae* and the flat, white ground of the first group of frescoes. Fra Angelico here expanded the repertory of exemplars to include other saints as well as Dominic. In the *Annunciation* (Cell 3), for example, St Peter Martyr observes the colloquy between the Virgin and the Angel with a gesture that was believed to induce humility, while the gesture of the same saint when he reappears in the *Presentation in the Temple* (Cell 10) indicates that he is interceding on behalf of the brethren. In the clerics' cells, therefore, as in the north corridor *Annunciation* or the *Crucifixion* in the chapter room, the friars were encouraged to identify with the mystical life of notable forerunners, mostly Dominican, as they meditated on the liturgical texts associated with the major feasts of the calendar.

At this period lay brothers were assumed to be untutored in Latin and would not have undergone even the minimal theological preparation required for ordination. Accordingly, the frescoes in their cells, on the south side of the north corridor, are devoid of the liturgical and even mystical references woven into the paintings made for novices and clerics. The compositions are fully narrative illustrations of various scenes from the *Life of Christ*, drawn mostly from the Passion cycle beginning with the *Last Supper* (Cell 35) and ending with the *Noli me tangere* (Cell 1). Here as elsewhere in the dormitory nothing determines the sequence of scenes from cell to cell. Fra Angelico, or perhaps his assistant Benozzo Gozzoli, seems intentionally to have based these frescoes on the didactic cycle in the chapter room, with its chapel of Corpus Domini, at S Maria Novella, Florence. As early as the S Domenico Altarpiece, Fra Angelico had made reference to the art of the mother house, as it was from there that the convent at Fiesole had been founded. A free variation of the S Marco chapter room *Crucifixion* embellishes the large Cell 37, indicating that the room served a parallel function for the lay brothers, who were not voting members of the Conventual Chapter itself. Finally, the cells along the north side of the north corridor display rather conventional Crucifixions with saints, indicating that, as guest cells, their programme was not designed to reinforce the mentality appropriate for each of the three segments of an Observant Dominican community.

4. *c.* 1446–55. Probably towards the end of 1445 Fra Angelico left Florence for a sojourn of about four years in Rome. In March 1446 Antonino Pierozzi, the former prior of S Marco, became Archbishop of Florence. According to Vasari, in an anecdote that has persisted as an example of the artist's legendary good nature, Pope Eugenius IV (*reg* 1431–47) offered the post first to Fra Angelico, who turned it down out of modesty and suggested instead the name of his former superior and novice master. A close relationship between Pope and painter undoubtedly existed, dating from the nine years when Eugenius IV's court had been housed in Florence at S Maria Novella. The only recorded commissions of the Roman years were for large-scale mural decorations, a task that the Pope could confidently entrust to the artist in view of his familiarity with Fra Angelico's Florentine works.

Fra Angelico was assigned a number of tasks in St Peter's and the Vatican Palace, although only one of them survives, the cycle of the *Lives of SS Stephen and Lawrence* (1448–9) in the private chapel of the humanist pope NICHOLAS V. Varying accounts of these commissions and the widespread reconstruction of the Vatican complex in

6. Fra Angelico: *St Lawrence Distributing Alms* (1448–9), fresco, chapel of Nicholas V, Vatican Palace, Rome

the 16th century all but obscure the number and location of the projects apart from this chapel. It has been argued that there were four papal commissions in all: the chapel of St Peter (1447), located near or on the site of the Sistine Chapel at that level, accessible from both the palace and the basilica; the chapel of Nicholas V in the palace (1448–9); a studio for Nicholas V (1449); and a chapel of the Sacrament in the palace, painted either in 1446 or 1452, during Fra Angelico's second Roman sojourn.

With the return of Eugenius IV to Rome in 1443, the popes established their major residence at the Vatican rather than at the Lateran, the official seat of the Roman pontiffs since the 4th century AD. The papal palace was therefore the site of constant building and renovation. Nicholas V expanded the palace and incorporated a 13th-century tower into the new edifice, and it was here that a small but lofty chapel (6.6×4 m) was built for his private use, dedicated to the deacon martyrs, SS Stephen and Lawrence. Entirely preserved except for the altarpiece, which probably depicted the *Deposition*, a sumptuous programme of decoration covers the vaulted ceiling and three walls in three horizontal zones. The *Four Evangelists* appear in the vault against a blue field studded with gold stars and the pilasters supporting the vault depict the *Eight Doctors of the Church* standing in tabernacles reminiscent of the classicizing Gothic style of the throne in Fra Angelico's *Coronation of the Virgin* (Paris, Louvre). Half-length figures alternate with rosettes in the pair of window mullions in one long wall and *trompe l'oeil* brocaded damask covers all three walls in the lower zone. In 1447 Fra Angelico's Roman shop included Benozzo Gozzoli and three other painters, all of whom may have worked in the chapel, though numerous restorations make it difficult to assign parts of the cycle to specific assistants.

Six scenes from the *Life of St Stephen* appear in the three lunettes of the upper zone, while five depicting the *Life of St Lawrence* follow in the rectangular fields below. The dedication to the two deacon martyrs reflects the Pope's desire to underscore the legitimacy of the Roman pontiffs in a period ridden with schisms. St Stephen's traditional tomb in S Stefano Rotondo was one of the major pilgrimage sites in Rome, as was the funerary basilica dedicated to the 3rd-century Roman martyr St Lawrence. Religious humanists of the 15th century, among whom Nicholas V was a leading figure, were especially interested in Christian antiquity, and Nicholas may have dedicated his chapel with propagandist purposes deriving from his own Christian antiquarianism. The correspondences between the two ordination scenes must be attributed to Nicholas: in the *Ordination of St Stephen* the bishop is depicted, appropriately, as St Peter; in the *Ordination of St Lawrence*, Nicholas V is portrayed as the bishop and thus shown to be the successor to St Peter, Bishop of both Jerusalem and Rome. Other interests of the Roman humanists in this period may be discerned in Fra Angelico's frescoes. Although many of the architectural backgrounds in the scenes may be traced directly to earlier panel paintings, others do not appear in Fra Angelico's work before his transfer to Rome. The strongly differentiated Classical orders and contemporary Roman architectural motifs in the *Ordination of St Stephen*, the *Ordination of St Lawrence* and *St Lawrence Distributing Alms* (see fig. 6) suggest that these scenes may have been inspired or even designed by the architect and humanist Leon Battista Alberti, then present at the papal court.

It is difficult to analyse the development of Fra Angelico's monumental narrative style because of the disappearance of the other three fresco cycles from the Vatican Palace. The more recondite, non-narrative paintings at S Marco are far removed from the active and even didactic manner of such episodes as *St Stephen Preaching* and *St Stephen Addressing the Council*, although these may be felt to recall the predella scenes from the S Marco Altarpiece. The expanse of space, the clarity of gesture and expression and the carefully adjusted light in the chapel of Nicholas V profoundly reveal Fra Angelico's long scrutiny of Masaccio's frescoes in the Brancacci Chapel, S Maria del Carmine, Florence. The poignantly humane sensitivity to the poor that informs Masaccio's *St Peter Healing with his Shadow* is also apparent in Fra Angelico's scene of *St Lawrence Distributing Alms*.

In the summer of 1447 Fra Angelico and his shop journeyed to Orvieto, where he had accepted a commission to paint the chapel of S Brizio in the cathedral, now better known for Luca Signorelli's wall paintings of the *Last Judgement* and the *End of the World* (1499–1503). Fra Angelico's contribution was confined to the vaults, where *Christ in Glory* appears in the compartment over the altar, with 16 *Prophets* appearing in the compartment to the right. Fra Angelico never returned to Orvieto and the contract was nullified in 1449.

By early 1450 Fra Angelico had returned to Tuscany from Rome to assume the priorate of S Domenico, Fiesole, for the standard period of two years. The altarpiece depicting the *Virgin and Child Enthroned with Two Angels and SS Anthony of Padua, Louis of Toulouse, Francis, Cosmas, Damian and Peter Martyr* (Florence, Mus. S Marco), commissioned by Cosimo de' Medici for the Observant Franciscans of S Bonaventura, Bosco ai Frati, near Florence, probably dates from this period. The church and convent, near Cosimo's favourite villa at Cafaggiolo, were designed by MICHELOZZO DI BARTOLOMMEO and are a simpler and more rustic version of S Marco. The general design of the altarpiece resembles both the Annalena Altarpiece and the S Marco Altarpiece, although its sumptuous surfaces, grander rhythms and more substantial figures reflect Fra Angelico's recent Roman experiences.

In the same period Fra Angelico accepted another Medici commission: to decorate, for SS Annunziata, Florence, a complex group of shutters (Florence, Mus. S Marco) covering the cabinet where the silver votive offerings to a miraculous image were stored. In 1448 Piero de' Medici, Cosimo's son, had assumed the patronage of the shrine, commissioning Michelozzo to erect, among other works, a magnificent marble tabernacle before the image. The 35 extant panels depicting scenes from the *Life of Christ* thus belonged to an ensemble. The compositions are related to those of similar subjects in the cells at S Marco, although the numerous biblical inscriptions demonstrate that a complex iconographic programme united an otherwise traditional array of episodes.

Fra Angelico's tenure as prior of S Domenico would have expired in the spring of 1452, and in March of that year he journeyed to Prato to discuss the fresco decoration for the main chapel of the cathedral. He declined the offer, and the commission subsequently went to Fra Filippo Lippi. Fra Angelico's decision not to accept what would have been not only a prestigious but lucrative commission must be weighed against the fact that he and his brother Fra Benedetto, until his death in 1448, were the main supporters of S Domenico. Unlike its sister convent at S Marco, S Domenico had no patron comparable with Cosimo de' Medici and although the bequest of Barnaba degli Agli had provided funds for the convent's construction, the friars of Fiesole lacked steady income and remained very poor throughout the period of S Marco's ascendancy. Fra Angelico's decision not to take the Prato commission was most probably made in light of some other opportunity and this is likely to have been in Rome. A possible theory is that he had another commission at the Vatican, or that he had been engaged to paint the cloister of S Maria sopra Minerva, Rome, the Dominican Order's main Roman foundation. At about this time, the distinguished Dominican jurist and Master of the Papal Palace, Cardinal Juan de Torquemada (*d* 1468), designed an extensive programme of decoration for the cloister, and it is plausible to assume that he wanted Fra Angelico to be responsible for it. The two men had been acquainted since the time of Torquemada's residence in Florence in the 1430s, and Torquemada owned the *Crucifixion* panel by Fra Angelico in which he is portrayed (Cambridge, MA, Fogg). The cloister has entirely disappeared, but its iconographical programme is preserved in a manuscript, probably in Torquemada's own handwriting (Rome, Vatican, Bib. Apostolica), and a woodcut edition was printed at Subiaco in the 1460s. Despite his long spiritual and artistic associations with S Domenico in Fiesole and S Marco in Florence, Fra Angelico died in Rome and was buried at S Maria sopra Minerva, where his tomb is now venerated as a shrine to his beatitude, which was implied in biographies of the artist since the 16th century and finally declared by Pope John Paul II (*reg* 1978–) in 1984.

II. Working methods and technique.

Considerable disagreement among scholars and often sparse documentation has made it difficult to establish a firm canon for Fra Angelico. For the great programmes in S Marco and in Rome, the difficulty is to disentangle the contribution of Fra Angelico from that of the various assistants who worked together as a team in his shop. Evidence for the existence of such teams dates from the early 1430s. A large number of works in all media and sizes can suddenly be assigned to Fra Angelico's shop between 1430 and 1437. So great an increase in production and of such high quality presupposes that his workshop underwent rapid expansion and that he was forced to employ not just *garzoni* (shop boys) and assistants, but skilled journeymen, painters in whom he could have great confidence even though they had come to him fully trained by others. Some assistants, mostly anonymous, appear to have remained attached to his workshop for considerable lengths of time. His closest follower was Benozzo Gozzoli. The names of those who assisted Fra Angelico at Orvieto and in Rome are not known.

Finding patrons was not Fra Angelico's responsibility. As a Dominican friar he was guaranteed his living, something that his secular colleagues had to wrest for themselves in the pressures of a competitive market. Unlike them, however, he was committed to developing an expressive repertory that would reinforce the theological and liturgical traditions of the Dominican Order. These traditions were both very strong and very old, and throughout his career they conditioned the artist's attitude to all Dominican commissions, including various parts of the S Marco complex.

Fra Angelico's facility in small-scale production, seen in the Missal (Florence, Mus. S Marco, MS. 558), led naturally to particularly lively and detailed predella scenes, but if thinking on a small scale came naturally to Fra Angelico, the major impulse of his self-education in the early years of his career was aimed at developing the skills necessary for painting on a monumental scale. This required the development of a system for representing volume that did not depend on the refined, calligraphic application of points of colour appropriate to manuscript illumination. For this reason the altarpieces of the 1420s reveal his close study of recent exercises in modelling in light and shade. However, for Fra Angelico the chief problem was that chiaroscuro implicitly made redundant the brilliance of local hues that characterized 14th-century painting, a quality he sought to retain in spite of the concomitant difficulty of rendering mass and space convincingly. Around 1432 he abandoned the chiaroscuro technique then current in Florence and turned instead to an invention of his own. This was a method of rendering the plasticity of solids in space by exploiting the opposition between complementary colours, particularly red and green. To achieve this, he studied early 14th-century Sienese painting, especially that of Duccio and Simone Martini, and was guided by his Sienese contemporary Sassetta. He seems to have met Sassetta in the early 1430s and to have remained in contact throughout the decade. This profound orientation towards a Sienese rather than a Florentine way of seeing accounts for the discontinuous nature of Fra Angelico's development from around 1429 to 1433.

Other visual effects whose extravagance is more closely allied with Sienese than Florentine taste may be seen in, for example, the Linaiuoli Tabernacle. Here, apart from the planes of prestigious and costly ultramarine blue and carmine red, which were themselves luxury ornaments in early 15th-century Florentine painting, the entire surface of the inner panel is covered with magnificent passages of complicated *sgraffito* work in no fewer than four separate patterns of cloth-of-gold damask, brocade and embroidered satin. The musicmaking angels around the frame are similarly executed in a rapidly changing sequence of costly pigments, the shimmer of their wings achieved by spreading transparent layers of colour thinly across the gold ground. These refined techniques were traditional painters' devices for conveying God's ineffable majesty, and as such none were new to Fra Angelico or his generation, although their most recent and most lavish appearance had been in Gentile da Fabriano's Quaratesi Altarpiece.

BIBLIOGRAPHY

G. Vasari: *Vite* (1550, rev. 2/1568); ed. G. Milanesi (1878–85)
J. Pope-Hennessy: *Fra Angelico* (Oxford, 1952, rev. London, 1972)
S. Orlandi OP: *Beato Angelico: Monografia storica della vita e delle opere con un' appendice di nuovi documenti inediti* (Florence, 1954)
U. Middeldorf: 'L'Angelico e la scultura', *Rinascimento*, vi (1955), pp. 179–94
Mostra delle opere del Beato Angelico nel quinto centenario della morte (1455–1955) (exh. cat., ed. M. Salmi and others; Florence, 1955)
U. Baldini: *L'opera completa dell'Angelico* (Milan, 1970)
A. Greco: *La Cappella di Niccolò V del Beato Angelico* (Rome, 1980)
G. Fallani: *Vite e opera di Fra Giovanni Angelico* (Florence, 1984)
Beato Angelico: Miscellenea di studi, Postulazione Generale dei Dominicani (Rome, 1984)
U. Baldini: *Beato Angelico* (Florence, 1986)
D. Dini and G. Bonsanti: 'Fra Angelico e gli affreschi nel convento di San Marco (*ca*. 1441–50)', *Tecnica e stile: Esempi di pittura murale del rinascimento italiani*, ed. E. Borsook and F. Superbi Gioffredi (Florence, 1986), pp. 17–24
L. Castelfranchi Vegas: *L'Angelico e l'umanesimo* (Milan, 1989)
G. Didi-Humberman: *Fra Angelico: Dissemblance et figuration* (Paris, 1990)
La chiesa e il convento di San Marco a Firenze, Cassa di Risparmio di Firenze, ii (Florence, 1990)
W. Hood: *Fra Angelico at San Marco* (New Haven, CT, 1993)

WILLIAM HOOD

Angelini, Costanzo (*b* Santa Giusta degli Abruzzi, 22 Sept 1760; *d* Naples, 22 June 1853). Italian draughtsman and painter. He trained in Rome under Marco Caprinozzi and was a pupil of Domenico Corvi at the Accademia di San Luca. The greatest influence on his work, however, was the style of Jacques-Louis David. Angelini soon distinguished himself as a skilled draughtsman and collaborated with the engravers Giovanni Volpato and Raphael Morghen on *Principi del disegno tratti delle più eccellenti statue antiche* (Rome, 1786), a work that was of fundamental importance in disseminating the Neo-classical style, particularly through the teaching of the academies. About 1790 Angelini travelled to Naples at the request of William Hamilton (i), the British Consul, in order to draw the antique vases in his collection (published Naples, 1791–5). His work was admired by several other collectors in Naples and in 1799 he was commissioned to draw the antique vases of the Marchese Vivenzio (published *c*. 1900).

With the introduction of French Neo-classicism in Naples, Angelini became the artist best able to respond to the demands of the new taste. In 1809 he painted a portrait of *Joseph Bonaparte* (Caserta, Pal. Reale) and drew a pastel of the *Battle of Aboukir* (Naples, Capodimonte), as well as designing a medal to commemorate the abolition of the feudal system (design in Naples, Mus. N. S Martino). He enjoyed great prestige as a teacher of drawing in the Naples Accademia di Belle Arti, where he was responsible for training a large number of artists. His commitment to the doctrines of Neo-classicism is recorded in his writings on the teaching of art (1820–21). Angelini is most notable for his portraits, which are characterized by a naturalistic style and a strong sense of psychological analysis, as in his *Self-portrait* (Naples, Accad. B.A.) and such works as *Mary Caroline of Bourbon* (1790) and *Domenico Venuti* (both Naples, Mus. N. S Martino). His son Tito Angelini (1806–78) was a sculptor.

WRITINGS

Alcune idee di Costanzo Angelini per promuovere le arti liberali (Naples, 1820)
Osservazioni sulle Accademie pittoriche per rendersi utili (Naples, 1821)
Relazione storica ove si mostra il vantaggio che reca lo studiare la pittura in Roma (Naples, 1821)

BIBLIOGRAPHY

V. Bindi: *Artisti abruzzesi* (Naples, 1883)
A. Caputi and R. Causa: *La Galleria dell'Accademia di Belle Arti* (Naples, 1971)
R. Cioffi: 'Per una storia del neoclassicismo a Napoli: Appunti su Costanzo Angelini', *A. Illus.*, lix (1974), pp. 374–82

ROSANNA CIOFFI

Angellis [Angélis; Angelles; Angillis], **Pieter** (*b* Dunkirk, 5 Nov 1685; *d* Rennes, 1734). Flemish painter, active in England. The fact that his style is heavily dependent on the work of David Teniers the younger suggests that Angellis may have been apprenticed to him. According to Walpole, the artist arrived in London in 1712, but in 1725 Vertue, who knew him, wrote in his notebook that Angellis was 40 years old, had been in England for nine years and had lived for a time before 1712 in Düsseldorf, where he had studied the collection of John William von Wittelsbach, the Elector Palatine. Van Gool, who had met Angellis in London, confirmed the visit to Düsseldorf. Angellis was first listed as a Master in the Antwerp Guild of St Luke in 1715–16, but in 1716 he was in London. The years 1719–28 were the most active of his career and his market scenes, conversation pieces (e.g. *c*. 1715–20; London, Tate) and still-lifes with vegetables proved popular in English aristocratic circles. The style of these works reflects his origins, combining the narrative vigour of

Teniers the younger with an elegant refinement derived from Watteau, resulting, as Walpole said, in 'more grace than the former, [and] more nature than the latter'. Queen Anne (*reg* 1702–14) commissioned a commemorative portrait of the *Knights of the Garter* from Angellis (London, N.P.G.) and in 1722 he contributed three canvases to a series depicting the life of Charles I, intended for engraving: *Charles I Seized by Joyce at Holmby House*, *Charles I's Escape from Hampton Court* and the *Trial of Charles I* (Ireland, priv. col., see Raines and Sharpe, pls 6–8); the engravings were published in 1728.

Angellis left England for Rome in 1728 with Pieter Scheemakers II and Laurent Delvaux. William Hoare joined them shortly after their arrival. Angellis stayed for 18 months, mainly devoting his time to study and producing only a few paintings. He left Italy with Scheemakers in 1730, but while the latter returned to London, Angellis obtained a number of official commissions in Rennes, where he died (the suggestion that he also revisited Düsseldorf cannot be confirmed).

BIBLIOGRAPHY

Meissner

J. van Gool: *De nieuwe schouburg* (1750–51), ii, pp. 138–40

H. Walpole: *Anecdotes of Painting in England* (London, 1762–71), iv, pp. 16–18

W. von Doe: 'Das flämische Sittenbild in der ersten Hälfte des XVII. Jahrhunderts', *Z. Bild. Kst* (1924), pp. 145–52

K. T. Parker: 'Mercier, Angélis and De Bar', *Old Master Drgs*, vii (1932–3), pp. 36–40

G. Vertue: 'Notebooks', *Walpole Soc.*, xxii (1934) [whole issue]

W. R. Juynboll: 'Pieter de Hoogh of Pieter Angilles', *Oud-Holland*, lii (1935), pp. 190–92

D. Sutton: 'Pieter van Angellis (1685–1734)', *Old Master Drgs*, xii (1938–9), pp. 67–9

R. Raines and K. Sharpe: 'The Story of Charles I', *Connoisseur*, clxxxiv (1973), pp. 38–46

D. Coekelberghs: *Les Peintres belges à Rome de 1700 à 1830* (Brussels and Rome, 1976), pp. 361–3

I. Roscoe: 'Peter Scheemakers at Rome. A Visit with Laurent Delvaux, Peter Angelles and William Hoare', *Gaz. B.-A.*, 6th ser., cx (1987), pp. 1–10

S. Trauzeddel: 'Angellis, Pieter', *Saur Allgemeines Künstler-Lexikon*, iv (Munich and Leipzig, 1992), pp. 18–19

CARL VAN DE VELDE

Ângelo, António (*fl c.* 1766; *d* Lisbon, 1814). Portuguese wood-carver and cabinetmaker. From 1766 he worked uninterruptedly on commissions from the royal family or under their patronage, even after the court had gone into exile in Brazil in 1807. His name is recorded from 1803 in the book of those receiving communion in Rua S Roque in the Encarnação parish where he, like many other wood-carvers, lived or had his workshop. He was licensed as a wood-carver of the Casa do Infantado and later of the royal palaces (1805). When he applied for the latter qualification, he made a list (possibly chronological) of his works prefaced by the statement: 'As I show here, I have been serving the royal household for thirty-three years'. This key document in Ângelo's own hand allows a fuller survey of his work than has previously been feasible (Correira Guedes, 1971). Ângelo worked principally in executing the designs of architects of the royal household or the Casa do Infantado, sometimes on his own with complete freedom and responsibility, as in the construction of the tower for fireworks on the occasion of the inauguration (1775) of the equestrian statue of *Joseph I* in the palace courtyard and in the tribunes for Évora Cathedral (1778), or in partnership with other carvers, as in the chests, candle-holders and confessionals (1789) for the new Estrela basilica (1763–90). As was often the case with cabinetmakers of stature, Ângelo left a wide range of work: furniture for the Court of Appeal in Lisbon (benches for the judges and thrones for the presidents), and for the Paço de Madeira in Ajuda, where the rooms of the Prince and the Queen Mother had bookcases in *pau santo* inlaid with *pau amarelo*. The palace was destroyed by fire in 1794, however, and all the furniture made between 1777 and 1781 was lost. A large number of works by him at Bemposta, Queluz and Mafra illustrate his employment as master wood-carver of the Casa do Infantado from 1791. They include furnishings for the apartments of Mary I and of the Infantes João and Carlota Joaquina (*c.* 1793). For the chapel in the royal palace of Queluz, where his work as carver included the provision of wooden moulds for casting candlesticks for the banqueting table. His work at Mafra (1792–1807) includes four book rests for the choir and the carving of the organ casing and balustrades, for which it is likely that he followed designs by the royal architects.

UNPUBLISHED SOURCES

Lisbon, Arquiv. Hist. Min. Finanças, MS. Casa Real, box 271, 1766

BIBLIOGRAPHY

C. Pires: *História do Palácio Nacional de Queluz*, 2 vols (Coimbra, 1925)

N. Correia Guedes: *O palácio de Queluz* (Lisbon, 1971)

A. de Carvalho: *A basílica da Estrela no segundo centenário da sua fundação* (Lisbon, 1979)

——: *Os três arquitectos da Ajuda* (Lisbon, 1979)

N. Correia Guedes: *António Ângelo entalhador setecentista* (in preparation)

MARIA HELENA MENDES PINTO

Angelo, Nicolaus de. *See* NICOLAUS DE ANGELO.

Angelo da Orvieto (*fl* 1317–*c.* 1337). Italian architect. He is first mentioned in 1317, working with Lorenzo Maitani on the restoration of the fortifications and aqueduct at Perugia. Two inscriptions testify to his authorship of some of the most important public buildings in Umbria. One, on the architrave of the Palazzo Comunale at Città di Castello, reads '. . . urbe de veteri Angelus architector . . .'. The other, on the arch over the main entrance to the Palazzo dei Consoli in Gubbio, reads '. . . struxit et immensis hoc Angelus urbsveterensis'.

The Palazzo Comunale at Città di Castello, begun in 1322 according to the damaged inscription, is stone-faced and was built only as far as the first floor. The original design must have included at least another row of windows, in keeping with the contemporary style of public and private buildings. The ground floor of the façade has a socle rising to a stone bench and two doors alternating with small, narrow single-light windows. The main door, which has a pointed arch with mouldings and a tympanum, is framed by pilasters with foliage capitals. The simpler secondary door has a pointed arch with heavy voussoirs. Above the string course that runs along three sides of the building are inserted a series of fine two-light windows with slender marble mullions supporting trilobed arches, and the same emphatic voussoirs. The ground-floor hall is divided by two massive octagonal piers with foliage capitals, which support the arches of the six heavily ribbed vaults.

At Gubbio the square, flanked by the Palazzo dei Consoli and the Palazzo Pretorio and built on a specially constructed terrace jutting from the hillside, is an outstanding example of medieval civil engineering. According to the inscription, it was carried out under Angelo's control from 1322 until at least 1337 and was subsequently completed by Matteo di Gattapone (*fl* 1345–76; Gurrieri, 1959). The austere Palazzo dei Consoli is a three-storey limestone building, articulated by four buttresses and crowned with a row of crenellation; the bell-tower has unequal sides like the tower of the Palazzo Vecchio in Florence (1302–10). The main entrance, up a flight of steps, has a round-headed arch like that of the entrance to S Ercolano at Perugia, on which Angelo probably collaborated *c.* 1326 (Gurrieri, 1959). The six windows on the second floor are linked by semicircular hood-moulds, and they rest on a cornice that runs across the entire width of the main façade. The first-floor windows are closer to those of the Città di Castello building: mullioned and decorated by columns with foliated capitals and trilobe arches (for illustration *see* GUBBIO, §1). In the unfinished Palazzo Pretorio can be found the massive octagonal piers already encountered in the Palazzo Comunale at Città di Castello, which unify and support the vaults and floors of the entire building.

A later work attributed to Angelo da Orvieto is the Palazzo del Podestà at Città di Castello, constructed about 1336, which seems to amalgamate individual elements from the earlier buildings. Above the ground floor, which is in the style of a Gothic-vaulted warehouse, the first floor has mullioned windows with large semicircular arches, similar to those of the Palazzo dei Consoli at Gubbio; the elegant decoration is close in style to that of the windows of the Palazzo Comunale at Città di Castello.

BIBLIOGRAPHY

Thieme–Becker
P. Laspeyres: *Bauwerke der Renaissance in Umbrien* (Berlin, 1873), pp. 8–9
A. Rossi: 'Lorenzo e Ambrogio Maitani al servizio del comune di Perugia', *G. Erud. A.*, ii (1873), pp. 57–9
G. Magherini-Graziani: *L'arte a Città di Castello* (Città di Castello, 1897), pp. 68–84
O. Gurrieri: 'Città di Castello: Todi', *Le cento città d'Italia* (Bergamo, 1939), p. 4
——: *Angelo da Orvieto, Matteo Giovanello Gattaponi e i palazzi pubblici di Gubbio e di Città di Castello* (Perugia, 1959), pp. 3–56

M. FABBRIZI

Angelo (di Pietro) del Macagnino (da Siena) [Parrasio, Angelo] (*fl* Ferrara, 1447; *d* 1456). Italian painter. He was court painter to Borso d'Este, Duke of Ferrara, and, with Cosimo Tura, decorated the Duke's *studiolo* at the Villa Belfiore (destr.) from 1447. The iconographic programme was provided by Guarino da Verona. In 1449 Cyriac of Ancona saw two finished paintings of *Clio* and *Melpomene* (both untraced) in Angelo's workshop, probably destined for the *studiolo.* No work by him has been identified.

BIBLIOGRAPHY

A. Lazzari: 'Il "Barco" di Lodovico Carbone', *Atti & Mem. Deput. Ferrar. Stor. Patria*, xxiv (1919), pp. 5ff
R. Longhi: *Officina ferrarese* (Rome, 1934); rev. in *Opere complete di Roberto Longhi*, v (Florence, 1963)
M. Davies: *The Earlier Italian Schools*, London, N.G. cat. (London, 1961, rev. 2/1961/*R* 1986), pp. 519–20

JANE MARTINEAU

Ângelo (César Cardoso) de Sousa (*b* Lourenço Marques, Mozambique, 1938). Portuguese painter. He studied at the Escola de Belas Artes in Oporto, where he taught from 1963. In the 1960s Ângelo worked in sculpture, photography and experimental cinema as well as painting. Having won a scholarship, he attended St Martin's School of Art and the Slade School of Fine Art in London from 1967 to 1968.

In the 1960s he painted simplified motifs drawn from nature, applying the paint thinly but unevenly, thus allowing a certain luminosity to show through the brushstrokes from the ground beneath. More interested in the mechanisms of perception than in their objects, Ângelo dispensed with figurative references from 1970, and henceforth his paintings dealt with light and spatial ambiguity. The formats comprise large, luminous, monochromatic fields of colour, applied in transparent, modulated layers and are usually divided into a few large geometric shapes by fine, incisive dark lines.

BIBLIOGRAPHY

B. F. Pinto de Almeida: *Ângelo de Sousa* (Lisbon, 1985)

RUTH ROSENGARTEN

Angelo di Pietro d'Assisi (*fl* 1345–*c.* 1362). Italian sculptor. He was previously thought to have sculpted the tomb of *St Margaret of Cortona* (*d* 1297; Cortona, S Margherita), then thought to date to *c.* 1362; it is now attributed to Gano di Fazio.

□

Angeloni, Francesco (*b* Terni, after 1559; *d* Rome, ? 29 Nov 1652). Italian writer, historian and collector. He produced about 38 novels and several comedies, although his literary works have been little studied. In Perugia he was a member of the Accademia degli Insensati, under the name Tenebroso. He is documented as having been in Rome in the late 16th century as secretary to Cardinal Ippolito Aldobrandini (later Pope Clement VIII) and chief Apostolic Notary. At his home on the Pincio hill he accumulated a substantial collection, containing scientific instruments, examples of flora and fauna, a picture gallery, a large collection of *Kleinkunst*, medals, and a vast assortment of drawings by contemporary artists especially Annibale Carracci. The collection was accompanied by a rich library. The organization and contents of the collection are described by Angeloni himself in a manuscript in Venice (Fletcher, 1974). From 1634 his nephew Giovanni Pietro Bellori lived in the house; Angeloni educated him in art, literature and antiquities, and introduced him into the circle of classicist artists with whom he had formed a relationship, more in the role of erudite mentor than that of patron.

Angeloni's contacts with Domenichino are amply documented by their correspondence (Bellori; and Bottari and Ticozzi) and it was through Nicolas Poussin and Paul Fréart that he obtained permission to dedicate to Louis XIII his most important work, the *Historia Augusta da Giulio Cesare infino a Costantino il Magno illustrata con la verità delle antiche medaglie* (1641). The second edition of this work (1685), edited by Bellori, was supplemented by a study of the numismatic collection of Queen Christina of Sweden. In 1646 Angeloni's *Historia di Terni* was published in Rome, with a portrait of the author by Giovanni Angelo Canini (1617–66). In his will Angeloni named Bellori as sole heir, stipulating that the collection was to remain intact. His relatives contested the will, however, and Bellori was left with only the house. A letter dated 1652 from the antiquarian Leonardo Agostini (1593–after 1669) states that after Angeloni's death 'his beautiful study came into the hands of Signor Prencipe Panfilio' (Bellori, intro.), and Cassiano dal Pozzo indicated that in the following year 'his study was dispersed' (Lumbroso, p. 72). Twenty years later a letter from Domenico Maria Corsi (1633–97) in Rome to Cardinal Leopoldo in Florence attests that 'Cirro [Ferri] and Morandi . . . again saw about 200 of Angeloni's drawings that were for sale . . . of which at least 20 were by Annibale Carracci and the others by excellent artists' (Bellori, intro.).

WRITINGS

Historia Augusta da Giulio Cesare infino a Costantino il Magno illustrata con la verità delle antiche medaglie (Rome, 1641), 2nd edn G. P. Bellori (1685)
Historia de Terni (Rome, 1646)
Description of the collection (Venice, Bib. N. Marciana, MS. Ital. Cl. XI Cod. CXI (7410); R. Symonds, London, BM, Egerton MS. 1635 cc. 50*v*–54*v*); quoted by J. Fletcher in 'Francesco Angeloni and Annibale Carracci's *Silenus Gathering Grapes*', *Burl. Mag.*, cxvi (1974), pp. 665–6

BIBLIOGRAPHY

DBI
G. P. Bellori: *Vite* (1672); intro. G. Previtali; ed. E. Borea (Turin, 1976), pp. xvi–xviii, xix–xxii, xxvii, xxix, xxxv, xlii, lxi-lxiii [intro], 354, 356, 370–72
G. Bottari and S. Ticozzi: *Raccolta di lettere sulla pittura, scultura e architettura*, 8 vols (Milan, 1822–5), i, pp. 387, 389; ii, p. 392; iii, pp. 48–9, 88–90
G. Lumbroso: *Notizie sulla vita di Cassiano Dal Pozzo, protettore delle belle arti e fautore della scienza dell'antichità nel secolo decimosettimo* (Turin, 1875)
K. Donahue: 'The Ingenius Bellori: A Biographical Study', *Marsyas*, iii (1943–5), pp. 107–38, esp. 110–13
D. Mahon: *Stories in Seicento Art and Theory* (London, 1947), pp. 119–21, 144–5, 148–9, 240–41
J. Fletcher: 'Filippo Napoletano's Museum', *Burl. Mag.* cxxi (1979), pp. 649–50

DONATELLA L. SPARTI

Angeluccio (*b* Rome, 1620–25; *d* Rome, 1645–50). Italian painter. He is the only known pupil of Claude Lorrain other than Claude's long-standing assistant Giandomenico Desiderii (*b* 1620–24; *d* after 1657). Pascoli, the only biographer to record him, claimed in his life of Claude that Angeluccio was Claude's most able student but had died young and was able to work little. Angeluccio appears to have lived in Rome and, like Claude, was exclusively a landscape painter. About 25 paintings and 35 drawings, all dated 1640–45, comprise his entire oeuvre. Claude's influence can be seen in such paintings as *Landscape with Figures and Bridge* (priv. col., see 1983 exh. cat., no. 88). This is a composition with centrally placed foreground figures framed by trees in the middle ground, which in turn stand before a bridge and a distant vista, and was borrowed directly from such paintings by Claude as *Pastoral Landscape* (1644–5; Merion Station, PA, Barnes Found.). Although Angeluccio shared Claude's approach to landscape, he was not merely an imitator. His paintings form a coherent stylistic group of wooded landscapes, rich in foliage and undergrowth and characterized by a blue-green tonality, which indicates that he also embraced the tradition of landscape painting brought to Rome in the 17th century by Dutch and Flemish artists. The *Landscape with Hunters* (Rome, Pal. Barberini), painted on an intimate scale and aligned vertically, like most of Angeluccio's paintings, betrays the artist's debt to this tradition. In the painting the pockets of sunlight and the highlighted foliage, indicated with the abbreviated white brushstrokes typical of Angeluccio's manner, provide sharp contrast to a dark, tunnel-like wood. The resulting sense of the landscape closing in on the figures is an effect often found in the landscapes of the Flemish artist Paul Bril. The distant vista, however, is similar to those that appear in works by Claude. The romanticism evoked by this blending of borrowed elements gives Angeluccio's works their distinguishing quality. His paintings frequently also contain rustic genre figures. For example, the *Garden Landscape* (priv. col., see Salerno, ii, p. 482) represents an assortment of people enjoying a day in a park; other canvases, such as the *Landscape with Attacking Bandits* (priv. col., see Roethlisberger, 1967, p. 135), with figures by Jan Miel, depict more spirited themes. Angeluccio's most frequent provider of figures was Michelangelo Cerquozzi (e.g. *Landscape with Figures under a Tree*, priv. col., see Salerno, ii, p. 483).

Most of Angeluccio's surviving drawings are landscapes, sketched out of doors in black chalk, lavishly heightened with white, on blue paper. His graphic technique lends a richness to his drawings of trees and foliage and to his close-up ground studies (many examples in Berlin, Kupferstichkab.), which is matched by the detailing of foliage and plants in his paintings.

BIBLIOGRAPHY

L. Pascoli: *Vite* (1730–36), i, pp. 29–30
M. Roethlisberger: *Claude Lorrain*, 2 vols (New Haven, 1961)
——: 'Drawings around Claude, ii: Drawings by Angeluccio', *Master Drgs*, iv (1966), pp. 375–83
——: 'Angeluccio', *Gaz. B.-A.*, lxix (1967), pp. 129–38
L. Salerno: *Pittori di paesaggio del seicento a Roma*, 3 vols (Rome, 1977–80) [bilingual edn, Eng. trans.]
Im Licht von Claude Lorrain (exh. cat. by M. Roethlisberger, Munich, Haus Kst, 1983)
Landscape Painting in Rome, 1595–1675 (exh. cat. by A. Sutherland Harris, New York, Richard L. Feigen, 1985)

PAUL SCOLARI

Angelus de Trivio. *See under* DRUDUS DE TRIVIO.

Angeren, Antoon Derkzen van. *See* DERKZEN VAN ANGEREN, ANTOON.

Angermair, Christoph (*b* Weilheim, Bavaria, *c.* 1580; *d* Munich, 6 June 1633). German ivory-carver and sculptor. He was the first in a line of 17th-century south German ivory-carvers who served the taste of princely and aristocratic patrons for small-scale carvings for their *Kunstkammern.* Angermair worked mainly at the Munich court of Duke Maximilian I of Bavaria; his works reveal a high degree of virtuosity, and minute details are worked with a precision reminiscent of goldsmith's work. As his style developed, the modelling became softer, but there was always a certain stiffness in his compositions.

Angermair was the son of a Swabian goldsmith, and he was first apprenticed to the Weilheim sculptor Hans Degler, through whom he would have had close contact with the Munich court sculptors Hans Reichle, Hubert Gerhard and Hans Krumpper. His first recorded work was a *Christ Child* (untraced) in ivory, carved in 1606 for the Innsbruck court of Anna Caterina Gonzaga (1566–1621), the widow of Archduke Ferdinand of Tyrol. It has been conjectured that Angermair might have worked in Hubert Gerhard's workshop at this time, since the latter is known to have been in Innsbruck in that year. In 1611 Angermair was working in Augsburg with Philipp Hainhofer on an ivory chess set (Berlin, Tiergarten, Kstgewmus.) for the *Kunstschrank* (collector's cabinet) Hainhofer was making for Duke Philip of Pomerania (*reg* 1606–18). This is one of a number of chess sets dating from Angermair's early years (e.g. St Petersburg, Hermitage; Brunswick, Herzog Anton Ulrich-Mus.) in which the rank of the figures is differentiated not only by their attributes but also by their bearing and gestures. In 1612 Angermair applied for citizenship of the town of Konstanz on Lake Constance. His intention of settling in Swabia was, however, forestalled by Maximilian I, who summoned him to Munich, where he is recorded as a court artist from 1613.

Further early works by Angermair are portrait medallions of *Duke William V of Bavaria* (h. 12.8 mm, *c.* 1610; Vienna, Ksthist. Mus.) and *Prince Sigismund Bathory* (h. 82 mm, 1613; Munich, Bayer. Nmus.), notable for their detailed depiction of physiognomy and dress; and reliefs of *St Sebastian* (boxwood, 160×124 mm; Frankfurt am Main, Liebieghaus) and the *Temptation of Christ* (ivory, 162×121 mm, London, BM; see fig. 1). The latter were carved between 1610 and 1620. In the way the landscape is represented the reliefs are very similar to those made in the 1520s by the Master I.P. who worked in the Bavaria–Salzburg area, an indication of the keen interest around 1600 in German Renaissance works. Angermair achieved the maximum effect of depth by the different treatment of foreground and background—the figures nearest to the viewer are sculpted almost in the round, whereas the other parts of the relief become flatter as they recede.

Angermair's most important and ambitious work is the coin cabinet made in 1618–24 for Duke Maximilian (850×440×347 mm; Munich, Bayer. Nmus.; see fig. 2). Its exterior is decorated with ivory reliefs and statuettes. Their complex programme was designed to emphasize that the Duke's interest in numismatics was primarily related to the history of ancient empires. Thus, the exterior panels have, in addition to reliefs of the Colosseum, Trajan's Column and a woman personifying Collecting, representations of Nimrod, the founder of Babylon, and Romulus, the founder of Rome (*see* GERMANY, fig. 78). Constantine, the model for the Christian monarch, is shown in the equestrian statuette (inspired by Giambologna) that surmounts the cabinet. His presence underlines the necessity of God's blessing on earthly empires. When opened, the cabinet displays the colours of Bavaria, blue and white, in lapis lazuli and ivory. The reliefs inside the doors are of music-making; their intimate tone contrasts with the exterior, and they may have held private allusions for Angermair's patron.

1. Christoph Angermair: *Temptation of Christ*, ivory, 162×121 mm, 1610–20 (London, British Museum)

Although much of Angermair's patronage came from Duke Maximilian, and his style was inspired by the court art of Munich, which was dominated by Netherlandish artists, he did not work exclusively for the court, nor were his sources exclusively Netherlandish. Several other small-scale items made in the 1620s have been preserved, including an ivory Crucifix (h. 500 mm; Munich, Bayer. Nmus.) and an ivory statuette of *Lucretia* (h. 110 mm; Munich, priv. col., see Gruenwald, pls 29–31). Although the statuette of *Lucretia* uses the repertory of the Netherlands, it is clearly influenced by the works of the early 16th-century German sculptor Conrat Meit. Similarly, *Das Tödlein* (1624; Vienna, Ksthist. Mus.), a skeleton on a clockwork mechanism in which the dramatic warning of the inexorable approach of death is heightened by the use of ivory, recalls the *vanitas* symbols used by artists of Albrecht Dürer's generation.

In addition to such works, Angermair also carved ivory decorative mounts for pieces of furniture, made ivory candelabra and worked on large-scale sculptures during these years. In 1621, for instance, he made four wooden busts of emperors (destr. World War II) for the Goldener Saal in the Augsburg Rathaus. Subsequently he produced large wooden statues for altars, including those of *St Catherine* and *St Barbara* (both 1626; Hirtelbach, nr Indersdorf, parish church), of *Christ the Redeemer*, the 12 *Apostles* and the *Virgin* (all after 1626; Aufkirchen, pilgrimage church) and of *St Catherine*, *St Dorothy* and the *Virgin* (all 1628–9; Tutenhausen, pilgrimage church).

Angermair's large statues in wood are in the Weilheim technical tradition: relief is built up with minimal carving into the depths of the block and the attachment of projecting forms by dowels or glue. Consequently the sculptures are built up from mass areas of drapery, and there is hardly any sense of a body beneath. He also created wooden fountain figures of *Neptune* (1628) and *Hercules* (1629) for the city council of Munich, although neither of these works has survived.

Several late reliefs in ivory by Angermair survive. Among them are a *Crucifixion* (418×495 mm; Munich, Residenz) based on an engraving by Aegidius Sadeler II after Jacopo Tintoretto's famous painting of the same subject in the Scuola Grande di S Rocco, Venice, but with the figure groups more symmetrically arranged; a *Holy Family* (178×130 mm; Munich, Bayer. Nmus.), which recalls 16th-century Italian reliefs in its calm, clear structure; and a *St Jerome* (235×154 mm; Munich, Bayer. Nmus.), which was for a long time attributed to Angermair's pupil Georg Petel because of its powerful modelling. The ivory figure of *Christ at the Column* (h. 299 mm; Munich, Residenz) dates from the master's final years, as does a second *Tödlein* (h. 210 mm; Dresden, Grünes Gewölbe). Around 1630, as the disturbances caused by the Thirty Years War drew nearer, the artist's financial position deteriorated. In 1631 he was released from court service at his own request, though he is known to have produced work for Duke Maximilian until the end of 1632, the year Gustavus Adolphus of Sweden entered Munich.

BIBLIOGRAPHY

K. Trautmann: 'Ein Holzrelief des Weilheimer Bildhauers Christoph Angermair', *Mschr. Hist. Ver. Oberbayern*, vii (1898), p. 87

M. D. Gruenwald: *Christoph Angermair*, Münchn. Ksthist. Abh., vii (Munich, 1975)

JOHANNES RAMHARTER

Angers. French city, prefecture of the Maine-et-Loire département, situated on the River Maine. By the late 20th century it was a city of *c.* 141,000 inhabitants, with growing suburbs and a number of industries, including slate-quarrying, which began there in the 9th century.

1. History and urban development. 2. Buildings. 3. Apocalypse Tapestries.

1. History and urban development. Located along the boundaries of the Armorican Massif and the Paris basin, Angers took shape on a rocky promontory east of the river dominating the small valley of the Maine. It was only after the Gallic Wars (58–51 BC) that the first town, Juliomagus, inhabited by the Gallic Andes, came into existence. The town was built on the Roman routes to Armorica and Normandy, and it expanded considerably from the 1st to the 3rd centuries AD; baths, a circus and an amphitheatre were built. Following the Germanic invasions, the settlement withdrew to the present site of the castle (*see* §2(iv) below) from the end of the 3rd century. Civitas Andecavorum was protected by a 1200 m-long wall (largely destr.) with four gates. It was incorporated into the Frankish Kingdom in 507, and the Angevin rulers, who emerged in the 9th century, were at their most powerful as feudal potentates during the 11th and 12th centuries under the Fulk and Plantagenet dynasties. The Plantagenet hegemony crumbled at the beginning of the

2. Christoph Angermair: coin cabinet for Duke Maximilian I of Bavaria, ivory and wood, 850×440×347 mm, 1618–24 (Munich, Bayerisches Nationalmuseum)

13th century after the long struggle between Philip II (*reg* 1180–1223) and the English crown, and Angers passed to the Capetians. It became a duchy in 1360 and experienced the brilliant artistic patronage of René I (*see* ANJOU, §II, (4)), the last Duke of Anjou, before coming under the control of Louis XI.

The late 10th-century Benedictine abbey of St Serge (*see* §2(iii) below) was one of the earliest religious foundations in Angers. Fulk III (*reg* 987–1040) founded the collegiate church of St Martin (partly destr.), St Nicholas Abbey (partly destr.; now a home for the elderly) and De Ronceray Abbey (now the Ecole des Arts et Métiers), the 11th-century tower of the last stands next to the church of La Trinité (1150–75; rest.). The Tour St Aubin (*c.* 1130; rest.) belonged to the powerful Benedictine abbey of St Aubin (*see* §2(ii) below). The Hôpital St Jean (now part of the Musée Jean Lurçat) was founded by Henry II of England and built in 1180–1210; it includes the 12th-century vaulted Salle des Malades, a chapel with traces of wall painting, and a cloister with two late 12th-century ranges. The present cathedral (*see* §2(i) below) was built largely in the 12th and 13th centuries. The university was founded in 1364 but was suppressed during the Revolution (1789–95).

During the Middle Ages Angers spread to the west bank of the Maine, where the Quartier de la Doutre prospered. The Tour des Anglais was built to fortify the city in the 13th century, and several 15th-century houses (rest.) still stand around the Place de la Laiterie. Back on the east bank there was an Augustinian canons' church (known as Toussaints Abbey; partly destr.), and Dominicans, Franciscans and Carmelites all built churches in the

14th and 15th centuries. The Maison d'Adam, next to the former Bishop's Palace, and the Logis Barrault (now the Musée des Beaux-Arts) survive from the 15th century.

The 16th century was characterized by the affirmation of municipal authority and by economic and cultural recovery. Such artists and humanists as the architect Jean de L'Espine, the jurist Jean Bodin (1530–96) and the poet Joachim Du Bellay (1522–60) were among the finest representatives of the Angevin Renaissance. L'Espine built the Hôtel Pincé (began 1523; rest.; now Musée Turpin de Crissé); he also added a tower (1540) to La Trinité, and a third range (1549) to the cloisters of the Hôpital St Jean. The Hôtel des Pénitentes and several houses also survive from the 16th century.

The religious wars of the second half of the 16th century had a great impact on the city. The cathedral was pillaged by the Huguenots in 1562, and the St Bartholomew's Day massacre on 24 August 1572 was particularly bloody in Angers. The castle remained a royal bastion during this period. Plagues, famines and widespread poverty also characterized the 16th century.

During the 17th century Angers recovered from its decline during the civil wars of the Fronde (especially in 1649 and 1651), but it was recaptured and pillaged by Louis XIV's armies in 1652. The crown seized communal power, the economy underwent a severe recession and cultural life was virtually moribund. The Neo-classical Ursuline Chapel (1637–47) is the only 17th-century religious building in Angers. In 1691 the Collège d'Anjou (now the Hôtel de Ville) was built.

1. Angers Cathedral, begun *c.* 1150; interior looking east

Captured by the Vendéens during the Revolution, Angers and its region suffered as a result of the long war of the Chouans. Following the flight of the Republican Army, the town was occupied by the Chouans from 20 June to 4 July 1794 and was besieged by them again in December of that year. This troubled period coincided with the beginning of the Reign of Terror with its trials and executions, an episode that ended a year later with the dissolution of the Revolutionary Tribunal. The city did not have an economic renewal or new urban projects until the beginning of the 19th century. In 1807 the ramparts were destroyed and replaced by the wide boulevards that give the city its present appearance. The Palais de Justice was built in 1883. The city was the birthplace of the sculptor David d'Angers, who was encouraged in his artistic ambitions by Jacques Deluse (1757–1833), painter and curator of the Musée des Beaux-Arts in Angers. He was also given a study grant by the municipal council of Angers in 1811 and sculpted a statue of *King René of Anjou* for the city (inaugurated 1846).

BIBLIOGRAPHY

C. Port: *Dictionnaire historique, géographique et biographique de Maine-et-Loire*, 3 vols (Angers, 1869–77)
Congr. Archéol. France, cxxii (1964) [issue dedicated to Anjou]
F. Dornic: *Histoire de l'Anjou* (Paris, 1971)
R. Favreau: *Monumenta historiae Galliarum: Atlas historique français—Le territoire de la France et de quelques pays voisins: Anjou* (Paris, 1973)
M. Provost: *Angers gallo-romain: Naissance d'une cité* (Angers, 1978)
Images du patrimoine, région des pays de Loire: Angers, Maine-et-Loire, Inventaire général des monuments et des richesses artistiques de la France (Angers, 1988)

PASCALE CHARRON

2. Buildings.

(i) Cathedral. (ii) St Aubin. (iii) St Serge. (iv) Castle.

(i) Cathedral.

(a) Architecture. The cathedral of St Maurice is a fine representative of the regional style known as Angevin Gothic. Its characteristic single-nave construction gives it a smoothly unified exterior broken only by the two west towers. This powerful spatial unity is also evident in the clarity of the cruciform plan, with a nave of three square bays, a single bay on each arm of the transept, and a square choir bay leading to a semicircular apse.

The design, however, falls into two principal phases. The nave, which is more than 20 m wide (see fig. 1), is attributed to Bishop Normand de Doué (*reg* 1149–53), and it formed the model for the transept and eastern parts, which were built seven decades later. The lower walls are articulated by large blind arcades surmounted by a moulded cornice on sculpted brackets. The cornice supports a passage in front of the walls, which runs through the back of the piers. The upper wall is filled by large two-light windows. Only the two rose windows of the transept arms and the continuous circle of windows in the apse break the formal unity of this majestic building. The Gothic sections were finished in 1240, when the liturgical choir was installed. In the mid-15th century ANDRÉ ROBIN repaired earlier glass and installed new glass after a fire in 1451.

BIBLIOGRAPHY

L. de Farcy: *Monographie de la cathédrale d'Angers: Les Immeubles* (Angers, 1910)

A. Mussat: 'La Cathédrale Saint-Maurice d'Angers: Recherches récentes', *Congrès Archéol. France*, cxxii (1964), pp. 22–36
G. Gilmore-House: *The Mid-fifteenth-century Stained Glass by André Robin in Saint-Maurice Cathédrale, Angers, France* (diss., Columbia, U. MO, 1982)

MARIE PASQUINE SUBES-PICOT

(b) Sculpture. Situated in the centre of the west façade is an important Early Gothic portal, which is associated with the nave campaign initiated by Normand de Doué. It has suffered greatly over the centuries. From the late medieval period until 1808 it was protected by a porch, depicted in an engraving of 1699, which ran the length of the façade. In 1617 the upper part of the portal was struck by lightning, necessitating the replacement of the *Evangelist Symbols* of saints Matthew and Mark, the angel and the lion on the tympanum. In 1745 the trumeau, carrying a statue of *St Maurice*, and the lintel were removed to enable elaborate processions to pass through the doorway. It is not clear how the terminals of the lost lintel would have been engaged with the portal structure. Finally, in 1830, the sculpture was incautiously restored by Danton, who replaced the heads of most of the figures.

The iconographic programme closely follows that of the central portal of the west front of Chartres Cathedral and so suggests that it may be dated *c.* 1155. On the tympanum (see fig. 2), *Christ in Majesty* is surrounded by the four *Evangelist Symbols.* There were eight *Apostles* depicted on the lost lintel; the remaining four are seated below architectural canopies on the springers of the inner two archivolts. These arches are otherwise occupied by threequarter-length angels emerging from clouds. Full-length angels stand on the springers of the two outer archivolts, which also bear the 24 *Elders of the Apocalypse.*

2. Angers Cathedral, west portal, *c.* 1155

The archivolts, which are distinctly pointed, are separated from one another by thin bands of flower heads. The label, carved with heads in foliage and edged with saw-tooth, recalls the labels of the Chartres Portal. It terminates, at springer level, in two colonnettes, which may indicate the original or intended solution at Chartres. The rather dessicated acanthus of the impost blocks has central ribs ornamented with bands of pearls: the curling acanthus foliage of the capitals has the same brittle character and continues across the arrises to form a horizontal frieze. Acanthus also curls around the continuous astragals. Only the inner pair of capitals are inhabited, incorporating caryatids and heads into the Corinthian-derived structure. Eight column statues occupy the unmodified recesses of the embrasures. As at Chartres, they probably represent Old Testament characters, but only *Moses* with the Commandments and *David* carrying a harp can be identified. The figures are squat compared with those at Chartres, but they are more liberated from the blocks from which they are carved. They stand on low, round socles arranged along a straight cornice. Below this, instead of stepped plinths, the lower zone of the embrasures is oblique and articulated by engaged colonnettes. As this feature does not occur on other portals before *c.* 1170, its appearance at Angers seems extremely precocious. Alternatively, it may not be original.

BIBLIOGRAPHY

A. Lapeyre: *Des façades occidentales de Saint-Denis et de Chartres aux portails de Laon* (Paris, 1960), pp. 85–90
A. Mussat: *Le Style gothique de l'ouest de la France* (Paris, 1963), pp. 184–7
W. Sauerländer: *Gotische Skulptur in Frankreich, 1140–1270* (Munich, 1970: Eng. trans., London, 1972), p. 399

KATHRYN MORRISON

(ii) St Aubin. In the 12th century the Benedictine abbey of St Aubin was one of the richest in Anjou, and its abbot enjoyed a position second only to that of the bishop. This was expressed in a series of building projects involving lavish sculptural decoration. There are few remains (the abbey was demolished in the 19th century), but they suffice to illustrate the changing fashions in sculpture in the middle years of the 12th century in a centre of Angevin patronage. The influence of forms from south-west France increased, in line with the region's long-standing connections with Poitou, and the chaotic arrangements of ornamental and figural motifs were gradually superseded by historiated compositions with a coherent religious message.

Successive building campaigns were marked by transfers of relics in 1070, 1128 and 1151. No sculpture survives from the first campaign. The chevet, completed either by 1128 or by 1151, is also lost, but a drawing and a description of the 19th century testify that it was rich in ornamental capitals. Construction of the claustral buildings probably began at the same time as the chevet, but it was completed later. Their remains are incorporated in the offices of the Préfecture, and they comprise the arcaded entrance wall of the chapter house, including a portal; and parts of the refectory, with another portal.

In the chapter house arcade, the capitals and arches are decorated with human figures, animals, monsters and foliage. The carved voussoirs form a repetitive pattern, with the motifs placed radially to the arches; the rows of identical human heads are particularly striking. This method of decorating an arch was common in western France in the first half of the 12th century but later largely abandoned. It represents a tendency to subordinate motifs to an architectural and ornamental framework. In the complex as a whole, there are two styles. In the arcade to the north of the portal, the shapes are simple, angular and purely decorative in a manner typical of Anjou (e.g. the chevet of Fontevrault Abbey, before 1119). A second style appears in the portal and the three twin arcades to its south, where rich decoration covers even some of the colonnettes, and ornamental sculpture competes with historiated compositions. This style represents the spread of artistic ideas from Angoumois and Saintonge to Poitou and Anjou, and eventually even to England. The figural capitals include the story of *Samson* (in the portal), and the spandrels of the twin arches contain reliefs of *David and Goliath*, a dragon combat and the *Virgin and Child*, the last accompanied by a painting of the *Magi*; the containing arches are carved with calendar themes, warriors and angels.

In the refectory portal, variously dated between *c.* 1140 and *c.* 1180, the emphasis on figural sculpture is increased at the expense of ornament, under the influence of new ideas from Poitou and Saintonge. The archivolts are carved with combats of animals and humans, the *Lamb of God* flanked by angels and Apostles and the *Psychomachia.* The figures, which follow the curve of the arch, are large and fully modelled. In this, they are proto-Gothic.

The western tower of the abbey, probably begun *c.* 1130 under Abbot Robert de la Tour Landry, also survives. Although much of the original sculpture was replaced during the restorations of 1904–5, it is known from photographs. There were foliate capitals, comparable to those of *c.* 1150 in the nave of Angers Cathedral and belonging to a tradition of Corinthian-derived capitals that had flourished in the Loire valley from the early 11th century.

BIBLIOGRAPHY

F. Henry and G. Zarnecki: 'Romanesque Arches Decorated with Human and Animal Heads', *J. Brit. Archaeol. Assoc.*, xx–xxi (1957–8), pp. 1–35; repr. in G. Zarnecki: *Studies in Romanesque Sculpture* (London, 1979)

S. R. Connolly: *The Cloister Sculpture of Saint-Aubin in Angers* (diss., Cambridge, MA, Harvard U., 1979)

——: 'A Proposed Dating for the Tour Saint-Aubin in Angers', *Gesta*, xix (1980), pp. 17–27

J. Mallet: *L'Art roman de l'ancien Anjou* (Paris, 1984), pp. 38–41, 138–53

ANAT TCHERIKOVER

(iii) St Serge. The abbey of St Serge was a Merovingian foundation, then dedicated to SS Sergius and Médard. It was situated north of the city in the flood-plain of the River Maine. It also suffered badly as a result of the Norman invasions. The abbey revived with Bishop Rainaud (*reg* 973–1005), who installed Benedictine monks. The earliest structural remains of the church date from his time, with traces of a lantern tower on brick piers in the present transept. Bishop Rainaud's building, now dedicated to the Syrian saints Sergius and Bacchus, was enlarged by Abbot Vulgrin (*reg* 1036–1040) and consecrated by his successor (1042). Evidence that the choir was raised is seen under the roof of the crossing, where there survives the beginning of a barrel vault that would have risen to over 12 m in height.

The present chevet and transept date from *c.* 1210. The choir is a vast rectangular aisled hall of 300 sq. m leading to a straight-ended axial chapel. The choir is flanked by two-bay chapels en echelon. There are round-headed lancet windows throughout. The Angevin vaulting, with multiple ribs applied to markedly domical webs (*see* MOULDING, §III, 2(ii)), was a decisive stage in the regional development of Gothic architecture, a clear response to the quadripartite vaults over rectangular bays associated with Capetian architecture on the Ile-de-France. One of the fundamental innovations in Angevin vaulting is the use of multiple ribs at the eastern corners of the choir. A homogeneous iconographic programme was introduced in the sculpture of the vault bosses (1215–25). The nave of St Serge was reconstructed between 1445 and 1480 in keeping with the earlier parts of the building. Its four thick-walled bays with interior passages and vaults with penetrating ribs demonstrate tenacious loyalty to Angevin Gothic forms. André Robin painted some glass for St Serge monastery from *c.* 1463.

BIBLIOGRAPHY

A. Mussat: *Le Style gothique de l'ouest de la France* (Paris, 1963)

J. Mallet: *L'Art roman de l'ancien Anjou* (Paris, 1984)

(iv) Castle. Around 850, in response to the Viking invasions, Odo, Count of Anjou, built his residence on the south-west of the rocky promontory dominating the River Maine. This building was probably a simple wooden fortress, the castle being essentially a ceremonial site, described in surviving documents as 'aula' (hall). The residential buildings occupied at least a quarter of the present castle site and lay mainly against the Gallo-Roman fortification. The hall, built on the earlier terrace, had adjoining rooms overlooking the Maine.

The earliest surviving remains date from the transformation of the castle in the 11th and 13th centuries. The first building to be erected outside the Gallo-Roman fortification was the St Laud Chapel (1150). Traces of the foundations of a donjon (8×11 m) and of a tower (3×4 m) are visible. Linked by a passage, they must have constituted the fortified gate-house of the count's castle. The castle fell to Philip II (*reg* 1180–1223) in 1204, and conflicts with Peter I of Dreux, the powerful Duke of Brittany (*reg* 1213–37), for the possession of Angers around 1230 encouraged Louis IX and his mother, Blanche of Castile, to build a castle at the head of the promontory, so that permanent troops could confront both the Bretons and the still-hostile town. The new castle covered the entire rocky spur, engulfing the earlier buildings. The 17 D-shaped towers joined by narrow curtain walls and the disappearance of the donjon placed it in the tradition of constructions built under Philip II, inaugurated *c.* 1202 at the Louvre in Paris: known as the 'château–cour', this type of building reflected the newly developed need for defence against siege and the latest developments in ballistics.

The faced rubble walls are powerfully reinforced against mining. They are strengthened around the towers with layers of limestone, in *opus mixtum.* The towers themselves are a striking combination of dark grey masonry and white stripes. The enclosure has a regular plan, the towers, 18 m in diameter, jutting prominently to avoid blind angles for the defenders. The upper wall-walk is protected by a crenellated parapet. The towers are pierced with arrow loops and are vaulted with domes and groin vaults, which not only limit the risk of fire but also reinforce the masonry. The tops, therefore, were all turreted except for the tower that contained a windmill (necessary for the subsistence of the garrison). The castle had two twin-towered gates, the Porte de l'Entrée from the city, and the Porte des Champs (see fig. 3) facing out to ensure the castle's independence of the city. The interior buildings, neatly arranged and built against the curtain walls, were principally intended for the use of the garrison. The central space was left clear for artillery movements.

In the 14th and 15th centuries the functions of the castle became more residential and administrative, as the rulers of Anjou tended to live in Angers. Towards 1370 the first Duke of Anjou, Louis I, ordered the construction of the Seneschal's apartments behind the Porte de l'Entrée and redecorated the old apartments overlooking the Maine, dividing the castle essentially into two, with the garrison area at the east and the seigneurial court to the west. Between 1400 and 1415 Louis II, Duke of Anjou, built the royal apartments and his wife, Yolande of Aragon, built the chapel of St John the Baptist. The latter was built in a traditionally Angevin style, consisting of a simple nave with a plain elevation. Towards 1450 René I, last Duke of Anjou, gave the royal apartments a vaulted gallery that linked the rooms and opened into the seigneurial court and the Seneschal's apartments. He created the gardens and kept a menagerie, and also commissioned the châtelet, or small castle, which became the main gate-house to the seigneurial court. The latter was then enclosed by a large administrative building. The troubles at the end of the 15th century triggered a new campaign of fortification. A bastion was built, and ravelins were added to the gates to give the castle control over movements by land and by river. The moat was gouged from the rock. At the end of the 16th century Donadieu de Puycharic, governor of the castle, adapted it to the new methods of warfare. Defying the decision in 1585 of Henry III of France (*reg* 1574–89) to destroy the castle, he reduced the towers to the level of the walls and installed stone platforms in them capable of holding light artillery pieces. Cannonières were then set into the 13th-century walls. To the south-west and the north-east earth platforms were raised to hold heavy artillery. A barracks and an arsenal completed these new defences.

The castle has remained in this last state. It was converted into a prison in 1779, and it remained in the army's possession until 1947 when it was handed over to the Monuments Historiques. The last addition was the gallery built by Bernard Vitry in 1950 to exhibit the *Apocalypse* tapestries (*see* §3 below).

BIBLIOGRAPHY

M. Deyres: 'Les Châteaux de Foulques Nerra', *Bull. Mnmtl*, cxxxii (1974), pp. 7–28

J. F. Fino: *Forteresses de la France médiévale: Construction, attaque, défense* (Paris, 1977)

A. Chatelain: *Châteaux et guerriers de la France au moyen-âge*, ii (Strasbourg, 1981)

——: *Châteaux-forts: Images de pierre des guerres médiévales* (Paris, 1983)

Le Château: Angers, Maine-et-Loire, Inventaire général des monuments et des richesses artistiques de la France (Nantes, 1991)

PASCALE CHARRON

3. Angers Castle (after 1230), Porte des Champs and part of the curtain wall

3. 'APOCALYPSE' TAPESTRIES. These form the largest surviving ensemble of historiated tapestries and the largest cycle of monumental images from 14th-century Europe in any medium. They were woven in six pieces (not seven, as earlier scholars maintained), each piece over 23 m long and over 4.5 m high, consisting of two rows of seven scenes prefaced by a large canopy rising the full height of the tapestry and sheltering a seated figure reading from a lectern. Originally, each scene also had a panel below it (h. *c.* 0.58 m) with an inscription, but so little evidence of these survives that their content cannot be ascertained; they were probably excerpts either from the text of Revelations or from a commentary on it. In addition, a ground strip along the bottom edge depicted a flower-strewn lawn, while at the top was a strip containing musician angels among heavenly clouds; these have survived only in part. Altogether, the set would have been over 130 m long, illustrating the Apocalypse in 84 scenes. Four of the reading figures and about sixty-nine scenes have survived. Since the tapestries have been cut into segments comprising at most two, and more usually one scene, and since some of the scenes have been lost, the reconstitution of the original sequence of scenes is problematic, particularly for the second piece. The difficulty is compounded by the fact that in two instances the scenes were woven in reverse sequence (scenes 6–5 and 55–54).

The creation of the tapestries is well documented. They were woven between 1373 and 1382 for Louis I, Duke of Anjou. For their design Louis 'borrowed' the services of JAN BOUDOLF, painter to his brother, King Charles V. Louis is also known to have borrowed an illuminated Apocalypse manuscript (Paris, Bib. N., MS. fr. 403) from Charles, but it cannot have served Boudolf as the principal model for the tapestry designs, which follow more closely the recension represented by another illuminated Apocalypse manuscript, now dismembered, the Burckhardt–Wildt cuttings (sold London, Sotheby's, 25 April 1983). Arrangements for weaving Boudolf's designs were put in the hands of the Parisian tapestry dealer, Nicolas Bataille, and at least some of the tapestries were woven in the Paris workshop of Robert Poinçon. They apparently cost over 6000 francs.

Based iconographically on a manuscript model, Boudolf's designs were transformed to register current artistic concerns. They were then used to create full-sized cartoons, from which the tapestries were woven. Although the documents make clear that the weaving method was '*haute lisse*', it is uncertain whether this refers to high-warp or low-warp looms. Except for the limited use of silver-gilt thread to create the background motifs of the reading figure on the fourth piece, dyed woollen weft threads on an unbleached woollen warp were used throughout. The density of the weft threads varies between 7 and 15 double passages per centimetre. During the cleaning and restoration of the tapestries (begun in 1981), the backing fabric was removed, revealing that the quality of the weaving is so exceptional that the back is a virtual mirror image of the front, and that, not being subject to the effects of light, the dye colours on the reverse have not faded substantially and provide a rare impression of original 14th-century tapestry colours (see fig. 4).

The tapestries rank among the highest accomplishments of contemporary French pictorial arts. The scenes display a limited but well-defined interest in pictorial space, with a shallow ground plane and consistent modelling of figures and objects in light and shade, from a generally centralized light source. The architectural structures represented, particularly the large canopies of the reading figures, display a surprisingly accomplished perspective. Boudolf's designs are far more vivacious and exciting than any known Apocalypse manuscript, using a variety of dramatic poses and gestures, several of which recall distinctive examples by the Master of the Parement de Narbonne, a remarkable range of highly emotive facial expressions and the depiction of contemporary clothing. Boudolf's designs also display an informed interest in Italian painting. The idea for arranging the scenes in two rows of elongated rectangular fields framed by fictive masonry mouldings must be derived from Italian wall painting, as must the *cangiante* draperies that occur throughout the tapestries. Occasional windswept flourishes of drapery (e.g. scene 81) may betray a specific interest in the work of Simone Martini.

The virtuosity of weaving, particularly in hands and faces, is remarkable, and pictorial effects are achieved through a variety of weaving techniques, notably the gimping, which emphasizes contours by means of rows of small holes in the fabric surface. Although in style and technique the Angers tapestries bear some relation to the slightly later *Nine Worthies* tapestries (*c.* 1385; New York, Cloisters; *see* GOTHIC, fig. 114), their layout in double

4. Angers, *Apocalypse* tapestry by Jan Boudolf, Nicolas Bataille and Robert Poinçon: *Those who Worship the Beast Warned of God's Torment by the Third Angel*, scene 51, 1.56×2.38 m, fourth piece, 1373–82 (Angers, Château et Galerie de l'Apocalypse, Collection des Tapisseries); view of the back of the tapestry with the negative reversed

rows of masonry-framed scenes is unique among surviving tapestries.

The backgrounds of the scenes are alternately red and blue. The earliest backgrounds are plain, but this changes at the beginning of the third piece, and all the later backgrounds are patterned, by either the repetition of a single motif or a continuous *rinceaux* pattern. This is indicative of a significantly different approach to design from this point. Besides the change to a patterned background, from this point the ground plane tends to rise up into coulisses, and the trees become less fantastic and more comparable to manuscript illumination; the scenes become generally busier, and more architecture is included. This change is difficult to evaluate, since it is not known whether Boudolf was responsible for both the designs and the cartoons (or the exact role of each of these stages). If it is assumed that he designed the whole series, then this could indicate a change of cartoon-maker. It is from this point, as well, that the reuse of cartoons becomes common. This is most noticeable in the last three large reading figures, but identical individual motifs and figures recur throughout the later parts of the series.

Narrative devices abound in the tapestries. Besides the 84 inscriptions, St John is represented in every scene, most often standing to one side and sometimes holding or writing in a book, looking on at the vision as it unfolds. The reading figures that prefaced each piece, once thought to represent the Seven Churches of Asia, have been related to the preface to the Apocalypse (Revelations 1:3): 'Happy is the man who reads, and happy those who listen to the words of this prophecy.'

There is little evidence of how the Angers tapestries originally functioned: they were certainly too large for the chapel in Louis of Anjou's castle in Angers, and not enough is known of the hall to judge. The only certain use that Louis is known to have made of the tapestries was for the marriage celebrations of his son, Louis II, Duke of Anjou, to Yolande of Aragon in 1400, for which purpose the entire set was carted to Arles where they were hung around the courtyard of the archbishop's palace. The tapestries were bequeathed to Louis II, and his widow Yolande bequeathed them to their son, René I, who in turn bequeathed them to Angers Cathedral, in which they were hung on important feast days until 1767. In 1782 the cathedral canons unsuccessfully tried to sell the tapestries as a set, and it was probably shortly after that date that they were disastrously dismembered. It was only in 1848 that a concerned custodian, Canon Joubert, made an effort to gather together all the remaining pieces, which were restored and sewn back together between 1849 and 1863. In 1902 the tapestries were classed among the Monuments Historiques, and they became the property of the state; from 1954 they were displayed in their own gallery in the castle at Angers.

BIBLIOGRAPHY

L. de Farcy: *Histoire et description des tapisseries de la cathédrale d'Angers* (Angers, 1889)

R. Planchenault: *L'Apocalypse d'Angers* (Paris, 1966)

D. King: 'How Many Apocalypse Tapestries?', *Studies in Textile History in Memory of Harold B. Burnham* (Toronto, 1977), pp. 160–7

F. Joubert: 'L'Apocalypse d'Angers et les débuts de la tapisserie historiée', *Bull. Mnmtl*, cxxxix (1981), pp. 101–10

M. Auzas and others: *L'Apocalypse d'Angers: Chef-d'oeuvre de la tapisserie médiévale* (Fribourg, 1985)

G. Henderson: 'The Manuscript Model of the Angers *Apocalypse* Tapestries', *Burl. Mag.*, cxxvii (1985), pp. 208–19

F. Muel, A. Ruais, C. de Mérindol and F. Salet: *La Tenture de l'Apocalypse d'Angers*, Cahiers de l'Inventaire, iv (Paris, 1987)

JAMES BUGSLAG

Angers, Pierre-Jean David d'. *See* DAVID D'ANGERS.

Angerstein, John Julius (*b* St Petersburg, 1735; *d* Blackheath [now London], 22 Jan 1823). Merchant, philanthropist and collector. He was supposedly the natural son of the Empress Anna of Russia and an English merchant. In the course of his career in the City of London he established Lloyd's on a new footing. He amassed a fortune that he expended on charity and, from about 1790, on collecting paintings, guided by Benjamin West and Thomas Lawrence. Angerstein's first acquisitions were English pictures: family portraits commissioned from Joshua Reynolds from 1765, and William Hogarth's *Self-portrait with a Pug* (1745; London, Tate), bought in 1789. After 1790 he took advantage of the dispersal of Continental collections after the French Revolution and the Napoleonic campaigns to secure Old Masters in prime examples, sometimes at record prices. His early purchase (1794) of Aelbert Cuyp's *Hilly River Landscape* (*c.* 1655–66; London, N.G.) proved to be untypical of a taste that inclined to figure paintings by Raphael, Titian, Correggio, the Carracci, van Dyck, Rembrandt, Rubens, Velázquez and Sebastiano del Piombo, whose *Raising of Lazarus* (1517–19; London, N.G.), bought from the Orléans collection in 1798, became the centrepiece of Angerstein's collection. He also had a liking for classical landscape, exemplified by masterpieces by Claude Lorrain (e.g. the *Embarkation of the Queen of Sheba* (1648; London, N.G.). Angerstein's interest in English painting was sustained in his purchase of Hogarth's *Marriage à la Mode* series (1743; London, N.G.) and three paintings from Henry Fuseli's Milton Gallery: the *Creation of Eve* (1793; Hamburg, Ksthalle) and two untraced works: *Satan Fleeing from Ithuriel's Spear* (1796) and the *Vision of the Deluge* (1796–1800; both known from prints, Zurich, Schweizer. Inst. Kstwiss.). This interest was further demonstrated in his subsequent patronage of David Wilkie and of Lawrence, to whom he was almost a father. On Angerstein's death the British Government purchased 38 of his pictures as the foundation of the National Gallery, and took over the lease of his town house, 100 Pall Mall, for their display, during the construction of the new building in Trafalgar Square.

BIBLIOGRAPHY

DNB

J. Young: *A Catalogue of the Celebrated Collection of Pictures of the Late John Julius Angerstein, Esq.* (London, 1823)

C. Holmes and C. H. Collins Baker: *The Making of the National Gallery* (London, 1924)

F. Herrmann: *The English as Collectors* (London, 1972)

John Julius Angerstein of Woodlands (exh. cat. by J. Bunston and C. Fry, London, Woodlands A.G., 1974)

DAVID BLAYNEY BROWN

Angerville, Seigneur d'. *See* PERRAULT, (1).

Anghel, Gheorghe (*b* Turnu Severin, 22 Aug 1904; *d* Bucharest, 7 April 1966). Romanian sculptor. He studied in 1923 with Dimitrie Paciurea at the Fine Arts School in Bucharest. Between 1924 and 1937 he lived in Paris, where he studied with Antoine Injalbert at the Ecole des Beaux-Arts, and for a short time frequented the studio of Brancusi, to whose work he was not sympathetic, however. To support himself Anghel worked in the studio in Paris of the Romanian architect Alexandru Delanof. He exhibited at the Paris Salon (1929, 1932, 1935) and at the Salon des Indépendants. In 1935 he had a one-man exhibition of terracotta sculpture. The only known portraits from this period are that of the actor *Jean Yonell* (1929; Paris, Mus. Comédie-Fr.) and a *Head of a Child* (Paris, Jean Delanof priv. col.).

Anghel established his reputation in Romania with his first exhibition at the Galeria de Artà Dalles in Bucharest (1943), when he showed clay sculptures of figures, influenced by Gothic work and with an emphasis on frontality and verticality (e.g. *Maternity*, bronze, h. 670 mm; Costeşti, Mus.). His work gradually developed towards a style similar to the French neo-classicism of the 1930s. He ignored the ideological pressures that were forcefully exerted in Romania in the 1950s and was unimpressed by Socialist Realism. He actively resisted the transformation of art into a propaganda instrument, producing work of formal austerity and an almost Byzantine asceticism, such as the commemorative statues of *Ion Andreescu* and *Ştefan Luchian* (both h. 2.75 m, 1954; destr.), which were displayed in front of the Simu Museum, Bucharest. A similar stance was shown by his exhibition of 1956, in which there were no concessions to official dictates concerning style and subject-matter. Instead Anghel continued to produce carefully modelled sculptures that owed much to Egyptian and Greek examples, and that succeeded in creating a feeling of spirituality and timelessness. Among these were bronze sculptures of the painter *Theodor Pallady* (h. 425 mm, 1955; Bucharest, N. Mus. A.) and the poet *Mihai Eminescu* (h. 460 mm, 1959; Craiova, Mus. A.). He also made a number of portrait busts of women, a large female nude (h. 2.19 m, 1956; Bucharest, N. Mus. A.), and the reliefs *From the Life of a Genius* (dedicated to Mihai Eminescu; first version 1938) as part of a coherent programme that drew on Classical ideals to produce works of great stylistic unity.

BIBLIOGRAPHY

G. Oprescu: *Sculptura românească* [Romanian sculpture] (Bucharest, 2/1965), pp. 160–61

P. Comarnescu: *Gh. D. Anghel* (Bucharest, 1966)

T. Enescu: 'Repere pentru o viitoare istorie a artei contemporane româneşti' [References for a future history of Romanian contemporary art], *Arta*, i–iii (1973)

I. Vlasiu: 'Momente din evolutia contemporana a sculpturii monumentale in Romania' [The evolution of contemporary monumental sculpture in Romania], *Stud. & Cerc. Tstor. A.*, xxv (1978), pp. 141–3

Expoziţia omagială G. D. Anghel [G. D. Anghel retrospective exhibition] (exh. cat. by R. Matei, Bucharest, Mus. A. Col., 1979)

A. Mândrescu: 'Gh. D. Anghel şi ideia de om' [Gh. D. Anghel and the idea of man], *Secolul 20*, xx/328–30 (1988), pp. 230–56

IOANA VLASIU

Anghelu Ruju. Group of 35 tombs cut in a sandstone bluff overlooking the Filibertu River, 10 km north of Alghero, Sardinia. The village to which they belonged has not been located, but the tombs, excavated in 1907–8 by A. A. Taramelli, shed valuable light on the form and decoration of the houses of the living. There are no radiocarbon dates for the tombs, but they have been dated to the 3rd millennium BC by the archaeological material recovered from them and now held in the Museo Nazionale G. A. Sanna in Sassari. These finds include Neolithic Ozieri and Bell Beaker pottery, a few copper daggers, flint and obsidian arrowheads and a variety of personal ornaments, beads and amulets of stone, bone and shell. The most notable artefacts are some stylized female statuettes in marble. The Ozieri pottery is well made and highly decorated with a variety of designs, of which hatched spirals are the most distinctive. The Bell Beaker pots are bell-shaped vessels of fine, hard-textured red pottery covered with neat, impressed ornament.

The tombs are varied in form and are approached either by a shaft or by a ramp cut in the level rock. Each has a main oval or rectangular chamber, sometimes entered through a small antechamber. Small burial chambers open off the main chamber; in more complex tombs these chambers themselves have subsidiary rooms. It was in these side chambers that the corpses or skeletons of the dead were laid out. The main chambers were occasionally carved in the form of contemporary houses. One example has a pair of pillars left in the solid rock to support the ceiling, and the inner doorways are often framed with ribs in relief, representing jambs and lintels. Other parts of the tomb walls were sometimes carved with reliefs of horned bulls' heads.

Anghelu Ruju is the largest and most accessible of such cemeteries, other examples of which, often with finer details, are scattered in smaller groups throughout the island. The tombs at Santu Pedru-Alghero yielded notable finds of statuettes, while at Sant'Andrea Priu-Bonorva chambers were carved to represent gabled or semicircular raftered roofs. Bulls' heads (bucrania) in relief are found at a number of sites, and a few tombs retain painted decoration in red ochre, though none survives at Anghelu Ruju itself. The most remarkable known paintings are at Mandra Antine-Thiesi; they include a panelled roof with white spirals on a black ground set between red 'rafters' and false doorways surmounted by sweeping red bulls' horns from which black pendants hang.

For further discussion of Neolithic European art and architecture *see* PREHISTORIC EUROPE, §IV.

BIBLIOGRAPHY

A. A. Taramelli: 'Nuovi scavi nella necropoli preistorica, Anghelu Ruju', *Mnmt. Ant.: Lincei*, xix (1909), col. 397

M. Guido: *Sardinia* (London, 1963), pp. 49–51

J. Hawkes: *Atlas of Ancient Archaeology* (London, 1974), p. 109

E. Atzeni: 'Aspetti e sviluppi culturali del neolitico e della prima età dei metalli in Sardegna', *Ichnussa: La Sardegna dalle origini all'età classica*, ed. E. Atzeni and others (Milan, 1981), pp. 21–51

DAVID TRUMP

Angicourt, Pierre d'. *See* PIERRE D'ANGICOURT.

Angiviller, Comte **d'** [Billarderie d'Angiviller, Comte de la; Flahaut, Charles-Claude] (*b* Saint-Rémy-sur-l'Eau, 24 Jan 1730; *d* Altona, nr Hamburg, 11 Dec 1809). French administrator. His brief but distinguished military career led to the Dauphin Louis, son of Louis XV, by whose side he had served at the Battle of Fontenoy (1745), entrusting him with the education of the royal princes, including the

Duc de Berry, the future Louis XVI. Flahaut's many years of faithful service were rewarded with his appointment as Directeur Général des Bâtiments du Roi after Louis XVI's accession in 1774. Although nothing in his background had prepared him for his new responsibilities—he was of pure military stock and unlike his predecessor, the Marquis de Marigny, had not been groomed in the arts—he proved an excellent civil servant: efficient, imaginative and, above all, devoted to the King. Of all 18th-century Directeurs des Bâtiments, he alone merits comparison with Jean-Baptiste Colbert, Louis XIV's great minister.

D'Angiviller is best known for his attempts to revitalize history painting and sculpture (*see* FRANCE, §§III, 4 and IV, 4), largely dormant since Louis XIV's death in 1715. This he did through a sustained programme of state patronage, in which eight history paintings and four life-size statues of illustrious Frenchmen (the 'Grands Hommes') were commissioned every two years from artists of the Académie Royale. The programme, begun in 1777, continued until the Revolution and produced many fine works of art, including Jacques-Louis David's *Oath of the Horatii* (1784) and *The Lictors Bringing Brutus the Bodies of his Sons* (1789; both Paris, Louvre) and Clodion's statue of *Montesquieu* (1783; Versailles, Château). In addition to stimulating high art in France, the paintings and sculptures were intended to edify the public through the subjects depicted. Paintings illustrated specific moral categories, while sculptures defined the hero as brilliant or courageous but at the same time dedicated to disinterested service of the state and humanity. The influence of the Enlightenment on the artists of these works is clear and not surprising in the light of d'Angiviller's personal friendships with many prominent *philosophes*.

Though these paintings and statues made their début at the Salon in Paris, they were destined for the museum d'Angiviller was planning for the Grande Galerie of the Louvre, Paris (*see* FRANCE, §XIV). In that setting, alongside Italian and Flemish Old Master paintings from the royal collection, they would have demonstrated recent French ascendancy in the arts, as well as the enlightened rule of the Bourbons. The museum was d'Angiviller's most ambitious project, the one for which he most wanted to be remembered by posterity. Financial difficulties in the 1780s and a number of nagging architectural problems prevented him from completing it before the Revolution broke out. When the Louvre museum opened to revolutionary fanfare in 1793, his efforts were nowhere acknowledged.

In addition to these outstanding accomplishments, d'Angiviller must be credited with significant reforms in the administration of the arts and architecture in Paris. After decades of mismanagement and financial starvation, the Bâtiments under his direction started to function as an efficient and politically effective branch of the monarchy (*see* MAISON DU ROI, §II). The Bâtiments archives are full of documents attesting to the Directeur-Général's conscientious supervision of the various royal palaces, gardens, academies and manufactories (Sèvres, Gobelins, Savonnerie) that fell under his jurisdiction. His interest in promoting the arts extended to support for scientific experiments on new paints, artistic techniques and restoration procedures. His numerous acquisitions for the royal collections included Peter Paul Rubens's *Adoration of the Magi* (Paris, Louvre), purchased in 1777 for 30,000 livres from a convent in Brussels. He was also actively involved in the construction of the Rennes Cathedral, a theatre in Marseille, baths at Bagnères-de-Luchon, law courts at Aix-en-Provence, waterworks for the gardens of the Château of Versailles and other works. His efforts to construct a Bourbon funerary chapel in the crypt of the abbey church of St Denis were foiled by the Revolution.

The corollary of d'Angiviller's commitment to making the arts 'an emanation of the throne', as an article in the *Journal de Paris* (1777) put it, was his vigorous suppression of organizations that threatened the Académie Royale's monopoly on the production and display of high art in the capital. For d'Angiviller the success of his principal projects—the museum and the history paintings and sculptures—depended on strict control of the art that was made and the art to which the public had access. His systematic deprivation of institutional support and recognition for the large number of artists outside the Académie Royale contributed to increased tensions in the art world in the years before the Revolution and helps explain the hostility that existed towards the Directeur-Général and the Académie after 1789.

Shortly after the fall of the Bastille in July 1789 d'Angiviller went into exile. He returned to France the following January but left again in the spring of 1791, never to return. He spent the rest of his life in exile, first in Russia then in Germany, living pseudonymously under the name of Trueman. He eventually settled in the town of Altona near Hamburg, where he died a virtual recluse. To the end he remained a loyal servant of the Crown.

In 1782 d'Angiviller married his former mistress, Mme de Marchais, at whose salon he had met many of the leading figures of the Enlightenment. He was a noted *amateur* of science and natural history and owned a good collection of shells as well as pictures. The latter included Giambattista Tiepolo's *Last Supper* and Salvator Rosa's *Archangel Raphael and the Young Tobias* (both Paris, Louvre). Following their confiscation in 1793 fifteen of his pictures were sold to the Louvre while the remainder were disposed of privately. Two fine portraits of him survive, one by Jean-Baptiste Greuze (1763; New York, Met.), the other by Joseph-Siffred Duplessis (1779; Versailles, Château).

BIBLIOGRAPHY

M. Furcy-Raynaud: 'Correspondance du comte d'Angiviller avec Pierre', *Nouv. Archvs A. Fr.*, 3rd ser., xix–xx (1905–6)

J. Locquin: *La Peinture d'histoire en France de 1747 à 1785* (Paris, 1912)

L. Bobé, ed.: *Mémoires de Charles-Claude Flahaut, comte de la Billarderie d'Angiviller: Notes sur les mémoires de Marmontel* (Copenhagen, 1933)

J. Silvestre de Sacy: *Le Comte d'Angiviller, dernier directeur général des Bâtiments du Roi* (Paris, 1953)

F. Dowley: 'D'Angiviller's *Grands Hommes* and the Significant Moment', *A. Bull.*, xxxiv (1957), pp. 259–78

J. L. Connelly: 'The Grand Gallery of the Louvre and the Museum Project: Architectural Problems', *J. Soc. Archit. Hist.*, xxxi (1972), pp. 120–32

B. Scott: 'The Comte d'Angiviller: The Last Directeur-Général des Bâtiments', *Apollo*, xcvii (1973), pp. 78–85

B. Jobert: 'The *Travaux d'encouragement*: An Aspect of Official Arts Policy in France under Louis XVI', *Oxford A. J.*, x (1987), pp. 3–14

A. McClellan: 'Two Neo-classical Designs for a Bourbon Chapel in Saint-Denis', *Burl. Mag.*, cxxx (1988), pp. 340–45

——: *Inventing the Louvre: Art, Politics and the Origins of the Modern Museum in Eighteenth-century Paris* (Cambridge, 1994)

ANDREW McCLELLAN

Angkor. Site in northern Cambodia, in a fertile plain to the north-east of the northern tip of the Tonle Sap (Great Lake) and near the modern town of Siem Reap. Angkor was the site of almost all the capital cities founded by successive rulers of the Khmer realm from the end of the 9th century AD until the mid-15th, when it was abandoned in the face of attacks from the neighbouring Thai kingdom of Ayutthaya. Each ruler built in the centre of his capital a state temple, usually in the form of a stepped pyramid representing Mt Meru, centre of the universe and abode of the gods, in accordance with the precepts of Hindu and Buddhist cosmology (*see also* CAMBODIA, §II, 1(ii)). This state temple was generally surrounded by a series of concentric enclosures bounded by walls, ditches, moats and embankments, laid out in accordance with the same cosmological precepts. Within the enclosures were the chief buildings of the city, including the royal palace and other temples founded by the king, members of the royal family or leading state dignitaries. All but the religious monuments were built of wood. Important adjuncts to many of these royal cities were the reservoirs (Khmer *baray*), canals, moats, ponds and other hydraulic works; these also were constructed according to strict cosmological rules. Scholars differ as to whether the chief function of the *baray* was symbolic and cosmological or whether they were made to provide water for the daily needs of the citizens and for the cultivation of irrigated rice (*see* CAMBODIA, §I, 1).

1. History and urban development. 2. Buildings.

1. HISTORY AND URBAN DEVELOPMENT. King Jayavarman II (*reg* 802–50), whose reign is generally considered to mark the beginning of the Angkor period of Khmer history, established his capital at Hariharalaya, near the town of Roluos, about 15 km to the south-east of Siem Reap. King Yashovarman I (*reg* 889–*c*. 900) abandoned Hariharalaya *c*. 900 and founded a new capital, about 15 km north-west of Roluos, which he called Yashodharapura. The centre of the city was the hill of Phnom Bakheng (see figs 1a and 2; *see also* §1(i) below), and round this he enclosed a vast area of about 16 sq. km, with earth ramparts, of which traces still remain, on the east and south. On the summit of Phnom Bakheng he constructed his state temple (*see* §2(i) below) and instituted there his cult of the *devarāja* (Khmer: 'the god who is king'), first instituted by Jayavarman II. He also initiated a number of important hydraulic works, including the creation to the east of the city of an immense reservoir,

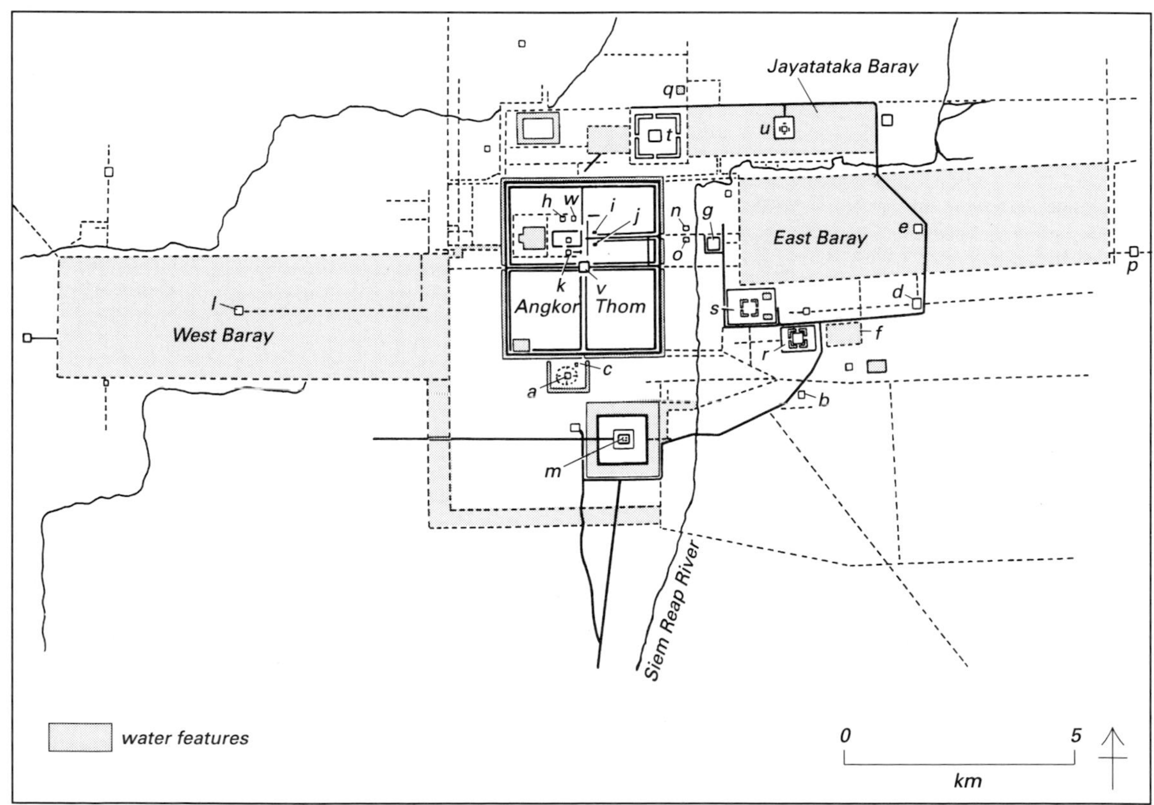

1. Plan showing principal monuments at Angkor, northern Cambodia: (a) Phnom Bakheng; (b) Prasat Kravan; (c) Baksei Chamkrong; (d) Pre Rup; (e) East Mebon; (f) Sras Srang; (g) Ta Keo; (h) Phimeanakas; (i) North Khleang; (j) South Khleang; (k) Baphuon; (l) West Mebon; (m) Angkor Vat; (n) Thommanon; (o) Chau Say Tevoda; (p) Banteay Samre; (q) Preah Pithu; (r) Banteay Kdei; (s) Ta Prohm; (t) Preah Khan; (u) Neak Pean; (v) Bayon; (w) Royal Square

7.5×2.5 km in area, known as the Yashodharatataka or East Baray.

In the first half of the 10th century two small but important monuments were built at Angkor: Prasat Kravan (ded. 921; see fig. 1b; *see also* CAMBODIA, fig. 17), a brick temple consisting most unusually of five towers in a row and with notable low reliefs sculpted in the brick showing Vishnu and his consort Lakshmi; and Baksei Chamkrong (see fig. 1c), completed *c.* 947 and consisting of a single brick tower on a laterite stepped pyramid, 27×27 m at the base.

Jayavarman IV (*reg* 921[928]–44) moved his capital to Chok Gargyar (modern Koh Ker, *c.* 100 km to the north-east of Angkor), but his successor, Rajendravarman II (*reg* 944–68), returned it to Angkor, where it remained continuously thereafter until the 15th century. Rajendravarman built his state temple, Pre Rup (see fig. 1d; *see also* CAMBODIA, fig. 5), a classical temple-mountain in the form of a stepped pyramid surmounted by five tower-sanctuaries in quincunx, on the southern shore of the East Baray (*see* CAMBODIA, §II, 1(ii)). He also built a temple, the East Mebon (see fig. 1e), consecrated in 953, on an artificial island in the middle of the East Baray. His palace seems to have been between Pre Rup and the *baray*, and his city was apparently never surrounded by dykes or moats. According to the inscriptions, the East Mebon and several other buildings, including the *baray* of Sras Srang ('Royal Pool'; see fig. 1f), were all the work of Kavindrarimathana, who is virtually the only Angkor architect whose name is known.

Rajendravarman's son and successor, Jayavarman V (*reg* 968–1001), laid out his capital, which he called Jayendranagari ('Capital of the Victorious King'), to the west of the East Baray, with his state temple, Ta Keo, at its centre (see fig. 1g). Ta Keo is a stepped pyramid with three tiers, clad almost entirely in sandstone and surmounted by five tower-sanctuaries in quincunx (*see* CAMBODIA, fig. 7). In 968 the exquisite and elaborately decorated temple of Banteay Srei, founded in the previous reign, was completed and consecrated (*see* §2(ii) below and CAMBODIA, fig. 6). Although Banteay Srei is situated some 20 km north of Angkor and so is not strictly on the site of Angkor, it is usually considered as belonging to it; it has also given its name to an art style characterized by many archaic features (e.g. the treatment of colonnettes and lintels) and some important innovations (e.g. the depiction of scenes from Indian mythology on the tympana).

Suryavarman I (*reg* 1002–50) was the first Buddhist ruler of Angkor and a prolific builder. His palace, which was to become the Royal Palace of the later city of Angkor Thom (*see also* §2(v)(c) below), was built on the axis of Phnom Bakheng and the East Baray. It was the first palace at Angkor to be surrounded by a fortified wall. In the centre of the enclosure Suryavarman I completed the temple of the Phimeanakas (see fig. 1h), possibly begun by Jayavarman V. This is a small, almost miniature temple, measuring only 35×28 m at its base and surmounted by a single central tower-sanctuary, instead of the more usual five towers in quincunx (*see also* CAMBODIA, §II, 1(ii)(c)). In front of the enclosure is the Royal Square, originally laid out by Rajendravarman II (*see also* §2(v)(c) below). Facing the square on the east are two rectangular sandstone buildings known as the North and South Khleang (see fig. 1i and 1j). '*Khleang*' means storehouse or treasury, but it is more likely that both buildings had a religious function. The North Khleang is the older of the two and contains several inscriptions of the usurper King Jayaviravarman (*reg* 1002–11). The South Khleang was evidently built by Suryavarman I, perhaps simply to balance the North Khleang, although the two buildings are not identical. Also attributed to Suryavarman I is the West Baray, the second great reservoir of Angkor.

Udayadityavarman II (*reg* 1050–66) built the Baphuon (see fig. 1k), one of the largest and most splendid of all the state temples of Angkor. It faces the Royal Square on the west, immediately to the south of the royal palace, on the north–south axis formed by the Phimeanakas and Phnom Bakheng. The enclosure is surrounded by a sandstone wall 120×100 m, and it is likely that outside this was a dyke enclosing approximately the area covered by the later city of Angkor Thom, although the building works of subsequent kings have obliterated it. Udayadityavarman II also built the West Mebon (see fig. 1l), a Vaishnavite shrine on an artificial island in the centre of the West Baray.

Early in his reign Suryavarman II (*reg* 1113–*c.* 1150) constructed his state temple, Angkor Vat (see fig. 1m; *see also* §2(iii) below, and CAMBODIA, figs 8, 9 and 20), generally considered to be the crowning achievement of Khmer architecture. The temple is enclosed by a laterite wall *c.* 1.03×0.84 km, and it is probable that Suryavarman II built a new royal palace in the northern part of this area. On either side of the great causeway known as the Avenue of Victory that leads from the Royal Palace of Angkor Thom to Jayavarman V's palace at Ta Keo, he built two small and very similar temples, Thommanon (see fig. 1n) and Chau Say Tevoda (see fig. 1o), which were probably not completed until the reign of his successor, Yashovarman II (*reg c.* 1150–*c.* 1165). During the same period one of the dignitaries at his court built the outstandingly fine 'flat' temple (built not as a temple-mountain, but all on one level) of Banteay Samre (see fig. 1p) about 400 m east of the south-east corner of the East Baray. Just to the north of the North Khleang and on the same side of the Royal Square is a group of five small, beautifully decorated temples known as Preah Pithu (see fig. 1q), some of which are thought to date from Suryavarman II's reign.

The Buddhist Jayavarman VII (*reg* 1181–*c.* 1220) began a frenzied programme of building at Angkor (*see also* CAMBODIA, §II, 1(iv)). Early in his reign he built Banteay Kdei (see fig. 1r; *see also* CAMBODIA, fig. 10) at the centre of a walled city to the west of the Sras Srang *baray*, which he entirely reconstructed. To the north-west of this he founded the great temple-monastery of Ta Prohm (see fig. 1s; *see also* CAMBODIA, fig. 11), originally known as Rajavihara ('Royal Monastery'). It was surrounded by an enclosure covering an area of 700×1000 m, which made it one of the largest in the Khmer empire. Jayavarman VII's first capital was Nagara Jayashri, about 1 km north-west of the East Baray. In the centre he built the temple-monastery of Preah Khan (see fig. 1t; *see also* §2(iv) below), a monument of great complexity; immediately to the east he constructed the Jayatataka, a *baray* 3700×900 m, in the middle of which he built the exquisite temple of Rajashri,

2. Angkor, temple-mountain of Phnom Bakheng, built *c.* AD 900, aerial view from the west

now known as Neak Pean ('Coiled Serpents'; see fig. 1u; *see also* CAMBODIA, fig. 12) on an artificial island, 350 sq. m in area. Early in his reign Jayavarman VII began the construction of Angkor Thom ('Great Capital'; *see* §2(v) below), the last and most magnificent of the royal cities of Angkor, in the centre of which he built his extraordinary state temple of the Bayon (see figs 1v and 3; *see also* §2(v)(b) below and CAMBODIA, figs 13 and 23). Angkor Thom was the last capital of Yashodharapura, and after Jayavarman VII's reign there was almost no building at Angkor. The only monument certainly built by Jayavarman VIII (*reg c.* 1243–95) during his long reign was the Mangalartha in the north-east of Angkor Thom; the small temple known as no. 486 also dates from about the same period (*see* CAMBODIA, §II, 1(iv)(e)).

In 1431/2 Angkor fell to the Thais, and by 1450 it had been more or less abandoned and the Khmer capital established at Phnom Penh. Between 1546 and 1564 King Ang Chan (*reg c.* 1510–*c.* 1560) had some of the low reliefs restored. His grandson Satha (*reg* 1576–before 1594) apparently lived there for a time and, according to an inscription, had 'the temple' (Angkor Vat) restored in its ancient form. Satha also altered and embellished some of the sanctuaries of Angkor Thom, and he may have restored some of the hydraulic works.

It seems that Angkor was completely forgotten in Europe, after the appearance of Diogo do Couto's description of Angkor and of other Spanish and Portuguese accounts in the 16th century, until it was 'rediscovered' in 1858 by the French botanist Henri Mouhot. Since then the site has been studied intensively, and almost all its many monuments have been meticulously documented and restored by the Ecole Française d'Extrême-Orient under the direction of a series of outstanding scholars, among them Henri Parmentier, Jean Commaille, Henri Marchal, George Coedès, Maurice Glaize, Jean Boisselier and George Groslier and Bernard-Philippe Groslier. In 1970 the overthrow of Prince Sihanouk and the outbreak of war in Cambodia compelled the Ecole Française to withdraw, and in the years following many of the monuments were damaged or vandalized, while all of them suffered from neglect.

JOHN VILLIERS

2. BUILDINGS.

(i) Phnom Bakheng. (ii) Banteay Srei. (iii) Angkor Vat. (iv) Preah Khan. (v) Angkor Thom.

(i) Phnom Bakheng. Temple-mountain built before AD 900 by King Yashovarman I and dedicated to the worship of Shiva in the form of a *liṅga* (Skt: symbolic representation of Shiva as a stylized phallus). It is built on the summit of Phnom Bakheng, the highest of the hills in the area, 1.3 km north of Angkor Vat and 400 m south of the southern gate of Angkor Thom, at the centre of Yashodharapura, the first city of Angkor. Its construction marks the establishment of the stepped pyramid form as the prototype for the Khmer temple-mountain (see fig. 2). The temple itself is a natural sandstone pyramid 65 m high and 76×78 m at its base, orientated to the east, with five terraces of decreasing height rising to a platform, on which stand five sandstone tower-sanctuaries in quincunx. Phnom Bakheng was excavated by Henri Marchal between 1919 and 1930.

The stepped pyramid of Phnom Bakheng is unique among Khmer temple-mountains in not being composed of backfill but cut from the rock and covered with a sandstone facing. It is also the earliest Khmer temple in which the central shrine has four real doors at the four cardinal points. Four axial staircases at an angle of 70° lead to the shrine. They mark the four points of the compass, with the principal approach on the east. The entire structure has the appearance of a succession of squares one inside the other round the central shrine, an arrangement that is simultaneously centrally and axially orientated, with the centre as the dominant feature (for the symbolism of this plan *see* CAMBODIA, §II, 1(ii)(a)). Each terrace has 12 small shrines on it, making a total of 60. Round the base of the pyramid is an additional ring of 44 secondary brick shrines, all facing east; in short, there are 109 shrines surrounding the pyramid or on its slopes. On either side of the main entrance is a rectangular building facing west; these are the so-called 'libraries'. At the foot of the pyramid three or four images of the sacred bull Nandi, the mount of Shiva, have been found. They were originally placed opposite the entrance stairways.

A quadrangular enclosure 120×190 m surrounds the entire structure. This is composed of a laterite wall punctuated by four doors facing the four staircases of the pyramid, and approached by four monumental staircases leading up from the foot of the hill. The base of each staircase is flanked by two seated lions, considered among the most beautiful in Khmer art. Phnom Bakheng hill is surrounded by a stone enclosure that is in turn surrounded by a moat with two entrance gates, one on the west and the other on the east.

(ii) Banteay Srei. Temple *c.* 20 km to the north-east of Angkor, founded at the end of the reign of Rajendravarman II by a high dignitary of the empire, the Brahman Yajnavaraha, and his younger brother Vishnukumara and consecrated in 968, the first year of the reign of Jayavarman V. It was dedicated to a Shiva *liṅga* under the vocable of Tribhuvanamaheshvara. Banteay Srei was excavated in 1924 by Henri Parmentier and Victor Goloubew and then restored by the anastylosis method by Henri Marchal in 1931. The temple is approached on the east by a causeway 70 m long, constructed on an east–west axis, which is in turn approached on the east by a cruciform *gopura* (entrance pavilion). The causeway is paved in laterite and bordered by 32 stone posts. On either side of the causeway and running parallel to it is a gallery, with a pillared arcade on the inside and a solid wall on the outside, forming an interior courtyard. The galleries are traversed in the middle by two vestibules which face north on to a long hall and south on to a group of three long halls set at right angles to the galleries. All these constructions were originally roofed with wooden beams and tiles.

The temple itself is a 'flat' temple composed of three quadrangular enclosures round the principal shrine; they measure respectively 95×110 m, 38×42 m and 24×24 m. The outermost enclosure is surrounded by a moat that is bounded in turn by a laterite wall. Access to the second enclosure is by two causeways, which cross the moat on the west and the east. The eastern one forms a continuation of the approach causeway. The second enclosure slopes slightly to the east and is surrounded by a laterite wall with a *gopura* on the east and the west. These *gopuras* have three fine triangular frontons with highly decorative volutes (*see* CAMBODIA, fig. 6). The innermost enclosure is surrounded by a brick wall and contains the three shrines of the central sanctuary, which are grouped together on a single platform and all face east. On either side of the sanctuary is a rectangular 'library' opening on the west towards the three shrines.

The central shrine is only 9.8 m high and contains a niche 1.7×1.9 m, while the door is a mere 1.08 m high and extremely narrow. These small dimensions are exceptional and have never been satisfactorily explained. Were they a limitation imposed on the founders, because they were only distant kinsmen of the king and were therefore obliged to build on a more modest scale and away from the royal temples? If so, this might also explain the choice of site for the temple more than 20 km from Angkor Thom.

The highly distinctive ochre colour of the various parts of Banteay Srei is due to their being built of a pink-brown sandstone in conjunction with brownish brick and laterite. These together create a harmonious blend of colour that is unique to Banteay Srei and sets it apart as an exceptionally picturesque temple. The quality and profusion of its decorations are also outstanding (*see also* CAMBODIA, §III, 2(ii)). The scenic richness of the pediments foreshadows the great pediments decorated with narrative scenes of Angkor Vat and the classical period of Khmer art. The most remarkable decorations are in the west entrance of the east *gopura* of the inner enclosure, representing the goddess Durga slaying the demon buffalo Mahisha; on the east pediment of the south 'library', Ravana, Rama's chief adversary in the Hindu epic the *Rāmāyana*, moving Mt Kailasa, Shiva's abode in the Himalayas; on the east pediment of the north 'library', the rain of Indra, god of war and of rain and guardian of the eastern direction; and on the west pediment, the murder of King Kamsa by Krishna (*see* CAMBODIA, fig. 18). This last scene is especially interesting because it takes place in a palace and thus gives an idea of the probable appearance of wooden domestic buildings in Cambodia in the 10th century.

(iii) Angkor Vat. Royal temple-mountain built by King Suryavarman II but not completed until after his death (*c.* 1150); it is the largest and most important of all the monuments of Angkor (see fig. 3). It is dedicated to the worship of Vishnu, one of the three principal gods of Hinduism, saviour and protector of the world, whose direction is the west, which explains the unusual westerly orientation of this temple. Located 1.7 km from the southern gate of Angkor Thom in the south-east quarter of the first capital of Angkor, Yashodharapura, it consists of a stepped pyramid on three levels surrounded by four enclosures one inside the other on an approximately square ground-plan. The pyramid is surmounted by five towers in quincunx (*see* CAMBODIA, fig. 8). Angkor Vat was first excavated (1908–13) by Jean Commaille.

The outermost enclosure covers an area of 1.3×1.5 km. It is surrounded by a laterite wall 4.7 m high, outside which

3. Angkor, royal temple–mountain of Angkor Vat, completed *c.* AD 1150; aerial view from the north–east

is a moat 190 m wide traversed on the west by a paved causeway raised on an embankment. This causeway leads to an entrance pavilion with five interconnected passages extending over a length of almost 250 m. The entrance consists of three *gopuras*, each surmounted by a tower replicating the central tower-sanctuaries of the temple itself and flanked on the north and south by galleries open on the outside that terminate in two further *gopuras* without staircases to permit carts and elephants to enter at ground level. The central *gopura* of the outermost enclosure opens on to a causeway 350 m long and 9.4 m wide, paved and faced with sandstone and with a *nāga* balustrade, that gives access to the *gopura* of the third enclosure. Six lateral stairways lead from the platform of the temple to the ground. Halfway along and 1.5 m below, the causeway is flanked by two 'libraries' and further along again by two ponds. The platform supporting the temple is about 1 m high and is surrounded by a sandstone wall with a *nāga* balustrade. In front of this is a cruciform terrace with three staircases on each side.

The third enclosure is entirely surrounded by a gallery, 187×215 m, consisting of a solid wall on the inside decorated with low-reliefs and a colonnade with square pillars on the outside. The low-reliefs illustrate scenes from the *Ramāyāna*, *Mahābhārata*, *Harivaṃsa* and other Hindu epics and sacred texts for the edification of the faithful, as well as depicting Suryavarman II reviewing his armies and marching in his posthumous form towards the kingdom of the dead (for a full description *see* CAMBODIA, §III, 3(i)(b)). Access to this gallery is gained from the west *gopura*, which faces east on to a cruciform cloister with four sections, situated between the second and third enclosures. This cloister consists of three east–west galleries that join the three passages of the *gopuras* of the second and third enclosures. Cutting across them at right angles is a north–south gallery, which with the east–west galleries divides the courtyard into four sections. The two intermediate galleries have three corridors resting on pillars on both sides. The two end galleries have two corridors, with a solid wall on the outside containing a door in the middle that gives access to the north and south 'libraries' of the third enclosure. The three west galleries and the *gopura* of the second enclosure are linked together by three stairways roofed with projecting vaults of a particularly felicitous design.

The second enclosure is raised above the level of the first enclosure to form a second storey and measures 100×115 m. It is only 2.45 m wide and is surrounded by a gallery with a solid wall on the outside, openwork doors and windows on the inside, giving on to the courtyard of the second enclosure. It is decorated on the inside with a great number of figures of *devatā* (deities) with a wide variety of rich adornments. From this courtyard on the second storey, 11 m above the first enclosure, there is an impressive view of the towers of the central mass. There are two small 'libraries' in the courtyard built on a north–south axis and linked with each other, with the western *gopura* of the second enclosure and with 12 stairways, one on each side and two at each corner, leading to the first enclosure by a sandstone gangway on short sandstone columns.

The gallery of this innermost enclosure is open on both sides, with balustered windows on the outer wall and pillars on the inside supporting a corbelled vault and half-vault pierced in the middle by a *gopura* with a single passage and in the corners by tower-sanctuaries, which are replicas of the central shrine. Galleries with three corridors, resting entirely on pillars, link the four cruciform *gopuras* to the central shrine. The linking galleries have in their centre two small staircases leading down into the courtyard. The shrine is 42 m high and has four real doors that have been walled in. The shrine once housed a sacred image of Vishnu in a square niche. Vestiges of relief carving of high quality testify to the care with which the central shrine was decorated. Traces of stucco remain in some of the hollow areas, and it may be assumed that the shrine was painted and perhaps gilded. Immediately beneath the pedestal in the central sanctuary is a pit, which goes down to ground level, in which the sacred foundation deposit, consisting of two circular sheets of gold leaf, 180 mm in diameter, has been discovered laid between two stones.

Among the characteristic architectural features of Angkor Vat is the treatment of the enclosure as a gallery and the extent to which it is associated with the terraces of the stepped pyramid. The gallery-enclosures make for a predominance of horizontal lines, which emphasize the steps of the pyramid and reinforce the verticality of the tower-sanctuaries. They also provide a natural continuation of the causeways leading up to the temple and so open it to worshippers. They impart to the whole composition a balance and harmony that make Angkor Vat the finest achievement of Khmer architecture. This balance is also achieved by the plan of the temple complex, which is at one and the same time centred and axial. Its centre is the central shrine, surrounded by successive enclosures which fit into each other like a nest of dolls, and its axis follows the alignment of the favoured west entry, which from the fourth enclosure inwards consists of a series of causeways that succeed one another into the cloister galleries.

Another notable feature of this temple is its decoration, in which there is an abundance of figures in very low relief (*see* CAMBODIA, fig. 20) portrayed either in a continuous frieze, as in the third enclosure, or individually, as in the tympana of the pediments. There are almost 2000 *devatās* throughout the temple, the finest being in the central shrine, in the *gopura* of the fourth enclosure and in the courtyard of the second storey. The distribution of this decoration is also remarkable. The shadows cast by the mouldings, which are always judiciously placed along the lines of force of the building, emphasize their mass. This is an architecture of light and shade, in which the decorated and plain surfaces alternate felicitously to underline the balance of the whole.

(iv) Preah Khan. 'Flat' temple built by Jayavarman VII in the north-east corner of Angkor Thom, in a direct line with Neak Pean and the Jayatataka. According to the foundation stele, it was consecrated in 1191 and dedicated to the memory of the King's father, Dharanindravarman II, in the form of an image of the *bodhisattva* Lokeshvara and to the sacred sword, symbol of the durability of the kingdom. In style, it is transitional between Angkor Vat and the Bayon and was the subject of numerous additions and alterations. It is a Mahayana Buddhist temple, although evidence that Brahmanic cults continued to flourish in Jayavarman VII's reign is provided by the large number of images of Hindu deities it contains. The temple probably occupies the site where Jayavarman VII inflicted a decisive defeat on the Chams. It may also have been the centre of the town of Nagarajayashri, which is mentioned in the inscriptions and served as a temporary residence for the King during the reconstruction of Angkor Thom. Preah Khan was first excavated in 1927 by Henri Marchal and again in 1939 by Maurice Glaize, who restored parts of it by the anastylosis method, using the original materials on the site.

The plan of the temple is extremely complex and consists of four quadrangular enclosures, one within the other, centred on the principal shrine. The enclosures tilt slightly to the east, emphasizing the orientation of the temple towards the rising sun. A series of porches, vestibules, chambers and galleries marks the two main east–west and north–south axes. The outer enclosure is bounded by a laterite wall and measures 700×800 m. On the east it has a *gopura* with three passages, the central one of which is on ground level to permit access to carts and elephants. Access to the east *gopura*, as to the three others, is gained by a causeway across the moats, approximately 100 m long and 10 m wide, flanked by 54 figures of giants, the sign of a royal city. This is in turn preceded by an imposing avenue of stone posts. To the east the causeway leads to a terrace facing the Jayatataka, in the centre of which on an artificial island stands Neak Pean, also dedicated to Lokeshvara (*see* CAMBODIA, fig. 12). About halfway up the east–west causeway leading to the third enclosure, on the north side, there is a well-preserved building that was used as a guest-house for pilgrims (*dharmasālā*). This building, which is mentioned in the inscriptions, is oblong in shape and has very thick walls and windows with a double row of balusters.

Entry to the third enclosure is through a *gopura* composed of three central towers and two end pavilions, all interlinked by five galleries. Overall it covers more than 100 m, and it recalls the west *gopura* with its four enclosures in Angkor Vat. Access to the second enclosure is through a covered cruciform courtyard, and matching this to the north, south and west are three miniature temples that together form a cloister. The second enclosure, which is very close to the first, was probably added subsequently, as its decoration is of a later date. The *gopura* of the first enclosure leads to a four-towered cloister, in which there are numerous ancillary shrines. In the centre is the principal shrine that houses a later stupa and the foundation stele, which was found intact under a pile of fallen rocks. The shrine is cruciform and was formerly covered on the inside with bronze plates; the holes that were made to fix these are still clearly visible.

The enormous dimensions of Preah Khan give it an essentially urban character. It is almost certain that the space between the fourth and third enclosures was filled with houses. In other words, there was a town round the temple, which was founded by Jayavarman VII to establish his political authority while his capital was being rebuilt. That it was only a temporary centre of power is implied both by its setting and its architecture. Preah Khan is also notable for the wealth of its epigraphy and the abundance of the data it supplies. The inscriptions refer to the installation of more than 500 statues, to the building of a hospital rest-house and of a *dharmaśālā* and state that 97,000 people, including 1000 female dancers, were assigned to serve in the temple. Preah Khan and its numerous additions give an impression of confusion, which is increased by the temple having been left by the Conservation d'Angkor in the state in which it was found at the beginning of the 20th century. Of all the temples of Angkor it is the most surprising and at the same time the most poetic.

GUY NAFILYAN

(v) Angkor Thom. The last of the royal capitals of Angkor. It appears from the evidence of the hydraulic construction works there that Yashodharapura, the city of Yashovarman I (*see* §1 above), was moved, probably after the 11th century, to a new site that must have occupied approximately the same area as the later city of Angkor Thom. Although it has not been possible to verify this hypothesis, it is certain that from the end of the 10th century several important monuments were erected around the space now known as the Royal Square of Angkor Thom. These included the temple of Phimeanakas (late 10th century) in the centre of the enclosure of the Royal Palace, the two Khleangs (early 11th century) and the Baphuon (mid-11th century). At about the same time the West Baray was laid out to the west of the city. In 1177 Yashodharapura was captured and pillaged by the Chams. King Jayavarman VII drove out the invaders in 1181 and began the work of rebuilding the capital slightly to the north of the city founded by Yashovarman I (*see also* CAMBODIA, §II, 1(iv)(c) and (d)). It was Jayavarman VII's city that became what is now known as Angkor Thom, although it retained the name of Yashodharapura until the end of the Angkor period. At its centre, to the south of the Royal Square, he built the Bayon. By the end of his reign (*c.* 1220) almost all the buildings of which the ruins can still be seen within the enclosure of Angkor Thom were already in existence.

(a) City walls and gates. The city walls of Angkor Thom form an almost perfect square, with each side more than 3 km in length. The ramparts, built of laterite, are almost 8 m high. At each corner is a small temple called Prasat Chrung containing a stele recording the founding of the city. The city wall is pierced by five monumental gates, all similar: one in each of the south, west and north walls, and two in the east wall (see fig. 4). The two last are known as the Gate of the Dead, which is axially aligned with the Bayon, and the Gate of Victories, which is aligned with the Royal Palace. The moat and ditches are traversed

4. Angkor, Angkor Thom, gateway in the city wall, late 12th century

by a causeway flanked on either side by a row of 54 giant guardian figures in sandstone. These figures supported two huge nine-headed *nāga* who confronted anybody entering the city.

The gateways, some 23 m high and 3.5 m wide, are also built in sandstone and are crowned by four heads representing deities; the two central heads form a single two-faced block, while the lateral heads, set somewhat lower, are detached from the centre. The heads crowning the gates are thought to represent the Guardians of the Four Quarters and share the task of protecting the city with the giant divinities of the *nāgas* and the images of Indra, king of the gods, riding his three-headed elephant, which are carved into the corners of the gates.

The interior has now been invaded by the forest, but the Chinese chronicler Zhou Daguan, who came to Cambodia at the end of the 13th century, reported that 'the palace, the official residences and the houses of the nobility are all orientated towards the east' and that 'the common houses and outlying lodgings are roofed with thatch; only family temples and private apartments may be roofed with tiles'.

(b) Bayon. Three-storey temple in the centre of Angkor Thom (*see* CAMBODIA, fig. 13). Galleries on the two lower floors surround a cruciform upper terrace, which supports the central tower-sanctuary as well as the secondary sanctuaries. The central sanctuary has a circular groundplan and from it radiates a sunburst of chapels open to the outside. The topmost point of the roof ridge is 43 m above ground level. Each sanctuary is crowned by towers adorned with four faces, and faces of equally colossal

proportions appear on the various levels of the central sanctuary. Several different hypotheses have been advanced to identify these faces, which appear to protect, or perhaps to assist, the deities worshipped in the sanctuaries. The rules of Buddhist cosmology and the epigraphic evidence suggest that the Bayon was conceived as a meeting-place of the gods, where Brahma in his aspect as head of the *Pancashikha gandhavas* ('celestial musicians') would come to sit next to each god during their 'ceremonies of good order'.

The two galleries running round the outside contain *gopuras* (entrance pavilions) at the axes of the building and further pavilions at the corners. The outer gallery measures 140×160 m, and the inner gallery 70×80 m. Since Jayavarman VII was himself a Buddhist, the Bayon is primarily a Buddhist temple. An image 3.6 m high of the Buddha, seated in meditation and protected by the *nāga* (Skt: mythical serpent dwelling in the underworld), was found in 1933 during an excavation in the pit under the central sanctuary and was erected on a small terrace to the east of the Royal Palace. The walls of the two surrounding galleries are decorated with low reliefs, the most famous of which represents the naval battle during which Jayavarman VII (*see* CAMBODIA, §III, 4(i) and fig. 24) crushed the Cham fleet.

(c) Royal Square, Royal Palace and Terraces. To the north of the Bayon lay the Royal Square, a vast esplanade 720×80 m, with monuments erected around its edges. To the east, a row of 12 towers in laterite, the Prasat Suor Prat ('Towers of the Cord Dancers'), was built in front of the Khleangs. Their true function is unknown, but they have been given this name locally in the belief that they may have served to support the cables on which rope dancers and tightrope walkers performed, by analogy with the wooden towers set up in Thailand on the occasion of great royal ceremonies.

The western edge of the Royal Square is marked by the outer, eastern *gopura* of the Baphuon, which stands at the end of a causeway 200 m long, raised on short columns, and the series of terraces linked with the Royal Palace. Apart from the temple of Phimeanakas, all that remains of the buildings of the Royal Palace is the surrounding wall with its *gopura*, some ponds and the remains of the terraces. These served as the bases for various buildings in light materials that have now completely disappeared. The richly decorated Royal Terraces in front of the palace on the edge of the Royal Square were built during the reign of Jayavarman VII. The central, highest part appears to have been supported by telamones in the form of royal beasts—lions alternating with *garuḍas* (mythical creatures, half-human and half-bird)—sculpted in relief on the side. On either side of this central block are the long Terraces of the Elephants, so called because they are decorated with a frieze of reliefs depicting elephants in war and hunting scenes.

To the north of the Royal Terraces stands the Terrace of the Leper King, which owes its name to a statue on its upper platform that is traditionally thought to represent a legendary Khmer ruler who suffered from leprosy but in fact represents a deity associated with death. The supporting walls are sculpted with images of deities arranged in registers that presumably correspond to the different levels of existence.

Zhou Daguan has left a succinct description of the buildings that once stood within the precincts of the Royal Palace, as they were at the end of the 13th century (Pelliot):

> The tiles of the private apartments are made of lead; those of the other buildings are of earthenware, and yellow. . .the long verandahs and the covered corridors are bold and irregular, without great symmetry. The council chamber has window-frames of gold; to the right and left are square columns bearing from 40 to 50 mirrors lined up on the sides of the windows. Below there are figures representing elephants. The council chamber was doubtless built on the Royal Terrace.

Zhou Daguan said little about the lives of the mass of the population in Angkor, but scenes of everyday life are depicted on the lower part of the great low relief at the Bayon illustrating Jayavarman VII's naval victory over the Chams. These include scenes of markets, workshops, entertainments and family life in modest houses.

After the reign of Jayavarman VII few foundations were made at Angkor except for the Mangalartha, a Brahmanic temple known simply as no. 486 (*see* §1 above). After 1351 Angkor Thom suffered from frequent attacks from the Thais, whose new capital of Ayutthaya was uncomfortably near, but the city appears only to have been finally abandoned as the royal capital in 1432 when the Khmer court moved first to Basan (Srei Santhor) and then in 1434 to Phnom Penh. In the mid-16th century it was occupied by a Khmer king who may have been Ang Chan (*reg c.* 1510–*c.* 1560; *see* §1 above), but hardly any new foundations were built in Angkor Thom during the last century of the Angkor monarchy. The most important building project was the erection to the north of the Terrace of the Leper King of the monumental Buddha of Tep Pranam, a statue some 6 m high depicting the Buddha gaining his victory over the tempter, Mara (*Māravijaya*). Some buildings and sculptures were also repaired or rebuilt in other temples, and a number of new reliefs were carved in the northern part of the Royal Terraces, notably in one of the five small Preah Pithu temples, which was converted into a Theravada Buddhist monastery. In Angkor Vat, some Buddha images were erected in the central sanctuary.

In his description of Angkor Thom at the end of the 16th century, Diogo do Couto wrote:

> As for the great moat, it is always full, for important and abundant rivers flow into it. . .each of these streets that goes from each of the gates is flanked by two other [channels] of water by which enter numerous small craft [loaded] with provisions, with firewood and other necessary produce, which they will unload at the very door of the inhabitants, who all have an access to the canal. . .and thus the city is cleaned of all the refuse which is carried outside to the moat; in this manner, after the king had discovered this city and transferred his court there, it became the most beautiful, the best-served and the cleanest of all the cities of the world.

MADELEINE GITEAU

BIBLIOGRAPHY

P. Pelliot: 'Mémoires sur les coutumes du Cambodge par Tcheou Takouan', *Bull. Ecole Fr. Extrême-Orient*, ii (1902), pp. 123–77 (rev. 1951; Eng. trans., Bangkok, 1967, 1987)

G. Coedès: *Un Grand Roi du Cambodge: Jayavarman VII* (Phnom Penh, 1935)
——: *Inscriptions du Cambodge*, 8 vols (Hanoi and Paris, 1937–66)
G. de Coral Rémusat: *L'Art khmer: Les Grandes Etapes de son évolution* (Paris, 1940, 2/1951)
G. Coedès: *Pour mieux comprendre Angkor* (Hanoi, 1943, rev. Paris, 2/1947); rev. with Eng. trans. by E. Gardiner as *Angkor: An Introduction* (London and New York, 3/1963)
P. Dupont: 'La Dislocation du Tchen-la et la formation du Cambodge angkorien (VIIe–IXe siècle)', *Bull. Ecole Fr. Extrême-Orient*, xliii (1943), pp. 17–55
G. Coedès: *Les Etats hindouisés d'Indochine et d'Indonésie* (Hanoi, 1944, 2/1963, rev. Paris, 3/1964); Eng. trans. by S. B. Cowing as *The Indianized States of South-east Asia* (Honolulu, 1958)
M. Glaize: *Les Monuments du groupe d'Angkor* (Saigon, 1944, rev. Paris, 4/1993)
L. P. Briggs: 'The Ancient Khmer Empire', *Trans. Amer. Philos. Soc.*, xli/1 (1951) [whole issue]
B.-P. Groslier: *Angkor: Hommes et pierres* (Paris, 1956)
B.-P. Groslier with C. R. Boxer: *Angkor et le Cambodge au XVIe siècle d'après les sources portugaises et espagnoles*, Annales du Musée Guimet, lxiii (Paris, 1958)
B.-P. Groslier: *Hinter Indien* (Baden-Baden, 1960); Fr. trans. as *Indochine: Carrefour des arts* (Paris, 1960); Eng. trans. as *Indochina: Art in the Melting-pot of Races* (London, 1962)
G. Coedès: *Les Peuples de la péninsule indochinoise* (Paris, 1962); Eng. trans. by H. M. Wright as *The Making of South East Asia* (London, 1966)
P. Stern: *Les Monuments du style khmer du Bayon et Jayavarman VII* (Paris, 1965)
J. Boisselier: *Le Cambodge* (Paris, 1966)
O. W. Walters: 'The Khmer Kings at Basan (1371–73) and the Restoration of the Cambodian Chronology during the Fourteenth and Fifteenth Centuries', *Asia Minor*, n.s., xii (1966), pp. 44–89
M. Gîteau: *Histoire d'Angkor*, Que sais-je? (Paris, 1975)
——: *Angkor: Un Peuple, un art* (Fribourg, 1976)
Nidhi Aeusrivongse: 'The Devarāja Cult and Khmer Kingship at Angkor', *Explorations in Early Southeast Asian History*, ed. K. R. Hall and J. K. Whitmore (Ann Arbor, 1976), pp. 107–48
D. P. Chandler: *A History of Cambodia* (Boulder, 1983)
J. Delvert: *Le Cambodge* (Paris, 1983)
J. Boisselier: *Il Sud-est asiatico* (Turin, 1986)
A. Le Bonheur: *Angkor: Temples en péril* (Paris, 1989)
B. Dagens: *Angkor: La Forêt de pierre* (Paris, 1989)
C. Jacques with R. Dumont: *Angkor* (Paris, 1990)
J. Lacouture and others: *Angkor: Sérénité bouddhique* (Paris, 1990); Eng. trans. by R. Sharman as *Angkor: The Serenity of Buddhism* (London, 1993) [phot. by Marc Riboud]

MADELEINE GITEAU, GUY NAFILYAN, JOHN VILLIERS

Anglada-Camarasa, Hermen(egild) (*b* Barcelona, 11 Sept 1871; *d* Port de Pollença, Mallorca, 7 July 1959). Spanish Catalan painter. He studied under Tomàs Moragas (1837–1906), but mainly under Modest Urgell (1839–1919) at the Escola de Belles Artes (Llotja) of Barcelona. In 1888 Anglada-Camarasa participated in the Exposició Universal in Barcelona. At his first one-man show, at the Sala Parés, Barcelona (1894), he exhibited Realist landscapes. In 1894 he settled in Paris and studied at the Académie Julian and Académie Colarossi. Between 1898 and 1904 he took part in numerous international exhibitions and won fame with his almost expressionistic scenes of Spanish dance (e.g. *Spanish Dance (Córdoba)*, 1901; St Petersburg, Hermitage) and iridescent nocturnal Parisian scenes (e.g. *Glow-worm*, 1904; Stockholm, Thielska Gal.), which influenced the young Picasso and Kandinsky. In 1904, after a trip to Valencia, he began painting folkloric subject-matter not out of interest in anecdote or naturalism but as a source of brilliant and colourful forms. He had a strong sense for the decorative and greatly admired fireworks. Until 1914 he lived in Paris, where his pupils included María Blanchard, Amadeu de Sousa Cardoso, Charles Ginner, Roberto Montenegro and Tito Cittadini (1886–1960), and he exhibited in cities in Europe and America. Maksim Gor'ky admired his work, and the theatre director Vsevolod Meyerhold (1874–1940) mounted a play in St Petersburg based on paintings by Anglada-Camarasa (1912). In 1914 he settled in Port de Pollença and predominantly painted landscapes, always in a more decorative rather than realistic style. In this period Anglada-Camarasa was very successful in the USA, exhibiting in many cities, including Pittsburg, Philadelphia, Chicago, Los Angeles and Washington, DC. He also showed work in Barcelona, Madrid, Buenos Aires, Palma de Mallorca, London and Liverpool. He lived in Barcelona and the Monastery of Santa Maria, Montserrat, during the Spanish Civil War (1936–9) and afterwards went into exile in Pougues-les-Eaux, near Nevers, until 1948. He was a member of various academies and societies. The Fundació La Caixa in Palma de Mallorca houses his largest painting, *Valencia* (5.80×6.12 m, 1910).

BIBLIOGRAPHY

S. Hutchinson Harris: *The Art of H. Anglada-Camarasa* (London, 1929)
F. Fontbona and F. Miralles: *Anglada-Camarasa* (Barcelona, 1981) [incl. cat. rais. and reproductions of all the known ptgs]
Anglada-Camarasa (exh. cat., ed. F. Fontbona and F. Miralles; Barcelona, Cent. Cult. Caixa Pensions, 1981)

FRANCESC FONTBONA DE VALLESCAR

Angler, Gabriel, the elder. *See* MASTERS, ANONYMOUS, AND MONOGRAMMISTS, §I: MASTER OF THE TEGERNSEE ALTAR.

Anglés, Juan Carlos (*b* Barcelona, 1755; *d* Barcelona, 7 Sept 1822). Spanish writer and painter. He was a member of the Real Escuela de la Junta de Comercio in Barcelona, where he was primarily active in a political capacity rather than as an artist and professor in its Escuela de Nobles Artes. He was expelled from the Junta in 1814 because he had taken the oath of loyalty to the usurper King Joseph Bonaparte, and as a result of accusations of favouring the French he spent his last years in total isolation from public life. His work as a writer on art is of considerable interest. He strongly defended French Neo-classicism and, in particular, the artists François Gérard and Jacques-Louis David. In a lecture he gave to the Junta de Comercio in 1810 he proclaimed the absolute validity of academic classicism, and this belief also pervades such manuscript pamphlets as the *Discurso sobre la enseñanza del dibujo*, *Máximas generales para la pintura* and *De la belleza* (both Barcelona, Mus. A. Catalunya; Nos. 6414–5). His importance as a theorist outweighs his career as a painter, which principally involved copying paintings by Correggio, Titian and Mengs. His best qualities were found in his use of composition, draughtsmanship and colouring, and his pupils included some of the earliest Romantic painters in Barcelona, including Ramón López Soler (*d* 1836) and José Arrau y Barba (1802–72).

BIBLIOGRAPHY

J. Ainaud de Lasarte: 'Juan Carlos Anglés: Pintor neoclásico', *An. & Bol. Mus. A. Barcelona*, ii (1944), pp. 7–29
J. A. Gaya Nuño: *Historia de la crítica de arte en España* (Madrid, 1975), p. 159

PILAR BENITO

Angles-sur-l'Anglin [Roc aux Sorciers]. Site in Vienne, France. It is important for its rock art of the Late Upper Palaeolithic period (*c.* 20,000–*c.* 10,000 BP; *see also* PREHISTORIC EUROPE, §II, 1 and 2). The rock-shelter of Angles-sur-l'Anglin runs for *c.* 50 m along the foot of a south-facing cliff, 20 m above the right bank of the Anglin river. Excavations by Dorothy Garrod and Suzanne de Saint-Mathurin in 1952 led to the discovery of some Palaeolithic sculpture dating to *c.* 14,000 BP. Subsequent investigation revealed that the entire back wall and ceiling of the shelter had originally been sculpted, but that the roof had collapsed and buried them in rubble and sediment. The finds from the site are housed in the Musée des Antiquités Nationales at St Germain-en-Laye, where some of the finest carved blocks from the shelter roof are displayed.

Two areas were cleared by the excavators: in the first, the Cave Taillebourg, a carved bison figure 700 mm in length remained *in situ* on the wall, while in the other, the Abri Bourdois rock-shelter 33 m away, a sculptured frieze *c.* 15 m long was uncovered. It is certain that the bas-reliefs continue in the unexcavated area between the two sites and extend beyond them on both sides. Excavated material of a Magdalenian culture layer was dated by radiocarbon analysis of burnt bone, providing an uncalibrated date of 14,160 BP. Artefacts included large stone picks and massive burins, which were probably the tools used to create the figures. Traces of pigment remain on the frieze, indicating that it was originally painted, a fact supported by the discovery of stones for grinding mineral colours (red ochre and manganese) and of pigment crayons. The carvings include remarkable renditions of ibex, bison and horses, but the most famous figures still *in situ* are four life-size 'Venuses'. Created without chest, head or feet, each figure is *c.* 1.2 m high, with normal hips and the vulva marked. Three are grouped together, the first being in half-profile, the second three-quarter face and the third full-face. A fourth figure near by had an ibex superimposed on it, and there are further examples of replacement and superimposition elsewhere on the frieze, although the timespan involved in these changes cannot be assessed. The fallen blocks now at the Musée des Antiquités Nationales, St Germain, include some fine carved horse heads, a superb bison head, and, most importantly, a fairly realistic life-size profile of a bearded man, which is sculpted, engraved and painted. As in ancient Egyptian profiles, his eye is shown from the front.

BIBLIOGRAPHY

S. de Saint-Mathurin and D. Garrod: 'La Frise sculptée du Roc-aux-Sorciers à Angles-sur-l'Anglin (Vienne)', *L'Anthropologie*, lv (1951), pp. 413–23

——: 'The Master Sculptors of 12,000 Years Ago Revealed', *Illus. London News*, ccxx (1952), pp. 454–7

S. de Saint-Mathurin: 'L'Abri du Roc-aux-Sorciers', *L'Art des cavernes* (Paris, 1984), pp. 583–7

——: 'Les Sculptures rupestres du Roc-aux-Sorciers', *Doss. Hist. & Archéol.*, cxxxi (1988), pp. 42–9

PAUL G. BAHN

Anglo-Saxon art. Art of the period in England between the Germanic invasions of the later 5th century AD and the Norman Conquest of 1066.

I. Introduction. II. Architecture. III. Sculpture. IV. Painting. V. Metalwork. VI. Ivories. VII. Stained glass. VIII. Textiles.

I. Introduction.

The invading Angles, Saxons, Jutes and possibly Frisians settled all over lowland England, bringing their Germanic culture (*see* MIGRATION PERIOD) and establishing kingdoms—the Jutes and Saxons in the south and the Anglians in the east, Mercia (the Midlands) and what became Northumbria, north of the River Humber. The native British were pushed into Wales and the far south-west, and paganism replaced the Christianity that had survived from late Roman times. Artefacts from this period consist largely of burial goods recovered from excavated cemeteries.

New Christian missions arrived in Kent from Italy and Frankish Gaul in the late 6th century (*see* CANTERBURY, §I) and in Northumbria from Ireland and Scotland in the 7th, resulting in the gradual conversion of all the kingdoms and the adoption of the Roman liturgy after 664. The conversion to Christianity encouraged not only the construction of stone buildings and crosses, but also the production of liturgical books, vessels and vestments, many of which survive. Although a Mediterranean-based culture was transmitted via the Merovingians (*see* MEROVINGIAN ART) and later the Carolingians (*see* CAROLINGIAN ART), artistic links to the Celtic regions remained so strong before the 9th century that the specific provenance within the British Isles of some works, particularly illuminated manuscripts (*see* §IV, 2 below), can be difficult to locate (*see* INSULAR ART). At the same time influences from Britain were reaching continental Europe through the Irish missions (*see* ECHTERNACH).

The political primacy enjoyed by the kingdoms of Northumbria from the late 7th century to the 8th, and Mercia from the mid-8th century to the mid-9th, was shattered by the Viking invasions (*see* VIKING ART, §II, 4(iii)), which began in 865. While East Anglia, Northumbria and Mercia sued for peace, Alfred, King of Wessex (*see* WESSEX, (1)), held out against them, and the country was unified under his son Edward the Elder (*reg* 899–924/5) and grandson Athelstan (*reg* 924/5–39; *see* WESSEX, (2)). The great Church reform movement of the late 10th century under such men as Dunstan, Archbishop of Canterbury, AETHELWOLD, Bishop of Winchester, and Oswald, Archbishop of York (*reg* 972–92), which was based on Lotharingian reform movements (*see* GORZE, ORDER OF), led to a new flowering of art and architecture. Except on metalwork, Viking influence was not strong even under the rule of the Danish kings between 1016 and 1042, and the upbringing of the Anglo-Saxon king Edward the Confessor (*reg* 1042–66) at the court of Normandy ensured cultural links between England and Normandy even before the Conquest.

BIBLIOGRAPHY

T. D. Kendrick: *Anglo-Saxon Art to AD 700* (London, 1938)

——: *Late Saxon and Viking Art to AD 900* (London, 1949)

D. Talbot Rice: *English Art, 871–1100* (Oxford, 1952)

D. M. Wilson: *Anglo-Saxon Art* (London, 1984)

The Golden Age of Anglo-Saxon Art (exh. cat., ed. J. Backhouse, D. H. Turner and L. Webster; London, BM, 1984)

The Making of England: Anglo-Saxon Art and Culture, AD 600–900 (exh. cat., ed. L. Webster and J. Backhouse; London, BM, 1991)

II. Architecture.

1. Introduction. 2. Building materials and organization. 3. Chronological survey.

1. INTRODUCTION. That there was something distinctive about Anglo-Saxon architecture was first recognized within a few years of the introduction of Romanesque architecture to England in the second half of the 11th century: contemporaries perceived that the new architecture was different from the old. Goscelin of St Bertin merely saw the old as deficient in the qualities he admired in the new. William of Malmesbury, the first English architectural historian, not only realized that a new style had been introduced with Edward the Confessor's Westminster Abbey and the buildings of the Norman conquerors; but he also tried to discern the relative antiquity of different Anglo-Saxon buildings that survived in his day, and in one case (that of King Alfred's Athelney Abbey) he saw a stylistic difference between one Anglo-Saxon church and others of earlier date.

The serious attempt to distinguish Anglo-Saxon architecture was taken up again only in the 19th century: first by Thomas Rickman, then by J. T. Micklethwaite and others. It was Baldwin Brown, however, who laid the academic foundation for the subject in his *Anglo-Saxon Architecture* (1903, rev. 1925), in which he not only defined various constructional characteristics of Anglo-Saxon buildings but also made comparisons with contemporary continental architecture, which enabled him to suggest a chronological framework for the study of the material, divided into three periods that he labelled A, B and C (following the standard archaeological practice of the time), a nomenclature that has been retained by a number of subsequent writers. Sir Alfred Clapham (1930) summarized Baldwin Brown's work and modified some of the emphases without fundamentally changing the picture.

A new impetus was given to the subject (1965–78) by Harold Taylor, who catalogued and described all the Anglo-Saxon churches known to him and analysed the features they contained, although he did not feel able to suggest a clear chronological development. Taylor's work stimulated a revival of interest in the subject, and the study of it from various points of view. Fernie's analysis (1983) emphasized the role of style-criticism, while others sought to apply archaeological method (e.g. Morris, 1983), being concerned to study buildings in their social and economic context as one aspect of Anglo-Saxon society.

Excavation since the 1950s has for the first time provided significant evidence of Anglo-Saxon secular buildings, the subject having been studied previously entirely on the basis of ecclesiastical architecture.

2. BUILDING MATERIALS AND ORGANIZATION. The Old English words for build and builder, *timbran* and *timbrend*, indicate that timber was assumed to be the natural building material. In the earliest period timber seems to have been almost the only material used, and when masonry construction was introduced from *c.* 600, it was seen to be exceptional, as something 'Roman', to be used for such special buildings as churches but not for general purposes. In this context 'Roman' meant both what was normal in the Roman Catholic churches of the Continent (a meaning that seems foremost in Bede's mind) and an evocation of the Romans, the surviving ruins of whose buildings in England struck a certain awe in the Anglo-Saxon spectator.

Evidence for the organization of the building trade is sparse. There is a late 7th-century record of masons and workers in allied trades being imported by patrons from Frankish Gaul to erect stone buildings, and it must be presumed that these helped to establish an indigenous tradition. At the same time, however, surviving Anglo-Saxon buildings suggest that masoncraft was never developed to a very high degree: the manufacture of bricks, which had been standard in the Roman period, was never revived. Building stone was often reused from earlier buildings rather than systematically quarried; where carefully dressed ashlar was employed, it was often given a meticulously polished surface that must have been produced by time-consuming techniques inappropriate to mass production. Certain categories of building were carried out with the aid of customary labour. There were public duties for building strongholds for the defence of the land, for making bridges and for work on the buildings of the royal estate, while a lord could expect customary service on his estate, and the local church was kept in repair by service from its parishioners. Nonetheless, while unskilled labour may have been used for certain categories of building work, there are specific references to masons and carpenters, which suggest specialized trades. Craftsmen could be attached to monasteries and to bishops by the grants of land tenancies, and into this pattern fits the 'church-wright' Teinfrith, who worked for Edward the Confessor on Westminster Abbey: yet it remains uncertain how far such craftsmen were specialists exclusively in masonry construction, rather than being general craftsmen in a number of the arts.

3. CHRONOLOGICAL SURVEY.

(i) 5th century AD to the early 9th. (ii) Mid-9th century to the mid-10th. (iii) Mid-10th century to the mid-11th. (iv) Second half of the 11th century.

(i) 5th century AD to the early 9th. The first type of Anglo-Saxon secular building to be excavated was represented by a sunken feature in the ground and a number of associated stake holes, and for this the German name *Grubenhaus* ('sunken-featured building') was adopted (*see* VIKING ART, §III, 1). The picture thus formed of the first English settlers living in squalid holes in the ground has since been revised, as the large numbers of *Grubenhäuser* that were subsequently excavated, dating from the 5th century onwards, seem in many cases to have been used for industrial or storage purposes; moreover, the sunken feature is interpreted as underlying a proper timber floor. Many genuine early Anglo-Saxon dwellings have been excavated: at Cowdery's Down (Hants) the 6th- to 7th-century buildings were substantial rectangular halls with timber-framed walls, in some cases having floors suspended above ground level. At Yeavering (Northumb.) a settlement documented as a royal centre, with buildings more splendid and diversified, was still of timber: a remarkable theatre was presumably for assemblies; a great hall in the centre of the complex went through several phases of rebuilding (the first had massive plank walls,

plastered internally, and paired internal posts to support the roof).

Of the first Christian missionaries who arrived in the late 6th and 7th centuries, those from Ireland and Scotland were accustomed to building in wood, but the missionaries from Italy and Frankish Gaul introduced the use of masonry construction. Evidence of these first churches is preserved at St Augustine's Abbey and St Martin's, both in Canterbury, and at St Peter by the Wall, Bradwell-on-Sea (Essex). They comprised an aisleless nave with the altar standing at its east end; beyond this was an apsidal chancel for the clergy, and flanking the nave were side chambers (porticus) for use as sacristies and providing space for burials. Another church of this type was the first church, later cathedral, in Winchester (*see* WINCHESTER, §III, 1(i)). This form of building was derived from late Roman architecture in Italy and Gaul but, once established in England, it continued unbroken right through the Anglo-Saxon period, even when more progressive architectural forms were adopted alongside it.

In the late 7th century, following the missionary activities of the preceding decades, a well-defined ecclesiastical structure was established throughout the Anglo-Saxon kingdoms of England, which endured as the basic pattern during the 8th century and into the 9th. Each of the kingdoms had one or more bishoprics, and beneath these was a network of 'minster' churches. Some of these minsters were monasteries observing an ascetic rule of life and, in many cases, comprising communities of both monks and nuns; other minsters housed communities of clergy that had the pastoral care of a large parish. Many of the most significant churches to survive from the mid-Anglo-Saxon period seem to have been minsters.

In south-east England the pattern already established continued into the late 7th century and early 8th at RECULVER ABBEY, and at St Pancras, Canterbury. In Wessex, St Peter, Titchfield (Hants), shows a plan with a long aisleless nave preceded by a western porch, and this can be seen also in Mercia at Deerhurst Priory (Glos), as well as in Northumbria at the monastic churches of Monkwearmouth (*see* MONKWEARMOUTH ABBEY) and Jarrow (Tyne and Wear). A subsidiary chapel survives at Jarrow, while the carefully planned monastic offices of Bede's monastery have been excavated. Documents indicate that the monastic churches of Bishop Wilfrid (*d* 709), HEXHAM ABBEY (Northumb.) and Ripon Minster (N. Yorks) were the most elaborate in Northumbria in the late 7th century, and of these the crypts survive; but the romantic reconstructions proposed by earlier writers for the main churches are not supported by the archaeological evidence.

The most impressive surviving mid-Anglo-Saxon church is Brixworth (*see* BRIXWORTH, ALL SAINTS' CHURCH), which perhaps dates to the mid- or late 8th century and shows a quasi-aisled plan. True aisled plans were adopted for the churches of St Mary, Wareham (Dorset; destr. 19th century), and Cirencester Abbey (Glos). The latter had a ring crypt and an outer crypt, which indicate Carolingian influence (for further discussion *see* CRYPT); such influence seems to date these buildings to the early 9th century.

1. St Peter, Britford, Wiltshire, archway to the north porticus, early 9th century

One notable characteristic of some early 9th-century churches is their extensive use of elaborate sculptured decoration ornamenting the openings or used as continuous friezes. Notable examples are at St Peter, Britford (Wilts; see fig. 1), All Saints, Ledsham (W. Yorks), and St Mary, Breedon (Leics); some of the motifs indicate continental Carolingian influence. In plan, however, Britford and Ledsham are simple, aisleless buildings with flanking porticus.

Secular buildings show continuity with the preceding period, as at the village of Catholme (Staffs) or the palace (possibly royal) at Northampton. At the latter a great timber hall (comparable to Yeavering) of the mid-8th century was replaced in the early 9th with a masonry structure of similar scale, suggesting an emulation of the stone palaces of the Carolingian kingdom. The period is also characterized by the development of incipient urban trading and industrial centres, called in Old English *wics.* At Hamwih, the port of Southampton (Hants), a regular layout of roads and buildings has been excavated.

(ii) Mid-9th century to the mid-10th. The difficulty of establishing accurate dates for 9th-century buildings has led some writers to suggest that building activities were halted by the Viking invasions, but this improbable view is also contradicted by some documentary evidence. A critical case is the important church of Deerhurst, which was substantially rebuilt on earlier foundations. A prominent feature is the use of animal-head sculptures to

decorate the openings, and these relate to well-dated 9th-century metalwork. Important features are also the hood-moulds around the arches, and the narrow strip-like pilasters and arcading that decorated the polygonal apse; a similar apse survives at All Saints, Wing (Bucks). At St Wystan, Repton (Derbys), archaeological work suggests that already before the Viking occupation of the site in 873 the church had attained a developed form including a chancel with pilaster decoration and an underlying crypt with a vault carried on four spiral columns. This crypt suggests continuing Carolingian contacts in the mid-9th century.

In the late 9th century the minster of St Oswald, Gloucester, looked back in plan to the earlier tradition of an aisleless nave with flanking porticus, but it incorporated also a Carolingian-style west apse. In a secondary phase in the early 10th century a four-pier crypt was added beyond the chancel, and a tower may have been raised over the east end of the nave. By contrast the early 10th-century New Minster at Winchester was a massive aisled building with transepts. The Gloucester church had elaborate sculptural decoration, which can be seen also on the early 10th-century tower at St John the Baptist, Barnack (Cambs; see fig. 2), which displays both pilaster decoration and inset panels of foliage and birds.

For domestic buildings of the period, excavations at Cheddar (Somerset) have shown a royal vill centering on a great timber hall, which was probably two-storey. At North Elmham (Norfolk) an existing settlement was laid out in the early 10th century with a group of timber buildings probably for the residence of the bishop. At Goltho (Lincs) a manorial centre was constructed between the late 9th century and the early 10th century with a timber hall and other buildings grouped within an enclosure defended by a bank and ditch.

2. St John the Baptist, Barnack, Cambridgeshire, west tower, early 10th century

Urban centres also developed further in this period. The first impulse towards this was probably military and lay in the policy of the West Saxon and Mercian rulers to provide *burhs* or strongholds to act as focal points in the defence against the Vikings. The rectangular earthen defences around Wareham are one of the best examples of this. At the same time, however, the *burhs* were planned internally with a grid of streets, suggesting the intention to develop them as centres of population and industry. Such street planning was not confined to new towns but was applied also to some of the former Roman cities, such as Winchester and London, which had not been properly urban since the 4th century.

(iii) Mid-10th century to the mid-11th. The reforming monk-bishops of the later 10th century established a number of monastic houses in their respective spheres of influence. Dunstan was responsible for work at Glastonbury (*see* GLASTONBURY ABBEY) and St Augustine's, Canterbury, at both of which he extended existing complexes of buildings for monastic use. Aethelwold followed a similar policy at Winchester, where he and his successors added to the church an extended chapel to the east, while at the west end they erected a great westwork deriving from Carolingian models. At Ely surviving inventories indicate the wealth of gold and silver plate and precious textiles that ornamented such churches. At Abingdon (Oxon), Aethelwold was associated with a new abbey church that seems from descriptions to have been a rotunda in the tradition of the palatine chapel at Aachen. The surviving church of St Peter, Barton-upon-Humber (S. Humberside), may be a private chapel built by Aethelwold: it comprised a tower with chapels on the east and west sides; the tower was decorated with pilaster stripwork. The third reformer, Oswald, founded a great monastery at Ramsey (Cambs), of which the church is described as having a great central tower with chapels to the east, north and south, while the nave to the west terminated in a second tower at the front.

Most surviving Anglo-Saxon churches probably belong to the last century before the Norman Conquest rather than to earlier periods, but they tend not to be the major documented buildings such as cathedrals and abbeys. One or two major buildings do survive, however; for example St Mary in Castro, Dover (Kent; see fig. 3), a church probably built for the community of minster priests in the town. It has an aisleless nave with a lofty central tower over the choir at its east end; further east is a rectangular chancel, and to north and south of the tower are two-storey porticus; the west end of the nave was linked to a Roman lighthouse, which was retained as a second tower. Generally similar buildings occur at a number of other places, such as St Mary, Breamore (Hants), and Norton (Cleveland). At St Nicholas, Worth (W. Sussex), a more primitive plan survives with no central tower, while at St Lawrence, Bradford-on-Avon (Wilts), a similar plan was used for a chapel executed in high-quality ashlar stone and decorated with blank arcading on its external walls. Elsewhere churches with no central tower enjoyed the provision of a west tower, such as that at St Bene't, Cambridge, or St Michael at the Northgate, Oxford; in the former the tower arch is decorated with elaborate mouldings and animal sculptures. Many humbler churches (and some important ones also) continued to be of timber, but only one Anglo-Saxon timber church survives, at Greensted (Essex), with its walls constructed of half tree-trunks, joined by fillets and tenoned into a wall-plate. However, timber buildings did receive rich internal paintings in some cases; while at St Andrew, Nether Wallop (Hants), a pair of angels in the style of the so-called Winchester school survives on the east wall of the masonry nave (*see* §IV, 1 and fig. 8 below).

Several secular sites have been excavated. The royal vill at Cheddar continued in use with new buildings: a timber-framed hall was built, but a chapel was provided in masonry. At Goltho the buildings were twice reconstructed but were still disposed within a defended enclosure; while at Sulgrave (Northants) another manorial site had buildings both of timber and stone construction, and the enclosing bank and ditch were secondary features. Urban life came into its own at this time, and excavations in cities such as London, Chester and York (*see* YORK, §1(i)) have thrown considerable light on the buildings associated with this. A pattern was already developing that is familiar in later medieval towns of buildings lying both along the street frontage and back from it behind the front ranges. Some of the buildings were built at ground level, others were sunken or partly sunken, while others had cellars. Most were of timber, and excellent conditions of preservation at Coppergate, York, have preserved some of the timber-lined structure below ground.

(iv) Second half of the 11th century. The extent to which Romanesque architectural ideas had already been introduced to England before the Norman Conquest is a matter of dispute (*see* ROMANESQUE, §II, 6). At St Mary, Stow (Lincs), the crossing arches of the church of *c.* 1050 show both the adoption of the regular crossing and also, in their decoration, the use of half-columnar shafts. At St Augustine's Abbey, Canterbury, on the other hand, the work of the 1050s involved the linking together of existing structures with a rotunda, which was modelled after the tradition deriving from the Carolingian model of the palatine chapel at Aachen (*see* AACHEN, §2(ii)(a)). The first decisively Romanesque building in England was the reconstruction of Westminster Abbey in the 1050s and 1060s by a workshop clearly linked with the Norman workshop responsible for the nave of Jumièges Abbey (*see* LONDON, §V, 2(i)).

Some lesser buildings reached a degree of sophistication, such as Holy Trinity, Great Paxton (Cambs), where the nave arcades are carried on fasciculated piers comparable to buildings in the Rhine and Meuse region. Other churches, such as All Saints, Wittering (Cambs), have archways with jambs and heads enriched with a variety of soffit and angle-roll mouldings; but it is difficult to tell whether the earliest examples of this fashion are pre-Conquest, while later examples, such as St John the Evangelist, Milborne Port (Somerset), date from *c.* 1090. Also of this later date are those buildings where roll mouldings are combined with cavetto mouldings, as at Holy Trinity, Bosham (W. Sussex). The taste for rich mouldings in these small buildings coincides to some extent with the development of a similar taste in some of the great Anglo-Norman Romanesque churches from *c.* 1090 onwards.

3. Church of St Mary in Castro, Dover, Kent, *c.* 1000, view from the south-east

See also ESCOMB CHURCH.

BIBLIOGRAPHY

Bede: *Ecclesiastical History*, XXI

Goscelin of St Bertin: *Liber confortatorius* (*c.* 1082–3); ed. C. H. Talbot, *Stud. Anselm.*, xxxvii (1955), p. 82

William of Malmesbury: *De gestis pontificum anglorum* (completed 1125); ed. N. E. S. A. Hamilton, Rolls Series (London, 1870), p. 199

——: *De gestis regum anglorum* (completed 1125); ed. W. Stubbs, Rolls Series (London, 1887–9), i, p. 280; ii, p. 306

T. Rickman: *An Attempt to Discriminate the Styles of English Architecture from the Conquest to the Reformation* (Liverpool, 1817)

J. T. Micklethwaite: 'Something about Saxon Church Building', *Archaeol. J.*, liii (1896), p. 293–351

G. Baldwin Brown: *Anglo-Saxon Architecture*, ii of *The Arts in Early England* (London, 1903, rev. 1925)

A. W. Clapham: *Before the Conquest*, i of *English Romanesque Architecture* (Oxford, 1930)

H. M. Taylor and J. Taylor: *Anglo-Saxon Architecture*, 3 vols (Cambridge, 1965–78)

D. M. Wilson, ed.: *The Archaeology of Anglo-Saxon England* (London, 1976)

B. Hope-Taylor: *Yeavering: An Anglo-British Centre of Early Northumbria* (London, 1977)

C. Ahrens and others: *Frühe Holzkirchen im nördlichen Europa* (Hamburg, 1981)

W. Rodwell: *Archaeology of the English Church* (London, 1981)

E. Fernie: *Architecture of the Anglo-Saxons* (London, 1983)

R. D. H. Gem: 'Towards an Iconography of Anglo-Saxon Architecture', *J. Warb. & Court. Inst.*, xlvi (1983), pp. 1–18

R. Morris: *The Church in British Archaeology*, Council for British Archaeology Research Report, xlvii (London, 1983)

R. D. H. Gem: 'L'Architecture pré-romane et romane en Angleterre', *Bull. Mnmtl*, cxlii (1984), pp. 233–72

J. Haslam, ed.: *Anglo-Saxon Towns in Southern England* (Chichester, 1984)

S. James, A. Marshall and M. Millett: 'An Early Medieval Building Tradition', *Archaeol. J.*, cxli (1984), pp. 182–215

L. A. S. Butler and R. K. Morris: *The Anglo-Saxon Church: Papers in Honour of Dr H. M. Taylor*, Council for British Archaeology Research Report, lx (London, 1986)

B. Ford, ed.: *Early Britain*, i of *The Cambridge Guide to the Arts in Britain* (Cambridge, 1988–91); rev. as *The Cambridge Cultural History* (Cambridge, 1992)

R. D. H. Gem: 'Architecture of the Anglo-Saxon Church, 735 to 870', *J. Brit. Archaeol. Assoc.*, cxlv (1993)

RICHARD GEM

III. Sculpture.

1. Introduction. 2. Regional survey.

1. INTRODUCTION. Owing to the nature and extent of the remains, sculpture is significant in the surviving arts of Anglo-Saxon England. Stone carvings are more durable and less intrinsically valuable than manuscripts or jewellery; they are more likely to have been made in their current locations than the many portable masterpieces of disputed origin. Stone sculpture was not practised by the pagan Anglo-Saxons, and it can therefore be firmly associated with the arts of the church imported from the Mediterranean world as part of the conversion of the English. It was used in an entirely ecclesiastical context to decorate churches and crosses, the main patrons being monasteries. The imported ornament was, however, soon modified by local taste; Anglo-Saxon sculpture shows a continuous conflict between Classical and native art. Much stone carving was painted in accordance with the Anglo-Saxon taste for bright and shining decoration.

As there are no securely dated monuments, chronology is uncertain. Some crosses have inscriptions thought to refer to historical personages, but their decipherment is doubtful; some carvings can be associated with buildings whose foundation date is known, but this only provides a *terminus post quem.* The decoration can often be compared to that on another medium, such as a manuscript, with a more secure date, but this does not allow for time lag in transmission or the fact that some workshops were innovative while others were deeply conservative. Quite different styles could be produced at the same time and the relative chronological sequence depends on the subjective judgement of style historians. Research on defining different workshops through the techniques of manufacture, such as the use of grids and templates, can contribute most to the problems of dating and origin.

The development of Anglo-Saxon sculpture follows the historical sequence of Northumbrian primacy in the late 7th and 8th centuries, being superseded by Mercia from the mid-8th century to the late 9th and by Wessex from the end of the 9th century to the Norman Conquest in 1066. The effect of the Viking invasions was felt mainly in the north, and it is now recognized not to have caused as much disruption to the style sequence as was previously thought.

2. REGIONAL SURVEY.

(i) Northumbria. (ii) Mercia. (iii) The Viking north. (iv) Wessex.

(i) Northumbria. Christianity and the arts of the Church were first established in Northumbria. Among the earliest centres were the twin monasteries of MONKWEARMOUTH ABBEY and Jarrow (Tyne and Wear), founded in 674 and 682 by Benedict Biscop, who had made several journeys to Rome and Gaul, bringing back not only books and relics but also masons to build and decorate the new churches and monasteries. There were also local Roman models in the form of the fragments of carvings, bricks and tiles dating from the Roman occupation, which were reused in early buildings. The first carved ornament was on church façades and furnishings, consisting of columns, friezes and panels, the closest parallels for which are found in 6th- and 7th-century Gaul and Italy. Naturalistic animals in deep relief used as friezes at Monkwearmouth and HEXHAM ABBEY (Northumb.) were inspired by Italian carving, but a more local subject was the motif of two serpentine beasts carved on the porch of St Peter's, Monkwearmouth, by AD 686; these were copied from the interlacing animals of pagan Anglo-Saxon jewellery.

Once stone carving had been learnt from foreign craftsmen, a range of local and imported patterns was adapted for use on the most typical monument of Anglo-Saxon sculpture, the cross, symbol of Christ's sacrifice and Christianity in general. Crosses of metal and wood are referred to in the historian Bede's account of the conversion from the beginning of the 7th century; the decoration of these was combined with the Celtic tradition of a commemorative stone pillar and the early Christian custom of stone grave markers. These were small rectangular slabs, incised or carved in relief with a cross and inscription, of Gaulish origin and found in the earliest monastic cemeteries at Lindisfarne (Northumb.), Hartlepool (Cleveland) and Monkwearmouth from the late 7th century.

There is a reference to a cross at Glastonbury commemorating a king who died in 685, probably Centwine, and it is established through a comparison with architectural motifs that crosses were certainly being made by 700 and were probably a fairly sudden development. The cross had several functions: it was a teaching aid and territorial marker as well as a memorial. Some crosses may have been erected in churches, with their decoration as part of the overall carved and painted designs; others may have preceded the building of a church.

Northumbrian crosses of the 8th century are firmly associated with monastic centres. The carving associated with the Monkwearmouth/Jarrow foundation, which was already rich in architectural motifs, tended to avoid Celtic interlace and adopted the Mediterranean vine scroll, a symbol of Christianity and the Eucharist. The scroll may be inhabited by birds and beasts, and may be used as the sole decoration or in conjunction with biblical iconography copied from imported manuscripts, paintings and ivories. The RUTHWELL CROSS is the most elaborate example of the school. It uses Mediterranean models in a distinctively Insular manner (*see* INSULAR ART, §4), combining vine scrolls with sophisticated figural ornament relating to the monastic life. Figures of *Christ, St John the Baptist, St Mary Magdalene* and others harder to interpret are carved in a deep and rounded relief with a monumental simplicity, together with descriptive texts and a runic poem, the *Dream of the Rood.* The cross can be dated to the first half of the 8th century. A closely related monument is the Bewcastle Cross (Cumbria; see fig. 4), which adds separate panels of abstract geometric design of Hiberno-Saxon type, showing the underlying influence of native art. Other

4. Stone cross, h. 4.4 m, Bewcastle, Cumbria, 8th century

products of the school are marked by their deep relief and use of fleshy vine scrolls, but always with the local tendency to make surface patterns out of representational motifs such as drapery or vegetation.

A different style of carving is seen at Hexham Abbey, whose founder, Bishop Wilfrid, had also made many journeys to the Continent. Early architectural remains include Gaulish and Visigothic motifs and reused Roman carving. The crosses, however, show neatly designed, uninhabited vine scrolls and interlace of manuscript type in a low relief; they are entirely non-figural but retain the naturalism of their Mediterranean models. The detailed leaves and berries on the crosses from Lowther (Northumb.) and Heversham (Cumbria) have no sign of the native tendency towards abstraction. The best-known example of the Hexham school is a cross (Hexham Abbey, Northumb.) traditionally connected with Bishop Acca (*d* 740).

A third centre was Lindisfarne, a remote and ascetic community retaining its links with the Celtic church that had founded it, unlike the Rome-orientated Hexham and Jarrow. The surviving crosses have no plant scrolls but show the combination of geometric ornament and interlacing animals that was the local contribution to early Christian art in Britain, placed in separate panels down the shafts.

Other monastic-based workshops produced the many surviving crosses, which show a blend of styles and influences that make attribution and dating difficult. The ornament remains a combination of Mediterranean and local elements, often uneasily mixed. Animals remained characteristic, with the inhabitants of the vine scroll becoming increasingly important, and their own bodies forming the supporting tendrils; plant details became less realistic. The Aberlady Cross (Edinburgh, Royal Mus. Scotland), for example, has entwined birds and beasts who dominate their berried scroll. The sculptors were never successful at the Classical depiction of human figures, although the copying of drapery, rounded reliefs and figures under arcades show a full awareness of Roman models. By the end of the 8th century, Northumbria was coming to the end of its 'Golden Age', but sculpture continued to be an integral part of art and teaching and the styles established in the 8th century were to continue to the end of the 10th.

(ii) Mercia. The new styles of sculpture to the south in the late 8th and 9th centuries relate to a change in the balance of power from Northumbria to Mercia. The Middle Anglian kingdom at its peak extended from south of the River Humber to south of the River Thames, but it was broadly concentrated on the east and west Midlands. Distinctive features included new types of monument and a revival of architectural decoration. While traditional ornament continued, there were also new subjects inspired by the political and cultural contacts between England and the Carolingian empire, including personal and family links between Offa, King of Mercia (*reg* 757–96), and Emperor Charlemagne. The Carolingian renaissance drew upon the early Christian art of Italy; English sculpture as a result reflected a further wave of Classical influence, which reinforced the earlier movement progressively weakened by the native Hiberno-Saxon tradition.

These features included rows of standing figures under arcades, copied directly from early Christian sarcophagi, which were being imported by Charlemagne from Rome; round-shafted crosses, inspired by the Roman columns that were also being imported; a very deep, almost undercut relief; a new range of fantasy birds and beasts in delicate scrolls; and figures with Classical hairstyles and deeply drilled eyes. There was also less use of the geometric interlace and spiral patterns of Northumbrian art, although this was matched by a greater interaction between the media, particularly in the use of animal and foliage ornament, which also appears frequently on manuscripts and metalwork.

The importance of architectural sculpture is exemplified in the carved friezes from the former monastic site of Breedon-on-the-Hill (Leics), now in the nearby church of St Mary. Designed to decorate the outside of a church, the long narrow strips are carved in deep relief. The ornament is of various types, including leafy scrolls far developed from the vine motif employed at Britford (see fig. 1 above), foliage inhabited by a lively range of slender birds and long-legged beasts, figural panels with pairs of birds, hounds, lions and huntsmen and some panels of geometric patterns. Such friezes find their closest parallels in Byzantine strip friezes from the eastern Mediterranean and Italy; many of the individual motifs could have reached England on the imported textiles and ivories that were also used as models in the Carolingian empire. They probably date from the early 9th century. The panels at Breedon include haloed figures under round arches, an elegant angel in Classical style (see fig. 5) and a Virgin of Byzantine type.

Similar friezes of animals in scrolls and busts under arcades are found further to the east near Peterborough, at St Margaret, Fletton, and St Kyneburg, Castor (Cambs). As Breedon was founded from the great monastery at Peterborough, these carvings may all be the product of the monastic workshop. Another example is the Hedda sarcophagus, now in Peterborough Cathedral. The sides are carved with Christ and the Apostles, full-length figures standing under arcades, copying those on early sarcophagi, but on the lid are animals of Anglo-Saxon type entwined in the interlace formed from their own extended bodies.

5. Stone panel depicting an angel, h. 910 mm, St Mary, Breedon-on-the-Hill, Leicestershire, 9th century

An uncharacteristic survival of Insular ornament occurs at St Mary and All Saints, South Kyme (Lincs), where a group of carved stones may have formed parts of a chancel screen; there are Celtic spirals and fretwork, and panels with creatures of manuscript type interlaced in leafy scrolls.

As with earlier Northumbrian sculpture, architectural and free-standing carvings shared the same subjects. Round-shafted crosses appeared from the beginning of the 9th century in Mercia, Kent and Northumbria. One example, the Wolverhampton Pillar (Wolverhampton, W. Midlands, St Peter), combines the deeply carved figures of Christ and Apostles with the spindly animals of contemporary metalwork. The fragments of the Reculver shaft, now in Canterbury Cathedral (*see* RECULVER ABBEY, §2), illustrate the Apostles, the *Ascension* and the *Sacrifice of Isaac*, together with busts and vine scrolls, and fit convincingly into a 9th-century context.

A shaft excavated in 1979 at St Wystan, Repton (Derbys), again illustrates the use of Classical models in its scene of a mounted warrior, inspired by a Late Antique emperor portrait; this has been identified as depicting King Aethelbald of Mercia (*reg* 716–59). The reverse of the stone shows a serpent devouring two humans, whose entwined bodies can be compared to interlacing figures in manuscripts. Another example of foreign influence occurs on the coffin lid at St Mary, Wirksworth (Derbys), which has *Passion* scenes of Byzantine or Syrian type and which is thought to have been inspired by an eastern liturgical calendar.

A group of carvings from the west Mercian area have exotic animals in clearly defined leafy scrolls treated in a far more naturalistic and asymmetrical manner than the earlier examples of the inhabited vine scroll. The shallow, almost sketchy carving is beginning to show again the Insular fondness for surface decoration in contrast to the more monumental qualities of the ultimate Classical models, a conflict that was always present in Anglo-Saxon sculpture. The carvings from St Giles, Acton Beauchamp (Hereford & Worcs), St Michael, Cropthorne (Hereford & Worcs), and St Mary, Newent (Glos), are not products of the same workshop but share the recurrent themes of birds and canine creatures in the foliage characteristic of southern manuscripts of the 9th century.

The influence of Mercian carving can be recognized in Northumbria. The deeper relief, expressive faces with deep-drilled eyes and fantastic animals are all features of later Northumbrian sculpture. The cross at Rothbury (Northumb.) may be assigned to the Monkwearmouth/Jarrow school on the basis of its complex iconography; it has the figure of Christ under a round arch, a crowd scene that exploits spatial recession for the first time and a biting beast of Mercian type in a slender scroll. A related cross from Easby Abbey (N. Yorks) again has a receding group of haloed heads of the Apostles on one face, with a bird and leaping quadruped in scrollwork on the back, and at

All Saints, Otley (W. Yorks), there is a row of busts under arcades. Other lively animals are used on shafts at St Michael, Croft (Leics), and Holy Trinity, Dacre (N. Yorks). The various regional workshops were therefore continuing to produce sculpture in the vigorous tradition established in the 8th century but incorporating the changes developed in Mercia in the 9th century.

(iii) The Viking north. Although the initial effect of the Viking raids was to cause great disruption to the monastic centres of patronage, subsequent Scandinavian settlement in the north of England (*see* VIKING ART, §II, 4(iii)(a)) inspired new forms of ornament marked by fresh emphasis on the animal form, different types of interlace and an iconography resulting from secular rather than ecclesiastical patrons. The art of stone carving was learnt for the first time by the Scandinavian settlers in their new homelands, so it is more appropriate to consider the effect on the Vikings of the powerful Anglian sculpture tradition than to look for the import of Viking art. The introduction of new motifs provides evidence of Viking patrons; stone carving would have been carried on by local schools drawing upon the patterns of contemporary metalwork and wood-carving. From the end of the 9th century, it is possible to recognize Scandinavian elements on the crosses, in particular the double-outlined animal body, distinctive eye and jaw, loosely interlaced shapes and new types of knots, ring-chains, pellets and tendrils. The figural ornament can show Viking warriors, but their very existence on memorial cross shafts proves the rapid conversion to Christianity and use of a local type of monument.

Despite the occupation, the Anglian tradition also continued. The community of St Cuthbert at Chester-le-Street (Durham) maintained the artistic standards of its home on Lindisfarne. A group of cross-heads from the chapter house of Durham Cathedral, which date from the end of the 10th century, are still in the traditional Northumbrian form, using deep relief, though with the addition of some new motifs. One Viking innovation was the introduction from Ireland of the ringed cross-head, which had not previously been used in England.

(iv) Wessex. With the newly prominent kingdom of Wessex following King Alfred's successful resistance to the Vikings and his encouragement of the revival of religion, learning and the arts, sculpture developed in further new ways. During the 10th century there was a great variety of styles and a considerable contrast between works made under court or monastic patronage and the simpler products of provincial schools.

An example of the new spirit is the lively carving of a man plucking fruit from a tree, from Codford St Peter (Wilts; see fig. 6). The mannered, angular figure and plump leaves are affected by the manuscript drawing of the developing Winchester school. Carvings tended to be in flattish relief with surface decoration of plant ornament and fine-lined interlace, but a new feature is the use of Carolingian acanthus leaves rather than the old vine scroll and its derivatives. The leaf forms, tendrils and dotted decoration are also seen on manuscripts and metalwork. Animals remained popular, but with an increasingly ornamental rather than symbolic character; they are treated as part of a pattern merging with leaves and interlace on a

6. Stone shaft depicting a man picking fruit, h. 1.25 m, Codford St Peter, Wiltshire, 10th century

group of carvings from St John the Baptist, Colerne (Wilts), St Mary, Bibury (Glos), and Holy Cross, Ramsbury (Wilts). Some features of these animals show that the sculptors were aware of art in the Viking north of England.

Renewed contacts with the Continent are suggested through the figural slabs that became more common in the 10th century. The Byzantine art that inspired that of Ottonian Germany can be recognized in the graceful flying angels of St Lawrence, Bradford-on-Avon (Wilts), and St Michael, Winterbourne Steepleton (Dorset). Such figures were applied to the inside or outside of buildings in a decorative rather than functional manner. Other applied architectural carvings are the Roods, or Crucifixion panels, such as those from Romsey Abbey (Hants) or Langford (Oxon), which again show the influence of Byzantine art through the medium of Carolingian and Ottonian ivory carvings. Other examples of architectural carving are the decorated shafts from, for example, Barnack, with trilobate tree scrolls.

A secular narrative tradition is suggested by the fragment (Winchester, City Mus.) from Winchester Old Minster, with a warrior and a man being licked by a wolf; this may have come from a frieze illustrating a Norse saga. It dates from the 11th century and shows the overlap of styles in the years leading up to the Norman Conquest. Romanesque elements were already present in a number of earlier 11th-century carvings, but the Anglo-Saxon tradition was sufficiently strong to carry on into the early 12th century. Final examples of the sculptor's art can be traced in the delicate foliage, enmeshed animals and decorative, linear quality on some of the tympana, lintels and capitals of the new wave of Norman churches and cathedrals.

BIBLIOGRAPHY

Bede: *Ecclesiastical History*

R. Cramp: 'Schools of Mercian Sculpture', *Mercian Studies*, ed. A. Dornier (Leicester, 1977), pp. 191–234

J. T. Lang, ed.: *Anglo-Saxon and Viking Age Sculpture*, British Archaeological Reports, British Series, 49 (Oxford, 1978)

R. N. Bailey: *Viking Age Sculpture in Northern England* (London, 1980)

Corpus of Anglo-Saxon Stone Sculpture in England, i: *County Durham and Northumberland*, ed. R. Cramp (Oxford, 1984); ii: *Cumbria, Westmorland and Lancashire*, ed. R. N. Bailey and R. Cramp (Oxford, 1988); iii: *York and East Yorkshire*, ed. J. Lang (Oxford, 1991)

R. H. Jewell: 'The Anglo-Saxon Friezes at Breedon-on-the-Hill', *Archaeologia*, cviii (1986), pp. 95–116

C. L. Neuman de Vegvar: *The Northumbrian Renaissance* (London, 1987)

For further bibliography *see* §I above.

CAROLA HICKS

IV. Painting.

Anglo-Saxon painting survives preponderantly in manuscript illumination, which was a significant art form from the arrival of the Christian missionaries in the late 6th century. Wall painting must also have been important, but the evidence is much more fragmentary.

1. Wall. 2. Manuscript.

1. WALL. Evidence is confined almost entirely to small excavated fragments and to documentary references to paintings now lost; nothing survives remotely comparable to such contemporary continental schemes as at Müstair and Reichenau (*see* CAROLINGIAN ART, §IV, 1 and OTTONIAN ART). Nevertheless, most of the material remains have been unearthed or recognized since 1960, and the documentary sources have also been analysed in detail. Taken together with the similarly increasing evidence for painted sculpture, textiles, window glass and coloured tiles, a much clearer idea of the polychromy of Anglo-Saxon buildings is now possible.

Particularly early fragments of painted plaster, dating from the late 7th century or the early 8th, have been excavated from monastic buildings at Monkwearmouth and Jarrow (Tyne and Wear), but these merely show stripes and arcs. Much more significant were the paintings brought back by Benedict Biscop from his visits to Rome *c.* 678 and 684/6 to decorate the churches of this great twin monastery. It seems clear that these were panel paintings, and the subjects included scenes from the Gospels and from the Apocalypse at Monkwearmouth, and Old Testament and New Testament types and antitypes at Jarrow. This subject-matter was probably influenced by some of the great Early Christian schemes in Rome, for example the typological programme in S Giovanni in Laterano, which thus found a reflection in the Northumbrian monastery. Imported panel paintings may have been far from uncommon in major churches at this period; the church at Kildare (Ireland) is also described in the 7th century as 'adorned with painted pictures', presumably panel paintings, and such panels may well have exerted a crucial influence on the iconography of the Irish high crosses.

Anglo-Saxon painted plaster has also been excavated from nine other sites, the majority providing evidence of figural schemes. Perhaps dating from the 8th century are a number of fragments recovered from St Patrick's Chapel, Heysham (Lancs), including two with painted lettering. These may have formed part of the inscription for a figural subject, similar to the tituli used in continental wall paintings from the Early Christian period onwards. At St Oswald's Minster, Gloucester, various fragments of figural and foliate painting are datable to the 10th century and appear to have belonged to a painting on the screen wall at the east end of the nave. An especially notable find was made in 1977, in a small timber-and-wattle structure immediately to the south of the Norman keep of Colchester Castle. Fragments of life-size figures were excavated from what seems likely to have been an early 10th-century royal chapel, but most of the plaster was left undisturbed, and it may, therefore, provide an opportunity in the future to recover this scheme almost completely.

By the mid-1990s the single most important fragment of Anglo-Saxon wall painting so far to have been excavated was that found in 1966 at Winchester (now in Winchester, City Mus.; see fig. 7). Discovered reused in the foundations of the New Minster, it is datable from the archaeological context to before *c.* 901–3. It shows the remains of three figures and of pelta ornament similar to that often seen in Carolingian manuscripts. The strong linear style—figures with staring eyes, narrow shoulders, and 'wig-like' hair—is comparable to painting in such manuscripts as Bede's *Life of St Cuthbert* (after 934; Cambridge, Corpus Christi Coll., MS. 183) and the additions (before 939) to the Athelstan Psalter (London, BL, Cotton MS. Galba A. XVIII; *see* §2(i)(a) below), and also to the embroidered stole (*c.* 909–16; Durham Cathedral Treasury; see fig. 15 below) and other pieces ordered for Bishop Frithestan of Winchester by Elfleda (*d* before 916), wife of King Edward the Elder. This suggests that this style had already appeared by the late 9th century. The subject of the paintings is unknown, but its row of figures suggests that the miniatures depicting heavenly choirs in the Athelstan Psalter, otherwise difficult to parallel, may perhaps have derived from a source in monumental painting at Winchester.

Later Anglo-Saxon wall painting at Winchester is doubtless reflected in the nearby parish church of Nether Wallop (Hants), which retains the only Anglo-Saxon wall painting known in any upstanding building. The painting is on the

7. Wall-painting fragment, 242×586 mm, from Winchester, before *c.* 901–3 (Winchester, City Museum)

nave east wall and, though partly destroyed when the chancel arch was later enlarged, clearly showed four angels supporting a mandorla (see fig. 8), probably enclosing a *Christ in Majesty*. Executed in a delicate, essentially linear manner, the painting is in the agitated style dependent on Carolingian manuscript painting of the Reims school, seen in such Winchester manuscripts as the Benedictional of St Aethelwold (*c.* 980; London, BL, Add. MS. 49598; see fig. 9 below). The wall painting is probably slightly later, perhaps *c.* 1000.

Bishop Aethelwold is likely to have supervised the reform of the royal nunnery at Wilton (Wilts) in the second half of the 10th century, and a major scheme of wall painting was executed there at that time. In the following century Goscelin of St Bertin related that one of the nuns, Edith, a daughter of King Edgar (*reg* 959–75), added a timber chapel to the south side of the main church, in which a cycle of *Passion* paintings was executed by Benna, a canon of St Maximin in Trier. The programme suggests that the chapel may have enshrined the relic of the Holy Nails that Benna is known to have brought to the abbey. It is likely that the paintings were purely Ottonian in style and layout, and although no wall painting from this period survives at Trier itself, the late 10th-century scheme at Reichenau-Oberzell (*see* REICHENAU, §2(ii)) may suggest something of the appearance of the Wilton paintings. It is possible that the Wilton scheme played a significant role in introducing Ottonian influences to English painting in the late 10th century. From the very end of the Anglo-Saxon period is the painted ceiling 'variously intermixed with gold with wonderful artistry' that Archbishop Ealdred (*reg* 1060–69) provided for Beverley Minster (N. Humberside). It may have been executed by a German artist, or at least have reflected German examples, since Ealdred also

8. Wall painting (fragmented, *c.* 1000), St Andrew, Nether Wallop, Hampshire

had a metal 'pulpitum' described as 'of German work' made for the minster.

Ottonian influences are very evident in such post-Conquest wall paintings as the 'Lewes Group', five closely related schemes of painting in the Sussex parish churches of Clayton, Hardham and elsewhere, dating from the years around 1100. Although various features of these paintings may have been derived, directly or indirectly, from Anglo-Saxon schemes, they illustrate the developments in English painting in the first half century after the Conquest. Nothing could be in greater contrast to the fluttering, linear style of Nether Wallop than these formal, monumental paintings, with their boldly striped draperies: the overall effect is purely Romanesque.

BIBLIOGRAPHY

F. Wormald: 'Anniversary Address', *Antiqua. J.*, xlvii (1967), pp. 162–5

——: 'The "Winchester School" before St Aethelwold', *England before the Conquest: Studies in Primary Sources Presented to Dorothy Whitelock*, ed. P. Clemoes and K. Hughes (Cambridge, 1971), pp. 305–13; repr. in *Collected Writings: I. Studies in Medieval Art from the Sixth to the Twelfth Centuries*, ed. J. J. G. Alexander, T. J. Brown and J. Gibbs (Oxford, 1984), pp. 76–84

P. Meyvaert: 'Bede and the Church Paintings at Wearmouth–Jarrow', *Anglo-Saxon England*, ix (1981), pp. 115–36

C. R. Dodwell: *Anglo-Saxon Art: A New Perspective* (Manchester, 1982)

S. Cather, D. Park and P. Williamson, eds: *Early Medieval Wall Painting and Painted Sculpture in England* (Oxford, 1990)

R. Stalley: 'European Art and the Irish High Crosses', *Proc. Royal Irish Acad.*, xc (1990), pp. 135–58

D. Park: 'Anglo Saxon Wall Painting: The Current State of Research', *Edifices et peintures aux V–XIe siècles: Proceedings of CNRS Symposium: Auxerre, 1992*

DAVID PARK

2. MANUSCRIPT. The production of illustrated manuscripts, both religious and secular, flourished in the last decades of the 10th century; liturgical books, in particular, were lavishly decorated. The products of this period are often referred to under the general title 'Winchester school', named after the place of origin of some of the most important manuscripts (for further discussion of the term and its wider usage *see* WINCHESTER, §II). The scope and variety of manuscripts illustrated, the diversity and originality of their iconography, and the skill and inventiveness of the artists involved, places manuscript production of Anglo-Saxon England in the 10th and 11th centuries at the very pinnacle of European achievement.

Manuscripts produced in the period before the 10th century are treated under Insular art (*see* INSULAR ART, §3).

(i) Religious. (ii) Secular.

(i) Religious.

(a) The reign of Athelstan, 924/5–39. (b) The period of monastic reform, *c.* 940–*c.* 1000. (c) Canterbury in the early 11th century. (d) Other 11th-century centres of production.

(a) The reign of Athelstan, 924/5–39. The Winchester school is foreshadowed by a handful of surviving works dating from King Athelstan's reign. Foremost among these is the earliest known copy of Bede's prose and verse *Life of St Cuthbert* (after 934; Cambridge, Corpus Christi Coll., MS. 183), which includes a full-page miniature (fol. 1*v*) of the King offering the book to the Saint. It was commissioned to commemorate Athelstan's visit to Cuthbert's shrine at Chester-le-Street in 934. Its figures are reminiscent of those on the embroidered stole (Durham, Cathedral Treasury; see fig. 15 below) also offered at Chester-le-Street by Athelstan. A decorated calendar and four full-page miniatures were added to a small continental 9th-century Psalter, which may have been Athelstan's personal property and which now bears his name (before 939; London, BL, Cotton MS. Galba A. XVIII; Oxford, Bodleian Lib., MS. Rawlinson B. 484, fol. 85). Two of the miniatures depict Christ enthroned among the heavenly choirs. The manuscript belonged throughout the Middle Ages to the Old Minster (now cathedral) at Winchester. Athelstan is known to have imported numerous books together with relics and other works of art from the Continent for distribution to various English churches, thus providing native English artists with direct access to continental models.

(b) The period of monastic reform, c. *940–*c. *1000.* Of the three bishops associated with the late 10th-century Church reform, DUNSTAN and AETHELWOLD were both extremely well connected at court and in the Church and are reputed to have been talented craftsmen in their own right. Dunstan, educated at Glastonbury Abbey, was appointed abbot of the house by King Edmund (*reg* 939–46) and later became Archbishop of Canterbury (959–88). A Latin classbook that once belonged to Glastonbury (Oxford, Bodleian Lib., MS. Auct. F. 4.32) contains a fine added drawing of a *Monk Kneeling at the Feet of Christ* (fol. 1*r*), which has been attributed to Dunstan's hand and dated to the middle of the 10th century. This drawing may be seen as the precursor of a number of monumental line drawings of individual figures, notably a *Christ* (Oxford, St John's Coll., MS. 28, fol. 2*r*) and a personification of *Philosophy* (Cambridge, Trinity Coll., MS. 0.3.7, fol. 1*r*), both of which are attributed to St Augustine's, Canterbury.

Two other manuscripts have traditionally been associated with Dunstan personally. One is the Bosworth Psalter (*c.* 975–1000; London, BL, Add. MS. 37517), made probably at Christ Church, Canterbury, and containing all the basic texts necessary for the performance of the Benedictine daily office. It is ornamented at the Psalter divisions with extremely impressive decorated initials and lines of coloured display capitals (*see* CANTERBURY, fig. 5). The other is the Sherborne Pontifical (Paris, Bib. N., MS. lat. 943), which includes full-page drawings of the *Crucifixion* (fol. 4*v*) and of the *Three Persons of the Trinity* (fols 5*v*–6*r*), all conceived on the same monumental scale as the drawing in the Glastonbury classbook. This second association with Dunstan, however, is no longer generally accepted, and the book is probably later than his death in 988; it may well have been written at Sherborne and was certainly there by the beginning of the 11th century.

One further manuscript from the last decade of the 10th century may be mentioned with this group: the Arenberg Gospels (New York, Pierpont Morgan Lib., MS. M. 869) contains elaborate canon tables, Evangelist portraits and initial pages executed in multicoloured line drawing against wash grounds of mauve, soft blue and green, with some gold. The coloured display capitals on the initial pages are reminiscent of the Bosworth Psalter, while the figure style seems to be derived from that in the Leofric Missal (Oxford, Bodleian Lib., MS. Bodley 579), which is a Glastonbury compilation of the third quarter of the century.

The manuscripts associated with Aethelwold, Bishop of Winchester, are more obviously luxury creations, designed for show. Aethelwold, like Dunstan, was educated at Glastonbury Abbey, and he was granted the derelict monastery of Abingdon, where he founded a new community (*c.* 954). It is thought that the script later regarded as typical of the Winchester school was probably developed in his scriptorium there. He was appointed Bishop of the royal city of Winchester in 963 and promptly undertook the reform of the communities both of the Old Minster (the cathedral) and of the New Minster, introducing monks from Abingdon as a nucleus in both places. The new regime at the New Minster is commemorated by the magnificent New Minster Charter (966; London, BL, Cotton MS. Vesp. A. VIII). Written out in book form in letters of gold and witnessed by leading Church and state figures, including King Edgar (*reg* 959–75) and his grandmother Eadgifu, widow of the founder, the document opens with a full-page miniature of the King, flanked by the Virgin and St Peter, offering the manuscript to Christ. This is the first known painting in the fully developed Winchester school style.

Aethelwold was the patron personally responsible for the outstanding masterpiece of the period, the Benedictional of St Aethelwold (London, BL, Add. MS. 49598), which must have been made before his death in 984 and probably dates from *c.* 980. No other surviving example of the type has such a wealth of illustration and decoration. According to a dedicatory poem written out in gold at the beginning of the manuscript, it was made for Aethelwold by his chaplain, Godeman, a monk of the Old Minster. It originally contained as many as 43 full-page miniatures, including a sequence showing the *Choirs of Heaven*, scenes from the *Life of Christ* and individual *Saints*. Among the latter, prominence is given to *St Etheldreda of Ely* (see fig. 9), patron of one of the monasteries refounded by Aethelwold. There are also 19 decorated text pages, all of which are lavishly enhanced with gold. Other pigments are thickly applied, with extensive use of white highlighting. The figures themselves convey a sense of great solidity, but there is a lively linear quality in the treatment of their draperies and of the surrounding decorative frames.

Three other manuscripts can be grouped with the Benedictional of St Aethelwold. One is a two-leaf fragment of a Gospel book (London, Coll. Arms, MS. Arundel 22), apparently in the hand of Godeman, in which is preserved a single decorative border. Another is the first portion of the erroneously named Ramsey Benedictional (Paris, Bib. N., MS. lat. 987), in a very similar if not identical script, containing text exactly parallel to that in the Aethelwold book. This has nine ornamental pages with initials and borders but no illustrations. The third is the Benedictional of Archbishop Robert (Rouen, Bib. Mun., MS. Y.7), so named from a 17th-century inscription. It contains three full-page miniatures from an original total of five, all very closely related to those in the Benedictional of St Aethelwold, and a related series of decorated text pages. It has been suggested that this book may originally have been intended for Aethelwold's contemporary Ethelgar of Abingdon, first abbot of the reformed New Minster, who

9. Manuscript illustration showing *St Etheldreda of Ely*; miniature from the Benedictional of St Aethelwold, 295×225 mm, *c.* 980 (London, British Library, Add. MS. 49598, fol. 90*v*)

was appointed Bishop of Selsey in 980 and Archbishop of Canterbury in 988. All four books are extremely grand and expensive products, reflecting the existence of first-class manuscript workshops in the monasteries of Winchester.

Oswald, the third bishop associated with the monastic reform movement, having spent several years at Fleury Abbey, was made Bishop of Worcester in 961 and Archbishop of York in 972. Under his leadership the community at Worcester Cathedral was placed under the Benedictine rule. He also re-established the monasteries at Winchcombe (Glos) and at Ramsey (Cambs). The latter in particular maintained a close relationship with Fleury, from which the great scholar Abbo came over to teach for two years before returning to France and becoming abbot in 989. No manuscript contains direct evidence of Oswald's patronage, but a very important group of late 10th-century manuscripts can be associated with connected foundations. Foremost is the Ramsey Psalter (London, BL, Harley MS. 2904). Although its script, decoration and certain textual features suggest that it may have been made at Winchester, in the litany a triple invocation of St Benedict, uniquely the patron of Ramsey, implies a connection with Ramsey or with Oswald. The anonymous artist of the superb coloured line drawing of the *Crucifixion* (fol. 3*v*) with which the manuscript opens, and also possibly of its magnificent Beatus initial (fol. 4*r*), provides through his varied and substantial work a very concrete illustration of the close relations maintained between England and the Continent at the end of the century. The

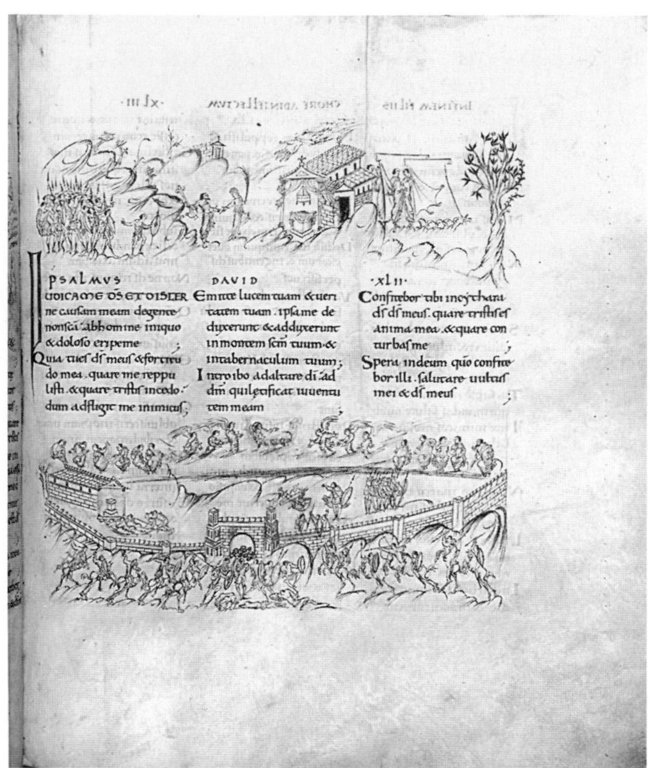

10. Manuscript illustration showing scenes illustrating Psalms 42–3; coloured line drawings from the Harley Psalter, 380×310 mm, first half of the 11th century (London, British Library, Harley MS. 603, fol. 25*r*)

style of his work leaves no doubt of his English training, but the Ramsey Psalter is the only one of his manuscripts that is entirely English in execution.

In two copies of the Gospels (New York, Pierpont Morgan Lib., MS. M. 827, and Boulogne, Bib. Mun., MS. 11) this artist's work appears alongside that of scribes and illuminators from northern France. The Boulogne manuscript, written by a continental scribe, contains an oustandingly rich scheme of fully coloured illustration, in which the traditional Evangelist portraits of *Matthew* (fol. 10*v*) and *Mark* (fol. 55*v*) are accompanied by scenes from the Christmas story, beginning with depictions of the ancestors of Christ. The book can be firmly associated with the abbey of St Bertin, Saint-Omer, as two of the lesser initials are attributable to Odbert, abbot of the house, a favourite staging-post for travellers crossing from England. Odbert had strong personal links with Canterbury and copies of his letters survive to Archbishop Ethelgar (*reg* 988–90) and Archbishop Sigeric (*reg* 990–94). The New York Gospels, also written by a continental scribe, has very similar Evangelist portraits to those in the Boulogne manuscript but without the accompanying narrative scenes; these are enclosed within Franco-Saxon style frames.

Two further manuscripts, recognizable as the work of this artist, are directly connected with Fleury. The first is a copy of Cicero's *Aratea* (*see* §(ii) below); the second, St Gregory's *Homilies on Ezekiel* (Orléans, Bib. Mun., MS. 175), includes a single drawing (fol. 149*v*) showing *Christ Enthroned with SS Gregory and Benedict*, the latter presenting the tiny figure of a monk kneeling at his feet. A dedicatory inscription places the volume at Fleury. Both these manuscripts display the same superb mastery of the line-drawing technique found in the Ramsey Psalter, implying that this particular artist was peripatetic.

(c) Canterbury in the early 11th century. Line drawing, often carried out in a variety of colours and sometimes set against backgrounds of delicately coloured wash, was a technique adopted widely by Anglo-Saxon artists. Several examples have already been cited. Towards the end of the 10th century the general development of the drawing style in England was very much influenced by the appearance of a major early 9th-century Carolingian manuscript, the UTRECHT PSALTER (Utrecht, Bib. Rijksuniv., MS. 32), brought to Canterbury at that time. At some point during the first two decades of the 11th century, artists from Christ Church, Canterbury, embarked upon the production of a grand Psalter (London, BL, Harley MS. 603; see fig. 10 and MANUSCRIPT, colour pl. II), which was originally planned as a direct copy of the Utrecht book, although the monochrome drawings in the original, studiedly emulating the Antique, were translated into the multicoloured version more popular with English craftsmen. Work on this ambitious enterprise continued well into the second quarter of the century, involving at least six different hands, and the manuscript, although incomplete, now contains more than a hundred separate drawings, almost all of which contain large numbers of lively figures as well as a wealth of other details. The drawings in the early work of the volume follow their model in translating the text of the psalms into visual form, although the scheme was simplfied as work progressed. One of the scribes involved in the book is identifiable as the Christ Church monk, Eadui, whose activities provide a link between a number of major Canterbury books of the early 11th century.

There is much to suggest that during the early part of the 11th century the scriptorium of Christ Church played an extremely active role in producing de luxe illuminated manuscripts, especially copies of the Gospels, for the use of other churches besides their own. It is not impossible that some part of this large number of books was commissioned by such important patrons as Knut (*reg* 1016–35) and his Norman queen Elfgyfu (Emma), possibly as gifts. Of the several manuscripts identifiable as containing Eadui's hand, two may have been both written and illuminated by him. One is a Psalter (London, BL, Arundel MS. 155), which includes, in addition to three large decorated initials, a full-page miniature of *Eadui* (fol. 133*r*) in the presence of the monastic community and prostrate at the feet of St Benedict, to whom he is offering the book (*see* BENEDICTINE ORDER, fig. 1). This is executed in a combination of full colour and coloured line drawing, introducing a subtle sense of hierarchy into the composition. The other is a Gospels (Hannover, Kestner-Mus., MS. WM XXIa 36) containing canon tables, Evangelist portraits and initial pages, all painted in full colour and lavishly enriched with gold. This manuscript includes a colophon in which Eadui is named.

Eadui is also recognizable as the scribe of the Grimbald Gospels (London, BL, Add. MS. 34890), which belonged to the New Minster at Winchester. The decorative scheme, which employs a great deal of now badly oxidized silver, features the choirs of heaven, already noted in two earlier Winchester books, the Athelstan Psalter and the Benedictional of St Aethelwold. This artist contributed to the York Gospels (York Minster, Chapter Lib., Add. MS. 1), which contains additions made at York as early as the 1020s. He added into a Gospels (London, BL, Royal MS. 1. D. IX), which may have been in use at Christ Church itself, Knut's solemn confirmation of the privileges of the house, made at the request of Archbishop Lyfing (*reg* 1013–20), presumably on the occasion of the King's visit sometime between 1016 and 1019. All these books are ornamented with varying combinations of canon tables, miniatures and initials, often partially lost, and involving a number of different illuminators.

The last of these manuscripts provides a link to a second related group, because it involves another, this time unnamed, scribe, presumably also working at Canterbury. As well as sharing in the writing of the Royal Gospels, he was responsible for the text of the Trinity Gospels (Cambridge, Trinity Coll., MS. B. 10.4), of the Kederminster Gospels (Langley Marsh, St Mary's, Kederminster Lib., no. 267; currently London, BL, Loan MS. 11) and of the Missal of Robert of Jumièges (Rouen, Bib. Mun., MS. Y.6). The decoration in both his Gospels follows the standard pattern, but the Missal has some of the most original and outstanding work of the period, worthy to be considered alongside the great Winchester manuscripts of the Aethelwold group. More properly to be described as a Sacramentary, comprising only those parts of the mass that are actually recited by the celebrant, this book contains thirteen full-page miniatures (see fig. 11) illustrating the principal feasts of the ecclesiastical year (three more are apparently missing) and four decorated pages at the beginning of the prayer of consecration. The work is extremely lively and expressive, carried out in bright colours enriched with gold. Like the Benedictional of St Aethelwold, the manuscript is unusual in its class for the richness of its decorative scheme. Textually it appears to be derived from an exemplar made for Peterborough, which was one of Aethelwold's foundations. It was probably made before 1023, as the translation of St Alphege, which took place that year, is not among its feasts. It takes its name from a subsequent owner, a friend of Edward the Confessor (*reg* 1042–66), Robert of Jumièges, who was successively Bishop of London (1044–51) and Archbishop of Canterbury (1051–2). He gave it to Jumièges Abbey in Normandy, of which he was abbot from 1037.

11. Manuscript illustration showing the *Annunciation to the Shepherds* and the *Flight into Egypt*; miniatures from the Missal of Robert of Jumièges, 340×220 mm, *c.* 1020 (Rouen, Bibliothèque Municipale, MS. Y.6, fol. 33*r*)

(d) Other 11th-century centres of production. Nothing as richly decorated as Canterbury's Gospel manuscripts can be linked to 11th-century Winchester, but one craftsman working there in the second quarter of the century is identifiable. A small-scale collection of personal devotions (London, BL, Cotton MSS Titus D. XXVI–XXVII) made for Aelfwine, Dean of the New Minster, immediately before 1032 contains the name of the scribe Aelsinus, who seems also to have been responsible for the New Minster *Liber vitae* (London, BL, Stowe MS. 944), which was made *c.* 1031. Both manuscripts contain illustrations in line drawing, heightened with green, the former including one very unusual example of iconography, the so-called *Quinity*, in which the Three Persons of the Trinity are accompanied by figures of the Virgin and Child (Cotton MS. Titus D. XXVII, fol. 75*r*). The *Liber vitae* has two major compositions, a *Last Judgement* (fols 6*v*–7*r*) and a presentation miniature (fol. 6*r*) in which Knut and his queen are seen giving an altar cross to the abbey. All illustrations in both books, together with a drawing of an *Evangelist* added to an earlier Winchester Gospels (Besançon, Bib. Mun., MS. 14, fol. 58*v*), are by a single hand, which may well be that of the scribe Aelsinus himself.

A number of splendid Psalters were made towards the middle of the 11th century. The most ambitiously decorated can apparently be assigned to Winchester (London, BL, Cotton MS. Tib. C. VI; *see* WINCHESTER, fig. 2), although the scriptorium cannot be specified. It is the earliest such manuscript known to contain a sequence of narrative illustrations before the Psalter text, a format that was to become very popular throughout Europe in later centuries. There are five full-page pictures illustrating the *Story of David* and eleven for the *Life of Christ*, all executed in multicoloured line drawing. Other illuminated Psalters of the period are associated with Crowland (Oxford, Bodleian Lib., MS. Douce 296), with Winchcombe (Cambridge, U. Lib., MS. Ff.1.23) and with Bury St Edmunds (Rome, Vatican, Bib. Apostolica, MS. Reg. lat. 12). The last includes, in addition to two fully illuminated initial pages, a series of 53 marginal drawings covering subjects from both Old and New Testaments.

Towards the middle of the century a number of expensive copies of the Gospels, linked with two contemporary noblewomen, were produced. One (Oxford, Bodleian Lib., MS. lat. liturg. F.5) belonged to St Margaret of Scotland, granddaughter of Edmund Ironside (*reg* 1016). Two others (New York, Pierpont Morgan Lib., MSS M. 708 and 709) and probably a third (Montecassino, Montecassino Abbey, Archv, MSS BB. 437 and 439) are associated with Countess Judith of Flanders, who came to England in 1051 as the bride of Tostig Godwinson, Earl of Northumbria, and returned to the Continent in 1064. All four manuscripts contain the traditional sequence of fully illuminated Evangelist portraits and decorated initial pages. In addition, M. 709 includes a memorable rendering of the *Crucifixion* (fol. 1*v*). The two manuscripts in New York retain their splendid 11th-century bindings of wooden boards covered with precious metals; that on M. 708 is now held to be English, while its companion is thought to be the product of a Flemish workshop. None of these four Gospels has been convincingly localized, although Winchester, Canterbury and centres in East Anglia have been variously proposed. It is at least possible that the craftsmen concerned in the making of Judith's books were directly recruited into her household for the purpose.

Two further mid-11th-century manuscripts, a Gospels (Cambridge, Pembroke Coll., MS. 302) and a Troper (London, BL, Cotton MS. Calig. A. XIV), have come to be associated with Hereford because there is evidence that the former belonged very early in its history to Hereford Cathedral. The four Evangelist portraits in the Gospels and the eleven surviving illustrations to the feasts in the Troper are particularly rich and intense in colouring and gilding. Their distinctive style has been characterized as Winchester school evolving towards an embryonic native English Romanesque, which, interrupted by the Norman Conquest, failed to develop its full potential.

(ii) Secular. There are a number of important illustrated Anglo-Saxon manuscripts that are secular in content. These include three more or less complete late 10th-century copies of Prudentius' *Psychomachia* (London, BL, Cotton MSS Cleop. C. VIII, Add. MS. 24199, and Cambridge, Corpus Christi Coll., MS. 23) and a fragment of a fourth (Munich, Bayer. Staatsbib., Clm. 29031b). This popular Latin poem on the fight between the virtues and the vices was illustrated with *c.* 90 line drawings, clearly dependent on originals going back to late antiquity and probably transmitted through Carolingian copies. On palaeographical grounds the Cotton manuscript has been located to Christ Church, Canterbury, to which the Cambridge example is also assigned, but the other two copies are of uncertain origin.

Two unique and outstanding Old Testament narrative cycles, both associated with vernacular texts, were produced for manuscripts within a secular context. The first, a series of some 48 line drawings by 2 artists, accompanies the Old English Genesis poem in the so-called Caedmon manuscript (Oxford, Bodleian Lib., MS. Junius 11). One of the artists was also responsible for the Cambridge Prudentius, which suggests that the manuscript may be a Christ Church product of *c.* 1000. The second cycle (substantially unfinished—it was to have been fully coloured but not gilded) illustrates Aelfric's Old English paraphrase of the Pentateuch and Joshua (London, BL, Cotton MS. Claud. B. IV). Its style is often crude by comparison with that of the major liturgical books, but the wealth of its iconography is astonishing. There are more than 400 separate scenes in the book, for some of which the artists clearly drew on Late Antique sources, although many obviously contemporary details are included. The book seems to have belonged in the later Middle Ages to St Augustine's, Canterbury, and may well have originated there, probably during the second quarter of the 11th century.

There are also some scientific books with notable illustrations. The late 10th-century *Aratea* manuscript (London, BL, Harley MS. 2506, fols 36*r*–44*v*) has 21 drawings of constellations by the Ramsey Psalter artist. A fine Carolingian version of the *Aratea* (London, BL, Harley MS. 647) had been brought to Canterbury before the end of the 10th century and it was copied to provide one of the items in a collection of scientific treatises put together at Christ Church, probably in the second quarter of the 11th century (London, BL, Cotton MS. Tib. B. V). In this volume the text is preceded by a calendar with a fine series of *Labours of the Months*, parallel to a series in line drawing in another, somewhat earlier, Christ Church calendar (London, BL, Cotton MS. Jul. A. VI; *see* CALENDAR, fig. 1), which has the distinction of being the earliest surviving example of such a cycle, adopted for the majority of decorated calendars during the remainder of the Middle Ages. Later, in the Tiberius manuscript, is a treatise on the *Marvels of the East*, accompanied by 38 illustrations of monsters and fabulous folk, and an extraordinarily early *Mappa mundi* (fol. 65*v*), attached to a copy of Priscianus' *Periegesise Dionysio*.

A fine mid-11th-century medical compendium (London, BL, Cotton MS. Vitell. C. III) includes the *Herbarium* of pseudo-Apuleius and portions of the *Liber medicinae ex animalibus* of Sextus Placidus. This contains two full-page miniatures and several hundred coloured drawings of plants and animals, which would have provided an often remarkably accurate aid to their identification. Opinions as to the place of origin of this book are divided. It has been compared both to the Cotton Prudentius from Christ Church and to the Tiberius Psalter, which is associated with Winchester.

BIBLIOGRAPHY

F. Wormald: *English Drawings of the Tenth and Eleventh Centuries* (London, 1952)

E. Temple: *Anglo-Saxon Manuscripts, 900–1066* (1976), ii of *A Survey of Manuscripts Illuminated in the British Isles*, ed. J. J. G. Alexander (London, 1975–) [with bibliog.]

F. Wormald: *Collected Writings: I. Studies in Medieval Art from the Sixth to the Twelfth Centuries*, ed. J. J. G. Alexander, T. J. Brown and J. Gibbs (Oxford, 1984)

M. Brown: *Anglo-Saxon Manuscripts* (London, 1991)

For further bibliography *see* §I above.

JANET BACKHOUSE

V. Metalwork.

1. Before the 8th century AD. 2. The 8th century and after.

1. Before the 8th century AD. From the earliest years of Anglo-Saxon settlement in England fine metalwork, especially jewellery, was an art form of major importance. The immediate continental Germanic ancestors of the Anglo-Saxons had absorbed a wide range of techniques, forms and decorative conventions from contact with late Roman provincial workshops and their products, adapting them to their own cultural requirements. Such late Roman motifs as running spirals, key and star patterns, animal motifs and images of gods and sea-beasts were seized upon and translated into a fresh decorative repertoire. Densely textured surfaces with gilded chip-carving were characteristic of the distinctive Germanic animal style of the late 5th century and throughout the 6th, known as Style I (*see also* Migration period and fig. 1). Its fractured, analytical treatment of animal and human forms, dissecting them into highly formulaic components, developed a distinctive and lively character in Anglo-Saxon hands. It predominates on buckles, brooches and other fine metalwork indicative of high status (for modern reconstruction drawing *see* Dress, fig. 9). The techniques of casting, repoussé work, stamping, gilding and niello inlay (*see* Gold, §2; Silver, §3 and Metal, §V) were augmented during this early period by the technique of garnet inlay, adopted from Frankish jewellers (*see* Merovingian art, §2). Thus by the time of the Christian mission of St Augustine in 597 Anglo-Saxon metalwork deployed both a distinctive, inventive stylistic vocabulary and a range of practical techniques of late Roman derivation.

In the kingdom of Kent greater access to resources had encouraged the development of more lavish and spectacular forms of ornament. Particularly striking is the use of garnet, shell, coloured glass and niello to create polychrome effects. More significant still was the increased availability of gold in the decades around 600 which, although short-lived, was intense and brought fresh opportunities for the Anglo-Saxon jeweller. Byzantine gold coinage reaching England through Frankish channels was the ultimate source of this gold glut, and, although the flow was to decline sharply as Byzantine political interests shifted eastwards, the new opportunities that the gold provided for craftsmen were to transform the character of Anglo-Saxon jewellery. In particular, the ductility of gold facilitated the development of sophisticated cloisonné inlays and, perhaps even more importantly, permitted the use of filigree, which was a major factor in the emergence of the more symmetrical, interlacing, sinuous zoomorphic style known as Style II, exemplified on the garment clasps (*c.* 600; London, BM) from the princely grave at Taplow (Bucks).

By the early 7th century in the courts of Kent and East Anglia these trends had led to the production of ceremonial jewellery of quite exceptional brilliance and luxury, as exemplified by the royal trappings from mound 1 at Sutton Hoo (London, BM; *see also* Sutton Hoo, §2 and fig. 1) and the great disc brooch from Kingston Down, Kent (Liverpool Mus.). In such pieces as these the extravagant use of gold and of complex polychrome inlays reflects both the influence of Byzantine tastes and the wealth and power of rulers at this unstable period. The 7th century was in many ways a watershed between a pagan Germanic past and a Christian medieval society. No aspect of society—political, economic, religious or cultural—was untouched; even the fashions in dress shifted, in emulation of Mediterranean customs, from brooches and beads to pins and pendants. One particular consequence of these processes was that the pagan tradition of burial with grave goods, a major source of information on Anglo-Saxon metalwork, gradually ceased under the strictures of Christianity.

2. The 8th century and after. From the early years of the 8th century, owing to the changes in burial rites mentioned above, the evidence for the development of metalwork is notably more scarce, since it comes from a more diverse and random set of sources. These include pieces that had found their way into Viking graves as loot, or that had been taken abroad and presented to continental churches. Given the altered parameters of retrieval, the nature of what survives is inevitably rather different from that of artefacts from earlier centuries. Yet even for the ill-represented 8th century an emergent picture is clear.

The sharp decline in the availability of gold after the early 7th century meant that fine metalwork of the 8th was, like the coinage, predominantly of silver. Gold seems to have been reserved for such small articles as finger-rings or for insets into large objects. Spectacular dress pins remained the primary costume jewellery for females, continuing the trend away from brooches. The decoration on these and on other fine 8th-century secular metalwork retains the zoomorphic element; here, sprightly creatures with pointed wings and speckled bodies clamber in and out of leafy interlace. The iconography is essentially that of the Christian inhabited vine scroll that entered the Anglo-Saxon repertoire in the 7th century and dominated sculpture in particular (*see* §III above); but the dynamics of this style reflect the long-standing Anglo-Saxon fascination with the manipulation of animal forms. This is equally evident in high-status ecclesiastical metalwork, as exemplified by the great standing Anglo-Saxon *Crux gemmata* (cross set with jewels; Salzburg, Dommus.), which was probably presented to Salzburg Cathedral during the episcopate of the Irish bishop Virgil (*reg* 756/7–84), who had been trained on Iona. Stylistically, the decoration of the cross has affinities with the sculpture and manuscripts of late 8th-century Northumbria, as well as with Northumbrian metalwork such as the Ormside Bowl (York, Yorks Mus.). It may even have been made by a Northumbrian craftsman, although in general it seems unwise to assign metalwork of this period to particular regional groups.

The tendency towards uniformity becomes even more marked in the metalwork of the 9th century, when the Trewhiddle style (*see* Trewhiddle hoard) became the predominant decorative style. Well before the middle of the century this distinctive style of ornament, well dated from its occurrence in coin hoards and on objects associated with historical figures, became current on secular and

12. Fuller Brooch, silver and niello, diam. 114 mm, late 9th century (London, British Museum)

ecclesiastical metalwork from the Scottish borders to Cornwall. A natural descendant of the spotted beasts enmeshed in interlace that populate late 8th-century metalwork, the Trewhiddle style is characterized by the use of panelled decoration teeming with quirky speckled animals and foliage, usually set against a ground of niello inlay on silver, which remained the favoured metal. The renewed popularity of the large disc brooch during the early 9th century gave jewellers the scope to produce effects of considerable elegance and sophistication, as demonstrated by the brooches from the Pentney Hoard (Norfolk), dated to the first third of the 9th century. By the closing years of the century the religious and intellectual reforms brought about by King Alfred were also encouraging an interest in more complex iconography, as the Fuller Brooch (London, BM), with its programme of the *Five Senses*, illustrates (see fig. 12). The splendid Alfred Jewel (Oxford, Ashmolean; see JEWELLERY, colour pl. IV, fig. 1), which has an inscription stating that it was commissioned by 'Aelfred' (almost certainly the King), exhibits a similar meditative or didactic purpose in its principal decoration, identified as either a personification of *Sight* or *Christ as the Wisdom of God*.

The Alfredian reforms were followed in the 10th century by the much more radical changes brought about by the monastic reform movement. A strengthening of ties with continental foundations brought renewed artistic influences from abroad, most notably the various aspects of Carolingian classicism that were to be integral to the Winchester style as it developed during the 10th century (*see* §IV, 2 above). Although this is a style primarily associated with manuscript illumination and ivory carving, it adapted well to metalwork, both in terms of high-relief versions of the characteristic acanthus and bird and beast ornament and in an agitated style of figure drawing. This tradition continued to develop throughout the first half of the 11th century and is seen in a reliquary cross (early 11th century; Brussels, St Michael) and a portable altar (second quarter of the 11th century; Paris, Mus. Cluny), but, with the arrival of a Danish dynasty on the accession of Knut, (*reg* 1016–35) Danish traditions became more influential, particularly in metalwork. Anglo-Saxon versions of Scandinavian styles became current in southern England as well as in the regions of the north and east under Scandinavian control, as is demonstrated by such splendid objects as two early 11th-century Ringerike-style mounts (Winchester, Cathedral Treasury, and London, Mus. London). The trend continued throughout the century, culminating in the wonderfully inventive Anglo-Saxon adaptation of the Urnes style (*see* VIKING ART, §II, 1(vii) and (viii)), best seen in a remarkable series of openwork metal ornaments, among which the Pitney Brooch (11th century; London, BM) foreshadows the elegance and vigour of English Romanesque.

BIBLIOGRAPHY

D. M. Wilson: *Anglo-Saxon Ornamental Metalwork, 700–1100, in the British Museum* (1964), i of *Catalogue of Antiquities of the Later Saxon Period* (London, 1964–)

D. A. Hinton: *A Catalogue of the Anglo-Saxon Ornamental Metalwork in the Department of Antiquities* (Oxford, 1974)

G. Speake: *Anglo-Saxon Animal Art and its Germanic Background* (Oxford, 1980)

C. R. Dodwell: *Anglo-Saxon Art: A New Perspective* (Manchester, 1982)

The Work of Angels: Masterpieces of Celtic Metalwork, 6th–9th Centuries AD (exh. cat., ed. S. M. Youngs; London, BM, 1989)

For further bibliography *see* §I above.

VI. Ivories.

During the Anglo-Saxon period some of the most exquisite early medieval ivories were produced. The earliest surviving decorative bone carvings date from *c.* 700, but there is plenty of evidence from the grave goods in pagan cemeteries to show that the 5th- and 6th-century Anglo-Saxons were competent bone and antler workers who could turn out combs, box fittings and the like with simple incised linear or compass-drawn motifs. Surprisingly, however, there is no hint that the plastic animal ornament so characteristic of much metalwork was ever transferred to bone, antler, or ivory objects, and although objects worked in these materials are perishable, enough examples of simply ornamented bone items survive from the early period to suggest that there may have been no established tradition of bone or ivory fine carving among the early Anglo-Saxons.

1. THE EARLY 7TH CENTURY AD TO THE LATE 9TH. A hint that Late Antique ivory carvings were among the material from the post-Classical Mediterranean world that arrived from Merovingian Gaul survives from the ravaged early 7th-century burial under mound 2 at Sutton Hoo, where a charred fragment of a small hardstone plaque carved with a winged *Victory* (London, BM) was found. The presence of such an item in the East Anglian royal burial ground suggests that by the beginning of the 7th century fine carving in the Classical manner was prized at court. The effect of such exemplars on indigenous bone

and antler carving is comparable to that of Mediterranean illuminated manuscripts on the development of the Insular manuscript tradition (*see* INSULAR ART, §3). Fresh techniques and forms gave new life to traditional Germanic motifs within a completely new set of intellectual and artistic conventions.

An elegant later 7th-century antler fragment from Southampton (Southampton, God's House Tower Mus.) is one of the earliest surviving examples of a new, more ambitious and accomplished style of carving. It is in delicate low relief with a procession of developed Style II animals (*see* MIGRATION PERIOD). These are related both to the traditional beasts of metalwork such as those on the Crundale sword pommel (London, BM) and to the classically ordered creatures seen in the Book of Durrow (second half of 7th century; Dublin, Trinity Coll. Lib., MS. 57; *see* INSULAR ART, §3).

The most striking example of the fusion of themes at this developmental period is the Franks Casket (with replica right-hand panel, London, BM; right-hand panel, Florence, Bargello; see fig. 13). This extraordinary box was probably made in a Northumbrian monastic milieu, in the first half of the 8th century. It is of whalebone and exhaustively carved in bold relief on the sides and lid with a programme of scenes from Germanic legend, Classical mythology, ecclesiastical history and the Bible. These are accompanied by explanatory runic inscriptions in two languages (Old English and Latin) and two scripts (runic and roman), with encoded passages and other displays of virtuosity. The programme is uncertain because of difficulties in identifying two of the apparently Germanic scenes, although in its use of antithesis, for example the *Foundation of Rome* contrasted with the *Fall of Jerusalem*, it reflects an exegetic tradition. The casket itself was clearly modelled on an early Christian reliquary similar to the 4th-century Brescia Casket (Brescia, Mus. Civ. Crist.; *see* RELIQUARY, §I, 2 and EARLY CHRISTIAN AND BYZANTINE ART, fig. 80). Though far from its classicizing models in its jostling, cluttered style, the Franks Casket illustrates in its uninhibited display of learning and its assimilation of Germanic and antique motifs the new direction that Anglo-Saxon bone and ivory carving was taking.

Surviving fine carving in bone or antler from the 8th and 9th centuries is, however, rare. This is perhaps a reflection of the fragility of the material and of the lack of access to such denser and more durable materials as walrus or elephant ivory; the Viking attacks of the 9th century must also have been a factor. Such rare survivals as the 8th-century Anglo-Saxon whalebone casket (Brunswick, Herzog Anton Ulrich-Mus.), formerly at Gandersheim Abbey, and the Larling bone plaque (Norwich, Castle Mus.) show exquisitely miniaturized versions of the inhabited vine scroll that dominated stone sculpture at this period (*see* §III above). This motif is combined with

13. Franks Casket, carved whalebone, 130×230×190 mm, first half of the 8th century (London, British Museum)

typically Insular beasts enmeshed in interlace and, in the case of the Gandersheim Casket, with running spiral motifs of Celtic descent. These two ivories reveal a fully mature technical virtuosity equal to that of the monumental stone carvers. Some hint of the prestige of Anglo-Saxon work at this time may be gained from surviving continental ivories such as the panel with animal interlace (London, V&A) and the Genoels-Eldoren 'diptych' (Brussels, Musées Royaux A. & Hist.), which exhibit features of the Insular stylistic repertory.

2. THE 10TH CENTURY AND AFTER. One reason why many more Anglo-Saxon ivories exist from the 10th century than from the 9th is suggested by a passage incorporated into the late 9th-century Old English translation (London, BL, Add. MS. 47967) of Orosius' *History against the Pagans*, which recounts how the Viking merchant Ohthere made a gift of walrus ivory to his protector, King Alfred, telling him how he had travelled to the Kola peninsula in search of walruses 'because they have very fine ivory in their tusks . . .'. The translator had to devise a new word, *horshwælum* ('horse-whale') for the walrus, which was evidently unknown to the Anglo-Saxons; yet after that time walrus ivory became the dominant medium for Anglo-Saxon fine carving. A much denser, more fine-grained medium than bone, antler or whalebone and available in more substantial thickness, it was durable and lent itself to the expressive figural iconography of the 10th-century monastic reform movement. The latter was to give a major impetus to the development of a brilliant and distinctive school of late Anglo-Saxon ivory carving that developed throughout the 10th and 11th centuries.

In the reign of King Athelstan, whose close connections with Europe brought the first currents of monastic reform, classicizing elements in Carolingian manuscripts and ivories (*see* CAROLINGIAN ART, §§IV, 3 and VI) were beginning to be emulated by Anglo-Saxon artists, but the continental reforms under Athelstan's successors and their effects on Anglo-Saxon foundations led to significant developments in ivory-carving as in manuscript illumination. Ivory-carving played a much enhanced role in the art of the reform movement, at its finest equalling the greatest manuscripts of the Winchester school style (*see* §IV, 2 above) in the controlled expression of religious sentiment. Two aspects of this style dominated in the late 10th century: a classicizing, monumental style that owed its inspiration largely to the late 9th- and early 10th-century Metz school (*see* CAROLINGIAN ART, §VI, (ii)), and a more impressionistic style in which fascination with the nervous energy of line dominated. The former is revealed in an ivory of *Adoring Angels* (Winchester, City Mus.) and in an outstanding walrus-ivory *Nativity* (Liverpool Mus.; see fig. 14); the second style is inspired by 9th-century manuscripts from Reims, such as the UTRECHT PSALTER (816–34; Utrecht, Bib. Rijksuniv., MS. 32), known to have been at Canterbury *c.* 1000, and finds its expression in the emotional intensity of such masterpieces as the figures of *St John* and the *Virgin* (Saint-Omer, Mus. Hôtel Sandelin). A close relationship with contemporary Anglo-Saxon manuscripts is evident in several of the late 10th-century ivories, as the striking stylistic similarities between the *Baptism of Christ* ivory (London, BM) and the version of the *Second Coming of Christ* in the Benedictional of St Aethelwold (London, BL, Add. MS. 49598; *see* WINCHESTER, §II) illustrate. Even more directly, the ivory *Christ* on a gold and enamelled crucifix reliquary (London, V&A) is a three-dimensional analogue to the powerful *Crucifixion* in the Ramsey Psalter (London, BL, MS. Harley 2904, fol. 3*v*). Other ivories reflect different aspects of the Winchester school style, such as the lush acanthus foliage and Franco-Saxon interlace embellishing the Alcester tau-cross (London, BM).

14. *Nativity*, walrus ivory, 80×65 mm, late 10th century or early 11th (Liverpool Museum)

Most ivories, like contemporary stone sculpture, were intended to be brightly painted, and sometimes were embellished with gold foil and inset dark glass eyes, as occasional fugitive traces show. Unlike metalwork, 11th-century ivory-carving was scarcely affected by Scandinavian influences but followed its own course. Small-scale *Crucifixion* panels and other small ivories—for example *Christ in Majesty* or the *Virgin and Child*—became popular; many of these may have come from book covers. One such plaque depicting *Christ in Majesty* framed in a mandorla (11th century; London, BM) illustrates the growing trend towards a more static and formal style and finds a close parallel in the commanding stone sculpture of the same subject at Barnack, Cambs. This and other Anglo-Saxon ivories from the period around the Norman Conquest such as a pencase (London, BM) are already at the threshold of Romanesque.

BIBLIOGRAPHY

A. Goldschmidt: *Die Elfenbeinskulpturen aus der Zeit der karolingischen und sachsischen Kaiser, VIII–XI Jahrhundert*, 2 vols (Berlin, 1914–18)

M. Longhurst: *Catalogue of Carvings in Ivory, Victoria and Albert Museum Department of Sculpture*, 2 vols (London, 1927–9)

J. Beckwith: *Ivory Carving in Early Medieval England* (London, 1972)

D. Gaborit-Chopin: *Ivoires du moyen âge* (Fribourg, 1978)
English Romanesque Art, 1066–1200 (exh. cat., ed. G. Zarnecki, J. Holt and T. Holland; London, Hayward Gal., 1984)
F. Wormald: *Studies in Medieval Art from the Sixth to the Twelfth Centuries* (1984), i of *Collected Writings*, ed. J. J. G. Alexander, T. J. Brown and J. Gibbs (Oxford, 1984–8)
For further bibliography *see* §I above.

LESLIE WEBSTER

VII. Stained glass.

Although window-glass had been used in Roman Britain, the technology of glazing had been lost by the time the Anglo-Saxon Church was established. Bede (chap. 5) described how BENEDICT BISCOP imported glaziers from Gaul to Northumbria in the late 7th century to glaze the windows of his monasteries of St Peter, Monkwearmouth (*see* MONKWEARMOUTH ABBEY), and St Paul, Jarrow (both Tyne and Wear), and to teach the English the art of glassmaking. Excavations on these sites have revealed over 450 fragments of coloured window-glass, together with lead calmes. The glass was cylinder-blown, in a range of colours, some produced by the technique known as flashing; it had been cut with a grozing iron (*see* STAINED GLASS, §I, 1, 3 and 7). There was no evidence of painting, and the glass may have been arranged as a mosaic, resembling cloisonné jewellery (*see* SUTTON HOO, §2). In the 670s Bishop Wilfrid glazed the windows of his church at York, and in the early 8th century the Bishop of Worcester replaced the wooden shutters in his cathedral with glass.

Glass fragments have been excavated at Escomb Church, All Saints, Brixworth, and St Wystan's, Repton (all 8th century). At Glastonbury Abbey evidence for a 9th- or 10th-century glass workshop has been found, including the remains of furnaces, coloured glass and leads. Other fragments, including blue and green pieces, have been excavated from the Old Minster at Winchester. Some were painted with foliage or drapery of 10th- and 11th-century manuscript type. Glass has also been found at secular sites, including the late 10th-century royal palace at Old Windsor, the 8th- to 10th-century port of Hamwih near Southampton and the 10th-century urban settlement at Thetford. Although no designs can be reconstructed, there was clearly an established Anglo-Saxon stained-glass tradition.

BIBLIOGRAPHY

Bede: *Lives of the Abbots of Wearmouth and Jarrow* [*c*. 716–26]; Eng. trans. in *The Age of Bede*, ed. D. H. Farmer (Harmondsworth, 1965, rev. 1983), pp. 185–211 [also Eddius Stephanus: *Life of Wilfrid*]
D. B. Harden: 'Domestic Window-glass, Roman, Saxon and Medieval', *Studies in Building History: Essays in Recognition of the Work of B. H. St J. O'Neil*, ed. E. M. Jope (London, 1961), pp. 39–63
R. Cramp: 'Decorated Window Glass and Millefiori from Monkwearmouth', *Ant. J.*, l (1970), pp. 327–35
D. B. Harden: 'Anglo-Saxon and Later Medieval Glass in Britain: Some Recent Developments', *Med. Archaeol.*, xxii (1978), pp. 1–24
M. Biddle: 'Glass', *The Golden Age of Anglo-Saxon Art* (exh. cat., ed. J. Backhouse, D. H. Turner and L. Webster; London, BM, 1984), p. 135

CAROLA HICKS

VIII. Textiles.

The textiles produced by and for Anglo-Saxons were of various types and materials. They ranged from garments and accessories to draperies and hangings—both secular and ecclesiastical—and they comprised woven cloths, narrow tablet-woven braids (see below), appliqués, embroideries and other forms of needlework, sometimes in combination. Materials included wool, linen, silk, gold and other metals, gemstones and pearls. Gold thread consisted of gold strips or strands in the early period and gold-wrapped threads with a core of silk or horse hair in the later period. Dyes were both native and imported and included madder, woad and kermes (*see* DYE, §2).

Techniques included twisting, carding, spinning, dyeing, weaving and needleworking. Distaffs for spinning had free-hanging spindles weighted by whorls. Sets of tablets for tablet-weaving were turned in sequences and had groups of holes through which the threads were passed. For weaving, a warp-weighted loom set against a wall or fixed upright in the ground was used until, in the 11th century, a free-standing horizontal loom made longer cloths possible. Various weaves had given way by the 11th century mainly to a three-shaft twill. Embroidery was worked using split stitch, stem stitch, laid-and-couched work and surface-couched gold threads. (*See* TEXTILE, §§I, 1 and 2; II, 1(i)(e) and (f); III, 1(i) and 2.) Evidence for production methods, decoration, makers, patrons and uses occurs in surviving objects, vocabulary, literature and documentary sources. Archaeological finds and relics from cemeteries, settlements and ecclesiastical sites include textiles, fibres, tools and such equipment as whorls and loom-weights. Textile production was a domestic craft practised by women of all social grades, as written sources show.

The most famous surviving textiles include the Maaseik embroideries (*c*. 800; Maaseik, St Katharinakerk), the Durham embroideries and braids (*c*. 909–16; Durham, Cathedral Treasury; see fig. 15) and the Bayeux Tapestry (*c*. 1066–97; Bayeux, Mus. Tap.; for discussion and illustration *see* BAYEUX TAPESTRY). The Maaseik embroideries are a set of matching panels intended as appliqués, perhaps for a chasuble or an altar cloth. According to medieval tradition, they were made by the early 8th-century Merovingian saints Harlindis and Relindis, founders of the abbey that owned the embroideries. However, the style is clearly southern English and later than their time. The Durham embroideries, a stole and matching maniple and small maniple, were presented *c*. 934–9 to St Cuthbert's community at Chester le Street by King Athelstan; inscriptions indicate that they were commissioned by Queen Elfleda (*d* 916) for Frithestan, Bishop of Winchester (*fl* 909–24). All these works carry figural and ornamental patterns characteristic of their periods (*see also* EMBROIDERY, §1). Some contemporary manuscripts show textiles and textile production. Notable examples occur in the Old English Hexateuch (first half of 11th century; London, BL, Cotton MS. Claud. B. IV) and the Junius Manuscript (*c*. 1000; Oxford, Bodleian Lib., MS. Junius 11), as well as on textiles themselves (e.g. the Durham stole and maniple and the Bayeux Tapestry). Many sources mention lost works, for example the tapestry or embroidery showing the deeds of Byrhtnoth, presented by his widow to Ely Cathedral after his death at the Battle of

15. Anglo-Saxon embroidered stole from the shrine of St Cuthbert, detail showing *Peter, Pope Gregory's Deacon*, silk and gold thread on linen, 1969×595 mm, *c.* 909–16 (Durham, Cathedral Treasury)

Maldon in 991. Anglo-Saxon textile production influenced the later medieval period and, in embroidery, led to the development of OPUS ANGLICANUM.

BIBLIOGRAPHY

C. F. Battiscombe, ed.: *The Relics of Saint Cuthbert* (Oxford, 1956)

C. R. Dodwell: *Anglo-Saxon Art: A New Perspective* (Manchester, 1982)

E. Crowfoot: 'The Textiles', *The Sutton Hoo Ship Burial*, ed. R. Bruce-Mitford, iii/1 (London, 1983), pp. 409–79

M. Budny: 'The Anglo-Saxon Embroideries at Maaseik', *Acad. Anlct.: Kl. S. Kst.*, xlv/ii (1984), pp. 55–133

M. Budny and D. Tweddle: 'The Maaseik Embroideries', *Anglo-Saxon England*, xiii (1984), pp. 65–96

C. Fell, C. Clark and E. Williams: *Women in Anglo-Saxon England and the Impact of 1066* (London, 1984)

D. M. Wilson: *The Bayeux Tapestry* (London, 1985)

G. R. Owen-Crocker: *Dress in Anglo-Saxon England* (Manchester, 1986)

P. Walton: 'Textiles, Cordage and Raw Fibre from 16–22 Coppergate', *Small Finds*, ed. P. V. Addyman (1989), xvii/5 of *The Archaeology of York*, 38 vols (York; xiv/1 (1976), xvii/8 (1992))

M. Budny: 'The Byrhtnoth Tapestry or Embroidery', *The Battle of Maldon, AD 991*, ed. D. Scragg (Oxford, 1991), pp. 263–78

MILDRED BUDNY

Ango [Angot], **Jean-Robert** (*fl* 1759–70; *d* after 16 Jan 1773). French draughtsman and painter. Most of the biographical information about him comes from the writings of his friend, the painter Jean-Antoine Julien, who established in his autobiography that Ango was already in Rome in November 1760; he also described Ango as a painter, although only drawings by him survive. In 1772, in correspondence with the Belgian painter Andries Cornelis Lens, Julien referred to an attack of apoplexy that had left Ango half-paralyzed and reduced to living on charity. Julien's last mention of him is on 16 January 1773. Dated drawings known to be by Ango are from the period 1759–70. Most of the surviving drawings are of paintings and decoration in Roman churches and palaces, but some attest to a knowledge of Naples, and it is recorded that on 18 March 1761 Ango and Jean-Honoré Fragonard were given permission to draw copies of the paintings in the gallery of Capodimonte there. Many of Ango's drawings are copies after Old Masters such as *St Lawrence Giving Alms to the Poor* (red chalk; Paris, Louvre), a copy of a painting by Guercino (untraced; ex-S Lorenzo fuori le Mura, Rome). Some are after his contemporaries Fragonard and Hubert Robert (e.g. the *Corpus Domini Procession*, black chalk, Paris, Gal. Cailleux after the original by Robert (London, priv. col.)), and in a number of instances he reworked counterproofs of drawings by Robert (e.g. the *Draughtsman of Antiques*, black and red chalk, 1762; Cambridge, MA, Fogg) after the original drawing by Robert (Valence, Mus.). Ango also recorded in drawings the paintings in the collection of Bailli de Breteuil, ambassador of the Order of Malta to the Holy See from 1758 to 1780, but he is best known for the 27 etchings and aquatints after his drawings engraved by the Abbé de Saint-Non for his *Recueil de griffonnis, de vues, paysages, fragments antiques et sujets historiques* (Paris, 1755–78), all of them copies of paintings located in Rome. Ango's draughtsmanship is characterized by strong contours and heavy modelling; he usually worked in red or black chalk.

BIBLIOGRAPHY

J. de Parme: *Vie de Julien de Parme, peintre, écrite par lui-même* (MS.; 1794); ed. C. Landon in *Précis historique des productions des arts: Peinture, sculpture, architecture et gravure*, i (Paris, 1801), pp. 114–48

A. Ananoff: 'Fragonard et Ango, collaborateurs de Saint-Non', *Bull. Soc. Hist. A. Fr.* (1963), pp. 117–20

——: 'Les Paysages d'Ango', *Bull. Soc. Hist. A. Fr.* (1966), pp. 163–8

M. Roland Michel: '"Un Peintre français nommé Ango . . ."', *Burl. Mag.*, cxxiii (1981), pp. i–viii

P. Rosenberg: 'La Fin d'Ango', *Burl. Mag.*, cxxiv (1982), pp. 236–9
J. de Parme and A.-C. Lens: *Correspondence*, ed. P. Rosenberg and D. Coekelberghs (in preparation)

M.-E. HELLYER

Angola, People's Republic of [República Popular de Angola]. African country bordered by Congo and Zaïre to the north, Zambia to the east and Namibia to the south. It has a long Atlantic coastline to the west. Officially included in the political area of Southern Africa, Angola is more closely linked by ancestral tradition to Central African culture. It has a total area of 1,246,700 sq. km and a population of *c.* 11 million (1995 estimate). The capital is Luanda. Angola consists mainly of savannah and sparse forest. The fertility of the soil is assured by a network of water-courses. The climate is characterized by alternate dry and rainy seasons. After the foundation of Luanda (1575) the port became the capital of the Portuguese colony of Angola, essentially limited to the Ambundu territory of the Ngola and ruled (except for a brief period of Dutch occupation between 1641 and 1648) in the name of the Portuguese kingdom by a succession of governors. The 19th-century 'scramble' in Africa originated a further conquest of land which, after the International Berlin Conference (1885), was confirmed as lying within official colonial borders. Angola became an overseas province of Portugal in 1951 and gained its independence in November 1975. This entry mainly covers the art produced in Angola since colonial times. For art of the region in earlier times *see* AFRICA, §VII, 6. *See also* CHOKWE AND RELATED PEOPLES, KONGO and YAKA.

1. INTRODUCTION. Most of Angola's population consists of settled Bantu-speakers whose ancestors arrived in the area *c.* 2000 years ago and gradually pushed the indigenous hunter-gatherers towards the Kalahari, although a few groups of the latter still survive near the border with Namibia. With the exception of some people in the south-west who practise herding, the peoples of Angola live exclusively by farming, work done by women, supplemented by hunting, which is considered men's work.

The area first came into contact with the West when the Portuguese navigator Diogo Cão put in at the mouth of the Zaïre river in 1483 and learnt of the existence of the Kingdom of the Kongo on its southern bank. During the 16th century, the rival Ambundu kingdom of the Ngola (or Ndongo) emerged. Profits from the slave trade encouraged the development of other kingdoms in the east and south of the territory. To the south of the Kwanza the great territories of the Ovimbundu chiefs enjoyed a period of economic growth beginning in the 18th century. The Ovimbundu (*see* CHOKWE AND RELATED PEOPLES, §4) came to specialize in long-distance trade and acted as intermediaries between the peoples living in the interior of the continent and the Portuguese, who, at least until the mid-19th century, were largely confined to the coastal strip. Towards the end of the 19th century, the lands beyond the Kwango were explored by large numbers of Europeans as new economic factors gradually increased the profits to be made from wax, ivory and rubber.

Traditional arts, which continue to flourish in Angola, can be divided into large cultural regions. The art of the Kongo and related peoples has a naturalistic tendency, revealing a certain Western influence. Unfortunately, ancient traditions of statuary have largely vanished from the area around Mbanza Kongo (formerly São Salvador), the capital of the ancient kingdom to the south of the Zaïre river. This is the result of 'idols' being burnt in large numbers after the conversion of the sovereigns to the Catholic faith. To the north of the river a great wealth of plastic art is still created by the Vili, the Woyo and the Yombe of Cabinda, and there is evidence of soapstone funeral effigies having been produced around the river mouth. Among the Chokwe, mask-making continues to flourish, and Angolan peoples still produce everyday objects made of pottery, basketwork, iron, wood and sometimes ivory, often decorated with geometrical designs. The aesthetic sense of these peoples, however, is principally expressed in the design of scarifications and adornments and, particularly, in the creation of truly remarkable hairstyles and headdresses for men and women that vary from one ethnic group to another.

2. ARCHITECTURE. The presence of the Portuguese in Angola dates from the 15th century. In accord with their preoccupation with evangelization, Portuguese influence can most clearly be traced in church architecture. By 1491 the king of the Kongo was baptized, and the first church, S Maria Nossa Senhora, was built at Mbanza Kongo using local stone, with the help of Portuguese labour. During the 16th century, the cathedral of São Salvador (1517 or 1526) was built in its place, and this later became the new name of the capital, which was also the episcopal see. Kongo kings were buried in this building, which was left almost completely in ruins at the end of the 18th century after a long series of wars. By the early 20th century nothing was left of it but the walls.

The Mbwila defeat and the death of the king in 1665 put an end to the pre-eminence of the Kongo, and the bishop's see was moved to Luanda. The fortress of S Miguel protected the burgeoning city, and its first parish church, dedicated to Nossa Senhora da Conceição, was built there in light materials by 1590. Although rebuilt in permanent materials in 1668, nothing now remains except the tower, where the Meteorological Observatory has since been installed. Several other churches in Luanda, often connected to convents, monasteries or hospices, also date from the 17th and 18th centuries. Made of materials from Portugal or Brazil, their style was typical of the period. The Baroque Igreja de Jesus (1636) had three doors in its façade and a number of paintings inside. The small church of Nossa Senhora da Nazaré (1664) is famous for two panels of decorative glazed tiles depicting the victory of Mbwila. Nossa Senhora dos Remédios (1679) was an imposing edifice with two towers and a façade decorated with volutes, in contrast to Nossa Senhora do Carmo (1689) with its charming décor in blue-and-white glazed tiles and delightful paintings of religious motifs on the walls and ceiling. By the end of the 18th century several of these buildings were in danger of falling into ruins, but they were restored a century later and were then classified as national monuments.

In 1579 the Portuguese began to use the valley of the Kwanza as their major route into the interior. Fortresses established at Calumbo, Muxima, Massangano and Cambambe were accompanied by the building of churches; a famous example is S Maria de Matamba, situated to the north-east, consecrated by the Capuchin chronicler Cavazzi on 12 August 1663 in the presence of Queen Nzinga.

The first churches built in Benguela, founded in 1617 to the south of the Kwanza, were made out of perishable materials, and the city had to wait until 1748 before the present Nossa Senhora do Pópulo—an imposing edifice in the Baroque style, with two towers and a pediment adorned with volutes—was built in a more lasting fashion. As a result of the earlier concentration of Christian missionary activity in the north of the country, it was only towards the end of the 18th century that a number of short-lived parishes with ad hoc churches were created on the Benguela plateau. Not until the last quarter of the 19th century were any churches built at Huambo, Bailundo, Bié or Caconda. Two cathedrals, ultra-modern in style, were built during the 20th century—one at Negunza (1969) and another at Benguela (1970); both have steeply pitched roofs, and the church at Negunza has a square tower.

In domestic architecture the oldest structures comprise a two-storey central section with two single-storey wings, often in ochre and pink, with white windows and doors. By the mid-19th century, ornate windows and balconies were common.

3. Sculpture. Beginning in the 16th century, European imagery, in the form of the insignia, emblems and statues of the Catholic Church, began to be used in indigenous arts and came to inspire a sincere reverence, which persisted even after the decline of Catholicism in the 18th century. Some of these objects were directly copied by the Kongo. For example, Crucifixes were given by the Kongo king Alfonso I (*reg* 1509–41) to clan chiefs and judges presiding over tribunals. Subsequently the Crucifix (*nkangi kiditu*) became a standard element of Kongo chiefly investiture ceremonies. Based on 14th–16th-century European examples, *nkangi kiditu* were produced in brass and wood and incorporated indigenous stylistic features. Objects not directly copied inspired the creation of new symbols used in traditional religious practices by, for example, the Holo. The Songo, the Shinji and the Chokwe honoured figurines representing Europeans in order to obtain their blessing.

European influence of quite a different order of magnitude affected the work of traditional sculptors when Europeans started to show an interest in acquiring 'souvenirs'. Already apparent by the end of the 19th century, this interest became marked from the 1930s onwards. A good example is provided by the figurine *The Thinker* made by Sazangwiyo, a Chokwe artist (see fig. 1). This is a modern interpretation of the miniature *kuku* divinatory symbol: the figure holding its head in its hands represents an ancestor lamenting that it has not been sufficiently honoured and was part of the ritual contents of the divination basket. Depicted on an enlarged scale and separated from its traditional function, it has become an official emblem of the modern state and is reproduced on a mass-production basis. During the first quarter of the 20th century, figurine production also flourished on the Benguela plateau, with small statuettes depicting anecdotal scenes of everyday life being executed for the European market.

1. Angolan sculpture by Sazangwiyo: *The Thinker*, wood, h. 168 mm, before 1949 (Luanda, Museu Nacional de Antropologia)

4. Painting. Artists active in Angola in the second half of the 20th century included such self-taught practitioners as José zan Andrade, known as Zan (*b* 1946), who

began working in Chinese ink and gouache before moving into acrylics in the early 1980s. Many Angolan artists received their training in Luanda, and of these some continued their education abroad. António Sallo (Sally), for example, went to study at the Khar'kov Fine Art School in the former USSR, while the large Académie des Beaux Arts at Kinshasa in neighbouring Zaïre has trained such artists as Matondo Afonso (*b* 1936), who painted under the name Mestre Bonga.

Other painters of this period include M'Vemba, A. Nzinga and M'Gombo, who were inspired by traditional themes, and Paulo Jazz (*b* 1940) and Tomas Vista (*b* 1957), who were influenced by modern art movements. A number of Angolan artists were featured in exhibitions in Stockholm in 1989 (see 1989 exh. cat.), in Britain and Ireland in 1990 (see 1990 exh. cat.), at the International World Exhibition at Seville in 1992 (see 1992 exh. cat.) and at the Johannesburg Biennale in 1995 (see 1995 exh. cat.). António dos Santos (Kida) (*b* 1961), from Dande, Bengo Province, was trained in graphic arts in Luanda (1980–81) and worked there as an engraver and painter. António Olé (*b* 1951) from Luanda was a film maker as well as a painter and sculptor. Vitor Manuel Teixeira, known as Viteix (*b* 1940), from Luanda studied art in Angola, Portugal and France. He was head of the Angolan branch of the International Association of Art Critics and was a founder member of União Nacional de Artistas Plásticos (UNAP). He produced colourful works on canvas. Francisco D. Van-Dúnem, known as Van (*b* 1959), from Bengo studied visual arts in Luanda. He worked as an urban designer for eight years. Also known outside Angola as António Olé, Fernando Alvim (*b* 1963) from Luanda explored the moral and emotional aspects of justice and human dignity through multimedia and innovative techniques.

5. WEAVING. Weaving is a traditional speciality of Angola that experienced a revival in the 1990s. Originally practised to meet domestic needs, the craft declined in the face of imported substitutes. During the 1980s and 1990s Angolan women revitalized the form, drawing on traditional decorative motifs. In her textile hanging *Sociedade* (see fig. 2) Marcela Costa (*b* 1957) revived a complex technique used by Kongo weavers that was admired by European collectors in the 16th century. In 1990 an exhibition in Luanda included the work of Maria Luiza da Silva. Having learnt to weave from her family, she later followed a six-month intensive course at the National Art School. Her tapestries are created from wool, sisal embroidery thread and hessian and are notable for their colours and motifs, as well as her subtlety of line.

6. ART INSTITUTIONS. After independence, the União Nacional de Artistas Plásticos encouraged contemporary artists by organizing national and international exhibitions, and the Humbiumbi Gallery, Luanda, is also extremely active. In 1990 the Empresa Nacional de Seguros de Angola (ENSA) created a painting prize for Angolan artists.

In the 1930s a museum was built at the head offices of the Angolan Diamond Company (DIAMANG), Dundo, and gradually acquired a rich collection. Most of its art collection (*c.* 2000 pieces) was transferred to Luanda at the end of 1974 and housed in an 18th-century building, which the company had originally acquired for office use. After independence this became the Museu Nacional de Antropologia and came under the jurisdiction of the Ministry of Culture, which is responsible for instigating and organizing cultural activities on a national scale and for supervising the organization of regional museums and schools of higher education where art is taught. Further assistance in this area is provided by the Departamento Nacional de Artes Plásticas (DINARTE).

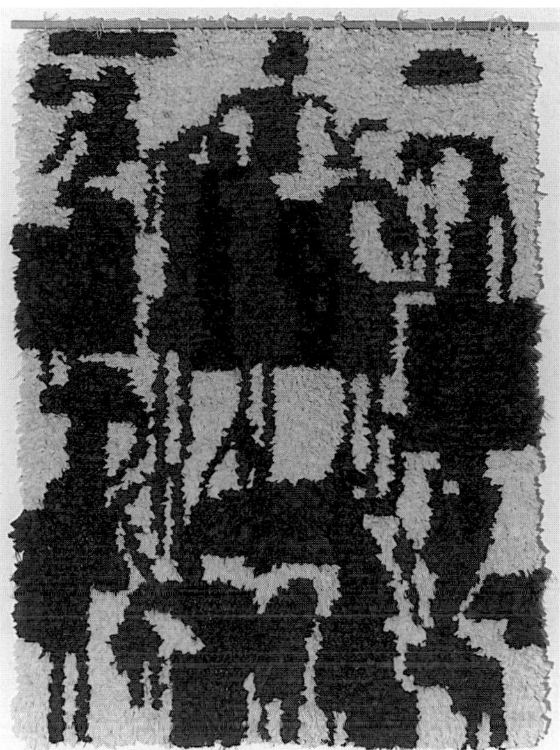

2. Angolan textile hanging by Marcela Costa: *Sociedade*, cotton, polyester silk and white nylon, 1.58×1.10 m, ?1980s (Glasgow, Art Gallery and Museum)

BIBLIOGRAPHY

F. Diniz: *Populações indígenas de Angola* (Coimbra, 1918) [Ethnographical and ethnological study: illus. and maps]

L. Kochnitzky: *Shrines of Wonder: A Survey of Ethnological and Folk Art Museums in Central Africa* (New York, 1952)

D. Birmingham: *The Portuguese Conquest of Angola* (London, 1965)

J. Vansina: *Kingdoms of Savanna* (London and Milwaukee, 1966)

D. L. Wheeler and R. Pélissier: *Angola* (London, New York and Washington, 1971)

J. C. Miller: *Kings and Kinsmen: Early Mbundu States in Angola* (Oxford, 1976)

D. M. N. Gabriel: *Padrões da Fé: Igrejas antigas de Angola* (Luanda, 1981)

A. Hilton: *The Kingdom of Kongo* (Oxford, 1985)

Artes Plásticas-87, União Nacional de Artistas Plásticos (Lubango, 1987)

Art/Images in Southern Africa (exh. cat., ed. B. Bjork, K. Danielsson and B. Sereander; Stockholm, Kulthuset, 1989)

S. Peters and others, eds: *Directory of Museums in Africa/Répertoire des musées en Afrique* (London and New York, 1990)

Art from the Frontline: Contemporary Art from Southern Africa (exh. cat., Glasgow, A.G. & Mus.; Salford, Mus. & A.G.; Dublin, The City Cent.; London, Commonwealth Inst.; 1990) [illustrates works by António dos Santos, António Sallo, Viteix, João Inglês and Marcela Costa]

A. M. de Oliveira: *Angola e a expressão da sua cultura material* (Rio de Janeiro, 1991)
N. Guez: *L'Art africain contemporain/Contemporary African Art: Guide Edition 92–94* (Paris, 1992)
Arte contemporânea angolana: Pintura/escultura, tecelagem artística, gravura, cerâmica (exh. cat., Seville, 1992) [52 colour illus. and biographies of the artists]
La Naissance de la peinture contemporaine en Afrique centrale (exh. cat. by J.-L. Vellut and others, Tervuren, Kon. Mus. Mid.-Afrika, 1992)
Sculpture angolaise: Mémorial de cultures (exh. cat. by M.-L. Bastin, Lisbon, Mus. N. Arqueol. & Etnol., 1994) [250 illus. of works from all Angola's ethnic groups]
'Angola', *Africus '95: Johannesburg Biennale* (exh. cat., Johannesburg, 1995) [colour illus. of modern paintings and sculpture]

MARIE-LOUISE BASTIN

Angolo [Agnolo; Angeli; Angelo] **del Moro, dell'.** Italian family of artists. (1) Battista dell'Angolo married the daughter of Francesco Torbido (called il Moro) and added her family nickname to his surname. Battista practised as a decorative fresco painter in the Veneto in the second half of the 16th century and was the first of an important group of etchers active in and around Verona and Venice at that time. His Mannerist style was perpetuated by his sons (2) Marco dell'Angolo del Moro and (3) Giulio dell'Angolo del Moro. Marco also followed in his father's footsteps as an etcher, whereas Giulio was active also as a sculptor.

(1) Battista dell'Angolo del Moro (*b* Verona, *c.* 1515; *d* ?Verona, 1573 or after). Painter, draughtsman and etcher. He was trained by his father-in-law, whose decorative painting style was much influenced by the work of Titian and Giulio Romano. Much of Battista's paintings, on the façades of churches and palazzi in the Marches, has been lost (due to the damp and salty coastal environment), but the recently restored façade of the Palazzo Pindemonti, Verona, reveals his talents as a fresco painter. There are other surviving paintings by Battista in the churches of S Eufemia (*Paul before Ananias*), S Stefano (*An Angel Presenting the Palms of Martyrdom to the Innocents*) and S Fermo Maggiore, all in Verona, and also in Mantua Cathedral. In 1557 Battista, assisted by his son Marco, painted fresco decorations in the Palazzo Treviso at Murano, where Veronese was also active.

Battista's style is more clearly revealed in his greater surviving output of drawings and particularly his lively and ingenious prints. A drawing of *St Roch* (Paris, Louvre) is characterized by the same crosshatching that appears in his prints. Bartsch compiled a catalogue of only 37 etchings, but Battista's oeuvre is probably nearer 70 prints; some of his etchings have been wrongly attributed to Giovanni Battista Fontana and to artists of the school of Fontainebleau, whose prints were highly influential in 16th-century Italy. Battista's Mannerist style, which can be traced to the Fontainebleau school prints and to a common source in the prints of Parmigianino, can be seen in the ornamental frame of his only known etched portrait, that of *Henry II, King of France* (B. 28). Battista's experiments with landscape etchings reflect the influence of Titian, one of several artists after whom he made reproductive prints; others include Schiavone, Raphael and Bernadino Campi.

For bibliography *see* (2) below.

(2) Marco dell'Angolo del Moro (*b* ?Verona, *c.* 1537; *d* after 1586). Painter, draughtsman and printmaker, son of (1) Battista dell'Angolo del Moro. He was taught by his father and collaborated with him in 1557 on fresco decorations in the Palazzo Treviso at Murano, where Marco was active for most of his career. Among his surviving altarpieces is one painted for S Bartolommeo, Murano (1570; Venice, Accad.). Like his father, Marco is now better known for the ten etchings confidently attributed to him. Among these, *Hercules and the Hydra* (B. 6) stands out for its bold lines and fantastic subject. The print of *Augustus and the Tiburtine Sibyl* (B. 3), which combines etching and engraving, exemplifies the importance of the landscape subject for Veronese etchers and the continuing influence of landscape prints after Titian (such as those by Cornelis Cort). Marco also made numerous reproductive prints.

BIBLIOGRAPHY

Bolaffi; Thieme–Becker
G. Vasari: *Vite* (rev. 2/1568); ed. G. Milanesi (1878–85), v, pp. 296–8
B. dal Pozzo: *Le vite de' pittori, scultori e architetti veronesi* (Verona, 1718)
G. Mazzotti: *Le ville venete* (Treviso, 1954)
L. Crosato: *Gli affreschi nelle ville venete del '500* (Treviso, 1962)
Disegni veronesi del cinquecento (exh. cat. by T. Mullaly, Venice, Fond. Cini, 1971)
G. Schweikhart: 'Battista del Moro (Verona, 1514–1573/4)', *Maestri della pittura veronese*, ed. L. Puppi (Verona, 1974), pp. 201–8
H. Zerner: *Sixteenth-century Italian Etchers* (1979), 32 [XVI/i] of *The Illustrated Bartsch*, ed. W. Strauss (New York, 1978–), pp. 275–312 [B.]
V. Sgarbi: 'Aspetti della maniera nel Veneto', *Paragone*, xxxi/369 (1980), pp. 65–80
G. Ericani: 'Battista del Moro, 1535', *A. Ven.*, xxxviii (1984), pp. 137–40
D. Landau: 'Battista del Moro', *Prt Q.*, iii/4 (1986), p. 347 [attributes three new etchings to Battista not included in Bartsch]
T. Mullaly: 'Battista del Moro in Perspective', *Prt Q.*, iv/4 (1987), pp. 403–7
——: 'Il Palazzo Pindemonti', *Affreschi del rinascimento a Verona* (Verona, 1987)
Italian Etchers of the Renaissance and Baroque (exh. cat. by S. Welch Reed and R. Wallace, Boston, MA, Mus. F.A., 1989), pp. 32–7

S. J. TURNER

(3) Giulio dell'Angolo del Moro (*b* Verona, 1555; *d* Venice, 21 July 1616). Sculptor and painter, son of (1) Battista dell'Angolo del Moro. He is recorded as a member of the Venetian painters' guild first in 1584 and for the last time in 1615. A connection with Alessandro Vittoria's workshop in the 1570s seems likely. The work necessitated by the fires in the Doge's Palace in that decade served as Giulio's entry to State patronage. Between 1584 and 1589 he carved the figures of *Diligence*, *Secrecy* and *Fidelity* in the Sala delle Quattro Porte and in 1585–90 painted the *Capture of Caffà* in the Sala del Scrutinio. His most prominent picture is *Doge Ziani Receiving Gifts from Pope Alexander III* (*c.* 1610) in the Sala del Maggior Consiglio, but perhaps his best painting is the awkward but animated *Ecce homo* (1595–1600) in S Giacomo dell'Orio, Venice. He has been credited with the sculpture on the Priuli Tomb in S Salvador, but in fact these figures seem to be by a certain Alvise Moro. The tomb of *Andrea Dolfin and Benedetta Pisani Dolfin* (completed *c.* 1605) in the same church contains his most significant sculpture, especially the figures of *St Andrew* and the *Risen Christ*. His last projects took place *c.* 1605–15 at S Giorgio Maggiore: the façade sculptures of *St George* and *St Stephen* and the busts of the doges *Sebastiano Ziani* and *Tribuno Memmo*, as well as the tomb of the doge *Marcantonio Memmo* on the inside façade. Although some of his work, for example the bust of *Giovanni da Lezze* (Venice, Gesuiti), shows Giulio at his most inspired, his surviving sculptures and paintings are largely dry and derivative.

BIBLIOGRAPHY

Thieme–Becker
A. Venturi: *Storia*, x/3, pp. 265–78
A. da Mosto: *I dogi di Venezia in particolare riguardo alle loro tombe* (Venice, 1939), pp. 43, 55, 174–5, 212
E. Comastri: 'Profilo di Giulio dal Moro', *A. Ven.*, xlii (1988), pp. 87–96

THOMAS MARTIN

Angoulême. City in Charente, western France. The name is derived from the Celtic Iculisma. The town was founded on a long limestone spur rising *c.* 75 m above the valleys of the rivers Charente and Enguienne. The Romans settled here, but the layout and function of the early Imperial city remain uncertain. At the end of the 3rd or beginning of the 4th century AD, a rampart was built, girdling the upper part of the spur. Some remains are still recognizable. Christianity was established in the suburb named St Ausone, after the man accepted by tradition as the city's evangelist; the remains of an Early Christian necropolis survive in the district.

In the early Middle Ages the city, seat of a bishopric and centre of a small comté, was sheltered within its ramparts in a fairly constricted space on the top of the spur ('le plateau'). The cathedral complex, comprising the cathedral (*see* §1 below), the bishop's palace, a baptistery, a church dedicated to Notre-Dame and a canons' close, was situated near the castle. Other churches were scattered throughout the city. Outside the ramparts there were three main suburbs. To the north, between the edge of the spur and the Charente, a quarter grew up around the monastery of St Cybard, founded in the 6th century. To the north-west extended the Faubourg St Ausone, near the necropolis and church of St Augustin. Finally, to the south, a third quarter grew up around St Martin and St Eloi.

Of the medieval castle, there remain two towers (13th and 15th centuries); the Renaissance style Hôtel de Ville was built on its site by Paul Abadie in the 19th century. In the old city several fine residences (e.g. the former bishop's palace, the 16th-century Hôtel St Simon) and 18th- and 19th-century middle-class houses survive. The modern city grew up largely outside the 'plateau' and the old suburbs. Angoulême was a centre of faience production from 1748 until the late 19th century.

1. CATHEDRAL. Dedicated to St Pierre, Angoulême Cathedral is one of the most distinguished buildings in western France, despite having been heavily restored and altered in the 19th century by Paul Abadie. It was built in the first half of the 12th century, with a consecration in 1128 during the episcopacy of the legate Girard d'Angoulême. The church has a cruciform plan with an aisleless nave of three bays, a transept and choir with radiating, apsidal chapels. The nave and crossing are spanned by large domes.

The west façade, which is *c.* 20 m wide, is decorated with an elaborate programme of Romanesque sculpture. Its general design is established by the five large arches, containing smaller, superimposed arcading, that constitute its lower and central zones. This ensemble represents the original scheme: the decision to place a further tier of small arches above the large lateral ones and to raise the central arch over the portal and single window above was probably taken in the course of construction. The unusual square form of the façade was altered during Abadie's restorations, when he added the gable and bell-towers and discreetly retouched the sculpture.

The iconographic programme of the façade combines the *Ascension* and the *Second Coming*. The upper zone is devoted to Christ, who stands in a mandorla surrounded by the Evangelist Symbols, angels and the Elect placed within small medallions. The sky stretches out above his head; the Tree of Life blossoms beneath his feet. Under the arcades of the central zone of the façade are the Apostles and the Virgin, who direct their gaze to Christ. Large angels on the window arch point to the triumphant Christ, while the damned are cast aside, showing the association of Christ's Second Coming.

The reliefs of *St George* and *St Martin* above the inner arches of the lower zone and the portal tympanum are modern, but the *St George* relief incorporates an original fragment depicting a seated woman, who may represent an allegory of Ecclesia, accompanying an equestrian figure of Constantine. In the blind tympana of the lower zone the Apostles, grouped in threes, are shown walking, to suggest their apostolic mission. Within the foliage friezes are hunting scenes and a cavalry battle outside a town. This has been interpreted as an episode from the *Song of Roland* and illustrates the Christian struggle against the forces of evil. Inside the church similar foliate interlace, sometimes inhabited by animals and monsters, dominates the decoration of capitals and friezes.

The sculptural decoration of the cathedral (*see* ARCHITECTURAL CONSERVATION AND RESTORATION, fig. 2) is abundant yet disciplined, the ground covered with rich ornament in multiple compositions. The participants in the iconographic programme are isolated and emphasized by their surrounding frames and high-relief carving. The forms are supple, the attitudes animated and varied, and the drapery of the figures extremely delicate. Nevertheless the differences in style show that there were several sculptors, either working side by side or in succession.

The most likely date for the sculpture is between 1110 and 1130. It is related to the regional style of the 11th century (especially the *feuilles gras*, or fat leaves, of Poitou) and the experiments of workshops in south-west France (e.g. St Pierre, Moissac, and Toulouse) at the turn of the 11th and 12th centuries, but it is also highly original. The sculptors must be associated with those who worked on the crossing of St Eutrope, Saintes, and, in the case of the large figure of Christ, with the sculptor of Cahors Cathedral. The cathedral workshop produced at least one studio in the Angoumois, and its influence was felt in others. Several sculptures from the cathedral are preserved in the Musée Archéologique.

BIBLIOGRAPHY

J. George: *Les Eglises de France: Charente* (Paris, 1933)
C. Daras: *Angoumois roman*, Nuit Temps (La Pierre-qui-vire, 1961), pp. 69–99

P. Dubourg-Noves: *Iconographie de la cathédrale d'Angoulême*, 2 vols (Angoulême, 1973)
——: *Les Sculpteurs de la cathédrale d'Angoulême* (diss., U. Poitiers, 1974)

M. T. CAMUS

Angran, Louis-Auguste, Vicomte de Fontpertuis (*fl* 1708; *d* Paris, 1747). French courtier, soldier and collector. Despite a Jansenist education, he entered wholeheartedly into the life of the royal court and won the favour of Philippe II, Duc d'Orléans. He developed his love of art through his maternal uncle, Du Vivier, who bequeathed him his remarkable collection, rich in curiosities, East Asian porcelain and paintings, which Angran augmented, not hesitating to resell in order to acquire the finest pieces. At his death, his collection was dispersed in sales between December 1747 and March 1748. It comprised fine landscapes, including works by Paul Bril, Jan Breughel I, Claude Lorrain and François Boucher, and numerous Flemish and Dutch genre scenes by such masters as Adriaen van Ostade, Gerrit Dou and Gabriel Metsu, which reflect the contemporary predilection for the Northern painters. The collection included such outstanding works as Breughel's *Abraham Sacrificing Isaac* (Geneva, Mus. A. & Hist.), Claude Lorrain's *Judgement of Paris* (*c.* 1645; Washington, DC, N.G.A.) and Metsu's *Woman Playing the Viola da Gamba* (1663; San Francisco, CA, de Young Mem. Mus.).

BIBLIOGRAPHY

DBF
E. F. Gersaint: *Catalogue raisonné des bijoux, porcelaines, bronzes, lacqs, lustres de cristal de roche et de porcelaine . . .tableaux, desseins, estampes, coquilles et autres effets de curiosité, provenans de succession de M. Angran, vicomte de Fontpertuis* (Paris, 1747)
C.-A. Sainte-Beuve: *Histoire de Port-Royal* (Paris, 1888–91), iv, pp. 489–90; v, pp. 589–90
K. Pomain: *Collectionneurs, amateurs et curieux, Paris, Venise: xvie–xviiie siècle* (Paris, 1987), p. 185

ANNE LECLAIR

Angrand, Charles (*b* Criquetot-sur-Ouville, Normandy, 19 April 1854; *d* Rouen, 1 April 1926). French painter. He was trained at the Académie de Peinture et de Dessin in Rouen, where he won prizes. Although he failed to gain entry to the Ecole des Beaux-Arts in Paris, Angrand began to win a controversial local reputation for canvases in a loosely Impressionist manner. In 1882 he secured a post as a schoolteacher at the Collège Chaptal in Paris. With this security he was able to make contacts in progressive artistic circles, and in 1884 he became a founder-member of the Salon des Indépendants. His paintings of this period depict rural interiors and kitchen gardens, combining the broken brushwork of Monet and Camille Pissarro with the tonal structure of Bastien-Lepage (e.g. *In the Garden*, 1884; priv. col., see 1979 exh. cat., p. 27).

By the mid-1880s Angrand had met Seurat through Signac and the literary salon of the writer Robert Caze. From 1887 Angrand began to paint in Seurat's Neo-Impressionist manner and adopted his tenebrist drawing style. Paintings such as *The Seine at Dawn* (1889; Geneva, Petit Pal.) typify Angrand's ability to distil poetry from the most banal suburban scene. In the early 1890s he concentrated on conté crayon drawings, producing rural scenes and mother-and-child subjects of dark Symbolist intensity, and on submitting illustrations to anarchist publications such as *Les Temps Nouveaux*. In 1896 Angrand retreated to Normandy, though throughout his life he remained loyal to the Salon des Indépendants. Returning to painting about 1906, Angrand took up the mosaic touch and sumptuous colours of Signac and Henri Edmond Cross in landscapes that verge on the non-representational (e.g. *Farmyard in Normandy*, *c.* 1907; Paris, Pierre Angrand priv. col.). Angrand always stressed that his art was concerned with 'an intellectual vision of harmony', and he single-mindedly pursued his disciplined humanitarian purpose.

BIBLIOGRAPHY

P. Angrand: 'Charles Angrand', *The Neo-Impressionists*, ed. J. Sutter (London, 1970), pp. 77–88
B. Welsh-Ovcharov: *The Early Work of Charles Angrand and his Contact with Vincent van Gogh* (The Hague, 1971)
Charles Angrand (exh. cat. by P. Angrand, Dieppe, Château-Mus., 1976)
Post-Impressionism: Cross-currents in European Painting (exh. cat., London, RA, 1979–80), pp. 27–8
F. Lespinasse: *Charles Angrand, 1854–1926* (Rouen, 1982)
F. Lespinasse, ed.: *Charles Angrand: Correspondances* (Rouen, 1988)

RICHARD THOMSON

Angrand, Léonce(-Marie-François) (*b* Paris, 8 Aug 1808; *d* Paris, 11 Jan 1886). French painter and draughtsman active in Peru. He served as the French Vice-Consul in Lima from 1834 to 1838 and while there produced albums of watercolours and drawings of cities such as Arica, Arequipa, Lima, Cuzco, Ollantaytambo, Urubamba and Tacna. His romantic spirit inclined him to the exotic, and he documented street scenes, the characters of city life, groups of buildings and archaeological monuments. Taken as a whole, these pictures bear witness to everyday life in Peru at that time.

BIBLIOGRAPHY

C. Milla Batres, ed.: *Léonce Angrand: Imagen del Perú* (Lima, 1972)
L. E. Tord: 'Historia de las artes plásticas en el Perú', *Historia del Perú*, ix (Lima, 1980)

LUIS ENRIQUE TORD

Anguiano, Raúl (*b* Guadalajara, 26 Feb 1915). Mexican painter, printmaker and teacher. He studied painting from 1927 at the Escuela Libre de Pintura in Guadalajara. He moved to Mexico City in 1934 and entered the Escuela de Pintura Escultura y Grabado 'La Esmeralda' in 1935. He was also a founder-member in that year of the Taller de Gráfica Popular in Mexico City, where he was able to develop his interest in engraving and lithography. He produced a vast body of work. His subject-matter, both in his prints and his paintings, focused on people's dramas, labours and fiestas (e.g. *The Circus*, 1937; artist's col.; see Crespo, fig. 14), the resignation and stoicism of Mexican women, and popular myths and folk wisdom, for example *Popular Sayings*, an album of 18 engravings. He also painted numerous portraits and produced a number of murals which expressed a typical local ideology (e.g. *Fascism and Clericalism, Enemies of Civilization*, fresco, 1937; Mexico City, Cent. Escul. Revol.). Later murals portray Pre-Columbian historical events (e.g. *Creation of Man in the Mayan World*, 1964; Mexico City, Sala Maya, Mus. N. Antropol.). He began to produce his series of ceramic items in the late 1950s.

WRITINGS

Dichos populares (Mexico City, 1944)

BIBLIOGRAPHY
Exposición retrospectiva 1930–1982 Raúl Anguiano (exh. cat., Mexico City, Inst. N. B.A., 1982)
J. J. Crespo de la Serna and others: *Raúl Anguiano* (Mexico City, 1985)
En la pintura de Raúl Anguiano (Mexico City, 1986)

ELISA GARCÍA BARRAGÁN

Anguier [Anguierre]. French family of sculptors. Honoré Anguier (*b* Eu, *fl c.* 1570–80; *d* Eu, 1648) was a carpenter, wood-carver and small-scale entrepreneur in Eu, Normandy. Local church archives document his work on doors, frames, balustrades and retables. His eldest son, (1) François Anguier, became noted for his funerary sculpture but also contributed to decorative schemes for ecclesiastic and secular buildings. His younger son, (2) Michel Anguier, worked in Rome before returning to Paris where he enjoyed royal and aristocratic patronage and became a distinguished teacher and lecturer at the Académie Royale. Both François and Michel introduced a new Roman influence, helping to form the classical style in France. A third brother, Guillaume Anguier (1628–1708), was a successful decorative painter, working at various royal residences; one of his daughters married the sculptor Domenico Cucci. Catherine Anguier, sister of François, Michel and Guillaume, was the mother of the sculptor David Bouderelle, who inherited the family house and studio.

(1) François Anguier (*b* Eu, 1604; *d* Paris, 8 Aug 1669). By 1621 he was apprenticed to a wood-carver, Martin Caron in Abbeville, and later he joined the Paris workshop of Simon Guillain. According to d'Argenville he went to England, where he was able to save enough to finance a stay of two years in Italy. Neither trip is documented, but his later work suggests an association with Alessandro Algardi, or at least the influence of the temperate style that Algardi and François Duquesnoy were practising as an alternative to the High Baroque of Bernini. By the late 1640s he was documented as a 'sculpteur ordinaire du roi' and was living in the Tuileries.

François Anguier's major works were funerary sculptures. He was praised in contemporary literature for his striking portrayals of character, but his success owed as much to the influences that he brought back from Rome, which enabled him to inject new life into traditional French monument types. In the 1640s he completed the tomb of Jacques-Auguste de Thou (Paris, Louvre) for St André-des-Arts, Paris. Originally de Thou was shown kneeling between his two wives on a long entablature supported by columns and two atlantes, the statue of the first wife having been carved more than three decades earlier by Barthélemy Prieur. Anguier's figures seem spirited, alert and psychologically vivid when viewed beside Prieur's. Between 1649 and 1652 he was working on the tomb of *Henri, Duc de Montmorency* (1595–1632), *and his Wife* for the chapel of the Couvent de la Visitation (now the Lycée Banville), Moulins (see fig.), for which he employed the services of his brother Michel and other assistants. The monument as a whole is based on the Aldobrandini tombs by Giacomo della Porta in S Maria sopra Minerva. The Duc's pose is that of the familiar *gisant*, but Anguier gave the body a sharp turn that is reminiscent of reliquary drawings by Algardi. For the

Michel and François Anguier: tomb of *Henri, Duc de Montmorency and his Wife*, marble, 1649–52 (Moulins, Lycée Banville)

church of the Couvent des Célestins, Paris, he executed the tomb of *Henri Chabot, Duc de Rohan* (1655; Versailles). The Duc is depicted dead, slumped back in the manner of heroes on ancient sarcophagi, a weeping genius supporting his head, another covering the lower half of his slender, youthful body with a mantle. Something of the same pagan spirit surrounds the tomb of *Jacques de Souvré* (*d* 1670), which was made in the years before 1667 for the church of St-Jean de Latran, Paris (fragments Versailles; Paris, Louvre and St Gervais, St Protais), although here the hero is represented at the instant before death. The Couvent des Célestins housed yet another of his memorials, the tomb of the *Ducs de Longueville* (1663–9; Paris, Louvre), which Bernini admired during his trip to Paris in 1665. This is his most allegorical monument and features a set of marble statues of the Cardinal Virtues, two battle reliefs in copper and a tall obelisk with reliefs of the military and cultural accomplishments of the Longueville family.

In addition to his funerary sculpture, François contributed to the decorative programmes of Porte St-Antoine (two statues), Val-de-Grâce (two statues and two reliefs intended for the high altar; model for the main door), the gardens of Versailles (models for two vases) and other private and religious settings in Paris. He refused to join the Académie, preferring instead to remain a member of the Communauté des Maîtres Peintres et Sculpteurs de Paris (known as La Maîtrise), later the Académie de St-Luc (*see* FRANCE, §XV).

(2) Michel Anguier (*b* Eu, 1612 or 1614; *d* Paris, 11 July 1686). Brother of (1) François Anguier. For a time he worked with an unknown sculptor in Eu until, aged 15, he settled in Paris, joining the studio of Simon Guillain. Around 1641 he went to Rome, where he lived in a colony of artists for ten years and seems to have been on good terms with François Duquesnoy and Nicolas Poussin. In 1648 he was one of 39 sculptors brought together by Gianlorenzo Bernini to carve the papal medallions and reliefs of putti on the pilasters along the nave of St Peter's. In 1648–9 he was a member of the team from Alessandro Algardi's workshop that modelled the large stucco reliefs for the nave of S Giovanni in Laterano; his three panels (and his terracotta models) reveal a mixture of Baroque and late Mannerist treatment that is very different from Algardi's own sculpture during this period. For the Holy Year of 1650 he made (after Algardi's designs) a float (untraced; drawing, Zurich, Graph. Samml. Eidgenöss. Tech. Hochsch.), in wood or papier-mâché, of the *Lamentation over the Dead Christ* for the Arciconfraternità del Gonfalone. Above all, however, he dedicated himself to the study of ancient statues and reliefs and to a careful reading of the ancient authors.

Michel returned to Paris in 1651, when the city was still engulfed in civil disturbances. His first commission was the seated marble statue of Hercules for the tomb of the *Duc de Montmorency and his Wife*, a work which clearly derives from a combination of classical models but which reveals for the first time an attempt on the part of the sculptor to correlate the psychology of a character with its physical nature and pose (for illustration *see* (1) above). During the next few years (but seldom thereafter) he had commissions for small-scale works, usually in bronze and silver, the most important example being a group of seven statuettes of the *Gods and Goddesses* (from 1652; *Neptune*, New York, Met.; *Mars*, Dresden, Skulpsamml.; *Pluto*, Dresden, Grünes Gewölbe; *Amphitrite*, New York, Met.; *Ceres*, London, V&A; *see* STATUETTE, fig. 3), commonly known as the Montarsis bronzes, for the family of royal jewellers that owned (and probably ordered) the original set. Five still exist in one state or another, and together they present a remarkable range of psychological and physical character.

From 1655 to 1657 Michel collaborated with Giovanni Francesco Romanelli and others on the decoration of a suite of four rooms in the summer apartment of Anne of Austria in the Louvre. Although required by contract to follow Romanelli's designs, Michel's gold and white stuccowork is most elegant, with elongated, elegant Fames, muscular, virile Rivers and playful genii forming an important link between the Italian Baroque of Pietro da Cortona, the schools of Fontainebleau and the special brand of French classicism that Charles Le Brun would soon formulate at Versailles. According to early sources he also at this time produced a series of 14 life-size statues of the *Gods of Olympus* (*Leda*, 1654; New York, Met.; *Amphitrite*; Toledo, OH, Mus. A.) for the sculpture gallery of the château of St-Mandé acquired by Nicolas Fouquet. The sculptures were admired for their proportion, grace and lively personalities and Michel became Fouquet's favoured sculptor. He was a major provider of outdoor works at VAUX-LE-VICOMTE, contributing a group of *Apollo and Cybele*, the parterre statues of *Clemency* and *Justice*, another of *Geometry*, three large animals, a group of busts, and other architectural and garden figures (*in situ*; rest.). He also played a vital role in the sculptural programme for the church of Val-de-Grâce (1645–67), built by Anne of Austria to celebrate the birth of her son Louis XIV. His contribution included four great medallions of the *Evangelists* in the pendentives that support the dome, the relief cycles above the arches of the nave and choir and on the vault, some of the architectural ornamentation, the wooden figures above the baldacchino as well as the marble altarpiece of the *Nativity* (Paris, St Roch) beneath it. These tend to be highly classical, although the tensions in some of the pendentive figures and in the altar figure of Joseph show the Baroque influence of his years in Rome.

Teaching and lecturing at the Académie dominated his life in the 1670s. He had joined the Académie de St-Luc in March 1663, but in March 1668 Colbert persuaded him to enter the Académie Royale, where he at once assumed the position of adjunct professor, becoming adjunct-rector in October 1669 and rector in June 1671. He took part in the new round of theoretical lectures and debates, which had been reintroduced in 1667, and in the next ten years developed the broadest theoretical framework of any practising sculptor in France.

BIBLIOGRAPHY

A.-N. Dezallier d'Argenville: *Vies des fameux architectes et sculpteurs* (1788)
G. de Saint-Georges: 'Michel Anguier', *Mémoires inédits sur la vie et les ouvrages des membres de l'Académie royale de peinture et de sculpture*, ed. L. Dussieux and others, 2 vols (Paris, 1854)
A. Sanson: *Les Frères Anguier* (Rouen, 1889)
H. Stein: 'Les Frères Anguier', *Réun. Soc. B.-A. Dép.*, xiii (1889), pp. 527–609
M. Beaulieu: 'Gabriel Le Duc, Michel Anguier et le maître-autel du Val-de-Grâce', *Bull. Soc. Hist. A. Fr.* (1945–6), pp. 150–61
A. Blunt: *Art and Architecture in France: 1500–1700*, Pelican Hist. A. (Harmondsworth, 1953, rev. 4/1980)
J. Monicat: 'Le Tombeau du duc et la duchesse de Montmorency dans la chapelle du Lycée de Moulins', *Gaz. B.-A.*, n. s. lxii (1963), pp. 179–98
M. Charageat: 'La Statue d'*Amphitrite* et la suite des dieux et des déesses de Michel Anguier', *Archvs A. Fr.*, n. s. xxiii (1968), pp. 111–23
J. D. Draper: 'For the Love of Leda', *Bull. Met.*, xxx (1971), pp. 50–58
C. Mignot: 'L'Eglise du Val-de Grâce au faubourg Saint-Jacques de Paris: Architecture et décor', *Bull. Soc. Hist. A. Fr.* (1975), pp. 101–36
I. Wardropper: 'Michel Anguier's Series of Bronze Gods and Goddesses: A Re-examination', *Marsyas*, xviii (1975–6), pp. 23–36
M. Harvey: 'The Tomb of Montmorency as Recompense du martyre', *Gaz. B.-A.*, cxiv (1989), pp. 63–80
B. Black and H.-W. Nadeau: *Michel Anguier's 'Pluto': The Marble of 1669* (London, 1990)

THOMAS F. HEDIN

Anguissola [Angosciola; Anguisciola; Angussola]. Italian family of painters. Six sisters from a noble family of Cremona, daughters of Amilcare Anguissola and Bianca Ponzoni, were painters of some renown: (1) Sofonisba Anguissola, (2) Lucia Anguissola, Europa (*c.* 1542–*c.* 1578), Elena (*fl* 1546–84), Minerva (*fl* 1558–69) and Anna-Maria (*c.* 1555–*c.* 1611) Anguissola. Sofonisba and Elena studied painting with Bernardino Campi from *c.* 1545 and with Bernardino Gatti from 1549. Elena entered the convent of S Vincenzo in Mantua, where she was recorded in 1585, and may be the subject of the *Portrait of a Nun* (1551; Southampton, C.A.G.) attributed to Sofonisba. Vasari, who visited the family in 1566, praised the sisters' work. He noted that Sofonisba's *Family*

Portrait (1560s; Nivå, Nivaagaards Malsaml.) shows Minerva, her father and her brother Asdrubale. Europa executed a portrait of their mother (untraced), according to Vasari, and she signed the *Calling of SS Andrew and Peter* (Vidiceto, Parrocchiale). The *Holy Family* (Cremona, Mus. Civ. Ala Ponzone) is signed by Anna-Maria.

(1) Sofonisba Anguissola (*b* Cremona, *c.* 1532; *d* Palermo, Nov 1625). The best known of the sisters, she was trained, with Elena, by Campi and Gatti. Most of Vasari's account of his visit to the Anguissola family is devoted to Sofonisba, about whom he wrote: 'Anguissola has shown greater application and better grace than any other woman of our age in her endeavours at drawing; she has thus succeeded not only in drawing, colouring and painting from nature, and copying excellently from others, but by herself has created rare and very beautiful paintings'. Sofonisba's privileged background was unusual among woman artists of the 16th century, most of whom, like Lavinia Fontana (*see* FONTANA (ii),(2)), FEDE GALIZIA and Barbara Longhi (*see* LONGHI (i), (3)), were daughters of painters. Her social class did not, however, enable her to transcend the constraints of her sex. Without the possibility of studying anatomy, or drawing from life, she could not undertake the complex multi-figure compositions required for large-scale religious or history paintings. She turned instead to the models accessible to her, exploring a new type of portraiture with sitters in informal domestic settings. The influence of Campi, whose reputation was based on portraiture, is evident in her early works, such as the *Self-portrait* (Florence, Uffizi). Her work was allied to the worldly tradition of Cremona, much influenced by the art of Parma and Mantua, in which even religious works were imbued with extreme delicacy and charm. From Gatti she seems to have absorbed elements reminiscent of Correggio, beginning a trend that became marked in Cremonese painting of the late 16th century. This new direction is reflected in *Lucia, Minerva and Europa Anguissola Playing Chess* (1555; Poznań, N. Mus.) in which portraiture merges into a quasi-genre scene, a characteristic derived from Brescian models.

Many of Sofonisba's works were self-portraits, and at least 12 survive, including examples in Boston, MA (1552; Mus. F.A.), Vienna (1554; Ksthist. Mus.), Naples (1559; Capodimonte) and Milan (*c.* 1555; Mus. Poldi Pezzoli). She depicted herself with various attributes, some relating to her artistic profession, some to the literary and musical accomplishments typical of contemporary noblewomen. In the latest dated *Self-portrait* (1561; Althorp House, Northants; see fig.) she is shown seated at a spinet, watched by a chaperone, also an allusion to her status. Although the rendering of perspective in the keyboard is not convincing, the background figure of the chaperone gives some illusion of space. Her approach to portrait painting was personal, not coldly realistic, and she showed an interest in the psychology of her sitters, although it was never fully realized. This interest is evident in a series of drawings and paintings that explore the physical expression of emotions, such as *Child Bitten by a Crayfish* (*c.* 1554; Naples, Capodimonte), which influenced Caravaggio, or *Old Woman Learning the Alphabet, Mocked by a Young Girl* (*c.* 1550; Florence, Uffizi). Anguissola's Cremonese

Sofonisba Anguissola: *Self-portrait*, oil on canvas, 812×635 mm, 1561 (Althorp House, Northants)

works also include a small number of religious paintings, mainly for private devotion, as is evident from the small size of the *Holy Family* (350×300 mm, 1559; Bergamo, Gal. Accad. Carrara), which is based on a prototype by Camillo Boccaccino (Glasgow, A.G. & Mus.); however, the *Pietà* (*c.* 1570; Milan, Brera), which is traditionally attributed to her, is not characteristic of her style and is certainly by Bernardino Campi. In 1559 Sofonisba was invited to the court of Madrid through the offices of Ferdinand Alvarez de Toledo (1508–82), Duke of Alba, and of the Duca di Sessa, the Governor of Milan, one of Campi's principal patrons. There, she was chosen by Philip II to be an attendant to the Infanta Isabella (1566–1633), and she also became lady-in-waiting to the queen, Elizabeth of Valois (1545–1568). In Spain, Sofonisba pursued her work as a portrait painter, although the Althorp *Self-portrait* is the only securely attributed work surviving from this period. In Madrid *c.* 1571 she married the nobleman Fabrizio de Moncada, brother of the Viceroy of Sicily, Francesco II, and she then settled in Sicily. In 1584, after his death, she married the Genoese nobleman Orazio Lomellino and moved to his native city. In both Palermo and Genoa she continued to paint and to preserve her links with the aristocracy, as is evinced by the visit of the Spanish Infanta, who was in Genoa in 1599, the date of her portrait of the *Infanta Isabella Clara Eugenia* (Vienna, Ksthist. Mus.). Anthony van Dyck visited Anguissola in Palermo in July 1624 and drew a portrait of her in his so-called Italian Sketchbook (London, BM), on which he noted that she was 96 (if true, this would alter her presumed birthdate) but still lucid and enthusiastic about painting.

In the few surviving paintings from her Genoese period there appears to be considerable borrowing from the work of Luca Cambiaso. Indeed, the *Virgin Suckling the Infant Christ* (Budapest, Mus. F.A.) was attributed to Cambiaso until cleaning revealed a signature that confirmed it as the work of Anguissola, dated 1588. The *Holy Family with St Anne and the Young St John* (1592; Coral Gables, FL, U. Miami, Lowe A. Mus.), which is signed, like the Budapest painting, with her husband's surname, Lomellino, is also based on the work of Cambiaso.

BIBLIOGRAPHY

DBI; Thieme–Becker
G. Vasari: *Vite* (1550, rev. 2/1568); ed. G. Milanesi (1878–85), v, p. 81; vi, pp. 498–502; vii, p. 133
A. Lamo: *Discorso intorno alla scoltura e pittura* (Cremona, 1584) [appended to Zaist, see below]
R. Soprani: *Le vite de' pittori, scultori et architetti genovesi* (Genoa, 1674/*R* Genoa, 1768–9), pp. 411–16
F. Baldinucci: *Notizie* (1681–1728); ed. F. Ranalli (1845–7), ii, pp. 619–36
G. B. Zaist: *Notizie istoriche de' pittori, scultori ed architetti cremonesi* (Cremona, 1774/*R* Cremona, 1975), pp. 227–36
I. Kühnel-Kunze: 'Zur Bildniskunst der Sofonisba und Lucia Anguissola', *Pantheon*, xx/2 (1962), pp. 83–96
E. Tufts: 'Sofonisba Anguissola, Renaissance Woman', *ARTnews*, lxxi (1972), pp. 50–53
L. Nochlin and A. Sutherland: *Women Artists, 1550–1950* (Los Angeles, Co. Mus. A.; Austin, U. TX., A. Mus.; 1976) [published in conjunction with travelling exhibition]
G. Greer: *The Obstacle Race: The Fortunes of Women Painters and their Work* (New York and London, 1979), pp. 3, 12, 69–70, 136, 180–85, 251
R. Parker and G. Pollock: *Old Mistresses: Women, Art and Ideology* (London, 1981), pp. 18, 47, 84–6
I Campi e la cultura artistica cremonese del cinquecento (exh. cat., ed. M. Gregori; Cremona, Mus. Civ. Ala Ponzone, 1985), pp. 171–8, 301–2
F. Caroli: *Sofonisba Anguissola e le sue sorelle* (Milan, 1987)
M. Kusche: 'Sofonisba Anguissola en España', *Archv Esp. A.*, lxii (1989), pp. 391–420
I. S. Perlinghieri: *Sofonisba Anguissola: The First Great Woman Artist of the Renaissance* (New York, 1992)
Sofonisba Anguissola e le sue sorelle (exh. cat., Cremona and Milan, 1994)

MARCO TANZI

(2) Lucia Anguissola (*b* Cremona, 1536 or 1538; *d* ?Cremona, ?1565, before 1568). Sister of (1) Sofonisba Anguissola. She probably trained with her sister, and her work, mainly portraits, is similar in style and technique. Her only signed painting, a portrait of a Cremonese doctor, *Pietro Maria* (early 1560s; Madrid, Prado), was praised by Vasari, who saw it when he visited the family after her death. It is a sensitive portrayal, in a restricted palette of greys and browns, and may be a pendant to Sofonisba's *Portrait of a Lady* (1557; Berlin, Gemäldegal.). Lucia also painted a *Virgin and Child* (untraced; for copy, see Caroli, 1973) and a half-length *Self-portrait* (*c.* 1557; Milan, Castello Sforzesco). A *Portrait of a Woman* (early 1560s; Rome, Gal. Borghese) is thought to be either a self-portrait by her or Sofonisba, or a portrait of Lucia by Sofonisba. Two portraits (Brescia, Pin. Civ. Tosio–Martinengo; Milan, Mus. Poldi Pezzoli), probably of Minerva Anguissola, may also be by Lucia.

BIBLIOGRAPHY

Thieme–Becker
G. Vasari: *Vite* (1550, rev. 2/1568); ed. G. Milanesi (Milan, 1878–85)
I. Kühnel-Kunze: 'Zur Bildniskunst der Sofonisba und Lucia Anguissola', *Pantheon*, xx/2 (1962), pp. 83–96
F. Caroli: 'Antologia d'artisti: Per Lucia Anguissola', *Paragone*, 277 (1973), pp. 69–73
——: *Sofonisba Anguissola e le sue sorelle* (Milan, 1987)
I. S. Perlinghieri: *Sofonisba Anguissola: The First Great Woman Artist of the Renaissance* (New York, 1992)

□

Angus [Cook]**, Rita** [Henrietta] **(Catherine)** (*b* Hastings, 12 March 1908; *d* Wellington, 26 Jan 1970). New Zealand painter. She studied at the Canterbury School of Art, Christchurch (1927–33). In 1930 she married the painter Alfred Cook and used the signature *Rita Cook* until 1946; they separated in 1934. Angus established her reputation in the 1930s with a hard-edged realist style of painting influenced by contemporary Canadian and American regionalism. An example of her landscapes of that period is *Cass* (1936; Christchurch, NZ, McDougall A.G.), a symbolic image of a small Canterbury railway station typifying the isolated and unpopulated character of rural New Zealand. Angus was also a painter of highly formalized portraits, which she often imbued with symbolic overtones. In her portrait of *Betty Curnow* (1942; Auckland, C.A.G.), Angus captured not only the likeness of the sitter but the essence of the period. Angus was a pacifist during World War II and gave to her paintings a degree of social and philosophical concern rare in New Zealand art of that time. Her later paintings are more strongly modelled and often incorporate composite imagery, as in *Flight* (1968–9; Wellington, Mus. NZ, Te Papa Tongarewa). Angus influenced a younger generation of New Zealand realists, including Robin White (*b* 1946) and Brent Wong (*b* 1945). The major collection of her works is in the National Art Gallery, Wellington.

BIBLIOGRAPHY

G. Docking: *Two Hundred Years of New Zealand Painting* (Wellington, 1970), p. 146
Rita Angus (exh. cat., ed. L. Bieringa; Wellington, N.A.G., 1983)

MICHAEL DUNN

Anhalt-Dessau, (Leopold III Frederick) Francis, Prince of [Anhalt, Duke of] (*b* Dessau, 10 Aug 1740; *reg* 1756–1817; *d* Dessau, 9 Aug 1817). German ruler and garden designer. After leaving the Prussian Army in 1757, he devoted himself to governing Dessau, instituting provision for the poor, public health and education. He made four journeys to England (1763–85) with FRIEDRICH WILHELM ERDMANNSDORFF, with whom he also travelled through Italy (1765–6). He studied for six months with JOHANN JOACHIM WINCKELMANN, whose 'mimetic theory of the Ancients' he realized in his garden designs. With Erdmannsdorff and his planters, he created gardens at Luisium (1774) and Sieglitzer Berg (1777) and most notably at WÖRLITZ (1764–1810), based on such English models as The Leasowes (Worcs), Stowe (Bucks), Kew Gardens (London) and Stourhead (Wilts). He was acquainted with William Chambers, Henry Holland, Sir William Hamilton (i) and possibly also Henry Flitcroft and 'Capability' Brown. As well as introducing the English landscape garden and Palladian country house to the Continent, the Prince also transplanted the Gothic Revival. The 'Country House' and 'Gothic House' at Wörlitz were possibly the earliest examples of continental 'Palladian' classicism and the New Gothic (known as 'Franz Gothic'). He even copied the first iron bridge over the River Severn in England as a monument to technology. Thus a 'pedagogic province', in Goethe's sense, was constructed in the gardens at Wörlitz. The Prince was inspired by the Classical works of the Roman emperor Hadrian when he designed the 'Stone', a grotto resembling the ruins of the Emperor's villa near Tivoli. He also promoted the graphic arts through the Dessau Chalkographische Gesellschaft.

BIBLIOGRAPHY

F. Reil: *L. F. Franz* (Dessau, 1845)
W. Hosäus: *Wörlitz* (Dessau, 1869, 3/1902)
A. F. Heine and L. Grote: *Die Chalkographische Gesellschaft in Dessau* (Dessau, 1930)
E. Hirsch: *Der Dessau-Wörlitzer Kulturkreis im Urteil der Zeitgenossen* (diss., Halle, Martin Luther-U., 1969)
——: *Dessau-Wörlitz* (Munich, 1985, 2/1987)
——: *Der Ursprung der deutschen Neugotik im aufgeklärten Dessau-Wörlitzer Reformwerk* (Dessau, 1987)
Die Chalkographische Gesellschaft zu Dessau (exh. cat., Coburg, Veste Coburg, 1987)
E. Hirsch: *Experiment Fortschritt. Praktizierte Aufklärung: Zum 250. Geburtstag L. F. Franz* (1990)
H. Günther, ed.: *Gärten der Goethezeit* (Leipzig, 1993)

ERHARD HIRSCH

Anhtoni [Anthonij], **Giovanni** [Johan] (*fl* Narol, 1663; *d* Stockholm, 1688). Italian stuccoist active in Sweden. He collaborated with HANS ZAUCH on ceilings in Skokloster Castle, Uppland (1663–4), and he created the ceiling in the great hall in Djursholm Castle (1668), near Stockholm. At Skokloster he may have executed two ceilings (1663–4) alone, in the antechambers of the apartment of Carl Gustaf Wrangel (1613–76) and his wife in the east wing. These ceilings are dominated by figurative motifs—flying putti in one ceiling, representatives of the Four Seasons in the other. The latter especially is marked by its somewhat naive but fine modelling and has lyrical scenes, such as the heavily clad young man warming his hands by a fire, typifying winter.

BIBLIOGRAPHY

E. Andrén: *Skokloster* (Stockholm, 1948)
S. Karling: 'Les Stucateurs italiens en Suède', *Arte e artisti dei laghi lombardi*, ed. E. Aslan (Como, 1964), pp. 291–302
G. Beard: *Stucco and Decorative Plasterwork in Europe* (London, 1983), p. 69

TORBJÖRN FULTON

Anhui school [Chin. Xin'an pai]. Term used to refer to a group of painters, mostly landscapists, active in Anhui Province chiefly in the second half of the 17th century, early in the Qing period (1644–1911). The Chinese name refers to the region of Xin'an in south-eastern Anhui, where the artists were mostly concentrated. Anhui was prominent in the production of craft and trade goods, including paper, lacquer, brushes and ink-cakes, before it became a centre for painters. From the early 17th century the finest woodblock cutting and printing were done here, rivalled only by nearby Nanjing. Some Anhui artists of the late Ming (1368–1644), notably Ding Yunpeng, contributed designs for pictorial prints, and the spare, precise linear patterns of Anhui printing must have been a factor behind the popularity of related painting styles among local artists (*see also* CHINA, §XIII, 19).

Another important factor in the formation of the school and the stylistic direction it took was the patronage of the wealthy Huizhou merchants, who by the late Ming period controlled most of the commerce in the lower Yangzi River area. Their passion for collecting antiquities, especially works of calligraphy and painting by prestigious masters of the past, is attested in writings of their time; the prices paid for certain kinds of paintings by respected literati masters of the Yuan (1279–1368) and Ming periods are said to have shot up tenfold as a result. Also in demand as status symbols were works by local artists in styles derived from such old masters as Ni Zan and Huang Gongwang. The early Qing collector and connoisseur Zhou Lianggong related that possession of paintings by the leading artist of the Anhui school, HONGREN, determined the status of families in the lower Yangzi region: those who had one were *ya*, or cultivated, those who did not were *su*, or uncultivated.

The character of the Anhui terrain, especially the spectacular scenery of Mt Huang, the range of mountains located some 65 km north-west of She xian, also influenced the Anhui school. Some of the artists' fondness for angular, geometricized forms must be based on their observations of similar forms in the craggy masses of its peaks. As a series of notable sights of Mt Huang—peaks, waterfalls, old pine trees—were established and given names, these became favoured subjects for the painters, and albums of Mt Huang scenes are among their typical productions.

A few painters of note had appeared in Anhui already by the late Ming period: the aforementioned Ding Yunpeng, Zhan Jingfeng (1520–1602), the landscapist Zheng Zhong (*fl c.* 1565–1630) and a few others. But the real rise of the school began at the very end of the Ming and in the early Qing, the 1630s and 1640s. Several secondary masters active at that time, among them Li Yungchang (*fl* 1630s–1640s), Wang Zhirui (*fl* 1640s–1650s) and Sun Yi (*c.* 1605–*c.* 1660), laid the foundations for developments that are distinguished sometimes by extremes of reductionism: linear renderings of highly simplified landscape forms with a minimum of wash and little detail. XIAO YUNCONG was a more versatile and serious artist, with a more solid foundation in traditional Wu school or Suzhou styles than most others of the Anhui group. He executed designs for two notable series of woodblock prints, the *Lisao tu* ('Illustrations to Qu Yuan's "Encountering sorrow"'; 1645) and the *Taiping shanshui tu* ('Landscapes of Taiping county'; 1648) and during the several decades of his activity produced an impressive number of paintings, especially in the album and handscroll formats.

The greatest master of the school was the Buddhist monk Hongren. In just 12 years between his return to She xian in 1651 or 1652 (he had fled to Fujian to escape the Manchu invaders) and his death in 1664, he painted numerous landscapes that established him as one of the major individualist masters of the early Qing and represent the full maturity of the Anhui school. Some of these works follow the model of Ni Zan, but many artists of the time imitated Ni with fair success, and Hongren's major achievement lies elsewhere. Preserving the essential qualities of the school manner—the dry brush-line and angular forms, the avoidance of rich ink-wash and of fine detail—he created spacious, substantial, even monumental landscapes. He became, for a time, the principal model for others of the school.

One of those most influenced by Hongren was ZHA SHIBIAO, who attempted an official career early in his life but abandoned it and lived chiefly by his painting. During his early period, from the 1650s into the 1670s, he followed

Hongren fairly closely, often with works in the manner of Ni Zan. In the 1670s he became more independent; an album of 10 landscapes (1674; Tokyo, N. Mus.) displays his new, broader range of styles and a greater individualism. His late works, after he had moved to Yangzhou, tend to be more quickly produced and sketchier.

A stylistic tendency among several masters of the school was towards a dry, crumbly brushstroke, not unlike charcoal drawing in effect; when the ink is richly black and brushed on dry, the technique is called *jiaomo* ('roasted, or dry, ink'). Two who used it extensively were Cheng Sui (1605–91) and Dai Benxiao. Cheng came from a prosperous She xian family and painted chiefly for his own pleasure, beginning late in life; genuine works by him are relatively scarce. His undated *Landscape* (see fig.) is an especially fine example; like a work of calligraphy or a seal, it arranges small, formally similar units into a flat design. The *jiaomo* technique, the tendency to geometricize the land masses, and the mountain landscapes with waterfalls and pine trees are school characteristics. Cheng remarked in his inscription that the 'high distance' (*gaoyuan*) mode, in which the composition is read vertically, was not favoured by artists of his time and region, who mostly employed the 'level distance' (*pingyuan*) mode of Ni Zan and other masters of the river landscape (*see* CHINA, §V, 3(iv)). The refinement of taste that Cheng developed through study of the family collection and deciphering old inscriptions imbues his calligraphy and seal-carving, as well as his painting, with an antiquarian flavour much admired by Chinese connoisseurs. They regard him as a forerunner of the Epigraphers' school (Jinshi jia) of practitioners of these three interlocked arts, a school that flourished in the late 18th century and the 19th.

DAI BENXIAO was from Hezhou (modern He xian), near the eastern border of Anhui Province and close to Nanjing; some of his works betray affinities with styles of the NANJING SCHOOL. Typically, his paintings, which sometimes portray Mt Huang and other places of notable scenery, depict tall earth masses that twist as they thrust upwards to fill most of the picture space. Figures, recluses or travellers, are seen in most of them, and his inscriptions indicate that the idea of landscape as a refuge from human affairs is the underlying theme of much of his work. The same is probably true of the other Anhui masters: their spare styles seem to suggest a longing for disengagement and purification.

Active in Xuancheng, further to the south, were MEI QING, Mei Chong (*fl c.* 1690; probably a nephew) andMei Geng (1640–*c.* 1716; perhaps a younger brother). Most of Mei Qing's painting is devoted to the scenery of Mt Huang. In the best of his works, a poetic inventiveness and delicacy of touch compensate for his technical deficiencies; other paintings, especially some of his hanging scrolls, are too awkwardly composed and routinely executed to be quite satisfying. His best paintings are mostly in album form, the finest an album of Mt Huang scenes painted in 1693 (Shanghai Mus.); it reveals how heavily he was influenced by his younger contemporary Daoji, who lived in the Xuancheng area during the 1670s. Other artists of the school worthy of note include Zheng Min (?1633–?1683) from She xian, whose reputation has improved as more excellent and original works by him have become known, and Yao Song (1648–after 1721), also from She xian, whose imitations of the Hongren manner bring the active period of the school to a close. Other, still later painters from Anhui whose works sometimes echo the regional style are Fang Shishu (1692–1751), Luo Ping and Huang Binhong.

Anhui school hanging scroll by Cheng Sui: *Landscape*, ink on paper, 1003×400 mm, Kangxi reign period, 1662–1722 (New York, C. C. Wang and family private collection)

For a discussion of the Xin'an yin pai, the Anhui school of seal-carvers, *see* CHINA, §XIII, 22.

BIBLIOGRAPHY

M. Shen and Shen Fu: *Studies in Connoisseurship: Chinese Paintings from the Arthur M. Sackler Collection in New York and Princeton* (Princeton, 1973), pp. 9–10, 140–51

Kuo Chi-sheng: *The Painting of Hung-jen* (diss., Ann Arbor, U. MI, 1980)

Shadows of Mt Huang: Chinese Painting and Printing of the Anhui School (exh. cat., ed. J. Cahill; Berkeley, CA, U. A. Mus., 1981)

JAMES CAHILL

Ani [Turk. Kemah]. Site (*c.* 162 ha) of an Armenian fortified city with religious and secular buildings of the 10th-14th centuries, situated on a high, triangular plateau at the confluence of the Arpa Chay and Alajai Chay Rivers near Kars in eastern Turkey, on the border with Armenia. It was founded as a fortress in the 5th century AD, and it became the capital of Armenia under the Bagratuni kings from 961 until 1045 when it fell to the Byzantines. Thereafter the city suffered many devastating attacks, and it was ruled consecutively by the Seljuks, their Shaddadid vassals and the Georgians; but in 1199 it was liberated by the Zak'arian princes. It flourished as an international trade centre on the route between the Far East and the West until the 14th century. In his history (1004) Matthew of Edessa describes Ani as 'the city of a thousand and one churches'. It was said to have 50 gates and 100 palaces within its towered stone walls, and in the 10th century it had been reported to have 10,000 houses and a population of over 100,000—much larger than contemporary medieval cities in Europe.

Stores, bazaars, factories, hotels, baths, warehouses and artisans' workshops were built on the surface of the plateau, while hollowed out of the cliffs below was an extensive underground city with approximately 400 dwellings, 30 churches, architectural complexes with chapels, storehouses, caravanserais, stables, tombs and 16 dovecotes. The original citadel on the southern edge of the plateau and the expanded part of the city to the north were protected by a fortification system built in the standard Armenian style in 961 by King Ashot III (*reg* 953–77) and reinforced by King Smbat II (*reg* 977–89) in 989. It includes double walls (h. 6–8 m), rounded towers (h. 8–12 m), which are incorporated into the wall system, and bent entrances. The city also had bridges with arch spans of more than 30 m, which were very advanced for their time. All buildings were of highly polished blocks of native tufa facing a rubble core. The walls, gates and towers are often ornamented with darker-coloured stone slabs forming checkerboard patterns, crosses and other geometric motifs. The inscriptions carved on all types of building in Ani are a rich source of political, religious, social, economic, commercial and juridical information, as well as of names, dates and events associated with building donations. Orbeli published more than 250, documenting about two dozen churches built between the 7th and 14th centuries.

Of the dozen or so churches that have survived, most were constructed in the 10th and 11th centuries. They are in varying states of repair. The most notable is the Cathedral of the Mother of God (Astvatsatsin; see fig.) begun by King Smbat II in 989 and completed in 1001 (or possibly 1010) by Queen Katranidē, the wife of King Gagik I (*reg* 989–1020). Trdat (*fl* 989–1001), the architect who in 989 also repaired the dome of Hagia Sophia in

Ani, Cathedral of the Mother of God (Astvatsatsin), 989–1001/10, view from the north-west

Constantinople, constructed a domed basilican-type church with pointed arches, clustered columns and stone vaults, features that prompted Josef Strzygowski and other scholars to claim Armenia as the source for similar features in Romanesque and Gothic architecture. The cathedral's graceful exterior blind arcades on the drum and lower walls are a characteristic of the so-called 'Ani school of architecture', examples of which appear in various parts of the region.

Another church is St Grigor, the Abughamrents family church, which was built before 994 by Prince Grigor Pahlawuni (*c.* 990–*c.* 1058) or his wife Princess Šušan, and which is a domed round building with six radiating apses. The Pahlawunis also commissioned other churches, including the Holy Apostles (Arak'elots'), which was built by 1031 and is a rectangular structure with four apses, four corner chapels and possibly five domes, and the church of the Holy Saviour (P'rkitch), a round domed building with eight radiating apses, which was completed in 1035/6 by Abgharip Pahlawuni, governor of Armenia, to house a fragment of the True Cross that he had brought from Constantinople.

In 1000 Trdat completed the church of St Grigor the Illuminator (destr.), a domed, three-level, aisled tetraconch based on the 7th-century cathedral at ZVART'NOTS and commissioned by King Gagik I, whose portrait statue (untraced) holding the church model was discovered by Marr. One of the most innovative churches was the small three-level chapel of the Shepherd (Hovvi; probably 11th century; destr. 1966). Its ground plan was star-shaped and was surmounted by an ingenious sytem of vaulting in which six arches terminated in a hanging keystone at the centre of the building. Among the other churches from the Bagratid period are several in the citadel, including the Palace Church, a tetraconch church, two hexaconch churches and the church of the Princely Children, while in the city proper are Ashot's Church (or Tomb) and the so-called Georgian Church. Another 10th- or 11th-century structure is a vaulted building that may have been a council hall, customs house, garrison or *gavit* (assembly hall next to church façade) but is now known as the Mosque of

Manuč'e (Turk. Minuchihr); in 1072 the Shaddadids built an octagonal minaret beside it. In the 13th century the wealthy merchant Tigran Honents' commissioned a church dedicated to St Grigor the Illuminator (completed 1215) and decorated it with lavish relief sculpture of birds and animals on the exterior walls and extensive frescoes on the interior. He also founded the Monastery of the Virgins (Kusanats'), of which only a round church survives (probably 13th century).

During the 14th and 15th centuries Ani suffered several severe earthquakes, and with the shift southwards of important trade routes, the town was gradually abandoned and fell into ruin. Brosset's descriptions of the site published in 1861 revived interest in Ani in the late 19th century. The excavations of Marr and T'ōramanyan followed in 1892–3 and 1904–17. In addition to architecture, the excavations produced thousands of such small finds as metalware, tools, glass, bricks, arms, coats of mail, coins, textiles, high quality silks, rug fragments and cotton goods.

BIBLIOGRAPHY

M. Brosset: *Les Ruines d'Ani* (St Petersburg, 1861)
G. Alishan: *Shirak* (Venice, 1881)
——: *Ayrarat* (Venice, 1890)
J. Strzygowski: *Die Baukunst der Armenier und Europa*, 2 vols (Vienna, 1918)
K. J. Basmadjian: *Les Inscriptions arméniennes d'Ani, de Bagnair et de Marmashen* (Paris, 1931)
J. Baltrushaitis: *Le Problème de l'ogive et l'Arménie* (Paris, 1936)
T'. T'ōramanyan: *Nyut'er haykakan tchartarapetut'yan patmut'yan* [Materials for the history of Armenian architecture], 2 vols (Yerevan, 1942–8)
G. Levonian: 'Tchartarapet Trdat Anets'in ev ir gordserê' [The architect Trdat of Ani and his works], *Ēdjmiadzin*, i (1949), pp. 55–66
V. M. Harut'yunyan: *Midjnadaryan Hayastani k'aravanatnern u kamurdjnerê* [The caravanserai and bridges of medieval Armenia] (Yerevan, 1960)
M. Thierry and N. Thierry: 'Ani, ville morte du Moyen Age arménien', *Jard. A.*, lxv (1960), pp. 132–45
S. Barkhudaryan: *Midjnadaryan hay tchartarapetner ev k'argords varpetner* [Medieval Armenian architects and sculptors] (Yerevan, 1963)
V. Harut'unyan: *Ani qaghaqê* [The city of Ani] (Yerevan, 1964)
H. A. Ōrbeli: *Divan hay vimagrut'yan—Corpus inscriptionum armenicarum*, i (Yerevan, 1966)
P. Cuneo: *L'architettura della scuola regionale di Ani nell'Armenia medioevale* (Rome, 1977)
A. A. Manutch'aryan: *K'nnut'yun hayastani iv–xi dareri shinararakan vkayagreri* [A study of building documentation in Armenia during the 9th–11th centuries] (Yerevan, 1977)
L. Der Manuelian: *Armenian Architecture*, i, ed. K. Maksoudian, 7 vols (Zug, 1981–) [in microfiche]
P. Cuneo and others: *Ani* (Venice, 1984)
P. Cuneo: *Architettura armena dal quarto al diciannovesimo secolo* (Rome, 1988)
L. Der Manuelian: 'Ani: The Fabled Capital of Armenia', *Ani Millenium Symposium, New York, 1989* (in preparation)

LUCY DER MANUELIAN

Anichini [Annichini; Nichini; Nichino]. Italian family of gem-engravers. Francesco Anichini (*b* Bagnacavallo, *fl* 1449–1526; *d* ?1545), active in Ferrara, was highly praised by his contemporaries, including Vasari and Jacopo Tagliacarne (*fl* late 15th century). He was also criticized for being self-willed and slow-working. From 1492 to 1497 he is recorded as having worked for Isabella d'Este, Marchioness of Mantua, who referred to him in a letter as 'il migliore maestro d'Italia'. Documents indicate that Francesco supplied her in 1492 with a turquoise *Head of a Child*, some rubies and a cameo, in 1494 with gems for rings and in 1496 with two turquoises with figures of *Orpheus* and *Victory*, after a design by the Marchioness, and a gem with a symbolic emblem (all untraced). For a physician from Ferrara, Francesco carved a glow-worm in lapis lazuli (untraced) in such a way that the natural gold veins of the stone appeared as the luminous parts of the insect's body. In 1500 Francesco moved his atelier to Venice; in a document of 1505 he is referred to as 'famigliare del Duca di Ferrara' and in 1519 the Anichini family received honorary citizenship of Ferrara. Francesco had five sons: Luigi Anichini (*b* Venice, ?1500–10; *d* Ferrara, after 1559); Andrea Anichini (*fl* 1526–53); Callisto Anichini (*b* Ferrara, before 1527; *d* Venice, ?1553); Alvise Anichini and Pietro Anichini, who were also gem-engravers and worked in Ferrara and Venice. Luigi has often been confused with his father and, like him, received lavish contemporary praise from Vasari and others. Until 1540 he had a house in Ferrara but lived most of the time in Venice, where his friends included Titian and Sansovino. In that year a *Ganymede* in lapis lazuli is recorded, in 1544 a carnelian with *Apollo* and a cameo portrait of *Giovanni delle Bande Nere* and in 1547 a seal with a head of *Medusa* for Pietro Aretino (all untraced). Luigi maintained the good relations established by his father with the court of Ferrara and Isabella d'Este. Of the other brothers, it is known that Callisto was also a jeweller and was probably active in Venice, where it is thought that he worked with his father.

BIBLIOGRAPHY

G. Baruffaldi: *Vite de' pittori e scultori ferraresi*, 2 vols (Ferrara, 1841–46)
E. Kris: *Meister und Meisterwerke der Steinschneiderkunst*, 2 vols (Vienna, 1929)
C. G. Bulgari: *Argentieri, gemmari e orafi d'Italia: Notizie storiche e raccolta dei loro contrassegni con la riproduzione grafica dei punzoni individuali e dei punzoni di stato*, 5 vols (Rome, 1958–74)

□

Anicia Juliana (*b* ?Constantinople, *c.* AD 461–3; *d* Constantinople, *c.* 527–9). Byzantine patron. As the great-granddaughter of Galla Placidia and daughter of Flavius Anicius Olybrius (Emperor of the West, *reg* 472) she was the last major figure of the Theodosian house. In 512, during a popular uprising against Emperor Anastasius I (*reg* 491–518), the imperial crown was pressed on her husband Flavius Areobindus Dagalaifus, an honour he avoided by flight. Her imperial connections and social standing gave her an important status at court and she was an active patron. She is chiefly remembered for the Dioskurides codex (Vienna, Österreich. Nbib., med. gr. 1), which was produced in Constantinople *c.* 512 (*see* EARLY CHRISTIAN AND BYZANTINE ART, §I, 2(ii)). The inscription around her portrait (fol. 6*v*) indicates that the manuscript was commissioned for her by the people of Onoratou, a suburb of Constantinople, in gratitude for a church she built for them.

An epigram of 76 lines in the *Palatine Anthology* (I, 10–17) describes her construction of the magnificent church of St Polyeuktos at Constantinople (524–7), in honour of her dynastic ancestry. Excavations in the 1960s and 1970s uncovered the church's remains on the south slope of a ridge between the Sea of Marmara and the Golden Horn. Among the finds were fragments of the poem that was originally carved on the entablature of the nave and outside the narthex. The church was square in plan (51.45×52 m) with an orientated apse and an atrium to the west, and was probably surmounted by a central dome. The most striking feature of the architectural sculpture, however, is its variety, abundance and technical quality (Istanbul, Archaeol. Mus.; *see* EARLY CHRISTIAN AND BYZANTINE ART, §IV, 2(i)). The combination of familiar Classical motifs with new and exotic designs deriving partly from Sasanian models has links with the sculptural decoration in SS Sergius and Bacchus and in Hagia Sophia. It has been suggested that the latter was Justinian's reply to the challenge of St Polyeuktos. Abandoned in the 11th century, the church was thoroughly looted during the Latin occupation of Constantinople (1204–61), and many fragments of architectural sculpture, such as the so-called Pilastri Acritani, were later placed in the Piazza S Marco, Venice.

BIBLIOGRAPHY

Theophanes: *Chronicle* (early 9th century); Eng. trans. by H. Turtledove (Philadelphia, 1982)
A. von Premerstein, K. Wessely and J. Mantuani: *Dioscurides: Codex Aniciae Julianae* (Leiden, 1906)
W. R. Paton, ed.: *The Greek Palatine Anthology*, Loeb Class. Lib. (London and New York, 1916)
C. Mango and I. Ševčenko: 'Remains of the Church of St Polyeuktos at Istanbul', *Dumbarton Oaks Pap.*, xv (1961), pp. 243–8
C. Capizzi: 'L'attività edilizia di Anicia Giuliana', *Orient. Christ. Anlct.*, 204 (1977), pp. 119–46
R. M. Harrison: *Excavations at Saraçhane in Istanbul*, i (Princeton, 1986)
——: *A Temple for Byzantium* (London, 1989)

L. JAMES

Anige. *See* ARNIKO.

Anikushin, Mikhail (Konstantinovich) (*b* Moscow, 2 Oct 1917). Russian sculptor. He studied (1935–41) at the Institute of Painting, Sculpture and Architecture in Leningrad (now St Petersburg), working under Aleksandr Matveyev, from whom he gained an unbiased attitude to nature and a well thought-out pictorial system to interpret it. He fought at the front during World War II and graduated from the Institute only in 1947, with his diploma work *The Soldier–Victor* (St Petersburg, Acad. A., Mus.), at the heart of which lay his impressions of the front. In 1949 he won the competition for a monument to Pushkin in Leningrad. Work on the realization of the monument overflowed into a series of portrait sculptures of *Pushkin*, both monumental and small-scale, in which the poet is represented at different ages and in a variety of emotional states, but always agitated and inspired (statue, 1952, Moscow U.; portrait bust, 1955, St Petersburg, Rus. Mus.). These culminated in the monument, executed in a severe classical style, which was erected in 1957 in Arts Square in Leningrad (*in situ*), and which was well suited to the surrounding early 19th-century architecture.

In the 1960s Anikushin worked enthusiastically on the project for a monument to Anton Chekhov in Moscow, and from this he created many different portrait sculptures, among them the luminous, lyrical representation of the young writer (*A. P. Chekhov*, bronze, 1961; St Petersburg, Rus. Mus.). His sculptures of *V. I. Lenin*, particularly the monument he designed to be erected in Moscow Square in Leningrad (bronze and granite, 1970; *in situ*) show a romantic and emotional approach. Anikushin led a vast project for the creation of the monument to the *Defenders of Leningrad* (concrete, bronze and granite; St Petersburg, Victory [Pobedy] Square), which he executed in 1975. In this work an important role is played by the overall architectural composition, which comprises a broad space (designed by the architects Sergey Speransky and Valentin Kamensky) enriched with sculptural groups, placed at the entrance and the centre, of generalized personifications of the dramatic events and the life of the residents and defenders of the blockaded town. Anikushin also made portrait sculptures of contemporary figures.

BIBLIOGRAPHY

Anikushin Mikhail Konstantinovich: Al'bom proizvedeniy [Anikushin Mikhail Konstantinovich: An album of his works] (Leningrad, 1960)
A. I. Zamoshkin: *Mikhail Konstantinovich Anikushin* (Leningrad, 1979)

R. YA. ABOLINA

Animalier sculpture. Term applied particularly to mid-19th-century French sculpture with animal subject-matter. The beginnings of this genre as a significant phenomenon may be located in 1831, when three sculptors, ANTOINE-LOUIS BARYE, C. Fratin (1801–64) and A. Guionnet (*fl* 1831–53), all exhibited animal pieces at the Paris Salon. The popularity of such sculpture, and its commercial exploitability through the production of serial bronzes and plasters, induced some sculptors, such as Barye et Cie, to cast and market their own animal statuettes. Antecedents are numerous, but a comparable degree of concentration on animal subjects in sculpture is found only at the end of the 18th century, in the work of the English painter and sculptor George Garrard. Garrard's animal pieces reflect contemporary concern with 'improved' stock-breeding, as well as the involvement with natural history of the encyclopedists. A much publicized debate in 1830 on comparative anatomy, between Etienne Geoffroy de Saint Hilaire and his pupil Georges Cuvier, stimulated widespread interest in zoology, as did the growth of the Paris Jardin des Plantes, where several generations of sculptors studied animals from life. They could observe dissections at the Musée National d'Histoire Naturelle, where Barye occupied the post of Professor of Zoological Drawing from 1854 until his death in 1875, when he was succeeded by another sculptor, Emmanuel Fremiet.

The power and cruelty of tropical species preoccupied Barye in a number of his influential early groups. This epic vision of a 'Nature, red in tooth and claw' (in Tennyson's words) was taken up by Auguste-Nicolas Cain, who made his Salon début in 1846, and who, like Barye, was a regular recipient of official commissions for large-scale animal statuary, such as the *Family of Tigers* in the Tuileries Gardens, Paris, commissioned in bronze by the State after the Salon of 1873. In the work of Pierre-Jules Mène, who first exhibited at the Salon of 1838, a distinct shift occurs in the mid-1840s from the tropical and epic towards hunting and equestrian subjects conceived in a nervous and luxuriant miniaturist style. In lesser hands, this branch of sculpture developed into a record of modern blood sports and racing achievements. Another alternative, espoused in particular by Rosa Bonheur in her occasional sculptures, and by her brother, Isidore Jules Bonheur (1827–1901), was the agricultural subject, sheep and cattle (see fig.). Barye, who set most of the standards in this area, provided an example, in his *Lion Crushing a Serpent*

Isidore Jules Bonheur: *Bull*, bronze statuette, h. 311 mm, mid-19th century (London, Victoria and Albert Museum)

(bronze, 1832), of an allegorical and philosophizing approach to animal subjects, which was followed by Emmanuel Fremiet. In his attempt to instil meaning into his animal pieces, Fremiet indulged occasionally in serious or comic anthropomorphism, but anthropocentricity was ironically reversed in some of his confrontations of man and beast, where the beast is seen to be taking the upper hand.

By the early 20th century, animal specialization in sculpture had become an international phenomenon, but by then its leading practitioners, the German August Gaul, the Italian Rembrandt Bugatti, and the Frenchman François Pompon, spurned the romantic tendency to identify with the animal world, and replaced pathos with a detached and elegant formalism.

BIBLIOGRAPHY

Lami

J. Horswell: *Bronze Sculpture of 'Les Animaliers'* (Woodbridge, Suffolk, 1971)

J. Mackay: *The Animaliers: A Collector's Guide to the Animal Sculpture of the 19th and 20th Centuries* (New York, 1973)

PHILIP WARD-JACKSON

Animal style. Term used to describe an art dominated by animal themes, associated with a series of 1st-millennium BC cultures of the Eurasian steppes, extending from Central Europe to the ORDOS region of north-west China.

1. INTRODUCTION. The Animal style is characteristic of a series of cultures, including the Thracians (north Balkans), Savromats (lower reaches of the Don and Volga rivers), a people of the south Ural Mountains who are perhaps identifiable as the Issedones (Herodotus: *Histories* IV.26), the cultures of Tasmola (central Kazakhstan), PAZYRYK (Altai Mountains) and Tagar (south Siberia), and other barrow (kurgan) burials in the Semirechiye (Seven Rivers) region of Kyrgyzstan and east Kazakhstan, the Pamirs and the Tien Shan Mountains. In Central Asia and the north Black Sea region, the Animal style is usually associated with nomadic tribes known in ancient Persian and Classical sources as the Sakas or Scythians (*see* SCYTHIAN AND SARMATIAN ART), a term which loosely appears to refer to an eastern Iranian linguistic group.

2. SUBJECT-MATTER. Although of diverse origins, these cultures are all associated with arms, armour and horse-trappings, and share a common range of motifs and iconographic themes. Zoomorphic images predominate. Influences from ACHAEMENID and Classical Greek sources also resulted in the occasional use of anthropomorphic images. The art was generally used to decorate functional items, such as weapons, horse-trappings, clothes and ritual objects. The choice of motifs was governed to some extent by the type and form of each object. Most examples are stamped gold and cast bronze pieces, either in relief or in the round. Unique permafrost conditions in some of the barrows (e.g. Pazyryk) have preserved an exceptional number of organic materials, which show that the same motifs were used to decorate

textiles, felt, leather, wood, bone (see fig. 1) and also tattooed on human bodies.

The repertory of images includes elements found throughout the entire region and purely local variants. Common motifs comprise three principal groups: herbivores (antlered stags, ibexes), feline predators and birds of prey. The pose of each group of animals is standardized, a few elements are strongly emphasized, and little attention is paid to smaller details. Herbivores are shown either standing or in a so-called 'flying gallop', with the legs drawn under the body (actually often merely a reclining pose). In early examples, deer are usually depicted in the latter pose, their heads stretched out in front with enlarged stylized antlers in the form of tendrils or volutes extending along their backs; for example gold appliqué discs from a quiver found in the Chiliktin burial, east Kazakhstan (St Petersburg, Hermitage). Predators are usually depicted crouching or coiled so that the head and tail meet, with the legs enclosed within the circle formed by the body (*animal enroulé*). The paws are either depicted realistically or terminate in small stylized rings, for example gold discs from the Chiliktin burial (St Petersburg, Hermitage); bronze horse harness rings from the Uygarak burial, north-east of the Aral Sea (Moscow, Hist. Mus.). In depictions of birds, the head and wings are emphasized; more usually, only the heads, with enlarged round eyes and curved beaks are represented.

Other motifs include boars, hares, horses, waterfowl and camels. Subsequently, fantastical beasts combining individual features of different animals were more widely used. A common method of stylization depicts details of the body as animal forms; for example antlers or claws may comprise the heads of birds of prey, while other animals are incorporated into the shoulders or hindquarters of a larger beast. This device, known as 'zoomorphic juncture', was used less often in Central Asia than in other regions.

During the early development of the style, compositions comprised individual animals juxtaposed on an object. Later specific themes were introduced, which concentrated on variations of the animals in combat postures: for example a predator, bird or mythical beast attacking its prey (see fig. 2); less frequently, a fight between predators; or, very rarely, a battle between hoofed beasts. More varied iconographical schemes included the widespread use of stylized contortions, such as quadrupeds with inverted hindquarters (e.g. openwork gold discs depicting an elk and a horse, from the Issyk Barrow, Semirechiye region; Alma-Ata, Kazak Acad. Sci.). A subsequent tendency towards greater ornamentation meant that the identity of the original animal was often obscured by a wealth of purely decorative detail.

1. Animal-style plaque in the form of a reclining horse, bone, l. 110 mm, from the tomb of *Sagly-Bazhy II*, western Tuva, 5th–3rd centuries BC (St Petersburg, Hermitage Museum)

2. Animal-style belt plaque showing a battle between a tiger and a wolf-like animal, cast gold, 92×168 mm, Sakic culture, 4th–5th centuries BC (St Petersburg, Hermitage Museum)

3. ORIGINS AND INTERPRETATION. The question of the immediate origins of the Animal style is a highly contentious subject. In the preceding Bronze Age (beginning of the 1st millennium BC), only the Karasuk culture of the Minusinsk region, southern Siberia, and the nearby regions of Mongolia appear to have had a developed tradition of rock painting and bronzework, both of which included an abundance of animal images. The full repertory of the Animal style cannot, however, derive from this particular tradition, for its influence is only evident locally in southern Siberia and the adjoining regions. The sudden appearance, over a wide area, of a relatively uniform style suggests that the art may have spread from a single source during the migration of its originators. Classical sources (e.g. Herodotus: *Histories* IV.1–142) describing the arrival of the Scythians in the northern Black Sea area, include within the group all the inhabitants of the Eurasian steppes, which implies that Central Asia was the historical homeland of all these peoples and may have been the area where the Animal style originated. Those in favour of this hypothesis consider the discovery of the Arzhan Kurgan in Tuva, which included superb objects in this style, of great significance. However, the date of Arzhan is still uncertain, with a disputed range of the 9th–6th centuries BC, while certain peculiarities apparent in the art from this site eliminate it as a possible source of many motifs that were popular in other regions during the Scythian period. A second hypothesis is that the Animal style originated from zoomorphic images borrowed by the Scythians from

an Ancient Near Eastern repertory (possibly from Assyria, Urartu or Luristan), with the ZIWIYEH hoard from Iranian Kurdistan considered in this context to represent an important stage in the formation of Scythian art (New York, Met., Tehran, Archaeol. Mus. and elsewhere).

A theory gaining increasing credence suggests that sources for the Animal style were polycentric. The basis of the art is thought to have originated from separate artistic traditions in different parts of Eurasia, for example in southern Siberia from the Karasuk culture. During the earliest phase of development these different sources can be distinguished, but the nomadic lifestyle of the various groups meant that an intensive exchange of artistic ideas and actual objects inevitably took place. The rapid assimilation of motifs resulted in the emergence of a fairly well-defined repertory of common themes throughout the region, although the art of individual cultures and periods nevertheless remained stylistically diverse. The possible significance of the images is also disputed. One hypothesis suggests that the zoomorphic images were associated with SHAMANISM, in that the depicted animals were supposed to bring their bearers the qualities they embodied. Alternatively, it is thought that these animals were seen as totems of individual Eurasian tribes, or that the animals represented a pantheon of gods in zoomorphic form. Finally, the animal motifs are interpreted as a specific system of cosmic signs associated with ideas relating to the creation of the world. The issue, however, remains open.

BIBLIOGRAPHY

M. Rostovtzeff: *The Animal Style in South Russia and China* (Princeton, 1929)

S. I. Rudenko: *Kultura naseleniya Tsentralnogo Altaya v skifskoye vremya* [The culture of the inhabitants of the Central Altai during the Scythian period] (Moscow, 1960); Eng. trans. as *Frozen Tombs of Siberia: The Pazyryk Burials of Iron-Age Horsemen* (London, 1970)

K. Jettmar: *Die frühen Steppenvölker: Die eurasiatische Tierstil, Entstehung und socialer Hintergrund* (Baden-Baden, 1964); Eng. trans. by A. E. Kemp as *Art of the Steppes: The Eurasian Animal Style* (London, 1967)

M. P. Gryaznov: *South Siberia* (London, 1969)

M. I. Artamonov: *Sokrovischcha sakov* [The treasury of the Shakas] (Moscow, 1973)

K. A. Akishev: *Kurgan Issyk: Iskusstvo sakov Kazakhstan* [The Issyk Kurgan: the art of the Shakas of Kazakhstan] (Moscow, 1978)

E. Jacobson: 'The Stag with Bird-headed Antler Tines: A Study in Image Transformation and Meaning', *Bull. Mus. Far E. Ant.*, lvii (1985), pp. 133–80

D. S. RAYEVSKY

Animal subjects. Although animals have been represented in the art of almost all cultures from prehistoric times, the depiction of animal subjects in painting and the graphic arts became a particularly well-established tradition in Western art following the Renaissance, as European explorers discovered new species, as the demand for illustrated books increased and as the traditional Christian interpretation of the relation between humanity and the rest of creation began to be reappraised. Moreover, while hunting, falconry and similar pursuits continued to provide artists with subjects, animals came to have a more complex relation to society, as curiosities, status svmbols or in a domesticated role. Animals continued to occupy an ambiguous role in 19th- and 20th-century Western art, as the subjects of human science, as opportunities to demonstrate technique, and as the instinctive, unrestrained vehicles for a range of Romantic and post-Romantic symbolic possibilities. It is this Western tradition that is discussed in this article; discussion of the depiction of animal subjects in the art of other cultures may be found in the respective regional and cultural surveys.

1. Before the 17th century. 2. The 17th century. 3. The 18th century. 4. 19th century and after.

1. BEFORE THE 17TH CENTURY. During the 15th century depictions of the animal world were often imbued with a complex symbolism, most notably in the sporting scenes painted by such artists as Paolo Uccello (e.g. *Hunt in the Forest*, *c.* 1460–70; Oxford, Ashmolean; *see* UCCELLO, PAOLO, fig. 4). Gradually, however, an increasing accuracy and realism began to appear in the treatment of animal subjects in the BESTIARY, in the drawings of Pisanello, in the works of Leonardo da Vinci and in Dürer's watercolours and woodcuts. While realistic representations of animals became important elements in some oil paintings in the 16th century, for example in Titian's *Charles V on Horseback* (1548; Madrid, Prado) or in the works of Jacopo Bassano, they rarely constituted the subjects of such works. One exception, however, is the *Still-life with a Dead Partridge* (1504; Munich, Alte Pin.) by Jacopo de' Barbari, in which the artist used an early form of *trompe l'oeil* to portray hanging game, a subject that became very popular in later centuries.

In media other than oil painting, however, artists became increasingly interested in the realistic depiction of animal subjects during the 16th century. Animals were already recognized by such artists as Giovanni da Udine and Pordenone as ideal subjects for graphic exercises, but the major impetus to this development came from a revival in scientific studies and extensive geographical discoveries, which aroused new interest in the systematic classification of the animal world. The arrival in Europe of increasing numbers of new species of animals, especially from the Americas, led to a fundamental revision of traditional zoological knowledge. Seeking a system of precise description and, more importantly, an accurate understanding of the interrelationships and peculiarities, scientists engaged artists to depict, under their supervision, the species that they were studying. Watercolour and tempera, which helped to emphasize their colouring, were the most common media, while drawings were often copied as engravings and used to illustrate the many natural history books that were being published. One of the earliest and most famous zoological images of the early 16th century is undoubtedly Dürer's woodcut of a *Rhinoceros* (1515; see fig. 1), which was made from a drawing 'from life' by a Portuguese painter in Lisbon of a specimen brought from Goa, India, to be presented to Pope Leo X, but which drowned in a shipwreck off Genoa and was later stuffed. Although it later became the object of innumerable reproductions, the picture was distinctly unrealistic, and its success was, from a 'scientific' point of view, decidedly undeserved.

The *Historia animalium* (5 vols, Zurich, 1551–87) by the Swiss naturalist Konrad Gessner was of fundamental importance to the evolution of zoological imagery. This vast encyclopedia was illustrated with 1200 woodcuts of

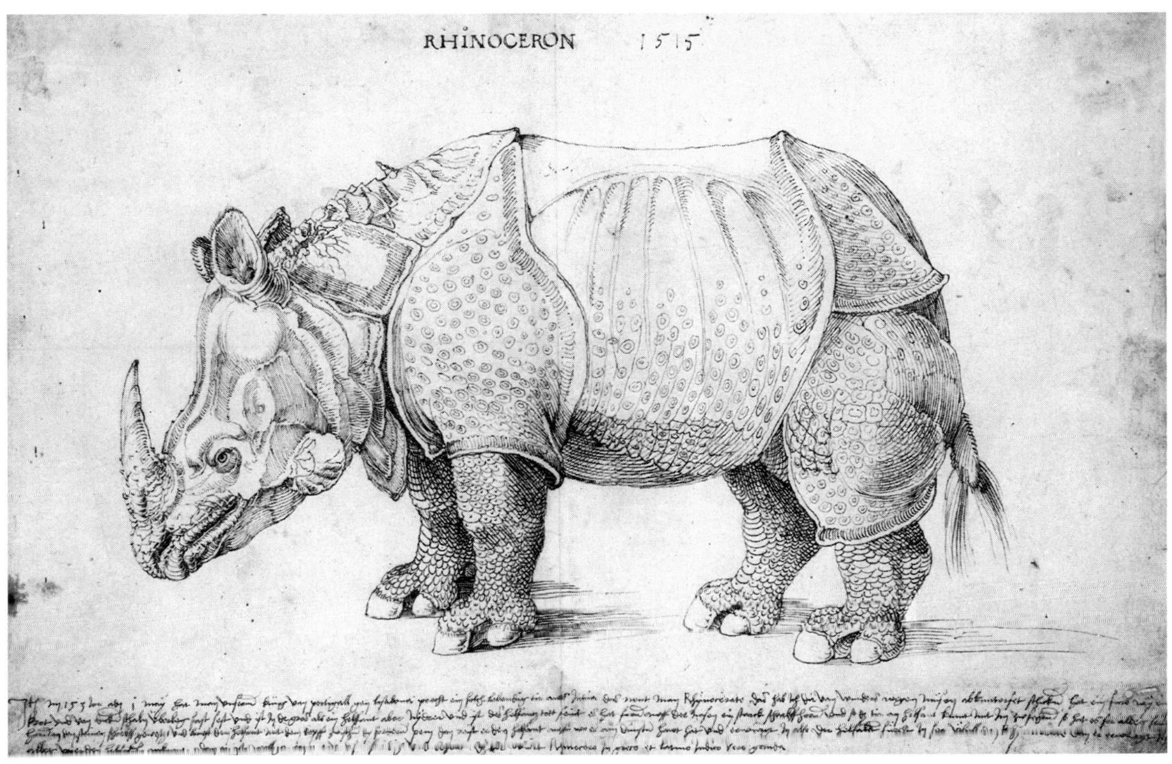

1. Albrecht Dürer: *Rhinoceros*, pen and brown ink, 274×420 mm, 1515 (London, British Museum)

quadrupeds, birds and fish, most of them made 'from life', but it also still contained various fantastical and monstrous creatures, indicating that the animal world had still not been freed from the symbolic and diabolic connotations that had characterized it during the Middle Ages. Gessner also referred to the legends, proverbs and symbols associated with each animal and maintained that his work could be of use and 'pleasure' not only to doctors and philosophers but also to grammarians, poets and men of learning in general.

Other texts focused attention on specific animal groups, particularly fish and birds. Examples of this genre include the *De piscibus marinis* (Lyon, 1554) by Guillaume Rondelet (1507–66) and the *Histoire de la nature des oiseaux* (Paris, 1555) by Pierre Belen, both of which are extensively illustrated with woodcuts. The latter includes the first likeness of the turkey, recently introduced from the New World. Nicolas Beatrizet made copper-engravings to illustrate the *Aquatilium animalium historia* (Rome, 1554) by the naturalist Ippolito Salviani, which contained 99 illustrations of fish and other marine species.

A figure of prime importance in the development of zoological illustration was Ulisse Aldrovandi (see ALDROVANDI, (1)), who taught at Bologna University in the late 16th century and who was convinced of the crucial importance of pictures in scientific research. He organized an artistic workshop in his home, where numerous painters and engravers, including Lorenzo Benini, Cornelio Swint and Cristoforo Coriolano (*d* after 1603), produced thousands of botanical and zoological studies. Aldrovandi also collected tempera works by the painter and miniaturist Jacopo Ligozzi, who worked for the Medici family in Florence and who was one of the most notable zoological artists.

Many accounts of travels and explorations were also illustrated with animal pictures. For example the *Historia de gentibus septentrionalibus* (Rome, 1555), published by Olao Magno, Bishop of Uppsala (1490–1557), contains woodcuts of marine organisms and sea monsters, and in his *America* (Frankfurt am Main, *c.* 1590) Theodor de Bry used pictures executed in Virginia by JOHN WHITE and watercolours painted in Florida by Jacques le Moyne de Morgues (*d* 1588).

Towards the end of the 16th century there was an increasing variety of publications illustrating animal subjects. The English naturalist Thomas Muffet (*d c.* 1600) concentrated on the insect world, illustrating his own manuscript *Theatrum insectorum* (London, 1634; New York, Amer. Mus. Nat. Hist. Lib.) with drawings of butterflies, beetles and arthropods (repr. in *The History of Four-footed Beasts and Serpents and Insects*, iii, London, 1967). The Neapolitan philosopher, naturalist and sorcerer Giovan Battista della Porta (*c.* 1535–1615) in his *De humana physiognomia* (Naples, 1586) investigated the relationship that he thought existed between human and animal physiognomy. His text is illustrated with woodcuts depicting quadrupeds, birds and fish, showing the reader how to interpret the relationship between animal and human features and so unveil deeper similarities in personality and psychology.

By the late 16th century many fine lithographs of animal subjects were also being produced, many of which became

2. Frans Snyders: *Bird Concert* (St Petersburg, Hermitage Museum)

the subject of frequent copies, replicas and variations. Some of these, together with examples taken from encyclopedic treatises, also became part of the emblematic repertory. Particularly remarkable are the hunting subjects depicted by JOANNES STRADANUS in the cartoons (1567–76) for the tapestries of the Medici Villa at Poggio a Caiano, near Florence, which were reproduced as engravings in 1578 by Phillip Galle. These were densely populated with exotic and native animals depicted in a typically Mannerist style, notably in the highly animated *Ostrich Hunt*.

The exotic nature of many of the new species naturally led to the collection by princes and nobles both of the animals themselves, in extensive menageries or as individual 'curiosities', and of depictions of animal subjects. Among the painters employed by the Holy Roman Emperor Rudolf II in Prague, for example, were Daniel Fröschl, whose ornithological pictures were highly prized, and JORIS HOEFNAGEL, who executed complex compositions of symbolically significant mammals, birds, shells and insects. The menageries of the wealthy offered important opportunities to artists and became particularly significant in the 17th century.

2. THE 17TH CENTURY. The fashion in many European cities and royal courts for menageries and aviaries filled with exotic and native species provided many 17th-century artists, particularly in the Low Countries, with subjects that they could paint from life. At Antwerp, for example, one of the earliest centres of animal painting, there was a famous den of lions, much admired at the end of the 16th century by the painter Roelandt Savery, who, on arriving at the court of the Holy Roman Emperor Rudolf II in Prague in 1603, embellished the traditional iconography of such subjects as the *Garden of Eden* (1625; priv. col.) and *Orpheus Charming the Animals* (1610; Frankfurt am Main, Städel. Kstinst. & Städt. Gal.; for illustration *see* SAVERY, (2)) with large numbers of animals. Jan Breughel I, who worked for the Archduke Albert of Austria and his wife Isabella Clara Eugenia of Spain, drew inspiration from the menagerie at Brussels for the portrayals of animals that appear in his paintings of the *Earthly Paradise* (1615, priv. col.; 1613–15, Budapest, Mus. F.A.). Rubens's studio in Antwerp was particularly important for the development of animal subjects. Rubens himself sometimes used animals as the focal point of his paintings, for example, in *Daniel in the Lions' Den* (*c*. 1615; Washington, DC, N.G.A.), where the prophet is almost made to appear of secondary importance to the nine lions surrounding him, the poses of which were perfected in numerous preparatory drawings (New York, Pierpont Morgan Lib.). FRANS SNYDERS and Paul de Vos (*see* VOS (i), (2)), both pupils of Rubens, also frequently gave pride of place to the animals in their paintings. Among the most memorable of Snyders's works are his *Three Greyhounds* (Brunswick, Herzog Anton Ulrich-Mus.) and, in particular, his *Bird Concert* (St Petersburg, Hermitage; see fig. 2), in which an owl leads a chorus of winged creatures, including a bat, a creature then still believed to be a bird. Works by de Vos include his complex portrayals of a *Stag Hunt* and *Deer Hunt* (Brussels).

Exotic animals were collected not only to adorn cages, aviaries and gardens; once dead, they were also often placed in the scientific laboratories and cabinets of famous naturalists, such as those belonging to Manfredo Settala in Milan and Olaus Worms (1588–1654) in Copenhagen. Throughout the 17th century there continued to be a close relation between the development of the natural sciences and the fine arts. Pictures documenting new discoveries became an important means of transmitting information, and scientists called on the services of painters and illustrators. For example, the naturalist Charles de L'Ecluse (1526–1609) employed Jacques de Gheyn II (*c.* 1565–1629), whose work included accurate drawings of animals. As the demand for exact observation increased, investigations began to be made into areas previously beyond the scope of the human eye and into the revelation of hitherto unknown natural phenomena. In the Accademia dei Lincei, Rome, the first scientific academy in Europe, Galileo Galilei used the microscope he had recently invented to examine tiny animals and even the structure of an insect eye (1626). In the academy's *Apiarium* (1615), the first work to show an animal and its anatomical parts as seen through a microscope, the German engraver Matthäus Greuter (*c.* 1564/6–1638) skilfully and elegantly portrayed the bee, which appeared on the coat of arms of the Barberini family, patrons of the academy. Bernini also carved the Barberini bees, on the funerary monument (1628–47) of *Urban VIII* (*see* BARBERINI, (1)) in St Peter's in Rome.

The illustrations of 17th-century books on zoological subjects were intended to fulfil varying functions: some had a predominantly scientific purpose, such as the *Historie of Fourefooted Beastes* (London, 1607) and *Historie of Serpents* (London, 1608) by the English naturalist Edward Topsell (1572–1625); the *Historiae naturales* (Frankfurt am Main, 1649–53) by Johannes Johnston (1603–75); the posthumous volumes on quadrupeds (Bologna, 1616) and fish (Bologna, 1613) by Ulisse Aldrovandi; and the treatise on the anatomy of the horse by the Bolognese Carlo Ruini (*Anatomia del cavallo*, Venice, 1602). An exceptional example of this genre is provided by the work of the German Maria Sibylla Merian (*see* MERIAN, (3)), a member of a famous family of engravers who devoted herself from childhood to the portrayal of the natural world, particularly insects, and who created the marvellous plates of the *Metamorphosis insectorum Surinamensium* (Amsterdam, 1705). Other works containing engravings were designed primarily with aesthetics in mind, such as Antonio Tempesta's *Raccolta di animali* (Rome, 1600) and the Uccelliera (Rome, 1622) of Giovanni Pietro Oliva, with illustrations by Giovanni Maggi (1566–1618) and Pietro da Cortona. The numerous albums of animal illustrations produced in northern Europe by such famous engravers as Justus Sadeler, Aegidius Sadeler II, Jan Sadeler (ii) and Crispin van de Passe I, also belong to this group. Travel accounts continued to be copiously illustrated with animal subjects, for example the *Historia naturalis Brasíliae* (Leiden and Amsterdam, 1648) by Willem Piso (1611–78) and Georg Margrav (1610–44), an account of a scientific expedition to South America organized by John Maurice, Count of Nassau Siegen. The woodcuts were taken from paintings and drawings executed on the spot by ALBERT ECKHOUT and Franz Post (*see* POST, (2)), one of which depicts the dodo.

Many artists during the 17th century tried to introduce animal subjects into still-life paintings, which were becoming increasingly popular as the taste for natural realism and detailed observation became more prevalent. Sometimes such subjects were 'posed' in conjunction with other objects in scenes depicting kitchens or markets; at other times they were portrayed in their natural environment. Among the most important examples of this genre are the paintings created for the grand dukes of Tuscany by Bartolomeo Bimbi, such as the *White Parrot* and the *Flamingo and White Vixen* (both Florence, Uffizi).

LUCIA TONGIORGI TOMASI, EDWARD J. NYGREN

3. THE 18TH CENTURY. The influence of the Dutch and Flemish artists who had dominated the treatment of animal subjects in the 17th century continued to be evident after 1700 in the work of such artists as Dirk Langendijk, AERT SCHOUMAN and Jacob van Strij. However, in the 18th century the most significant developments in the tradition took place in France and Great Britain. Throughout this period animals continued to grace many types of European paintings, including historical compositions, portraits, landscapes, genre scenes and still-lifes, but as a separate category animal subjects were considered to be imitative of nature and, therefore, of less artistic significance. They were devoted primarily to sporting scenes, military subjects, game pieces and illustrations of natural history. Eventually, however, the animal portrait, with its social and sentimental overtones, emerged as a popular sub-genre, particularly in Britain.

The history of French animal painting in the first half of the century revolves around François Desportes (*see* DESPORTES, (1)) and JEAN BAPTISTE OUDRY, painters of the chase to the French kings Louis XIV and Louis XV respectively. Their depictions of favourite animals, hunting scenes and still-lifes with game decorated royal palaces and châteaux such as Versailles and Vauré. Hunting compositions, such as Oudry's *Louis XV Hunting the Stag in the Forest of St Germain* (1730; Toulouse, Mus. Augustins), with their glorification of an élitist blood sport, tacitly acknowledged royal prerogatives at the same time as they alluded to military and social traditions.

Desportes and Oudry also created hunting scenes for use on Sèvres porcelain and in the production of Gobelins and Beauvais tapestries and upholstery. With their emphasis on violent confrontations, their compositions recall 17th-century Dutch and Flemish prototypes and share affinities with the images of their German contemporary JOHANN ELIAS RIDINGER. The tradition was continued in the second half of the century by JEAN-BAPTISTE HUET I and others. Animals also occur in the still-lifes of Jean-Siméon Chardin, the moralizing genre pieces of Jean-Baptiste Greuze and the pastoral fantasies of François Boucher, while towards the end of the century the equestrian portrait, a convention going back to antiquity, depicting the symbolic relationship between noble rider and powerful steed, was re-examined in such compositions as David's *Count Stanislas Potocki* (1781; Warsaw, N. Mus.).

In Britain animal painting enjoyed an unrivalled popularity in the 18th century. The number of painters active in this field multiplied, including such distinguished animal painters as JOHN WOOTTON, JAMES SEYMOUR and Sawrey Gilpin (*see* GILPIN, (2)), as well as Jacques-Laurent Agasse, Thomas Gainsborough, George Morland, Thomas Rowlandson and James Ward. Many sporting paintings were translated into prints for the British and continental markets, attesting to the international demand for such images. The growth of sporting art into one of the dominant forms of artistic expression reflects in part the growing interest in hunting and racing among a wide range of social classes. The early 18th-century rural attitude to sport, as healthy and virtuous, was somewhat tarnished by the excesses of the sporting world, but the subject-matter remained enormously popular. Thoroughbred racehorses, jockeys, trainers and owners, cited or implied, were recorded for posterity by Wootton, Seymour, George Stubbs and others in crisp profiles emphasizing their distinguishing traits and fine points, as in Stubbs's *Gimcrack with John Pratt up* (*c.* 1765; Cambridge, Fitzwilliam; *see also* SPORTING SCENES). Shooting scenes meanwhile hinted at existing tensions between city and country due to restrictive game laws. Towards the end of the century, portraits of breeds of cattle, sheep, pigs and poultry reflected nationalistic concerns and agricultural improvements in a period of international turmoil.

Among British animal painters of the 18th century, GEORGE STUBBS has no peer. From natural history pieces to portraits of champion or favourite animals, from sporting scenes to conversation portraits and from history paintings to violent animal combats with classical allusions, he invested traditional subject-matter with new vitality. In the theme of mares and foals, a subject he treated throughout the 1760s and 1770s, exemplified by *Mares and Foals in a River Landscape* (*c.* 1763–8; London, Tate), the rhythmic grouping of animals in pastoral settings movingly expresses the nurturing quality of gentle creatures close to man in the Great Chain of Being and essential to his happiness. Explored simultaneously, the violent theme of the *White Horse Attacked by a Lion* (1770; New Haven, CT, Yale U. A.G.) displays an interest in animal psychology and emphasizes the uncontrollable side of nature through powerful confrontations placed in a dramatic setting. Epitomizing the rational and irrational aspects of life, these two themes serve as a bridge to the artistic and philosophical concerns of the early 19th century.

4. 19TH CENTURY AND AFTER. With the gradual breakdown of the traditional hierarchy of painting in the early 19th century, artistic interest in animal subjects increased. Animals were used initially as expressions of the outer realities of life and later as symbols of the artist's inward reflections. The themes of the paintings often displayed national variations. In Britain the subjects that had dominated the 18th century still continued to appear. Some painters, such as Ben Marshall and John Ferneley, focused almost exclusively on sporting themes, depicting champion horses or favourite animals, as well as racing and hunting scenes. Others, such as JAMES WARD and Edwin Landseer, who had greater artistic ambitions (*see* LANDSEER, (4)), painted a wider range of subjects. Although the themes and compositions of the 19th century resembled those of the 18th, artists' treatment of them changed. The generalization of form favoured in the previous century gave way to particularization. Attention to detail was often combined with an intensification of colour and a vigorous application of pigment to capture an animal's specifics as well as its vitality (e.g. Ward's *Eagle*, 1809; New Haven, CT, Yale Cent. Brit. A.). New subjects appeared, such as the coaching scenes produced by James Pollard (*see* POLLARD, (2)) and anthropomorphic animal genre scenes (e.g. Landseer's the *Old Shepherd's Chief Mourner*, before 1837; London, V&A). Many artists, such as members of the Alken family, also produced watercolours of animals, either as independent compositions or as designs for prints.

Although sporting scenes were especially popular in Britain, artists in many other countries also undertook animal subjects. In the USA, for example, EDWARD TROYE painted horse portraits and racing views in the English manner. John James Audubon, the best-known American animal artist of the first part of the century, followed a visual tradition going back to the Renaissance in executing natural history illustrations of native birds and mammals, such as the *Golden Eagle* (1833; New York, NY Hist. Soc.; for illustration *see* AUDUBON, JOHN JAMES). Wilhelm von Kobell in Germany (e.g. *Hunt Scene by the Tegernsee*, 1824; Winterthur, Stift. Oskar Reinhart; for illustration *see* KOBELL (i), (2)) and THÉODORE GERICAULT in France were among European artists who gave new vigour to hunting and racing themes. In Gericault's the *Charging Chasseur* (1812; Paris, Louvre), painted at the height of the Napoleonic period, the presence of a powerful horse adds to the painting's dynamism and nationalistic fervour. Eugène Delacroix's compositions such as the *Lion Hunt* (see fig. 3), while consciously recalling the work of such 17th-century masters as Rubens, were also part of a widespread renewed interest in exoticism. By mid-century, oils and watercolours of North African or Near Eastern subjects were ubiquitous. Prominent among French artists of exotic scenes and animals were ANTOINE-LOUIS BARYE, Eugène Fromentin, Jean-Léon Gérôme and Horace Vernet. Painters from many other countries depicted similar images; they included John Frederick Lewis (*see* LEWIS (i), (1)) in England, Alberto Pasini (1826–99) in Italy and Adolf Schreyer (1828–99) in Germany. In the USA the portrayal of native life by Albert Bierstadt, George Catlin and others was a variation on this theme. Paintings glorifying the white man's conquest of the West and the defeat of the indigenous peoples were often brimming with animals; these subjects continued to be exploited in the 20th century by Charles M. Russell and Frederic Remington (for illustration *see* REMINGTON, FREDERIC).

A romantic viewpoint was fused with a realistic style in the examination of equine force by ROSA BONHEUR (e.g. the *Horse Fair*, 1853; New York, Met.) and in the pastoral visions of the Barbizon painters, particularly Constant Troyon and Charles Jacque. This development, at a time when rapid industrialization was altering the fabric of society, had parallels in other countries. In the Netherlands the artists associated with The Hague school emphasized the virtues of country life, for example in the works of Willem Maris and Anton Mauve, such as *Morning Ride on the Beach* (1876; Amsterdam, Rijksmus.; for illustration *see* MAUVE, ANTON); and compositions by Pieter van Os (1806–60) and Eugène Verboeckhoven, like those of their French counterparts, often recall Dutch and Flemish masters of the 17th century. In Munich, Anton Braith (1836–1905) and Frederick Voltz (1817–86) explored comparable pastoral subjects with a French flavour, while in Italy the MACCHIAIOLI, particularly Giuseppe Abbati

3. Eugène Delacroix: *Lion Hunt*, oil on canvas, 0.92×1.18 m, 1858 (Boston, MA, Museum of Fine Arts)

(1836–68) and Giovanni Fattori, treated similar themes in a more individualistic style. The brutally frank depictions of deer hunts by GUSTAVE COURBET, with their psychological intensity and possible symbolic significance (see Fried, p. 186), imbued traditional subjects with new content (e.g. *The Kill: Episode during a Deer Hunt in a Snowy Terrain*, 1866–7; Besançon, Mus. B.-A. & Archéol.). In the same vein was Winslow Homer's powerful *Fox Hunt* (1893; Philadelphia, PA, Acad. F.A.; *see* HOMER, WINSLOW, fig. 1), which comments ironically on a conventional theme in its depiction of a fox being hunted by crows in a snowy landscape. The symbolic or religious potential of animal imagery was tapped by such diverse artists as Albert Pinkham Ryder, Henri Rousseau and William Holman Hunt (e.g. *The Scapegoat*, 1854–5; Port Sunlight, Lady Lever A.G.; *see* HUNT, WILLIAM HOLMAN, fig. 2).

In the 1870s photography changed the presentation of animal movement as well as the attention to pictorial details. The photographic work of Edgar Degas and Thomas Eakins had a direct influence on their artistic vision. The serial images of animals and humans that Eadweard Muybridge produced with stop-action photography (for illustration *see* MUYBRIDGE, EADWEARD) affected the way in which motion was depicted; this is particularly apparent in horse-racing scenes. In the 18th and early 19th centuries such subjects had been the preserve chiefly of English artists, but Degas, Manet and Toulouse-Lautrec made it their own as, in the late 19th century, the race-course increasingly became a feature of fashionable French life. Although 20th-century artists continued to paint animal subjects, few major figures devoted themselves exclusively to the field; one exception was ALFRED MUNNINGS, who continued to depict racing themes in an impressionist style. In general, however, animals in 20th-century art are expressive of feelings rather than descriptive of the world, as in the intensely coloured compositions of Franz Marc and the dream-like fantasies of Marc Chagall. Roy Lichtenstein used the image of a bull to explore, among other things, the evolution of art history from representation to abstraction (*Bull Profile Series*, six line cuts with silkscreen and lithography, 1973; New York, MOMA), but perhaps because animals have become incidental to the modern mechanistic world, they are no longer regarded as central to artistic concerns. They tend to be used most effectively as archetypal symbols: thus the simplified equine forms of Susan Rothenberg (*b* 1945) recall prehistoric paintings (e.g. *Axes*, 1976; New York, MOMA), as they present a hazy collective memory of some forgotten primitive force.

See also SPORTING SCENES.

EDWARD J. NYGREN

BIBLIOGRAPHY
W. Gaillie-Grohman: *Sport in Art from the 15th to the 18th Centuries* (London, 1913)
J. Bouret: *The Barbizon School and 19th-century French Landscape Painting* (New York, 1972)
S. Walker: *Sporting Art: England, 1700–1900* (New York, 1972)
G. de Lastic: 'Desportes et Oudry: Peintres des chasses royales', *Connoisseur*, 196 (1977), pp. 290–99
P. S. Dance: *The Art of Natural History: Animal Illustrators and their Works* (London, 1978)
J. Egerton: *British Sporting and Animal Painting, 1655–1867* (London, 1978)
C. Nissen: *Die zoologische Bookillustration Geschichte*, 2 vols (Stuttgart, 1978)
Immagine e natura: L'immagine naturalistica nei codici e libri a stampa delle Biblioteche estense e universitaria di Modena, secoli XV–XVII (exh. cat., ed. P. Tongiorgi, L. Tongiorgi Tomasi and M. G. Tavoni; Modena, Pal. Ducale, 1984)
N. A. Finlay: *Animal Themes in the Painting of Eugène Delacroix* (diss., Princeton U., NJ, 1984)
The Orientalists: Delacroix to Matisse (exh. cat., ed. M. Stevens; London, RA, 1984)
N. Bronde: *The Macchiaioli: Italian Painters of the 19th Century* (New Haven and London, 1987)
S. Deuchar: *Sporting Art in 18th-century England* (London and New Haven, 1988)
M. Fried: *Courbet's Realism* (Chicago and London, 1990)
A. Potts: 'Natural Order and the Call of the Wild', *Oxford A. J.*, xiii (1990), pp. 12–33
LUCIA TONGIORGI TOMASI, EDWARD J. NYGREN

Anisfel'd, Boris (Izrailevich) (*b* Beltsy, Bessarabia [now in Moldova], 14 Oct 1879; *d* Waterford, CT, 4 Dec 1973). Russian painter and stage designer. He was a Symbolist artist who, like many of his colleagues in the World of Art group, made his foremost contribution to the development of Russian art in the fields of graphic art and stage design. He first studied at the Drawing School of the Odessa Society of Fine Arts (1895–1900) and then at the St Petersburg Academy of Arts (1901–9), where his tutors included Dmitry Kardovsky and Il'ya Repin. His participation in exhibitions included the World of Art (St Petersburg and Moscow, 1906–18), the Union of Russian Artists (Moscow and St Petersburg, 1906–10), the Salon d'Automne (Paris, 1906), Wreath (St Petersburg, 1908) and the Izdebsky International Salon (Kiev and Odessa, 1909–10). His painting attracted considerable critical acclaim for its exotic themes and colouring. Simultaneously, he worked as a caricaturist, creating grotesque and fantastic images for satirical magazines as well as executing wall paintings for houses in St Petersburg. His prolific career as a stage designer began in February 1907 when he designed the sets and costumes for Vsevolod Meyerhold's production of Hugo von Hofmannsthal's *Die Hochzeit der Sobeide* at the Kommissarzhevskaya Theatre in St Petersburg (designs now Moscow, Bakhrushin Cent. Theat. Mus.). These were marked by an atmospheric, psychological rendering of form, rather than attention to visual accuracy and detail. He subsequently collaborated on Serge Diaghilev's productions of *Boris Godunov* (1908) and *Sadko* (1911) with the Ballets Russes, as well as Fokine's *Islamei* (St Petersburg, 1912) and *Une Nuit d'Egypte* (Stockholm, 1913), where his designs formed an integral part of the producers' synthesist conceptions. Anisfel'd emigrated to the USA in 1918 and there continued to work in theatre, most notably at the Metropolitan Opera, New York, and with the Chicago Opera Company, as well as being professor of Advanced Drawing and Painting at the Chicago Art Institute from 1928.

BIBLIOGRAPHY
Boris Anisfeld, 1879–1973 (exh. cat., Chicago Gilman Gals, 1981–2)
J. E. Bowlt: *Russian Stage Design: Scenic Innovation, 1900–1930—From the Collection of Mr and Mrs Nikita D. Lobanov-Rostovsky* (Jackson, MS, 1982), pp. 54–60
JEREMY HOWARD

Anjar [Andjar, ʿAnjar, ʿAyn al-Jarr]. Late Antique and early Islamic settlement in the Beqaʿa Valley of Lebanon, 56 km east of Beirut. Excavations since 1953 have revealed a cardinally orientated rectangular enclosure (370×310 m) with dressed stone walls. Each side has regularly spaced half-round towers and a central gate. Two colonnaded avenues intersecting at right angles under a tetrapylon link the gates, a plan recalling that of Roman foundations in the Levant and in north Africa. Within the enclosure are the remains of two palaces and the foundations of three others in stone and hard mortar, as well as a mosque, two baths (one paved with mosaics) and a well. The western area has streets intersecting at right angles and housing units with private courts, and the eastern area has open fields beyond the palaces and mosque. The construction of the greater palace in alternating courses of stone and brick is a technique well known in Byzantine architecture. Reused architectural elements from the Roman and early Christian periods, some bearing Greek inscriptions, are found all over the site. A large quantity of archivolts and mouldings, carved with vegetal, geometrical and figural motifs, was found among the ruined palaces. Texts suggest that Anjar was founded in the time of the Umayyad caliph al-Walid (*reg* AD 705–15), but archaeological evidence points to an earlier date and a continuous occupation until the 14th century.

BIBLIOGRAPHY
J. Sauvaget: 'Les Ruines omeyyades de Anjarr', *Bull. Mus. Beyrouth*, iii (1939), pp. 5–11
M. Chehab: 'The Umayyad Palace at Anjar', *A. Orient.*, v (1963), pp. 17–25
S. Ory: 'Les Graffitis umayyades de Ayn al-Ğarr', *Bull. Mus. Beyrouth*, xx (1967), pp. 97–148
K. A. C. Creswell: *Early Muslim Architecture*, i (Oxford, 1969), pp. 478–81
H. K. Chehab: 'On the Identification of 'Anjar ('Ayn al-Jarr) as an Umayyad Foundation', *Muqarnas*, x (1993), pp. 49–56
HAFEZ K. CHEHAB

Anjou, House of. French dynasty of rulers, patrons and collectors. The first House of Anjou (*see* §I below) was founded by Charles of Anjou (1266–85) and was active mainly in Italy, notably as kings of Naples and Jerusalem. Members of the second House of Anjou (*see* §II below) lost Naples to the house of ARAGON but continued to style themselves as kings of Naples, Sicily and Jerusalem until the death of Charles, 5th Duke of Anjou, in 1481, when the titular kingdom passed to Louis XI, King of France.

I. First House.

In 1266 Charles of Anjou (1226–85), brother of Louis IX, King of France (*see* CAPET, (2)), defeated Manfred, King of Naples and Sicily (*reg* 1258–66), of the Hohenstaufen dynasty and established the Angevin dynasty in the kingdom of Naples. Charles I, as he became, also ruled in Sicily until 1282, when a rising against him led to the election of Peter of Aragon as king. In 1276–7 Charles also purchased a claim to the kingdom of Jerusalem, which was maintained by his successors. His son and successor (1) Charles II, King of Naples and Jerusalem, who, at his accession in 1285, was a prisoner of the Aragonese in Spain, established Naples as an important cultural centre through his extensive building campaigns in the city. These were continued by his son (2) Robert, King of Naples and Jerusalem, who also employed Giotto to decorate the Great Hall of the Castelnuovo in Naples.

Through the claims of Charles Martel (1271–95), Charles II's son, members of the first House of Anjou also ruled in Hungary. The patronage of Charles Martel's grandson (3) Louis, King of Hungary and Poland, largely consisted of donations of gold- and silversmiths' work and extensions to his various residences. His brother Andrew (*d* 1345) was married to Joanna I, Queen of Naples (*reg* 1343–82), who had succeeded her grandfather King Robert. Joanna adopted Louis I, 1st Duke of Anjou (*see* §II, (1) below), as her heir, but after protracted disputes the kingdom of Naples was conquered by the House of ARAGON in 1435.

(1) Charles II [Charles the Lame], King of Naples and Jerusalem [Count of Anjou and Provence] (*b* 1254; *reg* 1285–1309; *d* Naples, 5 May 1309). He was the son and successor of Charles I (*reg* 1266–85), the founder of the Angevin dynasty in the kingdom of Naples, and Beatrice of Provence. At his accession Charles was a prisoner of the Aragonese in Spain. Granted his liberty in 1288, he was crowned in Rieti in 1289. In 1270 he married Mary of Hungary (*d* 1323); their children included Charles Martel, titular King of Hungary (1271–95); the Franciscan Bishop of Toulouse, St Louis (*d* 1298; *can* 1317); and (2) Robert, who succeeded Charles in 1309.

From the outset it had been the policy of the House of Anjou to establish Naples as a great cultural and artistic centre. Charles II contributed to the advancement of these goals through his endowments to the University of Naples, the enhancement of the royal library through the acquisition and copying of fine manuscripts, and the ambitious building campaigns undertaken during his reign. Following the example set by his father, the King engaged artists, scribes and craftsmen from northern Italy and Europe to create works of art for the court; unlike his predecessor, he also employed Neapolitan masters.

Major civic projects that he initiated in Naples included the enlargement of the city walls and the expansion of the port and arsenals. A man of deep religious conviction, Charles also sponsored numerous ecclesiastical foundations. When construction was resumed on S Lorenzo Maggiore in the early 14th century, the Franciscan basilica begun by Charles I, the King broke with the precedent of importing architects from France and engaged Italian masters for its completion (*see* NAPLES, §IV, 2). As a benefactor of the Dominican Order, he erected the monastery of S Pietro a Castello and the churches and convents of S Pietro Martire and S Domenico Maggiore. Built in the Gothic style between 1289 and 1324, the last served as the headquarters for the Order in the Kingdom of Naples and became an important centre for the study of theology. In 1294 Charles II began the reconstruction of Naples Cathedral, an enterprise that lasted almost three decades. To honour St Gennaro, the titular saint, the King ordered a silver reliquary bust (chapel of St Gennaro). Three French goldsmiths, Stefano Godefroy (*fl* 1297–1312), Guglielmo di Verdelay (*fl* 1297-1309) and Milet d'Auxerre (*fl* 1297–1332), were charged with the execution of the bust, which was completed in 1306.

It was through the generosity of Mary of Hungary, Charles's consort, that the Franciscan church of S Maria Donnaregina was rebuilt. Completed in 1320, it was enriched with monuments of exceptional historic and artistic merit, including the beautiful marble tomb of *Queen Mary*, which was executed by the Sienese sculptor TINO DI CAMAINO in collaboration with the Neapolitan architect Gagliardo Primario (*d* 1348). The Roman painter PIETRO CAVALLINI, documented in Naples from 1308, contributed to the fresco decoration of the church. The Roman school of Cavallini, with the Sienese and Florentine schools, constitute the three major stylistic currents present in Neapolitan art during the first half of the 14th century. The patronage of Charles II and his successors gave this eclectic art its distinctive courtly character.

BIBLIOGRAPHY

DBI

F. Bologna: *I pittori alla corte angioina di Napoli, 1266–1414, e un riesame dell'arte nell'età fridericiana* (Rome, 1969) [bibliog.]

A. Lipinsky: 'Un reliquario napoletano del periodo angioina', *Napoli Nob.*, 3rd ser., xv/1 (1976)

B. B. Johannsen: 'Zum Thema der weltlichen Glorifikation des Herrscher und Gelehrtengrabmals des Trecentos', *Hafnia*, vi (1979), pp. 81–105

A. P. Saggesse: *I romanzi cavallereschi miniati a Napoli* (Naples, 1979)

S. Savarese: 'Il portale trecentesco della chiesa di S Domenico Maggiore in Napoli', *Scritti in onore di Ottavio Morisani* (Catania, 1982), pp. 131–45

P. L. De Castris: *Arte di corte nella Napoli angioina* (Florence, 1986) [full bibliog.]

A. Porzio: *Arte sacra di palazzo: La Cappella Reale di Napoli e i suoi arredi: Un patrimonio di arti decorative* (Naples, 1989)

(2) Robert [Robert the Wise], King of Naples and Jerusalem [Count of Provence] (*b* Naples, ?1278; *reg* 1309–43; *d* Naples, 19 Jan 1343). Son of (1) Charles II, King of Naples and Sicily, and Mary of Hungary. Archival records and extant monuments testify to the splendour of life in Naples during Robert's reign. In promoting the cultural aggrandizement of the Angevin capital, he invited many notable figures to his court, including the poets Petrarch and Boccaccio. The King lavished special care on the embellishment of the royal library and scriptorium. Inventories of the collection reveal not only the influence of the eminent scholars who frequented Naples but also the breadth and discernment of the monarch's interests, thus supporting the statement by the Florentine chronicler Giovanni Villani, who described him as 'a most wise king . . . [skilled] in Theology and Philosophy' (*Cronica*, ed. F. Gherardi Dragomanni, 4 vols, Florence, 1844–5, xii, 10, pp. 23–4). Robert himself contributed to the royal library; his predilection for composing sermons led Dante, in the *Divine Comedy*, to refer to him disparagingly as 'a king. . .fit for sermons' (*Paradise*, viii, 147).

During Robert's reign Naples became a haven for the dissident Spiritual Franciscans, whom the King defended against the condemnation of Pope John XXII. The church and convent of S Chiara was built for the Franciscans through the munificence of Robert's second wife, Sancia of Mallorca (*m.* 1304). Construction of the church was begun in 1310 and completed in 1328; the architecture, which combined Provençal and Gothic elements, has been attributed to a Neapolitan, Gagliardo Primario (*d* 1348). S Chiara became the necropolis of the royal family and contains the imposing tomb of *King Robert* designed by the Florentine sculptors Giovanni Bertini and Pacio Bertini between 1343 and 1345. Severely bomb damaged in 1943, the church has been restored, but many of its monuments were destroyed, including the tomb of *Charles of Calabria* (*d* 1328) by the Sienese master Tino di Camaino.

Monumental art and manuscript illumination in Naples in the 14th century was under the patronage of the House of Anjou and demonstrates a distinctly courtly character. Not only the style but also the subject-matter was determined by the ruling dynasty. The Malines Bible (*c.* 1340; Mechelen, Grand Sémin., Bib., MS. 1), illuminated by the Neapolitan artist CRISTOFORO ORIMINA, contains full-page frontispieces depicting the *Glorification of Robert of Anjou* (fol. 1*v*) and the *Genealogy of the Anjou of Naples* (fol. 2*r*). Two Neapolitan panel paintings with scenes from the *Apocalypse* (*c.* 1330–40; Stuttgart, Staatsgal.) are representative of works with iconography reflecting the profound religious preoccupations of Robert and Sancia. Of the numerous versions that derive from these panels, the most faithful reproductions occur in the Hamilton Bible (Berlin, Kupferstichkab., MS. 78.E.3), executed during the reign of Robert's successor Joanna I (*reg* 1343–81).

Three different schools contributed to the embellishment of Naples and its surroundings during Robert's reign. The Roman painter PIETRO CAVALLINI had been summoned to the capital by Charles II in 1308. The Sienese master Simone Martini was active there in 1317. At the invitation of the King, GIOTTO decorated the walls of the Palatine Chapel and the Great Hall of the Castelnuovo between 1328 and 1333 (destr.). A fresco fragment in the window embrasure of the chapel has been attributed on stylistic grounds to Giotto's disciple Maso di Banco. The influence of these masters left its mark on the artistic community in Naples, with the result that Roman, Sienese and Florentine characteristics merged with those from northern France and Avignon to produce an essentially eclectic style (*see* NAPLES, §II, 1). While Neapolitan artists were patronized by the court in increasing numbers, the policy of attracting foreign talent was maintained throughout the 14th century. It was Sienese art, however, with its expressive qualities and decorative richness, that found most favour with the House of Anjou in Naples.

BIBLIOGRAPHY

A. Schmitt: 'Die Apokalypse des Robert von Anjou', *Pantheon*, vi (1970), pp. 475–503

J. Gardner: 'Saint Louis of Toulouse, Robert of Anjou, and Simone Martini', *Z. Kstgesch.*, xxxix/1 (1976), pp. 12–33

B. Degenhart and A. Schmitt: 'Frühe angiovinische Buchkunst in Neapel: Die Illustrierung französischer Unterhaltungsprosa in neapolitanische Scriptorien zwischen 1290 und 1320', *Festschrift Wolfgang Braunfels* (Tübingen, 1977), pp. 71–92

O. Pujmanova: 'Robert of Anjou's Unknown Tabernacle in Brno', *Burl. Mag.*, cxxi (1979), pp. 483–91

A. P. Saggesse: *I romanzi cavallereschi miniati a Napoli* (Naples, 1979)

F. Avril: 'Un Atelier "picard" à la cour angevine de Naples', *Nobile claret opus: Festgabe für Ellen Judith Beer* (Zurich, 1980); also in *Z. Schweiz. Archäol. & Kstgesch.*, xliii/1 (1986), pp. 76–85

For further bibliography *see* ORIMINA, CRISTOFORO and ANJOU (i), (1).

JOAN ISOBEL FRIEDMAN

(3) Louis [Louis of Anjou; Louis the Great], King of Hungary and Poland (*b* 1326; *reg* Hungary 1342–82, Poland 1370–82; *d* 10 Sept 1382). Great-grandson of (1) Charles II. He was the son of Charles Robert I, King of Hungary (*reg* 1308–42) and Elisabeth Piast (*c.* 1305–80). He continued his father's policy of attempting to secure the succession of his younger brother Andrew, Duke of Calabria (1327–45), who was married to Joanna I, Queen of Naples (*reg* 1343–82), to the throne of Naples. To avenge Andrew's murder he led two military expeditions to Naples; in 1347–8 and in 1350. His first wife, whom he married in 1345, was Margaret of Luxembourg (1335–49), the daughter of the later Emperor Charles IV. In 1353 he married Elisabeth (*d* 1387), daughter of Stephen Kotromanić, Ban of Bosnia (*reg* 1322–53). In 1367 he founded a university at Pécs. He inherited the Polish throne on the death of Kasimir III in 1370 and three years later betrothed his daughter Maria (1370–95) to Sigismund of Luxembourg, the son of Emperor Charles IV. Louis's two royal seals show him sitting in state, an image also found on silver groats minted before 1370.

Of the books copied in his court, the best known is the manuscript referred to as the Illustrated Chronicle (Chronica Hungarorum; Budapest, N. Szechényi Lib., Cod. Lat. 404), copied in 1358, which depicts the King and his court in the frontispiece. The miniatures portray events from Hungarian history and rulers and ancestors of aristocratic clans up to the time of Charles Robert I. The main illuminator of this work, although almost certainly active in the Hungarian court and familiar with miniature painting as practised in Charles IV's court in Prague, worked in a Neapolitan style. Another product of the same workshop is the Secretum Secretorum (Oxford, Bodleian Lib., MS. Hertford College 2), a pseudo-Aristotle, which also contains a portrait of *Louis* on its frontispiece (fol. 1*r*).

Gold- and silversmiths' work from Louis's court is known primarily from gifts to institutions abroad. In most cases the donor was the King, although many objects are also connected with his mother, Elisabeth, the Queen Dowager. *Paramenta* (sacred implements) and other objects came to European great churches, such as St Peter's, Rome (in 1343), the Franciscan church in Marseille, S Nicola in Bari, the Stephansdom in Vienna and the cathedrals of Prague and Kraków. The donations served to propagate the cult of the Hungarian saints. The most significant group of donations, including candelabra, monstrances and votive icons with gold frames, went to the Hungarian chapel founded in 1367 (rebuilt 1756–67) next to Aachen Cathedral. These were supplemented in 1381 with two composite cloak-brooches adorned with the King's arms (Aachen, Domschatzkam.). In 1363 the pilgrimage church of Mariazell received a votive icon of the *Schatzkammerbild* (treasury picture) type, similar to those given to Aachen, and the jewels from a comparable picture (known as the 'crown-cross') have survived in the treasury of Kraków Cathedral. In court circles silver votive crowns on a standard model were produced in series;

several copies have survived, notably the crown (Budapest, N. Mus.) from Nagyvárad (now Oradea, Romania), which was originally donated for the head-reliquary of St Laszlo but later used in 1437 as the burial crown of King Sigismund. Another was attached to a mitre from the Serbian monastery of Krušedol (now Belgrade, Mus. Serb. Orthdx Ch.); a further crown was incorporated in the reliquary of St Simeon in the church dedicated to him in Zadar. A golden belt-buckle (Bucharest, Mus. A.) found in Curtea de Argeş, Romania, in the tomb of either Vladislav I (*reg* 1364–*c.* 1377) or Radu I Negru (*reg c.* 1377–*c.* 1383), is closely related in style to the cloak-brooches donated to the chapel at Aachen. In addition to these standardized products of the court jewellers there survive Louis the Great's reliquary in the form of a double cross (Vienna, Schatzkam.) and a chalice of silver and chased enamel, adorned with armorial bearings (Zadar, St Simeon). According to an extant contract of between 1377 and 1380 the jeweller Francesco da Milano (*fl* 1377–88) prepared the silver mask of St Simeon originally intended for the church of the Virgin in Zára (since 1632 St Simeon, Zadar) on commission from Queen Elisabeth, Louis's wife.

Louis's grandest buildings are all extensions of his various residences. VISEGRÁD Palace acquired its inner courtyards and terraces and was further embellished with ornamental fountains. After 1342 he had castles built in Zólyom and Diósgyőr to a regular, square plan. The southern part of the castle at Buda, where the court was held regularly from 1347, was built under Louis, who also established several monastic foundations. He provided donations for building the pilgrimage church at Mariazell, made, according to local tradition, after his victory over the Turks in 1377, which is represented in a votive relief from St Lambrecht Abbey (now Graz, Steiermärk. Landesmus.) and in the tympanum (1420s) of the west portal of the pilgrimage church at Mariazell. Louis had built a family burial chapel (destr. 1601) at Székesfehérvár to house the remains of his father. Apart from a few architectural fragments, some pieces of a red marble tombslab have survived (Székesfehérvár, Gdn Ruins), bearing two figures representing Louis and (probably) Princess Catherine (*d* 1374).

BIBLIOGRAPHY

D. Dercsényi: *Nagy Lajos kora* [The age of Louis the Great] (Budapest, 1941)

D. Dercsényi, ed.: *Képes Krónika* [Illustrated Chronicle] (Budapest, 1964) [facsimile edn]

L. Gerevich: *The Art of Buda and Pest in the Middle Ages* (Budapest, 1971)

Művészet I. Lajos király korában, 1342–1382 [Art in the age of King Louis I, 1342–1382] (exh. cat., ed. E. Marosi, M. Tóth and L. Varga; Székesfehérvár, István Király Mus., 1982)

ERNŐ MAROSÍ

II. Second House.

(1) Louis I, Count and later 1st Duke of Anjou, was the second son of John II, King of France (*see* VALOIS, (1)). His lavish patronage of French goldsmiths' work is recorded in two important surviving inventories of his possessions. His main interest in the field of architecture was the reconstruction of the castle of Saumur; this was continued by his son, (2) Louis II, 2nd Duke of Anjou. With his wife, (3) Yolande of Aragon, Louis II commissioned numerous manuscripts. Their second son, (4) René I, 4th Duke of Anjou, inherited the title after the death of his elder brother, Louis III, in 1434. He also received other titles through marriage and diplomacy, and briefly ruled in Naples (1438–42). His travels throughout Europe, due to territorial disputes, brought him into contact with artistic developments in the Netherlands and Italy, and, after he settled in Provence in 1471, his patronage of Italian artists led to the introduction of early Renaissance forms into this region. He also employed many notable French and south Netherlandish painters and illuminators. The patronage of one of the last rulers of the second House of Anjou, (5) René II, Duke of Lorraine, grandson of René I, was largely directed towards commemorating his victory over Charles the Bold, Duke of Burgundy, in 1477. (For information on the patronage and collecting of the descendants of René II *see* LORRAINE, House of.) After the death of René II's successor, Charles, Duke of Anjou (*d* 1481), the duchy of Anjou reverted to the French Crown.

(1) Louis I, 1st Duke of Anjou [Count of Provence; Titular King of Naples, Sicily and Jerusalem] (*b* Vincennes, 23 July 1339; *d* Biseglia, nr Bari, 20 Sept 1384). He was the second son of John II, King of France. He became Count of Anjou in 1356 and Duke from 1360; he was Count of Provence from 1382. Louis owned several residences in Paris, including the Hôtel d'Anjou; his three principal properties outside Paris were the castles of Saumur (largely destr.), Maine and Le Mans. Between 1360 and 1380 he undertook the reconstruction of Saumur; its appearance is preserved in the *September* miniature of the Très Riches Heures of Jean, Duc de Berry (Chantilly, Mus. Condé, MS. 65, fol. 9*v*). Much is known of the building history and the craftsmen employed there from the accounts (1 March 1367–1 Nov 1377; London, BL) kept by the Duke's Master of the Works, Macé Darne. In 1369 work began on the reconstruction of the north-east wing, and private apartments, a chapel, an oratory and a monumental staircase were built. Work was simultaneously carried out at the castles of Angers and Le Mans, although on a smaller scale than at Saumur.

Louis was a lavish patron and collector with a particular passion for goldsmiths' work, as is clear from the two surviving inventories of his possessions, which also record his ownership of the earliest significant collection of 14th-century royal plate. The first inventory (1365–8; Paris, Bib. N., MS. fr. 11861) lists almost 800 items. It also records 76 tapestries with chivalric, courtly, Classical and biblical scenes. Two of the tapestries (destr.), probably purchased by Louis in 1363, depicted scenes from the *Story of Troy*; they are the earliest known tapestries with this subject-matter. Accounts preserved for the years 1375–9 for the Hôtel d'Anjou show that Louis purchased about 20 tapestries during those years. The second inventory (1379–80; Paris, Bib. N., MS. nouv. acq. fr. 6338) lists approximately 3600 items, including around 380 ecclesiastical objects from Louis's chapel. The Duke was closely involved in compiling the inventories, dictating the descriptions to his secretary and even adding records of several items in his own hand. The meticulous descriptions are an invaluable document for understanding the techniques and terminology of 14th-century metalwork. Virtually nothing remains of the outstanding collection, which was either sold or destroyed to support Louis's military campaigns. Two gold mirror-cases (see fig.), decorated with *basse taille* enamel, are probably those listed as no. 3577 in the second inventory. The *Libretto* (Florence, Mus. Opera Duomo), a reliquary in the form of a small book, was given to Louis by his brother Charles V, King of France, and is described in the first inventory as formerly being in the treasury of Piero I de' Medici. A pair of kneeling donors on an enamel plaque attached to the reliquary is believed to represent Louis and his wife (Gaborit-Chopin, 1985). Among the exquisitely wrought objects described in the inventories is a gold goblet decorated with depictions of Louis, his wife and retinue against a floral background. Some of the secular objects had decoration with well-known themes, including the Labours of the Months, chivalric romances, Classical figures, hunting scenes and fantastic beasts. There were vessels in the form of a griffin, a monkey, a fox and a peacock, as well as a magnificent silver-gilt and enamel nef. Louis also possessed a cup with the arms of France, Navarre and Champagne, originally made for Philip IV, King of France. The cup is the earliest recorded example of the rare *plique à jour* enamel technique. The ducal accounts surviving for the years 1375–9 also record payments to a number of goldsmiths, including Simon de Dammartin, Pierre de Pons, Jehan Jolis, Laurencin Malequin and Claux de Fribourg. The latter received payment on 23 July 1377 for making a gold cross for Louis and on 28 July payment for a gold and gemstone circlet for the Duchess. Before 1375 Louis employed the goldsmith Henry Ambert at 100 francs per annum as the head of a small workshop, and during 1376–7 Ambert resided at Angers, where Louis had built a forge to assist him with his work. Ghiberti, in his *Commentaries*, relates how Gusmin of Cologne, a goldsmith, worked for the Duke and made him a 'tavolo d'oro', a gold altar; 'une très grande table d'autel d'or', possibly an antependium, is listed among the Duke's possessions. In 1376 Louis commissioned a series of tapestries (Angers, Château, Col. Tap.; *see* ANGERS, §3 and fig. 4) depicting scenes from the *Apocalypse* for his castle at Angers. The Netherlandish painter and manuscript illuminator Jan Boudolf produced designs, and the weaving was organized by the Parisian tapestry-maker Nicolas Bataille. During 1377–9 Louis had mounts made for a double-armed reliquary cross, the Croix d'Anjou or Cross of Lorraine (Baugé, Chapelle des Filles du Coeur de Marie). He also founded the Order of the True Cross during this period.

In the 1370s Louis commissioned an illustrated copy (Heidelberg, Ubib., Cod. Pal. Lat. 1969) of the allegorical poem *Le Pèlerinage de vie humaine*, written *c.* 1330–32 by Guillaume de Déguileville. Moreover, he had in his library a French Apocalypse manuscript borrowed from Charles V as a source for the designs of his tapestries. Also in his collection was a fine mid-14th-century illuminated manuscript of the *Statutes of the Order of Saint-Esprit* (Paris, Bib. N., MS. fr. 4274). After Charles's death (1380), Louis became effective head of state, with the power to acquire whatever volumes he desired. Although not a collector of books on the scale of his brother, in 1380–81 Louis acquired 40 books from Charles's library in the Louvre, including two Bibles, two Breviaries, two Books of Hours and a number of translations of such Classical authors as Aristotle, Seneca, Ovid and Valerius Maximus.

Louis was crowned titular King of Sicily and Jerusalem at Avignon on 30 May 1382 and in June of that year he left Provence with his army for Naples. In his last will (26 Sept 1383) he made a series of foundations and donations to the principal churches in France. He founded a chapel

Two mirror-cases of Louis I, Duke of Anjou, depicting (left) the *Virgin and Child with SS Catherine and John the Baptist*, (right) *God the Father with St John the Baptist and Charlemagne*, gold and *basse taille* enamel, diam. 68 mm (each), Paris, before 1379 (Paris, Musée du Louvre)

at the Cistercian convent of La Boissière and left provision for the foundation of a Charterhouse near Capoue. Louis died during his unsuccessful campaigns to conquer the kingdoms of Adria and Naples. His body was carried back to France and he was buried in Angers Cathedral.

BIBLIOGRAPHY

G. Ledos: 'Fragment de l'inventaire des joyaux de Louis I, duc d'Anjou', *Bib. Ecole Chartes*, i (1889), pp. 168–79

H. Moranvillé: *Inventaire de l'orfèvrerie et des joyaux de Louis I, duc d'Anjou* (Paris, 1903–6)

Les Fastes du gothique: Le Siècle de Charles V (exh. cat., Paris, Grand Pal., 1981), pp. 260–62, cat. nos 211–12, 300

R. Bergmann: *Die Pilgerfahrt zum himmlischen Jerusalem: Ein allegorisches Gedicht des Spätmittelalters aus der Heidelberger Bilderhandschrift Cod. Pal. Lat. 1969. 'Pèlerinage de vie humaine' de Guillaume de Déguileville* (Wiesbaden, 1983)

F. Robin: 'Art, luxe et culture: L'Orfèvrerie et ses décors à la cour d'Anjou, 1378–1380', *Bull. Mnmtl*, cxli/1 (1983), pp. 337–74

——: 'L'Orfèvrerie, art de cour: Formes et techniques d'après l'inventaire de Louis I d'Anjou', *Gaz. B.-A.*, xii (1983), pp. 60–74

——: 'Le Tabernacle d'or de l'inventaire de Louis I d'Anjou (vers 1378–1379)', *Gaz. B.-A.*, civ (1984), pp. 147–52

D. Gaborit-Chopin: 'La "Croix d'Anjou"', *Cah. Archéol.*, xxxiii (1985), pp. 156–78

F. Robin: 'Louis d'Anjou et le rayonnement de l'art parisien, 1360–1380', *J. Med. Hist.*, xii/1 (1986), pp. 55–80

□

(2) Louis II, Duke of Anjou [Count of Provence and Maine; Titular King of Naples, Sicily and Jerusalem] (*b* Toulouse, 7 Oct 1377; *d* Angers, 29 April 1417). Son of (1) Louis I. At the death of his father in 1384 he became Duke of Anjou and Count of Provence and Maine and in 1389 Titular King of Naples. He continued the construction of the castle of Saumur, for which he employed the royal architect Guy de Dammartin. In 1400 Louis married (3) Yolande of Aragon and in the same year ordered the rebuilding of the castle of Tarascon at an expense of over 33,388 florins. Through the merchant and banker Michel de' Pazzi he commissioned for his Paris residence white satin fittings embroidered with aviary scenes for one hall, and red ones for another. In Pierre de Beauveau's *Roman de Troyle et Criseida*, Louis is mentioned as having a collection of 'romans' secured in an isolated room at the château of Angers, where the titular king had ordered the construction (1405–12) of the still extant chapel dedicated to Ste Geneviève and apartments referred to as 'logis royaux'. Extant books expressly made for him include a copy of Boethius's *De consolatione* (Paris, Bib. N., MS. lat. 11856), a *Livre du trésor de vénerie* (Paris, Bib. N., MS. fr. 855) and a translation made for him by Eude Richart of Pietro da Eboli's *De balneis puteolanis* (Paris, Bib. N., MS. fr. 1313). In 1407 Louis II gave his uncle Jean, Duc de Berry, the Book of Hours in which John II, King of France, had learnt to read. Louis founded the university of Aix-en-Provence in 1409. A large watercolour profile bust of *Louis II* (Paris, Bib. N., Cab. Est.) is possibly by the Master of the Rohan Hours and datable to *c.* 1417.

BIBLIOGRAPHY

A. Lecoy de La Marche: *Extraits des comptes et mémoriaux du roi René pour servir à l'histoire des arts au XVe siècle* (Paris, 1873)

A. Coville: *La Vie intellectuelle dans les domaines d'Anjou–Provence de 1380 à 1435* (Paris, 1941)

J. Porcher: 'Le Portrait de Louis II d'Anjou', *A. France*, i (1961), pp. 290–92

S. Pressouyre: 'Le Château de Tarascon', *Congrès archéologique de France, CXXIe session: Avignon and Comtat-Venaissin, 1963*, pp. 221–43

H. Enguehard: 'Le Château d'Angers', *Congrès archéologique de France, CXXIIe session: Anjou, 1964*, pp. 9–21

(3) Yolande of Aragon (*b* Spain, 1380; *d* Angers, 1442). Wife of (2) Louis II. The daughter of John I, King of Aragon (*reg* 1387–95), and Yolande of Bar (*d* 1431), she married Louis in 1400. She was recognized by contemporaries for her intelligence and political acumen and as a protectress of the future king, Charles VII, who married her daughter Marie in 1422. Yolande's patronage was limited by the draining of family resources after the reconquest of the throne of Naples. Between 1400 and 1410 she ordered the building of the chapel of St John the Baptist at the castle at Angers. She may have been responsible for commissioning stained-glass windows (*c.* 1430–40) depicting members of the Anjou family, including herself, in Le Mans Cathedral. After the death of Jean, Duc de Berry (1416), she purchased his Belles Heures (New York, Cloisters; *see* LIMBOURG, DE, fig. 3). Around 1417 she engaged the MASTER OF THE ROHAN HOURS (*see* MASTERS, ANONYMOUS, AND MONOGRAMMISTS, §I) to be in her exclusive service. She made available to him the Belles Heures and a *Bible moralisée* (Paris, Bib. N., MS. fr. 9561), which her husband commissioned in Naples, as sources for the decoration of four manuscripts that the artist and his workshop produced for the family: the Hours of Isabella Stuart (Cambridge, Fitzwilliam, MS. 62), probably for her daughter Yolande (1412–40); the Grandes Heures de Rohan (Paris, Bib. N., MS. lat. 9471), a gift for either her son-in-law Charles VII or her son Louis III (*reg* 1417–34); the Hours of René of Anjou (Paris, Bib. N., MS lat. 1156A), begun for either Louis II or Louis III and containing the arms of René I; and a Book of Hours for the use of Angers (ex-col. Martin Le Roy; priv. col.).

BIBLIOGRAPHY

A. Lecoy de La Marche: *Le Roi René: Sa Vie, son administration, ses travaux artistiques et littéraires, d'après les documents inédits des archives de France et d'Italie*, 2 vols (Paris, 1875)

J. Porcher: 'Le Maître de Rohan: Un Grand Peintre français du XVe siècle', *Jard. A.*, 15 (1956), pp. 151–61

M. Meiss with S. O. Smith and E. Beatson: *French Painting in the Time of Jean de Berry: The Limbourgs and their Contemporaries*, 2 vols (New York and London, 1974)

PATRICK M. DE WINTER

(4) René I, 4th Duke of Anjou [Duke of Lorraine; Titular King of Naples and Sicily, Hungary and Jerusalem] (*b* Angers, 19 Jan 1409; *d* Aix-en-Provence, 10 July 1480). Son of (2) Louis II and (3) Yolande of Aragon. He was also the brother-in-law of Charles VII, King of France, and father-in-law of the English king Henry VI. As a second son René had few expectations but acquired prestigious titles through his mother's diplomatic skills (Duke of Bar, 1430), his marriage to Isabelle of Lorraine (*d* 1453) in 1420 (Duke of Lorraine, 1431) and the death of his elder brother Louis III in 1434 (Duke of Anjou and Count of Provence, 1434; Titular King of Naples and Sicily, Hungary and Jerusalem, 1435). The lands attached to the titles, however, proved either difficult to keep or unobtainable. René was twice made prisoner of Philip the Good, Duke of Burgundy, during his eventually successful struggles for Bar and Lorraine (1431–2, 1435–7), and he made repeated attempts to claim his favourite kingdom of Sicily and Jerusalem from Alfonso V, King of Aragon, but he managed to retain control of Naples for only four years (1438–42).

Much of René's personality as a patron was formed by the pattern of his inheritance. The plurality and variety of his domains, from western and eastern France to southern Italy, made him lead a peripatetic life and conditioned the types of buildings and objects he commissioned, although the frequent territorial struggles limited his ambitions as a patron. The contacts he made while claiming his territories contributed to the formation of his taste and influenced his choice of artists. His enforced stay in Burgundy probably brought him into contact with Netherlandish painters, and he became acquainted with early Renaissance motifs and artists while travelling in Italy. It has often been claimed that René was himself a painter, but there is little evidence to support this theory. What distinguishes René from most contemporary patrons, however, is his writing on a variety of subjects: tournaments (*Traité de la forme et devis d'un tournois*), religious morals (*Mortifiement de vaine plaisance*) and allegorical romance (*Livre du cueur d'amour espris*). The choice of subjects and the allegorical form in which they are written demonstrate how deeply René espoused contemporary ethics and chivalric ideals (in 1448 he created the exclusive Order of the Crescent).

By contrast, in the building and restoration of his castles and manors fortification was given less importance, and windows were enlarged. Terraces and gardens were created at his castles at Angers, Saumur and Tarascon; manors, while in the Late Gothic style, were built with emphasis on space and light and, like contemporary and later Italian villas, were often working farms, for example Baugé and Le Menitre (Maine-et-Loire) and Launay (Eure). Interior walls were painted with heraldic devices or stylized fruits, plants and fantastic animals in a manner familiar since the 14th century in France and Italy. Ornamental sculpture adorned architectural features (e.g. windows and fireplaces), but it was for his private chapels and some favourite churches that the more important sculptures were commissioned, most of which are known only through documents or occasionally drawings. This is the case of one of the major undertakings of his reign, the funerary monument (destr.) of René and his first wife Isabelle of Lorraine in Angers Cathedral. The tomb was executed in parts by Jacques Morel and probably remained unfinished at René's death; as part of its iconography René was depicted seated on a throne as a crowned skeleton (for references to drawings see Robin, p. 272). The image of the 'Roi Mort' was one specifically personal to René and part of a series of images (e.g. London, BL, MS. Egerton 1070, fol. 53*r*) and writings attesting to his fascination with death.

Having lost or given away most of his domains, René, King of Sicily (as he still styled himself), settled in Provence in 1471. There he commissioned a marble relief of the *Carrying of the Cross* (1479–81) for the church of the Célestins (now St Didier) in Avignon from Francesco Laurana, who made two lengthy stays in Provence (1461–6, 1475/7–83). Laurana also made several portrait medals with inscriptions and mottoes in the Italian manner for the King and various members of his family (e.g. the double-portrait medal of *René I and Joanna of Laval*, 1463; Paris, Bib. N., Cab. Médailles) and entourage, as did Pietro di Martino da Milano, who had also arrived in 1461 (e.g. the medals of *René I*, 1461, and *René I and Joanna of Laval*, 1462; both Paris, Bib. N., Cab. Médailles). The architectural character of much of Laurana's sculptures in Provence introduced an influential range of early Renaissance motifs to the art of the region. Possibly through his friendship with the Pazzi family of Florence, René acquired several works from the workshop of Luca della Robbia. The glazed terracotta coat of arms, which belonged to the Pazzi family (London, V&A), is similar to that known to have decorated René's palace at Aix-en-Provence (drawing, Paris, Bib. N., Cab. Est., Gaignières Pe 18, fol. 9). Another friend, Jacopo Marcello, Governor of Padua, sent René and his councillor Jean Cossa a copy of *De situ orbis*, a Latin translation of Strabo (1459; Albi, Bib. Mun., MS. 77), and a *Life and Passion of St Maurice* (Paris, Bib. Arsenal, MS. 940) respectively; both were illustrated by northern Italian painters. A few Italian artists are recorded to have worked for René, and he financed the trip to Rome in 1476 of his illuminator, Georges Trubert. Most of his painters and illuminators, however, were from Anjou or the Loire (e.g. Coppin Delf, Georges Trubert); others, for example the MASTER OF KING RENÉ OF ANJOU (*see* MASTERS, ANONYMOUS, AND MONOGRAMMISTS, §I), who illuminated René's *Livre du cueur d'amour espris*

Master of King René of Anjou: *Amour Comes to the Bed of the Lovesick King and Takes his Heart Away, Giving it to Desire*; frontispiece miniature from René I: *Livre du cueur d'amour espris*, 290×207 mm, *c*. 1465–70 (Vienna, Österreichisches Nationalbibliothek, Cod. 2597, fol. 2*r*)

(Vienna, Österreich. Nbib., Cod. 2597; see fig.), were of south Netherlandish origin but assimilated aspects of, and contributed to, Angevin and Provençal painting. The Provençal panel painter Nicolas Froment also provided an interesting stylistic link between Provençal and south Netherlandish painting in his *Burning Bush* altarpiece painted for René and his second wife Joanna of Laval (4.10×3.05 m; 1476; Aix-en-Provence Cathedral; for illustration, *see* FROMENT, NICOLAS). Most of the surviving paintings executed for the court are illuminated manuscripts. Many are Books of Hours containing René's coat of arms and mottoes, others translations of Boccaccio (e.g. the *Théséide*, Vienna, Österreich. Nbib., MS. 2617; *see* MASTERS, ANONYMOUS, AND MONOGRAMMISTS, §I: MASTER OF KING RENÉ OF ANJOU, fig. 1) or René's own writings. Usually René employed artists on a salaried basis, giving only a few (Trubert and Barthélémy d'Eyck) the coveted title of 'valet de chambre', as was common in French courts. One office at a time was given to a goldsmith, weaver, embroiderer and painter-illuminator. In his choice of artists René contributed to the introduction of both Netherlandish and Italian elements into France, particularly Provence. His discriminating taste ensured that after his death the poet Jean Robertet could sing the praise of the *peintres de feu le roy de Cecille*.

BIBLIOGRAPHY

A. Lecoy de la Marche: *Extraits des comptes et mémoriaux du roi René pour servir à l'histoire des arts au XVe siècle* (Paris, 1873)
——: *Le Roi René: Sa vie, son administration, ses travaux artistiques et littéraires, d'après les documents inédits des Archives de France et d'Italie*, 2 vols (Paris, 1875)
G. Arnaud d'Agnel: *Les Comptes du roi René publiés d'après les originaux inédits conservés aux Archives des Bouches-du-Rhône*, 3 vols (Paris, 1908–10)
O. Pächt: 'René d'Anjou et les Van Eyck', *Cah. Assoc. Int. Etud. Fr.*, viii (1956), pp. 40–67
——: 'René d'Anjou', *Jb. Ksthist. Samml. Wien*, lxix (1973), pp. 85–126; lxxiii (1977), pp. 7–106
J. J. G. Alexander: *Italian Renaissance Illuminations* (London, 1977)
J. J. Gloton: *Renaissance et Baroque à Aix-en-Provence*, 2 vols (Aix-en-Provence, 1979)
La Littérature angevine médiévale. Actes du colloque: Angers, 1980
M. T. Gousset, D. Poirion and F. Unterkircher, eds: *Le Cueur d'amour espris* (Paris, 1981)
Le Roi René (1409–1480): Décorations de ses chapelles et demeures (exh. cat., ed. C. de Merindol; Paris, Mus. Mnmts Fr., 1981)
Le Roi René en son temps, 1382–1481 (exh. cat., Aix-en-Provence, Mus. Granet, 1981)
N. Coulet, A. Planche and F. Robin: *Le Roi René: Le Prince, le mécène, l'écrivain, le mythe* (Aix-en-Provence, 1982)
F. Robin: *La Cour d'Anjou-Provence: La Vie artistique sous le règne de René* (Paris, 1985)
F. Avril and others, eds: *Le Livre des tournois du roi René de la Bibliothèque nationale* (MS. *frs 2695*) (Paris, 1986) [facsimile]
C. de Merindol: *Le Roi René et la seconde maison d'Anjou: Emblématique, art, histoire* (Paris, 1987)

A. DEMARQUAY ROOK

(5) René II (of Vaudemont), Duke of Lorraine (*b* Angers, 2 May 1451; *reg* 1473–1508; *d* 10 Dec 1508). Grandson of (4) René I. His mother, Yolande of Anjou (1428–*c.* 1483), the daughter of René I, abdicated in his favour. Two major preoccupations dominated his reign and influenced his patronage: the inheritance of the House of Anjou, which was contested by the kings of France, and, more urgently, the threat posed by Charles the Bold, Duke of Burgundy. René's victory over Charles near Nancy in 1477, his claim to the Kingdoms of Naples and Jerusalem and his membership of the House of France and that of Anjou inspired the iconography of the works he commissioned. He founded a church (1482) for the convent of the Cordeliers in Nancy, as well as a chapel (1498) in the collegiate church of St Georges, Nancy. A sculptural group of the *Annunciation* (*c.* 1505; destr.) was placed above the Porte de la Craffe. Other sculptural commissions were the tomb of *Charles the Bold* (1506–7; destr.) in St Georges, René's own tomb (1511; partly destr.) in the church of the Cordeliers, and two equestrian statues of *René II* (*c.* 1500), one (destr.) for the façade of the ducal palace, executed according to a design by René, and another (partly destr.) from the south portal of the west façade of the cathedral at Toul. The stained glass (*c.* 1483–6; fragments, Nancy, Mus. Hist. Lorrain) by Peter Helmmel von Andlau for the church of the Cordeliers and that (*c.* 1510; partly destr.) in the apse of St Nicolas-de-Port attributed to Nicolas Droguet of Lyon and Master Georges were commissioned by the Duke. Among the manuscripts made for him were a Diurnal (Paris, Bib. N., MS. lat. 10491), a Breviary (Paris, Petit Pal., MS. 42; Bib. Arsenal, MS. 601) and a Book of Hours (priv. col.), all illuminated by GEORGES TRUBERT between 1492 and 1494. Several of the Duke's coins and seals survive; their iconography and precise dates provide an outline of the Duke's artistic activities.

BIBLIOGRAPHY

P. Marot: 'Le Tombeau de Charles le Téméraire à Nancy', *Humanisme actif: Mélanges d'art et de littérature offerts à Julien Cain* (1968), pp. 345–58
N. Reynaud: 'Georges Trubert: Enlumineur du roi René et de René II de Lorraine', *Rev. A.*, 35 (1977), pp. 41–63 [docs, good bibliog. and pls]
C. de Mérindol: *Le Roi René et la seconde maison d'Anjou: Emblématique, art, histoire* (Paris, 1987)
——: 'La Politique du duc de Lorraine René II (1473–1508) à l'égard de la seconde maison d'Anjou, de la France et de la Bourgogne, d'après le témoignage de l'emblématique et de la thématique', *Les Pays de l'entre deux au moyen âge. Actes du 113e congrès national des sociétés savantes: Strasbourg, 1988*, pp. 61–114 [good bibliog. and pls]
——: 'Les Drapeaux du duc de Lorraine René II à la bataille de Nancy, la référence au roi de France et à Jeanne d'Arc', *Annu. Soc. Fr. Vexillologie* (1994)

CHRISTIAN DE MÉRINDOL

Ankara [Gr. and Lat. Ancyra; Mod. Gr. Angora]. Capital city of the Turkish Republic since 1923. Ankara lies near the northern edge of the central Anatolian steppe at the confluence of three small rivers, spreading down the slopes of a mountain on which stands the ancient citadel. It has been a centre of trade and administration since antiquity.

In 25 BC, then a large and prosperous Phrygian city on the Royal Road from Sardis to Persepolis, Ancyra was made the capital of the Roman province of Galatia. It was embellished with buildings, of which the white marble Temple of Roma and Augustus is the most important to survive. Inscribed on its walls is the *Monumentum Ancyranum*, the most famous of all antique inscriptions. Written in Greek (on the exterior) and Latin (on the interior), the text is an account by the emperor Augustus (*reg* 27 BC–AD 14) of his public life and works. Other Classical remains include the Bilkis Minaresi (a column of the emperor Julian (or Jovian)) and the foundations of a large Roman bath on the road to Çankırı.

St Paul is said to have visited Ancyra in AD 51 and addressed his *Epistle to the Galatians* to its inhabitants, although a Christian community there is not attested for another century. The temple was eventually converted into a church, and the walls of the citadel, frequently restored and extended, largely date from Byzantine times. The city was taken by the Persians in 620 and attacked by the Arabs in the 7th, 9th and 10th centuries. Some time after the Battle of Manzikert in 1071 it came under the rule of the SALJUQS OF RUM (*reg* 1077–1307), although it was held from 1101 to *c.* 1120 by crusaders. The wooden minbar (1197–8; *see* ISLAMIC ART, §VII, 2(iii)) in the Alaeddin Mosque in the citadel is an early and particularly fine example of the art of the Saljuqs of Rum. The Arslanhane Mosque (1289–90), located outside the fortress gate, was the congregational mosque for the city. A hypostyle wooden structure, it contains a beautiful wooden minbar (1290) and an important mihrab of glazed ceramic tile. The contemporary Kızılbey Mosque preserves a wooden minbar dated 1299–1300.

In the early 14th century the city was controlled successively by the Ilkhanids of Iran, the Eretnids of Sivas and the Ottomans, who took the city in 1361 and held it for over 500 years. Throughout the Ottoman period the city remained a major trading centre and administrative capital. Hajji Bayram Wali (1352–1429/30), a dervish and founder of the Bayramiyya Order, took over the old church; his tomb and mosque (15th century) stand beside the ruins. Ottoman mosques include the Imaret Mosque (1427–8), with an inverted T-shaped plan, and the mosque of Cenabi Ahmed Paşa, also known as the Yeni (New) or Kurşunlu Mosque, built in 1565–6 by Sinan (*see* SINAN (ii)). The Kurşunlu Caravanserai (endowed 1746) and the adjacent covered market (Turk. *bedesten*) have been restored for use as a museum of Anatolian civilization. The citadel, with its overhanging houses and narrow streets, preserves much of its medieval aspect. The city has long been famous for the white long-haired goats of central Anatolia, from whose silky wool mohair (Arab. *mukhayyar*, Turk. *tiftik*) is spun.

BIBLIOGRAPHY

Enc. Islam/2; *Islam. Ans.*
P. Wittek: 'Zur Geschichte Angoras im Mittelalter', *Festschrift für G. Jacob* (Leipzig, 1932), pp. 329–54
İslâm ansiklopedis (Istanbul, 1940–)
A. Galanti: *Ankara tarihi* [History of Ankara] (Istanbul, 1950–51)
G. Öney: *Ankara'da Türk devri dini ve sosyal yapıları* [Turkish period buildings in Ankara] (Ankara, 1971) [English summaries]
İ. H. Konyalı: *Ankara camileri* [The mosques of Ankara] (Ankara, 1978)

LALE H. ULUÇ

Anker, (Samuel) Albert [Albrecht] (*b* Anet, Berne, 1 April 1831; *d* Anet, 16 July 1910). Swiss painter and illustrator. An early interest in art was kindled by visiting the exhibitions of the Société des Amis des Arts in Neuchâtel in 1842, and he took private drawing lessons with Louis Wallinger (1819–86) between 1845 and 1848. However he began studying theology in Berne in 1851, continuing these studies at the university in Halle. During his stay in Germany he became acquainted with major German collections, notably the Gemäldegalerie in Dresden, which impressed him deeply. His father reluctantly consented to an artistic career, and in 1854 Anker moved to Paris, where he joined the studio of Charles Gleyre. He studied at the Ecole Impériale des Beaux-Arts in Paris from 1855 until *c.* 1860, meanwhile selling portraits. In 1861 he travelled in nothern Italy, copying Old Masters such as Titian and Correggio.

In the course of this training Anker started painting large original compositions, such as *Job and his Friends* (1856; see Kuthy and Lüthy, 1980) and *Village School in the Black Forest* (1858; Berne, Kstmus.). He exhibited with the Société des Amis des Arts in Neuchâtel from 1860, an involvement that lasted until 1905. In 1864 he married in Switzerland. In Paris, where he spent every winter from 1862 to 1890, he regularly showed works in the Salon from 1859 to 1885, winning the gold medal in 1866 for the paintings *In the Wood* (Lille, Mus. B.-A.) and the *Writing Lesson* (1865; see Kuthy, 1981). Despite this assured popularity, he continued for financial reasons to do paintings on faience for the manufacturer Joseph-Thédore Deck (1823–91) from 1866 until 1892. As he became more eminent, however, official duties increasingly took up Anker's time. In 1870 he was elected a member of the Bernese cantonal council; his one action as such was to recommend, in 1874, the establishment of a fine art museum in Berne. In the same year the Société Bernoise des Arts made him an honorary member, and from 1873 until 1883 he was on the editorial board of *Le Magasin Pittoresque.* He helped to organize many exhibitions, such as the Swiss section of the Exposition Universelle in Paris in 1878 and the Internationale Kunstausstellungen in Berlin and Munich in 1896 and 1897. He was also one of the first advisers in the creation of the Gottfried-Keller Stiftung (*see* KELLER, GOTTFRIED), in 1890.

The human figure was always central to Anker's work. His most characteristic works are scenes of Swiss village life, for example the *Village Tailor* (1885; Berne, Kstmus.) and the *Child's Funeral* (1863; Aarau, Aargau. Ksthaus), which go beyond mere anecdote to become general symbols of human behaviour. In all his pictures Anker sought to emphasize not a type or a profession but the psychology of an individual, as can be seen in his rural figures: *The Drinker* (1868; Berne, Kstmus.) and *Girl Feeding Hens* (1865; Neuchâtel, Mus. A. & Hist.). He painted portraits on commission but also by choice; many of these are of children, including his daughter *Louise Anker* (1874; Winterthur, Samml. Oskar Reinhart). His still-lifes were modelled on those of Jean-Siméon Chardin, whose work was accorded new favour during the later 19th century; they dwelt on humble subjects simply arranged, as in *Beer and Radish* (1898; Berne, Kstmus.).

In 1890 Anker agreed to provide a series of vignettes of Swiss rural life to illustrate Jeremias Gotthelf's *Ausgewählte Werke* (Chaux de Fonds, 1901–2). This work occupied him for several years and necessitated repeated stays in central Switzerland. In 1901 a stroke paralysed his right hand, forcing him to abandon oil painting for watercolours, for example *Old Peasant with Bread and Wine* (1909; Berne, Kstmus.), which he did with his left hand.

BIBLIOGRAPHY

Albert Anker: Katalog der Gemälde und Ölstudien (exh. cat. by M. Huggler, H. Wagner and K. von Walterkirchen, Berne, Kstmus., 1962)
M. Huggler: *Albert Anker: Le Peintre et son village* (Berne, 1977)

S. Kuthy and H. A. Lüthy: *Albert Anker: Deux Portraits d'un artiste* (Lausanne, 1980)
Anker in seiner Zeit (exh. cat. by S. Kuthy, Berne, Kstmus., 1981)
S. Kuthy: *Albert Anker: Faïences* (Lausanne, 1985)
R. Meister: *Albert Anker und seine Welt: Briefe, Dokumente, Bilder* (Berne, 1981)

ANNE PASTORI ZUMBACH

An Kyŏn [*cha* Gado, Tŭksu; *ho* Hyŏndong-ja, Chugyŏng] (*b* ?Sŏsan, South Ch'ungch'ŏng Province, *c.* 1400; *d* 1464–70). Korean painter. During the reign of King Sejong (1418–50) he was promoted from the sixth rank in the Bureau of Painting to the fourth rank. This was the first time an artist had been promoted to such a high rank in a period when artists were not allowed to advance beyond the lower sixth rank, an indication of the esteem in which An Kyŏn was held as a painter. The influence of An Kyŏn and his followers may be seen in Japanese ink landscape paintings of the Muromachi period (1333–1568; *see* JAPAN, §VI, 4(iii)).

The only direct evidence of An Kyŏn's work is his *Dream Journey to the Peach Blossom Land* (handscroll, ink and colours on silk, 387×1065 mm, 1447; Tenri, Cent. Lib.; *see* Ahn Hwi-joon, 1993, pl. 12) and the *Eight Views of the Four Seasons* (set of eight album leaves, ink and colours on silk, each leaf 358×285 mm; Seoul, N. Mus.; see 1979–81 exh. cat., pls 181a–d), which is attributed to him. His style is based on that of GUO XI, a Chinese artist of the Northern Song period (960–1127) and is characterized by unbalanced yet harmonious composition, the use of blank space, diagonal movement and distinctive brush technique. This style became tremendously influential in Korean landscape painting of the 16th and 17th centuries. The patronage of Prince Anp'yŏng, known as YI YŎNG, played an important role in the development of An Kyŏn's artistic talent. Prince Anp'yŏng owned a very large collection of Chinese paintings, including 17 works by Guo Xi and several by artists of the Li Guo school. In 1442 An Kyŏn painted a portrait of Prince Anp'yŏng at the age of 25. Indeed, many of An Kyŏn's paintings were commissioned by the Prince, most notably *Dream Journey to the Peach Blossom Land.*

BIBLIOGRAPHY

M. Takaaki and Ch'oe Sun-u: 'Richō no suibokuga' [Ink paintings of the Yi dynasty], *Suiboku bijutso taikei* [Compendium of ink painting arts], suppl. ii (Tokyo, 1977)
Ahn Hwi-joon [An Hwi-jun]: 'Jŏn an Kyŏn p'il sasi p'alkyŏng-do' [On the *Eight Views of the Four Seasons* attributed to An Kyŏn], *Kogo Misul*, cxxxvi–vii/3 (1978), pp. 72–8
5000 Years of Korean Art (exh. cat., ed. R.-Y. Lefebvre d'Argencé; San Francisco, CA, Asian A. Mus.; Seattle, WA, A. Mus.; Chicago, IL, A. Inst. and elsewhere; 1979–81)
Ahn Hwi-joon [An Hwi-jun]: *Hanguk hoehwasa* [History of Korean painting] (Seoul, 1980)
——: 'An Kyŏn and *A Dream Journey to the Peach Blossom Land*', *Orient. A.*, xxvi/1 (March 1980), pp. 59–71
——: *Han'guk hoehwa ŭi Jŏnt'ong* [Traditions of Korean painting] (Seoul, 1988)
——: 'Traditional Korean Painting/Hanguk chŏnt'ong hoehwa-ŭi byŏnch'ŏn', *Korean Art Tradition/Hanguk-ŭi yesul chŏnt'ong*, ed. Young Ick Lew [Ryu Yŏng-ik] (Seoul, 1993) [bilingual text], pp. 83–147, pls 12–14

AHN HWI-JOON

Anna, d'. Italian family of patrons. Probably from Brussels originally, the d'Anna family were wealthy merchants who settled in Venice at the beginning of the 16th century. Martin [Martino] d'Anna (*b* ?1475; *d* Venice, 11 Nov 1556) acquired Venetian citizenship in 1545. He bought a palace on the Grand Canal from Lodovico Talenti on 7 December 1538 (Venice, Archv Stato, Notarile atti, Ba. 3258, fols 126–8). Talenti, not Martin, must have commissioned from Pordenone the famous frescoes (*c.* 1534; destr., known from prints) that decorated the building's façade. Martin continued embellishing this residence, and in his will (1553, Venice, Archv Stato, Notarile testamenti, Ba. 1218/x42) he requested that his heirs neither destroy nor disperse the decorations and furniture.

The sons of Martin d'Anna, Daniele (*d* Venice, 26 Dec 1579) and Giovanni (*d* 1580), were also important patrons. They asked Leone Leoni to engrave several medals for them (e.g. portrait medals 1544–5; Milan, Castello Sforzesco). This sculptor was close to Titian at the time, and it was probably the latter who introduced him, as Giovanni d'Anna was also a friend of Titian. The latter painted several works for him in the style of Vasari, including the *Ecce homo* of 1543 (Vienna, Ksthist. Mus.), which features several members of the family. Daniele was the dedicatee of the *Praecipua aliquot romanae antiquitatis ruinarum monumenta* (Venice, 1561), a collection of prints by Battista Pittoni depicting views of the main ruins of Rome. In his dedication Pittoni asserted that Daniele was a great lover of painting and architecture. Giovanni's son Paolo (*d* 1582) is the last member of the family on whom there is any information. Francesco Sansovino dedicated to him his *Osservationi della lingua volgare* (Venice, 1562), praising his magnificence. In 1577 Paolo was appointed Guardian grande of the Scuola di S Rocco. The painter Baldassare d'Anna (*fl c.* 1560) was probably related to this family.

BIBLIOGRAPHY

G. Vasari: *Vite* (1550, rev. 2/1568); ed. G. Milanesi (1878–85), v, p. 115; vii, pp. 429–30, 457
C. Ridolfi: *Maraviglie* (1648); ed. D. von Hadeln (1914–24), i, p. 120
E. A. Cicogna: *Delle inscrizioni veneziane* (Venice, 1824–53), iv, pp. 197–9
M. Hochmann: *Peintres et commanditaires à Venise, 1541–1628* (Rome, 1991), pp. 201–4

MICHEL HOCHMANN

Anna Amalia, Duchess of Saxe-Weimar. *See* WETTIN, (10).

Annaba. *See* HIPPO REGIUS.

Annaberg. German city in Saxony. It is particularly known for its Late Gothic hall church, the Annenkirche. The church was built after the foundation of the city in 1496/7 by Herzog Georg of Saxony, following the discovery of silver near by. Herzog Georg endowed the church and personally appointed the architects. The building, which was integrated into the regular plan of the city, was probably begun in 1499 by CONRAD PFLÜGER, the highest-ranking Master of the Works in the Duchy. On Pflüger's death in 1508 direction of the works was taken over by Peter Ulrich von Pirna (*d* 1513–14); the roof was built in 1512, the piers from 1514 to 1517. In 1515 JACOB HAYLMANN took over as Master of the Works, and the galleries and the imaginative vaults with patterns of loops and stars were built following his designs (see fig.). The transept-like annexe to the south side, built in 1519, is also attributable to him. In 1519 an Expertise conducted by

Annaberg, Annenkirche, 1499–1525; interior view after restoration

Benedikt Ried, Hans Schickentanz (*fl* 1493–1528) and Hans Meltwitz investigated possible problems in the wall coping. The sculptures in the vaults were carved by Christoph Walther I, while the 100 gallery reliefs were made from 1519 to 1522 by Franz Maidburg (*fl* 1503–25). The church was dedicated in 1519, but the rich programme of paintings and furnishings was completed only in 1525. The most important elements are the altar of the miners and the smelters, and the high altar, with its early Renaissance features, made by Adolf Daucher in Augsburg in 1522. The building sequence can be established from inscriptions, account books and building chronicles begun as early as the 16th century, although the evidence is not complete for the first ten years.

The Annenkirche is a hall church with three aisles of seven bays, each terminated to the east by a polygonal apse. The west and north walls join at an acute angle, perhaps owing to the plan of the city. Square sacristies are attached at the second bay from the east, with polygonal choir galleries above. The exterior, which is constructed of gneiss, is simple and without projecting buttresses. The exterior dressings and the interior articulation are of sandstone. The building was originally plastered and topped with a curved roof covered in copper and supporting three turrets.

Although the design of the interior produces a unified visual effect, there were several changes during construction: the pilasters and galleries were not originally planned in their present form, and the southern sacristy, with its particularly imaginative vault forms, was the work of Haylmann, as were the galleries above the sacristies and the vault in the main church.

In 1577 the 'beautiful portal' built by MASTER HW (*see* MASTERS, ANONYMOUS, AND MONOGRAMMISTS, §III) at the Franciscan church in Annaberg was transferred to the Annenkirche. The roof was destroyed by fire in 1604 and replaced between 1688 and 1692 by a Baroque one. After the destruction of the spire by fire in 1813, the present classicizing termination was built. During the extensive historicist restorations carried out between 1879 and 1884 the walls were painted and stained glass introduced, but in 1927–8 the historicist paintings were partly removed, and from 1975 the original paint has been revealed and an attempt made to restore the earlier spatial effect.

In German art-historical literature of *c.* 1900 the Annenkirche was considered the culmination of a stylistic development that could be seen as a sort of independent Renaissance. More recently the building has been seen rather as the most mature achievement of Late Gothic architecture in Upper Saxony, enriched by stylistic elements from Bohemia and the Danube region. It represents the Upper Saxon type of hall church, characterized by a simple exterior and a richly articulated and dynamic interior. There are characteristic individual elements, such as the drawing of the buttresses into the interior, the gallery with its oriel-like extensions at each pier, octagonal piers with concave sides and a rib design extending uniformly over the ceiling without transverse arches. These forms were introduced here and at Freiberg Cathedral (and to some extent at St Thomas, Leipzig). The design of the east end is derived from that at SS Peter und Paul, Görlitz, but Haylmann's looped stellar vault is a development of forms used by Benedikt Ried in Bohemia, especially in the Vladislav Hall in Prague Castle. Individual early Renaissance details were also introduced by way of Bohemia, for example the southern sacristy portal.

BIBLIOGRAPHY

R. Steche: *Beschreibende Darstellung der älteren Bau- und Kunstdenkmäler des Königreichs Sachsen* (Dresden, 1885)

E. O. Schmidt: *Die St Annenkirche zu Annaberg* (Leipzig, 1908)

K. Gerstenberg: *Deutsche Sondergotik* (Munich, 1913, rev. Darmstadt, 2/1969), pp. 171–4

H. Schönemann: 'Die Baugeschichte der Annenkirche in Annaberg', *Wiss. Z. Martin-Luther U. Halle-Wittenberg, Ges. & Sprachwiss. Reihe*, xii (1963), pp. 745–56

F. W. Fischer: 'Unser Bild von der deutschen spätgotischen Architektur des XV. Jahrhunderts', *Sber. Heidelberg. Akad. Wiss.* (1964), pp. 43–4

W. Gross: *Gotik und Spätgotik*, Epochen der Architektur (Frankfurt am Main, 1969), p. 189

K. Kratzsch: 'Bergstädte des Erzgebirges: Städtebau und Kunst zur Zeit der Reformation', *Münchn.Ksthist. Abh.*, iv (1972), pp. 18–27

H. Magirius: 'Neue Ergebnisse zur Baugeschichte der Annenkirche in Annaberg', *100 Jahre Kunstwissenschaft in Leipzig* (Leipzig, 1975), pp. 140–46

——: *Die Sankt-Annen-Kirche zu Annaberg*, Das Christliche Denkmal 7/7A (Berlin, 2/1985)

HEINRICH MAGIRIUS

Anna Maria Luisa, Electress Palatine. *See* MEDICI, DE', (29).

Annan. Scottish family of photographers. Richard Annan was co-founder and business manager with his brother, (1) Thomas Annan, of the T. & R. Annan photographic studio in Glasgow in 1857. The firm was joined by

Thomas's sons, John Annan and (2) James Craig Annan, and became Annan & Sons in 1888.

(1) Thomas Annan (*b* 1829; *d* December, 1887). He lived for most of his life in Glasgow, and he trained and worked as a copperplate-engraver until 1853, when he started a calotype printing business, probably with the encouragement of his friend David Octavius Hill. Annan's business proved successful and led in 1857 to the establishment of a photographic studio, T. & R. Annan in Sauchiehall Sreet. At first, Annan's emphasis was on the photographic reproduction of works of art and on architectural photography, as in the collection of photographs of mansions around Glasgow, *The Old Country Houses of the Old Glasgow Gentry* (Glasgow, 1870). Having mastered the technical and practical difficulties of architectural photography, Annan turned his attention to portraits, at which he was equally gifted. The carbon prints contained in *Memorials of the Old College of Glasgow* (Glasgow, 1871) consisted of both portraits and views of buildings. The process, for which he had acquired the Scottish patent rights shortly after its invention by Joseph Wilson Swan in 1866, produced rich, dark brown prints through the incorporation of a permanent pigment in a gelatin layer. Annan first used the carbon process commercially in 1866 in his reproduction of D. O. Hill's painted group portrait, the *Signing of the Deed of Demission* (1843–65, Edinburgh, Free Church Assembly Hall) in which he himself featured. An astute businessman, Annan also acquired the British patent rights in the 'heliogravure' or photogravure process invented by William Henry Fox Talbot and developed by Karel Klíč (*see* PHOTOGRAPHY, §I), a photomechanical printing method that was employed to great effect by Annan's son, (2) James Craig Annan.

Annan was a technical perfectionist but he was not a purist. He did not consider it unethical to add to or alter a negative, or to combine negatives in order, for example, to insert clouds into an empty sky. In spite of the criticism attracted by these practices, he regarded the manipulation of the negative as essential for achieving the desired final result. Annan's reputation as one of the first to use photography as a form of documentation and as a tool for social change stems from his commission of 1868 from the Glasgow Improvement Trust to record the slums of the city shortly before their demolition. These images, published in three editions as *Old Closes and Streets of Glasgow* (Glasgow, 1871, albumen prints; 1877, carbon prints; and a posthumous photogravure edition in 1900) were taken in difficult circumstances, in dark narrow passageways between tall tenement buildings. Restricted spaces and poor lighting imposed severe limitations on camera angles and meant long exposure times. Annan's decision to include children and adults, often in large groups, added to his difficulties: figures are often visible only as ghostly shadows because of the problems of recording movement. A rare technical achievement, these photographs are not only picturesque, but powerful and affecting images.

BIBLIOGRAPHY

M. Harker: 'From Mansion to Close: Thomas Annan, Master Photographer', *Phot. Colr*, v/1 (1980), pp. 81–95

Masterpieces of Photography from the Riddell Collection (exh. cat. by J. Lawson and S. Stevenson, Edinburgh, N.P.G., 1986), p. 110, pls 1–2

J. Lawson: 'The Problems of Poverty and the Picturesque: Thomas Annan's *Old Closes and Streets of Glasgow*, 1868–1871', *Scot. Phot. Bull.*, ii (1990)

S. Stevenson: *Thomas Annan, 1829–1887* (Edinburgh, 1990)

(2) James Craig Annan (*b* Hamilton, 8 March 1864; *d* Lenzie, nr Glasgow, 5 June 1946). Son of (1) Thomas Annan. He studied chemistry and natural philosophy before entering the family photographic business, T. & R. Annan. In 1883 he was sent to Vienna to learn the technique of 'heliogravure' or photogravure from KAREL KLÍČ, for which his father had acquired the British patent rights and in which he was to produce most of his best work. James Craig Annan received no formal artistic training but associated with contemporary Glasgow painters and etchers, including his friends Sir David Young Cameron (1865–1945), Muirhead Bone and William Strang, whose work, like his, was influenced by the graphic style of Whistler. In 1892 Annan and Cameron visited the Netherlands. On his return Annan produced photogravures (or 'monotones' as he called them), influenced by the Hague school and by Dutch 17th century masters, such as *Utrecht Pastoral* (1892; see 1986 exh. cat., p. 39) and *On a Dutch Shore* (see M. Haworth-Booth, p. 170), both exhibited at the Annan Gallery at 230 Sauchiehall Street in Glasgow.

In 1894 Annan travelled with Cameron to Italy, where he used a hand-held camera, not merely because it was less cumbersome and obtrusive, but because it made a new sort of photograph possible. His practice was to select a view and then wait as long as necessary for an interesting visual event to occur within the frame. His *White Friars* (see M. Haworth-Booth, p. 174), praised when it was exhibited in New York in 1899, is an example of this calculated instantaneity. In 1896 Annan published 35 folios, each containing 11 Italian photogravures.

In the early 1890s James Craig Annan made prints from negatives by the Scottish photographers David Octavius Hill and Robert Adamson, who had known his father and whose example played a significant part in his education as a photographer. He helped to revive their reputations by sending some of their calotypes to an exhibition in Hamburg in 1899, and through their work may have clarified his view of photography as an art form, which he shared with the group of photographers known as the LINKED RING. On the occasion of their first exhibition in 1893, Annan was described by a critic in *The Studio* as a 'consummate artist'. Through the Linked Ring Annan's work acquired an international reputation and Alfred Stieglitz in particular emulated his use of the hand-held camera. Annan's stature in the movement known as PICTORIAL PHOTOGRAPHY was confirmed by his many exhibitions, including his first one-man show at the Royal Photographic Society (1900). In 1901 he organized the photographic section of the inaugural exhibition of the Glasgow Art Gallery and Museum. In 1913 Annan made a series of photogravures in Spain in the company of the artist William Strang. By this time the running of the family firm was taking precedence over his own photographic interests, and although he continued to supervise the work of assistants until his death in 1946, his reputation still rests on the work produced before World War I.

WRITINGS

'Photography as a Means of Artistic Expression', *Cam. Work*, 32 (1910), pp. 21–4

BIBLIOGRAPHY

W. Buchanan: 'The "Most Versatile and Artistic" James Craig Annan', *Phot. Colr*, v/1 (1980), pp. 70–80

M. Haworth-Booth, ed.: *The Golden Age of British Photography, 1839–1900* (New York, 1985)

Masterpieces of Photography from the Riddell Collection (exh. cat. by J. Lawson and S. Stevenson, Edinburgh, N.P.G., 1986), pp. 111–12, pls 3–6

W. Buchanan: *The Art of the Photographer: J. Craig Annan* (Edinburgh, 1992)

JULIE LAWSON

Annandale Imitation Realists. Australian group of mixed-media artists active in 1962. They formed for the purpose of staging an exhibition of the same name. Ross Crothall (*b* 1934), Mike Brown and Colin Lanceley worked together in Crothall's studio in Annandale, a suburb of Sydney, in 1961. They shared an interest in assemblage, collage, junk art, *objets trouvés* and in non-Western art. Brown, who had worked in New Guinea in 1959, was impressed by the use in tribal house decoration and body ornament of modern urban rubbish such as broken plates and bottletops. Crothall delighted in the altered *objet trouvé*, for example egg cartons unfolded to become the *Young Aesthetic Cow*, or pieces of furniture crudely gathered into frontally posed female icons, sparkling with buttons and swirling house-paint, with such titles as *Gross Débutante*. Lanceley was deeply influenced by his teacher John Olsen and through him by Jean Dubuffet. He covered impastoed surfaces with junk materials, often decorating distorted female forms with strings of pearls, broken plates and other items; in *Glad Family Picnic* (1961; Sydney, A.G. NSW) elements combine into a garish visual cacophony.

From 13 February to 1 March 1962 the three artists exhibited together as *Annandale Imitation Realists* at the Museum of Modern Art of Australia in Melbourne. An environment was created out of 212 works installed on chicken-wire structures, on the floor, walls and ceiling, forcing the viewers into direct experience. Each work was conceived as a pun and as an irreverence. Over the entrance was a quotation from W. B. Yeats's 'Sailing to Byzantium'. Hanging at the terminus of the maze was the largest work in the show, one of 32 collective works, presented as a welcoming monster shouting across the ceiling its title *Here in Byzantium*. At the end of the exhibition many of the works were hammered together into *The Scow*. From 23 May the exhibition was reinstalled at the Rudy Komon Gallery in Sydney and, with the group, was renamed *Subterranean Imitation Realists*. The exhibitions were a form of social satire prompted by a desperation to transcend the confines of both the established art world and everyday mundaneness. They were warmly received by many critics. Although critical discussion soon introduced international comparisons and precedents, in particular contemporaneous movements such as Pop art, Neo-Dada, and Nouveau Réalisme, the initial reception took local inspiration for granted, a sentiment on which the artists insisted. However, being an 'imitation' art event itself, which had been very consciously and ironically staged, the group disbanded before it could develop into a movement or programme.

Crothall went to New Zealand in 1965 and in July 1966 presented *Dayo*, an echo of the Annandale Imitation Realists, at the New Vision Gallery, Auckland, his last known exhibition. Lanceley won a travelling scholarship in 1964 and lived from the following year in London, travelling extensively in Europe until his return to Sydney in 1981. Brown's satirical work attracted both critical attention and the wrath of the law. In 1963 he reworked an Annandale Imitation Realist painting, *Mary Lou* (destr.), to include a bevy of cut-outs from pin-up magazines. This led to the expulsion of the painting from the travelling exhibition *Australian Painting Today*. In 1964 Brown launched a bitter attack on the Sydney art world and its key artists and critics. On his painting *Sydney, February 15, 1964 (Kite)* he scrawled such castigations as 'Colin Lanceley is there, having over the preceding two years refined a number of "Imitation Realist" clichés (such as plastic dolls, visual puns, gaping toothy mouths, and cutely naughty erotic references) and plugged them until they have become fashionably acceptable'. In 1965 Brown's exhibition *Painting a Go-go* at Gallery A, Sydney, led to a long and debilitating trial for obscenity and indecency. Brown was found guilty and fined £20.

WRITINGS

Annandale Imitation Realists (exh. cat., ed. E. Lynn; Melbourne, MOMA, 1962)

Arty Wild Oat (July, 1962) [contains contrib. by Lanceley and Crothall]

Subterranean Imitation Realists (exh. cat., Sydney, Rudy Komon Gal., 1962)

BIBLIOGRAPHY

E. Lynn: 'Pop Goes the Easel', *A. & Australia*, i (1963), pp. 166–72

T. Smith, N. Hutchson and T. McGillick: 'Interview: Colin Lanceley', *Other Voices*, i (1970), pp. 36–41

G. Catalano: 'The Aesthetics of the Imitation Realists', *Meanjin*, 35 (1976), pp. 175ff

Mike Brown: A Survey of Work, 1961 to 1977 (exh. cat., Melbourne, N.G. Victoria, 1977)

Irreverent Sculpture (exh. cat., ed. M. Plant; Melbourne, Monash U., A.G., 1985)

Colin Lanceley (exh. cat., intro. R. Hughes, interview W. Wright; Sydney, A.G. NSW, 1987)

TERRY SMITH

Annapolis. North American city and capital of the state of Maryland. It is situated on a peninsula in the Severn River (see fig.) and has a population of *c*. 31,500. It was founded as state capital in 1694. Originally called Providence, it was then named after Princess, later Queen, Anne, although it was also known at that time as Anne Arundeltown. Following the English Glorious Revolution of 1688, which brought William III and Mary II to the English throne, the formerly largely Catholic state of Maryland was divided into Anglican parishes by its new governor, Francis Nicholson. Although land had been set aside before 1694 on Annapolis's site, little development had occurred. The city plan (1695) is attributable to Nicholson: while several towns in the English colonies, including New Haven (founded 1638) and Philadelphia (founded 1682), had adhered earlier to formal design principles, none was as obviously Baroque as his plan. Although the original was lost, another exists from 1743, which retraced a survey made in 1718; the original layout

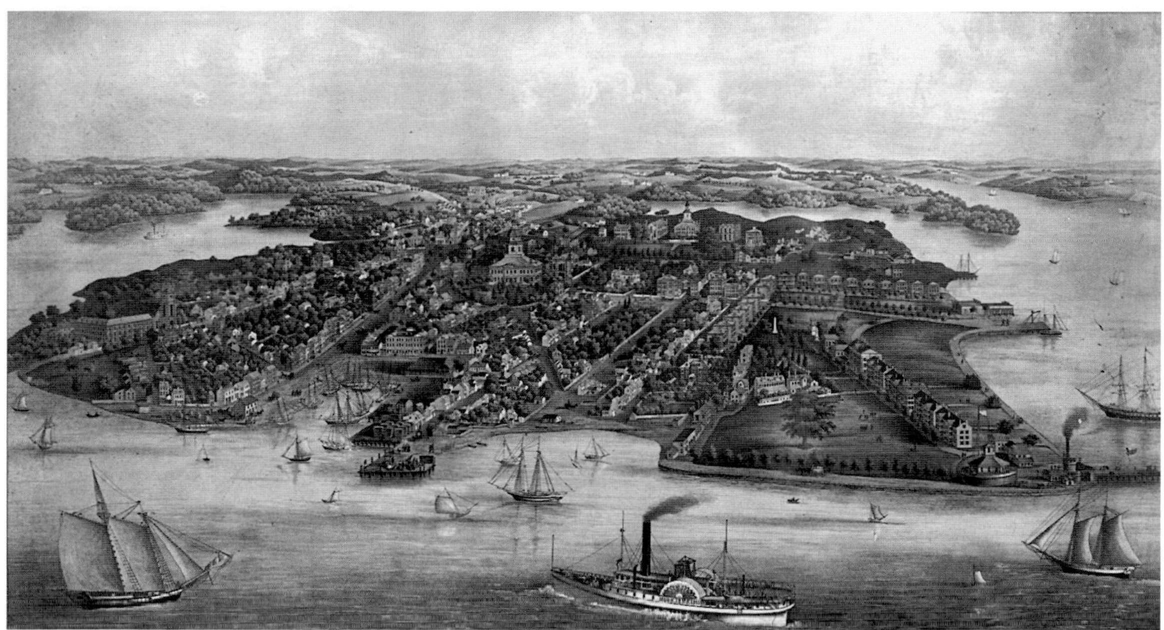

Annapolis, Maryland, view from the south-east, *c.* 1860; from a lithograph by E. Sachse and Company (Baltimore, MD, Maryland Historical Society Museum)

is believed to have been faithfully drawn but with additional streets to the north. Its Baroque character, with streets radiating out from two circles, affirms Nicholson's awareness of the plans by Christopher Wren and John Evelyn for rebuilding London after the Great Fire of 1666.

The firm connection between Church and State that the Glorious Revolution meant to effect is strongly expressed through the dominating Church Circle and Public Circle in the city plan. Nicholson intended each circle to house the Anglican church of St Anne and the statehouse respectively. Linking the two circles is the short School Street, on which was built King William's School (chartered 1696). Other features of the plan included Bloomsbury Square to the west of the circles and a market square to the east, neither of which survives. The main street, Church Street, led from Church Circle to the dock and harbour. Because of its constricted peninsular site and because Baltimore had surpassed Annapolis as Maryland's major town shortly after the Revolution, Annapolis never became a metropolis, and much of the character of the original town survives; government buildings lie to the west of the colonial city without destroying its intimacy. Although its first statehouse and churches are gone, the existing statehouse or capitol, begun in 1770 possibly by Joseph H. Sharpe, remains the oldest in continuous use in the USA. An unusual church was built to replace the first church in 1775–92, but it was destroyed by fire in 1858; a print of *c.* 1800 shows it as a two-storey brick rectangular structure with a pedimented roof and single bell-tower, the first storey ornamented with a series of blind arcades. A third significant colonial building in Annapolis was the house begun *c.* 1742 by Governor Thomas Bladen, intended to equal the Williamsburg Governor's Palace; due to its inordinate cost, however, funding was stopped, and it became known as Bladen's Folly. It was later remodelled on the campus of St John's College.

Annapolis has many high-quality houses dating to the mid-to-late-18th-century, at least five of which were worked on by WILLIAM BUCKLAND, who settled in Annapolis after 1771. These include the Chase-Lloyd House (1771), the James Brice House (*c.* 1772) and, the finest of all, the Hammond-Harwood House (1773–4). The last comprises five sections, with two end pavilions with octagonal bays. The United States Congress met in Annapolis in 1783–4, following the Peace of Paris (1783), and the city, with its central location, bid unsuccessfully to become the United Staes capital. Indeed, with nearby Baltimore's emergence as the USA's fifth largest city in 1790, Annapolis, with only 2000 inhabitants, had to fight to remain state capital. In 1808 the circular Fort Severn was built by the government at the tip of the peninsula to the north-east of the town; the site was later selected for the United States Naval Academy (1845). While the rate of restoration of the city's buildings may not have been as fast as in the colonial city of WILLIAMSBURG, a number of Victorian buildings that overshadowed important 18th-century sites have been removed, enabling the reconstruction of sites of interest.

BIBLIOGRAPHY

E. S. Riley: *'The Ancient City': A History of Annapolis, in Maryland, 1649–1887* (Annapolis, 1887)

W. B. Norris: *Annapolis: Its Colonial and Naval Story* (New York, 1925)

D. Davis: *Annapolis Houses, 1700–1775* (New York, 1947)

M. L. Radoff: *Buildings of the State of Maryland at Annapolis* (Annapolis, 1954)

H. C. Forman: *Maryland Architecture—A Short History* (Cambridge, MD, 1968)

J. W. Reps: *Tidewater Towns: City Planning in Colonial Virginia and Maryland* (Williamsburg and Charlottesville, 1972)

JAMES D. KORNWOLF

Anne, Duchess of Bourbon. *See* BOURBON, §I(4).

Annear, Harold Desbrowe (*b* Bendigo, Victoria, 16 Aug 1865; *d* Melbourne, 22 June 1933). Australian architect. He served articles with William Salway (1844–1902) in Melbourne and practised alone from the late 1880s to the early 1930s, with a circle of clients and friends drawn from varying levels of Melbourne society. As well as a commitment to the ideals of the Arts and Crafts movement, he aimed to create an Australian idiom and saw architecture as an art rather than a profession. His talent for sketching and his flair for writing on architecture were also recognized at an early stage in local building journals.

His earliest designs show the influence of H. H. Richardson, whom he greatly admired, but the Viennese Secession may have influenced the Springthorpe Memorial in Kew cemetery, Melbourne (1897). His well-known houses at 32, 34 and 38 The Eyrie, Eaglemont (1902–3), are free and decorative adaptations of a half-timbered, roughcast and Marseilles-tiled idiom fused with an Arts and Crafts approach, which he continued to develop in examples such as the Norman Macgeorge house at Alphington (1910) and 449 Glenferrie Road, Malvern (1920s). They are interesting internally because the principal spaces flow into each other but can be divided by closing sliding doors. Some of his designs with roughcast exteriors, such as Broceliande (1918; destr., see 'Domestic Architecture in Australia', pl. xxxi), have been misleadingly interpreted as proto-Functionalist forerunners of the International Style. They perhaps indicate an interest in Californian-Spanish designs, motivated by the desire to create an Australian architecture by adapting styles from countries climatically similar to southern Australia. Annear also designed buildings in a classical idiom, for example 1 Heyington Place (1925), and Cloyne, 611 Toorak Road, both in Toorak (1929).

WRITINGS

'The Recognition of Architecture', *A. Australia* (1919), pp. 19–24 [special issue: 'Domestic Architecture in Australia', eds S. U. Smith and B. Stevens]

ed.: *For Every Man his Home* (Melbourne, 1922)

BIBLIOGRAPHY

AUDB

R. Boyd: *Australia's Home* (Melbourne, 1962), pp. 160–63

GEORGE TIBBITS

Anneessens, Jan Andries (*b* Brussels, *bapt* 3 Dec 1687; *d* nr Aachen, 30 June 1752). Flemish architect and sculptor. He was the son of the influential Brussels guild-master Frans Anneessens (1660–1719), who was beheaded for his part in the Popular Rebellion. In 1705 he was accepted into the Guild of the Vier Gekroonden ('Four Crowned Ones') as a master mason. On 26 January 1709 he married Françoise van Troen, a relative of the sculptor and architect Cornelis van Nerven (*fl* 1696–1717), who was in charge of the work on the new rear wing of the town hall in Brussels from 1708 to 1717. Anneessens provided drawings and models for two fountains for the inner courtyard of this wing in 1714. These comprised marble river gods representing the *Scheldt* and the *Meuse* surrounded by bronze tritons and dolphins; they were executed by Pieter-Denis Plumier in 1715–17. He also supervised the restoration of the abbot's residence of the Norbertine abbey at Grimbergen, near Brussels, from 1710 to 1726 and in 1747 he added two chapels to the church of the Benedictine abbey at Affligem, Brabant, later rebuilt by Laurent Benoît Dewez in 1764–7. After his father had been exculpated, on 14 January 1733 Anneessens was appointed Court Architect. In this capacity he designed the horseshoe-shaped stables at Charles of Lorraine's country seat, the castle at Tervuren, near Brussels. His most important work, and his only extant building, is the south wing of the palace of the prince-bishop of Liège, built in 1736–40 for Georges-Louis de Berghes, which has a strictly classical monumental stone façade.

BIBLIOGRAPHY

BNB; Thieme–Becker

J.-P. ESTHER

Annenkov, Yury [Georges] **(Pavlovich)** (*b* Petropavlovsk, Kazakhstan, 23 July 1889; *d* Paris, 18 July 1974). Russian painter, draughtsman and stage designer. He studied at the University of St Petersburg (later Petrograd) in 1908 and in the private studio of Savely Zeidenberg (1862–1924). In 1909–10 he attended the studio of Yan Tsyonglinsky (1850–1914) in St Petersburg, where he became acquainted with the avant-garde artists Yelena Guro (1877–1913), Mikhail Matyushin and Matvey Vol'demar (1878–1914). In 1911–12 he worked in the studios of Maurice Denis and Félix Vallotton in Paris, then in Switzerland (1913) before returning to St Petersburg. As a painter he was a modernist, and his work developed rapidly towards abstraction, although he did not adhere to any particular branch of it. His works of the time use various devices of stylization and decorativeness, and some of them echo the free associations of Marc Chagall, but fundamentally they remain geometrically based compositions. In 1919–20 he made a series of abstract sculptural assemblages and a great number of abstract collages.

Annenkov became popular as an illustrator, producing elegant drawings for a number of magazines in Petrograd in 1913–17, including *Satirikon*, *Argus*, *Lukomor'ye* and *Solntse Rossii.* He designed and illustrated many books for Moscow and Petrograd publishing houses in the 1910s and 1920s. In the early 1920s he designed a great number of book covers in the Constructivist style. He illustrated children's books, especially for the private publishing house Raduga in Petrograd. But his most important illustrations were those for Aleksandr Blok's revolutionary poem *Dvenadtsat'* ('The Twelve'; St Petersburg, 1918), which were successful improvisations on the poem's themes, combining stylization and emotion. He also drew and painted a great number of portraits, especially of cultural and political figures. His monumental *Portrait of the Red Army Leader L. Trotsky* (1923; Moscow, Cent. Mus. Revolution), which has an urban background in Constructivist style, was particularly successful.

From 1913 Annenkov worked as a stage designer. He worked for the Krivoye Zerkalo (Distorting Mirror) Theatre in Petrograd (1914–15) and for the Komissarzhevsky Theatre in Moscow (1914–18). He then worked for a number of theatres in Petrograd, sometimes as designer and producer. He collaborated with Vsevolod Meyerkhold (e.g. Lev Tolstoy's *Pervyy vinokur*, 'First distiller', Hermitage Theatre, Petrograd, 1919) and with Nikolay Yeureinov. Annenkov's designs for *Bunt mashin* ('Revolt of the machines', Georg Kaiser adapted by Aleksey Tolstoy, Bol'shoy Dramatic Theatre, Petrograd, 1924) used a Constructivist-inspired mechanized set. Annenkov also designed a number of celebrations and pageants commemorating the Revolution of 1917, including the ambitious re-enactment of the storming of the Winter Palace, which took place in Uritsky (now Dvortsovaya) Square in Petrograd on 7 November 1920 and involved monumental scenery and *c.* 7000 performers. In 1922–4 he led the revival of the activities of the WORLD OF ART group and in 1924 worked towards the establishment of the SOCIETY OF EASEL PAINTERS. The same year he settled in Paris, where he aligned himself with the Ecole de Paris. He continued to design books, stage and film sets in France and Germany, and he exhibited at many joint Russian and French exhibitions. He also became active as an exhibition organizer himself, especially for the USA.

WRITINGS

Yu. Annenkov: *Dnevnik moikh vstrech* [Diary of my meetings], 2 vols (New York, 1966)

BIBLIOGRAPHY

Yu. Annenkov: Portrety [Yu. Annenkov: portraits], text by M. Babenchikov, M. Kuz'min and Ye. Zamyatin (Petrograd, 1922)

M. Babenchikov: 'Annenkov: Grafik i risoval'shchik' [Annenkov: draughtsman and painter], *Press and Revolution*, iv (Moscow, 1925), pp. 101–29

P. Courthion: *Georges Annenkov* (Paris, 1930)

V. RAKITIN

Anne of Beaujeu. *See* BOURBON, §I(4).

Anne of Bohemia. Queen of England. *See under* PLANTAGENET, (6).

Anne of Brittany. *See* VALOIS, (12).

Anne of Denmark, Queen of England and Scotland. *See* STUART, House of, (3).

Anne of France. *See* BOURBON, §I(4).

Annichini. *See* ANICHINI.

Annigoni, Pietro (*b* Milan, 7 June 1910; *d* Florence, 29 Oct 1988). Italian painter. He studied art at the Accademia di Belle Arti in Florence. Exhibitions of his drawings and paintings in 1929 and 1934 (Florence, Gal. Calvalensi & Botti) led to private and public commissions, including portraits and frescoes in the cloisters of S Marco, Florence. An exhibition in 1950 at Wildenstein & Co., London, introduced Annigoni's work to the English public, with whom he remained popular. He based his style on Leonardo da Vinci and Titian, working in tempera and oil to simulate old-master oils, or pen-and-ink to imitate silverpoint. His portraits include *Juanita Forbes* (Forbes priv. col.; see Cammell, 1954, pl. 2), *Margot Fonteyn* (1956; Panama, Arrias priv. col.; see Cammell, 1956, p. 112), the *Duchess of Devonshire* (1954; Chatsworth, Derbys) and a commission from the livery of the Fishmongers Company of the City of London to paint *Queen Elizabeth II* (1954; London, Fishmongers' Hall). This became a popular and much discussed image, and also a rallying point for conventional figurative painters in the 1950s.

In retrospect, Annigoni's work fits into the Neo-Romantic vein of the 1930s but introduces an Italian note. In later years he continued to teach individual pupils and to execute commissions in Florence where he lived. Annigoni's critical reputation has been overshadowed by more avant-garde artists and affected by the neglect of many artists who played little active part in World War II. He had little influence on his contemporaries but earned his reputation through his society portraits.

BIBLIOGRAPHY

C. R. Cammell: *Pietro Annigoni* (London, 1954)

——: *Memoirs of Annigoni* (London, 1956)

R. Wraight: *An Artist's Life, as Told to Robert Wraight* (London, 1977)

PHILIP CORE

Annulet [Lat. *annulus*: 'ring']. Narrow moulding, generally one of several that are typically semicircular in section, employed as a fillet beneath the ECHINUS of a Doric capital (*see* POLYCHROMY, colour pl. I, fig. 1).

Anonimo Magliabechiano. *See* MAGLIABECHIANO, ANONIMO.

Anonymous masters. *See* MASTERS, ANONYMOUS, AND MONOGRAMMISTS, §I.

Anovelo da Imbonate (*fl c.* 1395–1402). Italian illuminator. Two Sacramentaries in Milan are documented as his work. He was responsible for the illumination of all bifolios with historiation in the Coronation Missal of Gian Galeazzo Visconti (Milan, Bib. Capitolare S Ambrogio, MS. 6), which bears his signature below the miniature of *Christ in Majesty* (fol. 153*v*). The list of expenses incurred in the production of the Missal of S Tecla (1402; Milan, Bib. Capitolare Met., MS. II, D. I. 2, fol. 215*r*) records payment to Anovelo of 89 lire 6 soldi for illuminating the initials and canonical miniature. His style is a more schematic and crude version of that of the MASTER OF LATIN 757 (*see* MASTERS, ANONYMOUS, AND MONOGRAMMISTS, §I): decorative and detailed, with compact, round-headed figures with generalized features, often in patterned clothing set against patterned grounds. His most impressive work is on folio 8*r* of the Coronation Missal, which is remarkable for the accuracy with which it records the investiture of Giangaleazzo Visconti as 1st Duke of Milan in September 1395. It was in commemoration of this event that the Duke presented the manuscript to the basilica of S Ambrogio. Anovelo also illuminated two identical copies of the *Lives of SS Aimone and Vermondo*, founders of the monastery of S Vittorio de Meda outside Milan (Milan, Castello Sforzesco, MS. 509 and ex-Jeanson priv. col., sold Monaco, Sotheby's, 28 Feb–1 March 1987, lot 339). Like those in the Sacramentaries, these scenes are attractive and colourful, but artistically naive. The attribution of the frescoed decoration of some Lombard oratories to Anovelo has been suggested.

BIBLIOGRAPHY

P. Toesca: *La pittura e la miniatura nella Lombardia dai più antichi monumenti alla metà del quattrocento* (Milan, 1912/*R* Turin, 1966), pp. 148–9

Arte lombarda dai Visconti agli Sforza (exh. cat., Milan, Pal. Reale, 1958), pp. 41–3

R. Amiet: 'La Tradition manuscrite du Missel Ambrosien', *Scriptorium*, xiv (1960), pp. 40–44
M. G. Recanati: 'Una crocifissione del secondo trecento a Milano: Una proposta sulla committenza e sulla data', *A. Crist.*, lxxviii (1990), p. 18
L. M. Galli: 'Per la pittura lombarda del secondo trecento: Gli affreschi dell'oratorio Porro a Lentate e i suoi maestri', *A. Crist.*, lxxxi (1993), pp. 243–57

KAY SUTTON

An Qi [An Ch'i; *zi* Yizhou; *hao* Lucun] (*b* Tianjin, Shandong Province, 1683; *d* after 1742). Chinese art collector and connoisseur. Son of a wealthy salt merchant of Korean descent who was a bannerman (administrative official) in the house of the powerful Manchu statesman Mingzhu, he is best known for his collection of Chinese paintings and calligraphy. He used the family wealth to acquire works by old masters and to commission works by contemporary artists, assembling one of the finest of the collections of Chinese paintings of the Qing dynasty (1644–1911).

Many of the paintings known to have been in his collection had been previously owned by other well-known collectors, most notably Xiang Yuanbian and Liang Qingbiao (1620–91). But unlike Liang Qingbiao and many other earlier collectors, who concentrated their efforts on acquiring the works of old masters, An Qi was also an active patron of contemporary artists. In 1715 he commissioned a portrait of himself (Cleveland, OH, Mus. A.) from three artists, Wang Hui, Yang Jin (1644–after 1762) and Tu Luo. According to Wang Hui's inscription on the painting, Tu Luo painted An Qi's face. This is one of the earliest examples of a portrait being commissioned by a member of the increasingly powerful merchant class, and as such is an indication of their growing financial and social confidence.

In 1742, by which time An Qi had not only assembled a fine collection but had developed a profound appreciation and understanding of Chinese painting, he completed his famous catalogue, the *Moyuan huiguan*, in which he listed and described in detail paintings in his collection or others that he had seen and studied. Nevertheless, some of the finest paintings that bear the An family seal and were certainly acquired by An Qi were not included in the catalogue, for example *Fishermen*, attributed to XU DAONING. It is unclear why this is so, but it is possible that he was wary of making known to his contemporaries the exact contents of his collection. It is thought that part of An Qi's collection was sold in order to finance the construction of a massive fortified wall around Tianjin, begun in 1725. It is probable that many of the paintings from his collection made their way into the imperial collection at this time, while a significant number were subsequently acquired by the Qianlong Emperor (*reg* 1736–96).

BIBLIOGRAPHY

Hummel: 'An Ch'i'
An Qi: *Moyuan huiguan* [Annotated catalogue of An Qi's collection] (1742); repr. as *Moyuan huiguan fa shu*, (Shanghai, 1920)
Chinese Calligraphy and Painting in the Collection of John M. Crawford, Jr. (exh. cat. by L. Sickman, M. Loehr and Lien-sheng Yong, New York, Pierpont Morgan Lib.; Cambridge, MA, Fogg; Kansas City, MO, Nelson–Atkins Mus. A.; 1962)
Eight Dynasties of Chinese Painting: The Collections of the Nelson–Atkins Museum, Kansas City, and the Cleveland Museum of Art (exh. cat. by Wai-kam Ho and others, Kansas City, MO, Nelson–Atkins Mus. A., Cleveland, OH, Mus. A.; Tokyo, N. Mus.; 1980–81)

LAURA RIVKIN

Anquetin, Louis (*b* Etrepagny, nr Gisors, 26 Jan 1861; *d* Paris, 19 Aug 1932). French painter. He came to Paris in 1882 and studied art at the Ateliers of Bonnat and Cormon, where he was a contemporary and friend of Henri de Toulouse-Lautrec, Emile Bernard and Vincent van Gogh. His early work shows the influence of Impressionism and of Edgar Degas. In 1887 Anquetin and Bernard devised an innovative method of painting using strong black contour lines and flat areas of colour; Anquetin aroused much comment when he showed his new paintings, including the striking *Avenue de Clichy: Five O'Clock in the Evening* (1887; Hartford, CT, Wadsworth Atheneum) at the exhibition of Les XX in Brussels and at the Salon des Indépendants in Paris in 1888. The new style, dubbed Cloisonnisme by the critic Edouard Dujardin (1861–1949), resulted from a study of stained glass, Japanese prints and other so-called 'primitive' sources; it was close to the Synthetist experiments of Paul Gauguin and was adopted briefly by van Gogh during his Arles period. Anquetin's works were shown alongside Gauguin's and Bernard's at the Café Volpini exhibition in 1889, where they attracted considerable attention among younger artists.

Following this early success, Anquetin worked in close association with Bernard and Toulouse-Lautrec on subjects from the life of the city streets, cafés, theatres and racecourses. He exhibited work at Le Barc de Boutteville's gallery, at the Salon des Indépendants and even, in 1891, at a splinter salon of his own, the so-called Salon du Palais des Arts Libéraux, which he set up after the rejection of seven of his works by the jury of the Salon du Champ de Mars. In the mid-1890s, like Bernard, he reverted to the study of the techniques of the Old Masters and evolved towards a more Rubensian style; simultaneously he abandoned modern life subject-matter for traditional allegorical and decorative themes such as *Rinaldo and Armida* (see Bernard, p. 109), the subject of a large decoration commissioned by M. Empain of Brussels. During his later career he designed a number of tapestry cartoons for the Gobelins, and his curtain design for the Théâtre Antoine (1897), first exhibited at the Cubat restaurant in 1897, was bought by the City of Paris. He was awarded the Légion d'honneur.

WRITINGS

Rubens (Paris, 1924)

BIBLIOGRAPHY

E. Bernard: 'Louis Anquetin', *Gaz. B.-A.*, n.s. 5, xi (1934), pp. 108–21
Van Gogh and the Birth of Cloisonnism (exh. cat., Toronto, A.G. Ont.; Amsterdam, Rijksmus. van Gogh, 1981)
Louis Anquetin 'Rond Point des Champs-Elysées, 1889': Mémoire d'un tableau (exh. cat., Saint-Germain-en-Laye, Mus. Dépt. Prieuré, 1987)
Anquetin: La Passion d'être peintre (exh. cat., Paris, Brame & Lorenceau, 1991)

BELINDA THOMSON

Anraadt [Anraedt], **Pieter van** (*b* Utrecht, *c.* 1635; *d* Deventer, *bur* 13 April 1678). Dutch painter. He probably became a pupil of Gerard ter Borch (ii) in Deventer after 1654 and by 1660 he must have visited Amsterdam: the surprisingly mature *Still-life with Stone Jar and Pipes* (The Hague, Mauritshuis), signed and dated 1658, displays both the stylistic influence of ter Borch and an awareness of the work of the Amsterdam painters Jan Jansz. den Uyl (1595/6–1639/40) and Jan Jansz. Treck (*c*. 1606–52). This is the only still-life in van Anraadt's oeuvre, which otherwise consists mainly of portraits, chiefly of groups.

In 1660 he was confirmed in Utrecht, where in 1663 he married Antonia, daughter of the popular poet Jan van der Veen (1578–1659). During the 1660s van Anraadt appears to have painted little; only one dated work from these years is known, the *Departure of Capt. Hendrik de Sandra* (1661; Amsterdam, Rijksmus.), a large group portrait that includes van Anraadt's self-portrait. Thereafter his activity was confined to portraits and genre scenes. Although he lived in Deventer, his commissions came mainly from Amsterdam and Haarlem. In 1674 he painted *Four Regentesses of the Holy Ghost House in Haarlem* (Haarlem, Frans Halsmus.). One year later he completed another major work, *Six Regents and the Warden of the Old People's Hospital in Amsterdam* (Amsterdam, Hist. Mus.). These works demonstrate his ability as a fine craftsman, rather than the virtuoso that might have been anticipated by the still-life masterpiece of 1658.

BIBLIOGRAPHY

H. R. Hoetink: 'Beschouwingen naar aanleiding van een unicum' [Observations on a unique object], *Boymans bijdragen: opstellen van medewerkers en oud-medewerkers van het Museum Boymans-van Beuningen voor J. C. Ebbinge Wubben* (Rotterdam, 1978), pp. 104–9

B. P. J. BROOS

Anrion [Henrion]**, Adrien-Joseph** (*b* Nivelles, 14 Sept 1730; *d* ?Brussels, end 1771). South Netherlandish sculptor. He served his apprenticeship at Nivelles with Laurent Delvaux, with whom he collaborated on a series of statues of *Apostles* in oak for the collegiate church of Ste Gertrude. Between *c*. 1757 and *c*. 1761 he made a monumental stone group of *Neptune with Aeolus and Amphitrite*, commissioned by Claude Lamoral II, Prince of Ligne (1685–1766), for the ornamental lake of the château of Beloeil, Hainaut. In 1761 Anrion was given the title of Court Sculptor by Charles of Lorraine (1712–80), the Austrian Governor of the Netherlands. From 1766 he worked under the direction of the architect Laurent-Benoît Dewez on the decoration of Charles's new palace in Brussels. Anrion's most important contribution to the work was 12 low reliefs of the *Labours of Hercules* (gilt-bronze; untraced) for the main staircase. During the same period he executed sculptures for the high altar of the Benedictine abbey church of Afflighem in Brabant, which was being renovated by Dewez. These included marble statues of *Religion* (signed and dated 1769) and *St Peter* (both now Brussels, St Jacques sur Coudenberg). A terracotta model of 1765 for *Religion* is in the Musées Royaux des Beaux-Arts in Brussels. In 1769 Anrion executed, for the chapel of the château of Seneffe, Hainaut, a marble altar from a model by Dewez. In that year he received a commission for a chimney-piece for the Hôtel d'Ursel, Brussels, while in 1770 he worked for the abbey of Heylissem in Opheylissem, Brabant, and in 1771 for the collegiate church of St Salvator, Harelbeke, in West Flanders. Anrion's work announced the Neo-classical style.

BIBLIOGRAPHY

BNB

M. Devigne: 'De la parenté d'inspiration des artistes flamands du XVIIe et du XVIIIe siècle: Laurent Delvaux et ses élèves', *Mém. Acad. Royale Belgique: Cl. B.-A.*, n. s. 1, ii (1928), pp. 15–19

F. Leuridant: *Beloeil: Le Château, les jardins* (Paris, 1930)

X. Duquenne: *Le Château de Seneffe* (Brussels, 1978), p. 122

HELENA BUSSERS

Ansaldi, Innocenzio (*b* Pescia, nr Lucca, 12 Feb 1734; *d* Pescia, 16 Feb 1816). Italian painter and writer. His family came from Voltri, near Genoa, and his ancestors included the painter Andrea Ansaldo. He studied drawing at the Accademia Fiorentina and in November 1754 went to Rome, where he trained with the artist Agostino Masucci. In 1759 Ansaldi returned to Pescia to work with a local painter, Padre Alberico da Vellano. During the 1760s he made visits to Florence, Bologna, Genoa, Padua, Venice and Naples and in addition to looking at paintings, spent time studying history and classical mythology. He also published a book on art in Pescia, the *Descrizione delle sculture, pitture ed architettura della città e diocesi di Pescia* (Bologna, 1772). In 1772 he returned to Rome, where he studied the work of Raphael, Michelangelo and Annibale Carracci, among others, acquired some proficiency in architecture and became friendly with the German painter Anton Raphael Mengs. Ten years later Ansaldi returned to Pescia, where he enjoyed a modestly successful career. His training and inclination led him towards a classicizing, academic style of painting of the kind exemplified by Mengs, and his works decorate several of the local churches.

Ansaldi continued to write, and he translated Charles-Alphonse Du Fresnoy's 17th century poetical treatise *De arte graphica* into Italian, as *L'arte della pittura di C. A. du Fresnoy* (Lucca, 1813). He also composed his own poem-treatise, *Il pittore originale* (1816), which he addressed to Mengs. In the biography of Ansaldi by the writer Domenico Moreni (1763–1835) that prefaces the poem, Moreni referred to Ansaldi's extensive knowledge of art. This had enabled Ansaldi to help and advise art collectors and writers such as Moreni himself, Francesco Bartoli (1745–?1806), Luigi Crespi, Luigi Lanzi, Leopoldo Cicognara (1767–1834) and the Genoese art biographer Carlo Giuseppe Ratti, to whom Ansaldi had dedicated his translation of Du Fresnoy.

WRITINGS

Descrizione delle sculture, pitture ed architettura della città e diocesi di Pescia (Bologna, 1772)

trans.: *L'arte della pittura di C. A. du Fresnoy* (Lucca, 1813)

Il pittore originale, poemetto didascalico, del pittore e poeta Innocenzio Ansaldi di Pescia (Florence, 1816) [with biog. note by D. Moreni, pp. 1–54]

BIBLIOGRAPHY

DBI

JANET SOUTHORN

Ansaldo, (Giovanni) Andrea (*b* Voltri, 24 Aug 1584; *d* Genoa, 18 Aug 1638). Italian painter. His first teacher was Orazio Cambiaso, son of Luca Cambiaso, from whom he learnt the principles of design and acquired his proficiency in the use of colour. Ansaldo's appreciation of colour must also have owed something to Veronese, whose works he copied as a student. Orazio Cambiaso's large canvas of *St James Converting Josiah* (*c*. 1600; Genoa, Oratory of S Giacomo delle Fucine) is one of many sources for

Ansaldo's multi-figured and highly detailed compositions, set in a deep architectural space. The elegant figures and subtle tonalities of his early works are derived also from the work of Tuscan Mannerist artists in Genoa, such as Pietro Sorri (1556–1621), Ventura Salimbeni and Aurelio Lomi (1556–1622). The sumptuous draperies and strong chiaroscuro contrasts of Giovanni Battista Paggi, who had adopted the Tuscan manner after a period in Florence, influenced Ansaldo, as did the rich impasto of Bernardo Strozzi and Simone Barabbino (*b* 1585). In the 1620s the work of the more progressive Lombard artists Cerano and Giulio Cesare Procaccini, who visited the city between 1618 and 1621, had an impact on his art. Ansaldo was also indebted to the realism of the colony of Flemish artists who worked in Genoa at this time. From such rich sources he created a style justly described as 'elegant in design, well founded in perspective, intelligent in *sotto in sù*, expressive in effects, and soft and gentle in colouring' (Soprani, p. 200).

Although Ansaldo's dated or documented works are few, most of the paintings listed in Soprani survive. They span a period of over 20 years. The earliest dated picture is the *Beheading of St John the Baptist* (1615; Recco, S Giovanni Battista), in which the intense lighting and gleaming metals recall Paggi. The documented works of the 1620s, the *Martyrdom of St Sebastian* (1621; Cadiz Cathedral), the vault fresco of the *Apotheosis of St Charles Borromeo* (1622–3) and an altarpiece, the *Miracle of St Charles Borromeo* (1623; both Albisola, Nostra Signora della Concordia), show the increasing influence of Procaccini and Cerano. In the *Miracle* the elaborate candlesticks reveal Ansaldo's expertise in depicting shiny, brilliant metals. The *Apotheosis* shows his interest in illusionism and foreshortening, which is further developed in frescoes in the Villa Spinola di San Pietro in Genoa-Sampierdarena, which may be dated in the 1620s. In a series of rooms on the *piano nobile* he painted scenes from the *Story of Perseus*, the imprese of Ambrogio Spinola and, in the *salone*, a frieze of musicians behind an illusionistic balustrade.

Ansaldo was expert at defining perspectives and, like Lazzaro Tavarone, often set his figures in backgrounds that proclaimed not only the intricacies of the newly built palaces and churches in Genoa, so admired by Rubens, but also his skill in arranging architecture in deep perspective. From the late 1620s the settings became increasingly grandiose, and the deep space dominated the figures. An organ screen (Genoa, S Lorenzo) documented to 1635 shows, on one side and within a majestic temple, the *Charity of St Lawrence* and, on the other, further scenes from the *Life of St Lawrence* set against a rich display of elaborate architecture. Complex multi-levelled compositions also featured in altarpieces and in canvases made for private collectors, for example the *Allegory of Ferdinand II de' Medici* (*c.* 1629; Florence, Pitti) and the *Judgement of Solomon* (priv. col., see Newcome, 1987, fig. 49). His extravagant use of perspective and ornament is seen particularly in his altarpiece of the *Triumph in the Name of John the Baptist* (*c.* 1625; Loano, S Giovanni Battista) and in a painting from the 1630s, *St Thomas Baptizing the Three Kings* (Genoa, S Fede).

The architectural settings were also important in Ansaldo's many fresco cycles. Around 1633 he frescoed the ceiling of the crypt of Nostra Signora del Monte, Genoa, with many small scenes of the *Life of the Virgin*. In the

Andrea Ansaldo: *Head of St John the Baptist Brought to Herodias*, pen and brown ink and brown wash, heightened with white, 213×350 mm, *c.* 1635 (London, Victoria and Albert Museum)

fresco of the *Assumption of the Virgin* (*c.* 1635) on the small dome of the chapel in the Palazzo Airoli Negroni, Genoa, he experimented with ideas that he developed in his most celebrated work, the cupola fresco of the *Assumption of the Virgin* (*c.* 1636; Genoa, SS Annunziata del Vastato). This is a highly intricate and iconographically complex design. Around the drum elaborate *quadratura* settings frame the *Four Evangelists*; between them are scenes showing *Adam and Eve*, saints and prophets, and the *Virgin* ascending into the lantern to *God the Father*. The originality of the dome design caused his contemporaries to discredit it, and only after he had sent the design to the Florentine Accademia del Disegno, where it was praised by Jacopo da Empoli and Domenico Passignano, and had painted the design on a wall, did his patrons, the Lomellini family, permit him to start work. His concept, restored in 1700–05 by Gregorio de' Ferrari, inspired the integration of figures and *quadratura* framework in Giulio Benso's frescoes, the *Assumption of the Virgin* and the *Annunciation* (1640–47; Genoa, SS Annunziata).

Most of Ansaldo's known drawings, mainly in pen and brown ink, are compositional studies. They include elaborate, scenographic architectural perspectives, with small, compact figures, as in the *Presentation in the Temple* (1630s; Genoa, Pal. Rosso), which was a sketch for a fresco completed *c.* 1670 by Benso and Giovanni Battista Carlone I on the presbytery side wall in SS Annunziata, and the *Head of St John the Baptist Brought to Herodias* (*c.* 1635; London, V&A; see fig.). Ansaldo's students included Gioacchino Assereto, Orazio de' Ferrari, Bartolommeo Basso and Giovanni Raffaello Badaracco.

BIBLIOGRAPHY

DBI

R. Soprani: *Vite* (1674), pp. 141–6; ed. C. G. Ratti (1768–9), i, pp. 200–11

R. Longhi: 'Verso il riposo di Gio. Andrea Ansaldo', *Scritti giovanili* (Florence, 1961), pp. 345–6

V. Belloni: *Pittura genovese del seicento* (Genoa, 1969), pp. 155–80

Genoese Baroque Drawings (exh. cat. by M. Newcome, Binghamton, SUNY; Worcester, MA, A. Mus.; 1972)

E. Gavazza: *La grande decorazione a Genova*, i (Genoa, 1974)

Un pittore genovese del seicento: Andrea Ansaldo, 1584–1638 (exh. cat., ed. F. Boggero; Genoa, Commenda S Giovanni di Pré; Rome, Pal. Barberini; 1985)

F. R. Pesenti: *La pittura in Liguria: Artisti del primo seicento* (Genoa, 1986)

M. Newcome: 'Ansaldo Revisited', *Paragone*, xxxviii/449 (1987), pp. 61–74

Disegni genovesi dal XVI al XVIII secolo (exh. cat. by M. Newcome Schleier, Florence, Uffizi, 1989), pp. 73–4

M. NEWCOME

Ansano di Matteo. *See* SANO DI MATTEO.

Ansano di Pietro di Mencio. *See* SANO DI PIETRO.

Ansbach. German town in Bavaria, *c.* 40 km south-east of Nuremberg. Ansbach is known particularly as a centre of ceramics production. A faience factory was established by Matthias Baur and J. C. Ripp in Ansbach *c.* 1708–10. Wares included jugs and tankards at first decorated in blue and later in the *famille verte* (green, yellow, iron-red, blue and purple) palette. In 1757 a porcelain factory was established beside the faience factory at the behest of Margrave Karl Alexander (*d* 1806), who in 1763 transferred it to Schloss Bruckberg. The secret formula for porcelain was brought to Ansbach by Johann Friedrich Kändler (1734–91), a nephew of the Meissen Modellmeister Johann Joachim Kändler, who had worked at the factory of Wilhelm Caspar Wegely (1714–64) in Berlin, as had the superb miniaturist and colour specialist Johann Carl Gerlach (1723–86) and the modeller Carl Gottlob Laut (*d* 1802). The shapes produced at Ansbach are therefore reminiscent of Berlin wares. Meissen was the inspiration for the relief decoration developed by Kändler, which was retained throughout the 18th century. The 'Ansbach' pattern consisted of four symmetrically arranged landscapes within Rococo cartouches on a basketware border (e.g. plate, 1765–70; Hamburg, Mus. Kst. & Gew.). Rococo motifs with applied acanthus leaves were used as three-dimensional decoration on handles, and small ladies' heads were used to decorate handles and spouts (e.g. teapot, *c.* 1760; Hamburg, Mus. Kst. & Gew.). On teapots or chocolate-pots the spouts end in a dog or dragon's head. Painted motifs included flowers by Johann Wolfgang Mayerhöffer (1699–1771) and Johann Jakob Schreitmüller (*fl* 1779–1807), fruit and garlands by Alexander Telorac (1749–92), animals and birds by Gottlob Büttner (*fl* 1785–93) and Albrecht Hutter (*c.* 1754–1804), scenes after Watteau, and genre scenes and landscapes by Johann Melchior Schöllhammer (1745–1816) and Johann Eberhard Stenglein (*fl* 1765–95). In addition to utilitarian wares, services and ornaments, one of the main production lines was figures for the Margrave's court; the inspiration for these came from the work of such artists as Johannes Esaias Nilson, Claude Gillot, Jacques Callot and Johann Balthasar Probst (1673–1750). The faience factory closed in 1839 and the porcelain factory in 1860.

BIBLIOGRAPHY

A. Bayer: *Ansbacher Porzellan* (Brunswick, 1959)

WALTER SPIEGL

Ansdell, Richard (*b* Liverpool, 11 May 1815; *d* Farnborough, Hants, 20 April 1885). English painter. He was the son of an artisan and in 1835 entered the Liverpool Academy Schools, where he later became president (1845–6). One of his earliest and largest dated works is the *Waterloo Coursing Meeting* (1.4×2.4 m, 1840; Liverpool, Walker A.G.). This canvas demonstrates his considerable skill as a portrait painter and creates a detailed record of a major sporting event of the period which was attended by many members of the local aristocracy, some of whom, notably the 3rd Earl of Sefton, were his patrons. It was engraved and published in 1843, and other works were similarly popularized. *Shooting Party in the Highlands* (1840; Liverpool, Walker A.G.) was the first of 149 works exhibited at the Royal Academy. It shows huntsmen with their horses and dogs resting after a good day's sport, a theme that Ansdell often depicted. He also portrayed other rural scenes such as gamekeepers or shepherds with domestic and wild animals, often in historical settings. All are painted with precision and sensitivity and without sentimentality. Although based in London from 1847 until 1884, Ansdell owned houses in Lancashire and Scotland and found inspiration in northern landscape. He travelled to Spain with the painter John Phillip in 1856 and alone in 1857 and produced several works of Spanish inspiration, for example *Feeding Goats in the Alhambra* (Preston,

Harris Mus. & A.G.). He also collaborated with William Powell Frith and Thomas Creswick in rural genre scenes. Ansdell was commercially successful and was elected ARA in 1861 and RA in 1870. His animal subjects often rival those of Landseer, both in execution and composition, and place him in the forefront of Victorian sporting art. The contents of Ansdell's studio were sold at Christie's, London, 19 March 1886.

BIBLIOGRAPHY

Merseyside Painters, People and Places (exh. cat., ed. M. Bennet; Liverpool, Walker A.G., 1978)

Richard Ansdell: A Centenary Exhibition (exh. cat., London, Malcolm Innes Gal., 1985)

LUCINDA LUBBOCK

Anselmi, Michelangelo (*b* Siena or Lucca, ?1492; *d* Parma, 1556). Italian painter and draughtsman. He was arguably the most imaginative painter in Parma in the early 16th century after Correggio and Parmigianino. However, he was trained in Siena, though his only surviving work there, a *Visitation* in the church of Fontegiusta, shows the importance of Sodoma in the formation of his art. Anselmi's family was apparently from Parma, but he is not securely documented there until 1520. In that year he began to paint in S Giovanni Evangelista, where he decorated the ribs of the nave vaults, the apses of both transepts and at least two chapels: the chapel in the north transept, with frescoes of *SS Agnes and Catherine*, and the sixth chapel on the left of the nave, with frescoes of the *Four Doctors of the Church*. It has also been suggested that he executed the frescoes of *SS Nicholas and Hilary* in the fourth chapel on the left, which have been attributed to Parmigianino. In 1525 Anselmi was one of the group of prominent artists consulted about the construction of S Maria della Steccata, Parma, where his most extensive works in fresco were subsequently painted. These comprise the *Coronation of the Virgin* (1541–2, altered 1547) in the main apse, a commission that was given to him after the death of Parmigianino in 1540 and for which he was required to work from a 'coloured drawing' by Giulio Romano, and, on the facing apse and vault over the west door, an *Adoration of the Magi* and *Four Prophets*, which were completed by Bernardino Gatti.

In 1522 Anselmi was one of the select group who received commissions from the cathedral authorities; his task was to decorate the vault of the south transept, but the work was not completed until the signing of a second contract of 1548. The frescoes do not survive but were replaced by what appear to be accurate copies. As a fresco painter, he also decorated the dome and pendentives of the oratory of the Immaculate Conception in Parma, where the role of his collaborator Francesco Maria Rondani must have been a distinctly subsidiary one; he also executed a series of grisaille *Apostles* and four biblical narratives for the Palazzo Lalatta (now Collegio Maria Luigia) in Parma and a cycle of the *Church Fathers* for the chapel of the Immaculate Conception in the collegiate church at Busseto. Furthermore, both documents and preparatory drawings reveal that he executed a steady stream of coats of arms for external display.

In conjunction with his activity as a fresco painter, Anselmi produced a considerable number of altarpieces and smaller-scale religious works. The majority of the altarpieces seem to have been executed for churches in Parma. Three of the best remain *in situ*: *Christ Carrying the Cross* in S Giovanni Evangelista, and a *Virgin and Child with Four Saints* and a *St Agnes* both in the cathedral. The one notable exception outside Parma is the *Baptism* in S Prospero, Reggio Emilia (see fig.), which is probably his most successful altarpiece. A single *Cupid* (ex-Agnew's, London, see Ghidiglia Quintavalle, fig. 43) is his sole surviving generally accepted mythological painting, but the drawings of *Leda* and *Hercules and Cacus* (both Paris, Louvre) suggest a wider interest in this type of subject, as does a *Lucretia* (Naples, Capodimonte), traditionally given to Bedoli, which has all the hallmarks of Anselmi's style. A productive and extremely stylish draughtsman, he almost invariably employed red chalk, generally with great fluency and at times with extraordinary tonal richness (e.g. London, BM; Paris, Louvre).

The works from Anselmi's early years in Parma mark him as a genuine original, and it may be that between 1520 and 1525 he had more to teach Correggio and Parmigianino than to learn from them, especially concerning boldly luminous colour and daring *sfumato*. In terms of style he remained his own man, but later there are occasional compositional borrowings from Correggio and Parmigianino, as well as a gradual but undeniable fading of inspiration. His reputation has not been helped by the fact that his one major work outside Italy, an altarpiece of his maturity, the *Virgin and Child with SS John the Baptist and Stephen* (Paris, Louvre), is not usually exhibited.

Michelangelo Anselmi: *Baptism*, oil on panel, 2.58×1.87 m, 1530s (Reggio Emilia, S Prospero)

BIBLIOGRAPHY

A. E. Popham: *Correggio's Drawings* (London, 1957), pp. 107–13, 169–72

A. Ghidiglia Quintavalle: *Michelangelo Anselmi* (Parma, 1960)

F. Viatte: 'Dessins de l'école de Parme', *Rev. Louvre*, 5–6 (1982), pp. 351–5

Correggio and his Legacy: Sixteenth-century Emilian Drawings (exh. cat. by D. De Grazia, Washington, DC, N.G.A.; Parma, G.N.; 1984), pp. 194–207

The Age of Correggio and the Carracci (exh. cat., Bologna, Pin. N.; Washington, DC, N.G.A.; New York, Met.; 1986–7), pp. 53–5

D. Ekserdjian: 'Parmigianino in San Giovanni Evangelista', *Florence and Italy: Renaissance Studies in Honour of Nicolai Rubenstein*, ed. P. Denley and C. Elam (London, 1988), pp. 448–50

DAVID EKSERDJIAN

Anselmo, Giovanni (*b* Borgofranco d'Ivrea, Piedmont, 5 Aug 1934). Italian sculptor. After working as a painter from 1959 to 1964, he turned to conceptual art in 1965 and by 1968 was associated with the emergence of ARTE POVERA, of which he became one of the strictest and most coherent exponents. His limited output consisted largely of the staging of major physical processes whose long-term effects the audience was invited to imagine, in such a way that the non-material dimension of thought was brought to bear on bulky and spectacular physical phenomena. In *Direction* (150×500×800 mm, 1967–9; Paris, Pompidou), for instance, a magnetic compass is set within a circular recess of a slab of granite shaped like an arrowhead and displayed pointing north, thus proposing two different ways of expressing the concept alluded to by the title.

A consistent message in Anselmo's work is that one should not entirely believe one's eyes, since there is always a component that lies beyond appearances. In one sculpture, *Untitled* (1968; Paris, Pompidou), he presented two blocks of basalt separated by a space filled with lettuce leaves destined to perish within a short space of time; the viewer is thus led to envisage the hard elements in a state of reciprocal friction that will eventually wear them both away. In another work, *Towards a Groove in an Indefinite Number of Millions of Years* (1969; Turin, Christian Stein priv. col., see 1985 exh. cat., p. 38), a post protected by a layer of lubricant is leant against a wall, giving the impression that it will ultimately gouge a groove in it as the protective buffer is worn away and it is pulled downwards by the force of gravity. The conceptual element so fundamental to Anselmo's work has sometimes taken the form of words projected on slides into space, as in *Infinity* (1970; many versions, see 1985 exh. cat., p. 45): the messages could either be absorbed by the spectators by placing themselves in the rays of projected light, or lost in space by being left to pass unimpeded, giving rise to a disquieting sensation. Anselmo received an international award at the Venice Biennale of 1990.

WRITINGS

Leggere (Turin, 1972)

BIBLIOGRAPHY

U. Castagnotto: 'Giovanni Anselmo', *Data*, 18 (1975)

Giovanni Anselmo (exh. cat. by S. Pagé, Paris, Mus. A. Mod. Ville Paris, 1985)

Giovanni Anselmo (exh. cat. by B. Merz, Lyon, Mus. St Pierre A. Contemp., 1989)

For further bibliography *see* ARTE POVERA.

RENATO BARILLI

Anselmo da Campione. *See under* CAMPIONESI.

Anselmus (*fl* Milan, 1171). Italian sculptor. He signed, with Girardus, the reliefs of the Porta Romana in Milan (now Milan, Castello Sforzesco); he is described as *Dedalus alter*, while Girardus is mentioned as *pollice docto*. The reliefs, dated 1171, show contemporary scenes of warfare between the Milanese and inhabitants of Brescia, Cremona and Bergamo. Fra Jacobo holds a crusading standard; St Ambrose is fighting the Arians and Jews. These sculptures, relating both to the patron saints of the city-state and to contemporary life, are typical of civic commissions. The narrative style depends somewhat on that of Nicholaus, but the reliefs also show influences from Provençal Romanesque and the school of Wiligelmo, seen in the monumentality of the figures, the classicizing facial features and the complex relief technique. The sculptors formed part of the larger school of Campionesi masters, and according to some scholars the Anselmus active in Milan should be identified with Anselmo da Campione, who worked at Modena Cathedral (*see* CAMPIONESI).

BIBLIOGRAPHY

A. Venturi: *Storia* (1901–40/*R* 1967)

G. de Francovich: *Benedetto Antelami* (Milan, 1952)

A. W. Arslan: 'La scultura romanica', *Stor. Milano*, iii (1954), pp. 591–3

T. Binaghi Olivari: 'I rilievi di Porta Romana e alcune sculture milanesi del XII secolo', *Contrib. Ist. Stor. A. Med. & Mod.*, ii (1972), pp. 44–52

J. Gardner: 'An Introduction to the Iconography of the Medieval City Gate', *Dumbarton Oaks Pap.*, xli (1987), pp. 199–213

CHRISTINE VERZAR

Anseramo da Trani (*fl c.* 1276–92). Italian sculptor. He signed the tomb of the Falcone children placed against the lateral wall of S Margherita, Bisceglie (Puglia). The effaced date in the inscription was probably 1276. The monument has an ogee-shaped baldacchino with a trefoil arch. Anseramo also signed the portal of the collegiate church of Terlizzi (destr.), now immured in the church of the Madonna del Rosario in that city. The tympanum shows the *Last Supper*, the lintel the *Annunciation*, the *Three Magi*, the *Nativity* and the *Crucifixion*. Fragments found in Bari Cathedral (Bari, Pin. Prov.), including two bearing Anseramo's name, have been convincingly identified as the remains of two ciboria over the side altars of the Virgin and St John the Baptist. They were commissioned by Archbishop Romualdo Grisone (*reg* 1280–1309), who rededicated the church in 1292. A now untraced fragment of a tomb once standing against the collegiate church of Terlizzi was attributed by Bertaux to Anseramo on stylistic grounds. There is no reason to identify the sculptor with the *Anseranus protomagister* who signed an architrave of Emperor Frederick II's castle at Orta (destr.). Anseramo's work is, like much contemporary work in the region, characterized by rich ornament showing an elaboration of Romanesque Apulian forms. The portal of Terlizzi also shows an awkward treatment of the human figure. The Byzantine features of the iconography of the scenes point to two-dimensional models (e.g. illuminated manuscripts and frescoes). Apparently the sculptor had difficulties in transferring such designs into relief.

BIBLIOGRAPHY

Thieme–Becker

E. Bertaux: *L'Art dans l'Italie méridionale de la fin de l'empire romain à la conquête de Charles d'Anjou*, ii (Paris, 1904/*R* Paris and Rome, 1968), pp. 704, 756–61

J. Baltrušaitis: 'La Troisième Sculpture romane', *Formositas romanica: Beiträge zur Erforschung der romanischen Kunst Joseph Gantner zugeeignet* (Frauenfeld, 1958), pp. 47–84 (60–61)
H. Buschhausen: *Die süditalienische Bauplastik im Königreich Jerusalem von König Wilhelm II. bis Kaiser Friedrich II.* (Vienna, 1978), pp. 387–8
M. S. Calò Mariani: entry in *L'Art dans l'Italie méridionale: Aggiornamento dell'opera di Emile Bertaux*, ed. A. Prandi, V (Rome, 1978), pp. 958–62

VICTOR M. SCHMIDT

Anshan. *See* MALYAN, TALL'I.

Anshelm, Thomas (*fl* Basle, 1485; *d* 1524). German engraver and printer. He established himself in Basle in 1485 but subsequently worked as a printer in Strasbourg (1487, 1488), Pforzheim (1500–10), Tübingen (1511–17) and Hagenau (1516–22). Although a few of his prints bear dates between 1501 and 1506, stylistically his work belongs to the 15th-century tradition.

BIBLIOGRAPHY

Hollstein: *Ger.*
A. A. W. Goetze: *Die hochdeutschen Drucker der Reformationszeit* (Strasbourg, 1905), p. 33

JETTY E. VAN DER STERRE

Anshutz, Thomas (Pollock) (*b* Newport, KY, 5 Oct 1851; *d* Fort Washington, PA, 16 June 1912). American painter and teacher. In 1872 he moved to New York, where he enrolled at the National Academy of Design. By 1875 he had advanced to the life class but found the Academy 'a rotten old institution'. Moving to Philadelphia, Anshutz entered a life class taught by Thomas Eakins at the Philadelphia Sketch Club and transferred to the Pennsylvania Academy of the Fine Arts when it opened its new building in 1876. Continuing to study under Eakins and Christian Schussele (1824/6–79), Anshutz soon became Eakins's assistant demonstrator for anatomy courses taught by the surgeon William Williams Keen.

Anshutz's style quickly progressed from a tight linearity toward an emphasis on solid form, expressed through simplified modelling and a thorough knowledge of anatomy. For his first mature works he sought subjects in the active lives around him, whether in the lush pastoral setting of *The Father and his Son Harvesting* (1879; New York, Berry-Hill Gals) or the cruder homestead of *The Way They Live (Cabbages)* (1879; New York, Met.). The factual yet measured depiction of both outdoor setting and human activity in these works also characterizes Anshutz's finest painting, *The Ironworkers' Noontime* (1880; San Francisco, CA, de Young Mem. Mus.), a scene of factory workers at their midday break. Masterful in the arrangement and description of human form and industrial setting, the painting was groundbreaking for the choice of subject and the objectivity of the artist's approach. Curiously, Anshutz never attempted another work so bold or important, perhaps because his duties at the Academy were increasingly demanding of his energies.

By 1881 Anshutz had become Chief Demonstrator for life-class dissections at the Academy; two years later he became Assistant Professor in Painting and Drawing to Eakins. In 1884 he assisted Eakins and Eadweard Muybridge with their experiments in motion photography at the University of Pennsylvania. Yet by 1886 Anshutz had joined the students and faculty who charged Eakins with misconduct of the life class; after Eakins resigned, Anshutz succeeded him as Professor of Painting and Drawing. Thereafter teaching dominated his activities.

In 1892 Anshutz married and combined his honeymoon with a year's study at the Académie Julian, Paris. On his return he began working more in pastels and watercolour, showing a greater interest in light and colour, even while basing his compositions on photographic sources. He resumed teaching at the Academy in 1893; five years later he joined Hugh Breckenridge (1870–1937) in establishing a summer school for landscape painting. In 1909 Anshutz succeeded William Merritt Chase as Director of the Academy; the next year he was elected President of the Philadelphia Sketch Club. Anshutz's portraits and figural paintings from these later years demonstrate his characteristic concern for modelling and form, yet works such as *The Tanagra* (1911; Philadelphia, PA Acad. F.A.) also display more fluid brushwork and a hint of decorative flatness, suggesting the influence of Chase as well as study in Paris.

One of the most influential American teachers of the 19th century, Anshutz transmitted Eakins's emphasis on careful observation, solid form and comprehension of anatomy. While insisting on fundamentals, he encouraged individual expression. His instruction formed a bridge between the analytical realism of Eakins and the more expressive, experimental styles of the early 20th century. Anshutz's most successful students included the Pennsylvania landscape painter Edward Redfield (1869–1965), such members of the Ashcan school as Robert Henri and John Sloan, and artists who drew inspiration from European modernism, such as Charles Sheeler and John Marin.

BIBLIOGRAPHY

F. Zeigler: 'An Unassuming Painter: Thomas P. Anshutz', *Brush & Pencil*, iv (1899), pp. 277–84
R. Bowman: 'Nature, the Photograph and Thomas Anshutz', *A. J.* [New York], xxxiii/1 (1973), pp. 32–40
Thomas P. Anshutz, 1851–1912 (exh. cat. by S. D. Heard, Philadelphia, PA Acad. F.A., 1973)
L. Goodrich: *Thomas Eakins*, i (Cambridge, MA, 1982)
Thomas Anshutz: Artist and Teacher (exh. cat. by R. C. Griffin, Huntington, NY, Heckscher Mus., 1994)

SALLY MILLS

Ansuino da Forlì [Ansuyn da Furlì] (*fl* Padua, 1451). Italian painter. A document dated 30 Oct 1451 records a payment for a fresco, signed OPVS ANSVINI, that depicted *St Christopher Preaching* (destr. 1944; fragments survive) in the middle compartment of the right-hand wall of the Ovetari Chapel in the church of the Eremitani, Padua. Ansuino and others had been appointed in place of Giovanni d'Alemagna and Antonio Vivarini to produce six scenes from the *Life of St Christopher* after Giovanni's death in 1450. Scholars have identified the 'Ansuyn depentore' of the Ovetari document with the Ansuyn da Furlì mentioned by Marcantonio Michiel as Filippo Lippi's and Niccolo Pizzolo's collaborator in the decoration (1434–7; destr.) of the chapel of the Podestà, Padua. The style of the Ovetari fresco is fairly close to that developed in the workshops of Pizzolo and Mantegna around 1450. Schmarsow assigned to Ansuino the two scenes in the lunette at the top of the right-hand wall of the Ovetari Chapel depicting *St Christopher and the Devil* and *St Christopher Taking Leave of the King*. Longhi and Zeri, however, have assigned the latter to Girolamo di Giovanni da Camerino.

BIBLIOGRAPHY

DBI

M. Michiel: *Notizia d'opere di disegno* (MS.; *c.* 1520–40); ed. G. Frizzoni (Bologna, 1884), pp. 64, 76

A. Schmarsow: *Melozzo da Forlì* (Berlin and Stuttgart, 1886), pp. 302–8

——: 'Maîtres italiens à la Galerie d'Altenburg', *Gaz. B.-A.*, n.s. 2, xviii (1897), pp. 177–95

R. Longhi: *Lettera pittorica a Giuseppe Fiocco* (1926); also in *Saggi e ricerche, 1925–1928,* II/i of *Edizione delle opere complete di Roberto Longhi* (Florence, 1967), pp. 87–92

F. Zeri: *Due dipinti, la filologia e un nome* (Turin, 1961), pp. 75–6

Anta [antae]. Engaged column or pilaster terminating the side wall of a Classical building. When the columns of an end portico stand between projecting end walls terminating in *antae*, they are said to be *in antis* (*see* GREECE, ANCIENT, fig. 7a).

□

Antal, Frederick [Frigyes] (*b* Budapest, 21 Dec 1887; *d* London, 4 April 1954). Hungarian art historian. He studied art history in Vienna with Max Dvořák and wrote a thesis on French Neo-classical and early Romantic painting. After residing for brief periods in Budapest, Florence, Vienna and Berlin, he settled in London in 1933. He never held a regular teaching position but lectured occasionally at the Courtauld Institute of Art. He wrote on Florentine painting in relation to its social setting, on the origins and evolution of Mannerism and on the interaction of Romanticism and Classicism from the French Revolution to the death of Gericault. His interpretative stance, as set forth in 'Remarks on the Method of Art History' (1949), was Marxist. Style, for Antal, was not restricted to formal features but included subject-matter and the social, political and economic context of the artist and work of art. His outlook enabled him to give such artists as Hogarth and Fuseli, who had previously been considered of only limited interest, a context in art history. For instance, he demonstrated how Hogarth's thematically and formally innovative art revealed the views and tastes of a broad cross-section of English society. He followed Aby Warburg in his rejection of a view that valued 'art for art's sake'.

WRITINGS

Florentine Painting and its Social Background: The Bourgeois Republic before Cosimo de' Medici's Advent to Power: XIV and Early XV Centuries (London, 1948)

Fuseli Studies (London, 1956)

Hogarth and his Place in European Art (New York, 1962)

Classicism and Romanticism, with Other Studies in Art History (London, 1966) [includes the essay 'Remarks on the Method of Art History']

BIBLIOGRAPHY

J. Berger: 'Frederick Antal: A Personal Tribute', *Burl. Mag.*, xcvi/617 (1954), pp. 259–60

DEBORAH J. HAYNES

Antefix. Plaque closing the outer end of the final cover tile in each row of overlapping cover tiles running down from the ridge to the eaves of a sloped roof on Classical Greek and Roman and on Neo-classical buildings. Its practical functions were to prevent rain from penetrating below the cover tile and seeping through the opening

Palmette antefixes from Olympia, Greece, 5th–4th century BC, from *Die Baudenkmaler von Olympia* (Berlin, 1896)

between the adjacent pan tiles beneath, and to prevent wind from dislodging the row of cover tiles. Although functional in origin, the antefix soon also became a decorative element adorned with relief and/or painted decoration. The size and shape of early examples was determined by that of the cover tile, but by *c.* 550–525 BC the plaque had become larger than its tile in order to accommodate more decoration.

The earliest antefixes, from the first half of the 7th century BC, apparently formed part of undecorated terracotta roofs in the Corinthia of Greece. Decorated examples appeared in the second half of the century, taking forms that varied according to the region and roof type involved. Those on Corinthian roofs tended to have floral ornament (see fig.) while those on Lakonian roofs generally had geometric designs (for roof types *see* GREECE, ANCIENT, §II, 1(ii)(b)); other areas show an early predilection for figural decoration, particularly north-west Greece, Italy and Asia Minor. During the Classical period (*c.* 480–323 BC) Greek buildings regularly had marble antefixes with modest floral designs derived from their Corinthian terracotta precursors; in the Hellenistic period (323–31 BC) these often surmounted elaborate lateral simas with floral decoration and lion-head spouts, in both stone and terracotta. During the Roman period (31 BC–AD 330) terracotta antefixes again became common, but the decorative patterns are pallid imitations of their Classical and Hellenistic predecessors.

BIBLIOGRAPHY

Enc. A. Ant.: 'Antefissa'

H. Koch: *Dachterrakotten aus Campanien* (Berlin, 1912)

E. D. Van Buren: *Figurative Terra-cotta Revetments in Etruria and Latium* (London, 1921)

——: *Archaic Fictile Revetments in Sicily and Magna Graecia* (London, 1923)

——: *Greek Fictile Revetments in the Archaic Period* (London, 1926)

I. Thallon-Hill and L. S. King: *Decorated Architectural Terracottas* (1929), iv/1 of *Corinth* (Cambridge, MA, 1929–)

E. Buschor: *Stirnziegel* (1933), ii of *Die Tondächer der Akropolis* (Berlin, 1933)

A. Andrén: *Architectural Terracottas from Etrusco-Italic Temples* (Lund, 1940)

Å. Åkerström: *Die architektonischen Terrakotten Kleinasiens* (Lund, 1966)

C. Le Roy: *Les Terres cuites architecturales* (1967), ii of *Fouilles de Delphes* (Paris, 1967–)

N. A. Winter: *Greek Architectural Terracottas from the Prehistoric to the End of the Archaic Period* (Oxford, 1993)

NANCY A. WINTER

Antelami, Benedetto (*fl* 1178–?1233). Italian sculptor and architect. After Wiligelmo and Nicholaus, Antelami was the last of the great northern Italian sculptors working in the cities of the central Po Valley in the 12th century. Although he is referred to in the inscriptions as a sculptor, it is probable that he was also an architect, and that he belonged originally, as his name implies, to the guild of civic builders known as the 'Magistri Antelami', active in the region of Como. He worked mainly in Parma and its surroundings, although his influence was widespread.

His earliest recorded commission is the signed and dated *Deposition* relief (1178), now set in the south transept of Parma Cathedral, which may originally have formed part of a choir-screen (*see* PARMA, fig. 2). Other fragments (a badly preserved relief showing *Christ in Majesty*, several capitals, atlantes and column-supporting lions) are located in the cathedral and in the Galleria Nazionale, Parma. The *Deposition* relief includes iconographic elements from Byzantine sources, but its figure and drapery styles have been compared with those on the *Crucifixion* tympanum at Saint-Gilles-du-Gard Abbey in southern France. Typical of Antelami's style, the compositions are formed by a few vertical figures in a processional arrangement, separated from each other and set against a flat background. The solemn dignity and ceremonial attitudes of the figures are also characteristic features, reminiscent of Wiligelmo's Genesis reliefs at Modena Cathedral. Antelami combined the monumentality of Wiligelmo's work with increased narrative detail and surface naturalism, exceeding that of Nicholaus and indicating contact with the school of the Magistri CAMPIONESI, whose figure style is related to Provençal Romanesque sculpture. Antelami probably also carved the episcopal throne of the cathedral, with atlantes and lions supporting the seat and armrests.

The fragments of the large figural panels bearing the *Labours of the Months* and personifications of the Seasons now in the Baptistery at Parma are generally attributed to Antelami (see fig.). According to Quintavalle (1969), they were originally intended for the main entrance portal of the cathedral in an arrangement similar to the portal of St Trophîme, Arles. These genre scenes have a figure style comparable to that of the *Deposition* relief, but they are characterized by greater monumentality and expression and are therefore probably closer in date to the architectural sculpture of the Baptistery.

The Baptistery (*see* BAPTISTERY, fig. 3) was begun in 1196 (recorded in an inscription bearing Antelami's name on the lintel of the north portal) and was ready for use in 1216. Here, Antelami developed an extensive sculptural programme, which included three portals and an interconnecting frieze. On the north portal, the *Adoration of the Magi* on the tympanum and the prophets on the jambs recall Nicholaus's portal scheme at Verona Cathedral as well as the tympanum of the north-west portal at Saint-Gilles-du-Gard. Antelami's elaborate narrative vocabulary, unprecedented in the region, is evident in the *Last Judgement*, the *Six Acts of Mercy* and the *Parable of the Labourers in the Vineyard* on the west portal. The south portal bears a most unusual and inventive allegorical scene, while such features as the *Tree of Jesse* on the jamb of the north portal (*see* PARMA, fig. 3) suggest acquaintance with Early Gothic portals in the Ile-de-France.

Benedetto Antelami (attrib.): *Spring*, marble, *c.* 1196 (Parma, Baptistery)

Apart from the sculpture at Parma, the other significant attribution to Antelami is the architectural sculpture of the pilgrimage church of Borgo San Donnino (Fidenza) and the completion of the building itself. Most notable among the sculptures are the two large classicizing figures of prophets in niches on the façade. Antelami's workshop or school was active in both the north-west and the east: at S Andrea (1219–25), Vercelli, in the equestrian statue of Oldrado da Tressano (1233), Milan, at Forlì Cathedral and in the *Labours of the Months* from the Porta dei Mesi at Ferrara Cathedral. Its influence can also be seen in the work of the sculptors who produced the portals of S Marco, Venice. A close follower was Radovan at Trogir Cathedral in Dalmatia.

BIBLIOGRAPHY

A. Venturi: *Storia* (1901–40/*R* 1967), I, ii
A. K. Porter: *Lombard Architecture*, 4 vols (New Haven, 1917)
P. Toesca: *Storia dell'arte italiana*, I, ii: *Il medioevo* (Turin, 1927/*R* 1965)
G. de Francovich: *Benedetto Antelami: Architetto e scultore e l'arte del suo tempo*, 2 vols (Milan, 1952)
G. H. Crichton: *Romanesque Sculpture in Italy* (London, 1954)
O. Demus: *The Church of San Marco in Venice: History, Architecture, Sculpture*, Dumbarton Oaks Studies, vi (Washington, DC, 1960)
A. C. Quintavalle: *Romanico padano, civiltà d'occidente* (Florence, 1969)
——: *La cattedrale di Parma e il romanico europeo* (Parma, 1974)
C. Gnudi: 'Il maestro dei Mesi di Ferrara e la lunetta di San Mercuriale a Forlì', *The Year 1200. A Symposium: New York, Metropolitan Museum of Art, 1975*, iii, pp. 469–96
V. Gvozdzanovich: 'Master Radovan and the Lunette of the Nativity of Trogir', *Stud. Med. Cult.*, viii, ix (1976), pp. 85–98
Atti del convegno internazionale degli studi romanico padano, romanico europeo: Parma, 1977
S. Stocchi: *Emilie romane*, Nuit Temps (La Pierre-qui-vire, 1984)
A. C. Quintavalle: *Benedetto Antelami* (Milan, 1990)

CHRISTINE B. VERZAR

Antenor (*fl* Athens, *c.* 530–*c.* 510 BC). Greek sculptor. A statue base signed by Antenor, son of Eumares, and indicating a dedication by Nearchos (perhaps the potter of that name who was working in the 560s BC) has been matched almost certainly with an outstanding kore found on the Acropolis of Athens in 1886 and hence called the *Kore of Antenor* (h. incl. plinth 2.15 m; Athens, Acropolis Mus., 681). The kore is a conservative work of *c.* 520 BC. Both arms are held unusually far from the body, which is powerfully modelled, the strong vertical folds of its *himation* (cloak) giving a columnar effect. Such features as the inlaid eyes and thin ankles betray a bronze worker: Pausanias (*Guide to Greece* I.viii.5) recorded that Antenor produced bronze statues of the tyrannicides Harmodios and Aristogeiton, which were carried off by Xerxes in 480/479 BC and replaced by KRITIOS AND NESIOTES' famous group. The Antenor statues remained at Persepolis until Alexander the Great or one of his successors returned them to Athens, where they were placed in the Agora alongside the second group. A Roman head (London, BM) is perhaps a copy of Antenor's *Harmodios*. The generally accepted date for the group is 510 BC (following Pliny: *Natural History* XXXIV.xix.70), although the years after 488 BC have also been suggested. Resemblances between the *Kore of Antenor* and the architectural korai of the Archaic Temple of Apollo at DELPHI (?after 510 BC) have led to an association of Antenor with the latter project.

BIBLIOGRAPHY

H. Payne and G. M. Young: *Archaic Marble Sculpture from the Acropolis* (London, [1936]), pp. 31–3, 63–5, pls 51–3
G. M. A. Richter: *Korai: Archaic Greek Maidens* (London, 1968), pp. 69–70, figs 336–40
J. Floren: *Die geometrische und archaische Plastik* (1987), i of *Die griechische Plastik*, Handbuch der Archäologie (Munich, 1987–), pp. 295–7
A. Stewart: *Greek Sculpture: An Exploration*, i (New Haven and London, 1990), pp. 60, 86–9, 124, 249–50

KIM RICHARDSON

Antependium [Lat.: 'hung in front']. Covering for the front of an ALTAR, typically made of rich fabric and highly decorated. □

Antequera (i). District of Málaga, Spain, best known for its megalithic communal tombs of the later 4th millennium and the 3rd millennium BC. Located 2 km east of the town of Antequera and 70 m apart are Cueva de Menga and Cueva de Viera, while Cueva del Romeral lies 2 km to the north-east of these. Each tomb was partly recessed in a rock-cut trench and covered by a large, artificial mound. Cueva de Menga was first noted in 1675 and was excavated by Rafael Mitjana in 1842. It has a parallel-sided passage (8.7×2–3 m) leading to an ovoid chamber (16.25×2.2–5.4×3.2 m). The largest roof slab (6×8 m) weighs *c.* 170 tonnes. Engraved lines on the underside of the roofing slabs were used to position them accurately above the chamber and passage, and three pillars along the central axis of the chamber served to distribute the enormous weight of the roof. One orthostat in the passage is decorated with engravings of four anthropomorphic figures and a five-pointed star. Cueva de Viera and Cueva del Romeral were discovered by the Viera brothers in 1903 and excavated shortly afterwards. Cueva de Viera has an orthostatic passage (19×*c.* 1.3×2 m) containing two vertical 'door' or 'porthole' slabs, each with a large central perforation; one is situated towards the front and one towards the rear of the tomb. The chamber measures 1.75 sq. m and comprises three solid wall slabs and one porthole slab, all of which are carefully notched and joined to each other. Cueva del Romeral was built using slabs and drystone masonry and represents an excellent Iberian example of 'beehive' dome construction of the type used in the THOLOS TOMB architecture of Mycenae. It has a masonry passage (originally *c.* 30×*c.* 1.7×2 m) terminating in a narrow, slab-built entrance. Beyond this lies the principal chamber (diam. 4.8–5.2 m), with a beehive-shaped dome capped by an enormous slab. A short passage leads from this chamber to another, smaller chamber of similar form and construction, with a massive horizontal 'altar' slab in the rear wall. Despite looting prior to excavation, the tombs yielded finds of burnished pottery, stone vessels and axes, flint blades, shell, a copper awl, animal bones and human remains.

For further discussion of Neolithic European architecture *see* PREHISTORIC EUROPE, §IV, 2, and MEGALITHIC ARCHITECTURE.

BIBLIOGRAPHY

C. de Mergelina: 'La necrópolis tartesia de Antequera', *Actas & Mem. Soc. Esp. Antropol., Etnog. & Prehist.*, i (1922), pp. 37–90
G. Leisner and V. Leisner: *Die Megalithgräber der iberischen Halbinsel: Der Süden*, Römisch-Germanische Forschungen, xvii (Berlin, 1943), pp. 175–85

CLAY MATHERS

Antequera (ii). *See* OAXACA.

Antes, Horst (*b* Heppenheim an der Bergstrasse, nr Bensheim, 28 Oct 1936). German painter, sculptor and printmaker. He studied from 1957 to 1959 at the Staatliche Akademie für Bildende Künste in Karlsruhe, where he was taught by the figurative painter H. A. P. Grieshaber (*b* 1909). His early work, in which he favoured structures created from violently flung colour, was influenced by Art Informel and by Abstract Expressionism, particularly by the work of Willem de Kooning. Around 1960 he began to form such brushstrokes into a figure with firm contours that he referred to as the *Kopffüssler* because it consisted of only head and limbs with no torso; this image, which he used throughout his later work as a sign for the human form, was inspired in part by the Kachina dolls of the North American Pueblo Indians. Antes felt a spiritual bond with the Pueblo Indians and accepted the psychological interpretations made of his paintings; he was interested in particular in the visit made to the Pueblo Indians in New Mexico in the 1920s by the psychoanalysts Carl Gustav Jung and Hans Prinzhorn, and by the affinities that they outlined in Pueblo culture, in the subconscious and in aspects of Surrealism.

The invention by Antes of his unmistakable stock character allowed him to relate his work to traditions of Western painting rather than to stylistic trends of his own time and to breathe a new life into the depiction of the human figure. His recurring figure functioned as a kind of *alter ego* who could lead him to a deeper self-knowledge, since Antes regarded painting as a means of coping with dilemmas in his own life. His pictures are free of narrative, representing instead a condition or state of being as metaphors of human existence, defined in part by the associations of the accessories accompanying the figure: everyday objects such as furniture; animals and creatures resembling snakes or sperm; and geometric forms or archaic cult objects.

In the 1960s Antes favoured a profile view for his gnome-like creature, with colour subordinated to the modelled form, as in *Masked Figure with Yellow* (acrylic on canvas, 1.2×1 m, 1965; Hamburg, Ksthalle). Around 1970 he returned to a flatter conception of the figure, sometimes with a fully-formed torso, in works such as *Seated Figure with Disc and Egg* (1971; Zurich, Ksthaus). Antes also applied this imagery to lithographs and to sculptures, including massive and colourful painted steel sculptures in the 1960s and a series of *Votives* produced in 1983 (see 1983 exh. cat.), small perspex boxes (each between 470–810 mm in height) containing filigree-like objects and figures made of fine gold plate.

BIBLIOGRAPHY

Antes: Bilder, 1965–1971 (exh. cat., intro. K. Gallwitz; Baden-Baden, Staatl. Ksthalle; Berne, Ksthalle; Bremen, Ksthalle; Frankfurt am Main, Schirn Ksthalle; 1972)

Horst Antes: Der Kopf (exh. cat., intro. M. Schwarz; Karlsruhe, Bad. Kstver.; Lübeck, Mus. Dom; 1978)

Horst Antes: 25 Votive (exh. cat., intro. K. Gallwitz; Frankfurt am Main, Städel. Kstinst., 1983)

Horst Antes: Lithographien (exh. cat., Dresden, Kupferstichkab., 1985)

DOMINIK BARTMANN

Anthemion [honeysuckle; palmette]. Floral ornament, typically with alternating motifs. The term first occurs in a progress report commissioned in 409 BC on the building of the Erechtheion in Athens. Although the west side of the building was refurbished by the Romans in the 1st century AD, it is probable that the unfinished column bands referred to in the report were decorated with PALMETTE and lotus friezes comparable with those that decorate the Ionic columns of the north portico. In Classical architecture, anthemion ornaments are typical of the Ionic order, although they also occur in the decoration of a wide range of different artefacts, especially ceramics (see fig.). Alternation of motif is characteristic, but there is considerable variation in the type, form and detail of the constituents.

Anthemion ornament on a Red-figure krater depicting *Diomedes and Aeneas* by the Tyszkiewicz Painter, h. 452 mm, diam. 513 mm, *c.* 490–480 BC, from Vulci (Boston, MA, Museum of Fine Arts)

The characteristic anthemion composition comprises alternating palmette and lotus motifs, which in Classical ornament emerge from an acanthine calyx (*see* ACANTHUS) and are joined to one another by curving S-shaped scrolls. In the 5th century BC these features are found in conjunction with single palmettes in the architectural and funerary sculpture of Greece, but, with the exception of Neo-classical ornament, are not typical of anthemia in post-Classical periods. The alternation of palmette and lotus motifs is also the dominant composition of Byzantine and Western medieval anthemia. Unlike the earlier open ornament of fluent line, however, medieval anthemion friezes are densely packed compositions in which the lobes of the constituents are contiguous and fewer in number. An absence of linking scrolls and calyces is also characteristic of this period. In the 10th and 11th centuries, however, anthemion compositions were enriched by acanthine features, which produced a highly individualized ornament; the 'Winchester acanthus' is a prominent example (*see* WINCHESTER, §II).

Evidence of a return to the ornaments of antiquity is apparent in the Neo-classical revival of the 18th and 19th centuries. Both the taxonomy of ornament and a nomenclature for the various motifs of the Classical repertory were considered integral to the study of Classical art and architecture. In the case of the anthemion, the derivation of the term from the Greek *anthos* ('flower') and the similarities observed between the Classical palmette and the flower of the honeysuckle prompted many architects and craftsmen to consider the term anthemion appropriate to the palmette alone. Although the architect and designer OWEN JONES rejected the notion that the honeysuckle had served the Greeks as a model for the palmette, 'honeysuckle', 'anthemion' and 'palmette' gained currency as equivalent and interchangeable terms, as in the use of 'anthemion' to describe the conventional palmette design of late 18th-century English chair backs. Despite this confusion of nomenclature, alternation of motif (usually palmette and lotus) is now held to be axiomatic to the definition of anthemion.

BIBLIOGRAPHY

O. Jones: *Grammar of Ornament* (London, 1856/*R* 1972)
R. Sturgis: *Dictionary of Architecture and Building*, i (New York, 1901), cols 78–9
J. Fleming and H. Honour: *The Penguin Dictionary of Decorative Arts* (London, 1989), p. 30

JEFFREY WEST

Anthemios of Tralles (*b* Tralles [now Aydın, Turkey]; *fl* early 6th century AD). Greek architect, scientist and mathematician. Together with Isidoros of Miletus he was engaged by Justinian I (*reg* AD 527–565) to design Hagia Sophia (*see* ISTANBUL, §III, 1(ii)(a)). Prokopios (*Buildings*, I.i.24) called him 'the most learned man in the skilled craft which is known as the art of building' and described the dome of Hagia Sophia as 'suspended from heaven' (*Buildings*, I.i.47). Anthemios also had a deep knowledge of Hellenistic science: fragments of his treatises *On Burning Mirrors* and *Concerning Remarkable Mechanical Devices* survive.

BIBLIOGRAPHY

G. Downey: 'Byzantine Architects: Their Training and Methods', *Byzantion*, xviii (1946–8), pp. 99–118
G. L. Huxley: *Anthemios of Tralles: A Study in Later Greek Geometry* (Cambridge, MA, 1959) [with texts of the scientific treatises]

THOMAS E. RUSSO

Anthonij, Johan. *See* ANHTONI, GIOVANNI.

Anthonisz. [Teunissen; Theunissen; Thonisz.], **Cornelis** (*b* Amsterdam, *c.* 1505; *d* Amsterdam, 1553). Dutch printmaker, painter and cartographer, maternal grandson of JACOB CORNELISZ. VAN OOSTSANEN. He was the dominant figure in the creation of north Netherlandish woodcuts from the mid-1530s until his death. His monogram, which combines the initials 'C' and 'T' with the staff and bell of St Anthony, was probably inspired by his father's first name. The greater part of his career was apparently spent in his native Amsterdam, where he probably trained with his grandfather.

Cornelis Anthonisz.'s earliest extant work is a signed and dated panel painting known as the *Braspenningsmaaltijd* ('Banquet of the copper coin', 1533; Amsterdam, Hist. Mus.), which depicts 17 members of the Crossbowmen's Guild, one of Amsterdam's civic militia companies. Departing from the traditional isocephalic format for such paintings, Cornelis introduced a narrative element by arranging his subjects around a banquet table. The young man standing directly below the monogram and date at the upper left is probably a self-portrait. His next extant, autograph painting is a *Plan of Amsterdam* (1538; Amsterdam, Hist. Mus.; *see* AMSTERDAM, fig. 1), which was commissioned by the city for the town hall. The high viewpoint suggests Cornelis's familiarity with Jacopo de' Barbari's woodcut *Aerial View of Venice* (*c.* 1500; *see* VENICE, fig. 1). In 1544 Cornelis published a woodcut, *Bird's-eye View of Amsterdam* (Hollstein, no. 47), seen from the same high angle.

Most of the works associated with Cornelis Anthonisz. are princely portrait woodcuts. The Renaissance cult of personalities and a growing sensitivity towards the propagandistic possibilities of prints helped to popularize this form in the early 16th century. Cornelis designed two princely genealogies in woodcut: the *Lords and Ladies of Holland* (*c.* 1549–50; Hollstein, no. 55) and the *Lords of Brederode* (1550–51; Hollstein, no. 50). From *c.* 1538 to 1548 he was also involved in the creation of some 60 single-sheet equestrian, full-length and half-length portraits of various European kings, princes and noblemen, which generally recall images by Dürer, Jan Swart and Lucas Cranach the elder.

Another significant portion of Cornelis's oeuvre, unmatched by any of his predecessors, is the group of some 20 moralizing prints, generally in woodcut and notable for their inventive, often witty allegorical imagery. Recurring themes include the danger of spendthrift, dissolute habits (e.g. *Wealth and Idleness*; *Flighty Youth*; and the *Misuse of Prosperity*, Hollstein, nos 21, 27 and 19), man's proclivity for sinful behaviour (e.g. *St Aelwaer*; see fig.; the *Demon of Drink*; and *Nabal, Ceres and Bacchus*; Hollstein, nos 40 and 28) and the concurrent banishment of various virtues (e.g. *Concord, Peace and Love* and *Truth, Hate and Fear*; Hollstein, nos 2 and 36). Stressing moderation in every aspect of life, such prints were largely aimed at an ever-growing urban middle class. Frequently monumental in size (e.g. *Fable of the Father, Son and Ass*, 305×1480 mm; Hollstein, no. 45) and often provided with lengthy texts in the vernacular, many were doubtless used as an inexpensive and instructive form of interior decoration. Only a few of his moralistic prints are overtly religious, for example his woodcut series representing the *Parable of the Prodigal Son* (Hollstein, nos 5–10), which expresses a distinct, if moderate, Protestant viewpoint.

In addition to portraits and allegories, Cornelis produced a few topographical subjects. Besides the woodcut *View of Amsterdam* (1544), there are two woodcut panoramas of a military nature: one, the *City of Algiers* (1542; Hollstein, no. 43), representing Charles V's disastrous expedition against the Turks, the other (*c.* 1552–3) depicting Charles's more successful attack on the French town of Terwagne (Terwaen). Cornelis's known activity as a cartographer is difficult to assess since most of his work in this field has been lost. Two examples survive: his *Map of Eastern Lands* (695×955 mm, 1543; Hollstein, no. 48), a monumental woodcut showing the northern Netherlands, Germany and the Scandinavian countries, and

Cornelis Anthonisz.: *St Aelwaer*, woodcut, 370×280 mm, *c.* 1540 (Amsterdam, Rijksmuseum)

Onderwijsinge van der Zee ('Nautical instructions'; *c.* 1544), a navigation handbook with woodcut coastal profiles and assorted diagrams.

Efforts to trace Cornelis's stylistic development are hampered by the comparatively small size of his oeuvre—fewer than 100 surviving works (the largest single collection of his prints being in the Rijksmuseum, Amsterdam). Nevertheless, it is apparent that his debt to the prints of Jacob Cornelisz. and Lucas van Leyden amounts to little more than the appropriation of a few motifs—surprising not only in the light of his familial relationship to the former but also because these two artists would have provided the most significant native models for woodcut. In early prints (e.g. *Mutius Scaevola*, 1536; Hollstein, no. 42; and the *Allegory of Transitoriness*, 1537; Hollstein, no. 26), Cornelis seems to have experimented with an aggressively Italianate manner like that of Jan Gossart. But by the 1540s (e.g. in *Deathbeds of the Righteous and Unrighteous*; Hollstein, no. 16) he had shifted to a looser brand of Mannerism, more akin to that of Jan van Scorel.

BIBLIOGRAPHY

Hollstein: *Dut. & Flem.*, xxx (1986); *NKL*; Thieme–Becker

E. W. Moes and C. P. Burger: *De Amsterdamsche boekdrukkers en uitgevers in de zestiende eeuw*, 4 vols (Amsterdam, 1900–15)

H. Nijhoff-Selldorff and M. D. Henkel: *Nederlandsche houtsneden, 1500–1550* (The Hague, 1933–9)

F. J. Dubiez: *Cornelis Anthoniszoon van Amsterdam, 1507–1553: Zijn leven en werken* (Amsterdam, 1969)

R. Tooley: *A Dictionary of Mapmakers* (New York, 1979)

I. H. van Eeghen: 'Jacob Cornelisz., Cornelis Anthonisz. en hun familierelaties', *Ned. Ksthist. Jb.*, xxxvii (1986), pp. 95–133

B. Haeger: 'Cornelis Anthonisz.'s Representation of the Parable of the Prodigal Son: A Protestant Interpretation of the Biblical Text', *Ned. Ksthist. Jb.*, xxxvii (1986), pp. 133–50

C. Armstrong: *The Moralizing Prints of Cornelis Anthoniszoon* (Princeton, 1990)

CHRISTINE ARMSTRONG

Anthropology and art. In the broadest terms anthropology is the study and science of people. As such there are a number of branches, including archaeological, biological, physical as well as social and cultural anthropology. The study of artefacts and art practices is of relevance to all these branches, but since at least the 1950s to social and cultural anthropology in particular. Traditionally, anthropology has focused its attention on the non-industrial societies of indigenous peoples, such as Aboriginal Australians, Pacific Islanders and Native Americans. Although anthropologists no longer consider themselves restricted to studying non-industrial societies, the emphasis of the anthropology of art, as of anthropology in general, is still the pre-literate traditions of non-industrial societies. The most prominent theoreticians within the anthropology of art include FRANZ BOAS and CLAUDE LÉVI-STRAUSS.

Early European evaluations of the non-Western art traditions encountered during the era of colonial expansion assumed that they represented early stages in a universal developmental process that culminated in the European Renaissance. This assumption derives from the theory, developed by Dugald Stewart and others during the 18th century, that human societies pass through a series of obligatory stages. Such non-European art was seen as 'rude' or unsophisticated because it failed to use specific techniques such as linear perspective that were developed during the Renaissance. Thus Leonard Adam, a relatively sympathetic author, wrote as late as 1940 (p. 40), 'A good test case of art for art's sake is landscape painting. Generally speaking, it is very rare in primitive art.' Artists such as Picasso and Braque, who were inspired by works from the Côte d'Ivoire and other African colonies to regard 'primitive art' as possessing a natural, uninhibited vitality, also failed to consider how non-Western art traditions had their own history of development towards particular artistic goals, which had occurred within specific social environments. This trend has recently been subjected to critical reassessment by S. Price and S. Hillier.

The methods of contemporary anthropology were devised in reaction to the 'armchair' research of earlier academics, which included museum studies of ethnographic art. They facilitated instead long-term field research within non-Western communities, in order to study cultural behaviour and artefacts in their indigenous context. Anthropology has been termed comparative sociology or, alternatively, the translation of culture. These two concepts express different assumptions about what is possible in anthropology. In the first, certain general principles can be shown to underlie the enormous variation in human societies. In the second, cultures are built on convention alone and are the product of historical accident; the most an anthropologist can hope to achieve in this view is to translate the meanings embodied in one cultural tradition and render them comprehensible to members of another.

Most anthropological studies of art carried out since the 1950s have been based on a comparative theory. Two such theories have dominated anthropology, both derived ultimately from the writings of the French sociologist Emile Durkheim (1858–1917). One of these is functionalism, which for anthropologists explains the existence of a custom or belief in terms of its alleged function. The function of a custom (as expounded by Bronislaw Malinowski, 1884–1942) is to satisfy individual human needs in a socially ordered fashion. The orthodox version of functionalism that was promoted by A. R. Radcliffe-Brown (*fl* 1920–50) regards the function of a custom as its contribution to social solidarity and the persistence of harmonious community life. Although this approach reifies society as an entity with 'needs' that transcend those of the individual, it underlies a number of classic studies of art in small-scale societies. Daniel Biebuyck (1973) described the art of the Bwami cult of the Lega of Central Africa in such terms (*see* LEGA AND RELATED PEOPLES, §2). Initiates to higher levels in the cult are potential leaders, who must demonstrate their patience, piety and eloquence before admission. These ideals are expressed in proverbs and in sculptures that belong to high-ranking initiates. Biebuyck concluded that 'social cohesion, social solidarity and ritual autonomy are promoted by some sculptures and other initiation objects' (Biebuyck, p. 172). The Warlpiri of central Australia (*see* ABORIGINAL AUSTRALIA, §III, 2) trace both their laws and personal identity from the actions of totemic beings during the Creation Period, who established principles of reciprocity and group boundaries, and who are reincarnated in living people. The ancestors are therefore the foundation of social order. Each ancestor is represented by motifs that embody their creative power. Nancy Munn argued that 'collective representations [in Warlpiri art and ritual] are among the mechanisms through which the socio-cultural structure gets a "grip" on the individual' (Munn, p. 211).

The functionalist tendency to reify society can be overcome by examining what common interests lead people in a community to cooperate or to exchange resources. The role of art in facilitating such self-interested social interaction has been studied among the competitive societies of Highland New Guinea.

The other dominant theory is structuralism, with which Lévi-Strauss was closely associated. In this, cultural forms are explained in terms of structures that derive from characteristic modes of human thought; dual oppositions and tripartite structures are common features of this style of analysis. Ross Bowden explained the iconography of *yena* sculptures among the Kwoma of Papua New Guinea in structuralist terms (*see* PAPUA NEW GUINEA, §I, 1(vi)). Yena sculptures depict spirits in aggressively masculine form. They are carved to promote the growth of yams, and they express an ethos of male dominance in the ritual sphere. Bowden made the provocative claim that all cultures acknowledge such equations as male is to female, as culture is to nature, as higher is to lower (Bowden, pp. 84–5), but he conceded later that women's actual status is downplayed in male ideology and women's ideology probably expresses matters differently (p. 88). Joan Vastokas's analysis of art among the native peoples of the Northwest Coast of North America encapsulates the structuralist approach: 'Visual images reveal themselves as mechanisms for these latent cultural–cognitive tensions, the rivalry between one principle of order and another and a striving for integration and balance, never perfectly achieved' (Vastokas, p. 257).

While structuralist analysis readily finds apparently similar patterns of opposed symbols in diverse cultures, the extent to which these are genuinely intended by members of the culture under study is often problematic. The structuralist approach can also attach undue importance to inferred cultural systems and not enough attention to the actual performances of cultural life. A study that avoids this trap is Howard Morphy's analysis of symbolism in an Australian Aboriginal funeral rite. An exciting method for analysing the evolution of symmetrical and rhythmic patterns in art was presented by Dorothy Washburn. Contributors to Washburn's volume compare the work of different artists and variations in the works of particular individuals from the native Americas, Africa and New Zealand. Although concerned primarily with decorative form rather than iconography, Washburn placed her approach in the structuralist tradition.

The origins of anthropological method in the study of small-scale, non-literate, non-Western societies imposed what are now seen as unhelpful limitations on research. The lack of written records meant the study of change was long neglected, while the desire to study interaction within 'exotic' communities resulted in anthropologists underestimating the extent to which all communities are dependent, to a greater or lesser extent, on events and forces in the outside world. There are, however, some good studies of change in non-Western art. Marion Wenzel showed that the style of house decoration in villages about to be flooded by the Aswan Dam had not been transmitted unchanged for generations but instead developed rapidly, due to the innovations of a few artists. Harry Silver, who documented innovation among modern Asante carvers, argued that creativity is not a randomly conferred 'gift'; its manifestation is, rather, dictated by the different economic incentives and risks faced by carvers of high, middle and low status. Tourist art demonstrates dramatically the exposure of non-Western communities to the economy of the world market. Nelson Graburn showed that tourist art is subject to the buyers' desire to bring home evidence of their first-hand contact with the 'exotic', but that where indigenous artistic traditions have survived the onslaught of the West, works produced for sale can embody subtle symbolism and a complex aesthetic. Increased contact with the outside world can reinvigorate the art that members of such communities produce for their own use.

The question has arisen, however, of whether the very labelling of indigenous peoples' carvings and paintings as 'art' is the imposition of a Western concept on formerly autonomous traditions (*see also* ART, and ART HISTORY, §III, 4). From the 'translation of culture' perspective, one of the most vexed questions for anthropologists is whether art itself is a Western concept, with no equivalent in other cultures. It is alleged, for instance, that Australian Aboriginal cultures possess no category of 'fine art' as distinct from functional design, and that White Australian gallery owners created the concept of 'Aboriginal fine art' to increase their profits as middlemen. A challenge to the

Western assumption that all graphic traditions aim for naturalistic representation was provided by Alexander Alland, who asked children aged between two and eight, from six diverse cultures, to draw for him. Each study yielded *c.* 40 drawings. Alland found no uniform progression towards representation and, indeed, no universal lines of development at all. Each sample showed an internal unity of style, but these styles differed markedly from one community to another and appeared to be conditioned by the child's experience of local cultural norms. While Micronesian children started anywhere on the page, extending outwards in 'amoeboid fashion' from one point, the Taiwanese children constructed several discrete elements, separated by blank paper, which reminded Alland of Chinese written texts. Balinese children, like adult Balinese artists, liked to cover the surface of the paper completely. Some samples showed overlapping of forms, while others seemed deliberately to avoid overlap. Most importantly, the children did not seem primarily motivated to produce pictures that looked like objects in the real world. The desire to achieve representational art, Alland concluded, is particularly culture-specific: for example only 17% of the Micronesian sample contained representational figures compared with 60% of the Balinese sample. The study underlines the danger of elevating the values of Western culture to universal principles.

While there are classic studies in art history that converge with the interests of anthropology, for example Erwin Panofsky's 'Die Entwicklung der Proportionslehre als Abbild der Stilentwicklung' (1921) or Ernst Gombrich's *Art and Illusion* (1960), anthropological studies of art provide useful antidotes to a number of tendencies in art-historical analysis. They challenge models of changes in style that regard naturalistic representation as the pinnacle of achievement; the tendency to map artistic culture areas without reference to the social functions of art; and the focus on artists or schools of artists in isolation from their place in a wider community.

BIBLIOGRAPHY

E. Durkheim: *Les Formes élémentaires de la vie religieuse: Le Système totémique en Australie* (Paris, 1912; Eng. trans., London, 1915)
E. Panofsky: 'Die Entwicklung der Proportionslehre als Abbild der Stilentwicklung', *Mhft. Kstwiss.*, xiv (1921), pp. 188–219; repr. and Eng. trans. in *Meaning in the Visual Arts* (New York, 1955)
L. Adam: *Primitive Art* (London, 1940)
E. Gombrich: *Art and Illusion* (London, 1960, rev. 3/1977/*R* 1993)
D. Biebuyck, ed.: *Tradition and Creativity in Tribal Art* (Berkeley, 1969/*R* 1973)
A. Strathern and M. Strathern: *Self-decoration in Mount Hagen*, A. & Soc. Ser. (London, 1971)
M. Wenzel: *House Decoration in Nubia*, A. & Soc. Ser. (London, 1972)
D. Biebuyck: *Lega Culture: Art, Initiation and Moral Philosophy among a Central African People* (Berkeley, 1973)
A. Forge, ed.: *Primitive Art and Society* (London, 1973)
N. Munn: *Walbiri Iconography: Graphic Representation and Cultural Symbolism in a Central Australian Society* (Ithaca, NY, 1973)
N. H. H. Graburn, ed.: *Ethnic and Tourist Arts: Cultural Expressions from the Fourth World* (Berkeley, 1976), pp. 1–37
J. M. Vastokas: 'Cognitive Aspects of Northwest Coast Art', *Art in Society*, ed. M. Greenhalgh and V. Megaw (London, 1978), pp. 243–59
R. Layton: *The Anthropology of Art* (London, 1981, rev. Cambridge, 1991)
H. R. Silver: 'Calculating Risks: The Socioeconomic Foundations of Aesthetic Innovation in an Ashanti Carving Community', *Ethnology*, xx/2 (1981), pp. 101–14
A. Alland: *Playing with Form: Children Draw in Six Cultures* (New York, 1983)
R. Bowden: *Yena: Art and Ceremony in a Sepik Society*, Pitt Rivers Museum Monograph, 3 (Oxford, 1983)
D. K. Washburn, ed.: *Structure and Cognition in Art*, New Directions in Archaeology (Cambridge, 1983), pp. 1–7
H. Morphy: *Journey to the Crocodile's Nest: An Accompanying Monograph to the Film 'Madarrpa Funeral at Gurka'wuy'* (Canberra, 1984)
J. V. S. Megaw: 'Contemporary Aboriginal Art: Dreamtime Discipline or Alien Adulteration?', *COMA*, 18 (July 1986), pp. 31–42
P. Sillitoe: 'From Head-dresses to Head-messages: The Art of Self-decoration in the Highlands of Papua New Guinea', *Man*, n. s., xxiii/2 (1988), pp. 298–318
S. Price: *Primitive Art in Civilised Places* (Chicago, 1989)
S. Hillier: *The Myth of Primitivism in Modern Art* (Cambridge, 1991)
J. Coote and A. Shelton, eds: *Anthropology, Art and Aesthetics*, Oxford Studies in the Anthropology of Cultural Forms (Oxford, 1992/*R* 1994)
R. Finnegan: *Oral Traditions and the Verbal Arts* (Cambridge, 1992)
S. Lavie, K. Narayah and R. Rosaldo, eds: *Creativity/Anthropology* (Ithaca, NY, 1993)
H. Morphy: 'The Anthropology of Art', *Companion Encyclopedia of Anthropology: Humanity, Culture and Social Life*, ed. T. Ingold (London and New York, 1994), pp. 648–85

ROBERT LAYTON

Anthroposophy [from Gr. *anthropos*: 'man'; *sophia*: 'wisdom']. Philosophy formulated by RUDOLF STEINER from 1913, when he founded the Anthroposophical Society. Anthroposophy has been called a 'spiritual' or an 'occult' science, and Steiner felt that occult knowledge could be studied empirically and transmitted in the manner of any modern science. He developed anthroposophy in reaction to the Asian philosophical emphasis of THEOSOPHY, within which he crystallized his ideas. He combined his own experience with the idealism of Johann Wolfgang von Goethe, Rosicrucianism and esoteric Christianity. The notion of Karma and certain ideas about reincarnation and cosmic evolution were retained from the Hindu and Buddhist elements of theosophy. Anthroposophy is not only a theory of knowledge but also a detailed series of mental exercises designed to distract the human senses so that one can perceive higher levels of reality. Steiner described three stages through which the student must pass in order to gain knowledge of higher worlds: probation, enlightenment and initiation. This higher knowledge is possible by means of an empirical system because intellectual concepts are said to have an objective quality of their own. Steiner claimed to have perceived spiritual realms because of his refined cognitive abilities.

Such artists as František Kupka, Piet Mondrian, Kazimir Malevich, Paul Klee and Vasily Kandinsky were involved in the study and use of anthroposophy, as well as other occult and mystical systems. Early 20th-century artists were interested in anthroposophy in their search for a visual language for the connections between the seen and unseen and for the higher order of the transcendental world. They also sought a link between the spiritual and scientific data that were proliferating at the time.

BIBLIOGRAPHY

R. Steiner: *Die Geheimwissenschaft im Umriss* (Leipzig, 1910)
S. C. Easton: *Man and World in the Light of Anthroposophy* (Spring Valley, NY, 1975)

For further bibliography *see* STEINER, RUDOLF.

GERI DE PAOLI

Antichak [anc. Vikramashila, Vikramaśīla]. Site of Buddhist monastery on the River Ganga in Bhagalpur District, Bihar, India. Until recently, the location of the monastery of Vikramashila was known only approximately from Tibetan sources, but excavations at Antichak have almost surely revealed its remains. The monastery was founded by the Pala dynasty monarch Dharmapala (*reg c.* AD 781–812; *see* PALA AND SENA). At the middle of the site is a tall brick stupa with a cruciform plan, closely related in form and dimensions to the stupa at PAHARPUR, also part of a monastic complex built by Dharmapala. Both stupas are set on an elevated terrace for circumambulation and in both cases the lowest portion of the stupa wall (where it survives) is decorated with terracotta plaques. At Antichak these depict mostly animals, human figures and ritual devices (pots, conch shells etc). Although sometimes described as 'folk art', they are carefully rendered and appear to be arranged according to a systematic programme. A row of cells forms the site's outer perimeter, enclosing the large courtyard in which the stupa stands. These may have been intended as dwellings for monks or to accommodate images and likely functioned as the outer rim of the three-dimensional *maṇḍala* (Skt: 'spiritual diagram') created at the site. Close to the monastery, on a cliff overlooking the river, is a place known as Patharghata, where there are rock-cut reliefs of Viṣhnu and his incarnations (*c.* 5th century).

BIBLIOGRAPHY

A. P. Bannerji-Sastri: 'Keur, a Probable Site of Vikramaśīla', *J. Bihar & Orissa Res. Soc.*, xv (1929), pp. 263–76

M. H. Kuraishi: *List of Monuments Protected under Act VII of 1904 in the Province of Bihar and Orissa*, Archaeol. Surv. India, New Imp. Ser., li (Calcutta, 1931), pp. 205–7

R. C. Prasad Singh: 'Antichak, the Seat of Vikramaśīla University', *J. Bihar & Orissa Res. Soc.*, xlvi (1960), pp. 135–8

F. M. Asher: 'Vikramaśīla Mahāvihāra', *Bangladesh Lalit Kala*, i/2 (1975), pp. 107–13

B. S. Verma: 'Excavations at Antichak', *J. Bihar Puravid Parishad*, i (1977), pp. 192–201

F. M. Asher: *The Art of Eastern India, 300–800* (Minneapolis, 1980)

FREDERICK M. ASHER

Antichi [Scavezzi]**, Prospero** [il Bresciano; Prospero da Brescia] (*b* Brescia, 1555–65; *d* Rome, 1592). Italian sculptor. According to Baglione, he went to Rome from his native Brescia as a youth. He studied anatomy and the art of ancient Rome, and he gained fame for his anatomical models and small *bozzetti.* His skill as a modeller resulted in several commissions from Gregory XIII, including stucco angels (1580–81) for the Pauline Chapel and the Scala Regia in the Vatican. The success of these elegant, classicizing figures led to the commission (after 1585) for the sculptural components of the tomb of *Gregory XIII* in St Peter's, consisting of a seated statue of the Pope, allegorical figures of *Charity*, *Faith*, *Religion* and *Justice*, and two angels bearing the papal arms. The tomb has undergone numerous transformations and much of its sculpture has been lost; its original appearance is recorded, however, in several engravings and in a drawing by Ciro Ferri (Florence, Uffizi). The surviving stucco figures of *Religion* and *Justice*, which now adorn the tomb of *Gregory XIV*, exemplify Antichi's style. Standing in contrapposto poses and enveloped in broad masses of finely modelled drapery, these highly classicizing figures, reminiscent of the work of Andrea Sansovino, reveal the artist's profound debt to the art of antiquity.

Antichi also produced many works for Sixtus V, often in collaboration with other artists, as was typical of the Sistine period. Working with Francesco (Cecchino) da Pietrasanta (*fl* late 16th century), he provided the clay models for the bronze lions (1587) below the Vatican obelisk, and with the same sculptor he produced the marble *Nativity* group (1587) in the confessio of the Sistine Chapel at S Maria Maggiore. He also collaborated with Leonardo Sormani on the marble statues of *St Peter* and *St Paul* (1587–8) for the same chapel and on the much disparaged colossal marble statue of *Moses* for the Fountain of the Acqua Felice (1587–8). Although ridiculed by Baglione and many other critics, this ill-proportioned work was highly praised by Giambattista Marino and was the basis for the poet's inclusion of Antichi in his famous *La galeria* (Venice, 1630).

BIBLIOGRAPHY

DBI; Thieme–Becker

G. Baglione: *Vite* (1642); ed. V. Mariani (1935), pp. 42–4

A. Venturi: *Storia* (1901–40), X/iii (1937), pp. 574–7

A. Riccoboni: *Roma nell'arte: La scultura nell'evo moderno dal quattrocento ad oggi*, i (Rome, 1942), pp. 115–17

R. Montini: *Le tombe dei papi* (Rome, 1957), pp. 337–40

S. Pressouyre: *Nicolas Cordier: Recherches sur la sculpture à Rome autour de 1600*, 2 vols (Rome, 1984)

STEVEN F. OSTROW

Antico [Alari-Bonacolsi, Pier Jacopo di Antonio] (*b* ?Mantua, *c.* 1460; *d* Gazzuolo, 1528). Italian sculptor. An expert in goldsmith work, bronze sculpture and medals, he earned his nickname 'Antico' because of his 'astonishing penetration of antiquity' (Nesselrath). He achieved lasting fame through his small-scale re-creations (often also reinterpretations) of famous, but often fragmentary, statues of antiquity (e.g. the APOLLO BELVEDERE, Rome, Vatican, Mus. Pio-Clementino, and the SPINARIO, Rome, Mus. Conserv.). Most of these bronze statuettes were made for the Gonzaga family, notably for Ludovico, Bishop of Mantua, and for Isabella d'Este, wife of Francesco II Gonzaga, 4th Marchese of Mantua. Antico also restored ancient marble statues and acted as an adviser to collectors.

1. Life and work. 2. Working methods and technique.

1. LIFE AND WORK. A birth date of 1460 has been calculated on the basis of Antico's earliest recorded commission (1479), and he is presumed to have been born in Mantua because his father, a butcher, owned a house there and he himself was granted the privilege of owning a stall in the meat market by Federico I Gonzaga, 3rd Marchese of Mantua. A training as a goldsmith is inferred from the fact that he began as a medallist in relief and in intaglio. In addition, he is documented (see below) as the maker of a pair of silver gilt vases and later demonstrated great skill at casting and chasing bronze statuettes, and at gilding and inlaying them with silver. His restoration of antique marble statues also implies an expertise in working that material, but nothing is known of how he acquired this skill.

Antico's first recorded commission (1479) was for a pair of medals to celebrate the wedding of Gianfrancesco Gonzaga, Conte di Rodigo and Lord of Bozzolo, with Antonia del Balzo. These are signed with the abbreviated form of Antico, ANTI, implying that by this time his pseudonym was widely recognized. He was employed by Federico I Gonzaga, whose court included Andrea Mantegna, probably until Federico's death (1484). Antico seems to have then moved to the court of Federico's younger brother, Gianfrancesco, at Bozzolo for a period of *c.* 12 years. In November 1493 a letter was sent to Francesco II Gonzaga, commending Antico, and by June 1494 the artist was making a portrait of Francesco.

By 1495 Antico was in Rome, employed by Pope Alexander VI to work on the Castel Sant'Angelo. It was presumably during this period that he restored one of the antique sculptural groups known as the *Horse-tamers* (Rome, Piazza del Quirinale). In 1496 Gianfrancesco Gonzaga died at Bozzolo, and in the inventory of his possessions was listed a pair of silver gilt vases (untraced) by Antico. These were probably similar to the bronze Gonzaga Vase (Modena, Gal. & Mus. Estense), which bears Gianfrancesco's and Antonia's personal devices. The design of the bronze vase was probably influenced by Mantegna, who was recorded in 1483 as having designed vases to be produced by the goldsmith Gian Marco Cavalli.

1. Antico: *Apollo Belvedere*, bronze, h. 413 mm, ?*c.* 1498 (Frankfurt am Main, Liebieghaus)

Also listed, without giving the sculptor, were several *all'antica* bronzes, their titles in some cases matching those of surviving statuettes in Antico's inimitable style: *Meleager* (London, V&A) and *Hercules* (Madrid, Mus. Arqueol. N.). Others mentioned include a group of a *Horse-tamer* (untraced), doubtless a reduction after Antico's restoration of the original, and an equestrian *Marcus Aurelius* (untraced).

Antico may have returned to Mantua at this juncture, for in 1497 he was sent back to Rome by Francesco II Gonzaga, on a mission to acquire antiquities for Isabella d'Este. In 1498 Antico was again in Bozzolo, employed by Ludovico Gonzaga, Bishop of Mantua. A letter written by Ludovico in November of that year mentions two statuettes: an *Apollo Belvedere* (three examples survive, ?earliest: Frankfurt am Main, Liebieghaus; see fig. 1), for which Antico had to reconstruct the statue's missing arm (not restored on the original marble until later), and a *Venus Kneeling on a Tortoise* (Madrid, Mus. Thyssen–Bornemisza), after the statue that is now in the Museo del Prado, Madrid. By this time Antico was also working in marble, which his patron was busy acquiring from Venice. From this period date a *Hercules* (still unfinished May 1499; New York, Frick) and a *Head of Scipio* (1499; untraced), which was made for Bishop Ludovico. By 1499 Antico had also made a bronze statuette of the *Spinario* (New York, Wrightsman priv. col., see Allison, 1994, pp. 210–12, pls 165–8) and a *Satyr* (New York, Met.), which was intended as a companion piece to the *Venus Kneeling on a Tortoise.* Also from around this time date a group of *Hercules and Antaeus* and the *Fate Atropos* (both London, V&A).

In March 1500 Isabella d'Este (*see* ESTE (i), (6)) commissioned from Antico some bronzes to decorate her suite of rooms in the Castello di S Giorgio, Mantua, and by March 1501 Antico had provided a replica of his statuette of the *Spinario*, and two years later another seated figure, this time female: *Andromeda* (ex-Baron Gustave Rothschild priv. col., Paris, see Allison, 1994, pp. 183–4, pls 130–31). However, Antico was still working mainly for Ludovico and held a position at Gazzuolo as *camerero* (Gentleman of the Bedchamber) with a good salary (1501). From 1504 there survives an exchange of letters between the rival patrons and the artist about the production of a gold statuette of the *Young St John the Baptist* (untraced). Further surviving correspondence between Antico and Isabella mentions not only bronze statuettes but also the acquisition and restoration of ancient sculptures. Antico went on to make for Isabella a horse's head and an eagle for casting in silver, and in 1506 he restored Classical heads of a *Minerva* and a *Cupid* (all untraced). After Mantegna's death in 1506, Antico took over his role of general adviser to Isabella on artistic matters. Following the death of her husband Francesco (1519), Isabella decided to create a new *studiolo* and grotto in the Corte Vecchia of the Palazzo Ducale, Mantua, for which she requested from Antico casts of all the bronzes that he had produced 20 years earlier for Bishop Ludovico. In a letter to her (1519) he proposed to provide her with eight statuettes, of which five survive in the Kunsthistorisches Museum, Vienna; her posthumous inventory of 1542 mentions *Hercules and Antaeus* (see fig. 2), identified as

2. Antico: *Hercules and Antaeus*, bronze, h. 432 mm, *c.* 1519 (Vienna, Kunsthistorisches Museum)

being the version in the Kunsthistorisches Museum, Vienna, by the inscription on the base, and the equestrian *Marcus Aurelius* (untraced). The 1542 inventory also indicates how the statuettes were displayed: along a cornice running round the walls of the grotto, with bronze busts on another cornice, higher up. Unlike the original statuettes for Ludovico, none of those for Isabella was gilded or inlaid with silver eyes. After this commission, the actual casting of which was subcontracted, Antico seems to have turned more towards architecture, designing new sculptural decorations for Gazzuolo, which were much admired, but have long since been destroyed.

As with many neo-classical sculptors, Antico's work needs to be closely compared with its prototypes to discover where his sculptural talent lay, as distinct from a mere facility in copying what was before his eyes. So damaged were his models that great scope existed for the imaginative reintegration of missing arms, legs and attributes: these, as in the case of his *Apollo Belvedere*, may differ from the subsequent restorations that are familiar today. Antico had to use much imagination and archaeologically orientated surmise in order to re-create the imagined perfection of the lost or damaged originals. Through sometimes gross marble copies, his enthusiast's eye could discern the pristine magnificence of lost ancient Greek bronze originals.

His style is a sculptural counterpart to Mantegna's in painting, emphasizing the anatomical articulation and the smooth, rotund forms of the human body. He loved to contrast polished and darkly patinated surfaces with intricately chiselled details of hair, drapery and accoutrements, which are often gilded, with the eyes sometimes being inlaid with silver. His overtly opulent creations appealed to his courtly patrons, in contrast to the more intellectual and romantic evocations of ancient mythology by the other great sculptor of the bronze statuette, Andrea Riccio, whose clientele were sensitive humanists, the professors and learned clerics of Padua University.

Antico's talent may be likened to that of Canova, who centuries later gave a new lease of life to ancient forms through an instinctive understanding of the artistic ideals that they embodied.

2. Working methods and technique. Antico was the first sculptor to realize the commercial advantages of being able to cast identical replicas of his compositions. Previously, particularly in Florence, bronze statuary had been made directly from the master model in a unique cast, probably rather a rough one, which was then chased, hammered and filed into its final shape. This remained true until the time of Benvenuto Cellini. Antico departed from this method in making an original master model in wax around an iron armature and finishing it highly: from this he would take piece-moulds in plaster, which could be carefully removed (leaving the master model intact) and then reassembled. Wax could be poured or packed into the resultant cavity to make the actual casting model—often in separate components (e.g. head, torso and limbs)—which could then be assembled by slight melting at the joints and smoothing out any traces with a warm spatula. This secondary model would then of necessity be lost in the casting process. Antico used a steel burnisher to scrape the cast metal smooth, as can be seen or felt occasionally from parallel striations on the surface.

Despite the commercial potential of this approach to casting, Antico did not put it to use seriously, never casting more than three examples of a given composition, perhaps owing to the jealousy of his patrons. They would have set great store by the exclusiveness of their statuettes and permitted replicas only for close relations.

BIBLIOGRAPHY

DBI

W. von Bode: *Die italienische Bronzestatuetten der Renaissance* (Berlin, 1906; Eng. trans., London, 1907–12); rev. and ed. J. Draper (New York, 1980)

H. J. Hermann: 'Pier Jacopo Alari-Bonacolsi, genannt Antico', *Jb. Ksthist. Samml. Allhöch. Ksrhaus.*, xxviii (1909–10), pp. 219–20

A. Allison: 'Four New Busts by Antico', *Mitt. Ksthist. Inst. Florenz*, xx (1976), pp. 213–24

A. F. Radcliffe: 'Antico and the Mantuan Bronze', *Splendours of the Gonzaga* (exh. cat., ed. D. Chambers and J. Martineau; London, V&A, 1981–2), pp. 46–9, 132–40

A. Nesselrath: 'Antico and Monte Cavallo', *Burl. Mag.*, cxxiv (1982), pp. 353–7

R. Stone: 'Antico and the Development of Bronze Casting in Italy at the End of the Quattrocento', *Met. Mus. J.*, xvi (1982), pp. 87–116

C. M. Brown: *La grotta di Isabella d'Este: Un simbolo di continuità dinastica per i duchi di Mantova* (Mantua, 1985)

The Liechtenstein Collection (exh. cat., New York, Met., 1985), no. 133
Natur und Antike in der Renaissance (exh. cat., Frankfurt am Main, Liebieghaus, 1985), nos 3, 22–4, 94–5, 97–8, 104, 116, 120, 128
Die Bronzen der Fürstlichen Sammlung Liechtenstein (exh. cat., Frankfurt am Main, Liebieghaus, 1986), pp. 257–61, no. 58
Renaissance Master Bronzes from the Kunsthistorisches Museum, Vienna (exh. cat., Washington, DC, N.G.A., 1986), nos 8–10
L. N. Amico: 'Antico's *Bust of the Young Marcus Aurelius*', *Getty Mus. J.*, 16 (1988), pp. 95ff
K. Fittschen: 'The Bronze Bust of the *Young Marcus Aurelius* by Antico and its Antique Model', *Getty Mus. J.*, 18 (1990), pp. 113–26
A. H. Allison: 'The Bronzes of Pier Jacopo Bonacolsi, called Antico', *Jb. Ksthist. Samml. Wien*, 89–90 (1994), pp. 35–310
The Currency of Fame: Portrait Medals of the Renaissance (exh. cat., ed. S. K. Scher; New York, Frick, 1994), pp. 77–80, nos 16–17
M. Leithe-Jasper: 'Isabella d'Este und Antico', *Isabella d'Este, Fürstin und Mäzenatin der Renaissance* (exh. cat., ed. S. Ferino-Pagden; Vienna, Ksthist. Mus., 1994), pp. 317–61

CHARLES AVERY

Antigna, (Jean-Pierre-)Alexandre (*b* Orléans, 7 March 1817; *d* Paris, 26 Feb 1878). French painter. He was taught at the school of drawing in Orléans by a local painter, François Salmon (1781–1855). On 9 October 1837 he entered the Ecole des Beaux-Arts in Paris, first in the atelier of Sebastien Norblin de la Gourdaine (1796–1884). A year later he became a pupil of Paul Delaroche, from whom he acquired his understanding of dramatic composition.

Antigna exhibited at the Salon for the first time in 1841 with a religious canvas, the *Birth of Christ* (untraced), and showed there every year for the rest of his life. Until 1845 his exhibits were primarily religious scenes and portraits. Influenced by the effects of industrialization and the sufferings of the urban working class, which he witnessed at first hand while living in the poor quarter of the Ile St Louis in Paris, he turned towards contemporary social subjects dominated by poverty and hardship. The 1848 Revolution confirmed him in his allegiance to Realist painting, and he continued to paint in this style until *c.* 1860. During this period he produced his most important and personal works, which frequently dramatized natural or manmade disasters with bold lighting, dramatic poses and rich colour, almost exclusively on a large scale: for example *Lightning* (1848; Paris, Mus. d'Orsay), *The Fire*, his most famous painting (1850; Orléans, Mus. B.-A.; see fig.), the *Forced Halt* (1855; Toulouse, Mus. Augustins) and *Visit of His Majesty the Emperor to the Slate Quarry Workers of Angers during the Floods of 1856* (1856–7; Angers, Mus. B.-A.). In 1849 he painted *After the Bath*, a large canvas bought by the state and sent the same year to the Orléans museum. The sensuality of the nudes and the topical quality of the scene provoked a local scandal.

Alexandre Antigna: *The Fire*, oil on canvas, 2.62×2.82 m, 1850 (Orléans, Musée des Beaux-Arts)

Around 1860 Antigna moved from tragic Realism to a gentler Naturalism, and social subjects were replaced by anecdotal scenes, although he never lost his sense of compassion for the poor. He travelled in search of local colour and the picturesque: from 1857 onwards he made several journeys to Spain; in 1858 he stayed in Gargilesse and the Creuse. He visited Brittany many times over several years. Landscape, including the sea, appeared with increasing frequency in his works, which often had a moralizing or satirical flavour: the *Village Cock* (*c.* 1858; Bagnères-de-Bigorre, Mus. A), *Young Breton Sleeping* (*c.* 1858–9; Orléans, Mus. B.-A.), *Young Girls Reading a Lament* (1860; Nantes, Mus. B.-A.), *Summer Evening* (1862; Dinan, Hôtel de Ville) and *High Tide* (1874; Dunkirk, Mus. B.-A.).

At the same time Antigna also produced a number of canvases of mystical and sentimental inspiration and of a Symbolist tendency: for example *A Mother's Last Kiss* (*c.* 1865; Lille, Mus. B.-A.). Children appear in most of his works, and he painted them with sympathy, whether happy or sad. Antigna received numerous distinctions and honours, including the Chevalier of the Légion d'honneur in 1861. In the same year he married Hélène-Marie Pettit (1837–1918), who herself became a painter. Their son, André-Marc Antigna (1869–1941), was also a painter and miniaturist.

BIBLIOGRAPHY

Alexandre Antigna (exh. cat. by D. Ojalvo, Orléans, Mus. B.-A., 1978)
The Realist Tradition: French Painting and Drawing, 1830–1900 (exh. cat. by G. P. Weisberg, Cleveland, OH, Mus. A., 1980), pp. 265–6

DAVID OJALVO

Antigó, Joan (*b* Girona [Sp. Gerona], ?1409; *d* Girona, 1452). Catalan painter. He was trained in the workshop of the Borrassà family and collaborated with some of its members, working principally in the city of Girona and its surroundings. He had two sons, also painters, Miguel Antigó (*fl* 1452–6) and Rafael Antigó (*fl* 1458), as well as a daughter, Margarita. He is first mentioned in 1432, when he painted the altarpiece of *St Catherine* for the chapel of that name in Girona Cathedral and also completed an altarpiece of the *Virgin*, begun by Francesc Borrassà I (*d* 1427), for the chapel of Vilademany Castle. In 1435 he painted an altarpiece for the chapel of S Roc in the parish church of Vilablareix and another of *St Andrew* for the church at Sant Gregori. His last documented works are altarpieces for the churches of St Vicenç at Espinelves and of St Vicenç at Maià de Montcal (1442). All these works are untraced.

Joan Antigó's only surviving work is the altarpiece of the *Virgin of the Ladder* (1437–9), previously thought to be by an unknown master, in the monastery of S Esteve, Banyoles (Sp. Bañolas). It has 18 painted panels depicting the *Life of the Virgin*, from the *Annunciation* to the *Coronation of the Virgin*, and a sumptuous frame composed of depressed ogee arches, small pilasters and finials. On the predella are bust-length representations of four saints, an angel of the Passion and the Virgin. The central sections of the altarpiece, including its ornamental crown, remain untraced. The paintings show that Antigó was the most striking exponent of the second generation of the Girona school, working in the so-called International Gothic style of Franco-Flemish origin that was then at its peak in Catalonia.

BIBLIOGRAPHY

N. Roca: 'Las naves de la catedral de Gerona', *Rev. Gerona*, xii (1888), pp. 304–13

S. Sanpere i Miquel: *Los cuatrocentistas catalanes: Història de la pintura en Cataluña en el siglo XV* (Barcelona, 1906)

C. R. Post: *A History of Spanish Painting*, viii (Cambridge, MA, 1930)

J. Gudiol: *Història de la pintura gótica en Cataluña* (Barcelona, 1944)

G. L. Constans: *Dos obras maestras del arte gótico* (Barcelona, 1947)

J. Gudiol: *Pintura gótica*, A. Hisp., ix (Madrid, 1955)

J. Marquès i Casanovas: 'El retablo gotico de Bañolas', *Rev. Gerona*, xlix (1969), pp. 32–5

J. Sureda: *El gòtic català*, i: *Pintura* (Barcelona, 1983)

N. de Dalmases and A. J. Pitarch: *L'art gòtic: S. XIV–XV*, Historia de l'Art Català, iii (Barcelona, 1984)

M. Pujol i Canelles: 'El retaule de Sant Miquel de Castelló d'Empúries: Descoberta la identitat dels seus autors', *An. Inst. Estud. Gironins*, xxx (1988–9), pp. 233–59

PERE FREIXAS

Antigonos. *See under* ISIGONOS, EPIGONOS, STRATONIKOS AND ANTIGONOS.

Antigua (i) [formerly Santiago de Guatemala]. Guatemalan city, located in a valley at the foot of the Agua volcano, 1500 m above sea-level, with a population of *c*. 25,000. It was founded in 1527 as Santiago de Guatemala, but following a landslide in 1541 it was relocated in 1543 to the Panchoy Valley. It was the capital of the Audiencia de Guatemala, which included the present Mexican state of Chiapas and the five Central American countries (excluding Panama), until 1773, when the last in a series of devastating earthquakes led to its abandonment as the capital; GUATEMALA CITY became the new capital in 1776. The old city quickly began to grow again and gained the status of capital of the Sacatepéquez department, acquiring its present name in 1790.

Antigua was originally laid out on the typical Spanish grid plan centred around a main square; the plan is believed to have been executed by Juan Bautista Antonelli the elder (*d* 1588). Before its demise in 1773, the city had *c*. 30,000 inhabitants. As capital of an area of *c*. 500,000 sq. km and the main city between Mexico and Peru, it was a centre of economic, political and cultural life for a wide region. The finest artists were based there, with new artistic styles reaching it first from Spain before spreading out over the territory of the kingdom. One of the most notable painters of the early 18th century was TOMÁS DE MERLO. The architecture of the city possessed several striking aspects: there was minimum use of stone, with most buildings being made first from rubble, and later from brick, with a stucco surfacing; a second feature was the limited height of the buildings, with towers barely rising higher than the central elements of the façades. This feature, in addition to the thick walls and columns and groined vaults, among other things, was the result of the efforts of architects to make buildings withstand the earthquakes that periodically struck the city. Although they were not totally successful, they persisted in their search for solutions to the problem, producing the heavy dimensions that came to be termed 'earthquake baroque' by Pál Keleman.

Antigua, S José (formerly the cathedral) by Joseph de Porres, completed 1686

The repeated earthquakes between 1600 and 1773 destroyed most 16th-century and 17th-century buildings. The original cathedral, destroyed in 1541, was replaced (inaugurated 1680, completed 1686; see fig.) largely by Joseph de PORRES with a vaulted three-nave church; damaged in 1717, it was restored by his son Diego de Porres (1677–1741) in 1720–21 but was again damaged in 1773. Joseph de Porres was appointed Arquitecto Mayor in 1687 and began to adopt early Baroque forms in such buildings as the churches of S Francisco (1690) and La Compañía de Jesús (1698). A notable achievement of the Baroque architecture of the late 17th century and the 18th was the development of a series of new forms of pilaster, such as the frequently used bolster pilaster (*almohadillado*), seen, for example, in La Merced (1767) on the third storeys of the towers. Notable civil architecture of the mid-18th century included the Real Cabildo (1740–43), probably by José Manuel Ramírez, the Real Palacio, built by Luis Díez Navarro, and the Casa de Chamorro (1762), also by Díez Navarro, in a Baroque style with an arcaded patio. The polychromed wood carvings of Santiago de Guatemala were renowned for their high quality, and major sculptors in the 18th century included members of the GÁLVEZ family.

Although in the 20th century artistic activity tended to be concentrated in Guatemala City, three important museums were founded in Antigua: the Museo de Arte Colonial (founded 1936), housing work by such artists as Tomás de Merlo, the Museo de Santiago (founded 1957) and Museo del Libro Antiguo (1960). The city has retained its colonial appearance, with the ruins of churches and monasteries still present. In 1943, on the 400th anniversary of the city's foundation, Antigua was declared a national monument. Its main buildings were cleaned and a process of conservation was begun, with legislation establishing regulations for new buildings in the city. In 1965 it was declared a 'Monument of America' in the Congress of the Panamerican Institute of Geography and History, and in 1985 a 'Heritage of Humanity' by UNESCO. Its preservation is entrusted to a specific autonomous council. By the late 20th century the city had become an important centre of traditional craftwork, with maiolica, glazed pottery, carpentry, ironwork and textiles widely available. A number of commercial art galleries had also become established.

BIBLIOGRAPHY

P. Keleman: *Baroque and Rococo in Latin America* (New York, 1951), pp. 122–5

S. D. Markman: *Colonial Architecture of Antigua Guatemala* (Philadelphia, 1966)

V. L. Annis: *La arquitectura de la Antigua Guatemala, 1543–1773* (Guatemala City, 1968)

JORGE LUJÁN-MUÑOZ

Antigua (ii). *See under* ANTILLES, LESSER.

Antilles, Greater. Group of CARIBBEAN ISLANDS comprising CUBA, JAMAICA, PUERTO RICO and Hispaniola, the last divided into HAITI and the DOMINICAN REPUBLIC. Prior to contact with the Spanish colonists, the art of the Greater Antilles was relatively unified. However, after colonization traditions soon separated.

□

Antilles, Lesser. Group of CARIBBEAN ISLANDS comprising TRINIDAD AND TOBAGO, Barbados, the Netherlands Antilles and the Leeward and Windward Islands. These last include the French Overseas Departments of Martinique and Guadeloupe with their dependencies of St Martin, St Barthélémy, and the Saintes Islands; the American and British Virgin Islands; Dominica; Grenada; St Lucia; St Vincent and the Netherlands possessions of Saba, St Eustatius and St Maarten, among numerous smaller islands. The remotest islands of Aruba, Bonaire and Curaçao were all formerly Dutch colonies, but Aruba withdrew from the Netherlands Antilles in 1986. (For map, *see* CARIBBEAN ISLANDS, fig. 1.)

I. Introduction.

In geological terms the Virgin Islands form an eastern extension of the faultblock geology of the Greater Antilles, while the outer islands, such as Anguilla, Antigua and Barbuda in the Leeward Islands, Barbados, eastern Guadeloupe and the Aruba, Bonaire and Curaçao group are of coral limestone formation. The latter are generally low-lying and surrounded by white sand beaches and coral reefs. Rainfall is low, *c*. 0.5–1.15 m a year, and there is little surface water; the coastal areas are particularly arid. The inner islands are of volcanic origin and are more rugged: there are active volcanoes on St Vincent, St Lucia, Martinique, Guadeloupe, Dominica, Montserrat, and St Kitts and Nevis. The highest points are Soufrière on Guadeloupe (1467 m), Morne Diablotin on Dominica (1447 m) and Mont Pelée, Martinique (1397 m). These well-watered islands have lush vegetation, especially on the upper slopes of the central hills, and support several rare indigenous species of birds. The sugar industry was established by the mid-17th century, and, as a result, Caribbean life was at its most affluent between 1750 and 1840. However, the waning of the industry in the 19th century also had a great impact. Cotton was grown as an export crop from the 17th century and peaked during the late 18th century, stimulated by the demands of the English textile industry. However, cultivation was virtually abandoned during the 19th century, due to rapid growth of cotton production in the USA.

The earliest known inhabitants of the islands were the Arawaks. These were subsequently displaced by the Carib people (*see* §II, 1 below), who were in occupation at the time of the first European contact at the end of the 15th century AD. Traces of Carib and Arawak culture can be seen in the rock-carvings and pottery found on many islands. The earliest British colonists established principal permanent settlements on Barbados and St Kitts (1625), Nevis (1628), Antigua and Montserrat (1632), Anguilla (1650) and the British Virgin Islands a little later (e.g. the largest, Tortola, 1666). The French settled on Dominica (1632), Martinique and Guadeloupe (both 1635), St Barthélémy (1648) and Grenada (*c*. 1650). The Dutch established settlements at St Eustatius (1632), Saba (1640) and St Maarten (1648), and Curaçao, Bonaire and Aruba (1634). The Danish West India Company established itself on St Thomas in 1671, and occupied St John and St Croix in the Virgin Islands until the USA bought them in 1917. Several islands changed hands many times in the 17th and 18th centuries, but colonial control was finally settled in the early 19th century. A multi-cultural history has left its mark on the islands. Colonial architecture gives a distinctive appearance to many islands and *patois* based on various European languages with some African and Indian influences is widely spoken.

For bibliography *see* CARIBBEAN ISLANDS and individual island surveys.

JANET HENSHALL MOMSEN

II. Cultures.

1. AMERINDIAN. Most islands in the Lesser Antilles have small collections of prehistoric artefacts in their museums and libraries, but the majority of the large collections are overseas (e.g. London, BM; New York, Amer. Mus. Nat. Hist. and Mus. Amer. Ind.; Cambridge, MA, Harvard U., Peabody Mus.). The artefacts chiefly predate the Amerindian Caribs, who inhabited most of the Lesser Antilles at the end of the 15th century, when Columbus first explored the area. The only substantial surviving group of Amerindians live on the Carib reserve in Dominica. The Caribs' predecessors were said to have been the Arawaks, an Amerindian people originating in central South America, who by the 16th century occupied the Greater Antilles. Linguistic and, to a lesser degree, biological data suggest that the Island Caribs and Arawaks were virtually identical, but despite this, various attempts have been made to attribute different pottery styles to these two peoples. For example, because 'Suazey' ceramic figurines depicted people with flattened heads and pierced

ears they were linked with early European descriptions of Caribs, which included comments on their habit of distorting the skull in infancy. The earlier 'Insular Saladoid' pottery had complicated decoration, frequently including lugs representing animal heads. Zoomorphic stone figures were roughly contemporary with these, while anthropomorphic stone figures (see fig. 1) coincided with later Saladoid ceramics.

The prehistoric art of the Lesser Antilles is characterized by numerous rock drawings or petroglyphs. Because of their location, these are difficult to date stratigraphically, but stylistic analysis suggests that they are pre-Carib or at least pre-Suazey. However, this attribution is inconclusive, as the use of different media can produce different styles, particularly when they are employed by different individuals. The most typical Lesser Antillean petroglyphs represent anthropomorphic figures with rayed heads and/or swaddled bodies. Similar rayed heads are depicted in rock drawings in the Greater Antilles, although swaddled bodies are virtually absent except in Puerto Rico, which lies closest to the Lesser Antilles. As the major artistic heritage of Caribbean prehistory, these petroglyphs have had an impact on the vernacular arts of the Lesser Antilles and some 'Carib' themes derived from them appear in tourist art.

1. Stone pestle, 130×75 mm, from the Antilles, *c.* AD 800–1500 (London, British Museum)

Historical accounts of the Caribs and illustrations of their artefacts show that their art forms included wooden clubs decorated with geometric designs, painted hammocks, basketwork with black, brown and yellow geometric designs, ceramics, featherwork, body painting (mainly using red pigment with black for rays and moustaches), singing and dancing. Their metal jewellery was thought to have been produced outside the area, but Carib-style basketry was still produced in Dominica and Martinique in the late 20th century. Outside the region, the descendants of Vincentian Caribs deported to Central America in 1795/6, known as the Garifuna (*see* BELIZE, §I, HONDURAS and GUATEMALA, §II), have retained some of their ancestors' basketwork styles.

The Caquetios (also known as Caiquetios and Caiquetias) who inhabited Aruba, Bonaire and Curaçao also dwelt on the mainland in what is now Venezuela. They were Arawak speakers, and the records of early settlers also mention their body painting, pearl bracelets and calabash penis sheaths. Archaeologists have seen many parallels between their artefacts and those of other Amerindian populations of Venezuela and Colombia (*see* VENEZUELA, §II and COLOMBIA, §II). The Caquetios appear to have succeeded a fishing, hunting and gathering people who have sometimes been identified as Ciboney (*see* CUBA, §II, 1 and HAITI, §II, 1). Cave and rock drawings exist on all three islands, and local prehistoric artefacts are displayed in the Curaçao Museum in Willemstad.

See also CARIBBEAN ISLANDS, §II, 1 and SOUTH AMERICA, PRE-COLUMBIAN, §VII, 1.

BIBLIOGRAPHY

Proceedings of the International Congress for the Study of Pre-Columbian Cultures of the Lesser Antilles (1961–)

H. Huth: 'Agostino Brunias, Romano: Robert Adam's "Bread Painter"', *Connoisseur*, cli (Dec 1962), pp. 264–9

A. Bullen and R. Bullen: *Archaeological Investigations on St Vincent and the Grenadines West Indies*, William Bryant Foundation, American Studies Report, viii (Orlando, 1972)

The European Vision of America (exh. cat. by H. Honour, Washington, DC, N.G.A.; Cleveland, OH, Mus. A.; Paris, Grand Pal.; 1975–7)

F. Chiappelli and others, eds: *First Images of America* (Berkeley, 1976)

L. Allair: *Later Prehistory in Martinique and the Island Caribs: Problems in Ethnic Identification* (diss., New Haven, CT, Yale U., 1977; microfilm, Ann Arbor, 1977)

A. Boomert: 'The Cayo Complex of St Vincent', *Anthropológica*, lxvi (1986), pp. 3–68

P. Hulm: *Colonial Encounters: Europe and the Native Caribbean* (London, 1986)

I. Rouse: *The Taino* (New Haven, 1992)

2. AFRO-CARIBBEAN. From the beginning of the 16th century African slaves were imported into the Lesser Antilles to work on plantations. They came mainly from West Africa, where the major arts included dance, woodcarving, bronze- and brass-casting, goldwork, textiles and architecture. Metalworkers frequently belonged to a separate caste, and good carvers, potters and weavers could become full-time specialists. Others came from Western Central Africa, where fewer specialists were found, although the region was famous for raffia cloth and carvings in wood and ivory. Slaves who brought their craft skills with them from Africa practised those permitted by their masters; the most commonly reported were basketwork,

used to make containers and chairs; straw plaiting for ropes and bed mats; and leatherworking and pottery. Dance, which initially survived as a part of slave celebrations at Christmas and carnivals, also required costumes and accoutrements. Many Antillean slaves were later transferred to North America, and some of their arts and crafts travelled with them: for example, North American Afro-American pottery was influenced by Caribbean ceramics. Full emancipation of slaves in the British Caribbean took place in 1834.

Whether the slaves were generally permitted to build their own design of huts in the Caribbean is debated, but there appears to have been less African architectural input than in the Greater Antilles. Rural housing can be seen as the result either of a mixture of African and European influences or of modifications of European architecture. A major problem with such debates is the fact that the historical and archaeological study of the artefacts produced by Black Caribbeans in the Lesser Antilles is in its infancy. Early descriptions of items rarely give sufficient data, and there are problems with interpreting illustrations owing to the artists' stylistic and aesthetic conventions. As a consequence of this lack of hard data, African connections are frequently proposed to explain parallels between contemporary African and Caribbean crafts and designs. However, studies of 'Bush Negro' arts in Surinam have shown how inaccurate such arguments can be.

Afro-Caribbean craftwork in the Antilles is the work of both full-time specialists and part-time craftspeople, whose products cover a wide range of household, tourist and ritual items. Household products sometimes continue the traditions of the slave period, although many have been replaced by mass-produced or European-style products. For example, contemporary ceramics range from the highly African-influenced wares of Antigua to the uninfluenced pottery of Barbados. However, whereas in North America and Haiti some African traits persisted in Afro-American metalwork, little has survived in the Lesser Antilles. A minor art form of the region is the decoration of vehicles, especially vans, buses, trucks and hearses. Tourist arts include shell, straw and fibre works. Carved wood, bamboo products, cloth, ceramics and seed (bead) work are produced in most islands, and embroidery is sold in Trinidad and the French islands. Leatherwork is sold in the French islands and beaten metal products in Trinidad. Few, if any, of these artefacts can be seen as representing a continuation of slave traditions, and some types have recently been introduced from Africa. For example, Black Power-orientated cooperatives use 'African' themes to produce works emphasizing the Black population's African origins. As with the use of Amerindian themes in tourist art (*see* §1 above), this stresses the fact that Afro-Caribbean people were not the indigenous inhabitants of the region.

Antillean ritual arts include drawings used by various Pentecostal Christian sects to assist initiates on spiritual pilgrimages. However, these are of minor import when compared to the arts associated with Christmas and carnival celebrations. In general, those islands with a predominantly British and Protestant history celebrate Christmas, while those with a French and Roman Catholic past hold pre-Lenten carnivals. Islands with significant

2. 'Indian' carnival costume, St Kitts, Lesser Antilles, 1992

influences from both colonial powers tend to celebrate both occasions, and the Dutch islands celebrate both carnival and New Year, although the former is the more significant (*see* CARNIVAL). Most of the performing arts featured at these festivals can be traced back to local slave events and sometimes to Africa: the Martiniquan carnival, for example, includes performances and costumes very similar to those found in West Africa. However, in St Vincent the British suppressed most of the French-style carnival during the 19th century, and the modern version in Kingstown, the capital, is the result of a reintroduction of the event from Trinidad (*see* TRINIDAD AND TOBAGO, §II, 2). The Trinidadian influence similarly modified many of the carnivals in the southern Windward Islands. Before World War II, carnivals held on the islands to the north of Trinidad were generally performed by individuals and small groups using traditional costumes and dances. However, after the war they imitated the larger carnival bands of Trinidad. Such bands have costume designers who ensure that the costumes of their 'king', 'queen', 'prince', 'princess' and supporting players illustrate a common theme; the queen is usually the dominant figure. The topic changes annually, and the costumes and their relationship to the overall theme are judged on artistic grounds.

The islanders of St Kitts and Nevis similarly influenced the Christmas celebrations of their northern neighbours: for example, evidence suggests that the traditional St Kitts and Nevis Christmas dances involving 'Indians' were exported to the Dominican Republic and Bermuda along with labour migrants. The Indian masqueraders wear tall feather headdresses with trousers, shirts, aprons and capes decorated with beads and mirrors (see fig. 2). The costumes and dances changed little during the 20th century, although early masqueraders frequently wore European masks (made of wire mesh and imported from the Tyrol in the early 19th century) to make them appear white. The costumes are influenced by the dress of Native North Americans, but not to the extent of those worn by Indian carnival bands in Trinidad and actors in the Christmas cowboy play performed in Nevis. There are also similarities between the Christmas performances of the Lesser Antilles (especially the northern islands) with the Jamaican, Bahamian and Belizean *Jonkonnu* or *Junkanoo* (John Canoe) performances (*see* BAHAMAS, THE, §II, 2) and the Gombey celebrations of Bermuda, all of which are normally held at Christmas.

BIBLIOGRAPHY

R. D. Abrahams: *The Man-of-words in the West Indies* (Baltimore, 1956)

Carib. Q., iv/3–4 (1956) [special issue on carnival]

C. J. M. R. Gullick: 'West Indian Artefacts: A Bibliographical Essay', *Mus. Ethnographers Grp Newslett.*, xix (1985), pp. 26–53

J. W. Nunley and J. Bettelheim: *Caribbean Festival Arts* (Seattle, 1988)

C. J. M. R. GULLICK

III. Architecture.

1. PRE-COLONIAL AND VERNACULAR FORMS. Before the arrival of the Europeans the Amerindians built circular or oval thatched huts, typically with walls of timber staves spaced to allow ventilation: none of these now survives on the islands, but a characteristic pre-colonial Arawak dwelling has been reconstructed at the Arawak Indian Museum, St Catherine, Jamaica. After the largest islands were settled by the rival European powers, the Amerindian dwelling was subsequently developed in rectangular form for plantation-workers and slaves; it was probably the prototype of the chattel house (originally so called as a movable possession of transient workers in Barbados) or *casa*, in which many islanders live. The houses were usually built of timber, raised off the ground on stone (or later concrete) 'pillar trees'. Characteristically the chattel house had exposed timber corner-posts, weatherboarded walls and a steeply pitched roof covered in wood shingles. The weatherboarding was usually inset between the vertical frames, allowing each to be articulated by painting in a different colour, traditionally yellow ochre panels between dark red structural frames and door and window surrounds. Island preferences, however, have produced other colour combinations (e.g. blues and greens in Grenada, brown with yellow ochre in St Lucia). A timber-framed chattel house has been restored on the Welches plantation, north of Bridgetown, Barbados (see fig. 3). On islands where there was a shortage of timber, plantation houses were also built with stone walls, and in Curaçao (Netherlands Antilles), for example, thatch rather than shingles was common, but both were increasingly displaced by corrugated iron after it became available in the 19th century.

2. COLONIAL SETTLEMENT: 17TH AND 18TH CENTURIES. Though much influenced by the vernacular and

3. Chattel house, Barbados, Lesser Antilles

the available local craft skills, urban architectural character in the Lesser Antilles was largely derived from Europe. In the century and a half after the arrival of colonists, some of the islands were shared and others changed hands by conquest or political manoeuvre. Their architecture, therefore, shows evidence of mixed cultures: examples are British and French in St Lucia, Grenada, Dominica and St Kitts and French and Dutch in St Martin. Early building was concerned with defence: bastion-trace fortifications were small in scale. Examples include Fort Amsterdam (begun 1634) at Willemstad, Curaçao; Fort St Louis (Fort Royal; begun 1670s), Martinique; Fort St George (1680s), Grenada; and Fort Christian (begun 1671), Charlotte Amalie, St Thomas, US Virgin Islands. Fortifications were extended when nearly a hundred years of conflict between the British and French began in the second quarter of the 18th century. Examples include Fort Berkeley (1740s), Antigua, protecting the naval installations of English Harbour (1726–94), and the technically and architecturally sophisticated Prince of Wales bastion on Brimstone Hill, St Kitts, with its classicizing details.

Little survived the hurricanes and fires of the prosperous 17th century. St Nicholas Abbey (probably 1660s), Barbados, with its triple ogee gables, and Drax Hall, Barbados, built by Thomas Shettenden Drax (*d* 1702) in the last quarter of the century, are among the few surviving great houses that can be dated to the 17th century with any degree of certainty. A few examples from the 18th century remain: plantation houses, such as Romney Manor, or Rawlins above Dieppe Bay at the foot of Mt Misery, both in St Kitts; Château Murat, the severely classical French country house on Marie Galante, Guadeloupe; and the Danish Baroque Whin Plantation Museum on St Croix, US Virgin Islands. Characteristic Dutch-gabled urban houses were built at Punda (from 1706), Willemstad, Curaçao, where there are also merchants' houses, such as the Five Senses (begun 1750), neither of which types makes any concession to local climate or conditions. Smaller British and French estate houses, on the other hand, were carefully adapted to climate: metal- and timber-framed verandahs surrounded the houses at each floor level, and jalousies and louvred shutters gave protection from the sun and facilitated through-ventilation. Byde Mill, Barbados, is a fine mid-18th-century example, with a delicately framed and balustraded verandah at ground-level only; French examples with elegantly framed verandahs survive in both Guadeloupe and Dominica. Military housing also gives expression to both national and local factors: the barracks at Fort St George (before *c.* 1750), St George's, Grenada, is characteristic of French provincial buildings of the period, with simple stone surrounds to segmental window- and door-heads; British examples from later in the century, such as the ruined buildings on Shirley Heights, Antigua, and the garrison, Bridgetown, Barbados, reflect European academic classicism and recall contemporary British military buildings in South-east Asia.

Churches have been especially prone to hurricane damage and therefore much restored and altered. They were usually single-naved with a single square west tower. The ruined Dutch Reformed Church on St Eustatius is squat and forceful; towers are castellated (e.g. St Mary's, Bridgetown, Barbados), or have characteristic finials (St George's on the island of the same name); all have foundations of the late 17th century and early 18th. The fine Fort Church (1766–9; cupola, 1903), Willemstad, Curaçao, has Dutch Rococo overtones. The English architect Sir Thomas Robinson went to Barbados as Governor (1742–7), and the refining influence of his mid-Georgian Palladianism upon the design of government and public buildings is widely apparent on the islands: Government House, Bridgetown, has been attributed to him, as well as an armoury and arsenal. Jackson-Stops (1986) suggests that his influence extends to the mid-18th-century parts of such great houses as Clifton Hall, Barbados. Influences of this kind are widespread, ranging well into the 19th century, from such elegant classicizing urban façades as the western waterfront of St George's, Grenada (built after the arrival of the British in 1762), to the arcaded façades of Kingstown, St Vincent, and Charlotte Amalie, St Thomas.

3. NEO-CLASSICAL TO MODERN: 19TH AND 20TH CENTURIES. There are interesting 19th-century churches in both British and French traditions. The church at Parham (1840), Antigua, is an octagonal Neo-classical building of simple dignity; the cathedral of Fort-de-France (after *c.* 1875), Martinique, is built in iron to the design of Gustave Eiffel. The Roman Catholic cathedral at Castries, St Lucia, is another iron church of the same period, and Basseterre, St Kitts, has a 19th-century iron clock-tower in its main square. Among the finest domestic buildings of the 19th century and early 20th are those of the Netherlands Antilles, mostly in the academic classical manner. Examples include Belvédère House (1864–5), Otrabanda, Willemstad, Curaçao, built for the Governor by Lt W. F. H. van Riemedijk, an army engineer; imposing urban mansions in the Scharloo district, such as that built for David Senior in 1875, with a fine two-storey portico with coupled Doric columns; and, also at Willemstad, the elegant classical octagonal house, Groot Davelar (1873), by the Curaçoan architect Antoine Martis and the unique Bolo de Bruid (wedding-cake) house (begun 1916), built by Henry da Costa Gomez and a local amateur architect, Maurice Cardoze.

In the Netherlands Antilles during the 1930s developments parallel with those in Europe took place: for example a form of Art Deco appeared in such buildings as P. A. Stuyvenburg's streamlined cinemas, Cinelandia (1936) and West End (*c.* 1940), both Willemstad. Despite substantial development programmes, however, the unrest of the 1930s led to mass emigration to the UK after World War II. The growth of tourism in the 1950s created a demand for hotels, including Sandy Lane Hotel, Barbados, and La Toc, St Lucia, both by Robinson Ward of Barbados, reminiscent of the Georgian style associated with the colonial past. By the late 20th century many major buildings were still being designed by American or European consultants, although local practices were also active in many of the islands, including such major firms as Gillespie and Steel and such distinguished, small practices as that of Colin Laird (*b* 1924). Laird's work includes a number of major hotels, for example the Spice Islands Hotel (1960), Grande Anse, Grenada, and such public buildings as the

Government Administration Building (1961), St Kitts, and the five-storey Government Headquarters (1968), Dominica, both sophisticated Modernist buildings designed to respond to climate. Details of Ian Morrison's Barbadian vernacular houses of the mid-1980s were published internationally.

BIBLIOGRAPHY

A. W. Acworth: *Buildings of Architectural or Historic Interest in the British West Indies* (London, 1951)

M. D. Ozinga: *De monumenten van Curaçao in voord en beeld* (The Hague, 1959)

P. W. Gosner: *Plantation and Town: Historic Architecture in the US Virgin Islands* (Durham, NC, 1971)

R. Devaux: *Saint Lucia Historic Sites* (Castries, 1975)

Y. Attema: *St Eustatius: A Short History of the Island and its Monuments* (Zutphen, 1976)

V. Radcliffe: *The Caribbean Heritage* (New York, 1976)

G. Tyson: *An Inventory of the Historical Landmarks of St Kitts-Nevis* (Saint Thomas, 1976)

D. Buisseret: *Historic Architecture of the Caribbean* (London, 1980)

B. Hill: *Historic Churches of Barbados* (Barbados, 1984)

V. Hitchcock: 'Sun, Sieges and Sugar Cane', *Country Life*, clxxviii/4597 (26 Sept 1985), pp. 704–9

G. Jackson-Stops: 'A Future for a Colonial Past', *Country Life*, clxxx/4649 (25 Sept 1986), pp. 936–41

R. Marcorelles: 'Guadeloupe–Martinique', *Archit. Medit.*, 33 (Oct 1989), pp. 157–82

H. E. Coomans, M. A. Newton and M. Coomans Eustatia: *Building up the Future from the Past: Studies on the Architecture and Historic Monuments of the Dutch Caribbean* (Zutphen, 1990)

K. Howes: 'Barbadian Palladian', *House & Gdn*, xlvi/7 (July 1991), pp. 84–91

C. L. Temminck Groll and others: *Curaçao: Willemstad: City of Monuments* (Amsterdam, 1992)

JOHN NEWEL LEWIS

IV. Painting, graphic arts and sculpture.

The Lesser Antilles and their Carib inhabitants appeared or were described with varying degrees of accuracy in minor European illustrations, travel books, stage costumes and paintings from the 15th century onwards. Until the mid-20th century the majority of these were produced by Europeans: many early depictions were executed in Europe and were based on the descriptions and sketches of travellers and sometimes on artefacts. Most early prints accompanied sensational travellers' tales. Amerindians became equated with nakedness or exotic costumes comprising feather headdresses and imaginary feather skirts, as in the work of Albrecht Dürer (e.g. the illustration to Psalm 24 in the *Book of Hours of the Emperor Maximilian I*, fol. 41*r*; Munich, Bayer. Staatsbib.), and were mainly portrayed either as noble savages living a pastoral life or as inhuman cannibals. The Caquetios who inhabited Aruba, Bonaire and Curaçao were initially described as giants and tended to be depicted as towering noble savages. From the 17th century naturalists illustrated their accounts of the Lesser Antilles with depictions of tropical plants, crops and animals. This artistic theme reached its apex in the 19th century with, for example, the watercolours of Caribbean molluscs and plants by Hendrik van Rijgersma (1835–77).

The European artists who visited the region in the 18th and 19th centuries included both amateurs (mainly sailors, soldiers, priests and clerks) and itinerant professional artists. Significant among the latter was Agostino Brunias [Augustin Brunais] (1730–96), who painted Caribs in St Vincent and plantation life in Dominica; some of these works were reproduced in volume 3 of Bryan Edwards's *The History of the British Colonies in the West Indies* (1801). In general professional artists were employed to show the grandeur of their patrons' plantations and other possessions; the amateurs tended to illustrate other aspects of island life. While some of the works of the itinerant European artists were hung in the plantation houses, the majority of art on display in such mansions was imported from Europe. The collections are hinted at in the holdings of the Curaçao Museum, Willemstad, Sam Lord's Castle, St Philip, Barbados, and the Musée de la Pagerie, Trois Ilets, Martinique. Reports of slave life in both pictures and documents around the time of the abolition of slavery in the mid-19th century tend to be biased towards either the planters or the slaves. The arduous transatlantic passage and the plantation system had extirpated virtually all African graphic arts. However, the ritual drawings of such Pentecostal Christian sects as the Vincentian Shakers and Trinidadian Shouters may have African antecedents. Slavery and colonialism became a topic of the Afro-Caribbean art of the late 20th century.

Indigenous fine arts in the region began only during the late colonial period with art classes begun by expatriate teachers. This instruction was reinforced by further training for promising students in the colonial homeland, with consequent Dutch influences on the arts of Aruba, Bonaire and Curaçao, and French influences on those of Guadeloupe and Martinique. Conversely, Paul Gauguin's discovery of the tropics in Martinique in 1887 influenced French perceptions of the Caribbean. The Musée Gauguin, Le Carbet, Martinique, documents his visit but displays only reproductions of the paintings he produced there. Following independence, American influences replaced the British colonial influence in the majority of Caribbean Commonwealth states. As a result, early exhibitions of Caribbean art tended to include examples of most mainstream schools with little, except occasionally the subject-matter, to distinguish them as Caribbean. Local naive artists, however, were far more centred within their own cultural milieux. In the late 20th century artists from the Lesser Antilles were educated at the Jamaica School of Art (*see* JAMAICA, §XI), and distinctive Caribbean styles developed from the merging of local and foreign art traditions. Noteworthy naive artists of the area included Ivan Payne (1922–77) of Barbados, Canute Caliste (*b* 1916) from Carriacou (see fig. 4) and Hipólito Max Ocalia (1916–84) from Curaçao.

All the states of the Lesser Antilles experienced a flowering of indigenous naive and fine arts in the late 20th century, each island expressing its own individuality. For example, St Lucia has produced many sculptors as the consequence of Joseph Eudovic's tutorage. During its revolutionary phase Grenada developed, partially as a consequence of Cuban influences, a politicized version of its own naive school of art; in contrast, the presence of a large community of expatriate artists in Barbados may have swamped local talent. In St Vincent during the 1970s there was a trend to develop local 'Carib' themes, while Trinidadian artists, perhaps influenced by their island's carnival, have concentrated upon abstract paintings.

BIBLIOGRAPHY

B. Edwards: *The History, Civil and Commercial, of the British Colonies in the West Indies*, 3 vols (London, 1793–1801)

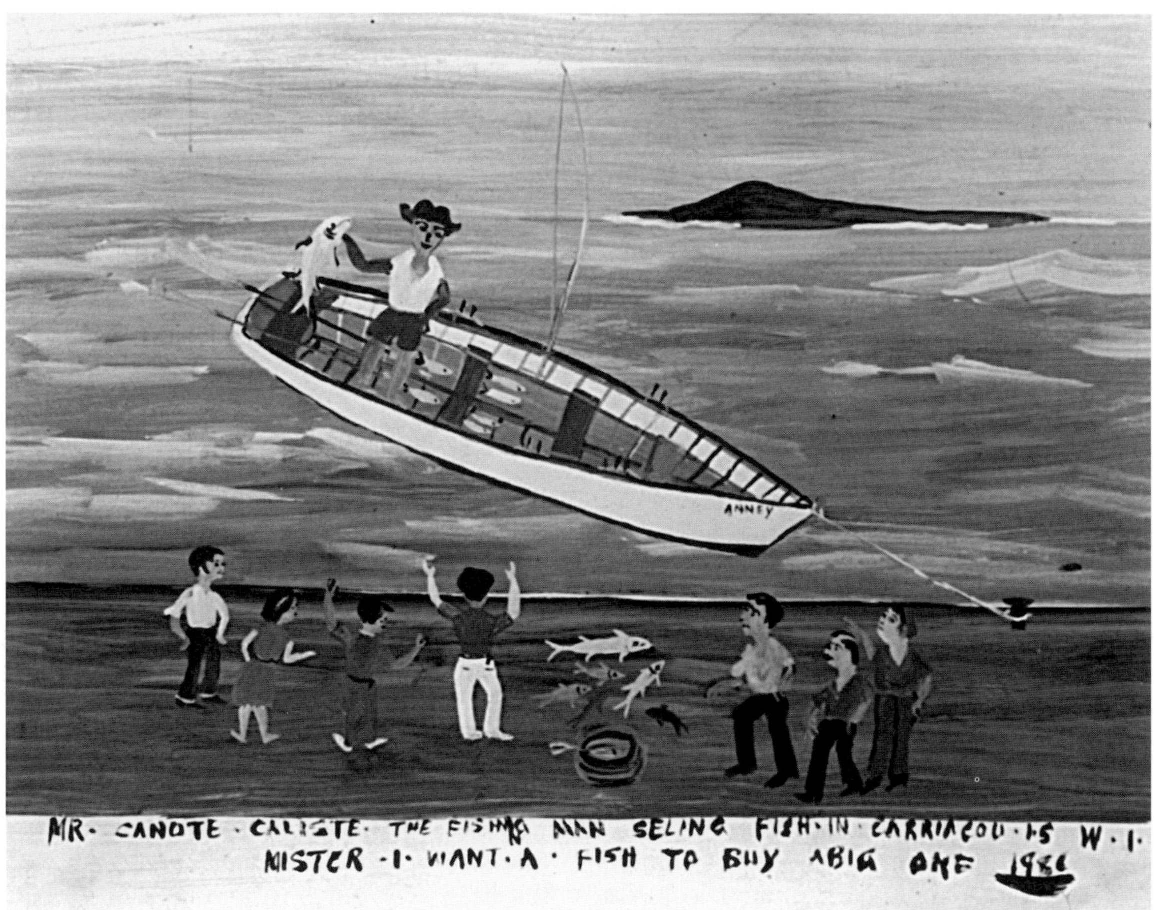

4. Canute Caliste: *Fisher Man Selling Fish*, acrylic on hardboard, 241×305 mm (Grenada, Yellow Poni Gallery)

N. Connell: 'Caribbean Artists, Paint, Action and Colour', *Studio Int.*, cliii/770 (1957), pp. 129–35
H. Huth: 'Agostino Brunias, Romano: Robert Adam's "Bread Painter"', *Connoisseur*, cli (1962), pp. 264–9
M. L. Vincent: 'Two Painters of the Tropics: Lafacio Hearn and Paul Gauguin in Martinique', *Carib. Stud.* (March 1970), pp. 177–9
F. Chiapelli, ed.: *First Images of America: The Impact of the New World on the Old* (Los Angeles, 1976)
B. L. Duke: 'Women, Art and Culture in the New Grenada', *Lat. Amer. Persp.*, xi/3 (1984), pp. 37–52
Caribbean Art Now: Europe's First Exhibition of Contemporary Caribbean Art (exh. cat. by E. Wallace, London, Commonwealth Inst., 1986)
H. E. Coomans and M. Coomans Eustatia: *Flowers from St Martin: The 19th Century Watercolours of West Indian Plants by Hendrik van Rijgersma* (Zutphen, 1988)
H. E. Coomans: *Antillean Seashells: The 19th Century Watercolours of Caribbean Molluscs Painted by Hendrik van Rijgersma* (Zutphen, 1989)
N. Henriques and J. Römer-de Vreese: *Ocalia: Schildert Curaçao* (Zutphen, 1992)

C. J. M. R. GULLICK

V. Decorative arts.

1. Interior design and furniture. 2. Textiles. 3. Ceramics. 4. Metalwork and jewellery.

1. INTERIOR DESIGN AND FURNITURE. Apart from written observations, inventories and wills, a few paintings from the late 18th century survive as documentation of the West Indian interior. The furnishings of the homes of the earliest settlers comprised woven cotton hammocks slung from eaves and crudely constructed stools, storage chests, tables and benches. By the 1640s small tobacco farmers had simple, undecorated wooden cabins furnished with the merest essentials. Roger Mills's deed of 1642 (Barbados) revealed that the lower of the two storeys was furnished with only a long table and two benches, and the upper bedchamber contained a bed, brass lamp, table and bench.

The introduction of stone structures in the mid-17th century influenced interior design, as did English Jacobean style. Drax Hall (*c.* 1655), St George, Barbados, is dominated by a fine mastic wood staircase and a broad elliptical arch, ornately carved with bold pendants of leaves. St Nicholas's Abbey (*c.* 1650) at St Peter, Barbados, has wooden floors throughout, and intricately carved mouldings enhance the cornices, main beams and arched doorways. A Chippendale-style staircase was installed in 1746, and Georgian-style sash windows and cedar panelling were added by the plantation carpenter in 1898. The Caribbean Georgian style became popular between *c.* 1750 and 1840, and importation of furniture from England (mahogany from Lancaster and Cork) and the USA (particularly Boston and Salem, MA) increased during the 18th century.

Nevertheless, late 18th-century newspaper advertisements for Barbados reveal a growing number of local craftsmen. John Mottley's notice (1783) identifying his runaway slave, Grigg, as 'an excellent good hand at the carpenter's and joiner's trade' is evidence of another source of furniture production before emancipation. Slaves were trained to produce copies of European furniture for the plantations. The introduction of mahogany to Barbados *c.* 1780 provided joiners with an excellent source of raw material. An example of the Caribbean Georgian style was the Olovaze Plantation near Basseterre, which had a hall, panelled in mahogany and finished with mirrors. Both drawing room and bedroom were typically 'entirely fitted up and furnished in the English taste'. The Villa on Calliaqua Estate, St George, St Vincent (destr. 1795), was unusually sumptuous in its décor, boasting a large ballroom and a painting by Agostino Brunias. In St Philip, Barbados, Samuel Hall Lord built Long Bay Castle (1831; later known as Sam Lord's Castle). The ground-floor rooms were decorated with late Georgian woodwork and fine plaster ceilings, the latter the work of Charles Rutter and two Italian assistants; many of the original furnishings remain, including elaborate crystal chandeliers, massive gilt-framed mirrors and several pieces of Sheraton-style mahogany furniture.

After the devastation caused by a hurricane in 1831, many houses were reconstructed or built in quite modest fashion. In furniture a distinctive local style developed, adapted from European pattern books for a middle-class market, and characterized by heavier proportions, coarse yet exuberant carving and a heavily lacquered dark finish. Tub chairs and 'berbice' or 'planter' chairs (a type of chair with broad arms and an extended leg-rest) were particularly popular, as were double- and single-ended couches with caned backs and seats. Reflecting the local practice of rum-drinking, the Barbadian cellaret (drinks cabinet) was a unique design, featuring a large tray-top, resting on a semicircular drawer section cradled in a curved X-frame (see fig. 5). Apart from the introduction in the 1920s of the popular Morris chair (with an adjustable backrest), this repertory remained virtually unchanged for over a century. In the 1940s industry was mechanized and new opportunities created for exporting furniture to neighbouring islands. By the 1950s and 1960s, however, Caribbean style had significantly changed, due in part to the introduction of American-influenced metal furniture and also influenced by the British stage designer OLIVER MESSEL. Through such projects as Maddox, Cockade House, and Mango Bay, St James, Barbados, he popularized an indoor–outdoor lifestyle, using open-plan rooms extending on to verandahs, loggias and terraces, and trelliswork, and the use of sage green walls, floors and shutters with white contrasting elements. After his death his associates Heather Aquilar, Arne Hasselqvist and Robert Thompson continued to create luxurious interiors, primarily for expatriates in Mustique and Barbados. The Barbados-based architect Ian Morrison combined pastel-coloured pickled pine floors and ceilings with curving coral walls, while Andrew Steel and Merwyn Avon have in different ways explored the texture, colour and versatility of indigenous wood. Avon's work also incorporates traditional jalousie shutters and 'gingerbread' decorative touches reminiscent of 19th-century Caribbean vernacular architecture.

5. Barbadian cellaret, mahogany, *c.* 1830 (St Michael, Barbados Museum)

2. TEXTILES. In spite of the Caribbean cotton industry, imported coarse linens and woollen and other textiles formed the bulk of material available for domestic use and clothing until the late 18th century. Sir Joshua Steele, founder of the Barbados Society of Arts, first encouraged the development and promotion of the local textile industry. He imported equipment for spinning, reeling, weaving and frame-knitting and brought over a Lancashire weaver and his wife to give public demonstrations of the newly invented engine for spinning on 20 spindles. Following the decline of the sugar industry, in the 19th century cotton cultivation first waned and was then revived in the latter half of the century, leading to the introduction of Sea Island cotton, remarkable for its length, lustre and fineness. Throughout the 20th century the industry experienced many vicissitudes so that a textile industry remained in a formative stage. During the 1960s a growing tourist industry encouraged the development of successful batik production, studios for which included Caribelle Batiks (St Kitts), Bagshaws (St Lucia) and Stella St John's Studio Gallery (Barbados), all of which based their designs on Amerindian motifs. In the 1970s the Spencer Cameron Gallery (St Kitts) established a successful silkscreen workshop, producing textiles printed with floral and tropical designs. Hilary Armstrong's lyrical silkscreened Caribbean

scenes and Judy Layne's colourful tie-dyed renderings of traditional culture have also attracted attention.

3. CERAMICS. Archaeological evidence from mid-17th- to 18th-century sites reveals widespread importation of primarily English tin-glazed and earthenware and Delftware. By the 17th century some plantations already had 'pot houses' to provide the conical sugar moulds used for the draining and storage of freshly refined sugar. Slave potters also produced red, African-inspired earthenware for domestic use on the plantation and possibly for barter. These early wares were often painted with a red slip and multi-directional striations were occasionally incised below the rim on the exterior. Emancipation of slaves gave impetus to the development of a cottage-based industry in all the islands. In general this was characterized by a predominantly female workforce producing handmade, open-fired pottery, which provided a secondary family income. There was no formal apprenticeship system, but skills were passed on through families.

In most islands the industry became localized around areas with a ready supply of clay, which have remained the production centres. Traditional pottery from Morne Sion, Pointe Caraibe and Fiette (St Lucia) is handcoiled and includes cooking vessels, flower pots and 'coal pots' (ceramic stoves). At Seaview Farm, Antigua, a traditional vessel with a flat bottom and handles is called variously 'pepper pot', 'mud pot' or 'jar pot'; a red-slipped earthenware griddle (*yabba*) was also produced. Newcastle and Brick Kiln (Nevis) produce hand-built 'monkey jars', cooking vessels, coal pots and large storage jars, usually painted and burnished. The same forms are produced at Chalky Mount and Turners Hall (Barbados), along with 'guglets' or 'goglets' and *conarees* with an interior glaze. These vessels were usually unadorned except for an incised line below the rim. By the 20th century large storage jars, flower pots with saucers and 'crimp pots' with indented rims and extended shoulders were also produced, as were small zoomorphic figures. Folk potters shifted their emphasis to more decorative pieces including ashtrays, vases, candlesticks, miniature monkeys and coal pots, primarily for the growing souvenir market.

During the late 1940s and 1950s island governments introduced gas-fired kilns and factory structures in an effort to industrialize and commercialize handicraft production. The pottery industry was revolutionized by the British ceramicist Christopher Russell's establishment of his potteries (1962–4) near Bridgetown, Barbados, which produced a range of tableware, lamps, tiled tables and trays with tropical motifs. With the Jamaican Denis Bell, Russell developed a technique of fusing coloured glass to a glazed ground to enhance his large-scale ceramic panels, such as *Mother and Child* (1962). Other ceramicists include Lionel Laville (Dominica), the best-known exponent of traditional forms, Helena Jones (Nevis) and Wilbert Harding (Barbados). Annie Kinsella (Antigua) produced popular glazed figurines, while Bill Grace (Barbados) expressed his fascination with music through ceramics; Ras Akyem Ramsey (Barbados) interpreted his symbiotic relationship with the natural environment, and Stanley Greaves reinterpreted traditional Native American imagery in his work. The potteries that have achieved some commercial success include the Marinica (Dominica), the Nevis near Newcastle (Nevis) and the Fairfield, Earthworks and Courtney Devonish (Barbados). Sarah Fuller Arawak Pottery is known for blue-and-white wares, and Cockleshell Pottery run by Ken Derrick for floral ceramic art in non-local clay.

4. METALWORK AND JEWELLERY. Despite the paucity of mineral resources in the region, 17th-century accounts mention jewellers and goldsmiths in the islands. By the 18th century gold jewellery had become an essential part of the costume of both Creole (native-born white) and mulatto (mixed-race) women. The Creole gold jewellery produced in Martinique was particularly popular, and the paintings of Agostino Brunias offer convincing evidence of a considerable trade in such metalwork. By the 19th century, most silverware and jewellery was imported from Europe. However, by the first half of the 20th century pewter, copper and iron were worked by a number of itinerant artisans, supplying basic domestic wares and construction services to the local community; these have since been overtaken by the ready availability of modern commodities, and only those expert artisans who cut and work metal drums for the thriving steel-pan music industry have gained significant recognition for their work. The Barbados Foundry, established during this period, was the only one of its kind in the Lesser Antilles, but its focus was on servicing industry, not on the creation of products. In the late 20th century Caribbean metalwork remained primarily confined to jewellery making, and professional metalworkers were few. In 1965 William Bertalan began to cast sculptures in bronze, aluminium and brass using the lost-wax process. In Antigua during the 1960s the metalsmith Frank Agard (1911–91) gained popular recognition for his carnival costumes, musical instruments and scale models in copper and brass; in the 1970s the Dutch goldsmith Hans Smit used the same technique to create his marine-inspired pieces. The silversmith Patricia Byer-Dunphy moved from Jamaica to Barbados to establish the Pat Byer Studio, producing starkly lyrical pieces inspired by the rhythms of Caribbean music, and the Barbadian goldsmith Disa Allsopp produced jewellery incorporating such local materials as black coral.

BIBLIOGRAPHY

N. Connell: 'Furniture and Furnishings in Barbados during the 17th century', *J. Barbados Mus. & Hist. Soc.*, xxiv (1957), pp. 102–21

E. M. Shilstone: 'Books and Pocket Almanacs', *J. Barbados Mus. & Hist. Soc.*, xxviii (1961), pp. 78–84

R. S. Dunn: *Sugar and Slaves: The Rise of the Planter Class in the English West Indies, 1624–1713* (Chapel Hill, NC, 1972, 2/London, 1973)

J. S. Handler: 'A Historical Sketch of Pottery Manufacture in Barbados', *J. Barbados Mus. & Hist. Soc.*, xxx (1973), pp. 129–53

L. Honychurch: *Our Island Culture* (Dominica, 1982)

K. R. Wernhart: 'Report of Ethno-technological Research', *Research in Ethnography and Ethnohistory of St Lucia: A Preliminary Report*, iii (1986), pp. 122–38

J. B. Petersen and D. R. Watters: 'Afro-Montserratian Ceramics from the Harney Site Cemetery, Montserrat, West Indies', *An. Carnegie Mus.*, lvii/1 (1988), pp. 167–87

ALISSANDRA CUMMINS

VI. Patronage.

Patronage has changed from European commissions for illustrations of the area to encouragement of the arts within the islands themselves. Partly as a result of these changes, the art of the region has become international. While the early European illustrators of the Lesser Antilles were employed to embellish travel books, few of them visited the area; they and their art remained in Europe, where Caribbean themes commonly featured in élite commissions, such as views of the Four Continents. In France, the Gobelins produced variations on this theme from 1687, with major revisions in 1735 (example in Valletta, Pal. Grand Masters, Tapestry Room). Planters were early patrons, at first importing European art and design, but later using their slaves to copy European models for their housing, furniture and furnishings (*see* §V above). Sir William Young, for example, a landowner in St Vincent, employed itinerant European artists, such as Agostino Brunias, to paint local personalities and scenes. Sir William edited the third volume of Bryan Edwards's *The History, Civil and Commercial, of the British Colonies in the West Indies* (1801) and included several engravings after Brunias's paintings. The majority of illustrations appear to have been designed to display patrons' status and wealth. In the debate over emancipation planters also used art to defend slavery, while their opponents encouraged illustrations of the barbarity of the transatlantic 'Middle Passage' and the life of the slaves.

The role of planters as patrons declined in the 19th century with emancipation and the collapse of the Lesser Antillean sugar industry. Items from planters' collections were sometimes preserved in local museums (e.g. Willemstad, Curaçao Mus., and Bridgetown, Barbados Mus.) and libraries, although some are still held by the companies that took over the plantations. During the last three decades of the 20th century local museums began to exhibit items produced by local artists, while the development of tourist art produced new patrons and galleries throughout the region. The owners of these frequently short-lived institutions found suitcase-sized pictures of sun, sea, palm trees and local festivals easiest to sell, and it was generally immaterial whether these were produced by locals or by expatriate artists. However, in the 1950s Barbados had a large influx of expatriate artists who encouraged and patronized local craftspeople and artists, even though they often overshadowed them. Because of their higher status expatriates tended to dominate local shows and collections. It was not until the 1980s that exhibitions of local artists began to be sponsored by institutions in Grenada and Barbados (e.g. Bridgetown, Barbados Mus.; Bridgetown, Queen's Park Gal.; Barbados A. Council). Another form of patronage involves the organization of cultural events such as carnivals. Such bodies as Carnival Development Committees comprise artists and members of the local élite who set the rules for major events and give prizes for artistic displays.

As many contemporary institutions for the distribution of the art of the Lesser Antilles are aimed at visitors, most locally produced art has been dispersed throughout the world. It is either in small, private collections, or part of major holdings of Caribbean art in the USA and Europe (e.g. London, BM; London, N. Mar. Mus.; Washington, DC, Lib. Congress; Leiden, Kon. Inst. Taal-, Land- & Vlkenknd.). Despite the widespread exportation of art, most islands maintain collections of local scenes and other works by local artists in their museums and public libraries (*see* §VII below) as do some commercial organizations (e.g. St John's, Montserrat, Mellon Col., Barclays Bank). Local art is sold at local markets or tourist shops or direct from studio-workshops. Galleries aimed primarily at tourists tend to have relatively short lifespans, but most are rapidly replaced. Some galleries, particularly in Antigua (e.g. Nonsuch Bay, Harmony Hall; St John's, Island A.; Falmouth, Seahorse Studios), Martinique (e.g. Fort de France, Carib. A. Cent. (Métiers A.)) and Barbados (e.g. Christchurch, Guardhouse Gal.; Christchurch, Coffee & Cream), sell pieces of higher quality. Most concentrate upon local scenes by both expatriates and local artists, and some upon the work of the latter.

BIBLIOGRAPHY

B. Edwards: *The History, Civil and Commercial, of the British Colonies in the West Indies*, 3 vols (London, 1793–1801)

C. Hampshire: *The British in the Caribbean* (London, 1972)

D. Devenish: 'On Collecting Caribbean Material', *Mus. Ethnographers' Grp Newslett.*, xix (1985), pp. 58–67

C. J. M. R. Gullick: 'West Indian Artefacts: A Bibliographical Essay', *Mus. Ethnographers' Grp Newslett.*, xix (1985), pp. 26–53

Caribbean Art Now: Europe's First Exhibition of Contemporary Caribbean Art (exh. cat. by E. Wallace, London, Commonwealth Inst., 1986)

C. J. M. R. GULLICK

VII. Museums.

Between 1847 and 1848 the Governor-in-Chief of the Windward Islands, Lt-Col., later Sir, William Reid, initiated the development of legislation to establish museums 'to which everyone may have access' in St Lucia, Barbados and Grenada. Although he was convinced that 'their establishment will at once give a great forward movement to general education', until the first decades of the 20th century they remained for the most part case collections housed in local libraries. The expansion of American archaeological activities within the region stimulated the rapid growth of 'museum' collections in even the smallest of islands, and by the 1920s libraries in St Vincent, St Kitts, Grenada, Guadeloupe, St Lucia and Antigua all held small collections. In 1933 a Museums Association survey of museums in the British Empire included a study of the Caribbean institutions in which Bather and Sheppard undertook to ascertain 'the status of museums in general in the West Indies and also to make suggestions as to the methods by which they could be improved'. The survey revealed very little Caribbean museum development. The only new museums were the Victoria Memorial Museum (1911) at Roseau in Dominica, Brimstone Hill on St Kitts and a historical museum at the Naval Dockyard at English Harbour in Antigua; the last was the first historic site museum in the region. The visit of the surveyors also gave impetus to the establishment of the Barbados Museum and Historical Society at St Michael, Barbados, in 1933.

A proposal for a Federal Museum in 1956 did not come to fruition. However, in the 1960s local historical and archaeological societies proliferated, and national trusts were established in most of the islands; all had plans to open new museums. This, combined with the fact that during the 1970s most of the islands achieved independence, triggered the establishment of several new institutions. These include the Grenada National Museum (1976) at St George's, Grenada; the Carriacou Museum (1976) at Carriacou, Grenada; the Montserrat National Museum

(1976); the Brimstone Hill Museum (1982) on St Kitts; the Fort Shirley Museum (1982) at Portsmouth, Dominica; the Hamilton House Museum (1983) on Nevis; the St Vincent Archaeological Museum (1979); the Eco Museum (1979), Marie-Galante, Guadeloupe; and the Museum of Antigua and Barbuda (1985), St John's, Antigua. In 1989 the Museums Association of the Caribbean (MAC) was founded.

BIBLIOGRAPHY

F. A. Bather and T. Sheppard: 'The Museums of the British West Indies', *Report on the Museums of Ceylon, British Malaya, the West Indies, etc to the Carnegie Corporation of New York*, Museums Association Report (London, 1933), pp. 27–58
Caribbean Community: *Report of Workshop on Museums, Monuments and Historic Sites* (Kingston, Jamaica, 1979)
J. Whiting: *Museum Focussed Heritage in the English-speaking Caribbean*, UNESCO Report (New York, 1983)
D. Devenish: 'Barbados Museum: Reminiscences of a Contract Appointment', *Mus. Ethnographers' Grp Newslett.*, xix (1985), pp. 58–67
A. Cummins: *The History and Development of Museums in the English-speaking Caribbean* (diss., U. Leicester, 1989)

VIII. Art education.

Following emancipation (1834) an apprenticeship system was introduced, which lasted until 1838, to train ex-slaves in various manual skills; art, however, did not form part of any curriculum for apprenticeship or basic education. During the first quarter of the 20th century a few institutions were established to provide technical and vocational training, and some craft unions emerged, though with only sporadic success. In 1932 the Marriot-Mayhew Commission, a West India Royal Commission to consider problems of primary and secondary education in Trinidad, Barbados, Leeward Islands and Windward Islands, carried out a comprehensive survey of educational services and recommended necessary changes in both curricula and teacher training. The Moyne Commission of 1945, a West India Royal Commission established to investigate thoroughly the social and economic conditions of the Caribbean labouring classes, recommended the organization of a handicraft industry. At the same time the British government established a colonial office of the British Council in Barbados to serve Jamaica and the eastern Caribbean. Art classes sponsored by the Council encouraged the development of an aesthetic consciousness and contributed to the establishment of Art Societies in most islands. In Barbados the plans of Neville Connell (1906–73) for an Art Education department at the Barbados Museum, St Michael, received a supporting grant. During the 1950s and 1960s moves towards independence in the islands triggered the realization that education would play a key role in the development of cultural identity. In 1963 the Barbados government appointed Hector Whistler (1905–78), from Britain, as the first Government Adviser on Art Teaching, and for the first time art education was fully incorporated into secondary school curricula. The provision of scholarships provided opportunities for student training overseas, especially in Britain. From 1950 the Jamaica School of Arts and Craft, later the Edna Manley School for the Visual Arts (*see* JAMAICA, §XI), was the major regional training institution for Caribbean students of Fine and Applied Arts. During the 1960s and 1970s technical colleges were established in most of the islands, including the Barbados Community College (1969) and the Samuel Jackman Prescod Polytechnic (1970), Wildey, St Michael, Barbados.

BIBLIOGRAPHY

C. Brock: 'Education and Multiculturalism in the Caribbean Region', *Education in Multicultural Societies*, ed. T. Corner (1978, 2/London, 1984), pp. 157–97
Hector Whistler (exh. cat. by A. Cummins, Bridgetown, Barbados Mus., 1988)
P. Ellis: *Adult Education in Barbados* (1991)

ALISSANDRA CUMMINS

Antimenes Painter. *See* VASE PAINTERS, §II.

Antin, Duc **d'** [Gondrin, Antoine-Louis de Pardaillan de] (*b* Paris, 5 Nov 1665; *d* Paris, 2 Nov 1736). French administrator and patron. He was the son of the Marquis de Montespan, whose wife, Françoise Athénais de Mortemart, became one of the mistresses of Louis XIV. During the prominence of her successor Mme de Maintenon, d'Antin pursued an undistinguished military career, and it was only after his mother's death in 1707 that his gifts as a courtier were rewarded with the post of governor of the Orléanais and, in 1708, with that of Directeur-Général des Bâtiments du Roi (*see* MAISON DU ROI, §II). His predecessor, Jules Hardouin Mansart, had been termed Surintendant; d'Antin held this amplified title from 1716 to 1726, but thereafter returned to his initial designation. His dukedom was from 1710. He inherited the châteaux of Bellegarde (Loiret), Oiron (Deux-Sèvres) and Petit-Bourg near Fontainebleau, and considerably embellished them.

As Directeur-Général, d'Antin's authority extended over all artists nominally attached to the royal household, over the Imprimerie Royale, the Mint, the Gobelins, the Observatoire and all the academies except the Académie des Sciences. During the last years of Louis XIV financial difficulties inhibited state patronage of the arts, but after his death in 1715 d'Antin—who joined the Council of Regency in 1716—helped with the return of political power from Versailles to Paris, overseeing the conversion of the Tuileries Palace to house the young Louis XV and the laying-down of the Avenue des Champs-Elysées, which opened in 1724. He also presided over improvements to the châteaux of Versailles (Cour des Cerfs, library, 1728; Salon d'Hercule, 1729) and Marly.

D'Antin took a particular interest in the Académie de France in Rome, establishing it in sumptuous surroundings in the Palazzo Mancini on the Corso in 1725, and corresponded copiously with its director Nicolas Vleughels. In 1727, in an attempt to revive the waning influence of the Académie Royale at a time when artists were more reliant on private than on public patronage and when history painting was going out of fashion, he ran a closed competition between 12 Academicians to produce a history painting. The size was specified (1.83×1.22 m) but not the subject. The resulting pictures were put on public exhibition in the Gallerie d'Apollon at the Louvre, the prize being shared between *Diana Resting* by Jean-François de Troy and the *Continence of Scipio* (both Nancy, Mus. B.-A.) by François Lemoyne, d'Antin's protégé, who was subsequently awarded the commission to paint the ceiling of the Salon d'Hercule at Versailles. Though d'Antin was made a Minister of State in 1733, his powers of awarding commissions passed over in 1735 to the King.

BIBLIOGRAPHY

DBF

A. de Montaiglon and J. Guiffrey, eds: *Correspondance des directeurs de l'Académie de France à Rome* (Paris, 1887–1908)

L. Hautecoeur: *Le Style Louis XV*, ii/1 of *Histoire de l'architecture classique en France* (Paris, 1950), pp. 2–5

P. Rosenberg: 'Le Concours de peinture de 1727', *Rev. A.* [Paris], xxxvii (1977), pp. 29–42

M. Antoine: *Le Gouvernement et l'administration sous Louis XV: Dictionnaire biographique* (Paris, 1978), p. 9

T. Crow: *Painters and Public Life in Eighteenth-century Paris* (New Haven and London, 1985), pp. 79–80

S. Jugie: 'Grandeur et décadence d'une famille ducale au XVIIIe siècle: La Fortune du duc d'Antin', *Rev. Hist. Mod. & Contemp.* (1990), pp. 452–77

OLIVIER MICHEL

Antin [née Fineman]**, Eleanor** (*b* New York, 27 Feb 1935). American performance artist. In the mid-1950s she studied acting at the Tamara Daykarhanova School for Stage, New York, and creative writing at the College of the City of New York. Her performances can be seen as autobiographical, with invented roles based partly on historical characters. Set-pieces recurring in performances from the early 1970s included the *King of Solana Beach*, inspired by a portrait of Charles I, King of England, by Anthony van Dyck; *Eleanor Antinova*, giving the recollections of a black dancer in Serge Diaghilev's Ballets Russes; and the *Angel of Mercy*, Florence Nightingale in the Crimea. Antin considered her performances as a means of self-definition as an artist and woman in the late 20th century. The presentations incorporated pithy commentaries on contemporary social and political issues. The spontaneous nature of her activity can be linked to the early years of American film-making, when participants devised dramatic scenarios in an ad hoc sequence. By interspersing her personal experience and vision with episodes from the past, Antin attempted to redefine traditional boundaries associated with women, power and art. From 1979 she was Professor of Visual Arts at the University of California, San Diego.

BIBLIOGRAPHY

Contemp. A.

Eleanor Antin, 'The Angel of Mercy' (exh. cat., La Jolla, CA, Mus. Contemp. A., 1977) [essays by J. Crary and K. Levin]

M. Roth, ed.: *The Amazing Decade: Women and Performance Art in America, 1970–1980* (Los Angeles, 1983)

□

Antinoöpolis [Antinoë; now el-Sheikh Ibada]. Egyptian site 75 km north of Asyut. The town was officially founded by the Emperor Hadrian in October AD 130 to commemorate his favourite, Antinous, who had been drowned there. However, there was a Late Predynastic (*c.* 3000 BC) cemetery on the site and Ramesses II (*reg c.* 1279–*c.* 1213 BC) built a temple there using decorated blocks and columns from buildings at Tell el-Amarna. The Roman town was designed on a grid plan and boasted an amphitheatre and hippodrome, a temple to the deified Antinous and a colonnaded main street with a triumphal arch: the last, now destroyed, was still standing when Edmé Jomard (1777–1862) visited and drew the site in 1803. The necropolis of Antinoöpolis has yielded important Roman artefacts, particularly illustrated papyri, textiles (e.g. Lyon, Mus. Hist. Tissus, 28.927; *see* ROME, ANCIENT, fig. 129) and encaustic mummy portraits of distinctive shape and technique. The last were produced by a local school of artists and often embellished with gilded wreaths and stucco jewellery before being bound into the mummy wrappings (e.g. Detroit, MI, Inst. A., 25.2); their style and iconography blends Egyptian and Hellenistic elements. Brick tombs of the 6th century AD at Antinoöpolis are reminiscent of contemporary churches, with short rectangular naves and semicircular apses, sometimes containing carved and painted decoration, such as an *orans* figure of the deceased between saints. The subjects of the Early Christian niche sculptures (e.g. New York, Brooklyn Mus., 62.44 and 63.36; Oxford, Ashmolean, 1971.993) are all figural and draw, apparently indiscriminately, from a repertory of pagan and Christian motifs: Daphne or Dionysos, for example, appears among vegetation surmounted by a cross in a nimbus. Also found were funerary stelae of the Terenuthis type (for illustration *see* KOM ABU BILLO), and some magnificent weavings, such as the wall hanging with 12 figural medallions (New York, Met., Harkness Bequest).

BIBLIOGRAPHY

LÄ: 'Antinooupolis'

E. Guimet: *Les Portraits d'Antinoë au Musée Guimet* (Paris, 1912)

E. Kuhn: *Antinoöpolis* (diss., U. Leipzig, 1913)

J. W. B. Barns, C. H. Roberts and H. Zilliacus: *The Antinoöpolis Papyri*, 3 vols (London, 1924–58)

S. J. Gasiorowski: 'A Fragment of a Greek Illustrated Papyrus from Antinoë', *J. Egyp. Archaeol.*, xvii (1931), pp. 1–9

M. Salmi: 'I dipinti paleocristiani d'Antinoë', *Scritti dedicati alla memoria di Ippolito Rosellini* (Florence, 1945), pp. 161–9

K. Parlasca: *Mumienporträts und verwandte Denkmäler* (Wiesbaden, 1966)

T. K. Thomas: *Niche Decorations from the Tombs of Byzantine Egypt: Visions of the Afterlife* (diss., New York U., 1990)

DOMINIC MONTSERRAT

Antioch (i) [now Antakya]. Greek and Roman city on the River Orontes in south-east Turkey (ancient Syria), which flourished from *c.* 300 BC to the 7th century AD.

1. Introduction. 2. Ancient. 3. Early Christian and after.

1. INTRODUCTION. Its advantageous site on the edge of the Amuk Plain at the foot of Mt Silpius, commanding important trade routes linking Anatolia with Palestine and the Mediterranean with inland Syria, attracted the attention of Seleukos I (*reg* 305–281 BC), who founded the city (*c.* 300 BC) as the capital of his Syrian empire. With its port at Seleucia and residential suburb at Daphne, Antioch prospered as capital of the Roman province of Syria from 64 BC. The city enjoyed the attentions of Roman benefactors from Julius Caesar onwards and attained the height of its prosperity during the 2nd to the 7th century AD, becoming the diocesan capital of Oriens. Its influence was particularly strong in early Christian affairs: Paul and Barnabas were active at Antioch, while Peter was regarded as its first bishop. Constantine endowed the city with its famous Great Church (AD 327–41; *see* §3 below), and the patriarch of Antioch ranked high in the Church hierarchy. The city's urban development reflected its vulnerability to earthquakes as well as its political and commercial importance; numerous ancient sources confirm repeated destruction and rebuilding. Repaired by Justinian after a Persian raid of AD 540, Antioch suffered a devastating fire and two earthquakes during the 6th century before being

captured by the Arabs in AD 637–8. It returned to Byzantine control in 969 and changed hands repeatedly in the 11th–13th centuries between Saljuqs, Crusaders and Armenians before falling under Mamluk control in 1268 (*see* §3 below).

Modern exploration of Antioch was conducted by a joint American–French expedition organized by Princeton University, which from 1932 to 1939 recovered many spectacular floor mosaics from domestic and public buildings, now in museums in Princeton (Princeton U., NJ, A. Mus.), Worcester, MA (A. Mus.), Washington, DC (Dumbarton Oaks), Baltimore, MD (Walters A.G.), Paris (Louvre) and Antakya (Hatay Mus.).

2. Ancient.

(i) Architecture. Both legend and excavation suggest that Antioch was first established on a rectilinear grid plan along the east bank of the Orontes. Under Seleukos II Kallinikos (*reg* 246–226 BC) it expanded on to an island in the river and reached its full extent under Antiochos IV Epiphanes (*reg* 175–164 BC), whose new quarter (Epiphaneia) included an agora, bouleuterion and temples. This urban centre, fortified under Tiberius (*reg* AD 14–37), formed the heart of Roman Antioch. Major earthquakes, however, repeatedly devastated the site and necessitated imperial intervention, and the frequent flooding of the Orontes and its tributaries have gradually buried parts of the Roman city to depths as great as 9 m. In addition, excavations at Antioch have revealed a site severely damaged by extensive plundering and overbuilding. Nonetheless, despite its disappointing condition, written accounts and a topographic mosaic from a house at nearby Yakto (mid-5th century AD; Antakya, Hatay Mus.) provide a detailed picture of the appearance of the ancient city. Antioch's primary axis from Hellenistic times was formed by a 3 km long street running parallel to the Orontes right through the city, from the Beroea gate at the north to the Daphne gate at the south. It was broadened and paved by Herod (*c.* AD 73–4), while Tiberius (*reg* AD 14–37) added flanking porticos to create an early example of a colonnaded street with covered sidewalks (w. almost 30 m including porticos). Secondary roads at right angles formed a grid of *insulae* (each *c.* 58×112 m), while major public squares along the main thoroughfare contained a nymphaeum, a column of Tiberius and an arch of Trajan (after AD 115). Towards its north end, under the later Forum of Valens (*c.* AD 370), stood the Kaisareion (*c.* 48 BC), the earliest imperial basilica in the eastern Mediterranean. The nearby theatre was built (*c.* 47 BC) on the site of a Hellenistic predecessor, as probably were the temples of Zeus (Tiberian), Ares (1st century BC) and Athena (rest. *c.* AD 180–*c.* 192).

Aerial photographs of modern Antakya reveal the general street plan of the ancient city and its slight shift in orientation on the island in the Orontes. A large public bath building on the island, Bath C, was erected in the 1st century AD and rebuilt in the 2nd and 4th centuries along similar lines. Its plan employs an axially organized sequence of octagonal, polygonal and domed spaces to accommodate the three stages of the bathing process. Several lavish villas, including that with the *Judgement of Paris* mosaic (1st century AD; Paris, Louvre), were also built in the 1st century, while the island's main residential structure, the Seleucid palace, was rebuilt by Diocletian before AD 298. In addition to apartments and baths arranged in a rectilinear plan, this later complex included a tetrapylon and a hippodrome.

About 8 km south of the city was the residential suburb of Daphne. Set on a plateau overlooking the plain of Antioch, it was renowned for its pastoral charms. An early 3rd-century BC temple was erected there to Apollo, whom myths associated with the site. There was also a large stadium (before AD 195) for the local games, with a shrine of Olympian Zeus (rebuilt *c.* AD 300) and a shrine of Nemesis (*c.* AD 300). Daphne repeatedly received imperial benefactions: Titus (*reg* AD 79–91) built a theatre there, Hadrian (*reg* AD 117–38) a large reservoir with nymphaeum to supply Antioch and Diocletian a summer palace (before AD 298). The quarter also contains several luxurious villas identified by excavation. The House of Menander, one of the largest, was built and remodelled between the early 2nd century AD and the 4th century. It was organized around two elegant, mosaic-floored triclinia complexes set

1. *Tyche* of Antioch, marble, h. 895 mm (Rome, Vatican, Galleria dei Candelabri); Roman copy of the original by Eutychides, *c.* 300 BC

at right angles to each other and included courtyards and elaborate fountains.

BIBLIOGRAPHY

K. O. Müller: *Antiquitates Antiochenae* (Göttingen, 1839)

Antioch-on-the-Orontes, 5 vols (Princeton, 1934–72)

G. Downey: *A History of Antioch in Syria from Seleucus to the Arab Conquest* (Princeton, 1961)

R. Stillwell: 'The Houses of Antioch', *Dumbarton Oaks Pap.*, xv (1961), pp. 47–57

J. Lassus: 'La Ville d'Antioche à l'époque romaine d'après l'archéologie', *Aufstieg und Niedergang der römischen Welt*, II/viii (Berlin, 1977), pp. 54–102

(ii) Sculpture. The once flourishing sculptural industry of Hellenistic and Roman Antioch survives today only in battered fragments. Its pagan monuments were purged to suit the Late Antique city's Christian tastes, and recurring earthquakes took further toll, as did later generations who quarried the Classical city for building material.

Throughout its history Antioch's artists looked to other eastern Mediterranean centres for material and artistic inspiration. Since the limestone massif of Mt Silpius affords no local supply of marble, sculptors relied on imported stone, primarily from Proconnesian and Pentelic quarries. Imperial models imported into the city were copied by sculptors trained in the Classical style of the Aegean cities. This strong Classical tradition lingered into Late Antique Antioch, but inland Syria remained largely untouched by urban Hellenized tastes. The work most closely identified with the city is the *Tyche* of Antioch, carved *c.* 300–*c.* 290 BC by EUTYCHIDES of Sikyon to commemorate its foundation. The work is mentioned by Pausanias (VI.ii.6–7) and is known by several copies, of which the Vatican example (Rome, Vatican, Gal. Candelabri; see fig. 1) is the best preserved. The draped personification of the city is seated on a rock, her legs crossed with one foot resting on the shoulder of a youthful swimming Orontes. Hellenistic Antioch and Daphne were further embellished with statues of Hellenistic kings and a famous statue of Apollo attributed to BRYAXIS (Pliny: *Natural History* XXXIV.lxxiii; Libanius: *Oratio* LX.vi.9–11). Most excavated sculpture dates from the 2nd century AD and later. One group, comprising three imperial portraits and several mythological sculptures (late 2nd century–early 4th; mostly Antakya, Hatay Mus.), came from a late Roman villa. The heads usually identified as Pertinax and Gordian III are apparently of Proconnesian marble and find their closest parallels with the workshops of coastal Asia Minor; a porphyry head identified as Constantius Chlorus (untraced) preserves a distinctive local interpretation of the radical Tetrarchic style (*see* ROME, ANCIENT, §IV, 2(ix)).

BIBLIOGRAPHY

Pausanias: *Guide to Greece*

G. W. Elderkin, ed.: *The Excavations of 1932* (1934), i of *Antioch-on-the-Orontes* (Princeton, 1934–72), pp. 49–51

F. Poulsen: 'Portrait hellénistique du Musée d'Antioche', *Syria*, xix (1938), pp. 355–61

R. Stillwell, ed.: *The Excavations, 1933–1936* (1938), ii of *Antioch-on-the-Orontes* (Princeton, 1934–72), pp. 170–79

W. A. Campbell and R. Stillwell, eds: *The Excavations, 1937–1939* (1941), iii of *Antioch-on-the-Orontes* (Princeton, 1934–72), pp. 116–34

T. Dohrn: *Die Tyche von Antiochia* (Berlin, 1960)

D. M. Brinkerhoff: *A Collection of Sculpture in Classical and Early Christian Antioch* (New York, 1970)

M. RAUTMANN

(iii) Mosaics. Antioch is famous for the many floor mosaics found there. Most came from private houses, especially in Daphne and Seleucia; others from baths, a few from tombs, and in the later period from churches. The preserved portions (mainly figured panels) are now divided between Antakya (Hatay Mus.), the Louvre and numerous museums in the United States. Levi (1947) established a chronological table for them, running from the early Empire (before the earthquake of AD 115) to the 6th century AD (before the Persian sack of 540); the general lines of this are normally still accepted, though a few specific dates have been questioned.

The earlier mosaics display continuity with the Hellenistic tradition. They are mainly in the form of pseudo-emblemata or independent panels, surrounded by multiple borders; several are often combined within one room. Figures and drapery are handled with fine effects of chiaroscuro; the illusion of space and depth is well indicated. Subjects of figural scenes are predominantly mythological as, for example, in the Atrium House, where mosaics from the late 1st century to the early 2nd century AD represent the *Drinking Contest of Dionysus and Hercules* (Worcester, MA, A. Mus.), *Judgement of Paris* (Paris, Louvre), and *Aphrodite and Adonis* (Princeton U., NJ, A. Mus.). The subject the *Drinking Contest of Dionysus and Hercules* is also represented in a notable early 3rd-century AD mosaic from the House of the Drinking Contest (Princeton U., NJ, A. Mus.; see fig. 2). Several have a marked literary aspect, including rare illustrations derived

2. Antioch, the House of the Drinking Contest, mosaic pavement depicting the *Drinking Contest of Dionysus and Hercules*, overall dimensions of floor 8.2×7.1 m, early 3rd century AD (Princeton, NJ, Princeton University, Art Museum)

from novels, such as the early 3rd-century AD *Ninus and Semiramis* (Princeton, U., NJ, A. Mus.) and *Metiochos and Parthenope* (Worcester, MA, A. Mus.). Ornamental patterns sometimes aim at three-dimensional effects but are less varied than contemporary examples in the West. Composition and subject-matter sometimes reflect the use of the room, principally in *triclinia* (dining-rooms), for example in the House of the Buffet Supper.

Changes appeared from the late 3rd century. There was an increasing use of personifications to represent such abstract ideas as Luxury, Time and the Ages, the Foundation (of a building), and Pleasure. Hunting scenes appeared in the Constantinian Villa and became common in the 5th and early 6th century AD, for example the *Megalopsychia Hunt* (Antakya, Hatay Mus.; see fig. 3 below) and the *Worcester Hunt* (Worcester, MA, A. Mus.). Composition of figural scenes departs from the single-viewpoint panel and adopts all-over systems; in the later hunt scenes, figures are distributed without depth across the surface and offer multiple viewpoints. Figural style became more linear, landscape elements more schematic. The greatest changes appeared in the range and treatment of ornamental patterns. The Rainbow style exploits effects derived from contrasting colours of the tesserae; 'carpet' patterns cover the entire floor with unbroken designs, often based on repeated floral elements and imbrications. A single large motif may be set at the centre of these, as in the mosaics of the *Phoenix* (*c*. AD 500; Paris, Louvre) and the *Striding Lion* (2nd half of the 5th century AD; Baltimore, MD, A. Mus.). Scrolls of vine and acanthus are common for borders; topographical borders, such as in the *Megalopsychia Hunt*, offer schematic views of buildings. The extent of eastern influence on these later floors is disputed. Individual motifs are undoubtedly of Sasanian origin (beribboned parrots, confronted rams' heads), but the general changes correspond to a widespread shift throughout the Empire. North African influence was posited by Lavin (1963) for the composition of the later hunt mosaics, but these too seem rather to reflect more general changes in the art of the late Empire.

BIBLIOGRAPHY

C. R. Morey: *The Mosaics of Antioch* (New York, 1938)

R. Stillwell, ed.: *The Excavations, 1933–1936* (1938), ii of *Antioch-on-the-Orontes* (Princeton, 1934–72), pp. 180–204

W. A. Campbell and R. Stillwell, eds: *The Excavations, 1937–1939* (1941), iii of *Antioch-on-the-Orontes* (Princeton, 1934–72), pp. 171–251

D. Levi: *Antioch Mosaic Pavements* (Princeton, 1947/*R* 1971)

I. Lavin: 'The Hunting Mosaics of Antioch and their Sources', *Dumbarton Oaks Pap.*, xvii (1963), pp. 179–286

J. Balty: 'La Mosaïque antique au Proche-Orient, i: Des origines à la Tétrarchie', *Aufstieg und Niedergang der römischen Welt*, II, xii/2 (1981), pp. 347–429

S. Campbell: *The Mosaics of Antioch* (Toronto, 1988)

KATHERINE M. D. DUNBABIN

3. EARLY CHRISTIAN AND AFTER. Antioch was one of the most important centres of Early Christian culture between the 4th and 6th centuries. Its development at this time is largely known from the writings of Eusebius of Caesarea (*c*. 265–340), Libanius (314–93), his pupil St John Chrysostom (*c*. 344–407) and Evagrius Scholasticus (6th century), who wrote a history of Antioch between 540 and 593. This is supplemented by the accounts of early visitors to the site and by the finds from the excavations of 1932–9 and 1962–5.

After fires, earthquakes and Persian raids in the 6th and 7th centuries, Antioch finally fell to the Arabs in 638 and remained in their hands until 969, when it was recaptured by Emperor Nikephoros Phokas (*reg* 963–9) and became an eastern outpost of the empire. It was taken by the Saljuq Turks in 1084, but was then seized by the Crusaders under Bohemond of Taranto (*reg* 1099–1111), who established the Frankish principality of Antioch (*see* JERUSALEM, LATIN KINGDOM OF), which lasted until the city came under Mamluk control in 1268. From this time its trade declined and the harbour at Seleucia-Pieria (now Mağaracık) silted up. An Ottoman army led by Sultan Yavuz Selim (*reg* 1512–20) captured Antioch in 1517, and it became subject to Aleppo. Its population had now diminished to 25,000, of which only 4000 were Christian. During World War I Antioch was occupied by the British, who afterwards gave it to Syria. The city became part of Turkey in 1939.

Under Constantine the Great (*reg* 306–37), Antioch served as an imperial residence. The principal monument of that time was the cathedral known from its gilded dome as the Golden Octagon, which the Emperor began to build in 327 near the imperial palace on the Orontes island. It was completed in 341 by his son, Constantius II (*reg* 337–61), and was dedicated to Harmony. Its plan is known only from references in literary sources, and its probable depiction in the topographical border of the *Megalopsychia*

3. Antioch, the Golden Octagon (with a white dome); detail from the topographical border of the *Megalopsychia Hunt* mosaic, Yakto complex, near Daphne, 5th century AD (Antakya, Hatay Museum)

Hunt mosaic (Antakya, Hatay Mus., inv. no. 1016; see fig. 3) in the Yakto complex (5th century) near Daphne. It was octagonal and surrounded by a niched ambulatory and gallery, presumably preceded by a two-storey narthex. The earliest church excavated at Antioch is the cruciform martyrium of St Babylas (*c.* 379) at Kaoussie, just outside the city (*see also* MARTYRIUM). The central square was covered in marble paving and probably surmounted by a pyramidal timber roof. The graves of the saint and of Bishop Meletius (*d* 381), who was probably responsible for the construction of the martyrium, are within the chancel enclosure. Colourful geometric mosaics decorate the floors of the cross-arms, next to which a baptistery and other annexes were added when the martyrium was later converted into a church.

Several other Early Christian buildings have been excavated in the surrounding region, including a late 5th-century quatrefoil (diam. 36 m) some 20 km west of the city in the suburb of Mağaracık. It is a double-shell design with colonnades supporting the inner quatrefoil and opening into a single-storey quatrefoil ambulatory. A deep chancel or apse projects from the east wall. The whole structure had a timber roof, and the floor was decorated with mosaic. A fragment in the north ambulatory consists of a frieze containing an assortment of fauna and flora within a vine-scroll inhabited by birds, which follows the lines of the architecture.

The remains of the monastery of St Simeon the Stylite the Younger (541–65) lie a short distance south-west of Antioch on the Wondrous Mountain (Samandağı). The monastery, which is partly cut into the rock, consists of a walled enclosure (approx. 167×122 m) with a complex of churches forming a rectangle (approx. 85×60 m). This in turn surrounds the central octagon with its radiating arms where the stylite's column stood. The church is clearly modelled on QALʿAT SIMʿAN, except that here three churches were placed side by side to the east of the octagon. The middle church is a three-aisled basilica dedicated to the Holy Trinity. Colonnades of six columns each flank the central nave, which terminates at the east in a semicircular apse. The south church was probably the martyrium of Simeon's mother, St Martha. It is a three-aisled basilica divided by two arcades, each resting on four piers and terminating in an eastern triconch. A small chapel attached to its south-east corner is supposed to be the burial place of mother and son. The north church, which is also a basilica, is divided into three aisles by two pairs of rectangular piers.

The early 6th-century monastery of St Barlaam was built on Mt Kasios (now Keldağ), 60 km south-east of Antioch. The main church is a three-aisled basilica with a semicircular apse inscribed within a rectangle and flanked by two chambers. Although the monastery was abandoned after an earthquake, it was refounded in the second half of the 10th century and functioned as a monastery until the 13th century.

There is hardly any evidence of building activity in Antioch after the 7th century. During the 10th and 11th centuries building was limited to the construction of monasteries on the slopes of the Black Mountains running parallel to the coast. Only one such foundation (1035–42), near Yoğun Oluk, south-west of Antioch, has partly survived. The main church is a domed cross-in-square with the bema and flanking chambers terminating in semicircular apses to the east. The west side is preceded by a narthex and a small open porch. In the 17th and 18th centuries the church was used by the Armenian community who dedicated it to St Thomas. In Antioch itself the 13th-century church of St Peter, its mosaic floors dating from the 4th or 5th century and noted for its 11th- or 12th-century façade, consists of an eastern section with a single, barrel-vaulted nave, carved into the rock, and a western masonry structure with a Gothic façade, divided into three bays and dominated by a domelike roof. Under Ottoman rule Antioch was a minor province, and the only record of any building activity is the conversion of what was probably a Byzantine church into the mosque of Habib Neccar Camii. The numerous alterations to the structure and the whitewashed walls make it difficult to distinguish the original plan. A Baroque minaret was added in the 17th century.

BIBLIOGRAPHY

H. W. Devreesse: *Le Patriarcat d'Antioche depuis la paix de l'église jusqu'à la conquête arabe* (Paris, 1945)

J. Lassus: *Sanctuaires chrétiens de Syrie* (Paris, 1947)

P. Petit: *Libanius et la vie municipale à Antioche au IVe siècle après J. C.* (Paris, 1955)

G. Downey: *A History of Antioch in Syria from Seleucus to the Arab Conquest* (Princeton, 1961)

——: *Antioch in the Age of Theodosius the Great* (Norman, OK, 1962)

W. Djobadze: 'Vorläufiger Bericht über Grabungen und Untersuchungen in der Gegend von Antiochia am Orontes', *Istanbul. Mitt.*, xv (1965), pp. 218–42

J. Mécérian: *Expédition archéologique dans l'Antiochène occidentale* (Beirut, 1965)

J. Lafontaine-Dosogne: *Itinéraires archéologiques dans la région d'Antioche: Recherches sur le monastère et sur l'iconographie de S. Symeon Stylite le Jeune* (Brussels, 1967)

J. H. W. G. Liebeschuetz: *Antioch: City and Imperial Administration in the Later Roman Empire* (Oxford, 1972)

W. Djobadze: *Archaeological Investigations in the Region of Antioch-on-the-Orontes* (Stuttgart, 1986)

MİNE KADİROĞLU

Antioch (ii) ['Pisidian']. Greek and Roman city in western Asia Minor (now Turkey) on a plateau above Yalvaç. It was founded by the Seleucids in the 3rd century BC and refounded as a colony for veteran soldiers by Augustus *c.* 25 BC; it flourished until the Early Christian period. The site was excavated in 1924 by D. M. Robinson and has more recently been the object of a detailed architectural survey. About 4 km south of the city Hellenistic remains survive at the sanctuary of Mên Askaênos, where an imposing temenos with porticos on four sides enclosed a mid-2nd-century BC Ionic temple (6 by 11 columns) on a high, stepped podium. The design of the temple was influenced by the layout of the temples of Zeus Sosipolis and Artemis Leukophryene at MAGNESIA ON THE MAEANDER, which had supplied Antioch with its original settlers.

The city site is dominated by a complex of buildings associated with the imperial cult, which were laid out on a monumental rectilinear plan (*c.* 25 BC–*c.* AD 50). A Corinthian tetrastyle prostyle podium temple (*c.* 10 BC–*c.* AD 30) stands at the east end of a colonnaded square, with a two-storey semicircular portico behind it. It was perhaps dedicated to Augustus and Mên, the Anatolian moon-god. Opposite the temple there was a three-arched gateway

(AD 50) at the top of a flight of stairs that led to a colonnaded street named after the Emperor Tiberius. The temple sculpture includes a bucranium and garland frieze, and one of acanthus, as well as a magnificent winged Victory acroterion; the gateway was decorated with reliefs of captured Pisidians and winged Victories commemorating Augustus' campaigns in the region. The quality of the sculpture is comparable with the best provincial work of the first half of the 1st century AD, and the architectural design shows Western influence. Together with contemporary buildings at Ankara and Pessinus, the central civic complex at Antioch clearly indicates that central Asia Minor in the 1st century AD was not an architectural backwater. The city also has a well-planned street system; a theatre whose *cavea* spanned the main north–south street that ran through a tunnel underneath it; an aqueduct that fed a large bath building and a nymphaeum; a gateway of the late 2nd century AD whose design and sculptures imitated those of the central gateway; an arch and colonnades of the early 4th century AD; and churches of the 4th and 5th centuries AD.

BIBLIOGRAPHY

D. M. Robinson: 'A Preliminary Report on the Excavations at Pisidian Antioch and at Sizma', *Amer. J. Archaeol.*, xxviii (1924), pp. 435–44

——: 'Roman Sculptures from Colonia Caesarea (Pisidian Antioch)', *A. Bull.*, ix (1926–7), pp. 5–69

S. Mitchell and M. Waelkens: *Pisidian Antioch: The Site and its Monuments* (in preparation)

STEPHEN MITCHELL

Antioch, Plain of. *See* AMUK REGION.

Antioch-on-the-Chrysorrhoas. *See* GERASA.

Antiparos [Andiparos; anc. Oliaros]. Small Greek island just to the south-west of Paros, in the Aegean Cyclades. It is the site of a number of finds from the Greek Bronze Age (*c*. 3600–*c*. 1100 BC), many of which come from excavations carried out by Tsountas and Bent in the 19th century (e.g. the cemetery of Krassades, which yielded important objects from the Early Cycladic (EC) I period), and in the 20th century by the Greek Archaeological Service. Items found by Bent, including a rare lead figurine, are in the British Museum, London.

The nearby islet of Saliagos is the site of the earliest excavated settlement in the Cyclades, dating to the Final Neolithic period (*c*. 4000–*c*. 3500/3000 BC). Among the finds were marble figurines, reflecting both the previous Neolithic tradition of squatting figures (e.g. the 'Fat Lady of Saliagos'; Paros, Archaeol. Mus.) and a standard EC type (the violin shape; *see* CYCLADIC, fig. 8). There are also some stone vases from the site. A few pieces of Saliagos obsidian come from a source on Antiparos that was barely exploited in antiquity. The islet of Despotikon (anc. Prepesínthos) has four known EC cemeteries, the largest at Zoumbaria, where a grave contained numerous beads in local stone, one or two in the form of birds or animals.

BIBLIOGRAPHY

J. T. Bent: 'Researches among the Cyclades', *J. Hell. Stud.*, v (1884), pp. 42–59

C. Tsountas: 'Kykladika', *Archaiol. Ephemeris* (1898), pp. 137–212

J. D. Evans and C. Renfrew: *Excavations at Saliagos near Antiparos* (London, 1968)

R. L. N. BARBER

Antiphanes (*fl c*. 414–*c*. 369 BC). Greek sculptor of the Argive school, student of Periklytos (who was himself a pupil of Polykleitos), teacher of Kleon of Sikyon, and thus in the circle of the elder Polykleitos (Pausanias: V.xvii.3). With no preserved sculpture, knowledge of Antiphanes derives entirely from Pausanias' description (X.ix) of three Delphic monuments and three signatures: first, a bronze *Trojan Horse* dedicated by the Argives for a battle over Thyrea, probably the battle of 414 BC referred to by Thucydides (VI.xcv); also a *Dioskouroi* dedicated by Sparta as spoils from the battle of Aigospotamoi (405 BC; Dittenberger, no. 115); and finally, statues of *Elatos*, *Apheidas* and *Erasos*, which Pausanias claimed were part of the Tegean spoils from a battle with Sparta. A 4th-century BC inscription on a black limestone base may indicate that the dedicants were Arcadians, not just Tegeans, and thus that the battle was the devastation of Lakonia in 369 BC, although Vatin refers to a new inscription indicating that Pausanias was correct. Fragments of the limestone base also preserve the name of Antiphanes as sculptor twice (Dittenberger, no. 160), while a signature from an Argive dedication reading 'Antiphanes from Argos made it' appears on a monument commemorating the founding of Messene in 369 BC (Dittenberger, no. 161).

BIBLIOGRAPHY

Pausanias: *Guide to Greece*; Pauly–Wissowa

W. Dittenberger: *Sylloge inscriptionum Graecarum*, i (Leipzig, 1915/*R* Hildesheim, 1960)

F. P. Johnson: *Lysippos* (Durham, NC, 1927/*R* New York, 1968), pp. 7–17

C. Vatin: 'Monuments votifs de Delphes', *Bull. Corr. Hell.*, cv (1981), pp. 429–59

GAIL L. HOFFMAN

Antiphilos (*fl* later 4th century BC–early 3rd). Greek painter. Born in Egypt, Antiphilos was a pupil of Ktesidemos. Although none of his works survives, he painted both large and small pictures and was famous for the facility of his technique (Quintilian: *Principles of Oratory* XII.x.6). Pliny (*Natural History* XXXV.114, 138) listed many of his pictures, which included portraits (*Philip II and Alexander the Great with the Goddess Athena*, in Rome in Pliny's day; *Alexander the Great as a Boy*, also taken to Rome; and *Ptolemy I of Egypt Hunting*) and mythological subjects (*Hesione*; *Dionysos*; *Hippolytos Terrified of the Bull*; and *Cadmus and Europa*), all of which were in Rome in Pliny's day. He also painted genre pictures: *A Boy Blowing a Fire*, a painting much admired for the reflections cast about the room and on the boy's face, and *Women Spinning Wool*. The Egyptian city of Alexandria was an artistic centre famous for the depiction of comic figures and grotesques in several media. In that context, Antiphilos contributed a picture of a man called *Gryllos* wearing a ridiculous costume, from which pictures of that sort came to be called *grylloi*, and a famous picture of a satyr (called *The Gazer*) raising his hand to shade his eyes as he performed the satyric dance called the *skopeuma*. According to Lucian (*Calumnies* 2), Antiphilos' rivalry with his more famous contemporary APELLES inspired the latter's picture of *Calumny*.

BIBLIOGRAPHY
J. Overbeck: *Die antiken Schriftquellen zur Geschichte der bildenden Künste bei den Griechen* (Leipzig, 1868/*R* Hildesheim, 1959), nos 1512 (4), 1838 (1), 1839 (6, 20, 25), 1870, 1874, 1904 (2), 1942–4

C. HOBEY-HAMSHER

Antiphonal. *See under* CHOIR-BOOK.

Antipodean group. Australian group of artists formed in Melbourne in February 1959 and active until January 1960. The founder-members were the art historian Bernard Smith (*b* 1916), who was elected chairman, and the painters Charles Blackman, Arthur Boyd, David Boyd (*b* 1924), John Brack, John Perceval and Clifton Pugh. They were joined subsequently by the Sydney-based painter Bob Dickerson (*b* 1924). Smith chose the name of the group and compiled the *Antipodean Manifesto*, the appearance of which coincided with the inaugural exhibition, *The Antipodeans*, held in the Victorian Artists' Society rooms in Melbourne in August 1959. The group's main concern was to promote figurative painting at a time when non-figurative painting and sculpture were becoming established as the predominant trend in Australia, as in the USA and Europe. To gain a more prestigious venue to show their work, the group asked Smith to enlist the support of Kenneth Clark, who responded by suggesting the Whitechapel Gallery in London. The Gallery's director, Bryan Robertson (*b* 1925), received British Council support and made a selection for an exhibition entitled *Recent Australian Paintings* (1961), which featured the work of the group alongside that of Jon Molvig, Albert Tucker, Sidney Nolan, Fred Williams and others. Although the members of the group had experienced much critical opposition, they felt vindicated by their inclusion in this exhibition, which established that contemporary Australian painting had a well-founded and powerful national identity.

WRITINGS
B. Smith: *The Antipodean Manifesto: Essays in Art and History* (Melbourne, 1976)

BIBLIOGRAPHY
The Antipodeans (exh. cat. by B. Smith, Melbourne, Victorian Artists' Soc., 1959)
Recent Australian Paintings (exh. cat. by B. Robertson and R. Hughes, London, Whitechapel A.G., 1961)

JANET SPENS

Antiquaries and antiquarian societies. An antiquary (Lat. *antiquarius*) is a lover, collector and student of ancient learning, traditions and remains. Antiquarianism originated from the revived interest in Classical antiquity during the Renaissance and became a scientific and historical method in the 17th century. The difference between literary and non-literary sources distinguishes humanism from antiquarianism, the latter being based on those tangible remains of antiquity (inscriptions, coins and ruins) related to literary sources. From the 16th century new attitudes towards antiquity were discussed in antiquarian circles, later giving rise to antiquarian societies. Thereafter, antiquarianism was firmly linked to archaeological excavations and to the study and collecting of ancient art. It was also linked to the search for a national identity in the arts and for the origins of Western culture and was sustained by a curiosity about civilizations outside Europe. Antiquarianism, in fact, was associated with the GRAND TOUR and with travel more generally. Antiquaries and artist–antiquaries were responsible for producing numerous drawings, prints and illustrated volumes. High-quality illustrations of archaeological sites and ancient sculpture contributed to the growth of art history as an autonomous discipline. They also contributed to the popularization of the Antique and to the transformation of commercial dealing in objects associated with antiquarian interests (*see* ART MARKET). During the 18th century the learned research of antiquaries created the conditions for the birth of various modern disciplines, including archaeology, aesthetics and art history. Subsequently, antiquarian studies coincided with historical research itself.

1. 16th century and before. 2. 17th century. 3. 18th and 19th centuries.

1. 16TH CENTURY AND BEFORE. From at least the 15th century in Italy the term 'antiquary' was associated with the work and travels of such humanists and amateur scholars as Ciriaco d'Ancona (*d* 1455), who kept visual records of antiquities in Greece, the Levant and Italy, Poggio Bracciolini, Felice Feliciano, Flavio Biondo and many others. The figure of the artist–antiquary originated in the growing interest in Classical architecture and sculpture among such artists as Brunelleschi, Donatello, Francesco di Giorgio Martini, Ghirlandaio, Giuliano da Sangallo and Raphael. In 1515 Pope Leo X appointed Raphael Commissario dell'Antichità di Roma, and he was charged with surveying the city. This appointment was partly inspired by the recent study of Vitruvius' *On Architecture* edited by Raphael's friend and adviser Fra Giovanni Giocondo (illustrated edition in Latin, 1511 and 1513) and translated into Italian by Marco Fabio Calvo at the instigation of Raphael. Vitruvius became the focus for a new generation of antiquaries in Rome, who met at the Accademia della Virtù. This was one of the earliest antiquarian institutions and was founded by Claudio Tolomei, who called for a new edition of Vitruvius, a survey of Roman urban planning and accounts of its antiquities. His plan was not carried out, although it influenced such works as those of the Netherlandish antiquary Stefanus Vinandus Pighius and the Neapolitan Pirro Ligorio. Pighius visited Rome *c*. 1548–55 and was responsible for assembling drawings by various anonymous hands in the Codex Pighianus, so providing important records of the exact state of ancient reliefs. This archaeological approach was also followed by the Florentine Giovanni Antonio Dosio, whose drawings formed the basis of Giovanni Battista de' Cavalieri's *Urbis Romae aedificiorum illustrium* (Florence, 1569). Ligorio used archaeological reconstruction for the two maps of Imperial Rome he produced in 1553 and 1561, which included precisely delineated buildings based on such primary sources as Roman coins.

The acquisition of books, manuscripts, coins, ancient statuary and other works of art was one of the duties of court antiquaries during the Renaissance. As Keeper, John Leland acquired monastic books for the library of King Henry VIII, Ligorio purchased antiquities for the Este collections and Jacopo Strada acquired antiquities for Hans Jakob Fugger (1516–75) of the Augsburg banking family and for Albert V of Bavaria. In 1568, after securing the collection of ancient sculpture formerly owned by Andrea Loredan for the court in Munich, Strada produced the architectural designs on which the Antiquarium in Munich was based. This building was specially designed to house antiquities.

There were many reasonable-size collections of Classical sculpture by this time, above all in Rome and Venice, but few were housed in buildings designed for that purpose. In Rome the predecessors of the Antiquarium in Munich were the courtyard of Palazzo della Valle, used as a showplace for ancient statuary from *c.* 1518, and the Antiquario of Cardinal Federico Cesi, which was in use in the early 1540s. The display of marbles in gardens and courtyards was fairly common in Rome, but none was as spectacular as the Vatican Belvedere, which was mentioned by Vasari and occasionally opened to visitors. By the second decade of the 16th century it included the *Apollo Belvedere*, *Laokoon*, *Cleopatra* (all Rome, Vatican, Mus. Pio-Clementino) and *Nile* (Rome, Vatican, Braccio Nuo.). Marbles were also housed in buildings originally designed for other purposes, as, for instance, with such early collections of ancient art as the Capitoline collection in Rome and that of the Statuario Pubblico in Venice. The Capitoline collection originated in 1471, when such works as the *She-wolf* (Rome, Mus. Conservatori) and the *Spinario* (Rome, Mus. Capitolino) were given by Pope Sixtus IV to the Conservators of Rome and housed in the Palazzo dei Conservatori. The Statuario of Venice originated in the legacy of the collections of Domenico Grimani (1523) and Giovanni Grimani (1593) and was later augmented by the gift of the collection of Giacomo Contarini, which was effective from 1713. Converted from the Antisala of the Libreria Marciana by Vincenzo Scamozzi, it was completed in 1596 and was then opened to visitors.

Antiquarianism developed to a greater extent in Rome than elsewhere. Numerous artists travelled to the city to study its ancient art, as is documented in drawings by the Bolognese Amico Aspertini, the Frenchman Jean-Jacques Boissard, the Portuguese Francisco de Holanda and the Dutchman Maarten van Heemskerck. The growth of collections led to the employment of such sculptor–restorers as Giovanni Angelo Montorsoli, who worked in the Vatican Belvedere in 1532–3, and Tiziano Aspetti (ii), who worked for Giovanni Grimani in Venice. It also stimulated the publication of such engravings as those by Hendrick Goltzius and the publication of works on ancient Rome: Giovanni Bartolomeo Marliani's *Topographia antiquae Romae* (Lyon, 1534), Cavalieri's *Antiquae statuae urbis Romae* (Rome, *c.* 1560–93) and Antoine Lafréry's prints forming the *Speculum Romanae magnificentiae* (which amounted to 107 works by 1567 and was continued after his death in 1577). In 1553 Lafréry had formed a partnership with Antonio Salamanca, a Spanish print dealer and publisher who worked in Italy, and the commercial activities of such men were vital to the growth of antiquarianism. On the other hand, the creation of the office of Commissario dell'Antichità in Rome contributed to the institutionalization of antiquarian research. Commissioners were at first leading artists (e.g. Raphael); later, during the 17th century, the office was held by such leading antiquaries as Leonardo Agostini (formerly Antiquary to the Barberini family) and Giovanni Pietro Bellori.

In Venice the collecting of Classical antiquities received such public adulation that the Statuario Pubblico was established and Venetian portraiture includes such strong statements of antiquarian interests as Lorenzo Lotto's *Andrea Odoni* (1527; London, Hampton Court, Royal Col.), Jacopo Tintoretto's *Giovanni Paolo Cornaro* (1561; Ghent, Mus. S. Kst.) and *Ottavio Strada* (1567; Amsterdam, Rijksmus.) and Titian's *Jacopo Strada* (1567–8; Vienna, Ksthist. Mus.). At the time, portraits of this type were unusual outside the Venetian territory, with the important exceptions of Parmigianino's *The Collector* (*c.* 1523; London, N.G.), a portrait probably commissioned by a collector–antiquary of the Baiardi family of Parma, and Bartolomeo Passarotti's *The Collector* (*c.* 1579; London, It. Embassy), a portrait painted in Bologna.

In Italy antiquarian research was monopolized by ancient Rome. Elsewhere, the study of Roman remains coexisted with studies of native, non-Classical and medieval antiquities. A principal preoccupation among English and French antiquaries was to collect material for accounts of the history and topography of their home countries. Leland's *De antiquitate Britannica* was written in 1534–50 (published as *Itinerary* by Thomas Hearne in Oxford in 1710–12), *Antiquités gauloises et françaises* by Claude Fauchet (1529–1601) appeared in Paris (1579–99) and William Camden's *Britannia* was published in London in Latin in 1586 and in English in 1610. Camden's work stimulated the formation of the first antiquarian society—the Society of Antiquaries of London—in 1586 (discontinued after 1604, re-established in 1717). By this time antiquarian interests had come to be seen as a prestigious pursuit among royalty and nobility all over Europe.

2. 17TH CENTURY. New meanings were attached to the word 'antiquary' during the 17th century, when such a figure was often referred to as a virtuoso. Regional tours, the Grand Tour and the Voyage d'Italie became popular, and antiquarian research became more clearly defined. In 1600 Camden and Robert Bruce Cotton made a six-month tour of northern Britain, which helped to establish the practice of visiting sites and making use of archaeological remains as evidence for historical research. In 1605 Francis Bacon (*The Advancement of Learning* II.ii.3) described antiquarian research as a scientific and historical discipline based on the distinction between original and derivative sources, a view later echoed by other authors. The new role attributed to non-literary evidence caused a radical change in historical method and marked a new beginning for antiquarianism. In 1679 Jacob Spon proclaimed the superiority of archaeological evidence in his *Résponse à la critique publiée par M. Guillet* (Lyon). In 1697 Francesco Bianchini demonstrated in his *La istoria universale provata con monumenti e figurata con simboli degli antichi* (Rome) that archaeological evidence was a more reliable source for history than literary evidence.

New views of history were paralleled by new attitudes towards the study and collecting of ancient statuary. Rubens (*De imitatione antiquarum statuarum*, first published in de Piles's *Cours de peinture par principes*, Paris, 1708) stated that painters should concern themselves with the art of the past and so collect ancient marbles, while noblemen and gentlemen could become 'virtuosos' out of their love for ancient statuary. In 1634 Henry Peacham (*Compleat Gentleman*, London, 2/1634), described the 'virtuoso' as a collector of ancient marbles, inscriptions, medals and coins. This definition can be perfectly applied to Thomas Howard, 2nd Earl of Arundel, with whom Peacham was connected and whose portrait (*c.* 1618; London, N.P.G., on loan to Arundel Castle, W. Sussex) by Daniel I Mijtens was staged in Arundel's gallery of statues. Arundel formed a magnificent collection of ancient statuary, which led him to encourage important research on both Classical antiquity and medieval architecture. A similar attitude is found among professional antiquaries. For example John Speed's *Theatre of the Empire of Great Britain* (London, 1611) was illustrated with engravings of Roman, Saxon and medieval coins. Similar developments also took place in Italy, especially from the 1670s. The Roman *Giornale de' letterati* (started in 1668) and the Accademia di Propaganda Fide (established as the Accademia dei Concili in 1671) contributed to the new discovery of early Christian and medieval antiquities.

The field of British antiquarianism was remarkably broad due to the expansion of the English trade in the Mediterranean, the activities of diplomats and the impact of the Grand Tour and travels to the East and to North Africa. British antiquaries pioneered the study of Etruscan antiquities: the Scottish Catholic émigré Thomas Dempster left a manuscript, *De Etruria regali* (published by Thomas Coke, 1st Earl of Leicester, in Florence, 2 vols, 1723–4), that anticipated the 18th-century interest in Etruria. They also pioneered studies of ancient Egypt (John Greaves, *Pyramidographia*, London, 1646) and Roman antiquities in North Africa (Abraham Seller, *The Antiquities of Palmyra*, 1696) and made contributions to Greek studies (John Potter, *Archaeologia Graecae*, 2 vols, Oxford, 1697–9). Elsewhere in northern Europe antiquarian studies were devoted mostly to Roman and Greek antiquities, as in Johannes Georgius Graevius's *Thesaurus antiquitatum Romanorum* (12 vols, Leiden, 1694–9) and *Thesaurus Graecarum antiquitatum* (12 vols, Leiden, 1697–1702) by Jakob Gronovius (1645–1716). It was in Italy and France, however, that illustrated works on antiquities reached their peak. The French artist François Perrier published illustrated volumes of the finest antique marbles (e.g. *Icones et segmenta illustrium e marmore tabularum quae Romae adhuc extant*, Paris and Rome, 1645, with a commentary on each plate by Bellori), while the Italian engraver Pietro Sante Bartoli produced such books as *Colonna Traiana* (Rome, 1665).

Rome was the centre for the arts, and it was there that a new classical style developed in Franco-Roman circles and that antiquarian studies were most closely linked to developments in the fine arts. In Rome artists, virtuosos and collectors from all over the world could visit spectacular collections of ancient marbles. One such was that of Marchese Vincenzo Giustiniani (i), who was among the earliest to have an illustrated catalogue of his collection published (*Galleria Giustiniani*, i, Rome, 1631; engravings by Joachim von Sandrart after drawings by various artists, including Pietro Testa). Important collections were housed in urban and suburban villas that were often conceived as semi-public museums. Statues were displayed in special rooms (e.g. Stanza dell'Ermafrodito, Villa Borghese) and archaeological gardens (e.g. Bosco delle Statue, Villa Ludovisi). Sometimes catalogues were printed for visitors (e.g. Jacomo Manili's *Villa Borghese fuori Porta Pinciana*, 1650). The most extraordinary of the collections in Rome was Cassiano dal Pozzo's Museum Chartaceum. Assembled during the second quarter of the 17th century, this museum was open to contemporary artists, scholars, collectors and virtuosos and included encyclopedic drawings after the Antique, in a similar manner to the work of Pighius and Ligorio. The owner intended to record all the remains of ancient Rome: relief sculptures, frescoes, religious implements, oil lamps, vases etc.

Antiquities were hunted, excavated, purchased, collected, viewed, studied and also, particularly in Rome, copied and restored. Since broken fragments alone could not possibly be displayed in the 17th century, a variety of restoration work was carried out by sculptor–restorers (e.g. Algardi, Bernini and François Du Quesnoy) and semi-professional and professional restorers (e.g. Orfeo Boselli, his son Ercole Boselli, Ippolito Buzzi (*d* 1634) and Nicolas Cordier). During the 17th century the demand for Classical sculpture had created a large market for plaster casts, marble copies and bronze statuettes. Charles I, King of England and Scotland, and Philip IV, King of Spain, formed collections of casts and copies, while that formed by Louis XIV, King of France, served the didactic needs of the Académie Royale de Peinture et de Sculpture in Paris (founded 1648) and the French Académie Royale in Rome (founded 1666). French students in Rome were obliged to make copies after the Antique, which were sent to Paris and used as models in the academy there or as ornaments in royal parks. Moreover, the Frenchman Girard Audran published an important book of proportions designed for a modern academy, *Les Proportions du corps humain mesurées sur les plus belles figures de l'antiquité* (Paris, 1683). Aesthetic preoccupations grew in Rome and Paris, especially at the time when Bellori was Commissario dell'Antichità di Roma (1670–94), and discussions about the Greek style and its different forms of expression in different Greek cities were started. These anticipated the ideas of Winckelmann and contributed to the transformation of antiquarianism, preparing the ground for the birth of modern archaeology, aesthetics and art history.

3. 18TH AND 19TH CENTURIES. From the 18th century historical research and discussion was centred on antiquarian academies and societies rather than colleges and universities. The Académie d'Inscriptions et Belles Lettres (founded 1663) issued its rules in 1701. These defined its purpose as being research into the medals, gems and other rare objects in the collection of the King and into the antiquities and monuments of France. The Society of Antiquaries of London was re-established in 1717, its aim being to collect and print material regarding prehistoric, Roman, Saxon and medieval British antiquities. This was illustrated in the Society's *Vetusta Monumenta*, prints that were circulated among fellows and published as volumes from 1747 to 1893. Leading antiquaries and their associates were elected to the Society, including Robert Adam (i), Thomas Jenkins, Richard Payne Knight, Giovanni Battista Piranesi, James Stuart, Charles Townley, Josiah Wedgwood and many others, including Marco Foscarini, the

historian of Venice, and Cardinal Alessandro Albani, one of the greatest collectors of antiquities of the day. Antiquarian institutions such as these were either educational, as was the Accademia degli Antiquari Alessandrini (which met at the Palazzo del Quirinale and was formed by Francesco Bianchini in 1700 for Albani, then aged eight), or learned societies, such as the Accademia di Antichità Profane (founded Rome, 1740). Antiquarian institutions fostered new fields of research, as did the Accademia Etrusca of Cortona (founded 1725), the first president of which was Filippo Buonarroti, and the Società Columbaria of Florence, founded by Antonio Francesco Gori in 1735. After the publication of Luigi Lanzi's *Saggio di lingua etrusca* in Rome in 1789, Etruscan studies entered a new phase that developed fully in the 19th century. Archaeological research, including studies on Etruria, contributed to the establishment of the Istituto di Corrispondenza Archeologica (later Istituto Germanico) at Rome in 1828.

The establishment of antiquarian institutions during the 18th century sometimes coincided with the discovery of ancient cities, as, for example, with the Accademia Ercolanese (founded 1755), which supervised the publication of *Le antichità di Ercolano esposito* (8 vols, 1757–92) and whose foundation was prompted by the discovery of Herculaneum (*see* HERCULANEUM, §VI). Excavations began in Herculaneum in 1738 and ten years later work began at Pompeii. New findings in the area of Naples and new values attached to the collecting of antiquities (increasingly an equivalent for art patronage and connoisseurship) were instrumental in attracting foreign visitors and in dictating a more active policy for the arts to the rulers. In 1754 Charles-Nicolas Cochin II and Jérôme-Charles Bellicard published their *Observations sur les antiquités de la ville d'Herculaneum*, made from memory. Charles VII, King of Naples (later Charles III of Spain), housed the finds from Herculaneum in a purpose-built suite of rooms in his new palace at Pórtici, which became a private museum of ancient art popular among foreign visitors. The collection of William Hamilton (i) was no less popular and was partly illustrated in Baron d'Hancarville's *The Collection of Etruscan, Greek and Roman Antiquities from the Cabinet of the Honble Wm Hamilton* (4 vols, Naples, 1766–76). This book provided new decorative patterns for modern objects *à l'antique* produced by Matthew Boulton, Wedgwood and other manufacturers, as did such other illustrated volumes as Piranesi's *Diverse maniere d'adornare i cammini* (Rome, 1769) and *Vasi, candelabri, cippi . . .* (Rome, 1778).

From the mid-18th century there was an enormous increase in Europe and the USA in the production of high-quality illustrations, copies, casts, furniture and other objects that attempted to re-create the world of antiquity. The restoration of ancient fragments often included the production of forgeries and copies, as was the case with the sculptor Bartolomeo Cavaceppi, the leading restorer in Rome at the time when the architect Matthew Brettingham the younger and the painter Gavin Hamilton provided British patrons and collectors with antiquities. The number of portraits revealing antiquarian interests became exceptionally high. Telling examples are found among the work of such painters as Pompeo Girolamo Batoni, but no other portraits convey such a powerful idea of the peaks reached by the antiquarian taste during the golden age of the Grand Tour as Johan Zoffany's *Tribuna of the Uffizi* (1771–8; Windsor Castle, Berks, Royal Col.) and *Charles Towneley's Library in Park Street* (1781–3; Burnley, Towneley Hall A.G. & Mus.; *see* ZOFFANY, JOHAN, fig. 2). What the study of the Antique meant to the poet is epitomized by Wilhelm Tischbein's *Goethe in the Roman Campagna* (1786–7; Frankfurt am Main, Städel. Kstinst.), and what it meant to the artist by Henry Fuseli's *Artist in Despair over the Magnitude of Antique Fragments* (1778–80; Zurich, Ksthaus). Fuseli's work is comparable with such earlier depictions of the artist before ancient art as Maarten van Heemskerck's *Self-portrait with a Draughtsman Studying Classical Remains* (1553; Cambridge, Fitzwilliam) and Antoni I Goubau's *Study of Art in Rome* (1662; Antwerp, Kon. Mus. S. Kst.). Topographical images and landscapes might also reflect antiquarian interests. Depictions of ruins (Egyptian, Greek, Roman and Oriental as well as Celtic, Druidic and medieval) flourished throughout the 18th and 19th centuries, leading to such works as Giovanni Paolo Panini's *Roma antica* (1757; Paris, Louvre) and Philipp Hackert's *Ruins of Pompeii* (1799; Attingham Park, Salop, NT). These paintings celebrate the triumph of antiquarianism and the Grand Tour.

The Grand Tour introduced a further category of antiquarian institutions: those established by artists who had travelled to Rome (e.g. the Roman Club, London, 1723–42) and those founded by noblemen and gentlemen who had made their Grand Tour (e.g. the Society of Dilettanti, London, founded 1732). In the early 1740s some of the Dilettanti and other travellers established the Egyptian Society and the Divan Club. The Dilettanti financed the expedition to Greece of James Stuart and Nicholas Revett in 1751–5 and that to Asia Minor of Revett, Richard Chandler and William Pars in 1764–6. These expeditions resulted respectively in the publication of the *Antiquities of Athens* (4 vols, London, 1762–1816) and the *Antiquities of Ionia* (2 vols, London, 1769–97). Such volumes fall into two important categories of illustrated publication of the period: those documenting ancient monuments and those documenting ancient statuary. The first group includes such important works as Robert Wood's *Ruins of Palmyra* (London, 1753) and *Ruins of Balbec* (London, 1757), Piranesi's *Antichità romane* (Rome, 1756) and *Il Campo Marzio dell'Antica Roma* (Rome, 1762), Julien-David Le Roy's *Les Ruines des plus beaux monuments de la Grèce* (Paris, 1758) and other publications that contributed to the development of the Greek and Gothic revivals. Among the second group are Paolo Alessandro Maffei's *Raccolta di statue antiche e moderne* (published in 1704 by Domenico de Rossi, the leading publisher of antiquarian books in Rome) and Bernard de Montfaucon's *L'Antiquité expliquée et représentée en figures* (10 vols, Paris, 1719; *Supplément*, 5 vols, Paris, 1724). These were followed by more rigorous works, for example the Comte de Caylus's *Recueil d'antiquités égyptiennes, étrusques, grecques, romaines et gauloises* (7 vols, Paris, 1752–67).

A novel aesthetic appreciation and a new archaeological view of the Antique grew rapidly after the publication of Winckelmann's works. Of no less importance were the closer inspections and cataloguing of museum objects carried out by such leading antiquaries and archaeologists as Giovanni Gaetano Bottari and Ennio Querino Visconti. New museums relevant to antiquarian and archaeological research opened in rapid succession. The Museo Pio-Clementino opened in Rome in 1734 and, as a result of the activities of Francesco Scipione Maffei, the Museo Lapidario opened in Verona in 1745. The Museo Borbonico in Naples (founded in 1816, renamed the Museo Nazionale in 1860 and now the Museo e Galleria Nazionali di Capodimonte) originated in the years 1787–1805, when the Farnese marbles were removed from Rome to Naples, and by the mid-19th century its collections were catalogued in the *Real Museo Borbonico* (16 vols, Naples, 1824–57). The Gustavus IIIs Antikmuseum, Stockholm, opened in 1794 as a memorial to the patronage of Gustav III, who had employed the Roman dealer and antiquary Francesco Piranesi to form his collection of marbles. The British Museum, London (founded 1753), underwent major transformations at the beginning of the 19th century: the Department of Antiquities was created (1807) and this was followed by the opening of the Townley Gallery (1808) and the temporary Elgin Room (1817). The first detailed catalogue of its collection of ancient statuary was also published at this time (Taylor Combe's *Ancient Marbles in the British Museum*, 3 vols, London, 1812–17).

The Musée Napoléon in Paris (founded 1799, now Musée du Louvre) is a case apart, since it originated in the largest spoil of Classical statuary of the modern era, especially from such collections in Rome as those of the Museo Pio-Clementino, the Palazzo dei Conservatori and the Museo Capitolino. This attracted Ennio Querino Visconti to Paris, where, with Toussaint-Bernard Emeric-David, he wrote the texts on the sculptures for *Le Musée français: Recueil complet des tableaux, statues et bas-reliefs qui composent la collection nationale* (4 vols, Paris, 1803–9). After the Battle of Waterloo (1815), Antonio Canova, who had been appointed Ispettore Generale delle Antichità e Belle Arti in 1802, was sent to Paris on a diplomatic mission and ensured that the marbles were returned to Rome (1816). A new illustrated catalogue of the Louvre collection was produced by Charles-Othon Clarac in the period from 1826 to 1853. The Louvre stimulated enormous interest from the 19th century onwards.

Although antiquarian research and societies continued beyond this, around the mid-18th century antiquarianism underwent major transformations that broadly affected historical disciplines. In the fine arts the publication of Winckelmann's works provided a major impetus to the birth of modern aesthetics and archaeology, fields initially developed mostly by German writers and scholars. In France the conflict between antiquaries and philosophers was most acute. The antiquaries were accused by Voltaire (*Remarques sur l'histoire*, Geneva, 1742, and *Nouvelles Considérations sur l'histoire*, Paris, 1744) of lacking a philosophical and critical spirit, and he described their historical accounts as pure erudition of no use. This view, echoed by others, had important consequences for the development of a type of history in which the author's own views counted for more than the collecting and analysis of data. On the other hand, empirical historians appropriated the antiquarian method of checking literary sources against non-literary evidence. An important component of modern art history has its origins in the works of those antiquaries who first attempted—George Vertue—and then succeeded—Luigi Lanzi—in writing the earliest national histories of the arts.

BIBLIOGRAPHY

A. Momigliano: 'Ancient History and the Antiquarian', *J. Warb. & Court. Inst.*, xiii (1950), pp. 285–315

J. Evans: *A History of the Society of Antiquaries* (Oxford, 1956)

E. Mandowsky and C. Mitchell: *Pirro Ligorio's Roman Antiquities* (London, 1963); review by C. Dionisotti in *Riv. Stor. It.*, lxxv/4 (1963), pp. 890–901

R. Weiss: *The Renaissance Discovery of Classical Antiquity* (Oxford, 1969, 2/1988)

F. Haskell and N. Penny: *Taste and the Antique: The Lure of Classical Sculpture, 1500–1900* (New Haven and London, 1981)

S. Settis, ed.: *Memoria dell'antico nell'arte italiana*, 3 vols (Turin, 1984–5)

P. P. Bober and R. O. Rubinstein: *Renaissance Artists and Antique Sculpture: A Handbook of Sources* (London, 1986)

K. Pomian: *Collectionneurs, amateurs et curieux: Paris, Venice, XVIe–XVIIIe siècle* (Paris, 1987; Eng. trans., Oxford, 1991)

I. Favaretto: *Arte antica e cultura antiquaria nelle collezioni venete al tempo della Serenissima* (Rome, 1990)

S. Howard: *Antiquity Restored: Essays on the Afterlife of the Antique* (Vienna, 1990)

ILARIA BIGNAMINI

Antique, the. Term used between the 15th and the 18th century to refer in a general way to the civilizations of ancient Greece and Rome. It was used to appeal to qualities and standards common, or thought to be common, to the art of that period. It was widely believed that such qualities should be revived, should inspire and (no less important) should control the productions of the modern artist. Progress in taste involved a return to the Antique. Such a vague index of excellence could not have survived for centuries had it not commanded general consent, and for this very reason it is fundamental to any understanding of European culture in this period. The Antique was indeed in many respects equivalent to the Classics—a category, quite as vague, that constituted the body of generally admired ancient Greek and Roman literature. These were also recommended as models, but for modern literature in the modern languages. Implicit in the pedagogic invocation of the Antique as a standard was the assumption that antique art was generally superior: it was not believed that all ancient Greek and Roman art and architecture were of the highest quality, but it was assumed that most of it was of high quality and worthy of special study. Moreover, within the four or more centuries of Greek and Roman civilization held up for special admiration, little development or variation was allowed for. This was certainly a false picture, but it is based on one important truth: patrons of high art of the Roman Empire and of the Hellenistic kingdoms seem to have acknowledged that certain models of excellence in art and architecture had been achieved that should be faithfully imitated and that could never be surpassed. It was indeed precisely because the concept of the superior ancient model was so powerful in antiquity that the Antique could reassume an equivalent role in the modern world.

1. 'ALL' ANTICA' DECORATION. In 15th-century Italy the new art inspired by the Antique was simply described

as *all'antica* (in the ancient mode). A whole new vocabulary of ornament was involved: trophies of Roman armour like those found on some ancient sculpture (e.g. the reliefs on the base of Trajan's Column, Rome) and also on some coins; skulls, masks and swags found in the friezes of ruined temples and on pagan altars; playful male nude children (putti) found on some marble carvings and on numerous engraved cameos. Such ornaments were rapidly adopted for all sorts of circumstances, including Christian altarpieces, but tended to be most richly on display where it was most appropriate, as, for example, in the finely illuminated first manuscript page of the *Life of Julius Caesar* by Suetonius (Paris, Bib. N., MS. lat. 5814; see fig. 1), which probably dates from the 1480s and may be the work of a Paduan artist, Lauro Padovano. Many Classical texts were rediscovered in the 15th century, but Suetonius' *Lives of the Caesars* had been known throughout the Middle Ages. What was new was the interest in illustrating, or at least complementing, the text with a revival of the visual art of the same period (see also MANUSCRIPT, colour pl. III). This may remind us that the careful study, the systematic collection and the imitation of ancient Roman coinage and inscriptions, which had been steadily increasing since the early 14th century, were closely associated with the restoration of Classical scholarship.

1. Antique ornament from Suetonius: *Life of Julius Caesar*, fol. 1, illuminated by ?Lauro Padovano, with capitals by Bartolomeo Sanvito, probably 1480s (Paris, Bibliothèque Nationale, MS. lat. 5814)

2. WRITING, LETTERING AND PRINTING. European writing, lettering and printing were profoundly affected by the passion of 15th-century Italian antiquarians for ancient Roman lettering. Something more or less Roman became standard throughout Europe, although Gothic lettering survived, mainly in Germany. The illuminated Suetonius manuscript reflects the tastes of the circle of learned artists who worked in Padua, chief among whom was Andrea Mantegna. The coloured epigraphic capitals of its first page, together with the Italic script of the text that follows, have been attributed to a Paduan scribe, Bartolomeo Sanvito. They reveal a careful study of the forms of letters used by the ancient Romans, for the student of Roman inscriptions had come to take an interest in style in a visual as well as literary sense. (Sanvito had copied the inscriptions collected by the noted antiquarian Fra Giovanni Giocondo of Verona.)

The capital A, the initial letter with which the text commences, is of special interest because it is represented as if of three dimensions and free-standing, and it has a golden brown colour in imitation of the separately cast bronze capital letters that the ancient Romans used for some of the inscriptions on the friezes of their great public buildings (*see* ROME, ANCIENT, §II, 1(iii)(c)). Such letters with their facets and sharp extremities represented reversals of the letters cut into bronze and marble by the Romans with gravers and chisels, which left a cut with a V section and tapered to a point. Implicit in this capital letter is admiration not only for the style of ancient Roman inscriptions but also for the superb quality of their casting in bronze.

In this same period and in the same area of north Italy the earliest known treatise on the design of ancient Roman letters, the *Alphabetum romanum* (*c.* 1460), was made by Felice Feliciano, a poet, printer, alchemist and, above all, antiquarian: indeed, he was known to his friends as *l'antiquario, the* antiquarian. In the famous epistolary description of an excursion (probably imaginary) on Lake Garda, made by Felice and Mantegna, an inscription cut on a marble column in 'the most handsome letters' excites quite as much enthusiasm as any sculpture. The first book to be printed in Roman type was Cicero's *De oratore* in 1465; probably the earliest competent imitation of the inscriptions of the late Republic or early Empire in an actual stone inscription is that on the tomb of *Pope Nicholas V* (*d* 1455; Rome, St Peter's); and the earliest notable revival of the monumental capitalized inscriptions on modern public buildings can be associated with Leon Battista Alberti a little earlier.

Feliciano's treatise, which was never published and is of uncertain date, was followed by the *Trattati delle lettere antiche* by Damiano Moille (*fl* 1480s), published in Parma in about 1480. Moille was primarily concerned to produce a pattern book for craftsmen and it was perhaps partly for this reason that he showed how the antique letters could be regulated by a geometric framework, inscribed within a square or circle and with segmental cusps. But this geometric aspect of the fascination of ancient Roman letters also reflects the convictions of the learned that there were laws that determined the pleasing shapes of such letters just as there were laws underlying the harmonious proportions of antique architecture, and this emerges clearly in Luca Pacioli's treatise *De divina proportione*, published in Venice in 1509.

3. ARCHITECTURE. The establishment of Roman lettering coincided with that of the orders, or different classes, of ancient Greek and Roman architecture, each with its own rules (*see* ORDERS, ARCHITECTURAL). By the end of the 15th century there was no major architect in Italy who was not employing the principal elements of antique architecture: cylindrical columns, fluted pilasters, Corinthian and Ionic capitals, domical vaults, semicircular arches, pediments and entablatures. That these were familiar all over Europe by the close of the 16th century was chiefly owing to the publications by two highly influential practising architects. The first of these was Sebastiano Serlio's *Regole generale*, published in Venice in 1537, which illustrated the range of ancient Roman architecture as studied from actual ruins and as imaginatively reconstructed not only by Serlio himself but by other earlier architects, most notably Baldassare Peruzzi, whose drawings (many Florence, Uffizi) he inherited. Serlio also expounded the idea of the orders.

Still more influential than Serlio's treatise of 1537 and far more cogent in expository style and lucid in presentation was Andrea Palladio's *I quattro libri dell'architettura*, which was published in 1570, also in Venice. Palladio's book was probably intended chiefly for other architects, although it certainly reached a much larger public. It had three interconnected aims: to expound the basic principles of building and design, to illustrate the exemplary masterpieces of antiquity and to publish Palladio's own buildings and projects. Behind this book and Serlio's, as also behind earlier writing on the architecture of antiquity, there lay the ten books *On Architecture* by Vitruvius (*see* VITRUVIUS, §§2; 3(ii)), the earliest surviving treatise on architecture known and the only literary work on architecture to survive from antiquity. Palladio had indeed collaborated with his patron, the Venetian nobleman Daniele Barbaro, in the publication (1556) of an illustrated edition of Vitruvius with a translation (apparently the earliest) and annotations. It was with reference to Vitruvius that Palladio and others

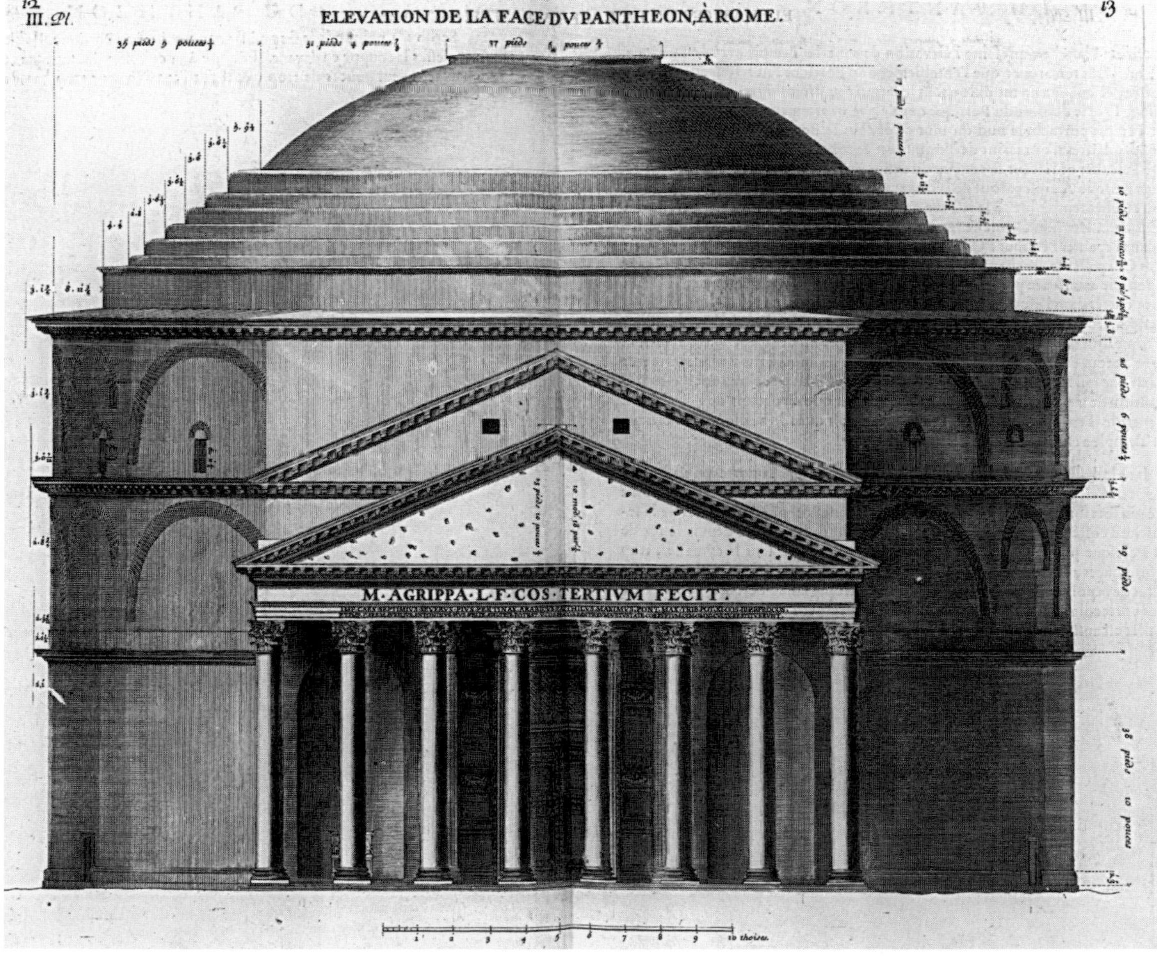

2. Pantheon, Rome; copperplate engraving from Antoine Desgodetz: *Les Edifices antiques de Rome dessinés et mesurés très exactement* (Paris, 1682), pl. III (London, British Library)

felt able to establish the rules behind the practice of antique architecture, to reconstruct whole buildings from surviving fragments and to create novel structures that had no direct relationship with any antique building but which they nevertheless felt to be antique in spirit.

Palladio's work remained influential throughout the 17th and 18th centuries, although in the latter century more for its presentation of Palladio's own buildings than for the information that it supplied on antique ones. In this latter respect it was superseded by Antoine Desgodetz's *Les Edifices antiques de Rome dessinés et mesurés très exactement*, published in Paris in 1682 and dedicated to Jean-Baptiste Colbert, who, as founder of the Académie de France and Surintendant des Bâtiments du Roi, had sent Desgodetz to Rome in 1674. Desgodetz's copperplates (see fig. 2) are far finer in detail than the woodblocks employed by Palladio, and he made more precise measurements, ceaselessly pointing out that he had corrected Palladio's and Serlio's errors. He did not permit himself the speculative reconstructions that were an important part of Palladio's work, observing that where an acanthus leaf on a Corinthian capital had broken off he felt it legitimate to restore it but that he was not in the business of composing a great temple on the evidence of three solitary columns.

Desgodetz's book set the standard that all subsequent serious archaeological publications sought to emulate before the 20th century. Editions of it were still being published in the early 19th century, and in the mid-18th century, when it was out of print but still in demand, Robert Adam (i) thought of reissuing it with some glamorous perspective views to extend its appeal and 'a smart preface', additional notes and corrections printed in red to advertise his own talents. More important than its influence on archaeologists, however, were the hundreds of builders' pattern books that were parasitic on it for over a century, making the buildings that he illustrated, almost all of them temples in Rome, canonical.

4. SCULPTURE. The buildings that Desgodetz published had all been known in the 15th century. With sculpture, however, the situation was different: the canon was constantly expanding as more statues were excavated.

(i) The rediscovery of ancient sculpture: collections and museums. (ii) Prints and plaster casts after the Antique. (iii) Artists and the Antique: from the 16th century to the early 18th.

(i) The rediscovery of ancient sculpture: collections and museums. The *all'antica* decoration of Suetonius' *Life of Julius Caesar* owed little to figural relief sculpture and free-standing statues, although the artist probably did have some knowledge, not necessarily first hand, of the battle narratives on sarcophagi and columns. One might suppose, too, that he had seen an antique statue of Victory inscribing a shield (but this motif is more likely to have been derived from a coin). Moreover, the Pegasus restrained by the two warriors at the top of the page may echo the colossal marble groups in the Piazza del Quirinale, Rome, the so-called *Horse Tamers*.

Yet few of the sculptures by which the Antique would come to be identified were known by the 1480s. In addition to the groups in the Piazza del Quirinale, the reliefs of Trajan's Column (*see* ROME, fig. 25) and those on the triumphal arches of Constantine (*see* ROME, fig. 30 and ROME, ANCIENT, fig. 83) and Titus (*see* TRIUMPHAL ARCH, fig. 1) were visible in Rome, as well as numerous sarcophagi in Rome and elsewhere, some of which had been reused as modern tombs. There was also an important group of bronzes that had been displayed near the Lateran Palace in Rome, but the Pope Sixtus IV had recently donated these to the Palazzo dei Conservatori on the Capitol (where they remain to this day): the *She-wolf* (*see* ROME, ANCIENT, fig. 60), the *Camillus* and *Spinario* (Rome, Mus. Conserv.; *see* STATUE, fig. 2). The largest and most important of all the ancient bronzes to have survived more or less complete from ancient times was the equestrian statue of *Marcus Aurelius* (Rome, Mus. Capitolino; *see* ROME, ANCIENT, fig. 61), which had long been mistaken for a statue of the first Christian emperor, Constantine. This remained at the Lateran until 1538, when it too was transferred to the Piazza del Campidoglio, as Sixtus IV had planned, and the placed on the pedestal designed for it by Michelangelo.

In the late 15th century and the early 16th a number of spectacular discoveries doubled the number of major antique statues known in Italy: the APOLLO BELVEDERE was excavated in the 1490s, the LAOKOON group in 1506 (both Rome, Vatican, Mus. Pio-Clementino) and the *Commodus as Hercules* (Rome, Mus. Conserv.) in 1507; the *Cleopatra* (Rome, Vatican, Mus. Pio-Clementino) was first recorded in 1512, the year in which the colossal *Tiber* (Paris, Louvre) was excavated and a year before the colossal *Nile* (Rome, Vatican, Braccio Nuo.). All these sculptures were taken to a courtyard with fountains and niches and orange trees, part of the Villa Belvedere built in the antique style by Bramante in 1503 for Pope Julius II, the nephew of Sixtus IV. The famous BELVEDERE TORSO (Rome, Vatican, Mus. Pio-Clementino) was also displayed here, and so too would be the statue believed to represent *Antinous* (Rome, Vatican, Mus. Pio-Clementino) after its discovery in 1543. The Palazzo dei Conservatori had been turned by Sixtus IV into a sort of public collection of sculpture. The Cortile di Belvedere was a museum of antique sculpture, the first such museum since antiquity itself.

Gradually other collections and other museums were formed in the palaces and villas of Rome, which enjoyed a similar esteem. The first of these consisted of the group of marbles assembled by the Farnese in their Roman palace during the last few years of the pontificate of the Farnese pope Paul III (*d* 1549): the colossal group of the FARNESE BULL, the colossal FARNESE HERCULES and Farnese *Flora*, and the *Callipygian Venus* (all Naples, Mus. Archeol. N.) were the most notable items. Then there were the statues assembled by the Medici in their villa on the Pincio towards the close of the century: these included the NIOBE GROUP, *The Wrestlers* and the VENUS DE' MEDICI (all Florence, Uffizi; see fig. 3). In the early 17th century the Medici Villa was equalled in fame by those of the Borghese and Ludovisi families, each of which acquired

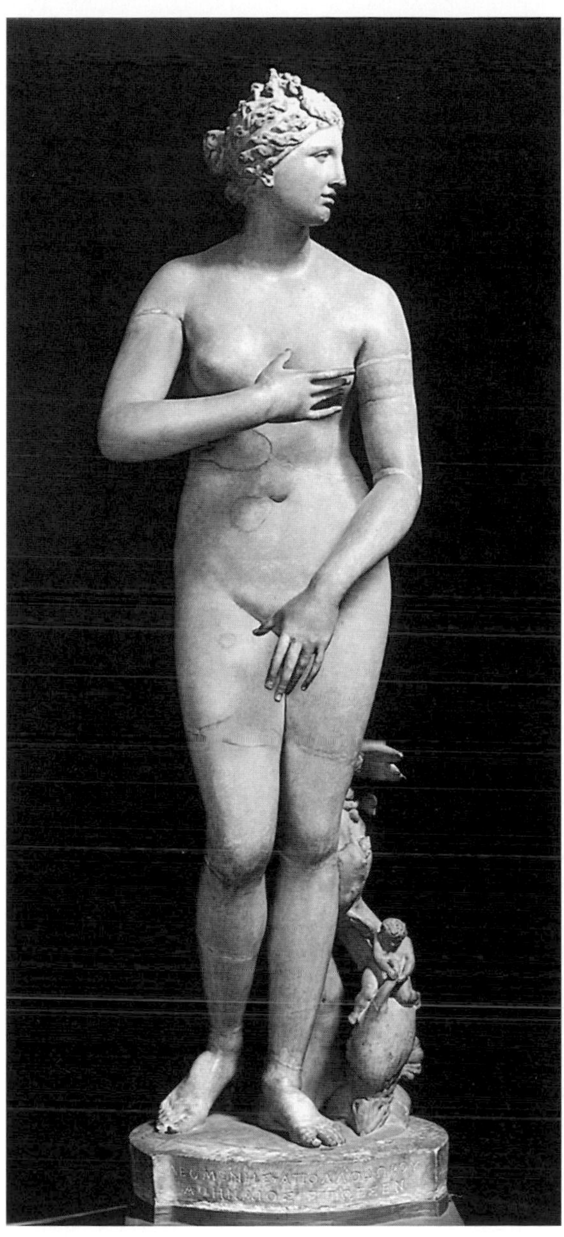

3. *Venus de' Medici*, marble, h. 1.53 m, ?1st century BC (Florence, Galleria degli Uffizi)

a group of antique statues. Most of these were newly acquired: the BORGHESE GLADIATOR, the Borghese *Hermaphrodite*, the Borghese Vase (all Paris, Louvre), the Ludovisi *Gaul* group (*see* PERGAMON, fig. 4), the Ludovisi *Mars* (both Rome, Mus. N. Romano) and the *Dying Gaul* (Rome, Mus. Capitolino; *see* GREECE, ANCIENT, fig. 67).

After 1630 the number of notable discoveries seems to have decreased in Rome. But about a century later excavations in the Emperor Hadrian's villa at Tivoli (*see* TIVOLI, §2(ii)) revealed a remarkable series of discoveries including the black marble centaurs, the faun of red marble, the Capitoline *Antinous* and Capitoline *Flora* (all Rome, Mus. Capitolino), which were purchased by Pope Clement XII (for the most part from Cardinal Alessandro Albani) to form the Capitoline Museum. Later in the 18th century more excavations at Tivoli and elsewhere were prompted by the insatiable demands of foreign, especially British, collectors. Although a great deal of high quality was exported, the finest works stayed in Rome, and after 1769 these were diverted to the new museum in the Vatican formed by Clement XIV and continued under the auspices of Pius VI. This museum, the Museo Pio-Clementino, which incorporated the Cortile Belvedere and is now a part of the Vatican museums, represents one of the most intelligent and imaginative combinations of architecture and sculpture ever devised.

Whereas in the mid-17th century almost all the most admired antique sculpture was to be seen in Rome, the situation had changed by the close of the 18th century. In 1679 the Medici had transferred their most famous sculptures to the Tribuna of the Uffizi. In the 1780s the King of Naples, who had inherited the Farnese collection, began to transfer the statues to his own kingdom, where they would be united with the sculpture excavated at Pompeii and Herculaneum. Nevertheless, it is striking that the Antique, in sculpture as in architecture, consisted not only of ancient Roman buildings and statues but also of buildings and statues that were mostly to be seen in Rome.

(ii) Prints and plaster casts after the Antique. Anthologies of prints of these antique statues were published in Rome in the 1560s and 1570s by ANTOINE LAFRÉRY and GIOVANNI BATTISTA DE' CAVALIERI. These may be regarded as equivalent to the publications of Serlio and Palladio. The much superior engravings published by Domenico de' Rossi (*fl* 1680–*c.* 1730) in Rome in the early 18th century may be thought to parallel the great publication by Desgodetz, and Girard Audran's *Les Proportions du corps humain mesurées sur les plus belles figures de l'antiquité* (1683) measures the thighs of the *Venus de' Medici* and the nose of the *Apollo Belvedere* with the same thoroughness that Desgodetz had devoted to the columns of the Pantheon or the abacus of the capitals of the Temple of Castor and Pollux. Prints of sculptures, however, although highly important for broadcasting their fame, were not as valuable to practising sculptors as the illustrations in Palladio or Desgodetz were to practising architects. Of far more significance were plaster casts.

Plaster casts after the Antique had played an important part in the studio equipment of artists (painters as well as sculptors) since the mid-15th century, at least in Italy, but they had, before the early 18th century, seldom taken the form of complete casts of life-size or over life-size statues. Such casts, which were both difficult and costly to make and transport, had been made for royal patrons—for Francis I, King of France, for Mary of Hungary, for Philip II, King of Spain, and for Charles I, King of England—and usually in connection with the casting of bronze copies, which served primarily as palace ornaments. But such casts had also by the late 17th century come to be regarded as essential equipment for an artistic academy. The Accademia di San Luca in Rome acquired a set in 1598, and one was acquired for the Milanese Academy in 1620. The most ambitious and influential of all academies of art, that established by Jean-Baptiste Colbert in France in 1649, initiated the campaign of making casts from the famous antique statues in Rome at the same date that Desgodetz was given the task of measuring and drawing the city's antique architecture. The casts were not needed exclusively for academic purposes: copies were made from them for the new gardens of the king's palace at Versailles. Nonetheless, in the Académie de France, as in the numerous European academies established on the same model, the study of such plaster casts played an important part.

(iii) Artists and the Antique: from the 16th century to the early 18th. The priorities of the official curriculum did not necessarily correspond with the deeper interests either of the students or even their instructors; certainly it is hard to think of a French sculptor or painter of the first half of the 18th century who was as sympathetic to the celebrated antique statues that they had had to study (and in many cases actually had to copy) as had been those French artists of an earlier generation who had not had an academic education. Moreover, there was often an element of lip service, or at least of pious exaggeration, in professions of esteem for the Antique. A particularly telling example of this is the pedagogic drawing, commissioned in 1682 by the 7th Marqués del Carpio from the most highly regarded painter in late 17th-century Rome, Carlo Maratti.

Maratti's drawing (Chatsworth, Derbys.; no. 646) was engraved by Nicolas Dorigny in 1728 with the inscription *A Giovani studiosi del disegno* (see fig. 4) and it is eloquent of the values behind the establishment of academies. Some elementary geometry is on the blackboard and some

4. *A Giovani studiosi del disegno*, engraving by Nicolas Dorigny after Carlo Maratti, 1728

perspective too. Further back, Leonardo demonstrates the muscles of an *ecorché* (a skinned, nude statue) to other eager students. In these parts of the print the message is written clearly three times: *Tanto che basti* ('in due measure'). It is implied that one could have too much of these exercises. However, behind these, and at a higher level, are three statues: a Hercules in a niche, and two other statues—a nude Venus, seen from behind, and an Apollo—in front of it. These must have been selected to represent the three principal types of antique figure: heroic male power, feminine beauty and elegant male grace. One cannot study these antique statues too much (*Non mai abbastanza* is written on the wall behind the Apollo) because from these figures all perfections of form are to be derived. To the right in the distance there is another niche matching that in which the Hercules is placed. It is occupied by a draped statue, but this is obscured by a cloud bank occupied by three graces with the motto *Senza di noi ogni fatica è vana* ('without us every effort is pointless'), alluding to the god-given feeling for gracious composition.

We can match the instructor's own practice against his precepts. Certainly a knowledge of geometry, perspective and anatomy is evident, but not excessively or even remarkably so. Maratti is known to have studied from the nude figure, and, although his draperies are copious, we can sense the articulation of the body below each one. He had also surely studied antique statues: the bearded head of the principal instructor suggests this, as do some of the hand movements. Nevertheless, the Antique plays less of a role in Maratti's own style than one might expect from the message of the print. Indeed, he seems to have been uncertain as to what was antique. The colossal Hercules is certainly based on the Farnese *Hercules* (or one of its variants), but the more prominent Venus is not an antique statue at all, and the Apollo is the god invented by Raphael to fill one of the niches in the *School of Athens* (*see* ITALY, fig. 32). Moreover, in his enthusiastic account of this drawing in his life of Maratti, Giovanni Pietro Bellori, the most powerful advocate of the study of the Antique, erroneously identified (or remembered) the Venus as the *Venus de' Medici* and the Apollo as the Belvedere *Antinous*.

In commending the artists of whom he approved, such as Maratti, Poussin, Andrea Sacchi and the Caracci, Bellori emphasized their debt to the study of antique sculpture, not their debt to antique painting. Very little ancient Roman and no ancient Greek wall painting was known; indeed, only one real figure composition, the *Aldobrandini Wedding*, a wall painting discovered in 1606, was known, and its merits were much disputed. The other paintings known were decorative grotesques that seemed to correspond with work of which writers in antiquity disapproved. In any case it was regarded as a virtue for the painter to study sculpture for it concentrated the mind on basic form as against superficial appearance. Critics of this point of view complained that the painters were encouraged to produce figures that were *statuino* (hard as statues), and Poussin, at least in some of his more severe works, would seem to have regarded this as a positive quality. Rubens is known to have been critical of this tendency and to have urged that the artist, in studying marbles, should be sure to reinvest these models with flesh and blood.

The study of antique statues was by no means a monopoly of the artists commended by Bellori. Luca Giordano, rival of Maratti, a dazzling performer whose success Bellori deplored, was famous for his adoration of the *Venus de' Medici.* Rubens certainly owed as much to his study of antique sculpture as did Poussin. Moreover, certain tendencies in 16th-century Italian painting that have been regarded as anti-Classical—most notably the disregard for clearly defined and logically constructed pictorial space and for planar compositions—were surely influenced by the study of Roman sarcophagi. Some of the daring novelties introduced into architecture by Francesco Borromini, to the distress of Bellori, were in fact inspired by archaeological evidence of idiosyncratic tendencies in antique architecture itself. The evidence of ancient practice could often be used to qualify or even subvert the precepts and rules that exponents of the orders propounded, for these exponents were as much influenced by the theoretical writings of Vitruvius as by the remains of a few Roman buildings.

From the moment that the Antique was promoted as an educational norm, anxiety was expressed that it would inhibit invention, that creative youth would be crippled by assertions that it is 'impossible to do or say anything in a way that has not been done or said better by the ancients'. This claim was made by Domenico da Prato in the *Invettiva contra certi calunniatori di Dante* . . . (1420); similar arguments were advanced in late 17th-century France by Charles Perrault in the famous QUARREL OF THE ANCIENTS AND MODERNS. That the Moderns could in some respects surpass the Ancients was often enough allowed: indeed, Desgodetz, in his hyperbolic dedicatory epistle, professed to look forward to the flowering of architecture in his own time, for the great men who raised the buildings of antiquity, 'les Augustes, les Trajans et les Antonins', had 'ceded the first place in the Temple of Glory to the invincible, the great and the magnanimous Louis'. But in retrospect it is remarkable how deeply the opponents of excessive deference to the Antique themselves respected it.

5. RESPONSE TO THE ANTIQUE: 18TH CENTURY AND LATER. The real challenge to the authority of the Antique came not from critics of its enthusiastic supporters but, inadvertently, from those supporters themselves. No-one had written about the Antique with more enthusiasm than JOHANN JOACHIM WINCKELMANN, but in his *Geschichte der Kunst des Altertums* (Dresden, 1763, dated 1764) he classified antique art in terms of its historical development, giving special attention to those sculptures that came from (or at least reflected) the earliest and purest periods; he also inquired into those circumstances in ancient civilization that had made such art possible. The result was that the Antique ceased to be an ideal residing outside history and became part of a historical process. The Antique thus became more marvellous but also more remote. Since it was the product of particular cultural circumstances, and since it was impossible that those circumstances would recur, it was inappropriate to attempt to replicate that product. One conclusion—not one that Winckelmann himself reached but one that he made possible—was that Christians living north of the Alps should adopt the Gothic rather than Greek or Roman models for their architecture.

The publication of the architectural ruins of Greece and Asia Minor (the first two volumes of *Antiquities of Athens* by JAMES STUART and NICHOLAS REVETT were published in 1762 and 1789) extended the models for antique architecture to include buildings outside Italy. The genuine Greek Doric and the early Greek forms of Ionic and Corinthian were now imitated and with a fanatical exactitude. One might argue that the Antique had never been more influential. In fact, however, the very exactitude acknowledged the alien nature of the art imitated: a beautiful language but not a living one.

Although Winckelmann's followers, first and chief among them his friend Anton Raphael Mengs, had begun to challenge the status of the statues in the Belvedere, the Tribuna, the Villa Ludovisi and so on, pointing out that they were but copies of lost Greek originals, the popular fame of these statues long survived, and plaster casts of them continued for more than a century to be central to the education of artists all over the Western world. New statues were discovered and greeted with rapture: the NIKE OF SAMOTHRACE, the VENUS DE MILO (both Paris, Louvre), the Prima Porta *Augustus* (Rome, Vatican, Braccio Nuo.), Praxiteles' *Hermes* (Olympia, Archaeol. Mus.), the bronze *Charioteer* (*see* DELPHI, fig. 5) and, most recently, the Riace bronzes.

Something had, however, begun to change before 1800. Alternative touchstones were available, and the idea also came to be popular that the modern world should not permit itself to be dominated by the past. Some of the finest architecture of the 19th and 20th centuries had been deeply inspired by the architecture of ancient Greece and Rome: Charles Robert Cockerell's St George's Hall (1851–6) in Liverpool or John Russell Pope's National Gallery of Art (1935–41) in Washington, DC, would certainly have been acknowledged as masterpieces by Lord Burlington, Palladio, Alberti and Vitruvius, but at the same dates equally great buildings were created without any reference to the Antique at all, and this was also true of some sculpture and much painting.

See also CLASSICISM.

BIBLIOGRAPHY

S. Serlio: *Regole generali di architettura sopra le cinque maniere de gli edifici cioè Thoscano, Dorico, Ionico, Corinthio, et Composito* (Venice, 1537)

M. P. Vitruvius: *I dieci libri dell'architettura* (Venice, 1556)

A. Palladio: *I quattro libri dell'architettura* (Venice, 1570)

G. P. Bellori: *Vite* (1672); ed. E. Borea (1976)

A. Desgodetz: *Les Edifices antiques de Rome dessinés et mesurés très exactement* (Paris, 1682)

C. Perrault: *Parallèle des anciens et des modernes en ce qui regarde les arts et les sciences* . . ., 4 vols (Paris, 1688–97)

J. Stuart and N. Revett: *The Antiquities of Athens*, 4 vols (London, 1762–1816)

J. J. Winckelmann: *Geschichte der Kunst des Altertums* (Dresden, 1763, dated 1764)

N. Pevsner: *Academies of Art Past and Present* (Cambridge, 1940)

B. Ashmole: 'Cyriac of Ancona', *Proc. Brit. Acad.*, xcv (1957), pp. 25–41

C. Mitchell: 'Felice Feliciano antiquarius', *Proc. Brit. Acad.*, xlvii (1961), pp. 197–221

J. Summerson: *The Classical Language of Architecture* (London, 1963/*R* 1980)

R. Weiss: *The Renaissance Discovery of Classical Antiquity* (Oxford, 1969)

H. Burns: *Andrea Palladio, 1508–1580* (London, 1975)

F. Haskell and N. Penny: *Taste and the Antique* (London and New Haven, 1981)

P. P. Baber and R. O. Rubinstein: *Renaissance Artists and Antique Sculpture* (London, 1986)

J. Onians: *Bearers of Meaning: The Classical Orders in Antiquity, the Middle Ages and the Renaissance* (Princeton, 1988)

For further bibliography *see* CLASSICISM.

NICHOLAS PENNY

Antiquity, Late. *See* LATE ANTIQUITY.

Antissa. *See under* LESBOS.

Antoine, Jacques-Denis (*b* Paris, 6 Aug 1733; *d* Paris, 24 Aug 1801). French architect. He was the son of a joiner and trained as a builder, becoming a mason and, by the age of 20, a building contractor. He received no formal education and did not undertake the conventional study tour abroad, preferring to pursue theoretical studies on his own, although he did eventually visit Italy in 1777–8. After competing unsuccessfully for the commission for the Halle au Blé (corn exchange) in Paris, which was built (1763–9) by Nicolas Le Camus de Mézières, in 1766 Antoine was appointed architect of the Hôtel des Monnaies (mint), Paris, for which his early rival Etienne-Louis Boullée also submitted designs. His reputation rests almost exclusively on this single prominently sited building (see fig.).

When Anges-Jacques Gabriel's Place Louis XV (later Place de la Concorde) was begun in 1755 at the western edge of Paris, it was proposed that a new mint be built around two courtyards behind the Hôtel de Coislin (later Hôtel de Crillon). After his appointment as architect of the mint, Antoine must have worked closely with Gabriel, acquiring much of the older architect's manner if not his elegance. Antoine's initial project was abandoned in 1767, when it was decided to build the new mint in a more central location next to Louis Le Vau's Collège des Quatre Nations (later the Institut de France) and across the Seine from the Louvre.

Jacques-Denis Antoine: main façade of the Hôtel des Monnaies, Paris, 1767–75

One of the two projects Boullée submitted for the new site resembled a large town house, with the main block separated from the Quai de Conti by a forecourt. Antoine's scheme reversed this disposition, placing the administration block along the river front and removing the high-security foundry and workshops to interior courtyards fitted within the irregular site of the old Hôtel de Conti. Antoine was careful to differentiate between the industrial and administrative sections: the low side elevation along the Rue Guénégard to the east has robust rustication and a defensive character associated with coinage at least since Jacopo Sansovino's Venetian mint 200 years earlier; the palatial elevation facing across the Seine to the Louvre was meant to convey the idea of national prosperity.

If the sumptuous interiors of the administrative wing are close in spirit to the inventive manner of Charles de Wailly, the exterior is typical of Antoine, who assimilated into the tradition of French classicism something of the character of the Roman Renaissance palazzo. The insistent horizontality of the façade, however, was innovative, with 27 bays extending *c.* 300 m along the river. The effect would have been emphasized by the intended rebuilding of the embankment with rustication and stairways as a podium for the new mint, but this was not carried out. The only vertical accent amid the horizontal reiteration of the windows is the projecting central pavilion with its Ionic columns above a rusticated ground floor. On the side wings the repetitive character of the fenestration is relieved only by the addition of balconies on consoles in front of every third window of the main floor. The planarity is exaggerated by the absence of shadows on this north front, a fact remarked by Le Camus de Mézières at the time. Above the strong cornice Antoine eliminated the high-pitched roofs of French tradition, and in place of a conventional pediment above the hexastyle frontispiece he substituted an attic, in front of which are six statues symbolizing Peace, Commerce, Prudence, Law, Strength and Abundance. The building is also notable for the use of a system of fire-resistant hollow tile vaulting, which Antoine is credited with perfecting.

The Hôtel des Monnaies established Antoine's reputation. In 1776, a year after its completion, he was named a member of the Académie Royale d'Architecture, and his official positions included that of Contrôleur des Hôtels des Monnaies du Royaume. Following a fire in 1776, he participated in the rebuilding of the Palais de Justice in Paris, for which he designed a new staircase, writing hall and record office. He also produced plans (unexecuted) for the redevelopment of the Ile-de-la-Cité, which included a Place Louis XVI, and he designed the façade (1780s) of the Hôtel de Ville in Cambrai, in association with Nicolas-Henri Jardin. In 1790–92 he built the mint in Berne. Antoine's numerous town houses, designed in a severe and cubic manner, included the Hôtel Brochet de Saint-Prest (1773; now part of the Ecoles des Ponts et Chaussées) at 28, Rue des Saints-Pères. He also designed such country houses as the Château de Herces (1770–72) in Berchères-sur-Vesgres and the Château du Buisson-du-Mai (1782) in Saint-Aquilin-de-Pacy, and he was responsible for remodelling and laying out the gardens of many more. Outside France he worked for José Alvárez de Toledo y Gonzaga, Duke of Alba, designing the staircase and other interiors as well as the gardens of the Palacio Alba y Berwick (1778) in Madrid; and in the 1780s for Friedrich Salm-Kyrsburg he designed the house and gardens of Schloss Kirn-Kyrsburg in the Palatinate. Antoine's ecclesiastical designs seem less constrained by considerations of taste and convention. The unusual façade of his early church of St Nicholas-du-Chardonnet (1765), Paris, was crowned with a pyramidal bell-tower, and his temple-front portico (*c.* 1780) for the chapel in the courtyard of the monastery of the Révérends Pères de la Charité on the Rue des Saints-Pères seems to have been one of the first examples in Paris of the use of the Greek Doric order and may have been inspired by the publication in 1758 of Julien-David Le Roy's *Ruines des plus beaux monuments de la Grèce.*

Always a careful and scrupulous administrator, in 1789 Antoine was appointed to replace Claude-Nicolas Ledoux as architect of the new Paris toll gates and to bring their finances under control. His supervision proved indispensable, and when he was imprisoned during the Revolution (on a charge of providing a facility in the mint for smuggling gold down the river) he was soon released in order that work might continue on the toll gates. In 1799 he was elected to fill the vacancy in the Institut de France left by the death of Boullée, and the last two years of his life were spent in reasonable comfort and honour.

BIBLIOGRAPHY

A. Renou: *Notice des ouvrages et de la vie du c[itoy]en Antoine* (Paris, n.d.)
C. Lussault: *Notice historique sur défunt Jacques-Denis Antoine* (Paris, 1801)
J.-G. Legrand and C.-P. Landon: *Description de Paris et de ses édifices* (Paris, 1806)
Plans des divers étages, . . de l'Hôtel des Monnaies, à Paris (Paris, 1826)
A.-C. Quatremère de Quincy: *Histoire de la vie des ouvrages des plus célèbres architectes* (Paris, 1830)
F. Mazerolle: *L'Hôtel des Monnaies,* Les Grandes Institutions de France (Paris, 1907)
L. Hautecoeur: *Histoire de l'architecture classique en France*, iii–v (Paris, 1950–53)
M. Gallet: *Paris Domestic Architecture of the Eighteenth Century* (London, 1972)
M. Mosser: 'L'Hôtel des Monnaies de Paris: Oeuvre de J.-D. Antoine', *Inf. Hist. A.*, vi (1972), 2, pp. 94–9
R. Middleton and D. Watkin: *Neoclassical and 19th Century Architecture* (New York, 1979)
A. Braham: *The Architecture of the French Enlightenment* (London, 1980)

RAND CARTER

Antoine de Grenoble. *See under* JACQUET.

Antoine-Marie-Philippe-Louis d'Orléans, Duc de Montpensier. *See* ORLÉANS, (11).

Antoine of Burgundy. *See* BURGUNDY, (4).

Antokol'sky, Mark (Matveyevich) (*b* Vil'no [now Vilnius], Lithuania, 2 Nov 1843; *d* Bad-Homburg, 9 July 1902). Russian sculptor of Lithuanian birth. He was the son of an innkeeper of modest means. From 1862 he studied under Nikolay Pimenov (1812–64) as an occasional student at the Academy of Arts (Akademiya Khudozhestv) in St Petersburg. While still a student he produced two high relief sculptures, which attracted attention for their realism and which were awarded silver medals: the *Jewish Tailor* (wood, 1864) and *The Miser* (wood and ivory, 1865; both St Petersburg, Rus. Mus.). In 1871 Antokol'sky left Russia for health reasons. He worked first in Rome and then, from 1877, in Paris. He gained fame in Europe mainly through a number of monumental statues on subjects drawn from Russian history: *Ivan the Terrible* (marble, 1875; Moscow, Tret'yakov Gal.), *Nestor the Chronicler* (marble, 1890) and *Yermak* (bronze, 1891; both St Petersburg, Rus. Mus.), and also on subjects connected with the history of religion and philosophy: *Christ* (marble, 1876; Moscow, Tret'yakov Gal.), *Death of Socrates* (marble, 1875–7) and *Spinoza* (marble, 1886–7; both St Petersburg, Rus. Mus.). He produced a whole series of sculpted portraits of his contemporaries, executed in a realistic style: *Vladimir Vasil'yevich Stasov* (marble, 1872–3; St Petersburg, Saltykov-Shchedrin Pub. Lib.), *Sergey Petrovich Botkin* (marble, 1874) and *Ivan Turgenev* (plaster, 1880; both St Petersburg, Rus. Mus.).

Antokol'sky was one of the most outstanding Russian sculptors of the second half of the 19th century. His naturalistic approach to historic subjects brought him success not only in Russia but also in Europe. Unlike most of his contemporaries, he addressed complicated historical and philosophical problems in his sculptural work. In this sense Antokol'sky was closely connected with the Russian painters of the time who formed the group known as the Wanderers (Peredvizhniki).

BIBLIOGRAPHY

V. P. Shalimova: *Mark Matveyevich Antokol'sky* (Leningrad, 1970)
E. V. Kuznetsova: *Mark Matveyevich Antokol'sky, 1843–1902* (Leningrad, 1986)
——: *M. M. Antokol'sky: Zhisn'i Tvorchestro* [Life and work] (Moscow, 1989)
Mark Antokol'sky: Vystavka proizvedeniy k 150-letiyu so dnya rozhdeniya [Mark Antokol'sky: an exhibition of his works to mark the 150th anniversary of his birth] (exh. cat., St Petersburg, Rus. Mus., 1994)

SERGEY ANDROSSOV

Antolínez (y Sarabia), Francisco (*b* Seville, *c.* 1644; *d* Seville, *c.* 1700). Spanish painter. A lawyer by training, he continued his profession while practising as a painter and was well educated in the humanities. Although he was a prolific artist, few of his paintings are signed; only one, the *Adoration of the Shepherds* (1678; Seville Cathedral, Sacristia de los Cálices), bears his name. This painting is characteristic of his style, depicting small, highly expressive figures in a setting with dramatic lighting effects. Antolínez painted spacious interior scenes and landscapes, always featuring small figures in lively attitudes. He specialized in modestly sized pictures, usually in series of eight or ten paintings of religious subjects, to which he gave a pleasing decorative effect by the addition of landscape backgrounds. Most of them were evidently painted in haste with an eye to a quick sale. His output includes many scenes of episodes from the lives of Jacob (Seville Cathedral, sacristy), Abraham and David from the Old Testament, scenes from the life of the Virgin, and New Testament scenes of the childhood of Christ (Madrid, Colegio S Anton) and of the life of Christ (Fuentes el Año, parish church). Many of these series have been dispersed into numerous different locations. Antolínez is thought to have been related to the painter JOSÉ ANTOLÍNEZ, who may have been his brother or his uncle.

BIBLIOGRAPHY

D. Angulo Iñiguez: *Pintura del siglo XVII*, A. Hisp., xv (Madrid, 1971), p. 384

——: *Murillo y su escuela* (Seville, 1975), p. 8

E. Valdivieso: *Historia de la pintura sevillana* (Seville, 1986), p. 229

A. E. Pérez Sánchez: *Pintura barroca española* (Madrid, 1992), p. 382

ENRIQUE VALDIVIÈSO

Antolínez [Antolín], **José** (*bapt* Madrid, 7 Nov 1635; *d* Madrid, 30 May 1675). Spanish painter. According to Palomino he was an arrogant and quarrelsome character. Although he came from a low social position the prestige he acquired procured him an important clientele: the Almirante of Castile hung works by him in a hall intended to exhibit the most important Spanish artists, and the Danish ambassador to Spain, Cornelius Lerche, gave him commissions. Although initially employing simple compositions, these became more complex during his career, and he also developed into a dynamic and brilliant colourist.

The son of a carpenter, at the age of 18 Antolínez married the daughter of the artist Julián González de Benavides, and his first apprenticeship was served with his father-in-law. He then joined the workshop of Francisco Rizi, with whom he collaborated. He became one of the most prominent Baroque painters of religious subjects, particularly that of the *Immaculate Conception.* This was a favourite theme in Spanish Baroque art, and the Spanish monarchy was closely connected with the proclamation of the dogma it embodied. Antolínez's earliest treatments of the subject were in the tradition established by Jusepe de Ribera, Francisco Pacheco and Alonso Cano, but his composition eventually became freer, and he added more cherubs around the Virgin. The first version (Palma de Mallorca, Col. March), showing the influence of Alonso Cano, was signed *José Antolín* and dated 1658; he later took the name Antolínez in an attempt to make his surname appear more aristocratic. The versions painted after the mid-1660s (e.g. Barnard Castle, Bowes Mus.; Oxford, Ashmolean; Munich, Alte Pin.) are more dynamic. Other than the *Immaculate Conception*, his favourite themes were scenes with the Virgin: the *Annunciation*, *Pentecost* and *Christ and the Virgin in Judgement*, and several with the Magdalene (e.g. *Penitent Magdalene*, 1673; Seville, Mus. B.A.).

Antolínez sometimes painted theatrical works, such as his fine *Esther and Ahasuerus* (Helsingør, Kronborg Slot). Usually, as in the *Crucifixion of St Peter* (1660; London, Dulwich Pict. Gal.), his religious scenes have a landscape background. One of his finest works is the *Apotheosis of St Rosa of Lima* (Budapest, Mus. F.A.), but his most interesting works are those of secular subjects. The conversation piece *Cornelius Lerche and his Friends* (1662; Copenhagen, Stat. Mus. Kst), commissioned by the Danish ambassador in the year he left Madrid, echoes the composition of some paintings by Gerard ter Borch (ii), whom Antolínez knew in Madrid. The Dane is shown preparing for departure, and a dog in the foreground shows Antolínez's naturalistic interest. Two portraits of young girls (both Madrid, Prado) exemplify his attention to the psychology of his sitters. The *Picture Seller* (*c.* 1670; Munich, Alte Pin.) shows his familiarity with Dutch painters and a preoccupation with the treatment of space similar to that of Velázquez, although it is unlikely that this picture portrays his own workshop.

Antolínez also painted mythological subjects, relatively rare in Spanish 17th-century painting. Two charming scenes of the *Education of Bacchus* are in Madrid collections. More important in terms of both subject and composition are the *Death of Lucretia* and *Suicide of Cleopatra*, which belonged to Sebastián Martínez Pérez, a collector from Cadiz and friend of Goya. These are early works, without the 'tinta atizianada' (Palomino) of his later paintings. José Antolínez is thought to have been related to the painter FRANCISCO ANTOLÍNEZ, who may have been his brother or his nephew.

BIBLIOGRAPHY

A. A. Palomino de Castro y Velasco: *Museo pictórico* (1715–24)

D. Angulo Iñiguez: *José Antolínez* (Madrid, 1957)

J. Rogelio Buendía: 'José Antolínez, pintor de mitologias', *Bol. Inst. & Mus. 'Camón Aznar'*, i (1980), pp. 45–57

Carreño de Miranda y la pintura madrileña de su tiempo (exh. cat. by A. E. Pérez Sánchez, Madrid, Prado, 1986), pp. 280–83

E. J. Sullivan: *Baroque Painting in Madrid: The Contribution of Claudio Coello, with a Catalogue Raisonné of his Works* (Columbia, 1986), pp. 22–6

J. ROGELIO BUENDÍA MUÑOZ

Antolini, Giovanni Antonio (*b* Castel Bolognese, Ravenna, 1756; *d* Bologna, 11 March 1841). Italian architect, engineer and theorist. He graduated from the University of Bologna in engineering and architecture. From 1775 to 1796 he was in Rome, where his design for the new sacristy of St Peter's (1775) was admired by Pius VI, although the commission was awarded to Carlo Marchionni. Antolini took part in the scheme to drain the Pontine Marshes (1776–7), but caught malaria and resigned his appointment. Devoting himself to the study and practice of architecture, he became involved in the artistic controversies of the day, including the debate on the use of the Doric order (*see* PIRANESI, GIOVANNI BATTISTA) and the changing attitudes towards the restoration of ancient monuments, his own position becoming progressively more conservative. He published his first important archaeological work on the Temple of Hercules at Cori in 1785 and began his studies on the Temple of Minerva at Assisi. During this period he also produced schemes for palaces, chapels and other buildings for noble foreign clients, including a design for the façade of the palace and court chapel of the Duke of Courland at Mitau (now Jelgava, Latvia). During the French intervention in Italy (1796–1815) Antolini, who sympathized with the revolutionary ideology, was summoned to Faenza (1796), where he designed a Doric triumphal arch to the glory of the French nation (inaugurated 1799; destr.). He planned a number of villas for the local gentry and carried out a series of hydraulic engineering surveys. For his expertise in this field he was invited to Milan (1799) to join the city's water board.

In 1801 Antolini secured the commission for a grandiose urban planning scheme in Milan to celebrate the 'independence' of the Cisalpine Republic, Napoleon's puppet government in Lombardy. Dubbed the Foro

Bonaparte, it was centred on the Castello Sforzesco, which was to be refaced in Doric style to become the centre of an enormous circular piazza (diam. *c.* 570 m) lined by a Doric colonnade, behind which were ground-floor shops with living-quarters above. These were interspersed with 14 civic buildings including a pantheon, museum, theatre, stock exchange, custom-house and baths. A navigable canal was to run round the piazza, 20 m in front of the colonnade, fed from the city's existing internal navigation system. Bridges were to give access to an enormous open space designed for republican celebrations and military parades. The inspiration for the Foro Bonaparte was the ideal city of Chaux (1773–9) as projected by Claude-Nicolas Ledoux on an elliptical plan. Antolini's scheme was submitted to Napoleon in 1801, but was abandoned the following year for lack of funds. It nevertheless greatly influenced those architects who were finally charged with replanning the city. Antolini's project (1806, 1807) for a royal palace to be erected between the Procuratie Vecchie and Procuratie Nuove at Piazza S Marco, Venice, on the site of Jacopo Sansovino's S Geminiano (1557–8; destr. 1807), was torn down shortly after commencement and replaced by a link block (the 'Napoleonic wing') to the designs of Giuseppe Maria Soli. From 1803 to 1815 he taught architecture and hydraulics in Bologna and performed the duties of surveyor to the fabric of various public buildings in Mantua, Bologna and Modena. In 1815 he was obliged for political reasons to move to Milan, where he taught architecture at the Accademia di Brera until his death, his hopes of succeeding to the chair left vacant on the death of Giuseppe Zania (1817) remaining unfulfilled. His style was representative of the Neo-classical taste of the late Roman 18th century, marked by the rationalist and functionalist influence of Francesco Milizia and the utopian outlook of the visionary French architects Etienne-Louis Boullée and Ledoux, although it contrasted with the more imaginative, sometimes eclectic approach of his contemporary GIUSEPPE PISTOCCHI, who produced many schemes to rival those of Antolini.

WRITINGS

L'ordine dorico, ossia, il Tempio d'Ercole nella città di Cori (Rome, 1785; rev. Milan, 2/1828)

Il Tempio di Minerva in Assisi confrontato colle tavole di Andrea Palladio (Milan, 1803, rev. 1828)

Opera d'architettura, ossia, progetto sul foro che doveva eseguirsi in Milano dal professore G. Antolini (Parma, 1806)

Idee elementari di architettura civile per le scuole del disegno (Bologna, 1813)

Osservazioni ed aggiunte ai principii di architettura civile di F. Milizia (Milan, 1817)

Le rovine di Veleja misurate e disegnate, 2 vols (Milan, 1819–22)

'Biografia dell'architetto Giovanni Antonio Antolini, scritta da sè medesimo', *G. Arcad. Sci. Lett. & A.*, xci (1842), pp. 342–9

BIBLIOGRAPHY

DBI

G. Mezzanotte: *Architettura neoclassica in Lombardia* (Naples, 1966), pp. 231–79

C. W. Westfall: 'Antolini's Foro Bonaparte in Milan', *J. Warb. & Court. Inst.*, xxxii (1969), pp. 366–85

F. Bertoni: 'L'architettura a Faenza dalla Repubblica Cispadana alla restaurazione: Giovanni Antonio Antolini e Pietro Tomba', *Giuseppe Pistocchi (1774–1814), architetto giacobino* (exh. cat., ed. E. Godoli and others; Faenza, Pal. Espos., 1974), pp. 61–76

R. Fregna and E. Godoli: 'Una raccolta inedita dei disegni del Foro Bonaparte', *Parametro*, 27 (June, 1974), pp. 4–15

A. Gambuti: 'Giovanni Antonio Antolini e la questione del "dorico"', *Architettura in Emilia Romagna dall'illuminismo alla restaurazione: Faenza, 1974*, pp. 43–54

E. Godoli: 'Progetti per Venezia di Giovanni Antonio Antolini', *Architettura e città in Emilia Romagna dall'illuminismo alla restaurazione: Faenza, 1974*, pp. 81–101

O. Rossi Pinelli: 'Il Foro Bonaparte: Progetto e fallimento di una città degli eguali', *Ric. Stor. A.*, 3 (1976), pp. 43–76

G. Kannès: 'Giovanni Antonio Antolini e l'ambiente milanese: Appunti sul carteggio Diedo Albertolli (1791–1803)', *Martinella Milano*, xxxiii/1 (1979), pp. 4–13

——: 'Il Foro Bonaparte tra l'Antolini e il Canonica: Un progetto di concorso ma non di esecuzione', *Milano Parco Sempione: Spazio pubblico, progetto, architettura, 1796–1980* (exh. cat., ed. M. G. Folli and D. Samsa; Milan, Pal. A., 1980), pp. 106–13

——: 'Un acquarello per il Foro Bonaparte in Milano ed altri inediti di Giovanni Antonio Antolini', *Stor. Città*, vii/2 (1982), pp. 81–8

LUCIO FRANCHINI

Antonakakis. Greek architects. Dimitris Antonakakis (*b* Chania, Crete, 22 Dec 1933) studied at the School of Architecture, National Technical University of Athens (1953–8). He began teaching there in 1959 and retired in 1992. His wife, Suzana (Maria) Antonakakis [née Kolokytha] (*b* Athens, 25 June 1935), also studied at the University (1954–9). In 1965 they co-founded the architectural partnership Atelier 66. Their work is influenced by Aris Konstantinidis's interpretation of vernacular forms through a rigid grid system and modern construction, as seen in the Archaeological Museum of Chios (with Eleni Goussi-Desylla, 1965) and the housing settlement (1969) at Distomon, probably the best example of low-rise, high-density housing in post-war Greece. Here the grid is transformed into a zoning scheme that regulates the allocation of domestic and public activities. Their debt to Dimitris Pikionis is evident in the emphasis given to movement within built space, the creation of path-like networks of spaces and the treatment of the courtyard as a selective collector of activities, as in two vacation houses (1973, 1977) at Oxylithos, Evvoia, as well as in the Archaeological Museum of Chios. They transformed the influences of Konstantinidis and Pikionis into a complex system, one of the best examples of which is the block of flats (1972) at Benaki 118, Athens, where the interior is an adaptation of the vernacular open-air courtyard. The vacation house (1973) at Spata, Attica, is an even clearer expression of the importance of movement. Beginning with the house (1977) at Oxylithos, they moved towards a more fragmented composition of volumes, as seen in a vacation house (1981–5) near Perdhika, Aigina.

BIBLIOGRAPHY

K. Frampton: *Modern Architecture: A Critical History*, World A. (London, 1980, rev. 1985)

K. Frampton, ed.: *Atelier 66: The Architecture of Dimitris and Suzana Antonakakis* (New York, 1985)

ALEXANDER KOUTAMANIS

Antonelli. Italian family of engineers and architects. They were active in Spain and Spanish America in the service of the Spanish Habsburgs from 1559 to 1650. The most prominent member of the family was Juan Bautista Antonelli the elder (*b* Gaeteo, Italy, *c.* 1530; *d* Madrid, 17 March 1588), who settled in Spain from 1559 while working in the employ of Charles V, Holy Roman Emperor. Most of his fortification works were carried out in the coastal south-east of Spain, where several members of his family settled, although he also worked in Oran and particularly in Portugal as a strategist and engineer. Many of his projects were not realized, including the creation of a navigable river network throughout the Iberian peninsula to facilitate the transport of merchandise from the ports to the interior. Several fortification plans for the Magellan Straits also failed to materialize.

Bautista Antonelli (*b* Rimini, 1547; *d* Madrid, 22 Feb 1616), brother of Juan Bautista Antonelli (with whom he is often confused), began working in Spain from 1570, participating in the fortification of Cartagena, Peñíscola and Alicante as well as various sites in Navarre, Catalonia and Portugal. In 1581 he travelled to the Americas for the first time, planning the fortification of the Cape Verde Islands, but soon returned from his main destination, the Magellan Straits, after an unproductive visit. In 1586 he went to Colombia, where he worked on the fortification of Cartagena de Indias, subsequently moving on to Tierra Firme (the provinces of Panama, Darien and Veraguas) and Cuba (*see* CUBA, §III) with the intention of studying how best to defend it against continuous attacks by pirates. On returning to Spain, he submitted a general plan of fortification for all Spain's overseas possessions to Philip II, who accepted it and charged Antonelli with putting his scheme into practice. With this objective he travelled again to the Americas in 1589, settling first in Puerto Rico, then moving on to Santo Domingo and Havana (Cuba), which had become the chief port of Spanish America after the sack of Santo Domingo by Sir Francis Drake in 1586. Here Antonelli began building the fortress of Los Tres Reyes del Morro. Later he went to Mexico and Tierra Firme to write reports on work in progress there to protect communication routes and the transport of merchandise. In San Juan de Ulua (Mexico) and along the Pacific coast, he analysed the problems inherent in shipping products out of Peru. He remained in Cuba until 1593, when he gave up directing the schemes he had in hand, moving on the next year to Cartagena de Indias, Portobelo and Panama, where he proposed various protective measures. In 1599 he returned to Spain to work on the fortification of Gibraltar and Larache. Other members of the Antonelli family who worked as military engineers include his son Juan Bautista Antonelli the younger (*c.* 1585–1649), his nephews CRISTÓBAL DE RODA and Cristóbal Garavelli Antonelli and the latter's son, Juan Bautista Garavelli Torres, who became known as Juan Bautista Antonelli on assuming control of the estate founded by the first Juan Bautista Antonelli.

BIBLIOGRAPHY

D. Angulo: *Bautista Antonelli: Las fortificaciones americanas del siglo XVI* (Madrid, 1942)

J. A. Calderón Quijano: *Fortificaciones de Nueva España* (Seville, 1953)

R. Segre: 'Significación de Cuba en la evolución tipológica de las fortificaciones coloniales de América', *Bol. Inst. Invest. Hist. & Estét.*, 13 (1972)

L. Toro Bariza: 'Juan Bautista Antonelli el Mayor', *Bol. Real Acad. B. Let.*, vii/7 (1979), pp. 41–56

J. M. Zapatero: *Historia de las fortificaciones de Cartagena de Indias* (Madrid, 1980)

J. Porres Martín-Cleto: *Toledo, puerto de Castilla* (Toledo, 1982)

MARIA CONCEPCIÓN GARCÍA SÁIZ

Antonelli, Alessandro (*b* Ghemme, Novara, 14 July 1798; *d* Maggiora, Novara, 18 Aug 1888). Italian architect and urban planner. He was the most prominent Neo-classical 19th-century architect in Piedmont, with a long and prolific career that included designs for houses, churches and major urban planning schemes. He trained at the Accademia di Brera, Milan, and the Politecnico, Turin, qualifying in 1824. Shortly afterwards he won a scholarship to Rome, where he remained until 1831. This long period of Classical studies profoundly influenced his career. One of his first commissions on his return to Piedmont was the completion of the church of S Agapito, Maggiora. Begun in 1817 by Giuseppe Zanoia (1752–1817), the church was completed in 1838; Antonelli's work included the portico and the complex Neo-classical interior, with richly coffered, decorated vaults and a dome on pendentives. His next work was the Santuario del Crocefisso at Boca, near Maggiora. Begun in 1830, the design underwent many revisions and was not completed until 1888. The chapel has an imposing octastyle portico, while the crossing is crowned by a dominating drum constructed externally entirely in brick. The building was slightly modified during its reconstruction after partial collapse in 1907. In 1835 Antonelli began building his own house at Maggiora. The completed villa has a monumental façade, comprising a series of superimposed Doric orders, a motif that became characteristic of his domestic work. At the same time he began his long association with Novara Cathedral, where his first work was a new high altar, with a tetrastyle Corinthian baldacchino, and a richly inlaid altar below.

In 1837 Antonelli began to remodel and enlarge the 16th-century church of S Clemente at Bellinzago, the interior of which anticipated the rebuilt cathedral at Novara. The style is Corinthian, with an elaborate interior including monolithic marble nave columns, rich vaulting and a dome on pendentives. This contrasts with the plain brick exterior, one of Antonelli's most characteristic features, which allowed him to exploit his interest in the structural properties of brickwork. In 1841 he began his own town house on the Corso S Maurizio, Turin, a substantial palazzo in a restrained classical form, with rather flat external modelling, and in the same year he started another major church project, S Gaudenzio, Novara. The early Baroque church lacked a central dome, and Antonelli's development of this extraordinary construction occupied him intermittently for the next 40 years. His first design consisted of a simple dome on a drum, but as his plans developed the design became taller and more complex. There followed a second, then a third scheme, the latter incorporating two superimposed drums with a crowning dome. What was built was based on a fourth version, which had become yet higher, finally rising 122 m from the ground. Structurally, it was surpassed only by the Mole Antonelliana in Turin (see below) and it stretched the capabilities of brickwork perhaps further than had been attempted since Classical times. The lantern was added in 1872–8. His next major scheme was the remodelling and enlarging (1850–64) of the Ospedale Maggiore della Carità at Novara; the scheme was formal and highly repetitive, based around large internal courtyards. During these years he designed a new cathedral (1854) for Novara; building work began at the west end with a noble atrium, surrounded by an imposing colonnade of unfluted Corinthian columns. The portico to the cathedral itself is richer, with fluted columns and fine classical detailing. This part was completed in 1863, when the medieval cathedral was demolished for the new one (completed 1869), in which Antonelli further developed his themes from Bellinzago, notably in the rich, barrel-vaulted nave.

In 1854 Antonelli presented a development plan to Turin's city council. Although he revised it in 1859, it never received formal approval. The city was growing rapidly and in 1861 was declared the capital of united Italy. The essence of the plan was the extension of the city's already rational grid plan of streets as far as the city walls. It was a formal solution, incorporating such urban features as churches within the axial street pattern. Also dating from the 1850s is the Casa Ponzio Vaglia in the Corso Matteotti, Turin, a large apartment block on four storeys above a ground-floor colonnade; the detailing is sparse and rational, a simple repetitive urban form. Only half the block was completed. In the later 1850s Antonelli built the Ospizio degli Orfani at Alessandria and the new church (1856–62) at Borgo Lavezzaro. The church façade has a broad, tetrastyle portico, the tympanum decorated with low reliefs. The elaborate interior has a barrel-vaulted nave, Corinthian columns to the narrow aisles and painted coffers and vaults. Another urban planning scheme followed in 1857 with his proposal to connect the town centre of Novara with its new railway station using paired colonnades, terminating in a great formal piazza, although only one block, at Porta Sempione, was executed. In 1862 he completed his development plan for Ferrara, taking his lead from the grid plan that had formed the basis of Ercole I d'Este's Addizione Ercolea (begun 1492) and extending the pattern further.

In 1863 Antonelli proposed a new cathedral for Alessandria (unexecuted) and in the same year he began his most notable work, the unique building today known as the Mole Antonelliana (see fig.) in the Via Montebello, Turin. Structurally developed from the dome of S Gaudenzio, Novara, the completed project was perhaps even more technically daring. The origins of the building date back to 1860, when the authorities at the Università Israelitica decided to build a large new synagogue. After an unsatisfactory competition, Antonelli was appointed its architect. The extensive vaults and lower storeys, including the main hall, were completed by 1877, when the unfinished structure was bought by the city council, which transformed it into a monument to King Victor-Emanuel II. The great 'dome' (49 m high) was begun in 1878 in the unusual form of four curved planes; in 1880 Antonelli designed the lantern (1881–5) surmounting the dome and in 1884 he designed the spire. The final height of this structure is 167.5 m. After Antonelli died, the work was continued by his son Costanzo Antonelli (1844–1923), an engineer, until 1900, when the pinnacle was finally completed. The interior decoration was executed in 1905–8 by Annibale Rigotti. In the 1930s the tower was strengthened with reinforced concrete, and stabilization continued in the 1950s, although in 1953 a storm destroyed the top 47 m of the pinnacle (rebuilt 1958–61). The Mole occupied much of the last 25 years of Antonelli's life. In 1874 he began the Asilo Infantile at Bellinzago, a simple restrained building with an external Doric order, but with the interior (notably the stairs and corridors) in a minimal classical style, devoid of sculptural detail. His last uncompleted project was a tower for the church at Bellinzago. This represents a reduced version of his great tower at Novara, a simple design with an open, classical bell chamber and above it a tall pinnacle.

Alessandro Antonelli: the Mole Antonelliana, Turin, 1863–1900

Antonelli's productive career incorporated several diverse elements. His urban planning schemes are formal solutions with grand colonnades; his churches, too, are rich, usually Corinthian Neo-classical works. The villas are simpler, usually Doric and often of Palladian derivation. Structural inventiveness, however, was his most remarkable quality. His desire to exploit masonry to its structural limits reached its peak at the Mole and S Gaudenzio, building to heights rarely achieved before. It is a measure of his success that both great structures have since become the symbols of their respective cities. Antonelli represents the survival of Neo-classicism, fused with the scientific spirit of enquiry of the Politecnico and of the new profession of the structural engineer.

WRITINGS

'Tempio israelitico', *A. Italia* (1873)

Ricordo storico nazionale a Vittorio Emanuele II: Relazione sui lavori (Turin, 1881)

BIBLIOGRAPHY

Portoghesi

A. Daverio: *La cupola di S Gaudenzio* (Novara, 1940)

V. Gregotti and A. Rossi: 'L'influenza del romanticismo europeo nell'architettura di Alessandro Antonelli', *Casabella*, ccxiv (1957), pp. 62–81

G. Gavinelli: *Novara e Antonelli* (Novara, 1976)

F. Rosso: *Alessandro Antonelli e la Mole di Torino* (Turin, 1977)

D. Biancolini, ed.: *Il secolo di Antonelli; Novara, 1798–1888* (Novara, 1988)

G. Pacciarotti: 'Itinerario No. 40: Antonelli e Novara', *Domus*, 699 (1988), Supplement, pp. xii–xv

R. Gabetti: *Alessandro Antonelli* (Milan, 1989)

F. Rosso: *Alessandro Antonelli, 1798–1888* (Milan, 1989)

RICHARD J. GOY

Antonello da Messina [Antonello di Giovanni degli Antonii] (*b* Messina, *c.* 1430; *d* Messina, between 14 and 25 Feb 1479). Italian painter. He was the greatest Sicilian artist of the 15th century and the only one to achieve international renown. His work combines Italianate concerns for form, structure and measured space with a south Netherlandish interest in the detailed depiction of surface and texture. Antonello is traditionally credited with the introduction into Italian art of the systematic use of oil glazing, developed in northern Europe by Jan van Eyck. His visit to Venice in 1475–6 enabled the technique to be disseminated there, and this had a crucial effect on the art of Giovanni Bellini and on late 15th-century Venetian painting in general. Antonello painted fashionable portraits as well as religious works, and his reputation among contemporaries must have been largely based on his skills in this field: he was instrumental in establishing a new, vital type of portraiture in Italy, again based on south Netherlandish models. He also played an important role in the development of the Venetian Renaissance altarpiece. Antonello established a workshop in Messina, in which his son JACOBELLO D'ANTONIO and his nephews Antonio and Pietro DE SALIBA and SALVO D'ANTONIO participated. In the work of these *Antonelleschi*, the provincial inheritance of his art can be seen.

1. Life and work. 2. Working methods and technique.

1. LIFE AND WORK.

(i) Training and early years, before *c.* 1465. (ii) Middle years, *c.* 1465–75. (iii) Trip to Venice, 1475–6. (iv) Last years: Sicily, 1476–9.

(i) Training and early years, before c. *1465.* Antonello was one of the four children of a stone mason of Messina. According to Vasari, who is not always reliable, he died at the age of 49. His death certainly occurred in 1479, between 14 February (when he made his will) and 25 February (when his son Jacobello renewed workshop contracts in his own name), and the fact that he was survived by both his parents, for whom he made provision in his will, might support the idea that he was then relatively young; a birthdate of *c.* 1430 is therefore usually accepted.

Antonello is first documented in 1457, when he was running his own workshop in Messina, but he appears to have received training in Naples: a letter dated 1524 from Pietro Summonte in Naples to Marcantonio Michiel in Venice describing the history of Venetian painting mentions that Antonello was the pupil of NICCOLÒ COLANTONIO, who (according to Summonte) had received instruction in the methods of Netherlandish painting at the court of King René I of Naples. This would seem to explain the south Netherlandish qualities of Antonello's style. It is possible, however, that Antonello received further instruction elsewhere: Wright (1980) argued that both stylistically and technically Colantonio's painting is almost entirely French, rather than Netherlandish, in character, most closely resembling the work of the Master of the Aix Annunciation. Moreover, only Antonello's very early *Crucifixion* (Bucharest, N. Mus. A.) resembles in technique the work of his supposed teacher; his other early works are much closer to finely glazed Netherlandish models. Although Antonello could have become familiar with Netherlandish paintings in Naples (there were a number of examples in collections there, including that of Alfonso I, who owned works by Jan van Eyck and Rogier van der Weyden), the Eyckian glazing technique was far too complex to be learnt by observation alone, and he may have travelled to the Netherlands for further study, an event perhaps underlying Vasari's improbable assertion that he was the direct pupil of Jan van Eyck, who had died in 1441. The hypothesis that Antonello received training in Milan under Petrus Christus is based only on the ambiguous appearance of the names 'Piero de Bruges' and 'Antonello de Sicillia' in the ducal payment records of 1456 under *provissionati* (those in receipt of a stipend), in the company of crossbowmen. The training under Colantonio would probably have taken place *c.* 1443–50, with the Bucharest *Crucifixion* presumably dating from the end of this period, *c.* 1450–53, before Antonello's postulated second phase of instruction.

A number of documents provide an outline of Antonello's activities from 1457 to 1465, but no dated works survive from these years. On 5 March 1457 he signed a contract to produce a *gonfalone* (untraced) for the confraternity of S Michele dei Gerbini in Reggio Calabria, and in April he was dealing with an assistant who had broken the terms of his contract. He subsequently left Sicily for the mainland, taking his family and his servants with him, for in January 1460 his father hired a brigantine to transport them back to Messina from Amantea on the Calabrian coast. The removal of his household suggests a prolonged absence, and conjectured destinations have included Calabria (the source of the *gonfalone* commission) and Rome (where Antonello could have seen works by Piero della Francesca, crucial to the formation of his mature style); apparent knowledge of the work of Enguerrand Quarton has also suggested contact with Provençal painting during this period. In January 1461 Antonello was re-established in Messina and had taken his brother Giordano di Giovanni (*fl* 1461–88) as an apprentice. From then until 1465 records survive of a number of contracts and payments, but the works to which they refer are untraced.

Paintings attributed to Antonello from this period include the finely glazed but badly damaged *Penitent St Jerome*, the fragment of the *Hospitality of Abraham* (both Reggio Calabria, Mus. N.) and *St Jerome in his Study* (London, N.G.; see fig. 1). The last is often thought to be a mature work of *c.* 1475, but its proximity in style, technique and iconography to Eyckian painting, which influenced Antonello in its purest form in his early career, places it more happily in the period before 1465. Its empirical method of perspective also suggests an early date; in his later works Antonello adopted the mathematically controlled system of Italian origin. The painting was first recorded by Michiel in the house of Antonio Pasqualino in Venice in 1529; significantly, it was then commonly believed to be by Jan van Eyck or Hans Memling, demonstrating its thoroughly Netherlandish character. Michiel, however, personally favoured an attribution to Antonello because the face was finished *alla italiana* (presumably a reference to the profile view). According to Puppi, Antonello may have taken the painting to Venice in 1475 as an example of his work. The composition is probably at least partly based on the wing

1. Antonello da Messina: *St Jerome in his Study*, oil on panel, 460×365 mm, *c.* 1460–65 (London, National Gallery)

of Jan van Eyck's Lomellini Triptych, which depicted *St Jerome in his Library* (untraced) and which, according to Bartolomeo Facio (*De viris illustribus*, 1456), was given to Alfonso I by Battista Lomellini in 1444; it apparently inspired a number of representations of the saint, of which the version attributed to Colantonio is the earliest (Naples, Capodimonte). Jolly demonstrated that Antonello's picture incorporated an extensive use of disguised symbolism, indicating the artist's understanding of complex Netherlandish programmes.

Further attributions to Antonello for the years up to *c.* 1465 include the *Virgin Annunciate* (Como, Mus. Civ. Stor. Garibaldi), the *Virgin Reading* (Venice, Forti priv. col.) and the Salting *Virgin and Child* (London, N.G.), which are often grouped with the *St Rosalie* (Baltimore, MD, Walters A.G.). Only the badly rubbed *St Rosalie* approaches the sensitivity and refinement of Antonello's work, however, in some respects resembling the Bucharest *Crucifixion.* The rest of this group can be better designated as by various *anonimi*, perhaps working in Antonello's circle and influenced particularly by Hispanic models popular in both Naples and Sicily at this time. The *St Zosimo* (Syracuse Cathedral, Treasury) is also often thought to be an early work, but it is more likely to be by a follower at a later date, and it can be associated by both scale and provenance with the *Virgin of the Uccelluzzo*, which has been attributed to various members of Antonello's workshop.

(ii) Middle years, c. *1465–75.* Antonello's mature style and character as an artist were formed in this period, from which some signed and dated works survive, including a number of portraits. The absence of documentary references to him in Sicily between 1465 and 1471 has led to speculation that he travelled abroad, possibly to Venice, which might explain some otherwise puzzling aspects of his career: his possible knowledge of Giovanni Bellini's *St Vincenzo Ferrer* altarpiece (Venice, SS Giovanni e Paolo) in the *St Gregory* polyptych of 1473, and the award of the important Venetian commission for the S Cassiano Altarpiece in 1475 to an apparently unknown foreigner (*see* §(iii) below).

Antonello's first signed and dated work may be the *Salvator mundi* (London, N.G.). It bears the date 1465, but this is qualified by the accompanying inscription *viije Indi* (8th indiction), which could refer to either 1460 or 1475 but not 1465 (the 13th indiction). Previtali favoured the later date (1475), but the contradiction is more reasonably explained by an error in calculation or a calligraphic slip, writing *viije* instead of *xiije* (13th). The use of a *cartellino* (label) for the inscription introduces a device derived from Netherlandish *trompe l'oeil* effects, which Antonello was to use throughout his later career to sign his works. It appears to be fixed to the front of the parapet behind which the figure is set, and its bottom edge curls forwards, rather wittily suggesting a projection from the picture plane into real space.

The frontal depiction of the bust of Christ suggests a northern source, possibly Petrus Christus's 'figure of Christ *in maiestate*', described in Summonte's letter and at that time in the Sannazzaro collection in Naples. The pose could also indicate knowledge of versions of the Christ Blessing type, which were ultimately derived from the central panel of Rogier van der Weyden's Braque Triptych (Paris, Louvre) of the early 1450s. An Italianate character is imposed on this essentially Netherlandish format, however, by the simplified, geometric forms (the fingers are rendered as cylinders lit from above and to the left) and by the placing of the blessing hand directly in front of the bust in strong foreshortening. This establishes clear spatial relationships in the picture and also suggests that Antonello was aware of the work of Piero della Francesca. He was evidently experimenting here: pentiments, seen in detail under infra-red light, show that Christ's neckline was originally higher and his blessing hand more vertical and less emphatically volumetric. A number of versions of the *Ecce homo* (New York, Met.; Genoa, Pal. Spinola) can be seen as developments of the Christ Blessing model, culminating in the signed picture of 1473 (Piacenza, Coll. Alberoni), Antonello's first dated work after the Sicilian documents begin again in 1471 when he appears to have been in Noto.

The signed and dated altarpiece of the *Virgin and Child with SS Gregory and Benedict* (1473; Messina, Mus. Reg.) has a badly damaged surface with some clumsy repainting. The missing central panel from the upper register almost certainly depicted a *Pietà*. A unified space is created in the three main panels—the *Virgin and Child*, *St Gregory* and *St Benedict*—by the extension of the cast shadows and the Virgin's raised dais behind the (lost) frame. The polyptych format was rare in southern Italy at this date, but it was fairly common in the north; whether or not Antonello knew Bellini's *St Vincenzo Ferrer* altarpiece, the *St Gregory* polyptych shows his own attempts, on a monumental scale, to fuse the surface effects of Netherlandish painting with the expression of forms as geometric volumes. This tendency is usually attributed to an increased awareness of the work of Piero della Francesca, and parallels have been drawn between the figures of *SS Gregory and Benedict* and the standing saints from Piero's *St Augustine* altarpiece (Lisbon, Mus. Gulbenkian; London, N.G.; Milan, Mus. Poldi Pezzoli; New York, Frick). An interest in illusionistic effects is demonstrated by the way in which the feet of the standing saints and the rosary on the semicircular projection of the dais overlap the edge of the platform to which the *cartellino* is attached. The work is lit from the left, but the viewpoint is slightly to the right of centre, creating a pleasing and subtle counterpoise.

The fine but badly damaged *Annunciation* (1474; Syracuse, Pal. Bellomo) shows a similar combination of Netherlandish and Italianate concerns. The setting, a domestic interior that opens on to an adjoining room on the right, with shuttered windows through which a landscape can be seen, is reminiscent of the work of the Master of Flémalle and Petrus Christus, but the trabeated colonnade in the foreground is Italian; the monumental column separating Gabriel from the Virgin seems to recall Piero della Francesca's frescoed *Annunciation* in S Francesco, Arezzo.

In this period Antonello also made significant innovations in portraiture. The 12 surviving examples, all of male sitters, constitute a radical departure for the genre in Italy.

2. Antonello da Messina: *Virgin and Child with SS Nicholas of Bari and Mary Magdalene, Ursula and Dominic* (detail), fragment of the S Cassiano Altarpiece, oil on panel, w. 1.33 m, 1475 (Vienna, Kunsthistorisches Museum)

Antonello understood not only the bone structure of the head but its relationship to the overlying muscles and sinews, and he could represent nuances of expression by accurately depicting the play of muscles across cheeks and jaws and around the eyes and mouth. His mastery of oil glazing also enabled him to model the heads continuously, imperceptibly blending light and shade. The portrait type that he evolved was again based on south Netherlandish models. The sitters are shown in three-quarter view and bust length, with the arms excluded. They face into the light, which falls diagonally from the left illuminating the right cheek and modelling the nearside of the face with chiaroscuro. They are depicted simply, wearing unostentatious contemporary dress, with no emblems or symbols to detract from the direct communication with the spectator in their steady gaze.

The dating of Antonello's portraits is hindered by their condition. The so-called *Pirate of Lipari* (Cefalù, Mus. Mandralisca) is generally thought to be the earliest, probably dating from the later 1460s. It establishes the general character of his portrait style, although the handling is more linear than in his later works. Nonetheless, the individuality of the sitter is strongly conveyed, in his twinkling eyes and half-smiling lips. Slightly later portraits probably include two of unknown male sitters (Pavia, Pin. Malaspina; Madrid, Mus. Thyssen-Bornemisza) and the Altman *Portrait of a Young Man* (New York, Met.). The last shows a softness of touch and subtlety of expression comparable with the *Virgin Annunciate* from the *St Gregory* altarpiece of 1473, suggesting a date of *c.* 1472–3. The signed and dated *Portrait of a Youth* (1474; Berlin, Gemäldegal.) shows a greater monumentality and assurance than the earlier examples. The carefully modulated tonal variations in the flesh create a powerfully defined sense of form, while the fully modelled pleats on the tunic lend robustness to the sitter, who has a direct gaze and slightly parted lips, subtly animating the face. This first dated portrait may be a little later than the expressive *Portrait of a Man* (Rome, Gal. Borghese), which is slightly more linear and tentative in handling. Although damaged and retouched, the Johnson *Portrait of a Man* (Philadelphia, PA, Mus. A.) shows signs of having been a work of great tonal richness. Like the Berlin portrait, to which it must be closely related in date, the fully modelled head and bust give a powerful sense of volume. A slightly chaotic personality is sympathetically evoked by the bemused expression, the wispy hair disarrayed by the pressure of the hatband, the doublet, which falls open to reveal a splendid fur lining, and the loosened, escaping shirt-tie. The *Portrait of a Man in a Red Cap* (London, N.G.) is similar in character but slightly more awkward in handling and must also date from *c.* 1473–4. On the back of the panel an early 18th-century inscription records a lost parapet and *cartellino*; it was thought to be a self-portrait, but the owner may have mistaken the artist's signature for a title.

(iii) Trip to Venice, 1475–6. Antonello arrived in Venice between November 1474, the contracted delivery date of the Syracuse *Annunciation*, and August 1475, when he received the commission for the S Cassiano Altarpiece. His conjectured earlier visit to Venice may have led to this

commission, but it is also possible that the patron Pietro Bon, who was elected Venetian consul to Tunisia in 1469, may have visited Messina on his way to North Africa and initiated the invitation to the artist there (Puppi).

Only fragments survive from the S Cassiano Altarpiece (Vienna, Ksthist. Mus.; see fig. 2), the *Virgin and Child* and four of the attendant saints, who are truncated at the waist—*SS Nicholas of Bari and Mary Magdalene, Ursula and Dominic.* Wilde proposed a reconstruction of the main figure group with the help of copies by David Teniers (ii) of fragments now lost (e.g. Princeton U., NJ, A. Mus.; Vienna, Ksthist. Mus.), as well as engravings made from these copies for his *Theatrum pictoricum* of 1658. The *Virgin and Child* were enthroned and raised above the surrounding saints in the interior of a building, and all were seen from a low viewpoint. The details of the architecture were unresolved, but Robertson indicated that the light source must have been within the choir and proposed a curved rather than a windowless, square-ended setting. Interest in the architectural background is particularly keen because it is debated whether this type of altarpiece, which was to become standard in Venetian painting in the last quarter of the 15th century, was introduced by Antonello, or whether he adopted the form from Giovanni Bellini, integrating with it his own understanding of the work of Piero della Francesca.

Antonello's portraits had an important influence on Venetian painters, particularly Bellini and Alvise Vivarini. Michiel praised two examples (untraced), said to be of the collectors Michele Vianello and Alvise Pasqualino, which were in the collection of Antonio Pasqualino in Venice in 1532, commenting on their 'great power and vivacity, especially in the eyes'. Two surviving portraits were painted during these years in Venice: the *Portrait of a Man*, known as *The Condottiere* (Paris, Louvre; see fig. 3), of 1475 and the Trivulzio *Portrait of a Man* (Turin, Mus. Civ. A. Ant.) of 1476. They demonstrate Antonello at the height of his powers as a portraitist and show compelling psychological power of expression.

Antonello's concern with volume and structure is combined with a technical virtuosity and an apparently renewed enthusiasm for the details of surface and texture, seen also in the exquisite little *Crucifixion* (1475; Antwerp, Kon. Mus. S. Kst.). The muscular tension across the cheek and jaw of the Condottiere, the slight pull of the flesh around the scar on his upper lip and the sensuous suggestion of moisture on his full lower lip are acutely observed. The Trivulzio portrait, sometimes thought to depict Pietro Bon, shows a similar immediacy in such details as the softly modelled, sagging jawline, the slightly hooded eyelids and unruly eyebrows.

The *St Sebastian* (Dresden, Gemäldegal. Alte Meister) is Antonello's most essentially Italianate work and represents the culmination of his attempts to integrate the figure in an architectural background. The Venetian square is carefully defined by the surrounding buildings, and courtiers and courtesans, merchants, churchmen, a mother and a soldier go about their daily lives apparently unaffected by the monumental vision of the martyred saint in the foreground. Antonello may have known Bellini's *Coronation of the Virgin* (Pesaro, Mus. Civ.) when he conceived the architectural setting, but it is equally likely

3. Antonello da Messina: *Portrait of a Man*, known as *The Condottiere*, oil on panel, 350×280 mm, 1475 (Paris, Musée du Louvre)

that both artists were independently inspired by Piero della Francesca, who may have created this type of composition (Longhi, 1914). Antonello must also have known Mantegna's versions of the theme (Paris, Louvre; Vienna, Ksthist. Mus.), and his handling of the setting may point to knowledge of Mantegna's frescoed *Martyrdom of St Christopher* in the Eremitani, Padua.

In 1581 Francesco Sansovino recorded a *St Christopher* by Antonello and a *St Sebastian* by Pino da Messina flanking a wooden sculpture of *St Roch* in S Giuliano, Venice. However, he may have accidentally transposed the names of the painters: the *St Sebastian* was probably this work by Antonello, while the *St Christopher* (untraced) may have been by Pino, probably Antonello's son Jacobello.

(iv) Last years: Sicily, 1476–9. Antonello was still in Venice in March 1476, completing the S Cassiano commission, when Gian Galeazzo Sforza, Duke of Milan (*reg* 1476–94), contacted Pietro Bon through his agent in Venice about the possibility of acquiring Antonello's services. The agent praised a painting, presumably a portrait, for its figure described as *cavata dal naturale.* It is not known whether Antonello went to Milan. By September 1476 he is documented back in Messina in connection with his daughter's dowry. Very few works are recorded in these final years: a commission for a *gonfalone* (June 1477), a record of a gift of barley and wheat in compensation for work done in Catania (October 1477) and a commission for a 'banner of red silk' for Ruggero de Luca di Randazzo (November 1478), all of which are untraced. Paolini (1979) proposed that the discrepancy between the numerous paintings attributed to Antonello's Venetian period and the few to his final years was due to a return trip to Venice

between October 1477 and November 1478, but there is no firm evidence for this.

A few works can, however, be attributed to Antonello's last years. The small *Crucifixion* (London, N.G.; see fig. 4) has a dated *cartellino* with an illegible final cipher. It is sometimes placed with the Antwerp *Crucifixion* of 1475, but the simple geometry of the composition and the eloquence of its controlled pathos suggest that it is the result of more mature reflection: it may belong to 1477. The *Virgin Annunciate* (Palermo, Gal. Reg. Sicilia) is often placed in the period before Antonello went to Venice, *c.* 1474, and compared with the Syracuse *Annunciation* and the Piacenza *Christ Blessing*, but the more confident and almost geometrically conceived depiction of the Virgin is closer to the monumental form of the *St Sebastian*, making a post-Venetian date more likely.

The *Portrait of a Man Set against a Landscape* (Berlin, Gemäldegal.) probably dates from 1478, because it can be associated with a work bearing that date seen by Zanetti in the Vitturi collection in the late 18th century. The landscape background, unique in Antonello's portraiture, is more schematic than his other landscapes (e.g. the Syracuse *Annunciation*), and Longhi (1953) suggested that it was a later addition, like the inscription beneath. The bust was evidently narrowed during the course of execution to allow for the inclusion of the landscape, however, and the stratification of the painting along the left-hand edge of the panel reveals that the green of the landscape and the blue of the sky are laid directly on to the whitish priming, so they must belong to the original conception (Wright, 1980). Whether or not the landscape was executed by Antonello, its inclusion perhaps reflects knowledge of the work of Hans Memling, whose painting was known in Italy by *c.* 1470.

4. Antonello da Messina: *Crucifixion*, oil on panel, 412×247 mm, 1475 or 1477 (London, National Gallery)

In this period Antonello's son Jacobello seems to have worked as his principal assistant. Previtali convincingly suggested that a number of works from Antonello's last years, such as the *Pietà* (Madrid, Prado) and the Benson-Mackay *Virgin and Child* (Washington, DC, N.G.A.), were collaborations between father and son; other works, for example the *Virgin and Child* (Bergamo, Gal. Accad. Carrara), were probably planned by Antonello but executed by Jacobello after his father's death. In the last, Jacobello paid final and fitting tribute to his father, signing himself 'the son of Antonello, a painter of no human kind'.

2. Working methods and technique. Antonello's assimilation of south Netherlandish techniques is best seen in such early works as the *Salvator mundi* (?1465; London, N.G.), which is almost entirely composed of very thin translucent layers of paint and glazes, with delicate and refined underdrawing. This technique, which closely resembles that of Jan van Eyck's portrait of a *Man in a Red Chaperon* (1433; London, N.G.; *see* Eyck, van, (2), fig. 2), enabled the artist to create subtle surface effects and to achieve continuity of modelling, and it contrasts with Colantonio's thicker, more opaque use of paint. It can also be seen in the central part of the London *St Jerome in his Study* and in the Berlin *Portrait of a Young Man* (1474), where the underpaint seems to have been applied in a thin scumble with feathery brushstrokes, again close to van Eyck's method. Nervous hatching strokes are particularly noticeable in Antonello's work. In subsequent paintings, however, he seems to have simplified the layer structure to produce work that was adequate to his needs but less time consuming. Only briefly in Venice, in 1475, perhaps freshly inspired by south Netherlandish paintings, did he return to the more complex technique of the *Salvator mundi*, resulting in such works as the Louvre *Condottiere.*

A drawing (London, BM) with studies for an altarpiece of the Virgin and Child (with sketches of individuals, animals and limbs, including a torso and legs, on the *verso*) may possibly be attributed to Antonello's workshop; it apparently conflates two works by Petrus Christus, the artist whom it would appear he is most likely to have known: the *Annunciation* (1452; Berlin, Gemäldegal.) and the *Virgin and Child* (*c.* 1450–60; Kansas City, MO, Nelson–Atkins Mus. A.).

BIBLIOGRAPHY

DBI; Thieme–Becker

B. Facio: *De viribus illustribus* (1456); ed. L. Mehus (Florence, 1745)

M. Michiel: *Notizia d'opere di disegno nella prima metà del secolo XVI* (MS.; 1524–43); ed. J. Morelli (Bassano, 1880; rev. Bologna, 1884)

G. Vasari: *Vite* (1550, rev. 2/1568); ed. G. Milanesi (1878–85), ii, pp. 563–89

F. Sansovino: *Venetia città nobilissima et singolare* (Venice, 1581)

G. Di Marzo: *Di Antonello da Messina e dei suoi congiunti* (Palermo, 1903/*R* 1983)
R. Longhi: 'Piero della Francesca e lo sviluppo della pittura veneziana', *L'Arte*, xvii (1914), pp. 189–221; repr. in *Opere complete di Roberto Longhi*, i (Florence, 1961), pp. 61–106
F. Nicolini: *L'arte napoletana del rinascimento e la lettera di Pietro Summonte a Marcantonio Michiel* (Naples, 1925), pp. 157–75
J. Wilde: 'Die *Pala di San Cassiano* von Antonello da Messina: Ein Rekonstruktionsversuch', *Jb. Ksthist. Samml. Wien*, n.s., iii (1929), pp. 57–72
J. Lauts: *Antonello da Messina* (Vienna, 1940)
S. Bottari: *Antonello da Messina* (Messina and Milan, 1953) [bibliog.]
G. Carandente: 'I restauri compiuti dall'Istituto Centrale del Restauro per la mostra di Antonello da Messina e del quattrocento siciliano', *Boll. Ist. Cent. Rest.*, 14–15 (1953), pp. 67–88
R. Longhi: 'Frammento siciliano', *Paragone*, xlvii (1953), pp. 3–44; repr. in *Opere complete di Roberto Longhi*, viii/1 (Florence, 1975), pp. 143–77
Antonello da Messina e la pittura del '400 in Sicilia (exh. cat., ed. G. Vigni and G. Carandente; Messina, Pal. Com., 1953); rev. by S. Bottari in *A. Ven.*, vii (1953), pp. 189–92; M. Davies in *Burl. Mag.*, xcv (1953), pp. 207–8; R. Longhi in *Paragone*, iv/47 (1953), pp. 3–44 and repr. in *Opere complete di Roberto Longhi*, viii/1 (Florence, 1975), pp. 143–77
M. Bernardi: *Antonello in Sicilia* (Turin, 1957)
S. Bottari: *Arte in Sicilia* (Messina and Florence, 1962)
R. Causa: *Antonello da Messina*, Maestri Colore (Milan, 1964)
G. Consoli: 'Ancora sull'Antonello de Sicilia: Precisazioni su alcuni documenti sforzeschi', *A. Lombarda*, xxi (1967), pp. 109–12
G. Robertson: 'The Architectural Setting of Antonello da Messina's San Cassiano Altarpiece', *Studies in Late Medieval and Renaissance Painting in Honour of Millard Meiss* (Oxford, 1977), pp. 368–72
M. Lucco: 'Due problemi antonelliani', *Antol. B.A.*, 9–12 (1979), pp. 27–33
M. G. Paolini: 'Antonello e la sua scuola', *Stor. Sicilia*, v (1979), pp. 3–61
——: 'Problemi antonelliani: I rapporti con la pittura fiamminga', *Stor. A.* (1980), pp. 151–84
G. Previtali: 'Da Antonello da Messina a Jacopo di Antonello', *Prospettiva*, xx (1980), pp. 27–34; xxi (1980), pp. 45–57
J. Wright: 'Antonello da Messina: The Origins of his Style and Technique', *A. Hist.*, iii (1980), pp. 41–60
S. Tramontana: *Antonello e la sua città* (Palermo, 1981)
Antonello da Messina (exh. cat., ed. A. Marabottini and F. Sricchia Santoro; Messina, Mus. Reg., 1981) [contains documents]
Atti del convegno di studi. Antonello da Messina: Messina, 1981 [incl. articles by M. Muraro, L. Puppi and J. Wright]
L. Castelfranchi-Vegas: *Italia e Fiandra nella pittura del '400* (Milan, 1983)
P. Howell Jolly: 'Antonello da Messina's *St Jerome in his Study*: An Iconographic Analysis', *A. Bull.*, xlv (1983), pp. 238–53
E. Battisti: *Antonello: Il teatro sacro, gli spazi, la donna* (Rome, 1985)
F. Sricchia Santoro: *Antonello e l'Europa* (Milan, 1986) [excellent pls and full bibliog.]
P. Humfrey: 'Competitive Devotions: The Venetian *Scuole piccole* as Donors of Altarpieces in the Years around 1500', *A. Bull.*, lxx (1988), pp. 401–23
J. Wright: 'Antonello in formazione: Un riesame della *Crocifissione* di Bucarest', *A. Ven.*, xlv (1994), pp. 21–31

JOANNE WRIGHT

Antonescu, Petre (*b* Rîmnicu Sărat, Brăila, 29 June 1873; *d* Bucharest, 22 April 1965). Romanian architect and teacher. He studied at the Ecole des Beaux-Arts, Paris, gaining a diploma in 1899. In 1900 he became a professor of history of architecture at the High School (later Academy) of Architecture, Bucharest. He was influenced by ION MINCU, whose principles of 'neo-Romanian' architecture he adopted and considerably developed, becoming, after Mincu, the best-known proponent of this national style. Initially his use of the 'neo-Romanian' vocabulary verged on the eclectic, with elements drawn from classicist and turn-of-the-century forms, as at the Kretzulescu Palace (1903; now headquarters of the UNESCO Centre for Higher Education), Bucharest, and the Casino and Palas Hotel (1903), Sinaia. At the end of World War I he became Rector of the High School of Architecture, and about this time he began experimenting in a style drawn from modern rationalist concepts, favouring reinforced concrete structures, but with Neo-classical decorative elements, for example in the University Building (1933–5; now the Law Faculty) and the Nicolae Iorga Institute of History (1939), both in Bucharest.

His restoration (1948) of his own Ministry of Construction Building (1910), Bucharest, which then became the Bucharest Municipal Council Building, demonstrated the possibilities of the 'neo-Romanian' style as a potent source of constructive solutions, particularly for decorative details of façades on a monumental scale. He adapted the style not only to projects for housing and leisure but also to official buildings. Typically the effects were concentrated in verandahs, loggias, highly protruding decorative mouldings, rhythmically alternating horizontal façades and decorative cornices in contrasting materials. He was also the first architect to adapt the style successfully to the requirements of multi-storey, multi-purpose urban buildings, often with shop premises at ground-floor and basement level, bow windows on many of the storeys and traditionally ornamented consoles. In 1944 he became a member of the Romanian Academy.

WRITINGS

Clădiri, construcţii, proiecte şi studii [Houses, constructions, projects and studies] (Bucharest, 1963)

BIBLIOGRAPHY

G. Ionescu: *Arhitectura pe teritoriul României de-a lungul veacurilor* [Architecture in Romania through the centuries] (Bucharest, 1982), pp. 554, 568, 580, 593

CODRUŢA CRUCEANU

Antoniazzo Romano [Antonio di Benedetto Aquilio] (*b* before 1452; *d* between 15 April 1508 and 1512). Italian painter. He was the leading painter of the Roman school during the 15th century. His first recorded commission dates from 1461 when he made a replica (untraced) of the miraculous *Virgin and Child of St Luke* in S Maria Maggiore, Rome, for Alessandro Sforza, Lord of Pesaro; by 1464 he was working for the papal court. Antoniazzo was influenced at first by the decorative manner of Benozzo signed and dated Gozzoli and by the local painters of Lazio. The central figures in his early signed and dated triptych of the *Virgin and Child with Saints* (1464; Rieti, Mus. Civ.) appear animated but stiff and artificially arranged. By the 1470s he had fully mastered the representation of three-dimensional form, stimulated by his contact with Melozzo da Forlì and Florentine artists. The Umbrian painters Perugino and Bernardino Pinturicchio, who were working in Rome, also influenced Antoniazzo; his figures acquired gentle expressions and their garments were ornamented with decorative patterns. Nevertheless, medieval features survived right into his later works. The fresco of the *Virgin and Child Enthroned* (*c.* 1470; Rome, S Maria della Consolazione) shows attention to the naturalism of form but also retains the gold background befitting a miraculous image. The signed triptych of the *Virgin and Child with SS Peter and Paul and a Donor* (*c.* 1474–9; Fondi, S Pietro) demonstrates Antoniazzo's skill as a portrait painter. The donor (probably Onorato II Gaetani, Lord of Fondi) is shown on a diminutive scale compared to the Virgin and saints, yet his features are striking. Antoniazzo was one of the three founders of the Compagnia di S Luca, the guild of painters in Rome, and signed the statutes in 1478. He participated in the fresco decoration of the Biblioteca Latina (now Biblioteca Apostolica) in the Vatican Palace with Domenico Ghirlandaio in 1475 and with Melozzo da Forlì in 1480–81.

Antoniazzo's reputation and production increased during the 1480s. The autograph painting of the *Virgin and Child with St John and Angels* (*c.* 1480; Cambridge, MA, Fogg) shows his ability to simulate the restrained emotion and design of an icon. In the signed *Virgin and Child with SS Paul and Francis* (?late 1480s; Rome, Pal. Barberini) he continued the medieval tradition of using a gold background. In 1491 he accepted a commission to produce a fresco cycle at the Castello Orsini (now Odescalchi) in Bracciano. Finished by 1493, this is his only known secular work. Part of the scheme consists of two scenes from the life of the patron, Gentil Virginio Orsini (now detached, but in the same castle). Of his numerous frescoes for chapels in the major Roman churches, the few surviving include the *Legend of the True Cross* in Santa Croce in Gerusalemme (after 1491; *in situ*) and those for S Pietro in Montorio (*c.* 1495; *in situ*). In his later years Antoniazzo varied his treatment of traditional themes. The signed and dated *Virgin Enthroned* (1494; Paris, Louvre) exhibits a naturalism and solidity of form suggestive of the High Renaissance. His authenticated works from the late 1490s are sparse. His last known paintings were commissioned in 1501, although he painted a banner (untraced) for a confraternity in Rieti in 1505. On 25 March and 15 April 1508 he dictated a will and codicil, but evidence of his death does not appear until 1512.

Apart from a brief absence in 1471–4, Antoniazzo lived in Rome throughout his career, though extant altarpieces show that he sometimes worked in outlying areas such as Velletri and Capua. Documents for fresco commissions provide evidence that he supervised the most prolific workshop in Rome at the time. It originated *c.* 1470, the principal members being the painter's relatives: his brother Nardo (*fl* 1452–78), his nephew Evangelista (*fl* 1480–1524) and others. During Antoniazzo's later years his assistants took over the execution of major projects. His school, including his eldest son, Marcantonio (*fl* 1505–21), and his second son, Bernardo (*fl* 1508–49), remained active after his death, primarily in Rome, though Marcantonio worked in Rieti. Various works have been associated with anonymous masters from his school, such as the Master of the Liverpool Madonna, the Master of the Avignon Altarpiece and, more recently, the Master of Tivoli. Relatively few frescoes can be attributed to Antoniazzo's hand, while the prevalence of workshop pieces has meant that his oeuvre is often associated with paintings of inferior quality. This problem is further compounded by the fact that Antoniazzo frequently collaborated with other artists. Nevertheless, he did successfully manage to forge a personal style, which combines the innovative with the archaic.

BIBLIOGRAPHY

R. van Marle: *Italian Schools* (1923–38), xv, pp. 244–304
F. Negri Arnoldi: 'Madonne giovanili di Antoniazzo Romano', *Commentari*, xv (1964), pp. 202–12
——: 'Maturità di Antoniazzo', *Commentari*, xvi (1965), pp. 225–44
V. Golzio and G. Zander: *L'arte in Roma nel secolo XV* (Bologna, 1968), pp. 275–85
G. Noehles: *Antoniazzo Romano: Studien zur Quattrocento Malerei in Rom* (diss., Münster, Westfäl. Wilhelms-U., 1973)
G. Hedberg: *Antoniazzo and his School* (diss., New York U., Inst. F.A., 1980)
A. Cavallaro: 'Antoniazzo Romano e le confraternite del quattrocento', *Ric. Stor. Relig. Roma*, v (1984), pp. 335–65
E. Howe: 'Antoniazzo and a Madonna of Santa Maria Maggiore', *Burl. Mag.*, cxxvi (1984), pp. 417–19
F. Floccia: 'Ancora un contributo, e un'ipotesi, per Antoniazzo Romano', *Stor. A.*, iii (1985), pp. 15–21
A. Cavallaro: *Antoniazzo Romano e gli Antoniazzeschi* (Udine, 1992)
A. Paolucci: *Antoniazzo Romano (1430/1435–1508/1512)* (Florence, 1992)

EUNICE D. HOWE

Antoninus Pius [before adoption, Titus Aurelius Fulvus Boionius Arrius Antoninus; as emperor, Caesar Aelius Hadrianus Antoninus Augustus Pius] (*b* Lanuvium [now Lanuvio], nr Rome, 19 Sept AD 86; *reg* 138–61; *d* Lorium, nr Rome, 7 March AD 161). Roman emperor and patron. His long reign was characterized by a rare security, peace and prosperity, but little architectural development in Rome compared with the reigns of his predecessors. Nevertheless, under Antoninus the monumental area of the Campus Martius was further enriched with a great octastyle peripteral temple in honour of the deified Hadrian (the Hadrianeum, ded. AD 145; *see* ROME, ANCIENT, §II, 2(i)(f)), which in part still exists. The interior decoration included reliefs personifying the provinces (most are in Rome, Mus. Conserv. and Naples, Mus. Archeol. N.) and emphasized the Emperor's policy of bringing peace and order to the Empire. In the old and crowded centre on the Via Sacra a temple was built to Antoninus' wife Faustina in the same year that she died and was deified (AD 141). When the Emperor died, the dedication was extended to include him. The temple, incorporated in the Middle Ages into the church of S Lorenzo in Miranda, stood on a high podium, approached by a stairway. Its façade displays six large columns of green cipollino marble with white marble Corinthian capitals, with three more columns behind on each side. On the two long sides of the cella, faced with squares of peperino tufa, runs a marble frieze with griffins flanking plant motifs.

BIBLIOGRAPHY

V. Passarelli: 'Rilievo e studio di restituzione dell'Hadrianeum', *Atti del III congresso nazionale di storia dell'architettura: Firenze, 1938*, pp. 123–37
G. A. Mansuelli: *Roma e il mondo romano*, ii (Turin, 1981), pp. 19, 43–57

LUCA LEONCINI

Antonio, Biagio d'. *See* BIAGIO D'ANTONIO.

Antonio, Francesco d'. *See* FRANCESCO D'ANTONIO.

Antonio, Jacobello d'. *See* JACOBELLO D'ANTONIO.

Antonio, Jacopo di. *See* JACOPO DI ANTONIO.

Antonio, Nicola di Maestro. *See* NICOLA DI MAESTRO ANTONIO.

Antonio, Salvo d'. *See* SALVO D'ANTONIO.

Antonio (Leonelli) da Crevalcore (*b* Crevalcore; *d* before 1525). Italian painter and musician. Although

Antonio da Crevalcore was highly regarded by his contemporaries as both a painter of still-lifes and a musician, his artistic oeuvre remains the subject of debate. It has been suggested that he trained in Ferrara, because of the stylistic similarities his work shares with other Ferrarese painters working in Bologna, such as Francesco del Cossa and Ercole de' Roberti. The influence of Cossa's Bolognese painting on Crevalcore is clear, especially of the *Pala dei Mercanti* (Bologna, Pin. N.), but the connection between Cossa's Ferrarese works or Ercole de' Roberti's later Ferrarese paintings and Crevalcore is less evident.

Crevalcore is first documented in Bologna in 1478 and recorded as 'Master Antonio, the painter of the Cappella S Proclo' in 1491. The date of his death has been deduced from his inclusion in Girolamo Casio de' Medici's book of epitaphs (1525). His only signed and dated painting was the *Holy Family* (1493; ex-Kaiser-Friedrich Mus., Berlin, destr.). Other works attributed to him include the portrait of the *Sacrati Family* (Munich, Alte Pin.), the *Holy Family with St John the Baptist* (Stuttgart, Staatsgal.), the *Portrait of a Young Man* with the sigil *A.F.P.* [?*Antonius Ferrariensis pinxit*] (Venice, Correr) and three large tempera paintings on canvas of the *Virgin and Child with an Angel*, *St Paul* and *St Peter* (London, priv. col., see Sgarbi, 1985).

BIBLIOGRAPHY

Thieme–Becker
G. P. Achillini: *Il viridario nel quale nomina litterati bolognesi e di altre città* (Bologna, 1513), p. 188
G. Casio de' Medici: *Libro intitulato: Cronica ove si tratta di epitaphii: di amore: e di virtute . . .* (Bologna, 1525)
L. Alberti: *Descrittione di tutta l'Italia* (Bologna, 1550), p. 304
A. Venturi: 'Nuovi documenti: Quadri di Lorenzo di Credi, di Antonio da Crevalcore e di un discepolo del Francia', *Archv Stor. A.*, i (1888), p. 278
L. Coletti: 'Über Antonio da Crevalcore', *Belvedere*, xiii (1928), pp. 9–11
G. Bargellesi: *Notizie di opere d'arte ferraresi* (Rovigo, 1954), pp. 37–9
F. Zeri: 'An Addition to Antonio da Crevalcore', *Burl. Mag.*, cviii (1966), pp. 422–5
F. Filippini and G. Zucchini: *Miniatori e pittori a Bologna: Documenti del secolo XV* (Rome, 1968), pp. 19–20
V. Sgarbi: *Antonio da Crevalcore e la pittura ferrarese del quattrocento a Bologna* (Milan, 1985)

KRISTEN LIPPINCOTT

Antonio da Fabriano [Antonio di Agostino di ser Giovanni] (*fl* 1451–89). Italian painter and sculptor. He worked mainly in the Marches, but it has been suggested that he was in Naples in 1440–45 and possibly trained there (Donnini). This is reinforced by the apparent influence of Antonello da Messina in his two dated autograph paintings, *St Jerome in his Study* (1451; Baltimore, MD, Walters A.G.) and a *Crucifixion* (1452; Matelica, Mus. Piersanti). The composition of another early work, the *Death of the Virgin* (Fabriano, Pin. Civ. Mus. Arazzi), also reflects prototypes produced in southern Italy. Works attributed to him include a fresco fragment of *St Bernardino of Siena* (1451) and a triptych of the *Virgin and St Anne with SS Joseph and Joachim* (both Gualdo Tadino, Pin. Com.), a panel of *St Jerome* and a double-sided standard of the *Virgin and Child* and *St Clement* (both Genga, S Clemente). From 1468 to 1471 he was in Sassoferrato, where for the Palazzo Comunale he painted a *Virgin and Child with Saints* (1468; destr.). Also from this period is a double-sided standard of the *Madonna della misericordia* and *SS Bernardino and John the Baptist* (Milan, U. Cattolica). A signed triptych of the *Virgin and Child with Angels and Saints* (Genga, S Clemente) is dated by documents to 1474. The frescoes of the *Crucifixion with Dominicans* and *Christ with Dominican Saints* (both Fabriano, Convent of S Domenico) have a suggested date of *c.* 1480 (Borgogelli). Antonio da Fabriano's approach to light and volume reflects the influence of Piero della Francesca, perhaps acquired through the work of Gerolamo di Giovanni da Camerino and Giovanni Boccati. Antonio's only signed work of sculpture is a marble tabernacle (Fabriano Cathedral).

BIBLIOGRAPHY

DBI
B. Molajoli: 'Un tabernacolo di Antonio da Fabriano', *Rass. March.*, vi (1927–8), pp. 301–3
G. Donnini: 'Sui rapporti di Antonio da Fabriano e di Matteo di Gualdo con Girolamo di Giovanni', *Ant. Viva*, x/1 (1972), pp. 4–7
A. Borgogelli: 'Antonio da Fabriano e gli affreschi di S Domenico', *Not. Pal. Albani*, ii/1 (1973), pp. 29–36
A. Tambini: 'Uno stendardo di Antonio da Fabriano', *Paragone*, xxxvi/429 (1985), pp. 77–9
P. Zampetti: *Pittura nelle Marche: Dalle origini al primo rinascimento* (Florence, 1988), pp. 336–7, 343–4, 382–5

HELEN GEDDES

Antonio da Mercatello Bencivenni. *See* BENCIVENNI, ANTONIO.

Antonio da Negroponte. *See* FALIER, ANTONIO.

Antonio da Trento (*b* Trent; *fl* Bologna, *c.* 1527). Italian printmaker. Of six documented chiaroscuro woodcuts by the artist (two signed, four mentioned by Vasari), five are skilfully cut in a very controlled two-block style, for example *Nude Man in a Landscape* (B. p. 148, no. 13). The sixth, the *Martyrdom of Two Saints* (B. p. 79, no. 28; for illustration *see* WOODCUT, CHIAROSCURO), is among the best of Italian multiple-block chiaroscuros. All are after designs by Parmigianino. According to Vasari, Parmigianino, arriving in Bologna after the Sack of Rome in 1527, stayed with a friend for several months and retained Antonio to instruct him in the cutting of two- and three-block prints. Although Vasari stated elsewhere that Parmigianino prepared many other designs to be incised in copper and printed, he implied that Antonio was employed for this purpose. The project foundered because of Parmigianino's painting obligations, whereupon Antonio stole all the prints (or possibly matrixes—Vasari is not clear) in copper and wood and as many drawings as possible and disappeared. Since the 18th century attempts have been made to rediscover him in the person of the etcher and painter Antonio Fantuzzi, active at Fontainebleau between 1537 and 1550. Four etchings (out of over 100) by Fantuzzi copy Parmigianino drawings and correspond to chiaroscuro designs. This overlap, the hiatus in Antonio da Trento's career, the mention of copperplates by Vasari and the likelihood that such highly prized designs would find a further use enhance the theory, which, however, lacks firm substantiation. All of Antonio's chiaroscuros were recut for later editions, though not those issued by Andreani.

BIBLIOGRAPHY

Thieme–Becker
Vasari: *Vite* (1550, rev. 2/1568); ed. G. Milanesi (1878–85)
A. von Bartsch: *Le Peintre-graveur* (1803–21), xii [B.]

G. Suster: 'Di Antonio da Trento e dei suoi chiaroscuri', *Archv Trent.*, xvii (1902), pp. 5ff
F. Zava Boccazzi: 'Antonio da Trento incisore (prima metà XVI sec.)', *Collana di artisti trentini* (Trent, 1962)
C. Karpinski: *Italian Chiaroscuro Woodcuts*, 48 [xii] of *The Illustrated Bartsch*, ed. W. Strauss (New York, 1971)
L. Lambertini and N. Rasmo: *L'incisione trentina dalle origini ai giorni nostri* (Trento, 1971), pp. 24–5

JAN JOHNSON

Antonio Dei, Pietro di. *See* BARTOLOMEO DELLA GATTA.

Antonio de Saliba. *See* SALIBA, DE, (1).

Antonio di Niccolò di Lorenzo (di Domenico) (*b* Florence, 1445; *d* Florence, 28 March 1527). Italian illuminator and stationer. He was trained in the climate created by such painters and illuminators as Zanobi Strozzi and Apollonio di Giovanni, who were important during the 1450s. Their influence accounts for the dynamism and the sculptural treatment of his figures, which gives them a courtly flavour reminiscent of the work of Andrea del Verrocchio or Antonio del Pollaiuolo. Antonio di Niccolò di Lorenzo's interest in larger-scale works—frescoes or panel paintings—is apparent from his repeated depiction, especially in border decoration, of metal objects, individually characterized interiors, portraits and contemporary fashions. He took his inspiration from scenes painted on cassoni, and from Apollonio's late work. Stylistic affinities between Antonio and Francesco di Antonio del Chierico have sometimes led to confusion between their work; however, enough of Antonio's works have been traced to distinguish him substantially from the del Foro *bottega*, Giovanni Boccardi and many other illuminators. The discovery of a catalogue recording the sale in 1468–9 of a Psalter (ex-De Marinis priv. col., Florence, MS. 261) for the convent of S Francesco in Fiesole shows the success of the artist, even in his youth. In a later Gradual (Lucca, Bib. Stat., MS. 2676) from the convent of S Francesco in Lucca, the monumentality and sculptural forms of the human figures, elaborated in the manner of panel painting, suggest that Antonio was familiar with the work of Sandro Botticelli, Filippino Lippi and Domenico Ghirlandaio. Antonio is known primarily for the documented graduals (1473–5; Florence, Bib. Capitolo, graduale A and F) executed for the Compagnia dei Servi of SS Annunziata in Florence; these were formerly the only known works of the artist. The *Fior di virtù* (Florence, Bib. Riccardiana, MS. 1711), in which allegorical and moralistic themes predominate, was illuminated by Antonio for Agnolo Bardi. Apart from the evident stylistic affinities with Botticelli's work, the presence in this codex of a drawing of *Urania* that was clearly influenced by Botticelli supports the hypothesis that the two were in direct contact. Antonio illuminated a copy of the *Storia fiorentina* (Florence, Bib. N. Cent., MS. II.III. 53–4), a translation (1473) by Donato Acciaiuoli (1429–78) of a Latin original, for the Strozzi family, in which his early interest in Verrocchio seems to have been revived. He made some bindings for Ripoli Monastery in 1480–82. The only known work produced by Antonio after 1484 is in the incipit page of a choir-book (Pisa, Mus. Sinopic Composanto Mnmtl, corale A).

BIBLIOGRAPHY

M. Levi D'Ancona: *Miniatura e miniatori a Firenze dal XIV al XVI secolo* (Florence, 1962), pp. 19–22
A. Garzelli: *Miniatura fiorentina del rinascimento, 1440–1525: Un primo censimento*, i (Florence, 1985), pp. 249–53

PATRIZIA FERRETTI

Antonio Maria da Villafora (*fl* Padua, 1469; *d* Padua, 1511). Italian illuminator. His place of origin is cited as 'Villa Fuora Territorii Policinis'; the surname Sforza, sometimes attributed to him, belonged only to his adopted son Bartolomeo. Antonio Maria is mentioned in a document of 1482 among the illuminators of the law faculty at Padua University, and numerous payments were made to him there during the years 1481–1511 for the decoration of philosophical and legal texts, mostly commissioned by Pietro Barozzi, Bishop of Padua (1487–1507). Although they were produced in the Veneto, these manuscripts have strong Ferrarese characteristics, which have convinced some scholars that the artist was of Emilian origin, but there is no evidence for his identification with the Antonio Maria Casanova documented in Ferrara in 1470 and 1475, nor for the inclusion of three Olivetan graduals (Modena, Bib. Estense, MSS lat. 1013, 1014, 1022) among his early works (Mariani Canova, 1987). There is no doubt, however, about the Ferrarese background to his work, which shows the influence of Guglielmo Giraldi and especially Franco dei Russi, in whose workshop he may have been trained. Antonio Maria was also evidently acquainted with the Roverella *Decretals* of Gratian (Ferrara, Mus. Civ. A. Ant. Pal. Schifanoia), which was printed in Venice by Jenson in 1474 and probably illuminated in the Veneto by Ferrarese artists.

Antonio Maria was probably responsible for a canon law book (Rome, Vatican, Bib. Apostolica, MS. Vat. lat. 4097), presented to Pope Sixtus IV (*reg* 1471–84), and for a Bible (Modena, Bib. Estense, MS. alpha B. 1. 15) published in Venice by Jenson in 1476, which is closely related in style and decoration to contemporary Emilian illumination. Shortly afterwards Antonio Maria must have decorated a Missal (Milan, Bib. N. Braidense, MS. AE. X. 30), perhaps for a Benedictine nunnery in Padua. Among the numerous manuscripts decorated for Pietro Barozzi are a Missal (Padua, Bib. Capitolare, MS. 260), which is identifiable with that published by Hamman in Venice in 1491, for which Antonio Maria received payment in 1494, and the *Commentary on the Twelve Prophets* of St Jerome (Padua, Bib. Capitolare, MS. 202), decorated in 1500. Although Levi D'Ancona considered that the payments for the Missal referred only to the filigree letters, attributing the rest of the decoration to Benedetto Padovano, the identification of this artist with BENEDETTO BORDON has enabled the attribution of the Barozzi Missal to Antonio Maria to be reaffirmed.

Towards the end of his life Antonio Maria decorated a Psalter (Padua, Mus. Civ., MSS CM 811–12), which came from S Giustina, Padua, and is mentioned in its necrology. A Missal (London, BL, Add. MS. 15813) is also cited; it was partly illuminated by Antonio Maria but finished by another artist, perhaps after his death (Mariani Canova, 1976).

BIBLIOGRAPHY

Thieme-Becker

M. Cionini Visani: 'Di alcuni codici quattrocenteschi della Biblioteca Capitolare di Padova: Il Maestro dei Delfini e Antonio Maria da Padova', *A. Ven.*, xxi (1967), pp. 45–56

M. Levi D'Ancona: 'Benedetto Padovano e Benedetto Bordone: Primo tentativo per un corpus di Benedetto Padovano', *Commentari*, xviii (1967), pp. 3–42

——: 'Precisazioni sulla miniatura veneta', *Commentari*, xix (1968), pp. 268–72

G. Mariani Canova: *La miniatura veneta del rinascimento, 1450–1500* (Venice, 1969), pp. 80–96, 130–36

L. Montobbio: *Miniatori, scriptores, rilegatori di libri della cattedrale di Padova* (Padua, 1972)

M. Billanovich Dal Zio: 'Bidelli, cartolai e miniatori allo studio di Padova nel secolo XV', *Quad. Stor. U. Padova*, vi (1974), pp. 59–72

G. Mariani Canova: 'Manoscritti miniati veneti nelle Biblioteche di Cambridge e Boston (Mass.)', *A. Ven.*, xxix (1975), pp. 97–104

Dopo Mantegna (exh. cat., Padua, Pal. Ragione, 1976), pp. 157–8 [entry by G. Mariani Canova]

G. Castiglioni: 'Di alcune miniature di Antonio Maria da Villafora nel Museo Civico di Verona', *Boll. A.*, lxvii/15 (1982), pp. 109–14

G. Mariani Canova: 'Libri miniati in Friuli e problemi di miniatura in Veneto: Franco dei Russi, Antonio Maria da Villafora, il Decretum Gratiani Roverella', *Miniatura in Friuli, crocevia di civiltà: Udine, 1985* (Pordenone, 1987), pp. 119–37

MILVIA BOLLATI

Antonio Veneziano [Antonio di Francesco da Venezia] (*fl* 1369; *d* ?Florence, ?after 13 March 1419). Italian painter. Documents dated 1369–70 record that he produced a series of paintings, including frescoes in two chapels, for Siena Cathedral (all untraced). On 20 September 1374 he was registered as a member of the Arte dei Medici e Speziali in Florence. He is documented from 1384 until 3 March 1388 in Pisa, where he painted three large frescoes in the Camposanto: the *Return of St Ranierus to Pisa*, the *Death and Burial of St Ranierus* and *Posthumous Miracles of St Ranierus* (1384–6; Pisa, Mus. Sinopie Camposanto Mnmtl; see fig.). Czarnecki has demonstrated that Antonio Veneziano was registered, with interruptions, in the Florentine tax records until at least 1393; he further suggested that the painter should be identified with the 'Antonio di Francesco dipintore' recorded there until 1419. Apart from the Camposanto frescoes, only one verified work by Antonio survives: a signed and dated panel of the *Flagellation* (1388; Palermo, Mus. Dioc.). A group of paintings can be attributed to the painter on the basis of stylistic comparisons with this and the frescoes, but their chronology is disputed.

Early works produced in Florence are thought to include the frescoes from the tabernacle of the Torre degli Agli, Novoli, near Florence (Florence, Uffizi); a *Coronation of the Virgin* (ex-Mrs Franklin Lawrence priv. col., New York) to which belong four small panels with half-figures of saints (ex-Richard Hurd priv. col., New York, and Berlin, Gemäldegal.); and the Boston polyptych, which includes a *Virgin and Child* (Boston, MA, Mus. F.A.), a *St Andrew* (ex-Otto Lanz priv. col., Amsterdam), a *St Bartholomew* (Auckland, C.A.G.), a *St Peter* and a *St Paul* (Florence, Pal. Vecchio). Works from the beginning of the artist's maturity, possibly produced in Pisa, are a *Virgin and Child Enthroned with Angels* (Hannover, Niedersächs. Landesmus.), the accompanying *Annunciation* and a *St James* (both Berlin, Gemäldegal.). Close stylistic connections with the Ranierus frescoes are evident in an *Assumption of the Virgin* from the convent of S Tommaso, Pisa (Pisa, S Tommaso, on dep. Pisa, Sopr. Gal.), a panel with *Six Kneeling Apostles* (Altenburg, Staatl. Lindenau-Mus.), and a processional standard showing the *Crucifixion* (front) and *Holy Hermits* (reverse; Pisa, Mus. N. & Civ. S Matteo). According to Czarnecki, Antonio Veneziano executed the *Madonna of Humility* (Montefiesole, S Lorenzo) after his return to Florence, which would make this the artist's last known work.

Antonio Veneziano: *Posthumous Miracles of St Ranierus* (detail), fresco, 1384–6 (Pisa, Museo delle Sinopie del Camposanto Monumentale)

A series of paintings in Toledo Cathedral, especially the fresco cycle illustrating the Creed in the Capilla de S Blas, show close links with Antonio Veneziano's style, and it has been suggested that he worked for a time in Toledo. The frescoes are heavily painted over, however, so no definitive judgement is possible. They were produced between 1395/6 and 1399, and, if the painter recorded as living in Florence from 1393 to 1419 is Veneziano, they would have to be attributed instead to an artist with a close knowledge of his work, possibly an assistant.

Veneziano was influenced both by Giotto's monumental style and by the Sienese artists Ambrogio Lorenzetti and Pietro Lorenzetti. A tension between superficial, decorative effect and spatial, plastic tendencies is characteristic of him. His significance derives from the attempts in his compositions to establish a continuous spatial context for individually characterized figures. This quality is apparent in the Ranierus frescoes and anticipates tendencies that were not to become current in Florence until after 1400.

BIBLIOGRAPHY

R. Offner: *Studies in Florentine Painting* (New York, 1927), pp. 67–81

M. Salmi: 'Antonio Veneziano', *Boll. A.*, viii (1929), pp. 433–52

K. Steinweg: 'Eine Verkündigung des Antonio Veneziano', *Berlin. Mus.: Ber. Staatl. Mus. Preuss. Kultbes.*, xv (1965), pp. 4–6

F. Bologna: 'Un altro pannello del "retablo" del Salvatore a Toledo: Antonio Veneziano o Gherardo Starnina?', *Prospettiva* [Florence], ii (1975), pp. 43–52

M. Boskovits: *Pittura fiorentina alla vigilia del rinascimento* (Florence, 1975), pp. 69–73, 280–83

J. Czarnecki: *Antonio Veneziano: A Florentine Painter of the Late Trecento* (Indiana, 1978)

CORNELIA SYRE

Anton of Worms. *See* WOENSAM, ANTON.

Anton Ulrich, Duke of Brunswick-Wolfenbüttel. *See* WELF, (5).

Antropov, Aleksey (Petrovich) (*b* 14 March 1716; *d* St Petersburg, 12 June 1795). Russian painter. He trained at the Construction Office in St Petersburg, where his teachers included Ivan Vishnyakov, in whose team of painters Antropov later worked. He participated in the decorative painting of the Winter Palace and other imperial residences in St Petersburg and its environs. In 1752 he embarked on painting Andreyevsky Cathedral in Kiev and produced icons for its iconostasis. He returned to St Petersburg in 1758 and then trained for two years with Pietro Antonio Rotari. Soon afterwards he was appointed principal supervisor of the artists and icon painters of the Synod.

Antropov is remembered primarily as a portrait painter who worked in a realistic style that retained many traditional elements. The most notable among his portraits is that of the lady-in-waiting *Anastasiya Izmailova* (1759; Moscow, Tret'yakov Gal.), which shows the best and most typical features of his work. He conveys the sitter's authority, energy and intelligence, suggesting the force of character of a significant figure at the court of the Empress Elizabeth. Antropov's style is typical of the Russian Baroque. His preference for vivid local colours and his careful reproduction of detail and texture link his work to the traditions of both Russian folk art and earlier Russian portrait painting. Also notable are the portraits of the Chieftain of the Don Cossacks, *Fyodor Krasnoshchokov* (1781; St Petersburg, Rus. Mus.), and of *Archbishop Silvestr Kulyabka* (1760; St Petersburg, Rus. Mus.) and the full-length ceremonial portraits of *Tsar Peter III* (1762; St Petersburg, Rus. Mus., and Moscow, Tret'yakov Gal.).

BIBLIOGRAPHY

I. Sakharova: *Aleksey Petrovich Antropov, 1716–1795* (Moscow, 1974)

G. KOMELOVA

Antunes, Bartolomeu (*b* Lisbon, 1688; *d* Lisbon, 1753). Portuguese decorative artist. He was highly active in the second quarter of the 18th century, during the period when High Baroque glazed tiles were produced in the Lisbon factories. His output was enormous, and his work was distributed throughout Portugal and Brazil. In partnership with his son-in-law, the painter Nicolau de Freitas (*c.* 1703–65), he continued the tradition of António de Oliveira Bernardes (*see* BERNARDES, (1)). Under the influence of Joanine wood-carving and silver, the decorative borders of their tiles became richer and more elegant, dominated by grimacing masks and cascading palm and acanthus foliage. The tile makers adapted the convention of using arched frames, which end in garlanded volutes often accompanied by cherubs, for their high dado panels.

Two chapels in the church of Vilar de Frades, Barcelos, dated 1736 and 1742 are decorated with scenes, signed by Antunes and Freitas, from the *Life of the Virgin.* In S Francisco, Salvador, Brazil, two large panels of *St Francis* are dated 1737 and signed by Antunes. Antunes and Nicolau de Freitas collaborated on the panels in four rooms of the Mitra Palace, Lisbon, in which they incorporated decorative subjects, landscapes and *fêtes galantes*; on the staircase, which has painted balustrades, shells and figures representing the elements (*c.* 1735–45); and in the Quinta dos Arcebispos in S Antão do Tojal, Loures, where three of the rooms contain tiles of the four seasons and an allegory of the arts (*c.* 1730–40). Some of Antunes's figurative panels, painted in perspective and framed by dramatically exuberant borders, are monumental and have great decorative impact: these include those with sculptural motifs, medallions, landscapes and religious figures (*c.* 1730–40) in the nave of the Albertas church, Lisbon, and some of the panels of scenes from the *Life of St Augustine* (*c.* 1740) in the Pópulo church, Braga, where more care and imagination appear to have been spent on the decoration than on the figures. Antunes carried out ornamental compositions with lovely Baroque motifs, such as the *Symbols of the Virgin*, with floral swags and Baroque ornament, in the sanctuary of the hermitage of Porto Salvo, Oeiras, in 1734.

BIBLIOGRAPHY

R. C. Smith: 'French Models for Portuguese Tiles', *Apollo*, xcvii (1973), pp. 396–407

J. M. dos Santos Simões: *Azulejaria em Portugal no século XVIII* (Lisbon, 1979)

J. Meco: 'A azulejaria do palácio da Independência, em Lisboa', *Bol. Cult. Assembl. Distr. Lisboa*, i (1981), pp. 5–76

——: *Azulejaria portuguesa* (Lisbon, 1985)

——: 'O palácio da Mitra em Lisboa e os seus azulejos', *Lisboa-Rev. Mun.*, 12 (1985), pp. 13–31; 13 (1985), pp. 25–40; 14 (1985), pp. 7–17

JOSÉ MECO

Antunes, João (*bapt* Lisbon, 30 Sept 1643; *d* Lisbon, 25 Nov 1712). Portuguese architect and master mason. He worked in the context of a national tradition marked by Mannerism and the Plain style (*see* PORTUGAL, §II, 2), but he also contributed to the progressive acceptance of new Baroque concepts of space in Portugal, as shown in the use of polygonal plans. He gave a festive and sumptuous treatment to the interiors of his buildings, using inlay of coloured jasper or marble, which is sometimes combined with carved and gilded woodwork (*talha*) and blue and white *azulejos* (glazed tiles). Antunes probably learnt these intarsia techniques from the examples of the decorations (*c.* 1665–92; destr. 1755) of the nave and chancel of the church of the convent of S Antão-o-Novo, Lisbon, and those (1668–*c.* 1707) of the sacristy of the convent church of S Vicente de Fora, Lisbon. In 1670 Antunes was admitted to the Irmandade de S José dos Carpinteiros e Pedreiros in Lisbon, which gave him professional status as master mason. In 1682 he began an apprenticeship at the Aula de Arquitectura Civil do Paço da Ribeira in Lisbon, where his master was Francisco Tinoco da Silva (*d* 1730) and he was responsible to the Provedor da Casa das Obras e Paços Reais.

Following an alleged act of sacrilege, the chancel of the first church of S Engrácia, Lisbon, was rebuilt in 1630 by a fraternity composed of leading members of the nobility, but in 1681 it collapsed. Antunes, still a master mason, won a competition for the plan of the new church in spite of rivalry from the court architects. Antunes's Greek-cross plan with a central dome and four apses (see fig.; *see also* PORTUGAL, fig. 4) was based on a Baroque reading of Baldassare Peruzzi's design for St Peter's, Rome, published in Serlio's treatise (Book III), which was itself inspired by Bramante's design (1506). Altering Peruzzi's plan, Antunes reduced the diameter of the dome by *c.* 17.7 m and the four lateral bodies by *c.* 11 m and opened the four large domed apses into the central space. He made square chambers in the four towers and used the thickness of the walls to create small compartments and labyrinthine corridors. The main entrance has four giant Doric columns framing three arches crowned by pedimented niches. Two twisted columns with composite capitals support a richly carved entablature and a broken pediment, while on the tympanum two angels bear the royal arms. Heavy mouldings are used to accentuate the undulating curves of the exterior elevations. The interior combines golden limestone with coloured marble in black, white and pink in contrasting geometrical patterns. After Antunes's death additional buttresses in the form of inverted volutes were built (1713). Work on the church was stopped in 1733, and it remained unfinished (lacking the tops of the towers and the ciborium) until 1966, when the building was adopted as the National Pantheon, with a restructuring that altered Antunes's original design.

João Antunes: S Engrácia, Lisbon, begun 1682; early 19th-century drawing of ground-plan and principal façade by José Honorato Correira (Lisbon, Academia Nacional de Belas-Artes)

In 1681 Antunes was commissioned by Francisco de Sousa (1631–1711), a member of the S Engrácia fraternity, to design the chapel of S Francisco for the Quinta do Calhariz (Arrábida, Sesimbra). Here the retable is made in inlaid Italian jasper with two pairs of twisted columns (a motif he used in all his subsequent altars). The decoration shows the influence of Flemish strapwork, which is combined with stylized foliage. In 1686 Veríssimo de Lencastre (*d* 1692), Superintendente das Obras at S Engrácia, commissioned Antunes to design the Capela dos Lencastre for S Pedro de Alcântara, Lisbon. The form and decoration of the retable is similar to that at Calhariz, except that there is no Flemish influence; instead, it contains foliage that resembles the patterns in Persian and Indian carpets, or the marquetry of Indo-Portuguese furniture. The floor and walls are also inlaid with motifs that Antunes repeated in later works.

In 1694 Antunes designed the church of the S Elói convent, Lisbon (destr. 1755), the first of a series of churches of similar plan. It had a rectangular plan (22.0×15.4 m) with truncated corners, eight nave chapels, two symmetrical pulpits and a very deep chancel. In 1696 he designed the sacristy of the church of S Antão-o-Novo convent (now the chapel of the Hospital de S José). The intarsia decoration is confined to small sections of the frieze and panels in the vault and does not detract from the basic classicism of the architecture. A small room, possibly an oratory, in the same convent is also attributed to him and is square in plan, with truncated corners and an interior decoration of inlaid marble. In 1698 the diplomat João Gomes da Silva (1671–1738), 4th Count of Tarouca, Superintendente das Obras de S Engrácia, commissioned from Antunes a design for a palace in Lisbon. All that is known of this building is that it was to have been constructed on such a scale as to have rivalled the royal palace in magnificence. This factor, among others, may have impeded the completion of the work (demolished after 1755).

Around 1695 Antunes became architect to the Casas da Rainha and in 1699 he was appointed Royal Architect (Arquitecto Real). Peter II commissioned him to design the tomb of the *Infanta Joana* and the interior of the ante-choir of the convent church of Jesus in Aveiro (1699–1711), in which it stands. The tomb is an enormous free-standing chest borne by four angels and two phoenixes and is crowned by two pairs of cherubs, who support the royal arms. Despite the decoration, the work shows the king's preference for archaicist styles. The colouring of the geometric patterns in inlaid marble is similar to that in his earlier retables and comprises red, pink and a yellow-orange set against backgrounds of black or ash-grey. Antunes had been architect of the military orders of Santiago de Espado and S Bento de Avis since 1697, and in 1700 they first commissioned him to design the church of Santiago in Alcácer do Sal. This patronage explains his choice of a Plain Style design. In 1701 he built the palace, the Paço da Bemposta (now the Military Academy, Lisbon), for Catherine of Braganza (1638–1705), the widow of Charles II of England. Little remains of this besides two square doorways crowned with the arms of England and Portugal.

The church of Senhor da Cruz, Barcelos (begun 1705), was Antune's last documented commission. He also designed a wooden retable in National Style (1709; sold 1736) for the church. It is not known when his career ended, although the fine church of the Menino Deus (1711–37; façade unfinished) in Lisbon is attributed to him on stylistic grounds. The work was a royal commission and with it the cycle of 17th-century courtly Baroque architecture was brought to a close.

BIBLIOGRAPHY

Viterbo
R. C. Smith: 'The Portuguese Woodcarved Retable, 1600–1750', *Belas A.*, n. s. 1, ii (1950), pp. 16–57
A. de Carvalho: *D. João V e a arte do seu tempo*, 2 vols (Lisbon, 1960–62)
G. Kubler: *Portuguese Plain Architecture between Spices and Diamonds, 1521–1706* (Middletown, 1972)
A. de Carvalho: *As obras de Santa Engrácia e os seus artistas* (Lisbon, 1973)
J. F. Pereira: *Arquitectura barroca em Portugal* (Lisbon, 1986)
P. V. Gomes: *A arquitectura barroca em Portugal* (Lisbon, 1987)
J. F. Pereira: 'Resistência e aceitação do espaço barroco', *História da arte em Portugal*, viii (Lisbon, 1987), pp. 9–65
João Antunes, Arquitecto, 1643–1712 (exh. cat., Lisbon, S Engrácia, 1988)
C. A. Ferreira de Almeida: 'Um retábulo de João Antunes', *Actas I Congresso Internacional do Barroco: Oporto, 1989*, ii, pp. 635–40
J. F. Pereira: 'Antunes, João', *Dicionário da arte barroca em Portugal*, ed. J. F. Pereira (Lisbon, 1989), pp. 33–6
J. F. Pereira, L. Ferrão and L. Arruda: *Percursos em Lisboa: Lisboa no tempo de D. João V (1689–1750)* (Lisbon and Paris, 1994)

LEONOR FERRÃO

Antunes Ribeiro, Paulo (*b* Rio de Janeiro, 1 Sept 1905; *d* Rio de Janeiro, 8 March 1978). Brazilian architect. He graduated in 1926 from the Escola Nacional de Belas Artes, Rio de Janeiro, where he won the gold medal; his contemporaries there included Lúcio Costa and Diógenes Rebouças. He then studied urban planning at the Institut d'Urbanisme, University of Paris (1928–9). Initially, like Costa and other contemporaries, he supported the neo-colonial movement in Brazil in the wide-ranging debate on the development of national art that dominated Latin America from the beginning of the century. Later, influenced by the tremendous growth taking place in American cities, he based his work on the rationalist modernism of Le Corbusier and CIAM, and its Brazilian adaptations, specializing in urban planning. An early example is the plan he drew up for the city of Goiânia (1933; with Attilio Corrêa Lima). Other important works include the Prudência office building (1946; also known as the Caramurú building), Salvador, covered with *brises-soleil* on panels arranged in a chequered fashion and with a roof garden and curved service towers and windbreaks on the roof and for which he won an honourable mention at the first São Paulo Bienniale (1951); and the Hotel da Bahia (1949–51; with Diógenes Rebouças), Salvador, a long, rectangular block of rooms above two floors of public rooms that curve out beyond the plan form in an exuberant manner. He was a versatile architect, designing houses, blocks of flats, public buildings and hospitals, and he made a significant contribution to the development of Brazilian architecture immediately after World War II. He was President of the Instituto de Arquitetos do Brasil (1953–6) and was its representative on the selection jury for the national competition to design the master plan for the new capital city of Brasília.

BIBLIOGRAPHY

'Edifice Caramurú A Bahia: Paulo Antunes Ribeiro Architecte', *Archit. Aujourd'hui*, xxiii/42–3 (1952), pp. 24–5
D. Paglia, ed.: *Arquitetura na Bienal de São Paulo* (São Paulo, *c.* 1952)
H. E. Mindlin: *Modern Architecture in Brazil* (Amsterdam and Rio de Janeiro, 1956)
Y. Bruand: *Arquitetura contemporânea no Brasil* (São Paulo, 1981)

JULIO ROBERTO KATINSKY

Antúnez, Nemesio (*b* Santiago, 1918; *d* June 1993). Chilean painter and printmaker. After studying architecture at the Universidad Católica de Chile in Santiago he won a scholarship that enabled him to continue his studies at Columbia University, New York, from 1943 to 1945. Having painted sensitive watercolours from nature while living in Chile, his journey to New York had a disquieting effect on him: he translated his experience of the concrete city, with its massive buildings dwarfing the anonymous inhabitants wandering the streets, into nearly abstract geometric compositions. He remained in New York to work with Stanley William Hayter from 1948 to 1950 and later travelled to Spain.

On his return to Chile in 1953 Antúnez founded Taller 99, a workshop modelled on Hayter's Atelier 17, which had far-reaching effects on the development of printmaking in Chile. His renewed contact in Chile with the natural landscape and its fields, beaches and mountains allowed him to return to intimate sensitively coloured scenes, as in the *Fishing-lines* and *Bicycles* series. He returned to the USA from 1964 to 1969, this time as cultural attaché in the Chilean Embassy in Washington, DC, which brought him back into contact with crowds; his paintings again featured volumes in perspective and geometric structures based on his vision of the modern city. He went back to Chile to work as Director of the Museo Nacional de Bellas Artes in Santiago, vigorously promoting the visual arts and extending the exhibition space by building the Sala Matta, but he went into voluntary exile in Europe after the military coup of 1973, spending time in England, Spain and Italy. In 1975 he painted a series entitled *The Black Stadia*, an allusion to the football stadium that served as a massive prison for political detainees under the military junta, in which he expressed his anguish at the dramatic events that had taken place in Chile after the fall of President Allende's government. He decided to settle again in Chile only in 1985.

Antúnez's work stems in general from a sensitive and emotionally detached contemplation of daily life, even when dealing with dramatic events. Within the apparent restrictions of line and colour he found all the expressive possibilities he needed, superimposing images of female figures, beds and tablecloths in intimate natural surroundings on to highly formal structures.

BIBLIOGRAPHY

E. Lihn: 'Antúnez', *Rev. A.* [Santiago], 3 (March–April 1956)

M. Ivelić and G. Galaz: *Chile: Arte actual* (Santiago, 1988)

Antúnez (exh. cat., Santiago, Gal. Praxis, 1988)

MILAN IVELIĆ

An Túr Gloine. *See* TOWER OF GLASS.

Antwerp [Flem. Antwerpen; Fr. Anvers]. Belgian city and port on the River Scheldt, *c.* 90 km from the sea, with a population of *c.* 465,000 (1992). In the 16th and 17th centuries it was one of the leading centres of art in northern Europe, with such painters as Quinten Metsys, Peter Paul Rubens and Jacob Jordaens. Prints were published there, and it was a centre for the production of ceramics, tapestry, furniture and objects of vertu, the last encouraged by the establishment of the European diamond trade from the late 15th century. Antwerp was considerably damaged in World War II. It is now a leading international port and a sprawling industrial town.

BIBLIOGRAPHY

F. Prims: *Geschiedenis van Antwerpen*, 29 vols (Brussels and Antwerp, 1927–49)

Antwerpen in de XVIIIde eeuw: Instellingen, economie, cultuur, Genootschap voor Antwerpse Geschiedenis (Antwerp, 1952)

H. Gerson and E. H. ter Kuile: *Art and Architecture in Belgium, 1600–1800*, Pelican Hist. A. (Harmondsworth, 1960)

Antwerpen in de XIXde eeuw, Genootschap voor Antwerpse Geschiedenis (Antwerp, 1964)

L. Voet: *Antwerp: The Golden Age: The Rise and Glory of the Metropolis in the Sixteenth Century* (Antwerp, 1973)

J. van Acker: *Antwerpen van Romeins veer tot wereldhaven* (Antwerp, 1975)

Antwerpen in de XVIde eeuw, Genootschap voor Antwerpse Geschiedenis (Antwerp, 1975)

K. van Isacker and R. van Uytven, eds: *Antwerp* (Antwerp, 1986) [good bibliog.]

Antwerpen in de XVIIde eeuw, Genootschap voor Antwerpse Geschiedenis (Antwerp, 1989)

I. History and urban development. II. Art life and organization. III. Centre of production. IV. Buildings.

I. History and urban development.

1. Before 1585. 2. 1585–1830. 3. After 1830.

1. BEFORE 1585. The city originated on an *aanwerp* (hence the name), a small spit of land that provided facilities for quays. A short-lived Roman settlement of the 2nd–3rd centuries AD was followed by a flourishing Carolingian port destroyed by the Vikings in 836. About 980 Emperor Otto II built a castle (of which the main gate is still preserved and known as the Steen), as the centre of a *mark* or fortified border zone, which, with the adjacent Vismarkt (Fish Market), became the nucleus of the new city. Settlement was confined to the right bank of the river (the left bank was developed as a residential district only after World War II); and the river acted as a boundary between Flanders and Brabant, to which Antwerp was incorporated in 1106, with a brief period of rule by the County of Flanders in the later 14th century. The Grote Markt became the civic centre. The parish church, named Onze Lieve Vrouw, was established near by in 1124, and between 1352 and 1521 the Romanesque building became one of the largest Gothic churches in the Netherlands; it achieved cathedral status under the reorganization of the bishoprics in 1561 (*see* §IV, 1 below).

The city is traversed by small watercourses, now all covered over, but traceable in street names ending in *rui*

1. Antwerp, view from the east; woodcut by Pauwels van Overbeke, 283×475 mm, 1568 (Antwerp, Stedelijk Prentenkabinet)

(canal), *vest* (moat) and *brug* (bridge); the largest, the Meir (marsh), is now the main street of Antwerp (for illustration of the Meir in the 16th century *see* VREDEMAN DE VRIES, HANS, fig. 1). Although the port remained in the shadow of Bruges until the latter declined in the 15th century, the settlement expanded throughout the Middle Ages, and the fortifications were continually rebuilt to encompass new suburbs. A circle of canals was replaced *c.* 1200 by moats with fortified bridges; *c.* 1300 more solid ramparts enclosed 158 ha. About 1400 the area was extended to 208 ha. With the military threats of the 1540s the walls were rebuilt with Italian-style bastions and including a small new section to the north (1543–5; see fig. 1).

In the meantime, *c.* 1500 the Portuguese had established Antwerp as the western European centre of the spice trade, with an immediate increase in commercial, industrial and artistic activity. Until the religious troubles of the later 16th century, the city became the financial centre of Europe. The building boom that began after 1500 swept away many structures, but, in addition to the cathedral, surviving Gothic churches include the St Jacobskerk (begun 1491; rest.), the St Andrieskerk (begun 1515) and the former Dominican church of St Paulus (begun 1520; many times damaged and rebuilt). The larger religious buildings were generally constructed of limestone, imported at first from Tournai but later replaced by Brabant stone. Some secular buildings were also of limestone, though brick was more common. Typically Brabantine was the use of brick alternating with rows of natural stone.

The Vleeshuis (Butchers' Hall; now the Museum of Applied Arts), with its prominent stepped gable, was built in 1501–3 by Herman de Waghemakere, while the Steen was largely rebuilt in 1520 by Domien de Waghemakere (now the National Maritime Museum). Some courtyard complexes survive: the Huis van Liere (*c.* 1515; now part of St Ignatius University) and the Oude Beurs (Old Exchange; *c.* 1515). The latter's replacement of 1531–3 (New Exchange, rebuilt 19th century; *see* §3 below) inspired similar buildings abroad, including that of London, begun in 1566. As the population swelled to *c.* 100,000, the city became a leading Renaissance centre. The Hessenhuis (1561–3) was built by Cornelis Floris, but the first truly monumental Renaissance building in the Netherlands is the Stadhuis, built by Floris in 1560–64 (*see* §IV, 2 below).

Limited numbers of Gothic and Renaissance private houses have been preserved, some with the slender corner towers, up to 26 m high with characteristic bulbous spires, which were a 16th-century status symbol for the rich. Ordinary houses were at first mostly of wood, but when closely crowded terraced housing was built in the 16th century the authorities forbade thatching (1503) and wooden gables (1546). The latter, however, remained very common until the 19th century, a very restored example surviving in Stoelstraat.

The city was badly affected by the 16th-century religious wars. It was a Calvinist stronghold in 1566–7; after the rebellion was crushed, a large, pentagonal, bastioned citadel (destr. 1874; see fig. 1) was built by FRANCESCO PACIOTTO and Bartolomeo Compi on open ground to the south, its outer bastions integrated with the city walls. The city was sacked by the Spanish in 1576. William I, Prince of Orange, gained control in the following year, but in 1585 the city was forced to capitulate to Spanish troops under Alessandro Farnese, Duke of Parma (*reg* 1578–92). Antwerp then became the foremost defender of the Catholic Counter-Reformation in the southern Netherlands.

2. 1585–1830. After 1585 Antwerp was much reduced, both by the emigration of half the population and by the rise of the United Provinces of Holland, which controlled the Scheldt estuary to its benefit by imposing customs dues on import and export (contrary to popular belief the river never was closed). Nevertheless, the city remained a significant outlet for exports from the southern Netherlands; it regained some prosperity and supported a substantial, wealthy upper class. Until *c.* 1700 Antwerp was a leading centre of north European Baroque. Its citizens restored those church interiors that had been vandalized by Protestant iconoclasts, but they retained the Gothic exteriors and built few new churches. The most important were constructed in the new, Italian-inspired Baroque style: the St Augustinuskerk (1615–18), still with a sober brick façade, and the Jesuit church of St Carolus Borromeus (1615–21; see fig. 2), a splendid example of ornate Baroque, designed by Peter Huyssens and Franciscus Aguilonius, and decorated largely by Rubens. The renewed Catholic fervour also led to the proliferation of statues of the Virgin on house gables.

In the depopulated city the rich could easily purchase groups of houses to be transformed into large hôtels—a phenomenon practically unknown in the golden age between 1500 and 1585. Limestone remained in great

2. Antwerp, St Carolus Borromeus by Peter Huyssens and Franciscus Aguilonius, west façade, 1615–21

3. Antwerp, Rubens's house, portico, *c.* 1610–*c.* 1620

demand for secular architecture, often with sandstone decoration. Baroque ornament became characteristic on the houses of the wealthy, but it was generally applied to existing Renaissance structures. Often the decoration on larger hôtels was concentrated around a courtyard, presenting an unobtrusive façade to the outside world. Fine examples are the pure Renaissance Plantin–Moretus House (now Museum; *see* PLANTIN, CHRISTOPH), the ornate Baroque houses of Rubens (*c.* 1610–*c.* 1620; see fig. 3; for the courtyard *see* ARTIST'S HOUSE, fig. 3) and Jordaens (1641), and the Huis Delbeke (1647–9). Typical of Antwerp are the many so-called 'Spanish doors' that have survived, with richly wrought Baroque decoration framing the main entrance of otherwise plain houses.

In the first half of the 18th century Jan Pieter van Baurscheit (ii) introduced a personal and refined Rococo style that combined rocaille motifs with rather severe structures, accentuating the horizontal for the first time in the architectural history of Antwerp (*see* BAURSCHEIT, (2)). Two fine examples are the Huis van Susteren–Roose (1745–*c.* 1750; later the Royal Palace, now the International Cultural Centre) and the Osterriethhuis (1749; now the Paribas Bank; *see* BELGIUM, fig. 28), both on the Meir. His style was superseded *c.* 1760 by the more classicist Louis XVI style. At first this was sober, for example on the façade (1761–3) of the Plantin–Moretus House, but later indulging in more decorated façades in blocked natural stone, such as the Huis della Faille (1789), with or without pilasters, such as those at the Huis van Ertborn (*c.* 1777; rebuilt 1884).

The French occupied the city between 1793 and 1814. Proposals were made to revive the port, but although such architects as François Verly drew up elaborate plans to improve the waterfront and street system, there is little architecturally to show from either those years or the Dutch occupation that followed until 1830. Instead, during the French period, many religious landmarks were destroyed (e.g. St Michael's Abbey and St Walburgiskerk).

3. AFTER 1830. As Antwerp began to develop again into a major international port, the emphasis lay at first on transport and business, with industry (largely concentrated around the harbour) winning greater importance only after World War II. The appearance of the city changed only slowly until it began to gain impetus in the 1850s, after which it developed rapidly. In 1860–63 the 16th-century ramparts, with their small number of narrow gates, were torn down and replaced by broad avenues. The easier access to the town favoured the rapid growth of the

suburbs, notably around the Cogels-Osylei, but the government had decided to retain Antwerp as a key bastion in the defences of Belgium. The resulting larger ring of fortifications (*see* MILITARY ARCHITECTURE AND FORTIFICATION, §III, 3) similarly restricted growth and was demolished *c.* 1909; its outline is reflected in the Singel, the highway that encompasses Greater Antwerp. The unlimited growth of the agglomeration now became possible. The Scheldt remained a formidable barrier to the west that was breached only by the construction of tunnels under the river in 1933 and 1969.

The harbour expanded in a most spectacular way. In the city itself the Scheldt was straightened in 1877–84 for the construction of quays and warehouses, which led to the destruction of the old nucleus of the town around the Steen. Most effort went into developing the area of polders to the north. Starting in the French and Dutch periods and gaining momentum from 1860, the network of docks and sluices advanced steadily until it reached the Dutch border about 1960.

Under the direction of PIERRE BOURLA, streets were widened and new ones laid out, altering the aspect of many quarters of the city. The most important change took place in the area known as the Zuid, where the 16th-century Spanish citadel was levelled (1874) and converted into a residential district. The new prosperity led to a profusion of building activities. Upper-class houses followed Neo-classical styles throughout the 19th century—sober structures, generally three storeys high, mostly with plastered or white-painted façades. Bourla's Koninklijke Nederlandsche Schouwburg (Royal Dutch Theatre; 1827–34) was inspired by the historicist Roman style of the First Empire. Gothic Revival was adopted for churches and Renaissance and Baroque Revival for public buildings, for example the Koninklijk Museum voor Schone Kunsten (1877–90) by Jean-Jacques Winders (*see* WINDERS, (1)) and Frederik van Dÿk (*see* §II, 3 below). Flemish Renaissance Revival (*see* BELGIUM, §II, 4) appeared in Antwerp in the work of Henri Beyaert, for example the Nationale Bank complex (1874–9). Metal construction was tried, the first example in Belgium being the roof of the Beurs (1852–4), rebuilt after a fire in 1869 by JOSEPH HENRI MARTIN SCHADDE. The monumental Centraal Station, built in 1895–1905 in Renaissance Revival style by Louis Dela Censerie, also employed metal construction.

De Passer (1883), Winders's town house, was also in Renaissance Revival, which, with Baroque Revival, was adopted for private housing around the turn of the century. There is a noteworthy ensemble on Leysstraat. Winders built several houses in the Zuid: both there and in the Cogels-Osylei they were accompanied by Art Deco, which appeared in the 1920s and 1930s. The Torengebouw (Tower building) of 1931, by Jean van Hoemacker, Joseph Smolderen (*b* 1899) and Ernest van Averbeke, was one of the earliest high-rise buildings in Europe. In Antwerp, however, it was one of the last, for few more were constructed in the inner city. Since the 1930s utilitarian styles have prevailed.

BIBLIOGRAPHY

J. H. Plantenga: *L'Architecture religieuse dans l'ancien duché de Brabant depuis le règne des archiducs jusqu'au gouvernement autrichien, 1596–1713* (The Hague, 1926)

A. de Lattin: *Evoluties van het Antwerpse stadsbeeld: Geschiedkundige kronijken*, 7 vols (Antwerp, 1940–53)

Antwerpen, 1860–1960 (exh. cat., Antwerp, Stadsfeestzaal, 1960)

L. Voet and others: *De stad Antwerpen van de Romeinse tijd tot de 17de eeuw: Topografische studie rond het plan van Virgilius Bononiensis, 1565* (Brussels, 1960)

Stad Antwerpen, 4 vols, Bouwen door de eeuwen heen in Vlaanderen: Inventaris van het Cultuurbezit in België, iii (Ghent, 1976–92)

II. Art life and organization.

1. Before 1585. 2. 1585–1830. 3. After 1830.

1. BEFORE 1585. Parallel to its economic and physical expansion, in the 16th century Antwerp grew into the leading art centre north of the Alps, attracting the brightest practitioners from all over the Netherlands, and, in the applied arts, some Italians. In this period it monopolized the most significant Netherlandish forms of artistic expression and exercised great influence abroad through the export of its products and, later in the century, the emigration of the artists themselves as they fled their troubled country.

In order to practise their craft, artists had to be citizens of Antwerp and join the Guild of St Luke. The ledgers of the Guild begin in 1453 and are continuous down to the closure of the organization in 1795. They are an immensely rich source of information on south Netherlandish artists. To the 35 names entered in the first year were added 303 by 1500; for the 16th century as a whole 1925 names are registered, a figure that does not reflect the total number of craftsmen working in the city, as bookbinders, printers, engravers and harpsichord-makers were forced to join from about 1550 only; and most gold- and silversmiths formed their own guild. The Guild of St Luke had a booth in the forecourt of Onze Lieve Vrouw, for the sale of sculptures, retables and paintings. The artists also sold them from their own houses.

Although Italian Renaissance influence was felt early on, at first it consisted of decorative elements; a more profound appreciation came only about 1540, together with an Italo-Flemish decorative style, the Grotesque, which was initiated by Cornelis Cort or Cornelis Floris and rapidly permeated all forms of art. Such artists as PIETER COECKE VAN AELST I and HANS VREDEMAN DE VRIES played an important part in the dissemination of Renaissance ideas through the publication of illustrated handbooks; and as the rise of Protestantism reduced the commissions by and for churches, profane subject-matter quickly gained currency. With 694 painters registered in the 16th century, painting was the dominant art form of Antwerp. From *c.* 1500 to *c.* 1530 the Antwerp Mannerists produced countless religious subjects mainly for export (*see* ANTWERP MANNERISM). Alongside them, however, worked painters of greater talent, including briefly Pieter Bruegel I.

The first great name in Antwerp painting is that of Quinten Metsys (*see* METSYS, (1)), who explored what were to become specialities of Antwerp painting: landscape (seen also in the work of Joachim Patinir; see fig. 4), genre and portraiture. In imitation of Hieronymus Bosch, some—Pieter Bruegel, Jan Mandijn and Pieter Huys (*see* HUYS, (1))—experimented with surrealism. These types of painting were the least affected by Italian influence, which

4. Quentin Metsys and Joachim Patinir: *Temptation of St Anthony*, oil on panel, 1.55×1.73 m, *c.* 1515–25 (Madrid, Museo del Prado)

permeated more deeply the larger religious, mythological and allegorical paintings. Pieter Coecke van Aelst brought the influence of Raphael, but that of Michelangelo, transmitted through the works of Frans Floris, was more durable, and not always for the best, for his dry, colourless style was imitated by many 'Romanists'. Only Marten de Vos, inspired by Venetian painting, used vivid colours.

Graphic art, in both prints and book illustration, became another virtual Antwerp monopoly. Early woodcuts were superseded by engraving, many engravers reproducing the designs of other artists. The sale of prints was largely centred on publishing houses, in particular those of Philip Galle and Hieronymus Cock, at whose House in the Four Winds Giorgio Ghisi worked for a while around 1550. Particular virtuosity was displayed by members of the WIERIX family.

Sculpture had a more chequered evolution. Early in the century the European market for polychrome or gilded wooden altarpieces was divided between Brussels and Antwerp, until demand fell away under the influence of Protestantism from about 1540. The crisis was only partly resolved by increasing secular commissions in both wood and stone, the latter dominated by Cornelis Floris. A number of fine bronze and copper monuments, for example the bronze statue of the *Duke of Alba* (1571; destr. 1577), were made by Jacques Jonghelinck, the Warden of the Antwerp Mint, who was one of a group of talented medallists working in the second half of the century, in an art tried first by Metsys.

Stained glass, particularly the work of DIRK VELLERT, was an important Antwerp craft, as were bookbinding, gold- and silversmithing, crystal, ceramics and, to a lesser degree, tapestry (*see* §III below). Hans Ruckers (*d c.* 1598) won international fame for his harpsichords.

2. 1585–1830. Despite the events of 1585, the relative prosperity of Antwerp that lasted through the 17th century enabled artistic activity to flourish. The Counter-Reformation led to a great increase in commissions for religious works, while demand for profane subjects remained high.

Painting continued to be the dominant art form in the city, painters greatly outnumbering other artists in the Guild of St Luke.

The Mannerism of the late 16th century was supplanted after the return of PETER PAUL RUBENS from Italy in 1608 by his blend of Flemish realism with the Italian Grand Manner, which introduced Baroque to the southern Netherlands in a colourful unity of power, movement and ornament. The style invaded all forms of art (*see* ARTIST'S HOUSE, fig. 3), and the Antwerp school was dominated by Rubens, Anthony van Dyck and Jacob Jordaens. A steady market was provided by the urban patriciate, including such collectors as the merchant CORNELIS VAN DER GEEST and the burgomaster NICHOLAAS ROCKOX, who commissioned large altarpieces and mythological and allegorical subjects. The new fashion for cabinet pictures created a great demand for portraits, genre pictures, landscapes, marine paintings, still-lifes and animal paintings (*see* CABINET PICTURE, §1). True Baroque, however, did not long survive the death of Rubens. Even his former pupils went over to classicism, and the number of painters dwindled rapidly. The two most interesting artists of the late 17th century were David Teniers (ii), who left Antwerp in 1647 to become court painter in Brussels, and Jan Siberechts, who emigrated to London. Many others joined the flight and were not replaced: by about 1700 the Antwerp school was finished.

A similar evolution marks the other great Antwerp speciality, printmaking. Christoffel Jegher was virtually the only Antwerp woodcutter (*see* JEGHER, (1)), and more painters than before tried etching, but the craft consisted essentially of professional reproductive engravers. The Galles and some minor firms continued to flood the market with engravings and albums, but gradually subsided into producing reprints of past works. About 1620 a new school developed of young artists engaged to reproduce Rubens's paintings and drawings; their work counts among the most brilliant ever executed (see fig. 5; *see also* ENGRAVING, §II, 4). By 1700, however, graphic art in Antwerp was no longer of any importance.

Production of sculpture increased with the growth of church commissions. Rubens was most influential in this, too, but at first the sculptors had difficulty in translating pathos and movement into wood and stone. Baroque sculpture reached fulfilment only after Rubens's death, and, unlike painting and engraving, sculpture continued to be practised in the 18th century with some success, although now in the Rococo style. The stylistic transition is perhaps best seen in the work of LOUIS WILLEMSSENS in the cathedral and the St Jacobskerk.

Some older art forms, including medallions and glasswork, declined quickly, but the manufacture of gold- and silverwork, stained glass and harpsichords retained its vitality for longer (*see* §III, 3 and 4 below). Some new art forms emerged, including lace and embroidery. Furniture-making now became very important, and such art dealers as the Forchoudt firm exported it all over Europe, together with paintings and sculptures. Only sculpture, lace and gold- and silverwork continued in the 18th century, albeit on a modest scale.

On the initiative of Teniers, the Academie voor Schone Kunsten was founded in 1663 (*see* BELGIUM, §XV) and was taken over by the city in 1749. Although in theory Antwerp artists were compelled to join the Guild of St Luke, the Austrian government had already excused painters, engravers, sculptors and architects from membership in 1773. The Academie inherited the guild's possessions in 1795, including its ledgers, and was to play an important role in the revival of art in 19th-century Antwerp.

5. Lucas Vorsterman I: *Deposition*, engraving, 562×429 mm, 1620 (Antwerp, Rubenshuis); after Peter Paul Rubens's triptych, 1612–14, in Antwerp Cathedral

3. AFTER 1830. Only from the establishment of Belgium in 1830 did Antwerp begin to resume leadership in artistic matters, although this has been concentrated on painting, engraving and sculpture. The Academie voor Schone Kunsten was instrumental in the revival, attracting talented teachers and many pupils. Societies 'for the propagation of fine arts' played their part by organizing salons and competitions. The Huis Plantin–Moretus was bought by the city in 1876 and established as a museum, and the Koninklijk Museum voor Schone Kunsten moved into its new building (1878–90; *see* §I, 3 above). After World War I the avant-garde disseminated their ideas in papers and exhibitions, small groups dissolving as quickly as they arose, but always followed by others, until in the 1950s and 1960s they had reached record numbers. The Museum Mayer van den Bergh was founded by Henriette Mayer van den Bergh (*d* 1920) to display the paintings and other works collected by her son Fritz Mayer van den Bergh (1859–1901). Rubens's house (*see* §I, 2 and fig. 3 above) was bought by the city in 1937 and opened as a museum in 1946; the 18th-century house and collections of Pieter Smidt vom Gelder (1878–1956) were presented

to the city in 1949, and from 1950 the Openluchtmuseum voor Beeldhouwkunst Middelheim was established in Nachtegalen Park.

The years to 1860 were dominated by the Antwerp school of historical Romanticism as practised by Nicaise De Keyser, Director of the Academie (1855–79), who was to paint a series of historical scenes (1862–72) for the Museum voor Schone Kunsten that was transferred to the new building, and HENRI LEYS, who developed the style and blended it with a realism that was particularly represented by Leys's nephew, Henri De Braekeleer (*see* DE BRAEKELEER, (2)). Realism in its turn gave way in the 1870s to a looser style, which became dominant in Antwerp to the virtual exclusion of Impressionism. Nevertheless, a number of painters, such as Frans Simons (1855–1919), became associated with the Brussels-based, Paris-orientated group Les XX, while others, notably Emile Claus and George Morren, both members of the Vie et Lumière circle, were affected by Impressionist and Post-Impressionist concerns with heightened chromatics. In the early 20th century the influence of Fauvism became apparent in the work of Ferdinand Schirren.

After World War I, Cubism, Futurism and Constructivism were all tried by JOZEF PEETERS, the founder of the Moderne Kunst group, and Paul Joostens, but the Flemish preferred Expressionism, represented in the work of Floris Jespers (1889–1965), combined from *c.* 1930 with the more Intimist tendencies of Albert Van Dyck (1902–51). After World War II, abstract art predominated until other currents filtered in from abroad.

Etching was revived about 1840 by Henri Leys, and it remained essentially a painters' hobby, along with lithography, although the latter was less popular. After World War I, the older generation continued etching, but younger artists rediscovered the woodcut, the black-and-white contrasts of which made a perfect medium for Expressionist ideas. The pioneers of the Flemish woodcut revival were known as The Five, of whom Joris Minne (1897–1988) and Henri Van Straten (1892–1944) worked in Antwerp. As Minne gradually moved towards a more Intimist and Surrealist style, he took up engraving. After World War II, graphic art followed the same course as painting, the main exponent of abstraction being Frans Dille (*b* 1909).

From *c.* 1830 countless figured and ornamental monuments were made in stone, marble and bronze, to adorn public buildings, squares, private houses and churches. Most were technically sound but uninspired, only the work of JEF LAMBEAUX (e.g. the Brabo Fountain in the Grote Markt, 1887) being in any way exceptional. After World War I, however, Oscar Jespers led a revival in quality, with works largely in Expressionist styles. Since World War II, sculpture has shown the same stylistic diversity as the other arts, but quality has remained high.

BIBLIOGRAPHY

GENERAL

P. Rombouts and T. van Lerius: *De liggeren en andere historische archieven der Antwerpsche Sint-Lucasgilde*, 2 vols (Antwerp and The Hague, 1864–72/*R* Amsterdam, 1961)

J. Denucé: *Bronnene voor de geschiedenis van de vlaamsche kunst*, 5 vols (Antwerp, 1931–49)

Le Siècle de Bruegel (exh. cat., Brussels, Musées Royaux B.-A., 1963)

Geschiedenis en uitstraling van de Koninklijke Academie voor Schone Kunsten te Antwerpen, 1663–1963 (exh. cat., Antwerp, Kon. Acad. S. Kst., 1964)

Le Siècle de Rubens (exh. cat., Brussels, Musées Royaux B. A., 1965)

G. von der Osten and H. Vey: *Painting and Sculpture in Germany and the Netherlands, 1500–1600*, Pelican Hist. A. (Harmondsworth, 1969)

Antwerp's Golden Age: The Metropolis of the West in the 16th and 17th Centuries (exh. cat. by L. Voet and others, Washington, DC, Smithsonian Inst. Traveling Exh. Serv., 1973–5)

PAINTING

F. J. van den Branden: *Geschiedenis der Antwerpsche schildersschool* (Antwerp, 1883)

R. Oldenbourg: *Die flämische Malerei des XVII. Jahrhunderts* (Berlin and Leipzig, 1922)

G. Marlier: *Hedendaagse vlaamse schilderkunst* (Brussels, 1944)

L. van Puyvelde: *La Peinture flamande au siècle de Bosch et de Breughel* (Brussels and Paris, 1962)

M. J. Friedländer: *Early Netherlandish* (1967–76)

G. J. Faggin: *La pittura ad Anversa nel cinquecento* (Florence, 1968)

Corpus Rubenianum Ludwig Burchard (Antwerp and London, 1968–)

Schilderkunst in België ten tijde van Henri Leys, 1815–69 (exh. cat., ed. J. F. Buyck and A. A. Moerman; Antwerp, Kon. Mus. S. Kst., 1969)

Z. Z. Filipczak: *Picturing Art in Antwerp, 1550–1700* (Princeton, 1987)

PRINTMAKING

Hollstein: *Dut. & Flem.*

A. J. J. Delen: *Le XVIe Siècle*, 2 vols (1934–5), ii of *Histoire de la gravure dans les anciens Pays-Bas et dans les provinces belges, des origines jusqu'à la fin du XVIIIe siècle* (Paris, 1924–35)

K. Renger: 'Rubens dedit dedicavitque: Rubens Beschaftigung mit der Reproduktionsgraphik', *Jb. Berlin. Mus.*, xvi (1974), pp. 122–75; xvii (1975), pp. 166–213

Antwerp Drawings and Prints, 16th–17th Centuries (exh. cat. by L. Voet, Washington, DC, Smithsonian Inst. Traveling Exh. Serv., 1976–8)

SCULPTURE

J. Duverger and M. J. Onghena: 'De Zuidnederlandse beeldhouwkunst gedurende de 16de eeuw', *De Middeleeuwen: De zestiende eeuw* (1954), i of *Kunstgeschiedenis der Nederlanden*, ed. H. E. van Gelder and J. Duverger (Utrecht and Antwerp, 1954–6)

A. Jansen: 'De beeldhouwkunst in de 17de en in de 18de eeuw', *Van het einde van de zestiende eeuw tot onze tijd in Zuid-Nederland* (1956), iii of *Kunstgeschiedenis der Nederlanden*, ed. H. E. van Gelder and J. Duverger (Utrecht and Antwerp, 1954–6), pp. 116ff

La Sculpture au siècle de Rubens dans les Pays-Bas méridionaux et la principauté de Liège (exh. cat., Brussels, Musées Royaux B.-A., 1977)

DECORATIVE ARTS

Grove 6: 'Ruckers'

J. Duverger and J. Versyp: 'De kunstnijverheid in de zeventiende en achttiende eeuw', *Van het einde van de zestiende eeuw tot onze tijd in Zuid-Nederland* (1956), iii of *Kunstgeschiedenis der Nederlanden*, ed. H. E. van Gelder and J. Duverger (Utrecht and Antwerp, 1954–6)

STAINED GLASS

J. Helbig: *De glasschilderkunst in België: Repertorium en documenten*, 2 vols (Antwerp, 1943–51)

LEON VOET

III. Centre of production.

1. Tapestry. 2. Ceramics. 3. Objects of vertu. 4. Gold and silver.

1. TAPESTRY.

(i) Before 1585. (ii) 1585 and after.

(i) Before 1585. Until 1415 the tapestry-weavers of Antwerp were part of the guild of linen-weavers, but in July of that year they formed their own guild with their own statutes, which included regulations concerning the duration of an apprenticeship, the fee for becoming a master and salary. In addition there were sanctions provided against weavers who produced inferior work or who lured apprentices away from another workshop. Nothing, however, is known about the number of members, as the membership books have not survived. In the aldermen's registers and other documents (Antwerp, Stadsarchf), however, various tapestry-weavers are mentioned by name.

No work of this period has survived, but it would be wrong to suggest that only *verdures* were woven in Antwerp in the 15th century.

In the 16th century the city underwent considerable expansion. The board of magistrates encouraged the maximum expansion of local crafts, including attempts to attract tapestry-weavers from such places as Enghien, Diest, Mechelen, Grammont, Sint-Truiden, Tirlemont, 's-Hertogenbosch, Lille, Tournai, Mons and Binche and entire workshops from Brussels. The tapestry-worker and painter Pieter van Uden settled in Antwerp in 1553 and brought 400 weavers with him from Brussels. His workshop contained 126 looms and employed 33 master weavers, all of whom were granted the freedom of the city. In order to aid the expansion of the trade in Antwerp the collegial act of 20 July 1559 extended this grant to all Brussels tapestry-workers who wished to settle in Antwerp. The imperial edict of 1544 was an attempt by the government to combat certain types of fraud and ensure the high quality of wall hangings. Weavers were required to work the mark of the city and a weaver's monogram into their tapestries; this regulation was not imposed in Antwerp until 1562. The influx of workers from Brussels included Michel de Bos (*fl* 1560–67) and the Brussels cartoon painter Jan Collaert, who arrived in 1563. They were followed by Joos van Herzeele (*fl* 1576–89), to whom the city granted a house near the castle to be used as a workshop for at least 40 workers.

The art of tapestry-weaving was encouraged in Antwerp not only by the municipal government, but also by the new school of painting. Numerous expert cartoon painters also settled in Antwerp. The earliest of these was Pieter Coecke van Aelst. In 1544 the Brussels cartoon painter Leonard Knoest gained the freedom of the city and enrolled himself in the Guild of St Luke. In the same year Karel de Riddere of Mechelen and Hans de Duytscher (pseud. Singher; *fl* 1544–58) from Hesse were also enrolled as cartoon painters in the guild. Other cartoon painters included Joris van Liecke (*fl* 1564), Maarten van Tiegem (*fl* 1580), Lucas Floquet (*fl* 1589), Artus Vermylen (*fl* 1589) and Otto van Veen (1556–1629); knowledge of their activities, however, is not as fully documented.

By the mid-16th century Antwerp had become the main centre of the international tapestry trade. The construction of the Pant, a tapestry hall, took place in 1550–54, and this became the main centre for the sale and display of tapestries, cartoons and sketches in Flanders. Extant documents supply little information about the local workshops and their production at this time. Makers' marks added to the borders of several wall hangings enable works to be definitely attributed to Antwerp. The city mark (a stylized image of the city castle flanked on either side by a hand) is clearly derived from the blazon of the Margrave of Antwerp. Sometimes the mark is highly simplified, as in a *Hunting Tapestry* (*c.* 1600; Stuttgart, Württemberg. Landesmus.), which has only a single hand and the letter A. In other cases, the city mark of Brussels was woven in an altered form into the underside of the Antwerp tapestries—instead of the initials B-B (Brabant-Brussels), with the traditional miniature red shield in the middle, the

6. Tapestry depicting *Hercules Killing Nessus* from the *Deeds of Hercules* series, made in the workshop of Michel de Bos, Antwerp, 1565–79 (Munich, Residenzmuseum)

initials B-A (Brabant-Antwerp) were woven into the borders of the work; this can be seen on two tapestries now in the château of Azay-le-Rideau, as well as on a *Grotesque Tapestry with Nebuchadnezzar and the Children in the Fiery Furnace* (*c.* 1585; Amsterdam, Rijksmus.). A weaver's monogram is sometimes woven into the border, which enables an accurate attribution. A few of the monograms have not yet been identified, such as that on the above-mentioned *Hunting Tapestry* and that on a scene from the *Life of Moses* and from the *Story of Esther* (*c.* 1560; Oxford, St John's Coll.). The borders of these tapestries are filled with flowers and fruit, as well as fantastic figures and personifications of Faith, Hope and Love.

Among the most characteristic Renaissance tapestries is a series depicting the *Deeds of Hercules* (see fig. 6), with its typical blue ground and fine grotesque borders. The series comprises 13 (originally ?14) wall hangings and 10 window hangings depicting the *Arms of Bavaria and Austria* (1567; Munich, Bayer. Nmus.). It was woven for Albert IV, Duke of Bavaria, and his Austrian consort in the workshop of Michel de Bos, whose name appears repeatedly in the borders of the *Hercules* tapestries. The mythological illustrations were derived from a fresco cycle by Frans Floris, which was published in part as engravings by Cornelis Cort in 1563. A monogram, IVH, appears on three of the four above-mentioned grotesque tapestries; this has been attributed (Göbel) to the Brussels weaver Jan van den Hecke (*fl c.* 1575–1600). It seems more logical, however, to associate the monogram with the Antwerp weaver Joos van Herzeele, whose initials consist of the same letters. The same monogram appears in three of the series of eight tapestries with scenes from the *Life of Alexander the Great* (last quarter of 16th century; Vienna, Ksthist. Mus.). These, too, may have come from the workshop of van Herzeele. In 1576, during the war with Spain, the Pant was closed after heavy looting of the tapestries, trade materials and designs. Economic activity revived in 1578, and the building was re-opened.

(ii) 1585 and after. In the early 17th century the weavers' guild was no longer effective; there was little or no supervision of the raw materials used or of the quality of work produced, and the training of apprentices was occasionally neglected. The principal aim of the masters was to prevent the emigration of their workforce, and in response to the problem they directed a petition to the city board of magistrates in 1606–7, in which they emphasized that every possible inducement had been offered to bring the art of tapestry-weaving to the city and keep it there. Such European rulers as the French king did their best to attract the most important workers and artists to their own tapestry industries. Already by 1586 van Herzeele is believed to have moved to Hamburg, and in December 1594 Frans Spierincx (*c.* 1550–1630) arrived in Delft; around 1607 Maarten Steurbout (*fl* 1591–1607) travelled to Moscow, although it is not certain whether or not he planned to work there as a tapestry-weaver. In 1619–20 the weavers realized that further measures were necessary to ensure the continued growth of the industry in Antwerp. They petitioned the board of magistrates to institute legislation for the masters and apprentices so that their business would flourish. Unfortunately, this document has not survived, but it appears to have been ineffective in stemming the flow of emigration: in April 1693 Balthazar Bosmans (*fl* 1687–1717) left for Paris; many weavers from Antwerp went to work at the Mortlake factory in England; and Jacques van der Goten (1659–1724) went to Madrid on 30 July 1720 and set up an important tapestry workshop, which continued to produce tapestries in the late 20th century (*see* SPAIN, §XI, 4).

In many of the workshops, wall hangings were produced, which were frequently sold through dealers or brokers. The latter made sure that monograms or weavers' signatures were excluded from the pieces sold, so that the buyers would not be able to trace the origin of the tapestry. The tapestry merchants also occasionally took the liberty of weaving their own names into the borders of the tapestries that they sold, to publicize their own businesses. In the wall hanging of a *Bacchanale* (*c.* 1650; Deurne, Prov. Mus. Sterckshof) the city mark of Antwerp and the subtitle *Anvers* are in the lower left-hand corner, and on the right there is a cartouche enclosing the words *Cura Simonis Bouwens.* Simon Bouwens was probably concerned only with the sale of tapestries; this is confirmed by the Latin tag in the cartouche, which is translated as 'under the supervision of Simon Bouwens'. Pieter Wouters (*fl* 1664–82), an important tapestry dealer and tapestry printer in the second half of the 17th century, signed his merchandise in this same way.

In many cases it is still difficult to determine who the weaver and/or dealer was. It often happened that an important tapestry-weaver, at the head of a busy workshop, was also an important dealer. The most significant dealers include the Vrancx, van Welden and de Bie families, as well as Jacob Tsantels (*fl* 1635–83), Hans Bos (*fl* 1626–46), Bernard Gerstelinck (*fl* 1629–53), Peter van Camp (*fl* 1679–89), Jan Frans Cornelissen (1640–78) and Joris Rombout (*fl* 1649–79). Another was Joost van Butsel (*b c.* 1609) of Enghien, who was active in Antwerp in the late 1640s. His son, Andries van Butsel, owned a series of cartoons depicting the *History of Tamburlaine and Bajazet* (1675–). After his death, these were probably passed to Maria Anna Wauters (1651–*c.* 1696), who had them made into tapestries. The wall hangings on this theme (Kremsmünster, Stiftsgal., and Vienna, Dom- & Diözmus.) may well have come from the workshop of van Butsel. The separate pieces in the Hermitage, St Petersburg, and the Kunsthistorisches Museum, Vienna, which were probably once part of the same series, may have been woven in the workshop of Wauters. The latter works rank both technically and artistically among the most beautiful products of the Antwerp workshops of this period.

Jan van der Goten (1642–1700) must also be considered one of the most important tapestry-workers in the second half of the 17th century. From 1677 he produced different series for the Antwerp dealer Nicolaas Nauwelaerts (*fl* 1677–1709), including the *History of Rinaldo and Armida*, *Perseus and Andromeda*, *Bacchic Feasts*, the *Four Continents* and *verdures* with small figures in conversation. The series of the *Story of Jephtha* (see fig. 7) carries the signatures of van der Goten and his brother-in-law Peter Kolvenaar. Balthazar Bosmans was also the head of an important workshop, the productions of which included

7. Tapestry of the *Fight of the Ammonites* from the *Story of Jephthah* series, made by Peter Kolvenaar, Antwerp, *c.* 1670 (Stockholm, Kungliga Husgerådskammaren)

the *Story of St Kilian* (1687–8; destr. 1945) made for the Chapter of the Dom in Würzburg.

The tapestry workshop of the brothers Michiel Wauters (*d* 1679) and Philip Wauters (1617–79) enjoyed an international reputation. The intervention of numerous dealers meant that their wall hangings were offered for sale in most of the principal cities abroad. They produced simple series, mentioned in the documents as 'rough' work, and also the 'royal' series, which could be used by their owners for purposes of display. In many cases production was adapted to local taste. They repeatedly produced low-pile tapestries, which they called the 'English' style. They also requested the aid of well-known painters for the production of cartoons: Giovanni Francesco Romanelli, for example, supplied the designs for the *Story of Dido and Aeneas* (*c.* 1675–1700; examples in Piacenza, Coll. Alberoni; Milan, Castello Sforzesco; Cleveland, OH, Mus. A.), and ABRAHAM VAN DIEPENBEECK made cartoons for the nine-piece *Story of Moses* and the *Story of Semiramis*. Others were active in the same way, either directly or indirectly, as cartoon painters for the firm, including Thomas Willebroirts Bosschaert (1614–54), Peter de Witte (1586–1651), Pieter Boel, Daniël Janssens (1636–82) and the French artist Philippe de La Hyre (1640–1718). In 1678 Michiel Wauters purchased no fewer than 29 cartoons from Jacob Jordaens.

At the beginning of the 18th century Cornelis de Wael (*d* 1723), Jacobus de Bock (*fl* 1693–1705) and Jan van der Goten were still active as producers and dealers in tapestries. The industry, however, was encountering increasing difficulties, including rising production costs, the closing of many foreign markets, growing competition from abroad and, above all, changes in taste and cheaper, alternative wall coverings, all of which contributed to the collapse of the industry. The death of de Wael marked the virtual end of the tapestry industry in Antwerp.

See also TAPESTRY, §§I and II.

BIBLIOGRAPHY

H. Göbel: *Wandteppiche, i: Die Niederlande* (Leipzig, 1923; Eng. trans., New York, 1924)

A. Coulin Weibel: 'Tapestries by Peeter Wauters', *Bull. Detroit Inst. A.*, xiv (1934–5), pp. 44–7

M. Crick-Kuntziger: 'Contribution à l'histoire de la tapisserie anversoise: Les Marques et les tentures des Wauters', *Rev. Belge A. & Hist.*, v (1935), pp. 35–44

J. Denucé: *Les Tapisseries anversoises: Fabrication et commerce* (Antwerp, 1936)

E. Duverger: 'Antwerpse tapijtkunst en tapijthandel', *Tentoonstelling Antwerpse wandtapijten* (exh. cat., Deurne, Prov. Mus. Sterckshof, 1973), pp. 17–43

——: 'Antwerp Tapestries of the Seventeenth Century', *Connoisseur* (April 1977), pp. 274–87

ERIK DUVERGER

2. CERAMICS. Antwerp was a major centre for faience production during the 16th century. About 1512 three Italian maiolica potters, Janne Maria de Capua, Jan Frans de Brescia and Guido Andries, settled in Antwerp. In 1520 Andries bought the Den Salm workshop in Kammenstraat. From 1545, at the height of Antwerp's faience production, Henric van Grevenbroeck of the Dmoelenyser workshop and Jan Bogaerts (*fl* 1552–71) of De Maeght van Gent had workshops in the same street. Andries's five sons also directed workshops in Antwerp and abroad. Jan Floris (Juan Flores; *d* 1567) was made a master craftsman of the Guild of St Luke in 1550 and was famous for his work as a faience painter; in 1563 Philip II of Spain summoned him and bestowed on him the title Maestro de Azulejos. From 1550 to 1626–7 some 30 faience potters were admitted to the Guild of St Luke as master craftsmen. During the Wars of Religion (1562–98) many potters emigrated and spread their craft to Spain, the northern Netherlands, England and Germany. During the 17th century the Antwerp factories went into a slow but inexorable decline because of the competition from Holland. Antwerp's faience production comprised floor- and wall-tiles, *albarelli*, tablewares and plaques. Forms and decoration were influenced by Italian maiolica and by Hispano-Moresque wares. Antwerp's finest wares are those decorated with biblical subjects, strapwork and grotesques inspired particularly by engravings by such Netherlandish artists as Enea Vico (e.g. tile-picture of the *Conversion of St Paul*, 1547; Antwerp, Mus. Vleeshuis).

BIBLIOGRAPHY

M. Laurent: 'Guido di Savino and the Earthenware of Antwerp', *Burl. Mag.*, xli (1922), pp. 288–97
N. Nicaise: 'Notes sur les faïenciers italiens établis à Anvers dans le premier tiers du XVIe siècle', *Rev. Belge Philol. & Hist.*, xvi (1937), pp. 189–202
A.-M. Mariën-Dugardin: 'Les Grotesques dans la majolique anversoise de la seconde moitié du XVI siècle', *Bull. Musées Royaux A. & Hist.*, xlv (1973), pp. 173–200
C. Dumortier: 'Les Ateliers de majolique à Anvers (1508–1585)', *Bull. Antwerp. Ver. Bodem- & Grotonderzoek*, i (1988), pp. 23–38

CLAIRE DUMORTIER

3. OBJECTS OF VERTU. Antwerp has been a trading centre for gemstones and pearls since the Middle Ages. A decree of 1447, the first of its kind, ordered the prosecution of merchants trading in fake stones. In the 15th century a number of Jews, including diamond-cutters who had been expelled from Spain and Portugal, migrated to Antwerp. In 1483 diamond-cutters are recorded as working in the city, and by 1577 the guild of diamond-cutters, which at this time included cutters of all gemstones, numbered between 30 and 40 members. The extent of the gemstone-cutting industry was such that from 1584 to 1642 the ruby-cutters (who cut all coloured gemstones) formed their own guild. During the 16th century Antwerp became the main centre of jewellery production in the southern Netherlands. Hans Collaert, for example, designed pendants that departed from the Renaissance style.

Exotic shells and pearls continued to be traded through Antwerp harbour (e.g. ewer, 1544; Moscow, Kremlin, inv. 2383; see Filimonov, 1894, plate 157); in the last decades of the 16th century nautilus cups were popular (e.g. double nautilus cup, *c.* 1550; Florence, Pitti; others in Brussels, Mus. Royaux A. & Hist.; Kassel, Staatl. Museen; London, BM), and from 1600 to 1610 there was a guild of pearl-drillers. Cameo-carving was also practised in the 16th century and the early 17th, although little is known about this trade. A large cup (gold, enamel, diamonds, emeralds, rubies and pearls, 1530–40; Vienna, Ksthist. Mus.) and a smaller cup (silver gilt, *c.* 24 cameos, 1625; Amsterdam, Rijksmus.) are thought to have been made in Antwerp. Intaglios in the style of Giovanni Bilivert were also produced, as were, probably, porphyry objects, for example a jar (mounted *c.* 1470; London, V&A) by Siger van Steynemeulen (1443–1508).

During the 17th century the trade in diamonds expanded, and by 1618 Antwerp had 164 workshops with an average of three employees per workshop. Towards the second half of the 17th century a lower demand for coloured gemstones led to a decline in the number of ruby-cutters, and by 1642 the ruby-cutters' and the diamond-cutters' guilds were amalgamated. The diamond trade also declined after the mid-17th century, and by 1670 only about 100 workshops were still operating. Many cutters emigrated to Amsterdam or to Paris, where Cardinal Jules Mazarin promoted the brilliant cut, which was introduced to Antwerp only from the end of the 17th century. During the 18th century the industry lost its creative energy, although a large amount of diamonds were still cut in Antwerp: in 1788, for example, the French crown jewels (destr.) were recut there.

During the 1820s, in the depression following the Napoleonic Wars, there were only about 20 or 30 gem-cutters in Antwerp, who were largely dependent on Amsterdam for their supplies of rough stones and for providing a market for the cut stones. From 1840 mechanization, introduced to Antwerp by the merchant J.-J. Bovie, made cutting on a large scale possible and led to the growth of the diamond-cutting industry during the second half of the 19th century. During the 20th century demand decreased, although craftsmanship of the stones continues to develop, and Antwerp remains the most important centre for the trading and processing of cut diamonds.

BIBLIOGRAPHY

G. Filimonov: *Opis Moskovskoj Oruzejni Palati*, ii (1893), pp. 14–16; iii (1894)
D. Schlugleit: *Geschiedenis van het Antwerpsche diamantslijpersambacht* (Antwerp, 1935)
G. Switzer: *Diamonds in Pictures* (London and Melbourne, 1967)
J. Walgrave and others: *Antwerp: World Diamond Center* (Antwerp, 1973)
Diamantjuwelen uit Rubens' tijd (exh. cat., Antwerp, Prov. Diamantmus., 1977)
I. Kockelbergh, E. Vleeschdrager and J. Walgrave: *The Brilliant Story of Antwerp Diamonds* (Antwerp, 1992)

G. VAN HEMELDONCK

4. GOLD AND SILVER. The earliest record of an organization in Antwerp that included workers in precious metals is an ordinance from 1382. An independent community of gold- and silversmiths was slowly growing, however, and its statutes were officially recognized on 24 February 1456, when, in addition to makers' marks, the use of the city mark, a crowned right hand, derived from the city's coat of arms, was made compulsory for works

of the prescribed gold or silver content. In addition, a mark depicting a smaller hand, without the crown, was also used on pieces with a lower gold or silver content.

During the 16th century, the golden age of Antwerp silverwork (*see* BELGIUM, fig. 40), the city boasted not only numerous expert goldsmiths who produced costly ornaments and jewellery but was also an important centre for the production of prints, used as models throughout Europe. In spite of a brief but serious decline as a result of the civil war that separated the northern and southern Netherlands in the second half of the 16th century, there was a new flowering of gold and silver production in the 17th century, when the Flemish Baroque style was at its height. There was, however, a gradual decline from the 18th century.

See also BELGIUM, §IX, 1(i) and (ii).

BIBLIOGRAPHY

D. Schugleit: *De Antwerpse goud- en zilversmeden in het corporatief stelsel, 1332–1798* (Wetteren, 1969)

Antwerps huiszilver uit de 17e en 18e eeuw (exh. cat., Antwerp, Rubenshuis, 1988)

Zilver uit de gouden eeuw van Antwerpen (exh. cat., Antwerp, Rockoxhuis, 1988)

LEO DE REN

IV. Buildings.

1. CATHEDRAL. The cathedral of Onze Lieve Vrouw is the most spacious religious building in Belgium and an important example of Brabantine Gothic architecture. In the 12th century a college of canons founded by Godfrey VI, Duke of Lower Lorraine (*reg* 1088–1100), was installed in an existing chapel, a Romanesque church preceded by a façade block with two towers. A new church was begun in 1352, but it was not completed until 1615.

The present building, of limestone, is 117 m long internally and 26 m to the crown of the vault. It has a three-bay choir with an ambulatory and five radiating chapels, a narrow transept of shallow projection and a nave with double aisles and side chapels, which is seven bays long including the façade block. There are a central lantern tower and two west towers. The eastern arm was built between 1352 and 1420, first under the direction of Jan Appelmans (*d* 1395) and, from before 1419, under his son, PETER APPELMANS. In 1422 the foundations of the north-west tower were laid, at a higher level than the choir, the floor of which was then raised 1 m to correspond. The lower parts of the nave and aisles were built from 1425 to 1472, the chapels being added in the late 15th century by Domien de Waghemakere. The nave was partly vaulted by 1508, but in 1521, after the completion of the north transept (1519) and the north-west spire, a new choir was projected, to be built by Domien de Waghemakere and Rombout Keldermans II. Emperor Charles V laid the foundation stone of the new work, which was to have seven radiating chapels (traces are visible); but building was halted by a fire that seriously damaged the nave in 1533. The transepts were vaulted and the lantern tower built in 1537; the nave was vaulted in 1614. The building was completed a year later by the construction of the transept portals, the south portal being by Cornelis van Mildert (*d* 1667). The north transept porch was rebuilt in 1896.

8. Antwerp Cathedral, west front, begun 1422

The choir of Onze Lieve Vrouw introduced a new type of elevation into Brabantine Gothic. It has two storeys, the clerestory windows having a balustrade fronting a wall passage, with the glass on the external plane of the wall. The arcades are supported on moulded piers with capitals so small that they give the impression of continuous mouldings. The arcade spandrels are covered with applied rectilinear panelled tracery. This form of tracery was used slightly earlier in Mechelen Cathedral, but the Antwerp design is more coherent; and the general design is derived not from Mechelen but from 13th-century Normandy, where this type of elevation is frequent (e.g. Bayeux Cathedral). At Antwerp the complete absence of superfluous decoration lends the interior a classic rigour, and the luminosity of the upper storey created by the huge traceried windows contrasts with the dim multiple spaces of the ground-storey aisles and chapels.

The elevation design was continued in the nave, where the continuous mouldings obviated the impression of width given by the aisles and chapels. The quadripartite rib vault of the choir is supported by a double span of flying buttresses, but that of the nave is buttressed by the transverse roofs of the aisles and chapels. Tierceron and lierne ribs were introduced only in the choir chapels and the transept. Of the façade towers (see fig. 8) only the north was finished, but not to the original plan. For technical reasons it was cut down by one storey. The lower part was crucial to the development of towers in Brabant. Above it a smaller octagon with pinnacles and little flying buttresses leads to an openwork spire. The central portal of the façade, which is topped by an ogee arch, has an early 20th-century sculpture of the *Last Judgement* (replacing two earlier versions, destroyed in the 16th century and the late 18th).

Important works of art in the cathedral include a 13th-century *Virgin and Child* (*see* GOTHIC, fig. 43) and, above all, paintings by Rubens: the *Raising of the Cross* (1610–11; *see* BAROQUE, fig. 2), the *Descent from the Cross* (1612–4; *see* RUBENS, PETER PAUL, fig. 3), the *Assumption of the Virgin* (1626) and *Coronation of the Virgin*.

BIBLIOGRAPHY

S. Leurs and L. J. M. Philippen: *De kathedrale kerk van O.-L.-Vrouw te Antwerpen*, A. Belg., ix (Antwerp, 1938)

J. Van Brabant: *Onze-Lieve-Vrouwkathedraal van Antwerpen: Grootste gotische kerk der Nederlanden* (Antwerp, 1972)

J. P. Boyazis: 'L'Espace intérieur dans l'architecture gothique-brabançonne au XVe siècle', *Bull. Comm. Royale Mnmts & Sites*, xii (1985), pp. 5–57

JACQUES THIBAUT

2. STADHUIS. The earliest city government of Antwerp (12th century) presumably met in the house of one of the aldermen. In the 13th and 14th centuries, however, municipal government was housed in the Broodhuis (destr.), a residence of the Dukes of Brabant. When Antwerp returned to the rule of Brabant in the early 15th century (*see* §I, 1 above), the municipal government was given its own aldermen's hall, south of the current town hall. Although relatively modest, it nevertheless demonstrated the city's growing importance. Owing to the vast increase in population after 1500, plans were made *c.* 1540–41 for a larger and more imposing town hall, to be built by Domien de Waghemakere in Gothic style on the south side of the Grote Markt. Political and military circumstances, however, required that the materials and money that had already been collected were used to build the new fortifications (*see* §I, 1 above).

Twenty years later, plans for a new town hall were renewed, but this time it was to be on the west side of the Grote Markt and in Italian Renaissance style (see fig. 9). The design of the Stadhuis is attributed to Cornelis Floris and Willem van den Broeck, who may have been assisted by advisers from outside the city. The building was inaugurated in 1565. When Antwerp was sacked in November 1576, the Stadhuis, the courtyard of which had served as an artillery arsenal, was gutted by fire; it was completely rebuilt in the original style in the succeeding years. It has four storeys, with a rusticated ground floor, pilasters between the windows, a central frontispiece with round-headed windows, Ionic columns and a tall, classicizing stepped gable. The design retains such northern

9. Antwerp, Stadhuis, attributed to Cornelis Floris and Willem van den Broeck, 1561–5

features as square-headed windows with mullions and transoms and a steeply pitched roof with dormers.

During the French occupation (1793–1814) various aspects of the building's interior were changed to accommodate the introduction of a new form of government. The most important alterations, however, came after the mid-19th century: the courtyard was roofed over, as at the Beurs (*see* §I, 3 above), and provided with a monumental state staircase leading to the so-called 'schoon verdiep' on the first floor, where the most beautiful and richly decorated chambers were located. The rooms were completely redecorated; the windows giving on to the courtyard were blinded, so that the resulting blank walls could be used for frescoes. These, begun by Henri Leys but unfinished at his death, portrayed the city's former greatness in trade, shipping and the fine arts, but they were also intended to emphasize the ancient privileges of Antwerp. In various parts of the building, elements of the earlier style remain, such as the chimneypiece (16th–17th centuries) in the Trouwzaal (Hall of Weddings), or the paintings (early 18th century) by Jacques de Roore and Balthazar Barbiers on the ceiling of the Raadzaal (Council Chamber).

The Stadhuis became a model for those (both destr.) at Vlissingen and Emden, both of which had close economic ties with Antwerp. It is likely that the town hall (1648–55; now Royal Palace) at Amsterdam was largely inspired by that of Antwerp.

For further discussion *see* TOWN HALL.

BIBLIOGRAPHY

A. Corbet: *Cornelis Floris en de bouw van het Stadhuis te Antwerpen* (Antwerp, 1937)

J. Duverger: 'Cornelis Floris en het Stadhuis te Antwerpen', *Gent. Bijdr. Kstgesch.*, vii (1941), pp. 37–72

F. Prims: *Het Stadhuis te Antwerpen: Geschiedenis en beschrijving* (Antwerp, 1941)

H. Bevers: *Das Rathaus von Antwerpen, 1561–1565: Architektur und Figurenprogramm* (Hildesheim, 1985)

JAN VAN ROEY

Antwerp Mannerism. Style of painting and drawing practised by artists working in Antwerp during the period from *c.* 1500 to 1530. The term was coined by Max Friedländer in 1915 in his article 'Die Antwerpener Manieristen von 1520'. In this and subsequent publications (1921, 1933 and 1937) he attempted to bring order into a large body of anonymous Antwerp paintings (and some drawings) that had been gradually gathered under the name of Herri met de Bles, after an *Adoration of the Magi* (Munich, Alte Pin.) bearing a false Bles signature. Only a small proportion of these works could be sorted into recognizable hands. The principal anonymous masters identified by Friedländer were PSEUDO-BLES (or Pseudo-Blesius), the author of the Munich painting, the MASTER OF THE VON GROOTE ADORATION, the MASTER OF THE ANTWERP ADORATION, the MASTER OF AMIENS (for all of whom *see* MASTERS, ANONYMOUS, AND MONOGRAMMISTS, §I) and the Master of 1518 (subsequently identified by Marlier as JAN MERTENS). The outstanding known artist of the group is JAN DE BEER. Friedländer also included ADRIAEN VAN OVERBEKE, the early work of JAN GOSSART and the putative oeuvre of Jan Wellens de Cock (*see* COCK, (1)) as part of Antwerp Mannerism. Despite its name, Antwerp Mannerism is unrelated to Italian or later Flemish Mannerism; its mannerism, instead, is an expression of Late Gothic art.

A work such as the *Beheading of St John the Baptist* (see fig.), attributed by Friedländer to Pseudo-Bles, exemplifies the main features of the style: histrionic figural groupings, flamboyant costumes, elegant chromatic effects, technical virtuosity and fantastical architecture freely combining Gothic and Renaissance elements. Decorative invention is the keynote. Another characteristic of Antwerp Mannerism is the marked tendency towards repetition, whether of themes (the Adoration of the Magi being a kind of signature subject), of stock motifs and figures, or of entire compositions (copies and variants exist in large numbers). This aspect, as often noted, is probably a result of production for the Antwerp market. Much of Antwerp Mannerist output was intended for export, particularly the large retables in which Mannerists either provided painted wings for sculpted shrines (e.g. Jan Mertens's work for the carved wooden altarpiece, 1518; Lübeck, Marienkirche) or painted the entire polyptych themselves (e.g. the altarpiece of 1516, Västerås Cathedral, Sweden). Collaboration and mass production appear to have been common. While this has a definite levelling effect, Antwerp Mannerism nonetheless is not an entirely homogeneous phenomenon. The range of quality among works is broad, from the sophisticated chiaroscuro and colouristic refinement of de Beer's *Nativity* and the *Flowering of St Joseph's Rod* (both U. Birmingham, Barber Inst.), and the dazzling virtuosity of the Master of Amiens's Puy panel *'Au juste pois véritable balance'* (1518; Amiens, Mus. Picardie), to the crude workmanship of van Overbeke's altarpiece in Kempen, Germany (1513; parish church of St Anne) and the even more routine work of the many anonymous painters practising the style.

Friedländer dated the onset of Antwerp Mannerism to the first decade of the 16th century, emphasizing the guild entrance dates of its named practitioners: Gossart and Jan van Leyden (whom he identified with Jan de Cock) in 1503, de Beer in 1504 and van Overbeke in 1508. The fact that the earliest extant dated work (van Overbeke's Kempen altarpiece) dates to 1513 has led some (e.g. von der Osten) to conclude that Antwerp Mannerism cannot be shown to have existed before then, but Friedländer and others regard the presence of Mannerist elements in Gossart's work during his Antwerp years (1503–7/8) as evidence of its earlier origin. With relatively few dated works surviving, and all of them from the second and third decades of the century, the origin and chronology of Antwerp Mannerism remains problematic. Silver has stressed the similarity of stylistic conventions found in Antwerp Mannerism and Brabantine sculpture of the late 15th century and the early 16th, finding indications of these conventions in Quentin Metsys's *Lamentation* altarpiece of 1508–11 (Antwerp, Kon. Mus. S. Kst.).

In its exclusive focus on religious themes and devotional iconography, and in its flamboyant style, Antwerp Mannerism was a manifestation of late medieval culture that did not survive beyond the third decade of the 16th century. In its day, however, it exerted a wide appeal among merchants and churchmen buying art in Antwerp

Pseudo-Bles (attrib.): *Beheading of St John the Baptist*, oil on panel, 480×350 mm, *c.* 1520 (Berlin, Gemäldegalerie)

and a broadly diffused influence on contemporary artists. In Antwerp itself, the impact of the style was occasionally registered on painters not otherwise associated with it: Gossart, Metsys, Joos van Cleve, Dirck Vellert, the Master of Frankfurt and Goswijnn van der Weyden. The early development of Pieter Coecke van Aelst shows connections with the work of Jan Mertens (the Master of 1518), who was perhaps his teacher (Marlier). Some of the paintings attributed to the Bruges artist Adriaen Isenbrandt incorporated Mannerist elements, and the influence of the style also extended to French stained-glass and manuscript production (Orth). Friedländer (1915) even detected traces of the style in contemporary German books. A more problematic case is Leiden painting of the period, particularly the work and circle of Cornelis Engebrechtsz., which shows striking connections with Antwerp Mannerism. Gibson suggests that influence may have been transmitted by the Master of the Vienna Lamentation, whom he believes arrived in Leiden from Antwerp *c.* 1512–14.

The term Antwerp Mannerism has often been regarded as unsatisfactory, and a number of attempts have been made to introduce alternative nomenclature (Baldass, Marlier, Faggin, Philippot). Of greater significance has been the recognition that the tendency towards mannered stylization was not limited to Antwerp but broadly characteristic of Late Gothic Netherlandish art as a whole (Baldass, Hoogewerff, Benesch). Closely related strains of Late Gothic Mannerism have also been identified in regional 16th-century French painting (Laclotte, Laveissière, Foucart). A complex phenomenon, Antwerp Mannerism has elicited strong and often conflicting responses from scholars. In iconography the style is generally conservative, and in execution it frequently betrays routine production values in the service of the market-place. At its best, though, Antwerp Mannerism is stylish, assured and extraordinarily vital, revealing a freedom of invention and technique that bears comparison with contemporary German Florid sculpture and Flamboyant Gothic architecture.

BIBLIOGRAPHY

M. J. Friedländer: 'Die Antwerpener Manieristen von 1520', *Jb. Kön.-Preuss. Kstsamml.*, xxxvi (1915), pp. 65–91

——: *Die niederländischen Manieristen* (Leipzig, 1921)

——: *Die altniederländische Malerei* (Berlin, 1924–37); Eng. trans. as *Early Netherlandish Painting*, 16 vols (Leiden, 1967–76)

L. Baldass: 'Die niederländischen Maler des spätgotischen Stiles', *Jb. Ksthist. Samml. Wien*, n.s., xi (1937), pp. 117–38

G. J. Hoogewerff: *De Noord-Nederlandsche schilderkunst*, ii (The Hague, 1938), pp. 12–14

G. von der Osten: 'Studien zu Jan Gossaert', *De artibus opuscula XL: Essays in Honor of Erwin Panofsky* (New York, 1960), pp. 454–75 (460–61) [argues that Antwerp Mannerism does not predate 1513]

O. Benesch: *The Art of the Renaissance in Northern Europe: Its Relation to the Contemporary Spiritual and Intellectual Movements* (rev. London, 1965), pp. 79–100

G. Marlier: *La Renaissance flamande: Pierre Coeck d'Alost* (Brussels, 1966), pp. 109–16

M. Laclotte: 'Quelques Tableaux bourguignons du XVIe siècle', *Studies in Renaissance and Baroque Art Presented to Anthony Blunt* (London, 1967), pp. 83–5

G. T. Faggin: *La pittura ad Anversa nel cinquecento* (Florence, 1968), pp. 17–19

S. Herzog: *Jan Gossart called Mabuse (ca. 1478–1532): A Study of his Chronology with a Catalogue of his Works*, 3 vols (diss., Bryn Mawr Coll., PA, 1968), pp. 18–39 [Gossart's Antwerp work and Antwerp Mannerism]

P. Philippot: *Pittura fiamminga e rinascimento italiano* (Turin, 1970), pp. 101–5

W. S. Gibson: *The Paintings of Cornelis Engebrechtsz.* (New York, 1977), pp. 171–207 [the 'Jan de Cock problem' and the Master of the Vienna Lamentation]

D. Ewing: *The Paintings and Drawings of Jan de Beer*, 2 vols (diss., Ann Arbor, U. MI, 1978)

J. Foucart: 'Nouvelles acquisitions de peintures des écoles du nord', *Rev. Louvre*, xxix (1979), pp. 370–80 (370–71, 378)

S. Laveissière: 'Un Volet de retable du XVIe siècle retrouvé', *Rev. Louvre*, xxix (1979), pp. 362–4

E. Starcky: 'A propos d'un dessin maniériste anversois', *Rev. Louvre*, xxxi (1981), pp. 96–102 [observations on the character of Antwerp Mannerism]

L. Silver: *The Paintings of Quentin Metsys, with a Catalogue Raisonné* (Montclair, NJ, 1984), pp. 45–7

M. W. Ainsworth and M. Faries: 'Northern Renaissance Paintings: The Discovery of Invention', *Bull. St Louis A. Mus.*, xviii (1986), pp. 3–47 (31–7) [study of underdrawings of Master of 1518 with attributions of drgs]

J. R. Judson: 'Jan Gossaert and the New Aesthetic', *The Age of Bruegel: Netherlandish Drawings in the Sixteenth Century* (exh. cat. by J. O. Hand and others, Washington, DC, N.G.A.; New York, Pierpont Morgan Lib.; 1986–7), pp. 13–24 (14–17)

M. D. Orth: 'Antwerp Mannerist Model Drawings in French Renaissance Books of Hours: A Case Study of the 1520s Hours Workshop', *J. Walters A.G.*, xlvii (1989), pp. 77–90

DAN EWING

Anunciação, Tomás José da (*b* Lisbon, 26 Oct 1818; *d* Lisbon, 3 April 1879). Portuguese painter. He belonged to the first generation of romantic artists in Portugal and specialized in paintings of landscapes and animals. From 1837 until 1844 he attended the Academia de Belas-Artes in Lisbon, where, with other pupils, he protested against the teaching methods of the Academia, which was dominated by the classical tradition of António Manuel da Fonseca.

Anunciação was to advocate the practice, new in Portugal, of painting out of doors. In fact, however, his landscapes were rather stiff and conventional, effects emphasized by his continued use of sepia glazes. They show the influence of the classical landscape tradition of Pierre Antoine Quillad and Jean Pillement, who worked in Portugal, on the one hand, and, on the other, that of the genre painting of Auguste Roquement (1804–52), whom Anunciação much admired. In his scenes of shepherds or herdsmen the landscapes are always subordinate to the main themes and are intended to complete the compositions with backgrounds of foliage and trees.

Anunciação sold a painting to King Ferdinand II in 1848 (subject and location unknown), and in 1852 he became a teacher at the Academia de Belas-Artes, Lisbon. He went to Paris for the Exposition Universelle (1867) and was able to study at first hand the naturalism of the Barbizon school. He visited the studios of Adolphe Yvon and Filippo Palizzi, the Neapolitan animal painter, and he admired the work of Constant Troyon (1810–65), whose influence is apparent in the *Calf* (1873; Lisbon, Mus. N. A. Contemp.). A comparison between this work and his earlier *View of the Penha de França in Lisbon* (1857; Lisbon, Mus. N. A. Contemp.) shows a development from a rigid and idealized landscape based on a study of nature to an animal painting in a more naturalistic setting. Increasingly his landscapes become more of a pretext, though his ability to take these naturalistic ideals further was limited.

In João Cristino da Silva's group portrait of the romantic generation of artists *Five Artists at Sintra* (1855; Lisbon, Mus. N. A. Contemp.), Anunciação appears at the centre, painting in the open air. This canvas was intended as a homage to Anunciação and also a manifesto and programme. Anunciação had asserted the value of contact with nature and had acted as a catalyst, and while he was esteemed by the movement he played no further part in its development. He became Director of the Ajuda Palace Gallery of Paintings in 1867 and gave painting lessons to Queen Maria Pia. He was appointed Director of the Academia de Belas-Artes in 1878, and in 1884 the Prémio Anunciação (Anunciação Prize) was created at the Academia for students of paintings of animals.

BIBLIOGRAPHY

Z. d'Aca: *Tomás José da Anunciação* (Lisbon, n.d.)

D. de Macedo: *Tomás José da Anunciação* (Lisbon, 1951)

——: *Tomás José da Anunciação: Chefe do romantismo* (Lisbon, 1955)

J.-A. França: *A arte em Portugal no século XIX*, i (Lisbon, 1966), pp. 260–64

LUCÍLIA VERDELHO DA COSTA

Anuradhapura [Anurādhapura]. Ancient city and religious centre in north-central Sri Lanka on the Malvatu Oya River. The site (see fig.) extends over an area of about 64 sq. km. At its centre are the vestiges of a fortified inner city, surrounded by several ancient Buddhist monastery complexes and four large, man-made lakes. The founding of Anuradhapura as a major urban complex is traditionally ascribed to the semi-historical figure of the pre-Buddhist period, King Pandukabhaya, in the 4th century BC. Recent excavations indicate the existence of settlement, import ceramics and early writing from a horizon of the 5th century BC or earlier, indicating the possibility of urbanization taking place from *c.* mid-1st millennium BC. The earliest rock shelter monasteries at the site date from the last few centuries BC.

Anuradhapura was the country's principal political and religious centre for nearly a millennium and a half, until the closing decades of the 10th century AD. It continued to be an important urban centre for nearly 300 years even after it was replaced as the island's principal city by the new capital at POLONNARUVA. The 'citadel' or central urban area (a) probably remained in continuous occupation for almost 2000 years. It has been described as 'one of the most durable centres of political power and urban life in South Asia' and 'one of the most stable, long-term urban sites in world history'.

The present remains of the city consist of an earthen embankment or rampart—in fact, a massive city wall, wholly or partly constructed of brick—enclosing an elongated asymmetrical quadrilateral area, the maximum dimensions of which are about 1,500 m from north to south and 900 m from east to west. The surviving embankment, nearly 30 m wide and about 4 km long, was originally surrounded by a moat and had four gateways. Connecting the gateways and traversing the city are traces of ancient roads in a rough grid layout. Monuments on the surface in this citadel area itself date mainly to the 8th–10th centuries and are relatively limited. They consist of the remains of two temples for the Tooth Relic (of the Buddha), the palladium of Sinhalese royalty, and two ruined palaces, one of which dates from the 11th century

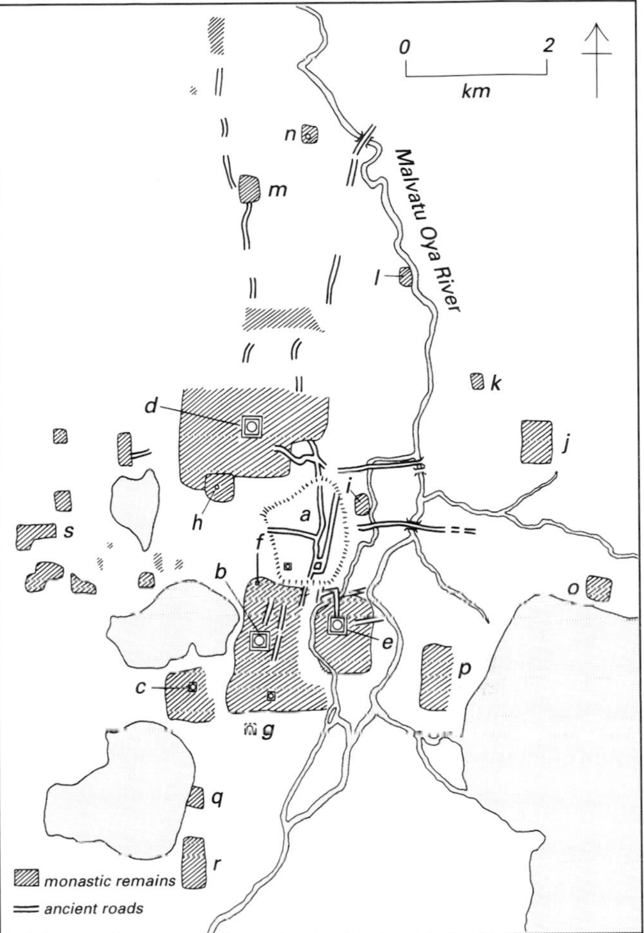

Anuradhapura, plan: (a) 'Citadel'; (b) Mahavihara; (c) Mirisavati Vihara; (d) Abhayagiri Vihara; (e) Jetavana Vihara; (f) Thuparama; (g) Dakkhina Vihara; (h) Lankarama; (i) Nakhavehera; (j) Puliyankulan; (k) Mullegaca; (l) Pankuliya; (m) Vijayarama; (n) Kiribatvehera; (o) Pachinatissapabbata; (p) Toluvila; (q) Surumuniya; (r) Vessagiriya; (s) Western monasteries

(i.e. the Polonnaruva period). Excavations indicate extensive buried structural remains in mud, brick and stone, belonging to various earlier phases.

The most extensive architectural remains of Anuradhapura are to be found in a number of major and minor monasteries ranged in a series of roughly concentric circles around the central urban core. The furthest of these lies *c.* 8 km north of the city centre. The largest are the four great monasteries—the Mahavihara (b), the Mirisavati Vihara (c), the Abhayagiri Vihara (d) and the Jetavana Vihara (e)—all located immediately around the citadel area. Each of these is centred around a colossal brick-built and freestanding stupa or *dāgaba* (from a period between the 2nd century BC and 4th century AD) and other ritual and monastic buildings. These include stupa-temples (*see* SRI LANKA, fig. 3), temples for sacred *bodhi* trees, image-houses, chapter houses, assembly halls, refectories, bathing pools and bathhouses, each constituting a distinctive Sri Lankan architectural type. Ranged around these monastery centres, as an integral part of each complex, is a series of monastic colleges (*piriveṇas*). Each monastic college is laid out in a variation on a basic plan, with a gatehouse, central avenue, principal and subordinate monastic residences and its own refectory, bathhouse and toilets. The central element in this plan is a group of five residential buildings with the principal structure in the middle, flanked by four subsidiary residences off its corners, reflecting the familiar *pañcāyatana* or *pañcaprāsāda* (five-shrine or five-mansion) concept of South Asian religious architecture.

Most of the estimated 3000 or 4000 buildings found on the surface or in the immediate sub-surface strata at Anuradhapura are extensively ruined. What survive today are the basal platforms and stone internal columniation of buildings that originally had timbered superstructures and tiled roofs. The basal platforms of the most elaborate monuments have ornate mouldings and highly decorated entrances, with intricately carved stone steps, wingstones, guardstones and a semicircular first step or 'moonstone' (*see* SRI LANKA, figs 2 and 8).

BIBLIOGRAPHY

S. Bandaranayake: *Sinhalese Monastic Architecture: The Vihāras of Anurādhapura* (Leiden, 1974)

R. Silva: *Religious Architecture in Early and Medieval Sri Lanka: A Study of the Thūpa, Bodhimaṇḍa, Uposathaghara and Paṭināghara* (diss., Leiden, Rijksuniv., 1988)

S. Bandaranayake: 'The Architecture of the Anuradhapura Period, 3rd Century BC to 10th Century AC', *Department of Archaeology: Centenary Commemoration Publication*, ed. N. D. Wijesekera, iii (Colombo, in preparation)

SENAKE BANDARANAYAKE

Anuszkiewicz, Richard (*b* Erie, PA, 23 May 1930). American painter, printmaker and sculptor. He trained at the Cleveland Institute of Art in Cleveland, OH (1948–53), and under Josef Albers at the Yale University School of Art and Architecture in New Haven, CT (1953–5). In his paintings of the late 1940s and early 1950s he depicted everyday city life, as in *The Bridge* (1950; artist's priv. col., see Lunde, pl. 66). In 1957 he moved to New York, where from 1957 to 1958 he worked as a conservator at the Metropolitan Museum of Art and from 1959 to 1961 as a silver designer for Tiffany and Co. During this period he began to produce abstract paintings, using either organic or geometric repeated forms, as in *Winter Recipe* (1958; New York, Mr and Mrs David Evins priv. col., see Lunde, pl. 100). These led in the early 1960s to asymmetric and imperfectly geometric works, such as *Fluorescent Complement* (1960; New York, MOMA), and then to more rigidly structured arrangements, for example *In the Fourth of Three* (1963; New York, Whitney), which consists of blue and green squares on a red ground. He often incorporated geometrical networks of coloured lines, thus exploring the phenomenon of optical mixtures in these mature works, with which he made his contribution to Op art, as in *Iridescence* (1965; Buffalo, NY, Albright–Knox A.G.), although these sometimes extend only a little way in from the edge of the picture. The strong internal structure of each work is the result not of a rigid system, however, but of a trial-and-error approach to composition; from the early 1960s he applied these methods also to screenprints, lithographs and prints made by intaglio techniques, still within the terms of Op art. In the late 1960s he turned to sculpture, characteristically making painted wooden cubes, sometimes on a mirror base, as in *Spiral* (1967; artist's priv. col., see Lunde, pl. 29). In his later works he remained faithful to the approach he established in the 1960s while developing more subtle colour modulations and sophisticated geometries (see COLOUR INTERACTION, colour pl. VII, fig. 2). These were extended into low relief, with a new monumentality, in the mid-1980s. His main concern continued to be with the perception of colours and with the exploration of a variety of effects.

BIBLIOGRAPHY

L. Lunde: *Anuszkiewicz* (New York, 1977)

Richard Anuszkiewicz: Prints and Multiples, 1964–79 (exh. cat. by D. Brooke and G. Baro, Williamstown, MA, Clark A. Inst.; New York, Brooklyn Mus.; 1979–80)

Richard Anuszkiewicz (exh. cat. by A. Stewart and E. H. Varian, Tallahassee, FL State U., F.A. Gal., 1981)

For further bibliography *see* OP ART.

KENNETH W. PRESCOTT

Anyang [An-yang]. Chinese city in Henan Province, near the site of the last capital of the SHANG or Yin dynasty (*c.* 1600–*c.* 1050 BC). The site is sometimes called Yinxu, 'Waste of Yin', an ancient name for the abandoned city.

At least as early as the Northern Song period (960–1127) Anyang was known to antiquarians as a source of ancient bronze ritual vessels. At the beginning of the 20th century archaeologists were led there by the realization that animal bones and turtle shells found by local farmers were carved with inscriptions in a form of Chinese script more archaic than any previously known (see fig.; for a discussion of the oracle-bone texts *see* CHINA, §IV, 2(i) and fig. 83). The bones had been used in divination rituals; their inscriptions, which showed the divinations to have been performed on behalf of the last nine Shang kings, secured the identification of the Anyang site. According to historical texts of the last few centuries BC, such as the *Shiji* ('Records of the historian', compiled in the 2nd

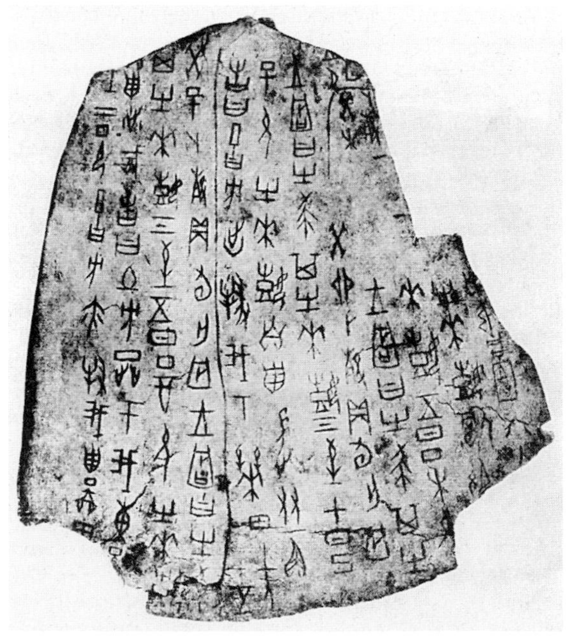

Anyang, inscribed oracle bone (ox scapula), h. 220 mm, reign of Wu Ding, 13th century BC (Beijing, Historical Museum)

century BC by Sima Qian), the last Shang capital was the seat of 12 kings who ruled for 273 years, a period now referred to as the historical Anyang period (*c.* 1300–*c.* 1100 BC).

Excavations at Anyang began under the direction of Academia Sinica in 1928 and have continued, apart from interruptions between 1937 and 1949 caused by the Sino-Japanese and civil wars. The remains of the Shang capital are spread over a large area on both sides of the River Huan, which has eroded parts of the site. There are no conspicuous monuments above ground and no trace of a city wall (Shang city walls are known from the pre-Anyang sites at Zhengzhou and Panlongcheng). South of the river, at the village of Xiaotun (*see* CHINA, §II, 2(i)), the pre-war excavations uncovered foundations of large buildings and a few associated human and animal sacrificial burials, including burials of chariots, horses and trappings. The foundations, which preserved impressions of wooden pillars, were constructed of rammed earth (*hangtu*). One of the most important discoveries at Xiaotun was an oracle-bone storage pit in which more than 300 inscribed turtle undershells, or plastrons, had been deposited, probably during the reign of Wu Ding (13th century BC), the fourth king to reign at Anyang.

North of the River Huan, at Xibeigang, near the village of Houjiazhuang, the pre-war excavators discovered a group of very large shaft tombs. Because of their size these are assumed to be royal tombs, but all had been stripped by robbers before excavation. Eight large tombs have been found in the western part of the Xibeigang cemetery and five more in the eastern part (north of the village of Wuguan cun). The tombs take the form of vertical shafts approached by ramps, usually two or four ramps aligned with the cardinal directions and sloping down into the shaft (*see* CHINA, fig. 51). In common with smaller Shang tombs, they have two important peculiarities of construction. First, part of the way down the shaft all four walls step inwards, forming a ledge (*ercengtai*). Second, at the bottom of the shaft, below the burial chamber, is a waist-pit (*yaokeng*), a small pit located approximately beneath the waist of the corpse. Mortuary offerings such as pottery and bronze vessels, carved bone and ivory, jades and bronze weapons were placed on the shelf and in the burial chamber along with human and animal sacrificial victims and attendant burials. The waist-pits contained sacrifices of a dog, or a man, or both; with a halberd. These were probably meant to serve as guardians. The walls and ledges of the Xibeigang tombs were made of earth that was pounded hard (*hangtu*); the tombs were subsequently filled with earth that was treated in the same way.

Sacrificial burials were found in large numbers in and near the Xibeigang tombs. Some of these were not placed there at the time of the royal entombments but instead represent later sacrifices periodically offered to the deceased. These later burials correspond with references made in the oracle-bone texts to victims sacrificed, sometimes by the hundred, to the reigning king's ancestors.

Many of the Anyang bronzes and jades in collections outside China must have come from the Xibeigang tombs, but the looting of the tombs deprived the artefacts of an archaeological context and at the same time left the tombs unimpressive and anonymous. The discovery in 1976 of an intact royal tomb, the occupant of which could be identified, was accordingly a major landmark in Shang archaeology.

The tomb was not in the Xibeigang cemetery but across the river at Xiaotun, and it contained many bronzes inscribed with the name Fu Hao. The identification of the tomb's occupant as a consort of Wu Ding is now generally accepted and secures a date of *c.* 1200 BC for the tomb. Compared with the enormous cruciform tombs at Xibeigang, this was a modest burial, consisting of a small pit without entrance ramps, measuring 8 m deep and 5.6×4 m along the sides. Nevertheless it yielded a greater wealth of funerary goods than all the pre-war Anyang excavations together: more than 200 bronze vessels and 200 bronze weapons and tools (totalling 1600 kg of metal), 750 jade and stone carvings, 500 carved bone and ivory objects, 4 bronze mirrors, 7000 cowrie shells (used as currency) and 16 sacrificial victims. For the study of Anyang bronzes and jades the tomb of Fu Hao was by far the most important archaeological discovery ever made (*see* CHINA, fig. 236).

Although bronze ritual vessels and jades are considered the chief artistic legacy of the Anyang civilization, the inscriptions on bronzes and oracle bones must also be remembered in this context. The Anyang oracle inscriptions were not mere archival documents but had some important commemorative purpose. They were incised with painstaking care, and the finest examples make it clear that writing was already an art form in China at the time of its earliest known appearance. The briefer inscriptions on bronze vessels give the same testimony.

The first excavations at Anyang were an unexpected revelation of the antiquity of Chinese civilization, but until the 1950s Anyang remained the only known Shang site of any importance, and archaeologists were puzzled by the sudden appearance in China of a fully developed bronze-using civilization. A few Western scholars, ignoring the distinctive character of that civilization, explained it as a wholesale transplant from the Ancient Near East. Excavations carried out since 1950 have provided local antecedents for the Anyang culture, however, and indicate that Anyang was heir to the flourishing Erligang phase of Shang civilization, represented most importantly by the Shang city at Zhengzhou as well as by other sites in the Zhengzhou area. The study of the early Chinese bronze age consequently centres not on Anyang but on other sites and earlier times.

BIBLIOGRAPHY

Li Chi: *Anyang* (Seattle, 1977) [pre-war excavations only]
D. N. Keightley: *Sources of Shang History: The Oracle-bone Inscriptions of Bronze Age China* (Berkeley, 1978) [with comprehensive bibliog.]
R. Bagley: 'The High Yinxu Phase (Anyang Period)', *The Great Bronze Age of China* (exh. cat., ed. Wen Fong; New York, Met., 1980), pp. 175–91
K. C. Chang: *Shang Civilization* (New Haven, 1980) [incl. full references to Chinese archaeological reports]
Yinxu Fu Hao mu [The tomb of Fu Hao at Yinxu] (Beijing, 1980, rev. 1984) [excavation report, with 228 pp. of pl.]

ROBERT W. BAGLEY

Aoki, Tomitarō. *See* HARA, SANKEI.

Aoki Mokubei [Hyakurokusanjin; Kokukan; Kukurin; Rōbei; Ryūbei; Sahei; Seirai; Teiunrō; Yasohachi] (*b* Kyoto, 1767; *d* Kyoto, 1833). Japanese potter, painter and scholar. He was born into the Kiya family of restaurateurs and adopted the surname Aoki only after becoming a painter. Mokubei, one of his many artist's names, was created by combining the Chinese characters for 'tree' and 'rice' (a character anagram of his given name Yasohachi). His most familiar studio name (*gō*), Rōbei ('deaf [Moku]bei'), dates from the time when he had become deaf from the clangour of his ceramic kilns. Despite his plebeian origins, he gravitated at a young age towards the arts and Chinese philosophy and poetry. At 18 he became a pupil of KŌ FUYŌ, from whom he learnt seal-carving, epigraphy, literati painting (*Nanga* or *Bunjinga*; *see* JAPAN, §VI, 4(vi)(d)), Confucianism and the arts and crafts of China. His first acquaintance with pottery also came through Fuyō, who owned a large collection of Chinese ceramics. After studying with Fuyō, he is said to have gone to Ise (now Mie Prefect.) to take up metalwork, and he later tried his hand at sculpture, but he was successful at neither. In 1796 he began to make pottery and in the same year submitted a landscape painting to an exhibition.

1. PAINTING. Mokubei is better known as a painter than as a potter, although little is known of his early painting, few of his works survive, and the literary record is also slim. Like fellow *Bunjinga* painters, Mokubei did not imitate or study the works of contemporary Japanese painters. Instead, he displayed an independent appreciation of Chinese painting manuals (Jap. *gafu*; Chin. *huapu*) such as *Shizhu zhai huapu* ('Ten bamboo studio manuals of painting'). *Falling Green Leaves* (*Hekitan suimozu*; 1804) is thought to reflect the style of the artist's early years up to *c*. 1820. Several of its features were to be characteristic of Mokubei's work: the leaves of the tree in clusters on each branch and the branches further grouped to form the tree, the ruggedness of tree-trunks and of mountains. Such features were employed early on to great effect, for example in *Mugwort Landscape at Dawn* (1781), and, although in time they became less marked, they never disappeared completely. When he depicts a clump of trees, the individuality of each tree is always evident. Mokubei's distinctive, emphatically kinetic style, with strong black outlines around rocks and trees and expressionistic composition and brushwork, emerged *c*. 1811–12 and was firmly established by 1818. So violent were his distortions that Mokubei and his contemporaries called his works 'demon landscapes' (*bakemono sansui*). Representative works from this period include *Mountain Stream in the Rising Sun* (1811) and *Landscape with Stupa* (hanging scroll, 1822). The composition of the latter is plain and straightforward, but the colouring is turbid, the paints having apparently been mixed with some impurity. The lines and pigments were painted with a hard stroke, made by working with a finely pointed bamboo implement. Mokubei would adapt a bamboo stick used in ceramic production to use as a paint brush. He sometimes liked to use ceramic pigments in his paintings, as well as ink. Towards the end of the Bunsei era (1824–9) Mokubei's paintings began to display an inexplicable sense of coldness, for example in *Morning Scene of a Rabbit Path* (1824) and *Ghost Scene* (1829).

Aoki Mokubei: *Morning Sunshine at Uji*, hanging scroll, ink and colours on paper, 486×594 mm, 1824 (Tokyo, National Museum)

The *Southern Star of Long Life* (*Senju nansei zu*; 1820) is representative of Mokubei's later work. Although small (166×263 mm), the painting suggests the vastness of nature by showing a god descending from the heavens as a diminutive figure in one corner. The painting may be a sign of Mokubei's submission to nature after his long years of dedication to the art of ceramics. The mountains and other land forms in his work have a strong presence and vertiginous energy not seen in the works of other painters.

From 1824 onwards Mokubei concentrated on painting. The previous year his friend RAI SAN'YŌ had introduced him to the literati artist TANOMURA CHIKUDEN, and this new friendship doubtless inspired the significant increase in his output. Works from this phase of his life include *Morning Sunshine at Uji* (Tokyo, N. Mus.; see fig.), *Landscape, Going Fishing in a Sunny Autumn* (all 1824), *New Green and Rain* (1826) and *Autumn Landscape* and *Demon Landscape* (both 1829). Although Mokubei moved in literati circles, his unique style is only faintly reminiscent of typical *Bunjinga* painting. In his final years Mokubei began to paint more small works for use in the *sencha* style of tea ceremony (*see* JAPAN, §XIV, 1), such as the *God of Longevity Rides Down on a Cloud* (1830), showing a figure enjoying eternal life in a fantastic land. He left a will requesting that his corpse and the ceramics he had stored be cremated together and the ashes interred in the northern hills of Kyoto, but this instruction was not carried out.

For bibliography *see* §2 below.

KŌZŌ SASAKI

2. POTTERY. Mokubei was most famous in his day as a potter. He appears to have learnt much from reading, particularly from manuals such as the *Taoshuo* (Jap. Tōsetsu; 'Ceramics explained'; 1774) by Chu Li-heng of the Qing period (1644–1911), which he had read and studied at the home of the literatus Kimura Kenkadō of Osaka, whom he met in 1796. After a short period of study under OKUDA EISEN, in 1805 Mokubei opened a

kiln at Awataguchi, one of the old pottery centres in the hills to the east of Kyoto, sponsored by Prince Shōren'in no Miya, to whom he was called into service as imperial ceramic master. From 1806 to 1808 he was invited to make ceramics at Utatsu and Kasugayama in Kanazawa, the latter at the behest of the daimyo of Kaga Province (now Ishikawa Prefect.). He also gave instruction in ceramics. His association with the literati artists of the period resulted in his producing numerous implements for the *sencha* (green tea) tea ceremony, such as teapots, freely potted stoneware teabowls and cooling hearths. He also made Korean- and Japanese-style pieces popular among *matcha* (whipped tea) devotees. He was the first potter in Japan in the late Edo period (1600–1868) to make celadon ware (*aoki*). By 1822 his reputation was such that he was included in the *Heian jinbutsushi* ('Records of famous personalities of Heian').

Mokubei mastered both Chinese and Japanese ceramic traditions, including *kōchi* (type of polychrome ware), *sometsuke* (underglaze cobalt blue, or blue-and-white porcelain), *iroe* (polychrome [overglaze] enamels), *hakuji* (porcelain), *kinrande* ('gold and enamel') and *Nanban* ('Southern barbarian') wares. Even the motifs and shapes based on clay types carry the distinctive stamp of Mokubei's technique. The relief decorations that appeared on his works such as braziers were also highly valued. The sheer range of Mokubei's work attracted many clients and influential patrons, yet he was known for his low rate of production. Clients and dealers had to pay a thousand *ryō* (gold pieces) for his works, for which they had to wait years; and such was his popularity that even the mother of his friend Rai San'yō had to wait a long time to obtain a single small teapot.

BIBLIOGRAPHY

Kodansha Enc. Japan
M. Takeda: *Nihon bijutsu egazenshu* [Complete collection of Japanese painting], xxi (Tokyo 1977)

HIROKO NISHIDA

Aoki Shigeru (*b* Kurume, Kyushu, 1882; *d* Fukuoka, Kyushu, 1911) Japanese painter. Although his family disapproved of his early interest in Western-style art (*Yōga; see* JAPAN, §VI, 5(iv)), he left home at 17 to pursue his studies in Tokyo, first with Koyama Shōtarō (1857–1916), a pupil of Antonio Fontanesi, an Italian painter who taught at the Kōbu Bijutsu Gakkō (Technical Art School) from 1877 to 1879, and then with KURODA SEIKI at the Tōkyō Bijutsu Gakkō (Tokyo Art School; now Tokyo University of Fine Arts and Music). Aoki finished his studies in 1904. A brilliant, rather eccentric young man, he showed precocious talent and while still a student exhibited his work with Kuroda's prestigious association of Western-style painters, the Hakubakai (White Horse Society), established in 1896.

Aoki showed a strong literary bent, and his interest in Japanese, Christian and Indian mythology led him to develop a romantic style, often recalling the British Pre-Raphaelite Brotherhood. A number of his most important paintings dealing with mythological and related subjects, among them the *Tenpyō Era* and *Harvest of the Sea* (both Tokyo, Bridgestone A. Mus.), were painted in 1904, shortly after his graduation, but Aoki's fascination with such themes continued throughout his brief life. Two of his most admired paintings (both Tokyo, Bridgestone A. Mus.), *Ōnamuchi no Mikoto* (1905) and *Palace under the Sea* (1907), drew on mythological subject-matter taken from the *Kojiki* ('Record of ancient matters'; AD 712). He also travelled with friends to the seaside north of Tokyo, where he painted several striking seascapes. His close relationship with the noted poet Kanbara Ariake (1876–1952) gave Aoki an opportunity to create a number of highly evocative book illustrations.

Unable to support himself, Aoki left the circle of his Tokyo friends and returned to Kyushu, where he led a nomadic life until his death from tuberculosis at 29. Forgotten at that time, his work was rediscovered after World War II, since when he has had an enormous reputation as an artist accomplished in Western-style painting.

WRITINGS

Kanshō no sōzō [Creativity of sentiment] (Tokyo, 1966)

BIBLIOGRAPHY

Shigeru Aoki and the Late Victorian Art (exh. cat., Kurume, Ishibashi A. Mus.; Tochigi, Prefect. Mus. F.A.; Tokyo, Bridgestone A. Mus.; Hiroshima, Mus. A.; 1983)
Paris in Japan: The Japanese Encounter with European Painting (exh. cat. by S. Takashina, J. T. Rimer and G. D. Bolas, Tokyo, Japan Found.; St Louis, MO, George Washington U.; 1987–8)

J. THOMAS RIMER

Aomen. *See* MACAO.

Aosta [anc. Augusta Praetoria]. City situated at the confluence of two ancient Alpine passes, the Great and Little St Bernard, in Piedmont, Italy. The medieval nucleus lies within the Roman walls and important monuments of both periods survive. Founded as a Roman camp in 24 BC, and later colonized under Emperor Augustus (22 BC), it soon also became a Christian bishopric. In 1025 the city was in the possession of Umberto Biancamano, the feudal lord under Rudolf, King of Burgundy, and founder of the ruling family of Savoy. It was the birthplace of St Anselm (*c.* 1033/4–1109), who became Archbishop of Canterbury in 1093.

Of the Roman remains, the Porta Praetoria, the theatre, bridge and Arch of Augustus are best preserved and bear testimony to Aosta's importance as a Roman Imperial city; there are also ruins of the Roman forum. From the period of St Anselm, two important monuments survive: the cathedral, dedicated to St John the Baptist, and the Benedictine abbey of S Orso, the latter with important 11th-century frescoes and 12th-century cloister capitals. The 12th-century mosaic pavement in the cathedral represents the *Labours of the Months*, surrounding the god Annus ('year') in a central medallion, and belongs to the small number of surviving Italian figured floor mosaics. The present architecture of the cathedral and S Orso dates from the 15th, 16th and 19th centuries, but the campanile and crypt of S Orso are Romanesque. The cathedral has a Neo-classical façade with a 16th-century sculptured portal and a 15th-century cloister. Having lost its Roman military and medieval ecclesiastical significance, Aosta is now an Alpine tourist centre.

CHRISTINE VERZAR

1. Augusta Praetoria. In 22 BC Emperor Augustus established the Colonia Augusta Praetoria, which replaced a Roman military camp located above a village of the conquered Celtic Salassi tribe, and transferred 3000 Praetorians and their families there from Rome. It is one of the best examples of an early Imperial fortified city and took the form of a rectangular gridded military camp (572×724 m; *see* Rome, ancient, fig. 57). The surrounding wall of concrete and local travertine rose over 10 m in height, with 20 squared towers at regular intervals, of which two survive. The four main gates had portcullises; that on the east, the Porta Praetoria, had a double curtain defining a large interior court. Seven north–south streets and seven east–west define a grid of 64 blocks; the plan remains intact. The main street was displaced one double block to the west to avoid dissecting the forum. The forum itself is rectangular in shape with a surrounding cryptoporticus; it opened on the north to a large porticoed temple enclosure. The city prospered in the early Imperial period, as attested by the construction of grand public buildings. West of the forum stands a bath complex (mid-1st century AD) and a roofed theatre (*c*. 27 BC–AD 14). A large amphitheatre (mid-1st century AD) nestles within the walls at the extreme north-east of the city. Excavations in the 1970s and 1980s uncovered houses, a Mithraeum (second half of 2nd century AD) and an Early Christian church. To the east along the main road into the city stands the Arch of Augustus, commemorating the Roman victory in 25 BC over the local Salassi; beyond, a single-arched Roman bridge is still in use. Augusta Praetoria remained strategically important during the late Empire and continued to receive Imperial patronage. In the cathedral is a remarkable ivory diptych (AD 406) with representations of the Emperor Honorius.

BIBLIOGRAPHY

P. Barocelli: *Augusta Praetoria*, Forma Italiae: Regio XI, 1: Transpadana (Rome, 1948)

I. Beretta: *La romanizzazione della Valle d'Aosta* (Milan, 1954)

V. Viale and M. Viale Ferrero: *Aosta romana e medievale* (Turin, 1967)

G. Manasse, G. Massari and M. Rossignani: *Piemonte, Valle d'Aosta, Liguria, Lombardia*, Guide archeologiche Laterza (Bari, 1982), pp. 96–115

DIANE FAVRO

2. S Orso. The present church, built in the late 15th century, contains earlier remains, including the crypt and traces of a fresco cycle from the 11th-century church. Its importance for sculpture lies in the cycle of narrative capitals in the cloister, which represents the most complete such cycle to survive in northern Italy. Of the 52 original marble capitals, 40 remain, now covered by a black patina.

Founded as a Benedictine abbey, the chapter was reformed into an Augustinian priory dependent on the pope by Bishop Erberto in 1133, and its first prior, Arnolfo di Avise, became Bishop of Aosta from 1149 to 1152. These events are recorded on the cloister capitals and accompanied by inscriptions, thus providing a date for the sculptures (1149–52). A rich cycle of scenes from the infancy of Christ and the lives of Jacob, David, Rebecca, Nebuchadnezzar and St Orso are carved on the other capitals. The figure style of these sculptures shows great affinity to the Lombard school, with stocky, stiff and large-headed figures carved in deep relief and arranged rather awkwardly around the sides of the capitals. These characteristics can be found on some of the figures at S Michele (*c*. 1125–30), Pavia, on the pulpit at S Giulio on Lago d'Orta and on the figures carved by the second master of the Zodiac portal of the Sagra di S Michele (*c*. 1120–30), near Turin. There are also distinctive features, however, such as the busts of prophets, the stylized treatment of foliage and some details closer to Provençal sculpture.

BIBLIOGRAPHY

R. Berton: *Les Chapiteaux du cloître de St-Ours: Un Bijou d'art roman en Val d'Aoste* (Novara, 1954)

N. Gabrielli: 'L'arte nella Valle d'Aosta: Lineamenti dal sec. XI al sec. XVI', *Relazioni e comunicazioni presentate al XXXI congresso storico-subalpino di Aosta. La Valle d'Aosta: Turin, 1956*, i, pp. 391–421

U. Chierici: 'Fra cultura padana e cultura francese', *Piemonte, Valle d'Aosta* (Milan, 1968), pp. 105–326

M. Magni: *Architettura religiosa e scultura romanica nella Valle d'Aosta* (Aosta, 1974), pp. 99–108

S. Chierici and D. Citi: *Il Piemonte, la Val d'Aosta, la Liguria*, Italia romanica, ii (Milan, 1979)

F. Hirsch: *The Sculptural Program at Sant'Orso in Aosta* (diss., New Haven, Yale U., 1987)

S. Barberi: *Il chiostro di Sant'Orso* (Rome, 1989)

CHRISTINE VERZAR

Aostalli [Aostallo; Austalis; Avostali]. Italian family of architects, active in Bohemia. The family helped introduce a more austere, Tuscan style into Bohemian architecture, replacing the decorative Lombard style but retaining such vernacular features as the pitched roof. The exact relationship between the family members is unclear. Giovanni Maria Aostalli (*b* Pambio; *d* Prague, 1567) assisted Giovanni Spazio in 1538 at the Belvedere Villa in Prague and succeeded him during its construction (1539–45). From 1545 to 1562 he was Master of the Works at the Hradčany in Prague, assisted in 1548 by his sons Pietro Aostalli and Andrea Maria Aostalli (*b* ?Pambio; *d* Prague, 1586–7), as well as by his relative Ulrico Aostalli (*b* Savosa; *d* Prague, 10 May 1597). In 1555 Giovanni Maria began the Hvezda at Bila Hora, outside Prague, to the designs of Archduke Ferdinand I (later Emperor). In 1559 he, Giuseppe Soldata and the mason Giovanni from Campione (*fl* 1537–63) produced a plan for the Diet Hall at the Hradcăny in Prague. This was rejected, however, in favour of plans by Bonifaz Wolmut. Giovanni Battista Aostalli (*b* Savosa; *d* Poděbrady, 31 July 1575) worked with a group of masons, including his brothers Antonio Aostalli, Francesco Aostalli and Stefano Aostalli, at the Hradčany in Prague, especially on the Belvedere, the garden palace. In 1550–64 Giovanni Battista remodelled and enlarged the royal castle at Poděbrady, adding loggias and open arcaded stairs, and later (1572) a rusticated gateway. He also rebuilt the Gothic church at Poděbrady, but his major work was the monumental, symmetrical west wing (1568–71) of the great Renaissance house at Litomyšl of the noble Pernštejn family. He may also have designed the palace of the noble Rožmberk family in Prague, built in 1545–56 by Giovanni Fontana, arcaded along two sides of the courtyard and with impressive gables, as at Litomyšl.

Ulrico Aostalli executed several designs between 1556 and 1576 by Bonifaz Wolmut, Master of the Royal Works in Prague, including the upper floor of the Belvedere. He succeeded Wolmut in 1574, after which he executed schemes designed by Pietro Ferabosco and Giovanni

Gargiolli, supervised the construction of royal castles in central Bohemia and furnished technical reports. Ulrico built houses in Malá Strana, Prague, and laid out a street for the Italian community there. With the mason Giovanni Antonio Brocco (*d* 1615) he participated in the construction of the aqueduct that supplied water to a lake in the old Royal Park in Prague, where he also remodelled (1578–80) the summer palace of Vladislav II for Rudolf II with arcading along both floors articulated by a colossal order of pilasters that runs through it. Other work in Prague included the Italian walled garden (1573–4) that he designed for the Rožmberk family, surrounded by arcades that support a gallery on one side, and the Lion Court (1582), built for the Emperor's animals. Ulrico was also involved in religious architecture: he reconstructed the Gothic chapel of All Saints at Hradčany Castle (*see* PRAGUE, §IV, 1), while in the Old Town he directed work on the Minorite monastery and church of St James (1586–96; remod. 1689) and supervised the work carried out by Bernardo de Alberto on the Augustinian church of St Thomas (1586–96; altered 1723–31) in Malá Strana. Outside Prague, Ulrico worked for various members of the Bohemian nobility. For the Pernštejn family he made plans (1571–2) for the enlargement of the castle at Pardubice, equipping it with massive arcades (executed 1574). He also finished (1581) their house at Litomyšl, begun by Giovanni Battista, adding three new wings that feature loggias, one of which opens on to a spacious courtyard on one side and to a garden on the other. The scheme also included a chapel, and the building became one of the most important Renaissance houses in Bohemia. His projected reconstruction (1595) of the fire-damaged castle at Domažlice as a town hall proved too expensive for the citizens.

BIBLIOGRAPHY

K. Chytil: 'Mistři lugánští v Čechách v XVI. století' [Artists from Lugano in Bohemia in the 16th century], *Roč. Kruhu Pěstování Dějin Umění* (1935), pp. 32–66

L. Brentani: *Antichi maestri d'arte e di scuola delle terre ticinesi*, i (Lugano, 1937), pp. 8–9, 66–9

F. Lašek: *Litomyšl* (Litomyšl, 1945), pp. 50–51, 105–6

J. Moravek: 'Ke vzniku Hvezdy' [The rise of the Star], *Umění*, ii (1954), pp. 199–211

F. Křivka: 'O stavbě litomyšlského zámku' [The construction of the château at Litomyšl], *Sborník příspěvků k dějinám Litomyšle* [Memorial collection of contributions to the history of Litomyšl] (Pardubice, 1959), pp. 107–22

J. Krčálová: 'Palác pánů z Rožmberka' [The palace of the Lords of Rožmberk], *Umění*, xviii (1970), pp. 469–85

——: *Centrální stavby české renesance* [Centrally planned buildings of the Renaissance in Bohemia] (Prague, 1974), pp. 48–50, 75–6

——: 'Arts in the Renaissance and Mannerist Periods', *Renaissance Art in Bohemia* (London, New York, Sydney and Toronto, 1979), pp. 49–147

P. Preiss: *Italští umělci v Praze* [Italian artists in Prague] (Prague, 1986)

J. Krčálová: 'Renesanční architektur, Rudolfinská architektura' [Renaissance architecture, architecture of Rudolf II], *Dějiny českeho výtvarného umění* [History of arts in Bohemia] (in preparation)

J. KRČÁLOVÁ

Apadana. Term from Old Persian used to describe a distinctive type of building, found in the royal Achaemenid Persian palaces at SUSA and PERSEPOLIS. It has a square columned hall with six rows of six columns and three columned porticos, each with two rows of six columns. *Apadanas* are thought to have been audience halls for the king and his court and for the reception of foreign vassals and ambassadors. The word is found in inscriptions of Darius II (*reg* 423–405 BC) and of Artaxerxes II (*reg* 404–359 BC) from Susa and from Hamadan, the old Median capital city, which was used as a royal residence by the Achaemenid kings. One of the texts from Susa was carved on the column bases of a building of this type constructed by Darius I (*reg* 521–486 BC) and restored by Artaxerxes II. A building of a similar size and with the same arrangement of stone columns, many of which stand *in situ* with their elaborate floral, volute and animal capitals in place, dominates the citadel terrace at Persepolis. It was built on a raised platform with square corner towers and rows of rooms along the south side of the building. Staircases on the north and east sides were decorated with low-relief friezes, which depict processions of courtiers and tributaries and are the most important of all Achaemenid Persian works of art. The building was started by Darius I and completed by his son Xerxes I (*reg* 485–465 BC). It has been suggested that this specific type of audience hall was distinctive of the reign of Darius I, but during this period various different types of columned hall were built, both with and without porticos, which are derived from earlier Achaemenid examples from Pasargadae that in turn probably derive from Median architecture.

In Old Persian the word *apadana* may have had a wider range of meanings, but the term is now restricted to buildings of this specific type. Two smaller buildings, each with square central columned hall and three columned porticos, which stand south of the terrace at Persepolis and were probably built in the reign of Darius I, have been described as a gate-house and a fire temple, although these identifications are uncertain.

For a discussion of the possible antecedents of the *apadana*, further bibliography and illustrations *see* IRAN, ANCIENT, §II, 3.

BIBLIOGRAPHY

D. Stronach: 'The *Apadana*: A Signature of the Line of Darius I', *De l'Indus aux Balkans: Recueil Jean Deshayes* (Paris, 1985), pp. 433–45

MICHAEL ROAF

Apameia [Lat. Apamea; Arab. Afāmiya, Fāmiya; now Qalʿat al-Muḍīq]. Hellenistic and Roman city in northern Syria, on a plateau on the south-west tip of Jebel Zawiye overlooking the valley of the Āsi (formerly the Orontes). It was founded in 300–299 BC by Seleukos I Nikator (*reg* 301–281 BC) on the site of an ancient Bronze Age capital; it was one of the four great cities known as the Tetrapolis. The disastrous earthquake of 15 December AD 115 carried away most of the original buildings, but in many places there remain powerful courses, solidly anchored on rock, of the Hellenistic walls, eloquent testimony to their 7 km circuit of the city. The Apameia that the excavations of a Belgian archaeological expedition brought to light from 1928 onwards is essentially a Roman city, capital of the province of Syria Secunda from *c*. AD 415. Apameia contributed greatly to the cultural life of the empire and a famous school of Neo-Platonic philosophy existed there from the 2nd to the 4th century AD. Despite systematic reconstruction, after the earthquakes of AD 526 and 528 the city never recovered its splendour. Abandoned by its élite at the time of the Arab conquest (AD 638), it was then 'ruralized' by an influx of villagers from the Massif Calcaire. The settlement continued in this form until the 12th century, as ceramics and coins testify (Apameia, Archaeol. Mus.), although there have been claims that it was ruined by the Persian incursions of the 6th century AD or the early 7th.

1. ARCHITECTURE. The *cardo maximus* (main avenue), or *plateia*, exactly orientated north–south, constitutes the backbone of the regular town plan, which in its present state dates to the 2nd century AD. The great width of this avenue (22.5 m for the single paved street and nearly 40 m from the back of the covered portico on one side to that on the other) and its length (nearly 2 km) make it one of the most extraordinary avenues in the ancient world. Inscriptions on the northern part of the portico honour the founder, Lucius Julius Agrippa, who dedicated it in AD 116 along with a *basilica thermarum* and baths. Crossed by two broad east–west arteries, it stamps the city plan with a cross of Lorraine and emphasizes the prominent position of a monumental temple to Zeus Belos (destr. *c.* AD 376). At the foot of the temple and its peribolus the forum stretches parallel to the *cardo maximus.*

Facing the acropolis in a fold in the ground is one of the largest theatres in the Roman world (diam. 139 m). Its plan is similar to that at ASPENDOS, but the ruin has served as a quarry and the *scenae frons* has lost most of its architectural decoration. In several quarters of the city there are luxurious houses (2nd–7th century AD), their principal rooms opening on to a large peristyle, their rich reception rooms paved with mosaic or *opus sectile.* One of these houses, the Triclinium Building (enlarged 5th–6th century AD), was probably the residence of the governor of the province and had an impressive hunting mosaic in one of its rooms (*see* §2 below). The city was the seat of an archbishop as early as the 5th century AD and is covered with churches. The cathedral, with its trefoiled central plan, took over the site of the school of philosophy; the atrium church was built on the site of a synagogue containing a remarkable mosaic pavement (*see* §2 below).

BIBLIOGRAPHY

Apamée de Syrie. Bilan des recherches archéologiques, 1965–1968 (Brussels, 1969)

Apamée de Syrie. Bilan des recherches archéologiques, 1969–1971 (Brussels, 1972)

J. C. Balty: *Guide d'Apamée* (Brussels, 1981)

Apamée de Syrie. Bilan des recherches archéologiques, 1973–1979: Aspects de l'architecture domestique d'Apamée (Brussels, 1984)

JEAN CH. BALTY

2. MOSAICS. The mosaics so far discovered—preserved in Brussels (Musées Royaux A. & Hist.), Damascus (N. Mus.) and Apamea (Archaeol. Mus.)—date from the 1st to the 6th century AD, but only the end of that period (4th–6th centuries) is well represented. An important group can be attributed to the school of Neo-Platonic philosophy and dates to the period of Julian the Apostate (*reg* AD 360–63). The best-known of these pavements represents Socrates surrounded by the Greek sages (Apamea, Archaeol. Mus.). Two other panels illustrate themes at first sight less philosophical: the *Return of Ulysses* and the *Servants* (*therapenides*) (both Brussels, Musées Royaux A. & Hist.) and *Thetis and Cassiopeia* (Apameia, Archaeol. Mus.). Comparison with texts (e.g. of Philo Alexandrinus, Porphyry, Proclus, Eusthasius), however, permits an interpretation of Ulysses embracing Penelope as the image of the wise man reuniting with Philosophy, of the *Servants* as representing the encyclical sciences and of Cassiopeia triumphing over the marine divinities and revealing her beauty as the symbol of man escaping matter and casting off his carnal fetters to reach the Absolute. This deeply pagan content is expressed in a perfectly Classical form, a 'retrospective' style very much characteristic of Julian's period: the figures, treated in the illusionistic manner of previous centuries, faithfully reproduce pictorial models whose origins go back to the great creations of the Hellenistic era. Through the use of geometrical decoration, however, in which the compositions and motifs of the Rainbow style dominate, these mosaics are good examples of the developments that occurred in the second half of the 4th century AD. This geometrical repertory is also found at the end of the century on the pavements of the synagogue (dated to AD 392 by two inscriptions). From this period, pavement mosaic came back into its own as carpet.

Owing to patrons' aversion to mythological themes, a new iconographic repertory was formed in the 5th century AD, which retained from the old one only vegetal and animal themes and scenes of everyday life. The style also changed: the illusionistic treatment inherited from the Hellenistic tradition was replaced by a tendency towards stylization and abstraction. These different characteristics are well illustrated in the mosaics of the covered porticoes of the *cardo maximus* (AD 469; Brussels, Musées Royaux A. & Hist.; Damascus, N. Mus.). On the white ground of the carpet, sometimes enlivened with small flowers, file in artistic disorder, caravans and camels, peasants at work, animal hunts and processions of birds. The same decorative approach appears in the mosaics of *Amazons Hunting* (3rd quarter of the 5th century AD; Apameia, Archaeol. Mus.) and *Meleager and Atalanta* (late 5th century AD; *in situ*), probably from the same workshop. The 'Great Hunt' of the Triclinium Building was executed in the same spirit of abstraction, even if the workmanship remains much more Classical (5th century AD; Brussels, Musées Royaux A. & Hist.; *see* ROME, ANCIENT, fig. 96). The fashion for large, free compositions gave way in the 6th century AD to a taste for the partition of surfaces and infilling; several pavements in the House of the Stag testify to this.

BIBLIOGRAPHY

J. Balty: *La Grande Mosaïque de chasse du triclinos* (Brussels, 1969)

C. Dulière: *La Mosaïque des Amazones* (Brussels, 1969)

——: *Mosaïques des portiques de la grande colonnade* (Brussels, 1974)

J. Balty: *Mosaïques antiques de Syrie* (Brussels, 1977)

J. Balty and J. Ch. Balty: 'Un Programme philosophique sous la cathédrale d'Apamée: L'Ensemble néo-platonicien de l'empereur Julien', *Actes du colloque international de Chantilly: Texte et image: Chantilly, 1982*

J. Balty: 'Les "Thérapénides" d'Apamée: Textes littéraires et d'iconographie', *Dial. Hist. Anc.*, 18.1 (1992), pp. 281–91

JANINE BALTY

Apap, Willie (*b* 1918; *d* Rome, 3 Feb 1970). Maltese painter, active in Italy. He studied painting in Rome at the Regia Accademia di Belle Arti, where his master was the Neapolitan artist Carlo Siviero. At the outbreak of World War II, he surrendered his British passport in return for a residence and work permit in Italy. Arrested after the capitulation of Italy in 1945, he was brought to Malta and tried for high treason, together with *c.* 25 other Maltese, but was acquitted. His release was followed by a period of intense activity during which he established himself as Malta's leading portrait artist. In 1955 he transferred himself permanently to Rome, where in June 1964 he organized a one-man exhibition at the Galleria L'Agostiniana in Piazza del Popolo, which won him very favourable comments. In 1961 he was invited to Windsor Castle to paint a portrait of *Princess Anne* (exh. 1962; London, Grabowski Gal.). In 1967 he had another successful show, at the Galleria Galeazzo in Alba. His work had by this time become profoundly religious in content, and the bright colours of his earlier paintings gave way to gloomy mauves and grey tones. His brother, Vincent Apap (*b* 1909), became Malta's leading sculptor. Among his works are several public monuments, which include the Tritons' Fountain at Valletta and the Dante Memorial at Floriana.

MARIO BUHAGIAR

Aparicio Inglada, José (*b* Alicante, 1770; *d* Madrid, 1838). Spanish painter. He studied at the Real Academia de S Fernando in Madrid (1792–8) and then completed his training as a *pensionnaire* in Paris with David (until 1807) and in Rome until 1815. Though having didactic and moralizing pretensions, his paintings are, in fact, rhetorical, theatrical and sycophantic, factors that explain his constant success in official circles. His works include his scholarship submission, *Godoy Presenting Peace to Charles IV* (1796; Madrid, Real Acad. S Fernando); his triumph in the Paris Salon of 1804, *Athaliah and Jonah*; and his presentation piece to the Accademia di S Luca in Rome, *Ransom of Prisoners in the Reign of Charles III* (1815). His appointment in 1815 as Pintor de Cámara was marked by his painting of the *Glories of Spain*. He also achieved popular recognition through such patriotic and nationalistic works as *Famine of Madrid* (1818; Madrid, Mus. Mun.). His carefully drawn compositions were well suited to engraved reproductions, and this led to their wider circulation. *Ferdinand VII Disembarking at Puerto de Santa Maria* (1827, destr.) was intended as an expression of loyalty to the monarch and epitomized Aparicio Inglada's style. Despite his popular success, critics were not so convinced of his talent, and after his death his work was rapidly consigned to oblivion. Nevertheless, together with José de Madrazo y Agudo and Juan Antonio Ribera y Fernández, he is the most representative artist of Spanish Neo-classicism.

BIBLIOGRAPHY

M. Ossorio y Bernard: *Galería biográfica de artistas españoles del siglo XIX* (Madrid, 1868, 2/1883–4/*R* Barcelona, 1975), pp. 40–43

A. Espi Valdes: 'José Aparicio: Pintor alicantino y de Corte', *Rev. Inst. Estud. Alicant.*, n. s. 1, xxiii (1978), pp. 5–33

JESÚS GUTIÉRREZ BURÓN

Aparici y Soriano, Federico (*b* Valencia, 1832; *d* Madrid, 1917). Spanish architect, teacher and writer. He studied at the recently established Escuela de Arquitectura in Madrid and received his degree in 1855. He was noted for the historical knowledge that he was able to apply to the theories of eclecticism in the pursuit of pure historicism. He was more a theoretician than a practising architect, devoting 50 years to teaching at the Escuela de Arquitectura as Catedrático de Construcción. He was director of the Escuela between 1896 and 1910 and bequeathed his library to it.

Aparici y Soriano's early architectural works, such as the monument to *Mendizábal, Argüelles and Calatrava* (1857) in the cemetery of S Nicolás, Madrid, shows his scholarly interests. Immediately after, however, his style came under the influence of Viollet-le-Duc, of whom he became a fervent follower, as is apparent in his few completed projects. The most important of these was the sober and monumental basilica of Nuestra Señora de Covadonga (1877–1901) at Covadonga (Asturias), which he based on the Romanesque architecture of Normandy, such as at St Etienne (begun 1073), Caen. The work replaced an unrealized Neo-classical design by Ventura Rodríguez. In 1877 Roberto Frasinelli began work on the crypt of Covadonga, but Aparici y Soriano subsequently reorganized the plan of the church with a nave, aisles and a transept. He collaborated with Enrique Fort (*d* 1909) on the design of the Hospital de Epilépticos at Carabanchel (Madrid province) and also built a few private residences.

WRITINGS

Elementos fundamentales de construcción (Madrid, n.d.)

Apuntes de construcción (Madrid, 1885–6)

BIBLIOGRAPHY

J. A. Gaya: *Arte del siglo XIX*, A. Hisp., xix (Madrid, 1966)

P. Navascues: *Arquitectura y arquitectos madrileños del siglo XIX* (Madrid, 1973)

D. Benito: *La arquitectura del eclecticismo en Valencia* (Valencia, 1983)

ALBERTO VILLAR MOVELLÁN

Apartis [Apartoglou]**, Thanassis** (*b* Smyrna [now Izmir], 24 Oct 1899; *d* Athens, 1 April 1972). Greek sculptor. From 1919 to 1926 he studied in Paris, at the Académie Julian, the Ecole des Beaux-Arts and the Académie de la Grande Chaumière under Emile-Antoine Bourdelle. He exhibited at the Salons d'Automne, des Indépendants, des Tuileries and at the Petit Palais. The French state bought a number of his works, and in 1939 he was awarded the Légion d'honneur. In 1940 he moved to Athens, and from 1945 to 1956 he shared his time between Athens and Paris. Apartis excelled in sensitive and realistic portraits with emphasis on individual character. He also made some sculptures of animals, reliefs and monuments, including the Monument to the Unknown Sailor at Khíos. His thorough knowledge of ancient and modern art helped him assimilate influences from archaic and Classical Greek art and from medieval French sculpture in a distinctive personal idiom. He was awarded the Order of the Phoenix by the Greek government in 1960.

Between 1938 and 1969 he participated in both group and solo exhibitions. In 1950 he was one of the Greek representatives at the Venice Biennale; in 1953 he participated in *Seven Greek Sculptors* at the Petit Palais, Paris. The French Institute organized a posthumous one-man show in Athens, Lárisa, Sparta and Kalámata (1977–80); the National Gallery and the Alexandros Soutzos Museum, both Athens, organized a major retrospective in 1985.

WRITINGS

Apo tin anatoli sti dusi [From east to west] (Athens, 1962/*R* 1984)

BIBLIOGRAPHY

Apartis—Athens, 1977 (exh. cat. by Dimitre Tsouchlou, Athens, N.G., 1977)

S. Ludakis: *I neoelliniki gluptiki istoria tupologia lexico glupton* [Neohellenic sculpture, history and typology: a dictionary of sculptors] (Athens, 1981), pp. 113–15, 274–7

C. Chrusanthos and others: *Neoelleniki gluptiki, 1800–1940* [Neohellenic sculptors, 1800–1940] (Athens, 1982), pp. 87, 107–10, 141, 166 n., 177, 178 n., 240, 253, 255, 264, 270, 272–3, 277

G. Kalognomou: *To ergo tou glupti Thanasi Apartis (1899–1972)* [The work of the sculptor Thanassis Apartis] (Athens, 1984)

Thanassis Apartis (exh. cat., Athens, N.G. and Mus. Alexandros Soutzos, 1984)

ANGELA TAMVAKI

Apartment [flat]. Term used originally to describe a suite of rooms reserved for the use of a particular individual or group within a great house or palace, but now also used more broadly to denote a set of rooms comprising middle- or upper-class accommodation within a larger building; this apartment block may contain several such apartments and is usually several storeys high. The apartment is distinguished by its more elevated social status from the tenement, which provides low-rent accommodation units (*see* TENEMENT BUILDING). While the origins of the tenement can be traced back to the insulae of ancient Rome (*see* INSULA), multiple dwellings that provided a solution to population pressures and rising land values within city fortifications from the 2nd century AD, the early development of the apartment is closely associated with the urbanization of western Europe from the 16th century. As fortified residences diminished, the château becoming associated with opulence and leisure rather than any defensive military purpose and the urban palace or palazzo replacing the castle, the apartment emerged as a private suite of rooms set aside for the wealthy inhabitant and comprising such rooms as a chamber, antechamber, bedchamber and cabinet (*see* CABINET (i)).

It was on the model of the aristocratic suite that the first middle-class apartments were built. In 18th-century France such architects as FRANÇOIS DEBIAS-AUBRY, who specialized in designing residential architecture for a wealthy clientele of aristocrats and middle-class financiers, began designing blocks comprising numerous apartments (e.g. Debias-Aubry's Maison Cotelle, 1739; in the Rue St André-des-Arts in Paris). Outside France, however, the apartment was slow to gain acceptance as a middle-class housing type. As the Industrial Revolution gained pace in Great Britain, for example, the idea of living in flats rather than individual houses became associated with the urban working class, and it was only in the mid-19th century that housing reformers in Britain began to introduce the concept of the upper middle-class apartment block (e.g. in Victoria Street, London, 1852–4). Towards the end of the century, however, a number of apartment blocks were built in London, usually as second homes for the fashionable upper middle classes, the 'flat set', or as bachelor flats. One of the earliest developments, Queen Anne Mansions (1877), St James's Park, London, was 14 storeys high and included hydraulic lifts, a restaurant and room service. Other examples included the Prince Teck Buildings (1881) in Earl's Court and Prince's Mansions (*c.* 1884) in Victoria Street. In the USA there were similar developments around the same time. The first apartment block to be built in New York, for example, was the French-inspired Stuyvesant Building (1869–70; destr.) by Richard Morris Hunt. By the 1880s, however, stylish apartment blocks were being built in New York for the middle classes (e.g. the Dakota Apartments, 1880–86; by HENRY JANEWAY HARDENBERGH).

To some extent the rejection of urbanization by the Arts and Crafts Movement and the Garden City movement at the end of the 19th century and the beginning of the 20th militated against the apartment gaining universal acceptance. Nevertheless, in the early 20th century some of the most significant innovations, at least in the field of domestic architecture, took the form of apartment buildings. In New York at the turn of the century the Beaux-Arts style dominated, while in Europe the eight-storey apartment block built in 1903–5 by Auguste Perret at 25, Rue Franklin, Paris (*see* PARIS, fig. 11), for example, represented an important moment in the development of rationalist architecture, and Antoni Gaudí's Casa Milà (1906–10; *see* GAUDÍ, ANTONI, fig. 1) in Barcelona was a significant example of domestic Art Nouveau. All these buildings, however, continued to serve a wealthy middle-class clientele, as did the block at 998 Fifth Avenue, New York, built in 1910–12 by McKim, Mead & White. During the 1920s and 1930s apartment blocks came to be associated with the avant-garde and modernity, exemplified by Wells Coates's Lawn Road Flats (1932–4; for illustration *see* COATES, WELLS) in London or the streamlined Kelvincourt (1937), Glasgow. In the period immediately after World War II multi-storey living perhaps became less fashionable among the middle class in some countries because of its associations with low-cost public housing, but this did not prevent the conversion of three- and four-storey terrace mansions in such areas as Belgravia in London into exclusive blocks of flats or the creation of new blocks (e.g. Palace Green, Kensington, London) as land prices soared in the late 20th century.

BIBLIOGRAPHY

A. Sutcliffe, ed.: *Multi-storey Living* (London, 1974)

J. A. Wilkes, ed.: *Encyclopedia of Architecture: Design, Engineering and Construction*, i (New York, 1990), pp. 219–40

□

Apel, Otto (*b* Vatterode, Hessen, 30 Dec 1906; *d* Frankfurt am Main, 19 March 1966). German architect. He studied at the Baugewerbeschule in Kassel (1925–7) and in Berlin (1929–32). He worked from 1933 to 1943 as an assistant to Albert Speer for the Berlin Generalbauinspektion. After 1945 he worked for the Frankfurter Aufbau AG in the field of residential building. In the 1950s Apel's buildings were very much modelled on the modern architecture that came back to Germany from the United States. In the context of a building programme for the American state department, the architectural partnership Skidmore, Owings & Merrill were responsible for designing a considerable number of buildings—embassies, consulates—for the overseas representation of the USA. Apel collaborated with Skidmore, Owings & Merrill on the Consulate General of the United States (1952–3) in Bremen. The building is based on functional considerations, follows a strict constructional grid and is constructed from prefabricated building components. Two building cubes are joined vertically to form a steel structural framework, into which infill walls of glass or travertine panels are inserted. Living accommodation for consulate officials built in 1953–4 refers back to the blocks of flats with access balconies common in German domestic architecture of the 1920s and 1930s. The American Consulate General in Düsseldorf was also built by Skidmore, Owings & Merrill with the participation of Apel. Like the building in Bremen it is a steel-frame building with the ground floor designed as an open hall.

Not only do Apel's commercial, office and residential buildings as social institutions take up the forms and types of the Modern Movement but they are also to some extent rationally based on precast construction. From 1960 to 1966 he worked in association with the architects Hansgeorg Beckert (*b* 1927) and Gilbert Becker (*b* 1925). They were involved in building extensions at the Rhine-Main airport (1961–3) at Frankfurt am Main, the Intercontinental Hotel buildings at Frankfurt (1963) and Hannover (1965), the jointly planned theatre and opera (1960–63) in Frankfurt and the centre (1965–8) for Nordweststadt, Frankfurt. The centre of this satellite town is planned as a pedestrian area over a lower level carrying road traffic. A small-scale grid enables commercial premises and social and cultural institutions to be closely linked in building terms.

BIBLIOGRAPHY

J. Joedicke: *Geschichte der modernen Architektur* (Stuttgart, 1958)
W. Pehnt: *Neue deutsche Architektur 3* (Stuttgart, 1970)
W. Durth: *Deutsche Architekten, biographische Verflechtungen, 1900–1970* (Brunswick, 1986)

ROLAND WOLFF

Apelles (*b* Kolophon, Ionia; *fl* late 4th century BC–early 3rd century BC; *d* ?Kos). Greek painter. Ancient sources stating that he was born at Kos (Pliny XXXV.xxxvi.79) or Ephesos (Strabo: *Geography* XIV.i.25) apparently confused his correct place of birth (*Suidas*: 'Apelles') with cities where he was later active. According to Pliny, Apelles flourished in the 112th Olympiad (332 BC), and his association with Philip II of Macedon implies that his career began before 336 BC. His work for Ptolemy I of Egypt suggests that it lasted until after 304 BC, when Ptolemy declared himself king. No painting by Apelles survives, however, and his works are known only from literary sources.

Apelles studied painting first under Ephoros of Ephesos, then under Pamphilos of Sikyon (*Suidas*). According to Plutarch (*Aratos* xiii), however, he was already much admired before he went to Sikyon and enrolled at the school simply to share in its reputation. This is borne out by his probable collaboration with MELANTHIOS on an important commissioned painting of the *Victory Chariot of the Tyrant Aristratos* while in Sikyon. Apelles' fame was later based primarily on his portraits, especially of Philip II and Alexander the Great. Several sources, including Pliny (XXXV.xxxvi.85), state that Alexander allowed no artist but Apelles to paint him, and two anecdotes apparently confirm his privileged status. The first relates that Apelles silenced Alexander, who was giving an ill-informed discourse on painting, by telling him that the boys grinding paint were laughing at him. This may be apocryphal, since it is also told of other artists and patrons. The second recounts that when Apelles fell in love with Alexander's favourite concubine, Pankaspe, while painting her nude portrait, Alexander gave her to him.

Apelles' most famous portrait of Alexander was probably *Alexander Holding the Thunderbolt* in the Temple of Artemis at Ephesos, considered extraordinary because the thunderbolt and Alexander's fingers seemed to project out of the picture. To achieve this, the figure of Alexander was apparently darkened so that the thunderbolt, which may have been given highlights, stood out. This feat was particularly remarkable because the painting was in the four-colour palette (black, white, yellow and red), deliberately chosen by some artists of this period, despite the availability of other colours (*see* GREECE, ANCIENT, §VI, 2(iii)). Though no examples of the technique survive, the *Alexander Mosaic* (2nd century BC; Naples, Mus. Archeol. N.; *see* POMPEII, fig. 7), representing the Battle of Issus between Alexander the Great and Darius, is undoubtedly based on a four-colour painting and gives an impression of the sophisticated results that could be achieved. Certain painters gained particular fame through their use of the four-colour palette, which seems to have been an important aspect of Greek painting. Though the date of the technique's invention is disputed, Apelles and his contemporaries were confirmed as having perfected it. Apelles was also noted for the use of a thin black varnish, a technical innovation that both protected his paintings and enhanced their brightness (Lat. *claritas*).

According to Pliny (XXXV.xxxvi.90), Apelles was also the first artist to paint portraits in three-quarter view, a scheme originally developed to hide the missing eye of Alexander's general Antigonos Monophthalmos (Gr.: 'one-eyed'), later king of Macedonia (*c*. 382–301 BC). Apelles painted portraits of many of Alexander's entourage, as well as death-bed portraits and one self-portrait. The likenesses were said to be so exact that one fortune-teller (Gr. *metoposkopos*) could tell the precise ages of sitters and predict their dates of death. In addition to portraits, Apelles produced more than a dozen other works recorded by ancient sources. Mythological subjects and personifications predominated, but there was also a painting of a nude hero, and a painting of a horse was alleged to have won a competition for realism actually judged by horses.

Apelles' *Aphrodite Anadyomene* (Aphrodite rising from the sea) was considered a masterpiece, and Pankaspe may have modelled for it (Pliny XXXV.xxxvi.86,91). Athenaeus (*Deipnosophists* XIII.590) named Phryne, the mistress of Praxiteles, as the model, but this is less likely. The pose of Apelles' Aphrodite may be reflected, if imprecisely, in several later sculptures of Aphrodite wringing water from her hair. The painting was taken to Rome and dedicated by Augustus in the Temple of Julius Caesar. When it was damaged, however, no-one could restore it, and it continued to decay until it was replaced by a copy during the reign of Nero. Apelles had begun his copy or revised version of the work on Kos, but it was unfinished at the time of his death. Another famous work was *Calumny*, apparently painted in response to the slanderous accusation of his rival, Antiphilos, that Apelles had participated in a plot to overthrow Ptolemy I. This was a complex allegorical work in which the beautiful female figure of

Calumny, led by Jealousy and accompanied by Treachery and Deception, approached a man with huge ears, flanked by Ignorance and Suspicion. Behind Calumny came a tearful Repentance, who turned towards Truth. Lucian's description of *Calumny* (*Calumniae non temere credendum* iv–v) inspired Botticelli's *Calumny of Apelles* (Florence, Uffizi) and, through it, the whole European tradition of allegorical painting.

Ancient critics regarded the most notable quality of Apelles' work as its grace (Gr. *charis*, Lat. *venustas*), in the sense both of outward beauty and of an inner spiritual radiance. In his lost treatise on painting, referred to by ancient authors (e.g. Quintilian: *Institutio oratoria* XII.x.6), Apelles himself claimed superiority over other artists in *charis*, while conceding that some showed greater skill in the, to him less important, fields of composition (Lat. *disposito*) and perspective (Lat. *mensurae*). He attributed his success to a knowledge of the right moment to stop work on a painting, while other artists used too much detail. Discipline and practice were also necessary; the proverb 'Never a day without a line' was attributed to him and may come from his treatise.

BIBLIOGRAPHY

Pliny: *Natural History*
J. Overbeck: *Die antiken Schriftquellen zur Geschichte der bildenden Künste bei den Griechen* (Leipzig, 1868), pp. 344–58, nos 1827–906
J. J. Pollitt: *The Ancient View of Greek Art: Criticism, History and Terminology* (New Haven, 1974), pp. 297–301
J. Bruno: *Form and Colour in Greek Painting* (London, 1977), pp. 53–87
D. Cast: *The Calumny of Apelles* (New Haven, 1981)

SUSAN B. MATHESON

Apergis, Achilleas (*b* Corfu, 1909; *d* Athens, 1986). Greek sculptor. He studied drawing briefly in Corfu and in 1937 enrolled at the School of Fine Arts, Athens, where he studied sculpture under Thomas Thomopoulos, Kostas Dēmētriadēs and Mikhaēl Tombros. His first works were academic in nature and included busts and statues such as the *Standing Female Nude* on the tomb of Dem. C. Verellis at the First Cemetery in Athens. After World War II, and increasingly after 1950, he turned towards abstract compositions; his first exhibition was held in Athens in 1955. He used iron rods to create compositions based on Constructivism, but which include strong Expressionist elements (e.g. *Don Quixote*, iron, 1958; Athens, Min. Cult. Affairs). After 1960 he started using bronze rods, at first combining them vertically to make his sculptures seem worn by time and space, and giving an impression of deterioration, as in *Composition* (bronze, 1963; Athens, N.G.); later the rods were used horizontally (e.g. *Drunken Boat*, bronze, 1975; London, priv. col.), and finally diagonally (e.g. *Bronze Rods*; Athens, N. Bank of Greece). In 1976, influenced by the theories of Hegel and the poetry of Edgar Allan Poe, he became involved with environmental and conceptual art and began using different objects, inscriptions, sound and lighting in his work. This direction was further expressed with his *Ladders*, mainly wooden and in various sizes, perceived as symbols of ascension, effort and of the quest for knowledge. In 1985 his 10 m high ladders were placed in Faliron, near Athens. Apergis took part in numerous one-man and group exhibitions in Greece and abroad.

BIBLIOGRAPHY

C. Christou and M. Koumvakali-Anastasiadi: *Modern Greek Sculpture, 1800–1940* (Athens, 1982), pp. 119–21, 215
B. Spiliadi: *Apergis* (Athens, 1984)

TONIA P. GIANNOUDAKI, with EVITA ARAPOGLOU

Aphrodisias. Hellenistic and Roman site in south-west Caria, Asia Minor (modern Turkey), on a plateau in the Baba Dağ mountains above a tributary valley of the Maeander (Büyük Menderes).

1. INTRODUCTION. As its name suggests, Aphrodisias was a major cult centre of a goddess of nature and fertility, originally of local character but eventually influenced by other similar Anatolian and Near Eastern divinities. She was identified with Aphrodite only in late Hellenistic times, so the use of the name Aphrodisias for the site must also be dated to that time; Stephanos of Byzantium indicated that it was also known by other names (*Nations* cdlxxvi.6–7). Access to the site was for a long time difficult. From the late 18th century several archaeologically inclined travellers, including members of the Society of Dilettanti, described visible remains and copied inscriptions. Early excavations, undertaken by a French amateur archaeologist, Paul Gaudin, in 1904–5 and by an Italian mission under G. Jacobi in 1937, were short-lived. The current series of investigations, inaugurated in 1961 under the aegis of New York University and continued annually ever since, has made a large number of artistic and archaeological discoveries.

Excavations in two prehistoric mounds in the later city have revealed that habitation here went back at least to the 5th millennium BC. In Archaic and Classical times (*c.* 600–323 BC) Aphrodisias was essentially a sacred site and developed into a fully-fledged city only in the late 2nd century BC to the 1st. Ancient textual references are limited, and much of its history must be reconstructed from epigraphical and other archaeological evidence. The growth and prosperity of the city owed much to the patronage of Republican and Imperial Rome. In the troubled 1st century BC its loyalty to Rome and Julius Caesar resulted in special status and privileges, granted by senatorial decree and confirmed by Augustus (*reg* 27 BC–AD 14). Under the Julio-Claudian emperors (*reg* AD 14–68) close ties with Rome were continued, and consequently Aphrodisias developed into a cultural and artistic centre of great prosperity and renown. A remarkable school of sculpture flourished here from the 1st century BC to the 5th century AD. The creations of these artists owed much to the ample supplies of excellent marble quarried in the mountains to the east of the city. The sculptures were exported to many parts of the Empire, including Rome itself, where a workshop may have been active. Despite the turmoils of the 3rd century AD and the subsequent ascendancy of Christianity, which was hostile to the cult of its patron goddess, Aphrodisias continued to prosper until the 7th century AD, but damaging earthquakes, internal dissensions, plagues and invasions accelerated its decline after that date. Nevertheless Byzantine records and archaeological evidence show that modest habitation continued as late as the 13th century.

2. ARCHITECTURE. The site lies on a plateau inclined slightly to the south-west, featuring a conical hillock *c.* 20 m high (the 'acropolis') in its central eastern portion and a gentle ground irregularity at its east end (see fig. 1a). These are the mounds of accumulated prehistoric habitation. A 3.5 km circuit of fortifications of Byzantine date, often restored and including earlier architectural fragments and inscriptions, enclosed an area of *c.* 250 acres. This formed the core of the ancient city, while beyond these walls stretched extensive necropoleis (1b).

No formal city plan is recognizable in the layout of monuments uncovered so far, except at the main public areas such as the agora (1c) and its vicinity. The chief landmark was the Temple of Aphrodite (1d). Fourteen Ionic marble columns of its peristyle are still standing; it was originally an octastyle structure with 13 columns on the sides. Many of its architectural features were obscured by drastic modifications during its conversion into a Christian basilica in the late 5th century AD. Present evidence suggests two building phases in the 1st century BC for the pagan shrine, preceded by a sanctuary that was Archaic at the latest (6th century BC). All these constructions freely reused architectural elements of earlier dates. To the south of the temple is a well-preserved odeion-bouleuterion (1e; many odeia in the Greek-speaking world doubled as places of civic assembly). Once roofed, its lower *cavea* consisted of 9 tiers of seats; its upper *cavea* was supported by 11 vaulted chambers. Its backstage opened on to one of the two porticoed areas forming the agora (1st century AD). The adjacent colonnaded unit to its south, the Portico of Tiberius (1f), was so called after its dedication to that emperor (*reg* AD 14–37). On its western side are the large Baths of Hadrian (2nd century AD; 1g), decorated with panelled pilasters carved with

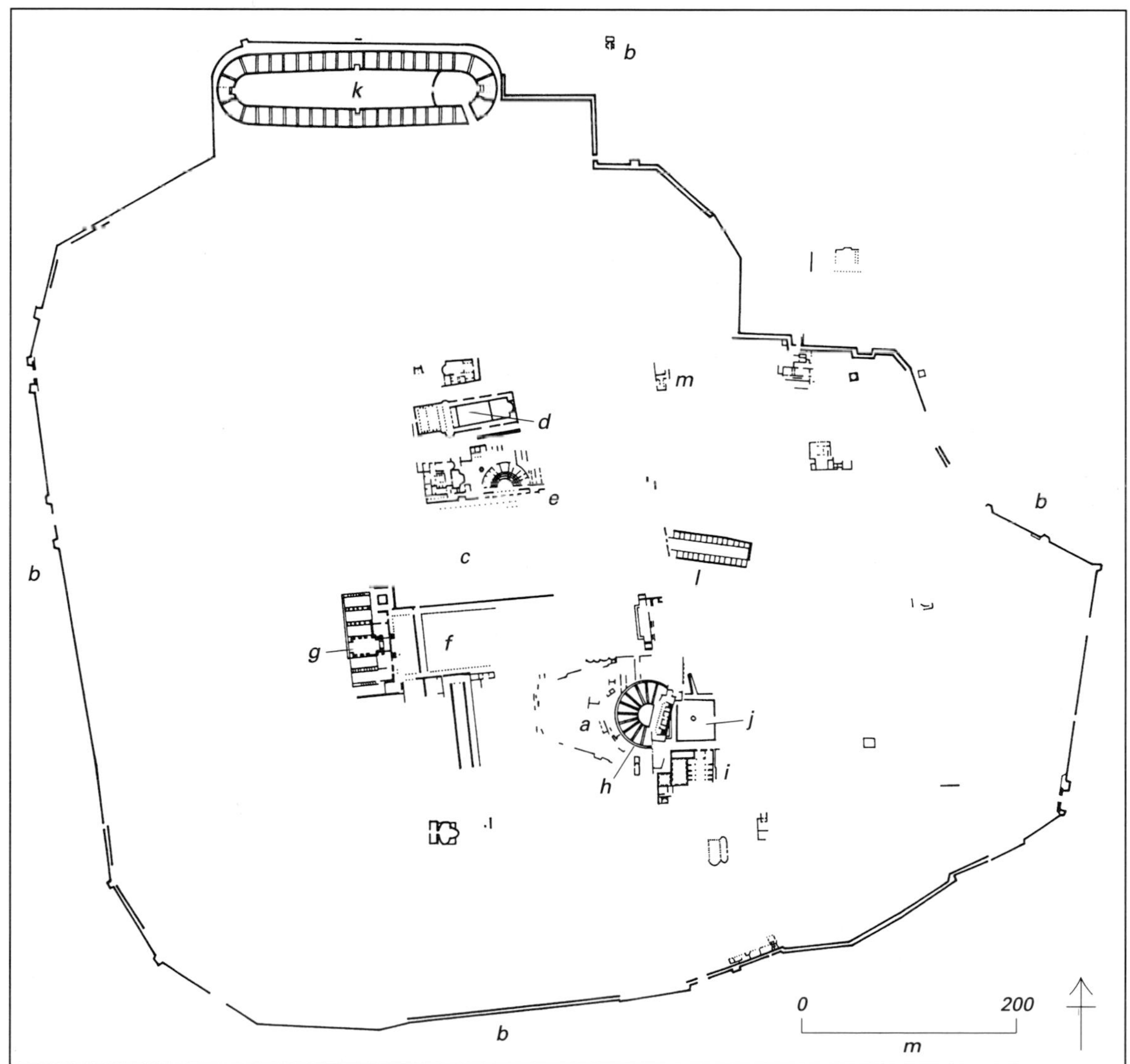

1. Aphrodisias, plan: (a) 'acropolis'; (b) necropoleis; (c) agora; (d) Temple of Aphrodite; (e) odeion-bouleuterion; (f) Portico of Tiberius; (g) Baths of Hadrian; (h) theatre; (i) bath complex; (j) market area; (k) stadium; (l) Sebasteion; (m) tetrapylon

figured acanthus scrolls, while to the east a monumental gateway (2nd century AD), its façade adorned by aediculae, stood between the portico and a major north–south street.

A large theatre (1h) was constructed in the 1st century BC on the eastern slope of the 'acropolis'. Its horseshoe-shaped *cavea* is typical of theatres in Asia Minor; many rows of seats have been preserved in excellent condition. A large number of important 2nd- and 3rd-century AD inscriptions were found on the wall of the stage building. To its south-east another bath complex was built (later 2nd century AD; 1i). In the later 4th century AD earthquakes led to the creation of a wide public market area (1j) behind the theatre's stage, probably because of flooding in the earlier agora. Attempts at stemming such floods are discernible in several other lower-lying monuments of the city.

The most arresting of Aphrodisias' public buildings is a large stadium (1st or 2nd century AD, capacity 30,000; 1k) which nestles in the northern sector of the later Byzantine fortifications. It measures 262×59 m and has 30 tiers of seats. In Byzantine times an arena was created at the east end. The most unusual monumental discovery is the Sebasteion (first half of the 1st century AD; 1l), a building complex dedicated to the cult of Augustus (Gr. *sebastos*), and to those of his Julio-Claudian successors, Aphrodite and Rome. It consisted of two long parallel porticos facing each other, with a temple to the east and a monumental gateway to the west, and was lavishly decorated with relief panels and statuary. Other buildings of note include a decorative gateway east of the precinct of Aphrodite that incorporates spirally fluted columns (the tetrapylon, *c*. mid-2nd century AD; 1m) and several late Roman and early Byzantine houses adorned with mosaic floors and wall frescoes.

KENAN T. ERIM

2. Aphrodisias, marble relief panel from the Sebasteion (probably the north portico) depicting the young Nero being crowned with a wreath by his mother Agrippina, 1.72×1.42 m, *c*. AD 54–9

3. SCULPTURE. Long before excavations were resumed in Aphrodisias in 1961, evidence of the importance of Aphrodisian sculptors and sculpture had been provided by numerous signed works of art found around the Mediterranean (*see* ROME, ANCIENT, fig. 78). The amount of the recently discovered statuary dating from the 1st to the 6th centuries AD greatly outnumbers the finds from neighbouring towns. The origins of the Aphrodisian sculptural tradition seem linked with the construction of a new temple for Aphrodite during the late Hellenistic period (323–31 BC) and the inexhaustible supply of high-quality marble from the nearby mountains. Several fine panels from a monument dedicated shortly after 30 BC by Gaius Julius Zoilos, a freedman of Octavian, are among the earliest sculptural remains of Aphrodisias. They show allegorical figures glorifying Zoilos, through whom the town had gained a special status. Reliefs (*in situ* and Aphrodisias Mus.) inserted into the walls of the Sebasteion, begun about half a century later, reflect the local understanding of Roman rule. They represent cosmic and ethnic allegories and Julio-Claudian emperors as lords over land, sea and vanquished enemies (see fig. 2). Some panels refer to the Imperial family's mythical ancestors, on others gods are seen and Greek myths are illustrated.

The original context of reliefs dating from the late 2nd century AD with scenes of the major mythical battles is unknown. They were later incorporated into a fountain house in the agora. A statue of Antoninus Pius (*reg* 138–61) and bases for statues of other emperors were retrieved from a complex near by. As expected, the odeion and the theatre provided rich finds: among them are statues of poets or philosophers, of Apollo and Melpomene (the Muse of Tragedy), of Victories, of Demos (People), of an athlete and of the Emperor Domitian (*reg* 81–96), as well as honorific portraits of dignitaries, benefactors and professional boxers. Many impressive portraits, several of them representing high officials, were found in various public areas. The statue of Flavius Palmatus, a 5th-century governor who is shown equipped with the insignia of his rank, is a striking example of the quality of Aphrodisian sculpture. Among the statues from the portico behind the odeion stage are other portraits of members of the Aphrodisian aristocracy, such as those of Diogenes, wearing a crown to indicate his high-priesthood of Aphrodite, and his wife (both Aphrodisias Mus.), both erected late in the 2nd century. The Baths of Hadrian, already partly excavated at the beginning of this century, have yielded further statuary, among them a colossal female head with a stellar diadem, heads of Apollo and Aphrodite and groups with scenes from the Trojan War (Achilles and Penthesilea and Menelaos dragging the dead body of Patroklos). The fragmentary colossal statue of Aphrodite of Aphrodisias was recovered to the south of the goddess's precinct (all first half of the 2nd century AD; Aphrodisias Mus.).

Striking features of Aphrodisian sculpture are the use of bichrome marble and the many shield-portraits. The rich imagination, thematical sophistication, creative originality and stylistic exuberance of the Aphrodisian sculptors are also reflected in the ever-increasing amount of sarcophagi found in the area, even though by the early 1990s systematic exploration of the cemeteries had not yet begun. Most of the artefacts discovered on the site are displayed at the Aphrodisias Museum.

BIBLIOGRAPHY

Enc. A. Ant.; Stillwell

M. Collignon: 'Note sur les fouilles exécutées à Aphrodisias par M. Paul Gaudin', *Acad. Inscr. & B.-Lett.: C. R. Séances* (Nov-Dec 1904), pp. 703–11

G. Jacopi: 'Gli scavi della Missione Archeologica Italiana ad Afrodisiade', *Mnmt. Ant.: Lincei*, 38 (1939–40)

J. M. R. Cormack: *Notes on the History of the Inscribed Monuments of Aphrodisias* (Reading, 1955)

W. M. Calder and J. M. R. Cormack, eds: *Monuments from Lycaonia, the Pisido-Phrygian Borderland, Aphrodisias* (1962), viii of *Monumenta Asiae Minoris Antiqua* (Manchester and London, 1928–)

K. T. Erim: 'Aphrodisias (Karia) Kazılari ikinci Kampam-yaya ait rapor (Hazuran-Eylül 1962)', *Türk Arkeol. Derg.*, xii/1 (1962), pp. 14–18

——: 'Aphrodisias 1963 Mafriyati', *Türk Arkeol. Derg.*, xiv (1964), pp. 86–92

——: 'Aphrodisias and its Marble Treasures', *Nat. Geog.*, 132 (Aug 1967), pp. 286–94

——: 'Aphrodisias: Results of the 1967 Campaign', *Türk Arkeol. Derg.*, xvii (1967), pp. 67–80

——: 'De Aphrodisiade', *Amer. J. Archeol.*, lxxi (1967), pp. 233–43

J. M. Reynolds: *Aphrodisias and Rome* (London, 1982)

K. T. Erim: *Aphrodisias: City of Venus Aphrodite* (London, 1986)

M. S. Joukowsky and others: *Prehistoric Aphrodisias: An Account of the Excavations and Artifact Studies*, 2 vols (Providence, RI and Louvain-la-Neuve, 1986)

C. Roueche and K. T. Erim, eds: *Aphrodisias Papers: Recent Work on Architecture and Sculpture: 2nd International Aphrodisias Colloquium: London, 1987*

R. R. R. Smith and K. T. Erim, eds: *Aphrodisias Papers 2: The Theatre, a Sculptor's Workshop, Philosophers and Coin Types: 3rd International Aphrodisias Colloquium: New York, 1989*

KALINKA HUBER

Aplomata, hill of. *See under* NAXOS, §1.

Apocalypse [Gr.: 'revelation' or 'unveiling']. The last book of the New Testament, also known as Revelation, written by John, traditionally identified as the Evangelist. The Apocalypse is unique among the books of the New Testament in that it comprises descriptions of the author's visions, each signalled by the words 'I saw' or 'In my vision I heard'. Generated by the opening of seven seals, the sounding of seven trumpets and the pouring of seven vials, the narrative flows outside the boundaries of operative causes and effects since its events lie beyond time. The thrust of the text is prophetic and admonitory. Abstract forces of good and evil are inexorably caught up in a series of catastrophes and horrific battles waged between angels and demonic beasts, interspersed by ecstatic glimpses of celestial bliss, which ends in a vision of the heavenly Jerusalem. The text was a frequent subject of illustration in different media during the Middle Ages down to the 16th century; there was a particularly strong tradition in illuminated manuscripts and early printed books.

BIBLIOGRAPHY

J.-L. D'Aragon: 'The Apocalypse', *The Jerome Bible Commentary*, ed. R. Brown and others (Englewood Cliffs, 1969), pp. 467–614

J. Ford: *Revelation* (1975), xxxviii of *The Anchor Bible* (Garden City, 1964–77)

G. Quispel: *The Secret Book of Revelation: The Last Book of the Bible* (New York, 1979)

1. Manuscript. 2. Printed.

1. MANUSCRIPT. About 140 illustrated Apocalypse manuscripts survive from the Middle Ages, with 35 other manuscripts containing illustrated texts of the book of Revelation. Unlike the manuscript traditions for other biblical books, extended cycles of pictures render not only each episode but every moment and gesture recorded in the text. John is present throughout as author–seer and protagonist, serving as the human intermediary between the reader and divine revelation; his stance and gestures register awe-struck terror and joy as he is commanded, comforted, warned, admonished and reassured by angels and finally by the Lord himself.

The earliest illustrated Apocalypses (9th century; Trier, Stadtbib., MS. 31, see fig. 1; Valenciennes, Bib. Mun., MS. 99) contain 75 and 40 miniatures respectively. As creations of the Carolingian *renovatio* they demonstrably represent a revival of Late Antique designs from the 5th century. Modest in scale, they comprise pages of text facing full-page coloured ink drawings on plain or lightly washed grounds and were probably created in Benedictine houses for the monks' private reading. A replica (Cambrai, Bib. Mun., MS. 386) of the Trier Apocalypse dates from the 10th century; Valenciennes MS. 99 was later copied (Paris, Bib. N., MS. nouv. acq. lat. 1132) and also inspired a magnificent expanded version (Bamberg, Staatsbib., MS. Bibl. 140) with 50 illustrations fully painted on gold and coloured grounds, presumably for liturgical use, which

1. Apocalypse manuscript: *Fall of Satan*, tinted ink drawing, 250×210 mm, *c.* 820 (Trier, Stadtbibliothek, MS. 31, fol. 38*r*)

2. Apocalypse manuscript: *John Commanded to Eat the Book*, painted ink drawing, 146×110 mm, *c*. 1270–75 (Oxford, Bodleian Library, MS. Douce 180, fol. 33)

was given by Emperor Henry II *c*. 1020 to the collegiate church of St Stephan in Bamberg.

A tradition developed in Spain to illustrate the commentary on the Apocalypse composed in three editions between 776 and 786 by the Asturian monk Beatus of Liébana (*d c*. 798). Represented by 25 extant manuscripts dating between the latter half of the 10th century and the beginning of the 13th, the Beatus Apocalypses are often of immense size, perhaps destined for liturgical use at the altar. The fourth Council of Toledo (633) required the continuous reading and explanation of the Apocalypse from Easter to Pentecost. Although their patronage was sometimes royal, such as the Facundus manuscript (Madrid, Bib. N., MS. Vit. 14–2) made in 1047 for Ferdinand I (*reg* 1035–65) and Queen Sancha (*d* 1067), the illustrated Beatus commentaries were produced for monastic communities. Sixty-four glossed articles (*storiae*) from Revelation are preceded by framed miniatures heavily painted in strong colours, ranging in size from small, square pictures enframed within the text to double-page openings. Larger Beatus manuscripts (e.g. Girona, Mus. Catedralici; London, BL, Add. MS. 11695; New York, Pierpont Morgan Lib., MS. M. 644) contain prefatory miniatures, prologues and tracts as well as an illustrated text of Jerome's commentary on Daniel.

In a wide variety of Romanesque Apocalypse manuscripts the illustrations are either relegated to historiated initials, for example in a German copy of the commentary by Rupert of Deutz (*c*. 1075–1129; Heiligenkreuz, Stiftsbib., MS. 83), or they are unframed ink-drawn or painted vignettes within the text columns or margins (e.g. Berlin, Staatsbib. Preuss. Kultbesitz, MS. theol. lat. fol. 561; Rome, Vatican, Bib. Apostolica, MS. lat. 39). Most notable are the picture books in which the text is reduced to captions and speech scrolls, for example a German manuscript of Haimo of Auxerre's commentary (*c*. 870), prefaced by 68 Apocalypse illustrations fully painted in several registers on full pages (first half of the 12th century; Oxford, Bodleian Lib., MS. Bodl. 352), and the *Liber floridus*, which survives in six manuscripts. The earliest example containing the *Apocalypsis depictus* (*c*. 1150–70; Wolfenbüttel, Herzog August Bib., MS. Guelf. 1. Gud. lat. 2) has illustrations for the first 13 chapters presented in several registers on full pages; the only complete copy (Paris, Bib. N., MS. lat. 8865) bears an inscription (*c*. 1260) of Blanche of Castile, Queen of France. Also associated with the patronage of Queen Blanche and King Louis IX is the *Bible moralisée* with its cycle of over 300 miniatures for the book of Revelation, comprising the last component of a monumental glossed Bible in which both the scriptural text and glosses are copiously illustrated (*see* BIBLE, §I, 3(i)).

A singular group of German Apocalypses from the late 13th century and the 14th illustrates a contemporary commentary written by Alexander the Minorite (e.g. Cambridge, U. Lib., MS. Mm. 5.31; U. Wrocław, Lib., MS. I.Q.19). The pictorial cycle is uniquely characterized by a series of double-headed figures that reflect the commentary's identification of the figures in John's visions as rulers and popes from Constantine the Great to Innocent IV (*reg* 1245–54).

The Anglo-French manuscripts form the largest and most influential corpus of medieval illustrated Apocalypses, comprising almost 80 surviving English, French and Netherlandish codices and fragments dating from the mid-13th century to the 16th. Designed in England in the second half of the 13th century, picture cycles containing between 78 and 100 half-page framed miniatures were created for Latin and Anglo-Norman texts accompanied by excerpts from the 12th-century commentary by Berengaudus (e.g. London, Lambeth Pal. Lib., MS. 209; Malibu, CA, Getty Mus., MS. Ludwig III.1; Oxford, Bodleian Lib., MS. Douce 180, see fig. 2). A notable pair of 13th-century English Apocalypses (Lisbon, Mus. Gulbenkian, MS. L.A. 139; London, BL, Add. MS. 42555) contains full cycles of miniatures for the Berengaudus commentary as well as Revelation. Although painting tends to supplant tinted outline drawing, the half-page format remains remarkably consistent throughout the development of the Berengaudus cycles, notwithstanding anomalous manuscripts (e.g. Cambridge, Trinity Coll., MS. R.16.2) and the importance of the so-called 'aristocratic' picture books (e.g. New York, Pierpont Morgan Lib., MS. M. 524), in which the illustrations are arranged in double registers and an abbreviated text is incorporated within the framed picture space.

Anglo-French cycles were also designed for an anonymous vernacular gloss in which illustrations are inserted irregularly within the text columns, as represented by the group of 13th- and 14th-century English Apocalypses constituting the Corpus–Lambeth stem (e.g. London, Lambeth Pal. Lib., MS. 75; Paris, Bib. N., MS. fr. 9574) with later sub-groups. The Corpus–Lambeth cycle also influenced the production of continental manuscripts. Although the 13th-century English cycles were probably created initially for clerical use, Anglo-French Apocalypses came to be made increasingly for the private devotions of aristocratic lay readers such as Jean, Duc de Berry (New York, Pierpont Morgan Lib., MS. M.133), and Margaret of York, Duchess of Burgundy (New York, Pierpont Morgan Lib., MS. M.484).

New manuscript cycles continued to be produced in the 15th century, most notably those for the *Bible historiale* (*see* BIBLE, §I, 3(iii)) compiled by Guyart des Moulins, the cycle of more than 300 text and commentary illustrations in the Bedford Hours (London, BL, Add. MS. 18850) and a south Netherlandish Apocalypse (Paris, Bib. N., MS. néerl. 3) containing full-page miniatures summarizing the 22 chapters of Revelation.

For further illustration *see* MANUSCRIPT, fig. 15.

BIBLIOGRAPHY

L. Delisle and P. Meyer: *L'Apocalypse en français au XIIIe siècle*, 2 vols (Paris, 1901)
M. R. James: *The Apocalypse in Art* (London, 1931)
W. Neuss: *Die Apokalypse des hl. Johannes in der altspanischen und altchristlichen Bibel-Illustration: Das Problem der Beatus-Handschriften*, Sp. Forsch. der Görres-Ges., ii–iii (Münster, 1931)
R. Freyhan: 'Joachism and the English Apocalypse', *J. Warb. & Court. Inst.*, xviii (1955), pp. 211–44
G. Henderson: 'Studies in English Manuscript Illumination', *J. Warb. & Court. Inst.*, xxx (1967), pp. 71–137; xxxi (1968), pp. 103–47
F. Van der Meer: *Apocalypse: Visions from the Book of Revelation in Western Art* (London, 1978)
P. Klein: 'Les Cycles de l'Apocalypse du haut moyen âge (IX–XIIIe s.)', *Apocalypse de Jean. Actes du colloques de la Fondation Hardt: Geneva, 1979*, pp. 135–86
——: *Endzeiterwartung und Ritterideologie: Die englischen Bilderapokalypsen der Frühgotik und MS. Douce 180* (Graz, 1983)
R. Emmerson and S. Lewis: 'Census and Bibliography of Medieval Manuscripts Containing Apocalypse Illustrations, *c.* 800–1500', *Traditio*, xl (1984), pp. 337–79; xli (1985), pp. 367–409; xlii (1986), pp. 443–72
S. Lewis: 'Tractatus adversus Judaeos in the Gulbenkian Apocalypse', *A. Bull.*, lxviii (1986), pp. 543–66
N. Morgan: *The Lambeth Apocalypse* (London, 1990)
S. Lewis: 'The English Gothic Illuminated Apocalypse, *Lectio divina*, and the Art of Memory', *Word and Image*, vii (1991), pp. 1–32
——: 'Beyond the Frame: Marginal Figures and Historiated Initials in the Getty Apocalypse', *Getty Mus. J.*, xx (1992), pp. 53–76
——: 'Exegesis and Illustration in Thirteenth-century English Apocalypses', *The Apocalypse and the Middle Ages*, ed. R. K. Emmerson and B. McGinn (Ithaca, 1992), pp. 259–75
J. Williams: *The Illustrated Beatus* (London, 1994)

2. PRINTED. Block-book Apocalypses represent the last phase of the Anglo-French tradition, making the illustrated text available to wider, less affluent and often semi-literate audiences. Printed from single carved woodblocks, six editions were produced between 1430 and 1470, the first three in the Netherlands, the rest in Germany (*see* BLOCK-BOOK, fig. 1). They are based on a manuscript model (descending from New York, Pierpont Morgan Lib., MS. M.524) and may be represented by two 15th-century German Apocalypses (London, Wellcome Inst., Mus. Medic. Sci., MS. 49; New York, Pub. Lib., MS. De Ricci 15), which consist of *c.* 50 pages of pictures in two registers, executed in a simple, bold style demanded by the new medium, with the Latin text relegated to captions and speech scrolls. In the Netherlands these popular devotional books were promoted and often produced by the Brethren of the Common Life.

In the later 15th-century printed Bibles, the Apocalypse was the first part to be illustrated (*see* BOOK, fig. 6), but the cycles were reduced to a series of eight or nine woodcuts, as in the Cologne Bible published by Heinrich Quentell (*fl* 1478–1501) in 1479 and republished by Anton Koberger (*d* 1513) in Nuremberg in 1483 and the Strasbourg Bible of 1485 issued by Johann Grüninger (*c.* 1455–1533). These abbreviated sequences provided the models for the Woodcut Apocalypse of 1498 (see fig. 3) by Albrecht Dürer (*see* DÜRER, (1)), in which John's visions are condensed into 15 complex images of great dramatic power, with the vernacular text from the Nuremberg Bible printed on the back of each sheet. Dürer's designs served as models for the Apocalypse woodcuts by Giovanni Andrea Vavassore (*fl* 1510–72) in the Latin Bible published in Venice by Alessandro de Paganini (*fl* 1519–38) in 1515–16. With the publication of Martin Luther's

3. Apocalypse illustrated by Albrecht Dürer: *The First Vision*, woodcut, 610×433 mm, 1498 (Washington, DC, National Gallery of Art)

Wittenberg Bible of 1522, an expanded cycle of 21 scenes designed by Lucas Cranach the elder under the influence of Dürer's series proclaimed the message of the Reformation to wide masses of people. The Wittenberg model proved to be a potent instrument for the dissemination of Dürer's new Renaissance conception to major artists such as Hans Holbein the younger and Hans Burgkmair I, as well as to the minor masters Hans Brosamer and Sebald Beham, who produced five engraved editions of the Apocalypse from 1539 to 1558. The last new cycle descending from Dürer's model was created by the French goldsmith and engraver JEAN DUVET in 22 plates and issued in Lyon in 1561.

BIBLIOGRAPHY

Hollstein: *Ger.*
G. Bing: 'The Apocalypse Block-books and their Manuscript Models', *J. Warb. & Court. Inst.*, v (1942), pp. 143–58
F. Juraschek: *Das Rätsel in Dürers Gottesschau: Die Holzschnittapokalypse und Nikolaus von Cues* (Salzburg, 1955)
The Apocalypse (exh. cat. by K. Henkel, College Park, U. MD A.G., 1973)
C. Eisler: *The Master of the Unicorn: The Life and Work of Jean Duvet* (New York, 1979)

SUZANNE LEWIS

Apodyterium. Ancient Greek or Roman changing-room.

Apol, Louis [Lodewijk Franciscus Hendrikl] (*b* The Hague, 6 Sept 1850; *d* The Hague, 22 Nov 1936). Dutch painter. He was a pupil of Johannes Franciscus Hoppenbrouwers (1819–66) and Pieter Stortenbeker (1828–98) and studied at the Koninklijke Academie van Beeldende Kunsten in The Hague. His first exhibited work, in 1869, was a summer landscape, but he made his name with *A January Evening in the Hague Woods* (*c.* 1875; Amsterdam, Rijksmus.). He specialized in winter landscapes; his works became extremely popular in the last quarter of the 19th century. In views such as *Wood in Winter* (*c.* 1884; Haarlem, Teylers Mus.) staffage, in the shape of skaters, horse-drawn sleighs and so on, is subordinated to the overall mood. In this respect he differs from other Dutch painters of winter scenes such as Andreas Schelfhout and Hoppenbrouwers. Apol had a broad, pronounced manner of painting and was considered one of the minor masters of the Hague school. He made many drawings on a trip to Novaya Zemlya in 1880 (Amsterdam, Rijksmus.; Amsterdam, Ned. Hist. Scheepvaartsmus.). The journey resulted in a number of paintings of arctic scenes, including *Ship in the Ice near Novaya Zemlya* (untraced; ex-de Geus van Heuvel priv. col., Nieuwe Sluis) and a panorama, *Nova Zembla* (1892; destr.; small replica Amsterdam, Ned. Hist. Scheepvaartsmus.). Apol also painted a number of summer landscapes and river and town views, some dating from 1886 to 1892, when he left The Hague temporarily to live in Roosendaal near Arnhem.

BIBLIOGRAPHY

Scheen
W. J. de Gruyter: *De Haagse School*, ii (Rotterdam, 1968–9)
J. Ubbens: 'Louis Apol (1850–1936) en zijn foto's', *Tableau*, xi (1988), no. 3, pp. 49–51 [incl. summary in English]

ANNEMIEKE HOOGENBOOM

Apollinaire, Guillaume [Apollinaire de Kostrowitzky, Guillaume Albert Wladimir Alexandre] (*b* Rome, 26 Aug 1880; *d* Paris, 9 Nov 1918). French poet and writer. He loved to hint at his 'dark' origins: he was the illegitimate son of Angélique-Alexandrine Kostrowitzky, an eccentric beauty from a Polish noble family under the protection of the Roman Curia, and Francesco Flugi d'Aspermont, a former officer in the Royal Army of the Kingdom of the Two Sicilies. When the liaison ended Apollinaire was placed under the wing of the Bishop of Monaco, Monseigneur Theuret, and went through an exciting period of travel and education in Catholic schools on the French Riviera, where his mother had settled. Apollinaire liked to ascribe his genesis to a cardinal or even to Pope Pius IX himself.

While still a schoolboy, Apollinaire took a keen interest in literature and poetry, not only in the work of the Symbolists Stéphane Mallarmé (1842–98) and Paul Verlaine (1844–96) but also in the writings of the Naturalist school. In 1897, with his school-friend Toussaint-Luca, he founded his first (anarchic and unpublished) magazine, *Le Vengeur*, under the impact of Emile Zola's intervention in the Dreyfus Affair. In 1899 Mme Kostrowitzky moved from the Côte d'Azur to Paris with the Jewish financier Jules Weil. Because of his mother's extravagance, Apollinaire had to work in badly paid secretarial posts, although the most important aim of his life was still to become a poet. His active imagination was fired by the myths and legends of the Ardennes landscape during a short stay at Stavelot, which he had to abandon owing to lack of money. His first incursion into the literary world was as one of the ghost-writers of a mystical, pseudo-scientific novel *Que faire?* (Paris, 1950)—published in instalments in *Le Matin* during 1900 and written in the style of Jules Verne (1828–1905) and H. G. Wells (1866–1946)—and as the outspoken author of pornographic works published under a pseudonym, a practice to which he returned throughout his life in order to supplement his income. His financial position improved only when he became a private tutor in the household of Baroness Milhau, whose daughter he also had to accompany in 1901–2 to the small Rhenish castle of Neu-Glück, in Bennerscheid near Bad Honnef. While staying in the Rhineland, he fell in love with the family's English governess, Annie Playden, who, even after he had visited her in London twice, finally felt unable to respond to his advances. As a result of this experience, he wrote the *Chanson du mal-aimé* (1903) and created his first important poems, all of which he later included under the title of *Rhénanes* in his volume of poetry *Alcools* (Paris, 1913). On his return to Paris, Apollinaire worked in a bank and also made contact with poets. At the beginning of 1903 he took part in literary evenings organized by the magazine *La Plume*, where he became acquainted with the most important new writers, including Alfred Jarry and André Salmon. His own magazine, the *Festin d'Esope*, appeared that year, and he was already working for two other magazines. During the winter of 1903–4, thanks to Jean Mollett, Apollinaire also met Picasso (*see* PICASSO, PABLO, §2(ii) (v)), which led to a long friendship and to his first art criticism. Between 1907 and 1910 Apollinaire established himself as the most experienced writer on art in the new avant-garde; he wrote regularly on art for *L'Intransigeant* (from 1910 onwards), also producing a column called 'Echos' for *Paris-Journal* and collaborating on several other periodicals. His first great articles on Matisse, Picasso and Braque appeared, opening discussion on Cubism, which Apollinaire took every opportunity to defend as 'new art'. Marie Laurencin, a less gifted painter, whom Apollinaire nevertheless ranked as a first-rate Cubist, was his lover until 1912.

The Cubist group found a champion in Daniel-Henry Kahnweiler, who published Apollinaire's early stories under the title *L'Enchanteur pourrissant* (Paris, 1909), with woodcuts by Derain. The book contained a long prose poem, *Onirocritique*, in the tradition of the late 19th- and early 20th-century works by Arthur Rimbaud, the Comte de Lautréamont and Alfred Jarry, which seemed to anticipate Surrealism. Apollinaire first enjoyed literary recognition with his prose poem the *Chanson du mal-aimé*, which appeared in the *Mercure de France* on 1 May 1909, and with the volume of stories *L'Hérésiarque et Cie* (Paris, 1910), which won three nominations for the Prix Goncourt. The year 1911 marked the first highpoint of Apollinaire's career: he had his own column, 'La Vie anecdotique' in the *Mercure de France*, and his volume of poems *Bestiaire ou cortège d'Orphée* (Paris, 1911) appeared in a de luxe edition with woodcuts by Raoul Dufy. Apollinaire was still obliged to write articles in every conceivable style under a number of pseudonyms; moreover, he continued to write pornographic novels and edited a 14-volume *Bibliothèque des curieux* (Paris, 1909–13), including an edition of Baudelaire's *Fleurs du mal*, as well as a reference-bibliography of the Bibliothèque Nationale's 'enfer' (erotic literature on the Index). Yet by now he could also look back on a steeply ascending career as a French poet.

In September 1911 Apollinaire was arrested on suspicion of complicity in the theft of Leonardo's *Mona Lisa* (*c.* 1500–04) from the Musée du Louvre. A former acquaintance had previously given Apollinaire a small statuette he had stolen from the Louvre, and the publicity caused by the theft of the *Mona Lisa* led to the police discovering this and other statuettes in Apollinaire's home. He was sent to La Santé prison, where he had to spend several days on remand. Although he was later acquitted, arrest led to a serious crisis in Apollinaire's life and work, which was intensified when several old friends, including Marie Laurencin, turned away from him. Even when the poet André Billy founded the *Soirées de Paris* (with Salmon and René Dalize as co-editors) in 1912, and Apollinaire was able to publish his challenging views on the development of art openly, it stimulated his mood only briefly. A trip to the Jura Mountains, with Francis Picabia and his wife and Marcel Duchamp, gave him a change of scene.

The Picabias offered Apollinaire financial support for his long-projected book on the new artists, whose work Apollinaire wanted to unite under the heading 'cubisme écartelé'. A number of other artists had emerged from the original Cubism of Picasso and Braque and sought fresh paths for the form and content of the new art. In October 1912 Apollinaire made the inaugural address for the painters of the Section d'or (*see* SECTION D'OR (ii)), which included Albert Gleizes, Jean Metzinger, Duchamp, Picabia and Roger de La Fresnaye, proclaiming a new art invented by Robert Delaunay. He baptized this art ORPHISM, with particular reference to the *Fenêtres* (window-pictures) by Delaunay, such as *Window on the City No. 4* (1912; New York, Guggenheim). In November and December 1912, when Apollinaire had his flat renovated, he sought refuge with the Delaunays, which in the short term resulted in a close collaboration. The Orphism that Apollinaire had launched found passionate support in inaugural addresses, manifestos and articles, which made an especially strong impact on the Blaue Reiter and *Der Sturm* circles in Berlin. At the Delaunays', Apollinaire also met the poet Blaise Cendrars, who made a deep impression on him by reading his poem *Les Pâques à New York* (Paris, 1912).

Apollinaire's poem *Zone*, published in *Alcools* in 1913, marked the beginning of a new phase of innovation in both the form and content of his work because of its suppression of punctuation and its bold synthesis of vastly different sensory impressions and fragments of perception. 'Simultaneity' was not only the catch-phrase and operating principle of Robert Delaunay's circle, but also an inspiration for the Futurists, who were gaining more and more importance in Paris through Filippo Tommaso Marinetti's manifestos. Apollinaire also found himself drawn into the vortex of Futurist propaganda and wrote his own manifesto, *L'Anti-tradition futuriste* (Milan, 1913). The friendship between Delaunay and Apollinaire finally broke down because of the controversy over Delaunay's and Boccioni's use of the concept of 'simultaneity'. A few incautious remarks by Apollinaire concerning the priority of the 'métier simultané', his flirting with Futurist aesthetics and his unquenchable inquisitiveness put paid to his commitment to Orphism. Nor did his projected book about Delaunay materialize; instead, he published an anthology of various articles about the new painters, *Les Peintres cubistes: Méditations esthétiques* (Paris, 1913; repr. in Chipp, 1968, pp. 220–48), which presented Delaunay and Orphism as merely an offshoot of 'cubisme écartelé'.

In June 1914, before the outbreak of war, the *Soirées de Paris* published the first of Apollinaire's ideograms: creations of words and images full of complex references, which count among Apollinaire's most original works. Wishing to be acknowledged as a French citizen, Apollinaire volunteered for military service and on 5 December 1914 was assigned to an artillery regiment. During a train journey to his regiment in Nîmes, he met Madeleine Pagès, who inspired him to conduct a long amatory correspondence published as *Tendre comme le souvenir* (Paris, 1952). On 9 March 1916, news reached him at the Front that he was now officially a French citizen; on 11 March, a fragment of shell caused him a severe head-wound. He was discharged after a trepanation, which temporarily restored him to health, and soon resumed his journalistic activity with undiminished energy. He worked on new Dadaist, pre-Surrealist magazines, such as *Sic, Nord-Sud* (founded by Pierre Reverdy) and *391* (founded by Picabia). The *Mercure de France* published a new collection of stories, *Vitam impendere amori: Poèmes et dessins* (Paris, 1917). His friends published his collection of stories *Le Poète assassiné* (Paris, 1916) and held an enormous banquet in 1916 to celebrate Apollinaire's return to the Parisian art world. Apollinaire's surrealistic theatre-play, the *Mamelles de Tirésias*, aroused a great deal of interest when it was performed at the Théâtre Renée-Maubel in Montmartre on 24 June 1917; in the programme notes Apollinaire coined the word 'surréalisme', defining it as the point of departure for the manifestation of a new, joyous spirit that would modify both art and life. In 1918 the *Mercure de France* published more ideograms under the title of *Calligrammes*, including, in April 1918, one of Apollinaire's most beautiful poems, the *Jolie Russe*; it had been inspired over a period of two years by Jacqueline Kolb, whom Apollinaire married on 2 May 1918. The collection of ideograms *Calligrammes* was also published in Paris in that year (see fig.). He was working on many new projects when he died unexpectedly in the Spanish influenza epidemic that was raging through Europe.

Apollinaire was the great 'impresario of the French avant-garde'. He allowed everything new to sweep him along unconditionally and found inspiration everywhere — in literature, in art and even in the newly created genre of film. (Because of its fantastic adventures, *Fantômas* (1913–14) was Apollinaire's favourite film series.) He advocated Fauvism, Cubism, Orphism, Simultanism and finally even Surrealism (audaciously in advance of his time) with the same degree of enthusiasm and inspiration. He was outstanding not so much for his deep pictorial understanding as for his unique flair for everything anarchistically new, that 'esprit nouveau' that he propagated to the last in his lecture of 26 November 1917, published after his death in the *Mercure de France* on 1 Dec 1918.

Douces figures poignardées Chères lèvres fleuries
MIA MAREYE
YETTE LORIE
ANNIE et toi MARIE
où êtes-
vous ô
jeunes filles
MAIS
près d'un
jet d'eau qui
pleure et qui prie
cette colombe s'extasie

Tous les souvenirs de naguère
O mes amis partis en guerre
Jaillissent vers le firmament
Et vos regards en l'eau dormant
Meurent mélancoliquement
Où sont-ils Braque et Max Jacob
Derain aux yeux gris comme l'aube
Où sont Raynal Billy Dalize
Dont les noms se mélancolisent
Comme des pas dans une église
Où est Cremnitz qui s'engagea
Peut-être sont-ils morts déjà
De souvenirs mon âme est pleine
Le jet d'eau pleure sur ma peine

CEUX QUI SONT PARTIS A LA GUERRE AU NORD SE BATTENT MAINTENANT
Le soir tombe O sanglante mer
Jardins où saigne abondamment le laurier rose fleur guerrière

Guillaume Apollinaire: *La Colombe poignardée et le jet d'eau*; ideogram, from his *Calligrammes* (Paris, 1918)

WRITINGS

Oeuvres poétiques, ed. M. Adéma and M. Décaudin (Paris, 1956)
Chroniques d'Art (1902–18), ed. L.-C. Breunig (Paris, 1960; Eng. trans. as *Apollinaire on Art: Essays and Reviews, 1902–18* (London, 1972))
Oeuvres complètes, ed. A. Balland and J. Lecat, 4 vols (Paris, 1965–6)
Apollinaire zur Kunst, ed. H. Düchting (Cologne, 1989)

BIBLIOGRAPHY

A. Billy: *Apollinaire vivant* (Paris, 1923/*R* 1949)
A. Breton: *Les Pas perdus* (Paris, 1924)
E. Aegerter and P. Labracherie: *Au temps de G. Apollinaire* (Paris, 1943)
G. Lemaitre: *From Cubism to Surrealism in French Literature* (Cambridge, 1947/*R* 1978)
M. Adéma: *Guillaume Apollinaire, le mal-aimé* (Paris, 1952)
P. Pia: *Apollinaire* (Paris, 1954)
A. Rouveyre: *Amour et poésie d'Apollinaire* (Paris, 1958)
J. Golding: *Cubism: A History and Analysis 1907–1914* (London 1959, 2/1968)
R. Shattuck: *The Banquet Years: The Origins of the Avant Garde in France, 1885 to World War I: Alfred Jarry, Henri Rousseau, Erik Satie, Guillaume Apollinaire* (New York, 1959/*R* 1968)
C. Mackworth: *Guillaume Apollinaire and the Cubist Life* (London, 1962)
F. Steegmuller: *Apollinaire: Poet among the Painters* (New York, 1963)
M. Davies: *Apollinaire* (London, 1964)
H. B. Chipp, ed.: *Theories of Modern Art* (Berkeley, 1968)
L. C. Breunig: *Guillaume Apollinaire* (London, 1969)
H. Buckley: *Apollinaire as an Art Critic* (Ann Arbor, 1981)
K. Samaltanos: *Apollinaire: Catalyst for Primitivism, Picabia and Duchamp* (Ann Arbor, 1984)

HAJO DÜCHTING

Apollinopolis. *See* EDFU.

Apollo Belvedere. This statue of the Greek sun-god Apollo (h. 2.24 m) in the Octagonal Courtyard of the Belvedere of the Museo Pio-Clementino, the Vatican, may be a marble copy made in the time of the Roman emperor Hadrian (*reg* AD 117–38) of a bronze original by the Greek sculptor Leochares. It represents the god stepping forwards lightly on his right foot and looking to his left, his left arm outstretched and supporting his cloak. When it was found the figure probably lacked most of the left forearm and part of the right hand. These and other parts were restored by Giovanni Angelo Montorsoli between 1532 and 1533, although the restored portions have now been removed. It is likely that in his left hand Apollo was holding the arrows that were the usual attributes of the sun-god. There is also a tradition identifying the statue with the Apollo Venator, the god of the hunt; perhaps for this reason he is often shown beside the huntress Diana. The date and place of the statue's discovery are uncertain, although Pirro Ligorio advanced the theory that the *Apollo* was discovered at Anzio, near Rome. It almost certainly belonged to Cardinal Giuliano della Rovere (later Pope Julius II, *reg* 1503–13) and was at the Vatican by 1509 and in the Cortile del Belvedere in 1511. It appears in the garden of the church of S Pietro in Vincoli in a drawing made before 1509. It remained at the Vatican until 1798, when, under the terms of the Treaty of Tolentino, it was transferred to Paris, where it was displayed from November 1800 in the Musée Central des Arts. After the fall of Napoleon, thanks to the diplomatic efforts of the sculptor Antonio Canova, the *Apollo* was returned to the Vatican, and in February 1816 it was replaced in the Octagonal

Courtyard of the Belvedere. From the moment of its discovery the *Apollo* has been one of the most celebrated ancient Greek statues; as early as 1523 it was described as 'famous throughout the world'. Its beauty and elegance have been celebrated by poets, artists and writers. The presumed Greek origin of the work was the subject of a lively dispute among 18th-century antiquarians.

BIBLIOGRAPHY

W. Helbig: *Führer durch die öffentlichen Sammlungen klassischer Altertümer in Rom*, i (Tübingen, 1963), pp. 170–72
F. Haskell and N. Penny: *Taste and the Antique: The Lure of Classical Sculpture, 1500–1900* (New Haven and London, 1981), pp. 148–51
F. Pinter: 'Der Apollo von Belvedere', *Jb. Ksr. Dt. Archäol. Inst.*, vii (1982), pp. 164–77

LUCA LEONCINI

Apollodoros (*fl* last quarter of the 5th century BC). Greek painter. Nicknamed the 'Shadow Painter', he is famous for his experiments with chiaroscuro, although none of his works survives. Pliny (*Natural History* XXXV.xxxvi.60) placed Apollodoros in the 93rd Olympiad (408–405 BC) and credited him with being the first painter to give his figures the appearance of reality and to bring true glory to the brush. Plutarch (*De gloria Atheniensium* II) was more specific and attributed to him the discovery of mixing colours, as well as the indication of light and shade in his work. Pliny saw Apollodoros as the precursor of ZEUXIS, while Quintilian (*Principles of Oratory* XII.x.4) stated that the younger painter invented chiaroscuro. Among Apollodoros' paintings were a *Priest at Prayer* and, still surviving at Pergamon in Pliny's day, an *Ajax Struck by Lightning*. A scholiast of the comic playwright Aristophanes (*Wasps*, 385) attributed to Apollodoros a picture of the *Daughters of Herakles and Alkmene Coming as Suppliants to the Athenians*, although Aristophanes himself attributed the picture to Pamphilos. Apollodoros was said to have been the first artist to give Odysseus his distinctive peaked hat, the *pilos*. The painter's pride in his work is reflected in the epigram recorded by Plutarch (*De gloria Atheniensium* II): 'It is easier for one to find fault than to imitate'.

BIBLIOGRAPHY

J. Overbeck: *Die antiken Schriftquellen zur Geschichte der bildenden Künste bei den Griechen* (Leipzig, 1868/*R* Hildesheim, 1959), nos 1109(5), 1641–6, 1647(7)

C. HOBEY-HAMSHER

Apollodoros of Damascus (*b* Damascus; *d* Rome, *c.* AD 125). Roman architect. His first known work, and possibly his training, was in military engineering. He constructed the 1135-m-long bridge across the Danube (nr Turnu Severin, Romania) in AD 103–5, between Trajan's two Dacian campaigns. It had a timber superstructure and arches on huge masonry piers and is represented on Trajan's Column in Rome. Apollodorus' treatise on the bridge remains untraced. His other major achievements were in Rome. Dio (LXIX.iv.1) recorded that he built the Baths and Forum of Trajan and an odeum. Substantial remains of the first two survive. The forum, built in AD 107–13 and famous in antiquity for its magnificence, was a boldly conceived project that involved the removal of part of the Quirinal Hill (*see* ROME, §V, 2). Apollodoros was probably also architect of the adjacent Markets of Trajan, since its masterly adaptation to its site seems integral with the forum's design (*c.* AD 100–12; *see* ROME, ANCIENT, §II, 1(i)(e) and fig. 30). The broken pediments of the stuccoed brick façade of the markets' hemicycle of shops, an eastern Mediterranean feature, may thus be one of the rare references to his Syrian origins among buildings that are otherwise thoroughly metropolitan. According to Dio (LXIX.iv), Hadrian ordered the death of Apollodoros following an argument about the proposed design of the Temple of Venus in Rome (*see* ROME, ANCIENT, §II, 2(i)(e)).

BIBLIOGRAPHY

Dio: *Roman History*
Procopius: *On Justinian's Buildings* IV.vi.11–13
W. L. MacDonald: *The Architecture of the Roman Empire*, i (New Haven and London, 1965), pp. 129–37

T. F. C. BLAGG

Apollona. *See under* NAXOS, §2(ii).

Apollonia [now Pojan]. Site in Albania, *c.* 20 km north-east of Kerce. The city was founded about 600 BC as a colony of Corinthians and Corcyreans on low hills bordering the coastal plain of the Aoos River (now Vojussa). In the 3rd and 2nd centuries BC Apollonia supported the Romans in their Macedonian wars, and in the civil war the city was one of Julius Caesar's bases against Pompey (48 BC). Augustus (*reg* 27 BC–AD 14), who had studied there, rewarded the city by granting it autonomy, and Greek remained its official language during the Roman Empire. Its prosperity declined after the 2nd century AD, and it was abandoned during the 6th century AD. The first city defences of fine ashlar masonry (mid-5th century BC) were extended in the following century with external towers and a brick superstructure. The acropolis is flanked by a terrace wall with a corbelled gate with a pointed arch, west of which is a 4th-century BC stoa with a niched wall. South of the gate is a complex of 2nd-century AD buildings including an odeion, a triumphal arch, what was probably a library, and the bouleuterion. The last has a façade of six Corinthian columns surmounted by a pediment, reconstructed in the 1970s, and contained seats arranged in an extended semicircle, its plan resembling that of the bouleuterion at Miletos. These buildings were uncovered by the French Archaeological Mission in 1922–33. Subsequently, Albanian archaeologists have uncovered Roman houses and a gymnasium to the south, and a fine nymphaeum (4th century BC) terraced into the hillside below the acropolis. South of the bouleuterion is the monastery church of St Mary (13th century); its outer narthex, rebuilt by 1350, has Romanesque-style sculptural details. The refectory has notable frescoes (1261–1328), including the *Marriage at Cana*. The monastery buildings, restored in 1985, now house the archaeological museum, where there is a good collection of material from the necropolis, but some of the best sculpture is in the National Museum of Archaeology, Tiranë.

BIBLIOGRAPHY

L. Rey: 'Fouilles de la mission française à Apollonie d'Illyrie', *Albania*, i (1925), pp. 9–32; ii (1927), pp. 11–23; iii (1928), pp. 13–37; iv (1932), pp. 7–27; v (1935), pp. 7–13, 47–8, 51–7; vi (1939) [whole issue]
H. Buschhausen and H. Buschhausen: *Die Marienkirche von Apollonia in Albanien* (Vienna, 1976)

T. F. C. BLAGG

Apollonio di Giovanni (di Tomaso) [Dido Master; Master of the Jarves Cassoni; Virgil Master; Compagno di Pesellino] (*b* Florence, *c.* 1416; *d* Florence, 1465). Italian painter and illuminator. He was trained by illuminators in the circle of Bartolomeo di Fruosino and Battista di Biagio Sanguini (1393–1451) and became a member of the Arte dei Medici e degli Speziali in 1442 and of the Compania di S Luca in 1443. Apollonio was influenced by Filippo Lippi, Lorenzo Ghiberti and Paolo Uccello. For much of his working life, from *c.* 1446 to 1458 and perhaps later, he was in partnership with Marco del Buono di Marco (?1403–after 1480). Apollonio specialized in work for the secular sphere, painting cassoni (chests; *see* CASSONE), *deschi da parto* (birth trays), *spalliere* (panels attached to furniture or set into wall panelling; *see* SPALLIERA), images for private devotion and other furnishings, as well as illuminating manuscripts. His clients were Florentine merchants, bankers, notaries and others.

In 1902 Heinrich Brockhaus found a 17th-century copy of Apollonio di Giovanni's and Marco del Buono's workshop book, a fragmentary record of commissions, which Schubring published in 1915. Stechow (1944) identified one of its entries as *Xerxes' Invasion of Greece* (Oberlin Coll., OH, Allen Mem. A. Mus.) on the basis of coats of arms painted on the panel, thus enabling him to link the bulk of those works previously grouped under various names (Virgil Master, Master of the Jarves Cassoni, Dido Master and Compagno di Pesellino) to the workshop of Marco del Buono and Apollonio di Giovanni. Gombrich (1955) was able to ascribe the two cassone panels with scenes from Virgil's *Aeneid* (New Haven, CT, Yale U. A.G.)—those formerly in the Jarves collection to which two of the above names allude—to Apollonio on the basis of a poem by the contemporary humanist Ugolino Verino (1438–1516). This describes in detail a lost painting of the *Aeneid* by Apollonio. As a consequence, all the panels associated with the workshop are in fact in Apollonio's style, leaving Marco del Buono's hand unknown, although his life is well documented.

Apollonio di Giovanni: *Scenes from the Odyssey* (detail), tempera on panel, 420×1317 mm, *c.* 1440 (Chicago, IL, Art Institute of Chicago)

The framework for Apollonio's stylistic development is provided by two dated works; the autograph manuscript of 1442 in which he painted three initials for Dante's *Divine Comedy* and six illustrations to Petrarch's *Trionfi* (Florence, Bib. Medicea-Laurenziana, MS. Med. Pal. 72) and a shop piece, the cassone with the *Conquest of Trebizond* (New York, Met.; *see* CASSONE, fig. 2) painted under his direction between late 1461 and the summer of 1465. Apollonio's earliest work, a *desco* with the *Allegory of Music* (ex-priv. col., see Callmann, 1974, no. 1) from the late 1430s, abounds in characteristics of the Late Gothic style. Yet here and in the *Trionfi* of 1442 he already employed the facial types he was to keep throughout his life—sweet, youthful visages with only an occasional beard to indicate age. Under the influence of the early Renaissance masters, however, he soon adopted classical proportions and anatomical detail. Moreover, he created a figural style and compositions notable for their histrionic expressiveness and narrative force, as in the Virgil Codex (Florence, Bib. Riccardiana, MS. 492). In his works of the 1440s he espoused the light palette of Fra Filippo Lippi's and Domenico Veneziano's work of those years, as, for example, in cassoni illustrating scenes from the Homeric epic, the *Odyssey* (pair, Chicago, IL, A. Inst.; see fig.; panel, Pittsburgh, PA, Frick A. Mus.; fragments of a single panel, Cambridge, MA, Fogg). By the 1450s, like other Florentine painters, he had turned to deeper, more sombre tones, as in the *Aeneid* cassoni at New Haven. In his last years he discarded the flat, frieze-like composition characteristic of contemporary cassoni in favour of a more flowing movement and a deeper and more integrated space, as can be seen in the Oberlin panel and its pendant, the *Triumph of the Victorious Greeks* (ex-Wittmann priv. col., Bath, destr.), the *Triumph of Scipio Africanus* (Cambridge, Fitzwilliam) and the *Conquest of Trebizond.*

The organization and working methods of this large workshop may be reconstructed through an analysis of its oeuvre and is informative about 15th-century artistic practices. Though Apollonio painted little himself, he had firm control over the shop's output. He seems to have devised the basic composition for each subject himself and probably executed the first example of it; thus, the early, autograph *Tournament in the Piazza Santa Croce* (New Haven, CT, Yale U. A.G.) has his lively inventiveness, while the later cassone of the same subject (London, N.G., 4906) is a stiff shop piece. Once a basic composition was established, variants could be left to assistants because they were guided by a set of model drawings consisting of a large assortment of figures, horses, hats etc, of which no example has survived. At other times Apollonio did the underdrawing and others laid in the colours; thus, the painted portraits in MS.Strozz.174 (Florence, Bib. Medicea-Laurenziana) are mediocre, but where paint has flaked off the underdrawings are outstanding. The ability of assistants and apprentices varied greatly and their assignments accordingly; hence the less prominent backs, insides of lids and end panels of cassoni are usually of comparatively low quality.

Apollonio introduced a host of new subjects to Renaissance painting. He may have been the first to illustrate Petrarch's *Trionfi* and to depict recent events of personal significance to the patron. He was the first Renaissance painter to illustrate scenes from ancient Greek and Roman mythology and history, and he created an extensive new repertory of previously unknown compositions.

Most of the works Apollonio executed himself illustrate the *Aeneid* or the *Odyssey*, presumably reflecting his personal taste. Scenes of Roman battles and triumphs, as well as biblical stories, tales from Boccaccio, devotional images etc were left to assistants. More than 60 cassoni panels, some half dozen *deschi* and an equal number of devotional images and manuscripts survive from this prolific shop, and there is documentary evidence of other types of work for the interior—painted ceilings, mouldings, *spalliere* set above chests etc—and even frescoes. Apollonio played a formative role in the creation of the sumptuous domestic interiors that evolved during the second half of the 15th century.

BIBLIOGRAPHY

P. Schubring: *Cassoni, Truhen und Truhenbilder der italienischen Frührenaissance* (Leipzig, 1915, Suppl., 1923)

W. Stechow: 'Marco del Buono and Apollonio di Giovanni, Cassoni Painters', *Bull. Allen Mem. A. Mus.*, i (1944), pp. 5–21

E. H. Gombrich: 'Apollonio di Giovanni: A Florentine Cassone Workshop Seen through the Eyes of a Humanist Poet', *J. Warb. & Court. Inst.*, xviii (1955), pp. 16–34, also in E. H. Gombrich: *Norm and Form* (London, 1966), pp. 11–28

E. Callmann: *Apollonio di Giovanni* (Oxford, 1974)

——: 'An Apollonio di Giovanni for an Historic Marriage', *Burl. Mag.*, cxix (1977), pp. 174–81

F. W. Kent and D. Kent: 'Messer Manno Temperani and his Country Cousins', *Rinascimento*, xxiii (1983), pp. 246–7

A. Garzelli: 'Micropittura su temi virgiliani prima e dopo Apollonio di Giovanni, Apollonio, Giovanni Varnucci, Mariano del Buono e altri', *Scritti di storia dell'arte in onore di Federico Zeri* (Milan, 1984), pp. 147–62

——: *Miniatura fiorentina del rinascimento, 1440–1525*, Inventari e cataloghi toscani, i (Florence, 1985), pp. 41–8

E. Callmann: 'Apollonio di Giovanni and Painting for the Early Renaissance Room', *Ant. Viva*, xxvii/3–4 (1988), pp. 5–18

ELLEN CALLMANN

Apollonios and Tauriskos (*b* ?Tralles, Asia Minor; *fl* ?2nd century BC). Greek sculptors. They were active in the Hellenistic period. Pliny (*Natural History* XXXVI.iv.34) mentioned a large sculpted group by Apollonios and Tauriskos portraying the *Punishment of Dirke*, which was brought to Rome from Rhodes in the time of Augustus (*reg* 27 BC–AD 14). A Roman copy of the work, the so-called FARNESE BULL, was excavated in the Baths of Caracalla in Rome in 1545 (Naples, Mus. Archeol. N.); it is probably contemporary with the baths, which were built in the mid-3rd century AD. Small copies on gems prove that this marble copy is more elaborate than the original group. Thus it is impossible to date Apollonios' and Tauriskos' activity. Pliny provided the names of both their natural father, Artemidoros, and their adopted father, Menekrates. Attempts to identify Menekrates with the Menekrates of Rhodes who worked on the 'Great Altar' at Pergamon are unsuccessful: the Pergamene inscription is so fragmentary that the name of Menekrates cannot be restored with certainty.

BIBLIOGRAPHY

F. Studniczka: 'Die farnesische Stier und die Dirkegruppe des Apollonios und Tauriskos', *Z. Bild. Kst*, n. s. 14 (1903), pp. 171–82

G. Lippold: *Kopien und Umbildungen griechischer Statuen* (Munich, 1923), pp. 48–9

VIRGINIA C. GOODLETT

Apophyge [Fr *congé*: 'scape']. Concave sweep of a Corinthian or Doric column shaft at its junction with the upper or lower ANNULET. The term also refers to the curved profile of the annulets that join the Doric column shaft to the ECHINUS of the capital.

□

Apostool, Cornelis (*b* Amsterdam, 6 Aug 1762; *d* Amsterdam, 10 Feb 1844). Dutch museum director and painter. He was a student at the Tekeningen Akademie in Amsterdam from 1784 to 1786. His teacher was the landscape painter Hendrik Meijer (1738–93), with whom he travelled to England in 1786. Between 1790 and 1795 Apostool produced some 80 aquatints after other masters. From 1796 he occupied a number of posts that once again took him to England, and to New York in 1806. The pen drawing made there, *Flatland on Long Island* (1806; Amsterdam, Hist. Mus.), is a valuable document within his sparse oeuvre.

Apostool's career in artistic politics began in 1807. He was appointed secretary to the Legation to Naples, from where he travelled to Paris to report on the Dutch Prix de Rome artists working there. In Italy he made one of his few oil paintings, still entirely in the heroic 18th-century mode: the *Anio Valley with the Waterfalls of Tivoli* (Amsterdam, Rijksmus.). In 1808 he became the first Director of the Koninklijk Museum in Amsterdam (from 1815 the Rijksmuseum), where he remained until his death, compiling the first printed catalogue of the collection in 1809. In 1816 he was given the responsibility of recovering the works of art taken to Paris from the governor's collection by the French occupiers in 1795 and 1812. Following the success of his mission he was appointed in 1816 Curator of the Prentenkabinet (Print room), which was moved to Amsterdam from The Hague in that year. In 1822 Apostool recommended that William I buy Vermeer's *View of Delft* (The Hague, Mauritshuis), but it was assigned to the Mauritshuis rather than the Rijksmuseum. Frustrated by lack of funds and royal support, Apostool became increasingly apathetic during his last years as Director of the Rijksmuseum, which were a barren period for acquisitions. Apostool was also a member of various academies, in particular the Koninklijk Instituut voor Wetenschappen, Letterkunde en Schoone Kunsten, which was influential in artistic politics.

UNPUBLISHED SOURCES

Amsterdam, Ubib. [MS. biog.]

WRITINGS

Catalogus der schilderijen, oudheden enz op het Koninklijk Museum te Amsterdam [Catalogue of paintings, antiquities etc in the Koninklijk Museum of Amsterdam] (Amsterdam, 1809, rev. 19/1853)

BIBLIOGRAPHY

Scheen

G. J. Hoogewerff: 'Nederlandsche Kunstenaars te Rome in de XIXde eeuw', *Meded. Ned. Hist. Inst. Rome*, n.s. 2, iii (1933), pp. 147–96

P. J. J. van Thiel and others: *All the Paintings of the Rijksmuseum in Amsterdam: A Completely Illustrated Catalogue* (Amsterdam, 1976), pp. 15–21

M. Jonker: 'Cornelis Apostool (1762–1844): Cultureel ambtenaar', *Bull. Rijksmus.*, xxv/3 (1977), pp. 97–112

Reizen naar Rome: Italië als leerschool voor Nederlandse kunstenaars omstreeks 1800 [Journeys to Rome: Italy as a school for Dutch artists around 1800] (exh. cat., Haarlem, Teylers Mus.; Rome, Ist. Olandese; 1984) [with It. trans.]

FRANSJE KUYVENHOVEN

Karel Appel: *From the Beginning*, oil on canvas, 2.30×3.00 m, 1961 (Amsterdam, Stedelijk Museum)

Appel, (Christiaan) Karel (*b* Amsterdam, 25 April 1921). Dutch painter, sculptor, designer, printmaker and writer. He was first encouraged to paint by an uncle, who gave him a set of paints for his 15th birthday, and he also took painting lessons. From 1940 to 1943 he studied at the Rijksakademie of Amsterdam, where he became friendly with Corneille. His earliest works recalled the painting of George Hendrik Breitner; during World War II, however, he began to paint with a more vigorous palette, with a clear interest in German Expressionism and above all in the work of van Gogh. There was a turning-point in Appel's style *c.* 1945 when he found inspiration in the art of the Ecole de Paris and in particular of Matisse and Picasso. This influence remained visible in his work until 1948, for example in a series of plaster sculptures that he made at this time. From 1947, his completely personal, brightly coloured universe of simple, childlike beings and friendly animals populated gouaches, oil pastel drawings, painted wood sculptures and, gradually, oil paintings. His sense of humour comes to the fore in grotesque assembled pieces and wooden reliefs and paintings such as *Hip, Hip, Hooray* (1949; London, Tate).

In July 1948 Appel, Constant and Corneille were among the founders of the Experimentele Groep in Holland; in Paris in November of the same year Appel was also one of the founders of the international Cobra movement. The contacts resulting from this movement, especially with the Danish members, encouraged Appel to continue in the primitivistic vein in which he had already embarked. His most important source of inspiration during this period was children's art. His work aroused both indignation and revulsion in the Netherlands. A mural, *Children Asking Questions* (for illustration see W. Stokvis: *Cobra: An International Movement in Art after the Second World War*; New York, 1988; fig. 72), which he painted in the cafeteria of the former city hall in Amsterdam in early 1949, was hidden behind a layer of wallpaper for ten years because the public found it intolerable.

At the end of 1950 Appel moved to Paris. In 1952, with better painting materials at his disposal (thanks to the support of the writer and art promoter Michel Tapié), his work became more fluent. Somewhat rigid, thinly applied areas of colour linked by a few thick lines had dominated his compositions since 1950, making them strongly reminiscent of the work of Miró, but from 1952 to 1960 he increasingly adopted a passionate style in which colour and line fused into an agitated mass of paint so as to take precedence over the motifs. Animals and human beings were still recognizable in these paintings, although they assumed an unchained, demonic character. The turbulence of the paint and the riot of colour gradually controlled enormous areas of canvas, for example in *From the*

Beginning (1961; Amsterdam, Stedel. Mus.; see fig.). From 1956 Appel painted portraits such as *César* (1956; Belfast, Ulster Mus.), some of them large scale, and a series of female nudes, both in the same manner. When he travelled to New York for the first time in 1957, he painted jazz musicians such as Miles Davis and Count Basie; for Appel, as for many of the former members of Cobra, jazz had always been an important source of inspiration. He divided his time from then on between New York and Paris, and from 1964 he lived also at the castle that he had acquired in Molesmes, in central France.

From the mid-1950s Appel began to acquire a considerable international reputation. Martha Jackson exhibited his work regularly from 1954; Appel also had one-man shows in Paris at Studio Facchetti, and at Galerie Rive Droite from 1956. Willem Sandberg provided him with powerful support from the Netherlands, and, through Sandberg's intervention, Appel took part in a series of international group shows, also having retrospectives of his work in prominent museums in various countries. In 1960 he received the international Guggenheim award for his painting *Woman and Ostrich* (1957; Amsterdam, Stedel. Mus.). The following year the Dutch journalist Jan Vrijman made a film about Appel, *De werkelijkheid van Karel Appel* (The reality of Karel Appel), in which the left-handed artist was filmed attacking enormous canvases as if possessed; the film was accompanied by music composed by Appel and the jazz trumpeter Dizzy Gillespie.

In France in summer 1961, Appel produced a series of sculptures from olive trunks, which he painted in brilliant colours. In 1963 he was briefly influenced by Pop art and incorporated all sorts of objects, including plastic toys, in his paintings, for example *Motherhood* (1963; priv. col., see 1970 exh. cat., p. 43). Around 1966 he began to make an increasing number of wooden reliefs, which soon became free-standing objects, such as *Three Figure Triptych* (1967–8; Amsterdam, Stedel. Mus.). These works, with their cut-out and therefore strongly outlined forms, which he then superimposed and painted, and the childlike motifs, which he chose for the objects that he produced, recall Appel's artistic vocabulary during the period of Cobra's existence. He extended this style *c.* 1968 to polyester and in the early 1970s to aluminium. From the mid-1950s he also produced reliefs and free-standing pieces in ceramic. While he preferred acrylic paints for his canvases in these years, he began again to use oil paints in 1976, at which point he attempted a conscious renewal of his style. To this end he spent some time in painting compositions in thick parallel strokes; his subjects included masklike faces, cats and still-lifes.

Around 1980 Appel rediscovered the turbulent expressionistic language with which he had reached a high point in the second half of the 1950s. Working in turn in his studio in New York and from 1979 in his house in Monaco, he began to paint, in a muted palette, first a series of *Windows*, followed by *Crimes* (e.g. *Crime I*, 1980; priv. col., see 1987 Bristol exh. cat., p. 23) and a varied assortment of dramatic subjects, with human figures as the central theme. Some of these works recalled contemporary German Expressionism, the so-called 'Neue Wilde', and revealed, in the case of certain landscapes, his love for the art of van Gogh. He also produced sculpture in the form of windmills in earthenware combined with other materials. In 1986–7 Appel made sculptures of *Standing Nudes* from large Polaroid photographs and wood (e.g. *Standing Nudes* nos 2–4; artist's col., see 1987 New York exh. cat., pp. 12–13).

Appel was famed for his flamboyant self-promotion and was tireless in his exploration of new media; after World War II he even wrote poetry. He received many large-scale commissions, including mural paintings, sculptures, stained-glass windows, carpets and tile pictures, which were produced either by Appel or by assistants. He also wrote the plot and designed the scenery for the ballet *Can We Dance a Landscape?*, performed at the Opéra, Paris, in 1987.

PUBLISHED WRITINGS

Karel Appel over Karel Appel, intro. A. Rikmans (Amsterdam, 1971)
Océan blessé (poèmes et dessins) (Paris, 1982; Amsterdam, 1986)

BIBLIOGRAPHY

C. Dotremont: *Appel*, Bibliothèque de Cobra (Copenhagen, 1950) [Dan. and Fr.]
H. Claus: *Karel Appel: Painter* (New York, 1962)
Sculture di Karel Appel, intro. W. Sandberg (Turin, 1962)
Karel Appel (exh. cat., Amsterdam, Stedel. Mus., 1965)
Karel Appel: Reliefs, 1966–1968 (exh. cat., Paris, Cent. N. A. Contemp., 1968)
Appels Oogappels (exh. cat., Utrecht, Cent. Mus., 1970)
Appel's Appel's (exh. cat., intro. L. Rombout; Toronto, Rothmann's of Pall Mall; Stratford, Rothmann's A.G.; 1972)
N. Koster and E. Wingen: *Het gezicht van Appel* (Venlo, 1977)
Appel: Works on Paper, foreword M. McLuhan; essay J.-C. Lambert (New York, 1980)
A. Frankenstein: *Karel Appel* (New York, 1980)
E. Reinhartz-Tergau: 'Het monumentale werk van Karel Appel', *Karel Appel* (exh. cat., The Hague, Gal. Nova Spectra, 1981)
Ecrits sur Karel Appel (Paris, 1982)
The New Work of Karel Appel: Paintings, 1979–1981 (exh. cat., intro. W. A. L. Beeren; Rotterdam, Boymans-van Beuningen, 1982)
F. de Vree: *Karel Appel* (Schelderode, 1983)
P. Restany and A. Ginsberg: *Karel Appel: Street Art, Ceramics, Sculpture, Wood Reliefs, Tapestries, Murals, Villa el Salvador* (New York, 1985)
F. Towarnichi and A. Verdet: *Propos en liberté de Karel Appel, 1974–1984* (Paris, 1985)
A. Verdet: *Fenêtres de Karel Appel* (Paris, 1985)
Karel Appel (exh. cat., intro. S. Hunter; New York, del Re Gal., 1986)
Karel Appel: Paintings, 1980–1985 (exh. cat., ed. R. Martin; Bristol, Arnolfini Gal.; Dublin, Trinity Coll., Hyde Gal.; 1987)
Karel Appel: Recent Paintings and Sculpture (exh. cat., essay D. Kuspit; New York, del Re Gal., 1987)
Karel Appel: Rétrospective (exh. cat., Nice, Poinchettes-Art Contemporain, 1987)
Appel (exh. cat., Osaka, N. Mus. A.; Tokyo, Seibu Mus. A.; Tochigi, Prefect. Mus. F. A.; Hiroshima, City Mus. Contemp. A.; 1989)

WILLEMIJN STOKVIS

Appelmans [Appelman], **Peter** (*b* Antwerp, before 1373; *d* Antwerp, 15 May 1434). South Netherlandish architect. He was the son of Jan Appelmans (*d* Antwerp, between 1 April and 28 Sept 1395), who worked on the St Joriskerk, Antwerp. Peter was one of the most important representatives of Brabantine Gothic. His known career was confined to Antwerp Cathedral (*see* ANTWERP, §IV, 1): in 1406 he was among its leading masons, and he became Master of the Works before 1419, a post he held until his death. The west façade (1419), which, with its two towers (only the north of which was completed) and portals, follows the French model, must be attributed to him. Its design may be compared with the virtually contemporary west façade of Brussels Cathedral. He designed the nave, the foundations of which were begun in 1431, and also made some additions to the cathedral choir; the present St Jozefskapel on the north side and the sacristy, robing room and library on the south side of the choir entrance were begun in 1433.

BIBLIOGRAPHY

S. Leurs and L. J. M. Philippen: *De kathedrale kerk van O.-L.-Vrouw te Antwerpen*, Ars Belgica, ix (Antwerp, 1938)

R. Lemaire: 'De O.-L.-Vrouwekerk van Antwerpen in het kader van de Brabantse gothiek', *Miscellanea Historica in honorem Alberti de Meyer* (Leuven and Brussels, 1946), ii, pp. 667–96

J. Van Brabant: *Onze-Lieve-Vrouwkathedraal van Antwerpen: Grootste gotische kerk der Nederlanden* (Antwerp, 1972)

Stad Antwerpen, Bouwen door de Eeuwen heen in Vlaanderen: Inventaris van het Cultuurbezit in België, iii (1976–9), pp. 84–95

KRISTA DE JONGE

Appian, Adolphe(-Jacques-Barthélémy) (*b* Lyon, 28 Aug 1818; *d* Lyon, 29 April 1898). French painter and printmaker. He was a student of François Grobon (1815–1901) and Augustin Thierriat (1789–1870) at the Ecole des Beaux-Arts, Lyon. Appian made a speciality of charcoal studies from nature in which colours were transposed into tonal values. From 1852 he worked from nature at Crémieu, together with Corot, Charles-François Daubigny, Auguste Ravier, Louis-Hector Allemand (1809–86) and Louis Carrand. He had by this time achieved financial independence and devoted himself completely to painting.

Appian depicted an enormous range of subjects, visiting the Pyrenees, the Auvergne, the Bugey and Italy: he often favoured views of still waters and the Mediterranean such as *The Beach* (1870; Lyon, Mus. B.-A.). His scenes are frequently dotted with little figures in the style of his friend Corot. The style of this prolific and meticulous production remained rather static until 1877, when Appian abandoned his earlier sombre palette and became a virtuoso colourist, producing work with a glistening enamel-like quality. In 1885 he painted in the environs of Fontainebleau. His work as a whole is regional in outlook, with its frequent concentration on the landscape of the Lyon area, and can be found in the collections of the Musées des Beaux-Arts at Dijon and Lyon. His studio in the Villa des Fusains came to symbolize 19th-century landscape painting in the region. Appian was also a notable printmaker; from 1863 he belonged to the Société des Aquafortistes, producing etchings for Alfred Cadart and working in drypoint. He also produced work for the *Gazette des beaux-arts*, the *Revue du Lyonnais*, *Le Fusain* and *Paris Salon*. His son Jean-Louis Appian (1862–96) was also a painter and printmaker.

BIBLIOGRAPHY

A. Curtis and P. Prouté: *Adolphe Appian, son oeuvre gravé et lithographié* (Paris, 1968)

COLETTE E. BIDON

Appiani, Andrea (*b* Milan, 31 May 1754; *d* Milan, 8 Nov 1817). Italian painter and designer. He had been intended to follow his father's career in medicine but instead entered the private academy of the painter Carlo Maria Giudici (1723–1804). He received instruction in drawing, copying mainly from sculpture and prints. He studied Raphael through the engravings of Marcantonio Raimondi, as well as the work of Giulio, Anton Raphael Mengs and, again from prints, the compositions in Trajan's Column. He then joined the class of the fresco painter Antonio de' Giorgi (1720–93), which was held at the Ambrosiana picture gallery in Milan, where he was able to study Raphael's art directly from the cartoon of the *School of Athens* and the work of Leonardo's followers, particularly Bernardino Luini. He also frequented the studio of Martin Knoller, where he deepened his knowledge of painting in oils; and he studied anatomy at the Ospedale Maggiore in Milan with the sculptor Gaetano Monti (1750–1847). His interest in aesthetic issues was stimulated by the classical poet Giuseppe Parini, whom he drew in two fine pencil portraits (Milan, Brera; Milan, Mus. Poldi Pezzoli). In 1776 he entered the Accademia di Belle Arti di Brera to follow the painting courses of Giuliano Traballesi, from whom he received a mastery of the fresco technique and the encouragement to make copies after Domenichino and Correggio.

Appiani made his début with the fresco dedicated to *SS Gervasio and Protasio* executed in 1776–7 for the church at Caglio (nr Como). In 1782 he painted the altarpiece of the *Nativity* for the collegiate church of S Maria Nascente at Arona (nr Novara). Between 1783 and 1784 he worked successfully in Florence as a stage designer. Dating from 1786 is the architectural project (completed in 1798) for the high altar of Monza Cathedral, which was followed by frescoes with mythological subjects for the Palazzo Busca Arconati, Milan. In 1788 he painted the portrait of *Alessandro Litta Arese* and carried out the decorations, in collaboration with Traballesi, for the Palazzo Orsini Falcò, Milan. In 1788 he had also begun for the Congregazione degli Osti, Milan, the great *Supper at Emmaus* (destr; engraved by Jacopo Bernardi, *b c*. 1808), which was finished only in 1796.

In 1789 Appiani produced his first masterpiece, the cycle of frescoes depicting the *Story of Psyche* in the Rotonda of the Villa Reale at Monza, commissioned by the Habsburg Archduke Ferdinand and influenced by Raphael's decorations in the Villa Farnesina, Rome. From the study of antique lamps and cameos he derived the inspiration for *Venus and Cupid* (1789–90; destr.; engraved by Michele Bisi), painted for Giovanni Battista Sommariva. During this period Appiani was also active as a designer of fashionable Neo-classical furniture (*see* ITALY, §VI, 3). In 1791 he made a nine-month journey to study in Bologna, Florence, Rome and especially in Parma, where he studied the frescoes of Correggio. On his return to Milan, he was entirely occupied between 1791 and 1795 on the frescoes for the cupola and pendentives of the church of S Maria presso S Celso (see fig.), which are considered his masterpieces (many of the drawings and preparatory cartoons are kept in Milan, Brera and Castello Sforzesco). In 1795 he was a guest at the Palazzo Moriggia in Balsamo, where he executed frescoes on mythological subjects, of which the surviving portions are preserved in the Villa Ghirlanda at Cinisello (nr Milan).

In 1796, on the entry of Napoleon into Milan, Appiani made a splendid pencil portrait of him (Milan, Brera), which won him the favour of the General and numerous commissions within the Cisalpine Republic. He designed many medals and the headings for official papers and was put in charge of choosing the works of art to be requisitioned and transferred to France. In 1798 he produced the fresco for the *salone* of the Palazzo Castiglioni in Milan, adorned with putti and mythological scenes, and a painted drop-curtain for the Teatro Patriottico, Milan, which represents *Virtue Putting Vice to Flight*. In 1799–1800 he completed the cycle of frecoes with the *Myths of Apollo* at the Casa Sannazzaro, Milan, later the Casa Prina (Milan, Brera; Milan, Gal. A. Mod.), and executed a beautiful posthumous portrait of *General Desaix* (Versailles, Château).

Appiani was sent to the Assembly at Lyons in 1801 and he also travelled to Paris, where he made numerous portraits of members of the Bonaparte family. Returning to Milan the same year, he frescoed two ceilings in the palazzi Litta and Passalacqua with a depiction of *Aurora*, inspired by Guido Reni. In 1802, having been nominated Commissario Generale delle Belle Arti, Appiani drew attention to the need to restore Leonardo's *Last Supper*; from 1803 he worked with Giuseppe Bossi on the preparation of the Pinacoteca di Brera. Also in 1803 he painted the celebrated portraits of *Napoleon* and of *Francesco Melzi* (both Bellagio, Villa Melzi-d'Eril). The same year he began work on the *Fasti di Napoleone*, a series of 35 monochrome canvases for the Sala delle Cariatidi in the Palazzo Reale, Milan, which were completed in 1807 (destr.; engraved under the supervision of Appiani himself and the direction of Giuseppe Longhi).

In 1804 Appiani went to Paris for the coronation of Napoleon and met Jacques-Louis David. In 1805 he painted the portrait of *Napoleon, King of Italy* (Vienna, Ksthist. Mus.), and the same year he completed the canvas of the *Meeting of Jacob and Rachel*, which he had begun in 1795 (Alzano Maggiore, basilica of S Martino). His activity as a decorator at the Palazzo Reale in Milan was notable; he painted frescoes for a series of staterooms (destr. 1943). The only ones to survive (Tremezzo, Villa Carlotta) are those for the Sala di Trono, completed in 1808: the *Apotheosis of the Emperor Napoleon* (*see* MILAN, fig. 11) on the vault and four lunettes representing *Justice*, *Prudence*, *Fortitude* and *Temperance*. In the Sala delle Udienze Solenni he represented *Minerva Showing the Shield of History to Clio* on the vault and the *Four Continents* in the lunettes (1809), and in the Sala della Rotonda he painted *Peace and Hymen* (1810) to commemorate the wedding of Napoleon with Maria Luisa. Appiani died before completing the decorations of the Sala della Lanterna, where he had completed two frescoes with the *Continence of Scipio* and *Mucius Scaevola* and where he had planned the *Death of Lucretia*, the *Pacification between the Romans and the Sabines*, as well as *Veturia and Coriolanus* (preparatory drawings Milan, Castello Sforzesco).

Appiani, who was perhaps the chief exponent of Italian Neo-classical painting, was valued for his impeccable technique and for his superb handling, whether in drawings, oil paintings or frescoes. His distinctive style, which was based chiefly on gentle chiaroscuro passages and on a delicate gradation of tone inspired by Correggio and by the school of Leonardo, differs from the severe and statuesque manner of David and resembles more closely that of Pierre-Paul Prud'hon. His paintings, particularly his frescos, were preceded by numerous preparatory drawings carried out in pencil or charcoal. The effects of extreme softness and luminosity that characterize his drawings are also found in the paintings, which appear to

Andrea Appiani: *St Luke* (1791–5), pendentive fresco, S Maria presso S Celso, Milan

have been executed with an extraordinary facility and grace. In particular in the portraits, where he was able to overcome the formal conventions of his time, he eliminated over-attention to the surroundings, through a refined feeling for colour and atmosphere. He was able to achieve similar results in his grand decorations in fresco, where the iconographic allusions to Classical antiquity or the requirements of political allegory are resolved in compositions that are lively and refined.

BIBLIOGRAPHY

DBI

Catalogo delle pitture, dei cartoni e dei disegni più ragguardevoli del defunto cavaliere Andrea Appiani e di varie altre pitture, stampe e libri figurati esistenti presso gli eredi (Milan, 1818)

G. Longhi: *Elogio storico di Andrea Appiani* (Milan, 1818)

M. Bisi: *Incisioni delle opere di Andrea Appiani* (Milan, 1820)

G. Beretta: *Le opere di Andrea Appiani* (Milan, 1848)

M. Borghi: *I disegni di Andrea Appiani dell'Accademia di Brera* (Milan, 1948)

Andrea Appiani pittore di Napoleone (exh. cat., ed. M. Precerutti Garberi; Milan, Villa Reale, 1969)

M. Precerutti Garberi: 'Aggiunte ad Andrea Appiani', *A. Illus.*, lii (1973), pp. 15–21

G. L. Mellini: 'Apologia di Andrea Appiani', *Labyrinthos*, iii–iv (1983), pp. 208–39

Mito e storia nei 'Fasti di Napoleone' di Andrea Appiani (exh. cat., ed. F. Mazzocca and M. E. Tittoni; Rome, Mus. Napoleonico, 1986)

FERNANDO MAZZOCCA

Appiani, Giuseppe (*b* Porto, nr Milan, ?1701; *d* Triefenstein, Franconia, ?1785–6). Italian painter, active in Germany. As a youth he assimilated the decorative traditions of Lombard painting and was deeply influenced by Venetian artists, chiefly Giambattista Tiepolo. He probably left Italy as a young man, travelling to Bavaria, where he was attracted to the art of Carlo Innocenzo Carlone, and then, perhaps between 1720 and 1730, to that of Jacopo Amigoni. Appiani's earliest confirmed works are four preparatory studies (three pairs of Classical figures and the *Parnassus*, all *c.* 1743; priv. col., see Zubeck, figs 1–4) for frescoes in the castle (destr. 1793) at Saarbrücken. From 1745 he lived in Mainz, where he became the foremost court painter, and between 1748 and 1751 he executed frescoes of sacred subjects in churches in Lindau and Oberdorf. His two most notable surviving early fresco cycles are that in the refectory of the former Premonstratensian monastery of SS Peter and Paul, Obermarchtal (including the *Triumph of St Norbert*; 1750–51), and the mythological scenes (e.g. *Neptune*, *Flora* and *Venus*; 1751–2) at the castle of Seehof (nr Bamberg). About 1757–8 he started an academy of painting in Mainz. Although much of his fresco work is now severely damaged or destroyed, his mature and robust Rococo manner is particularly well represented in three existing fresco cycles at the Neues Schloss in Meersburg (profane and mythological subjects, including a portrait of his patron *Franz Konrad von Rodt, Bishop of Konstanz* (*reg* 1750–57); the Domkirche in Arlesheim (*Glorification*, *Annunciation* and *Assumption of the Virgin*; 1759–?61); and the sanctuary of the pilgrimage church at Vierzehnheiligen (e.g. *Fourteen Saints*, the *Nativity*, *Jacob's Dream* and *Moses and the Burning Bush*; *c.* 1764–9). Appiani is thought to have executed numerous altarpieces, but only one has been identified (Voss): the *Suffering Job* (*c.* 1764–9; Nuremberg, Ger. Nmus.), which originated from the Vierzehnheiligen programme. During his late career he worked in Höchst, Würzburg, Camberg and Heidenfeld, and in Triefenstein after 1784. He also executed engravings, the most notable being the *Four Muses among Clouds*.

BIBLIOGRAPHY

Bolaffi; *DBI*

H. Leiterman: 'Joseph Appiani: Kurfürstlicher Hofmaler und Akademiedirektor', *Mainz. Z.*, xxx (1935), pp. 1–31

E. Lavagnino: *Gli artisti italiani in Germania*, iii of *I pittori e gli incisori* (Rome, 1943), pp. 100–07, 159

H. Tintelnot: *Die barocke Freskomalerei in Deutschland* (Munich, 1951), pp. 169, 302, 304, 312

H. Voss: 'Giuseppe Appiani: Versuch einer Würdigung', *Pantheon*, xxi (1963), pp. 339–53

P. Zubeck: 'Vier neuentdeckte Zeichnungen Giuseppe Appianis', *Pantheon*, xxvii (1969), pp. 480–85

□

Appius Claudius Pulcher. *See* CLAUDIUS PULCHER, APPIUS.

Apple, Billy [Bates, Barrie] (*b* Auckland, 1 Jan 1935). New Zealand sculptor and conceptual artist. He studied at the Royal College of Art in London in the early 1960s and first showed his work alongside that of fellow students such as David Hockney and Derek Boshier, helping to mark the emergence of British Pop art. The pseudonym that he adopted in 1962 reflected his obsession with different ways of representing fruit. On moving in 1964 to New York he began to produce neon versions of popular icons. In 1970 he established Apple as one of New York's first artist-run 'alternative' art spaces.

The conceptual element in Apple's early Pop work became dominant in the late 1960s and 1970s. From 1975 to 1980 he concentrated on the deconstruction of the 'white cube' gallery exhibition space, proposing alterations to or actually changing existing interiors, notably at the Leo Castelli Gallery in New York (1977, 1978, 1980) and at a number of public galleries in New Zealand (1975, 1979–80). In 1981 he instigated a new series concerned with the provenance of the art object with a series of commissioned canvases, *From the Collection*, which apparently rejoice in their context of ownership.

BIBLIOGRAPHY

From Barrie Bates to Billy Apple, 1960–1974 (exh. cat., London, Serpentine Gal., 1974)

W. Curnow: 'Report: The Given as an Art-Political Statement', *A. NZ*, 15 (1980), pp. 26–33

WYSTAN CURNOW

Applebroog, Ida (*b* New York, 11 Nov 1929). American painter. She attended the New York State Institute of Applied Arts and Sciences (1947–50) and in 1958 moved to Chicago, where she was a student at the School of the Art Institute of Chicago (1966–8). In 1974 she moved to New York. Applebroog's paintings were best known for their collision of imagery based on specific everyday experiences, news items and endemic social ills. She first became known in the 1970s for small books, such as *Galileo Works* (1977), in which her own 'narratives', consisting of leaps and jumps between ideas and images, represent a disjunction associated with social critique and a questioning of the ideologies implicit in representation. She posted them to friends and people in the art world. They were the precursors to larger sequential works such as *Sure I'm Sure* (ink and rhoplex on vellum, 2.56×1.72 m, 1980; artist's col.), comprising six panels, much like sinister comic-strips, combining irony and intense tenderness. She is best known for her multi-partite paintings that, as part of the legacy of feminist practice in the 1970s, deal with the 'trivial details' of everyday life as if they had the scale and weight of subject-matter of traditional history painting. By giving prominence to ordinary events or to groups of people whom she saw as victimized or marginalized, she attempted to empower such groups, especially women, by revealing those elements in their experience that she saw as common to all (e.g. *Pull Down the Shade*, oil on canvas, 2.18×1.52 m, 1985). Her paintings place the viewer in an uncomfortable moral position, as they demonstrate Applebroog's moral outrage and social conscience.

BIBLIOGRAPHY

Applebroog (exh. cat. by R. Feldman and others, New York, Ronald Feldman F.A. Inc., 1987)

Art at the Edge: Ida Applebroog (exh. cat. by S. Krane, Atlanta, GA, High Mus. A.; Pittsburgh, PA, Carnegie–Mellon U. A.G.; 1989)

Ida Applebroog (exh. cat. by M. Schor, Londonderry, Orchard Gal.; Dublin, Irish MOMA; 1993)

Appleton, Thomas (Gooch) (*b* Shalford, Essex, 1854; *d* 1924). English mezzotint engraver. He worked in London from the late 1870s until 1903. His early work includes prints after Luke Fildes (e.g. *Roses*, exh. RA 1877) and Frederic Leighton. Although he continued to engrave contemporary work, he achieved prominence with his prints after 18th- and early 19th-century English portrait painters, copying works by, among others, Thomas Lawrence and George Romney. He exhibited 13 engravings at the Royal Academy between 1877 and 1893 and by 1894 had over 30 prints registered with the Print Sellers Association. The majority of his work was commissioned and published by the leading dealers Henry Graves (1806–92) and Arthur Tooth. The British Museum and the Victoria and Albert Museum, both in London, hold examples of his work.

BIBLIOGRAPHY

H. Beck: *Victorian Engravings* (London, 1973)

R. K. Engen: *Dictionary of Victorian Engravers, Print Publishers and their Works* (Cambridge and Teaneck, NJ, 1979)

Appliqué. Technique of decorating textiles with motifs cut from one material, which are attached or 'applied' to another with embroidery stitches (*see* AFRICA, fig. 155 and TEXTILES, §III, 2).

Apse. Semicircular or polygonal vaulted space, usually at the end of a basilica nave (*see* CHURCH, fig. 2).

Apsidiole. *See* ABSIDIOLE.

Apteral. Term applied to a building with no columns along the sides, though it may have a portico at the front and/or back. □

Apulia, Nicolaus de. *See* NICCOLÒ DELL'ARCA.

Aqa Buzurg [Āqā Buzurg] (*b* Shiraz; *fl* *c*. 1840–60). Persian painter. His portrait of the Qajar ruler Nasir al-Din (*reg* 1848–96) as Crown Prince (untraced) was done in 1846, as was a painting of a pheasant and partridge in the Churchill Album (London, BM, Or. MS 4938). His finest piece is a varnished ('lacquered') penbox dated 1853 (Tehran, Mus. Dec. A.) decorated with penetrating portraits of the ministers of Prince Farhad Mirza, governor of Shiraz. The butt end of the penbox contains a self-portrait of the artist, showing him painting a penbox. Portraits continued to be his main subject, as on a pair of varnished book covers (priv. col., see Robinson, 1979, fig. 235) attributed to the end of his career. His portraits are notable for their realism and are similar in spirit to the work of his contemporary, the court painter Abu'l-Hasan Ghaffari (*see* GHAFFARI, (2)).

BIBLIOGRAPHY

B. W. Robinson: *Persian Miniature Painting from Collections in the British Isles* (London, 1967)

——: 'Persian Painting in the Qajar Period', *Highlights of Persian Art*, ed. R. Ettinghausen and E. Yarshater (Boulder, 1979), pp. 331–62

M. A. Karimzada Tabrizi: *Aḥvāl u āthār-i naqqāshān-i qadīm-i īrān* [The lives and art of old painters of Iran] (London, 1985), no. 10

L. S. Diba: 'Lacquerwork', *The Arts of Persia*, ed. R. W. Ferrier (New Haven and London, 1989), pp. 243–54

B. W. Robinson: 'Qajar Lacquer', *Muqarnas*, vi (1989), pp. 131–46

——: 'Persian Painting under the Zand and Qājār Dynasties', *From Nadir Shah to the Islamic Republic*, vii of *The Cambridge History of Iran* (Cambridge, 1991), pp. 870–90

□

Aqa Mirak [Sayyid Aqā Jalāl al-Dīn Mīrak al-Ḥasanī (or al-Ḥusaynī) al-Iṣfahānī] (*fl* Tabriz, *c*. 1520–55; Mashhad, *c*. 1555–65; Qazvin, 1565–?75; *d* before 1576). Persian illustrator and painter. He was painter, purveyor and boon companion to the Safavid shah Tahmasp I and was well known in contemporary circles. The contemporary chronicler Dūst Muhammad mentioned that Aqa Mirak along with MIR MUSAVVIR did wall paintings for Prince Sam Mirza's palace in Tabriz and illustrations for royal manuscripts of Firdawsi's *Shāhnāma* ('Book of kings') and Nizami's *Khamsa* ('Five poems'). Qazi Ahmad wrote that he had no peer in artistic design and was an incomparable painter, very clever, enamoured of his art, a bon vivant, an intimate [of the Shah] and a sage. A manuscript (London, BL, Or. MS. 2265) of the *Khamsa* done between 1539 and 1543 has four illustrations bearing attributions to Aqa Mirak. Dickson and Welch have attributed other paintings to Aqa Mirak in the monumental copy (dispersed; ex-Houghton priv. col.) of the *Shāhnāma* made for Tahmasp, and have used these attributions to define four periods in the artist's life. Works ascribed to a youthful period in the 1520s have tautly composed landscapes inhabited by a few large-scale figures. A transitional period in the early 1530s was followed by mature works produced from the late 1530s to *c*. 1555, in which the compositions are more complex and the colouring more subtle. In the view of Dickson and Welch, at the end of his life the artist returned to his youthful style in two paintings (fols 169*v* and 291*r*) for Ibrahim Mirza's copy (Washington, DC, Freer, 46.12) of Jami's *Haft awrang* ('Seven thrones') produced between 1556 and 1565.

BIBLIOGRAPHY

Enc. Iran.

Dust Muḥammad: 'Preface to the Bahram Mirza Album' (1544); Eng. trans., ed. W. M. Thackston, in *A Century of Princes: Sources on Timurid History and Art* (Cambridge, MA, 1989), pp. 348–9

Qāżī Aḥmad ibn Mīr Munshī: *Gulistān-i hunar* [Rose-garden of art] (*c*. 1606); Eng. trans. by V. Minorsky as *Calligraphers and Painters* (Washington, DC, 1959), p. 185

L. Binyon: *The Poems of Nizami* (London, 1928), pls 8–10, 13

S. C. Welch: *Persian Painting: Five Royal Safavid Manuscripts of the 16th Century* (New York, 1976), pp. 22–7, pls 19–20, 22–3, 30–31

Wonders of the Age: Masterpieces of Early Safavid Painting, 1501–1576 (exh. cat. by S. C. Welch, London, BM; Washington, DC, N.G.A.; Cambridge, MA, Fogg; 1979–80), nos 4, 62

M. B. Dickson and S. C. Welch: *The Houghton Shahnameh* (Cambridge, MA, 1981), pp. 95–115 [many pls]

SHEILA R. CANBY

Aqa Riza (i) (*b* ?Mashhad; *fl* *c*. 1580–*c*. 1610). Iranian painter active in India. He joined the service of Prince Salim (later the Mughal emperor Jahangir (*reg* 1605–27)) sometime before 1588; his son was the great painter ABU'L-HASAN. Various inscriptions tell us that Aqa Riza came from Mashhad and that another of his sons was the painter ʿABID. Whereas Abu'l-Hasan developed consistently as a painter, Aqa Riza's style remained basically consistent with his Safavid origins, a style of calligraphically drawn lines and surface pattern-making, with a few gestures—such as facial modelling—towards the naturalism for which Mughal painting was aiming under the direction of Akbar (*reg* 1556–1605). Prince Salim, perhaps out of filial antagonism, tended to favour the Safavid tradition, so that it is no surprise that Aqa Riza gravitated to his service.

Little of Aqa Riza's work survives from the period before Prince Salim removed himself from his father's control in 1599 and took up residence at Allahabad. Here some of his artists joined him, including Aqa Riza and Abu'l-Hasan. The *Muraqqaʿ-i gulshan* or Gulshan Album (Tehran, Gulistan Pal. Lib.) contains three elaborate signed or attributed pages depicting a prince enjoying a feast in his court, a princess watching ladies bathe and the young Jahangir (Salim) with Shaykh Salim Chishti. While their composition is Iranian, the figures match Aqa Riza's securely dated work for Jahangir of 1604, as do the delicately modelled features of the faces. The same album also contains four pages of marginal illumination signed by Aqa Riza (one dated 1600). These are early examples of the marginal illuminations around calligraphy in Jahangir's albums, of freely drawn landscapes in gold against which are set delicately coloured figures. Many of the other unsigned pages are very probably also Aqa Riza's work. A painting of a gardener in the Binney Collection (San Diego, CA, Mus. A.) is datable to the years at Allahabad: Aqa Riza designed the garden known later as the Khusrau Bagh outside the city.

The most important of the illustrated manuscripts begun at Allahabad is the fable-book *Anvār-i Suhaylī* ('Lights of Canopus'; London, BL), to which Aqa Riza contributed five signed paintings, two of them dated AH 1013 (AD 1604–5). The small, narrow format of these miniatures caused him some problems. As he was unable or unwilling to express recession in paint, his figures, buildings and landscape are piled on top of one another, unlocated in space and unrelated to each other; his boneless figures float in front of the richly tiled pavilions or deeply coloured Safavid-type mountains. The rounded, smooth faces are still in the Safavid manner but are gently modelled as a concession to Mughal taste. In many of Aqa Riza's inscriptions he calls himself the 'disciple' or 'devoted disciple' of his master. When Jahangir's taste developed beyond this sort of style, however, Aqa Riza could make little contribution, and his work disappeared early in Jahangir's reign.

See also INDIAN SUBCONTINENT, §V, 4(i)(c).

BIBLIOGRAPHY

J. V. S. Wilkinson: *The Lights of Canopus, Anvar-i Suhaili* (London, 1929)
Y. A. Godard: 'Les Marges du Murakka Gulshan', *Āthār-é Īrān*, i (1936), pp. 11–33
A. K. Das: *Mughal Painting during Jahangir's Time* (Calcutta, 1978)
The Grand Mogul: Imperial Painting in India, 1600–1660 (exh. cat. by M. C. Beach, Williamstown, MA, Clark A. Inst., 1978)

J. P. LOSTY

Aqa Riza (ii). *See* RIZA.

Aqar Quf [Arab. ʿAqarqūf; anc. Dur Kurigalzu]. Site in Iraq of the ancient capital city of the KASSITEs, which flourished *c.* 1400–1157 BC (*see also* MESOPOTAMIA, §I, 2). The ruins of ancient Dur Kurigalzu are 15 km west of modern Baghdad, at the point where an outcrop of soft limestone marks the northern extremity of the alluvial plain. The eroded core of its ZIGGURAT (see fig.; now partly rest.) is visible from the highway leading west to Ramūdī and the desert crossing to Jordan. The mud-brick fabric of its structure is reinforced with deep layers of reed-matting and faced on all sides with kiln-baked brick.

Iraqi excavations at Aqar Quf in 1942–5 under Taha Baqir led to the discovery of a complex of temple buildings at the foot of the ziggurat itself. A Kassite dynasty ruled Babylonia from the 16th century to the 12th century BC, apparently maintaining the ancient civic and religious traditions of Mesopotamia. The architecture of this temple precinct was therefore characteristic of the period (*see* MESOPOTAMIA, §II, 5), apart from certain features such as small rectangular platforms supporting individual shrines. King Kurigalzu, whose name appears here on pivot-stones and tablets, was at first identified as the

Aqar Quf, eroded ruin of the ziggurat, Kassite dynasty, 15th–12th centuries BC

traditional founder of the city. The palaces were, however, frequently rebuilt by other kings, at least one of whom bore the same name.

A group of secular buildings, comprising at least three 'palaces', was discovered on a separate site 1 km to the north-west. The planning and appointments of these civic buildings were interesting and the finds more plentiful than in the temple. The largest, although least well-preserved, palace had a central courtyard, around which multiple doorways created a cloister in the Hittite manner. The piers between them were decorated with low friezes of mural painting representing Kassite courtiers, a feature lacking in the two subsidiary palaces, the courtyards of which were surrounded by double ranges of side chambers with light wells between. In the corner of one, a group of three chambers, lined on either side with vaulted recesses, was identified as the treasury. The central pedestals in these three chambers were surrounded by the debris of looting. Elsewhere in the palaces, at convenient points, small chambers contained stairways leading to an upper storey or to the flat roof. One such chamber seems to have been the scene of fierce fighting and looting, since broken weapons and fragments of valuable objects were found, scattered among the charred woodwork of the stairs.

Finds from Dur Kurigalzu, now in the Iraq Museum, Baghdad, provide rare examples of Kassite craftsmanship.

They include a sculptured macehead, a gold bracelet with paste inlay and many fragments of gold granulation, and glass ornaments. The painted head of a bearded man and the sensitively modelled figure of a lioness (for illustration *see* KASSITE), both of terracotta, seem to resemble the style of art in 18th-Dynasty Egypt.

BIBLIOGRAPHY

T. Baqir: 'Excavations at 'Aqar Qūf, 1942–1943', *Iraq* (1944) [supplement]
——: 'Excavations at 'Aqar Qūf', *Iraq* (1945) [supplement]; viii (1946), pp. 73–93

SETON LLOYD

Aqqoyunlu [Akkoyunlu]. Islamic dynasty that ruled in eastern Anatolia, Iran and Iraq from 1378 to 1508. The Aqqoyunlu (Turk.: 'White Sheep') were a group of Sunni Turkomans that rose to power by supporting Timur, eponym of the Timurid dynasty, against the Ottomans in western Anatolia. By allying with Timur, the first Aqqoyunlu ruler Qara Yülük (who had a Greek mother and married a Byzantine princess) was granted the region of Diyar Bakr in south-eastern Anatolia. In 1467 the Aqqoyunlu ruler Uzun Hasan (*reg* 1453–78) killed the QARAQOYUNLU leader Jahanshah in battle and moved the capital from Amid (now Diyarbakır in Turkey) to Tabriz in Iran. The Aqqoyunlu then took control of Azerbaijan and, briefly, much of Iraq and northern Iran. They became a power of international significance and opened diplomatic relations with Venice. The position of the Aqqoyunlu was not seriously threatened under Uzun Hasan's son Ya'qub (*reg* 1478–90), but conflicts among his successors allowed Isma'il I, the founder of the SAFAVID dynasty, to usurp the throne in 1501. By 1508 all the remaining Aqqoyunlu princes had been eliminated.

The Aqqoyunlu princes were noted patrons of architecture, metalwork and the arts of the book. The only surviving building is the mausoleum of Zaynal Beg, a son of Uzun Hasan killed in battle with the Ottomans in 1473, at Hisn Kayfa (now Hasankeyf) in south-eastern Anatolia. Built of brick with tile decoration in the style of contemporary Iranian work, it may reflect lost constructions in Tabriz, such as the palaces of Uzun Hasan and Ya'qub Beg, known from travellers' accounts (*see* ISLAMIC ART, §II, 6(i)(b)). Uzun Hasan's patronage is also represented by an elaborate bronze lampstand (h. 1.21 m; priv. col.; *see* Melikian-Chirvani, pls VII–VIII) of eclectic form and decoration (*see* ISLAMIC ART, §IV, 3(i)(b)). Other metal wares in the VENETO-SARACENIC style may be attributed to the Aqqoyunlu domains. The finest extant Aqqoyunlu manuscript is a copy (Istanbul, Topkapı Pal. Lib., H. 762) of Nizami's *Khamsa* ('Five poems'), which was begun for the Qaraqoyunlu prince Pir Budaq and taken over by Uzun Hasan's older son Khalil (*reg* 1478). The text was completed in 1481 under Ya'qub and supplied with 11 paintings in the colourful and vigorous style of painting that scholars have attributed to Tabriz (*see* ISLAMIC ART, §III, 4(v)(e); *see also* COLOUR, colour pl. V).

BIBLIOGRAPHY

Enc. Iran.; *Enc. Islam/2*: 'Aḳ Ḳoyunlu'
J. E. Woods: *The Aqquyunlu: Clan, Confederation, Empire* (Minneapolis, 1976)
B. W. Robinson: 'The Turkman School to 1503', *The Arts of the Book in Central Asia, 14th–16th Centuries*, ed. B. Gray (London and Paris, 1979), pp. 215–47
A. S. Melikian-Chirvani: 'The Lights of Sufi Shrines', *Islam. A.*, ii (1987), pp. 117–36
J. W. Allan: 'Metalwork of the Turcoman Dynasties of Eastern Anatolia and Iran', *Iran*, xxix (1991), pp. 153–9

□

Aquae Sulis. *See* BATH (i), §1.

Aquae Tarbellicae. *See* DAX.

Aquamanile. Type of ewer, usually of metal, used for the washing of hands in a liturgical or secular context. It is often zoomorphic in form and usually has two openings, one for filling with water and the other for pouring. In their original usage aquamanilia expressed the symbolic significance of the lavabo, the ritual washing of the hands by the priest before vesting, before the consecration of the Eucharist and after mass. The earliest production of aquamanilia is associated with Mosan art of the Meuse Valley in northern France, and with Lower Saxony in north-east Germany. The majority of surviving examples are made of a variety of bronze that resembles gold when polished, while nearly all those made of precious metals are known only from church inventories.

Church documents refer to aquamanilia as early as the 5th century, when canon regulations stipulated that on ordination the subdeacon should receive such a vessel. Various documents from the 5th century to the beginning of the 11th sometimes use the term to denote both the ewer and its basin. Sometime after the beginning of the 11th century the term became transferred to a type of vessel, usually in the shape of an animal (e.g. lion, stag, horse), bird (cock, dove) or fantastic beast (dragon, griffin, unicorn), but sometimes also shaped as a human figure, bust or head. Some aquamanilia have clear iconographic

Aquamanile in the form of Aristotle and Phyllis, bronze, h. 335 mm, Mosan, *c.* 1400 (New York, Metropolitan Museum of Art)

meaning, for example those in the shape of a dove symbolize spiritual cleansing (Psalm 26:6), those in the shape of a hart signify the celebrant's spiritual devotion (Psalm 42:1), while aquamanilia in the form of demonic creatures served as exhortative warnings to the clergy to remain obedient to their vows and to live virtuous lives.

Non-liturgical aquamanilia were increasingly widespread from the 12th century until the late 16th and were used in banquets, monastic refectories, inns and private homes, for hand ablutions after meals. Monastic refectory aquamanilia were cast in the form of creatures such as those carved on the capitals in the cloisters from which the water was drawn. There is evidence that aquamanilia were only used at the superior's table; other members of the religious community used ablution fountains. The earliest examples of secular aquamanilia were cast in the form of mounted knights, a form that may have reflected the assertion of nobility by divine right, inspired by the ideas of the Investiture Contest (1074–1122). The allegorical connection to ablutions would have served as a warning to remain honourable and just. Later, some aquamanilia evolved into sculptural table decorations, while others took on humanistic subjects such as the humiliation of Aristotle by Phyllis (New York, Met.; see fig.). In the 14th century they began to influence dinanderie ewers, which, although usually referred to as ewers rather than aquamanilia, often had figured spouts, lids, handles and feet. German bellarmines (a type of Rhenish stoneware wine decanter) imitated the secular aquamanilia, as did English pottery. In the 19th-century Gothic Revival, German workshops began to reproduce aquamanilia, many of which have been confused with authentic pieces and have found their way into both private and public collections.

BIBLIOGRAPHY

J. Braun: *Das christliche Altargerat in seinem Sein und in seiner Entwicklung* (Munich, 1932), pp. 531–51, figs 423–43

O. van Falke and E. Meyer: *Bronzegeräte des Mittelalters*, i (Berlin, 1935), pp. 38–96, 106–18 [pls and bibliog.]

G. Swarzenski: 'Romanesque Aquamanile of the Guennol Collection', *Brooklyn Mus. Bull.*, x (1949), pp. 1–10

E. Meyer: 'Romanesque Aquamanile in the Form of a Dragon', *Burl. Mag.*, xcii (1950), pp. 102–5

Medieval Art from Private Collections: A Special Exhibition at the Cloisters (exh. cat., ed. C. Gomez-Moreno; New York, Cloisters, 1968)

K. Niehr: 'Horaz in Hildesheim—Zum Problem einer mittelalterlichen Kunsttheorie', *Z. Kstgesch.*, i (1989), pp. 1–24

JOHN N. LUPIA

Aquatint. Term used to describe either the intaglio process or the print made by etching a plate through a special etching ground composed of particles of resin. During the confused early history of the technique, the term *manière de lavis* was used. However, this led to a misleading broad definition that included any printmaking process emulating the effect of a flat wash. The strict definition above is now generally preferred.

See also PRINTS, §III, 2.

1. Aquatint and etching, with hand colouring, by Joseph Constantine Stadler: *Fishermen Going out at Worthing*, 440×580 mm, 1801; after a pen-and-ink and watercolour drawing by Philippe Jacques de Loutherbourg (Manchester, University of Manchester, Whitworth Art Gallery)

1. Materials and techniques. 2. History.

1. MATERIALS AND TECHNIQUES. After stopping-out (with varnish) areas that are to remain white, the image is formed by applying the aquatint ground of resin (or a substitute of asphalt, bitumen or pitch) using one of two methods. The first is to allow the resin to settle on the plate as a dry dust, usually by inserting the plate at the bottom of a box in which the dust has previously been shaken. The plate is then heated so that each separate grain of the dust-ground melts and adheres to the metal. The second method is to dissolve the resin or asphalt in alcohol (or equivalent distillate); this spirit-ground is then poured over the plate. The alcohol evaporates, leaving a thin film of resin which cracks in the final stages of drying.

The plate is then immersed in acid, which etches the metal in the gaps around the grains of resin, thus forming a very fine crazed pattern of etched lines. Like an ordinary line ETCHING, the ground is then cleaned off the plate, to which ink is applied. The ink penetrates the etched depressions, and when the plate is printed, it creates a very fine network of lines that gives the effect of a soft grain or wash. The process produces areas of only a single tone, but the density of the tone varies depending on how finely the dust was ground and how thickly it covered the plate. Because it cannot produce lines, the process is often combined with etching (see fig. 1).

Gradations of tone for modelling forms can be achieved by using different densities of ground on the same plate, by burnishing the aquatint after it has been etched or by etching some areas of the plate longer than others to give a darker tone (either by tilting the plate out of the acid or by successively stopping-out areas with varnish). Another method of drawing an aquatint, more suited to making an artist's print, is called LIFT-GROUND ETCHING (or sugar-lift etching). In this the artist draws directly on the plate with a brush using a sugar solution, which swells when immersed in warm water and lifts the varnish to leave the brushed design as exposed metal; an aquatint ground is then applied in the usual way (or it can be applied to the whole plate before the sugar solution is brushed on), but it will affect the plate only in the exposed areas. When etched and printed, this gives the effect of a brush drawing.

Aquatints can be printed in colour in two ways: different coloured inks can be applied to the plate *à la poupée* (i.e. with a rag stump or 'dolly'), or a separate plate can be made for each colour and the several plates aligned for printing by a system of registration pins. Colour can also be added to aquatints by hand with considerable success due to the affinity between aquatint tone and watercolour washes.

2. HISTORY.

(i) Experiments and prototypes, *c.* 1650–*c.* 1760. (ii) Development, *c.* 1760–*c.* 1800. (iii) Subsequent use, *c.* 1800 and after.

(i) Experiments and prototypes, c. *1650–*c. *1760.* The first known resin-ground aquatints were made by Jan van de Velde IV (1610–86) in the Netherlands in the 1650s, at the same time as Ludwig von Siegen was developing another tonal intaglio process, the mezzotint. The process, however, did not catch on, and these isolated experiments seem to have had no successors until the aquatint was re-invented in France in the mid-18th century, stimulated by the search for better tonal printmaking processes in response to the demand for reproductions of drawings. Various processes then invented were grouped under the term *manière de lavis* and have since been mistaken for aquatint proper. In certain early examples it is impossible to discern whether an aquatint ground was used.

In the early 1720s reproductions of drawings were made using mezzotint and wooden tone blocks by Elisha Kirkall (1685–1742). These were followed by facsimiles that used etching and wooden tone blocks, most notably the first volume of the *Cabinet Crozat* (1729) by the Comte de Caylus, and the *Imitations of Drawings* (1732, 1736) by Arthur Pond and Charles Knapton (1700–60). Pond also invented the method called CRAYON MANNER, which used a roulette through an etching ground to reproduce the effect of chalk drawings. But crayon manner became widely established only after it was re-invented by Jean-Charles François in 1757 in France, where it was more suited to the taste for chalk drawings among artists and collectors. Many 18th-century prints, including the celebrated colour prints of Jean-François Janinet and Philibert-Louis Debucourt (which were initially called *manière de lavis* and have also been called aquatints), are actually refinements of the crayon manner method. They were made using a vast array of special stippling tools and roulettes through an etching ground, or directly to the plate (as in mezzotint), to build up a patchwork of dots that imitated the manner of a wash.

Several artists, including Paul Sandby in England *c.* 1750 and François in France in 1758, experimented with the distinct but related tonal process of *lavis* (open-bite etching), which consisted of brushing pure acid directly on to the plate. This technique had been in limited use in the 17th century, for instance by Stefano della Bella, but in the 18th century attempts were made to make *lavis* more controllable. The method invented by the Nuremberg engraver Johann Adam Schweikart (1722–87) used an acidic paste that could be brushed on to the plate in a more controlled fashion than pure *lavis*, etching the plate in irregular patterns similar to those produced by etching through an aquatint ground. Schweikart's technique was used from the late 1750s onwards by a school of engravers in Florence to make facsimiles of drawings, most notably in the *Disegni originali d'eccellenti pittori esistenti nella R. Galleria di Firenze* (Florence, *c.* 1766) of Andrea Scacciati (1725–71) and Stefano Mulinari (*c.* 1741–*c.* 1790).

(ii) Development, c. *1760–*c. *1800.* The first prints to be made in France with an actual aquatint ground were probably those made in 1761–2 by François-Philippe Charpentier (1734–1817) and his Swedish pupil Per Gustaf Floding. An examination of the prints suggests the application of a very fine aquatint ground to the whole plate and the subsequent use of stopping-out varnish to define the areas of shading. Floding returned to Sweden in 1764 and made no more prints in this manner. Charpentier continued to use the method between 1763 and 1766, including a large number of plates for the second edition of the *Cabinet Crozat* (1763), and then again in 1778–9. The next group of aquatints was made probably in 1766 by the Abbé de Saint-Non, who learnt it from somebody else (presumably Floding or Charpentier) and was sworn

to secrecy. Whereas Charpentier was restricted by the need to draw negatively with a stopping-out varnish, Saint-Non must have made use of some equivalent to lift-ground, which enabled him to brush his design positively on the plate.

Although preceded by Charpentier and Saint-Non, the artist usually credited with the invention of the resin-ground aquatint process is Jean-Baptiste Le Prince. In 1769, after experimenting with various methods of achieving tone, including drypoint hatching, *lavis* and uncontrolled resin tone, he arrived independently at a highly individual method of aquatint. After the outlines were etched, he covered the plate with a new ground, then brushed his design with a special solvent ink that weakened the ground so that it could be wiped off. The patches of exposed metal plate were then brushed with a sticky solution of soap and sugar on to which pulverized resin was shaken from a silk bag held above the plate. The resin was held by the sticky solution until it was fused to the plate by heating. The plate was then etched in the normal way. The process could be repeated many times, and sometimes stopping-out varnish was also used. The considerable success of Le Prince's aquatints was due to the freedom of drawing that resulted from the positive brush process. His method found no real followers in France, perhaps because the wash drawings it was best suited to reproducing were not popular there. The most extraordinary aquatints produced by a Frenchman in the last decade of the 18th century were actually made in Sweden by Louis Jean Desprez.

The first British aquatint artist was Peter Perez Burdett (*fl c.* 1770–73), who exhibited his first aquatints in 1772. His technique varied from any of the French methods, suggesting that he developed it himself. He drew by brushing acid on to an aquatint ground, using stopping-out varnish merely to define large areas of flat tone. Other early aquatints were made in England by François-Xavier Vispré in 1774, Francis Jukes in 1775, Philippe Jacques de Loutherbourg in 1776, James Barry, whose long series of aquatints began in 1776, and Thomas Gainsborough, who used the process by 1780. But the most important early aquatint artist in Britain was Paul Sandby, who made his first prints in the medium in 1774 and published them in the *Twelve Views in South Wales* (1775). He learnt the basic technique from the Hon. Charles Greville (1749–1809), who in turn may have learnt it in France (from Charpentier or Saint-Non) or from Burdett. Sandby himself introduced significant developments to the aquatint process. He was the inventor of the spirit-ground, which he laid over the entire surface of the plate. He then brushed his design on to the ground with a sugar solution and laid a coat of varnish over the top. The varnish lifted off when the plate was immersed in water. This is the basic lift-ground technique, which was subsequently preferred to Le Prince's more complicated method, itself brought to Britain by Robert Adam when it was first made public in 1782. Although the spirit-ground became popular, since the end of the 18th century most aquatint artists have preferred the dust-ground.

Britain has the strongest tradition of aquatinting because the technique was ideally suited to the reproduction of late 18th-century British watercolours, usually made up of outlines and flat washes. In some cases a specialist aquatint artist would add aquatint to the lines etched by another printmaker. Most of these prints were topographical and many illustrated the series of colour-plate books published in large numbers throughout this period, such as the three-volume *Microcosm of London* (London, 1808–11). After 1780 aquatint was often combined with etching in satirical caricatures. Thomas Rowlandson was a notable exponent in both fields.

In the last 30 years of the 18th century the technique of resin-ground aquatint spread rapidly to most European countries. Although it is not clear how the information was disseminated, it is likely that it stemmed from France. The earliest practitioners in Germany worked at the Leipzig academy. They were the architect Johann-Friedrich-Karl Dauthe (1749–1816) in 1770, Ernst Gottlob (1744–89) in 1772, Johann Gottlieb Prestel (1744–89) and Maria Prestel (1747–94) in 1775. In Italy the only notable 18th-century practitioner was Giovanni David; his *Divers portraits à l'eau-forte* were published in 1775, although the aquatint may have been added later.

(iii) Subsequent use, c. *1800 and after.* The invention of lithography in the final years of the 18th century produced a technique better suited to the reproduction of certain types of drawings, particularly those in ink and chalk. Aquatint thus began to lose its status as a reproductive medium everywhere except Britain, where watercolour imitations continued to be produced in the first half of the 19th century. Aquatinted plates wore out too quickly for a wide commercial application, especially in comparison with steel-engraving and lithography, and by the second or third decade of the 19th century lithography was also more popular as an original printmaking medium. That aquatint survived at all as an artist's medium has much to do with the inspiration of Francisco Goya, who used it with etching for most of his print series: the *Caprichos* (1799; see fig. 2), the *Disasters of War* (*c.* 1810–20), the *Tauromaguia* (1816) and the *Disparates* (1820). Only the *Caprichos* and the *Tauromaguia* were published during his lifetime. It is not known how Goya learnt the basic technique displayed in his earliest aquatints (1778), but it has been suggested that he was inspired by Giovanni David. Goya developed his range of techniques to include acid washes and the extensive use of burnishing. One plate, *The Colossus* (*c.* 1812), is one of the few in the history of printmaking to be made entirely in burnished aquatint. Goya's aquatints are unparalleled in their expressive strength. Few other aquatints have used chiaroscuro to such dramatic effect. In the *Disasters of War* even the substandard plates available to Goya in wartime were exploited to produce aquatints of technical imperfection but profound power.

The influence of Goya's aquatints was most strongly felt in 19th-century France, first in the work of Eugène Delacroix, particularly in *The Blacksmith* (1833), and later in the work of Edouard Manet. Towards the end of the 19th century aquatint again became more widely used when its delicacy was exploited for Impressionistic and then Symbolist purposes. Degas used it for its flat tonal properties, while it was the more subtle atmospheric effects that appealed to Pissarro. In Germany Max Klinger was

2. Aquatint and etching by Francisco Goya: *The Sleep of Reason Produces Monsters*, 215×150 mm; pl. 43 of *Los Caprichos*, 1799 (Cambridge, Fitzwilliam Museum)

the most effective exponent of aquatint. In 1891 Mary Cassatt made a set of ten colour-printed aquatints 'in imitation of Japanese prints' which exploited the medium's potential for the effect of delicate flat washes. Partly in response to the popularity of colour lithographs, around 1900 several other artists made colour aquatints, some of the best and most sophisticated being those by Jacques Villon. At the same time the growing school of professional reproductive engravers in France also started to use colour aquatint. The plates could be steel-faced to print a large edition.

In the 20th century aquatint has been either used for its painterly properties or subsumed in mixed method prints. Georges Rouault started to rework photogravures for which he made drawings in 1916, but it was only in the mid-1930s that the printer Roger Lacourière (*d* 1967) showed him how colour might be added to his prints by means of aquatint plates. Lacourière actually made the colour plates in the same way as he did when making a reproduction of a watercolour. Rouault simply drew the black plates, usually in lift-ground etching. It was also Lacourière who in 1936 introduced aquatint to Picasso, who used it for the last of the *Vollard Suite* (assembled 1937, but offered for sale only in 1950) and a number of subsequent prints (*see* PICASSO, PABLO, fig. 10). Picasso also favoured lift-ground, which he used with dust-ground resin and also with *lavis* (or open-bite etching as it has become known in the 20th century). In 1938–9 Picasso attempted colour-printed aquatints of his companion, the Surrealist artist Dora Maar (*b* 1909).

Picasso's use of aquatint can be related both to the expressive tradition deriving from Goya and to the narrative use of the technique, for it has been employed to a large extent in 20th-century book illustration (many of Rouault's colour aquatints, for example, were book illustrations). David Hockney, some of whose earliest and most impressive prints used aquatint, employed it to great effect in his *Illustrations for Six Fairy Tales from the Brothers Grimm* (1969). The flat wash properties exploited in these prints also led to the increased use of the medium by abstract artists in the 1970s. The most subtle aquatints ever made are those of the North American Minimalist artists Robert Mangold, whose flat geometric shapes are enlivened only by the texture of the aquatint, and Robert Ryman, whose white aquatints depend for their variety solely on the density of the ink and its edges. At the opposite extreme, artists such as Gerhard Richter have used aquatint to modify photo-engravings of the real world. Aquatint has also been used in commercial photomechanical printmaking, particularly in photogravure.

BIBLIOGRAPHY

P. Deleschamps: *Des mordants, des vernis et des planches dans l'art du graveur: Traité complet de la gravure* (Paris, 1836)
T. H. Fielding: *The Art of Engraving, with the Various Modes of Operation* (London, 1841)
S. T. Prideaux: *Aquatint Engraving: A Chapter in the History of Book Illustration* (London, 1909)
A. M. Hind: 'Notes on the History of Soft-ground Etching and Aquatint', *Prt Colr Q.*, viii (1921), pp. 397–401
B. F. Morrow: *The Art of Aquatint* (New York, 1935)
A. Griffiths: *Prints and Printmaking* (London, 1980)
E. Rebel: *Faksimile und Mimesis* (Mittenwald, 1981)
B. Gascoigne: *How to Identify Prints* (London, 1986)
A. Griffiths: 'Notes on Early Aquatint in England and France', *Prt Q.*, iv (1987), pp. 255–70
C. MacKay: 'An Experiment to Follow the Spirit Aquatint Methods of Paul Sandby', *Prt Q.*, iv (1987), pp. 271–3
A. Stijnman: 'Jan van de Velde IV and the Invention of Aquatint', *Prt Q.*, viii (1991), pp. 153–63

CRAIG HARTLEY

Aqueduct. Bridge that carries a water channel. Strictly speaking the term simply means water channel (Lat. *aquaeductus*) and can be applied to any conduit intended for water supply, irrigation or transport, although in English it generally designates the bridge that supports the water channel itself where it crosses a valley. (Although often similar in appearance, a VIADUCT carries a road or a railway.)

Rudimentary aqueducts were probably features of irrigation works at an early date. The oldest known example was built by the Assyrian king Sennacherib in 690 BC to carry a canal to Nineveh across a river. Its remains reveal a structure 300 m long and 12 m wide on five corbelled arches. Ancient Greek engineers frequently built water supplies but rarely aqueducts; they apparently preferred the security of conduits at or near ground-level and used pipelines to cross valleys. Early Roman systems of water supply followed this pattern, and the use of aqueducts was avoided wherever possible. At Rome itself ten water-supply systems were constructed between 312 BC and

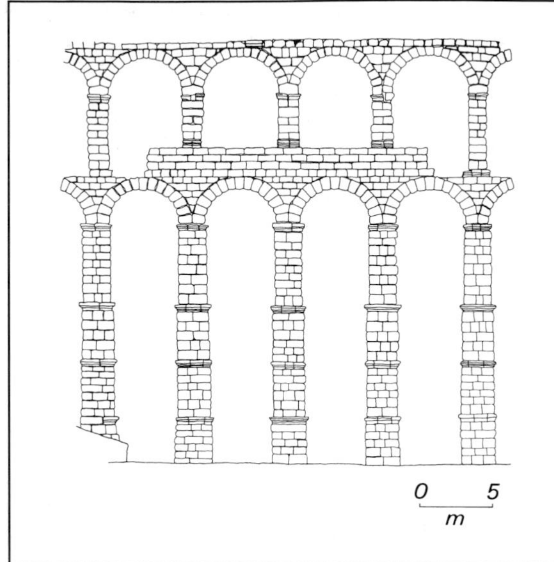

Roman aqueduct, Segovia, ?mid-1st century AD; reconstruction drawing

AD 226, and almost from the beginning, aqueducts were needed to bridge the deep gorges between Tivoli and Palestrina and to cross the low-lying Campagna on superb arcades as much as 1500 m long in one section. To economize on construction costs, however, both the Aqua Tepula and the Aqua Julia near Rome were carried on the Aqua Marcia's arcade, while the Aqua Avio Novus shared an arcade with the Aqua Claudia (*see also* ROME, ANCIENT, §III, 3). Rome's aqueducts were emulated throughout the Roman Empire. Among the most impressive are the huge Pont du Gard near Nîmes (*see* NÎMES, §2) in southern France (late 1st century BC) and the more structurally refined aqueduct at Segovia in Spain (?mid-1st century AD; see fig.; *see also* SEGOVIA, fig. 1), which is still in use. The ultimate development of Roman aqueduct building, expressive of the most elegant structural concepts, is represented by examples at Mérida in Spain (anc. Augusta Emerita) and at Cherchel in North Africa (both ?early 2nd century AD).

The Roman legacy in aqueduct building is difficult to trace with certainty, but in the 4th–6th centuries AD in Byzantium existing Roman aqueducts were rebuilt and new ones constructed on the traditional pattern. In the central Islamic lands, which are normally quite arid, Roman systems were maintained and new systems built for irrigation and to supply palaces and cities. The provision of water for drinking and bathing was considered a meritorious act in Islam, and many of the water systems built to supply the holy cities of Mecca and Medina are described in medieval texts. Some of the earliest surviving examples are the stone aqueducts that supplied water to the palaces of KHIRBAT AL-MAFJAR near Jericho (early 8th century AD), where a large arch supports two tiers of smaller arches, and MADINAT AL-ZAHRA' (936) near Córdoba, where three horseshoe arches carry the channel across the valley. The repairs and additions made by the 16th-century architect SINAN (ii) to the great aqueduct system of Istanbul are arguably his most significant contribution to the city. He repaired the aqueduct of Valens during the reign of Süleyman (*reg* 1520–66). The Uzun ('long') aqueduct in Belgrade Forest to the north-west of the city has tiers of tall pointed arches and may have been executed to Sinan's plan. A superb, although ruined, French example near Coutances (13th century) reveals its medieval origins in its Gothic arches, and similar pointed arches figure in the 14th-century aqueduct at Spoleto in central Italy. Aqueducts were commonly constructed in Spain for irrigation work, and Spanish engineers introduced these techniques to the Americas, where highly 'baroque' structures were developed, especially in Mexico. Large water-supply aqueducts were, however, uncommon in Europe for some centuries. In France in 1684 Louis XIV's engineer Vauban began and then gave up (1688) a 4600 m aqueduct across the River Eure at Maintenon, as part of a grandiose attempt to solve the perennial water-supply problem at the palace of Versailles. In the next century Henri Pitot (1695–1771), rebuilt and widened the Pont du Gard and built the magnificent Aqueduc St Clément, nearly 1 km long and 22 m high, at Montpellier.

The first aqueduct for a navigation canal dates from *c.* 1470 and was constructed near Milan on the Martesana Canal; two centuries later the Canal du Midi included three aqueducts. In the 18th and 19th centuries navigable aqueducts became commonplace as transport canals proliferated. In Britain traditional masonry aqueducts were built for the Lancaster, the Peak Forest and the Kennet and Avon canals. More innovative aqueducts were built by THOMAS TELFORD. He experimented with cast-iron construction at Longdon-on-Tern and Chirk, and, with the engineer William Jessop (1745–1814), fully developed the new material at Pontcysyllte on the Ellesmere Canal in 1795. Here a metal channel 300 m long was carried on bolted-up iron arch elements supported by masonry columns 37 m high: it is as beautiful and daring a canal structure as any in Britain. In the USA even wood was used in the heyday of canal construction before railways took over. In France canal building flourished throughout the 19th century, and many new aqueducts were built. A few (for example on the Canal du Berry) are now abandoned, but most are still in use. There are large and elegant aqueducts at Agen, at Digoin on the Canal du Centre and, on the Canal Latéral à la Loire, at Guétin. At Briare the finest of all such *ponts canaux* was built by Gustave Eiffel in the 1890s; it crosses the River Loire at a length of 662 m.

In Europe after the Roman period aqueducts were seldom again used for urban water supply until the 19th century, when essentially Roman engineering concepts were revived in the effort to bring water to the cities' burgeoning populations. In Britain, where pressurized iron pipelines were more economic, aqueducts for water supply remained rare, and the traditional aqueduct achieved its final flourish elsewhere: in the USA in the water supply of New York; in Italy in and around Genoa; and in France, where two 19th-century examples are especially impressive, at Arcueil and Roquefavour. At Arcueil the Romans had built an aqueduct; a 17th-century replacement initiated by Marie de' Medici (1573–1642) became the lower tier of a much grander edifice built in 1874, 1057 m long and

38 m high. At Roquefavour a more magnificent aqueduct still was built in 1847 to bring the waters of the River Durance to Marseille. Although only 400 m long, the aqueduct achieves its arresting appearance from three tiers of masonry arches reaching a combined height of 82.5 m, with the top arcade barely one-third as high as either of the other two. The whole design deliberately evokes the Pont du Gard; although some 1900 years apart, these two aqueducts are stylistically closely related, constructionally similar and functionally identical.

BIBLIOGRAPHY

G. Rennie: 'Description of the Bridge-aqueduct of Roquefavour, on the Line of the Canal of Marseilles', *Proc. Inst. Civ. Engin.*, xiv (1854–5), pp. 190–238

T. Ashby: *The Aqueducts of Ancient Rome* (Oxford, 1935)

K. A. C. Creswell: *Early Muslim Architecture*, ii (Oxford, 1940/*R* New York, 1979), pp. 329–32

E. C. R. Hadfield: *The Canal Age* (Newton Abbot, 1968, 2/1981)

C. Fernandez-Casado: *Acueductos romanos en España* (Madrid, 1972)

P. Cohen: 'Origins of the Pont Cysyllte Aqueduct', *Trans. Newcomen Soc.*, li (1979–80), pp. 129–42

G. M. Binnie: *Early Victorian Water Engineers* (London, 1981)

C. Hadfield: *World Canals* (Newton Abbot, 1986)

M. Prade: *Ponts et viaducs au XIXe siècle* (Poitiers, 1988)

NORMAN A. F. SMITH

Aquila. *See* L'AQUILA.

Aquila, Silvestro dell'. *See* SILVESTRO DELL'AQUILA.

Aquila de Rakerspurga, Johannes. *See* JOHANNES AQUILA DE RAKERSPURGA.

Aquileia. Roman and Early Christian city at the east end of the plain of the Veneto, *c.* 90 km north-east of Venice and 5 km from the Adriatic coast. Founded as a Roman colony in 181 BC, it received full town status in 89 BC and became the regional capital of Venetia et Histria. It was strategically sited on the River Natissa, which was navigable to the sea, and at the intersection of routes leading north-west over the Alps and north-east to the Balkans. Written sources indicate that several emperors, including Constantine the Great, had a residence in Aquileia; from AD 294 to the 5th century it also had its own mint. In 313 it became a bishopric and in 381 it was the venue of a council before which followers of Arianism were tried. Civil wars and the invasions of the Huns (452) and the Lombards (568) led to the migration of most of the population and the transference of the see to Grado.

Excavations have revealed a grid-plan street system and several Roman buildings, including a forum, a harbour of the mid-1st century AD along the banks of the Natissa, an amphitheatre and a circus. Finds also indicate that Aquileia was a manufacturing centre for sarcophagi, glass, ceramics and mosaics (e.g. Aquileia, Mus. Archeol. N.). Roman houses have produced outstanding mosaic pavements, the decorative themes of which, such as shepherds tending their flocks and scenes of fishermen and the sea, are not exclusively Christian but illustrate the predilection of Late Antiquity for idyllic and peaceful scenes (Schumacher). Early Christian mosaic floors (Aquileia, Mus. N. Paleocrist.) have also been uncovered in two basilicas: one (late 4th century) lies beneath the Museo Nazionale Paleocristiano in the former Benedictine monastery of S Maria and the other (*c.* 600) comes from the south of the town.

The most important monument in Aquileia is the cathedral, which stands on the site of an Early Christian church complex. An inscription states that it was founded by a Bishop Theodor (*reg* 313–19), thus making it one of the oldest datable churches outside Rome. It was formed out of three small, ashlar buildings, which may originally have served as Christian meeting houses: the two main halls (each *c.* 20×37 m) running parallel east–west were aisled, with seven bays of columnar arcading, and connected at their west end by a transverse hall. Ceilings were flat; only the east bay of the south hall had a transverse barrel vault built of cane, under which stood the bishop's throne and the bench for the clergy. The interior decoration comprised wall paintings of garden scenes, and floor mosaics, large sections of which have survived. In the north hall geometric fields inhabited by various animals cover the pavement; the floor of the south hall is divided into nine roughly equal-size rectangular panels with all-over geometric patterns framing symbolic animals, personifications (e.g. the Seasons) and donor portraits (see

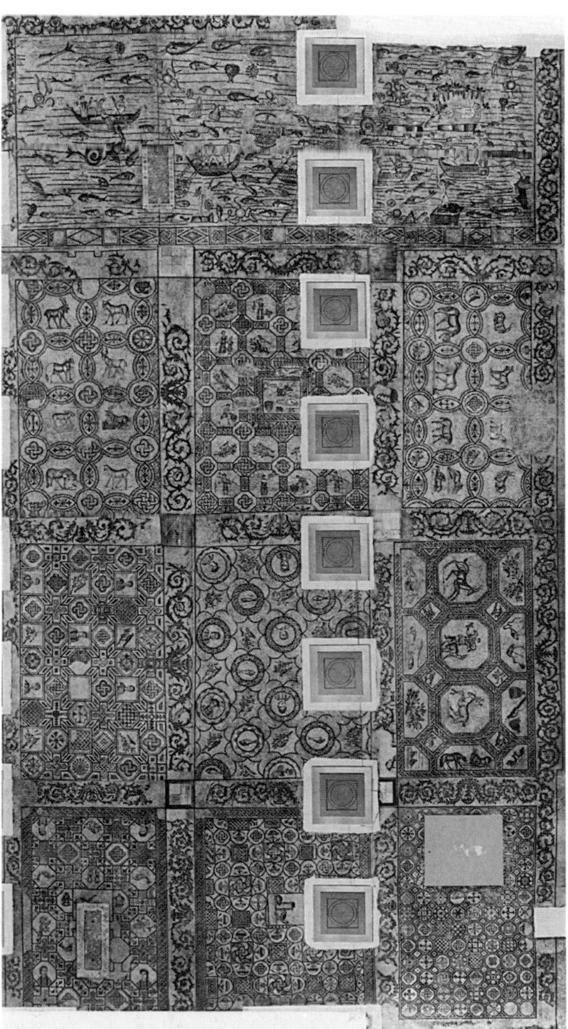

Aquileia Cathedral, mosaic floor in south hall, AD 313–19

fig.). A larger panel across the east quarter of the floor depicts scenes from the *Life of Jonah*, which were set into an earlier neutral seascape at the time of the buildings' conversion to a cathedral. The north hall was enlarged eastwards and widened *c.* AD 345 and divided into a wide nave and two narrow aisles; a square baptistery was added to the west in the late 4th century.

The present cathedral was built under Archbishop Poppo (*reg* 1021–31). A dedicatory inscription and frescoes in the apse show him with a model of the church, King Conrad II (*reg* 1026–7), his consort Gisela of Swabia and their son Prince Henry (later Henry III, *reg* 1027–42) standing before the Virgin and Child and six patron saints. The late 12th-century frescoes in the crypt, below the presbytery, depict scenes from the lives of Christ, the Virgin and the local martyrs SS Hermagoras and Fortunatus. A low-relief (after 1170) shows Christ between SS Peter and Thomas à Becket.

BIBLIOGRAPHY

Reallex. Ant. & Christ.; *RBK*

V. Scrinari: 'Aquileia', *Enciclopedia dell'arte antica classica e orientale*, ed. R. B. Bondinelli, i (1958), pp. 511–20

H. Kähler: *Die Stiftermosaiken in der konstantinischen Südkirche von Aquileia* (Cologne, 1962)

G. C. Menis: *I mosaici cristiani di Aquileia* (Udine, 1965)

W. N. Schumacher: *Hirt und 'Guter Hirt'* (Rome, Freiburg and Vienna, 1977), pp. 217–307

N. Himmelmann: *Über Hirten-Genre in der antiken Kunst* (Opladen, 1982), pp. 168–72

G. C. Menis: *Il complesso episcopale Teodoriano di Aquileia e il suo battistero* (Udine, 1986)

C. Jäggi: 'Aspekte der städtebaulichen Entwicklung Aquileias', *Jb. Ant. & Christ.*, xxxiii (1990), pp. 158–96

FRANZ RICKERT

Aquileia, Patriarchs of. *See* GRIMANI.

Aquilio, Antonio di Benedetto. *See* ANTONIAZZO ROMANO.

Aquinas, Thomas. *See* THOMAS AQUINAS.

Aquincum. *See under* BUDAPEST, §I, 1.

Arabesque. Distinctive kind of vegetal ornament that flourished in Islamic art from the 10th to the 15th century. The term 'arabesque' (and the obsolete form *rebesk*, It. *rebesco*) is a European, not an Arabic, word dating perhaps to the 15th or 16th century, when Renaissance artists used Islamic designs for book ornament and decorative bookbindings. Over the centuries the word has been applied to a wide variety of winding and twining vegetal decoration in art and meandering themes in music, but it properly applies only to Islamic art.

ALOIS RIEGL was the first to characterize the principal features of the arabesque by noting the geometrization of the stems of the vegetation, the particular vegetal elements used and the fact that these elements can grow unnaturally from one another, rather than branching off from a single continuous stem. Riegl also pointed out that the arabesque has infinite correspondence (Ger. *unendliche Rapport*), meaning that the design can be extended indefinitely in any direction. Riegl's analysis is the basis for most later art-historical descriptions of the arabesque.

Most of what Riegl wrote about the arabesque fails to mark it off as a category of design distinct from other vegetal decoration, such as the vegetal ornament of Late Antiquity. It is the infinite correspondence of the arabesque that is unique in world art: the structure of the arabesque gives sufficient information for the viewer to imagine how the design would appear were it extended beyond its actual limits. This infinite correspondence in the arabesque was an outcome of artistic interest in such geometric constructions as the complex geometric frameworks popular in Late Antique architecture and art. However, while vegetal elements may appear as fillers within geometric designs in Late Antique art, they are separate from the geometric framework. Such geometric constructions were also popular in Islamic art on their own account, appearing without vegetal elements as a distinct type of decoration (*see* ORNAMENT AND PATTERN, §IV). In the case of the arabesque, however, the repeating axes of the geometric construction allow the viewer to extend a vegetal design in his imagination. The actual vegetal elements of the arabesque were drawn from Sasanian and Late Antique art. They include, and for many centuries were limited to, acanthus and grape leaves, grape clusters and the derived, abstracted form usually known as the PALMETTE. These elements became standard, and only in the 14th century were other vegetal forms such as flowers introduced into the arabesque, particularly in Persian and Turkish art.

The fully geometrized arabesque appeared no earlier than the mid-10th century, when foliate motifs such as the vine or acanthus scroll were made to interlace with geometric frames; at roughly the same time the stem pattern of the vegetal scroll was assimilated to the geometric framework: the stems of the scroll were given the shape of what had formerly been a non-vegetal pattern, or conversely, the geometric framework came to life and leaves sprouted directly from it. The arabesque was probably invented in Baghdad, the cultural capital of the Islamic world in the 10th century, as the arabesque was disseminated quickly to all Islamic lands. The earliest datable example of this distinctive and original development may be found in carved marble panels flanking the mihrab of the Great Mosque of Córdoba (see fig.).

The full arabesque has infinite correspondence along all the axes of the underlying geometry, but there are many examples of Islamic vegetal ornament that do not have full infinite correspondence. Some such designs are turned inward at their edges, limiting their extensibility. Continuous scrolls, which often appear as borders, usually have a regular geometric basis but are extensible only to their sides. The same limitation applies to arabesque cresting, such as that seen in the borders of illuminated manuscripts and relief stuccowork. Full or partial, the arabesque became one of the mainstays of Islamic art, along with strictly geometrical designs and calligraphy.

The arabesque was displaced from the 14th century, both by freer designs employing chrysanthemum, peony and lotus motifs from Chinese art and by the new fantastic foliage of the Saz style, which became popular under the Ottomans in the 16th century. Both kinds of foliage can be made into arabesques but generally were not treated in that fashion. By the late 17th century the arabesque fell

Arabesque decoration on a carved marble panel flanking the mihrab of the Great Mosque, Córdoba, *c.* AD 965

out of use as Baroque vegetal forms were imported into Islamic art and became extremely popular. In the 19th century, with the rise of Western interest in Islamic arts and crafts, traditional techniques and motifs, including the arabesque, were revived in the Islamic world. In some cases these revivals proceeded openly, and objects were made in historical styles; in other cases historical styles were revived for the purpose of producing forgeries. Both of these trends have continued into the 20th century, most arabesques being based on historical examples, rather than rendered in a new style.

The arabesque has been seldom copied in Western art; its appearance in the 15th and 16th centuries seems to have been associated with Venetian craftsmen imitating Islamic metalwork (*see* VENETO-SARACENIC) and bookbinding, which in turn was connected with the influence of Islamic techniques and sources of materials (e.g. 'morocco' leather). Although the famous intertwining illumination of the Book of Kells and related manuscripts (*see* INSULAR ART, §3) was in some ways a development parallel to the arabesque, such illumination remained without a strict geometric basis and employed animate rather than vegetal motifs.

BIBLIOGRAPHY

Enc. Islam/2

A. Riegl: *Stilfragen* (Berlin, 1893); Eng. trans. by E. Kain as *Problems of Style* (Princeton, 1992)

E. Kühnel: *Die Arabeske* (Wiesbaden, 1949); Eng. trans. by R. Ettinghausen as *The Arabesque: Meaning and Transformation of an Ornament* (Graz, 1976)

S. Morison: 'Venice and the Arabesque Ornament', *Selected Essays on the History of Letter-forms in Manuscript and Print*, ed. D. McKitterick (Cambridge, 1981), pp. 142–58

T. Allen: *Five Essays on Islamic Art* (Sebastopol, CA, 1988), pp. 1–9, 52–4

□

Arabesque style. Term used, mainly in France, to describe painted ornament in the late 18th century incorporating grotesques, STRAPWORK and the foliate scrollwork inspired by the Moresque style. Contemporaries referred to the style, which was in evidence from 1775 and developed until the collapse of the *ancien régime*, as 'goût étrusque' (*see* ETRUSCAN STYLE) or 'genre arabesque', or sometimes used the double appellation 'goût arabesque et étrusque'. It derives in part from surviving examples of the grotesque in Rome (*see* GROTESQUE and fig. 1) and is characterized by naturalistically shaped ornamental motifs, which pivot on a central axis to form a mirror image (*see* ARABESQUE and fig.). The principle of composition of the style lies in the curvilinear ACANTHUS scroll, symmetrically aligned on an axis and rolling up to form a spiral. Spirals are also found in the scroll friezes, in scroll motifs turning in on themselves to become spirals and in flutings. This naturalistic imagery is diametrically opposed to the heavy forms, sober abstract friezes and the severe and solemn pictorial inventions of early Classicism and the *goût grec*.

One of the earliest examples of the style was the decoration by Charles-Louis Clérisseau for the salon of the Hôtel Grimod de la Reynière, Paris (1774; for illustration *see* CLÉRISSEAU, CHARLES-LOUIS). A contemporary account in the *Almanach des artistes* (Paris, 1977, pp. 84–6) describes the highly coloured decoration 'dipping into the maxims of the ancients, it is very easy to find a genre that suits us perfectly though it is very different from the ones we have adopted.' Clérisseau also used arabesque decoration for the salon of another mansion (1779–81; now probably London, V&A) on the Rue Boissy d'Anglas for Laurent Grimod de la Reynière. The court did not begin to adopt the arabesque style until after 1785. In 1787 Rousseau de La Rottière decorated a games-room and a boudoir with a 'cabinet turc' at Fontainebleau for Marie-Antoinette. These rooms represent the apogée of the French 'style arabesque', and some of the motifs employed in them formed a transition to Pompeian decoration (*see* POMPEIAN REVIVAL). In its late phase the arabesque style corresponds closely to the DIRECTOIRE STYLE.

BIBLIOGRAPHY

L. Hautecoeur: *Rome et la renaissance de l'antiquité à la fin du XVIIIe siècle* (Paris, 1912)

E. Croft-Murray: 'The Hôtel Grimod de La Reynière: The Salon Decorations', *Apollo* (1963), p. 377

H. Ottomeyer and P. Pröschel: *Bronzearbeiten des Spätbarock und Klassizismus*, i (Munich, 1986), p. 217

HANS OTTOMEYER

Arabia, pre-Islamic. Region in which diverse cultures and civilizations flourished from *c.* 4500 BC to the rise of Islam in the early 7th century AD. Throughout history the term Arabia has varied according to changing political and cultural conditions. In this article it denotes the Arabian peninsula as far north as the borders of Jordan and Iraq.

For regions north of this modern boundary *see* SYRIA-PALESTINE and MESOPOTAMIA.

A supraregional survey is not always possible for the art forms discussed below, either because of distinct regional diversity or because archaeological excavation is more advanced in some parts of the peninsula than in others. In some cases, therefore, this article simply discusses those works of art and architecture that are most noteworthy, either stylistically, technologically or iconographically. Generally, the earliest material considered dates to the latter part of the late prehistoric period, *c.* 4500–*c.* 3400 BC. Thereafter there is a range of sites and finds that span the protohistoric (*c.* 3400–*c.* 2300 BC), early historic (*c.* 2300–*c.* 300 BC) and late pre-Islamic, including Hellenistic and Roman, periods (*c.* 300 BC–*c.* AD 600). For later periods *see* ISLAMIC ART §I, 1; BAHRAIN; KUWAIT; OMAN; QATAR; SAUDI ARABIA; UNITED ARAB EMIRATES; and YEMEN.

I. Introduction. II. Architecture. III. Sculpture. IV. Other arts. V. Museums and exhibitions.

I. Introduction.

An irregularly shaped plateau that slopes slightly towards the east, Arabia is bounded in the west by the Gulf of Aqaba and the Red Sea, in the south by the Gulf of Aden and the Arabian Sea and in the east by the Gulf of Oman and the Persian/Arabian Gulf (see fig. 1). Arabia contains the largest uninterrupted sand desert in the world. With an area of *c.* 416,670 sq. km (larger than the Netherlands, Belgium and France combined), the Empty Quarter or Rubʿal-Khali dominates a large portion of the southern

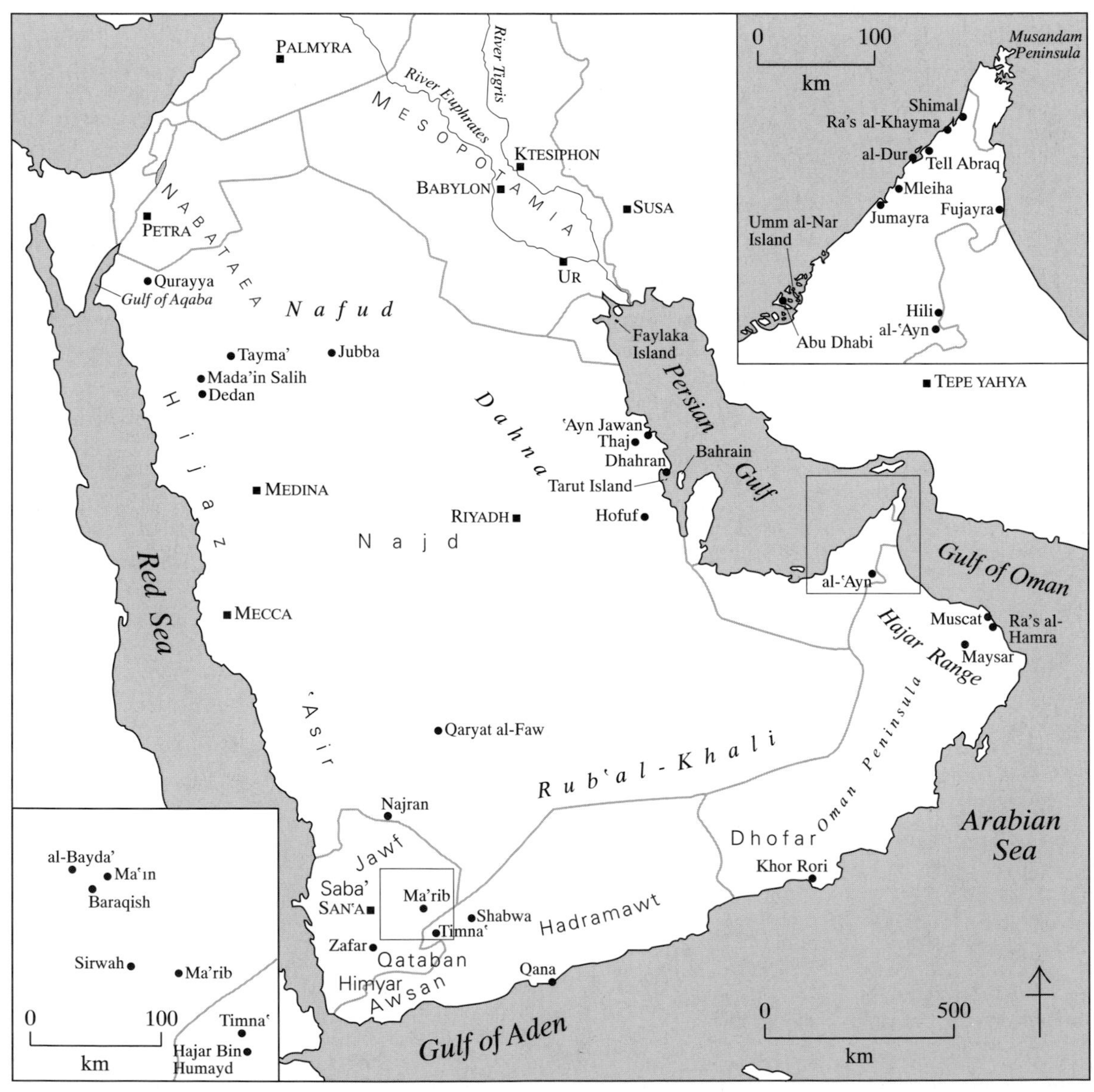

1. Map of pre-Islamic Arabia; those areas with separate entries in this dictionary are distinguished by CROSS-REFERENCE TYPE

part of the peninsula. Nor is this the only major desert, for the Nafud in the north and Dahna in the north-east are also considerable in their extent. Nevertheless the popular image of Arabia as nothing but sand is quickly dispelled when the inhabited zones outside these great deserts are examined. It was in these environmentally diverse areas that artistically rich and variegated cultural forms emerged in pre-Islamic times.

In north-western Arabia a steep mountain escarpment, reaching elevations of over 2000 m, runs abruptly down to the Red Sea coast. To the east of the escarpment is a series of deeply incised valleys and spring-fed oases where important towns grew up in antiquity, such as MECCA, MEDINA, Dedan (Khurayba in al-ʿUla oasis) and Tayma'. This area, known as the Hijaz, was important long before the formative years of Islam. It was the home of the biblical Midianites and Dedanites and the target of the westward, expansionist policies of the Assyrian and Babylonian empires. The Lihyanite state flourished here in the late 1st millennium BC and the Nabataean kingdom expanded into the Hijaz from Petra (now in southern Jordan; *see* NABATAEA) by the 1st century BC. The Hijaz is easily accessible from Palestine, Jordan, Syria and Egypt, which influenced cultural developments in the region.

On the eastern side of the peninsula the low-lying coastal plain, which today includes the Eastern Province of Saudi Arabia, Kuwait and Qatar, barely rises above sea level. This is the area known traditionally as al-Bahrayn, a name that was applied to the offshore island group only in the Middle Ages. Although it is an arid area with little rainfall, it is underlain by a rich system of aquifers, and both natural springs and hand-dug wells have ensured numerous coastal settlements throughout history. Moreover, the availability of marine resources, coupled with the potential for inter-regional contact and trade afforded by direct access to the Persian Gulf, resulted in the development of a rich cultural tradition. From the early 3rd millennium BC this area, known in Mesopotamian cuneiform sources as Dilmun, was in touch with Babylonia, Elam (south-west Iran), Magan (the Oman peninsula) and the Harappan civilization of the Indus Valley. It continued to play an important role during the Hellenistic (late 4th century BC–late 1st), Parthian (mid-3rd century BC–AD 220s) and Sasanian (*c.* AD 224–651) periods and has been reasonably well investigated by archaeologists.

The centre of the peninsula is archaeologically the poorest known part of Arabia. It has been called the heart of Arabia and is traditionally known as Najd (Arab.: 'highland'). The area is dominated by the Tuwayq escarpment, a roughly 830 km-long rock shelf that cuts an arc through the centre of the peninsula. In antiquity a major caravan route from South Arabia towards al-Bahrayn and on to Mesopotamia ran north through a string of oasis settlements in Najd, the most important of which, from an art historical point of view, was Qaryat al-Faw.

South Arabia, or al-Yaman, is anomalous in many ways. With its generally much higher altitudes and rainfall, the region has a different flora, fauna and architecture from most of Arabia. It was home to the great South Arabian kingdoms—Saba', Hadramawt, Awsan, Qataban, Maʿin (the Minaean kingdom) and, lastly, Himyar—that flourished in the 1st millennium BC and 1st millennium AD in part through the lucrative trade in frankincense and myrrh. As the most literate portion of the peninsula in pre-Islamic times, it has yielded thousands of pre-Islamic inscriptions which provide enormous insight into the political history, economy, society and religion of the region. Such sites as Ma'rib, Baraqish, Shabwa and Timnaʿ have yielded important works of art.

The Oman peninsula, comprising the modern nation states of the Sultanate of Oman and the United Arab Emirates, juts out into the Indian Ocean like a great appendage. Geographically, the low-lying coast of the Emirates is not unlike much of al-Bahrayn, but the desert foreland is backed by a fertile gravel plain and an impressive mountain massif, the Hajar range, which runs from the Musandam peninsula in the north down the centre of the Oman peninsula like a great spine. Altitudes and rainfall are much higher here than in the rest of eastern Arabia, particularly in the Jabal Akhdar, and the vegetation is accordingly different from the more desertic and steppic regions further west. At the same time there is a strong maritime orientation along the extensive coasts of Oman and a natural exposure to the Indian Ocean and subcontinent. Throughout antiquity Oman's distinctive material culture (ceramics, stone vessels, metalwork) distinguished it from that of its Arabian neighbours. Known in Mesopotamian cuneiform sources as Magan or Makkan, Oman was a principal source of copper for Sumer and Akkad. Furthermore, it always enjoyed close ties with the opposite shores of Iran and Baluchistan and had considerable links with the Indus Valley and Gujarat as well.

BIBLIOGRAPHY

B. Moritz: *Arabien* (Hannover, 1923)
W. C. Brice: *South-West Asia* (London, 1966)
An Introduction to Saudi Arabian Antiquities (Riyadh, 1975)
W. Daum, ed.: *Yemen: 3000 Years of Art and Civilisation in Arabia Felix* (Innsbruck, 1987)
D. T. Potts: *The Arabian Gulf in Antiquity*, 2 vols (Oxford, 1990)

II. Architecture.

1. Domestic. 2. Funerary. 3. Palatial. 4. Military. 5. Religious.

1. DOMESTIC. It is impossible to generalize about the domestic architecture of pre-Islamic Arabia since environmental conditions in each part of the peninsula conditioned the appearance of different architectural forms. The availability of building materials and the climatic suitability of different sorts of constructions varied from region to region. From the late prehistoric period into the modern era perishable houses of date palm fronds (*barasti*) have been built in coastal areas (e.g. on the Gulf coast, the Batina coast of Oman and the Tihama plain in Yemen). These are cool constructions which, when properly maintained, can last for many years. The particular manner of plaiting the palm fronds gives plenty of scope for decorative patterns, not unlike those found in basketry. Patterns depicted in Mesopotamian art, particularly on Protoliterate (late 4th millennium BC–early 3rd) cylinder seals and Early Dynastic II–III (*c.* 2600–*c.* 2340 BC) carved soft-stone vessels, so closely resemble those in use in these areas until recent times that some continuity in this tradition stretching back into prehistoric and early historic periods can be considered certain.

Another building material available on the Gulf coast is beach-rock (*farush*), a carbonate sediment which forms offshore and can be broken up into slabs suitable for use as building stone. Although it was no more decorative than the modern cinder-block, buildings made of beach-rock could be plastered on the outside and thus made to appear highly decorative (*see* §5(i) below). Dry-stone construction was used extensively in prehistoric South Arabia, early historic north-western Arabia and throughout the Oman peninsula. Where the outer faces of walls were made of ashlar (the kind of stone used depending on the location), the interior of the walls was often made of a rubble core, probably what was left after cutting the ashlar. Gypsum mortar was widely used as a bonding material. Mud-brick, or sand-brick, was also used widely, often with a mud or gypsum plaster coating for protection. This was commonly employed in Oman from *c.* 3000 BC to the sub-modern era. In Bahrain and the Oman peninsula, as well as in South Arabia, dry-stone foundations were often made for house walls, the upper portions of which were made of mud-brick or pisé.

For all these types of house construction the trunks of locally available date palm, tamarisk and mangrove were used to provide roof-beams, while imported woods such as Indian teak and East African mangrove poles were probably also employed in more wealthy houses. Late Early Dynastic (*c.* 2500 BC) royal inscriptions from the Sumerian city state Lagash, in southern Mesopotamia, record the arrival of ships of Dilmun (north-eastern Arabia) bearing 'timber from foreign lands'. Much of this presumably originated in the East. The *Periplus of the Erythraean Sea*, a ?1st-century AD maritime handbook describing the sea-route between Egypt and the Indian subcontinent, specifically refers to the import of sandal-wood, timbers of teak and logs of blackwood and ebony at Ommana, an Arabian port possibly to be identified with al-Dur in Umm al-Qaywayn (UAE), from Barygaza in the Indian subcontinent.

House-plans varied greatly in pre-Islamic Arabia. Circular or oval dwellings of dry-stone are attested on Bronze Age sites in Yemen (2nd millennium BC); rectangular stone houses, often multi-roomed, are known throughout Oman and north-western Arabia in all periods; while in Bahrain, during the period *c.* 2000–*c.* 1700 BC, there seems to have been great standardization in the construction of generally square houses consisting of a large, L-shaped room with a smaller, almost square room which was perhaps used as a storage facility. Orientation seems to have suited the individual location and was probably determined by such factors as prevailing winds and the sun. Windows are attested in private houses, for example at al-Dur, where thin slabs of alabaster have also been found. A comparison with sub-modern Yemeni architecture suggests that these probably represent fragments of window-panes.

BIBLIOGRAPHY

A. de Maigret: 'The Yemeni Bronze Age', *Yemen: 3000 Years of Art and Civilisation in Arabia Felix*, ed. W. Daum (Innsbruck, 1987), pp. 38–40

D. T. Potts: *The Arabian Gulf in Antiquity*, i (Oxford, 1990)

2. FUNERARY.

(i) Oman peninsula. Since 1958, when archaeological excavations began in the region, the funerary architecture of the Oman peninsula has been well investigated. Apart from simple pit burials of the early 4th millennium BC at Ra's al-Hamra near Muscat, the earliest monumental graves are cairns of Hafit type, so named because the first examples excavated, which date to *c.* 3000–*c.* 2700 BC, were located near Jabal Hafit, close to the border between Oman and Abu Dhabi. These were single-inhumation burials consisting of an inner and an outer ring of stone walling heaped up to form a dome, with a narrow entrance leading to a small, interior space. A variant which may have been contemporary or only slightly later than the Hafit burials is the 'beehive' grave. These are better built than the Hafit graves and employ flat slabs of stone set horizontally, without mortar, so as to form a carefully constructed tholos.

By the mid-3rd millennium BC a much larger, architecturally more elaborate, collective form of burial appeared. So-called Umm al-Nar graves are circular, ranging in size from *c.* 5 to *c.* 13 m in diameter. Unlike the Hafit and beehive graves, the Umm al-Nar graves consist of a dry-stone wall set on a plinth which is clad with well-masoned, limestone ashlars. The ashlars can be truly cyclopean in their proportions. The walls of the grave probably stood to several metres above ground-level, and the whole construction appears to have been unroofed. Access was gained by an apsidal hole in the wall. Graves of this sort have been known to contain the remains of up to 200 individuals; anthropological investigations of the skeletal material found in the graves on the eponymous Umm al-Nar Island, opposite the modern city of Abu Dhabi, indicate such close genetic relationships between the individuals buried within a tomb that they must have belonged to the same family or clan. (*See also* §III, 1(i)(a) below.)

In the early 2nd millennium BC collective graves continued to predominate, although sub-surface, single inhumations in stone-lined cists are also known, and considerable architectural variety is now found. Grave forms include 40 m-long, narrow, semi-subterranean structures with a pitched or saddle-back roof made of unworked boulders (e.g. at Qattara nr al-ʿAyn, Bidya between Dibba and Khor Fakkan, and al-Qusays nr Dubai); long (9–27 m), narrow, above-ground Shimal graves with rounded ends; subrectangular Ghalila graves with a long, central plinth in the middle; and similarly shaped Khatt graves, which are Shimal graves that have been encircled with an extra wall, probably to accommodate more burials. T-shaped, subterranean chambers, often several metres deep and lined with stone, have also been found at such sites as Dhaya (nr Rams) and Bithna near Fujayra town. Most of these grave types are attested in the north of the Oman peninsula, particularly in Ra's al-Khayma and Fujayra, where large, locally available boulders were used without any attempt at working or bonding them.

By the end of the 2nd millennium BC large, circular and horseshoe-shaped graves appeared (e.g. at Rafaq south-west of Kalba and Qidfa south of Khor Fakkan). These were also collective and largely subterranean. Shaft graves consisting of a vertical opening widening to an oval chamber have also been found at al-Qusays in Dubai. Finally it should be noted that the Iron Age population of the region routinely reused earlier Umm al-Nar and 2nd-millennium BC graves, pushing aside the remains of earlier inhumations to make room for new ones.

An altogether different tradition, which appeared at Mleiha in Sharjah during the Hellenistic period and at Qaryat al-Faw in central Arabia during the first few centuries AD, involved the excavation of a subterranean chamber which was surmounted by a standing, rectangular tower of mud-brick. The tower was generally decorated with architectural elements which functioned like acroteria and ornamented gables. These latter ornaments took the form of simple, stepped pyramids, much like the parapets shown in depictions of fortresses on Neo-Assyrian reliefs (883–612 BC).

During the 1st century AD a type of monumental grave was in use at al-Dur and Mleiha that is reminiscent of contemporary monuments at Parthian Assur in northern Iraq. The grave consisted of a subterranean, rectangular, walled chamber made of locally available beach-rock (on the coast) or other stone (in the interior). The floor was paved with flagstones or cobbles and often covered with grey gypsum plaster. The chamber was roofed over with a barrel vault of the same stone and it was entered via a well-made, walled shaft entrance, which also had a vaulted roof. While the actual grave chamber was under the ground, the barrel vault and entrance stood above ground.

(ii) North-eastern Arabia. From the late 3rd to the 1st millennium BC a widespread tradition of burying the dead in stone chambers of varying, though usually rectilinear, shape was practised, in contrast to the Oman peninsula in this period. The stone chamber was often semi-subterranean and was encircled by a low ring-wall of stone. The entirety was buried beneath an earthen mantle, so that the grave appears from the surface like a barrow. It is estimated that over 100,000 burials of this type once existed in Bahrain, while several thousand once encircled the modern city of Dhahran in eastern Saudi Arabia. Although differences of scale can be observed through time (e.g. the early, so-called 'royal' mounds near ʿAli in Bahrain are much larger than the lower, flattened Iron Age mounds), the principles of construction varied little from period to period.

For whatever reasons, the tradition of burial mound construction dominant in Bahrain for almost 2000 years was replaced in the Hellenistic and Parthian periods by a pattern of necropoleis composed most often of single-chamber, stone-lined, subterranean cist graves. These are well represented in Bahrain at such sites as Janussan, Abu Saybi and Karrana and usually contained a single individual together with a variable number of grave goods (e.g. ceramic vessels possibly for food offerings, personal jewellery and weaponry). In eastern Saudi Arabia, on the other hand, burial mounds continued to be the norm at such Hellenistic sites as Thaj, whereas cist graves were common at the slightly later, Parthian period site of ʿAyn Jawan.

(iii) South Arabia. Most of the evidence for funerary practices in South Arabia comes from the area of south Yemen. There are at least five forms of burials that typify this region. The simplest are pit burials dug into the alluvial deposits in the midst of irrigated fields. Stone cairns, not unlike those made during prehistoric periods in the Oman peninsula, are found on high ground in some areas. Another form of burial often found on the heights overlooking nearby settlements is a necropolis consisting of rock-cut cists intended for individuals. Free-standing stone sarcophagi, sealed with flat stone slabs, are also attested, both individually and in groups. When grouped together these were sometimes encircled by a 1.5–2.0 m-high wall, often up to 6–8 m in diameter, the whole covered with flat stone slabs which rested on the coverings of the sarcophagi. Rock-cut chambers with multiple wall niches which probably functioned as ossuaries are also attested. South Arabia is distinguished from the rest of the Arabian peninsula by the use of funerary buildings, such as the ones excavated at Timnaʿ, ancient capital of Qataban. These consist of a central corridor from which generally eight to ten narrow crypts were provided for the interment of the dead.

(iv) North-western Arabia. The funerary monuments found in north-western Arabia display a diversity almost equal to that found in South Arabia, yet are devised in markedly differing fashion. Simple pit burials were often distinguished by an upright, stone grave stele bearing a stylized pair of human eyes, nose and eyebrows. Burials consisting of small stone cairns mounded over the deceased, the entirety encircled by a ring of stones, are also attested. Stepped burial mounds crowned with a rectangular, above-ground burial cist are found at Tayma'. At Dedan rectangular cists were cut into the sheer cliff face, sometimes with internal divisions so that more than one corpse could be interred, and in several cases accompanied by large, frontally depicted lions carved in low relief (*see* §III, 1(i)(b) below).

The tradition of a rock-cut chamber in the face of a cliff reached its highest degree of elaboration under the Nabataeans, who adorned what had been in the Dedanite case a simple opening, with elaborate architectural ornamentation. Treating the opening to the burial chamber as if it were the doorway to a building, the entrances to Nabataean tombs were decorated with both zoomorphic (e.g. lions, eagles) and architectural elements (e.g. curving pediments, architraves, rosettes, triglyphs, funerary urns, cornices, capitals). The doorway was then framed in a cleanly cut façade, flanked by engaged columns and topped by a series of cornices, often culminating in an inverted, stepped-pyramid frieze. In this way the tomb façade assumed the grandeur of a large, public building.

In Arabia the most striking examples of Nabataean funerary architecture (dating to the 1st century AD) are to be found at Mada'in Salih, a site in the Hejaz *c.* 25 km north of al-ʿUla. The rock face of Qasr al-Bint at Mada'in Salih contained twenty-three such tombs (see fig. 2), while the smaller outcrop called Hreba contained thirteen and the Hremat outcrop contained at least four complete and one unfinished tomb. Unlike their counterparts at PETRA,

2. Nabataean tomb façade, Qasr al-Bint, Mada'in Salih, Saudi Arabia, 1st century AD

the Nabataean tombs of Mada'in Salih are often characterized by the presence of a *tabula ansata*, frequently situated above the entrance to the tomb. This was a framed and recessed panel on which a Nabataean inscription was carved which, typically, named the builder of the tomb, the year of the entombed person's death and juridical conditions relating to the use of the tomb by members of the deceased's family and others.

BIBLIOGRAPHY

A. Grohmann: *Arabien* (Munich, 1963)

B. Doe: *Southern Arabia* (London, 1971)

R. Boucharlat and J.-F. Salles: *L'Arabie orientale, Mésopotamie et Iran méridional* (Lyons, 1984)

R. Boucharlat and others: 'The European Archaeological Expedition to ed-Dur, Umm al-Qaiwayn (UAE): An Interim Report on the 1987 and 1988 Seasons', *Mesopotamia*, xxiv (1989), pp. 5–72

D. T. Potts: *The Arabian Gulf in Antiquity*, 2 vols (Oxford, 1990)

K. Frifelt: *Third Millennium Graves*, The Island of Umm an-Nar, i (Århus, 1991)

3. PALATIAL. Between 1953 and 1964 a Danish archaeological expedition in Bahrain excavated part of a large residential complex at Qal'at al-Bahrain, on the north coast, built of 1.1 m-thick, plastered walls of ashlar masonry. The plan of the building, which stood to a height of 5 m in places, is reminiscent of the Neo-Assyrian palace at NIMRUD known as Fort Shalmaneser (mid-9th century BC), the provincial Assyrian palace at ARSLAN TASH in Syria (mid-8th century BC) and the 'Summer Palace' of Nebuchadnezzar II (*reg* 604–562 BC) at BABYLON. Although relatively little of the Bahrain building has been exposed, enough is there to recognize part of the central courtyard, the reception/throne-room, the 'retiring chamber' and a lavatory (*see also* §5(i) below). Similar arrangements can be identified in house complexes at Babylon and UR that are not considered palatial but that clearly represent substantial residences. In this case, although the names of several rulers of ancient Dilmun (Bahrain) who reigned in the late 8th century BC and 7th are known, it is not known whether the building in question served as a palace for one of them. The functional similarities between the Bahraini building and the Neo-Assyrian and Neo-Babylonian houses/palaces mentioned above are, nevertheless, striking.

Three buildings excavated in the early 1970s at Jumayra, a suburb of Dubai, appear to have been public. These include a complex of square 'shops' on either side of a street, a 'governor's palace' and a 'hunting lodge'. This last building appears to have been an elaborate residence consisting of rectangular rooms grouped around a central courtyard. In plan it shows some similarities to the hunting lodges of the Umayyad period (AD 661–750) in Jordan and Iraq (*see* ISLAMIC ART, §II, 2 and 3(iii)). Circular corner bastions, semicircular buttresses and quarter-circular projections flanking internal and external doorways were undoubtedly more important for display than for structural support. Yet the building does not resemble true fortifications (*see* §4 below) and should probably be considered a palace or grand residence. Decoration took the form of plaster and stucco reminiscent of that found typically in Sasanian palaces in Iran and Mesopotamia (*c*. AD 224–651; *see* SASANIAN and §IV, 9 below).

BIBLIOGRAPHY

G. Bibby: *Looking for Dilmun: The Search for a Lost Civilization* (London, 1970/*R* 1984)

P. Lombard: 'Iron Age Dilmun: A Reconsideration of City IV at Qal'at al-Bahrain', *Bahrain through the Ages: The Archaeology*, ed. H. A. al-Khalifa and M. Rice (London, 1986), pp. 225–32

D. T. Potts: *The Arabian Gulf in Antiquity*, 2 vols (Oxford, 1990)

4. MILITARY. Defensive architecture in pre-Islamic Arabia can be broadly divided into two categories: walled enclosures and true fortified buildings. By walled enclosures are meant large areas of civil space that have been walled in as a defence from enemy attack. Perhaps the most impressive structure of this sort is the city wall of Tayma', which encloses an area *c*. 8 sq. km and is over 3 km long. It was built of locally available dry-stone and probably dates to the 6th century BC.

A walled enclosure dating to the 3rd century BC exists at Thaj, the largest site of the Hellenistic period in eastern Arabia. Built entirely of cut limestone ashlars, with a rubble core, the wall is 4.5 m thick and runs for just over 2.5 km. It is shaped like an irregular parallelogram and has square to diamond-shaped towers at each corner, as well as semicircular turrets along the east wall and smaller buttresses on the south wall. Likewise, a *c*. 3 m-high enclosure wall runs around the site of Najran in south-west Saudi Arabia, while a more regular pattern of projecting and receding segments, all made of dry-stone masonry, is preserved at many South Arabian sites, such as Ma'rib and

Baraqish. The circuit of the rectangular walled enclosure at Ma'rib is *c.* 4.5 km.

Fortresses or fortress/palaces are much more common than city walls of the sort found at Tayma' and Thaj. Examples of fortresses, which may also have functioned as the élite residences of political leaders and their families, are known from a number of sites dating to between the 3rd century BC and the 6th century AD. The earliest of these, dating to the early Hellenistic period, were found on Faylaka Island (anc. Ikaros), Kuwait and at Mleiha. Like many fortifications of this period, the basic shape is square to rectangular, with square corner towers and projections guarding the main entrances. While the plan of the building on Faylaka is complete and shows evidence of several phases of rebuilding, only a small portion of one side of the fortress at Mleiha has been excavated.

At Qaryat al-Faw a large building (30.25×25.20 m), interpreted by the excavator as a market, has massively thick walls, square corner towers, and square projections in the middle of three walls. The interior is marked by a complex of rooms built around the four sides of an open courtyard, with a large cistern in the centre fed by an external water channel. In layout this building seems more likely to have had a military or defensive, rather than a commercial, purpose.

In the Parthian era (mid-3rd century BC–AD 220s) an architectural innovation appeared in Near Eastern fortress construction which had its roots in the Central Asian Bronze Age. Under the Parthians themselves, and during the period of their supremacy, round corner towers, semicircular buttresses and quarter-circular pilasters replaced square or diamond-shaped features. These rounded forms were then picked up in later, Sasanian architecture (*c.* AD 224–651) and became standard features of Islamic architecture. In fact, however, such round towers can already be seen on such Central Asian sites as Togolok 1 and 21 (located in the Morghab River delta in eastern Turkmenistan), of the late 3rd millennium BC and early 2nd. It is thought that the Parthians, whose original homeland lay in Central Asia, brought this innovation with them when they moved into western Asia.

In eastern Arabia, fortresses built of stone that have round corner towers are known at al-Dur (1st century AD), at Qal'at al-Bahrain (?2nd century AD) and at Jumayra (5th or 6th century AD). These buildings vary greatly in size. For example the fortress at al-Dur is only 20 m on a side, with walls 0.7 m thick and towers 4 m in diameter at each corner, whereas the much more massive fortress in Bahrain measures 52.5 m on a side. Internally the Bahrain fortress is divided into a complex of rooms around a central courtyard, generally comparable in plan to the fortress at Qaryat al-Faw.

BIBLIOGRAPHY

A. R. al-Ansary: *Qaryat al-Fau: A Portrait of Pre-Islamic Civilisation in Saudi Arabia* (London, 1982)

P.-A. Beaulieu: *The Reign of Nabonidus, King of Babylon, 556–539 BC* (New Haven and London, 1989)

D. T. Potts: *The Arabian Gulf in Antiquity*, 2 vols (Oxford, 1990)

J.-F. Breton: *Les Fortifications d'Arabie méridionale du 7e au 1er siècles avant notre ère* (Mainz, 1993)

5. RELIGIOUS. Unlike Mesopotamia, where a tradition in temple plan, construction techniques and decoration can be followed over the course of nearly 5000 years, pre-Islamic Arabia is characterized by regional diversity and heterogeneity through time.

(i) Eastern Arabia. The earliest excavated religious monument in the Arabian peninsula is the Barbar Temple in Bahrain (see fig. 3). Constructed *c.* 2200 BC and still in use as late as *c.* 1700 BC, the Barbar Temple originally consisted of a parallelogram-shaped platform (23/25×15/17 m) capped by a small, rectangular shrine, which was, early in the 2nd millennium BC, surrounded by an oval retaining wall enclosing an area *c.* 70×58 m. The temple was sited on a low hill close to a natural spring, and the spring was eventually incorporated into the temple complex by means of a perimeter wall and steps of well-cut, limestone ashlars. Temple ovals are rare in the Near East, the most famous examples being the Oval Temple at Khafajeh (north-east of Baghdad; *see* DIYALA REGION) and the oval precinct wall at Tell al-Ubaid in southern Iraq, both of which date to the Early Dynastic period (*c.* 2900–*c.* 2340 BC).

A different type of temple excavated at Sar, also in Bahrain, dates to *c.* 2000–*c.* 1700 BC. In plan, the dry-stone building is roughly rectangular (16.50×9.25/6.15 m), with one end wider than the other. Internal features include a square altar in the centre, flanked by one square and one circular column support, a podium in the north-east corner, a trough along the north wall and a second altar along the south wall. Another temple in Bahrain of the same period, at Diraz, shows elements of a similar plan.

The existence of any later 2nd-millennium BC temples in Arabia has not been established, although a number of stone vessel fragments from Faylaka bearing incised, votive inscriptions name the temples to which they had been dedicated. It is not until the Iron Age that the next examples appear. Once again Bahrain provides an example in the form of the western half of the palatial building complex at Qal'at al-Bahrain (*see* §3 above). This building, made of cut limestone ashlars, consists of an entrance leading to an area for performing ablutions, with basins for washing. Beyond this is a larger, roughly square room, with two square column bases, and to the east of this is a smaller chamber with an altar in the centre.

Faylaka contained a number of temples during the Achaemenid Persian period (538–331 BC), at least one of which, sacred to Artemis or her Arabian equivalent, is mentioned by Arrian (*Campaigns of Alexander* VII.xx.2–3). Unfortunately the excavation of what is probably a contemporary shrine at Tell Khazna, near the centre of the island, produced no coherent plan.

Within the fortified enclosure on Faylaka (*see* §4 above) were two temples. Temple A was a small, rectangular building (11.5×7.5 m) with a doorway framed by two columns *in antis*. While the columns show a mixture of Greek and Achaemenid elements, which could be called Ionic-Achaemenid, other elements, such as the acroteria, cornices and gables, are more Greek in appearance. The smaller Temple B, which shows a similar plan to that of A but had Doric column capitals, measured just over 7 m on each side. A small, two-roomed shrine consisting of a naos and pronaos, which was probably sacred to Artemis (as indicated by traces of a dedication in paint on an altar

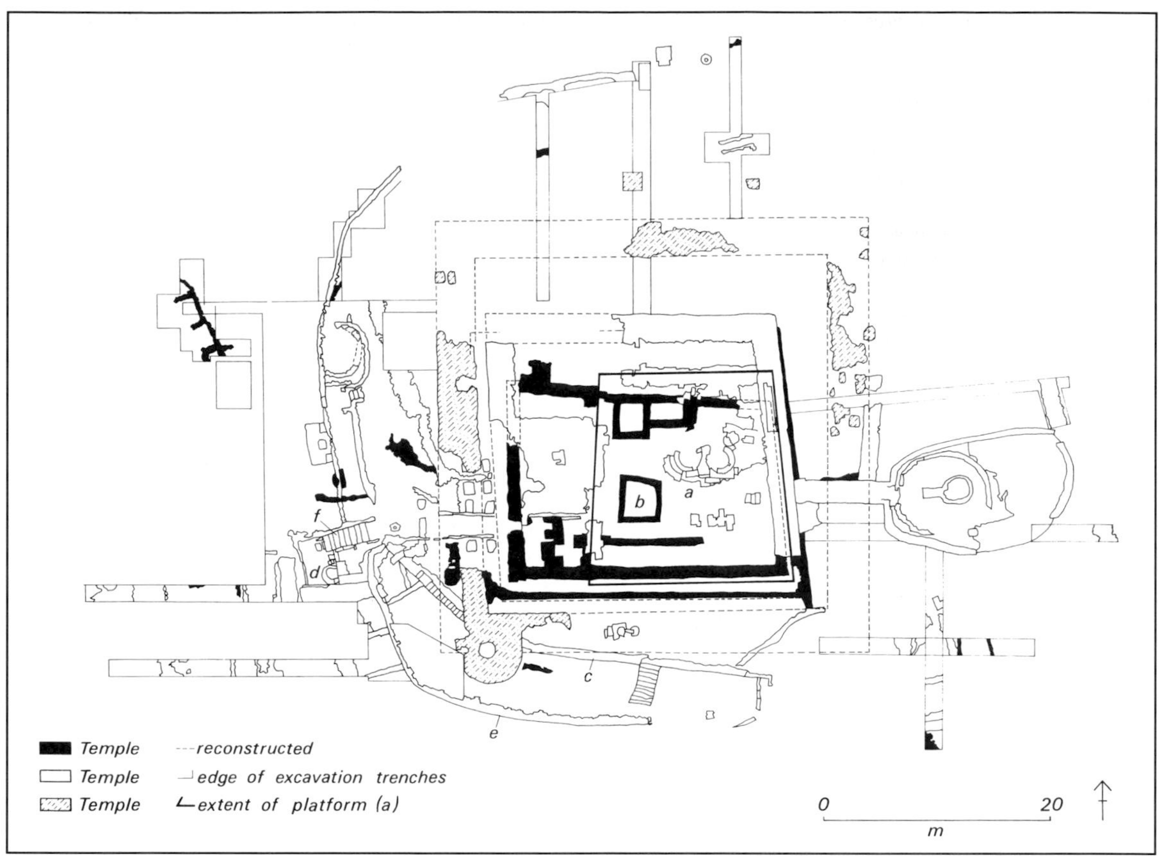

3. Barbar Temple, Bahrain, *c.* 2200–*c.* 1700 BC, plan: (a) platform; (b) shrine; (c) retaining wall; (d) spring; (e) perimeter wall; (f) steps

found there), was excavated near the present shoreline to the south-east of the Hellenistic enclosure.

In 1987 excavations at al-Dur brought to light an almost square (8.3×8.0 m) building made of beach-rock, which stood to a height of over 2 m. The exterior was coated with a thick façade of white gypsum plaster which had been artfully scraped and incised in imitation of marginally drafted and pecked stone masonry. A running, vertical swastika frieze ran up either side of the main, south entrance, which was flanked by two socles. These may have originally supported a pair of statues of eagles (*see* §III, 1(ii) below). Because of an inscribed incense burner or basin found resting on one of three altars just outside it, the building is identifiable as a temple to the pan-Arabian solar deity Shamash. The altars took the form of truncated pyramids. The interior of the shrine, which had no floor, was empty except for a massive block of limestone found near the centre of the room. This had a circular depression on one side. The al-Dur temple dates to the 1st century AD.

The existence of numerous Nestorian Christian communities throughout eastern Arabia is well documented in written sources, and the existence to this day of certain toponyms, such as *Dayr* or *Darin* in Bahrain and eastern Saudi Arabia, points to the presence there at one time of cloisters or monasteries (Aramaic *dayr*). The remains of a small church have been found at Jabal Barri (nr Jubayl) in eastern Saudi Arabia; the discovery at Thaj of a large ashlar with several incised crosses points to the existence of a Christian community there as well.

Excavations at al-Qusur, on Faylaka, revealed the plan of a Christian church which may date to the late 5th century AD or early 6th. The building measured 35×19 m and has a tripartite plan, comprising a narthex (15.6×2.6 m) leading to a central nave (19.0×5.6 m) flanked by two galleries (19.0×3.4–5.0 m; 17.0×3.4 m). A cruciform chapel (9.0×3.4 m) was located at the east end of the building. Two large stucco panels with crosses in the centre (*see* §IV, 9 below) confirm the Christian nature of the building, which, in its tripartite layout, shows striking parallels to much earlier Mesopotamian religious architecture.

D. T. POTTS

(ii) South Arabia. According to Pliny (*Natural History* VI.xxxii.154–6), there were 60 temples at Shabwa, and it is known that there were at least that many at Ma'rib. However, it may be that these figures include other religious structures, such as monumental altars. Three of the oldest temples in South Arabia lie in the area of the ancient kingdom of Saba': the temple of the moon god Almaqah at Masajid south-west of Ma'rib, the temple of the same god at Sirwah—both built by the priest-king Yada'il Dharih in the 8th century BC—and the temple of Wadd Dhu Masmaʿ in Wadi Qututa, between Ma'rib and Sirwah.

Typologically these represent the classical Sabaean ground-plan: an enclosed rectangular structure divided into a three-chambered cella on the far side of an open courtyard. The courtyard was surrounded by a U-shaped pattern of monolith supports, which formed a covered gallery. The entrance lay on the narrow side, aligned with the central axis of the building and usually preceded by a gateway. This plan survived relatively unchanged for some time. It is also found in areas that formed part of the Minaean kingdom, as in the temple of ʿAthtar (god of the planet Venus) at Maʿin, probably built at the end of the 5th century BC, as well as in the temple of Huqqa, just north of Sanʿa, which dates to the 1st century BC. A variant of this plan seems to be represented by the temple of Almaqah at Bar'an near Ma'rib, also known as ʿArsh Bilqis (Throne of Bilqis). The apparently atypical ground-plans seen at the Awwam Temple (also known as Mahram Bilqis) near Ma'rib and at Sirwah are examples of temenos walls not temple walls; the former is ovoid, the latter rectangular with an apsidal end wall.

Another type of temple has been found only in the Minaean area, for example at Maʿin. The basic plan consists of a rectangular building with six or eight supports spread evenly over the floor surface. A variant was made by increasing the number of crossbeams to make a hypostyle structure, as seen, for example, in the fragmentary remains of a temple at Baraqish. A different type of temple structure exists at al-Bayda (anc. Nashq), also near Maʿin. The temple is roughly square in plan, with a symmetrical entrance and gateway. Here the interior space is not divided at all and it was probably unroofed. A conspicuous feature of this building, otherwise unknown in South Arabia, is the façade, which is decorated with an expressively architectonic high relief.

The masonry of South Arabian temples consists predominantly of carefully dressed limestone ashlars. At Almaqah-Masajid and Wadd Dhu Masmaʿ the roof supports, the roofing itself and the face of the cella are made of limestone, while the circuit walls consist of dry-stone slabs of gneiss. As a rule, roof supports are monoliths, cut as square or subrectangular pillars. One form has the same cross-section all the way up; another is conical, tapering downwards. The pillars either have no capitals at all or are provided with so-called denticulated capitals. Hexagonal pillars probably appeared for the first time in the early centuries of the Christian era; in the later pre-Islamic period octagonal pillars began to be used as well as columns with surface channelling and, less commonly, with fluted channelling. Late period capitals were varied in form, though mostly round.

The masonry blocks of the early and classical periods have both smoothly worked, drafted surfaces and roughened, pecked centre panels to give a decorative effect. The entablatures contain denticulated friezes, occasionally doubled one above the other, and animal friezes (*see* §III, 1(i)(c) below). The most common motif was a stylized row of ibex heads. The ceilings above the roof supports had simple coffering. The configuration of ancient South Arabian architecture was generally developed from an abstract language of geometrical forms to which everything else was subordinated. In the later period, under the influence of Hellenistic and Roman art, naturalistic representations and vegetal forms appeared.

BIBLIOGRAPHY

A. Grohmann: *Arabien* (Munich, 1963)

G. Bibby: *Looking for Dilmun: The Search for a Lost Civilization* (London, 1970/*R* 1984)

H. H. Andersen: 'The Barbar Temple: Stratigraphy, Architecture and Interpretation', *Bahrain through the Ages: The Archaeology*, ed. H. A. al-Khalifa and M. Rice (London, 1986), pp. 166–77

P. Lombard: 'Iron Age Dilmun: A Reconsideration of City IV at Qalʿat al-Bahrain', *Bahrain through the Ages: The Archaeology*, ed. H. A. al-Khalifa and M. Rice (London, 1986), pp. 225–32

J. Schmidt: 'Ancient South Arabian Sacred Buildings', *Yemen: 3000 Years of Art and Civilisation in Arabia Felix*, ed. W. Daum (Innsbruck, 1987), pp. 78–98

R. Boucharlat and others: 'The European Archaeological Expedition to ed-Dur, Umm al-Qaiwayn (UAE): An Interim Report on the 1987 and 1988 Seasons', *Mesopotamia*, xxiv (1989), pp. 5–72

K. Jeppesen: *The Sacred Enclosure in the Early Hellenistic Period*, Ikaros: The Hellenistic Settlements, iii (Århus, 1989)

D. T. Potts: *The Arabian Gulf in Antiquity*, i (Oxford, 1990)

V. Bernard, O. Callot and J.-F. Salles: 'L'Eglise d'al-Qousour Failaka, Etat de Koweit', *Arab. Archaeol. & Epig.*, ii/3 (1991), pp. 145–81

R. R. Killick and others: 'London–Bahrain Archaeological Expedition: 1990 Excavations at Saar', *Arab. Archaeol. & Epig.*, ii/2 (1991), pp. 107–37

E. Haerinck, C. Metdepenninghen and K. G. Stevens: 'Excavations at ed-Dur (Umm al-Qaiwain, UAE): Preliminary Report on the Third Belgian Season (1989)', *Arab. Archaeol. & Epig.*, iii/1 (1992), pp. 44–60

J. SCHMIDT

III. Sculpture.

This section discusses reliefs as well as free-standing sculpture; for rock art *see* §IV, 6 below.

1. Stone. 2. Bronze. 3. Terracotta.

1. STONE. Although relief-carving was widespread in the peninsula, examples of free-standing stone sculpture are few and widely dispersed in space and time. Carved stone reliefs occurred on graves, funerary stelae and buildings; most extant examples are from South Arabia.

(i) Relief. (ii) Free-standing.

(i) Relief.

(a) Oman peninsula. The earliest examples of relief-carving in Arabia are those found on two Umm al-Nar graves in Abu Dhabi (*see* §II, 2(i) above) dating to *c.* 2500 BC. The exterior of these circular, monumental collective tombs with their finely masoned, limestone ashlar block cladding provided an ideal surface for relief decoration. Nevertheless, the occurrence of low reliefs on Umm al-Nar graves appears to be the exception rather than the rule and seems only to have occurred early in the Umm al-Nar period (*c.* 2500–*c.* 2000 BC).

The first reliefs were discovered in 1960–61 during the excavation of Cairn II on Umm al-Nar Island opposite Abu Dhabi town. This grave (diam. 12 m) was originally constructed of nearly 400 ashlar blocks, only five of which bore relief decoration. One of them (900×400×350 mm) shows a dromedary camel and an Arabian oryx. A second (780×430×300 mm) shows a short-horned bull with a perfectly straight back and tail running perpendicular to it. A third block (670×490×450 mm) has a single dromedary, notably more stylized than that found on the first stone. The fourth relief (310×380×270 mm) was decorated with a form composed of a semicircle on top of an elongated rectangle with a slightly narrowing 'waist'. This has been interpreted as an idol and may represent a stylized human figure. The fifth relief, a deeply grooved, semi-cylindrical stone, which has been interpreted as a gutter stone but may have been part of a broken offering table (resembling similar objects in South Arabia), is decorated with a meandering snake on each side carved in high relief.

The second group of reliefs was found on a large (diam. 12 m) grave excavated by the Danish team at Hili (1964–8) in what is today a suburb of al-ʿAyn, in the interior of Abu Dhabi. Three of the four reliefs found here were situated on the north side of the tomb around a semi-oval, porthole-like entrance which stood *c.* 0.5 m above ground-level. Closest to the ground, just beneath the northern entrance, was a contest scene consisting of two diametrically opposed quadrupeds with long, curving tails above their backs (? lions, wild cats), attacking a long-horned caprid (? gazelle). Above and to the left of the doorway was a male riding a donkey, accompanied by a second male holding a spear or staff in one hand and a sword or club in the other. Above and to the right of the doorway was a depiction of a standing couple having sexual intercourse. The south side of the tomb was decorated with a single, highly symmetrical scene of two men holding hands, flanked by two oryx.

All the Umm al-Nar period reliefs are characterized by their simplicity. While the shapes are generally realistic enough to permit identification, no attempt has been made to represent the physical features of either animals or humans in any detail. Thus the figures appear as if drawn in outline without the addition of distinguishing marks on them, giving them an almost modern quality of abstraction.

4. Stone relief-carving, sandstone, 370×370 mm, from Qasr al-Hamra, Tayma', Saudi Arabia, mid-6th century BC (Riyadh, Museum of Archaeology and Ethnography)

Both groups of reliefs are now displayed in the al-ʿAyn Museum, Abu Dhabi.

(b) North-western Arabia. The earliest examples of relief-carving in this region come from the oasis town of Tayma' (bibl. Tema), north-east of Mada'in Salih, where Nabonidus (*reg* 555–539 BC), last king of the Neo-Babylonian dynasty, resided for ten years. Several important reliefs have survived from this period and, not surprisingly, they show a blend of iconographic elements.

The well-known Tayma' Stone or stele, which Charles Huber and Julius Euting found at Tayma' in 1884 (0.43×1.10×0.12 m; Paris, Louvre), has two panels of low relief on one of the narrow sides, just above an Aramaic inscription. The larger, upper relief panel shows a tall, standing, bearded figure, facing right, who holds a staff or sceptre in his left hand. He wears a tiara and is clothed in a long, wrapped robe. Above him is a winged sun-disc. His identity is not known: it has been suggested by some scholars that he is a deity, while on analogy with several stelae of Nabonidus from Harran, in south-east Turkey, others suggest that this is Nabonidus himself engaged in an act of prayer. The lower, smaller panel depicts a bearded priest, similarly clothed, with raised hands, standing to the side of an altar topped by a bucranium (bull's head). Both figures look decidedly Assyro-Babylonian. The bucranium is a distinctly South Arabian device, while the winged sun-disc is an emblem used widely in the Ancient Near East, from Egypt, the Hittite empire (Anatolia) and the kingdom of Mitanni (northern Mesopotamia) to Assyria, Babylonia and the Achaemenid empire (e.g. *see* MESOPOTAMIA, §I, 3(ii)).

In 1979 excavations at Tayma' in a complex known as Qasr al-Hamra uncovered a stone cube (each side 370 mm), two sides of which were decorated with relief (Riyadh, Mus. Archaeol. & Ethnog.). Iconographically the cube evinces many links with the Tayma' Stone. One (see fig. 4) depicts a priest standing to the side of a stepped altar on which a bucranium rests, clearly reminiscent of the Tayma' Stone. There are, however, many more details visible in this scene, including a winged, specifically Egyptianizing sun-disc above the priest's head; a sun-disc between the bull's horns, which suggests that the bucranium is meant to be understood as an Egyptian Apis bull; a second altar or incense burner to the right of the central altar; and a crescent moon and eight-pointed star, symbols of the Babylonian lunar deity Sin and Ishtar, the goddess of the planet Venus, respectively, above the second altar. The opposite side of the cube shows a priest holding a bowl up to the mouth of a striding Apis bull. Above the bull's back is a large, winged sun-disc, topped by the star symbol of Ishtar.

A second, more fragmentary piece of relief (Paris, Louvre) discovered by Huber and Euting at Tayma' is technically similar to the Tayma' Stone. It shows the legs of a man in a short kilt or skirt, standing above a stylized date palm. The palm is flanked by two large double-handled vessels. To the right is a grapevine with five bunches of hanging grapes; to the left is an altar or offering table. Generally, this piece shows Assyrianizing tendencies, although the crudeness of the workmanship suggests that it was locally made, perhaps influenced by provincial Assyrian art styles then prevalent in Syria.

Several centuries after the Tayma' reliefs, Minaean colonists at Dedan (in al-ʿUla oasis) buried their dead in rock-cut tombs often adorned on the outside with stylized lions or wild cats. The figures (900×300 mm) are carved in low relief (*c.* 100 mm). They are depicted frontally, with a criss-cross pattern of incised lines beneath the eyes which runs across the animals' faces, and a series of ten registers of vertically incised layers of hair. The heads are round, with pointed, triangular ears and stylized, circular eyes. The forelegs are stocky and show no attempt at realism.

During the course of several centuries there developed a tradition in north-western Arabia of decorating grave stelae in low relief. These rectangular stelae, examples of which are known from Mada'in Salih, Tayma' (Amman, Jordan Archaeol. Mus.) and many sites in Jordan (Riyadh, Mus. Archaeol. & Ethnog.), show an abstract face consisting of a pronounced, rectangular nose, often linked to two curving eyebrows, and either square or almond-shaped eyes cut in fairly high relief. Accompanying inscriptions sometimes identify this face as a particular deity, such as the goddess al-ʿUzza or the god Helal. In South Arabia comparable stelae are known on which the face has been incised rather than carved in relief, along with the name of a dedicant rather than that of a deity.

(c) South Arabia. Relief-carving was used extensively in South Arabia, both in the decoration of public buildings and on funerary stelae. Generally, all the reliefs are characterized by a simplicity of execution that stands in stark contrast to the sophistication of the architectural monuments of South Arabian cultures. In their crude representation of the human form, the rendition of dress and the treatment of animal anatomy, they resemble Early Christian or early medieval art and lack the accomplishment of contemporary Hellenistic or Roman sculptural and relief carving. Architectural decoration falls broadly into two groups, zoomorphic and floral. Zoomorphic elements used extensively include both horizontal and vertical rows of couchant ibexes; horizontal rows of stylized, frontally depicted ibex or gazelle *protomes* (busts); and bucrania. Vertical panels and architraves decorated with intertwining grapevine tendrils and symmetrically opposed bunches of grapes are common, and the acanthus leaf design was sometimes used on column capitals. Floral and zoomorphic elements were also combined, for example in repeated scenes of rearing ibexes flanking a date palm, or winged griffins flanking a tree.

Columns were sometimes decorated with extensive low relief. An example from the Temple of ʿAthtar at Maʿin, probably from the 5th century BC, has eight registers covering one face (0.60×1.25×0.40 m). Proceeding downwards these comprise: a row of seven open circles; a row of five ibexes facing left; a zigzagging chevron pattern; a row of six ibexes facing right; the chevron pattern repeated; a broad band of stylized ?trees, which appear like spearheads on shafts, over a crosshatched background; a row of nine couchant oryx in antithetical pairs; and nine pairs of intertwined snakes. Similar decoration has been found on the column of a gateway at al-Haẓm, west of Maʿin, which has, in addition, two female dancers standing beneath a double row of suspended amphorae.

As in north-western Arabia, relief-carving in South Arabia was frequently added to funerary stelae. Many fine examples made of marble or alabaster have survived (e.g. London, BM; Paris, Louvre; Sanʿa, Yemen N. Mus.). One example in the Louvre (550×290 mm, 2nd century AD) bears a Sabaean inscription at the top identifying it as the grave stele of ʿIdjl, son of Saʿdlat. Beneath the inscription is a recessed panel on which a banquet scene is carved. On the left a musician holds a lute; the largest figure, seated right (presumably the deceased ʿIdjl), holds a cup in his right hand, which he takes from a table attended by a smaller figure, perhaps a servant. A band of vine tendrils and grapes separates this scene from the lower panel, in which a male figure mounted on horseback wields a spear and pursues a camel. Many reliefs of this type show the deceased riding a camel. A second stele in the Louvre, unfortunately very fragmentary, once bore at least three panels of decoration. The main panel shows a male figure with a whip in one hand driving a team of oxen. Beneath the ground-line are three male figures preserved only from the chest up. These are presumably 'Yalmad Qashafriqan, Hassat and Khalkarib', the three individuals named in an inscription above the oxen scene.

The stele of Saʿad-Awwam (photographed in Rome in the early 1870s, known from lithograph pubd 1876; untraced) is divided into four registers. The top register shows the deceased holding a staff and walking, accompanied by a smaller, servile figure. The second register depicts the deceased riding a camel, accompanied by his servant who rides behind him. The third shows the deceased with his arms around the horns of a galloping bull, his torso hanging off the side of the animal. He is accompanied by two figures, one in front of and one behind the bull. The fourth register shows Saʿad riding a horse, again accompanied by his servant. A famous Sabaean stele (1st century BC–1st century AD; London, BM) shows, in the upper register, a woman seated under a portico supported by columns. She plays a lyre and is flanked by two smaller, servile figures. In the lower register the deceased is on her deathbed, accompanied by a secondary figure. A Qatabanian relief (Bombay, Prince of Wales Mus.) shows the upper body of a woman in high relief, with two armbands above the elbow on each arm. Her hair is in braids, her right hand is raised and she holds a bird in her left hand.

One of the most difficult reliefs to interpret is that known as the Hombrechtikon Plaque, acquired in Yemen in 1913 and built into a house at Hombrechtikon, Zurich (pubd in *Iraq*, xvi, 1954; see fig. 5). This rectangular piece of alabaster is divided into three fields. The upper field shows, on the left, two South Arabian letters; on the right, a South Arabian monogram. If the two letters are the beginning of a proper name then the plaque was clearly part of a larger decorative programme, without which the figural elements below it cannot properly be understood. Beneath the letters is a corrugated band of four raised ridges. Below this, carved in deep relief, is an architectural frieze consisting of three archways supported by four Corinthian columns. Under each arch is a figure: a lion rampant to the left; a nude male in the centre; a mostly

5. Stone relief carving known as the Hombrechtikon Plaque, alabaster, 400×250×40 mm, ?2nd–4th centuries AD (Switzerland, private collection)

nude female wearing a skirt on the right. The areas immediately beneath each arch are decorated with a male's head in profile facing left (left); a bucranium (centre); a female head portrayed frontally (right). The lion and nude figure may be related to the myth of Herakles and the Nemean lion; the female possibly represents a local deity; the bucranium could be a symbol of the male solar god Almaqah. Clearly, without the adjacent panels, no coherent understanding of this fascinating piece is possible. A date somewhere between the 2nd and the 4th century AD has been suggested.

Portable objects found in sanctuaries are often decorated with relief-carving. Simple solar and lunar symbols, such as a plain disc and a crescent, were sometimes carved on the faces of incense burners (e.g. Paris, Louvre), while bucrania, perhaps symbolizing the god Almaqah, were frequently employed as a terminus on one end of an offering table. Small, rectangular, alabaster plaques with the name of a dedicant in the lower half, often show in the upper half a human face carved in high relief. This is usually assumed to represent the dedicant. In many cases the eyes are hollow and were presumably filled with another material, such as bitumen, shell or a hardstone.

(d) North-eastern Arabia. Early in the 20th century a number of funerary reliefs were discovered at Darin, on Tarut Island, off the east coast of Saudi Arabia. Similar pieces were later found in Bahrain (Manama, Bahrain N. Mus.). These are generally small, rectangular objects (*c.* 210–240×240–410×90–110 mm) with a rounded upper surface. They show a human figure, portrayed frontally, framed by an arch supported by two columns. As in the Qatabanian relief (*see* §(c) above), the figure holds his or her right hand up, palm forward. The left hand, however, is generally shown holding the figure's garment, which is usually a flowing, toga-like tunic. Technically these are quite crude. They are probably pre-Christian and may be contemporary with Parthian, Hatran (*see* HATRA, §2) or Palmyrene (*see* PALMYRA, §2) statuary. It is likely that the hand gesture denoted blessing and that the stelae were funerary in nature.

BIBLIOGRAPHY

A. Grohmann: *Arabien* (Munich, 1963)
R. L. Cleveland: *An Ancient South Arabian Necropolis: Objects from the Second Campaign (1951) in the Timna' Cemetery* (Baltimore, 1965)
B. Doe: *Southern Arabia* (London, 1971)
S. Dalley: 'The God Salmu and the Winged Disk', *Iraq*, xxxxviii (1986), pp. 85–101
S. Y. Bersina: 'In the Ways of Sarapis, Isis and Harpokrates', *Ancient and Mediaeval Monuments of Civilization of Southern Arabia* (Moscow, 1988), pp. 92–113
P.-A. Beaulieu: *The Reign of Nabonidus, King of Babylon, 556–539 BC* (New Haven and London, 1989)
P. Lombard and M. Kervran, eds: *A Selection of Pre-Islamic Antiquities*, Bahrain National Museum Archaeological Collections, i (Manama, 1989), pp. 130–31
D. T. Potts: *The Arabian Gulf in Antiquity*, ii (Oxford, 1990)
K. Frifelt: *Third Millennium Graves*, The Island of Umm an-Nar, i (Århus, 1991)
D. T. Potts: 'Tayma and the Assyrian Empire', *Arab. Archaeol. & Epig.*, ii/1 (1991), pp. 10–23

D. T. POTTS

(ii) Free-standing. The earliest example of free-standing sculpture found in Arabia is a limestone statue of a nude male from al-Rufaya on Tarut Island (see fig. 6). Both the conception and execution of this figure were strongly influenced by Early Dynastic Sumerian sculpture and it probably dates to *c.* 2500 BC. The standing figure is unclothed except for three incised striations at his waist which recall the triple-belt worn by the cast copper figure of a male on an offering stand from Khafajeh in the Diyala region of Mesopotamia (U. Chicago, IL, Orient. Inst. Mus.). His arms are held close to his sides and are bent at the elbows; his hands are crossed in front of his chest in a typically Mesopotamian gesture of devotion. The head is bald and the eyebrows are pronounced. A row of diagonal striations running off the collar-bone may be meant to suggest a collar or ribbon worn around the neck. The penis is clearly shown, and the feet of the statue are missing. Unfortunately, the statue does not come from controlled excavations (see Potts, 1989).

An early 20th-century survey at Dedan (in al-'Ula oasis; capital of the Lihyanites in the late 1st millennium BC) found several over life-size, fragmentary limestone statues (Riyadh, Mus. Archaeol. & Ethnog.). The largest of these (h. 2.26 m), broken off at the knees, depicts a beardless male, nude from the waist up, who wears a short belted kilt or skirt. His long hair is bound in the Egyptian style with a band. The upper body is well modelled, and the statue, like all surviving Lihyanite sculpture, shows the influence of Ptolemaic Egyptian types (*c.* 332–30 BC) in the representation of the human form. Fragments of legs,

6. Stone statue of a nude male, limestone, h. 940 mm, from al-Rufaya, Tarut Island, Saudi Arabia, *c.* 2500 BC (Riyadh, King Saud University, Archaeology Department)

as well as a head broken off at the neck, have also been found at Dedan (Al-Ula Mus.). The frequent references to sculptors and statues in the Lihyanite inscriptions from Dedan suggest that these pieces were manufactured locally. Moreover, the fact that the Lihyanite sculptors mentioned in these texts have Arab names indicates that, while Egyptian influence is clear, a local school of sculpture existed in north-western Arabia during the late 1st millennium BC.

Few sculptures have survived from Faylaka, one of the most important Hellenistic sites in eastern Arabia. One piece (Kuwait City, N. Mus.), which is without parallel in the peninsula, is a limestone dolphin (350×680 mm). Its snout is blunt and porcine when viewed from the front; the eyes are shown as two incised circles, and two small circular depressions mark the air holes. The front flippers are clearly indicated; the rear portion was broken off in antiquity. Assuming this to be the work of a Greek craftsman, it is hardly one of great accomplishment. However, it clearly does not represent *Delphinus delphis*, the Mediterranean dolphin which would have been familiar to a Greek artist, but is rather *Tursiops aduncttus*, the bottle-nosed dolphin which inhabits the waters of the Persian Gulf. In view of this, the depiction must be considered a success, if not an aesthetic triumph.

Excavations in Area F at al Dur in the UAE brought to light two headless, limestone statues of eagles (h. *c.* 450 mm; Umm al-Qaywayn, Ruler's Office). They may originally have stood in front of the temple in Area M (*see* §II, 5(i) above), where two socles were found on either side of the main, southerly entrance. The eagles are portrayed facing front. Each is hewn out of a single piece of rock and stands upon a flat plinth. Stylistically, however, they are different. One is realistically portrayed, with incised markings to indicate the feathers. The other is more stylized: the feathers are crosshatched and appear more like a cloak; the legs are incised so as to suggest greaves, and the eagle stands above a bucranium. The bucranium may be a link with South Arabian iconography and recalls a stamp seal from Zafar, the Himyarite capital (*fl* 2nd century BC–4th century AD), on which an eagle stands above a bucranium. The eagle in pre-Islamic Arabia was widely identified with the deity Nasr; the bucranium may represent the South Arabian deity Almaqah. The only other free-standing eagles that are known in Ancient Near Eastern sculpture come from Hatra in northern Iraq (*fl* 2nd century BC–3rd century AD). There is little stylistic resemblance, however, between these and the al-Dur statues.

Free-standing South Arabian sculpture in the round of greatly varying quality has survived from antiquity, comprising works by both common and master craftsmen. Materials ranging from the finest alabaster to the coarsest limestone were employed. Many examples of fine alabaster heads, ending at the base of the neck, are known. These may have been dedicated in temples as votive statues or in memory of a deceased person. Numerous pieces were discovered in the funerary building at Timnaʿ (e.g. Munich, Staatl. Mus. Vlkerknd.). Despite the obvious differences in the quality of execution, all are distinguished by their abstract, symmetrical frontality, angular features and mask-like quality. The eyes were either inlaid with, for example, bitumen, shell or hardstone, or were crudely incised, with only the pupils being inlaid. In some cases the busts were mounted on inscribed socles; occasionally the top of the head was cut off, perhaps so that the bust would fit into an existing niche. Generally, the heads are small, ranging between *c.* 100 and *c.* 250 mm in height.

Related to this group is a class of alabaster statues of both males and females shown either standing or sitting on a plain socle (e.g. Aden, N. Mus. Ant.). In all cases the heads are rendered as above. The typical posture of these stylized statues is one of a frontally facing figure with arms bent at the elbows, forearms projecting forward and fists clenched. The body is abstract, monolithic and stocky; the only individual features indicated, apart from those of the face, are the fingers, toes and hair. Some of the standing figures show the line of a garment below the knees, and the hands are occasionally perforated, suggesting that they once held something thin and tubular. While most of the figures are depicted barefoot, some wear sandals. In some cases the front of the socle on which the figure stands bears an inscription.

Coarse limestone was used to produce a large class of so-called *Pfeilerbeinestatuen* ('pillar-leg statues'): seated figures with their arms bent at the elbows, and their forearms resting on their thighs (e.g. Cambridge, MA, Harvard U., Peabody Mus.). These are normally 200–250 mm tall and of poor artistic quality, appearing almost to have been mass-produced. They are thought to represent ancestors; the stiffness of their seated posture may reflect Egyptian influence. At the same time, more realistic sculpture is also attested in South Arabia. One particularly fine example is the statue of Yaduq'il Fari' Sarah'at, King of Awsan (h. 780 mm; Aden, N. Mus. Ant.), which probably dates to the last centuries BC or first centuries AD. Yaduq'il wears a long, draped garment not unlike a toga. He has long hair, hanging down to his shoulders and parted in the middle. His arms, broken off at the elbow, were bent, with the forearms pointing forward. His face is realistically portrayed, and the effect is that of a statue of an individual, even if his posture is identical to that of the full-body, standing alabaster statues described above. An alabaster torso of a female figure from Timnaʿ (Falls Church, VA, Amer. Found. Stud. Man; on dep. Washington, DC, Sackler Gal.) wears a tunic fastened in a knot across the chest, exposing the breasts; this style has been identified as the 'knot of Isis'. This undoubtedly local product was probably fashioned after a late Egyptian representation of the ancient Egyptian goddess Isis who, in the Hellenistic period, became identified as the mate of Sarapis, a deity widely represented in Hellenistic iconography. The Timnaʿ Isis is unlikely to pre-date the mid-2nd century BC.

BIBLIOGRAPHY

W. Caskel: *Lihyan und lihyanisch* (Cologne, 1954)

A. Grohmann: *Arabien* (Munich, 1963)

R. L. Cleveland: *An Ancient South Arabian Necropolis: Objects from the Second Campaign (1951) in the Timna' Cemetery* (Baltimore, 1965)

B. Doe: *Southern Arabia* (London, 1971)

R. Boucharlat: 'Documents arabes provenant des sites "hellénistiques" de la péninsule d'Oman', *L'Arabie préislamique et son environnement historique et culturel: Actes du colloque de Strasbourg: Strasbourg, 1987*, pp. 109–26

J. -F. Breton: 'L'Orient gréco-romain et le Hadhramawt', *L'Arabie préislamique et son environnement historique et culturel: Actes du colloque de Strasbourg: Strasbourg, 1987*, pp. 173–85

S. Y. Bersina: 'In the Ways of Sarapis, Isis and Harpokrates', *Ancient and Mediaeval Monuments of Civilization of Southern Arabia* (Moscow, 1988), pp. 92–113

J. -F. Breton: 'Arabie méridionale et Orient hellénisé', *L'Arabie et ses mers bordières* (Lyons, 1988), pp. 191–9

D. T. Potts: *Miscellanea Hasaitica* (Copenhagen, 1989)

J. Gachet and J. -F. Salles: 'Iconographie et cultes à Failaka, Koweit', *Mesopotamia*, xxv (1990), pp. 193–215

D. T. Potts: *The Arabian Gulf in Antiquity*, 2 vols (Oxford, 1990)

PAOLO M. COSTA, D. T. POTTS

2. BRONZE. The casting of both life-size and miniature anthropomorphic and zoomorphic bronze figures was widespread throughout Arabia in pre-Islamic times but South Arabia is the only area that has as yet produced evidence of the casting of large-scale statuary in bronze.

7. Bronze statue of Maʿadkarib, h. 930 mm, from Ma'rib, Yemen, 5th–4th centuries BC (Sanʿa, Yemen National Museum)

The lost-wax technique was used, and larger statues were often assembled in sections. One of the finest examples (see fig. 7) is the statue of Maʿadkarib found in Mahram Bilqis (the Awwam Temple) at Ma'rib. An inscription on the shoulder of the statue identifies him as Maʿadkarib, but the posture and attributes are clearly those of Herakles. He is shown striding and bearded with a lion skin draped over his shoulders, the arms of the pelt crossed over his chest, its legs curving around his thighs. The origin of this imagery can be sought in Cyprus, where depictions of Herakles clothed in the pelt of the Nemean lion, symbol of victory in the greatest of his labours, first appeared in the 6th century BC. The orthography of the boustrophedon dedicatory inscription on the statue suggests a date in the 5th or 4th century BC. At this time finished examples of Greek statuary were imported into South Arabia from workshops in the eastern Mediterranean, such as a fine Archaic bronze statuette of a helmeted Greek warrior, probably manufactured *c.* 530 BC, which was found south of Shabwa (priv. col.).

By the beginning of the Christian era a marked Greco-Roman influence is detectable, particularly that of Hellenistic and Ptolemaic models. This is typified by two figures of a nude boy riding a lion (each 610×520 mm) from Timnaʿ. These were cast with their rectangular bases, each of which bears a South Arabian inscription, strongly suggesting that they were manufactured in South Arabia. The moulds used for the figures, however, are thought to have been imported from Egypt; the nearest prototypes for the Timnaʿ figures are to be found among the Ptolemaic statuary placed in the Memphis Serapeum during the reign of Ptolemy I (*reg* 305–283 BC).

Another important work from Timnaʿ is the statue of a seated female known as *Lady Barat* (h. 520 mm, ?1st century BC; Aden, N. Mus. Ant.). She has a stocky figure and wears a short-sleeved tunic, anklets, sandals and a diadem, which is triangular in section. Her arms are bent at the elbows and she holds a baton. The unusual folds of cloth around her breasts are probably an attempt to represent the 'knot of Isis' (*see also* EGYPT, ANCIENT, §IX, 3(xii)(a)); her diadem is surely an attribute of a deity or deified personage. It is striking how similar the features of Lady Barat's face, as well as her diadem, are to those found on coins bearing the portraits of Ptolemaic queens, particularly Arsinoe III (235–205 BC), mother of Ptolemy V. The deification of deceased queens under the Ptolemies would explain the use of the divine diadem. It is possible that a statue or statuette of Arsinoe/Isis, brought to South Arabia in the 2nd century BC, served as a model for Lady Barat.

Another notable sculpture of cast bronze is a large horse (1.06×1.02 m; Washington, DC, Dumbarton Oaks), which seems to have been inspired by Roman models of the 2nd or 3rd century AD. The statues of the Himyarite ruler Damar alay Yuhabirr (h. 2.37 m) and his son Tharan (both Sanʿa, Yemen N. Mus.; see fig. 8), found at Nakhlat al-Hamra in 1931 are the most impressive examples of over life-size statuary yet discovered in the region. They date to the late 3rd century AD and, according to a Greek inscription on one of the statues, were cast by a Greek metalworker named Phokas and then riveted together by a local South Arabian named Lahayʿaman. Typologically

8. Bronze statue of Tharan (detail), h. 2.38 m, from Nakhlat al-Hamra, late 3rd century AD (Sanʿa, Yemen National Museum)

these statues are akin to those of Roman emperors that stood in front of temples (*see* ROME, ANCIENT, §IV, 1(iv)(a)), although the South Arabian statues may have stood in the palace at Nakhlat al-Hamra. This type of representation goes back to a tradition begun at the time of Alexander the Great which continued throughout the Hellenistic era.

Excavations at Qaryat al-Faw in central Arabia have yielded a number of small human and animal figures, including a draped female with the upper arms shown close to the body, the forearms projecting forward from the elbow; a draped female (a goddess?) with one hand extended, palm down, as if in blessing, the other hand clenched around an opening where a sceptre, staff, trident or spear may once have stood; an ibex, several camels, a goat and a dolphin. Several small bronzes of foreign origin were also found, such as a kneeling male wearing a kilt, shown in prayer, which has Egyptianizing characteristics; it represents a type of Egyptian cult figurine typical of the Late Period (*c.* 750–*c.* 332 BC) and was undoubtedly produced in Egypt. One of the finest discoveries, a statuette of a winged Harpokrates, holds a cornucopia of grapes; his chubby figure and face framed by curls are characteristics of Eros, but he wears the double crown of Egypt and is an Egyptian product of the 1st or 2nd century AD. The finds are in the Archaeology Department, King Saud University, Riyadh.

Finally, cast bronze tablets are known from South Arabia on which, in addition to the inscriptions, friezes of relief decoration occur. These include sphinxes flanking a central plant, or Tree of Life, framed by date palms (e.g. a Sabaean tablet, 2nd–3rd century AD; London, BM). Decorative elements such as rosettes, guilloche and lotus blossoms were used to frame and divide the inscribed panels.

BIBLIOGRAPHY

A. Grohmann: *Arabien* (Munich, 1963)

G. Bibby: *Looking for Dilmun: The Search for a Lost Civilization* (London, 1970/*R* 1984)

K. Weidemann: *Könige aus dem Yemen: Zwei spätantike Bronzestatuen* (Mainz, 1983)
A. Hauptmann: *Die Entwicklung der Kupfermetallurgie vom 3. Jahrtausend bis zur Neuzeit* (Bochum, 1985)
J.-F. Breton: 'L'Orient gréco-romain et le Hadhramawt', *L'Arabie préislamique et son environnement historique et culturel: Actes du colloque de Strasbourg: Strasbourg, 1987*, pp. 173–85
S. Y. Bersina: 'In the Ways of Sarapis, Isis and Harpokrates', *Ancient and Mediaeval Monuments of Civilization of Southern Arabia* (Moscow, 1988), pp. 92–113
D. T. Potts: *The Arabian Gulf in Antiquity*, i (Oxford, 1990)

3. TERRACOTTA. Simple human figurines, dating to the early 1st millennium BC, with bent arms, hands held in front of the chest, stylized faces consisting of incised lines for eyebrows and nose, and impressions for the eyes, were found at Hajar Bin Humayd in South Arabia. Camel figurines with painted bands around the neck and other long-necked animals are also attested, although the form of the ears and head make identification of the latter uncertain. In north-eastern Arabia, female and 'Persian rider' type figurines (Kuwait City, N. Mus.) were found on Faylaka from the Neo-Babylonian or Achaemenid period (*c.* 600–*c.* 330 BC). The latter are hooded horsemen with skilfully modelled faces, which are typologically comparable to finds from sites in Mesopotamia (e.g. Seleucia-on-the-Tigris, Nippur and Babylon). The riders were generally meant to sit on modelled clay horses; more rarely, the two figures were modelled as one. The horses tend to be stylized, with curving necks, dropped heads, ears and appliqué eyes. Camel figurines were also found, though in smaller numbers.

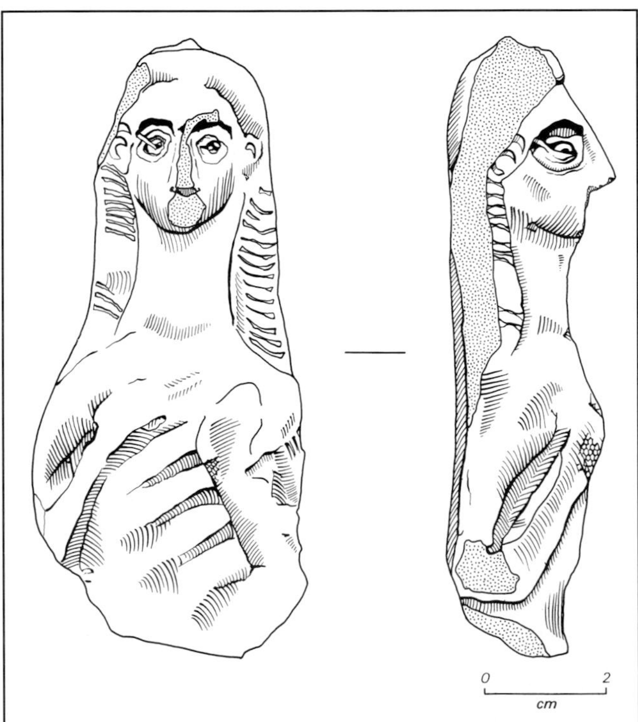

9. Terracotta figurine of nude female, (105 mm×44 mm), from al-Dur, Umm al-Qaywayn, United Arab Emirates, 1st century AD (Umm al-Qaywayn, Ruler's Office)

Faylaka has also yielded a large corpus of mould-made Hellenistic figurines, as well as fragments of moulds. One house excavated in 1958 was named the 'terracotta workshop' because it contained 14 moulds, five times as many as were found in any of the other houses excavated on Faylaka. The Danish and French excavators recovered over 400 figurine fragments, including a male head thought to be that of the young Herakles, a number of female-headed thymiateria (incense burners), Alexander portraits, draped males and females, satyrs and a Nike.

An indigenous Arabian coroplastic tradition is also known in the Hellenistic period in Bahrain and the Eastern Province of Saudi Arabia, particularly at Thaj (Riyadh, Mus. Archaeol. & Ethnog.). Here virtually identical examples of both male and female figurines have been found, although the female figurines are more numerous. The latter are crudely modelled, with a pinched head and depressions or punctations for eyes. The breasts, however, are well defined, and the arms are bent at the elbows, the hands supporting the breasts. The torso is usually large and crudely formed, and the pubic triangle is marked by incisions. Judging by the more complete examples of this type, the figures were modelled in a seated position. A pair of mould-made, nude, female figurines (1st century AD) found at al-Dur in the UAE (see fig. 9) also have arms bent at the elbows and hands cupping the breasts. The hair is long, falling to the shoulders, and is incised diagonally to provide definition. There are traces of black paint on the eyebrows and red paint around the mouths. The posture is similar to that of one of the figurines found at Hajar Bin Humayd.

Free-standing camel figurines of local manufacture, dating to the Hellenistic period and 1st century AD, are well known in north-eastern Arabia (e.g. Thaj). Technically, these approximate the locally made anthropomorphic figurines, although they are characterized by more attention to anatomical detail. Skin folds on the muzzle, for instance, are routinely shown. The camels normally stand with outstretched legs, as if they were running. Examples from al-Dur are almost certainly of north-east Arabian manufacture.

BIBLIOGRAPHY

G. W. Van Beek: *Hajar Bin Humeid: Investigations at a Pre-Islamic Site in South Arabia* (Baltimore, 1969)
H. E. Mathiesen: *The Terracotta Figurines*, Ikaros: The Hellenistic Settlements, i (Copenhagen, 1982)
J.-F. Salles: 'Tell Khazneh: Les Figurines en terre cuite', *Failaka, fouilles françaises, 1984–1985* (Lyon, 1986), pp. 143–200
J. B. Connelly: 'Votive Offerings from Hellenistic Failaka: Evidence for Herakles Cult', *L'Arabie préislamique et son environnement historique et culturel: Actes du colloque de Strasbourg: Strasbourg, 1987*, pp. 145–58
R. Boucharlat and others: 'The European Archaeological Expedition to ed-Dur, Umm al-Qaiwayn (UAE): An Interim Report on the 1987 and 1988 Seasons', *Mesopotamia*, xxiv (1989), pp. 5–72
D. T. Potts: *Miscellanea Hasaitica* (Copenhagen, 1989)
J. B. Connelly: 'The Terracotta Figurines: Greek Types and Cult', *Failaka, fouilles françaises, 1986–1988* (Lyon, 1990), pp. 209–20
D. T. Potts: *The Arabian Gulf in Antiquity*, ii (Oxford, 1990)

IV. Other arts.

1. Coins. 2. Glass. 3. Jewellery. 4. Metalwork. 5. Pottery. 6. Rock art. 7. Seals. 8. Stone vessels. 9. Stucco. 10. Wall painting.

1. COINS. Until the 1960s little was known about coinage in the Arabian peninsula outside of north-western

and south-western Arabia. The north-western region will be dealt with only cursorily as it did not produce any indigenous coinage that we know of, although it was an area in which Nabataean coins circulated. Nabataean coinage, most of which was struck in Palestine (e.g. at Petra in Jordan) rather than in Arabia proper, was not minted until the 1st century BC, originating most probably with Aretas III (*c.* 110–62 BC) who, like his successors, relied largely on Seleucid models of coinage for inspiration. Portraits of the reigning king or king and queen facing right usually decorate the obverses, while the reverses show portraits, deities (Tyche), horns-of-plenty, eagles, hands and wreaths. Legends in both Greek and Nabataean are known. The minting of autonomous Nabataean coinage ceased in AD 106 with the Roman annexation of the Nabataean kingdom and its transformation into the Roman province known as Arabia Provincia.

(i) North-eastern Arabia. The Danish (1958–63) and French (1983–90) expeditions to Faylaka and Bahrain discovered four pre-Islamic hoards, and amateur collectors in eastern Saudi Arabia have found thousands of pre-Islamic coins at such sites as Thaj, Jabal Kenzan, al-Sha'aba, 'Ayn Jawan, Jabal Barri, Dhahran and Hofuf.

Iconographically, east Arabian coinage borrowed heavily from the coinage of Alexander the Great (*reg* 336–323 BC) and his Seleucid successors. The volume and quality of Alexander's own issues were so great that they became the model for many provincial issues throughout the Classical world and the Near East (*see* GREECE, ANCIENT, §X, 2(iii)). In the silver archetype the obverse shows the head of Herakles wearing the pelt of the Nemean lion, while the reverse shows a seated Zeus, his left arm curled about a sceptre, his outstretched right hand supporting an eagle. The legend 'Alexandrou' runs vertically down the right side of the coin face, behind the sceptre. Although the model used was the Alexander tetradrachm (four-drachma piece), many smaller denominations occur in the east Arabian corpus as well. In addition to the many series that were based on this archetype, there exist others that were clearly copying Seleucid prototypes, for in place of a head of Herakles, these coins often bear a diademed, youthful portrait, resembling that of Seleukos I (*reg* 305–281 BC) or Antiochos III (*reg* 223–187 BC).

More than 50 variant series are known from this area that were based on these prototypes (principally the Alexander model). They range from faithful copies of the original to thoroughly debased, geometric abstractions with a blank obverse and a stick-figure on the reverse. Even in the most abstract cases, however, a fragment of the name of Alexander can often still be identified. The 'stages' of debasement that can be recognized do not necessarily represent a chronological sequence of minting. As is known from other parts of the world, copies of highly variable quality can be produced concurrently and may have no chronological significance.

Occasionally on some of the more faithful representations the name Shams, in South Arabian letters, appears in front of the reverse figure's knees. Shams was one version of the name given to the pan-Semitic solar deity, known in Mesopotamia as Shamash. Often a vertical or horizontal South Arabian letter *shīn*, the first letter of the name Shams, is found in front of the reverse figure's knees. In a number of cases one of three rulers' names has supplanted that of Alexander, and certain iconographic details have been altered. In one group, the name Abyatha is written in South Arabian characters, and a South Arabian *alif* appears as a monogram in front of the seated figure's legs. On these coins the seated figure no longer supports an eagle but seems to hold a thin reed between his thumb and forefinger. Coins of this type are best known from Faylaka and Jabal Kenzan, although one has been found at Thaj and several at Gordion and Mektepini in Anatolia.

A second group, which is thought because of its iconography to originate in eastern Arabia but which is only represented at Susa in south-west Iran, bears the name Harithat, 'king of Hagar', written in South Arabian characters. The name Hagar may be at the root of the Greek toponym Gerrha, via an hypothesized Aramaic form Hagara. Classical sources state that Gerrha was the wealthiest city in eastern Arabia during the Hellenistic period; it is possibly to be identified with the site of Thaj.

A third group, which differs substantially from the others, shows a seated figure on the reverse supporting a horse in his outstretched right hand, with a small date palm in front of his knees. In place of the name of Alexander there is an Aramaic legend, which, thanks to better preserved examples found at Mleiha (*see* §(ii) below), can be read 'Abiel, son of (BR) BGLN'. A large number of debased variants of this type exist, and 77 examples were found in a hoard discovered in 1970 in Bahrain (Manama, Bahrain N. Mus.), but the source of this group is probably the Oman peninsula.

Two groups fall outside the parameters described above. One group, best represented at Jabal Kenzan, has a reverse figure supporting an eagle, but instead of a date palm in front of his knees, a standing Nike is shown proffering a wreath. This usage can also be observed on a number of 2nd-century BC Seleucid issues and on an unusual issue of Alexander himself from Babylon (New York, Amer. Numi. Soc.). The second group shows, on the obverse, a frontal head framed by ringlets of hair, and an eagle and vertical South Arabian *shīn* on the reverse.

As most of the coins are surface finds, it is difficult to be precise in dating them. The evidence of the Faylaka and Bahrain hoards, however, suggests that some of the more Classical issues date to the late 3rd century BC and 2nd, while the evidence from al-Dur, in south-east Arabia, shows that coins of the more debased, geometric variety were still in circulation in the 3rd century AD or early 4th.

(ii) Oman peninsula. Most of the coins found at Mleiha (1st century BC) and al-Dur (1st century AD) are variants of the coinage of Abiel (*see* §(i) above). That they are later than the 'classical' Abiel issue found in Bahrain is likely because the legend is in many cases markedly rectilinear or 'lapidary' in appearance, a feature of the Aramaic used in later Characene coinage (1st–2nd centuries AD). Excavations at Mleiha have brought to light fragments of at least three moulds for the manufacture of this coinage, confirming its local production. There is no evidence of minting at al-Dur, however, despite the fact that several hundred examples of this group have been found there.

10. Coin with head of Herakles (obverse) and seated figure (reverse), debased silver, 16.02 g, diam. 22 mm, from Mleiha, Sharjah, United Arab Emirates, 1st century BC (private collection)

A number of typological variants have been identified in the coinage of Mleiha and al-Dur. All show a markedly more abstract head of Herakles on the obverse, in which the pelt of the Nemean lion appears as a series of stylized chevrons or zigzags. The seated figure on the reverse supporting a horse is accompanied by one of a number of monograms. These include what appears to be a derived form of the Seleucid anchor, often pointing towards the chest of the seated figure (see fig. 10); a ?letter resembling a Greek lambda placed in front of the figure, with the anchor behind him; and a large, cone-like object in place of the lambda. There are great differences in the degrees of abstraction in these coins, ranging from modelled realism to geometric abstraction.

Another, apparently unrelated, series is distinguished by its blank obverse. The reverse shows a seated figure supporting an eagle. A fragment of the legend 'Alexandous' can be read behind the figure, and a large, vertical *shīn*, topped by a separate monogram composed of several Greek letters, is placed in front of the figure's knees. There is a date in Greek (37) beneath the ground-line; it is not known according to which era this date should be calculated (e.g. ?Parthian, Seleucid) and it may relate to a local calendar. These coins are all of the tetradrachm class.

(iii) South Arabia. South Arabian coinage has been studied since the mid-19th century yet, because of the uncertainties of South Arabian chronology and the difficulties of exploration and excavation, little progress has been made beyond the classification achieved in 1922 by G. F. Hill.

The earliest coins struck in South Arabia were Sabaean issues which imitated 'old style' Athenian tetradrachms. These show, on the obverse, a helmeted head of Athena, and on the reverse the letters alpha, theta, epsilon, with an olive branch, crescent moon and owl. The beginnings of this coinage are unlikely to pre-date 300 BC. Coins of different denominations belonging to this group are characterized by a value mark on the cheek of Athena, using the South Arabian *n* for whole pieces, *g* for halves, *t* for quarters and *shīn* for eighths. A related and probably later group of Sabaean coins shows a more debased owl on the reverse and a variety of South Arabian monograms in the form of individual letters and letter combinations.

Another series on which the reverse owl and South Arabian monograms were retained shows, on the obverse, the unbearded portrait of a male with curly hair. This may be one of the first portraits of a local ruler to appear in South Arabian coinage. A slightly more stylized but not wholly dissimilar obverse portrait appears on series thought to represent the earliest Qatabanian coinage. Here, however, the reverse shows the bust of a bearded male, South Arabian monograms and the name of the mint location, Harb.

The 'new style' Athenian coinage was introduced in the 2nd century BC and lasted until *c.* 85 BC. This, too, was imitated in South Arabia, probably by the rulers of Himyar. The obverse of these coins shows a diademed, unbearded portrait of a male with long hair, encircled by a double wreath, while the reverse still shows the owl flanked by various South Arabian monograms, and a border of what appear to be handleless amphorae. As well as a large number of silver issues of this sort, there are several gold pieces (London, BM).

Another iconographic innovation probably occurred in the 1st century AD. This time the coinage of the Roman emperor Augustus (*reg* 27 BC–AD 14) served as the model for issues that show, on the obverse, an unbearded male bust wearing a wreath-like diadem, encircled by a wreath border, and a reverse like that of the imitations of 'new style' Athenian issues. This has been seen as a by-product of Aelius Gallus' invasion of South Arabia in 25–24 BC, but it is unlikely that local rulers would have depicted the head of their enemy's emperor on their own coinage. Instead, it appears from the *Periplus of the Erythraean Sea* (?1st century AD) that commercial relations between Rome and South Arabia were close and amicable during the later 1st century AD, which might explain the adoption of a Roman model by a Himyarite ruler.

A different series has a diademed male head, facing left, on the obverse, and on the reverse a bucranium flanked by South Arabian monograms. Opinions differ as to whether the obverse portrait is that of a ruler or deity. The wreath of amphorae around the portrait is highly stylized, and the reverse bucranium, possibly a symbol of the male South Arabian solar god Almaqah, has supplanted the Athenian owl.

In the early centuries of the Christian era a new series of coins was struck by the Himyarite 'kings of Saba' and Dhu Raydan', which typically show, on the obverse, a male head flanked by monograms, and a second and generally similar male head on the reverse, around which the ruler's name and the place of minting, usually Raydan (the name of the Himyarite castle in their capital Zafar), are written in South Arabian script. On some of the smaller denominations the ruler's name is omitted on the reverse, probably for lack of space. It is not known whom the obverse portrait depicts, whether a deity, an ancestor of the king who minted the coins or a co-regent.

A major group of bronze coins (London, BM) about which little is known shows, on the obverse, a male portrait with long hair hanging down the neck, flanked by two large South Arabian monograms. The reverse shows an eagle and a monogram. These coins tend to be of poor quality and are generally considered late pre-Islamic.

As archaeological work progresses in South Arabia new issues and variants keep appearing, but the difficulty of interpreting the monograms and distinguishing between rulers' portraits, deities and Greek or Roman models continues to make the study of South Arabian coinage problematic.

BIBLIOGRAPHY

G. F. Hill: *Catalogue of the Greek Coins of Arabia, Mesopotamia and Persia* (London, 1922)

G. Dembski: 'The Coins of Arabia Felix', *Yemen: 3000 Years of Art and Civilisation in Arabia Felix*, ed. W. Daum (Innsbruck, 1987), pp. 125–8

O. Callot: 'Les Monnaies dites "arabes" dans le nord du Golfe arabo-persique à la fin du IIIe siècle avant notre ère', *Failaka, fouilles françaises, 1986–1988* (Lyons, 1990), pp. 221–40

D. T. Potts: *The Arabian Gulf in Antiquity*, ii (Oxford, 1990)

C. Arnold-Biucchi: 'Arabian Alexanders', *Mnemata: Papers in Memory of Nancy M. Waggoner* (New York, 1991), pp. 101–15

D. T. Potts, ed.: *The Pre-Islamic Coinage of Eastern Arabia* (Copenhagen, 1991)

2. GLASS. The use of vitreous materials has a long history in the Arabian peninsula. During the late 2nd millennium BC on Faylaka blue glass was in use, some of it compositionally similar to Egyptian blue glass of the 18th Dynasty (Kuwait City, N. Mus.). At Hajar Bin Humayd in South Arabia the base of a glass vessel was recovered in Stratum J which compares closely with Mesopotamian products of the 8th–5th century BC.

A variety of glass beads, as well as a glass vessel, was found in the tombs at Hurayda in South Arabia, dating approximately to the Achaemenid or early Hellenistic period (*c.* late 6th century BC–3rd; Washington, DC, Freer). Simple, hemispheric bowls are attested in Hellenistic graves at Mleiha in the UAE (Sharjah, Mus. Archaeol.), but it is only later, during the Roman era, that the first influx into Arabia of considerable quantities of glass can be detected. Roman glass has been found in many of the late graves in Bahrain (Manama, Bahrain N. Mus.); in the tomb at 'Ayn Jawan on the Saudi Arabian mainland; in both graves and private houses at al-Dur; in the Hadramite settlement of Khor Rori on the coast of Dhofar; and at Qaryat al-Faw in the Arabian interior. Typologically, considerable variety is present in the corpus of glass. Pillar-moulded bowls in a variety of colours are extremely common; pear-shaped unguentaria are found; small pitchers with applied trails are known from a grave at Dhahran (Riyadh, Mus. Archaeol. & Ethnog.); handled jugs, grape-bunch and fish-shaped vessels are attested at al-Dur.

Sasanian glass of the 3rd and 4th centuries AD was found in a group of late graves at al-Dur (Umm al-Qaywayn, Ruler's Office), including simple, open bowls of a type well attested on Sasanian sites in Mesopotamia (e.g. Uruk, Nineveh, Assur and Babylon). It has been suggested that glass manufacture was introduced into South Arabia following the Sasanian conquest of that region in the 6th century AD. Kawd am-Sayla (Washington, DC, Freer), a site not far from Shaykh 'Uthman near Aden, shows abundant evidence of glass wasters and at least four kilns, suggesting it was a glass manufactory. Most of the site's occupation seems to be Islamic, however, and it is difficult to tell how much glass manufacture, if any, took place there during the pre-Islamic period.

BIBLIOGRAPHY

G. Caton-Thompson, ed.: *The Tombs and Moon Temple of Hureidha (Hadhramaut)* (Oxford, 1944)

G. W. Van Beek: *Hajar Bin Humeid: Investigations at a Pre-Islamic Site in South Arabia* (Baltimore, 1969)

A. M. Pollard: 'Report on the Analysis of Failaka Glass, Glazed Pottery and Faience', *The Bronze Age Pottery*, Failaka/Dilmun: The Second Millennium Settlements, ii (Århus, 1987), pp. 185–95

R. Boucharlat and others: 'The European Archaeological Expedition to ed-Dur, Umm al-Qaywayn (UAE): An Interim Report on the 1987 and 1988 Seasons', *Mesopotamia*, xxiv (1989), pp. 5–72

3. JEWELLERY. The earliest jewellery found in the Arabian peninsula comes from the site of Wadi Wutayya, just inland from the Omani capital Muscat, and dates to between *c.* 5000 and *c.* 4000 BC. Flat, circular beads of shell, limestone and soft-stone, often less than 10 mm in diameter, have been recovered, as well as pierced gastropod shells, which were probably strung into necklaces. The slightly later site of Khor Milkh 1, on the Omani coast near Qurayyat, has yielded tubular beads and lunate earrings of soft-stone, as well as perforated and incised shell bracelets. The roughly contemporary cemetery (RH 5) at Ra's al-Hamra, near Muscat, shows that, in addition to the use of flat, circular soft-stone beads and shell bracelets, shell pendants in the form of bay leaves and sharks' teeth were manufactured (all Muscat, Oman N. Mus.).

During the 3rd–1st millennium BC, a wide variety of soft-stone, cornelian, agate, shell and clay beads is attested on sites in eastern Arabia (e.g. Umm al-Nar; Abu Dhabi, al-'Ayn Mus.), most of which were probably of local manufacture. Frit or paste beads appear as well, but these are more likely to have been imported from Mesopotamia;

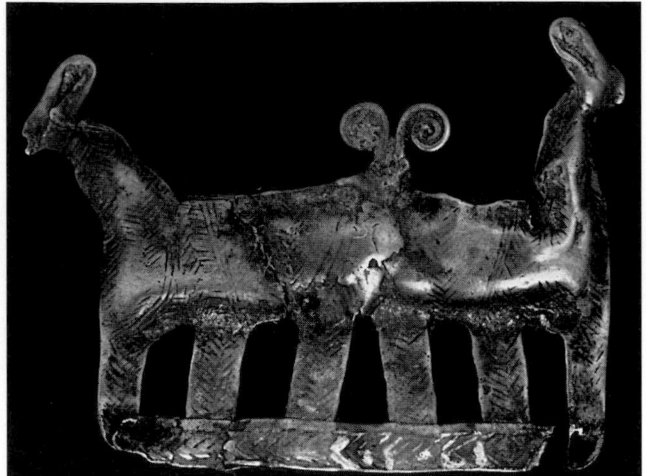

11. Gold ornament, *c.* 40×60 mm, from Qattara, Abu Dhabi, United Arab Emirates, early 2nd millennium BC (Abu Dhabi, al-ʿAyn Museum)

lapis lazuli and serpentine beads may have entered the region from Iran (the lapis originating ultimately in Afghanistan).

By the mid-3rd millennium BC contacts between eastern Arabia and the Indus Valley began to occur. One of the surest indicators of such contact is the appearance of etched cornelian beads on sites in the Gulf region (Abu Dhabi, al-ʿAyn Mus.). While not all cornelian beads need have originated there (some may have come from Iran), the practice of etching cornelian beads by applying an alkaline paste to the bead and then heating it has always been peculiar to the Indian subcontinent.

Early 2nd-millennium BC monumental graves in the Oman peninsula belonging to the Wadi Suq period (*c.* 2000–*c.* 1200 BC) have yielded a small corpus of unusual animal ornaments (Abu Dhabi, al-ʿAyn Mus.; Ra's al-Khayma, N. Mus.) which appear to have no close parallels outside the region. At least four examples found on sites in Ra's al-Khayma (Shimal) and Abu Dhabi (Qattara) consist of an identical pair of quadrupeds, facing in opposite directions, which are joined at the hindquarters (see fig. 11). They are made of hammered gold, with simple, engraved decoration in the form of diagonal lines to show the animals' hair. Solitary gold and silver goats and bulls are also shown (e.g. Abu Dhabi, al-ʿAyn Mus.). It is thought that these objects were worn as attachments on clothing.

During the Iron Age (*c.* 1200–*c.* 400 BC) a distinctive class of flat, rectangular or subrectangular, bifacial soft-stone amulets appeared in the Oman peninsula. Four have been found at Tell Abraq, and individual examples are known from Rumayla and Shimal. On some, the only decoration is a pattern of crisscrossing lines; one example has a boat with a sail; others show semi-demonic, anthropomorphic figures with claw-like hands and feet. A piece with a demon figure on one side bears a pair of diametrically opposed feet on the reverse (Umm al-Qaywayn, Ruler's Office). In analogy with *lamashtu* amulets in Mesopotamia, those which show a demonic figure may have been worn to ward off an evil spirit thought to bring sickness or bad luck.

By the Hellenistic and Roman periods, gold jewellery of the type found in parts of the Mediterranean and elsewhere in the Near East is attested in eastern and South Arabia. A hoard of gold jewellery found buried in a jar on a large site near Dhahran airport, in eastern Saudi Arabia (priv. col.), includes a hollow gold bracelet with antelope-head finials; an elaborate pair of earrings showing crouching lions above a row of pendent pomegranates; a second pair depicting a crouching sphinx on a beaten trapezoid of gold; and numerous barrel-shaped, circular and square gold beads, all with fine granulation. Close parallels exist for these latter beads in the Muncherjee Collection of gold jewellery (Aden, N. Mus. Ant.). Cut gemstones showing such Classical figures as Nike striding with an olive branch, or the helmeted Athena, are known from Dhahran and al-Dur.

BIBLIOGRAPHY

G. Turner: 'South Arabian Gold Jewellery', *Iraq*, xxxv (1973), pp. 127–39; pls XLVIII–LIV

E. Isetti and P. Biagi: 'The Polished Stone Earrings of Site RH5 and the Distribution and Chronology of the Prehistoric Earring of Coastal Oman', *Riv. Archeol.*, xiii (1989), pp. 5–17

D. T. Potts: *Miscellanea Hasaitica* (Copenhagen, 1989)

——: *The Arabian Gulf in Antiquity*, i (Oxford, 1990)

E. Haerinck, C. Metdepenninghen and K. G. Stevens: 'Excavations at ed-Dur (Umm al-Qaiwain, UAE): Preliminary Report on the Second Belgian Season (1988)', *Arab. Archaeol. & Epig.*, ii/1 (1991), pp. 31–60

D. T. Potts: *Further Excavations at Tell Abraq: The 1990 Season* (Copenhagen, 1991)

M. Uerpmann: 'Structuring the Late Stone Age of Southeastern Arabia', *Arab. Archaeol. & Epig.*, iii/2 (1992), pp. 65–109

4. METALWORK. This section discusses copper-bronze and silver vessels and other utilitarian items; for bronze statuary *see* §III, 2 above.

The mountain range that extends the length of western Arabia into South Arabia has modest supplies of mineral deposits, and several ancient mines have been located there. The Yemeni historian al-Hamdani, writing in the 10th century AD, described a major mine called al-Radrad, north-east of Sanʿa, which yielded *c.* 3000 kg of silver annually. Copper sources have been found near Taʿizz and in south-east Yemen. The mountains of the Oman peninsula are rich in sulphidic copper ore. Since the 4th millennium BC these deposits have been exploited to produce a variety of utilitarian items, vessels, jewellery and weaponry. The discovery, since the early 1970s, of over 150 documented smelting sites in Oman boasting concentrations of slag ranging from 1 to 150,000 tonnes confirms the substantial scale of the copper industry in the pre-modern era.

While the early medieval period surely ranks as one of the most productive in the history of Omani metallurgy, ample evidence confirms the presence of a local industry during the late prehistoric period, the Bronze Age, the Iron Age and the later pre-Islamic era. In addition to slag concentrations, anvil and crushing stones, fragments of furnace lining, casting moulds and bun-shaped ingots have been recovered from such sites as Maysar in the Wadi Samad (north-east Oman). The Maysar ingots (*c.* 2300–*c.* 2000 BC) represent the sort of refined copper that was acquired by Mesopotamian merchants in exchange for textiles, oil and other commodities. Throughout the 3rd millennium BC, when it was known in cuneiform sources as Magan, the Oman peninsula was probably Mesopotamia's principal southern supplier of refined copper.

A number of votive offerings made of copper-bronze and dating to the late 3rd millennium BC and early 2nd were found in Bahrain, under Barbar Temple IIa. These include a cast bull's head (200×75 mm; Manama, Bahrain N. Mus.) with symmetrically curving horns, blunt muzzle and hollow eyes, which were probably once inlaid. The curvature of the horns recalls the horned headdress worn by deities on cylinder seals of the Akkadian period (*c.* 2334–*c.* 2193 BC). More distant parallels can be drawn to bulls' heads found in Mesopotamia (e.g. at Ur, Khafajeh, Telloh and Tell al-Ubaid; London, BM; Baghdad, Iraq Mus.) from the Early Dynastic period (*c.* 2900–*c.* 2340 BC). A second piece of note from the foundation deposit is a cast bronze anthropomorphic mirror-handle (Manama, Bahrain N. Mus.) (h. 160 mm). Originally attached by rivets to a circular bronze mirror, the male figure, who is shown with arms bent and hands clasped beneath his chest, is undoubtedly an import from Central Asia or the Indo-Iranian borderlands. Similar mirror-handles are known at Mehi in Baluchistan, but they are most common on Bronze Age sites in Bactria (northern Afghanistan/southern Uzbekistan).

Graves of the 2nd and 1st millennia BC in the Oman peninsula have yielded a number of copper-bronze vessels (Fujairah, N. Mus.; Dubai Mus.). One of the most common shapes is a bucket with separately hammered strap-handles attached to the body by rivets. Goblets with a flaring, high-kick base and cordon at the intersection of the bowl and stand have also been found. Vessels with long, straight, open spouts running horizontally off the lip are known in Iron Age contexts, for example at al-Qusays (Dubai Mus.). These are similar to contemporary, spouted ceramic vessels on such sites in Iran as Tepe Sialk (*see* IRAN, ANCIENT, §VI, 2).

The production of wine in pre-Islamic Arabia is well attested in both epigraphic and literary sources, and wine drinking is confirmed by the discovery of several bronze wine sets on east Arabian sites. The earliest set comes from one of the many Iron Age ceramic 'bathtub' coffins that were buried in the ruins of the large building complex at Qalʿat al-Bahrain after it had been abandoned. The wine set consists of a shallow cauldron, a loop-handled situla, a deep, long-handled ladle and a strainer with handles. Good parallels for the specific shapes of these implements exist in the western Achaemenid empire (e.g. at Devehöyüğü, west of Carchemish on the Turkish–Syrian border), particularly in the 5th century BC.

In the 1st century AD a type of wine set appeared in eastern Arabia that differed from its predecessors in two ways. Outwardly the east Arabian wine sets were modelled closely on Roman wine sets. Iconographically, however, it is clear that these were local, Arabian products made in a non-Roman, Arabian style. The Arabian character of the wine sets is evident in the use of animals' heads as spouts on the wine cauldrons, which has no parallel in the Roman world. At al-Dur a bull's head was affixed to one cauldron, and a horse *protome* was found on another. Identical horse *protomes* have been discovered at Mleiha, Samad al-Shan

12. Underside of a gold and silver ladle (l. 140 mm) showing hunting scenes, from Wadi Dura, South Yemen, 4th century AD (Aden, National Museum of Antiquities)

in Oman and Jabal Kenzan in eastern Saudi Arabia. Roman wine ladles typically end in the heads of swans, ducks or wolves (London, BM; Toronto, Royal Ont. Mus.; Nijmegen, Stadhuis). At al-Dur, two ladles with snake-headed terminals have been discovered (Umm al-Qaywayn, Ruler's Office), and the handles of a wine strainer found there were made in the form of a snake, its back engraved with chevrons in imitation of snakeskin.

Both silver and bronze were employed extensively in Arabia for the manufacture of small, often highly decorated bowls and other implements (see fig. 12). Excavations at Mleiha have yielded four bronze examples (Sharjah, Mus. Archaeol.). These are generally simple, open bowls, sometimes with engraved lines running just beneath the rim, occasionally augmented by a row of diamonds. The engraved scenes always adorn the interior of the bowl. One bowl shows a procession consisting of a camel ridden by a man wielding a camel stick, and an armoured horseman throwing a spear from the back of a rampant horse. The spearman appears to be riding straight towards another figure, no longer visible because of a break in the bowl, who defends himself with a shield. A second bowl shows a lion attacking a man holding a shield. The lion is itself being attacked from the rear by a man who appears to be driving a sword into the lion's hindquarters. The bowl also bears a personal name engraved in South Arabian characters. A third, more fragmentary piece depicts what is unmistakably a griffin. All three examples date to the 3rd or 2nd century BC. The fourth bowl dates to the 1st century AD. It has a more concentric design, with a floral motif in the centre, flanked by three registers of decoration.

The innermost register consists of four human figures; the next depicts lions and other quadrupeds; the outermost register shows rearing lions. A large date palm rises out of the ground-line of the middle register and continues into the third register.

From the cemetery of Hajar am-Dhaybiyya in South Arabia (Aden, N. Mus. Ant.) comes a silver bowl decorated with a frieze of animals and an incised dedication to the god Sin Dhu Ilim. Several bowls have also been found at Qaryat al-Faw in south central Arabia. A silver example (Riyadh, King Saud U., Dept Archaeol.) bears an incised personal name in South Arabian characters just beneath the rim, while a bronze bowl has a longer inscription below the rim but cast in relief.

It is probable that all these bowls were local, Arabian products. The South Arabian inscription on the second Mleiha bowl need not imply that it originated in South Arabia since epigraphic South Arabian was used in eastern Arabia during the Hellenistic period, and the evidence for craft areas at Mleiha makes it likely that the bowl was produced at the site. Decorated bowls made of silver or bronze have also been found in South Arabia and at Qaryat al-Faw in central Arabia.

BIBLIOGRAPHY

A. Grohmann: *Arabien* (Munich, 1963)

G. Bibby: *Looking for Dilmun: The Search for a Lost Civilization* (London, 1970/*R* 1984)

A. Hauptmann: *Die Entwicklung der Kupfermetallurgie vom 3. Jahrtausend bis zur Neuzeit* (Bochum, 1985)

R. Boucharlat: 'Documents arabes provenant des sites "hellénistiques" de la péninsule d'Oman', *L'Arabie préislamique et son environnement historique et culturel: Actes du colloque de Strasbourg: Strasbourg, 1987*, pp. 109–26

C. Robin: 'The Mine of ar-Raḍrāḍ: Al-Hamdānī and the Silver of the Yemen', *Yemen: 3000 Years of Art and Civilisation in Arabia Felix*, ed. W. Daum (Innsbruck, 1987), pp. 123–4

R. Boucharlat and M. Mouton: 'Cultural Change in the Oman Peninsula during the Late 1st Millennium BC as Seen from Mleiha, Sharjah Emirate (UAE)', *Proceedings of the Seminar for Arabian Studies: Oxford, 1990*, xxi, pp. 23–33

D. T. Potts: *The Arabian Gulf of Antiquity*, i (Oxford, 1990)

5. Pottery.

(i) Oman peninsula. The oldest pieces of pottery found in south-eastern Arabia are fragments of imported vessels of Ubaid type from southern Mesopotamia, which date to *c.* 4500–*c.* 3800 BC (*see also* MESOPOTAMIA, §V, 1). The appearance of small quantities of imported pottery at sites on the coast of the UAE, extending from Abu Dhabi in the south to Ra's al-Khayma in the north, is part of a wider phenomenon that has been observed in Qatar, Bahrain and eastern Saudi Arabia. Presumably these vessels were brought south by traders seeking to acquire such local products as pearls. It has been suggested that the earliest pottery in Oman is a fragment of a carinated, black burnished cooking pot from Ra's al-Hamra 5 (Muscat, Oman N. Mus.), near Muscat, which the excavators dated to the late 4th millennium BC on the basis of parallels in eastern Iran. This attribution, however, remains controversial and cannot be verified until more material of this sort has been found.

By *c.* 3000 BC small quantities of imported vessels again appear, this time in the Hafit graves near Jabal Hafit (Abu Dhabi, al-ʿAyn Mus.). Both in form and decoration these squat, biconical vessels with black and plum-red painted geometric decoration on the shoulders are closely paralleled at sites of the Jemdet Nasr period (*c.* 3100–*c.* 2900 BC) in southern Mesopotamia. Several unpainted examples with a slightly different shape are probably later, for they find good parallels in the Early Dynastic I–II repertory (*c.* 2900–*c.* 2600 BC) in the Diyala region of north-eastern Mesopotamia.

It is possible that this renewed contact with Mesopotamian ceramics provided the impetus for the development of an indigenous pottery tradition in south-eastern Arabia. At Hili 8, in al-ʿAyn oasis, a ceramic sequence extending for almost 1000 years began, according to corrected, radiocarbon dates, *c.* 3000 BC. The local clays, when fired, turned a pale orange colour. Decoration often takes the form of black paint applied in meandering, wavy lines, spirals, chevrons and zigzags. Short-necked jars (Abu Dhabi, al-ʿAyn Mus.) with everted rims are most common, and decoration was usually applied to the shoulder of the vessel. The standard of workmanship varied, and there appears to have been an élite as well as a household level of production. Examples of the former category appear most often in graves but they have also been found in settlement contexts (e.g. at Tell Abraq on the coast; see fig. 13). This material is extremely well fired, the clay having been finely levigated. Coarser, sandier fabrics were reserved for daily use. Pottery within this tradition, known as Umm al-Nar, continued to be produced throughout the 3rd millennium BC. Around the mid-3rd millennium true imports from southern Mesopotamia (as deduced from physicochemical paste analyses) appear on Umm al-Nar Island in the form of torpedo-based storage jars, with close parallels at Nippur, Ur, Tell al-Ubaid and Abu Salabikh, which may originally have held wine or oil.

Early in the 2nd millennium BC there are signs of a significant technological change in the ceramic industry. This Wadi Suq style (*c.* 2000–*c.* 1200 BC) is characterized by a more vegetal tempering, with the addition of such inorganic temper as crushed shell and grit. The pottery was less well fired than Umm al-Nar ceramics, and the clay less well prepared. The repertory of shapes changed, as did the patterns of decoration. On the basis of both form and decoration, and with the help of imports from Mesopotamia, three sub-groups have been distinguished. Heavier jars, often with sloppily applied, zigzagging or meandering decoration in brown paint, are common. Small beakers with simple bands (Ra's al-Khayma Mus.) beneath the rim are found in both funerary and settlement contexts. Large jars with straight spouts or channel spouts running off the rim and geometric decoration in black or brown, consisting of concentric semicircles, bands of lines and zigzagging chevrons, also occur. Imported wares include Barbar pottery from Bahrain (*see* §(ii) below) and chaff-tempered, green-buff jars from Mesopotamia and Susiana ranging from Old Babylonian to Middle Elamite types (18th–12th century BC).

By *c.* 1200 BC another major change occurred in the repertory. Coarse, friable, grit-tempered wares appear at several coastal sites in the UAE (e.g. Tell Abraq and Shimal nr Ra's al-Khayma town), which represent the earliest Iron Age pottery in the region. It rapidly gave way to a more widespread tradition of heavy, grit-tempered pottery, often decorated with incised, geometric patterns

13. Umm al-Nar pottery from a tomb at Tell Abraq, *c.* 3000 BC (clockwise, from top left): (a) black-on-fine gritty orange ware, h. 90 mm; (b) black-on-fine orange ware, h. 101 mm; (c) fine red-slipped orange ware, h. 64 mm; (d) fine red-slipped orange ware, h. 52 mm; (e) black-on-fine gritty orange ware, h. 69 mm; (f) black-on-fine orange ware, h. (incomplete) 64 mm

and wavy lines on the surfaces of the rims and on raised cordons. Such 'classic' Iron Age pottery has been found at over 150 sites throughout the Oman peninsula and is perhaps best represented at Rumayla, in al-ʿAyn oasis, during period I (*c.* 1000–*c.* 500 BC). A third and final Iron Age phase is represented in period II at Rumayla (*c.* 500–*c.* 300 BC). Finer forms occur, including carinated bowls with red slip, which recall Achaemenid forms in Iran, and handled jugs in a coarse grey ware also appear.

During the Hellenistic and Roman periods there was an evolution of the indigenous Iron Age industry with the admixture of forms derived from the Hellenistic repertory. Mleiha is the principal site for the earlier, Hellenistic period (Sharjah, Mus. Archaeol.); al-Dur provides the most material from the 1st century AD. Purely Greek forms, such as fish-plates, double-handled amphorae and double-handled drinking cups (skyphoi) appear. Greek Black-glaze ware, as well as Rhodian amphorae fragments, are attested at Mleiha. Small quantities of Eastern *Terra sigillata* (a smooth red ware with a glossy sintered slip) have been found at al-Dur. Namord ware, a black-painted, highly fired, red-orange ware covered with geometric and floral motifs, which originated in south-eastern Iran, appears at al-Dur in the 1st century AD, and a later variety is attested at Jazirat al-Ghanam, in the Musandam peninsula (Oman), several centuries later. Similar forms, including handled pitchers, continued in use during the later pre-Islamic era, contemporary with the Sasanian empire (*c.* AD 224–651). Certain pieces from Area F at al-Dur are almost certainly true Sasanian imports, such as large storage jars with wavy incised and punctate decoration from Jazirat al-Ghanam.

(ii) North-eastern Arabia. Apart from fragments of imported Ubaid pottery of the late 5th millennium BC from about 40 sites in eastern Saudi Arabia, Bahrain and Qatar, the earliest pottery in north-eastern Arabia is represented by several dozen storage jars, some with raised rope-ridge decoration, which are almost certainly imports from southern Mesopotamia (Riyadh, Mus. Archaeol. & Ethnog.). These have been found at sites in eastern Saudi Arabia, including Tarut Island, Abqayq, Umm al-Ramadh and Umm al-Nussi, and date to the Early Dynastic I–II era (*c.* 2900–*c.* 2600 BC).

The earliest indigenous ceramic industry appeared *c.* 2400 BC in Bahrain and on the adjacent Saudi Arabian mainland. So-called Chain-ridged ware (Manama, Bahrain N. Mus.), belonging to City I in the Qalʿat al-Bahrain sequence, is made of a coarse, friable, red ware tempered with small particles of lime grit which exploded during firing, leaving a tiny ring of yellow on the surface of the ware. By the end of the 3rd millennium BC the Chain-ridged ware, which was used particularly for large vats and storage jars, had been supplanted by a product of similar paste but different decoration known as Red-ridged or Barbar ware. Large-bodied jars with short necks are common; *c.* 300 fragments, perhaps comprising an exported commodity, were found at Tell Abraq in levels dating to *c.* 2000–*c.* 1700 BC. Red-ridged ware is also widespread on the coast of Saudi Arabia and, above all, on

Faylaka, which was founded as an outpost of Bahrain *c.* 2000 BC.

By the mid-2nd millennium BC Bahrain had come under the control of a governor imposed by the Kassites in Mesopotamia. This brought about a major change in pottery production, and Kassite shapes, including typical tall goblets or beakers, appear in great numbers in Bahrain (Manama, Bahrain N. Mus.) and the grave mounds on the mainland at Dhahran (Riyadh, Mus. Archaeol. & Ethnog.). Chaff-tempered types of the late 2nd millennium BC are perhaps most closely related to South Arabian wares (e.g. from Hajar Bin Humayd, nr Timnaʿ), while in the Iron Age in Bahrain there was a reversion to earlier traditions and the production of a ware known as Pseudo-Barbar because of its superficial resemblance to Red-ridged pottery. The jar forms of Pseudo-Barbar ware, however, which are often characterized by a distended belly and elongated neck, recall Neo-Babylonian forms in Mesopotamia.

In the Hellenistic and Roman eras there was massive pottery production both in Bahrain and on the mainland. In paste the wares are akin to the earlier, Barbar pottery. The most common form is a hole-mouthed, round-bottomed cooking pot with shallow ridges on the body. The pots are undecorated, except for a white or black slip and sometimes rocker stamping around the rim. A class of fine bowls with sharply incurving sides and straight rims, which appears at such sites as Thaj, ʿAyn Jawan and Faylaka, seems to imitate Roman *Terra sigillata* forms of the 1st century AD. As at Mleiha, many Hellenistic Greek forms were also adopted at this time, and the use of glazed pottery became common. A form of late glazed ware dating to the 1st century AD has been called BI-ware after the sector on Faylaka (Kuwait City, N. Mus.) where it was first discovered during the Danish excavations. BI-ware has also been found in Bahrain and al-Dur. Little is known of pottery production during the Sasanian period in this region, although certain large storage jars with incised decoration recall contemporary forms known on sites in Iran and Mesopotamia.

(iii) North-western Arabia. In comparison with the rest of the peninsula, north-western Arabia has scarcely been investigated. Most information comes from limited surveys and soundings at such sites as Qurayya, Mada'in Salih, Khurayba (al-ʿUla oasis) and Tayma'. However, its proximity to southern Palestine has meant that certain types could be more readily identified than was the case in eastern Arabia during the early years of exploration.

The earliest major ceramic complex is represented by so-called Midianite or Qurayya painted pottery, best known from the type site of Qurayya in the Hejaz, east of the Gulf of Aqaba. This pottery (Riyadh, Mus. Archaeol. & Ethnog.), which has been dated to the late 2nd millennium BC, is thought to have been produced by the biblical Midianites because it occurs in that area of Arabia thought to have been their homeland. It is characterized by a pale-coloured fabric (buff, orange, cream), the occasional use of a thick slip (cream, orange, grey) and red and black painted decoration, such as chevrons, hatched diamonds, lozenges, pendent semicircles and running spirals, as well as birds, camels and lotus patterns. Inspiration for the decoration may be traced back to the eastern Mediterranean, with specifically Aegean and Egyptian influence. The discovery of kilns at Qurayya, however, confirms that the wares were produced locally.

The Iron Age tradition of the Hejaz is best known from the survey and soundings undertaken at Tayma' (Riyadh, Mus. Archaeol. & Ethnog.). Shallow, open bowls are common. Decoration often takes the form of black paint on a cream slip and includes hatched, pendent triangles, crosshatched bands, chequer-board bands and zigzagging or wavy lines. A slightly later Iron Age complex characterized by bichrome pottery, called Dedanite after biblical Dedan, is attested at Khurayba and Khif al-Zahra in al-ʿUla oasis. This group is characterized by less decoration than on the Tayma' pottery and is usually restricted to wavy or zigzagging lines between horizontal lines on the outside of open bowls.

In the last century BC and beginning of the Christian era fine Nabataean and Roman pottery appears in the region. The ultra-thin Nabataean pottery, made of finely levigated orange clay and decorated with elaborate floral motifs, represents one of the high points of ceramic production in the ancient world (*see* NABATAEA). Later Byzantine wares with raised ribs, similar to those found on sites in Palestine and Syria, are also attested. Excavations at the site of Zubayda further east yielded evidence of a ceramic complex dating to the first centuries AD. A variety of shapes and fabrics was found, some of which show clear links to the ceramic assemblages of eastern Arabia (e.g. Thaj, ʿAyn Jawan), central (e.g. Qaryat al-Faw) and South Arabia (e.g. Hajar Bin Humayd and Hurayda).

D. T. POTTS

(iv) South Arabia. Evidence of a culture between the Neolithic and Sabaean periods was discovered in South Arabia by Italian excavators in the 1980s. This Bronze Age occupation of the region, beginning *c.* 3000 BC, was found at several sites south-west of Sanʿa (e.g. Khawlan al-Tiyal, al-Hada); the globular jars, round-bottomed bowls and large plates have typological links with Early Bronze Age ceramics of Palestine (*see* SYRIA-PALESTINE, §I, 2(iv)(a) and (b)). Technically much of the pottery of this period is inferior, consisting of more sand temper than clay, and consequently having a friable and easily breakable fabric. The paste is frequently red, and decoration usually consists of multiple bands of incised, wavy lines beneath horizontal lines; some punctate decoration is also found.

Classical South Arabian ceramics (Sanʿa, Yemen N. Mus.) are widespread both in space and in time, showing little variation from the earlier Sabaean period (?early 1st millennium BC) until the later Himyarite period (first centuries AD) and no significant variation between historically attested states (e.g. Saba', Maʿin, Qataban, Awsan, Himyar). The fabric is usually chaff-tempered, and vessel forms often include a ring-base. The use of a burnished red slip is common. Excavations have shown that certain forms, such as carinated bowls and vessels with wavy, 'pie crust' rims, went out of favour; others, including storage jars on tripod bases and jars with horizontal, lug handles, came in late in the pre-Islamic sequence.

Many foreign wares also circulated in South Arabia from the 1st century AD as a result of trade with the eastern Mediterranean. Excavations at Qana on the south coast of Yemen brought to light imported amphorae from North African, Aegean and Palestinian (Gaza) workshops, Nabataean pottery and Eastern *Terra sigillata.* Heavy storage jars made of a dense, black paste with raised cordons probably represent imports from such sites as al-Dur in south-eastern Arabia.

Throughout Arabia fired clay was used with limestone in the manufacture of squat, square, four-legged incense burners. These were sometimes inscribed, as in South Arabia, with the name of a particular type of incense (e.g. London, BM). In other cases, as at Thaj or in Bahrain, the incense burners were decorated with rocker stamping or incised lines imitating architecture. Such 'Arabian' incense burners had a wide distribution, extending from Palestine and southern Iraq to the Oman peninsula and South Arabia.

BIBLIOGRAPHY

L. Hannestad: *The Hellenistic Pottery*, Ikaros: The Hellenistic Settlements, ii (Århus, 1983)

A. de Maigret: 'A Bronze Age for Southern Arabia', *E. & W.*, xxxiv (1984), pp. 75–106

F. Højlund, ed.: *The Bronze Age Pottery*, Failaka/Dilmun: The Second Millennium Settlements, ii (Århus, 1987)

A. de Maigret: 'The Yemeni Bronze Age', *Yemen: 3000 Years of Art and Civilisation in Arabia Felix*, ed. W. Daum (Innsbruck, 1987), pp. 38–40

P. J. Parr: 'Aspects of the Archaeology of North-West Arabia in the First Millennium BC', *L'Arabie préislamique et son environnement historique et culturel: Actes du colloque de Strasbourg: Strasbourg, 1987*, pp. 39–66

——: 'Pottery of the Late Second Millennium BC from North West Arabia and its Historical Implications', *Araby the Blest: Studies in Arabian Archaeology*, ed. D. T. Potts (Copenhagen, 1988), pp. 73–89

D. T. Potts: *The Arabian Gulf in Antiquity*, 2 vols (Oxford, 1990)

A. V. Sedor: 'New Archaeological and Epigraphical Material from Qana (South Arabia)', *Arab. Archaeol. & Epig.*, iii/2 (1992), pp. 110–37

ALESSANDRO DE MAIGRET, D. T. POTTS

6. ROCK ART. Engraved or pecked petroglyphs of widely varying age are found in all parts of the Arabian peninsula that are dominated by rock formations. In sandier areas, such as north-eastern Arabia, where only isolated rock outcrops occur, there is less true rock art, and most of what has been found can be subsumed under the rubric of relatively recent bedouin *wusūm*, or tribal monograms. Much of the finest rock art occurs in northern Arabia and in the Jabal Akhdar of north Oman. Its dating is, however, highly problematic, for the association of artefacts on the ground around a rock art site is no indication of the age of the rock art itself. Scholars who plead for early dates based on the discovery of late prehistoric chipped stone tools around outcrops with rock art ignore the fact that more recent drink cans may occur on the same site, and yet these are not used for dating purposes. New scientific techniques for dating rock art, however, are being developed. Human blood residue recovered from the pecked surfaces of a petroglyph can, for example, be dated by means of radiocarbon. This promises to be of great utility if it can be applied in the Arabian peninsula. Patina alone, most scholars agree, is no clear indicator of age. Cultural features in rock art depictions may also be chronologically diagnostic but can rarely be dated with any precision. Thus the appearance of such hunting weapons as the bow and arrow may suggest antiquity but does not allow for fixing a date within more than a couple of millennia. In addition, the occurrence of a particular species of animal no longer found in a given area today may indicate that the rock art is pre-modern, but the potential date range may be millennia, and cannot be narrowed down further simply on the basis of such presence–absence indicators.

(i) Northern and central Arabia. One of the richest areas of petroglyphs in the Arabian peninsula is located at Jubba in the midst of the great Nafud desert of northern Arabia, where a massive rock outcrop known as Jabal Umm Silman is covered with thousands of petroglyphs and inscriptions, which can be divided broadly into two groups. The first group, in what is known as the Jubba style, is characterized by large (over 1 m tall in some cases), abstract, flat-headed male figures with elongated bodies. There are indications of headdresses, belts, circular decorations on the chest and stripes on the stomach. The arms are normally extremely thin, while the legs and torso are better proportioned.

The figures are usually shown standing in profile, sometimes in rows, with the legs bent slightly at the knees, and the arms bent at the elbows (see fig. 14). Females with long, braided hair, flaring skirts and decorated breasts have also been identified. The figures often have such equip-

14. Rock art in Jubba style showing a human figure with caprids and canids (*c.* 4500–*c.* 3800 BC), Jabal Umm Silman, Jubba, Saudi Arabia

ment as a bow and arrow, a quiver slung over one shoulder, a throwing stick and club and are usually accompanied by animals, including canids, caprids such as gazelle or oryx, and long- or short-horned cattle, frequently with areas of body marking. Equids, with manes and pecked patches on their hides, are also attested.

The second group at Jubba is iconographically similar to the more primitive wall-painting style found at Qaryat al-Faw (*see* §10 below) and in parts of Yemen and Dhofar. Stick-figure men on horseback wielding spears and pursuing camels are common. Camels are also shown being ridden, and individual hands, feet, palm trees and geometric motifs occur. This sort of rock art is widespread throughout northern Arabia and is clearly distinguishable from the Jubba style: the depiction of the human form is completely different; large bovids are absent; and the camel, never found in the Jubba-style petroglyphs, is common.

There is no evidence for the domestication of the camel in northern Arabia before the mid- or late 2nd millennium BC: camel-riders are thus unlikely to be earlier than this; wild cattle would have been found in this largely desertic region only during times of higher rainfall. Although there are great gaps in our knowledge of the palaeoclimate of this region, it is clear that there were several periods in the 5th and 4th millennia BC, and perhaps again in the late 2nd millennium BC, when climatic conditions were moister. The disparity between the bovid-dominated Jubba style and the camel-dominated second group suggests a chronological discrepancy and makes a late prehistoric date (*c.* 4500–*c.* 3800 BC) for the Jubba style likely. This remains only an hypothesis, however, until reliable dating techniques can be applied. The second group may be considerably later than the 2nd millennium BC because of the association of some of this rock art with pecked inscriptions in Thamudic and Safaitic scripts. These must have been produced in the late 1st millennium BC and early 1st millennium AD.

While Jubba is perhaps the foremost site at which the Jubba style has been discovered, similar rock art was found in the 1950s by the Philby–Ryckmans–Lippens expedition in the ʿAsir in south-west Saudi Arabia. Similar material has also been discovered in the southern Nejd near Qaryat al-Faw and Najran. Some particularly fine examples occur at the site of Bir Hima. Comparable rock art also exists in Yemen and Dhofar.

(ii) Oman peninsula. Petroglyphs have been discovered throughout the Hajar or Oman mountains, with the largest concentration of rock art being in the Jabal Akhdar, the great mountain massif south-west of Muscat. Its mountainous wadis, with their walls of smooth, cretaceous limestone, formed an ideal field on which to peck images by making repeated blows with a hammerstone. The rock art was produced over a long period, making dating difficult. Technically, few of the Omani examples reach the level of sophistication of the Jubba style. Mounted horsemen with spears are found, as in northern Arabia, but with crude stick-figures. It is unlikely that the horse was being ridden here before the late pre-Islamic period. Standing stick-figures with swords or daggers at their waists can be compared with the demonic figure on an Iron Age amulet from Tell Abraq (*see* §IV, 3 above), suggesting a date in the early to mid-1st millennium BC. Large images of bovids with short, curving horns, long tail and raised hump are of the zebu variety, a species introduced into the region from Baluchistan or the Indian subcontinent in the 3rd millennium BC. The resemblance between these depictions of the zebu and that shown on a stamp seal from Maysar (*see* §7 below) makes it likely that some of the rock art showing the zebu should be dated to *c.* 2300–*c.* 2000 BC, although the continued presence of the zebu in the region means that a later date cannot be ruled out.

One of the most unusual examples of rock art in Oman is found at Hasat Bin Salt, a site known locally as Coleman's Rock after its discoverer, an American geologist. Four life-size human figures, of uncertain date, have been carved in low relief, rather than pecked. They have round heads with schematic features and massive, muscular shoulders. One of the figures wears a skirt or kilt and wields a weapon in his raised hand; another wears a headdress. These depictions are as yet unique in Arabian rock art.

BIBLIOGRAPHY

P. Lippens: *Expédition en Arabie Centrale* (Paris, 1956)
C. Clarke: 'The Rock Art of Oman', *J. Oman Stud.*, i (1975), pp. 113–22
K. Preston: 'An Introduction to the Anthropomorphic Content of the Rock Art of the Jebel Akhdar', *J. Oman Stud.*, ii (1976), pp. 17–38
P. J. Parr and others: 'Preliminary Report on the Second Phase of the Northern Province Survey, 1397/1977', *Atlāl*, ii (1978), pp. 29–50
J. Zarins and others: 'Preliminary Report on the Survey of the Central Province, 1978', *Atlāl*, iii (1979), pp. 9–42
M. C. A. Macdonald: 'Camel Hunting or Camel Raiding?', *Arab. Archaeol. & Epig.*, i/1 (1990), pp. 24–8

7. SEALS. Seal use was far more limited in Arabia than elsewhere in the Ancient Near East, and most of the information derives from eastern Arabia. From the 3rd to the 1st millennium BC the cylinder seal was the predominant type of seal used in Mesopotamia, Syria and Iran (*see* ANCIENT NEAR EAST, §II, 1(ii)). In eastern Arabia, cylinder seals of Mesopotamian origin, as well as locally manufactured imitations of Mesopotamian and Elamite types, are attested. The largest group comes from Faylaka (Kuwait City, N. Mus.), where the earliest imported seals are a pair of Ur III type (*c.* 2112–*c.* 2004 BC), which show the classic presentation scene in which a worshipper is led before an enthroned deity by a second, minor deity. Cylinder seals of Old Babylonian, Mitanni, Kassite, Pseudo-Kassite and Elamite types are also present in the Faylaka group, as is at least one seal blank, suggesting the presence of a seal-cutting workshop on the island. Indeed, one of the Faylaka cylinder seals shows both a carving technique and iconography that closely approximates that of the Dilmun stamp seals (see below) and is almost certainly a local product. The proximity of Faylaka to the Mesopotamian mainland, however, accounts for the prevalence of seals of actual Mesopotamian manufacture on the island.

Elsewhere in eastern Arabia, a badly worn Isin–Larsa (early 2nd millennium BC) cylinder seal showing a presentation scene is known from the surface of Thaj (Riyadh, Mus. Archaeol. & Ethnog.), and a group of Kassite (2nd millennium BC) and Neo-Assyrian (883–612 BC) cylinder seals has been found in the al-Hajjar graves in Bahrain (Manama, Bahrain N. Mus.). A Middle Elamite (14th–12th century BC) cylinder seal was discovered at the Salt

Mine site in eastern Saudi Arabia, and a pseudo-Middle Elamite seal, with close parallels in Iran at Susa and Chogha Zanbil (south-east of Susa) in the 14th century BC, has been excavated at Tell Abraq in the UAE. A handful of Neo-Assyrian cylinder seals in both the Late Cut and Linear Styles has also been found at the Salt Mine site (priv. col.).

The earliest indigenous sealing tradition in Arabia is represented by several late 3rd-millennium BC stamp seals from the Oman peninsula. A triangular prism seal from Maysar (Muscat, Oman N. Mus.) in east Oman shows what appears to be a dog and goat on one face; a humped bull (zebu) and scorpion on a second face; and two goats on the third face. The seal is pierced longitudinally. Two much cruder stamp seals from Maysar depict simple human stick-figures with outstretched arms. A small bronze stamp (Abu Dhabi, al-ʿAyn Mus.), with a pattern of concentric circles on the sealing face, is known from a late 3rd-millennium BC site on Ghanada Island, off the coast of Abu Dhabi.

In the area of Bahrain, Faylaka and north-eastern Arabia there was a development of a local stamp seal tradition *c.* 2100 BC, known as Persian Gulf seals, with a seal form unparalleled in the ancient world. A circular form was chosen with a high back or 'boss', perforated longitudinally and generally decorated with a single incised line. The material used was almost always soft-stone, and the scenes depicted were usually simple, eschewing the human form in favour of animals, including the bull, gazelle, scorpion and goat. It is striking that, out of the 29 seals known (London, BM; Manama, Bahrain N. Mus.) that belong to this category, no fewer than 11 bear the representation of a bull shown in profile together with a short inscription in the Harappan or Indus Valley script. This suggests a strong Harappan influence on Bahrain at this time, with direct input into the development of sealing there.

Between *c.* 2000 and *c.* 1700 BC there was an evolution from the simpler Persian Gulf seals to the more complex Dilmun seals, in which a much more sophisticated and generally deeper carving technique can be observed. The iconographic repertory is greater, encompassing a wide variety of human figures, often wearing long, kilt-like shirts; animals, most commonly the gazelle; and objects, often of uncertain function, resembling altars, standards, doors etc. Lunar and solar symbols also appear. The boss of the seal is usually decorated with three parallel, incised lines, flanked by two pairs of double dotted circles.

Over 400 seals of this class have been found on Faylaka (Kuwait City, N. Mus.), the northern outpost of the land known in cuneiform sources as Dilmun; the number known from Bahrain itself, thought to have been the centre of Dilmun, is probably under 150. Seal impressions have also been found in Bahrain, as have the remains of what has been interpreted as a seal-cutter's workshop. Dilmun seals have also been found on sites in Iraq, Iran, Afghanistan, Saudi Arabia, the UAE and India. A small group of bitumen seals that obviously imitate Dilmun seals is known from Susa (Paris, Louvre) in south-west Iran; a soft-stone seal from Tell Abraq is probably not so much an imitation as a local product inspired by the Dilmun glyptic tradition.

Throughout much of the Near East the cylinder seal became less popular during the Iron Age and there was a reversion to various forms of stamp seal. In the Oman peninsula, conoid and pyramidal stamp seals appear, in shape not unlike their counterparts in Syria–Palestine and Anatolia. The sealing surfaces show simple stick-figures of men and animals, and these seem to date to *c.* 1200–*c.* 400 BC.

Little research has been done into the glyptic tradition of South Arabia, but it is clear that one existed there as well. Broadly, two streams of influence can be discerned. Scaraboid seals with South Arabian inscriptions (Vienna, Ksthist. Mus.) bear witness to close contacts with Egypt, and ovoid and subrectangular disc seals recall Neo-Babylonian and Achaemenid glyptic in Mesopotamia (7th–4th century BC). Eagle-headed demons, the master of animals (a human or deity holding on to an animal in each hand), an eagle standing above a bucranium, and rampant ibexes are found on seals of this type. The fact that these seals often bear South Arabian inscriptions suggests that they were locally made.

BIBLIOGRAPHY

H. Frankfort: 'Note on Two Seal Stones', *The Tombs and Moon Temple of Hureidha (Hadhramaut)*, ed. G. Caton-Thompson (Oxford, 1944), pp. 101–3

P. Kjærum: *The Stamp and Cylinder Seals*, Failaka/Dilmun: The Second Millennium Settlements, i/1 (Århus, 1983)

P. Lombard and M. Kervran, eds: *A Selection of Pre-Islamic Antiquities*, Bahrain National Museum Archaeological Collections, i (Manama, 1989), pp. 135–64

D. T. Potts: *The Arabian Gulf in Antiquity*, i (Oxford, 1990)

K. G. Stevens: 'Four "Iron Age" Stamp Seals from Qarn Bint Sa'ud (Abu Dhabi Emirate, UAE)', *Arab. Archaeol. & Epig.*, iii/3 (1992), pp. 173–6

8. STONE VESSELS. The mountainous regions of south-eastern and western Arabia contain several forms of soft-stone (e.g. talc, steatite, chlorite) which have been used since the 3rd millennium BC for the production of a wide range of vessels and other objects of daily life. In its natural state, soft-stone is extremely soft (1 on the Mohs scale of hardness, capable of being scratched with the fingernail) and therefore easily carved, yet it can withstand temperatures of up to 1400°C and when heated becomes extremely hard. The name 'steatite', from the Greek word for 'fat', suggests the uses to which soft-stone vessels may have been put in antiquity, such as holding unguents, oils, pigments and other fatty substances. Numerous decorative styles have been documented in eastern Arabia, from the mid-3rd millennium BC to the late pre-Islamic era.

(i) 3rd millennium BC. The earliest carved soft-stone in Arabia is undecorated and consists of simple, open bowls and slightly trumpet-shaped, bell-shaped bowls (Riyadh, Mus. Archaeol. & Ethnog.), which have clear parallels in southern Mesopotamia during the Jemdet Nasr and Early Dynastic I–II periods (*c.* 3100–*c.* 2600 BC). Over 300 fragments have been found on Tarut Island, in eastern Saudi Arabia, and individual examples have been found on such sites in the UAE as Umm al-Nar and Tell Abraq. The oldest group of decorated soft-stone vessels belongs to the *série ancienne* of Intercultural style, which dates to *c.* 2500–*c.* 2200 BC. Almost 200 pieces are known from Tarut (Riyadh, Mus. Archaeol. & Ethnog.), where they had probably been housed in a temple. Physicochemical

analyses suggest that two major stone quarries, named Arabian A and B, were exploited in the production of the Tarut vessels. One of these is probably a source *c.* 300 km south-west of Riyadh. A few vessels in similar style were made of muscovite schist, almost certainly originating in western Arabia, near Jedda. Workshops manufacturing similar vessels also existed in south-eastern Iran. The distribution of the *série ancienne* was wide, extending from Mari on the Middle Euphrates in Syria to the Ferghana Valley in Uzbekistan. Objects that chemical analyses suggest were made of Arabian stone have been found on Faylaka, at Mari and at Bismaya, Khafajeh, Nippur, Kish and Ur in Iraq, usually in temple contexts.

Among the most common vessel forms used in the *série ancienne* are tall, flaring beakers with concave sides, low canisters, simple and carinated bowls and squat jars. Decoration was often applied in low relief to most of the outer surface of the vessel; sometimes it was used more sparingly on only part of a vessel. It falls into two broad categories, naturalistic and geometric/architectural, and in each case includes types not found on Tarut. Naturalistic motifs found in the Tarut material include the guilloche pattern (which probably represents stylized, intertwined snakes), zebu bull, Anzu bird (lion-headed eagle), rosette or eight-pointed star (symbol of the goddess Inanna-/Ishtar), combatant snake and lion/leopard, and date palm. Geometric/architectural motifs include mat-weave, imbricate, bevelled square and hut or temple façade. These were clearly élite objects for a particular market, which included the temple estates of southern Mesopotamia. It has also been suggested that they were exchanged by high-ranking individuals to cement social links between distant groups. Certainly their circulation, judging by the contexts in which they have been found, was very restricted.

During the Umm al-Nar period (*c.* 2500–*c.* 2000 BC, and especially after *c.* 2300 BC) a new type of decorated soft-stone vessel appeared in the Oman peninsula, and production on Tarut (or wherever the north-eastern Arabian workshops were located) ceased. The new group, called the *série récente*, is characterized by a wider variety of forms than its predecessor. Plain, shallow bowls; deep, rounded bowls; straight-sided and round-bellied canisters with lids; and single- or double-compartmented and lidded vessels, rectangular in shape, became common. Decoration, however, was far more restricted and none of the earlier motifs survived. Almost all the decoration was done with a tube-drill, which produced a double dotted circle. This was applied in single rows beneath the rims of plain bowls, around the perimeters of lids and in vertical rows down the sides of canisters and compartmented vessels. Examples of *série récente* soft-stone have been found at many sites in the Oman peninsula (Abu Dhabi, al-ʿAyn Mus.; Sharjah, Mus. Archaeol.; Muscat, Oman N. Mus.; Ra's al-Khayma Mus.; Ajman, N. Mus.) as well as in Bahrain (Manama, Bahrain N. Mus.), on Tarut (Riyadh, Mus. Archaeol. & Ethnog.) and Faylaka (Kuwait City, N. Mus.); in Iran they are known from Susa, Bandar Bushire and Tepe Yahya; in Pakistan a single piece comes from the Harappan site of Mohenjo-daro; and an inscribed example from Telloh, in southern Iraq, bears a Neo-Sumerian dedication from one Ur-Baba to an unnamed governor (*ensi*) of Lagash (Paris, Louvre).

(ii) 2nd millennium BC. The earliest examples of 2nd-millennium BC soft-stone in the Oman peninsula belong to the *série intermédiaire*. They are closely related to the *série récente* and differ only in the prevalence of small, round-bodied suspension vessels with four lugs spaced around the body, and accompanying lids, which were decorated with a single dot-in-circle, rather than the double dotted circle. These probably date to the first centuries of the 2nd millennium BC and have been found on relatively few sites in south-eastern Arabia, such as Shimal (Ra's al-Khayma Mus.), Wadi Suq, Hili 3 and Maysar 9 (Muscat, Oman N. Mus.), as well as on Tarut (Riyadh, Mus. Archaeol. & Ethnog.) and in Bahrain (Manama, Bahrain N. Mus.).

By the mid-2nd millennium BC the *série intermédiaire* had given way to the *série tardive*. A wider range of vessel form appears, including many round-bodied canisters with lids; squat jars with rounded base, slightly carinated body and small mouth, often with four unpierced lugs near the base; shallow, flat-bottomed bowls; and shallow dishes with protruding lips, which were probably oil lamps. The decoration is often crudely applied, consisting of bands of crosshatching or parallel, diagonal lines, alternating with rows of single dotted circles, usually divided by crudely incised pairs or bunches of horizontal lines. More effort was made to cover the entire body of the vessel with decoration, crude though it may have been, than in any of the earlier styles except for the *série ancienne*. Enormous numbers of *série tardive* vessels are known from sites (particularly burials) in the Oman peninsula; exports have also been recovered in Bahrain, on Tarut and Faylaka, as well as at Bandar Bushire in Iran, and Ur and Tell al-Ubaid in southern Iraq.

(iii) 1st millennium BC. During the Iron Age (*c.* 1200–*c.* 300 BC) soft-stone vessel production in the Oman peninsula was vast: excavated graves have yielded hundreds of examples. The carinated, hole-mouth form of the *série tardive* was common, but the section of the vessel is more severe and triangular. Carinated jars also appear, as do tall suspension canisters with lugs evenly spaced around the middle of the vessel. Shallow bowls, lamps and compartmented, open bowls with a rectangular shape occur. Unlike those of the *série récente* to the *série tardive*, Iron Age vessels were not normally decorated with incised circles. Patterns of parallel, zigzagging lines; chevron or herringbone decoration; scalloped gadroons (?in imitation of metal vessels); and rocker stamp incised lines now appear. While most of the decoration is geometric, applied in varying combinations, attempts at depicting naturalistic forms using the rocker stamp incised lines (e.g. leaves, trees, animals, griffins) are also attested. For all their frequency in the Oman peninsula, vessels of this type do not seem to have circulated much outside the area. Several pieces are known from the al-Hajjar grave mounds in Bahrain (Manama, Bahrain N. Mus.), and a tall canister (Baghdad, Iraq Mus.) with close parallels to a piece from Rumayla, in al-ʿAyn oasis of Abu Dhabi, was found at Nippur in southern Iraq; this, however, was made of alabaster.

While soft-stone was the preferred stone in south-eastern Arabia, alabaster or calcite was also used to a limited extent. Most of the evidence for this comes from the Iron Age and late 2nd millennium BC at al-Qusays in Dubai (Dubai Mus.). Extensive use of alabaster, however, occurred in South Arabia, where there are abundant sources of the raw material. Such sites as the Timnaʿ cemetery have yielded hundreds of alabaster examples (Washington, DC, Sackler Gal.), including simple bowls and compartmented vessels. One of the most common shapes is a small, lidded, beehive canister, often with two pierced lugs symmetrically positioned on the sides. The lids frequently have handles carved in the form of a couchant lion or ibex. Examples have been found as far afield as Thaj, Mleiha (Sharjah, Mus. Archaeol.) and Qaryat al-Faw (Riyadh, King Saud U., Dept Archaeol.). Incense burners were also made of alabaster, as well as of commoner stones such as limestone (Cambridge, MA, Harvard U., Peabody Mus.). Some of the limestone examples take the form of a circular, tripod dish with squat legs.

By the Hellenistic and Roman periods the lathe was used to turn soft-stone vessels in the Oman peninsula. This can be seen clearly in the decoration, which often consists of multiple lines around the rims or along the sides of shallow bowls. Small depressions in the bases of these bowls indicate where they were affixed to the lathe. Most examples come from Mleiha and al-Dur.

BIBLIOGRAPHY

R. L. Cleveland: *An Ancient South Arabian Necropolis: Objects from the Second Campaign (1951) in the Timna' Cemetery* (Baltimore, 1965)

P. L. Kohl: 'The Balance of Trade in Southwestern Asia in the Mid-Third Millennium BC', *Curr. Anthropol.*, xix (1978), pp. 463–92

J. Zarins: 'Steatite Vessels in the Riyadh Museum', *Atlāl*, ii (1978), pp. 65–93

P. Lombard: 'Iron Age Stone Vessels from the Oman Peninsula: A Preliminary Note', *Proceedings of the Seminar for Arabian Studies: Cambridge, 1981*, xii, pp. 39–48

C. C. Lamberg-Karlovsky: 'The "Intercultural Style" Carved Vessels', *Iran. Antiq.*, xxiii (1988), pp. 45–95

R. Boucharlat and M. Mouton: 'Cultural Change in the Oman Peninsula during the Late 1st Millennium BC as Seen from Mleiha, Sharjah Emirate (UAE)', *Proceedings of the Seminar for Arabian Studies: Oxford, 1990*, xxi, pp. 23–33

D. T. Potts: *The Arabian Gulf in Antiquity*, 2 vols (Oxford, 1990)

9. STUCCO. Carved stucco was widely employed by the Sasanians (*c.* AD 224–651) as a form of interior architectural decoration (*see* SASANIAN). Parts of eastern Arabia were at times under the direct political control of the Sasanians or their Arab vassals, the Lakhmids of al-Hira on the Lower Euphrates, and examples of stucco decoration have survived from a number of sites in the region. At al-Hira itself stucco from the late Sasanian period (6th century AD–early 7th) has been found in two churches. It is very white and hard and shows steep-cut rows of triangles, rosettes, pine cones and vine leaf decoration. The drill was used extensively in carving the floral motifs and their accompanying, chain-like borders.

Excavations in 1989 at the site of al-Qusur, in the centre of Faylaka, uncovered the remains of a Nestorian church (*see* §II, 5(i) above) and associated settlement. While its exact date is not known, it is thought that the complex was originally founded in the 5th or 6th century AD. Two large stucco panels (each 800×600 mm) were recovered which bore deeply cut crosses with accompanying decoration (Kuwait City, N. Mus.). On one, the cross sits on a pedestal out of which two bands arise, perhaps symbolizing the fountain of resurrection. Palmettes occur in the upper right- and left-hand corners of the central rectangle holding the cross. This is framed by a border consisting of rosettes, palmettes and chevron decoration. On the second panel (see fig. 15) the cross, pedestal and bands are framed within an oval or subrectangular frame. This is enclosed by a pattern of curving vine leaves on the sides and floral motifs within diamonds at the top and bottom of the panel.

15. Stucco panel, 800×600 mm, from the Nestorian church at al-Qusur, Faylaka, Kuwait, 5th–6th centuries AD (Kuwait City, National Museum)

Darin on Tarut Island is known from Nestorian sources to have been the seat of a bishopric and to have figured prominently in the history of eastern Arabia during the Sasanian period. Unlike al-Hira and Faylaka, however, Darin has yielded evidence of decorative stucco that is almost certainly secular and may have come from the residence of a prominent citizen. One fragment shows a five-pointed fleur-de-lis, a lenticular leaf, and a bird in flight shown in profile. A second fragment shows a couchant ram with short, curved horns, its neck twisted so that the head is shown in profile, facing to the rear. Portions of floral decoration are visible above the ram's head (both priv. col.). Similar stucco is known from the Sasanian palaces at Kish, Chal Tarkhan and Ctesiphon.

Another example of decorative stucco from a secular context was found in the 'governor's palace' at Jumayra in Dubai (*see* §II, 3 above). Steep-cut triangles were found, similar to those in the churches at al-Hira, as well as rosettes and floral motifs used in a running frieze. The excavator compared his Jumayra stucco with that of the Sasanian palace at Tepe Hissar in north-east Iran.

BIBLIOGRAPHY

D. Talbot Rice: 'The Oxford Excavations at Hira, 1931', *Antiquity*, vi (1932), pp. 276–91

D. T. Potts: *Miscellanea Hasaitica* (Copenhagen, 1989)

——: *The Arabian Gulf in Antiquity*, 2 vols (Oxford, 1990)

V. Bernard, O. Callot and J.-F. Salles: 'L'Eglise d'al-Qousour Failaka, Etat de Koweit', *Arab. Archaeol. & Epig.*, ii/3 (1991), pp. 145–81

10. WALL PAINTING. Little evidence remains of the wall painting in pre-Islamic Arabia that must have existed at one time. However, excavations at Qaryat al-Faw have revealed a significant number of well-preserved wall paintings (some in Riyadh, King Saud U., Dept Archaeol.), which represent the first sizeable corpus of paintings found in the peninsula. They were discovered on the walls of a room in the fortress (*see* §II, 4 above) and in the so-called palace. Analyses of these works show that the scenes were painted using inorganic mineral, as opposed to vegetal-based, pigments. Red, yellow, brown, black and white were the commonest colours used, and most of the minerals crushed to make the pigments, such as haematite, were available locally within the catchment of the Tuwayq escarpment. The discovery of small amounts of animal glue in one of the buildings suggests that this may have been the binding medium used to make the paint. A small amount of dried red paint was also discovered. The paintings were done on a 2 mm-thick layer of fine, white gypsum plaster applied over a coarser gypsum plaster which covered the walls of the Qaryat al-Faw buildings.

Iconographically and stylistically two broad groups within the Qaryat al-Faw corpus can be distinguished. In the fortress are crude, unprofessional paintings showing figures that resemble those in much Arabian rock art (*see* §6 above). Generally comparable painted figures have been observed in red ochre on the sides of large boulders in South Arabia, which may be the work of ancient herdsmen who also left behind much painted graffiti. One Qaryat-al-Faw scene is of camel raiding, in which a man wielding a spear on horseback pursues a camel. Above the man, painted in South Arabian characters, is the personal name Salim ibn Kaʿb. The figures comprise opaque, black stick-men and animals, showing no artistic accomplishment. Another panel depicts a more stylized man with triangular torso mounted on a red horse with raised forelegs. He is shown pursuing a camel with an exaggerated hump. Other animals, probably an oryx and dog, are shown above him, and the word 'king' is painted in outline above his head. Such a scene appears more like a graffito than a painting, and the occurrence of incised South Arabian scribbling near by suggests this was the casual production of someone in the fortress, rather than a wall painting as such. The name Kahl, the chief deity of Qaryat al-Faw, occurs repeatedly on this panel.

These contrast with the highly skilled paintings from the 'palace'. Given their level of technical expertise, they are obviously by professional artists. One of the largest panels (see fig. 16), unfortunately fragmentary, shows a Dionysiac figure with curly dark hair, moustache and beard, flanked by two figures holding fruit. A bunch of grapes hangs from a vine above the main figure's head. The better preserved flanking figure wears a garment that resembles a Roman toga, and the whole scene seems

16. Wall painting of a Dionysiac scene (early 1st millennium AD), from the 'palace' at Qaryat al-Faw, Saudi Arabia (*in situ*)

inspired by a Roman image, despite the fact that the central figure's face and beard give a decidedly Arab cast to his Dionysiac features. The name Zaky occurs alongside the painting. This panel is distinguished by the use of reds for the skin of the figures; by the accomplished rendering of the shine on each grape; and by the use of black for the outlines of eyes, eyebrows, noses and mouths. The visage of the main figure (?Dionysos) is turned slightly to the right and has been realistically portrayed by an artist who understood perspective.

Fragments of other wall paintings from the palace show the hoofs and lower legs of at least two horses, apparently standing by a pond in which two fish swim. The fish are realistically rendered in red and black, with considerable attention to their dorsal and ventral fins. As the excavator of Qaryat-al-Faw, al-Ansary, noted, the discovery of these paintings underscores how little is known of central Arabian art in the first centuries AD, and how false it would be to attribute all the important developments in early Islamic art to Byzantine and Sasanian influence. It is clear that central Arabian artists included some who were as sophisticated as their northern counterparts.

Additional evidence for wall painting in Arabia has been discovered at Shabwa, ancient capital of Hadramawt, by French excavators. At least one depiction of a draped female figure from the 3rd-century AD palace suggests a level of sophistication comparable to that at Qaryat al Faw. Other scenes depict riders, fish and vegetal motifs. Excavations at al-Hira in south Iraq in 1931 uncovered traces of painting (floral pattern, circles and a small bird) on the walls of a church of the early 7th century AD, which represent a continuation of the Arabian tradition attested to at Qaryat al-Faw and Shabwa.

BIBLIOGRAPHY

D. Talbot Rice: 'The Oxford Excavations at Hira, 1931', *Antiquity*, vi (1932), pp. 276–91

A. R. al-Ansary: *Qaryat al-Fau: A Portrait of Pre-Islamic Civilisation in Saudi Arabia* (London, 1982)

J.-F. Breton: 'Ancient Shabwa, the Capital of Ḥaḍramawt', *Yemen: 3000 Years of Art and Civilisation in Arabia Felix*, ed. W. Daum (Innsbruck, 1987), pp. 111–15

V. Museums and exhibitions.

Only a few international exhibitions of pre-Islamic Arabian art and antiquities have been organized, such as one on Yemen held at the Staatliches Museum für Völkerkunde in Munich in 1987–8, which included Islamic art. Several Western museums hold collections donated by 19th and early 20th-century explorers, in particular Vienna (Ksthist. Mus.), London (BM), Berlin (Staat. Mus. Dahlem), Birmingham (Mus. & A.G.), Brussels (Mus. Royaux A. & Hist.), Hamburg (Mus. Vlkerknd.), St Petersburg (Hermitage), Marseille (Mus. Borély), Oxford (Ashmolean), Rome (Mus. N.), Washington, DC (Dumbarton Oaks) and Paris (Louvre). Most finds since the mid-20th century are housed in national museums in the peninsula. Museums devoted primarily to archaeology, ethnography and Islamic art exist in Riyadh (Saudi Arabia), San'a (Yemen), Kuwait City (Kuwait), Doha (Qatar), Manama (Bahrain) and Muscat (Oman). In the UAE most of the individual emirates have their own museums. These are located in al-'Ayn (Abu Dhabi), Dubai, 'Ajman, Sharjah and Ra's al-Khayma. Museums have also been planned for both Fujayra and Umm al-Qaywayn. Saudi Arabia also has an extensive system of provincial museums close to important archaeological sites. These are located at Hofuf, al-Jawf (nr the site of Dumat al-Jandal, anc. Adummatu), al-'Ula, Tayma', Jizan (in the Tihama plain) and Najran. A smaller museum is located in Dammam with antiquities from sites in the Eastern Province.

BIBLIOGRAPHY

A. Grohmann: *Arabie* (Munich, 1963)

An Introduction to Saudi Arabian Antiquities (Riyadh, 1975)

P. M. Costa: *Pre-Islamic Antiquities at the Yemen National Museum* (Rome, 1978)

P. Lombard and M. Kervran: *A Selection of Pre-Islamic Antiquities from Excavations 1954–1975*, Bahrain National Museums Archaeological Collections, i (Manama, 1989)

A. Caubet: *Aux sources du monde arabe: L'Arabie avant l'Islam*, Collections du Musée du Louvre (Paris, 1989)

D. T. POTTS

Aragon, House of. Spanish dynasty of rulers, patrons and collectors, active in Italy. The county of Aragon was established as a kingdom in 1035 under Ramiro I (*reg* 1035–63), son of Sancho III the Great, King of Navarre (*reg* 1000–35). In the 13th century James I the Conqueror, King of Aragon (*reg* 1213–76), extended the kingdom by taking control of Valencia and the Balearic islands. His son, Peter III, King of Aragon (*reg* 1276–85), also became King of Sicily in 1282, following a revolt against the rule of the House of Anjou (*see* ANJOU). Separate branches of the Aragonese dynasty, which included (1) Peter IV, King of Aragon (*reg* 1336–87), ruled the two kingdoms until 1409, when Martin, King of Aragon (*reg* 1395–1410), succeeded to the kingdom of Sicily. On his death in 1410 both kingdoms were given to his nephew, Ferdinand (*reg* 1412–16), son of John I, King of Castile (*reg* 1379–90). Ferdinand's successor, (2) Alfonso (who ruled as Alfonso V, King of Aragon and Sicily), was the adopted heir of the Queen of Naples and seized control of the kingdom of Naples in 1442, becoming Alfonso I. He and his descendants (who reigned until 1504), including (3) Ferdinand I and (4) Alfonso II, embarked on extensive programmes of building in the city, the most notable work being the improvements to the fortress of Castelnuovo.

On the death of Alfonso I in 1458 the kingdoms of Aragon and Sicily passed firstly to his brother John II (*reg* 1458–79) and then to his nephew (5) Ferdinand II. Through his marriage to (6) Isabella, Queen of Castile and Léon, and the subsequent conquest of the Moorish kingdom of Granada, the regions of Spain were unified under central rule. The power of the Spanish monarchy was strengthened through comprehensive internal reforms and a series of marriage alliances between Ferdinand and Isabella's children and those of other European rulers, most notably that of Joanna of Castile and Philip the Fair, Duke of Burgundy (later Philip I, King of Castile; *reg* 1504–6), son of the Holy Roman Emperor Maximilian I. Ferdinand and Isabella's patronage of architecture was extensive; the fusion of Netherlandish, Renaissance and Mudéjar forms that Isabella, in particular, favoured led to the development of the so-called HISPANO-FLEMISH STYLE. In 1516, on the death of Ferdinand (who had assumed control of Castile after his son-in-law's death and his daughter's madness), his grandson Charles inherited the territories of the Spanish kingdoms, both in the peninsula and in Italy. In 1519 he was elected Holy Roman Emperor, thus ensuring that the fortunes of Spain were linked with those of the Habsburg dynasty until the end of the 17th century.

(1) Peter IV ['el Ceremonosio'], King of Aragon (*b* 1319; *reg* 1336–87; *d* 1387). His surviving commissions include examples of goldwork, such as the reliquary monstrance by Pere Moragues for the Capilla de los Corporales in the parish church at Daroca (1384–6; Daroca, Mus. Santísimo Misterio). He also was responsible for building work at POBLET ABBEY, where he erected royal tombs. Untraced commissions include an altarpiece (*c.* 1383) painted for the convent of S Damian, Barcelona, by Lluís Borrassà, while surviving inventories record that he had a large collection of manuscripts of romances (narrative poems) in his library at Toledo.

□

(2) Alfonso I [Alfonso the Magnanimous], King of Naples [Alfonso V, King of Aragon and Sicily] (*b* Medina del Campo, 1396; *d* Naples, 27 June 1458). In 1416, on the death of his father, Ferdinand, he became King of Aragon and Sicily. In 1421 he was welcomed in Naples as the adopted son and heir of Joanna II of Anjou, Queen of Naples (*reg* 1414–35); he was disinherited in 1423 but claimed Naples by force on 6 June 1442, thereby ensuring that the Spanish dominated southern Italy for the next half-century.

Alfonso embarked on an ambitious campaign to reconstruct and embellish his new capital. Work began in 1443 to rebuild and modernize the former Angevin fortress of Castelnuovo (*see* NAPLES, §IV, 4), which Alfonso had chosen as his chief residence. The design was completed under the supervision of the Catalan architect and sculptor Guillem Sagrera and his assistants and incorporates Spanish and Italian elements; it is considered the most important representative of Renaissance architecture in southern Italy. An outstanding feature is the monumental marble Triumphal Arch (*c.* 1452–71; *see* NAPLES, fig. 5) that serves as the chief entrance to the castle. Flanked by two medieval towers, the arch has an elaborate sculptural programme distributed over four registers, surmounted by a rounded pediment and a crowning statue. A major component of the arch is a frieze commemorating the King's victorious entry into Naples on 26 February 1443. The ceremonial procession is carved in high relief, with the regally attired sovereign shown seated on an imposing chariot drawn by four chargers *all'antica*, accompanied by courtiers and musicians. A drawing (*c.* 1448; Rotterdam, Mus. Boymans–van Beuningen) attributed to Pisanello is considered the earliest design for the arch. Attempts to identify the author of the final version have been inconclusive, although Pere Joan and Francesco Laurana were among the sculptors who collaborated on the arch, while Pietro di Martino da Milano is credited with its completion in 1466. Castelnuovo became the site of a splendid court that was famed as a centre of Renaissance art and humanist learning. The court was frequented by such scholars as Lorenzo Valla and Bartolomeo Facio. The latter's *De viris illustribus*, written in tribute to the King in 1546, contains a chapter on painters and sculptors that provides insight into the sovereign's artistic preferences; the author also discusses works of art in Alfonso's collection that have been lost, including paintings by Jan van Eyck and Rogier van der Weyden.

The art produced in southern Italy during Alfonso's reign was directly linked with his personality. It was heterogeneous in style, drawing on diverse elements: the King particularly favoured Netherlandish works but also patronized artists from Spain (e.g. Jacomart), Italy (e.g. Francesco di Antonio del Chierico) and Dalmatia (e.g. Francesco Laurana). Laurana's marble portrait bust of *Alfonso I* (*c.* 1453; Detroit, MI, Inst. A.) immortalizes the features of this Renaissance ruler.

BIBLIOGRAPHY

DBI
R. Filangieri di Candida: *Castel Nuovo reggia angioina ed aragonese di Napoli* (Naples, 1934, 2/1964)
M. Baxandall: 'Bartholomaeus Facius on Painting: A Fifteenth-century Manuscript of the *De viris illustribus*', *J. Warb. & Court. Inst.*, xxvii (1964), pp. 90–107
E. Driscoll: 'Alfonso of Aragon as a Patron of Art', *Essays in Memory of Karl Lehmann*, ed. L. Freeman Sandler (New York, 1964), pp. 87–96
G. Hersey: *Alfonso II and the Artistic Renewal of Naples, 1485–1495* (New Haven, 1969)
——: 'The Arch of Alfonso in Naples and its Pisanellesque "Design"', *Master Drgs*, vii (1969), pp. 16–24
——: *The Aragonese Arch at Naples, 1443–1475* (New Haven, 1973)

JOAN ISOBEL FRIEDMAN

(3) Ferdinand [Fernando; Ferrante] **I**, King of Naples (*b* Valencia, 2 June 1423; *reg* 1458–94; *d* Naples, 25 Jan 1494). Illegitimate son of (1) Alfonso I, King of Naples. He was educated by the humanists Antonio Beccadelli and Bartolomeo Facio; he did not enjoy a reputation for magnanimity, as his father had done, although artistic patronage in Naples continued on a generous scale under his rule. In 1448 he was made Duca di Calabria, official heir to the throne of Naples and by 1 December 1458 he had been crowned King of Naples.

Pietro di Martino da Milano continued work begun under Alfonso I on the triumphal arch (*see* NAPLES, fig. 10) at Castelnuovo, Naples. A relief (damaged) on the inner arch, with the *Coronation of Ferdinand*, depicted the King crowned and holding an orb and sceptre. His equestrian portrait relief (destr.) was formerly on the Porta Capuana, a city gate in Naples. In 1466 he commissioned for the upper niche of the triumphal arch a heart-shaped gilded copper and silver vessel (destr.) to contain the embalmed heart of Alfonso I. Ferdinand also commissioned a set of bronze doors (?1474–5; *in situ*) for the inner portal at Castelnuovo. They are signed by Guglielmo lo Monaco and decorated with six narrative panels depicting episodes from the King's military career. Portrait medallions of *Ferdinand I* and his wife *Isabella di Chiaromonte* were formerly situated above the doors. Girolamo Liparolo [Luparello] (1462–97), the royal die and seal engraver at the Neapolitan Mint, also produced inscribed portrait medallions (e.g. Oxford, Ashmolean) of *Ferdinand I*. In 1468 the King ordered the rebuilding of the Castello del Carmine (formerly the Forte dello Sperone), Naples, and was also involved with the restoration of the great park at the Castelnuovo. In 1484 a fragment of an antique marble statue of a horse was discovered, and Ferdinand had it restored and erected, where it is still *in situ*, over the entrance to the Castel dell'Ovo, Naples.

Ferdinand I encouraged the production of Italian translations of Classical literature: in 1444–5 Bartolomeo Facio prepared an Italian version of Isocrates' *Ad Nicoclem*, and the Florentine Neoplatonist Cristoforo Landino dedicated an Italian version (*c.* 1460s–70s) of Pliny's *Natural History* to Ferdinand. In 1465 the Studio, an educational institute, was reopened and restructured; under Ferdinand's encouragement the first printing shop was set up in Naples *c.* 1470. He also greatly increased the royal library and *c.* 1486 appropriated at least 260 manuscripts and books from confiscated property of the Neapolitan barons.

BIBLIOGRAPHY

E. Pontieri: *Per la storia del regno di Ferrante I d'Aragona re di Napoli* (Naples, 1947, 2/1969), pp. 128–33

——: 'La Puglia nel quadro della monarchia degli Aragonesi di Napoli', *Atti del congresso internazionale di studi sull'età aragonese: Bari, 1972*, pp. 19–52

G. d'Agostino: *La capitale ambigua: Napoli dal 1458 al 1580* (Naples, 1979), pp. 7–107

J. H. Bentley: 'Il mecenatismo culturale di Ferrante I d'Aragona', *Esperienze letterarie*, xii (1987), pp. 3–19

——: *Politics and Culture in Renaissance Naples* (Princeton, 1987), pp. 21–34, 62–80

(4) Alfonso II, King of Naples (*b* 4 Nov 1448; *reg* 1494–5; *d* Messina, 18 Dec 1495). Son of (3) Ferdinand I, King of Naples. He was educated by the humanists Antonio Beccadelli and Giovanni Pontano (1426–1503) and later had a successful military career. His victory over the Florentines at the siege of Poggio Imperiale was commemorated in 1479 with a medal (e.g. Oxford, Ashmolean) attributed to Francesco di Giorgio Martini, while the Battle of Otranto (1481) was commemorated in two medallions (e.g. Oxford, Ashmolean) by Andrea Guacialoti.

In the 1480s Alfonso began the extensive remodelling of Naples: streets were straightened, an aqueduct was built to supply new fountains throughout the city, and a number of churches were constructed or remodelled. In 1485 a city gate, the Porta Capuana, was designed by Giuliano da Maiano, and in 1488 Giuliano da Sangallo produced designs (unexecuted) for a palace complex for Alfonso. He also commissioned the country villa of Poggio Reale (1487–9; destr. late 18th century), located outside the eastern walls of the city. The plan, symmetrical and cross-axial, is attributed to Giuliano da Maiano, although Francesco di Giorgio Martini and Fra Giovanni Giocondo were also involved. It is considered to be one of the most important villa designs of the early Renaissance. La Duchesca (destr. ?16th century), a garden casino also attributed to Giuliano da Maiano and intended for Alfonso's wife, Ippolita, was built in the gardens surrounding his official residence, the Castel Capuano, within the eastern walls near the Porta Capuana. Work on the garden began in July 1487, and by September 1488 part of the interior of the casino was decorated, but Ippolita died before it was completed.

In 1494 Francesco di Giorgio was put to work on the fortifications (mostly destr.) of the Castelnuovo and possibly the new fortress at the Castel S Elmo, Naples. Alfonso is depicted as Joseph of Arimathea in Guido Mazzoni's life-size terracotta group of the *Lamentation* (1492–4; Naples, S Anna ai Lombardi di Monte Oliveto; for illustration *see* MAZZONI, GUIDO). He was crowned King of Naples on 8 May 1494 in Naples Cathedral, but owing to his repressive policy towards the Neapolitan barons, he became so unpopular that he was forced to abdicate (23 Jan 1495). Shortly after, he took several boatloads of treasure and works of art with him to Sicily, where he spent the rest of his life in the Olivetan monastery at Mazara del Vallo.

BIBLIOGRAPHY

DBI

G. L. Hersey: 'Alfonso II, Benedetto e Giuliano da Maiano e la Porta Reale', *Napoli Nob.*, 3rd ser., iv (1964), pp. 77–95

——: *Alfonso II and the Artistic Renewal of Naples, 1485–1495* (New Haven and London, 1969)

V. Juren: 'Le Projet de Giuliano da Sangallo pour le palais du roi de Naples', *Rev. A.* [Paris], xxv (1974), pp. 66–70

□

(5) Ferdinand [Fernando] **II** [the Catholic], King of Aragon and Sicily [Ferdinand V, King of Castile; Ferdinand, King of Naples] (*b* Sos, 10 May 1451; *reg* 1479–1516; *d* Madrigalejo, 23 Jan 1516). Nephew of (1) Alfonso I, King of Naples.

(6) Isabella [the Catholic], Queen of Castile and León (*b* Madrigal de las Altes Torres, 20 April 1451; *reg* 1474–1504; *d* Medina del Campo, 26 Nov 1504). Wife of (5) Ferdinand II, King of Aragon and Sicily. Ferdinand married his cousin Isabella in Valladolid on 19 October 1469. Isabella became Queen of Castile and León on the death of her brother, Henry IV (*reg* 1454–74), and Ferdinand became King of Aragon and Sicily on the death of his father, John II (*reg* 1458–79). Together they unified the country and created the basis of modern Spain, as well as pursuing a policy of expansion that resulted in the establishment of an empire.

With the two crowns united and firmly established, Ferdinand and Isabella launched campaigns outside their kingdoms that had important consequences. They regained the Moorish Nasrid kingdom of Granada (1481–92) after eight centuries, and their initiative in the Americas in 1492 opened a vast new territory for Spanish enterprise. Confrontation with France resulted in a policy of pacts and marriage alliances: their youngest daughter Catherine of Aragon, married Henry VIII, King of England; Joanna (later Queen of Castile; *see* HABSBURG, §II (1)), the second daughter, married Philip the Fair, Duke of Burgundy (*d* 1506), and Isabella (1470–98), the eldest, became Queen of Portugal. Political and military intervention in Italy resulted in the conquest and annexation of the kingdom of Naples in 1504 (after the line of rulers descended from (1) Alfonso I died out). This expansionist policy was completed in 1512 with the annexation of Navarre, which became part of the kingdom of Castile.

Internally, Ferdinand and Isabella strengthened the institution of monarchy, making agreements with the nobility and the clergy, creating a state administration and restoring the economy. For the work of reforming the clergy they depended on Cardinal FRANCISCO JIMÉNEZ DE CISNEROS. They sought religious unity, resulting in the expulsion of the Jews from Spain in 1492, and created the Tribunal of the Holy Office of the Inquisition (1478). The title of 'Catholic Kings' was conferred on Ferdinand and Isabella by Pope Alexander VI in 1494.

The deaths of several of Ferdinand and Isabella's sons, the madness of their daughter Joanna and the sudden death of Philip I in 1506, together with the unconditional support of Cisneros and part of the Castilian states, allowed Ferdinand to govern the kingdom of Castile after Isabella's death and to pursue the same internal and external policies. His grandson, Charles (*see* HABSBURG, §I (5)) thus became the most powerful ruler in 16th-century Europe through his inheritance of the territories of Spain as well as those of the Holy Roman Empire.

Ferdinand concentrated his energies on politics and war and showed less interest in the arts than Isabella, who enjoyed a European reputation for her patronage of scholars and wide cultural interests; she had her own library and a refined taste in sculpture and painting as well as in the decorative arts. Her splendid art collection, the most important part of which is in the sacristy of the Capilla Real, Granada, was composed of religious paintings, including those by such Spanish Gothic artists as Bartolome Bermejo (e.g. the double-sided panel of the *Adoration of the Magi* and the *Head of Christ*) and Pedro Berruguete (e.g. *St John the Evangelist*). Works by 15th-century Flemish artists include two panels of the *Nativity* and *Pietà*, which are copies of the *Miraflores* Triptych (Berlin, Neue N.G.) by Rogier van der Weyden and said to have been painted in Spain by a court painter trained in the Netherlands; the altarpiece of the *Deposition*, with the *Crucifixion* and *Resurrection* on the wings (1450s), a *Virgin and Child*, a *Virgin and Child Enthroned between Angels* and the *Head of Christ* by Dieric Bouts I; and a *Virgin and Child, Descent from the Cross, Pièta* and the *Holy Women* by Hans Memling. Isabella also owned Italian religious paintings, including the *Agony in the Garden* (*c.* 1495–1500) by Botticelli and the *Dead Christ before the Tomb* by Perugino (all Granada, Capilla Real).

Capilla Real, Granada, by Enrique Egas, 1506–21

The greater part of Ferdinand and Isabella's patronage was predominantly Gothic architecture covered with elaborately carved surface ornament overlaying the structure. This style, known as the HISPANO-FLEMISH STYLE or the *Estilo Reyes Católicos*, is a characteristically Spanish form of decorated Gothic and often combines Gothic, Mudéjar and Renaissance motifs. The only palace architecture that has been preserved from their reign is the Cuarto Real in the convent of S Tomás, Avila (1482–94), built by Martín de Solórzano. The building is arranged around an enormous square Gothic patio, and, as on all buildings commissioned by Ferdinand and Isabella, is decorated with royal heraldic emblems and devices. The civic foundations of their reign include the Hospedería Real in Guadalupe (1486; destr.), described in contemporary accounts as one of the richest and most splendid buildings in Spain. Similar in style are two buildings by ENRIQUE EGAS: the Hospital Real (now the Hospital de los Reyes Católicos), Santiago de Compostela (1499), organized around two Renaissance patios in the centre of which is the chapel with decorated columns and star vaults, and the Hospital Real, Granada (founded 1504, built 1511–1640; now part of the university), which is a Renaissance building with fine Plateresque windows and a square plan divided in the form of a Greek cross into four patios with wide corridors.

Isabella commissioned a number of religious buildings: as a memorial to her parents she ordered the completion of the Charterhouse of Miraflores, near Burgos (1454–99; *see* BURGOS, §1); the single nave and star vaults of the church (completed 1488) by Simón de Colonia are covered with rich decoration. Gil de Siloé executed the wooden high altar retable (1496–9; *in situ*) with a central tondo depicting the *Crucifixion*, and the alabaster tomb (1486–93; for illustration *see* SILOÉ, DE, (1)) before the high altar of Isabella's parents, *John II, King of Castile* (*reg* 1406–54) and *Isabella of Portugal* (*d* 1496) in the form of an eight-pointed star. Siloé also designed the tomb (1489–93) of their son, the *Infante Don Alfonso* (1453–68), which is set in a recessed arch. Siloé's work forms one of the most elaborate sculptural ensembles in the decorated Gothic style in Spain.

Isabella also founded the convent of S Juan de los Reyes in Toledo (1476–1504) to commemorate the victory at the Battle of Toro (1476) and with the intention of making a royal pantheon. The church and cloister (*see* TOLEDO, fig. 3), designed and begun by Juan Guas and completed by Simón de Colonia, display great structural and decorative variety, making the monastery fundamental in the evolution of Spanish Gothic at the end of the 15th century and in the early 16th. The culmination of royal patronage was the Capilla Real, Granada (1506–21), the mausoleum of the Spanish royal family, including the Catholic Kings, until the founding of the Escorial by Philip II. The influence of Cisneros is evident in the severe plainness of the building, although the splendid vaults and portals (*see* GRANADA, fig. 1) are among the finest in the Hispano-Flemish style.

The works commissioned by the Catholic kings show a taste for rich and splendid Gothic art, although their acceptance of the Renaissance is seen in the tomb (completed 1513) of their son *Prince John* (1478–97; Avila, S Tomás) by DOMENICO FANCELLI in Carrara marble, a catafalque in the form of a truncated pyramid with the recumbent effigy at the top. The sculptor returned to this form in the tombs of *Ferdinand II and Isabella* (executed 1514–17) in the Capilla Real (see fig.), which is Fancelli's finest work and is significant in the introduction of the Renaissance style to Spain. The ornate interior of the Capilla Real, with the royal tombs, the great retable by Felipe Vigarny (1521), the fine grille and the superb collection of paintings, make it one of the most important historic and artistic buildings in Spain.

BIBLIOGRAPHY

M. Gómez Moreno: 'Sobre el Renacimiento en Castilla', I, *Archv. Esp. A. & Arqueol.*, i (1925), pp. 1–40

——: 'Sobre el Renacimiento en Castilla', II, *Archv. Esp. A. & Arqueol.*, iii (1925), pp. 245–88

F. J. Sánchez Cantón: *Libros, tapices y cuadros que coleccionó Isabel la Católica* (Madrid, 1950)

J. V. L. Brans: *Isabel la Católica y el arte hispano-flamenco* (Madrid, 1952)

A. Gallego y Burín: *La Capilla Real de Granada* (Madrid, 1952)

L. Torres Balbás: *Arquitectura gótica*, A. Hisp., vii (Madrid, 1952)

J. Gudiol Ricart: *Pintura gótica*, A. Hisp., ix (Madrid, 1955)

J. Camón Aznar: 'Fernando el Católico y el arte español de su tiempo', *V Congreso de la corona de Aragón* (Saragossa, 1956), pp. 14–30

A. Durán Sanpere and J. Ainaud de Lasarte: *Escultura gótica*, A. Hisp., viii (Madrid, 1956)

A. Hernández Perera: *Escultores florentinos en España* (Madrid, 1957)

J. M. de Azcárate: *La arquitectura gótica toledana del siglo XV* (Madrid, 1958)

C. Félez Lubelza: *El Hospital Real de Granada: Los comienzos de la arquitectura pública* (Granada, 1979)

F. Checa: *Pintura y escultura del Renacimiento en España, 1450–1600* (Madrid, 1983)

M. Morán y F. Checa: *El coleccionismo en España* (Madrid, 1985)

J. Y. Luaces: *Los Reyes Católicos. Paisaje artístico de una monarquía* (Madrid, 1993)

A. BUSTAMANTE GARCÍA

Aragon, Louis (*b* Paris, 3 Oct 1897; *d* Paris, 24 Dec 1982). French writer. He took up writing as a career after studying medicine during World War I. He was mobilized in 1917 at the same time as his friend André Breton, with whom he had contributed poems to Pierre Reverdy's *Nord-Sud*. His first critical article, 'Du décor', published in *Le Film* (16 Sept 1918), praised the novelty of the cinema and the aims of modern life, which he defined as progress, novelty of experience, liberty of artistic expression and inspiration of love. These were his main concerns when he founded the review *Littérature* (1919), together with Breton and the French writer Philippe Soupault. Fascinated by Tristan Tzara and by the collages of Max Ernst, he wrote his poems *Feu de joie* (Paris, 1920) and his parodic stories *Anicet* and *Les Aventures de Télémaque* (both Paris, 1922) under the influence of Dada, whose techniques he borrowed and to which he added his own insolence. Experimentation with subconscious motivations led to the formation of the Surrealist group around the three poets; it was officially launched in October 1924. With his essay 'Une Vague de rêves' (1924) Aragon provided Surrealism with its first historical and theoretic text, and he became one of the most dynamic contributors to their periodical, *La Révolution surréaliste* (1924–9). He considered the transforming power of passion in his ambiguous novels *Le Libertinage* (Paris, 1924) and *Le Paysan de Paris* (Paris, 1926), which contained in embryonic form his programme for Realism and the New Novel. He interpreted the group's position in such poems as *Le Mouvement perpétuel* (Paris, 1926) and *La Grande Gaîté* (Paris, 1929), and through polemical writings on art, such as the *Traité de style* (Paris, 1928) and *La Peinture au défi* (Paris, 1930). He considered that painting was based on moral concerns, a view that explains his invectives against de Chirico, who he felt had renounced the ideals of his youth, and his intolerance of Dalí.

Aragon himself turned his back on some of his early enthusiasms after joining the Communist Party in 1927 and visiting the USSR in 1930–31; he broke with the Surrealists in 1932 and celebrated the rise of Socialism in his poems, for example *Hourra l'Oural* (1934). In this he was inspired by Elsa Triolet (*d* 1970), whom he met in 1928 and subsequently married. As a Marxist he depicted French society at the beginning of the century in a Romanesque cycle of novels that he called 'Le Monde réel': *Les Cloches de Bâle* (Paris, 1934) and *Les Beaux Quartiers* (Paris, 1936) are the best-known of these, and they give a vivid picture of bourgeois life in capitalist Paris and in a small town in the Midi, seen through the eyes of a militant Marxist. During World War II he became the most popular poet of the Resistance movement, celebrated for his patriotic poems *Le Crève-coeur* (Paris, 1940) and his love poems *Les Yeux d'Elsa* (Paris, 1942). At the same time he led a fierce battle against non-figurative art and in support of Soviet painting. However, in the journal *Les Lettres françaises*, for which he was responsible, he published a portrait of Stalin by Picasso sufficiently far from reality for Aragon to be forced to express his doubts publicly. Though his faith in the Soviet leadership was shaken by disclosures in the 1950s and 1960s he remained a party member and strove to demonstrate in all his writings the permanence of his convictions. His writing on art was largely confined to monographs on Klee (1925), Pierre Roy (1926), Matisse (1943) and Picasso (1953), though his championship of Socialist Realism emerged in *L'Exemple de Courbet* (Paris, 1952) and in *Fougeron* (Paris, 1957). He paid tribute to his friend Matisse in *Henri Matisse, roman* (Paris, 1971).

WRITINGS

Anicet (Paris, 1922)

Les Aventures de Télémaque (Paris, 1922)

'Une Vague de rêves', *Commerce*, i (Oct 1924), pp. 89–122

Le Libertinage (Paris, 1924)

Le Paysan de Paris (Paris, 1926)

Traité de style (Paris, 1928)

La Peinture au défi (Paris, 1930)

Les Cloches de Bâle (Paris, 1934)

Les Beaux Quartiers (Paris, 1936)

L'Exemple de Courbet (Paris, 1952)

Fougeron (Paris, 1957)

Les Collages (Paris, 1965)

Henri Matisse, roman (Paris, 1971)

Escrits sur l'art moderne (Paris, 1981)

BIBLIOGRAPHY

R. Garaudy: *L'Itinéraire d'Aragon* (Paris, 1961)

Y. Gindine: *Aragon, prosateur surréaliste* (Paris, 1966)

L. F. Becker: *Louis Aragon* (New York, 1971)

P. Daix: *Aragon, une vie à changer* (Paris, 1975)

H. J. Neyer: *Kunst und Politik bei Aragon: Vom Surrealismus zur Poésie de Circonstances* (Frankfurt am Main, 1984)

HENRI BÉHAR

Aragón, Martín Gurrea y, Duque de Villahermosa. *See* GURREA Y ARAGÓN, (1).

Aragón, Pedro Antonio de. *See* SEGORBE Y CARDONA.

Aragón y Pino, Gasper Galcerán de Gurrea, Conde de Guimerá. *See* GURREA Y ARAGÓN, (2).

Arai, Alberto T. (*b* Mexico City, 29 March 1915; *d* Mexico City, 25 May 1959). Mexican architect, theorist and writer, of Japanese descent. The son of a Japanese ambassador in Mexico, he studied philosophy, espousing neo-Kantianism and becoming politically a socialist. He became a supporter of Functionalism, with its emphasis on the social applications of architecture, and was a founder, with Enrique Yañez, of the Unión de Arquitectos Socialistas (1938), helping to draw up a socialist theory of architecture. He was one of the most active participants in the Unión and attempted to put his socialist theory into practice on two unexecuted projects: the building for the Confederación de Trabajadores de México and the Ciudad Obrera de México, both with Enrique Guerrero and Raúl Cacho in the same year. Later, when Mexico opted for a developmental policy, Arai became a standard-bearer for nationalism in architecture. He re-evaluated traditional building materials, such as tree trunks, bamboo, palm leaves and lianas, using them in a plan for a country house that was adapted to the warm, damp climate of the Papaloapan region. The building of the Ciudad Universitaria, Mexico City, gave him his greatest architectural opportunity when he designed the Frontones (1952). In these he used the volcanic stone of the area to great effect in truncated pyramid shapes inspired by Pre-Columbian pyramids. His numerous books and articles addressed conceptual problems in Mexican architecture.

WRITINGS

La nueva arquitectura y la técnica (Mexico City, 1938)
Nuevo urbanismo (Mexico City, 1940)
Filosofía de la arquitectura (Mexico City, 1944)
Caminos para una arquitectura mexicana (Mexico City, 1952)
Qué orientaciones fundamentales debe seguir la arquitectura en México? (Mexico City, 1956)

BIBLIOGRAPHY

M. L. Cetto: *Moderne Architektur in Mexico* (Stuttgart, 1960; Eng. trans., New York, 1961)
E. X. de Anda: *Evolución de la arquitectura de México* (Mexico City, 1987)

RAMÓN VARGAS

Arakan. Kingdom on the east coast of the Bay of Bengal existent from at least the mid-4th century AD. It was independent until 1784 when it was conquered by the Burmese: in 1826 it was annexed by the British. When Burma gained its independence in 1948 it became one of the constituent states of the Union of Burma. Its geographical position (see fig. 1) favoured both land and sea links with Burma, India and, less directly, with China, and facilitated the spread of Buddhist, Hindu and Islamic influence from India along the trade routes across the bay and up the Kaladan River, along which a series of cities arose from about the 5th century. The architecture and sculpture of these cities shows the influence of the great Indian schools of art of both north and south, from the Gupta period in the 4th century to the 17th century, reinterpreted in a South-east Asian cultural context.

The earliest of the Indianized cities, Dhannavati (Dinnyawadi), was throughout the history of Arakan, from at least the 2nd century BC, the centre of the cult of the Mahamuni image. Aerial photographs of the Mahamuni shrine, north-east of the palace, show a rectangular wall with an opening to the east, surrounding a square temple set on two terraces. The sculptural remains suggest Mahayana influence from north-east India and connections with China and the Pyu cities of Burma. The architectural fragments suggest Gupta influence. A series of high reliefs illustrating the life of the Buddha and exhibiting a knowledge of perspective and abstraction otherwise unknown in the sculpture of South-east Asia has been discovered in the Selagiri shrine, on the pilgrimage path to the Mahamuni. To the south, the city of Vesali, where a Hindu or Indianized dynasty was ruling in the 2nd century BC and which in the mid-4th century AD became the capital of the kings of the Chandra dynasty, has numerous Buddhist Shaivite and Vaishnavite remains. The Thingyang-taung, reputedly a royal burial site, is an image shrine in the form of a stupa, with brick vaulting in the manner of the Pyu shrines of Srikshetra. A royal shrine centred on a statue of a reclining bull, the emblem of the Chandra dynasty, has been excavated, along with the remains of an ordination hall. Little remains of Pyin-sa, Parein, Cheik and Launggyet, a series of small cities built in the Lemyo Valley between the 12th and the 14th century, when Arakan was dominated by the powerful kings of Pagan and subsequently attacked by the Mons of Pegu. Massive Buddha images attest the dominance of Theravada Buddhism.

Arakan rose to power again with the founding of the city of Myohaung (Myauk U; Arakanese Mrohaung, Mrauk U) in 1433. It was built in a commanding position between the Kaladan and Lemyo rivers and became a prosperous port open to overseas influence. It is said to have been constructed with the aid of Portuguese and Bengali engineers and architects, and was defended by a network of ramparts and a complex hydraulic system that could check the approach of enemy armies by flooding. The architectural remains date chiefly from the 15th to the 17th century. They have survived better than similar monuments in Burma proper because most of them were built of sandstone, rather than brick and stucco, and the blocks were joined by a strong lime mortar that rendered them less vulnerable to the elements and to encroaching vegetation. The palace, near the city centre, has three concentric, tiered enclosures of sandstone, of which the topmost is about 15 m higher than the lowest. Only the gate at the south-west corner remains, as does a tank reputed to have been used for royal ablutions.

The northern approaches to the palace were protected by a series of shrines, some of which doubled as fortresses. Built mainly during the reign of King Minbin (*reg* 1531–53), these are unique in the architecture of South-east Asia. To the north of the site of the royal palace is the Shitthaung ('shrine of 80,000 images') which was built by Minbin as a refuge for the royal family and their retainers. Built on a hill, its vulnerable sides were fortified by massive stone walls, the outer one forming a rampart commanding the valley, so that the temple premises could accommodate a large garrison. A flight of steps at the southern end leads to the first platform. The next principal platform, which is entered through a vaulted gateway, is surrounded by a wall, on which are circular, turret-like pagodas built of brick, interspersed by stone slabs sculpted in high relief, on the outer side with *kīrttimukha*s (Skt: 'demon masks'), *nāga*s (serpent deities) and other creatures of the underworld, and on the inner side with Buddha images. The shrine itself consists of an inner temple court, a gallery all round the structure, intricate secret passages and chambers in the body of the pagoda and a central image chamber with a passage leading to it from the east. The vaulted passage round the inner court has on its outer side 28 arched passages, each containing two Buddha images, seated in *bhūmisparśa mudrā* (calling the earth to witness) back to back, facing the inner and outer court respectively. The inner wall has six tiers of figures sculpted in high relief, the lowest tier showing dancing, boxing and other scenes from everyday life, the middle tiers possibly representing *jātaka*s (stories of previous lives of the historical Buddha) and the upper tier praying figures. These are interspersed with a series of larger sculptures including the Buddha seated under the *nāga*, or surmounted by a *garuda* (mythical half-bird, half-human creature). At the corners are the king riding an elephant, or a four-armed deity surrounded by Brahmans and ministers. (For sculpture at Myohaung *see also* BURMA, §IV, 3.)

To the north of the Shitthaung is the An-daw-thein, which contains a tooth relic of the Buddha. The shrine was built by King Minyazagyi (*reg* 1593–1612), and the principal part of the building consists of an octagonal core inset with eight Buddha shrines, circled by two internal concentric passages. A little to the west of the An-daw-thein is the Htokkan-thein ('shrine of misery'), built by King Miuphalaung (*reg* 1571–93). It is surrounded by a square enclosure and is rectangular in plan with an apsidal bulge on the west side. Its flat roof is crowned by a central turret-like cupola surrounded by four smaller ones in the corners. A labyrinth winds through the shrine, open to the east, relieved at intervals by seated Buddha images in niches and ending in an image chamber containing a seated Buddha and a prostrate Sumedha. The Le-myet-hna is a square structure, with projecting porches at each cardinal point and surmounted by a massive circular dome constructed of stone. Niches in the octagonal central chamber contain seated Buddha images. Similar shrines were common in the contemporary capitals of the Burmese kings. A Muslim mosque, the Santikan, built by the followers of King Min Sawmun (Narameikhla) after his return from exile in Bengal in 1430, is rectangular in plan and surmounted by a low hemispherical cupola constructed on the same principles as the Shitthaung and Htokkan-thein.

By the 17th century Myohaung architecture had become more Burmese in style. Buddhist stupas were designed in the form of a spire, solid throughout, rising from a circular, square or octagonal base in a succession of tiers or bands, tapering to a point at a height usually one and a half times or twice the width of the base. Porches were attached to the sides or niches let into the wall for images. The monument was surmounted by a *hti* (Burm.: 'tiered umbrella') of metal (often copper).

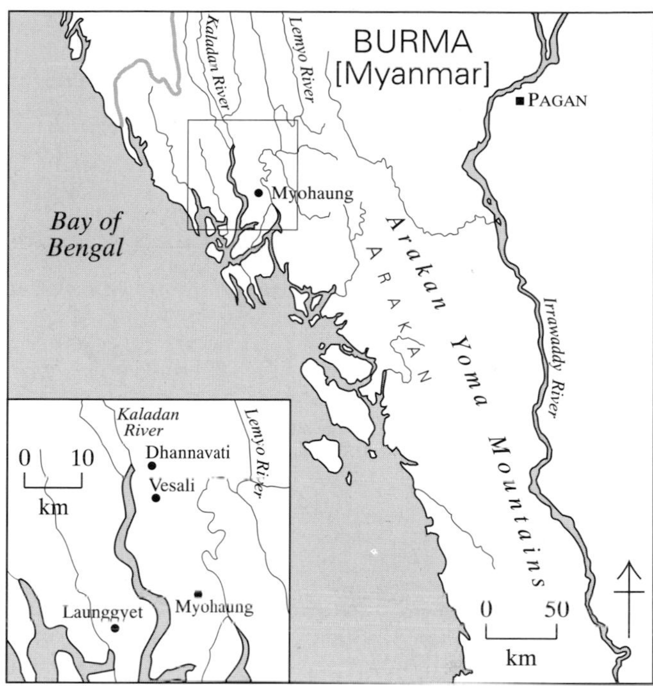

1. Map of Arakan; those areas with separate entries in this dictionary are distinguished by CROSS-REFERENCE TYPE

The stone Pitaka-taik, used as a repository for Buddhist scriptures received from Sri Lanka by King Narapatigyi (*reg* 1638–45), has a square base, and the main body of the structure widens in a curved line to the top, so that the upper part is broader and wider than the base. The entrance is an arched passage, opening to the east, and the roof, judging from the scattered stones, was a hemispherical cupola. The ornamentation is Burmese in inspiration, decorated with stone reliefs and leaf-shaped terracotta tablets, glazed in red, blue, yellow and white. The Lin-ban-maung Stupa, a massive stone structure with an octagonal base, is similarly decorated. On the first tier there were originally porches with niches above them containing Buddha images. Similar in concept are the Mingala-man-aung and Thet-kya Man-aung stupas. The latter dates from 1629. The Yadana Man-aung Stupa is also octagonal but it lacks niches and porches and has instead a small square entrance chamber to the east leading to an inner sanctum containing a massive seated Buddha image. Remains of a *nay* (spirit) shrine can be seen on Wunti Hill, with low-relief sculptures of female deities which show some Bengali influence.

The Kadaw-thein, erected by King Sandawizaya in 1723, south of Launggyet, is square in plan with indented corners. A vaulted passage leads from the east to a chamber with a seated Buddha image on the west side, and the roof is a hemispherical cupola. The outer stone surface of the shrine is covered with intricate ornamental designs (see fig. 2) derived ultimately from Pagan, and was originally gilded. The inner temple court was surrounded by a double

2. Arakan, Launggyet, façade of the Kadaw-thein, 1723; from E. Forchhammer: *Papers on Subjects Relating to the Archaeology of Burma* (Rangoon, 1891, rev. 1895), pl. xxxvi (London, British Library)

stone wall and paved with square tiles, glazed in blue, green and brown with etched floral and animal motifs.

Sittwe (Akyab), which became a garrison town under British rule, has a few modern temples remarkable in that their style is a combination of the Burmese pagoda and the Muslim four-cornered minaret, surmounted by a hemispherical cupola, and that they have been regularly frequented by both Muslims and Buddhists.

BIBLIOGRAPHY

E. Forchhammer: *Papers on Subjects Relating to the Archaeology of Burma* (Rangoon, 1891, rev. 1895)

——: *Report on the Antiquities of Arakan* (Rangoon, 1892)

U. Aung Thaw: *Historical Sites in Burma* (Rangoon, 1972/*R* 1978)

P. Gutman: *Ancient Arakan, with Special Reference to its Cultural History between the 5th and 11th Centuries* (diss., Canberra, Austral. N.U., 1977)

San Tha Aung: *The Buddhist Art of Ancient Arakan* (Rangoon, 1979)

Pagan Newslett. (Paris and Pondicherry, 1982–) [esp. 1985 issue]

J. Boisselier: *Il sud-est asiatico* (Turin, 1986)

S. Fraser-Lu: 'Ancient Arakan', *A. Asia*, xvii/2 (1987), pp. 96–109

M. Gatelier: 'Le Temple Shittaung á Myohaung, dépositaire des traditions de l'Arakan', *A. Asiatiques*, xlviii (1993), pp. 110–26

T. Kine: *A Guide to Mrauk-U, an Ancient City of Rakhine, Myanmar* (Rangoon and Sittway, 1993)

PAMELA GUTMAN, with PIERRE PICHARD

Arakawa, Shusaku (*b* Nagoya, 6 July 1936). Japanese painter, performance artist and film maker active in the USA. He studied medicine and mathematics at Tokyo University (1954–8) and art at the Musashino College of Art in Tokyo, holding his first one-man exhibition at the National Museum of Modern Art in Tokyo in 1958 and contributing to the Yomiuri Independent exhibitions from 1958 to 1961. In 1960 he took part in the 'anti-art' activities of the NEO-DADAISM ORGANIZERS in Tokyo and produced his first Happenings and a series of sculptures entitled *Boxes*, which consisted of amorphous lumps of cotton wads hardened in cement; many of these were put in coffin-like boxes, though one entitled *Foetus* was laid on a blanket. In pointing to the sickness of contemporary society, these works caused a great scandal in Tokyo.

In 1961 Arakawa settled in New York, where soon afterwards he addressed himself to the idea of a work being 'untitled'. In taking as his subject this apparent lack of subject, he emphasized the areas of the picture surface where the subject 'ought to be' by means of a few well-placed coloured framing marks, as in *Untitledness No. 2* (1961–2; see 1979 exh. cat., pl. 1). These were followed by another series of paintings entitled *Diagrams*, which consist of the sprayed silhouettes of banal objects such as tennis- rackets, combs and gloves (e.g. *A Card Becomes a Foot*, 1964; see 1979 exh. cat., pl. 7). After thus alluding to the shadows cast by objects, he moved even further away from actual objects by replacing them with their names and cursory outlines, as in *Alphabet Skin No. 2* (1966; see 1979 exh. cat., pl. 23). Characteristically this work incorporates a 'mistake' in the scrubbing out of one label and its replacement with the correct word with which to identify it. This laying bare of mistakes and second thoughts as a recurrent feature of his paintings underlines the fact that he conceives of them as visualizations of thought processes, and it acts as a reminder that any interpretation might be erroneous. Arakawa continued to explore the interrelationship between different forms of representation in a series of drawings and paintings entitled *Webster's Dictionary* (1965–6; see 1979 exh. cat., pls 13, 14 and 18), in which reproductions of dictionary pages were altered so that only the initial word was legible. The definitions were scribbled out in various colours, paradoxically suggesting both that words were meaningless and also that they might have an equivalent in colour.

Many of Arakawa's works from 1963 to 1971 formed part of *The Mechanism of Meaning*, a series made in collaboration with the American poet Madeline H. Gins (*b* 1943). A set of reproductions of these works with short captions was published in book form in 1971: divided into 16 subsections, with titles such as 'The Energy of Meaning' and 'Degrees of Meaning', this was Arakawa's most concentrated treatment of the nature of thought, language and representation. Real objects and stencilled texts were incorporated in some works of this period, often suggesting that the viewer engage in an apparently nonsensical activity; one instruction, for instance, found beneath a piece of cloth attached to the canvas, demands: 'Before lifting this decide whether you have ever seen what is underneath.' Arakawa also experimented with film making during this period, producing *Why Not* in 1969 and *For Example (A Critique of Never)* in 1971. Soon after *The Mechanism of Meaning* his paintings settled into a more consistent style characterized by intricate networks of lines, stencilled words and pale, transparent colours. These have the rational look of technical drawings and, like his previous works, defy complete understanding, as in the diptych *Afternoon and Evening* (1974; see 1979 exh. cat., pls 43–4), which on the afternoon panel contains the faint words: 'THE AFTERNOON OF/EACH CLEAVING AIR/EVERY AIR OF CLEAVING/ON THE SAME AFTERNOON/OF "TO CLEAVE"/SHAPE AS "A NOTHING"/OR SHAPE IN NOTHING'. After producing other works, sometimes very large in scale, in a similar style, in the late 1970s and early 1980s he again investigated the idea of blankness, this time by using arrows and fragments of street maps, as in *Blank Dots* (1982; New York, Met.).

WRITINGS

with M. H. Gins: *Mechanismus der Bedeutung (Werk im Entstehen: 1963–1971)* (Munich, 1971), intro. L. Alloway; rev. as *The Mechanism of Meaning: Work in Progress (1963–1971, 1978)* (New York, 1978)

BIBLIOGRAPHY

Arakawa (exh. cat. by M. H. Gins, Düsseldorf, Städt. Ksthalle, 1977)
Shusaku Arakawa (exh. cat. by M. H. Gins, Tokyo, Seibu Mus. A., 1979)
Arakawa (exh. cat. by D. Rice, Chicago, A. Club, 1981)
Arakawa: Bilder und Zeichnungen, 1962–1981 (exh. cat. by A. Zweite, Munich, Lenbachhaus; Hannover, Kestner-Ges.; 1981–2)
Arakawa (exh. cat. by J.-F. Lyotard, Milan, Padiglione A. Contemp., 1987)

□

Araki, Nobuyoshi (*b* Tokyo, 25 May 1940). Japanese photographer. He graduated from the engineering department of Chiba University in 1963 and in the same year received the Taiyō prize for *Satchin* (Tokyo, 1964), a photographic series whose title was the pet name of a little girl. In 1971, he published the privately printed photographic collection *Senchimentaru na tabi* ('Sentimental journey'; Tokyo, 1971) in which his own private life, in particular his wedding and honeymoon, was displayed in diary form. At first glance they seem to be naive records but in fact are staged. He also gave a performance in 1972 called the Super-Photo concert in which these photographs were reproduced on a photocopier, bound and sent, as a collection, by post. He later became very popular through photographs that skilfully anticipated public demand, accompanied by essays written in a risqué style. A prolific worker, he published many collections of essays and photographs, including *Otoko to onna no aida ni wa shashinki ga aru* ('There is a camera between man and woman'; Tokyo, 1977), *Waga'ai Yōko* ('Yoko, my love'; Tokyo, 1978), *Shashin shōsetsu* ('Photograph novel'; Tokyo, 1981), *Tōkyō ereji* ('Tokyo elegy'; Tokyo, 1981), *Shojo sekai* ('World of girls'; Tokyo, 1984) and *Tōkyō wa aki* ('Autumn in Tokyo'; Tokyo, 1984). Beneath his boisterous photographs runs an undercurrent of cool detachment regarding human life and death.

BIBLIOGRAPHY

Kōen Shigemori, ed.: *Nude Photography*, Complete Hist. Jap. Phot., vi (Tokyo, 1986), pp. 140–44

IIZAWA KOHTARO

Arakou, Panagia tou. *See* LAGOUDERA, PANAGIA TOU ARAKOU.

Aramaean. Term for an ancient people of the Near East, prominent in the 1st millennium BC. Their origins are obscure; they were probably semi-nomadic tribesmen driven from the Syrian steppe by drought. By about 1000 BC they had occupied an arc of land from Babylonia to southern Lebanon. In the east the ancient local culture absorbed them. In the west they took over the cities and turned many of them into autonomous tribal centres, principally Aram (Damascus), Arpad (Bit-Agusi) to the north of Aleppo, Bit-Adini east of the bend of the River Euphrates, and Bit-Bahiani at Guzana (TELL HALAF) on the River Khabur. The earlier inhabitants mixed with the newcomers, and at Hamath (Hama) on the River Orontes a local Neo-Hittite dynasty retained control until *c.* 800 BC. Hardly had Aramaean kings taken power than they had to fight the Assyrians, who campaigned westwards from *c.* 900 BC, taking Damascus in 732 BC.

The chief recognizable characteristic of the Aramaeans is their West Semitic language, written in the 'Phoenician' alphabet. There is no clearly definable Aramaean art. Inscribed stone sculptures of the 9th and 8th centuries BC from Tell Fekheriyeh near Guzana and Sam'al (ZINCIRLI), inland from the Gulf of Alexandretta, imitate Assyrian styles. Others from sites in north Syria show clear Hittite influence. Occasionally local craftsmen produced their own styles, as at Guzana. Ivory-decorated furniture was popular. Some pieces bear Aramaic letters to guide assembly, but no feature can be recognized as particularly Aramaean. The distinctive plan of Aramaean palaces, named *bit hilani*, derives from the Bronze Age (*see* SYRIA-PALESTINE, §II and ANATOLIA, ANCIENT, §II).

BIBLIOGRAPHY

H. Frankfort: *The Art and Architecture of the Ancient Orient* (London, 1954, rev. 4/1970), pp. 164–201
G. Garbini: 'Il problema dell'arte aramaica', *Riv. Stud. Orient.*, xxxiv (1959), pp. 141–7
A. Malamat: 'The Aramaeans', *Peoples of Old Testament Times*, ed. D. J. Wiseman (Oxford, 1973), pp. 134–55

A. R. MILLARD

Aranda, 10th Conde de [Abarca de Bolea, Pedro Pablo] (*b* Sietano, 1 Aug 1719; *d* Epila, 9 Jan 1798). Spanish statesman and patron. He belonged to a noble Aragonese family and received a military education. Philip V made him an infantry colonel at an early age; he took part in the Italian campaign (1743–6) and was promoted to field marshal by Ferdinand VI. In 1755 he was first appointed ambassador to Lisbon and was then sent by the Bourbon Charles III as ambassador to Poland. In 1762 he was recalled to Madrid, where he held various political offices such as President of the Council of Castile. He was hostile to the Jesuits, who were expelled from Spain in 1767. In the role of enlightened politician, Aranda reformed military regulations (Ordenazas Militares) and in 1767 he re-established public events, such as the Carnival, which had previously been forbidden. In 1770 he wrote the national anthem.

In 1773, then head of the Aragonese party, he was removed from domestic politics by the minister, the Conde de Floridablanca, José Monino, and was appointed ambassador to Paris (1773–87), where he distinguished himself by his taste for luxury and his influential friendships at the French court. Recalled to serve as minister to the Bourbon Charles IV, he was soon removed from political life altogether, by the favourite Manuel Godoy, Principe de la Paz. He was confined first to the Alhambra in Granada in 1794 and then successively to Alahama and Sanlúcar de Barrameda until for health reasons he was allowed to return to his estates at Epila, where he died.

Aranda was distinguished by his love of the arts. In 1727 his father Don Buenaventura de Urrea Abarca de Bolea, 9th Conde de Aranda (*d* 1742), had founded a ceramic works at Alcora, which his son enlarged and made into a porcelain factory, importing German craftsmen and their technical expertise from Meissen. Aranda promoted the construction of the Imperial Canal in Aragón (1768–90) and was involved in a project for navigation on the River Ebro. In 1776 he was a founder-member of the Sociedad Económica de Amigos del País in Aragón, an enterprise that encouraged arts and sciences and led to the establishment of many schools and academies. He assisted in the founding in 1792 of the Real Academia de Bellas Artes de S Luis in Saragossa. Aranda was well known abroad as a cultivated Spaniard of the Age of Enlightenment and was praised by the Marquis de Condorcet (1743–94) and by Voltaire (1694–1778). The accusations of anti-Jesuitism and freemasonry made against him by 19th-century historians have been proved to be unfounded.

BIBLIOGRAPHY

Conde de Casal: *Historia de la cerámica de Alcora* (Madrid, 1919)

J. A. Ferrer Benimeli: *El Conde de Aranda y la Real Sociedad Económica Aragonesa de Amigos del País* (Saragossa, 1978)

R. Olaechea and J. A. Ferrer Benimeli: *El Conde de Aranda* (Saragossa, 1978)

Y. Bottineau: *L'Art de cour dans l'Espagne des lumières, 1746–1808* (Paris, 1986)

MERCEDES AGUEDA

Aranda, José Jiménez. *See* JIMÉNEZ ARANDA, JOSÉ.

Aranjuez Palace. Spanish palace that stands beside the rivers Tagus and Jarama in the province of Madrid, 47 km south of the capital. It was intended as a spring and summer residence for the royal family and is renowned for its gardens and fountains. The summer residence built at Aranjuez in 1387 by Lorenzo Suárez de Figueroa, Grand Master of the Order of Santiago, became royal property under Ferdinand II, King of Aragon, and Isabella, Queen of Castile and León. In the reign of Charles V improvements were carried out by Luis de Vega (from *c.* 1537) and the palace was extensively enlarged by Philip II. The chapel was designed by JUAN BAUTISTA DE TOLEDO and completed by Jerónimo Gili and JUAN DE HERRERA. It was built in a combination of white stone from Colmenar de Oreja and brick, giving a two-toned effect that was adopted for the rest of the palace. In 1571 work began on the *cuarto nuevo*, as the new palace was described, beside the chapel. The overall plan was probably by Juan Bautista de Toledo and is known to have been drawn up at the Escorial. Herrera was responsible for the lead roof (1577). The materials and mouldings of the palace were similar to those of the chapel, maintaining further links with the style of Bautista de Toledo. The ground-plan of the palace was square, with a square central courtyard, but the lack of towers with pinnacles at each corner, more usual at this date, gave the building a more classical appearance. The principal façade was elongated by wings, and at the end of one stands the chapel. This meant that the more usual plan of a block with four equal sides was replaced in favour of a design with one principal block, an emphasis that was to acquire greater importance with successive renovations. The separate Casa de Oficios, quarters for the courtiers and servants, was begun in 1577 after the design of Herrera, and the angled forms and sense of volume characteristic of his style are seen in the order of the cloister. This work was continued by Juan Gómez de Mora (i) in a more austere style.

Aranjuez Palace, aerial view of the palace complex from the west, begun 1571

Aranjuez Palace as planned in the 16th century was not completed. From 1715, under Philip V, a north wing was added by Pedro Caro Idogro. GIACOMO BONAVIA was commissioned to rebuild the palace, which had been damaged by fire, and restore the town. He was responsible for the vestibule, the great imperial staircase and the main façade (1744), in the centre of which is a portico surmounted by the ceremonial balcony of honour. Bonavia added a third storey and the frontispiece that gave weight to the main entrance. The statues on the balustrade of *Philip II*, *Philip V* and *Ferdinand VI* by Pedro Martinengo were added in 1752. The general style of this façade, combining designs that are both French and Italian, can be associated with that of the Spanish Bourbons. The palace was enlarged under Charles III in order to meet the increasingly elaborate etiquette of the court. Two wings at right angles to the main façade, forming a U-shaped entrance courtyard in the French manner, were added by Francesco Sabbatini (wings dated 1772 and 1777; see fig.).

The gardens at Aranjuez are among the most important in Spain. They were first created by Philip II and their continued development was made possible by the plentiful supply of water. An initial design was made by Juan Bautista de Toledo in 1560, but Herrera carried out the planning. Philip II first created a garden behind the main façade, ornamented with busts of Roman emperors. The Flemish naturalist Juan Holveque was employed from 1561 for the planting, and fountains were imported from Italy, such as that of *Venus* (1571). Conservatories, for example the Casa de los Naranjos (1571), were also built after the design of Herrera. The beauty of Philip II's gardens, with their groves, flowerbeds, fountains and statues, has been praised in literature (Ambrosio de Morales, 1565) and in music (*Concierto de Aranjuez* by Joaquin Rodrigo). In 1620 Philip III sent 27 bronze and marble statues for their embellishment. In 1622, under Philip IV, many more statues were taken from the Alcázar, Madrid, to be installed at Aranjuez; these included a series of portraits of emperors and works by Leone Leoni and

Pompeo Leoni, including Leone Leoni's bronze *Charles V and Fury Restrained* (1549–55; Madrid, Prado). From 1660 the design of the gardens was modified by Sebastián de Herrera Barnuevo. Among the garden fountains, some incorporated musical devices, others delighted with surprisingly devised waterworks. The fountain of *Hercules and the Hydra* (1661) was by Martinio Regio; that of *Trypolemus* (sculptor unknown) was set in the Jardín de la Isla (designed by Herrera Barnuevo, 1669). Others included the late 16th-century *Bacchus* by the Flemish Jacques Jonghelinck; *Diana* and *Neptune* (both by unknown sculptors) and the *Harpies* (1615) by Juan Fernández and Pedro de Garay. Under the Bourbons further improvements were made to the gardens, and in 1744 a bridge adorned with statues was built (attributed to Bonavia); in 1732–3 the formal Jardín del Parterre was laid out by Etienne Boutelou (*d* 1734), a gardener of French origin who was succeeded in this work by his son Etienne Boutelou.

The planning of the Jardín del Príncipe was initiated by Ferdinand VI in 1750, but it was officially founded in 1772 under Charles III (plan dated 1784). It is the largest garden at Aranjuez, sited with an attractive wharf beside the Tagus, and was designed, as were the pavilions, by Juan de Villanueva. This informal garden, with fountains and statues, incuding the fountain of *Narcissus* (1789–95) by Joaquín Dumandré, surrounds the Casa del Labrador, which was begun in the reign of Charles III and completed (*c.* 1792–1800) under Charles IV by Villanueva assisted by Isidro González Velázquez. The Casa del Labrador, decorated under Charles IV in Neo-classical style, was conceived in the same spirit as the Petit Trianon at Versailles, a retreat for the heirs to the throne, the Princes of the Asturias. It contains a collection of busts of Roman emperors once owned by Queen Christina of Sweden and installed there *c.* 1800.

The interior of Aranjuez was adorned during the 18th century with a considerable collection of paintings, statues, furniture, mirrors and chandeliers. One of the most decorative rooms is the Gabinete de la Porcelana (1763–5), which was sumptuously decorated in the Japanese style for Charles III with plaques of porcelain made in the Fábrica del Buen Retiro by Giuseppe Gricci of Naples. Since the reign of Philip II only those belonging to the royal household had been allowed to reside at Aranjuez. Under Ferdinand VI, therefore, a town adjacent to the palace was laid out on a perfectly regular plan designed and executed by Bonavia (1750–52). A triple avenue extends the axis of the gardens in a design resembling the trident at Versailles. The Plaza de S Antonio was aligned with the avenue, and to the south stands the church of S Antonio (plan by Bonavia, 1748), linked to the palace by a long covered passageway of a type often used in Spanish urban planning. The church has a circular plan, and a tribune for the royal family, thus allowing the public some proximity to the monarch.

See also SPAIN, figs 30 and 31.

BIBLIOGRAPHY

A. de Morales: *Las antigüedades de las ciudades de España* (Alcalá de Henares, 1565), p. 94

J. A. Alvarez de Quindós y Baena: *Descripción histórica del Real Bosque y Casa de Aranjuez* (Madrid, 1804)

Y. Bottineau: *L'Art de cour dans l'Espagne de Philippe V, 1700–1746* (Bordeaux, 1960)

J. J. Martín González: 'El Palacio de Aranjuez en el siglo XVI', *Archv Esp. A.*, xxxv (1962), pp. 237–52

C. M. Correcher: 'Jardines de Aranjuez: II Jardín del Príncipe', *Reales Sitios: Rev. Patrm. N.*, lxxiii (1982), pp. 21–38

P. Junquera and M. T. Ruiz Alcón: *Palacio de Aranjuez: Casa del Labrador y Jardín del Príncipe* (Madrid, 1985)

C. Díaz Gallegos: 'El real sitio de Aranjuez, ejemplo de urbanismo barroco en España: Sus calles y plazas', *Reales Sitios: Rev. Patrm. N.*, lxxxviii (1986), pp. 29–36

A. González: 'El Palacio de Aranjuez: Nueva estructura entre 1626 y 1750', *Reales Sitios: Rev. Patrm. N.*, lxxxix (1986), pp. 57–64

M. Estella: 'Sobre las esculturas del Jardín de la Isla en Aranjuez', *Velázquez y el arte de su tiempo* (Madrid, 1991), pp. 333–48

J. J. MARTÍN GONZÁLEZ

'Araq el-Emir. *See* 'IRAQ AL-AMIR.

Araujo, Ceferino (*b* Santander, 1824; *d* Madrid, 1897). Spanish painter and writer. He was a pupil of the landscape painter Carlos de Haes at the Escuela Superior in Madrid and exhibited at the National Fine Arts Exhibitions of 1858, 1860, 1862 and 1866. His artistic career, however, is less significant than his profound knowledge of art. He published articles in *La Ilustración española y americana*, *El Día*, *Arte en España* and the *Revista de bellas artes* (all published in Madrid), at a time when art criticism, understood as 'a commentary on work, made with some degree of authority', was still in its infancy in Spain. He gave several lectures at the Ateneo Cientifico, Literario y Artístico in Madrid, such as: 'Observaciones sobre el concepto del Arte' (15 May 1884), 'Los desenvolvimientos de la pintura—López, Madrazo, Rosales, Fortuny' (1887) and 'La España del siglo XIX: Goya y su época' (1895). His publications include the monographs *Goya* (1896) and *Palmaroli y su tiempo* (1897), and in the field of art criticism and theory, *Categoria y excelencias del arte barroco* (1886). In *Los Museos de España* (1875) he drew attention to the carelessness and neglect that most of the Spanish museums, especially the Prado, were suffering and proposed a series of steps for their improvement and restoration.

WRITINGS

Los Museos de España (Madrid, 1875)

Categoria y excelencias del arte barroco (Madrid, 1886)

Goya (Madrid, 1896)

Palmaroli y su tiempo (1897)

Regular contributions to *A. España*, *El Día*, *Ilus. Esp. & Amer.* and *Rev. B.A.*

BIBLIOGRAPHY

J. A. Gaya Nuño: *Historia de la crítica de arte en España* (Madrid, 1975)

PILAR BENITO

Araujo, César de. *See* POUSÃO, HENRIQUE.

Araújo, José Álvares de (*d* Braga, 10 March 1762). Portuguese wood-carver and designer. He designed the carved altarpieces, pulpits and valances for the church of the Third Order of St Francis in Ponte de Lima. The carving was completed in 1756 by António da Cunha Correia Vale and Manuel da Cunha Correia Vale from Guimarães. It is a fine example of carving in the new Rococo style. In 1756 Araújo was contracted to carve the arch of the frame of the altarpiece of Nossa Senhora dos Prazeres in the church of the Colegio de S Paulo in Braga, after designs by ANDRÉ RIBEIRO SOARES DA SILVA. A comparison between Soares's design and that by Araújo for the Third Order in Ponte de Lima shows the marked lack of plasticity in the latter, although Araújo used elements taken from the work of Soares and the designs of Nicolau Nasoni. Both these works, however, were completed before the redecoration carried out by Araújo in the church of S Martinho in the Benedictine monastery of Tibães. Araújo carved Soares's designs for the main altarpiece here as well as retables for the transept and sacristy; he also worked on the pulpits and valances in the nave. This carved ensemble was the most distinguished of the period. Araújo completed the high altar *c.* 1758; it was later gilded by João Gonçalves Ribas.

The spirit of the carving at Tibães was developed more fully in the designs by Soares for the immense altarpiece of Nossa Senhora do Rosário in the church of the Dominican convent of S Domingos in Viana do Castelo. In 1761 Araújo was commissioned by the Brotherhood of Nossa Senhora do Rosário to carve Soares's designs; the work was completed and gilded by 1764, after his death. The rosary altarpiece is one of the most monumental schemes of carving of the period. It was Araújo's last work and displayed his technical ability to the full. He was assisted by his gifted pupil, the Benedictine lay-brother Frei José de Santo António Ferreira Vilaça.

BIBLIOGRAPHY

R. C. Smith: 'A verdadeira história do retábulo de Nossa Senhora do Rosário da igreja de S Domingos de Viana do Castelo', *Belas A.*, n. s. 2, 23 (1967), pp. 19–38

——: *Frei José de Santo António Ferreira Vilaça: Escultor beneditino do século XVIII* (Lisbon, 1972), p. 761

Araújo, Marceliano de (*b* Braga, *c.* 1690; *d* Braga, 10 March 1769). Portuguese sculptor and carver. He was one of the most gifted of the wood-carvers who created Portuguese Baroque church interiors in the 18th century, lined with carved, gilt wood and glittering with gold. He used vigorous and imaginative ornament, in which plume-like displays of acanthus foliage, shells, dolphins and tritons mingle with angels, nude children, vases of flowers, bearded faces and masks with exotic coiffures, all framed and supported by distinctive carved brackets. Many of these motifs are enlarged versions of those in the engravings by Jean Berain I, known to have been in circulation at this time in Portugal.

This type of decoration is seen in Araújo's first important work (1716–19) in the Benedictine monastery of S Bento da Vitória, Oporto, where the towering frames of the choir-stalls contain sculptured panels made of gilt chestnut wood representing scenes from the *Life of St Benedict.* Between 1719 and 1734 Araújo's name appears on contracts as a guarantor for other artists, an indication of his professional standing in Braga. His most important work in Braga includes the carved triple retable, in gilt and silvered polychrome chestnut wood, for the church of the S Casa da Misericórdia (1734–9). In the lower section of the retable statues of saints, angels and allegories are set in niches; above they are incorporated into the ornament in a strong rhythmic design that is characteristic of Araújo's work. The twin organ cases of gilt and polychrome chestnut wood (1737–8) in the nave of Braga Cathedral, with their elaborately dressed allegorical figures, including the Virtues, show the theatricality of his style.

On 19 December 1751 Araújo became a member of the Brotherhood of S Maria Madalena, Monte da Falperra, near Braga, and from 1755 his name is linked with the Fraternity of Bom Jesus do Monte, near Braga. In 1758 he collaborated with others on the carving of two angels for the chancel of the church of São Vicente, Braga. Works attributed to Araújo in Braga include the Pelican Fountain (*c.* 1740–45), the pulpit of the church of Nossa Senhora da Penha de França (*c.* 1740–45), the retables of Nossa Senhora da Conceição and of Nossa Senhora das Dores (both *c.* 1745–50), both in the church of Nossa Senhora do Pópulo. Also attributed to him are the design of the title pages of the Statutes of the Confraria do Apóstolo S Tiago, Braga (1739; Braga, Arquiv. Irmandade Santa Cruz), and *Braga triunfante na real eleição* by Manuel José Correia e Alvarenga (Coimbra, 1742).

BIBLIOGRAPHY

R. C. Smith: *Cadeirais de Portugal* [Portuguese choir-stalls] (Lisbon, 1968), p. 49

——: *Marceliano de Araújo, escultor bracarense* (Oporto, 1970)

NATÁLIA MARINHO FERREIRA ALVES

Arausio [now Orange]. Roman town in south-west France, 7 km east of the river Rhône. It is famous for its theatre and triumphal arch. The Roman colony of Arausio was founded *c.* 35 BC for veterans of the 2nd Gallic Legion beside the Saint-Eutrope Hill, probably a stronghold of the native tribe of the Tricastini, which Strabo (IV.i.12) described as the most Romanized in southern Gaul. The Roman city included most of the hill, the regular street grid beginning at the foot of its steep northern slopes. The alignment of the streets was continued in the road system that divided the territory into equally sized plots of land allocated to each colonist. This is attested by the remarkable discovery in a limekiln near the theatre of fragments of three cadastral surveys carved on marble tablets (Orange, Mus. Mun.), the earliest set up in the city's record office in AD 77, the second and most informative probably made in the reign of Trajan (AD 98–117), the third of later but unknown date. The surveys identify the roads in numerical sequence relative to the *decumanus* and *cardo* (the north–south and east–west axes) and name the holder of each plot, as well as showing the course of a river and the marginal territory still occupied by the native Tricastini.

The main buildings known within the town are on the north slopes of the Saint-Eutrope Hill. Next to the theatre on the west, and also cut into the hillside, was a smaller semicircular walled structure 74 m in diameter, of Augustan date (27 BC–AD 14). Within this is the podium of a large octastyle peripteral temple facing north, variously dated as Augustan or 2nd century AD. The walls of a rectangular enclosure to the north may have joined the semicircular structure to form the forum and temple precinct. There may have been a smaller theatre on that site prior to the construction of the temple and the present theatre. There are also remains of a smaller temple and of another monumental building higher up the hillside.

The triumphal arch at Arausio was the most elaborate and impressive in Gaul, built a short distance beyond the city's north gate. It is a triple-arched structure, 17.80 m high and 19.58 m wide (see fig.). Of the two main elevations, similarly decorated, the north face is the better preserved. The central larger arch is flanked by pilasters carved with spirals of foliage. The voussoirs over the passages are carved with oak branches, and the stone-cut vaults are elaborately coffered. Four engaged fluted Corinthian columns on pedestals, placed at the corners and between the passages, carry an entablature, with a pediment over the central arch. The spaces above the side arches were filled with carvings of oval and trapezoidal Celtic and Germanic shields (some bearing names), weapons, helmets, standards and war trumpets. The attic is divided into two stages of equal height. The lower attic contains the pediment, with carvings of ships' prows, anchors, tridents and other naval tackle to each side. The upper attic, a feature not known on any other Roman arch, has three projecting socles. The higher central socle, which would have supported a statuary group, is carved with a cavalry battle between Romans and Gauls. Of the smaller socles above the side passages, only the north-east and south-east ones are original, and show sacrificial implements and a draped female figure respectively. The short sides of the arch (the west side is largely a restoration) have four Corinthian columns supporting a pediment with a central arched niche recessed into it, a late Hellenistic feature rarely found in Roman architecture in the West. Between the columns are relief carvings of bound captives standing beneath trophies of arms. The frieze has Roman and Celtic warriors. In the east pediment arch there is a bust of Sol, the Roman sun god, and there are two tritons on the lower attic below the pediment. The date and purpose of the arch have been much debated, despite the uniquely elaborate and apparently specific representation of triumph by land and sea, and the inscription on the architrave, restored on the basis of the holes for the lettering as naming the emperor Tiberius (*reg* AD 14–37) with his titles for AD 26–7. The battle scenes have been linked with the suppression in AD 21 of the revolt of Julius Sacrovir by the 2nd Augustan Legion, but Gros (1986) argued that the arch was intended to commemorate the achievements of Germanicus (15 BC–AD 19), the nephew and adopted son of Tiberius.

The Roman theatre at Arausio, together with those at ASPENDOS and SABRATHA, is one of the most complete Roman theatres surviving (*see* THEATRE, fig. 2). The *cavea* could seat 7000 spectators and was cut into the hillside; it therefore lacked the internal stairways of theatres built with vaulted substructures, and an external stair gave access to the upper seats through the surrounding portico at the top. The stage building survives to its full height of 37 m. Its façade, the *scaenae frons*, has a wide curved central recess, from which the main entrance projects, and a shallow rectangular recess for the stage entrances on each side. These features were embellished with three orders of marble sculpture, of which only a few pieces survive; some have been re-erected, and a restored statue of Augustus stands in the large niche above the central entrance. The inclined line of the sounding-board over the stage is visible in the masonry at the top of the wings that project at the ends of the *scaena*. The street frontage of the *scaena* (103 m long) is of rusticated ashlar and has two rows of brackets at the top to house masts from which awnings were suspended over the theatre. Below the brackets the plain appearance of the wall is only slightly relieved by shallow

Arausio (Orange), triumphal arch, begun *c.* AD 21

pilasters and a blind arcade. The open arcade carried on piers at the bottom originally had a portico in front of it, with a porch in the centre, at the entrance to the building.

BIBLIOGRAPHY

A. Grenier: *Manuel d'archéologie gallo-romaine*, III/ii (Paris, 1958), pp. 754–65

R. Amy and others: *L'Arc d'Orange* (Paris, 1962)

A. Piganiol: *Les Documents cadastraux de la colonie romaine d'Orange* (Paris, 1962)

P. Gros: 'Une Hypothèse sur l'arc d'Orange', *Gallia*, xliv (1986), pp. 191–201

T. F. C. BLAGG

Arazzeria Medicea. *See under* FLORENCE, §III, 3.

Arbeitsgruppe 4. Austrian group of architects formed in 1952 by Wilhelm Holzbauer, Friedrich Kurrent (*b* 1931) and Johannes Spalt (*b* 1920) at the Akademie der Bildenden Künste, Meisterschule Clemens Holzmeister, Vienna, after participating in a competition with Otto Leitner. It emerged early with its programmatic and innovative works such as the Wohnraumschule and community housing projects. Early buildings such as the church of Parsch, Salzburg (1953–6; *see* AUSTRIA, fig. 10), still deal in Clemens Holzmeister's romantic architectural concept made relative by the central and northern European Modernism of the 1950s. Participation in the Sommerakademie, Salzburg, at which Kurrent and Spalt were assistants to Konrad Wachsmann, led the group on the one hand to push on with the rational and constructivist interest, and on the other to start to deal systematically with the history of Viennese Modernism—from Otto Wagner to Josef Frank. Although the pastoral care complex of Steyr-Ennsleiten (1958–61; in cooperation with Johann Georg Gsteu, *b* 1927) still remains a constructivist manifestation, the theology college in Aigen, Salzburg (1961–4), built in steel, not only challenged the prevalent aesthetics of Mies van der Rohe, but also demonstrated a more liberal space-related use (in the sense of the Viennese tradition) of the material, the design and its meaning. Holzbauer had distanced himself from the architectural aims of the group following a lengthy stay in the USA (1956–60) and left the group in 1964. In Floridsdorf, Vienna, from 1970 to 1974 Kurrent and Spalt created an exemplary bank extension building, which showed great sense of freedom and a balance of architectural means.

BIBLIOGRAPHY

Johannes Spalt, Katalog (Gmunden, 1976)

F. Achleitner: *Österreichische Architektur im 20. Jahrhundert,* 3 vols (Salzburg, 1980–90)

Wilhelm Holzbauer, Bauten und Projekte, 1953–85 (Salzburg, 1985)

FRIEDRICH ACHLEITNER

Arbeitsrat für Kunst. Association of radical German architects, artists and critics founded in Berlin in December 1918 by Bruno Taut and dissolved on 30 May 1921. The membership grew rapidly and included the architects Otto Bartning, Walter Gropius, Paul Mebes, Erich Mendelsohn, Hans Poelzig, Paul Schmitthenner, Max Taut and Heinrich Tessenow; the painters César Klein, Erich Heckel, Käthe Kollwitz, Ludwig Meidner, Max Pechstein, Karl Schmidt-Rottluff and Lyonel Feininger; the sculptors Rudolph Belling, Oswald Herzog and Gerhard Marcks; and such critics and patrons as Adolf Behne (1885–1948), Mechtilde von Lichnowsky (1879–1958), Julius Meier-Graefe, Karl Ernst Osthaus and Wilhelm Worringer.

Bruno Taut initially conceived the group as a political pressure group, the artistic equivalent to the workers' and soldiers' councils that held power in November and December 1918. The founding manifesto demanded: 'Art and the people must form a unity. . . . From now on the artist alone, as moulder of the sensibilities of the people, will be responsible for the visible fabric of the new state'. The hope of achieving direct political responsibility proved a chimera, however, and an embittered Taut resigned from the leadership of the group at the end of February 1919, to be replaced by Walter Gropius. More pragmatic than Taut, Gropius abandoned any political aspirations and turned the group in on itself, suggesting that the association should regard itself as a community of radical artists who should work together on an ideal building task, the *Bauprojekt,* a temple-like construction that would serve as a focus for social and cultural regeneration. It would also offer the means to achieve the group's prime artistic aim: 'the fusion of the arts under the wing of a new architecture'. Political instability, gathering inflation, material shortages and a lack of artistic direction within the group condemned this noble project to remain on paper.

The hopes for an artistic revival led by architecture were not abandoned, however, and provided the basis of Gropius's programme for the newly established Weimar BAUHAUS in April 1919. With Gropius in Weimar, the administration of the Arbeitsrat für Kunst was taken over by the critic Adolf Behne. Although the *Bauprojekt* was retained as an ultimate goal and linked to schemes for rebuilding in the devastated battle zones in France, the group's only practical activity was limited to publications and exhibitions. In addition to the founding manifesto and Taut's 'Architektur-Programm', which were published in various journals, the group also published two books: *Ja! Stimmen des Arbeitsrates für Kunst in Berlin* (Berlin, 1919), the results of a survey conducted among the membership on such questions as art and design education, exhibition policy, state support of the arts and public architecture; and *Ruf zum Bauen* (Berlin, 1920).

Among the exhibitions organized by the Arbeitsrat were the *Ausstellung für unbekannte Architekten* (April 1919), an exhibition of art by workers and children (January 1920), and *Neues Bauen* (May 1920). The group also arranged exhibitions in Antwerp and Amsterdam. Several of the architects and painters involved in the Arbeitsrat exhibitions were also invited to join Bruno Taut's correspondence circle, the Gläserne Kette. Although the exhibitions were successful and provoked vigorous critical debate, the finances of the group became increasingly strained during 1920, leading to the final dissolution of the Arbeitsrat für Kunst.

BIBLIOGRAPHY

U. Conrads: *Programmes and Manifestos on 20th-century Architecture* (London, 1970)

M. Franciscono: *Walter Gropius and the Creation of the Bauhaus in Weimar* (Urbana, 1971)

Arbeitsrat für Kunst (exh. cat., ed. M. Schlösser; Berlin, Akad. Kst., 1980)

I. Boyd Whyte: *Bruno Taut and the Architecture of Activism* (Cambridge, 1982)

——: *The Crystal Chain Letters: Architectural Fantasies by Bruno Taut and his Circle* (Cambridge, MA, 1985)

IAIN BOYD WHYTE

Arbois, Jean [Jehan] **d'** [Arbosio, Giovanni d']. *See* JEAN D'ARBOIS.

Arboleda, Carlos (*b* Chilibre, Panama, 16 Jan 1929). Panamanian sculptor and painter. He studied at the Accademia di Belle Arti in Florence (1949–54) and at the Real Academia Catalana de Bellas Artes de San Jorge in Barcelona (1955–60). On his return to Panama City he became the first professor of sculpture at the Escuela Nacional de Artes Plásticas from 1961 to 1964, and in 1964 he founded the Casa de la Escultura, a government-supported centre for the teaching and promotion of the fine arts that he continued to direct after it was renamed the Centro de Arte y Cultura. Arboleda exhibited often and established his reputation as a young man with academic works such as *Serenity* (marble, 1950; Panama City, Mus. A. Contemp.). Most of his work was figurative, but he later developed a more symbolic style and produced his most original sculptures on indigenous themes, as with the bronze head of a Chocó Indian entitled *Under the Skin* (1961; Panama City, R. Durán priv. col., see E. Wolfschoon: *Las manifestaciones artísticas en Panamá,* Panama City, 1983, p. 286), with which he won the Prix Georges Roudier at the Paris Biennale of 1961.

BIBLIOGRAPHY

M. Martínez de Lahidalga: *Carlos Arboleda: Pintor y escultor panameño* (Madrid, 1974)

Encuentro de escultura (exh. cat., ed. M. E. Kupfer; Panama City, Mus. A. Contemp., 1987), pp. 4–5

MONICA E. KUPFER

Arbós y Tremanti, Fernando (*b* Rome, 22 Oct 1844; *d* Madrid, 18 Dec 1916). Spanish architect. He was the son of the watercolourist and printmaker Manuel Arbós y Ayerbe (*d* 1875) and studied at the Ecole des Beaux-Arts in Paris (1862–5). In 1865 he entered the Escuela de Arquitectura in Madrid, where he received a bursary to train in Paris (1867). He was awarded the title of Architect in 1869 and in 1884 was appointed Architect to the Ministry of Justice. In 1898 he became a member of the Real Academia de Bellas Artes de S Fernando, Madrid; his acceptance speech was entitled *Transformaciones más culminantes de la arquitectura cristiana.*

Arbós y Tremanti's work represents the pure eclecticism characteristic of architecture in the period after the restoration of Alfonso XII in 1874. The differences between his style, which reveals Italian and French influences mixed with a Byzantine type of orientalism, and that of his contemporaries may be explained by his training in Rome, Paris and Madrid.

Early work includes the Monte de Piedad y Caja de Ahorros (1870), Madrid, which shows considerable French influence, whereas his mature works are Italianate in style. Among the latter is his design for the Necrópolis del Este (1877), Madrid, which was revised in 1905 by Francisco García Nava (1877–*c.* 1950). Arbós y Tremanti's major work in Madrid was the great basilica of Atocha (1890), designed for official ceremonies; he completed only the tower. His contrasting aesthetics or eclecticism are seen in SS Manuel y Benito (*c.* 1900), Madrid.

BIBLIOGRAPHY

J. A. Gaya: *Arte de siglo XIX*, A. Hisp., xix (Madrid, 1966)
P. Navascués: *Arquitectura y arquitectos madrileños del siglo XIX* (Madrid, 1973)
Guia de arquitectura y urbanismo de Madrid, 2 vols (Madrid, 1982–3)
S. Cortés and others: *El arquitecto Fernando Arbós y Tremani (Roma, 1844–Madrid, 1916)* (Madrid, 1988)

ALBERTO VILLAR MOVELLÁN

Arburo [Arburu] **(y) Morell, José** (*b* ?Havana, 1864; *d* Paris, 17 Aug 1889). Cuban painter. He was one of the most prominent students of Miguel Melero (1836–1907), the first Cuban-born director of the Academia de S Alejandro in Havana (founded 1818). Morell also studied at the Academia de S Fernando in Madrid. Morell's portraits, with their natural poses in domestic settings, reflect an ease with effects of light and texture not seen in the work of his Cuban contemporaries, with the exception of Guillermo Collazo. One of his most significant works is *In the Garden* (1888; Havana, Mus. N. B.A.), in which the use of light is reminiscent of the naturalism of *plein-air*, with which Morell would almost certainly have come into contact in Spain. His promising career was cut short by typhus when he was 25.

BIBLIOGRAPHY

J. Mañach: 'La pintura en Cuba: Desde sus orígenes hasta 1900', *Las bellas artes en Cuba*, xviii of *La evolución de la cultura cubana (1608–1927)*, ed. J. M. Carbonell y Rivero (Havana, 1928), pp. 239–40
Enciclopedia del arte en América, iii (Buenos Aires, 1968)

RICARDO PAU-LLOSA

Arbus [née Nemerov]**, Diane** (*b* New York, 14 March 1923; *d* New York, 26 July 1971). American photographer. She was educated at the Ethical Culture School and Fieldston School until 1940. In this year she married Allan Arbus with whom she formed a successful partnership in fashion photography. She studied photography with Alexey Brodovitch *c.* 1954 and with Lisette Model *c.* 1955–7. Model encouraged Arbus as an artist and particularly as a maker of powerfully individualistic portraits. In 1963 Arbus visited a nudist camp for the first time. *Retired Man and his Wife at Home in a Nudist Camp One Morning, NJ* (1963; see Arbus and Israel, 1972, p. 27) juxtaposes the domestic, furnished environment with a middle-aged couple whose only clothing is their footwear, enhancing the overall air of incongruity.

In 1963 and 1966 Arbus received Guggenheim fellowships for a project entitled 'American Rites, Manners, and Customs'. A group of images from this work was featured in the exhibition of 1967 at the Museum of Modern Art, New York, entitled *New Documents*, alongside work by Lee Friedlander and Garry Winogrand.

Arbus's apparent interest in what the exhibition curator, John Szarkowski, referred to as society's 'frailties' aroused great controversy and debate. Some saw her as characterizing to perfection the disinterested, amoral voyeur potentially lurking in every photographer, taking pictures of, for example, transvestites, as in *Young Man with Curlers at Home on West 20th Street, New York City* (1966; see Arbus and Israel, 1972, p. 21). Others lauded her for her psychological authenticity, her evident empathy with disadvantaged subjects, such as the mentally handicapped, in the *Untitled* series (1970–71; see Arbus and Israel, 1972, pp. 165–74). Arbus was troubled by the notoriety her work achieved. She often felt that her imagery was misunderstood, excessively praised or vilified.

A very successful posthumous retrospective (New York, MOMA) confirmed Arbus's reputation as one of the most important photographers of the 1960s. Not only did her work extend notions of acceptable subject-matter and violate canons of 'decent' distance between photographer and subject, but it was also characterized by a psychological intensity rare in photographic portraiture and an obvious awareness of the photographer on the part of the subject.

Arbus exemplified clearly the shift during the 1960s from objectivity to subjectivity in documentary photography. Her portraits are an exposition of her personal fascination with American mores as seen through outsiders such as dwarfs, giants, twins and the elderly. Arbus did exploit her subjects in that she used them as metaphors of her own sense of what it was to be an individual, but her self-searching was not mere self-indulgence; her cri de coeur was a collective one that encompassed not only the stigmatized members of society but also the 'normal'.

Although Arbus captured an emotional rawness and undoubted aggression in her work, she was a highly intelligent photographer. Subtleties and sly ironies appear in works such as *House on a Hill, Hollywood, CA* (1963; see Arbus and Israel, 1972, p. 163), in which an elegant, abandoned false mansion front is seen in an overgrown setting. There is an ineffable sense of falling short in life and in society too—the grim gap between what is given and what is intended.

In her dark and compelling works Arbus created a memorable gallery of American characters, perhaps perverse but certainly not perverted. On a much narrower yet comparably intense scale, her imagery echoes August Sander's epic characterization of Weimar Germany. Arbus was dealing primarily with a psychological rather than overtly societal profile. Nevertheless, she encapsulated a remarkably vivid sense of the *Zeitgeist* of the 1960s.

BIBLIOGRAPHY
D. Arbus and M. Israel, ed.: *Diane Arbus: A Monograph* (Millerton, NY, 1972)
I. Jeffrey: 'Diane Arbus and American Freaks', *Studio Int.*, clxxxvii/964 (1974), pp. 133–4
——: *Diane Arbus: Magazine Work* (Millerton, NY, 1984)
G. Badger: 'Notes from the Margin of Spoiled Identity: The Art of Diane Arbus', G. Badger and P. Turner: *Phototexts* (London, 1988), pp. 162–73

GERRY BADGER

Arca, Niccolò dell'. *See* NICCOLÒ DELL'ARCA.

Arcade. Single arch or series of arches carried on piers or columns. In antiquity arcades were used most prominently in the architecture of the Roman Empire, which took advantage of the greater load-bearing capacity of arches over the trabeated system that dominated Greek architecture. In medieval architecture arcades became one of the principal structural components of church interiors, both dividing and linking the principal and subsidiary spaces, notably nave and aisles (*see* CHARTRES, fig. 1; for illustration *see also* SECTION); similar structural systems were employed in the interiors of many large secular buildings, including variations using the new iron technology of the 19th century (e.g. Bibliothèque Sainte-Geneviève, Paris; 1843; *see* LABROUSTE, HENRI, fig. 1). Arcades, sometimes in the form of dwarf galleries, were also used to articulate the façades of Romanesque and Gothic churches; at Lucca Cathedral (13th century), for example, rows of smaller, superimposed arcades entirely cover the façade above the principal portico arcade at ground level (*see* LUCCA, fig. 2). In addition, arcades serve to support the roofs of covered walks (*see* CLOISTER, fig. 1), porticos and loggias, being a common feature of a secular urban architecture in medieval and Renaissance Italy (e.g. Brunelleschi's Ospedale degli Innocenti, 1419; *see* FLORENCE, fig. 1). The use of arcades as covered walks in secular architecture led to the term 'shopping arcade' later being applied to city streets covered with glazed roofs and lined with shops (e.g. Galleria Vittorio Emanuele II, Milan; begun 1863; for illustration *see* MENGONI, GIUSEPPE).

See also BLIND ARCADE.

BIBLIOGRAPHY
RDK

DORIS KUTSCHBACH

Arcagnuolo. *See* CIONE, (1).

Arcangelo di Cola (di Vanni) da Camerino (*fl* 1416–29). Italian painter. From Macerata, he is first documented in 1416, when he received a payment for frescoes (destr.)

Arcangelo di Cola da Camerino (attrib.): *Virgin and Child Enthroned with Angels*; *Crucifixion*, diptych, each panel 305×175 mm (New York, Frick Collection)

in the Sala del Maggior Consiglio in the Palazzo Pubblico, Città di Castello. By 1420 he was in Florence, where he enrolled in the Arte dei Medici e degli Speziali and the Compania S Luca. In June 1421 he was commissioned by Ilarione de' Bardi to execute an altarpiece (untraced) for S Lucia dei Magnoli, Florence. A predella panel of the *Martyrdom of St Lawrence* (Venice, Fond. Cini) and two pinnacle panels of the *Archangel Gabriel* and the *Virgin Annunciate* (New York, priv. col.) may be from this altarpiece. Around the same time he received payments for a painting intended for the parish church at Empoli, but this was never completed. He was in Rome in 1422, where he executed work (untraced) for Pope Martin V and may have contributed to the decoration of the nave of S Giovanni in Laterano for the Jubilee of 1423. Arcangelo returned to the Marches early in 1423, and his last documented painting was a signed triptych of the *Crucifixion with Saints* (1425; destr. 1889) for the monastery of Isola di Cessapalombo, Macerata: it is recorded in a photograph (Venturi). A fresco fragment of *St George and the Dragon* in the church portico of the monastery has also been attributed to him. He is last documented in Camerino, in 1429.

Although none of Arcangelo's documented works survives, several paintings have been assigned to him on the basis of the photograph of the destroyed triptych and a diptych of the *Virgin and Child Enthroned with Angels* and the *Crucifixion* (New York, Frick; see fig.), attributed to him in an inscription on the reverse. These include a triptych of the *Virgin and Child Enthroned with Saints* (Urbino, Pal Ducale); a fragment of the *Virgin and Child Enthroned with Four Angels* (New Haven, CT, Yale U. A.G.); a *Virgin and Child with Six Angels* (Bibbiena, SS Ippolito e Donato); a *Virgin and Child Enthroned with Two Angels* (Camerino, Mus. Pin. Civ.); five predella panels (Modena, Gal. Mus. Estense) and two panels of *Saints* (Prague, N.G., Kinský Pal.). His style reflects Late Gothic painting in the Marches, in particular that of Carlo da Camerino (*fl* 1396), which combined naturalism with decorative preciosity. This may be seen, for example, in the *Madonna of Humility* (Ancona, Pin. Com.) attributed to Arcangelo (Zeri, 1950). Familiarity with the innovations of Masaccio and Lorenzo Ghiberti can be seen in the treatment of volume in the *Virgin and Child* at Bibbiena and the central panel of the Urbino Triptych. Another strong influence was the work of Gentile da Fabriano, seen, for example, in Arcangelo's refined facial types and elegant drapery, and it has been suggested that the two may have met and even worked together (Venturi).

BIBLIOGRAPHY

DBI
A. Venturi: 'Di Arcangelo di Cola da Camerino', *L'Arte*, xiii (1910), pp. 377–81
F. Zeri: 'Arcangelo di Cola: Due tempere', *Paragone*, 7 (1950), pp. 33–8
G. Vitalini Sacconi: *Pittura marchigiana: La scuola camerinese* (Trieste, 1968), pp. 97–8
F. Zeri: 'Opere maggiori di Arcangelo di Cola', *Ant. Viva*, vii/6 (1969), pp. 5–15
P. Zampetti: *Pittura nelle Marche*, i (Florence, 1988), pp. 222–6
La pittura in Italia, ii (Milan, 1988), pp. 565–6
A. De Marchi: 'Arcangelo di Cola a Firenze', *Prospettiva*, 53–6 (1988–9), pp. 190–99 [issue dedicated to Giovanni Previtali]

HELEN GEDDES

Arcangelo di Jacopo, Jacopo. *See* JACOPO DEL SELLAIO.

Arce, José de [Arche, Jozef de] (*b* ?Flanders; *d* Seville, 1666). Flemish sculptor, active in Spain. He arrived in Seville sometime before 1637, having had experience of both the Flemish and the Italian Baroque traditions. He introduced important changes to Andalusian sculpture, which departed from the naturalism characteristic of early national Baroque to convey figures in movement, clothed in flowing robes, with wind-blown hair. Arce's work in Seville led to a movement away from the imitative style of the pupils of Juan Martínez Montañés.

In 1637 Arce received an important commission for the principal altarpiece of the Carthusian monastery of Jerez de la Frontera, a retable composed of sculpture and paintings (1638–9) by Francisco de Zurbarán. The completed scheme must have been one of the most beautiful in 17th-century Spain. It was dismantled in the 19th century, when the paintings were dispersed to various museums and the large, richly polychromed figures by Arce, including the fine *Twelve Apostles*, were retained in the monastery.

In 1641 Arce completed for Martínez Montañés some work on the high altar of S Miguel, also in Jerez. He carved four reliefs: an *Annunciation*, a *Nativity*, an *Adoration of the Magi* and a *Circumcision*, and four sculptures in the round (all completed 1647; *in situ*). In 1657 he carved the monumental stone figures, clearly inspired by Italian models, of the *Four Doctors of the Church* and the *Four Evangelists*, which adorn the balustrade of the church of the Sagrario, Seville.

BIBLIOGRAPHY

M. E. Gómez-Moreno: *Escultura del siglo XVII*, A. Hisp., xvi (Madrid, 1963)
J. J. Martín González: *Escultura barroca en España, 1600–1770* (Madrid, 1983)

JUAN NICOLAU

Arce, Pedro de (*bapt* Madrid, 1 March 1607; *d* after 1678). Spanish collector and patron. He was a court functionary closely connected with commerce in precious objects, silver, gold and jewellery. His interesting picture collection indicates his decidedly Italianate taste and connoisseurship. It grew from a modest but select group of works in 1643 to a large collection in 1664 of tapestries, jewellery, *objets d'art* and over 200 paintings, including Diego de Velázquez's *'The Weavers' (Fable of Arachne)* (*c.* 1657; Madrid, Prado; see VELÁZQUEZ, DIEGO, fig. 9), first recorded in an inventory of Arce's collection in 1664, and a *Holy Trinity* by Jusepe de Ribera (possibly the painting of 1632–6; Madrid, Prado). Arce was also a patron of the Italo-Spanish painter Angelo Nardi (he had five to eight works by 1657).

The extensive documents of Arce's financial affairs offer a glimpse into Spanish middle-class life in the 17th century. Included are matters relating to his custody of the children of his first wife by a previous marriage; the elaborate arrangements separating his estate from those of his two wives, their children by him and by previous husbands, and other relatives; and the attempts of his son to enter the ranks of the lesser aristocracy.

BIBLIOGRAPHY

M. L. Caturla: 'El coleccionista madrileño don Pedro de Arce, que poseyó *Las Hilanderas* de Velázquez', *Archv Esp. A.*, xxi/84 (1948), pp. 292–304

M. Burke: *Private Collections of Italian Art in 17th-century Spain* (diss., New York U., 1984; microfilm, Ann Arbor, 1986), i, pp. 227–51; ii docs 5.60–5.66f

MARCUS BURKE

Arch. An opening or frame, which may be either load-bearing or decorative, with a profile based on the segment of a circle or series of segments. A true brick or masonry arch is a composite structure, the wedge-shaped constructional blocks (voussoirs) of which are disposed radially and held together in compression (*see* MASONRY, §III, 2(ii)).

1. Structure. 2. Types. 3. History.

1. STRUCTURE. An arch (see fig. 1) is composed of the following elements:

Arc. The curved segment forming half or one side of an arch (1a): hence arcature, the line or profile of an arch.

Archivolt. The exposed face of an arch or arches, when arranged concentrically, and framing a door, window or opening (1b). It is sometimes decorated. The term is also used of the exposed faces of the voussoirs (see below) and is sometimes applied to the underside, intrados (see below) or soffit of an arch.

Centre. See *Geometrical centre.*

Dosseret. A rectangular, thick impost block (see below) placed immediately above a capital and supporting an arch. It is an alternative to the usual abacus. It was common in Late Antique, Early Christian and Byzantine architecture, for example at S Vitale (*c.* 540), Ravenna, and was sometimes decorated. In French, the term is used for the square pilaster backing a half-shaft forming a respond (see below).

Extrados. The outer curve (1c), or upper edge, of an arch or voussoir.

Geometrical centre. The notional compass point, also known as the centre, from which an arc, or segment of a circle, is drawn in elevation.

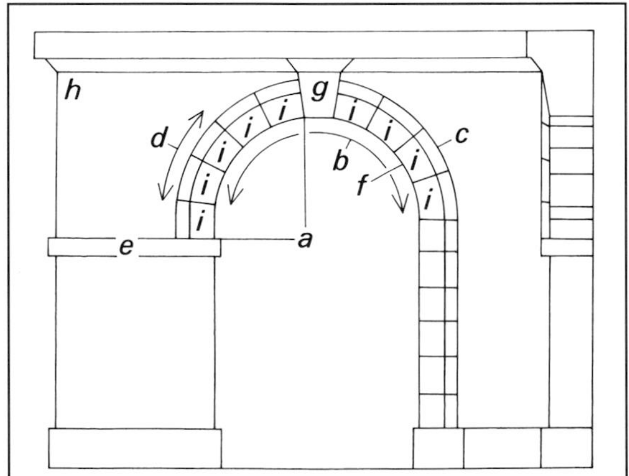

1. Arch structure, constituent parts: (a) arc; (b) archivolt; (c) extrados; (d) haunch; (e) impost; (f) intrados; (g) keystone; (h) spandrel; (i) voussoir

Haunch. A term occasionally used to describe the section of an arch passing through *c.* 45° (1d).

Impost. A block replacing the classical capital form, usually projecting from the top of a pier or respond, from which an arch might spring (1e). Sometimes the word is also used to describe the abacus block on top of a capital.

Intrados. The inner curve, or lower edge (1f), of an arch or voussoir (see below). Also known as a soffit.

Keystone. The central block or voussoir at the apex of an arch (1g), usually a round arch.

Lunette. The triangular area enclosed within the head of a blind arch of any form.

Soffit. See *Intrados.*

Spandrel. The triangular wall plane (1h) enclosed by the extrados of an arch and any horizontal division above.

Springing line. The level at which an arch springs in a curve, not necessarily at capital or impost height.

Voussoir. A wedge-shaped building block (1i), one component of an arch.

2. TYPES.

Basket. A depressed or chop arch, having three geometrical centres, of which some are below the springing line (see fig. 2a). It was popular in late Gothic architecture, for example in the Palais de Justice (1499–1526), Rouen, and in Baroque architecture.

Blind. A filled-in arch, denying access for light or passage. It is usually decorative and was much used on the exteriors of Early Christian buildings, for example at S Simpliciano (4th century AD), Milan, and in Romanesque architecture, as at Castle Acre (*c.* 1120), Norfolk. It is also found in Islamic architecture, as on the exterior of the Dome of the Rock (AD 691–2), Jerusalem, or the tomb towers at Kharragon (1067–8 and 1093), Iran.

Catenary. A parabolic arch, the profile based on the principle of the inverted hanging chain (*see* MASONRY, §III, 3(iv)). Arches approximating to this shape can be found in Egypt from the 13th century BC (e.g. the 'Ramesseum', Thebes). The most famous surviving example is that of the reception hall (?mid-6th century AD) of the great palace at KTESIPHON. It is often found in the webbing of Romanesque and Gothic vaults, and it was the basis for the structure of the dome of St Paul's Cathedral (*c.* 1680; *see* MASONRY, fig. 5), London.

Containing. An arch enclosing one or more smaller arches (2b), not necessarily of the same profile. It was sometimes used as a relieving arch (see below) for structural support. Containing arches are common in galleries in Romanesque and Gothic church architecture, for example at Jumièges (*c.* 1050; *see* JUMIÈGES ABBEY, fig. 1) and Amiens Cathedral (*c.* 1230).

Corbelled. Although a true arch in shape it is not structurally true; it is made by extending corbels at either side of an opening one above the other until they meet (2c). The profile tends to be triangular rather than curved. It was

2. Types of arch: (a) basket; (b) containing; (c) corbelled; (d) cusped; (e) diaphragm; (f) flat; (g) four-centred; (h) horseshoe; (i) interlace; (j) joggled; (k) nodding; (l) ogee; (m) pointed; (n) ramping; (o) relieving; (p) round; (q) segmental; (r) shouldered; (s) skew; (t) stilted; (u) transverse; (v) trefoil; (w) triangular; (x) Tudor; (y) two-centred; (z) two-tiered

used by the Mycenaeans (*c.* 1300 BC) in, for example, the tholoi outside the citadel of Mycenae, and in Egyptian architecture (e.g. the grand gallery of the Great Pyramid; 2551–2528 BC). It is also found with a curved profile in Islamic India at the Quwwat al-Islam Mosque (1198), Delhi, and in Mayan architecture (e.g. *c.* AD 900; Kabáh, Mexico). See also *False* below.

Curtain. A pointed arch consisting of two convex curves that meet at the apex. It was used in German Late Gothic and early Renaissance architecture for windows and doorways, especially in Saxony between 1480 and 1520 under the influence of Arnold von Westfalen.

Cusped. An arch composed of several, independent sections of a circle in series, usually arranged in a scalloped profile (2d). The cusps are usually decorative rather than structural. It is common in Islamic architecture, for example at the Great Mosque, Córdoba, Spain (961–76), and the Diwan-i-Khass of the Lal Qui'l, Delhi (1639–48; *see* INDIAN SUBCONTINENT, fig. 100), and is also found occasionally in Romanesque and Gothic architecture, as in the Founder's Chapel (1426–34) at the monastery of Batalha, Portugal. It was also popular in Late Gothic architecture in northern Europe, for example in Ghent Town Hall (1518; *see* GHENT, fig. 5). See also *Trefoil* below.

Depressed. See *Basket.*

Diaphragm. An arch carrying a section of wall, placed transversely across an interior in order to brace the side walls (2e), to create modular spatial effects, and to separate or support sections of a high roof or vault, such as in S Miniato al Monte (second half of the 12th century; *see* FLORENCE, fig. 21). It occurs in Islamic architecture, for example the Great Mosque (836–62), Kairouan, Tunisia. It was popular in Carolingian, Ottonian (e.g. from 961; Gernrode, St Cyriakus) and Romanesque architecture, for example in the nave of Jumièges Abbey (*c.* 1050) and 12th-century churches of the Auvergne, France, where they are pierced by groups of arches, such as at Notre-Dame-du-Port (1120), Clermont-Ferrand.

Drop. See *Basket.*

Equilateral. A two-centred, pointed arch, where the geometrical centre of each arc is taken from the base of its partner. It was a common form in European Gothic (*c.* 1150–1500) and in Islamic architecture.

False. An arch-shaped profile or recess, without structural value. It is employed in the proscenium arch drawn above a square stage opening in many European theatres, for example the London Coliseum (1904), by Frank Matcham. It is sometimes found on exterior façades, such as the Gruuthuse Hof (1425), Bruges. The term is also applied to corbelled openings (see above).

Flat. A structural arch but with the horizontal profile of a lintel, made up of irregular voussoir blocks, only the central keystone being truly wedge-shaped (2f). A Roman device in imitation of the Greek lintel, used, for example, on the porticos in the Forum (before AD 79), Pompeii, it was taken up by Michelangelo in his palaces (1530s) on the Capitoline Hill in Rome. The flat arch was used in Islamic architecture, as on the Bab al-Nasr (Gate of Victory; 1087) in Cairo and it was also common in Western medieval civil and domestic building, for example, the hall of Kenilworth Castle (1380s), Warwicks; it continues in use particularly in brick, square-headed window openings.

Four-centred. An arch in which the profile of each arc is drawn from two distinct geometrical centres, usually having a pronounced curve near the springing level, while becoming straighter nearer the apex (2g). It is a characteristic profile of European Gothic architecture from *c.* 1190, as on the west front of Peterborough Cathedral, England. Often, as in the chapter house of Old St Paul's (1331; destr.), London, the upper segments may appear to be almost triangular. The four-centred arch was the most popular form in the English Perpendicular style. It is also very common in Islamic architecture, appearing, for example, in the Dome of the Rock (691–2), Jerusalem, the mihrab of the Mosque of Ibn Tulun (876–9), Cairo, and the Taj Mahal (1631–48; *see* AGRA, fig. 1).

Horseshoe. An arch based on more than a semicircle, occasionally pointed at the apex (2h). It is very common in Islamic architecture, for example the Great Mosque (784–987), Córdoba (*see* ISLAMIC ART, fig. 45), and is also found in Christian architecture in such areas of Islamic influence as Spain (e.g. ?*c.* 1000; San Cebrián de Mazote), southern France and Italy. A variant with a pointed apex is the most common form in Afghanistan *c.* 1000–*c.* 1250 (e.g. the Arch at Bust; early 11th century; *see* ISLAMIC ART, fig. 33). The horseshoe profile is occasionally found in Gothic vault ribs around an apse, as in the Trinity Chapel (1184) of Canterbury Cathedral. Also known as a keyhole arch, it was popular for the front doors of English semi-detached houses between the two World Wars.

Interlace. The syncopated superimposition of two arches or series of arches, which may be round (2i) or pointed. They are usually blind and decorative but not always, as, for example, in the cloisters (*c.* 1120) at Soria Cathedral, Spain. Interlaced arches were probably of Islamic origin, for example in the Mosque of Bab Mardum (999–1000; now the church of El Cristo de la Luz), Toledo, and they were very popular in Romanesque and Gothic architecture and decoration. The English were particularly fond of this decorative form, such as at St Botolph's Priory (*c.* 1130; ruined), Colchester, Essex. Perhaps the most famous English Gothic examples are the eccentric interlaced arcades of the aisles of St Hugh's choir (*c.* 1195) in Lincoln Cathedral.

Inverted. A term sometimes used to describe an arch built upside down and therefore of little structural value. As a strainer (see below) designed as a form of buttress, however, as at Wells Cathedral (*c.* 1340), it may have considerable structural effect. The term may also refer to an ogee, or reversed curve arch (see below).

Joggled. An arch in which the voussoir blocks are shaped to interlock through right-angles or curves (2j). The use of alternating coloured stones sometimes gives a decorative effect. It is common in Islamic architecture, for example on the Bab al-Nasr (Gate of Victory; 1087), Cairo.

Keel. An arch resembling the profile of an upturned ship, the haunches usually straight, sometimes with a tiny ogee, or reversed curve, at the apex. It is probably Islamic in origin, for example the arcades around the court of the Mosque of al-Azhar (1130–49), Cairo, and may also be found in late Gothic architecture and design, and in Florentine palazzi, such as the Palazzo Guadagni (?1503–6), by Cronaca.

Keyhole. See *Horseshoe.*

Lancet. A two-centred arch, developed in early Gothic architecture in France, as at Saint-Denis Abbey (*c.* 1140). In its sharply pointed form it is particularly characteristic of English architecture of the late 12th century and early 13th, for example at Salisbury Cathedral (from *c.* 1220).

Nodding. An arch, usually an ogee (see below) that projects forwards beyond the wall plane of its springing line as it approaches the apex (see 2k). It was common in early 14th-century England, as in the pulpitum (*c.* 1330) in Southwell Minster, Notts, the Lady chapel (1321–48) of Ely Cathedral and the Great Gate (*c.* 1330) at Bury St Edmunds, Suffolk. It was not normally structural. See also *Skew* below.

Ogee. A sinuous and flowing arch with at least four geometrical centres, where each arc consists of two or more segments of a circle, the upper in inverse relationship to those below, so that the highest geometrical centre lies above and beyond the extrados (2l). Occasionally found in Islamic architecture, as in the Ak Medrese (1409), Niğde, Turkey, it appeared in Europe *c.* 1250 on the west front of S Marco, Venice, and in England on the Eleanor Crosses (*see* CROSS, §II, 3) from 1291. It was an essential element in the later English DECORATED STYLE (*c.* 1300–60), the French Flamboyant (*c.* 1380–1550), in Venetian Gothic after 1280 and all the other Late Gothic styles in Western Europe.

Parabolic. See *Catenary.*

Pointed. An arch composed of two or more segments of a circle, with a point at the apex (2m). Found first in Syrian architecture, as at Qasr Ibn Wardan (AD 561–4), it became common in Islamic buildings, for example the Mosque of Ibn Tulun (876–9), Cairo, and was introduced into Western Europe from *c.* 1060, as at Montecassino (destr.), and Cluny Abbey (from 1088). Despite these examples the pointed arch continues to be cited as a particular characteristic of Gothic architecture.

Ramping. An arch, usually pointed, where the springing line of one arc is considerably higher than its pair (2n). It was sometimes employed in the aisles of Romanesque churches for buttressing purposes, as at Vaison-la-Romaine Cathedral (*c.* 1100), France.

Rear-arch [rere-arch]. Any arch framing an opening on the internal face of an external wall. It was sometimes provided to retain the wooden door.

Relieving. An arch that takes the weight of the superstructure so that the wall area thus enclosed may be thinned for some purpose, as for a large window or gateway (2o), such as on the Arch of Augustus (*c.* 100 BC), Perugia (*see* ROME, ANCIENT, fig. 20). Relieving arches are common in Roman brick buildings, where they permit the upper section of the wall to be thickened for the support of the high roof or vault; and, in the Pantheon (*c.* AD 120), Rome, they enable the thrust exerted by the dome to be directed on to a series of strong points. They are very common in Ottonian and Romanesque architecture, for example in the west block (*c.* 1080) of Trier Cathedral. Islamic examples include the Bab al-Nasr (Gate of Victory; 1087), Cairo.

Round. A semicircular arch, and the most common arch form (2p). It is found as early as *c.* 800 BC in the stone vaults of the tomb chapels of the divine adoratrices of Amun (*c.* 712–525 BC) at Medinet Habu, Thebes, and was common in Roman architecture from the 4th century BC, such as in the Cloaca Maxima (*c.* 200 BC). It is usually, though not quite accurately, used to characterize Romanesque architecture.

Segmental. An arch formed by a single segment of less than a semicircle (2q). Rock-cut examples occur very early in Egyptian architecture, as at Beni Hasan (*c.* 2100 BC). True segmental arches are occasionally found in Greek temple architecture, such as in the Temple of Apollo (*c.* 330 BC) at Didyma, Turkey. The segmental arch is occasionally found in Islamic architecture, for instance the Great Mosque at Dera'a, Syria, of uncertain date. Segmental pediments are common over doors and windows in Renaissance buildings, for example the Palazzo Bevilacqua (*c.* 1530), Verona, by Michele Sanmicheli.

Shouldered. A three-part arch consisting of a central section raised above two quadrant or quarter arches by short uprights (2r). It is a variant of the trefoil arch (see below). The central section may be flat or pointed (see above), trefoil (e.g. Ribat-i Sharaf, Iran; 1114; rest. 1154) or even an ogee (see above), as in the main entrance portal of the Doge's Palace (14th century), Venice. Shouldered arches were often used in medieval Europe for doorways and in late Gothic architecture for more ornamental openings, as in the cloisters of S Juan de los Reyes (begun 1476; *see* TOLEDO, fig. 3) in Toledo. The shouldered arch first appeared in Iranian architecture of the 12th and 13th centuries, but it became common only in the 14th, for example in the exterior arcades of the tomb of Uljaytu (1305–15) at Sultaniyya. It was adopted in the architecture of Ottoman Turkey, such as the Yeşil Cami (Green Mosque; 1424), Bursa.

Skew. An arch that turns through more than one dimension or plane (2s), as in the curving bays of an apsidal arcade, or where, for some reason, the apex is distinctly off-centre, as in the north-east transept (1180) of Canterbury Cathedral.

Stilted. An arch, the springing line of which is raised well above the capital or impost level (2t). It existed in Islamic architecture by the 8th century AD, in, for example, the bath hall (724–43) at Khirbat al-Mafjar, near Jericho, and was used in Romanesque and Gothic architecture, particularly where arcade arches have different dimensions, as in the turning bays of an apse. Stilting is a way of equalizing the apexes of arches of different span. St John's Chapel in the Tower of London (*c.* 1080; *see* LONDON, fig. 39) is a particularly good example of stilting.

Strainer. As a structural arch or bracket placed between two opposing walls or masonry piers in order to prevent their imploding, it was a common remedial measure in medieval Europe, the best examples being in Wells Cathedral (*c.* 1340) and Canterbury Cathedral (1495). Despite their essential structural function, they are usually designed to look deceptively decorative. To create supports of the requisite height, strainer arches are used at the Great Mosque (AD 784–6) of Córdoba. See also *Inverted* above.

Surbased. A form of depressed arch.

Transverse. An arch crossing an interior space from one side to another at a right-angle to the lateral walls, and commonly employed to subdivide and compartmentalize bays of stone vaulting (2u). Transverse arches were common in the West from Carolingian times. Unlike diaphragm arches (see above), transverse arches have no exposed masonry wall above them.

Trefoil. A triple arch composed of three sections of a circle, arranged scallop-fashion, the central being the highest (2v). It may be pointed or round. Common in Islamic architecture, and areas of Islamic influence, for example in S Pau del Camp (?*c.* 1100), Barcelona, it is also found in some Romanesque and Gothic portals, such as in the Capelas Imperfeitas (1435) at Batalha Abbey, and is a common device in Mosan metalwork designs of the 11th and 12th centuries. Trefoil arches enjoyed a revival in northern European late Gothic architecture, usually in decoration, as on the exterior elevations of Ghent Town Hall (1515) and on the tomb of *Margaret of Austria* (*c.* 1525) in the priory church at Brou, Bourg-en-Bresse, France.

Triangular. Not a true arch, but a straight-sided opening formed by leaning two slabs against each other (2w). It was very common in Anglo-Saxon England, surviving until *c.* 1100, as in the tower of St Mary Coslany (*c.* 1096), Norwich. It was also used decoratively, as on the Lorsch Torhalle (for illustration *see* LORSCH ABBEY).

Tudor. A straight-sided, triangular arch of low profile, with tight curves at the springing line (2x). It was commonly used in England *c.* 1480–1600, for example in Henry VII's Chapel (*c.* 1503) in Westminster Abbey, London. The profile was also widely used in Islamic architecture from its beginning, as in the Dome of the Rock (AD 691–2), Jerusalem.

Two-centred. A pointed arch composed of two arcs, each struck from one centre (2y). See also *Lancet* and *Pointed* above.

Two-tiered. Superimposed arches, usually decorative (2z). They are found occasionally in Islamic architecture, as in the Great Mosque (AD 784–6 and later) at Córdoba.

3. HISTORY. The arch has a long history, but its popularity as a structural and decorative form was ensured only by its use in Roman times. In much of Asia and the Indian subcontinent, and in Central and South America, the structural arch was introduced either by invaders or by other contacts with Europe. Traditions based on wooden construction tend to avoid the arch, as in Scandinavian Viking architecture, although even thoroughly stone-based styles—Hindu Indian and Aztec Central American—also developed without the structural arch. The type of decorative, rock-cut, arch-shaped openings that appeared at Karle (?1st century BC) spread to China.

(i) Ancient Egypt, the Near East and the eastern Mediterranean. (ii) Ancient Greece and Rome. (iii) Indian subcontinent and Islamic lands. (iv) Western Europe and its influence.

(i) Ancient Egypt, the Near East and the eastern Mediterranean. The true structural arch originated in the Nile Valley. It was never popular in major religious Egyptian building, although it was probably very common in less durable, mud-brick, domestic structures. The earliest known arches were the brick barrel vaults (w. *c.* 2 m) dating from *c.* 3500 BC recorded by Flinders Petrie at Dendara. Standing mud-brick arches in Egypt are scarce; they were used mainly in domestic structures from the 3rd Dynasty (*c.* 2650–*c.* 2575 BC), but never externally. Although structural arches, their voussoirs were not wedge-shaped, but mortared into place. Corbelled arches were used in the inner chambers of the pyramid of King Huni (*reg c.* 2600–*c.* 2575 BC) at Maidum and the Bent Pyramid of King Sneferu (*reg* 2575–2551 BC) at Dahshur.

It is clear, however, that this was no conscious, aesthetic rejection of the arch form. The Egyptians considered the arch a semi-sacred shape, signifying a shrine or relic. Portable shrines are often depicted with arched roofs, and rock-cut tombs from all periods have arched or barrel-shaped vaults, for example in the tomb of Sennedjem (*c.* 1200 BC) at Deir el-Medina (*see* THEBES (i), fig. 10). The only surviving, free-standing building to adopt this form is the South Building (*c.* 2650 BC; rest.) in the Heb Sed Court at Saqqara, Lower Egypt. The roof has a segmental exterior profile in the manner of a shrine. Brick arches were common, however, although prone to collapse. The earliest examples still standing are probably the catenary arches over the magazine at the 'Ramesseum' (mid-13th century BC), Thebes. Stone arches do not appear to have survived from before the 8th century BC, the earliest being in the tomb-chapels of the divine adoratrices of Amun at Medinet Habu, Thebes, which have small, stone-built barrel vaults over the sanctuaries. The arch remained uncommon in Egyptian temple building even after the conquest of Egypt by the Romans.

The Mycenaean Greeks did not develop the true arch but did produce two closely related forms, 'beehive' domes and triangular openings, both dependent on corbel techniques but representing an attempt to create a clear span wider than can be achieved by post-and-lintel construction (*see* DOME, §3). The finest examples of both forms can be seen in the tholos tombs (?*c.* 1500–*c.* 1250 BC) outside the walls of Mycenae (for illustration *see* THOLOS TOMB). The Hittites also experimented with the arched form about the same time. Although not true arches, their parabolic profile and their builders' attempts to combine corbelled techniques with horizontal blocks, carved away on their undersides into curves, indicate at least visual knowledge of Egyptian arches. The finest Hittite examples are the King's Gate (*c.* 1400–*c.* 1200 BC) and the postern tunnels that pierce the walls at Bogazköy (*see* ANATOLIA, ANCIENT, fig. 7). Assyrian architecture in the Tigris Valley accommodated the true arch *c.* 800 BC. Several brick examples are known from the city gates and the palace and temple complexes at Khorsabad, which was built by Sargon II (*reg* 721–705 BC). The slightly pointed profile again denotes the influence of Egypt.

(ii) Ancient Greece and Rome. The ancient Greeks were well aware of the structural advantages of the arch (*see* GREECE, ANCIENT, §II, 2(iv)). Although it was not used on the superstructures of Greek temple architecture, concealed structural arches exist over the stairways of the Temple of Apollo (late 4th century BC onwards) at Didyma. In civil and domestic buildings, important examples are the arched entrances to the stadium (4th century BC) at Olympia and the entrance to the agora (2nd century BC) at Priene. A relieving arch supports the superstructure of the outer gate (3rd century BC) at Perge, Turkey (for illustration *see* PERGE), while the substructure of the stoa (?2nd century BC) at Alinda (now Karpuzlu, Turkey) has rounded arched windows. Like the Egyptians, the Greeks were prepared to expose arches on secular buildings, but seem not to have shared the Egyptian view of the arched form as something sacred.

The Romans established the arch as their pre-eminent element of design (*see* ROME, ANCIENT, §II, 1(iii)(a)), building arches from Syria to Scotland, as a result of which the popularity of the arch has endured in all European architectural styles and their dependants. The Romans and the Etruscans appear to have adopted the true structural arch from the 4th century BC, employing the round or semicircular arch from the beginning. Its earliest use was civic, for drains and city gates, many of which still stand, for example in Italy at Cosa (now Ansedonia; *c.* 272 BC) and Falerii Novi (*c.* 240 BC). The Roman preoccupation with the arch was connected with their development of stone, and later concrete, vaulting techniques, and its most obvious and common use was in major civic buildings. Aqueducts, bridges and the façades of theatres and amphitheatres across the Empire demonstrate the enormous advantage of the structural arch, especially when combined with piers capable of carrying its greater mass. The Colosseum (*c.* AD 80; *see* ROME, fig. 24 and ROME, ANCIENT, fig. 28) is the most famous example of this Roman arcade form. Other exceptional arched structures are the aqueduct (mid-1st century AD) at Segovia (for illustration *see* AQUEDUCT) and the Pont du Gard (*see* NÎMES, §2).

The monumental triumphal arch, a purely ceremonial structure, was invented under the Roman Republic, although one of the earliest standing examples is the Imperial Arch of Augustus (*c.* 8 BC) at Susa, while the Arch of Titus (*c.* AD 81) in Rome became the model for many others (*see* TRIUMPHAL ARCH, fig. 1). The triumphal arch consists of a semicircular arch within a square-headed, post-and-lintel design, the latter merely grafted on to a masonry superstructure. Like the Greeks, the Romans at first avoided showing obvious arched forms on their religious architecture, but the Pantheon (AD 118–24), Rome, is covered by a curved, concrete dome and the interior elevation has several arched openings (*see* ROME, ANCIENT, fig. 31). The arch, however, was to remain unusual in temple designs within the capital (although the early 4th-century 'Temple of Minerva Medica' is an arched and vaulted structure (*see* ROME, ANCIENT, fig. 36)). Outside the immediate influence of the capital, however, arches soon appeared on religious buildings. The small Temple of Hadrian (AD 117) at Ephesos combines a round arch with a trabeated portico. This unusual combination may reflect Syrian tendencies to mix arches and lintels in fora and market complexes, for example at Palmyra, Syria. In the North African provinces, relieving arches appeared on temple façades from *c.* AD 150, for example at Sbeïtla, Tunisia, and in the temple to the Severan family (AD 229) at Djemila (*see* ROME, ANCIENT, fig. 6).

In the late Roman period Hellenistic 'temple' porticos were added to domestic structures, as at the Palace of Diocletian (*c.* AD 300) at Split.

After the official recognition of Christianity in AD 313, the Christians, anxious to avoid architectural parallels with pagan temples, adopted exposed brick walls and the arch as major elements of their religious buildings, creating the classic basilican church of the late Roman period, for example S Sabina (*c.* 425), Rome, and S Apollinare in Classe (534–6; *see* RAVENNA, fig. 4). By the late 5th century the arcade was an essential feature of Christian architecture, in both the east and west. It remained so until the 20th century.

(iii) Indian subcontinent and Islamic lands. Although the arch has a history of more than 2000 years in India, the form was not significant in the architecture of the subcontinent before the 12th century AD. Some early masonry arches were found in the excavations at KAUSAMBI, but the continuous history of the arch in India begins only with the Lomas Rishi cave at Barabar (3rd century BC; *see* BARABAR AND NAGARJUNI; *see also* INDIAN SUBCONTINENT, fig. 25). While rock-cut, it copies wood-joinery in every detail, the arch itself consisting of laminated planks crowned by a finial. The buildings depicted in the low reliefs at Sanchi (1st century BC; *see* INDIAN SUBCONTINENT, fig. 17) show similar arches. The early cave-temples of western India often have rock-cut ogee arches leading to barrel-vaulted halls: at BHAJA (*c.* mid-2nd century BC) the hall has retained its original wooden rafters fitted into the rock-cut vault, but at KARLE (*c.* 1st century BC) the features are reproduced completely in stone. The decorative devices include dormers (*gavākṣa*, 'bull's-eye window'), which, in structural architecture from the 5th century AD, were progressively reduced to ogee-shaped devices (particularly in northern India). Apart from this usage, pointed arches seem to have been used continuously in brick architecture to provide internal support, for example at BHITARGAON (5th century AD). With the Islamic conquest from the 12th century, and repeated waves of influence from west Asia, the arch became a dominant feature of architecture in India, but post-and-lintel construction remained the preferred technique.

Most of the architectural forms used in the design of early mosques were adapted from the local Roman architecture, notably the arch (*see* MOSQUE). From the first, however, Islamic designers were far more adventurous than their Roman forebears. Pointed arches, of various profiles, appeared as early as AD 691–2 at the Dome of the

Rock, Jerusalem (*see* ISLAMIC ART, fig. 17), while near-straight-sided arches, trefoil, interlaced and joggled arches can all be found between 785 and 987 at the Great Mosque, Córdoba, which is a veritable catalogue of Islamic arch forms (*see* CÓRDOBA (i), fig. 2; ISLAMIC ART, fig. 45) and in the Mosque of Ibn Tulun (878–9), Cairo, which has both four-centred and stilted pointed arches (*see* ISLAMIC ART, fig. 24). The round arch all but disappeared from Islamic architecture after *c.* 700. Islam was probably responsible for the introduction of pointed and ogee arch forms into western Europe, the pointed arch at Montecassino (1066–71; destr. 1349), Italy, and later at Cluny, France, and the ogee *c.* 1250 in Venice.

(iv) Western Europe and its influence. After the collapse of the Western Roman Empire in the 5th century, the Christian Church was responsible for most new building, and the styles that emerged—whether Visigothic, Carolingian, Ottonian or Anglo-Saxon—all depended on ideas from Imperial and Early Christian Rome. The round arch, in brick, stone or rubble, remained the pre-eminent form until *c.* 1130. The increased use of rubble construction, and the poor quality of stone cutting, made thicker walls inevitable, requiring arches of greater depth (*see* ROMANESQUE, §II, 1). By *c.* 1000 masons had begun to experiment with ways of enlivening and utilizing the depth of arches for decorative purposes. The most obvious and popular method was the introduction of orders, whereby the arch consists of a series of concentric openings, diminishing by means of rebates, and giving the impression of space receding through the wall. This decorative form was later extended to include a variety of continuous mouldings and, eventually, sculptural decoration.

It was the Romanesque builders who first experimented with the pointed arch, especially in Italy and in Burgundy at Cluny Abbey (1088; *see* CLUNIAC ORDER, §III, 1(ii)). By *c.* 1130, workshops in several areas were taking up the form, for example in the choir (before 1104) of Durham Cathedral in England (*see* DURHAM, fig. 1) and in the Ile-de-France. The pointed arch became almost a trademark for the Cistercians, again prompted by the profile of their high barrel vaults, for example at FONTENAY ABBEY (*c.* 1139–47). At Durham Cathedral, pointed transverse arches were used in the high rib vaults, perhaps as early as 1120, while the west block of Saint-Denis Abbey (begun *c.* 1135) has pointed arches of several profiles (*see* SAINT-DENIS ABBEY, fig. 2). In both the latter examples, the pointed arch is used for structural advantage. The width of an arch with a pointed apex may be varied considerably without affecting its height. Thus it is possible to group together several pointed arches of different span but of the same overall height without the use of stilting, a discovery exploited with advantage in the early Gothic period.

Various types of pointed arch were introduced into medieval Europe, all based on Roman or Islamic prototypes, but what was new was the European application of the various arch forms, especially the use of the pointed arch in rib vaults, to which all other structural forms were subservient. The pointed arch was never fully accepted in Italy, and already by *c.* 1400 the newly self-conscious city-states had begun to experiment with the revival of their Roman past. For stylistic and political reasons the round arch prevailed, and in the 16th century the new Renaissance version of the old Roman style spread to most of Europe and was taken in varying forms to all the lands newly discovered: America, India and Asia. The dominance of the European empires and the longevity of the Classical Revival has ensured that the arch is the most familiar architectural form in the world. More recently building techniques involving cast iron, steel and concrete have threatened the supremacy of the arch, but it still enjoys immense popularity with architects and clients alike.

BIBLIOGRAPHY

B. Fletcher and B. Fletcher: *A History of Architecture . . . Being a Comparative View of the Historical Styles from the Earliest Period* (London, 1896, rev. 5/1905 as *A History of Architecture on the Comparative Method*, rev. J. Musgrove, 19/1987)

W. M. F. Petrie: *Dendereh, 1898*, Memoirs of the Egypt Exploration Fund, xvii (London, 1900)

K. A. C. Creswell: *Early Muslim Architecture: Ummayads, Early 'Abbāsids & Tūlūnids*, 2 vols (Oxford, 1932–40, rev. 2/1969)

N. Pevsner: *An Outline of European Architecture* (Harmondsworth, 1942)

K. A. C. Creswell: *The Muslim Architecture of Egypt*, 2 vols (Oxford, 1952–9)

A. Boëthius: *Etruscan and Early Roman Architecture*, Pelican Hist. A. (Harmondsworth, 1970; ed. R. Ling and T. Rasmussen; rev. 2/1978)

J. B. Ward-Perkins: *Roman Imperial Architecture*, Pelican Hist. A. (Harmondsworth, 1970, rev. 2/1981/*R* 1983)

M. Raeburn, ed.: *Architecture of the Western World* (London, 1980)

J. C. Harle: *The Art and Architecture of the Indian Subcontinent*, Pelican Hist. A. (Harmondsworth, 1986)

FRANCIS WOODMAN

Archaeology. The study of Man's past by means of his material remains. Archaeology provides the only record of ancient culture prior to the appearance of written documents (around 3000 BC in western Asia and much later in many other areas; *see* PREHISTORIC ART) and also contributes a great deal to the understanding of 'historic' periods (after the development of writing). The subject is both an art and a science: it aims to provide an understanding of Man's past, and thus, like history, is classified as one of the humanities. Many archaeological artefacts, however, supply no direct information, forcing the archaeologist to become a scientist as he collects data, conducts experiments, formulates hypotheses and finally draws conclusions. The scientific aspects of archaeology became increasingly important in the mid- and late 20th century, due to the development of such methods of analysis as radiocarbon dating.

1. History. 2. Site discovery and survey. 3. Excavation. 4. Dating techniques.

1. HISTORY. The history of archaeology is commonly seen in terms of great discoveries, for example the tomb of Tutankhamun in Egypt, the lost Mayan cities of Central America or the Terracotta Warriors in China. More important, however, is the progression of ideas that has allowed a better appreciation of what the remains of past societies can reveal. Such Greek and Roman writers as Herodotus (5th century BC), Pliny (1st century AD) and Pausanias (2nd century AD) were the first to discuss extensively all aspects of natural history, geography and antiquity, and the earliest known museum was set up by Nabonidus (*reg* 555–539 BC), last native king of Babylon. During the European Renaissance aristocrats began to

collect and display curiosities of all kinds, including ancient artefacts, and scholars began to study the relics of ancient Greece and Rome, as well as the monumental remains of other societies (*see* CYRIAC OF ANCONA). Such antiquarians as William Stukeley, the surveyor of STONEHENGE, began to produce systematic studies of some of these monuments.

Excavation of prominent sites began in the 18th century. Most, however, such as those at Herculaneum (*see* HERCULANEUM, §VI) and Pompeii (*see* POMPEII, §VI), both buried by Mt Vesuvius in AD 79, were little more than treasure hunts, designed not to answer questions about the past but to provide spectacular objects to adorn the houses of the rich. One exception was the excavation in 1784 of a burial mound in Virginia by Thomas Jefferson, arguably the first 'scientific excavation' ever conducted. (*See also* ANCIENT NEAR EAST, §III, 1, for discussion of changes in archaeological approaches over time.)

Until well into the 19th century archaeology was hampered by the belief, based on the Bible, that the world had been created in 4004 BC, a restriction that required all discoveries to be artificially constricted into an extremely limited timescale. It was not until the middle of the 19th century that the modern discipline of archaeology evolved, when advances in geological thought and, in particular, acceptance of the theory of evolution, freed it from the shackles imposed by the biblical calendar. The Scottish geologist James Hutton (1726–97), in his *Theory of the Earth* (1785), had established the principle of 'uniformitarianism', a concept confirmed by Charles Lyell (1797–1875) in his *Principles of Geology* (1833). They showed that the stratification of rock, that is, its arrangement in superimposed layers or strata, was due to processes identical to (or 'uniform' with) those continuing to produce layers in rivers, streams and lakes. This concept, applied to the history of Man, has become one of archaeology's most fundamental principles.

Partly as a result of this principle came acceptance of the considerable antiquity of Man. In 1841 James Boucher de Perthes (1788–1868) published manmade artefacts discovered in the gravels of the River Somme in association with the bones of extinct animals. His view that this was proof of Man's antiquity did not gain wide acceptance until, in 1859, he was able to convince two British scholars, Sir John Evans (1823–1908) and Joseph Prestwich (1812–96). The concept of 'prehistory' thereafter gained rapid currency with the publication of John Lubbock's *Prehistoric Times* (1865).

Equally helpful to the fledgling discipline was widespread acceptance of the ideas of Charles Darwin (1809–82), whose *On the Origin of Species* was published in 1859. He postulated the idea of natural selection, or survival of the fittest, as the most logical explanation for the origin and development of all plant and animal life; his *Descent of Man* (1871) made it clear that humans, too, had emerged as a result of this evolutionary process. Furthermore, his ideas suggested to such scholars as General Augustus Pitt-Rivers (1827–1900) and Sir John Evans that human cultures might also evolve in much the same way as species. From this came the idea of 'typology', the arrangement of artefacts in a relative chronological sequence, developed by Oscar Montelius (1843–1921).

A system for the subdivision of the prehistoric period had already been devised by various Scandinavian scholars and applied by C. J. Thomsen (1788–1865), who, between 1816 and 1819, arranged the Nationalmuseet of Copenhagen according to the Three Age System, i.e. Stone Age, Bronze Age and Iron Age (*see also* PREHISTORIC ART). Although not a new idea—for ancient Greek and Roman, as well as Chinese, writers appreciated the succession of stone, bronze and iron—it was an important step in establishing a relative chronology for the prehistoric period. The classification gained wide acceptance following the publication of Thomsen's guidebook to the museum in 1836, and its subsequent appearance in English as *A Guide to Northern Antiquities* in 1848, although many scholars initially tried to work within a timescale beginning at 4004 BC. The scheme was later elaborated: the Stone Age was divided into the Old and New Stone Ages (Palaeolithic and Neolithic), and subsequently a Middle Stone Age, the Mesolithic, was added. Each Age was also subdivided into Early, Middle and Late periods (except the Palaeolithic, which was divided into Lower, Middle and Upper), and a Copper Age was inserted between the Neolithic and Bronze Ages. The system, soon confirmed by stratigraphical investigations, had its disadvantages, however: it provided only a relative progression, and individual periods could occur at vastly different times in different regions. Much of Australia still had a Palaeolithic culture in the 19th century, and parts of South America were in the Neolithic period. Furthermore, some areas missed certain stages altogether—the Sahara moved directly from the Stone to the Iron Age—while boundaries between periods were also frequently blurred. Although the system has in many ways outgrown its usefulness, its classifying labels continue to be used for lack of a better system.

These advances in archaeological thought were accompanied by a number of important developments resulting from archaeological discoveries. A chance find during Napoleon's expedition to Egypt (1798–1800) provided the clue to ancient Egyptian hieroglyphic writing: the Rosetta Stone (London, BM) bears a matching inscription in Greek and Egyptian that Jean-François Champollion (1790–1832) finally deciphered in 1822, after 14 years' work (*see also* EGYPT, ANCIENT, §XVIII, 2). The secrets of the cuneiform script of ancient Mesopotamia were unravelled in similar fashion in the 1850s by Henry Rawlinson (1810–95), who spent 20 years working on a trilingual inscription of the 6th century BC carved on to a cliff-face between Tehran and Baghdad (*see also* ANCIENT NEAR EAST, §III, 1(i)). Perhaps the most spectacular discoveries of the 19th century, however, were those of HEINRICH SCHLIEMANN, who, inspired by Homer's *Iliad*, discovered and excavated the sites of TROY and MYCENAE in the 1870s and 1880s.

Schliemann's excavations, although important, and 'modern' in that they were undertaken to test a particular hypothesis, were crude and destructive, with none of the meticulous recording techniques developed by the next generation of archaeologists. Prominent among the latter were General Pitt-Rivers, FLINDERS PETRIE and MORTIMER WHEELER. Pitt-Rivers brought military precision to surveying and excavation on his private estates at Cranborne Chase in southern England. He demanded thorough record-keeping, an insistence reflected in his four volumes of excavation reports (1887–98). Flinders Petrie also insisted on the complete recording and publication of his excavations in Egypt and Palestine and developed his own technique of 'seriation', or sequential dating. Wheeler, well known for the excavation of such sites as MAIDEN CASTLE hillfort in Dorset, was, like Pitt-Rivers, an exponent of military precision and developed a technique of excavation that involved dividing the site into grid-squares, which, separated by vertical sections, were subsequently excavated independently (*see* §3 below).

Other well-known archaeologists in the 19th century and early 20th included Alfred Maudslay (1850–1931), a leading figure in Mayan archaeology; MAX UHLE, excavator in the 1890s of the Peruvian site of PACHACAMAC and one of the greatest figures of South American archaeology; HOWARD CARTER, discoverer in the 1920s of Tutankhamun's tomb in Egypt; Sir ARTHUR EVANS, discoverer of the Minoan civilization on Crete and excavator of the Minoan palace at KNOSSOS; and LEONARD WOOLLEY, excavator of Ur in Mesopotamia, biblical city of Abraham's birth and later capital of Sumeria.

During the late 19th century and the early 20th great effort went into building up regional sequences of artefacts and relative chronologies based on them. Absolute dates were established through 'cross-dating', that is by establishing a link between one sequence and another. The Swedish archaeologist responsible for the subdivisions of European prehistory, Oscar Montelius, provided absolute dates for the various periods by cross-dating across Europe from Egypt, a region for which dynastic lists provided an established timescale.

1. Aerial photograph showing Iron Age and Romano-British settlement indicated by cropmarks, Standlake, Oxfordshire

Gordon Childe (1892–1957), among others, concentrated on building up sequences of associated artefacts in an attempt to identify particular assemblages of objects that might represent the 'culture' of a particular people. He also attempted to explain the origins of these cultures: whereas Montelius, influenced by major discoveries being made in the Near East, had believed that all aspects of civilization had spread ('diffused') from the Near East into Europe, Childe argued in his *Dawn of European Civilization* (1925) that, while the major cultural changes within Europe were the result of Near Eastern influence, there had nonetheless been some indigenous development. Later, influenced by Marxist ideas, he suggested that a Neolithic revolution had prompted the development of farming and an urban revolution the development of towns and cities.

Dramatic advances in archaeology after World War II transformed the discipline, as whole new branches of research developed. Such environmental archaeologists as Grahame Clark (*b* 1907), for example, who excavated Starr Carr in Yorks, England, in the 1950s, broke away from the artefact-dominated approach to study, through painstaking analysis of organic remains, the way in which human populations adapted to their environments. Gordon Willey (*b* 1913) and Philip Phillips (*b* 1900), in *Method and Theory in American Archaeology* (1958), argued for the adoption of a wider 'processual interpretation' within archaeology, the study of the general processes at work in the development and spread of culture. Following them, and led by such scholars as Lewis Binford, the 'new archaeologists' of the 1960s and 1970s attempted to explain rather than just describe these processes, within a framework of scientific reasoning that allowed the testing of interpretations and conclusions.

Many other advances centred on the development and increasing availability of a host of scientific techniques that have allowed the establishment of accurate absolute timescales. The development of radiocarbon dating (*see* §4 below), which complements the more traditional evidence of cross-association, helped extend the scope of archaeological interpretation, and the rapid development of accurate techniques of quantitative analysis, as well as advances in computer technology, continue to lead to further developments in archaeological theory.

2. SITE DISCOVERY AND SURVEY. A number of techniques may be used to locate sites. The Bible and the Homeric epics, for example, have assisted in the discovery and identification of Near- and Middle-Eastern sites and such cities as Ur (Tell el-Muqayyar in southern Iraq) and Troy (Hissarlik in western Turkey); clues derived from place-names and early maps can be similarly used. Many sites are discovered by chance, and many more as a result of 'salvage' or 'rescue' archaeology, which aims to locate and record as many sites as possible in advance of modern development, ideally before work begins but more frequently by means of a 'watching brief' as development goes ahead.

Aerial photography, primarily used for the recording and interpretation of sites, is, nonetheless, a useful tool for site discovery, often revealing sites invisible from the ground. The first archaeological aerial photographs were made in the early 20th century, using balloons and box-kites; after World War I increasing use was made of photographs taken from aircraft. Whereas pictures taken vertically are most useful for mapping and planning, photographs taken at an angle, with the benefit of oblique sunlight, can be used to locate 'shadow' sites, highlighting slight slopes and depressions. Aerial photographs can also reveal cropmarks—differential growth patterns caused by features underlying the surface (see fig. 1)—and soilmarks formed, for example, by the ploughing out of a burial mound. In addition, satellite images, such as those from the LANDSAT (Earth Resources Technology) satellites, can be used to trace relatively large-scale features.

Archaeological sites and human remains of all kinds may also be discovered through reconnaissance survey work. Some sites are readily visible, while others are revealed by means of scattered artefacts disturbed by the plough or other action. Careful and systematic fieldwalking by teams of archaeologists, coupled with equally systematic recording, can result in the identification of new sites, as well as producing valuable information about entire regions.

Once a site has been discovered, the next step is site survey. Various techniques are available to supplement the initial recording of surface finds and drawing of plans. The simplest and most traditional technique is the use of probes or augurs; although useful, this inevitably involves some disturbance of, and damage to, the site. There are, however, various non-destructive methods of subsurface survey, which involve passing energy through the soil to detect anomalies within it or measuring variations in the Earth's magnetic field.

Seismic or acoustic survey requires the passage of sound through the soil. At its simplest this involves striking the ground with a wooden mallet (bowsing) and noting changes in the resultant echo. More sophisticated forms of echo-sounding can be extremely useful, particularly in the rapidly expanding field of marine archaeology. Radio waves can be used in much the same way: soil-sounding radar sends short radio pulses through the soil, and different readings reflect the changing soil conditions encountered, caused, for example, by the presence of walls or ditches. More widely available and used, however, is the technique of measuring electrical resistivity. A resistivity meter attached to electrodes placed in the soil measures the resistance to a current passed between the electrodes. Since damper soil conducts electricity better than drier, this technique can detect, for example, buried ditches and pits that retain moisture and walls and roads that do not.

Even more widely used than these are magnetic survey methods to detect pits and ditches, iron objects and such fired clay structures as hearths. These features produce slight distortions in the Earth's magnetic field that can be measured using various instruments; the most widely used is the proton magnetometer, though it has the disadvantage of considerable background interference from such electrical sources as power lines. In the differential fluxgate magnetometer and the fluxgate gradiometer, both of which work on the same principle, this problem has been eliminated.

Metal detectors, which employ both magnetism and conductivity, can also be used to locate buried objects. Metal artefacts and sometimes also buried features can be detected by measuring the distortions in an alternating magnetic field produced by passing an electric current through a transmitter coil. Metal detectors have been used by some to vandalize sites but, responsibly used, can be valuable for discovering objects buried near the surface.

3. Excavation. Excavation is by its very nature destructive and is also extremely costly. In many instances non-destructive survey methods obviate the need to dig, and the excavation of sites not threatened by development is normally undertaken only to investigate specific problems or with specific research objectives in mind. One of the main purposes of site survey, therefore, is to select areas for excavation that are both relatively undisturbed and likely to provide the information required.

Excavation is based on the principle of stratigraphy, the general assumption that where one layer rests on another, the lower level will have been deposited earlier than the upper one (see fig. 2). Strata can occasionally become inverted, however, and it is important to study the vertical section of the site, to gain an impression of the changes that have taken place through time. Similarly, artefacts and features found within the same stratigraphic layer are assumed to be roughly contemporary one with another, so that a horizontal section provides a picture of the site at a particular time. Few layers are reliably sealed from each other, however, and material can be transferred from one layer to another, for example by burrowing animals; in addition, such later features as modern drains are frequently cut into earlier levels.

There are various methods of excavation that must be adapted to the particular site in question. All require the introduction of a grid and the establishment of a datum point to ensure the accurate recording and plotting of finds and features. At the two extremes are excavations that concentrate primarily on revealing the vertical sections and those that concentrate on the horizontal. Mortimer Wheeler's 'box-grid' system is a means of revealing both sections at once by excavating grid-squares but retaining baulks between them to show the vertical stratigraphy (see fig. 3). The baulks can be removed once the overall layout of the site is established. Some excavators argue, however, that this system does not reveal the complete horizontal and vertical sequence, and that it obscures ephemeral structures that are only visible in plan. They prefer the 'open-area' excavation in which the stratigraphic relationship of all layers is recorded, not just those that occur in the sections (see fig. 4). In this case it is usual to reproduce the vertical stratigraphy in plan from three-dimensional measurements taken during excavation, a task made increasingly less laborious by the rapid development of computer technology. No excavation is of use unless it is carried out with good recording techniques and accompanied by efficient processing and classifying of finds and samples. Ideally, conservation of artefacts should be followed by swift and efficient analysis of the material and by timely publication of the findings and their interpretation..

4. Dating techniques. The stratigraphy of a site allows the relative dating of artefacts both in relation to

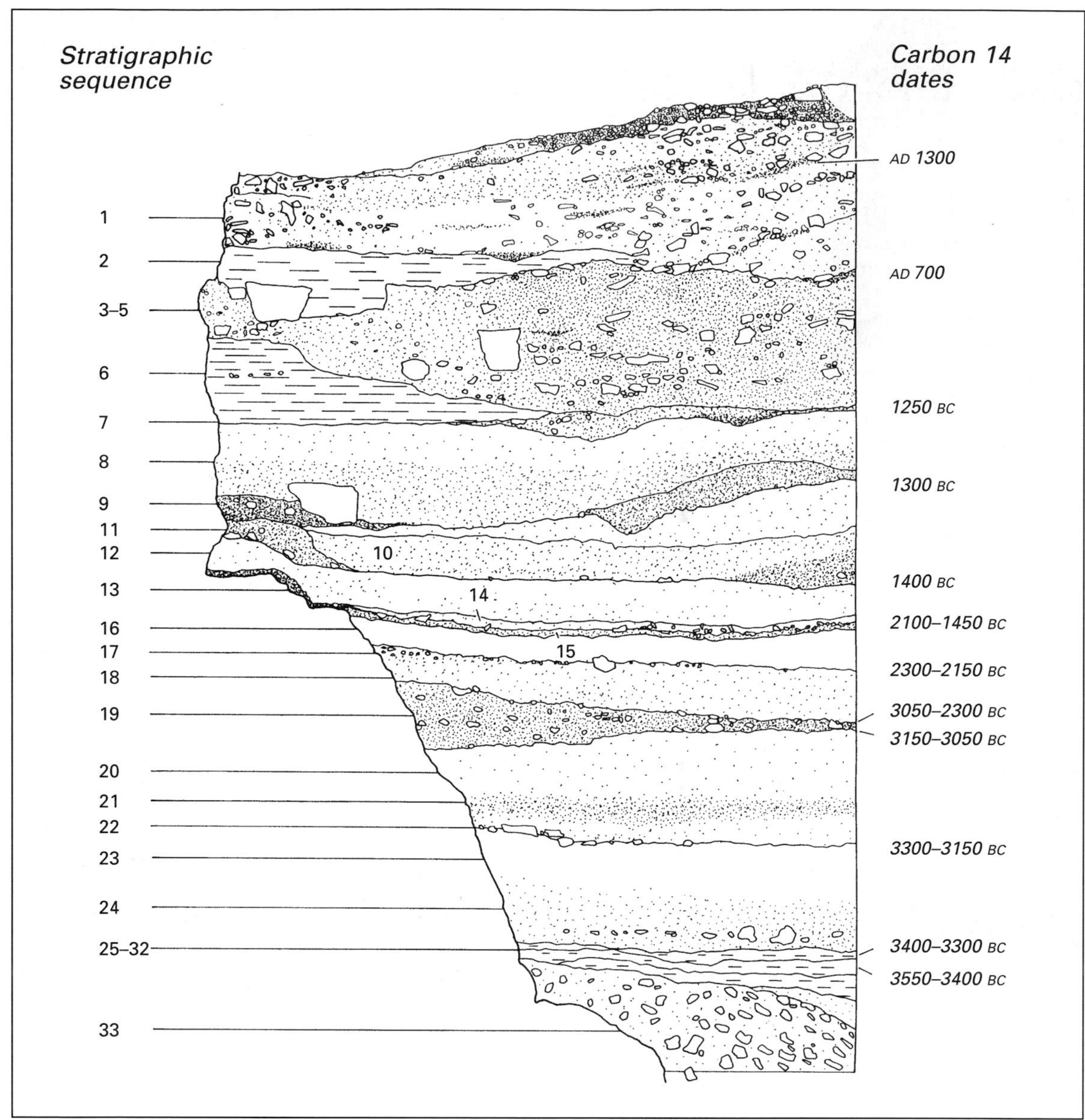

2. Stratigraphic profile showing how radiocarbon dates are consistent with the stratigraphic sequence, Gatecliff Shelter, Nevada

the site and by association with one another. Thus, if an object from a particular layer can be dated, by radiocarbon analysis, for example, the finds associated with it can also be dated. Typological sequences of artefacts can be established when, for instance, one type of axe-head is found in a level stratigraphically later or earlier than another.

To these methods of relative dating can be added a considerable array of absolute dating techniques. In 1878 the Swedish geologist Baron Gerard de Geer (1858–1943) recognized that layers of clay were deposited in lakes around the edges of Swedish glaciers by the annual melting of the ice sheets. As the layers varied in thickness, depending on the climatic conditions, it was possible to compare series of layers in nearby areas, and to build up overlapping sequences that were eventually linked together to extend as far back as the end of the last Ice Age, *c.* 12,000 BP. Although this dating technique is of limited use to the archaeologist, it displays the same principle as that of dendrochronology, or tree-ring dating.

Tree-ring dating was developed by the American A. E. Douglass (1867–1962) in the early 20th century. He based his work on the principle that a tree's annual growth-rings vary in size according to climatic conditions, and that particular sequences of growth-rings can be recognized among trees of a particular species in a specific region. Overlapping sequences can be identified in successively older timbers, allowing the establishment of a master series

3. Archaeological excavation using Mortimer Wheeler's 'box-grid' method, Sutton Walls, Hereford & Worcester

from which other timbers can be dated. Once several such series had been established, by the 1960s, dendrochronology became an extremely valuable method of dating, as well as a means of checking and calibrating radiocarbon dates. The technique can only be applied to trees outside the tropics, however, where seasonal differences are sufficiently pronounced to produce clear annual rings. In addition, tree-ring dates are available only for those species for which a master series exists, for example the American bristlecone pine, the Douglas fir in the south-west USA and the European oak; the German oak sequence stretches back to around 7500 BC.

The most spectacular breakthrough for scientific dating was the announcement by Willard Libby (1908–80) in 1949 of the new process of radiocarbon (carbon-14) dating, which for the first time enabled the establishment of absolute dates that were not dependent on cross-dating with other cultures or regions. The technique is based on the principle of radioactive decay: that on the death of a plant or animal it ceases to absorb carbon from the atmosphere, and the unstable carbon-14 within it thereafter decays at a standard rate. Thus the age of plant or animal tissue can be calculated by measuring the amount of carbon-14 left within it against the known rate of decay. To avoid confusion, AD 1950 was adopted as the 'present', and all radiocarbon dates are given in years BP, i.e. before the 'present'. Radiocarbon analysis became the main dating tool for organic remains dating as far back as 50,000–80,000 BP. One of the assumptions, however, made in the initial stages of research, that the concentration of carbon-14 in the atmosphere had remained constant over time, proved to be incorrect. Comparison between radiocarbon

4. 'Open-area' excavation showing smaller squares in which detailed stratigraphy is studied, Sutton Hoo, Suffolk; in the centre is an earlier 'box-grid'-style excavation of the 1960s

and tree-ring dates revealed that radiocarbon dates before *c.* 1000 BC were progressively too young; as a result, radiocarbon dates are normally corrected using a calibration curve produced from tree-ring dates.

The technique of thermoluminescense dating also measures radioactive decay and, unlike radiocarbon, can be used on pottery, the most common inorganic material recovered from archeological sites of the last 10,000 years. It is less precise than radiocarbon analysis but can extend further back in time. Radioactive elements within ceramic material emit radiation at a known rate, displacing electrons that are then released when the ceramic is heated to more than 500°C. Measurement of an object's thermoluminescence, the light emitted by escaping electrons, allows a calculation of the elapse of time from the last heating (i.e. the firing of the pottery). Another dating tool, Electron Spin Resonance, dates bone or shell by measuring the trapped electrons without the heating that thermoluminescence requires.

Two other dating techniques use the principle of radioactive decay: potassium-argon dating and uranium-series dating. The former can only be used on volcanic rocks over 100,000 years old, while the latter is particularly useful for dating rocks between 500,000 and 50,000 years old that are rich in calcium carbonate. Fission-track dating also involves the use of uranium isotopes, measuring the spontaneous fission of uranium-238 present in many rocks and minerals, and can usefully be used on samples more than 300,000 years old.

See also TECHNICAL EXAMINATION, §VII.

BIBLIOGRAPHY

G. Daniel: *150 Years of Archaeology* (London, 1950, rev. 2/1975)
W. Bray and D. Trump: *The Penguin Dictionary of Archaeology* (Harmondsworth, 1970, rev. 1982)
P. Barker: *Techniques of Archaeological Excavation* (London, 1977, rev. 2/1982)
K. Greene: *Archaeology: An Introduction* (London, 1983)
B. G. Trigger: *A History of Archaeological Thought* (Cambridge, 1989)
C. Renfrew and P. Bahn: *Archaeology: Theory, Methods and Practice* (London, 1991)

R. J. BRICKSTOCK

Archambo, Peter (*b* Parish of St Martin's in the Field, Middx; *fl* 1710–*c.* 1750; *d* 1759). English goldsmith. He was the son of Peter Archambo, a Huguenot refugee who worked in London as a staymaker. In 1710 he was apprenticed to the goldsmith Jacob Margas (*c.* 1685–after 1730) and, like Margas, became a freeman of the Butchers' Company (rather than the Goldsmiths' Company) on 7 December 1720. He first registered his mark at Goldsmiths' Hall, London, in 1721, when he gave his address as the Golden Cup in Green Street. One of his apprentices was Thomas Heming. He produced fine quality domestic silver, and a wide range of objects, including cups, candlesticks, cream jugs and cake baskets, bearing his mark survives. His work is French in influence, and he is often credited with helping to introduce the Rococo style into England. His approach to the Rococo was, however, more restrained than that of some of his contemporaries, for example Paul de Lamerie. His work also often incorporates marine motifs. His most important patron was George Booth, 2nd Earl of Warrington (1675–1758), who commissioned such pieces as a wine-urn (1728; London, Goldsmiths' Co.), chased with masks, shells and strapwork, a wine-cistern (1729; Dunham Massey, Ches, NT) and six sconces (1730). Other surviving works are a hot-water urn and a set of three caddies (Los Angeles, CA, Gilbert priv. col., on loan to Co. Mus. A.) and a plain ewer (New York, Met.). It is thought that Archambo retired around 1750, as very little silver bearing his mark is extant after that date.

BIBLIOGRAPHY

A. Grimwade: *Rococo Silver, 1727–1765* (London, 1974)
——: *London Goldsmiths, 1697–1837: Their Marks and Lives* (London, 1976, rev. 3/1990)
T. Schroder: *The Gilbert Collection of Gold and Silver*, Los Angeles, CA, Co. Mus. A. cat. (Los Angeles, 1988)

EMMA PACKER

Archanes [Arkhanes]. Site in northern Crete 15 km south-east of Herakleion. Occupied in Neolithic times, it flourished in the Minoan period (*c.* 3500/3000–*c.* 1500 BC). Arthur Evans was the first to excavate in the area after World War I, and work continued from the early 1960s under the direction of Y. Sakellarakis and E. Sakellarakis, who have investigated three major sites. At Turkogeitonia, in the middle of the modern town, were found the remains of a palace built at the start of the Middle Minoan (MM) IB (*c.* 1900–*c.* 1800 BC) and destroyed by earthquake *c.* 1650 BC. The settlement around the palace can also be dated to *c.* 1900 BC, as can the construction of the peak sanctuary on nearby Mt Juktas, where numerous clay idols—offerings placed within clefts in the rocks—and evidence of bonfires have been found. Around 1650 BC a new palace, one of the most important in Minoan Crete, was built on top of the old one. Finely cut tufa, marble and schist were among the materials used, and its walls were decorated with frescoes (*see* MINOAN, §IV, 2(i)) and reliefs. At least three storeys high, the complex included interior courtyards, sanctuaries, archives containing Linear A tablets, a theatre and a water cistern. The sanctuaries, and fixed altars positioned outside the palace, reveal its strongly religious character, which is also evidenced by the stone ladle of Archanes and the 'libation formula' in Linear A discovered in the settlement area. The palace was destroyed by earthquake *c.* 1425 BC, but it continued to be occupied during the period of Mycenaean control (*c.* 1425–*c.* 1360 BC). Among the remnants of this period are numerous ceramics of great beauty, kylikes and other vessels equal in quality to those discovered at Mycenaean centres on the mainland.

The Minoan cemetery on the hill at Phourni, 3 km north-west of Archanes at the foot of Mt Juktas, is the most important burial site in the Bronze Age Aegean. On the eastern side of the hill, five tholos tombs have been found, as well as fifteen burial buildings, a tumulus and a building that was inhabited by the living. The two earliest tholos tombs date from the middle of the 3rd millennium BC and contained many Cycladic idols (indicating early contact with the world outside Crete; *see* CYCLADIC, §IV), gold jewellery, faience, rock crystal and many obsidian blades. A third tholos tomb is of the MM period; the fourth and fifth date from the Mycenaean period and produced a treasure of gold rings, necklaces and seals made of hardstones, as well as copper utensils, alabaster vessels and pieces of carved ivory (*see* MINOAN, §VI, 3). There is also a Mycenaean-type grave circle of seven shaft graves. The tumulus was built towards the end of the MM period and, judging from its tear-drop shape and descending staircase, it was not a burial structure but a place of worship, which was in use until the end of Minoan times. The building inhabited by the living, which dates from *c.* 1600 BC, was probably the priests' residence, where weaving and the preparation of wine and oil were carried out in ceremonies dedicated to the worship of the dead.

Lying on the northern slope of Mt Juktas at Anemospilia is the only free-standing Minoan temple ever discovered, a tripartite building decorated with the horns of consecration and featuring step altars, rectangular benches and lustral basins. In this temple (destr. *c.* 1650 BC) was found the first evidence that human sacrifice was practised in Minoan Crete.

The Archanes area was inhabited in the Greek and Roman eras, as evidenced by archaeological finds (Herakleion, Archaeol. Mus.) and written sources. Notable among later structures are the 14th-century Byzantine churches in the villages of Archanes and, a little distance away, Asomatos.

BIBLIOGRAPHY

Y. Sakellarakis: 'Ysterominoiko kenotaphio stis Archanes' [Late Minoan cenotaph at Archanes], *Archaiol. Deltion*, xx (1965), pp. 110–18

Y. Sakellarakis and E. Sakellarakis: 'Archaiotites kai mnimeia kentrikis kai anatolikis Kritis' [Ancient finds and monuments from central and eastern Crete], *Archaiol. Deltion*, xx (1965), pp. 557–67, xxi (1966), pp. 411–19

——: 'Archanes, 1965', *Kadmos*, iv (1965), pp. 177–80

Praktika Athen. Archaiol. Etaireias (1966–)

Y. Sakellarakis and E. Sakellarakis: 'Anaskaphes stis Archanes' [Excavations at Archanes], *Architektoniki* (Aug–Sept 1966), pp. 64–7

Y. Sakellarakis: 'Die neuen Hieroglyphensiegel vom Phourni, Archanes 1,' *Kadmos*, v (1966), pp. 109–14

Y. Sakellarakis and E. Sakellarakis: 'The First Untouched Royal Burial Found in Crete', *Illus. London News* (26 March 1966), pp. 247–61

Y. Sakellarakis: 'Found a Gold Ring', *Horizon* (Winter, 1966), pp. 73–86

——: 'Mason's Marks from Archanes, Europa', *Festschrift für Ernst Grumach* (Berlin, 1967), pp. 277–88

——: 'Minoan Cemeteries at Archanes', *Archaeology*, xx (1967), pp. 276–81

——: 'Elaphantosta ek ton Archanon' [Ivories from Archanes], *Atti e memorie del I congresso internazionale de micenologia: Roma, 1968*, pp. 245–61

——: 'Das Kuppelgrab A von Archanes und das kretisch-mykenische Tieropferritual', *Prähist. Z.*, xlv (1971), pp. 135–218

——: 'Gruppen monoischer Siegel der Vorpalastzeit aus datierten geschlossenen Funden', *Jb. Röm.-Ger. Zentmus.*, xxvii (1980), pp. 1–12

Y. Sakellarakis and E. Sakellarakis: 'Drama of Death in Minoan Temple', *N. Geog.* (Feb 1981), pp. 205–22

Y. Sakellarakis: 'Protogeometriki–geometriki karameiki apo tos Archanes' [Protogeometric–geometric pottery from Archanes], *Kritika Chron.* (1986), pp. 145–63

Y. Sakellarakis and E. Sapouna-Sakellarakis: *Archanes* (Athens, 1991)

Y. Sakellarakis and E. Sakellarakis: 'Archanes-Anemospilia' and 'Archanes-Phourni', *The Aerial Atlas of Ancient Crete*, ed. J. Wilson Myers, E. Emlen Myers and G. Cadogan (Berkeley, 1992), pp. 51–8

E. SAPOUNA-SAKELLARAKIS

Arche, Anton [Antonín] **Alois** (*b* Lobositz [now Lovosice], 27 May 1793; *d* Kremsier [now Kroměříž], 7 Nov 1851). Bohemian architect, active in Moravia. He studied at the Royal Professional Polytechnical Institute in Prague under Georg Fischer (1768–1828), in whose office he subsequently worked. During the 1820s he worked on two Bohemian estates of the Chotek family, becoming involved in the final stages of building their country house at Kačina (1802–22), by Christian Friedrich Schuricht (1753–1832) and building some of the many follies in the park at Veltrusy. From 1832 until his death Arche worked in the office of works of the archdiocese of Olmütz (now Olomouc) at Kremsier, in Moravia, becoming director (1833) and later counsellor (1838). Arche worked in two styles, the Neo-classical, for which he derived his ideas from contemporary engravings and particularly the Leipzig *Ideenmagazin*, and the Gothic Revival, which he used in some of his remodellings. Soon after his arrival at Kremsier, he remodelled (1833) the Baroque gardens of the bishop's palace into a landscaped park and continued to add decorative buildings during the rest of his life. These included the fishing pavilion (1839), Maximilian's Court (1841–5), a model farm disguised as a porticoed country house, the Lantern, Vase and Silver bridges (all *c.* 1845–50) and the Pompeian Colonnade (1845–6), a gallery containing Classical busts. Other Neo-classical works included the addition of the attached portico (1835–41) to the archdiocesan seminary and the civic shooting-gallery (1838) at Olmütz, the latter designed as a rotunda, and the church of SS Peter and Paul (1843–7) at Újezd u Brna, Moravia, which has a severe Neo-classical plan. He also used the Rundbogenstil in the *cour d'honneur* (1840–45) of the Květná (Bishop's Flower Garden) at Kremsier and the country house of Jindřichov (1844) in Silesia. For Romantic effect he used delicate Gothic Revival ornament, as in his designs for remodelling the Mill Gate (1833) at Kremsier, the church of the Blessed Virgin (1835) at Stará Ves and a country house (*c.* 1847) at Třemešek. This aspect of his work culminated in his restoration and remodelling (1836–51) of the church of St Maurice in Kremsier, which was decorated by artists from Vienna.

BIBLIOGRAPHY

Thieme-Becker

Mitt. Ksr.-Kön. Mähr.-Schles. Ackerbauges. (1852), p. 27

V. Tomášek: 'Architekt Antonín Arche', *Věstník Mus. Kroměříži* (1964), pp. 17–22

P. Zatloukal: *Historismus. Architektura 2. poloviny 19. století na Moravě a ve Slezsku* [Historicism: architecture of the second half of the 19th century in Moravia and Silesia] (Olomouc, 1986), pp. 14–16, 22

PAVEL ZATLOUKAL

Archer. English collectors, curators and art historians.

(1) William George Archer (*b* London, 11 Feb 1911; *d* London, 6 March 1979). After studying history at Emmanuel College, Cambridge, from 1926 to 1930, he joined the Indian Civil Service. Unexpectedly, his service as a District Officer in India provided a vital stimulus to his intense interest in art and poetry. During a tour in Shahabad District in 1931, he discovered wood and stone images of the cattle god Birnath, which he described in *The Vertical Man.* In 1947 he ended his official career in the Naga Hills, where he collected examples of woodcarving and textiles. From 1935 to 1946 he edited the anthropological journal *Man in India* with Verrier Elwin, but the most crucial period of his service was as District Magistrate of Patna in 1941–2, when he became a close friend of such Indian collectors and connoisseurs as RAI KRISHNADASA of Varanasi, GOPI KRISHNA KANORIA of Patna and the barrister P. C. Manuk. His constant meeting with them to study their collections and discuss problems of Indian art proved an excellent preparation for his subsequent career as Keeper of the Indian Department of the Victoria and Albert Museum, London, following the end of British rule in India in 1947. During this period much exciting ancestral material was released in India, and Archer regularly returned there to work on it, travelling in the Punjab Hills with the scholar M. S. Randhawa, meeting dealers and renewing friendships with Indian scholars and collectors. In 1952–4 the museum acquired the Gayer-Anderson, J. C. French and Sir William Rothenstein collections of Indian miniatures, which provided Archer with much new research material. During his keepership (1949–59), he not only modernized the Victoria and Albert collection of Indian art but also published numerous books and articles, most notably on Mitthila (Madhubani) painting.

WRITINGS

The Blue Grove (London, 1940)
The Vertical Man (London, 1947)
Kangra Painting (London, 1952)
Garhwal Painting (London, 1954)
Central Indian Painting (London, 1958)
with P. Vitana: *Ceylon Painting from Temple, Shrine and Rock* (1958)
India and Modern Art (London, 1959)
Indian Painting in Bundi and Kotah (London, 1959)
Indian Miniatures (London, 1960)
Kalighat Painting (London, 1962)
Paintings of the Sikhs (London, 1966)
Indian Painting in the Punjab Hills (London, New York and Delhi, 1973)
The Hill of Flutes: Life, Love and Poetry in Tribal India (London, 1974)

MILDRED ARCHER

(2) Mildred (Agnes) Archer [née Bell] (*b* London, 28 Dec 1911). Wife of (1) William George Archer. She read history at St Hilda's College, Oxford, from 1931 to 1934, during which time she developed a general interest in the study of art. After their marriage in 1934 she accompanied her husband on his postings and tours in India. There, in Patna in 1941–2, she met the barrister P. C. Manuk, who introduced her to paintings and drawings made by Indian artists for British patronage. In *Patna Painting* she became the first scholar to identify this genre, which, through her publications, became known as the 'Company' school (*see also* INDIAN SUBCONTINENT, §V, 4(ix)) in reference to the employees of the East India Company, who were its primary patrons. Following India's independence in 1947, the Archers returned to England. From 1954, Mildred was employed by the India Office Library, London, to identify and care for their works of art, formerly held with the printed books; the Department of Prints and Drawings was set up under her direction. Although she became known as the prime authority on Company paintings, the lives and works of British painters in India subsequently superseded this subject as her primary area of research. She was created an Officer of the Order of the British Empire in 1979.

WRITINGS

Patna Painting (London, 1947)
with W. G. Archer: *Indian Painting for the British* (Oxford, 1955)
Tippoo's Tiger (London, 1959)
Natural History Drawings in the India Office Library (London, 1962)
British Drawings in the India Office Library, 2 vols (London, 1969)
Company Drawings in the India Office Library (London, 1972)
India and British Portraiture (London, 1979)
Early Views of India: The Picturesque Journeys of Thomas and William Daniell (London, 1980)
Company Paintings (exh. cat., London, V&A, 1992)
Regular contributions to *Apollo*, *Connoisseur*, *Country Life*, *Geog. Mag.* and *Hist. Today*

TOBY FALK

Archer, John Lee (*b* Ireland, 26 April 1791; *d* Stanley, Tasmania, 4 Dec 1852). Australian architect of Irish birth. He trained in the London office of the architect Charles Beazley and worked for five years for John Rennie, before spending eight years in architectural and engineering work in Ireland. In 1826 he was appointed Civil Engineer for Van Diemen's Land (now Tasmania), and he arrived at Hobart Town in 1827. He served as colonial architect as well as civil engineer for eleven years, during the first nine of which he was responsible for all government buildings, including military and penal works. His design for the Ordnance Stores, Hobart (1834), shows the austere and megalomaniac stamp of late 18th-century Neo-classicism, but only the less important sections were built, in 1834–8. His Customs House, Hobart (now Parliament House), begun in 1835 and completed by James Blackburn, shows the influence of the Greek Revival, and his monument to *Lieutenant-Governor David Collins* (1837–8) is Greek in the manner of John Soane. His churches show Regency and Tudor characteristics and are less sophisticated. Archer's finest engineering work was the bridge on the Midland Highway at Ross, designed on principles derived from Rennie's work, and enhanced by the fantastically carved voussoirs executed by convict stonemasons.

Archer's responsibility for military works was removed in 1836, and in 1838 his position was abolished as a cost-cutting measure. He was then appointed police magistrate for the district of Horton in north-west Tasmania and lived at Stanley, where he continued a small architectural practice until his death.

BIBLIOGRAPHY

AUDB
R. S. Smith: *John Lee Archer: Tasmanian Architect and Engineer* (Hobart, 1962)
E. G. Robertson: *Early Buildings of Southern Tasmania*, 2 vols (Melbourne, 1970)

MILES LEWIS

Archer, Thomas (*b* ?Umberslade, Warwicks, ?1668; *d* London, 22/23 May 1743). English architect. He was the son of a Warwickshire country gentleman and was an accomplished amateur who did not depend on architectural practice for his living. He did not hold any architectural posts under the Crown but his appointment as Groom Porter to Queen Anne in 1705 gave him the lucrative responsibility for the licensing of gaming as well as providing him with the connections at court that enabled him to build up a substantial domestic practice.

The nature of Archer's training is unknown, but it is clear that a period of European travel in 1691–5 instilled in him a taste for the continental Baroque that was to set his designs apart from those of his most important English contemporaries. Although his itinerary is not known, his presence is recorded in Padua in 1691, and it might be presumed on the evidence of his subsequent works that he visited Rome; it is likely that his passage to Italy took him through Austria. In the absence of solid documentation for a large number of buildings, Archer's first-hand experience of the work of the architects of the mature Roman Baroque has led critics to attribute to him several works simply because they employ motifs beloved of Gianlorenzo Bernini and Francesco Borromini: the giant order, lugged architraves, broken and inverted pediments and curved surfaces. While these features are all present in Archer's work, they were equally readily available to non-travelling Englishmen through the medium of Domenico de Rossi's *Studio d'architettura civile* (1702), a publication probably used by Archer himself to reinforce the preferences developed during his travels.

Archer began to practise architecture in his mid-thirties, announcing himself in 1705 as a country-house designer with the accomplished north front of Chatsworth, Derbys, where the bowed centre effectively disguised the irregularity of the ranges that lay behind it. He followed this with his most important country house, Heythrop House (1707–10; see fig.), Oxon, designed for Charles Talbot, 1st Duke of Shrewsbury, who returned to England early in 1706 after spending five years in Rome and shortly afterwards set about the building of his Baroque palace.

At Heythrop the influence of Bernini's designs for the Louvre, Paris, was mediated for Archer by William Talman's south front of Chatsworth to achieve an effect that places the house historically in the mainstream of the European late Baroque style, inviting comparison with Filippo Juvarra's slightly later Palazzo Madama (1718–21) in Turin. It was at Heythrop that Archer first employed certain motifs that were to be recurrent in his work: the use of colonnades to link the house with the service ranges; the raising of massive broken pediments, based on the model of the Villa Aldobrandini (1598–1603) at Frascati, which at Heythrop enlivened the skyline of the kitchen and stable blocks; and the breaking forward, at each end of the façade, of two bays bisected by a giant pilaster (rather than the usual three) to frame the composition of the main block of the house. This classically incorrect feature, uncommon in England, was employed in France by Louis Le Vau, and in Vienna by Johann Bernhard Fischer von Erlach in a building that Archer might well have seen on his travels, the Palais Stratmann (1692–3). Archer later used the two-bay framing device at Harcourt House (*c.* 1725; destr.), Cavendish Square, at Russell House (1716–17), 43 King Street, Covent Garden, and, in combination with the broken pediment roofline, at Roehampton House (1710–12) and Monmouth House (1717–18; destr. 1773), Soho Square. In these London houses Archer stressed the verticality of the design in the central bays as well by providing architectural links between the porch and the upper windows to achieve the most vigorously modelled of English town-house façades.

Archer's use of colonnades was also inventive: at Heythrop they formed a right angle, at Roehampton they were on a convex plan, and at Cliveden (*c.* 1705), Bucks, Hurstbourne Priors (*c.* 1712), Hants, and Aynho (1707–11), Northants, they were all quadrants, linking the houses with Archer's new service wings. At Aynho, the old columns of the colonnade survive, reused by John Soane in the triumphal arches that took their place.

Archer's plans were generally less inventive than his façades, although at Heythrop he contrived a remarkable central, apsed vestibule, and at Chettle (after 1711), Dorset, he complemented the convex curves at the corners of the building with concave curves in the projecting hall. Archer

Thomas Archer: Heythrop House, Oxfordshire, 1707–10

might have been restrained by his patrons from producing more spatially complex plans: he was certainly more innovative away from the constraints of domestic convenience, in his churches and garden buildings.

As a member of the Fifty New Churches Commission under the Act of 1711, Archer designed two churches in London: St Paul's (1713–30; *see* ENGLAND, fig. 6), Deptford, and St John's (1713–28), Smith Square. Like Nicholas Hawksmoor in his church designs, in both of these he was concerned to exploit the potential for variety and movement in intersecting axes. The main alignment of each was west to east in accordance with liturgical requirements, but prominent central entrances in the north and south sides made for axial contrast. Archer's designs are further complicated by the introduction of curves at the corners of the interior, which do not face each other diagonally across the central space. At St Paul's, especially, the effect is the closest achieved by any English architect to the Roman Baroque. Indeed, St Paul's has been read as an anglicized version of S Agnese (1652–5) in the Piazza Navona, Rome. The influence of Borromini can be discerned also in Archer's other great church, St Philip's (1710–25), Birmingham, which is spatially less adventurous than the London churches but retains its idiosyncratic detailing at the east and west doors and a splendid, concave-sided tower.

It was in his garden buildings, however, that Archer achieved his finest effects. The Cascade House (1702) at Chatsworth and the domed pavilion (1709–11) at Wrest Park, Beds, testify to his delight in spatial complexity. The pavilion is hexagonal with semicircular and rectangular projections on alternate sides. Another pavilion at Wrest, the demolished Cain Hill House (1715–17), had four straight sides alternating with four concave ones. These small-scale buildings demonstrate that Archer was alone among English architects of the Baroque in having seen and appreciated on the Continent the best that the style could offer.

BIBLIOGRAPHY

Colvin
K. Downes: *English Baroque Architecture* (London, 1966)
J. Lees-Milne: *English Country-houses: Baroque* (London, 1970)

J. Summerson: *Architecture in Britain, 1530–1830*, Pelican Hist. A. (Harmondsworth, 1970)
M. Whiffen: *Thomas Archer: Architect of the English Baroque* (Los Angeles, 1973)
E. Marsden: 'Thomas Archer's Creative Autumn', *Country Life*, clxxiii (12 May 1983), pp. 1268–72
T. Mowl: 'Thomas Archer and the Hurstbourne Park Bee House', *Archit. Hist.*, xxx (1987), pp. 77–82

JOHN BOLD

Archerius, Johannes. *See* ALCHERIUS, JOHANNES.

Archermos of Chios (*fl* 550 BC or later). Greek sculptor. The son of Mikkiades and father of the sculptors Bupalos and Athenis, Archermos was credited with creating the first winged figure of Nike (Victory) in Greek art; his works were apparently to be seen on Delos and Lesbos. A column signed by Archermos, that may have supported a *Nike*, was dedicated on the Athenian Acropolis in the late 6th century BC, and a badly damaged statue base from Delos has a much-restored inscription (written in the script of the island of Paros) suggesting that Mikkiades and his son Archermos dedicated the statue to Artemis after they had left their homeland of Chios. A statue found in the same general area as the base, and like it datable to *c.* 550 BC, is the so-called (and originally winged) *Nike* of Delos (Athens, N. Archaeol. Mus.; *see* DELOS, fig. 4). It is, however, not absolutely certain that the *Nike* belongs to the base, or, if it does, that it stood there alone. Assuming the *Nike* is both the work and the dedication of Mikkiades and Archermos, and that the Archermos who signed the late 6th-century BC Acropolis column is the same man, there is an unusually large chronological overlap between the careers of Archermos and his sons Bupalos and Athenis, who were themselves apparently active as early as *c.* 540 BC. Finally, it has been forcefully argued that the *Nike* of Delos is not Nike at all, but Artemis, who can also appear winged in Archaic art, and that Archermos first gave Nike her wings while working in Athens, where, with other well-known island sculptors, he enjoyed the commissions of the local aristocracy.

BIBLIOGRAPHY

Pliny: *Natural History* XXXVI.11–13
P. Scherrer: 'Das Weihgeschenk von Mikkiades und Archermos auf Delos', *Jhft. Österreich. Archäol. Inst. Wien*, liv (1983), pp. 19–25
B. S. Ridgway: 'The Nike of Archermos and her Attire', *Chios: A Conference at the Homereion: Chios, 1984*, pp. 259–74
K. Sheedy: 'The Delian Nike and the Search for Chian Sculpture', *Amer. J. Archaeol.*, lxxxix (1985), pp. 619–26
A. F. Stewart: *Greek Sculpture: An Exploration*, i (New Haven and London, 1990), pp. 116, 124, 243–4

JEFFREY M. HURWIT

Archibald, John S(mith) (*b* Inverness, 14 Dec 1872; *d* Montreal, 2 March 1934). Canadian architect of Scottish birth. From 1887 to 1893 he was an apprentice in the architectural office of William MacIntosh in Inverness. He settled in Canada in 1893, joining the office of Edward Maxwell in Montreal, where he was employed as draughtsman and assistant.

From 1897 to 1915 he formed a partnership with Charles Jewett Saxe (1870–1943), in which Archibald's role was predominantly administrative. The partnership's work included schools, large residences, residential blocks and office buildings. Early commissions in Montreal included the F. H. Anson Residence (1904), 466 Côte St Antoine, Westmount; Montreal Technical School (1909); and several additions to the Queen's Hotel (1909–13; destr. 1988), 700 Peel Street. After 1915, in his own independent practice, Archibald built the Baron Byng High School (1921); the Masonic Memorial Temple (1928); and St Mary's Memorial Hospital (1932), all in Montreal. In the 1920s Canadian National Railways commissioned him to design a chain of hotels, including hotels in Vancouver (1928–38), Halifax (1928), the Bessborough Hotel (1931), Saskatoon, and a major extension (1928) to the Chateau Laurier, Ottawa. For Canada Steamship Lines, he also built the new Manoir Richelieu (1928–9), Murray Bay, Quebec. Archibald's style of restrained classicism suited the conservative taste of Montreal, where traditional styles were in demand. While his buildings express a sensitivity to the client's taste, Archibald also adapted these traditional styles to local conditions. His architecture is dignified and restrained in ornamentation, with exteriors built of local material, usually stone or brick. His attention to detail is evident in the stone carvings, bronze grilles, interior woodwork and choice of interior fixtures. He also stressed the need for architectural teaching to be more practical and to address everyday matters of economics as well as design, and he pioneered a method of calculating the precise amount of steel required for a project. He was also active in numerous professional associations.

BIBLIOGRAPHY

'The New Chateau Laurier, Ottawa', *J. Royal Archit. Inst. Canada*, 7 (1930), pp. 393–411
W. S. Maxwell: 'John S. Archibald, 1872–1934', *J. Royal Archit. Inst. Canada*, 11 (1934), p. 44
I. Murray: *John S. Archibald and his Associates: A Guide to the Archive* (Montreal, 1990)
I. Puchalski: 'John S. Archibald: Architect, 1872–1934', *J. Can. A. Hist.*, xiv/2 (1991), pp.94–113
——: 'Bishop Court Apartments: Symbol of a Lifestyle', SSAC Bull., xvii/3 (1992), pp. 77–80

IRENE PUCHALSKI

Archigram. English architectural periodical, group and stylistic tendency of the 1960s. The periodical began as a student 'alternative' information sheet (Architecture+gram) founded in 1960 by PETER COOK, while he was working (1960–62) in the office of James Cubitt and Partners, with the aim of ensuring that student projects would be published. Most of the material illustrated was avant-garde with a strong bias towards what would be called HIGH TECH. Emboldened by the invitation to stage an exhibition, *Living City*, at the Institute of Contemporary Arts (ICA), London, in 1963, Cook and his associates became more ambitious and in 1964 they produced their fourth issue under the title 'Amazing Zoom Archigram 4'.

The success of this issue was immediate and striking. In a manner unabashedly indebted to the pioneer British Pop artists of the ICA Independent Group, it included a highly coloured pop-up tower city in the centre spread. Pages were reproduced in other magazines worldwide and became the model for other radical-formalist movements (e.g. the Italian ARCHIZOOM group). By 1964 Archigram consisted of Cook, together with Warren Chalk (*b* 1927), Dennis Crompton (*b* 1935), Ron Herron (1930–94), David Greene (*b* 1937) and Mike Webb (*b* 1937). In 1966 they organized a conference in Folkestone, Kent, under the

Archigram project (unexecuted) by Ron Herron: *Walking Cities* (detail), collage, ink and pencil drawing on photograph, *c.* 300×600 mm, 1964 (untraced)

title IDEA (International Dialogues on Experimental Architecture), whose speakers included most of the younger talents of visionary architecture, among them Hans Hollein, Claude Parent and Yona Friedman. Archigram's members were internationally in demand to give lectures, and they were invited to stage a section in the 1968 Triennale di Milano and again at Expo '70 in Osaka, Japan. The high point of their success was marked by their winning a major international competition (1970) for an underground entertainment centre on the sea-front at Monte Carlo.

The characteristic quality of the projects of their most productive period (1963–70), the 'age of Megastructures', apart from high quality draughtsmanship and the use of modern techniques such as photocopying, was an increasing emphasis on the transience and expendability of physical equipment and its direct response to human desires. The sequence of major projects began with the monumental scale of Cook's *Plug-in City* (1963–4; infinitely changeable by plugging or unplugging habitable capsules by means of cranes carried on tracks across vast multi-storied structures) and his *Entertainments Tower* project of the same date. Bryan Harvey (*b* 1936) and Ron Herron's *Walking Cities* project (1964; see fig.) envisaged very large urban structures set in motion on mechanical legs and was denounced as 'inhuman' by Siegfried Giedion and Constantinos Doxiadis. In 1967 Mike Webb proposed 'cushicle', a technically sophisticated single-seat environment vehicle, and 'suitaloon', a private one-person environmental bubble, which could be worn like a suit when not inflated for occupation. *Archigram 7* carried the warning that 'There may be no buildings at all in *Archigram 8!*'.

The Monte Carlo project, though it proposed the construction of a very flat dome more than 40 m in diameter, continued the anti-monumental theme by placing it entirely underground, so as not to obstruct the view of the Mediterranean, in striking contrast to most of the other entries that silhouetted (ironically) Archigram-inspired megastructures against the sea. In the end none of these structures was executed and in the changing intellectual and financial climate of the 1970s, which saw a general loss of confidence in large-scale planning and advanced technology, the direct influence of Archigram faded. Cook's Archigram exhibition at the ICA in 1972 marked the end of the group's significant collective activities, although its members all remained active as designers and teachers.

The true influence of Archigram has been most visible in the period since its demise. Habitable capsules were realized in Japan (*see* JAPAN, §III, 5), the basic ideas and formal vocabulary were thoroughly absorbed into the mainstream of modern architecture. Both Richard Rogers and Norman Foster publicly acknowledged its contribution to the development of their high-tech approach to design. The elaborate precision and mechanistic detailing of Archigram draughtsmanship find their most convincing realization in the detailing of buildings such as Foster's Renault spare part centre, Swindon, Wilts (1983), or Rogers's Lloyds of London building, London (completed 1987), while it has become accepted wisdom that Piano & Rogers's 'Pompidou Centre, Paris, is Archigram's Plug-in City, with its exposed structure and mechanical equipment painted in French blues and reds' (Charles Jencks). This is not surprising, as many of the junior members of the Piano & Rogers design team had been students of Cook and Herron.

BIBLIOGRAPHY

'A Clip-on Architecture', *Des. Q.*, lxv (1965) [special issue]

P. Cook: *Experimental Architecture* (London, 1970)

——, ed.: *Archigram* (London, 1972)

R. Banham: *Megastructure: Urban Futures of the Recent Past* (London, 1976)

For further bibliography *see* COOK, PETER.

REYNER BANHAM

Archinto. Italian family of patrons and collectors. They were one of the wealthiest and most celebrated patrician families of Milan. The earliest records of them date from 1228, when they made lavish donations to the monastery of Chiaravalle, near Milan. Giuseppe Archinto (i) (*d* 1476), Chancellor under Duke Galeazzo Maria Sforza (*reg* 1466–76), added to the family's wealth. His grandson Francesco Archinto (*d* 1551), a jurist, was the favoured commissary of Louis XII in the area of Chiavenna; a portrait of him, preserved by the family, is attributed to Leonardo da Vinci.

Francesco's cousin Filippo Archinto (1500–58) was appointed Senator by Duke Francesco Maria Sforza and in 1530 represented Milan at the coronation of the Emperor Charles V in Bologna. Filippo held various Imperial posts, including that of Ambassador to Rome, where Pope Paul III ordained him Bishop. In 1566 the Pope appointed him Archbishop of Milan, in which capacity his portrait (*c.* 1557; New York, Met.) was painted by Titian. In this evocative and emblematic work the bearded face and the figure are largely veiled by a light transparent curtain, which probably alludes to the fact that Filippo, opposed by the Spanish and by members of the local clergy, had to retire to Bergamo within the borders of the Venetian Republic. One of Filippo's descendants, Ottavio or Ottaviano (*d* 1656), gathered, among other things, a collection of epigraphs, adding to those already in the family; between 1648 and 1652 he produced a catalogue of these, which was later used by the historian Theodor Mommsen. Ottavio displayed his collections, as well as important paintings and sculptures, in the family palace in Via della Passione, Milan. His son Orazio Archinto (*d* 1683) had his portrait painted by Simon Vouet. In 1731 Giambattista Tiepolo frescoed ceilings in the Palazzo Archinto with profane and mythological subjects (largely destr. 1942; see Levey, pls 58, 59, 62). Ottavio's descendants died out in 1783 and all their property passed to the surviving branch of the family. In 1808, however, the palace left the family's possession and came to house a college for girls founded by Napoleon.

The surviving branch of the family was descended from Ottavio's cousin Carlo Archinto (i) (*d* 1665). His son Giuseppe Archinto (ii) (1651–1712) was ordained Bishop in 1685 and Cardinal and Archbishop of Milan in 1699. In 1701 Giuseppe Vismara of Milan (1633–1703), who until 1677 had been employed as a sculptor by the Fabbrica del Duomo, modelled two large medals with a portrait of the Cardinal, in a style reminiscent of Bernini. Carlo Archinto (ii) (1670–1732), grandson of his namesake, was a Cavaliere del Toson d'Oro and a grandee of Spain. He was highly accomplished, especially in the fields of medicine and pharmacy. He added to the family library, which he opened to scholars, and founded an academy to which he donated a substantial collection of scientific instruments. With Donato Silva, Carlo also formed the Società Palatina, which from 1733 was responsible for publishing the *Rerum Italicarum Scriptores* by Ludovico Antonio Muratori. Carlo's son Alberigo Archinto (*d* 1758) was a Papal diplomat and became Cardinal and Secretary of State; his portrait was painted by Anton Raphael Mengs. His nephew Giovanni Archinto (*d* 1799), a member of the Accademia della Crusca in Florence and the Accademia delle Scienze in Bologna, was the third and last Cardinal in the family. Giuseppe Archinto (1783–1861), Giovanni's cousin, was also prominent in public life and had a medal struck in 1819 by Francesco Putinati (*c.* 1755–*c.* 1853) to commemorate his marriage to Cristina Trivulzio. The fortunes of the Archinto family began to decline rapidly during the 19th century and their numerous and important works of art were dispersed, as was their library. A few other collections were sold privately in 1865 and later given to the museums of Milan; the manuscript relating to the epigraphs is in the museum of the Palazzo Venezia, Rome.

BIBLIOGRAPHY

Enc. It.; *EWA*: 'Tiepolo'; *EWA*: 'Titian'

P. Litta: *Archinto di Milano*, Famiglie celebri italiane, xlvi (Milan, 1843)

F. Arese: 'Genealogie patrizie milanesi', *La demografia del patriziato milanese nei secoli XVII–XIX*, ed. D. E. Zanotti (Pavia, 1972) [appendix]

D. Giorgetti: 'Silloge Archinto', *Accad. & Bib. Italia*, xlviii (1980), pp. 262–71

M. Levey: *Giambattista Tiepolo* (London, 1986)

□

Archipenko, Alexander [Aleksandr] (*b* Kiev, Ukraine, 30 May 1887; *d* New York, 25 Feb 1964). Ukrainian sculptor, active in Paris and in the USA. He began studying painting and sculpture at the School of Art in Kiev in 1902 but was forced to leave in 1905 after criticizing the academicism of his instructors. In 1906 he went to Moscow, where, according to the artist, he participated in some group exhibitions (Archipenko, p. 68). In 1908 he established himself in Paris, where he rejected the most favoured contemporary sculptural styles, including the work of Rodin. After only two weeks of formal instruction at the Ecole des Beaux-Arts he left to teach himself sculpture by direct study of examples in the Musée du Louvre. By 1910 Archipenko was exhibiting with the Cubists at the Salon des Indépendants, and his work was shown at the Salon d'Automne from 1911 to 1913.

A variety of cultural sources lies behind Archipenko's work. He remained indebted throughout his career to the spiritual values and visual effects found in the Byzantine culture of his youth and had a strong affinity for ancient Egyptian, Gothic and primitive art that co-existed with the influence of modernist styles such as Cubism and Futurism.

The decade following Archipenko's arrival in Paris was his most inventive and includes works produced during his residence at Cimiez, near Nice (1914–18), and throughout a period of extensive travel in Europe (1918–21). His first sculptures, such as *Woman with Cat* (1911; Düsseldorf, Kstmus.), in their stress on solid mass, showed the impact of Pre-Columbian art. By 1912 he had opened his own art school in Paris, and works such as *Walking Woman* (1912; Denver, CO, A. Mus.), a bronze female figure made up of interlocking convex and concave pieces on a flat supporting shape, were more directly related to Cubism. Influenced by the Cubist notion of integrating the figure with surrounding space, by 1914 Archipenko had begun to interchange solids and voids by incorporating effects of light in his sculpture, so that protruding elements seemed to recede and internal features to advance. In *Woman Combing her Hair* (bronze, 1914; New York, MOMA), the massive head is pierced by a hole, an absolute reversal of solid and void that took one step further Archipenko's characteristic exchange of concave and convex forms. His use of voids as positive forms, in doing away with the traditional monolithic concept of sculpture, had broad-ranging implications for other artists. *Boxing Match* (painted plaster, 1914; New York, Guggenheim) is one of Archipenko's most renowned sculptures of the Cubist years. It is nearly abstract in form, but, as the title suggests, its subject is the tension and struggle of opposing forces; depending on the viewpoint, the cylindrical shapes look like the heads and torsos of two combatants or like silhouetted fighters engaged in dynamic opposition.

Further sculptural innovations were initiated by Archipenko in his first constructions in painted materials, influenced both by the collages of Picasso and Braque and by the Futurist concepts published in Boccioni's *La scultura futurista* (1912). *Medrano II* (1914; New York, Guggenheim; see fig.) describes the volumes of a figure in articulated planes. The circus clown represented here is attached to a coloured back panel that serves to clarify the composition. The main volumes of the body are represented by intersecting planes, curving planar forms and wedge- and cone-shaped elements. Colour articulates structure and helps to distinguish the varying materials. In 1914 Archipenko developed a form that he called sculpto-painting, which he defined as 'a new character of art, due to its specific interdependencies of relief, concave or perforated forms, colours, or textures' (Archipenko, p. 40). He felt that this art form was more adaptable to artistic invention than traditional painting and sculpture in that it emphasized the inherent qualities of form and colour, bringing pictorial surfaces and sculptural volumes into a dynamic unity and exploiting new technical means and materials. He made almost 40 sculpto-paintings before 1920, and another concentration of these works appeared in the late 1950s. In *The Bather* (1915; Philadelphia, PA, Mus. A.) a woman holds a towel in her upraised arms as she steps from a tub. The figure is composed mainly from wooden and metal elements and is integrated with the surrounding drawn and painted space through conic sections, Archipenko's idiosyncratic version of Cubist facets.

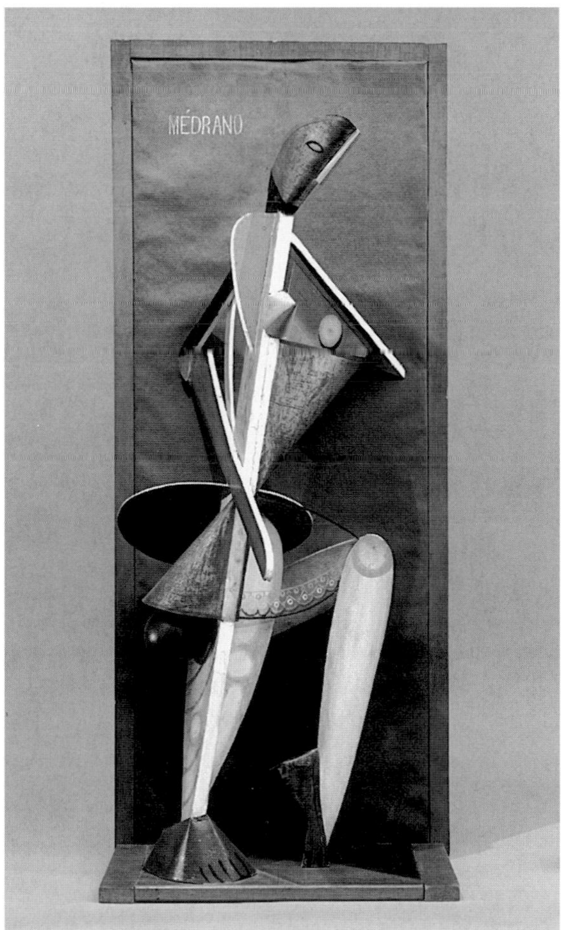

Alexander Archipenko: *Medrano II*, painted tin, glass, wood and oil cloth, h. 1.25 m, 1914 (New York, Solomon R. Guggenheim Museum)

Archipenko was represented in the New York Armory Show of 1913 and in many international Cubist exhibitions. In 1921 he moved to Berlin and opened an art school. In 1923 he settled in the USA and established a school in New York City. He initiated a summer programme in Woodstock, New York, in 1924, which continued until his death. In 1927 he was granted a patent for his invention of the 'peinture changeante' (or Archipentura), a motorized mechanism for the production of variable images in sequence. This machine (which in his view combined the scientific with the emotional), as well as his incorporation of electric light and actual movement into his work, revealed his continued attraction to the Futurist urge to represent the dynamism of the modern era.

In the 1930s and 1940s Archipenko's style changed to a classicizing naturalism, and he turned to traditional sculptural materials such as bronze, marble and ceramics to produce more restrained and elegant works. Bronze sculptures included his *Torso in Space* (1935; Jerusalem, Israel Mus.), and ceramic works included the terracotta *The Bride* (1937; Seattle, WA, A. Mus.). During this period he also lectured and taught art at numerous colleges and universities throughout the USA and Canada. In the 1950s he again concentrated on industrial materials, in which he demonstrated his taste for dazzling polychromy, for example in the series of reliefs initiated in 1957 in polychrome wood and bakelite, including works such as *Oval Figure* (1957; artist's estate, see Karshan, 1974, p. 153). Notable features of work of his late years were his indebtedness to his cultural origins and a deep spirituality. It is, however, for the freshness of his explorations of sculptural mass and space and for his innovative multi-media constructions that Archipenko received his greatest acclaim.

WRITINGS

Archipenko: Fifty Creative Years, 1908–1958 (New York, 1960)

BIBLIOGRAPHY

H. Hildebrandt: *Alexander Archipenko* (Berlin, 1923)
E. Wiese: *Alexander Archipenko* (Leipzig, 1923)
D. Karshan: *Archipenko: International Visionary* (Washington, DC, 1969)
——: *Archipenko: The Sculpture and Graphic Work* (Tübingen, 1974)
K. Michaelsen: *Archipenko: A Study of the Early Works, 1908–1920* (New York, 1977)
D. Karshan: *Archipenko: Sculpture, Drawings, Prints, 1908–1964* (Danville, KY, 1985)
J. Marter, R. Rosenblum and L. Weintraub: *Archipenko: Drawings, Reliefs and Constructions* (New York, 1985)
Alexander Archipenkos Erbe Werke von 1908 bis 1963 (exh. cat. by G. W. Költzch, Saarbrücken, Saarland-Mus., 1986)
K. Michaelsen and N. Guralnik: *Alexander Archipenko: A Centennial Tribute* (Washington, DC, 1987)

JOAN MARTER

Architect. Designer of buildings, responsible also in varying degrees for the supervision of their erection. The term is derived from the Greek word *architekton* ('craftsman' or 'master carpenter'). From this came the Latin word *architectus*, used by the theorist Vitruvius, whose treatise *On Architecture* was written *c.* 17 BC. The first use of the word in English came in John Shute's *First and Chief Grounds of Architecture*, published in 1563. The role and cultural status of the architect have been differently understood at different periods of history. In the modern Western world the architect is generally held to be something more than an artisan or manual worker and is in practice often a chief executive or director of works as well as a designer. This concept, however, dates only from the Renaissance, the period during which a distinction came to be drawn between the architect as designer and the master craftsman, who not only designed but also built. Outside the West, different traditions have emerged, with the architect not generally receiving the same individual recognition as his or her Western counterpart.

1. Ancient and Classical world. 2. Western world. 3. Islamic world. 4. Indian subcontinent. 5. East Asia.

1. ANCIENT AND CLASSICAL WORLD. The first architect of the Greek world of mythology was the legendary Daidalos, said to have designed the labyrinth in Crete (probably based on the palace at Knossos). His name meant 'the cunning or skilful one', and the attribution of cunning occurred in several later periods of history. No architects' names have been preserved for the great buildings of the first civilizations in the Mesopotamian plain. Records suggest that the kings were responsible for the palaces and that they kept control by keeping the measurements secret. The first designer recognizable as an architect was the Egyptian Imhotep, who designed (*c.* 2700 BC) the stepped pyramid at Saqqara as the tomb of his patron, King Djoser, creating the first great structure of cut stone. Although names are few, it is known that many lesser architects worked under Imhotep, and their working methods are known, as well as their instruments of design: the ruler, the square and the triangle. The education of architects in Egypt was probably based on a system of apprenticeship, and the official or state architects had high social status (*see* EGYPT, ANCIENT, §VIII, 1(iii)). Imhotep achieved particular importance (he was posthumously deified and worshipped as a god and the patron of wise men and scribes), while Senmut, under Queen Hatshepsut, was 'Guardian of the King's Daughter . . . and Governor of the Royal Palace'. Measurements were based on human dimensions, while plans were expected to follow tradition. In formal public buildings with a central axis and symmetry, the architect was expected to use a modular system based on human dimensions and a geometric system of exact precision, of which he was expected to be a master.

The ancient Greek architect was essentially a master craftsman (*see* GREECE, ANCIENT, §II, 1(iv)). Drawings by architects have not survived, but it is known that they used models, usually made of wax, especially for such details as the acanthus used on Corinthian capitals (*see* GREECE, ANCIENT, §II, 3(ii)). Vitruvius wrote about plans, elevations and perspective views and insisted that the designer must be skilful with the pencil. In both ancient Greece and ancient Rome architects often became known because of their preparation of trade books and learned treatises. Theodoros of Samos was one such Greek architect in the 6th century BC; he was consulted about problems of stability on a wet site. Chersiphron, one of the architects of the Temple of Artemis at Ephesos (*c.* 560–460 BC), wrote a treatise in partnership with his son Metagenes. When Athens became the centre of artistic production under Pericles, its architects, such as Iktinos, not only designed but also wrote. They were particularly busy under Alexander the Great, when new cities and towns were founded during the Hellenistic period. The most celebrated Greek architect and urban planner was Hippodamos of Miletos, who is credited with inventing the grid or chequer-board as the basis of city planning. He laid out Miletos and Peiraeus, dividing the land into three parts: sacred, public and private (*see* GREECE, ANCIENT, §III, 2(i)). Architects tended to be of elevated social status and to keep their profession within the family. Some were also contractors, such as Kallikrates, one of the designers of the Parthenon. As architects, they commanded substantial fees (possibly 20 times as much as a craftsman).

The most celebrated ancient Roman architect was VITRUVIUS, whose fame, however, rests not on his built work but on his treatise, the only one to have survived from antiquity. Many architects working in ancient Rome had practised in Greece; they might have trained in the liberal arts and through service with a master, or through military service and engineering works or in the civil service. Vitruvius insisted that an architect should be familiar with many branches of study; his knowledge was born from both practice and theory (*see also* ROME, ANCIENT, §II, 1(iv)).

Nero's architect was Severus, responsible for subtle interplays of curved and straight surfaces. The architect-in-chief to the emperor Trajan was Apollodoros of Damascus, architect, engineer and possibly also a sculptor. An architect, often descended from a family of architects, was expected to be expert in the production of plans, elevations and perspectives. A major part of architectural work was the supply of water and the construction of aqueducts. Architects carried out surveying work as well as building dams, ports and reservoirs and making town plans. Legionary architects laid out camps, fortifications and even towns. In the 3rd century AD the emperors Severus Alexander (*reg* 222–35) and Aurelian (*reg* 270–75) tried to promote architectural studies by making grants to teachers, and in AD 334 Constantine the Great found himself in difficulties through the lack of architects in the newly founded city of Constantinople. To cope with this situation, he issued a decree encouraging young men in the province of Africa to take up the study.

The term *architectus* became devalued in the 4th century AD, coming to mean simply a master builder, and it was superseded by *mechanicus*. This is the term used in Book VIII of the *Synagoge* of Pappos of Alexandria (*fl* AD 320), which proposes a syllabus for the instruction of architects. *Mechanici* in the later Roman Empire were persons of great technical standing, and sometimes of high rank: Cyriades, who worked for Theodosios I, is referred to by Symmachus as 'Count and sometime Consul'. In Procopius' book on Justinian I's buildings, *De aedificiis* (*c.* AD 550), the role of the architect as designer and organizer is played down in order to magnify that of the Emperor. Contemporaneously with Procopius' account, however, Flavius Magnus Aurelius Cassiodorus, who acted as secretary to most of the Gothic rulers of Rome, depicts the architect in a very different light, in Book VII of his *Variae* (*c.* AD 540). Describing all the work that the architect must specify and supervise, he observed, with regard to the tradesmen involved, that 'if you direct them rightly, while theirs is the work, yours is all the glory'.

2. Western world.

(i) *c.* 1100–*c.* 1400. (ii) *c.* 1400–*c.* 1800. (iii) After *c.* 1800.

(i) c. *1100*–c. *1400.* The architects of the medieval period have often been mistaken for the patrons who commissioned great buildings and were recorded as the persons responsible for them. The architects were celebrated master masons who frequently travelled from one job to another (*see* MASON (i), §§II and III). VILLARD DE HONNECOURT is best known through his portfolio, a textbook he may have been commissioned to make for a masonic lodge, although this claim is unsubstantiated. Architecture became an empirical skill learnt through apprenticeship. Abbots, bishops and kings might—and did—take credit for their commission, but the architects, such as William of Sens, who was brought to England to rebuild Canterbury Cathedral after the fire of 1174, were also known and honoured.

The symbol of a medieval architect is often a set of compasses in the hand, and God as the 'architect of the universe' was often drawn in that way (see fig. 1). Essentially, however, the medieval architect was the master builder who rose from the ranks of the building crafts. What marked him out was his mastery of geometry, which was expected to form part of his education, along with arithmetic, astronomy, physics and some manual work, especially in painting and metals. Much of this education was provided by monastic orders such as the Cistercians. Plans, such as that of St Gall Abbey (*c.* 820; for illustration *see* ST GALL ABBEY), were thought out in the architect's head through the process of what in the 13th century was called *cogitatio*, the thinking that led to a plan. The architect would then direct the work of travelling craftsmen: masons, glassmakers, mosaicists and others. The chief was called *lathomus* or *caementaus*, or *ingeniator* if he also undertook military engineering. Architects were buried with honours in the churches they had designed, in recognition of their role in these major constructions.

1. *God as the Architect of the Universe*, parchment, 344×260 mm; miniature from a *Bible moralisée*, *c.* 1230 (Vienna, Österreichisches Nationalbibliothek, cod. 2554, fol. 1*v*)

(ii) c. *1400*–c. *1800.* In the Renaissance, public taste was transformed by the 'rediscovery' in early 15th-century Italy of Vitruvius' manuscript (*see* VITRUVIUS, §3(ii)). However, the status and background of the architect also took on a new shape during this period. A craft-based apprenticeship was no longer a prerequisite for the architectural designer. Brunelleschi, for example, trained as a goldsmith, and the painter Raphael, who took over the design of St Peter's, Rome, in 1514, also received no formal training as an architect. Again, publications were important. In 1550 Giorgio Vasari published his *Vite*, which took as its model artist the scholar and architect Leon Battista Alberti, exceptional in the breadth of his knowledge and a famous example of 'theory and practice being united in one person'. Alberti himself insisted on the architect's need for a breadth of knowledge, a combination of skills rather than a mastery of a craft or technique, in the preface to his treatise *De re aedificatoria* (1485):

> An architect is not a carpenter or joiner . . . the manual worker being no more than an instrument to the architect. Him I call an architect who by sure and wonderful skill and method is able, both with thought and invention, to devise and . . . to complete his work . . . To be able to do this, he must have a thorough insight into the noblest and most curious sciences.

Brunelleschi filled his notebooks with measured drawings of Classical buildings and details and noted their proportions. Alberti also found models for new buildings in Classical examples. Architecture was a collaborative and continual process between a group of experts, in which an erudite client might also take an active part. The architect was the man who applied knowledge and learning and who gave instructions on site, but as an insistence on Classical forms replaced the tradition and practice of the medieval workshop it became less important that he should understand structure. As the role of the architect changed, such design aids as the ARCHITECTURAL DRAWING and the ARCHITECTURAL MODEL took on a new importance.

The emergence during the Renaissance of the architect as his own master with his own skill and training is most clearly seen in France. Philibert de L'Orme, anticipating the achievements of the 19th century, envisaged a self-governing profession of specialists with accepted standards of training and responsibilities, and he defined the role of the architect in his *Premier Tome de l'architecture*

(1567), stating that he was not to be also a builder. Also influential on the development of the modern architectural office was the Service des Bâtiments du Roi (*see* MAISON DU ROI, §II), whose regulations governing the length of apprenticeship and examination were important moves towards the establishment of a profession. The administration also introduced architectural advisers who had administrative duties: de L'Orme, for example, who had been trained as a mason and worked his way up to be an administrative architect, became surveyor of the royal works in 1548. In addition, the Bâtiments exercised control over building work and produced a building code for Paris, with uniform regulations for fireproof construction. Under Louis XIV the Finance Minister, Jean-Baptiste Colbert, became Surintendant et Ordonnateur Général des Bâtiments, Arts et Manufactures in 1664 and founded the Académie Royale d'Architecture in 1671. If the King thus had ultimate control over the architectural profession, it was Colbert who decided on the way architects should be trained. It was only after a period of many years learning abstract principles of design in the Académie that any practical experience was gained.

In England the first man to call himself an architect was John Shute in the 16th century. Like his continental contemporaries, Shute expected an architect to be a universal man, proficient in drawing, surveying, geometry and arithmetic, as well as optics, literature, history, philosophy, medicine and astronomy. The first recognizable Renaissance architect in England, however, was Inigo Jones (see fig. 2), who had travelled in Italy and acquired a profound understanding of Classical designs. In 1615 Jones became Surveyor of the King's Works (*see* OFFICE OF WORKS), an office that influenced architectural thought

2. *Inigo Jones* by Anthony van Dyck, black chalk, 241×197 mm, *c.* 1635 (Chatsworth, Derbys)

more than any other. At this time, however, the idea of the architect as a single figure responsible for both design and supervision was still unknown: more common was the gentleman-architect, such as Roger Pratt, who designed Coleshill (*c.* 1658–62; destr. 1952), Berks. The dominant figure in the mid-17th century, though, was Christopher Wren, who had been an astronomer and a brilliant academic and mathematician before becoming an architect. Wren was Surveyor General in the Office of Works, coordinating the work of a huge collection of craftsmen as well as designing a vast number of buildings. His office also trained major architects. Wren's contemporaries included Nicholas Hawksmoor and John Vanbrugh, who first achieved fame as a playwright and was untrained as an architect. Vanbrugh's partnership with the professional Hawksmoor resulted in some of the greatest buildings in England in the English Baroque style.

By the 18th century there were three types of architect: the gentleman-architect, the artist-architect and the craftsman-architect, with professionals such as Hawksmoor a rarity. The best-known gentleman-architect was the enormously influential Richard Boyle, 3rd Earl of Burlington, whose publications established Palladio's principles and designs as the correct and fashionable style of the day. Other important publications of the 18th century included writings by Colen Campbell, William Kent, James Gibbs and Isaac Ware. Gibbs's *Book of Architecture* (1728) and Ware's *Complete Body of Architecture* (1756) were followed by many pattern books and manuals that enabled lesser-known and provincial architects to design in the fashionable style and effectively to transform the urban scene (*see* PATTERN BOOK, §I, 2(ii)). The architect's learning was even more important in the second half of the 18th century, when Palladianism was superseded by Neoclassicism. Architectural competitions became common as a means of selecting architects for public projects (*see* COMPETITION, §I), and private commissions were abundant as estates were enclosed and transformed, and as new large mansions as well as towns and villages were created. Architects were usually trained as articled pupils in an established office but might at the same time have learnt drawing at an art school. Recognition came by membership of the Architects' Club, established in London in 1791. Architects became more independent when the surveyors formed their own Surveyors' Club in 1793, although some individuals, especially in provincial England, continued to combine the two activities.

(iii) After c. *1800.* The major definition of the role of the architect came with the founding in 1834 of the Institute of British Architects (from 1866 the Royal Institute of British Architects). Membership of the Institute was the sign of an architect's arrival as a professional and a guarantee of competence and integrity. In a very short time, the job of an architect was seen as essentially separate from that of a builder, and builders began to form their own organizations. The new role of the architect was defined by John Soane in *Plans, Elevations and Sections of Buildings* (London, 1788):

> The business of the architect is to make the designs and estimates, to direct the works and to measure and value the different parts; he is the intermediate agent between the

> employer, whose honour and interest he is to study, and the mechanic, whose rights he is to defend. His situation implies great trust; he is responsible for the mistakes, negligence and ignorance of those he employs; and above all, he is to take care that the workmen's bills do not exceed his own estimates. If these are the duties of an Architect, with what propriety can his situation, and that of the builder or the contractor, be united?

This distinction subsequently remained crucial to the status of an architect, even if in the late 20th century it was beginning to be eroded.

The architect's special role was insisted on by A. W. N. Pugin, whose books as well as his designs demanded care in planning, expression and choice of materials. The reputation of the architect was further enhanced by new forms of architectural journalism, such as *The Builder* (est. 1842) in England and the *Revue générale de l'architecture* (est. 1840) in France. Moreover, the nature of the architect's work was dramatically changed by the emergence of new or enlarged building types, such as prisons, commercial buildings and railways (which, by greatly facilitating the use of transported materials, effectively brought an end to locally based vernacular styles). The architect now offered a distinctive expertise. Architects were trained in England in offices; in France they could attend the Ecole Polytechnique and the Ecole des Beaux-Arts, Paris. The RIBA imposed uniformity over fees, publishing its guidelines on *Professional Practice and Charges of Architects* in 1862. It also began to control competitions and to examine candidates for associateship of the Institute. By 1887 it had established three stages of membership—probationary, intermediate and final—achieved through examination. Full-time courses in architecture also became available at King's College, London, in 1892.

The development of the architectural profession in Britain and the example of the Ecole des Beaux-Arts in France influenced the training and the status of architects in many parts of the world. Even after the foundation of the first school of architecture in the USA (1865; at the Massachussetts Institute of Technology), American architects often went to Paris to study classical principles and examples. Generally, though, American architects in the 19th century had little formal education and were either builders, contractors or former draughtsmen. Eventually, however, the founding of schools and courses led to the recognition in the USA of architecture as a profession, with the American Institute of Architects resolving in 1900 that members must have trained in an approved school. For many years the American schools remained under the influence of the Ecole des Beaux-Arts, but increasingly they produced what the American Institute of Architects' Committee on Education called in 1906 'the gentleman of general culture with special architectural ability'. In spite of developments in architectural training, some of the most notable American architects of the early 20th century, such as Frank Lloyd Wright (see fig. 3), trained as engineers or underwent a form of apprenticeship.

The first registration for American architects was enacted by law in Illinois in 1897. The first atelier, however, had been set up in New York 40 years earlier. It was a system that influenced all American architects. The most celebrated examples were the atelier of H. H. Richardson and the office of McKim, Mead & White. As practices got larger in the second half of the 19th century, it became necessary to delegate responsibility and to divide the various areas of work. Decision-making became divorced from specialized architectural tasks, and this affected the pattern of an architect's life. 'My idea', said Daniel H. Burnham, 'is to work up to a big business, to handle big things, deal with big businessmen, and to build a big organization, for you can't handle big things unless you have an organization' (quoted in Louis Sullivan's *Autobiography of an Idea*, New York, 1924). The American Institute of Architects' survey of the profession in 1950 concluded that there were three types of office: small (fewer than 10 employees), medium (10–50) and large (more than 50). Practices also began to specialize in particular building types. Collaboration in the office between individuals with different specializations became a crucial test of its efficiency. It was necessary to work in teams, with the senior architect being responsible for overall coordination. The firm of Skidmore, Owings & Merrill became archetypal of American practice in the 20th century. Founded in 1939, within a few years it reckoned to provide a full professional architectural service within one office. The firm eventually established four regional centres, each of which provided a total design service.

3. *Frank Lloyd Wright*, photograph, *c.* 1950

By 1950 there were 19,000 registered architects in the USA plus 90,000 unregistered assistants in architectural offices. Large offices such as Skidmore, Owings & Merrill remained an exception, and about one-tenth of all registered architects had one-man practices, a situation not markedly different from that in Britain. It was the big offices, however, that carried out most of the work. The architect's new role as the manager of a business inevitably affected the type of person entering the profession, who generally became more businesslike and less idealist. Some architects, notably John Portman in the USA, also became developers; although generally disapproved of by the profession, this combined role would, he claimed, extend the control of architects over large-scale projects, an approach famously adopted in the 18th century by John Wood the elder in Bath (*see* PROPERTY DEVELOPMENT). Increasingly, however, the architect known by name was more a leader among equals than a master of works. Decision-making was shared, and as the architectural office displaced the individual architect the results naturally became more anonymous than in earlier periods. The architect as artist had become a rarity.

BIBLIOGRAPHY

C. M. Butler: *The Society of Architects* (London, 1925)
J. Harbeson: *The Study of Architectural Design* (New York, 1926)
M. S. Briggs: *The Architect in History* (Oxford, 1927/*R* New York, 1974)
N. Pevsner: *Pioneers of Modern Architecture* (1936); rev. as *Pioneers of Modern Design* (Harmondsworth, 1960)
F. Baldwin Smith: *Egyptian Architecture as Cultural Expression* (London, 1938)
J. Summerson: *The Architectural Association* (London, 1947)
H. A. Meek: 'The Architect and his Profession in Byzantium', *J. RIBA*, xlix/6 (1952), pp. 216–20
J. Harvey: *English Medieval Architects* (London, 1954)
B. Kaye: *The Development of the Architectural Profession in Britain* (London, 1954)
D. Watkins: *Architecture and Morality* (London, 1957)
R. Banham: *Theory and Design in the First Machine Age* (London, 1960)
J. Fitchen: *The Construction of Gothic Cathedrals* (Oxford, 1961)
F. Jenkins: *Architect and Patron* (Oxford, 1961)
S. Giedion: *Space, Time and Architecture* (Oxford, 1963)
P. Collins: *Changing Ideals in Modern Architecture, 1750–1950* (London, 1965)
R. Carpenter: *The Architects of the Parthenon* (Harmondsworth, 1970)
R. Macleod: *Style and Society: Architectural Ideology in Britain, 1835–1914* (London, 1971)
B. Ashmole: *Architect and Sculptor in Classical Greece* (New York, 1972)
S. Kostof, ed.: *The Architect: Chapters in the History of the Profession* (Oxford, 1977) [the only comprehensive modern book on the subject]
P. Burgess, ed.: *The Role of the Architect in Society* (Pittsburgh, 1983)
J. Gimpel: *The Cathedral Builders* (Suffolk, 1983)
J. James: *Chartres: The Masons who Built a Legend* (London, 1983)
P. Nuttgens: *The Story of Architecture* (Oxford, 1983)
J. J. Scott: *Architectural Practice* (London, 1985)
N. Coldstream: *Masons and Sculptors* (London, 1991)

PATRICK NUTTGENS

3. ISLAMIC WORLD. Architects in the Islamic lands of North Africa, the Middle East and western Central Asia initially continued the practices of designer-contractors in late antiquity. Some were known in the medieval period as *bannā'* (Arab.: 'builder'), suggesting that they were master craftsmen. Some architects rose from other professions, such as Husayn ibn Talib al-Damghani, who worked at Bistam, Iran, in the early 14th century and was known as a *jissās* ('plasterworker'). Others were known as *muhandis* ('engineer'), suggesting that they had mathematical training. Indeed the well-known astronomer Ahman ibn Muhammad al-Faraghani (Alfraganus) was sent by the caliph al-Mutawakkil (*reg* 847–61) to restore the Nilometer in Egypt; he called himself *al-ḥāsib* ('the mathematician') in the restoration inscription, although he is known in other sources as an engineer. Architects in the medieval period were also in charge of estimating costs and distributing payment. The profession seems to have become increasingly specialized: by the 14th century architects came to be known as *mu'allim* or *ustādh* ('master'). *Mi'mār*, the Arabic (and later Persian and Turkish) word that most closely approximates to 'architect', became common from this period (*see also* ISLAMIC ART, §II, 1(v)).

The profession, like many others in medieval times, passed from father to son, as for example with the Ibn Babawayh family, who worked in Iran from 1175 to 1335, or the al-Munif family, who worked in Sfax in Tunisia from 1640 to 1738. Architects were valued for their skills and moved from one city to another, as in the case of the architects who moved from Edessa (now Urfa in south-east Turkey) to Cairo to design the 11th-century walls and gates of the city. The careers of few architects before *c*. 1400 can be established with certainty, and rarely can their work be identified by purely stylistic criteria. One of the first is QAVAM AL-DIN SHIRAZI, who was active in Khurasan for three decades in the early 15th century. In addition to his signed works, his activities were recorded by contemporary historians, and this corpus allows other works to be attributed to him.

The profession of architect was particularly encouraged under the Ottoman dynasty (*reg* 1281–1924), and the names of Ottoman architects are recorded from the late 14th century. The enormous growth of the empire in the 15th century and the desire for a uniform architectural style led to the creation in the 1520s of the imperial corps of court architects (*see* ISLAMIC ART, §II, 7(i)). The corps approved and supervised all major architectural projects throughout the empire; their work included design, procuring materials and keeping accounts. The chief court architect might carry out this responsibility himself, use the branch offices in major provincial centres or send someone from the central office in Istanbul to the site. The corps also trained apprentices, who assisted court architects in their tasks before being allowed to design small-scale works independently. The most celebrated of all Ottoman and indeed Islamic architects is SINAN (ii), chief architect (Turk. *mimarbası*) under the Ottoman sultans Süleyman (*reg* 1520–66) and Selim II (*reg* 1566–74). Sinan is credited with designing nearly 500 buildings, of which the masterpiece is the Selimiye mosque in Edirne (1567–75; for illustrations *see* EDIRNE and ISLAMIC ART, fig. 64).

Unlike their counterparts in 16th-century Italy, architects in the Islamic lands did not write treatises on architecture. Architectural knowledge was transmitted largely by gesture and example. The earliest treatise is Ca'fer Efendi's *Risāla-yi mi'māriyya*, which recounts the life and work of MEHMED AĞA, chief court architect from 1606 to *c*. 1622. Judging from the few plans that have survived, Ottoman architects rarely drew elevations, but they did use models.

BIBLIOGRAPHY

Ca'fer Celebi: *Risāla-yi mi'māriyya* [Treatise on architecture] (1614–15); Eng. trans. by H. Crane as *An Early Seventeenth-century Ottoman Treatise on Architecture* (Leiden, 1987)

L. A. Mayer: *Islamic Architects and their Works* (Geneva, 1956)
D. Wilber: 'Builders and Craftsmen of Islamic Iran: The Earlier Periods', *A. & Archaeol. Res. Pap.*, x (1976), pp. 31–9
R. Lewcock: 'Architects, Craftsmen and Builders: Materials and Techniques', *Architecture of the Islamic World: Its History and Social Meaning*, ed. G. Mitchell (New York, 1978), pp. 112–43
S. S. Blair: 'A Medieval Persian Builder', *J. Soc. Archit. Historians*, xlv (1986), pp. 389–95
G. Necipoglu-Kafadar: 'Plans and Models in 15th- and 16th-century Ottoman Architectural Practice', *J. Soc. Archit. Historians*, xlv (1986), pp. 224–43
A. Kuran: *Sinan: The Grand Old Master of Ottoman Architecture* (Washington, DC, and Istanbul, 1987)
J. M. Bloom: 'On the Transmission of Designs in Early Islamic Architecture', *Muqarnas*, x (1993), pp. 21–8

□

4. INDIAN SUBCONTINENT. The nearest equivalent in Indian culture to the Western architect is the *sthapati*, whose role is described in *vastu śāstras*, treatises on building, engineering and associated subjects (*see* INDIAN SUBCONTINENT, §I, 9). The *Manasara* (14th–15th century), one of the major treatises, traces the *sthapati*, along with all other kinds of artist, to a descent from Vishwakarma, the heavenly architect. The *Mayamata* (11th century) includes a note on the qualifications—the knowledge and the moral qualities—of the *sthapati*. The *Manushalaya chandrika* urges the twice-born castes (the three higher castes in classical Indian society) to patronize the *sthapati* and artisans in the construction of houses and so on. These architect–builders would have been linked by training and class with the building trades, although temple-building also involved high-caste priest–architects. The practices described in the *vastu śāstras*—organization in guilds and in regionally diverse forms—continued until the consolidation of British rule and still survive for temple-building. Successive Muslim dynasties from the end of the 1st millennium, most significantly the Mughals (1526–1712), introduced new architectural principles and devices that were assimilated by indigenous architect–builders working under the direction of a court architect or master of works. The names of some of these figures are known (e.g. Ustad Ahmad, who according to one account was put in charge of the works on the Taj Mahal), but it remains impossible firmly to identify individual architects responsible for buildings before the British period.

The majority of civic buildings erected during British rule were designed by engineers in public works departments rather than by architects. However, the work of a handful of architects, most notably Edwin Lutyens and Herbert Baker, introduced a European conception of the role of the architect, eventually leading to the establishment of an architectural profession and a system of training on the British model. The Indian Institute of Architects dates from 1917 and by Independence (1947) had 300 members.

See also INDIAN SUBCONTINENT, §§I, 9, and III, 1(iii).

BIBLIOGRAPHY

P. K. Acharya: *Indian Architecture according to Manasara-Silpasastra* (Oxford, 1934/*R* New Delhi, 1981)
Mayamata: An Indian Treatise on Housing Architecture and Iconography (New Delhi, 1985)
G. H. R. Tillotson: *The Tradition of Indian Architecture: Tradition, Continuity, Controversy and Change since 1850* (New Haven and London, 1989)

SUNAND PRASAD

5. EAST ASIA. In China, architecture was not admired as an art in the same way as calligraphy, poetry and painting, and the master builders who were responsible for most construction did not possess the education or social status of post-medieval Western architects. Senior court officials were often responsible for supervising the construction of imperial palace buildings and tombs. One such scholar–official, Li Jie, of the Song Dynasty (960–1279), actually learnt the skills of a practising master builder and published (in 1100) the *Yingzao fashi* ('Building standards'), China's first architectural treatise. Nevertheless, Chinese architecture has traditionally been shaped not so much by individual architects as by well-established rules of construction and the handing down of skills to sons and apprentices.

In Japan too, until the mid-Edo period (1600–1868), craftsmen and master builders were generally responsible for supervising new buildings (*see* JAPAN, §VIII, 1(iv)). The master carpenter (*daiku*) was responsible for the overall design and execution of a building; he also determined the work parameters of the other professions (e.g. fellers and sawyers, smiths, masons, plasterers, papermakers, roof tilers, thatchers and cabinetmakers). He was thus both artist and artisan, architect and builder, comparable to the master masons of medieval Europe. The Mokuryō (Construction Bureau) was established in AD 728 to construct temples and public buildings and to coordinate urban planning for Nara (then the capital). The Todaiji, a temple in Nara, also had its ministry for construction. Later, aristocratic families such as the Fujiwara had their own craftsmen. Generally, craftsmen were organized in family workshops, and few builders achieved individual recognition, the exceptions including Kōra Munehiro Bungo (the hereditary head of the Kora family) and Heinouchi Masanobu, who in 1608 compiled the *Shōmei* ('The elucidation of craft'), a five-part treatise detailing the secret tradition of his family's practice.

See also CHINA, §II, 1(i) and 2(v) and (ix), and JAPAN, §III, 1(v).

BIBLIOGRAPHY

Shokunin no rekishi [A history of craftsmen] (Tokyo, 1956, rev. 1965)
E. Glahn: 'Chinese Building Standards in the 12th Century', *Sci. Amer.*, ccxliv/10 (1981), pp. 162–73
W. Coaldrake: *The Way of the Carpenter: Tools and Japanese Architecture* (Tokyo and New York, 1990)

Architecta. Finnish association of women architects, founded in 1942. The first female architect to graduate with a degree in Finland was Signe Homborg (1862–1916), who trained as an 'extra student' at the Polytechnic Institute of Helsinki from 1887 to 1890. By the mid-1980s there were some 500 women in a profession numbering 1500 practitioners, and the foundation of Architecta, the first such national women's architectural association, marked the growing importance of women in the profession. Noted members have included Elna Kiljandend (1889–1970), who mostly designed interiors and furniture; Kerttu Rytkönen (*b* 1895), who advanced a Nordic classical style of building; Elsi Borg (1893–1958), designer of numerous ecclesiastical buildings; and Märta Blomstedt (1899–1982), an influential designer of Functionalist architecture. Individual practitioners found great success in their professional careers: Martta Martikainen-Ypä (*b* 1904), who designed factories, schools, hospitals, housing areas and offices throughout Finland, received no less than 29 awards in international competitions between 1930 and 1960.

BIBLIOGRAPHY

R. Nikula and R. Jallinoga, eds: *Profiles: Pioneering Women Architects from Finland* (Helsinki, 1983)

□

Architectengroep de 8. Dutch association of architects, based in Amsterdam from 1927 to 1942. It was founded by six former pupils of the School voor Bouwkunde, Versierende Kunsten en Ambachten in Haarlem: BEN MERKELBACH, J. H. GROENEWEGEN, Charles Karsten (1904–79), Hans van den Bosch (*b* 1900), Henri E. van de Pauwert (1895–1981) and Pieter Jan Verschuyl (1902–83). The name, probably coined by van de Pauwert during his military service, derived from the command to attention used in the Dutch army—'geef acht', 'acht' in Dutch meaning either 'attention' or 'eight'. In the manifesto of De 8, published in the journal *I 10* (1927), the young architects presented themselves as pragmatic and international, thus taking a stand against the expressive architectural outlook of the Amsterdam school to which their former teachers belonged. The declaration of intent, stimulated by the ideas of H. P. Berlage, De Stijl and contacts with functionalism in Belgium and Germany, attracted other Dutch architects and engineers connected with the Nieuwe Bouwen ('new building') movement of the 1920s. In 1928 Albert Boeken, Johannes Duiker and Jan Gerko Wiebenga (1886–1974) joined the group, the latter two already having designed a number of functionalist buildings. Boeken was mainly active as a publicist. The avowedly functionalist architect CORNELIS VAN EESTEREN joined in 1929 and introduced urban planning to the group. They took an active part in international CIAM congresses from 1929, van Eesteren becoming chairman of CIAM in 1930. De 8 soon took a stand in Amsterdam in favour of high-rise building and modern social housing construction (*see* AMSTERDAM, §II, 5). In 1932 De 8 officially joined forces with the Rotterdam group of modern architects DE OPBOUW, whose members included Johannes Bernardus van Loghem and Leendert Cornelis van der Vlugt. While members of the two groups continued to practise individually in the two cities, an editorial team was formed to produce the journal *De 8 en Opbouw*, an important forum for new architecture in the Netherlands. Their ideas gained increasing resonance, and in 1934 the younger architects of Groep 32 joined, as did Mart Stam, Gerrit Rietveld and Sybold van Ravesteyn. The group debated functionalist principles at the end of the 1930s, and a number of members left, including Rietveld and van Ravesteyn. The German occupation paralysed the architects' activities as a group, and publication of *De 8 en Opbouw* ceased in 1942.

BIBLIOGRAPHY

De 8 & Opbouw (1935–42)
G. Fanelli: *Moderne architectuur in Nederland, 1900–1940* (The Hague, 1978) [with Eng. summary]
B. Rebel: 'De Amsterdamse architectenvereniging *de 8*', *Het Nieuwe Bouwen, Amsterdam, 1920–1960* (exh. cat., Amsterdam, Stedel. Mus., 1983), pp. 8–51
De 8 en Opbouw, 1932–1943 (*R* Amsterdam, 1985) [essay by M. Bock]

OTAKAR MÁČEL

Architects' Co-Partnership. English architectural practice founded in London in 1939 as the Architects' Co-Operative Partnership (ACP). It originally consisted of 11 members from the Architectural Association who wished to work without office hierarchies and on projects of a predominantly social character. They were influenced by the methods and organization of Tecton in Britain and GATEPAC in Spain, while their attitudes paralleled those of their American contemporaries, TAC. Kenneth Capon (*b* 1915), Peter Cocke (*b* 1917), Michael Cooke-Yarborough (*b* 1915), Anthony Cox (*b* 1915), Michael Grice (*b* 1917), A. W. Nicol, Anthony Pott, Michael Powers (1915–94), Greville Rhodes (*b* 1916), Leo de Syllas (1917–64) and John Wheeler were the original partners. World War II and its aftermath reduced this to eight.

ACP's first and most original building was the Brynmawr Rubber Factory (1947–52; later Dunlop Rubber Factory, now derelict), South Wales, an idealistic project commissioned by Lord Forrester to relieve unemployment in a badly depressed town. Ove Arup & Partners acted as engineers for this building, which included a cluster of nine dramatic domes in shell concrete. ACP also contributed to the *Festival of Britain* (1951), but the staple of their early practice was building for educational establishments. The 'beehive' building at St John's College, Oxford (1960), and Dunelm House and an adjacent bridge at the University of Durham (1965–7), where Arup & Partners again acted as important coadjutors, were all praised for their elegant humanity. The University of Essex (from 1963), for which ACP produced a master plan and designed almost all the buildings, was untypically formalistic and correspondingly less successful. Work in Nigeria came to the firm through the influence of Leo de Syllas. Many of the partners taught in architectural schools, teaching being a strong component of the liberal ACP's philosophy. In due course the organization and operations of ACP became more conventional. It became a limited company in 1970; a substantial practice also grew outside Britain.

BIBLIOGRAPHY

Contemp. Architects
'Architects' Co-Partnership', *J. RIBA*, lxxiv (1967), pp. 229–38
O. Arup and others: 'The Brynmawr Rubber Factory', *AA Files*, x (1985), pp. 3–12

□

Architectural conservation and restoration. The stabilization, repair or reconstruction of buildings of historic, cultural or architectural significance. The history of building conservation is beset with ideological and aesthetic problems, including whether it should be practised at all and, if so, to what extent restoration should supervene in the original structure. Modern conservation principles, as set out in the Venice Charter (1964; *see* §3 below), are based on specific alternative approaches. Preservation involves minimal intervention, ensuring the stabilization and maintenance of remains in their existing state and retarding further deterioration. Restoration involves returning the fabric to a known earlier state of greater significance by removing accretions or by reassembling existing components, but without the introduction of new material. Reconstruction involves returning the fabric as nearly as possible to a known earlier state and is distinguished by the introduction of materials—new or old—to the fabric. Architectural conservation may include any of these approaches or a combination of more than one, as well as the adaptation or modification of a building to suit proposed new and compatible uses.

The following survey discusses the historical development of largely Western attitudes towards architectural conservation, which culminated in the above principles. In other areas of the world, such as East Asia, restoration involving the incorporation of materials into older fabric (*see* CONSERVATION AND RESTORATION, §I, 4) and even replacement are regarded as valid ways of dealing with wear and damage. Information on the technical conservation of specific materials, for example brick, concrete, stone and wood, may be found in the relevant articles on such materials. For information on the general principles and techniques of conservation of other art forms *see* CONSERVATION AND RESTORATION.

1. Before *c.* 1800. 2. *c.* 1800–*c.* 1900. 3. After *c.* 1900.

1. BEFORE *c.* 1800. The desire to preserve significant monuments from the past is not an invariable concomitant of high civilization. Ancient Egyptian kings, while anxious to keep their own funerary chambers intact, had little compunction in defacing the buildings of their predecessors for political reasons, or in adapting them to serve other purposes. Greek monuments were sedulously preserved by the emperors Augustus and Hadrian, while, after the fall of the Western Empire, Flavius Magnus Aurelius Cassiodorus acted as custodian of ancient monuments to Theodoric the Great, the Ostrogothic ruler of Italy (*reg* 493–526). Charlemagne appointed EINHARD superintendent of public buildings. During the Middle Ages, however, theatres, baths and tombs in Rome were adapted as fortifications by rival aristocratic families, such as the Fabi, who took over the Theatre of Marcellus (13–11 BC; *see* ROME, ANCIENT, fig. 10) in 1150. More than 140 of these structures were damaged in 1257 by the senator Brancaleone degli Andalò (*d* 1258) in a drive against nobles' towers, with consequent injury to the underlying monuments.

The continuing deterioration of the remains of Classical antiquity proved a source of anguish to the early humanists, most notably Petrarch, who protested to Cola di Rienzo (1313–54) in 1347 against the destruction of buildings and the export of art treasures. A similar outlook is evinced by Raphael at the pinnacle of the High Renaissance. In a celebrated letter (1519) to Pope Leo X, who had appointed him Romanarum Antiquitatum Praeses, Raphael deplored the current state of the remains of antiquity, as compared with the descriptions of them in the ancient authors. He urged the Pope to protect them, the Forum Romanum in particular, and to attempt a reconstruction, either in fact or at least on paper. Despite Raphael's plea, the spolia—ancient building material—continued to be used as a quarry (*see* ROME, §VII, 1), and not just the spolia. The Temple of Vesta in the Forum Romanum was still in a fair state of preservation at the end of the 15th century; it was destroyed by Michelangelo and his successors, who used the materials, in whole blocks or burnt for lime, to build St Peter's. As late as 1624 Gianlorenzo Bernini, at the behest of Urban VIII, stripped the original cladding from the portico beams of the Pantheon to provide bronze for the baldacchino in St Peter's.

A proclamation issued in 1666 by the Swedish regents for the protection of all the country's monuments was the harbinger of a fundamental change in attitude to the restoration of historic architecture that began to develop in the 18th century. Great care was taken at Orléans Cathedral to ensure that the rebuilding work conformed with the prevailing Flamboyant style (*see also* GOTHIC SURVIVAL). The study of Classical antiquity was given strong impetus by the discoveries from 1738 at Pompeii and Herculaneum, by the four volumes of *Antiquities of Athens* (London, 1762–1816) by James Stuart and Nicholas Revett, which describe the city's surviving Classical buildings, and by Johann Joachim Winckelmann's *Geschichte der Kunst des Altertums* (Dresden, 1764). In England the *Gentleman's Magazine* started to issue warnings from the early 1790s, notably in many articles by JOHN CARTER, about the destruction of medieval buildings. Various European administrations began to legislate for the conservation of antiquities, but a setback came with the French Revolution. In 1792 the Legislative Assembly ordained 'the destruction of all monuments of a kind to recall the memory of feudalism, and the obliteration of everything liable to revive the remembrance of despotic rule'. A number of valuable monuments were lost or damaged in consequence, as they were in China almost two centuries later during the Cultural Revolution, at its most frenzied in the years 1966–8, when the Red Guards pursued an identical policy.

2. *c.* 1800–*c.* 1900. The first complete official scheme for the care of monuments was formulated in a decree (1818) issued by Ludwig I, Grand Duke of Hesse-Darmstadt (*reg* 1806–30). This required the compilation of a graphic survey of the duchy's historical buildings. Thereafter no alterations or demolitions were to be permitted without prior notification to a Higher College of Building, and schemes for repair and preservation had to be submitted for official approval. Ludwig's decree was given wider publicity in *Denkmäler der deutscher Baukunst* (Darmstadt, 1815–51) by his court architect GEORG MOLLER. In this form it was seen by and undoubtedly influenced Arcisse de Caumont, who was agitating for a government grant for the protection of ancient monuments in France and the setting up of a Historical Monuments Commission. His allies included Victor Hugo, whose manifesto *Guerre aux Démolisseurs* (1825) urged the protection and rescue of medieval monuments. The campaign was successful. In 1830 the Ministry of the Interior voted funds for the care of ancient monuments, a practice continued ever since. The Commission des Monuments Historiques was set up in 1837 and elaborated a method of listing monuments of national importance as the basis for a system of protection, conservation and research. Other European states followed and the foundations were laid for many of the historic monuments' services in operation throughout the world.

The establishment of official provision for conservation coincided with the emergence of a new ethic of restoration.

In the 15th century the Colosseum (completed AD 80; *see* ROME, §V, 6) had served as a travertine quarry from which stones were robbed to build the Palazzo Venezia (begun 1455), the Cancelleria (*c.* 1483–1514) and later St Peter's. When Pope Leo XII (*reg* 1823–9) ordered the outer wall of the amphitheatre's west end to be shored up in 1825 to save it from collapse, strong brick buttresses were built (*see* STERN, (2)). No attempt was made to imitate the original structure, and the material used was completely different from that employed in antiquity. A different approach was adopted, however, for the repair of the Arch of Titus (AD 81) at the eastern end of the Forum Romanum. When it was freed in 1819–21 from its medieval encumbrances in the Torre Cartularia (see fig. 1), it was found to require lateral support. This was supplied to a design by Giuseppe Valadier, who extrapolated side panels and outer pairs of Corinthian columns by analogy with other more completely preserved arches. Valadier left the shafts of the new columns unfluted, however, and simplified the capitals (*see* TRIUMPHAL ARCH, fig. 1), establishing a compromise between a restoration that sought to imitate the missing parts exactly, albeit conjecturally, and one that aimed to consolidate, like the Colosseum buttress, without reinstating the unity of the structure. At the same time, it had been determined that the medieval fortress of the Frangipani family, into which the arch had been incorporated, had to be dismantled and removed. A historic townscape that showed the working of time and society

1. Arch of Titus, Rome, AD 81, before restoration in 1819–21; pen and brown ink wash by Bartholomeus Breenbergh, 270×200 mm, *c.* 1625–9 (London, British Museum)

on architecture was thereby destroyed in favour of restoring a Classical monument, which was then exposed without its ancient context.

The first explicit theory of restoration was formulated by EUGÈNE-EMMANUEL VIOLLET-LE-DUC, who worked for the new Commission des Monuments Historiques in France from 1840. In the eighth volume of his *Dictionnaire raisonné de l'architecture française du XIe au XVIe siècle* (Paris, 1854–8) he expressed the view that to restore a building was not to repair or rebuild it, but to re-establish it in its original state. The resultant work would then conform as closely as possible to its ideal prototype. In pursuance of this doctrine he reconstructed in a uniform style buildings that had developed by accretion over the centuries, retaining forms he thought typical and altering others to conform with them by stylistic analogy. Major restorations in this spirit were effected at Ste Madeleine (1840–59), Vézelay, St Sernin (from 1860), Toulouse, and Clermont-Ferrand Cathedral (from 1862), where a new Rayonnant west front was supplied. His pupils took these doctrines to the logical extremes. Erveuf proposed erecting spires on the twin towers of Notre-Dame, Paris, and removing the decoration (1708–25) of the choir. Other followers replaced the Flamboyant balustrades of Amiens Cathedral with parts copied from Chartres. At Angoulême Cathedral, a scheme for simple conservation (1842) grew into a major project, directed by PAUL ABADIE from 1849 to 1880, involving a new pitched roof, which required new gables to support it. 'No risks of interpretation or of creating lost portions are involved', Abadie wrote in 1862, but the west front's present appearance features a gable with five stepped windows, flanked by twin-light belfries surmounted by conical spires (see fig. 2), which is purely a work of Abadie's invention superimposed on an early 12th-century elevation. Even less compunction was displayed in dealing with post-medieval features. Simon-Claude Constant-Dufeux swept away the entire Renaissance façade of St Laurent, Paris, and replaced it with a Flamboyant design (1863–6) of his own.

Viollet-le-Duc's theory of restoration found a sympathetic response in England among the members of the Cambridge Camden Society, which had been founded in 1839 for the study of ecclesiology. They were intimately concerned with questions of church restoration, which they classified as destructive, conservative or eclectic. Destructive restoration would preserve nothing of the original building; conservative would keep everything down to the Tudor period; while eclectic, the Society's choice, would sometimes restore, sometimes remodel. 'To restore,' the *Ecclesiologist* declared, 'is to revive the original appearance. . .lost by decay, accident or ill-judged alteration' (i, 1842, p. 70), although such action, it was later admitted, might in fact produce an ideal state that the building had never enjoyed in the first instance.

Much work in this spirit is attributable to George Gilbert Scott I, who, although he maintained in *A Plea for the Faithful Restoration of our Ancient Churches* (London, 1850) that 'as a general rule it is highly desirable to preserve those vestiges of the growth and history of buildings which are indicated by the various styles and irregularities of its parts', in practice acted quite differently (*see* SCOTT (ii), (1)). His tendency was to reconstruct in a uniform style a

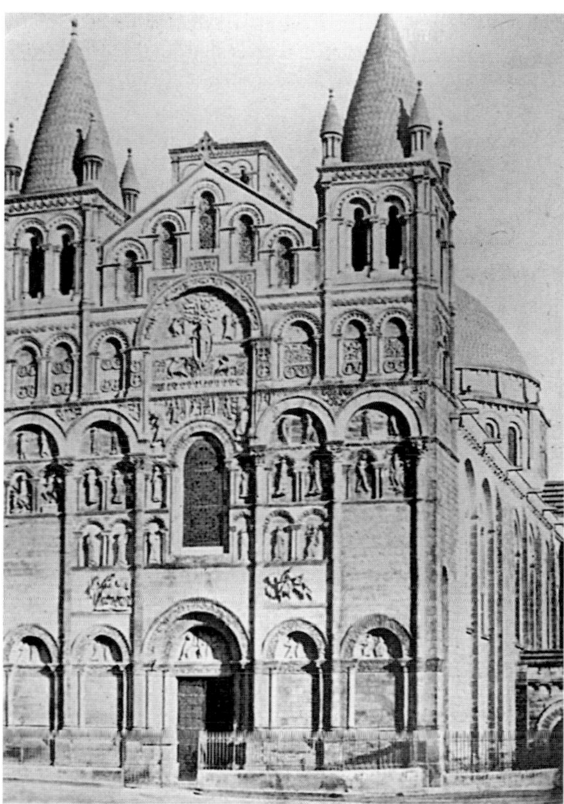

2. Angoulême Cathedral, west front: (left) before restoration, mid-1840s; (right) after restoration by Paul Abadie, 1849–80

medieval church that exhibited work of different epochs, sometimes on the evidence of a single surviving early feature. Most notoriously, he pulled down the whole east end of Christ Church Cathedral, Oxford, and rebuilt it (1870–76) in the Norman style. The work of Scott and his school provoked an early reaction from John Ruskin, who in *The Seven Lamps of Architecture* (London, 1849) declared unequivocally that 'it is impossible, as impossible as to raise the dead, to restore anything that has ever been great or beautiful in architecture'. Ruskin's attitude influenced the Society of Antiquaries of London, which urged at the Council meeting of 1 May 1855 that 'no restoration should ever be attempted, otherwise than. . .in the sense of preservation from further injuries'.

Notwithstanding these objections, the tide of inventive restoration flowed unabated. It was helped by the critical research into the nature of Gothic architecture that was evoked by the Gothic Revival and by the confidence that the new knowledge inspired in architects. It culminated in the completion, after a hiatus of 300 years, of Cologne Cathedral (1842–80) to designs by ERNST FRIEDRICH ZWIRNER (*see also* COLOGNE, §IV, 1, and fig. 5), an extraordinary episode in which nationalism battled with scholarship in a manner reminiscent of the Greek and Roman controversy of Giovanni Battista Piranesi's day. Few amenders of the mistakes and mishaps of ancient buildings exceeded the boldness of JOSEF MOCKER. Among many other works, not least those at Prague Cathedral (*see* PRAGUE, figs 13 and 14), he reconstructed Křivoklát Castle (from 1882) in the Jagiellonian style and undid the Renaissance remodelling (1587–96) of Karlštejn Castle by Gothicizing it again (1887–94; *see* CZECH REPUBLIC, fig. 2). Finally, in 1889 he gave the early 14th-century castle at Konopiště its present admired appearance.

It was the prospect of Scott intervening in similar fashion at Tewkesbury Abbey that led William Morris to found the Society for the Protection of Ancient Buildings (SPAB) in 1877 and write its manifesto (*see* MORRIS, WILLIAM, §4). This urged all who might be responsible for the upkeep of historic buildings 'to put Protection in place of Restoration', and in the work of maintenance only to employ 'such means as are obviously meant for support or covering, and show no pretence of other art'. The extreme reserve of this outlook took some time to attract support, but ultimately its diffusion was widespread and long-lasting: its traces may be observed in such dicta as that of Camillo Boito: 'It is better to consolidate than to repair, better to repair than to restore' (*Questioni pratiche di belle arti*, Milan, 1893; *see also* BOITO, CAMILLO, §3).

H. A. MEEK

3. AFTER *c.* 1900. The influence of the Society for the Protection of Ancient Buildings (*see* §2 above) remained strong in Great Britain in the early 20th century and its advice on conservation matters was sought by government departments. Many great monuments were restored in conformity with SPAB practice, including Fountains Abbey and Dover Castle. Similarly, the DEUTSCHER WERKBUND, founded by Hermann Muthesius in 1907, combined

a thorough study of historic buildings with the wish to revive standards of craftsmanship. In 1908 the Royal Commission on Historical Monuments was established in England (with similar bodies in Scotland and Wales) to provide inventories of ancient monuments and historic buildings dated before 1714, a date that has been progressively advanced. Even though the surveys still do not cover the whole of the British Isles, they have provided a quality and quantity of knowledge that has enhanced the basis on which conservation takes place.

Major works of historical architecture in Belgium and France destroyed during World War I were generally restored in faithful imitation of the original design. At Arras, for example, the historic core of which was reduced to rubble by German artillery, the squares were restored in the 1930s by Pierre Paquet (1875–1959). The scale of the damage was obviously beyond the scope of restrained SPAB-type interventions. The alternative would have been what Ruskin called the 'necessity of destruction'. 'Accept it as such', he had written, 'pull the building down, throw its stones into neglected corners, make ballast of them, or mortar if you will' (*The Seven Lamps of Architecture*). But the death of buildings as contemplated by Ruskin was occasioned by irreversible decay, not apocalyptic bombardment. At all events, no government was prepared to abandon its nation's heritage for the sake of conservational purism. Where, on the other hand, damage, or its threat, was occasioned by the inroads of decay, greater reserve was still displayed. In particular, where ancient façade sculpture began to show signs of dilapidation, the tendency was to put it indoors and substitute simplifed replacements, instead of pastiche re-creations of ancient statuary, in the manner of Viollet-le-Duc.

In the USA the large-scale restoration of colonial WILLIAMSBURG was initiated in 1926 when John D. Rockefeller bought 173 acres of the town with the intention of restoring it to its layout and appearance in 1775. Existing, run-down buildings were subsequently restored and those that were in ruins or completely built over were reconstructed, the latter involving the removal of several hundred 19th- and 20th-century buildings. An unusual feature of the exercise was the archaeological and archival research put into each property, with the foundations of each house being excavated before rebuilding. By the end of the 20th century more than 100 major buildings had been restored, 50 of which were reconstructions. The authenticity of the whole is as careful as a

3. Coventry's cathedrals from the south-east

mixture of old and new can be, much enhanced by mature trees and gardens. It is the yardstick by which other folk museums are judged, although very few can boast original house plots on the scale of Williamsburg.

After World War II many countries took stock of their losses and chose various paths. In England, Coventry Cathedral, at the heart of a city centre almost totally demolished in November 1940, was left as a consolidated ruin beside Basil Spence's new cathedral (1954–62; see fig. 3) and surrounded by shops and offices. The precise restoration of the destroyed centre of Warsaw owed more to sentiment than any idea of conservation (*see* WARSAW, §II, 2). In Cologne, a voluntary tithe was collected from the citizens and almost every church destroyed by bombing was reconstructed with painstaking accuracy over a period of nearly half a century, each reconstruction publicly accounted for with photographs and drawings placed at the entrance. This campaign was helped through the application of photogrammetry, by which measured drawings of elevations are produced from photographs.

Loss or damage through fire, for example at Hampton Court, near London, and York Minster in 1984 and at Windsor Castle in 1992, flood, as at Florence in 1966, and earthquake, such as struck Tuscania in Latium in 1971, has led to the growth of international establishments to coordinate work during such disasters, to study techniques and to teach them; the best known of these is the International Centre for the Study of Preservation and Restoration of Cultural Property (ICCROM) in Rome. International funding and advice for World Heritage Sites is provided through the United Nations Educational, Scientific and Cultural Organization (UNESCO). In the 1960s, for example, a series of Egyptian temples in the Upper Nile region was moved above the flood level behind the Aswan Dam, the construction of which was then considered essential to the feeding of the nation. Here the rock-cut temples built at ABU SIMBEL by Ramesses II (*reg c.* 1279–*c.* 1213 BC) were cut away from the living rock in blocks and reassembled. By the mid-1990s, however, the temples of the complex were at a second crisis, suffering from severe wind erosion. World funds and advice have also been used for all the 5th-century BC buildings on the Acropolis in Athens (*see* ATHENS, §II, 1(i)). The Parthenon, Propylaia and Erechtheion were all built of Pentelic marble, the exact placing of every feature, the pattern of light and shade, and the quality of each piece of sculpture having been the subject of intense consideration during their construction. The explosion of gunpowder stored in the Propylaia (1645) and the Parthenon (1687), and further erosion owing to time, visitors, deteriorating iron ties and pollution have, however, severely altered the view. Repairs and reconstructions have involved years of discussion and extensive computer studies to determine the original place of each major stone. At the Parthenon indeed, as at the prehistoric sites of LASCAUX and Stonehenge, visitors may no longer approach or touch the monument, to avoid abrasion.

Anastylosis, the resurrection of monuments at sites where the fallen pieces have remained close to their original position, has been seen as the simplest form of repair, especially for Classical temples. The drums used by Greek and Roman builders to make up large columns were pinned together at their centres by wooden blocks and iron pins that rotted over time. Hundreds of sites are littered with the collapsed but comprehensible remains of temples, agora, fora—and indeed whole towns—not only in Greece and Rome but also in Tunisia, Turkey, Israel and France. The opportunity to study preserved sites throughout the Greek and Roman empires has greatly enhanced understanding of the quality of architecture of the Classical world and the structures chosen for reconstruction are no longer confined to temples. Anastylosis, however, is not always aesthetically pleasing. If stones are unevenly worn from the time they were collapsed, resurrection could be unstable. If the deficit is made up in artificial materials rather than matching stone, the effect tends to be honest but ugly. There also remains a risk of incorrect reconstruction. In Rome, the Arch of Titus is generally considered to be a successful anastylosis but the Arch of Constantine (AD 315) is marred by obtrusive infill (*see* ROME, §V, 12 and fig. 30). Anastylosis is widely accepted as ethical provided that a full visual record is kept showing the state of the building before and after restoration, and that only insertions or other action that can be reversed without harming the fabric is taken.

The ethics of restoration, including anastylosis, were debated in 1964 at the International Congress for Conservation in Venice. A summary of the ideas raised was published as the Venice Charter, and the International Council on Monuments and Sites (ICOMOS) was established to promote its principles. The Venice Charter has been accepted by many countries but has no legal standing and has received widely varying interpretations. Its principles are most applicable to archaeological sites and are not always suited to buildings in use. Where a building is of great antiquity or unique, total preservation is the aim. No-one today would require the Tower of London, for example, to meet modern building regulations, although European Community Health and Safety regulations are applied. Most buildings, however, need to be in use to guarantee their conservation. Social change has caused vast numbers of important buildings to become redundant or face ideological opposition. In countries under Communist rule, for example, some churches were maintained as historic buildings but their care was not always paramount and their contents were sometimes gathered in museums, lost or stolen. Wooden churches were particularly vulnerable. In Muslim countries, conversion into mosques has guaranteed the maintenance of some buildings, such as SS Sergios and Bakchos in Istanbul, but lack of finance and interest has threatened many churches, especially in rural areas.

The decline of the Church's wealth and support has led to large numbers of churches becoming redundant: in England, for example, there were 16,500 Anglican churches in 1968, but within 20 years 1147 had been declared redundant. To prevent wholesale demolition, many were converted into music and theatre workshops, old people's day centres, bookshops, libraries or heritage centres. Uses that require an open space can be compatible, but some schemes preserve only the outer appearance of the building and carve up the interior. The extra floors and rooms that were inserted when the imposing SS Thomas and Swithun (1845–6), Winchester, designed by E. W. Elmslie (*fl* 1843–72), was converted to house the

Hampshire County Records Office did little for either church or record (see fig. 4). Social and economic change has also altered the circumstances for the maintenance of other types of buildings. Manor houses, châteaux and palazzi were built to be run by armies of servants who lived on the premises. By the end of the 20th century few individuals, aristocratic or otherwise, were able to devote their lives to such properties. A select few are maintained by the state or by public trusts. Some became schools, agricultural colleges, sports clubs and hotels, but the necessary adaptive treatment is rarely in keeping. In 1977 there was public outcry when the 7th Earl of Rosebery allowed the contents of Mentmore House (1852–4, by Joseph Paxton and G. H. Stokes) to be sold at auction, but no legislation existed in Britain to deal with assemblages of furniture and paintings that belong to the architecture.

In the urban environment economic growth creates pressure for change and demolition. In the 1950s and 1960s bombed areas were redeveloped and there was expansion into green-field areas, but from the 1970s the increasing demands of traffic, changes in manufacturing requirements and even the marketing of vegetables have sometimes led to inner city decay and congestion. In France, the Loi Malraux (1962), named after André Malraux, the then minister of cultural affairs, introduced the concept of conservation areas (*secteurs sauvegardés*), where city districts or entire historic villages would be surveyed and their reinstatement systematically planned. This would be financed by a mixture of state grants, loans and private investment. The areas selected, such as the Marais district in Paris and much of the city of Chartres, have subsequently been magnificently cared for regardless of the owners' wishes. Although France has sometimes been accused of being too selective in the areas conserved, its standards are high.

4. SS Thomas and Swithun, Winchester, by E. W. Elmslie, 1845–6; converted to house the Hampshire County Records Office, 1972–5

In England and Wales the Civic Amenities Act (1967), which was clearly inspired by the French initiative, required local authorities to designate Conservation Areas. The aim was to recognize that the value of a street or square is created not only by its individual buildings of quality, but also by the attention to scale and the care taken with the minor properties, spaces and street furniture. Chester, Bath, Chichester and York were selected for pilot studies that helped develop ways of funding and organizing repairs in buildings with multiple occupancy, such as the Circus (1754–8), by John I Wood (i) in Bath or the Rows in Chester. The Edinburgh New Town Conservation Committee, faced with similar problems, formed an agency to inspect their terraces quinquennially and has protected the ability to pay with insurance policies. Some of the schemes promoted under French and British legislation have been accused of 'gentrification', pushing out old people and small shops from the Marais or York city centre and attracting rich tenants who can afford to maintain the properties. A similar charge is often laid against the conversion of market buildings. In Boston, MA, the businesses that operated around Faneuil Hall Market (Faneuil Hall, 1742; additional rows, 1824–6, by Alexander Parris; rest. by Benjamin Thompson Associates) were moved away from their 18th- and 19th-century arcades and replaced by cafes and expensive shops. Similarly, in 1974 the fruit and vegetable market (1828–30, by Charles Fowler) in Covent Garden, London, and the Piece Hall (1775–9, by Thomas Bradley), the former cloth hall in Halifax, W. Yorks, were abandoned, restored with care and converted into successful commercial ventures.

Imaginative conversions of dock warehouses abound, saving magnificent buildings with a variety of uses. The scheme in 1980 to convert St Katharine Docks in London, built by Philip Hardwick in 1827–9, into luxury apartments and a hotel was followed by numerous other projects, including the neighbouring Tobacco Dock (1811–14, by David Asher Alexander and John Rennie), now a shopping centre. In Liverpool, Albert Dock (1839–45), built by Jesse Hartley (1780–1860), has been turned into a recreation area with museums, an art gallery, a TV station, shops, boating pools and apartments (for illustration *see* DOCK). In Amsterdam, 84 warehouses built between 1708 and 1829 were converted into council apartments above offices and shops. Copenhagen Docks, built in the late 18th century and largely disused by the 1970s, became hotels, condominiums, a conference centre and an exhibition centre for architecture.

The difference between adaptive reuse and the careful preservation of every stone in a cathedral or castle has been frequently debated. 'Façadism', in which only the street frontage is preserved in the belief that only the façade is in the public domain, has allowed much of value to be demolished through misattribution. The practice of facing medieval timber-framed buildings with fire-resistant brickwork has often disguised the structures' true origins, such as in several buildings in Salisbury, Wilts, which were listed as 19th-century, but which proved to be well-preserved timber-framed merchants' houses erected between the 14th and 17th centuries and which were saved largely because representatives from the Royal Commission on Historical Monuments pleaded their case.

The destruction of vast areas in two world wars encouraged a comprehensive approach to redevelopment. Even after the loss of many precious town centres, there continued to be arguments based on the premise that any buildings could be demolished provided that a substitute of sufficiently high quality was proposed. This argument was hotly refuted by conservationists on the grounds that there will never be another 18th- or 19th-century building and therefore the stock is always dwindling. Until the 1970s penalties for the demolition of a protected building were derisory, especially when compared with the cost of land in expensive city-centre locations. European Architectural Heritage Year in 1974 did much to influence public awareness. Craft skills that had been endangered by large-scale, post-war building booms made a modest revival, and the manufacture of specialist products in clay, ironmongery and lead has been resumed. Some types of building stone became rare, however, and France set up an international stone supplies organization to fill the need.

It has sometimes been difficult to ensure that old and new buildings in historic cities are compatible. In Jerusalem, for example, all buildings must be stone-clad, requiring vast quantities of stone for its skyscrapers. In Bath, height restrictions reduce the demand, and correctly coloured stone substitutes are permitted in many situations. No height restrictions were imposed in Boston, MA, and several key buildings, including the King's Chapel (1750, by Peter Harrison) and the Old State House (1713), are dwarfed by skyscrapers. In Chicago, however, the Loop area, close to the Stock Exchange, with buildings by H. H. Richardson, Louis Sullivan and Frank Lloyd Wright, was protected by transferring 'air rights': skyscrapers were forbidden within the historic core, and in exchange the city authorities allowed extra storeys outside the protected area. Recognition of the earlier skyline's value can be expensive, as for example at Philadelphia, where surroundings were not protected at first, but there was a change of heart in the 1970s and tall buildings were demolished at great cost.

Whole districts of smaller houses abandoned as unfit or unwanted have been reconditioned by both public and private means. The National Trust for Scotland bought a number of neglected villages, including Culross, Fife, restored them and leased the properties. Historic Hill, Newport, RI, has been similarly restored. Trinity, an area of 17th-century weavers' houses in Frome, Somerset, was condemned for demolition in the early 1970s but was reprieved and restored after a prolonged campaign (Pearce). Tall terraces of stone tenements in the Gorbals of Glasgow were saved by careful reuse of open space between the rows. Smaller terraces ripe for redevelopment were 'enveloped', given new roofs, identical kitchens and bathrooms in the 1980s. At this level the conservation gain is small, but it demonstrates a preference for rehabilitation rather than the construction of new tower blocks.

Architectural conservation in the late 20th century has drawn on a wide range of attitudes and techniques. At its most sophisticated it has supported such projects as the floating of York Minster's central tower on self-adjusting hydraulic jacks. This may be contrasted with controversial schemes to move timber-framed buildings to museums or other locations to aid development. Very few technical problems remain, but the finance is not always available.

MARION MEEK

BIBLIOGRAPHY

G. B. Brown: *The Care of Ancient Monuments: An Account of Legislative and Other Measures Adopted in European Countries for Protecting Ancient Monuments and Objects and Scenes of Natural Beauty, and for Preserving the Aspect of Historical Cities* (Cambridge, 1905)

P. Léon: *Les Monuments historiques: Conservation, restauration* (Paris, 1917)

La ricostruzione del patrimonio artistico italiano (Rome, 1950)

P. Léon: *La Vie des monuments français: Destruction, restauration* (Paris, 1951)

A. Ciborowski: *Warsaw: A City Destroyed and Rebuilt* (Warsaw, 1964)

Il monumento per l'uomo: Atti del II congresso internazionale di restauro: Venezia, 1964

F. Mielke: *Fremdenverkehr, Altstadt und Denkmalpflege* (Bonn, 1971)

J. Harvey: *Conservation of Buildings* (London, 1972)

Architects' J. (May 1974) [special issue on tourism and conservation]

J. Fawcett: *The Future of the Past: Attitudes to Conservation, 1174–1974* (London, 1976)

New Life for Old Churches (London, 1977)

D. Hodges: *The Care and Conservation of Georgian Houses* (Edinburgh, 1978)

E. R. Chamberlin: *Preserving the Past* (London, 1979)

M. W. Thompson: *Ruins: Their Preservation and Display* (London, 1981)

B. M. Fielden: *Conservation of Historic Buildings* (London, 1982)

D. Pearce: *Conservation Today* (London, 1989)

HAROLD MEEK, MARION MEEK

Architectural drawing Representation in graphic form of a building or part of a building, either as a stage in the planned construction of an actual edifice or as an imaginative act in its own right. The development of the form in Western art has reflected not only developments in architectural and graphic techniques but also broader developments in the status and role of the architect.

1. Medieval. 2. Renaissance and after.

1. MEDIEVAL. In the Middle Ages architectural drawings served to visualize a building design and to establish its dimensions; they depicted the whole or part of a building, individual details and the architectural ornament of church furnishings such as choir-stalls or sedilia. The earliest surviving medieval architectural drawing is the monastic plan made *c.* 820 of St Gall Abbey, which was probably produced as an 'ideal' rather than as a working plan (for further discussion and illustration *see* ST GALL ABBEY, §2). Romanesque and Early Gothic churches were normally built without preliminary drawings, but a few architectural drawings survive from the 13th century, among them the portfolio of VILLARD DE HONNECOURT, the Reims Palimpsest (Reims, Archvs Ville; a palimpsested manuscript of *c.* 1250, with the incised outlines of arches and tracery visible beneath the later writing) and Strasbourg Design A (*c.* 1260; Strasbourg, Mus. Oeuvre Notre-Dame). A larger number survive from the late medieval period; a few of these are from Italy, but the majority are associated with the masons' lodges of northern Europe and therefore tend to be concentrated in such centres as Ulm, Strasbourg and Vienna. An ambitious mason usually learnt to draw after his apprentice and journeyman years, hiring himself to a Master of the Works, to be taught either by him or his foreman. The style of the lodge could transcend that of the individual, and a drawing remained

the possession of the lodge where it was made: in a contract or instructions for Masters of the Works it was often expressly stated that they were not allowed to take drawings with them when they left the lodge.

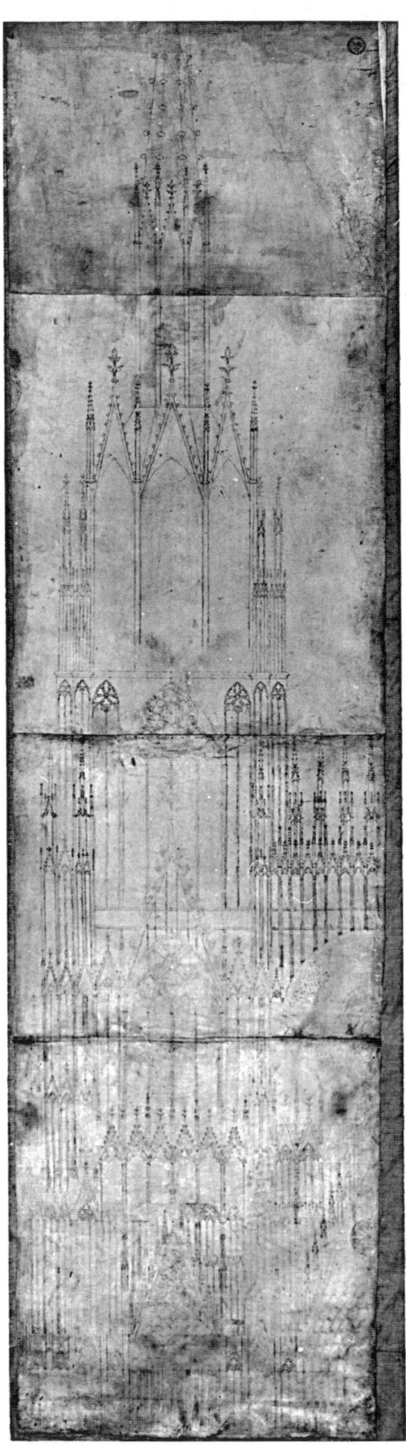

1. Architectural drawing, Strasbourg Design B, ink on parchment, 2.74×0.70 m, *c*. 1275 (Strasbourg, Musée de l'Oeuvre Notre-Dame)

The purpose of earlier drawings can be difficult to establish but was different from that of the architects' notebooks, which contained exemplary prescriptions and methods of squaring up or instructions for the following generation (*see* LODGEBOOK and MASON (i), §IV, 4). It is not certain, for example, whether Strasbourg Design B (see fig. 1) was made at Strasbourg or taken there as a finished work. It shows half of a two-tower façade, with tracery derived from the transept façades of Notre-Dame, Paris, although the forms are vastly more refined. Yet, as the drawing is not based on the proportions of the nave of Strasbourg Cathedral, the design could not have been executed as drawn. Cologne Plan F (see fig. 2) is 4.05 m high and drawn on eleven sheets of parchment; it is a design for the entire façade of Cologne Cathedral, showing five storeys with five axial directions. As a façade design the Cologne drawing was clearly intended to surpass all its predecessors in both size and height.

Drawings of the later period fall into several categories: at the extremes are working drawings intended as the basis for construction, and studies that were never intended to be used. Some of the latter are of existing buildings, represented either as they are or with imagined variations, while some are purely theoretical designs, such as the numerous studies for vault patterns. In between are drawings whose designs were evidently revised before execution, and some that were never realized because a different plan was adopted or because that part of the building was never constructed. The surviving fraction of what must once have existed is an indication of the many interesting designs that were never executed.

Drawings were made with basic tools such as compasses, the square and straight-edge; it is not clear whether medieval draughtsmen possessed simple mechanisms for making parallel lines. The drawing medium was usually a light, portable material such as parchment, which was later superseded by paper (*see* §2(i) below); if the drawing were on a large scale several pieces were joined together. If it had to be made on a scale of 1:1, it was done on the tracing floor on the building site (*see* TRACING FLOOR and YORK, §III, 1(i)). The principal lines were first drawn in with a thin metal point, which was also used for lesser lines such as arches. Even small circles were usually produced with compasses; only ungeometric forms such as leaf patterns were drawn freehand. The main lines were then gone over with pen and ink. Lines produced by the straight-edge were hatched or given ink washes. The 'blind tooling' made by the metal points is still visible on the plans and can be used to distinguish between incised plans and tracings. The latter were made by stretching the original on a frame and lighting it from below to make it translucent; the tracing sheet would then be placed over the top.

Drawings were constructed by means of orthogonal projections: 'flat' two-dimensional projections in which the line of sight is vertical to the principal surfaces. Orthogonal plans, elevations and sections are drawn parallel to the drawing surface without distortion and can be made to scale. Medieval orthogonal projections stand in a fixed, measurable relationship to the building. In contrast to modern architectural drawings, medieval ground-plans represent a section through all storeys at once (see fig. 3). This had the advantage of allowing the

2. Architectural drawing of the façade of Cologne Cathedral, Cologne Plan F (detail), ink on parchment, 4.05×1.70 m, *c.* 1310 (Cologne Cathedral, Dombauarchiv)

dispositions of superimposed elements to be controlled but makes the drawings difficult for a modern eye to read (*see also* MASON (i), §IV,4). The section specified the vertical dimensions. Intersecting lengths of wall were usually shown, as on fol. 30*v* of the portfolio of Villard de Honnecourt, where the intersecting vault surfaces of the choir chapel at Reims Cathedral are shown as wavy lines. Sections of wall at another level are often included in the drawings as separate views. An elevation drawing, however, normally shows the exterior: elevations, particularly of façades, such as Strasbourg Design B and the façade drawings for Cologne Cathedral (Cologne Cathedral, Dombauarchv), are, because of their clarity, among the most famous medieval drawings. A 'show' drawing, made for demonstration purposes, usually consisted of an orthogonal drawing of an elevation, enhanced with shading, colour or elements in perspective to make them clearer. Although artificial perspective was unknown at this period, occasional attempts were made to represent buildings, or parts of buildings, in space.

BIBLIOGRAPHY

R. Wortmann: *Der Westbau des Strassburger Münsters von 1275 bis 1318* (diss., U. Freiburg im Breisgau, 1957)

R. Branner: 'Drawings from a Thirteenth-century Architect's Shop: The Reims Palimpsest', *J. Soc. Archit. Historians*, xviii (1958), pp. 9–21

——: 'Villard de Honnecourt, Reims and the Origin of Gothic Architectural Drawing', *Gaz. B.-A.*, lxi (1963), pp. 129–46

F. Bucher: 'Design in Gothic Architecture: A Preliminary Assessment', *J. Soc. Archit. Historians*, xxvii (1968), pp. 49–71

H. Koepf: *Die gotischen Planrisse der Wiener Sammlungen* (Vienna, 1969)

K. Hecht: 'Mass und Zahl in der gotischen Baukunst', *Abh. Braunschweig. Wiss. Ges.*, xxi (1969), pp. 215–325; xxii (1970), pp. 105–263; xxiii (1971/2), pp. 25–236

P. Pause: *Gotische Architekturzeichnungen in Deutschland* (diss., U. Bonn, 1973)

H. Koepf: 'Die gotischen Planrisse der Ulmer Sammlungen', *Forsch. Gesch. Stadt Ulm*, xviii (1977)

A. Wolff: 'Der Kölner Fassadenplan F', *Die Parler und der schöne Stil, 1350–1400: Europäische Kunst unter den Luxemburgern* (exh. cat., ed. A. Legner; Cologne, Schnütgen-Mus., 1978), i, pp. 146–8

F. Bucher: *Architector: The Lodgebooks and Sketchbooks of Medieval Architects*, i (New York, 1979)

L. R. Shelby and R. Mark: 'Late Gothic Structural Design in the "Instructions" of Lorenz Lechler', *Architectura* [Munich], ix (1979), pp. 113–31

A. Seeliger Zeiss: 'Studien zum Steinmetzbuch des Lorenz Lechler von 1516', *Architectura* [Munich], xii (1982), pp. 125–50

B. Schock-Werner: *Das Strassburger Münster im 15. Jahrhundert* (Cologne, 1983)

C. Gerlach: *Vorzeichnungen auf gotischen Planrissen*, Diss. Kstgesch., xxiii (Cologne, 1986)

Les Bâtisseurs des cathédrales gothiques (exh. cat., ed. R. Recht; Strasbourg, Anc. Douane, 1989)

BARBARA SCHOCK-WERNER

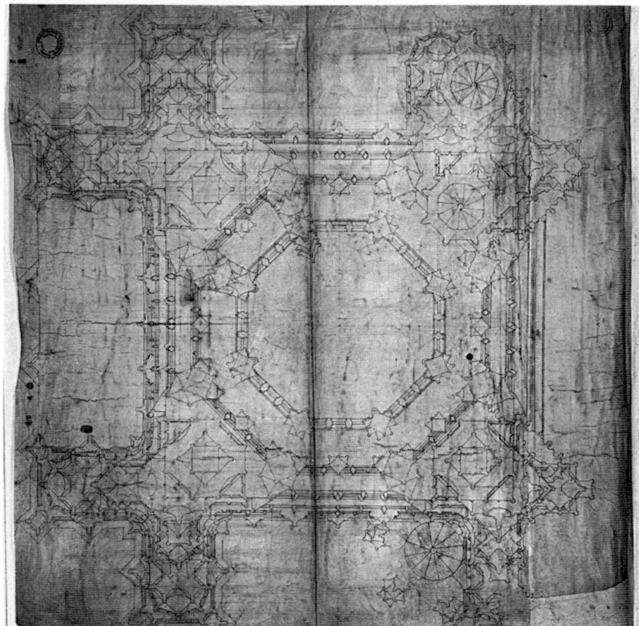

3. Ground-plan of the north tower of the Stephansdom, Vienna, ink on parchment, 835×820 mm, 1440s (Vienna, Gemäldegalerie der Akademie der Bildenden Künste)

2. Renaissance and after.

(i) 15th and 16th centuries. (ii) 17th and 18th centuries. (iii) 19th century and after.

(i) 15th and 16th centuries. One of the most profound changes in architectural drawing occurred in the second half of the 15th century, when the production of paper was hugely increased as a result of the invention of printing. As paper replaced expensive parchment, it encouraged a greater freedom in design and drawing methods, with communication between architect and builder coming gradually to depend less on oral and written instructions. It was in Renaissance Italy that the most significant developments in architectural drawing took place, for while all medieval architects were trained as building craftsmen, some notable Italian architects of the later 15th century were also painters and sculptors and received their initial training in those arts. Leonardo da Vinci, Donato Bramante, Baldassare Peruzzi and Raphael were among the artist–architects who invented or perfected new ways of representing architectural designs during this period.

Very few architectural drawings made in Italy before the 16th century survive, however: only two minor drawings by Leon Battista Alberti are known, for example (see fig. 4), and none by Filippo Brunelleschi. These two architects played a vital role in the development of drawing by formulating the laws of linear perspective in the early 15th century. It seems that most designs at this time were represented by a ground-plan and, often, by an Architectural model. Elevations were usually unnecessary since the builder, by means of simple geometrical and modular formulae, could determine the disposition and measurements of the major vertical elements of a design from the proportions inherent in the ground-plan. Models gave the general form and scale of a proposed building and were the basis for discussion between architect, patron, mason and advisers. It is likely that full-size details of capitals, architraves and other classical elements were made by the mason from measured drawings taken by the architect from antique examples. The ruins of Roman buildings were an important source for Renaissance architecture, and their construction, plans, proportions and details were studied and recorded in sketchbooks and portfolios by architects from Brunelleschi's generation onwards.

Alberti, in *Della pittura* (1436), his book for painters, was the first to codify the system of one-point perspective devised by Brunelleschi a decade earlier. However, in his architectural treatise *De re aedificatoria* (1485), written *c.* 1450, he advised architects against 'illusionistic' perspective drawing, because it could be inaccurate and misleading; instead he recommended the use of a model together with plans and elevations drawn orthogonally and on separate sheets. All the same, while the need to convey to the builder accurate information based on proportion and measurement is best achieved by the rational and methodical system of orthography, perspectives, because of their greater realism, are often more easily understood by the patron and are also cheaper and quicker to produce than models. Because they depict three-dimensional form they also help the architect at the early stages of a project to work through various design solutions and to picture the inter-relationship of a ground-plan, exterior and space (for further discussion *see* Perspective, §II).

The bird's-eye view (a type of perspective drawn from a high vantage-point) was introduced into architectural drawing *c.* 1490 by Leonardo da Vinci, who also used it for anatomical and engineering studies as well as for relief maps. It shows an object as an entity and when used with a bird's-eye view section answered the problem of explaining the multi-domed, centralized buildings proposed by Leonardo. Thus, as late 15th-century architecture became more complex and more plastic, new methods of representation developed. In Bramante's circle the form and volume of an interior space (extant or proposed) might be shown by a bird's-eye view section in which shade and light were used to model the projections and recesses of walls. Another perspectival sectional method, used by Giuliano da Sangallo for a drawing of an antique circular temple (see fig. 5), employed the novel convention of 'ruinizing' the building so as to reveal its interior.

Although both methods of representation were suited to the plain centralized interior of a circular temple (e.g. the Pantheon in Rome), they were inadequate for larger, more complex centralized buildings or for those with a longitudinal interior—that is to say, having intricate spaces that cannot be taken in at a glance but need 'the cumulative effect of many impressions'. Experiments were made with multiple perspective, in which more than one vanishing point is used, and with drawings that mixed orthography and central perspective. An example of the latter is Peruzzi's 'ideal view' of St Peter's, Rome, a drawing of *c.* 1515 that daringly combined plan, section, perspective and horizontal sections and which came close to isometric projection. Peruzzi, who was associated with St Peter's until his death in 1536, continued his experiments with

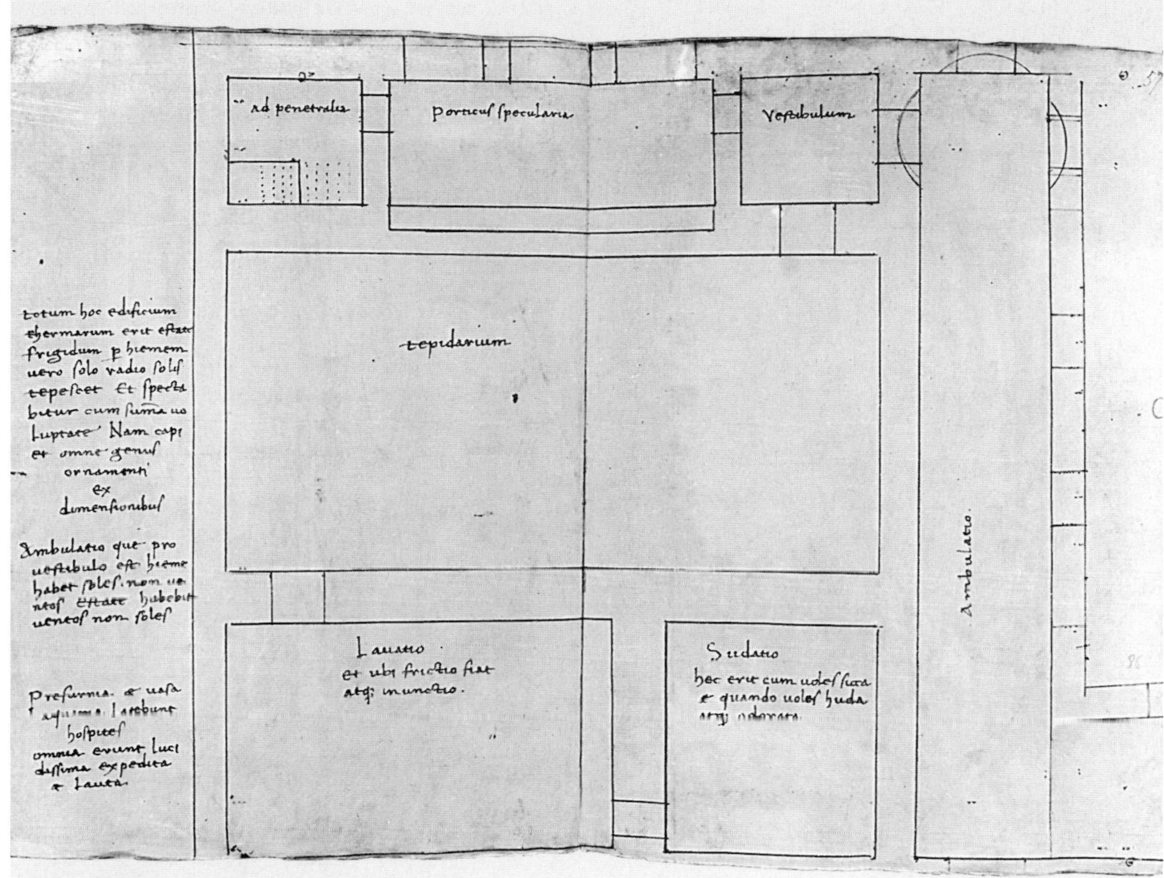

4. Architectural drawing (275×195 mm) by Leon Battista Alberti: project for a bath complex, *c.* 1470 (Florence, Biblioteca Medicea-Laurenziana, MS. Laur. App. 1828, cc. 56*v*–57*r*)

both perspective and 'mixed' projections all his life. St Peter's, with its changing programme for a Greek or Latin cross plan, became a kind of forcing house for the resolution of architectural drawing practice. Building work began in 1506 under Bramante, and subsequent architects included Giuliano da Sangallo, Raphael, Antonio da Sangallo (ii) and, from 1546, Michelangelo. The need for consistency in drawing up designs was appreciated by Raphael, and in a letter of 1519 to Pope Leo X he argued (much as Alberti had) for a three-fold system of plan, elevation and section all drawn to the same scale, a system probably first fully explored by Antonio da Sangallo (ii). Orthogonal drawing gradually became the architect's way of seeing and representing, and since it is less illusionistic and more abstracted than perspectival drawing it can be said to mark the separation of architects from artists. The standardization of drawing practice helped free the architect from the need for day-to-day site supervision and laid the foundations for the architectural office, with its assistants and draughtsmen.

From the evidence of the 330 or so drawings that survive (examples at Chatsworth, Derbys; London, RIBA; and elsewhere) of the thousands he must have made, ANDREA PALLADIO used only orthogonal projection (see fig. 6). Two-thirds are studies of Roman buildings rather than design drawings for new buildings (the majority of extant 16th-century Italian drawings are *of* rather than *for* buildings), and this can perhaps be explained by the importance of Roman buildings as sources of design both for the architects who measured and drew them and for their successors. Almost all Palladio's initial sketch designs are lost, as are the working drawings that must have been worn out through use on the building site. It is certain that Palladio used models for his important projects and that he prepared full-size profiles of mouldings from which masons made their templates. His preliminary designs were first drawn freehand, while in drawings made to scale the main elements were first drawn without ink, using a stylus and compasses. A quill pen was then used to draw over the incised construction lines and to complete the drawing, either freehand or with a straight-edge. Sometimes the first or under-drawing was made in red or brown chalk or in lead and then traced over with pen and ink. Palladio's drawing instruments must have included styluses (of wood or ivory, or of metal with a rounded point), quill pens, holders for chalk and lead, compasses, dividers, straight-edges and set-squares. He would also have had a magnetic compass, a level, a plumb-line and a case of

5. Architectural drawing (diam. 380 mm) by Giuliano da Sangallo: antique circular temple, *c.* 1500 (Rome, Vatican, Biblioteca Apostolica, Cod. Barb. Lat. 4424, fol. 32)

travelling instruments for measuring and drawing the remains of Roman buildings.

Palladio's enormously influential *Quattro libri dell' architettura* was published in 1570. The clear woodcut illustrations, with a plan and elevation often together on the same page, not only demonstrated his design principles but also his preference for orthography over perspective. A very different book, *Les Plus Excellents Bastiments de France* (1576–9) by Jacques Androuet Du Cerceau (i) (*see* DU CERCEAU, (1)), introduced in a published form the bird's-eye topographical view. Its large engraved plates showing some of the great royal and private châteaux of France set in their gardens is the first systematic (though not very accurate) survey in this form. It was presumably a development from map-making since most town plans until the mid-18th century were drawn as bird's-eye views, despite Leonardo's invention *c.* 1502 of ichnography. With this method all topographical features are drawn as if reflected on a single horizontal plane: the map-maker's equivalent of orthography. Other developments during the 16th century in astronomy, military engineering and land surveying, calling for exact measurement and accurate draughtsmanship, effectively marked the beginning of technical drawing. By 1600 drawing scales, protractors, adjustable set-squares, parallel rulers, proportional compasses and dividers, wing-compasses and dividers and other measuring and drawing instruments were all available to draughtsmen.

(ii) 17th and 18th centuries. The introduction of GRAPHITE in the late 16th century was almost as important to drawing as the introduction of paper. The advantages of graphite lie in its fluency and the ease with which it can be erased (usually done with breadcrumbs until it was discovered *c.* 1770 that india-rubber was more effective). The English architects Robert Smythson and John Smythson used graphite for their drawings from *c.* 1600, and INIGO JONES used it in his architectural designs from 1616. Jones used only orthogonal projections for his architectural drawings (examples in London, RIBA, and elsewhere), though his very early elevations have the characteristic Elizabethan and Jacobean perspective elements found in some of the Smythsons' drawings. Jones's second tour of Italy (1613–14) and his purchase there of many of Palladio's drawings became a key source for Renaissance classicism in England. An architecture controlled by proportional relationships (whether classical or otherwise) is best expressed orthographically rather than through perspectives. Thus it was inevitable that Jones would adopt Palladio's drawing practice as well as his design principles. Jones varied his drawing style, and he worked with great freedom, rapidity and assurance. Rather tellingly, he seems never to have

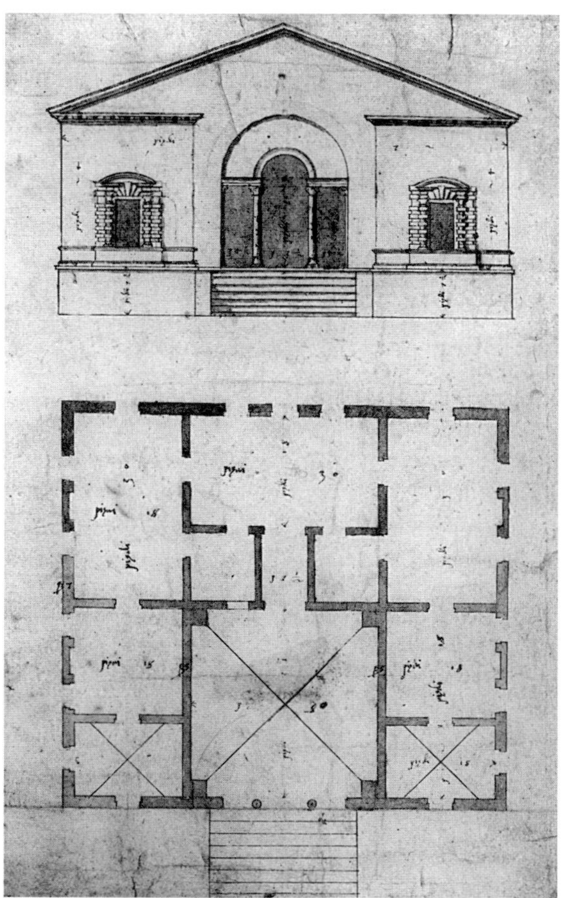

6. Architectural drawing by Andrea Palladio: plan and elevation for the Villa Valmarana, Vigardolo, 1541 (London, Royal Institute of British Architects)

used a metal ruling-pen, which achieved a constant thickness of line, preferring instead the more flexible quill pen.

The use of drawing instruments, however, tends to depersonalize drawing style, and, in an office where a drawing may be worked on by two or three minds and hands, an office style of draughtsmanship and handwriting as well as design will evolve. The Office of Works in London under Christopher Wren was the first professionally organized office for architects in England, and it was something of a training school too. Architectural offices, or studios, had been established earlier in Italy and France, and the need for them can be seen as the inevitable result of the complex nature of Baroque architecture: more preliminary design studies had to be made, and many more working drawings were required for the builder. Both Jules Hardouin Mansart in Paris and Carlo Fontana (iv) in Rome had studios with pupils as well as paid assistants. Fontana's drawings, indistinguishable from those by others in his studio, were neatly made, with each design isolated in the middle of its sheet. Colour washes were used to distinguish existing and new work and in a limited way also served to indicate materials and function. A general characteristic of Baroque draughtsmanship is the careful rendering in ink or coloured wash of the walls of a plan so as to emphasize their curvaceous and massive qualities, while the use of shade and, in particular, of cast shadow to model elevations achieved the same end.

The introduction *c.* 1700 by Ferdinando Galli-Bibiena of the *scena per angolo* in stage design, in which a central axis gives way to one or more diagonals each with further vistas opening off, helped to develop perspective, although the general tendency was still towards a standardized orthography. This was probably reinforced both by the increasing number of illustrated books of architecture and architectural prints, and by the academies. The oldest of these was the Accademia di S Luca in Rome (*see* ROME, §VI). Architecture, including drawing, was taught there on a kind of Sunday school basis from as early as 1593. The Accademia's influence grew after 1676, when it was united with the Académie de France in Rome and with the fame of its student competitions. For these a plan, shaded elevations and section to the same scale on separate sheets with ruled borders were generally submitted. There were many exceptions, however, such as the plan for a palace by Filippo Juvarra, illusionistically drawn as if on a scroll (1705; Rome, Accad. N. S Luca, 141).

During the 18th century Rome remained Europe's artistic centre and the culmination of the Grand Tour, that essential component of an ambitious architect's training. From the 1740s onwards many visitors returned home with etchings by GIOVANNI BATTISTA PIRANESI; his views of the city and his archaeological reconstructions and architectural fantasies were enormously influential. Using the diagonally receding perspectives of Galli-Bibiena's *scena per angolo* for his etchings, Piranesi exploited light and shade, made dramatic use of scale and narrative and emphasized the pictorial values of texture and tone; he also provided landscape settings for his buildings and

7. Architectural drawing by William Chambers: design for a mausoleum for Frederick, Prince of Wales, 1751–2 (London, Sir John Soane's Museum)

exposed the relentless effects that the passage of time wrought on them. All these ideas were taken up and explored by painters as well as by such architects as Charles-Michel-Ange Challe, Charles-Louis Clérisseau, Louis-Jean Desprez and William Chambers.

Chambers's design for a mausoleum (1751–2; London, Soane Mus.; see fig. 7) for Frederick, Prince of Wales, is the first English example of a finished architectural design in which the building is set within a landscape, though William Kent gave his elevational drawings (or occasionally sketch perspectives) a landscape setting with added figures, animals or trees. Uncharacteristically, Chambers's design is drawn in perspective, for he generally used a kind of false perspective in which both foreground and background, with sky, trees and figures, were added to an elevational drawing. Nor did Robert Adam (i) make much use of design perspectives except for the few he published in the *Works in Architecture* (1773, 1779, 1822). Nevertheless, the tendency towards finished perspectives developed in England from the 1770s, coinciding with an interest in the Picturesque, that is, with architecture as scenery. Movement, variety, irregularity, texture and a sense of place are best conveyed by perspectives. There was also the influence of the Royal Academy, London, where architectural drawings were exhibited with paintings from its foundation in 1768. The tendency towards large, gilt-framed perspectives with plenty of anecdotal detail (often added by another more painterly hand) also became increasingly common.

(iii) 19th century and after. Architectural drawing in the early 19th century was influenced by the watercolour revolution of the 1790s, in which painting took the place of tinted drawing (*see* WATERCOLOUR, §2). The traditional (and architectural) convention of indicating light and shadow with grey washes, for example, gave way to shadows painted as darker tones of the same colour as the form on which they fell. The greatest influence was probably that of J. M. W. TURNER, whose early training was as an architectural draughtsman and who from 1807 was Professor of Perspective at the Royal Academy. His exploration of cloud formations, reflections in water (and in window-panes) and the effects of light and atmosphere, as well as a sublime use of contrasting light and shade, were taken up by JOSEPH MICHAEL GANDY in particular, who became the most important English architectural perspectivist of the early 19th century (examples in London, Soane Mus.). A quite different style of drawing was the pure outline style. This was derived from Greek vase painting, and initially it was used for archaeological and other illustration by the artists John Flaxman and Wilhelm Tischbein (from 1790). Soon after, the architects Charles Percier and Pierre-François-Léonard Fontaine adopted this unshaded linear style for the plates of their *Recueil de décorations intérieures* (1801); it was also used for Thomas Hope's *Household Practice and Decoration* (1807). The most notable exponent was KARL FRIEDRICH SCHINKEL, who used it for his published designs.

8. Architectural drawing by Louis Duc: detail of a Corinthian capital, Colosseum, Rome, 1829 (Paris, Ecole des Beaux-Arts)

The Ecole des Beaux-Arts in Paris, which developed from the old Académie Royale d'Architecture (*see* PARIS, §VI, 2), is associated with a particular style of drawing partly characterized by the use of carefully cast shadows at 45° on plans as well as on elevations, sections and details (see fig. 8). Shading can give added legibility and is found in architectural drawings from the Middle Ages onwards; shadows to indicate curved walls and vaults were used on drawings from the late 15th century. A consistent theory of shadow projection was developed and published in France in the mid-17th century and thereafter widely disseminated throughout the academies of Europe. Once it was established, the Beaux-Arts draughting style became particularly influential in the USA and remained so well into the 20th century. It was also well received in England in the 20th century, where architectural education for much of the 19th century depended largely on the varying standards of articled pupilage.

An important change in drawing-office practice in the 19th century was brought about by the establishment of the general building contractor. The competitive tendering system that resulted meant that costing was from then on based on bills of quantity calculated by the new profession of estimator, from the architect's working drawings and detailed specifications; bills of quantity were probably first used by Robert Smirke in the 1830s for the British Museum, London. New materials, new construction techniques, new building types, more complicated services and the introduction of unfamiliar Gothic Revival ornament as well as the needs of the contractor and his estimator greatly increased the number of working drawings that had to be produced. To cope with this, architects' offices became larger (that of George Gilbert Scott I had 27 pupils, assistants and clerks in 1858), and various methods of copying drawings were involved. Pricking, in which the main outlines of a drawing were pricked through to a sheet beneath and the pinholes thus made joined up, was a method used by architects from the 16th century, and it continued in use during the 19th. Methods of making tracing-paper had been described by Cennino Cennini in his *Libro dell'arte* (*c.* 1390), but commercially produced tracing-paper and tracing-cloth did not become available until the 1850s. Various printing methods including anastatic (a method of transfer lithography) and LITHOGRAPHY were available from 1830 onwards. The ferro-prussiate or blue-print method, though described in 1842, was not common until the 1870s; it was supplanted by the diazo or dye-line process from the 1920s. Both methods make use of light-sensitive paper.

Drawings proliferated; they also became much larger and more detailed. Antiquarian-size paper (1340× 780 mm), manufactured by James Whatman from 1773 for engraving purposes, was used by such architects as Gandy from the early 19th century. Large (antiquarian-size) drawing-boards with sizeable tee-squares and wooden, triangle set-squares (introduced in the 1780s) were used with drawing instruments that were scarcely different from those of the 18th century, although there was a wider selection. By the end of the century some English drawings were scaled to fractions of an inch though earlier, decimal ratio divisions of an inch were more usual. Lettering on drawings became more formal, and further inscribed information, including the architect's office address, was included. Charles Barry followed the example of John Soane, who used sanserif lettering from 1784. A. W. N. Pugin sometimes used black letters, and William Burges's inventive Gothic lettering, which he used from the 1850s, began a trend towards unconventional lettering that was later taken up by R. Norman Shaw, C. F. A. Voysey and Charles Rennie Mackintosh in Britain, and elsewhere by Frank Lloyd Wright, Otto Wagner and many others. Stencilled lettering was in use in England by the 1840s. Whereas before the 19th century working drawings were usually monochrome, and construction materials were indicated to a very limited extent, from the mid-19th century formal colour-coding to indicate different building materials became essential. By 1887, when he published his *Architectural Drawing*, Richard Phené Spiers (1836–1916) was able to include a list of colours generally accepted in architects' offices, for example Venetian or light red for brickwork or Prussian blue for iron and steel.

The importance of the perspective for presentation, exhibition and for an increasing number of competitions was firmly established from the 1830s. Though some architects were excellent draughtsmen and well able to draw their own, others employed perspective artists who were usually architects by training, for example JOSEPH MICHAEL GANDY, Thomas Allom (1804–72), Axel Herman Haig, Howard Gaye and, in the 20th century, William Walcot, Cyril Farey and Raymond Myerscough-Walker (1908–84). A further stimulus to perspective drawing was publication, particularly in the professional architectural journals that began to appear in Britain from 1842 (*The Builder*), France from 1840 (*Revue générale de l'architecture*) and the USA from 1876 (*American Architect and Building News*). Methods of reproduction had an important effect on the development of perspective draughtsmanship. In *The Builder* first wood-engraving and then lithography were used. The introduction in *Building News* of photolithography in 1868 meant that pen drawings could be reproduced without being engraved or re-drawn. The result was that pen drawing flourished from the 1870s, becoming increasingly mannered towards the end of the century, as revealed by CHARLES RENNIE MACKINTOSH and other exponents of the GLASGOW STYLE, Art Nouveau architects and those connected with the Vienna Secession. Naturally there was a reaction against this, and some architects of the Arts and Crafts Movement made only working drawings, although these were drawn, colour-washed, lettered and laid out with great discrimination.

The rejection of pictorialism in architectural drawing was a characteristic of the Modern Movement, whose adherents favoured orthography but also used axonometric projections. Axonometric is a generic term describing all forms of parallel projection, including isometric. It is often used to describe what is more accurately known as planometric, in which the plan is drawn to true shape and scale, and the plan form is then tilted to 45° to provide the third dimension—height—which is drawn to the same scale as the plan. Axonometric drawing has the advantage

9. Architectural drawing by Ludwig Mies van der Rohe: *Glass Skyscraper*, charcoal, brown chalk and crayon on brown paper, 1385×832 mm, 1922 (New York, Museum of Modern Art)

of representing both plan and volume and is constant in measurement since, unlike central perspective, there are no converging lines. The method is also useful for detail drawings because it shows clearly how parts join together. Axonometry has a long though intermittent history and has been used for military engineering, descriptive geometry, cartography, technical drawing and painting as well as in architecture; its revival in the early 1920s is owed to the De Stijl movement and to the Bauhaus. Under the leadership of Walter Gropius (1919–28) and Ludwig Mies van der Rohe (1930–33) the Bauhaus assumed the influential role previously enjoyed by the Ecole des Beaux-Arts. With Le Corbusier, Gropius and Mies dominated the architectural world of the first half of the 20th century. For them and other architects of the Modern Movement, drawing was a means to an end, and this they expressed by a conscious simplicity. Indeed, Le Corbusier advised students to develop a 'loathing of drawings', by which he meant 'a shimmering display of illustrations'. His design sketches, familiar to many through their publication, were spontaneously drawn, a record of ideas that, taken together with the working drawings, were a reaction to the highly finished drawings made in the Beaux-Arts manner. Mies, the best architect–draughtsman of the period, achieved 'maximum effect with minimum means'; using chalk, charcoal and crayon, his drawings graphically expressed the economy of his architecture (see fig. 9). From 1910 he also made use of photomontage, an earlier example of which is Charles Garnier's use of the medium in 1861 for the Paris Opéra.

When the International Style lost ground in the 1970s, Post-modernism revived interest in more elaborate forms of drawing and the use of colour (for illustration *see* GRAVES, MICHAEL). Yet the influence of individual or collective styles on architectural draughtsmanship in the 20th century was of little significance in comparison with the effect of computer-aided drawing systems. Developed from experimentation in computer graphics during the 1950s, computer-aided design (CAD) was used by an increasing number of architects from 1980 onwards. By the 1990s there were some offices that used only CAD, turning to drawing machines only when competition conditions required them. The advantages of CAD include greater speed, accuracy, easier coordination and revision and, perhaps above all, the facility for endless permutations of three-dimensional visualization or modelling. As well as working drawings, presentation drawings in a variety of techniques can be produced by CAD, including information for the perspective artist. It seems unlikely that manual drawing will now survive beyond the initial sketch design and perhaps the occasional PRESENTATION DRAWING.

BIBLIOGRAPHY

GENERAL

W. Burges: 'Architectural Drawings', *Trans. RIBA*, 1st series, xi (1861), pp. 15–28

RIBA Drawings Series, 8 vols (London, 1968)

J. Lever, ed.: *Catalogue of the Drawings Collection of the Royal Institute of British Architects*, 20 vols (Farnborough, 1969–89) [mainly British material]

S. Kostof, ed.: *The Architect: Chapters in the History of the Profession* (Oxford, 1977)

C. Cable: *The Architectural Drawing: Its Development and History, 1300–1950* (Monticello, IL, 1978) [bibliog.]

H. Powell and D. Leatherbarrow, eds: *Masterpieces of Architectural Drawing* (New York, 1982)

J. Lever and M. Richardson: *Great Drawings from the Collection of the Royal Institute of British Architects* (London, [1983])

S. Lambert: *Drawing: Technique and Purpose* (London, 1984)

J. Lever and M. Richardson: *The Art of the Architect* (London, 1984)

TECHNIQUES

J. Dubreuil: *Perspective Practical* (London, 1672)

R. Brown: *The Principles of Practical Perspective* (London, 1815)

H. van Buren Magonigle: *Architectural Rendering in Wash* (New York, 1928)

C. A. Farey and A. Trystan Edwards: *Architectural Drawing, Perspective and Rendering* (London, 2/1949)

H. Jacoby: *New Techniques of Architectural Rendering* (London, 1971)

T. Da Costa Kaufmann: 'The Perspective of Shadows: The History of the Theory of Shadow Projection', *J. Warb. & Court. Inst*, xxxviii (1975), pp. 258–71

Y.-A. Bois: 'Metamorphosis of Axonometry', *Daidalos*, i (1981), pp. 41–59

M. Scolari: 'Elements for a History of Axonometry', *Archit. Des.*, iv (1985), pp. 73–8

MEDIA AND INSTRUMENTS

R. A. Skelton: 'Colour in Mapmaking', *Geog. Mag.*, xxxii (1960) pp. 534–53

P. Collins: 'The Origin of Graph Paper as an Influence on Architectural Designs', *J. Soc. Archit. Historians*, xxi (1962), pp. 159–62

M. Darby and D. van Zanten: 'Owen Jones's Iron Buildings of the 1850s', *Architectura* [Munich], 111 (1974), pp. 53–65 [note on photomontage]

M. B. Cohn: *Wash and Gouache: A Study of the Development of the Materials of Watercolour* (Cambridge, MA, 1977)

M. Hambly: *Drawing Instruments: Their History, Purpose and Use for Architectural Drawings* (London, 1982)

R. D. Harley: *Artist's Pigments, c. 1600–1835: A Study in English Documentary Sources* (London, 2/1982)

J. Krill: *English Artists' Paper: Renaissance to Regency* (London, 1987) [overview of types of paper available to artists from the late 16th century to the early 19th]

M. Hambly: *Drawing Instruments, 1580–1980* (London, 1988)

J. Lever: 'Color in English Architectural Drawings', *Color in Architectural Illustration*, ed. R. Rochon and H. Linton (New York, 1989), pp. 10–21

HISTORY

Italy

J. White: 'Developments in Renaissance Perspective', *J. Warb. & Court. Inst.*, xii (1949), pp. 58–79

J. S. Ackerman: 'Architectural Practice in the Italian Renaissance', *J. Soc. Archit. Historians*, xiii (1954), pp. 3–11

H. Saalman: 'Early Renaissance Architectural Theory and Practice in Antonio Filarete's *Trattato di architettura*', *A. Bull.*, xii (1959), pp. 89–106

S. Y. Edgerton jr: 'Florentine Interest in Ptolemaic Cartography as a Background for Renaissance Painting, Architecture and the Discovery of America', *J. Soc. Archit. Historians*, xxxiii (1974), pp. 275–92

P. Marconi, A. Cipriani and E. Valeriani: *I disegni di architettura dell'archivio storico dell'Accademia di San Luca*, 2 vols (Rome, 1974)

J. A. Pinto: 'Origins and Development of the Ichnographic City Plan', *J. Soc. Archit. Historians*, xxxv (1976), pp. 35–50

W. Lotz: *Studies in Italian Renaissance Architecture* (London, 1977)

C. Cable: *Architectural Drawing and Architectural Practice during the Late Fifteenth and Early Sixteenth Centuries in Italy* (Monticello, IL, 1979) [bibliog.]

J. A. Gere and P. Pouncey: *Italian Drawings in the Department of Prints and Drawings in the British Museum: Artists Working in Rome,* c. *1550–*c. *1640* (London, 1983)

Drawing in the Italian Renaissance Workshop (exh. cat. by F. Ames-Lewis and J. Wright, London, V&A; Nottingham, A.G.; 1983)

Great Britain

R. P. Spiers: *Architectural Drawing* (London, 1887)

H. S. Goodhart-Rendel: 'Architectural Draughtsmanship of the Past', *J. RIBA*, lviii (1951), pp. 127–36

H. M. Colvin: *Architectural Drawings in the Bodleian Library* (Oxford, 1952)

J. Harvey: 'Early Tudor Draughtsmen of the Past', *Connoisseur Coronation Book* (1953), pp. 97–101

H. M. Colvin: *A Catalogue of the Architectural Drawings of the 18th and 19th Centuries in the Library of Worcester College, Oxford* (Oxford, 1964)

J. Summerson, ed.: 'The Book of Architecture of John Thorpe in Sir John Soane's Museum', *Walpole Soc.*, xl (1964–6)

K. Downes: *English Baroque Architecture* (London, 1966), pp. 14–15
——: *Hawksmoor* (London, 1979), pp. 49–51
J. Harris and A. A. Tait: *Catalogue of the Drawings by Inigo Jones, John Webb & Isaac de Caus at Worcester College, Oxford* (Oxford, 1979)
K. Baynes and H. Pugh: *The Art of the Engineer* (Guildford, 1981)
G. Stamp: *The Great Perspectivists* (London, 1982)
M. Hambly: *Twentieth-century Architectural Drawings: The Technical Background to their Preparation, Storage and Reproduction: RIBA Drawings Collection Research Project, 1982–1984*, (1985)
J. Harris: *The Artist and the Country House: A History of Country House and Garden View Painting in Britain, 1540–1870* (London, 1985)
——: *The Design of the English Country House, 1620–1920* (London, 1985) [drgs for country houses]
L. Stainton and C. White: *Drawing in England from Hilliard to Hogarth* (London, 1987)
K. Downes: *Sir Christopher Wren: The Design of St Paul's Cathedral* (London, 1988) [reproduces the drgs and discusses drg practice]
L. Jacobus: 'On "Whether a Man Could See before him and behind him Both at Once": The Role of Drawing in the Design of Interior Space in England, *c.* 1600–1800', *Archit. Hist.*, xxxi (1988), pp. 148–65
Turner & Architecture (exh. cat., London, Tate, 1988)
J. Harris and G. Higgott: *Inigo Jones: Complete Architectural Drawings* (London and New York, 1989)

France and USA

A. Drexler: *The Drawings of Frank Lloyd Wright* (New York, 1970)
E. Michels: 'Late Nineteenth-century Published American Perspective Drawings', *J. Soc. Archit. Historians*, xxxi (1972), pp. 291–308
A. Drexler, ed.: *The Architecture of the Ecole des Beaux-Arts* (New York, 1977)
D. Gebhard and D. Nevins: *200 Years of American Architectural Drawing* (New York, 1977)
D. Nevins and R. Stern: *The Architect's Eye: American Architectural Drawings from 1799–1978* (New York, 1979)
J. Guiton: *The Ideas of Le Corbusier on Architecture and Urban Planning* (New York, 1981), pp. 71–83
Le Corbusier: *Sketchbooks*, 4 vols (i–ii, London, 1981; iii–iv, Cambridge, MA, 1981–2)
Y. Futagawa, ed.: *Frank Lloyd Wright in his Renderings, 1887–1959* (Tokyo, 1984)

JILL LEVER

Architectural model. A small-scale three-dimensional structure used to test, clarify or illustrate part or all of an architectural design or building. Although frequent references to the use of models can be found from Classical antiquity onwards, because of their often fragile materials (e.g. wood, gesso, papier-mâché and balsa wood), few have survived in proportion to their extensive use. Those that remain date chiefly from the end of the 15th century, or shortly after, and tend to represent monumental rather than intimately scaled buildings. Moreover, documentary references from the Renaissance, when a fresh interest in the use of models emerged, are sometimes misleading. The term 'model', derived from the Italian *modello*, frequently refers to a drawing rather than a three-dimensional aid for the designer (*see* MODELLO, §I). With the advent of a wide range of specialized drawings in the late 18th century, the value of the model as a presentational and didactic device was first seriously undermined. Nevertheless, it continued to prove useful up to the late 20th century, when holography and sophisticated computer graphics began to replace it as a source of three-dimensional information for architects and clients.

1. Types. 2. History.

1. TYPES. The many functions and types of architectural model may be divided into three broad categories: design models, *post factum* models and symbolic models; the first two can be further subdivided as described below.

(i) Design models.

Conceptual models. These isolate a specific aspect of design, such as formal composition or structural solutions to a problem. Accordingly, decorative details, textures and colours are usually excluded from these highly simplified objects. Moholy-Nagy used models of this kind to undertake 'experiments in space' in his teaching at the Bauhaus in Weimar and Dessau in the 1920s.

Sketch models. These have a function similar to a painted or drawn sketch, with the designer using clay, wax or easily altered materials, such as plaster or soft wood, to evolve an overall design. Michelangelo designed a façade (unexecuted) for St Peter's, Rome, in this way.

Experimental models. These are used to explore technical problems such as structure and the distribution of light. In the 20th century, advanced methods of assessing the effect of high winds or degrees of stress by means of wind tunnels and electronic measurement gave these aids a highly sophisticated role.

Detail models. These are produced to explore or demonstrate specific structural techniques or ornamental parts of a total design.

Presentation or demonstration models. These constitute the largest category of surviving examples. They reproduce a total design in considerable detail for a client or committee to judge or for builders and workmen to follow. The more elaborate examples can be opened to reveal a sectional view of their interiors; services and decorative schemes can also be revealed by opening up the façade or roof.

Full-scale or mock-up models. These represent portions and (rarely) entire buildings in temporary materials for site trials.

Site models. These show the setting or immediate urban context of a particular building; they also indicate the ground contours and the relationships within a designed complex of separate buildings.

Urban models. These similarly involve the broadest application of model usage, in depicting an entire townscape, or parts of it, occasionally providing the context of a projected building within it.

Ideal or project models. These give scope to the architect's fantasy for impracticable buildings or visionary conceptions. This category includes unexecuted proposals as well as projected or alternative designs.

(ii) Post factum *models.*

Documentary or facsimile models. These record destroyed buildings for posterity or provide souvenirs of famous buildings. The 18th-century Grand Tour provided a demand for the latter type.

Teaching models. These are used for didactic purposes in schools of architecture, as documented in Jacques-François Blondel's school in 18th-century Paris.

Reconstruction models. These attempt to create the original appearance of ruined or totally vanished buildings and are frequently used in exhibition or museum display.

Control models. These were extensively used before the era of photography and provide the basis of information for later repairs, alterations and extensions to a particular building.

(iii) Symbolic models. This category covers the widest and most elusive forms of model, both in pictorial as well as three-dimensional terms. Among the earliest are votive models of houses in Egyptian and Etruscan tombs, and a wide variety of structures, held by saints or donors, are to be found in religious paintings. Few of the latter are likely to portray actual designs with any degree of accuracy, but they often provide valuable information about ornamental fashions and structural systems.

2. History.

(i) From antiquity to the Renaissance. Symbolic roles apart, the recorded history of the architectural model goes back at least to Ancient Greece. Models were undoubtedly of great value in periods of major structural innovation, such as Imperial Rome and the Gothic era. During the Middle Ages they were used to work out and test systems of masonry vaulting and for setting patterns of decorative carving through templates and full-scale prototypes. Among the earliest to survive, however, is the wood and papier-mâché model for St Maclou, Rouen (Rouen, Mus. d'Art Normand), now thought to date from the early 16th century. Other surviving models from this period include a conceptual one in wood for the Luginsland Tower of Augsburg's defences (1514; Augsburg, Maximilian Mus.) and an elaborate demonstration model, also in wood, by Hans Hieber for the Neupfarrkirche, the pilgrimage church dedicated to Our Lady, Regensburg (1519/20; Regensburg, Stadtmus.; *see* Germany, fig. 4).

The Italian Renaissance gave new prominence to models with the emergence of the architect as the coordinator of building operations as well as the sole author of a design. Brunelleschi used a variety of model functions in creating his dome for Florence Cathedral, ranging from the presentation model that helped him to win the competition to the many improvised ones (even cut out of lumps of rutabaga) used for instructing workmen in technical details. It is now doubted whether the surviving wooden model (Florence, Mus. Opera Duomo) is the one known to have been left at Brunelleschi's death in 1446 to guide the completion of the lantern. Alberti discussed the importance of models in *De re aedificatoria* (1485) but added a cautionary note, repeated by theorists for centuries thereafter: 'I would not have the model too exactly finished, nor too delicate and neat, but plain and simple, more to be admired for the contrivance of the inventor than the hand of the workman.'

By the 16th century models had entered standard practice in Western architecture and inevitably played key roles in the protracted building history of St Peter's, Rome. Antonio da Sangallo (ii)'s large 1/24 scale presentation model, commissioned in 1539 (*see* Sangallo, (4)), took several years to make, and Michelangelo's sectional dome model of the 1560s (both Rome, Vatican, Mus. Stor. A. Tesoro S Pietro) guided Giacomo della Porta in completing the structure. Michelangelo also used models as aids to demonstrate formal composition. His surviving façade model of 1517 for S Lorenzo, Florence (Florence, Casa Buonarrotti; *see* Florence, §IV, 5) set the fashion for the many façade competition models that followed, such as those of the 1580s and 1590s for Florence Cathedral (Florence, Mus. Opera Duomo). He also used clay models to design the shape of the steps of the Biblioteca Medicea-Laurenziana, Florence, and to explore the spatial innovations of S Giovanni dei Fiorentini, Rome. In 1546 a full-scale wooden section of his cornice for Palazzo Farnese, Rome, was placed *in situ* to determine its appearance. Elsewhere models also assisted a lay decision in 1576, when Palladio submitted models of alternative designs to the Venetian Senate for both a longitudinal and a central plan for his church of Il Redentore.

Inevitably, the use of models accompanied the spread of Renaissance design to northern Europe. Domenico da Cortona made models for several of Francis I's châteaux, including Chambord (begun 1519). In 1567 Philibert de L'Orme discussed their various advantages at length in his *Premier Tome de l'architecture.* Jacques Androuet Du Cerceau (i), moreover, stressed the need for site models to include garden design in his *Les Plus Excellents Bastiments de France* (1576–9). The use of urban models was also established in the 16th century, with a model of Florence being constructed in 1529 in order to study the siege defences and Albert V of Bavaria having models made of his principal towns between 1568 and 1574. Meanwhile in England, one of the earliest references to a model dates from 1576, when the French joiner Adrian Gaunt made one for Longleat, Wilts, a country house built for Sir John Thynne.

(ii) The Baroque and Neo-classical periods. The concern for spatial complexity and dramatic lighting that began to develop in the 17th century found particular expression in those types of model that explored as well as represented solutions for interiors. Bernini, like Michelangelo, made sketch models in wax and clay for structures as well as sculpture. While it is uncertain whether Borromini used them as extensively, models devised to reveal elaborate internal systems were used well into the 18th century; a fine example is that for Balthasar Neumann's church of the Vierzehnheiligen (1744; Bamberg, Hist. Mus.).

In England, Christopher Wren's technological cast of mind contributed to his exploiting models widely throughout his career; surviving examples extend from the one of 1663 for Pembroke College Chapel, Cambridge (Cambridge, Pembroke Coll. Lib.), to those of the 1690s for the Royal Naval Hospital, Greenwich, London (site model and sectional detail model for one of the domes, London, N. Mar. Mus.). Models were created at all stages of the design of St Paul's Cathedral (*see* London, §V, 1(ii)(a)). The 18-ft-high Great Model of 1673 (London, St Paul's Cathedral), made to a scale of 1 inch to $1\frac{1}{2}$ feet by the Cleer brothers and a team of craftsmen, portrays the interior in as much detail as the exterior. Wren's pupil Nicholas Hawksmoor used models extensively for their creative value, as shown by alterations to his surviving one for Easton Neston, Northants (*c.* 1702; *in situ*). Others survive for King's College, Cambridge, and the Radcliffe Library, Oxford (1713 and 1735; both *in situ*); others once existed for the architect's remarkable London churches built as a result of the Fifty New Churches Act of 1711. Indeed, many outstanding models still survive for church designs in 18th-century England, including a pair of highly finished presentation wooden models for James Gibbs's St Mary-le-Strand, London, and St Martin-in-the-Fields, London (1713 and 1722; both London, RIBA).

Throughout continental Europe and particularly in France, a wide range of models survive from the 18th century, indicating the continuing importance as well as the widening range of their uses. The Musée des Plans–Reliefs in Paris contains a collection of model designs for fortifying the eastern frontier of France by the military engineer Sébastien Leprestre de Vauban. The Musée Carnavalet in Paris also possesses an exceptional group of models for major public buildings such as the façades of Pierre Contant d'Ivry's church of La Madeleine and Giovanni Niccolano Geronimo Servandoni's St Sulpice, Jean-Rodolphe Perronet's Louis XVI bridge and Jacques-Denis Antoine's foyer of the Law Courts. A large sectional model in plaster demonstrating Jacques-Germain Soufflot's dome structure (1757) for Ste Geneviève survives in the crypt of what later became the Panthéon. Nearly 30 years later, when the architect Charles-Louis Clérisseau helped Thomas Jefferson design the new Virginia Capitol, a plaster model (1786; Richmond, VA State Lib.) was sent from Paris to Richmond to aid the construction.

Towards the close of the 18th century models began to appear along with presentation drawings at the annual exhibition of the Paris Salon; the model exhibited in 1771 for Charles de Wailly's staircase at the Château de Montmusard, near Dijon, is an early example. Teaching models, meanwhile, had already been used in the academies for

Architectural model by John Soane: proposed Law Courts next to the Palace of Westminster, wood, 736×347×508 mm, *c*. 1823 (London, Sir John Soane's Museum)

many years, and Jacques-François Blondel gave special emphasis to models of 'significant buildings' in his *Cours d'architecture* (Paris, 1771–7). Similarly, documentary models recording or reconstructing celebrated monuments or sites were produced in lightweight materials, such as plaster or cork, for connoisseurs on the Grand Tour or travelling professionals. This didactic aspect is strikingly illustrated by cork models of the temples at Paestum and the excavations at Pompeii held at Sir John Soane's Museum, London, which has the largest and most diverse collection of models to survive from any architect's career. At his death in 1837, Soane left over 150 models covering 40 years of practice and representing virtually every function of the architectural model. The most elaborate models were devoted to commissions of particular complexity, such as the Bank of England (1788–1830) and the Westminster Law Courts (*c*. 1823; see fig.). Soane, as Professor of Architecture at the Royal Academy from 1806, regularly used models for teaching and gathered some of the most important examples in a special Model Room at the Museum, now restored to its original purpose.

(iii) The Romantic period and after. Predictably, models were often associated with innovative buildings of the Romantic era where pictorial values were of prime importance. A striking papier-mâché model (*c*. 1810; priv. col.) of the bizarre mansion Fonthill Abbey, Wilts, was probably used to guide the patron, William Beckford, and his builders after the unexpected death of the designer, James Wyatt; this model registers the Picturesque silhouette and ornamentation of this Gothic Revival masterpiece. At about the same time, Frederick Augustus Hervey, the eccentric Bishop of Derry, had a wood and papier-mâché model made of his equally strange residence at Ickworth, Suffolk (*in situ*), sent to him in Rome for his comments before its construction under the direction of Francis Sandys (*fl* 1796–1814). Portions of the model can be removed to show directions indicated within for colour schemes in the main interiors.

By the start of the 19th century a new range of specialized drawings had begun to undermine the more exploratory functions of the model. Most of the surviving models are of the presentation type, directed at committees and juries, caught up in the controversy over the choice of an appropriate style, known as the Battle of the Styles, where façades were often of greater concern than internal functions. Despite the attractive perspectives drawn by specialist artists, models continued to be required in major competitions involving public buildings of complexity, such as the London Law Courts scheme of the 1860s, won in competition by G. E. Street in 1866.

Through such idiosyncratic and diverse designers as Antoni Gaudí, Rudolf Steiner, Erich Mendelsohn and Theo van Doesburg, the creative roles of the conceptual and sketch models returned during the 20th century. Most recently, this basic function continued in the work of such architects as Denys Lasdun, who developed a design from its earliest stages using the three-dimensional potential of models to the full. The aid of full-scale models to test a design on site was revived by designers as various as Mies van der Rohe (Kröller House, The Hague, 1912) and Edwin Lutyens (Castle Drogo, Devon, begun 1910).

Advances in technology also enabled the experimental model to provide exceptionally sophisticated data using computers, as well as photographic or optical aids, such as Endoscopes and Relatoscopes, which enlarge images from model scale to actual size. Vincenzo Scamozzi's warning (*L'idea dell'architettura universale*, 1615; Eng. trans., 1669), however, continues to be relevant:

> Manie modells, being but inanimate and breathlesse things, have need of the Architect's, or some other worthy, & Knowing purson's speech, to expresse with words, and demonstrate with reasons, what they are, and to give them life, & motion. For thereby minds are excited, and inflamed, whereby resolutions may be taken in matters of moment ... Yet modells are like young birds, mongst which one cannot discerne the males from ye females, but being growen bigger are Showen whither they be Eagles or Ravens: And therefore the owners of the workes may easily be deceaved by Modells.

BIBLIOGRAPHY

RDK

M. S. Briggs: 'The Architectural Model', *Burl. Mag.* (1935), pp. 174–83, 245–52

T. W. Hendrick: *The Modern Architectural Model* (London, 1957)

J. Wilton-Ely: 'The Architectural Model', *Archit. Rev.*, cxli (1967), pp. 26–32

——: 'The Architectural Model: English Baroque', *Apollo*, l (1968), pp. 250–59

——: 'The Role of the Architectural Model in Church Design', *Country Life Annu.* (1968), pp. 76–9

——: 'The Architectural Models of Sir John Soane', *Archit. Hist.*, xii (1969), pp. 5–38

S. Hohauser: *Architectural and Interior Models* (New York, 1970)

J. Wilton-Ely: 'A Model for Fonthill', *The Country Seat: Studies in the History of the British Country House Presented to Sir John Summerson* (London, 1970), pp. 199–204

M. S. Van Treeck: *La Relatoscopie* (Paris, 1973)

S. Buttolph, ed.: *Great Models: Digressions on the Architectural Model*, Student Publication of the School of Design, North Carolina State University, 27 (Raleigh, NC, 1978)

M. Mosser: 'Models of French Architecture in the Age of Enlightenment', *Daidalos*, ii (1981), pp. 83–97

H. Reuther: 'The Origin and Development of the Architectural Model in Germany', *Daidalos*, ii (1981), pp. 98–111

M. Scolari: 'L'idea di modello', *Eidos*, 2 (June 1988), pp. 16–39

J. Wilton-Ely: 'Wren, Hawksmoor and the Architectural Model', *English Architecture, Public and Private: Essays for Kerry Downes*, ed. J. Bold and E. Chaney (London, 1993), pp. 147–58

JOHN WILTON-ELY

1. ?Giotto (or his workshop): *Expulsion of the Devils from Arezzo* (late 13th century or first quarter of the 14th), fresco, Upper Church, S Francesco, Assisi

Architectural pictures. Paintings in which a building or a group of buildings or ruins constitutes either the main subject of the composition or plays an important role in it. The term is modern and owes much of its currency to Jantzen's fundamental survey (1910) of 16th- and 17th-century Netherlandish architectural paintings (*see* bibliography under §2 below). Works most commonly described as architectural paintings include views of church interiors, both real and imaginary; interior and exterior views of imaginary palaces and, occasionally, country estates; and exterior views of important buildings, such as cathedrals, town halls and country houses. In some cases, especially in earlier periods, a TOWNSCAPE is referred to as an architectural picture. Indeed, there is a considerable body of Italian Renaissance paintings devoted to general urban views, in which such picturesque architectural elements as turreted walls, cupolas, bell-towers, palazzi, porticos and temples are emphasized (usually arranged according to artistic licence rather than by strict adherence to topographical accuracy). Whereas in the Middle Ages the image of the city had generally served simply as a background for religious narrative scenes, by the early Renaissance increasing interest in both ancient and contemporary architecture meant that it came to be seen as an appropriate subject for painting in its own right. It is not always possible to make a clear distinction between a townscape and an architectural picture: views such as that by Gerrit Berckheyde of the new mansions on the *Herengracht in Amsterdam* (1685; Amsterdam, Rijksmus.) and many of Jan van der Heyden's pictures, with their close study of architectural style and conspicuous use of linear perspective, are so strongly related to the tradition of architectural painting that they may be considered part of it, while Vermeer's *View of Delft* (*c.* 1661; The Hague, Mauritshuis; *see* DELFT, fig. 2) shares essential qualities with landscape paintings, as do many other townscapes, which had a very different significance for contemporary viewers than did architectural views.

See also TOPOGRAPHY and URBAN LIFE.

WALTER LIEDTKE, DANIELA COIA

1. Before *c.* 1550. 2. *c.* 1550–*c.* 1700. 3. After *c.* 1700.

1. BEFORE *c.* 1550. In the late 13th century and the beginning of the 14th, Giotto and artists in his circle employed an original and innovative pictorial interpretation of architectural space in such works as the painted cycle of the *Legend of St Francis* (1296–1304) in S Francesco, Assisi (*see* ASSISI, §II, 2(iv)). The enormous variety of views and representations of buildings introduced in the narrative scenes clearly shows the influence

of ancient painting. A memorable example is the *Expulsion of the Devils from Arezzo* (see fig. 1), in which a city on a hillside is suggested through the juxtaposition and interweaving of elements (houses, towers, chimneys, roofs etc), each of which is seen from two sides to avoid a flattening effect. The complex civic life of the great medieval communes thus became a subject for painting: the city was represented in condensed form, with rather crowded buildings appearing above high surrounding walls fortified with gates and towers. An example of this is the fresco by Ambrogio Lorenzetti, the *Allegories of Good and Bad Government* (1338–9; Siena, Pal. Pub.; *see* SIENA, fig. 12). The artists of this period were mainly concerned with the rediscovery of nature and a new sense of space; they aimed to depict the real world and took their inspiration from it. Houses and furnishings thus became valid subjects for painting, and these works provide a valuable record of city life (*see also* URBAN LIFE). This can be seen with particular clarity in certain works, for example the frontispiece of a manuscript (*c.* 13th century) in the Bodleian Library, Oxford, which shows the *Departure of Marco Polo from Venice*. The city of Venice, seen panoramically from above, is represented in an ingenuous and fantastic way, but with realistic details such as bridges, canals, the winged lion, and houses with front doors barely above the water.

At the end of the 14th century and the beginning of the 15th, the vast industry of illuminated manuscript painting also produced a great many architectural views, enclosed, as always, within turreted walls. An example is the famous TRÈS RICHES HEURES (*c.* 1411/13–16; Chantilly, Mus. Condé, MS. 65) of the Duc de Berry, created by the Limbourg brothers (*see also* LIMBOURG, DE, figs 2 and 4) who concentrated on the accurate rendering of scenes and costumes and made an early attempt at perspective using architectural backgrounds (*see* MILITARY ARCHITECTURE AND FORTIFICATION, fig. 1). In the early 15th century the representation of architecture in Renaissance paintings became precise and competent in response to the desire for formal perfection. The new science of perspective led painters and architects to paint views of cities, squares and perspective backgrounds for their own sake, often with no human figures, as pure abstract experimentation (e.g. the paintings of Francesco di Giorgio Martini and Luciano Laurana); everything was based on a principle of scenic harmony, on the search for a perfect balance between mass and space that was typical of Renaissance architecture itself.

Whereas in medieval painting, buildings and cities were represented with no attention to proportion and with naive juxtapositions that did not always correspond to reality, Renaissance artists based their designs on calculated proportions and tried to follow a principle of symmetry and equilibrium between volumes. A composition was mainly based on one-point perspective, so that the buildings faced each other in parallel lines. In the frescoes by Masolino and Masaccio in the Brancacci Chapel, S Maria del Carmine, Florence, the squares, porticos and façades of Florence were set along the horizon to give the painted narratives a sense of actuality (*see* MASOLINO, fig. 2). In this period, architecture had close links with the theatrical world: often in a painting an important episode would be enclosed within an architectural frame. Idealized buildings in these paintings often had an unreal aspect. This resulted from the complex figurative culture of the period: not only were decorative elements freely borrowed from Classical architecture, but the imagination of the artist himself played an important part, as can clearly be seen in the eponymous works of the Master of the Barberini Panels (New York, Met., and Boston, MA, Mus. F.A.).

Flemish painting in the 15th century, exemplified by the works of Rogier van der Weyden, Jan van Eyck and Petrus Christus, among others, presents buildings, architecture and city views reproduced in minute detail, including windows, chimneys and decorative elements even at a great distance (*see* EYCK, VAN, (2), fig. 5). Dürer produced at least two strange views of mountain cities: in the

2. *Field of the Cloth of Gold* by an anonymous artist, oil on canvas, 1.69×3.47 m, 1520 (London, Hampton Court, Royal Collection)

Adoration of the Magi (1504; Florence, Uffizi; *see* DÜRER, (1), fig. 6) and a detail of a fortified town in the *Lamentation* (1500; Munich, Alte Pin.). In the former the city is still represented in a traditional way, with northern architecture; in the latter work the buildings, set vertically like so many crystals, give the impression of a fantastic city.

In the 16th century architectural paintings no longer represented urban scenes, as in the early Renaissance, but turned to the Classical settings of tragic, comic or satiric theatre. Stage design was, in fact, the field of experimentation for painters, and angled views, oblique and lateral arrangements and dislocated perspectives characterize the architecture in Mannerist paintings and frame the narrative works of such artists as Titian, Tintoretto and Giulio Romano. In 1526 Albrecht Altdorfer painted *Susanna at the Bath* (Munich, Alte Pin.). The protagonist of this large panel is the architecture of a city in the form of a Renaissance palazzo with various Gothic elements in the decoration. The relationship created by the artist between architecture and landscape accentuates the vertical character of the masses and thus of the whole composition. The use of the architectural frame for historical and religious narratives continued, however, in the first half of the 16th century. In the works of Vittore Carpaccio an attentive architectural rendering of real buildings produces an image at once exotic and fabulous (*see* CARPACCIO, (1), figs 2 and 4); the same can be said of a painting of the *Field of the Cloth of Gold* (1520; London, Hampton Court, Royal Col.; see fig. 2) by an anonymous artist.

BIBLIOGRAPHY

E. Garin: *Medioevo e rinascimento* (Bari, 1954)

H. Kiel and D. Neri: *Paesaggi inattesi nella pittura del rinascimento* (Milan, 1958)

C. Buttafava: *Visioni di città nelle opere d'arte del medioevo e del rinascimento* (Milan, 1963)

D. Gioseffi: *Giotto architetto* (Milan, 1963)

G. Contessi: *Architetti-pittori e pittori-architetti* (Bari, 1985)

D. Mazzoleni: *La città e l'immaginazione* (Rome, 1985)

M. Milman: *Architecture peinte en trompe-l'oeil* (Geneva, 1986)

C. de Seta, M. Ferretti and A. Tenenti: *Imago urbis* (Milan, 1986)

G. Massobrio and P. Portoghesi: *L'immaginario architettonico nella pittura* (Bari, 1988)

DANIELA COIA

2. *c.* 1550–*c.* 1700. From the mid-16th century, the production of architectural pictures formed a coherent development that began in Antwerp and spread through the southern and northern Netherlands, with Dutch and Flemish artists active also in parts of Germany, Italy, the Habsburg empire and England.

(i) Introduction. In the past the question of meaning in architectural painting in this period was overshadowed by stylistic analysis. This was encouraged by the importance to the genre of linear perspective; by the fact that some artists painted palace views, grand domestic settings and church interiors in the same style; and by the emphasis of Jantzen and others on regional styles, such as the 'schools' of Antwerp, Haarlem and Delft. Certainly, many architectural pictures, whether of secular or religious buildings, reflect an interest in architectural styles and the practice of perspective; both subjects were discussed extensively in contemporary treatises. Furthermore, the Flemish type of church interior or palace view is often referred to as a 'perspective' in 17th-century inventories. However, Dutch inventories distinguish clearly between a scene of elegant society in a stately setting, and a church interior that might be identified as 'the Great Church seen from inside', or even as a 'Sermon' when a preacher and congregation are shown. Furthermore, Flemish architectural paintings after 1600 almost always represent a church interior, frequently with significant staffage and with worship, acts of charity or ceremonies such as christenings placed conspicuously in view. Finally, Dutch church interiors, while sometimes imaginary, very often represent known buildings of great importance to the religious, civic and sometimes even national sentiments of likely patrons or purchasers.

(ii) Flemish artists. The early development of architectural painting in the Netherlands was centred in Antwerp and was an integral part of the Flemish response to Italian Renaissance art and architecture. Jan Gossart's extraordinary architectural settings for religious and mythological subjects reveal a fascination with the forms, if not the principles, of the ideas he had encountered in Rome, where he worked in 1508–9: for instance, the deep, centralized recession of his *St Luke Drawing the Virgin* (*c.* 1515; Prague, N.G., Šternberk Pal.) looks like an extravagant, eclectic echo of Raphael's Vatican murals. It is such works that must have inspired the perspective prints and paintings of the mid-16th-century artist HANS VREDEMAN DE VRIES. Vredeman de Vries, like his teacher Pieter Coecke van Aelst and his colleague Cornelis Floris, was a universal designer whose architectural ideas also owed much to the books of Sebastiano Serlio. There is a direct line of development from Serlio's Classical temples and stage designs to Coecke's decorations in 1549 for the triumphal entry into Antwerp of Charles V and his son, the future Philip II of Spain, and to Vredeman's *Scenographiae, sive perspectiva* (1560; *see* VREDEMAN DE VRIES, HANS, fig. 1). This treatise and the better known *Perspective* (1604) served as pattern-books for architectural painters and introduced two of the most common subjects, the extended view down the centre of an imaginary church and the palace court with views through arcades and archways. (Later artists turned to other, more modern architectural treatises, as well as to those of Vredeman de Vries, but their sources remain to be fully explored.) Hans Vredeman de Vries's paintings, and those by his son Paul Vredeman de Vries (1567–after 1630), are highly detailed, colourful, decorative works in which Gothic and Renaissance motifs are freely mixed. The figures are usually numerous, fashionably dressed and unencumbered by moralizing themes. Most of these works on canvas are fairly large and must have been intended for patrician homes, where they would have served as enchanting surrogates for a kind of architecture that was entirely impractical and unaffordable. A good example is Hans Vredeman de Vries's *Imaginary Palace with a Musical Company* (1596; Vienna, Ksthist. Mus.; *see* VREDEMAN DE VRIES, HANS, fig. 2), which was in the gallery of Rudolf II in Prague.

The Flemish tradition descending from the Vredeman de Vries family was remarkably coherent, in part because it was sustained by a number of master–pupil relationships. According to Karel van Mander, Hendrick van Steenwijk the elder was Vredeman's pupil, and van Steenwijk's *Interior of Aachen Cathedral* (1573; Munich, Alte Pin.)

3. Bartholomeus van Bassen: *Interior of the St Cunerakerk, Rhenen*, oil on panel, 611×805 mm, 1638 (London, National Gallery)

dates from a period when Vredeman de Vries probably lived in Aachen. Views of Antwerp Cathedral, the entire interior from the west, were painted by van Steenwijk in the early 1580s and established the type represented so often by Hendrick van Steenwijk the younger and by Pieter Neeffs the elder and Pieter Neeffs the younger. The Antwerp views depend on the plates in Vredeman de Vries's *Scenographiae* in so far as they employ a nearly centralized recession set off by the repoussoir of an arched elevation parallel to the picture plane. However, many of the elder van Steenwijk's known paintings depict actual churches and are remarkable for their realistic effects of light and atmosphere. The palette is tonal and the drawing softer than in most architectural pictures of the next 40 years. Wide-angle effects in the foreground, such as an arch stretching to the side, and a low horizon give the viewer some sensation of being in the interior, rather than seeing it from a distant, ideal vantage-point.

Hendrick van Steenwijk the younger worked in Frankfurt am Main (where his father had moved by 1586), Antwerp, London (by 1617, until after 1637) and, finally, at The Hague. He carried on his father's practice of executing cabinet pictures (*see* CABINET PICTURE, §I), works on a smaller scale, with meticulous drawing, varied colours and striking, rather than subtle effects of light and shade. On the whole, this is also true of Pieter Neeffs the elder, the leading Flemish specialist of the 17th century. His paintings range enormously in size and usually represent Antwerp Cathedral or an imaginary Gothic church of similar design. His son, Pieter Neeffs the younger, seems to have worked mostly for his father and was the lesser artist, lacking, for example, the elder Neeffs's fine line and subtle shading. Both Neeffs collaborated with the figure painters Frans Francken (ii) and Frans Francken (iii).

(iii) Dutch artists. Both imaginary palace views and church interiors flourished as subjects in the northern Netherlands, in Middelburg with Dirck van Delen and his follower Daniël de Blieck (*c.* 1630–73) and at The Hague and Delft with Bartholomeus van Bassen and his pupil Gerrit Houckgeest. By *c.* 1640 van Bassen, van Delen and Houckgeest, and to some extent the Rotterdam painter Anthonie de Lorme (*c.* 1610–73), became proponents of the 'realistic imaginary church' (Liedtke, 1982), which in its subdued palette, refined illumination and more accessible arrangements of space recalls the promise of Hendrick van Steenwijk the elder. A panel in this manner by van Bassen represents, exceptionally, a real church, the *Interior of the St Cunerakerk, Rhenen* (1638; London, N.G.; see fig. 3). Other paintings by these artists incorporate real elements in imaginary arrangements, a practice taken much further in the mature work of Emanuel de Witte.

The important Haarlem painter Pieter Saenredam (*see* SAENREDAM, (2)) was probably inspired by his association with practising architects and by the drawings he executed for Samuel Ampzing's *Beschryvinge ende lof der stad Haerlem* (Haarlem, 1628), and he became the first Dutch artist who made a career of depicting existing churches. His sketches faithfully record some of the greatest churches in the northern Netherlands (*see* SAENREDAM, (2), fig. 1), and reveal a sophisticated understanding of the perceptual problems inherent in recording architecture close at hand. His stylized and subtly toned paintings, many of them depicting only sections of a church (*see* SAENREDAM, (2), fig. 2), were not adaptable as models by other painters, although his more conventional ideas influenced a few contemporaries and the younger generation of Haarlem painters Job and Gerrit Berckheyde (for illustration *see* BERCKHEYDE, (2)), and Isaac van Nickele (*fl* 1659–1703).

The last period of architectural painting in the northern Netherlands began in Delft, where *c.* 1650 Gerrit Houckgeest, followed quickly by Emanuel de Witte and Hendrick van Vliet, painted realistic views of the Oude Kerk (for illustration *see* WITTE, EMANUEL DE) and the Nieuwe Kerk (for illustration *see* HOUCKGEEST, GERRIT). Both churches included tombs of national heroes, and the catalyst of the Delft development may have been Hendrick de Keyser's tomb of *William the Silent* (*c.* 1618, *in situ*) in the choir of the Nieuwe Kerk. Houckgeest employed a 'two-point' perspective scheme that allowed him to place columns in the immediate foreground and to record, with surprising fidelity, the complicated juxtapositions of near and far forms. His partial views inside the Delft churches, dating mostly from 1650 and 1651, inspired the rest of van Vliet's career, although the latter freely modified the proportions and some details of the architecture and also depicted a number of churches in other towns. Anthonie de Lorme's views of the Laurenskerk in nearby Rotterdam depend on the compositional innovations of Houckgeest and van Vliet, as do the small number of church interiors by the Delft artist Cornelis de Man (1621–1706).

The culmination of architectural painting in the Netherlands is embodied in the work of Emanuel de Witte, who freely borrowed designs from other artists, especially Houckgeest, but painted in a fluid manner without precedent in architectural views. By the time he moved to Amsterdam, *c.* 1652, de Witte had refined his early, crude, painterly manner into a style superbly suited to his main interests, which were impressions of light, shade, atmosphere and the free flow of extensive spaces, rather than the structure and substance of monumental architecture. His views of real and imaginary churches can be grand and intimate at once. Optical qualities evoke the still serenity of a Dutch church. De Witte had one minor follower, Hendrick van Streek (1659–1713). It is consistent with the strongly conventionalized nature of architectural painting in the 17th century that its two greatest practitioners, Saenredam and de Witte, stand out in isolation from their predecessors, contemporaries and followers.

BIBLIOGRAPHY

RDK: 'Architekturbild'

H. Jantzen: *Das niederländische Architekturbild* (Leipzig, 1910/*R* Brunswick, 1979)

W. Liedtke: *Architectural Painting in Delft* (Doornspijk, 1982)

Perspectives: Saenredam and the Architectural Painters of the 17th Century (exh. cat. by J. Giltaij and G. Jansen, Rotterdam, Mus. Boymans–van Beuningen, 1991)

WALTER LIEDTKE

3. AFTER *c.* 1700. Architectural pictures in the 18th and 19th centuries, which became very popular with connoisseurs and collectors, emerged from two separate traditions: 17th-century Dutch architectural painting and townscape paintings by such artists as Johannes Vermeer, Jan van Goyen, Gerrit Berckheyde and Jan van der Heyden (*see* §2 above) and the classicizing landscapes produced in Italy from 1640 to 1660 by the French painters Nicolas Poussin and Claude Lorrain. In fact, it is in Claude's landscapes that ancient monuments, ruins and mythical Greek cities regularly appear for the first time. Archaeological data and monumental ruins were seen as proof of a past as fascinating as nature itself and equally worthy of artistic representation. This interest grew throughout the 18th century as more and more discoveries were made. In the 18th century the fashion for VEDUTA painting prevailed, especially in Italy. In the cosmopolitan climate of that century the Grand Tour became increasingly popular. The rise of the veduta was directly connected with this custom, especially in such Italian cities as Venice, Rome and Naples, the obligatory points of call. The veduta involved a faithful representation of monuments, cities and landscapes in perspective. This type of painting obviously fitted in with the Enlightenment theme of accuracy, and it also met the demand from international patrons for pictorial souvenirs of their travels. Its most important Italian exponents, following the lead of Gaspar van Wittel, were Giovanni Paolo Panini, Canaletto, Bernardo Bellotto and Francesco Guardi (for illustrations *see* WITTEL, GASPAR VAN; PANINI, GIOVANNI PAOLO, fig. 2; CANALETTO, figs 1, 2, 3 and 4; BELLOTTO, BERNARDO, figs 1 and 2; and GUARDI, (2), figs 1 and 2). Especially popular with English travellers were the famous Venetian scenes painted by Canaletto, with their minute depictions of squares, *campielli*, canals and embankments (see fig. 4). Canaletto was one of many artists, including Bellotto, Guardi, Joseph Vernet, Thomas and Paul Sandby, Samuel Prout and John Ruskin, among others, to use the CAMERA OBSCURA as a tool for refining and correcting the focus of the architectural composition. Such architectural pictures are characterized by precise outlines and the smooth, uniform application of colour; the views are rigidly frontal.

In the 19th century, with the rise of interest in THE SUBLIME and the PICTURESQUE, painters began to depict spectacles designed to excite the imagination and stimulate fantasies. While architectural elements still featured in the landscapes, they tended to be mock ruins and allusive constructions, especially 'temples' and 'Gothic cathedrals', as, for example, in the work of Caspar David Friedrich. These structures were placed in natural settings or forests, and their role was highly symbolic. With Corot landscape painting returned to an attitude of direct and faithful representation of the natural scene, but the architectural elements inserted into these works no longer had any meaning; what interested him were simply the relationships between shades of colour. Moreover, although architecture continued to provide important subject-matter for later artists, such as Monet (e.g. his series devoted

4. Canaletto: *View of the Piazzetta S Marco with the Libreria*, oil on canvas (Rome, Palazzo Corsini)

to Rouen Cathedral), as with Corot, the primary concern was with other aspects of the painted composition.

BIBLIOGRAPHY

Paesisti e vedutisti a Roma nel seicento e nel settecento (exh. cat. by N. di Carpegna, Rome, Pal. Barberini, 1956)

G. Briganti: *Gaspar van Wittel e l'origine della veduta settecentesca romana* (Rome, 1966)

Vedutisti veneziani del settecento (exh. cat. by P. Zampetti, Venice, Accad., 1967)

For further bibliography *see* §1 above.

DANIELA COIA

Architectural proportion. Proportion is the general term used to describe the dimensional relationships among the constituent elements of an artefact and between those elements and the whole composition. As the only factor in design that significantly affects aesthetic outcomes and yet is susceptible to quantification, it has been the subject of various attempts at systematization. These ranged from elementary applications of Pythagorean geometry to the idealized simplicity of numerical progressions in Plato's cosmology: aesthetic perfection was sought for the latter in the musical analogy and in the former in systems based upon the golden section. At the most general level, proportional systems might be expected to offer precise reproducibility. But it is perhaps Panofsky's generalizations that describe proportion best for both plastic arts and architecture (*Meaning in the Visual Arts*, p. 56):

> The history of the theory of proportion is the reflection of the history of style;. . .when dealing with mathematical formulations, it may even be looked upon as a reflection which often surpasses the original in clarity. One might assert that the theory of proportions expresses the frequently perplexing concept of *Kunstwollen* in clearer or at least more definable fashion than art itself.

JOHN MUSGROVE

I. Before *c.* 1450. II. *c.* 1450–*c.* 1800. III. *c.* 1800 and after.

I. *Before* c. *1450.*

1. The problem and the method. 2. Late medieval evidence. 3. Masonic drawing. 4. Mathematical precedents. 5. Conclusion.

1. THE PROBLEM AND THE METHOD. It is possible to read magisterial studies of ancient and medieval buildings without ever encountering the notion that their designs might have been based on principles of proportion; and the very existence of such studies implies that even if proportions were present, their contribution to the proper understanding of the design was minimal. This is in marked contrast to the treatment of proportion in Renaissance and Baroque architecture, where its central importance has always been recognized. The difference is

easy enough to explain. From the Renaissance onwards specific evidence is abundant and unambiguous; before the Renaissance it hardly exists. That is why discussions of proportion in architecture before the Renaissance, in so far as they occur at all, tend to be either special pleading or polemical in tone, and largely taken up with the elementary question of whether any such thing existed. Dismissive or sceptical attitudes are not at all misconceived. The presence of proportions in a building can be asserted with confidence, but they are notoriously difficult to demonstrate, at least on the evidence of the building alone. Monuments of great age hardly ever survive intact or unchanged, and, even if they are well-enough preserved for their mathematical properties to be detected, few were built to standards of exactitude high enough to resolve the problem beyond all doubt. A building may seem to fulfil all the expectations of a particular theory, but that seldom constitutes a proof. Other theories may also pass the test of compatibility. A more stringent criterion is the ability to account for a whole series of buildings; but where the issue is whether Classical and medieval architects thought in terms of proportion, what is required is not so much inductive hypotheses as independent confirmation, preferably verbal. Texts and documents are, however, scarce and uninformative. For antiquity there is one substantial treatise, Vitruvius' *On Architecture* (*see* VITRUVIUS, §2), which does have things to say about proportion and illustrates them by reference to Roman or Hellenistic temples in which they were exemplified (*see also* ROME, ANCIENT, §II, 3(ii)). Yet few Classical buildings conform to Vitruvius' rules, and for the great period of Doric temples they are no use at all (*see* GREECE, ANCIENT, §II, 2(ii)(b)). Vitruvius provides a long list of monographs that Greek architects wrote about their buildings, but all have been lost, as also were the works of Marcus Terrentius Varro (116–27 BC) and Heron of Alexandria (*fl* AD 62), who were ostensibly far more authoritative than Vitruvius. In the Middle Ages the silence was unbroken almost to the end: only on the eve of the Renaissance were a few enigmatic disclosures made public in Germany by Mathes Roriczer and Hanns Schmuttermayer, which, it has been alleged, can be construed as clues that rules of proportion were part of the stock-in-trade of medieval masons. If so, they require a great deal of interpretation before general theory can be extracted from them (*see* §2 below).

Those little tracts were virtually ignored until the beginning of the 19th century, when they were promoted by Romantics and Freemasons, convinced that medieval architects had been the guardians of ancient and secret mysteries (*see* §III, 1 below). The French rationalist Eugène-Emmanuel Viollet-le-Duc, who had views of his own about proportion, preferred to trust his intuition that the principle of stability in properly constructed buildings was most adequately expressed by the equilateral triangle. Some evidence for interest in the equilateral triangle exists in the records of debates in the 1390s about the design of Milan Cathedral (*see* MASON (i), §IV, 3(iii)), and Viollet-le-Duc claimed to find equilateral triangles everywhere among medieval churches. Yet the views of those who actually measured the cathedrals were well summed up by Georges Durand in his monumental *Monographie de l'église Notre-Dame cathédrale d'Amiens* (Amiens, 1901–3): 'The proportions of Gothic churches vary infinitely and there are no two, even among those most alike in style and dimensions, that have identical proportions.' It is small wonder that most reputable historians of medieval architecture should have been content to adopt Durand's agnostic position and leave proportions to the lunatic fringe.

The dilemma facing Classical archaeology was even more acute. It was axiomatic for the Renaissance that proportions were an indispensable aspect of the excellence that made the architecture of antiquity superior to that of the Middle Ages. The whole point of measuring ancient buildings was to discover the correct rules, yet intensive research between 1550 and 1750 by French and Italian scholars produced no conclusive answers. When the range of the evidence was extended in the 19th century to include Classical Greek temples, the shift of attention to the minutiae of the orders and the subtleties of refinements was in effect a tacit admission of defeat. Yet no architecture was ever so patently mathematical as that of the Greeks (*see* GREECE, ANCIENT, §II, 3(v)). Whether mathematics and proportions were synonymous for Greek architects remains an open question, but the instinct that led Renaissance antiquaries to suppose that the formal qualities of Classical architecture were expressed in proportional terms was sound, even if their results were disappointing.

There is an overwhelming case for placing proportion once more high on the agenda of Classical archaeology; and it is clearly improbable that the Middle Ages were marked by indifference between two periods of intense interest. Yet the only firm foothold in documentary history occurs at the point where the Middle Ages were already giving way to the Renaissance. Everything else is a matter of inference, an attempt to answer the question: where did the ideas of the late medieval masons originate? This quest leads back to the Greeks or even beyond. Contrary to what is still perhaps the received opinion, the period of the Middle Ages, to a far greater extent than the Renaissance allowed, was the true heir of Classical antiquity, in this respect if no other. There was no rupture; from which it follows, paradoxically, that one of the strongest arguments for supposing Greek or Roman architects would use particular proportions is that medieval architects did likewise. The rest of this section will set out in greater detail the thesis outlined above. Procedure will be retrospective. Verification lies in the buildings themselves, or what is left of them.

2. LATE MEDIEVAL EVIDENCE. Before the 14th century medieval authors occasionally mentioned proportions when they wrote about aesthetics, but they never singled out specific ratios for special approval. Thus for Thomas Aquinas it was enough to name proportion, alongside integrity or perfection, and brightness or clarity, as one of the three conditions of beauty (*Summa theologiae*, I.xxxix.8). Proportion in the sense of a mathematical relation between numbers first featured as a key concept in the studies on velocities in motion made by the so-called Merton calculators at Oxford during the first half of the 14th century; this was to become the science of

mechanics. The necessary competence in practical arithmetic had become widespread during the 13th and 14th centuries, especially in Italy, and this had disturbing repercussions on the professional status of masons (*see* MASON (i), §IV, 2(i)). Before calculation became common, architects had some claim to be the most (in some places the only) numerate members of medieval society; afterwards they were increasingly exposed to the charge of being mathematically incompetent. It was against this background that the theorists of the Renaissance could write with some justification, as though they had rediscovered proportion, and reintroduced it into art and architecture for the first time since antiquity.

The real difference, however, between the Middle Ages and the Renaissance lay in the elevation of the subject of proportion from the realm of practice to that of theory. Medieval craftsmen, who had a deferential attitude to what their fathers taught them, had no need of theory to justify what they did. The Renaissance wanted to know what made good art good, and felt the need to discuss proportion in the context of beauty. Yet much Renaissance theorizing about proportion was little more than medieval practice smartened up and restated in the more sophisticated language of the day. This makes it possible to call Renaissance as well as medieval witnesses to testify about the state of the proportion question at the end of the Middle Ages.

Four works from the second half of the 15th century, three of them Italian, the other German, bring out the salient features. The latest was the *De divina proportione* by LUCA PACIOLI (MS. completed 1497; Venice, 1509). This work is in three parts: the first extols the special excellence of the GOLDEN SECTION, the divine proportion; the second deals with constructions derived from the five regular solids; and the third with rules for architects based on the proportions of the human body (*see also* HUMAN PROPORTION). Pacioli's main concerns were the section and the solids. There was nothing new in what he had to say about either. The mathematical chapters are in effect an extended commentary on Book XIII of the *Elements* by Euclid (*fl c.* 300 BC), and the proof that there are no more than five solids is taken directly from the scholium to proposition 18. In much of this Pacioli was anticipated by Piero della Francesca, who wrote at length not only about the solids but also about the ratios and polygons involved in their construction. Pacioli was Piero's literary executor and, if Vasari was right, published Piero's work as his own. Piero's *Libellus de quinque corporibus regularibus* (*c.* 1440; Rome, Vatican, Bib. Apostolica, Cod. Urb. 273) was not published until the early part of the 20th century (Rome, 1916; ed. G. Mancini). Behind Euclid loomed the charismatic figure of Plato himself, who in the *Timaeus* had identified four of the solids with the four elements of the physical world: earth with the cube, water with the icosahedron, air with the octahedron and fire with the pyramid. It was Aristotle who, for the sake of consistency, postulated the heavenly, quintessential fifth element, ether, to go with the dodecahedron, which was the solid associated with the golden section: hence its divinity.

Piero and Pacioli give the impression that they were exploring a new geometrical world. So far as the solids were concerned this was perhaps true, but the ratios and polygons needed no such rediscovery. Polygons had been staple items of Gothic tracery patterns for more than three centuries and of apse plans for even longer. Piero and Pacioli were simply tracing medieval knowledge back to its ultimate Classical sources, which Gothic masons seem to have forgotten.

Where Piero and Pacioli did improve upon their immediate medieval predecessors, and even their ancient sources, was in the quality of their arithmetic. Piero calculated that the side of a polygon inscribed in a circle with a diameter of 12 was $\sqrt{(90-\sqrt{1620})}$ (7.05342308), which is exactly right. Pacioli knew that the golden section of 10 can be expressed as $\sqrt{125}-5$. Both had a firm grasp of the notion of an irrational number. These attainments put them in a different league from all medieval craftsmen, who, although they were familiar with such ratios as the golden section and could construct polygons accurately enough, were often content to make do with crude approximations and almost certainly found irrational numbers beyond their comprehension. Pacioli was excited by the mystery of incommensurability, but others, while recognizing the distinction between rational and irrational ratios, concluded that works of art that aimed at perfection should use only rational ratios, since the irrational was by definition never complete or perfect. It was this line of thought that inclined Alberti towards the musical ratios.

Unlike Pacioli, Alberti wrote *De re aedificatoria* as a practical manual for architects, and his comments on the aesthetics of architecture are characteristically to the point (*see* ALBERTI, LEON BATTISTA, §II, 2). He saw beauty as 'a kind of harmony and concord of all the parts to form a whole that is constructed according to a fixed number, and a certain relation and order, as symmetry, the highest and most perfect law of nature, demands' (IX.v). The concepts of harmony and concord were borrowed from music: Alberti wrote as though the musical ratios, which seem to have represented for him one of the ways in which the architecture of the future could improve on the architecture of the past, were not used by contemporary architects. The practical advantage of the musical ratios was that they were entirely compatible with Vitruvius' module systems. All the numbers were integral and all the ratios commensurable. Irrational ratios could be used only with modules in the imperfect form of approximation. This was anathema to Alberti, and they played little part in Renaissance architecture. The only exception Palladio was prepared to countenance was the ratio between the side and the diagonal of a square ($1:\sqrt{2}$), presumably because Vitruvius had sanctioned it as a possible shape for an atrium. Designing by modules, that is proceeding from small units to large aggregates, was the exact antithesis of Late Gothic practice, which was to start with one large dimension, such as the *choresmaas* of Lorenz Lechler (*see* LECHLER, LORENZ, §2), and to derive other dimensions from it by a process of subdivision. If this is what Alberti had in mind, his proposals for the reform of architecture were radical indeed. Yet although his remedy was in a sense the opposite of Pacioli's, the diagnosis was the same. The vitiating flaw in Late Gothic was mathematical imprecision, which had its roots in the use of irrational ratios.

The first printed edition of *De re aedificatoria* (Florence, 1485) appeared more than 30 years after it was written. It is most unlikely that the near simultaneous publication of the first printed edition of Vitruvius (Rome, 1486–92) by Sulpizio de Veroli and of the first German masonic tract, Mathes Roriczer's *Büchlein von der Fialen Gerechtigkeit* (Regensburg, 1486; *see* RORICZER, (3), §2), was coincidental. The latter sets out the successive stages through which the design of a finial or pinnacle passed (see fig. 1)—a somewhat recherché subject, for which the only ostensible readership was unlikely to have needed instruction. Nevertheless persistent claims have been made that Roriczer was revealing more than meets the eye, and that the finial was only a special instance of a method used by medieval designers at every stage of their work (*see* MASON (i), §IV, 2 and fig. 3). The real purpose of the work can be deduced from its dedication to Wilhelm II von Reichenau, Bishop of Eichstätt (*reg* 1464–96). Eichstätt was then a well-known centre of humanist learning in south Germany, and the Bishop was godfather to the Nuremberg humanist Willibald Pirckheimer. Roriczer addressed the Bishop as a patron of the liberal art of geometry, and it is the geometry of the finial, based on a succession of rotated squares, that matters. As an exercise involving the sides and diagonals of squares, Roriczer's finial was mathematically identifiable with Vitruvius' atrium, thus the *Fialenbuch* was staking a

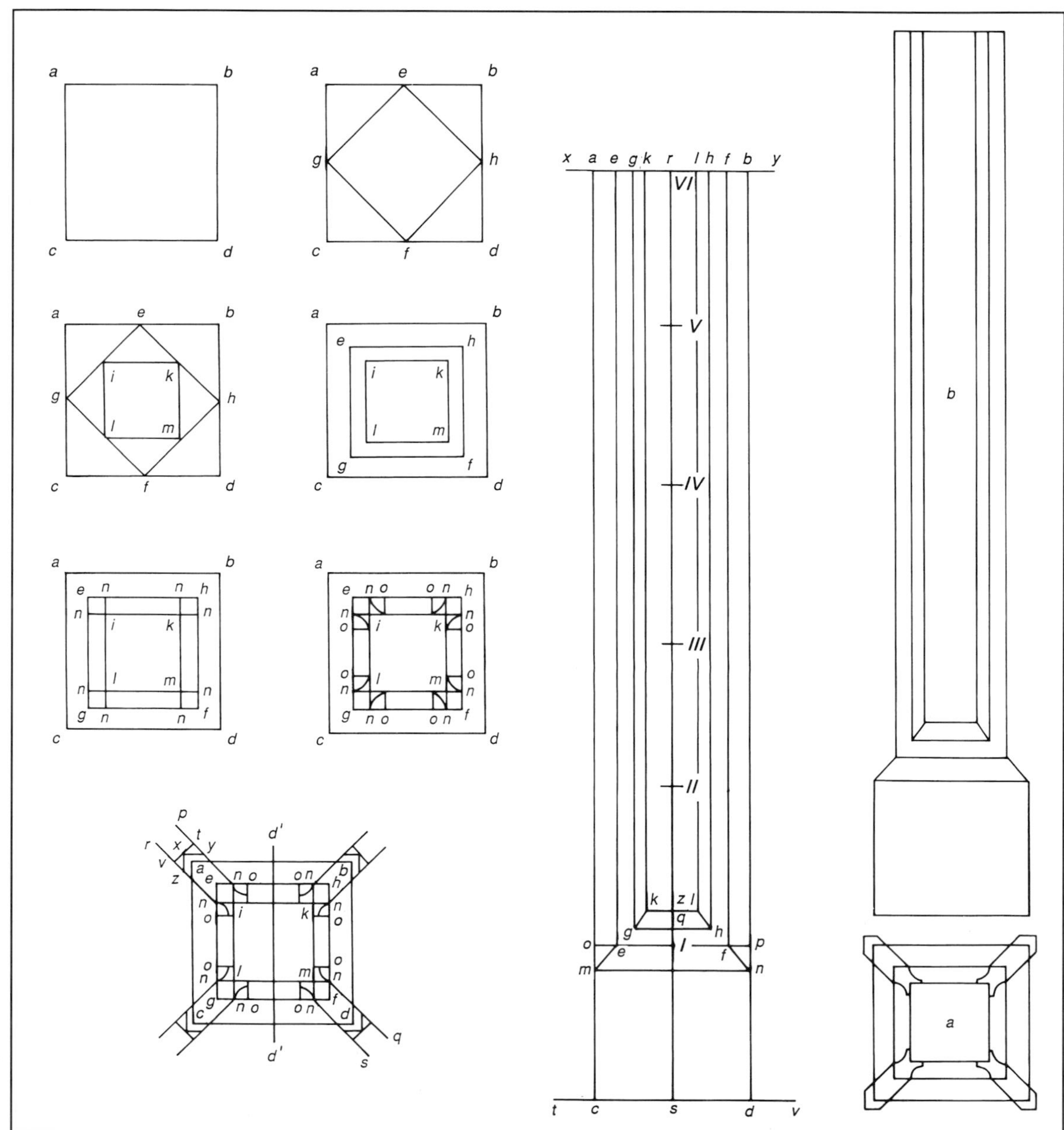

1. The main steps in drawing a pinnacle, following Mathes Roriczer: *Büchlein von der Fialen Gerechtigkeit* (Regensburg, 1486)

claim on behalf of Gothic architecture for a place in the estimation of learned humanists. In spite of the strictures emanating from Italy, Gothic too was in the line of descent from Classical antiquity. Roriczer was almost certainly put up to it by a member of the Eichstätt *literati*, perhaps even the Bishop himself.

The *Fialenbuch* gives very little away beyond the principle relating the squares. Nor was much added by Schmuttermayer's *Fialenbüchlein* (Nuremberg, late 1480s; *see* SCHMUTTERMAYER, HANNS, §2; *see also* MASON (i), fig. 4). But when these are read in conjunction with Roriczer's so-called *Geometria deutsch*, the squares do begin to look like the tip of a geometrical iceberg. *Geometria deutsch* demonstrates ways to draw three of the regular polygons: the pentagon (see fig. 2), the heptagon and the octagon. Three other polygons (the square, equilateral triangle and hexagon) were omitted, presumably because they were too easy to require instruction; as was the enneagon, conversely because it was too difficult. The methods recommended provide real insight into the state of masonic mathematics. Neither the pentagon nor the heptagon is strictly accurate, but they enabled masons to sidestep awkward calculations involving incommensurables. It may seem extraordinary that architects (or indeed goldsmiths, such as Schmuttermayer) with such rudimentary mathematical talents should have become entangled with sophisticated concepts that eventually were bound to expose their limitations. The real explanation is that they were the prisoners of their own traditions and unable to choose otherwise. Even so, the true state of affairs was not common knowledge for a long time. Medieval masons could be justifiably proud of their achievements, and, if they chose to attribute these to their geometrical prowess, only the most perceptive critics were in a position to appreciate that the claim was based on very slender foundations. So long as masons managed to keep themselves secluded in their lodges, there was no one to tell them that their little rules of thumb were not mathematics at all; and until there were mathematicians of the calibre of Piero and Pacioli to put them in their place, they seem to have been taken at their own evaluation by the world at large. Only rarely were there flickers of anxiety within the profession. One such occasion occurred in Milan in 1392 when the local masons, having elected to build the new cathedral *ad triangulum*, based on an equilateral triangle, took the precaution of hiring Gabriele Stornaloco, a professor of mathematics, to do their sums for them, even though they must have been familiar with equilateral triangles when they made their decision.

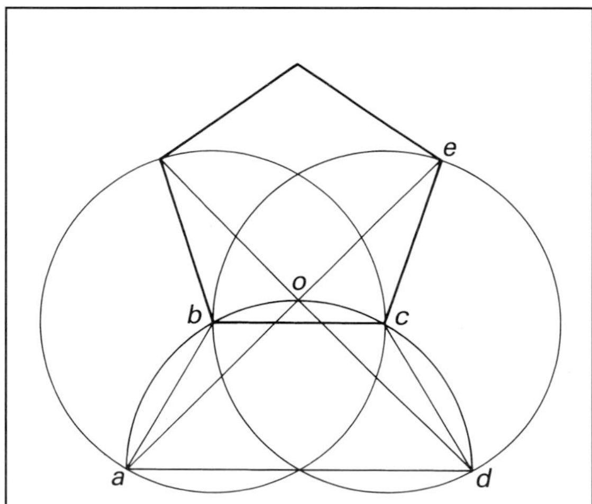

2. Construction of a pentagon, following Mathes Roriczer: *Geometria deutsch*: a, b, c, d forms half a hexagon; a, o, d forms half a square; angle b, c, e ought to be 108° (actually 108.36612°)

3. MASONIC DRAWING. Regular polygons, mostly equilateral triangles, squares, pentagons, hexagons and octagons, occur frequently among the several hundred Late Gothic architectural drawings preserved in Vienna in the Akademie der Bildenden Künste and the Historisches Museum der Stadt Wien (*see also* ARCHITECTURAL DRAWING, §2). They also show that apses might be parts of polygons, for example five sides of an octagon, and that two sides of a pentagon embracing 108° (see fig. 2) could be made into a porch, such as that beneath the south tower of the Stephansdom, Vienna. These abbreviations suggest that polygons may have been more versatile than is immediately apparent. There was an obvious connection between the drawing of polygons and the invention of bar tracery at the beginning of the 13th century: sexfoiled and cinquefoiled oculi figure prominently among the earliest traceried windows (*see* TRACERY, fig. 2). If Viollet-le-Duc's restoration of the 12th-century elevation of Notre-Dame, Paris, was correct, pentagons were already in the repertory by the 1180s, and one of the nave chapel windows (*c.* 1240) has a heptagonal oculus nearly 250 years before *Geometria deutsch*.

Masonic interest in polygons, however, was older than architectural drawing. The proof is to be found in Early Gothic apses. The apse (*c.* 1140–44) of the abbey church at Saint-Denis began as seven sides of a thirteen-sided polygon (*see* SAINT-DENIS ABBEY, fig. 1). At Sens Cathedral (begun *c.* 1140) the apse was constructed around the angles of an enneagon (*see* SENS, fig. 1), a rarity that occurred again at Canterbury Cathedral (begun 1174), presumably on the initiative of William of Sens. At Notre-Dame the starting point was a heptagon, and the similarity to the construction in *Geometria deutsch* is close enough to suggest that this was the ultimate source of Roriczer's short cut. The correct derivation of true heptagons and enneagons requires knowledge of the trisection of angles, and it remains a mystery how this was done successfully in the 12th century, if not by trial and error. In the second campaign (late 1230s–1240s) at Beauvais Cathedral the angle subtended at the centre by two sides of a regular pentagon (i.e. 144°) was even divided into five equal parts to form the basis of the apse (*see* BEAUVAIS, fig. 1). By comparison the most common Early Gothic apse, which comprised five sides of a decagon, was child's play: the side was simply the golden section of the apse radius.

An interest in polygons may have originated from the symbolic properties of centrally planned shapes, but it rapidly became an exercise in mathematical dexterity for its own sake. There is an understandable temptation to connect this with the appearance in western Europe of the first Latin translations of Euclid associated with the names of Adelard of Bath (*c.* 1070–after 1142) and Gerard of Cremona (*c.* 1114–87). Euclid, however, belonged strictly to the schools and the liberal arts; and to judge by *Geometria deutsch* not much school-learning spilled over into the masons' yard. In any case, Euclid did not discuss polygons that depended on the trisection of angles. Applied geometry was *sui generis*, and while it had much to do with the emergence of Gothic, the two were neither synonymous nor mutually dependent. The origins go back further still.

In Romanesque Italy the entire art of the Roman *marmorarii* was based on simple, regular shapes: squares, circles, equilateral triangles (*see* COSMATI). The papal throne (*c.* 1260) signed by Vassallettus in Anagni Cathedral, for example, has inlaid roundels that echo on a miniature scale compositions executed in the 1170s on the exterior of the apse of Monreale Cathedral (*see* MONREALE, fig. 1). Perhaps the most telling example of all is the floor (1207) in the nave of S Miniato al Monte, Florence, which has the decorative motif of squares inside squares, exactly as Roriczer prescribed for his finial. From there, although a thousand years intervened, the derivation from the ancient world is not seriously in question. The designs of pavements (*in situ*) at Ostia and pebble mosaics (*c.* 300 BC; Pella, Archaeol. Mus.) take that theme back almost to the time of Plato.

Such squares are too slight and superficial to bear the weight of a general theory linking the Middle Ages to Classical antiquity. It may be inferred from the corpus of Gothic drawings that they were fundamental to the design of towers; and Villard de Honnecourt's portfolio connects them with the planning of cloisters. These were serious operations, extending far beyond the world of patterns; yet squares as such fail to shed any light on the recurrent features of the plans, sections and elevations of ordinary churches. All that can be said is that they surfaced at regular intervals over a long period, as though they were never far from the main current of architectural thought.

Another Gothic drawing that takes the enquiry on to a more elemental plane appears among the outlines scratched in the plaster surface of the tracing floor of York Minster (*see* TRACING FLOOR). This bears the shape of the arched head of the windows in the aisles of the Lady Chapel and must date from after 1361. From this it transpires that the radius was related to the width of the window or the span of the arch as the diagonal to the side of a square. In other words, the ratio at the heart of Roriczer's finial construction was being used here in a way that had nothing to do with the square shape as such. What was true of squares could equally be true of equilateral triangles and pentagons (see fig. 3). The ratios were more fundamental than the polygons and could be entirely separated from them. Their primary function was simply to relate dimensions, and in that capacity there was no limit to what could be done with them. When the Milanese talked about 'building to the triangle', they meant a ratio between width and height. In principle all the dimensions of a building could be related to one another and form a single system; and in this sense the ratios could permeate a design from the space frame down to finials and surface patterns. They also provided a substitute for scale. The York drawing was at full scale and demonstrably

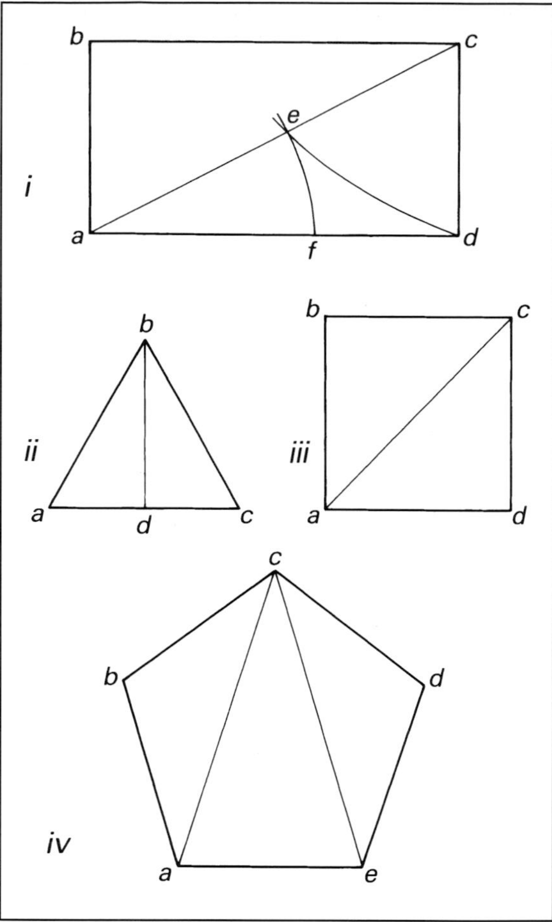

3. The relation of irrational ratios to plane figures: (a) 2ab=bc, ce=cd, ae=af, af is the golden section of ad; (b) ad:bd=1:√3; (c) ad:ac=1:√2; (d) ae is the golden section of ac

connected with actual windows. The German lodge drawings were miniatures; yet they were composed in exactly the same way as a real building, and, to the extent that they incorporated ratios, they could be said to be mathematical models of potential structures. Some were little more than training exercises; others the equivalent of *sinopie* in contemporary painting.

The canonical list of the architectural ratios included 1:√2, 1:√3, 1:√5 and the golden section. Other ratios, such as 1:2, 2:3 and 3:4, were also used, but the irrationals were exclusive to architecture. If it is assumed that the ratios were used in compounds or in combinations, most of the masonic drawings make sense; their ability to explain the drawings is perhaps the most effective confirmation of the hypothesis that they were in general use.

Given the limitations of masonic arithmetic, it is natural to presume that irrational ratios were always worked out geometrically. There is, however, one notable exception, namely the space frame. Complete sections of churches are conspicuously absent from the drawings at Vienna: either they have all been lost, or space frames were executed in some other way. It is often forgotten that drawing was introduced late in the medieval period. It did not usher in a new era but was the last refinement of a long-established tradition; and it is to be understood as a method for extending design by ratios to levels of detail that were otherwise the province of sculpture or painting. There was no essential break between early Gothic and late Gothic; but if this was so the question arises: how were ratios handled before masonic drawing became general? Unless it is supposed that there were techniques of which nothing is known, the only alternative to geometry is arithmetic. We shall now consider whether architects always fought shy of numbers and calculations.

4. MATHEMATICAL PRECEDENTS. The correspondence between Gerbert of Aurillac (Pope Sylvester II, *reg* 999–1003) and Adelbold, later Bishop of Utrecht (*reg* 1010–26), concerning the calculation of the area of an isosceles triangle, mentions the ratio 26/15 as an adequate expression of the sense of √3. A few years later two pupils of Fulbert of Chartres (*c.* 960–1028), who had been one of Gerbert's pupils, discussed the relative merits of 7/5 and 17/12 for √2. Not only are these fairly accurate approximations, but they were arrived at by a method for computing square roots current in late antiquity. This can best be illustrated by the √2 approximations that come from the table of side and diagonal numbers published by Theon of Smyrna (*fl c.* AD 115–40) as a contribution to the mathematics needed to understand Plato. The side and diagonal numbers are successive integral solutions to the equation $2x^2 2-y^2 2=\pm1$. They start with two units and then proceed by a process of differential addition, each x being the sum of the previous x and y, and each y the sum of twice the previous x and the previous y:

x	y
1	1
2	3
5	7
12	17 etc

Theon's procedure could be applied to any irrational square root simply by varying the number of times the previous x was included in the successive y. Thus for √3 the formula is $3x^2 2-y^2 2$:

x	y
1	1
2	4
1	2
3	5
8	14
4	7
11	19
30	52
15	26 etc

For √5 the formula is $5x^2 2-y^2 2$:

x	y
1	1
2	6
1	3
4	8
1	2
3	7
10	22
5	11
16	36
4	9
13	29 etc

From the √5 figures integral values can be obtained for the golden section. The golden section is (√5–1):2, so, substituting 9/4 for √5, the golden section is approximately 5:8, and using 29/13 it is 16:26 or 8:13. These numbers form themselves into the so-called Fibonacci series (1, 1, 2, 3, 5, 8, 13, 21, 34, 55 etc), in which each item is the sum of its two predecessors, and any pair an integral approximation for the golden section.

This method for obtaining working values for irrational square roots was not invented by Theon of Smyrna. When Heron of Alexandria wanted a value for √2 in order to calculate the area of an octagon, he used 17/12. When Archimedes (*c.* 287–212 BC) needed a really accurate value for √3, he declared it to be larger than 265/153 and smaller than 1351/780, both of which he obtained by refining 26/15. The ultimate source of these approximations was the mathematics of ancient Mesopotamia.

Although Gerbert and his school may have made contact with the mathematicians of antiquity, perhaps through Arab intermediaries, they may equally have picked up the formulae from architects. The designers of Early Christian, Carolingian and Romanesque churches were as interested in √2 and the golden section as their Gothic successors: examples abound in the St Gall plan (*c.* 820; St Gall, Stift.-Bib.; for illustration *see* ST GALL ABBEY). Early Christian basilicas were extremely simple buildings. The ratios were virtually confined to the space frame and its subdivisions into nave and aisles, arcades and clerestories. The magnitudes involved were substantial, and the evidence suggests that √2 was commonly represented by 7/5 or 17/12, and the golden section by 5:8. The fact that there were several values for each ratio meant that it was possible to turn them into a simple calculus by adding like to like or by subtraction, a procedure that could meet a surprisingly large number of eventualities. Most masons at most times could add and subtract even if they found it difficult to multiply or divide. Such practices would go a long way to explain the consistently generous margins of tolerance that seemed to have prevailed over centuries, as much as 1% or 2% in well-designed buildings.

There is a virtual proof that architects were using approximations for the irrational ratios during the critical period when the Roman Empire was in the process of turning into medieval Europe. It can be shown that the ratios were instrumental in converting the measures of Classical antiquity into the metrological standards of the Middle Ages. Thus the English fathom, of which the yard and the foot are subdivisions, originated as the golden section (strictly 34:55) of the Classical Roman *decempeda* or perch; and the Classical Roman foot was the golden section (strictly 5:8) of the Italian *piede Liutprando.* The Rhenish foot was related to the Classical Roman cubit as 1:√2 (strictly 17:24, a variant of 12:17), and √3 and √5 were involved in the genesis of the neo-Roman *staiolo* and the neo-Roman foot. The only context in which such transformations make sense is architecture. It has to be supposed that there was a long period when the care of measures was almost exclusively in the hands of architects, and that when medieval governments set up new standards, it was the architects who supplied them.

This argument presupposes that the irrational ratios were an established feature of the architecture of late antiquity, and that the conversion to Christianity made no difference except to add churches to the list of commissions. Despite the Renaissance myth about the deleterious effects of barbarian invasions, the architectural profession suffered no catastrophic disruption, at least in Italy. Architects set about designing churches in much the same ways that they had designed basilicas, baths and temples. In Rome the width of the nave of Old St Peter's (completed AD 337), like that of the Basilica Ulpia (early 2nd century; destr.) in the Forum of Trajan, was a √2 function of the Classical Roman *actus* (a measure of 120 feet). Similarly the dome (diam. 105 Roman feet) of Hagia Sophia (*see* ISTANBUL, §III, 1(ii)(a)) was related by √2 (derived as 7/5) to the diameter of the Pantheon (147 Roman feet). The vaulted halls of Imperial Rome, of which Hagia Sophia was in a sense the last, were the work of specialist engineers—the so-called 'mechanicians of Heron's school', who presumably used Heron of Alexandria's (lost) treatise on vaults as their theoretical handbook. It can be inferred from surviving vaults that the idea of applying ratios to arches and vaults was learnt from Heron.

By contrast with Heron, Vitruvius seems to have had little influence on Imperial Roman architecture. Moreover, although he cites an impressive list of earlier authors, there is little evidence that he had read them; so his value as a source of information about Classical views on proportion in architecture is not easy to judge. His habit of expressing ratios in terms of modules (*see* ROME, ANCIENT, §II, 1(iv)) had the effect of deflecting his Renaissance admirers away from the irrational ratios, and the instances he cites of pycnostyle, diastyle and araeostyle intercolumniations in Roman temples certainly convey the impression that his contemporaries did not use them. On the other hand, the conclusion to be drawn from his declared preference for the eustyle interval of 4:9 (i.e. 1:√5), which he said he derived from Hermogenes and of which there were as yet no examples in Rome, is that he cast himself in the role of missionary, preaching the true faith of Hellenistic theory to his unregenerate countrymen. The eustyle and the atrium show that Vitruvius was no stranger to the irrational ratios. The architects of Republican Rome may have managed without them, but there are no grounds for inferring that they were discovered after the time of Vitruvius. All the threads lead back from Rome to Greece.

Despite much recent wishful thinking to the contrary, Honorius of Autun (*d c.* 1156), Durandus of Mende and other medieval writers who touched upon the symbolism of church building kept well away from numbers and ratios, which almost certainly means that for the Christian era they carried no specifically religious overtones. The only intellectual underpinning the irrational ratios ever received is found in Plato, whose cosmology, as set out in the *Timaeus*, was grounded in the analogy between the creator and the architect. The building bricks of the physical world are the regular solids. Behind these are the three regular polygons, which can be broken down into three elementary triangles. Two of these are right-angled, one being half a square embodying the √2 ratio, the other half an equilateral triangle and the √3 ratio. The third triangle, in which one side is the golden section of the other two, gets a rather perfunctory mention, perhaps because it was not right-angled, but Plato's argument presupposes its role in the construction of pentagons.

Plato took a poor view of the mimetic arts, but he was careful to distinguish them from craftsmanship of another kind:

> I do not mean by beauty of form such beauty as that of animals or pictures. . .but straight lines and circles and the plain and solid figures that are formed out of them by turning-lathes and rulers and measures of angles; for these I affirm to be not only relatively beautiful like other things, but they are eternally and absolutely beautiful (*Philebus*, 51c).

Whatever the philosophical meaning of this passage, it had no point unless Plato's contemporaries, pre-eminently architects, actually produced such shapes. The *demiourgos* who fashioned the physical universe out of the mathematical forms may have been a god, but the operations he performed were those of a stone mason. The picture of God the Father in the act of creation in the medieval *Bible moralisée* is a purely Platonic image (e.g. *c.* 1220–30; Vienna, Österreich. Nbib., Cod. 2554, fol. 1*v*; *see* BIBLE, fig. 8). The cosmology of the *Timaeus* was not newly invented in the 4th century BC. It had been taking shape slowly in the minds of Pythagorean thinkers for the better part of two hundred years. If the coping stone of the whole edifice was the elegant proof, attributed to Plato's younger contemporary Theaetetus (*c.* 414–369 BC), that there were only five regular solids—a discovery that must have focused attention firmly on √2, √3, √5 and the golden section—the starting-point was the craftsman's distinction between form and matter, and the belief that all form could be expressed ultimately in terms of number. The existence of magnitudes that refused to conform to the system of integral numbers, however, presented a serious stumbling block, and the cosmological part of the programme never got off the ground until the notion of incommensurability had been rationally contained within the logical framework of Greek mathematics. Paradoxically, perhaps, domestication emasculated their emotive power. In their unexplained state irrational ratios were surrounded by a numinous aura that brought them into the orbit of primitive religion. For two thousand years before Pythagoras, Babylonian and Egyptian priests, teased and tantalized by the thought of numbers that could not be expressed by number, had hunted for pairs of integrals that would resolve the riddle. Their search produced the approximations, but it was their failure that nourished the conviction that the irrationals were clues to the ultimate secrets to the physical world. This may equally have applied to the Middle Ages. Anyone who wished to honour divinity by constructing temples or churches attuned to the cosmic mystery could hardly do better than to co-opt these esoteric enigmas for the purpose. It may be surmised that such were the circumstances in which the ratios entered architecture.

So far as the Greeks were concerned, the only period when this might have happened was when they first took to building temples, that is during the Geometric period (*c.* 900–*c.* 700 BC) or even late Mycenaean times (before *c.* 1100 BC). There is no intrinsic reason why the pursuit of origins should not be pushed back further still to Anatolia, Mesopotamia and the Nile Valley, since it is unlikely that no one before the Greeks had thought of making buildings in the image of the cosmos. The proof is hard to find, however, and whether the Greeks derived the idea from someone else or not, it is necessary to postulate a long, formative period in the early 1st millennium BC, during which their instinct for giving mathematical definition to their sense of form gradually hardened into clear ideas about what could or could not be done. The architectural evidence for any such experimental episode has effectively disappeared, but from the moment when the remains of their earliest stone temples survive in a state from which deductions can be made (*c.* 600 BC), the ratios were already being used in ways that remained hardly changed until the end of the Middle Ages, that is, not just as a collection of favoured shapes but as a method for generating dimensions and making a system out of them. A few, easily verified illustrations must suffice. The stylobate of the early Temple of Olympian Zeus (*c.* 550 BC) outside Syracuse measures *c.* 22.1×62.4 m, which is 1:2√2. At Paestum in the second Temple of Hera ('Temple of Neptune'; *c.* 460 BC; for further discussion and illustration *see* PAESTUM), the height of the columns plus the entablature (12.65 m) is virtually √2 times the height of the columns alone (8.88 m). In the Temple of Aphaia (early 5th century BC) on Aigina the width of the *naos* is given as 8.01 m and of the stylobate 13.8 m; the ratio here is 1:√3 (strictly 11:19; *see* AIGINA, §2(i) and fig. 1). At Olympia the corresponding measurements (16.03 m and 27.68 m) in the Temple of Zeus (*c.* 470–456 BC) are double those at Aigina, but the ratio remains the same. The terrace of the old Heraion at Argos, which is very early indeed, is said to be a rectangle 34.4×55.8 m; the former is the golden section of the latter (strictly 8:13).

The Parthenon (*c.* 447–432 BC) at Athens demonstrates the interweaving of ratios. It is well known that the plan and the façade are both 4×9 rectangles. The height of the entablature is one third of that of the columns, from which it follows that the column height comprises one third of the temple's width. This rather unusual fact was presumably mentioned in the monograph by IKTINOS, from which it seems to have been extracted and turned into a general rule that found its way into the *Etymologiae* by Isidore of Seville (AD 560–636). The cella corresponds to 5×14 intercolumniations, which makes it 1×2√2. The wall between the naos and the Parthenon chamber coincides with the golden section of the long side of the stylobate; the internal width of the naos is the golden section of the short side; and the external width of the naos (i.e. five intercolumniations) is the short side divided by √2. The famous contraction of the corner intercolumniations simply followed as a matter of course and, *pace* Vitruvius, was not done for the sake of the triglyph–metope sequence. It was the other way round.

5. CONCLUSION. Long before the Parthenon was built, the irrational ratios were being used as means to aesthetic ends, the mathematical instruments through which architects pursued the form of the ideal temple. Then, when temple building ceased to be the primary business of architecture, they were extended to every sort of design and became in effect the language of the art. When medieval architects took them over, they were so hallowed by the weight of precedent that any suggestion of dispensing with them would have seemed as unthinkable as using a language other than Latin for the liturgy.

There were three critical episodes in the life of this long tradition. When the principal focus of attention shifted from exterior to interior and the need for vaulted halls set a higher premium on the ability to construct arches of great span than on extensive colonnades, the ratios provided the mathematical framework within which the practical expertise of the 'mechanicians of Heron's school' was encapsulated. Structural theory was inextricably bound up with the geometry of shapes. That was the first great crisis faced by the intellectual resources of the architectural profession of the Greco-Roman world, and it rose to the occasion magnificently, as the monuments of Imperial Rome testify. The second came during the Middle Ages when architects, operating with what was still essentially the same set of ideas, took up the challenge to put a vault over a type of building that Roman and Early Christian experience had declared to be unvaultable, namely the basilican church. The result was Gothic. Again the revolution was effected without the method being questioned. There is no better vindication of the medieval conviction that the ratios were the timeless first principles of all architecture than the effortless transition to Gothic. As late as 1400 it was still possible for a French consultant at Milan, Jean Mignot (*d* 1410), to lecture the Milanese about the *scientia* of architecture as though it were something sacrosanct. What he meant by science on that occasion was not spelt out, but the rules of thumb of applied geometry are likely to have been part of it. By then, however, the third crisis was already looming, and this time the threat came from the mathematicians as well as the patrons of architecture. Scholastic mechanics were on an altogether different theoretical plane from the curiosity about machines exemplified by Vitruvius or Villard, and the long-term effect on the scientific pretensions of Gothic architecture can only have been humbling. As the prestige of the new mathematics grew, so the masons and their ratios must have seemed like Beckmesser defending the rules in Richard Wagner's *Mastersingers of Nuremberg.* In the end they had no answer.

BIBLIOGRAPHY

C. L. Stieglitz: *Von altdeutscher Baukunst* (Leipzig, 1820)

S. Boisserée: *Geschichte und Beschreibung des Doms von Köln* (Stuttgart, 1823, rev. Munich, 2/1842)

E.-E. Viollet-le-Duc: *Dictionnaire raisonné de l'architecture française du XIe au XVIe siècle* (Paris, 1854–68), vii, pp. 532–61

L. R. Shelby, ed. and trans.: *Gothic Design Techniques: The Fifteenth-century Design Booklets of Mathes Roriczer and Hanns Schmuttermayer* (Carbondale, IL, 1977)

Age of Chivalry: Art in Plantagenet England, 1200–1400 (exh. cat., ed. J. Alexander and P. Binski; London, RA, 1987), p. 406 [York Minster tracing floor]

P. Kidson: 'A Metrological Investigation', *J. Warb. & Court. Inst.*, liii (1990), pp. 71–97

T. Coke and P. Kidson: *Salisbury Cathedral: Perspectives on the Architectural History*, Royal Comm. Anc. & Hist. Mnmts & Constr. England (in preparation)

P. Kidson: *From Greek Temples to Gothic Cathedrals: Religious Architecture in the Classical and Medieval Periods* (in preparation)

PETER KIDSON

II. c. *1450*–c. *1800.*

1. Introduction. 2. The Vitruvian model. 3. 15th century: Alberti and the musical analogy. 3. 16th century: Codification and Palladio's method. 5. 17th and 18th centuries: revival and decline.

1. INTRODUCTION. Mathematical systems of proportion have been espoused by architects of many periods in the West. Renaissance architects based them on the model provided by the human figure (created by God in his own image and thus expressive of a higher order; *see* HUMAN PROPORTION) or on a standard module of their own selection, both recommended by Vitruvius, the only contemporary Classical authority directly available to them. From simple precedents more extensive patterns of proportionally related dimensions could be developed. Whatever the theoretical concepts, however, whether regulated by the overall application of idealized Platonic (regular geometric) figures, by limiting and co-ordinating the number of dimensional ratios in the building elements themselves or their aggregations, or by selecting numerical equivalents of musical consonances, they were generally overtly commensurable. Unlike the more esoteric practice-based applications of irrational ratios of Pythagorean origin used in medieval building, which to Neoplatonists must have smacked of the intellectually lowering effects *banausia* associated with manual work, Renaissance methods embraced an intellectually stimulating *theoria*, based on the manipulation of rational numbers and inductive techniques. The latter called for dimensional series with additive properties: that is to say, numerical progressions with as many terms as possible which, when combined (added), gave numbers that already appeared sequentially at higher levels in the series. Preferred dimensions derived in this way would produce designs whose overall proportions, as well as those of their constituent parts, were wholly co-ordinated, and, if Vitruvius was to be believed, harmonious.

The power of the mathematical system of proportionality seemed to lie in the integration of equal numerical ratios throughout the design of buildings. Ratios of the simplest kind:

$$1:2=7:14=23:46 \quad . \; . \; . \; . \; . \quad \frac{a}{b}=\frac{p}{q}=\frac{x}{y}$$

gave rectangles of equal proportion, random in size and without compatible additive properties. When made continuously proportional, however,

$$1:2 = 2:4 = 4:8 \quad . \; . \; . \; . \; . \; . \quad \frac{w}{x}=\frac{x}{y}=\frac{y}{z}$$

such ratios generated simple geometric series such as

$$\begin{array}{llllllll} 1 & 2 & 4 & 8 & 16 & 32 & \ldots\ldots & \rangle \\ 1 & x & x^2 & x^3 & x^4 & x^5 & \ldots\ldots & \rangle \end{array}$$

but gave few relevant additive terms—the latter only 1+1=2, 2+2=4 etc. The properties of a single progression were improved, however, by superimposing others of similar derivation upon it:

$$\begin{array}{llllllllll} 1 & 2 & 4 & 8 & 16 & 32 & \ldots\ldots\ldots & \rangle & & \\ & & 3 & 6 & 12 & 24 & 48 & \ldots\ldots & \rangle & \\ & & & & 9 & 18 & 36 & 72 & \ldots\ldots & \rangle \end{array}$$

to give many more additive terms, here including, for example

$$\begin{array}{lll} 1+2=3 & 2+\ 4=\ 6 & 4+\ 8=12 \text{ etc} \\ 1+3=4 & 2+\ 6=\ 8 & 4+12=16 \text{ etc} \\ 1+8=9 & 2+16=18 & 3+\ 6=\ 9 \text{ etc} \end{array}$$

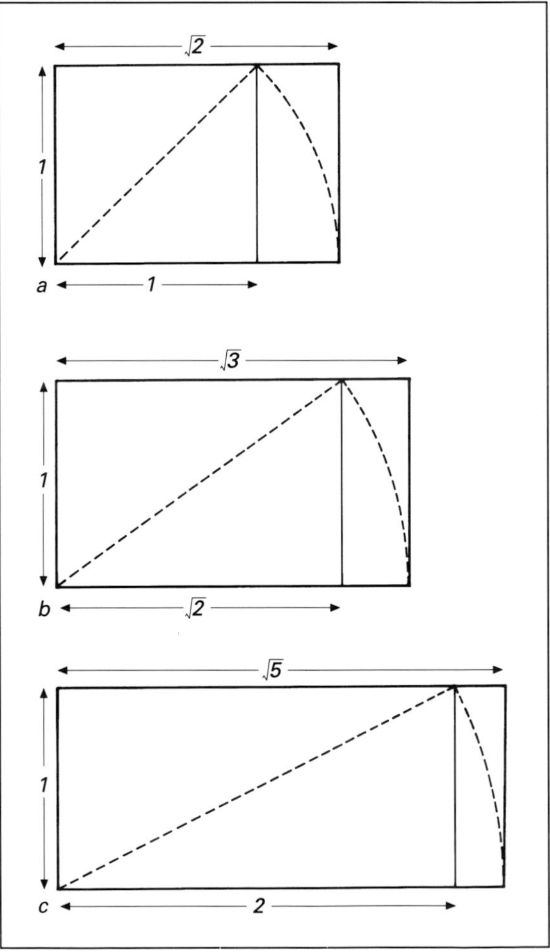

4. Proportional systems: (a) √2 rectangle; (b) √3 rectangle; (c) √5 rectangle

Systems of this kind could be applied, for example, where design was based on the square or double square: other commensurable values could be gained by superimposing further progressions, and could be extended to form double geometrical progressions such as those expressed in horizontal and vertical columns below:

$$\begin{array}{ccccc} 1 & x & x^2 & x^3 & \ldots\ldots \rangle \\ y & xy & x^2y & x^3y & \ldots\ldots \rangle \\ y^2 & xy^2 & x^2y^2 & x^3y^2 & \ldots\ldots \rangle \\ y^3 & xy^3 & x^2y^3 & x^3y^3 & \ldots\ldots \rangle \\ \vdots & \vdots & \vdots & & \vdots \\ \vee & \vee & \vee & & \vee \end{array}$$

Renaissance architects were not, however, ignorant of the irrational ratios. Even from Vitruvius they would have learnt the use of √2 dimensions relating the diagonal of a square to the length of its sides (see fig. 4a): in detailing the orders (*On Architecture*, IV.i.11); to double the area of a square, after Plato's *Meno* (IX.Intro.4 and 5); or as an acceptable length for one side of an atrium (VI.iii.3); and developed into a geometrical series,

$$1 \quad \sqrt{2} \quad 2 \quad 2\sqrt{2} \quad 4 \quad \ldots\ldots \rangle$$

√2 could provide ratios other than merely those related to the square itself: its additive terms include 1+√2 (the side of a square added to its diagonal, 2.414 ...), which was sufficiently widely used eventually to be given the single symbol, θ, and this too could be used to generate progressions related to the √2 series:

$$\begin{array}{ccccc} 1 & \theta & \theta^2 & \theta^3 & \ldots\ldots \rangle \\ \sqrt{2} & \sqrt{2}\theta & \sqrt{2}\theta^2 & \sqrt{2}\theta^3 & \ldots\ldots \rangle \\ 2\sqrt{2} & 2\sqrt{2}\theta & 2\sqrt{2}\theta^2 & 2\sqrt{2}\theta^3 & \ldots\ldots \rangle \\ \vdots & \vdots & \vdots & \vdots & \\ \vee & \vee & \vee & \vee & \end{array}$$

Thus many more additional proportional values were obtained. The other widely used incommensurable ratio was based on √5, the hypotenuse of the triangle formed by the adjacent sides and diagonal of the double square (4c), long used (e.g. Euclid: *Elements* II.xi) to generate the constant Θ, known since the 19th century as the GOLDEN SECTION:

$$\Phi = \frac{1 + \sqrt{5}}{2} = 1.618 \ldots$$

The progression 1, Θ, Θ²2, Θ²3 ... generated even more numerous useful additive terms, of which the most important, 1+Θ=Θ²2, could be combined with other series (e.g. as illustrated for the θ double progression above); this provided a high degree of flexibility in proportionally related dimensions. The √3 and 1+√3 ratios, which are related to the use of the equilateral triangle (4b) generate few additive terms and were less widely used.

Incommensurable series had found substitute approximations to facilitate practical application in the Middle Ages. The best known example is the Fibonacci series,

$$1, 1, 2, 3, 5, 8, 13, 21 \quad \ldots\ldots \rangle$$

in which each term is equal to the sum of the two preceding it, and though not a true geometric progression, approximates more and more closely to the golden section as it is extended. Many examples of division and aggregation of planar figures on the bases of the irrational ratios (geometrical method) and of the additive terms generated in related progressions (analytical method) have been prepared by 20th-century writers on proportion. Notable among them are Scholfield, upon whose work some of the above examples have been modelled, and Hambidge, some of whose examples are also reproduced by Scholfield (pp. 129–46).

2. THE VITRUVIAN MODEL. Although Vitruvius' treatise *On Architecture* (*see* VITRUVIUS, §2) was not printed until 1486, it had long been available in manuscript and was the principal source of architectural theory in the Renaissance. Paradoxically, Vitruvius was not a theorist, but a practical man, and for him the rules of proportion seem to have been concerned with building function and structure as much as, if not more than, aesthetics. Nevertheless, it was he who provided the Renaissance architects' authority for the use of proportions related to those of the human body (*see also* HUMAN PROPORTION). In the much-studied opening paragraphs of Chapter i, Book III, he asserted that the successful design of temples depended upon proportion (*proportio*), defined as 'a correspondence among the measures of the members of an entire work and of the whole to a certain part selected as standard'. Only through proportion could the desired symmetry (*symmetria*) be achieved. Without proportions and symmetries it would not be possible to attain to that 'precise relationship between members as is the case with those of a well-shaped man', and, by implication, to the desired harmony that lay in *eurythmia*. There followed the brief cursive listing of human proportions in terms of total height—the specification for 'Vitruvian man'.

Wittkower asserted, however, that it was because *On Architecture* 'contains no real theory of proportion' (p. 120) that Daniele Barbaro (*see* BARBARO, (1)) was constrained in his Italian translation of Vitruvius (Venice, 1556) to insert 'a circumstantial discourse on proportion', which concludes with 'compound ratios which he considers of the utmost importance'. Scholfield was in good company, therefore, when he proposed a similar process—using the evidence in the book itself—based on the view that Vitruvius intended the human figure as little more than a convenient scale—as 'a vivid diagram, so familiar that it does not need to be drawn' (p. 21). He went on to express the body proportions as described by Vitruvius as submultiples down to 1/10 of a man's height (M), to form a harmonic series which can be written:

$$\frac{M}{1} \quad \frac{M}{2} \quad \frac{M}{3} \quad \frac{M}{4} \quad \frac{M}{5} \quad \ldots\ldots \quad \frac{M}{10}$$

Of itself this does not constitute a system of proportion, of course, and would provide only a scale of preferred dimensions without additive properties. Scholfield then suggested that Vitruvius' subdivision of the face into three further parts (each 1/30 of the man's height) pointed the way to similar division of each term in the harmonic set, and thus generated a double geometric progression. He demonstrated its application in precisely this way by Vitruvius in his example of the Attic base (*On Architecture*, III.v.2). Such a flexible system of proportion could be developed into further double and triple progressions (*see* §1 above) with the necessary additive qualities to provide an adequate range of dimensions of related proportions to cover the principal parts of the most complex building.

Symmetry, on the other hand, as achieved through the proper use of the system of proportion, was defined by Vitruvius as 'a harmony between. . .small parts. . .[which] may be calculated from the thickness of a column, from a triglyph, or even from a module' (I.ii.4). This would make for internal consistency of appearance and order between constituent parts of the larger elements associated with the leading dimensions of the plan, section and elevation of the design as previously determined under the system of proportion.

It also made sense in terms of another of Vitruvius' desirable qualities, *commensus*, the Latin root of which suggests comparability of size, or, in this context, compatibility of scale within the whole proportional system. Scholfield (pp. 24–31) evolved a plausible (if less tenable) comprehensive system which included both symmetries and proportions, and was able also to relate his proposals logically to Vitruvius' apparently almost irrelevant paragraphs on metrology and perfect numbers (III.i.5–8). The former he treated as a system of measurement that would have been easily understood on Roman building sites, the latter as giving the essential choice of bases of numeration.

At best Vitruvius' method of presentation may be said to conform to the second part of his own definition of symmetry, i.e. 'calculated from the thickness of a column. . .or a module' (I, ii, 4) or indeed simply by relating leading dimensions by proportion to an adjacent feature or member (e.g. III.v.10–13). Intercolumniations are ostensibly anthropometric—unless the 2.25:1 spacing recommended for the preferred eustyle temple ('the most approved class. . .arranged with a view to convenience, beauty and strength', III.iii.6) is indeed an approximation for 1:√5 (2.236 . . .), as has been suggested (*see* §I, 4 above, and ORDERS, ARCHITECTURAL, §I, 2(i)(c)). Also, from the point of view of proportion, the recommendations for houses and other building types were established according to function, precedent and experience rather than theoretical precept.

Inscrutable as it was, *On Architecture* had a powerful influence throughout the Renaissance (and beyond) simply because of the vital part it played in establishing in the minds of Quattrocento architects that perfection—eurythmia, beauty, harmony, however it was expressed—could be achieved through the application of theory. Overt rules would govern the proportional dimensions of the parts of a building rather than artistic vision allied to experience. Even the misapprehension initiated as early as the middle of the 16th century by Jerome Cardan (Book XIII, p. 494), that Vitruvius' notes on acoustics for the better design of theatres provided a system of relating aural to visual harmony, persisted, and was principally responsible for the pursuit of the musical analogy by Renaissance architects.

3. 15TH CENTURY: ALBERTI AND THE MUSICAL ANALOGY. There were other 'straws in the wind' of burgeoning 15th-century humanism in Italy that fostered the development of analytical methods of determining proportion. Nicholas of Cusa (Cusanus; 1401–64), the German mathematician and mystic who held that without proportion there could be no form, and who stressed the relationships between number and the harmonic intervals in music, was writing in the 1440s when Alberti was preparing *De re aedificatoria*. At the same time the biographer of his friend and mentor Brunelleschi, Antonio di Tuccio Moretti, wrote after 1471 that Brunelleschi attempted to rediscover the musical proportions. Marsilio Ficino's translation of Plato was completed in 1482, also the year of the first printed version of Euclid in Latin; and the work of Boethius (*c.* AD 480–524) on arithmetic and music, developed from the Greek writings of Nikomachos of Gerasa (*fl c.* AD 100) on number and harmony, was published in 1492.

Though critical of his presentation, Alberti modelled his own Ten Books on those of Vitruvius (*see* ALBERTI, LEON BATTISTA, §II, 2), and dealt with proportionality through parallel though different parameters. For Alberti, it was what Leoni translated as the 'finishing' (*finitio*) that represented the 'mutual correspondence of those several lines by which the proportions are measured, . . . length, . . .breadth, and. . .height' (IX.v), which with number (*numerus*) and position or placement (*collocatio*) produced a mutual harmony (*concinnitas*) in architecture. Vitruvius was no Platonist, but the common ground was the inherent Neoplatonic certainty that beauty could be achieved objectively, and that the application of a theory of proportion was essential to the process.

Michel claimed a seminal role in this for Alberti, whose very definition of beauty was 'a harmony of all the parts. . ., fitted together with such proportion and connexion that nothing could be added, diminished or altered but for the worse' (VI.ii). More importantly perhaps, he followed Vitruvius in expressing proportions as submultiples of overall dimensions for whole buildings (e.g. VII.xiv) as well as for the orders and their constituent parts (e.g. VII.vii). This resulted in harmonic dimension series—in the latter case the geometric progression 1, 3, 9, 27, etc—significant in Plato's cosmology and thus to mid-century humanism. And Alberti was also well aware of the irrational ratios and their geometrical origins (IX.iv), but set the seal on humanist attitudes to proportionality in the late 15th century and 16th by relegating them to only a brief passing mention of their existence (IX.vi).

Alberti's crowning achievement in the theory of proportion, however, was his systematization for use in architecture of the harmonic musical intervals on the basis of spatial ratios, originally related to the physical length of open vibrating cords by Pythagoras, and handed down through Nikomachos and Boethius. The table below (after Scholfield) lists Alberti's 'musical consonances' (IX.v) alongside the harmonic ratios and their associated Latin terms:

Ratio	Latin terms	Musical interval
1:1		Unison
4:3	Sesquitertius	Fourth (*diatessaron*)
3:2	Sequialter	Fifth (*diapente*)
16:9		
2:1	Duplus	Octave (*diapason*)
9:4		
8:3		Eleventh (*diapason cum diatessaron*)
3:1	Triplus	Twelfth (*diapason cum diapente*)
4:1	Quadruplus	Fifteenth (*bisdiapason*)

The ratios established two-dimensional proportions generally intended as the first and third terms in groups of three numbers representing the ratios between length, height and breadth: each three-term progression was listed separately (IX.vi: abstracted below after Scholfield):

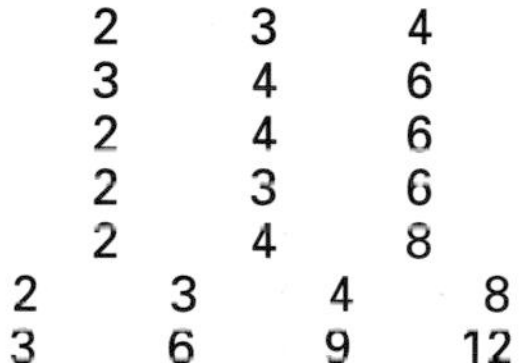

2 3 4
3 4 6
2 4 6
2 3 6
2 4 8
2 3 4 8
3 6 9 12

The inclusion of two rows of four instead of three numbers seems to have been aimed at providing alternative values for height (IX.vi). The ratio of any two of these values (or its equivalent) also appeared in the list of selected musical intervals: Alberti suggested that usually, though not necessarily always, the intermediate number would represent height—architects were to 'make use of [them]. . .in such manner as to be constantly and every way agreeable to Harmony'.

In describing Alberti's method of forming the number groups or progressions, Wittkower, who called it 'ratio generation' (pp. 100–103) used a development of the linear scale, presented by the Franciscan monk Francesco Giorgio (*b* 1460) in his book *De harmonia mundi* (Venice, 1525), and cited (pp. 90–94) its use by Giorgio in his *Memorandum for S Francesco della Vigna* (Venice, 1535), when Jacopo Sansovino's proportions for the church were in dispute. The latter was also quoted in full by Wittkower (pp. 136–7) as evidence of the Pythagorean and Platonic origin of the use of the musical analogy. The linear method of presenting complex proportions helped to clarify the relative positions of other significant features in the buildings to which they related. Giorgio used higher numbers (6, 12, 24, 48 etc) to avoid fractions, but as Scholfield has pointed out, the whole series of numbers come together with those given by Alberti to form the double geometric progression 1:2:4:8. . .3:6:12:24. . .etc. Alberti also gave instructions on how to provide the third dimension, where the ratio already selected represented the highest and lowest values of the three, by the use of arithmetic, geometric or harmonic means. In the examples he gave,

4 [6] 8 (arithmetic)
4 [6] 9 (geometric)
3 [4] 6 (harmonic)

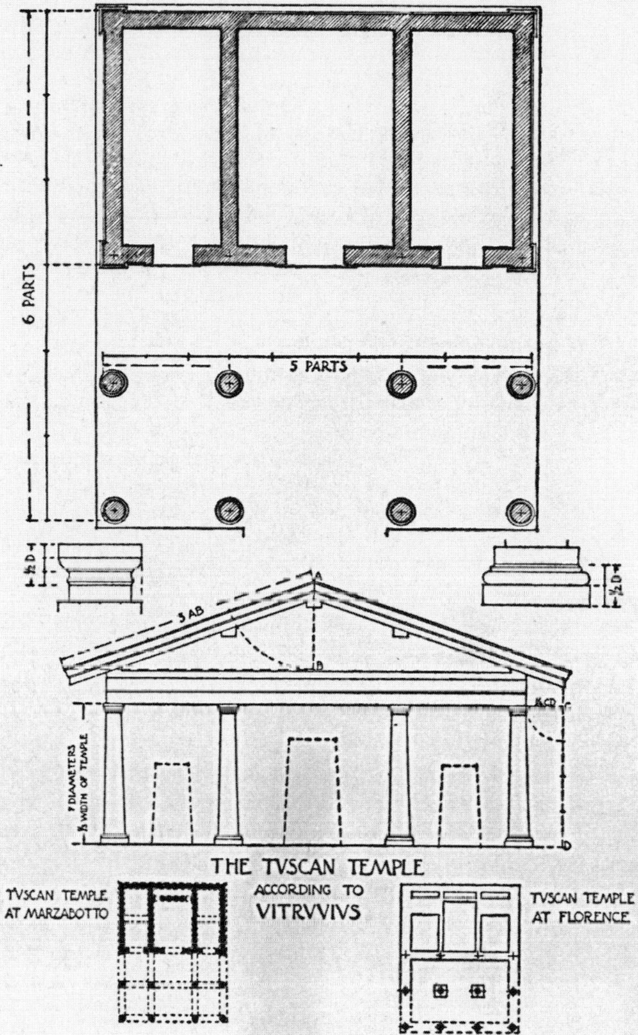

5. Proportions of the Etruscan temple according to Vitruvius in *On Architecture* (1st century BC); from the English translation by M. H. Morgan: *The Ten Books on Architecture* (Cambridge, MA, 1914), p. 121

the means are also consistent with the musical intervals; and in the groups of three numbers giving Alberti's recommended proportions for length, breadth and height (abstracted above and derived by the 'ratio generation' method), the intermediate number in each case is also one of the three recommended means.

It is clear how Alberti's concern with systematic commensurable proportionality related, for example, to the well-documented 1:1 overall proportion of the elevations of his designs in Mantua for S Sebastiano (begun 1460) and S Andrea (begun 1472), both designed after *De re aedificatoria* was completed in mid-century; it is less clear, however, how they related to the leading internal proportions, with the possible exception of the internal elevational proportion of the chapels in S Andrea of 3:4, to which Wittkower drew attention (p. 47). Although Alberti may have intended, however, to revive the form of the Etruscan temple (Wittkower, p. 47, n. 4), the proportions of the nave of S Andrea bear no resemblance to those referred to either by Vitruvius (IV.vii.1; see fig. 5) or in his own treatise (VII.iv; see fig. 6).

Writings by Filarete (*Trattato di architettura*, 1461–4) and Francesco di Giorgio Martini (*Architettura civile e militare*, after 1480), both near in date to Alberti's *De re aedificatoria*, failed to find publication during the Renaissance. Both owe debts to Alberti, but neither moved far away from the anthropomorphism of Vitruvius. The former, writing in the vernacular and in dialogue form, used the human head as his module for the orders and even as a superimposed model for the proportions of an entablature; the latter—who was also one of the early translators of Vitruvius—literally derived the proportions of the orders from the human body and is thought to have inspired Diego de Sagredo's *Medidas de Romano* (Toledo, 1526), which was wholly concerned with architectural proportion and the orders on Vitruvian lines, and circulated widely in 16th-century Spain. *De divina proportione* (Venice, 1509), by the Franciscan monk and mathematician Luca Pacioli, brought together a number of matters of contemporary interest to architects. He wrote of the $\sqrt{5}$ ratios, and his title is said to be responsible for one of the names given to the golden section; his instructions on architectural proportions remained conventionally Vitruvian (*see also* §I, 2 above).

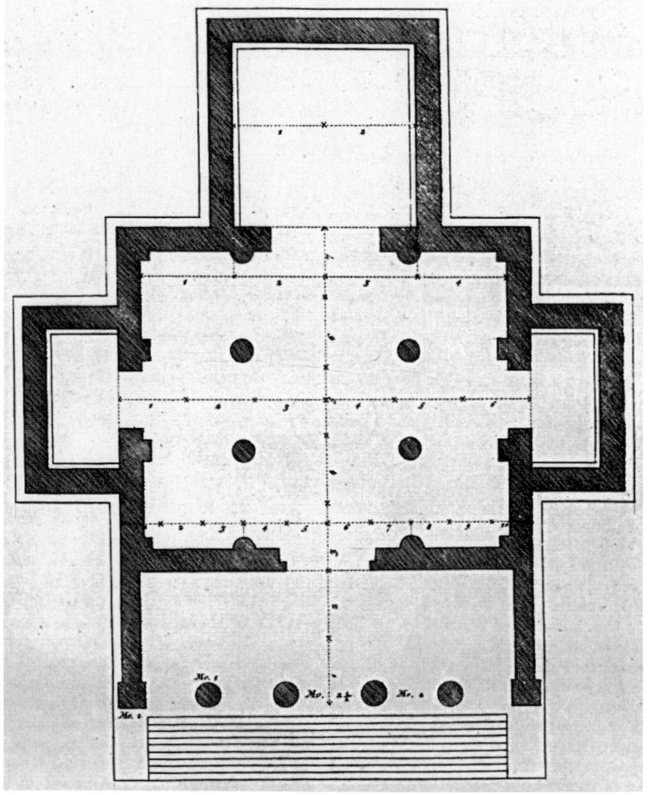

6. Proportions of the Etruscan temple according to Leon Battista Alberti in *De re aedificatoria* (Florence, 1485); from the English translation by J. Leoni: *The Ten Books of Architecture* (London, 1726), pl. 22

4. 16TH CENTURY: CODIFICATION AND PALLADIO'S METHOD. The use of the human figure in systems of proportion, whether by the harmonic method (division of large measures) or by the arithmetic (modular) method (aggregation of small measures), retained its fascination well into the 16th and even the 17th century: Pomponius Gauricus (*De scultura*, 1504) preferred harmonic division of the figure, Albrecht Dürer tried both arithmetic and harmonic methods in an empirical study (*De symmetria . . .*, Nuremberg, 1532). In his translation of Vitruvius, Daniele Barbaro used Jerome Cardan's Vitruvian figure with the head one tenth of overall height: Cardan divided the whole into 180 equal parts, and Barbaro's proportional system consisted of incomplete geometric progressions, also given in terms of the submultiples of total height:

$$(1)\ \frac{1}{180} \quad (2)\ \frac{1}{90} \quad (4)\ \frac{1}{45}$$
$$(6)\ \frac{1}{30} \quad (12)\ \frac{1}{15}$$
$$(18)\ \frac{1}{10} \quad (36)\ \frac{1}{5}$$

Others such as Leonardo and Gauricus had divided the face into nine parts and introduced the significant 1, 3, 9, 27 progression.

In the *Regole generali di architettura* (Venice, 1537), Sebastiano Serlio, the first of the great 16th-century codifiers, drew attention to Vitruvius' shortcomings but insisted on his method being followed wherever possible. He espoused the harmonic system and in his descriptions of the orders produced what must have seemed curiously confusing instructions for division (as opposed to multiplication or addition of parts). Serlio's writings formed the basis of Hans Blum's *Säulenbuch* (Zurich, 1550), widely popular in Germany where it greatly improved the accessibility of Renaissance theory by tabulating the related proportions as well as illustrating the orders; it was translated into Dutch, French and English. A little later John Shute also followed Serlio in his *First and Chief Groundes of Architecture* (London, 1563); like Francesco di Giorgio Martini, Shute took the derivation of proportion for the orders directly from the human body. The first French book on the orders, *Reigle générale d'architecture des cinque manières de colonnes* (Paris, 1564) by Jean Bullant, which attempted to reconcile the Vitruvian approach to proportion with his own measurements of the Antique, owes little to Serlio, but was reprinted well into the 17th century. Jacopo Vignola's *Regola delli cinque ordini d'architettura* (Rome, 1562) was a set of illustrations with instructions for a range of orders of standard size. Their simplicity ensured widespread popularity on a worldwide basis.

The gradual change to arithmetic methods from the harmonic, which characterized the many examplars and parallels of the orders published in the 16th and 17th centuries (*see also* ORDERS, ARCHITECTURAL, §I, 2(iii)) has been attributed to the difficulties experienced in trying to reconcile the Vitruvian proportional system with the dimensions of the Classical monuments. The need to re-establish the authority of the Vitruvian system and with it the Quattrocento ideal of objectively attainable harmony coincided with the appeal to authority of the Counter-Reformation. It was Palladio (*see* PALLADIO, ANDREA, §I, 2) who answered that appeal. His canonical *I quattro libri dell'architettura* (Venice, 1570), at once a theoretical manual and exemplar of application, assumed the authoritative stamp of Vitruvius while introducing 'measures and proportions' taken directly from the Antique (I.xii.11). Before the end of Book I he listed the simplest of recommendations on how to achieve 'the most beautiful and proportionable manners of rooms. . .round (tho' but seldom) or square, or their length will be the diagonal line of the square, or of a square and a third, or of one square and a half, of one square and two thirds, or of two squares' (I.xxi.27; Isaac Ware's trans., 1738). Instructions were given on the use of mean values between plan dimensions to determine the heights of rectangular vaulted rooms: the height of rooms with flat ceilings 'must be equal to their breadth' (I.xiii.28–9). Thus, square and circle apart, he used five prescriptive and to all intents and purposes commensurable ratios: √2:1, 4:3, 3:2, 5:3 and 2:1, all to be found in Vitruvius. To Vitruvius also he admitted conformity in the measures used for the orders, but he divided his column-diameter modules into 60 minutes as a standard measure (I.xiii.13).

At the theoretical level, therefore, only the restricted use of mean values seemed to owe anything to Alberti. Palladio's *I quattro libri*, however, also contained numerous dimensioned examples of his own buildings, as well as measured drawings of antiquities. Also, it was in the dimensioned illustrations of his own buildings, not the didactic text, that the rigorous and often complex applications of proportionality demonstrated his indebtedness to Albertian theory. Palladio put into his designs a theoretical sophistication he did not try (or wish) to justify theoretically or codify. The interlocking musically consonant ratios of the Book II villas (Godi, Malcontenta, Emo, Thiene, Pisano, Sarego, etc) have been explored in some detail by Wittkower and aptly named 'Palladio's "fugal" System of Proportion' (p. 110). Each pair of room dimensions conforms to musical intervals, and together they form related geometrical progressions. A selection of the latter has been set alongside some of the drawings by Scholfield (pp. 64–77). His incomplete triple progression for the Villa Sarego, Pedemonte, is given here as an example, and may be related to fig. 7:

4	8		16		
		12		24	
	9		18		
				27	
	10		20		40
		15			

The Villa Sarego is also one of the examples in which Wittkower has shown (p. 117) that dimensional ratios reduced to musical intervals such as 5:6 (minor third) and 3:5 (major sixth), unknown to Alberti, were used by Palladio, who was aware of 16th-century developments in musical theory in northern Italy.

A remarkable contrast with Palladio's oeuvre is provided by his contemporary Philibert de L'Orme, also a successful practising architect, whose book *Le Premier Tome de l'architecture* predated *I quattro libri* by three years. He separated mathematics and geometry (Books III and IV) but suggested no direct applications, and while he, too, gave his own measurements of the antiquities and relied on Vitruvius (and Serlio) for his treatment of the orders (Books V–VII), he prescribed no proportions. He held proportion to be God-given and comprehensible only with His inspiration. Vincenzo Scamozzi's monumental treatise, *Dell'idea dell'architettura universale* (Venice, 1615), the last of the great 16th-century codifications, took up the concept of the *idea* translated into artefact by *disegno* from Giovanni Paolo Lomazzo and Federico Zuccaro, whose Mannerist aesthetics had seemed to threaten Neo-platonic rationalism some 25 years earlier when the treatise was begun. Though methodologically different, Scamozzi followed Serlio in his treatment of proportion but gave parallel scales for drawing the five orders. Like Palladio, however, he published many of his own works as exemplars of style rather than applications of a system.

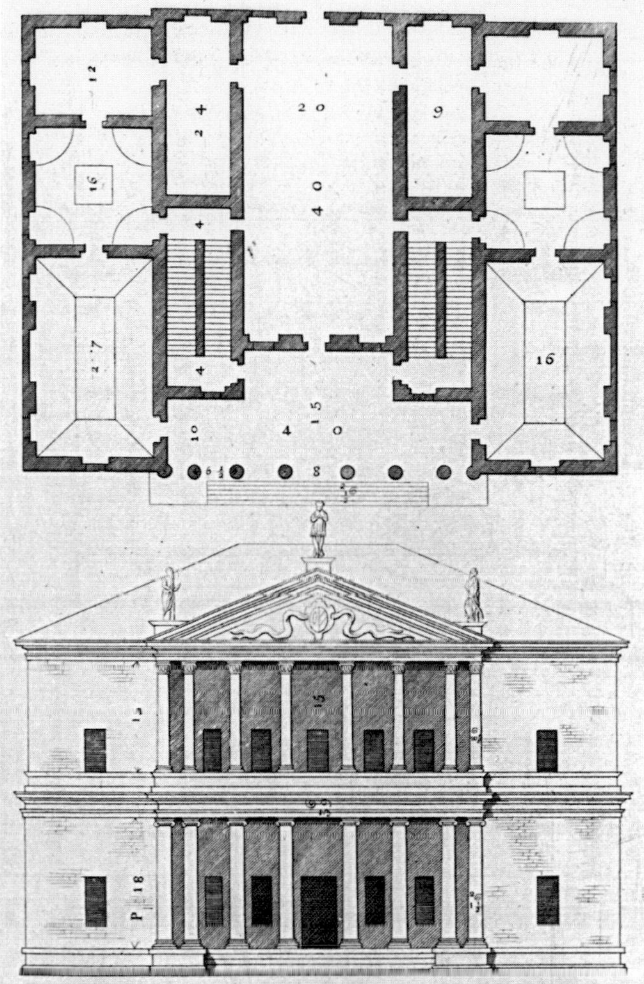

7. Proportional design by Andrea Palladio for the Villa Sarego, Pedemonte, from *I quattro libri dell'architettura* (Venice, 1570); from the English translation by Isaac Ware (London, 1738), pl. L(50)

5. 17TH AND 18TH CENTURIES: REVIVAL AND DECLINE. The immediate influences of Palladio and Scamozzi

were evident in the simple harmonic proportions used by Inigo Jones in London (e.g. the two-storey cube of the hall of the Queen's House, Greenwich, 1616–38, and the 2:1 proportions of the plan of St Paul's, Covent Garden, 1630–31) and a little later in Holland by Jacob van Campen and others.

Although the development of an objective theory of proportion atrophied during the Baroque period in Italy, the Classical (Vitruvian) concept of the human basis of architectural form remained current and spread outside Italy through the numerous books on the orders, usually applied through the simple column-shaft module of 60 minutes favoured by Palladio. Guarino Guarini, however, prefigured the coming changes by asserting a subjective attitude to proportion in his *Architettura civile* (Turin, 1737).

In France, on the other hand, there was an active renewal of interest in and a debate on the validity of the musical analogy in architectural proportion. In his *Cours d'architecture* (Paris, 1675–83) François Blondel, director of Jean-Baptiste Colbert's newly established Académie Royale d'Architecture (1671), based his recommendations on proportion on Alberti, deduced simple commensurable progressions and cited Palladio's buildings.

Claude Perrault, whose translation of Vitruvius (Paris, 1673; commissioned by Colbert in 1664) was used in the Académie, published his *Ordonnance des cinq espèces de colonnes* in 1683 and took issue with the concept of equating aural with visual harmony. He went much further, however, and denied the aesthetic value of proportion or that good proportion was inherent in nature. He held that acceptability of proportion was established by custom, and that preferences would change with taste. The position of the contemporary Sir Christopher Wren lay between these extremes and was nearer to the Neoplatonists (*Parentalia*, Tracts I–IV): he placed proportion amongst the attributes of natural beauty, which arose from geometry, in contrast with customary beauty which arose from familiarity and might apply to objects not intrinsically beautiful.

It was not until he was 92 that Charles-Etienne Briseux, somehow converted from excesses of Rococo in earlier manifestations, took up the cudgels of Classicism against Perrault in his *Traité* (published in 1752): beauty was determined mainly by proportion, for which no ideal system was specified, although he cited Palladio's musical consonances, Scamozzi and the elder Blondel. Unlikely support came a few years later from Marc-Antoine Laugier, whose lay *Observations sur l'architecture* (The Hague, 1765) posited a new architecture, the proportion of which would be philosophically determined according to the buildings' *caractère*.

Neither here nor in the Vitruvian tradition of 18th-century Italy, however, was there any significant development of proportional theory. The harmonic system of proportion continued in use by architects in parts of the Veneto, as in the work of the Neo-classicist Francesco Maria Preti in Treviso. It is, however, indicative of rapidly changing attitudes that in the early 1760s Preti was constrained to take issue with Tommaso Temanza, a biographer of Palladio, to defend the Renaissance ideal of universal harmony through an objective fixed rule of proportion based on the simple harmonic ratios. Temanza, however, although he supported overall commensurability, asserted the subjective view that the observer's perception (perspective) should take primacy over the orthogonal application of harmonic ratios, a position taken also by Francesco Milizia, whose *Principi* (1781) and other works were translated into the principal European languages before the end of the century. Also, a year or two later the prominence of proportion as a factor in design had so far diminished that in a major study of Palladio (1776–83) Ottavio Bertotti Scamozzi could believe he had rediscovered the musical analogy in Palladio's drawings, as Robert Morris had done in England *c.* 40 years earlier.

Paradoxically, in Britain the Palladian revival merged into 18th-century classicism and was accompanied by the eclipse of Renaissance theory, and thus of whatever status proportionality may have enjoyed as an objective determinant of beauty. In the mid-18th century William Hogarth deplored any suggestion of a mathematical base to beauty, and Henry Home, Lord Kames, denied the validity of the musical analogy, referred to the changing visual effects of perspective upon a moving observer, and settled for a wholly subjective judgement of proportionality. Towards the end of the century Archibald Alison related proportion to function and its aesthetic effects to subjective association. Interestingly, Richard Payne Knight, the theoretician of the Picturesque movement, supported the latter view and in a sense reflects the ambivalent attitude to proportional systems of architects such as Sir William Chambers, who believed that perspective concealed actual proportions, and Robert Adam (*see* ADAM (i), (3)), whose theory, enshrined in the phrase 'variety of movement' was concerned with 'the picturesque of the composition' (Adam, i, p. 46) rather than with ideals of Classical architecture and concepts of proportionality (see, e.g., Watkin, pp. 323–5). It was perhaps Sir John Soane, however, who prefigured the new and open attitudes to proportion of the ensuing centuries: architecture 'has no fixed proportion', but architects would 'apply harmony and justice of relative proportion. . .[to achieve] correlation of the parts with the whole, and of the whole with each part' (see Bolton, p. 753).

BIBLIOGRAPHY

EARLY SOURCES

Vitruvius: *On Architecture* (1st century BC); Eng. trans. by M. H. Morgan as *The Ten Books on Architecture* (Cambridge, MA, 1914/*R* New York, 1960)

Nikomachos of Gerasa: *Introductio arithmetica* (*c.* AD 100); Eng. trans. by M. I. d'Ooge as *Introduction to Arithmetic* (New York, 1926)

L. B. Alberti: *De re aedificatoria* (Florence, 1485); Eng. trans. by J. Leoni as *The Ten Books of Architecture* (London, 1726/*R* New York, 1986)

L. Pacioli: *De divina proportione* (Venice, 1509)

S. Serlio: *Regole generali di architettura sopra le cinque maniere degli edifici* (Venice, 1537); Eng. trans. by S. Peake as *The Five Books of Architecture* (London, 1611)

J. Cardan: *De subtilitate* (Lyons, 1559)

J. B. da Vignola: *Regola degli cinque ordini d'architettura* (Rome, 1562)

P. de L'Orme: *Le Premier Tome de l'architecture* (Paris, 1567)

A. Palladio: *I quattro libri dell'architettura* (Venice, 1570); Eng. trans. by Isaac Ware as *The Four Books of Architecture* (London, 1738)

V. Scamozzi: *Dell'idea dell'architettura universale* (Venice, 1615)

C. Perrault: *Les Dix Livres d'architecture de Vitruve corrigés et traduits nouvellement en français* (Paris, 1673)
F. Blondel: *Cours d'architecture enseigné dans l'Académie royale d'architecture* (Paris, 1675–83)
C. Perrault: *Ordonnance des cinq espèces de colonnes selon la méthode des anciens* (Paris, 1683)
R. Morris: *Lectures in Architecture* (London, 1734–6)
C. Wren: *Parentalia: Or, Memoirs of the Family of the Wren* (London, 1750)
C.-E. Briseux: *Traité du beau essentiel dans les arts appliqué particulièrement à l'architecture* (Paris, 1752)
W. Hogarth: *Analysis of Beauty* (London, 1753)
H. Home: *Elements of Criticism* (Edinburgh, 1762)
R. Adam and J. Adam: *The Works of Architecture*, 3 vols (London, 1773–1822)
O. B. Scamozzi: *Le fabbriche e i disegni di Andrea Palladio*, 4 vols (Vicenza, 1776–83)
F. Milizia: *Principi di architettura civile*, 3 vols (Bassano, 1781)
A. Alison: *Essays on the Nature and Principles of Taste* (Edinburgh, 1790)
R. P. Knight: *Analytical Inquiry into the Principles of Taste* (London, 1805)
A. T. Bolton, ed.: *Lectures on Architecture by Sir John Soane* (London, 1929)

MODERN WORKS

E. Panofsky: 'Die Entwicklung der Proportionslehre als Abbild der Stilentwicklung', *Mhft. Kstwiss.*, xiv (1921), pp. 188–219; Eng. trans. as 'The History of the Theory of Human Proportions as a Reflection of the History of Styles', *Meaning in the Visual Arts: Papers in and on Art History* (Garden City, NY, 1957), pp. 55–107
P. H. Michel: *La Pensée de L. B. Alberti* (Paris, 1930), pp. 331–41
M. Ghyka: *Geometrical Composition and Design* (London, 1952)
R. Wittkower: *Architectural Principles in the Age of Humanism* (London, 1952)
M. Borissavlievitch: *The Golden Number and the Scientific Aesthetics of Architecture* (London, 1958)
P. H. Scholfield: *The Theory of Proportion in Architecture* (London, 1958)
K. Freckmann: *Proportionen in Architektur* (Munich, 1965)
F. Borsi: *Per una storia della teoria delle proporzioni* (Florence, 1967)
A. M. Finoli and L. Grassi, eds: *Antonio Averlino detto il Filarete: Trattato di architettura*, 2 vols (Milan, 1972)
F. Borsi: *Leon Battista Alberti* (Milan, 1975); Eng. trans. by R. G. Campanini (Oxford, 1977)
G. Jouven: *L'Architecture cachée: Tracés harmoniques* (Paris, 1979)
G. Doezi: *The Power of Limits: Proportional Harmonics in Nature, Art and Architecture* (London, 1981)
H.-W. Kruft: (Munich, 1985); Eng. trans. by R. Taylor, E. Callander and A. Wood as *A History of Architectural Theory from Vitruvius to the Present* (London, 1994)
D. Watkin: *A History of Western Architecture* (London, 1986)

JOHN MUSGROVE

III. c. 1800 and after.

1. THE 19TH CENTURY. There was a range of new approaches to proportion in this period. One of these is exemplified by the work of Jean-Nicolas-Louis Durand, the most influential of the European architectural theorists of the early 19th century. While he inherited much from the classical tradition, he modified it very substantially. His numerous projects, dating from 1779 onwards, for a wide range of building types, reveal the influence of his master Etienne-Louis Boullée and of Claude-Nicolas Ledoux in their large scale and bold simplifications. Durand departed from them in his greater concern for the functional requirements of specific architectural programmes and in his avoidance of the rhetorical symbolism exemplified by Ledoux's '*architecture parlante*'. Durand's strictly axial plans are based on a square module, with frequent use of circles and semicircles, and they create a repetitive pattern of units. This contrasts markedly with Palladio's development of the Vitruvian tradition, in which plans comprise a range of ratios (e.g. 2:3, 3:5, 1:2) organized hierarchically. While a Palladian elevation displays varied elements, each of which is significant in its proportional relationship to the whole, Durand followed Boullée in emphasizing such dominant features as colonnades, undecorated domes and large areas of plain wall surface, to which all details are subservient. This 'rationalization' is also apparent in his attitude to and use of the orders; in his most important theoretical work, the *Précis*, he reduced them to two only, Doric and Corinthian. He was accordingly little concerned with the complex rules of Palladio and his followers for the correct proportions of the orders. For Durand proportion became a matter of the employment of simple formulae, exemplified by his use of squared paper for drawing plans and his aim to develop a virtually 'styleless' architecture. Such beliefs and practices, the basis of his teaching at the Ecole Polytechnique in Paris, were continued in the methods of the Ecole des Beaux-Arts throughout the century.

A similar proportional system was used in one of the masterpieces of Neo-classical architecture, Karl Friedrich Schinkel's Altes Museum in Berlin (1823–30; *see* GERMANY, fig. 9), the great columnar portico, domed central rotunda and severe axiality of which echo Durand's projects for large public buildings. However, for Schinkel the example of Greek architecture, especially in the proportioning of the Ionic order of the portico, was far more important than for Durand, and in the plan there is a more subtle use of varied relationships, notably the 2:3 ratio used in the portico, which contrasts with Durand's mechanical square grids. Many of the buildings and projects of this phase of Neo-classical architecture can be considered, either precisely or more loosely, as Greek Revival in style. Schinkel's belief in the intrinsic superiority of Greek to Roman architecture had been held by many architects since the 1760s; far more was learnt of Greek systems of proportion following the publication of James Stuart and Nicholas Revett's *Antiquities of Athens* in 1762. Serious archaeological research into Greek architecture continued through much of the 19th century, leading to increased awareness of Greek principles of optical correction and entasis, and deviations from simple arithmetical ratios. While some theorists, notably Joseph Gwilt (1784–1863) in England, echoed Durand in their interpretation of Greek architecture in terms of modular units, there was a growing belief that the Greeks had employed geometrical systems as well as arithmetical ones based on whole numbers.

The growth of the Gothic Revival led to intensified interest in geometric proportions. Such concerns with geometry and the incommensurable were clarified by Viollet-le-Duc, who based his analysis of Gothic architecture on various kinds of triangle that generate further geometrical figures. In particular, he considered the equilateral triangle to be the basis of all structure. Viollet-le-Duc's remarks in the *Entretiens* on the laws of growth and structure were aligned to a belief that it was Gothic architecture above all that conformed to such principles. His theory of architecture was thus, like Durand's, 'rationalist' by intention, but giving primacy to structure rather than to planning. While some Gothic Revival architects in England, for example J. L. PEARSON, emulated Viollet-le-Duc's concern for the proportional and geometric logic of Gothic structures, others took the lead from Ruskin (who believed that architects should be guided by 'feeling and experience') in considering rules of proportion unnecessary.

2. THE 20TH CENTURY. The 'functional' basis of much 19th-century thinking on architecture and Ruskin's objections to proportional rules found support in the writings of the English architect and craftsman W. R. Lethaby. Lethaby stressed the need for 'fitness for purpose', and wrote in 1915 of the 'pretentious nonsense about proportion, style and the grand manner', a clear attack on academic training and Beaux-Arts principles, which were gaining ground in Britain at that time. Edwin Lutyens was outstanding among those who upheld such traditions, and showed a particular interest in devising subtle and complex systems of proportion. In total contrast to the common-sense functionalism that Lethaby represented after 1915, Lutyens took up what he called the 'high game' of Palladio in his country houses after about 1908, and he based much of his later work of the √2 rectangle, which relates to the square and the octagon and their use in expanding sequences. In the Cenotaph (1919–20) in Whitehall, London, he based the entasis on that of the Parthenon, and designed the horizontals as curves of circles, the centres of which are 900 feet (274.32 m) below the ground. Lutyens's memorial to the *Missing of the Somme* (1927–32; *see* LUTYENS, EDWIN, fig. 4) at Thiepval, France, has a hierarchy of arches in the ratio of 2.5:1, and his design (1929–41; only crypt executed) for Liverpool Roman Catholic Cathedral further developed interlocking proportional ratios.

In the first half of the 20th century systematic approaches to proportion were employed by modernist architects, notably by Frank Lloyd Wright, Mies van der Rohe and Le Corbusier, no less than by traditionalists. Wright, in such early works as the Martin House (1904), Buffalo, developed the Beaux-Arts concern with axiality while introducing calculated asymmetries into basically symmetrical plans. Much later, in his Ralph Jester House project (1938), he based the plan on an expanding sequence of circles with radii of 2, 4, 8, 12, 20 and 32 feet. The plan of Mies van der Rohe's Farnsworth House (1945–50; *see* MIES VAN DER ROHE, LUDWIG, fig. 3) at Plano, IL, retains, like all his later work, the disciplined rectilinearity of his canonic German (or Barcelona) Pavilion (1929; destr.; reconstructed 1985; *see* MIES VAN DER ROHE, LUDWIG, fig. 1) at Montjuïc, Barcelona. The Farnsworth House is based on a modular unit of 24×33 ins, the size of a paving tile, and all elements within the house are multiples of those two dimensions. Architectural coherence was thus achieved both by Wright and by Mies through the repetition of particular ratios. Perhaps the most widely admired of Mies's American buildings, Crown Hall (1952–6) of the Illinois Institute of Technology, has clear classical implications while employing a modernist vocabulary and structural system; it is a kind of minimal steel and glass 'temple' (*see* MIES VAN DER ROHE, LUDWIG, fig. 2).

In his early writings, including *Vers une architecture*, Le Corbusier revealed a particular interest in 'regulating lines'. In late 19th-century books by Auguste Choisy and Heinrich Wölfflin, diagonal lines are superimposed on façades of classical buildings, revealing the repetition of rectangles of the same proportions but of different sizes, and the 'place of the right angle' that determines these diagonals. Thus variety of area is shown to combine with unity of proportions. Le Corbusier used regulating lines in the design of the façades of early houses, for example the Villa Stein–de-Monzie (1926–7) at Garches, Paris, where the overall dimensions of the north façade form a golden section rectangle, and numerous smaller elements are of the same proportion (*see* LE CORBUSIER, fig. 2). The façade is further subdivided horizontally creating a 2:1:2:1:2 rhythm, and subtle asymmetries are introduced into the fundamentally symmetrical ordering. Thus the façade combines geometric with arithmetical ratios. Le Corbusier's early houses have been compared with the villas of Palladio; they share the concern for order and system, but in contrast to Palladio, Le Corbusier aimed for the unexpected, the considered contradiction or inversion of traditional formal schemata.

Le Corbusier's Modulor, devised in 1946, is the most frequently discussed of 20th-century proportional systems (see fig. 8). It is based on the height of a man 6 ft (1.83 m) tall, whose solar plexus is 1.13 m above the ground; with arm raised, his total height to fingertips is 2.26 m. These measurements provide the basis for two Fibonacci sequences (i.e. sequences in which each number is the sum of the two numbers immediately preceding it), the 'red series' (...27, 43, 70, 113, 183 cm...) and the 'blue series' (...86, 140, 226 cm...); the blue series measurements double the dimensions on the red scale. Points on the blue scale also correspond to a scale given in inches thus linking the metric system to that of feet and inches. All the measurements of a building could be determined from the

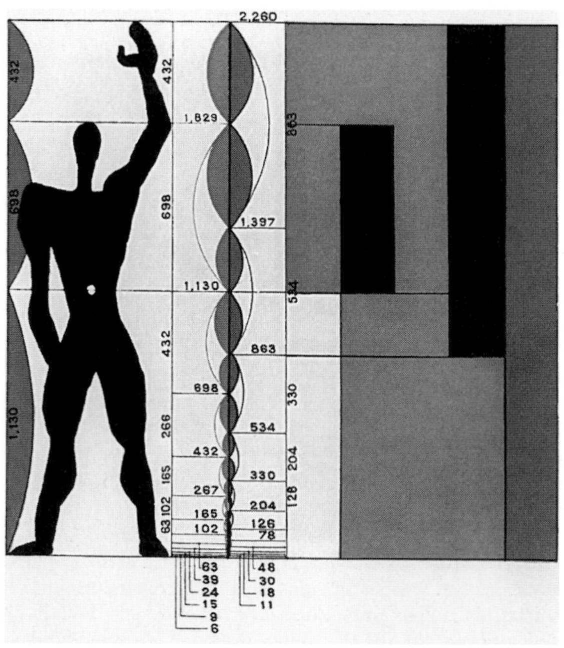

8. Proportional system known as the Modulor, devised by Le Corbusier in 1946

red and blue series, and an explicit reference to human scale was maintained throughout.

Le Corbusier devised the Modulor as he felt that both the traditional means of measurement by feet and inches and the modern metric system were inadequate as a basis for a proportional method, the former being clumsy and difficult to calculate, while the latter was abstract and devoid of any specific relationship to the body. Le Corbusier believed that the golden section and the related Fibonacci sequence could provide the framework for a system that ensured flexibility and variety and was linked to human scale. He also criticized Beaux-Arts formalism and asserted the dynamic quality of the Modulor, emphasizing the generative capacity of the golden rectangle (whereby a square added to a golden section rectangle produces a further rectangle of the same proportions, thus an expanding series of similarly proportioned rectangles can be readily created). This capability for progressive expansion can be contrasted with the more static rectilinearity of the proportions of buildings by Le Corbusier's one-time master Auguste Perret, who united reinforced concrete construction with a severe 'stripped classicism'.

Le Corbusier used the Modulor systematically in his subsequent work, for example in the Unité d'Habitation block (1945–52) in Marseille, where all dimensions of rooms, windows, doors, fitted furniture, etc, as well as the overall dimensions of the entire building, are based either on the red or the blue scale or on the two scales used in combination. Le Corbusier was convinced of the ergonomic, practical and aesthetic advantages of such a system. It is a measure of the Modulor's flexibility that Le Corbusier used it not only in the Marseille block and later 'Unités' (e.g. *see* LE CORBUSIER, fig. 4) but also in the 'anti-rational' chapel (1950–55) at Ronchamp (*see* LE CORBUSIER, fig. 6). In spite of its wide publicity, it appears to have had few adherents since Le Corbusier's death in 1965. Nevertheless its creation led to the emphasis on 'modular coordination' in architecture and design after 1950, for example in the standardization of mass-produced building components, and to a more thoroughgoing development of ergonomics. The primary concerns of such research were thus practical, aimed at simplifying and claryifying processes of specification and manufacture, and tended to promote a language of design essentially rectilinear, spare and 'universal', as did the work of those who followed the principles of Mies van der Rohe. Alison and Peter Smithson's school (1950–54) at Hunstanton, Norfolk, a landmark in the development of New Brutalism owing to its frank statement of structure and exposure of services, has an equally clearcut formalism and axiality, indebted both to Mies and to the publication in 1949 of Rudolf Wittkower's *Architectural Principles in the Age of Humanism.* In contrast to the rectilinear aesthetic that pervaded so much modern architecture are the geodesic dome structures originally devised by R. Buckminster Fuller, geometric rather than arithmetical in their design systems, and based, like Viollet-le-Duc's interpretation of Gothic, on the equilateral triangle (for illustration *see* GEODESIC DOME). A renewed interest in the geometry of Gothic and Islamic buildings was also revealed in the writings of architectural theorists, including Keith Critchlow (*b* 1933) in England.

The values of modernism were increasingly questioned and criticized after *c*. 1970. Subsequent architecture was characterized by pluralism; multiple contrasting design ideologies were current, and 'Post-modern classicism' was dominant. This produced on the one hand a revival of concern for Palladian proportional theory and attention to the detailing of the orders, as in the work of Quinlan Terry in England, and numerous revivals of Beaux-Arts axial planning, for example in the schemes of Rob and Leon Krier for Berlin and elsewhere. On the other hand there have been wilful and sometimes bizarre revisions or parodies of classical language. The work of the Spanish architect Ricardo Bofill in France provides a striking instance. While the plan of his Antigone complex (1979–83) at Montpellier combines the golden section with the square and the circle, the buildings themselves show a consummate disregard for proportional 'sense', with their overscaled giant orders and pseudo-Mannerist features. Similar characteristics are to be found in his Les Echelles du Baroque housing scheme (1979–85), Paris, and in the Les Espaces d'Abraxas scheme (1978–83; for illustration *see* BOFILL, RICARDO). This kind of assertiveness and rhetoric, combined also with coarse precast concrete detailing, are such as to make Giulio Romano's departures from classical orthodoxy appear as models of subtlety and discretion. In view of the essentially fluid and eclectic state of late 20th century architecture, it is difficult to imagine any newly devised proportional system acquiring the status and authority once given to the writings of Vitruvius, Alberti and Palladio.

See also ORDERS, ARCHITECTURAL, §I, 2(iii), and GREEK REVIVAL.

BIBLIOGRAPHY

J.-N.-L. Durand: *Précis des leçons d'architecture données à l'Ecole polytechnique*, 2 vols (Paris, 1802–5)

J. W. Gwilt: *The Rudiments of Architecture* (London, 1826)

E. Viollet-le-Duc: *Entretiens sur l'architecture*, 2 vols (Paris, 1863–72; Eng. trans., London, 1959)

Le Corbusier: *Vers une architecture* (Paris, 1923); Eng. trans. by F. Etchells as *Towards a New Architecture* (London, 1927)

C. Rowe: 'The Mathematics of the Ideal Villa', *Archit. Rev.* [London], ci (1947), pp. 101–4; repr. in *The Mathematics. . . and Other Essays* (Cambridge, MA, and London, 1976)

Le Corbusier: *Le Modulor* (Boulogne-sur-Seine, 1948; Eng. trans., London, 1954)

C. Hussey: *The Life of Sir Edwin Lutyens* (London, 1950)

Le Corbusier: *Le Modulor 2* (Boulogne-sur-Seine, 1955; Eng. trans., London, 1958)

P. H. Scholfield: *The Theory of Proportion in Architecture* (Cambridge, 1958)

C. Alexander: 'Perception and Modular Co-ordination', *RIBA J.*, lxvii (Oct 1959), pp. 425–9

R. Wittkower: 'The Changing Concept of Proportion', *Daedalus* (Winter 1960), pp. 199–215

P. Collins: *Changing Ideals in Modern Architecture* (London, 1965)

L. March and P. Steadman: *The Geometry of Environment* (London, 1971)

W. Szambien: 'Durand and the Continuity of Tradition', *The Beaux-Arts*, ed. R. Middleton (London, 1982), pp. 19–33

R. A. M. Stern: *Modern Classicism* (London, 1988)

Karl F. Schinkel: A Universal Man (exh. cat., ed. M. Snodin; London, V&A, 1991)

H. W. Kruft: *A History of Architectural Theory from Vitruvius to the Present* (London and New York, 1994)

GEOFFREY NEWMAN

Architecture. Term, denoting the art of building, derived from *architekton* (Gr.: 'master carpenter'), which was first used by the historian Herodotus (*d c.* 420 BC; III.lx). Its derivative, *architectus*, appeared *c.* 17 BC in Vitruvius' *On Architecture* (I.i). The word 'architecture' was first used in English in the early years of the reign of Queen Elizabeth I with the publication of John Shute's *The First and Chief Groundes of Architecture* (London, 1563).

Architecture is one of the most universal as well as elementary of mankind's activities. It arises from the basic human need for shelter and security. It takes place on a variety of scales and spans the crudest form of accommodation in a cave and the most complex kind of sophisticated modern environment. Its meaning and scope have changed with its use and social relevance throughout history. The earliest manifestations of architecture were ordinary dwellings for the majority of people. There are, and always have been, only two ways of erecting such a building: putting one block on another or making a skeleton and covering it with a skin. Blocks can be made from almost anything but are commonly made from mud or clay (bricks) or stone (the most universal and influential material in architecture). The most obvious example of skeleton and skin is the Native American Indian tepee. Such elementary buildings are generally described today as VERNACULAR ARCHITECTURE; they occur throughout history and can be classified according to the uses they satisfy and the spaces provided for them. What is generally recognized as architecture has the additional (and ultimately decisive) characteristic of aesthetic quality, which transforms the fundamental need for shelter into one of the grandest manifestations of the human spirit.

Great architecture originated, however, not from the house but from the tomb and then the temple; the pyramids of ancient Egypt are the most celebrated example of this (*see* PYRAMID, §1). In its varied and always fascinating development, great architecture reflects not only functional needs but also the aspirations of the architect and the patrons of the building and the aesthetic sensibilities of their time. In that sense architecture is the most basic of all the arts. It has come to be known as 'the mother of the arts' in that it encloses all the other arts and can be the most total and expressive. Its definition implies the architect's need to combine artistic sensitivity and theoretical learning on the one hand with practice and technology on the other. Any discussion of architecture has to reflect its practical and utilitarian aspect, and that makes it more difficult to define simply than any other art.

A definition of architecture must allow for these two essential elements, and most distinguish between them. Nikolaus Pevsner wrote in the introduction to *An Outline of European Architecture* (Harmondsworth, 1943): 'A bicycle shed is a building: Lincoln Cathedral is a piece of architecture. Nearly everything that encloses space on a scale sufficient for a human being to move in is a building; the term architecture applies only to buildings designed with a view to aesthetic appeal.' The difficulty with such a definition is that 'aesthetic appeal' is even more elusive a term than 'architecture', and it is subject to more changes in taste. But it helps to make a distinction that might otherwise be unclear from definitions of architecture as an art: the distinction between architecture and sculpture. That architecture should 'enclose a space on a scale sufficient for a man to move around in' is helpful but not decisive. Constructions such as small tombs, the rock-cut monolithic shrines (7th–8th centuries AD) of the Pallava kingdom at Mamallapuram in southern India, or such forms as the sphinx and the obelisk in Egypt, are usually accepted as works of architecture yet do not fulfil this condition. By the same definition, Edwin Lutyens's *Memorial to the Missing* (1926), the monument to the dead of the battles of the Somme at Thiépval in northern France, can be accepted as architecture since it is possible to move among its interlocking arches to read the names inscribed on the stone faces of the pillars; the Cenotaph (1919) in Whitehall, London, by the same architect, would be accounted as sculpture since it is a solid monument. Both are in practice regarded as architecture.

The multipurpose nature of architecture was recognized by Vitruvius, whose work has influenced every theorist of architecture since his time. In *On Architecture* (VI.viii.9–10) he identified three qualities that characterize good architecture: *firmitas* (structural soundness), *utilitas* (function) and *venustas* (beauty). English students are usually introduced to his dictum through the writings of the 17th-century scholar Sir Henry Wotton. In his *Elements of Architecture* (1624) he wrote: 'In architecture as in all other operative arts the end must direct the Operation. The end is to build well. Well-building hath three conditions: Commodity, Firmness and Delight.' This trinity forms the underlying brief for all architectural designs today: any commission must supply the type of building required, containing the required accommodation, suitably sited and orientated; the building must be structurally sound; and it must satisfy aesthetic needs or intentions, whether of designer, user or viewer.

What has constantly changed throughout the ages is the interpretation of these conditions, the emphasis on each and the balance between them. For instance, commodity was of no great account as regards the internal arrangements of the Classical Greek temple, since it provided little more than housing for an image with sometimes a treasury room near by (*see* TEMPLE, §I, 4); the Greek concern was predominantly with delight, a concern amounting to a passion that spurred the architects to evolve as perfect a visual form as possible, helped by the invention of entasis, a device that shapes the outlines of columns and horizontal features so as to correct any optical distortions that might detract from perfection. The opposite emphasis is apparent in some of the work of the 20th century. In the British Brutalist school of the 1960s and 1970s (*see* BRUTALISM), aestheticism was deliberately replaced by the rough and the crude. Nevertheless, awareness of all three 'conditions' persists. The American architect Buckminster Fuller, the inventor of geodesic domes, said of his work in Charles Knevitt's *Perspectives: An Anthology of 1001 Architectural Quotations* (London, 1986): 'When I am working on a problem, I never think about beauty. I think only of how to solve the problem. But when I am finished, if the solution is not beautiful, I know it is wrong.'

At some periods what does or does not constitute architecture has depended on the status of the person considered responsible for the idea of the building, whether the client or patron, the architect or designer, or the builder or mason. In other areas the granting of the accolade of the term 'architecture' to a building has depended on the judgement of later critics. What has transformed the meaning of architecture in the later 20th century has been the coincidence of two factors. The effect of the Industrial Revolution and its aftermath in the late 18th century and the 19th was to introduce into building—and therefore to architecture—new materials, new kinds of structure and thus new forms, which produced works of architecture unprecedented in shape and scale. Modern communications, from travel to photography and film, have made available to the West aspects of Eastern architecture and its associated decorative arts, while at the same time introducing to Eastern countries structures and forms previously unknown there. Architecture is now an international phenomenon in every sense, however architecture itself has *always* been an international phenomenon in a more limited sense.

At a time of drastic and continuing change, it may be difficult to isolate and identify the elements that make a work of architecture different from any other art form. The approach that sees the functional programme of the building as the only key to its form and therefore to its design is inadequate. What architecture ultimately does—and does alone—is to create space for the accommodation and satisfaction of people's needs. The purpose of architecture is to make a space expressive and a complex of spaces fascinating and memorable. In that sense architecture is the most distinct as well as the most fundamental of all the arts. It can be defined as an expression of human experience in the form of usable space.

BIBLIOGRAPHY

Vitruvius: *De architectura libri decem* [*c.* 17 BC]; ed. & Eng. trans. F. Granger, Loeb Class. Lib. (London and Cambridge, MA, 1934)
H. Wotton: *The Elements of Architecture* (London, 1624)
R. Fréart: *Parallèle de l'architecture antique et de la moderne: Avec un recueil des dix principaux auteurs qui ont écrit des cinqs ordres* (Paris, 1650; Eng. trans., London, 1733)
J. Ruskin: *The Seven Lamps of Architecture* (London, 1849); also in *The Works of John Ruskin*, ed. E. T. Cook and A. Wedderburn (London, 1903–12), viii, pp. 19–272
B. Fletcher: *A History of Architecture . . . being a Comparative View of the Historical Styles from the Earliest Period* (London, 1896); rev. as *A History of Architecture on the Comparative Method* (London, 5/1905); rev. by J. Musgrove (London, 19/1987)
G. Scott: *The Architecture of Humanism* (London, 1914, rev. 3/1980)
Le Corbusier: *Vers une architecture* (Paris, 1923); Eng. trans. as *Towards a New Architecture* (New York and London, 1927/*R* 1970)
E. Panofsky: *Gothic Architecture and Scholasticism* (Latrobe, 1951/*R* 1957)
R. Banham: *Theory and Design in the First Machine Age* (London, 1960)
L. Mumford: *The City in History* (London, 1961)
R. Wittkower: *Architectural Principles in the Age of Humanism* (London, 1962)
J. Summerson: *The Classical Language of Architecture* (London, 1963/*R* 1964)
G. Jellicoe and S. Jellicoe: *The Landscape of Man* (London, 1975)
S. Kostof: *The Architect: Chapters in the History of the Profession* (Oxford, 1977)
D. Watkin: *Morality and Architecture* (Oxford, 1977)
P. Nuttgens: *The Story of Architecture* (Oxford, 1983)
——: *Understanding Modern Architecture* (London, 1988)

PATRICK NUTTGENS

Architecture parlante. Term applied to the architecture of the French Revolutionary period. *Architecture parlante* was supposed to express the purpose and character of a building at first glance.

Architext. Informal Japanese architectural group founded in 1971 by Takefumi Aida, Takamitsu Azuma, Mayumi Miyawaki, Makoto Suzuki and Minoru Takeyama. The members of Architext emphasized their lack of a common philosophy other than their mutual interest in publishing the magazine *Architext* in support of highly individual, experimental and sometimes unconventional architecture. While the publication echoed the visionary texts of the avant-garde group Archigram, the name was an ironic comment on architectural doctrines and theoretical writings. All five members of Architext were born in the 1930s and grew up during World War II and the reconstruction that followed. They were particularly concerned with the relationship of the individual to the environment and to tradition, and they advocated pluralism and radicalism. Of the group, it was primarily Takeyama who stressed in his buildings the analogy between architecture and semiology that the name Architext suggested. The magazine was published five times between summer 1970 and winter 1972 as *Architext 00, 0, 1, 2,* and *Extra*, designed as a series of five posters (one per architect); these were cut into five 21 cm-square pages and bound as 'posteresque statements'. *Architext* functioned as a forum for publishing individual buildings (the group built no collective architecture), philosophies and architectural fantasies in drawings, photographs and texts, mainly in Japanese.

WRITINGS

Architext Extra (1972) [inserted in *Toshi-Jutaku*, 58 (1972)]

BIBLIOGRAPHY

'Architext', *Japan Architect*, 232 (1976) [whole issue]
M. F. Ross: *Beyond Metabolism: The New Japanese Architecture* (New York, 1978)

JACQUELINE E. KESTENBAUM

Architrave. Lowermost portion of an entablature, principally used in Classical architecture, comprising a horizontal beam that spans the columns or piers in the manner of a lintel (*see* GREECE, ANCIENT, fig. 9b and ORDERS, ARCHITECTURAL, fig. 1vi). The term was subsequently applied to the moulding around a door or window.

□

Archives. Collections of original records.

1. Types. 2. History. 3. Modern examples.

1. TYPES. There are primarily two types of archives. Single-agency or institutional archives are repositories of primarily non-current records, retained for legal and historical purposes, of the past activities of an institution, company or person. Archivists and administrative staff responsible for record management establish procedures and timetables for the transfer of materials no longer needed for current transactions. Government agencies, museums and academic institutions usually have archives that include the documents of their own affairs, for example correspondence, financial statements, minutes of meetings and news clippings. Single-agency archives are often referred to as 'fonds'. Multiple-collection archives are repositories of original materials believed to be worth preserving for future study or exhibition; these may come from a variety of sources, public or private, and are usually on a subject related to the overall interests of the institution

that holds the collections. Archives of this type are often affiliated with large institutions, such as libraries, and may or may not hold the institutions' administrative files.

Art archives encompass a variety of repositories and publications related to the arts. There are six main categories of art archives, outlined below; this article will concentrate on the first three. First, there are archives that contain original records of artists, collectors, dealers, art critics, authors and publishers, museums, societies and any agency related to the arts; they may include correspondence, diaries, financial papers, reviews and exhibition records. The Tate Gallery Archives of 20th Century British Art, London, and the Archives of American Art, Washington, DC, are examples of this type of archive. Second, there are collections of original works of art, mostly graphic art (drawings, etchings, lithographs and photographs), which may include sketches for paintings, sculptures, architecture and industrial design, as well as original book illustrations. These two types of archives range from public archives, such as the Picture Division of the National Archives of Canada, Ottawa, to the private archives of Frank Lloyd Wright at Taliesin West in Scottsdale, AZ, USA; or from the collections of medieval illustrations in monasteries to the archives of museums and academic institutions. Such archives, which are generally non-commercial, preserve their holdings for research and general art information. The third type of archive, public and frequently commercial, includes collections of photographs, prints and microforms of works of art gathered primarily for reference and teaching purposes; when commercial, such collections may be devoted to the distribution of reproductions. The photographs are not valued works of art in themselves, unlike a photograph by Julia Margaret Cameron or Henri Cartier-Bresson, but are reproductions of works of art. The UNESCO *International Directory of Photographic Archives of Works of Art* (1950) lists over 600 collections in 87 countries.

Among other types of archives are commercial collections of all kinds of visual images including some in the arts, such as the Bettmann Archive in New York, which primarily sells reproductions, worldwide, to book publishers, advertising agencies and the mass media; and published collections of original papers and drawings of artists and architects and out-of-print illustrations. These may be facsimile editions of original documents (e.g. the Garland series of *Architectural Archives*) or popular reprint publications on specific subjects (e.g. the *Dover Pictorial Archives*). Finally, there are journals with 'Archives' or 'Archiv' in their title (e.g. the *Archives of Contemporary Art*); most of these are published by a repository or an organization interested in original art documents, and they report on recent acquisitions and projects.

Archives, libraries and museums all acquire, house, organize and make available documents and/or artefacts, and produce information about their holdings and their services. The difference between these agencies usually lies in the character of their materials and their organization. Most art libraries describe, arrange and catalogue individual items according to a predetermined classification system (*see* BIBLIOGRAPHY OF ART, §II). Museums also describe items but arrange their collections in accordance with their individual programmes, usually by period, theme, medium or artist. Archives have traditionally arranged their holdings by provenance (that is, in the order in which individual collections entered the repository) since it is not only the individual items but also the manner in which the material was gathered by its original owner that constitute important historical evidence.

New scholarly and public interests and new technologies are beginning to bring closer the organization and services of individual agencies that have overlapping constituencies, leading to an increase in networks. In order to use common indexes and databases, art libraries, archives and museums are beginning to coordinate the terminology used to describe art works. Archives are considering alternatives to the arrangement by provenance, in descriptive tools if not in physical arrangement; and the publication of directories of collections, similar to those of special libraries, is enhancing the sharing of information and resources. On the local level, public libraries, museums and academic institutions—in some instances linked by being part of the same university—have for some time cooperated by coordinating their collections, journal subscriptions and reference services. Larger public libraries often have an art division that may include special archives, videotapes and picture files, as well as books, journals and collections of artefacts with exhibition space. On the national and regional level cooperation varies greatly; there are lively networking activities in the USA, Canada, Australia and some European countries. In Britain the Museums Association Council and the Society of Archivists, subsequently joined by the Library Association, agreed in 1976 to establish a joint working party to explore the common ground between these institutions. Even in those regions where conditions do not yet permit formal cooperative arrangements, the close relationship between the major information and documentation agencies is becoming recognized. UNESCO and its affiliates encourage exchanges across countries and across organizations to harmonize the professional interests of archives, libraries and museums.

2. HISTORY.

(i) General archives. The earliest remnants of organized archival collections have survived, in the form of clay tablets inscribed in cuneiform characters, from the Sumerian, Assyrian, and Babylonian civilizations of Mesopotamia (3rd millennium BC) and from other sites, especially in the Mediterranean region and Central and South-east Asia. Such early collections also served as libraries; depending on whether they were part of a palace, temple, museum or school, they contained official state and business records, religious texts or literary documents. In Egypt under the rule of the Ptolemies (3rd century BC) the literary manuscripts held by the Museum in Alexandria (a combination of museum, library, archive and centre of scholarship) were systematically copied and catalogued. The lost works of some Greek artists, such as Apelles, are known only through references in Alexandrian and Roman manuscripts. Imperial Rome paid much attention to the administration of public records, as well as to the production and presentation of literary and scholarly texts.

There was no clear distinction between libraries, archives and museums until the late Renaissance and the dawn of the Age of Reason. In the second half of the 15th century the invention and rapid spread of printing made it possible to produce multiple identical copies of a text, free from scribal variations. A lively book trade developed; under the stimulus of the Reformation, small local public and school libraries began to appear.

In France the preservation of local and regional public records was carried out in archives established by the Church and a few public agencies. In most of these the original arrangement, as well as the subsequent care, varied from total neglect to responsible but idiosyncratic organization. The systematic development of public archives began during the French Revolution (1789–95), with the foundation in 1789 of the Archives Nationales in Paris. In accepting responsibility for the nation's documentary heritage, the government developed procedures based on the principle of *respect des fonds*—the preservation of records in chronological order of creation. In 1796 regulations for regional archives, the Archives Départementales, were issued, and a unified national system was established to include also the record-producing public agencies. The French system with its centralized administration became a model for many nations; its policies and principles of arrangement were followed not only by public agencies but also by all types of single- and multiple-collection repositories. In England the Public Records Act of 1838 initiated a policy concerning public records. In other countries, including the USA, historical societies and special libraries promoted the collection and retention of historically valuable documents. The establishment of history departments in universities in the later part of the 19th century gave impetus to the development of archives.

Canada created its Public Archives in Ottawa in 1872. From the beginning acquisition was not limited to records of the government and its agencies; the archives included historical documents and particularly pictorial records of individuals and corporate bodies. In the USA it was only in 1934 that the National Archives was established. In addition to governments other agencies, both public and private, established archival collections in the 19th and 20th centuries. As new archives were founded, some old ones suffered from the ravages of war, fire and flood, and from prolonged neglect. Since the severe damage caused by the floods in 1966 in Florence, Italy, special attention has been paid all over the world to the protection and preventive care of archives.

In 1950 the first International Congress of Archives was held in Paris, and the International Council on Archives (ICA) was founded, with headquarters in the city. The International Congress is held in a capital city every four years, and its proceedings are published in *Archivum*.

(ii) Art archives. The establishment of art archives as distinct collections within libraries or general archives followed the development of museums and academies; and especially the development of art history as an academic discipline. Museums such as those of Alexandria, Pergamon, Rome and—since the 15th century—the Vatican have usually contained archival documents. In the 16th century Vasari drew up the plans for the Uffizi in Florence, the first building specifically designed as a museum. In the 16th and 17th centuries there were art archives in Italian churches and public libraries. Since that period museums and art academies have come to publish catalogues of their holdings and accumulated records of their activities. The files of the Preussische Akademie der Künste in Berlin, founded in 1696, contain documents of many of its members, as well as records of proceedings and correspondence from the 18th century to the present. The Germanisches Nationalmuseum in Nuremberg lists Dürer's *Unterweisung der Messung* among the early manuscripts in its archives. An increasing number of museums have created archives and opened them to research. National art library and museum associations, together with UNESCO, have contributed much to this development. Since World War II, and especially since the 1970s, conferences, seminars, journal articles and directories of art resources have increased steadily.

Individual art historians and connoisseurs have also played a major role in the development of art archives and libraries. Many have collected or encouraged the establishment of collections, and some, such as Wilhelm von Bode or Aby Warburg, donated their personal papers and visual materials, which became the nucleus of important art resources. In 1873 Hermann Grimm (1828–1901), shortly after his appointment as Professor of art history at the University of Berlin, set out to supplement the museum's holdings in Berlin, especially the collection of the Royal Print Gallery (Sammlungen des Königlichen Kupferstich Kabinetts) with an archive of 'manual and technical' reproductions (that is, drawings, prints and photographs). In Italy the Alinari brothers, having started as engravers, in 1854 turned to photography in order to document works of art; in 1892 they founded the Ufficio Fotografico. These were probably the beginnings of picture archives of works of art and of photoarchives.

Artists and their students or heirs have also founded art archives. The houses in London of William Morris and Frederic Leighton and Franz von Stuck's villa in Munich are examples of artists' homes that are now open to the public as museums and archives. Art dealers, galleries and auction houses have often preserved the files of the artists whom they represented. Such important auction houses as Christie's in London or M. Knoedler & Co. in New York contain invaluable original and well-organized papers. Liberty & Co. in London and other producers of the Arts and Crafts Movement have their own company archives; those of Thomas Ross & Son, copper- and steelplate printers in London since 1833, are a rich source for research into the history of art prints. Art publishers also have archives containing correspondence and manuscripts from art historians and critics. The artist-archives of Peter A. Juley (1862–1937) and Paul Juley (1890–1975) in New York are perhaps unique: commissioned by the American Academy of Design these two, father and son, photographed the work of virtually every American artist between 1896 and 1975. The Juley Archives were transferred in the 1970s to the Smithsonian Institution, Washington, DC, where they received proper preservation treatment and are now accessible for research. Private art archives from the 19th century and early 20th are increasingly being transferred to public archives for protection and easier access.

It is difficult to establish when the term 'art archives' was first used for collections. It has been used in titles of journals, but not for collections, at least since the middle of the 19th century; examples are the *Archives de l'art français* (1851-62); the *Archiv für zeichnende Künste*, Leipzig (1855-70); and the *Archiv für Christliche Kunst* (1833-1929). Monographs publishing documentary materials, such as Lionello Venturi's *Les Archives de l'impressionnisme* (1939), a collection of the letters of Renoir, Monet and others, have also used the term. In the case of archival collections, the term was apparently first used to designate an archive of art-related photographs in 1913, when Richard Hamann founded the Bild Archiv Foto-Marburg in Germany. In subsequent years the term appeared in the annual reports of museums and libraries, with reference to their institutional records and to artists' documents and other materials gathered for exhibitions.

Carl Zigrosser (1891–1975), Curator of Prints at the Philadelphia Museum of Art, was probably the first to propose the foundation of a multiple-collection art archive when, in 1942, he encouraged the trustees of his institution to create a central repository of documents relating to the arts of the USA. In 1954 a similar project was launched at the Library of the Art Institute of Detroit. The Archives of American Art, affiliated since 1970 with the Smithsonian Institution of Washington, DC, is now a major research centre. It distributes the *Museum Archivists' Newsletter* to more than 300 museums.

In 1964 seven major European art libraries, sited in Berlin, Munich, Cologne, Nuremberg, Rome (2) and Florence, joined to form the Arbeitsgemeinschaft der Kunstbibliotheken, with the financial support of the Fritz Thyssen Foundation. The members, all possessing major art archives of photographs and manuscripts, coordinate their acquisitions, funding policies and services, as well as such bibliographic activities as the production of catalogues, indexes and directories. It could well be that most art archives will come to be linked with libraries, as is already the case with many museum archives.

This account of the development of art archives may appear to be biased towards American and western European practice; this is because the establishment of museums and the study of fine arts in many other countries is of comparatively recent date. It is therefore difficult to ascertain where and what kind of art documentation may exist. However, as the demand for original sources gains momentum, librarians, archivists and museum professionals in many countries are taking the initiative in creating art archives.

3. Modern examples.

(i) Uses. (ii) Sources and methods. (iii) Ordering and access. (iv) Conservation. (v) Staff training. (vi) Publications. (vii) Funding. (viii) Principal art archives. (ix) Other archival resources. (x) Future developments.

(i) Uses. A broadening of disciplines and interests, new fields of study that lean heavily on the arts for documentation, and new methods of interpretation have all affected research methods and resources in all disciplines and made increasing intellectual demands on archivists. Many new subjects have, for example, been added to the original concept of the fine arts. Since the 1950s the term has come to encompass folk art and ethnic art, decorative arts, photography and industrial design, as well as social, economic and legal aspects of the arts. Such new topics as women in the arts, museum studies and the arts and the law have greatly extended both the size and the cultural and linguistic diversity of the clientele of art libraries and art archives.

An additional reason for the surge of interest in archives, expressed on the Continent and in Canada more often than in the USA and Britain, is the notion that the artistic property and production of a nation constitute its cultural heritage. The national inventories of art properties that have been undertaken in the Romance cultures are evidence for this assumption. The Roman Catholic Church has likewise established several organizations of ecclesiastical archivists to guard its documentary and artistic patrimony. National festivals and celebrations, such as the Bicentennial of the Constitution of the USA, also tend to generate an interest in the nation's art.

Before the mid-19th century, archives collected almost exclusively retrospective records, deposited primarily by prearranged schedules. A major policy change has been the inclusion of contemporary documentation. While the accession of historical documents continues, many repositories seek out current materials. Archivists may also initiate the production of records: they plan interviews with artists and make video films of exhibitions and other events documenting current art activities. The inclusion of contemporary documents also affects preservation methods. Preventive care has been added to the customary problems of conservation and restoration of fragile documents: every item has to be analysed to determine the best way to minimize deterioration. This is of special concern to art archivists, because visual materials come in a great variety of media and formats, and the concept of the original is an important concern. Posters, photographs and other images produced on plastics and with chemicals of unknown lifespan constitute a major challenge.

(ii) Sources and methods. As well as traditional art-historical studies of style, connoisseurship and iconography, art history now encompasses treatises on the social, political, intellectual and economic milieux in which works of art have been produced. This kind of research relies heavily on such documentary evidence as the records of institutions connected with works of art: for example, contracts and commissions, records of wages paid to artisans, correspondence between patrons and artists, or architectural drawings. The use of such evidence heralds a new reliance by art historians on scientific method. In France, the intense interest in the maintenance of documentary evidence has resulted in the development of ARCADE, a database constructed by the Archives Nationales to contain information on official records of art patronage, schools, museums and the like.

A significant amount of contemporary art-historical research consists of the compilation and editing of archival records for the consumption of other scholars. Many collections of documents, such as the Barberini archives or the Orsini inventories, are being published. In addition, numerous archival publications are now available in microform. This format is used primarily for pictorial material, as in Christie's Pictorial Archive, the Alinari Archive of 19th-century photographs of Rome, and the Marburger Index, a set of images of works of art owned by Germany before World War II, derived from the archives of numerous photographers and institutions. Much of the documentation in the Archives of American Art is also available in microfilm; these collections are housed in five regional centres.

Advances in optical scanning technology are gradually making more and more archives available on computer screens. Computers have been used to compile documentary evidence from archives relating to Medici gold- and silverwork, and are used to organize the Marburger Index. Video disc technology is being used experimentally in the AVIADOR project of Columbia University, New York, to catalogue architectural drawings, many of which form archival groupings; it has also been used in experimental projects at the Library of Congress in Washington, DC. The most important role of computers has been in cataloguing and indexing documents; it is the cooperative potential of archival cataloguing and the standardization of description that holds the greatest promise. Through 'piggy-backing' on library networks, the archival community in North America has developed an Archives and Manuscripts Control (AMC) system of description, in machine-readable (MARC) format, which allows the sharing of data. For example, an art historian can pose a query about records relating to Winslow Homer to a general library terminal that has the AMC database (specifically the Research Library Information Network or RLIN system) and find out which record groups relating to this artist have so far been reported by the 40 or so participating repositories. The database is constantly being augmented by the addition of new records and new participants.

The first step in archival research is to compile a list of likely archival record groups and establish their location. There are many published guides to the location of collections (*see* bibliography below). It is very probable that a part of the records relating to an art-historical topic, such as an artist's life, will be lodged in general, and not specifically historical, archives. Finding aids, which play a major role in the accessibility of resources, are available in three categories: international and regional directories to archives, manuscript collections and libraries; guides to the holdings of specific archives, with a general description of the major collections and their arrangement; and guides to the individual collections, which usually include inventories, registers, calendars and other lists or indexes.

(iii) Ordering and access. The great diversity of material that an art archive may contain poses problems of ordering. The art archive of an institution such as the Pennsylvania Academy of Fine Arts may contain letters from the institution's founders, the minutes of the board of trustees, the charter and acts of incorporation; membership files, student records, prize information, curators' and registrars' files on de-accessioned works of art; annual reports, exhibition catalogues, architectural plans of the building, financial files, office files of the director and curators; correspondence with artists; clipping files, scrapbooks and publicity records. An art archive may also hold an artist's working drawings; an architect's office files; audio and videotapes of a scholar's interviews with craftspeople; or, in the case of the British Public Records Office, a manufacturer's scrapbooks of samples and designs.

Archival principles require that material from a particular source should be kept together, in order to respect provenance and to preserve the collection's organicity, and that its original order should be retained if possible, since much archival material is fragmentary and virtually meaningless out of its original context. For example, the text of a picture postcard might mean little in itself, but its place in a chronological correspondence file might indicate when the writer was in the place depicted, and adjacent letters might clarify the message, and so might substantiate the meeting of two artists or explain the evolution of a work of art in the artist's mind. The original order is therefore preferable to a 'logical' order that an archivist might impose by filing together all the postcards in an artist's records. It is particularly important to respect archival order in the case of pictorial material: the individual drawing, undated and unidentified, may convey little information, but a collection of sketches on the same subject in the artist's own order can indicate the evolution of his ideas.

A related problem is that of description. The historical archives of an institution are generally arranged in record groups that reflect its organizational structure; and it is these groups, not the items they contain, that are 'described'—the term 'catalogued' is not used. Typically the basic description of a group of documents indicates not their content but the organization or individual who created or compiled the records, thus recording their context. Ancillary indexing may list persons or organizations mentioned in the documents. (However, with the growing use of computers, this practice is gradually changing.) A significant advance in the description of archival holdings has been the development of the AMC format (*see* §(ii) above), which offers an outline of descriptive categories; it was developed in part by members of the Society of American Archivists, based largely on developmental work in the MARC (machine-readable) formats at the Library of Congress in Washington, DC, and is leading in the USA and Canada to considerable standardization of approach, as well as to a modest exchange of records through RLIN. In Europe other communication formats, such as the CCC, are preferred; yet other descriptive systems are gradually being defined in other countries and regions. *A Manual of Archival Description* (2/1989) deals with these issues from the British point of view.

While such generic codes, intended to describe all types of art works and documents, may make a useful starting-point for describing collections, the particular kinds of material handled by art historians require individually designed methods of description. For example, architectural drawings as a genre have received considerable attention from the Society of American Archivists, from the Architectural Drawings Advisory Group at the National Gallery in Washington, DC, and from the AVIADOR project at the Avery Architectural and Fine Arts

Library of Columbia University, New York, for cataloguing architectural drawings in the RLIN system of the Research Libraries Group. Other organizations active in this area are the Society for the Study of Architecture in Canada, the Centre Canadien d'Architecture in Montreal, the British Architectural Library and the project for the Cooperative Preservation of Architectural Records (COPAR). The archival principle of organicity is particularly useful in organizing and describing architectural material: all the drawings for a specific project are kept together, whether drawn by the architect or an assistant. Ralph E. Ehrenberg, among others, has proposed a hierarchy of categories for drawings. The broadest level would be 'activity', a term that might include design, site survey, compilation etc, for a particular project. The second level would contain working drawings, shop drawings, and so on; the third level would be mechanical, electrical and structural drawings. Further divisions, analogous to record groups, would be based on the generation of particular kinds of drawings, prepared by an architectural firm's subsections. Closely related to description is the creation of finding aids. The essential ones are accession registers, descriptive inventories and 'bridging aids' relating a variety of research topics to the archive's structure. Highly desirable finding aids are detailed indexes to records, detailed guides to collections, and publications announcing acquisitions or describing the research potential of older material.

Policies for shaping museum archives are receiving increased attention in the USA and Great Britain. Beginning with Claudia Hommel's significant article on the Detroit Institute of Art (1979), American museums are changing their procedures from passive storage to active programmes of retention schedules and selection processes, and are developing a new terminology (see Fleckner) that includes such terms as 'activist archivist', 'proactive selection', 'collections strategies' and 'interinstitutional cooperation'. In the areas of access and service art archives are beginning to develop effective policies and practices. Such factors as the ownership of information, privacy and discretion, demands on staff and traditional assumptions about appropriate service to the public make difficult the opening of archives, particularly those containing records of museum operations, although scholars can usually overcome these restrictions.

(iv) Conservation. Preservation work in archives can be divided into three categories: protection of the original material, its transfer to other formats and preventive care for new acquisitions. Advice on these can be found in the publications of such organizations as the Society of American Archivists, the American Association for State and Local History, the Museums Association of Great Britain, the British Society of Archivists, and UNESCO. In modern archival conservation the emphasis is on preservation: the retention of intellectual content and original physical property. This represents a shift from earlier interest in restoring the aesthetic appearance and qualities of deteriorated documents. Current thinking demands that the object should retain its value as evidence; treatment should therefore be documented, reversible and minimal and undertaken primarily to ensure the object's survival. The conservator's technical operations include restoring material, providing advice, running workshops on techniques, monitoring the environment and overseeing the transfer of contents to alternative formats. All of these operations are especially complex in an art archive, because of the difficulties of preserving art works on unstable materials (for example photographs and pencil drawings on acidic paper) and the desirability of retaining the original, often for aesthetic as well as documentary reasons.

Preservation has been widely interpreted as comprising a wide variety of managerial activities, including selecting storage facilities, establishing methods for handling materials, developing appropriate environmental conditions and surveying the condition of materials. Modern conservation also seeks to prevent the unnecessary handling of objects by developing policies for use and by reproducing the original through publication, microfilming or computer-aided reproductive technology.

(v) Staff training. There is no single accepted approach to education for archival work. In Britain the apprentice system has been the norm; the French and German models include formal advanced study in institutions of higher education. In the USA archivists used to come from academic disciplines, mostly history, art history and social sciences; however, some graduate departments in these fields have now added courses and programmes in archival work, and librarianship training schemes have developed similar courses and certification programmes. Although it is still common for archival skills to be picked up through attendance at workshops, self-education, apprenticeships and on-the-job experience, the professional degree in museology is becoming the norm for those taking administrative positions in museums and other art agencies.

The new demands made on the profession have generated new training requirements. In 1973 the Society of American Archivists (SAA), founded in 1936, published its first *Education Directory*, containing articles on archival careers and guidelines for graduate archival education programmes, together with a list of curricula. Schools for archival education may be independent, such as the Ecole des Chartes in France, or attached to national or state archives, as in Germany and India, or they may be departments of schools of library and information studies, as in Spain, Britain and the USA. The curricula are fairly similar, but most European schools include auxiliary subjects, such as paleography.

(vi) Publications. Professional journals are published primarily by national and state archives and by organizations of archivists. A few art archives publish their own journals, such as the quarterly *Archives of American Art Journal*. Some organizations publish occasional books or pamphlets, as well as newsletters. Other literature on art archives may be found in the journals of libraries and museums and of general archives. Publications such as those of the Museum Documentation Association in Britain or the research series *The Archive* of the Center for Creative Photography of the University of Arizona in Tucson are important sources.

(vii) Funding. With the emergence of special collection archives that serve a broader clientele, funding has become a major issue. Whereas single-agency archives are usually maintained by their parent institutions (e.g. governments, churches and companies) to fulfil legal obligations, multiple-collection archives—the category into which most art archives fall—can rarely count on such support and must procure external funding. Thus public and private foundations have become essential to the operation of art archives. In the USA the National Endowment of the Humanities, the National Endowment of the Arts, National Historical Publications, the Records Commission of the National Archives and state councils give grants to art archives that have professional staff. Private foundations are of equal significance; the J. Paul Getty Trust, for example, not only supports American archival projects of preservation and microfilming but is also involved in bibliographic enterprises of archival significance. The Ford Foundation's support was essential in the formative stages of the Archives of American Art.

In 1953 the Bibliotheca Hertziana in Rome, with its rich library, archives and photographic library, became a branch of the German government-sponsored Max-Planck-Institut. The Stiftung Volkswagenwerk supports the Marburger Index of the Bildarchiv Foto-Marburg, and the Robert Bosch and Fritz Thyssen foundations support research related to the arts and archives. Publishers such as Chadwyck-Healy and Mindata in Britain and K. G. Saur in Germany contribute to the development of art archives through their publications of high-quality microforms of visual archives. Art archives in local and regional museums and in universities are sometimes able to procure funding from companies in their area or from community foundations. Art archives have also benefited from special events such as centennial celebrations and major exhibition programmes. Thus since 1964 the publicly supported Neue Galerie of Kassel, Germany, has housed the Dokumenta Archiv, a valuable source for the study of contemporary international art. The Australian Bicentenary celebrations of 1988 have stimulated and financed programmes there, including national art inventories.

International organizations have played a major part in contemporary archival activities. From its beginning UNESCO has recognized the importance of archives; in 1950 the International Council on Archives (ICA) was established under the auspices of UNESCO, with a standing committee on literature and art archives. This organization, the UNESCO-supported International Federation of Library Associations and Institutions (IFLA) and the International Council of Museums (ICOM) have exerted an incalculably wide influence, through conferences, symposia and publications. Thus individual art archives, as they develop their own collections, become part of an international network that provides scholars with information about the great variety of national archival resources.

(viii) Principal art archives. Few countries have central or regional art archives. Documentary materials may be found in a great variety of repositories, from national archives and national museums to historical societies, academies, institutes, art schools, libraries, churches and private institutions. Since the 1950s several countries have established special sections in their national archives for the arts: for example Bulgaria, Canada, Denmark, Finland and Norway. Other countries, such as Russia, have founded independent archives for literature and art. These government agencies not only collect and provide services but also provide archival training programmes.

Material in public art archives may be acquired through government agencies; in France and Finland, for example, arrangements exist for some auction houses to offer the government first refusal. Countries whose archives have no special art division frequently hold records related to art in their general collections. These are, however, seldom accessible by artists' names or by subjects, being generally arranged by provenance or location. In some countries—for example Brazil, Japan, Peru, the Philippines and Spain—national art information centres have been established; these do not have archival collections but provide information about their country's art resources.

As a rule, museums of all types have some institutional files; many individual curators keep files of exhibitions and correspondence with artists. The museum library supplements these and may also be able to provide information about the institution's own documents. Museums devoted to one artist, such as the Museé Horta in Brussels, or to one subject, such as the Textile Museum in Washington, DC, generally have strong archival resources, listed with their library holdings. The archives of art academies and of general academies that have artists as members are important sources of information about individual artists, and many of them are open to researchers. Equally important are the files of art schools and organizations: artists' equity associations, artists' welfare funds, gallery associations, crafts councils, museum associations and the files of individual art galleries, auction houses and publishers.

The following list includes all types of art archival collections, arranged alphabetically by country, with a brief indication of their collection emphasis. Most of the institutions provide reference and photographic services; for specific research conditions, their staff, as well as current directories, can be consulted.

Argentina. The Archivo General de la Nación Departamento Documentas de Imagen y de Sonido has materials relating to Argentina; the Centro de Arte y Comunicación includes all of Latin America.

Australia. The library of the Australian National Gallery (now National Gallery of Australia) in Canberra began in the 1980s to collect on a national scale newspaper reviews, art society catalogues, advertisements and other ephemera as the beginning of a national art archival collection. The National Library of Australia in Canberra maintains special collections of original art works, including photographs. The pictorial records are included in the Australian National Data Base, which will eventually include such records from other collections. All Australian state galleries and libraries hold pictorial archives and other art-related documentation. A number of recently founded art institutions, such as the Australian Centre for Photography in Sydney, the Print Council of Australia in Melbourne and the Women's Movement Library in Canberra, maintain files related to their specific interests.

Austria. Rich art archival documentation from the Middle Ages to the *Jugendstil* and later movements is held in five repositories in Vienna: the Graphische Sammlung Albertina, the Historisches Museum, the Kunsthistorisches Museum, the Österreichisches Museum für Angewandte Kunst and the Wiener Stadt- und Landesarchiv. The archives of the Egon Schiele Gesellschaft in Tulln are a fine example of documentary collections focusing on one artist and his period.

Belgium. The Institut Royal du Patrimoine Artistique in Brussels is preparing a photographic inventory of art in Belgian collections, with iconographic, name and place indexes. Also in Brussels, the Archive de l'Art Contemporain en Belgique, as part of the Musées Royaux des Beaux-Arts, collects documentation for art works of the Flemish part of Belgium. In Antwerp the Rubenianum includes a library and documentation of the Nationaal Centrum voor de Plastische Kunsten.

Brazil. The Centro de Documentação e Informaçās Sobre Arte Brasileira Contemporânea in São Paulo with its library serves the art research needs of Brazil and, to some extent, of Latin America.

Canada. The National Archives of Canada, founded in Ottawa in 1827, began to acquire pictorial documents in 1906. Today the Picture Division and the Photography Collection constitute major visual art archives, while the artists' documents are in the general archives. The library and archives of the National Gallery of Canada, founded in Ottawa in 1880, serve as a collection and information centre for art documentation. There are also considerable collections in Toronto at the Art Gallery of Ontario and the University of Toronto.

Denmark. The Nordjyllands Kunstmuseum (North Jutland Museum of Art), founded in Ålborg in 1972, has developed an archive of Scandinavian art and in particular for the documentation of exhibition materials. The Kunstakademiets Bibliotek in Copenhagen, founded in 1827, maintains collections of manuscripts, ephemera and audiovisual documentation.

Egypt. Both the Coptic Museum and the Egyptian Museum in Cairo maintain archival files.

France. In Paris several institutions have significant art archives: the Bibliothèque Centrale des Musées Nationaux; the Ecole Nationale Supérieure des Beaux-Arts; the Bibliothèque des Arts Décoratifs; the Bibliothèque Forney; the Centre Georges Pompidou, with its Documentation du Musée National d'Art Moderne; and the Musée d'Art Juif, with archival records of Jewish artists and popular art from North Africa and Eastern and Central Europe. Also in Paris, the International Council of Museums (ICOM) maintains archives on international art activities, especially preservation. In Marseille the archives of the Musée des Arts et Traditions Populaires du Terroir Marseillais and the Centre d'Etude et de Documentation sur l'Image (CEDDCI) are typical examples of a regional collection of original documents in the arts. Documents of prominent French artists are often preserved in special museums devoted to their work, in communities with which they were associated: examples are the Musée Ingres in Montauban and the Musée National Marc Chagall and the Musée Matisse, both in Nice.

Germany. The Archiv der Preussischen Akademie der Künste in Berlin dates from 1696. In addition to the documents of its own transactions (including the fine arts, literature, and music), the documents of such 20th-century artists as George Grosz and Käthe Kollwitz are maintained as special collections. Also in Berlin is the Bauhaus-Archiv housed since 1979 in the Gropiusbau, which in addition to its own records contains documents from the Wiener Werkstätte and other 20th-century art movements. In Kassel the Dokumenta Archiv für die Kunst des 20. Jahrhunderts contains the files of the Dokumenta exhibitions and other records of 20th-century art. The Staatsgalerie in Stuttgart contains archives of individual artists, and the Bayerisches Hauptstaatsarchiv in Munich contains major pictorial collections, artists' documents and records of art institutions in Bavaria. The Staatliche Kunstsammlungen in Dresden administers the Zentrale Kunstbibliothek, with its archival collections.

The Bundesverband der Bildarchiv is a federation of pictorial archives, mostly related to the arts, in Germany and Austria. Members are the Deutsche Fototek in Dresden, the Bildarchiv Foto-Marburg, the Rheinische Bildarchiv in Cologne, the Landesstelle für Bild Dokumentation in Hamburg and the Bildarchiv der Österreichischen Nationalbibliothek in Vienna. The members of the Arbeitsgemeinschaft der Kunstbibliotheken are the Kunstbibliothek in Berlin; the Bibliothek of the Germanisches Nationalmuseum in Nuremberg; the Kunst-und-Museumsbibliothek at the Wallraf-Richartz-Museum in Cologne, which holds archives on art of the Benelux countries; the Bibliothek of the Zentralinstitut für Kunstgeschichte in Munich, which specializes in the Renaissance and humanism; the Bibliotheca Hertziana, with its photographic library of Italian art, and the Deutsches Archäologisches Institut, both in Rome; and the Kunsthistorisches Institut in Florence, which concentrates on source materials of Italian art from the 15th century to the present.

Greece. The Benaki Museum in Athens has a department of historic archives and one of photographic archives.

Iraq. The National Library Department in Baghdad maintains original sources from prehistory to the 20th century.

Israel. The Israel Museum in Jerusalem and the Museum of Ethnography and Folklore in Tel Aviv both maintain documentary sources.

Italy. In addition to the German library-archives, the Bibliotheca Hertziana in Rome and the Kunsthistorisches Institut in Florence, there are several noteworthy indigenous art archives. Rome has the Fototeca Unione Archive (founded in 1957) at the American Academy and the archives of the Biblioteca Apostolica Vaticana, as well as the Vatican museums with collections ranging from the 4th century to the present. Florence is the home of the Museo della Fotografie Fratelli Alinari. In Venice the

Archivio di Stato spans the years 1030–1805 and includes an inventory of the art of the late 18th century. The Archivio Storico dell' Arti Contemporanea della Biennale di Venezia preserves the Biennale records. Local community archives, in places such as Siena where major artists have lived, provide rich sources.

Japan. The Department of Archives at the Tokyo National Research Institute of Cultural Properties and the National Museum of Modern Art in Tokyo both contain art records of Japanese art and artists.

Mexico. The Instituto de Investigaciones Estéticas in Mexico City serves as the major centre for art archival documentation and information.

The Netherlands. The Rijksdienst Beeldende Kunst in The Hague, with its office for fine arts, serves as a central information agency for the preservation of collections in the Netherlands. This is complemented by the Rijksbureau voor Kunsthistorische Documentatie, also in The Hague. Among the museums, the Stedelijk Museum with its division for scholarly documentation, and the Rijksmuseum (both in Amsterdam), and the Nederlands Textiel Museum in Tilburg, maintain archival collections.

New Zealand. The National Art Gallery in Wellington bears the main responsibility for collecting archival documents relating to New Zealand.

Nigeria. The Centre for Black and African Arts and Civilization in Lagos collects original artefacts and documents.

Peru. The Centro de Arte in Lima serves as an information agency for art research, and the Archivo Nacional includes art documentation.

The Philippines. The Cultural Center for the Philippines Museum and Gallery Department in Manila has permanent collections and provides information on Philippine art.

Poland. Eight regional museums, among these the National Museum (Muzeum Narodowe) in Kraków and the National Museum (Muzeum Narodowe) in Wrocław, maintain archival collections in their libraries.

Russia. In 1941 the government of what was then the USSR established the Central Archives of Literature and Art in Moscow. It is strong in records of cultural organizations, publishers, journals, newspapers, artists' committees, unions and societies of artists. Also in Moscow, the Pushkin Museum of Fine Arts collects records of non-Russian art, in addition to its own files. In St Petersburg the Hermitage Museum, the Academy of Arts and the M. E. Saltykov-Shchedrin Public Library maintain research libraries with archival materials.

Spain. The Centro Nacional de Información Artística, Arqueológica y Etnológica in Madrid includes a major art archive and provides information on art in Spain.

Sweden. The Arkiv för Dekorativ Konst in Lund and the Nordiska Museets Bibliotek in Stockholm maintain archival collections.

Switzerland. The Kunsthaus and the Zentralbibliothek, both in Zurich, have archival collections and provide information. The university libraries in Basle, Geneva and Lausanne, as well as some of the libraries of the Swiss cantons, also have manuscript holdings in the arts.

United Kingdom. The archival holdings, worldwide in scope, encompass materials from the Middle Ages to the present. In addition to public records offices and museums, archival documents can be found in academies, churches, the houses of landed families and universities. There exist some guides to these repositories, such as Foster and Sheppard's *British Archives: A Guide to Archive Resources in the United Kingdom* (1983), which includes 26 references to fine arts archives and 21 to art history archives. The Museum Documentation Association, founded in 1977, initially interested in the recording of museum items, is now also concerned with documentation related to artists and artefacts. The major art archival collections in London are the Royal Society of Arts, where transactions and correspondence in the archives date back to the society's foundation in 1754, and the Tate Gallery Archive (established in 1970), the national archive of 20th-century British art. For earlier periods the manuscript collections of the British Museum and the British Library contain rich resources. The archives of the Victoria and Albert Museum focus on the decorative arts. Such research centres as the Courtauld Institute and the Warburg Institute, now part of the University of London, contain major photographic archives and the working papers of Aby Warburg and other prominent scholars.

United States of America. The Archives of American Art, founded in 1954 in Detroit and since 1970 affiliated with the Smithsonian Institution in Washington, DC, collect the original records and oral histories of artists, dealers, publishers, collectors and historians, as well as those of related societies, institutions and business firms. With five regional research centres in New York, Washington, DC, Detroit, Boston and San Marino, CA, as well as an office in Rome, this archive is a unique, active repository for the art documentation of one country; it offers fellowships to enable scholars to utilize its resources. Its collections are supplemented by the archives of the National Museum of American Art, also affiliated with the Smithsonian Institution; the latter houses the inventory of American paintings from colonial times to 1914, and the Peter and Paul Juley archives. Other important archival collections in Washington, DC, are in the Library of Congress, with its pictorial archives and manuscript collections; the National Archives, with pictorial documentation from colonial times to the present; and the Center for the Advanced Study in the Visual Arts at the National Gallery of Art. In addition to its manuscript and ephemera collections, the Center has a photographic archive (established in 1971), which holds over a million photographs and three million microform images of works of art.

In New York the Metropolitan Museum of Art has several major archival collections, some of which are recorded with the Archives of American Art and in the RLIN database. The Museum of Modern Art's special collections include major papers of art-historical importance. The reference library and archives of the M. Knoedler Company contain 19th- and 20th-century auction catalogues and exhibition catalogues with reviews, cuttings and annotations. The Bettmann Archive has the largest commercial pictorial collection, with over five million images, including several thousands depicting works of art. The Brooklyn Museum Archives, established in 1985, hold materials dating back to 1823, including many documents relating to exhibitions and public art projects.

The photographic archives of the George Eastman House–International Museum of Photography in Rochester, NY, contain prints and negatives by over 8000 photographers from Louis Daguerre to the present, supplemented by a comprehensive reference library with rare serials. In Scottsdale, AZ, the Frank Lloyd Wright Foundation at Taliesin West holds the architect's documents, including thousands of letters and drawings. *The National Union Catalog of Manuscript Collections* lists more than 100 general repositories holding art documents.

(ix) Other archival resources. Historical societies, as well as regional and municipal agencies, often collect documents and news items on artists who have lived in their communities, and on museum activities and art in public buildings. Church records may have correspondence and drawings related to artists in their congregation and to sculptures, liturgical objects and stained-glass windows. Companies have files with illustrations of their product designs and advertisements and posters. Newspapers keep back issues, and radio and television stations have records of their programmes. Special-interest groups have files of their activities. All of these repositories contain source material, such as reviews of exhibitions and biographical data, not available elsewhere. Religious archives, such as those of seminaries and monasteries, or of church organizations and their historical societies, contain a wealth of resources. In Germany the Arbeitsgemeinschaft für das Archiv und Bibliothekswesen in der Evangelischen Kirche coordinates the activities of the major Protestant church archives. *The Parish Register of England* (1974) provides a good introduction to collections, offering a valuable guide to artists' social and cultural backgrounds. Roman Catholic repositories can usually be found at diocesan offices and at universities and seminaries. An outstanding example of a Jewish archive outside Israel is at the Leo Baeck Institute in New York, which includes documents of prominent artists and art historians.

Further information can be found in general bibliographies and directories, such as the *International Directory of Arts*, and in national and regional reference works; most museums have archival files related to their interest.

(x) Future developments. New technologies will allow more precise indexing, with resulting improvement in access to records, and facilitate communication about holdings. Although the technical means for the exchange of data already exist, there must first be agreement on record structures and vocabulary control. Sophisticated computer programmes can overcome some incompatibility of data, but basic field definitions and authority work have to be carried out. The numbers of users and the volume of their demands will increase, necessitating an improved information delivery service. The Archives and Special Collections Task Force of the North American Research Libraries Group, which manages the RLIN database, is considering guidelines for access policies. Clearer statements of policy for the management and appraisal of current art records should also emerge.

It is probable that art researchers will see closer cooperation among the various professionals concerned with art archives; this was heralded by the *International Symposium on Harmonization of Education and Training Programmes in Information Science, Librarianship and Archival Studies*, published by UNESCO (Paris, 1984). In 1982 the Museums Association of Great Britain produced a *Statement of Policy Relating to Archives* and has published guidelines for archivists in its 1992 *Yearbook*. Electronic communications between archives will increase; an example of a new and experimental electronic network is the European Remote Access to Museum Archives (RAMA) project, which involves the Museo del Prado in Madrid, the Beazley Archive in the Ashmolean Museum, Oxford, the Musée d'Orsay, Paris, and others. Finally, the definition of scope of collections is likely to be approached cooperatively, with an increasing awareness of what others are collecting. Archives are already becoming part of networks and are developing closer ties between the producers of documents and their archival keepers.

See also CATALOGUE, LIBRARY and the 'Art libraries and photographic collections' sections of country surveys.

BIBLIOGRAPHY

The World of Learning (London, 1947, 36/1986)
Répertoire international des archives photographiques d'oeuvres d'art (London, *c.* 1950)
L. Ash: *Subject Collections: A Guide to Special Book Collections and Subject Emphases as Reported by University, College, Public and Special Libraries and Museums in the United States and Canada* (New York, 1958, 3/1993)
National Union Catalog of Manuscript Collections (Washington, DC, 1959–)
Archvs Amer. A. J. (1960–)
J. Gadille: *Guide des archives diocésaines françaises* (Lyon, *c.* 1970)
D. Zidouemba: *Directory of Documentation, Libraries and Archives Services in Africa* (Paris, 1977)
Directory of Archives and Manuscript Repositories in the United States (Washington, DC, 1978)
C. Hommel: 'A Model Museum Archives', *Mus. News*, lviii/2 (1979), pp. 62–9
UNESCO J. Inf. Sci., Librsp & Archvs Admin. (1979–)
The Card Catalog of the Manuscript Collections of the Archives of American Art, 10 vols (Wilmington, DE, 1980)
R. E. Ehrenberg: *Archives and Manuscripts: Maps and Architectural Drawings* (Chicago, 1982)
R. Berner: *Archival Theory and Practice in the United States: A Historical Analysis* (Seattle and London, 1983)
J. Foster and J. Sheppard: *British Archives: A Guide to Archive Resources in the United Kingdom* (London, 1983)
W. Deiss: *Museum Archives: An Introduction* (Chicago, 1984)
International Symposium on Harmonization of Education and Training Programmes in Information Science, Librarianship and Archival Studies: Paris, 1984
M. Cook and K. Grant with P. Starkey: *A Manual of Archival Description* (London, 1985); 2nd edn M. Cook and M. Proctor (Aldershot, 1989)
P. Walne, ed.: *Modern Archives Administration and Records Management* (Paris, 1985)
J. A. Fleckner: 'An Archivist Speaks to the Museum Profession', *Mus. News*, lxv/1 (1986), pp. 17–25
Archvs & Mus. Inf. (1987–)
Mus. Archivist (1987–)
A. Pederson: *Keeping Archives* (Sydney, 1987)
A. Giral: 'At the Confluence of Three Traditions: Architectural Drawings at the Avery Library of Columbia University', *Lib. Trends*, xxxvii/2 (1988), pp. 232–42
A. B. Lemke: 'Art Archives: A Common Concern of Archivists, Librarians and Museum Professionals', *A. Libs J.*, xiv/2 (1989), pp. 5–11

ANTJE B. LEMKE, DEIRDRE C. STAM

Archivolt. Continuous curved moulding framing the face of an arch (*see* ARCH, fig. 1).

Archizoom (Associati). Italian architectural and design partnership formed in 1966 by Andrea Branzi (*b* 1939), Gilberto Corretti (*b* 1941), Paolo Deganello (*b* 1940) and Massimo Morozzi. These were joined by Dario Bartolini and Lucia Bartolini in 1968. They were based in Florence and were influenced initially by the utopian visions of the English architectural group Archigram. They achieved international prominence following appearances at the *Superarchitettura* exhibitions of radical architecture held at Pistoia (1966) and Modena (1967) and organized with the SUPERSTUDIO group. Numerous projects and essays reflected the group's search for a new, highly flexible and technology-based approach to urban design, and in the late 1960s exhibition and product design began to form a significant part of their work. The Superonda and Safari sofas, designed for the Poltronova company, combine modular flexibility with kitsch-inspired shiny plastic and leopard-skin finishes. Their central aim of stimulating individual creativity and fantasy was the focus of installations such as the *Centre for Electric Conspiracy*, with its closed, perfumed meditation areas housing exotic objects from different cultures, and the empty grey room presented at *Italy: The New Domestic Landscape*, an exhibition held at MOMA, New York, in 1972. In the latter a girl's voice describes the light and colour of a beautiful house that is left to the listener to imagine. Dress is the theme of the two films (*Vestirsi è facile* and *Come è fatto il capotto di Gogol*) that the group made shortly before disbanding in 1974 to follow separate careers.

WRITINGS

A. Branzi: *The Hot House: Italian New Wave Design* (London, 1984)

BIBLIOGRAPHY

A. George: 'Archizoom Hydra', *Archit. Des.*, xliii (1972), pp. 2–16
C. Jencks: *Modern Movements in Architecture* (Harmondsworth, 1973)
P. Navone and B. Orlandoni: *Architettura radicale* (Milan, 1974)
M. Pidgeon: 'Archizoom', *Space Des.*, 121 (1974), pp. 124–36

□

Arcimboldo [Arcimboldi], **Giuseppe** (*b* ?Milan, ?1527; *d* Milan, 11 July 1593). Italian painter, draughtsman and tapestry designer, active also in Austria and Bohemia. He came from a distinguished Milanese family that included a number of archbishops of the city; his father was the painter Biagio Arcimboldo. Giuseppe is first documented in 1549, working with his father for Milan Cathedral; he received payments until 1558 for supplying paintings, designs for an altar baldacchino and stained-glass windows for the cathedral: the *Story of Lot* and the *Life of St Catherine* in the south transept windows are usually attributed to him. He collaborated with Giuseppe Meda in designing the *gonfalone* of St Ambrose in Milan, probably sometime soon after 1558. In 1556 he received a commission to paint the south wall and vault of the south transept of Monza Cathedral, also in Lombardy, a work that must have been completed by 1562. Portions of a fresco of the *Tree of Jesse* on the south wall there can be attributed to him. In 1558 he was paid for designing tapestries for Como Cathedral (*in situ*). On the basis of stylistic comparison with the windows in Milan and the frescoes in Monza, the design of a tapestry representing *St John the Baptist Preaching and Baptizing* (Monza, Mus. Duomo) can be attributed to Arcimboldo. The Archbishop of Milan, Carlo Borromeo, probably paid for this tapestry.

Arcimboldo was therefore an established painter when he was called to the Viennese court of Emperor Ferdinand I in 1562. Nothing in his previous works, however, prepares the way for his most famous invention: the series of composite heads made up from objects pertaining to them, first exemplified in the *Four Seasons*, such as *Spring* (probably 1563; Madrid, Real Acad. S Fernando, Mus.) from spring flowers or *Summer* (1563; Vienna, Ksthist. Mus.) from grain that blooms then. He entered imperial service as a portrait painter, first recorded there in 1564 as *Hofconterfetter* of Emperor Maximilian II. However, with the exception of his own *Self-portrait* (*c.* 1570; untraced; see Kaufmann, 1985, *L'Ecole de Prague*, p. 214), no painted portraits can be convincingly attributed to him, though several examples have been suggested (e.g. Innsbruck, Schloss Ambras) and a number of portrait drawings survive (two portraits of *Rudolf II*, 1575, Prague, N. Mus.; and a *Self-portrait*, Prague, N.G., Convent of St George; see fig. 1). The composite heads were certainly the most celebrated in Arcimboldo's own time, and, along with his festival designs, made his name.

1. Giuseppe Arcimboldo: *Self-portrait*, pen and blue ink, blue wash, 230×157 mm, *c.* 1575 (Prague, National Gallery, Convent of St George)

Further interpretation of the composite heads is possible thanks to surviving poems (Vienna, Österreich. Nbib.) by Giovanni Battista Fontana (ii), who was possibly an artistic collaborator at court from *c.* 1568 to 1571 (as is suggested by a drawing for a tournament; Berlin, Dt. Staatsbib.). These poems were presented at court along with the series of the *Seasons* of 1563 and the first versions of the *Elements* (1566; *Water* and *Fire*, Vienna, Ksthist. Mus.; *Earth* and *Air*, priv. cols; see Kaufmann, 1987, pp. 92 and 98) and show that the paintings were intended as allegories on imperial rule. Individual pictures, adorned with numerous Habsburg symbols and imprese, are related to each other according to an elaborate string of associations suggesting that as the Habsburgs ruled the world of states, the body politic, and hence claimed dominion over the microcosm, so too they may be seen to hold sway over the macrocosm, the universe.

Whereas Arcimboldo's paintings may now be considered witty plays of artifice in the way that they harmonize seemingly disharmonious elements to make their point, these series, as well as further sets sent to other European courts (e.g. to Dresden: *Four Seasons*, 1573; Paris, Louvre), may best be regarded as serious jokes. This notion is an expression of the Renaissance love for paradox, according to which serious content could be presented in fanciful form. Jokes were long employed to present a serious point entertainingly; this idea among others was discussed in another treatise on laughter by Fontana (*De risu*, Vienna, Österreich. Nbib.). Moreover, from antiquity it was thought to be a sign of a ruler's *urbanitas* that he could take and tell a joke. The wit of Arcimboldo's inventions continued in the tournaments that he designed for the court. Descriptions and programmes are known for celebrations he organized in Prague (1570) and Vienna (1571). A volume of drawings (Florence, Uffizi) given to Rudolf II in 1585 represents Arcimboldo's designs, some dateable to 1571, in which he again adopted allegorical imagery to glorify the Habsburgs.

Apart from visiting Italy in 1566 and to record his will in Milan in the 1570s, Arcimboldo remained at court in Vienna and Prague. He was frequently rewarded by special payments, and his noble status was confirmed by Rudolf II in 1580. In 1582 he was sent to Germany to buy antiquities and rare objects for the imperial collections. He is also said to have designed water works, ciphers and a colour cembalo. Around 1587 he submitted drawings depicting the process of silk manufacture (Boston, MA, Mus. F.A.) for the central field of a grotesque decoration proposed to adorn the Prague palace of the president of the imperial *Hofkammer*, Baron Ferdinand Hoffmann (1540–1607). A letter accompanying the drawings reveals that Arcimboldo was familiar with several topics of contemporary theoretical dispute and that he assumed a 'modern' stance in the perennial dispute of 'ancients and moderns'.

Arcimboldo's connection with learned circles and discussions continued after he returned to Milan in 1587. The paintings of *Flora* and *Vertumnus* he did for the Emperor, in whose employ he remained and who made him a Count Palatine in 1592, were celebrated by many Italian writers, including Gregorio Comanini, Giovanni Paolo Lomazzo, Paolo Morigia (1524–1604), Gherardo Borgogni (1526–1608) and Bernardino Baldino (1556–1637). In particular the portrait of *Rudolf II as Vertumnus* (*c.* 1591; Skokloster, Skoklosters Slott; see fig. 2), which plays off a poem by Propertius (*c.* 55–16 BC) in several clever ways, represents the culmination of the imagery of Arcimboldo's composite heads in its glorification of the Emperor. Arcimboldo was much copied and imitated in his lifetime; his composite heads established a type that was often used subsequently (e.g. by Anton Mozart), and he was rediscovered in the 20th century by the Surrealists and other fantastic painters or followers of Dada.

2. Giuseppe Arcimboldo: *Rudolf II as Vertumnus*, oil on panel, 700×580 mm, *c.* 1591 (Skokloster, Skoklosters Slott)

BIBLIOGRAPHY

B. Geiger: *I dipinti ghiribizzosi di Giuseppe Arcimboldo* (Florence, 1954)
F. C. Legrand and F. Sluys: *Giuseppe Arcimboldo et les Arcimboldesques* (Brussels, 1955)
S. Alfons: 'Giuseppe Arcimboldo', *Symbolistor*, ii (1957), pp. 21–153
P. Preiss: *Giuseppe Arcimboldo* (Prague, 1967)
T. DaCosta Kaufmann: 'Arcimboldo's Imperial Allegories', *Z. Kstgesch.*, xxxix (1976), pp. 275–96
——: 'Arcimboldo au Louvre', *Rev. Louvre*, xxvii (1977), pp. 337–42
R. Barthes: *Arcimboldo* (Parma and Geneva, 1978)
T. DaCosta Kaufmann: *Variations on the Imperial Theme in the Age of Maximilian II and Rudolf II* (New York and London, 1978)
F. Porzio: *L'universo illusorio di Arcimboldi* (Milan, 1979, rev. 2/1987)
Drawings from the Holy Roman Empire, 1540–1680 (exh. cat. by T. DaCosta Kaufmann, Princeton U., NJ, A. Mus.; Washington, DC, N.G.A.; Pittsburgh, Carnegie; 1982–3), pp. 134–7
A. Beyer: *Giuseppe Arcimboldo Figurinen Kostüme und Entwürfe für höfische Feste* (Frankfurt am Main, 1983)
T. DaCosta Kaufmann: 'Arcimboldo and Propertius: A Classical Source for *Rudolf II as Vertumnus*', *Z. Kstgesch.*, xlviii/1 (1985), pp. 117–23
——: *L'Ecole de Prague: La Peinture à la cour de Rodolphe II* (Paris, 1985; rev. Eng. trans., Chicago and London, 1988)
S. Rasponi and C. Tanzi: *Effetto Arcimboldo* (exh. cat., ed. P. Hulten; Venice, Pal. Grassi, 1987)
T. DaCosta Kaufmann: 'A Tapestry Design by Giuseppe Arcimboldo', *Burl. Mag.*, cxxx (1988), pp. 428–30

Prag um 1600: Kunst und Kultur am Hofe Rudolfs II (exh. cat., ed. J. Schultze; Essen, Villa Hügel, 1988), cat. nos 111–14, 188–93
T. DaCosta Kaufmann: 'Arcimboldo's Work in Monza and the Artist's Early Career', *Stud. Monzesi*, iii (1989), pp. 5–17
——: 'Mysterious but Long Meaning: Taking Arcimboldo's Jokes Seriously', *The Visual and the Verbal Essays in Honor of William Heckscher* (New York, 1990), pp. 57–86
——: *The Mastery of Nature: Aspects of Science, Art and Humanism in the Renaissance* (Princeton, 1993)

THOMAS DACOSTA KAUFMANN

Arciniega [Arziniega]**, Claudio de** (*b* Burgos, 1526–7; *d* Mexico City, 1593). Mexican architect and sculptor of Spanish birth. In 1541 he moved from his native city to Madrid, where he served as an apprentice to Luis de Vega, one of the architects working in the High Renaissance style for Emperor Charles V. Arciniega worked with Vega in the remodelling of the Alcázar at Madrid. At intervals between 1542 and 1548 he worked under the direction of Rodrigo Gil de Hontañón as a sculptor on the plateresque façade of the university at Alcalá de Henares. He was possibly also responsible for the main retable in the church of Santiago at Guadalajara.

In 1554 Arciniega arrived in New Spain (now Mexico) with his brother Luis de Arciniega (1537–99), who was also an architect. He settled in Puebla de los Angeles (now Puebla) and worked there between 1554 and 1558, primarily engaged in a large number of public works as master mason. However, he established his reputation with the fountain that he constructed (1556–7) in the centre of the city's main plaza. After seeing the fountain, the viceroy engaged Arciniega to work for him in México (now Mexico City). Arciniega's career in the viceregal capital began in 1558, and a year later he designed the *Túmulo Imperial*, a temporary monument for the obsequies of Charles V (an engraving of 1560 of the design is preserved in Seville, Archv Gen. Indias). In the harmonic proportions, structural use of Classical orders and simplicity of ornamentation, the design displays a genuine High Renaissance style. Arciniega was thus one of the earliest exponents of the mature Renaissance in New Spain. In 1559 the viceroy appointed him Maestro Mayor for the viceregal capital, and 19 years later King Philip II bestowed on him the title of Obrero Mayor for New Spain. This was the highest honorific title to which an architect could then aspire. In 1578 Arciniega had reached the peak of professional glory.

As chief architect for México, Arciniega was involved, in one way or another, in all of the major projects of the city, which comprised at least five churches, two convents, three hospitals and one school for girls. He was the main architect for the construction of the Viceregal Palace (1563–76, destr. 1692). Outside México, he possibly designed the Franciscan church at Tecali, near Puebla (1568–9). In 1591 he made the plans for the church of S Mateo, Atenco, near México. He was also involved in 1576 in the design of the fortress of S Juan de Ulúa (Veracruz) and made recommendations concerning a projected relocation and new urban plan for the city of Veracruz. Arciniega also made assessments and recommendations on the project to construct the cathedral at Pátzcuaro (1560) and for rebuilding Puebla Cathedral (1564).

Arciniega's greatest architectural achievement, however, was his contribution to the cathedral of México, the largest church building in the western hemisphere until the 20th century (*see* MEXICO, fig. 3). In his capacity as Maestro Mayor, Arciniega was entrusted with designing the cathedral. By 1563 he had completed the ground-plan and elevation, based on those of various Spanish cathedrals, especially of Segovia and Salamanca. Serious problems relating to the stabilization of the building site delayed construction, but by 1570 the ground was consolidated; construction began in 1573, and by 1585 the foundations and boundary walls were well advanced. At the time of Arciniega's death, most of the exterior walls had been completed. Also concluded were the buttresses forming the peripheral chapels, some of the niches serving as altars for the latter, many of the interior piers and a few of the rib vaults on the eastern end of the building. Construction came almost to a halt after Arciniega's death. Between *c.* 1600 and 1610 Arciniega's scheme for the vaults was modified, possibly by Juan Miguel de Agüero (*fl* 1574–?1613). This was a more modern design, calling for saucer vaults and dome instead of the original rib vaulting scheme. The interior of the building was completed incorporating these modifications by 1667.

BIBLIOGRAPHY

H. Berlin: 'Artífices de la Catedral de México', *An. Inst. Invest. Estét.*, xi (1944), pp. 19–39
D. Angulo Iñiguez: *Historia del arte hispanoamericano*, i (Barcelona, 1945)
E. Marco Dorta: *Fuentes para la historia del arte hispanoamericano*, i (Seville, 1951)
M. Toussaint: *Claudio de Arciniega: Arquitecto de la Nueva España* (Mexico, 1981)

FRANÇOIS-AUGUSTE DE MONTÊQUIN

Arcis, Marc (*b* Cunq, Tarn, 1655; *d* Toulouse, 26 Oct 1739). French sculptor. He trained in Toulouse, where he received his first official commission in 1677. This was for 30 terracotta busts representing famous men of Toulouse, together with a bust of *Louis XIV* for the Galerie des Illustres of the Capitole (Hôtel de Ville; 21 still *in situ*). From 1678 to 1688 Arcis was employed by the Bâtiments du Roi, collaborating on the sculptural decorations for the château of Versailles. These included a stone statue personifying *Reason of State* on the south wing, as well as a marble vase and term figure of *Flora* for the gardens (all *in situ*). In 1684 he was received (*reçu*) by the Académie Royale on presentation of a marble low relief of *St Mark* (Versailles, Notre-Dame). The following year the city of Toulouse commissioned a bronze equestrian statue of *Louis XIV*, raised on a high base with four low reliefs and four seated statues of slaves; this did not progress beyond a terracotta model (Toulouse, Mus. Augustins). In 1688 Arcis began for the city of Pau a bronze standing statue of *Louis XIV*, based on a model by François Girardon; this was completed in 1697 and destroyed in 1792.

From 1690 Arcis settled permanently in Toulouse, where he set up a free drawing school, and was much in demand in Languedoc. He produced numerous works of sculpture for Toulouse: these included religious and secular sculptures (untraced) commissioned from 1693 to 1710 by the Archbishop of Toulouse, Jean-Baptiste Colbert de Villacerf; the high altar (1720) and baldacchino (1736) in St Sernin; marble statues of *St Mark* and *St Matthew* (1727) in the cathedral; and ten stucco low reliefs representing *Virtues* (before 1734) in St Jérôme (Chapelle des Pénitents Bleus). He was also responsible for a great secular decoration, that of the Toulouse Opéra (1725), of which the wall at the back of the stage, with a low relief in stucco of *Apollo and the Muses*, survives. His main project outside Toulouse was to provide ten monumental stone statues of *Evangelists*, *Church Fathers* and *Virtues* (1715–22; 6 *in situ*) for the façade of Montauban Cathedral.

A considerable proportion of Arcis's substantial oeuvre survives in reasonably good condition, as do a large number of terracotta models (Toulouse, Mus. Augustins). His sculpture, which is not without charm, was scarcely affected by the classicizing spirit of Versailles and demonstrates a free and original style tending towards the Baroque.

BIBLIOGRAPHY

Guiffrey; Lami; Mariette; Souchal

Biographie toulousaine ou dictionnaire historique, i (Toulouse, 1823), pp. 19–21

A. Fontaine: *Académiciens d'autrefois* (Paris, 1914), pp. 230–47

R. Mesuret: *Evocation du vieux Toulouse* (Paris, 1960)

M. Martin: *Monuments équestres de Louis XIV* (Paris, 1986), pp. 171–7

FRANÇOISE DE LA MOUREYRE

Arco, Alonso del (*b* ?Madrid, ?1635; *d* Madrid, 9 Aug 1704). Spanish painter. Born deaf and dumb, he was a pupil of Antonio de Pereda and was known as 'el sordillo de Pereda'. He was a prolific artist, although his many signed works are of unequal quality, largely because in his mature years his wife frequently obtained commissions at a low price. These compositions were copied from prints in his studio and were then only retouched or signed by Arco. Other works of higher quality and excellent technique show Pereda's influence, particularly in the treatment of still-life objects. The human figures that he portrayed, however, usually represent a characteristic type, with a triangular-shaped face and large, bulging eyes. He was a typical representative of the Madrid school and was also a good colourist.

Arco painted mainly in oil but also used tempera and fresco, e.g. his fresco decoration of the Camarín of the hermitage of La Virgen de la Oliva, Almonacid de Toledo, with scenes from the *Life of the Virgin* and the *Story of La Virgen de la Oliva* (1689; *in situ*).

The best of Arco's religious paintings are the altarpieces of *St John the Baptist* (*c.* 1675–85; Atienza, Guadalajara, S Juan del Mercado) and *St Filippo Neri* (*c.* 1675–85; Madrid, church of the Trinitarians). He painted several versions of the *Immaculate Conception*, the finest of which (1683) is in the Universitat de Barcelona. Also notable are the *Annunciation* (*c.* 1670–80; Madrid, Mus. Lázaro Galdiano) and the late work, *The Infant Jesus Asleep on the Cross* (1681; Madrid, Real Acad. S Fernando, Mus.), with its fine still-life detail. Arco was an excellent portrait painter, as is apparent in *Mariana of Austria* (1696; Toledo, Mus. Santa Cruz).

BIBLIOGRAPHY

Ceán Bermúdez

A. Palomino: *El Parnaso español pintoresco laureado* (Madrid, 1724, rev. 1947), pp. 1077–9

N. Galindo: 'Alonso del Arco', *Archv Esp. A.*, xlv (1972), pp. 347–85

——: 'Alonso del Arco: Un fresquista inédito', *Bol. Semin. Estud. A. & Arqueol.*, xlvi (1980), pp. 451–60

NATIVIDAD GALINDO

Arconati [Arconato], Conte **Galeazzo (Maria)** (*b* Milan, before 1592; *d* after 4 Oct 1648). Italian collector. He is best known for his collection of works by Leonardo da Vinci. He owned 12 small Leonardo notebooks as well as the *Codex Atlanticus*, which he donated to the Biblioteca Ambrosiana, Milan, in 1637, and several cartoons, among them the *Virgin and Child with St Anne*, known as the Burlington House Cartoon (London, N.G.), and a standing *Leda* (untraced). Inventories of the Arconati collection and Edward Wright's travel diary (1730) reveal that he had also owned the 11 coloured chalk drawings (e.g. Chapel Hill, U. NC, Ackland A. Mus.; Melbourne, N.G. Victoria) after Leonardo's *Last Supper* (Milan, S Maria delle Grazie), attributed to Giovanni Antonio Boltraffio (Brown), and also paintings by Raphael and Andrea del Sarto. During the 1630s Arconati corresponded with Cassiano dal Pozzo, who was trying to procure Leonardo manuscripts for the Barberini library and to prepare compilations of Leonardo's writings for publication. Passages on mechanics, hydraulics, light and shadow and perspective and additional chapters on painting were collected into 'treatises' by Arconati with the help of his son, Francesco (Brother Luigi Maria, *b* 1600; *d* after 1644), and one Father Gallo and sent to dal Pozzo. Only the *Treatise on Painting* was eventually published (Paris, 1651), but a volume of notes on hydraulics, compiled by Francesco, was presented to Cardinal Francesco Barberini in 1643 (*Dal moto e misura dell'acqua*; Rome, Vatican, Bib. Apostolica, MS. Vat. Lat. Barb. 4332). Around 1620 Arconati built an elegant villa at Castellazzo, for which he amassed a considerable collection of sculpture, including a colossal antique statue of *Pompey the Great*; he also had parts of the tomb of *Gaston de Foix* by AGOSTINO BUSTI, in particular the seven bas-reliefs, which he is believed to have bought (Beltrami).

BIBLIOGRAPHY

DBI

E. Wright: *Some Observations Made in Travelling through France, Italy, etc. in the Years 1720, 1721 and 1722* (London, 1730)

'Istrumento della donazione di dodici manoscritti di Leonardo da Vinci fatta alla Biblioteca Ambrosiana . . . 1637', *Ricerche intorno a Leonardo da Vinci*, ed. G. Uzielli (Rome, 1884), pp. 235–54

L. Beltrami: 'La villa di Castellazzo dei Conti Sormani-Busca', *Ville e castelli d'Italia, Lombardia e Laghi* (Milan, 1907), pp. 65–82

E. Carusi: 'Lettere di Galeazzo Arconati e Cassiano del Pozzo per lavori sui manoscritti di Leonardo', *Accad. & Bib. Italia*, iii/6 (1929–30), pp. 503–15

D. Brown: *Precedents and Reflections*, iii of *Leonardo's 'Last Supper': Before and After* (Washington, 1983)

JANIS CALLEN BELL

Arconio, Mario (*b* Rome, ?1575; *d* Rome, 1635). Italian painter and architect. He was a courtier–artist in the service of Cardinal Camillo Borghese, whose patronage he had the misfortune to abandon just before the latter's election as Pope Paul V in 1605. Arconio remained in the town of Cori, of which he was governor, during most of the pontificate but returned to Rome in 1620 and submitted a design (unexecuted) for a new house and oratory for the Congregation of the Oratory. He painted a fresco over the door of the church of S Maria in Campo Carleo (destr. 1862), finished the convent and high altar of S Isidoro begun by Felice Antonio Casone (1559–1634), decorated the Cappella Merenda in S Maria della Vittoria (*c.* 1630), the portal of S Eufemia (destr. early 19th century), restored S Urbano ai Pantani (1634) and built the adjacent convent (destr.) under the patronage of Cardinal Francesco Maria del Monte. He also worked on the Villa Sannesi (destr.) on the Via Flaminia and created the portal (destr.) of the Sannesi garden in the Borgo district of Rome. Exact building dates for his works, the attributions of which are based on Giovanni Baglione's lists, are unknown, and Arconio remains an enigmatic personality.

BIBLIOGRAPHY
G. Baglione: *Vite* (1642); ed. V. Mariani (1935), pp. 327–9
J. Connors: *Borromini and the Roman Oratory* (Cambridge, MA, and London, 1980), pp. 13–14
L. A. R. de Amicis: 'Studi su città e architettura nella Roma di Paolo V Borghese (1605–1621)', *Boll. Cent. Stud. Stor. Archit.*, xxxi (1984), pp. 1–97

Arcucci, Camillo (*b* ?Sigillo, nr Nocera; *d* Rome, ?6 Feb 1667). Italian architect. He is representative of the conservative and decorative current in 17th-century Roman architecture that co-existed with the spatial innovations of the Baroque masters. Early in his career, in 1652, he replaced Borromini as the architect of the Casa dei Filippini in Rome, rebuilding the high altar of the Oratory (1653–64) and completing the long residential wing of the building (1659–62), more or less following Borromini's plans. The ornate marble revetment of this altar and some of the elaborate mouldings in the main staircase in this wing reflect Arcucci's decorative style, as does the campanile built to his design (1666) for the Oratorian church S Maria in Vallicella (the Chiesa Nuova). His major commissions for the Roman aristocracy are the Palazzo Gottifredi-Grazioli and the façade of the Palazzo Pio di Carpi near the Campo dei Fiori, both presumably built during the pontificate of Alexander VII (1655–67). Between 1646 and 1658 he designed the Piazza di 16 Viale, with the Eagle and Triton fountain at Villa Mattei, a commission in which Bernini may have been marginally involved.

Arcucci drew up his will on 6 February 1667. Although he was buried in an unmarked grave at S Maria in Vallicella, Arcucci left funds for the completion of a small suburban church, S Maria del Rosario (or della Febbre) on Monte Mario, Rome, which he had been rebuilding to serve as his memorial. To his adopted son, Giuseppe Brusati Arcucci, he left his architectural instruments and volumes of drawings of vases, candelabra, fountains, cornices and tombs. He possessed a handsome library covering the subjects of fortification, artillery, mechanics, hydraulics, geometry and measurement, alongside the usual exemplars of Alberti, Vitruvius, Serlio and Vignola.

BIBLIOGRAPHY
J. Connors: *Borromini and the Roman Oratory* (Cambridge, MA, 1980), pp. 53–4, 226–7, 270–71
A. Blunt: *A Guide to Baroque Rome* (London, 1982), pp. 110, 182, 190
C. Benocci: 'Il rinnovamento seicentesco della Villa Mattei al Celio: Francesco Peparelli, Andrea Sacchi, Andrea Lilli ed altri artisti', *Stor. A.*, lxvi (1989), pp. 187–96, esp. p. 196
J. Connors: 'Virgilio Spada's Defence of Borromini', *Burl. Mag.*, cxxxi (1989), pp. 76–90

JOSEPH CONNORS

Ardabil [Ardabīl; Ardebil]. City in Azerbaijan in north-west Iran *c.* 180 km east of Tabriz, situated on the eastern slopes of Mt Sabalan, an extinct volcano, and with a population of *c.* 222,000. Founded in the pre-Islamic period, it flourished after the Arab conquest in the 7th century, often serving as the capital of Azerbaijan. It was sacked by the Mongols in 1220 and was subsequently overshadowed by Tabriz, but its partial recovery was marked by the erection of a new congregational mosque in the early 14th century. Now ruined, this consisted of a rectangular hypostyle prayer hall with a square domed 'sanctuary' in front of the mihrab.

Ardabil became one of Iran's holiest cities under the SAFAVID dynasty (*reg* 1501–1732), which was descended from a local mystic, Shaykh Safi al-Din Ishaq (*d* 1334). Through the patronage of the Safavid shahs, his tomb and the associated hospice (*khānaqāh*) became an important shrine. The main buildings are clustered around a rectangular paved courtyard. On the north side is the Jannatsaray (*c.* 1540), a domed, octagonal building intended for Sufi gatherings and prayer. To the east lies the Dar al-Huffaz (begun 1334), a large rectangular hall for Koran reading, with an apsidal extension leading south to the cylindrical tomb tower of Shaykh Safi al-Din, built in 1334–44. East of this is the domed square tomb of his son Muhyi'l-Din (*d* 1324/5). Beyond the Dar al-Huffaz is a large, domed, octagonal building that has been known as the Chinikhana ('House of Porcelain') since a thousand pieces of Chinese porcelain were deposited there by Shah ʿAbbas I between 1607 and 1611. Shah ʿAbbas also donated a great library to the shrine, but this was plundered by the Russians in 1828, and its contents, which included many rare manuscripts, are now in the St Petersburg Public Library. Two of the most spectacular carpets of the Safavid period were purportedly made for the shrine. Known as the Ardabil carpets (London, V&A, and Los Angeles, CA, Co. Mus. A.; *see* ISLAMIC ART, §VI, 4(iii)(c) and fig. 200), they were woven in 1539–40 as a matched pair. In the nearby village of Kalkhuran is the tomb of Safi al-Din's father, Shaykh Jabra'il (*d* 1258/9). It consists of a pentagonal entrance and a square tomb chamber surmounted by a tall, bulbous dome and is mainly the work of Shah ʿAbbas, who ordered its repair and redecoration in 1620–21.

BIBLIOGRAPHY
Enc. Iran.
J. A. Pope: *Chinese Porcelains from the Ardebil Shrine* (Washington, DC, 1956)
A. H. Morton: 'The Ardabīl Shrine in the Reign of Shāh Ṭahmāsp I', *Iran*, xii (1974), pp. 31–64; xiii (1975), pp. 39–58
R. Stead: *The Ardabil Carpets* (Malibu, CA, 1974)

ABBAS DANESHVARI

Ardagh Treasure. A treasure hoard (now in Dublin, N. Mus.) discovered in 1868 within the rath (circular earthwork) called Reerasta Rath, near Ardagh in Co. Limerick, Ireland. The objects were buried slightly less than 1 m deep and partly protected by an upright stone. The hoard consists of a splendid two-handled chalice, a smaller bronze chalice and four gilt silver brooches. The probable dates of manufacture range from the 8th century AD to perhaps the early 10th.

The silver chalice (h. 178 mm; max diam. 195 mm) has a broad, almost hemispherical bowl, a copper-alloy stem cast in three parts, and a large, sub-conical foot with a broad, flat foot-ring (see fig.). A band of filigree ornaments and gem-set enamel studs girdles the bowl below the ring.

Ardagh Chalice, silver, gilt-copper, enamels, gold, hardstones, h. 178 mm, ?mid-8th century (Dublin, National Museum of Ireland)

Below this are two applied medallions with filigree and enamels. The strap handles spring from applied escutcheons decorated with enamel, filigree and granulation. The stem carries superb cast gilt *kerbschnitt* (chip-carved) ornaments; curvilinear, Ultimate La Tène designs and animal patterns are noteworthy. The upper- and underside of the foot-ring are heavily decorated. The bowl, foot and stem are united by a large copper-alloy pin with a split ending. The catch plate for its spread leaves is concealed on the underside by a magnificent roundel of *kerbschnitt* ornament and a band of filigree animals around a large central rock crystal.

On the body of the bowl, just below the girdle, are the names of 11 Apostles and St Paul in lightly incised lettering set off by the stippled background. The style of the letters is similar to that of the LINDISFARNE GOSPELS. Animal and human heads are also lightly incised on the surface of the bowl. Stamped motifs, knitted wire mesh, malachite, amber and mica are also used in the ornament. The style of the chalice is similar to that of the Derrynaflan paten (*see* DERRYNAFLAN TREASURE), and it was probably made in the mid-8th century. Like the paten, it is a complex structure, and the two may stem from the same workshop tradition. Like the Derrynaflan chalice, the bowl is an adaptation of a traditional form to liturgical use. The large foot, bowl girdle, stem construction and elaborate strap handles make the Derrynaflan and Ardagh chalices each the other's closest analogue. They are presumably the sole survivors of a type that was originally more widespread.

The bronze chalice was damaged at the time of discovery and was originally *c.* 110–120 mm high. It is 138 mm in diameter and appears to have had a short funnel-shaped foot. Three of the silver brooches belong to the pseudo-pennanular type and are of cast silver gilt. The largest bears, on the obverse, zones of cast interlace and three large applied birds (that formerly on the pinhead is now missing); it may date to *c.* 800. The other two are smaller and decorated on their margins with animals, in one case openwork beasts, a feature characteristic of 9th-century brooches. The fourth brooch is a pennanular form of thistle brooch with ball-shaped terminals. The type appears to have become current in the later 9th century and to have remained in use until well into the 10th. The Ardagh hoard, therefore, represents an accumulated treasure that may have been deposited in the 10th century, perhaps, like the Derrynaflan Treasure, as a result of Viking activity.

See also INSULAR ART, §2.

BIBLIOGRAPHY

Earl of Dunraven: 'On an Ancient Chalice and Brooches Lately Found at Ardagh in the County of Limerick', *Trans. Royal Irish Acad.*, xxiv (1874), pp. 433–54

L. Gogan: *The Ardagh Chalice* (Dublin, 1932)

R. Organ: 'Examination of the Ardagh Chalice: A Case History', *Application of Science in Examination of Works of Art*, ed. W. J. Young (Boston, 1973), pp. 238–71

Treasures of Ireland: Irish Art, 1500 BC–1500 AD (exh. cat., ed. P. Cone; New York, Met., 1977)

Treasures of Ireland: Irish Art, 3000 BC–1500 AD (exh. cat., ed. M. Ryan; Dublin, Royal Irish Acad., 1983), pp. 124–32

M. Ryan: 'The Derrynaflan and other Irish Eucharistic Chalices', *Ireland and Europe: The Early Church* (Stuttgart, 1984), pp. 135–48

——: *Early Irish Communion Vessels: Church Treasures of the Golden Age* (Dublin, 1986)

MICHAEL RYAN

Ardalan, Nader (*b* Tehran, 9 March 1939). Iranian architect, urban planner and writer. He studied architecture at the Carnegie Institute of Technology, Pittsburgh (BA, 1961) and at Harvard University, Cambridge, MA (MArch, 1962). He worked in several firms in the USA, including Skidmore, Owings & Merrill, before returning to Iran to work for the National Iranian Oil Company (1964–6). In 1966 he became Design Partner for Iran's largest archictectural firm, Abdul Aziz Farman Farmaian & Associates, in Tehran, and in 1972 he set up his own practice in Tehran, the Mandala Collaborative. Ardalan, whose work ranges from private residences to master plans for new towns, is one of the most important architects to emerge from Iran in the recent past. His work reflects his particular concern for cultural and ecological aspects of architecture; in Iran it is strongly rooted in an understanding of the traditions and forms of Iranian Islam, although his buildings are in a totally contemporary idiom. Perhaps his best-known work is the Iran Centre for Management Studies (1972) in Tehran, which consists of four iwans, or vaulted structures arranged formally around a central courtyard. His use of geometry, the enclosed courtyard and the vault are drawn from Islamic tradition; other traditional concepts reinterpreted in his work include the use of water and light, symbolic axes and the 'paradise garden'. Other innovative works in Iran include the Behshahr Home Offices (1974), Tehran (now used as the Ministry of Industry), as well as plans for Bu Ali Sina University (1977, with Georges Candilis) in Hamadan and several new towns such as Nutan, near Isfahan (1978), designed with a traditional paradise garden as its axial spine. In 1977 Ardalan moved to the USA, continuing his practice in Boston and undertaking work in Pakistan, France, Israel and Turkey, for example the Old City Preservation Plan for Jerusalem (1984) and the Ankara Sheraton Hotel Centre (1985). He joined Jung/Brannen International, Boston, in 1983 and became a Principal Associate. His work in the USA covers planning, interior design and architecture. He was appointed Principal in charge of planning for the clean-up of Boston Harbour during the 1990s, including the creation of new land forms containing a sewage plant; other projects included a prizewinning competition entry for the Citizens' Plaza Office (1989), a triangular-shaped building set in the context of a historic site in Providence, RI. He was appointed Visiting Professor at Harvard and at Yale University, New Haven, CT.

WRITINGS

with L. Bakhtiar: *A Sense of Unity: The Sufi Tradition in Persian Architecture* (Chicago, 1973)
Blessed Jerusalem (Cambridge, MA, 1983)
'On Mosque Architecture', *Architecture and Community: Building in the Islamic World Today*, eds R. Holod and D. Rastorfer (Millerton, NY, 1983), pp. 55–6

BIBLIOGRAPHY

R. Beny: *Iran: Elements of Destiny* (Toronto, 1978)
J. M. Dixon: 'Cultural Hybrid—Tehran Museum of Contemporary Art', *Prog. Archit.*, lix/5 (1978), pp. 68–71
Y. Pontoizeau: 'Architectures iraniennes', *Archit. Aujourd'hui*, cxcv (1978), pp. 5–8, 17–24

HASAN-UDDIN KHAN

Ard el-Na'am. *See under* HELIOPOLIS (i).

Ardemans, Teodoro (*b* Madrid, 1664; *d* Madrid, 15 Feb 1726). Spanish architect, painter and writer. He was trained in architecture by the Jesuits and in painting by Claudio Coello and worked mainly as an architect. Two overdoors showing multiple allegorical scenes of the *Battle of Lepanto* (1721; Madrid, Pal. Arzobisp.) and a *St Barbara* (1723; Madrid, Mus. Lázaro Galdiano) reveal Ardemans as a talented painter working in the tradition of Francisco Rizi, Juan Carreño de Miranda and Francisco de Herrera the younger, and partially influenced by Luca Giordano. His debt to Coello is apparent in a ceiling fresco attributed to him in the Capilla del Cristo de los Dolores of the Venerable Orden Tercera de San Francisco, Madrid, which shows St Francis riding in a chariot of fire with figures watching from a balcony. Also attributed to Ardemans is the portrait of *Pedro Atanasio Bocanegra* (*c.* 1689; Granada, Pal. Arzobisp.).

As an architect, Ardemans belongs to a period of transition, continuing into the 18th century the Baroque tradition of the Madrid school. He worked in Granada (1689–91) as chief architect of the cathedral, also advising on civil and engineering works. He returned to Madrid in 1691 as deputy municipal architect, becoming municipal architect in 1700. The doorways and towers of the Casa de la Villa, the Ayuntamiento in Madrid, remodelled by him *c.* 1690, are a good example of his bold manner and cosmopolitan taste. The doorways are Italianate and the heraldic pedestals are reminiscent of the style of John Vanbrugh in England. The capitals of the Ayuntamiento in Toledo (1693) were built following a design of Ardemans, who was in charge of the cathedral works in that city from 1694. He became chief designer of the royal works in 1702 and Pintor de Cámara in 1704.

From 1719 Ardemans was involved in the first great building of the Spanish Bourbon dynasty, the palace of La Granja in San Ildefonso, near Segovia, built on the site of a farm and Jeronimite monastery founded in 1477 and acquired by Philip V in 1718. Ardemans was required to design a palace and chapel using the 16th-century cloister as a nucleus. Work started in April 1721 and both palace and chapel were ready for benediction and consecration in 1723. Ardemans designed a very simple Alcázar-type palace. Square in plan and set around a central courtyard, the Patio de la Fuente, it has four towers at the corners. The Baroque capitals of the towers are still visible despite the recasing (1735–9) of the whole structure by Filippo Juvarra and Giovanni Battista Sacchetti. The palace chapel, the Colegiata, elevated to collegiate church status in 1723, is in a Latin cross plan crowned by a dome. Modelled on the parish church of Alpagés, Aranjuez (1681–1705), it follows the traditional style of Baroque churches in Madrid and is set at an axis to the palace façade, its dome rising above the palace towers to form a picturesque grouping. In its original form, Ardemans's design recalled the Escorial, which offered a similar view of a church flanked by the palace towers. Like the palace, the chapel was subsequently given a grander appearance (1727–34 and 1736–80). For the chapel he also designed the high altar dedicated to San Ildefonso, an elaborate construction in bronze and such rich materials as jasper, which was unfinished at his death. Ardemans's interest in urban planning and engineering is reflected in his two treatises (*see* Writings below).

WRITINGS

Declaración y extensión sobre las ordenanzas de Madrid, que escribió Juan de Torrija, y de las que se practicaban en Toledo y Sevilla, con algunas advertencias a los alarifes (Madrid, 1719)
Fluencias de la tierra y curso subterráneo de las aguas (Madrid, 1724)

BIBLIOGRAPHY

Ceán Bermúdez
E. Llaguno y Amirola: *Noticias* (1829), iv, pp. 110–14, 217–18
G. Kubler and M. Soria: *Art and Architecture in Spain and Portugal and their American Dominions, 1500–1800*, Pelican Hist. A. (Harmondsworth, 1959), pp. 21, 33, 38, 43, 298
J. del Corral: *Teodoro Ardemans, maestro mayor de las obras de Madrid y su fontanero mayor* (Madrid, 1974)

□

Ardenti, Alessandro (*fl* 1539; *d* Turin, 20 Aug 1595). Italian painter. Probably a native of Faenza, although sometimes thought to have been from Pisa or Lucca, he worked in a Mannerist style and enjoyed a long and prolific career. Ardenti's earliest known work is a *Nativity* in the parish church, Antraccoli, near Lucca, signed *Alexander Ardentius faventinus* and dated 1539. Other extant dated paintings bearing the same signature are the *Virgin and Child with Saints* (1565; Lucca, S Paolino), the *Madonna of Mercy* (1565; Lucca, S Salvatore) and an *Assumption* (1567; Sesto, parish church). The signature *Alexander Ardentius lucensis* appears on a canvas depicting *St John the Baptist with SS Jerome and Joseph* in the parish church, Lunata, near Lucca. About 1572, Ardenti moved to Turin where he was employed as a painter and sculptor to the Savoys, first by Duke Emanuel-Philibert (*reg* 1558–80) and then by his successor Duke Charles-Emanuel I (*reg* 1580–1630). Documents confirm Ardenti's marriage in 1583 and a journey to Milan the following year. His widow and children received a pension after his death. While a noticeable hardness is evident in his work at Lucca, the Turin paintings reveal an affinity with the Roman school (Lanzi). Stylistic differences between some of the paintings possibly indicate the hands of two different artists, both named Alessandro Ardenti, perhaps a father and son (Sardini).

UNPUBLISHED SOURCES

Lucca, Archv Stato [Arch. Sardini, MS. 124 n. 14—MS. of G. Sardini: *Notizie dei due Ardenti*]

BIBLIOGRAPHY

DBI; Thieme–Becker

L. Lanzi: *Storia pittorica della Italia* (Bassano, 1795–6; Eng. trans., London, 1847)

G. M. Valgimigli: *Dei pittori e degli artisti faentini dei secoli XV e XVI* (Faenza, 1871), p. 162

A. Baudi di Vesme: 'L'arte alla corte di Emanuele Filiberto e di Carlo Emanuele I nei primi anni del suo regno', *Atti Soc. Piemont. Archeol. & B.A.*, xi (1929), pp. 146–66

SUSANNE JULIANE WARMA

Ardistan [Ardistāni; Ardestān]. Iranian town in the province of Isfahan, just east of the road from Natanz to Na'in. It occupies an ancient site and preserves the ruins of a Sasanian fire-temple, but the most important monuments date from the medieval period, when Ardistan was a flourishing agricultural centre, renowned for its silk. By the 10th century the town was fortified and had five gates. Its congregational mosque, which now has a four-iwan plan, was first built during this period; a tunnel-vaulted arcade in the south-west corner with a fragmentary kufic inscription and polylobed piers can be attributed to the 10th century, when similar work was done on the Friday Mosque at Isfahan (*see* ISLAMIC ART, §II, 5(i)(a)). In 1158–60 the mosque was remodelled on the orders of Abu Tahir Husayn ibn Ghali ibn Ahmad by the master Mahmud ibn al-Isfahani known as al-Ghazi (*see* ISLAMIC ART, §II, 5(i)(b)). The domed bay in front of the mihrab and the adjacent qibla iwan date from this rebuilding and are notable for their original decoration, which includes three stucco mihrabs, brickwork highlighted in red and white and plaster decoration in purple, yellow, white and blue. In 1539–40 the mosque was greatly enlarged, the three other iwans were rebuilt (for illustration *see* IWAN) and a corridor was added along the east side. Near the congregational mosque is the ruined mosque of Imam Hasan (*c.* 1150); its main portal is surmounted by twin minarets, an early example of this form.

BIBLIOGRAPHY

Enc. Iran.: 'Ardestān'; *Enc. Islam/2*

A. Godard: 'Ardistān et Zawārè', *Āthār-é Īrān*, i (1936), pp. 296–309

J. Sauvaget: 'Observations sur quelques mosquées seldjoukides', *An. Inst. Etud. Orient. U. Alger*, iv (1938), pp. 81–120

A. P. Mihrābādī: *Ātashkada-yi ardistān* (Tehran, Iran. Solar 1382/1953–4), i, pp. 28–40

L. Hunarfar: *Ganjīna-yi āthār-i tārīkhī-yi Isfahān* [Treasury of the historical monuments of Isfahan] (Isfahan, 2/Iran. Solar 1340/1961–2), pp. 210–27

ABBAS DANESHVARI

Arditi [di Ardito]**, Andrea** (*fl* 1324–38). Italian goldsmith. A native of Antella (near Florence), he had moved to Florence by 16 August 1324, when he was registered in the goldsmiths' guild. His sole extant autograph work, incorrectly attributed by Vasari to Cione Aretino, is the reliquary bust of *St Zenobius* (Florence, S Maria del Fiore), which is inscribed: ANDREAS ARDITI DE FLORENTIA ME FECIT. An inventory of the sacristy of S Reparata, compiled in 1418, describes the bust and dates it to 1331. It was restored in 1704 and 1812 and has lost much of its original enamel. The figure's mitre (detachable) and collar are decorated with quatrefoil plaques of *basse-taille* (translucent) enamel on silver relief depicting *Angels*, winged *Virtues* and *Saints*. The plaques are among the earliest examples of the use of this technique, of which Andrea appears to have been a leading exponent, by a Florentine goldsmith.

Five other works by Andrea are recorded. The inventory of 1418 describes two chalices with patens (both untraced). The first bore the arms of St Zenobius and was signed; its paten was enamelled with the *Ascension*. The second, decorated with enamels of *Saints*, was produced in 1331. The appearance of a third silver gilt and enamel signed chalice (h. 225 mm; ex-Spitzer priv. col., 1893) is known from engravings and a description (1847): its base was decorated with medallions depicting the *Crucifixion*, *St John the Evangelist*, *St John the Baptist*, *Justice* (or *St Michael*) and the *Virgin*. Rossi has suggested that this chalice could be one of the two referred to in the 1418 inventory. In 1338 Andrea was commissioned by the abbot of S Miniato al Monte and the Arte della Calimala in Florence to make a silver cross (untraced) for the altar of S Giovanni Gualberto. A 15th-century inventory of the sacristy of Santo Spirito, Florence, records a signed silver chalice (untraced) decorated with 12 enamels and a paten enamelled with the *Pietà*.

BIBLIOGRAPHY

DBI

F. Rossi: *Capolavori di oreficeria italiana* (Milan, 1956), no. 20

M. M. Gauthier: *Emaux du moyen âge occidental* (Fribourg, 1972), p. 392

A. Guidotti: *L'oreficeria nella Firenze del quattrocento* (Florence, 1977), pp. 176–7

C. Strocchi: 'Lo smalto traslucido a Firenze: Prime osservazioni sulla bottega di Andrea Arditi', *An. Scu. Norm. Sup. U. Pisa*, n. s. 2, xviii/1 (1988), pp. 137–50

□

Ardizzone, Edward (Irving Jeffrey) (*b* Haiphong, French Indo-China [now Vietnam], 16 Oct 1900; *d* Rodmersham, Kent, 8 Nov 1979). English illustrator and author. From 1905 he grew up in England, becoming a professional artist in 1926 after part-time study at the Westminster School of Art, London. He became known as an illustrator of genre scenes in a variety of media, often with a comic Victorian flavour. He was best known for illustrated stories, the first of which, *Little Tim and the Brave Sea-captain* (Oxford, 1936), was followed by numerous imaginative and popular children's books and by many other illustrated books. *Baggage to the Enemy* (London, 1941) reflected his appointment in 1940 as an Official War Artist, recording the German invasion of France, and the North African and Italian campaigns. His freelance career continued after the war with a steady production of illustrative and ephemeral work in an instantly recognizable style that relied on ink line and delicate washes.

WRITINGS

The Young Ardizzone: An Autobiographical Fragment (London, 1970)

Diary of a War Artist (London, 1974)

BIBLIOGRAPHY

B. Alderson: 'A Preliminary Hand-list of Illustrated Books', *Priv. Lib.*, v/1 (1972)

Edward Ardizzone: A Retrospective Exhibition (exh. cat., London, V&A, 1974)

G. White: *Edward Ardizzone: Artist and Illustrator* (London, 1979)

E. Booth-Clibborn: *My Father and Edward Ardizzone: A Lasting Friendship* (London, 1983)

ALAN POWERS

Ardon, Mordecai [Bronstein, Max] (*b* Tuchów, Poland, 13 July 1896). Israeli painter of Polish birth. As a young boy he greatly admired El Greco, Goya and Rembrandt. From 1920 to 1925 he studied at the Bauhaus, Weimar, under Klee, Kandinsky, Johannes Itten and Lyonel Feininger and the following year studied painting techniques at the Akademie der bildenden Künste in Munich under Max Doerner. During the 1920s he changed his name from Max Bronstein to Mordecai Ardon. He taught at the Kunstschule Itten in Berlin from 1929 to 1933, when Nazi persecution forced him to flee to Jerusalem. Though he had been an active Communist in Germany, in Jerusalem he soon found a great affinity with Jewish religion and culture. In 1935 he was made a professor at the Bezalel School of Arts and Crafts in Jerusalem, and was its Director from 1940 to 1952.

Ardon's early paintings show the influence of Expressionism, as in *Seated Woman in a Straw Chair* (1937; Haifa, MOMA). He had his first one-man show in 1940 at the Jewish Museum in New York. After the 1950s his work moved away from Expressionism towards a more poetic, symbolic style, while still drawing on Jewish history and culture. Though always deeply involved with reality his paintings range from the more figurative works, such as the triptych *Missa Dura* (1958–60; London, Tate), to the more abstract, such as the triptych *Yom Kippur, 1973* (1974; Tel Aviv Mus.). From 1952 to 1963 Ardon was artistic adviser to the Ministry of Education and Culture in Jerusalem, and in 1963 he was awarded the Israel Prize. From 1982 to 1984 he worked on the stained-glass window *Isaiah's Vision of Eternal Peace* for the Jewish National University and Library in Jerusalem. After 1965 he divided his time between Jerusalem and Paris.

BIBLIOGRAPHY

M. Vishny: *Mordecai Ardon* (New York, 1973)

Ardon: A Retrospective (exh. cat. by Z. Amishai-Maisels and others, Tel Aviv Mus., 1985)

□

Arellano, Cristóbal Ramírez de. *See* RAMÍREZ DE ARELLANO, CRISTÓBAL.

Arellano, Francisco Chávez y. *See* CHÁVEZ Y ARELLANO, FRANCISCO.

Arellano, Juan de (*b* Santorcaz, *bapt* 3 Aug 1614; *d* Madrid, 13 Oct 1676). Spanish painter. He was the pre-eminent painter of flower-pieces in 17th-century Spain. Although Spaniards of the previous generation had painted such works, it was the inspiration of Flemish and Italian examples in Madrid that from *c.* 1650 encouraged Arellano's success as a specialist in this genre. According to Palomino, who moved to the Court shortly after the artist's death and befriended many painters who had known him, Arellano began to paint flowers only in his thirties after a beginning that showed little promise. When asked why he devoted himself to flower-pieces and had abandoned figures, he replied that it was because with them he worked less and earned more (Palomino).

Arellano was apprenticed at a very early age to an unknown painter in Alcalá de Henares until around the age of 16, when he went to Madrid and entered the studio of Juan de Solís. He emerged from this training a competent but undistinguished figure painter, as is seen in two signed but undated religious pictures (Santorcaz, parish church). His earliest signed and dated work is *Garland of Flowers with Vanitas* (1646; Seville, priv. col., see 1983 exh. cat., p. 118), where the large wreath of flowers surrounds a cartouche depicting putti blowing soap bubbles and other *vanitas* symbols in a landscape. The *vanitas* scene is signed by Francisco Camilo and the wreath by Arellano. The painting recalls the type of composition by Daniel Seghers that was popular in Spain, and the wreath also reveals a northern inspiration in its dense naturalism. *Flowers and Landscapes*, a pair dated 1652 (Madrid, Prado), show garlands of flowers and cartouches that enframe beautifully atmospheric landscapes. Possibly also executed in collaboration, they demonstrate Arellano's mastery and great decorative skill.

Much of Arellano's output consisted of paired works depicting bouquets arranged in baskets or in crystal or metal vases supported on free-standing, rough stone plinths. Often internally asymmetrical, such works, when paired, imply a central axis that reveals their fundamentally decorative function as flanking elements on a wall. In most of these, the colours of red, white, blue and yellow are carefully balanced in a way that is characteristic of Arellano's work. His compositions of the 1660s and 1670s, with their full-blown blossoms and curling leaves, are more agitated than his early flower-pieces and are painted with a greater breadth. This change has been attributed to the influence of the Italian artist Mario Nuzzi, whom Palomino says he admired and copied. However, the Baroque exuberance of Nuzzi's style finds a more direct echo in flower-pieces by the following generation of painters in Madrid, such as Bartolomé Pérez and Gabriel de la Corte (1648–94). Arellano's own style developed out of his initial emulation of Flemish models.

Arellano maintained a workshop across from S Felipe el Real, which Palomino described as 'one of the most famous painting shops in this Court'. Among his apprentices and collaborators were his son José (*b* 1655) and a son-in-law, BARTOLOMÉ PÉREZ, who sometimes painted the figures to accompany Arellano's garlands of flowers. The inventory of Arellano's studio (Madrid, Archv Hist. Protocolos, Francisco de Roa, 1676, no. 10431) suggests that Arellano may also have acted as a dealer in pictures.

BIBLIOGRAPHY

A. A. Palomino de Castro y Velasco: *Museo pictórico* (1715–24/*R* 1747), pp. 963–4

J. Cavestany: *Floreros y bodegones en la pintura española* (Madrid, 1936–40), pp. 82–3

I. Bergström: *Maestros españoles de bodegones y floreros del siglo XVII* (Madrid, 1970), pp. 60–64

E. Valdivieso: 'Una *vanitas* de Arellano y Camilo,' *Bol. Semin. Estud. A. & Arqueol.*, xlv (1979), pp. 479–82

I. Martín: *Juan de Arellano and Flower Painting in Madrid* (MA thesis, Dallas, TX, S. Methodist U., Meadows School A., 1980)

Pintura española de bodegones y floreros de 1600 a Goya (exh. cat. by A. E. Pérez Sánchez, Madrid, Prado, 1983), pp. 98–9, 118–22

M. Duque Oliart: 'Pintura de flores: La obra de Juan de Arellano', *Goya*, 191 (1986), pp. 272–9

WILLIAM B. JORDAN

Arena, Giuseppe d' [il Romano] (*b c.* 1633; *d* 1719). Italian painter, active in Malta. He worked exclusively in Malta, moving in the circle of Mattia Preti. Contemporary documents refer to him as 'il Romano', suggesting that he was of Roman origin. He was in Malta by 1666, the year in which he married. Certain of his paintings, such as *St Sebastian before the Pope* (Valletta, St John's Mus.), reveal some knowledge of the work of Guercino. His output was prolific, but with a few notable exceptions his compositions are dull and his drawing weak. The *Adoration of the Magi* (Valletta, church of the Carmine) and the *Virgin of the Rosary* (Spinola Bay, church of the Immaculate Conception) are among his best works but his supreme achievement is the *Last Supper* (Gozo Cathedral), his last documented work. It shows him in complete control of the Baroque idiom, exploiting its theatrical possibilities, while nonetheless conveying genuine religious feeling, which is Roman rather than Neapolitan in its sobriety. D'Arena enjoyed considerable prestige and was received into the Order of St John as a lay brother. In old age he became blind. There are works by him in most Maltese churches.

BIBLIOGRAPHY

M. Buhagiar: *The Iconography of the Maltese Islands, 1400–1900* (Valletta, 1987), pp. 108–9 [with bibliog.]

MARIO BUHAGIAR

Arenas, Diego López de. *See* LÓPEZ DE ARENAS, DIEGO.

Arenberg. Flemish (Belgian) family of collectors and patrons. The ancient county of Arenberg, situated between the duchy of Juliers, archbishopric of Cologne and county of Blankenheim, was raised to a principality in 1576 and a duchy in 1664. Members of the family played important roles in the politics of the Netherlands, France and Germany. Louis Engelbert, 5th Duke of Arenberg (1750–1820), made major acquisitions of prints and drawings, especially of views, towns and statues, during visits to France, Italy and Switzerland. He also acquired drawings by Lambert Lombard, 400 of which form part of the Arenberg Album (Liège, Cab. Est. & Dessins), and commissioned painters and sculptors. His brother, Auguste-Marie-Raymond, 6th Duke of Arenberg (1753–1833), was a connoisseur and a great bibliophile and was the first member of the family to create a gallery of paintings. By 1808 he had begun to purchase works of art at sales in Holland, London and Paris, as well as through such dealers as Jean-Baptiste-Pierre Le Brun and direct commissions from C. G. E. Dietrich, Watteau and others. Within 15 years he owned over 100 paintings and 15,259 books. The collection, which was open to the public in the Arenberg Palace, Brussels, was known for its Dutch and Flemish paintings and included works by Paulus Potter, Gabriel Metsu, Philips Wouwerman, Meindert Hobbema, Allart van Everdingen, Philips Koninck, Nicolaes Maes and Adriaen Brouwer. Among the most important works were Rembrandt's *Tobias Healing his Father's Blindness* (1636; Stuttgart, Staatsgal.) and Johannes Vermeer's *Head of a Young Woman* (1672–4; New York, Met.). The Duke left his collection to his nephew, Prosper-Louis, 7th Duke of Arenberg and Duke of Arschot (1785–1861), who refined it with new acquisitions of works by, among others, Pieter de Hooch, Peter Paul Rubens, Anthony van Dyck, Adriaen van Ostade and Jan Steen, including Steen's *Wedding Feast at Cana* (1676; Pasadena, CA, Norton Simon Mus.; *see* STEEN, JAN, fig. 3). Prosper-Louis's son Engelbert-Auguste, 8th Duke of Arenberg (1824–75), further enriched the Brussels palace with paintings, vases, laceworks, ivories, manuscripts and rare books, focusing on Netherlandish literature. In 1902 his son, Englebert-Marie, 9th Duke of Arenberg (1872–1949), sold (London, Christie's, 14–17 July) 40,000 individual prints from his vast collection, which remained in the Brussels family palace until 1914. The prints, which represented all periods and schools, included editions of van Dyck's *Iconography* and works by Albrecht Dürer, Rembrandt, Jacques Callot and Lucas van Leyden, the 'cabinet of the king' (a collection of prints produced by order of Louis XIV), portraits of the Arenberg family and important printed books of hours. The Duke's primary residence was in Brussels, but in 1904 he purchased the Schloss Nordkirchen, 'the Versailles of Westphalia', which housed the library of the Plettenberg family. In 1918 the palace in Brussels was sold to the city; it was later transferred to the state. In 1921 the Belgian government confiscated the paintings of the Duke of Arenberg, who was alleged to have been a German partisan during World War I. Some of the paintings entered the Musée d'Art Ancien in Brussels. Of the 20,000 volumes sold from the library at Brussels in 1929, the Bibliothèque Royale Albert 1er, Brussels, which was given first choice, acquired 175. The 20 cases of books and manuscripts that the Duke donated to the University of Leuven in 1939 were destroyed during World War II. In 1952 Engelbert Charles, 10th Duke of Arenberg (1899–1974), sold the illuminated manuscripts: more than 33 were bought by the Bibliothèque Royale Albert 1er; others were acquired by Harvard University and by Lessing Rosenwald (ex-Alverthorpe Gal., Jenkintown, PA), who later gave many to Cornell University, Ithaca, NY, and the Library of Congress, Washington, DC. In 1959 the 10th Duke sold Schloss Nordkirchen and donated the manuscripts from the Plettenberg collection to the University of Münster.

BIBLIOGRAPHY

Illuminated Manuscripts (11th Century through the 16th Century) from the Bibliothèque of Their Highnesses the Dukes d'Arenberg (exh. cat., New York, Jacques Seligmann Gal., 1952)

Engravings from the Celebrated Collection of the Dukes d'Arenberg (exh. cat., New York, Jacques Seligmann Gal., 1955)

M. E. Kronenberg: 'De verspreiding van de Arenberg-collectie' [The dispersal of the Arenberg Collection], *Het Boek*, xxxiii (1958), pp. 16–31

H. Neu: *Die Münzen und Medaillen des Herzogtums und des herzoglichen Hauses Arenberg* (Bonn, 1959)

Oude drukken uit de Nederlanden: Boeken uit de collectie Arenberg thans in de verzameling Lessing J. Rosenwald [Old editions from the Netherlands: books from the Arenberg Collection now in the Lessing J. Rosenwald collection] (The Hague, 1960)

Livres anciens des Pays-Bas: La Collection Lessing J. Rosenwald provenant de la Bibliothèque d'Arenberg (exh. cat., ed. L. Brummel and H. Liebaers; The Hague, Rijksmus. Meermanno-Westreenianum; Brussels, Bib. Royale Albert 1er; 1960)

C. Lemaire: 'La Bibliothèque des ducs d'Arenberg: Une Première Approche', *Liber amicorum Hermann Liebaers*, ed. F. Vanwijngarden and others (Brussels, 1984), pp. 81–106

□

Arendtz, Cornelius (*fl* Sweden, 1608–55). Dutch painter, active in Sweden. The son of the painter Arendt Lambrechts (*fl* 1585; *d* 1623), he is best known for his copies of a 16th-century series of portraits of Swedish monarchs of the House of Vasa, which he was commissioned to do in the 1620s; their location, the mansion of Bysta in Närke, caused him to be known as the Bysta Master before he was identified (Steneberg, 1935). The finest of the portraits is that of *Gustav I, King of Sweden*, showing him as ponderous, suspicious and bad-tempered, playing irritably with his gold chain; this picture is a psychological study, although forced into the formal stiffness of state-portrait style. As Arendtz was also a portrait painter in his own right, he may have improved on the series of pictures that he took as his models. Notable among his own works are his portraits of *Carl Bonde* (1616; Närke, Esplunda) and *Gabriel Gustavsson Oxenstierna* (*c.* 1640; Mariefred, Gripsholm Slott), and an equestrian portrait of *Gustav II Adolf, King of Sweden, at Lech* (1636; Uppsala U., Västmanlands-Dala). The portrait of *Carl Bonde* depicts a tense, anxious, sensitive face, which contrasts with the still, formal posture of the body and the characteristic flatness and absence of volume and perspective in the rest of the canvas. The vivid intensity of the faces in Arendtz's works, at variance with the playing-card, abstract quality of the picture as a whole, is peculiar to this period in both Sweden and other European countries.

BIBLIOGRAPHY

SVKL
K. E. Steneberg: *Vasarenässansens porträttkonst* [Portrait painting of the Vasa Renaissance] (Stockholm, 1935)
——: *Kristinatidens måleri* [Painting in the time of Christina] (Stockholm, 1955)

TORBJÖRN FULTON

Arens, Johann August (*b* Hamburg, 2 Oct 1757; *d* Pisa, 18 Aug 1806). German architect, draughtsman, landscape designer and painter. He studied from 1778 to 1783 at the University of Göttingen and the Royal Danish Academy in Copenhagen, where he was awarded four prizes. His early designs included drawings for the hothouse of the botanic gardens in Copenhagen and a lecture room at Schloss Charlottenburg, Berlin. While visiting Paris in 1784–5 he devoted himself to the study of Revolutionary architecture, and in England and Italy (1786) he studied landscape design and ancient sites. In Rome in 1787 he met Johann Wolfgang von Goethe, who later summoned him to WEIMAR to rebuild the prince's Schloss. In addition to a number of designs for the palace at Weimar he produced drawings for various summer-houses. In 1790 he moved to Hamburg, his plans for the Schloss at Weimar still largely unexecuted. By the end of his life he had designed numerous public buildings and private houses in Hamburg, including the house for Bürgermeister Bartel, the church in Wandsbek (1795–1800; destr. 1898), the school and workhouse (1795–1800) of the Institute for the Poor, and chapels for the churches of St Nikolai, St Katharinen and St Petri. Between these works he made repeated journeys to Italy. Arens was the major exponent of Neo-classicism in Hamburg and his buildings were quite distinct from the traditional houses of the city.

BIBLIOGRAPHY

E. Rump: *Lexikon der bildenden Künstler Hamburgs, Altonas und der näheren Umgebung* (Hamburg, 1912)
W. Scheidig: *Das Schloss in Weimar* (Erfurt, 1951)
G. Wietek: *Untersuchungen über Goethes Verhältnis zur Architektur* (diss., U. Kiel, 1951)
——: 'Der Hamburger Architekt Johann August Arens als Baumeister Goethes', *Die Bau- und Künstlerdenkmale der Freien und Hansestadt Hamburg*, ed. G. Grundmann (Hamburg, 1953)
J. Gerhardt and W. Gramberg, eds: *Bewahren und Gestalten: Festschrift zum 70. Geburtstag von Günter Grundmann* (Hamburg, 1962), p. 165–76
Architekt Johann August Arens, 1757–1806 (exh. cat., ed. C. Knupp; Altonaer Mus., 1972)
A. Jericke and D. Dolgner: *Der Klassizismus im Baugeschehen Weimars* (Weimar, 1975)
D. Dolgner: *Weimar: Schloss* (Leipzig, 1983)

ANDREAS KREUL

Arensberg. American collectors and patrons. Walter (Conrad) Arensberg (*b* Pittsburg [now Pittsburgh], PA, 4 April 1878; *d* Los Angeles, CA, 29 Jan 1954) and his wife, Louise [née Mary Louise Stevens] (*b* Dresden, 15 May 1879; *d* Los Angeles, CA, 25 Nov 1953), lived in New York from 1914 to 1921. During this period their apartment at 33 W. 67th Street was an unofficial salon for the American DADA movement, where French expatriate artists such as Marcel Duchamp and Francis Picabia mingled with American writers, artists, musicians and others. Although Walter Arensberg enjoyed financial com fort for a while, owing to financial assistance from his father, this soon ended. Walter's support of such journals as *Others* and *Blind Man* and of the Marius de Zayas Gallery was short-lived and ended in financial failure. In contrast, his wife, Louise (whom he had married in 1907), had inherited substantial wealth from her parents, which provided the means to acquire the majority of works the couple amassed from the 1920s.

While the Arensbergs lived in New York, their entire holdings of art, furniture and rugs comprised fewer than 70 items but it grew to over 1500 items by the time of their deaths. The expansive display of these works in their apartment in New York was dramatically altered in their house in Hollywood, CA, where they settled permanently in 1927: paintings were hung frame to frame, floor to ceiling, on the staircases and even in the bathrooms; oriental and Middle Eastern rugs were piled three to four on top of one another; Shaker furniture, purchased with the assistance of Charles Sheeler, was displayed with Chippendale and other types. In May 1933 an extension designed by Richard Neutra and Gregory Ain was completed in an attempt to relieve the overcrowding.

The Arensbergs' collection comprised two main sections, avant-garde art and non-Western artefacts, a pattern of acquisition begun in the 1910s. The majority of modern works, most dated between 1910 and 1914, were centred around the aesthetic impact of European modernism, in particular Cubism, first seen in the USA at the ARMORY SHOW (1913). The Arensbergs felt that this art heralded a new perception, and with singular commitment they sought particular works that they believed demonstrated its effect on the very premise and process of art. Their collection was dominated by Cubist works, the works of forerunners of Cubism and works by artists influenced by the movement, including paintings, prints and drawings by Georges Braque, Paul Cézanne, Marc Chagall, Robert Delaunay, Albert Gleizes, Juan Gris, Fernand Léger, Henri Matisse, Jean Metzinger, Francis Picabia, Pablo Picasso, Henri Rousseau and Jacques Villon. One of the Armory

Show's most notorious works, Duchamp's *Nude Descending a Staircase No. 2* (1912), was eventually acquired with ten other works from the show. Duchamp's art became the focus of the collection, which contained over 35 of his works. (Among the other artists who were substantially represented were Constantin Brancusi and Paul Klee.) From the 1930s the Arensbergs expanded this initial concentration in Cubist works to acquire works by Klee, Surrealist paintings, including those by such artists as Max Ernst, Joan Miró and Salvador Dalí, and contemporary Mexican artists such as Diego Rivera.

Out of more than 65 modern artists represented in the collection, only a small number were American. Most of these works were produced in the mid-1910s by members of the Arensbergs' circle in New York, such as Walter Arensberg's cousin John R. Covert (1882–1960), Charles Demuth, Charles Sheeler and Morton Livingston Schamberg. Their small photographic collection was dominated by the works of such Americans as Sheeler and Edward Weston.

The section devoted to ethnic artefacts, which eventually included more than 300 items, changed after the Arensbergs moved to California. They ceased buying wooden African works in favour of Pre-Columbian objects (primarily of stone), Mexican retables, native American items (baskets, rugs, spearheads) and some Asiatic and Indian works. The display of the large number of items in this section in their homes in New York and Hollywood continued the aesthetic interrelationships and cultural juxtaposition of 'primitive' to modern promoted in the 1910s by such dealers in New York as Alfred Stieglitz and Marius de Zayas.

Although the Arensbergs purchased directly from individuals, their major dealer and art adviser was MARCEL DUCHAMP, whom they met on his arrival in the USA in 1915. Not including gifts such as *Boîte-en-valise*, Duchamp sold the Arensbergs approximately 50 works, the majority being by either him or Brancusi. Duchamp and the Arensbergs also made a conscious effort to have the majority of Duchamp's works in their collection, including '*The Bride Stripped Bare by her Bachelors, Even*' ('*The Large Glass*'; Philadelphia, PA, Mus. A.), which they sold to Katherine S. Dreier in 1921, and *Sad Young Man on a Train* (Venice, Guggenheim).

The Arensbergs were committed to the public dissemination and display of modern art, especially in the Los Angeles area, which at that time lacked both a museum devoted solely to art and in particular a museum devoted to the modern period. They supported the Modern Institute of Art and American Arts in Action, Inc., both public galleries of modern art. Their activities in Los Angeles were, however, more isolated and restricted than they had been in New York. Entrance to their Hollywood home was by invitation and recommendation, although apparently no-one interested in seeing the collection was refused access. Their collection had little impact, however, on art life in Los Angeles, beyond shared interests with other modern collectors such as Ruth Maitland.

The Arensbergs' original intention was for their collection to remain in the Los Angeles area. An initial offer made to the County Museum of Art in 1938 was, however, never acknowledged. Negotiations took place with over 30 institutions in the USA, including the University of California at Los Angeles and Stanford University, CA, as well as with institutions in Paris and Mexico City. The primary negotiating problems were twofold. The Arensbergs insisted that a research institute be part of the bequeathal of the art collection. The institution established by them in 1937 as The Francis Bacon Foundation (in Claremont, CA, from the 1960s), its aim being to promote Walter Arensberg's theory that the English statesman and philosopher Francis Bacon (1561–1626) wrote the plays and poems attributed to William Shakespeare, was the immediate beneficiary of the art collection. The other criterion was that the entire art collection be displayed as a unit for a substantial period. After almost three years of discussions, and after relinquishing the idea of such a research institute from the negotiations, the Board of Trustees of The Francis Bacon Foundation approved the offer made by the Philadelphia Museum of Art (bequeathed 1950). In 1954, 22 galleries housing the collection in the Philadelphia Museum of Art opened to the public.

Walter Arensberg also received recognition as a writer and took an active role in promoting modernism in the USA. His early sporadic writings on art were on established artists or movements, but by the mid-1910s he was writing articles on Dada artists for various journals and joined the literary vanguard of Imagist writers with the publication of two books of poetry (*Poems*, 1914; *Idols*, 1916). By the time the Arensbergs moved to the Los Angeles area, Walter Arensberg was less actively involved in writing or commenting publicly about art. The only occasions on which he expressed any view were when he considered publicity a necessity for demonstrating the importance of the collection, in particular during the Art Institute of Chicago's exhibition of a major portion of their 20th-century holdings (1949), and shortly after its bequeathal to the Philadelphia Museum of Art.

UNPUBLISHED SOURCES

Philadelphia, PA, Mus. A., Arensberg Archv

San Marino, CA, Huntington Lib. & A.G., Arensberg Archv

WRITINGS

'Mr Pennell's Etchings of London', *Evening Post* (1 March 1906); *R* in book form (New York, 1906)

W. C. Brensberg [*sic*]: 'Art in America: The Art Season in New York', *Burl. Mag.*, x/46 (1907)

'The National Academy of Design', *Burl. Mag.*, x/47 (1907), p. 336

'Partie d'échecs entre Picabia et Roché', *391*, vii/7 (1917), p. 3

BIBLIOGRAPHY

A. Norton: 'Walter's Room', *The Quill* (June 1919), pp. 20–21 [describes the Arensbergs' salon in New York]

H. McBride: 'Modern Forms (The Arnsbergs) [*sic*]', *Dial* (July 1920), pp. 61–4

J. T. Soby: 'Marcel Duchamp in the Arensberg Collection', *View*, v/1 (1945), pp. 11–12

J. Langsner: 'The Arensberg Riches of Cubism', *Artnews*, xlvii/7 (1949), pp. 24–5, 61–2 [incl. quotes from interviews with Walter Arensberg]

20th-century Art from the Louise and Walter Arensberg Collection (exh. cat., Chicago, IL, A. Inst., 1949)

'The Louise and Walter Arensberg Collection', *Modern Artists in America*, 1st ser. (1950–51), pp. 124–31 [contains phot. of the col. in the Arensbergs' home in Los Angeles]

The Louise and Walter Arensberg Collection, 2 vols (Philadelphia, 1954)

F. Kimball: 'Cubism and the Arensbergs', *ARTnews Annu.*, xxiv (1955), pp. 117–22, 174–8 [contains personal reminiscences of the Arensbergs by their friends]

W. H. Higgins: *Art Collecting in the Los Angeles Area, 1910–1960* (diss., Los Angeles, U. CA, 1963), pp. 621–81

K. Kuh: 'Walter Arensberg and Marcel Duchamp', *The Open Eye: In Pursuit of Art* (New York, 1971), pp. 56–64
L. H. Lincoln: *Walter Arensberg and his Circle* (MA thesis, Newark U. DE, 1972)
A. d'Harnoncourt: 'A. E. Gallatin and the Arensbergs: Pioneer Collectors of Twentieth-century Art', *Apollo*, n.s., xclx/149 (1974), pp. 52–61
F. M. Naumann: 'Walter Conrad Arensberg: Poet, Patron, and Participant in the New York Avant-garde', *Bull. Philadelphia Mus. A.*, xxvi/328 (1980), pp. 2–32
R. E. Kuenzli, ed.: 'Bibliography on Dada, 1978–1983', *Dada Surrealism*, xiii (1984), pp. 164–93 [contains section on Walter Arensberg's writings and works about him and the art col.]
R. E. Kuenzli and T. Shipe, eds: 'Bibliography on New York Dada', *Dada Surrealism*, xiv (1985), pp. 126–64
F. M. Naumann, ed.: 'Marcel Duchamp's Letters to Walter and Louise Arensberg, 1917–1921', *Dada Surrealism*, xvi (1987), pp. 203–57; also in *Marcel Duchamp: Artist of the Century*, R. E. Kuenzli and F. M. Naumann, eds (Cambridge and London, 1989)
N. Sawelson-Gorse: *'For the Want of a Nail': The Disposition of the Louise and Walter Arensberg Collection* (MA thesis, Riverside, U. CA, 1987)
——: 'Hollywood Conversations: Duchamp and the Arensbergs', *West Coast Duchamp*, B. Clearwater, ed. (Miami, 1991), pp. 24–45

NAOMI SAWELSON-GORSE

Arentsz. Dutch family of architects. (1) Arent Arentsz. van 's Gravesande was one of the most prominent members of the group of craftsmen who quickly assimilated the classicizing Baroque style of Jacob van Campen into their own designs and thus contributed to the presence of Dutch classicism in the mid-17th century. Façades in the style of Arent Arentsz. may be found in every Dutch town, although not all of them have a central stone bay. Some of his designs, including that for the town hall at Middelharnis (1649), were carried out by his brother (2) Pieter Arentsz. Noorwits.

(1) Arent Arentsz. van 's Gravesande (*b* ?1600; *d* Middelburg, *bur* 8 Feb 1662). From 1632 he worked as a cabinetmaker and draughtsman for the stadholder Frederick Henry at various palaces in the area around The Hague. In 1636 he was appointed city architect of The Hague and in the same year built the St Sebastiaansdoelen there, adjacent to the Mauritshuis, designed by JACOB VAN CAMPEN in 1633. In this first building Arentsz. demonstrated a mature classicism in the style of van Campen. The St Sebastiaansdoelen is constructed mainly of brick in two storeys. The broad façade of the corner building has a monumental central stone section with a colossal order of Ionic pilasters, crowned by a pediment with sculpture.

In 1639 Arentsz. became city architect of Leiden, where he had already designed the imposing Lakenhal and Marekerk. The Lakenhal or Cloth Hall (1639) has a recessed central block with wings, consisting of a single upper storey raised on an open colonnade, on both sides of a forecourt, which is closed off on the street side by a wall with a portal. The plan of the building has similarities with the urban palace (*c.* 1634) in The Hague, owned and designed by Constantijn Huygens, and also with the Oude Hof in The Hague, which was rebuilt by van Campen in 1639. The central section of the Cloth Hall corresponds with that of the St Sebastiaansdoelen, but at Leiden Arentsz. enriched the façade with niches, festoons and reliefs. Used for its original purpose until 1823, in 1866 the Cloth Hall became the Stedelijk Museum 'De Lakenhal'. A new wing was added on the east side in 1920, constructed in the same style.

The Protestant Marekerk (1639) was the first church in Holland to have a dome. An octagonal building with an ambulatory, its dome rests on a high drum, the corners of which are supported by scrolled buttresses. When the municipal authorities, who had commissioned the church, invited van Campen to give his opinion of the design, he praised it but made several recommendations, including the removal of the large windows in the ambulatory. On van Campen's advice, Arentsz. also added a monumental sandstone portal with pilasters and a pediment, which takes the place of a free-standing portico. In the interior, the ambulatory around the domed space is articulated by eight Ionic columns, which support the drum. The square pulpit to the side of the central area is free-standing. In Leiden Arentsz. also built several stately dwellings with pilastered façades, including the Hofje van Brouckhoven (1640), which has an ornate central pavilion. Faced with stone, flanked by low brick wings and articulated by a disproportionately giant order of Ionic pilasters surmounted by a pediment, the pavilion encompasses the main entrance and the Regent's Hall on the first floor. In 1657 Arentsz. was appointed city master carpenter of Middelburg, where he completed the Oostkerk, an octagonal building with a cupola designed by Bartholomaeus Drijfhout in 1647 in collaboration with Pieter Post. In 1655 Arentsz. was dismissed from his post of city architect of Leiden for reasons that are now unknown.

BIBLIOGRAPHY

Thieme–Becker
F. A. J. Vermeulen: *Handboek tot de geschiedenis der Nederlandsche bouwkunst* [Handbook of the history of Dutch architecture], ii (The Hague, 1941)
J. J. Terwen: 'De ontwerpgeschiedenis van de Marekerk te Leiden', [The history of the design of the Marekerk in Leiden], *Opus Musivum* (Assen, 1964), pp. 231–56
W. Kuyper: *Dutch Classicist Architecture* (Delft, 1980)

(2) Pieter Arentsz. [Aaronsz.; Adriaensz.; Arontssen] **Noorwits** [Noorwittus; Norwisz.; Norwits] (*fl* 1637; *d* The Hague, Jan 1669). Brother of (1) Arent Arentsz. van 's Gravesande. He is recorded in 1637 as a carpenter in The Hague. On 7 July 1645 he was appointed architect of the auditor's office of the Court of Holland, the provincial government. In 1649 he was commissioned with Bartholomeus van Bassen to build the Protestant Nieuwe Kerk in The Hague, to his own design. The ground-plan of the free-standing church consists of a rectangle with two apses against each of the long sides and one against each short side, thus creating a 'preaching' church with a centralized nave. The exterior is constructed of brick and articulated by Tuscan pilasters in stone, and the high-rising pavilion roof is crowned with a little open turret. The Nieuwe Kerk is the only known work by Pieter Arentsz., but in this design he proved himself an extremely competent architect, who introduced the idea of doubling up a centralized building. For the interior he recalled the scheme of Hendrik de Keyser I—the combination of two Greek crosses on plan—reworking this in a Baroque manner, with the pulpit placed at the point of maximum constriction. The Nieuwe Kerk attracted much attention both in Holland and abroad and may have served as a model for the Burgkirche in

Königsberg, East Prussia (now Kaliningrad, Russia), which was built by Johann Arnold Nering between 1687 and 1701.

BIBLIOGRAPHY

Thieme–Becker

M. D. Ozinga: *De Protestantse kerkenbouw in Nederland* [The architecture of Protestant churches in the Netherlands] (Amsterdam, 1929)

F. A. J. Vermeulen: *Handboek tot der geschiedenis der Nederlandsche bouwkunst* [Handbook of the history of Dutch architecture], iii (The Hague, 1941)

PAUL H. REM

Arequipa. Peruvian city and capital of the department of Arequipa. The city (population *c.* 634,500) is situated on the River Chili in a fertile valley in the foothills of the Andes and on the slopes of a volcanic range. It dates back to the Early Horizon (*c.* 900–*c.* 200 BC), and there have been archaeological finds at San Juan de Siguas, Santa Isabel de Siguas (to the north), and in the Vítor Valley (to the west of Arequipa). The Lupaca people first settled in the area around what is now Arequipa *c.* AD 800–1200. By the 1350s provincial Inca settlements had been established near the present-day city. Arequipa would have been a *tambo* (Quechua: 'road-side inn') on the route between the highlands and the coast. The Spaniards founded the city of Villahermosa de Arequipa (or Villa Hermosa de la Asunción) on 15 August 1540. The proximity of the volcanic range has ensured the supply of easily dressed but strong, white volcanic tufa, or sillar; however, it has also led to disastrous earthquakes (in particular, 1582, 1600, 1687, 1715, 1784 and 1868), which have defined the phases of the city's architectural development. These may be referred to generally as rural development (1540–82), Baroque (1582–1784), Rococo and Neo-classical (1784–1868), and Colonial Revival and modern (1868–1960). In efforts to withstand earthquakes, architects used wide-based, buttressed and supported walls; these give a sense of volume, bulk and static mass, broken only by the vitality of the carvings. Unfortunately, few early colonial buildings survive; many are 18th-century reconstructions. Arequipa does, however, retain its characteristically colonial grid plan.

The present church of La Compañía (1650–98; tower rebuilt 1919 and 1966) represents the Mestizo Baroque style that developed in the 1600s. It has a characteristic Arequipeño relief, carved by incising the surface rather than by working in the round, creating a tapestry-like effect. The main façade (1698; see fig.) was initially planned by Gaspar Báez (*fl* 1569–73) in 1573, and in 1590 Diego Felipe (*fl* 1590–95) planned the main entrance. The portal has two registers crowned by a trilobate arch, with indigenous decorative elements. A number of church and house façades feature Hispanicized forms of such Pre-Columbian motifs as cantuta flowers, maize, leaves, birds, fish and masks. The design of the portal is ascribed to Agustín de Costa, and it was probably executed by the mason Agustín de Adrián. The side portal (1654) and other parts of the church were by Simón de Barrientos (*fl* 1654–90). The importance of this church lies in its incorporation of Creole and Mestizo traditions, as in the side portal, where the Hispanic saint Santiago Matamoros is supported by winged mermaids, who had a symbolic value in Pre-Columbian times. The main cloisters have arches supported on substantial square columns, crowned by pediments containing medallions displaying the Jesuit monogram. They were begun at the end of the 17th century by Lorenzo de Pantigoso and Juan de Ordoñez and completed in 1738; the style and ornamentation are the same as those on the façade. Similar traditions of masonry and decoration were also used on La Merced (rebuilt 1657; rest.), S Agustín (early 18th century) and the suburban churches of S Miguel (*c.* 1719–30), Cayma, by Pérez del Cuadro (*fl c.* 1719), with a dome (1782) by Carlos Aranchi, and S Juan Bautista (1750; partly destr.), Yanahuara. Polychrome paint was sometimes applied, for example on the façade of S Juan Bautista.

Arequipa, façade and main portal of the church of La Compañía, 1698

S Domingo (1677-80) is another of the city's oldest churches and follows the scheme of La Compañía. The façade of two registers was finished in 1647 and the polygonal tower in 1649, both under Juan de Aldana (*fl* 1643–56). The nave was remodelled in 1784, and the vaults were rebuilt in 1873. Earthquakes in 1958 and 1960 destroyed a large section of the main portal, but the lateral portal remains as a good example of the contribution of local carvers, who combined the human form and geometric, floral designs. Damaged sections, including the tower, have been restored in sillar and brick. Viceregal Arequipeño architecture can also be found in the townships of Ayaviri, Asillo, Lampa, Juli, Pomata, Juliaca, Puno and Zepita. Additionally, there are at least 16 parish churches in the Colca Valley along the main route to the Collao that reveal its influence (e.g. churches of Yanque and Maca).

The first convent in Arequipa was S Catalina (1576), officially founded in 1580. The plans were drawn up by Juan de la Torre, Gómez de Hernández and Francisco Espinoza. It was built within huge, fortress-like, buttressed walls and still occupies nearly 2.5 ha, an area equivalent to a whole block on the city's grid plan. In 1582 the convent was badly damaged by an earthquake; it was rebuilt in 1662 and restored in 1758. Following the earthquake of 1784 large sections were reconstructed following the old ground-plans, and further restoration took place in 1874. The miniature citadel of arcaded galleries, small squares and individual houses was opened to the public in 1970, a small section being retained for the remaining nuns. The walls within are washed in crimson, red, orange, golden-yellow and cobalt-blue, and such architectural details as cornices are picked out in natural sillar. The convent of S Teresa (1700–*c.* 1784) retains its original character, although the associated church and its façade have been altered. The convent of S Rosa (founded 1747) likewise retains its original design, despite a total reconstruction following the earthquake of 1868.

Construction of the cathedral (founded 1612) began in 1621 and continued for several decades under the architect Moscoso; it was completed under Juan de Aldana in 1656. Following a fire in 1844 and the 1868 earthquake it was rebuilt by Lucas Poblete, and it retains much of the original plan. It is a long, low building, with a façade occupying the entire north end of the city's main square, the Plaza de Armas. It is divided into two, largely undecorated, registers, each supported by a series of columns. Surrounding the Plaza de Armas are two-storey Neo-classical arcades built in sillar, which complement the cathedral and give the square a sense of architectural unity. The second storey (post-1900) was added in the Republican period.

Secular architecture in Arequipa includes the multiple-arch Puente Bolognesi (1577–1608), which was built in sillar and spans the Chili. Fine Mestizo carving was applied to the portals, windows, cornices, gargoyles and lintels of seigneurial houses and mansions. These are usually of one storey with thick walls supporting vaulting and a small patio. In the Casa del Moral (mid-18th century; formerly owned by Arthur Williams, now by Banco Industrial) elements of Arequipeño mestizo Plateresque are combined with aspects of religious architectural design. The original owner's coat of arms fills the central ground of the portal tympanum. The protruding bay-like windows resemble those found in coastal towns, although they have much more decorative detailing. Heraldic elements include keys, lions, towers, cocks and crowns, which are complemented by puma gargoyles, cantuta flowers, drums and indigenous elements. The Casa Ugarteche (1738; originally Seminario de San Jeronimo, now Casa Gibbs-Ricketts, offices of Banco Continental) has similar proportions to the Casa del Moral, although its decoration is more formal and complex. Other seigneurial houses include the Casona Irriberry (1793), Casa de la Moneda (1794) and Casa Goveneche. It has been suggested that such single-storey houses in Arequipa are closer to the civilian architecture of the Canary Islands than to that of mainland Spain (Keleman). Furthermore, Juan de Mesa y Lugo (1605–65), Governor of Arequipa, had been a member of the council of Santa Cruz de Tenerife, Canary Islands.

From the Republican period onwards there has been an urge to conserve the city's characteristic architecture and even to replicate it using Baroque and Rococo Revival styles, for example in the late 1950s the Teatro Municipal, various public buildings and the Hotel de Turistas. In the 1960s purely functional, modernist structures were built, such as the Beneficencia Pública, Hospital del Empleado and American-style housing associations; sillar facing was sometimes used. In the 1970s and 1980s, following a massive influx of peoples from the Altiplano (Juliaca, Puno, Cuzco), sections were added to the University of S Agustín (1990s). The suburbs expanded rapidly, with large shanty towns and some houses built of brick, cane, matting and sillar blocks.

BIBLIOGRAPHY

H. E. Wethey: *Colonial Architecture and Sculpture in Peru* (Cambridge, MA, 1949), pp. 140–75

P. Keleman: *Baroque and Rococo in Latin America* (New York, 1951)

E. Harth-Terré: *Perú: Monumentos históricos y arqueológicos* (Mexico City, 1975), pp. 69–87

Prehistoria de Arequipa (exh. cat. by E. Linares Málaga, Arequipa, Casa Ricketts, 1983)

J. B. Ballesteros: *Historia del arte hispanoamericano: Siglos XVI a XVIII*, ii (Madrid, 1987), pp. 277–81

J. A. de Lavalle and others: *Arequipa* (Rio de Janeiro, 1988)

W. IAIN MACKAY

Aretino [del Tura], **Pietro** (*b* Arezzo, 19 or 20 April 1492; *d* Venice, 1556). Italian art critic, writer, poet and collector. He was one of the most engaging literary figures of the Italian Renaissance, known not only for his famous *Lettere* but also for political lampoons, erotic books and religious writings. He was the son of a shoemaker, Luca del Tura. From before 1510 until 1517 he lived in Perugia. A book of poems that he published during these years, *Opera nova* (1512), suggests by its subtitle, in which the author is called 'Pietro pictore Aretino', and by a note to the first sonnet in which he claims to be 'studioso . . . in pictura', that he had some training as an artist. About 1517 he moved to Rome, after a short period in Siena, and joined the household of Agostino Chigi. He became friendly with Raphael, Michelangelo, Sebastiano del Piombo and Jacopo Sansovino. At this time too he became known for his political lampoons. For a period Aretino was a valet to Pope Leo X; on Leo's death in 1522 he left Rome and entered the service of Giovanni dalle Bande Nere, but returned to Rome in 1523.

In 1524 one of Aretino's friends, Marcantonio Raimondi, was imprisoned by Bishop Giovanni Matteo Giberti for making and circulating 16 engravings after *'modi'* or sexual positions drawn by Giulio Romano (9 fragments, London, BM), whereupon Aretino wrote the *'sonetti lussuriosi'* (describing the *'modi'*), which were published with another edition of Raimondi's prints *c.* 1525. This edition seems to be extinct but at least one copy of an edition of 1527, printed in Venice and containing woodcut illustrations instead of Raimondi's prints, survives in a private collection. For this defiant act Aretino was obliged to leave Rome to escape imprisonment. On his return, however, he was attacked and stabbed, at the instigation of Bishop Giberti. He departed from the city once more (1525), this time for good, briefly staying at the court of Duke Federico Gonzaga at Mantua before moving to Venice in 1527, where he lived for the rest of his life.

In Venice, Aretino became friendly with Titian and other artists working there and began to write the letters (*Lettere*, Venice, 1538–57), some of them to the publisher LODOVICO DOLCE, that established his reputation as a writer. Over 600 of the letters are about art or artists, and some of them have been widely discussed, such as those of 16 September 1537 and November 1545 to Michelangelo, concerning his *Last Judgement* (1535–41; Rome, Sistine Chapel), and one dated May 1544 to Titian, which evocatively describes the view of the Grand Canal at sunset. Other letters reveal his unusual sympathy with Venetian art, particularly that of Titian, whose use of colour Aretino often praised.

It can be seen in his *Lettere* that Aretino practised essentially two kinds of criticism, as did other Renaissance writers on the subject of art. One kind is analytical and prescriptive, as in the letter of 1545 concerning Michelangelo's *Last Judgement*, a work that Aretino knew only from an engraving. The critic praised the painting's beauty of invention, but censured the artist for representing the genitalia of his figures in so holy a place as the Sistine Chapel; he even suggested that the offending anatomical parts should be painted over. The other kind of criticism practised by Aretino and his contemporaries is known as EKPHRASIS, and is laudatory and evocative in nature. In a letter of 9 November 1537 describing Titian's *Annunciation of the Birth of Christ* (untraced), for example, Aretino conveys something of the dramatic action of the figures, the quality of the composition, the beauty of the colouring and the power and sense of the illusion. On occasion Aretino broadened the range of his ekphrastic descriptions to include his practical or analytical criticism, thereby creating a third mode of criticism. It can be seen in the letter of 15 December 1540 praising Vasari's cartoon of the *Fall of Manna*, or in that of August 1545 about a print after Francesco Salviati's *Conversion of Saul* (Rome, Gal. Doria-Pamphili). In these examples Aretino evoked the scenes before him but also praised the invention of the compositions, the grace of the figures and the expressiveness of their gestures.

Aretino's associations with artists resulted in numerous portraits of him, some of them no longer extant. He commissioned an engraved portrait from Raimondi (Paris, Bib. N.) and painted portraits from del Piombo (Arezzo, Pal. Comm., Sala Consiglio) and Titian (Florence, Pitti; New York, Frick), which served as models for a number of woodcuts. He was also painted by Francesco Salviati. He is portrayed on medals (Brescia, Mus. Civ. Armi Marzoli) by Alessandro Vittoria and Leone Leoni, and his likeness appears in works by Titian (*Ecce homo*, 1543; Vienna, Ksthist. Mus.), Sansovino (bronze doors of the sacristy, Venice, S Marco) and others.

Aretino possessed a relatively small collection of works of art. Ceiling paintings by Tintoretto showing *Apollo and Marsyas* (1545; Hartford, CT, Wadsworth Atheneum) and *Mercury and Argus* (untraced) adorned his residence in the Ca' Bollani, Venice, but were left behind in 1551, when he moved to his much grander quarters of the Ca' Dandolo. In 1549 Giorgio Vasari sent him the cartoon of his *Fall of Manna* (untraced) which the critic had praised, and at Aretino's request drew for him two of Michelangelo's sculptures in the Medici Chapel, S Lorenzo, Florence.

The art of contemporary painters seems to have been influenced by Aretino's religious books, the imagery of which had been at times influenced by his knowledge of works of art. A description of the Last Judgement in his version of the first book of the Bible, *Il Genesi* (Venice, 1538), may have inspired the composition of Titian's *Trinity* (*c.* 1554; Madrid, Prado), painted for Emperor Charles V. And Veronese's *Marriage at Cana* (1562–3; Paris, Louvre), which contains a portrait of Aretino, seems to rely on his description of the same event in *La humanità di Christo* (Venice, 1535).

WRITINGS

Lettere, 6 vols (Venice, 1538–57)

F. Pertile and E. Camesasca, eds: *Lettere sull'arte di Pietro Aretino*, 3 vols (Milan, 1957–60)

G. Bull, ed. and trans.: *Selected Letters* (Harmondsworth, 1976)

L. Lawner, ed. and trans.: *I Modi—The Sixteen Pleasures: An Erotic Album of the Italian Renaissance* (Evanston, IL, 1988)

BIBLIOGRAPHY

P. Fehl: 'Veronese's Decorum: Notes on the *Marriage at Cana*', *Art the Ape of Nature: Studies in Honor of H. W. Janson*, ed. M. Barasch and L. F. Sandler (New York, 1981), pp. 344–58

L. A. Palladino: *Pietro Aretino: Orator and Art Theorist* (diss., New Haven, Yale U., 1981) [extensive bibliog.]

D. Rosand: *Painting in Cinquecento Venice: Titian, Veronese and Tintoretto* (New Haven and London, 1982), pp. 195–7

D. Rosand, ed.: *Titian: His World and his Legacy* (New York, 1982), pp. 16–22, 73–133

J. Anderson: 'Pietro Aretino and Sacred Imagery', *Interpretazioni veneziane: Studi di storia dell'arte in onore di Michelangelo Muraro*, ed. D. Rosand (Venice, 1984), pp. 275–90

N. E. Land: 'Ekphrasis and Imagination: Some Observations on Pietro Aretino's Art Criticism', *A. Bull.*, lxviii (1986), pp. 207–9

N. Land: 'Pietro Aretino's Art Criticism', *The Viewer as Poet: The Renaissance Response to Art* (University Park, PA, 1994), pp. 128–50

NORMAN E. LAND

Aretusi, Cesare (*bapt* Bologna, 1 Sept 1549; *d* Bologna, 4 Oct 1612). Italian painter. His early training was influenced by Bagnacavallo and Venetian painters. His earliest known work, the altarpiece of *St Bartholomew Worshipping the Virgin* (1570–75; Bologna, S Bartolomeo), is in a Mannerist style, with clear references to the work of Bartolomeo Passarotti, Lorenzo Sabatini and Orazio Samacchini. The austerity of the early Counter-Reformation, introduced in Bologna by Cardinal Gabriele Paleotti, is reflected in the slightly later *Crucifixion with the Virgin and Saints* (Bologna, Santa Trinità). From *c.* 1576 he collaborated with Giovanni Battista Fiorini (*d* after 1599) on such projects as the frescoes of *Christ Giving the Keys to St Peter* (1579; Bologna, Metropolitana S Pietro) and the *Coronation of the Virgin* (1588; Bologna, S Michele in Bosco). Also with Fiorini he painted numerous altarpieces for churches in Bologna, including the *Birth of the Virgin* (1577–82; S Giovanni in Monte), the *Miraculous Procession of St Gregory the Great* (1580; S Maria del Baraccano), the *Mass of St Gregory the Great* (*c.* 1580; S Maria dei Servi) and the *Deposition with SS Benedict and Francis of Paola* (S Benedetto) documented in 1593. These altarpieces have a luminosity derived from Prospero Fontana and also reflect Tuscan and Roman art. The partnership was interrupted in 1586 when Aretusi was called to Parma to make a copy of Correggio's fresco of the *Coronation of the Virgin* for the apse of S Giovanni Evangelista. The contract indicates that he was not the son of the painter Pellegrino Aretusi (1465–1523). He was also known as a portrait painter (e.g.

the portraits of *Paolo Ricci* and *Pomponio Torelli*; both Parma, G.N.). For Alfonso II d'Este, Duke of Ferrara, he painted portraits of women on small copperplates (untraced).

BIBLIOGRAPHY

DBI

D. Benati: 'L'attività bolognese di Cesare Aretusi (1549–1612)', *Il Carrobbio*, vii (1982), pp. 37–50

——: 'Cesare Aretusi', *Pittura bolognese del '500* (Bologna, 1986), ii, pp. 709–22

C. Spantigati: 'Aretusi Cesare', *La pittura in Italia: Il cinquecento* (Milan, 1987), ii, p. 689

MARIO DI GIAMPAOLO

Arezzo [anc. Arretium]. Italian city and diocese in Tuscany, *c.* 75 km south-east of Florence. Set on a small hill on the plain between the upper Arno and Valdichiana valleys, it stands on one of the principal ancient routes between Rome, Florence and Emilia-Romagna. A flourishing town in Antiquity, it also contains many fine works of art from the Gothic and Renaissance periods. In Etruscan and early Roman times, Arezzo owed part of its prosperity and fame to bronze, earthenware and gold products (the latter industry still thrives today). By the 5th century BC Arezzo was walled and had become one of the 12 most important Etruscan towns. Examples of characteristic black-glazed pottery from this period survive, as do some exceptional bronze statues, including the *Chimaera* (early 4th century BC) and a later *Minerva* (both Florence, Mus. Archeol.), which were discovered in 1553 and 1541 respectively and appropriated by Cosimo I, Grand Duke of Tuscany, for whom they helped legitimize the importance of the art of Etruria/Tuscany. Linked to Rome by the Via Cassia, Arezzo became a Roman municipium during the Republican period, and its fame as a centre for pottery grew with the production of a variety of red-glazed vases, known as *corallini* (*see* ROME, ANCIENT, §X, 8). Celebrated Aretines of this period included Caius Cilnius Maecenas (*d* 8 BC), friend of the Emperor Augustus and of the poet Horace, whose name provides the Italian word for patronage of the arts, *mecenatismo*. Ruins of a late 1st-century BC amphitheatre survive on the south side of the city.

After centuries of decline, the diocese of Arezzo expanded from the 8th century AD to within a few miles of Siena and Florence, and the power of its bishop-lords during the Middle Ages was expressed in the building of an imposing cathedral outside the city walls (consecrated 1032; destr. 1561) and the fine Romanesque Pieve di S Maria (early 12th century), with an unusual colonnaded façade and campanile (early 14th century; see fig.). The city's principal mendicant churches, S Domenico and S Francesco (both late 13th century–early 14th), contain two interesting monumental painted crucifixes from the late 13th century: one by the young CIMABUE in the former and another, attributed to an Umbrian master, in the latter. Dominating the city from the top of the hill, from which the streets fan out in a hemispherical pattern towards the city gates, is the Gothic cathedral (1280s–early 16th century), which contains two important monuments of this period: the *Arca di S Donato* on the high altar by 14th-century Florentine sculptors and the tomb of *Bishop Guido Tarlati* (1330) by the Sienese sculptors AGOSTINO DI GIOVANNI and Agnolo di Ventura. Links with Sienese

Arezzo, Pieve di S Maria, façade and campanile, early 14th century

Gothic painting stretch from Guido da Siena (*Virgin and Child*, *c.* 1270; Arezzo, Mus. Dioc.) to Pietro Lorenzetti (*see* LORENZETTI, (1)), whose important polyptych of 1320 adorned the Pieve (main panel, *in situ*).

A local school of painting flourished in Arezzo *c.* 1350–1450 with Andrea di Nerio, Spinello Aretino (*see* SPINELLI, (1)) and his son Parri Spinelli. In 1384 the city came under the dominion of Florence and commissions to 15th-century masters reveal the influence of Florentine culture, which was enriched by the presence in Florence of such Aretine humanists and chancellors as Leonardo Bruni and Carlo Marsuppini. BARTOLOMEO DELLA GATTA was among the painters active in Arezzo at this time, and PIERO DELLA FRANCESCA painted his greatest work in Arezzo: the fresco cycle of the *Legend of the True Cross* (after 1447) in the choir of S Francesco. In architecture, a link between the Gothic and early Renaissance vocabularies can be seen in Bernardo Rossellino's upper storey (1433–5) of the Palazzo della Fraternità (*see* ROSSELLINO, (1)), the seat of the Fraternità di S Maria della Misericordia (founded in 1262 and still active) in the main square of Arezzo, the Piazza Grande. Also in the mid-15th century was built the Palazzo Bruni-Ciocchi, later extended and now housing the Galleria e Museo Medioevale e Moderna). During the last quarter of the 15th century S Maria delle Grazie, built *c.* 1440 outside the city gates, was provided with a graceful loggia and porticoed piazza—for which

Benedetto da Maiano provided a design (*c.* 1478)—to accommodate large crowds of church-goers, and from the 1490s the 14th-century SS Annunziata was enlarged, partly by Antonio da Sangallo (i).

The Roman High Renaissance was brought to Arezzo by the stained-glass maker and painter, GUILLAUME DE MARCILLAT, who lived in Arezzo from 1519. He painted several works for the cathedral, SS Annunziata and S Francesco. His pupils included Giorgio Vasari (*see* VASARI, (1)), possibly the most famous Aretine native since Petrarch. The legacy of Vasari, whose chauvinist praise for Arezzo echoes throughout his *Vite* (1550), includes the decoration (1542–8) that he produced for his own house (now Mus. Casa Vasari; *see* ARTIST'S HOUSE, fig. 1), and also the loggias (1572) that he designed for the Piazza Grande. A huge defensive system was commissioned by Cosimo I at the beginning of the 16th century from Giuliano da Sangallo and Antonio da Sangallo (i), with a large fortress (destr. *c.* 1800) on the site of an old Roman castle at the top of the hill and a bastioned wall a short distance out from the 14th-century enceinte. Within these walls was built the monastery of S Bernardo (*c.* 1550; now the Museo Archeologico Ciao Cilnia Mecenate) from the ruins of the ancient amphitheatre near by. The fortunes of Arezzo nevertheless began to decline thereafter and it came to be overshadowed by Florence. Despite extensive damage in World War II, the city centre has retained its medieval character, still evident in its streets and churches.

BIBLIOGRAPHY

P. Farulli: *Annali ovvero notizie istoriche dell'antica nobile valorosa Juan città di Arezzo in Toscana* (Foligno, 1717/*R* Bologna, 1968)

U. Pasqui and U. Viviani: *Guida illustrata storica e artistica di Arezzo e dintorni* (Arezzo, 1925/*R* Rome, 1981)

M. Salmi: *Civiltà artistica della terra aretina* (Novara, 1971)

A. Tafi: *Immagine di Arezzo: Guida storico-artistica* (Arezzo, 1978)

——: *Immagine di Arezzo: La città oltre le mura medicee e il territorio comunale* (Cortona, 1985)

V. Franchetti Pardo: *Arezzo*, Le città nella storia d'Italia (Bari, 1986)

FRANK DABELL

Arezzo, Margarito d'. *See* MARGARITO D'AREZZO.

Arfe [Arphe]. Spanish family of artists, of German origin. They were the most important dynasty of gold- and silversmiths active in Spain in the 16th century.

(1) Enrique de Arfe [Heinrich von Harff] (*b* Julich or Harff, nr Cologne, *c.* 1475; *d* León, 1545). Goldsmith. He established himself in León, Spain, *c.* 1505. He introduced new types of ecclesiastical silver into Spain, for example the so-called 'seated' monstrances, transforming tower-shaped structures into free-standing objects. He executed monstrances for León Cathedral (begun 1506; destr.), the monastery of S Benito, Sahagún (Sahagún, Ayuntamiento, Mus.), Córdoba Cathedral (1518; *in situ*) and possibly also that in Cádiz Cathedral (1528; *in situ*). Cardinal Francisco Jiménez de Cisneros, Archbishop of Toledo, commissioned from de Arfe a magnificent processional cross (1515–24; Toledo Cathedral) decorated with silver-gilt statuettes. De Arfe also executed a number of silver pieces for the diocese of León, for example the processional cross of Villamuñio, the shrine of S Froilán (1519–20; *in situ*) in León Cathedral and the processional cross and the Reliquary of the Holy Cross of the Colegiata de S Isidoro, León. He also made the four sceptres (1527) in Oviedo Cathedral. His style is idiosyncratic, as he used a complex Gothic style found in contemporary German silver. Despite producing the same types of object throughout his career, he developed variations of form and style, although the architectonic conception of all his pieces is outstanding. He gradually adopted Renaissance ornamental elements in his work without abandoning the Flemish style of northern Europe. His son Antonio de Arfe (*c.* 1510–75) was also a notable silversmith and was active in Valladolid from 1547. Antonio's work is in the Plateresque style, for example large silver tabernacles in Santiago de Compostela Cathedral (1539–45).

BIBLIOGRAPHY

C. Justi: 'Die Goldschmiedefamilie der Arphe', *Miscellaneen aus drei Jahrhunderten spanischen Kunstlebens*, i (Berlin, 1908), pp. 269–90

E. Díaz Jiménez y Molleda: 'Enrique de Arfe: Nuevos datos para su biografía', *Rev. Castell.*, 8 (1916)

F. J. Sánchez Cantón: *Los Arfe: Escultores de plata y oro, 1501–1603* (Madrid, 1920)

E. Díaz Jiménez y Molleda: 'El arte en España. Enrique de Arfe: Nuevos datos para su biografía', *Erud. Ibero-Ultramarina*, 8 (1931)

A. Cortes: *Noticias de los Arfes* (Madrid, 1951)

R. Rodríguez: 'Enrique de Arfe en la catedral de León', *Archvs Leoneses*, 10 (1951)

M. V. Herraez: *Enrique de Arfe y la orfebrería gótica en León* (León, 1988)

JAVIER RIVERA

(2) Juan de Arfe (y Villafañe) (*b* León, 1535; *d* Madrid, 1 April, 1603). Goldsmith, sculptor and writer, grandson of (1) Enrique de Arfe. He spent his early life in Valladolid, where his father, Antonio de Arfe (*c.* 1510–75), was active as a silversmith and where Juan himself married in 1562. Juan carried out works in both Valladolid and Avila. His book on assaying, *Quilatador* (1572), was intended for the use of artists engaged in similar work. He moved to Seville in 1580, when he was commissioned to make the *custodia* (portable tabernacle) for Seville Cathedral (sacristy; *in situ*). Signed and dated, it was completed in 1587. It was altered in the 17th century, but its original form is known from de Arfe's description of it in *Descripción de la traça y ornato de la custodia de plata de la Sancta Iglesia de Sevilla* (1587), accompanied by engravings. Its decoration conforms iconographically to the programme drawn up by Canon Francisco Pacheco (1540–99); this is apparent in the pictorial reliefs showing figures and landscape settings. *De varia commensuración* (Seville, 1585), an influential work that was widely circulated, reflected de Arfe's aesthetic ideas as well as his theoretical and practical knowledge. It covers both the elements of geometry and the anatomical proportions needed by an artist. Juan de Arfe advocated the more stylized proportions introduced by Gaspar Becerra and Alonso Berruguete. The book also discusses the depiction of animals, as well as of architecture and the way it is related to the art of the goldsmith.

In 1587 Juan de Arfe returned to Valladolid. In a dispute with the Burgos guild of silversmiths, he described himself as *'Escultor de oro y plata'*, indicating his sense of the dignity of his art. This pride was later reflected in the magnificent funerary statues of the *Duque and Duquesa de Lerma* (Valladolid, Mus. N. Escul.). Another important work was the *custodia* (1564–71; *in situ*) of Avila Cathedral. It has a hexagonal plan, which creates a star-shaped base, and is composed of six superimposed sections with Classical orders combined with alternating circular and polygonal forms; these characteristics are repeated in other works in silver by de Arfe. The *custodia* is decorated with reliefs and free-standing figures, and in the centre is a group that movingly depicts the *Sacrifice of Isaac*. The *custodia* (1587–90; *in situ*) of Valladolid Cathedral, which is signed and dated, measures 1.64 m high and is designed in four stages. The group of *Adam and Eve* appears below the series of arches of the first section. De Arfe made a smaller *custodia* (commissioned 1592; Toledo, Mus. Santa Cruz) for the church of Carmen, Valladolid. He also executed the *custodia* (commissioned 1588; untraced) of Burgos Cathedral and restored the cathedral's processional cross. His *custodia* (1588–92; not completed; untraced) for Segovia Cathedral was made when he was appointed Ensayador de la Casa de la Moneda of the city (1589). In 1596 he was summoned to court to restore damage to the bronze sepulchres in El Escorial that had been made by Leone Leoni and Pompeo Leoni, and from 1596 he was commissioned to execute other works there, such as a series of 64 coloured reliquary busts in bronze plate (1597–1605), including a bust of *St Martha* (1599–1603; Madrid, Escorial). Other works by de Arfe include the *custodias* of Burgo de Osma (1599), of S Sebastián de los Reyes (commissioned 1596; possibly that in the cathedral of Lugo) and that of the church of S Martín, Madrid (1599; all untraced). His last works before his death (1603) were for the Lerma family, who commissioned him in 1602 to complete and cast in bronze the funerary statues of the *Duque and Duquesa de Lerma* (Valladolid, Mus. N. Escul.), the plaster models for which had been made in 1601 by Pompeo Leoni, and to make the funerary statues in bronze of the Duque's uncle *Cardinal Bernardo de Sandoval y Rojas, Archbishop of Toledo* (may have been unfinished; untraced) and of *Don Cristóbal de Rojas, Archbishop of Seville* (Lerma, Colegio S Pedro), which was finished after the artist's death by his son-in-law, the silversmith Lesmes Fernández del Moral (*fl* 1590–1608).

De Arfe's work as a goldsmith established the high quality of this art at the end of the 16th century, and his use of architectural forms was highly influential. His ability as a sculptor is apparent in his decoration, including reliefs and free-standing figures depicted with skilled Mannerist foreshortening. The valuable theoretical works of this important figure also express his humanist views.

WRITINGS

Quilatador de la plata, oro y piedras (Valladolid, 1572) [with engravings]; facs. & intro. by A. Bonet Correa (Madrid, 1976)

De varia commensuración para la esculptura y architectura (Seville, 1585, 2/1587) [with engravings]; facs. of books I & II, ed. A. Bonet Correa (Madrid, 1974)

Descripción de la traça y ornato de la custodia de plata de la Sancta Iglesia de Sevilla (Seville, 1587); ed. C. Bermúdez (Madrid, 1864), pp. 174–6

BIBLIOGRAPHY

Ceán Bermúdez

J. Martí y Monsó: *Estudios histórico-artísticos relativos principalmente a Valladolid* (Valladolid, 1901), pp. 12, 121, 169–300, 307, 386, 476, 523, 527, 531, 601, 657–9

C. Pérez Pastor: 'Quiénes fueron los escultores de las estatuas que mandaron hacer los duques de Lerma para . . . San Pablo de Valladolid?', *Rev. Archivs Bib. & Mus.*, 5 (1901), p. 281

C. Justi: 'Die Goldschmiedefamilie der Arphe', *Miscellaneen aus drei Jahrhunderten spanischen Kunstlebens*, i (Berlin, 1908), pp. 269–90

F. J. Sánchez Cantón: *Los Arfe: Escultores de plata y oro, 1501–1603* (Madrid, 1920)

J. García Marin: 'Juan de Arfe y la custodia de Avila', *Bol. Semin. Estud. A. & Arqueol.*, 8 (1941–2), pp. 257–68

M. J. Azcárate: *Escultura del siglo XVI*, A. Hisp., XIII (Madrid, 1958), pp. 144, 168, 350, 353

J. Camon Aznar: *La arquitectura y la orfebrería españolas del siglo XVI*, Summa A.: Hist. Gen. A. (Madrid, 1964), pp. 386–7

C. Oman: *The Golden Age of Hispanic Silver, 1400–1665* (London, 1968)

J. M. Cruz Valdovinos: 'La custodia de Juan de Arfe del Museo de Santa Cruz de Toledo', *Archv Esp. A.*, 197 (1977), pp. 9–29

M. J. Sanz Serrano: *Juan de Arfe y Villafañe y la custodia de Sevilla*, Arte Hispalense, xvii (Seville, 1978)

M. T. Maldonado Nieto: 'La cruz metropolitana de la catedral de Burgos y un nuevo aspecto de la obra de Juan de Arfe', *Archv Esp. A.*, 235 (1986), pp. 304–19

IV Centenario de la terminación de El Escorial (exh. cat., Madrid, Escorial, 1986), pp. 181–2

MARGARITA ESTELLA

Arfvidson, André-Louis (*b* Boulogne-sur-Seine, 3 May 1870; *d* Paris, 14 Aug 1935). French architect. He trained at the Ecole des Beaux-Arts under Paul-René-Léon Ginain and Louis-Henri-Georges Scellier de Gisors, receiving his architectural diploma in 1892. His early work included S. Bing's Art Nouveau pavilion (destr.) at the Exposition Universelle of 1900 (inspired by Louis Bonnier's initial project), blocks of flats in Paris in ashlar work, for example 236–238 Boulevard Raspail, 105 Rue Raymond Poincaré (both 1906) and the corner site of the Avenues du Bois de Boulogne et Malakoff (*c.* 1908), as well as regionalist constructions (garage in Neuilly and rural buildings in Herqueville and Heilly). He participated regularly in the competitions organized by the City of Paris, building low-cost housing schemes in the Rue Brillat-Savarin (1914–30) and the garden city at Chatenay-Malabry (1920–32) in collaboration with Joseph Bassompierre and Paul de Rutté. Following World War I he was named architect for the reconstruction schemes for the districts of Aisne and Pas-de-Calais.

Arfvidson's most innovative work is the block of flats for artists at 31 Rue Campagne Première in Paris (1911), in which each of the flats is arranged in a duplex form, with the living room overlooking the studio. The façades were decorated by the ceramicist Alexandre Bigot. After World War I Arfvidson's work evolved towards Art Deco, incorporating massive volumes, a Neo-classical vocabulary and interiors luxuriously faced in mosaic and marble. Among his most prestigious commissions are the First National City Bank Complex (1929–31) and the Hotel Prince de Galles (1929) on the Avenue Georges V in Paris.

BIBLIOGRAPHY

Petites Maisons pittoresques, 4 vols (Paris, n.d.), i, pl. 25; iv, pls 18–19

E. Rivoalen: *Maisons modernes de rapport et de commerce*, 27 (Paris, n.d.)

'Immeuble pour ateliers d'artistes', *Architecture* [Paris], 3 (Jan 1912), pp. 20–22, pls 4–5

'Cité jardin à Châtenay-Malabry', *Archit. Aujourd'hui*, 8 (1931), pp. 57–8

B. Lemoine and P. Rivoirard: *Paris, l'architecture des années trente* (Paris, 1987), pp. 52–4

A. Dugast and I. Parizet: *Dictionnaire par noms d'architectes des constructions élevées à Paris au XIXe et XXe siècles*, i (Paris, 1990)

SUSAN DAY

Argan, Giulio Carlo (*b* Turin, 17 May 1909; *d* Rome, 12 Nov 1992). Italian art historian, critic and politician. He enrolled to study law at the University of Turin, but was soon drawn to art history by the lectures of Lionello Venturi, to whom he submitted his thesis on Sebastiano Serlio in 1931. At university he was inspired by the anti-Fascist idealism of Benedetto Croce; in the Fascist period he campaigned to defend the cultural heritage, and during the German occupation he participated in the Resistance. In the early 1950s, with Roberto Longhi and Giuliano Briganti (*d* 1993), he served on the committee for the restitution of works of art removed to Germany during the war. He began teaching at the University of Palermo in 1954 and five years later succeeded his mentor Venturi at the University of Rome. He served as the Mayor of Rome between 1976 and 1979, years of terrorist activity and student unrest, subsequently joining the Communist Party, which he later represented in the Italian Senate.

Argan was a prolific writer and published studies on art from the Middle Ages to the present, including painting, sculpture, architecture, design, urbanism, photography and restoration. His approach to art history was pluralistic, encompassing iconographic, structuralist and social historical methodologies. As a Marxist, he stressed the dependence of art on the structure of production and treated such styles as Mannerism as periods of artistic decline in his influential *Storia dell'arte italiana.*

WRITINGS

L'architettura protocristiana a preromanica e romanica (Florence, 1936, 2/Bari, 1978)
Henry Moore (Turin, 1948)
Borromini (Milan, 1952)
with J. Lassaigne: *The Fifteenth Century: From van Eyck to Botticelli* (New York, 1955)
Brunelleschi (Milan, 1955, 2/1978)
Fra Angelico: Biographical and Critical Study (Lausanne, 1955)
Botticelli: Biographical and Critical Study (Geneva, 1957, 2/1967)
L'Europa delle capitali (Geneva, 1964)
Progetto e destino (1965)
Storia dell'arte italiana (1968–70, Florence, 2/1988)
The Renaissance City (London, 1969)
L'arte moderna, 1770–1970 (Florence, 1970)
Studi e note dal Bramante al Canova (Rome, 1970, 2/1980)
Die Kunst des 20. Jahrhunderts, 1880–1940 (Berlin, 1977)
with M. Fagiolo: *Guida a la storia dell'arte* (Florence, 1977)
Leonardo, la pittura (Florence, 1977)
L'architettura italiana del duocento e trecento (Bari, 1978)
Walter Gropius et le Bauhaus (Paris, 1979)
Da Hogarth a Picasso: l'arte moderna in Europa (Milan, 1983)
Classico–anticlassico: Il rinascimento da Brunelleschi a Bruegel (Milan, 1984)
with B. Contardi: *Michelangelo: Architect* (London, 1993) [excellent illus]

BIBLIOGRAPHY

E. Hüttinger: 'Aspekte der modernen italienischen Kunsthistoriographie: Zum Werk von Giulio Carlo Argan', *Ars auro prior: Studia Ioanni Białostocki sexagenario dicata* (Warsaw, 1981), pp. 39–42
Studi in onore di Giulio Carlo Argan (Rome, 1984–5)
Obituary, *NY Times* (14 Nov 1992), p. 27
A. B. Oliva: Appreciation, *A. Newspaper*, iii/23 (Dec 1992)
M. E. Vetrocq: Obituary, *A. America*, lxxxi (1993), p. 126

□

Argead. *See* ALEXANDER THE GREAT and PHILIP II, KING OF MACEDONIA.

Argenson, Marc-René d'. *See* VOYER, Marquis de.

Argenta, Jacopo Filippo d'. *See* JACOPO FILIPPO D'ARGENTA.

Argenta, l'. *See* ALEOTTI, GIOVANNI BATTISTA.

Argentina, Republic of [República Argentina]. South American country. It borders to the north with Bolivia and Paraguay, to the north-east with Brazil and Uruguay, to the east with the Atlantic Ocean and to the west with Chile (see fig. 1). Buenos Aires is the capital city, and the country is divided administratively into several areas. The mild and fertile Pampa region in the centre accounts for the country's agricultural wealth; the Andes in the west range from dry, hot, northern peaks to sub-Antarctic Patagonia; the arid north-west is rich in mineral reserves. The north is covered by subtropical forest, known as the Chaco. Mesopotamia, to the north-east, is enclosed by two great rivers, the Paraná and the Uruguay, which the Spanish expeditioners followed in search of the gold and silver that they believed Argentina ('the land of silver') concealed. This varied hinterland has, nevertheless, remained underdeveloped at the expense of the over-populated capital; around a third of the total population of 32,609,000 lives there and in the surrounding province. The majority of the population is of European, particularly Spanish and Italian, origin, although there are also communities of East Asian immigrants. The population of African descent that was introduced through slavery during colonial rule has all but disappeared, not least as a result of an epidemic of yellow fever in 1871.

This article discusses the art and architecture of Argentina after Spanish colonization. For a discussion of Pre-Columbian art and architecture, *see* SOUTH AMERICA, PRE-COLUMBIAN, §§IV, 2 and VII, 3.

I. Introduction. II. Architecture. III. Painting, graphic arts and sculpture. IV. Gold and silver. V. Textiles. VI. Patronage and art institutions. VII. Art education. VIII. Art libraries.

I. Introduction.

The settlement of Argentina by the Spanish conquistadors was a gradual and faltering process: Juan Díaz de Solís first set foot on Argentine territory in 1516; after Díaz's death at the hands of the indigenous peoples, Sebastian Cabot followed in his trail in 1526, but only in 1536 was BUENOS AIRES founded by Pedro de Mendoza (only to be abandoned and refounded in 1580 by Juan de Garay). Little evidence remains of the indigenous population, which probably numbered *c.* 300,000 at the time of the Spaniards' arrival. The most prolific people in terms of surviving indigenous art was the north-western Diaguita people, who were able potters and basket-makers and who were acquainted with basic metalwork and stone-carving techniques. Their stone fortresses or *pucará* still stand on the old Inca road that the Spanish later followed on their way to the Atlantic. The Guaraní people in the north-east were taken in by the missionaries once the Jesuits became established in Paraguay in 1585. The ruins of San Ignacio Miní mission in the province of Misiones testify to their technical and artistic abilities.

The Viceroyalty of Peru was given control of all Spanish possessions south of Lima in 1543, and in that year expeditions were sent from both Peru and the Captaincy of Chile to those territories. The oldest Argentinian towns were therefore founded along the expeditions' routes: along the north route these were Santiago del Estero (1551), Tucumán (1565), Córdoba (*see* CÓRDOBA (ii); 1573), Salta (1582), La Rioja (1591) and Jujuy (1592); while expeditions from the west founded Mendoza (1561), San Juan (1562) and San Luis (1598). Settlers followed, as well as the religious orders of the Merced, Jesuits (*see*

1. Map of Argentina; those sites with separate entries in this dictionary are distinguished by CROSS-REFERENCE TYPE

JESUIT ORDER, §4(ii)), Dominicans and Franciscans. Settlements grew into cities, and a local Baroque style developed in architecture, painting and devotional sculpture that was to prevail throughout the 17th and 18th centuries.

In the 19th century the growing weakness of the Spanish crown under Napoleonic control and two attempted British invasions (1806, 1807) strengthened local independence movements. A revolt in 1810 established a locally elected government in Buenos Aires, leading to a formal declaration of independence in 1816 by the Congress of Tucumán. In 1853 the national constitution was drawn up, settling the civil war between Buenos Aires and the provinces that had raged since independence and abolishing the slave trade. Visual records of this period survive in the paintings and etchings of contemporary foreign artists such as EMERIC ESSEX VIDAL exploring the newly independent South American countries. Art education was furthered by the formation of drawing and painting schools. In the second half of the 19th century the arrival of European immigrants, mainly from Italy and Spain, heralded a period of stability. Painting and architecture flourished with the adoption of European trends. The indigenous community, however, suffered a final blow when the nomadic peoples of Araucanos, Querandíes, Tehuelches, Onas and Yaganes were systematically exterminated and all their crafts destroyed during the Conquista del Desierto campaign (1877–81). The remaining population began to increase again only in the 20th century.

With the two world wars and the economic depressions of the 1930s another wave of immigrants arrived from Europe. At the same time developments in European and North American art and architectural styles attracted a new generation of young Argentinians. The Instituto Torcuato di Tella (founded 1958; *see* §VI below) played a significant role in focusing interest on the modernization of Argentine art. Cultural development was hindered by a series of military dictatorships from the 1930s to the early 1980s; democracy was finally restored in 1983.

BIBLIOGRAPHY

J. León Pagano: *Historia del arte argentino* (Buenos Aires, 1944)
W. Parish: *Buenos Aires y las provincias del Río de la Plata desde su descubrimiento y conquista por los españoles* (Buenos Aires, 1957)
J. Luis Romero: *Breve historia de la Argentina* (Buenos Aires, 1979)

IRENE FANNING, with MARIO TESLER

II. Architecture.

1. Colonial period, before *c.* 1810. 2. *c.* 1810–*c.* 1920. 3. After *c.* 1920.

1. COLONIAL PERIOD, BEFORE *c.* 1810. In 1536 Pedro de Mendoza founded the first settlement of Buenos Aires, but it was demolished in 1541. In 1580 it was refounded permanently on the River Plate by Juan de Garay. By 1617 the importance of Buenos Aires had been recognized by Spain, who made it the capital of a new province of the same name within the Viceroyalty of Peru. By 1776 the city was declared the capital of the newly created Viceroyalty of the River Plate, the last of Spain in America. Other new establishments were made between 1553 and 1588 when Spanish expeditions out of Lima and Santiago, Chile, established a series of cities in Argentine territory, including Santiago del Estero, Mendoza, San Juan, Tucumán, CÓRDOBA (ii), Salta, La Rioja, Jujuy, San Luis, Concepción del Bermejo and Corrientes. The cities founded by the Spaniards were characterized by their grid-plans, with a *plaza mayor* in the centre surrounded by the government house, the town hall and the principal church. The relative poverty of Argentinians until the 18th century prevented the construction of great places of worship or sumptuous residences, however. In Salta and Jujuy the first houses were of rough stone with timber roofs; in Santiago del Estero and Córdoba they were of adobe and thatch, as in the eastern zone and Buenos Aires; in their north-eastern missions the Jesuits made use of a more solid system, *pisé*, earth construction within a wooden framework. An early 18th-century temple at Molinos in Salta is typical; it has an adobe and brick church and cloister. Squat twin towers are crowned with simple cupolas and bridged by a deep barrel vault.

Numerous chapels with Hispanic influence were constructed in Salta and Jujuy, including the Yaví Chapel (1690), Jujuy. Other notable buildings include the church of S Francisco (1657–80), Santa Fe, attributed to Fray Francisco Arias, and the later S Pedro de Fiambalá (1770, Catamarca). The front of the *posta* (rest-house) at Sinsacate, near Córdoba City (18th century), is shaded by a verandah with closely spaced piers flanking a small adobe chapel with a freestanding bell tower. By comparison the *estancia* of S Catalina, also near Córdoba, is more sophisticated. The church has a Baroque façade and a dome with much simplified scroll buttresses. It was completed in 1763 with the help of the German architect–priest Anton Harls but may also show the influence of Jesuit architects ANDREA BIANCHI and GIOVANNI BATTISTA PRIMOLI, who both arrived in 1717.

Córdoba City was the most outstanding centre of colonial architecture, a position that it owed to the Jesuits, among whom there was an abundance of good architects. The Society's first chapel was established there *c.* 1596, and La Compañía (1645–74) was the mother church of the town. Its vaulting, constructed in Paraguayan cedar, is due to the Belgian Jesuit Felipe Lemer; it was partially damaged by fire in 1965. The cathedral (1697–1787) was inspired by Jacopo Vignola's Il Gesù in Rome. It was begun by José González Merguete of Granada who came to Córdoba from Bolivia in 1697; and Bianchi took over *c.* 1729. The curious dome (1752) attributed to the Franciscan Fray VICENTE MUÑOZ refers to the Late Romanesque cupolas of the Old Cathedral at Salamanca and the cathedrals at Zamora and Toro in Spain. A good example of the architecture of Jesuit *reducciones* (hamlets for converted Indians) in north-eastern Argentina is offered by the ruins of San Ignacio Miní (Misiones prov.), the constructions of which were designed by fathers Giuseppe Brasnelli and Angelo Petragrassa (*c.* 1700–24). The splendid church of San Ignacio Miní shows the presence of Indian artisans in the elaborate ornament of its Baroque façade of red stone.

In Buenos Aires the Jesuit church of S Ignacio was begun in 1712 by the architect–priest Johann Kraus, of Pilsen, Bohemia. Bianchi worked in a number of churches in Buenos Aires, including El Pilar (1716–32), La Merced (1721–33) and S Francisco (1730–54). The cathedral (1755–1791) is a three-aisled church with chapels along both sides, a dome at the crossing and a three-bay choir designed by Antonio Masella. The town hall by Bianchi was inaugurated in 1740, although building work finished only in 1765. Domestic architecture was built of brick and tiles until sometime in the second half of the 18th century. At this time the first flat-roofed dwellings of Hispanic origin were constructed. A turn-of-the-century example is the villa of Gen. Juan Martín de Pueyrredón at San Isidro (near Buenos Aires), with an elegant verandah with a simple Tuscan order. After restoration, by 1944 it had opened as a museum.

2. *c.* 1810–*c.* 1920. Little new building had taken place in the period of the War of Independence (1810–19). The government then recruited European architects to work in Argentina. The French architects Tomás Prosper Catelin (1764–1842) and Pierre Benoit, along with Antonio Masella, designed the great Neo-classical Corinthian dodecastyle portico of Buenos Aires Cathedral (1822–7; see fig. 2) with reference to the Palais Bourbon, Paris. With the hexastyle portico of S José de Flores (1830–33; destr. 1883), Buenos Aires, by the Catalan Felipe Senillosa (1783–1858), it marks the wider acceptance of Neo-classicism, which had already taken in Córdoba, Mendoza and Santa Fe before the end of the 18th century. Senillosa's Palermo de San Benito, the villa of Juan Manuel de Rosas (1838; destr. 1899), however, reintroduced nostalgic references to the colonial tradition eschewed since independence.

Other architects and engineers who came to Buenos Aires in the 1820s included James (Santiago) Bevans, Edward Taylor, Richard Adams and Charles Rann from Britain, CARLOS ENRIQUE PELLEGRINI from France, and Carlo Zucchi and Paolo Caccianiga from Italy. The Neo-classical Presbyterian church of St Andrew (1829–30) and the Anglican cathedral of St John the Baptist (1830–31), both in Buenos Aires, were built by Adams. Renewed confidence was symbolized by the enhancement (1856–7) by PRILIDIANO PUEYRREDÓN of the Pirámide de Mayo, an obelisk 15 m high, made in 1811 to commemorate the first anniversary of the Revolution, and since then placed in the Plaza de Mayo. Other buildings in Buenos Aires include Edward Taylor's Gothic Revival German Evangelical Church (1850–51), his somewhat Mannerist Customs House (1855–7; destr. 1894) and the Club del Progreso (1856; destr. 1971); and Henry Hunt's and Hans Schroeder's Stock Exchange (1861), which now belongs to the Central Bank of Argentina.

The building of the suburb of Adrogué by Nicolá Canale (1807–74) and his son Giuseppe (1833–83)—who came from Genoa in 1855—was part of the development of Buenos Aires. They designed the churches of La Inmaculada Concepción (1865–78) and La Piedad (1866–95), which has a circular plan, both in Buenos Aires. Juan Antonio Buschiazzo (1846–1917) was the first architect to graduate in architecture from the Universidad de Buenos Aires (1878). He designed the town hall (1869–72), Belgrano, now a museum, and completed La Piedad. Pietro Fossati from Lombardy transformed the Palacio San José (1848–59) in Entre Ríos into a Renaissance Revival palace for the Urquiza family, and built the mother

2. Tomás Prosper Catelin, Pierre Benoit and Antonio Masella: portico of Buenos Aires Cathedral, 1822–7

3. Francesco Tamburini: Casa de Gobierno (Casa Rosada), Buenos Aires, 1885–98; finished by Juan Antonio Buschiazzo and Vittorio Meano

church at Concepción del Uruguay (1856–9) and the Palladian residence of Santa Cándida (1858–64). Cathedrals were built at Tucumán (1845–56) by Pierre Dalgare Etcheverry, at Salta (1876–86) by Francisco Righetti; and at Corrientes (1854–64) by master mason Nicola Grosso. Increased building activity in Paraná during the seven years that it remained capital (1854–60) included new government buildings, mainly by the Italian Salvatore Danuzio in a Renaissance Revival style: the Chamber of Deputies (1855), the Senate (1859) and the Government House (1854–5). Before architectural education began at the Universidad de Buenos Aires, the few Argentinian architects included Jonás Larguía (1832–91) of Córdoba, who studied in Rome and designed the first Congreso Nacional (1864) in the Plaza de Mayo, and Ernesto Bunge (1839–1903), educated in Germany, who built the church of S Felicitas (1879) in Buenos Aires.

In 1880 Buenos Aires was federalized as capital. During a period of the greatest and most sustained economic growth in history, it became transformed into the overwhelming image of the new Argentina, which increased its powers on all levels, to the point that it almost became the Nation itself. Architecturally it rushed to emulate Haussmann's Paris, and a Beaux-Arts classicism first took root. Buschiazzo opened up the Avenida de Mayo (1888–94) and demolished older buildings. Spacious vistas were opened up and gave credence to the cognomen 'Paris of South America'. The Italian Vittorio Meano (1860–1904) designed the Congreso Nacional (1898–1906), and, until his untimely death, was responsible for the rebuilding of the Teatro Colón (completed 1908; for illustration *see* BUENOS AIRES). It was designed by the Italian Francesco Tamburini (*d* 1891), who also built the Casa de Gobierno (Casa Rosada, 1885–98; see fig. 3), and finished by the Belgian architect Jules Dormal (1846–1924).

Characteristic of *fin-de-siècle* eclecticism is much of the work of ALEJANDRO CHRISTOPHERSEN. It includes the elegant Palacio Anchorena (1909; now the Foreign Office), in the Plaza San Martín and the Stock Exchange (1916), Avenida Alem, and the two-storey *petit hôtel* (1903), Calle Libertad 1270. Among architects working in the Art Nouveau idiom were Louis Dubois (1867–1916); Francesco Gianotti; Enrique Rodríguez Ortega, who designed the four-storey façade of Calle Rivadavia 2031 (1905); and Emile Hugé (1863–1918), whose Casa Moussion (1908; now Fundación Banco Patricios) features a highly decorated giant order and shop-front canopies reminiscent of Hector Guimard's work. Julián Jaime García Núñez (1875–1944) was educated in Barcelona and worked under Luis Domènech i Montaner. He designed many buildings in Buenos Aires, including Calle Chacabuco 78 (1910) and Calle Luis Sáenz Peña 274 (1913). His Hospital Español (1908; partly destr.) has suggestions of Moorish influence and a central dome with Gaudíesque fish-scale tiles.

3. AFTER *c.* 1920. A Neo-colonial movement flourished during the 1920s with such works as the Museo de Arte Isaac Fernández Blanco (1924) in Buenos Aires, by Martín Noel (1888–1963). But the outstanding personality of the period is ALEJANDRO VIRASORO, a forerunner of Art Deco and a bridge to early Modernism. Le Corbusier visited Argentina in 1929 to give a series of ten lectures later published in *Précisions sur un état présent de l'architecture et de l'urbanisme* (1930). These had little immediate effect, but his influence grew over the next 20 years. The local pioneer of the Modern Movement was Alberto Prebisch, whose Gran Rex cinema (1937), Calle Corrientes 857, Buenos Aires, is one of the most significant buildings of Modernist architecture. Other rationalists include ANTONIO UBALDO VILAR, designer of the multi-storey flats of Avenida del Libertador 3590 and the office building of Calles Florida and M. T. de Alvear (both 1935; Buenos Aires); Jorge Kalnay (1894–1957); and Léon Dourge

(1890–1969). Mention is due to the first skyscrapers of Buenos Aires—the Comega (1932), Safico (1933) and Kavanagh (1936), all of them Modernist. In June 1939 the Austral group published their manifesto 'Voluntad y acción' [Will and action] in Buenos Aires's *Nuestra arquitectura*, in which they assumed the defence of Rationalism against what they denounced as the dehumanization and lack of social engagement of the International Style. The group included ANTONIO BONET, Juan Kurchan (1913–72) and Jorge Ferrari Hardoy (1914–77). The three had met a year before at Le Corbusier's studio in Paris, where they helped Le Corbusier with his far-reaching masterplan for Buenos Aires (completed by 1940 but made known only in 1947), which was never brought to fruition. The principles of the 1939 manifesto were realized, however, in such works as the apartment house at Calle Virrey del Pino 2446 (1943). AMANCIO WILLIAMS exhibited in Paris in 1947, under the auspices of Le Corbusier and was later patronized by Walter Gropius and Ludwig Mies van der Rohe. The principle of his work was to make optimum use of air, light and space, which was realized in the House over the Brook designed for his father at Mar del Plata (1943–5; for illustration *see* WILLIAMS, AMANCIO). Eduardo Sacriste (*b* 1935) employed a rationalist language to create an architecture responsive to Argentina's social and aesthetic demands. Sacriste's Critical Regionalism is evident above all in a dozen one-family residences he built (1939–83) in the province of Tucumán.

Rationalism was also the starting-point of three distinguished practices founded in Buenos Aires in the late 1930s. The first, chronologically, was that of José Aslán and Héctor de Ezcurra, whose work includes the apartment house (1968) at Calle M. T. de Alvear 534 in Buenos Aires and the Lever factory (1978–82) in Pilar, north of Buenos Aires. The second, SEPRA, Santiago Sánchez Elía, Federico Peralta Ramos and Alfredo Agostini, designed the Telephone building (1951–64) in Buenos Aires and the town hall (1954–61) and the football stadium (1977) in Córdoba City. The third was that of MARIO ROBERTO ALVAREZ, whose extensive work ranges from the elegant Teatro General San Martín (1956) and the IBM offices (1983), to the Galeria Jardin (1974) and the Le Parc apartment tower (1993), all in Buenos Aires. SEPRA was associated with CLORINDO TESTA in one of the most notable contemporary buildings of Buenos Aires; the Banco de Londres y América del Sur (1959–66; now Lloyd's Bank; for illustration *see* TESTA, CLORINDO). Testa was also responsible for the civic centre (Government House, ministries and legislature; 1958–63 and 1972–6), Santa Rosa, province of La Pampa, and the Biblioteca Nacional (1962–92), Buenos Aires.

Claudio Caveri designed the church of Our Lady of Fatima (1957, with Eduardo Ellis) in Martínez and two one-family residences, Casa Caveri (1962), his own house in San Miguel, and Casa Moores (1963), San Isidro. Located near Buenos Aires, these are examples of an architecture concerned with local traditions and materials. Among the important buildings of the practice of Flora Manteola, Javier Sánchez Gómez, Josefina Santos and Justo Solsona is the ATC (the State Television Network) headquarters (1978) and the Prourban office circular tower (1982), both in Buenos Aires. Other innovative practices include those of: Juan Manuel Bortagaray, Mario Gastellu and Carlos Marré (Escuela Carlos della Penna, 1971; apartment house in Avenida del Libertador and Calle Blanco Encalada, 1981); Juan Llauró and José Urgell (Hospital Regional S Vicente de Paul, Orán, Salta prov., 1963; Villa Argentina Permanente of Yacyretá, Corrientes prov., 1982); Antonio Antonini, Gerardo Schon, Eduardo Zemborain and Associates (football stadium and multisports complex in Mar del Plata, 1977; Club Hotel DUT, nr Nahuel Huapi Lake, Neuquén prov., 1981); Miguel Baudizzone, Jorge Erbin and Alberto Vara (Estuario building, 1979; 25 de Mayo tower, 1981, both in Buenos Aires, with Jorge Lestard and Antonio Díaz); Angela Bielus, Jorge Goldemberg and Olga Wainstein-Krasuk (social housing quarters in Florencio Varela, 1978, nr Buenos Aires, and Formosa, 1985, Formosa prov.); and Miguel Ángel Roca (Paseo Azul, 1980; Office Centre, 1993, both in Córdoba City).

The members of the 'Generation of 1970', developed under the aegis of rationalist teaching, followed the architectural paths of the preceding decades. They included the practices of Rosina Gramática, Juan Carlos Guerrero, Jorge Morini, José Gregorio and Juan Ricardo Pisani and Eduardo Urtubey (Nuevocentro shopping centre, 1991, Córdoba City); Berardo Dujovne and Silvia Hirsch (apartment building at Calle Salguero 2150, 1983, Buenos Aires), Raúl Lier and Alberto Tonconogy (Paseo Alcorta shopping centre, 1992, Buenos Aires); Juan Carlos López (Alto Palermo, 1990, and Galerías Pacífico, 1992, both shopping centres, Buenos Aires). They indicate the range of late 20th-century trends.

BIBLIOGRAPHY

J. A. Pillado: *Buenos Aires colonial* (Buenos Aires, 1910)
A. Christophersen: 'Nuevos rumbos', *Rev. Arquit.* (July 1915), p. 7
M. J. Buschiazzo: *Las viejas iglesias y conventos de Buenos Aires* (Buenos Aires, 1937)
J. Giuria: *Apuntes de arquitectura colonial argentina* (Montevideo, 1941)
A. Lascan Gonzálaz: *Monumentos religiosos de Córdoba colonial* (Buenos Aires, 1941)
D. Angulo Iñíguez, E. Marco Dorta and M. J. Buschiazzo: *Historia del arte hispanoamericano*, 3 vols (Barcelona, 1945–56)
P. Keleman: *Baroque and Rococo in Latin America* (New York, 1951), pp. 126–64
C. Sanz: *Relación histórico-bibliográfica de la conquista del Río de la Plata y fundación de Buenos Aires* (Madrid, 1958)
F. Bullrich: *Arquitectura argentina contemporánea* (Buenos Aires, 1963)
——: *Arquitectura latinoamericana, 1930–1970* (Barcelona, 1969)
——: *New Directions in Latin American Architecture* (London, 1969), pp. 15–17, 30–35, 104–17
D. Bayón and P. Gasparini: *The Changing Shape of Latin American Architecture* (Chichester and New York, 1979), pp. 10–37, 234–7
J. Glusberg, ed.: *Arquitectos de Buenos Aires* (Buenos Aires, 1979)
M. J. Buschiazzo: *Arquitectura en Argentina* (Buenos Aires, 1982)
T. Dagnino: *Manteola, Sánchez Gómez, Santos, Solsona* (Buenos Aires, 1984)
S. Borghini, H. Salama and J. Solsona: *1930–1950: Arquitectura moderna en Buenos Aires* (Buenos Aires, 1987)
R. Gutiérrez, M. Martín and A. Petrina: *Otra arquitectura argentina* (Bogotá, 1989)
A. Irigoyen and R. Gutiérrez: *Nueva arquitectura argentina: Pluralidad y coincidencia* (Bogotá, 1990)
J. Glusberg: *Breve historia de la arquitectura argentina* (Buenos Aires, 1991)
R. Gutiérrez: *Buenos Aires: Evolución histórica* (Bogotá, 1992)

JORGE GLUSBERG

III. Painting, graphic arts and sculpture.

1. Colonial period, 1536–1816. 2. After 1816.

1. COLONIAL PERIOD, 1536–1816. Despite the fact that Buenos Aires and a number of other cities were founded on Argentinian territory during the 16th century, no art of any consequence was produced during this period; indeed, throughout the entire colonial period artistic activity in Argentina was less significant than in other parts of Latin America. Nevertheless, the country did come to conform with the general Latin American trend of forming regional styles. These were centred in the north on Jesuit schools in Buenos Aires, Santa Fe and Córdoba, where workshops produced paintings that were essentially religious in theme. However, rather than encouraging a production with purely local characteristics, models were sought in Peru and Europe, and European styles, subjects and techniques were adopted. It was also commonplace to import paintings from Spain, Italy, Flanders, Peru and Upper Peru (now Bolivia); those from Upper Peru were produced in the workshops of Cuzco and Potosí and went on to enjoy wide dissemination in the 18th century. Of particular interest were highly imaginative paintings of arquebus angels, probably executed in Cuzco, for which there was no known European prototype.

Notable local artists included Fray Luis Berger, who painted the *Virgin of the Miracles* (1636) in the church of La Compañía in Sante Fe; Juan Bautista Daniel painted foliage and figurative decorations in the interior of the church of La Compañía (1645–71) in Córdoba. Although there must have been painters at the Jesuit missions in addition to the sculptors, gilders and wood-carvers, only written documentation survives. The first examples of engraving in Argentina came from the Jesuit missions. The earliest preserved book, *Diferencia entre lo temporal y lo eterno* by Fray Nieremberg, was illustrated with woodcuts by indigenous artists, one of which was signed by the Indian Joan Yapaí. The second Argentinian printing press reached Buenos Aires in 1780, when the first engravings were made in the city (e.g. *Holy Trinity*, 1781; Buenos Aires, Mus. Saavedra). In Buenos Aires Spaniards and Italians were the most active artists. They included José de Salas, who painted the portrait of *Canon Riglos* (Luján, Mus. B.A.), Martino di Pietro, who painted the earliest miniature (1794) in Buenos Aires, and Angelo María Camponeschi, perhaps the most important painter of the colonial period, who executed the portrait of *Fray Zemborain* (1804; Buenos Aires, Conv. S Domingo; see fig. 4). Camponeschi's achievements earned him the praise of the Cabildo, which proclaimed him as 'the best artist of his time'.

Retables and pulpits were an important complement to religious architecture; *retablos mayores* in particular, as the focal point at the high altar, were a fundamental element of church interiors, although in Argentina their style was simpler than the Baroque theatricality of those in other Latin American countries. Outstanding examples in the north are found in the Jujuy, Quebrada and Altipiano regions, in churches at Humahuaca, Yavi and Uquía; also noteworthy is the *retablo mayor* of the church of La Compañía in Córdoba. In Buenos Aires, where the old Baroque retables were later replaced by Rococo and Neo-classical ones, those in the cathedral and the churches of S Ignacio and La Merced are of interest. Some Argentinian pulpits are among the best examples in Latin America, and include those of Jujuy Cathedral, which was carved by Indians and gilded, and La Merced in Córdoba, also in gilded wood. Figurative carvings were often imported from Spain, Portugal, Italy, Peru, Quito and Brazil; local production was in the north and north-east, the Jesuit missions, Buenos Aires and Córdoba. Each region had special characteristics, but the most original sculpture was produced by indigenous artists at the Jesuit missions. Sculptures from Peru and Upper Peru pre-date the European imports and were carved in wood or made of maguey, glued cloth and paste. Some of those created by mestizo and creole craftsmen using wood or stone are remarkably expressive. The oldest surviving Spanish statues are from the 17th century, and Italian examples arrived in the 18th century, generally carved in wood and painted in the exaggerated style of Italian academic Baroque. A fine example of an 18th-century work from Quito is a group

4. Angelo María Camponeschi: *Fray Zemborain*, 1804 (Buenos Aires, Convento de S Domingo)

in the Convento de Clarisas, intended to be clothed, with brilliantly painted lead faces. One of the most striking features is the predominance of sculptured mass, as in the 18th-century *Archangel Gabriel* (priv. col.) carved in wood with traces of original polychrome.

2. AFTER 1816. As in other parts of Latin America, in the first half of the 19th century a number of foreign artists visited Argentina, attracted by the possibility of exploring the newly independent republic. One of the first to arrive, in 1817, was the Swiss artist Josef Guth, who settled in Buenos Aires. Within a year he had set up a drawing school, and he went on to teach drawing at the Universidad de Buenos Aires from 1822 to 1828. Many became known as 'traveller–reporter' artists, recording in oil, watercolour, drawing and engraving what they perceived as the characteristic and picturesque qualities in the people and landscapes of the Río de la Plata area. Foremost among them were EMERIC ESSEX VIDAL and Johan Moritz Rugendas; Carlos Enrique Pellegrini, also an architect, settled in Argentina and expanded the typical subject-matter of the traveller–reporter–landscapes, exotic fruit and Amerindians—in his depictions of daily life in Buenos Aires, which he included with letters to friends in Europe. In the second half of the 19th century these artists were instrumental in forging a new sense of national identity following independence from Spanish rule and after centuries of emulation of European iconography.

In the mid-19th century Argentinian-born artists began to gain in stature. Among the leading figures were PRILIDIANO PUEYRREDÓN who produced portraits and nudes, as well as landscapes and street scenes; CARLOS MOREL, a painter, miniaturist and lithographer who had studied under Josef Guth; and CÁNDIDO LÓPEZ, who portrayed the War of the Triple Alliance (1865–70) against Paraguay with great detail and spontaneity. From the 1870s the art life in Buenos Aires gained momentum, firstly with the creation of the Sociedad Estímulo de Bellas Artes by, among others, Eduardo Sívori. Then in 1878 the Escuela Nacional de Bellas Artes 'Prilidiano Pueyrredón' was founded, followed in 1895–6 by the Museo Nacional de Bellas Artes. This period was a cultural and economic highpoint in the country's history, and the work of such artists as ERNESTO DE LA CÁRCOVA, EDUARDO SÍVORI and ANGEL DELLA VALLE combined European training with local vernacular subjects. At the turn of the century a number of artists began to adopt Impressionism, including Martín Malharro (1865–1911) and Fernando Fader (1882–1935), who had studied in Munich. Prominent sculptors in the late 19th century included FRANCISCO CAFFERATA, who began to break with academic style in his depictions of the African descendants in Argentina. Lucio Correa Morales (1852–1923) taught, among others, Pedro Zonza Briano (1866–1941) and ROGELIO YRURTIA, the first great Argentine sculptor, who, while influenced by European trends, avoided copying them. In the early 20th century Lola Mora (1867–1936) became the first successful woman sculptor in Argentina, with such works as the Nereidas Fountain.

Pío Collivadino (1869–1945), who was director of the Escuela Nacional de Bellas Artes in Buenos Aires from 1908, set up the first workshop for the teaching of engraving. In 1915 the Sociedad de Acuarelistas, Pastelistas y Grabadores was founded and held its first salon, and in 1916 the engraver Mario Canale (1890–1951) founded the first specialist engraving periodical, *El grabado.* The medium was boosted in the 1920s by the appearance of the so-called Artistas del Pueblo, who treated social themes; as well as writers, painters and sculptors, the group included such printmakers as Guillermo Facio Hébequer, José Arato, Antonio Vigo and Adolfo Bellocq, who formed what came to be known as the Grupo de Boedo. Their approach was one of merciless realism and sharp social criticism, expressing through lithographs, etchings and woodcuts the more sombre aspects of the world of the working and disadvantaged classes. Similar subjects were taken up in the woodcuts of Víctor Rebuffo (1903–83), while the Expressionism of Pompeyo Audivert (1900–77) and the imaginative and formal invention of Fernando López Anaya (1903–88) displayed different responses to the medium. Printmakers working in the provinces included Víctor Delhez (1901–85) and Sergio Sergi (1896–1973) in Mendoza, Gustavo Cochet (1904–79), Juan Grela (*b* 1914), Agustín Zapata Gollán (1895–1986) in Santa Fe and Alberto Nicasio (1902–80) and Oscar Meyer in Córdoba.

AGUSTÍN RIGANELLI and Luis Falcini (1889–1973) were among the sculptors who depicted working-class subjects in a Social Realist style in the 1920s. PABLO CURATELLA

5. Emilio Pettoruti: *Argentinian Sun*, oil on canvas, 995×650 mm, 1941 (Buenos Aires, Museo Nacional de Bellas Artes)

MANES, meanwhile, moved from Cubist sculpture to totally abstract works, and SESOSTRIS VITULLO depicted gauchos and Argentinian landscapes using blocks of stone or wood; both spent periods living in Europe. The work of their contemporaries José Fioravanti (1896–1977) and Alfredo Bigatti (1898–1964) was monumental, while ANTONIO SIBELLINO was one of the first Latin American sculptors to use abstract forms.

Painting took on new forms with the generation active during the 1920s and 1930s, who had been influenced by Cubism and Fauvism from France. Perhaps the first important figure was EMILIO PETTORUTI, who first introduced Cubism to the country to an initially bemused public, and who remained with the style for some time (e.g. *Argentinian Sun*; Buenos Aires, Mus. N. B.A.; see fig. 5). Other figures experimenting with the avant-garde styles were Ramón Gómez Cornet (1898–1964), LINO ENEAS SPILIMBERGO, RAQUEL FORNER, HORACIO BUTLER, HÉCTOR BASALDÚA, JUAN DEL PRETE, who worked successively with abstraction and *Art informel* styles, and EMILIO CENTURIÓN. The periodical *Martín Fierro* was launched in 1924, and its manifesto, published in the fourth issue in May, in many ways reflected Marinetti's views on Futurism; in addition, it acknowledged the paradoxical situation whereby, in spite of the need to assert Latin American independence, artistic influence from Europe was unavoidable. A leading contributor to the periodical was Argentina's celebrated writer Jorge Luis Borges, and among the artists that grouped themselves around it was XUL SOLAR, whose abstract and mythical paintings prefigured Surrealism and broke new ground in Argentina; Solar also translated Dadaist poetry and illustrated a number of books by Borges. This cosmopolitan generation of artists was known collectively as the Grupo de Florida; aside from their interest in the European avant-garde, they were also united by a concern for social issues, a subject that was to become more prominent as the century progressed. Some painters concentrated on aspects of life in Buenos Aires, among them Onofrio Pacenza and Horacio March who gave a metaphysical view of some districts. MIGUEL DIOMEDE, Leónidas Gambartes (1909–63), Juan Grela (*b* 1914) and, in Córdoba, LUIS SEOANE were all influenced by European trends.

In 1928 the Argentinian critic Aldo Pellegrini formally introduced Surrealism to the country through the poetry review *Qué*. JUAN BATLLE PLANAS was quick to identify with the movement (e.g. in *The Message*), and he remained with it for many years. He was followed in 1939 by Grupo Orión, whose members included Orlando Pierri, Luis Barragán and Leopoldo Presas. Batlle Planas's student ROBERTO AIZENBERG achieved considerable success with paintings that combined Surrealism, Symbolism and geometric abstraction; it was this lack of clear definition in his work and that of countless Latin American artists that contributed in a fundamental way to the richness of their art, free as it was from the categorizations imposed on European art. Other artists who used elements of Surrealism in their work included RAÚL ALONSO, MILDRED BURTON and VÍCTOR CHAB; a member of the group Siete Pintores Abstractos, Chab oscillated between geometric abstraction and Surrealism. In the 1940s a strong Constructivist trend developed, initially through the group calling themselves the ASOCIACIÓN ARTE CONCRETO INVENCIÓN. Its members included Tomás Maldonado (*b* 1922), GYULA KOŠICE, the rigorously logical and rational sculptor ENNIO IOMMI, Raúl Lozza (*b* 1911), Claudio Girola (*b* 1923) and the Uruguayan artists Rhod Rothfuss (*b* 1920) and Joaquín Torres García. The last contributed a text to the only issue of the periodical *Arturo* (1944) enunciating the group's commitment to abstract art; Rothfuss in turn advocated the use of irregularly shaped canvases, expressing the desire to break away from what was seen as the restrictive tradition of the rectangular format. The Asociación's membership increased, and the original members broke away, coining the name ARTE MADÍ for their new grouping. Principal among them was Košice, who wrote the Arte Madí manifesto in 1946 (see 1989 exh. cat., p. 330), and whose irregularly shaped canvases displayed ideological similarities with the Asociación. Also of prime importance to the group were the involvement of the spectator, movement and articulation and the use of new materials and technology, seen in Košice's *Madí Aluminium Structure No. 3* (neon, 1946; artist's col.; see fig. 6): these were significant elements in the inventiveness and playfulness that the movement had in common with Dada. Another break occurred in 1947 when Raúl Lozza separated from the Asociación Arte Concreto Invención to form the group *Perceptismo*; still concerned with promoting Constructivism, Lozza typically used large backgrounds on which he placed dynamically shaped planes of colour. Another line of development was

6. Gyula Košice: *Madí Aluminium Structure No. 3*, neon, 560×410×180 mm, 1946 (artist's collection)

represented by the *Manifiesto blanco* (1946) of LUCIO FONTANA and his followers, which set out the concept of *Spazialismo*; Fontana's work in steel and mixed media explored the boundaries between painting and sculpture.

Argentina increasingly synchronized with developments in European art, and in the 1950s various groups and trends emerged. In 1952 four semi-abstract painters, José Antonio Fernández Muro, Sarah Grilo, Miguel Ocampo (*b* 1922) and Hans Aebi (*b* 1923), formed the group Artistas Modernos de Argentina, and in 1959 *Art informel* arose in opposition to the rationality of Arte Concreto, led by such artists as KENNETH KEMBLE and ALBERTO GRECO, whose work included gestural painting, assemblage and performance art, which had no local precedents. Prominent sculptors in the 1950s included NOEMÍ GERSTEIN, who used welded metal and later bronze tubes, and Líbero Badii. Badii's works ranged from rounded forms symbolizing fecundity to specifically Argentinian themes and portraits and, from the late 1960s, polychromed wooden doll figures; the Museo Badii was opened in Buenos Aires in 1988. Geometric abstraction continued to be favoured by a number of artists. The term ARTE GENERATIVO was coined in 1959 by EDUARDO MACENTYRE and MIGUEL ANGEL VIDAL, and in 1960 they published a manifesto to support their aims. Other artists associated with the style included the painter and sculptor Ary Brizzi, the painters CARLOS SILVA, MARÍA MARTOREL, and ROGELIO POLESELLO and the painter, draughtswoman and printmaker ANA KOZEL. Most Argentinians interested in kinetic and Op art were working in Paris, and in 1960 the Groupe de Recherche d'Art Visuel was formed around JULIO LE PARC, among those associating with Le Parc was the Minimalist GABRIEL MESSIL. During the same period ALEJANDRO PUENTE used unconventional shaped canvases, and César Paternosto used geometric symbols from Pre-Columbian cultures in a constructivist spirit.

In the 1960s many avant-garde activities were centred on the Centro de Artes Visuales di Tella at the Instituto Torcuato Di Tella (founded 1958) in Buenos Aires, which promoted, among other things, the Argentinian equivalent of Pop art. Among those who exhibited their work at the Instituto were Carlos Squirru, the performance artist and sculptor MARTA MINUJÍN, and MARTHA PELUFFO; as a result of political pressure and financial problems the centre closed in 1970. In 1962, also in Buenos Aires, the Nueva Figuración group emerged, comprising RÓMULO MACCIÓ, LUIS FELIPE NOÉ, JORGE DE LA VEGA and ERNESTO DEIRA; they worked in a variety of media with a combination of neo-Expressionism, gestural and geometric painting, Pop art and *Art informel.* The last was also used by the painter and printmaker ANTONIO SEGUÍ, whose work contained elements of humour, and JOSEFINA ROBIROSA, who was part of an *Art informel* group centred on the periodical *Boa*; Robirosa later turned to Op art and figuration and, eventually, abstraction in her paintings and drawings. Another group formed round the Centro de Arte y Comunicación in Buenos Aires, taking its name from the centre founded in 1969 by Jorge Glusberg, Grupo CAYC was made up of artists working in a variety of media. They included the painter and sculptor LUIS BENEDIT, the sculptors JACQUES BEDEL and VÍCTOR GRIPPO and the architect and painter Clorindo Testa. Happenings publicizing ecological concern were organized by, among others, the conceptual artist and architect Nicolás García Uriburu.

By the late 20th century an abundance of artistic styles was being simultaneously expressed. Worthy of note are Guillermo Kuitca, the abstract painter Eduardo Médici, Jean Lecuona, Alfredo Prior, who produced neo-figurative landscapes, the Expressionist Duilio Pierri, Fernando Fazzolari, Ana Eckell and the painter, draughtsman and graphic designer Juan Pablo Renzi. Initially involved with Nueva Figuración, Renzi combined figurative and Abstract Expressionist elements in his work before developing a more rational style; he also worked with other artists from Rosario on *Tucumán arde*, a multimedia event using image, sound and movement, which expressed the desire for an alternative to institutionalized culture. JUAN CARLOS DÍSTÉFANO, one of the major figures in painting and sculpture in the late 20th century in Argentina, projected his profound humanism through the use of man-made materials and strong colours; JORGE MICHEL produced both modern and archaicizing combinations of carved wood or stone and bronze, iron or steel; and HERNÁN DOMPÉ pursued a regional identity with his evocations of Aztec, Inca and Maya civilizations.

BIBLIOGRAPHY

E. Schiaffino: *La pintura y la escultura en la Argentina, 1783–1894* (Buenos Aires, 1933)

El grabado en la Argentina, 1705–1942 (exh. cat., Rosario, Mus. Mun. B.A., 1942)

J. L. Pagano: *Historia del arte argentino desde los aborígenes hasta el momento actual* (Buenos Aires, 1944)

A. Pellegrini: *Panorama de la pintura argentina contemporánea* (Buenos Aires, 1967)

C. Córdoba Iturburu: *80 años de pintura argentina* (Buenos Aires, 1978)

Cien años de pintura y escultura en la Argentina, 1878–1978 (exh. cat. by A. Ribera, N. Perazzo and G. Whitelow, Buenos Aires, Banco Ciudad, 1978)

H. Schenone and A. L. Ribera: *Historia general del arte en la Argentina*, 2 vols (Buenos Aires, 1982–3)

Arte argentina. Dalla indipendenza ad oggi, 1810–1987 (exh. cat., Rome, Ist. It.–Lat. Amer., 1987)

N. Perazzo: 'Constructivism and Geometric Abstraction', *The Latin American Spirit: Art and Artists in the United States, 1920–1970* (exh. cat., New York, Bronx Mus. A., 1988–9)

Art in Latin America: The Modern Era, 1820–1980 (exh. cat., ed. D. Ades; London, Hayward Gal., 1989)

R. Brughetti: *Nueva historia de la pintura y escultura en la Argentina* (Buenos Aires, 1991)

120 años de pintura en Córdoba, 1871–1991 (exh. cat., foreword by N. Perazzo; Córdoba, Argentina, Mus. Prov. B.A. 'Emilio A. Caraffa', 1991–2)

NELLY PERAZZO

IV. Gold and silver.

Silversmiths were among the earliest settlers in the River Plate region, but they discovered that the gold and silver deposits of the region were limited compared to the riches of Peru and Mexico. Some mines were established in the Mendoza region, but the sparse indigenous population meant that, unlike in Potosí (now in Bolivia), there was little slave labour available to make large-scale mining of gold and silver viable. Nevertheless, there was considerable demand for both ecclesiastical and domestic gold- and silverwork in wealthy Buenos Aires on account of its position on the trade routes, and by the mid-17th century the city supported a thriving colony of silversmiths. Unlike their counterparts in Peru and Mexico, however, they were subjected to few regulations. Periodic attempts were made to force them to use a maker's mark and to submit their work for assay, but an almost total lack of surviving marked pieces shows how unsuccessful these attempts were. A small group of silver pieces, which appear to date from the early 19th century, survive stamped with a town mark consisting of the conjoined initials BsAs within the 'Pillars of Hercules' (similar to the official and more widespread marks used in Mexico). Such official hallmarks should not be confused with stamps bearing owners' names, which sometimes appear on 19th-century domestic articles.

A rare survival from the mid-17th century is a pair of silver lanterns (Buenos Aires, Mus. Hist. N. Cabildo Ciudad) made in Buenos Aires and dated 1642. They are chased with strapwork and foliage, but 17th- and 18th-century silver produced in the River Plate region is generally plainer than that produced in Peru, with a distinct emphasis on line rather than ornament, even when the piece is highly decorated. A good example is a candelabrum of 1796 (Orán Parish Church), on which exotic foliage enclosing cartouches and coats of arms is contained within severe, plain borders. As in Peru, Baroque ornament continued to be used throughout the 18th century with the occasional addition, late in the century, of such Rococo motifs as rocaille. Unlike contemporary Peruvian work, however, the ornament on pieces made in the River Plate region never dominates the form: a silver altar-frame (*c.* 1760; Buenos Aires, S Ignacio), though elaborately chased with Baroque and Rococo motifs, lacks the exuberance of contemporary Peruvian examples.

Work produced in the central regions and the north in the 17th and 18th centuries generally shows Peruvian influence in its more forceful decoration, while perfectly plain pieces, for example a cylindrical ciborium of *c.* 1680 (Córdoba, Convento de S Francisco), were inspired by the work of River Plate silversmiths. An architectonic tabernacle (*c.* 1800; Córdoba Cathedral) by Cayetano Albares is virtually unique in Argentinian silverwork on account of its scale; it follows the form of 17th-century Spanish examples.

Argentinian metalwork of the 18th century was often influenced by the work of European silversmiths, some of whom worked in South America. In the early 18th century the Jesuits brought with them skilled workers from Germany, as well as quantities of tools, but little of the silverwork produced in their missions to the Guaraní tribe has survived, although an altar-frame of *c.* 1750 (Buenos Aires Cathedral) shows the assured use of such Baroque elements as twisted pilasters, baluster columns and roundels incorporating sacred scenes, which are typical of their work. Another important influence was that of the Portuguese silversmiths who had settled in Brazil. After 1766, when the manufacture of gold and silver in Brazil was prohibited, many emigrated to the River Plate area, bringing with them superior techniques and new forms and designs. The work of Francisco da Silva Lemos (*fl c.* 1770–1810) from Rio de Janeiro, for example, shows assured use of Rococo forms and ornament (e.g. chalice, *c.* 1790; Buenos Aires Cathedral).

Neo-classicism was introduced at the beginning of the 19th century, largely due to works imported from Antonio Martínez Barrio's Real Fábrica de Platería in Madrid and mass-produced plated articles, such as candlesticks, from Sheffield and Birmingham. A monumental inkstand showing the vertical fluting typical of Martínez's work is in the Complejo Museo Gráfico 'Enrique Udaondo', Luján. A series of columnar candlesticks (Buenos Aires, S Francisco), decorated with a mixture of classical motifs, is marked with the Buenos Aires town mark. In the 1820s a more ponderous style was introduced in domestic silver, often utilizing castings of fauna and foliage evidently imported from Europe; the silversmith from Buenos Aires who marked his work CONEH appears to have specialized in domestic articles of this kind, such as a perfume burner (Buenos Aires, Mus. Saavedra) in the form of a tree surrounded by deer. Jeronimo Martínez (*fl* 1790–1826) also worked in this monumental style, illustrated by his perfume burner surmounted by an eagle (*c.* 1825; Buenos Aires, Mus. N. B.A.).

Typical vessels produced in the 19th century include the silver cups used to drink *mate*, often formed of gourds or polished nuts mounted in silver. At the beginning of the 19th century they became much more elaborate, often supported on a circular dish and accompanied by a silver tube (*bombilla*). Rectangular kettles with compartments to hold coal, used for infusing the *mate* leaves, were also popular; some were made in the form of animals, while others are circular and raised on three legs. Silver boxes in the form of shells, their interiors fitted with vials and spoons, are often described as chrysmatories; they may have been used, however, for storing coca leaves, on account of the lack of religious motifs in their decoration.

Such plain, utilitarian domestic objects as mugs and platters were made in large quantities, while articles for the horse and rider were especially important. Throughout the 19th century great wealth was expended on silver and even gold horse trappings, for example stirrups, saddles, reins and bridles were often mounted with precious metal. Gauchos carried a dagger in an elaborately decorated silver sheath, as well as a similarly ornamented whip, a silver-mounted drinking horn (*chifle*) and a gold or silver *yesquero* or flint-striker, profusely chased with decoration often incorporating nationalist symbols. Silver spurs, which became larger during the 19th century, are usually characterized by large rowels and decoration of foliate scrolls.

BIBLIOGRAPHY

A. Taullard: *Platería sudamericana* (Buenos Aires, 1941)
J. Torre Revello: *La orfebrera colonial en Hispanoamerica y particularmente en Buenos Aires* (Buenos Aires, 1945)
A. Perez-Valiente de Monctezuma: *Platería colonial* (Buenos Aires, 1960)
El arte luso brisileno en el Río de la Plata (exh. cat., Buenos Aires, 1966)
A. L. Ribera and H. H. Schenone: *Platería sudamericana de los siglos XVII–XX* (Munich, 1981)
H. Schenone and A. L. Ribera: *Historía general del arte en la Argentina,* 2 vols (Buenos Aires, n.d.)
Platería americana (exh. cat. by A. L. Ribera and others, Rosario, 1986)
G. de Urgell and others: *El mate de plata* (Buenos Aires, 1988)

CHRISTOPHER HARTOP

V. Textiles.

The sources of Argentinian textile production are both pre-Hispanic (with corresponding ethnic diversities) and

Spanish; styles and techniques therefore reflect these influences. In the rural zones of the northern province of Jujuy a style displaying native influences is common, which is a feature repeated only among some weavers of the Calchaqui valleys and in Patagonia. In other regions there is evidence of a markedly Hispanic tradition.

In the period of the Viceroyalty of Peru, Santiago del Estero was an important centre for textile production. At the end of the 16th century the cotton and wool industry became increasingly important in Santiago, and such items as tapestries, quilts and blankets, some of which were exported to Brazil by the bishop of Victoria in 1587, were woven. From the end of the 18th century textiles were also manufactured in Córdoba (examples in Córdoba, Argentina, Convent of Sta Catalina; Mus. Teresas). During the Viceroyalty tapestry hangings or very heavily embroidered carpets were made, which generally depicted local flora (e.g. Buenos Aires, Cabildo). Domestic textiles with bold designs and motifs representing local plants and flowers were also made particularly in Santiago del Estero, Córdoba and San Luis.

The *caranchado* from Santiago del Estero is a checked fabric made using contrasting techniques and colours and is one of the characteristic textiles made in the late 20th century. The quilts made in central and north-western Argentina featuring shaggy, uncut pile are produced using a technique called *caracolillo*, which made use of extra wefts. In the Chaco area plant fibres are employed to make fabrics. The geometric designs in *chahua* textiles refer to mythical animals. In the north-east, cotton is woven. The manufacture of *ñanduty* (a filmy lace) links it to production in Paraguay. In Tucumán a Spanish technique is used to manufacture cotton *randas* (lace borders). The most important centre of production for this type of weaving is Monteros. Manually produced braidwork or 'semi-fabrics' is a traditional craft in Argentina. It continued to be used in the manufacture of rough blankets for horses and saddle padding.

In the northwest the hair of the indigenous vicuña is woven into fabrics, and the best weavers are in the area around Catamarca. In addition to the 'wool' of cameloids, which continued to be very prestigious in the late 20th century, wool from sheep, goat hair, cotton and other indigenous vegetable fibres were more extensively used.

The poncho is very much associated with Argentina. This garment first became popular during the colonial era. The first references to it date from the 17th century (1983 exh. cat.). In the 18th century it became popular as an outer garment for riders on long journeys. In Upper Peru (now Bolivia) during the 18th century striped ponchos already featured mestizo elements. At the beginning of the 19th century the poncho was an indispensable garment during the War of Independence, forming part of the 'uniform' of the soldiers. There are different styles of poncho depending on which region they come from and what materials, colours and designs are used; the Catamarcan vicuña poncho, for example, was left undyed, and if it was embroidered, the thread was of the same colour and occasionally combined with silk. The ponchos made in Salta are red with a black border, which according to tradition is a mark of respect for the death of the regional chief Guemes.

7. Pampa poncho, warp ikat technique, wool, natural and dyed blue, 1.66×1.54 m, 19th century (Buenos Aires, Museo de Motivor Populares Argentinos José Hernandez)

During the 18th century, when the Araucanians ruled vast regions of Argentina from Patagonia to Buenos Aires, the use of the ikat Pampa poncho (see fig. 7) made of sheep's wool dyed in indigo and decorated with pre-Hispanic designs became increasingly extensive. At the beginning of the 19th century industrially made ponchos, which reproduced traditional Argentine designs, were imported from England. In the late 20th century the hair of the vicuña was being replaced by that of the alpaca. The ikat design continued to be popular in the north-west. Since the end of the 19th century the modernization of Argentina marked the decline of the traditional textile industry. Some contemporary tapestry artists, however, among them Antoinette Galland (*b* 1926), Beatriz Bodigliani (*b* 1933), Gracia Cutulli (*b* 1937) and Carola Segura (*b* 1944), derived inspiration from traditional Argentinian textiles.

BIBLIOGRAPHY

F. L. May: *Hispanic Lace and Lace Making* (New York, 1939)

D. Millán de Palavecino: *El tejido en la Argentina* (Buenos Aires, 1981)

A. Geijer: *A History of Textile Art* (London, 1982)

Aymara Weavings: Ceremonial Textiles of Colonial and 19th Century Bolivia (exh. cat. by L. Adelson and A. Tracht, Washington, DC, Smithsonian Inst. Traveling Exh. Serv., 1983)

R. Faccaro: *Arte textil argentino hoy* (Buenos Aires, 1986)

R. de Corcuera: *Herencia textil andina* (Buenos Aires, 1987)

RUTH DE CORCUERA

VI. Patronage and art institutions.

In the years following the Spaniards' arrival, artistic activity in Argentina was centred on the missions, where the Indians learnt from European priests to build churches and to engrave religious images; it was a long time before the educated and wealthy classes began to patronize any form of art. When they did start collecting art in the 19th century, they sought only European art, in particular

French, to adorn their houses, estates or small palaces. The first exhibition in Argentina is believed to have been one that took place at the Colegio de Ciencias Morales, Buenos Aires, in March 1829. It was organized by the Spanish businessman and collector José Mauroner, who risked his fortune to bring works over from Europe. These included paintings by Titian, Tintoretto, Rubens and Murillo—more than 300 paintings in all, representing French, Spanish, Flemish and Italian schools. They were probably not all authentic, but Mauroner intended to sell them to the state to found a museum; this never took place, however, and, partly as a result of unstable political and economic conditions in the country, he returned to Europe in 1830 with his cargo.

The first Argentinian collector was probably Manuel J. de Guerrico of Buenos Aires, whose collection of paintings was later increased by his son José Prudencio de Guerrico and later became part of the collection of the Museo Nacional de Bellas Artes, Buenos Aires. A large part of this collection comprised 19th-century Spanish paintings, which were very popular with Argentinians at the time. Public interest in the arts continued to be stimulated by various exhibitions in the 1870s and 1880s, such as the one organized in 1878 in the former Teatro Opera, Buenos Aires, by the Sociedad Damas de Caridad, at which indigenous pottery, fabrics, arms, drawings, portraits, coins and medals, among other things, were exhibited to raise money for charity. In September 1888 an exhibition of 326 paintings by Spanish artists was held in Buenos Aires, organized under the auspices of the Spanish Chamber of Commerce; in the same year an exhibition of French paintings was held at the Jardin Florida in the capital, although this was unsuccessful. The Galería Witcomb, established in 1868, went on to hold important exhibitions of French and Italian painting, and in the early 20th century Argentinian artists began to gain recognition as they returned from Europe, versed in the latest artistic movements and styles.

The Museo Nacional de Bellas Artes was created by decree in 1895 during the presidency of José E. Uriburu; it was officially inaugurated in 1896, in the Bon Marché building at Calle Florida 783 in Buenos Aires. Its first collection comprised 40 pictures donated by Aristóbulo del Valle, pictures from the Biblioteca Nacional and acquisitions made by Eduardo Schiaffino. On the top floor of the building the Sociedad Estímulo de Bellas Artes held classes in drawing and painting. In 1910 the directorship of the museum was entrusted to Carlos Zuberbühler, and it began to operate from the Argentinian pavilion in the Retiro. Various collections were donated to the museum, including those of Adriano Rossi and José Prudencio de Guerrico, who had specified that the legacies they left to the State should serve solely as the basis for a national art museum. Further donations of works were made by Emilio Furst and his wife, Antonio and Mercedes Santamarina, the di Tella family, Alfredo and Elizabeth Hirsch and Simón Scheinberg. By 1914 there were 3000 works in the museum, a level that was maintained for 20 years until the move was made to the permanent site, for which the former Casa de Bombas de la Recoleta was converted. By the late 20th century the museum housed an important collection of 2500 paintings, over 1000 drawings and engravings, 2590 coins and medals, 300 sculptures and a number of singularly valuable Flemish tapestries from the 17th century. The collection is fundamentally orientated towards modern art, and, although not as rich as some, it was the first major collection in Latin America and is perhaps one of the most complete. Ribera, Manet and Goya are among the most important artists represented, and of particular interest is the collection of French Impressionist works. There is also an annexed workshop and a specialist library. Important group and one-man shows are periodically organized by the museum. The important work of art lovers and collectors such as José Prudencio de Guerrico, Andrés Lamas, Adriano Rossi and Aristóbulo del Valle was later supplemented by such groups as El Ateneo (*fl* 1893–8), which supported, disseminated and promoted the work of Argentinian artists. Between *c.* 1910 and 1929 the Cooperativa Artística operated in Buenos Aires with the aim of helping young artists. The Boliche de Arte was set up in 1927 under direction of the critic Leonardo Estarico to provide financial assistance for avant-garde artists.

The Museo de Calcos y Escultura Comparada shares a site in Buenos Aires with the Escuela Superior de Bellas Artes 'Ernesto de la Cárcova'. Housed in a former veterinary quarantine site converted by the school's founder, Ernesto de la Cárcova, the museum and the various workshops of the school were officially established by decree in 1921, and activities began in 1923. The museum is one of only two of its kind in Latin America (the other is in Mexico City), and its importance stems from the fact that the casts contained in it were taken with moulds directly from the originals, thus faithfully preserving their markings. The casts were brought to Buenos Aires from such places as the Musée du Louvre and Musée Guimet, Paris, the British Museum, London, the National Archaeological Museum in Athens and the Glyptothek in Munich between 1923 and 1930, and the Comisión Nacional de Bellas Artes combined them with another group of casts that had arrived between 1911 and 1913, sent from the Königliche Museum, Berlin. The collection was distributed between various schools, with the largest number remaining in the Escuela Superior de Bellas Artes.

The Museo Provincial de Bellas Artes 'Rosa Galisteo de Rodríguez' in Sante Fe was built in 1922 and donated to the province by Martín Rodríguez, who also donated his rich private collection of art to provide the basis for the museum; its long-standing director was Horacio Caille Bois. The institution grew to contain more than 1000 works by Argentinian artists, and it is committed to the development and cultivation of all art forms: its 22 rooms hold paintings, sculpture, engravings and numismatics, and it also has a print room, a restoration workshop, a photographic laboratory and a public library specializing in both antiquarian and new books on art; there is also a large concert hall. Acting under the auspices of the provincial Dirección General de Bellas Artes, Museos y Archivos, the museum is the focus of all the main artistic activities in the province, and every year since 1922 the Salón de Pintura, Escultura, Dibujo y Grabado de Santa Fe, one of the most important national art exhibitions in the country, has been held there. Among the most valued collections on display is a group of paintings by Cesáreo

Bernaldo de Quirós, which depict the region of Entre Ríos in the second half of the last century.

In Buenos Aires, the Museo Municipal de Arte Colonial was initially operated from a site at Calle Suipacha 1422, in the private residence of Carlos and Martín Noél. In 1937 the Buenos Aires City Council acquired the museum, and it was opened to the public in 1938. It is the only museum in the country dedicated to Latin American colonial art. In its original form the building attempted to revive an ideal Peruvian palace from the viceregal period; the distribution of the rooms was therefore planned so as to respect the original residential structure, and the museum's Chilean ironwork, Spanish tiles and ceramics, numerous pieces of furniture and items from Peru, Ecuador, Colombia, Bolivia, Chile and northern Argentina were distributed on this criterion when the site was organized, under the honorary direction of Rómulo Zabala and the secretary Enrique de Gandía. In 1942, under the municipal leader Carlos A. Pueyrredón, a part of this museum was moved to the Saavedra park and combined with the collections of the Museo de Arte Colonial to form the Museo Municipal Brigadier General Cornelio de Saavedra. The task of organizing this musuem was given, in an honorary capacity, to Silvia de Pueyrredón, and its first director was José Marco del Pont. The collections of religious, silver and numismatic pieces are distributed between 11 rooms.

In 1911 the architect Tené Sergent, with the collaboration of the landscape painter Achille Duchesne, built a palace on Avenida Alvear (later Avenida Libertador) for Matías Errázuriz and his wife Josefina de Alvear. The building contains a gothic chapel that is an important example of French-inspired, 20th-century Neo-classical architecture; the chapel façade was inspired by that of the Petit Trianon in the palace of Versailles. In 1937 the building was turned into the Museo Nacional de Arte Decorativo, containing the collections of the Errázuriz family in addition to various other collections, comprising paintings, sculpture, furniture, porcelain, tapestries, glass, musical instruments and silverware. The Museo de Arte Moderno was founded in Buenos Aires in 1956; its collection of Latin American paintings focuses especially on the work of Argentinian artists. The collection of Ignacio Pirovano was donated to the museum.

A large number of galleries was established from the 1950s onwards, and such groups as Ver y Estimar, made up of artists and critics, continued the work of investigation and dissemination of the arts; of particular importance was the Centro de Artes Visuales di Tella at the Instituto Torcuato di Tella, which provided space for all new forms of artistic expression. Founded in 1958, the centre was led from 1963 by Jorge Romero Brest, and it became critically important to the development of Argentinian art, not least by trying to overcome the confines on artistic production imposed by military dictatorship. Brest championed the work of young Argentinians, as well as popularizing international art and increasing public awareness through exhibitions and discussion. At a national level the State operated the Fondo Nacional de las Artes in the late 20th century, which encouraged in particular the work of young artists through grants, loans for exhibitions, study trips, research work, the purchase of materials etc. On the whole, however, the State has rarely been a benefactor of the arts in Argentina, with the result that institutions and cultural groups have had to seek private finance. Nevertheless an active art market is supported by a fair number of galleries in the country's major cities, and museums stimulating public interest in the arts are widespread; most museums have established foundations or associations of friends that support their growth.

BIBLIOGRAPHY

J. L. Pagano: *El arte de los argentinos*, i (Buenos Aires, 1937)
J. Mantovani: *La cultura, el arte y el estado* (Santa Fe, 1939)
E. Maglione: 'Las galerías de arte bonaerenses', *Lyra*, xv/171–3 (1958) [whole issue]
F. Palomar: 'Primeros salones de arte de Buenos Aires: Reseña histórica de algunas exposiciones desde 1829', *Cuad. Buenos Aires*, xviii (1962)
Los 15 años del Fondo nacional de las artes (Buenos Aires, 1973)
R. Squirru: *Arte argentino hoy* (Buenos Aires, 1983)
Colección Ignacio Pirovano (exh. cat., Buenos Aires, Mus. A. Mod., 1983)
M. de Riglos, G. Whitelaw and M. Mújica Lainez: *Colección Ignacio Pirovano: Donación Sra Josefina Pirovano de Mihura* (Buenos Aires, 1983 and 1992)
Argentina y sus museos (Buenos Aires, 1986)

NELLY PERAZZO, MARTA ARCIPRETE DE REYES, JULIETA ZUNILDA VAQUERO

VII. Art education.

With European art as the model, various religious orders, and the Jesuits in particular, offered the indigenous Argentinians the opportunity to produce their own architecture, sculpture and painting; this activity ceased, however, when the Jesuits were expelled in 1767. The earliest formal attempts to foster art education include the plan of Manuel Belgrano (1770–1820), Secretary to the Consulate of Buenos Aires, to establish the Academia de Dibujo in 1799, but this had barely started to operate when it was closed by the Court in the same year. In 1815 Fray Castañeda opened two small academies in the Monastery of La Recoleta, with 'the purpose of propagating ... the custom of graphic arts', and *c.* 1818 Josef Guth ran a drawing school in the capital, as well as teaching drawing at the Universidad de Buenos Aires in the 1820s. There was considerable activity in the 1870s: firstly, in 1876 the Sociedad Estímulo de Bellas Artes was created through the efforts of Carlos Gutiérrez, Eduardo Schiaffino and Eduardo Sívori; it was a further 30 years, however, before the society, effectively a forerunner of art education, was officially recognized by the government. At that time it had more than 600 pupils. Formal education was stimulated in 1878 by the foundation in Buenos Aires of the Escuela Nacional de Bellas Artes 'Prilidiano Pueyrredón', with departments of painting, sculpture and engraving. The first faculty of architecture was also opened in the Universidad de Buenos Aires in the 1870s, and this meant that students no longer had to go to Europe to study.

Various initiatives were taken in the early 20th century to increase the availability of training in the arts, notably with the foundation in 1904 of the Escuela Nacional de Bellas Artes 'Manuel Belgrano', the Escuela Superior de Bellas Artes 'Ernesto de la Cárcova' in 1923 and the Academia Nacional de Bellas Artes in 1936, all in Buenos Aires. In the 1950s an interest in the possibilities of educating through art led to the establishment in 1958 of the Instituto Vocacional de Arte (IVA) in Buenos Aires. Under the leadership of Marta Calvo the institute went on in 1979 to incorporate the techniques of teaching children through workshops. By the late 20th century the Dirección General de Enseñanza Artística had been established under the Ministerio de Educación y Justicia, and a three-tier system of training was created, with a basic level, teacher training and advanced specialization. Political instability in the country, however, prevented the development of a more specific programme. Nevertheless, courses are offered in ceramics and other decorative arts, drawing, design, stage design, sculpture, graphic arts, history of art and painting in 13 universities throughout the country, and architecture is taught at 18 universities.

BIBLIOGRAPHY

I. Córdoba Iturburu: *80 años de pintura argentina* (Buenos Aires, 1978)

J. Cáceres Freyre, M. J. Buschiazzo and H. H. Schenone: *Historia general del arte en la Argentina* (Buenos Aires, 1982)

MARTA CALVO

VIII. Art libraries.

The creation of libraries that specialized in the visual arts and architecture followed the establishment of educational institutions and art museums. The library of the Museo Nacional de Bellas Artes was created together with the museum in 1895–6, and by 1911 it had 2253 books. By 1931 it had 2560 and a further 2500 exhibition catalogues and periodicals. It was enriched in 1944 by the donation of Antonio Santamarina's valuable collection of books. A new site was inaugurated in 1983, with specially constructed and refurbished rooms, and the collection grew to 40,000 books, 600 periodical titles, 400 bulletin titles and *c.* 120,000 leaflets and catalogues from major museums, private institutions and galleries throughout the world, making it one of the most important specialist art libraries in Latin America. Many other art museums in Argentina have specialist libraries, including the Museo de Arte Moderno in Buenos Aires, which has 2000 items, the Museo Nacional de Arte Decorativo, also in Buenos Aires, with 2000, and the Museo Provincial de Bellas Artes 'Rosa Galisteo de Rodríguez' in Santa Fe, with over 30,000.

The library of the Escuela Nacional de Bellas Artes 'Prilidiano Pueyrredón' initially comprised almost entirely those books donated by the architect Pío Collivadino, who directed the Escuela Nacional de Bellas Artes from 1908. The collection grew to *c.* 11,000 books, covering all aspects of the arts, aesthetics, history of art and architecture. The first inventory of the library of the Escuela Superior de Bellas Artes 'Ernesto de la Cárcova' (as the Escuela Superior de Bellas Artes came to be known) dates from 1929. It was formed with the donations of lecturers, the greater contribution being made after 1944. The collection was later increased by acquisitions made by the Ministerio de Educación, as well as through donations from institutions. Aside from books the library also houses collections of French, English and German periodicals, as well as a substantial collection of prints and reproductions, an archive of work by pupils in the engraving workshop and a cabinet of engravings.

BIBLIOGRAPHY

Repertorio de bibliotecas especializadas y centros de información (Buenos Aires, 1979)

JULIETA ZUNILDA VAQUERO

Argenville, Dezallier d'. *See* DEZALLIER D'ARGENVILLE.

Argos. Principal city in the Argolid, southern Greece. It was built around the Larissa and Aspis hills dominating the Argive plain, about 8 km from the sea, and flourished throughout Classical antiquity. The modern town occupies the site of the ancient city. Argos was a major power in the Peloponnese from the Bronze Age. Rivalry with Sparta culminated in King Pheidon's victory in the 7th century BC, which made Argos pre-eminent in Greece. After Pheidon's death, however, Sparta and the rising power of Corinth held Argos in check. Argos was included in the Roman province of Achaia in 146–5 BC. POLYKLEITOS was the most famous of several renowned Argive sculptors (the 'Argive school') of the High Classical period (*c.* 450–*c.* 375 BC). Argive architecture, although firmly within the Hellenic tradition, had various distinctive local characteristics and took many innovative forms, especially under the early Roman Empire. Excavations in and around Argos were made by the Dutch archaeologist Wilhelm Vollgraff in 1902–30 and the French School from 1952; Prosymna and the Sanctuary of Hera (Heraion) 9 km north-east of Argos were excavated by the American School (1892–5), Carl Blegen (1925–8) and P. Amandry and J. Caskey (1949), among others.

1. GREEK. The only structures known from the Middle Helladic period (*c.* 2050–*c.* 1600 BC) are the cemeteries and a dwelling on the Aspis, which appears not to have been fortified. The earliest monumental structures are the Mycenaean tombs at Deiras, which are notable for the early use of sand-and-lime mortar (if this is not part of a later alteration), the four-colour fresco decoration on their stuccoed door frames and the inclusion of a dromos with a double door. The only extant Geometric building is the first Temple of Hera (?early 7th century BC) in the Heraion (see fig. (a)), which is probably the oldest peripteral structure in the Peloponnese. It was destroyed by fire in 423 BC. The principal buildings of the Archaic period (*c.* 675–*c.* 480 BC) are also mainly in the Heraion. Among them is the 'West Building' (*c.* 525–*c.* 500 BC; (b)) which has dining chambers and one of the earliest extant peristyle courts, doubtless derived from Mycenaean buildings, such as the House of Columns at Mycenae; while capital 'C', perhaps from the North Stoa, is among the first Doric capitals in stone (7th century BC).

In the Classical period (*c.* 480–323 BC) Argos received a wide variety of new buildings and was more coherently planned. Of the 29 or 30 temples seen by Pausanias (*Guide to Greece* II.xviii–xxiv), however, only a few blocks from one, that of Aphrodite to the south of the odeion, have survived. The most notable remains in the city belong to a double stoa (?early 4th century BC), and a neighbouring hypostyle hall (*c.* 460 BC) in the agora. The former had tufa columns, fine limestone orthostats and a trapezoidal pi-shaped plan which is still not entirely clear. The latter, which was a squarish structure 100 ft long with a Doric porch and outer entablature, and 16 internal Ionic columns, was built on a grid pattern related to the axial spacing of both its inner and façade columns. It may have been a temple of Demeter, since it resembles the Telesterion at Eleusis. Alternatively, it was perhaps a political meeting-place, like two theatral buildings, one with straight rows of seats beneath the Roman Imperial odeion, built

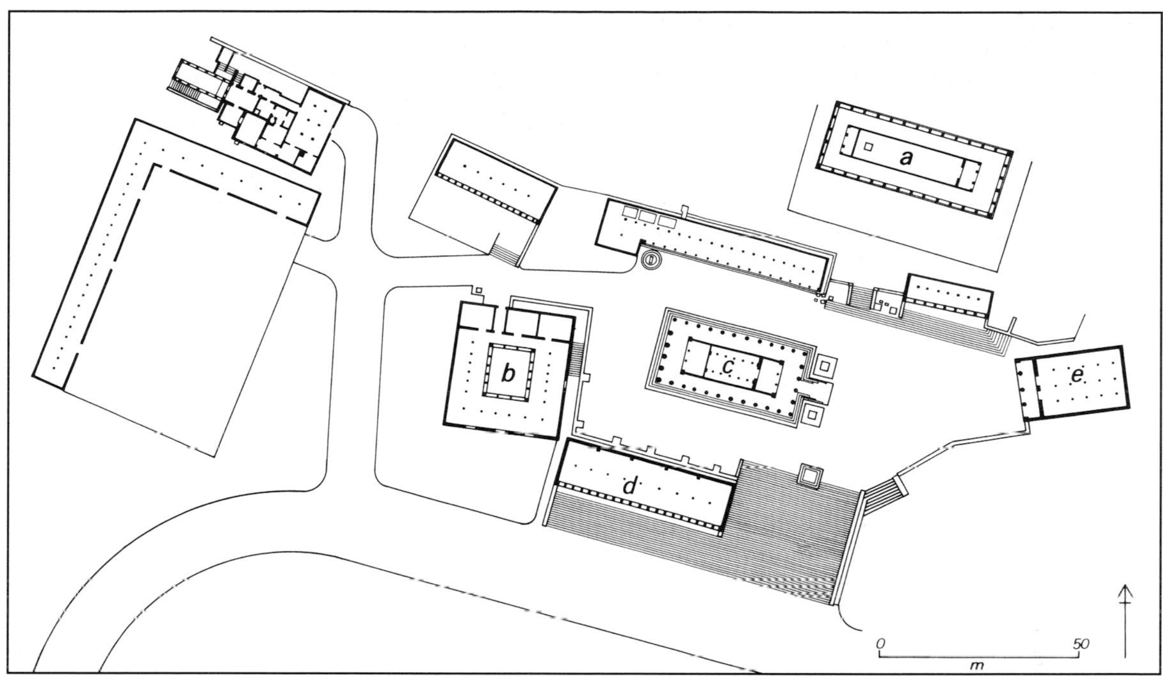

Argos, plan of the Sanctuary of Hera (Argive Heraion): (a) first Temple of Hera, ?early 7th century BC; (b) 'West Building', *c.* 524–*c.* 500 BC; (c) second Temple of Hera, 420–405 BC; (d) South Stoa, *c.* 450–425 BC; (e) hypostyle building, *c.* 450 BC

when democratic rule was established, and another with a unique seating arrangement in an extended semicircle that was discovered more recently next to the North Stoa in the agora (Moretti; Pariente, Aupert and Moretti), which was used by the Council of Eighty or for performances by chorae. The theatre, which is of early Hellenistic date, seated around 20,000 spectators. The entire central section of its 87 rows of seats, with a horizontal gangway and five staircases, is hewn into the rock, and several deep cavities show that a canopy was installed, doubtless in Roman Imperial times. The *orchestra* is defined by an unusual stone circle and has a subterranean passage.

In the Heraion the democratic government erected several important sacred structures between 460 and 400 BC. These included a new Temple of Hera (c) with a peristyle of 6 by 12 columns and an internal colonnade (420–405 BC). It was the last Argive temple to exhibit Athenian influence, with sculpted metopes on its exterior instead of above the pronaos and opisthodomos, and Attic-inspired mouldings. Its terrace was approached from the south by means of a vast stairway partly occupied by the two-aisled South Stoa (d) and closed at its east end by an unusual retaining wall with its courses set back in a series of steps. The architect was Eupolemos. The chryselephantine cult statue was by Polykleitos, who may also have designed the architectural sculpture (both are Argive). The terrace itself is delimited to the north by a stoa and to the east by a large hypostyle building (e) of unknown function. The complex's stepped arrangement has few apparent precursors (e.g. the acropolis at Selinus and, on a far smaller scale, the treasury terrace at Olympia), but resembles some Egyptian schemes and prefigures the vast terraces of Hellenistic sanctuaries. It testifies to Argos' ambition and wealth, and to the inventiveness of its architects, who were influenced but not enslaved by Athenian practices.

Argive originality is also apparent in several unusual Hellenistic structures. These include what appear to be small forts scattered over the Argive plain (?late 4th century BC), which are mainly in polygonal masonry and have a pyramidal form unknown elsewhere. Similarly, altars with low-level triglyphs were also common at Argos in the 3rd century BC, although originally developed at Corinth. One occurs in the agora, another at the Heraion, to the east of the Classical temple. A starting line in the agora, an unusual setting, indicates that there was once a race-course there. The only large-scale building project of this period was the remodelling of the Sanctuary of Pythian Apollo at the foot of the Aspis. A long Ionic altar was built near the Archaic temple, of which nothing now remains, while the temple terrace was connected to a higher level by a wide rock-cut staircase recalling the arrangement at the Heraion. The building at the east side of the upper terrace has a peristyle court derived from the 'West Building' of the Heraion and foreshadowing that of the Serapieion/Asklepieion near the theatre. It may also be an Asklepieion, while the nearby tholos, of which only the foundations remain, may be the temple of Athena Oxyderkes.

2. ROMAN. The establishment of Roman domination in the 1st century AD led to the introduction of new architectural forms and new building techniques, such as the use of kiln-baked bricks and concrete. A tomb in the south cemetery with a cruciform interior was imitated on the agora by a rare type of fountain with a baldacchino

and probably a cupola, while a little later the palaestra of the stoa in the agora was converted into baths. The most innovative building was undoubtedly the great temple near the theatre (*c.* AD 100). Its nucleus was a cella with a podium in a huge apse, presumably for an acrolithic cult statue, fronted by a deep porch flanked by two square chambers. The Corinthian façade of the porch interrupted the west wing of an arcaded Ionic peristyle surrounding a courtyard 3 m below, linked to the porch by a wide staircase. The presence of an oracular crypt, or basin for water from the River Nile, and the use of Egyptian-style pitched-brick vaults, imply that this was a temple of Serapis/Asklepios. The span of the vaults (*c.* 10.6 m) is unparalleled in Greece at this period, while the technique of construction became more common only in late Imperial times. The roofing system is unique in Roman Imperial architecture. The vault and the tops of the side walls bore four low cross walls with sloping tops supporting a pitched roof formed by two long concrete slabs, an ingenious device for separating the vaulting from the roof and so lightening its load. The monumental use of arcades around the courtyard was another of the building's unusual features, which later figured prominently in Byzantine architecture.

At the same time, or early in the 2nd century AD, a rectangular odeion was built on the site of the theatral building with straight rows of seats. Building projects initiated by Hadrian (*reg* AD 117–38) included the transformation of the courtyard of the Serapieion/Asklepieion into baths (the cella doubtless continuing to be used for worship), the erection at the foot of the Larissa of a nymphaeum, doubling as a castellum distributing water to the city, and the construction of two water mains, one incorporating an aqueduct. The nymphaeum, completed under Antoninus Pius (*reg* AD 138–61), was also a remarkable structure, with a vaulted chamber deeply recessed into a rock face. At the centre of its rear wall was a high niche containing a statue of the naked *Hadrian* (Argos, Archaeol. Mus.), from beneath which the water flowed out in two successive pools behind the Ionic colonnade of the façade. The central intercolumniation of the façade may have been spanned by a curved architrave, or 'Syrian arch', as in other Hadrianic monuments, while two rectangular fountains on a lower terrace also formed part of the structure. Another unusual nymphaeum of similar date in the centre of the agora consisted of an octastyle tholos on a square base that distributed the water into a circular surrounding channel. The channel was intersected by a tunnel running under the building with a spiral staircase at its inner end giving access to the cella of the tholos. At some later date the cella walls were replaced by four columns.

During the 3rd century AD few funds were available for either public or private building projects. Gordian III (*reg* AD 238–44) constructed two vast halls decorated with mosaics on either side of the cella of the Asklepieion, and a monumental ramp supported by half-vaults between its façade and the agora. The *orchestra* of the theatre was transformed into a pool for aquatic displays, and, probably following the Gothic raids of AD 267, the odeion was rebuilt on a semicircular plan, with ambitious roof spans. Later Roman works chiefly involved alterations to existing structures, such as the baths, which were repaired, as well as such small-scale projects as the building of villas, including the Villa of the Months (*c.* AD 500), and the construction of churches at Deiras and underneath the present church of St Constantine. An earthquake followed by the invasion of the Slavs in AD 585 brought about the ultimate demise of the Roman city. Subsequent building projects carried out by successive conquerors were largely confined to alterations to the fortifications on the Larissa and to the construction of churches, of which hardly a trace remains.

BIBLIOGRAPHY

C. Waldstein: *The Argive Heraeum*, 2 vols (Boston and New York, 1902–5)
C. W. Blegen: *Prosymna* (Cambridge, 1951)
P. Amandry: 'Observations sur les monuments de l'Héraion d'Argos', *Hesperia*, xxi (1952), pp. 222–74
W. Vollgraff: *Le Sanctuaire d'Apollon pythéen à Argos*, Etudes Péloponnésiennes (Paris, 1956)
G. Roux: 'Le Sanctuaire argien d'Apollon pythéen', *Rev. Etud. Gr.*, lxx (1957), pp. 474–87
W. Vollgraff: 'Le Flanc oriental de la Larissa', *Bull. Corr. Hell.*, lxxxii (1958), pp. 516–70
G. Roux: *L'Architecture de l'Argolide aux IVe et IIIe siècles avant J-C* (Paris, 1961)
J. Deshayes: *Argos: Les Fouilles de la Deiras*, Etudes Péloponnésiennes, iv (Paris, 1966)
R. Ginouvès: *Le Théâtron à gradins droits et l'odéon d'Argos*, Etudes Péloponnésiennes, vi (Paris, 1972)
R. A. Tomlinson: *Argos and the Argolid* (London, 1972)
S. G. Miller: 'The Date of the West Building at the Argive Heraion', *Amer. J. Archaeol.*, lxxvii (1973), pp. 9–18
G. Åkerström-Hongen: *The Calendar and Hunting Mosaics of the Villa of the Falconer in Argos* (Stockholm, 1974)
P. Aupert: 'Un Sérapieion argien?', *Acad. Inscr. & B.-Lett.: C. R. Séances* (1985), pp. 151–75
P. Aupert and R. Ginouvès: 'Une Toiture révolutionnaire à Argos', *The Greek Renaissance in the Roman Empire: A Colloquium: London, 1986*, pp. 151–5
P. Aupert: *Etudes d'architecture et d'histoire grecque à l'époque impériale: La Ville d'Argos aux Ier et IIe siècles* (diss., U. Paris X, 1988)
A. Pariente, P. Aupert and J.-C. Moretti: 'Rapport sur les travaux de l'Ecole Française en Grèce en 1987', *Bull Corr. Hell.*, cxii (1988), pp. 697–791 (697–720)
M. Piérart, ed.: 'Polydipsion Argos', *Bull. Corr. Hell.*, suppl. xxii (1992)
J.-C. Moretti: *Théâtres d'Argos* (Paris, 1993)
J.-F. Bommelaer and J. des Courtils: *La Salle hypostyle d'Argos*, Etudes Péloponnésiennes, i (Paris, 1994)
P. Aupert: *L'Edifice A1 d'Argos: Sérapieion–Asclépieion?* [in preparation]

PIERRE AUPERT

Argote de Molina, Gonzalo (*b* Seville, 1548; *d* Las Palmas, Canary Islands, 1596). Spanish soldier, writer and collector. As a reward for his military achievements, Philip II appointed him Alférez Mayor of Andalusia, and he also received honours from the kings of France, Portugal and Poland. He became royal chronicler, which gave him access to numerous libraries throughout Spain, in which he discovered rare Spanish books dating from the Middle Ages. These were important for his *La historia de la nobleza de Andaluzia*, only the first part of which was published (1588). Among other things, this includes histories of Seville, Ubeda and Baeza and a genealogy of Argote de Molina's family. Argote de Molina was also Veinticuatro of Seville, a commissioner of the Inquisition and first Provincial de la Santa Hermandad. In addition he was a member of the circle of humanists and writers around the Duques de Gelves in their villa, called La Merlina. His marriage to the daughter of the Marqués of Lanzarote obliged him to move to that island, and on the death of his wife he settled in Gran Canaria. His humanist interests led him to create a private museum in his home, a typical example of a 16th-century collection of art and exotic objects, a *Wunderkammer*, which was visited by Philip II in 1570. It contained printed books and manuscripts, antique and modern weapons, stuffed animals and natural curiosities, coins and antiquities, curios from the East and West Indies, and a fine library. The paintings included portraits of famous men by Alonso Sánchez Coello and mythological scenes. On his death Argote de Molina's manuscripts and papers were dispersed, some going to his nephew and heir Don Garci López de Cárdenas, who allowed them to become destroyed through neglect. The little that survived passed to several collectors, including the historians Ortiz de Zúñiga and Ximena y Jurado.

WRITINGS

Libro de elogios de varones ilustres (untraced)

'Descripción del bosque y casa real del Pardo', in *Libro de la Montería* (Seville, 1582)

La historia de la nobleza de Andaluzia (Seville, 1588)

BIBLIOGRAPHY

F. Pacheco: *Libro de descripción de verdaderos retratos de ilustres y memorables varones* (Seville, 1599); ed. P. M. Pinero Ramirez and R. Reyes Cano (Seville, 1985)

Comte de Puymaigre: 'Un Savant espagnol du XVIe siècle, Argote de Molina', *Rev. Hisp.*, ii (1895), pp. 147–80

C. Fernández Duro: 'Memoria autobiográfica de Gonzalo Argote de Molina para su hijo Agustín', *Bol. Real Acad. Hist.*, xxxviii (1901), pp. 232–3 [discusses MS. of Argote de Molina's autobiography]

A. Millares Carlo: 'La biblioteca de Gonzalo Argote de Molina', *Rev. Filol. Esp.*, x (1923), pp. 137–52

A. Palma Chaguaceda: *El historiador Gonzalo Argote de Molina. Estudio biográfico, bibliográfico y crítico* (Madrid, 1949)

NATIVIDAD SÁNCHEZ ESTEBAN

a.r. group [Pol. artysci rewolucyjni: 'revolutionary artists']. Polish group of avant-garde artists that flourished between 1929 and 1936. Its members were the sculptor Katarzyna Kobro, the painters WŁADYSŁAW STRZEMIŃSKI and Henryk Stażewski, and the poets J. Brzękowski and J. Przyboś. It was founded by Strzemiński after he, Kobro and Stażewski left the Praesens group. The group's programme chiefly reflected the views of Strzemiński. In two leaflets entitled *Kommunikaty a.r.* ('a.r. bulletins') the group declared itself in favour of a 'laboratory' version of Constructivism and an avant-garde art that influenced social life in an indirect and gradual manner. It opposed the politicization and popularization of art, which it regarded as a debasement of artistic expression, but the group also believed that rigorous, formal discipline, the organic construction of a work, its coherence, effectiveness and economy of means, made art somewhat synthetic or contrived. From 1933 the group's announcements regarding its programme appeared in the Łódź art magazine *Forma*.

Among the most important initiatives of the group was the publication of the 'a.r. library' (Biblioteka a.r.) series (Łódź, 1930–36), seven works in all, including the poems of Przyboś and Brzękowski with text designed by Strzemiński and illustrations by Hans Arp and Max Ernst; the theoretical essay by Kobro and Strzemiński, *Kompozycja przestrzeni* ('Composition of space'); and Strzemiński's *Druk funkcjonalny* ('Functional printing'). Even more significant was the creation of the International Collection of Modern Art, which was presented to the municipal museum in Łódź (later the Museum of Art) in 1931. It contained 75 works donated by representatives of the avant-garde of the period (including members of the group Cercle et Carré): Hans Arp, Willi Baumeister, Alexander Calder, Serge Charchoune, Theo van Doesburg, Max Ernst, Albert Gleizes, Jean Gorin, Jean Hélion, Vilmos Huszar, Fernand Léger, Piet Mondrian, Louis Marcoussis, Amédeé Ozenfant, Pablo Picasso, Enrico Prampolini, Kurt Schwitters and Georges Vantongerloo, among others. It was the second public collection of modern art after Hannover. It was conceived by Strzemiński and started with the considerable assistance of Brzękowski, who lived in Paris and was on friendly terms with Cercle et Carré, along with the publishers of the avant-garde journal of painting and poetry, *L'Art contemporain*.

BIBLIOGRAPHY

R. Stanisławski and others, eds: *Grupa a.r.: 40-lecie Międzynarodowej Kolekcji Sztuki Nowoczesnej w Łodzi* [The a.r. group: 40th anniversary of the International Collection of Modern Art in Łódź], Łódź, Mus. A. cat., 2 vols (Łódź, 1971) [also contains ess.]

Constructivism in Poland, 1923–1936 (exh. cat., ed. R. Stanisławski and others; Essen, Mus. Flkwang, 1973)

A. Turowski: *Konstruktywizm polski: Próba rekonstrukcji nurtu, 1921–1934* [Polish Constructivism: an attempt to reconstruct its development, 1921–34] (Wrocław, 1981)

EWA MIKINA

Argunov, Ivan (Petrovich) (*b* St Petersburg, 1729; *d* Moscow, 1802). Russian painter and teacher. He came from a family of serfs, belonging to the Counts Sheremetev, that produced several painters and architects. In about 1746–7 he was a pupil of Georg Christoph Grooth (1716–49), who painted portraits of the Sheremetev family. With Grooth, Argunov worked on the decoration of the court church at Tsarskoye Selo (now Pushkin). A full-length icon of *St John of Damascus* (1749; Pushkin, Pal.-Mus.), in Rococo style, is distinguished by its secular, decorative character. *The Dying Cleopatra* (1750; Moscow, Tret'yakov Gal.) is typical of Rococo decorative painting of the mid-18th century, with its striking combination of light, soft tones. Argunov subsequently painted in a quite different style, mainly producing portraits, of which about 60 are known. Among the first of these are pendant portraits of *Ivan Lobanov-Rostovsky* and his wife (1750 and 1754; St Petersburg, Rus. Mus.), in which the sitters are idealized, as in ceremonial court portraits. The colour schemes of the two portraits are complementary, a device Argunov was to favour, and the feel of materials is admirably rendered. A certain flatness and stiffness in the figures recalls the old tradition of *parsun* (semi-iconic) painting.

Argunov had his greatest success and was at his most prolific at the end of the 1750s and during the 1760s. Most of his works from this time are intimate portraits, a type then beginning to appear in Russia, for example the companion portraits of *Koz'ma Khripunov* and his wife (1757; Moscow, Ostankino Pal. Mus. Serf A.), who are seen in domestic surroundings holding, respectively, a newspaper and a book. The works skilfully depict the inner dignity of educated members of Russian society at this period. The tonal range of these portraits is characteristically reserved: greyish-brown and light blue predominate, animated with bright patches of colour in the details.

Ivan Argunov: *Peasant Girl in Russian National Costume*, 1784 (Moscow, Tret'yakov Gallery)

In the same period Argunov painted a *Self-portrait* (late 1750s) and a portrait of his wife *Marfa Argunova* (mid-1760s; both St Petersburg, Rus. Mus.). The latter is decorative in style and has a rich chromatic range of lemon yellow and medium blue tones. Argunov's work was characterized throughout by the warmth and directness of his portrayal of individuals. The portrait of the *Kalmyk Girl Annushka* (1767; Moscow, Mus. Cer. & Kuskovo Estate), a ward of Countess Sheremeteva, renders with admirable skill the girl's national character, her liveliness, her childlike directness and charm.

Among Argunov's more intimate portraits are those of the Lazarev family, leading members of the Armenian colony in Moscow, in particular the merchant head of the family, *Lazar Nazarovich Lazarev* (1700–1782), who founded the Moscow Institute of Oriental Languages, and his wife *Anna Ekimovna Lazareva* (1710–1770) (both 1769; Moscow, Pushkin Mus. F.A. and Ostankino Mus.). The portrait of Anna Lazareva in her brocaded national dress is extremely colourful, and her face with its wrinkles and lively eyes is depicted in a captivating manner. The largest group of Argunov's portraits, however, shows members of the Sheremetev family. The portrait of the Count's daughter *Varvara* (1766; Moscow, Mus. Cer. & Kuskovo Estate) is one of his most charming works and is executed with a light touch in shades of pale pink and pearly grey.

Argunov's ceremonial portraits (e.g. *Catherine II*, 1762; St Petersburg, Rus. Mus.) follow the usual formulae for this genre. He produced interesting 'historical' or posthumous portraits, however, relying on both engraved and painted records. Argunov produced few portraits in the 1770s, the most notable among them being *Rear-Admiral Samuel Greyg* (?1772–3; St Petersburg, Rus. Mus.). He was more active in the early 1780s, when he painted one of his best works, the remarkably simple and poetic portrait of a *Peasant Girl in Russian National Costume* (1784; Moscow, Tret'yakov Gal.; see fig.), which anticipates the paintings of peasants produced by Aleksey Venetsianov. Argunov subsequently ceased painting. Remaining a serf until the end of his life, at Count Sheremetev's request, he moved to Moscow, where he was fully occupied in managing the Sheremetev estates.

Argunov was of considerable importance as a teacher. Among his pupils were other serfs of the Sheremetevs, and, from 1758, Anton Losenko. Among Argunov's last pupils were his sons Pavel Argunov (1768–1806) and Nikolay Argunov (1771–after 1829), the latter a painter of portraits.

BIBLIOGRAPHY

T. Selinova: *Ivan Petrovich Argunov, 1729–1802* (Moscow, 1973)

Zhivopis' 18–nachala 20-go veka: Katalog [Catalogue of paintings, 18th-early 20th century], Leningrad, Rus. Mus. cat. (Leningrad, 1980)

G. KOMELOVA

Arias Fernández, Antonio (*b* Madrid, *c.* 1614; *d* Madrid, 1684). Spanish painter. He trained in Madrid with Pedro de las Cuevas, an excellent teacher who instructed many contemporary painters. Arias was a precocious artist; he painted the altarpiece (destr.) of the Carmelitas Calzados in Toledo at the age of 14. In 1639 he collaborated with other painters of his generation in the decoration of the *salón grande*, or Sala de las Comedias, in the Alcázar, Madrid. His painting of *Charles V and Philip II, Kings of Spain* (1639; Madrid, Prado, on dep. U. Granada) shows his individual style, which is sculptural, with firmly drawn outlines and broad areas of light colours, all of which is archaic in character.

Arias Fernández established a studio in Madrid in 1645 and began accepting apprentices. His most important works belong to this decade, including the *Tribute Money* (1646; Madrid, Prado), which exemplifies his best qualities: precise outlines, angular drapery, light colouring in the predominantly cool tones reminiscent of Juan Bautista Maino and intensely naturalistic detail. The *Pietà* (1658; León, Las Carvajalas Convent), inspired by the *Pietà* of Quinten Metsys, a late 15th-century Flemish composition, shows how remote he was from other artists then working in Madrid in ignoring Baroque developments and persisting in rendering a sense of monumental solemnity that recalls the style of painting at the Escorial of almost a century earlier. The *Virgin of Montserrat with SS John the Baptist and Mary Magdalene* (*c.* 1640–50; Barcelona, Mus. Marés) seems to evoke late 15th-century Venetian models, such as the work of Giovanni Bellini, Cima or Marco Basaiti. His style remained at odds with the general development of taste and he died in poverty.

BIBLIOGRAPHY

D. Angulo Iñiguez and A. E. Pérez Sánchez: *Pintura madrileña del segundo tercio del siglo XVII* (Madrid, 1983), pp. 13–34

ALFONSO E. PÉREZ SÁNCHEZ

Arias Montano, Benito (*b* Fregenal de la Sierra, Badajoz, *c.* 1527; *d* Seville, 6 July 1598). Spanish theologian and poet. He studied humanities in Seville from 1546 to 1547 and Latin, rhetoric and theology at Alcalá de Henares from 1548 to 1552. In 1559 he retired to a hermitage in Castaño del Robledo (Huelva) called La Peña de Aracena, where he devoted himself to the study of Greek, Hebrew and oriental languages. In 1560 he was ordained a priest in the Orden Militar de Santiago at the Convent of S Marcos, León. He attended the Council of Trent from 1562 to 1563 and in 1564 was appointed chaplain and Historiador Real (royal historian) to Philip II.

The King, as patron of the projected *Biblia políglota*, a multilingual Bible that was to be published by the Flemish printer, Christoph Plantin, appointed Montano director of this extensive project with the title of Doctor theologus delegatus. In May 1568 Montano arrived in Antwerp having first travelled in Ireland and England, where he visited the University of Oxford. The *Políglota Regia*, completed 1572, comprises seven volumes; vols VI–VII contain the Apparatus, which is Montano's most significant contribution to learning and which includes his philological and archaeological treatises: *De mensuris*, *De sacris fabricis* and *Sanctorum ornamentorum summa descriptio*. The beautiful typography of the Bible was enhanced with engravings made by leading Flemish artists including Jan Wierix, Pieter van der Heyden and Philip Galle.

Montano was later employed by Philip II as adviser to the 3rd Duque de Alba, Governor of the Netherlands, 1567–73. He was also charged with acquiring books and manuscripts in Flanders for the royal library of the Escorial, and many of these came from monasteries abandoned because of the religious conflicts. He returned to Spain in 1576 and held the position of director of the library of the Escorial for a total of about four years at various times between 1577 and 1592. He was responsible for purchasing and for the classification of books and manuscripts, and he also advised on the programme for the decoration of the library, which he hung with portraits of saints and learned men. He taught Greek, Hebrew, mathematics and astronomy to students at the Escorial, including his follower, José de Sigüenza. Montano spent his last years at La Peña de Aracena, devoted to a life of piety and to writing his great theological works. He was a gifted poet in Latin, as is evident in *Rhetoricorum libri IV* (Antwerp, 1569) and *Humanae salutis monumenta* (Antwerp, 1571), which contains 71 odes illustrated with engravings after his own design as well as verses that were used later by Philip Galle for his engravings. Galle also executed 88 engravings to decorate Montano's *Davidis regis* (Antwerp, 1574).

There are engravings as well as many recorded portraits of Montano, including one painted in the studio of Peter Paul Rubens in 1633 (Antwerp, Mus. Plantin–Moretus). One of the finest is a full-length portrait attributed to Francisco de Zurbarán (Madrid, Escorial, Bib. Monasterio S Lorenzo). The best likeness is the portrait by Francisco Pacheco (1593) which appears in his *Libro de descripción de verdaderos retratos de ilustres y memorables varones* ('Gallery of illustrious persons', 1599). A silver-plated medal engraved with Montano's portrait (1569) shows him aged 42 (Madrid, Prado). At his death Montano left the Escorial an important collection of Greek, Hebrew and Arabic manuscripts.

WRITINGS

Biblia sacra hebraice, chaldaice graece et latine, 8 vols (Antwerp, 1568–73)
Rhetoricorum libri IV (Antwerp, 1569)
Humanae salutis monumenta (Antwerp, 1571)
Davidis Regis ac prophetae aliorumque... (Antwerp, 1574)
Dictatum christianum (Antwerp, 1575)
Hymni et saecula (Antwerp, 1593)

BIBLIOGRAPHY

F. Pacheco: *Libro de descripción de verdaderos retratos de ilustres y memorables varones* (Seville, 1599), p. 90
T. González Carvajal: *Elogio histórico del doctor B. Arias Montano*, Memorias de la Real Academia de la Historia, vii (1832)
F. C. A. Bell: *Benito Arias Montano* (Oxford, 1922)
F. J. Sánchez Cantón: *Catálogo de las pinturas del Instituto de Valencia de D. Juan* (Madrid, 1923), pp. 71–2
C. Doetsch: *Iconografía de Benito Arias Montano* (Madrid, 1927)
L. Morales Oliver: *Arias Montano y la política de Felipe II en Flandes* (Madrid, 1927)
B. Rekers: *B. Arias Montano* (London, 1972) [unpubd works by Montano listed pp. 191–4]

GREGORIO DE ANDRÉS

Ariccia, Duca di. *See* CHIGI, (2).

Ariha. *See* JERICO.

Arikha, Avigdor (*b* Rădăuţi, Bukovina, 28 April 1929). Israeli painter, draughtsman, printmaker and writer, of Romanian birth, active in France. The drawings he made in deportation from Nazi labour camps at the age of 13 and 14 saved his life by attracting attention to his precocious talent. In 1944 he emigrated to Israel, living in a kibbutz near Jerusalem and studying art at the Bezalel School in Jerusalem; after being severely wounded in 1948 in the Israeli War of Independence, he continued his studies in Paris (which he made his home in 1954) at the Ecole des Beaux-Arts (1949–51). He first made his name as an illustrator, for example of an edition of Rainer Maria Rilke's *The Way of Love and Death of Cornet Christopher Rilke* (Jerusalem, 1953), for which he was awarded a gold medal at the Milan Triennale in 1954. From 1957 to 1965 he produced abstract paintings, such as *Noir basse* (1959; Jerusalem, Israel Mus.), which had something in common with Art Informel but were characterized by his particular sensitivity of touch and sumptuousness of colour. During this period he also designed stained-glass windows, including a series of 30 windows for the Bnei Israel Synagogue in Woonsocket, RI.

Arikha stopped painting in 1965, feeling that it was impossible to continue in the same vein, and he restricted himself until 1973 first to drawing and then to etching in black and white; notable examples include a sustained series of portraits of the Irish playwright Samuel Beckett, one of his closest friends, such as *Samuel Beckett with Cigar* (brush and sumi ink on gessoed paper, 1970; Paris, Pompidou). He resumed painting in 1973, this time working exclusively from life, painting quickly in oil on canvas on an intimate scale well-suited to his generally domestic subjects. He often painted his wife, as in *Going out* (1981; Jerusalem, Israel Mus.), the view from his flat in Paris, as in the *Square in June* (1983; Washington, DC, Hirshhorn), still-lifes, interiors and landscapes. His rare commissioned portraits include *H.M. Queen Elizabeth, the Queen Mother* (1983; Edinburgh, N.P.G.).

Wary of his own virtuosity and always receptive to the shocks of emotion and chance, Arikha practised a kind of dynamic realism motivated in part by the work of Edgar Degas and Alberto Giacometti, who were among the artists whose work he studied in depth; as a scholar he was also known for his publications on Nicolas Poussin and Jean-Auguste-Dominique Ingres, among others. Arikha's paintings from life after 1973, calm and endowed with a feeling of plenitude arising from his mastery of colour and amplitude of gesture, also have a muted drama because of the vibration of the marks, tonal contrasts and spatial ambiguities, which together assure the modernity of his work within a long tradition.

WRITINGS

Nicolas Poussin: The Rape of the Sabines (exh. cat., Houston, Mus. F.A., 1982)

J. A. D. Ingres: Fifty Life Drawings from the Musée Ingres at Montauban (exh. cat., Houston, Mus. F.A., 1986)

BIBLIOGRAPHY

Avigdor Arikha: Dessins, 1965–1970 (exh. cat., preface S. Beckett, essay B. Rose; Paris, Cent. N. A. Contemp., 1970)

S. Beckett and others: *Arikha* (Paris and London, 1985)

□

Arimaddanapura. *See* PAGAN.

Arinbjarnar, Snorri (*b* Reykjavík, 1 Dec 1901; *d* Reykjavík, 31 May 1958). Icelandic painter. He was self-taught, and he took part in several exhibitions of the Society of Friends of Icelandic Art, Listvinafélag Islands, exhibiting works incorporating motifs from fishing villages on the northern coast, rather than more traditional landscapes. After studying intermittently at the Kongelige Kunstakademi in Oslo (1928–31), Arinbjarnar became one of the pioneers of 'social expressionism', dealing with subjects from everyday life on the Icelandic coast. This expressionism, which lasted throughout the Depression (until 1940–42), was never politically engaged, but aimed rather at the heroic interpretation of daily life. Arinbjarnar's works are notable for their strongly constricted composition, which expresses the hardships of the time. After 1940 Arinbjarnar's work moved steadily towards abstraction, but still incorporated discernible motifs from everyday life (e.g. *Girls with Doll*, 1943; Reykjavík, N.G.). The younger generation of artists who instigated the Septemberhópurinn (Septembrists') exhibitions in 1947–52 welcomed Arinbjarnar into their group as one of the pioneers of modern Icelandic art. His status as a popular artist was guaranteed by a retrospective exhibition of his work held in Reykjavík in 1952 by the Felag Islenskra Myndlistarmanna (Icelandic Artists' Union), an association of painters, sculptors and other pictorial artists with their own exhibition hall in Reykjavík.

BIBLIOGRAPHY

B. Th. Björnsson: *Íslenzk myndlist á 19, og 20, öld* [Icelandic art in the 19th and 20th centuries], ii (Reykjavík, 1973), pp. 7–30

BJÖRN TH. BJÖRNSSON

Arinobu. *See* TAKUMA, (2).

Ariosto, Ludovico (*b* Reggio Emilia, 8 Sept 1474; *d* Ferrara, 6 July 1533). Italian poet. His father was a captain in the service of the ruling Este family at Ferrara and Ariosto studied Latin literature and philosophy at the *studium* (university) there. From 1503, he served first Cardinal Ippolito I d'Este and then his brother, Alfonso I d'Este, Duke of Ferrara, in various administrative and diplomatic capacities, finally retiring around 1526. His supervision (1526–33) of the ducal theatre at Ferrara enabled him to collaborate with, among others, Dosso Dossi and Battista Dossi, who designed sets for several of his comedies. Despite the brilliance of these and of his seven *Satires* (1517–25), Ariosto's fame rests on his romance-epic in Italian, *Orlando furioso* (Ferrara, 1516, 1521, 1532). The poem, begun in 1502 and completed only shortly before his death, uses Charlemagne's war against the Saracens as a backdrop to explore typical Renaissance themes such as love, madness and fidelity. It highlights Ariosto's interest in art in several ways, containing many ekphrases (for example iii, xxxiii, xlii, xlvi) and a detailed description of a woman (vii, 11–15), often cited in subsequent theoretical discussions of descriptive poetry, for example Lodovico Dolce's *Dialogo della pittura* (Venice, 1557) and Gotthold Ephraim Lessing's *Laokoon* (Berlin, 1766). The poem praises nine contemporary artists at xxxiii, 2, and its structure, according to some scholars, mirrors the classical harmony found in the art of the period (Gnudi). The definitive third edition includes a woodcut portrait in profile of Ariosto said by contemporary sources to be after a drawing by Titian. Published in over 60 different, often illustrated, editions before 1600, *Orlando furioso* has been a source of inspiration for leading European painters and anonymous craftsmen alike since the 16th century. In the 1780s, for example, Jean Honoré Fragonard prepared over 150 drawings for an edition that was never published, and a noteworthy later edition (Paris, 1879) contains over 500 drawings by Gustave Doré. In Italy its characters and themes have often been used for the decoration of artefacts.

BIBLIOGRAPHY

M. Catalano: *Vita di Ludovico Ariosto*, 2 vols (Geneva, 1930–31)

P. Barocchi: 'Fortuna dell'Ariosto nella trattatistica figurativa', *Critica e storia letteraria: Studi offerti a Mario Fubini*, i (Padua, 1970), pp. 388–405

C. Gnudi: 'L'Ariosto e le arti figurative', *Congresso Internazionale Ludovico Ariosto: Rome, 1975*, pp. 331–401

R. W. Lee: *Names on Trees: Ariosto into Art* (Princeton, 1977)

R. Cesarani: 'Ludovico Ariosto e la cultura figurativa del suo tempo', *Studies in the Italian Renaissance*, ed. G. P. Biasin and others (Naples, 1985), pp. 145–66 [extensive bibliog.]

Signore cortese e umanissimo: Viaggio intorno a Ludovico Ariosto (exh. cat., ed. J. Bentini; Reggio Emilia, 1994)

DENNIS LOONEY

Arisbe. *See under* LESBOS.

Aristeides [Aristides] (*fl* 4th century BC). Greek painter(s) from Thebes. There appear to have been two painters named Aristeides, perhaps grandfather and grandson; none of their works survive. According to Pliny (*Natural History* XXX.75) an Aristeides was a pupil of Euxenidas, a contemporary of Parrhasios and Timanthes. The same author named the painter and sculptor Euphranor among his pupils (XXXV.111). This Aristeides would have flourished in the first half of the 4th century BC. Elsewhere, however, Pliny (XXXV.110) mentioned an Aristeides who was a pupil of his father Nikomachos of Thebes. He must be the Aristeides who was a contemporary of Apelles and whose style and works the author described (XXXV.98–100). This Aristeides would have worked in the second half of the 4th century BC. Pliny criticized the younger Aristeides for using colours that were a little harsh but praised him for being the first painter to depict the soul and to give expression to the affections and emotions. Many of the paintings ascribed to that Aristeides suggest the emotional quality of his work: *The Suppliant*, so moving that his voice could almost be heard; the *Girl Dying for Love of her Brother*; and the much-praised picture of a *Sick Man*. Henry Fuseli (*Lecture* I) pointed to the balance of pity and disgust inherent in Aristeides' painting of a *City Sacked*, in which a mother dying from a wound fears that her baby will drink blood rather than milk from her breast. Aristeides also painted a portrait of *Leontion*, the pupil and mistress of Epicurus, which perhaps gave rise to his reputation as a pornographer. Aristeides' pictures sold for vast sums. Attalos II, King of Pergamon (*reg* 160–139 BC), tried to buy for 600,000 denarii a painting of *Dionysos* that fell to the Romans when Corinth was sacked in 146 BC. Roman soldiers had been using the picture as a dice-board. When the Roman general L. Mummius learnt the value Attalos placed on the painting, however, he removed it to the Temple of Ceres in Rome, where it was later destroyed in a fire (31 BC). Pliny (XXXV.24) believed it to have been the first foreign painting dedicated at Rome.

BIBLIOGRAPHY

J. Overbeck: *Die antiken Schriftquellen zur Geschichte der bildenden Künste bei den Griechen* (Leipzig, 1868/*R* Hildesheim, 1959), nos 1295, 1745, 1762, 1772, 1775, 1778–85

C. HOBEY-HAMSHER

Aristotile da Bologna [Aristotele di Fieravanti]. *See* FIORAVANTI, ARISTOTELE.

Aristotle (*b* Stagira, 384 BC; *d* Khalkis, 322 BC). Ancient Greek philosopher. Born to a physician at the Macedonian court, Aristotle travelled to Athens in his 18th year to study philosophy at PLATO's Academy. He remained for nearly twenty years until Plato's death in 348 BC; he was then forced to leave Athens: probably he had come under suspicion because of his Macedonian connections. He went first to Assos, then to Mytilene, doing the original biological research on which his later scientific writings are based. During this period, he spent some time as tutor to the young Alexander the Great (*reg* 336–323 BC); the relationship does not seem to have been a warm one. Returning to Athens in 335 BC, he set up his own philosophical school, later called the Lyceum. From the colonnaded path, or *peripatos*, attached to the building, his followers were later called 'Peripatetics'. Here he taught, and wrote most of his surviving works. After Alexander's death in 323 BC, anti-Macedonian feeling once again forced Aristotle to leave Athens; he died in exile of a stomach ailment about a year later.

Aristotle's writings cover every major area of philosophy: logic, metaphysics, philosophy of nature and the sciences, philosophy of life and mind, ethics, politics, rhetoric and poetry. In every area his thought has had a ubiquitous and pervasive influence in the Western tradition—especially through medieval Aristotelianism (*see* AESTHETICS §II, 2 and 4, and MANUSCRIPT, colour pl. III). However, as his works were not edited in their present form until *c.* 30 BC, in some cases there may be a whole made from inconsistent parts, and his thought was not always represented faithfully by medieval Aristotelianism.

Aristotle argued that all knowledge must be based upon prior perceptual experience. He attacked the Platonic view that intelligible universal forms exist apart from perceptible particulars, holding that the mind apprehends universals *in* the perceptible things of this world. In the *Categories*, he argued that the primary objects of knowledge and definition are particular substances such as this human being, this horse. Substances, i.e. members of natural kinds and some artefacts, are prior to qualities, quantities and relations, which can be known and spoken of only as attached to some substance. In every category particulars are prior to generic and specific universals. The *Metaphysics* refines this position further, arguing that the form or structure of a particular thing, not its matter or its incidental properties, is what is truly essential to the thing and the basis for an understanding of it. Scientific understanding, Aristotle argued elsewhere, takes the form of valid deduction from first principles that are true, necessary and primary; insight (*nous*) into the explanatory role of first principles is gained through experience and practice in making arguments.

The substance or form of living things (plants, animals, humans) is the *psuche* or 'soul'. Aristotle argued that *psuche* is neither simply matter nor an immaterial object, but rather the 'organization-to-function' of a living body. To be alive is to be in a condition capable of functioning in the ways appropriate to the species. The most important functions in living things are self-nutrition, reproduction, perception, imagination, desire and thinking, the last belonging only to humans and to God.

In his ethical works Aristotle held that the good life for a human being (*eudaimonia*) consists in virtuous action. Virtue is defined as an ordered state of the person, which results in his being able to choose the appropriate action, and to carry it out with the right motives and feelings. Aristotle placed considerable emphasis on the value of social life and training in the arts for the development of character. Friendship plays a central role in both education and the good life generally. For these reasons and others, the good human life requires support from the external world and cannot be achieved in isolation. Several chapters in the last book of Aristotle's *Nicomachean Ethics* suggest that only intellectual contemplation has intrinsic worth, but these remarks are contradicted by many others elsewhere in the text, and scholars agree in finding a serious interpretative problem here.

Aristotle's surviving work on art focuses on poetry but begins with some general observations about artistic *mimesis* (representation/imitation/expression), which is vindicated against Plato's attack in the *Republic*. The *Poetics* mentions painting only glancingly, but always as a *mimesis* comparable to poetry. The ubiquitous human interest in *mimesis* is held to stem from an interest in learning and recognizing. The notoriously obscure claim that the function of tragic poetry is 'through pity and fear to accomplish a catharsis concerning experiences of that sort' is probably to be understood in connection with that more general thesis. The common meaning of *katharsis* in Greek is 'cleaning up' or 'clearing up'. Aristotle was probably saying that our pity for the tragic hero, and our fear when we notice that the events of the drama are 'such as might happen' to ourselves, are sources of clarification or illumination concerning our possibilities as human beings and our deepest values. Similarly, Aristotle's strong interest in the structure of the tragic plot seems to be an ethical one; the possibilities for all human lives may be learnt when the reversals (*peripeteiai*) that may happen to a good person are witnessed. The famous concept of *hamartia*—the 'mistake' through which the hero's fall comes about—was later interpreted to be a character defect. A more credible interpretation is a 'missing of the target'; some way, perhaps blameworthy, in which a person with well-directed character fails to achieve the goal or 'target' of *eudaimonia.*

Aristotle's great treatise on rhetoric argues, against Platonic strictures, that rhetoric is a subject that can be treated systematically. Defining rhetoric as 'the capability of recognizing in each case the possible means of persuasion', he argued for its autonomy and went on to offer a comprehensive discussion of persuasion through speech; the treatise includes probing discussions of psychology.

Aristotle's influence on artists and theorists of art has been multifaceted and ubiquitous, although this influence can be based on misreading and distortion. In general, the medieval Aristotelians left posterity an Aristotle who was far more dogmatic and hierarchical, far more rigidly systematic, than the real Aristotle, eclipsing the tentative, flexible and searchingly reflective character of Aristotle's thought.

WRITINGS

For editions of the works see Oxford Classical Texts, Teubner Library and Loeb Classical Library.

J. Barnes, ed.: *The Complete Works of Aristotle*, Bollingen Series (Princeton, 1985)

BIBLIOGRAPHY

L. Cooper: *The Poetics of Aristotle: Its Meaning and Influence* (London, 1923)

W. D. Ross: *Aristotle* (London, 1923)

G. F. Else: *Aristotle's Poetics: The Argument* (Cambridge, MA, 1957)

B. Weinberg: *A History of Literary Criticism in the Italian Renaissance*, i (Chicago, 1961)

D. W. Lucas: *Aristotle: Poetics* (Oxford, 1968)

J. L. Akrill: *Aristotle the Philosopher* (Oxford, 1981)

M. Nussbaum: 'Aristotle', *Ancient Writers*, ed. T. J. Luce (New York, 1981)

J. Barnes: *Aristotle* (Oxford, 1982)

S. Halliwell: *Aristotle's Poetics* (Chapel Hill, 1986)

MARTHA C. NUSSBAUM

Arita. Region in Japan, now part of Saga Prefecture, and the name of a type of porcelain first produced there during the early Edo period (1600–1868). The ware was originally known as *Imari yaki* ('Imari ware') because it was shipped from the port of Imari (Saga Prefect.). During the Meiji period (1868–1912) porcelain was produced throughout the country. The need to distinguish it from other porcelain wares led to the use of the name Arita (*Arita yaki*). As a result, the names Imari and Arita wares were used interchangeably. In the West, Arita porcelain was known by several names, including Imari, Amari, Old Japan and Kakiemon (*see* JAPAN, §VIII, 3(iii)).

Porcelain production is said to have begun in Japan in 1616, when the Korean ceramicist Ri Sanpei [Jap. Kanagae Sanbei] (1579–1655), who had been brought to Japan after Toyotomi Hideyoshi's invasions of Korea (1592 and 1597), discovered porcelain clay near Arita in Izumiyama. The earliest wares, which were *sometsuke* ('blue-and-white'; cobalt underglaze decorated porcelain) imitations of late Ming period (1368–1644) wares, are called *Shoki Imari* ('Early-period Imari'). From *c.* 1660 Arita ware was extensively exported, and *Kakiemonde* ('Kakiemon style'; *see* KAKIEMON WARE) and *somenishikide* ('polychrome style') overglaze enamels (*iroe*) wares were popular. They were exported for about 80 years. In addition to blue-and-white wares, overglaze enamels, which were called *Koimari keibutsu* ('Old Imari-patterned objects'), and which imitated the technique of *kinrande* ('gold-brocade style') wares of the Ming period, were highly appreciated in foreign markets. At the end of the Edo period, kilns principally producing overglaze enamels became more active, with the production of large plates. After the Meiji period and the accompanying modernization, pieces that frequently retained a sense of handmade production became a special feature of this ware.

BIBLIOGRAPHY

R. Cleveland: *Two Hundred Years of Japanese Porcelain* (St Louis, 1970)

HIROKO NISHIDA

Aritthagiri. *See* RITIGALA.

Ark. Decorated repository in a synagogue for Torah scrolls (*see* JEWISH ART, §§III and V, 1, and fig. 14).

□

Arkadia. Park near Łowicz, Poland. The best-preserved 18th-century Romantic landscape park in Poland, it was founded in 1778 by the patron and collector Princess Helena Radziwiłł (1749–1821). She competed as a patron with Princess Izabela Czartoryska, and Arkadia was a response to the latter's park (destr.), also called Arkadia, at Powązki, outside Warsaw. Princess Helena Radziwiłł conceived the literary and philosophical idea of the park, and in order to realize her project she employed Simon Bogumił Zug as designer.

The park covers *c.* 30 ha on the banks of an artificially formed lake, with the Isle of Sacrifices and the River Łupia. An area of wild, unimproved nature, the Elysian Fields, is laid out on the west bank. An English-style park, complete with pavilions, classical ruins, tombs, altars and grottoes, is situated on the east bank. The park is so designed and landscaped that the footpaths, lined with trees and shrubs, lead the visitor to its main feature, the Neo-classical Temple of Diana, from where there is a panoramic view of the lake and the park. The temple, designed by Zug in 1783, freely combines elements of a Greek temple, a square cella with Ionic portico at the front and a circular colonnade at the back. The ceiling fresco representing *Aurora Leading Apollo's Horses* (*c.* 1785) was painted by Jan Piotr Norblin de la Gourdaine, who also decorated the temple with *Views of Powązki* (destr.). Besides the overall design of Arkadia, Zug was responsible for the Gothic Cottage (1791–2), the Aqueduct (1784; destr.; rebuilt 1952) and the High Priest's House (before 1783 and after 1821). Built of bricks and turf, this last incorporates parts taken from the dismantled tomb and chapel of Primate *Jakub Uchański*, designed (1580–83) by Jan Michałowicz z Urzędowa for the collegiate church in Łowicz. The architect Henryk Ittar (1773–*c.* 1850) designed the Tomb of Illusions (*c.* 1799; destr.), patterned on a Roman cinerary urn, the Amphitheatre and the Circus (before 1804; destr.), both inspired by drawings by Piranesi. Since 1945 Arkadia has been run by the National Museum in Warsaw.

BIBLIOGRAPHY

H. Radziwiłł: *Le Guide d'Arcadie* (Berlin, 1800)
J. Wegner: *Arkadia* (Warsaw, 1963)
W. Piwkowski: 'Et in Arcadia ego: Program Arkadii nieborowskiej na przełomie XVIII/XIX wieku i dzisiaj' [The meaning of Arkadia near Nieborów at the turn of the 18th and 19th centuries and today], *Roc. Muz. N. Warszaw./Annu. Mus. N. Varsovie*, xxxi (1987), pp. 95–160

ANNA BENTKOWSKA

Arkalochori [Arkalokhori]. Minoan sacred cave in central Crete, which flourished *c.* 1650–*c.* 1425 BC. Situated 33 km south-east of Herakleion, on the west slope of Profitis Elias, a mountain to the east of the modern village of Arkalochori, it was a cult centre throughout the Minoan era (*c.* 3500–*c.* 1100 BC). Excavations by Joseph Hazzidakis (*c.* 1911), Spiridon Marinatos and Nikolaos Platon (1935) uncovered prolific finds despite previous plundering.

The earliest, scanty remains are ceramic and date from the periods Early Minoan I and II (*c.* 3500/3000–*c.* 2200 BC) and Middle Minoan I (*c.* 2050–*c.* 1800 BC). Material from Neo-Palatial times (*c.* 1650–*c.* 1425 BC) was also found, but a roof collapse severely curtailed worship thereafter. Low walls may have been constructed to give the cave an architectural focus, but all that survive are a passage and a possible cell. Most of the finds are Neo-Palatial metal votive artefacts. A heap at the north end was estimated to contain hundreds of bronze double axes, some of immense size, hundreds of knives or daggers and dozens of swords. Some small silver and gold double axes were also discovered (Herakleion, Archaeol. Mus.).

The swords, which have a small tang, and rounded shoulders and midrib, are of serviceable size and proportions, but several may have been made specifically as offerings, since their tangs are not pierced to receive handles and their blades are unsharpened. The double axes are of sheet metal and so clearly designed only for votive purposes. They were constructed in various ways, the gold ones being regularly provided with small shafts and wire suspension loops. Cedar of Lebanon was used for the larger axe-shafts. Chased decoration is common on the axes and not infrequent on the swords. On the axes it follows a regular pattern, with the blade outlined by one or more groups of lines, and further bands running diagonally across it. Sometimes the bands are enlivened by foliate motifs, while spiral and scroll-based designs occasionally infill the blade. One axe is adorned with several vertical zones, of which the central three contain Linear A characters (Herakleion, Archaeol. Mus.).

The nature of these votive offerings suggests that the presiding deity was one of war. That it was also female might be implied by a Neo-Palatial seal from Knossos depicting a woman (?priestess) carrying a sword (Herakleion, Archaeol. Mus.). The unfinished nature of some finds and the presence of raw materials (a possible 'ox-hide' ingot fragment and undoubted bun-ingots of copper/bronze) have given rise to the theory that priests actually produced votive objects in the vicinity of the cave.

After the collapse of its roof, the cave's importance as a cult centre effectively ended. Later Minoan deposits, including Late Minoan IIIA–B (*c.* 1390–*c.* 1190 BC) wares and even part of a potter's wheel (Herakleion, Archaeol. Mus.), are restricted to the outer chambers. Occasional finds of Greek pottery, for example of Archaic and Hellenistic (*c.* 700–480 BC and 323–27 BC), do not imply continuity of worship.

BIBLIOGRAPHY

J. Hazzidakis: 'An Early Minoan Sacred Cave at Arkalokhori in Crete', *Annu. Brit. Sch. Athens*, xix (1912–13), pp. 35–47
S. Marinatos: 'Arkalokhori', *Praktika Athen. Archaiol. Etaireias* (1935), pp. 212–20
S. G. Spanakis, ed.: *Kentriki-anatoliki* [Central and eastern] (1964), i of *I Kriti* [Crete] (Herakleion, 1964–73), pp. 143–9
A. Kanta: 'The Late Minoan III Period in Crete: A Survey of Sites, Pottery and their Distribution', *Stud. Medit. Archaeol.*, lviii (Göteborg, 1980), p. 80

D. EVELY

Árkay. Hungarian family of architects.

(1) Aladár Árkay (*b* Temesvár [now Timişoara, Romania], 1 Feb 1868; *d* Budapest, 2 Feb 1932). He studied painting under Bertalan Székely, Károly Lotz and Károly Kernstok. In 1886 he enrolled in the faculty of architecture at the Technical University, Budapest, but he continued to study painting with Székely and Lotz from 1886 to 1888. In 1892 (and again in 1900) he studied painting and architecture in Paris. After 1893 he worked in Vienna as site architect for the partnership of Ferdinand Fellner and Herman Helmer. On his return to Budapest he first worked with Alajos Hauszmann on the extension (1891–1905) of the Royal Palace. With his father-in-law, Mór Kallina (1844–1913), he then produced numerous eclectic designs, including the Concert Hall (1897; now Institute for Adult Education), Budapest, with a Palladian façade and richly executed interior in the Secessionist style. His first independent work was the Babochay Villa (1905; altered), on the corner of György Dózsa Street and Andrássy Road, Budapest. The single-storey residential part of the villa adjoins a two-storey office wing. With a domed corner turret, softly undulating gable covered in ceramic tiles from the ZSOLNAY CERAMICS FACTORY and ornamental motifs recalling both Hungarian folklore and Moorish architecture, the building is a typically eclectic example of Hungarian Secessionism. In 1910–14 he executed a housing estate for judges and lawyers on Kis-Svábhegy, a hill in Budapest. Although the 'nationalist style' can be felt throughout, the estate gives an impression of heterogeneity, with elements from Transylvanian vernacular architecture and the Renaissance architecture of Carpathia (now Slovakia). Aladár's major work of this period is the 1000-seat Reformed Church (1911–12), Budapest. It has a Greek-cross plan, and its centre is spanned by a cupola, 15 m in diameter, resting on reinforced-concrete arches. In façade and distribution of mass it resembles the churches of Károly Kós, as well as Lars

Sonck's Tampere Cathedral (1900–07) and Eliel Saarinen's church of St Paul (1915–17), Tartu. The main façade is composed of a sturdy belfry and a simple triangular gable with ceramic tiles in the Secessionist style, which is pierced by a large semicircular window and rests on the low columns of the shallow portico.

Following a study trip to Germany and the Netherlands in 1928, Árkay built a Roman Catholic church at Győr in fine-textured red stone, which contrasts with the grey concrete apertures; a memorial church (1929–41), Mohács, near Pécs; and a Roman Catholic church (1932–3), Buda City Park (Városmajor), Budapest, all using a reinforced-concrete frame. The latter two were completed by his son (2) Bertalan Árkay. The church in Buda City Park is among the first and most beautiful examples of Hungarian church design to show the influence of Italian Rationalism. The three-aisled, flat-roofed design has chapels abutting longitudinal walls. Between these the walls are pierced by stained-glass windows by Bertalan Árkay's wife, Lili Sztehlo (1897–1959), while the frescoes (1938) on the aluminium ceiling panels are by Vilmos Aba-Novák.

(2) Bertalan Árkay (*b* Budapest, 3 April 1901; *d* Budapest, 23 Nov 1971). Son of (1) Aladar Árkay. He received his diploma of architecture from the Technical University, Budapest, in 1925. In 1926 he attended the Académie des Beaux-Arts, Paris. After 1927 he studied at the Akademie der Bildenden Künste, Vienna, under Peter Behrens. In 1929 he was awarded a scholarship by the Hungarian Academy in Rome, where he spent a year. Returning to Budapest he worked in his father's studio until the latter's death, when he set up his own practice. He built *c.* 60 villas in Budapest, many of which—notably the villas on Diószegi Road (1929), on Branyiszkó Road (1932) and on Tárogató Road (1940)—clearly show the influence of the Dutch Expressionists, especially J. J. P. Oud. His tenement-block complex for the National Health Insurance Organization, Köztársaság Square, Budapest, designed with numerous other architects, including József Fischer, Farkas Molnár and Móric Pogány (*see* POGÁNY & TŐRY), has a functionalist ground-plan and façade and is a rare European example of buildings developed in parallel rows in an urban, as opposed to suburban, environment. Bertalan won international acclaim for his Hungarian exhibition pavilions at an international exhibition of ecclesiastical art (1936), Rome, at the Esposizione Triennale (1936), Milan, and at the Biennale (1937), Venice. He also produced several designs for urban development projects, but most of them remained unrealized, including a project for the redevelopment of Vitézek Square and Szent Korona Road, Budapest, conceived in the style of the Italian urban architecture of the 1930s. His most significant activity after World War II was the renovation of historic monuments, such as the reconstruction (1948) of the Museum of Fine Arts in Budapest.

BIBLIOGRAPHY

J. G. Wattjes: *Moderne villa's en landhuizen in Europa en Amerika* (Amsterdam, 1927), pls 107–25

B. Dercsényl: *Árkay Aladár* (Budapest, 1967)

L. Pusztai: 'Árkay, Bertalan, 1901–1971', *Magyar Építőművészet*, lxxxiii/5 (1972), pp. 60–61

N. Pámer: *Magyar építészet a két világháború között* [Hungarian architecture between the two World Wars] (Budapest, 1986)

ÁKOS MORAVÁNSZKY, KATALIN MORAVÁNSZKY-GYÖNGY

Arkel, Gerrit van (*b* Loenen, 3 April 1858: *d* Abcoude, 11 July 1918). Dutch architect. He trained as a carpenter's assistant and took evening classes at the Society for the Workers, afterwards becoming a draughtsman for Jan Galman. From 1876 he worked in the office of Gerlof Bartholomeus Salm, where he was involved in, among other projects, the design of the building for the Vrije Gemeente (built 1879–80) on the Weteringschans, Amsterdam. In 1882 van Arkel set up as an independent architect. Rather than adopt Salm's eclectic style, he was influenced by Netherlandish Renaissance architecture. His preferred Renaissance Revival style is particularly apparent in his early smaller works, such as the shop at Kalverstraat 200, Amsterdam. Following H. P. Berlage's ideas, van Arkel also became more sparing in his use of decorative elements. An example of this sober style, related to Jugendstil, is the photographic studio at Spui 15–19, Amsterdam. He always remained active as a draughtsman and had a great interest in historic buildings, illustrating the book by A. W. Weissman, *Nord-Hollandse oudheden beschreven en afgebeeld* (Amsterdam, 1891–1905). In 1914 he took into partnership H. J. Breman, who continued the practice after van Arkel's death.

WRITINGS

Uitgevoerde gebouwen, projecten enz. (platen en afbeeldingen met tekst) [Executed buildings, projects etc (plates and illustrations with text)] (Bussum, 1917)

BIBLIOGRAPHY

A. W. Weissman: Obituary, *De Bouwwereld*, xvii (1918), p. 247

H. J. F. Roy van Zuidewijn: *Amsterdamse bouwkunst, 1815–1940* (Amsterdam, 1970)

M. Bock: *Anfänge einer neuen Architektur: Beilages Beitrag zur architektonischen Kultur der Niederlände im ausgehenden 19. Jahrhundert* (Wiesbaden, 1983)

M. Brekelmans: *Gerrit van Arkel* (diss., U. Amsterdam, 1988)

DIANNE TIMMERMAN, FRANK VAN DEN HOEK

Arkesilaos (*fl* Rome, mid-1st century BC). Greek sculptor. He was one of the greatest masters of his time, though referred to only by Pliny. A contemporary of PASITELES, like him he worked in a variety of media (marble statuary, marble and/or metal vessels) and believed in the value of preliminary models, which were themselves sold at high prices. Arkesilaos was commissioned by L. Lucullus or his son to make a statue of *Felicitas* (Pliny: XXXV.clv–clvi), which was never completed. His most famous work was the cult statue for Caesar's Temple of Venus Genetrix (ded. 46 BC). Hadrianic coin representations of this deity show a figure close to the late 5th century BC Fréjus Aphrodite type (*see* GREECE, ANCIENT, fig. 59). If these represent Arkesilaos' cult statue, then it must have been classicizing in style. The Temple of Venus, however, was extensively rebuilt in Trajanic times, so the statue depicted may have been a 2nd-century AD replacement. Only two other works are mentioned: a group of *Centaurs Carrying Nymphs* in the collection of Asinius Pollio (Pliny: XXXVI.xxxiii) and a group owned by Varro of *Winged Cupids Playing with a Lioness* (Pliny: XXXVI.xli), the latter especially suggesting a mood less serious than that of the cult statue. This is not a problematic inconsistency since in so eclectic a time as the 1st century BC master artists must have displayed considerable stylistic versatility.

BIBLIOGRAPHY

Pliny: *Natural History*
M. Bieber: 'Die Venus Genetrix des Arkesilaos', *Röm. Mitt.*, xlviii (1933), pp. 261–76
M. Borda: 'Arkesilaos', *Bull. Comm. Archeol. Mun. Com. Roma*, lxxiii (1949–50), pp. 189–204
G. M. A. Richter: *Ancient Italy* (Ann Arbor, 1955), pp. 112–16

MARK D. FULLERTON

Arkesilaos Painter. *See* VASE PAINTERS, §II.

Arkesine. *See under* AMORGOS.

Arkhanes. *See* ARCHANES.

Arkhangel'skoye. Estate situated 20 km west of Moscow. It was first recorded in 1537 as the village of Upolzy, and renamed Arkhangel'skoye after a brick church dedicated to the Archangel Michael was built in 1667 to replace a wooden one. From 1703 to 1810 the estate belonged to the princes Golitsyn and from 1810 to 1917 to the princes Yusupov, notably NIKOLAY YUSUPOV. In 1919 it became a museum-estate.

One of the finest Russian palace and park ensembles, Arkhangel'skoye has as its nucleus a Neo-classical palace, connected to the two wings set in front of the main façade by powerful Tuscan colonnades. It was built by local serf craftsmen between 1780 and 1790 to a plan by the French architect Charles de Guerney. The strict symmetry of the palace's architecture is underscored by the severe belvedere and central portico with four Ionic columns; on the opposite side, overlooking the park, the projection of an oval room, decorated with a pair of Ionic columns, echoes the portico. In 1815–17 the architects S. P. Mel'nikov and Vasily Strizhakov added a storey to the wings and built a gate between them in the style of a triumphal arch, thus creating an enclosed parade courtyard. The lower storey of the palace is occupied by a suite of state apartments, redecorated in the 1820s with stuccowork, paintings and bronze lamps to a design by the architect Yevgraf Tyurin (1792–1870). The rich Empire-style interior of the lower storey contains Gobelins tapestries, pictures by van Dyck, Giambattista Tiepolo, Hubert Robert and Boucher, and sculptures by Etienne-Maurice Falconet, Ivan Vitali and others, from the collection of Nikolay Yusupov. The palace also houses Yusupov's library of *c.* 16,000 volumes.

The park is situated to the south of the palace and is compositionally related to it by two artificial terraces, set out in 1790 to a plan by Giacomo Trombarro. The terraces are surrounded by marble balustrades and decorated with over 200 vases, statues and busts of Classical heroes and philosophers. A staircase connects the lower terrace with the huge parterre, framed by copses. To the south the parterre encloses a viewpoint that looks over the former channel of the Moskva river; to the east and west it is flanked by small areas of landscaped parkland.

Spread around the park area are pavilions such as the Caprice (1819; architect Tyurin) and the Tea House (1829; architect F. I. Pettondi), the temple-monument in honour of Catherine II (designed by Tyurin), obelisks, trellises and fountains. The theatre (1817–18; designed by Osip Bove and Pietro di Gottardo Gonzago) has a luxurious Palladian-style interior that contrasts with the simple exterior. Between the church of St Michael the Archangel in the south-east and the parterre is the mausoleum of the Yusupov family (1910–14; designed by Roman Kleyn).

BIBLIOGRAPHY

S. V. Bezsonov: *Arkhangel'skoye* (Moscow, 1937)
V. V. Poznansky: *Arkhangel'skoye* (Moscow, 1966)
Kuskovo, Ostankino, Arkhangel'skoye (Moscow, 3/1981)

M. I. ANDREYEV

Arkhipov [Pyrikov], **Abram (Yefimovich)** (*b* Yegorovo, Ryazan province, 15 Aug 1862; *d* Moscow, 25 Sept 1930). Russian painter. He trained at the Moscow School of Painting, Sculpture and Architecture under Vasily Perov, Aleksey Savrasov, Vladimir Makovsky and Vasily Polenov and joined the WANDERERS (*Peredvizhniki*) in 1889 and the Union of Russian Artists in 1903. While indebted to the realist painting of Perov, Arkhipov also gave particular attention to effects of light, rhythm and texture, even in his most didactic canvases, such as *Washerwomen* (late 1890s; two versions Moscow, Tret'yakov Gal. and St Petersburg, Rus. Mus.). Arkhipov found a rich and diverse source of inspiration in the Russian countryside and the peasantry; he painted peasants at work, the melting of the snow, the local church and priest, the villages of the far north and the White Sea. Works such as *The Lay Brother* (1891) and *Northern Village* (1903, both Moscow, Tret'yakov Gal.) are evidence of Arkhipov's important position in the history of late 19th-century Russian landscape painting. His concentration on *plein-air* painting was shared to a considerable extent by other representatives of the Union of Russian Artists such as Baksheyev, Leonard Turzhansky (1875–1945) and Sergey Vinogradov (1869–1938).

Like Filipp Malyavin, Arkhipov is perhaps best remembered for his dynamic pictures of peasant women, a constant theme in the 1910s and 1920s, in which the bravura of his brushstroke, rendered with a heavy impasto of bright red and orange paint, communicates the energy and the earthiness of his subjects—a quality lacking in the more sombre works of the Critical Realists. Like Baksheyev and Konstantin Korovin, Arkhipov was a major artistic force in the intermediary generation that assimilated the narrative, often tendentious, approach of the Critical Realists before embracing a more lyrical, more Impressionist style of painting. Paintings such as *Guests* (1914) and *Girl with a Bowl* (1927; both Moscow, Tret'yakov Gal.) are typical of Arkhipov's optimism and *joie de vivre*, and they often served as models for the young artists of the 1920s and 1930s who founded the Association of Artists of Revolutionary Russia (AKhRR).

BIBLIOGRAPHY

N. Shchekotov: *Abram Yefimovich Arkhipov* (Moscow, 1927)
I. Barsheva: *Abram Yefimovich Arkhipov* (Leningrad, 1974)
I. Nenarokova: *Solnechnye polotna Abrama Arkhipov* [The sunny canvases of Abram Arkhipov] (Moscow, 1982)

JOHN E. BOWLT

Arlaud, Jacques-Antoine (*b* Geneva, 18 May 1668; *d* Geneva, 25 May 1743). Swiss miniature painter and collector, active in France. He is said to have shown precocious signs of great talent. In 1688 he established himself in Paris as a miniature painter; his talent secured him the protection of such patrons as Philippe II, Duc d'Orléans and later Regent of France, and his mother, Elisabeth-Charlotte, Duchesse d'Orléans. Arlaud advised the Duc d'Orléans on the purchase of paintings from the collection of Christina, Queen of Sweden. Later, he himself acquired various works of considerable quality, eventually building up an interesting collection. As he was in contact with Hyacinthe Rigaud and Nicolas de Largillierre, his style naturally reflected their manner, as well as the prevailing taste. He generally executed miniatures in gouache, such as *Madame de la Baume* (Geneva, Mus. Horlogerie & Emaillerie), sometimes adding highlights in pastels, as in the case of his *Self-portrait* (1727; Florence, Uffizi). This technique, which was a novelty when Arlaud adopted it, has unfortunately aged badly, and the effect achieved, which was much appreciated at the time, has since become blurred. Arlaud was received at the English court in 1721 and executed a number of portraits there. In that same year his brother Benjamin Arlaud (*c.* 1670–1721) died in London, where he had settled some time previously. Despite failing eyesight, Jacques-Antoine Arlaud managed in 1724 to complete a number of works intended for the *Bibliothèque publique* of Geneva, which inherited most of his collection, including both works of art he had executed himself and those by other artists. A number of his miniatures are preserved in various museums in Geneva.

BIBLIOGRAPHY

T. Heyer: *Documents inédits sur Jacques-Antoine Arlaud*, xv (Geneva, 1865), pp. 213–31

D. Foskett: *A Dictionary of British Miniature Painters*, i (London, 1972), p. 140

VINCENT LIEBER

Arles, aerial view showing the amphitheatre, second half of the 1st century AD, with the theatre in the background

Arles [Lat. Arelate]. French town in Bouches-du-Rhône, *c.* 25 km from the Mediterranean coast and *c.* 25 km from Nîmes. It lies on a ridge south of a bend in the River Rhône.

1. History and urban development. 2. St Trophîme.

1. HISTORY AND URBAN DEVELOPMENT. Originally a Greek settlement, it was refounded with the name Arelate in 46 BC by Julius Caesar as a colony for army veterans. Christianity was established by Bishop Trophimus in the late 3rd century AD, and one of the first Councils of the Church was held in the city in AD 314.

(i) Arelate. The walls were among the first structures of Arelate; the east gate was interrupted by the foundations of a new building constructed above. Much broken early Imperial sculpture, no doubt from the forum, was deposited there. Two columns of the building with an arcaded entablature remain as part of the structures in the modern Place du Forum.

The theatre and the amphitheatre are both well preserved (see fig.). The theatre was built soon after the colony was founded, probably early in the reign of Augustus (*reg* 30 BC–AD 14). The three external orders of the *cavea* (auditorium) combine Corinthian with Doric elements in a manner not common later. Although it stood on a hillside, the seating was entirely built on vaulted substructures. The stage-building, now largely ruined, had a central doorway projecting from a curved exedra, but there were no exedrae at the sides, as found in the more fully evolved theatres of the western type at ARAUSIO (Orange) and Vienne (*see* VIENNE, §1). The columns, two of which are still standing, were of coloured marble imported from Greece and Asia Minor. The Venus of Arles (Paris, Louvre) and the head of a large marble statue of Augustus (late 1st century BC; Arles, Mus. Réattu) were among the sculptures found there.

The amphitheatre is very similar to that at Nîmes (*see* NÎMES, §1) and was probably built in the late 1st century AD. Externally it has two tiers, each of 60 arches, decorated with engaged columns. Its substantial survival is due to use as a fortification in the 8th, 9th and 12th centuries, of which three rectangular towers remain.

The first cathedral, a basilica, was built near the south-east ramparts in the early 4th century. It was rivalled by Les Alyscamps, the Roman necropolis that became one of the pilgrimage centres of Europe. In the mid-4th century there was a great florescence of marble funerary sarcophagi, many of which survive in Les Alyscamps. Arelate's importance in the 4th century is reflected also in the large public baths of Imperial type, constructed near the river of coursed rubble masonry with interval courses of brick. The remains include the apse of one of the heated rooms with its vaulting complete. About 392 the city became the capital of the praetorian prefecture of the Gauls and the diocesan centre of Britain, Spain and Gaul. Its rising spiritual influence was unimpeded by the Visigothic invasion of 427; Bishop Hilarius (*reg* 429–49) built a new cathedral at the centre of the Roman city.

BIBLIOGRAPHY

L. A. Constans: *Arles antique*, Bibliothèques des écoles françaises d'Athènes et de Rome, cxix (Paris, 1921)

A. Grenier: *Manuel d'archéologie gallo-romaine*, III/ii (Paris, 1958), pp. 612–39, 742–53
J. Formigé: 'L'Amphithéâtre d'Arles', *Rev. Archéol.*, ii (1964), pp. 25–41, 113–63; i (1965), pp. 1–46
R. Amy: 'Les Cryptoportiques d'Arles', *Les Cryptoportiques dans l'architecture romaine*, Collections de l'Ecole Française de Rome, 14 (Rome, 1973), pp. 275–91

T. F. C. BLAGG

(ii) Modern town. The history of Arles from the 6th to the 8th century is obscure, as little survived repeated barbarian incursions. The Roman theatre had been partially demolished in a fit of early Christian fervour, but in the 9th century the amphitheatre was fortified by the Saracens with added towers. After the formation of the kingdom of Arles–Burgundy in 933, Arles was the first city to recover. Although it was subsumed by the Holy Roman Empire in 1038, the archbishops had their own mint, controlled the port and administered justice. The city was divided into four, each quarter with its own seigneur and, in the 12th century, its own walls. Arles was one of the first *consulats* in southern France, ruled by the archbishop and the commune.

The rebuilding of the abbey church of St Caesarius began in 897. Only two chapels survive, the 9th century Romanesque St Jean-du-Moustier and St Blaize, with an early 12th-century nave, domed crossing and narrow aisles, an early 13th-century bay and a 14th-century bay with acoustic jars. A set of 9th–10th-century sarcophagi in Les Alyscamps attests to the recovery of the city and the continued veneration of the site. In the mid-11th century the monks of St Victor of Marseille founded the priory of St Honorat in Les Alyscamps and built a Romanesque church. The east and west ends survive, as does the transept covered by a semi-dome and decorated with arcading. A massive lantern-tower, with two stages pierced by large arcades, dominates the exterior. Early in the 12th century, building began on a replacement cathedral (*see* §2 below) near the Roman theatre, rededicated to St Trophimus, and on the church of Notre-Dame-la-Major, near the eastern ramparts. Like much of medieval Arles, it was built of limestone ashlar removed from the Roman remains. In 1152 the relics of St Trophimus were translated from Les Alyscamps to the new cathedral.

By the end of the 12th century the area enclosed by the city walls had doubled to 38 ha, and all the medieval parishes had been established. The amphitheatre, refortified with rectangular watch-towers (see fig.), enclosed a town with two parish churches, described as late as 1724 as 'crowded with beggarly tenements' (*see* URBAN PLANNING, fig. 1). These buildings were finally cleared in 1825 to provide a bullfighting arena.

The crusades in Spain and the Middle East, and the growing power of Pisa and Genoa, brought about a commercial revival. With their increasing wealth, the bourgeoisie wanted greater freedom from the burden of taxes, and 1232–4 marked a period of bitter civil disturbance and violent anticlericalism. Intervention first by Frederick II, and then Charles, Duke of Anjou (*reg* 1246–85), eroded the privileges of both the archbishop and the commune. From 1251 onwards the merchants of Arles became mere agents of the Italian companies that followed the papacy to Avignon (1309–77). Court prelates became absentee archbishops, and plague, war, floods and famine swept through Provence. Yet, despite the lack of a university, the Dominicans chose Arles as the centre of reform in Provence and built a new church (ded. 1484; now a storehouse) in lofty southern Gothic style, its high nave of five bays decorated with pierced arcading. At the same time the Augustinians rebuilt the 12th-century church of St Caesarius with a rib-vaulted four-bay nave and a chapel in each bay of the north and south aisles. A flat-roofed chevet and a crossing covered with an octagonal cupola and a lantern-tower were added in the 17th century.

Les Alyscamps lost many of its finest marble carvings to Renaissance collectors, and its churches and chapels were despoiled to build the city walls, houses and churches. At the same time new funerary chapels were built. A cube-shaped nave covered with rib vaults and an elaborately carved portal was endowed by the wealthy Porcellet family in the early 14th century, and the chapel of St Accurse (1521–9) was founded to expiate the death of a duelling opponent. Its Gothic nave is covered with lierne and tierceron vaults.

The Jesuits arrived in Arles in 1636 and remodelled the Hôtel de Laval (now Musée Lapidaire d'Art Chrétien) near the cathedral, giving it a wooden ceiling carved with imitation rib vaulting. Louis XIII endowed the Provençal Gothic church of Ste Anne (now Musée Lapidaire d'Art Païen) in the square facing St Trophîme. The Hôtel de Ville, with its classical façade, was rebuilt (1673–5) to plans by Jules Hardouin Mansart. A grand staircase leading up to the superb, flat-vaulted vestibule gives access to the medieval Plan de la Cour and Hôtel des Potestats (12th–15th century).

An outbreak of plague in 1720–21 killed nearly a third of the population. By the time the archbishopric was suppressed in 1801, Arles had passed into obscurity. With the exception of one long avenue, ending at St Honorat, and the Porcellet and St Accurse chapels, Les Alyscamps—celebrated by Dante and Ariosto—was destroyed in 1848 to make way for a marshalling yard. The town was heavily bombed in 1944.

BIBLIOGRAPHY

F. Benoit: *Les Cimetières suburbains d'Arles dans l'antiquité chrétienne et au moyen-âge*, Studi di Antichità Cristiana, xi (Rome and Paris, 1935)
P.-A. Fevrier: *Le Développement urbain en Provence de l'époque romaine à la fin du XIVe siècle* (Paris, 1964)
J. Brosse, ed.: *Dictionnaire des églises de France*, ii (Paris, 1966)
B. Montagnes: *Architecture dominicaine en Provence* (Paris, 1979)
L. Stouff: *Arles à la fin du moyen-âge*, 2 vols (Aix-en-Provence, 1986)

E. B. SAREWITZ

2. ST TROPHÎME. The outer walls of the present cathedral of St Trophîme are normally assigned to the Carolingian period. The church was reconstructed with a nave and aisles in the Romanesque style during the first quarter of the 12th century, and a new Gothic choir was built in the mid-15th. The cloister consists of two Romanesque galleries, dating from the 12th century, and two Gothic galleries dating from the 14th, which have attracted little attention. The Romanesque sculpture can be divided into four distinct groups: the nave capitals, the façade and the north and east cloister galleries. The cloister walks and the façade are all closely related, but there is no general agreement about the order of work or its date. The main

church and its capitals represent the earliest Romanesque phase; the building is one of a similarly decorated group in Provence, the earliest of which is the cathedral of Notre-Dame-des-Doms, Avignon. The nave capitals, which derive from late antique Corinthian forms, have been dated on stylistic grounds to *c.* 1120.

St Trophîme has the best-known example of a typical Provençal cloister, with barrel-vaulted galleries and arcades richly decorated with sculpture (*see* CLOISTER, fig. 1). The north and east walks are Romanesque, but they are not of the same date. The best and earliest work is in the north gallery. Each gallery is arcaded, with paired colonnettes and capitals, many of which are historiated. The piers at the corners and dividing the arcades have large-scale figure sculpture and reliefs. A variety of Old and New Testament subjects is represented on the capitals, but there is no clear iconographic programme. The figure style is related to that found on the west portal, and it can be argued that the work on the façade was carried out between the north and east galleries of the cloister. All the Arles sculpture is closely related to the façade of SAINT-GILLES-DU-GARD ABBEY, although the stylistic relationship is closest in the north gallery, one artist of which may have worked in both places. The façade and east gallery are both later than Saint-Gilles, but inevitably the dates of the two buildings must be related. Since no firm dates are accepted for either monument, the Arles work has been placed as early as 1120 and as late as the early 13th century.

The main sculpture in the north gallery consists of Apostle figures and *St Trophîme* on the piers, with relief panels at the corners showing the *Three Marys*, the *Ascension* and the *Stoning of Stephen.* At least two sculptors can be distinguished, both working in a highly classical manner and closely related to the style of Brunus at Saint-Gilles. The artist who carved the figures of *St Peter* and *St John* may well have been a member of the Saint-Gilles workshop. All the sculpture in the north gallery is of very high quality, and the historiated capitals show a fully developed and expressive narrative style. The foliage capitals are mostly Corinthian, with richly ornamented abaci.

The technical excellence of the north gallery sculpture is again evident on the façade. None of the cloister artists worked on the façade, however, although the closeness of the links is apparent if one compares the cloister reliefs with the façade frieze. The façade sculpture lacks the fluidity and expressiveness of the north gallery, and, despite its virtuosity, it has a mechanical and mass-produced appearance, which suggests that it was carved very rapidly. The single portal, flanked by large figures of eight Apostles and *St Trophîme* and set within a classically inspired portico, has a tympanum of *Christ in Majesty*, with a frieze below representing the *Last Judgement.* A secondary lower frieze bears *New Testament* scenes. Much Roman-based ornament is also included.

The progressive degeneration of the Arles sculpture continues in the east gallery of the cloister. This follows the general form of the north gallery, but the style of the larger figures has become stiff and somewhat crude, although a number of the historiated capitals are well handled and of better quality. The difference in quality between these galleries has led some to date them widely apart, but the overall cohesion of the Arles style argues against this. The earliest firmly dated epitaph in the cloister is 1183; but this proves only that the wall then existed. It has also been suggested that the façade was hurriedly completed for the coronation of Frederick Barbarossa in 1178. The most likely date for the north gallery is in the mid-12th century. The east gallery probably dates from the 1170s or 1180s.

Arles was an important centre of influence for the development of later Provençal Romanesque. It established the fashion for decorated cloisters and popularized the use of Roman decorative motifs. Artists from Arles carved the apse capitals at Saintes-Maries-de-la-Mer and the west window at St Gabriel, and worked at St Paul-Trois-Châteaux. More controversially, the influence of Arles has been traced in Italian sculpture, notably at Pisa and Parma, and it has been suggested that Benedetto Antelami worked on the east cloister gallery. This is difficult to accept, but the full nature of the Italian connection still awaits proper study.

BIBLIOGRAPHY

L. Labande: 'Etude historique et archéologique sur St Trophîme d'Arles du IVe au XIIIe siècle', *Bull. Mnmtl*, lxvii (1903), pp. 459–97; lxviii (1904), pp. 3–42

H.-A. Von Stockhausen: *Die romanischen Kreuzgänge der Provence* (Marburg, 1932)

R. Hamann: *Die Abteikirche von St Gilles und ihre künstlerische Nachfolge*, 3 vols (Berlin, 1955)

A. Borg: *Architectural Sculpture in Romanesque Provence* (Oxford, 1972)

W. Stoddard: *The Façade of St Gilles: Its Influence on French Sculpture* (Middletown, 1973)

J.-M. Rouquette: *Provence romane: La Provence rhodanienne*, Nuit Temps, 40 and 46 (Saint-Léger-Vauban, 1974)

ALAN BORG

Armagnac, Jacques d'. *See* JACQUES D'ARMAGNAC.

Arman [Fernandez, Armand] (*b* Nice, 17 Nov 1928). American sculptor and collector of French birth. He lived in Nice until 1949, studying there at the Ecole des Arts Décoratifs from 1946 and in 1947 striking up a friendship with Yves Klein, with whom he was later closely associated in the NOUVEAU RÉALISME movement. In 1949 he moved to Paris, where he studied at the Ecole du Louvre and where in an exhibition in 1954 he discovered the work of Kurt Schwitters, which led him to reject the lyrical abstraction of the period. In 1955 Arman began producing *Stamps*, using ink-pads in a determined critique of *Art informel* and Abstract Expressionism to suggest a depersonalized and mechanical version of all-over paintings. In his next series, the *Gait of Objects*, which he initiated in 1958, he took further his rejection of the subjectivity of the personal touch by throwing inked objects against the canvas.

Arman's willingness to embrace chance was indicated by his decision in 1958 to change his name in accordance with a printing error, having already stopped using his surname in 1947. The attitude was consistent with that of his work, which by the late 1950s had moved away from traditional painting and sculpture in favour of the object and specifically of the ready-made as defined in the Dada movement by Marcel Duchamp. In his *Accumulations* he piled up identical salvaged objects, modifying their meaning by repetition and giving the construction an ironic title, as with the accumulation of gas masks, *Home Sweet Home* (1960; Paris, Pompidou). He continued this aesthetic of detritus and scrap in another particularly provocative group of works, the *Dustbins*, transparent containers in which he placed either rubbish he had collected or objects that had belonged to a friend, as in *Robot-portrait of Yves Klein, The Monochrome* (1960; Paris, priv. col., see 1986 exh. cat., p. 117).

In response to Yves Klein's installation of an empty room, *The Void* (Paris, Gal. Iris Clert, 1958), Arman exhibited *Fullness* (Paris, Gal. Iris Clert, 1960), a gigantic accumulation of refuse that filled the same space from floor to ceiling; both works were important early examples of ENVIRONMENTAL ART. He soon widened his vocabulary by choosing both to cut the objects into thin strips, revealing their internal structure, and to destroy them violently during *Rages* held in public as a kind of performance art. The objects used by Arman were extremely diverse, but they were always familiar things collected in considerable quantities. Among those he favoured were those deriving from domestic consumption, such as coffee grinders and beer glasses, as well as musical instruments, which he subjected to all kinds of violence and destruction, as in *Chopin's Waterloo* (see fig.). In 1963 he began another series, *Combustions*, using fire as his basic material. Arman's ill-treatment of objects, especially in his early work, was due less to a systematically destructive will than to a desire to provoke new aesthetic effects. The subsequent development of his art largely confirms this view, as in his *Inclusions*, such as *Venus of the Shaving Brushes* (1969; London, Tate), which consist of transparent polyester containers holding objects embedded in resin; this became a standard form for many of his works. In the mid-1960s he used tubes of paint dribbling colour as a parody of abstract painting, especially of the impasto effects of Tachism, and he also began using polyester to preserve perishable rubbish for a new series of *Dustbins*.

From the mid-1960s Arman made numerous visits to New York, and he soon came to regard the USA as his second home, taking American citizenship in 1972. The stocks of new objects that he discovered there directed him towards new and more abstract accumulations. These culminated in 1967–8 in the *Renault Accumulations* (e.g. *Renault Accumulation No. 106*, 1967; see 1986 exh. cat., p. 221), highly sculptural works made from separate pieces supplied by the Renault car factory, and in large-scale commissioned monuments such as *Long Term Parking* (h. 18 m, 1982–3; Jouy-en-Josas, Fond. Cartier Mus.), a gigantic tower consisting of 60 cars embedded in concrete. In his later work he also recast some of his earlier *Rages* and *Combustions* in bronze, and in another series, *Armed Objects*, he used concrete as a base in which to fix the object, somewhat in the way he had previously used transparent plastic. He broadened his imagery to include tools while remaining faithful above all to objects symbolising the excesses of the consumer society. Arman was also an avid collector of objects, artefacts and works of art, including watches, radios, cars, European pistols, African carved sculpture (especially Kota guardian figures) and Japanese armour.

Arman: *Chopin's Waterloo*, broken piano fragments on wood panel, 1.86×3.00×0.48 m, 1962 (Paris, Pompidou, Musée National d'Art Moderne)

BIBLIOGRAPHY

O. Hahn: *Arman* (Paris, 1972)

H. Martin: *Arman* (New York, 1973)

Arman, Parade der Objekte (exh. cat., Hannover, Sprengel Mus., 1982)

J. van der Marck: *Arman* (New York, 1984)

1960: Les Nouveaux Réalistes (exh. cat. by B. Cotenson and others, Paris, Mus. A. Mod. Ville Paris, 1986)

For further bibliography *see* NOUVEAU RÉALISME.

ALFRED PACQUEMENT

Armando [Dodeweerd, H. D. van] (*b* Amsterdam, 1929). Dutch painter, draughtsman, writer and sculptor. In 1950 he studied art history at the University of Amsterdam. He had his first one-man show at the Galerie Le Canard in Amsterdam in 1954, the year in which he began to write poetry. Influenced by the Cobra group, his early drawings of the 1950s are spontaneous and have a tendency towards abstraction; he often drew them in the dark or with his left hand, as in *Drawing* (1954; Berlin, Alte N.G.). From 1954 to 1959 he produced a number of largely abstract works that were influenced by Dubuffet and Jean Fautrier; for these he used thickly impastoed paint, as in *Criminal Painting* (1957; Venlo, Mus. Van Bommel–Van Dam). In 1957 he was one of the founder-members of the Nederlandse Informele Groep (Informelen), with the Dutch painters Kees van Bohemen (1928–85), Jan Henderikse (*b* 1937), Henk Peeters (*b* 1925), Jan Schoonhoven and others.

In the early 1960s Armando, instead of painting, produced a number of relief works comprising mounted tin, bolts and barbed-wire, as in *Six Times Black* (1962; Utrecht, Blotkamp priv. col., see 1984 Biennale exh. cat., p. 15). These were created during his membership of NUL, a group he founded with members of the earlier Informele group in 1960 and which he left in 1965. After a period of neglect Armando resumed painting in 1971. The works of the 1970s, such as the triptych the *Enemy on its Way* (1978–9; Utrecht, Cent. Mus.), were black-and-white Expressionist works in which paint covered only a small area of the canvas. Later, covering the whole canvas while retaining the black-and-white style, he produced a number of series on fixed themes, as in *Outskirts of the Forest* (1983–4; Kiel, Christian Albrechts-U., Ksthalle), from a series of that name. In title and content the themes often recall the German Nazi past. After 1967 Armando resumed drawing, using a spontaneous style with few lines. On occasion he included photographs in his drawings, as in the triptych the *Unknown Soldier* (1975; Amsterdam, Stedel. Mus.). After 1979 he lived in Berlin.

BIBLIOGRAPHY

Armando (exh. cat. by R. Fuchs, Berlin, daad gal.; Eindhoven, Van Abbemus.; 1979)

Armando (exh. cat. by P. Hefting, Venice, Biennale, 1984)

Armando: 100 Zeichnungen, 1952–1984 (exh. cat., foreword by W. Beren; Rotterdam, Mus. Boymans–van Beuningen, 1984)

Armando (exh. cat. by K. Blotkamp, Edinburgh, Fruitmarket Gal., 1989)

□

Armant [anc. Gr. Hermonthis; Copt. Ermont]. City in Egypt, on the west bank of the Nile, some 10 km south of Luxor. It was at first called Iunu-Shema (Egyp.: 'the southern Heliopolis') and Iunu-Montu (Egyp.: 'Heliopolis of the war-god Montu'), from which subsequent names derive. It was the capital of the fourth nome (administrative province) of Upper Egypt throughout the Old Kingdom (*c.* 2575–*c.* 2150 BC), until the rise of the city of Thebes. Armant was the original home of the Mentuhotpe family, the founders of the 11th Dynasty. Preliminary excavations in the town area (1935–7) uncovered stone relief blocks of many periods; a few delicate reliefs of the 11th Dynasty show Sankhkare Mentuhotpe III in the company of Montu and his consorts the goddesses Iuniyt and Teneniyt. Some lower courses of a New Kingdom temple were uncovered, including the base of an 18th Dynasty Pylon bearing a depiction of a lively procession of Nubian captives headed by a rhinoceros. A granite stele, found near by, records various exploits, such as the capture of a rhinoceros by Tuthmosis III.

The Ptolemaic and Roman temples of Montu and his later consort, Rattawy, were demolished in the mid-19th century to build a sugar factory. The scant remains (see fig.) include a MAMMISI (Copt.: 'birth-house') erected by Cleopatra to commemorate the birth of Ptolemy Caesarion, her son by Julius Caesar. During the Coptic period, Armant was the seat of a bishopric; only a few granite columns are left of the once large and handsome church. In the desert beyond the town is the BUCHEUM, burial place of bulls (which were thought to be incarnations of the god Buchis) and cows (the 'mothers of Buchis'). This cemetery was in use for about six and a half centuries (*c.* 360 BC–AD 305), from Nectanebo II to Diocletian.

Armant, view of the temple from the west; engraving from V. Denon: *Description de l'Egypte*, i (Paris, 1820), pl. 92 (London, British Library)

BIBLIOGRAPHY

C. R. Lepsius: *Denkmäler aus Aegypten und Aethiopien*, iv (Berlin, 1849–59), pp. 1–11

P. E. Newberry: 'The Temple of Erment As it Was in 1850', *Proc. Soc. Bibl. Archaeol.*, xxvii (1905), p. 100

R. Mond and O. H. Myers: *The Bucheum*, 3 vols (London, 1934)

——: *Temples of Armant*, 2 vols (London, 1940)

M. S. DROWER

Armas, Ricardo (*b* Caracas, 1952). Venezuelan photographer. He was a self-taught photographer and dedicated himself to photography from 1972, first working for the magazine *Escena* (1974–6) and then for the Galeria de Arte Nacional in Caracas (1976–8). His first exhibition,

Acercamiento a Zitman, was held at the Museo de Arte Contemporáneo Sofía Imber, Caracas, in 1976. He lived in New York from 1979 to 1983 and studied at the International Center of Photography; from then on technical and formal growth and transformation became evident in his work, demonstrating a particular taste for the dramatic effects of the medium and for the narrative power of black-and-white photography. He went on to work as a photographer for the Museo de Arte Contemporáneo Sofía Imber in Caracas.

BIBLIOGRAPHY

Caracas, Fond. Gal. A. N., Archvs [File A-71]

GUSTAVO NAVARRO-CASTRO

Armature. Structural ironwork used especially in medieval buildings to reinforce slender columns or to consolidate canopies, bosses or tracery. The term refers also to the wooden or metal framework that supports a large work of sculpture.

□

Armenia, Republic of [Hayasdan; Hayq; anc. Pers. Armina]. Country in the southern part of the Transcaucasian region; its capital is EREVAN. Present-day Armenia is bounded by Georgia to the north, Iran to the south-east, Azerbaijan to the east and Turkey to the west. From 1920 to 1991 Armenia was a Soviet Socialist Republic within the USSR, but historically its land encompassed a much greater area including parts of all present-day bordering countries (see fig. 1). At its greatest extent it occupied the plateau covering most of what is now central and eastern Turkey (*c*. 300,000 sq. km) bounded on the north by the Pontic Range and on the south by the Taurus and Kurdistan mountains. During the 11th century another Armenian state was formed to the west of Historic Armenia on the Cilician plain in south-east Asia Minor, bounded by the Taurus Mountains on the west and the Amanus (Nur) Mountains on the east. Its strategic location between East and West made Historic or Greater Armenia an important country to control, and for centuries it was a battlefield in the struggle for power between surrounding empires. Periods of domination and division have alternated with centuries of independence, during which the country was divided into one or more kingdoms.

I. Introduction. II. Architecture. III. Painting. IV. Sculpture. V. Carpets. VI. Other arts. VII. Patronage and collecting. VIII. Museums and institutions.

I. Introduction.

The Armenians were referred to as Armenoi by the Greek historian Hecataeus of Miletus (*c*. 550–476 BC) and their

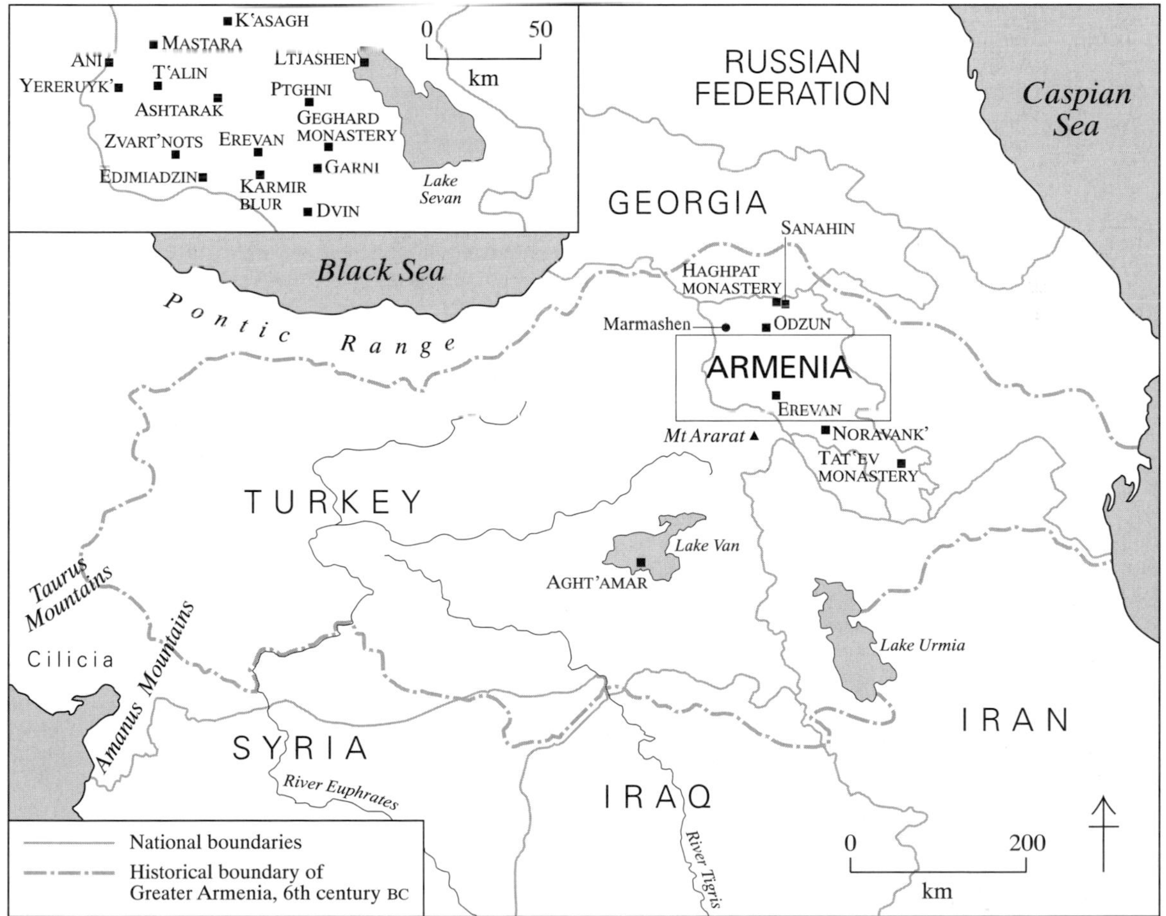

1. Map of Armenia; those sites with separate entries in this dictionary are distinguished by CROSS-REFERENCE TYPE

country identified as Armina in an inscription (520–519 BC) of Darius at Bisitun, Iran. Herodotus related (VII.73) that they migrated from Phrygia south-east towards the River Euphrates. Following this migration they probably merged with the people of Hayasa-Azzi, settled in Urartu (*see* URARTIAN) and later replaced the Urartian kingdom. According to Armenian tradition, their legendary hero Hayk (from which is derived the term by which the Armenians refer to themselves) was a descendant of Noah's son Japheth; he travelled north to the land of Ararat after the destruction of the Tower of Babel. Recent scholarship has suggested, however, that the Armenians were indigenous to Asia Minor and did not migrate from elsewhere. During the 6th and 5th centuries BC Armenia was part of the Persian empire, becoming an independent state *c.* 330–300 BC. It reached its apogee under Tigran the Great (*reg c.* 95–55 BC), but after his death, it was fought over by the Romans and Parthians until in AD 226 the Sasanians overthrew Parthia and invaded Armenia.

As early as the time of the Apostles Thaddeus and Bartholomew, from whom the Armenian Apostolic Church traditionally derives its name, segments of the Armenian population began to convert to Christianity. Under the guidance of St Grigor the Illuminator (239–325/6), King Trdat III (*reg* 287–330) declared Christianity the official religion (*c.* 314) and constructed the first churches. Armenia was partitioned in 387 between the Byzantines and Sasanians. In 451, the Armenians could not attend the council of Chalcedon due to their rebellion againt the Sasanians' attempt to reimpose Zoroastrianism on them. At a later date they refused to accept the decisions of the council, and in these and other church matters they practised their particular form of Christianity. They adhered closely to the Holy Scriptures, the first three ecumenical councils, the writings of the pre-Chalcedonian patristic authors and local church councils. The structure of the Armenian church also allowed feudal lords to participate with the clergy in councils on doctrinal and disciplinary matters. The church remained at the core of their sense of national identity and is reflected in their art. Another important factor affecting the development of Armenian art from the 4th century was the formation of a feudal class, in which the feudal lords (*nakharar*s) ruled their lands, usually separated from the neighbouring ruler by mountains, almost autonomously. When there was a king, he was only *primus inter pares.* As a result there were many patrons in different parts of the country who commissioned a wide variety of churches, sculpture and painting, as well as metalwork, carpets, textiles and illuminated manuscripts, especially of the Gospels.

The classical period of Armenian art, mainly between the 4th and 7th centuries, was the most creative in terms of architecture. Many forms of churches were built (*see* §II below). Some churches are decorated with figural relief sculpture over the portals and exterior walls (*see* §IV, 1 below). Wall painting, architectural sculpture, carved stelae and illuminated manuscripts also survive from the classical period and contain a mixture of Christian and pagan motifs that often reflect the Armenian emphasis on the theme of salvation (*see* §III, 1(i) below).

The first flowering of Armenian art was brought to an end by the Arab invasions, beginning in 640. Armenia became a province of the Caliphate and for the next 200 years was fought over by the Arabs and Byzantines. Building and artistic activity revived with the establishment of the Bagratid kingdom of King Ashot Bagratuni (*reg* 884–90). With their capital at ANI, the Bagratids ruled until the Saljuq invasions in the 1060s devastated the country. In the 10th century the Ardsruni family established the kingdoms of Vaspurakan (908–1021) and Siunik' (*c.* 970–1170). During the Bagratid period of Armenian art from the 9th to the 11th century new architectural and art forms appeared, many Gospel manuscript were copied and illustrated and numerous important churches were built. Monasteries were flourishing cultural and religious centres, the wealth of which was founded on donations and the possession of extensive feudal lands.

With the increasing invasions by the Saljuq Turks in the second half of the 11th century, many feudal nobles and their followers migrated to the Cilician plain in south-east Asia Minor, where they later established the Armenian kingdom of Cilicia (1198–1375), also known as the Kingdom of Lesser Armenia with the coronation of Leo I. It was one of the most important Christian states in the region and played a significant role during the Crusades, until it was destroyed by the Mamluks of Egypt. The reigns of the Cilician kings are marked by the construction of many almost impregnable castle-fortresses and by richly illuminated manuscripts. Although the images reflect increased contact between the Armenians and the West, both Western and Eastern elements are often modified to express the independence of the Armenian Church and rite. Meanwhile, in greater Armenia the Zak'arid princes Zak'are and Ivane succeeded in liberating the north-eastern regions from the Saljuqs. During the Zak'arid period from the 11th to the early 14th century, they, their descendants and other feudal families rebuilt the monasteries, commissioned many new churches, *gavit*'s and other structures, architectural sculpture and illuminated manuscripts in all parts of Armenia. In the 1220s the Mongols invaded Armenia and the country later ceased to be an independent political entity. There was a general decline in architectural and artistic production, although some traditional forms survived.

In 1828 the eastern part of Historical Armenia became part of the Russian empire, and Armenian culture came under the influence of Russia and Europe. The Russification of Armenia was greatly increased by its becoming the Armenian Soviet Socialist Republic on 29 November 1920. This also resulted, however, in the foundation of numerous state institutions that encouraged artistic development, for example in 1921 the Art College (from 1922 to 1936 the Art and Industry Technical College) and the Armenian State Museum (from 1941 the Armenian State Art Gallery) in Erevan; in 1932 the Artists' Union; and in 1945 the Art Institute of the Armenian Academy of Sciences (from 1953 the Art and Theatre Institute) in Erevan. With the break-up of the Soviet Union in 1991–2, Armenia gained independence.

In addition to the territories mentioned, an Armenian diaspora has existed for centuries in Europe and Asia

Minor, later spreading to many other parts of the world. As early as the 4th century an Armenian presence is recorded in Jerusalem, for example from Armenian inscriptions on seven surviving floor mosaics and medieval manuscripts donated to the monastery of St James by Armenian pilgrims. References to Armenian ecclesiastics are also known from the 6th century in Italy, France and Ireland. During the Middle Ages and later some of the diaspora communities played an active role in the revival of Armenian art and culture, especially manuscript illumination in the Crimea, New Julfa (Isfahan, Iran) and Constantinople (now Istanbul). During the 19th century and the early 20th the largest centre of Armenian culture was Tbilisi, and there were Armenian communities in L'vov (now L'viv), Kaminets' Podil'sky, Baku, Rostov-on-Don, Moscow and St Petersburg.

BIBLIOGRAPHY

J. Baltrusaitis: *Etudes sur l'art médiéval en Géorgie et en Arménie* (Paris, 1929)
O. Avedissian: *Peintres et sculpteurs arméniens du 19ème siècle à nos jours précédé d'un aperçu sur l'art ancien* (Cairo, 1959)
Corpus inscriptionum Armenicarum—Divan Hay Vimagrut'yan, 6 vols (Erevan, 1960–82)
S. Der Nersessian: *The Armenians* (New York, 1969)
N. Stepanian and A. Tchakmakchian: *L'Art décoratif de l'Arménie médiévale* (Leningrad, 1971)
V. Harouthiounian and M. Hasrathian: *Monuments of Armenia* (Beirut, 1975)
S. Der Nersessian: *L'Art arménien* (Paris, 1977/*R* 1989; Eng. trans., London, 1978)
T. S. R. Boase: *The Cilician Kingdom of Armenia* (Edinburgh and London, 1978)
B. Narkiss and M. Stone: *Armenian Art Treasures of Jerusalem* (New Rochelle, 1979)
B. Brentjes, S. Mnazakanjan and N. Stepanjan: *Kunst des Mittelalters in Armenien* (Berlin, 1981)
L. Der Manuelian: *Armenian Architecture*, 4 vols (Zug, 1981–6)
Armenien. Wiederentdeckung einer alten Kulturlandschaft (exh. cat., Bochum, Mus. Bochum Kstsamml., 1985)
A. Alpago-Novello and others: *The Armenians* (Milan, 1986)
J.-M. Thierry and P. Donabedian: *Les Arts arméniens* (Paris, 1987; Eng. trans., New York, 1989)

LUCY DER MANUELIAN

II. Architecture.

Between the 7th century BC and *c.* AD 300 the architecture of Armenia was heavily influenced first by the URARTIAN and later by the Greeks, Parthians, Romans and Syrians. After the adoption of Christianity (AD 314), Armenia produced a national architectural style, the genesis of which lies in the cross-fertilization of ideas from Cappadocia, Mesopotamia and Iran between the 1st and 3rd centuries AD. This is evidenced by the construction of such towns as Artashat and Van, and of cult and secular buildings, such as the sanctuaries at Bagavan and Ashtishat, and the temple and baths of Garni (late 3rd century AD; *see* GARNI). As in Mesopotamia (*see* DURA EUROPOS, §4), Christian worship in this period was probably organized in individual palaces and houses. Surviving buildings from the period after the 4th century AD are mostly mausolea and churches.

1. 4TH–8TH CENTURIES AD. The earliest surviving Christian monument is the two-storey royal mausoleum (364 AD) at Aghts'. Although the upper level is ruined, the crypt below survives as a vaulted chamber with an apse at one end. The image of a similar two-storey, tower-like mausoleum appears on one of the low reliefs decorating the east face of the south stele (?7th century AD) at Odzun. This type of structure was probably in existence as early as the 1st century BC.

The prevalent architectural forms were vaulted basilicas and centrally planned, domed churches. In the 4th and 5th centuries AD single- and three-aisled basilicas predominated. Their walls are of tufa or basalt ashlars facing a rubble core and are usually set on stepped podia, as in the single-aisled basilicas at Djrvezh (4th century AD) and Voghdjaberd, and the three-aisled basilicas at Yereruyk' (5th–6th centuries) and Tsitsernavank'. The interior of a single-aisled basilica is subdivided into equal bays by attached pilasters supporting arched ribs and is lit by windows in the thick, unadorned walls. Cornices and frames rarely interrupt the transition from the straight sides to the vaulted roof. A semi-dome covers the eastern apse, which is usually horseshoe-shaped but occasionally square, as in the 5th-century basilica at Ara.

The exterior of the apse is either enclosed in a straight wall (e.g. Zovuni and Shirvandjough) or, if it protrudes from the east façade, is often pentagonal (e.g. Tsoghakert, 4th–5th centuries), more rarely semicircular (e.g. Verishen, 5th century) or three sided (Voghdjaberd). Some single-aisled basilicas also have colonnaded porticos extending along one side or along three sides of the building and terminating in apses, as at Djrvezh. The porticos were used by catechumens as gathering places.

The three-aisled basilicas have free-standing piers, which are usually T-shaped but occasionally cross-shaped, as at Yereruyk'. Some basilicas, such as the church at K'ASAGH (4th–5th centuries), are a hall type with pitched roofs extending over the nave and aisles, but others have a higher central vessel, thus allowing for a clerestory, for example Tsitsernavank' and Yereruyk'. Horseshoe-shaped decorative niches were frequently inserted in interior and exterior walls of domed buildings, for example at Voskepar.

From as early as the 4th century AD Armenian architects were experimenting with problems relating to the construction of domes. Excavations have indicated that the first cathedral at ĒDJMIADZIN (anc. Vagharshapat), which was built in AD 301–3 by St Grigor the Illuminator (239–325/6), was centrally planned with a dome. It was rebuilt *c.* 484–5 by Vahan Mamikonian (*reg c.* 485–505) to a square plan with four protruding apses and four free-standing central piers supporting the dome. During the 6th and 7th centuries, the 'classical period', Armenian architects continued to develop designs for domed, centrally planned and basilican buildings. The use of increasingly elaborate vaults led to the creation of domed, cruciform structures, in which four free-standing piers form a domed central square; flanking barrel-vaulted bays absorb the thrust of the dome. Among the finest examples of centrally planned, cruciform churches are the cathedral (rest. 618 and 650) and Gayane Church (630–41) at Ēdjmiadzin and the church of Bagaran (613). Cruciform churches in which the basilican plan predominates include those of Odzun (6th–7th centuries), Bagavan (631–9) and Mren (639). From the 7th century domes were also added to existing

2. T'alin Cathedral, Armenia, mid-7th century AD

basilican churches, for example at Tekor and SS Paul and Peter, Zovuni.

Before beginning the construction of a church, an architect would first make a model, which constantly changed and grew more intricate as more options for its design and decoration were presented. This approach partly explains the sculptural quality of these buildings. In their development of centrally domed structures Armenian architects increased the number of symmetrically arranged axes. In its simplest form, this plan appears with three rectangular arms, each terminating in an apse. This type was widespread between the 5th and 7th centuries, for example at Tsrviz, Tayk' and Hogevank'. The cathedral at T'ALIN (mid-7th century; see fig. 2) combines this trefoil plan with a three-aisled, basilican structure. The cross, also a result of the use of central planning and symmetrical axes, was a particularly favoured motif in Armenian art, appearing on thousands of *khatchk'ar*s (stone slabs engraved with crosses; *see* CROSS, §§II, 4, and IV, 1(ii) below) as well as in architectural planning. The preference for centrally planned buildings led, further, to the development of multifoil plans, such as in the church of the Holy Trinity at Aragats (6th–7th centuries), which has six apses. This tendency continued into the 9th and 10th centuries with the construction of churches with a hexafoil plan, for example at Bagaran (9th century), or an octafoil plan, such as at Irind, Vartsakhan and the Zoravar near Yeghvard. The church at ZVART'NOTS, which was surrounded by a circular ambulatory, probably had a quatrefoil plan related to Syrian and Georgian churches of the 6th and 7th centuries.

Another type of centrally planned building to develop in the 6th and 7th centuries had a central dome with an octagonal drum resting on squinches that were arranged above an interior articulated by four large, axial apses and four smaller, diagonal niches. Among the earliest examples of this type are the Armenian churches of Okht Drnevank' at Artsagh (5th–6th centuries) and St Ēdjmiadzin at Soradir (early 6th century), and the Georgian church of Ninotsminda (late 6th century). One of the most important and original buildings is the church of St Hovhannes (6th–7th centuries) at Mastara, a large, square hall with a dome over the entire interior, buttressed by four semicircular axial apses and squinches. Similar designs were later used in the Byzantine monastery churches of Nea Moni (1045) on Chios (*see* CHIOS, §2) and Antiphonitis (12th century) on Cyprus.

Church building declined during the period of Arab domination in the second half of the 7th century and the subsequent struggle over Armenia in the following century between the Arabs and Byzantines. Instead, numerous fortresses were built by the Armenian *nakharar*s (feudal lords), extending from Nakhdjavan to Kharberd and from Karin to T'arsus. Under Arab rule caravanserais and bridges were built, and roads between the cities were improved; bazaars became the social and economic centres of urban life.

2. 9TH–15TH CENTURIES. From the late 9th century the formation of the independent Armenian kingdoms of the Bagratids (885–1045), the Ardsrunis in Vaspurakan (908–1021), the Kyurikians in Tashir-Dzoraget (966–1113) and the Syunyats (987–1170) led to a marked revival in Armenian architecture. The accompanying development of urban civilization was evident in such important political, administrative and commercial centres as ANI, DVIN, Kars, Artsn, Shirakavan and Van, as well as the more feudal cities of Ayrarat, Siunik', Artsagh, Gugark', Tayk' and Vaspurakan. The fortified city built by the Ardsruni King Gagik (*reg* 908–36) on the island of AGHT'AMAR in Lake Van is an exceptional example of a royal foundation, having its own harbour, palaces (all destr.) and the church of the Holy Cross (915–21; see fig. 7 below). The last was built by the architect Manuel as a variant of the quatrefoil plan with a 16-sided drum and angle niches covering three-quarters of a circle.

The revival and elaboration of ancient forms by royal architects is also evident in the church of St Grigor the Illuminator (*c.* 1001–15) at Ani, which was built by Trdat for King Gagik I (*reg* 989–1020) in imitation of the 7th-century church at Zvart'nots. New forms were also created, as in the small, three-storey church of the Shepherd (11th century; destr.) near Ani, the thick walls of which had six pointed niches cut into the interior and twelve triangular recesses framed by ribbed arches and colonnettes on the exterior. The hexagonal second storey was circular inside, and above it rose a circular drum surmounted by a conical dome. The monastery cathedral at Marmashen (986–1029; see fig. 3) represented another new type, having a domed cross-in-square plan with a pair of two-storey corner chapels.

The use of the *gavit'* or *zhamatun*, a portico-like roofed atrium built next to the main façade, is characteristic of Armenian church architecture from the 9th century to the 11th. They are derived from secular architecture and feature a complex roofing system of arches and vaults resting on the walls and four central piers, which support a dome with a central opening for light. The use of the *gavit'* as an assembly hall for large religious and secular gatherings required the development of roofing systems without intrusive piers, a problem solved by the introduction of subsidiary arches. One of the simplest systems,

3. Marmashen Monastery, Armenia, 986–1029

used in the square library (1063) at SANAHIN MONASTERY, has a respond in the middle of each side of the hall, which is connected by semicircular arches that support the dome. In the library (second half of the 13th century) at HAGHPAT MONASTERY two pairs of intersecting arches spring from pillars abutting the walls. A third system is found in the 13th-century *gavit‘* of the church of the Holy Apostles at Ani, where the rectangular space is divided into two bays by six engaged columns, from which pointed arches spring over each bay and intersect one another diagonally. A further elaboration appears in the great hall of Hamazasp (1254) at Haghpat, where four centre columns divide the area into nine equal sections. The arches connecting the columns and supporting the dome are higher than those between the columns and the eight engaged pillars on the side walls.

In 1045 Ani fell to the Byzantines, and many Armenians began to migrate towards Cilicia and the Crimea. The strategic position of the Armenian kingdom of Cilicia (1170–1375) at the crossroads of military and trade routes between the Mediterranean and Mesopotamia is reflected in its numerous powerful fortresses. Those built in the mountains either follow the site's topography, as at the capital Sis (now Kozan; *c.* 1200), Djandjiberd, Kantchiberd and Levonkla, or are rectangular in plan, as at Guglak. Fortresses on valley sites, such as at Maraş (anc. Germaniceia), have a regular geometric plan with walls dominated by rectangular towers. The castles at Anazarba (now Anavarza), Sis, Lambron (now Namrun) and Levonkla also contained palaces and chapels, which were usually on the first floor of octagonal towers and decorated with frescoes, although at Levonkla they were hewn out of the rock. The cities in the valleys were protected by a system of fortresses, while T‘arsus was defended by a moat and a double stone wall pierced by six gates. The walled coastal cities of Ayas (now Yumurtalık) and Korykos were protected by separate fortresses, that at Ayas being on the coast. At KORYKOS a fortress was built on a nearby promontory (Korykos Kale; 12th century) and another on an offshore islet (Kızkalesi; 1104); they were originally connected by a causeway.

In the Crimea many churches and monasteries were built in traditional Armenian forms, such as the churches of St Sargis (13th century), T‘eodosia, and the Holy Cross (1358) at Surkhat‘. Further west the Armenian cathedral (1356–63) at L'VIV is reminiscent of the architectural school of Ani, while the influence of Armenian traditions is also evident in the architecture of the Moldovan and Romanian cities of Botoshan (now Botoşani), Yash (now Iaşi), Sutchava (now Suceava) and Galats (now Galaţi).

The study of medieval Armenian architecture began in the 19th century when French and English travellers published their descriptions, sketches, plans and photographs of medieval Armenian churches and attracted the attention of art historians. The vaulted churches were a revelation to scholars because Armenian architects displayed a technical mastery of the problems of stone construction much earlier than their counterparts in the

West. The stone churches were built according to an extraordinary variety of ground-plans, with domes supported by squinches or pendentives, and naves and aisles with horseshoe-shaped and pointed arches pre-dating their use in Romanesque and Gothic architecture. The structures were conceived of as frame systems, and architects used geometric forms to direct the weight and thrust of the stone vaults and domes and minimize the damage from earthquakes.

At first Armenian architecture was misassessed as being a provincial branch of Byzantine architecture, and it later became part of a great debate among scholars as to whether Christian art originated in the East or in Rome. Studies were published that tried to explain the similarities in construction between Armenian church architecture of the 4th century onwards and the medieval architecture of western Europe built later. With the help of palaeographic and documentary evidence, T. T'oramanyan made a major contribution to the field through his excavations, structural analyses and reconstructions of buildings. His studies were extensively used in Strzygowski's two-volume work on Armenian architecture (1918), which proposed that the Armenians were the first to build churches with stone domes, subsequently playing a major role in the origins and development of Christian architecture through their influence on Byzantine, Romanesque, Gothic and even Renaissance architecture. Many scholars do not accept Strzygowski's wide-reaching claims and consider that the techniques used in medieval European architecture developed independently, particularly since more is now known about Early Christian churches outside Armenia. At the same time, however, the available information concerning the extent and quality of early Armenian churches has been greatly increased through the research and archaeological excavations of recent decades, as on the foundations of the cathedral of St ĒDJMIADZIN, now dated to the 4th century.

3. 16TH CENTURY AND AFTER. With the suppression of the Armenian kingdoms, architects of Armenian descent were employed throughout the Seljuk and Ottoman territories. They also settled in Persia, where they established the New Julfa district of Isfahan in 1606, which was built to a regular street plan with some two dozen domed churches (*see* ISFAHAN, §3(ix)). There the influence of Iranian art is apparent on the façade of All Saviour's Cathedral (Amenap'rkitch; 1656) and inside the dome of the Bethlehem Church (1627). Between the second half of the 18th century and the early 20th, members of the Armenian Balyan family served as royal architects in Constantinople (now Istanbul), building palaces and mosques. Later Armenian architects also worked in Madras, Calcutta, Cairo and Alexandria, and designed churches and Neo-classical secular buildings in Moscow, Tbilisi and Baku.

Following the union of Armenia with Russia (1828) and the closer contacts with western Europe, many Armenian cities, including EREVAN and Kars, were rebuilt according to the principles of urban planning and architecture imported from Russia and the West. Public architecture was influenced successively by the 19th-century classical revival, Eclecticism and Art Nouveau, although domestic buildings retained certain Iranian features.

Contact with European architecture was strengthened following the Russian Revolution of 1917 and the establishment of the Soviet Socialist Republic of Armenia in 1920. Avant-garde theories and styles, particularly those of the BAUHAUS, DE STIJL, Soviet Constructivism (*see* CONSTRUCTIVISM, §1) and Neo-Futurism, were influential. Socialist and revolutionary aims became important, and such Armenian architects as Karo Halabyan, Gevork B. Kochar (1901–73) and M. Mazmanyan all attended VKHUTEMAS. Large-scale urban planning was undertaken with the emphasis on architectural integrity and the construction of collective houses and rectangular 'superblocks' containing houses, nurseries, schools, garages and a sports centre. The reconstruction of Erevan (1924) to a plan by ALEK'SANDR T'AMANYAN was an important example of this approach, in which the circular centre, with intersecting principal arteries and a grid-plan of rectangular blocks, was conceived as an 'ideal city' enclosed within a wide circular belt of gardens. T'amanyan later applied the same principles when planning the reconstruction of Ēdjmiadzin, Leninakan (now Kurnayri) and Stepanakert (now Xankändi).

A faculty of architecture was established at the new Karl Marx Polytechnic Institute of Erevan in 1930, followed two years later by the foundation of the Architects' Union of Armenia. Numerous attempts were made to create a forward-looking plan for Erevan's housing and services, but these were later abandoned in favour of Stalinist urban planning (*see* STALINIST ARCHITECTURE), with its emphasis on monumentalism. Plans for Erevan culminated in 1961 in one for Greater Erevan by Mazmanyan, E. Papian and G. Murza. Progressive architects tended to see urban-planning problems as largely territorial, and, in this sense, the building of the hydroelectric power station at Lake Sevan (1930–69) was of great importance for Armenia since it allowed linkage to the Caucasian energy system. Allied to this is the reclamation of the Araratian valley, the urbanization of the Lori, Noyemberyan and Zangezur regions and the industrialization of Leninakan, Kirovakan and Erevan.

Beginning in the 1960s, plans were prepared for Leninakan, Ēdjmiadzin, Goris, Kirovakan, Ashtarak, Idjevan and other places, based on a common 'international' style with little individuality, as can be seen in the extensive use of tower blocks. More individual approaches to architectural projects began to appear in the 1970s, however, particularly in public buildings such as the Zvart'nots airport (1976–81) in Erevan by D. T'orosyan. Although after 1970 some Armenian architects were still influenced by Soviet Constructivist tendencies, there was a second dominant trend based on traditional Armenian architecture. The third and most widespread trend, however, was still characterized by monotonous mass-building projects attempting simplistic solutions to socio-economic problems resulting from the movement of large numbers of people from villages to the city.

BIBLIOGRAPHY

G. Millet: *L'Ecole grecque dans l'architecture byzantine* (Paris, 1916)
J. Strzygowski: *Die Baukunst der Armenier und Europa*, 2 vols (Vienna, 1918)

J. Baltrusaitis: *Le Problème de l'ogive et l'Arménie* (Paris, 1936)
T. T'oramanyan: *Nyut'er Haykakan tjartarapetut'yan patmut'yan* [Studies in the history of Armenian architecture], 2 vols (Erevan, 1942–8)
E. Utudjian: *Les Monuments arméniens du IVe siècle au XVIIe siècle* (Paris, 1967)
Architettura medievale armena (exh. cat., Rome, Pal. Venezia, 1968)
L. K. Dolukhanyan: *Arkhitektura sovetskoy Armenii: 20-yye gody* [The architecture of Soviet Armenia: the 1920s] (Erevan, 1980)
L. Der Manuelian: *Armenian Architecture*, 4 vols (Zug, 1981–7)
A. G. Grigoryan: *Sovremennaya arkhitektura Armenii* [Modern architecture in Armenia] (Erevan, 1983)

ARMEN ZARIAN

III. Painting.

1. Before 1828. 2. 1828 and after.

1. BEFORE 1828. The two main types of painted decoration in the earlier Christian period are wall paintings and illuminated manuscripts. Examples of the closely related art form of mosaic are rare. Apart from the Urartian wall paintings (8th century BC; *see* URARTIAN) recovered at Erebuni (Arinberd, now Erevan), the only surviving monumental decoration from pre-Christian Armenia is the floor mosaic with sea gods, nereids and allegorical figures from the baths (2nd half of the 3rd century AD) at GARNI. Mosaic fragments discovered in the 5th-century AD basilica at Dvin and the 7th-century cathedral of Zvart'nots would suggest that some of Armenia's Early Christian churches were decorated with mosaics. Other examples are the seven floor mosaics with Armenian inscriptions unearthed in Jerusalem, which belonged to Armenian churches constructed there during the Early Christian period. The largest is the Musrara mosaic (6th century) near the Damascus Gate, which consists of a large vine scroll inhabited by many different kinds of birds.

(i) Wall paintings. (ii) Manuscripts.

(i) Wall paintings. According to the Armenian theologian Vrt'anes K'ert'ogh (*c.* 610; see J.-M. Thierry, p. 80), Armenian churches were decorated with wall paintings of scenes from the Gospels and the lives of SS Grigor the Illuminator, Hrip'sime and Gayiane. Although many 7th-century churches preserve traces of wall painting, the recognizable compositions at Lmbat, T'alin, Aruch (T'alish), Karmravor, Mren and Gosh do not represent Gospel cycles, except for the one interpreted as depicting the *Entry into Jerusalem* at T'alin. The apses of the churches of Lmbat, T'alin, Mren and Gosh were decorated with the Old Testament theophanic vision inspired by Ezekiel and Isaiah. In depicting this vision Armenian artists adopted alternatives to the usual Early Christian formula of showing Christ surrounded by the four symbols of the Evangelists, as in the Book of Revelation. At Lmbat, Christ is shown in an aureole, seated on a gem-encrusted throne, and flanked by a tetramorph, a six-winged seraph and double wheels surrounded by flames. At T'alin, Christ reigns in glory on a pedestal holding a long scroll written in Armenian, but instead of sitting he is shown standing. Other paintings include portraits of saints, again depicted standing, as at Aruch (T'alish), T'alin and Mren, and within medallions, as at T'alin and Mren. Although these may indicate the existence of a systematic method of decorating early Armenian churches, in general too few examples of early wall paintings survive to form any conclusions except to indicate the probable independent attitude of the Armenian Church.

Under the Bagratids (885–1045) the church of SS Paul and Peter (895–906) at TAT'EV MONASTERY was decorated with wall paintings in 930 (now Erevan, N.A.G.) by Frankish painters, who worked with Armenian assistants under the direction of the Armenian Bishop Hakob of Dvin. The paintings show a seated Christ flanked by three prophets and four saints, an enormous *Last Judgement* from the west wall and a *Nativity* from the north wall. Several other 10th-century churches in the Siunik' region in Armenia are reported to have had frescoes, including Gndevank', erected by a Princess Sophia, with scenes (931) painted by 'Yeghishe, priest and painter'. The most important and well-preserved wall paintings are in the church of the Holy Cross (915–21) at AGHT'AMAR; they include a *Genesis* cycle in the upper zone of the drum with some unique iconographical details such as the angel witnessing the creation of Eve, and the unusual expressions of intimacy between the Creator, Adam and Eve. The lower walls have scenes from the *Life of Christ* including the *Entry into Jerusalem* (see fig. 4) and the *Adoration of the Shepherds and Magi*, a characteristic Armenian feature in the depiction of the Nativity. As in Armenian architectural sculpture, Aght'amar's paintings demonstrate the Armenian preference for Early Christian types and the ways in which religious cycles were changed to fit Armenian ritual. Other interesting wall paintings are found in the church of the Holy Sign at HAGHPAT MONASTERY; the church of the Holy Saviour (P'rkitch'; 1035–6) at Ani; St Grigor (1215), erected in Ani by the merchant Tigran Honents with a cycle including scenes

4. Armenian wall painting showing the *Entry into Jerusalem*, western apse, church of the Holy Cross, Aght'amar, 915–21

from the *Life of St Grigor the Illuminator*; and the apse of Kat'oghike Church (*c.* 1282), in Kobayr.

BIBLIOGRAPHY

S. Der Nersessian: 'Une Apologie des images du septième siècle', *Byzantion*, xvii (1944–5), pp. 58–87; also in *Etudes byzantines et arméniennes*, i (Leuven, 1973), pp. 379–403

——: 'Image Worship in Armenia and its Opponents', *Armen. Q.*, i (1946), pp. 67–81; also in *Etudes byzantines et arméniennes*, i (Leuven, 1973), pp. 405–15

N. Thierry and M. Thierry: 'Peintures murales de caractère occidental en Arménie: L'Eglise St-Pierre et St-Paul de Tat'ev (début du Xe siècle). Rapport préliminaire', *Byzantion*, xxxviii (1968), pp. 180–242

S. Der Nersessian: 'La Peinture arménienne au VII siècle et les miniatures de l'évangile d'Etchmiadzin', *Etudes byzantines et arméniennes*, i (Leuven, 1973), pp. 524–32

N. Thierry and M. Thierry: 'La Peinture médiévale arménienne', *Corsi Cult. A. Ravenn. & Biz.*, xx (1973), pp. 397–407

B. N. Arakelian: 'Armenian Mosaic of the Early Middle Ages', *Atti del Primo Simposio Internazionale di Arte Armena: Bergamo, 1975*, pp. 1–9

N. Thierry: 'Survivance d'une iconographie palestinienne de la Pentecôte au Vaspourakan', *Atti del Primo Simposio Internazionale di Arte Armena: Bergamo, 1975*, pp. 709–22

N. G. Kotandzhyan: *Khudozhestvennyy yazyk archskoy rospisi i rannesrednevekkyye freski Armenii* [The artistic language of Arouch wall paintings and early medieval Armenian frescoes], *Second International Symposium on Armenian Art: Erevan, 1978*, iii, pp. 164–72

——: *Tsvet v rannesrednevekovoy zhivopisi Armenii/Hayastani vagh mijnadaryan geghankarch't' yunum* [Colour in early medieval Armenian painting] (Erevan, 1978)

I. R. Drambyan: *K'obayri Ormnankarnere/Freski Kobaira* [The frescoes of Kobayr] (Erevan, 1979)

A. Ja. Kakovkin: 'Il significato degli affreschi della chiesa di S Gregorio di Tigran Honents (1215) ad Ani', *Atti del Terzo Simposio Internazionale di Arte Armena: Milano & Vicenza, 1981*, pp. 339–42

T. M. Mathews: 'The Genesis Frescoes of Aght'amar', *Rev. Etud. Armén.*, xvi (1982), pp. 245–57

J.-M. Thierry: *Les Arts arméniens* (Paris, 1987)

LUCY DER MANUELIAN

(ii) Manuscripts. Armenian illustrated manuscripts constitute one of the most important groups of codices produced by the Eastern Christian churches, both in their artistic quality and in the number of surviving examples. The corpus of extant manuscripts (*c.* 26,000) provides an uninterrupted series of examples from the 9th century to the 18th. Most Armenian illuminations are found in copies of the Gospels, the complete Bible and liturgical books for church use. The principal elements of this book decoration include calligraphy, the Letter of Eusebios, the canon tables, portraits, headpieces and cycles of Gospel scenes.

The illumination of manuscripts in Armenia probably started soon after the invention of the Armenian alphabet in AD 406. In a treatise called *Yaghags patkeramartits* ('Concerning images', 604–7), which was directed against Armenian iconoclasts, the author Vrt'anes K'ert'ogh (550–620) defended the practices of the Armenian church and the sumptuous decoration of Gospel books with illuminations and bindings of gold, silver, ivory and purple parchment. The oldest surviving Armenian illuminations, the final four in the ĒDJMIADZIN GOSPELS, belong to this period and, together with the Gospels' ivory covers, provide eloquent testimony to Vrt'anes's statements. Stylistically these illuminations, such as the *Annunciation*, resemble the wall paintings in the churches of Lmbat (7th century), Aruch (T'alish; 661–82) and Mren (629–40).

The second flowering of Armenian painting (862–1064) coincides with the apogee of material prosperity and cultural revival in Armenia under the Bagratids and Ardsrunis. Works of outstanding quality mark the resumption of artistic activity after centuries of Arab occupation; the GOSPELS OF QUEEN MLK'E, the Gospel of Kars (Jerusalem, Gulbenkian Lib., MS. 2556), copied for King Gagik I (*reg* 990–1020), and the Gospels of Trebizond (Venice, Lib. Mekhitharists, MS. 1400) show the skill of the painters in figural representations and rich ornamental designs. In these examples the main trends in manuscript illumination are combined to include decorated arcades, elaborate gold-lettered title pages, cycles of full-page illuminations and marginal illuminations within the text.

The choice of subjects and the style of the painting vary considerably in 11th-century manuscripts. Some works draw heavily on images from the classical period of Armenian art (6th–7th centuries) such as the crocodile hunt, frequently used by late Roman painters and mosaicists, and a 6th-century scheme showing two seated and two standing Evangelists set against an architectural background reminiscent of a *scaenae frons*. Other Armenian painters rejected the classical tradition and replaced it with a more decorative style, as in the Mughni Gospels (Erevan, Matenadaran Inst. Anc. Armen. MSS, MS. 7736) and the Gospels of 1053 (Erevan, Matenadaran Inst. Anc. Armen. MSS, MS. 3593). Instead of creating an illusion of reality, the figures are painted as two-dimensional forms with drapery folds indicated by shaded lines; the grounds are uniformly blue; there is little use of gold; and even the nimbi of the angels are painted red, blue or green. Certain features, such as the inclusion of Eve as midwife in the *Nativity* or the naked Christ in the *Crucifixion*, indicate that the painters drew their inspiration from Armenian apocryphal sources. The Vehap'aṙ's Gospels (1088) contain the earliest examples in Armenian manuscript illumination of narrative miniatures set into the columns of the text at the exact point where they illustrate the story, as in the depictions of the *Betrayal of Christ* and *Peter Cutting the Ear of Malchus* (see fig. 5). They are similar in style to illuminations in the Melitine group of manuscripts. The figures are drawn in ink and filled in with light washes; sometimes the lines have been painted over. The heads are large with staring wide open eyes, their whiteness emphasized by the swarthy colouring of the faces.

The increasing threat of Saljuq invasion in the second half of the 11th century resulted in a break in manuscript illumination as in other areas of Armenian art. With the resumption of artistic activity in the late 12th century, lavish manuscripts were produced, including the Awag Vank' Gospels of 1200–21 (London, BL, Or. MS. 13654), the large *Homily of Mush* (1204; Erevan, Matenadaran Inst. Anc. Armen. MSS, MS. 7729), the Gospels of Haghpat (1211; Erevan, Matenadaran Inst. Anc. Armen. MSS, MS. 6288) and the Targmantchats (Translator's) Gospels (1232; Erevan, Matenadaran Inst. Anc. Armen. MSS, MS. 2743), named after the monastery where it was kept until 1900. These particular manuscripts are noted for the force of their artistic expression and the monumental character of their composition.

The 13th century was the great period of Cilician manuscript illumination. Already in the 12th century the Armenians had founded scriptoria in different monasteries, principally at Drazark, Skevra, Akner, and at Hṙomkla where the patriarchal see had been transferred in 1151.

5. Armenian manuscript illumination of the *Betrayal of Christ* and *Peter Cutting the Ear of Malchus*, vellum, 325×245 mm, from the Vehap'aṙ's Gospels, 1088 (Erevan, Matenadaran Institute of Ancient Armenian Manuscripts, MS. 10780, fol. 71*r*)

The art that flourished in these centres had its roots in the luxurious Byzantinizing style of 11th-century illuminated manuscripts from Greater Armenia. Cilician painting, however, soon developed along original lines under the leadership of renowned painters such as T'OROS ROSLIN, Grigor Mlitchetsi (1150–1215) and Sargis Pidsak (1290–1355), all of whom produced manuscripts for prelates and princes. Among T'oros Roslin's distinctive traits of style is the sculptural modelling of the slender figures combined with a slight tendency to schematize the draperies, as in the *Presentation of Christ in the Temple*. The soft, subtle colours that predominate in the compositions are heightened by the occasional vivid touches of red, and by the gold background in full-page illuminations.

From the late 13th century onwards, despite difficult social and political conditions, a regional school of illuminators was active in Vaspurakan and neighbouring regions such as the city of Khizan, south-west of Lake Van. Illuminated manuscripts were still being produced in the 17th century in the Armenian colonies at Constantinople, in the Crimea and in Isfahan. These artists drew their inspiration mainly from Cilician works of the 13th and 14th centuries.

BIBLIOGRAPHY

S. Der Nersessian: *Manuscrits arméniens illustrés des XIIe, XIIIe et XIVe siècles de la Bibliothèque des Pères Mékhitaristes de Venise*, 2 vols (Paris, 1936–7)

——: 'Une Apologie des images du septième siècle', *Byzantion*, xvii (1944–5), pp. 58–87

——: *The Chester Beatty Library: A Catalogue of the Armenian Manuscripts*, 2 vols (Dublin, 1958)

——: *Armenian Manuscripts in the Freer Gallery of Art* (Washington, DC, 1963)

L. A. Dournovo: *Haykakan manrankartchut'yun* [Armenian miniatures] (Erevan, 1967)

S. Der Nersessian: *Armenian Manuscripts in the Walters Art Gallery* (Baltimore, 1973)

H. Buschhausen and H. Buschhausen: *Die illuminierten armenischen Handschriften der Mechitaristen-Congregation in Wien* (Vienna, 1976)

D. Kouymjian: *Illuminated Armenian Manuscripts to the Year 1000 AD* (Fresno, 1977)

B. Narkiss and M. E. Stone: *Armenian Art Treasures of Jerusalem* (Jerusalem, 1979)

E. Korkhmazyan, I. Drampyan and H. Hakopyan: *Armenian Miniatures of the 13th and 14th Centuries from the Matenadaran Collection, Yerevan* (Leningrad, 1984)

Armenien: Wiederentdeckung einer alten Kulturlandschaft (exh. cat., Bochum, Mus. Bochum Kstsamml., 1985)

S. Der Nersessian and A. Mekhitarian: *Miniatures arméniennes d'Ispahan* (Brussels, 1986)

V. Nersessian: *Armenian Illuminated Gospel-Books*, London, BL cat. (London, 1987)

T. F. Mathews and A. K. Sanjian: *Armenian Gospel Iconography: The Tradition of the Glajor Gospel* (Washington, DC, 1990)

S. Der Nersessian: *Miniature Painting in the Armenian Kingdom of Cilicia from the Twelfth Century to the Fourteenth Century*, 2 vols (Washington, DC, 1993)

T. F. Mathews and R. S. Wieck: *Treasures in Heaven: Armenian Illuminated Manuscripts* (New York, 1994)

VREJ NERSESSIAN

2. 1828 AND AFTER. Following the union of the eastern part of Armenia with Russia, contacts with western Europe increased dramatically, and painters adopted traditional Western genres and styles. Among the most important Armenian artists of the early to mid-19th century were Akop Hovnat'anian the younger (*see* HOVNAT'ANIAN, (1)), who painted portraits, for example *Natalia Teumian* (1840s; Erevan, Pict. Gal. Armenia), and Stephan Nersisian (1815–84). They were followed by the landscape painter Gevorg Bashindjaghyan (1857–1925) and the history and genre painter Vardyes Surenyants (1860–1921), whose work clearly reflects the influences of *Jugendstil* and the Munich School. The landscape paintings of Egishe T'adevosyan (1870–1936) show the influence of Impressionism.

The most accomplished Armenian painter of the early 20th century was MARTIROS SARYAN, who had played an important role in the Blue Rose group in Moscow, and who, together with the painters Stephan Aghadjanyan (1863–1940), Gabriel Gyurdjyan (1892–1989), Hakob Kodjoyan (1883–1959) and P'anos T'erlemezyan (1865–1941), returned to Armenia following the Russian Revolution of 1917 and the establishment of the Armenian Soviet Socialist Republic in 1920. This period is marked by its diversity of schools and movements and the establishment of numerous institutions and groups. A group of artists, for example, left the Fine Art Workers' Society in 1927 to set up the Armenian branch of the ASSOCIATION OF ARTISTS OF REVOLUTIONARY RUSSIA, with the aim of producing pictures that depicted the new life of the people. Genres typical of Armenian painting, however—landscapes, portraits and still-lifes—were still produced in the 1920s and early 1930s.

Saryan played an exceptional role in shaping the new representational school. His powerful and colourful landscapes over the years came to be identified with Armenia itself. The monumentality, generalization and decorative brilliance of his work was in part a response to the concept of beauty prevailing in folk art. A more lyrical approach to landscape painting was developed by T'adevosyan. He also painted portraits, such as that of the composer *Komitas* (1936), with landscape backgrounds. The lyrical and genre landscapes of Sedrak Arak'elyan (1884–1942) were among the first to be based on contemporary themes, as in *Taking Culture to the Mountains* (1936; Erevan, Pict. Gal. Armenia). Other artists, such as Gabriel Gyurdjyan, T'erlemezyan and Vahram Gayfetjyan (1879–1960), produced some of the earliest examples of industrial landscapes (e.g. Erevan, Pict. Gal. Armenia). Stephan Aghadjanyan played an important role in the development of portrait painting with his realistic images of ordinary people, such as *Grandpa Sedrak* (1926; Erevan, Pict. Gal. Armenia). His work influenced that of several other artists including Efrem Savayan (1909–74) and Arp'enik Nalbandyan (1916–64).

Graphic art of the early 1920s mainly took the form of political posters and caricatures, but by the mid-1920s Hakob Kodjoyan was producing watercolours for books as well as compositions on historical revolutionary subjects, as in the *Shooting of the Communists in Tat'ev* (1930; Erevan, Pict. Gal. Armenia). While the production of illustrations, posters and lampoons grew along with publishing, the establishment of permanent theatres was a boost to stage design. Following early performances in Constructivist style, the designs of Georgy Yakulov (e.g. for Aleksandr Shirvanzade's comedy *Kum Morgana*, 1927) had a great influence on the development of Armenian stage design, as did those of Saryan.

During the 1930s there was a gradual rediscovery of Armenian art and an awakening of interest in older art forms, but Armenian artistic development was curtailed by World War II, when propagandist work predominated, for example by Dmitry Nalbandyan (*b* 1906). The diversity of visual forms was restored in the post-war years, but until the mid-1950s subject-matter tended to be officially correct and ostentatious. However, from the late 1950s Armenian art enjoyed an upsurge, which was partly a result of the establishment of the Institute of Art in Erevan in 1945 (from 1953 the Art and Theatre Institute) and partly because in the late 1940s Armenian artists, such as Harut'yun Kalents (1910–66), Armine (Paronyan) Kalents (*b* 1920), Petros Konturadjyan (1905–65) and Bart'ugh Vardanyan (1897–1989), began returning from abroad. Foremost among them was Harut'yun Kalents, whose subtle mastery of colour had a profound impact on the development of a new style of painting. Another influential artist was Hovhannes Zardaryan (1918–92), who produced large-scale thematic paintings, such as the *Victory of the Builders of the Sevan Hydroelectric Power Plant* (1947; Moscow, Mus. Orient. A.), which was the first in a series of works in the 'severe style', as well as symbolic historical works.

6. Minas Avetisyan: *Djadjur*, oil on canvas, 1.0×0.75 m, 1960 (Erevan, Picture Gallery of Armenia)

At this time Armenian artists also began to show an interest in decorative colour, expressive drawing and individual statements. The use of the traditional landscape genre in order to convey the emotional meaning of events became a feature of Armenian painting of the time, as in Zardaryan's *Spring* (1956; Moscow, Tret'yakov Gal.), in which the depiction of a peasant girl in a rural setting symbolizes the native land bursting with life. Some artists, such as Sargis Muradyan (*b* 1927) and Grigor Khandjyan (*b* 1926), attempted to re-evaluate the events of the early 20th century through their history painting.

One of the most notable painters from this period on was Minas Avetisyan (1928–75), who reinterpreted the dramatic capabilities in Saryan. Avetisyan's works, such as *Djadjur* (1960; see fig. 6), deal with timeless issues, and the characters have a rare beauty and determination. The emotional impact of this confessional type of painting lies in the powerful combination of colours and the expressive but simply drawn forms. Avetisyan also produced important series of paintings as designs for ballets (Ravel's *Bolero* and Khachaturian's *Gayane*). Another trend in Armenian painting was represented by the more theatrical and poetic works of artists such as Robert Elibekyan (*b* 1941), Varuzhan Vardanyan (*b* 1948) and Karo Mkrtchyan (*b* 1951), who all to some extent reinterpreted the work of Aleksandr Bazhbeuk-Melikyan, a resident of Tbilisi.

An experimental trend in Armenian art was very much based on the work of Ervand Kotchar, and it was represented by the work of Ruben Atsalyan (*b* 1948), Genrikh Elibekyan (*b* 1936), Martin Petrosyan, Vruyr Galstyan (*b* 1924) and Ruben Abovyan (*b* 1929). From the mid-1980s there was a tendency to adopt international art practices as a means towards individual expression. A nostalgia for historical themes was also notable in the work of Grigor Khandjyan, and there were urban primitivist painters, such as Gevorg Grigoryan (1897–1975), Iosif Karalyan (1897–1981) and Hakob Ananikyan (1919–78), with their intimate depictions of life and acute sense of longing for home. Contrasting images of Armenia appear in the laconic and severe landscapes of Hakob Hakobyan (*b* 1923) and in the gentle and lyrical paintings of Rafayel Atoyan (*b* 1931).

BIBLIOGRAPHY

M. A. Ayvazyan and T. A. Izmailova: *Iskusstvo Armenii* [Armenian art] (Moscow, 1962)

S. I. Daniyelyan: *Chetvert veka: Iz istorii Yerevanskogo khudozhestvenno-teatral'nogo instituta* [Quarter of a century: from the history of the Erevan Art and Theatre Institute] (Erevan, 1971)

A. A. Kamensky: *Etyudy o khudozhnikakh Armenii* [Studies of Armenian artists] (Erevan, 1979)

N. S. Stepanyan: *Ocherk izobrazitel'nogo iskusstva Armenii* [An outline of Armenian fine arts] (Moscow, 1985)

A. V. Agasyna: *Molodyye khudozhniki Armenii* [Young Armenian artists] (Erevan, 1987)

N. S. Stepanyan: *Iskusstvo Armenii* [Armenian art] (Moscow, 1989)

NONNA S. STEPANYAN

IV. Sculpture.

1. Before 1828. 2. 1828 and after.

1. BEFORE 1828. The few surviving examples of sculpture that pre-date the official adoption of Christianity reflect Iranian, Achaemenid, Parthian and Hellenistic influences, as well as having Armenian features. They include such pieces as a marble statuette of *Aphrodite* (2nd–1st century BC; Erevan, Hist. Mus. Armenia), found at Artashat, and the stone heads from Dvin (1st century AD; Erevan, Hist. Mus. Armenia). The ancient capitals of Armavir, Ervandashat, Tigranocerta and Artashat, together with their pagan idols and temples, were destroyed by King Trdat III (IV) (*reg c.* 298–*c.* 330) and St Grigor the Illuminator after 314. Only the temple (1st century AD) at GARNI preserves its relief sculpture, in which Hellenistic influence is particularly strong. The practice of adopting and transforming images from neighbouring cultures is recurrent in Armenian sculpture of the earlier period, most of which survives as reliefs carved on the walls of churches and monasteries, on stelae (4th–mid-14th centuries AD) and on wooden doors.

(i) Architectural. Armenian architectural sculpture of the earlier Christian period is of particular interest to the history of Christian art because Armenia has an almost continuous tradition of carving figural images in stone on the exterior of churches, apparently beginning as early as the 4th century. This contrasts with Byzantine art and with Western art, which did not adopt the practice until the Romanesque period. The earliest dated examples (364) are reliefs on the walls of the royal hypogeum at Aghts' and include a depiction of a naked man thrusting a lance into a wild boar. Generally reliefs are used to decorate the tympana and lintels of portals, window arches, the drums supporting domes, cornices, under the gables and the lower elevations of churches and other religious structures. On interior walls reliefs are found in the apse, on the face of the bema platform, the ceiling, and on the pendentives and squinches at the base of the drum. There seems to have been little interest in portraying human figures realistically, but rather as abstract and stylized forms. A characteristic feature, however, is the inclusion of historic personages dressed in contemporary attire, with great attention paid to details of the texture, design and ornament of their clothing.

Although the images and themes depicted are similar to those in pagan, Christian and Islamic art, they are adapted to illustrate the teachings, history and spirit of the Armenian Church with its emphasis on the individual and the message of eternal salvation. Despite the apparent diversity of motifs, Armenian relief sculptors consistently focused on salvation and portrayed Armenian princes as exemplars of the faithful. The cross is ubiquitous, whereas the *Crucifixion* seldom appears except in a few later examples (see below).

There are also no images of the damned in the few surviving representations of the *Last Judgement*. The surviving reliefs contain sacred and secular figures, real and mythical birds and animals, miscellaneous objects such as wine bottles, and compositions of which the iconography remains obscure. Sacred figures include Christ, the Virgin and Child, saints, angels, Evangelists and apostles. On some churches, *Christ* or the *Virgin and Child* are accompanied by Armenian ecclesiastics and the building's donors, sometimes identified by inscription as kings and princes. Portraits of other secular figures, such as architects, masons (e.g. Zvart'nots; *c.* 650–59) and praying figures, also appear in the niches, spandrels, above the windows, next to portals or carved on the interior.

Although some of the figural scenes that appear between the 4th and 7th centuries are drawn from the traditional repertory of biblical scenes, certain additions and changes were made to reflect Armenian religious practice, such as on the church at PTGHNI and the cathedral of ODZUN (both 6th or 7th century). Although the composition on the window cornice of the south façade at Ptghni resembles an Early Christian image, with low-relief medallions of Christ and two angels presiding over six medallion portraits of the apostles, the sculptor has placed two hunting scenes below the composition, each depicting an Armenian martyr-prince, who is either a donor or an ancestor of the donors. The spirit and emphasis of the composition is thus focused on the mounted princes, who serve as both exemplars for the faithful and images of Christian triumph. They are pictured here in the company of saints, just as they are treated during the Armenian liturgy. The earliest Armenian example of a hunting scene on a Christian structure seems to be the slab inserted into an interior wall in the royal mausoleum of Aghts' (364), which may not have been made specifically for this structure. In addition to the example at Ptghni, similar scenes appear at the cathedral of ZVART'NOTS and as part of donor images on the churches of the Holy Sign (Nshan; early 14th century) at T'anahat, the Mother of God (Astvatsatsin; 1321) at Spitakavor and the *gavit'* (*see* §II, 2 above) at the monastery of NORAVANK' at Amaghu.

Depictions of single figures also contain certain distinctive features, as in the image of Christ holding the Gospel of St John on Odzun Cathedral. The opening words of the text are carved in Armenian letters, while Christ is flanked by angels holding snakes, the bodies of which intertwine and end in palmettes. The church of SS Paul and Peter (895–906) at TAT'EV MONASTERY has several windows decorated with portrait heads, probably of donors, each flanked by snakes or dragon-serpents. The cathedral at Mren (completed *c.* 639–40) and the church of the Holy Apostles (Arak'elots', now Kümbed Camii; 928–53) at Kars each have a similar image over a window; the church at Kars also has 12 full-length figures on its dome drum, possibly apostles, one of whom is flanked by snakes.

7. Aght'amar, Armenia, church of the Holy Cross, 915–21; view from the south

Evangelist portraits appear in unusual locations, which illustrates their mission of preaching to the four corners of the world, as well as the Armenian practice of reading the Gospels in different parts of the church. At the church of St Hovhanes (late 7th century) at Sisian, the four Evangelists are portrayed on the cornice, one on each side of the church. At the church of the Holy Cross (915–21) at AGHT'AMAR, an Evangelist portrait is placed under the gable of each elevation. Later, Evangelists' symbols replace the portraits, and are carved on the pendentives and squinches of monastery churches such as those of the Mother of God (929–51) at Sanahin, Gndevank' (936), the Holy Apostles at Kars (*c.* 955), the Mother of God (1321) at Areni, the Mother of God (1321) at Spitakavor and the Mother of God (1339) at Noravank'.

Another characteristic feature of Christian architectural relief sculpture is the frequent use of donor images. Four types appear and are used throughout the 4th century to the mid-14th. At Odzun, Mren, Sisian and Pemzashen (Mahmudjugh; 6th or 7th century), donors are shown individually or as part of a portal composition with Christ or the Virgin and Child. A third type, which occurs frequently, shows the donor holding a model of a church, as though to present it to God, as on the cathedral of Tekor (5th century) and the church of the Holy Cross (915–21) at Aght'amar. The church (1216–38) at Gandzasar has two such portraits on the drum, while the two-storey church (1339) at Noravank' preserves a similar image on the column of a rotunda. A more usual form of this type of donor portrait shows two figures, usually princely brothers, supporting the church model between them. On the churches of the Redeemer of All (Amenap'rkitch; 966) at Sanahin and the Holy Sign (976) at HAGHPAT MONASTERY their founder, Queen Khosrovanoush, placed portraits of her two sons under the east gable. A similar example appears on the church at Harichavank' (1201), where the Zak'arid princes Zak'are (the donor) and Ivane are portrayed. These images, together with their accompanying inscriptions, recall the exhortation by the historian Moses Khorenats'i (5th or 8th–9th century) that Armenian princes must record their deeds so as to inform and instruct others. The compositions also reflect such Armenian traditions as the participation by feudal lords in Armenian church councils and the emphasis on the individual's responsibility for his own salvation. The inscriptions further ensured that the names of the donors, for whom the churches served as intercessors, were inscribed forever in the 'Register of Life', as expressed in the 7th-century canons attributed to Sahak Part'ev and Grigor Narekats'i.

A further distinguishing feature of Armenian relief sculpture on churches is the manner and frequency with which birds and animals appear: eagles, small birds, pelicans, lions, bulls, stags, horses, griffins, harpies, sphinxes, and snakes or dragon-serpents. They may be shown on walls and portals singly, in confrontation or conflict, or as part of a frieze. One of the most outstanding examples of this decoration is the church of the Holy Cross at Aght'amar (see fig. 7), the oldest surviving Christian church to be entirely covered on the exterior with figural reliefs in stone. In addition to its donor portrait, Evangelist figures and multitude of biblical scenes, the church is encircled by friezes of animals under the domed roof and eaves, and by a vine scroll with scenes of hunting and daily life. Individual real and mythical animals form a horizontal band roughly midway up the exterior wall. From the 11th to the 13th centuries three motifs of conflict appear prominently on a number of important churches: an eagle holding a lamb or ram in its claws, a large bird biting a smaller bird, and a lion triumphing over a bull. The churches with these reliefs were founded by the Zak'arid princes and their feudal vassals, for example at the Kat'oghiké (1215) at Geghard (*see* GEGHARD MONASTERY), the main church (1205) at Makaravank' and St Step'anos at T'anahat (1273).

Some of the compositional schemes of the 13th and 14th centuries include images of the *Virgin and Child* with iconographic features that reflect Western influences, yet others are specifically Armenian in character. In the church of the Mother of God (1339) at Noravank', for example, the *Virgin and Child* are seated on a fringed rug with a lion beneath Christ's feet. Similar depictions appear at Areni (1321), where they are again seated on a rug, and at Spitakavor (1321) and the church of St John the Baptist (1216–38) at Gandzasar. In the *gavit'* of the monastery of Horomos (1038), *Christ Enthroned* is surrounded by Evangelist symbols and presides over portraits of Armenian catholicoi, including St Grigor the Illuminator. Variant forms of the *Wise and Foolish Virgins* appear in the tympana at the churches of the Forerunner (Karapet; 1216–21) at Hovhannavank' Monastery and St Step'anos (1212–17) in the monastery of Aghjots' St Step'anos. A unique composition that expresses the spirit of the Armenian form of Christianity is preserved in the tympanum relief over the window of the *gavit'* (1321) at Noravank', in which a compassionate God is shown holding the head of Adam tenderly in his hand, while to his right is a *Crucifixion*. This and other Armenian compositions omit the frightening elements in Western art, such as in Last Judgement scenes.

Following the Tatar–Mongol invasions and Armenia's later loss of statehood in the late 16th century, architectural work declined, although stone-carving continued, and there was some renewed building activity in the 17th and 18th centuries.

(ii) Non-architectural. The earliest surviving examples of non-architectural sculpture date from the Middle and Late Bronze Age and the Early Iron Age (2nd millennium–10th century BC) and feature geometric, plant and animal motifs. Among the various forms are the prehistoric fish-shaped megalith known as a *vishap* (dragon), decorated with reliefs of birds and animals and associated with the worship of water (e.g. from Imirzek, *c.* 2000 BC; *in situ*).

In the Early Christian period two types of commemorative stele were produced: tall, obelisk-shaped columns and smaller, quadrangular stele. Examples of the former type (6th–7th century AD) are found next to the cathedral at ODZUN and at the church at Brdadzor. They are covered with reliefs of Christ, the Virgin, saints, angels, apostles, ecclesiastics and salvation scenes from the Old Testament. Those on the two stelae at Odzun, for example, would appear to illustrate Armenia's conversion to Christianity, and include the *Virgin and Child*, the *Baptism*, the *Three Hebrews in the Furnace*, apostles standing in pairs, and a figure identified as King Trdat III (IV) (*reg c.* 298–*c.* 330) in the form of a boar before being healed by St Grigor the Illuminator. Similar scenes appear on the quadrangular stelae (7th century AD) from T'alin, Harich, Kharabavank' and Agarak. The stele from the latter site also shows a donor figure holding a church.

In the late 9th century the stele was superseded by the *khatchk'ar* (*see* CROSS, §II, 4), a uniquely Armenian art form consisting of a stone slab (*k'ar*) carved with a large cross (*khatch*) on one side. The earliest dated *khatchk'ar* is at Garni, erected in 879 by Queen Katranide. In the 9th

8. Armenian *khatchk'ar* (stone slab carved with a cross) in the precinct of Ēdjmiadzin Cathedral, commissioned by Grigor Khaghbakian, 1233

and 10th centuries the cross is represented as the Tree of Life or winged cross with two large leaves sprouting from the base and two bunches of grapes or other forms flanking the upper stem, for example at Mets Mazra (881). Later the *khatchk'ar* developed into an elaborately carved stone with intricate, lacelike ornamentation framing the central cross, at the base of which is a round medallion representing Golgotha. Examples include those at Noravank' Monastery (1308) by the sculptor Momik, and at Goshavank' (1291) by Poghos. Some *khatchk'ar*s have sacred images on the top frame or beside the cross, and a donor image, such as that at the base of Grigor Khaghbakian's *khatchk'ar* (1233; see fig. 8) on the grounds of Ēdjmiadzin Cathedral, where it was brought from Imirzek'. The *khatchk'ar* of the Redeemer of All (Amenap'rkitch) type shows Christ on the cross and was believed to have miraculous powers, such as that by Vahram at Haghpat (1273) and Mamikon's *khatchk'ar* (1279) at Ēdjmiadzin. The *khatchk'ar* is found in cemeteries, beside church portals and inside churches (e.g. Haghpat, 976; Geghard, 1215) and *gavit*'s (e.g. at Sanahin, 1181; Goshavank', 1197; and Makaravank', 1224). They were also inserted into building façades and erected as free-standing monuments in open country. Some, such as the Tuteordi *khatchk'ar* (1184) at Sanahin, have an inscription on the east side, and these indicate that they usually served as offerings for the salvation of the soul of the departed or the donor. Others commemorate the completion or restoration of a church, *gavit'*, fountain or bridge, such as the Sanahin monastery bridge (*c.* 1192) erected by Queen Vaneni. They may also record a significant donation, historical event or military victory, for example that of the Zak'arid princes at Amberd Castle (1202).

Other surviving forms of non-architectural relief sculpture from this period include wooden objects such as the doors at Mush Monastery (1131), lecterns, the wooden capitals at Sevan Monastery (874), and a panel showing the *Deposition* given to Havuts T'ar Monastery by the Armenian writer Grigor Magistros in 1031.

BIBLIOGRAPHY

G. Hovsep'ian: *Khaghbakeank' kam Prosheank' Hayoc' patmut'yan mej* [The Khaghbakeans or Prosheans in Armenian history], 3 vols (Vagharshapat and Jerusalem, 1928–42, rev. Antelias, 2/1969)
N. Marr and J. Smirnov: *Les Vichaps* (Leningrad, 1931)
G. Hovsep'ian: 'Sepulchral Steles and their Archeological Value for the History of Armenian Art', *Materials and Studies for the History of Armenian Art and Culture*, iii (New York, 1943), pp. 30–54
B. Arak'elyan: *Haykakan patkerak'andaknerē IV–VII darerum* [Armenian figurative bas-reliefs of the 4th to 7th centuries] (Erevan, 1949)
S. Barkhudaryan: *Midjnadaryan Hay tjartarapetner ev k'argords varpetner* [Armenian architects and sculptors of the Middle Ages] (Erevan, 1963)
N. Stepanian and A. Tchakmaktchian: *L'Art décoratif de l'Arménie médiévale* (Leningrad, 1971)
M. Thierry and N. Thierry: 'La Cathédrale de Mren et sa décoration', *Cah. Archéol.*, xxi (1971), pp. 43–77
L. Azaryan: *Khatchkars arméniens* (Ēdjmiadzin, 1973)
——: *Vagh midjnadaryan Haykakan k'andagke* [Armenian sculpture of the early Middle Ages] (Erevan, 1975)
S. Der Nersessian: 'Deux Tympans sculptés arméniens datant de 1321', *Cah. Archéol.*, xxv (1976), pp. 109–22
S. Mnatsakanyan: *Haykakan ashkharhik patkerak'andake IX–XIV darerum* [Armenian secular sculpture, 9th–14th centuries] (Erevan, 1976)
R. Thomson, trans.: *Mores Khorenati'l, History of the Armenians* (Cambridge, MA, 1978)
C. Kane: 'The Enthroned Virgin and Child in the Ojun Church', *Proceedings of the First Dr H. Markarian Conference on Armenian Culture: Philadelphia, 1979*, pp. 159–75
L. Der Manuelian: 'Armenian Sculptural Images, Fifth to Eighth Centuries', *Proceedings of the First Dr H. Markarian Conference on Armenian Culture: Philadelphia, 1979*, pp. 176–207
——: *The Monastery of Geghard: A Study of Armenian Architectural Sculpture in the 13th century* (diss., U. Boston, 1980)
——: *Armenian Architecture*, i–iv (Zug, 1981)
——: 'Armenian Sculptural Images, Part II: Seventh to Fourteenth Centuries', *Proceedings of the Third Dr H. Markarian Conference on Armenian Culture: Philadelphia, 1982*, pp. 96–119
——: 'Some Observations on the Carved Images of Classical and Medieval Armenia', *Acta Jutland*, lvi (1982), pp. 83–102
S. Mnatsakanyan: *Haykakan vagh midjnadaryan memorial hushardzannerē* [Armenian memorial monuments of the early medieval period] (Erevan, 1982)
——: *Varpetats' varpetner Manuel, Trdat, Momik* [Master sculptors Manuel, Trdat and Momik] (Erevan, 1982)
——: *Hayastani midjnadaryan kot'oghayin hushardzannerē IX–XIII dareri khatch'k'arerē* [The stelae monuments of medieval Armenia: khatchk'ars of the 9th to 13th centuries) (Erevan, 1984)
A. Ayvazyan: *Nakhijevani kot'oghayin hushardzannern u patkerak'andaknerē* [The stelae monuments and relief sculpture of Nakhchyvan] (Erevan, 1987)

LUCY DER MANUELIAN

2. 1828 AND AFTER. After the union with Russia the nature of Armenian sculptural activity changed radically, under the influence of Western trends. In Tbilisi, then the largest centre of Armenian culture, sculptural work reflected the main artistic tendencies of western Europe, including realist portraiture and Art Nouveau. In the early 20th century sculpture was represented by portrait busts and small-scale works, as in the work of Mik'ayel Mik'ayelyan (1879–1943) and Andreas Ter-Maruk'yan (1875–1919), for example Ter-Maruk'yan's portrait sculpture of *K. Abovyan* (1913, erected 1933; Erevan, Abovyan House Mus.).

There were strong contacts with Moscow and St Petersburg, and, following the Russian Revolution of 1917 and the establishment of the Armenian Soviet Socialist Republic in 1920, numerous sculptors who had been forced into exile returned to Armenia, including Ara Sargsyan (1902–69), Suren Step'anyan (1895–1971) and Aytsemnik Urartu (1899–1974), who all settled there during the 1920s. With the establishment of institutions to support and encourage the arts, and along with the new political situation, diverse types of sculptures were produced. Monumental sculptures and decorative reliefs, in particular, appeared in association with the rapid development of urban construction. Monumental sculpture was a particularly important emotional and visual component in the replanning of EREVAN by ALEK'SANDR T'AMANYAN in 1924 (*see* §II, 3 above). Among the sculptures created were the obelisk bust of *Azizbekov* (1932) by Suren Step'anyan, the monument to the *Heroes of the May Uprising in Leninakan* (1931) by Ara Sargsyan and the monument to the young Communist hero *Ghukasyan* in the University Square (1934), also by Step'anyan. Their generalized, static forms are imbued with an internal dynamism, which also characterizes the work of the Constructivist architects in the 1920s. The use of stone relief work on Erevan's main buildings, such as that on T'amanyan's Armenian SSR Government House (1926–41) by the sculptors Step'anyan and Taragros (or Ter-Vardanyan; 1878–1953), shows the return to the legacy of medieval Armenian architecture. During the 1930s, however, a more psychological approach was shown, and works began to deal with more ordinary subjects. In line with the concern to make art more accessible to the general public, group compositions were developed, and statues of *Step'an Shahumyan* (1932) and *V. I. Lenin* (bronze, 1940), both by SERGEY MERKUROV, were erected in the centre of Erevan.

During World War II military themes predominated, and throughout the 1950s the subject-matter conformed to official policies. Some sculptors, including Ghukas Tchubaryan (*b* 1923), Sergey Baghdasaryan (*b* 1923), Ara Hrut'yunyan (*b* 1928) and Khatchatur Iskandaryan (*b* 1923), generated an interest in stylized decorative reliefs. From the late 1950s, however, changes occurred in the concept of civic monuments. Although statues continued to be erected on the traditional site in the centre of the town or city square, others were set up in less orthodox places. The equestrian statue of *David of Sasun* (1959), for example, by ERVAND KOTCHAR rises above a crag in a hollow directly in front of the Erevan Railway Station, and the statue of *Alek'sandr T'amanyan* leaning over his drawing board (1969) by Artashes Hovsep'yan (*b* 1931) is placed at pedestrian eye-level; there are other examples by Nikolay Nikogesyan (*b* 1918). There was also an increase in decorative works (e.g. by Hripsime Simonyan, *b* 1916, and Ruzanna Kyurkchyan, *b* 1930) during this period, which is connected to the changes in methods of construction in architecture, especially the building of mass housing and the transition to standard planning schemes.

The work of Kotchar in particular served as the basis of an experimental trend in Armenian art. From the mid-1980s especially there was a noticeable move towards individuality of expression, and sculpture from this period is characterized by an uninhibited use of form and a feeling of spaciousness, even in small-scale works by such artists as Levon Tokmadjan (*b* 1934), Ara Shiraz (*b* 1941) and Kamo Gyandjyan. At the same time the extensive spread of military memorials has again drawn attention to the problems of synthesizing sculpture with architecture.

For bibliography *see* §III above.

N. STEPANYAN

V. Carpets.

It has been suggested that Armenians were prolific weavers from Classical times and wove the earliest surviving carpet, found in the 1940s in a frozen south Siberian tomb, the Pazyryk rug (now St Petersburg, Hermitage), generally attributed to the 5th century BC. Since few carpets of undoubted Armenian authorship have survived from before 1880, however, some scholars (e.g. Pope) have taken a sharply opposing view, denying that Armenians ever were substantial rug producers and claiming instead that they merely marketed the rugs. During the 1980s, thanks to the efforts of the Armenian Rug Society in the United States, this latter view was largely dispelled. Its members catalogued and photographed hundreds of rugs with Armenian inscriptions, many of which explicitly identify the weaver as Armenian and also provide the date or place of origin. Indeed, it is difficult to imagine that any group inhabiting those parts of eastern Anatolia and the southern Caucasus that were the homelands of the Armenians for at least 3000 years would not have been rug weavers, as sheep and their wool have long been significant in the local economy. Greek, Roman and Arab geographers, historians and travellers all mentioned Armenian woollen fabrics, even if it is not always clear which of the surviving early Near Eastern carpets are Armenian.

1. ARMENIAN WORKS. In the early 20th century a group of rugs was found in the Alaeddin Mosque in Konya, Turkey (now Istanbul, Mus. Turk. & Islam. A.), and, although usually described as 13th-century Seljuk work, they may have been woven by those Armenians and Greeks who, according to Marco Polo (*c.* 1254–1324; *Travels*, ed. Latham, p. 4), 'intermingled among the Turkomans ... weave the choicest and most beautiful carpets in the world'. An Armenian origin has been claimed for several other early surviving carpets, including a group of bird and animal rugs (one New York, Met.; one Stockholm, Stat. Hist. Mus.; one Berlin, Pergamonmus.) dating to the early centuries of the Ottoman Empire. The carpet alleged to be from the shrine of ARDABIL in Iranian Azerbaijan (15th–16th centuries; London, V&A) has also been at times attributed to Armenian weavers, although its elaborate Persian inscription provides insufficient support for this idea.

A group of *c.* 175 carpets of the 17th–18th centuries from the Caucasus (now New York, Met.; Washington, DC, Textile Mus.; London, V&A; Istanbul, Mus. Turk. & Islam. A.; Istanbul, Vakiflar Kilim & Flat-Woven Rug Mus.; Tokat, Mosque of Ali Pasha; Erzurum, Mosque of Lala Mustafa Pasha), known as 'dragon rugs', because of their highly stylized renditions of dragons and other mythical beasts, has also been the subject of considerable controversy. They were formerly used in east Anatolian mosques in areas that were once inhabited by Armenians, and several early 20th-century writers, including F. R. Martin (pp. 116–17), believed that they were woven by Armenians, although this was vigorously rebutted by A. U. Pope (pp. 147–58) and later by other scholars. A closer look at these complete and fragmentary carpets does, however, suggest that they are of Armenian workmanship, and they are among the most powerfully drawn and dramatically coloured early rugs to have survived into modern times. Evidence favouring an Armenian origin relates to both the design and the weave of the carpets. Some 19th-century rugs from the Karabagh (Karabakh) region of the former Soviet Azerbaijan show designs suggestive of the dragon rugs. Most prominent of these motifs is the 'sunburst', a medallion found in at least one surviving dragon rug (18th century; priv. col., ex-Textile Mus., Washington, DC) and another related but later piece (19th century; Hannover, Kestner-Mus.). With the compilation of data on inscribed Armenian rugs, it has become clear that the 'sunburst', as it appears on 19th-century carpets, is an Armenian design; it is therefore reasonable to assume that rugs with designs showing earlier forms of this motif are also Armenian. There are also some structural features of the dragon rugs that indirectly relate them to Armenian production. While all of them are symmetrically knotted on a wool foundation, the largest group shows the unusual feature of an extra thick weft strand, of unknown purpose, at intervals of every few centimetres along the length of the rug. This peculiarity relates the dragon rugs to other types of large Caucasian rug, those that include palmette and leaf designs known as 'afshan' and 'harshang'. Although none of the dragon rugs with an extra weft strand is inscribed, one rug of this type but with an afshan design (untraced; see 1984 exh. cat.) is inscribed with Armenian names. Another rug with a border system identical to that of the largest group of afshan rugs, the Kirakos rug (untraced; see 1984 exh. cat.), has an elaborate Armenian inscription, which apparently localizes its weaving to a village near the city of Gandja (Azerbaijan), one likely source of the dragon rugs. The cryptic date on this carpet has been read by some as 1202, but this seems extremely unlikely as it is stylistically so similar to 18th-century carpets.

While not conclusive, the similarities of design and weave between 19th-century Armenian rugs and the dragon rugs and the structural resemblance between them and some contemporary rugs with Armenian inscriptions strongly suggest that the latter were woven by Armenians. The large towns of the southern Caucasus in Azerbaijan most likely to have been their place of origin are Shusha and Gendje, both known to have had large Armenian populations when these rugs were woven. Another carpet that is similar in design to the dragon rugs is the Gohar rug (USA, priv. col.; see fig. 9), named after the weaver identified by the elaborate Armenian inscription. The most likely reading of the date, about which there is controversy, is 1700, which would make it the oldest surviving inscribed Armenian carpet. It is still intact, with vibrant colours, and it is clearly related in design to the 'Kasim Ushag' type, with a central medallion and palmettes, made during the 19th century in the Karabagh area. Several of these later rugs with Armenian inscriptions are also known (e.g. 1909; Lemyel Amirian priv. col.).

The types of problem connected with Armenian weaving before 1800 are more easily solved for rugs in the 19th century, when production can be documented through a study of rugs with Armenian inscriptions. Most of these pieces were woven in the Karabagh region, where many Armenians have lived for centuries, and others were settled from Persia during the early 19th century. Some of the rugs have extremely brief inscriptions, perhaps just a few Armenian letters, while others bear only Christian dates. Most, however, have more detailed inscriptions, thus confirming their Armenian origin. They usually fall into the mainstream of Caucasian rugs from this area and include such classic designs as the 'cloudband' (two stepped medallions and S-shaped figures) and the 'lampa' (medallions repeated on a vertical axis). A group of pictorial rugs and others showing European-type floral motifs (priv. cols) appear to be late 19th-century Armenian products from Shusha. The more finely woven rugs of the eastern Caucasus known as Quba and Shirvan were probably not woven by Armenians. Kazakh rugs (e.g. early 20th century; A. T. Gregorian priv. col.) from the western Caucasus and eastern Anatolia, on the other hand, undoubtedly included many of Armenian origin. Much of this area was inhabited by both Azeri Turks and Armenians, and it is often impossible to determine which people wove particular types of rugs, although those with Islamic dates are most likely to be Turkish work. Another possible clue to the Armenian origin of a particular Caucasian rug is the presence of the cooler red shades from cochineal or a similar dye, rather than the brick-reds obtained from the more common madder used throughout most of the Near East. Armenians were known to use dyes made from scale insects gathered from the exposed roots of shrubs and from imported cochineal.

9. Gohar rug, wool, 3.47×1.95 m, from the Karabagh region, Azerbaijan, Armenia, probably 1700 (USA, private collection)

2. Works from the Diaspora. Armenian rugs woven within the Persian Empire are even more difficult to identify, as here inscriptions are less common than in those from the Caucasus. A colony of Armenians was established by Shah Abbas I (*reg* 1588–1629), at Julfa, across the river from his capital at Isfahan, where they probably engaged in carpet weaving. Also from the 17th century is a highly accomplished pile-woven chasuble showing a *Crucifixion* (London, V&A), which, if of Armenian workmanship, would suggest that they were engaged in other court-style weaving. Armenians also settled in villages of the Chahar Mahal, a region west of Isfahan in the foothills of the Zagros Mountains, and in

villages around the town of Dilijan. The modern rugs (late 19th century–early 20th; examples in J. M. Keshishian and A. T. Gregorian priv. cols) woven by Armenians in both these areas show designs and technical features of the non-Armenian rugs woven by neighbouring peoples. There has probably not been a rug type identifiable as Armenian during the 20th century in Iran, although it may be that the small crosses woven into rugs from Iran and occasionally Turkey and the Caucasus indicate Armenian weavers.

Many rugs were also apparently woven by Armenians living within the Ottoman Empire, and there inscriptions are rare, presumably because of proscriptions against such labelling. It is not, therefore, surprising to find that several rugs survive with inscriptions woven along the ends, outside the border design. This would allow the letters to be removed without damaging the rug, should it be sold commercially. A number of rugs surviving from the Kirşehir area in Turkey (e.g. 19th century; P. Sharian & J. M. Keshishian priv. col.) have been found with Armenian inscriptions, but few appear from the regions of eastern Anatolia known to have had large Armenian populations during the 19th century. The existence of Armenian workshops is recorded near Kayseri and Sivas in Turkey, where pictorial rugs and rugs with designs like those made in Tabriz, Iran, were produced.

Between the late 19th century and the early 20th Armenians settled in and around Istanbul were engaged in weaving rugs. This production, which usually sold under the label of Kumkapu, seems unrelated to the indigenous village weaving of eastern Anatolia and the Caucasus, as both the designs and weaving technique were adapted from other sources. The rugs are usually of silk, at times with some of the field brocaded in metal-wrapped thread, and the weave often exceeds 600 asymmetrical knots per square inch (93 per square cm), placing them among the finest rugs ever produced. The designs on the Kumkapu rugs vary within a range of motifs derived from earlier Persian court rugs or from a group of rugs now thought to have been woven for the Topkapı Palace during the 18th century. Many appear in the form of prayer rugs, with a horseshoe-shaped arch design, and in some respects may be seen as predecessors to the present-day manufactured rugs from Hereke in Turkey.

After the mass Armenian exodus from Turkey in 1915, rugs were woven by refugees in Greece, Syria and other locations around the eastern Mediterranean. As the refugees took up other occupations, this gradually diminished, and now the only Armenian weaving to survive on a significant scale is found in the (former Soviet) Armenian Republic, where the state agency in charge of carpet production had its headquarters in Erevan and also maintained workshops in Leninakan, Kamo, Eghegnadzor, Dilijan, Bassarguechar, Arti, Idjevan, Artsvashen, Martuni and Shakhorazar. Rugs from these sources are based on 19th-century designs, usually of the type that would be described in the trade as 'Kazak' rugs. While these are competently woven, they lack the subtle colour variations of the 19th-century pieces, which are naturally dyed, and because of their cotton foundation yarns they feel quite different from the more blanket-like quality of the all-wool rugs.

BIBLIOGRAPHY

F. R. Martin: *A History of Oriental Carpets before 1800* (Vienna, 1908)
A. U. Pope: 'The Myth of the Armenian Dragon Carpets', *Jb. Asiat. Kst*, ii (1925), pp. 147–58
R. Latham, trans. and ed.: *The Travels of Marco Polo* (New York, 1958)
Early Caucasian Rugs (exh. cat. by C. G. Ellis, Washington, DC, Textile Mus., 1975)
H. H. Gayayan: 'Armenian Loan Words Used in the Turkish Language', *Lraber*, 8 (1977), pp. 85–99
M. L. Eiland: *Oriental Rugs: A New Comprehensive Guide* (Boston, 1981)
U. Schurmann: *The Pazyryk: Its Uses and Origin* (Munich, 1983)
Weavers, Merchants and Kings: The Inscribed Rugs of Armenia (exh. cat. by L. der Manuelian and M. L. Eiland, Fort Worth, TX, Kimbell, A. Mus., 1984)

MURRAY L. EILAND

VI. Other arts.

1. Ceramics. 2. Jewellery. 3. Metalwork. 4. Textiles, embroidery and lace.

1. CERAMICS. A large number of ceramic idols (h. 7 to 15 cm) dating from the 3rd millennium BC, perhaps associated with fertility, have been excavated in recent years at the sites of Mokhlablur, Art'ik, Shengavit and Mecamor (Erevan, Hist. Mus. Armenia). Late 3rd and 2nd millennium BC high-quality burnished redware, with painted and incised geometric and animal designs, was made in Armenia; it may have originated there before spreading throughout the Near East. Characteristic of the immediate pre-Urartian period were large (h. 100 cm, diam. 100 cm) burnished jars, sharply tapering at the top and bottom, with serpent designs in high relief, perhaps associated with a cult. These date from the 12th century to the 10th BC and originate from Sanahin, Dvin and Mecamor. The ceramics of the Urartian period (mid-9th century BC–*c*. 590 BC; *see* ANATOLIA, ANCIENT, §V, 2) show great skill and diversity. Ceramic rhyta (Erevan, Hist. Mus. Armenia; Sardarabad, Mus. Ethnog. Armenia) from the 9th century to the 7th BC were found at Karmir Blur and Armavir. Potters cleverly imitated metal vessels, such as the silver rhyta (5th–4th centuries BC; Erevan, Hist. Mus. Armenia) from Erebuni (Arinberd, now Erevan). There are, however, few convincing examples of locally produced pottery for the period between the fall of the Urartian kingdom and the 5th century AD. The excavations at Dvin and Ani have uncovered much interesting pottery from the 5th century onwards, some of which followed fashions prevalent in surrounding regions. Yellow and green splashed ware and turquoise blue faience, for example, were also produced in substantial quantities between the 8th and the 9th centuries in Islamic centres in Iran and Central Asia (*see* ISLAMIC ART, §V, 3(iv)). Ceramics painted with light green on a white or light yellow ground with figures of birds are derived from Byzantine ceramics found throughout the east Mediterranean (*see* EARLY CHRISTIAN AND BYZANTINE ART, §VII, 1(iii) and (iv)). More typically Armenian in style are the many pots and dishes, some with Armenian inscriptions, painted with human, animal and hybrid motifs (Erevan, Hist. Mus. Armenia). Between the 11th and 13th centuries the production of ceramics in Armenia, especially at Ani, was important and of high quality. An example in green and brown against a white ground shows a woman in national costume holding a spindle (Erevan, Hist. Mus. Armenia).

By the 15th century the city of Kütahya, *c.* 200 km south-east of Istanbul, had become a flourishing centre of Armenian ceramic production. The earliest dated pieces, inscribed on the bottom in Armenian, are from the early 16th century and have characteristic blue-and-white decoration (London, BM). By the 17th century brightly coloured faience was produced with yellow, green and a brilliant 'tomato' red made from Armenian bole. The potters created vessels in widely varying shapes for diverse uses.

Kütahya's main competitor in the production of ceramics was Iznik, the renowned centre for Ottoman pottery and architectural tiles (*see* ISLAMIC ART, §V, 5(ii)). Potters at Kütahya also produced square tiles to decorate the walls of numerous mosques, mostly in Constantinople (now Istanbul), and churches. The most spectacular display appears in the Armenian monastery in Jerusalem, where various parts of the complex are decorated with thousands of Kütahya tiles, notably a series of polychrome Old and New Testament scenes, accompanied by an inscriptional band in Armenian, in the Ēdjmiadzin chapel of the Armenian Patriarchate. These tiles were originally commissioned in 1718 for the renovation and decoration of the Church of the Holy Sepulchre, but, owing to a dispute between the competing Christian denominations, the work was never undertaken.

Among the most popular ceramic forms to originate from Kütahya were the egg-shaped ornaments that hang from the chains of oil lamps suspended in churches and mosques. These ceramic eggs are variously decorated, but the most common motifs are seraphim (e.g. Jerusalem, Gulbenkian Lib.). Other popular forms include demi-tasse coffee-cups without handles, saucers, monogrammed plates, rose-water flasks, incense burners and lemon squeezers; these often bear Armenian inscriptions (e.g. Edinburgh, Royal Mus. Scotland; London, BM and V&A; Brussels, Mus. Royaux A. & Hist.; Venice, S Lazzaro degli Armeni, Bib.; Athens, Benaki Mus.). The production of Armenian ceramics flourished in Kütahya until the expulsion of the Armenians during World War I. Several families settled in Jerusalem, where they continue to manufacture polychrome ceramics.

Another centre of Armenian tile production was New Julfa, the Armenian suburb of Isfahan, founded in the early 17th century. Large pictorial panels made of square blue-and-yellow painted tiles are found *in situ* in some of the city's Armenian churches. A fine example is the *Adoration of the Magi* depicted on 28 tiles (1719) in the church of St George (1610/11). Functional pottery continued to be made in Greater Armenia until the 20th century and is still produced in Armenia, where the traditional forms known from pottery finds at Dvin and Ani persist.

BIBLIOGRAPHY

J. Carswell and C. Dowsett: *Kütahya Tiles and Pottery from the Armenian Cathedral of St. James, Jerusalem*, 2 vols (Oxford, 1972)
Armenian Ceramic Art (exh. cat. by P. Bedoukian, V. Bedoukian and T. Hazarian, New York, Armen. Mus., 1982)
Treasures of Etchmiadzin (Ēdjmiadzin, 1984) [trilingual text]
Armenien: Wiederentdeckung einer alten Kulturlandschaft (exh. cat., Bochum, Mus. Bochum, Kstsamml., 1985)
Sale Catalogues: Islamic Works of Art, London, Sotheby's: 'Armenian Works of Art', 13 April 1988; 12 Oct 1988; 12 April 1989; 22 April 1990; 10–11 Oct 1990; 24–5 April 1991
D. Kouymjian: *The Arts of Armenia* (Lisbon, 1992), pp. 46–8

2. JEWELLERY. Though Armenia was one of the world's first centres of metallurgy, the little that has survived of early jewellery in precious metals was found through excavations (unless otherwise stated, all objects mentioned below are in the State Historical Museum of Armenia, Erevan). A medallion (3rd millennium BC) found at Shengavit is decorated with linear ornament and two small gold balls. Gold beads made by the double-thread and embossed granular techniques and a gold frog-shaped brooch covered with an embossed granular design were uncovered at the site of Ljashen (2nd millennium BC). Horseshoe- and crescent-shaped earrings were found at Getashen and Karmir Blur, the latter an Urartian site of the 8th–7th century BC at which was also found a twisted gold bracelet with snakes' heads at each end. In the post-Urartian period, a gold necklace (*c.* 6th–4th century BC) was uncovered at Armavir, an old Urartian site that in the immediate pre-Christian era became the capital of Armenia. The necklace, decorated with filigree work and bluestones and in places covered with black glasspaste, portrays birds and a schematized *Tree of Life*. At Armavir, medallions depicting relief busts of women with children's heads resting on their breasts show a Classical influence. A medallion showing a winged goddess, possibly Isis (2nd–1st-century BC), was found in the Sisian region. Cast earrings from the same period were excavated at the old capital of Artashat and the fortress of Garni.

The only items of Armenian jewellery preserved from the early medieval period have been those excavated after World War II at DVIN, capital of Christian Armenia in the 5th and 6th centuries AD and administrative centre of the Arab conquerors after the 7th century. Among them are a small gold cross; twisted gold bracelets with snake ends, one of which is enhanced with precious stones; earrings with long hanging pendants of crescents, birds and figures; a necklace with dangling gold ball pendants; and a ring with a large turquoise, and engraved fishscales on its sides. The major examples of the jeweller's art surviving from the Middle Ages are gold or silver reliquaries, church plate and manuscript covers for Gospels (*see* §4(ii) below). Manuscript illuminations, especially those featuring portraits of royalty from the Armenian kingdom of Cilicia (12th–14th century), provide glimpses of sumptuous dress and jewellery. At least two gold rings from royal households have survived: one ring (Venice, Monastery of the Mekitarists) may have belonged to Prince T'oros II (*reg* 1145–68) and depicts the Lamb of God surrounded by an inscription *T'oros Servant of God*; the other has a motif of a lion and is attributed to a later prince and King T'oros (*reg* 1293–7). Occasionally, simply designed twisted silver bracelets and small silver Armenian crosses with flaring arms and small balls at their points have been found in large hoards of Cilician Armenian silver coins.

From the 17th century jewellery-making was one of the most prominent craft industries. Thousands of silver medallions, tiaras, bracelets, necklaces, earrings, mirrors, purses, belts and rings survive in collections of Armenian and Ottoman artefacts. The objects have been hammered, moulded and cast and often have been worked with a niello technique known in Armenia since the pre-Christian era. Many are characterized by filigree work. Large numbers of crosses were also fashioned, as well as snuff-boxes and small pieces of jewellery. Large and carefully arranged displays of such items are in the Museum of Armenian Folk Art and the State Historical Museum in Erevan. The art of jewellery-making, following traditional designs and techniques, survives into the late 20th century, and museum collections display the work of the best contemporary craftspeople. As well as in Erevan, Armenian jewellery and artefacts in precious metals are in such collections as those of S Lazzaro degli Armeni, Venice; the Catholic Armenian Congregation Treasury, Vienna; the Musée Arménien de France, Fondation Nourhan Fringhian, Paris; the Armenian Library and Museum of America, Watertown, MA; the Armenian Patriarchate Museum, New Julfa, Isfahan; the Metropolitan Museum, New York; and the Hermitage, St Petersburg.

BIBLIOGRAPHY

A. Sakisian: 'L'Orfèvrerie arménienne à l'influence de Constantinople aux XVIIIe et XIXe siècles', *Pages d'art arménien* (Paris, 1940), pp. 87–95

B. Arak'elian: 'Metalwork', *Arbestnere Hayastanum, IV–XVIII dd* [The crafts in Armenia, 4th–18th century] (Erevan, 1956), esp. pp. 90–156

——: 'Metalwork', *Kaghakner ew arbestner Hayastanum, 9–13 dd* [Cities and crafts in Armenia, 9th–13th century], i (Erevan, 1958), pp. 133–86

S. Der Nersessian: 'Le Reliquaire de Skévra et l'orfèvrerie cilicienne aux XIIIe et XIVe siècles', *Rev. Etud. Armén.*, n. s. i (1964), pp. 121–43; repr. in *Etudes byzantines et arméniennes*, i by S. Der Nersessian (Leuven, 1973), pp. 705–20

J. Guevrekian: 'The Mystery of a Royal Ring', *Der Ararat*, viii/3 (1967), pp. 58–9

C. Dowsett: 'An Armenian Gold Pyx (Kayseri, A.D. 1687)', *Rev. Etud. Armén.*, n. s. vii (1970), pp. 171–86

N. G. Akolian: *Khudozhestvennyy metal' srednevekovoy Armenii, IX–XIII vv.* [Metallic art in medieval Armenia, 9th–13th century] (diss., U. Erevan, 1972)

B. Ananian and S. Djemdjemian: 'Toros ishxani oski matanin' [The gold ring of Prince T'oros], *Essays on Armenian Numismatics in Honor of Fr. Clement Sibilian*, ed. D. Kouymjian and Y. Nercessian (Los Angeles, 1980), pp. 97–103

D. Kouymjian: 'Islamic Metalwork with Armenian Inscriptions: Annex II', *Islamic Metalwork from the Iranian World, 8th–18th Century*, ed. A. S. Melikian-Chirvani (London, 1982), pp. 403–7

V. Abrahamian: *Yuvelirnoe iskusstvo Armenii s drevneyshikh vremyon do nashikh dney/Armenian Jewelry Art from Ancient Period to Present Days* (Erevan, 1983) [bilingual text]

M. Ghazarian, ed.: *Treasures of Etchmiadzin* (Ēdjmiadzin, 1984) [trilingual text]

Sale Catalogues: Islamic Works of Art, London, Sotheby's: 'Armenian Works of Art', 12 April 1989, pp. 58–9; 10–11 Oct 1990, pp. 79–83; 24–5 April 1991, pp. 268–82

D. Kouymjian: *The Arts of Armenia* (Lisbon, 1992), pp. 49–54

3. METALWORK. The Armenian plateau is rich in metallic ores, and its people have been master metalworkers and jewellers since the 1st millennium BC. The main categories of artefact that survive are items in base metals and items (mainly cult objects) in precious metals. A third category, coins, were produced in both bronze and silver. Under the successive Orontid and Artaxiad dynasties (4th–1st centuries BC), there was an uninterrupted flow of coins. Notable are the splendid tetradrachmas of Tigran II the Great (*reg c.* 96–56 BC) showing on the obverse the King in profile wearing the conical headdress known as the Armenian tiara, which has a pair of addorsed birds flanking a star. After this, the numismatic tradition was aggressively renewed, only later, under Cilician Armenian dynasties of the 12th to the 14th centuries. These coins are loosely modelled on those of the Holy Roman and Byzantine empires, with the addition of certain Armenian motifs representing Christianity and royal authority (e.g. a cross flanked by two rampant lions wearing crowns; New York, Amer. Numi. Soc.).

(i) Base metals. The first major artistic use of metals was in the 9th–6th centuries BC under the URARTIAN. The excavations at Toprakkale, Erevan and Karmir Blur have yielded quantities of weapons, including ceremonial shields with elaborate processional designs in repoussé, domestic objects and votive statues (e.g. London, BM; St Petersburg, Hermitage; Ankara, Mus. Anatol. Civiliz.; Erevan, Erebuni Mus.). The excavations at Dvin and Ani have produced most of the medieval bronze metalwork (Erevan, Hist. Mus. Armenia) including many utilitarian objects such as knives, scissors and jugs, animal-shaped candleholders, large cauldrons, a church chandelier from Ani, and censers (12th–13th centuries). The latter are moulded with scenes from the life of Christ and copy Early Christian models.

Later bronze, copper, and occasionally pewter vessels mostly date from the 17th century onwards. Tokat and Caesarea were among the main centres of production. Although hundreds of plates, bowls, jugs and trays of tinned copper with Armenian inscriptions have been preserved in private and public collections (e.g. Erevan, Hist. Mus. Armenia) they have received little attention. Many are dated, such as a large tray (1477; Erevan, Hist. Mus. Armenia) from Old Julfa, on the Arax River, and are thus useful for a chronological study of style and motif. Cast bronzes also survive from this later period, some in traditional Iranian shapes, for example horn-shaped rhyta (e.g. Erevan, Hist. Mus. Armenia) and massive cylindrical candlesticks; others with characteristic Armenian forms, for example the *khatch'kar* (cross stone), the flowering cross, and the Armenian cross, with small circles at the two flaring points of each arm of a cross with shorter latter arm. Numerous pewter pilgrim flasks bearing the figure of a warrior saint killing a dragon (as well as some silver Gospel covers) were mass-produced with pre-stamped plates.

(ii) Precious metals. Items in precious metals were made for royalty, the church and wealthy individuals. The earliest examples are several silver rhyta of the 5th–3rd centuries BC from Erzinjan (formerly Erez; London, BM, and Paris, Louvre) and Arinberd (Sardarapat, Mus. Ethnog. Armenia); two from the latter site are in the shape of a rider in Iranian costume (5th century BC) and an animal head with drinkers and musicians (3rd century BC). Armenia was one of the first wine-producing areas, which explains the popularity of these drinking vessels. Among gold medallions from the ancient capital of Armavir is one of the 2nd–1st centuries BC with a woman holding a child to her breast (Erevan, Hist. Mus. Armenia). Virtually nothing survives of precious metalwork or jewellery from the Christian centuries until the establishment of the Cilician kingdom. From the 13th century onwards there is a continuous series of Gospel bindings, reliquaries, chalices, patens and other vessels in silver, often washed with gold,

and occasionally in solid gold (Ēdjmiadzin Cathedral, Sacristy; Jerusalem, Armen. Patriarch.).

One of the oldest and finest silver bindings (1254; Ant'ilias, Beirut, Armenian Catholicate) has the *Crucifixion* accompanied by busts of the Virgin, St John the Evangelist and the Apostles on the front cover and *Christ Enthroned* on the back. Another cover chased in gold (1255; Erevan, Matenadaran Inst. Anc. Armen. MSS) shows a *Deësis* on the front and the four Evangelists on the back. Among surviving reliquaries, the most famous are the silver triptychs of Skevra (1293; St Petersburg, Hermitage) and of the Holy Cross of Khotakerats' (Armen.: 'grass eaters', i.e. monks; 1300; Ēdjmiadzin Cathedral, Sacristy), commissioned by the feudal lord Eatchi Proshian. The latter displays a large jewelled cross in the central panel with Christ resting on the beasts of the Apocalypse at the top of the cross and the donor shown in prayer at the bottom; the leaves covering the central panel have the archangels Gabriel and Michael on the inner sides, and St Grigor the Illuminator and St John the Baptist on the outer sides.

The most common scene depicted on silver bindings is the *Crucifixion*. Other scenes include the *Adoration of the Magi* surrounded with delicate grape bunches studded with jewels (1475; Baltimore, MD, Walters A.G.) and a monumental *Ascension* (1496; Erevan, Matenadaran Inst. Anc. Armen. MSS). The scores of silver bindings from the 15th to 19th centuries display great variations of style and decoration. Among chalices and liturgical vessels, the gold pyx (1687; Lisbon, Mus. Gulbenkian) made in Caesarea is remarkable for its elegant workmanship. The central panel depicts the *Last Supper*, the others, pairs of Apostles. Another notable work is a bejewelled gold chalice (1749; Jerusalem, Armen. Patriarch.) from Constantinople (now Istanbul). Many luxurious chalices decorated with enamelling and filigree were made by Armenians working there. In the 18th and 19th centuries large quantities of silver belts, buckles, earrings, purses and communion boxes were manufactured in Armenian centres such as Van, where the black and silver niello technique was popular, and metalworking to a high standard continued in the Armenian Republic.

BIBLIOGRAPHY

G. Hovsép'ian: *Mi edj hay arvesti ev mshakoyti patmut'iwnits'* [A page from the history of Armenian art and culture] (Aleppo, 1930)

A. Sakisian: 'L'Orfèvrerie arménienne à l'influence de Constantinople aux XVIIIe et XIXe siècles', *Pages d'art arménien* (Paris, 1940), pp. 87–95

B. Arak'elian: 'Metalwork', *Kaghakner ev arhestner Hayastanum, 9–13 dd* [Cities and crafts in Armenia, 9th–13th centuries], ed. L. Xacikyan, i (Erevan, 1958), pp. 133–86

P. Bedoukian: *Coinage of Cilician Armenia* (New York, 1962)

E. Musheghyan: *Hayeren ardzanagrut'yanb ararkaner* [Objects with Armenian inscriptions], Erevan, Hist. Mus. Armenia cat., i (Erevan, 1964)

S. Der Nersessian: 'Le Reliquaire de Skévra et l'orfèvrerie cilicienne aux XIIIe et XIVe siècles', *Rev. Etud. Armén.*, i (1964), pp. 121–43; repr. in *Etudes byzantines et arméniennes*, i (Leuven, 1973), pp. 705–20

C. Dowsett: 'An Armenian Gold Pyx (Kayseri, A.D. 1687)', *Rev. Etud. Armén.*, vii (1970), pp. 171–86

Armenian Coins and Medals (exh. cat. by P. Bedoukian and V. Bedoukian, New York, AGBU Gal., 1971)

N. G. Akolian: *Khudozhestvennyy metal' srednevekovoy Armenii, IX–XIII vv* [Metallic art in medieval Armenia, 9th–13th centuries] (diss., U. Erevan, 1972)

P. Bedoukian: *Coinage of the Artaxiads of Armenia* (London, 1978)

Thirty Centuries of Armenian Metal Art (exh. cat. by P. Bedoukian and V. Bedoukian, New York, AGBU Gal., 1978)

D. Kouymjian: 'The Iconography of the "Coronation" Trams of King Levon II', *Essays on Armenian Numismatics in Honor of Fr. Clement Sibilian*, ed. D. Kouymjian and Y. Nercessian (Los Angeles, 1980), pp. 67–74

P. Z. Bedoukian: *Selected Numismatic Studies of Paul Z. Bedoukian* (Los Angeles, 1981)

D. Kouymjian: 'Islamic Metalwork with Armenian Inscriptions', *Islamic Metalwork from the Iranian World, 8th–18th Century*, ed. A. S. Melikian-Chirvani (London, 1982), appendix ii, pp. 403–6

K. Musheghian: *Dramakan shrjanarut'yune Hayastanum (M.t'.a. V d–m.t'. XIV d.)* [Monetary circulation in Armenia (5th century BC–14th century AD)] (Erevan, 1983)

Y. Nercessian: *Armenian Numismatic Bibliography and Literature* (Los Angeles, 1984)

D. Kouymjian: *The Arts of Armenia (Accompanied by a Collection of 300 Slides in Color)* (Lisbon, 1992), pp. 49–54

4. TEXTILES, EMBROIDERY AND LACE. Despite a rich and ancient tradition, few serious studies of these Armenian art forms have been undertaken. Catalogues and complete inventories of the rich textile collections in the Armenian monasteries of Ēdjmiadzin, Jerusalem, Venice and Vienna are also lacking. Carbonized fragments of woven textiles have been found in excavations in Armenia, but they offer little information about design and style. Evidence for woven textiles before the 17th century is mainly derived from representations in monumental painting, sculptural reliefs, for example on the church of the Holy Cross (915–21) at AGHT'AMAR (see fig. 7 above), manuscript illustration and textile pieces used to hide the wood left exposed on the inside of most manuscript bindings from the 13th to the 17th centuries. The latter may be cotton, silk, linen or some other fabric, and have both woven and stamped patterns. Many are from cloth fashioned outside Armenia: Iran, India, Byzantium and the West. When fully published, they will provide invaluable evidence for the history of textiles in Armenia.

Almost all the comparatively large quantities of brocades, embroidery and other textiles surviving from the late 17th century onwards were used as church furnishings or vestments. The most important textiles in terms of size are the stamped and embroidered altar curtains (Ēdjmiadzin Cathedral, Sacristy; Jerusalem, Armen. Patriarch.). Most 18th-century examples are rich in colour and form and were produced in Madras, India, a major centre of stamped fabrics where Armenians had established themselves in the 16th century. Although these altar curtains have long Armenian inscriptions and purely Armenian designs, often depicting the *Life of St Grigor the Illuminator* and the conversion of Armenia to Christianity (314), they were probably manufactured by Indian workers using cartoons supplied by Armenian artists. Altar curtains produced in other centres include a stamped curtain (1663; Ēdjmiadzin Cathedral, Sacristy) from Suceava, Romania, with a central *Crucifixion* and an upper band devoted to the *Life of Christ*, two of dark blue cloth (1756 and late 18th century; Ēdjmiadzin Cathedral, Sacristy) both showing the *Crucifixion* and probably made in Tokat. Other curtains were made at Karin-Erzerum, Tbilisi, Lim on Lake Van and Constantinople.

Richly embroidered textiles have survived in much greater numbers than plain or printed textiles. These embroideries are mostly found on ecclesiastical vestments (e.g. chasubles, copes, mitres, stoles), altar curtains and chalice covers. Major collections with pieces from the 17th to the 20th century are housed in the Armenian monasteries of Ēdjmiadzin, Jerusalem, the Mechitarist monasteries on S Lazzaro, Venice, and in Vienna, and in Bzummar, Lebanon. Rich figural designs on silk, velvet, satins and less expensive materials are sewn in vivid colours, the most lavish employing gold and silver threads, pearls, other precious gems and hardstones. The astounding variety of designs and styles reveals an expert rendering of figures, garments and faces. The earliest surviving embroidery is a large 13th-century fragment from Ani showing a pair of asymmetrical lions (Erevan, Hist. Mus. Armenia). The most famous example is the ceremonial banner (1448; Ēdjmiadzin Cathedral, Sacristy) with full-length portraits of *St Grigor the Illuminator* flanked by *King Trdat III* (*reg* 287–98) and the female martyr *St Hrip'sime* (*d c.* 300) on one side and, on the reverse, *Christ Enthroned with the Symbols of the Evangelists* (see fig. 10).

Other outstanding embroideries (all Ēdjmiadzin Cathedral, unless indicated otherwise) include a cope (1601; Erevan, Hist. Mus. Armenia) showing *Christ Enthroned* with the symbols of the Evangelists; a crown (1651); a stole (1736); a series of shirt collars in the form of short stoles (1734) made of embroidered silver and gold thread on a red ground, the most elaborate of which depicts the *Last Supper* on the back and *St John the Baptist, Grigor the Illuminator and St James* on the front; the so-called eagle carpet of Catholicos Philippos (1651) made of silk embroidered with silver thread; and a chalice cloth (1688) with a central floral motif on a yellow ground with crosses and seraphim in the border. Several embroidered altar cloths also survive: one of 1613 from Karin-Erzerum shows St Grigor; another of 1619 (Jerusalem, Armen. Patriarch.) from Constantinople is on a rich emerald green ground with silver and gold thread and shows the *Virgin being Presented with the Head of St James* bordered by scenes from the *Life of Christ* (Jerusalem, Armen. Patriarch.); one of 1620 (Jerusalem, Armen. Patriarch.) from Constantinople has a monumental scene of the *Last Supper* bordered by scenes from the *Life of Christ*; one of 1704–14 from Constantinople shows *Christ, the Apostles, St Grigor and King Trdat*; and one of 1741 depicts *St Grigor's Vision of Christ.*

10. Enbroiderd processional banner showing *Christ Enthroned with the Symbols of the Evangelists*, 1448 (Ēdjmiadzin, Alex and Marie Manoogian Museum)

Embroidery was commonly used to decorate towels, bags, stockings, kerchiefs, tablecloths and various textiles. Some of the most renowned work was produced at Marash and is characterized by polychrome geometric and floral designs on dark or coloured backgrounds. The stitching follows various grid patterns, as well as designs based on star, cross and braided motifs. Many of the richly decorated elements on vestments were votive offerings donated by pilgrims.

Armenian lace is executed with a single needle using techniques passed down through many generations of women, although few pre-19th-century examples have survived. Different styles and stitches were developed in the various regions of Armenia, such as the Aintab stitch, Vaspurakan stitch, Baghesh (Bitlis) stitch and Kharpert stitch. Its delicacy and intricacy has long been recognized; early laces of silk and gold thread or decorated with pearls and precious gems, depicted in 17th-century miniatures, were used as chalice covers and as cross and Gospel holders; surviving examples are from the 17th century. Lace borders were often added to embroidered articles, while many scarves and kerchiefs were fringed with miniature lace flowers. Many scholars believe that the origin of Venetian lace-making, which was well established by the second half of the 16th century, should be sought in Armenia. The merchant cities of Italy were in close touch with Armenians during the late medieval period, so there was ample opportunity to import lace and lace-making techniques.

BIBLIOGRAPHY

L. Dournovo: *Armyanski naboki* [Armenian textiles] (Moscow, 1953)

B. Arak'elian: *K'aghak'nere ev arhestnere Hayasranum IX–XIII dd.* [Cities and crafts in Armenia, 9th–13th centuries], 2 vols (Erevan, 1958–64)

S. Davtyan: *Haykakan janyak* [Armenian lace] (Erevan, 1966)

——: *Haykakan Aseghnagorcoutiwn* [Armenian embroidery] (Erevan, 1972)

——: *Marashi Aseghnagorcoutiwne* [The embroidery of Marash] (Erevan, 1974) [with Eng. and Rus. summaries]

Z. R. Tarayan: *Naboïka v Armenii* [Armenian textiles] (Erevan, 1978)

B. Narkiss and M. E. Stone, eds: *Armenian Art Treasures of Jerusalem* (Jerusalem, Oxford and New Rochelle, NY, 1979)

Armenian Woven Art (exh. cat. by P. Bedoukian and V. Bedoukian; New York, Armenian Mus., 1980)

A. Odian Kasparian: *Armenian Needlelace and Embroidery* (McLean, VA, 1983)

Armenian Costumes through the Centuries (Fresno, CA, [1985])

D. Kouymjian: 'Les Tapis à inscriptions arméniennes', *Tapis et textiles arméniens*, ed. H. Kevorkian and B. Achdjian (Marseille, 1991), pp. 247–53

——: *The Arts of Armenia* (Lisbon, 1992), pp. 55–60

Armenien: Wiederentdeckung einer alten Kulturlandschaft (exh. cat., Bochum, Mus. Bochum, Kstsamml., 1995)

DICKRAN KOUYMJIAN

VII. Patronage and collecting.

Whenever relative political tranquillity prevailed in Armenia, the great feudal families—the Bagratuni, Ardsruni, Orbelian, Proshian and Zak'arian—took under their protection the monasteries situated on their estates and encouraged the work done there. They built religious edifices and educational centres, which they endowed with lands, properties and financial resources, as well as precious gifts. It was customary for the nobility to safeguard their holdings by offering them, either temporarily or in perpetuity, to monastic institutions, whose tax exempt status was, in the main, honoured by the conquerors. The transfer of property ownership was frequently inscribed upon the walls of the churches in the presence of witnesses, the text of the inscription emphasizing that the grant had been made free from all tax obligations. The GOSPELS OF QUEEN MLK'E were offered to the monastery of Varag in the province of Vaspurakan at the beginning of the 10th century AD. In 989 King Smbat II (*reg* 977–89) invited the architect Trdat to ANI to build the cathedral (989–1001). The 10th-century historian Thomas Ardsruni described in great detail the churches and palaces built by King Gagik (*reg* 908–36) including the palatine church of the Holy Cross (915–21; *see* ARMENIA, fig. 7) built by the architect Manuel on the island of AGHT'AMAR. The east façade of the church of the Saviour at Sanahin (*see* SANAHIN MONASTERY), erected by King Ashot III (*reg* 952–77) and Queen Khosrovanush in 966–72, is decorated with the portraits in high relief of their two sons Gurgen and Smbat holding a model of the church. The library at Sanahin was founded by Queen Hranush in 1063, and although originally it may have been to house relics, its collection of manuscripts became one of the largest in Armenia. Among the art treasures produced under Cilician royal patronage are such manuscripts as the Lectionary of King Het'um II (1286; Erevan, Matenadaran, Inst. Anc. Armen. MSS, MS. 979), the Gospels of Queen Keran (1272; Jerusalem, Gulbenkian Lib., MS. 2563), the Gospels of Prince Vasak (13th century; Jerusalem, Gulbenkian Lib., MS. 2568) and the Gospels of Queen Mariun (1346; Jerusalem, Gulbenkian Lib., MS. 1973), and the silver reliquary of Skevra (1293; St Petersburg, Hermitage).

The Catholicoses were just as active as were the influential members of the clergy in endowing the country with beautiful churches. Catholicos Nerses III (*reg* 641–61) was particularly diligent in this and was known as 'the builder'; his most elaborate foundation was undoubtedly the church of ZVART'NOTS. Patronage is closely connected with the concept of the Church as 'heaven on earth' as is evident in the many inscriptions on churches and in manuscripts derived from two verses in the Scriptures: Luke 10:20 and Hebrews 12:31. In his canons, Catholicos Sahak (*reg* 387–438) commented on both these verses and refers to the church as the meeting place of the faithful together with the first-born citizens of heaven whose names are written in the 'register of life'.

Some of the most distinguished art connoisseurs and collectors operating in the first half of the 20th century include the Armenians Calouste Sarkis Gulbenkian, Tigran Khan Kelekian (1868–1951), Harut'iwn Hazarian (1886–1981), Dr Paul Z. Bedoukian (*b* 1912) and Alex Manoogian (*b* 1901), all of whom were devoted to the recovery of the Armenian treasures, thus helping Armenians retain their identity as a national group.

BIBLIOGRAPHY

An Exhibition of Armenian Books: Early Printing, 1512–1700, from the Collection of Dr. P. Z. Bedoukian (exh. cat. by P. Bedoukian and V. Bedoukian, Watertown, MA, Armen. Lib. & Mus., 1975)

Thirty Centuries of Armenian Metal Art: An Exhibition from the Collection of Dr. P. Z. Bedoukian (exh. cat. by P. Bedoukian and V. Bedoukian, New York, AGBU Gal., 1978)

P. J. de Azeredo: *Calouste Gulbenkian collectionneur* (Lisbon, 1979)

Armenian Woven Art: An Exhibition from the Collection of Dr Paul Z. Bedoukian (exh. cat. by P. Bedoukian and V. Bedoukian, New York, AGBU Gal., 1980)

Armenian Ceramic Art: An Exhibition from the Collection of Tina and H. Hazarian and Dr Paul Z. Bedoukian (exh. cat. by P. Bedoukian and V. Bedoukian, Watertown, MA, Armen. Lib. & Mus., 1982)

Catalogue Fundação Calouste Gulbenkian (Lisbon, 1982)

A. T. Gregorian and J. Gregorian-Hampshire: *Armenian Rugs from the Gregorian Collection* (Cambridge, MA, 1987)

VIII. Museums and institutions.

Medieval museums in Armenia were divided into three categories—royal, princely and monastic—and were called *ganjatun* or *avandatun* ('treasury'). The 7th-century historian Hovhannēs Drasxanakertc'i testified that under Catholicos Movsēs Eghivardec'i (*reg* 574–604) the author Vrt'anes K'ert'ogh (550–620) was the *avandapah* of the catholicate's museum. This role corresponds to that of a curator in a modern museum. The monasteries of Sanahin, Haghpat, Ēdjmiadzin and Tat'ev each had a *ganjatun* or *avandatun* that housed their art treasures.

In modern times museums were founded by Khatchatur Abovyan (1809–48) in the provincial school, Erevan, in 1846, Khrimian Hayrik (1820–1907) in the monastery of Varag, Vaspurakan, in 1858 and Vahan Bastamyan in the monastery of St Gayanē, Ēdjmiadzin, in 1872. In 1869 Catholicos Gevorg IV (*reg* 1866–82) built a sacristy of three galleries adjoining the east side of Ēdjmiadzin Cathedral to house its treasury; the basement preserves the site of a Zoroastrian fire altar. In 1982 the Alex and Marie Manoogian Treasury Museum was built near the residence of the Catholicos at Ēdjmiadzin for the display of Armenian religious objects including relics, chalices, crosses, staffs, fans, reliquaries, carpets, embroidered vestments and altar curtains. Treasury museums also exist in the Armenian Patriarchate of St James at Jerusalem, the Armenian Catholicate of Cilicia at Antilias (Lebanon), the Armenian Patriarchate in Istanbul, the Armenian Monasteries in Venice (1717) and Vienna (1811), and All Saviour's Armenian Cathedral (1906) in Isfahan.

In 1921 the artists of Erevan and the Armenian Cultural Society of Tbilisi organized an exhibition of paintings, most of which were purchased by the Armenian government on 20 August 1921 and became the core of the State Historical Museum of Erevan. In 1921–2 the Ethnographic Society of Tbilisi founded in 1895 by Ervand Lalayan (1864–1931) transferred its museum and library to Erevan, thus forming the archaeological and ethnographic departments of the State Historical Museum. The finds made by N. Marr and T. T'oramanyan during excavations at ANI 1892–3 and 1904–17 were deposited in the Ani Treasury (*Anii hnadaranē*; destr. 1918), from which 2344 items were salvaged and deposited in the State Museum by 1926. By 1936 the museum had departments of history, archaeology, ethnography, arts and letters. The arts department grew to such an extent that it was transformed into a separate museum and from 1947 was known as the State Gallery of Armenia; in 1991 it was renamed the National Gallery of Armenia. Its collection contains more than 20,000 Armenian, Russian and west European works. In 1937 part of the State Museum's ethnographic material was transferred to the Museum of the Ethnography of Armenia in Sardarapat. In 1954 the State Museum's sections on literature, theatre, music and fine art were separated to form the Museum of Literature and Art in Erevan, which holds 600 manuscripts by Armenian writers, as well as the private archives of actors, musicians and composers.

In 1914 the collection of manuscripts (begun in the 5th century AD) from the Catholicate of Ēdjmiadzin was transferred to Moscow for safekeeping against the Turkish threat. Under the supervision of the newly created State Cultural Historical Institution the collection was returned to Ēdjmiadzin in 1921 together with the manuscript collection of the Lazarian Institute (1802) in Moscow. These collections were enriched by the historian and art critic Ervand Shahaziz (1856–1951) with the addition of the manuscript collection from the Armenian Museum in Naxijevan, Azerbaijan. In 1939 the manuscripts were moved to the Alexander Myasnikyan Public Library in Erevan (founded 1832; renamed National Library of Armenia, 1990) and remained there until 1959 when they were deposited in the Matenadaran Library of Ancient Manuscripts (now Matenadaran Institute of Ancient Armenian Manuscripts) built by MARK GRIGORYAN. The collection holds 16,089 manuscripts of which 13,623 are in Armenian and 2466 in other languages. Erevan's other major library is the Central Library of the Academy of Sciences of Armenia which was established in 1935.

Other museums in Erevan are the Martiros Saryan Gallery (1967), the Children's Art Gallery (1970) and the Erebuni Urartian Citadel, which was excavated in the 1950s and turned into a museum in 1968. Museums outside Armenia include the Musée Arménien de France in Paris, which was established by the Fondation Nourhan Fringhian, the Armenian Library and Museum of America, Watertown, MA, and the Alex and Marie Manoogian Museum (1992) in Detroit, Michigan.

BIBLIOGRAPHY

K. Ghafadaryan, ed.: *Ughec'uyc' Hayastani Petakan Patmakan T'angarani* [Guide to the State History Museum of Armenia] (Erevan, 1961)

G. W. Abgaryan: *The Matenadaran* (Erevan, 1962)

G. Aznavuryan, ed.: *Ughec'uyc' grakanut'yan ev arvesti tB±R angarani grakan fonderi* [Guide to the literary archives in the Museum of Literature and Art] (Erevan, 1962)

K. Ghafadaryan: 'Hayastani Petakan Patmakan T'angaranĕ' [The State History Museum of Armenia], *Patma Banasirakan Handes*, ii (1962), pp. 207–15

J. Carswell: *New Julfa: The Armenian Churches and Other Buildings* (Oxford, 1968)

J. Carswell and C. J. F. Dowsett: *Kutuhya Tiles and Pottery from the Armenian Cathedral of St James, Jerusalem*, 2 vols (Oxford, 1972)

K. Ghafadaryan: 'Hayastani thangaranneri patmut'yunic' [From the history of the museums in Armenia], *Lraber Hasasrakakan gitut'yunneri*, x (1972), pp. 20–35

G. A. Madoyan: *E. Tcharenc'i anvan grakanut'yan ev arvest t'angaran* [The Museum of Literature and Art named after E. Tcharanc'] (Erevan, 1972)

N. Mazmanian, ed.: *The Art Gallery of Armenia* (Leningrad, 1975)

B. Narkiss, ed.: *Armenian Art Treasures of Jerusalem* (Oxford, 1980)

M. Ghazaryan, ed.: *Treasures of Etchmiadzin* (Ēdjmiadzin, 1984)

S. Der Nersessian and A. Mekhitarian: *Armenian Miniatures from Isfahan* (Brussels, 1986)

Hayastani Azgayin Patkerasrah, Galerie Nationale d'Arménie, National Gallery of Armenia, Friends of the Museums of Armenia (Paris, 1992)

VREJ NERSESSIAN

Armenini, Giovanni Battista (*b* Faenza, *c.* 1525; *d* Faenza, April 1609). Italian painter and writer. He probably began his apprenticeship at Faenza and at the beginning of the 1550s settled in Rome, where he worked as a copyist of ancient and modern works. Around 1556 he made a series of journeys across Italy before settling in Faenza in 1564, where he took orders. Of his artistic works, which he himself held in low esteem, we know only an *Ascension of the Virgin* (Faenza, Pin. Com.) and a few leaves from an album of drawings, dating from the 1550s, which show Raphael's Logge. His most important contribution to the history of art is his treatise entitled *De' veri precetti della pittura* (1587).

With this book Armenini wished to revive painting, which he felt had declined. He attributed its downfall to three main causes: the indifference of the great masters of the early 16th century to teaching, the lack of artists of sufficient stature to succeed them and a general depreciation of the art of painting. The *De' veri precetti* takes these three factors as its starting-point. The aim of the work is not only to prove the nobility of painting, but also to lay the foundations of a training designed to encourage new talents to develop. The text is divided into three books: the first two examine the practical aspects of painting while the third treats of iconography and ends with some reflections on the perfect painter.

Armenini defined painting as the imitation of nature. He subdivided it into five main parts, *disegno*, *lume*, *ombra*, *colorito* and *componimento*. *Disegno*, or the power to conceive an idea visually, relies on the mastery of all the technical means that make possible the immediate expression and the gradual realization of an image. It cannot be dissociated from *buona maniera* and *invenzione*. The first is acquired gradually through the daily practice of drawing; the second is concerned with the organization of a composition and of each of its figures. It results from constant intellectual activity stimulated by the practice of sketching and observation. *Lume* and *ombra* mean relief as indicated by variations of natural and artificial light. The chapter on *colorito* treats at length of pigments and their properties in the three main techniques of painting (oil, fresco and *a secco*). Finally, *componimento*, which is reminiscent of Alberti's *historia* (*see* ALBERTI, LEON BATTISTA, §I, 2), brings all these aspects together. It is presented as the ultimate fusion wherein all the elements of the pictorial vocabulary converge towards the appropriate and personal expression of a given subject. To his treatment of these five aspects of painting, Armenini adds comments on foreshortening, perspective, proportions, anatomy, making brushes and preparing grounds. The third book of *De' veri precetti* concentrates on iconography and surveys the subjects that are suitable for both sacred and secular use for churches, chapels, libraries, refectories, palaces, loggias, studies, façades, villas and gardens.

The sources of Armenini's treatise, the first drafts of which date from the author's stay in Rome, are to be found in the most important texts on art of the Renaissance (by Alberti, Vasari, Paolo Pino, Lodovico Dolce, Sebastiano Serlio). Yet it is based on experience and oriented towards training, and the author's constant insistence on the necessity of a practical knowledge of the art means that he avoids dogmatic theory. The work's didactic intent links it to the first academies of art, founded in Rome, Florence and Bologna at the same period (*see* ACADEMY). Despite its limited influence (there were only four editions before the 19th century), *De' veri precetti* therefore constitutes one of the most complete accounts of 16th-century art.

WRITINGS

De' veri precetti della pittura (Ravenna, 1587/*R* New York, 1971; Eng. trans., New York, 1977, with annotated bibliog.)

BIBLIOGRAPHY

DBI

L. Grassi: 'G. B. Armenino e alcuni motivi della storiografia artistica del cinquecento', *L'Arte*, n. s., xviii (1948), pp. 40–54

A. C. Ferretti, ed.: *Dipinti d'altare in età di Controriforma in Romagna* (Bologna, 1982), pp. 6–9

B. F. Davidson: 'The Landscapes of the Vatican Logge from the Reign of Pope Julius III', *A. Bull.*, lv (1983), pp. 587–602

FRANÇOIS QUIVIGER

Armitage, Edward (*b* London, 20 May 1817; *d* Tunbridge Wells, Kent, 24 May 1896). English painter. He came from a wealthy Leeds family owning estates and coal mines. Private means enabled him to study in Paris at the Ecole des Beaux-Arts under Paul Delaroche from 1835 to 1842. He gained valuable experience assisting Delaroche on the decoration of the hemicycle at the Ecole, adopting his master's correct style of drawing. His first exhibit at the Salon was *Prometheus Unbound* (*c.* 1842; untraced), described by a contemporary critic as 'well drawn but brutally energetic'. On his return to England Armitage won a premium for his cartoon *Caesar's First Invasion of Britain* (*c.* 1843) in the competition to decorate the new Houses of Parliament. Subsequently he carried out two frescoes (now in poor condition) in the House of Lords: *The Personification of the Thames* from Pope and *The Death of Marmion* from Scott. In 1847 Queen Victoria purchased his painting *The Battle of the Meeanee* (1847; London, St James's Pal., Royal Col.). Apart from classical and biblical subjects, Armitage painted some contemporary events from the Crimean War and also the strikingly large *Retribution* (2.67×2.89 m, 1858; Leeds, C.A.G.), an allegory depicting the suppression of the Indian Mutiny of 1857. Armitage was elected ARA in 1867, RA in 1872 and professor and lecturer in painting in 1875. His lectures on painting, published in 1883, placed history painting at the summit of art. This ideal he followed in his own full-scale compositions, correctly drawn, with a fine sense of colouring. He was well placed to paint scenes of Empire but never quite realized his early potential in the hierarchy of late Victorian artists.

WRITINGS

Lectures on Painting, Delivered to the Students of the Royal Academy (London, 1883)

BIBLIOGRAPHY

Pictures and Drawings Selected from the Works of Edward Armitage (exh. cat., ed. J. P. Richter; London, RA, 1898)

T. S. R. Boase: 'The Decoration of the New Palace of Westminster 1841–1863', *J. Warb. & Court. Inst.*, xvii (1954), pp. 319–58

A. Robertson: 'Three Paintings by Edward Armitage RA', *Leeds A. Cal.*, lxix (1971), pp. 29–32

ALEXANDER ROBERTSON

Armitage, Kenneth (*b* Leeds, 18 July 1916). English sculptor. He attended Leeds College of Art (1934–7) and won a scholarship to study at the Slade School of Fine Art, London (1937–9). In World War II he served in the British Army, and between 1946 and 1956 he was head of the sculpture department at the Bath Academy of Art, Corsham, Wilts; he also held a Gregory Fellowship in sculpture at Leeds University in 1953–5. Armitage's first works were carved in stone, in emulation of Henry Moore and Barbara Hepworth, but in the post-war years he modelled with plaster on metal armatures, then cast in bronze. He first attracted international attention as one of a group of young British sculptors, including Reg Butler, Lynn Chadwick, Eduardo Paolozzi and William Turnbull, who showed at the 26th Venice Biennale in 1952 and whose work signalled a new, anti-monumental, expressionist approach. Armitage's preoccupation was with the human figure, combined with an interest in vertical and horizontal structure. He created small-scale figures, full of droll humour, with broad, flattened bodies, pinheads and sprouting, stick-like limbs. Descended from the figures of Giacometti and Picasso, they gesture, stroll, link arms, roll on their backs or simply sit. His groups sometimes appear to 'move' in unison on spindly legs, which protrude from the screen-like planes of their joined clothing, as in *People in the Wind* (bronze, h. 652 mm, 1951; Venice, Guggenheim) or *Family Going for a Walk* (bronze, h. 740 mm, 1951; New York, MOMA). The hieratic, frieze-like aspect of his work was also developed in such sculptures as *Diarchy* (bronze, 1.71×1.09×1.0 m, 1957; London, Tate). Armitage's first solo exhibitions were held at Gimpel Fils Ltd, London (1952), and at the Bertha Schaefer Gallery, New York (1954). In 1955–7 he changed to working in clay, and in the 1960s he employed wax, resins and aluminium, and his pieces became darker in mood and more abstract. In the late 1960s and early 1970s he made a series of disembodied limbs (e.g. *Both Arms*, bronze, h. 2.35 m, 1969; Hakone-machi, Hakone Open-Air Mus.) and 'furniture-figures'. He also experimented with drawn, screen-printed and photographic figural images on three-dimensional surfaces (e.g. *Folding Screen*, 1972; U. Nottingham A.G.). Between 1975 and 1986 he moved from the figure to nature in his series of sculptures and drawings of oak trees in Richmond Park, London.

BIBLIOGRAPHY

N. Lynton: *Kenneth Armitage* (London, 1962)

C. Spencer: *Kenneth Armitage* (London, 1973)

British Sculpture in the Twentieth Century (exh. cat., ed. S. Nairne and N. Serota; London, Whitechapel A.G., 1981–2), pp. 124–33, 248

Armleder, John (*b* Geneva, 24 June 1948). Swiss draughtsman, performance artist, painter and sculptor. He studied at the Ecole des Beaux-Arts, Geneva (1966–7) and at the Glamorgan Summer School, Britain (1969). Armleder is known primarily for his involvement with

Fluxus during the 1960s and 1970s, which included performances, installations and collective activities. He was a member of the Groupe Luc Bois, based in Geneva in 1963. In 1969, with Patrick Lucchini and Claude Rychner, he was a founder-member of the Groupe Ecart, Geneva, from which stemmed the Galerie Ecart (1973) and its associated performance group (1974) and publications. Armleder's first exhibition was at the Galerie Ecart in 1973, followed in the same year by one at the Palais de l'Athénée, Geneva. The anti-establishment and anti-formalist philosophy of the Fluxus groups continued in Armleder's mixed-media works of later years, which include the *Furniture Sculpture* of the 1980s. In works that couple objects (second-hand or new) with abstract paintings executed by Armleder himself, and which often refer ironically to earlier modernist abstract examples, he questioned the context in which art is placed and the notion of authenticity in art. Such concerns continued to appear in his work. Armleder's *Pour Paintings* (exh. 1992, Utrecht, Cent. Mus.) are commonly seen in conjunction with his mixed-media works. His work is in the collections of the Kunstmuseum, Basle, the Musée d'Art et d'Histoire, Geneva, and the Musée de Grenoble.

WRITINGS

Lézards sauvages (Geneva, 1973)

BIBLIOGRAPHY

John Armleder: Paintings & Furniture Sculpture (exh. cat., essay by S. Morgan, London, Lisson Gal., 1986)

John M. Armleder: Furniture Sculpture, 1980–90 (exh. cat., Geneva, Mus. Rath, 1990)

John M. Armleder: Pour Paintings (exh. cat., ed. M. Bosma; Utrecht, Cent. Mus., 1992) [Dut. and Eng. text]

□

Armory. *See* HERALDRY.

Armory Show [International Exhibition of Modern Art]. Exhibition of art held between 17 February and 15 March 1913 in New York at the 69th Regiment Armory, Lexington Avenue, Manhattan, from which it derived its nickname. The exhibition then travelled to the Art Institute of Chicago (24 March–16 April) and Copley Hall, Boston (28 April–19 May). Its importance was primarily as the first large-scale show of European modern art held in the USA (*see* UNITED STATES OF AMERICA, §III, 3), although two thirds of the 1300 works were by American artists. It resulted from the independent campaign of the Association of American Painters and Sculptors, a group of progressive artists formed in 1912 to oppose the National Academy of Design. Arthur B. Davies, the President of the group, and Walt Kuhn (1877–1949) were determined to present an international survey for the first in what was to have been a series of exhibitions. The Armory Show was modelled on the *Sonderbund* exhibition in Cologne (1912) and on the two Post-Impressionist exhibitions organized by Roger Fry in London. In 1912 Kuhn travelled to Cologne, The Hague, Amsterdam, Berlin and Munich to make selections and was joined by Davies in Paris and London. Assisted in Paris by Walter Pach, they succeeded in borrowing significant examples of Impressionism, Post-Impressionism, Fauvism and Cubism from leading European artists and dealers.

The organizers attempted in the Armory Show to trace the development of modern art movements from the 19th century to contemporary work. Selections ranged from Jean-Auguste-Dominique Ingres to Post-Impressionists such as Paul Cézanne, Paul Gauguin and Vincent van Gogh, as well as Picasso, Georges Braque, Henri Matisse, Vasily Kandinsky and Marcel Duchamp. The European section of the exhibition reflected Davies's preference for French art. German Expressionism was not adequately represented, and the Italian Futurists refused to participate. American entries ranged from the late Impressionism of Childe Hassam to the Ashcan realism of John Sloan and the Post-Impressionist modernism of Arthur B. Carles, Alfred H. Maurer and Joseph Stella.

The publicity campaign for the exhibition ensured that modern art reached a broad public. Aided by the journalist Frederick James Gregg, the organizers produced posters, badges, postcards and educational brochures. They adopted the pine-tree flag from the American Revolution as their emblem and 'The New Spirit' as their motto. Around 300,000 people attended the exhibition during its three-city tour. Revenues from the sale of works amounted to £44,148.75. The Metropolitan Museum of Art acquired Cézanne's *The Poorhouse on the Hill* for £6700. Despite its success, the Association of American Painters and Sculptors did not survive to sponsor other exhibitions.

Although the Armory Show was not the first exhibition of modern art in the USA, it was unmatched in its scope and significance. With galleries and collectors of modern art flourishing in its wake it transformed the art market in New York and thereby marked the advent of modernism in the USA.

BIBLIOGRAPHY

Association of American Painters and Sculptors: *For and Against: Anthology of Commentary on the Armory Show* (New York, 1913)

A. & Déc., iii (March 1913) [special issue]

Armory Show: 50th Anniversary Exhibition, 1913–1963 (exh. cat., Utica, NY, Munson–Williams–Proctor Inst., 1963)

M. Brown: *The Story of the Armory Show* (New York, 1963, rev. 1988)

The Armory Show: International Exhibition of Modern Art, 3 vols (New York, 1972) [anthol. of primary doc.]

J. Zilczer: '"The World's New Art Center": Modern Art Exhibitions in New York City, 1913–1918', *Archv Amer. A. J.*, xvi/3 (1974), pp. 2–7

R. Tarbell: 'The Impact of the Armory Show on American Sculpture', *Archv Amer. A. J.*, xviii/2 (1978), pp. 2–11

J. Zilczer: 'The Armory Show and the American Avant-garde: A Re-evaluation', *A. Mag.*, liii/1 (1978), pp. 126–30

G. McCoy, ed.: 'The Seventy-fifth Anniversary of the Armory Show', *Archv Amer. A. J.*, xxvii/2 (1987), pp. 2–33

M. Green: *New York, 1913: The Armory Show and the Paterson Strike Pageant* (New York, 1988)

JUDITH ZILCZER

Arms and armour. Military equipment. The study of arms and armour falls between that of the fine and decorative arts and that of technology, between scholarship catered for by a few museums (and almost no universities) and the self-taught collector and dealer. Although it is usually regarded as a highly specialist discipline, it covers every period of history and all cultures throughout the world. The history of arms and armour is one of continual development, characterized by the evolution of forms not from the simplest to the most complex but towards those most appropriate to the rapidly changing nature of warfare; there has been constant competition between the armour-maker and the weapon-maker, the one continually nullifying an advantage gained by the other through technological advances.

The historical survey in this article covers European arms and armour. The development of arms and armour elsewhere is discussed under 'Other arts' in individual culture and civilization surveys in this dictionary.

I. Introduction. II. Europe.

I. Introduction.

1. Terminology. 2. Types and materials. 3. Sources and collections. 4. Antiquarianism and historiography.

1. TERMINOLOGY. The terminology used to describe arms and armour is one of the reasons why the discipline is often inaccessible for the non-specialist. This is partly because there is a great deal of specialist vocabulary, much of it in the language of origin of the type of arms and armour, as seen particularly in the case of Japanese armour and weapons (*see* JAPAN, §XVI, 1), the study of which is rendered more difficult by the use of Japanese terms alone, without translation, in most publications. There is no single, accepted and published system of controlled vocabulary for anything other than Japanese material, and many older publications use terminology differing wildly from the current standard. The vocabularies used are so extensive that it would be useless to try to enumerate them in this introductory essay, and the detailed articles below provide examples of the current orthodoxy in the study of European arms and armour. In general, however, scholars attempt to describe a piece of armour or a weapon with the term by which it was known at the time of its use. In the study of European material this has been complicated by several factors, one being the inconsistency of contemporary users, both in terminology and in orthography. The term for the head defence of a horse, for example, has undergone many changes in spelling: from cheveronne, shawfron, shamfron, chaufrayne, chaufrain, shaffron, chieffront, chaufrain, shafferoon, shafrone (all examples from the period of use) to chamfron, chamfrain, champfrein, and more recently to chanfron (some of which, at least, are misreadings of MSS). The current standard version is shaffron, which seems to have been the most popular spelling among military writers in England during the 16th century. In general the various publications by Claude Blair can be taken to express the current terminological orthodoxy at the time of writing.

2. TYPES AND MATERIALS. The practical nature of arms and armour means that materials and applications have been fairly uniform across the world. Weapons can be divided into two groups: hand-to-hand and projectile. Hand-to-hand or *mêlée* weapons can be divided into concussive and cutting or thrusting (i.e. edged) weapons. The first group comprises only maces and hammers. Cutting weapons include swords (many of which were also designed for thrusting) and daggers, axes and a complex array of weapons wielded in two hands, for example such staff-weapons as halberds and glaives. Despite the importance afforded to swords in the study of arms and armour, they were usually carried as secondary weapons. Thrusting weapons include various different types of spears, including the pike, wielded by the infantry with two hands, and the lance. The latter term is usually applied to heavy spears used by mounted troops, though it originates in the Roman *lancea*, a short, light, throwing or thrusting spear used by cavalry or infantry. The group also includes the bayonet, used to convert the firearm into a *mêlée* weapon.

Projectile (or missile) weapons fall into two groups: those propelled by hand, for example stones, knives and spears or javelins, and those propelled by other means. A small group of weapons in which the power of the throwing arm is enhanced by direct leverage, as in the sling, falls between the two. Among the second main group of projectile weapons are bows, in which kinetic energy is built up quite slowly, stored in a set of levers until the moment of release, then transmitted quickly through the bowstring to the missile. This group includes crossbows, in which manual power is not used directly to draw back the bowstring, and the catapults or ballistae commonly used in the ancient world. The most important group of projectile weapons are firearms, in which a charge of gunpowder or other propellant is used to release the missile.

The primary purpose of armour for protection means that its development has been closely related to that of weapons. There is a series of priorities in the use of armour: head wounds are the most disabling, the next being thoracic injuries; the lowest proportion of disabling wounds occurs on the limbs and other parts of the body. Thus there is a natural hierarchy of protection: head, body, limbs. In the wearing of armour the relationship between cost, protection and mobility must be taken into account, since the more armour of any type that is worn, the more the wearer will be impeded in movement, and the more time and cost will have been spent on its production. Armour is generally made of metal, but fabrics, wood and leather have also been used.

Metal armour can be classified according to metal and technique. The most common metals used were copper alloys and iron or steel, the latter group universally displacing the former as soon as was technically possible within a culture. There are four main techniques for metal armour: mail, scale, lamellar or laced plate and plate. In mail defences a flexible mesh of interlocked links of wire is produced and is always used in conjunction with a padded or quilted fabric garment underneath. Scale defences are characterized by the use of small metal plates pierced along their upper and side edges with holes for attachment to each other or more commonly to a fabric lining; this type of armour is readily identifiable by the feature of the scales overlapping downwards. Lamellar defences, which characteristically overlap upwards, are made by lacing together horizontally long, thin plates of metal or hardened leather, pierced with numerous pairs of holes, into flexible strips and then vertically into complete garments, which might or might not be lined. These three types are defences with a degree of flexibility inherent in their construction and function, relying for their operation on the dissipation of the kinetic energy of an impacting weapon. Plate defences, on the other hand, have smooth, rigid surfaces that deflect or simply stop an impacting weapon. The flexibility for parts of the body that need to move is supplied by the use of narrow plates (lames), which are articulated together by rivets or by internal leathers.

In general, metal defences fall within quite well-defined weight ranges, head defences usually weighing about 2.5 kg, while the weight of body defences ranges from about 7 kg for a mail shirt to about 27 kg for a complete field armour of steel plate (although some armours intended for special functions, usually for sieges or for the tournament, where the usual mobility was unnecessary, could weigh up to 48 kg). One prevalent idea in ill-informed literature suggests that a man in complete plate armour was incapable of mounting his horse, save with the aid of a crane or some other form of hoist, because of the weight of his armour, and that once fallen to the ground he was unable to stand again unassisted. It is clear from contemporary sources, however, that men-at-arms were able to vault fully armed into the saddle without even using their stirrups, and experiment has shown that a man wearing complete armour can comfortably walk, run, fall down and stand up again.

It is perhaps because of the importance of warfare in human history and the high status of the warrior in most societies that weapons and armour have from the earliest times been decorated, often with highly valuable materials, including precious metals and precious gemstones. In many societies the cost and beauty of a warrior's equipment were a necessary adjunct to his status as a king or leader. Some armours, with decoration designed or executed by the most prominent craftsmen, were of such exquisite workmanship that they were not intended for any actual use other than in a parade, though such examples are relatively rare. Throughout history arms and armour have also been at the forefront of technological development. The screw, for example, was probably first used in Europe as a method of fastening together plates on jousting armours made for the court of the Holy Roman Emperor Maximilian I, and etching was used as a method of sword and armour decoration before it became a printing medium.

Advances in scientific analysis, which have revolutionized dating in an archaeological context, have had very little impact on the study of arms and armour. The main reason for this is that most of the material concerned is made of iron or steel, on which few of the available methods of non-destructive analysis have any useful application. The use of X-radiography, X-ray fluorescence analysis and similar techniques has, however, provided a certain amount of information, particularly in the analysis of wrought-iron cannon and of pattern-welded sword blades. Connoisseurship has, in general, remained the most important aspect of the discipline, though as in any other area of the arts, attribution of arms and armour remains a matter of scholarly consensus rather than one of fact.

3. SOURCES AND COLLECTIONS. The quantity of arms and armour from Europe that can be dated to before 1400 is very small, and scholarship relies on artistic representations and written accounts for information. Without actual objects for comparison, interpretation of these sources can be difficult. It is also necessary to note that the equipment illustrated is normally that of the period of execution of the work of art and not that of the period depicted. Thus most illustrations of battles of the Hundred Years War from Froissart provide useful material for the equipment used in the mid- to late 15th century but are unhelpful for the period of the war; similarly the latten effigy of *Richard Beauchamp, Earl of Warwick* (1382–1439) in the church of St Mary, Warwick, is very clearly of 1453, when it was cast, and does not depict any armour actually used by the Earl.

A large proportion of the surviving corpus of medieval and later European arms and armour comes from arsenals, either wholly or partly comprising material assembled at the time of its use. These range in size from national institutions, often incorporating royal collections, for example the Royal Armouries in the Tower of London, the Musée de l'Armée, Paris, the Real Armería, Madrid, and the Waffensammlung of the Kunsthistorisches Museum, Vienna, to town arsenals, for example the Landeszeughaus, Graz, and to such smaller family arsenals as that of the Counts Trapp at Schloss Churburg (Castello Coira) in the Italian Tyrol. Many arsenals have been lost, particularly the smaller family ones, through, for example, remodelling of a house at a time when arms were seen as inappropriate for interior decoration or by dispersal on the art market when such material was in demand.

Many surviving examples of arms and armour have also been retrieved through archaeology. The bulk of extant European material made before 1300 comes from archaeological sites, though the majority is the product of chance finds or tomb-robbing rather than scientific excavation. Several large finds have also contributed substantially to the surviving corpus of later periods, three important examples being the Wisby find of 14th-century armour (Stockholm, Nmus.), the Rhodes group of 15th- and early 16th-century armour from the garrison of the Knights of St John (New York, Met., and London, Tower) and the Chalkis find of early to mid-15th-century armour (Athens, N. Archaeol. Mus., and New York, Met.).

Religious contexts provide a third major source of arms and armour. From at least 1327 arms and armour of the deceased were set up over the tomb as an 'achievement', adjuncts to the heraldry of a dead knight. These groups of arms usually comprised the helmet, gauntlets, spurs, shield, sword and coat-armour. In a few instances, for example the achievement on the tomb of *Edward the Black Prince* (*d* 1376; Canterbury Cathedral), the whole group survives, but more commonly the helmet is the only surviving piece. Such survivals are numerous in England but less so in continental Europe, though the single largest corpus of 15th-century Italian armours survives at the sanctuary of S Madonna della Grazie at Curtatone, near Mantua.

In Japan (*see* JAPAN, §XVI, 1) many works survive for religious reasons, since, according to Shinto belief, the armour and the sword continue to be inhabited by the spirit of the warrior after his death and thus have been preserved and venerated over the centuries. Despite the fragility of the armours and the vulnerability of the swords to the hostile climate, more than 30 complete armours made before 1400 have been preserved in Japan (there being, in contrast, not one complete European example), and the number of early Japanese swords surviving in near perfect condition must run into hundreds. The main locations of such works are Shinto shrines, notably Itsukushima Shrine (Hiroshima Prefecture) and Oyamazumi Shrine (Ehime Prefecture).

Military conquest has formed an important means of moving historic arms and armours around the world. By far the largest single source of Islamic arms and armour (*see* ISLAMIC ART, §VIII, 1) was the great trophy set up in the Hagia Eirene just outside the Topkapı Saray in Istanbul as a monument to Ottoman victories, surviving intact until 1840. It formed the basis of the present armoury of the Topkapı Palace Museum and the Military Museum in Istanbul, as well as most of the European and American collections of Turkish arms and armour. The movement of material to and from Paris in the course of the Napoleonic Wars, together with the later purchase of the great European collections by American private collectors (e.g. the collection of Karl Otto von Kienbusch, now in Philadelphia, PA, Mus. A.) and public institutions (e.g. New York, Met.), have set scholars the most extraordinary puzzles of reunion and provenance tracing.

4. ANTIQUARIANISM AND HISTORIOGRAPHY. Of the cultures of the world, only the Japanese regarded armour and weapons, particularly the sword, as a subject for scholarship before the 18th century, partly because of the association through Shinto of the military equipment of earlier times with the souls of the heroes who used it. In Europe the study of historical arms and armour began in the 1780s with the work of Francis Grose and J. B. L. Carré and in the 1820s was placed on a more scholarly footing by SAMUEL RUSH MEYRICK. However, the nature of the trade in arms and armour, particularly in armour, militated against true academic study. In the 19th century, with the development of the Gothic Revival led by Sir Walter Scott, it became essential to complete the interior of a Gothic country house or castle with medieval armour (for illustration *see* SCOTT, WALTER; *see also* DISPLAY OF ART, §IX), the very material that was in the shortest supply. In order to satisfy this demand, complete 'composite' armours were constructed from surviving fragments of different original harnesses, and, from the early 19th century, additional elements were extensively modified and faked. The celebrated 'Fico' group, for example, contains eight full armours and the head defences (shaffrons) for seven horses; originally, however, there was a single armour, but its elements were divided between four of the present armours, the remaining elements of which were modified from heterogeneous original material or faked in Nuremberg *c.* 1805 (now dispersed between Philadelphia, Mus. A.; London, Tower; Brussels, Kon. Mus. Leger & Krijgsgesch.; Berlin, Mus. Dt. Gsch.; Kassel, Löwenburg; Worcester, MA, Higgins Armory Mus.; Nuremberg, Ger. Nmus.).

In addition to the composition of armours for interior decoration, the demand for medieval armour in the 19th century was met by faking entire works. The collection of 'early medieval' helms assembled by Lord Curzon (Robert Curzon, 14th Baron of Harringworth, 1810–73), at Parham House, W. Sussex, in the mid-19th century, comprising at its height some 50 helmets, was composed mainly of fakes, which had been produced for the dealer Samuel Luke Pratt of London and sold to Curzon as genuine objects. Such pieces frequently had elaborate provenances invented to emphasize their apparent authenticity. Although armour probably suffered most from this phenomenon, weapons, particularly swords, were also extensively faked in the 19th century. Nor was the phenomenon limited to England: the most notorious fakers, for example Anton Konrad (1879–1938) and Ernst Schmidt (*c.* 1875–1930), worked on the Continent.

The practical nature of the subject dictated that most of the important early scholars were amateurs and, quite frequently, collectors. Most of the published scholarship of the 19th century, however, was produced by writers with a great knowledge of artistic representations of their subject but little familiarity with the actual pieces, and many of the misunderstandings were the result of attempts to interpret directly what were, in fact, merely artistic conventions. Perhaps the best example of this is the attempt of William Burges and others to model the construction of mail on the representations of it in manuscripts and on sculpture, giving rise to the hypothetical 'banded mail', 'mascled mail' and various other types, none of which was ever produced in reality.

One of the first attempts at a scholarly approach was the *Exhibition of Helmets and Mail*, organized by the Baron C. A. de Cosson and William Burges in 1880. This exhibition brought together a wide variety of material, and it was examined on a constructional basis, revealing practical differences between bogus and real pieces. The process was taken further by the encyclopaedic *Record of European Arms and Armour* published by Guy Laking in the 1920s. In the USA the work of Bashford Dean and his successor Steven Grancsay at the Metropolitan Museum of Art, New York, was of considerable importance, as was that of Wendelin Boeheim and his successors Bruno Thomas and Ortwin Gamber at the Kunsthistorisches Museum in Vienna. In Britain the scholarly tradition of John Hewitt and Harold Arthur, 17th Viscount Dillon, was continued by Charles ffoulkes and Sir James Mann, while the expansion of museums after World War II enabled such professional scholars as Claude Blair and John Hayward to extend this tradition.

In Europe, edged weapons continued to be used long after they had ceased to be important weapons on the battlefield, both in the context of dress uniforms and, in a stylized form, in fencing. Scholarship on historic weapons did not parallel this continued use, and sword scholarship was previously as underdeveloped as that of armour. The major advances have appeared in relatively recent times, through such luminaries as Claude Blair, John Hayward, Heribert Seitz, A. V. B. Norman and Ewart Oakeshott.

The study of European firearms presents a very different story. Military and civilian training in shooting has produced a huge body of interest in both modern and historical guns, and the sporting tradition, focused on the gun-rooms of country houses, has continued unabated. Historic guns are the most widely collected of arms and armour, with by far the widest corpus of literature, both scholarly and popular, and with the best-informed collectors and scholars, at least in terms of their practical experience of shooting. The list of important scholars in this field is huge but must include Arne Hoff, Torsten Lenk, Nolfo di Carpegna and Howard Blackmore.

BIBLIOGRAPHY

F. Grose: *A Treatise on Ancient Armour and Weapons* (London, 1786)
J. B. L. Carré: *Panoplie* (Châlons-sur-Marne and Paris, 1795)
S. R. Meyrick: *A Critical Enquiry into Antient Armour* (London, 1824)
J. Hewitt: *Ancient Armour and Weapons in Europe* (London, 1855–60/R Graz, 1980)
E. E. Viollet-le-Duc: *Dictionnaire raisonné du mobilier français*, v–vi (Paris, 1874)
Baron C. A. de Cosson and W. Burges: 'Catalogue of the Exhibition of Ancient Helmets and Examples of Mail', *Archaeol. J.*, xxxvii (1881)
W. Boeheim: *Handbuch der Waffenkunde* (Leipzig, 1890)
C. ffoulkes: *The Armourer and his Craft* (London, 1912)
G. F. Laking: *A Record of European Armour and Arms through Seven Centuries*, 5 vols (London, 1920–22)
G. C. Stone: *A Glossary of the Construction, Decoration and Use of Arms and Armor* (Portland, ME, 1934)
B. Thordemann: *Armour from the Battle of Wisby, 1361*, 2 vols (Uppsala, 1939–40)
C. Blair: *European Armour* (London, 1958)
H. L. Blackmore: *British Military Firearms* (London, 1961)
C. Blair: *European and American Arms* (London, 1962)
J. Hayward: *The Art of the Gunmaker*, 2 vols (London, 1962, rev. 1965)
J. G. Mann: *European Arms and Armour*, Wallace cat. (London, 1962); suppl. by A. V. B. Norman (London, 1982)
J. F. Hayward and others: *The Kretzmar von Kienbusch Collection of Arms and Armor*, intro. by C. O. von Kienbusch (Princeton, 1963)
E. Oakeshott: *The Sword in the Age of Chivalry* (London, 1964)
H. Seitz: *Blankwaffen*, 2 vols (Brunswick, 1965–8)
A. Hoff: *Feuerwaffen*, 2 vols (Brunswick, 1969)
H. Nickel: *Ullstein Waffenbuch* (Frankfurt am Main, 1974)
B. Thomas: *Gesammelte Schriften zur historischen Waffenkunde* (Graz, 1977)
C. Blair and L. Tarrasuk: *The Complete Encyclopaedia of Arms and Armour* (London, 1982)
Arms and Armor: Collected Essays . . . from the Metropolitan Museum of Art Bulletin, 1920–64 (New York, 1984)
D. La Rocca: 'The Fico Armours: A Study in Connoisseurship and Secular Iconography', *J. Arms & Armour Soc.*, xiii/1 (1989), pp. 1–72

TOM RICHARDSON

II. Europe.

1. Edged weapons. 2. Projectile weapons. 3. Armour.

1. Edged weapons.

Edged weapons fall into two main categories, the first covering swords and daggers (including sheath-knives) and the second staff-weapons, or arms that consist of a blade mounted on a staff, usually of wood. From the art-historical point of view the two categories are almost indistinguishable, though staff-weapons were, on the whole, less frequently decorated than swords and daggers and very seldom so elaborately. The present entry therefore concentrates mainly on the more important first category, with the main emphasis on swords, since there are few technical or decorative differences between these and daggers.

(i) Before 1450. (ii) 1450–1630. (iii) After 1630.

(i) Before 1450.

All swords and daggers consist basically of a blade with a handle (grip), which may be an entirely separate feature attached to the blade but which is usually either formed as an extension of its upper end or, more commonly, built round such an extension. In addition, a guard for the hand may be formed or fitted at the point where the grip and top of the blade proper meet. This feature became normal from the Migration Period, as did the pommel, a shaped counterweight for the blade at the top of the handle. The whole assembly of guard, grip and pommel is now called the hilt. Until the end of the 15th century the guard was never more—and, in earlier periods, usually much less—than a simple cross-bar, either straight or arched, while the most popular blade form was straight and double-edged, though single-edged and curved swords were also used, the latter especially in Eastern Europe.

Because the outline of these weapons remained simple, the aesthetic qualities of swords and daggers dating from the Bronze Age until the end of the Middle Ages often have as much to do with form and proportion as with decoration. Bronze examples from the beginning of this period include the long slender 'rapiers' from Mycenae and Crete (*c.* 2000–1500 BC) and the leaf-shaped northern and central European swords of the period *c.* 1500–600 BC. Applied ornament of considerable sophistication had already appeared in Greece by the 2nd millennium BC. A well-known group of short-swords and daggers found in the shaft graves at Mycenae (*c.* 1600–1300 BC; Athens, N. Archaeol. Mus.; *see* MYCENAE, §4 and fig. 3) have blades inlaid in gold, silver and electrum with both figure scenes and geometric designs, and they originally had handles of organic material (wood, bone or ivory) with gold and silver mounts chased with foliate and geometric ornament. Applied ornament of this general kind, which did not interfere with function, was the norm on swords, daggers and their scabbards and other fittings until the end of the Middle Ages. In detail it followed current decorative styles, especially those of goldsmiths' work, since goldsmiths were often responsible for executing it. The technique of inlaying precious and other metals also continued to be used, but, until the Renaissance, apparently never with the level of sophistication found on the blades of the Mycenaean swords.

Iron swords were being made as early as the 11th century BC in Crete and Athens and therafter gradually came into general use in the Mediterranean countries. The Late Bronze Age–Early Iron Age HALLSTATT culture provides the earliest evidence of their manufacture north of the Alps about the 7th century BC. The Hallstatt swords were at first copied directly from the bronze ones, but, as it was realized that less iron was needed to produce the same effect, thinner blades began to be made. The tradition of the Bronze Age short-sword was continued by the Greeks and Romans, who mainly used short, stabbing swords, but the long sword, designed to be used from horseback or from a chariot, later became the most widely used type. The prototype of this was developed in or before the 2nd century BC by the swordsmiths of the Celtic LA TÈNE culture. Such hilts as have survived on these are plain, but the more elaborate scabbards, which are usually of copper alloy, are finely engraved with geometric, zoomorphic and cursive designs (*see* CELTIC ART, §II, 3 and fig. 1). Some of the blades also show the earliest form of pattern welding, the basis of which was a bar formed of iron and steel rods twisted and welded together to form patterns in the finished product (for further discussion of this technique *see* METAL, §V and fig. 12). Blades of this kind continued to be made until the 10th century AD or the early 11th and were much esteemed, though modern research has suggested that their functional qualities were no greater than those produced by more conventional methods.

The late Roman long cavalry sword, the *spatha*, was apparently derived directly from these La Tène swords and from it, during the Migration Period, evolved the straight, double-edged, cruciform sword that was the most characteristic 'knightly' weapon of the Middle Ages. An exceptionally rich example (London, BM) of its early form, with a short, straight cross-guard, found in the early 7th-century Anglo-Saxon SUTTON HOO ship burial, has a pattern-welded blade and gold mounts set with garnets and glass in the same technique as other objects from the same source. Other Anglo-Saxon and Viking swords of almost equal richness, with mounts of chased precious metal or fire-gilt bronze, inlaid with precious metal, have been found both in Britain and on the Continent, especially in Scandinavia.

1. Sword mounted in gold set with gemstones, German, l. 955 mm, 11th century (Essen, Münsterschatzmuseum)

The simple cruciform hilted sword remained in general use until the end of the Middle Ages, and its typological development during this period consisted merely of variations on this shape. Pommels and grips of hardstone or crystal are sometimes found, but decoration was mainly applied, and most of the techniques of the goldsmith—casting, chasing and enamelling—were used for this purpose. Surviving works from among the many rich examples mentioned in documents are rare but include an 11th-century sword (see fig. 1), the two imperial coronation swords (early 13th century; Vienna, Schatzkam.) and the swords of Sancho IV, King of Castile and León (*c.* 1284; Toledo Cathedral), Henry, Earl of Derby, later Henry IV, King of England (*c.* 1390–99; Dublin, City Hall; used since 1403 as the civic sword of Dublin), the Holy Roman Emperor Frederick III (1440–52; Vienna, Ksthist. Mus.) and Charles the Bold, 4th Duke of Burgundy (*c.* 1470; Vienna, Schatzkam.), of which the last has a hilt and scabbard of narwhal's horn mounted in enamelled gold. The sword of Sancho IV has an inscription on the blade that appears to be the earliest-known example of the use of etching, while the silver-gilt decoration on the sword of Henry IV is unique in England for its period in being attributable to a known goldsmith, Herman van Cleve. Similar decoration was applied to daggers, but since they often formed part of civil dress and were not required to be as functional as swords, their hilts tended to vary more in shape and were sometimes of carved ivory or boxwood.

(ii) 1450–1630. At the beginning of this period there was no dramatic change in the development of the sword, and the simple cruciform hilt remained the most widely used type until the early 16th century, its decoration being mostly applied, as before. A magnificent example is the sword (see fig. 2) of Duke Christopher of Bavaria (*d* 1493), of which the hilt and the scabbard-mounts are of silver-gilt, cast and chased with running Gothic foliage and with small figures in niches in the grip. Of equal magnificence are the highly distinctive, and now extremely rare, Hispano-Moresque swords, known as *espadas jinetas*, of which the best-known example (Madrid, Mus. Ejército) is that of Abu ʿAbdallah Muhammad XI ('Boabdil'; *reg* 1482–3), the last Nasrid king of Granada, on which the pommel- and scabbard-mounts are of silver-gilt with partly enamelled filigree ornament. Originally from the same source but also widely used in Christian Spain and, to a lesser extent, elsewhere, was the so-called 'ear-dagger', of which the distinguishing feature is a pommel formed of two ear-like lobes set at an angle to each other. An example (Madrid, Real Armería) formerly owned by Boabdil has a scabbard with mounts decorated in a similar manner to that of his sword.

The cruciform sword survived in regular use until the 17th century, and, for ceremonial purposes, until modern times. In the mid-15th century in Italy the first swords showing the influence of the Renaissance in their design were produced. An example is the hilt of the sword (Madrid, Real Armería) given to John II, King of Castile and León (*reg* 1406–54), by Pope Eugenius IV in 1446–7, the earliest surviving example of the papal swords that were presented annually to Christian rulers. By the beginning of the 16th century these swords had succumbed completely to Renaissance styles and were being fitted with silver-gilt hilts that were splendid, but quite impractical, pieces of goldsmiths' work, for example the hilt by the papal goldsmith Domenico da Sutri on the sword (Edinburgh Castle) presented in 1507 to James IV, King of Scotland (*reg* 1488–1513), by Pope Alexander VI and subsequently used as the Scottish Sword of State. By this date some Italian sculptors were working with the decoration of swords: a number of hilts survive with pommels involving or set with gilt-bronze plaquettes, while the gilt-bronze cruciform hilt of a sword (Turin, Arm. Reale) bearing a spurious Donatello signature is attributed to Andrea Riccio.

During the second half of the 15th century, again in Italy, blades decorated with fire-gilt etching appeared and became common by *c.* 1500. On the most elaborate specimens the etching consisted of Classical motifs and scenes, executed in fine lines, of the same general type as those found on other contemporary Italian works of art and often derived from the same graphic sources. It is probable that a number of artists were involved in decorating blades in this way. The style is, however, particularly associated with the artist whose signature, OPVS HERC(VLIS), appears in the decoration on the blade of a sword (Rome, Fond. Camillo Caetani) made for Cesare Borgia between 1493 and 1498 and also on a finely tooled leather sword sheath (Paris, Mus. Armée). The 19th-century identification of this Hercules with a goldsmith of Ferrara named Ercole dei Fedeli is no longer accepted, and he remains anonymous.

Another decorative technique used on blades (and armour) and introduced at the same period, probably in Germany, was *Goldschmelz*, whereby designs with broad gold surfaces were set against a blued background. The bluing was a natural—though controlled—result of the heating of the steel blade; the gold surface was produced by filling the shallowly etched designs with fire gilding. The technique is particularly associated with Hans Summersperger of Hall, Tyrol, who was supplying swords (Vienna, Schatzkam. and Ksthist. Mus.) to the Holy Roman Emperor Maximilian I in the 1490s.

The major development during this period was the introduction of the rapier, the civilian sword. During most of the Middle Ages a dagger was commonly worn with civilian dress, but a sword was not, except when travelling or on ceremonial occasions. From *c.* 1500, however, it was increasingly the practice, for some reason that has yet to be explained, for men to wear a sword as part of their everyday dress. By the 1520s this had become normal all over Europe, and, until the second half of the 18th century, the wearing of a sword came to be regarded as a badge of gentility. There is some evidence to suggest that the fashion for wearing a sword regularly with civilian dress had started in the Iberian Peninsula, probably as early as the 1430s, and it is reasonable to assume that the Spanish term *espada ropera* ('robe sword'), first recorded in 1468, refers to a sword used for this purpose. The term rapier, first recorded in a Scottish document of 1505, almost certainly derives from this, via the late 15th-century French *épée rapière.* The rapier was, therefore, essentially a civilian sword, though for reasons mentioned below, it has come to be regarded as specifically a sword designed for fencing. The general adoption of the rapier produced three important results. Firstly, it and the sword designed for use in warfare or the tournament began to follow separate, though mutually influential, lines of development. Secondly, the fact that gentlemen carried swords regularly meant that they might have to use them at short notice and also encouraged the practice of duelling; this stimulated the development of systems of fencing, which, in turn, affected the design of the rapier. Thirdly, for the same reason, the rapier become a dress accessory as well as a weapon, and in consequence many gentlemen demanded that it should be decorative as well as functional.

2. Sword of Duke Christopher of Bavaria, mounted in silver gilt, German, l. 1360 mm, *c.* 1480 (Munich, Residenz)

So long as the sword was chiefly used in battle in conjunction with armour, the simple cross-guard was adequate. In the late 14th century, however, as a result of the practice of hooking the forefinger over one arm (quillon) of the cross, a small semicircular guard was sometimes added at the base of one side of the blade. During the second half of the 15th century two such guards were introduced, to which, from the end of the 15th century, a curved knuckle-bar was sometimes added. The developments in fencing already mentioned, with the need to provide better protection for the unarmoured hand, led from about 1520 to the addition of further bars, both above and below the cross, so producing by about 1550 the complex guard, involving diagonal curved bars, to which the modern term 'swept hilt' is applied.

The early rapier was a rather cumbersome weapon, with a long, double-edged blade designed for slashing as well as thrusting. The fencing systems of the 16th century and the early 17th led to its employment mainly for attack, parrying being carried out with the left hand, which was either protected by a gauntlet or by a cloak wrapped round it, or which held a parrying-dagger (poignard). Such daggers normally had a simple cross-guard, often arched so that it could be used to trap an opponent's blade and also often fitted with a small, central side-ring.

Rapiers and daggers were normally made *en suite* as sets, while it is known from written records that the richer examples, which were, in effect, masculine jewellery, were often accompanied by alternative scabbards, girdles and hangers made to match different suits of clothing. Every technique and virtually every material known to the goldsmith and jeweller was used in the decoration of their hilts and mounts, some of which, under Mannerist influence, were highly impractical in shape, though the weapons remained functional in design. Decoration of this kind was not confined to rapiers and their accompanying daggers but was also applied to other forms of dagger, hunting-swords and what can only be described as 'parade' swords, worn on semi-theatrical occasions by rulers and their nobility and which by this period included a moderate number of curved sabres, a type derived from eastern Europe. Staff-weapons, notably those carried by princely bodyguards, also became more decorative, although, apart from trimmings on the staff, the decoration was normally confined to etched designs, often gilt, on the blade.

Very few examples of the richest of these swords survive outside the remaining armouries of European princely houses, among which the Austrian imperial armoury (Vienna, Ksthist. Mus.) and that of the Electors and kings of Saxony (Dresden, Hist. Mus.) are outstanding. The most splendid example is the Spanish or Italian rapier (see fig. 3) with an enamelled gold hilt, presented to the future Emperor Maximilian II about 1550, but equal in quality, if perhaps not in design, are the rapier and dagger (Dresden, Hist. Mus.), with enamelled gold hilts by the Spanish goldsmith Pery Juan Pock, presented by the same Emperor to Augustus, Elector of Saxony, in 1575. Both collections contain many comparable rapiers and swords, which, though functional in design, are rendered unsuitable for serious practical use by the fragility of the material or the decoration of their hilts (some hilts are even made of rock crystal). Examples of such decoration on weapons other than rapiers are a series of hunting sets (Dresden, Hist. Mus.) with silver-gilt mounts by the goldsmith Gabriel Gipfel (*fl* 1591–*c.* 1615/20) decorated with applied, cast scenes of the chase and set with precious and semi-precious stones. It should be emphasized that weapons of this kind are, and always were, enormously outnumbered by entirely functional swords and daggers, modestly decorated or not decorated at all.

Two decorative techniques that became popular during the 16th century were damascening with gold or silver, and chiselling, probably because they were not only particularly appropriate for decorating iron (and steel) but could be used without weakening it. Neither technique was new, and damascening especially has a very long history, though it does not appear to have been much employed in the West during the late Middle Ages. It survived, however, in Islamic lands and was used, for example, on the blades of some of the Hispano-Moresque swords and daggers mentioned above. There are two forms: the first—often referred to as true damascening—involves engraving designs, with lines of dove-tail section, into the metal and then filling these with thick gold or silver wire. The second form, known as counterfeit or false damascening, involves hatching all over the surface of the iron, which can be heat-blued first, with a special tool that roughens it sufficiently to retain designs formed of fine gold or silver wire or, for simple plating, thin sheets of gold or silver, applied with a burnisher. Counterfeit damascening was the form used almost entirely throughout the West, and its production in the form of tourist souvenirs has been one of the main industries of Toledo, Spain, since the beginning of the 20th century. Counterfeit damascening is less durable than true damascening, but it permits greater flexibility in the treatment of designs. A technique related to damascening, and often used with it, is what is now known as encrustation, in which small pieces of gold or silver are keyed into recesses punched into the surface of the metal in such a way as to leave them standing proud and are then chiselled into decorative shapes.

3. Rapier of Emperor Maximilian II, with enamelled gold hilt, l. 1.22 m, Spanish or Italian, before 1550 (Vienna, Kunsthistorisches Museum)

Damascened decoration seems to have become popular again in Europe from the 1530s and was thereafter widely used for the decoration of arms of all kinds, but especially swords and daggers, and also, to a more limited extent, of armour. It is possible that the technique was reintroduced into the rest of Europe from Moorish Spain. One of the earliest-known references to it is in a letter of 1524 from Federico II Gonzaga, Marchese of Mantua, about obtaining the services of a Spaniard who 'works in damascening [*azamino*] extremely well'. This may refer to Diego de Çaias, the earliest-known damascener whose work can be identified and who is recorded as working for Francis I, King of France, from 1538 to 1542 and for Henry VIII and Edward VI, kings of England, from 1543 to after 1549. He is described as a Spaniard in English records, and his damascened ornament includes minute figures, many of Spanish type, and sometimes Kufic lettering and the coat of arms of the Nasrid kingdom of Granada. Pieces signed by or attributed to him include a hunting-sword (Windsor Castle, Berks, Royal Col.) made for Henry VIII, two maces made for the future Henry II, King of France (signed, New York, Met.; unsigned, Paris, Mus. Armée), an ear-dagger of Spanish type (New York, Met.) and a signed cross-hilted dagger (Dresden, Hist. Mus.). The hilt of a rapier (Vienna, Ksthist. Mus.) of the same period, decorated in an identical style, is signed DAMIANUS DE NERVE[N?], an otherwise unrecorded artist.

Chiselling involved, in effect, sculpting the iron or steel, either into a three-dimensional shape or relief decoration or both. Very simple chiselled linear ornament occurs on some medieval and early 16th-century hilts. After 1540, however, more elaborate motifs, such as foliage, strapwork, masks and small human figures, were increasingly employed and had become the norm by *c.* 1560. They were often gilded or silvered and picked out with, or accompanied by, damascening or encrustation in gold or silver, for example on the two swords, a mace and a boar-spear accompanying the Milanese Armour (Vienna, Ksthist. Mus.) bought by the Archduke Ferdinand of Austria in 1559 from Giovanni Battista Serabaglio and Marc Antonio Fava of Milan. Unadorned chiselled ornament was, however, equally popular. Among the finest surviving examples of the technique are the hilts of two rapiers chiselled with minute scenes, those on one taken from the Old Testament and on the other from the New, which are merely blued: the former (New York, Met.) is signed M.I.F., which, it has been suggested, rather doubtfully, is for Mathieu Jacquet (Fecit), sculptor to Henry IV, King of France, while the other (Paris, Mus. Armée) bears chiselled portraits of the same King and the date 1599. Similarly, the work of the steel-chisellers of Dresden and neighbouring Torgau during the second half of the 16th century is often simply blued (examples, Dresden, Hist. Mus.).

The most distinguished steel-chisellers of the late 16th century and the early 17th in the field of arms (though they also decorated other objects) were craftsmen who worked for the Dukes and Electors of Bavaria in Munich and who were known collectively as the Munich school: Ottmar Wetter (*d* 1598), Emanuel Sadeler (*d* 1610), his brother Daniel Sadeler (*d* 1632) and Casper Spät (*d* 1691). With the work of the two Sadelers in particular, the art of the steel-chiseller probably reached its apogee in Europe (*see also* §2(ii) below). Their work is characterized by minute figures—often after designs by the French engraver and medal die-cutter Etienne Delaune—chiselled in high relief and brilliantly blued against a gold background (examples, Munich, Bayer. Nmus.; Vienna, Ksthist. Mus.; New York, Met.; London, V&A).

No surviving graphic designs specifically for arms and their decoration dating from before the second quarter of the 16th century are known. Thereafter, however, they become available for study in increasing numbers. Some are manuscript, but the majority are engraved, forming part of the stream of such designs for all the decorative arts from the mid-16th century onwards. Most of the artists responsible were of comparatively minor stature, but among the important artists was Hans Holbein the younger, who produced a number of designs for swords and daggers, including some for a distinctive type of early 16th-century Swiss civilian dagger with a hilt shaped like a letter I and a scabbard covered in gilt brass, cast, chased and pierced with scenes (examples, Zurich, Schweiz. Landesmus.; London, Wallace). For this reason these daggers are sometimes now called 'Holbein daggers', though there is no evidence to suggest that he originated the type. A unique collection of mid-16th-century goldsmiths' lead patterns (Basle, Hist. Mus.) includes patterns for such scabbards as well as other sword- and dagger-mounts.

The earliest recorded artist specializing in designs for arms and armour appears to have been Filippo Orso or Urso of Mantua, who produced a volume of such designs, including many for sword-hilts, of which two slightly differing manuscripts dated respectively 1554 and 1558–9 exist (London, V&A; Wolfenbüttel, Herzog-August Bib.). Nothing is known about him apart from his own description of himself as *Pictor Mantuanus*. An exact contemporary was Pierre Woeiriot, an artist from Lorraine working during the mid-16th century in Lyon, where he produced eight sheets of designs (six in 1552) for hilts and scabbard-mounts. In addition to Etienne Delaune, already mentioned, other artists—some well known, others obscure—who either produced designs for swords and their decoration, or actually decorated them, were the painter, engraver and goldsmith HEINRICH ALDEGREVER of Soest, Westphalia, the engraver Hans Collaert the elder of Antwerp, the engraver Ambrosius Gemlich (*fl* 1527–42) of Munich, the engraver, embosser and damascener Giorgio Ghisi of Mantua, the printmaker and designer Daniel Hopfer of Augsburg, the goldsmith and engraver Erasmus Hornick of Prague, the goldsmith Wenzel Jamnitzer of Nuremberg, the goldsmith Jakob Mores (*d* before 1612) of Hamburg, the painter Hans Mielich of Munich and the engraver and painter Virgil Solis of Nuremberg. Mention must also be made of the designs (Barcelona, Inst. Mun. Hist.) for masterpieces submitted to the goldsmiths' guild of Barcelona, which include a number for sword-hilts and daggers, dating from 1537 onwards.

(iii) After 1630. In the early 17th century in France new and much faster fencing techniques were developed—the direct precursors of modern ones—in which the rapier blade was used for parrying as well as for attack. This led to the abandonment of the left-hand dagger and the development, by about 1630, of a much shorter, lighter rapier with a much simpler guard (see fig. 4), though the

older forms lingered until the 1640s. In Spain and in Naples, where Spanish influence was strong, a long rapier with a cup-hilt, often chiselled and pierced, and a matching left-hand dagger with a solid triangular guard for the back of the hand, remained in use until the early 18th century. Elsewhere, the light form of rapier with a slender blade and simple hilt, known as the small-sword, came increasingly into use from the 1640s and within a decade or so had been universally adopted for wear with civilian dress. The development of the military sword followed similar lines during the same period, though its blade remained much heavier and its guard normally more complex. From the mid-18th century, however, the light cavalry of a number of countries adopted the curved sabre, which had a simple cross-guard, of the Hungarian and Polish hussars.

4. Rapier with a cast and chased silver hilt with the maker's mark TH in a shield, l. 991 mm, English, *c.* 1640 (London, Victoria and Albert Museum)

From the second quarter of the 17th century there was a fashion for more restrained decoration, which also influenced arms. The decorative techniques described in §(ii) above continued to be used, however, and the small-sword continued the role of its predecessor as masculine jewellery, many hilts and mounts being made by the same craftsmen who produced snuff-boxes and similar objects. The most remarkable surviving examples of this are the swords in the sets (*c.* 1720; Dresden, Hist. Mus.) made by Johann Melchior Dinglinger, the prominent Saxon goldsmith, for Frederick-Augustus I, Elector of Saxony, which are decorated with gemstones and enamelled and accompanied by costume jewellery and such accessories as snuff-boxes, watches and stick handles, all *en suite*.

At a more modest level, steel chiselling became especially popular, and numerous exponents of it, mostly anonymous, appeared in various parts of Europe. The steel-chisellers of Brescia—among whom Carlo Botarelli (*fl c.* 1660–65) was outstanding—had a particularly high reputation, but there were many artist-craftsmen elsewhere whose work was superior, for example Pietro Ancino (*fl c.* 1660–70) of Reggio Emilia, Matteo Acqua Fresca (*d* 1738), of Bargi, Bologna, the medallist and sculptor Gottfried Christian Leygebe of Berlin, and the medallist Franz Matzenkopf (*d* 1776) of Prague and Salzburg. A distinctive form of steel chiselling that must be mentioned is cut-steel work, which, in effect, involves the use of faceted, highly polished steel studs in the same manner as brilliants. Possibly first used in Russia in the late 17th century, the technique is particularly associated with the factory at Soho, Birmingham, of Matthew Boulton in partnership with John Fothergill (*d* 1782) and, later, James Watt (1736–1819), during the period 1762–1800. Some of the cut-steel small-sword hilts and jewellery produced there incorporate Wedgwood jasperware cameos (examples, London, V&A). One new material occasionally used for mid-18th-century sword-grips was porcelain. These were produced by a number of factories, including Meissen.

In the second half of the 18th century, probably in the 1760s, gentlemen began to give up wearing swords with civilian dress, and by the 1780s the small-sword had gone generally out of use, except for special purposes, such as accompanying ceremonial dress. A few such occasions survive: new members of the Académie Française, for example, are presented with a sword, often designed by a distinguished artist. Because of these and the practice of presenting swords of honour for meritorious naval and military service (see fig. 5), finely decorated weapons continued to be made regularly until the end of the Napoleonic Wars, in France notably by Nicolas Noël Boutet (*d* 1833), of the Manufacture de Versailles, and occasionally since. The great industrial exhibitions of the 19th century also led to the production of a crop of 'exhibition pieces' that were commonly in a pseudo-Renaissance style, often technically the equal of the originals but rarely so in design. In this connection special mention must be made of the work of Eusebio Zuloaga

5. Small-sword by James Morisset of London, presented to Lt-Col. James Hartley by the Honourable East India Company, 1781 (London, Victoria and Albert Museum)

(*d* 1898) and his son Plácido Zuloaga (*d* 1910), both of Eibar and Madrid.

BIBLIOGRAPHY

A. Bertolotti: *Le arti minori alla corte di Mantova* (Milan, 1889)

A. Bruhn: *Der Schwertfeger Gottfried Leygebe* (Copenhagen, 1945)

H. L. Peterson: *The American Sword, 1775–1945* (Philadelphia, 1954, rev. 1965) [incl. 1965 exh. cat.]

American Silver Mounted Swords, 1700–1800 (exh. cat., Washington, DC, Corcoran Gal. A., 1965)

J. D. Lavin: 'The Zuloaga Armourers', *J. Arms & Armour Soc.*, xii (1968–8), pp. 63–148

J. Southwick: 'Patriotic Fund Swords', *J. Arms & Armour Soc.*, xii (1968–8), pp. 223–84, 291–311

C. Blair: 'A Royal Swordsmith and Damascener: Diego de Çaias', *Met. Mus. J.*, iii (1970), pp. 149–98

C. Burns: *Golden Rose & Blessed Sword* (Glasgow, 1970)

C. Blair: *Three Presentation Swords in the Victoria and Albert Museum and a Group of English Enamels* (London, 1972)

J. F. Hayward: *Virtuoso Goldsmiths and the Triumph of Mannerism, 1540–1620* (London, 1976)

H. Schneider: *Der Schweizerdolch* (Zurich, 1976)

A. V. B. Norman: *The Rapier and Small-sword, 1460–1820* (London, 1980)

A. Radcliffe: 'The Sword of Donatello in "Ricciana"', *Burl. Mag.*, cxxiv (1982), pp. 415–17

V. Harris, ed.: *Sword and Hilt Weapons* (London, 1989)

For further bibliography *see* §I above.

CLAUDE BLAIR

2. Projectile weapons.

(i) Before *c.* 1590. (ii) *c.* 1590–*c.* 1650. (iii) *c.* 1650–*c.* 1700. (iv) After *c.* 1700.

(i) Before c. *1590.* European hand arms and fire-arms were not vehicles for artistic ornament until the end of the 15th century. Prior to that time their purpose was wholly military. Early military guns were all long-arms with wooden stocks, designed to be fired with the butt against the shoulder, as is done today, or with the stock held against the cheek, the recoil being absorbed by the arms. The first system was popular in Mediterranean countries, while the latter was used in Germany and other northern European countries. A third and unusual form of stock, termed (probably improperly) a 'petronel', was held against the chest; it had only a limited popularity in France, the Low Countries and England at the end of the 16th century. The hand fire-arm, designed neither for beauty nor for sport, was an awkward weapon: it could be ignited only through the use of open fire in the form of a smouldering matchcord applied either manually or by a rude lever to a manually opened priming pan. The mechanism could not be reduced to a smaller scale for pistols, nor could it be used practically from horseback. Consequently, this unwieldy arm, relegated to use by the infantry, acquired equal status with the pike and crossbow, weapons not employed by gentlemen.

Ground troops received their arms at the expense of their commanders. This system did not encourage the application of decoration, and when rudimentary ornament was added, it was produced with the blacksmith's tools, the hammer, the file and, sometimes, the chisel. These could cut facets, mouldings and channels and could even be used for primitive engraving, which added visual interest but had little artistic value. The addition of such ornament was an afterthought by a non-specialist artisan for a consumer whose appreciation of the design was incidental to the purpose of the object. Conversely, armour and edged weapons, as knightly attributes, were from earliest times objects of the most sophisticated ornament. Until the end of the 15th century this social division in the use of arms was well defined; thereafter, their artistic importance came as the result of their acceptance by the upper class as fashionable, personal accessories, rather than as the weapon of the ordinary foot soldier.

About 1500 a new self-igniting mechanism, known as the 'wheel-lock' and based on the mechanical tinder lighter employing a steel wheel rotated against quartz or pyrites to produce a spark, was applied to fire-arms. The mechanism was operated by a large internal mainspring that rotated a steel wheel, originally mounted externally. The outer face of the lockplate also supported the appropriately named 'dog' or *cane*, the jaws of which held the stone and its large V-spring. To the rear of the wheel was mounted a safety lever with its spring. Because of its complexity and cost, this mechanism had limited military use, but, through the elimination of the need for open-fire ignition, it allowed fire-arms to be made comfortably small and portable. From then on the hand gun acquired importance as a status symbol, rivalling the sword, while the wheel-lock's complex machinery caught the fancy of those who were also intrigued by mechanical intricacies. From the

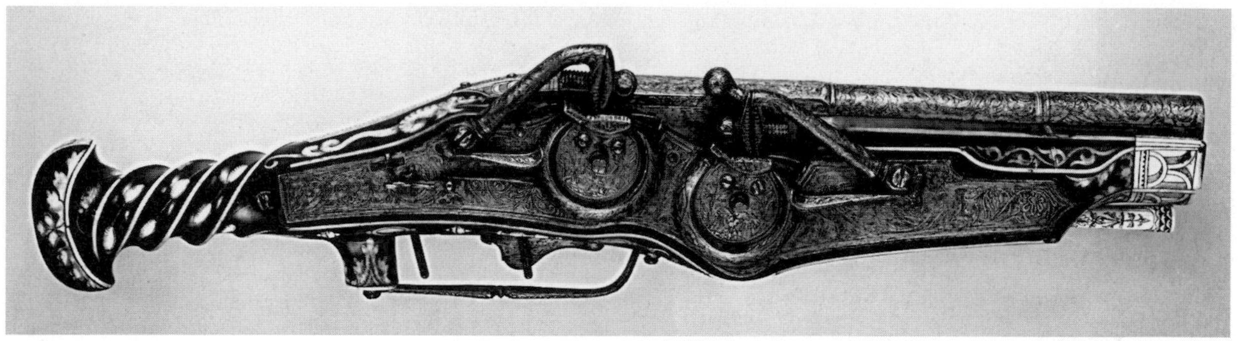

6. Double-barrelled wheel-lock pistol made by Peter Peck for Emperor Charles V, lock, barrel and triggerguard chiselled and gilded, cherry-wood stock inlaid with engraved ivory and staghorn, Munich, *c.* 1540 (New York, Metropolitan Museum of Art)

1520s European royalty, foremost among them the Holy Roman Emperor Charles V, began to adopt a miniature version of the long musket or arquebus, the precursor of the pistol.

Because it was in the Middle Renaissance that the hand gun was developed, the earliest examples to be decorated are in a conventional Renaissance style. Decorated projectile arms surviving from this period include the combination crossbow/wheel-lock gun (Munich, Bayer. Nmus.) made for Archduke Ferdinand of Austria, later Emperor Ferdinand I (*reg* 1558–64), possibly as early as 1521, and the series of single pistols (examples in Madrid, Real Armería) belonging to Charles V. During the first half of the 16th century, as the hand fire-arm was becoming an adjunct to dress, its design and decoration were in a state of flux. While its necessary components—lock and barrel—determined its overall shape, the stock that joined these into a unit had as yet no standardized form for decorated fire-arms. The Archduke's combination arm has its iron wheel-lock, barrel and bow etched, engraved and fire-gilded in the manner of contemporary armour decoration. Its wooden stock is like that of a crossbow and is thus related in its manner of use to the German cheek stock. It is painted red overall as a background for painted gold vegetal tracery in the Renaissance style. Subsequent 16th-century stock decoration used the natural surface of unfigured fruit-wood as a background for inlaid ornament.

The 15 pistols of Charles V illustrated in watercolour in his *Inventario iluminado* (?1540; Madrid, Real Armería) are quite plain, even severe. Some barrels and locks are shown dark, possibly indicating that they were fire-blued; others, shown light, were presumably of polished iron. Most stocks have the colour of natural wood, and only two show some sparse inlay of horn or bone. White stocks are shown on six pistols, one surviving example of which suggests that, like it, their stocks may all have been covered in ivory veneer engraved with foliage and trophies of Renaissance design. The stocks of 12 pistols in the *Inventario* are miniature versions of the German arquebus cheek stock. One, a small gun that the Emperor purchased from Bartholomaus Marquart in Augsburg in 1530, illustrates the vacillation in the manner of firing, as it is fitted with a threaded iron butt extension allowing it to be held to the shoulder. Other pistols, dating from around 1540, have a straight grip like that of a sword, thus permitting their one-handed use. Charles's inventories show only single pistols, thus supporting the idea that the concept of pistols in pairs had not been formulated before the middle of the 16th century.

Although considerably more portable than earlier fire-arms, the weight and size of these unwieldy weapons precluded their being carried on the body as an adjunct to or a substitute for the sword. That they were still considered diminutive versions of shoulder arms or arquebuses is shown in the Valladolid inventories, where they are called *arcabucillos* ('small arquebuses'), often with the qualifier *de arzón* ('for the saddlebow'), indicating their accepted place. Titian's equestrian portrait of *Charles V at Mühlberg* (1547; Madrid, Prado) shows the Emperor with a plain wheel-lock pistol about 450 mm long hanging fully exposed at his right against the cantle plate of his saddle. Small hooks set in the left-hand side of the stock of numerous surviving *arcabucillos* of the period show that the saddle holster was not yet in use.

The increased variety of applied ornament used on fire-arms from the late 15th century and the early 16th required the involvement of specialist craftsmen both within and outside the gunmaking field. Although in theory the master gunmaker might be expected to be responsible for his product from beginning to end, fire-arms production, from at least the late 15th century, commonly employed three specialists in the volume manufacture of military arms: the barrelmaker, the lockmaker, and the stocker, who finished the piece; these specializations were often retained, especially in areas with strong guilds, even in the manufacture of individual luxury arms. To them were added the specialist trades of steel chiseller, engraver, founder, chaser, gilder and *ébéniste*, the last skilled in the inlay of wood with bone, horn and metal. At the highest level, the manufacture of a fire-arm certainly involved the movement of many of its elements from workshop to workshop, all presumably under the supervision of the master who had contracted for the work. The most important of Charles V's pistols, for example, were made by Peter Peck of Munich in the 1540s. His wheel-locks, barrels and iron mounts can be quite ornate, with chiselling and engraving in Renaissance foliate designs covered overall with fire-gilding. The stocks, executed by an anonymous specialist craftsman whom Peck is known through records to have employed, have engraved staghorn inlay usually in the form of stylized acanthus leaves and vines. A double-barrelled pistol (see fig. 6) is an excellent example of Peck's work for Charles V.

Many elements of Renaissance design could be combined, sketched and executed in metal and wood for fire-arms with no recourse to published sources, although, like other artists and craftsmen, gunmakers would have collected prints of fashionable, often generic, patterns for use in the workshop. Early sources for fire-arms decoration were frequently patterns published for the decoration of such other media as silver. The legitimization of fire-arms as a medium for decoration was eventually followed by ornament designed exclusively for use on such weapons. Small engraved patterns, attributed to Jacques Androuet Du Cerceau (i), for the decoration of the French wheel-lock mechanism may be dated as early as *c.* 1550. During the second half of the 16th century some French and German designers included in their repertory patterns devoted to the decoration of elements of pistols and long-arms, including a few designs for the engraving of horn and bone stock ornament. While some patterns were executed in ink and wash, apparently intended for one-time use, a small number of engraved sheets, such as those by Du Cerceau, were made for distribution. Formal patterns were devoted principally to the decoration of iron parts, leaving the creation of most stock ornament to the woodworker; this was a system that did not always promote decorative unity.

By the second half of the 16th century, national and regional schools of fire-arms manufacture had emerged. Although influenced by earlier German predominance and the unifying standard of Renaissance design, an overlay of local tradition was evident. These styles, as distinctive as clothing fashions in their day, were easily recognized and are referred to in inventories. Arms made in different countries became the souvenirs of wealthy travellers and were a major means for the transmission not only of styles but also of constructional methods, which were not illustrated on pattern sheets. By 1550 the pistol had become an essential gentlemanly accessory and, viewed solely as an investment, was more important than the sword. The significant difference between them, however, was that the sword, worn on the person, was a more intimate accessory. Pistols, beginning to be used in pairs, were now carried in saddle holsters, with only their butts visible. They usually remained with the horse, and their decorative value was related to that of the cantle plates, stirrups, bit and even the horse itself.

By virtue of its mechanical construction, the wheel-lock mechanism presented a large and awkwardly arranged element difficult to render visually pleasing. With the addition of applied ornament, no matter how tasteful, it could easily become an overwhelming feature. The German wheel-lock gun, with its box-like long-gun cheek stock, never overcame its appearance of geometric massiveness. Bulk and solidity, however, must have had their appeal, for they also characterize late 16th-century German pistols. By then, these had acquired often disproportionately large, spherical and often elaborately inlaid wooden pommels, obviously designed to be displayed above saddle holsters and perhaps to give a better grip when drawing them (e.g. London, V&A). In the late 16th century German fire-arms began to suffer from a surfeit of applied ornament, especially in stock inlay, which was almost always comprised of smooth bone and staghorn plaques and enhanced with black-line engraving. The decoration included the standard Renaissance vocabulary of motifs—arabesques, grotesques and wreaths with classical busts—as well as the more common running dogs and game. On the whole, metal parts were relatively plain. A significant number of German fire-arms of this date, of better than average quality, show evidence of having mass-produced horn inlay applied in flat panels; this is most evident where the inlay was altered to fit the available space. Germanic design and decorative trends were also predominant in better-quality Scandinavian fire-arms until well into the 17th century.

The disproportionate wheel-lock mechanism seems to have been less acceptable to the French, who, towards the end of the 16th century, successfully reduced its size by separating the large mainspring from the lock and mounting it within its own recess in the wooden stock. This allowed a significant reduction in the size of the lock, which ceased to be an awkward feature. At the same time the manual safety disappeared from the French wheel-lock, possibly for aesthetic reasons. During the 16th century French pistol stocks may have incorporated a large ball pommel similar to those on German examples, but this perception is based only on a single surviving pair (New York, Met.). These French pistols have cherry-wood stocks delicately inlaid with engraved staghorn in foliate designs incorporating figures from Classical mythology. French long-arms of the same period have shoulder stocks that curve slightly downwards from the rear of the barrel. These stocks are thinner and more slender in profile, and their ornament usually consists of staghorn, often coloured, engraved in floral designs.

Sixteenth-century Italian fire-arms were frequently plain, but the Italians also developed a smaller wheel-lock, which, unlike the French version, had the mainspring mounted externally where it extended below the stock. However, this was not overwhelmingly popular to judge from the scarcity of surviving examples, and large, lozenge-shaped locks, in contrast to the German rectangular wheel-lock, were the standard. Their ornament consisted of relief chiselling, often only of the external moving parts and the lockplate border. Stocks were usually of walnut rather than cherry or other fruit-woods; when they were inlaid it was usually with pierced and engraved iron sheet. Some luxury Italian snap matchlocks of the 16th or early 17th century have their stocks covered in velvet decorated with rosette-headed silver-gilt nails.

(ii) c. *1590–*c. *1650.* The 17th century must be regarded as the golden age of European gunmaking. This was a period of great experimentation in design and ornament, especially at the luxury level. While during the 16th century function was the ultimate determinant of form, and applied ornament wholly conformed to this, there was in the 17th century an intelligent union of the two, as well as a heightened consciousness of the aesthetic. During the late 16th century both the gun and rifle had acquired status as hunting arms, and their social importance equalled that of

the pistol. In the same period a new ignition system, the flintlock, appeared, which, under various names and forms, also used the principle of flint struck against steel to produce a spark—and did so with a much simplified mechanism. The rapid, almost simultaneous, appearance of several flintlock systems in various parts of Europe may indicate a number of independent inventions. The collective result, however, was the same: the new gunlock was relatively compact, and it did not dominate the design of the arm as did the wheel-lock.

While the German states seem to have dominated in the production of wheel-locks during the 16th century, in the 17th century French gunmakers were pre-eminent. Two circumstances contributed to this: the invention in the 1620s of the French flintlock, eventually the dominant European gunlock, which was extremely simple and consequently relatively small and compact; and the unbounded interest of the young Louis XIII in every type of fire-arm, which inspired gunmakers and designers. The most prominent of these was Marin Le Bourgeois (*d* 1633) of Lisieux, who is traditionally regarded as the inventor of the French flintlock. He is first recorded in 1583 as designing decorations in Lisieux for the reception of the Duc de Joyeuse. He was appointed Valet de Chambre to Henry IV in 1598 and served as 'a worker on movable globes, sculpture and other mechanical inventions', although on one occasion, in 1605, he was referred to as a gunmaker (*harquebuzier*). He does not seem to have been a manufacturing gunmaker, but he can be identified as the designer of at least three surviving royal fire-arms. These include a magnificent flintlock hunting gun (see fig. 7) apparently made for Louis XIII during the 1620s; this was number 152 in the King's Cabinet d'Armes and epitomizes the finest of French gunmaking. Its most striking feature is its cherry stock, the butt of which is in the form of a stag's foot with an etched and gilt-metal hoof. Above this, serving as the stock's comb, is a cast, gilt-bronze *gaîne* or Hermes post. Engraved and punch-decorated gilt-metal plaques are fastened to the stock behind the barrel and the lock. Inlaid silver wire runs lengthwise down the stag's foot and elsewhere on the stock forms designs of leaves, flowers and curling tendrils in a manner hitherto unknown in gunstock ornament. The barrel is blued overall, covered with damascened gold ornament, which repeats the themes of the silver stock inlay. The iron flintlock, of the earliest form, shows evidence of its original blued finish; the lockplate has an etched design that continues that of the stock. The signature M LE BOVRGEOYS A LISIEVL is on one of the bronze straps of the stock ornament; there are no marks on the barrel or lock. The importance of this gun is due not only to its opulence, but also because it is an early example of the concept of the gun as an object with unified decoration.

Marin Le Bourgeois's concept of stock design was daring. There was no established tradition guiding the form of luxury gunstocks other than that the French preferred the shoulder stock to the German cheek stock. In an attempt to lighten visually the traditional musket form of butt, Marin built up the butt of the gun of Louis XIII with several free elements joined at their extremes. This innovation was his trademark, which was soon imitated. The delicate silver wire inlay breaks the solid wooden surfaces of the stock without giving the impression of massiveness, as seen on so many German stocks heavily inlaid with plaques of staghorn. A closely related gun designed by Marin Le Bourgeois and also made for Louis XIII is in the Metropolitan Museum of Art, New York.

Marin Le Bourgeois was given lodgings in the Galeries du Louvre, Paris, in 1608, but he seems to have spent considerable time in his native Lisieux, where he was involved in the manufacture of fire-arms probably with his brother Pierre Le Bourgeois until the latter's death in 1627. Their brother Jean Le Bourgeois worked there during the early 17th century. Both Pierre and Jean are considered to have been active as gunmakers; the barrel stamps PB and JB over a crossbow appear on the barrels of several Lisieux-made guns and are attributed to them. The prominence of Lisieux as the most important French centre of fire-arms in the early 17th century was certainly due to the Bourgeois family.

In Paris Marin Le Bourgeois seems to have acquired a disciple in François Duclos, who continued to design and decorate in the Lisieux style for some years after Marin's death. Evidence of this relationship is a second casting of the bronze *gaîne* from the St Petersburg hunting gun, which Duclos used, reversed, on the comb of a gun (1636; Paris, Mus. Armée) that he undoubtedly made for Louis XIII. Its stock is so like those of Marin that it could be attributed to him. While Duclos continued the Lisieux or Bourgeois style in his fire-arms, the engraver Thomas Picquot, also from Lisieux, with whom Duclos shared his workshop and lodging in the Louvre, codified it. In 1638

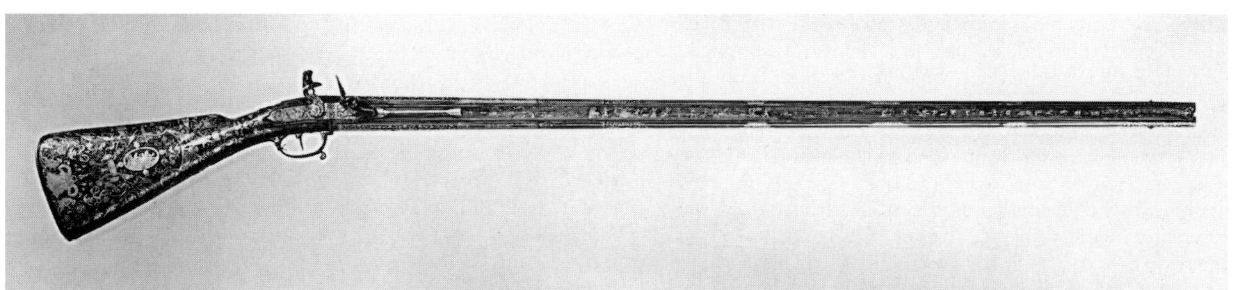

7. Hunting gun of Louis XIII, cherry-wood stock inlaid with silver wire and engraved horn, gilt-bronze mounts, designed and possibly made by Marin Le Bourgeois of Lisieux, early 1620s (St Petersburg, Hermitage Museum)

Picquot published in Paris a small pattern book of designs for gun ornament, including three for flintlocks, in the manner of Marin Le Bourgeois. Duclos is known to have left the Louvre in 1659, but by that date the Lisieux fashion had disappeared.

Other French schools contemporaneous with that of Lisieux produced fire-arms with different types of decoration. The engraver and gunmaker Jean Henequin, for example, working in Metz in the 1620s, not only made fire-arms for Louis XIII but also produced a series of plates illustrating the decoration of wheel-locks and flintlocks, which was probably based on ornament that he applied to his own fire-arms (examples in Munich, Bayer. Nmus.). The plates reflect the decoration on his known work: relief chiselling of all iron parts in Renaissance designs, combining vegetal themes, dogs in the form of grotesque animal heads holding the stone in their jaws, human figures, cherubs and putti. Such bold chiselled forms are absent from arms made in Lisieux.

The best French ornament of the first half of the 17th century tended to be delicate, showing great attention to finish and detail. Fine silver and brass inlay was combined with engraved bone, horn and mother-of-pearl stock inlay, but with great restraint. Concurrently, however, in another French style, probably originating in Paris but quite diffuse, emphasis was placed on the inlay, through its profuse covering of the entire stock. Its quality varied greatly; most often engraved mother-of-pearl plaques dominated, possibly an economic factor, since their engraving and inlay involved significantly less labour than that for inlaying an equal amount of wire. The resulting decoration was quasi-Germanic in style: it is found on a great number of extant long (over 750 mm) wheel-lock holster pistols of slender profile and very small bore (*c.* 0.35 calibre). Their pommels are lemon-shaped and much smaller than those of German pistols. These French pistols are frequently unmarked and cannot be associated with one particular centre of production.

Philippe Cordier Daubigny was a French gunmaker and designer who worked at least throughout the second quarter of the 17th century. From the mid-1630s to the mid-1640s he produced a series of 16 patterned plates, published in Paris probably around 1644, the date of the latest plate. Daubigny's patterns are marked by the extravagance of their design, the figures of which are mainly unrelated to the purpose of the objects. They consist of flowers with exaggerated blossoms, *rinceaux*, grotesques and biblical and Classical scenes. Only two show hunting scenes, both of which appear on lockplates for the flintlock. Daubigny concentrated only on the gunlock, as opposed to Marin Le Bourgeois, who left this plain. Unlike Jean Henequin, who chiselled in bold relief, Daubigny's plates provide patterns for engraving; only his first plate shows any designs for chiselling.

Both Daubigny's wheel-lock and flintlock patterns and the three flintlock plates by Picquot show no external springs or slotted screw heads. Immediately following the popularity of the Marin Le Bourgeois style, French gunmakers further simplified the flintlock mechanism by moving the steel spring from the exterior to the interior of the lockplate and by eliminating not only visible screws but all indication of the manner of attachment of parts. The latter was done by substituting bolts with decorated heads for slotted screws to join metal to metal and by fastening parts to the stock through the use of tiny transverse pins, rather than by wood-screws with visible heads.

A rubbing (*c.* 1630; Paris, Bib. N.) by Daubigny of an engraved lock is an example of the standard workshop method of recording a design produced there. Rubbings were also the source for subsequent published engravings, such as Daubigny's own series. This explains the sequence of dates covering an entire decade on Daubigny's patterns and also accounts for a significant delay in the transmission of formal designs when published patterns became the sole source of decoration for fire-arms. This delay became more apparent during the reign of Louis XIV, especially in French provincial and other European work, the decoration of which was unfashionable when compared with Parisian work. Curiously, Daubigny's patterns were reissued in the 1660s, at which time the plates were redated 1664–5; by then their designs, according to Paris standards, were obviously passé.

Little is known about English luxury fire-arms made before the end of the 16th century, because of the paucity of surviving examples or depictions in art. An English snaphaunce (flintlock) gun (1584; Copenhagen, Nmus.) with heavily inlaid breast stock and a pair of English snaphaunce pistols (1593; Konopiště, Schloss) are of considerable importance in advancing knowledge of early English fire-arms decoration. Their engraved horn and mother-of-pearl running foliate stock inlay, geometric borders, horn ramrod holders and, in the case of the pistols, large, faceted, apple-shaped butts owe much to 16th-century German ornament, apparently with some French influence. The iron locks of these arms are file-decorated and deeply engraved but are totally devoid of chiselling. In the case of the pistols, punch decoration forms a background to the engraving. The gun's barrel is blued and damascened in silver and gold. On the basis of affinities in its decoration with that of the arms mentioned above, a wheel-lock pistol at Belchamp Hall, Essex, is also considered to be English. The form of its stock is quite like those of the Konopiště pistols, and all of these arms are fitted with German-style left-hand manual safeties.

During the late 16th century the English gunstock butt became triangular in profile, its upper and lower edges being slightly concave. There was a pronounced small to the stock, marked by a deep, angled recess for the thumb. By the early 17th century the triangular profile was broadened into what is currently called a 'fishtail'. The most elaborate versions of this stock, combined with both matchlocks and snaphaunce locks, are inlaid with engraved bone, horn, mother-of-pearl and brass wire, definitely of German inspiration. The visual impact of these guns was mostly dependent on their stock ornament, since the majority of surviving examples have plain iron components. In decoration, form and mechanism, these English guns and similarly decorated pistols are virtually identical to contemporary Dutch fire-arms, and consequently the style is often referred to as 'Anglo-Dutch'.

Outstanding exceptions to the more conventionally ornamented early 17th-century English arms were the magnificent arms given as part of two gifts from James I to Philip III of Spain in 1604 and 1614. These consisted of a total of eight fowling pieces (fowlers) and eight crossbows, some covered 'with massive gould'. The decorated fowlers were broken up in the 18th century, undoubtedly in order to retrieve their gold stock inlay. One detached snaphaunce lock, two barrels, a triggerguard and six crossbows, their stocks picked clean of inlay (all Madrid, Real Armería), offer good evidence of the original appearance of these heavily decorated arms. All iron parts are chiselled in high relief, with gold overlay in the form of cherubs' and monsters' heads connected by running foliage over a blued or blackened ground. Blair indicated the similarity of this ornament to that produced by decorators working for the cutlers Robert South and Nathaniel Matthew of London.

From the end of the 16th century Scottish fire-arms, especially pistols, took a distinctive form. Most were made entirely of metal, as their stocks were also usually of brass or iron. Less frequently, stocks were wooden, their grips and pommels flattened and terminating in a scrolled fishtail, having some sheet-iron or brass inlay (e.g. London, Tower). Lemon-shaped pommels, not unlike those of contemporary French pistols, were most common on all-metal stocks (e.g. Stockholm, Livrustkam.). In some instances the lockplate and barrel were also of brass. Locks were invariably snaphaunce (flintlock) with flat surfaces. Except for the barrels, the overall decoration comprised engraving of imbrication, basket weave, rosettes and geometric cable borders; there was little reflecting the Renaissance ornament so popular on the Continent, although in the earliest Scottish examples there is often a mix of debased Renaissance ornament with Romanesque running foliage. Barrel decoration consisted of flared muzzles of stylized thistle form and filed relief mouldings; those of cast brass often had Baroque relief acanthus. Scottish pairs of pistols frequently had locks mounted on opposite sides. Both pistols and guns had button triggers without triggerguards, and pistols were fitted with long iron belthooks along the side opposite the locks. Such elaborate English arms as those given to Philip III would have offered a striking contrast to the extremely plain guns and crossbows made in Spain for early 17th-century monarchs. Certainly these indigenous arms were severe in style through royal preference, since many highly decorated foreign arms were in the royal collections. Philip IV chose a severely plain fowler with which to be portrayed by Velázquez in 1636. In fact, only one highly decorated Spanish gun that may have belonged to this monarch is known: a breech-loading Spanish-lock (flintlock) fowler (Paris, Mus. Armée) by Atienza. Its metal decoration consists of the engraving, relief chiselling and piercing of all iron parts with the motif of lions surrounded by running foliage in a loose interpretation of Renaissance *rinceaux*. The wooden stock, of traditional musket form but with a thumb groove, is heavily inlaid with iron wire, in a naive depiction of hunting scenes, and with engraved plaques, one consisting of Philip IV's arms surmounted by the Habsburg eagle. There is an overall coarseness in the execution of the ornament. Philip's monogram combined with that of Elizabeth Bourbon (1602–44) dates the gun to before 1644. Atienza was not a royal gunmaker, nor is this arm recorded in any of the royal inventories; this indicates that it was possibly intended as a gift to the monarch.

During the first half of the 17th century in Italy the wheel-lock ignition was retained much longer than in France, England, Scotland and Spain, where local versions of the flintlock replaced it. In terms of decoration, however, both northern and southern gunmaking centres responded to Spanish and French influences. This may be seen in the form of gun and pistol stocks, the most traditional of which emulate the musket shoulder stock in form but have pierced and engraved iron stock inlay, which, on the most elaborate pieces, covers most of the surface of the wood. Neither Italian nor Spanish arms-makers inlaid stocks with horn, bone or mother-of-pearl. Extensive collections of early Italian fire-arms are in the Armeria Reale, Turin, and the Museo e Gallerie Nazionali di Capodimonte, Naples.

From the 1590s a distinctive style of chiselled steel ornament was developed by the Sadeler family of Antwerp. In 1594 William V, Duke of Bavaria, brought the iron-worker Emanuel Sadeler to Munich; about the same time, Emanuel's brother Daniel Sadeler emigrated to Prague. They had been apprenticed to their father in Antwerp, and both worked in an identical style. Their designs, consisting of standard Renaissance vegetal motifs and classical themes, were executed in chiselled relief on wheel-locks, barrels and mounts. The originality of their works lies in the total blackening of the iron and the emphasis on the chiselled black relief by surrounding it with a matt gold background. In contrast to the heavily ornamented iron, the stocks, of both cheek and shoulder type, were either plain and ebonized or white overall, the latter being covered with ivory veneer inlaid with sparse black tracery. The black, gold and white decoration stands in dramatic contrast to all other types of European fire-arms decoration of this date. On Emanuel's death in 1610, Daniel was persuaded to come from Prague to Munich, where he died in 1632. A single wheel-lock pistol and a pair of pistols with iron ornament by Daniel Sadeler are in the Wallace Collection, London. He was succeeded by his follower Casper Spät (*d* 1691), who continued to work in this distinctive style until 1665.

Contemporaneous with the work of the Sadeler brothers, but in direct contrast to their style, were wheel-lock rifles having profusely relief-carved wooden stocks. These, often inlaid with staghorn plaques covered in high relief, were popular in southern Germany and Austria. Outstanding among the stockers working in this style was the so-called Master of the Animal-head Scroll, who presumably worked at the imperial court in Vienna. This master's name derives from his use of relief-carved Renaissance style tendrils terminating in monsters' heads. The carving on this type of stock may be accompanied by carved or engraved horn plaques and/or inlaid silver wire. Judging from the more than 50 surviving pieces (several in Vienna, Ksthist. Mus.; one in London, Wallace), however, there is enough variation in execution to indicate that several masters were working in the same style. A small number of fire-arms are linked to the same workshop through the identity of their metal parts.

(iii) c. *1650–*c. *1700.* In the mid-17th century the arts of France, and of Paris in particular, were pre-eminent in Europe and reflected the power and status of Louis XIV. In Paris the dominant figure in fire-arms decoration was undoubtedly the designer, painter and engraver Jean Berain I. His uncle Claude Berain (*d* 1729) and possibly also his father, Jean Berain, both gunmakers, worked in Paris during the 1640s and 1650s. The younger Jean, who in 1674 became Dessinateur de la Chambre et du Cabinet du Roi to Louis XIV, was the author of a well-known pattern book for fire-arms, first issued in Paris in 1659. His plates principally illustrate ornament for metal parts, concentrating on Baroque grotesques, both human and animal, surrounded by acanthus leaves, fruit swags and pierced work in the round, the last applied to triggerguard posts, cock necks and rear sights. Berain made a conscious attempt to integrate the ornament of metal parts into that of the wooden stock by offering a few patterns for relief carving around the barrel tang, which, in their design, correspond exactly to those for steel chiselling. He also included a few patterns for stock inlay: these continued the theme of grotesques in engraved sheet silver, often surrounded by foliage with silver-wire tendrils. The intended execution of these designs is not obvious from the engraved plates but is apparent on surviving arms of the period, for example a double-barrelled gun made by Le Conte of Paris (see fig. 8), which was a gift from Louis XIV to Karl IX of Sweden in 1673. Its elaborate silver stock inlay is signed by Berain, who may also have been responsible for the steel engraving. The 1659 edition of Berain's album consists of seven sheets and covers a developmental period of at least a decade, judging from stylistic changes in the arms depicted. These include a move from flat to rounded surfaces, and also combinations of both, and a gradual lengthening of pommel spurs. Besides depicting his own designs, Berain may also have illustrated arms produced by his father and uncle. The 1659 album was published in at least two subsequent editions: one was possibly issued later the same year; the other, dated 1667, includes two additional sheets.

Around the same time other albums with many designs similar to those of Berain were produced in Paris. One, by the gunmaker François Marcou (*b* 1595) and engraved by C. Jacquinet, consists of 13 plates, of which the last is dated 1657. Only the dated plate approaches contemporary style; the others form a retrospective of fire-arms design and ornament from the late 1630s to about 1650; the patterns even include several for wheel-locks. Marcou's patterns illustrate variations in design from flat, engraved surfaces with apparently stippled backgrounds, to plain line engraving and to chiselling in the round of the style of the 1640s. In fact, most seem to be a direct continuation of the style of plates from the 1620s to the 1640s by Jean Henequin and Philippe Daubigny (*see* §(ii) above). Marcou's themes are varied: Classical mythology on his earliest works, warriors and military trophies, some grotesques, hunting scenes and a profusion of large blossoms and tendrils. In his selection of flowers, Marcou was obviously influenced by the 'tulipomania' of the 1630s. What influence this odd album might have had in the late 1650s is not known, since there is no evidence of its having been directly used for the decoration of any surviving fire-arm of this date. Only the heavily chiselled and blued lock of a gun (Stockholm, Livrustkam.) given by Carl Gustaf Wrangel to Karl X of Sweden has decorative elements from three of Marcou's plates. This lock, however, pre-dates the album's publication by more than a decade and would more logically have been a source for, rather than a result of, this album.

The fact that such albums represented earlier works often had an archaizing effect on fire-arms ornament produced beyond Paris. A substantial number of fire-arms, all decorated in the manner of Marcou's plates and representing the period 1640–50, are variously attributed to the manufacturing centres of Paris, Liège and possibly Amsterdam. These include a gun (Copenhagen, Tøjhusmus.) with heavily chiselled lock and barrel, having its cock in the form of a monster holding its lower jaw in its forepaws, a lion in defensive posture on its lockplate and a monkey on its frizzen, in exactly the form shown in Marcou's early plates. Its decorative elements, however,

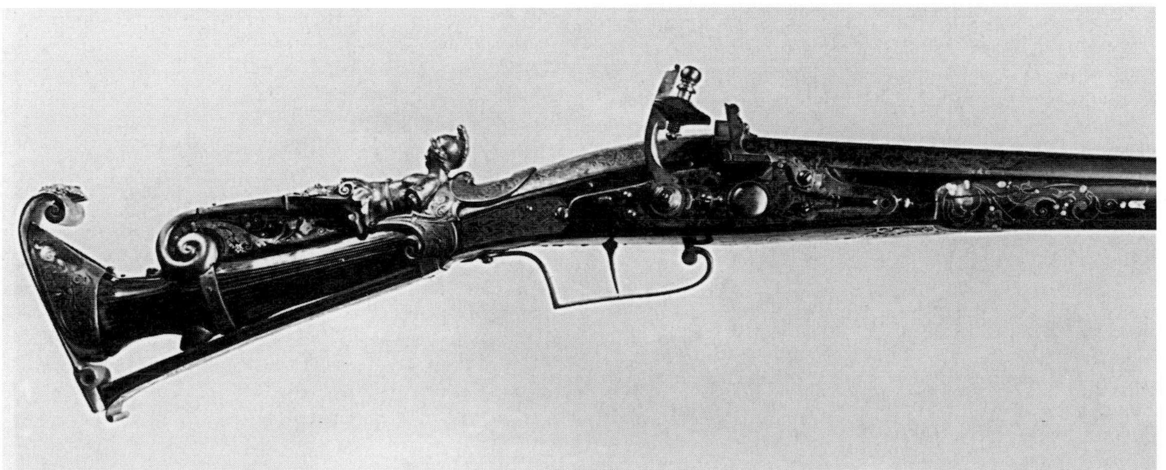

8. Double-barrelled gun made by Le Conte, silver stock inlay signed by Jean Berain I, l. 1.6 m, Paris, before 1673 (Stockholm, Livrustkammaren)

are not found in Marcou's plates. A similar gun (Bålsta, Skoklosters Slott), with elements on its lock and a hunting scene on its barrel identical to those of the Copenhagen gun, also survives, but differences in the execution of its ornament and the more modern form of its lockplate rule out a common place of manufacture. At this time the highest quality decoration was more influenced by the dissemination of fire-arms than that of the pattern books.

A third pattern book, based on the works of the gunmakers Thuraine and Le Hollandois (the latter believed to be Adrien Reynier), appeared in Paris around 1660. Its engraver, also C. Jacquinet, showed basically the same forms and ornament as those of Berain. The firm of Thuraine and Le Hollandois were appointed royal gunmakers about 1650. There are only two known extant arms (both *c.* 1660; Copenhagen, Tøjhusmus.) by them; one has rounded surfaces, the other is flat and faceted. The decoration of these arms is restrained, consisting principally of engraved ornament in the style of the makers' pattern book, with only the slightest relief chiselling and piercing. Both barrels are faceted, but one is covered with engraved gold damascening, in designs of large blossoms and a mascaron conforming to the pattern book, over its extreme breech and barrel tang. The walnut stocks are totally plain, lacking either inlay or carving.

The albums of Berain and Thuraine and Le Hollandois and a single plate from Marcou illustrate the classical Louis XIV style in decorated fire-arms. With only slight modification in the 1680s, this style dominated European fire-arms design and ornament for more than 150 years. While Paris albums were extremely influential, at the highest level of production their designs were infrequently copied exactly. Rather, they served as a point of departure, or, more often, designs were based on elements drawn from several different sheets. Only contemporary forgeries of famous makers' works embody exact translations from the albums. The most blatant of these is a Dutch gun (Stockholm, Livrustkam.) with the spurious signature of the royal gunmaker Laurent Le Languedoc, the maker of which misinterpreted the rendition of much of the ornament.

The Louis XIV style spread quickly to the Netherlands and was well established by the mid-17th century. Contrary to the earlier practice of inlaying with horn and mother-of-pearl, Dutch stocks became quite plain; ebony and full ivory stocks were common for pistols, which were of French form overall. In Maastricht and Utrecht especially a regional type of pommel, in the form of a human or animal head, was developed. The latter type was most frequently of hollow silver and depicted lions or dogs, while human heads were of ivory, most commonly depicting helmeted warriors, and were associated with full ivory stocks. These pommels seem to have been produced by specialist craftsmen. Curiously, the silver lion's-head pommels were imitated in Spain only in the Igualada-Manresa area of Catalonia, concurrently with their popularity in the Netherlands. Engraving in the Netherlands followed the styles of the French albums, and the Utrecht gunmaker Jan Knoop actually employed Berain's album in his workshop. Some Dutch guns have silver mounts finely decorated in the Louis XIV style, but in France and elsewhere cast metal mounts were considered inferior to those of forged iron. Silver mounts were often accompanied by engraved silver damascening in floral designs over the barrel breech, which contrasted with the dark blue finish of the iron.

In the mid-17th century Spanish and English gunmakers maintained the decorative traditions of half a century earlier. By the 1660s a few Spanish gunmakers had begun to experiment with the French practice of the concealed attachment of parts. They also copied relief steel chiselling, but these innovations were applied to traditional Spanish or non-French forms. In England response to the Louis XIV style was found in the lock style, but aside from cock shape and a brief period of concealing the frizzen spring by moving it to the lock's interior, the influence of this style was minimal. A few English arms of the 1670s have engraving inspired by Berain and Marcou and fluted forends in the French manner. Since the latter element is not illustrated in the French albums, it probably reached England through Dutch examples.

The style of Scottish fire-arms underwent no obvious change during the second half of the 17th century; the snaphaunce lock was retained, but on a few examples the engraving seems to show an awareness of Berain and Marcou. The butts of long guns continued to be gouge-decorated, but sometimes with stop-fluting, suggesting an awareness of classical ornament, which is supported by an occasional use of bead-and-reel moulding. On the whole, however, the flat chip-carving imitates the decoration of contemporary joined furniture.

German long guns, with their peculiar horn-inlaid cheek stock and wheel-lock, survived into the late 17th century and well into the 18th, by which time they must have been considered as antiquated and traditional as the Scottish pistol. A magnificent rifle (*c.* 1695; Woburn Abbey, Beds), made in Landshut, probably for Karl IX of Sweden, is the finest example of the persistence of this style. Concurrently, the French-style shoulder stock and French flintlock were made in Germany. The stock was distinguished by a broader and thicker butt and lacked horn inlay.

Italian gunmakers responded to the Louis XIV fashion by adopting its external forms and even applying these to the so-called 'Florentine' version of the snaphaunce lock. In the northern gunmaking centres of Brescia-Gardone and Bologna the emphasis was on steel chiselling, from low relief on all metal elements to three-dimensional on moving lock parts. Themes of decoration varied from scenes taken from Classical mythology, to portrait and classical busts, *rinceaux* and acanthus, occasionally combined with engraving in the Berain style. Gun stocks were of walnut and varied in form from adaptations of the earlier musket type to those showing some French influence; pistols more frequently show the influence of French fashion, but their iron mounts were heavier and broader in order to provide greater surface area for relief chiselling. Inlaid chiselled plaques, not found on French arms, were frequently added in the forend and around the barrel tang (e.g. London, Wallace). A distinctive form of steel chiselling is found on 17th-century guns and pistols whose manufacture is generally considered to be southern, possibly Neapolitan. The style is epitomized by a pistol (London, Wallace), whose figured root walnut stock follows the traditional Spanish gun-butt style and whose 'miquelet' flintlock is also Spanish-inspired; there, however, foreign inspiration ends, as all iron parts—mounts, lock and barrel—are heavily chiselled in relief and pierced in foliate designs containing rather naively executed human figures. This decoration is taken to the extreme of having non-functional projections on the lock simply to expand the area for chiselling and piercing. While the apparent Spanish influence on the form of this pistol supports a Neapolitan origin, some similar northern (Brescian) examples suggest a common decorative source for the chiselling.

Plain fruit-woods, of which cherry was the most valued for its strength and suitability for carving, were the traditional woods used for stocks throughout most of Europe, while walnut was a distant second in popularity, except for military arms. There was, however, especially in the north, a brief flirtation with such exotic but plain woods from Africa and the New World as ebony and jacaranda. In the 1670s the appreciation of the inherent decorative value of the wood itself seems to have begun in France, where highly figured maple, often with its grain artificially enhanced, replaced woods with plainer grains. The fad for figured woods spread throughout Europe, apparently through the dissemination of French arms, since this feature does not appear in the pattern books. English stockers used maple during the reigns of William III (*reg* 1689–1702) and Anne (*reg* 1702–14), while in Spain it did not become acceptable until the 1710s, and, even then, cherry with an artificial maple grain was preferred. In Italy, elaborately grained root walnut continued to fulfil the demand for figured wood for stocks, but this was a highly unstable material and often separated with the passage of time. By the mid-18th century the fad for fancy wood had passed, and reasonably plain walnut became the wood of choice throughout most of Europe, except Spain, where cherry was still favoured.

In 1684 a new pattern book appeared in Paris, the influence of which rivalled that of Berain. It consisted of eight plates engraved and printed by Claude Simonin, whose source was the works of Laurent Le Languedoc; the patterns were undoubtedly taken from Le Languedoc's workshop designs, and some reflect fashions of the 1670s. A second pattern book, consisting of 12 plates, appeared in 1693 as a collaboration between Claude and his son Jacques Simonin. It essentially continues the style of Claude's 1684 designs, but battle themes supplant many of the earlier classical elements. While by 1695 the second album had passed through three editions, its influence is barely apparent on surviving arms.

Both albums illustrate an existing tendency towards gently curved profiles and convex surfaces (see fig. 9), contrasting with the flat and faceted surfaces covered with Baroque relief chiselling popularized by Berain. Some of the finest of this ornament appears on the purely ornamental sideplates that were chiselled in the most elaborate designs and pierced to achieve maximum contrast with the wood into which they were inlaid. Pommel bosses in the form of masks were introduced in the designs, reflecting an innovation in fire-arms ornament of the late 1670s; these were probably derived from the mid-17th-century head-shaped pommels. The former became the most durable of design elements, remaining in vogue until

9. Designs for pommels, a lock, sideplates and escutcheons, from a pattern book by Claude Simonin (Paris, 1684), pl. 6 (private collection)

well into the 19th century. While chiselled masks (and other ornament) on barrels were oriented so as to be seen upright by the person holding the arm, pommel masks were turned so as to be upright when the pistol was held vertically with the muzzle down. Pistols were carried butt forward in saddle holsters so that these masks were visible. Graceful lines, gentle curves and slightly rounded surfaces epitomized French fire-arms from the 1670s and proved to be universally attractive judging from the rapid international adoption of this French style, which overall, however, still adhered to the fashion defined by Berain.

French style was most successfully interpreted by French masters, for example Bertrand Piraube, gunmaker to Louis XIV from 1670, who worked extensively in the style of Simonin and le Languedoc (e.g. gun, 1682; Windsor Castle, Berks, Royal Col.). While Simonin's patterns show ornament for relief chiselling, engraving, stock carving and wire and plate inlay, the actual execution of the ornament on an arm, as with earlier French designs, required a foreknowledge of the practices of Paris gunmakers. Otherwise, the flat, engraved patterns could be misleading: stock carving could be confused for wire inlay, or vice versa, and relief chiselling with engraving, as seen on the counterfeit Languedoc gun mentioned above. Thus, improbable interpretations of such details are occasionally found on English, Spanish and Italian arms, even where the gunmakers carefully followed Simonin's patterns. The one foreigner whose interpretation and execution equalled those of the great Paris makers of his day was the German Armand Bongarde, who worked in Düsseldorf from about 1668 until his death in 1727 (see Gusler and Lavin, plates, pp. 149–51). While he worked in the style of the albums then available, these seem only to have provided inspiration, since there is no evidence of direct copying. In style and decoration, however, his works are about ten years behind those made in Paris, suggesting at least some dependence on published patterns. Bongarde made a fine flintlock fowler (Vienna, Ksthist. Mus.) in the Louis XIV style for Charles Leopold, Duke of Lorraine.

French fashions were also introduced to other European countries by emigrant gunmakers. Both before and

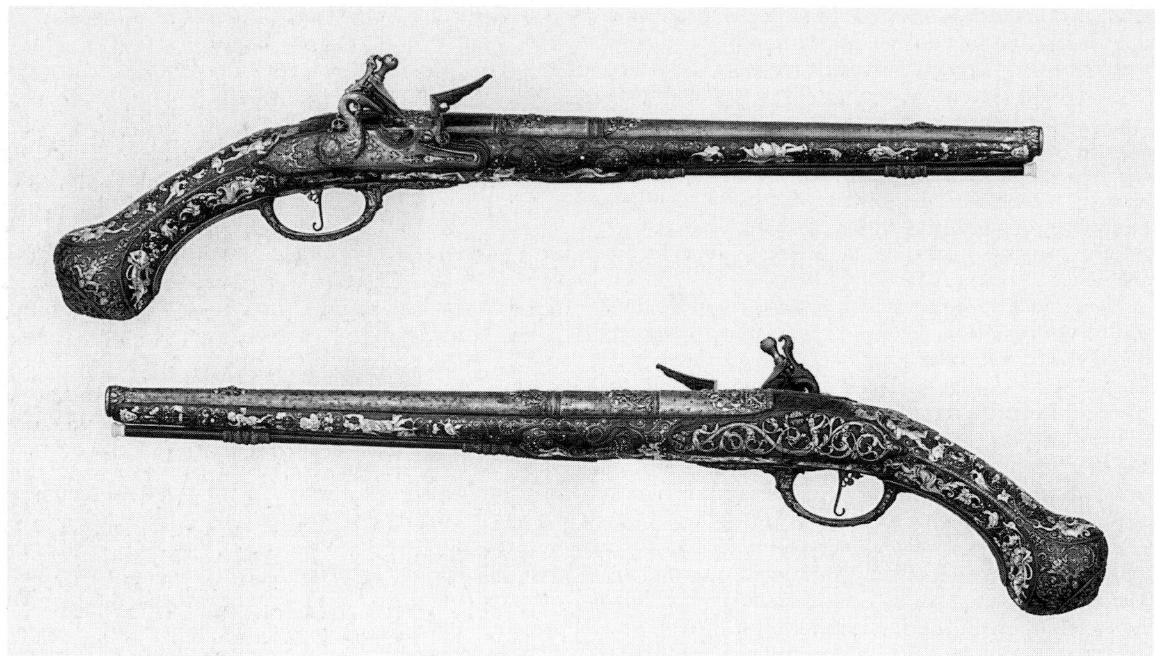

10. Pair of pistols made by Pierre Monlong, gunmaker to William III, stocks inlaid with silver wire and engraved sheet silver, mounts and barrels of chiselled iron, the barrels overlaid with gold, barrel l. 353 mm, London, *c.* 1695 (Leeds, Royal Armouries Museum)

after the revocation of the Edict of Nantes in 1685 many Huguenot craftsmen moved to England, among them both Parisian and provincial gunmakers. The best known of these was Pierre Monlong who had been appointed Arquebusier to Louis XIV in 1664. In England, where French style still clashed with archaic English fashion, the Huguenots were opposed and harrassed by the Gunmakers' Company of London. Some Huguenots, however, acquired noble and even royal patronage, and eventually their avant-garde fashion was accepted throughout England. In 1689 Monlong became Gentleman Armourer in Ordinary to William III, for whom he made what are considered the finest pair of 'English' pistols (Leeds, Royal Armouries Mus.; see fig. 10) in existence. Despite their date of *c.* 1695, they epitomize the best of the Louis XIV style of the late 1670s.

The manufacture of high-quality guns in Spain under the mentally unstable Charles II (*reg* 1665–1700), who, unlike either his predecessors or his successors, showed little interest in this area, stagnated stylistically during the late 17th century. The royal gunmaker Nicolás Bis experimented with French fashion in a gunlock (untraced) dated 1692, and in 1694 Diego Esquibel made a plain, French-type flintlock gun (Madrid, Real Armería), which was modernized by restocking in the early 18th century.

By the late 17th century gunmakers in Italy had assimilated the major aspects of the Simonin style without totally renouncing Italian features of half a century earlier. Thus, in northern Italy the new curved profile and convex surfaces were combined with relief chiselling of Renaissance grotesques, engraving after Philippe Daubigny and lacy iron sheet and silver sheet stock inlay. The earlier Italian snaphaunce gave way to the French-type flintlock. Production in southern Italy, however, remained ultra-conservative, even to the retention of the archaic snaphaunce until well into the 19th century, although some high-quality Louis XIV style guns were produced in Naples in the second half of the 18th century.

The style of Simonin and Le Languedoc remained dominant in European fire-arms until the advent of machine production in the 19th century. Such changes as the introduction of an alternate pommel form called 'bird's head' and the shortening of the stock's forend to mid-barrel enjoyed limited popularity. More important was the greater use of cast brass, silver and even silver-gilt mounts to replace those of steel. Despite the cost of precious metals, cast mounts represented a saving in labour, compared to the forging, chiselling and engraving of steel. Casting patterns were retained for future use, while steel mounts had to be individually forged. In some areas, such as Spain (except Catalonia), castings were disparaged until, in the final years of the 18th century, this innovation was grudgingly accepted.

(iv) After c. *1700.* The third edition of Simonin's album in 1705 consisted of the original eight plates and five additional plates by de la Collombe, whose first name is unknown. The later plates reflect a change in fashion: the flat and faceted surfaces of Berain's earlier patterns were revived. The earliest surviving example of this 'Berain revival' is a pair of pistols dated 1696 (Lenk, pl. 85) by Bertrand Piraube. All Parisian makers had espoused the style by 1700. Following the distribution of Simonin's 1705 edition, possibly the most popular pattern book for gunmaking ever, the flat and faceted surfaces of the new Berain revival style began to dominate European arms

fashion. This occurred with varying delay: gunmakers in Germany, Bohemia, Austria and the Netherlands took up the style in the 1720s, while in England little response was evident until about the 1740s. The result was that by the mid-18th century there was considerable conformity among European fire-arms. After his accession in 1700 Philip V, the new Bourbon king of Spain and Louis XIV's grandson, immediately disposed of all the Spanish and old-fashioned guns he had inherited, and Spanish gunmaking at court level was forced immediately to conform to the newer Louis XIV style, as defined by Simonin and Le Languedoc. Philip V retained Nicolás Bis, who made, shortly after 1705, a pair of pistols (London, Tower) for him; these were inspired almost entirely by two plates from the third edition of Simonin's album.

The first album to reflect completely the Berain revival was Nicolas Guérard's *Diverses pièces d'arquebuserie*, which appeared in Paris about 1720. Its designs, supposedly taken from contemporary Parisian gunmakers' work, are characterized by the addition, to already familiar Baroque elements, of strapwork in the manner of the designer Claude Gillot (who produced an unsuccessful album) and recessed panels apparently intended for gilding. Guérard also offered several elaborate patterns for engraved silver stock inlay, elements of which appear on a number of surviving guns. The renewed emphasis on profuse stock inlay signalled the demise of the stock made of heavily figured wood.

Accompanying the changes brought by the Simonin and Berain revival styles was the application of Rococo ornament to fire-arms. This began in the 1720s in Austria and Germany, passing to France only shortly thereafter. Again, pattern books reflected this new fashion only after a considerable time lapse. An album (1730) by de la Collombe, consisting of only six plates, continues the strapwork and recessed panels seen in Guérard's earlier work and offers several Baroque sideplate patterns, but it shows little to herald the birth of the Rococo. This work was continued almost 20 years later by de la Collombe's disciple Giles de Marteau, who added only four plates, dated 1743, 1744 and 1749. These all show full-blown Rococo patterns, an unusually large proportion of which are pure ornament: details for such non-functioning parts as sideplates, finials and rear sights and for relief stock carving around the barrel tang. Only one partial lock is depicted. De Marteau's interest in the non-mechanical is reinforced by his publication of a small album of 20 plates solely for the carving of tang surrounds. Evidence of the actual use of these designs is indicated by a bound copy (London, V&A) bearing the bookplate of the gunmaker Gauvain of Bordeaux, but these patterns have never been compared with actual carving. De la Collombe's and de Marteau's plates were, however, employed by gunmakers to the Spanish royal family.

Except for court fashion, gunmaking in Spain remained conservative. In Catalonia, in fact, the trend was regressive, as 17th-century styles were favoured. Not until the late 1740s did French-style fire-arms begin to be manufactured in Barcelona. An outstanding exception to the conservatism of gunmaking in southern Italy was the royal factory at Naples established in 1757 by Charles VII (later Charles III of Spain), which became the centre for the production of the most cosmopolitan arms in southern Italy during the latter half of the 18th century. These showed no Italian features but were frequently of a composite style resembling a Spanish interpretation of the Louis XIV style. Foremost among the factory's gunmakers was Michele Battista, who, during the 1770s, worked in a decorative style that owed more to Simonin than to his French contemporaries (e.g. New York, Met.).

After 1750 English gunmakers adopted the flat and faceted surfaces of the Berain revival, and these remained the only fashionable forms for the next 75 years. Cast silver mounts, with grotesque masks often comprising the entire pistol pommel, tendril-like silver-wire stock inlay and precise engraving of iron parts, the edges of which were decorated with stylized leaf borders, became the characteristics of nearly every English fire-arm. Barrels were frequently blued. So alike did English fire-arms become that it was no longer possible to distinguish the work of individual makers.

Scottish pistols of the same period were influenced by their 17th-century forebears, with the addition of Celtic ornament. After 1750 they were still being made with engraved all-metal stocks, usually iron, but sometimes brass or silver, terminating in a stylized ramshorn or rounded pommel. The latter feature was perhaps influenced by contemporary English fashion. These pistols retained the early button trigger and were fitted with archaic belthooks. Engraving on stocks, locks and barrels usually combined earlier motifs with current designs, and only locks conformed to contemporary fashion. Scottish long-arms, on the other hand, were no different from their English counterparts.

In southern Spain *c.* 1750 a reaction against French fire-arms fashion began, leading to a revival of 17th-century Baroque chiselled ornament, stock forms and even the traditional Spanish ignition mechanisms. This style soon spread to the court, where it was enthusiastically received, although the Baroque decoration was considerably more restrained. At the end of the 18th century Basque gunmakers had adopted the new style, and, with only slight modification, it endured well into the 19th century.

Unlike the Spanish, the French began to use silver mounts around the 1720s, and by the mid-18th century this feature was well established for fine fire-arms. Later cast and chased designs were predominantly Rococo. Surfaces in the Berain revival style continued to be preferred, and iron barrels were frequently inlaid with gold damascening over a blued background. Stocks on the whole became plainer, having less inlay, and their carved ornament was frequently limited to the area around the barrel tang. There was no significant change in this style until the Napoleonic empire, and even then change was minor: the incorporation of such Empire style elements as the sphinx, a right-angled pistol grip ending in a broad, flat pommel, decorative chequering, frequently in the form of scales, and the frequent use of gold or silver-gilt mounts. Nicolas Noël Boutet, gunmaker to Louis XVI and later to Napoleon, was the principal force in the development of the Napoleonic style in fire-arms (e.g. London, Wallace). Without a single pattern book being published, the style spread quickly during the early years of the 19th century, eventually affecting all European fire-arms design. In fact, the most popular published source of Empire ornament was the revived album of Simonin and de la Collombe.

During the period of Boutet's dominance in France there was little reaction to French influence in England; what there was affected pistols (e.g. London, Tower). Sideplates and pommel caps began to disappear completely, and the wooden pommel itself was either flat or rounded below chequered grips. Barrels were chemically browned, often with a visible damascus twist, mounts blued and locks case-hardened with a mottled finish. Restrained engraving tended to be innocuous against these darkened backgrounds. Gold inlay was most often the only obvious decoration; this was normally used for the maker's name and occasionally that of the city, on barrel, lock or both, and for a narrow stripe across the barrel breech. Only the finest arms were occasionally damascened in gold on their locks. This calculated decorative understatement continued until the advent of machine-made fire-arms (e.g. London, Tower, XII.4746-9). Rare instances of the impact of Napoleonic fashion in England are found on presentation fire-arms that often have cast-silver mounts with chased Empire style elements.

The numerous European and international exhibitions from the 1820s gave impetus to the decorative arts, but the Industrial Revolution and development of machine production quickly put an end to the high status of the individual artist–craftsman. Pattern books had effectively disappeared, to be replaced by catalogues illustrating the designs of exhibitors at these international trade fairs. One by Charles Claesen illustrating ornamented fire-arms received awards at the Brussels Industrial Arts Fair of 1856 but shows the paucity of original design for the decoration of machine-made fire-arms. Most heavily represented are Gothic Revival, Renaissance Revival and Rococo Revival styles. An armsmaker and decorator who did make a significant contribution to European design of this period was Eusebio Zuloaga of Madrid, Armourer of the Real Armería during the reign of Isabella II of Spain. He was an accomplished gunmaker, steel chiseller and damascener who worked in the Renaissance Revival style but also attempted to create a distinctive Spanish style by using Moresque gold damascening (see Gusler and Lavin, pp. 208–10), a revival of which was barely in its infancy in Toledo. Zuloaga worked with his eldest son, Plácido Zuloaga, at his factory in Eibar, near Bilbao, and Plácido's work is indistinguishable from his father's.

BIBLIOGRAPHY

J. Hayward: *The Art of the Gunmaker*, 2 vols (London, 1962, rev. 1965)
T. Lenk: *Flintlåset: Dess uppkomst och utveckling* [The flintlock: its origin and development] (Stockholm, 1939; Eng. trans., London, 1965)
A. Hoff: *Feuerwaffen*, 2 vols (Brunswick, 1969)
W. Gusler and J. Lavin: *Decorated Firearms* (Williamsburg, 1977)
C. Blair, ed.: *Pollard's History of Firearms* (London, 1983)
J. Lavin: 'The Gift of James I to Felipe III of Spain', *J. Arms & Armour Soc.*, xiv/2 (1992), pp. 64–88

JAMES D. LAVIN

3. Armour.

(i) Before 1450. (ii) 1450 and after.

(i) Before 1450. Following the fall of the Roman Empire in the West in the 5th century AD there appears to have been a long period in which there were few developments in the production of armour in western Europe. Since armour is primarily designed to protect the user against the weapons systems in use (*see* §§1 and 2 above) with the minimum impairment to the user's mobility, it follows that in a period when there is little advance in the technical development and tactical use of weapons, there will be a parallel continuity in the types of armour employed.

The most important type of metallic armour in early medieval Europe was mail, worn over a padded or quilted garment. Garments of mail were constructed from thousands of interlocking rings or links. Each link was made by drawing an iron wire through an aperture of the appropriate size and shape, then winding the wire in a coil on a mandril of the desired size (usually about 10 mm in diameter).

Individual links were then snipped off the coil, and the overlapping end of each link was placed in the jaws of a swage and hammered to make a flattened, conjoined section, often with a medial rib on the side that was to be on the exterior of the finished garment. The overlapped section was then pierced with a small rivet hole, and the overlapping pieces prised apart. The link could then be inserted through two links on the garment, and the tiny, wedge-shaped rivet, held in pliers, hammered into the rivet hole. Sometimes rows of riveted links were fitted at either side of alternate rows of hammer-welded links. Although expensive and time-consuming to produce, mail provided an effective, completely flexible defence, which weighed between about 10 and 16 kg.

The mail shirt (hauberk) in use in 11th-century Europe usually had elbow-length sleeves, an opening at the front of the neck and knee-length skirts split at the front and rear to permit the wearer to move about on foot or sit astride a horse. The shirt was extended upwards in the form of a mail hood (coif), which was later made as a separate item.

Over this coif was worn a conical iron helm made either of one piece of metal or of four triangular plates either riveted directly together or to narrow iron bands at the front, rear and either side (for an 8th-century example *see* England, fig. 83). It was fitted with a defence for the nose (nasal). This type of helmet, now described as a *Spangenhelm*, was derived directly from those used in the late Roman period (*see* Rome, ancient, §X, 1(iii)). The legs were usually unprotected, other than by fabric defences, though occasionally mail leggings (chausses) were worn. The man-at-arms was protected additionally by a long, kite-shaped, wooden shield, supported by straps (enarmes) for the left arm and suspended round the neck by a longer strap (guige).

Virtually all evidence for the armour of the early medieval period comes from illustrative and written sources, as the surviving armour of the period is scarce: only one early hauberk, possibly of the 10th century, is known (Prague, Cathedral Treasury); the earliest datable complete mail shirt is of the early 14th century. The earliest group of shields (Marburg, Umus. Kultgesch.) must be dated to about 1250, and, with two exceptions, all the surviving early helms are of the 14th century. Likewise, no examples of the fabric defences (aketon) worn under mail or as a separate defence survive.

From the 11th century until the end of the 13th the forms of armour developed gradually. After about 1150 illustrations of mail chausses become common. These consist either of a strip of mail covering the front of the leg and fastened at the rear with straps or laces, or a complete stocking of mail, most probably fastened to a pair of hose and gartered at the knee. At about the same time, probably under the influence of the dress of the Islamic troops encountered on the Crusades, a long, sleeveless, fabric coat (surcoat or coat-armour) began to be worn over armour.

By the 12th century the sleeves of the hauberk had been extended to the wrist and by about 1200 had been extended further into mittens (mufflers) covering the thumb and the backs of the hands. After 1150 a round-topped version of the helm, without a nasal, also became popular, and from about 1180 a flat-topped helm appeared, together with a defence for the face pierced with slits for vision (sights) and ventilation holes (breaths). These face defences were augmented in the early 13th century by defences for the rear of the neck, so that by about 1240 the 'great helm', a cylindrical defence protecting the whole head, had become the standard type of head defence for the knightly classes. The mail coif, supplemented by a padded arming cap worn over or under it, continued to be worn with the great helm. From about 1200 the brimmed kettle-hat became one of the characteristic head defences for the infantry, though it was also used extensively by the knightly classes. The other important development in helmet types was the evolution of the basinet, a simple, hemispherical headpiece worn either in conjunction with or as the upper part of the mail coif. The basinet was also used by infantry, on its own, and by men-at-arms, under their helms.

Despite the predominance of mail, other metallic defences were in use throughout the medieval period, especially in Scandinavia and eastern Europe. Scale armour, formed of small iron plates fastened to each other or to a fabric lining in rows that overlapped each other downwards, was used extensively in the Roman period, particularly from the late 1st century BC, and continued to be employed, albeit rarely, throughout the Middle Ages. Lamellar armour was formed of rectangular plates of iron or leather laced together horizontally in strips, which were in turn laced to each other vertically, the rows characteristically overlapping upwards. It originated in Central Asia and reached Europe in the Roman period. It enjoyed some popularity in Scandinavia, although it was more widely used in eastern Europe. Defences of these kinds, worn over mail, were also common in the Near East.

The earliest reference to an iron-plate defence for the body appears *c.* 1225, and in the mid-13th century there are references to 'cuiries', defences of hardened leather worn over the mail but under the surcoat. Only one surviving element of the hardened-leather limb defences of this period is known (probably early 14th century; London, BM); it has superb tooled decoration, as depicted on such armour in contemporary effigies and monumental brasses. By the end of the 13th century 'pairs of plates' or 'coats of plate' seem to have become common; these were fabric garments, inside which iron plates were riveted, worn over mail but under surcoats, so that only rarely are they illustrated in contemporary art. Such defences survive in quantity only in the grave finds from the site of the Battle of Wisby (1356) in Sweden (Stockholm, Nmus.).

The widespread introduction in the period *c.* 1320–50 of complete defences of iron plate worn over mail was rapid. Limb defences of iron plate became popular; initially these were made in individual elements and tied by points and straps to the body. The arm defences (vambraces) were made in upper and lower sections (cannons), with an additional elbow defence (couter), and leg defences were of similar arrangement, the thigh defence (cuisse) being joined to the knee defence (poleyn), which was strapped over the top of the defence for the lower leg (greave). Gauntlets and sabatons of plate were produced for the hands and feet respectively.

During the second half of the 14th century the manufacture of plate limb defences was refined. The main plates were articulated together by smaller iron plates or lames, either directly by rivets, sometimes fitted in slots in order to give greater movement, or by bands of leather riveted inside the plates. At the same time the plates in the coats of plate protecting the chest became larger and eventually formed the one piece breastplate. Coat armours continued to be worn over armour and were often used to display the owner's heraldry. The shield, which had become gradually shorter until it assumed the familiar heater ('flat-iron') shape, was also used for heraldic display (*see* HERALDRY, fig. 6), as were crests attached to the top of the helm by points.

Although the great helm continued to be used in the tournament, from about 1370 it ceased to be important on the battlefield, perhaps because of the increasing tactical use of men-at-arms in a dismounted role and the need for enhanced vision. It was replaced by the basinet, which had been worn under it; this headpiece was fitted with a visor with sights and breaths and attached to the skull by pivots at either temple or at the centre of the brow (the *Klappvisier* type). By the end of the 14th century the 'pig-faced' basinet was the most widely used helmet of the knightly classes throughout Europe.

About 1410 it became fashionable for the various coverings of armour to be discarded, thus revealing the complete 'white' armour of plate. The coat of plate was replaced by a back and breastplate, each composed of an upper and lower plate, attached together at the centre by a strap and buckle. When the solid breastplate appeared, it was fitted with a bracket on the right of the chest on which to rest the lance, so that when the lance struck something the impact did not shoot it backwards. The basinet was replaced in popularity by the great basinet, in which the mail aventail of the former was replaced by a solid defence of plate. From about this time such craftsmen as the Italian Masters IO and P can be identified by their makers' marks.

Before the 15th century the forms of armour had been remarkably homogeneous throughout Europe, but at this time differences appeared between armour made in Italy (predominantly Milan) and Germany. The advent of complete armour of plate made the use of the shield unnecessary on the battlefield, though it continued to be used in the joust. Instead, Italian arm defences were

11. Armet, steel, 4.2 kg, North Italian, *c.* 1440 (New York, Metropolitan Museum of Art)

reinforced on the left arm, making the armour asymmetrical. Otherwise defences were of smooth, rounded forms. Large defences, known as pauldrons, were worn at the shoulders, overlapping the cuirass at the front and rear; the left pauldron was large and fitted with a reinforce, while the right pauldron was smaller and cut out at the armpit to accommodate the lance. Two new, characteristically Italian helmets were introduced: one, described by modern scholars as an armet (see fig. 11), fitted with large, hinged cheekpieces fastening at the front and with a pivoted visor; and the open-faced barbuta, which closely resembles the ancient Greek Corinthian helmet. Italian armour of this period is quite well represented by surviving examples, primarily in the Trapp family armoury at Schloss Churburg (Castello Coira) in the Italian Tyrol, which contains by far the greatest quantity of early medieval European armour in the world, but also from a number of archaeological finds.

Unlike Italian armour, German armour in the first half of the 15th century remained symmetrical in form. The breastplate was fitted with a deep fauld (skirt) extending almost to the knees. Very few examples of German armour of this period survive, so knowledge of it comes mainly from artistic representations. In northern Europe a new open-faced helmet, the sallet, also appeared and became by far the most commonly used headpiece in this region.

(ii) 1450 and after. By the mid-15th century plate armour was used in one form or another by the great majority of troops on the battlefield. It was, in its finest form, an extremely expensive commodity, the manufacture of which was at the forefront of technological advance and on which the finest artists and craftsmen were engaged. By the mid-17th century, however, technical developments in fire-arms had led to a decline in the use of armour, and complete plate armour at least had disappeared from the battlefield.

In the second half of the 15th century German armour was made in the Gothic style, with all the elements embossed with fluting that imitated the pleating of fashionable garments, and with an overall tendency to slender, elongated forms. On the finest examples internal edges were cusped and fretted, and external edges were often decorated with applied brass borders, similarly cusped. The most important examples of this type are the armours (*c.* 1480; Vienna, Ksthist. Mus.) of Archduke Maximilian of Austria (later Holy Roman Emperor Maximilian I) and Archduke Sigismund, Count of Tyrol (1427–96; see fig. 12)), both made by Lorenz Helmschmied (*d* 1517) of Augsburg. As early as 1485 such armourers at Innsbruck as Kaspar Rieder (*fl* 1482–99), Hans Prunner (*fl* 1482–99) and various members of the Treytz family were producing

12. Armour of Archduke Sigismund, Count of Tyrol, by Lorenz Helmschmied, steel and brass, h. 1.72 m, Augsburg, *c.* 1480 (Vienna, Kunsthistorisches Museum)

armour that, though following German methods of construction, incorporated Italian forms and was probably the precursor of the synthesis of the German and Italian styles in the early 16th century. Milan remained the most important centre of armour production in Italy, and the dominant armourers there were members of the Missaglia family, identification of whom remains difficult despite a proliferation of makers' marks. The style of Italian armour remained constant throughout the second half of the 15th century.

Maximilian I was probably the greatest patron of armourers in the late 15th century and the early 16th, and his influence on the stylistic development of armour was profound, particularly on that of tournament armour. With the codification of the rules for the types of joust, foot combat and tourney within the tournament, different types of armour were needed for the various events. Jousts were divided into jousts of war (*Rennen*), in which sharp lances were used and for which armours of great weight, fitted with sallets and closely fitting shoulder-shields of wood and leather, were made, and jousts of peace (*Gestechen*), in which rebated (coronel-tipped) lances were employed and for which armours with frog mouthed helms were produced. Within these basic divisions there were numerous different forms of joust, for each of which a particular form of armour was made, and the same applied to the foot combat and tourney.

As well as patronizing armourers at Augsburg, those such as Matthias Deutsch (*fl* 1479–97) at Landshut and others at Nuremberg, Maximilian set up in 1504 an imperial workshop at Innsbruck. In the early 16th century the so-called 'Maximilian' style of armour, consisting of overall fluted decoration, usually found on every element of an armour except the greaves, started to be produced in the German centres. This style dominated central European production from about 1505 to 1530 and was also evident in Italian armour. A small number of armours exhibit a transitional style, with rounded breastplates and symmetrical limb defences, but with no fluting.

An important development during this period was the use of etching for the decoration of armour. In this method the plates were firstly either covered in a resist and the required design scratched through the coating, or the basic design was painted in reverse in wax and the details filled in by scraping; the plates were then placed in weak acid until a satisfactory etching of the uncovered surface had taken place. The first surviving example of etching on armour is the decoration of the horse armour (1477; Vienna, Ksthist. Mus.) of the Emperor Frederick III, though the technique was in use earlier for swords (*see* §1(i) above). By about 1510 the technique had become the most common method for decorating armour. Italian etchers tended to use either a plain, hatched or cross-hatched background, while German artists tended to use a stippled ground. Etched decoration is usually confined to the borders of plates or to bands running vertically or diagonally; it is also usually combined with fire-gilding of either the back or the foreground, and sometimes with niello or occasionally enamelling.

Towards the end of the 15th century a number of Milanese armourers seem to have emigrated to Flanders, where armour of reasonable quality had always been produced, and by this time an important workshop existed, probably centred on Brussels, where imperial commissions could be carried out and armour of the highest quality was produced. The most important craftsmen there included the Master of the Orb and Cross, the Master H and most possibly Martyn van Royne (*fl* 1515–40), who later moved to England. Other significant centres were Ghent, Bruges, Liège and Antwerp, though few of their products are certainly identified. A 15th-century breastplate probably associated with Liège is now in the Brussels Koninklijk Museum van het Leger en van Krijgsgeschiedenis. Work

13. Armour, probably made for Henry VIII of England, etched and gilded steel, brass, leather and velvet, Greenwich, 1527 (New York, Metropolitan Museum of Art)

14. Parade burgonet by Filippo Negroli, steel, damascened in gold and embossed, max. w. 185 mm, 1.9 kg, Milan, 1534 (New York, Metropolitan Museum of Art)

of conservative 15th-century Italianate style was produced in Flanders. The identification of much armour to Flemish workshops has been made only quite recently, and the history of the industry there is incompletely understood. Even less well known is the Spanish school, producing armour related in style to that of Flanders and thought in the 19th century to have been centred on Calatayud.

Armour produced in England is also difficult to identify. A guild of armourers existed in London as early as 1347, but none of its products of the 15th or 16th centuries can be positively identified. In 1515, however, Henry VIII brought to England 11 'Almains' (Flemings and Germans) and established a royal workshop in Greenwich Palace under the mastership of Martin van Royne to produce personal armour for him. Van Royne was succeeded after 1517 by the German Erasmus Kyrkenar (*d* 1567), who in turn was followed from 1567 to 1576 by the Englishman John Kelt (*d* 1577) and from 1577 to 1607 by the German Jacob Halder (*fl* from 1553). Milanese craftsmen were also employed. The Greenwich workshop produced armour (see fig. 13) of an individual style—a combination of the Italianate Flemish work and German influence—which remained of the highest quality throughout the 16th century.

As early as 1510 extra pieces began to be provided for an armour in order to render it suitable for the tourney, and from about 1530 this practice was extended, so that an armour could be used for the joust and foot combat, as well as for the field and tourney, thus obviating the need for owning a number of these exceedingly expensive different forms of armour. These extended armours are now known as garnitures, a term devised by modern German scholars. Many of the important surviving 16th-century armours were originally made as garnitures.

A derivation of the coat of plates was the brigandine, produced by a similar technique, by riveting columns of small, overlapping plates inside a fabric doublet. Manufacture of these defences continued until the mid-16th century, mainly in Italy. Brigandines were primarily worn by infantry, but also, together with complete defences of plate for the rest of the body, by men-at-arms. Another defence, produced mainly in England and Scotland, was the jack of plate, consisting of small, square plates sewn with twine inside a quilted doublet (jack). These were worn almost exclusively by infantry, including longbowmen, and were most popular during the mid- to late 16th century.

After 1450 the use of plate armour for the infantry became more common, and from the late 15th century a number of light, half armours with long, laminated tassets and no lance rest survive. German examples of the first half of the century, made mostly in north Germany and described in England as 'Almain rivets', had simple arm defences, protecting only the outside of the arm and back of the hand. These infantry armours were worn with open-faced helmets: during the 15th century and the early 16th sallets, and from the mid-16th century burgonets or morions. The burgonet is an open-faced helmet with a peak, neckguard (sometimes articulated) and hinged cheekpieces. It was often fitted with a buffe: a face and throat defence composed of articulated lames. The morion, the descendant of the kettle-hat, was an open-faced helmet with a broad brim, usually dipping down at the sides, and fitted with cheekpieces on internal leathers. By the mid-16th century half armours with open-faced helmets had become the normal equipment for the heavy infantry pikeman or halbardier. In England the great majority of these half armours (corslets) were imported from Flanders or Germany, although many were produced in Italy; the latter were often decorated with so-called 'Pisan' etching of very poor quality. The development of the form of 16th-century armours is particularly evident in that of the breastplate, the shape of which followed that of the civilian doublet: it remained globose until *c.* 1535, then took on a deep, bellied form from *c.* 1540 to *c.* 1560, then a peascod shape that was at its most extreme *c.* 1585, and then attenuating into the vestigial peascod form of the 17th century.

In Italy the Missaglia family was superseded in importance in the mid- and late 16th century by the Negroli family, also of Milan. They specialized in embossed decoration and damascening (see fig. 14). In the early 16th century another important Milanese armourer was Niccolo de Silva (*fl* 1511–49). In the late 16th century, however, production of armour of any quality in Italy virtually ceased except for that of Pompeo della Chiesa (*fl* 1585–93) of Milan.

German centres continued to produce fine armour in the 16th century. At Innsbruck Konrad Seusenhofer (*d* 1517) was followed by his brother Hans Seusenhofer (*d* 1555), the latter's son Hans Seusenhofer (*d* 1580) and Jakob Topf (*d* 1597). At Augsburg Lorenz Helmschmied was followed by his son Koloman Helmschmied (1471–1532) and Koloman's son Desiderius Helmschmied (1513–*c.* 1578). Other important armourers in Augsburg were Matthias Frauenpreiss (*d* 1549) and Anton Peffenhauser (1525–1603). In Nuremberg the most important master was Kunz Lochner the younger (*c.* 1510–67), though much of the production in that city was restricted to black and white munition armours. At Landshut a large amount of armour of the highest quality was made by Wolfgang Grosschedel (before 1515–63), who had also worked in the royal workshop at Greenwich, and Franz Grosschedel (*d* 1580). The Flemish centres continued to be important but after *c.* 1520 mainly for the production of munition armour. Armour of high quality with embossed decoration by Elisius Libaerts (*fl* 1557–64) was made in Antwerp *c.* 1560 for royal patrons (see fig. 15), and a small group of decorated pieces was produced in the 1580s by a member of the Collaert family, probably Hans Collaert (1566–1628), in the same city.

In the mid-16th century technical advances in fire-arms ignition systems brought about major changes in the tactics of warfare, and these had a significant impact on the development of armour. The availability of wheel-lock pistols led to the introduction of a new type of cavalry, known in Germany as *Reiters*, who were equipped with three-quarter armour, similar to that of the infantry, and open-faced burgonets. This type of cavalry largely replaced the completely armoured lancers in battle, though the need for some shock cavalry led to the retention of some lancers in three-quarter armour, known in England as demi-lances. The increasing importance of fire-arms and a type of warfare in which greater mobility was necessary

15. Pageant shield decorated by Elisius Libaerts, steel, h. 690 mm, Antwerp, *c.* 1560 (Vienna, Kunsthistorisches Museum)

led to the heavy infantry discarding, quite literally, their arm defences.

By the early 17th century the pikeman's armour comprised only headpiece, gorget, backplate and breastplate. The breastplate had tassets, each made in one piece and embossed to simulate the articulated lames of which they would have been made a generation earlier. About 1620 the fastening of shoulder-straps was improved, straps and buckles being replaced by straps with terminal plates pierced with holes, which fitted over pierced studs with swivel hooks. From about 1630 the headpieces used by infantry were known in England as potts, though they were merely versions of the comb morions that survived in northern Europe.

The heavy cavalry or cuirassiers were similar to the demilances of the late 16th century but were armed with pairs of pistols. These troops were the most heavily armoured of this period, having three-quarter armour usually fitted with a close helmet. Far more numerous were the light cavalry harquebusiers, armed with sword and carbine, and protected with an open-faced pott, and a cuirass or buff coat or both. English harquebusiers' potts had characteristic triple-bar face-guards, while their continental counterparts, known as *Zischägge* after the Turkish *çiçak* ('chichak') from which they had evolved, had single nasal defences.

While armour of high quality continued to be produced at Greenwich until 1635 and at Innsbruck, the finest armours in western Europe were produced in France, where enamelled decoration was sometimes employed, and in the Netherlands under the patronage of Maurice, Prince of Orange. Dutch armours, only recently identified, are characterized by punched and incised decoration combined with gilding, sometimes with sheets of gold leaf. Complete armours were still made for the tournament, which survived in a vestigial form beyond 1650 in Germany and until the end of the 17th century in Scandinavia, but which lost popularity in France in the mid-16th century and in England in the early 17th. Most armours, however, were intended primarily for ceremonial purposes.

In western Europe infantry armour had become redundant by 1650, although light cavalry armour for the harquebusier, comprising a cuirass (breastplate and backplate), pott and sometimes a long elbow gauntlet, continued to be made until the end of the 17th century. The finest example of this type is probably the armour (London, Tower) of James II, King of England (*reg* 1685–8), made by Richard Holden of London (*fl* 1658–1709). In general, however, the buff coat became the only common form of body armour, and the pott was replaced by the secret, a skull defence worn under a hat. After the 17th century body armour continued to be worn by a small number of continental cuirassiers (*see* POLAND, fig. 23) and forms part of ceremonial uniforms even in the 20th century; it was reintroduced in the uniform of the British Household Cavalry for the coronation of William IV in 1830. Although helmets were worn by many units of both infantry and cavalry during the 19th century, these were largely fashionable pieces of headgear and lacked any serious defensive properties.

With the changes in the character of warfare in the late 19th century a number of different types of thoracic defences, for example the Dayfield body shield, were used experimentally. During World War I the prevalence of shrapnel injuries led to the reintroduction on a large scale of protective helmets, and some quite heavy body armour was developed by the German forces. By World War II the need for body defence for key, immobile personnel, particularly air-crew, led to the development of the flak jacket. This was consciously based on the 16th-century jack of plate, and the research of such scholars of medieval armour as Bashford Dean was influential in the development of many new body defences. In the second half of the 20th century the invention and application of polyaramid fibres (kevlar) and light ceramic trauma pads considerably expanded the effectiveness of defences for the body and led to their more extensive use on the battlefield than at any time since the 17th century.

BIBLIOGRAPHY

Conde Valencia de don Juan: *Catalogo histórico-discriptivo de la Real Armería de Madrid* (Madrid, 1898)
E. Haenel: *Kostbare Waffen aus der Dresdner Rüstkammer* (Leipzig, 1923)
O. Trapp and J. G. Mann: *The Armoury of the Castle of Churburg* (London, 1929)
F. H. Cripps-Day: *Fragmenta armamentaria*, 5 vols (Frome, 1934–51/*R* London, 1952–6)
B. Thordemann: *Armour from the Battle of Wisby, 1361* (Uppsala, 1939–40)
Exhibition of Armour Made in the Royal Workshops at Greenwich (exh. cat., ed. J. G. Mann; London, Tower, 1951)
M. Burgess: 'The Mail Maker's Technique' and 'Further Thoughts on the Construction of Mail Garments', *Antiqua. J.*, xxxiii (1953), pp. 48–55, 193–202
Die Innsbrucker Plattnerkunst (exh. cat., ed. B. Thomas and O. Gamber; Innsbruck, Tirol Landesmus., 1954)
C. Blair: *European Armour* (London, 1958)
H. Nickel: *Der mittelalterliche Reiterschild des Abendlands* (Berlin, 1958)
A. Reitzenstein: 'Die Nürnberger Plattner', *Beitr. Wirtschaftesgesch. Nürnbergs*, ii (1967), pp. 700–25
H. Müller and F. Kunter: *Europäische Helme* (Erfurt, 1971)
Landshuter Plattnerkunst (exh. cat., ed. A. Reitzenstein; Landshut, Stadtmus., 1975)
B. Thomas and O. Gamber: *Katalog der Liebrüstkammer*, Vienna, Ksthist. Mus. cat., i (Vienna, 1976), ii (Busto Arsizio, 1990)
L. G. Boccia, F. Rossi and M. Morin: *Armi e armature lombarde* (Milan, 1980)
L. G. Boccia: *Le armature di S Maria delle Grazie di Curtaone di Mantova, e l'armatura lombarda del '400* (Busto Arsizio, 1982)
F. Mazzini: *L'Armeria reale di Torino* (Busto Arsizio, 1982)
D. Edge and J. M. Paddock: *Armour of the Medieval Knight* (London, 1988)

For further bibliography *see* §I above.

TOM RICHARDSON

Armson, William Barnett (*b* London, 1832 or 1833; *d* Christchurch, New Zealand, 22 Feb 1883). New Zealand architect of English birth. In 1862, after a lengthy apprenticeship in Melbourne, Australia, Armson arrived in New Zealand. He spent two years (1862–4) in the engineering department of the Otago provincial government, Dunedin, and from 1866 to 1870 he practised in Hokitika on the West Coast. Christchurch, where he finally settled in 1870, nurtured the most productive phase of his career. Inspired by Victorian London's palazzo-style clubs and Venetian Gothic office blocks, Armson transformed the commercial heart of Christchurch. In Hereford Street alone he designed 12 substantial buildings, but only the Fisher Building (1880), a wedge-shaped structure in Italian Gothic, survives. Elsewhere in Christchurch the former Library (1875), Boys' High School (1879), Girls' High School (1880), Anderson's Shops, Borough Hotel and Butterworth's Warehouse (1881) demonstrate his versatility in handling historicist vocabularies, while the Loan and Mercantile Company's Store (1881) is noteworthy as an exercise in functional design.

Further afield, the church of St Mary's (begun 1880), Timaru, appears ponderous as an essay in High Victorian Gothic. But the Bank of New Zealand (1879–83), Dunedin, a richly modelled palazzo in the Venetian High Renaissance style, is very pleasing. The banking chamber features a magnificent coffered ceiling with ornate plasterwork in exceptionally high relief.

BIBLIOGRAPHY

I. J. Lochhead and J. N. Mané, eds: *W. B. Armson: A Colonial Architect Rediscovered* (Christchurch, 1983)
J. N. Mané: 'A Colonial Architect Rediscovered: William Barnett Armson, 1834–1883', *Historic Places in New Zealand*, 3 (Dec 1983), pp. 18–19
——: 'Lost and Found: The Architecture of W. B. Armson', *A. NZ*, 29 (1983), pp. 54–7

J. N. MANÉ-WHEOKI

Armstead, Henry Hugh (*b* London, 18 June 1828; *d* London, 4 Dec 1905). English sculptor, silversmith and illustrator. He was the son of a chaser and attended the Royal Academy Schools, London. At first he gave his attention equally to silverwork and to sculpture, exhibiting at the Royal Academy from 1851. An early bronze, *St Michael and the Serpent*, cast in 1852 for the Art Union, shows him conversant with the style of continental Romantics, and his debut in metalwork coincided with the introduction into England of virtuoso repoussé work by the Frenchman, Antoine Vechte (1799–1868). In the *Outram Shield* (London, V&A), Armstead displayed the full gamut of low-relief effects in silver, but its reception at the Royal Academy in 1862 disappointed him, and he turned his attention to monumental sculpture. Among a number of fruitful collaborations with architects, that with George Gilbert I Scott (ii) included a high degree of responsibility for the sculpture on the *Albert Memorial* in Kensington Gardens, London. Here Armstead's main contribution was the execution of half of the podium frieze (1863–72), with its portraits of artists, writers and musicians from earliest times to the present. His church monuments, whether effigies or Renaissance-derived wall tablets, were admired for their naturalism. This quality, dominated by a taut sense of design, as well as his abilities as a craftsman in a variety of media, led to his being hailed as a forerunner of the New Sculpture movement. In 1903 he exhibited at the Royal Academy a marble figure of *Remorse* (London, Tate), whose expressive symbolism bears comparison with the work of a younger generation.

BIBLIOGRAPHY

G. White: *English Illustration in the Sixties* (London, 1897; *R* Bath, 1970) [contains examples of his illustrations]
M. H. Spielman: *British Sculpture and Sculptors of Today* (London, 1901)
B. Read: *Victorian Sculpture* (London, 1982)
S. Beattie: *The New Sculpture* (London, 1983)

PHILIP WARD-JACKSON

Armstrong, Elizabeth (Adela). *See* FORBES, (2).

Armstrong, Thomas (*b* Manchester, 19 Oct 1832; *d* Abbots Langley, Herts, 22 April 1911). English painter, designer and administrator of art education. When he left school he embarked on a business career in Manchester. In 1853 he travelled to Paris, where he became a pupil in the studio of Ary Scheffer. The semi-bohemian life that Armstrong led in Paris from 1853 to 1856, with his artist friends E. J. Poynter, T. R. Lamont (1826–98) and Whistler, is described in George Du Maurier's novel *Trilby* (1894; the character Taffy is modelled on Armstrong). During the later 1850s Armstrong travelled and painted in Europe and in Algiers; after *c.* 1860 he settled in London.

Armstrong's early paintings (e.g. *A Street Scene in Manchester*, 1861; Manchester, C.A.G.), which were exhibited at the Royal Manchester Institution, the British Institution and the Royal Academy, generally treat themes of social deprivation. In the later 1860s Armstrong joined the circle of painters associated with the emergent Aesthetic Movement. He painted bland but harmonious figurative pictures without narrative subject or contemporary references, such as *Haytime* (1869; London, V&A). Pictorial devices of Neo-classicism are apparent in the decorative schemes he created in the 1870s; surviving examples include the two principal canvases, *Woman with Lilies* (Newcastle upon Tyne, Laing A.G.) and *Women Watching a Tortoise* (sold Sotheby's, London, 21 June 1983), from the house of Eustace Smith, MP, in Princes Gate, London, and the paintings from Bank Hall, Derbys (1872–3; sold Sotheby's, London, 6 Oct 1980), carried out in collaboration with Randolph Caldecott.

Although Armstrong was considered a progressive artist by his contemporaries and exhibited at the Grosvenor Gallery from its inception in 1877 until 1881, his career as a professional artist did not prosper. From *c.* 1876 he gave up decorative schemes and concentrated on portraiture and landscape subjects; the latter may be seen as products of the Etruscan school and show the influence of Giovanni Costa, to whom Armstrong was introduced by George Howard, later 9th Earl of Carlisle, in 1879.

In 1881 Armstrong was appointed Director of the Art Division of the Department of Science and Art; based at the South Kensington Museum, he was responsible for the organization and supervision of art education throughout Britain. He also acquired original works of art and replicas for the collection of what is now the Victoria and Albert Museum. Armstrong retired from his post at South Kensington in 1898 and moved to Hertfordshire, where he painted and worked on various sculpted monuments, including the memorial to his son Ambrose (*d* 1894) in Abbots Langley parish church.

BIBLIOGRAPHY

F. G. Boyles: 'Mr Thomas Armstrong', *A. J.* [London] (1891), pp. 271–3
L. M. Lamont, ed.: *Thomas Armstrong, C.B.: A Memoir, 1832–1911* (London, 1912)
A. Smith: *Thomas Armstrong (1832–1911): His Works in their Context, 1852–1881* (diss., U. London, 1985)

CHRISTOPHER NEWALL

Armstrong Jones, Anthony. *See* SNOWDON.

ARMU. *See* ASSOCIATION OF REVOLUTIONARY ART OF UKRAINE.

Arnal, Enrique (*b* Catavi, Potosí, 1932). Bolivian painter. He was self-taught as a painter and had his first one-man show in Cuzco in 1954, which was followed by 25 one-man shows in La Paz and by exhibitions in North American cities and in Paris. Arnal was the principal exponent of the Generación del 52. In the 1950s he painted still-lifes with subjects drawn from the open-air markets that included potatoes, roosters and dogs, as in *The Inn* (1960; La Paz, Mus. N. A.). In the early 1960s he painted towns of earth and stone, and at the end of the 1960s he portrayed *Aparapitas*, the stevedores of La Paz, as well as condors and recumbent female nudes, which in the 1980s became *Mountains*, especially during the period 1985 to 1988. He then portrayed the galleries of *Mines* with a progressive stylization and abstraction, and also repeated all the themes he had treated throughout his career in a number of series under the overall title the *World of My Memory* (1989; La Paz, Banco Hipotecario N.). His paintings, with their nervous brushstrokes, are in sober colours: greys, earthen shades and especially black. Arnal won seven national prizes for painting, including that of the Salón Municipal de Pintura in 1955, the Salón Nacional de Artes prize in 1960 and the first INBO (Inversiones Bolivianas) Biennale prize in 1975. He worked as a painting instructor in the Faculty of Plastic Arts in the Universidad Católica Boliviana in La Paz.

BIBLIOGRAPHY

Museum of Modern Art of Latin America: Selections from the Permanent Collection (exh. cat., Washington, DC, Mus. Mod. A. Latin America, 1985)
P. Querejazu: *La pintura boliviana del siglo XX* (Milan, 1989)

PEDRO QUEREJAZU

Árnason, Jón Gunnar (*b* Reykjavík, 15 May 1931; *d* Reykjavík, 21 April 1989). Icelandic sculptor. He studied at art school (1945–50), graduated as a mechanic from the Technical School (1952) in Reykjavík and also studied at Hornsey College of Fine Arts, London (1965–7). Árnason was an influential figure in Icelandic art from 1960 onwards, as a result both of his intelligent reworking of a wide spectrum of artistic ideas and of his organizational abilities. In 1965 he was one of the founders of the radical group SÚM, and in 1967 he was a co-organizer of the first open-air exhibition of sculpture in Iceland; in the 1970s and 1980s he helped to found a centre for Icelandic sculptors as well as the Living Art Museum (Nýlistasafnið) in Reykjavík.

In 1959 Árnason was introduced to kinetic art by Dieter Roth, and movement, actual or implied, continued to be a guiding principle in his art. In the early 1960s he created metal reliefs that could be moved by hand and in 1967 his first motorized sculptures. By the end of the decade he was making threatening, fantastic creations. Movement-as-energy is largely the theme of Árnason's three-dimensional work of the 1970s, culminating in his *Mind Power Plant* of 1980, where spectators are invited to step on to two metal discs and transfer their thoughts elsewhere. In the 1980s his emphasis on materiality was exemplified by his series of monumental steel and aluminium boats that are clearly not seaworthy, yet brimming with energy.

BIBLIOGRAPHY

G. Bergsson: 'Jón Gunnar Árnason', *Íslensk list* (Reykjavík, 1981), pp. 62–7, 77–8, 130–39
Northern Poles (Copenhagen, 1986)

Sól, hnífar, skip [Sun, knives, ship] (exh. cat., ed. G. B. Kvaran; Reykjavík, Nordic House, 1987)
'Hugarorka og Sólstafir'—Jón Gunnar Árnason (exh. cat. by A. Ingólfsson, Reykjavík, N.G., 1994) [Eng. summary]

AÐALSTEINN INGÓLFSSON

Arnau de la Peña (*fl* Barcelona, 1357–*c.* 1390). Catalan illuminator. He was responsible for the illumination of the *Llibre Vert* (Barcelona, Arxiu Mun.), a four-volume compilation of juridical documents commissioned by the Council of Barcelona and datable to the early 1380s. The text was written by the notary Ramón Ferrer in 1345/6. A document (untraced) cited by Gudiol Ricart in *Els trecentistes* (Barcelona, n.d.) recorded that Arnau de la Peña decorated the first volume of the *Llibre Vert* in 1380, but the phrasing of the document did not make it clear whether he was responsible for the illumination of initials or for miniatures, which has caused some debate as to the nature of his activities. Evidence for Arnau's work as a miniaturist is found, however, in documents in the Municipal Archive of Barcelona that attest to payments made to him for both initials and miniatures. In 1357, for example, he was paid for the execution of nine *istorie* in a Book of Hours. The relationship of the *Llibre Vert* to a duplicated undated manuscript known as the *Usatges de Ramón Ferrer* (Barcelona, Arxiu Mun.), which also contains work attributed to Arnau de la Peña, is disputed. Arnau's place in the development of illumination in Barcelona has yet to be firmly established, but, like Ramón Destorrents, he worked in a Gothic style that blended French and Italian elements, under the influence of Simone Martini.

BIBLIOGRAPHY

J. Gudiol Ricart: *Documents per l'historia de la cultura catalana mig-eval*, ii (Barcelona, 1921), pp. 118, 156, 162
J. Domínguez Bordona: *Exposición de códices miniados españoles* (Madrid, 1929), p. 221
——: *La pintura gótica a Catalunya* (Barcelona, 1938), p. 10
M. Meiss: 'Italian Style in Catalonia and a Fourteenth Century Catalan Workshop', *J. Walters A.G.*, iv (1941), pp. 45–87
Spanish Painting (exh. cat., Toledo, OH, Mus. A., 1941), pp. 15–18

LYNETTE BOSCH

Arneberg, Arnstein (Rynning) (*b* Fredrikstad, 6 July 1882; *d* Biri, 9 June 1961). Norwegian architect. He was trained as a draughtsman at the Royal School of Design in Christiania (now Oslo) from 1899 to 1902, and as an architect at the Royal Polytechnic in Stockholm from 1904 to 1906. He worked as an assistant to Erik Lallerstedt in Stockholm (1906–7) and in partnership with Ole Sverre (1865–1932), in Christiania (1907–8), where he afterwards started his own practice. Some of his larger projects were carried out in collaboration with MAGNUS POULSSON, including his best-known works, the Telegraph building (1916–24) and the Town Hall (1916–51; *see* OSLO, fig. 1), both in Oslo. Like Poulsson, Arneberg was a major exponent of the National Romanticism that developed after Norway gained complete independence in 1905. His project for the Royal Hunting Lodge at Voksenkollen (second prize with Sverre, 1905) represented the first clear break with the then-dominant 'Dragon style' (*see* MUNTHE, HOLM), and pointed to a more straightforward use of national forms, particularly the older manor houses of the plains of south-east Norway. The Eidsvold College (1908; destr. 1980) was his first executed work in this style. Even as it became popular, Arneberg, drawing on his experience in Sweden, became increasingly influenced by the Renaissance and Baroque architecture of Scandinavia as a whole. The Villa Elsero (1918–23), Oslo, considered a masterpiece of modern domestic architecture, exemplifies Arneberg's increasing tendency towards simplification in the post-war, neo-classical architectural milieu. The villa's three wings enfold an irregularly shaped rose garden. The five-bay main block has a granite base that follows the uneven terrain. Above this, white-plastered brick rises smoothly, broken only by the windows and a grand, neo-classical entrance portal with a broken pediment. This and other sophisticated and articulate designs were much appreciated by the well-to-do.

With its square central tower, from which four rectangular wings with steeply pitched roofs project, the Vikingskipshus in Oslo (first wing 1926; tower and two more wings 1929; final wing 1954; all by Arneberg), looks like a church. Arneberg wanted to build a 'burial church' for the important excavation finds in the museum. His later works, from after the advent of the modern movement, do not have the same quality: although he used modern techniques and materials, he never embraced the Functionalist style. He was active as a restoration architect: at Oslo's Akershus Castle (of which the oldest part dates from the 14th century) he restored the east wing and royal burial chapel, and most of the interiors are his work (1929–62). His own development can be seen clearly in his various projects for the Town Hall, Oslo.

BIBLIOGRAPHY

NKL
C. Just: *Rådhuset i Oslo* [The town hall in Oslo], i–ii (Oslo, 1950–52)
G. Eliassen, A. Pedersen and O. Platov: *Arnstein Arneberg* (Oslo, 1952)
C. Norberg-Schulz: *Modern Norwegian Architecture* (Oslo, 1986)

CHRISTIAN NORBERG-SCHULZ

Arnheim, Rudolf (*b* Berlin, 15 July 1904). American psychologist and writer of German birth. He studied with Gestalt psychologists at the University of Berlin in the 1920s. His secondary studies in art history and musicology, together with Gestalt psychology, were the basis for his subsequent research into the mechanisms of perception. During the 1930s he studied film, finding in the silent film's unadorned method of reproduction an artistic interpretation of perceptible reality. He wrote film reviews and published the book *Film als Kunst* (Berlin, 1932). In 1940, he settled in the USA, where he taught psychology and the psychology of art at Sarah Lawrence College, Bronxville, NY; in 1968 he was appointed professor at the Harvard University Carpenter Center of Visual Arts, Cambridge, MA.

Arnheim was responsible for the revision of the prevailing opinion that perception was a primary, physiological function and thought a secondary, interpretative one; he did this by discovering an inseparable mutual interaction between perception and thought. Arnheim considered pictorial art the highest expression of visual thought, or thought in images, and, using Picasso's sketches for *Guernica*, he demonstrated that the visual thought was the beginning of the creative process, and that its power persisted into the completed work of art. Taking perceptual psychology as a point of departure, Arnheim strove, on a broader basis, to establish a comparative vision of art by characterizing the basic perceptual structures of works of art. In this way he made a contribution to the development of a historical morphology that supplemented the research methods of art history.

WRITINGS

Art and Visual Perception: A Psychology of the Creative Eye (Berkeley, CA, 1954; rev. 1974)

The Genesis of Painting: Picasso's Guernica (Berkeley, CA, 1962)

Visual Thinking (Berkeley, CA, 1969)

The Power of the Center: A Study of Composition in the Visual Arts (Berkeley, CA, 1982)

BIBLIOGRAPHY

'Visual Thinking: On Rudolf Arnheim', *Salmagundi*, 78–9 (Spring-Summer 1988), pp. 43–143 [special issue]

ANNEKE E. WIJNBEEK

Arniko [Chin. Anige; A-ni-ke; A-ni-ko] (*b c.* 1244; *d c.* 1306). Nepalese sculptor, architect and possibly painter who worked in Tibet and China. A Newar from the Kathmandu Valley, Arniko is now honoured in his native land as Nepal's most famous artist of early times. He left his home at the age of 17 or 18, joining the myriads of wandering Newar artists who served the courts of the great lamas and emperors of Tibet and China. He so impressed his patrons at the court of the Mongol Yuan dynasty (1279–1368) that he eventually rose to a position of prominence as the director of the imperial workshops at the capital of Dadu, now Beijing.

No trace of Arniko's life and works has survived in Nepal, but this is not surprising given the dearth of historical records (as is the case throughout the Indian subcontinent), and the fact that artists were generally anonymous. Further, as Arniko left the valley at a young age, his artistic distinction was almost entirely achieved in foreign lands.

Arniko's name and background have been the subject of some speculation. He is usually referred to in the Chinese sources as either Arniko or Anige; most scholars have now agreed that this most likely represents the Sanskrit 'Aneka' ('not one, many'), which was then, and still is, a popular name among the Newars of the Kathmandu Valley. The Chinese sources imply that he was a descendant of the Nepalese royal family, but this may be a historical hindsight used to help justify the high titles later conferred on him. Then as now most of the work in bronze-casting was carried out by the high-status Buddhist group, the Shakyas, who claim descent from the monkhood or from the Shakya clan of the Buddha himself.

Information on Arniko's career comes mainly from Chinese sources, the most important being an inscribed tablet (now lost) set up near his tomb near the village of Hsiang-shan in the district of Yuan-p'ing, west of Peking. Composed by Ch'eng Chu-fu five years after Arniko's death, the inscription recounts his life in some detail (Petech, p. 100, note 21). His official biography was also recorded in the *Yuan-shi* ('History of the Yuan dynasty'). These sources indicate that Arniko must have been born between 1243 and 1245. He thus entered the world at a time when the remarkable symbiotic relationship between the great Yuan emperors and the high Tibetan lamas was being forged. Kublai Khan (1215–94) had developed a close relationship with his imperial tutor, the powerful Sakya hierarch Phagspa (1235–80), chief of the great SAKYA monastery of south-central Tibet. When Kublai ascended the throne in 1260, he commissioned the Sakya abbot to erect a golden stupa either at the monastery or in north-eastern Tibet. It was this commission that prompted Phagspa to send to Nepal for the finest artists available. Shortly after Kublai's ascension to the throne, Arniko was selected to lead a contingent of some 80 artists to answer Phagspa's call.

Arniko completed the construction of several stupas in Tibet (these are no longer identifiable). The work impressed the Sakya hierarchy, and Arniko's reputation grew and spread. Phagspa took him on as his protégé and encouraged him to present himself at the imperial court of Kublai, which he reached in 1265. There he was asked to test his skill in the repair of a bronze figure of the Song period (AD 960–1279), which he managed with ease (Lan, p. 127). Soon Arniko was entrusted with major sculptural and architectural projects. He became director of all the court bronzeworkers in 1274, and in 1278 he was appointed controller of the imperial workshops (Petech, p. 101). His renown increased until his death in 1306, and was such that he received several posthumous titles, the foremost being Duke of Liang (Petech, p. 101).

The most famous surviving structure built by Arniko is the large stupa (h. *c.* 36 m, diam. 51.3 m) known as the 'White Pagoda' in the Miaoying Ysi, a monastery in Beijing's western district, which was constructed between 1271 and 1279 (*see* CHINA, fig. 25). The structure was designated a historical treasure after the founding of the People's Republic and was closed during the Cultural Revolution; in 1979 it was restored. The stupa clearly reflects the traditional Indo-Nepalese model on which it was based.

Though it is known that Arniko was a highly skilled sculptor, it has proved difficult to trace his work. A remarkable stone depiction of the great Buddhist protector Mahakala (France, Lionel Farnier priv. col., see Beguin, no. 21) has been attributed to Arniko (Stoddard). Although the inscription on the sculpture does not mention the artist, the date, 1292, is during the period of Arniko's career, and the mention of Phagspa (although some ten years after his death) and Kublai in the inscription would similarly place the image in the realms where Arniko worked. Even if not made personally by the master, the work shows a virtuosity and closeness to Nepalese style that suggest it is at least of his school. It is likely that Arniko also tried his hand at painting; the *Yuandai huasu ji* (*Yüantai huasu chi*), a record of materials used by artists of the Mongol court, implies that he was commissioned to paint a portrait (Karmay, p. 23).

See also NEPAL, especially §§IV, 3 and VI, 4 and TIBET, §I, 7.

BIBLIOGRAPHY

S. Beal: *Si-yu-ki: Buddhist Records of the Western World* (London, 1884)

S. Levi: *Le Népal: Etude historique d'un royaume hindou*, 3 vols (Paris, 1905–8/*R* Delhi, 1990)

L. Petech: *Medieval History of Nepal* (Rome, 1958, rev. 1984)

D. R. Regmi: *Medieval Nepal, i: 750–1530* (Calcutta, 1965)

M. Ishida: 'Gendai no kōgeika Neparu no ōzoku Anika no den ni tsuite' [On the biography of Aniko, artist and member of the Nepalese royal family during the Yuan dynasty], *Toa Bunkashi Sāko* [Studies in the cultural history of Eastern Asia] (Tokyo, 1973), pp. 371–94

H. Karmay: *Early Sino-Tibetan Art* (London, 1975)

Lan Hai: 'Beijing's White Dagoba: A Link with the Past, a Symbol of Friendship', *Souvenir on the Occasion of the 31st National Day of the People's Republic of China* (Kathmandu, 1980)
——: 'Arniko's Architectural Legacy', *Souvenir on the Occasion of the 33rd National Day of the People's Republic of China* (Kathmandu, 1982)
Satyamohan Joshi: *Kalākār Arniko: The Well-known Nepalese Architect Arniko* (Kathmandu, 1987)
H. Stoddard: 'A Stone Sculpture of mGur mGon-po, Mahakala of the Tent, Dated 1292', *Orient. A.*, xxxi/3 (1988)
G. Beguin: *Art ésoterique de P'Himalaya: La Donation Lionel Fournier* (Paris, 1990), p. 52

IAN ALSOP, KASHINATH TAMOT

Arnim, Ferdinand (Heinrich Ludwig) von (*b* Treptow an der Rega, 15 Sept 1814; *d* Potsdam, 25 March 1866). German architect and watercolourist. He studied at the Bauakademie in Berlin (1833–8) and from *c.* 1841 was head of works in the Hofbaukommission. He was therefore given the task after 1845 of completing the projects in Sanssouci left unfinished at the death of Ludwig Persius (including the Paradeisgärtl, Wachturm am Ruinenberg, and the Friedenskirche). His own Potsdam projects included the Friedhofs cemetery buildings (1851), the Villa von Hacke (Jägerallee 1; 1847), villas at Zeppelinstrasse 172 (1850) and Friedrich-Ebert-Strasse 63 (1860–61), and his own villa at Weinbergstrasse 20 (1858: illustrated in nine lithographs published in 1865), as well as several villas and country houses in the area. They were still designed in the Italianate villa style favoured by Persius, but the structures are more solid and the forms more classical. In this way Arnim, who had also been teaching at the Bauakademie since 1846, passed on to the next generation the formal language of the Schinkel school, his pupils including Friedrich Adler (1827–1908), his assistant. Arnim's commissions in Berlin included two houses in the Regentenstrasse (1860–62), but he also built Schloss Nennhausen in the Mark Brandenburg (1860) and palaces and hunting-lodges in Silesia. As court architect to Prince Charles of Prussia he built at Schloss Glienicke three entrance lodges (1849–54), the 'Klosterhof' (1850) for the Prince's medieval collection and the Swiss chalets on the Böttcherberg (about 1865). He reconstructed the Baroque Jagdschloss (1859–62), abandoning Schinkel's influence in favour of a style derived from early French Baroque. Arnim is also known for his watercolours. He made some watercolours of the Pfingstberg-Schloss, an unfinished architectonic plan by the king of Prussia, Frederick William IV, and published most of his own designs in the *Architektonisches Skizzenbuch* from 1852.

BIBLIOGRAPHY

Thieme–Becker
Kunstchronik, iii (1868), pp. 128, 134
J. Sievers: *Bauten für den Prinzen Karl von Preussen* (Berlin, 1942), in P. Rave and M. Kühn, eds: *Schinkel Lebenswerk* (Berlin, 1939–), pp. 159–64
I. Wirth: *Die Bau- und Kunstdenkmäler Berlins: Bezirk Tiergarten* (Berlin, 1955), p. 163
E. Börsch-Supan: *Berliner Baukunst nach Schinkel, 1840–1870*, Studien zur Kunst des neunzehnter Jahrhunderts (Munich, 1977)
H. Drescher and others: *Die Bau- und Kunstdenkmale in der DDR: Bezirk Potsdam* (Berlin, 1978)
A. Bernhard: 'Die Bautätigkeit der Architekten v. Arnim und Petzholtz', *Schloss Glienicke: Bewohner, Künstler, Parklandschaft* (exh. cat., W. Berlin, Schloss Glienicke, 1987), pp. 81–108

EVA BÖRSCH-SUPAN

Arnold, Christian Friedrich (*b* Drebach, 12 Feb 1823; *d* Dresden, 16 March 1890). German architect, teacher and writer. He attended the Gewerbeschule in Chemnitz and studied architecture (1841–50) at the Dresden Kunstakademie under Gustav Heine (1802–80) and Gottfried Semper. In 1849 he was awarded a travel scholarship and visited southern Germany, Italy, France and Belgium. From 1853 he worked as a lecturer in architectural science at the Dresden Kunstakademie, where he was later professor (1861–85). His buildings include the church (1859–64) at Lengefeld, near Plauen-Vogtland, an aisleless Romanesque Revival building with a gallery and flat ceiling; Schloss Eckberg (1859–61) at Loschwitz, near Dresden, built in the Tudor Revival style; the Villa Löschke (1860) in Tolkewitzer Strasse, Dresden, which resembles a manor house in the German Renaissance style; a Romanesque Revival church (1861–3) at Staucha, near Riesa; the Kreuzschule (1864–6), Dresden, in a strict High Gothic style; and the rebuilding of the Sophienkirche (1864–8; destr. 1945), Dresden, where the medieval twin-nave hall church was recased and given a pair of west towers with pierced cupolas. Other buildings by Arnold include the church (1865–9) at Falkenstein, near Auerbach-Vogtland, a Gothic Revival hall church with a gallery, a narrow chancel and a slender west tower; the church (1869–72) at Johanngeorgenstadt, a vaulted Gothic Revival hall church; the rebuilding of the west gallery (1869–71) of Meissen Cathedral; a new church nave (1883–4) at Eschdorf, near Dresden; and the Gothic Revival Friedenskirche (1889–91) in Löbtau, near Dresden. Arnold was preeminently an academic architect who took the buildings of the 14th century as his model, leaving their execution to others. He was the most important Gothic Revival architect in Dresden between 1860 and 1880, and an influential member of the Verein für Kirchliche Kunst im Königreich Sachsen.

WRITINGS

Der herzogliche Palast zu Urbino (Leipzig, 1857)
ed.: *Die Renaissance: Musterbuch nach monumentalen Schöpfungen für Architekten und Kunstgewerbe* (Leipzig, 1860)

BIBLIOGRAPHY

Thieme–Becker
H. A. Müller: *Künstlerlexikon der Gegenwart* (Leipzig, 1882)
V. Helas: *Architektur in Dresden, 1800–1900* (Brunswick, 1985) p. 194

VOLKER HELAS

Arnold, Josef, the elder (*b* Stans, Tyrol, 14 March 1788; *d* Innsbruck, 23 Feb 1879). Austrian painter. He was apprenticed to a house painter in Schwaz and was noticed by Father Eberhard Zobel (1757–1837) of Fiecht, a Benedictine well known as a collector and patron of the arts, who encouraged him to embark on a career as an artist. His first work is a fresco (1813) in the presbytery at Stans (*in situ*); this was soon followed by several altarpieces for various parish churches, among them that of St Margarethen in Wattens. These early works clearly reveal the influence of Josef Schöpf, but there is no evidence that Arnold was his pupil. In 1816 he went to Munich and made copies after such Old Masters as Raphael, Reni and Murillo in the painting collections. From 1818 to 1825 he trained at the Akademie der Bildenden Künste in Vienna, winning prizes for the panel paintings *David and Abigail* (1824) and *Death of Saphira* (both Innsbruck, Tirol.

Landesmus.). In 1825 he settled in Innsbruck and, as a successor to Schöpf, painted a prolific number of frescoes and altarpieces for churches in Innsbruck and the surrounding area. Examples of his frescoes are the *Transfiguration* (1832; rest. 1946–50; Innsbruck, Pfarrkirche St Jakob), scenes from the life of *St John the Baptist* (1841; Axams, Pfarrkirche zu den heiligen Johannes der Täufer und Johannes Evangelist) and scenes from the life of *St Catherine* (1852; Längenfeld, Pfarrkirche zur heilige Katharina). His altarpieces are to be found in such churches as the Kapuzinerkirche, Servitenkirche and Pfarrkirche St Johann in Innsbruck, as well as in churches in such Tyrolean towns and villages as Ladis, Imst, Karres, Stams im Oberinnental, Kufstein im Unterinnental and Gries am Brenner. His style of painting in the altarpieces inclined to the style of the Nazarenes. In his frescoes, however, the reflection of Baroque illusionistic painting is clearly discernible, although the presence of Greek architecture and the severely drawn figures reveals his interest in classicism. Arnold was also a portrait painter and was commissioned to paint a portrait of *Francis-Joseph I* (1863) for the Landhaus in Innsbruck (*in situ*). His son Josef Arnold the younger (1823–62) was a fresco painter, working with his father on several church commissions, and also painting interior scenes and landscapes.

BIBLIOGRAPHY

ÖKL; Thieme–Becker

E. Egg: *Kunst in Tirol: Malerei und Kunsthandwerk* (Innsbruck, Vienna and Munich, 1972), pp. 242–3

F. FORTER

Arnold, Sir **Thomas (Walker)** (*b* Devonport, 19 April 1864; *d* London, 9 June 1930). English Orientalist and historian of Islamic painting. He was attracted to Oriental studies while reading classics at Magdalene College, Cambridge, where he was inspired by Edward Cowell and William Robertson Smith. From 1888 he taught philosophy at the Anglo-Oriental College at Aligarh, India. With the appearance of his *Preaching of Islam* (1896), an account of the spread of Islam, he achieved high academic acclaim and in 1898 became professor of philosophy in the Indian Educational Service, teaching at Government College, Lahore. He returned to London in 1904 to become assistant librarian at the India Office Library, where he studied illustrated manuscripts and made significant purchases. He also taught Arabic at University College. In 1909 he was appointed Educational Adviser for Indian Students in Britain and after 1917, as secretary to the Secretary of State, was responsible for Indian students. When he retired from the India Office in 1920, he became professor of Arabic and Islamic studies at the School of Oriental and African Studies, and in the following decade, when he had more time to write, he showed a particular interest in the history of Islamic painting. His first contribution, *The Court Painters of the Grand Moguls*, was a collaborative effort with LAURENCE BINYON. In *Survivals of Sasanian and Manichaean Art in Persian Painting*, Arnold examined the recurrence of pre-Islamic artistic motifs in Persian painting after a lapse of six or more centuries and suggested the importance of the Manichaean tradition. This was followed by *Painting in Islam*, an outstanding study of the status of painting in Islamic culture. Remaining active despite fatal illness, he died two weeks after returning from Egypt, where he had been visiting professor at Cairo University.

WRITINGS

with L. Binyon: *The Court Painters of the Grand Moguls* (London, 1921)

Survivals of Sasanian and Manichaean Art in Persian Painting (Oxford, 1924)

Painting in Islam (Oxford, 1928/*R* 1965)

with A. Grohmann: *The Islamic Book* (London and Paris, 1929)

Bihzād and his Paintings in the Zafar-nāmah MS. (London, 1930)

The Old and New Testaments in Muslim Religious Art (Oxford, 1932) [British Academy Schweich Lectures, 1928]

BIBLIOGRAPHY

DNB

Obituary, *The Times* (11–14 June 1930)

I. Stchoukine: 'Un Historien de l'art musulman: Sir Thomas W. Arnold', *Rev. A. Asiat.*, vi (1930), pp. 188–90

M. Aurel Stein: 'Thomas Walker Arnold, 1864–1930', *Proc. Brit. Acad.*, xvi (1932)

S. J. VERNOIT

Arnoldi, Alberto (*fl* 1351–64). Italian sculptor. He was one of the most important sculptors in Florence of his day. According to the contemporary poet Sacchetti, Arnoldi was in Milan for a long period, but there is no other evidence for this. He is first mentioned in 1351 in the cathedral works in Florence, where he was working as a mason on marble inlay for the campanile. In 1355 and 1358 he was listed as one of the advisers for the construction of the cathedral. There were two other principal master builders in the cathedral works, and Arnoldi was briefly promoted to be a third, with responsibility for executing the decorative work. On the basis of his documented work, however, he cannot be described as an architect.

Between 1359 and 1364 Arnoldi made the near-life-size statues of the *Virgin and Child* and two angels above the altar in the oratory of the Bigallo, Florence, and in 1361 he was paid for the relief of the half-length *Virgin and Child* for the lunette of the entrance door. The sculptures are marked by a certain rigidity of pose and are deeply chiselled; even the statues are related to the backgrounds, giving the impression of being in high relief. These are the only works that can be reliably attributed to Arnoldi, although Frey argued convincingly in favour of ascribing the reliefs on the Loggia del Bigallo (1352–9) to him; Kreytenberg (1977) also attributed to him two statues of angels on the north flank of Florence Cathedral. The widely accepted attribution of the reliefs of the *Seven Sacraments* on the campanile of Florence Cathedral (Becherucci) has been proved untenable, however; the sculptures are probably the work of Maso di Banco (Kreytenberg, 1979).

BIBLIOGRAPHY

Meissner

C. Frey: *Die Loggia dei Lanzi zu Florenz* (Berlin, 1885), p. 105

L. Becherucci: 'I rilievi dei Sacramenti nel campanile del duomo di Firenze', *L'Arte*, xxx (1927), pp. 214–23

H. Kiel: *Il Museo del Bigallo a Firenze* (Milan, 1977), pp. 3–6, 125–6

G. Kreytenberg: 'I rilievi della Loggia del Bigallo a Firenze', *Prospettiva*, 11 (1977), pp. 27–33

——: 'The Sculpture of Maso di Banco', *Burl. Mag.*, cxxi (1979), pp. 72–6

G. KREYTENBERG

Arnold von Westfalen [Bestürling; Westfal; Westfäling von Meissen; Westphalen; Westveling] (*b* ?Leipzig, 1425; *d* Meissen, 4 May 1480). German architect. He probably came from the respected Leipzig family of Westfal; there is no evidence to support the long-held assumption that he originated from Westphalia. He served his apprenticeship and did his first work under Hans Kumoller at St Nicholas's Church (completed 1447), Zerbst. In 1456 he was Master of the Works at the Archbishop's Palace and St Stephen's Church at Calbe an der Saale, and in 1460–66, under the direction of Kumoller, he was building bridges over the River Elbe at Dresden and Meissen. Work at Schloss Hinterglauchau (1460–70) and on the choir of the church of the Holy Cross at Dresden are also attributed to his early period. In 1470 he was summoned to the Wettin court at Meissen and worked first under Hugo von Schleinitz on the renovation of Rochsburg Castle, and from 1471 on Kriebstein Castle. When the state administration of architecture in Saxony was created, he was appointed Oberlandbaumeister, and at various times directed building works at the Elector's castles at Dresden (west wing from 1471), Torgau and Leipzig (1478/80).

Also dating from this period is Arnold's major work, the Albrechtsburg (so-called in 1676) in Meissen (1471 onwards, completed 1525; *see* MEISSEN, §1; *see also* GOTHIC, fig. 17), one of the most important German Late Gothic buildings, commissioned by the brothers Elector Ernest (*reg* 1464–86) and Duke Albrecht (*reg* 1464–85) of Saxony as their main residence and seat of government.

1. Arnolfo di Cambio: marble tomb of *Cardinal Guillaume de Braye*, detail showing a deacon drawing a curtain, 1280s (Orvieto, S Domenico)

The Albrechtsburg is the best example of Arnold's original and innovative style in the transition from the medieval to the modern era: here, the fortified nature of the medieval castle gave way to the splendour of a modern palace complex. The buttresses are turned inwards, the piers have strong concave mouldings and no capitals, and the vault springers rise directly from the socles. The unusually large windows have arches shaped like a gathered curtain. This decorative feature, known as a 'curtain arch', was characteristic of Arnold and his workshop. The uniquely rich and fantastic vaults in the interior of the Albrechtsburg, especially in the Great Hall, have earned Arnold the epithet 'master of vaulting technique'. Almost all the rooms have cell vaults of a type first used in larger rooms in the Albrechtsburg, which quickly spread throughout Saxony and the neighbouring regions to the east. There are also vaults of original design in the Wappensaal, where the ribs cross at different levels, and the stone Princes' Stairs, called the 'Grosser Wendelstein'.

Arnold also worked on Meissen Cathedral (the west end and towers from 1479), the church of Unsere Liebe Frau auf dem Berge (*c.* 1472) at Penig, and the east gatehouse of Rochlitz Castle. In 1476 he assumed overall control of the building of Tharandt Castle (largely destr.), near Dresden, and Leipzig Castle (1478/80), and in 1479 he presented a design for the Drapers' Hall at Leipzig. He was also involved in strengthening the towers of Zwickau Cathedral and in building various town houses in Meissen. From Arnold's workshop emerged the so-called 'Lausitz Lodge', of which PAUL PREUSSE and BRICCIUS GAUTSZKE were members.

BIBLIOGRAPHY

Thieme–Becker
T. Distel: 'Meister Arnold, der Erbauer der Albrechtsburg', *Archv Sächs. Gesch.*, n.s., iv (1878); v (1879)
M. Radova-Stikova: 'Architectura Arnolda Vestfalskeho', *Archit. ČSR*, xxxi (1971)
J. Białostocki: *Spätmittelalter und beginnende Neuzeit*, Propyläen-Kstgesch., vii (West Berlin, 1972)
E.-H. Lemper: 'Arnold von Westfalen', *Die Albrechtsburg zu Meissen*, ed. H. J. Mrusek (Leipzig, 1972), pp. 41–55
W. Braunfels: 'Meissen', *Festschrift für H. Siebenhuhner* (Würzburg, 1978)
N. Nussbaum: *Deutsche Kirchenbaukunst der Gotik* (Cologne, 1985), pp. 260ff

VERENA BEAUCAMP

Arnolfo di Cambio (*b* Colle di Val d'Elsa, nr Siena; *fl* 1265; *d* Florence, ?8 March 1302). Italian sculptor and architect. The identification of Arnolfo the sculptor, who is documented as Nicola Pisano's pupil and who worked principally in Rome, with the architect Arnolfo, who worked in Florence, is no longer doubted, although it was once strongly contested by Frey (Thieme–Becker). In the first edition of his *Vite* (1550), Vasari mentioned Arnolfo only briefly as the builder of Florence Cathedral, but in the second edition (1568) he praised him as an architectural innovator and a precursor of the Renaissance, who had the same pioneering significance for architecture as Nicola Pisano for sculpture and Cimabue for painting.

1. Life and documented sculptural works. 2. Attributed sculptural works. 3. Architecture.

1. LIFE AND DOCUMENTED SCULPTURAL WORKS. Vasari was mistaken in describing Arnolfo as the son of the German mason Lapo (Jacopo Tedesco), to whom he

attributed the building of S Francesco, Assisi; Arnolfo is referred to in a Florentine document of 1 April 1300 as *Arnolphus de Colle filius olim Cambii*, which confirms both his place of birth and his father's name. Vasari's citation of the year of his birth as 1232 must also be mistaken, because this would be too early. Arnolfo is first mentioned in a document of 29 September 1265, when, as Nicola Pisano's assistant (*discipulus*), he collaborated with Lapo, Donato and Giovanni Pisano on the marble pulpit for Siena Cathedral. It is unlikely that he was first apprenticed in a Cistercian masons' workshop (Romanini, 1983), because he would have learnt nothing of figure portrait sculpture there, and, insofar as any retrospective conclusion can be drawn from Arnolfo's later works, they tend to confirm his training under Nicola Pisano.

Arnolfo is next heard of in Rome in 1277, in the service of Charles I, King of Naples and Sicily (*reg* 1266–85). This can be inferred from the fact that in August 1277 the Consiglio dei Savi in Perugia addressed the King requesting that he grant 'Arnolfo of Florence, a most subtle and ingenious master' (*subtilissimus et ingeniosus magister*) permission to go from Rome to Perugia to build a fountain on the Piazza Maggiore there. This was granted on 10 September 1277 in a letter written in Lagopesole, in which Charles also gave consent for Arnolfo to supply himself in Rome with the materials required for the work. Records of payments for the fountain do not appear, however, until 4 February 1281, when Arnolfo was paid for 24 days' work and the return journey from Rome to Perugia. Five figures from the fountain, which had evidently been removed by 1301, survive (Perugia, G.N. Umbria). A reconstruction of the fountain was proposed by Santi (1960).

In the 1280s and 1290s Arnolfo lived mainly in Rome, where he was in charge of a moderate-sized workshop. Several signed works from this period survive, the earliest being the tomb of *Cardinal Guillaume de Braye* (*d* 1282) in S Domenico, Orvieto, which is inscribed HOC OPUS FECIT ARNOLFUS. The tomb was dismantled in 1680 and reassembled in 1934, but in an incomplete form; the architectural frame survives only in fragments (Orvieto, Mus. Opera Duomo; for a reconstruction of the original monument see Romanini, 1969 and 1990). With the *de Braye* monument Arnolfo not only created one of the most important and lavish tombs of the Duecento but he also introduced a new type of wall tomb, surpassing in both size and richness of decoration the slightly earlier wall tombs of *Clement IV* (*reg* 1265–8) and *Adrian V* (*reg* 1276) in S Francesco, Viterbo. The decorative richness is principally evident in the increased use of figure sculpture and the animated scenes involving groups of figures. The centre of the tomb consists of a chamber enclosing the effigy, with curtains swept back by two deacons on either side (see fig. 1). In the upper section are the Virgin and Child enthroned, with the kneeling figure of the deceased accompanied by St Mark (the patron saint of the Cardinal's titular church) and St Dominic, forming a monumental, triangular composition. Both the overall structure and the individual motifs of this tomb were still being followed in the 14th century: a particularly faithful imitation is the tomb of *Benedict XI* (*reg* 1303–5) in S Domenico, Perugia.

2. Arnolfo di Cambio: high altar ciborium, 1285 (Rome, S Paolo fuori le Mura)

The ciborium above the high altar of S Paolo fuori le Mura, Rome, is dated 1285 and inscribed HOC OPUS FECIT ARNULFUS CUM SUO SOCIO PETRO. The *socius Petrus* named on the inscription has been identified as both Pietro Cavallini and Pietro di Oderisio, but there is no supporting evidence for either attribution. The ciborium was donated by Abbot Bartolomeo, who is shown presenting St Paul with a model of the ciborium in the spandrels of the western arch. The Gothic canopy is supported on antique porphyry columns and is richly ornamented with superb foliate capitals, small corner statues in a classicizing style, relief figures and Cosmatesque mosaic decoration (see fig. 2). It differs radically from the earlier, much simpler Roman ciboria, but its similarity to the ciborium (rest.) of the Sainte-Chapelle in Paris, on which it has been said to have been modelled, is slight. Arnolfo's ciborium is much richer in its figural ornamentation, and the architecture is also more strongly directed towards the accommodation of figure sculpture, in corner niches and on spandrel and gable surfaces. Another distinctive feature is the way in which current Gothic architectural motifs (pinnacles, gable crockets, trefoil arches) are independently articulated and transformed into solid, geometric forms. In both the synthesis of elements drawn from diverse sources and the strict rectilinearity of its architecture, the ciborium is a characteristic early example of Arnolfo's architectural style. The ciborium over the high altar of S Cecilia in Trastevere is similar in type but simpler in construction and somewhat modified in both its form and proportions. It is inscribed HOC OPUS FECIT ARNULFUS ANNI DNI M CCLXXXXIII M NOVEBER D XX on the pedestal of the front left-hand column, although this is now hidden by Baroque alterations.

The last Roman work that can be certainly attributed to Arnolfo is the tomb of *Pope Boniface VIII* (Rome, Grotte Vaticane), which was completed by 1300, and possibly as early as 1296. It is more simply constructed than the *de Braye* tomb and is more unified, the relationship between the sarcophagus and recumbent effigy showing stronger compositional control. The effigy was flanked at head and foot by angels holding a curtain. The sarcophagus and sculpted figures were originally installed in a rectangular niche above the altar to St Boniface IV on the entrance wall of Old St Peter's; there was a mosaic above by Jacopo Torriti showing the Pope kneeling before the Virgin and Child, accompanied by SS Peter and Paul. The original appearance of the tomb and the chapel of St Boniface in which it stood is reproduced in the *Album* of Giacomo Grimaldi (Rome, Vatican, Bib. Apostolica, Archv Capitolare S Pietro). Soon after its completion, the tomb was being used as a model for those of several other Roman prelates, for example the tombs of *Bishop Durandus* (*d* 1296) in S Maria sopra Minerva, *Cardinal González García Gudiel* (*d* 1298) in S Maria Maggiore and *Cardinal Matteo d'Acquasparta* (*d* 1302) in S Maria in Aracoeli (Gardner, 1973). The novel positioning of Boniface's tomb above or directly behind the altar was also soon imitated (e.g. in the tomb of *Giangaetano Orsini* (*d* 1292) in the Cappella di S Nicola, S Francesco, Assisi).

According to Vasari, the chapel of St Boniface, which was consecrated on 6 May 1296, bore the inscription HOC OPUS FECIT ARNOLPHUS ARCHITECTUS. This would be the first time that Arnolfo was described as an architect, the principal activity of his later years (*see* §3 below). Although he was probably summoned to Florence as early as 1294 or 1296 (for the cathedral there was started at about that time), he is not expressly mentioned in Florence until 1 April 1300, when he was exempted from taxes and lauded for his great abilities as a mason: 'he is a more famous master and greater expert in the building of churches than any other who is known in neighbouring parts'. Arnolfo is again named as the builder of Florence Cathedral in an inscription on its south nave wall, which probably dates from 1368 (ISTUD AB ARNULFO TEMPLUM FUIT EDIFICATUM). Arnolfo could have directed the cathedral's construction only in its early stages, however, as he died before 1310 (probably in 1302).

3. Arnolfo di Cambio: *Virgin and Child Enthroned*, marble, h. 1.73 m, *c.* 1300 (Florence, Museo dell'Opera del Duomo)

Arnolfo's artistic development is difficult to assess, not only because of the fragmentary state of many of his works, their uncertain chronology and the extensive participation of assistants, but also because his style was based on a synthesis of sources, reflecting his training in Nicola Pisano's workshop, his association with French patrons and the many years spent working in Rome. Especially distinctive features of his work are the monumentality and axial arrangement of his figures and the tendency towards geometric forms; the severity and firmness of his contours; the sober, grave pathos and the restrained yet expressive use of gesture; and the often astonishingly naturalistic details (particularly in the faces) and close dependence on antiquity. Despite the contrasts that are often made between Arnolfo's classicizing style and the more 'Gothic' and expressive work of Giovanni Pisano, however, it is clear that Arnolfo was also indebted to French Gothic models, as is demonstrated by the architectural motifs on his tombs and ciboria and by their figure sculpture. Arnolfo not only influenced the following generation of sculptors, especially members of the Cosmatus family (Johannes and Deodatus), but also Giotto, in whose early work is to be seen the impact of his highly individual figure style.

2. ATTRIBUTED SCULPTURAL WORKS. While working with Nicola Pisano in the 1260s Arnolfo may have collaborated not only on the Siena Cathedral pulpit but also on the Arca di S Domenico in S Domenico, Bologna (1265–7). Since Venturi (1906), several attempts have been made to identify accurately the young Arnolfo's contribution to these two works, and the *Nativity* relief on the pulpit in Siena and the reliefs on the rear and two end panels of the Arca di S Domenico have been attributed mainly to him. Arnolfo's style was, however, still too dominated by the discipline of the workshop and by Nicola Pisano's work to enable these attributions to be made with complete conviction (De Francovich).

The extremely expressive *Thirsting Figures* and *The Writer*, monumental in effect despite their small scale, which were made between 1277 and 1281 for the fountain in Perugia, and the sculptures created *c.* 1300 for the façade of Florence Cathedral (now mainly in Florence, Mus. Opera Duomo, and Berlin, Bodemus.) are well authenticated works. Of these, the large *Virgin and Child Enthroned* from the main portal tympanum in Florence Cathedral occupies pride of place as a late masterpiece by Arnolfo (see fig. 3).

Although Arnolfo's known works are not uniform in style and quality of execution, clearly revealing a heavy reliance on assistants, they provide a starting-point for the attribution to him of a large number of other works, most of which were already included by Vasari in Arnolfo's oeuvre. They belong exclusively to his time in Rome and most have survived in a fragmentary state. The first is the tomb of *Pope Adrian V* in S Francesco, Viterbo, which was probably made soon after the Pope's death in 1276. Arnolfo's responsibility for this work, first suggested by Venturi in 1905, has more recently been questioned, but both the architectural forms and the figure sculpture support the attribution (Poeschke, 1972), even if this relatively early work is less richly ornamented with figures than Arnolfo's later tombs.

4. Arnolfo di Cambio: *Charles I, King of Naples and Sicily, Enthroned*, marble, 1280s (Rome, Museo Capitolino)

Only fragments survive from the *Annibaldi* monument (now in the cloister of S Giovanni in Laterano, Rome). It was not, as previously supposed, erected for Riccardo Annibaldi (*d* 1276), the Cardinal Deacon of S Angelo in Pescheria, but for his nephew of the same name, a notary and subdeacon who died in 1289 (Herklotz, 1985). One distinctive feature of this monument, which recalls French Gothic tombs (Gardner, 1972), is the funeral procession of clerics on the frieze at the rear of the death chamber. This scenic enrichment of the centre of the tomb surpasses even the ornamentation of the *de Braye* monument.

The statue of *Charles I, King of Naples and Sicily, Enthroned* (Rome, Mus. Capitolino; see fig. 4) must have been made at about the same time, possibly in connection with Charles's renewed appointment as Roman senator in 1281. Doubt has quite unjustifiably been cast on its attribution to Arnolfo, first by Wickhoff (1890). Arnolfo's work is suggested not only by the sobriety of expression, the solidity of form and the dry, angular handling of the drapery, but also by the detailed and unusually naturalistic treatment of the features, which is closely paralleled in the *de Braye* monument. Also in the 1280s, probably during the reign of Pope Honorius IV (1285–7), Arnolfo created the *Praesepe* (crib) group for S Maria Maggiore (in the oratory of the Presepio, beneath the Cappella Sistina, since 1586, when the figures of the Virgin and Child were replaced). About 1287 he made the tomb of *Honorius IV*, but only the recumbent effigy and the sarcophagus survive (formerly in St Peter's; since 1545 in the Cappella Savelli, S Maria in Aracoeli).

Works dating from the 1290s include the marble relief bust of *Pope Boniface VIII* (Rome, Vatican Mus.) and the magnificent bronze figure of *St Peter* in St Peter's, Rome, which was based on the antique statue of a philosopher, remodelled to represent Peter, which used to stand in the atrium of Old St Peter's (now Rome, Grotte Vaticane). The long-disputed dating of the bronze figure to the late 13th century, first advocated by Wickhoff (1890), was confirmed by an analysis of the bronze alloy undertaken by Bruno Bearzi in 1957 (Salmi, 1960).

3. ARCHITECTURE. Although Arnolfo's architectural activity is now less clearly defined than his work as a sculptor, in Vasari's view his reputation was based on his architecture. The only documentary evidence of Arnolfo's work as an architect relates to the rebuilding of Florence Cathedral, plans for which were being made from 1294 (*see* FLORENCE, §IV, 1). The foundation-stone was consecrated in 1296, and in the document of 1 April 1300 cited above the enterprise is described as a *magnifico et visibili principio . . . operis ecclesie.* Construction ceased after Arnolfo's death and was resumed only after 1355; the cathedral was not finally completed until the 15th century. The question of how far the building conforms to Arnolfo's original project, and in particular whether he planned the octagonal, domed choir, has been largely resolved by the excavations carried out between 1965 and 1974 (Toker, 1978, 1983), which showed that the present building has essentially the same ground-plan as that envisaged by Arnolfo. His cathedral would have been considerably smaller, however, which ties in with the *piccolo modello* mentioned by Antonio Manetti in connection with Arnolfo's project. Arnolfo's nave was as wide as the present one, with a broader central vessel and narrower aisles; and, although it was shorter, there were to be five bays instead of four. An open-truss roof was planned. An octagonal choir directly adjoining the nave was to extend to about the middle of the present choir, but there is no evidence that the three polygonal conches were envisaged by Arnolfo, although this probably was the case. The nave piers begun by Arnolfo were polygonal, as are those in the present building. Three façade portals corresponded to the aisles, and their marble facing and figure sculpture were partly executed under Arnolfo. The rich façade decoration did not extend far above the portal zone and was removed in 1587; its appearance is known from pictorial records (the earliest is the fresco in the Loggia del Bigallo of 1342, but the most detailed and reliable is the late 16th-century drawing in the Opera del Duomo, Florence). The organization of the pilasters at the western end of the exterior nave wall, in which two exterior bays were intended to correspond to one internal bay, was also Arnolfo's responsibility.

Vasari attributed a number of other important buildings, renovations and urban development projects in Florence and its territory to Arnolfo: the third city wall; the Loggia of Orsanmichele (Vasari here refers to an earlier building than that reconstructed in the 14th century), the Loggia dei Lanzi, the Palazzo Vecchio and the Piazza della Signoria; the choir of the Badia with its flanking chapels; the Franciscan church of Santa Croce and the older cloisters of the monastery attached to it; the marble facing on the Baptistery; and the castles of S Giovanni and Castelfranco in the Arno Valley. Only the Badia and Santa Croce are now seriously regarded as Arnolfo's work; Paatz (1919–32; 1937) in particular attempted to justify fully their attribution to Arnolfo.

According to Giovanni Villani (*Cronica* VII, 98), the reconstruction of the Badia was started in 1284; its high altar was consecrated in 1310. The Gothic building was altered in 1627, but its exterior walls and parts of the choir and open-truss roof survive. It was originally an aisled basilica of two bays, with the central vessel extending beyond the aisles to the west, and three straight-ended, rib-vaulted chapels at the east end (Middeldorf and Paatz, 1919–32). Arnolfo's responsibility for the design is suggested by the broad choir façade, which is subdivided into rectangles by pilaster strips and string courses to create a well-proportioned system of clearly defined surfaces; the sparing insertion of details suggesting the influence of the Antique, and the simple way in which the window openings and masonry patterns are cut, with careful thought for the unified effect of the façade as a whole, are the most important indications of Arnolfo's work.

These features have their closest counterparts in the slightly later building of Santa Croce. Begun in 1294 or 1295, the church was not completed until the 15th century, although it was built substantially to a unified plan. It is an aisled basilica with a timber roof, transepts, and five rectangular chapels on either side of the polygonal choir. The ground-plan, deriving ultimately from Cistercian models, in some respects follows that of the Dominican church of Florence, S Maria Novella, but the proportions and the organization of the interior are completely different (*see* FLORENCE, §IV, 4). Many features of Santa Croce are reminiscent of Arnolfo's project for Florence Cathedral. These include the wide central vessel and narrow aisles, the broad span of the main arcade arches, the polygonal piers and the open-truss roof. The clear articulation of the interior, the deliberate emphasis on wall surfaces and their rectilinear, thoughtfully proportioned organization by means of narrow window openings, pilaster strips and horizontal gallery also indicate Arnolfo's responsibility for the work. The calm, harmonious effect, recalling the clarity of Early Christian basilicas, and the Gothic elements in the ground-plan and elevation form a combination unique for its time, and the same fusion, with a preference for balanced proportions, severe contours and a clear organization of volumes is also characteristic of the figure sculpture and architecture of Arnolfo's ciboria in Rome.

Arnolfo's contribution to the Palazzo Vecchio is harder to assess. Completed in 1310, it was started in 1299 at a time when he was Master of the Cathedral Works. It can therefore be safely assumed that Arnolfo had some influence on the building of the town hall of Florence, although scholars are overwhelmingly inclined to doubt, or accept only with reservations, the claim made by Vasari that he was the designing architect. In addition to Vasari's attributions, Orvieto Cathedral has occasionally been associated with Arnolfo (EWA) on the basis of some stylistic similarities with Santa Croce. His direct participation in this building, which was planned in 1284 with building work starting in 1290, must be discounted (Romanini, 1969); unlike Arnolfo's church buildings, it incorporates some decidely archaic features. This also applies to the alterations and extensions carried out at S Maria in Aracoeli, Rome, in the second half of the 13th century, which were evaluated as early evidence of Arnolfo's work as an architect by Cellini (1955).

BIBLIOGRAPHY

EWA; Thieme-Becker
A. Manetti: *Vita de Filippo Brunelleschi* (*c.* 1487); ed. D. De Robertis and G. Tanturli (Milan, 1976)
G. Vasari: *Vite* (1550, rev. 2/1568); ed. G. Milanesi (1878–85)
F. Baldinucci: *Notizie* (1681–1728); ed. F. Ranalli (1845–7)
C. Boito: *Architettura del medioevo in Italia* (Milan, 1880)
F. Wickhoff: 'Die bronzene Apostelstatue in der Peterskirche', *Z. Bild. Kst*, n.s., i (1890), pp. 109–14
A. Venturi: 'Frammenti del presepe di Arnolfo nella basilica romana di S Maria Maggiore', *L'Arte*, viii (1905), pp. 107–12
——: 'Arnolfo di Cambio: Opere ignote del maestro a Viterbo, Perugia e Roma', *L'Arte*, viii (1905), pp. 254–65
——: *Storia*, iv (Milan, 1906/*R* 1967)
U. Middeldorf and W. Paatz: 'Die gotische Badia zu Florenz un ihr Erbauer Arnolfo di Cambio', *Mitt. Ksthist. Inst. Florenz*, iii (1919–32), pp. 492–517
R. Barsotti: 'Problemi insoluti di scultura pisana: L'arca di S Domenico di Bologna e il pulpito di Pistoia', *Illus. Vatic.*, v (1934), pp. 336–40, 380–84, 561–5
H. Keller: 'Der Bildhauer Arnolfo di Cambio und seine Werkstatt', *Jb. Preuss. Kstsamml.*, lv (1934), pp. 205–28; lvi (1935), pp. 22–43
E. Carli: 'La giovinezza di Arnolfo di Cambio', *Boll. Stor. Pisa.*, xv (1936), pp. 7–50
W. Paatz: *Werden und Wesen der Trecento-Architecktur in Toskana* (Burg bei Magdeburg, 1937)
R. Salvini: 'Arnolfo e la cupola di S Maria del Fiore', *Atti del I congresso nazionale di storia dell'architettura: Florence, 1938*, pp. 25–36
G. De Francovich: 'Studi recenti sulla scultura gotica toscana: Arnolfo di Cambio', *Arti: Rass. Bimest. A. Ant. & Mod.*, ii (1939–40), pp. 236–51
M. Salmi: 'Arnolfiana', *Riv. A.*, xxii (1940), pp. 133–77
M. Weinberger: 'The First Façade of the Cathedral of Florence', *J. Warb. & Court. Inst.*, iv (1940–41), pp. 67–79
V. Mariani: *Arnolfo di Cambio* (Rome, 1943)
C. Gnudi: *Nicola, Arnolfo, Lapo: L'arca di S Domenico in Bologna* (Florence, 1948)
G. Nicco Fasola: 'La fontana di Arnolfo', *Commentari*, ii (1951), pp. 98–105
P. Toesca: *Il trecento* (Turin, 1951)
P. Cellini: 'Di fra Guglielmo e di Arnolfo', *Boll. A.*, xl (1955), pp. 215–29
M. Salmi: 'Una precisazione su Arnolfo architetto', *Palladio*, n.s., vii (1957), pp. 92–4
——: 'Il problema della statua bronzea di San Pietro nella basilica vaticana', *Commentari*, xi (1960), pp. 22–9
F. Santi: 'Considerazioni sulla fontana di Arnolfo a Perugia', *Commentari*, xi (1960), pp. 220–30
S. Bottari: 'L'arca di San Domenico in Bologna', *Studi di storia dell'arte in onore di Mario Salmi*, i (Rome, 1961), pp. 391–415
G. Kiesow: 'Zur Baugeschichte des Florentiner Domes', *Mitt. Ksthist. Inst. Florenz*, x (1961), pp. 1–22
H. Saalman: 'Santa Maria del Fiore, 1294–1418', *A. Bull.*, xlvi (1964), pp. 471–500
A. M. Romanini: 'Il "dolce stil nuovo" di Arnolfo di Cambio', *Palladio*, xv (1965), pp. 35–66
M. Salmi: 'Una statua di Arnolfo', *Commentari*, xvi (1965), pp. 17–22
M. Weinberger: 'Arnolfo und die Ehrenstatue Karls von Anjou', *Studien zur Geschichte der europäischen Plastik: Festschrift Theodor Müller* (Munich, 1965), pp. 63–72
P. Sanpaolesi: 'Sulla antica facciata di Santa Maria del Fiore', *Arte in Europa: Scritti in onore di E. Arslan* (Milan, 1966), pp. 309–23
V. Mariani: *Arnolfo e il gotico italiano* (Naples, 1967)
F. Santi: 'Un altro "scriba" di Arnolfo per la fontana perugina del 1281', *Paragone*, 225 (1968), pp. 3–10
A. M. Romanini: *Arnolfo di Cambio e lo 'stil nuovo' del gotico italiano* (Milan, 1969)
——: 'Nuove tracce per il rapporto Giotto-Arnolfo in S Gottardo a Milano', *Scritti in onore di Roberto Pane* (Naples, 1969–71), pp. 149–85
L. Becherucci and G. Brunetti: *Il Museo dell'Opera del Duomo a Firenze*, i (Florence, 1970)
J. Poeschke: 'Arnolfos Madonna mit dem Kind in der Florentiner Domopera', *Argo: Festschrift für Kurt Badt* (Cologne, 1970), pp. 164–75
V. Mariani: 'Una testa di apostolo dalla "Dormitio Virginis" di Arnolfo a Firenze', *Ant. Viva*, x (1971), pp. 28–34
J. Gardner: 'The Tomb of Cardinal Annibaldi by Arnolfo di Cambio', *Burl. Mag.*, cxiv (1972), pp. 136–41
J. Poeschke: 'Betrachtung der römischen Werke des Arnolfo di Cambio', *Röm. Qschr.*, lxvii (1972), pp. 175–211
J. Pope Hennessy: *Italian Gothic Sculpture* (London, 2/1972)
J. Gardner: 'Arnolfo di Cambio and Roman Tomb Design', *Burl. Mag.*, cxv (1973), pp. 420–39
V. Martinelli: 'La statua arnolfiana del pontefice sul faldistorio', *Boll. A.*, lviii (1973), pp. 88–94
M. Seidel: 'Der Marientod des Arnolfo di Cambio', *Forsch. & Ber.: Staat. Mus. Berlin*, xv (1973), pp. 41–4
G. Kreytenberg: *Der Dom zu Florenz* (Berlin, 1974)
W. Messerer: 'Zur Rekonstruktion von Arnolfo di Cambios Praesepe-Gruppe', *Röm. Jb. Kstgesch.*, xv (1975), pp. 25–35
B. Scharioth: *Arnolfo di Cambio und Giotto* (Essen, 1976)
F. K. B. Toker: 'Florence Cathedral: The Design Stage', *A. Bull.*, lx (1978), pp. 214–31
H. M. Dixon: *Arnolfo di Cambio: Sculpture* (diss., U. MI, Ann Arbor, 1979)
A. M. Romanini: 'Arnolfo e gli "Arnolfo" apocrifici', *Roma anno 1300: Rome, 1983*, pp. 27–52
——: 'La cattedrale gotica: Il caso di Arnolfo e Santa Maria del Fiore', *Storia dell'arte italiana*, III, v (Turin, 1983), pp. 3–45
——: 'Nuove ipotesi su Arnolfo di Cambio', *A. Med.*, i (1983), pp. 157–213
——: 'Il ritratto gotico in Arnolfo di Cambio', *Akten des XXV. internationalen Kongresses für Kunstgeschichte in Wien: Vienna, 1983*, vi, pp. 203–9
F. K. B. Toker: '"Magnifico et visibili principio dicti operis": Arnolfo di Cambio a Santa Maria del Fiore', *Roma anno 1300: Rome, 1983*, pp. 73–86
A. M. Romanini: 'I cistercensi e la formazione di Arnolfo di Cambio', *Studi di storia dell'arte in memoria di Mario Rotili* (Naples, 1984), pp. 235–41
I. Herklotz: *'Sepulcra' e 'monumenta' del medioevo* (Rome, 1985)

JOACHIM POESCHKE

Arnoult de Nimègue [Aert de Glaesmakere; Aert Ortkens; Arnold of Nijmegen; Arnoult de la Pointe; Arnoult van der Spits; Arnt Nijmegen; Artus van Ort de Nieumegue] (*fl c.* 1490; *d c.* 1536). South Netherlandish glass painter. He was one of the most productive and influential stained-glass artists of the early 16th century and according to Guicciardini invented the technique of firing enamel colour into glass (*see* STAINED GLASS, §I, 5). He began his career in Tournai, where his most famous works are the transept windows of the cathedral (*c.* 1500), over-restored by Jean-Baptiste Capronnier *c.* 1845. Shortly after 1500 Arnoult was called to Rouen, where he influenced a generation of Norman glass painters. His work is exemplified in windows in Rouen Cathedral; the *Crucifixion* now in York Minster, England, originally from St Jean, Rouen; and windows in St Vincent or St Godard, Rouen.

Arnoult's figures have small heads and long bodies swathed in layers of richly worked materials, seen, for example, in a magnificent *Tree of Jesse* (*c.* 1506) in St Godard, Rouen, and in the window of *SS Romanus and Adrian* (*c.* 1510) donated by Guillaume Toustain de Frontebosc in Ste Foy, Conche-en-Ouche (Eure). Arnoult then returned to the southern Netherlands, where he was admitted as a member of the Guild of St Luke in Antwerp (1513). The window of the *Three Marys* (*c.* 1520) in Notre-Dame, Louviers (Indre-et-Loire), which was shipped from Antwerp, continues to display his exquisitely delicate draughtsmanship in the elaborate clothing and intricate architectural settings, and the brilliant contrast of deeply saturated colours and silver-stain yellows. The influence of Dürer's graphic work is apparent but subsumed into grandiose compositions exploiting both the graphic surface and unique colour impact of stained glass. Although Friedländer attributed a number of drawings and designs to the artist, these are now thought to be the work of different artists, known as the PSEUDO-ORTKENS group (*see* MASTERS, ANONYMOUS, AND MONOGRAMMISTS, §I).

BIBLIOGRAPHY

L. Guicciardini: *Descrittione di . . . tutti i paesi bassi* (1567)
J. Helbig: 'Arnold de Nimègue et le problème de son identité', *A. & Vie*, iv/9 (1937), pp. 279–90
A. Van der Boom: 'Een Nederlands glasschilder in den vreemde: Aert Ortken van Nijmegen', *Ned. Kstbist. Jb.*, ii (1948–9), pp. 75–103
J. Lafond: 'Le Peintre-verrier Arnoult de Nimègue et les débuts de la Renaissance à Rouen et à Anvers', *Actes du XVIIe Congrès international d'histoire de l'art: Amsterdam, 1952* (The Hague, 1955), pp. 333–44
——: 'La Renaissance', *Le Vitrail français*, ed. M. Aubert and others (Paris, 1958), pp. 215–17
M. J. Friedländer: *Early Netherlandish* (1967–76)

VIRGINIA CHIEFFO RAGUIN

Arnoux, (Charles-)Albert d'. *See* BERTALL.

Arnt, Master (*fl* 1460; *d* Zwolle, 1492). Netherlandish sculptor. He is first mentioned in Kalkar (Germany) in 1460, moving to Zwolle (Netherlands) in 1484. In records he is always given the professional title 'Beeldesnider' (sculptor). His style was influenced by the paintings of Rogier van der Weyden and by the sculpture of Utrecht (stone sculpture in the cathedral and works by Adriaen van Wesel); some connections with painting in the Duchy of Guelders have also been established. His main extant works are sculptures in oak, many of which were commissioned by the Liebfrauenbruderschaft (Brotherhood of the Virgin) in KALKAR, ST NIKOLAI.

Documented works are the *Entombment*, delivered to Kalkar from Zwolle in 1487, and the design and some parts of the high altar in Kalkar, which was commissioned in 1490 but remained unfinished at his death. The *Ymago Salvatoris*, delivered to Xanten in 1476, may also be Arnt's work and may be identical with the *Ascension* (priv. col.). The two angels with the *Instruments of the Passion*, delivered to Xanten in 1477, are also ascribed to Arnt. His oldest surviving work is the choir-stalls in the former Franciscan church in Cleve: these are decorated with twelve saints on the end pieces (among them seven Franciscans) as well as drolleries and misericords. The style of the female saints, in their courtly elegance and linear tension, is still under the influence of Rogier van der Weyden. The same ornate yet childlike and lovable attitude characterizes two images of St Lucy (priv. col.), which were originally coloured. They show freedom of movement, clear differentiation between body and drapery and a painterly treatment of the folds on the surface. Figures from a Franciscan altar (untraced; statues in the parish churches at Birten and Eibergen) and from the Dominican church in Kalkar (Brussels, Musées Royaux A. & Hist., and Düsseldorf, Kstmus.) can be related to these sculptures. One of Arnt's finest compositions, a figure of St Bernard of Clairvaux (Münster, Westfäl. Landesmus.), follows the style seen in the choir-stalls in the unusually sensitive modelling of the saint's hand, which is holding a book.

The private altar (Paris, Mus. Cluny), donated by a Carthusian, is a compositional precursor of the monumental *Pietà* (Bedburg, parish church) with the *Lamentation* placed in the centre.

The most important work attributed to Arnt is the altar of St George in the church of St Nikolai, Kalkar (before 1484), given by Peter Ghiesen, the mayor. The central panel contains what might be called a carved painting: a unified landscape made up of three blocks of wood in which nine scenes from the life of the saint are set, distinguished from one another only by the grouping of the figures. This principle of differentiating scenes solely by divisions in the background recalls pictures by Hans Memling. The only easily distinguishable scene among the throng of small figures is the most important episode, St George's battle with the dragon, because of its position at bottom centre, larger scale and the way in which the figures are worked in high relief. The landscape is enriched with many carved flowers and plants, and the scenes are full of tension. The surviving polychrome increases the impression of profusion. Wings depicting the legend of St Ursula were later added to the shrine. A recently discovered relief of the *Adoration of the Magi* (Cologne, Schnütgen-Mus.) is closely connected to the style of the St George's retable.

Arnt's last work for Kalkar was the high altar, commissioned by the Brotherhood of the Virgin in 1490 and uncompleted at his death. Only the relief of *Christ Washing the Feet* in the predella is probably his own work; the others were partly completed to his design by other artists (two further reliefs on the predella by Jan van Halderen in 1498) and partly worked over and completed to designs by other people (1498–1500 by LUDWIG JUPAN). In *Christ Washing the Feet*, Arnt's wealth of variation in the characterization of the Apostles in conversation, the precision of details and folds and the sharply accentuated composition are captivating.

Arnt's style dominated Netherlandish sculpture until well into the 16th century: Jan van Halderen was his assistant in Zwolle as early as 1491. An extensive group of works is ascribed to the 'Master of the Emmerich Chandelier', Dries Holthuys worked in stone and wood in Cleve around 1500, and Henrik Bernts (*d* 1509) produced the Kalkar choir-stalls in 1505–08 in a coarse version of the style of those at Cleve.

BIBLIOGRAPHY

J. Leeuwenberg and F. Gorissen: 'De meester van het St Jorisaltaar te Kalkar', *Oud-Holland*, lxxiii (1958), pp. 18–42
Die Klevischen Beeldesnijder, niederrheinländische Holzbildnerei, 1474–1508 (exh. cat., ed. F. Gorissen; Cleve, 1963)

Der Meister von Varsseveld. Kerstken Woyers gen. van Ringenberg, zwei niederrheinländische Beeldensnijder (exh. cat., ed. F. Gorissen; Grubbenvorst-Nimwegen, 1965)
H. Meurer: *Das Klever Chorgestühl und Arnt Beeldesnider* (Düsseldorf, 1970)
G. de Werd: *Die St Nicolaikirche zu Kalkar* (Munich, 1983)
——: 'Das Altarfragment mit der Anbetung der Hl. Drei Könige: Ein Hauptwerk des Meisters Arnt von Kalkar', *Schnütgen-Museum, Arnt von Kalkar und Zwolle: Das Dreikönigsrelief* (Cologne, 1993), pp. 11–45

HERIBERT MEURER

Arntzenius [Arttzenius]**, Floris** [Flor; Pieter Florentius Nicolaas Jacobus] (*b* Surabaya, Java, 9 June 1864; *d* The Hague, 9 June 1925). Dutch painter, illustrator and printmaker. He moved to the Netherlands *c.* 1875, and was taught first by Johan Hendrik Frederik Conrad Nachtweh (1857–1941). He attended the Rijksacademie van Beeldende Kunsten in Amsterdam from 1883 to 1888, studying under August Allebé and Barend Wijnveld (1820–1902). He then spent a year studying life drawing at the Koninklijke Academie voor Schone Kunsten in Antwerp under Charles Verlat before returning to Amsterdam, where he initially applied himself to painting landscapes in the countryside around The Hague and in Nunspeet in Gelderland in the style of the HAGUE SCHOOL.

Arntzenius settled in The Hague in 1892. He was particularly active as a painter of Impressionist townscapes in both oil and watercolour from *c.* 1890 to 1910. His crowded street scenes with their misty, rainy atmosphere, such as *The Spuistraat* (The Hague, Gemeentemus.), were particularly successful and despite their greater emphasis on intimacy and tonality are reminiscent of the work of George Hendrik Breitner and Isaac Israëls. Arntzenius may have collaborated with Breitner, as a watercolour, *Market with Flower Stalls* (Amsterdam, Rijksmus.), is signed by both artists. Arntzenius also painted café scenes, portraits and still-lifes; his beach scenes painted between 1899 and 1908 are similar in style to works by Willem de Zwart and Johan Akkeringa (1864–1942). In 1910 he opened a studio for pupils in The Hague and applied himself to portrait painting. After 1917 he again turned to townscapes in oil and watercolour. His style became less detailed and descriptive than it had been at the turn of the century. Subjects were recorded as a series of coloured blobs of paint, and this resulted increasingly in a somewhat dreamy atmosphere. Arntzenius was a member of Arti et Amicitiae, Pulchri Studio and the Hollandsche Teekenmaatschappij (Dutch Sketching Society). He was one of the principal representatives, together with de Zwart, Akkeringa and others, of the late Hague school.

BIBLIOGRAPHY

P. A. Haaxman: 'Floris Arntzenius', *Elsevier's Geïllus. Mdschr.*, xiii/3 (1903), pp. 159–68
C. Harms Tiepen: 'Flor Arntzenius schildert weder "straatjes"' [Flor Arntzenius is painting *straatjes* again], *Morks Mag.*, xix (July 1917), pp. 325–32
A. Wagner: 'Floris Arntzenius 1864–1925', *Antiek*, iii/5 (1968), pp. 258–71
W. J. de Gruyter: 'Floris Arntzenius (1864–1925)', *De Haagse School*, ii (Rotterdam, 1969), p. 92
Floris Arntzenius 1864–1925: Het Haagse leven van gisteren [Floris Arntzenius: life in The Hague of yesteryear] (exh. cat. by A. Wagner, The Hague, Gemeentemus., Laren, Singer Mus., 1969)

R. W. A. BIONDA

Arnulphy, Claude (*b* Lyon or Grenoble, 1697; *d* Aix-en-Provence, 22 June 1786). French painter. He was trained by his father, Charles Arnulphy (*fl* 1688), and, apart from the traditional study visit to Rome, whence he returned in 1722, he spent his life in Aix-en-Provence. Among his earliest works was a *Crucifixion* (1722; priv. col.), which was his only historical subject, except for an altarpiece of *Christ Showing his Heart to the Blessed Margaret Mary Alacoque* (1742) for the chapel of the Visitation in the church at Meyreuil, near Aix. Otherwise, Arnulphy worked exclusively as a portrait painter; his clients were the *haute bourgeoisie* and aristocracy of Provence. In 1783 he was appointed a 'Peintre du Roi'; in 1765 he established in Aix an art school, in which he played a leading role. Arnulphy's works, such as the informal portrait of *Mme Simiane and her Granddaughter* (1735; priv. col.) and the more official *Portrait of a Magistrate* (1745; Paris, priv. col., see Boyer, p. 39), are realistically detailed and employ a virtuoso technique but also have a certain stiffness and provincial quality.

BIBLIOGRAPHY

Thieme–Becker
L. Dimier: *Les Peintres français du XVIIIe siècle*, i (Paris, 1928), pp. 300–10
J. Boyer: 'La Peinture et la gravure à Aix-en-Provence, 1530–1790', *Gaz. B.-A.*, n. s. 5, lxxviii (1971), pp. 39, 84

CATHRIN KLINGSÖHR-LE ROY

Aroch, Arie (*b* Kharkiv, Ukraine, 1908; *d* Jerusalem, 15 Oct 1974). Israeli painter of Ukrainian birth. His family settled in Palestine in 1924 and he then studied at the Bezalel School of Arts and Crafts in Jerusalem for a year and a half. In 1934 he travelled to Paris where he studied at the Académie Colarossi under Léger, returning to Tel Aviv in 1935. In 1937 he produced stage designs for the Habimah and Ohel theatres in Tel Aviv and the following year had his first one man show at the Santee Landwer Gallery in Amsterdam. He worked with Zvi Mairovich at Zichron Yaacov in 1942 and also exhibited landscape works with the Group of Seven. Typical of his paintings of this period is *Street in a Rural Settlement* (1942; Tel Aviv Mus. A.).

From 1942 to 1946 Aroch fought with the British army and on his discharge settled in Tel Aviv. In 1948 he was one of the founder-members of the NEW HORIZONS group, which included such artists as Mairovich, Yehezkel Streichman and Yossef Zaritsky and which first exhibited at the Tel Aviv Museum in 1948. In contrast to those others in the group who developed a lyrical abstract style, Aroch's work in the 1950s was of a naive appearance with scribbled, spontaneous lines, as in *Bus in the Mountains* (1955; Tel Aviv Mus. A.). In the 1960s he began to use found images in his work, as in *The High Commissioner* (1966; Jerusalem, Israel Mus.), in which he derived the central figure from that on an old rug. In his last works of the late 1960s and early 1970s Aroch worked with abstract forms under the influence of Constructivism, as in *Exercise with Line 8* (1969; Jerusalem, Israel Mus.).

From 1950 to 1971 Aroch worked for the Israeli diplomatic service and in 1971 he was awarded the Israel Prize.

BIBLIOGRAPHY

Arie Aroch: Paintings, 1953–1968 (exh. cat. by Y. Fischer, Jerusalem, Israel Mus., 1968)

Arie Aroch: Itineraries and Forms (exh. cat. by Y. Fischer, Tel Aviv Mus. A., 1976)

□

Arp, Hans [Jean] **(Peter Wilhelm)** (*b* Strassburg, Germany [now Strasbourg, France], 16 Sept 1886; *d* Basle, Switzerland, 7 June 1966). French sculptor, painter, collagist, printmaker and poet of German birth. The son of a German father and French Alsatian mother, he developed a cosmopolitan outlook from an early age and as a mature artist maintained close contact with the avant-garde throughout Europe. He was a pioneer of abstract art and one of the founders of Dada in Zurich, but he also participated actively in both Surrealism and Constructivism. While he prefigured junk art and the Fluxus movement in his incorporation of waste material, it was through his investigation of biomorphism and of chance and accident that he proved especially influential on later 20th-century art in liberating unconscious creative forces.

1. Training and early work, to 1915. 2. Dada period, 1916–20. 3. Links with Surrealism and Constructivism, 1920s and 1930s. 4. Sculpture, 1930s to the 1960s.

1. TRAINING AND EARLY WORK, TO 1915. Following a brief period at the Kunstgewerbeschule in Strasbourg (1900–01), Arp received instruction from 1901 from a friend and neighbour, the painter and printmaker Georges Ritleng (1875–1972). He then attended the Kunstschule in Weimar (1904–7) and the Académie Julian in Paris (1908–9). In spite of his opposition to academic training as sterile, his treatment of pictorial space remained conventional in early paintings such as *Still-life* (1903; Basle, Kstmus.), with heavily applied colour. A plaster *Head* (*c.* 1903; priv. col., see Poley, p. 173), notable for the indistinctness of its features, is reminiscent of sculpture by Medardo Rosso and Auguste Rodin. Other surviving works by Arp from the Weimar period include traditional nude drawings, rounded and full of movement, a self-portrait dating to 1904 and a landscape of *Weimar Park* (watercolour, 1906–8; Hamburg, Ksthalle), in a Neo-Impressionist style. Around 1909, in Weggis, Switzerland, Arp was taught techniques of plaster work by the Swiss sculptor Fritz Huf (1888–1970). His first essays into abstract painting, later described by him as grey monochromes covered in lines and dark blotches, date from the same period. The incomprehension with which these were greeted led him to destroy them and to revert temporarily to conventional figurative art.

Arp was a founder-member of the Moderne Bund in Lucerne, participating in their exhibitions from 1911 to 1913. He exhibited caricatures, heads and female nudes painted or drawn in a spontaneous, swift and simple style. The same expressive and graphic quality characterized his woodcuts and vignettes for their catalogues and for *Der Blaue Reiter Almanach*. In *Bathers* (1913; Basle, Kstmus.) and *Three Women* (1912; Clamart, Fond. Arp), the human anatomy is perceived in a very basic way: the bodies are painted in thick colours and silhouetted in black lines, giving them a dense and laboured quality that is almost sculptural with all unnecessary detail eliminated in the neutral backgrounds. Through his collaboration with the BLAUE REITER in Munich and DER STURM in Berlin Arp developed his international contacts; through the Munich group, in particular, he renewed his passion for German Romanticism and developed an interest in antiquity and primitivism. Around 1914, under the influence of Cubism and Futurism, Arp created collages in which he juxtaposed different materials, as in *Untitled* (1915; Berne, Kstmus.) and *Wallpaper* (1915; Basle, Kstmus.), but he limited himself to paper and fabric, never extending the shapes with drawn or painted features. The collages made at this time as illustrations for *Phantastische Gebete* (Zurich, 1916) by Richard Huelsenbeck are symmetrical in form and reminiscent of Native American totems.

In the spring of 1915 Arp sought refuge from World War I in Zurich, where an exhibition of his work was held at Galerie Tanner in November. In the preface to the catalogue he set out his view that art must express spiritual truths exclusively by means of form, line and colour, an aspiration that linked him to Art Nouveau, Expressionism and the Blaue Reiter. He rejected academic ideas such as naturalism, perspective and all forms of representation. He also stressed the virtues of anonymity and impersonality in the creative act. During the exhibition he met Sophie Taeuber (*see* TAEUBER-ARP, SOPHIE), whose personality and work greatly influenced him and whom he married in 1922. Impressed by the abstract pictures of squares and rectangles that she had begun to make in 1915, especially as he was unfamiliar at that time with the non-objective compositions of Malevich, Mondrian and Theo van Doesburg, he began collaborating with her on collages and embroideries patterned exclusively in squares, with rhythms established by the non-symmetrical use of sombre colours. These *Duo-Collages* of 1916 to 1918, with their anonymity of execution and their pure formalism, were exercises in purification for both artists. These vertical–horizontal compositions, while having no representational function, symbolized for them the equal and fundamentally conflicting forces of the world's dualism. By means of these mandala-like compositions they sought to express a profound interior reality, which was strengthened by a search both for the absolute and also for a new order, following the disorder and chaos of war. This geometric and rational order served Arp as a catalyst for his later work.

2. DADA PERIOD, 1916–20. The effervescence of the DADA movement, to which Arp belonged from its very beginning in February 1916, went far beyond polemics and challenges aimed to shock the bourgeoisie: it enabled ideas and new forms to develop and grow in a climate that was free from prejudice and academic conventions, and it also encouraged inventive spontaneity. It proved to be a fertile soil for the systematic evolution of Arp's typical style, conditioned by two factors, those of terrestrial form and the concept of chance. He exploited the potential of accidental conjunctions of forms in works such as *Collage with Squares Arranged According to the Laws of Chance* (1916–17; New York, MOMA). His investigation of BIOMORPHISM in shapes that he later referred to as 'moving ovals' (*see* DADA, fig. 1) was inspired by natural forms, especially by the debris thrown up on the beach at Ascona, such as roots, twigs and shingle. Giving free rein to his brush and to his imagination in irregular and slashed contours outlined in India ink, he developed a direct form

of pictorial expression that allowed him to abandon himself to subconscious forces and to the laws of chance. These forms became the basis of his Dada and Surrealist reliefs and of the free-standing sculptures that he initiated some 13 years later. Both the appearance and the structure of his forms were infinitely variable, as they are in nature, their continuous evolution symbolizing the cyclical metamorphosis of all earthly life as growth, decline and rebirth (e.g. in the three woodcuts published in *Dada*, 3, Dec 1918). Arp's work came very close at this time to that of Kandinsky, whom he knew and admired through the Blaue Reiter. Arp soon carved such biomorphic forms in wood, superimposing them in bright polychromatic reliefs such as *Forest* (1916; Clamart, Fond. Arp; see fig. 1), so full of movement that they seem to overflow their frames. These works have a genuine rather than illusionistic depth, with up to four separate layers appearing to project themselves into space.

At the end of World War I Arp renewed his contacts with the avant-garde in Germany, France and Italy, and helped to spread Dada in Berlin, Cologne, Hannover and Paris. For Arp, Dada represented the reconciliation of man with nature and the integration of art into life. From 1917 he and Taeuber had also become involved in a utopian community, Monte Verità, at Ascona; in 1918 they rejoined the NEUE LEBEN group in Basle (signing their *Manifeste des artistes radicaux* in 1919), which was also seeking to give the artist a social function, as Dada was doing in Berlin. In Arp's view, Dada was 'a moral revolution'. In tandem with his abstract compositions inspired by organic forms, he continued to conceive works derived from the human body, such as *Figure* (1915; Locarno, Fond. Arp) and *Madame Torso with Wavy Hat, Woman* (1916; Berne, Kstmus.). Subsequently human elements appeared in his abstract works, in the fragmentary form of eyes, heads or other body parts (e.g. *Flake Bois II–V*, 1920; see Arntz, cat. nos 52–5), and in greatly simplified reliefs, such as *Mask* (1918; Paris, Ruth Arp priv. col., see Rau, cat. no. 23).

1. Hans Arp: *Forest*, painted wood relief, 325×195×70 mm (3 layers), 1916 (Clamart, Fondation Arp)

3. LINKS WITH SURREALISM AND CONSTRUCTIVISM, 1920S AND 1930S. Following the splitting up of the human body, which projected the image of an increasingly fragmented world, Arp set out a complex and elaborate repertoire of half-real objects, which had irregular but supple contours. This was highly schematic, and it already contained the germ of his future sculpture. He set these into an empty spatial context and added to them elements derived from nature and the everyday environment, once again placing them in frames. His preferred motifs were: moustache, navel, mask, shirt-front, tie, bird, frog, flower, leaf, cloud, star, amphora and bottle. These strange symbols were used with a verve that was both comical and moving, as in *Navel-Bottle* (New York, MOMA) and six other lithographs, *7 Arpaden*, published by Kurt Schwitters in *Merz*, 5 (1923; see Arntz, cat. nos 305 and 311). Arp caricatured human beings by breaking them down into small pieces and putting them into the same framework as the symbols of their daily life; no longer the measure of all things, they were thus brought closer to their environment. Arp transformed people into objects; conversely, objects became humanized. The amoeba-like forms of Arp's 'object language' evoked cellular life and cosmic images with equal vividness. He wanted their universal application to be apparent to everyone through their simplicity, their interchangeability linking them directly to language. In his reliefs as well as in his poetry, Arp devoted himself to a game of unlimited combinations, to a succession of images and associations in consistently fresh variations as in the series of reliefs known as *Clocks* (1924; see Rau, cat. nos 57–61) and *Lips* (1926; see Rau, cat. nos 86–9). These ambivalent pictographs changed their form and underwent mutations in a totally unpredictable way depending on their context. The most typical form was the navel: amoeboid, it was either circular or oval, static or moving, a sun or an eye, a button or a nipple, a leaf or a cloud. For Arp, who had been strongly influenced by the pre-Socratic philosophers, it was a model of the primitive in an unchanging world that was nevertheless in a permanent state of flux. The navel, the very well-spring of the world, was also the basis of his creative strength: everything stemmed from it, and it in turn could be transmuted into everything. It was the 'symbol of metamorphosis and development of bodies' (*Jours effeuillés*, p. 357). Towards the end of the 1920s he produced many *Constellations*, in white, based on this primordial ovoid form, suggesting both cellular life and planetary movement, as in a group of reliefs entitled *Objects Arranged*

According to the Laws of Chance, Navel (1930; see Rau, cat. nos 222–7).

In 1925 Arp rented a studio in the rue Tourlaque, in Montmartre, and in 1926 he and Taeuber-Arp became French nationals. In 1928, after collaborating with THEO VAN DOESBURG for two years on the renovation of the Café de l'Aubette in Strasbourg, they built a house for themselves (to Taeuber-Arp's designs) at Clamart, near Paris; this later became the centre of the Fondation Arp. Right from the beginning Arp exhibited his work with the Surrealists. His adherence to the movement did not fundamentally change his style, since he had been using incongruous juxtapositions as early as 1920. Surrealism encouraged his exploration of subconscious and irrational impulses and his concern with the symbolic value of images. In particular it accentuated the intuitive, absurd and dream-like aspects of his work, his dependence on free association and automatic writing, and his inquisitive need to try out unusual methods and materials; these experiments included hollowed reliefs such as *Lunar Frog* (1925; see Rau, cat. no. 56), and reliefs made from pieces of driftwood (e.g. *Travel Kit of the Shipwrecked*, 1923; see Rau, cat. no. 33), old newspapers (e.g. *Disabled and Stateless Person*, 1936; Venice, Guggenheim) or string stitched on to canvas (e.g. *Man at the Window*, 1930; see Rau, cat. no. 198). From 1932 Arp produced torn drawings and prints in which a significant role was ascribed to chance. In addition to his use of poetic and descriptive titles as a way of linking his pictures to the written word, Arp described his pictorial compositions as 'calligraphies', as in *Calligraphy of Navels* (1928; see Rau, cat. no. 161).

In spite of his involvement with the Surrealists, Arp, like his wife, had close links with Constructivist groups such as DE STIJL, CERCLE ET CARRÉ, *Art Concret* and ABSTRACTION–CRÉATION, all of which had in common a desire to create a counterbalance to Surrealism as well as to change society and prepare the way towards a better future for mankind. Under these influences, and inspired above all by Taeuber-Arp's work, Arp began to introduce straight lines and sharp-angled notches into his curvilinear reliefs, as in *Constellation* (1934; see Rau, cat. no. 272) and *Amadryade* (1934; see Rau, cat. no. 274).

4. SCULPTURE, 1930S TO THE 1960S. Arp's first sculptures, such as *Fruit of a Hand* (1929; Zurich, Ksthaus), were assembled into reliefs from pieces of sawn wood and then positioned on an ornamental base. These transitional pieces led around 1930 to his first sustained group of sculptures in the round, known as *Concretions*, modelled in plaster or carved in wood or stone. The malleability of plaster enabled him to create forms that palpitate with exuberant life; these were later cast in bronze. Their sheer volume gives them a solid presence, the full spread of their sensual rounded contours invariably calling to mind the female body. In spite of their commandingly solid, even earthy, appearance, these works seem to be virtually weightless, endowed with an aerial and almost transcendental quality. On the same principle that his reliefs dispensed with a frame, Arp preferred his sculptures not to be mounted on a base, so that they could simply take their place in nature. A number of them were conceived without a predetermined orientation and could be positioned in any direction. In place of the term abstract art, he and other artists, notably van Doesburg, referred to their work as Concrete art, maintaining that their aim was not to reproduce, but simply to produce more directly (*see* CONCRETE ART). In such works as *Human Concretions on Oval Bowl* (1935; Clamart, Fond. Arp) Arp aimed to incorporate physical essence, with one part equated to the whole, concentrating form so as to increase the sculpture's domination of space and its impact on the spectator.

The rich profusion of Arp's sculpture was dependent in part on his repeated use of existing forms, as with his dozens of variations on torsos from 1930 to 1965. A fragment of an existing work sometimes gave rise to a new one, as with the transformation of *Torso* many years later into *Torso–Sheaf* (1958; see fig. 2). Mutations also occurred through the enlargement of a form, by cutting it into two, by amputating it or even by making use of accidental breakage, as in the transformation of *Winged Entity* (1961; see Trier, cat. no. 252) following an exhibition into *Angel's Torso* (1963; see Trier, cat. no. 287) and *Nocturnal Glance* (1964; see Trier, cat. no. 315). In his sculpture, as in his other work, Arp linked together humans and animals, vegetable and inanimate objects, the organic and the inorganic. Such surprising fusions occur, for example, in *Pagoda Fruit* (1934; Clamart, Fond. Arp) and *Mirror Leaf* (1962; Locarno, Pin. Casa Rusca), while in *Three Graces* (1961; priv. col., see Trier, cat. no. 263) the figures of a woman and a column are brought together. Elastic curves sometimes alternate with geometric shapes and sharp lines, as in *Cypriana* (1931; see Giedion-Welcker, cat. no. 9) or *Conjugual Sculpture* (1937; see Giedion-Welcker, cat. no. 35), one of a series of notched wood-carvings made in collaboration with his wife. After her death in 1943, he paid tribute to her in numerous works combining geometric crystallization with natural fluidity (e.g. *Oru*, 1948; see Giedion-Welcker, cat. no. 125).

Arp increasingly sought comfort in religion and in the mystics. His later work was no longer filled with radical inventiveness; instead he developed variations on his favourite themes, with darting forms becoming increasingly frequent. Finding symmetry in nature and the human body, Arp produced a series of collages cut from paper folded in the middle, known collectively as *Dolls*, representing figures that gaze at us with an unchanging stare. These works, and closely related sculptures such as *Amphora Woman* (1962; see Trier, cat. no. 280), have the quality of religious images. The search for a greater renunciation linked to verticality and symmetry gave an archetypal dimension to his later works, expressing his search for a deeper spirituality through stability, peace and a longing for the sacred.

WRITINGS

On my Way (New York, 1948) [Eng., Ger. and Fr. text]
Dreams and Projects (New York, 1951) [Eng., Ger. and Fr. text]
Gesammelte Gedichte, 3 vols (Zurich and Wiesbaden, 1963–84)
Jours effeuillés (Paris, 1966); Eng. trans. as *Arp on Arp* (New York, 1972)

BIBLIOGRAPHY

G. Buffet-Picabia: *Jean Arp* (Paris, 1952)
C. Giedion-Welcker: *Hans Arp* (Stuttgart, 1957); Eng. trans. as *Jean Arp* (London, 1957) [with cat. of sculptures and bibliog. by M. Arp-Hagenbach]
M. Seuphor: *Arp* (Paris, 1957)
Arp (exh. cat. by J. T. Soby, New York, MOMA, 1958)
J. Cathelin: *Jean Arp* (Paris, 1959)
G. Marchiori: *Arp: Cinquante ans d'activité* (Milan, 1964)

2. Hans Arp: (left) *Torso*, white marble, h. 600 mm, 1931 (Basle, private collection); (right) *Torso–Sheaf*, bronze, h. 670 mm, 1958 (private collection)

M. Seuphor: *Arp: Sculpture* (Paris, 1964)
R. Döhl: *Das literarische Werk Hans Arps, 1903–1930* (Stuttgart, 1967)
H. Read: *The Art of Jean Arp* (London, 1968)
E. Trier: *Hans Arp: Skulpturen, 1957–66* (Stuttgart, 1968; Eng. trans., London, 1968) [with cat. of late sculptures and bibliog. of M. Arp-Hagenbach]
R. Last: *Hans Arp, the Poet of Dadaism* (London and Chester Springs, 1969)
I. Jianou: *Jean Arp* (Paris, 1973)
S. Poley: *Hans Arp: Die Formensprache im plastischen Werk* (Stuttgart, 1978)
W. Arntz: *Hans Arp: Das graphische Werk, 1912–1966* (The Hague, 1980) [cat. of prints]
J. Hancock: *Form and Content in the Early Work of Jean Arp* (diss., Cambridge, MA, Harvard U., 1980)
B. Rau: *Hans Arp: Die Reliefs, Oeuvre-Katalog* (Stuttgart, 1981)
F. Usinger: *Huldigung für Hans Arp* (Merzhausen, 1981)
Hans Arp: Nach dem Gesetz des Zufalls geordnet (exh. cat. by J. Zutter and M. Stucky, Basle, Kstmus., 1982)
A. Bleikasten: *Arp Bibliographie*, 2 vols (London, 1983)
Hans Arp/Jean Arp: Le Temps des papiers déchirés (exh. cat., ed. C. Deronet; Paris, Pompidou, 1983)
Arp, 1886–1966 (exh. cat. by J. Hancock and S. Poley, Stuttgart, Württemberg. Kstver.; Strasbourg, Mus. A. Mod.; Paris, Mus. A. Mod. Ville Paris; and elsewhere; 1986–8)
S. Fauchereau: *Arp* (Paris, 1988)
Arp: Sculptures, reliefs et papier de 1913–1966 (exh. cat., PACA, 1992)
Hans Arp (exh. cat., ed. G. Hatje; Nuremberg, Ksthalle, 1994)

GRETA STROEH

Arp, Sophie Taeuber-. *See* TAEUBER-ARP, SOPHIE.

Arpachiyah. Prehistoric site in northern Iraq situated *c.* 6 km north-east of Nineveh and 9 km east of the River Tigris. Its low mound (120 m in diameter and 11.5 m high) was excavated by Max Mallowan in 1933 and by Ismail Hijara in 1976. These excavations show that Arpachiyah was occupied during the Halaf (*c.* 5200–*c.* 4500 BC) and Ubaid (5th millennium BC) periods (*see* MESOPOTAMIA, §§I, 2(i)(a) and V,1). The finds made in 1933 were divided between the Iraq Museum in Baghdad and Mosul and various other institutions, including the British Museum, London, and the Institute of Archaeology, London University. The finds of 1976 are all in Iraq.

The Halaf settlement is represented by a deposit 7.5 m deep occupying the whole site. On the basis of the finds in this deposit a framework for the classification of Halaf pottery was first established, which has since been elaborated. Arpachiyah provides most of the evidence for the Halaf sequence and is therefore a key site for comparative studies with other sites. Such an accumulation presumably reflects a lengthy occupation and may represent the full extent of the Halaf cultural period. It is the only site so far to yield a wide range of stratified pottery of the Early Halaf period.

Eleven Halafian building levels were distinguished by Hijara in the centre of the mound, of which the five upper levels correspond to Mallowan's TT6–10 levels. Hijara has identified four successive phases. In Phases One (the earliest) and Four (levels XI–IX and I/TT6 respectively) buildings were rectangular, but Phases Two and Three (levels VIII–VI and V–II/TT10–7) were characterized by circular structures (tholoi), which, in Phase Three, had stone foundations and antechambers. These buildings may have had beehive roofs of a type still found in northern Iraq and Syria. It is possible that the tholoi had a public—perhaps a religious—function, since burials were associated with some of them. In Phase Four a workshop, which had been destroyed by fire, was found to contain clay figurines of the 'mother-goddess' type, stone vases, amulets (in the shape of bull's head and hoof, double axe etc), flint and obsidian tools, pigments, palettes and pottery.

Early Halaf pottery is generally buff-coloured with designs of birds, fish, stylized animal heads and geometric motifs in red-brown paint. It was found in layers where there were no architectural remains, and also in association with Phase One and Two buildings. Middle Halaf pottery is technically superior with distinctive, shallow, carinated vessels with flaring rims ('cream-bowls'), which are beautifully painted. Late Halaf pottery was found in connection with Phase Four buildings and the polychrome decoration is applied to shallow bowls with red, brown and white paint on an apricot slip (see fig.). Analysis has shown that pottery was manufactured at Arpachiyah for export to other sites.

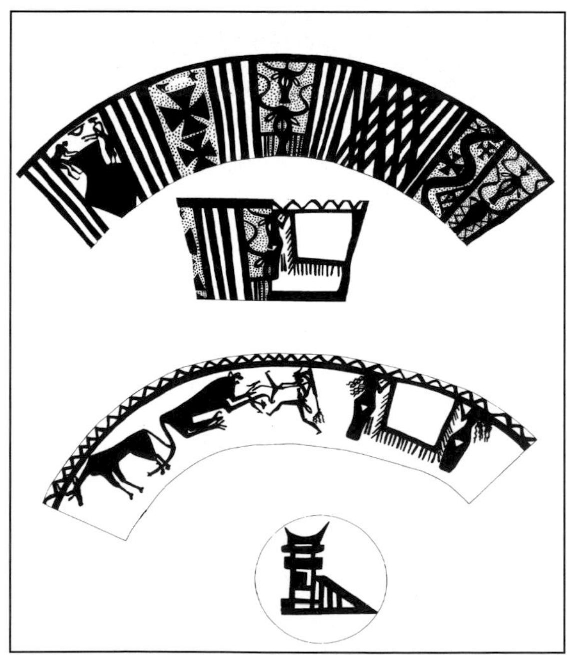

Arpachiyah, Halaf bowl from ritual burial G2, tholos area, h. *c*. 190 mm, *c*. 5000 BC (Baghdad, Iraq Museum)

There is probably a gap between Phase Four buildings and the later Ubaid-period levels excavated in 1933 (TT5–1). These are characterized by poorly built houses concentrated in the centre of the mound. Fifty Ubaid graves were discovered on the site, of which 45 were found in a cemetery. These included 15 fractional and thus possibly secondary burials. This may be further evidence of a continuing tradition of sanctity associated with the site. Much of the distinctive northern Ubaid pottery from Arpachiyah, with its bold designs on a light ground, was found in these graves.

BIBLIOGRAPHY

M. E. L. Mallowan and J. Cruikshank Rose: 'Excavation at Tall Arpachiyah, 1933', *Iraq*, xi (1935), pp. 1–178

I. Hijara: 'Three New Graves at Arpachiyah', *World Archaeol.*, x (1978), pp. 125–8

I. Hijara: *The Halaf Period in Northern Mesopotamia* (diss., U. London, 1980)

I. Hijara and others: 'Arpachiyah 1976', *Iraq*, xlii (1980), pp. 131–54

ISMAIL HIJARA

Arphe. *See* ARFE.

Arpino, Cavaliere d' [Cesari, Giuseppe] (*b* Arpino, nr Sora, 1568; *d* Rome, 3 July 1640). Italian painter and draughtsman. His father, Muzio Cesari, was probably a painter; his brother, Bernardino Cesari (1571–1622), became his principal assistant. Giuseppe's precocious talent for drawing led his mother to take him to Rome in 1581–2, where he became a colour mixer under Niccolò Circignani, then directing the decoration of the third of the great Vatican Logge for Gregory XIII. Circignani promoted him to the painting team; a tiny figure of *Abundance* on the vault of the seventh compartment has been identified as his earliest known work. During 1583 Giuseppe also worked at the Vatican on the monochrome figure of *Samson with the Gates of Gaza* in the Sala Vecchia degli Svizzeri and the restoration of the *Prophets* and *Virtues* painted by the Raphael workshop in the Sala dei Palafrenieri. Towards the end of the year the Pope granted Giuseppe a salary. Probably in 1584–5 he contributed a fresco of the *Canonization of St Francis of Paola* to the decoration of the cloister of Trinità dei Monti, Rome, begun by Cristoforo Roncalli. The painting is very damaged but still visible; among the figures in the crowd is probably Giuseppe's first self-portrait. There are also some beautifully realized foreground figures: a chalk study of a Michelangelesque nude for one of these survives (Florence, Uffizi).

In 1585 Giuseppe returned to the service of Gregory XIII, painting decorative friezes (destr.) in the newly built Palazzo del Quirinale. His standing in Rome now seemed assured: he was a member of the Accademia di S Luca, and in 1586 he was admitted to the Confraternity, the Virtuosi al Pantheon. He had been commissioned by Cardinal Giulio Santori to paint frescoes of the *Crucifixion* and the *Assumption of the Virgin* in S Atanasio dei Greci

(1588–91; *in situ*) and the decoration (destr.) for Santori's palazzo (now part of the Palazzo di Montecitorio). A more important commission of the same period was for frescoes in S Lorenzo in Damaso for Cardinal Alessandro Farnese. These included two narrative scenes (untraced): a vivid *bozzetto* (London, priv. col.; see 1973 exh. cat., pp. 68–71, fig. 1) and a pedestrian copy (Rome, Boncompagni, priv. col.; see 1973 exh. cat., pp. 71–2, fig. 3) of *St Lawrence among the Sick* show dignified groups dominated by elaborate architecture in a classicizing composition reminiscent of contemporary Florentine Mannerism. A third fresco of three angels (damaged and detached, but *in situ*) is fresher and more immediate.

In 1589 Giuseppe's most influential current patron, Cardinal Farnese, died. As he had no introduction to the court of Sixtus V, he eagerly accepted an invitation to decorate the vault of the choir of the Certosa di S Martino, Naples. He completed a canvas of the *Crucifixion* (1591; *in situ*), in which the simplicity of Counter-Reformation *arte sacra* combines with the grace and vivid colour of Federico Barocci to create a movingly original work. His scenes from the *Life of Christ*, with attendant *Prophets* and *Carthusian Saints*, were unfinished when he returned to Rome in 1591; they were completed by his brother, Bernardino, in 1592–3. On his return to Rome, Giuseppe received the commission to paint the vault of the Contarelli Chapel in S Luigi dei Francesi with small scenes in elaborate stuccowork. It was probably at this time that Caravaggio became a member of his studio: he certainly owned two of Caravaggio's early works (Rome, Gal. Borghese).

In 1592 Clement VIII was elected pope, and Giuseppe became his principal painter. The artist's re-entry into court circles was perhaps due to Bernardo Olgiati, the papal treasurer. The frescoes in the Olgiati Chapel (Rome, S Prassede), although commissioned in 1587, were probably executed at this time. Among his most important works, these combine his reassessment of the High Renaissance models in the Vatican, and possibly those found on a journey to northern Italy, with a restriction of the purely decorative aspects of Mannerism to a minor role. In a simple architectural framework by Giovanni Alberti, Giuseppe painted seated *Prophets*, *Sibyls* and *Doctors of the Church*; the eastern lunette contains a superbly realized *Resurrection*. Dominating the whole is the central scene of the *Ascension*, in which a consistent but separate illusion with a *di sotto in sù* perspective enlivens a radically simple composition. The whole has a consistency that presages the Baroque, and its references to the combined influences of Raphael, Titian, Correggio and Michelangelo make it a true forerunner of Annibale Carracci's Galleria in the Palazzo Farnese, Rome (begun 1597); a similar style informed Giuseppe's decoration of a loggia in the palazzo of Corradino Orsini (1594–5; Rome, Pal. Sodalizio Piceni) with light-hearted frescoes of the *Loves of the Gods* and *Labours of Hercules*, completing a scheme begun by Federico Zuccaro in 1589.

In the mid-1590s Giuseppe gained commissions from members of the papal family, particularly the Pope's powerful nephew, Cardinal Pietro Aldobrandini. He provided an altarpiece of *St Barbara* (1594–7) for the chapel of the Bombardieri in S Maria in Traspontina, Rome, built by the Cardinal; the saint's figure and attendant angel display an elaborated yet direct classicism, which moves the style of Raphael quite clearly in the direction of Guido Reni. He also painted the altarpiece of the *Annunciation* and frescoes of the *Adoration of the Shepherds* and the *Adoration of the Magi* (1596) for the funerary chapel of the Cardinal's uncle, another Pietro Aldobrandini (*d* 1587), in S Maria in Via, Rome. Giuseppe's most important commission from Cardinal Aldobrandini was the fresco decoration of the Palazzo dei Conservatori on the Capitoline Hill in Rome with a series of *Histories of Ancient Rome*, which occupied him intermittently for the rest of his life. The *Discovery of Romulus and Remus* (1595–7; see fig.), a superb composition full of life and movement, has graceful figures brilliantly disposed before and within a landscape setting that is both decorative and realistic. The *Battle between the Romans and the Men of Veii and Fidenae* (1597–1601) is more conventional, directly recalling Raphael but again enlivened with charmingly naturalistic landscape details.

In 1598 for the Pope's episcopal church, S Giovanni in Laterano, Giuseppe painted two canvases for the Baptistery: *St John the Evangelist Led to his Tomb* (Old Sacristy), a sombre scene of large figures before a bleak landscape, and *St John Drinking the Tyrant's Poison* (untraced). The following year he began supervising the decoration of the main church's transepts; he personally contributed a large fresco of the *Ascension* (1599–1601; *in situ*). For these works he was made Cavaliere di Cristo by Clement VIII; he had also been elected president of the Accademia di S Luca in 1599. He decorated Cardinal Pietro Aldobrandini's magnificent villa at Frascati with seven Old Testament scenes in fresco (1602–3), which, despite their quality, demonstrate a retreat to Mannerist norms. The high-point of Cavaliere d'Arpino's papal patronage was his undertaking in 1603 to design the mosaics of the dome of St Peter's (*see* ROME, fig. 38). This vast project occupied most of the following decade. The repetitious display of *Apostles*, *Saints*, *Angels* and other figures is pictorially disappointing, but the overall effect enhances the architecture.

In 1605 Clement VIII was succeeded by Paul V, whose nephew, Cardinal Scipione Borghese, had Arpino arrested in 1607 and confiscated his collection of 105 pictures, which still hang in the Cardinal's villa, now the Galleria Borghese. Arpino's humiliation appears to have affected his art, as can be gauged by another fresco at the Palazzo dei Conservatori, the *Fight between the Horatii and the Curatii* (1612), in which the rich liveliness of his previous scenes has been reduced to a dignified but melancholy stasis. From 1610 he was in charge of the decoration of the Pope's future funerary chapel, the Cappella Paolina in S Maria Maggiore. Here he supervised important contributions from Guido Reni and Ludovico Cigoli and painted turgid figures of *Prophets* in the pendentives and a schematic *Virgin with St Gregory* above the altar. A tender and beautiful drawing for the figure of *St Gregory* (Frankfurt am Main, Städel. Kstinst. & Städt. Gal.) shows that Giuseppe's artistic ideas, if not their execution, were still fresh.

In 1613–14 Arpino supervised the decoration, by Agostino Tassi and Orazio Gentileschi, among others, of the new casino of Cardinal Alessandro Peretti-Montalto's villa at Bagnaia (now Villa Lante). The extent of his own

Cavaliere d'Arpino: *Discovery of Romulus and Remus* (1595–7), fresco, Palazzo dei Conservatori, Rome

contribution is difficult to determine, but some friezes of animals and putti have been convincingly attributed to his hand. In 1617 he was involved in similar work (destr.) at the Palazzo del Quirinale. The explosion of artistic activity in Rome under Urban VIII drew Arpino once more into prominence. In 1629 he painted scenes of the *Birth of the Virgin* and *Death of the Virgin* for the choir of S Maria di Loreto (oil; *in situ*). In 1629 he was elected for a third term as president of the Accademia di S Luca. He resumed his series of frescoes in the Palazzo dei Conservatori, though with even less success. The *Institution of Religion*, *Rape of the Sabine Women* (much restored) and *Foundation of Rome* (all 1635–40) display disappointingly rigid compositions and lifeless figures, although some felicitous landscape features in the last recall the time when his confident, colourful, lively and lavish art prefigured elements of the Baroque.

BIBLIOGRAPHY

DBI; Thieme–Becker: 'Cesari, Giuseppe'

K. van Mander: *Schilder-boeck* ([1603]–1604)

G. Baglione: *Vite* (1642); ed. V. Mariani (1935), pp. 367–75

A. Venturi: *Storia* (1901–40), ix/5, pp. 921–39

I. Faldi: 'Gli affreschi della Cappella Contarelli e l'opera giovanile del Cavalier d'Arpino', *Boll. A.*, xxxviii (1953), pp. 45–55

S. J. Freedberg: *Painting in Italy, 1500–1600*, Pelican Hist. A. (Harmondsworth, 1971), pp. 460–62

Il Cavalier d'Arpino (exh. cat., ed. H. Röttgen; Rome, Pal. Venezia, 1973)

J. A. Gere and P. Pouncey: *Italian Drawings in the Department of Prints and Drawings in the British Museum: Artists Working in Rome, c. 1550–c. 1640* (London, 1983), i, pp. 29–33

□

Arpo, Guariento di. *See* GUARIENTO.

Arquitectonica. American architectural firm incorporated in 1977 by Bernardo Fort-Brescia (*b* Lima, Peru, 19 Nov 1950), Laurinda Hope Spear (*b* Rochester, MN, 23 Aug 1950), Hervin Romney (*b* Havana, Cuba, 9 Feb 1941), Andres Duany (*b* New York, 7 Sept 1949) and Elizabeth Plater-Zyberk (*b* Bryn Mawr, PA, 10 Dec 1950). The latter two members of the firm left in 1980 to start their own practice. The firm's early sketches displayed an interest in the surrealistic place-making of Giorgio de Chirico, which Arquitectonica transformed to exercises in geometric abstraction at the layered and orderly Spear house (1977–8), Miami, FL. In its first decade of practice Arquitectonica transformed speculative housing developments, office buildings and shopping centres—normally banal architectural projects—into dramatic, expressive 'high tech' forms marked by flashy, sensual and commercially attractive styling. It single-handedly transformed the Biscayne Bay–Brickell Boulevard skyline in Miami with its Helmsley Palace (1979–80), Babylon (1979–82), the Imperial (1979–83) and especially the witty housing block Atlantis (1980–82), achieving international recognition. Work in other cities included the Horizon Hill Center (1981–2), San Antonio, TX, which echoed the theatrical scale of the Soviet Constructivists' images of the 1920s, while the Casa Los Andes (1988), Lima, employed freer forms inspired by Matisse collages. At the Rio Shopping Mall (1988–9), Atlanta, GA, Arquitectonica ornamented a brightly coloured corrugated metal skin with elements of structural steel framing, a geodesic dome and, just for fun, a parade of adoring frogs in formation in a pond. Functionalism remained the underlying catalyst informing such later work as the Banco de Credito (1988), La Molina, Lima, whose independent forms for foyer, boardroom, auditorium and cafeteria slice through or slide under the four-storey courtyard block. Arquitectonica adapted the universality of Modernist abstraction to the local climate of time and place, especially in Miami where its chic, late-Modernist buildings reflected both the optimism of the 1980s and the regional colour and festive unconventionality of subtropical south Florida.

BIBLIOGRAPHY

'Romantic Modernism', *Process: Archit.*, 165 (1986) [issue dedicated to Arquitectonica]

W. McQuade: 'Glamour, Inc. Architecture with the Latino Flash, by Arquitectonica', *Connoisseur*, ccxviii (1988), pp. 146–55

B. Dunlap: *Arquitectonica* (New York, 1991)

ROBERT M. CRAIG

Arrabona. *See* GYŐR.

Arraiolos. Portuguese centre of carpet production; also the name applied to carpets made elsewhere in the same tradition. Arraiolos carpets are embroidered with strands of thick wool, or more rarely silk, on linen, jute or hemp canvas, using a large-eyed needle and a long-armed cross stitch, which gives the effect of braiding. The reverse side of the carpet shows no trace of finishing off and appears to be hatched. The pattern is drawn on squared paper, and then the main points of reference are marked on the canvas by counting the threads. The border and all the motifs are first outlined and then filled; the background is embroidered last. The carpet is finished with a continuous plain or polychrome edging of looped or cut fringe. In the days when natural dyes were used, the colours were predominantly red, blue and yellow, obtained from brazilwood, indigo, dyer's weed or spurge respectively. Originally the carpets were used to cover the floor of the hall or bedroom in noble houses and were surrounded by a strip of polished wooden floor.

These carpets have been made in the Alentejo region since the early 17th century, particularly around Arraiolos, where their production became a cottage industry. The oldest examples date from the early 17th century and were perhaps produced in monastic houses. They are executed on linen and show clearly the influence of Persian carpets (common in noble and monastic houses from the 15th century) in their use of colour, symmetry of design (with floral and animal motifs) and Oriental symbols (e.g. lotus flowers, pomegranates, birds of paradise and clouds). During the 18th century the carpets became larger, and Persian motifs gradually gave way to European ones: carnations, palms, tulips, narcissi and sometimes stylized human figures. They were embroidered in a medium-sized stitch using thinner wool, and the choice and variety of colours became greater, sometimes as many as 18 shades being used. During the 19th century the Persian theme almost totally disappeared, and the quality of the carpets gradually declined.

Carpet manufacture was revived in the middle of the 20th century, and examples are now made almost everywhere in Portugal, retaining the generic name Arraiolos. Similar carpets are made in centres of Portuguese emigration such as Brazil and Canada. The largest collections of Arraiolos carpets are in the Museu Nacional de Arte Antiga, Lisbon, the Museu Nacional de Machado de Castro, Coimbra, and the Palacio Nacional de Queluz, Queluz.

BIBLIOGRAPHY

D. J. Pessanha: *Tapetes de Arraiolos* (Lisbon, 1906)

D. S. Pessanha: *Tapetes de Arraiolos* (Lisbon, 1917)

M. J. de Mendonça: 'Tapetes de Arraiolos', *As artes decorativas* ([1953]), i of *Arte Portuguesa*, ed. J. Barreira, 3 vols (Lisbon, [1953-4]), pp. 265–320

F. Baptista de Oliveira: *História e Técnica dos Tapetes de Arraiolos* (Lisbon, 1973)

NATALIA CORREIA GUEDES

Arras [Lat. Nemetacum]. French city and préfecture of the Pas-de-Calais, now the major city of the Artois region in north-east France.

1. HISTORY AND URBAN DEVELOPMENT. The history of Arras has been particularly unstable. First inhabited by the Atrebates, it was destroyed in AD 407, rebuilt by St Vaast (its first bishop) in 500, and razed by the Normans in 880. It remained under the authority of the Counts of Flanders from 863 to 1180, when, with the marriage of Philippe II Auguste (*reg* 1180–1223) and Isabella of Hainault (1170–90), it became part of France. By 1384, when it was annexed by Burgundy, Arras consisted of a Gallo-Roman town to the west and the medieval Bourg-Neuf to the east. It was a thriving commercial centre and acquired an international reputation for its tapestries (*see* §2 below); the city was briefly occupied by the French in the late 15th century. In 1659, as a consequence of the Treaty of the Pyrenees, Louis XIV reclaimed Arras from Spain and surrounded the city with fortifications by Sébastien Leprestre de Vauban.

Arras developed around the Benedictine abbey of St Vaast, founded in the 7th century. Rebuilt from 1746 by Cardinal Armand Gaston Maximilien de Rohan (1674–1749), its austere and monumental buildings now house the Musée des Beaux-Arts. Its church, built from 1733 to the designs of Pierre Contant d'Ivry, became the cathedral on its completion in 1833 (for the destroyed medieval cathedral *see* §3 below). The city's most distinguished urban and architectural features are its two squares, located a short distance apart. The Petite Place (now Place des Héros; 60×100 m) was the traditional market-place from the Middle Ages. It is bordered to the west by the Town Hall (1517) and dominated by its belfry (h. 75 m), which was rebuilt in the 18th century. The less regular Grand' Place (area *c.* 2 ha) was built on the site of the abbey orchard, which in the 12th century became the main meeting-place in the thriving city, the location for military parades, festivities and executions. An ordinance of 19 July 1692 required new owners on both squares to match the façades of their gabled homes to those of the Maison de l'Ecu d'Or (destr.) which had only just been completed. In 1718 a new ordinance required that all rebuilt façades be identical 'brick for brick or stone for stone'. The result is a unique residential ensemble in the Flemish style, with slight variations brought by the different widths of the arcades and varied ornamentation. Owing to its strategic position, Arras was heavily bombed during World War I. Almost entirely demolished in 1915, the squares were carefully restored in the 1930s by Pierre Paquet (1875–1959).

BIBLIOGRAPHY

J. Lestocquoy: 'Etudes d'histoire urbaine: Villes et abbayes: Arras au moyen âge', *Mém. Comm. Ant. Dépt. Mnmts Hist. Pas-de-Calais*, XII/ii (Arras, 1966)

H. Gruy, ed.: *Regards sur Arras au cours des âges* (Le Coteau Horvath, 1982)

P. Bougard, Y.-M. Hilaire and A. Nobilos, eds: *Histoire d'Arras* (Dunkirk, 1990)

ISABELLE GOURNAY

2. CENTRE OF TAPESTRY PRODUCTION. High-warp tapestries were first produced in Arras at the beginning of the 14th century. Good-quality raw materials, together with the presence of artists and such rich merchants as the Cosset and Walois families, encouraged production. The reputation of Arras tapestries spread to the extent that the name Arras came to mean tapestry in several languages (It.: *arrazzi*). The story of *SS Piat and Eleuthère* (1402; Tournai, Cathedral) made by PIERROT FERÉ is the only remaining piece that can definitely be attributed to Arras, although the scroll, which bore the date and an inscription, no longer exists. Stylistically, however, the tapestries of the *Romance of Jourdain de Blaye* (early 15th century; Padua, Mus. Civ.) and the *scènes galantes* linked to the *Roman de la rose* (Paris, Mus. A. Déc.) and the *Annunciation* (*c*. 1400; New York, Met.; *see* TAPESTRY, fig. 5) can be tentatively attributed to the same place of production. The Walois workshop specialized in hunting scenes, and the *Devonshire Hunting Tapestries* (1430; London, V&A; *see* SPORTING SCENES, fig. 1) are recorded as being ordered from there. During the second half of the 15th century the production of high-warp tapestries spread to the north. It is therefore difficult to establish attributions, particularly as the cartoons were used in more than one centre. The *Story of St Peter* (1460; examples in Beauvais, Cathedral; Boston, MA, Mus. F.A.; Paris, Mus. Cluny; Washington, DC, N.G.A.) has been attributed to Arras. The town declined as a centre of tapestry production after the mid-15th century: in 1477 it was besieged by Louis XI and the repression that followed discouraged tapestry production.

BIBLIOGRAPHY

R. A. d'Hulst: *Tapisseries flamandes du XIVe au XVIIIe siècle* (Brussels, 1960; Eng. trans., 1967)

J. Lestocquoy: 'L'Art de l'Artois: Etudes sur la tapisserie, la sculpture, l'orfèvrerie, la peinture', *Mémoires de la commission départementale des monuments historiques du Pas-de-Calais*, xvi (Arras, 1973)

ANNICK DAVY-NOTTER

3. CATHEDRAL. The episcopal see at Arras certainly existed by *c*. 500 when St Vaast was bishop, but it was soon combined with that of Cambrai. The union of the two dioceses lasted until 1094, when, under the influence of the Investiture Contest, Arras once more became an autonomous seat. Nothing survives from the first buildings except for some capitals from the Romanesque cathedral, built *c*. 1030 but renovated at the end of the century. They were reused in the foundations of the Gothic cathedral, and, with those from St Bertin at Saint-Omer and Cambrai Cathedral (destr.), they show the high degree of skill attained by the Romanesque sculptors of northern France.

Work on the Gothic cathedral began *c*. 1160, and the choir and transepts were built at this time. In the 13th century only the main walls of the nave and façade were built and the main vessel was not vaulted until the 15th century. The building was never finished, the south-west tower always remaining a stump. In the restoration following a serious fire of 1571 or 1572, the nave was covered with two roofs of different heights; the eastern section was certainly rebuilt at that time; the lower, western section either represents the original roof or more probably frugal repairs.

The cathedral was appropriated at the Revolution to the cult of Reason and then became a provisions store; it was finally sold to businessmen in 1798 to be demolished and in 1804 Napoleon had the remains razed. The building is known through documents and especially through excellent visual sources, among which are a 17th-century watercolour by Adam Frans van der Meulen (see fig.) and the relief model of the city made around 1716 (Arras, Mus. B.-A.).

The cathedral was *c*. 120 m long and *c*. 30 m high, and was built of limestone. The plan of the choir was relatively simple, comparable to the first choir of Laon Cathedral. Raised over a crypt built to compensate a fall in ground level, the choir had an ambulatory with quinquepartite vaults giving access to two lateral chapels (the axial chapel visible in the views was evidently added later). These lateral chapels, each of two storeys, were the distant heirs of the pre-Romanesque oratories flanking the sanctuary, and were designed for the cult of relics. The transept was strongly projecting, then the customary practice in northern France. Its north façade was flanked by two projecting towers; the south façade, facing the episcopal buildings, was treated more simply. The transept arms had aisles on three sides, giving access to rectangular chapels on the east and west, a concession to Cistercian usage no doubt due to the fact that the two bishops who were in office when the transepts were being built were Cistercian monks. The west façade of the cathedral opened on to a triangular area at the entrance to the episcopal buildings. As in England, the principal entrance was on the aisle; a monumental portal was erected on the north side of the nave at the end of the 13th century or at the beginning of the 14th. Other northern French buildings, such as the cathedrals of Thérouanne and Cambrai, also adopted this solution.

The cathedral had a four-storey elevation. Over the arcade was a gallery with two openings under a relieving arch, then a triforium and clerestory. In the choir and transepts the piers were distributed in a ternary strong and weak rhythm: a pair of cruciform piers and two piers composed of slender, paired columns capped with fine, bell-shaped capitals sculpted by French artists in Tournai 'marble' (some capitals survive; Arras, Mus. B.-A.). Two master masons seem to have been responsible for the work: the first, a man of fairly traditional temperament, built the crypt and the outer wall of the ambulatory; his successor, on the contrary, was an innovator. Aiming to harmonize the width of the straight bays with those of the hemicycle, he gave the former an intercolumniation equal to the necessarily narrow ones of the apse. This squeezing of the bays must have accentuated the effect of verticality: the vaults, raised on narrow oblong bays, were already *c*. 33 m high. The strong piers must have provided both internal stiffening and suggested an element of strength in an elevation that otherwise would have appeared too

Arras Cathedral, begun *c.* 1160 (destr. 1804); detail from a watercolour by Adam Frans van der Meulen, 0.45×2.42 m, 1667 (Paris, Mobilier National)

spindly. The clerestory windows were made up of triple arches; in the choir only the middle arch was glazed but all three were glazed in the transepts. In the design of the eastern parts of the building the clerestory was linked to the triforium by mullions rising from each pair of triforium arches, as at St Remi in Reims. As in the nave of Cambrai Cathedral, the galleries and the embryonic flying buttresses assured the equilibrium of the structure. These high galleries were each covered by a small transverse roof bounded laterally by buttressing walls and to the exterior by a small gable built up at the top of the outer wall. This arrangement, possibly deriving from the nave of Durham Cathedral, must have given the gallery roofline an elegant, staccato rhythm.

The nave, built slowly and in many campaigns, was far less revolutionary in style. The four-storey elevation was retained even though galleries were no longer fashionable. The unfinished west front is of interest in the development of façade blocks. As at St Germer-de-Fly (Oise), Mont-Notre-Dame (Aisne) or Noyon Cathedral, the towers rest on an enormous, hollow block open to the nave, in this respect similar to a western transept. This type of façade was rare in northern France. The central portal was decorated with a late 13th- or 14th-century tympanum representing the *Coronation of the Virgin*.

The eastern parts of Arras Cathedral were influential; with the nave and transepts of Cambrai Cathedral they played a determining role in the formation of the architecture of the Scheldt Valley (e.g. the collegiate church of Notre-Dame in St Omer, St Martin in Ypres and St Nicholas in Ghent). The influence of Arras spread as far as Roskilde Cathedral in Denmark. The cathedrals of Arras and Cambrai also show the importance of English influences in the genesis of Early Gothic.

BIBLIOGRAPHY

P. Héliot: 'Les Anciennes Cathédrales d'Arras', *Bull. Comm. Royale Mnmts & Sites*, iv (1953), pp. 7–109

——: 'Les Oeuvres capitales du gothique français primitif et l'influence de l'architecture anglaise', *Wallraf-Richartz-Jb.*, xx (1958), pp. 85–114

J. Thiébaut: *L'Architecture médiévale du Nord-Pas-de-Calais* (Lille, 1983) [with a plan of the vault reconstruction]

JACQUES THIEBAUT

Arras, Jean d'. *See* JEAN D'ARRAS.

Arras, Mathias of. *See* MATHIAS OF ARRAS.

Arredondo, Isidoro (*b* Colmenar de Oreja, Madrid, *c.* 1657; *d* Madrid, 1702). Spanish painter. He trained in Madrid with José García Hidalgo and later in the studio of Francisco Rizi. He was Rizi's most frequent collaborator in the last years of his master's life, and he married a godchild of Rizi. Rizi obtained for Arredondo the title of Pintor del Rey, without salary, and on his death in 1685 Arredondo succeeded him in that capacity. In his will Rizi named him heir and left him sheets of drawings and his books relating to painting, sculpture and architecture. A large part of Arredondo's activity under Rizi's direction was painting scenery for the plays staged at El Buen Retiro, the palace on the outskirts of Madrid; he also contributed to temporary street decorations, notably those erected in Madrid in 1690 for the entry of Queen Mariana von Neuburg, the second wife of Charles II. On the death of Charles II (1700), Arredondo, Luca Giordano and Francisco Ignacio Ruíz de la Iglesia were appointed valuers of the King's possessions.

Among the few works by Arredondo that have survived are the signed paintings of *St Clare* and *St Louis of Toulouse* (1693; Madrid, Prado), executed for the Convent of Monjas Franciscanas de Nuestra Señora de Constantinopla, Madrid, both of which show a stylistic and formal dependence on Claudio Coello rather than on Rizi. They are strongly dynamic compositions, spiral arrangements that suggest the influence of Rubens and the impact he had on Baroque painting in Madrid in the second half of the 17th century. The same characteristics are seen in *St Eligius Giving Alms* (1693; Madrid, Patrm. N.), from the former church of El Salvador, Madrid, which shows Arredondo's skill in depicting architectural backgrounds in strict perspective, an ability derived from his theatrical decorations.

BIBLIOGRAPHY

A. E. Pérez Sánchez: 'Un lienzo de Arredondo para el Prado', *Bol. Mus. Prado*, i (1980), pp. 17–22

ALFONSO E. PÉREZ SÁNCHEZ

Arretium. *See* AREZZO.

Arricio [*arricciato*; It.: 'wrinkle']. In a FRESCO, the rough coat of plaster on which the preliminary composition sketch or *sinopia* is drawn.

□

Arrieta, (José) Agustín (*b* Santa Ana Chiautempan, near Tlaxcala, 28 Aug 1803; *d* Puebla, 22 Dec 1874). Mexican painter. He was one of the first students at the Escuela de Dibujo de la Real Casa de la Academia y Junta de Caridad para la Buena Educación de la Juventud, founded in Puebla in 1813, which eventually became the local Academia de Bellas Artes. He is the most representative artist of the Puebla school in the mid-19th century.

Arrieta concentrated at first on portraits, but *c.* 1840 he began to specialize in *costumbrista* paintings and still-lifes, for which he acquired a large local clientele. He exhibited paintings of both kinds from 1851 at the academies in Puebla and Mexico City. His genre paintings, like the Flemish and Dutch works from which they are derived, often have a moralizing intention. There are scenes of flirtation and seduction in kitchens, taverns and markets, in which he avoids sentimentality and condescension in the treatment of his predominantly lower-class subjects. His still-lifes are hybrid compositions in which he combined a variety of luxurious and ordinary Mexican and European foods, including fruits and vegetables, live and dead animals, and regional and foreign dishes. The best public collections of his work are held by the Museo Nacional de Historia in Mexico City and the Museo Bello and Galerías Bello in Puebla.

BIBLIOGRAPHY

F. J. Cabrera: *Agustín Arrieta: Pintor costumbrista* (Mexico City, 1963)
F. Pérez Salazar: *Historia de la pintura en Puebla* (Mexico City, 1963), pp. 105–8
F. Ramírez: *La plástica del siglo de la Independencia* (Mexico City, 1985), pp. 46, 58–9
F. J. Cabrera: *Puebla y los poblanos* (Mexico City, 1987), pp. 91–115
B. Olivares Iriarte: *Album artístico: 1874* (Puebla, 1987), pp. 51–4 [notes by E. Castro Morales]

FAUSTO RAMÍREZ

Arrieta, Pedro de (*b* Real de Pachuca, Mexico, *c.* 1670; *d* Mexico City, 1738). Mexican architect. He qualified as an architect in 1691. Between 1695 and 1709 he worked on the Basílica of Guadalupe, Mexico, which is mainly interesting for its broken lines and for the octagonal form used in the dome, in the section of the towers and the lintels of the doors. His activities were concentrated mainly in Mexico City, where he worked as Maestro Mayor for the Inquisition and the cathedral. He was responsible for the churches of S Gregorio and S Bernardo, the church and convent of S Teresa la Nueva, the monastery of S José de los Carmelitas Descalzos, the church of El Amor de Dios and the church, sacristy and sacristy entrance hall of S Domingo, as well as the Palace of the Inquisition and Customs, all in Mexico City. He also collaborated on the churches of S Clara, Jesús Nazareno, S Francisco, S Miguel and La Profesa, all in Mexico City, and worked on the Colegio Seminario of the cathedral. His non-ecclesiastical works include the S Juan del Río, Mariscala and Alhóndiga bridges. He used a white stone from Chiluca and *tezontle* (dark red volcanic rock), polychromy being fundamental to his work. In 1736 he was among the Mexican architects who drew up new regulations for the guild.

BIBLIOGRAPHY

H. Berlin: 'El arquitecto Pedro de Arrieta', *Bol. Archv Gen. Nación*, xvi (1945), pp. 73–94
D. Angulo Iñiguez, E. Marco Dorta and J. y Buschiazzo: *Historia del arte hispanoamericano*, 3 vols (Barcelona, 1945–56)
H. Berlin: 'Three Master Architects in New Spain', *Hisp. Amer. Hist. Rev.*, xxvii (1947), pp. 375–83
M. Toussaint: *Arte colonial en México* (Mexico City, 1962; Eng. trans., 1967)
G. Gasparini: *América, barroco y arquitectura* (Caracas, 1972)
C. Amerlinck: 'Pedro de Arrieta', *Bol. Mnmts Hist.*, vi (1981), pp. 27–40
G. Tovar de Teresa: *El barroco en México* (Mexico City, 1981)
R. Gutiérrez: *Arquitectura y urbanismo en Iberoamérica* (Madrid, 1983)
M. Fernández: *Arquitectura y gobierno virreinal: Los maestros mayores de la ciudad de México, siglo XVII* (Mexico, 1985)

MARIA CONCEPCIÓN GARCÍA SÁIZ

Arrigo, Giuliano d'. *See* PESELLO.

Arrigo Fiammingo [Paludano]. *See under* BROECK, VAN DEN, (3).

Arrigucci, Luigi (*b* Florence, 1575; *d* after 1652). Italian architect. In 1624 he restored and considerably enlarged the convent of S Maria Maddalena dei Pazzi in Florence. The work was paid for by Pope Urban VIII (Barberini), also a Florentine, who shortly afterwards called Arrigucci to Rome and, on 26 June 1630, named him Architect of the Papal Camera. By August 1630 Arrigucci was engaged in the first of a series of renovations of Roman churches for his Barberini patrons, the small 10th-century church of S Maria in Pallara (now called S Sebastiano al Palatino). In 1632 he renovated SS Cosma e Damiano, raising its floor-level and making it a two-storey building. In 1636 he provided a new façade with twin towers for S Anastasia and saw to the restoration of its roof. The façade of S Giacomo alla Lungara followed in 1641 and the renovation of the Romanesque interior of Spoleto Cathedral was carried out in 1644.

Arrigucci's name is often linked with those of other architects similarly employed on papal and other Barberini undertakings, including Domenico Castelli and Gianlorenzo Bernini. His work is quite distinct from theirs, however, in its cool and precise linearity and its avoidance of plasticity in either detail or overall composition. His involvement in the building industry in Rome included dealing in large timbers. Between 1634 and 1644 he is documented as having supplied beams of fir imported from Tuscany for various buildings, including the Barberini 'Casa Grande' in Via de' Giubbonari, the theatre of Palazzo Barberini, the Palazzo del Quirinale, the oratory of the Filippini and Bernini's campanile for St Peter's.

BIBLIOGRAPHY

G. Baglione: *Vite* (1642); ed. V. Mariani (1935), pp. 179*v*–180*r*

O. Pollak: *Die Kunsttätigkeit unter Urban VIII* (Vienna, 1928–31), i, pp. 21, 205, 344–5, 367, 370, 443–4; ii, p. 121

R. Battaglia: 'Luigi Arrigucci, architetto camerale d'Urbano VIII', *Palladio*, vi (1942), pp. 174–83

F. Borsi: *Bernini architetto* (Rome, 1980), pp. 222, 302–3, 306–7

J. Connors: *Borromini and the Roman Oratory* (New York, 1980), p. 52

PATRICIA WADDY

Arron Group. *See* NEEL, EDRIC.

Arrost, Jan [Janni; Giovanni]. *See* ROST, JAN.

Arrowsmith, John (*b* Monceaux-sous-Paris, 1790; *d* 1849). French dealer, print-publisher and collector, of English descent. His father, William Arrowsmith, was an agent for members of the Orléans family. Through his brother-in-law Louis Daguerre, John Arrowsmith was instrumental in negotiating the installation of the Diorama in Park Square East, Regent's Park, London, opened in 1823 (*see* DIORAMA). In 1822, on one of his frequent visits to London, he saw Constable's *Hay Wain* (1821; London, N.G., *see* LANDSCAPE PAINTING, fig. 10) at the British Institution and shortly after began negotiations to buy it in order to exhibit it in Paris. He purchased it in 1824, along with *View on the Stour near Dedham* (San Marino, CA, Huntington Lib. & A.G.) and a smaller seascape, and in June 1824 exhibited them at his premises at 1, Rue Grange-aux-Belles, Paris. He sent the two larger landscapes to the Salon of 1824, as well as a view of Hampstead Heath. He was one of a small group of dealers attempting to specialize in the sale of works by living artists, and his contacts with England were particularly useful during the 1820s, when an enthusiasm for English literature and art was widespread among young French artists who were part of the Romantic movement. Between 1824 and 1827 approximately 22 paintings by Constable were brought to France through the dealings of Arrowsmith and his colleague Claude Schroth or occasionally through such collectors as Ambroise Firmin-Didot. In November 1825 Arrowsmith's arrangements with Constable came to an abrupt and acrimonious end. His precarious financial situation forced him to hold a sale of his stock on 20 February 1826, the results of which were apparently disappointing.

Arrowsmith's name was associated with a young generation of landscape painters, but he was also an admirer of Paul Delaroche and owned his *Joan of Arc in Prison* (Rouen, Mus. B.-A.) when it was shown at the Salon of 1824. He is known to have commissioned at least one painting from Delacroix, whom he knew for several years. His activities as a publisher of prints began in the early 1820s; the English artist S. W. Reynolds engraved Delaroche's *Joan of Arc in Prison* for him, as well as other subjects. After 1826 Arrowsmith concentrated on the publication of prints. He had ADOLPHE GOUPIL as his business partner when the latter was 21 (1827 or 1830) and by the end of the 1820s was briefly associated with the newly established print publisher J. H. Rittner (1802–40). He later opened a restaurant on the model of an English tavern; this went bankrupt in 1840. However, he continued to make occasional purchases of pictures until his death in 1849. Among his close friends was Alexandre-Gabriel Decamps, from whom he is said to have commissioned the artist's first singeries (*see* SINGERIE) and with whom he maintained a regular correspondence. In 1847 he organized an exhibition of French painting in London. His last-known association with artists occurred in 1848, when correspondence with Delacroix revealed that he was assisting a group of artists with their plans to set up an exhibiting association. His brother Charles Arrowsmith (*b* 1798) specialized in the painting of church interiors.

BIBLIOGRAPHY

R. B. Beckett, ed.: *John Constable's Correspondence*, iv (Ipswich, 1966)

LINDA WHITELEY

Arroyo, Eduardo (*b* Madrid, 26 Feb 1937). Spanish painter, sculptor, potter, printmaker and stage designer. As a painter he was mainly self-taught. After working as a journalist in 1957, he left Spain in 1958 to avoid military service, settling in Paris. There he continued to work both as a journalist and painter. From 1968 to 1972 he lived in Milan, returning to Paris in 1973. His work developed from expressionism to realism (*Nueva figurina*), which reflected on the pictorial language and function of painting and the artist's role in society. He manipulated ready-made images, words and elements derived from commercial art and the work of other painters. His pieces formed series whose titles referred to the legacy of the Spanish Civil War and the contemporary political situation to help make their critical point. His work frequently provoked controversy, for example his series *Arcole Bridge and St Bernard's Pass* (1962–6) was based on the theme of Napoleon Bonaparte as a symbol of imperialism (e.g. *Arcole*, 1964; priv. col., see Astier, p. 12). He presented dictators, bullfighters, soldiers and Spanish gentlemen (e.g. *Spanish Gentleman*, 1970; Paris, Pompidou; *see* SPAIN, fig. 19) as a metaphorical list of his dislikes. Through his work he attacked such political figures as Winston Churchill and Adolf Hitler as well as Miró and perpetrators of uncommitted painting (e.g. *Blind Painters*, 1975; priv. col., see Astier, p. 77). From 1976 he painted portraits of such artist friends as Gilles Aillaud (*b* 1928), Aldo Mondino (*b* 1938) and Antonio Recalcati (*b* 1938). In 1980 Arroyo produced a series of mask-like bronze heads of chimneysweeps (e.g. *Chimneysweep I*, 1980; priv. col., see 1987 exh. cat., p. 148).

BIBLIOGRAPHY

Eduardo Arroyo: Blinde Maler und Exit (exh. cat. by A. Zweite, Munich, Lenbachhaus, 1980)

P. Astier: *Arroyo* (Paris, 1982)

Arroyo (exh. cat. by G. Gassiot-Talabot and C. Derouet, Paris, Pompidou, 1982)

Eduardo Arroyo: Theater–Boxen–Figuration (exh. cat., ed. W. Spies; Dortmund, Mus. Kst & Kultgesch., 1987)

INMACULADA JULIÁN

Arruda. Portuguese family of architects and master builders. From the middle of the 15th century to the end of the 16th four generations of the Arruda family held key posts in Portugal and overseas, ensuring their position by a wise policy of marriages. They had a decisive impact on Portuguese architecture, especially on military architecture, and their history represents the change from medieval mason to the role of architect in the modern sense. João de Arruda (i) (*d* ?1490) became master of works at Batalha Abbey and Évora and was employed in the building of the palace of the Duques de Beja (1485), later the residence of Manuel I. His sons were: João de Arruda (ii), clerk of building works (1531) and superintendent (1538) at Batalha; (1) Diogo de Arruda; (2) Francisco de Arruda; and António de Arruda, who was working in 1514 under the direction of his brothers. João (ii) was probably the father of (3) Miguel de Arruda and of Pedro de Arruda (*d* 1543), who was appointed master of works at the royal palaces at Santarém in 1526. Pedro's son was perhaps Dionísio de Arruda (*d* 1576) of Santarém, who became master of works at Batalha. Joâo Dias de Arruda, Miguel Fernandes de Arruda and others who worked at Azamor in Morocco in 1516 were probably kinsmen.

(1) Diogo de Arruda (*b c.* 1470; *d* Évora, 1531). He probably trained under his father João de Arruda (i) at Batalha. Diogo's youthful experience of court life under Manuel I, with its atmosphere of luxury and exoticism, made him its greatest interpreter and the creator of the MANUELINE STYLE, named after the King and characterized by decoration based on naturalistic forms. His first known work was a new royal palace in Lisbon, the Paço da Ribeira (1508; destr. 1755), built over the warehouses for African and Asian spices and to which he added a stronghold at the river end of the building. He was selected by the King to carry out the work of extending the church of the Convento de Cristo, Tomar, and a large new vaulted nave was added (1510–14), with a magnificent window (see fig.) decorated with ornament symbolic of discovery and Portugal's oceanic tradition. Diogo also directed work on the fortifications of the garrisons in Morocco at Safim (1512), Mazagão (1513) and Azamor (1516).

Diogo settled in Évora, where he built the Castelo Novo (1518–25), a solid building 60 m square with four square towers at the corners, perhaps after a design by Andrea Sansovino, who was in Portugal *c.* 1480. In the last decade of his life Diogo received a succession of prestigious appointments, as well as being the architect of the Duque de Braganza: in 1521 he was appointed Surveyor of Royal Works and Master of Royal Works in the Alentejo district, two posts created especially for him; and in 1525 he was appointed Master of Works for the Royal Palaces in Évora. After the death of King Manuel in 1521 he confined his activity to arbitration and valuation.

Diogo de Arruda: west window, church of the Convento de Cristo, Tomar, 1510–14

(2) Francisco de Arruda (*b c.* 1480; *d* Évora, 30 Nov 1547). Brother of (1) Diogo de Arruda. From 1506 he was employed in repairing the castles at Portel, Moura and Mourão in the Alentejo and in 1512 was working at Tomar with Diogo, whom he later accompanied to North Africa. There he made four innovative circular bastions with embrasures for cannon (1516) at the Castelo do Mar, Azamor. He was recalled by King Manuel I to construct a defensive tower (1514–21) at the entrance to the River Tagus at Belém (for further discussion and illustration *see* BELÉM (i), §2). The design of the tower of Belém combines medieval traditions with Moorish influences (the melon-shaped domes show a knowledge of Islamic architecture learnt in North Africa), and it incorporates ideas from the Italian system of fortification, with angle bastions, described in Francesco di Giorgio's *Trattato di architettura civile e militare* (*c.* 1482–92). The highly naturalistic ornament on the fortress includes the cross of the Order of Christ, the chief symbol of the Portuguese voyages of discovery, and rope mouldings associated with shipping and the sea.

Francisco, settling in Évora, constructed fortifications for the Duque de Braganza: the Castelo Artilhero at Vila Viçosa (*c.* 1525), in which it has been suggested that he followed a design by Leonardo da Vinci (Bury), and the castle and bastions of Évoramonte (*c.* 1531), where he owned property. It was a period of intense humanistic study, encouraged by the presence of the court in Évora, where his technical ability made Francisco the leading architect in the city and his interest in antiquity led to a commission to study and reconstruct the Roman Agua de Prata aqueduct (1531, inaugurated 28 March 1537). At Diogo's death in 1531, Francisco inherited all his brother's commissions; he was honoured by John III and made a knight, with permission to live in the palace at Évora (1534), later becoming a member of the Order of Christ and curator of the aqueduct (1542). His only daughter, Catarina de Arruda, married Diogo de Torralva, who succeeded him as architect to the King. The aqueduct at Elvas (begun 1543; completed 17th century) has been attributed to him; so have Elvas Cathedral (now the parish church) and the church of Madalena, Olivença, but there is no documentary evidence.

(3) Miguel de Arruda (*b c.* 1500; *d* Lisbon, 3 Jan 1563). Nephew of (1) Diogo de Arruda and (2) Francisco de Arruda. He replaced João de Castilho as master of works at the monastery of Batalha in 1533, and he already had sufficient prestige to be commissioned to build the prisons of the Inquisition in Lisbon and to be made a shield bearer (*escudeiro*) of the royal household. Since he is recorded as resident in Évora, he probably worked there with Francisco, thus receiving a sound training in the art of fortification. He worked with Nicolau Chantarene on the Augustinian convent of Nossa Senhora da Graça (church, 1532–40; convent, 1524–49; for illustration *see* ÉVORA); here, the church has a remarkable façade with four statues of sprawling giants at the corners of the pediment, a design inspired by engravings from Cesar Cesarino's edition (1521) of Vitruvius. Miguel's familiarity with humanistic circles in Évora is confirmed by his marriage with Isabel Mendes, a member of a wealthy family of the city; in 1535 his first-born daughter was baptized in the presence of the antiquary André de Resende (1498–1573) and Diogo de Castilho. Miguel also knew Dom João de Castro (1500–48), Viceroy of India, for whom he built the round temple of the Quinta da Penha Verde (1542) at Sintra, which has a Latin inscription between Hindu low reliefs on the foundation-stone.

Miguel was described as a 'great engineer' by the historian Frei Luís de Sousa (1555–1632), and his talents and ability were of great service to the King's brother, the Infante Dom Luis, in the modernization of Portuguese fortresses. Miguel was responsible for introducing the full Italian system of angle bastions into Portugal in the 1540s. He was part of the *junta* set up in April 1541 to formulate a defence policy for North Africa, and in this capacity he went to Ceuta and Mazagão in May 1541 with Charles V's engineer, Benedetto da Ravenna (*fl c.* 1500–*c.* 1560). Miguel designed the fortress at Mazagão (1542–5) in the form of a star with four bastions, with an impressive cistern and an impregnable harbour, as well as the wall across the isthmus of Ceuta (1543). His designs for the fortifications of the Portuguese colonies at Tangier, Mozambique, Diu in India and Bahia in Brazil (1546) are the first examples of the curtain wall with bastions to be built outside Europe.

Miguel enjoyed an unprecedented position at court, and in 1543 he succeeded his brother Pedro as master of works at the royal palaces of Santarém, Almeirim and Muge. Besides being responsible for the planning of the principal state projects, he was involved also with important civil and religious buildings. He drew plans for S Antão, Évora (1548; unexecuted); the convent of Santana (1565), Lisbon; the Hieronymite monastery at Valbenfeito (1540–55), near Óbidos; the Misericórdia Church at Santarém (1559); and for the royal palace of Xabregas (Lisbon), the construction of which he supervised (1556–9; unfinished; destr.), perhaps incorporating designs obtained in Rome in 1551 for John III. His design for the cathedral at Miranda do Douro (1548) shows a hall-church plan of pure cubic forms. It is probable that he designed the cathedrals for the three new bishoprics created by John III, since that of Leiria (1551) was built by his pupil and son-in-law, Afonso Álvares, and that of Portalegre (1556) echoes the classical nature of the Xabregas façade. The small palace chapel (1555) at Salvaterra de Magos, near Muge, a property of the Infante Dom Luis, is close to his style in its complex geometric combinations.

Miguel's last work is the most exploratory: the enormous fortress of S Julião da Barra (1553–75) at Oeiras, near Lisbon, at the mouth of the Tagus. A symmetrical pentagon, like the Fortezza da Basso in Florence, with round bastions and great Serlian gateways, its central nucleus, the cistern, is a gigantic Tuscan colonnade with three aisles half cut into the rock, with the same flat rib-vaulting he used at Leiria and Santarém. With this fortress, praised by Vincenzo Scamozzi and Cervantes, the architect perfected his massive 'Plain' style, combining military severity and mathematical sophistication, which is one of the essential features of mid-16th-century Portuguese architecture.

One of Miguel's children, Belchior de Arruda, was supervisor in 1564 of the fortress of Baçaim in India, and Brites de Arruda, probably his daughter, married Afonso Álvares, his pupil and successor. Another pupil was his apprentice (*criado*) Jerónimo de Ruão.

BIBLIOGRAPHY

Viterbo
R. dos Santos: *A torre de Belém* (Coimbra, 1922)
V. Correia: *Lugares d'Além* (Oporto, 1923)
R. dos Santos: *O estilo manuelino* (Lisbon, 1952)
G. Kubler: *Portuguese Plain Architecture* (Middletown, CT, 1972)
R. Moreira: 'Arquitectura', *The Portuguese Discoveries and the Europe of the Renaissance* (exh. cat., Lisbon, Mus. N. A. Ant., 1983)
J. Bury: 'A Leonardo Project Realized in Portugal', *Burl. Mag.*, cxxvi (1984), pp. 499–500

RAFAEL MOREIRA

Ars acustica. *See under* SOUND AND ART.

Arsenal. Building or group of buildings for the manufacture and storage of warships, weapons or ammunition. The term (from the Arabic *dar accina'ah*: 'workshop') was first used at the Arsenale in Venice, where both the military and the commercial ships of the Venetian Republic were built. According to tradition, the Arsenale at Venice was founded in 1104, although recent research has suggested a later date at the beginning of the 13th century. As

Venetian maritime power increased, the Arsenale grew in size, particularly during the 15th and 16th centuries, eventually occupying 46 ha, surrounded by walls and canals (*see* VENICE, fig. 2). The Arsenale's importance was emphasized by its monumental architecture, including one of the city's first Renaissance buildings, the Great Gateway (1460), attributed to Antonio Gambello, which is in the form of a triumphal arch. Despite the scale of the Arsenale at Venice, Venetian naval power was successfully challenged by the Ottoman Empire, whose own arsenal in Istanbul became the greatest in the world during the 16th and 17th centuries.

While the arsenals at Venice and Istanbul were the most magnificent of their time, important examples were also built in other parts of Europe. The Duc de Sully supervised the completion of Philibert de L'Orme's scheme for an arsenal in Paris, while the site of the Royal Arsenal at Woolwich in London was used for military stores as early as the 16th century. It was not until 1695, however, that the Royal Laboratory for making gunpowder was moved to Woolwich from Greenwich, followed in 1717 by a foundry for casting guns, with red brick buildings attributed to John Vanbrugh. Other contemporary arsenals included the Baroque Zeughaus (now the Deutsches Historisches Museum) in Berlin, begun in 1695 by Johann Arnold Nering and completed (1706) by Martin Grünberg, Andreas Schlüter and Jean de Bodt. A magnificent structure, it was decorated with numerous works of art, including Schlüter's *Heads of Dying Warriors* on the keystones of the windows (*see* SCHLÜTER, ANDREAS, fig. 1).

During the 18th and 19th centuries new arsenals were created throughout Europe and North America. They included establishments in Moscow (completed 1736) and St Petersburg, where the arsenal moved to new premises in the 1840s. In New York an armoury (1843) by Martin E. Thompson was built on East 64th Street, replacing an earlier one nearer the centre of town. The weapons that it contained were intended to meet the threat of civil disorder, although it was claimed that the arsenal was too far from central New York to provide prompt action in the event of a riot. Other existing arsenals also grew dramatically in size during this period. The development of the Royal Arsenal at Woolwich, for example, prompted by the American War of Independence and the Napoleonic Wars, led to the construction of a large number of mostly utilitarian buildings, with limited classical decoration. By the beginning of the 19th century the Royal Arsenal occupied 139 acres, and by 1855 this had almost doubled.

In the 20th century the historical arsenals gradually declined: for example, production at the Woolwich Arsenal fell after reaching a peak during World War I and stopped completely in 1967. Armament factories gradually replaced the old arsenals, but as it became less acceptable (and too expensive) for modern states to enhance their prestige through impressive buildings associated with arms manufacture, these generally lacked the monumental appearance and decoration of their predecessors. One of the last attempts to create an impressive arsenal was made in Nazi Germany, as part of Albert Speer's plans for the reconstruction of Berlin. Hans Hermann Klaje's design for a new armoury represents a classical arcaded building of intimidating scale. As a result of the Nazi defeat in World War II, Klaje's proposal fortunately never got beyond the stage of a model. It is, nonetheless, a reminder of a culture of ostentatious militarism that was to be challenged, if not completely defeated, by succeeding generations.

BIBLIOGRAPHY

B. Barbiche: *Sully* (Paris, 1978)

B. Cherry and N. Pevsner: *London, 2: South*, Bldgs England (Harmondsworth, 1983), pp. 286–9

E. Concina: *L'Arsenale della Repubblica di Venezia* (Milan, 1984)

G. Nehring: *Johann Arnold Nering: Ein preussischer Baumeister* (Essen, 1985)

Progetto Arsenale: Studi e ricerche per l'Arsenale di Venezia (exh. cat., ed. P. Gennaro and G. Testi; Venice, Scu. Grande S Giovanni Evangelista, 1985)

R. M. Fogelson: *America's Armories: Architecture, Society and Public Order* (Cambridge, MA, and London, 1989)

P. Adam: *The Arts of the Third Reich* (London, 1992), p. 270 [illus. of Klaje's proposal for Berlin]

□

Arsenalists [Pol. Arsenałowcy]. Term used to refer to the participants in the *Ogólnopolska wystawa młodej plastyki* ('Polish exhibition of young artists'), which was held in the Arsenal, Warsaw, between July and September 1955 and had as its theme the slogan 'Against War—Against Fascism'. The exhibition was organized on the occasion of the Fifth World Festival of Youth and Students, the first such large-scale international gathering following the period of Stalinist isolation in Poland. The exhibition catalogue lists 249 exhibiting artists and 499 pictures, graphic works and sculptures. The idea of the exhibition was conceived in 1954 by the painters Jan Dziędziora, Marek Oberländer and Jacek Sienicki and the art historian Elżbieta Grabska, all graduates of the Academy of Fine Arts, Warsaw. All the exhibitors made their débuts during the period of Polish Socialist Realism (1950–54). Setting themselves against the imposed doctrine, the organizers resolved during the growing thaw to set up an all-Polish review of the work of young people. Most young artists and exhibitors regarded it as the first demonstration against Socialist Realism, while its enemies saw it as being a more refined continuation of Stalinist doctrine because of the state's sponsorship of the event.

The exhibition was characterized by the expressionist canvases, which were dramatic in both form and content. In contrast to the other exhibitions at the festival, the show at the Arsenal created a stir in the press and in art circles and prompted a wave of discussion about the new artistic situation. The following names were mentioned most frequently by the critics: Marek Oberländer, Izaak Celnikier, Przemysław Brykalski, Waldemar Cwenarski, Barbara Jonscher, Jan Lebensztejn, Jan Tarasin and Jacek Sempoliński. Although it is difficult to find a common denominator in their later work, there was evidence in this group of artists of a tendency towards non-avant-garde art opposed to colourism and Socialist Realism. With the growth of political freedom and the appearance in the mid-1950s of abstract works deeply concerned with Polish life and existential questions, the pictures of the Arsenalists lost their significance. They were not to regain it until the late 1970s and 1980s, when Polish artists of the middle and younger generations were once again able to confront artistic and political problems simultaneously.

BIBLIOGRAPHY

Ogólnopolska wystawa młodej plastyki [Polish exhibition of young artists] (exh. cat., Warsaw, Arsenal, 1955)

A. Osęka: *Poddanie Arsenału* [Surrender of the Arsenal] (Warsaw, 1971)

W kręgu Arsenału [About the Arsenal] (exh. cat., Gorzów Wielkopolski, Distr. Mus., 1981)

W. Włodarczyk: *Socrealizm: Sztuka polska w latach, 1950–54* [Socialist realism: Polish art, 1950–54] (Paris, 1986)

WOJCIECH WŁODARCZYK

Arseven, Celal Esad (*b* Istanbul, 1875; *d* 1971). Turkish art historian. The son of the grand vizier Ahmed Esad Pasha (1828–75), he was forced in 1891 to follow family tradition and enrol at the Military Academy rather than at the Academy of Fine Arts in Istanbul as he desired. Nevertheless, he pursued his artistic interests among a group of military artists and resigned shortly after he was graduated. He then travelled extensively, researching and writing about Turkish art until 1912, when he became a civil servant. In 1920 he started teaching municipal administration, town planning and architectural history at the Academy of Fine Arts. A highly versatile intellectual, he was also an administrator, academician, editor, film director, musician, painter, photographer, novelist and translator. He wrote about the functioning of municipalities, urbanism, the history of Istanbul, modern architecture, the history of Turkish art and music, photography, painting techniques and librarianship, as well as his memoirs, a dictionary and an encyclopedia of art. His most significant contribution to the history of culture was his effort to establish Turkish art as distinct from Islamic art.

WRITINGS

Constantinople: De Byzance à Stamboul (Paris, 1928)

Türk sanatı [Turkish art] (Istanbul, 1928)

L'Art turc depuis son origine jusqu'à nos jours [Istanbul, 1939)

Turklerde mimari [Architecture of the Turks] (Ankara, 1939)

Sanat ansiklopedisi [Encyclopedia of art] (Istanbul, 1943–52)

Les Arts décoratifs turcs (Istanbul, [1952])

Türk sanatı tarihi [History of Turkish art], 3 vols (Istanbul, 1954–9)

BIBLIOGRAPHY

D. Kuban: 'Celal Esad Arseven ve Türk sanatı kavramı' [Celal Esad Arseven and the idea of Turkish art], *Mimarlık*, lxxii (1969), pp. 18–20

Ş. Eyice: 'Celal Esad Arseven', *Belleten*, xxxvi (1972), pp. 173–202

LALE H. ULUÇ

Arslankaya. *See under* PHRYGIAN.

Arslan Tash [Turk.: 'lion-stone'; anc. Hadatu]. Site in Syria, *c.* 35 km north-east of TIL BARSIP on the Harran–Euphrates road. It was an Assyrian town: its ancient name, preserved in two inscriptions from the site, is mentioned elsewhere only in the 'Harran Census' (7th century BC). The site was excavated by François Thureau-Dangin in 1928; finds are in the Louvre, Paris, and in the National Museum, Aleppo. The Assyrian features recovered were a town wall with three gates, a palace, a large house and a small temple dedicated to the goddess Ishtar. Later remains included a small Hellenistic temple. The town wall (l. *c.* 2 km) enclosed a roughly oval area of 30 ha. Two colossal basalt lions in the east gate gave the site its modern name, and fragments of another two were also found in the west gate. A cuneiform inscription on one fragment mentions Hadatu. Another, originally against the wall, is inscribed with a lengthy Aramaic text that includes a fragmentary personal name *šmš*. Reade has suggested that this could be Shamshi-ilu (?780–752 BC), governor of Til Barsip. Fourteen basalt wall reliefs of a procession of Assyrian soldiers and officials, carved in the local North Syrian style, were removed from the gate in 1886 (Istanbul, Archaeol. Mus.). Eckhard Unger attributed them to the time of Tiglath-pileser III (*reg* 744–727 BC) on the basis of similarities to that king's sculptures from Nimrud (London, BM). Further reliefs showing the delivery of tribute were found widely scattered and may have originated either in the west gate or in the palace courtyard. The palace (*c.* 150×65 m) comprised at least 56 rooms, with a throne-room suite, residential suite, administrative and service areas, and a double-shrine temple, probably dedicated to the god Nabu and his consort Tashmetum. The layout of the throne-room suite seems to predate that at KHORSABAD, and Tiglath-pileser III is the most likely builder. Next to the palace was a large house known as the Bâtiment aux Ivoires from the hoard of ivories found there; its plan combined Assyrian and North Syrian features. The architectural remains of the Ishtar Temple were badly disturbed, but included an outer gate with two inscribed basalt bulls and a shrine with two basalt lions at its entrance (Aleppo, N. Mus.; Paris, Louvre). The better-preserved bull inscription identified this as the Ishtar Temple at Hadatu and named Tiglath-pileser III as its builder. A free-standing Assyrian statue of a deity carrying a box (Aleppo, N. Mus.) and three similar fragmentary examples were found out of context but probably originally belonged to the Ishtar Temple.

BIBLIOGRAPHY

E. Unger: *Die Reliefs Tiglatpilesers III aus Arslan Tasch* (Constantinople, 1925)

F. Thureau-Dangin and others: *Arslan-Tash*, 2 vols (Paris, 1931)

G. Turner: 'The Palace and Bâtiment aux Ivoires at Arslan Tash: A Reappraisal', *Iraq*, xxx (1968), pp. 62–8

J. Reade: 'The Neo-Assyrian Court and Army: Evidence from the Sculptures', *Iraq*, xxxiv (1972), pp. 87–112

F. M. Fales: *Censimenti e catasti di epoca neo-assiria* (Rome, 1973)

P. Albenda: 'The Gateway and Portal Stone Reliefs from Arslan Tash', *Bull. Amer. Sch. Orient. Res.* (Aug 1988), pp. 5–30

JOHN M. RUSSELL

Arslantepe [Malatya]. Site in eastern Turkey, in the Malatya Plain on the right bank of the River Euphrates. It is a large artificial mound (h. *c.* 30 m) formed by the superposition of successive dwellings from about the 5th millennium BC to the Islamic period, *c.* 12th century AD. It was a strategic political and economic centre, especially in the Late Uruk period (*c.* 3300–*c.* 2900 BC), and was important in the cultural contexts of both MESOPOTAMIA and ANCIENT ANATOLIA. Finds from the excavations are housed in the Malatya Museum and the Museum of Anatolian Civilizations, Ankara.

1. BEFORE *c.* 3000 BC. Excavations in the southern area of the mound have revealed a stratified succession of four monumental public buildings of mud-brick at a depth of *c.* 8 m; radiocarbon dating has suggested that these structures were built *c.* 3300–3000 BC. Most have thick walls and stone foundations, and contain several rooms. Many niches, plastered and painted white, or more rarely red, are set in the interior walls. Building I, the most recent,

has a recognizable temple plan with a rectangular cella containing a central podium and a basin for sacrifices against the end wall; on one side are two communicating rooms for storage. The walls of the main room are richly decorated with concentric ovals stamped with a mould, comparable to an example from southern Mesopotamia (now Iraq) in Uruk itself.

The largest and oldest building of this period (Building IV), the walls of which are preserved to a height of more than 2 m, appears to be of the palace type: the excavated part contains a complex of storerooms and is not directly connected with religious activities. The building was entered through a great rectangular doorchamber and a wide corridor giving access to a complex of adjacent storerooms. The end wall of the central room (the only one with direct access from the corridor) contains a large niche flanked by wall paintings (see fig.). These are painted in red and black against a cream-coloured background, on the first of several successive layers of plaster. They depict two stylized human figures with similar characteristics: triangular faces with large eyes, wavy red and black lines coming from the heads (probably stylized hair or hats), hourglass-shaped bodies and long arms bent upwards. In front of each figure is a table with raised sides, perhaps an altar. In the left-hand painting the figure is placed under a sort of canopy, richly decorated with volutes, fringes and geometric motifs. The same elements are discernible in the right-hand painting, although this has lost its upper part. The right-hand figure has male genitals and in each hand he holds a peculiar object with teeth like a comb (not preserved in the left-hand painting). These remarkable late prehistoric paintings are exceptional for their state of preservation and the context in which they were found. Apart from the specific interpretation of the two figures, the style is of particular interest, for links with a northern and western tradition emphasize the autonomy of this local aspect of the Late Uruk culture of Mesopotamia. Evidence for the administrative organization of the Arslantepe storehouses is provided by the numerous sealed lumps of clay that were applied to various types of containers and stamped to guarantee their closure. A collection of these sealings was found in one of the storerooms, some alongside the vessels that they had originally sealed, and more than 2000 were recovered from a special waste deposit dug out of the west wall of the wide corridor of the palace, where they had been dumped, together with other refuse, as discarded administrative material. The designs of more than 100 seals have been reconstructed from their impressions on the clay sealings; their iconography and style provide information about the relations of this northern centre with Mesopotamia and its great capacity for autonomous development. The seals contain many animal figures, some marked by a particular geometric style in the figures and the composition. A different tendency appears in the naturalistic representation of animals in movement, both on cylinder and large, circular stamp seals (*see* ANCIENT NEAR EAST, §II, 1). Another type, closer to the south Mesopotamian repertory, shows animal figures, often lions, arranged in a *tête-bêche* (head-to-tail) configuration. Connections with southern Mesopotamia are also evident in the representation of porters bearing sacks and vases. The cylinder seals are generally naturalistic in style, although there is a preference for symmetry in the composition of the figures. One outstanding seal shows a scene in which a 'royal' figure rides in a canopied 'sledge' or chariot with runners instead of wheels (Malatya Mus.); this resembles a representation on a Mesopotamian plaque (London, BM), and although the style is different it clearly shows how symbols associated with power spread among the élite of different centres.

Arslantepe, wall painting from Building IV, red and black on cream plaster, 515×570 mm, *c.* 3300–3000 BC (*in situ*)

Excavations in Building III, of slightly later date than the palace, produced nine swords (the earliest known to date), twelve spearheads and a plaque with a quadruple spiral. These weapons, which comprise one of the largest and most ancient collections of metal arms, are made of an alloy of copper and arsenic. One of the swords and two smaller weapons have handles richly decorated with inlaid silver (Malatya Mus.). This discovery provides new information on the development of metallurgy and on particular forms of organized combat, and brings out the role of the metal-producing regions of eastern Anatolia in the inter-regional trade of the period.

2. *c.* 3000–*c.* 700 BC. The Mesopotamian proto-urban tradition came to an end in the second phase of the Early Bronze Age (*c.* 3000 BC) and was replaced by a typically east Anatolian culture, the development of which continued until the end of the 3rd millennium BC. The rise of Hittite influence in Late Bronze Age I (*c.* 1500–*c.* 1300 BC) was marked by the construction of a monumental city gate flanked by two towers of rectangular plan, following a typically central Anatolian architectural model. The outstanding architectural features from the latter part of the imperial Hittite period (Late Bronze Age II; 13th century BC) include the Imperial Gate, with a central chamber of a type well known in central Anatolia, and a gallery with a vault constructed of large stone blocks, which shows structural affinities with the posterns of Alişar Hüyük and Boğazköy. The monumental complex of the Lion Gate dates from the Neo-Hittite period (12th–8th century BC).

The gate is flanked by two figures of lions in relief, but with projecting heads in the round. The date of the lions and of other reliefs (Ankara, Mus. Anatol. Civiliz.) set in the surrounding walls has been disputed, but they may belong to the 12th–11th centuries BC. They depict a local king pouring a libation before several deities, including the Storm, Sun and Moon gods, and various mythological scenes (*see* ANATOLIA, ANCIENT, fig. 5).

BIBLIOGRAPHY

L. Delaporte: *Arslantepe: La Porte des Lions*, Malatya: Fouilles de la mission archéologique française (Paris, 1940)

E. Akurgal: *Remarques stylistiques sur les reliefs de Malatya* (Istanbul, 1946)

S. M. Puglisi and others: *Malatya*, 3 vols (Rome, 1964–75)

P. Amiet: 'Aperçu préliminaire sur la glyptique archaïque d'Arslantepe', *Origini*, vii (1973), pp. 217–24

A. Palmieri: 'Scavi nell'area sud-occidentale di Arslantepe', *Origini*, vii (1973), pp. 55–215

——: 'Scavi ad Arslantepe (Malatya)', *Quad. Ric. Sci.*, c (1978), pp. 311–73

——: 'Excavations at Arslantepe (Malatya)', *Anatol. Stud.*, xxxi (1981), pp. 101–9

P. Ferioli and E. Fiandra: 'Clay-sealings from Arslantepe: Administration and Bureaucracy', *Origini*, xii/2 (1983), pp. 455–509

M. Frangipane and A. Palmieri, eds: 'Perspectives on Protourbanization in Eastern Anatolia: Arslantepe (Malatya)', *Origini*, xii/2 (1983), pp. 287–668

——: 'A Protourban Centre of the Late Uruk Period', *Origini*, xii/2 (1983), pp. 287–454

C. Caneva, A. M. Palmieri and M. Frangipane: 'I metalli di Arslantepe nel quadro dei più antichi sviluppi della metallurgia vicino-orientale', *Quad. Ric. Sci.*, cxii (1985), pp. 115–37

A. Palmieri: 'Eastern Anatolia and Early Mesopotamian Urbanization: Remarks on Changing Relations', *Studi di Paleontologia in onore di S. M. Puglisi*, ed. M. Liverani, A. Palmieri and R. Peroni (Rome, 1985), pp. 191–214

——: 'Scavi ad Arslantepe (Malatya), 1976–79', *Quad. Ric. Sci.*, cxii (1985), pp. 75–114

A. Palmieri and M. Frangipane: 'Assetto redistributivo di una società protourbana della fine del IV millennio', *Dial. Archeol.*, n. s. 2 (1986), pp. 35–44

M. Frangipane and A. Palmieri: 'Urbanization in Perimesopotamian Areas: The Case of Eastern Anatolia', *Studies in the Neolithic and Urban Revolutions: The V. Gordon Childe Colloquium: Mexico, 1986*, Brit. Archaeol. Rep., Int. Ser. (Oxford, 1987), pp. 295–318

——: 'Aspects of Centralization in the Late Uruk Period in Mesopotamian Periphery', *Origini*, xiv (1988–9), pp. 539–60

A. Palmieri: 'Storage and Distribution at Arslantepe-Malatya in the Late Uruk Period', *Anatolia and the Ancient Near East*, ed. K. Emre and others (Ankara, 1989), pp. 419–30, pls 125–6

M. Frangipane: 'Dipinti murali in un edificio palaziale di Arslantepe-Malatya: Aspetti ideologici nelle prime forme di centralizzazione economica', *Studi Micenei ed Egeo-Anatolici*, xxx (1992)

MARCELLA FRANGIPANE

Art. According to some, art is all but a universal feature of human society, inhibited only by the extreme exigencies of life. According to others, art is a rare feature of society, confined perhaps to post-medieval Western culture so that, for instance, when artefacts of other societies are displayed in Western museums this generally involves imposing inappropriate categories and values on the material. Disagreement about the right answer to the question 'Does or did this society produce art?' is paralleled by a more fundamental disagreement about what makes an answer right, and the methodology of the question.

To historians of ideas of a positivistic bent it has seemed necessary that for a society to produce art there must be a word for art in that society. To this proposal, which has the apparent advantage of making the issue decidable, it might be countered that the question of whether a word current in another society does translate the English word 'art' raises the original issue all over again. This complexity apart, the requirement has been considered too stringent, and a more moderate demand is that the society should possess not the word but the concept, art. An equally vexed, but more constructive, question concerns the possession of a concept. Even if there is no one-to-one correspondence of concept to word, must not possession of a concept manifest itself in language, albeit in a diffused way, or does it suffice that the concept should guide practice? If the latter is the case, then whose practice? In other words, does possession of the concept of art lead the artificer to produce, for example, beauty, expression or meaning in his work, or does it, rather, lead the spectator to set some value, for example mystery or life-enhancement, on the artefact? Or is the relevant practice distributed in some subtly collusive way between artificer and spectator? To some the foregoing considerations will seem excessively individualistic, for, surely, if a society possesses the concept of art, this must manifest itself not only in the individual mind but also in certain institutions or social practices. To insist on certain specific practices, for example the establishment of a museum, would obviously be parochial, but it might nevertheless be contended that there must be some such institutions, each society forming its own. Finally, it may be questioned whether the criteria for the possession of the concept of art can be exclusively synchronic or if they must also be diachronic in that there have to be recognizable ways in which the skills of artificer and spectator can be transmitted across the generations. With this latter view, art is essentially historical.

Scholars from whom some contribution to these questions might have been anticipated have been unforthcoming. Anthropologists have mostly taken refuge in a form of relativism, according to which the activities that flourish in any particular society can be classified as, for example, religion, law or art only by reference to the aims, functions and structure of that society. From this it is inferred that, although anthropology can identify, for example, Yoruba art, Eskimo art, Byzantine art—even French 19th-century salon art—it can do this without a general concept of art. This may be a way of pointing to the difficulties inherent in aesthetics, but taken literally it offends against the compositional nature of thinking. Whatever else Yoruba art is, it is surely a form of art. Again, psychologists, for whom the issue of a general human nature might seem crucial, have not been declarative.

It is philosophers, particularly philosophers of language, who have maintained that a belief in a general human nature and a common conceptual scheme are assumptions that we must make if we are to claim to understand one another. However, this argument leaves open the exact depth to which the commonality of human nature goes, and the level at which it ceases and social or cultural particularity takes over. For this reason, the question of whether art is or is not *ceteris paribus* an integral part of human society remains undecided. One of the reasons why the question remains in such an unsettled state is that it has been common practice, over a wide range of disciplines on which it impinges, to ignore it.

See also AESTHETICS; ANTHROPOLOGY AND ART; for concepts of art in individual cultures *see under* country surveys.

BIBLIOGRAPHY

I. Kant: *Kritik der Urteilskraft* (Berlin, 1790; Eng. trans. by J. C. Meredith, Oxford, 1952)

G. W. F. Hegel: *Vorlesungen über die Ästhetik* (Berlin, 1835, rev. 1842); Eng. trans. by T. M. Knox as *Lectures on Fine Art*, 2 vols (Oxford, 1975)

L. Tolstoy: *Chto takoye isskustvo?* [What is art?] (Moscow, 1898; Eng. trans. by A. Maude, Indianapolis, 1960)

J. Dewey: *Art as Experience* (New York, 1934)

M. Schapiro: 'Style', *Anthropology To-day*, ed. A. L. Kroeber (Chicago, 1953)

C. Lévi-Strauss: *La Penseé sauvage* (Paris, 1962; Eng. trans., London, 1966)

M. Mead, J. B. Bird and H. Himmelfarb: *Technique and Personality* (New York, 1963)

W. Tatarkiewicz: 'The Classification of the Arts in Antiquity', *J. Hist. Ideas*, xxiv (April 1963), pp. 231–40

E. Wind: *Art and Anarchy* (London, 1963)

N. Chomsky: *Language and Mind* (New York, 1968, 2/1972)

R. Wollheim: *Art and its Objects* (New York, 1968, rev. Cambridge, 1980)

A. Forge, ed.: *Primitive Art and Society* (Oxford, 1973)

M. Schapiro: 'On the Aesthetic Attitude in Romanesque Art', *Romanesque Art* (New York, 1977)

D. Davidson: 'On the Very Idea of a Conceptual Scheme', *Inquiries into Truth and Interpretation* (Oxford, 1984)

RICHARD WOLLHEIM

Art, work of. Any consideration of the nature of the work of art as an object introduces a number of basic questions concerning what sort of object, or entity, it is: whether it is a physical thing, a mental thing, or perhaps neither of these; whether there is a necessary bond between the identity of a work of art and the identity of its maker; how in general we identify a given work of art as the thing it is; and how we distinguish it from other works of art of the same kind. This is quite distinct from considering the essential nature of art, i.e. that which a philosophical definition of art would aim to capture (*see* ART).

1. THE PHYSICAL OBJECT HYPOTHESIS. If we review the principal fine arts, it is natural to think that the work of art in such art forms is, simply, a particular physical object: a piece of coloured canvas, a hunk of bronze, a marked-up sheet of paper. There are, however, at least three objections commonly against this natural answer. The first two seem misplaced, but the third must be acknowledged to require some refinement in what can be called, following Wollheim (1968), the 'physical object hypothesis'.

The first objection is that works of art have distinctive expressive, symbolic and aesthetic properties that cannot belong to mere physical objects and so must attach to something more rarefied and immaterial, an 'aesthetic object' (see Pepper, 1955, and Beardsley, 1958). What force this has seems to reside partly in the rhetorical emphasis on 'mere', and partly in conveniently overlooking the intentional, cultural and historical context, which must be present for anything, physical object or not, to possess the rich set of properties that works of art typically have. The second objection is that what we are interested in *vis-à-vis* a painting, for example, is not the concrete object itself but the specific pattern of colour, line, tone, mass and texture it presents, and thus that this pattern *per se* is what we should regard as being the work of art (see, for example, Zemach, 1986). This view, however, cannot reasonably account for the deeply entrenched notion of the numerical uniqueness of many objects of fine art, paintings in particular, and for the related phenomenon of FORGERY.

The third, and soundest, objection is that in some fine arts, for example etching, lithography and cast sculpture, the work of art does not seem clearly identifiable with any particular physical object or objects. If we take an etching, we cannot say the work—the etching—is any given impression, for that would be completely arbitrary. Neither, however, can it be identified with all the impressions as a whole, nor with the original copper plate, for one can know and experience the etching, and do so fully, without contact with either the original plate or the totality of impressions pulled from it. Furthermore, if no impressions are ever pulled from the plate, or if there are impressions but they are destroyed, there is, according to the view proposed, no etching. These problems, among others, undermine the proposal by Goodman (1968) that an etching be identified with the class of its impressions. Finally, there are numerous specific properties of the plate (e.g. being metallic), of the complete run of impressions (e.g. typically, having a particular surface area) and of any single impression (e.g. being pulled on a particular date) that cannot be made out to be properties of the etching *tout court*; conversely, many of the most important properties of the etching itself, in particular aesthetic ones such as its specific transparency, delicacy, luminosity or grace, clearly do not belong to the plate and can only with awkwardness be thought to attach to the complete run of impressions, or primarily to any single one.

2. MULTIPLE ARTS. What this points to is that some of the recognized fine arts are singular in nature, while others are multiple. Singularity or multiplicity has to do with whether only one, or instead more than one, individual physical object does or can count as a genuine exemplar of the work of art in question. Thus, the individual impressions of, say, an etching all exemplify that etching; each as much as any other. With painting, by contrast, the sole exemplar of the work is the painting itself. Of the commonly discussed fine arts, painting, drawing, fresco, collage, assemblage and carved or modelled sculpture would be singular arts, while etching, engraving, lithography, woodcut and cast or moulded sculpture would be multiple arts. If we expanded the list to include ceramics and photography, the former would be largely in the first category and the latter in the second. Architecture poses special problems, associated with the fact that usually only one realization of a plan or blueprint is ever effected or even envisaged, which makes it difficult to assign it unequivocally to either category.

This still leaves unanswered the question of what the work, which the impressions of an etching, the castings of a sculpture or the prints of a photograph exemplify, is. To begin with, we can say that the work is some sort of abstract—at any rate, non-physical—entity, akin, perhaps, to a poem or a piece of music. But what sort of abstract object might, for example, an etching, be? The notion encountered earlier of a visual pattern or structure—a type whose instances are its tokens—would seem to be a reasonable candidate (see Wollheim, 1968, and Wolterstorff, 1975). This suggestion must, however, be qualified. In the first place, an etching cannot be a *pure* structure, since that is neither what an artist directly creates nor what he can be assured of creating; and there is nothing tethering such a pure structure to the person of the artist and the particular historical circumstances of creation in the way that its specific aesthetic, expressive and stylistic character requires (see Walton, 1970). We should instead think of an etching as a pattern-in-relation-to-a-given-archform, the archform (template, matrix) being the copper plate on which the artist actually worked and which was directly patterned by him (see Levinson, 1980). Thus, nothing counts as an instance of an etching merely in virtue of instantiating the pure visual structure it involves; it must also do so in virtue of having been pulled from a particular plate, one causally traceable to the artist himself.

Secondly, the structure we can identify with an etching must, in addition to involving a certain archform, be conceived as more than a strictly *visual* structure, since it typically and essentially requires, within a certain range, a particular kind of ink and a particular kind of paper. Thirdly, even though there is a kinship between etchings on the one hand and poems and sonatas on the other, in that these are all abstract entities not identical with any physical particulars and capable of existing in multiple tokens or instances, there is a significant difference between the one type and the other. The characteristic pattern or structure of an etching is not defined in a 'digital' manner, or given in a notation. The limits of rightness of visual structure among candidate instances of an etching are looser, and more 'analogical' in nature, involving close qualitative similarity to an unspecifiable extent.

In summary, an etching appears to be an analogically defined, archform bound, visual/material structure, such that all its true instances have a certain specific though not notationally circumscribed look, a certain material composition and a certain physical provenance. This formula also applies, with little modification, to works in the other multiple graphic arts. It is a formula that ensures the creatability of such works, acknowledges the physical nature of the media they involve, anchors them as the personal products of individuals operating in specific cultural contexts at specific times and underwrites for them, as for the works of singular arts, the distinction between authentic and inauthentic. The crucial point is that such works, although not themselves physical objects, are ontologically rooted in datable physical objects resulting from concrete acts of human invention or design. As such, although abstract, they are far from Platonic forms in that they are neither timeless nor indestructible.

It is important to realize that the several impressions of an etching are not copies of it, in the sense of even the most exacting art student's assigned drawing in a museum, nor are they reproductions of it, in the sense of a photograph in an art history book or, more loosely, another etcher's admiring imitations. Such copies and reproductions, unlike true impressions, are not in any way the etching itself; they are not, as we say, originals (*see* AUTHENTICITY and REPRODUCTION OF WORKS OF ART). It is clearly a mistake, one perhaps derived from Walter Benjamin, to think either that everything made in an artistic manner by hand is genuinely art, or that nothing produced by a mechanical process, at least at a certain stage, can be a fully fledged example of a work of art. Even if individual impressions, castings and so on are occasionally regarded as works of art in their own right, which in some contexts seems appropriate, especially where there are striking differences among authorized instances, we still invariably recognize as well the overarching works to which they belong and of which they are representatives.

3. SINGULAR ARTS. As regards paintings, drawings and carved sculptures, and their earlier characterization as single-location, concrete, physical particulars, they are, as many philosophers have noted, hardly the most ordinary or uncomplicated of physical objects. A number of additional considerations should be borne in mind, the most important of which is that a painting or sculpture is naturally not a brute object, of the order of a hunk, mass or conglomeration, but rather a specifically articulated one. If, for example, a painting is a piece of canvas and an amount of paint, it is only that canvas and that paint conditioned and configured in a specific way and preserving a certain appearance, and not those things in any state or arrangement. The continued identity of a painting, and its individuation from its surroundings, are crucially dependent on this. There still remain problems concerning whether or how, given the ever-present fact of physical deterioration, a work of fine art can possess its salient aesthetic properties unchanged throughout the course of its existence.

A second consideration is that a painting or sculpture that is an artwork is an intentioned or projected physical object, a physical object-as-intended-or-projected-for-a-certain-regard-or-treatment (see Levinson, 1990). In other words, a certain role or aim is an intrinsic aspect of its identity. Like other artefacts, a work of art is a physical object of a sort that comes into existence, typically, when a more ordinary object or set of materials is transformed or 'transfigured' (see Danto, 1981) by a certain human intention or purpose. This feature of an object's identity as a work of art becomes especially prominent, not to say acute, within certain minimalist and appropriationist modes of sculpture.

A third consideration is the matter of titles and their relation to such works of art as paintings; if paintings are to be wholly physical, then, since titles as strings of words are not, we would have to say that titles stand to paintings as properties, rather than integral components, of them (see Levinson, 1990). Finally, it should be noted that at least the second of these considerations affects the full story of the nature of the work of art in multiple art forms as well.

4. THE IDEALIST HYPOTHESIS. Some philosophers have proposed that works of art in all categories of the fine arts are in fact neither physical entities nor abstract ones, but instead mental or experiential, existing first,

foremost, and perhaps exclusively, in the minds or imaginations of artists. This doctrine was advanced prominently by Benedetto Croce and R. G. Collingwood in the early 20th century and was possibly held in another form by Jean-Paul Sartre. Aside from its implausibility and the damage it does to the notion of the public character of art and its integral involvement with physical media, the view does little to illuminate the differences between singular and multiple art forms, although it may have a bearing on the idea of the work of art in certain avant-garde practices.

5. AVANT-GARDE ART. The nature of the work of art in the spheres of conceptual art and performance art is obviously—and purposely—rather problematic, and what has been said here about the ontology of objects in the ordinary fine arts would not apply without some modification (see Wollheim, 1965, and Binkley, 1977). This is also true, to a lesser extent, of the work of art within certain less radical developments, such as land art and kinetic art. It is clear, at any rate, that the categories of concept, action and event would play a role in any philosophical elucidation of the ontology of such modes of art, supplementing those of physical object and physically tethered pattern or structure relied on above.

BIBLIOGRAPHY

M. Dufrenne: *Phénoménologie de l'expérience esthétique* (Paris, 1953)
S. Langer: *Feeling and Form* (New York, 1953)
S. Pepper: *The Work of Art* (Bloomington, 1955)
M. Beardsley: *Aesthetics: Problems in the Philosophy of Criticism* (New York, 1958, rev. Indianapolis, 1981)
R. Wollheim: 'Minimal Art', *A. Mag.*, xxix (1965), pp. 26–32
N. Goodman: *Languages of Art* (Indianapolis, 1968)
R. Wollheim: *Art and its Objects* (New York, 1968, rev. with suppl. essays, Cambridge, 1980) [esp. suppl. essay III]
K. Walton: 'Categories of Art', *Philos. Rev.*, lxxix (1970), pp. 334–69
G. Dickie: *Art and the Aesthetic* (Ithaca, 1974)
N. Wolterstorff: 'Toward an Ontology of Art Works', *Nous* [USA], ix (1975), pp. 115–42
T. Binkley: 'Piece: Contra Aesthetics', *J. Aesth. & A. Crit.*, xxxv (1977), p. 265–77
J. Margolis: 'The Ontological Peculiarity of Works of Art', *J. Aesth. & A. Crit.*, xxxvi (1977), pp. 45–50
M. Sagoff: 'On Restoring and Reproducing Art', *J. Philos.*, lxxv (1978), pp. 453–70
J. Levinson: 'Autographic and Allographic Art Revisited', *Philos. Stud.*, xxxviii (1980), pp. 367–83
N. Wolterstorff: *Works and Worlds of Art*, pt 2 (Oxford, 1980)
A. Danto: *The Transfiguration of the Commonplace* (Cambridge, MA, 1981)
E. Zemach: 'No Identification without Evaluation', *Brit. J. Aesth.*, xxvi (1986), pp. 239–51
J. Leninson: 'Zemach on Paintings', *Brit. J. Aesth.*, xxvii (1987), pp. 278–83
G. Currie: *An Ontology of Art* (London, 1989)
J. Levinson: *Music, Art and Metaphysics* (Ithaca, 1990)

For further bibliography *see* BENJAMIN, WALTER; COLLINGWOOD, R. G.; CROCE, BENEDETTO; DEWEY, JOHN; HEGEL, GEORG WILHELM FRIEDRICH; SARTRE, JEAN-PAUL; SCHOPENHAUER, ARTHUR.

JERROLD LEVINSON

Arta [anc. Ambrakia]. Capital of the Arta district in south Epiros, Greece, on the east bank of the River Arachthos, 16 km north of the Ambrakian Gulf. The town occupies the site of Ambrakia, which was colonized by Corinth in 625 BC. Pyrrhos, King of Epiros (*reg* 319–272 BC), transferred his capital to Ambrakia in 292 BC. It first appears with the name of Arta in 1082. The state (better known as the Despotate) of Epiros, with its capital of Arta, was founded by Michael I Angelos Doukas Komnenos (*reg* 1205–15) after the Latin conquest of Constantinople in 1204. His state included the whole of north-west Greece, New Epiros (part of modern Albania), north-west Macedonia and parts of Thessaly. Arta fell to the Turks in 1449, regaining its independence in 1881 when it was incorporated into the Greek state.

1. HISTORY AND URBAN DEVELOPMENT. The town was laid out on a grid plan and was surrounded by impressive walls, large parts of which survive. Remains of the Doric temple of Pythian Apollo (*c.* 500 BC) stand in the centre of the modern town; in 1976 a small theatre (early 3rd century BC) was discovered near by.

Although there is no written record of medieval Arta before 1082, several churches dating to the 9th century survive, including those of Hagios Demetrios Katsouris (early 9th century; *see* §2 below) and Hagios Vasilios of the Bridge (tis Gephiras; second half of the 9th century). In the 12th century the town became the seat of a bishopric and had a sizeable Jewish community.

Michael II (*reg* 1231–67/8), son of Michael I, fortified Arta and founded the monasteries of Kato Panagia and the Pantanassa. Between 1318 and 1335, Arta was ruled by the Italian Orsini family, against the rival claims of the Byzantine Empire and the Neapolitan kingdom of Anjou. The town suffered several sieges and many disasters: in the mid-14th century it was totally destroyed by fire; in 1374 it was captured by the Albanians; and in the early 15th century it was conquered by Carlo I, Count of Kephallonia (*reg c.* 1370; Despot Tocco, 1411–29).

The written records suggest that the medieval town around the fortified stronghold contained impressive buildings; the large number of existing Byzantine churches and the fact that Arta was the capital of the Despotate of Epiros suggest that it was more extensive than is indicated by the archaeological finds. Surviving monuments reflect its importance as an artistic centre in north-west Greece in the 13th to 15th centuries when it created its own 'school' of ecclesiastical architecture, which combined local building tradition with Constantinopolitan, Macedonian and Western architectural features. This school influenced the architecture of the rest of Epiros, as well as areas to the north and west.

Most churches were built of cloisonné masonry, with rich brickwork patterns, inscriptions and ceramic dishes decorating the outer walls. This polychrome ornament reflected the ostentatious tendencies of the local aristocracy, whose ambition was to recapture Constantinople.

The sculpture decorating the 13th-century churches of the Vlacherna (*see* §2 below) and the Pantanassa of Philippias so closely follows Constantinopolitan forms and technique that it may be the work of craftsmen who fled there from Constantinople after 1204. By the end of the 13th century, however, Western influence had arrived, detectable in such details as the pairs of intertwined columns and crocket capitals in the Parigoritissa church (*see* §2 below). As at this time the rulers of Arta were trying, by means of military alliances and marriages, to maintain good relations with Western rulers, it is likely that this is the work of artists from Italy. Most wall paintings survive only in fragments and it is not possible to form a proper understanding of painting in this period.

2. BUILDINGS. The oldest Byzantine monument in Arta is the cross-in-square church of Hagios Demetrios Katsouris in the village of Plisioi, 5 km south of the town. Once part of a monastery first mentioned in 1229, the church itself dates from the early 9th century; its clumsy proportions and construction faults attest to this early date. Its interior is decorated with wall paintings of the 17th–18th centuries, covering a painted layer of the 12th–13th centuries, as can be seen in the partially revealed figures of bishops in the sanctuary apse. Two marble slabs from the 13th-century templon form part of the present iconostasis.

One of the most renowned monuments in Arta is the former monastic church of Panagia Vlacherna, where several members of the ruling Komnenodoukoi family are buried. Today it serves as the parish church of Vlacherna village opposite Arta on the west bank of the Arachthos. The present building was constructed on the site of a 10th-century church and is a three-aisled basilica, originally barrel-vaulted, with the subsequent addition of three domes. The marble reliefs built into the walls around the doorways are from the original templon (13th century), which has been replaced. These reliefs, with their well-executed figures, are thought to be the work of artists from Constantinople.

The wall paintings in the main body of the church are dated *c.* 1250, while those in the narthex are late 13th century. The scene depicted in the south-west corner is of particular interest, since it shows the litany being performed before the icon of the *Hodegetria* ('Virgin who points the way') in Constantinople, which is known to have taken place every Tuesday. This is a rare representation and, apart from the iconographic interest in the details of its market-place scenes, it may be seen as a direct reference to the relations between Arta and Constantinople.

The monastery of Kato Panagia (mid-13th century) was probably founded by Despot Michael II and is the only Byzantine monastery in Arta that continues in its original function. The church is dedicated to the Birth of the Virgin and is a three-aisled, cross-vaulted basilica with a tetragonal dome, a characteristic of the architecture of the Despotate. The church is built of spolia and decorated with brickwork ornament, such as dogtooth bands and chequerwork patterns, which is noteworthy for its symmetry. The poorly preserved interior wall paintings (1715), noteworthy for their good design and colour and the fact that they are among few 18th-century extant examples depicting contemporary artistic life in Arta, cover a 13th-century layer, a small part of which has been exposed in the sanctuary. The monastery also has a small collection of icons.

The three-aisled basilica of Hagia Theodora (12th century) is named after the town's patron saint, who was the wife of Despot Michael II and a member of the Petraleipha family. The church was originally dedicated to St George and belonged to a monastery, the gateway of which has been preserved. The remains of the prytaneum of Ambrakia were uncovered on the north-west side of the church. In the mid-13th century Theodora paid for repairs to the church and the construction of a narthex. A few years later a porch was added to the south side. Theodora played an important part in Epirote politics and made a significant contribution to the peace negotiations between the Despotate and the Byzantine Empire of Nicaea (now Iznik, Turkey; 1204–61). Her tomb in the church was opened in 1873 and reconstructed from sculpted reliefs found inside. One of these reliefs (second half of the 13th century) shows two figures in imperial dress, identified as Theodora and her son Nikephoros, and is the work of local artists.

Not far to the north-east of Hagia Theodora is the church of Hagios Vasilios. It is a single-aisled basilica to which the chapels of St John Chrysostomos and St Gregory were later added on the north and south sides. The church is built in cloisonné masonry and is decorated externally with brick ornament. The two maiolica relief icons (14th century) embedded into the wall of the church's gable are a unique feature. They depict the *Crucifixion* and the *Three Hierarchs* (i.e. St Basil, St Gregory and St John Chrysostomos).

The church of the Parigoritissa (late 13th century) is the most imposing monument in north-west Greece. It was built by Nikephoros I (*reg* 1271–96) and his wife Anna Palaiologina as a monastery church; 16 monastic cells survive as well as the refectory, which now houses a small collection of finds from ancient Ambrakia. The church plan is most unusual for its time: the ground floor resembles an octagon, while the upper level resembles a cross-in-square church. The north and south sides are surrounded at ground- and first-floor level by side chapels

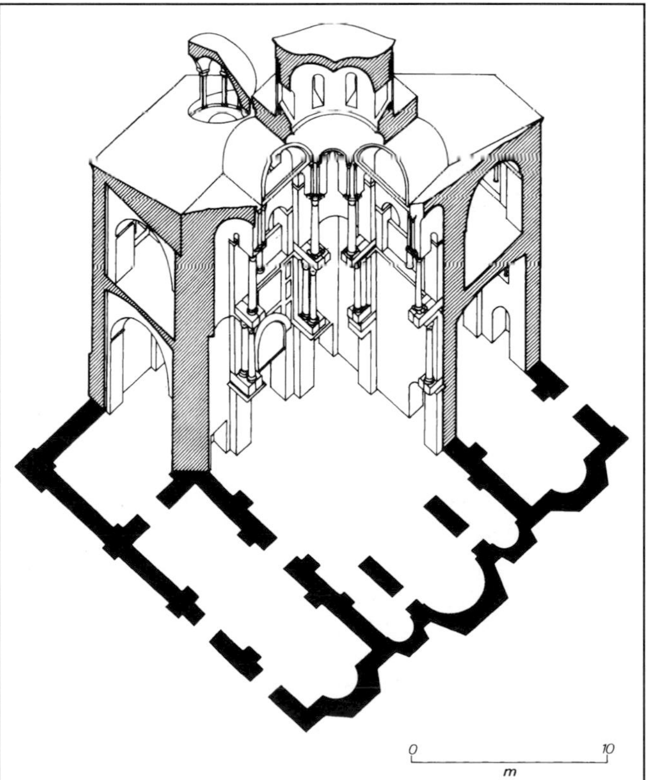

Arta, church of the Parigoritissa, late 13th century; isometric projection

that fuse with the western narthex and its gallery, thus creating an imposing cubic mass. The most striking feature in the main body of the church is the unique way in which the dome is supported by three superimposed levels of columns resting on eight piers at ground-floor level; each succeeding level projects slightly beyond the one below while leaving the central space free (see fig.). The dome is decorated with a mosaic (*c*. 1290) of the *Pantokrator* and the prophets. The sculpted figural reliefs that decorate the north and west arches of the vaults beneath the dome reflect Western influence in their techniques and subject-matter. In the centre of the north arch is a *Nativity*, with the archangels, the Magi, the shepherds, Joseph, St Luke and the prophets arranged down the sides. The west arch has the *Holy Lamb* in the centre with the Evangelist symbols of SS John and Matthew, and various prophets down the sides. The monument reflects the adoption of Constantinopolitan models by provincial craftsmen (for further illustration *see* EARLY CHRISTIAN AND BYZANTINE ART, fig. 27).

Other surviving Byzantine monuments in Arta and the surrounding area include those of Panagia of Koronisia (late 10th century), Hagia Paraskevi tou Drakou (second half of the 11th century), Hagios Nikolaos of Rodia (early 13th century), the Panagia of Vryoni (1238), the Red Church (*c*. 1290) and the 13th-century fortress.

BIBLIOGRAPHY

RBK: 'Epiros'

A. Orlandos: *Byzantina mnimeia tis Artis* [Byzantine monuments in Arta] (1936), ii of *Archeion ton byzantinon mnimeion tis Ellados* [Archive of Byzantine monuments in Greece] (Athens, 1935–)

D. Nicol: *The Despotate of Epiros* (Oxford, 1957)

A. Orlandos: *I Parigoritissa tis Artis* [The Parigoritissa church in Arta] (Athens, 1963) [with Fr. summary]

P. Vocotopoulos: 'Arta', *Alte Kirchen und Klöster Griechenlands*, ed. M. DuMont-Schauberg (Cologne, 1972), pp. 135–61

——: *I ekklisiastiki architektoniki eis tin dytikin sterean Ellada kai tin Ipeiron apo tou Telous tou 7ou mechri tou Telous tou 10ou Aionos* [Ecclesiastical architecture in western mainland Greece and Epirus, from the end of the 7th century to the end of the 10th] (Thessaloniki, 1975)

M. Acheimastou-Potamianou: 'The Byzantine Wall-painting of Vlacherna Monastery (Area of Arta)', *Praktika tou 15 diethnous synedriou byzantinon spoudon* [Proceedings of the 15th international conference on Byzantine studies]: *Athina, 1976*, ii, pp. 1–14

P. Soustal and J. Koder: 'Arta', *Nikopolis und Kephallenia, tabula imperii Byzantini*, iii (Vienna, 1981), pp. 113–15

D. Nicol: *The Despotate of Epiros, 1267–1479: A Contribution to the History of Greece in the Middle Ages* (Cambridge, 1985)

K. Tsouris: *O keramoplastikos Diakosmos ton ysterobyzantinon mnimeion tis voceiodytikis Ellados* [Brickwork patterns in post-Byzantine monuments of north-west Greece] (diss., U. Thessaloniki, 1988)

G. Velenis: '13th Century Architecture in the Despotate of Epiros: The Origins of the School', *Proceedings of the Conference: Studenica et l'art byzantin autour de l'année 1200: Beograd, 1988*

B. Papadopoulou: 'Nea archaeologika stiheia gia tin vizantini poli tis Artas' [New archaeological finds in the Byzantine town of Arta], *Proceedings of the International Symposium: The Despotate of Epirus: Arta, 1990*

BARBARA PAPADOPOULOU

Art Abstrait. Belgian art group designed to propagate abstract art. It was formed in April 1952 as a successor to JEUNE PEINTURE BELGE by the artists Jean Milo (*b* 1906), Jo Delahaut (*b* 1911), Pol Bury, Georges Carrey (1902–53), Léopold Plomteux (*b* 1920), George Collignon (*b* 1923) and Jan Saverys (*b* 1924), who were joined later that year by Jan Burssens (*b* 1925) and Hauror. The group first exhibited in 1952 at the Cercle Artistique in Ghent, the Galerie Le Parc in Charleroi and the Galerie Arnaud in Paris and also travelled to Britain. The following year it exhibited at the Palais des Beaux-Arts in Brussels, the Association pour le Progrès Intellectuel et Artistique de la Wallonie in Liège and at the Salle Comité voor Artistieke Werking in Antwerp. The members of the group had no unifying style or aesthetic apart from being non-figurative. The abstract styles within the group ranged from thickly impastoed informal works such as Carrey's *Composition* (1953; Brussels, Musées Royaux A. & Hist.) to hard-edged works such as Delahaut's *Besoar* (1953; see 1981 exh. cat., p. 25). In 1954 Delahaut, Bury and the writers Jean Séaux and Karel Elno published a manifesto that introduced the concept of SPATIALISME, thus marking the end of Art Abstrait. Delahaut's ideas about abstraction led to his co-founding the group Formes with the writers Séaux and Maurits Blicke in 1956. This was designed to realize the ideas of the *Spatialisme* manifesto, as shown, for example, in the abstraction of Delahaut's *Recall to Order* (1955; see 1981 exh. cat., p. 32). Again short-lived, the Formes group exhibited in 1956 at Morlanwelz-Mariemont in Hainaut and in 1957 at the Galerie Accent in Antwerp.

BIBLIOGRAPHY

Jo Delahaut (exh. cat. by B. Kerber and others, Ludwigshafen, Hack-Mus. & Städt. Kstsamml., 1981)

K. J. Geirlandt: *L'Art en Belgique depuis 45* (Antwerp, 1983)

□

Art à la Rue. Term used to refer to a movement or set of concerns espoused by a small number of left-wing artists and architects in the 1890s and early 1900s, mainly in Brussels and Paris. A significant number of leading Art Nouveau artists and architects, including Victor Horta, Héctor Guimard and Frantz Jourdain (the main spokesman for the movement) were involved. Art à la Rue, which focused specifically on bringing art to the working classes, was part of a broader movement aimed at social reform, whose roots were in the French socialist movement, the political theories of the Russian anarchist Prince Kropotkin and William Morris's later essays. In challenging the élitist status of art, it urged those in the arts to forget the world of museums and collectors and to concentrate instead on relating art to everyday life, so that it assumed a more socially responsive role in society. The main arena for this was the street, where ordinary people spent most of their leisure time. Proponents of Art à la Rue, therefore, urged that the streets should be enlivened with bright colours by means of lithographic posters (e.g. those of Jules Chéret and Théophile-Alexandre Steinlen) and by artistically designed signs, lights and drinking fountains, in order to make the city a more pleasing place to live; the process would help to shape aesthetic sensibility. Such art was to be deliberately popular in appeal, accessible and intelligible to people of all ages and educational backgrounds. Decorated building façades and shop fronts, too, were singled out as an especially good means of transforming sombre streets into free outdoor museums. With its aim of social reform and its focus on the street as a means of bringing art to the people, to lift morale and to elevate popular taste, the Art à la Rue movement suggests that Art Nouveau was not just a new aesthetic ideal: it also had a strong urbanistic, moral component, which helped to set the stage for the modernists' social utopianism of the 1920s.

BIBLIOGRAPHY

F. Jourdain: 'Art dans la rue', *Rev. A. Déc.*, xii (1891–2), pp. 211–14

L. Magne: 'L'Esthétique de la rue', *Mercure France*, lvi (1905), p. 170

M. L. Clausen: 'Architecture and the Poster: Toward a Redefinition of Art Nouveau', *Gaz. B.-A.*, n.s. 7, cvi (1985), pp. 81–94

MEREDITH L. CLAUSEN

Artamonov, Mikhail (Illarionovich) (*b* Vygolevo, Tver' Province, 5 Dec 1898; *d* Leningrad [now St Petersburg], 29 July 1972). Russian archaeologist and art historian. He began studying archaeology at the Archaeological Institute in Petrograd (now St Petersburg) in 1921 and subsequently at the University in that city. He became a postgraduate student in 1926, then joined the staff of the State Academy for the History of Material Culture, where he studied aspects of Old Russian art, including the miniatures of the Königsberg (Radziwill) Chronicle (St Petersburg, Acad. Sci., Lib.). He became a professor in 1935 and was appointed head of the faculty of archaeology at Leningrad State University in 1949. He was director of the Institute for the History of Material Culture from 1938 to 1945 and curator of the State Hermitage Museum from 1951 to 1964. His most important works deal with the history, archaeology and art of the Scythians, Slavs and Khazars and include a study of the Hermitage's collection of Scythian art (1970); he also conducted research into the Scythian–Siberian Animal Style. He directed excavations of numerous ancient and early medieval monuments in the Don region, the Ukraine and the northern Caucasus, including excavations of the Khazar Sarkel fortress (Rus. Belaya Vezha). The art of medieval nomads is discussed in his monograph on the history of the Khazars.

WRITINGS

Istoriya Khazar [History of the Khazars] (Leningrad, 1962)

Treasures from Skythian Tombs (London, 1969)

Goldschatz der Skythen in der Ermitage [The Skythians' golden treasure in the Hermitage] (Prague, 1970)

Sokrovishcha sakov [Saka treasures] (Moscow, 1973)

BIBLIOGRAPHY

Nauchnaya deyatel'nost M. I. Artamonova: Issledovanniya po arkheologii SSSR [The scholarly work of M. I. Artamonov: research into the archaeology of the USSR] (Leningrad, 1961)

L. S. Kleyn: 'K semidesyatiletiyu M. I. Artamonova' [On the occasion of the 70th birthday of M. I. Artamonov], *Sovet. Arkheol.*, iv (1968), pp. 151–6

A. Stoljar and others, eds: *Problemy arkheologii* [Problems of archaeology], ii (Leningrad, 1978), pp. 3–7

V. YA. PETRUKHIN

Artan (de Saint-Martin), Louis (Victor Antonio) (*b* The Hague, 20 April 1837; *d* Nieuport, 23 May 1890). Dutch painter. He began his painting career at the age of 20 in Spa, where he took lessons from the Romantic landscape painters E. Delvaux (1806–62) and H. Marcette (1824–90). From 1858 he went every winter to Paris, where he was overwhelmed by the masterpieces in the Louvre. He worked in the Fontainebleau area and along the Seine, and became friendly with Courbet and Corot. In 1868, with his friend Louis Dubois, he founded the Société Libre des Beaux-Arts to defend free artistic expression. During this period he painted landscapes, views of the suburbs and some figurative works, with great subtlety of colour.

He was inspired by a stay in Brittany (1867–8) to paint the grandeur of the sea, and from then on he was primarily a marine painter. From 1873 to 1874 he painted the Escaut coast at Antwerp. Then he went back to the coastline of his childhood and, breaking with the conventional style of contemporary marine painting, he created the Realist seascape, for example with *Marine* (Antwerp, Kon. Mus. S. Kst.), his only predecessor being P. J. Clays. Fascinated by the fleeting effects of nature, he educated himself in the researches of the Impressionists and also became a painter of light and shade. In 1887 he exhibited the large *My Studio at De Panne* (ex-Mus. S. Kst., Ghent; destr.). It showed his studio suspended above the water on wooden stilts, from which he could paint over, rather than in front of his subject. This direct contact enabled him to create an authentic image of the sea, capturing both its physical and atmospheric qualities. His small spontaneous sketches were as important as his full-scale canvases.

BIBLIOGRAPHY

T. Hannon: *Louis Artan* (Brussels, 1892)

G. Van Zype: *Maîtres d'hier* (Brussels, 1922), pp. 97–109

Louis Artan (exh. cat., Brussels, 1932)

D. Lambillon: 'Louis Artan de Saint Martin (1837–90), peintre de la mer', *Rev. Archéologues & Historiens A. Louvain*, iv (1971), pp. 278–9

BERNADETTE THOMAS

Art and Freedom [Arab. Al-fann wa'l-ḥurriyya]. Egyptian group of Surrealist writers, artists and intellectuals founded on 9 January 1939 by the poet Georges Hunain (1914–73). The group included the Egyptian painters Ramsis Yunan (1914–66), Fu'ad Kamil (1919–73) and Kamil al-Talamsani (1917–72). Inspired by the work of André Breton, whom Hunain met in Paris in 1936, the aim of the group was to defend freedom in art by stressing the liberating role of the individual imagination. On 22 December 1938 Hunain and his colleagues signed a manifesto entitled 'Vive l'Art Dégénéré', which protested against Fascism, particularly Hitler's claim that modern art was degenerate. The manifesto was followed by further writings, conferences and debates. Artists from the group exhibited work in June 1939 at the premises of Art and Freedom at 28 Shari' al-Madabigh in Cairo. In January 1940 the magazine *al-Taṭawwur* was launched, which presented ideas behind modern art to an Egyptian audience. This was followed in February 1940 by the first Exposition de l'Art Indépendant in Cairo, which provoked lively polemics from the press. A second exhibition was held in March 1941, and further exhibitions were held in the following years. The activities of the Art and Freedom group were responsible for reviving cultural life in Egypt in the late 1930s and early 1940s, especially by challenging pictorial and literary academicism. Although Surrealism continued to inspire Egyptian artists in the following decades, with the founding of the Contemporary Art Group in 1946 many artists turned to examine the heritage of Egyptian folklore.

BIBLIOGRAPHY

S. Gharieb: *Surrealism in Egypt and Plastic Arts*, Prism Art Series, iii (Giza, 1986)

L. Karnouk: *Modern Egyptian Art: The Emergence of a National Style* (Cairo, 1988), pp. 30–34

S. J. VERNOIT

Art and Language [Art & Language]. English group of conceptual artists founded in 1968 by Terry Atkinson (*b* 1939), Michael Baldwin (*b* 1945), David Bainbridge (*b* 1941) and Harold Hurrell (*b* 1940). In May 1969 they established the journal *Art–Language*, which was edited from 1971 by the critic Charles Harrison (*b* 1942), who had met them in 1969. They rapidly acquired associates outside England, especially in New York; by 1969 Joseph Kosuth, the Australian Ian Burn (*b* 1939) and another English artist, Mel Ramsden (*b* 1944), were affiliated to the group, as were many others for varying periods of time over the succeeding years. Motivated essentially by a sceptical interest in modernist art and its concomitant ideology, they produced discursive texts intended as a critique of modernism and the interrelationships between art, the art market and society. Some of these appeared in their journal, while others were printed as limited editions and sold as art works. The frequent allusions to philosophy and linguistics mark these texts, paradoxically, with an introverted élitism typical of much modernist art.

In 1972 Art & Language installed *Index* at *Documenta 5* in Kassel, Germany, and also at the Hayward Gallery in London. This consisted of a series of filing cabinets containing all the writings by the group, arranged by an index that allowed the sections to be read in a logical order. When the New York wing of the group collapsed in 1979 after internal disputes, Burn returned to Australia and the remaining members followed their own careers, apart from Ramsden, who returned to England and continued to work with Baldwin under the group's name, with Harrison still as their apologist. In 1979 they turned to painting, producing works that examined the relationship between style and content; in *Gustave Courbet's Burial at Ornans* . . . (1981; London, Tate), for example, they reworked Courbet's imagery in a quasi-Abstract Expressionist style.

WRITINGS

A.–Lang., i/1 (1969–)

BIBLIOGRAPHY

Art and Language (exh. cat., Eindhoven, Stedel. Van Abbemus., 1980)

C. Harrison and F. Orton: *A Provisional History of Art & Language* (Paris, 1982)

C. Harrison: *Essays on Art & Language* (Oxford, 1991)

For further bibliography *see* CONCEPTUAL ART.

□

Artaria. Austrian family of publishers of Italian descent. The family originally came from Blevio, near Como, in northern Italy, and in the mid-18th century worked as itinerant art dealers in Germany and Austria, offering an extensive range of English and French prints to the public. Francesco Artaria (*b* Blevio, 1744; *d* Vienna, 1808) and his cousin Carlo Artaria (*b* Blevio, 1747; *d* Vienna, 1808) settled in Vienna in the 1760s, establishing the firm Artaria & Co. in 1770. In 1774 they took over a subsidiary firm based in Mainz that had been founded in 1765 by their uncle Giovanni Casimiro Artaria (1725–97). Shortly after 1793, however, this branch relocated to Mannheim, where it eventually became Artaria & Fontaine. In Vienna, Artaria & Co. established its headquarters in the Kohlmarkt and began to specialize in the publication of prints. In 1775–6 it published its first large volume of copper engravings, *Zeichnungen nach dem gemeinen Volke besonders der Kaufruf in Wien* (Vienna), after works by Johann Christian Brand. Its most enduring art publication was *Collection de 50 vues de la ville de Vienne* (Vienna) by Carl Schütz (1745–1800), Johann Ziegler (*c.* 1750–*c.* 1812) and Lorenz Janscha (1749–1812). This was first published in 1779 and appeared in several new editions well into the 19th century. Artaria & Co. incorporated into the original copperplates the various topographical and scenic changes that had occurred in Vienna during these years, resulting in views recorded in up to eight states. The company's trade in fine art prints was expanded to include engravings of printed sheets of music, and it published scores by Mozart, Haydn and Beethoven. Its other interest was in the production of maps, including school atlases and maps of Vienna. The firm became famous throughout Europe under the management of Domenico Artaria (*b* Blevio, 20 Nov 1775; *d* Vienna, 5 July 1842), who became director in 1802. In 1813 Artaria & Co. organized its first art auction, following the examples of art publishing houses in London, and in 1838 it was the first to hold an auction of original manuscripts. By 1933, however, the firm's efforts were concentrated in the area of cartography, and, after amalgamation with Freytag & Berndt during World War II, it existed under the name Kartographische Anstalt Gustav Freytag & Berndt und Artaria.

BIBLIOGRAPHY

A. Weinmann, ed.: *Vollständiges Verlagsverzeichnis Artaria & Comp: Beiträge zur Geschichte des Alt-Wiener Musikverlages* (Vienna, 1952, rev. 1985)

Geschichte der Firmen Artaria & Compagnie und Freytag-Berndt und Artaria: Ein Rückblick auf 200 Jahre Wiener Privatkartographie, 1770–1970 (Vienna and Innsbruck, 1970)

R. Hilmar: *Der Musikverlag Artaria & Comp.: Geschichte und Probleme der Druckproduktion*, Publikationen des Instituts für Österreichische Musikdokumentation, vi (Tutzing, 1977)

Der Verlag Artaria: Veduten und Wiener Alltagsszenen (exh. cat., ed. G. Düriegl; Vienna, Museen Stadt, 1981)

G. TOBIAS NATTER

Artaria, Paul (*b* Basle, 6 Aug 1892; *d* Heiden, 25 Sept 1959). Swiss architect, teacher and writer. He was initially apprenticed as a construction draughtsman (1906–8), then spent time in the Gewerbeschule, Basle (1909–10), before working in various offices in Basle and Lausanne. From 1913 to 1920 he worked for Hans Bernoulli, an experience that was crucial to his development, and was involved with the building of low-cost housing and the planning of housing estates. In 1920 he began to work with Karl Zaeslin (1886–1936), for example on the 'Nur-Dach-Holzhaus' (1920), Prêles, and they practised together formally from 1922 to 1924; a notable achievement was their competition-winning house design (1922; unexecuted), Kriens. After a major success in the competition for the Habermatten estate (1923) in Riehen, conceived in an innovative terraced style—though the project was designed by HANS SCHMIDT in Artaria's name—Artaria then set up a practice (1926–30) with Schmidt, one of the leading exponents of *Neues Bauen* in Switzerland. With Schmidt he built the first flat-roofed houses in Switzerland, using steel construction methods (e.g. the Colnaghi House (1927) and the Schaeffer House (1928–9), both Riehen). Schmidt was involved more with the conceptual design and planning of buildings, while Artaria worked on the execution of the technically new projects and on interiors and furniture. Artaria's significance lies in the fact that he committed himself to *Neues Bauen*, but more at the technological and practical rather than theoretical level. Through his knowledge of wooden buildings he was able to contribute to *Neues Bauen* in the use of such modern wood building technology as gusset construction (e.g. Haus Mooshalde (1926), Riehen, by Artaria and Schmidt). He also carried out independent competition projects, for example Petersschule (1926; unexecuted), Basle. After his partnership with Schmidt ended, Artaria designed some steel-framed buildings, such as the Rebgasse House (1931), Biningen, and a competition entry for the Swiss Pavilion (unexecuted) at the Exposition Internationale des Arts et Techniques dans la Vie Moderne (1937), Paris. During the Depression of the 1930s, however, he developed a renewed interest in timber construction and produced some important examples, such as the projected Malerhaus (1933; unexecuted), Saignelégier, the Malerhaus Vierjuchartenweg (1935), Riehen, the holiday house built for the Landesausstellung (1939), Zurich, and the Malerhaus Albert Schnyder (1946), Delémont. In 1928 Artaria had participated in the first meeting of CIAM (*see* CIAM, fig. 1); in 1933 he became a founder-member of Gruppe 33 and participated in collective competition projects and urban plans, including the Gewerbeschule (1939; unexecuted), Basle, and the plan for the Gellertquartier of Basle (1951; unexecuted). In 1947 he began to teach perspective drawing and interior design at the Gewerbeschule, Basle. He also published numerous books on architecture and interior design.

WRITINGS

Schweizer Holzhäuser (Basle, 1935, rev. 2/1947)
Vom Bauen und Wohnen (Basle, 1939, rev. 2/1948)
Ferien- und Landhäuser (Zurich, 1947)

BIBLIOGRAPHY

P. Degen: 'Paul Artaria', *Gruppe 33* (exh. cat., ed. Y. Höfliger; Basle, Gal. Zem Specht, 1983), pp. 193–202

URSULA SUTER

Artaud, Antonin [Antoine Marie Joseph] (*b* Marseille, 4 Sept 1896; *d* Ivry-sur-Seine, 4 March 1948). French writer, draughtsman, stage designer, actor and director. He learnt to draw and paint in 1918–19 while staying in an establishment near Neuchâtel where he had been sent suffering from a nervous complaint that had begun in 1914. There he was prescribed opium in May 1919. He arrived in Paris in the spring of 1920 and visited salons, galleries and studios, produced art criticism (see *Oeuvres complètes*, ii), continued to sketch small portraits of himself or his family and composed poems. In the atelier of Charles Dullin (1885–1949), where he trained as an actor, he was asked to design the costumes for several performances. Nevertheless, after an attempt in 1923 to paint the portrait of a young friend and her father, he abandoned painting and drawing. Through the painter Elie Lascaux (*b* 1888), whom he knew from Max Jacob's circle, he met the art dealer Daniel-Henry Kahnweiler and the artists of his gallery. He became a friend of André Masson in particular and soon became a regular visitor at Masson's studio in the Rue Blomet, then also frequented by other painters such as Joan Miró, Jean Dubuffet and Georges Malkine and visited by writers Robert Desnos (1900–45), Michel Leiris (*b* 1901) and many others.

Artaud's first major text, 'Correspondance avec Jacques Rivière', was published in 1924. It went unnoticed by the critics, but not by more attentive readers, including André Breton, and Artaud was taken as a supporter of the Surrealist Movement (*see* SURREALISM). He became an active member of the group and published articles in *Révolution surréaliste* in 1925. Although he did not act on the stage after 1923, he continued to act in films. In September 1926, he founded the Théâtre Alfred Jarry partly perhaps as a result of his growing disillusionment with the Surrealist group (in particular, with Breton's political views), from which he was expelled in November 1926. He put on four shows in 1927 and 1928, which he designed and directed and which aimed at a 'total spectacle', integrating lighting, sets, props and acting, and at increasing audience involvement. From 1931 to 1935 he wrote a series of theoretical essays on the theatre; these were later published as *Le Théâtre et son double* (1938), which became the standard reference work for avant-garde theatre shortly after his death and earned him international fame. To put his ideas into practice, he founded the Théâtre de la Cruauté and in 1935 he wrote and put on *Les Cenci*, for which his friend Balthus designed the sets and costumes. The play did not run for long but was regarded as a revolutionary theatrical event. Afterwards Artaud travelled to Mexico (where he witnessed the peyote ceremony of the Tarahumaras Indians) and Ireland (from which he was forcibly repatriated in a straitjacket). Suffering from ill health and the effects of drug-taking he was taken to the general hospital at Le Havre on arrival on 30 September 1936. He spent the next nine years interned in various psychiatric hospitals and was released in May 1946.

Artaud spoke of the theatre in terms of an immense coloured painting in motion, which the actors peopled with living signs, and he considered all large paintings in terms of a finished spectacle, taking his inspiration from Paolo Uccello, André Masson, Lucas van Leyden and Edward Burne-Jones. He fitted Francisco de Goya, Hieronymus Bosch, Pieter Bruegel the elder, El Greco, Johannes Vermeer, Leonardo da Vinci and Henri Matisse into his own frame of reference, and painting is rarely absent from his writing, as is brilliantly demonstrated in one of his last texts, *Van Gogh, le suicidé de la société* (1947). Artaud had himself started drawing again in 1939 in the letters he sent from the asylum of Ville-Evrard, combinations of conjuration and malediction with calligraphy and patterns and streaks of bright colours occupying a page burnt in various places with a match or a cigarette (e.g. 1939, Dr Léon Fouks priv. col., see 1987 exh. cat., no. 10). It was in 1945, however, in the Rodez asylum that Artaud began to draw again seriously. His large compositions in colour, in which the page is filled with objects, organic shapes, truncated bodies and bones interspersed with writing, date from this period. These works can be seen as attempts to 'reassemble a new human body', as in *Execration of the Father–Mother* (see fig.). Drawing and writing became inseparable, co-existing in these compositions and in his manuscripts from then on, both of them having the same poetic function and the same explosive power. Artaud continued writing and drawing until his death. He undertook a series of large portraits that are

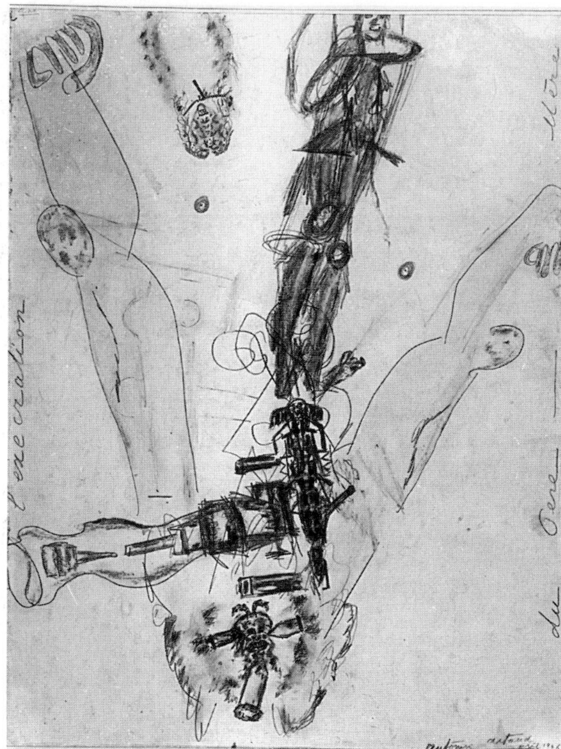

Antonin Artaud: *Execration of the Father–Mother*, pencil, pastel and watercolour, 640×490 mm, 1946 (Paris, Pompidou, Musée National d'Art Moderne)

striking in their expressiveness, with the contained violence of their strokes and the gentle vibrance of their shapes (e.g. the portrait of *Minouche Pastier*, charcoal and pastel, 1947; Paris, Pompidou). The gaze in these portraits is almost impossible to meet; Artaud made the human face the field of a desperate search, which turns each portrait into 'the explosive fuse of the beating of a shattered heart'. The poetry of the portraits and other drawings, which he was adamant should not be considered as works of art, is intense and overwhelming. Although the exhibition held in his lifetime, in July 1947 at the Galerie Pierre in Paris, attracted only his friends and a few rare admirers, the strange beauty and importance of the drawings were later widely recognized.

WRITINGS

'Correspondance avec Jacques Rivière', *Nouv. Rev. Fr.*, 132 (1924); as book (Paris, 1927); also in *Oeuvres complètes*, i; Eng. trans. in *Selected Writings*

Le Théâtre et son double (Paris, 1938; Eng. trans., New York, 1958/*R* London, 1970)

Van Gogh, le suicidé de la société (Paris, 1947); also in *Oeuvres complètes*, xiv; Eng. trans. in *Selected Writings*

Le Visage humain... (exh. cat., Paris, Gal. Pierre, 1947); also in *L'Ephémère*, 13 (1970)

Oeuvres complètes, 16 vols (Paris, 1956–81; rev. 1970–)

Collected Works, 4 vols (London, 1968–75)

S. Sontag, ed.: *Selected Writings* (New York, 1976)

'Dix ans que le langage est parti...', *Luna-Park*, 5 (1979)

BIBLIOGRAPHY

'Antonin Artaud', *Cah. Abbaye Ste-Croix*, 37 (1980) [whole issue to coincide with exhibition at Les Sables d'Olonne, Mus. Abbaye Ste-Croix]

F. Mèredieu: *Antonin Artaud: Portraits et gris-gris* (Paris, 1984)

P. Thévenin: 'Antonin Artaud: Autoportrait', *A. Press*, 101 (1986)

——: 'Dessin, peinture, théâtre', *Théât. Europe*, 11 (1986)

P. Thévenin and J. Derrida: *Antonin Artaud: Dessins et portraits* (Paris and Munich, 1986)

Antonin Artaud: Dessins (exh. cat., Paris, Pompidou, 1987)

PAULE THÉVENIN

Artaud de Montor, Jean-Alexis-François, Chevalier (*b* Paris, 21 July 1772; *d* Paris, 12 Nov 1849). French diplomat, collector and writer. As a diplomat, in Rome, he represented the French royal princes exiled during the Revolution. Later, under the Consulate he was assistant to the diplomat and collector François Cacault in the negotiation of the Concordat with the papacy. From 1804 to 1807 he was *chargé d'affaires* to Queen Marie-Louise of Etruria, and after the Bourbon restoration he was secretary at the French embassies in Vienna, Madrid and, most importantly, in Rome from 1819 to 1830. His love of Italy found expression in a number of published works on Italian history and a translation of Dante's *Divina commedia*. Influenced by the taste and writings of Jean-Baptiste Séroux d'Agincourt—and constrained by his limited financial means—Artaud assembled a collection of Italian primitives that was quite original in its day. It was chiefly made up of Sienese and Florentine pictures and included works then attributed to Fra Mino Turrita and to the Master of San Gaggio (e.g. Washington, DC, N.G.A., Chambéry, Mus. B.-A.), as well as to Giotto, Andrea di Cione, Nardo di Cione (*Virgin and Child with Saints*; New York, Hist. Soc.), Masaccio and Paolo Uccello, among others. He brought his collection to public attention most effectively by publishing his *Considérations sur l'état de la peinture dans les trois siècles qui ont précédé Raphaël* (1808). Artaud also owned a number of medals and a collection of portraits that illustrated his interest in Italy and the Renaissance. These included images of Machiavelli, Raphael, Bianca Capello and Louis XII. Artaud's involvement with circles interested in Italian archaeology and art were indicated by the presence in his collection of drawings by Jean-Auguste-Dominique Ingres, François-Marius Granet and Jean-Baptiste Wicar, among others. The collection was dispersed at auction in Paris in 1850 (2–3 April) and 1851 (16–17 January).

WRITINGS

Considérations sur l'état de la peinture dans les trois siècles qui ont précédé Raphaël (Paris, 1808); as *Peintres primitifs: Collection de tableaux rapportée d'Italie et publiée par M. le Chevalier Artaud de Montor* (Paris, 1843)

BIBLIOGRAPHY

DBF

Biographie des hommes vivants (Paris, 1816), p. 115

F. Haskell: *Rediscoveries in Art: Some Aspects of Taste, Fashion and Collecting in England and France* (London, 1976), p. 40, pls 100–01

□

Art autre [Fr.: 'other art']. Term coined in a book published in 1952 by French writer and critic Michel Tapié to describe the kind of art many intellectuals and artists deemed appropriate to the turbulent mood of France immediately after World War II. He organized an exhibition entitled *Un Art autre* for the Studio Facchetti, in Paris, also in 1952. Inspired in part by the ideas of Vasily Kandinsky, by Existentialist philosophy and by the widespread admiration for alternative art forms (notably child art, psychotic art and 'primitive' non-Western art), Tapié advocated an art that worked through 'paroxysm, magic, total ecstasy', in which 'form, transcended, is heavy with the possibilities of becoming'. He wrote of the need for 'temperaments ready to break up everything, whose works were disturbing, stupefying, full of magic and violence to re-route the public. To re-route into a real future that mass of so-called advanced public, hardened like a sclerosis around a cubism finished long ago (but much prolonged), misplaced geometric abstraction, and a limited puritanism which above anything else blocks the way to any possible, authentically fertile future'. Although the term has been used more or less interchangeably with ART INFORMEL and TACHISM as embodied in the expressive and non-geometric abstract work of artists such as Georges Mathieu, Henri Michaux and Wols, it also embraced the more figurative concerns of artists such as Jean Fautrier, Victor Brauner and Jean Dubuffet.

For illustrations *see* MATHIEU, GEORGES and WOLS.

BIBLIOGRAPHY

M. Tapié: *Un Art autre* (Paris, 1952)
——: *Morphologie autre* (Paris, 1960)

MONICA BOHM-DUCHEN

Art belle époque. *See* ART NOUVEAU.

Art brut [Fr.: 'raw art']. Term used from the mid-1940s to designate a type of art outside the fine art tradition. The commonest English language equivalent for *art brut* is 'Outsider art'. In North America, the same phenomenon tends to attract the label 'Grass-roots art'. The French term was coined by Jean Dubuffet, who posited an inventive, non-conformist art that should be perfectly *brut*, unprocessed and spontaneous, and emphatically distinct from what he saw as the derivative stereotypes of official culture. In July 1945 Dubuffet initiated his searches for *art brut*, attracted particularly by the drawings of mental patients that he saw in Switzerland. In 1948 the non-profit-making Compagnie de l'Art Brut was founded, among whose partners were André Breton and the art critic Michel Tapié. The Collection de l'Art Brut was supported for a while by the company but was essentially a personal hobby horse of Dubuffet and remained for three decades an almost entirely private concern, inviting public attention only at exhibitions in 1949 (Paris, Gal. René Drouin) and 1967 (Paris, Mus. A. Déc.). In 1971 Dubuffet bequeathed the whole collection to the City of Lausanne, where it was put on permanent display to the public at the Château de Beaulieu. At the time of opening (1976), the collection comprised 5000 works by *c.* 200 artists, but it grew thereafter.

Dubuffet's criteria for *art brut* were elaborated in a stream of texts, many polemical, some analytical, which include prefaces and letters, studies of individuals published in the house journal *L'Art brut*, and the abrasive tract *Asphyxiante culture* (1968). Dubuffet's ideal of autonomous inspiration rests on a model of the creator being somehow insulated from all social and cultural influences,

Guillaume Pujolle: *The Broken Violin*, watercolour, ink and coloured pencils, 475×635 mm, 1946 (Lausanne, Collection de l'Art Brut)

devoid of all schooling in the arts, and unaware of traditions or preset compositional formulae. The authentic specimen of *art brut* should be the unsolicited fruit of its maker's personal resources, being of value precisely as an index of the fertility and independence of individual vision. It should furthermore be made without thought of financial gain or public recognition. In due course Dubuffet had to relax his more stringent stipulations, conceding that even the most self-sufficient artist could hardly avoid some exposure to external influences. Nonetheless, he insisted, the concept of *art brut* remained an 'ideal pole' and a significant point of orientation. In practice the selection of items for his collection was sometimes determined by Dubuffet's prejudices and hunches: thus he would occasionally attribute excessive virtue to lacklustre work that happened to meet his other criteria or would somewhat spitefully exclude exciting work by individuals who had transgressed his 'rules' by exhibiting commercially. Although the phenomenon of *art brut* is incontrovertible, debate seems likely to persist with regard to the precise delimitation of its territory. Some difficulties arise because Dubuffet's thinking was focused on the status or posture of the creator rather than on the finished work. A purely aesthetic standard for evaluating works of *art brut* has never been agreed.

If Dubuffet's definition avoided singling out any one medium or style, it can be shown that a remarkable proportion of the artists falling into the category were ill-educated, retiring persons whose impulse to create arose late in life, often under the pressure of an emotional trauma, and took the form of a compulsive proliferation such that an isolated piece is often less telling than the cyclical ensemble. The Swiss psychotic ADOLF WÖLFLI, for example, spent some 30 years amassing in his asylum cell an enormous pictorial autobiography in which imaginary travels on a galactic scale are represented in colourful, tautly knit designs backed by florid captions and a ceaseless textual commentary. The London housewife Maud Ethel [Madge] Gill (1882–1961) claimed inspiration from the spirit world and over four decades produced an astonishing profusion of ink drawings that depict staring female faces caught in uncanny, asymmetrical interiors. The French mental patient Guillaume Pujolle (1893–*c.* 1965) translated his deliriums into watercolours in which recognizable forms dipped in eerie tints of black and pink dissolve amid quivering arabesque lines, to create a strong visionary effect (see fig.). The French farmer Emile Ratier (1894–1984) had to stop work at the age of 66 because he was going blind. His reaction to disability was to fashion toys out of rough wood and nails, and in due course he succeeded in constructing such large-scale working models as a two-metre high Eiffel Tower complete with moving lift and roundabouts on each floor. These crudely finished yet curiously assertive mechanisms have an ambiguous appeal. Whereas the Collection de l'Art Brut is predominantly composed of pictures and relatively small carvings and assemblages, it would seem legitimate to extend the term *art brut* to cover extensive environmental works fashioned in a similar spirit by creators such as Le Facteur (Ferdinand) Cheval (1836–1924) and Simon Rodia. Far removed from the mimetic aspirations of much naive art (with which it has erroneously been bracketed), *art brut* should above all be seen as an art of the subjective, the engrossed pursuit of inner obsessions, sign-systems and configurations. As such, its appeal is idiosyncratic and offbeat, although its marginal position on the general map of art does not preclude its products from exhibiting genuine power and a strange beauty.

BIBLIOGRAPHY

A. Brut, 1–9 (Paris, 1964–73), 10– (Lausanne, 1977–)
J. Dubuffet: *Asphyxiante culture* (Paris, 1968)
H. Raynal: 'Un Art premier', *Critique*, 258 (1968), pp. 965–83
R. Cardinal: *Outsider Art* (London, 1972)
J. Dubuffet: *L'Homme du commun à l'ouvrage* (Paris, 1973)
C. Lascault: 'La Pensée sauvage en acte', *L'Herne*, 22 (1973), pp. 218–33
H. Raynal: 'Le Personnage infini', *L'Herne*, 22 (1973), pp. 234–59
M. Thévoz: *L'Art brut* (Geneva 1975; Eng. trans., 1976)
G. Presler: *L'Art brut: Kunst zwischen Genialität und Wahnsinn* (Cologne, 1981)
G. Schreiner, ed.: *European Outsiders* (New York, 1986)
C. Delacampagne: *Outsiders: Fous, naïfs et voyants dans la peinture moderne (1880–1960)* (Paris, 1989)
W. Morgenthaler: *Madness and Art: The Life and Works of Adolf Wölfli* (London, 1992)
A. S. Weiss: *Shattered Forms,* Art brut, *Phantasms, Modernism* (Albany, 1992)
N. Wacher: *Peinture à partir du matériel brut et le rôle de la technique dans la création d'art* (Paris, 1993)

ROGER CARDINAL

Art Contemporain [Flem. Kunst van Heden]. Belgian exhibiting society of artists founded on 1 March 1905 in Antwerp and active from 1905 to 1955. Its founder, the dealer François Franck (1872–1932), was motivated by the many short-lived attempts by Antwerp artists to set up an artistic forum alongside or in opposition to the Société pour l'Encouragement des Beaux-Arts (founded in 1788) and the Cercle Artistique (founded in 1852). The society organized annual exhibitions in which the work of one or several late 19th century or contemporary artists was featured on a spectacular scale (e.g. Alfred Stevens in 1907), with artist-members often showing alongside representative groups of foreigners. Between 1918 and 1939 Art Contemporain gained a dominant position in the artistic life of Antwerp through its membership structure. The enterprise was financially supported by enthusiasts: dealers such as Henri Fester (1849–1939) and politically committed intellectuals such as G. Serigiers (1858–1930), Louis Franck (1869–1937), Pol De Mont (1857–1931) and Emmanuel De Bom (1868–1953). This group regarded the promotion of 'sincere and remarkable works of art, to whichever movement they might belong' as a prestigious mission to society. The multifarious, sometimes precarious composition of the society made it wary of particularly innovative art, and after exhibiting work by the Ecole de Paris there was open internal conflict, which brought further criticism from Antwerp's avant-garde artists. Nevertheless the work of members such as Jakob Smits, Albert Servaes, Georg Minne, Léon Spilliaert, Rik Wouters, Auguste Oleffe, Gustave Van de Woestyne, Edgard Tytgat, Gustave De Smet, Constant Permeke, Jean Brusselmans and others received ample attention. James Ensor was particularly fortunate to be promoted by Art Contemporain both at home and abroad. The close collaboration between the society and the Koninklijk Museum voor Schone Kunsten in Antwerp has a continuing significance as a result of the museum's purchases at the time, the gifts given by Friends of Modern Art (after 1925) and those of individuals, of which Charles Franck (1870–1935) and François Franck were the most prominent.

BIBLIOGRAPHY

Art Contemporain produced catalogues for its annual exhibitions at the Koninklijk Museum voor Schone Kunsten, Antwerp, in 1905–14, 1920–44, 1947–54.

W. Koninckx and M. Gevers: *Trente années au service de l'art* (Antwerp, 1935)

L'Art contemporain/Kunst van Heden (exh. cat., Antwerp, Kon. Mus. S. Kst., 1955)

R. Avermaete: *Een eeuw Antwerps mecenaat* [A century of patronage in Antwerp] (Brussels, 1974), pp. 93–119, 150–64

In dienst van de kunst: Antwerps mecenaat rond 'Kunst van Heden' (1905–1955) [In the service of art: Antwerp's patronage of *Kunst van Heden* (1905–1955)] (exh. cat. by M. Browaeys and others, Antwerp, Kon. Mus. S. Kst., 1991)

HERWIG TODTS

Art criticism. Term that may be defined loosely as writing that evaluates art, although there is no universally agreed meaning. The difficulty in its definition arises from fundamentally antithetical usages. While on the one hand art criticism is understood as a historical practice, embracing such writers as Pliny and Giorgio Vasari and continuing to the present, on the other it represents a kind of writing that is potentially independent of historical conditions. There is still no reliable history of art criticism, and virtually no literature on its nature. Some philosophers deny that art criticism exists as such, and others say it subsumes art history. The disparity of views as to the concept's nature makes appropriate separate discussions of the alternate definitions.

1. Art criticism as a kind of writing. 2. Art criticism as a historical practice.

1. ART CRITICISM AS A KIND OF WRITING. When treated in this way, art criticism has normally been considered evaluative or judgemental rather than descriptive. As such it may be contrasted with art history. The distinction between the two has, however, been criticized on at least three grounds. First, each definition of art criticism that opposes it to the ostensibly more neutral, descriptive work of art history represses both the inherent and continuous judgements in all historical writing and the philosophic argument that description and evaluation are inevitably mixed in all writing. Much art history depends on such a refusal, maintaining its ostensibly neutral position in part by excluding art criticism and defining it as judicative. The complementary exclusion can be observed in art criticism. Lionello Venturi called the distinction between art history and criticism a 'grave error', adding 'if a fact referred to is not considered as a function of judgement, it is perfectly useless' (Venturi, p. 20). Similarly, Grassi and Pepe's *Dizionario della critica d'arte* contains a brief entry on art criticism, noting that it is inseparable from historical writing.

Second, art criticism has also been distinguished from art history by noting that criticism has a different rhetorical purpose, since it is intended to persuade rather than inform. This does not, however, provide a stable definition, since no art-historical text leaves its reader unaffected by its implicit judgements regarding value and significance (Fried). Some of the most eloquent art historians, such as Roberto Longhi, have created persuasive re-evaluations of past art at least as much as they produce authoritative compilations of facts. Although Heinrich Wölfflin insisted that there was 'no question' of judgement in his work, his descriptions are persuasive precisely because they are such strong judgements.

Third, the historiography of art history provides evidence that many of the practices that gave rise to art history were conceived as critical enterprises that mixed evaluation and description (*see* ART HISTORY, §I). Vasari's writing is frequently cited as an example of mixed critical and factual narrative (Alpers). There is also the 17th-century practice of *ars critica* (von Dunin Borkowski, pp. 136–308), which laid the foundations for the higher biblical criticism and furnished 'the example for classical, and later modern, philology' (McKeon, p. 163) that in turn proved so fruitful for the developing discipline of art history. Thus for these reasons it is philosophically, rhetorically and historiographically untenable to maintain the distinction between art history and art criticism on the grounds that one evaluates and the other describes.

The problem is symmetrical: like most art history, some art criticism is conceived as non-judgemental and for the sake of knowledge only. In particular, criticism can be understood as imaginative re-enactment of creation or perception, with no determinate relation to evaluation. EKPHRASIS can function in this way and has done, from ancient times, with Pliny, Callistratus (*fl c.* 365 BC) and the Philostratus family, through to Vasari in the 16th century AD (see Mitchell, pp. 151–81). In German aesthetics at the turn of the 20th century, the doctrine of empathy (*Einfühling*), as first used by Robert Vischer (1847–1933), provided a foundation for writing that critically re-imagined the bodily experience of works of art (Vischer in Mallgrave and Ikonomou, p. 22). In the 1930s the American John Dewey proposed that criticism should not appraise or judge, but that 'we lay hold of the full import of a work or art only as we go through in our own vital processes the processes the artist went through in producing the work' (Dewey, p. 325). Benedetto Croce's concept of imaginative understanding had been similar (Croce, p. 42). Venturi's *History of Art Criticism* can be read as a second-order work of this kind, since he aimed in part to relive older critical experiences without judging them.

When art criticism is considered as an evaluative activity, it can be conceived either as personal response without explicit purpose or thesis, or as measured judgement governed by premeditated principles. The two provide divergent genealogies for the juridical aspect of art criticism. The first strategy comes from Romantic poetry, confession and reverie, and yields texts that can be read as the potentially idiosyncratic exercise of individual sensibility (*see also* AESTHETICS, §II, 4(i)); in general the second derives from Enlightenment philosophy and results in texts that aim to present an ostensibly true, universal or reliable assessment of the value of a work of art. In this first, more personal response, writers have characteristically pointed to the intimacy of writing about art. They have emphasized its dependence on the idea of sensibility or taste: thus Charles Baudelaire called for criticism that would be 'partial, passionate and political' (Baudelaire, p. 87), and FRIEDRICH NIETZSCHE practised a personal and psychological criticism of philosophy and art. Ultimately these tendencies could be traced back to

Plato's dialectic criticism, in which dialogue and opinions constitute the medium from which critical judgements emerge, as opposed to Aristotle's 'scientific' criticism, which is based on expository description and the rational unfolding of knowledge (McKeon, p. 162). Contemporary art criticism that depends on sensibility, personal reflection and taste is, however, more often understood as a fundamentally Romantic and post-Romantic enterprise (de Man).

A limitation of this approach is that it restricts the history of art criticism to certain strains of 19th- and 20th-century writing, excluding such writers as Johann Joachim Winckelmann and Denis Diderot in the 18th century and even Clement Greenberg in the 20th, because each of them proposed to speak according to explicit principles as much as from personal sensibility. In addition, this way of construing art criticism risks blurring the line between art criticism and any writing with a strong personal content. In the 20th century there have been various attempts to question the distinction between philosophy and writing, and more specifically to produce hybrids of art criticism that are partly philosophic, depending on the rational unfolding of principles, and partly literary in this sense (Deleuze and Guattari, 1991; Deleuze, 1993). It could perhaps be asked whether such forms of writing fail to take seriously the conventional and institutional divisions that continue to distinguish art criticism from art history.

Regarding the second strategy, in the Englightenment philosophic tradition, the word *Kritik* took on a specific meaning: the principled negotiation between destructive scepticism and constructive systematics (Schneiders; Ricoeur). A critique in this sense is neither purely critical nor merely hortative but uses explicitly developed principles and assumptions in order to achieve a moderated position. Argument takes the place of assertion, and doubt replaces dogma (Booth). This orientation produces texts that are governed by 'the philosophic principles assumed in the critical judgements', the 'conception of artistic purpose' and of art, and the selection and application of critical criteria and evidence (McKeon, p. 130). In other words, the rational examination of argument comprises part of the structure and meaning of the text. This form of inquiry continues to be common in philosophy, but relatively little art criticism makes important or consistent use of named principles, although contemporary counter-examples exist (Danto; McEvilley). Nor is such writing usually a continuation of the Enlightenment tradition of critiques as measured negotiations between conflicting propositions, so that contemporary art criticism sometimes becomes more dogmatic, excoriative or advisory than exploratory (or Socratic). Instead of seeking to navigate between conflicting assumptions to produce moderate solutions, such writing takes on the more rigid rhetorical forms of dogmatic criticism (Kramer). For both these reasons evaluative art criticism that proceeds from named principles is less frequent than criticism that works in a more intimate, personal way.

2. ART CRITICISM AS A HISTORICAL PRACTICE. In the West art criticism has been considered a historical practice in two potentially contradictory ways: by its description as a collection of texts and passages, without reference to any strong organizing principle; and by its restriction to times and places when the term 'art criticism' or its cognates were used by the writers themselves. In the latter, art criticism is a relatively recent practice, since the distinction between criticism and history was not made in modern terms until the early 18th century by such writers as Jonathan Richardson. Most histories of art criticism concentrate, however, on the first interpretation, assembling a diverse range of writings from different periods in Western culture. Thus the modern, Western sense of art criticism may be discerned in Western ancient, medieval and Renaissance texts, and also texts outside the Western world. Grassi opened his history of art criticism with Plato, and Venturi began his in the 3rd century BC with Xenocrates of Sikyon and Antigonos of Karystos, and continued with Roman authors, including Vitruvius and Lucian of Samosata, and on to St Augustine, Theophilus, the Polish student of optics Witelo (*c*. 1233–78) and Dante's observations about Cimabue and Giotto. A difficulty with such an approach is that critical writings about art can be found practically anywhere. The Latin author Heraclius (*c*. 575–641) wondered how the Romans incorporated gold into their glassware, and Venturi mentioned him along with more philosophic questions of expression raised by Theophilus, and Witelo's preference for almond-shaped eyes.

Such application becomes more convincing for later periods, since there is a continuity of preferences among Renaissance writers from Lorenzo Ghiberti and Filarete to Vasari. Critical literature after the Renaissance is recognizable as a genre, especially in such writers associated with the French Académie as Charles Le Brun, Charles Perrault, Roger de Piles and Denis Diderot. The criticism of the Salons in Paris forms a large resource for historians of the late 18th century and the 19th, and the reception of Impressionism (*see* IMPRESSIONISM, §6) helped consolidate the practice into a profession. The clarity begins to weaken again, however, when moving from the late 19th century and into the 20th. Even in the early 19th century, such philosophers as Georg Wilhelm Friedrich Hegel and August Wilhelm Schlegel had begun to challenge distinctions between the criticism, philosophy and history of art. The span from Jonathan Richardson's definition of art criticism to Schlegel's re-evaluation is only 80 years—a somewhat short time when the term 'art criticism' was both explicit and relatively unchallenged. The problem is exacerbated in the 20th century, not least because in the late 20th century art criticism no longer took place within the nationalist, academic and anti-academic discursive frames that first gave it meaning, but became combined with cultural criticism in general and with pieces of formerly unrelated kinds of writing: an art critic might write about journalism or shopping as much as about art, and it can be difficult to see how such writing can sensibly be described as a descendent of 18th- or 19th-century practice.

In addition to this problem of historical focus, historical definitions of art criticism are also difficult to apply to writings about art outside the Western world (*see also* ART HISTORY, §III, 4). Several cultures developed aesthetic discourses about their own art independent of Western influence, but none has terms strictly comparable to 'art criticism'. Instead the discourses constitute collections of critical practices. For African art there is a large literature reporting the ways that sculptors judge their work, but much of it either involves non-verbal judgements, as in a study of Kwele preferences (Child and Sirotto, in Jopling), or linguistically simple assessments requiring only comparative adjectives (Crowley, in Jopling). When indigenous words are applied to the evaluation of art, as in the Yoruba concept of *iwa* or the Fang concepts of opposition and vitality, they tend to be common also to various areas outside specifically art experience, making it difficult to assess whether their meanings are adequately reported by researchers who necessarily bring other concepts to their research. Because art criticism does not constitute a separate discourse in African traditions, it can be called art criticism only in the rudimentary sense of 'discourse about art' rather than for any more coherent correspondence to Western aesthetics and criticism. (For further discussion of African concepts of art *see* AFRICA, §II, 2).

In China, writing about visual art began at least as early as the 4th century AD (*see* CHINA, §V, 5). Treatises by such writers as Xie He (*fl c.* 500–35), Zhang Yanyuan (9th century), Guo Ruoxu (11th century) and Xia Wenyuan (14th century) include descriptive, critical, formal and philosophical terms (Sirén), so that it would be no less inappropriate to say that they were writing amalgams of art history and criticism than to say Vasari was writing in those genres without being fully aware of the fact. Several key concepts, such as *qiyun shengdong* ('spirit consonance'), have no adequate correlates in Western languages, making it difficult to find common ground. The *Lidai minghua ji* ('Record of famous painters of all periods') by Zhang Yanyuan begins with descriptions of painting's power to promote Confucian ethical values and its magical connection with the 'divine permutations' of nature. This is a double origin that places the remainder of the author's critical terms, no matter how familiar they might appear, outside the domain of Western aesthetics—even though Zhang distinguishes between criticism and history in the same way.

In the Islamic tradition, such texts as Qazi Ahmad ibn Mir Munshi's compendium *Gulistān-i hunar* ('Rose-garden of art', AD 1606; for others *see* ISLAMIC ART, §III, 2(i)(c)) mingle theological concepts with graphical, historical and critical terms. The concept of the *qalam*—the calligrapher's pen and the painter's brush—is at once a divine creation, since it was made by God: a term in historical narrative, since it was passed on from one style and one artist to the next; and a critical tool, because it enables the author to speak about the particular beauties of each artist's work. In each of these cases, the specific differences between the texts and traditions militate against a parallel with Western art criticism, and the task for a more reflective historiography would be to find other categories to put in its place.

BIBLIOGRAPHY

R. Vischer: *Über das optische Formgefühl: Ein Beitrag zur Aesthetik* (Leipzig, 1873)
F. Nietzsche: *Ecce homo* (Leipzig, 1908); Eng. trans. by W. Kaufmann (New York, 1989)
B. Croce: *Problemi di estetica* (Bari, 1910)
C. Baudelaire: 'Curiosités aesthétiques', *Oeuvres complètes* (Paris, 1923)
J. Dewey: *Art as Experience* (New York, 1934)
S. von Dunin Borkowski: *Spinoza*, iv of *Aus den Tagen Spinozas* (Münster, 1936)
O. Sirén: *The Chinese on the Art of Painting* (Beijing, 1936)
R. McKeon: 'The Philosophic Bases of Art and Criticism, Part Two', *Mod. Philol.*, xli (1944), pp. 129–71
S. Alpers: '*Ekphrasis* and Aesthetic Attitudes in Vasari's Lives', *J. Warb. & Court. Inst.*, xxiii (1960), pp. 190–215
C. Gilbert: 'Lionello Venturi', *A. Mag.*, xxxvi/5 (1962), pp. 58–60
L. Venturi: *History of Art Criticism*, Eng. trans. by C. Marriott (New York, 1936; It. edn, Florence, 1945; rev. Eng. edn, New York, 1964)
C. F. Jopling, ed.: *Art and Aesthetics in Primitive Societies* (New York, 1971)
W. Booth: *Modern Dogma and the Rhetoric of Assent* (Chicago, 1974)
J. J. Pollitt: *The Ancient View of Greek Art: Criticism History and Terminology* (New Haven, 1974)
L. Grassi and M. Pepe: *Dizionario della critica d'arte*, 2 vols (Turin, 1978) [esp. vol. 1, pp. 135–6]
T. S. R. Boase: *Giorgio Vasari: The Man and the Book* (Princeton, 1979)
M. Podro: *The Critical Historians of Art* (New Haven, 1982)
A. Potts: 'Winckelmann's Construction of History', *A. Hist.*, v/4 (1982), pp. 377–407
P. de Man: *Blindness and Insight: Essays in the Rhetoric of Contemporary Fiction* (1983), vii of *Theory and History of Literature*, ed. W. Godzich and J. Schulte-Sasse (Minneapolis, 1983)
H. Kramer: *Revenge of the Philistines: Art and Culture, 1972–1984* (New York, 1985)
W. Schneiders: 'Venünftiger Zweifel und wahre Eklektik: Zur Entstehung des modernen Kritikbegriffes', *Stud. Leibnit.*, xvii/2 (1985), pp. 143–61
C. Parsons: *A Bibliography of Salon Criticism in Second Empire Paris* (Cambridge, 1986)
S. Vogel: *African Aesthetics* (New York, 1986)
M. Fried: *Courbet's Realism* (Chicago, 1990)
P. Ricoeur: *Soi-même comme un autre* (Paris, 1990); Eng. trans. by K. Blamey (Chicago, 1992)
G. Deleuze and F. Guattari: *Qu'est-ce que la philosophie?* (Paris, 1991); Eng. trans. by H. Tomlinson and G. Burchell (New York, 1994)
N. McWilliam: *A Bibliography of Salon Criticism in Paris from the Ancien Régime to the Restoration, 1699–1827* (New York, 1991)
——: *A Bibliography of Salon Criticism in Paris from the July Monarchy to the Second Empire, 1831–1851* (New York, 1991)
A. Danto: *Beyond the Brillo Box: The Visual Arts in Post-historical Perspective* (New York, 1992)
G. Deleuze: *Critique et clinique* (Paris, 1993)
T. McEvilley: *The Exile's Return: Toward a Redefinition of Painting for the Post-modern Era* (New York, 1993)
Empathy, Form, and Space: Problems in German Aesthetics, 1873–1893, trans. H. F. Mallgrave (ed.) and E. Ikonomou (Santa Monica, CA, 1994) [6 essays *c.* 1870–1900]
W. J. T. Mitchell: *Picture Theory: Essays on Verbal and Visual Representation* (Chicago, 1994)

JAMES ELKINS

Art Deco. Descriptive term applied to a style of decorative arts that was widely disseminated in Europe and the USA during the 1920s and 1930s. Derived from the style made popular by the Exposition Internationale des Arts Décoratifs et Industriels Modernes held in Paris in 1925, the term has been used only since the late 1960s, when there was a revival of interest in the decorative arts of the early 20th century. Since then the term 'Art Deco' has been applied to a wide variety of works produced during the inter-war years, and even to those of the German Bauhaus. But Art Deco was essentially of French origin, and the term should, therefore, be applied only to French works and those from countries directly influenced by France.

1. FRANCE. The development of the Art Deco style, or the *Style moderne* as it was called at the time, closely paralleled the initiation of the 1925 exhibition, and in many ways it was the product of it. The exhibition was originally conceived in 1907, and, unlike the Expositions

Universelles that had preceded it in Paris, it was a government-sponsored project aimed specifically at developing export markets for French decorative and applied arts. It was also an attempt to find solutions to a broad range of problems experienced by French art industries since the mid-19th century, when the machine and the division of labour had been introduced into the artistic process. The issues that the exhibition was to address included: cooperation between artists, craftsmen and commercial manufacturers; increasing international competition in the luxury goods trade (of which France traditionally had been a leader); professional training for artisans; and apprenticeship legislation. These concerns were extremely important for Paris, which then had the highest concentration of artisans of any European city. The issues at stake, however, were not only artistic and economic but also cultural and nationalistic: the luxury crafts were considered one of the nation's traditional sources of prestige. Although its programme stipulated that everything included had to be 'modern', the exhibition in fact had conflicting goals: encouraging a union between art and industry, while at the same time finding modern applications for traditional handicrafts that would otherwise be destined to disappear.

Preparations for an international decorative arts exhibition, first scheduled for 1915 but later postponed until 1925, led to a concerted effort on the part of French designers to define and develop a modern, specifically French style of decorative arts. Thus, many of the constituent elements of the Art Deco style were in place before 1914. Even though they sought a style that was outwardly modern, the artists of the Art Deco movement generally paid more attention to maintaining high-art traditions of luxury and quality than to exploring the functional aspects of domestic design. Formally, the Art Deco style was both a reaction to, and an emanation of, the French ART NOUVEAU style. Like Art Nouveau, the decorative repertory of Art Deco was based on nature, but, whereas the former often derived its formal language from exotic flowers and plants whose twisting and climbing stems were usually integrated into the structure of an object, the latter was much more restrained, rejecting running motifs and climbing stems for stylized and geometricized flower blossoms, often roses, gathered up and tied into bouquets or in baskets.

The Art Deco style was also influenced by the elegance and refinement of Viennese decorative arts and by the exoticism and strong vibrant colours of the BALLETS RUSSES, which had made its début in Paris in 1909. The couturier Paul Poiret and the architect and decorator Louis Süe visited the WIENER WERKSTÄTTE and were impressed by its strikingly original and cosmopolitan style of design, as well as by its emphasis on making the environment, from domestic furnishings to clothing and jewellery, a total work of art. Poiret returned from Vienna and founded the Ecole d'Art Décoratif Martine and Atelier Martine in 1911. The furnishings he produced combined the Orientalism and warm colours of the Ballets Russes with the French Empire style. Poiret's clothing and decorative designs were widely diffused in magazines and luxurious reviews such as the *Gazette du bon ton* (1912–25), most notably through the illustrations of Paul Iribe (1883–1935) and Georges Lepape (1887–1971).

Louis Süe founded the Atelier Français in Paris in 1912 and tried to create a modern style that made explicit references to the French tradition. Many of the characteristics of what was to become the Art Deco style were presented in a manifesto written by one of Süe's associates, the landscape artist and garden theorist André Vera (1881–1971). Entitled 'Le Nouveau Style', this was published in *L'Art décoratif* in January 1912: in it Vera contended that a modern style of decorative arts should reject internationalism and also pastiche but nevertheless continue French traditions, especially the rationalism of the Louis XVI period and the more comfortable and bourgeois Louis-Philippe style. For decoration, contrasts of rich, bold colours should supplant the pale tones typical of Art Nouveau, and baskets and garlands of flowers should replace the 18th-century repertory of torches, bows and arrows. The decorator Paul Follot created one of the earliest designs with these characteristics, which is deemed one of the first Art Deco works: a dining-room ensemble in sycamore, ebony and amaranth, which was exhibited at the Salon d'Automne of 1912 (Paris, Mus. A. Déc.). The chair backs were sculpted in an openwork design representing a basket of fruit and flowers.

This decorative and rather traditional current continued after 1918, reinforced by notions of a *retour à l'ordre*, which was the leitmotif of much post-war art in France. References to French classical art could be seen especially in

1. Art Deco armoire by Jacques-Emile Ruhlmann, amaranth, ivory, ebony and macassar, h. 1.26 m, *c.* 1922 (Paris, Musée des Arts Décoratifs)

decorative painting, sculpture and ceramics. The Art Deco movement was then led by Süe and the decorator André Mare (1885–1932), through their Compagnie des Arts Français (founded in 1919), together with André Groult (1884–1967), Clément Mère (*b* 1870), Paul Follot and the master cabinetmaker Jacques-Emile Ruhlmann. Their work continued the traditions of French *ébénisterie* and featured unusual combinations of luxurious and exotic materials, especially those from French colonies in Africa and Asia, such as ebony, palm-wood, rose-wood and shagreen (e.g. the armoire by Ruhlmann; see fig. 1). They based their aesthetic on contrasts of textures, colours and materials and on complicated techniques such as lacquer-work, marquetry and inlaid work using such materials as ivory and mother-of-pearl. Other references to the *ébénistes* of the Louis XVI period can be seen in the ingenious devices incorporated into furnishings, such as swivelling or inclinable desktops, drawers and flaps (e.g. the desk by Mère, *c.* 1923; Paris, Mus. A. Déc.). Influenced by Japanese art, these decorators tended to give a pictorial treatment to such large pieces of furniture as armoires and buffets, applying the decoration all over the surface rather than restricting it to joints or mouldings (e.g. Ruhlmann, cabinet, 1925; Paris, Mus. A. Déc.; and Süe and Mare, cabinet, 1927; Richmond, VA Mus. F.A.; *see* FRANCE, fig. 62).

The Art Deco movement encompassed a wide variety of decorative arts that were characterized by a certain sensuousness of curving forms, a lavish employment of luxurious materials and bold combinations of colours and floral patterns. The lacquered screens and furniture by Jean Dunand (1877–1942), who was also a master of *dinanderie* (*see* FRANCE, fig. 84), were often engraved or sculpted and decorated with incrustations of mother-of-pearl or eggshell. In the work of the most important silversmith of the period, Jean Puiforcat, the clean lines and smooth surfaces, occasionally decorated with semi-precious stones, testify to a new architectural approach that departs from the exaltation of surface decoration typical of traditional silverwork. The painter Charles Dufresne brought the Art Deco style to tapestry; many of his designs were produced by the Beauvais factory. Georges Fouquet (1862–1957), Jean Fouquet (1899–1984), Louis Cartier (1875–1942), Raymond Templier (1891–1968) and Gérard Sandoz (*b* 1902) were the master jewellers of Art Deco. They replaced traditional precious stones and naturalistic floral settings with hardstones such as onyx, coral and jade in compositions of stylized motifs with strong colour contrasts (e.g. the pendant by Georges Fouquet; see fig. 2). Decorative forged ironwork, with lively motifs of stylized roses and arabesques, was popular in domestic and public interiors of the period. Raymond Henri Subes (1893–1970) and Edgar Brandt (1880–1960) were two of the major exponents of this medium.

The Art Deco style reached its apogee at the Exposition Internationale des Arts Décoratifs et Industriels Modernes of 1925. In the climate of a post-war return to normality the exhibition lost much of its original emphasis on a union between art and industry and became instead a showcase for the finest products of the French luxury-goods industries. The most popular French pavilions were those devoted to a specific theme that demanded the collaborative effort of a group of artists. Among them was the sumptuous Hôtel d'un Collectionneur presented by Ruhlmann, its architecture by Pierre Patout. It featured furniture by Ruhlmann, lacquerwork by Dunand, forged ironwork by Brandt, sculpture by Joseph-Antoine Bernard, François Pompon and Emile-Antoine Bourdelle, and the large decorative painting *The Parrots* (New York, priv. col.) by Jean Dupas (1882–1964), one of the few painters to whom the appellation Art Deco can justly be applied. The Société des Artistes Décorateurs presented decorative ensembles destined for a French embassy. Paul Poiret

2. Art Deco pendant by Georges Fouquet, diamonds, precious stones and mother-of-pearl, 1927 (private collection)

presented his collections in three *péniches* (barges) entitled *Amours*, *Délices* and *Orgues* decorated by Raoul Dufy. In the pavilion entitled Musée d'Art Contemporain, Süe and Mare presented a grandiose music-room furnished with a desk in ebony and bronze and a grand piano with curved legs in a modernized Louis XV style. The interior decoration studios of the major department stores in Paris—Au Printemps (Primavera), Galeries Lafayette (La Maîtrise), Au Bon Marché (La Pomone) and the Grands Magasins du Louvre (Studium)—each had their own pavilions and were important in diffusing the Art Deco style.

Art Deco began to decline in France after the exhibition of 1925, as a more functionalist and internationalist group of designers emerged who were opposed to the decorative extravagance, nationalism and traditionalism of Art Deco. They formed the Union des Artistes Modernes in 1929. It could be argued that the influence of Art Deco continued in France during the 1930s in such ensembles as the liner *Normandie* (1935), but by 1930 proportions were becoming more monumental and forms heavier and fuller, without the ornamental exuberance so characteristic of Art Deco.

2. USA. Because of the popularity of the 1925 exhibition, and through the diffusion of luxurious government-sponsored publications featuring the works displayed in the French section, the Art Deco style had a widespread international influence, especially in the USA. The Metropolitan Museum of Art in New York made numerous purchases from the exhibition and a display of 400 objects travelled to major American cities in 1926. The New York department store Lord & Taylor held yet another exhibition of the *Style moderne* in 1928. In spite of this, little that was produced in the USA during the late 1920s and early 1930s truly corresponds to the French works dating from 1920 to 1925, so the term 'Art Deco' should be used with caution. The USA simply did not have the luxury craft tradition that lay at the heart of Art Deco. Most of the best designers working in the USA from 1926 to 1930, and whose work has been labelled 'Art Deco' in popular publications, were industrial designers born and trained in Europe. Joseph Urban, Paul Frankl and Kem Weber (1889–1963), for example, were from Vienna, and the rationalism and geometry of the furnishings produced by the Wiener Werkstätte, rather than the French *Style moderne*, are clearly the source of their design. Frankl integrated the Viennese style with a specifically American skyscraper aesthetic (e.g. the 'Skyscraper' bookcase, *c.* 1928; Cincinnati, OH, A. Mus.). Other designers in America incorporated the rich colours and decorative geometries of the French *Style moderne* with a machine aesthetic. The interiors designed by Donald Deskey (1894–1989) for Radio City Music Hall (1931) testify to the pervasive influence of French Art Deco, especially in their refinement and polychrome decoration, but they were infused with a rationalism, urban sophistication and modern use of materials that were not prevalent in France until the 1930s. Art Deco, in addition, should not be used to describe a style of architecture, but rather its surface ornament. If the Chrysler Building (William Van Alen, 1929; *see* SKYSCRAPER, fig. 2) in New York displays certain Art Deco influences in the decorative stainless-steel sunburst of the upper floors, its mechanistic iconography referring to automobiles was not part of the Art Deco repertory. The lobby, however, with its expensive marbles and richly decorated elevator doors with an intarsia design in the form of a papyrus flower, is a masterpiece of the Art Deco style. One can find the decorative motifs of the French *Style moderne* applied to the entrance of the Goelet Building (E. H. Faile, 1930) at 608 Fifth Avenue, New York, and to the top floors of the Kansas City Power and Light Company Building (Hoit, Price & Barnes, 1932).

A highly exaggerated and commercialized version of Art Deco was popular in cinemas and theatres during the late 1920s, notably in the Pantages Theatre (Marcus B. Priteca, 1929–30) in Los Angeles. By the mid-1930s the Art Deco influence on American design gave way to the horizontal, flowing, streamlined style that was evocative of speed and a technological Utopia.

BIBLIOGRAPHY

Encyclopédie des arts décoratifs et industriels modernes au XXe siècle, 12 vols (Paris, 1932/*R* New York and London, 1977) [official edition for the Paris *Exposition internationale des arts décoratifs et industriels modernes*, 1925]
B. Hillier: *Art Deco of the 20s and 30s* (London, 1968)
G. Veronesi: *Style 1925: Triomphe et chute des 'Arts-Déco'* (Lausanne and Paris, 1968)
Y. Brunhammer: *The Nineteen-twenties Style* (London, 1969)
Art Deco: Schmuck und Bücher aus Frankreich (exh. cat., foreword by F. Falk; Pforzheim, Schmuckmus.; Munich, Villa Stuck; Hamburg, Mus. Kst & Gew.; 1975–6)
C. Bizot and M. Béranger: *Bibliographie 1925* (Paris, 1976)
Cinquantenaire de l'Exposition de 1925 (exh. cat. by Y. Brunhammer and others, Paris, Mus. A. Déc., 1976–7)
V. Arwas: *Art Deco* (London, 1980, rev. 1992)
A. Duncan: *Art Deco Furniture: The French Designers* (London, 1984)
W. Uecker: *Art Deco: Die Kunst der zwanziger Jahre* (Munich, 1984)
P. Cabanne: *Encyclopédie Art Déco* (Paris, 1986)
A. Duncan: *American Art Deco* (London, 1986)
P. Frantz Kery: *Art Deco Graphics* (London, 1986)
Y. Brunhammer and S. Tise: *French Decorative Art, 1900–1942* (Paris, 1990)
M. Dufrene, ed: *Authentic Art Deco Interiors* (Woodbridge, Suffolk, 1990) [illustrates the 96 interiors in the 1925 *Exposition internationale des arts décoratifs et industriels modernes*]

SUZANNE TISE

Arteaga, Sebastian López de. *See* LÓPEZ DE ARTEAGA, SEBASTIAN.

Arteaga y Alfaro, Matías de (*b* Villanueva de los Infantes, Ciudad Real, 3 Nov 1633; *d* Seville, 12 Jan 1703). Spanish painter and etcher. He is first documented in Seville in 1652 and entered the painters' guild there on 16 June 1656. His mature style is predominantly influenced by the work of Murillo and, to a lesser extent, that of Juan de Valdés Leal. In 1675, with Bernardo Simón de Pineda, Arteaga y Alfaro designed the new altarpiece in the Royal Chapel in Seville Cathedral. His first independent commission dates from 1676, yet his finest work is the set of nine Old Testament scenes from 1690 (Seville Cathedral). Although he also worked as a gilder, the trade in painting with the New World was an important source of income for him. He was a prolific but not gifted etcher, producing prints from 1661 until the year of his death. His exact relationship to the etcher Bartolomé Arteaga (*fl* 1627) is unclear. Francisco de Arteaga (*d* 1679), Matías's son (not his brother), was also an etcher. In Seville, Arteaga y

Alfaro served the guild and the Real Academia de Santa Isabel de Hungría in various posts.

BIBLIOGRAPHY

Ceán Bermúdez

A. de la Banda y Vargas: 'Pinturas de Matías de Arteaga en la parroquia del Sagrario, Sevilla', *An. U. Hispal.*, xix (1959), pp. 75–87

——: 'Matías de Arteaga, grabador', *Bol. B.A. Real Acad. S Isabel Hungría*, vi (1978), pp. 75–131

D. Kinkead: 'Tres documentos nuevos del pintor don Matías de Arteaga y Alfaro', *Bol. Semin. Estud. A. & Arqueol.*, xlvii (1981), pp. 345–58

J. C. Agüera Ros: 'Nuevas aportaciones a la obra de Matías de Arteaga', *Goya*, clxix–clxxi (1982), pp. 133–7

A. de la Banda y Vargas: 'Nuevos datos para la biografía de Matías de Arteaga', *Archv Hispal.*, lxiv (1982), pp. 63–8

D. Kinkead: 'Nuevos datos sobre los pintores Juan de Valdés Leal y Matías de Arteaga y Alfaro', *Archv Hispal.*, lxv (1982), pp. 175–98

DUNCAN KINKEAD

Art education. Training in the practices and/or principles involved in making works of art. From the earliest times such practical knowledge has been passed on by demonstration and advice. The different systems of art education are discussed in sections of the various surveys of regions, countries and cultures, and this survey concentrates on a brief history of the development of art education in Western culture.

1. ANCIENT AND MEDIEVAL, BEFORE THE 16TH CENTURY. There is limited evidence for the nature of training in the ancient world. Crafts appear to have been family affairs, passed down from parents to children. The Babylonian tablet of legal codes laid down by King Hammurabi (*reg* 1792–1750 BC), which required the craftsman to teach his craft to the young, suggest a form of apprenticeship. Canons of proportion were devised and learnt: the Egyptian models were simpler but less flexible than the later, more subtle Greek ones, such as that of the sculptor POLYKLEITOS. The Greek painter Zeuxis is known to have taken pupils in the 5th century BC, and another, PAMPHILOS, had a school of painting at Sikyon. It is likely that his pupils would have been instructed in drawing, geometry, symmetry and the golden section, as well as in a canon of proportion.

Trade guilds arose in the 8th or 9th century AD and with them more organized systems of apprenticeship. A beginner, aged about twelve, would be bound to a master craftsman for two to seven years, living in his house. If training in painting, under instruction and supervision he would begin with menial tasks, such as grinding, straining and mixing pigments, before being entrusted with work requiring skill. CENNINO CENNINI described a course of drawing, and something similar probably existed in the best workshops at the beginning of the 15th century. If at the end of the apprentice's time his work was judged by the guild wardens to be of sufficiently high standard, he would be given a guild certificate and be allowed to practise as a journeyman. After a few years he could submit his MASTERPIECE to the guild and, if successful, set up shop as a master craftsman. Alongside this system, it was possible in the 16th century for a youth of good family, such as Benvenuto Cellini, to receive training without being formally apprenticed, so that he escaped the menial work of the shop and might leave when he wished. Alternatively, medieval craftsmen were members of monastic communities and were trained in their workshops. Scribes and illuminators, in particular, learnt their arts in the scriptorium, a room set aside, particularly in Benedictine monasteries, for the production of manuscripts.

2. THE RISE OF THE ACADEMY, 16TH AND 17TH CENTURIES. The Renaissance brought changes in the artist's social position allied to the notion that painting, sculpture and architecture were not mechanical but liberal arts. They were considered to differ from such arts as pottery, weaving and stained glass in that their practice demanded intellectual understanding of such matters as anatomy, perspective and Classical culture. Around 1490 Lorenzo de' Medici appointed the sculptor Bertoldo di Giovanni to instruct any outstanding apprentice in Florence. His teaching is presumed to have included the study of the ancient and contemporary sculpture in the Medici collection (*see* FLORENCE, §V, 2). Shortly afterwards the first academies were founded (*see* ACADEMY): informal gatherings, initially, of those interested in study and discussion of Classical culture, but with no teaching role. The Accademia del Disegno, set up in 1563 (*see* FLORENCE, §V, 1), did have teaching among its objectives, as proposed by Giorgio Vasari among others, but there little, if anything, was achieved in practice. The first to have education as its primary aim was the Accademia di S Luca (*see* ROME, §VI), founded in the 1590s under Federico Zuccaro. Its curriculum, taught by visiting tutors, consisted of copying from drawings or engravings, drawing from plaster casts and male models and lectures on subjects of aesthetic concern. Prizes were awarded. It was the model for future academies in other Italian towns and later elsewhere in Europe.

The academic curriculum was turned into a national institution in France when the Académie Royale de Peinture et Sculpture was founded in 1648 (*see* PARIS, §VI, 1). This was to be a model for countries as far apart as Mexico and Russia. In France architecture was taught as a separate subject after the foundation in 1671 of the Académie Royale d'Architecture (*see* PARIS, §VI, 2). Students of these academies spent a high proportion of their time in lectures and discourse and learning drawing; they also had access to a reference library. The French academies' rigid control of opinion and taste ensured that drawing was done only in an approved manner—so that the academy, initially a place for debate and research, was turned into the opposite of its original conception. As with the vast majority of academies until the end of the 19th century, no practical work in painting, modelling or carving was carried out in the academy itself; students still learnt these skills in the workshop or studio. Apart from a few isolated cases, female artists were not admitted into the academies (*see also* WOMEN AND ART HISTORY).

3. THE GROWTH OF ART SCHOOLS, 18TH AND 19TH CENTURIES. Two quite different factors brought about far-reaching changes in art education in the late 18th century. First, the virtual disappearance of the guilds brought workshop training to an end and encouraged artists to take fee-paying pupils (*see* STUDIO, §II, 3). For a long time there cannot have been much difference between what was taught in a painter's studio and in a medieval workshop, but by the mid-18th century a new pattern had

emerged: in Joseph-Marie Vien's studio, for instance, models were permanently at the pupils' disposal. The studio of Jacques-Louis David at the end of the century typified what was to come: there was no elementary teaching, and as many as 40 pupils drew and painted directly from casts or from life, with daily criticism of their work at noon by David. Later Parisian studios, such as those of Ingres, Thomas Couture, or the Académie Suisse and the Académie Julian, were run along similar lines. Some of these provided separate tuition for female pupils, although there was a long controversy over their access to life drawing.

Second, the young artists of the Romantic movement, who believed that nature and feeling should be the artist's guides, rather than rules and the art of the past, attacked everything that the academy stood for. It was increasingly seen as irrelevant and out of touch with modern life. Some academies responded with such reforms as introducing classes in landscape or raising the age of admission from 12 to 16 or 18. Several German schools instituted *Meisterklassen* where the student, after reaching a particular standard, could choose to work under one professor, rather than several.

In the early 18th century the notion that art should make a contribution to a country's commerce became increasingly important. New schools were established and new classes for artisans in the furnishing trades were added to existing academies, with the aim of improving the quality of manufactures and public taste. Among the first and certainly the most influential was the Ecole Royale Gratuite de Dessin (later Ecole Nationale des Arts Décoratifs), opened in Paris in 1767 under Jean-Jacques Bachelier. This had 1500 pupils and afternoon classes with the standard academic curriculum, except that pupils copied prints of flowers and historical ornament. Several guilds provided scholarships. In Britain the state became involved in art education when it was realized that mechanization had brought about a serious decline in the standard of industrial art, and that British manufactures were relying on imported designs, particularly from France. A School of Design was opened in London in 1837, under William Dyce, with branches in the provinces, but it failed to meet expectations. Renewed doubts about British design occasioned by the Great Exhibition (1851) led the government in 1852 to set up the Department of Practical Art (later Department of Science and Art, or DSA), run on academic lines under Henry Cole; this again had almost no influence on industrial art. Although women began to be more accepted in art institutions in the mid-19th century, they were still segregated and were associated more with applied art than fine art. A trade school of art for women was established in London in 1842.

The Arts and Crafts Movement, which owed its success primarily to the influence of WILLIAM MORRIS, brought about a radical transformation of art education. Morris taught that designer and maker should be one: that good design resulted from a practical understanding of the materials from which an object is made and the process of its manufacture. Art could not, as the DSA supposed, simply be applied to industry. Among the first public art schools to be influenced by the movement were the Birmingham School, which established practical classes for silversmiths and jewellers in 1893, and the Glasgow Design School, which added classes in decorative design. Until nearly the end of the 19th century there was little separate education for architects, who, generally speaking, learnt their trade as clerks in the offices of practising architects in much the same way as an apprentice, although some were able to attend academic drawing classes. Practical instruction started with the opening of arts and crafts schools. The Central School of Arts and Crafts was opened in London in 1896 under W. R. Lethaby, exclusively for those employed in the building and allied trades—architects, designers and craftworkers in glass, furniture, printing, metalwork etc. There students were taught the whole of a craft by practising craftsmen and craftswomen in specially equipped workshops. This proved an extremely influential model throughout Europe.

4. DEVELOPMENTS IN THE 20TH CENTURY. The German design school the BAUHAUS (1919–33) was influenced by the Arts and Crafts Movement, but here the emphasis was more with industry than craft. Under the direction of its founder, the architect Walter Gropius, all arts, crafts and design were theoretically integrated as one under architecture, with a foundation course (the *Vorkurs*) preceding full-time courses towards trade certificates. Workshop practice was emphasized, and new technologies were embraced. Although the Bauhaus was forced to close by the Nazis, its influence spread to the USA (for example to BLACK MOUNTAIN COLLEGE) and to many other countries. In the 20th century there were also major changes in the way in which the developing artistic ability of children was viewed, which led to different systems of teaching in some schools and in general a reassessment of the naivety in children's art as being untainted rather than defective (*see* CHILD ART, §2). The Jugendkunstklasse of Austrian art teacher Franz Cižek was instrumental in the idea that 'child-centred drawing' should be encouraged in schools. This approach contributed to a greater freedom of expression in later art schools but did not become prevalent. In the late 20th century art education in the Western world became largely based on university and college courses, with architecture completely separate from fine art and design, which in turn were generally kept as separate faculties. There might be individual courses in, for example, furniture, photography, painting, printmaking, jewellery etc, or a more cross-media emphasis as, for example, in a three-dimensional design course. In such institutions, students' time is divided into practical work done within the institution or sometimes as a placement with a commercial operation, and theoretical work in the form of lectures, seminars and written papers. Art history is sometimes included in studies. Many institutions encourage the use of technology in art, obtaining, for example, computers to be used in each faculty. A formal qualification is attained at the end of each course.

BIBLIOGRAPHY

C. Cennini: *Il libro dell'arte* (MS.; *c.* 1390s); trans. and notes by D. V. Thompson jr (1933)

F. Blondel: *Cours d'architecture enseigné dans l'Académie royale d'architecture* (Paris, 1675)

W. Smith: *Art Education* (Boston, 1873)

British Government Reports of the Royal Commission on Technical Education (1882–)

J. Gaudet: *Eléments et théorie de l'architecture: Cours professé à l'Ecole nationale et spéciale des beaux arts* (Paris, 1909)
J. Guiffrey: 'L'Histoire de l'Académie de St Luc', *Archv. A. Fr.*, n. s., ix (1915) [whole vol.]
S. MacDonald: *The History and Philosophy of Art Education* (Cambridge, 1940, rev. New York, 1973)
N. Pevsner: *Academies of Art Past and Present* (London, 1940, rev. New York, 1973)
A. C. Weatherhead: *The History of Collegiate Education in Architecture in the United States* (New York, 1941)
L. W. Rochowanski: *Die Wiener Jugendkunst: Franz Cižek und seine Pflegestätte* (Vienna, 1946)
Q. Bell: *The Government Schools of Design* (London, 1963)
G. Sutton: *Artisan or Artist* (London, 1967)
G. Naylor: *The Bauhaus* (London, 1968)
A. Boime: *The Academy and French Painting in the Nineteenth Century* (London, 1971)
A. Burford: *Craftsmen in Greek and Roman Society* (London, 1972)
J. Milner: *The Studios of Paris: The Capital of Art in the Late Nineteenth Century* (Yale, New Haven and London, 1988)
W. Chadwick: *Women, Art and Society* (New York, 1990)

GODFREY RUBENS

Arte generativo. Style of Argentine painting named in 1959 by EDUARDO MACENTYRE and MIGUEL ANGEL VIDAL to describe their work, with its power to generate optical sequences by circular, vertical and horizontal displacement, and based on their studies of Georges Vantongerloo. Developing the tradition of geometric abstraction that had emerged in Argentina in the 1940s with groups such as Arte Concreto Invención, Movimiento Madí and Perceptismo, the aim of these artists was to extol the beauty and perfection of geometry through line and colour. They and the collector Ignacio Pirovano (1919–80), who acted as their theorist, were soon joined by the engineer and painter Baudes Gorlero (1912–59), who as well as creating his own work also analysed its development mathematically. All three artists were awarded prizes in 1959 in the Argentine competition *Plástica con plásticos* by a jury that consisted of the French critic Michel Ragon, the American museum director Thomas Messer (*b* 1920), the French painter Germaine Derbecq (1899–1973) and the Argentine critic Aldo Pellegrini (1903–75), shortly after which Gorlero died. MacEntyre and Vidal produced the *Arte generativo* manifesto in 1960, not as a theoretical statement but as a 'clarification of ideas'. They distinguished the adjective 'generative' ('able to produce or engender') from the verb 'to engender' ('to procreate, to propagate the same species, to cause, occasion, form') and from the noun 'generatrix' ('a point, line or surface whose motion generates a line, surface or solid'). After exploring these ideas more fully they suggested that shapes 'produce *power* through the sensation of breaking free from and wishing to penetrate the basic plane and *energy* from the displacements and vibrations that they produce'. Both MacEntyre and Vidal relied on an analytical process, organizing basic units (curved lines for MacEntyre, straight lines in Vidal's case) in accordance with constant laws and subjecting them to inventive variations characterized by an impeccable technique, splendid colour and surprising power.

WRITINGS

E. MacEntyre and M. A. Vidal: *El arte generativo* (Buenos Aires, 1960)
I. Pirovano: 'Arte generativo: Eduardo MacEntyre, Miguel Angel Vidal', *Arte argentino contemporáneo* (Madrid, 1979)

Arte Madí. Argentine movement of the 1940s based in Buenos Aires and led by Gyula Košice and the Uruguayan artists Carmelo Arden Quin (*b* 1913) and Rhod Rothfuss (*b* 1920). Together with Joaquín Torres García and the Argentine poet Edgar Bayley (*b* 1919), they were responsible for the publication in early 1944 of a single issue of a magazine, *Arturo*, which heralded the development of the Constructivist movement in Argentina, stressing the importance of pure invention and of interdisciplinary links. Tomás Maldonado, who designed the cover, and Lidy Prati (*b* 1921), who was responsible for most of the vignettes, soon dissociated themselves from their colleagues to help set up the ASOCIACIÓN ARTE CONCRETO INVENCIÓN; the editorial content of the magazine, however, suggested a coherent aesthetic that was also promoted in booklets published by Košice and Bayley in 1945 and in two exhibitions, *Art Concret Invention* (which opened on 8 Oct 1945 in the house of the doctor and patron Enrique Pichon Rivière) and *Movimiento de Arte Concreto Invención* (from 2 Dec 1945 in the house of the photographer Grete Stern). Articles by Arden Quin and Košice stressed the pure quality of plastic images free of naturalistic or symbolic connotations, whose radical character was distinguished by Bayley from what he termed the falsity of such movements as Expressionism, Realism and Romanticism. Rothfuss's exposition of his ideas about shaped canvases, prefiguring by more than a decade devices taken up by American abstract painters, proved particularly influential.

An exhibition of manifestos, paintings, sculptures, poems and architectural maquettes, together with recitals of music and dance performances, titled simply *Madí*, was held in August 1946 (Buenos Aires, Inst. Fr. Estud. Sup.). It was followed by further group exhibitions entitled *Arte Madí* in October 1946 (Buenos Aires, Salón Altamira, and Buenos Aires, Bohemien Club, Gal. Pacífico) and 1948 (Paris, Salon Realités Nouv.) and by Košice's *Manifiesto Madí* of February–March 1947, which refers to drawing, painting, sculpture, architecture, music, poetry, theatre, novels, stories and dance. A journal, *Arte Madí Universal*, was also published from 1947 until June 1954. Košice's work, particularly his use of shaped canvases, light and movement, typified Arte Madí's emphasis on spectator participation and on new technologies and materials.

WRITINGS

E. Bayley: *Invención 2* (Buenos Aires, 1945)
G. Košice: *Invención 1* (Buenos Aires, 1945)
——: *Arte Madí* (Buenos Aires, 1982)

BIBLIOGRAPHY

Vanguardias de la década del 40, Arte Concreto–Invención, Arte Madí, Perceptismo (exh. cat., intro. N. Perazzo, Buenos Aires, Mus. Mun. A. Plást. Sívori, 1980)

NELLY PERAZZO

Arte Metafisica. *See* PITTURA METAFISICA.

Artemision Bronzes. Three ancient Greek bronze figures, now in the National Archaeological Museum, Athens. They were recovered in 1926 and 1928 from the sea-bed site of an ancient shipwreck off Cape Artemision at the northernmost point of Euboia, Greece. The most famous is the bronze statue identified as *Zeus* or *Poseidon* (h. 2.09 m), datable to the second quarter of the 5th century BC (*see* GREECE, ANCIENT, fig. 43). It is attributed to an Attic artist, perhaps Kalamis, who made the Omphalos *Apollo*. The figure represents a bearded man with long hair tied up at the back of his neck. He is poised to throw either a thunderbolt or a trident, depending on which of the two gods he portrays. The position of the fingers of the right hand suggests that the statue originally held a trident rather than a bolt of lightning, though Zeus is represented in a similar pose in numerous bronze statuettes (see Stewart, ii, pls 287–9). The hypothesis that this was the pose of an earlier cult statue in the Temple of Zeus at Olympia before Pheidias created his colossal chryselephantine *Zeus* (destr. in antiquity) should probably be discounted, since the god is represented at the moment of striking a blow, an unsuitable pose for the cult statue of a deity in his own temple. The suggestion that the figure represents not a god but the hero Erechtheos, possibly by Myron, from a group on the Acropolis, also seems unacceptable. There is a certain imprecision in the positioning of the lower part of the legs, but this may reflect damage from long submersion on the sea-bed and does not compromise the powerful sense of form achieved in this splendid figure. The two other bronzes, also important though later works, are a bronze statuette (h. 840 mm; late 2nd century BC–early 1st) of a *Young Negro Jockey* and part of a statue of a horse (h. 2.3 m). The latter was for some time thought to be unconnected with the *Jockey* and was dated to the 4th century BC, but both are now exhibited as a single work (see Stewart, ii, pl. 816).

BIBLIOGRAPHY

H. G. Beyen: *La Statue d'Artémision* (The Hague, 1930)
J. D. Beazley and B. Ashmole: *Greek Sculpture and Painting* (Cambridge, 1932), fig. 67
E. Buschor: *Die Plastik der Griechen* (Berlin, 1936), pp. 4, 105
M. Robertson: *A History of Greek Art*, 2 vols (Cambridge, 1975), i, pp. 196, 289, 330, 558–9; ii, figs 57b, 177c
A. Stewart: *Greek Sculpture: An Exploration*, 2 vols (New Haven and London, 1990)

LUCA LEONCINI

Arte nucleare [It.: 'nuclear art']. Term applied to a style of Italian painting prevalent in the 1950s. The Movimento Nucleare was founded in 1951 by ENRICO BAJ and Sergio Dangelo (*b* 1931), with Gianni Bertini (*b* 1922), to promote a gestural, fantastical style of avant-garde art. In their first manifesto (1952) the artists introduced the idea of 'nuclear painting' and made it clear that they were striving for a relevant representation of post-War man and his precarious environment. *Arte nucleare* stood in opposition to the powers unleashed in the atomic age and expressed the general fear of imminent and uncontrollable damage from nuclear physics. The artists also reacted against the pictorial disciplines of De Stijl and all forms of geometric abstraction, pursuing instead the unpredictable effects of Surrealist automatism. This included gestural experiments similar to action painting and Tachism. Various *Arte nucleare* artists, including Gianni Dova, helped produce the magazine *Phases* in the mid-1950s. In 1955 Baj and other *Arte nucleare* artists joined the Mouvement International pour une Bauhaus Imaginiste (MIBI), founded by Asger Jorn. A further manifesto was released by the *Arte nucleare* artists in January 1959. This warned against the negative application of new technology and also found possibilities of a positive, aesthetic development from some aspects of atomic fission. Although a few *Arte nucleare* exhibitions were held, the movement did not gain the currency enjoyed by its rival, *Art informel*, and by the early 1960s had faded from the international arena.

BIBLIOGRAPHY

E. Baj and S. Dangelo: *Manifeste de la peinture nucleare* (Brussels, 1952)
T. Sauvage: *Arte nucleare* (Milan, 1962)

□

Arte Povera [It.: 'impoverished art']. Term coined by the Genoese critic Germano Celant in 1967 for a group of Italian artists who, from the late 1960s, attempted to break down the 'dichotomy between art and life' (Celant: *Flash Art*, 1967), mainly through the creation of happenings and sculptures made from everyday materials. Such an attitude was opposed to the conventional role of art merely to reflect reality. The first Arte Povera exhibition was held at the Galleria La Bertesca, Genoa, in 1967. Subsequent shows included those at the Galleria De'Foscherari in Bologna and the Arsenale in Amalfi (both 1968), the latter containing examples of performance art by such figures as MICHELANGELO PISTOLETTO. In general the work is characterized by startling juxtapositions of apparently unconnected objects: for example, in *Venus of the Rags* (1967; Naples, Di Bennardo col., see 1989 exh. cat., p. 365), Pistoletto created a vivid contrast between the cast of an antique sculpture (used as if it were a ready-made) and a brightly coloured pile of rags. Such combination of Classical and contemporary imagery had been characteristic of Giorgio de Chirico's work from *c.* 1912 onwards. Furthermore, Arte Povera's choice of unglamorous materials had been anticipated by more recent work, such as that of Emilio Vedova and Alberto Burri in the 1950s and 1960s, while Piero Manzoni had subverted traditional notions of the artist's functions (e.g. *Artist's Shit*, 1961, see 1989 exh. cat., p. 298). Like Manzoni's innovations, Arte Povera was also linked to contemporary political radicalism, which culminated in the student protests of 1968. This is evident in such works as the ironic *Golden Italy* (1971; artist's col., see 1993 exh. cat., p. 63) by LUCIANO FABRO, a gilded bronze relief of the map of Italy, hung upside down in a gesture that was literally revolutionary.

As well as expressing their interest in social issues, the Italians were preoccupied with creating various forms of physical interaction between the work of art and its viewer. From the early 1960s Pistoletto had been making life-size images of people that were attached to mirrored surfaces so that the reflections of the spectator became part of the work, for example *Vietnam* (1965; Houston, TX, Menil Col.; see 1989 exh. cat., no. 198), which represented demonstrators holding a banner. GILBERTO ZORIO began in the late 1960s to create installations that registered the actions of visitors or other changes in the work's immediate environment by such means as flashing lights. Other artists pursued more esoteric conceptual interests. GIULIO PAOLINI created replicas of historic sculptures or paintings, which are given the status of original works of art by the ideas behind them, if not by their form. In *Mimesis* (1976; artist's col., see 1989 exh. cat., p. 364), Paolini placed two plaster casts of the same Classical statue opposite each other as if they were in conversation. This transforms the viewer's perception of the original sculpture by depicting the figures in silent dialogue with each other, rather than with the onlooker, and by shattering the concept of a work of art as being a unique creative act. *Mimesis* presents the duplicates as if they were ready-mades rather than the products of an individual artist. Fragments of plaster casts were also used by the Greek exile JANNIS KOUNELLIS, who was particularly concerned with expressing the disintegration of culture in the modern world (e.g. a performance held 1973; Rome, Gal. Salita; see 1986 exh. cat., p. 139).

The Arte Povera artists did not restrict themselves to allusions to Western civilization; from 1968, for example, MARIO MERZ made igloos (e.g. *Double Igloo*; see fig.; *see also* ITALY, fig. 65), referring to nomadic societies, which he admired particularly for being flexible and well adapted to their environments. He himself emulated these qualities in the ease with which he built the igloos from a wide range of both technological and 'natural' materials, including metal, glass, neon, slate, wax, earth and wood. This eclecticism in fact emphasized the essential difference between homogeneous traditional cultures and pluralistic modern ones. Around 1970 Merz also became preoccupied with the Fibonacci series of numbers, which he presented as the mathematical structure underlying a wide range of natural and manmade objects. A more active interference with nature was achieved by GIUSEPPE PENONE: in *The Tree Will Continue to Grow Except at This Point* (1968; see 1978 exh. cat., p. 33), an iron impression of Penone's fist was fitted around the trunk of a sapling so as to affect but not prevent the tree's growth. The involvement of natural processes is also a feature of the work of GIOVANNI ANSELMO. In *Structure that Eats* (1968; New York, Sonnabend Gal., see 1989 exh. cat., p. 368) vegetables were put between two stone blocks with the expectation that one would fall when the organic material rotted. This emphasis on the sculpture's impermanence shattered conventional notions of how art can transcend the normal processes of mortality. Anselmo pursued his interest in such phenomena as gravity into the 1980s, often using blocks of granite. In general, his colleagues also showed remarkable consistency in both their themes and imagery, although from the late 1970s the prevailing trend towards figurative art was reflected in some of the artists' work: for example, while still producing igloos, Merz painted animal forms, often combined with neon lights (e.g. *Crocodile in the Night*, 1979, Toronto, A.G. Ont.). Other artists created highly complex installations, which, in the case of Kounellis, often combined earlier pieces with new motifs (e.g. *Metamorphosis*, 1984; Schaffhausen, Hallen Neue Kst). Despite competition from the figurative Transavanguardia artists in Italy, Arte Povera remained a vigorous movement, responsible for some of the most innovative and sophisticated Italian art of the period.

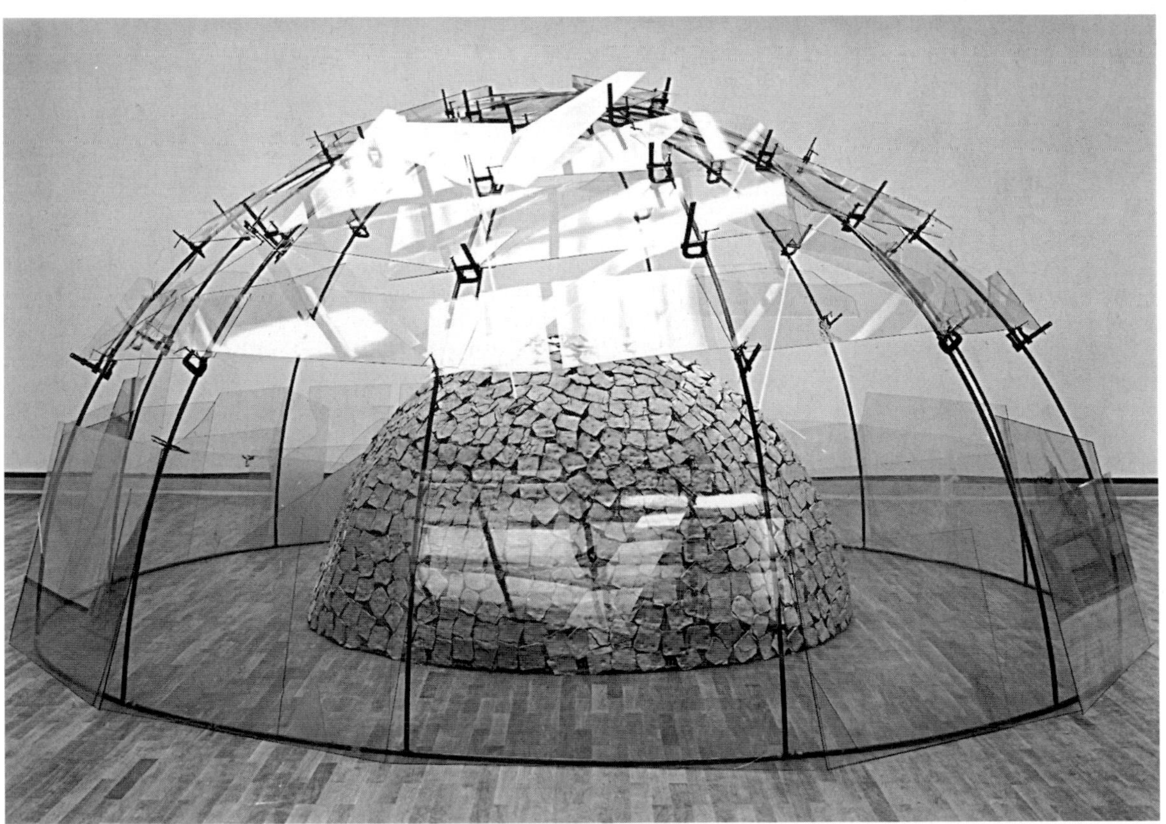

Arte Povera sculpture by Mario Merz: *Double Igloo*, steel, glass, earth and neon lights, h. 2.74 m, diam. 5.47 m, 1968–81 (Stuttgart, Staatsgalerie)

BIBLIOGRAPHY

G. Celant: 'Arte Povera: Appunti per una guerriglia', *Flash A.*, 5 (Nov–Dec 1967), p. 3
Arte Povera (exh. cat., ed. G. Celant; Genoa, Gal. La Bertesca, 1967)
G. Celant: *Arte Povera* (Milan, 1969)
Conceptual Art, Arte Povera, Land Art (exh. cat., ed. G. Celant; Turin, Gal. Civ. A. Mod., 1970)
Fabro, Kounellis, Merz, Paolini (exh. cat., Berne, Ksthalle, 1980)
Identité italienne: L'Art en Italie depuis 1959 (exh. cat., ed. G. Celant; Paris, Pompidou, 1981)
The Knot: Arte Povera (exh. cat. by G. Celant, New York, Inst. A. & Urb. Resources, P.S.1, 1985)
Jannis Kounellis (exh. cat., intro. M. J. Jacob; Chicago, IL, Mus. Contemp. A., 1986), p. 139
Italian Art in the 20th Century: Painting and Sculpture, 1900–1988 (exh. cat., ed. E. Braun; London, RA, 1989)
Gravity and Grace: The Changing Condition of Sculpture, 1965–1975 (exh. cat., London, Hayward Gal., 1993)

Arte programmata [It.: 'programmed art']. Term given to the work of various Italian artists active during the early 1960s who were primarily interested in KINETIC ART and OP ART. The phrase was used by Umberto Eco in 1962 for an exhibition that he presented at the Olivetti Showroom in Milan. This show included works by BRUNO MUNARI, Enzo Mari and members of GRUPPO N and GRUPPO T (both founded 1959). The artists produced objects by a procedure analogous to the methods of technological research, creating a prototype that was then developed through a series of closely related artefacts. This practice was exemplified by Munari, whose mass-produced 'multiples' took the form either of hand-operated objects or simple machines (e.g. *X Hour*, 1963; see Tanchis, pp. 72–3). The 'multiples' required the participation of members of the public in order to function and were intended to explore optical and physical phenomena, concerns that also dominated the work of other *Arte programmata* artists. Giovanni Anceschi (*b* 1939) created remarkable dynamic images with coloured liquids, while Gianni Colombo (*b* 1937) made reliefs constructed out of blocks that moved mechanically. *Arte programmata* gained an international reputation and in 1964 was the subject of exhibitions at the Royal College of Art, London, and at various venues in the USA. In the late 1960s, however, the artists became less closely associated, even though most continued to pursue their interests in kinetic and optical effects.

BIBLIOGRAPHY

Arte programmata: Kinetic Art (exh. cat. by B. Munari, New York, Loeb Student Cent., 1964)
Arte italiana, 1960–1982 (exh. cat. by C. Tisdall and others, London, Hayward Gal. and ICA, 1982–3)
Arte programmata e cinetica, 1953–1963: L'ultima avanguardia (exh. cat. by L. Vergine, Milan, Pal. Reale, 1983–4)
A. Tanchis: *Bruno Munari* (Milan, 1986; Eng. trans., London, 1987)

CHRISTOPHER MASTERS

Artes. Group of Polish avant-garde artists active in Lwów (now Lviv, Ukraine) between 1929 and 1935, from 1933 known as 'Neoartes'. Among its members were painters who studied in Lwów, Kraków and Paris: Otto Hahn (1904–42), Jerzy Janisch (1901–62), Henryk Streng (who after 1939 used the pseudonym Marek Włodarski), Margit Sielski (*b* 1903), Roman Sielski (*b* 1903), Mieczysław Wysocki (1899–1930), the self-taught painter Ludwik Lille (1897–1957) and the architect Aleksander Krzywobłocki (1901–79). Between 1930 and 1932 they held 11 exhibitions in Lwów, Warsaw and other cities. They searched for new, modern art, but they never defined it or formed any programme. Their art was heterogenous and covered various disciplines: painting, drawing, graphic art, collage and photomontage. Some of them were students of Léger and followed his style, but most of them moved towards Surrealism, for example Wysocki in his *Fantasy of a Fight* (1930) and Hahn in his lithograph *Composition with Leaves* (1930; both Wrocław, N. Mus.). They explored subjects popular among Surrealists, such as the journey, sea and dreams, as in Roman Sielski's *Seascape* (1931; Warsaw, N. Mus.). But they also made use of everyday subjects and depicted simple objects. Finally they broke with the timelessness and unreality of Surrealist visions and called for involvement in socio-political art. In 1933 Streng organized an opinion poll on new realism in art, and in 1936 he published in the monthly magazine *Sygnały* an article entitled 'Fighting for Live Art'. The move to realism was characteristic of the majority of Artes members. After the break-up of the group only Jerzy Janisch remained faithful to Surrealism; the others, for example Roman Sielski and Tadeusz Wojciechowski (1902–82), turned to Polish Colourism or, in the case of Streng, to abstraction.

BIBLIOGRAPHY

P. Łukaszewicz: *Zrzeszenie artystów plastyków Artes, 1929–35* [The 'Artes' association of mixed-media artists, 1929–35] (Wrocław, 1975)

ANNA BENTKOWSKA

Artesonado. Spanish term for a type of intricately joined wooden ceiling in which supplementary laths are interlaced into the rafters supporting the roof to form decorative geometric patterns. *Artesonado* ceilings were popular in the Islamic architecture of North Africa and Spain from the 13th to the 15th century and were also used widely in Jewish and Christian architecture. They continued to be popular into the 16th century when they were effectively integrated with Renaissance motifs.

Artesonado ceilings developed from horizontal coffered ceilings, which were used in Spanish Islamic architecture as early as the 10th century AD (*see* ISLAMIC ART, §II, 5(iv)). The Umayyad caliph al-Hakam II (*reg* 961–76) ordered a carved and painted coffered ceiling for the Great Mosque of Córdoba (*see* CÓRDOBA (i), §3(i)(a)). It was suspended from the ceiling joists and tie-beams of the pitched roofs covering the aisles. The halls of MADINAT AL-ZAHRA', the palace–city built by the Umayyads outside Córdoba, were also covered with coffered wooden ceilings, the horizontal beams of which were supported by carved, prow-shaped wooden consoles. This early type continued to be used in MUDÉJAR ceilings of the 12th and 13th centuries, such as the splendid coffered ceiling on the Romanesque church of S Millán in Segovia (mid-12th century; rest. 1669) and the chapter house of the monastery of Sigena (destr. 1936–9), in which large beams resting on corbels were decorated in the caliphal style of Córdoba. Coffered ceilings of this type continued to be constructed in Spain until the late 17th century.

The tie-beams on the underside of a hipped roof could be replaced in part by collar-beams, to form a popular type of ceiling shaped like an inverted trough with an increased amount of usable space under the roof. The

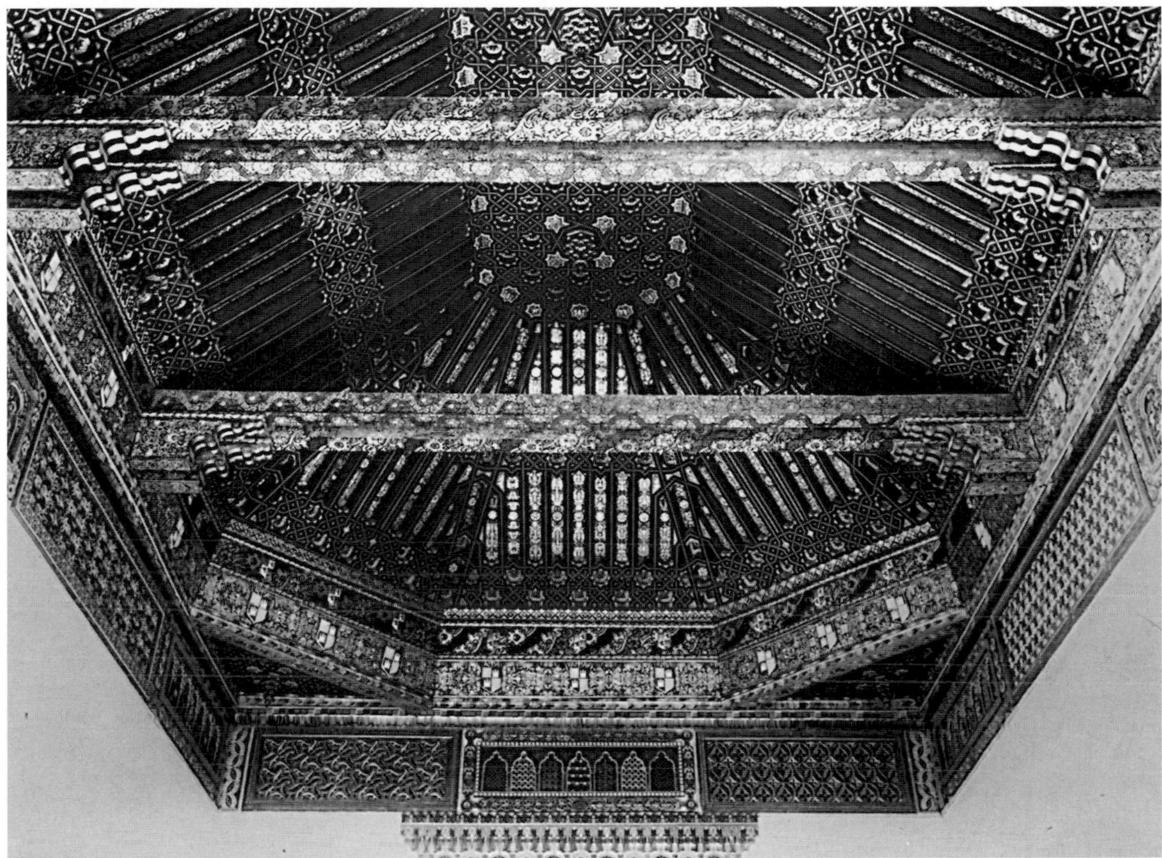

Artesonado ceiling in the great hall of the Archbishop's Palace, Alcalá de Henares, Spain, late 15th century

rafters of the four inclined faces rested on the wall plates, and single or double hip rafters marked the ridges between the faces. Pairs of opposite rafters were connected by collar-beams, to which horizontal panels were attached, and pairs of tie-beams resting on prow-shaped corbels stretched between the walls. This type of ceiling is first seen in ALMOHAD mosques in North Africa (e.g. the Kutubiyya Mosque in Marrakesh, 1158). In Spain, this basic rectangular structure formed the typical armature for the *artesonado* ceiling and could be modified for square, octagonal or even circular and oval roofs.

Both types of ceilings were decorated either with panels applied to the underside of the structure or with supplementary laths inserted between the structural members. The panels, which were nailed or glued to the rafters and collar-beams and concealed the entire roof structure, were usually decorated with elaborately carved and joined strapwork. The laths, which left the rafters and collar-beams visible, were usually painted. The oldest extant rafter and collar-beam roofs are found in the church of Santiago del Arrabal and the former Ibn Shoshun synagogue, later transformed into the church of Santa Maria la Blanca in Toledo (third quarter of the 13th century). The central nave of the cathedral of Teruel (mid-13th century) has a ceiling of exposed rafters and collar-beams, decorated with both supplementary laths and paint. The rich and varied decoration on the hip sheds and central panels includes geometric strapwork ornament, Arabic inscriptions and figural motifs illustrating contemporary Christian and Mudéjar society. Wooden ceilings of proverbial richness are preserved in the Alhambra and other palaces of GRANADA. Particularly fine examples are the ceiling of the throne-room of the Palacio de Comares (*c.* 1333–54), in which thousands of individual wooden elements are joined together to represent the seven heavens of Islam (*see* ISLAMIC ART, fig. 217), and the rounded ceiling of the Sala de la Barca (destr. 1890; rest.), named for its boatlike shape. MUQARNAS elements could be placed in various parts of the ceiling, such as squinches, pendentives and lanterns, to create an even more spectacular effect.

Magnificent ceilings of the same type adorned many palaces, monasteries and chapels of the 15th and 16th centuries. At Alcalá de Henares, near Madrid, splendid ceilings were erected under the patronage of Cardinal Francisco Jiménez de Cisneros in the great hall of the Archbishop's Palace (see fig.), the chapel of S Ildefonso and the Paraninfo (assembly hall) of the university. In the 16th century, when Renaissance styles of architecture were imported from Italy, they were incorporated into traditional *artesonado* ceilings. Islamic strapwork and Renaissance floral themes are blended in the coffered ceilings of the chapter house of the cathedral of Toledo and in the throne-room of the Aljafería at Saragossa.

BIBLIOGRAPHY

D. López de Arenas: *Breve compendio de la carpintería de lo blanco* (Seville, 1727)

L. Torres Balbás: *Arte almohade. Arte nazarí. Arte mudéjar* (1949), iv of *Ars Hispaniae* (Madrid, 1947–81)

B. Pavón Maldonado: *El arte hispanomusulmán en su decoración geométrica* (Madrid, 1975)

B. Martinez Caviró: 'Carpintería mudéjar toledana', *Cuad. Alhambra*, xii (1976), pp. 225–66

BASILIO PAVÓN MALDONADO

Art for Art's Sake [Fr. *L'Art pour l'art*]. Concept that emphasizes the autonomous value of art and regards preoccupations with morality, utility, realism and didacticism as irrelevant or inimical to artistic quality. It was the guiding principle of the AESTHETIC MOVEMENT.

In France the phrase 'l'art pour l'art' first appeared in print in 1833, but the concept had been popularized earlier by Madame de Staël's *De l'Allemagne* (Paris, 1813) and Victor Cousin's philosophy lectures at the Sorbonne, *Du vrai, du beau et du bien* (1816–18; pubd Paris, 1836). Théophile Gautier was its main literary publicist, especially in the preface to his novel *Mademoiselle de Maupin* (Paris, 1835). Studies of *l'art pour l'art*, such as Cassagne's, concentrate on the Second Empire literary movement (1851–70) that included Charles Baudelaire, Gautier, Edmond and Jules de Goncourt and the Parnassian poets. The application of the term to art criticism and visual art is uncharted, but it seems to have been used sufficiently loosely to embrace stylistically opposed artists. Sloane linked it to Edouard Manet and his circle—Manet was technically innovative, treated his subjects with moral neutrality and was defended by Emile Zola in *L'Evénement* in 1866 in formalistic terms: 'He does not know how to sing or to philosophize: he knows how to paint, and that is all.' Classicizing painters of the 1840s and 1850s, including Paul Baudry, William Bouguereau, Alexandre Cabanel and Jean-Léon Gérôme, probably also upheld *l'art pour l'art*: they opposed realism and cultivated 'pure art' and 'style', and for this reason Gautier supported them.

The phrase 'Art for Art's Sake' first appeared in English in Algernon Charles Swinburne's *William Blake* (London, 1868) and in Walter Pater's review of William Morris's poetry in the *Westminster Review* (Oct 1868). The end of the review became the 'Conclusion' to Pater's *Studies in the History of the Renaissance* (London, 1873), a key book in the Aesthetic Movement. The concepts of aestheticism had been introduced to Britain from France around 1860 by Frederic Leighton, James McNeill Whistler and Swinburne. They became current in the tightly knit group of painters, poets and art critics around Whistler and Dante Gabriel Rossetti and were controversial and avant-garde in the 1860s. Those who espoused Art for Art's Sake suggested that artistic quality lay in a work's formal organization rather than in its subject-matter. Aesthetic paintings therefore aimed at a decorative effect through composition and harmonious colour and frequently through the depiction of richly patterned surfaces and luxurious objects.

The exoticism associated with Art for Art's Sake became unfashionable by the late 19th century, but aestheticism influenced the development of formalist art criticism in the 20th century and the general acceptance of the autonomy of art.

BIBLIOGRAPHY

W. Pater: *Studies in the History of the Renaissance* (London, 1873, rev. 4/1893); rev. as *The Renaissance: Studies in Art and Poetry* (Berkeley, 1980)

A. Cassagne: *Le Théorie de l'art pour l'art en France chez les derniers romantiques et les premiers réalistes* (Paris, 1906)

R. F. Egan: 'The Genesis of the Theory of "Art for Art's Sake" in Germany and England', *Smith Coll. Stud. Mod. Lang.*, ii/4 (1921), pp. 5–61; v/3 (1924), pp. 1–33

A. Guérard: *Art for Art's Sake* (New York, 1936)

J. C. Sloane: *French Painting between the Past and the Present: Artists, Critics and Traditions from 1848 to 1870* (Princeton, 1951)

J. Wilcox: 'The Beginnings of *l'art pour l'art*', *J. Aesth. & A. Crit.*, ii (1952–3), pp. 360–77

HILARY MORGAN

Art history. Knowledge or study of the visual arts within a historical framework, the nature and breadth of which have been the subject of much discussion. Although earlier accounts of art and of aesthetics had suggested or implied the appropriateness and possibility of tracing patterns of historical development within the visual arts, it was perhaps only in the 19th century that a concerted attempt was made to give art history a philosophical basis. As art history subsequently became increasingly linked to and rooted in academic and educational institutions, it was accompanied by a shift in the status of the art historian, who came to be seen as the exponent of an increasingly sophisticated and specialized professional practice. Partly as a result of this increased specialization, and partly as a result of cross-fertilization with other disciplines, at the end of the 20th century art history in the Western world was characterized by a pluralism of approaches and by an acceptance of this pluralism as a corrective to what some perceived as a misguided earlier attempt to give a single comprehensive and universal account of art. This article therefore examines art history from three viewpoints: first, through a brief account of the development of art history as an intellectual discipline; second, through an account of art history as a modern institutional practice, mostly within the Western world; and third, through an analysis of some recent areas of contention within the discipline. It should be stressed that the analysis of issues must be seen as only one possible critique of art history. It should also be noted that art history generally flourishes in advanced industrial societies, counting as a luxury in the less industrially developed nations. Some developing countries, such as Nigeria, Thailand and India, have also emphasized the cultivation of the study of their own artistic heritage as a spur to the formation of a national identity. (In India art history is most typically considered part of the discipline of archaeology, art generally referring to material of the artists working within a 'modern art' framework in the Western sense.) In such contexts the role of the art historian is naturally very different and relatively well defined.

I. Historical development.

1. BEFORE THE 15TH CENTURY. The earliest surviving work that can be described as a history of art is the account

of the unfolding of Greek painting and sculpture found in the *Natural History* (XXXIII–XXXVII) written by Pliny the Elder (*see* PLINY, (1)) in the 1st century AD. From this Roman work, which interprets art in terms of progress, modern scholars have recovered the ideas of the Greek who appears to have been the first art historian, XENOKRATES of Sikyon (his own writings remain untraced). Having trained as a sculptor, Xenokrates sought to formulate criteria whereby the development of art could be measured. To judge from indications in Pliny, by the time of Xenokrates a canon of the great masters of Greek sculpture and monumental painting had already emerged. Moreover, the idea of decline had made its presence felt: in the early Hellenistic period, when Xenokrates was writing, the sense that the great epoch of Greek art was ebbing became widespread. A participant–observer, Xenokrates typifies the artist–critic who regarded his own time (even if somewhat disappointing, as it may have been in his case) as part of a continuously unfolding story. By contrast, the aristocratic Pliny took a purely retrospective view: he largely ignored Roman painters, so that art essentially belonged to 'long ago'—a lost Golden Age. This contrast between art as a continually developing process and art as the product of a past age was to echo down the centuries, with those critics who themselves began as artists tending to be more sympathetic to recent or contemporary works. In later Roman times two important genres were fostered: the guidebook tradition, of which the major landmark is the 2nd-century *Description of Greece* by PAUSANIAS (*see* GUIDEBOOK, §2), and the EKPHRASIS, a mode of vivid description of works of art, sometimes imaginary ones. With alterations responding to new religious interests, these two genres of writing about art continued into the Middle Ages, which introduced no fundamental innovations in the history of art.

While European art history marked time, an extraordinary independent awareness developed in China (*see* CHINA, §V, 5). The first landmark was the pithy Six Laws of Painting set forth by Xie He (*fl c.* 500–35). Subsequent Chinese art history was carried forward by the scholar–official class, whose members, like Xie He, were required to be adept in calligraphy, regarded as closely akin to painting, which they often practised as well. During the 11th and 12th centuries connoisseurs, basing themselves on earlier schemes, consolidated a standard three-category ranking of painters from the past: inspired, excellent and competent—sometimes supplemented by a fourth, extraordinary group, the untrammelled. Other scholars explored the contrast between the Northern and Southern Song schools, which show marked differences in style. The Chinese thus formulated a canon of worthy artists, who were then ranked by status, and they explored formal differences based on school and geography. These Chinese theories of art seem to have evolved entirely independently, although they bear similarities with ancient and later European ones. They declined during the Qing dynasty (1644–1911), however, and played little role in the West, except in the 20th-century study of Chinese art itself (*see also* §III, 2 below).

2. 15TH CENTURY TO THE LATE 19TH. The revived Western tradition of art history stems from the Italian Renaissance, with its renewed interest in the works of Classical antiquity and striving for fame, a lure to artists as well as to writers and political figures. This sense of fame as a kind of earthly immortality counts as one of the roots of the concept of individual genius, which was to be important in the later cult of the great masters. Combining the example of Pliny with his own enquiries, the sculptor Lorenzo Ghiberti (*see* GHIBERTI, (1)) created the first sketch of the history of Italian art in his *Commentarii* (*c.* 1450). After his death, several writers compiled notes containing a good deal of miscellaneous information, while oral reports of the undertakings of artists continued to circulate. This data remained unsynthesized, however, until the publication in 1550 of Vasari's monumental work *Le vite de' più eccelenti architetti, pittori, et scultori italiani*, which was followed by an enlarged edition in 1568 (*see* VASARI, (1)). This Italian painter, architect and scholar wrote as the intensity of the Renaissance art effort was waning. Although Vasari was avidly read in his own day and subsequently for the vivid details he supplied about individual works and their creators, he also propounded an overarching theory of the history of art. From 1250 to his own time, he believed, there had been three main eras: a modest, though hopeful, beginning; an improved, but still imperfect, intermediate stage; and the final attainment (which became known as the High Renaissance). This summit of perfection posed a dilemma: since it was not possible to go higher, art could only maintain itself on a plateau or begin to descend in quality. This second possibility became part of a discourse of decadence that continued to haunt cultural historians (*see also* DECADENCE AND DECLINE). Vasari entertained a normative concept of three styles: the 'good' *all'antica* style (whereby affinities could be traced between Renaissance art and its Greco-Roman predecessor), and the 'bad' Gothic and Byzantine styles. Finally, although he was a rationalist and a believer in adherence to the rules, Vasari suggested that a few artists were endowed with *grazia*, an ineffable excellence.

Vasari's model long ranked as paradigmatic. Gradually over the next two centuries his ideas spread first through Italy and then throughout Europe and became the dominant way of organizing information about art. Such writers as Karel van Mander (*see* MANDER, (1)), JOACHIM VON SANDRART, ROGER DE PILES and Antonio Palomino (*see* PALOMINO, (1)) took over Vasari's conceptual framework, adding much data from their own national records. Slowly, however, a new type of art historian also emerged, as great collectors began to employ learned functionaries. Two prominent examples are FILIPPO BALDINUCCI, who worked for the Medici, and the archaeologist JOHANN JOACHIM WINCKELMANN, who was in the service of Cardinal Alessandro Albani. Winckelmann's elegant writings, most notably his *Geschichte der Kunst des Alterthums* (1764), marked a new phase of art history, characterized by German dominance. Winckelmann held that scholars should sternly avoid personalities and write of art as a product of inexorable forces. In his rapturous accounts of the culture of ancient Greece, which he had earlier studied in the Classical texts, he emphasized the enabling factors of climate and political freedom, and he may thus be regarded as a proto-historicist. He also represented a beholder-centred (rather than artist-centred) historiography. Although he claimed competence only in ancient art, Winckelmann also disparaged the Baroque styles that continued to exert a powerful influence on 18th-century art and thereby helped (with such contemporaries as GOTTHOLD EPHRAIM LESSING) to foster the rise of the antithetical trend of Neo-classicism. In addition to his effects on art history and archaeology, Winckelmann gave impetus to the nascent field of art criticism (Denis Diderot acknowledged his influence), and from that point onwards the more contemporary-minded field of art criticism began to diverge from art history proper.

During the early decades of the 19th century historical research enjoyed enormous prestige in Germany. Discarding earlier models that expressed universal normative preferences, the new trend, sometimes termed historicism, emphasized the unique character of each individual epoch. Above all, the scholar embracing this ideal was required to resist anachronistic longings to project his or her own preferences on to the past. With regard to art research there were two main versions of historicism: a universal model derived from the philosopher and university professor GEORG WILHELM FRIEDRICH HEGEL, in which art—from the ancient Egyptians to Hegel's own time—moves from the symbolic to the classic to the romantic mode in accordance with the historical development of *Geist* or Spirit; and a particularist version, spearheaded by the independent scholar Karl Friedrich von Rumohr (1785–1843), which stresses the collection of discrete facts and the critical scrutiny of individual paintings. This last preoccupation fuelled the trend towards connoisseurship exemplified by GIOVANNI MORELLI, BERNARD BERENSON and MAX JACOB FRIEDLÄNDER—a major theme of 19th-century art history (*see* CONNOISSEURSHIP, §1(ii)).

Another important development in the 19th century was the institutionalization of art history as an academic discipline, beginning with the appointment in 1834 of Franz Kugler (1800–58) to the chair of art history at the Universität in Berlin. Professorial chairs were subsequently created at the universities of Bonn, Strasbourg, Leipzig and Prague, which were all occupied by German speakers. Slowly the institution spread to other countries, and there were also separate appointments in Classical archaeology. This development was accompanied by the establishment of a new approach to the study of art, placing it within the framework of a broader study of cultural history and thereby allowing such figures as JACOB BURCKHARDT to mediate between the two different versions of historicism. Other scholars meanwhile found employment in the great museums that were founded in many European capitals in the 19th century (*see* MUSEUM, §I). GUSTAV FRIEDRICH WAAGEN, who became Director of the Gemäldegalerie in Berlin in 1830, was the first distinguished figure of this type, closely followed by Charles Eastlake, who developed the National Gallery in London.

3. LATE 19TH CENTURY AND AFTER. It was only from the 1880s that modern art history crystallized into a new synthesis, which remained influential until the 1960s. The Swiss HEINRICH WÖLFFLIN created a formalist system based on the contrast between two 'modes of beholding', the first dominant during the Renaissance, the second during the Baroque. He also introduced a series of terms to characterize this contrast; of these, the linear and its antithesis, the painterly, are probably the most important. The linear mode brings out discrete separations between depicted entities by introducing clear lines and contours, while the painterly approach tends to merge individual elements into a single whole, the fluidity of which denies any clear boundaries. During the following decade the Viennese art historians FRANZ WICKHOFF and ALOIS RIEGL developed similar models, though with more allowance for cultural factors. This Vienna school (like Wölfflin) was influenced by new discoveries in experimental psychology, especially in the study of perception, and was important in 'rehabilitating' such neglected eras of art history as Roman art, Early Christian art, Mannerism and the Baroque (*see also* AUSTRIA, §XVII). Links between the new openness signalled by these scholarly advances and the artistic avant-garde of the Post-Impressionists, though often posited, are not easily demonstrable.

In turn-of-the-century France the medievalist EMILE MÂLE emphasized content over form, leading to the maturation of a new approach to subject-matter. These endeavours were carried further by his younger Hamburg contemporary ABY WARBURG, who founded a widely influential research institute, which later moved to London. Both figures gave important impetus to the study of iconography, the subdiscipline that addresses stable patterns of meaning in visual schemata and is therefore akin to semiotics. One of Warburg's protégés was the prodigiously learned ERWIN PANOFSKY. Sometimes misrepresented as a Formalist, Panofsky sharply criticized both Wölfflin and Riegl. He was interested chiefly in medieval and Renaissance art and brought to bear a range of sources, both visual and literary, intended to produce a holistic reading of individual works of art in keeping with a method that he termed 'iconology' (*see* ICONOGRAPHY AND ICONOLOGY). In 1933 the application of Hitler's racial laws compelled Panofsky to settle in the USA. From the Institute for Advanced Study in Princeton, NJ, he exercised a beneficent ascendancy over a maturing American art history. In fact, with the work of ARTHUR KINGSLEY PORTER and CHARLES RUFUS MOREY, American art history had begun to develop auspiciously during the second decade of the 20th century. In the mid-20th century, reinforced by a transatlantic migration comprising some 400 art scholars (many, though not all, of Jewish origin), it achieved international prominence. Meyer Schapiro (*b* 1904) integrated approaches derived from anthropology, psychoanalysis, philosophy and other disciplines, while Leo Steinberg (*b* 1920) combined close visual analysis with a careful reading of texts to provide flexible and subtle models of interpretation. Institutional art history, however, tended to neglect modern and contemporary art, and the first great strides in this area were made by scholars outside academia, such as JULIUS MEIER-GRAEFE, ROGER FRY and ALFRED H. BARR. Also neglected by the mainstream was Asian art, although cultivated by such figures as ERNEST FRANCISCO FENOLLOSA (China and Japan), JOSEPH STRZYGOWSKI (western Asia), K. A. C. CRESWELL (Islam), ANANDA KENTISH COOMARASWAMY (India and Sri Lanka) and STELLA KRAMRISCH (India).

After World War II the discipline was eager to find its way back to positive values. Panofsky's emphasis on philosophy, religion and traditional humanism seemed particularly relevant in the immediate post-war period, yet with the maturation of the secular post-war culture, with its consumer society and new media, this appeal dimmed. Political attitudes also changed: a new spirit of revolt found Panofsky too traditionally humanistic, out of tune with the yearning for innovation and transgression. Moreover, untrained in the strict canons of Classical philology, many of the German polymath's disciples experienced difficulty in emulating his achievements. Other problems reflected a changed emphasis in academia itself: a broader decline in the humanistic tradition gradually smothered the intellectual environment that had sustained his teachings, and within art history many felt that Panofsky's disregard of contemporary art was short-sighted. A new pluralism in art history was fostered by other factors, including a sense that art and the study of art should be socially significant. As in other fields of the humanities, new influences came from a renewed interest in MARXISM, psychoanalysis (*see* PSYCHOANALYSIS AND ART), SEMIOTICS and the set of views known loosely as DECONSTRUCTION. This New Art History, as it is sometimes termed, was more an alliance of interests than a single doctrine (*see* §II below). Sustained study of the arts of Africa, Oceania and the Pre-Columbian Americas also began to flourish in the second half of the 20th century. After the 1960s, however, such scholars as Edward Said questioned the appropriateness of imposing Western standards on other cultures. The task of creating a universal history of art, first glimpsed by Hegel, had thus not been realized by the end of the 20th century.

BIBLIOGRAPHY

M. Shapiro: 'Style', *Anthropology Today: An Encyclopedic Inventory*, ed. A. L. Kroeber (Chicago, 1953), pp. 287–312

E. Panofsky: *Meaning in the Visual Arts* (Garden City, NY, 1955)

J. Schlosser Magnino: *La letteratura artistica* (Florence, 1964)

C. Eisler: '*Kunstgeschichte* American Style: A Study in Migration', *The Intellectual Migration: Europe and America, 1930–1960*, ed. D. Fleming and B. Bailyn (Cambridge, MA, 1969), pp. 544–629

W. E. Kleinbaurer, ed.: *Modern Perspectives in Western Art History* (New York, 1971)

H. Dilly: *Kunstgeschichte als Institution* (Frankfurt am Main, 1979)

E. Arntzen and R. Rainwater: *Guide to the Literature of Art History* (Chicago, 1980)

D. Watkin: *The Rise of Architectural History* (Chicago, 1980)

J. Alsop: *The Rare Art Traditions* (New York, 1982)

W. E. Kleinbauer and T. Slavens: *Research Guide to the History of Western Art* (Chicago, 1982)

U. Kultermann: *Geschichte der Kunstgeschichte* (Frankfurt am Main, 1982; Eng. trans., New York, 1993)

M. Podro: *The Critical Historians of Art* (New Haven, 1982)

M. A. Holly: *Panofsky and the Foundations of Art History* (Ithaca, NY, 1984)

M. Barasch: *Theories of Art: From Plato to Winckelmann* (New York, 1985)

S. Bush: *Early Chinese Painting Texts* (Cambridge, MA, 1985)

H. Dilly and others, eds: *Kunstgeschichte: Eine Einführung* (Berlin, 1985)

L. Dittmann, ed.: *Kategorien und Methoden der deutschen Kunstgeschichte, 1900–1930* (Stuttgart, 1985)

G. Bazin: *Histoire de l'histoire de l'art de Vasari à nos jours* (Paris, 1986)

H. Dilly, ed.: *Altmeister moderner Kunstgeschichte* (Berlin, 1990)

M. Sitt, ed.: *Kunsthistoriker in eigener Sache* (Berlin, 1990)

F. Haskell: *History and its Images: Art and the Interpretation of the Past* (New Haven, 1993)

I. Lavin: *Past–present: Essays on Historicism in Art, from Donatello to Picasso* (Berkeley, 1993)

V. H. Minor: *Art History's History* (New York, 1994)

II. Modern institutional practice.

The institutionalization of art history as a professional discipline from the 19th century was accompanied by the development of professional organizations, a system of professional training and shifts in the perception of its relation to other academic disciplines. Parallel to these were developments in the dissemination of information, necessary to sustain the discipline at a professional level and at a more general level.

1. PROFESSIONAL ASPECTS. The first international art historians' association was formed in Vienna in 1873 on the occasion of the Weltausstellung there. Except for interruptions owing to war, meetings have taken place every three years. In the USA a quest for status led to the creation of a host of professional organizations around the turn of the century, for example the American Historical Association (1884) and the American Sociological Association (1904). The founding of the first professional grouping of academically employed artists and art historians, the College Art Association, came in 1911. This group, with its huge annual meetings and prestigious publications, provided a model for others. The (American) Society of Architectural Historians was formed in 1940, and in 1948 German art historians reorganized themselves as the Verband Deutscher Kunsthistoriker. Similar organizations appeared in Britain and France during the 1970s. There are hundreds of smaller organizations around the world, many of them catering for specialist areas, such as the societies for Oriental ceramics, Egyptian antiquities and so on. The maturation of a new profession, that of art librarian, was signalled by the formation of ARLIS/NA (Art Libraries Association/North America) in 1972; the British counterpart is ARLIS/UK. Until the last decades of the 19th century almost all art historians were self-taught, perfecting themselves through travel and personal contact with mentors. This informal method yielded to the German seminar system, whereby the tiro art historian learnt his or her craft from an established master, the 'Doktorvater'; variations of this procedure are still employed in Central Europe, the United Kingdom and North America. As a terminal credential, the PhD is now obligatory for most art-historical employment. The labour required to acquire the concluding document that confers the degree varies in intensity: in France it is the *thèse d'état*; in the UK and the USA, the PhD thesis; in Germany, the *Dissertation*; and in Italy, the *tesi di laurea*. At one time graduate students were expected to know Greek and Latin in addition to modern languages; now an Asian language may be required in addition to French and German. Museum work affording contact with original objects is often regarded as essential; there is sometimes the possibility of intern service. Under the aegis of some universities and museums, excavation experience abroad is possible. In the late 20th century the student and art historian must be computer-literate, not only for his own work but also to gain access to an increasing array of electronic data

bases; consultation with the specialized art reference librarian is often essential.

Modern art historians may specialize in a period, medium or even an individual artist, or they may be generalists. Among the specialists, some cherish a sense that the particular styles and types of art they favour are objectively privileged, that they are in effect superior to other kinds of art, while others share with generalists a sense of value-neutrality. One group of art historians, the uniformitarians, tend to view historical development as a gradual process; others, who might be termed the saltationists, detect clear breaks or discontinuities, which may take the form either of qualitative advances, sudden spurts, or of setbacks and even actual catastrophes. Finally, some art historians favour dualistic systems, stipulating the alternating domination of opposing principles (such as the linear vs. the painterly mode), while others minimize such fundamental contrasts.

There are also different views on the appropriate relation of art history to other academic disciplines. The contemporary organization of knowledge assigns the history of art and architecture to the sphere of the humanities (along with the study of literature, music and philosophy) as distinct from the social sciences and the natural sciences. The practice of art history involves a range of auxiliary disciplines and expertise, from PALAEOGRAPHY and chronology to radiocarbon dating and chemical analysis. ARCHAEOLOGY and art history, though originally closely allied, have grown apart; this distinction is particularly evident in Pre-Columbian studies, where archaeologists allege that art historians are interested only in prestige objects rather than the reconstruction of the entire culture, which archaeologists and anthropologists seek. On the other hand, anthropologists of the calibre of Franz Boas and Claude Lévi-Strauss have made their own contributions to the study of art, and there are useful collaborations between art historians, who are interested in subject-matter and cultural context, and anthropologists, with their interest in myth and social structures (*see* ANTHROPOLOGY AND ART). Sociology is another discipline from the social sciences with which an alliance with art history can open perspectives (*see* SOCIOLOGY OF ART), including the study of art historians themselves, their training, motivations and group interactions. The study of non-Western art has often flourished in the context of what are called area studies (of East Asia, South Asia, Islam and so on), although the findings of these interdisciplinary researches need to be integrated. Finally, art history has long had a problematic relationship with art criticism, and the links between the two are subject to alternating patterns of consolidation and estrangement.

2. DISSEMINATION OF INFORMATION. Access to good reproductions has long been of great importance for art historians, both for research and as standard teaching aids. There were four main developments in this, the first being the technique permitting prints made on paper from engraved plates. This practice, popular in many parts of Europe from the 15th century onwards, lent itself to both original and reproductive engravings. Reproductions were made of the more or less contemporary masterpieces of the Renaissance and Baroque, as well as the admired statues of Classical antiquity. The second major development stemmed from the introduction of still photography in the mid-19th century. The new medium was considered to provide an objective rendering of the subjects and was more convenient, allowing an art historian to document his or her research visits. Insertion of illustrations in books became much easier; new firms sprang up, offering huge selections of images of art and architecture. The third development was the use of photographic transparencies or slides. A two-slide method became common in public lectures in Munich during the 1890s, although this method of comparison did not become prevalent in American classroom teaching until the 1960s. Colour slides were also used after the 1950s. A further development in the late 20th century is digital imaging. Improvements in storage and retrieval through the polycarbonate compact discs called CD-ROM (Read Only Memory), open the possibility of creating huge banks of reliable digital images for study and comparison. Archaeological excavations, for example, can be monitored and the sites reconstructed through the use of computer imaging.

Locating and accessing existing literature about art is as important to the art historian as the access to reproduced images, and there are a number of reference genres for this purpose, all of which have long histories. Encyclopedias and dictionaries often form the first point of reference (*see* ENCYCLOPEDIAS AND DICTIONARIES OF ART), and the role played by art bibliographies is of great significance, from selected works listed in art books to such cumulative, ongoing works of the 20th century as the *Art Index*, *The Bibliography of the History of Art* (BHA), which is also in French, and the RILA (*Répertoire internationale de la littérature de l'art*), which is now absorbed into the BHA (*see* BIBLIOGRAPHY OF ART). The major cumulative bibliographies are available in both hard copy (printed volumes) and electronic retrieval modes (CD-ROM) and include classifications of the articles in many of the scholarly art journals that proliferated in the 20th century (*see* PERIODICAL, §II, 2). Catalogues, often illustrated, list the items of particular collections or temporary exhibitions, while catalogues raisonnés concentrate on particular artists (*see* CATALOGUE).

For the most part the above resources are consulted by specialists. Museums, on the other hand, have taken the lead as a source of dissemination for the general public as well as art historians; indeed, many major European museums were created by the opening up of private, princely collections to the public in the 17th and 18th centuries (*see* MUSEUM, §I). Most modern museums provide lecturers, with some offering tape-recorded commentary on particular exhibitions and galleries so that the visitor, stopping and starting the machine, may take them at his or her own pace. Many museums emphasize work with young people so as to educate a new generation of enthusiasts. In addition, in an increasing number of art galleries and museums, visitors can consult a computer library. In the National Gallery, London, for example, there is a Micro Gallery, or computer information room, which gives visitors access to over 4500 pages of material covering every painting and artist in the Gallery. Visitors may choose up to 10 paintings and print out a free floor-plan that lists the selections and highlights their locations in the Gallery. It is also possible to print out black-and-white photocopies of any of the Gallery's holdings.

After World War II the USA took the lead in publishing well-illustrated general textbooks on the history of art; the best known are those of Horst Woldemar Janson, Helen Gardner and Frederick Hartt. For the layperson interested in art history, the medium of the 'coffee-table' book became popular. While some specialists disparage this commerce-driven dissemination, such volumes communicate much information in an easily digestible form. The medium of television has perhaps achieved less in promoting art history than might have been expected, although the series *Civilization*, hosted by Kenneth Clark in 1969, was widely successful and set a high standard. Produced by private firms, thousands of video documentaries have become popular in the classroom and elsewhere, while the increasing number of television channels may afford greater scope for art programmes.

BIBLIOGRAPHY

M. W. Chamberlin: *Guide to Art Reference Books* (Chicago, 1959)

L. Corti, ed.: *Census: Computerization in the History of Art*, i (Pisa and Los Angeles, 1984)

L. S. Jones: *Art Information: Research Methods and Resources* (Dubuque, IA, 1990)

WAYNE R. DYNES

III. Contemporary issues.

The successful institutionalization of art history should not be taken to indicate universal consensus among art historians as to the method, value and nature of their discipline. Indeed, critical debate concerning these issues has continued to provide an important impetus to the development of art history as an academic subject and has been seen by some as an index of its health. In the late 20th century particularly, debate among art historians focused on issues concerning the cultural and epistemological assumptions inherent in the very idea of a history of art. While art history thus came to be regarded by some as 'in crisis', others suggested that the plurality of approaches did not reflect an unfortunate temporary state of affairs that would eventually be resolved but the necessary failure of and antidote to an over-ambitious attempt to give a unified account of widely heterogeneous practices.

1. DIVERSE APPROACHES. The roots of the plurality that characterizes modern art history can perhaps be said to lie in the 19th century, when the institution of the first university chairs in art history and the creation of public museums and galleries naturally stimulated two parallel lines of development within art history: between those (such as Wölfflin, Warburg and Panofsky) who dealt with questions of form, content, context, historical development and interpretation and were based principally in the universities, and those (such as Morelli, Friedländer and Berenson) who concerned themselves with problems of attribution, classification, restoration, documentation, presentation and evaluation and were based principally in museums (*see* §I above). As Friedländer pointed out in *Of Art and Connoisseurship* (1942), the 'historian' and the 'expert' failed to engage in a productive dialogue, divided as they were by different preoccupations and methods. Moreover, among those who shared a concern with the problems of interpretation there evolved such a multiplicity of issues and methods that the field of art history became fragmented and opened up as an arena for competing systems of explanation.

(i) Formalism. HEINRICH WÖLFFLIN, who succeeded Jacob Burckhardt as professor of art history at the University of Basle, made it clear in his preface to the second edition of *Classic Art* that art history should not be merely 'illustrative of the history of civilization' but should 'stand on its own feet as well'. For Wölfflin this meant a 'return to specifically artistic questions' and placing emphasis on the 'artistic content' of the work, which 'follows its own laws'. Wölfflin defined artistic content as the expression of a mode of 'imaginative beholding' developed from the range of 'formal possibilities' that a period has at its disposal. Against subjective criticism that approached the works by asking 'How do these works affect me?' and those that treat art as 'the emanation of various individuals considered as personalities, or as a product of differing historical circumstances and national peculiarities', Wölfflin advocated an enquiry into the conditions of possibility of artistic styles.

Wölfflin saw the philosophical treatment of art history as an improvement, for it provided a more rigorous account of stylistic changes based on an in-depth analysis of individual styles. However, for projecting abstract categories on to the infinite variety of artistic styles and for confining his analyses within the realm of formal considerations, Wölfflin's work has been severely criticized by contextualists as 'formalist' and anti-historical. WALTER BENJAMIN, who attended Wölfflin's lectures in Munich in 1915, was very critical of both his teaching and his method and, in an article entitled 'Rigorous Study of Art' (1933), praised the lesser known work of ALOIS RIEGL as pointing the way towards the future. In his 'Remarks on the Method of Art History' (1949), Frederick Antal, who studied under both Wölfflin and MAX DVOŘÁK, deplored the fact that 'Wölfflin's very lucid analyses . . . reduced the wealth of historical evolution to a few fundamental categories, a few typified schema', avoiding economic and social questions. Today, in assessing Wölfflin's contribution to the subject, we must remember that his 'formalism' was a direct consequence of his desire to bring back 'some aesthetics' into art history, and we must acknowledge that even if his system is now obsolete, his insights and the rigour of his analyses remain challenging.

In his introduction to *La Réalité figurative* (1965), Pierre Francastel took Wölfflin to task for isolating the history of form from other areas of social life. Informed by semiotics, Francastel's sociology of art set out to avert the formalism and essentialism of pure visibilism, by pointing out that because they are not 'systems of meanings constituted once and for all', forms cannot be credited with a fixed meaning independent of the context in which they occur. Francastel summarized his objection by stating that Wölfflin treated forms as objects, whereas he should have dealt with them as structures. By affirming the autonomy of art as a major form of human and social expression, Francastel nevertheless situated himself in the tradition of Wölfflin. Wölfflin's legacy can be traced down to ROGER FRY, BERNARD BERENSON and, more recently, CLEMENT GREENBERG, who has been at the focus of the debate between formalist and contextualist approaches, most noticeably in his polemic with T. J. Clark.

(ii) Contextualism. Among the historians who have concerned themselves with issues of context, one must distinguish between those who interpret context as essentially cultural (bringing, like Warburgian iconology, the history of ideas, religion, philosophy and literature to bear upon art historical interpretation) from those who, since Hippolyte Taine's *Philosophie de l'art* (1865), view context as encompassing social, political and economic factors as well. This is the path followed by the sociology of art and, more generally, by Marxist approaches.

(a) Culture as context. Antal recalled how, by studying 'the inter-dependence between the pictorial and literary evidence, the relation of the artist to the patron, the close connection between the work of art, its social milieu and its practical purpose', Aby Warburg rescued 'the work of art from the isolation with which it was threatened by a purely aesthetic and formal approach'. Erwin Panofsky's *Meaning in the Visual Arts* (1955), Edgar Wind's *Pagan Mysteries in the Renaissance* (1958), the work of FRITZ SAXL and RUDOLF WITTKOWER and, more generally, the method associated with the Warburg Institute illustrate this tendency.

In the wake of the structuralist revival of linguistics and the redefinition of the notions of sign and semiosis, however, iconology has come under attack in the more prominent formulation given by Panofsky in his *Studies in Iconology* (1939). In his introduction to *Etudes de sociologie de l'art* (1970), Francastel objected that, by its restrictive interpretation of images, iconology reduced artistic meanings to a linguistic formulation, thus eluding the specificity of visual modes of 'signification' (which he contrasted with modes of 'communication'). Referring to a contemporary debate about whether the visual arts were to be the legitimate object of study of a semiology of communication (following the model of verbal language) or of a restricted semiology of signification (together with those representations that did not display the presence of a code), Francastel emphasized the need to take the work of interpretation beyond the identification of its subject to encompass what he termed 'figurative thought' and its infinite ramifications; for it is through the work of the sign that Francastel identified the productive relation between painting and society.

If Francastel insisted in *Peinture et société* (1951) that 'a painting is not a double of reality, but a sign', thus privileging social and psychological factors in the interpretation of the visual arts, it could be objected that like Wölfflin, whom he criticized, Francastel confined interpretation to a restricted autonomous sphere irreducible to language, in which art was generated and fulfilled an immanent function. However, in his desire to avert what, in *La Figure et le lieu* (1967), he termed a 'xxth-century nominalism', Francastel acknowledged that the structures revealed by analysis are 'partial systems which suggest modes of approach of reality rather than things themselves, that they do not reveal immutable laws in the natural or in the spiritual order'.

(b) Social background as context. Contextual approaches set out to define meaningful relations and forms of interaction between the visual arts and external factors. From the Vasarian 'conditions of the times', which implied a deterministic action of context upon the work, to Taine's affirmation that artistic development is subject to 'specific conditions and fixed rules' that need to be unravelled, one deals with the chief assumption that artistic development is not autonomous but subject to the same laws that determine the course of human history as a whole. This totalizing view can express itself in the rather vague and under-theorized notions of background or in the dogmatic Marxist notion of economic determinism.

The interest in social background has manifested itself in several studies of the social position of the artist. Anthony Blunt included a chapter entitled 'The Social Position of the Artist' in his *Artistic Theory in Italy: 1450–1600* (Oxford, 1940), where he described 'the arguments about the liberal arts' as 'the theoretical side of the artist's struggle for a better position', while, 30 years later, Andrew Martindale documented *The Rise of the Artist in the Middle Ages and Early Renaissance* (1972). In 1948 Antal's *Florentine Painting and its Social Background* showed how information about economic, social and political history and ideas could be combined with the study of religion, philosophy, learning and literature to further define the context in which paintings were produced and used in Florence during the 14th and 15th centuries. Although the main emphasis of the book is on the cultural climate, Antal also discussed the interaction between painters and patrons and the social position of 'artists' (bringing in the notion of class), and he attempted a description of the social basis of stylistic differences through a detailed analysis of themes, for he believed that the theme or subject-matter of a picture shows more clearly than anything else how completely the picture as a whole is but part of the outlook, the ideas, of the public, expressed through the medium of the artist. In this way he hoped to transcend the limitations of formalism and link the 'development of styles' with 'other aspects of historical development'.

Antal's remarks, however, that 'knowledge historically grounded is the only sure means of neutralizing our subjective judgment on the quality of works of art of the past, even on the significance of individual styles' gives a measure of the optimism that accompanied the rise of the social history of art. For the purpose of genealogy, Antal could be described as continuing and extending the early work of Dvořák, who, as early as 1904, had called upon economic history to elucidate the sudden emergence of the van Eycks.

(c) The search for structural correlations. In 1933, when Antal was still working on *Florentine Painting*, Max Raphael (1889–1952) published a critique of Prud'hon's sociology of art and a critical overview of the Marxist theory of art in his *Prud'hon, Marx, Picasso: Trois Etudes sur la sociologie*

de l'art (Paris). Acknowledging the complexity of the interaction between the ideological and the material base, Raphael noted that the elaboration of a sociology of art required not only 'mastery of the materials of the history of art all over the world' but also 'the joint collaboration of several special sciences (economics, sociology, politics, psychology, theory of knowledge, history of religions, philosophy, etc.)'. Raphael went on to point out that due to these inherent difficulties, dialectical materialism had in the past produced only 'fragmentary investigations' but could, if 'applied correctly', help in the elaboration of 'a theory and a sociology of art'. It is ironic that the remark he made at the beginning of his essay on *The Marxist Theory of Art*—that traditional approaches neglected 'the phenomenon of art itself'—converged with the beliefs of Wölfflin, who, in his preface to the first edition of *Classic Art* (1898), deplored the fact that 'historical learning has almost abandoned the greater theme of "art" and has passed it over to a separate study—the philosophy of art'. It is unfortunate that Raphael's book, which includes an exemplary summary of Marx's theory of art, was not published in English until 1980, for its critique of Marxist generalizations and forced analogies between artistic developments and economic and political systems would have been particularly relevant in the 1970s, when a new art history was in the making.

A more influential attempt at establishing structural correlations between the visual arts and society was devised by ARNOLD HAUSER in his *Social History of Art* (1951), where the emergence of artistic styles is rooted in broad socio-political categories. This sociological reductionism is reflected in chapter titles such as 'The Baroque of the Protestant Bourgeoisie'. In spite of its excessive reductionism, severely criticized by Gombrich in his *Meditations on a Hobbyhorse* (1963), Hauser's *Social History of Art* substantially extended the neo-Vasarian perspective of standard survey courses—including Gombrich's *The Story of Art* (1950)—and focused students' attention on social aspects of the history of visual representations. In his *Philosophy of Art History* (1958), Hauser reviewed his position in a more theoretical way, pointing out that 'the sociological view of art is to be rejected if it claims to be the sole legitimate point of view, and if it confuses the sociological importance of a work with aesthetic value'. Taking issue with Wölfflin's 'lack of sociological sense and his abstract logical conception of history', Hauser insisted that 'the stimulus for change always comes from without, and is logically contingent'.

Meanwhile, the search for structural correlations between art and developments in other areas produced different systems of explanations, from the history of art seen as the history of civilization (Burckhardt) to the genetic formalism of Wölfflin or Elie Faure, the iconology of Panofsky or the perspectivism of Riegl's *Denkmalkutus* (1903). Thus the framework was established for art history to unfold toward its present condition. In an article entitled 'The Conditions of Artistic Creation' (*TLS*, 24 May 1974), T. J. Clark called for 'an archaeology of the subject in its heroic period: a critical history, uncovering assumptions and allegiances'. Responding to a text by Lukacs, which listed Riegl, Dilthey and Dvořák as examples of 'really important historians', Clark underlined the 'need to rediscover the kind of thinking that sustained art history at that time'. Clark's suggestion, written at a time when art history was experiencing an epistemological crisis, called for a re-examination of the terms of art historical practice on firmer theoretical grounds. His conclusion, however, that 'in art history—and I believe, elsewhere—it is precisely the Hegelian legacy that we need to appropriate: to use, criticize, reformulate', is somewhat ambiguous and problematic, as it could be read as a call either to establish the 'social history of art' as a 'scientific' discipline (an alternative to 'traditional' or 'bourgeois' art history, 'the place,' as Clark put it, 'where the questions have to be asked, and where they cannot be asked in the old way') or to re-examine art history on the basis of extensive critical work. In the late 20th century the need for a critical history of art history remains, for although the texts currently on offer (e.g. Venturi, 1936; Podro, 1982; Bazin, 1986) provide useful bio-bibliographical guidelines, they fail, with a few exceptions (e.g. Didi-Huberman, 1990), to engage their material in epistemological terms.

In the wake of successive redefinitions of the terms of artistic practice (from 19th-century Realism and Impressionism to Cubism, Expressionism, Dada, Surrealism, Constructivism and abstraction), and given the multiplication of competing interpretive positions (drawing from recent developments in anthropology, Marxism, linguistics, semiotics, hermeneutics and psychoanalysis), the Hegelian legacy has lost much of its attraction, especially in the light of the recent demise of Marxism, structuralism and other totalizing systems. This, of course, is not to say that the history of art cannot benefit from a careful re-reading of Hegel, nor of those texts singled out by Clark as significant, for considering the history of art history as a problem in its own right is an effective way of engaging in self-criticism.

(iii) Structuralism. Despite this theoretical pluralism, art history remained until the 1970s a more or less conservative discipline enshrined in universities, art schools, museums and the offices of auction rooms. During the 1960s the emergence of the intellectual movement STRUCTURALISM, which challenged established forms of knowledge across the disciplines, could have helped art history make a decisive epistemological break from its conservative stance. This, however, did not happen, except in some exceptional philosophical writings engaged in theoretical decentrings. In 1966 the emphasis was on language and SEMIOTICS, for example Pierre Macherey's recommendation in *Pour une théorie de la production littéraire* (Paris, 1966) that 'various disciplines such as linguistics, the theory of art, the theory of history, the theory of ideologies, the theory of unconscious formations, must all collaborate'. The publication of *Les Sciences humaines et l'oeuvre d'art* (by B. Teyssedre and others; Brussels, 1969) also made it clear that new forms of knowledge about the visual arts could be produced only with the collaboration of neighbouring disciplines—as Max Raphael himself had pointed out in 1933. In *Les Sciences humaines*, however, is the implicit prescription that new knowledge about visual practices can come only from outside the history of art, through the import of concepts and methods elaborated

from new sets of concerns. The essays in *Les Sciences humaines* do not attempt to alter the institutional order of the discipline but instead indicate theoretical possibilities that can be explored in the margins of art history. Unfortunately, in the same way that delays in translation had retarded the impact of Panofsky's writings outside the English-speaking world earlier in the 20th century, so the impact of structuralism was similarly delayed, with the additional hindrance of ideological distortions and resistances, and owing to institutional pressures, lack of time and specialist knowledge and diverging interests, much was lost in the many attempts to import critical and philosophical theories into art history.

2. THE ROLE OF THEORY. In the 1980s the New Art History gained currency, particularly in Great Britain, as a collective term for the cross-disciplinary approaches to art found within Marxism, feminism, psychoanalysis, structuralism and various other socio-political concerns. Thus, the term includes seminal French theoretical writings and the approaches adopted by, for example, T. J. Clark, Svetlana Alpers and Norman Bryson (*b* 1949). Although the New Art History displays all the symptoms of having been rushed in under the pressure of fashion and ideological trends, the high level of theory used by many modern art historians to justify their position and pre-empt misguided criticism gives a measure of the significant increase in theoretical sophistication achieved within the discipline itself since the 1970s. The work of T. J. Clark is a case in point. The opening pages of his introduction to *The Painting of Modern Life* (New York, 1984) seem intent to avert or at least close the ground for anticipated objections. This is also a reminder of the polemical context in which art-historical differences are increasingly enacted in public, in the emotionally charged atmosphere of conferences and symposia. Feminist writings are another example of this, with the 'intervention of feminism' working on several levels (*see also* FEMINISM AND ART and WOMEN AND ART HISTORY). Following a strategy of reversal, the first set of contributions by feminists set out to bring the work of neglected women artists to public attention, within the same parameters used for the appreciation of traditional 'male' art. The next step identified a new set of concerns. In a seminal article published in 1971, Linda Nochlin posed the question 'Why Have There Been No Great Women Artists?'. Ten years later, in *Old Mistresses: Women, Art, Ideology*, Griselda Pollock and Roszika Parker significantly extended the scope of feminist art history, setting themselves in deliberate opposition to 'the history of women in art as merely a fight against exclusion from, and discrimination by, institutions such as academies' that would judge women's histories merely 'against the norms of male history'. They displaced the emphasis from 'individual biographies of women' to 'serious consideration of works of art by them' and emphasized in their preface that the book was 'not a history of women artists, but an analysis of the relations between women, art and ideology'.

A few years later, Pollock's *Vision and Difference: Feminity, Feminism and the Histories of Art* (London, 1988) replaced the notion of a 'feminist art history' by that of 'feminist intervention in the histories of art'. Here, the emphasis moves into the language of art history. As Lisa Tickner pointed out: 'A feminism that does not contest the principal terms of the dominant discourse will be tamed by what it leaves unquestioned.' These concerns place feminism at the forefront of contemporary attempts to question the assumptions and renew the 'problematique' of the discipline. For Tickner (1989): 'The category of "art", the boundaries, concepts and language of historical enquiry, the privileging of the artist, and the invisibility of the viewer must be reworked, not in some abstract theoretical space, but as part of the understanding of objects and relations that are locally and historically specific.'

3. EPISTEMOLOGICAL ISSUES. The increasing sophistication of modern theory has served to open up considerably the areas of visual practice to be studied and to question the epistemological basis of art history. This conventionally rests on two fundamental assumptions: first, the recognition of a discrete area of practice, 'art', concerned with the production of a specific class of objects, 'works of art', and second, the belief in the continuity of that area of practice throughout human history (*see also* ART and ART, WORK OF). Nevertheless, in late 20th-century practice, following the global commodification of artefacts and images from all cultures and periods of human history, the concepts of 'art' and 'artist' were still being applied anachronistically and indiscriminately to as wide a range of contexts as prehistory, ancient Egypt, Greece, China, India, medieval Europe, feudal Japan, post-colonial Africa, Oceania and South America. Although the labelling of these objects as 'art' is not likely to be reversed, the specificity of the historical conditions under which these terms and the institutionalization of art-historical practices arose should be acknowledged. The heuristic projection of the concept of 'art' on to cultures that structured the production and perception of images in different terms has played an important part in preserving the myth that art has a universal value. Translators are partly to blame for this, as they have since the 19th century forced these concepts indiscriminately on to texts in a collective enterprise of cultural appropriation of the past (an example being the common mistranslation of *artefice* as 'artist' in English editions of Vasari). In the 1990s, apart from a few isolated objections raised mostly from within the New Art History (Mermoz, 1989), the concept of 'art' remains largely unchallenged, conferring on the history of 'art' the coherence of an autonomous discipline, be it 'traditional', modernist, Marxist, formalist, feminist or post-structuralist. The persistence of the idea of 'art' also serves to legitimize all those practices—from dealing and collecting to displaying and viewing works, writing and reading about them—that promote a sense of global cultural identity. Extending the notion of 'national heritage' on to a world scale, the concept of 'art' now offers, alongside the notions of culture, spirituality and progress, a universal paradigm through which different visual practices can be appropriated and their significance redefined, from the seemingly objective standpoint of a universal history of 'art'. Thus, the demise of modernism has facilitated the assimilation of Marxist, feminist, Post-modernist, black, gay and other alternative artistic practices

into an enlarged art-historical canon, with the result that such practices ironically situate themselves largely within the ideology of 'art' operating within and seeking recognition from art institutions and often retaining the conventional format of exhibitions of 'works of art'. While such practices may claim to displace the aesthetic into the political, there is an intrinsic contradiction in the attempt to theorize a political 'art' practice along the lines advocated by Marxist, feminist, black and gay artists, critics and art historians.

4. THE PROBLEMS OF A UNIVERSAL ART HISTORY. One problem with seeking to embrace all 'art'-historical traditions arises from the very diverse conceptualizations through which different cultures have appropriated their past. In China, for example, 'art-historical' periodization follows a classification model based on the chronological sequence of political dynasties. When a Western scholar is confronted with this material, it is tempting, as OSWALD SIRÉN admitted, to look for patterns of recurrences and to posit in Hegelian fashion that 'every epoch is characterized by certain prevailing ideals, which are brought out in the writings of the time' (*The Chinese on the Art of Painting*; Beiping (Beijing), 1936; New York, 1963, p. 4). Through searching in this way, Western scholars might claim to find that Chinese writings on the visual arts developed themes similar to those found in European writings and to use these parallels as guidelines (*see also* §I, 1 above). Thus, among Chinese writers, as in the Plinian and Vasarian traditions, speculations about the origins and nature of painting can be found. For example, Zhang Yanyuan wrote in AD 845 that painting 'originated from Nature and not from any decrees or works of men' (Sirén, p. 224), but that 'the art of painting should be sought for beyond outward likeness' (p. 227). In the *Lidai minghua ji* (II.iii), Zhang Yanyuan outlined a model for the assessment of pictures based on the relation between the 'idea' and its realization (Sirén, p. 231). An alternative to finding such parallels is to classify as culturally specific any differences found in Chinese 'aesthetics', for example the close relation between painting, theories of representation, philosophy and religion, and, likewise, the conceptual continuity across long periods of time, as indeed Sirén did.

In fact, a Western scholar may feel altogether uneasy about interpreting another culture from the standpoint and through the paradigms of Eurocentrism, using such recent Western terms as 'art', 'artist', 'critic' and the related expressions 'art history', 'art criticism' and 'aesthetics'. At present, a global perspective on world 'art history' is too problematic to be attempted, for it rests on too many questionable assumptions. It assumes, for instance, the existence of 'world art' and a 'world art history' by forcing modern categories on to contexts with explanations that are posited rather than demonstrated. This situation, sanctioned by the anachronistic use of these concepts by artists, dealers, collectors, curators, writers, teachers and others, culminates in the totalizing project of the 'history of art'—and the commodification of an ever-increasing range of artefacts—against the theoretical pluralism implicit in an alternative notion of histories of visual practices.

The reluctance of scholars to acknowledge the epistemological implications on which the project of a general history of 'world art history' rests indicates the power of logocentrism and ethnocentrism. It is not only Western writers who find it hard to escape their specific cultural perspective, even while attempting a universal account. This becomes apparent when an Asian writer seeks to establish correlations between Eastern and Western modes of thought. In *The Transformation of Nature into Art* (1934, 2/1956), for example, ANANDA KENTISH COOMARASWAMY set out to define an 'Oriental aesthetic theory based mainly on Indian and partly on Chinese sources', which could be used as a basis for 'a general theory of art coordinating Eastern and Western points of view' (p. 3). After pointing out that 'what is called the appreciation of Asiatic art is mainly based on categorical misinterpretations' (p. 4), Coomaraswamy indicated that his purpose was 'to place the Asiatic and the valid European views side by side, not as curiosities, but as representing actual and indispensable truth' (p. 4). His own ideological motivation becomes apparent in his statement that 'there was a time when Europe and Asia could and did actually understand each other very well'. At this point periodization is called on to inscribe ideology; thus, the suggestion that 'European art' is of 'two very different kinds, one Christian and scholastic, the other post-Renaissance and personal', postulates a break in 'the European consciousness', which would have led to a 'preoccupation with surfaces', to the effect that 'it has become more and more difficult for European minds to think in terms of unity, and therefore more difficult to understand the Asiatic point of view' (p. 3).

What the approach outlined by Sirén and the example of Coomaraswamy make clear is that the writing of cultural history is bound by ideological assumptions and theoretical presuppositions anchored in specific historical conditions. The historian of visual representations works within these constraints; no historian can escape them. The argument presented here—that it is impossible to write a 'general history of world art history'—rests on two convictions: first, that the concept of 'art' is inadequate to describe the variety of visual practices currently encompassed by this term, and second, that this inadequacy calls for a systematic re-examination of the concepts and practices through which the 'history of art', as an academic discipline, continues to present ideological constructs as historical facts. A possible alternative to the mystifying discourse of 'art history' would take the form of a multidisciplinary approach to visual representations (using concepts and methods from such disciplines as history, anthropology, semiotics, psychoanalysis and hermeneutics), never losing sight of the processes through which interpretation defines and constantly re-creates its object.

BIBLIOGRAPHY

L. Venturi: *History of Art Criticism* (Milan and New York, 1936/*R* 1964)
F. Antal: 'Remarks on the Method of Art History', *Burl. Mag.*, xci (1949), no. 551, pp. 49–52; no. 552, pp. 73–5
B. Teyssedre: *L'Histoire de l'art vue du grand siècle* (Paris, 1964)
N. Hadjinicolaou: *Histoire de l'art et lutte des classes* (Paris, 1973; Eng. trans., London, 1978)
T. J. Clark: 'The Conditions of Artistic Creation', *TLS* (24 May 1974), pp. 561–2
C. Maltese: *Guida allo studio della storia dell'arte* (Milan, 1975)
M. Roskill: *What Is Art History?* (London, 1976)
G. C. Argan and M. Fagiolo: *Guida a la storia dell'arte* (Florence, 1977)

J. Tagg: 'Marxism and Art History', *Marxism Today* (June 1977), pp. 183–92
E. Kris and O. Kurz: *Legend, Myth and Magic in the Image of the Artist* (New Haven and London, 1979)
G. C. Sciolla: *Materiali per la storia della critica d'arte del novecento* (Turin, 1980)
C. R. Sherman and A. M. Holcomb: *Women as Interpreters of the Visual Arts, 1820–1979* (Westport, 1981)
M. Podro: *The Critical Historians of Art* (New Haven and London, 1982)
M. Baxandall: *Patterns of Intention* (New Haven and London, 1985)
O. Calabrese: *Il linguaggio dell'arte* (Milan, 1985)
J. Tagg: 'Art History and Difference', *Block*, x (1985), pp. 45–7
G. Bazin: *Histoire de l'histoire de l'art* (Paris, 1986)
A. L. Rees and F. Borzello, eds: *The New Art History* (London, 1986)
N. Bryson, ed.: *Calligram: Essays in New Art History from France* (Cambridge, 1988)
W. M. Johnson: *Art History: Its Use and Abuse* (Toronto, 1988)
T. Y. Levin: 'Walter Benjamin and the Theory of Art History', *October*, xlvii (1988), pp. 77–90
G. Mermoz: 'Rhetoric and Episteme: Writing about "Art" in the Wake of Post-structuralism', *A. Hist.*, xii/4 (1989), pp. 497–509
D. Preziosi: *Rethinking Art History: Meditations on a Coy Science* (New Haven, 1989)
M. Roskill: *The Interpretation of Pictures* (Amherst, 1989)
L. Tickner: 'Art History Differently', *New Formations*, vii (Spring 1989), pp. 111–17
G. Didi-Huberman: *Devant l'image* (Paris, 1990)
G. Mermoz: 'Desire of Language', *A. Hist.*, xiii/3 (1990), pp. 404–7
N. Broude and M. D. Garrard, eds: *The Expanding Discourse: Feminism and Art History* (New York, 1992)
A. Jones: 'Artful Rewritings and Interpretive Repressions in New Feminist Art Histories', *A. Hist.*, xv/2 (1992), pp. 253–62

GÉRARD MERMOZ

Arthois [Artoes; Artoies; Artois; Artoos; Artoys]**, Jacques d'** (*bapt* Brussels, 12 Oct 1613; *d* between 26 April and 17 June 1686). Flemish painter, draughtsman and collector. He was apprenticed to Jan Mertens on 11 January 1625 and became a master in the Brussels painters' guild on 3 May 1634. On 10 July 1636 he married Marie Sampels, who bore him eight children. Besides his son Jan Baptist d'Arthois (*b* 1638) and his brother Nicolaes d'Arthois (*b* 1617), Jacques had six pupils; one of them, Cornelis van Empel, came from Mechelen, indicating that d'Arthois's fame extended beyond his native city. He was made chartered tapestry cartoon designer of the city of Brussels in 1655. At the time of his death he owned several houses and a substantial paintings collection, though an expansive lifestyle had left him severely in debt.

D'Arthois, the leading figure of the Brussels landscape school of the second half of the 17th century, is best known as the painter of the Forêt de Soignes, where one of his houses was located. His painted and drawn landscapes, with their bushes, ponds, hollow paths, clay banks and sandy hills, are dominated by tall trees crowned with luxuriant foliage (e.g. *Wooded Landscape with Flock*, Vienna, Ksthist. Mus.). Powerful colour contrast in the paintings, introduced all too often at the expense of nuance, is developed mainly within the framework of the traditional Flemish brown–green–blue scheme. The brushwork in his large compositions follows the supple lines of the vegetation, employing a breadth and boldness of touch that suggest some influence of Rubens. A number of smaller compositions feature more meticulous brushwork and a subtler, more varied use of colour. Three of d'Arthois's landscape paintings bear the monogram of David Teniers (ii), who painted the figures, and eight were engraved by Wenceslas Hollar (1648–52; Hollstein: *Dut. & Flem.*, ix, p. 70).

BIBLIOGRAPHY

Y. Thiéry: *Le Paysage flamand au XVIIe siècle* (Paris and Brussels, 1953), pp. 136–47
M. Kervijn de Meerendré: 'Jacques d'Arthois (1613–1686)', *An. Fed. Cerc. Archéol. & Hist. Belg.*, xliv (1976), pp. 841–7
Le Paysage brabançon au XVIIe siècle: De Brueghel le jeune à d'Arthois (exh. cat. by W. Laureyssens, Brussels, Mus. A. Anc., 1976)
Y. Thiéry and M. Kervijn de Meerendré: *Les Peintres flamands de paysage au XVIIe siècle: Le Baroque anversois et l'école bruxelloise* (Brussels, 1986), pp. 125–44
The Age of Rubens (exh. cat., ed. P. C. Sutton; Boston, MA, Mus. F.A.; Toledo, OH, Mus. A.; 1993–4), pp. 483–5, *passim*

HANS DEVISSCHER

Arthur III, 9th Duke of Brittany. *See* BRITTANY, (2).

Arthur, Eric (Ross) (*b* Dunedin, 1898; *d* Toronto, 1982). Canadian teacher, writer and historian of New Zealand birth. He studied architecture in New Zealand, and after service in World War I, he went to the University of Liverpool in 1919 as the Lord Kitchener National Memorial Scholar. He then emigrated to Canada (1923) and began to teach at the University of Toronto, where he spent almost his entire professional life. Arthur was an ardent supporter of the Modern Movement but also promoted an awareness of Canada's historic colonial buildings, which were derived from the English Georgian style: the simple lines and sparing ornament typical of such buildings dating from the late 18th century, as described in his book *The Early Buildings of Ontario* (1938), seemed to anticipate the goals of modern architecture. He was the architect for the restoration in 1937 of St Andrew's Church, Niagara-on-the-Lake, and became a pioneer of the conservation movement in Ontario. His survey of Toronto architecture, *No Mean City*, which appeared in 1964 after many years in preparation, was regarded as a celebration of Canadian heritage and a weapon for the conservation movement. At the same time he continued to support modern architecture; he was chairman of the committee that produced a master-plan (1953) for the University of Toronto and of the committee that selected Viljo Revell as the architect of the new town hall (1959), Toronto, a modernist design. He received several honours and awards during his career, including the Companion of the Order of Canada.

WRITINGS

The Early Buildings of Ontario (Toronto, 1938)
Toronto: No Mean City (Toronto, 1963, rev. 3/1986 by S. A. Otto)
with J. Acland: *Buildings by the Sea* (Toronto, 1963)
with D. Witney: *The Barn: A Vanishing Landmark in North America* (Toronto, 1972)

BIBLIOGRAPHY

'St Andrew's Church, Niagara-on-the-Lake', *J. Royal Archit. Inst. Canada*, xv/1 (1938), pp. 277–81
'University of Toronto Master Plan', *J. Royal Archit. Inst. Canada*, xxx/10 (1953), pp. 286–9

ALAN GOWANS

Artificial stone. Material most commonly used as a cheaper alternative to stone. Occasionally, its special properties make it a preferred but more expensive choice to stone. In its simplest form, artificial stone is an ashlar covering for buildings (e.g. 18th-century terraced houses by John Nash). It is found in its most sophisticated form as the component of numerous 19th-century terracotta or cement-based sculptures.

1. Materials and techniques. The earliest and simplest form of artificial stone is the lime-and-gypsum plaster used to decorate the walls of Egyptian tombs. These facings were predominantly of gypsum plaster lined and painted to simulate the texture of stone. In ancient Rome, renders (first coats of plaster) had a similar design and purpose, although they were applied to a wider variety of buildings. The incorporation of lime, pozzolana, additives of volcanic ash, sherds of pottery and brick dust strengthened the mortars and gave them greater durability. The renders were often painted to increase the illusion that actual stone was used (*see also* Rome, ancient, §VII). In 16th- and 17th-century Italy, recipes for stucco included marble dusts, lime and glue to aid in the imitation of stone and to ensure the strength of the mix. In the 18th century the interiors of Neo-classical buildings often featured stuccowork modelled to appear carved, and were coated with a light blue-grey overpaint to enhance the appearance of artificial stone, as seen for example in reliefs (*c.* 1764) by Thomas Carter (*d* 1795) in Henry Flitcroft's Pantheon (1754) at Stourhead, Wilts.

With the arrival of the Industrial Revolution and the increasing market for durable architectural decoration and statuary, recipes for harder and more dense artificial stone were created. In 1767 Daniel Pincot showed specimens of artificial stone at the Free Society of Artists Exhibition, London, and Eleanor Coade set up her manufacture in Lambeth, London, in 1769. Both produced stone far superior in strength and durability to white marble or ordinary rock stone. Strictly a terracotta material, the highly successful recipe and manufacturing technique for Coade stone was never published; neither Pincot nor Coade took out a patent. When analysed, Coade stone revealed a predominance of clay, silica and grog of flint and feldspar fired at high temperatures over a long period. As with most terracotta pieces produced from moulds, elements were interchangeable from one composition to the next. John Sealy (1749–1813) became Coade's partner, and later William Croggon (*fl* 1814–35) took over as manager. Other companies that manufactured artificial stone in Britain were run by Blashfield and John Doulton (1793–1873). Cement-based artificial stones, though not as sharply defined, weather well in the climate of Britain and have the appearance of natural stone. Pulham stone and Haddon stone, produced in the 19th century, are composed mainly of cement and aggregate cast and were used to make garden ornaments and statuary of great durability.

See also Stucco and plasterwork.

2. Uses. In ancient times artificial stone was widely used as a facing for houses and monuments when quarried stone was not easily available. In the 3rd and 4th centuries BC towns of the Roman Empire contained buildings built predominantly of brick with concrete walls faced with stucco polished to 'shine like marble'. Emperor Augustus (*reg* 30 BC–AD 14) boasted that he found 'Rome of brick and left it in marble' (Suetonius: *Augustus*). Scagliola, a type of imitation marble or pietra dura, was popular from the 16th century and was used for table-tops and as a moulding on walls and door panels. In the 17th and 18th centuries it was especially used as part of the design of monasteries in Italy.

Artificial Coade stone sculpture by John Bacon (i): *River God*, *c.* 1777–9 (Ham House, Surrey, NT)

In the 18th and 19th centuries Neo-classical façades of buildings were cheaply and quickly built with renders lined to look like stone entablatures, this having been made possible at the time by means of various formulae for the manufacture of cement. Prince Albert had Osborne House (begun 1845), Isle of Wight, inexpensively constructed with the latest of building technology: the house is faced with artificial stone. In the UK the demand for a more durable type of sculpture and ornament for out of doors frequently led to artificial stone being chosen as a preferred material. In the 19th century approximately 25 British manufactories produced artificial stone for statuary and garden ornaments. The fashion for Neo-classical façades and gardens, combined with existing skilled building technology, resulted in the manufacture of cast ornament of the highest standard. The most successful producer of artificial stone ornament was the Coade Artificial Stone Manufactory (*see* §1 above). Between 1769 and 1843 the company, through a combination of suitably fine mixtures of terracotta and the best contemporary craftsmanship, produced Coade stone (see fig.), which is as resilient today as it was in the 18th and 19th centuries.

BIBLIOGRAPHY

G. E. Bessey: 'The Maintenance and Repair of Regency Painted Stucco Finishes', *RIBA J.*, n.s. 2, lvii/4 (1950), pp. 143–5

Proceedings of the International Symposium, The Conservation of Stone, I: Bologna, 1975

A. Kelly: *Mrs Coade's Stone* (Hanley Swan, 1990)

J. P. S. Davis: *Antique Garden Ornament: 300 Years of Creativity, Artists, Manufacturers and Materials* (Woodbridge, 1991)

TREVOR PROUDFOOT

Artifort. *See under* WAGEMANS MAASTRICHT.

Artiga, Francisco (*b* Huesca, *c.* 1650; *d* Huesca, 1711). Spanish engraver, painter, architect, mathematician and astronomer. He founded the chair of mathematics at the University of Huesca, designed the façade of the university and from 1690 was responsible for overseeing the whole of its construction. He executed an etching of this façade, as well as others showing allegories referring to the city and the university. Artiga wrote scientific and literary works, including an unpublished treatise entitled *Fortificación elemental*, which he illustrated. He also illustrated Vicencio Juan de Lastanosa's *Tratado de la moneda jaquesa* (Saragossa, 1681) and engraved some further architectural views as well as images of antique Roman fragments and archaeological remains. In addition, he produced religious engravings, and a number of paintings have been attributed to him by Ceán Bermúdez.

BIBLIOGRAPHY

Bénézit; Ceán Bermúdez
A. Gallego: *Historia del grabado en España* (Madrid, 1979), p. 192
E. Páez Ríos: *Repertorio* (Madrid, 1981–3), i, pp. 70–71
C. Guitart Aparicio: 'Geografía de la arquitectura barroca en Aragón', *Actas de III coloquio de arte aragonés: Huesca, 1983*, pp. 26–7

BLANCA GARCÍA VEGA

Artigas. Spanish Catalan family of ceramicists. Josep Llorens Artigas (*b* Barcelona, 16 June 1892; *d* Barcelona, 11 Dec 1980) studied art in Barcelona at the Escuela de Artes y Oficios de la Lonja, at the Cercle Artístic de Sant Lluc and in 1915 at the Escola Superior de Bells Oficis. In 1923 he went for a lengthy stay to Paris, where he carried out a profound reconsideration of his pottery, divesting it of all decoration. In 1941, once more in Barcelona, he joined the Escuela Massana as a teacher, giving new impetus to Spanish pottery. His vessels, made of monochrome earthenware on the wheel, were not particularly unusual in their shape, but they were distinguished by the extraordinary quality of their glazes.

Llorens Artigas exhibited widely internationally and received several major awards. He collaborated with several major painters, beginning in 1923 with Raoul Dufy in Paris and later with Georges Braque (1948–9), and above all with Joan Miró, whom he met as early as 1912 and with whom he developed a close friendship. Artigas was spokesman for the Agrupación Courbet, a short- lived breakaway group from the Cercle Artístic de Sant Lluc, active in Barcelona in 1918–19; the founder-members included E.-C. Ricart, Miró and Francisco Domingo y Marqués. With Miró, too, he produced pots, sculptures and large ceramic murals, such as those for the UNESCO building in Paris (1955–6, installed 1958), which won the Guggenheim Foundation's first prize; for Harvard University (1960); and for Barcelona Airport (1971). Six of his vases (all 1969) are in the collection of the Fondation Maeght at Saint-Paul-de-Vence.

His son Joan Gardy Artigas (*b* Boulogne-Billancourt, Seine-et-Oise, 1938) studied at the Ecole du Louvre in Paris in 1958. In 1959 he started a ceramics studio in Paris, where he worked with Georges Braque and Marc Chagall. In 1960, the year in which he met Alberto Giacometti, he made his first sculptures, but he also continued working as a ceramicist, notably in collaborations with Miró in 1961, 1967 and 1969.

WRITINGS

J. Llorens Artigas: *Les pastes ceràmiques: Les esmalts blaus de l'Antic Egipte* (Barcelona, 1922)
——: *Formularios y prácticas de cerámica* (Barcelona, 1948)
——: *Esmaltes y colores sobre vidrio, porcelana y metal* (Barcelona, 1950)
J. Llorens Artigas, with J. Corredor-Matheos: *Cerámica popular española* (Barcelona, 1970)

BIBLIOGRAPHY

J. Corredor-Matheos and J. Pierre: *Céramiques de Miró–Artigas* (Paris, 1974)
Gardy Artigas: Sculptures-reliefs (exh. cat., Zurich, Maeght, 1975)
P. Courthion: *Llorens Artigas* (Barcelona, 1977)
F. Miralles: *A l'entorn de Llorens Artigas* (Barcelona, 1981)
Josep Llorens Artigas (exh. cat. by J. Teixidor and others, Madrid, Mus. A. Contemp., 1982)

JOSÉ CORREDOR-MATHEOS

Artigas, João B(atista) Vilanova (*b* Curitiba, 23 June 1915; *d* São Paulo, 6 Jan 1985). Brazilian architect, teacher and writer. He graduated as an engineer–architect from the Escola Politécnica of the University of São Paulo (1937) and became a partner in the design and construction firm Marone & Artigas. Like many architects he sought to move away from the academic electicism that dominated São Paulo at the time, and his first projects were influenced by the work of Frank Lloyd Wright; for example, the Rio Branco Paranhos house (1943) was clearly inspired by Wright's prairie houses. In 1944 he opened his own design office in São Paulo; he was increasingly influenced by the rationalist modernism of Le Corbusier that began to spread from Rio de Janeiro and often used pilotis, *brises-soleil* and roof gardens at this time, as in the Louveira block of flats (1948) and the Mario Bittencourt house (1949), São Paulo, and the bus station (1950), Londrina.

During this period Artigas was also heavily involved in cultural and political activities; he became a teacher of architecture at the Escola Politécnica, São Paulo (1940–56), where he was a pioneer of modern teaching, and in 1943 he helped form the São Paulo division of the Instituto de Arquitetos do Brasil and was one of its first directors. In 1945 he joined the Brazilian Communist Party and was one of the principal organizers of the first Brazilian Congress of Architects. He travelled in the USA for a year (1946–7) on a grant from the Guggenheim Foundation, and in 1948 he helped to establish the Faculty of Architecture and Urbanism at the University of São Paulo (FAUUSP). He then published his two most important critical essays on architecture: 'Le Corbusier e o imperialismo' and 'Os caminhos da arquitetura moderna' (1951 and 1952); both are pioneering analyses of the ideology behind modern architectural thinking.

In 1953 Artigas won a competition for the São Paulo football club stadium, his first large-scale work. After this project, he began to develop an architectural style of his own; in buildings in São Paulo such as the Olga Baeta house (1956), the José Mario Taques Bittencourt house (1959), the boat-house for the Santapaula Yacht Club (1960) and his most influential work, the new FAUUSP building (1961; see fig.), he searched for the dissociation of the building from its surrounding site, emphasized monumentality and used heavy construction elements both as means of architectural expression and as ethical metaphors for social conflict. This resulted in a brutalist approach, but it was based more on Wright's spatial experiments as seen in the Larkin Building (1904), Buffalo, NY, than on Le Corbusier's *manière brute*, although Artigas shared the latter's philosophy. In the 1960s and 1970s the rather limited vocabulary of this language, characterized by the extensive use of *béton brut* (Fr.: 'raw concrete') to define compact, regular volumes, blank walls supported by irregularly shaped pillars, and rectangular roofs covering a series of spaces, became the definitive model for architecture in São Paulo, adopted by many architects for a wide variety of buildings.

Artigas produced some of his most significant projects in the late 1960s, for example the Elza Berquó house (1967), a poetic work in which he used tree trunks as supports, and the housing complex Parque Cecap (1967), a plan for 10,000 low-cost flats based on the idea of the neighbourhood unit. He also presented his influential essay 'O desenho' in the opening lecture at FAUUSP in 1967. However, this was also the most troubled period of his political life. His influence on the architectural students of São Paulo had been growing since the mid-1950s, and he was involved in new proposals to reform the teaching of architecture at the FAUUSP (1962), which became the model followed by most schools in Brazil. After the military coup in 1964, however, the persecution of communists intensified, and in 1969 he was compulsorily retired from the university.

The only official commissions Artigas subsequently received were those for the Território Federal do Amapá in the far north, including the Presidente Costa e Silva gymnasium (1971) and the territorial guard barracks (1971). From 1972 he designed a series of elevated pedestrian walkways for the Empresa Municipal de Urbanização de São Paulo using a composite structure of reinforced concrete and steel, and in 1973 he designed the bus station for the Prefecture of Jaú with an immense reinforced concrete roof resting on huge columns like tree trunks. In his design for the Conceiçãozinha state school (1976), Guarujá, he returned to his earlier interest in materials and textures; the unusual combination of brick arcades, concrete block walls, wood latticework and tiled roofs make this his most creative project of the period. In 1979 Artigas returned to the University of São Paulo and was awarded a special doctorate from the FAUUSP in 1984. He received many other honours and awards during his career, including the Jean Tschumi Award (1972) and the Auguste Perret Award (1984), both from the Union Internationale des Architectes. His architecture and his teaching both had an enormous influence on a generation of architects in Brazil.

WRITINGS

'Le Corbusier e o imperialismo', *Fundamentos*, 18 (1951), pp. 8–9, 27

'Os caminhos da arquitetura moderna', *Fundamentos*, 24 (1952), pp. 20–25

O desenho (São Paulo, 1967)

Caminhos da arquitetura (São Paulo, 1981)

Memorial, 2 vols (São Paulo, 1981)

BIBLIOGRAPHY

H. E. Mindlin: *Modern Architecture in Brazil* (Amsterdam and Rio de Janeiro, 1956)

'Rapporto Brasile', *Zodiac*, 6 (1960), pp. 97–107

S. Ficher and M. M. Acayaba: *Arquitetura moderna brasileira* (São Paulo, 1982)

João B. Vilanova Artigas: Faculty of Architecture and Urbanism building, University of São Paulo, 1961

SYLVIA FICHER

Art informel [Informalism; Lyrical Abstraction]. Term coined in 1950 by the French critic Michel Tapié, primarily in relation to the work of Wols, and subsequently applied more generally to a movement in European painting that began in the mid-1940s and flourished in the 1950s as a parallel development to Abstract Expressionism (especially action painting) in the USA. Sometimes referred to as TACHISM, ART AUTRE or Lyrical Abstraction, it was a type of abstraction in which form became subservient to the expressive impulses of the artist, and it was thus diametrically opposed to the cool rationalism of geometric abstraction. Antecedents can be found in the work of Vasily Kandinsky, Paul Klee and Jean Dubuffet and particularly in the Surrealist current of AUTOMATISM, such as that practised by André Masson. In its more precise historical sense its pioneers were artists based in Paris, such as Jean Fautrier, Wols (e.g. *Composition*, 1947; Hamburg, Ksthalle, or *Yellow Composition*, 1946–7; Berlin, Neue N.G.; for illustration *see* WOLS) and Hans Hartung (e.g. *T. 1949-9*, 1949; Düsseldorf, Kstsamml. Nordrhein-Westfalen); Hartung in particular was producing paintings with many of the features of *Art informel* by the mid-1930s, as in *T. 1935-1* (1935; Paris, Pompidou; for illustration *see* HARTUNG, HANS). The movement came to include Jean-Michel Atlan, Jean Bazaine, Roger Bissière, Camille Bryen, Alberto Burri, Charles Lapicque, Alfred Manessier, Georges Mathieu, Henri Michaux, Serge Poliakoff, Pierre Soulages, Nicolas de Staël, Antoni Tàpies and others. Following the lead of Surrealist automatism, current in Surrealism, *Art informel* pictures were executed spontaneously and often at speed so as to give vent to the subconscious of the artist. Though embodying a wide range of approaches to abstraction, the brushwork in such works is generally gestural or calligraphic, as in Michaux's *Untitled* (1960; New York, Guggenheim; see fig.) or Mathieu's *Capetians Everywhere* (1954; Paris, Pompidou; for illustration *see* MATHIEU, GEORGES). Sometimes there is an emphasis on the texture or tactile quality of the paint, leading to a variant of *Art informel* referred to as MATTER PAINTING. Certain artists, such as Bazaine, Manessier and

Art informel drawing by Henri Michaux: *Untitled*, India ink on paper, 740×1099 mm, 1960 (New York, Solomon R. Guggenheim Museum)

Poliakoff, produced paintings that appeared less spontaneous and more controlled, with a more consciously mediated composition and use of colour, as in Manessier's *Barrabas* (1952; Eindhoven, Stedel. Van Abbemus.).

The roots of *Art informel* lay in the climate of 'art politics' that pervaded the period just after World War II in France. In seeking a dominant role within the avant-garde, its exponents were primarily in competition with the champions of geometric abstraction, who in 1946 attempted to reassert their earlier dominance by founding an exhibiting society, the Salon des Réalités Nouvelles. Although at this stage there was little cohesion among the practitioners of *Art informel*, some of whom even took part in the initial exhibitions of the Salon des Réalités Nouvelles, they soon came together in a series of exhibitions organized by Mathieu, who also coined the alternative term 'Lyrical Abstraction'. The first of these was an exhibition entitled *L'Imaginaire* (Paris, Gal. Luxembourg, 1947), which united the work of Atlan, Bryen, Hartung, Mathieu, Jean-Paul Riopelle and Wols with that of Picasso, Hans Arp, Victor Brauner and others, a fairly heterogeneous mixture; the catalogue preface by Jean-José Marchand adopted the oppositional tone that marked *Art informel* in its early years, calling for a battle against Constructivism and Neo-plasticism so as to free art from 'all enslavement and pseudo problems'. A second exhibition organized by Mathieu, *H.W.P.S.M.T.B.* (Paris, Gal. Colette Allendy, 1948), took its title from the names of its participants: Hartung, Wols, Francis Picabia, François Stahly, Mathieu, Tapié and Bryen. Tapié himself later organized several *Art informel* exhibitions, including three at Studio Facchetti in Paris: *Signifiants de l'informel* (1951 and 1952) and *Un Art autre* (1952). The Galerie Drouin in Paris also presented important group exhibitions, having shown Fautrier's *Hostages* series as far back as 1945 and Wols's first *Art informel* oils in 1947. A one-man show of Hartung's works was held at the Galerie Lydia Conti in Paris in 1947. Very quickly, therefore, *Art informel* achieved a high profile in the cultural life of Paris. The momentum of *Art informel* was further bolstered by exhibitions illustrating the links between contemporary French art and that of other countries, beginning in 1948 (Paris, Gal. Montparnasse) with an incompletely realized attempt by Mathieu to point out the similarities. *Véhémences confrontées* (1951; Paris, Gal. Nina Dausset), organized by Tapié, linked works by Hartung, Wols, Bryen and Mathieu with the work of North American painters such as Jackson Pollock (then little known in Paris), Willem de Kooning and Jean-Paul Riopelle. The first group show in Paris of the Northern Europeans known as Cobra also took place in 1951, organized by the French writer Michel Ragon; their style was similar to *Art informel* in its spontaneous handling, but more violent in tone and with a greater emphasis on figurative content.

The cohesive identity of *Art informel* as a fully formed movement was marked by the publication in the early 1950s of two books espousing its aims and charting its development. These were Ragon's *Expression et non-figuration* (1951) and Tapié's *Un Art autre* (1952), the latter emphasizing the radical break from tradition achieved by *Art informel.* The critic Charles Estienne, formerly a supporter of geometric abstraction, insistently attacked its inflexibility in *L'Art abstrait est-il un académisme* (1950). Having established their dominance within the avant-garde by the 1950s, the proponents of *Art informel* became involved in internal wrangles as soon as external struggles became superfluous; in 1954, for instance, Estienne introduced the term Tachism to refer to the work of those second-generation French painters whom he had gathered together at the Salon d'Octobre in Paris from 1950, including Marcelle Loubchansky (*b* 1917), Jean Degottex, Simon Hantaï and others. Further fragmentation followed as each of the leading critics—Tapié, Ragon, Estienne and Julian Alvard—formed his own faction.

Once established in France, *Art informel* spread to many other countries. The most notable exponents abroad included Tàpies, Modest Cuixart, Antonio Saura and Manolo Millares in Spain and Alberto Burri, Emilio Vedova and Antonio Corpora in Italy, though the work of Tàpies and Burri had a gravity and severity at odds with most *Art informel* painting. Related work was produced in West Germany by members of Quadriga, the Zen 49 group and Gruppe 53, and in particular by painters such as Willi Baumeister, Julius Bissier, Karl-Otto Götz, Karl Fred Dahmen (*b* 1917), Emil Schumacher and Theodor Werner; in Britain by Alan Davie, Patrick Heron, Roger Hilton and William Scott; in the Netherlands by Ger Lataster; in Belgium by Louis Van Lint (*b* 1909), René Guiette (*b* 1893) and Jean Milo (*b* 1906); and in Greece by Yannis Spyropoulos. Sam Francis, one of the most European of American painters, was also associated with these developments, and there were exponents of *Art informel* as far afield as Japan, Poland, Yugoslavia, Czechoslovakia and Latin America. In his book *L'Art informel* (1962) Jean Paulhan argued that this movement broke with all previous techniques and philosophies of art. Linking it to the work of philosophers and poets who had questioned the foundations of reality and the relation between the self and the world, he suggested that *Art informel* afforded insights into a half-world inaccessible to rational thought and beyond all experience. Nevertheless, he pointed to the similarities between certain microscopic images and *Art informel* works, making a connection, for example, between a picture by Wols and a photograph of nerve cells.

The popularity of *Art informel* immediately after World War II owed much to the fact that it was perceived as an attempt to shake off tradition and (in that it was an expression of artistic freedom) as a break from the atmosphere of political authoritarianism that had led to the war. For those artists still oppressed by political tyranny, as in Franco's Spain and Eastern Europe, it remained a permissible symbol of liberation. As an aesthetic, however, it represented a form of inward retreat in which reality was allowed only a concealed appearance. Thus by the early 1960s it was forcefully challenged by movements such as Nouveau Réalisme and Pop art, which sought a more direct engagement with everyday life and rejected the idea of art as the subjective expression of personality.

For additional illustrations *see* FAUTRIER, JEAN, and TÀPIES, ANTONI.

BIBLIOGRAPHY

C. Estienne: *L'Art abstrait est-il un académisme* (Paris, 1950)
M. Ragon: *Expression et non-figuration* (Paris, 1951)
J. Alvard and R. van Gindertael: *Témoignages pour l'art abstrait* (Paris, 1952)
M. Tapié: *Un Art autre* (Paris, 1952)
J. Paulhan: *L'Art informel* (Paris, 1962)
G. Mathieu: *Au-delà du tachisme* (Paris, 1963)
M. Ragon: 'Lyrical Abstraction from Explosion to Inflation', *Abstract Art since 1945*, by W. Haftmann and others (London, 1971), pp. 72–102
M. Seuphor and M. Ragon: *L'Art abstrait*, iii (Paris, 1973)
A. Pohribny: *Abstract Painting* (Oxford, 1979)
Paris-Paris: Créations en France 1937–1957 (exh. cat., ed. G. Viatte; Paris, Pompidou, 1981), pp. 216–41, 252–69
W. Schmalenbach: *Der expressive Elan in der Malerei nach 1945* (Duisburg, 1987) [parallel German/English text]

PHILIP COOPER

Artisan Mannerism. Term introduced by John Summerson to identify an architectural and decorative style, largely derived from north European MANNERISM, adopted by English artisans in the mid-17th century. Lugged architraves, broken pediments, grand and ornate gables, hipped roofs, heavy eaves-cornices and strongly demarcated string courses are among the idiosyncracies and embellishments that typify the style. More through available pattern books and the work of immigrant craftsmen than through travel abroad, English artisans, particularly in London, became increasingly aware during the 1620s and 1630s of recent developments in architectural design on the Continent. They took their ideas from such books as Jacques Francart's *Premier livre d'architecture* (Brussels, 1616), Rubens's *Palazzi di Genova* (Antwerp, 1622) and Salomon de Bray's *Architectura moderna* (Amsterdam, 1631)—which illustrates the work of Hendrik de Keyser—but did not treat them as authoritative, although precise borrowings can be traced. Instead, individual workshops developed their own versions, regional differences grew and persisted, and early sources of design, such as the engraved books of Jacques Du Cerceau the elder, continued to be influential. Nicholas Stone, at his Goldsmiths' Hall in London (1635–8; destr.), was also among those who followed their own inclinations. The giant pilasters of several buildings in Kent, for example Sir George Sondes's Lees Court (begun *c.* 1640), near Faversham, the hipped roof of Sir John Harris's Balls Park (*c.* 1640), Herts, and the tall rectangular façade and mullioned windows of Thorpe Hall (1653–6), Cambs, built by PETER MILLS for Oliver St John, are examples of the coarse classicism that characterizes the style. The period overlaps with the career of Inigo Jones, who had produced far purer forms of Renaissance architecture for more sophisticated courtly patrons.

Recent studies point to an interdependence of ideas and patronage—from London merchants and the Cromwellian regime—between these city builders and the later work of Jones and his successor John Webb. Their eclectic style began to decline after 1660. The Great Fire of 1666 provided the last opportunities for the style in London during wholesale rebuilding there, although the influence of Artisan Mannerism persisted in the provinces for a further generation.

BIBLIOGRAPHY

J. Summerson: *Architecture in Britain, 1530–1830*, Pelican Hist. A. (London, 1969, rev. 7/1983), pp. 157–72
H. J. Lowe: 'Anglo-Netherlandish Architectural Interchange, *c.* 1600–1660', *Archit. Hist.*, xxiv (1981), pp. 1–23

C. Hind, ed.: *Inigo Jones and the Spread of Classicism* (London, 1987)
G. Worsley: 'Thorpe Hall in Context', *Georgian Group Journal* (1993), pp. 4–12

T. P. CONNOR

Artistas Modernos de la Argentina. Argentine group of artists formed in 1952 and active until 1954. It was founded on the initiative of the art critic Aldo Pellegrini (1903–75) as a union of Constructivist painters belonging to the ASOCIACIÓN ARTE CONCRETO INVENCIÓN—Tomás Maldonado, Alfredo Hlito, Lidy Prati (*b* 1921), Ennio Iommi and Claudio Girola (*b* 1923)—and four independent semi-abstract artists: José Antonio Fernández Muro, Sarah Grilo, Miguel Ocampo and Hans Aebi (*b* 1923). Pellegrini's main concern was with the quality of the artists' work rather than with a shared programme. They were the first abstract artists in Argentina to exhibit together as a group abroad: in 1953 they showed both at the Museu de Arte Moderna in Rio de Janeiro and at the Stedelijk Museum in Amsterdam.

Pelligrini was pleased with the genuine interaction within the group. The work of the independent artists became more rigorous and economical, inclining progressively towards geometric abstraction, and their lack of dogmatism in turn led the Constructivists to adopt a more flexible approach. The group disbanded on Maldonado's move to Germany in 1954, but the former associates continued to work separately with great success.

BIBLIOGRAPHY

A. Pellegrini: *Panorama de la pintura argentina contemporánea* (Buenos Aires, 1967), pp. 60–61
N. Perazzo: *El arte concreto en la Argentina* (Buenos Aires, 1983), p. 106

NELLY PERAZZO

Artistic Forum [Czech. Umělecká Beseda]. Czech society of artists, literary figures and musicians, active from 1863 to 1973. Founded in 1863 with the objective of establishing a unified national programme with which artists in different fields would be associated, its most active section became the Artists Group (Výtvarný), which brought together the outstanding contemporary figures in Czech art. Its first president was Josef Mánes (*see* MÁNES, (2)), and its early members included KAREL PURKYNĚ (*see* CZECH REPUBLIC, fig. 17) and the sculptor Václav Levý (1820–70). The group's original participation in the National Reawakening reached its climax in the early 1880s, when it was involved in the building and the decoration of the National Theatre in Prague. In the 1890s Artistic Forum became conservative and lost its earlier significance: while younger Czech artists joined the MÁNES UNION OF ARTISTS, older ones seceded in 1898 and founded the Union of Artists (Jednota Umělců Výtvarných). In 1909 Artistic Forum was revivified by the new membership of VÁCLAV RABAS and Karel Boháček, graduates of the Academy of Fine Arts, who were preoccupied with landscape painting and with social themes. They subsequently persuaded members of the so-called 'Mayer Club', whose leader was J. Jareš, to join as well, the Club's special interest being Slovakia's history and traditions. From this time until the 1920s Artistic Forum underwent its period of greatest activity, organizing exhibitions, lectures and commemorative occasions. In 1914 Jareš and B. Malthesius published the periodical *Život a mythus* ('Life and myth'). After World War I Artistic Forum offered an alternative to the modernist and cosmopolitan hegemony of the Mánes Union of Artists. Various authors who espoused the national tradition joined the Forum, as did JAN ZRZAVÝ and JOSEF ČAPEK, both of whom had been members of the Mánes Union for a short time. In 1921 the Forum began to publish the annual journal *Život* ('Life'); from 1933 it was published monthly and acquired great prestige in the 1930s. From 1930 the Forum organized exhibitions of the work of such artists as Zrzavý, JOSEF ŠÍMA (*see* CZECH REPUBLIC, fig. 18) and De Chirico; *Ecole de Paris*, a show of contemporary Parisian art, was held in 1931. In the early 1940s, František Hudeček, František Gross and Václav Boštík, young members of the 42 Group, became members of the Forum. It survived the Communist putsch of 1948 in Czechoslovakia, but its activity was henceforth considerably limited. The Artistic Forum's demise was officially announced at its centenary celebrations in 1963, but it was not until 1973 that it finally ceased to exist.

WRITINGS

Život & Mythus (1914)
Život (1921–48)

BIBLIOGRAPHY

H. Jelínek: *50 let Umělecké besedy, 1863–1913* [50 years of the Artistic Forum] (Prague, 1913)
F. Skácelík, ed.: *Sedmdesát let Umělecké besedy 1863–1933* [70 years of the Artistic Forum] (Prague, 1933)
K. Krejčí: *Sto let Umělecké besedy* [100 years of the Artistic Forum] (exh. cat., Prague, N.G., Valdštejn Riding Sch., 1963)

LENKA BYDŽOVSKÁ

Artists Association of Pest [Pesti Műegyesület; Pesther Kunst-Verein]. Hungarian association of artists, active in Pest from 1839 to 1869. It was established to organize fine art exhibitions. In 1838 Agoston Trefort (1817–88), with László Serenyi, Miklós Jósika (1796–1865) and József Eötvos (1813–71), began to plan an association that would support Hungarian artists and that would operate as a joint stock company. In November 1839 Trefort was made the first President, with László Szalay (1813–64) as Secretary. Although its primary task was to help those artists who wished to be free of the academic constrictions of the Vienna and Munich Artists Associations, it also wanted to awaken an interest in contemporary art and public art. Vince Grimm took on the role of dealer, since he had many connections with the Viennese art market. The association's first exhibition opened on 7 June 1840 in the Vigado Concert Hall in Pest. The organizers exhibited works by the most famous contemporary Hungarian artists, including Miklós Barabás (1810–98), Jakab Marastoni (1804–60), Bálint Kiss, János Rombauer (1782–1849) and Pál Balkay (1785–1846), and a larger number of works by well-known foreign painters (Carl Rottmann, Josef Danhauser, Friedrich von Amerling, Ferdinand Georg Waldmüller, Franz Jaschke) and by Károly Márkó (i), who was Hungarian but lived in Italy. Almost 9000 visitors were able to see the work of these foreign artists for the first time in Pest. The number of shareholders rose to 1200 after the success of the exhibition.

In 1841 the Association's leadership changed: András Fay became President, with Sándor Wagner as Committee President, Lajos Kossuth (1802–94) as Vice-President and

Dániel Szekrényessy as Secretary. The Association's greatest achievement was its declaration of support for the National Picture Gallery Association (Nemzeti Képcsarnokot Létesítő Egylet), formed in 1845. The Artists Association of Pest bought paintings, mainly through public subscriptions, directly from artists and not only strengthened the links between those artists and the National Museum in Pest, but also donated works to the museum's collection. The Association published the paper *Évkönyv* every year, which helped to popularize the art of the period. The shareholders, for an annual membership fee, had the right to buy some of the pictures exhibited: this was done by holding a raffle. People who could not attend the exhibitions were free to view the exhibits in the Association's premises in Pest, where work was on display between shows. The greatest number of members at any time was 500.

From its inception the Association was severely criticized. The organizers were accused of being unpatriotic and of working in the interests of foreign artists instead of Hungarian ones; they were criticized for having a Pest warehouse for Viennese art dealers. This view was subsequently taken up by many art historians; not until the late 20th century has the Association been seen in a more favourable light. As a result of divisions within the Association it began to disintegrate in 1859 and finally broke up in 1869. Its role was taken on by the National Hungarian Fine Art Society (Országos Magyar Képzőművészeti Társulat), which had been formed as a rival to the Association in 1861.

BIBLIOGRAPHY

J. Bayer: *A 'Pesti Műegylet' és első Kiállítása, 1840-ben* [The Artists Association of Pest and its first exhibition in 1840] (Budapest, 1916), pp. 257–76

B. Biró: *Pesti művészeti közélet száz év előtt* [Art life in Pest 100 years ago], *Képzőművészeti szemle*, xii (1930), pp. 234–42

G. Szvoboda: 'A Pesti Műegylet megalakulása és első Kiállítása 1840-ben' [The foundation of the Artists Association of Pest and its first exhibition in 1840], *A. Hung.*, ii (1980), pp. 281–321

K. Lyka: *Nemzeti romantika: Magyar művészet, 1850–1867* [National romanticism: Hungarian art, 1850–1867] (Budapest, 1982), pp. 13–14

JÚLIA PAPP

Artist's house. House designed and/or decorated by an artist in a manner reflecting his or her interests, social aspirations and aesthetic tastes.

1. BEFORE THE 19TH CENTURY. During the Renaissance individual artists began to reject the craft distinctions imposed on them by the system of town guilds. Such artists as Andrea Mantegna and Giulio Romano in Mantua and Raphael in Rome were able to exploit their privileges as court artists to build town houses for themselves that were in no way inferior to those of the nobility, even surpassing them in their advanced architecture. Inevitably, painter–architects in particular used pictures to enhance the expressive power of their houses. Federico Zuccaro had his guests step through the jaws of demons to enter the garden of his Roman town palace (see fig. 1), a flight of fancy that even became a matter of concern to

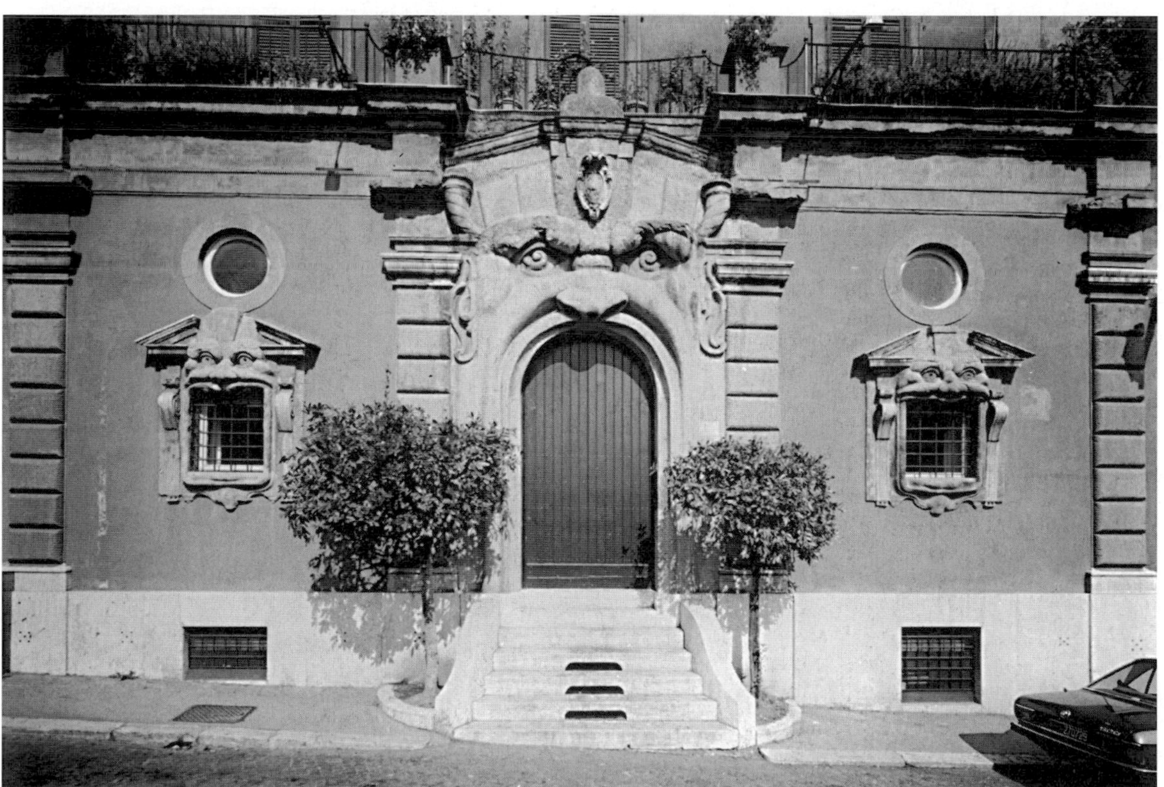

1. Palazzo Zuccari by Federico Zuccaro, Rome, 1591; former garden entrance

2. Giorgio Vasari's house, Arezzo, 1540–48; the Sala Grande with the statue of Diana of Ephesos

3. Peter Paul Rubens's house, Antwerp, *c.* 1610–*c.* 1620; inner courtyard and façade of the studio

4. Villa Stuck by Franz von Stuck, Munich, 1897–8; the Music Room

international diplomacy. Giorgio Vasari decorated his houses in Florence and Arezzo (see fig. 2) with paintings that illustrate the artistic theories of the period.

The earliest artists' houses, located significantly in the early absolutist principalities of northern Italy, were intended to demonstrate the courtly competence of their owners to the town and the ruler through their programme of design and were consequently highly individual in approach. The next generation exploited its experience at court to call for a higher social status for artists in general, on the hypothesis that artists and princes were equal in function. In this connection such artists as Raphael and Leone Lioni incorporated into the programme of their mansions in Rome and Milan the political theory developed by Niccolo di Bernardo dei Machiavelli (1469–1527) that it was the duty of the 'new prince' to transform the inchoate matter of 'society' into the cultivated form of the 'state'.

The call for the social emancipation of the fine arts voiced by the Italian artists through their palazzi also made itself felt among the artists of central and western Europe, culminating in the programme established by Peter Paul Rubens for his mansion in Antwerp (see fig. 3). The house was decorated with a pictorial programme that very subtly defined the relationship between public and private life, innovation and tradition, nature and art, a web of interconnections that still determines the function of some art. Many more grand houses were of course built during the 17th and 18th centuries, such as that of the Swedish architect Nicodemus Tessin, but their message was purely affirmative, aimed at safeguarding what had been gained and placing art completely at the service of courtly ceremonial.

5. John Soane's house (now Sir John Soane's Museum), London, 1817; sectional drawing through the dome and Breakfast Room by F. Copland

6. Frank Lloyd Wright's house, Taliesin West, Paradise Valley, near Phoenix, Arizona, begun 1938; drawing by Hugh Ferriss

2. THE 19TH CENTURY. In the course of the 19th century the history of the development of the artist's house separated into two clearly distinct social channels. On the one hand the trend whereby the artist's house was adapted to the ideal of an aristocratic mansion developed further, reaching a final nostalgically motivated climax in the houses of the Munich artist-princes Franz von Lenbach and Franz von Stuck (see fig. 4). The house in Lincoln's Inn Fields, London, of the English architect John Soane occupies an intermediate position (see fig. 5); he attempted to collect and display in his house, which was quite deliberately conceived as a memorial building (now Sir John Soane's Museum), a diverse selection of objects that together showed the unity of the arts.

Coexisting with these trends from very early in the 19th century are mature examples demonstrating that the renewal of life through art and architecture had become the idea behind the new concept of the artist's house, rather than a nostalgic harking-back to idealized élites from the past. An example is William Morris's Red House, Kent, designed in 1859 by the architect Philip Webb for the founder of the Arts and Crafts Movement. For those painters whose subject-matter was everyday life, such a programmatic approach was not explicit, as the house was simply an additional source of inspiration. This was true of Claude Monet's house and garden at Giverny and continued through to Vanessa Bell and Duncan Grant's Charleston, E. Sussex. The struggle to achieve relative prosperity was an unequal one for artists outside the fashionable mainstream. Many, such as van Gogh with his Yellow House at Arles, managed to establish only temporary spaces, which speak as eloquently for their art as the permanence of their more successful colleagues. The vast majority, however, continued to pass through anonymous spaces, although in the second half of the 19th century these were increasingly purpose-built studio buildings, such as those in Montparnasse, Paris, which fostered a sense of community and encouraged the establishment of rural counterparts, such as the artists' colonies at Pont-Aven, Brittany, or Worpswede, near Bremen. Of the prosperous artists of the later 19th century, a number (such as Mariano Fortuny y Madrazo in Venice and Frederic Leighton in London) used their studio houses to display collections that confirmed the erudite sources of their work. Implicit in this tendency was a belief (also associated with writers) in the individual genius of the artist, which was bound to a particular site. The gift of the Casa Buonarroti to the city of Florence in 1877 by a descendant of Michelangelo served to confirm this tendency and to encourage the collection of works in individual artistic 'shrines'. Rapidly taken up by descendants securing the artist's posthumous fame in an era of growing tourism, it encouraged such established artists as Auguste Rodin and Gustave Moreau in Paris to arrange their own corpus of works. In addition to the Renaissance purpose of establishing a contemporary reputation, the artist's house thus became a means for perpetuating that reputation for future generations.

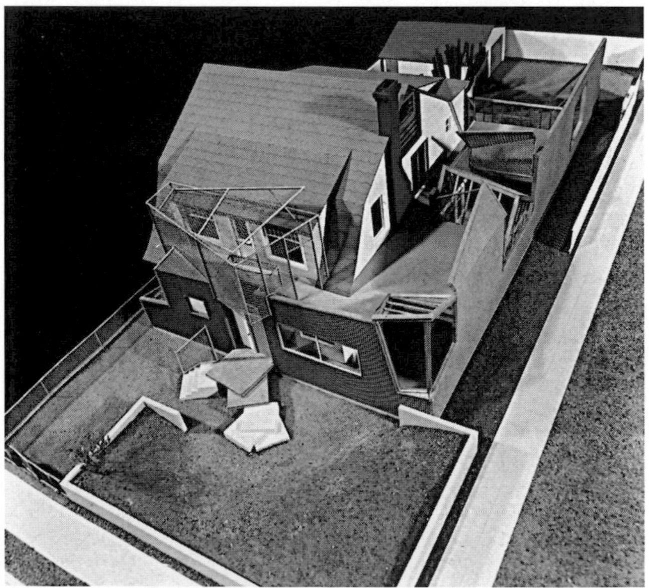

7. Model of Frank O. Gehry's house, Santa Monica, California, 1979

3. THE 20TH CENTURY. The chain of examples of artists and architects who have used their own house to demonstrate the harmony of artistically created space and life continued into the 20th century by way of Victor Horta and Otto Wagner to the architectural manifestos of such architects of the Modern Movement as Frank Lloyd Wright (see fig. 6), Konstantin (Stepanovich) Mel'nikov and Walter Gropius. Between the World Wars the studio-house once again became a declaration of allegiances. Le Corbusier designed buildings for Georges Braque and Amadée Ozenfant, and Gropius provided the studio-houses for the teachers at the Bauhaus, including Paul Klee, Vasily Kandinsky and Lyonel Feininger. These buildings demonstrated a unity of purpose between the arts in establishing a new, rationally determined environment. Some artists advertised their detachment from society through their houses. In Switzerland Ernst Ludwig Kirchner created a totally personal environment by carving all the surfaces of his wooden cabin, while in Hannover Kurt Schwitters's massive structure of ephemera, the Merzbau, engulfed his whole house.

By the 1950s architects were no longer able to present manifestations of a universally valid architectonic doctrine. Their own houses remained nonetheless as fields for experiment for architectonic and to some extent social Utopias. The house of the Californian architect Frank O. Gehry (see fig. 7), which is to some extent the building on which the architectural trend of Deconstructivism was founded, in fact bears eloquent witness to this, as do the Austrian Steinhaus of Günter Domenig, laden with the most private obsessions, and the house built for Thom Maine by the Californian architectural partnership Morphosis, outwardly modest but inside crammed with the most advanced technology.

BIBLIOGRAPHY

F. Wackernage: *Der Lebensraum des Künstlers in der florentinischen Renaissance* (Leipzig, 1938)

E. H. Kantorowicz: 'The Sovereignty of the Artist', *De Artibus Opuscula XL. Essays in Honour of Erwin Panovsky*, ed. M. Meiss, i (New York, 1961), pp. 267–79

F. Württemberger: *Der Manierismus* (Vienna and Munich, 1962), pp. 165–90
U. Nebbia: *La casa degli omenoni* (Milan, 1963)
R. Wittkower and M. Wittkower: *Künstler: Aussenseiter der Gesellschaft* (Berlin, 1965)
D. Heikamp: 'F. Zuccari a Firenze, 1575–1579', ii, *Paragone*, xviii (1967), no. 207, pp. 3–34
K. W. Forster and R. J. Tuttle: 'The Casa Pipi', *Architectura* [Munich] (1973), pp. 104–30
J. von Krüdener: *Die Rolle des Hofes im Absolutismus* (Stuttgart, 1973)
W. Kemp: 'Disegno: Beiträge zur Geschichte des Begriffs zwischen 1547 und 1607', *Marburg. Jb. Kstwiss.*, xix (1974), pp. 219–40
A. M. Maetzke: *Restauri della Casa del Vasari: La sala del camino* (Arezzo, 1977)
E. McGrath: 'The Painted Decorations of Rubens's House', *J. Warb. & Court. Inst.*, xli (1978), pp. 245–77
K. Herrmann-Fiore: 'Die Fresken des Federico Zuccari in seinem römischen Künstlerhaus', *Röm. Jb. Kstgesch.*, xviii (1979), pp. 35–112
N. S. C. Leopold: *Artist Homes in 16th-century Italy* (diss., Baltimore, MD, Johns Hopkins U., 1979)
C. Hoh-Slodczyk: *Das Künstlerhaus im 19. Jahrhundert* (Munich, 1985)
E. Hüttinger: *Künstlerhäuser von der Renaissance bis zur Gegenwart* (Zurich, 1985)
M. Warnke: *Hofkünstler* (Berlin, 1987)
Künstlerhäuser: Eine Architekturgeschichte des Privaten (exh. cat., ed. H.-P. Schwarz; Frankfurt am Main, Dt. Architmus., 1989)
H. P. Schwarz: *Künstlerhäuser: Anmerkungen zur Sozialgeschichte des Genies* (Brunswick, 1990)
G. Walkley: *Artists' Houses in London, 1764–1914* (Aldershot, 1994)

HANS-PETER SCHWARZ

Artists International Association [AIA]. English group founded in London in 1933 as the Artists International to promote united action among artists and designers on social and political issues, and active from 1953 to 1971. In its original formulation it pursued an identifiably Marxist programme, with its members producing satirical illustrations for *Left Review* (e.g. see exh. cat., pp. 20–21) and propaganda material for various left-wing organizations. Reconstituted as the AIA in 1935, it avoided identification with any particular style, attracting broad support from artists working in both a traditional and modernist vein in a series of large group exhibitions on political and social themes, beginning with *1935 Exhibition (Artists Against Fascism & War)* in 1935 (London, 28 Soho Square). Support was given to the Republican cause in the Spanish Civil War (1936–9) and to the Artists' Refugee Committee through exhibitions and other fund-raising activities, and efforts were made to increase popular access to art through travelling exhibitions, public murals and a series of mass-produced offset lithographs entitled *Everyman Prints*, published by the AIA in 1940 (see exh. cat., p. 57).

The AIA published a journal sporadically and in different formats from 1934, beginning with *Artists International Bulletin* (1934–5) and continuing with *Artists International Association Bulletin* (1935–6 and 1939–47), *Artists Newssheet* (1936–8) and *Artists International Association Newsletter* (1947–64). Its early political stance was also affirmed in a book of essays, *5 on Revolutionary Art* (London, 1936), edited by the sculptor Betty Rea (1904–64), an AIA member, with contributions by Herbert Read, Francis Klingender, Eric Gill, A. L. Lloyd and Alick West.

During World War II the AIA mounted a number of exhibitions to promote the ideological objectives of the war, notably *For Liberty* (1943), which was held in a basement canteen of the John Lewis department store in London; this included a number of specially commissioned works, for example *What We Are Fighting For* (1943; Zurich, Ksthaus) by Oskar Kokoschka. After the war exhibitions were held at the AIA Gallery, established in Lisle Street, London, in 1947, and there were further important theme exhibitions, such as the *Mirror and the Square* (1952; London, New Burlington Gals), which reviewed the range of current British art from forms of realism to abstract art.

The designer Misha Black (1910–77) and the painters James Boswell (1906–71) and Richard Carline (1896–1980) were successive chairmen of the AIA. Others prominent in the AIA's administration included the art historian Francis Klingender (the most influential of the Marxist intellectuals in the AIA) and the artists James Fitton (1899–1982), Paul Hogarth (*b* 1917), James Holland (*b* 1905), Victor Pasmore, Laszlo Peri, Cliff Rowe (1904–88) and Carel Weight (*b* 1908). Picasso, who had visited England to address the Sheffield Peace Congress in November 1950, was among the major artists, including Fernand Léger and Henry Moore, who participated in AIA exhibitions. The AIA officially abandoned its political objectives in 1953, but it continued as an exhibiting society until 1971, when it was dissolved.

BIBLIOGRAPHY

D. D. Egbert: *Social Radicalism and the Arts: The West* (New York, 1970)
T. Rickaby: 'The Artists International', *Block*, 1 (1979), pp. 5–14
The Story of the Artists International Association, 1933–1953 (exh. cat. by L. Morris and R. Radford, Oxford, MOMA, 1983)
R. Radford: *Art for a Purpose: The Artists International Association, 1933–1953* (Winchester, 1987)

ROBERT RADFORD

Art legislation. Multilateral treaties and bilateral agreements made largely in the latter part of the 20th century, entered into by nations in response to an unprecedented combination of political, economic and technological changes affecting the art world, and to the tension between the demand for a free international art market on the one hand and the need for countries to protect their own resources on the other. This is manifested in two important legislative areas: an increasing demand by developed nations for global recognition of their intellectual property rights, and an increasing demand by emerging nations for legislation to protect their cultural properties.

1. Protection of intellectual property. 2. Protection of cultural treasures.

1. PROTECTION OF INTELLECTUAL PROPERTY. 'Intellectual property' is the legal term used to describe statutorily protected intangible rights of artists to their creations. Intellectual property rights are separate from the property rights that follow the tangible work (i.e. painting, sculpture etc) when it is sold or transferred, and belong exclusively to the creator unless they are expressly transferred. The three most important intellectual property rights are copyright, moral rights (*le droit moral*) and resale royalty rights (*droit de suite*).

Copyright protects the artist from unauthorized copying, sale or distribution of a work, and provides the artist with a means of participating in the economic exploitation of art. For example, copyright gives the artist the exclusive right to manufacture and sell prints of an original work. Nearly every developed nation has some form of national copyright legislation, and the vast majority of nations are members or signatories of one of the multilateral treaties discussed below.

Moral rights protect the continuing relationship between artists and their works, even after a work has been sold. The most important moral rights are the right of disclosure (to decide whether or not to disclose a work), the right of attribution (to be publicly recognized as the creator of the work) and the right of integrity (to prevent the mutilation or destruction of the work). Legislation on moral rights provides a remedy for the artist's damaged reputation when a work of art is intentionally defaced. For example, in a notorious case in the USA, the city of Pittsburgh altered a mobile by Alexander Calder installed in its airport—immobilizing the parts, motorizing it to rotate 40 times per hour and changing its original black-and-white scheme to green and gold, the official colours of Pittsburgh. If the USA had recognized the concept of moral rights at that time, Calder would have been able to enjoin the city from displaying the defaced work and might have been able to collect monetary damages from the city. Artists' moral rights have been recognized in at least 63 countries throughout the world and have been codified in the Berne Convention (see below).

Copyright protects the economic rights of artists only on the original sale of a work of art. Resale royalties (*droit de suite*) give artists the right to share in the appreciation in value of their works by receiving a percentage of the profits when their works are resold in the market-place. The significance of this economic right cannot be overstated, especially in times of spiralling art prices. For example, in 1986, *Out the Window*, a painting by Jasper Johns, was auctioned at Sotheby's in New York for £3.63 million, setting a record as the highest sum paid for a work by a living American artist. The painting had been acquired in 1960 for £2250. In the absence of resale royalty legislation, the seller was the only one to benefit from the artist's enhanced reputation during the intervening 26 years.

Like moral rights, the *droit de suite* is a product of 19th-century France; there, royalties on all works of art sold at public auction are collected and paid by the Société de la Propriété Artistique et des Dessins et Modèles (SPADEM). Although not as widely accepted as moral rights, some form of resale royalties are also allowed in Germany, Italy, Belgium, Tunisia and Sweden. Resale royalties have also been enacted in the former Czechoslovakia (1926), Poland (1935) and Uruguay (1937), and are under study in Austria, Spain, Great Britain, Norway, Holland, Portugal, Switzerland and the USA.

Global intellectual property rights are governed by two important multilateral treaties: the Berne Convention and the Universal Copyright Convention. The Berne Convention, originally enacted in 1886, is the oldest multilateral copyright treaty in existence and provides the highest recognized standard of copyright protection. It has been periodically modernized through six revisions, and was last amended in 1979. In the early 1990s it had 77 signatories including the USA, all members of the European Community and most industrialized nations of the world with the exception of the former Soviet Union and the People's Republic of China. On 16 January 1992 China entered into a Memorandum of Understanding on the Protection of Intellectual Property with the USA. The Memorandum, which became effective on 16 March 1992, will have the same force and effect as a treaty, and provides that China will accede to the Berne Convention to protect American films, books, music and software effective from 15 October 1992 (Cobe, 1992).

The Berne Convention is founded on a policy of 'national treatment', which means that authors enjoy in other countries the same protection for their works as those countries accord their own authors. In addition to protecting nationals or domiciliaries of member countries, the Berne Convention also protects works by any author first published in a member country. In addition to national treatment, the Berne Convention imposes certain minimum standards on member nations: they must grant authors exclusive rights of reproduction, adaptation, public recitation and public performance of their works for a term that lasts the life of the author plus 50 years. Other central features of the latest revision of the Berne Convention include its prohibition of formalities as a condition of copyright protection, and its recognition of the concept of moral rights, requiring member nations to protect the rights of disclosure, paternity and integrity.

International copyright is also governed by the Universal Copyright Convention (UCC) and a number of smaller multilateral treaties and bilateral agreements. The UCC, promulgated by UNESCO in 1952, initially included only 12 nations, but by the early 1990s it had 80 members. Protection under the UCC requires a statutorily prescribed copyright notice, but, like the Berne Convention, member nations are prohibited from making copyright protection conditional on other formalities.

At the Paris Convention of 1971 the texts of the Berne Convention and the UCC were both revised, and priority was expressly given to the Berne Convention for nations that are party to both treaties. However, the UCC remains an important source of global copyright protection. In 1988, 25 member nations of the UCC (including what was then the Soviet Union) were not parties to the Berne Convention. In nations that do not belong to either the Berne Convention or the UCC, copyright protection for artists is available only under national laws or bilateral treaties, if at all.

Most of the later developments in intellectual property law were stimulated by innovations in the field of high technology. Copyright is the primary means of protecting software applications. As the computer technology market became increasingly international, the technologically developed countries began to demand a global approach to safeguarding these economically significant intellectual property rights.

Developments in the European Community (EC) in the 1980s provide a good illustration. Although the principle that goods may move freely within the Community applies to intellectual property, trade restrictions were found to be necessary to protect intellectual property rights, for example when one member nation's copyright laws did not offer the same level of protection as those of another. Although all member countries of the EC are also signatories to the Berne Convention, the Convention allows considerable differences in implementation, and member states' copyright laws vary greatly. In addition, two member states (Belgium and Ireland) were operating under an old version of the Berne Convention and had not yet signed the 1971 Paris Act, which made significant changes.

The need for harmonization of EC nations' intellectual property laws was addressed in the 1988 'Green Paper on Copyright: The Challenge of Technology—Copyright Issues Requiring Immediate Action'. The Green Paper calls for a two-fold policy on intellectual property. One goal is to ensure that intellectual property is adequately protected, both internally and externally. The second goal is to harmonize national legislation on intellectual property rights to remove trade restrictions among member nations. To this end, the Green Paper contains a draft proposal that copyright protection runs for the same length of time in all member states. In addition, on 14 May 1992 the Internal Market Council adopted a resolution calling on all member states to accede to the Berne Convention (as revised by the 1971 Paris Act).

Although the impetus for harmonization came from technology, the impact will be equally beneficial in the arts market. With regard to the issues of most significance to the arts community, the EC reserved the right to introduce harmonizing legislation on moral rights at a later date and will examine the resale royalty rights offered in some countries to see if they should be extended to all member states.

Another important issue for global protection of intellectual property rights revolves around the emerging nations of Eastern Europe. Although the Soviet Union had been a signatory to the UCC, some of the now-independent nations may not consider themselves bound by this treaty, and by the early 1990s many had not enacted their own internal intellectual property laws. Protection for artists in these nations will probably fluctuate until such laws are codified.

2. PROTECTION OF CULTURAL TREASURES. It was the Romans, in about 400 BC, who first glorified the plunder of art. The Roman conquerors believed that collecting booty from a vanquished nation was a legitimate by-product of war. The ancient Roman practice of wartime looting continued long after the fall of Rome, with little effort by the world community to do anything to protect national patrimony from plunder and destruction until the Hague Convention (1899 and 1907).

The Hague Convention established basic moral and legal principles, acceded to by all the major powers, which were designed to protect the world's greatest treasures in accordance with their origins. These principles were severely tested by World War II, when Adolf Hitler gathered a wealth of cultural objects, of which most were preserved for the instruction and edification of his 'superior race'; others were considered degenerate and were therefore destroyed. The Convention reconvened in 1954 for the purpose of re-establishing principles that had been neglected during the war. Its provisions allow for total protection of the cultural properties of any nation, either from the ravages of war or the pillages that occur during times of peace. By 1990 the Convention had been ratified by 72 nations, excluding the USA and Great Britain, which would not become party to any agreement without a provision allowing for withdrawal of immunity for military necessity.

It is not only during wartime that works of cultural significance are exported. In 1816 THOMAS BRUCE, 7th Earl of Elgin, who was serving as the British Ambassador to the Ottoman court, removed 88 sculpted sections from the wall of the Parthenon and shipped the marbles to England, where they were purchased by the British government and placed in the British Museum, London. Lord Elgin received permission from the Turkish government, which controlled Greece at the time, to make his acquisitions. However, the proposal that the British government should purchase them generated lively debate in the House of Commons. Should the Elgin marbles be returned to the Parthenon as part of Greek cultural heritage or ensconced in the British Museum, where they would be preserved and enjoyed by more people? The decision to keep the Elgin marbles was opposed by the English Romantic poet Lord Byron, whose poetry castigated Lord Elgin as a violator of shrines. Most politicians and scholars of the time, however, did not see anything wrong with transferring the antique treasures of poor nations to the museums and collections of richer nations more able to protect them.

In 1982 the actress Melina Mercouri, then the Greek Minister for Culture, demanded the return of the Elgin marbles. She did not file a lawsuit but tried to embarrass Britain by making her plea before a UNESCO conference of cultural ministers in Mexico City. UNESCO urged the British Museum to return the Elgin marbles, but Britain rejected the plea. David Wilson, Keeper of the British Museum, said: 'To rip the Elgin marbles from the walls of the British Museum is a much greater disaster than the threat of blowing up the Parthenon.' He accused all those supporting the Greeks of 'cultural fascism'.

Unlike Lord Elgin's 'legal plunder', many international sales of art in the late 20th century were a result of illegal theft and looting. The Italian government estimated that in Italy alone, art treasures worth a total of some £50 million were stolen each year. Interpol statistics showed an increase in art thefts across Europe and stories of grave robberies in Mexico and Central American countries were common. No one really knows how much stolen art was sold, but most experts believe that plundered treasures remained in wide circulation. In an extensive study of plunder in the early 1970s, however, archaeologists reported that 90% of the objects found in digs were duplicates that could easily be allowed to leave the country (Meyer, 1973).

After World War II, the leaders of many countries became increasingly concerned about the loss of national treasures and works of art that form part of their homeland's cultural heritage and enacted laws to protect these objects and keep them within their borders. Most countries of the modern world have some form of export restrictions on works of art. For example, Britain introduced the Waverley regulations in 1947 (codified in 1950), which stipulate that licences must be obtained for certain types of art to be exported (*see* ART MARKET). By 1983, many communist countries and developing nations, including Brazil, Bulgaria, China and Zaire, had established wholesale embargoes on all art from their borders. Others, such as Greece, Iran, Mexico, Turkey and the countries of Central and South America, adopted wide-ranging restrictions covering art and artefacts from certain areas and dating back to a certain number of years. Many European countries decide on a case-by-case basis.

The problem facing drafters of such legislation is how to balance the desirability of allowing unrestrained international commercial freedom and cultural exchange against a government's wish to protect cultural property within its borders. On the one hand, the international movement of art is a good ambassador, generating goodwill and international understanding. In addition, many curators argue that museums have the means to preserve art that might be ruined by the elements if left in place. On the other hand, the argument can be made that it robs countries and their people of cultural heritage.

The growing recognition of the importance of cultural property is exemplified by an important court decision handed down in the USA in 1989, ordering an American art dealer to return four rare Byzantine Christian mosaics to the Greek Orthodox Church of Cyprus. The case arose in 1988, when Peg L. Goldberg, an art dealer in Indianapolis, arrived in Amsterdam and was shown photographs of four sections of a large Byzantine mosaic dating from the 6th century. A Dutch art dealer told Goldberg that the mosaics had been removed from the rubble of a church on the island of Cyprus that had been destroyed in the fighting between Turkish and Greek Cypriots. He claimed that they were owned by a Turkish archaeologist who had received permission from the Turkish Cypriot government to take them with him to Munich. Goldberg got a loan and bought the mosaics for £1.08 million. About six months later she offered them to the J. Paul Getty Museum, Malibu, CA, which not only refused the offer but also alerted the government of Cyprus. The Greek Orthodox Church of Cyprus, joined by the Cypriot government, filed suit in a district court in the USA demanding return of the masterpieces, which it claimed were chiselled from Panagia Kanakaria, an ancient Cypriot church. They claimed that the mosaics disappeared after Greek-speaking residents were forced from the village in 1976 by Turkish forces. In 1989 District Judge James Noland ruled that the Greek Orthodox Church of Cyprus was the rightful owner of the mosaics, rejecting Goldberg's claim that she purchased them in good faith. The decision was hailed by art experts as a landmark in the international art trade, discouraging museums and collectors from acquiring works of art of questionable provenance.

After the 1960s, international concern over the destruction of archaeological sites and the looting of art treasures resulted in numerous international treaties and laws to stem the black-market trade. In 1970 UNESCO adopted a convention prohibiting 'the illicit import, export and transfer of ownership of cultural property'. The UNESCO Convention makes it illegal under international law for cultural artefacts to be plucked from their homelands for sale to another country. The UNESCO treaty has no retroactive effect, however, and does not demand the return of art that has already been stolen. It applies only to museums and similar institutions that are financed by governments, not to private museums. The country that has been robbed must prove that the stolen object is an endangered national treasure.

In 1979 the United Nations General Assembly adopted a resolution encouraging governments to accede to the UNESCO Convention and to return cultural property to the countries of origin. The Secretary General's report stated that one of the chief difficulties in the return of cultural property is that many countries do not have proper facilities to care for the works of art if they are returned. UNESCO therefore requested the International Committee of Museums (ICOM) to study problems raised by the return of cultural property lost during colonial or foreign occupations. The ICOM suggested that repository nations give an absolute priority to returning only objects of ethnographic interest or of historical or religious importance. The ICOM also suggested that, before a repository nation returns cultural property, it should satisfy itself that the requesting nation can ensure the property's conservation, security and display.

By 1993, 65 nations had signed the convention, but only one, the USA, is a major purchaser of Classical and archaeological art, and the USA subsequently dropped its membership of UNESCO. Because the USA was a strong supporter of the UNESCO convention, the American Senate ratified it unanimously in 1972, although it took 11 years for Congress to pass legislation implementing the act: the Cultural Properties Implementation Act to stop illegal trade in cultural artefacts was signed by President Reagan in 1983. Despite this, however, some experts say that the USA is still the largest market in the world for trade in illicit antiquities.

The UNESCO convention has been criticized because of its cumbersome procedures and ineffectiveness in protecting the cultural property of member countries. In response, UNIDROIT (the International Institute for the Unification of Private Law at Rome), an international organization of some 70 nations dedicated to harmonizing the laws of different countries, has prepared a draft convention that contains some innovative approaches to the cultural property problem. The preliminary draft UNIDROIT convention would considerably expand the rights of foreign governments seeking the return of cultural property from private as well as public entities, and in certain circumstances would allow compensation to be paid to a good-faith purchaser of stolen or illegally exported cultural property (Lerner and Brissler, 1992). There are several other multilateral art conventions, including the European Cultural Convention, the Pan-American Treaty of 1936 (binding only Pan-American nations) and a similar convention approved by the Organization of American States (OAS) in 1976. UNESCO's international treaty was also followed by several bilateral agreements that helped reduce smuggling by tightening up security at customs. For example, the USA adopted a bilateral treaty with Mexico in 1970, which resulted in *c.* 300 artefacts being returned to Latin America in two hauls. In 1972 the USA also enacted a law authorizing the Customs Bureau to confiscate any Pre-Columbian sculpture or murals imported from Latin America without a permit from its country of origin.

Despite all the legislation, spectacular thefts continue. For example, on Christmas Day 1985 thieves broke into

Mexico City's Museo Nacional de Antropología and stole its greatest treasure, a burial mask from a Maya pyramid–platform in Palenque (*see* JADE, colour pl. II, fig. 1). It is to be hoped that the taking of antiquities has become rarer, however, and responsible art collectors are becoming more cautious about acquiring works of questionable origin.

At the end of the 20th century the cutting edge of the debate regarding cultural artefacts, as with intellectual property law, was taking place in the EC and the emerging nations of Eastern Europe. Article 36 of the EC's founding Treaty of Rome urges a free flow of trade among member nations but allows member states to prohibit or restrict trade in 'national treasures of artistic, historic or archaeological value'. There was much concern among some member countries of the EC, however, that its free-movement rules would nevertheless lead to massive exports of cultural heritage, especially through a proposal to abolish all trade controls for works of art less than 50 years old and valued at under £64,000. From 1 January 1993, the EC relinquished all border controls to create one single market. From 1 April 1993, a harmonized EC licence system for exporting works of art beyond the EC entered into operation. The EC regulation requires exporters of works of art located in a member state and falling within certain categories and above a certain value to obtain a licence from the Department of National Heritage (DNH). For intra-Community trade, national systems apply as before. The DNH has worked out a special system for Britain, whose categories and monetary limits are not identical to the EC, and has given assurances that British historic portraits, textiles, arms and armour more than 50 years old will continue to receive extra protection (Marsan, 1993).

The process of *glasnost* in the former Soviet Union allowed the possibility for an open, pan-European art market to emerge. Opportunities presented by the opening of borders in Eastern Europe, however, did not go unnoticed by thieves and crime syndicates. A UNESCO report (Boyes, 1991) starkly illustrated the reality of smuggling and black markets created by the plundering of the art heritage of Central and Eastern European countries. The robbery of four works of art by Picasso in Prague was the most spectacular of the thefts that revealed lax security in Eastern European galleries. The black market in Russian icons also flourished as export regulations were often no longer enforced. In response to the plunder, the Russian Parliament passed the first law governing the export of cultural objects, banning the export of works more than 100 years old, along with objects claimed as part of the national heritage of any of the ethnic groups of the Russian Federation and the works of art belonging to Russian museums. All works of art must have documented proof that they were acquired legally, and export licences must be obtained from a special board of experts, thus recognizing the need for effective law to protect cultural property in Eastern Europe.

BIBLIOGRAPHY

A. L. Bogsch: *The Law of Copyright under the Universal Convention* (Leiden and New York, 1968)

K. Meyer: *The Plundered Past* (New York, 1973)

L. D. DuBoff: *The Deskbook of Art Law* (Washington, DC, 1978)

C. Masouye: *Guide to the Berne Convention* (Geneva, 1978)

S. Ricketson: *The Berne Convention for the Protection of Literary and Artistic Works: 1886–1986* (London, 1987)

M. Nimmer and P. Geller, eds: *International Copyright Law and Practice* (Albany, 1988)

R. Lerner: *Art Law* (New York, 1989); update ed. R. Lerner and J. Brissler (New York, 1992)

S. Meisler: 'Art & Avarice: In the Cutthroat Art Trade, Museums and Collectors Battle Newly Protective Governments over Stolen Treasures', *Los Angeles Times Mirror* (12 November 1989), mag. p. 8

Basic Documents of International Economic Law (Oxford, 1990)

R. Boyes: 'Eastern Europe Plunders for Art Treasures', *The Times* (30 May 1991), p. 20

D. J. Cobe: 'People's Republic of China to Protect Copyrights', *Client & Times* (Oct 1992), pp. 2–3

M. B. Nimmer and D. Nimmer: *Nimmer on Copyright: A Treatise on the Law of Literary, Musical and Artistic Property, and the Protection of Ideas*, 4 vols (New York, 1992)

Copyright Laws and Treaties of the World, WIPO and UNESCO, 3 vols (1992)

J. Marsan: 'European Community Law: How to Get your Art Export Licence as from April', *A. Newspaper*, 27 (April, 1993), p. 23

LAURIE A. MORIN

Art market. The arena in which a buyer seeks to acquire, either directly or through an agent, a particular work of art for reasons of aesthetics, connoisseurship, investment or speculation. The historical beginnings of the art market lie in patronage. With the growth of COLLECTING for aesthetic and worldly motives rather than religious ones came a corresponding growth in dealing, with the dealer acting as middleman as the number of artists and collectors increased and spread geographically. The dealer, often an artist, discovered and promoted other artists and persuaded collectors to buy at a price determined by him. His role was strengthened by the 16th-century distinction between artist and artisan and the concept of a MASTERPIECE. This precept, allied to a growing antiquarian interest, reinforced the position of the dealer as arbiter of taste, and his status was further enhanced as great collections were amassed and disposed of in the 16th and 17th centuries. During this period collecting became popular with the middle classes and the art market expanded accordingly; the sale of art by AUCTION became commonplace and in the mid-18th century auction houses were established in London. In the 19th century private and institutional buying flourished. Dealers' galleries multiplied rapidly throughout Europe and the USA, and major museums and national collections were established. The aristocratic patron was superseded by those who saw art as an area for INVESTMENT or speculation, a trend heightened in the 20th century, when increased private and corporate investment have made historical and contemporary works of art part of the commodities market.

I. Before 1500.

Evidence of an East–West trade in art objects from as early as 2000 BC is provided by the presence in Etruscan and Italian tombs of bronze objects from Asia Minor and vases of Phoenician glass respectively, both of which were produced solely for export. There was a flourishing art trade between Greece and Rome after the fall of Corinth in 146 BC, when Roman generals brought back booty in the form of Greek statuary. Copying industries sprang up in such cities as Athens to meet the demands of those buyers who could not obtain originals, and such writers as Horace (65 BC–8 BC) and Martial (AD *c.* 40–*c.* 104) described the art dealers' headquarters in the Via Sacra, Rome. The trade in copies of Greek sculpture continued during the reign of the Emperor Hadrian (AD 117–38), one of the great collectors of the Classical world, and Egyptian antiques and other booty from colonization were collected and traded from late Republican times. The fashion in collecting, and therefore in trade, was for works of art from the past, for trophies from cultures that had been destroyed rather than for contemporary work. The art of collecting was highly regarded in China in the Song period (AD 960–1279), and from the 13th century copies of older artefacts were made specifically for collectors (*see* FORGERY).

During the Middle Ages the artist was seen as an anonymous craftsman. In the second half of the 13th century in Italy, however, the individual personalities of such artists as Giotto and the Pisani began to emerge, and in the 15th century the Italian Renaissance produced unparalleled artistic activity in such cities as Florence. The concept of secular art emerged and collectors were motivated primarily by aesthetic appeal, although personal and political prestige still played their part. There was a flourishing trade in both historical and contemporary masters. Artists became the friends and intimates of connoisseur princes and dukes who began to collect paintings by living artists to hang on the walls of their palaces. Individual artists were fought over by various patrons; thus, Isabella d'Este at the end of the 15th century ordered her agent in Venice to obtain a piece by Giovanni Bellini; any piece would do as it was Bellini rather than the particular piece that was important.

II. 1500–1700.

In the 16th and 17th centuries such great European monarchs as Philip II of Spain and Charles I became passionate collectors and their agents scoured Europe for additions to their collections. In 16th-century Italy art sales began to be made through middlemen in a market still dominated by the courts and aristocracy. The sack of Rome in 1527 resulted in many Italian works being taken north across the Alps and the subsequent economic and social decline in Italy boosted the European art market with artists frequently acting as dealers between impoverished Italians and wealthy north European clients. Vasari's hagiography of Michelangelo in the *Vite* (rev. 2/1568) popularized the idea of the creative artist, a man of genius and vision, as opposed to the artisan, which, together with the concept of the masterpiece, enhanced the role of those who bought and sold works of art with a guarantee of AUTHENTICITY. Dealers, who were often artists, would also sell genuine (or what passed for) antiquities. Collectors were depicted with their Classical treasures, as in the portrait by Lorenzo Lotto of *Andrea Odoni* (1527; London, Hampton Court, Royal Col.) surrounded by both contemporary and Classical sculpture, including a small figure of Diana of the Ephesians and a prominently placed bust of Hadrian, a reference to the Emperor's passion for collecting.

Rubens was a highly successful artist–dealer, acting both for himself and for such distinguished connoisseurs as Charles I. In 1619 he bought a sardonyx vase (Baltimore, MD, Walters A.G.), probably carved in Asia Minor *c.* AD 400, in the St Germain market in Paris, which he sent *c.* 1628 to be sold in India, a lucrative market for such pieces. The Spanish ship carrying the vase was captured by privateers, however, and the vase disappeared until it was bought by WILLIAM BECKFORD *c.* 1822, passing subsequently through the collection of his son-in-law, Alexander Douglas-Hamilton, 10th Duke of Hamilton. Rubens advised Charles I in 1623 to buy Raphael's seven tapestry cartoons of the *Acts of the Apostles* (1515–16; London, V&A) for use at the new royal tapestry factory at Mortlake. In 1629 Charles bought the entire collection of Vicenzo Gonzaga, Duke of Mantua, which included the great series by Andrea Mantegna of the *Triumphs of Caesar* (*c.* 1486–94; London, Hampton Court, Royal Col.) and other works that were subsequently sold, such as Caravaggio's *Death of the Virgin* (1605–6; Paris, Louvre), Titian's *Deposition* (Vienna, Ksthist. Mus.) and Raphael's *St George and the Dragon* (1504–5; Washington, DC, N.G.A.).

The art market conflict between the high prices and high esteem accorded to the work of dead artists as opposed to the low prices and ignorance of the work of living artists began during this period. Michelangelo's *Sleeping Cupid* (1496; subsequently in the collection of Charles I; now untraced) is said to have been deliberately buried in order to be unearthed by connoisseurs who pronounced it antique Roman and subsequently sold it as such. It was certainly bought as an antique by Cardinal Raffaele Riario, who returned it as soon as he realized it was a fake.

During the 16th and 17th centuries Flanders and Holland began to rival Florence as centres both of artistic innovation and production, and of the art market. In the 16th century Antwerp became a prosperous trading centre and rich, middle-class merchants began collecting avidly. In the 17th century the focus moved north to Amsterdam. The first example of the practice of dealers buying works by contemporary artists speculatively and selling them to clients from their shops was in 17th-century Holland. Prints in particular changed hands rapidly and profitably, and the naming of Rembrandt's *One Hundred Guilder Print* (*c.* 1643–9; B. 74) was an optimistic indication of the market price. Paintings and prints were also sold by 'Dutch' auction, a system (no longer used for art sales) in which the lot is offered at a high price and the auctioneer reduces the bids until one is finally accepted. In 17th-century France the art market was seen as part of the comprehensive trade and diplomatic strategy of Jean-Baptiste Colbert, designed to encourage the French to buy native products and to sell abroad. The mainspring of this policy was the GOBELINS—La Manufacture Royale des Meubles de la Couronne—which made furniture, silverware and tapestries for the court but also sold goods through Paris dealers. These marchands–merciers dealt with French and foreign clients and acted as dealers, furnishers and subcontractors.

III. 1701–1850.

In 18th-century France the art market still catered mainly for the aristocracy and the court, with a growing emphasis on elegant furniture and ceramics. The sale of contemporary work through marchands-merciers was commonplace throughout the 18th century; it helped to obviate the complex restrictions that made it almost impossible for members of different guilds to work together. Watteau's *L'Enseigne de Gersaint* (1721; Berlin, Schloss Charlottenburg) depicts Edmé-François Gersaint's shop, where a portrait of *Louis XIV* is being symbolically packed while connoisseurs admire the paintings of varying degrees of salaciousness on show (*see* DRESS, fig. 43). The portraits appear to be 17th-century Dutch or Spanish; the other paintings look to be late Italian Baroque or contemporary French work. The furniture includes contemporary pieces in the Régence style. DOMINIQUE DAGUERRE succeeded Simon-Philippe Poirier at his premises in the Rue St Honoré, which was an established centre for the art trade; the shop attracted such customers as Horace Walpole and William Beckford, who bought furniture, paintings and Savonnerie carpets, often specially ordered through Daguerre. After the Revolution, Daguerre established himself in London, where he sold the goods of many émigrés to English customers, notably the Prince Regent (later George IV). In England, a similar role was undertaken by furniture-makers, who would completely equip a house with pictures, carpets, fittings and furniture, both old and new. They would also 'undertake' to bury deceased clients, organize their funerals and auction their effects.

In the 18th century the Grand Tour became an essential part of the education of such young English aristocrats as Richard Boyle, 3rd Earl of Burlington and 4th Earl of Cork (*see* BOYLE, (2)), who brought back works of art from abroad, thus expanding the international art market. Professional *ciceroni* would also act as dealers, as did James Byres and Joseph 'Consul' Smith, who acted as intermediaries between such artists as Canaletto, Giovanni Antonio Pellegrini and Sebastiano Ricci and their British clients. Smith's own collection of works of art and books was bought by George III: the paintings remain in the Royal Collection while the books became the nucleus of the British Library, London. In Rome, Baron Philipp von Stosch combined the role of *cicerone* and collector of gems with that of a Hannoverian spy at the court of James, the Stuart Pretender.

In the mid-18th century auction houses, with regular, catalogued sales, became established in London. Sotheby's, which was founded in 1745 by Samuel Baker (1713–78), dealt largely with books until the mid-19th century. Christie, Manson & Woods, founded in 1766 by James Christie, dealt with all aspects of art. Salerooms in Paris, Antwerp and Hamburg were equally sophisticated. The practice of selling by auction was popular, however, and not confined to the world of antiques: such contemporary ceramics as Chelsea and Longton Hall porcelain were also sold by auction. The establishment of such organizations as the Académie Royale des Inscriptions et Belles-Lettres in Paris, the Society of Antiquaries of London (1717) and the Society of Dilettanti (London, 1732) reflected the desire of collectors and connoisseurs to codify and improve their knowledge, thereby heightening their abilities to authenticate works of art and purchase with more discrimination. One of their stated aims was to produce academic, encyclopedic catalogues such as the Comte de Caylus's *Recueil d'antiquités égyptiennes, étrusques, grecques, romaines et gauloises* (Paris, 1752–67) and James Stuart and Nicholas Revett's *Antiquities of Athens* (4 vols, London, 1762–1816). Such marchands–amateurs as Sir William Hamilton dealt in both contemporary art and antiquities, often in concert with James Byres and Joshua Reynolds, who continued the tradition, started by Rembrandt, of collecting paintings and drawings by past masters.

A widening of the international art market became apparent with such sales as that of the collection formed by Sir Robert Walpole, 1st Earl of Orford, to Catherine II, Empress of Russia, in 1779 (now in St Petersburg, Hermitage). Negotiations via Christie's caused a general outcry, spurring the politician John Wilkes to propose that the collection be made the foundation of a national gallery to be contained in the British Museum, London. The French Revolution and subsequent wars had a dramatic impact on the art market at the end of the 18th century and the beginning of the 19th. The sale from 1792 onwards of the collection of Louis Philippe Joseph, Duc d'Orléans, which included important works from the collection of Queen Christina of Sweden, is one of the watersheds of the art market. It occurred just when rich English collectors were beginning to take an informed interest in Old Masters and it attracted such enthusiasts as John Julius Angerstein, who bought works that were to be the nucleus of the National Gallery, London, including the *Raising of Lazarus* by Sebastiano del Piombo (1517–19; London, N.G.). The Peace of Amiens (1801–2) encouraged further dealing, and in 1815 much Napoleonic loot was retrieved or sold. George IV was offered the Classical sculptures pillaged from the Vatican, which were then in the Louvre, Paris, since the Pope could not afford to transport them. George IV declined and had the sculptures, which included the *Laokoon*, the *Apollo Belvedere* and the Belvedere *Torso*, returned to Rome at his own expense.

IV. 1851–1945.

In the mid-19th century the art market received fresh impetus, especially in Paris, from a new international clientèle. Many new galleries were established, for example the WILDENSTEIN gallery, M. Knoedler & Co. (*see* KNOEDLER, M.), Georges Petit (*see* PETIT, (2)) and JACQUES SELIGMANN. The Academy structure worked in a symbiotic way with the dealers who emerged to sell modern works. The support and promotion of the Barbizon school and Impressionists by Paul Durand-Ruel (*see* DURAND-RUEL, (2)) is a good example. His relationship with his artists has become the norm; he kept the prices of his protégés at a high level and created a virtual monopoly. He also instituted the policy of buying from older, established artists whose prices had not kept up with the times. His famous coup was the direct purchase of 70 paintings from Théodore Rousseau in 1866, which was followed by a selling exhibition of the artist's work the following year. Durand-Ruel also introduced the Impressionists to the USA with his first exhibition in New York in May 1886. The market for historical works also flourished, however, as this was the century of museum growth. In Paris the Louvre continued as a national museum after the restoration of the *ancien régime*; in

London the British Museum was rehoused in the Neo-classical building designed by Robert Smirke and the National Gallery was established in 1824. In Berlin in 1830 the Altes Museum and the Königlichen National Galerie were opened, the latter being based on the collection of Edward Solly, which had been bought by Frederick William III in 1821. Other major galleries were founded: the Alte Pinakothek in Munich (before 1848), the Hamburger Kunsthalle, Hamburg (1869), and the Kunsthistorisches Museum, Vienna (1871). Museums and galleries were also being established in the USA: the Metropolitan Museum of Art, New York (1870), the Boston Museum of Fine Arts (1870), the Philadelphia Museum of Art (1876) and the Art Institute of Chicago (1879). All these institutions needed works of art and this competition in the art market drew out works from many private collections, especially in England, where landowners were experiencing severe agricultural depression. The great Hamilton Palace sale of 1882 (London, Christie's, 17 June), which included Old Masters and pieces from William Beckford's collection, is an outstanding example.

The emergence of a new, highly professional breed of curators, such as Wilhelm von Bode in Berlin, led to a more scientific attitude that resulted in rigorous reattributions and a more sceptical view of authenticity. Documentation and provenance acquired new importance as the discipline of academic art history superseded CONNOISSEURSHIP. The pioneering scholarship of Guido Morelli, Joseph Arthur Crowe and Giovanni Battista Cavalcaselle encouraged attribution based on documentary evidence combined with close stylistic analysis. The use of accurate engravings of works followed by the amassing of photographic archive material further spurred the science of attribution. Museums began to hang collections by chronology and by national or regional school. Such precision spread into the commercial world, which rapidly employed, subsidized and at times bribed acknowledged scholars to give written 'opinions'. One egregious partnership was that between BERNARD BERENSON and the dealer JOSEPH DUVEEN. Berenson would provide Duveen with certificates of authenticity, on the strength of which pictures would be sold, while Berenson would ensure the discussion of such works in his books. Duveen presided over the next great exodus of art from English private collections to galleries and private collectors in the USA.

By the turn of the century, and especially after World War I, agricultural depression, heavy taxation and death duties compelled many English families to sell off their collections. In 1921 Mary, Lady Kinloss (1852–1944), the daughter of the 3rd Duke of Buckingham and Chandos, sold off Stowe House, Bucks, its contents and the entire estate. In the same year Henry Somerset, 10th Duke of Beaufort (1900–84), and Henry Pelham-Clinton-Hope, 8th Duke of Newcastle (1866–1941), also sold their patrimonies. Between 1920 and 1929 many of the antiquities (especially Egyptian), paintings and American books were sold from Blenheim Palace. From such sales Henry Clay Frick, Samuel Kress, Andrew Mellon, J. Pierpont Morgan, the Rockefeller family and Isabella Stuart Gardner amassed their collections of Old Masters. Frick's town house in New York became the home of the Frick Collection, and Gardner's Venetian folly in Boston became a museum. Mellon, after an astute purchase from the impoverished Russian Bolshevik Government in 1922, which included the *St George* by Raphael that had been in the collection of Charles I, endowed the National Gallery of Art in Washington, DC; Kress bequeathed his collection to a number of American museums. The Wall Street crash (1929) led to a general collapse of the art market, although those who still had money did continue to buy, especially after 1933 when Nazi Germany began to sell what it described as 'decadent' art, which had been either confiscated or taken from museums. The Metropolitan, New York, for example, acquired a self-portrait by van Gogh from Munich, in a sale of 125 paintings in Lucerne on 30 July 1939. The trade in contemporary works of art was boosted by the establishment of such museums as MOMA, New York (1929), with the financial backing of Abby Aldrich Rockefeller. The collecting of modern art, especially in the USA, became the alternative to the amassing of increasingly rare and expensive Old Masters. The trend was led by such magnates as Solomon Guggenheim and his daughter Peggy Guggenheim. In pre-war Europe collectors of modern art were less ambitious: Kenneth Clark secretly subsidised Henry Moore and Graham Sutherland with his salary as Director of the National Gallery, London; Edward James was a constant support to such struggling painters as Salvador Dalí.

During World War II the open art market in Europe disappeared; looting by such collectors as HERMANN GOERING became commonplace and there was also wholesale confiscation by Russia of German collections. Schliemann's Trojan collection is thought to be in Moscow; nearly 500 Old Master drawings, taken by the Germans from the Museum Boymans in Rotterdam and subsequently lost to the Russians, are still missing. As a by-product of the British Government's intention to restrict exports of valuable objects, the Waverley regulations (named after Viscount Waverley, first president of the Committee for Export of Works of Art), which required export licences for art objects above a certain value, were introduced in 1947. 'Culturally significant' objects could be refused licences and could be bought by British institutions at the export price. This system, codified in 1950 and governed by the Board of Trade and subsequently the Department of Trade and Industry, was the first legislation in Britain to regulate the export of works of art; it continues to operate (*see also* ART LEGISLATION, §2).

V. After 1945.

There have been fundamental changes in the art market following World War II. In the 1950s London became the international centre of art trading, and the market began to be dominated by the auction houses rather than the dealers. Two factors contributed to this situation: first, the restrictions imposed by successive French governments on the commissaires-priseurs in Paris resulted in the decline of that city as a centre for international sales; and second, the dynamic management of Christie's by Ivan Chance (1910–84) and of Sotheby's by Peter Wilson (1913–84), together with the less stringent regulations on the import and export of works of art in Britain, Monaco and Switzerland, established both auction houses as an effective duopoly in London, New York, Monte Carlo and Geneva. In the 1960s the volume of trade in the art market was enormous, prices rose rapidly and new price records were set, in particular for Impressionist paintings. The *Times*–Sotheby index calculated that between 1951 and 1969 the prices of Old Masters multiplied by 7 times, of Impressionists by $17\frac{1}{2}$ times and of 20th-century paintings by 29 times. In the late 1960s the Japanese entered the market, and in 1969 Sotheby's and Christie's held sales in Tokyo. This golden era reached its peak in the late 1980s with sales of Impressionist and Post-Impressionist works at record prices to American, Australian and Japanese clients (e.g. £83,900,000 for van Gogh's portrait of *Dr Gachet* (1890) by Christie's, New York, in 1990). In 1989 the collapse of the international stock market, accompanied by the revelation that Sotheby's had lent the Australian entrepreneur Alan Bond (*b* 1938) the money to buy van Gogh's *Irises* (1889), produced a similar loss of confidence in the art market.

Frequent attempts have been made to inflate the market artificially or to persuade buyers, especially at times of high inflation, that investment in fine art gives a better yield than more conventional commodities. Generally, however, works of art have not kept above even median stock market indices, and the vagaries of taste continue to affect art market prices. For example, in Britain in the late 1980s corporate clients invested in modern art. Such young graduates from the Glasgow School of Art as Adrian Wiszniewski (*b* 1958) and Steven Campbell (*b* 1954) were achieving higher prices than established names. The impetus came from Charles Saatchi and Doris Saatchi, who sold works by such artists as Anselm Kiefer, Julian Schnabel, Francesco Clemente and Sandro Chia to buy what they considered 'blue chip' British works to add to their collection. The international economic recession of the early 1990s made buyers reluctant to invest in anything other than established names; while the prices for contemporary works remained lower than expected, Titian's *Venus and Adonis* (1555), which was last sold by Christie's in 1884 for £1764 (when it was considered to be only of the school of Titian), was sold by their London saleroom in December 1991 for £7,480,000 to a consortium buying for stock (now Malibu, CA, Getty Mus.). The finest pieces of decorative art more than kept their place in the market. Since the scholarship formerly applied only to the fine arts was extended to this area, there has been both a greater appreciation of and enhanced prices for objects, especially furniture, that can be attributed to a specific maker or given an exact provenance. Eighteenth-century French and English furniture and American furniture of provenance have followed this trend, although the price of £8,580,000 paid in 1990 for the Badminton Cabinet (1732; ex-Badminton House, Glos; Philadelphia, PA, Johnson priv. col.) is as exceptional as the piece itself.

During the 1970s and 1980s nations with a wealth of artefacts but a floundering economy became aware of the threatened disappearance of their cultural patrimony. This has resulted in strict legislation, usually poorly enforced, to attempt to prevent exports of works of art or archaeological specimens. In Europe, Greece and Italy have been particularly affected; most countries in Africa and South America have had similar problems, especially as a result of the fashion for 'primitive' ethnographic art. The possibility of compulsory registration of objects of art and further uniform restrictions throughout the European Community was discussed at a conference in Strasbourg in 1988; no firm conclusions were reached, although in June 1992 Britain decided against any listing of objects of art. Of equal concern is the diminishing supply of goods for the market. Such large new institutional buyers as the J. Paul Getty Museum, Malibu, CA, and the Yasuda Fire and Marine Insurance Co. of Japan, which acquired van Gogh's *Sunflowers* (1888) for £39,000,000 in 1987, will always bring items on to the market by inflating prices. The Getty Museum has shown remarkable restraint in its purchasing policy and in 1992 even sold some of its lesser paintings; however, as an increasing number of works of art become the property of nations, museums or trusts and are thereby effectively removed from the art market, dealers and auctioneers fear a decline in saleable objects, although this fear is partly offset by a widening of what constitutes 'collectable' art. Another factor is the 'de-accessioning' forced on museums by economic exigency. The possibility of large museum sales, combined with the opening up of markets in Eastern Europe, may well influence the art market of the late 20th century and early 21st.

BIBLIOGRAPHY

G. Redford: *Art Sales* (London, 1888)

W. Roberts: *Memorials of Christie's*, 2 vols (London, 1897)

G. Reitlinger: *The Economics of Taste*, 3 vols (London, 1961–70)

R. H. Rush: *Art as an Investment* (Englewood Cliffs, 1962)

F. Haskell: *Patrons and Painters: A Study in the Relations between Italian Art and Society in the Age of the Baroque* (London, 1963)

G. Agnew: *Agnew's, 1817–1967* (London, 1967)

C. Tomkins: *Merchants and Masterpieces: The Story of the Metropolitan Museum of Art* (London, 1970)

G. Keen: *The Sale of Works of Art: A Study based on the* Times–*Sotheby Index* (London, 1971)

F. Herrmann: *The English as Collectors: A Documentary Commentary* (London, 1972)

T. J. Clark: *The Absolute Bourgeois: Artists and Politics in France* (London, 1973)

F. Haskell: *Rediscoveries in Art: Some Aspects of Taste, Fashion and Collecting in England and France* (London, 1976)

F. Herrmann: *Sotheby's: Portrait of an Auction House* (London, 1980)

S. Schama: *The Embarrassment of Riches: An Interpretation of Dutch Culture in the Golden Age* (London, 1987)

A. Braham: 'Towards a National Gallery', *NACF Rev.* (1989), pp. 79–92

A. Distel: *Collectionneurs des impressionnistes* (Paris, 1989); Eng. trans. by B. Perroud-Benson as *Impressionism: The First Collectors* (New York, 1990)

A. MacGregor, ed.: *The Late King's Goods: Collections, Possessions and Patronage of Charles I in the Light of the Commonwealth Sale Inventories* (London and Oxford, 1989)

C. Wainwright: *The Romantic Interior: The British Collector at Home, 1750–1850* (London and New Haven, 1989)

Conference Proceedings of the Law and Business Forum: Collecting and Investing in Fine Art: London, 1990

BRUCE TATTERSALL

Art mobilier [Fr.: 'furnishing art']. Portable art objects used for decorative purposes.

□

Art Nouveau [Fr.: 'new art']. Decorative style of the late 19th century and the early 20th that flourished principally in Europe and the USA. Although it influenced painting and sculpture, its chief manifestations were in architecture and the decorative and graphic arts, the aspects on which this survey concentrates. It is characterized by sinuous, asymmetrical lines based on organic forms; in a broader sense it encompasses the geometrical and more abstract patterns and rhythms that were evolved as part of the general reaction to 19th-century historicism. There are wide variations in the style according to where it appeared and the materials that were employed.

1. Introduction. 2. Britain. 3. Belgium. 4. France. 5. Germany. 6. Austria. 7. Other. 8. Conclusion.

1. INTRODUCTION. Art Nouveau has been held to have had its beginnings in 1894 or 1895. A more appropriate date would be 1884, the year the progressive group Les XX was founded in Belgium, and the term was used in the periodical that supported it, *Art Moderne*: 'we are believers in Art Nouveau'. The origin of the name is usually attributed to S. Bing, who in December 1895 opened a gallery in Paris that he called L'Art Nouveau (*see* §4 below). The variety of other names by which the style is known are an indication of its multifarious character. They include: Glasgow style (Scotland); *Modern style*, *Style nouille*, *Style coup de fouet* (Belgium); *Style Jules Verne*, *Style Métro*, *Style 1900*, *Art fin de siècle*, *Art belle époque* (France); *Jugendstil* (Germany and Austria); *Sezessionstil* (Austria); *Arte joven* (Spain); *Modernisme* (Catalonia); *Arte nuova*, *Stile floreale*, *Stile Liberty* (Italy); *Nieuwe kunst* (the Netherlands); *Stil' modern* (Russia); Tiffany style (USA).

In each country there was a determination to break with the past and create a new style that could be incorporated into the design of objects in everyday use as well as architecture and interior decoration. Like those associated with PRE-RAPHAELITISM and the ARTS AND CRAFTS MOVEMENT in Britain, the proponents of Art Nouveau rejected the academic tradition and all forms of ornament based on Classical or Renaissance precedent. They believed, with WILLIAM MORRIS, in the unity of all the arts and crafts and wanted to abolish the distinction between the major and minor arts. The influence of Japan is evident in the regard for simple outlines and asymmetry (*see* JAPONISME).

The decorative repertory of Art Nouveau was derived principally from the observation and imitation of nature, in particular of exotic flowers and plants. This is epitomized in the work of Victor Horta in Belgium and Emile Gallé and Hector Guimard in France. From EUGÈNE-EMMANUEL VIOLLET-LE-DUC in France and JOHN RUSKIN and Morris in Britain came the idea of the alliance of form with need: that all the arts should have their roots in utility. The more angular manner of the later phase of Art Nouveau, after about 1904, apparent in the work of the Belgian, Henry Van de Velde, active in Germany, and the Austrian, Josef Hoffmann, looks forward to modernism.

The forms and designs of Art Nouveau were disseminated through the numerous periodicals that existed and were founded at the time; the best-known of these were *The Yellow Book*, *The Studio*, *The Savoy*, *La Plume*, *Jugend* and *Dekorative Kunst*. Such international events as the Exposition Universelle of 1900 in Paris and the Esposizione Internazionale d'Arte Decorativa Moderna of 1902 in Turin brought the style, in its various guises, to the notice of the public as well as architects, artists and designers.

2. BRITAIN. Among the earliest examples of the flowing asymmetry associated with Art Nouveau are the book illustrations of A. H. MACKMURDO, AUBREY BEARDSLEY and WALTER CRANE, in particular Mackmurdo's title page for his *Wren's City Churches* (1883). Mackmurdo, together with C. R. ASHBEE, C. F. A. VOYSEY and M. H. BAILLIE SCOTT, all of whom practised as designers as well as architects, provide the link between the Arts and Crafts Movement and Art Nouveau in Britain; Voysey, however, later despised the continental version of the style that he so strongly influenced. In Scotland, the GLASGOW STYLE was a manifestation of Art Nouveau. CHARLES RENNIE MACKINTOSH (*see* CUTLERY, fig. 2), HERBERT MACNAIR and the sisters Margaret Macdonald and Frances Macdonald (*see* MACDONALD) were all students of the Glasgow School of Art, the director of which, Francis Newbery (1855–1946), was much influenced in his ideas by the Arts and Crafts Movement. They came together as the Four. Their cool, attenuated designs for interiors, furniture, bookbindings and needlework were much admired on the Continent and particularly in Vienna (*see* §6 below), where they were an important influence on the development of a geometrical version of Art Nouveau. Mackintosh was an exhibitor at the international exhibition of 1902 in Turin, and his work was illustrated in the German magazine *Dekorative Kunst*.

3. BELGIUM. In 1881 the lawyer Octave Maus co-founded the magazine *Art moderne*, the chief aim of which was to introduce art into every aspect of everyday life. The editors called themselves 'the Art Nouveau faithful'. In 1884 the first exhibition took place in Brussels of Les XX (*see* <VINGT>, LES), a group of 20 artists seeking to show their work outside the official Salon. They chose Maus as General Secretary; in 1893 he organized the dissolution of Les XX and the foundation in its place of the LIBRE ESTHÉTIQUE. Those invited to exhibit in the first year included Toulouse-Lautrec and Seurat, and of singular importance to the development of Art Nouveau was the fact that Morris's and Beardsley's book illustrations and objects designed by Ashbee were given equal prominence to the paintings. With Claude Debussy playing his music at the opening, the exhibition was seen as an attempt to establish a relationship between all the arts.

The architect VICTOR HORTA is regarded as the 'father' of Belgian Art Nouveau. A disciple of Morris, he took charge of the interior decoration as well as the furnishings of his buildings. He made designs for woodwork, glass, textiles and, most notably, ironwork, in which the ideas put forward by Viollet-le-Duc are discernible. The inspiration for his style was nature itself (the only source of imitation he considered permissible), on which he based the interlacing *coup de fouet* (whiplash) that characterizes his work. Throughout the 1890s Horta worked towards the twin goals of creating a new type of formal expression and finding a logical and clear solution to the problems of construction. He achieved the first in the curvilinear, non-representational style of the Maison Tassel (1893; *see* HORTA, VICTOR, fig. 1), taking it a step further in the Hôtel Solvay (1894), both in Brussels. The second he achieved in the Maison du Peuple (1895–9; destr. 1964), Brussels, which incorporated the first iron and glass façade in Belgium. In this building Horta put into practice Viollet-le-Duc's theory that the future of architecture lay in the honest use of iron.

PAUL HANKAR, another of the creators of Belgian Art Nouveau, was influenced both by Japanese art and the Arts and Crafts Movement. His early work was in a traditional neo-Renaissance manner; the most important Art Nouveau characteristic of his later work was his treatment of façades as decorative ensembles, as in the façade (1897) of Niguet's Shirt Shop in Brussels.

The other leading figure in Belgian Art Nouveau was HENRY VAN DE VELDE, who became a member of Les XX in 1888. He gave up painting for design in 1892 and, much influenced by Ruskin and Morris, was one of the most important forces in Europe for the reform of design from the late 19th century. In 1895—without experience as an architect—Van de Velde built his own house, Bloemenwerf (completed 1896), near Brussels, and was himself responsible for even the smallest details, including all the furnishings. The house represents a manifesto against the 'lies' constituted by the use of forms borrowed from historic styles. Van de Velde had a particular feeling for harmony without symmetry, and the outstanding feature of his work is the use of a dynamic line that ensures the homogeneity of his forms. Conscious of the disparity between his social and political convictions and his love of craftsmanship (by means of which only unique and expensive pieces could be produced), he set up a company in Brussels in 1898 in an attempt to coordinate the production and distribution of his work. He is remarkable for the multiplicity of his talents, being as successful as a designer of furniture (*see* BELGIUM, fig. 33) as of lamps, wallpaper, textiles, fashion, silverware, porcelain and jewellery. He moved to Germany in 1899, and his style grew more sober and less ornamental after about 1902.

4. FRANCE. French Art Nouveau flourished most fully in the field of the applied arts rather than in architecture. Providing encouragement in the development of the style was the well-established tradition of craftsmanship in France and the support that the well-to-do gave to it. Another factor that contributed to its development was the existence of the Union Centrale des Beaux Arts Appliqués à l'Industrie (later the Union Centrale des Arts Décoratifs), founded in 1864, which from the outset professed the aim of 'supporting in France the cultivation of those arts that pursue the creation of beauty in utility'. The two centres where French Art Nouveau was created and from which the style was disseminated were Nancy and Paris and they witnessed the development of two

1. Art Nouveau table lamps by Emile Gallé, triple-overlay glass, after 1890 (private collection)

rather different tendencies: while the former leaned towards the floral, the latter favoured the more symbolic aspects of Art Nouveau.

The Union Centrale exhibition of 1884 marked the birth of the floral style and proved to be a showcase for the ceramics and glassware of EMILE GALLÉ. He wasted no time after winning two gold medals, one for ceramics and one for glass, at the exhibition in promoting his work and that of his colleagues. A glassmaker, potter and cabinetmaker, Gallé combined a poetic spirit with determined industrial enterprise. At the same time as he developed techniques for creating his unique and expensive pieces, he set up a business for the commercial production of his glassware (see fig. 1), using one activity to finance the other.

An interest in nature lies at the heart of the style associated with Nancy, but there were two other factors that played a role of undeniable importance: a pronounced taste for the Rococo (Nancy was substantially built during the reign of Louis XV) and for Japanese art. The latter was introduced to Nancy in the most direct manner, when, in 1885, the Japanese scholar Takasima came to study botany at the school of forestry. Takasima was both a scientist and an artist, and he and Gallé became friends.

In 1901 the Alliance Provinciale des Industries d'Art (later called the Ecole de Nancy) was founded, under Gallé's direction. Other important figures included the designer Victor Prouvé (*see* PROUVÉ, (1)) who replaced Gallé as head of the Ecole de Nancy on the latter's death; the glassmakers Auguste Daum and Antonin Daum (*see* DAUM); the *ébéniste* LOUIS MAJORELLE, who, in describing the source of his inspiration, remarked 'my garden is my library'; and the furniture designer and architect EUGÈNE VALLIN. After the Villa Majorelle was built in 1901 by HENRI SAUVAGE the Nancy group of 'botanist-decorators' concentrated on architecture. EMILE ANDRÉ, Lucien Weissenberger (1860–1929) and Vallin created the first Art Nouveau ensembles in France, and they never forgot the words of Gallé, who had told his colleagues in 1901 that 'painters and ornamental artists, we are one and all priests serving the same religion, worshippers of natural beauty spread through the world'.

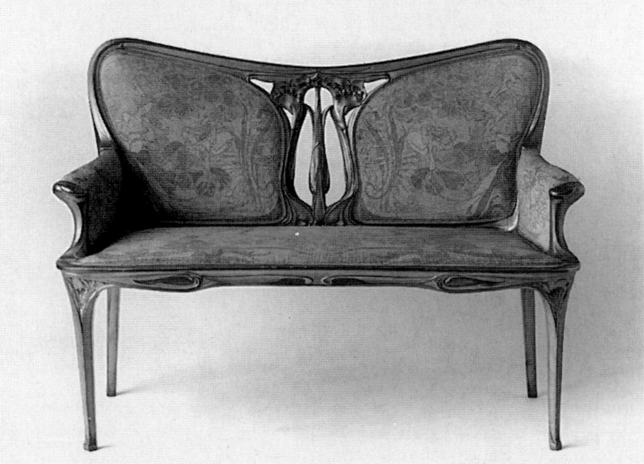

2. Art Nouveau sofa by Georges de Feure, gilt-wood with upholstery, 0.90×1.17×0.40 m, exhibited in 1900 (Copenhagen, Danish Museum of Decorative Art)

From the beginning of the 19th century architecture in Paris had been dominated by Neo-classicism. HECTOR GUIMARD, who studied at the Ecole des Beaux-Arts, instead of undertaking the traditional pilgrimage to Greece and Rome, went to Britain to study architecture and in 1895 visited Brussels, where he met Horta. On his return he re-worked a project begun in 1894, which he completed in 1897—the Castel Béranger, an apartment block in Paris. Here Guimard broke with the character of the surrounding buildings to give pride of place to sculpture and to colour, both on the exterior and in the interior. He designed every detail—the stained glass, ceramic panels, doors, locks, wallpaper and the furniture. The profusion of detail and the twisting and turning of lines is more pronounced than in the work of Horta or Van de Velde. All the contradictions that Guimard tried to resolve during the course of his career as an architect were expressed in the Castel Béranger: the opposition of structure and ornament, of abstract and figurative design, and the tension between rationalism and its relationship with naturalism. Although nature was the only model that could be evoked to find some unity in Guimard's designs, his was not the nature of Gallé and the Ecole de Nancy but rather that of Horta, who wrote 'I discard the flower and the leaf, but I keep the stalk'. Although he did not win the competition in 1896 to design the Métro stations in Paris, Guimard was nonetheless awarded the commission. The entrances are remarkable for the integration of decorative elements into the structure (for illustration *see* METRO STATION). Their appearance was halfway between that of a pavilion and a pagoda constructed of glass and iron. They were to make Guimard a household name and gave rise to the term *Style Métro*. Other architects, among them Frantz Jourdain (*see* JOURDAIN, (1)), who created the Samaritaine department store (1905–10) in Paris, and JULES LAVIROTTE, designed buildings that belong to Art Nouveau, with leanings towards the Rococo or a floral style, but only Guimard left a consistent body of work amounting to a true expression of architectural conviction.

At the end of 1895, S. BING opened his new gallery in Paris, *L'Art Nouveau*, for which Van de Velde designed three rooms and Louis Comfort Tiffany executed the stained glass. It became a rallying-point for the creators and devotees of Art Nouveau. Bing, one of the principal promoters of the style, brought together a number of artists and designers, among them GEORGES DE FEURE, EDOUARD COLONNA and EUGÈNE GAILLARD. All three designed rooms for Bing's pavilion (destr.) at the Exposition Universelle in Paris in 1900: de Feure's furniture for the model sitting room of a modern house included a gilt-wood sofa (see fig. 2), its undulating lines abstracted from plant shapes. Their work was greeted with enthusiasm by the *Revue des arts décoratifs*: 'The contrast of their modernism excites the eye and seduces the intellect . . . nothing in the foreign or French displays of decorative art, nothing is superior to this exhibition of Art Nouveau.' An article such as this and the enormous success of the exhibition led Parisians to believe that Art Nouveau was a typically

3. Art Nouveau buckle in the shape of a water-nymph by René Lalique (Lisbon, Fundação Calouste Gulbenkian)

French style; it was not a coherent style, though, but rather a juxtaposition of individual elements.

After 1900 the Art Nouveau style in France was expressed mainly in interior decoration, notably in the shop (1900–01; destr.) in Paris designed by ALPHONSE MUCHA for the jeweller Georges Fouquet. Art Nouveau restaurants, such as Maxim's (remodelled 1899; architect Louis Marnez, painter Léon Sounier), and boutiques proliferated until about 1910. Edouard Niermans introduced Art Nouveau to the architecture of brasseries, restaurants and casinos (1894–1914) and also theatres, particularly in Paris and on the Côte d'Azur. Originality in French Art Nouveau culminated in objects of vertu, such as those designed by Félix Bracquemond (*see* BRACQUEMOND, (1)), and the sublime jewellery and accessories designed by René Lalique (e.g. a buckle in the shape of a water-nymph; see fig. 3; *see also* LALIQUE, RENÉ, and JEWELLERY, colour pl. II, fig. 1).

5. GERMANY. Art Nouveau in Germany came into being as a reaction to the historic eclecticism epitomized by the castles built for Ludwig II, King of Bavaria. In the 1890s there was activity in various quarters. Van de Velde received a series of commissions, including one for the Havana Cigar Shop in Berlin, in 1899 where he settled. Also in Berlin, ALFRED MESSEL began work on the building of the Wertheim department stores in Berlin, taking his ideas for the second of them, in the Leipzigstrasse (1896–7; destr. 1944; *see* GERMANY, fig. 11), from buildings constructed in iron and glass in France and Chicago. At the same time a minor event in diplomatic circles occurred that was to have important repercussions: HERMANN MUTHESIUS was sent to London as technical attaché at the German embassy with the specific brief of gathering information about architecture and the decorative arts in Britain.

New periodicals played a more significant role in Germany than elsewhere, and they appeared in considerable numbers: in Berlin in 1895 the critic JULIUS MEIER-GRAEFE founded *Pan*, a magazine devoted to the fine and applied arts in Europe. In January 1896 *Jugend: Illustrierte Wochenschrift für Kunst und Leben* was launched; this was to give its name to the Art Nouveau movement in Germany, *Jugendstil*. This was a pacifist, anti-clerical magazine advocating a new art and aesthetic freedom, a national rebirth drawing inspiration from international currents in art. Almost in parallel with *Jugend*, the famous satirical magazine *Simplizissimus* was founded, giving space to the artists of the Art Nouveau movement. This was followed in 1897 by *Deutsche Kunst und Dekoration* and *Dekorative Kunst*, and in 1899 by *Die Insel*; support for modernity among intellectuals and in the media flourished with astonishing vigour.

Although Germany lagged behind the rest of Europe as far as painting was concerned, there were sudden developments in the graphic and applied arts, occurring almost simultaneously in all the major cities but in particular in Munich, Berlin, Weimar and Darmstadt. Most of the important figures associated with *Jugendstil* followed Morris and Van de Velde in abandoning painting to devote themselves to decorative art. OTTO ECKMANN was, with PETER BEHRENS, AUGUST ENDELL, HERMANN OBRIST, BRUNO PAUL and RICHARD RIEMERSCHMID, one of the founders of *Jugendstil* in Munich. He stopped painting in 1894 and began to study nature; some of his imaginative floral compositions were published in *Pan* and *Jugend*. He became interested in printer's type and made his name by developing the typeface known as the Eckmann type. The newly established periodicals promoted the move into graphic art, *Jugend*, for example, employing 75 illustrators during its first year of publication. In the first issue of *Deutsche Kunst und Dekoration*, its founder, ALEXANDER KOCH, appealed for the integration of all the arts and a return to craftsmanship. *Jugendstil* manifested itself in the designs that appeared not only in magazines but in programmes and posters, revolutionizing the country's graphic art to such effect that it soon acquired an international reputation.

In glass, jewellery and ceramics German craftsmen generally did not compare favourably with the French, although there were a few exceptions, among them the glassmaker Karl Kaepping (1848–1914) and the potters Max Laeuger (1864–1952) and Julius Scharvogel (1854–1938). They excelled in furniture-making, however: Riemerschmid, Endell and Obrist were all part of the tendency that strove for overall unity in interior decoration, one of the principal aims of Art Nouveau internationally. All three made interesting sets of furniture, like Van de Velde eventually abandoning a floral style for simpler forms. Each of this group practised as architects, Riemerschmid

4. Art Nouveau façade of the Elvira photographic studio, Munich, by August Endell, 1896–7 (destr.)

building a house for himself in 1896, but only Endell designed buildings of any note: the most remarkable was the Elvira photographic studio (1896–7; destr.) in Munich, which had a splendid asymmetrical motif across the façade (see fig. 4) and fantastical decorations in the stairwell. The group in Munich broke up around 1899–1900, and its members dispersed to Berlin, Weimar and Darmstadt.

A feature of *Jugendstil*, one that enabled the movement to extend from the graphic arts into other media, was the patronage it received from the ruling families and from leading industrialists. In Weimar, Graf Harry Kessler was behind Van de Velde's decision to move there in 1902 from Berlin. In Darmstadt, Ernest Ludwig, Grand Duke of Hesse-Darmstadt, commissioned Baillie Scott and Ashbee to decorate several rooms in the Neue Palais in the Art Nouveau style, which caused something of a stir. Encouraged by Koch, he promoted the idea of establishing an artists' colony and offered both land at Mathildenhöhe and money for this purpose. Several artists joined the Künstler-Kolonie, including the Austrian Joseph Maria Olbrich (*see* §6 below), who designed the Hochzeitsturm (1905) at Mathildenhöhe, Hans Christiansen (1866–1945), known for his designs for textiles and carpets, the architect and designer Patriz Huber (1878–1902) and Behrens.

At the Esposizione Internazionale d'Arte Decorativa Moderna of 1900 in Turin the German contribution stood out thanks to Behrens's Hamburg Vestibule. In 1903 Muthesius returned from London and brought current British ideas to the attention of German designers by means of such publications as *Das Englische Haus* (1904–5). In 1907 Behrens became artistic adviser of AEG in Berlin: the electricity company's founder, Emil Rathenau, supported avant-garde artists. Behrens, by this time, was moving towards a more rationalist, abstract and geometrical style.

6. AUSTRIA. Art Nouveau made its appearance in Austria (*see* VIENNA, §III, 4) later and more abruptly than elsewhere in Europe in the form of the *Sezessionstil*. It was dominated by two figures: GUSTAV KLIMT, in his decorative paintings, and OTTO WAGNER, in his architecture. On 25 May 1897 Klimt and 18 other artists left the Künstlerhaus in Vienna to found the Vereinigung Bildender Künstler Österreichs, the Viennese Secession (*see* SECESSION, §3); Klimt was its first President. From the first this new association, which gave its name to the *Sezessionstil*, took note of artistic currents abroad and was receptive to new ideas in every branch of art. An exhibition hall was constructed under the direction of JOSEPH MARIA OLBRICH and was ready for the second Secession exhibition in 1898. Over the entrance was the inscription 'To each age its art, to art its freedom'. One of the first statements published by the group of artists set out principles very close to those of Viollet-le-Duc and Morris: 'We do not recognize any difference between great and minor art,

between the art of the rich and that of the poor. Art belongs to all.'

The magazine *Ver Sacrum* was founded by the Secession in January 1898, with one of the artists responsible for designing the cover for each issue. They also produced the illustrations inside, which are of exceptionally high quality. Although publication of *Ver Sacrum* ceased in 1903, its impact on the spread of Art Nouveau in Austria was considerable; here as in Germany, the style began as a revolution in the graphic arts and in surface decoration. The same principles of spatial organization in a page from *Ver Sacrum* are present in the design of the Majolikahaus (1898) in Vienna by Otto Wagner, for example.

Wagner joined the Secession in 1898. He developed a very personal approach in his architecture, combining traditional elements with revolutionary practices and use of materials in order to meet contemporary requirements. He had believed since 1890 that the 'style of the future' would be the *Nuzstil*, or utility style, and in 1896 had brought out the magazine *Moderne Architektur*, in which he wrote that 'nothing that is not practical can ever be beautiful'. In his apartment houses in Vienna at 38–40 Linke Wienziele (1898–9) he demonstrated what a modern house should look like. He expressed himself best, as did Guimard, in a project that was primarily functional—the Vienna Stadtbahn, a major public commission that occupied him and a large team for several years. Here he achieved what he would like to have seen everywhere; as he wrote in the magazine *Der Architect*, 'not a station, not a shop, not a viaduct, not a bridge should be built without having been designed in the studio in an artistic and modern fashion'. Wagner made his mark on the centre of Vienna with this project, in particular with the Karlplatz station (1894; *see* WAGNER, OTTO, fig. 1), but his most important buildings were the church of St Leonard in the Am Steinhof Lunatic Asylum (1904–7) and the Postsparkasse building (1904–6, 1910–12; *see* WAGNER, OTTO, fig. 2) in Vienna, for which he also designed the furniture. Olbrich, a founder-member of the Secession, was Wagner's assistant from 1893 to 1898, the year he completed the Secession building, and was involved in illustrating *Ver Sacrum*. He left Vienna in 1899 for Darmstadt, where he executed several buildings for the artists' colony (*see* §5 above). In spite of his connections with the Viennese Secession, he remained in Germany and took part in the foundation of the DEUTSCHER WERKBUND in Düsseldorf.

In 1892 JOSEF HOFFMANN entered the Academie der Bildenden Künste in Vienna, where Wagner was his teacher. In 1898 he was employed on the Stadtbahn project and joined the Secession. He taught architecture and interior decoration at the Kunstgewerbeschule, and in 1900 he designed the Secession display at the Exposition Universelle of 1900 in Paris. He discovered the work of Mackintosh (*see* §2 above) on a visit to Scotland, and Mackintosh was to be an important influence on the WIENER WERKSTÄTTE, founded by Hoffmann and KOLO MOSER in 1903. Moser was a prolific designer of furniture, textiles (*see* AUSTRIA, fig. 42), posters, stamps and jewellery, among other items. He was one of the most productive of the collaborators on *Ver Sacrum* and designed the windows and altar of Wagner's church at Steinhof. The character of his work was stimulated by trips to Germany, Belgium, France and Britain. He was the organizer of more than 20 exhibitions and contributed to changes in interior decoration through his involvement with the Werkstätte.

The principal aim of the Wiener Werkstätte was to reintroduce art into objects of everyday use, revitalize the workers' love of their craft and give them a role in the design and distribution of the objects they made, all of which was close to the theories of Morris. In addition to manufacturing utilitarian objects, clothing, postcards and furniture, the Werkstätte executed such buildings as the sanatorium at Purkersdorf (1903–5; remodelled; *see* HOFFMANN, JOSEF, fig. 1) and the Palais Stoclet (*see* HOFFMANN, JOSEF, fig. 2 and BELGIUM, fig. 29) in Brussels between 1905 and 1911 from designs by Hoffmann. The latter, conceived as an aesthetic whole, was the most perfect expression of the group's true inclinations, partly due to the fact that the financier Baron Adolphe Stoclet, who commissioned the building, gave the designer *carte blanche*.

The last purely ornamental and curvilinear elements in Austrian Art Nouveau disappeared with Adolf Loos, who spent three years in the USA before settling in Vienna in 1896. He returned strongly influenced by American architecture, culture and lifestyle in general. His career was a succession of confrontations, one of the first being an article published in 1898 in *Ver Sacrum* entitled 'Die Potemkinsche-stadt', which comprised a violent polemic against historicism. He was the architect of various houses and apartments in Vienna, for some of which he designed the furniture as well. One of his most important projects at the beginning of the 20th century was the Goldman & Salatsch Building (Looshaus, 1910; *see* LOOS, ADOLF, fig. 1), Vienna; by 1910 the bare outlines of his Steiner Haus in Vienna foreshadowed the architecture of the 1930s.

7. OTHER. Art Nouveau left its mark on the whole of the Western world and on some European colonies, but its effects were less coherent and much less deeply felt outside the five countries referred to above. The presence of nationalist elements, particularly in Eastern Europe, gave rise to hybrid developments. Only a few isolated and atypical artists proved exceptions to this rule, but their work did not lie wholly within the historical and stylistic framework of Art Nouveau.

In Italy, where the version of Art Nouveau was known as *Arte nuova*, *Stile floreale* or *Stile Liberty* (after Liberty & Co., the shop in London), GIUSEPPE SOMMARUGA, designer of the Palazzo Castiglioni (1900–03), Milan, was the most important representative in architecture; other designers and architects who should be mentioned include CARLO BUGATTI, Gino Coppede (1866–1927), noted for his use of extravagant detail, and RAIMONDO D'ARONCO, who worked in Turkey for a while and was more influenced by Orientalism. Architecture in the Netherlands and Scandinavia was little touched by Art Nouveau, although in interior decoration and furniture there was a tendency within Dutch *Nieuwe Kunst* that related to curvilinear Art Nouveau elsewhere in Europe, exemplified in the work of GERRIT WILLEM DIJSSELHOF. H. P. BERLAGE left some interesting work belonging to the alternative, more austere tendency. In Russia the workshops in the artistic centre of TALASHKINO deserve mention; and the countries of the Austro-Hungarian empire are studded with buildings by students of Wagner.

In Spain there emerged the isolated phenomenon of Catalan *Modernisme*, closely associated with the city of Barcelona. The last years of the 19th century were dominated there by the figure of ANTONI GAUDÍ. His contribution to Art Nouveau was highly personal and original. The Palau Güell (1885–9; see MOSAIC, colour pl. IV, fig. 2), the Casa Batlló (1904–6) and the cathedral of the Sagrada Familia (taken over by Gaudí in 1883 and incomplete at his death) exemplify his fantastical style incorporating encrusted organic forms, which came from nowhere and were copied by nobody.

In the USA, Louis Comfort Tiffany (*see* TIFFANY, §2) was the leading designer and interior decorator in the Art Nouveau style, often known there as the Tiffany style. Many of his designs for electric lamps, made of bronze, his own 'Favrile' glass or mosaics of opalescent glass are based on natural forms. He was an influential designer of furniture, textiles, wallpaper, silver and jewellery as well as glass. In architecture the contribution of LOUIS SULLIVAN extended far beyond the swirling ornament of the entrance to his Carson, Pirie, Scott & Co. department store (1903–4) in Chicago, but the decorative elements in his work that relate to Art Nouveau are an isolated phenomenon.

8. CONCLUSION. Art Nouveau was born of the desire by a section of society to reject historicism and to abolish the distinction between the major and minor arts. It was to lead on the one hand to ART DECO and on the other to MODERNISM in architecture. The end of Art Nouveau came with World War I, but there had been some strong opposition to it much earlier. In 1901 Guimard had been criticized for the 'extravagance' of his designs for the Métro, for example; in 1903 Art Nouveau was described by Crane in the *Magazine of Art* as 'this strange decorative disease'; and the editors of *Art et décoration* were of the opinion that the Glasgow style, as represented at the Esposizione Internazionale of 1902 in Turin, 'does not appear to be in harmony with our artistic aspirations or our everyday needs'. Gaudí, like Mackintosh, thought little of Art Nouveau, although both had played a part in its development. In the 1920s and 1930s in France it was referred to dismissively as the *Style branche de persil* (stick of parsley style) or the *Style guimauve* (marshmallow style). It was not until the 1960s, through a series of exhibitions, that the reputation of Art Nouveau was re-established and that it was seen as more than a transitory phase linking 19th-century historicism and 20th-century Functionalism.

BIBLIOGRAPHY

F. Schmalenbach: *Jugendstil: Ein Beitrag zu Theorie und Geschichte der Flächenkunst* (Würzburg, 1935)
J. Grady: 'A Bibliography of Art Nouveau', *J. Soc. Archit. Hist.*, xiv/2 (1955), pp. 18–27
S. Tschudi Madsen: *Sources of Art Nouveau* (Oslo and New York, 1956, rev. New York, 1976)
H. Seling: *Jugendstil: Der Weg ins 20. Jahrhundert* (Heidelberg, 1959)
Les Sources du XXe siècle (exh. cat., intro. J. Cassou; Paris, Mus. N. A. Mod., 1960)
J. Cassou, E. Languy and N. Pevsner: *Les Sources du XXe siècle* (Paris, 1961; Eng. trans., London, 1962)
C. E. Schorske: *Fin-de-siècle Vienna: Politics and Culture* (New York, 1961/*R* London, 1980)
R. Schmutzler: *Art Nouveau: Jugendstil* (Stuttgart, 1962)
Henry Van de Velde, 1863–1957 (exh. cat. by R.-L. Delevoy, Brussels, Pal. B.-A., 1963)
R.-H. Guerrand: *Art Nouveau en Europe* (Paris, 1965)
M. Rheims: *L'Art 1900 ou le style Jules Verne* (Paris, 1965)
R. Barilli: *Il Liberty* (Milan, 1966); Eng. trans. as *Art Nouveau* (Feltham, 1969)
N. Pevsner: *The Sources of Modern Architecture and Design* (London, 1968)
F. Borsi and P. Portoghesi: *Victor Horta* (Rome, 1969)
G. C. Argan: *L'arte moderna, 1770–1970* (Florence, 1970)
F. Borsi and H. Weiser: *Bruxelles: Capitale de l'Art Nouveau* (Brussels, 1971)
Pionniers du XXe siècle: Guimard, Horta, Van de Velde (exh. cat. by Y. Brunhammer, M. Culot and R.-L. Delevoy, Paris, Mus. A. Déc., 1971)
R. Bossaglia: *Le Mobilier Art Nouveau* (Paris, 1972)
F. Borsi: *Bruxelles 1900* (Brussels, 1974, rev. 1979)
S. Tschudi-Madson: *Sources of Art Nouveau* (New York, 1975)
L. V. Masini: *Art Nouveau: Un'avventura artistica* (Florence, 1976)
R. Kempton: *Art Nouveau: An Annotated Bibliography* (Los Angeles, 1977)
R. Billcliffe: *Charles Rennie Mackintosh: The Complete Furniture, Furniture Drawings and Interior Designs* (Guildford, 1979, rev. London, 3/1986)
F. Russell, ed.: *Art Nouveau Architecture* (London, 1979)
F. Loyer: *Le Siècle de l'industrie* (Geneva, 1983)
J.-P. Bouillon: *Journal de l'Art Nouveau* (Geneva, 1985)
Vienne, 1880–1938: Naissance d'un siècle (exh. cat., Paris, Pompidou, 1986)
K. J. Sembach: *L'Art Nouveau* (Cologne, 1991)
Guimard (exh. cat., ed. P. Thiebaut; Lyon, Mus. A. Déc.; Paris, Mus. d'Orsay; 1992)

MICHÈLE LAVALLÉE

Artois, Charles, Comte d'. *See* BOURBON, §I(14).

Artois, Mahaut, Countess of. *See* CAPET, (4).

Arts and Crafts, John Th. Uiterwijk, & Co. Dutch company of art dealers and interior design and furniture workshop. The Arts and Crafts interior design and furniture workshop was set up in The Hague in 1893. The Art Nouveau character of the furniture produced by the workshop set it very much apart from its competitors. Designs were produced by the artist Johan Thorn Prikker and the architect Chris Wegerif (1859–1920). During the early years of the workshop the Belgian artist Henry van de Velde exercised a strong influence on its designs. After 1900 the designs became more austere, any Art Nouveau character being confined to woodwork and batik upholstery fabrics. In order to ensure the unity of each interior, an effort was made to have all the objects designed by the same artist. The workshop fostered a close relationship with The Hague school of painting.

BIBLIOGRAPHY

F. Netscher: 'Arts and Crafts', *De Hollandsche Revue* (1902), p. 211
J. de Mooy: 'Kunsthandel Arts and Crafts in Den Haag, 1898–1904', *Kunstlicht* (1982), pp. 19–23

MONIQUE D. J. M. TEUNISSEN

Arts and Crafts Movement. Informal movement in architecture and the decorative arts that championed the unity of the arts, the experience of the individual craftsman and the qualities of materials and construction in the work itself.

1. Introduction. 2. British Isles. 3. Europe. 4. USA. 5. Conclusion.

1. INTRODUCTION. The Arts and Crafts Movement developed in the second half of the 19th century and

lasted well into the 20th, drawing its support from progressive artists, architects and designers, philanthropists, amateurs and middle-class women seeking work in the home. They set up small workshops apart from the world of industry, revived old techniques and revered the humble household objects of pre-industrial times. The movement was strongest in the industrializing countries of northern Europe and in the USA, and it can best be understood as an unfocused reaction against industrialization. Although quixotic in its anti-industrialism, it was not unique; indeed it was only one among several late 19th-century reform movements, such as the Garden City movement, vegetarianism and folksong revivals, that set the Romantic values of nature and folk culture against the artificiality of modern life.

The movement was not held together by a statement of ideas or by collective goals and had no manifesto; its members simply shared, more or less, certain attitudes. The scalding critique of industrial work by JOHN RUSKIN in *The Stones of Venice* (1851–3) taught them to see factory work as soulless and degrading; the pleasure in working in the traditional crafts was the secret of the object's beauty. They condemned the decorative arts of their own day as revivalist in style, machine-made and heavy with meaningless ornament, and looked instead for fresh, unpretentious design, honest construction and appropriate ornament. They wanted to break down the hierarchy of the arts, challenging the supremacy of painting and sculpture and rejoicing in the freedom to work in wood, metal, enamel and glass. The philanthropists among them saw the crafts as therapy for the poor, educationalists saw them as a way of learning about materials. It was in some ways a serious movement, in others merely playful and self-indulgent, and its professed ideals did not always accord with its practices.

2. BRITISH ISLES. The earliest, and perhaps the fullest, development of the movement was in the British Isles, where its history falls into four phases. Its beginnings, in the 1850s, 1860s and 1870s, can be seen in the encouragement of church craftsmanship by GOTHIC REVIVAL architects, in the growth of a public taste for progressive decorative arts during the AESTHETIC MOVEMENT, in such art potteries as that of the Martin brothers and above all in the work of WILLIAM MORRIS, who was an inspiration to the whole movement, less for his pattern designs than for his exploration of old or abandoned craft techniques and his lecturing on the decorative arts. In 1883 Morris became an active Socialist. He was, arguably, taking Ruskin's critique of industrial society to its proper conclusion, but only a few Arts and Crafts people followed him.

In the 1880s the pace quickened; the movement acquired its name—the phrase 'Arts and Crafts' was coined by T. J. Cobden-Sanderson (1840–1922) in 1887. In addition, some of its principal organizations were founded: the ART WORKERS' GUILD (1884), a club that served as the social focus of the movement in London; the Arts and Crafts Exhibition Society (1888), which brought members' work before the public in its annual and later roughly triennial exhibitions; and the Home Arts and Industries Association (1884), which encouraged craft classes for the urban poor and the revival of such rural industries as lacemaking. Alongside the named designers there were many anonymous workers, including amateurs and middle-class women excluded from the world of work by the code of gentility.

In its third phase, during the 1890s and 1900s, the movement grew in extent, but it did not change its character greatly. Important workshops were started, such as that of Ernest Gimson, Ernest Barnsley and Sidney Barnsley (1865–1926). The movement influenced teaching in art schools, particularly at the Central School of Arts and Crafts in London under W. R. Lethaby, and it flourished outside London, for example in Haslemere, Surrey, and in Birmingham. In Scotland there was an extraordinary flowering of Arts and Crafts talent at the Glasgow School of Art, marked by the separate character of the GLASGOW STYLE, while the Arts and Crafts in Ireland, though dependent on the movement in England for guidance and expertise, was a vehicle for Irish nationalism.

The work produced while the movement was at its height did not all look alike. Unlike Art Nouveau, the Arts and Crafts cannot be identified with a single style. There were debts of style in Arts and Crafts work to India, Japan, the Middle East, Scandinavia, Celtic Ireland, Byzantium, medieval Europe, Renaissance Italy and most of all to 16th- and 17th-century England. Many styles were used, but there were also common qualities, and there is a consistent, if not very precise, meaning in the phrase 'Arts and Crafts' when it is applied to objects.

Arts and Crafts people usually liked their designs to show how they worked and what the objects were made of: they thought of this as honesty. In Arts and Crafts houses the loose massing of the parts, irregular fenestration and ad hoc arrangement of gables, bays and other features are meant to suggest a house designed from the inside out, a relaxed assembly of different and comfortable spaces. In furniture and metalwork the jointing is often made obvious, in contrast to the long craft tradition of concealing it. In stained glass designers preferred a coarse and gritty glass that draws attention away from the pictorial and translucent qualities to the material of the window itself. Similarly ornament in metalwork is often confined in such a way as to direct the eye to the plain surfaces of silver, copper and brass.

The Arts and Crafts Movement looked both to the past and to the future, and the objects reflect this. The 'old work' that Arts and Crafts people sketched in the countryside and studied in museums provided them with models and meanings for their designs: the tradition and aura of the small English manor house stands behind many Arts and Crafts houses. They revived and adapted archaic decorative techniques, such as lustre painting and so-called Limoges enamelling. Yet they also looked forward. The mature furniture designs of M. H. Baillie Scott, C. R. Ashbee and C. F. A. Voysey were usually deliberately fresh in style and anxious to underline their modernity. Taking old work as a point of departure, these designers used such novel forms as simple squared-off timbers and, in the case of Voysey, delicately tapered verticals. In the Arts and Crafts, tradition and modernity were not necessarily at odds. While most Arts and Crafts books, printed on handmade paper with dense typography, seem archaic, almost medievalizing, the Renaissance-inspired typography of the books printed at the Doves Press, though no less traditional, was so clear and fresh that it exercised a wide influence on English typography in the early 20th century.

There was much talk of the need for simplicity in design in Arts and Crafts circles and a streak of puritanism in Arts and Crafts taste. But not all Arts and Crafts designs were simple and austere. Most Arts and Crafts interiors were light and reserved, decorated with panelling and perhaps some plasterwork, but Baillie Scott and the architects Joseph Crouch (1859–1936) and Edmund Butler designed interiors hung with tapestries, gleaming with beaten metalwork and glowing with stained glass. The early metalwork of the Arts and Crafts was generally simple in character: W. A. S. Benson, in particular, produced tableware and lamps in brass and copper assembled from simple machine-made parts, while the silver tableware designed by Ashbee in the 1890s was sparingly decorated with coloured stones or enamel plaques. In the late 1890s and early 1900s, however, Henry Wilson, John Paul Cooper (*d* 1933), Alexander Fisher (1864–1936) and others began designing ceremonial silver encrusted with exotic materials and heavy with ornament. In pottery, conversely, the early work by William De Morgan and the Martin brothers was decorative, pots and tiles covered with naturalistic and figurative ornament; but then in the early 1900s W. Howson Taylor (1876–1935) and Bernard Moore (1850–1935) produced pots decorated with random, abstract glaze patterns in austere emulation of Oriental pottery.

Arts and Crafts objects are often rich in associations, carrying suggestions in their structure and decoration of things beyond themselves. Most ornament consisted of natural forms conventionalized, but in the work of Morris and many others it is a nature somehow so fresh and real that it carries the mind out to the country. Gimson and Sidney Barnsley incorporated details from hay rakes and farm wagons in their sophisticated furniture with something of the same effect. Narrative ornament was also used, the stories being drawn from myth and legend, particularly the *Morte d'Arthur.* It is not surprising that the imagery of the movement should refer to the twin Romantic dream-worlds of the countryside and the past, for the Arts and Crafts was, in many ways, a late expression of Romanticism.

The Arts and Crafts was also an avant-garde movement and, as such, a movement of reaction against prevailing middle-class taste. Arts and Crafts designers looked at what was in the shops, condemned it as 'commercial' and went away and designed the opposite. Late 19th-century jewellery, for instance, was dominated by the diamonds mined in great quantities in South Africa, usually set in small gold mounts and surrounded by other pale stones. Arts and Crafts designers despised diamonds as a vulgar display of wealth. Their designs had large silver mounts set with enamel or cheap and colourful stones, the difference proclaiming them as art. The sturdy and often uncomfortable-looking furniture of the Arts and Crafts can also be seen as a gesture of protest against the spindly upholstered furniture of late Victorian drawing-rooms.

These qualities can be found, overlapping one another, in most Arts and Crafts objects. The decanter designed by Ashbee (see fig. 1), for example, is simple in its construction, the silver wires being soldered into place without disguise or even refinement. Ornament is concentrated around the finial, and otherwise the metal is left plain, the hammermarks on its surface witness to the fact that it was handmade. It belongs to the type of late Victorian handled decanter sold in the shops as a claret jug, all but the cheapest of which were decorated by faceting or cutting of the glass; Ashbee's design makes a point of being plainer. The design is both old and new, for it was based on some glass bottles, probably of the late 17th century, that Ashbee found on the site of a house he was building in London. Yet with its linear elegance and hint of Art Nouveau, it is unmistakably *c.* 1900. Ashbee was able to add a further dimension to the design, for he thought the bottles he had found were Elizabethan, bringing with them connotations of bluff English hospitality—a clumsy and romantic view of history that was a characteristic feature of the Arts and Crafts.

The fourth and last phase of the movement in the British Isles ran from *c.* 1910 into the 1920s and 1930s. These were years of transition, for the Arts and Crafts movement was going out of fashion around 1910. Little radically new work was seen at Arts and Crafts Exhibitions, and in 1912 the Exhibition lost a good deal of money. The Arts and Crafts was edged out of the public mind by new developments, Post-Impressionism in art, the admiration for French classicism in architecture and in design by

1. Arts and Crafts decanter designed by C. R. Ashbee, green glass and silver, h. 253 mm, diam. 130 mm, 1904 (London, Victoria and Albert Museum)

those associated with the Design and Industries Association, who wanted to apply the standards of the craft movement to the productive power of industry. The essence of the Arts and Crafts, however, was not to be fashionable, and after World War I it carried on in an altered mood. Some major figures, such as Eric Gill, went on working, and a second generation continued the decorative traditions. There were also important new figures, particularly among weavers, such as Ethel Mairet (1872–1952), and studio potters, such as Bernard Leach and Michael Cardew. They were more exclusively concerned with materials and technique, and there was no longer any hint of the anti-industrialism of Ruskin. Their work was essentially revived hand-craftsmanship, done for the sake of creative satisfaction.

3. EUROPE. The picture of Arts and Crafts activity in Europe is less clear than it is in the British Isles or the USA. The earliest continental Arts and Crafts activity was around 1890 in Belgium, where such artists and architects as Gustave Serrurier-Bovy and Henry Van de Velde were inspired by the freshness of English Arts and Crafts work and the example of artists taking up the crafts: this seemed to be a less precious, more democratic art than easel painting. In 1894 the group of avant-garde artists known as Les XX reformed themselves as La Libre Esthétique with a new commitment to the decorative arts, and their first exhibition included work by Morris, Walter Crane, T. J. Cobden-Sanderson and Ashbee. Stylistically their work was influential in France, but it is not clear how large a part specifically Arts and Crafts ideas and practices played in the decorative arts in France, or indeed Spain or Italy. The main developments were in northern and central Europe.

The Arts and Crafts Movement in Germany was coloured by the strong spirit of nationalism following unification in 1871. The Arts and Crafts cult of the primitive and the vernacular was attractive to Germans, whose sense of national identity was rooted in a vigorous German culture of the past; local crafts, for example, were fostered by the Bund für Heimatschutz, founded in 1903 to preserve the traditional life and fabric of Germany. A progressive Arts and Crafts Movement could also contribute to Germany's struggle for industrial supremacy. Arts and Crafts workshops were set up in many parts of Germany; the two most important were the Vereinigte Werkstätten für Kunst im Handwerk, founded in Munich in 1897 by a group of artist–designers of whom Richard Riemerschmid and Bruno Paul were the most prolific, and the Dresdener Werkstätten für Handwerkskunst, started at Hellerau in 1898 by Karl Schmidt (1873–1954); both produced furniture, lighting, textiles and ceramics. Although modelled on English workshops, they had none of the scorn for trade that inspired and confined English Arts and Crafts, and they quickly developed into large commercial undertakings. In 1905 they both began producing standardized machine-made furniture with the idealistic purpose of reaching a larger public. Their business realism and experiments in standardization gave support to the reforming programme of Hermann Muthesius, who believed that if German industry could perfect pure, standardized Germanic designs, supremacy in world trade would follow, though in fact the Werkstätten themselves remained attached to the values of craft rather than industry, with machine production firmly under the control of the artist–designers.

The principal centre of Arts and Crafts in Austria was Vienna, a city whose cultural life, though long and distinguished, had become parochial in the late 19th century. Its younger artists looked eagerly to France, Belgium and the Netherlands and to English Arts and Crafts; they wanted to enlarge the scope of painters to include the decorative arts, and they made Viennese Arts and Crafts to some extent a painters' movement. In 1900, at the eighth exhibition of the Vienna Secession, the work of Charles Rennie Mackintosh and Ashbee was greeted with enthusiasm. In 1903 two leading Secessionists, Josef Hoffmann and Koloman Moser, set up craft workshops known as the Wiener Werkstätte. They were organized along the lines of the English and German Arts and Crafts, and their manifesto spoke of the dignity of everyday objects, pleasure in work and the value of fine workmanship. Their work, which consists of furniture, metalwork, jewellery and bookbinding, is in a distinctive manner, a stylish rectilinear version of Art Nouveau that contrasts with the deliberate naivety of English Arts and Crafts and with German experiments in cheap furniture; the Wiener Werkstätte catered to the luxury trade. There were also Arts and Crafts workshops in Prague, notably Artěl, founded in 1907, in whose work the influences of folk art and Cubism were mixed.

Folk art influenced Arts and Crafts design in other parts of central Europe and also in Scandinavia, partly because the movement in these countries was inspired by nationalism: where political independence was at stake, folk art became an emblem of national identity. This was the case in Hungary, dominated by Austria and the Habsburg emperors during the last quarter of the 19th century, and in Finland, which was an unwilling part of the Russian Empire. The nationalist impulse fostered both the practice of folk crafts in their traditional form and the incorporation of folk-art motifs in original designs. At Hvittrask, for example, in the idyllic colony of artists' houses near Helsinki, designed by Gesellius, Lindgren & Saarinen, peasant motifs decorate the interiors.

4. USA. In the USA there was the same mixture of social concern and dilettantism and the same rejection of historical styles in favour of a traditional simplicity. Many of the same groups of people, too, were involved: social reformers, teachers and women's organizations, as well as architects and designers. Ruskin and Morris were the prophets of craftsmanship for Americans as for Britons, though Thoreau, Ralph Waldo Emerson and Walt Whitman provided a sympathetic intellectual climate. Morris was also influential in book design and Voysey and Baillie Scott in architecture and furniture, and French artist–potters influenced their American counterparts. The Americans, however, were bolder than the British in making and selling large quantities. 'The World of Commerce', wrote Elbert Hubbard, 'is just as honorable as the World of Art and a trifle more necessary' (see 1987 exh. cat., p. 315). Compared with Europe, the American Arts and Crafts movement was much less influenced by Art

2. Arts and Crafts table and chairs designed by Charles Sumner Greene, mahogany and leather, table h. 760 mm, l. 1663 mm, chairs h. 921 mm, 1906 (Pasadena, CA, David B. Gamble House)

Nouveau. There was a sturdy, four-square quality about much American Arts and Crafts that appealed, as Theodore Roosevelt appealed, to an American ideal of strong, simple manliness.

The movement in craftsmanship started in the 1870s and 1880s, in response to a demand from such architects as H. H. Richardson. The art pottery movement began in Cincinnati, OH, in the 1880s; in quantity and quality the work of, among others, the Rookwood Pottery, the Van Briggle Pottery and the Grueby Faience Co. claims pride of place alongside furniture in American Arts and Crafts. The East Coast was always more aware of British and European developments, and the first Arts and Crafts exhibition in America was held at Copley Hall in Boston in 1897. This was followed by the foundation of the Boston Society of Arts and Crafts, which sponsored local exhibitions, sale-rooms and workshops with great success. The Society's Handicraft Shop produced fine silverware, but it was in printing that Boston excelled: the city's tradition of fine printing fostered outstanding Arts and Crafts presses, notably the Merrymount Press run by Daniel Berkeley Updike. In Philadelphia the architects of the T-Square Club looked particularly to England and exhibited Arts and Crafts work in the 1890s, and in 1901 the architect William L. Price founded an idealistic and short-lived craft colony at Rose Valley, outside Philadelphia, devoted to furniture, pottery and amateur theatricals.

Upper New York State was another important centre of the Arts and Crafts, partly perhaps because of the attractions of the Catskill Mountains. At the Byrdcliffe Colony in Woodstock, for example, pottery, textiles, metalwork and furniture were produced in a romantic backwoods setting; the Arts and Crafts shared some of the pioneering mystique of the log cabin for Americans. The most important figure in the area, and arguably in American Arts and Crafts as a whole, was Gustav Stickley, a furniture manufacturer in Eastwood, Syracuse, who began producing simple so-called Mission furniture about 1900. The design of Stickley's furniture was not as important as the scale of his operations and his power of communication. From 1901 he published *The Craftsman* magazine, which became the mouthpiece of the movement in America, and in 1904 he started the Craftsman Home-Builders Club, which issued plans for self-build bungalows; by 1915 it was estimated that ten million dollars' worth of Craftsman homes had been built. The furniture, house-plans and magazine together presented the Arts and Crafts as a way of life instead of a specialist movement. Simple, middlebrow, traditional, slightly masculine and slightly rural, it appealed to a large American market. The most flamboyant figure in New York State was Elbert Hubbard. At his Roycroft works in East Aurora, he produced metalwork, printed books and furniture very like Stickley's and published *The Philistine* magazine. Hubbard, too, created a powerful image for his craft enterprise, a slightly ersatz blend of bonhomie and culture which made him seem almost a parody of Stickley or, more subtly, of himself.

In Chicago the focus of the movement was at first at Hull House, the settlement house run by the social reformer Jane Addams (1860–1935), where the Chicago Society of Arts and Crafts was founded in 1897. Here immigrants were encouraged to practise their native crafts, such as spinning and weaving, less to perfect the craft than to soften the shock of the new city. There were more Arts and Crafts societies and workshops in Chicago than in any other American city, a witness to its aspiring culture. Perhaps the most distinguished of the workshops were those of the metalworkers and silversmiths, such as the Kalo Shop, which was started in 1900 and continued production until 1970. It was in Chicago, also, that the Arts and Crafts made one of its most important contributions to American architecture, for Arts and Crafts influence can be seen in the work of the Prairie school architects Walter Burley Griffin, George Washington Maher (1864–1926), Purcell & Elmslie and most notably Frank Lloyd Wright. In their sense of materials, their creation of a regional style echoing the horizontals of the prairies and their interest in designing furniture, metalwork and decorative details in their interiors, they continued the Arts and Crafts tradition.

Arts and Crafts workshops and activities in California began only in the early 1900s and were often stimulated by architects and designers from the East settling in California. Although Californian Arts and Crafts showed a debt to the beauty of the landscape and to the building traditions of the Spanish Mission, it had no single stylistic character. It ranged from the richly carved and painted furniture made by Arthur Mathews (1860–1945) and his wife Lucia in San Francisco, through the simple, almost monumental, copper table-lamps of Dirk van Erp (1859–1933), to the outstanding work of the architects Charles Sumner Greene and Henry Mather Greene. Between *c.* 1905 and 1911 the Greene brothers designed a number of large, expensive, wooden bungalows in and around Pasadena and equipped them with fine handmade furniture (see fig. 2). These houses lie along the contours of their sites, inside and outside merging in the kindness of the climate. Their timber construction, panelling and fitted and movable furniture all show the gentle and authoritative ways in which the Greenes could make one piece of wood meet another, with Japanese and Chinese jointing techniques transformed into a decorative Californian *tour de force*. Although most products of the American Arts and Crafts are strong and simple in character, the Greenes' finest houses, the masterpieces of American Arts and Crafts architecture, are delicate and exquisite.

5. CONCLUSION. In 1936 Nikolaus Pevsner published *Pioneers of the Modern Movement*, in which he traced the origins of Modernism among various European movements of the late 19th century and the early 20th, including the Arts and Crafts. Pevsner's book has influenced the study of the Arts and Crafts Movement more than any other, and much writing on the subject has concentrated on the movement's progressive elements, the tentative acceptance of machine production by some Arts and Crafts writers and the simpler designs that seem to reject ornament and historical styles in favour of functionalism. The Modernist view has subsequently come to seem incomplete; it ignored the fact that Arts and Crafts designs, without being any less modern in spirit, are almost always informed by a sense of the past, that ornament is central to much Arts and Crafts designing and that, whatever some theorists may have said, the practical bias of the movement, with its little workshops set apart from the world of industry, was anti-industrial. If the Arts and Crafts Movement is seen in its own time and context, and not just as part of the story of Modernism, it appears as a deeply Romantic movement with its roots in the 19th century, a movement that belongs as much to the history of anti-Modernism as of Modernism.

The most distinctive feature of the Arts and Crafts Movement was its intellectual ambition. Ruskin's attack on factory work uncovered a fundamental malaise in modern industrial society, which Karl Marx identified as alienation. When Morris tried to make art more accessible, giving as much attention to a table and a chair as to an easel painting, he challenged the whole esoteric tendency of modern art. Arts and Crafts objects carry special, idealistic meanings; they tell the viewer about the value of art versus money, about how they are made, about nature or modernity or the satisfactions of hand work. Such idealism is incompatible with the world of manufacture, and if the Arts and Crafts Movement flourished it did so at the price of compromise and contradiction. It drew strength from Ruskin's words but ignored the fact that they applied to all kinds of mechanized and factory work: Arts and Crafts confined its attentions to the small (and relatively unmechanized) world of the decorative arts. Artists and designers of the movement rejected the world of commerce for that of art, but then found that their difficult ambition of making everyday objects was thwarted as the objects were absorbed into the art world and became fodder for galleries and exhibitions. Although its hopes of changing the world were high and honourable, Arts and Crafts never managed to be more than just another movement in the decorative arts.

BIBLIOGRAPHY

PRIMARY SOURCES

J. Ruskin: *The Seven Lamps of Architecture* (London, 1849)
——: *The Stones of Venice*, 3 vols (London, 1851–3)
Catalogues, Arts and Crafts Exhibition Society (London, 1888–)
W. R. Lethaby: *Architecture, Mysticism and Myth* (London, 1891)
W. Crane: *The Claims of Decorative Art* (London, 1892)
Arts and Crafts Essays, Arts and Crafts Exhibition Society (London, 1893)
The Studio (1893–)
H. Van de Velde: *Déblaiement d'art* (Brussels, 1894/*R* 1979)
——: *Aperçus en vue d'une synthèse d'art* (Brussels, 1895)
The Philistine (1895–)
Art and Life and the Building and Decoration of Cities, Arts and Crafts Exhibition Society (London, 1897)
Dek. Kst (1897–)
Dt. Kst & Dek. (1897–)
Kst &Ksthandwk (1898–)
H. Muthesius: *Die englische Baukunst der Gegenwart* (Leipzig, 1900)
D. Cockerell: *Bookbinding and the Care of Books* (London, 1901)
H. Van de Velde: *Die Renaissance in modernen Kunstgewerbe* (Berlin, 1901)
The Craftsman (1901–16)
H. Wilson: *Silverwork and Jewellery* (London, 1903)
The Artsman (1903–7)
H. Muthesius: *Das englische Haus* (Berlin, 1904)
T. J. Cobden-Sanderson: *The Arts and Crafts Movement* (London, 1905)
C. Whall: *Stained Glass Work* (London, 1905)
M. H. Baillie Scott: *Houses and Gardens* (London, 1906)
W. Crane: *An Artist's Reminiscences* (London, 1907)
C. R. Ashbee: *Craftsmanship in Competitive Industry* (London and Chipping Campden, 1908)
E. Johnston: *Writing and Illuminating and Lettering* (London, 1909)
T. Raffles Davison, ed.: *The Arts Connected with Building* (London, 1909)
H. Waentig: *Wirtschaft und Kunst* (Jena, 1909)
W. Morris: *Collected Works*, ed. M. Morris, 24 vols (London, 1910–15)
W. Crane: *From William Morris to Whistler* (London, 1911)
W. R. Lethaby: *Form in Civilization: Collected Papers on Art and Labour* (London, 1922)
W. R. Lethaby, A. H. Powell and F. L. Griggs: *Ernest Gimson: His Life and Work* (London, 1924)
W. Rothenstein: *Men and Memories*, 2 vols (London, 1931)
W. R. Lethaby: *Philip Webb and his Work* (London, 1935)
H. J. L. J. Massé: *The Art-Workers' Guild, 1884–1934* (Oxford, 1935)

SECONDARY SOURCES

N. Pevsner: *Pioneers of the Modern Movement: From William Morris to Walter Gropius* (London, 1936); rev. as *Pioneers of Modern Design: From William Morris to Walter Gropius* (Harmondsworth, 1974)
G. Naylor: *The Arts and Crafts Movement: A Study of its Sources, Ideals and Influence on Design Theory* (London, 1971)
The Arts and Crafts Movement in America, 1876–1916 (exh. cat., ed. R. J. Clark; Princeton U., NJ, A. Mus., 1972)
California Design, 1910 (exh. cat., ed. T. J. Andersen, E. M. Moore and R. W. Winter; Pasadena, A. Mus., 1974)
P. Vergo: *Art in Vienna, 1898–1918* (London, 1975)
S. O. Thompson: *American Book Design and William Morris* (New York, 1977)
A. Callen: *Angel in the Studio: Women in the Arts and Crafts Movement, 1870–1914* (London, 1979)
P. Davey: *Arts and Crafts Architecture: The Search for Earthly Paradise* (London, 1980)
J. Sheehy: *The Rediscovery of Ireland's Past: The Celtic Revival, 1830–1930* (London, 1980)
The Arts and Crafts Movement in New York State, 1890s–1920s (exh. cat., ed. C. L. Ludwig; Oswego, SUNY, Tyler A.G., 1983)
M. Richardson: *Architects of the Arts and Crafts Movement*, RIBA Drawings Series (London, 1983)
A. Crawford, ed: *By Hammer and Hand: The Arts and Crafts Movement in Birmingham* (Birmingham, 1984)
The Glasgow Style, 1890–1920 (exh. cat., Glasgow, A.G. & Mus., 1984)
P. Stansky: *Redesigning the World: William Morris, the 1880s, and the Arts and Crafts* (Princeton, 1985)
E. Boris: *Art and Labor: Ruskin, Morris and the Craftsman Ideal in America* (Philadelphia, 1986)
F. Borsi and E. Godoli: *Vienna, 1900: Architecture and Design* (London, 1986)
J. Heskett: *Design in Germany, 1870–1918* (London, 1986)
'The Art that is Life': The Arts and Crafts Movement in America, 1875–1920 (exh. cat., ed. W. Kaplan; Boston, Mus. F.A., 1987)
E. Cumming and W. Kaplin: *The Arts and Crafts Movement* (London, 1991)

ALAN CRAWFORD

Artschwager, Richard (*b* Washington, DC, 26 Dec 1924). American sculptor and painter. He studied art in 1949–50 under Amédée Ozenfant in New York. During the 1950s he designed and made furniture in New York, but after a fire that destroyed most of the contents of his shop in 1958 he turned again to art, initially painting abstract pictures derived from memories of the New Mexican landscape.

Artschwager continued to produce furniture and, after a commission to make altars for ships in 1960, had the idea of producing sculptures that mimicked actual objects while simultaneously betraying their identity as artistic illusions. At first these included *objets trouvés* made of wood, overpainted with acrylic in an exaggerated wood-grain pattern (e.g. *Table and Chair*, 1962–3; New York, Paula Cooper priv. col., see 1988–9 exh. cat., p. 49), but he soon developed more abstract or geometrical versions of such objects formed from a veneer of formica on wood (e.g. *Table and Chair*, 1963–4; London, Tate). His preference for synthetic materials considered to be in debased taste together with his references to everyday objects were central to his response to Pop art. Similarly his blocklike sculptures had much in common formally with Minimalism.

From 1962 Artschwager also painted grey acrylic monochrome pictures, basing his images on black-and-white photographs, characteristically of modern buildings as shown in property advertisements, as in *Apartment House* (1964; Cologne, Mus. Ludwig). Gradually his paintings became more complex and mysterious, the surface subsumed in a pattern of flickering light, for example in *The Bush* (1.22×1.79 m, 1971; New York, Whitney). His emphasis, however, remained on ambiguities of perception—on the interaction of observation and illusion—especially in sculptures conceived as hybrids of recognizable objects, such as *Book III (Laokoon*; formica on wood with metal handles and vinyl cushion, 1981; Paris, Pompidou), part lectern and part pew.

BIBLIOGRAPHY

E. C. Baker: 'Artschwager's Mental Furniture', *A. News*, 66 (1968), pp. 48–9, 58–61

Richard Artschwager's Theme(s) (exh. cat., essays R. Armstrong, L. C. Cathcart and S. Delehanty; Buffalo, Albright–Knox A.G.; Philadelphia, U. PA, Inst. Contemp. A.; La Jolla, CA, Mus. Contemp. A.; Houston, TX, Contemp. A. Mus.; 1979)

Artschwager, Richard (exh. cat. by R. Armstrong, New York, Whitney; San Francisco, CA, MOMA; Los Angeles, CA, Mus. Contemp. A.; 1988–9)

MARCO LIVINGSTONE

Arttzenius, Floris. *See* ARNTZENIUS, FLORIS.

Artula von Villach, Thomas [Master of Gerlamoos] (*b* Thörl, nr Villach, *c.* 1435–40; *d* Villach, 1523–9). Austrian painter. Known formerly for his frescoes at St George, Gerlamoos (Carinthia), he was identified in 1939–40 by the name Thomas, which during restoration work was found inscribed by a *Crucifixion* painted by the same hand in St Andreas, Thörl; this name was in turn linked with a Thomas von Villach mentioned in a register of tenants of 1468 and described by the chancellor to the patriarch of Aquileia in 1486 as a 'second Apelles' who had painted altar retables in Villach (these are untraced). Further documents indicate he was a town magistrate of Villach in 1520.

Thomas appears to have trained in the workshop of Friedrich of Villach, and his earlier work displays a Carinthian version of the mannered figure poses and cascading drapery of the 'Soft Style', which had originated in Bohemia in the late 14th century. His painting, however, perhaps influenced by 14th-century North Italian work and by the *Knitterstil* ('creased style') of Salzburg painters, has harder outlines and stiffer figures than that of his predecessors. This earlier work includes the frescoes at Gerlamoos, of the *Life of Christ* and *St George* (*c.* 1470–80), and at Thörl, where he painted, among others, an allegorical *Crucifixion* surmounted by orders of angels (*c.* 1470–90); these are large-scale devotional works with elaborate iconography. It also includes some panels painted before 1480 (Klagenfurt, Landesmus. Kärnten; Villach, Mus. Stadt; Bolzano, Mus. Civ.). On the outer wall of Graz Cathedral he painted *c.* 1485 a mural of God the Father brandishing the arrows of his wrath, Famine, War and Plague.

Later work by Thomas shows a conservatively two-dimensional but highly individual melancholy style, seemingly influenced by Rogier van der Weyden: for example the votive fresco (1493) in the Stiftskirche of St Paul im Lavanttal, and the panel of the *Lamentation* (*c.* 1490–95; Klagenfurt, Landesmus. Kärnten), showing its donor Abbot Jöbstl. After 1500 Thomas mainly confined himself to running a workshop; the last work done partly in his hand and recognized as such by Demus, the high altar (*c.* 1512), originally in the old Marienkirche in Heiligengestade near Ossiach and now in the Deutschordenkirche at Friesach, shows traces of the influence of Rueland Frueauf the elder. Demus's researches confirm the theory advanced by Neumann about the artist's long life.

BIBLIOGRAPHY

Thieme–Becker ['Meister von Gerlamoos']

O. Demus: 'Der Meister von Gerlamoos', *Jb. Ksthist. Samml. Wien*, xi (1937), pp. 49–86; xii (1938), pp. 77–116

W. Frodl: *Die gotische Wandmalerei in Kärnten* (Klagenfurt, 1944)

A. Stange: *Deutsche Malerei der Gotik*, xi (Munich, 1961/*R* Nendeln, 1969), pp. 89–96, pls 197–209

J. Höfler: *Die gotische Malerei Villachs*, 2 vols (Villach, 1982)

W. Neumann: 'Der bedeutendste Maler der Kärntner Spätgotik - Thomas Artula von Villach', *Neues aus Alt-Villach: 20. Jahrbuch des Stadtmuseums* (Villach, 1983), pp. 59–98

J. Höfler: *Die Tafelmalerei der Gotik in Kärnten, 1420–1500* (Klagenfurt, 1987)

O. Demus: *Die spätgotischen Altäre Kärntens* (Klagenfurt, 1991)

JANEZ HÖFLER, NIGEL J. MORGAN

Artuqid [Ortukid]. Islamic dynasty that ruled in south-east Anatolia from 1098 to 1408. The Artuqids were descendants of a Turkoman military commander in the service of the Saljuq dynasty; his family settled in Diyarbakır and carved out two principalities, one in Diyarbakır and the other in Mardin and Mayyafariqin. The branch in Diyarbakır fell to the AYYUBID dynasty in 1232, but the other branch survived, sometimes in vassalage, until it was extinguished by the QARAQOYUNLU dynasty. In the 12th century the Artuqids battled against the crusader County of Edessa; it was an Artuqid who took captive Baldwin at Harran in 1104.

Four large Artuqid congregational mosques survive, at Diyarbakır, Mardin, Mayyafariqin (now Silvan) and Dunaysir (now Kiziltepe), all with plans based on that of the Great Mosque of Damascus (*see* ISLAMIC ART, §II, 5(ii)(e)). The one at Diyarbakır (12th century) has a courtyard in the Classical Revival style then in vogue in Syria, but the other buildings, of the late 12th century and early 13th, show a synthesis of Syrian and Anatolian decoration, as does the architectural style of the Saljuq dynasty of Anatolia. This style is continued at Mardin in the Sultan 'Isa Madrasa (1385) and several others. Like all Islamic dynasties of the period in eastern Anatolia, the Artuqids minted figural bronze coins, with original types as well as imitations of Classical and Byzantine coins. The only medieval Islamic enamel securely attested is a gilded bronze bowl (Innsbruck, Tirol. Landesmus.) made for Da'ud ibn Sökmen (*reg c.* 1109–44); it may represent a syncretic workshop of Byzantine craftsmen working under the Artuqids (*see* ISLAMIC ART, §VIII, 3). Other inlaid brass vessels attributed to Artuqid patronage are more Islamic in style. The Artuqids employed Ibn al-Razzaz al-Jazari (*fl* 1205) to make and write about complex mechanical automata, and an early copy of his book (Istanbul, Topkapı Pal. Lib., A. 3472) was copied and illustrated at Diyarbakır.

BIBLIOGRAPHY

Enc. Islam/2

A. Gabriel: *Voyages archéologiques dans la Turquie orientale*, 2 vols (Paris, 1940)

D. S. Rice: 'Inlaid Brasses from the Workshop of Aḥmad al-Dhakī al-Mawsilī', *A. Orient.*, ii (1957), pp. 283–326

G. Fehérvári: 'Working in Metal: Mutual Influences between the Islamic World and the Medieval West', *J. Royal. Asiat. Soc. GB & Ireland* (1977), pp. 3–16

M. Oluş Arık: 'Turkish Architecture in Asia Minor in the period of the Turkish Emirates', *The Art and Architecture of Turkey*, ed. E. Akurgal (New York, 1980), pp. 111–36

J. Raby, ed.: *The Art of Syria and the Jazira, 1110–1250* (Oxford, 1985)

T. Allen: *A Classical Revival in Islamic Architecture* (Wiesbaden, 1986)

E. Whelan: 'Representations of the *Khâssakîyah* and the Origins of Mamluk Emblems', *Content and Context of Visual Arts in the Islamic World*, ed. P. P. Soucek (New York, 1988), pp. 219–53

S. Redford: 'How Islamic Is It? The Innsbruck Plate and its Setting', *Muqarnas*, vii (1990), pp. 119–35

□

Arturo. Argentine art magazine published as a single issue in Buenos Aires in early 1944. Its avant-garde stance proved influential on the development of Constructivism in Argentina, leading directly to ARTE MADÍ and to ASOCIACIÓN ARTE CONCRETO INVENCIÓN.

Art Workers' Guild. English group of artists, designers, architects and craftsmen formed in 1884. In 1883 five young assistants from R. Norman Shaw's office formed the St George's Art Society. The Society discussed its worries about the growing practical and ideological separation of art and architecture, and the indifference to their ideas for reform in architecture, shown by the official institutions such as the Royal Academy and the Royal Institute of British Architects. They soon realized that there was a need for a larger, broader society. In 1884 these same architects—Gerald Horsley (1862–1917), W. R. Lethaby, Mervyn Macartney (1853–1932), Ernest Newton and E. S. Prior—joined with another group, The Fifteen, led by Lewis F. Day and Walter Crane, to form the Art Workers' Guild. The Guild actively promoted the theory of the interdependence of the arts, and its members were encouraged through lectures and discussion to understand each other's profession. Designers, artists, architects and craftsmen were brought together as equals.

The Guild was never a studio or workshop, although its members often collaborated and continue to do so. In 1888 the Arts and Crafts Exhibition Society was formed by some members after the Guild had rejected the idea that they should sponsor exhibitions of designers' work. For over a hundred years, however, the Guild has provided an influential forum for discussion of techniques, styles and current issues in design, architecture and industry. Early Guild members included distinguished names from every artistic field, most of whom played a crucial role in the Arts and Crafts Movement: C. R. Ashbee, Edward Burne-Jones, Ernest Gimson, Edwin Lutyens, William Morris, J. D. Sedding and C. F. A. Voysey. The Guild had a number of temporary homes until a house in Queen Square, Bloomsbury, was purchased in 1913, where meetings are still held fortnightly.

BIBLIOGRAPHY

H. J. L. J. Massé: *The Art Workers' Guild, 1884–1934* (Oxford, 1935)

I. Anscombe and C. Gere: *Arts and Crafts in Britain and America* (London, 1978), pp. 112–13

Beauty's Awakening: The Centenary Exhibition of the Art Workers' Guild, 1884–1984 (exh. cat., Brighton, A.G. & Mus., 1984)

MARTA GALICKI

Artz, (David) Adolphe (Constant) (*b* The Hague, 18 Dec 1837; *d* The Hague, 5 Nov 1890). Dutch painter and collector. From 1855 to 1864 he trained with Johannes Egenberger (1822–97) and Louis Royer (1793–1868) at the Amsterdam Academie. There he met Jozef Israëls, whose fishing subjects were to be a lasting source of inspiration for Artz. Unlike Israëls, however, Artz depicted only the more cheerful sides of the fisherman's life. Technically, he distinguished himself from Israëls in his use of sharp outlines and bright colour. Between 1866 and 1874 Artz stayed in Paris where he set up his own studio at the suggestion of Courbet. Here he maintained close contacts with his colleagues Jacob Maris and Frederik Kaemmerer (1839–1902) as well as the art dealer Goupil & Co. During this period Artz produced mainly fashionable genre scenes and a number of Japanese subjects. His control over line and colour became more powerful.

In 1874 Artz moved permanently to The Hague where he took up the fisherman genre again. In the early 1880s he established his reputation definitively with such works as *In the Orphanage at Katwijk-Binnen* (Amsterdam, Rijksmus.). One of his most famous paintings was *Grandmother's Sweetheart* (Rijswijk, A.-G. Oenema), an interior with an old woman offering an apple to a young child. During this period Artz also painted a number of variations on the theme of courtship. *Potato Harvest* (untraced) shows Artz's compositional strength towards the end of his life. His large watercolours were particularly popular collectors' items.

In his own time Artz was a well-respected artist of the HAGUE SCHOOL. He was awarded several medals both in Holland and abroad and became chairman of The Hague artists' society, the Pulchri Studio. In 1899 he was a member of the jury at the Paris Exposition Universelle. Artz himself collected Hague school paintings and prints after modern French masters.

BIBLIOGRAPHY

F. S[mit] K[leine]: 'Artz', *De Huisvriend* (1885), pp. 132, 134–5

J. Gramm: 'David Adolphe Constant Artz', *Eigen Haard* (1890), pp. 778–81

R. Heath: 'Adolphe Artz', *Mag. A.*, (Dec 1896), pp. 80–85

P. A. Haaxman jr: 'David Adolphe Constant Artz, geb. 18 December 1837, gest. 8 November 1890', *Elsevier's Geïllus. Mdschr.*, xv (1898), pp. 297–312 [repr. in M. Rooses, ed.: *Het schildersboek*, iii (Amsterdam, 1899), pp. 137–54]

J. de Gruyter: *De Haagse school*, ii (Rotterdam, 1969), pp. 83–4

The Hague School: Dutch Masters of the Nineteenth Century (exh. cat., Paris, Grand Pal.; London, RA; The Hague, Gemeentemus.; 1983), pp. 157–9

DIEUWERTJE DEKKERS

Arundel, Countess of. *See* HOWARD (i), (2).

Arundel, 2nd Earl of. *See* HOWARD (i), (1).

Arundel, 12th Earl of. *See* FITZALAN, HENRY.

Arundel Society. Association for the publication of reproductions of works of art. It was founded in 1848 and issued its first prospectus in 1849. Its founders included John Ruskin, Giovanni Aubrey Bezzi, Alexander Lord Lindsay (later 25th Earl of Crawford), Edmund Oldfield and Samuel Rogers. Although the Society was named after a great private collector, Thomas Howard, 2nd Earl of Arundel, it was intended to reach the largest possible public through the publication of reproductions that were to be truthful, rather than merely attractive or decorative. From the start the society focused on early Italian painting, particularly works in fresco; it also published some early Flemish and German altarpieces. Members were also offered reproductions in fictile ivory after Antique and medieval ivories, and reduced plasters and bronze electrotypes after details of the Elgin marbles. The Arundel Society popularized a growing taste for early Renaissance art, which had been nourished by Alexis-François Rio's *De la poésie chrétienne dans son principe, dans sa matière et dans ses formes* (Paris, 1836), Lord Lindsay's *Sketches of the History of Christian Art* (London, 1847) and sections of the second volume of Ruskin's *Modern Painters* (London, 1846). The Society's first publications included engravings (1849–69) after Fra Angelico's frescoes (1448–9) in the Chapel of Nicholas V in the Vatican, and robust wood-engravings (1852–60) after Giotto's frescoes (*c.* 1305) in the Arena Chapel, Padua. From 1857, on the advice of the collector and politician Sir Austen Henry Layard, the Society adopted chromolithography as its principal reproductive medium. It subsequently tended to favour the more accessible Quattrocento Masters, in particular Ghirlandaio, Perugino and Pinturicchio. A Copying Fund in 1857 was set up to record a remarkable range of frescoes in Italy that were in danger of decay and destruction; these copies, together with the watercolours on which the chromolithographs were based, were deposited in the National Gallery, London. The Victoria and Albert Museum, London, holds a collection of the Society's prints and further watercolours. The Society's monographs, which were popular rather than pioneering, included Ruskin's *Giotto and his Works in Padua* and numerous works by Layard. From 1866 the Society acted as publishers of a range of books and reproductions for the South Kensington Museum, London, now the Victoria and Albert Museum.

At the height of its popularity in the 1860s the Arundel Society had over 2000 members. The beauty of its chromolithographs, which were characteristically framed and glazed, brought early art into the heart of the Victorian home. From the early 1860s, however, the accuracy of the Society's watercolours, mostly executed by professional Italian copyists, was called into question in reviews in the *Saturday Review*, the *Art Journal* and the *Athenaeum*. The Society ceased its activities in 1897 for three reasons: by the 1890s there was a thriving market in second-hand prints; the Society's work was being undermined by progress in the field of photographic reproductions; and by the 1890s the art the Society had sought to popularize had been comprehensively 'rediscovered'. By the end of the 19th century, to admire Trecento, Quattrocento and early Northern art was the norm in educated circles.

BIBLIOGRAPHY

A. H. Layard: 'Publications of the Arundel Society', *Q. Rev.*, civ (1858), pp. 277–325

W. Gregory: 'The Arundel Society', *19th C.* [London], xv (1884), pp. 610–25

V. F. Marchese: *Ultimi scritti* (Siena, 1889)

W. N. Johnson: *A Handbook to the Collection of Chromolithographs from Copies of Important Works of Ancient Masters Published by the Arundel Society* (Manchester, 1907)

A. Smart: 'Some Unpublished Copies of Frescoes at Assisi', *Apollo*, xciv (1974), pp. 228–31

R. Cooper: 'The Popularisation of Renaissance Art in Victorian England', *A. Hist.*, i (1978), pp. 263–92

T. Ledger: *A Study of the Arundel Society, 1848–1897* (diss., U. Oxford, 1978)

T. Ledger Harrod: 'John Ruskin and the Arundel Society', *Apollo*, xciv (1988), pp. 180–88

TANYA HARROD

Arundell, Henry, 8th Baron Arundell of Wardour (*b* 31 March 1740; *d* Wardour, Wilts, 4 Dec 1808). English patron and collector. A leading Roman Catholic, he made a Grand Tour to Italy in 1758. In 1763, having already inherited the estate and part ruinous castle at Wardour, Arundell married Mary Conquest; soon after he commissioned a full-length portrait of himself from Joshua Reynolds (*c.* 1764–7; sold London, Robinson & Fisher, 21 June 1900) and another of *Mary, Lady Arundell of Wardour* (*c.* 1764–7; sold London, Christie's, 6 March 1914, lot 112). He employed the landscape gardener Richard Woods in 1764–8, but in 1770–76 the architect James Paine built for Arundell a magnificent new Wardour Castle in the Palladian style, while Lancelot Brown made further improvements (1774–5) to the grounds, adding new plantations and a lake. Wardour's interiors include Paine's finest staircase and, on the music-room ceiling, a copy by Pompeo Batoni of Guido Reni's fresco *Aurora* (1613–14; Rome, Pal. Rospigliosi–Pallavicini, Casino dell'Aurora). In Rome the Jesuit priest John Thorpe (*d* 1792), Arundell's agent there for the acquisition of Old Master paintings, engaged the architect Giacomo Quarenghi to provide designs for Wardour's chapel, which was intended for Catholic worship; these, however, were rejected by Arundell in favour of Paine's proposals, except for the altar (1772–4) by Quarenghi. The chapel is a richly decorated top-lit hall, and Thorpe's acquisitions for its furnishings included an altarpiece by Giuseppe Cades, the *Deposition* (*c.* 1776–9), and Pierre-Etienne Monnot's white marble relief of the *Virgin and Child*, once the altarpiece of the Jesuit-General's private chapel in Rome until Pope Clement XIV's suppression of the order in 1773. Wardour's chapel was extended at its sanctuary end in 1790 by the architect John Soane.

Arundell's collection of pictures and other objects, predominantly devotional in character and recorded in Rutter's catalogue, was dispersed after his death at sales in 1889 and 1935. Wardour Castle was sold in 1948 to the Society of Jesus and was then used until *c.* 1990 by Cranborne Chase School, where several family portraits were on loan, including *Thomas, 2nd Baron Arundell*, by John Michael Wright and *Henry, 7th Baron, and Lady Mary Arundell* by George Knapton.

BIBLIOGRAPHY

J. Rutter: *An Historical and Descriptive Sketch of Wardour Castle* (Shaftesbury, 1822), pp. 25–51

C. Hussey: 'Wardour Castle, Wiltshire', *Country Life*, lxviii (22 Nov 1930), pp. 646–52; (29 Nov 1930), pp. 676–82

E. K. Waterhouse: 'A Note on the Pictures at Wardour Castle', *Archaeol. J.*, civ (1947), p. 177

A. Rowan: 'Wardour Castle Chapel, Wiltshire', *Country Life*, cxliv (10 Oct 1968), pp. 908–12

M. Cowan: 'The Wardour Castles and their Landscape', *Hatcher Rev.*, iii/25 (1988), pp. 211–16

NIGEL SURRY

Arup, Sir **Ove (Nyquist)** (*b* Newcastle upon Tyne, 16 April 1895; *d* London, 5 Feb 1988). English engineer and structural consultant. He studied philosophy at Copenhagen University (BA, 1916) and engineering at the Polyteknisk Laereanstalt, Copenhagen (BSc, 1922), where he specialized in reinforced concrete. In 1922 he began work in Hamburg with Christiani & Nielsen, a Danish firm, expert in the design of reinforced concrete structures, and in 1924 moved with them to London as chief engineer. In the early 1930s he met Berthold Lubetkin and worked as structural consultant to the Tecton partnership, notably in London on the Penguin Pool (1934; see fig.) for the Zoological Gardens, Regent's Park, and on Highpoint One (1933–6), Highgate. Tecton's progressive attitude to building techniques impressed Arup, but he realized that the traditional subordination of engineer to architect in the design process impeded effective collaboration. He therefore moved to a building firm, J. L. Kier & Co. in London, where as director and chief designer (1934–8) he had greater control. This integration of professional roles

Ove (Nyquist) Arup, in collaboration with the Tecton partnership: Penguin Pool, Zoological Gardens, Regent's Park, London, 1934

formed the basis of Arup's lasting concern to link construction and design. During the 1930s he also worked with Wells Coates, Ernö Goldfinger, E. Maxwell Fry, Marcel Breuer and Yorke, Rosenberg & Mardall. He was a keen propagandist for the new architecture and served on the executive committee of MARS from 1935.

During World War II Arup studied air-raid protection for the government and was Finsbury Borough Council's adviser on shelter construction. In 1949 he formed Ove Arup and Partners, an engineering firm whose working practice demonstrated Arup's belief in the importance of teamwork. The members of the firm reflected the many specialized branches of engineering (for example acoustic, electrical and civil), and Arup was thus able to offer a complete service to architects. This was particularly useful on major buildings with complex structural and servicing requirements, such as the Brynmawr Rubber Factory (1947–52; Architects' Co-Partnership), Wales, Coventry Cathedral (1951–62; Basil Spence), Sydney Opera House (1956–73; Jörn Utzon), Australia, and the Centre Georges Pompidou (1971–7; Renzo Piano and Richard Rogers), Paris, and Lloyd's of London Headquarters (1978–85; Richard Rogers). In 1973 Arup achieved his aim to integrate the design team into one cohesive unit with the formation of Arup Associates, a multi-disciplinary firm of architects, engineers and surveyors. Their design work was characterized by the articulation of structural and service elements.

WRITINGS

Design, Cost, Construction and Relative Safety of Trench, Surface, Bombproof and Other Air Raid Shelters (London, 1939)
Safe Housing in Wartime (London, 1941)
'Reinforced Concrete', *Architect's Y-b.* (London, 1945)
'The Architect and the Engineer', *J. Inst. Civ. Engin.* (Aug 1959)

BIBLIOGRAPHY

M. Brawne: *University Planning and Design* (London, 1967)
H. Sharoum: 'Arup's First Ten Years', *Archit. Plus* (Nov–Dec 1974)
'Arup Associates', *A. & U.* (Dec 1977)
O. Arup: 'Arup Associations', *Archit. Rev.* [London] (Nov 1979)
M. Brawne: *Arup Associates* (London, 1983)

MALCOLM READING

Arvatov, Boris (Ignat'yevich) (*b* Wylkowyszki, Poland [now Vilkaviškis, Lithuania], 3 June 1896; *d* Moscow, 14 June 1940). Russian theorist and critic. Having studied physics and mathematics at the University of Petrograd (now St Petersburg), he became a member of PROLETKUL'T in 1918 and in 1921 joined the Moscow INKHUK and Russian Academy of Artistic Sciences. Together with other supporters of industrial design such as Osip Brik, Boris Kushner, Lyubov' Popova and Nikolay Tarabukin, he influenced the new identification of Inkhuk with the Production art movement (*see* CONSTRUCTIVISM, §1). He was one of the founders of LEF (Levyy Front Iskusstv: Left Front of the Arts), which promoted a utilitarian and organizational notion of art and provided a revolutionary platform for the Constructivists and Formalists. He was a contributor to the LEF art journals in the 1920s, writing on the theatre, Constructivism and Production art. Constructivism was regarded as no more than a transitional stage on the path to Production art, which involved the essential restructuring of life. He promoted the concept of 'engineer–constructor' as the sole instigator of creative work in the new Soviet society. Art was to be the product of skilled craftsmanship rather than an expression of the artist's psyche: like other forms of technology it was part of society's material culture. From 1923 until his death Arvatov lived in a psychiatric hospital suffering from a mental illness that originated from a concussive blow received while serving in the Red Army during the Russian civil war. During these years he still contributed to the journals of LEF. His theories comprised a skilful combination of socio-political and formalist analysis, as he advocated the apparently contradictory principles of non-objective aesthetics and utilitarian art.

WRITINGS

Iskusstvo i klassy [Art and the classes] (Moscow and Petrograd, 1923)
Natan Al'tman (Moscow, 1924)
Iskusstvo i proizvodstvo [Art and production] (Moscow, 1926)
Ob agitatsionnom i proizvodstvennom iskusstve [On agitational and production art] (Moscow, 1930) [collected writings]

BIBLIOGRAPHY

V. Friche: 'Arvatov, Boris Ignat'yevich', *Literaturnaya entsiklopediya*, i (Moscow, 1929), pp. 224–6
H. Stephan: '*Lef* and the Left Front of the Arts', *Slav. Beitr.*, cxlii (1981) [whole issue]
C. Lodder: *Russian Constructivism* (New Haven and London, 1983)

JEREMY HOWARD

Aryballos. Ancient pottery form, used to contain oils and perfumes (*see* GREECE, ANCIENT, figs 71(v)a, 88 and 89). □

Arzawa. *See under* BEYCESULTAN.

Arziniega, Claudio de. *See* ARCINIEGA, CLAUDIO DE.

Asʿad Yasārī. *See* ESAD YESARI.

Asai, Chū [Mokugo; Mokugyo] (*b* Edo [now Tokyo], 21 June 1856; *d* Kyoto, 16 Dec 1907). Japanese painter. He was the leading Western-style (*Yōga; see* JAPAN, §VI, 5(iv)) landscape painter of the Meiji period (1868–1912) and one of the founder-members of the Meiji Bijutsukai (Meiji Fine Arts Society, established 1889; later absorbed into the Taiheiyō Gakai [Pacific Painting Society]), the first association of Western-style painters in Japan. Asai was born into a samurai family retained by the Sakura clan. He was originally trained in Japanese bird-and-flower painting (*kachōga*) in the literati (*Nanga* or *Bunjinga*) style, but turned later to oil painting and at the age of 19 entered the Shōgidō, a private school of Western-style painting. The school had been opened in Tokyo the previous year by the artist Shinkurō Kunisawa (1847–77), who had studied painting under John Wilcolm in London.

When the government-sponsored Kōbu Bijutsu Gakkō (Technical Art School) was opened in Tokyo in 1876, Asai enrolled and studied painting under the Italian painter ANTONIO FONTANESI. After Fontanesi's departure in 1878, Asai and ten other of Fontanesi's students left the school and founded the Jūichikai (Society of Eleven). The following decade was notable for a distaste for *Yōga* and a concomitant rise in *Nihonga*, traditional Japanese-style painting (*see* JAPAN, §VI, 5(iii)). At the end of the 1880s, however, interest in *Yōga* began to revive, stimulated by the return of Japanese artists who had studied in Europe. The Western-style painters of the Meiji Fine Arts Society successfully challenged the dominant position of *Nihonga*, until the return of KURODA SEIKI in 1893 and his promotion of the luminous, *plein-air* palette of French Impressionism divided the world of *Yōga* into progressive and conservative camps, either for or against *plein-air* painting. Asai remained aloof from the debate until 1898, when he accepted a faculty post at Tōkyō Bijutsu Gakkō (Tokyo Art School, now Tokyo University of Fine Arts and Music) and taught alongside the 'progressive' Kuroda as a representative of 'conservative' interests.

An example of Asai's early landscape painting is *Fields in Spring* (1888; Tokyo, N. Mus.). Although close to Fontanesi's dark, earthy palette, it reveals Asai's profound ability to control the medium of Western oils and convey the gentle mood of nature in Japan.

In 1899 Asai was awarded a grant by the Monbushō (Ministry of Education) to study painting in France. He remained abroad from 1900 to 1902, dividing his time between Paris and the picturesque and tranquil suburb of Grez-sur-Loing, south of Paris. *Autumn in Grez-sur-Loing* (1901; Tokyo, N. Mus.) demonstrates the graceful chromatic concessions he made to the light Impressionist palette.

Asai travelled in Italy, Germany and England before returning to Japan, when he immediately went to Kyoto to teach Western-style painting at the newly opened Kyōtō Kōtō Kōgei Gakkō (Kyoto School of Design). He was the first official instructor in *Yōga* in the culturally conservative city of Kyoto. Western-style painting thus found favour in Kyoto and spread throughout western Japan. In 1903 Asai opened his own private academy, the Shōgoin Yōga Kenkyūjo (Shōgo Institute of Western Art) in Kyoto, which in 1905 became the Kansai Bijutsuin (Kansai Art Institute). Important painters from western Japan who studied *Yōga* with Asai were Ishii Hakutei (1882–1958), Sōtarō Yasui and Ryūzaburō Umehara. As well as paintings Asai executed designs for woodblock-printed books: especially noteworthy was the *Tōsei fūzohu gojūban uta awase* ('Collected poems of fifty views of Western manners', 1907; see Hillier, pls 660–61).

BIBLIOGRAPHY

M. Harada: 'Meiji no *yōga*' (Tokyo, 1968), *Nihon no bijutsu* [Arts of Japan]; Eng. trans. by A. Murakata as *Meiji Western Painting* (New York and Tokyo, 1968)

'Asai Chū', *Kindai no bijutsu* [Modern art], v (1971) [whole issue]

J. Hillier: *The Art of the Japanese Book*, 2 vols (London, 1987)

Paris in Japan: The Japanese Encounter with European Painting (exh. cat. by S. Takashina, J. T. Rimer and G. D. Bolas, Tokyo, Japan Found.; St Louis, MO, George Washington U.; 1987–8)

AYA LOUISA MCDONALD

Asam [Asamb; Asum]. German family of artists. (1) Hans Georg Asam, a Bavarian painter familiar with the Italian High Baroque, helped train his sons (2) Cosmas Damian Asam and (3) Egid Quirin Asam to become outstanding exponents of German Baroque art in the earlier 18th century. His wife Maria Theresia and daughter Maria Salome (*b* Benediktbeuren, 7 Feb 1685; *bur* Munich, 24 June 1740) worked with them on occasion. Cosmas Damian specialized in painting ceiling frescoes and altarpieces while Egid Quirin specialized in stuccowork and sculpture. Both also worked as architects, and Egid painted, but in their realizations of the GESAMTKUNSTWERK or total work of art, combining all categories, it is sometimes impossible to say who did what. Their principal collaborations to this end, at Weltenburg Monastery (1716–35), St Johann Nepomuk in Munich (1729–45) and the Ursulinenkirche at Straubing (1736–9), are discussed in §II below.

I. Family members. II. Collaborations on the *Gesamtkunstwerk*.

I. Family members.

(1) Hans Georg Asam (*b* Rott am Inn, 10 Oct 1649; *d* Sulzbach, *bur* 7 March 1711). Painter. The son of Christoph Asam, a master brewer at the Benedictine abbey at Rott am Inn, in 1679–80 he was apprenticed in Munich to the court painter Nikolaus Prugger and in 1680 married Prugger's daughter Maria Theresia. She frequently assisted him in his commissions, which were mainly for monasteries, painting stucco, woodwork and sculpture. In 1682–3 Hans Georg painted his largest commission, 58 portraits of abbots for Benediktbeuren Abbey and 8 pictures showing the monastery's history; then until 1687 he decorated the ceiling of its abbey church with frescoes of the *Life of Christ* and the *Last Judgement*. Subsequently he spent several months in Italy, visiting Venice and possibly Rome. Italian influence shows in his work in the abbey church (now St Quirin) at Tegernsee, where for the first time he painted the interior of a cupola (1689–93; see fig.).

Hans Georg Asam: cupola fresco (1689–93), St Quirin, Tegernsee

Cosmas Damian Asam: ceiling frescoes (1718–20), central aisle of Weingarten Abbey

He then worked in Munich and the Upper Palatinate. Between 1700 and 1707 he painted frescoes (destr.) depicting biblical, historical and mythological scenes for the castle of Graf Lorenz von Tilly in Helfenberg. In 1708–10 he collaborated with his sons on the Maria-Hilf-Kirche in Freystadt. Hans Georg was chiefly inspired by Italian High Baroque painting, such as the richly figured, perspectival ceiling frescoes of Andrea Pozzo. He was also influenced by 16th-century Venetian painting (Titian, Tintoretto and Veronese). Asam's painting is sometimes decorative, with much use of *quadratura.* Besides frescoes, Hans Georg also painted altarpieces, for instance those in the church (1690) of Rottach-Egern and in the Hofkapelle (1710–11) at Sulzbach-Rosenberg. The altarpiece for St Egidius, Harenzhofen, was completed by his wife Maria Theresia in 1710, while that at St Andreas, Helfenberg, was completed by Cosmas Damian in 1711.

Hans Georg's daughter Maria Salome worked as her father's assistant, for example at Harenzhofen (1708–09), where she and her mother Maria Theresia painted all the woodwork and stucco on the main altar and side altars of St Egidius. In 1721 Maria Salome married the painter and merchant Johann Philipp Bornschlegel from Würzburg. She later assisted her brothers at Weltenburg Monastery (1723–4) as a painter of stucco and woodwork.

(2) Cosmas Damian Asam (*b* Benediktbeuren, *bapt* 28 Sept 1686; *d* Munich, 10 May 1739). Painter and architect, son of (1) Hans Georg Asam. As a youth, he worked as his father's assistant, for example at Schloss Schönach (1704) and at the Maria-Hilf-Kirche (1708), Freystadt. After his father's death in 1711, Cosmas Damian went to Rome, studying at the Accademia di S Luca under Carlo Maratti; he was awarded the academy's first prize for his brush drawing of the *Miracle of St Pius* (Rome, Accad. N. S Luca) in 1713. That year he returned to Germany. In 1717 he married Maria Anna, daughter of the engraver Franz Anton Mörl (1671–1734); their son, Franz Erasmus Asam (1720–95), produced few works of his own, acting mainly as an assistant to his father. In 1724 Cosmas Damian bought an estate he named Asamisch-Maria-Einsiedel-Thal in Munich-Thalkirchen, even building a chapel of his own there in 1739. Throughout his life Cosmas Damian worked mainly on large commissions, painting and sometimes also acting as architect, sometimes collaborating with his brother Egid Quirin; his work took him to the Upper Palatinate, Upper and Lower Bavaria, Baden and Swabia as well as to the Tyrol, Switzerland, Bohemia and Silesia. Besides church dignitaries, his patrons included the court and the aristocracy. He was given the protection of the Elector's court in Munich in 1719 and subsequently some minor offices at various other courts. On large-scale commissions he always employed workshop assistants as well as members of his family. His pupils included Thomas Christian Scheffler (1699–1756), Matthäus Günther, Joseph Gregor Winck, Johann Adam Schöpf (1702–72) and Johann Adam Müller (*fl* 1718–38).

The first substantial commissions Cosmas Damian undertook after returning from Rome were for the abbey church of St Jakob (1714) at Ensdorf and for the Dreifaltigkeitskirche in Munich in 1715. Both were dominated by cupola frescoes. Hosts of drastically foreshortened figures in light, almost transparent colours surround illusionistic openings in the architecture. The way light is directed plays an important role. The influences of Roman ceiling painting—Carlo Maratti, Benedetto Luti and Pietro da Cortona—are unmistakable. In 1717–18 Cosmas Damian painted frescoes in the Maria-Hilf-Kirche in Amberg and St Johannes Evangelista in Michelfeld; the latter was his first collaboration with his brother Egid Quirin.

The interior (1718–20) of the newly built WEINGARTEN ABBEY was a major early achievement: his colouring was becoming bolder. Six large panels and many smaller ones, the cupola above the crossing and a mock cupola in the choir are all his work. Frescoes in the central aisle show his familiarity with the illusionism of Andrea Pozzo and Giovanni Battista Gaulli, using *quadratura* to extend the space into infinity (see fig.). In the fresco in the first bay of the nave, the *Veneration and Assistance of the Relic of the Holy Blood,* boldly painted architectural structures penetrate a picture-field flocked by figures seen *di sotto in sù*. The middle *Glory of St Benedict* is bathed in a sea of light and colour, with painted pillars supporting an open cupola that corresponds with the actual church building, and the cycle culminates in the shallow cupola above the choir with the *Miracle of Pentecost,* closely based on Pozzo's book *Perspectiva* (1693).

In 1720 Cosmas Damian again collaborated with Egid Quirin in the Cistercian abbey church of Mariae Himmelfahrt at Aldersbach. The ceiling there offered him his first opportunity for a single, continuous fresco: *St Bernard's Christmas Vision*. Here again the actual building opens via a simulated architecture, part paint part stucco, to reveal the visionary apparition. After Aldersbach came several other large commissions in which the Asam brothers could put their illusionistic ideas into practice, including Freising Cathedral (1723–4) and EINSIEDELN ABBEY (1725–6; *see* SWITZERLAND, fig. 2), where the crowning achievement is the fresco in the 'Christmas cupola', showing Mary and the Christ Child surrounded by shepherds and angels and bathed in an unearthly light, set against a nocturnal hilly terrain with bushes and trees. Starting with a dark bluey-green, the colours shade through light blue and red to an all-pervading golden brightness. Cosmas Damian was here at the height of his powers. Working again at the abbey church of St Margaretha in Osterhofen (1730–32) and at St Emmeram in Regensburg (1732–3), the brothers combined painting, sculpture and stucco in an ideal way, transcending the boundaries between being and seeming.

Among the secular buildings on which Cosmas Damian Asam worked are the castles in Schleissheim (1720), Mannheim (1728; destr. World War II) and Alteglofsheim (1730) and the Haus der Tiroler Landmannschaft (1734; now the Landhaus), Innsbruck. He also painted several altarpieces indebted to Roman Baroque painting, characterized by greater chiaroscuro than his frescoes. They include the early *SS Teresa of Avila and Peter of Alcántara* (1713; Straubing, Franciscan church) alluding to Bernini's *Ecstasy of St Teresa* (Rome, S Maria della Vittoria; *see* BAROQUE, fig. 1); the high altarpiece (1720–21) at St Johannes Evangelista, Michelfeld; two paintings (*c.* 1720) at St Laurentius, Tittmoning; *Leave-taking of SS Peter and Paul* (*c.* 1732) in the Benedictine abbey church at Rohr; and one of his most convincing altarpieces, the *Martyrdom of St Margaret* (1732) for St Margaretha at Osterhofen.

For Cosmas Damian's work as an architect *see* §II below.

(3) Egid Quirin [Aegidius Quirinus] **Asam** (*b* Tegernsee, *bapt* 1 Sept 1692; *d* Mannheim, 29 April 1750). Sculptor, stuccoist, painter and architect, son of (1) Hans Georg Asam. After working with his father, he was apprenticed to Anton Faistenberger in Munich to learn sculpture. He presumably accompanied his brother (2) Cosmas Damian Asam to Rome (1711–13), where he studied works by Bernini. In 1724 he became a valet and court stuccoist to the Prince-Bishop of Freising and in 1730 a valet to the Elector of Bavaria.

Egid Quirin undoubtedly collaborated on some of his brother's frescoes, while the frescoes (*c.* 1740) in the vault of the pilgrimage church of Maria Dorfen are his own creation, and he was also responsible for the designs and models of the church and the stuccowork in the choir. In the Ursuline church in Straubing he obviously completed Cosmas Damian's frescoes. There are also some surviving altarpieces by him, such as *Christ and Mary Magdalene* (1738) in the Carmelite church at Straubing (*in situ*). However, Egid Quirin Asam is more important as a sculptor and stuccoist, famous in particular for his altars, which are transformed into a Baroque theatrical stage by the pathos of their figures, enlisting the involvement of the onlooker in the events represented. As in Cosmas Damian's painting, the use of lighting and the setting also play a crucial role in Egid Quirin's sculptural work. Their first collaboration, at Michelfeld (1717–18), was followed by the decoration of Mariae Himmelfahrt (1720) at Aldersbach, where rich stuccowork adorns the pillars and vaulting, not merely providing a framework for the frescoes, but forming a connection with the paintings. Egid Quirin's stuccowork is often markedly three-dimensional, with clouds and figures seeming to spring out from the architecture. Only stucco sculpture is capable of conveying the movement of bodies and robes so as to reach out into space in this way.

Egid Quirin executed the architectural design, the construction of the altars, the figural decoration and ornamentation of a new abbey church in Rohr (1717–23). If frescoes by Cosmas Damian were envisaged, they were never implemented. The architecture and the decoration are vibrant with energetic modelling. Egid Quirin lavished special care on the interior stuccowork: richly ornamented composite capitals support the elaborately profiled entablature. The wall arches are covered with a charming alternation of framed panels, awaiting frescoes, and vegetal tendril-work. Putti and angels in the round are harmoniously inserted into the ornamental ensemble. The whole scheme, marked throughout by the rich profiling of cornices and entablatures, culminates in the design of the high altar and the larger-than-life statues there, a freely sculpted *Assumption of the Virgin* (*see* ALTARPIECE, fig. 6). The stage-like presentation at the colourful altar is framed within a structure of marbled columns and a blue-gold curtain, setting the altar area strongly apart from its predominantly white surroundings. In the lower part stands the Virgin's open sarcophagus, its lid propped up against one of the columns behind. The *Apostles*, sculpted in white stucco, express their wonder with powerful gestures in a broad spectrum of emotions. Such extremes of movement could be executed only with the lightness of stucco, using a core of wood, straw and cloth, while free-moving arms and parts of garments are supported by thin armatures of wire. The drapery runs in deep folds, reinforcing the Baroque pathos with strong shadows. In the centre the Virgin, borne by partly gilded angels, floats up towards a coronet. Above, the Trinity can be seen, lit through yellow glass; thus, aided by the lighting, the composition rises from a terrestrial white to a celestial gold.

At St Margaretha in the former Premonstratensian abbey of Osterhofen, built to Johann Michael Fischer's designs from 1729, Egid Quirin completed the stuccowork in 1731 and the interior furnishing in 1735, though the church was not consecrated until 1740. The nave is articulated by chapels and galleries, with a variety of mouldings, framings and balustrades using convex and concave curves. The stuccowork on the pillars and pilasters offers an array of red, green and gold, as well as variegated marbling, while the architectural structure is left brilliant white, set against the colour in the stucco and in Cosmas Damian's frescoes. Despite this variety of ornament and colour, scarcely any of the Asams' interiors has such concise unity of decoration and furnishing. The nave chapel altars are also by Egid Quirin: in that dedicated to St Norbert of Xanten (1734), the stucco figures are painted in a variety of colours, with a liberal use of gold, and glow with a lustre coating that gives them the appearance of precious, fragile porcelain. Egid Quirin also created the high altar area: four solomonic columns reminiscent of Bernini's tabernacle in St Peter's, Rome, provide the framework for several sculpted groups. On the plinths of the columns are gilded reliefs with scenes of the *Life and Martyrdom of St Margaret.* On the actual altar is a tabernacle with a relief of the *Supper at Emmaus* surrounded by angels and crowned by a golden aureole behind the Cross and encircling it.

Egid Quirin created another superb altar in Freising Cathedral (1735–8), again in collaboration with Cosmas Damian. The round shape of the apse of the chapel of St Johann in the south aisle there is taken up by the altar. Above a recessed construction with light-red marbled columns there is a round window with panes of dull yellow glass encircled by a golden aureole. The three stucco statues of saints, John the Baptist on the left, John Nepomuk in the middle and John the Evangelist on the right, in brilliant white, stand out against the gold and red tones. Two white angels sitting on the altar cornice provide a transition to the ceiling painted by Cosmas Damian.

Egid Quirin was a deeply religious man who never married, and from 1729 he dedicated his entire fortune to the construction and furnishing of a private church, St Johann Nepomuk in Munich. He bought four houses in Sendlinger Strasse in Munich: he occupied the southernmost, the middle two were given over to a new church and the northernmost was intended for the priest (*see* §II below). After his brother's death in 1739, he mainly devoted himself to completing this church. He then accepted a commission to do the stuccowork and frescoes for the Jesuit church in Mannheim (destr. World War II). Legend has it that while working there he fell to his death from the scaffolding. Of this work, only a design remains (Washington, DC, N.G.A.). Egid Quirin's art as a sculptor is primarily determined by his skill in organizing groups of statues: what is important is not the single figure but the whole group, acting out its story on the stage of the *theatrum sacrum*, with the light as director, and ultimately becoming a component in the *Gesamtkunstwerk.*

II. Collaborations on the Gesamtkunstwerk.

With their superb new decorative schemes for the buildings of others, the Asam brothers won a glowing reputation for themselves in south German church art. The idea of the *Gesamtkunstwerk*, however, in which they alone carried out the architecture, painting and ornamentation according to their own ideas, was the basis of their primacy and renown in German Baroque art.

1. WELTENBURG MONASTERY. On 29 June 1716 the foundation stone of the new church at the Benedictine monastery of Weltenburg an der Donau was laid, with Cosmas Damian as architect, and the shell of the building was consecrated in autumn 1718. The building opens from a porch into a lengthwise oval leading up to Egid Quirin's high altar. Around this oval eight columns support the dome, with four larger and four smaller recesses between. The extension of the façade and the provision of a pulpit, side altars and confessionals dragged on until 1735, though Cosmas Damian Asam signed the ceiling fresco of the *Church Triumphant* (see fig. 1) in 1721. This painting seems almost to 'float' above the drum of the cupola and a windowed area incorporated into it. Above the darker church interior and the dome with its gold stuccoing, the painted heaven full of saints opens up in radiant golden yellow hues, which, being indirectly lit, seem to imbue the groups of figures with light—a theological concept is given form through artistic means.

The high altar at Weltenburg is like a stage set (*see* LIGHTING, fig. 2): under a high arch the figure of St George on horseback in shimmering armour appears on a pedestal; as he pierces the dragon, the king's daughter shrinks away in vivid terror. They are framed by statues of *St Martin* and *St Maurus* looking on. Behind this triumphal arch can be glimpsed the fresco of the *Immaculate Virgin* on the globe with the serpent coiled round it, looking like a theatre backdrop. The dazzle created by looking against the light and the reflections on the gilded and silver stucco sculptures add to the miraculous impression. The reliefs in the inner surface of the dome are also by Egid Quirin. They form the transition from the architecture to the painting: placed above the side arches, the *Evangelists*, sculpted in the round, form a link with the lower storey, while the finer reliefs above them, with their painted background, lead into the ceiling frescoes by Cosmas Damian. Their theme, of the Church represented by the Benedictines, struggling to save pagan souls, connects with the *Church Triumphant* on the ceiling. The architecture, sculpture, ornamental work and painting in this area form a perfect unity.

2. ST JOHANN NEPOMUK, MUNICH. The façade of this unique private church, constructed between the adjoining houses bought by Egid Quirin in 1729, is based around a triple portal: in the lower stage there is the door surround and above it the frame of the large window; finally, the whole façade can be viewed as a portal with huge side pilasters supporting the curving gable that soars above the adjoining houses. The proportions of the interior (see fig. 2) are unusual; the width is just 9 m, while the length is 28 m. The roof had to surmount those of the adjoining houses so that the ceiling fresco by Cosmas Damian above the cornice could be directly lit by a window area. In their private church the Asam brothers created a superb *Gesamtkunstwerk* based on the combined effects of the architecture, painting, sculpture and ornament. In the high, narrow area all four arts work together, with none taking precedence. Each is carefully coordinated in colour with the others, making it a jewel among late Baroque religious buildings in Bavaria: red, gold and white, everything emanates a festive brilliance in honour of God. The crowning glory above the altar is the freestanding group representing the *Seat of Mercy*: painted in gold and silver, it draws the eyes up from the darker lower stage towards the fresco flooded in light where the Church personified appears within a *quadratura*, with the Virtues and temporal power paying her tribute. The furnishing of the Asam church was not completed until 1746.

1. Cosmas Damian Asam and Egid Quirin Asam: the *Church Triumphant* (1721), ceiling fresco, 19.4×14.5 m, SS Georg und Martin, Weltenburg Abbey; gilded and silver stucco illustrating the role of the Benedictine Order in the saving of souls

2. Cosmas Damian Asam and Egid Quirin Asam: interior of St Johann Nepomuk, Munich, 1729–46

3. URSULINE CHURCH, STRAUBING. The final glorious achievement of the brothers' collaboration before Cosmas Damian's death in 1739 was the decoration of the Ursuline church in Straubing; Egid Quirin was responsible for designing the building and the stuccowork, while Cosmas Damian painted three altarpieces but was unable to complete his frescoes. Green, red, gold and white predominate in Egid Quirin's inventive and imaginative stuccowork; for the high altar he produced statues of *St Ignatius* and *St Carlo Borromeo*, which stood beside twisted columns framing Cosmas Damian's high altarpiece. In the design of the interior, light is again channelled to raise the eyes of the faithful from darkness on the earthly level up to the highest heavenly spheres, where sacred events are enacted in illusionistically rendered buildings. Baroque pathos, the idea of the *Gesamtkunstwerk* and of a *theatrum sacrum* went hand in hand. In this the deep piety of both artists was likewise central—it was no accident that, with a few exceptions, they worked principally for church patrons, most of them in the Benedictine Order.

See also ILLUSIONISM, §3(v).

BIBLIOGRAPHY

Macmillan Enc. Architects; Thieme–Becker
E. Baumeister: 'Zeichnungen von Hans Georg Asam', *Das Münster*, iii (1950), pp. 156–61
——: 'Die Zeichnungen des Egid Quirin Asam', *Das Münster*, iv (1950), pp. 207–18
K. Mindera: 'Die Frühzeit des Hans Georg Asam in Benediktbeuren und sein Erstlingswerk', *Das Münster*, iii (1950), pp. 146–56
E. Baumeister: 'Zeichnungen des Cosmas Damian Asam', *Das Münster*, vi (1953), pp. 245–59
E. Hanfstaengel: *Die Brüder Cosmas Damian and Egid Quirin Asam* (Munich, 1955)
G. Hojer: *Die frühe Figuralplastik E. Q. Asams* (Witterschlick bei Bonn, 1967)
H. R. Hitchcock: *Rococo Architecture in Southern Germany* (London, 1968)
E. von Knorre: *Die Weltenburger Klosterkirche im Werk der Brüder Asam* (Weltenburg, 1972)
A. J. Weichslgartner and N. Molodovsky: *Die Familie Asam* (Munich, 1977)
A. Schirer: *Die Reliefstruktur Egid Quirin Asams* (MA thesis, U. Erlangen, 1979)
G. Dischinger: 'Zu Leben und Werk der Künstlerfamilie Asam', *Ars Bavar.*, xix/xx (1980), pp. 23–46
J. Hotz: 'Die Künstlerfamilie Asam—Versuch einer Werkliste', *Ars Bavar.*, xix/xx (1980), pp. 214–18
B. Rupprecht: *Die Brüder Asam* (Regensburg, 1980)
B. Bushart: 'Unbekannte Werke aus Cosmas Damian Asams früherer Meisterzeit', *Jb. Staatl. Kstsamml. Baden-Württemberg*, xix (1982), pp. 27–44
R. E. Penzlin: *Stil- und Motivquellen im Werk des Cosmas Damian Asam* (diss., U. Bonn, 1983)
E. Wagner-Langenstein: 'Georg Asam 1649–1711: Ein Beitrag zur Entwicklung der barocken Deckenmalerei in Bayern', *Misc. Bavar. Monacensia*, cxx (1983)
B. Bushart and B. Rupprecht, eds: *Cosmas Damian Asam, 1686–1739: Leben und Werk* (Munich, 1986)
H. J. Sauermost: *Die Asam als Architekten* (Munich and Zurich, 1986)
H. Trottmann: *Cosmas Damian Asam, 1686–1739: Tradition und Invention im malerischen Werk* (Nuremberg, 1986)
J. H. Biller: 'Zu Familiengeschichte der Brüder Asam', *Ars Bavar.*, xlix/l (1988), pp. 85–92

C. HÖPER

Asante [Ashanti] **and related peoples.** Largest of the Akan-speaking subgroups, concentrated in the forest areas of south-central Ghana around their capital, Kumasi. They number *c.* 2 million (1985).

1. Introduction. 2. History. 3. Regalia. 4. Religious arts. 5. Secular arts.

1. INTRODUCTION. The rich and highly varied subject-matter of Asante art represents in different contexts virtually the entire realm of the zoological and botanical environment; domestic, religious and political scenes from Asante society; and a wealth of objects drawn from Asante material culture, both indigenous and imported. Meaning in Asante art, however, extends well beyond mere representational imagery, for most images are typically paired with verbal expressions that can be metaphorically applied to various situations in Asante life. These verbal forms include folk-tales, proverbs, praise names, jokes, riddles, boasts and insults. Although proverbs and folk-tales are the inspiration of certain visual arts elsewhere in Africa, the verbal–visual nexus of Asante and other Akan arts is unique in its variety and pervasive influence.

Many of the visual images and their verbal counterparts are highly conventionalized and are displayed on a wide range of art objects, often regardless of their functional context. For example, one of the most frequent depictions is the porcupine, which commonly represents the saying 'If you kill a thousand, a thousand will come'. In popular thought the porcupine is a metaphor for the Asante army and is viewed as having the ability to shoot its spines and generate them anew to continue the battle. Other subjects in the enormous corpus of Asante motifs are similarly given meaning through their association with traditional sayings.

The verbal arts associated with Asante visual arts range from religion, politics and war to farming, marriage and childrearing. Most deal either directly or indirectly with intelligent and proper behaviour and help codify traditional customs and values. The strong ethical and moral content of many Asante arts give them an immediacy and relevance rarely found among African peoples.

2. HISTORY. Like most AKAN, the Asante were traditionally organized into a series of states, each headed by a paramount chief. At the end of the 17th century the Asante states were consolidated under the power of a king (Asantehene). The kingdom expanded through military conquest throughout the 18th century, eventually controlling most of their Akan neighbours. The Asante economy was traditionally based on agriculture, especially the cultivation of yams, plantains and maize, and they exported gold to both the Islamic peoples in the north and the Europeans on the coast in return for metalware and cloth from both areas and for European firearms.

In the early 19th century separate visits by two British envoys, Thomas Bowdich and Joseph Dupuis in 1817 and 1819, respectively, resulted in detailed publications on much of the art and culture of the Asante. These expeditions were intended to establish direct trade relations with the Asante, who controlled access to the interior of the Gold Coast and maintained an intermittent presence on the coast, frequently fighting with their Fante rivals, who were allies of the British, for access to European commerce at the trading forts scattered along the Atlantic. This eventually led to the British Asante war of 1874, in which Asantehene Kofi Kakari (*reg* 1867–74) was defeated and Kumasi sacked. Much of the finest Asante regalia housed outside Ghana (especially in the British Museum, London) was exported at this time along with a wealth of other objects. In 1896 Asantehene Prempeh I (*reg* 1888–96) and many senior chiefs and officials were exiled by the British, thus effectively bringing the confederacy to an end. After its defeat in a second war with the British (1900), the Asante were declared a Crown Colony in 1901. The Asante people revived with the return from exile of the Asantehene in 1924 and the restoration of the confederacy in 1933 under Prempeh II. In the early 1990s the Asante had 14 officially recognized paramount chiefs united under the Asantehene, who also serves as one of the paramount chiefs.

3. REGALIA. Asante arts are dominated by a wide array of royal regalia, much of it made of or featuring gold, designed to enhance and validate the position of ranking chiefs in society and to identify their senior officials. Unlike many African cultures, the Asante have no traditional masquerades, partly owing to the dominance of the institution of chieftaincy, which discouraged the introduction of masking cults that might rival their power. Secular leadership arts also tended to overshadow those more firmly rooted in religion, although the latter occupy a significant niche in Asante life. While the Asantehene cannot be characterized as a 'divine king', some of his regalia is invested with both political and spiritual significance. The regalia discussed below is generally seen as the property of the state rather than belonging to an individual chief, each of whom was expected to add to the collection of political heirlooms amassed by his predecessors.

(i) Golden Stool. Oral traditions help elucidate the most important political and religious art object in Asante culture, the Golden Stool (see fig. 1). According to these traditions the great priest Okonfo Anokye brought the stool down from the heavens to land gently on the knees of Osei Tutu (*reg* 1697–1731), the chief of Kumasi who founded the Asante empire and became its first king. Anokye claimed that the stool embodied the spirit of the entire Asante nation and the power of the state depended on its security. Although legend decrees that the stool is solid gold, in the early 1990s the stool consisted of a carved wooden core covered with gold plate. Unlike most rectangular Asante stools, the Golden Stool is basically circular with semicircular upward extensions on either side of the seat. The base and seat are connected by diagonal struts.

Numerous symbolic attachments amplify the stool's significance. Three European-style bells are used to announce its coming and to summon the Asante people to important state occasions. Several anthropomorphic bell-like images represent defeated enemies of the Asante. The fetters are said to bind the 'soul' of the Asante to the stool. Several protective Islamic amulets complete the assemblage. Owing to its considerable spiritual power the Golden Stool was never sat upon: on state occasions it is displayed next to the Asantehene, lying on its side on its own ceremonial chair, which is placed on an elephant skin. The whole ensemble is sheltered under its own umbrella.

While the Golden Stool is the premier emblem of the Asante empire, each Asantehene or chief commissions his own royal stool upon his installation or enstoolment. As his enstoolment approaches, the new ruler selects a design appropriate to carry a visual message about his forthcoming rule. A stool attributed to the reign of Asantehene Kofi Kakari features a circular support system identified as 'circular rainbow' (Kansas City, MO, Nelson–Atkins Mus. A.). This is a visual metaphor for the Asantehene

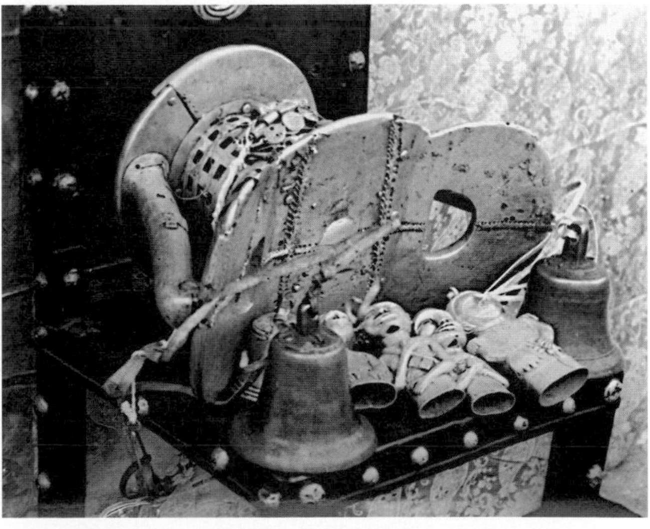

1. Asante stool, gold, wood, glass, brass and leather (Kumasi, State Treasury of the Asantehene)

and refers to the saying 'The rainbow surrounds everyone' (i.e. the king controls and unites his people).

Among the Asante, stools embody the traditions of figurative ancestral sculpture that exist in many African cultures. After the death of a celebrated individual, whether the Asantehene, another paramount chief or the head of a family, his stool is 'blackened' through a complicated process of ritual sacrifices. The stool is then placed in a 'stool room' where it is venerated in memory of the deceased with periodic offerings and sacrifices. Both royals and commoners may also possess artistically embellished domestic stools with supports that range from geometric or highly abstract designs to fully rendered images of certain animals, such as the elephant or porcupine, as well as human figures.

(ii) Chairs. Asante royalty also developed three chair types that are items of prestige used on ceremonial occasions and based on European 17th-century farthingale chairs. Although Muslim amulets are occasionally suspended underneath, the chairs are not venerated as are the stools. The chair in most widespread use, the *asipim* ('I stand firm'), is low and armless with an inclined back. Brass furniture tacks are used to hold the leather seat and back in place and to decorate the stretchers, legs and back. Usually the back has a stamped, incised and repoussé panel in sheet brass with geometric and figurative motifs, most commonly the crocodile, and is topped by cast brass finials.

The *hwedom* ('facing the enemy'), a chair traditionally used in military and judicial contexts, is also armless and leather-covered. It differs from the *asipim* in having a straight back and knob- or spiral-turned stretchers and legs, and lacks the embellished sheet brass decoration. The tacks and bosses on this chair are usually silver-coloured. The *akonkromfi* ('praying mantis') chair invariably has arms, an openwork back and legs that cross diagonally on each side; although rigid, the leg configuration is based on European articulated folding chairs. It is usually ornamented with a profusion of brass tacks and is used for festivals.

(iii) State swords. The second most important category of Asante regalia is that of the gold-ornamented state swords (*afenatene*; see fig. 2). Their numbers and function vary from chief to chief, but the attachment of cast gold ornaments to the scabbard is the exclusive prerogative of the 14 paramount chiefs and certain divisional chiefs of the Asantehene. Outmoded as weaponry after the introduction of firearms, most extant swords lack both cutting edges and a point with any capacity to pierce. The wooden handle typically has a cylindrical grip with globular pommel and hilt, and is covered with gold leaf. The sheath may be made of ray skin, antelope or, more rarely, leopard skin.

The various swords have different ritual functions. One sword is usually designated for use in the installation of a new paramount chief when he swears allegiance to his people and to the state. A second sword might be used by

2. Asante state swords (*afenatene*) of an unidentified paramount chief

lesser chiefs to acknowledge fidelity to the newly enstooled leader. Further swords might be used in oath-taking, in rituals to purify the chief's soul, or to identify couriers or other officials acting on behalf of a chief. On public occasions these swords are displayed by their bearers in two rows fanning out from the chief as he sits in state. When the chief is carried in procession in a palanquin the sword-bearers rest the sword hilts on either side of the litter, and after his death the swords are propped against his funeral bed. On these occasions the massing of swords with their gold ornaments is intended to affirm the wealth and power of the institution of chieftaincy and of the state itself. Cast gold ornaments (*abosodee*) are the artistic focus of the most important state swords and are the largest items produced by Asante goldsmiths.

One of the two principal swords of the Asantehene, known as Mponponso ('Responsibility'), is traditionally identified with Opaku Ware II (*reg* 1731–42), who is said to have pledged his life to his people with it. A 19th-century version of this sword was confiscated by the British in 1874 (London, BM); its replacement, which has a leopard skin hilt and scabbard, is used by senior chiefs in swearing allegiance to the Asantehene. The casting of a viper with a hornbill in its mouth on both swords refers to a lengthy folk-tale concerning the viper's persistent pursuit and eventual capture of the hornbill, with the message that 'patience triumphs'. A smaller sword attached to the hilt of this ritual weapon illustrates the proverb, 'Some swords are more powerful than others', in reference to the king's authority over the other paramount chiefs.

The second principal sword of state (*bosumuru*) is said to have been made for Osei Tutu, the founder of the Asante empire. Its ornament depicts the skull of a mangabey, referring to an oral tradition that describes one of the miracles of the priest Okomfo Anokye, in which he retrieved the magical skull from the heavens. A smaller version is also attached to the gold-covered hilt and scabbard. The *bosumuru* is used by the Asantehene at a special swearing-in rite upon his enstoolment and, together with another sword, in rites for the purification of the souls and spirits of deceased kings. At least 32 different motifs have been identified on cast gold sword ornaments belonging to Asante paramount chiefs, of which at least 18 are associated with the Asantehene. One of the most common motifs is that of a trophy head; the finest example, taken from Kumasi in 1874 (London, Wallace; see fig. 3), is said to represent Worasa, a chief of the state of Banda, north-west of Kumasi, who was defeated by Asantehene Osei Kwadwo *c.* 1765. Other ornaments depict vanquished enemies of the Asante.

(iv) Linguist staffs. The principal counsellors of a chief, referred to as 'linguists', are identified at public displays by their carved wood and gold-leaf staffs. In 1980 the Asantehene had 16 linguists, many paramount chiefs commonly had 12, while town and village chiefs had fewer. Linguist staffs were developed in the 19th century from the spokesmen's staffs used for several centuries to designate the official representatives of the European powers based in the trading forts along the coast. Asante staffs generally have a two-piece shaft and a figured finial portraying a proverb or saying. The most common finial

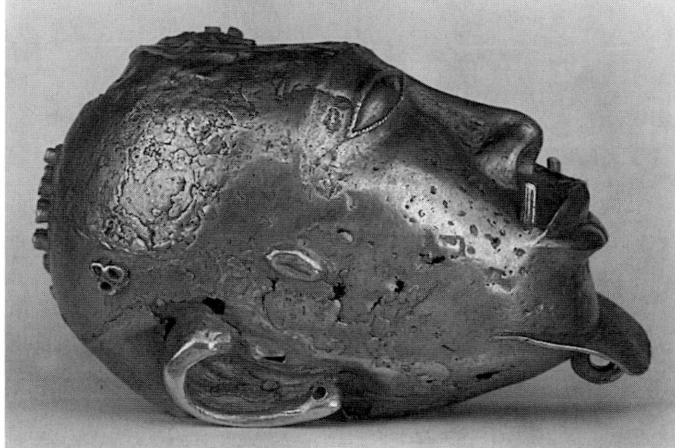

3. Asante sword ornament (trophy head of Worasa), gold, 202×132mm, before 1874 (London, Wallace Collection)

motif, found on one of the Asantehene's staffs, depicts two men seated at a table with a bowl of food, one man typically grasping his stomach while the other reaches into the bowl (*see* AFRICA, fig. 42). The image represents the maxim 'The food is for the man that owns it, not for the man who is hungry', meaning that chieftaincy belongs to the rightful heir and is not just for anyone who hungers for power.

The principal theme of many staff finials is the power of the chief, and the elephant is frequently used as a metaphor for royal power. Its invincibility is emphasized on a staff in the Asantehene's treasury that features one standing on a trap, illustrating the saying 'When the elephant steps on a trap, there is no more trap'. Another common motif represents a man standing, usually in regal dress, holding an egg in his right hand. It deals with the delicate role the chief plays in exerting power over his subjects and recalls the saying 'If the egg is held too tightly it will break, if it is held too loosely it will also break'.

(v) State umbrellas. Asante festival occasions are dominated visually by a profusion of brightly coloured umbrellas, generally made of such imported fabrics as velvets, silk, brocades, chintzes, damasks and, more rarely, locally woven kente cloth, often used in combination. Both domed and flat canopies have been documented among the Asante, although the former are much more common and may range up to *c.* 3.6 m in diameter. The exterior surface is typically divided into three contrasting fields; a small square surrounds the finial and a valance hangs from the edge of the dome. The predominant colour is red, with yellow the next most commonly used.

Paramount chiefs have varying numbers of umbrellas; there are at least 23 in the Asantehene's treasury, most of which are identified with one of his predecessors. Although umbrellas are generally named after the motif on their finials, three of the most important examples displayed with the Asantehene are named independently of the finial: Boaman ('destroyer of nations') is associated with Osei Bonsu (*reg* 1800–24); Oyokoman, named after the clan of the ruling lineage and traced to Osei Tutu, is a rare example of an umbrella made from indigenous hand-woven kente cloth; Nyankowton ('God's Rainbow') is also associated with Osei Tutu and is characterized by a surface of multicoloured velvets.

The finials of these three umbrellas are stylized representations of bamboo (*babadua*), the most common finial motif in Akan regalia. Bamboo was widely admired for its strength and resilience as a building material, hence it serves as an effective metaphor for both chief and state. The *prekese*, a fragrant fruit, the appealing scent of which is likened to the king's impact on his subjects, is also commonly depicted on finials. Another of the Asantehene's umbrellas, Akokobaatan, is named after the depiction of a hen with her chicks on its finial. Here the Asantehene is likened to the hen as a nurturing force in the state, at times appearing harsh but providing guidance. This motif is also found on one of the Asantehene's state swords and is often represented on the linguist staff finials of other chiefs.

(vi) Palanquins. On certain festival occasions most of the regalia is displayed in procession and important chiefs are carried on palanquins through the streets. The most common form of litter is a basketwork structure suspended between two poles and ornamented with a rich display of foreign and indigenous cloths that emphasize the chief's importance. A second type is basically a wooden chair, suspended from front and back, and profusely decorated with brass furniture tacks. The latter version is frequently identified with queen mothers, but it is also used by a few chiefs.

(vii) Personal adornments. The personal adornment of important Asante chiefs includes a variety of crowns, sandals, armlets, anklets, necklaces and finger rings made in part or entirely of gold leaf or cast gold. Smaller versions of many of the images represented on swords and as finials on linguist staffs are also found on all or most of these. Some armlets also incorporate Muslim charms in gold or leather-covered casings. The British Museum, London, the Musée Barbier-Mueller, Geneva, and the Alfred C. Glassel, Jr Museum of Fine Arts, Houston, have the largest collections of this material outside Ghana.

4. Religious arts.

(i) Akua'ba. Apart from the traditions of ancestral veneration through the medium of blackened stools (*see* §3(i) above), the best-known spiritually effective sculptural form of the Asante is the wooden *akua'ba* ('Akua's child'; see fig. 4), named after the first woman who conceived with the aid of such a figure. Typically a woman consulting a priest about infertility would be told to commission an *akua'ba* and care for the sculpture as if it were an actual infant, giving it beads and carrying it on her back beneath a wrapper, just as a young child would be carried. After a successful birth, the carving would usually be placed in the priest's shrine as an offering and a sign of the priest's powers, although sometimes the *akua'ba* would be given to the new-born child as a toy.

Asante *akua'ba* are invariably female and feature a flat disc-shaped head with facial features confined to the lower half. The resulting high forehead may represent an Asante ideal of feminine beauty. The head usually surmounts a legless cylindrical torso with short arms projecting at right angles close to the neck, although rare examples have a more fully realized naturalistic torso with legs. The equivalent of *akua'ba* are also found among other Akan groups, differentiated primarily by the shape of the head. *Akua'ba* are the most common form of tourist art in southern Ghana.

4. Asante *akua'ba*, wood, glass and pigment, h. 420 mm, *c.* 1920 (private collection)

(ii) Shrine sculpture. The Asante believe in a supreme god and creator, Nyame, who is venerated through prayers and sacrifices; however a series of lesser deities, often named after major rivers, is the focal point of active worship. They are acknowledged in shrines with sacrificial offerings and accumulations placed in brass, ceramic or gourd vessels. Sometimes these shrines are enhanced by the presence of figurative sculptures, of which the most common are female figures, mothers suckling children, executioner figures and images of priests or priestesses. Regardless of the image, most are identified as 'spirit helpers', whose existence also visually amplifies the powers of the enshrined deity. In the first four decades of the 20th century the introduction of shrines from northern Ghana that represent witch-catching deities further stimulated the production of shrine sculpture in many of the same forms.

(iii) Kuduo. Cast brass ritual vessels, known as *kuduo*, are created in many shapes for various functions, although there appears to be little or no relationship between their form and function (see fig. 5). Two of the most important contexts are connected to rituals involving a man's *ntoro*, a concept related to hereditary groupings associated with a man's father (in the otherwise matrilineal Asante society) and to rituals associated with a man's soul (*kra*). *Kuduo* were also used as containers for valuables included in men's burials and as receptacles for offerings at burial sites, shrines and in ancestral stool rooms. Although *kuduo* functioned primarily in male arenas, there is also documentation that they played a role in girls' puberty ceremonies (Rattray, 1923).

5. Asante *kuduo*, cast brass, h. 223 mm, 19th century (private collection)

The shape and decoration of the earliest *kuduo* are undoubtedly based on Arabic-inscribed Islamic prototypes from 14th-century Mamluk Egypt, traded across the Sahara into northern Akan areas and eventually into Asante. It is likely that casting techniques by the lost-wax method were also introduced about this time. Five basic shapes that can be traced to Mamluk prototypes have been identified: bowls or basins, cup-bowls, buckets, waisted forms and caskets (Silverman, 1983). Most share a common vocabulary of surface decoration that includes simulated Arabic script, rosettes, chequer-work patterns, pinwheel forms and groups of triangles or semicircular forms. A sixth basic shape, which constitutes the largest single grouping and has been referred to as a cylinder *kuduo* (Silverman), has no direct Islamic precedents. While the Islamic-inspired forms may date from the beginning of the 15th century, the cylinder *kuduo* probably developed about a century later and numerically dominated the earlier types between the 17th century and the late 19th when *kuduo* production virtually ceased.

The surfaces of the earliest Akan *kuduo* bear linear representational motifs, comprising mainly crocodile and bird forms. Figural relief decoration followed somewhat later and free-standing castings of animals and human depictions on the lids were probably produced in the 18th and 19th centuries. Crocodiles and birds remained popular motifs, but single leopards, leopards attacking antelopes, occasional elephants and equestrian figures, and multi-figured court scenes are also found. It is likely that many *kuduo* motifs represented proverbs and other verbal forms, but the meaning of *kuduo* imagery has not yet been documented by researchers.

(iv) Ceramics. Asante potters created a wide variety of food and water containers of considerable aesthetic merit as well as modelled ceramic oil lamps embellished with human and other representational images. Most of the artistic attention, however, was devoted to the family or clan pots (*abusua kuruwa*), which serve as ritual vessels at burial sites, in ancestral stool rooms and in shrines. Many are based on the forms of domestic wares, but are distinguished by representational relief decoration covering much of the surface. The frequent motif of a ladder, illustrating the proverb 'It is not only one man who climbs the ladder of death', emphasizes the inevitability of death. Some royal clan pots are further elaborated with full-figured representations of such court officials as drummers and sword-bearers.

Of the terracotta heads, busts and free-standing figures that were created for the burial sites of Akan notables (*see* AKAN) and erroneously labelled Asante, only those from the Adanse Fomena area have any claim to this description. Even so, although Fomena was, in the 1990s, identified among the 14 Asante paramouncies, its elders and chief have staunchly maintained their independence from the confederacy.

5. SECULAR ARTS.

(i) Gold weights. Cast brass gold weights, used as counterbalances in the weighing of gold-dust, are probably the most numerous and diverse of all African arts. The first Akan examples were probably made in the early 15th century and based on Islamic weight standards. Nearly all the 15th- and 16th-century weights are geometric in shape, including cones, polyhedrons, cog-wheels, stepped pyramids and embellished rectangles. About 1,600 figurative weights were introduced and the range of subjects steadily expanded to include the entire zoological environment and material culture of the Akan, including ritual, political and domestic scenes with one or more human figures, most usually *c.* 25–50 mm in height. Geometric weights continued to be produced in increasingly elaborate forms alongside figurative weights until the demise of the tradition *c.* 1900.

Attempts to identify the meaning of the geometric weights have been unconvincing, but the figurative weights, often known as proverb weights, draw their metaphorical subject-matter from the same body of oral literature that informs most Asante and other Akan arts. Except for very complex scenes, most figurative weights refer to, or at least suggest, a variety of proverbs, thus multiplying the symbolic content of the image. For example an isolated leopard may depict among other sayings: 'The leopard should never be considered old and feeble', 'Rain wets the spots on a leopard's skin but does not wash them off' and 'No one teaches a leopard's cub how to spring'. Thematically, these sayings address respect for political power and the elders, triumph over adversity, and education and heredity.

(ii) Forowa. Sheet brass containers for a vegetable fat called *shea* butter, which has various culinary, cosmetic and ritual uses among the Asante and other Akan groups, are known as *forowa.* Occasionally they were also used as containers for medicines or for such valuables as jewellery or gold-dust. Some fine examples have a hinged lid with a clasp and a hidden, subsidiary container in the base. They are made from imported mill-rolled sheet brass and developed from the shape of cylinder *kuduo* in the last two decades of the 18th century, when sheet brass became readily available on the coast. There is some evidence that the tradition began among the southern Akan, especially the Fante, although Asante workshops undoubtedly produced them.

Forowa are decorated with a combination of incised, stamped and repoussé techniques. Geometric designs predominate on the more modest cans, while larger, more elaborate examples usually feature representational motifs. The most common image is the *sankofa* bird with its head turned to its back, which illustrates the saying 'Pick it up if it falls behind', emphasizing that mistakes can be corrected and instructive. A European padlock with one or two keys and an Akan double-bladed sword are the next most frequently depicted images. Both probably serve symbolic protective functions, since proverbial sayings have not been documented for either, despite their regular appearances.

(iii) Combs. Asante and other Akan wooden combs are perhaps the most elaborately decorated African examples, often featuring ornate openwork handles with considerable incised surface decoration or fully sculptured heads, busts or even full human figures. These human images often echo the form of the *akua'ba* (*see* §4(i) above) and reflect the role of the comb in enhancing feminine beauty. Such elaborate combs were used exclusively by women, but they were often commissioned by men as gifts to commemorate puberty celebrations, weddings, births and a variety of traditional and Christian festivals. Although many traditional proverbial images are represented on the combs, Christian motifs are especially prevalent, suggesting that many combs were produced in areas with strong missionary influence. Hearts are also common, evoking the specific relationship involved in the comb as a gift.

(iv) Pipes. Nearly all Asante pipes are ceramic and were not restricted to royal use, although there are a few examples of cast gold pipes from the treasuries of chiefs. Tobacco pipes first appear in excavated Akan sites dated *c.* 1620 and, shortly after, smoking quickly spread throughout the Gold Coast. By the end of the 19th century pipe-bowls in the shape of birds, leopards, stools, game-boards and human figures in a variety of poses were common, and most were based on traditional proverbs. Pipes were also commonly placed as grave goods and traded with Europeans.

(v) Drums and ensembles. Although the five or six drum types used in royal drum orchestras do not bear any significant decoration, the traditional popular bands are often arranged around an elaborately ornamented master drum (h. *c.* 0.6–1.2 m). These voluntary musical organizations perform at such occasions as the naming of babies, puberty celebrations, weddings, the installation of chiefs and funerals. The master drums are distinguished by two or more female breasts projecting from the body of the drum. More complex examples may have carved human legs or a fully sculptured female figure supporting the body of the drum. The female imagery reflects the Asante identification of the drum as 'the mother of the group'. Other breasted examples are supported on the backs of such animals as lions (see fig. 6) and elephants. The surfaces of these drums are generally covered with a profusion of relief decoration drawn from Asante folklore; the subject-matter of those images runs the gamut of Asante thought, but themes relating to games and festivity are especially prominent.

The performances of Asante popular bands are often presented in conjunction with displays of polychrome figurative sculpture representing a chief and his court, including linguists, sword-bearers, executioners, local police and handcuffed prisoners. These secular 'stage props', designed to enhance the musical presentation, are often misidentified as 'shrine figures'.

BIBLIOGRAPHY

T. E. Bowdich: *Mission from Cape Coast Castle to Ashantee* (London, 1819)

J. Dupuis: *Journal of a Residence in Ashantee* (London, 1824)

R. S. Rattray: *Ashanti* (London, 1923)

——: *Religion and Art in Ashanti* (London, 1927)

K. Antubam: *Ghana's Heritage of Culture* (Leipzig, 1963)

A. A. Y. Kyerematen: *Panoply of Ghana* (New York, 1964)

6. Asante drum carved by Osei Bonsu, wood and pigment, h. 1232 mm, 1930s (private collection)

P. K. Sarpong: 'The Sacred Stools of the Ashanti', *Anthropos*, xxvi/1–2 (1967), pp. 1–60

B. Menzel: *Goldgewichte aus Ghana* (Berlin, 1968)

A. A. Y. Kyerematen: 'Royal Stools of Ashanti', *Africa*, xxxix/1 (1969), pp. 1–10

M. Swithenbank: *Ashanti Fetish Houses* (Accra, 1969)

P. K. Sarpong: *The Sacred Stools of the Akan* (Tema, 1971)

B. Menzel: *Textilien aus Westafrika*, 3 vols (Berlin, 1972–3)

W. Fagg: 'Ashanti Gold', *Connoisseur*, clxxxv/743 (1974), pp. 41–8

D. H. Ross: 'Ghanaian Forowa', *Afr. A.*, viii/1 (1974), pp. 40–49

H. M. Cole: 'The Art of Festival in Ghana', *Afr. A.*, viii/3 (1975), pp. 12–24, 60–62, 90

V. Lamb: *West African Weaving* (London, 1975)

M. Ehrlich: *A Catalogue of Ashanti Art Taken from Kumasi in the Anglo-Ashanti War of 1874*, 2 vols (diss., Bloomington, IN U., 1976)

D. H. Ross: 'The Iconography of Asante Sword Ornaments', *Afr. A.*, ix/1 (1977), pp. 16–25, 90–91

The Arts of Ghana (exh. cat. by H. M. Cole and D. H. Ross, Los Angeles, UCLA, Wight A.G.; Minneapolis, Walker A.G.; Dallas, Mus. F.A.; 1977–8)

M. D. McLeod: 'Three Important Royal Kuduo', *Akan-Asante Studies* (London, 1979)

T. F. Garrard: *Akan Weights and the Gold Trade* (New York, 1980)

S. F. Patton: *The Asante Stool* (diss., Evanston, IL, Northwestern U., 1980)

T. F. Garrard: 'Figure Cults of the Southern Akan', *IA Stud. Afr. A.*, i (1981), pp. 167–90

M. D. McLeod: *The Asante* (London, 1981)

D. H. Ross: 'The Verbal Art of Akan Linguist Staffs', *Afr. A.*, xvi/1 (1982), pp. 56–67

R. A. Silverman: 'Akan kuduo: Form and Function', *Akan Transformations: Problems in Ghanaian Art History*, ed. D. H. Ross and T. F. Garrard, Museum of Cultural History Monograph Series, xxi (Los Angeles, 1983), pp. 10–29

T. F. Garrard: 'Akan Silver', *Afr. A.*, xvii/2 (1984), pp. 48–53, 89

D. H. Ross: 'The Art of Osei Bonsu', *Afr. A.*, xvii/2 (1984), pp. 35, 90

——: 'Queen Victoria for Twenty-five Pounds: The Iconography of a Breasted Drum from Southern Ghana', *A. J.* [New York], xlvii/2 (1988), pp. 114–20

Gold of Africa: Jewellery and Ornaments from Ghana, Côte d'Ivoire, Mali and Senegal in the Collection of the Barbier-Mueller Museum (exh. cat. by T. F. Garrard, Washington, DC, Smithsonian Inst., 1989)

DORAN H. ROSS

Asbaşin Kalesi. *See* ÇAVUŞTEPE.

Asbrugg, Franciscus. *See* ASPRUCK, FRANZ.

Aschaffenburg. German town in Bavaria on the River Main, with a population of *c*. 65,000 (1986). It is first documented (AD 974) in relation to the collegiate church of SS Peter and Alexander, founded *c*. 950 by the ruling Ottonian dynasty. The church belonged to the archbishopric of Mainz from *c*. 980 until 1803. Aschaffenburg consequently became the second residence of the prince-bishops of Mainz (*see* §1 below) and played a significant role politically, economically and culturally. The church was rebuilt between the 12th and 15th centuries, and was stylistically influenced by Reformation architecture. It has a beautiful three-winged cloister (1220–40) and chapter house (now Stiftsmuseum). Its rich furnishing includes a life-size Romanesque crucifix (*c*. 1100); two pieces by MATTHIAS GRÜNEWALD (the frame, 1519, for the Virgin of the Snows Altarpiece (paintings dispersed), and the *Lamentation*, *c*. 1525); and works by Peter Vischer the younger, Hans Vischer (*see* VISCHER (4) and (5)) and Hans Juncker (*see* JUNCKER, (2)).

The former Jesuit church (1619–21) is an early example of the Roman Baroque style in Germany. The aristocratic, collegiate and bourgeois houses of the 15th to the 18th century were largely destroyed in World War II, but the Schönborner Hof (1661–81) was rebuilt. The palace (1778–82) and park (from 1785) of Schönbusch are by Emanuel von Harigoyen (1746–1817) and Friedrich Ludwig von Sckell respectively. Archbishop Karl Theodor von Dalberg (*reg* 1806–13) founded a university (1808) and a theatre (1810). Aschaffenburg became part of Bavaria in 1814. Under Ludwig I, the Pompejanum (1841–4) was built by Friedrich von Gärtner. After the destruction of the town during World War II a number of buildings were rebuilt.

1. SCHLOSS JOHANNISBURG. The former official residence of the prince-bishops of Mainz, it is one of the most splendid examples of German castle construction during the Renaissance and Baroque eras. The original medieval citadel (*c*. 1100–*c*. 1400) was almost completely destroyed in 1552 during the second Margrave war; only the 14th-century donjon survived. The new castle was

built on the same site, and derived its name from the citadel chapel of St John the Baptist. In 1605 Johann Schweikart von Kronberg, Archbishop and Elector of Mainz (*reg* 1604–26), summoned GEORG RIDINGER to Aschaffenburg to plan and supervise the castle reconstruction. Work began in February 1614 and was completed nine years later at the enormous cost of one million guilders. Ridinger's scheme consists of four long ranges, each 51 m in length and three storeys high to the eaves, disposed around a square inner courtyard. In planning Schloss Johannisburg, Ridinger used as his basis the main dimensions of the medieval donjon, which he incorporated in the north range of his new building as a symbol of tradition and the continuity of power and dominion exercised by the prince-bishops.

The four corner towers on the exterior of Schloss Johannisburg have eight storeys and are 52 m high; the smaller stair-towers on the interior of the corners have four storeys and rise above a square ground floor into an octagon. The ground floor of the east wing and the north-west corner formerly had a vaulted arcade on the courtyard side (destr. 18th century), which formed a terrace accessible from the first floor. With the exception of the stuccoed walls of the donjon, the elevations are faced in uniform courses of red sandstone ashlar. The quoins of the *corps de logis* are emphasized by diamond faceting. The three storeys, treated almost identically, are articulated horizontally by powerful string courses that also run round the towers, and vertically by axially located windows that have distinctive jambs and are capped by pediments that vary according to floor. Apart from the northern range with its towering donjon, the other three façades are surmounted by richly ornamented *Zwerchgiebel*: scrollwork, strapwork, mask consoles, decorative obelisks, niches, pilasters etc. display decorative forms of the German Renaissance as well as Italian influences.

In 1616 Ridinger published his illustrated *Architektur des . . . neuen Schlossbaues St Johannesburg*, which contains details of the layout and usage of the rooms. The chapel, which consists of a nave only, with a Gothicizing fan vault, is furnished with galleries on its narrow side; the west gallery was originally reserved for the emperor or the elector, the east gallery for the singers and musicians. The magnificent altar and pulpit were made (1609–18) by Hans Juncker (*see* JUNCKER, (2)): together with the figurative decoration of the portal in the castle courtyard (*c.* 1618), these are Juncker's masterpieces and at the same time key works of early Baroque sculpture in Germany. Schloss Johannisburg was severely damaged in World War II, but between 1954 and 1964 the exterior and chapel were restored following the 17th-century model. The interior was, however, adapted to suit the requirements of the state and municipal museums, as well as the court library and other institutions. A series of landscape paintings of Schloss Johannisburg, the Aschaffenburg cycle by Ferdinand Kobell (*see* KOBELL (i), (1)), was commissioned by the Elector Charles Joseph, Freiherr von Erthal, in 1786 (Munich, Neue Pin., and Aschaffenburg, Schloss Johannisburg Staatsgal.).

BIBLIOGRAPHY

F. Mader: *Die Kunstdenkmäler des Königreichs Bayern, Unterfranken*, xix (Munich, 1918)

G. Dehio: *Handbuch der deutschen Kunstdenkmäler, Bayern I: Franken* (Munich, 1979)

B. von Roda: *Schloss Aschaffenburg und Pompejanum* (Munich, 1982)

E. Schneider: *Aschaffenburg: Stift, Schloss und alte Gärten* (Amorbach, 1982)

I. Jenderko-Sichelschmidt and H. Murawski: *Die Museen der Stadt Aschaffenburg* (Brunswick, 1985)

H. Beseler and N. Gutschow: *Kriegsschicksale deutscher Architektur, Verluste-Schäden-Wiederaufbau: Eine Dokumentation für das Gebiet der Bundesrepublik Deutschland*, ii (Neumünster, 1988), pp. 1317–25

INGRID JENDERKO-SICHELSCHMIDT

Ascher (Oved), Daisy (*b* Mexico City, 25 April 1944). Mexican photographer. She studied art at the Universidad Motolinía and at the Universidad Anáhuac, both in Mexico City, and undertook specialist studies at the Club Fotográfico de México. Ascher's work showed the influence of such photographers as Yousuf Karsh, Sam Haskins (*b* 1926) and Richard Avedon, but it was also more generally stimulated by the work of Eugène Atget, Alfred Stieglitz, Paul Strand, Manuel Alvarez Bravo and Henri Cartier-Bresson. She made frequent trips to New York where she acquired experience from photographers and artists that not only enriched her own visual concepts but also the technical aspects of her work. Ascher consolidated her position in Mexican photography through her work, particularly in the acute sensitivity of her many portraits of personalities from the artistic and cultural world. Her series of José Luis Cuevas and Juan Rulfo are among her most outstanding works. After several years of work she collected the material that was published as *Revelando a Cuevas.*

BIBLIOGRAPHY

J. Rulfo and others: *Cien retratos por Daisy Ascher* (Mexico City, 1981)

JULIETA ORTIZ GAITÁN

Ascoli Piceno [Lat. Asculum Picenum]. Italian city, a provincial capital in the Marches built at the confluence of the Castellano and Tronto rivers and on the ancient Via Salaria, which links Rome with the Adriatic Sea. After being conquered and destroyed by the Romans in 89 BC, Ascoli Piceno was rebuilt on a rectangular grid, which it has retained to this day. Because of its geographical position, the city always enjoyed a certain economic well-being, and the River Castellano provided the energy for mills and paper factories from the Middle Ages. Throughout the city's history this wealth favoured the production of many noteworthy works of art. Its architectural monuments, built of the local Travertine marble, are set in a medieval and Renaissance urban fabric of considerable interest.

Important remains of the Roman period have survived in Ascoli, including the Solestà bridge and gate (originally the Augustan gate; partially rebuilt 1230); the 'di Cecco' bridge (1st century BC); Porta Gemini, a two-arched gate from the same period; parts of the theatre, which was remodelled in the Augustan age; and remains of temples incorporated in the church of S Gregorio Magno (13th century, temple 1st century BC). The cathedral (almost totally transformed in the 15th century) was originally medieval, as were the baptistery and a number of churches: SS Vincenzo ed Anastasio (of early Christian origin; enlarged in the 10th and 11th centuries and drastically remodelled in the 14th century, when it acquired its

Ascoli Piceno, Piazza del Popolo (*c.* 1509), with, left, the Palazzo del Capitano del Popolo (12th–13th centuries; door with the monument to Paul III, 1549) and, in the background, the side of the church of S Francesco (1290, remodelled 14th century), with the monument to *Julius II* above the door

panelled façade, decorated with interlaced mouldings), S Maria Intervineas (also early Christian; enlarged 12th and 13th centuries), and S Tommaso Apostolo (*c.* 1064; rebuilt 13th century).

Ascoli Piceno has some interesting civic buildings, among them the Casa Longobardo, a small palazzo built in the 12th century, and the contemporary adjoining tower, the Torre degli Ercolani, which is one of the few tower houses to survive of the many that once existed in Ascoli. In Piazza del Popolo, on the site of the Roman forum, the church of S Francesco (1290; remodelled 14th century) features a Lombard-style portal with columns resting on the backs of lions and holding up a stone porch, and the huge Dominican church of S Pietro Martire (begun *c.* 1280) exhibits both Romanesque and Gothic features, as does the church of S Agostino, which has a complex building history from the 12th to the 16th century. The Palazzo del Capitano del Popolo was first erected in the 12th and 13th centuries, then transformed in the 16th; and the Fortezza Malatesta, built in 1349, was modernized by Antonio da Sangallo the younger in 1540.

In the 15th and 16th centuries numerous architectural projects and paintings were commissioned in Ascoli Piceno and the surrounding area. Even the simplest houses were often embellished with portals and windows of notable artistic quality. Renaissance architecture was brought to the city mainly by Lombard sculptors, who took their inspiration from the decorative motifs of the Ducal Palace in Urbino and the nearby Sanctuary of Loreto. The small palazzo of Francesco Calvo (later Palazzo Bonaparte) dates from 1507. With its richly carved main door, flanked by pilasters and surmounted by a lunette, and its mullioned and transomed windows on the first floor, this is one of the most important examples of Ascoli's domestic architecture. Shortly afterwards, *c.* 1509, the Piazza del Popolo (see fig.) was laid out with porticoed buildings around three sides (broken by the Palazzo del Capitano del Popolo and the side of the church of S Francesco); these were probably planned by an architect from the Po valley. To the same period belong the monument to *Julius II* on the side door of the church of S Francesco (1510); the Loggia dei Mercanti (1509–19), a light, elegant structure, still showing the influence of Filippo Brunelleschi; and the Papal *cartiera* or paper mill (1512). This last was the work of Alberto da Piacenza (*fl* 1501–16), a collaborator of Donato Bramante.

Bramante's style of Roman classicism reached Ascoli Piceno through the work of COLA DELL'AMATRICE, whose work on such structures as the Palazzo del Capitano del Popolo and the cathedral (where he designed the façade,

1525) brought about a significant change in building styles during the 16th century. Among the most notable works of that century are the Palazzo Roverella (begun 1532); part of the Bishop's Palace, with frescoes by the Venetian painter Marcello Fogolino; and the imposing Palazzo Malaspina (1535–83), which has an unusual loggia motif of columns in the form of trunks with cut-off branches in the manner of Bramante's loggia at S Ambrogio, Milan. The portal of Palazzo del Capitano del Popolo, surmounted by a monument to *Paul III*, dates from 1549, and the Fortezza Pia was completed in 1564.

The 17th and 18th centuries were dominated by the work of the Giosafatti, a family of architects and sculptors who brought to Ascoli the styles of the late 16th century and the Roman Baroque, executing in particular altars and interior decorations for religious buildings. In 1679 Giuseppe Giosafatti, who was born in Ascoli Piceno and trained in Rome in the circle of Gianlorenzo Bernini, began the remodelling of the medieval Palazzo Anzianale, elaborating a design produced in 1610 by Giovanni Battista Cavagna. This work, in late Mannerist style, was completed only in 1745. The façade of the unfinished church of the Angelo Custode was begun in 1684 and the upper part of the façade of the church of the Madonna del Carmine was built by Giuseppe Giosafatti. The designer in both cases was Carlo Rainaldi. In 1704–8 Giosafatti carried out alterations on the cathedral crypt, and in 1716 he built the Tempietto di S Emidio alle Grotte, modelled on the façade of the church of S Maria della Pace in Rome.

In the field of painting the most important works in Ascoli Piceno are those of the Renaissance: Carlo Crivelli (*see* CRIVELLI, (1), fig. 2), Pietro Alemanno, Marcello Fogolino and Cola dell'Amatrice are the most illustrious representatives of a throng of artists who left numerous panels and frescoes throughout the territory of Ascoli. These works reflect various influences, from Venetian to Umbrian painting, and also show evidence of contact with the art of the Abruzzi. Sculpture, on the other hand, reached its greatest importance during the Baroque period, through the work of the Giosafatti, who were strongly influenced by Roman sculpture of the Bernini school. The major sculptors were again Giuseppe Giosafatti and his uncle Lazzaro Morelli, a collaborator of Bernini who was active mostly in Rome.

In the 18th and 19th centuries, but especially after the unification of Italy in 1861, Ascoli Piceno lost much of its importance and suffered from changes affecting its ancient role as a centre of transport and commerce.

BIBLIOGRAPHY

T. Lazzari: *Ascoli in prospettiva* (Ascoli Piceno, 1724)

B. Orsini: *Descrizione delle pitture, sculture ed architetture dell'insigne città di Ascoli nella Marca* (Perugia, 1790)

G. B. Carducci: *Su le memorie e i monumenti di Ascoli nel Piceno: Discorso* (Fermo, 1853)

C. Mariotti: *Ascoli Piceno* (Bergamo, 1913)

G. Fabiani: *Ascoli nel quattrocento*, 2 vols (Ascoli Piceno, 1950–51)

——: *Cola dell'Amatrice secondo i documenti ascolani* (Ascoli Piceno, 1952)

E. Sisi: 'Caratteri urbanistici: Ascoli Piceno', *Urbanistica*, xxvi/20 (1956), pp. 142–5

L. Benevolo: *Ascoli Piceno* (Milan, 1957)

G. Fabiani: *Ascoli nel cinquecento*, 2 vols (Ascoli Piceno, 1957–9)

W. Lotz: 'Italienische Plätze des 16. Jahrunderts', *Jb. Max-Planck-Ges. Förderung Wiss.* (1968), pp. 41–60; Eng. trans. as 'Sixteenth-century Italian Squares', *Studies in Italian Renaissance Architecture* (Cambridge, MA, and London, 1977), pp. 74–92

L. Leporini: *Ascoli Piceno: L'architettura dai maestri vaganti ai Giosafatti* (Ascoli Piceno, 1973)

A. Ghisetti Giavarina: *Cola dell'Amatrice architetto e la sperimentazione classicistica del cinquecento* (Naples, 1982)

Ascoli e il suo territorio: Struttura urbana e insediamenti dalle origini ad oggi (Cinisello Balsamo, 1984)

ADRIANO GHISETTI GIAVARINA

Asensi, Manuel Montfort y. *See* MONFORT Y ASENSI, MANUEL.

Ashanti. *See* ASANTE AND RELATED PEOPLES.

'Ashârah, Tell. *See* TERQA.

Ashbee, C(harles) R(obert) (*b* Isleworth, Middx, 17 May 1863; *d* Godden Green, Kent, 23 May 1942). English designer, writer, architect and social reformer. He was educated at King's College, Cambridge. As a young man he was deeply influenced by the teachings of John Ruskin and William Morris, and particularly by their vision of creative workmanship in the Middle Ages; such a vision made work in modern times seem like mechanical drudgery. Ashbee played many parts and might be thought a dilettante; but his purpose was always to give a practical expression to what he had learnt from Ruskin and Morris. An intense and rather isolated figure, he found security in a life dedicated to making the world a better place.

In 1888, while he was training to be an architect in the office of G. F. Bodley and Thomas Garner (1839–1906), Ashbee set up the Guild and School of Handicraft in the East End of London. The School lasted only until 1895, but the Guild, a craft workshop that combined the ideals of the Arts and Crafts Movement with a romantic, apolitical socialism, was to be the focus of Ashbee's work for the next 20 years. There were five guildsmen at first, making furniture and base metalwork. In 1891 they moved to Essex House, an 18th-century mansion in the Mile End Road, and work was expanded to include jewellery, silverwork and enamelling. The last workshop to be added, in 1898, was the Essex House Press, which took over staff and equipment from William Morris's Kelmscott Press. The Guild was in theory, and to some extent in practice, a cooperative workshop with arrangements for self-government and profit-sharing. By 1900 it numbered about 30 men, and its life was not confined to workshop hours: evenings and weekends would often be spent in communal singing, sports or amateur theatricals, under Ashbee's educational eye. The years around 1900 were the high point in the story of the Guild. It was registered as a limited company with enlarged capital in 1898, it exhibited successfully in Britain, Europe and America, and at the same time it seemed to be flourishing as a social experiment.

The products of the Guild were designed mostly by Ashbee, whose talents reached maturity *c.* 1900. His early work was uncertain in design, and the details often incorporated 16th- or 17th-century motifs in a prominent, ill-digested way. But in the early 1890s he began to design jewellery that was simple in form and radical in taste; made out of silver wire and cheap coloured stones, and without obvious historical precedents, it was the first distinctly Arts and Crafts jewellery (see fig.). In the later 1890s he designed some marvellously assured silver table

C. R. Ashbee: circular brooch, copper, dark blue enamel, silver wire and pearl, diam. 72 mm, *c.* 1895 (London, Victoria and Albert Museum)

ware, including dishes and decanters (*see* SILVER, fig. 4 and ARTS AND CRAFTS MOVEMENT, fig. 1); he chose to work with a few simple elements, such as plain hammered silver, coloured stones set sparingly and fluent wirework. He produced a remarkable variety of designs, which had a wide and enduring appeal (examples in London, V&A).

Ashbee was a designer who seemed to thrive on limitations, and the houses he built on Cheyne Walk in Chelsea, London, usually for artists, demonstrated the same fruitful puritanism; seven were built, but only two survive, numbers 38 and 39 (1898–9). Using a loose and asymmetrical grouping of parts, plain and rendered brickwork and a few allusions to old London, Ashbee created houses that were at once enigmatic and ordinary, subtle and appropriate.

In 1902 Ashbee moved the workshops of the Guild of Handicraft to Chipping Campden, Glos, a small town with a wealth of fine stone buildings and almost no experience of the Industrial Revolution. It was a bold move, inspired by current concerns over degeneracy in cities and by the rural nostalgia of the Arts and Crafts Movement. At first it was a success and an enlargement of Ashbee's ideals; he repaired local buildings and started a craft school. He seemed to be creating a rural utopia, but when trade declined around 1905 he felt unable to lay men off as he would have done in London, and they went on making unsaleable stock. The limited company went into liquidation at the end of 1907, and although the Guild of Handicraft continued in a reduced form until 1919, Ashbee's career lost direction for a time. In 1919 he was appointed Civic Adviser to the city of Jerusalem, with responsibility for repairing the fabric of the old city, fostering local crafts and planning new development. It was a marvellous opportunity for Ashbee to use all his old skills, a second, and exotic, chance to reach utopia; but it was short-lived. He resigned in 1922 and retired to Godden Green, Kent.

Ashbee's career was one of the most important in the Arts and Crafts Movement in Britain, and also one of the most varied. He was honest, generous and imaginative, and, as he turned his hand to architecture, design, craftsmanship, teaching and planning, his life became a stubborn protest against specialization. His commitment made him much more than an architect and designer; in 1894, for instance, he started an ambitious scheme for recording all historic buildings in London, because they were so often threatened with destruction. He had only amateur helpers and his own enthusiasm, but the project took hold and has grown into the continuing and scholarly record known as the *Survey of London.*

WRITINGS

A Few Chapters in Workshop Re-construction and Citizenship (London, 1894)
An Endeavour towards the Teaching of John Ruskin and William Morris (London, 1901)
Craftsmanship in Competitive Industry (London, 1908)
Modern English Silverwork (London, 1909, rev. 1974)
Should we Stop Teaching Art (London, 1911)
Where the Great City Stands: A Study in the New Civics (London, 1917)

BIBLIOGRAPHY

F. MacCarthy: *The Simple Life: C. R. Ashbee in the Cotswolds* (London, 1981)
A. Crawford: *C. R. Ashbee: Architect, Designer and Romantic Socialist* (London, 1985)

ALAN CRAWFORD

Ashburnham, Bertram, 4th Earl of Ashburnham (*b* 23 Nov 1797; *d* Ashburnham Place, nr Battle, E. Sussex, 22 June 1878). English collector. He was educated at St John's College, Cambridge, and travelled extensively in his youth, collecting many examples of fine art in Italy and Eastern Europe. After he succeeded his father, George, 3rd Earl of Ashburnham (1760–1830), he remained at Ashburnham Place, the family seat in Sussex, for which his grandfather, John, 2nd Earl of Ashburnham (1724–1812), had commissioned drawings and plans (*c.* 1767) for improvements to the park from 'Capability' Brown, and his father had commissioned extensive improvements to the house from George Dance the younger (*see* DANCE, (3)). He occupied himself with his collections and the running of the estates. The extensive library of rare books and manuscripts that he accumulated contained four main sections. In 1847 he bought from Guglielmo Libri (1803–69) a collection of ancient codices, works of medieval literature and illuminated manuscripts from the schools of England, France, Italy, Flanders and Germany. These included the Ashburnham Pentateuch (early 7th century; Paris, Bib. N., MS. nouv. acq. lat. 2334, *see* EARLY CHRISTIAN AND BYZANTINE ART, §V, 1) and two volumes of notes and drawings by Leonardo da Vinci (Paris, Bib. N., MS. It. 2037–8). The Barrois manuscripts, bought in 1849 from the French collector Jean-Baptiste-Joseph Barrois (1784–1855), comprised works of Old French poetry and romances, illuminated manuscripts and some fine specimens of bindings, including seven ivory covers. The Stowe collection, purchased in 1849 by private treaty from the estate of Richard Temple-Nugent-Brydges-Chandos-Grenville, 1st Duke of Buckingham and Chandos, contained historical documents, letters and charters relating to English and Irish history as well as many important books and manuscripts, for example the New Minister Register (*c.* 1031; London, BL, MS. Stowe 944). The fourth section, known as the 'Appendix', included most of the finest illuminated manuscripts of Ashburnham's collection, acquired from miscellaneous sources. After the Earl's death, the collection was dispersed: the Stowe manuscripts were bought by the British Museum, London, in 1883 for £45,000; in 1884 the Italian government paid £23,000 for the larger portion of the Libri collection and the Dante manuscripts from the 'Appendix' for the Biblioteca Medicea-Laurenziana in Florence; and in 1888, the Bibliothèque Nationale in Paris bought the remainder of the Libri and the Barrois collections.

BIBLIOGRAPHY

The Manuscripts of the Earl of Ashburnham, Reports of the Royal Commission of Historical Manuscripts, viii/3 (London, 1881)
E. A. Bond: *Description of the Ashburnham Manuscripts and Account of Offers of Purchase* (London, 1883)
C. Paoli: *I Codici Ashburnhamiani della R. Biblioteca Medicea-Laurenziana di Firenze* (Rome, 1887)
L. V. Delisle: *Catalogue des manuscrits des fonds Libri et Barrois de la Bibliothèque Nationale* (Paris, 1888)
B. Quaritch, ed.: *Contributions towards a Dictionary of English Book Collectors* (London, 1969), pp. 14–24

□

Ashburton, 1st Baron. *See* BARING, (3).

Ashby, Thomas (*b* Staines, 14 Oct 1874; *d* nr Raynes Park, Surrey, 15 May 1931). English archaeologist and collector. He began his study of Classical archaeology at Winchester; his father moved to Rome in 1890, and during holidays they explored the Campagna with the archaeologist Rodolfo Lanciani. Having read Classics at Christ Church, Oxford (1898), he became the first student at the British School at Rome in 1901 and its director in 1906. His earliest articles, on the topography of the aqueducts and roads of Rome and the Campagna, were later developed into books. Tomassetti listed 323 publications (including excavation reports) by Ashby on the Campagna, many of them pioneering works. Ashby's studies of 16th-century and later drawings of Roman monuments include his publication (1904, 1913) of the Coner Sketchbook (London, Soane Mus.), while his interest in Renaissance collections of ancient statues enabled him to identify works that had once stood in the Villa d'Este at Tivoli (1908) and led him to produce a bibliographical analysis of the engravings by Giovanni Battista de Cavalieri and his followers (1920). Retiring from the British School in 1925, he completed his and S. B. Platner's *Topographical Dictionary of Ancient Rome* (1929). He died by falling from a train while on his way to Oxford. Ashby's substantial collection of prints and drawings, mostly topographical views of Rome and the Campagna, is now in the Biblioteca Apostolica Vaticana, Rome.

WRITINGS

'Sixteenth-century Drawings of Roman Buildings Attributed to Andreas Coner', *Pap. Brit. Sch. Rome*, ii (1904), pp. 1–96; 'Addenda and Corrigenda', ibid., vi (1913), pp. 184–210
'The Villa d'Este at Tivoli and the Collection of Classical Sculptures which it Contained', *Archaeologia*, lxi (1908), pp. 219–56
'Antiquae Statuae Urbis Romae', *Pap. Brit. Sch. Rome*, ix (1920), pp. 107–58
The Roman Campagna in Classical Times (London, 1927, rev. with intro. by J. B. Ward-Perkins, 1970)
with S. B. Platner: *A Topographical Dictionary of Ancient Rome* (London, 1929)
The Aqueducts of Ancient Rome, ed. I. A. Richmond (Oxford, 1935)

BIBLIOGRAPHY

F. Tomassetti: 'Scrittori contemporanei di cose romane: Thomas Ashby', *Archv Soc. Romana Stor. Patria*, l (1927), pp. 77–123
A. H. Smith: 'Thomas Ashby (1874–1931)', *Proc. Brit. Acad.*, xvii (1931), pp. 515–41
D. Bodart: *Dessins de la collection Thomas Ashby à la Bibliothèque Vatican* (Rome, 1975)
Thomas Ashby: Un archeologo fotografa la campagna romana tra '800 e '900 (exh. cat., Rome, Brit. Sch., 1986)
Views of Rome from the Thomas Ashby Collection in the Vatican Library (exh. cat. by R. Keaveney, Washington, DC, Smithsonian Inst. Traveling Exh. Serv., 1988)
R. Hodges: *Visions of Rome: The Life and Times of Thomas Ashby* (in preparation)

RUTH OLITSKY RUBINSTEIN

Ashcan school. Term first used by Holger Cahill and Alfred Barr in *Art in America* (New York, 1934) and loosely applied to American urban realist painters. In particular it referred to those members of the Eight (i) who shortly after 1900 began to portray ordinary aspects of city life in their paintings, for example George Luks's painting *Closing the Café* (1904; Utica, NY, Munson-Williams-Proctor Inst.). Robert Henri, John Sloan, William J. Glackens, Everett Shinn and George Luks were the core of an informal association of painters who, in reaction against the prevailing restrictive academic exhibition procedures, mounted a controversial independent exhibition at the Macbeth Galleries, New York (1908).

Sloan, Glackens, Shinn and Luks had all worked for the *Philadelphia Press*. It was in Philadelphia, where Henri had trained at the Academy of Fine Arts, that he convinced them to leave their careers as newspaper illustrators to take up painting as a serious profession. In an explicit challenge to the 'art for art's sake' aesthetic of the late 19th century, Henri proposed an 'art for life', one that

Ashcan school: *Hairdresser's Window* by John Sloan, oil on canvas, 810 × 660 mm, 1907 (Hartford, CT, Wadsworth Atheneum)

would abandon the polished techniques and polite subject-matter of the academicians; it would celebrate instead the vitality that the painter saw around him in everyday situations.

In 1904 Henri set up his own school in New York in a Latin quarter on Upper Broadway. He was joined there by Sloan, Glackens, Luks and Shinn; George Bellows, Glenn O. Coleman (1887–1932) and Jerome Myers (1867–1940) also associated themselves with Henri's new urban realism. Henri and his followers were initially referred to as the 'revolutionary black gang', a term that alluded to the dark subdued palette that characterized much of the group's early paintings. They drew subject-matter from life in the Bowery, Lower Sixth Avenue and West 14th Street. Among the typical works of the Ashcan school were images of street urchins, prostitutes, athletes, immigrants and boxers, as in Bellows's *Stag at Sharkey's* (1909; Cleveland, OH, Mus. A.) and *Dempsey and Firpo* (1924; New York, Whitney; for illustration *see* BELLOWS, GEORGE). Such figure studies, together with street scenes such as *Hairdresser's Window* (see fig.) by Sloan, convey a vivid impression of life in New York in the early years of the century.

Their choice of such picturesque contemporary motifs was generally considered bold, but as William B. McCormick, writing in the *New York Press* in 1908, observed, there were clear precedents in European art:

> 'Surely it is not "revolutionary" to follow in the footsteps of the men who were the rage in artistic Paris twenty years ago. Nor is it "a new departure in American art" to paint after the manner of Manet, Degas, and Monet.'

BIBLIOGRAPHY

I. Forrester: 'New York Art Anarchists', *N Y World Mag.* (10 June 1906), p. 6

B. B. Perlman: *The Immortal Eight, American Painting from Eakins to the Armory Show, 1870–1913* (New York, 1962)

W. I. Homer: 'The Exhibition of "The Eight": Its History and Significance', *Amer. A. J.*, i/1 (1969), pp. 53–64

——: *Robert Henri and his Circle* (Ithaca, 1969)

M. S. Young: *The Eight* (New York, 1973)

B. B. Perlman: 'Rebels with a Cause – The Eight', *ARTnews*, lxxxi/18 (1982), pp. 62–7

J. Zilczer: 'The Eight on Tour, 1908–1909', *Amer. A. J.*, xvi/64 (1984), pp. 20–48

M. SUE KENDALL

Ashfield, Edmund [Edward] (*fl* from 1660; *d* 1690). English painter and pastellist. He worked in London and was probably from a Buckinghamshire family. His cousin Sir Thomas Lawrence described Ashfield as an 'ingenious painter' in a speech at Oxford on 11 July 1669. He trained under the portrait painter John Michael Wright and copied in oils portraits by Lely, van Dyck and others, examples of which survive in the Bodleian Library and Merton College, Oxford.

Ashfield's reputation was chiefly as a pastellist. Although Lely and his followers had drawn in coloured chalks, Ashfield raised the medium to a new distinction, using richer colours, often very thickly and in combination with wash, so that his work ceased to look like drawing and took on something of the density and finish of oil painting; Bainbridge Buckeridge wrote, 'Our countryman, Mr. *Ashfield*, multiply'd the number and variety of *tints*, and painted various complexions in imitation of oil; and this *manner* has been so much improved among us, that there is no subject which can be express'd by oil, but the *crayons* can effect it with equal force and beauty'.

Ashfield's work in pastels survives only from the period 1673–6 and is uneven in quality. The earliest extant example, the signed *Portrait of an Unknown Young Man* (1673; Oxford, Ashmolean), illustrates his painterly approach to the medium and is one of the masterpieces among English pastel portraits. Ashfield was the teacher of Edward Lutterell, whose more numerous pastels, comprising copies after the Old Masters as well as portraits, date from 1684 and after. They are more brightly coloured and are less sensitive than those of his master.

BIBLIOGRAPHY

B. Buckeridge: 'An Essay towards an English School of Painters', add. R. de Piles: *The Art of Painting*, Eng. trans. (London, 1695, rev. 3/1750) of *De arte graphica* (Paris, 1668); dedication and p. 355

C. H. C. Baker: 'Notes on Edmund Ashfield', *Walpole Soc.*, iii (1914), pp. 83–7

J. Woodward: *Tudor and Stuart Drawings* (London, 1951), p. 38

E. Croft-Murray and P. Hulton: *British Drawings, XVI and XVII Centuries*, London, BM cat., i (London, 1960), pp. 93–4

DAVID BLAYNEY BROWN

Ashford, William (*b* Birmingham, *c.* 1746; *d* Dublin, 17 April 1824). Irish painter. Although he was later to become one of Ireland's finest landscape painters, Ashford did not go to Ireland until 1764, when he took up an appointment at the Ordnance Office in Dublin. He worked at the office for over 20 years and travelled widely throughout the country. His earliest known works as a painter date from 1767 when he exhibited two flower pieces (Dublin, N.G. and priv. col.) at the Dublin Society of Arts. He exhibited his first landscapes in 1772 and was awarded the second premium from the Dublin Society. One of these exhibits, the earliest known example of the country house views for which he later became so celebrated, was a view (untraced) of Mount Kennedy, General Cunningham's great house near Dublin (later view of the house, 1785; New Haven, CT, Yale Cent. Brit. A.). The next year he exhibited seven further paintings and won the Society's first prize. In 1775 he made his first appearance at the Royal Academy in London, where at various dates until 1811 he exhibited a total of 25 works, mainly Irish landscapes. He left the Dublin Ordnance Office in about 1788 and travelled to London via North Wales, and for two years his exhibits in London included a number of Welsh views.

In 1791 Ashford moved back to Dublin and settled at Sandymount, near Dublin, in a house built for him by James Gandon. Although henceforth living permanently in Dublin, he continued to exhibit in London, at both the Royal Academy and the British Institution. He also exhibited regularly in Dublin between 1800 and 1821, became President of the Irish Society of Artists in 1813, and played a significant role in the foundation of the Royal Hibernian Academy, becoming its first president in 1823. Ashford's early landscapes show a marked Dutch influence, but his favourite subjects were his sets of views of the seats of Irish landowners, a number of which were engraved for Thomas Milton's *Views of Seats in Ireland* (1783–93). He had an impressive group of patrons, including Richard, 7th Viscount Fitzwilliam (1745–1816), for whom he painted views of *Mount Merrion Park* (Cambridge, Fitzwilliam), Charles Bury, 1st Earl of Charleville (1764–1835), Charles Moore, 1st Marquis of Drogheda (1730–1822), William, 2nd Duke of Leinster (1749–1804), Bernard Ward, 1st Viscount Bangor (1719–81), and William, 2nd Earl Fitzwilliam (1748–1833). He eschewed the wilder aspects of Irish scenery and is shown at his best when depicting a well-ordered estate. His fine topographical views are imbued with a characteristic warm tone giving his landscapes a peculiarly Continental atmosphere.

BIBLIOGRAPHY

Strickland
A. Crookshank and The Knight of Glin: *The Painters of Ireland, c. 1660–1920* (London, 1978), pp. 133–6; figs 120–22; pls 31–2
A. Crookshank: 'A Life Devoted to Landscape Painting: William Ashford (c.1746–1824)', *Irish A. Rev.* (1994)

DAVID MOORE-GWYN

Ashihara, Yoshinobu (*b* Tokyo, 7 July 1918). Japanese architect and writer. He graduated from the University of Tokyo in 1942 and in 1946–7 he worked in the office of Junzō Sakakura in Tokyo. After receiving a master's degree from Harvard University, Cambridge, MA (1953), he worked in the office of Marcel Breuer in New York (1953–6). In 1956 he returned to Japan and opened his own office in Tokyo. One of Ashihara's principal concerns was the use of logical structural systems to create flexible, integrated space within buildings. He developed the use of split levels or 'skip' floors to combine spaces of various sizes, as in the Chūō Koron building (1956), Tokyo, for which he was awarded the Architectural Institute of Japan prize in 1960. The Sony building (1966), Tokyo, was designed as a cubic spiral of skip floors, creating organic spatial continuity throughout the building with spaces that interrelate with each other and with their environment. A similar concept was used for the Japanese pavilion at Expo '67 in Montreal, for which he received an award from the Ministry of Education. The continuity and flow of space between interior and exterior, and in the spaces between buildings, were also addressed, for example in the Komazawa Olympic Gymnasium (1964), Tokyo, which received a special award from the Architectural Institute of Japan. His National Museum of Japanese History (1980), Sakura, also won a prize, from the Japan Institute of Art. Ashihara received a PhD from the University of Tokyo in 1961 and was appointed professor at several universities, both in Japan and overseas. He was a vice-president of the Architectural Institute of Japan (1976–8) and president of the Japan Architects Association (1980–82).

WRITINGS

Exterior Design in Architecture (New York, 1970)
Aesthetics in Townscape (Cambridge, MA, 1983)

BIBLIOGRAPHY

Ashihara Yoshinobu, Gendai Nihon kenchikuka zenshū [Complete collection of modern Japanese architects], xv (Tokyo, 1971)
Ashihara Yoshinobu, Nihon gendai kenchikuka shirīzu [Modern Japanese architects series], vi (Tokyo, 1983)

TOSHIAKI NAGAYA

Ashikaga. Shogunal dynasty that ruled Japan during the Muromachi period (1333–1568). According to the anonymous *Taiheiki* ('Chronicle of great peace'; ?1370–71), Ashikaga, the name of a town in Shimotsuke Province (now Tochigi Prefect.), was taken as a family name by a branch of the military Minamoto family. The Ashikaga came to power when the first Ashikaga shogun, Takauji (1305–58), overthrew the Hōjō regents in Kamakura and installed the ambitious Emperor GoDaigo (*reg* 1318–39) in Kyoto. When GoDaigo refused to name Takauji as shogun, the latter deposed him and replaced him by his own candidate. GoDaigo fled to Yoshino (Nara Prefect.), where he set up a rival court. The schism continued during the early Muromachi period, which is also known as the Nanbokuchō ('Northern and Southern Courts'; 1336–92) period. Takauji and his son, the second shogun Ashikaga Yoshiakira (1330–67), paid respect to the old aristocracy in Kyoto, but the third shogun, Ashikaga Yoshimitsu (1358–1408), asserted the political and cultural hegemony of the samurai class. Yoshimitsu built his palace in the Muromachi district of Kyoto, just north or 'above' the imperial palace. He followed his grandfather's lead as a patron of Zen Buddhist temples and used the Gozan ('Five Mountains'; hierarchy of Zen temples in Kyoto) system as a means of legitimizing Ashikaga rule. Yoshimitsu founded Shōkokuji near his palace and used the Zen temple as a bureaucratic resource, a trading house with Ming-period (1344–1568) China and an unofficial painting academy.

The evolution of *suibokuga* (ink painting; *see* JAPAN, §VI, 4(iii)) under Ashikaga patronage can be traced through the careers of the Shōkokuji ink painters JOSETSU, TENSHŌ SHŪBUN and TŌYŌ SESSHŪ. The relationship between these artists and the shogunate is illustrated by Josetsu's *Hyonenzu* ('Catching a catfish with a gourd'; *see* JAPAN, fig. 92), which was probably commissioned by the fourth shogun, (1) Ashikaga Yoshimochi, an accomplished ink painter in his own right. The artistic adviser to the eighth shogun, Yoshimasa (1436–90), the painter–connoisseur Shinsō Sōami (*see* AMI, (3)), produced *Kundaikan sōchōki* (a catalogue of the shogunal collection with display instructions). While the championing of ink painting by the shoguns led to the prominence of the KANŌ SCHOOL, patronage was also extended to exponents of *Yamatoe* (traditional Japanese painting; *see* JAPAN, §VI, 4(ii)), such as Tosa Mitsunobu (*see* TOSA, (1)). The Muromachi period is marked by a diversity of painting styles, themes and formats. In addition to hanging scrolls (*kakejuku*) and handscrolls (*emaki*), folding screens (*byōbu*) and sliding door panels (*fusuma*) were important formats. The Ashikaga shogun's patronage of the arts was manifested in many ways but most dramatically in architecture. After abdicating in favour of his son, Yoshimochi, Yoshimitsu retired to Kinkakuji ('Golden Pavilion'; *see* KYOTO, §IV, 6), a specially constructed villa in the Kitayama district of Kyoto.

Despite a brief period of political calm following Yoshimasa's rule, the second half of the 15th century was marked by a rapid decline of Ashikaga power, culminating in a century of civil war following the Ōnin Wars (1467–77). Yoshimasa built Gingakuji ('Silver Pavilion'; *see* KYOTO, §IV, 8) in a garden modelled on the moss-and-rock garden of Saihōji (*see* KYOTO, §IV, 2). Ginkakuji and the companion Tōgudo ('Hall of Eastern Quest') epitomize the elegant restraint when compared with Yoshimitsu's Kinkakuji. Tōgudo is noted for the Dōjinsai room, the earliest room in the *shoin* style (*see* JAPAN, §III, 4(ii)(a)) that was to flourish a century later. Two of Yoshimasa's interests, *renga* (linked verse) and the tea ceremony, were to be major elements of SEN NO RIKYŪ's *wabi* ('plain' or 'simple taste') aestheticism that dominated the Momoyama period (1568–1600). Ashikaga rule ended when the last shogun, Yoshiaki (1537–97), was driven into exile by the warlord ODA NOBUNAGA. Despite little real power in politics or artistic patronage after the time of Yoshimasa, the Ashikaga shogun's cultural legacy was passed on to their vassals and successors.

BIBLIOGRAPHY

S. Shimizu and C. Wheelwright, eds: *Japanese Ink Painting* (Princeton, 1976)

KEN BROWN

(1) Ashikaga Yoshimochi [Kenzan, Dōsen] (*b* Kyoto, 1386; *d* Kyoto, 1428). Patron, painter and shogun. Yoshimochi succeeded his father, Ashikaga Yoshimitsu, as fourth Ashikaga shogun in 1394, but did not actually take power until Yoshimitsu's death. He built a magnificent residential compound at Sanjōbōmon in Kyoto, with gardens and buildings rivalling those of the Zen temple Saihōji (*see* KYOTO, §IV, 2). A student of the Zen abbot Zekkai Chūshin (1336–1405), he took the tonsure in 1423 and abdicated in favour of his son Yoshikazu (1407–25), but became shogun for a second time in 1425 when Yoshizaku died.

Yoshimochi's period of activity coincided with the flowering of Chinese literary culture in Kyoto's Zen monasteries. He founded several retreats at Shōkokuji and Nanzenji and sponsored numerous poetry gatherings of Zen abbots. Yoshimochi is thought to be the 'Great Minister' (Daishōkō) mentioned as the sponsor in Daigaku Shūsū's (1345–1423) preface inscribed on Josetsu's *Hyōnenzu* ('Catching a catfish with a gourd'; *c.* 1413–15; Kyoto, Myōshinji; *see* JAPAN, fig. 92). Yoshimochi especially favoured Daigaku and several other prominent Zen abbots whose inscriptions appear on numerous poem–paintings (*shigajiku*) of the period. As an avocation, Yoshimochi painted figures in monochrome ink in an abbreviated brush manner reminiscent of the works of the Chinese painters MUQI and Yintuoluo (*fl* mid-14th century), both of whom were represented in his father's collection of Chinese paintings. Approximately a dozen extant paintings bear Yoshimochi's cipher or seal, and several are self-inscribed and dated. His subjects include the Buddhist deities Avalokiteshvara (Jap. Kannon) and Kshitigarbha (Jap. Jizō), the Zen patriarch Bodhidharma (Jap. Daruma), and the Zen eccentrics Budai (Jap. Hotei) and Hanshan (Jap. Kanzan).

A representative work is the *Byakue Kannon* (White-robed Kannon; 1413; hanging scroll, ink on silk; 610×280 mm; Atami, MOA Mus. A.). Executed entirely in soft grey ink, the deity's contemplative face is carefully drawn in fine line; the garment is sketched with heavier, fluctuating line; and the weighty triangular rocks are rendered in a combination of wash and textured strokes. Yoshimochi's six-line inscription appears in the empty sky below an ink-silhouetted moon.

Ashikaga Yoshimochi's patronage was not limited to temples of the Zen sect. He was devoted to the native deities (*kami*) Hachiman and Kitano Tenjin and made regular visits and donations to several Hachiman and Tenjin shrines. An anonymous portrait of Yoshimochi, dated 1414, at Jingoji attests to his patronage of that Shingon-sect temple. In the same year he joined several of his notable contemporaries, including retired Emperor GoKomatsu (*reg* 1382–1412), in the making of a lavish picture scroll set, *Yūzū nenbutsu engi* ('Miraculous origins of the all-permeating *nenbutsu*'; Kyoto, Seiryōji), for which Yoshimochi himself wrote one of the texts.

BIBLIOGRAPHY

T. Matsushita: *Muromachi suibokuga* [Muromachi ink painting] (Tokyo, 1960)
Japanese Ink Paintings from American Collections: The Muromachi Period (exh. cat. by Y. Shimizu and C. Wheelwright, Princeton U., NJ, A. Mus., 1976)
T. Matsushita: *Josetsu, Shūbun*, Nihon bijutsu kaiga zenshū [Complete collection of Japanese painting], ii (Tokyo, 1979)
S. Shimada and others, eds: *Suibokuga* [Ink painting] (1979), iii of *Zaigai Nihon no shihō* [Japanese art treasures abroad] (Tokyo, 1979–81)

KAREN L. BROCK

Ashkhabad [Pers. ʿAshqābād; formerly Askhabad, Poltorack]. Capital city of Turkmenistan. Lying in an oasis south of the Karakum Desert, the city was founded in 1881 on the site of a mountain village (Rus. *aul*). It was linked by rail with the Caspian coast in 1885 and developed rapidly as the centre of the Transcaspian region at the turn of the 20th century. It became the capital of the Turkmen republic in 1924. It suffered greatly from earthquakes in 1893, 1895 and 1929; following complete destruction by the earthquake of 6 October 1948, the city was rebuilt during the 1950s and 1960s.

The region has long been settled. The archaeological site at Anau, lying 6 km to the east, has yielded items dating from the 5th to the 1st millennium BC and has given its name to the Bronze Age culture of southern Turkmenistan (*see* CENTRAL ASIA, §I, 2(iii)(a)). The complex of shaykh Jamal al-Din (1455–6; destr. 1948) comprised a mosque and two domed structures, possibly a hospice and a madrasa, arranged around a court. The Parthian capital at NISA was situated 18 km to the west. The Turkmenistan History Museum (1927) at Ashkhabad houses archaeological finds and objects of applied art, and other archaeological finds are in the Institute of History of the Academy of Sciences. The Turkmenistan Museum of Fine Arts (1938) contains examples of Turkmen, Russian and western European art, of which the collection of Turkmen rugs is particularly fine, and there is also a museum of local history and culture.

BIBLIOGRAPHY

Enc. Iran; *Enc. Islam/2*: 'Ashḳābād'
A. Babayev and Z. G. Freykin: *Ashkhabad* (Ashkhabad, 1957)
V. V. Zhmuyda: *Ashkhabad* (Moscow, 1957)

A. A. IVANOV

Ashlin, George C(oppinger) (*b* Carrigrenane, Co. Cork, 28 May 1837; *d* Killiney, Co. Dublin, 10 Dec 1921). Irish architect. He received his early education at the Collège de St Servais, Liège. While at St Mary's College, Oscott (1851–5), with which A. W. N. Pugin was strongly associated, he studied drawing and perspective and developed an interest in architecture. Between 1856 and 1860 he was articled to E. W. Pugin (whose sister Mary he married in 1860) and in 1858 he entered the Royal Academy Schools, London. When in 1859 E. W. Pugin received the commission for SS Peter and Paul, Cork, he made Ashlin a partner with responsibility for their Irish work, a position he retained until about 1870 (*see* PUGIN, (3)). Their practice was primarily ecclesiastical, the remodelling (1869) of Enniscorthy Castle for Isaac Newton Wallop (1825–91), 5th Earl of Portsmouth, being one of their few domestic projects. They worked on some 25 religious buildings. The Augustinian church of SS Augustine and John, Thomas Street, Dublin (commissioned 1860, opened 1874), in a style inspired by French architecture, is one of their most successful designs. The site drops towards the river, so that while the entrance is at street level the nave and chancel are raised considerably above the surrounding streets, a dramatic effect enhanced by the soaring spire. Other large churches by Pugin & Ashlin include the Sacred Heart (1863), Donnybrook, and St Joseph's (1866), Glasthule. Their churches in the countryside, mainly in counties Wexford, Cork and Kerry, are simpler, with straightforward Latin-cross plans, good quality stonework and simple bellcotes. The church at Lady's Island, Co. Wexford, adjoins the parish of Tagoat, the church of which was designed by A. W. N. Pugin in 1846. Ashlin's greatest work with E. W. Pugin is St Colman's Cathedral (completed 1919) at Queenstown (now Cóbh), Co. Cork. Ashlin practised on his own from 1870 and in 1902 entered a partnership with his former pupil Thomas Aloysius Coleman (*d* ?1950). His nephew, Martin Ashlin (*d* 1942), became a partner in 1908.

Stylistically, Ashlin is primarily associated with the Gothic Revival, which was dominated in Ireland by J. J. McCarthy. Although particularly inspired by French Gothic architecture, he also followed other styles. The Redemptorist Convent Chapel of St Alphonsus (1873), Drumcondra, Dublin, is in a Romanesque Revival style, with silver granite ashlar exterior and a small, lavish interior combining inlaid marble, mosaic, rich carving and painted figurative panels in the chancel. The large granite-faced church of St Columba (1905), Glasnevin, is more influenced by transitional Gothic architecture and in addition incorporates motifs inspired by the contemporary Celtic Revival, such as the fretwork on the soffits of crossing arches that is treated as a series of Celtic interlace panels. Ashlin generally employed a classical style for his commercial work, such as the Sinn Fein office in St Andrew Street, Dublin. The tripartite Corinthian portico (Wicklow granite, 1902) that he added to St Audeon's (1841), High Street, Dublin, however, was determined by the arrangement of Patrick Byrne's existing building. With Coleman, Ashlin was responsible for Clery's Department Store (1919; interior much altered), O'Connell Street, Dublin, which includes an almost completely glazed ground-floor and two upper storeys articulated with a range of giant Ionic columns supporting a deep entablature and an attic storey; it is clearly dependent on Selfridge's Department Store (1909), Oxford Street, London, by Waring & Gillow.

BIBLIOGRAPHY

'Our Interviews, no. 5: George C. Ashlin', *Irish Bldr*, xliii (30 Jan 1902), pp. 1018–19

D. S. Richardson: *The Gothic Revival in Ireland* (New York, 1984)

P. Costello: *Dublin Churches* (Dublin, 1989)

F. O'Dwyer: 'A Victorian Partnership: The Architecture of Pugin and Ashlin', *150 Years of Architecture in Ireland: RIAI 1839–1989*, ed. J. Graby (Dublin, 1989), pp. 54–62

HUGH MAGUIRE

Ashmole, Bernard (*b* Ilford, 22 June 1894; *d* Peebles, 25 Feb 1988). English archaeologist. One of the most distinguished Classical scholars of the 20th century, specializing in Greek and Roman sculpture, he was equally well-known for his skills as an administrator and teacher. He was appointed Assistant Curator of Coins at the Ashmolean Museum, Oxford, in 1922, leaving the post to become Director of the British School in Rome in 1925. Tempted by the opportunity of proximity to the British Museum collections and library, Ashmole returned to England in 1929 to take up the Yates Chair of Classical Archaeology at the University of London (1929–48), soon arranging a transfer to the university of the museum's collection of plaster casts. As Keeper of Greek and Roman Antiquities at the British Museum (1939–56), he was largely responsible for the eventual display of the Elgin Marbles in the Duveen Gallery. He returned to Oxford in 1956 as Lincoln Professor of Classical Archaeology, from which post he retired in 1961, although he continued to take up visiting professorships and lecturing engagements in Britain and abroad. As advisor to J. Paul Getty, he was instrumental in gathering a nucleus of Classical sculptures for the J. Paul Getty Museum in Malibu, CA.

Ashmole's antiquarian interests were complemented by a taste for Modernism, which he demonstrated by commissioning from Amyas Connell the first concrete-framed house in England, High and Over, at Amersham (1928). He was himself a fine photographer of ancient sculpture, and his collection of photographs and negatives is now housed in the Ashmole Archive at King's College London.

WRITINGS

A Catalogue of the Greek and Roman Antiquities at Ince Blundell Hall (Oxford, 1929)

The Classical Ideal in Greek Sculpture (Cincinnati, 1964)

with N. Yalouris and A. Frantz: *Olympia: The Sculptures of the Temple of Zeus* (London, 1967)

Architect and Sculptor in Classical Greece (New York, 1972)

BIBLIOGRAPHY

M. Robertson: 'Bernard Ashmole', *Proc. Brit. Acad.*, lxxv (1989), pp. 313–28

GEOFFREY WAYWELL

Ashmole, Elias (*b* Lichfield, 23 May 1617; *d* London, 18/19 May 1692). English antiquary, collector and writer. He was the son-in-law of William Dugdale and the beneficiary and legatee of the collections of John Tradescant the elder and younger (*see* TRADESCANT). The Tradescants were the first in Britain to create a cabinet of curiosities, both natural and artificial, with a European reputation. In 1656 Ashmole and John Tradescant the younger compiled a printed catalogue of the Tradescant rarities called *Musaeum Tradescantianum*, the first catalogue of its kind. In 1662 Tradescant the younger left Ashmole his cabinet. In 1666 Ashmole completed a catalogue of the collection of Roman coins in the Bodleian Library, Oxford, and in 1672 he published *The Institution, Laws and Ceremonies of the Most Noble Order of the Garter* with plates by Wenzel Hollar. In 1675 Ashmole began negotiations with the University of Oxford about donating his collections. In the spring of 1679 work began on what has come to be known as the Old Ashmolean Building, following the designs of Thomas Wood (1664/5–95). It consisted of a fireproof chemical laboratory in the basement, a lecture theatre at ground level, and a room for the rarities (17.06 m×7.62 m) on the first floor. The museum was opened by James, Duke of York (1633–1701), on 21 May 1683. The exterior was engraved by Michael Burghers (1640–*c.* 1723) around 1685. Ashmole's foundation consisted of an extraordinary variety of artefacts including Native American Indian clothes, Buddhas, rare shells and stuffed birds, ivories, manuscripts, pictures of the Tradescants and their circle, a hawking glove of Henry VIII and antique medallions. Much of the collection survives at Charles Robert Cockerell's 19th-century Ashmolean Museum in Beaumont Street, Oxford. The Ashmolean Museum constituted the first public museum in Britain and the word 'museum' was first used in English to describe this foundation.

BIBLIOGRAPHY

DNB

J. Cambell: *Biographia Britannica*, i (London, 1747)

C. H. Josten: 'Elias Ashmole, F. R. S. (1617–1692)', *Notes & Rec. Royal Soc. London*, xv (1960), pp. 221–30

A. MacGregor, ed.: *Tradescant's Rarities: Essays on the Foundation of the Ashmolean Museum 1683* (Oxford, 1983)

DAVID HOWARTH

Ashmunein, el-. *See* HERMOPOLIS MAGNA.

Ashraf. *See* 'ALI ASHRAF.

Ashtarak. Town on the banks of the K'asagh River, 20 km north-west of Erevan, Armenia. It is the site of several churches (5th–19th centuries) and a cemetery with khatchk'ars (*see* ARMENIA, §IV, 1; CROSS, §II, 4) of the 12th to the 14th century.

The earliest church is the three-aisled basilica of Tsiranavor, which was built in the 5th century and partially reconstructed in the 6th, probably by Catholicos Nerses II (*reg* 538–57), a native of Bagravand. It subsequently underwent numerous alterations and was finally left a ruin in 1815. Restoration work in 1963 revealed that the exterior walls, the apse area, the north pier bases and the south aisle and nave arcade have survived. Traces of the beginnings of the main vault can be seen at the west end.

The walls are of tufa ashlars, facing a rubble core. The plan was defined by three pairs of T-shaped piers, a characteristic of 5th-century Armenian architecture (*see* ARMENIA, §II), as in the basilicas of K'asagh (4th–5th centuries), Tsitsernavank (5th–6th centuries) and Yereruyk' (5th–6th centuries). Tsiranavor's horseshoe-shaped eastern apse is flanked by two rectangular chambers, all three embedded in the rectilinear exterior wall, as at Yereruyk' and Aghts'.

The 7th-century church of the Mother of God (Astvatsatsin), also known as Karmravor (Arm.: 'red coloured'), is located in an ancient cemetery. An undated single-line dedicatory inscription beginning on the south elevation and ending on the north wall names the priests Grigor and Manas as its founders. It is a domed building (5.97×7.97 m) in the shape of a free-standing cross on the exterior and preserves its original roof of clay tiles, the only medieval Armenian church to do so. The eastern apse is horseshoe-shaped and embedded in the rectangular east end, but the other three apses are rectangular on both exterior and interior. The transition from the square central bay to the octagonal drum was made by four squinches at the base and eight smaller squinches above them. There are traces of wall painting on the interior of the drum. Among the many similar small cruciform churches of the 6th to the 7th century are the church of the Mother of God at T'ALIN, St Step'anos at Lmbat, St Sargis at Shenik, St Mariam at Bujakan and St Grigor at Nor Kyank.

The small domed church of St Mariné (1281; partially rebuilt 1838), once part of a monastery, is located west of Tsiranavor and Karmravor. It has an almost square ground-plan with two-storey chambers at each corner and a central dome on a tall drum. The latter has a cylindrical interior and 12-sided exterior decorated with a blind arcade. The window frames have trefoil extensions that create the effect of a cross, a motif seen in a number of 13th-century Armenian churches.

Finally, there is the ruined church of Spitakavor (Arm.: 'white-coloured'; 13th–14th centuries): a small, almost square building that may originally have had a dome.

BIBLIOGRAPHY

W. D'Onofrio: *Le chiese di Drin* (Rome, 1973), pp. 13–28 [Eng. text, pp. 71–86]

S. Der Nersessian: *L'Art arménien* (Paris, 1977/*R* 1989; Eng. trans., London, 1978)

L. D. Manuelian: *Armenian Architecture*, intro. by K. Maksoudian, Armenian Architectural Archives, ed. V. L. Parsegian, i (Zug, 1981)

F. Gandolfo: *Le basiliche armene: IV–VII secolo* (Rome, 1982), pp. 77–84

P. Cuneo: *Architettura armena dal quarto al diciannovesimo secolo*, i– (Rome, 1988–), pp. 194–6

J.-M. Thierry and P. Donabedian: *Les Arts arméniens* (Paris, 1987; Eng. trans., New York, 1989)

LUCY DER MANUELIAN, ARMEN ZARIAN

Ashton, Julian (Rossi) (*b* Alderstone, England, 27 Jan 1851; *d* Bondi, Sydney, 27 April 1942). Australian painter and writer. He attended the West London School of Art and, following the end of the Franco-Prussian War in 1871, the Académie Julian in Paris. In 1878 the newspaper owner David Syme invited Ashton to Melbourne to produce black-and-white illustrations for the *Illustrated Australian News*. After a disagreement with the management he transferred to the rival *Australasian Sketcher*. In 1883 he went to Sydney, where he joined the staff of the *Picturesque Atlas of Australia* and also contributed to the Sydney *Bulletin*. Ashton was an ardent disciple of Impressionist painting and claimed to have executed the first *plein-air* landscape in Australia: *Evening, Merri Creek* (1882; Sydney, A.G. NSW). Much of his work, as in the watercolour *A Solitary Ramble* (1888; Sydney, A.G. NSW), had a strong sentimental streak. In addition to his outdoor works Ashton painted a number of portraits, such as that of *Helen Ashton* (*c.* 1890; Canberra, N.G.). After teaching at the Art Society of New South Wales School from 1892 to 1896, he founded the Sydney Art School in 1896 (since 1975: Sydney College of the Arts). It became a centre of activity for aspiring young Australian artists and among its alumni were George W. Lambert, Sydney Long, William Dobell and John Passmore. In Sydney, Ashton attracted a circle of artist-disciples that included Charles Conder,

Alfred James Daplyn (1844–1926) and Albert Henry Fullwood (1863–1930), and he often worked with them in the scenic Hawkesbury River area. He continued to produce Impressionist-style portraits and landscapes throughout his life and influenced ideas of national patronage for Australian art. He encouraged government purchases and in 1913 lobbied for the foundation of the Education Department Gallery in Sydney.

WRITINGS

Now Came Still Evening On (Sydney, 1941) [autobiography]

BIBLIOGRAPHY

Genesis of a Gallery, Part 2 (exh. cat., intro. J. Mollison; Canberra, N.G., 1978), pp. 60–61

A. McCulloch: *Encyclopedia of Australian Art* (Melbourne, Sydney and London, 1984), vol. 1, pp. 49–50

□

Ashur. *See* ASSUR.

Asia, Central. *See* CENTRAL ASIA.

Asine [now Kastraki]. Coastal site in the north-eastern Peloponnese in southern Greece, 8 km south-east of Navplion. Centred around an easily defended rocky promontory (acropolis), the settlement is remarkable for its long, almost uninterrupted history of habitation, from at least *c.* 4000 BC to *c.* AD 400. It flourished during the Bronze Age (*c.* 4000–*c.* 1050 BC) and in the Geometric and Hellenistic periods (*c.* 900–*c.* 725 BC and 336–27 BC). First mentioned in the Homeric epic *The Iliad* (II.560; Catalogue of Ships), it was identified in modern times by E. Curtius in 1852 and excavated by Swedish expeditions in 1922–30 and 1970–90. The finds are in the Navplion Archaeological Museum, among them a terracotta head of less than life-size from the 12th century BC, known as the Lord (or Lady) of Asine (*see* HELLADIC, §V, 2(i)).

On the north-west slope of the acropolis there was an almost continuous habitation: especially remarkable are an apsidal house of the Early Helladic period (*c.* 3600/3000–*c.* 2050 BC), rectangular buildings of the Middle Helladic period (*c.* 2050–*c.* 1600 BC) (interspersed with graves) and a building complex with a cultic function of the 12th century BC (the terracotta head was found here in a room with two columns along the main axis and a cult bench in its north-east corner). The Late Geometric/Archaic (8th–6th centuries BC) Temple of Apollo on the Barbouna Hill has yielded few remains. In Hellenistic times the acropolis and the lower city were surrounded by a fortification wall with square towers in fine masonry. A small Roman bath (*c.* AD 400) is the latest impressive structure on the site.

BIBLIOGRAPHY

A. W. Persson, O. Frödin and A. Westholm: *Asine: Results of the Swedish Excavations, 1922–1930* (Stockholm, 1938)

Excavations in the Barbouna Area at Asine, ed. I. Hägg and R. Hägg (Uppsala, 1973–)

Asine II: Results of the Excavations East of the Acropolis, 1970–1974 (Stockholm, 1976–)

ROBIN HÄGG

Asinou [Gr. Panagia Phorbiotissa: 'Our Lady of the Pastures']. Byzantine church in Cyprus, situated on the west side of the island, 4 km south-west of the village of Vizakia. The church was originally part of the monastery of the Phorbia (destr.), and a marginal note in a synaxarion copied in Cyprus or Palestine in 1063 indicates that the manuscript once belonged to this monastery. The church is renowned for its well-preserved cycles of wall paintings and painted inscriptions, two of which attribute the foundation and decoration of the church to Nicephoros Ischyrios, the Magistros, in 1105–6. A third, damaged inscription mentions a certain 'Theophilos' and 'the people', who were probably responsible for a programme of redecoration in 1332–3. The wall paintings were cleaned and restored in 1965–8 by Ernest Hawkins and David Winfield under the auspices of the Center for Byzantine Studies at Dumbarton Oaks, Washington, DC.

The church is a single-aisle structure with a semicircular apse and barrel-vaulted nave supported by transverse ribs and engaged piers, forming three blind niches in the north and south walls. In plan it resembles the parekklesion of the Cypriot monastery of St John Chrysosthomos, but it does not have a dome. Although the original walls were of stone mortared with mud, probably in the late 12th century, yellow sandstone of better quality was used for the construction of a domed narthex with north and south absidioles; this arrangement is found elsewhere in Cyprus, at the monasteries of St John Chrysosthomos, and the Panagia Apsinthiotissa. The church was later given a secondary steeply pitched wooden roof of a type common among the Cypriot mountain churches.

In the naos the original paintings of 1105–06 reflect the 'sensitive linearism' (Megaw) of the best Comnenian painting of the time. They depict scenes from the *Life of Christ* and the *Virgin*, a host of saints and Church Fathers. The fine equestrian portrait of *St George* in the narthex may be dated to the late 12th century. An accompanying inscription identifies the donor as Nicephoros, a tamer of horses, and mentions the monastery of the Phorbia. The depictions of the *Virgin Pantanassa* and the *Sacrifice of Isaac* in the main apse and those of *St Anastasia* (the 'Poison Curer') and the *Virgin and Child* between Western donors in the narthex may be dated between 1200 and 1300. The other paintings in the narthex, including a striking *Last Judgement*, the *Virgin Phorbiotissa* and numerous saints and donors, belong to the redecoration of 1332–3. A contemporary, or slightly later, series in the naos is thought to reproduce faithfully the original 12th-century paintings of the *Life of Christ* and a portrait of *Nicephoros* presenting a model of the church to Christ and the Virgin.

See also EARLY CHRISTIAN AND BYZANTINE ART, §III, 4.

BIBLIOGRAPHY

Bishop of Gibraltar and others: 'The Church of Asinou, Cyprus and its Frescoes', *Archaeologia*, lxxxiii (1933), pp. 327–50

J. Darrouzès: 'Notes pour servir à l'histoire de Chypre', *Rev. Etud. Byz.*, xv (1957), pp. 85–6, 92–6

M. Sacopoulo: *Asinou en 1106 et sa contribution à l'iconographie* (Brussels, 1966)

D. Winfield and E. J. W. Hawkins: 'The Church of Our Lady at Asinou, Cyprus: A Report on the Seasons of 1965 and 1966', *Dumbarton Oaks Pap.*, 21 (1967), pp. 260–66

D. Winfield: *Asinou: A Guide* (Nicosia, 1969)

A. H. S. Megaw: 'Byzantine Architecture and Decoration in Cyprus: Metropolitan or Provincial?', *Dumbarton Oaks Pap.*, 28 (1974), pp. 85–6

F. Drossoyianni: 'Some Observations on the Asinou Frescoes', *Kleronomias*, x (1978), pp. 53–77

S. H. Young: *Byzantine Painting in Cyprus during the Early Lusignan Period* (diss., University Park, PA State U., 1983), pp. 321–81
A. Stylianou and J. Stylianou: *The Painted Churches of Cyprus: Treasures of Byzantine Art* (London, 1985), pp. 114–40

SUSAN YOUNG

Asís Cambó y Batlle, Francisco de. *See* CAMBÓ Y BATLLE, FRANCISCO DE ASÍS.

Askhabad. *See* ASHKHABAD.

Asklepiades (*fl c.* 100 BC). Mosaicist from Arados, Phoenicia. The fragmentary inscription...*piades Aradios epoiei* (Gr.: '...piades of Arados made') is set in two lines of black tesserae on the white ground of a tessellated floor still *in situ* in the House of the Dolphins on the island of Delos (see Bruneau, fig. 210). The beginning of the name is lost, but 'Asklepiades' is the most probable. The square floor, which occupies the central court, can be dated to *c.* 100 BC. It has an outer border of black crenellation and within that a series of pattern bands in concentric circles surrounds a rosette, each corner being occupied by an Eros riding a dolphin and leading a second on the rein. Most of the floor is worked in *opus tessellatum*, but these corner groups are in *opus vermiculatum* (using very fine tesserae). The inscription lies between two of the pattern circles. One of these has horned heads, alternately characterized as griffins and lions, that grow out of arcs of ornament. Animal ornament is rare in Greek art, but there is a close parallel on an Orientalizing vase of the 7th century BC from Crete (Herakleion, Archaeol. Mus.). Another floor in the house has the ankh-shaped symbol of the Punic goddess Tanit, suggesting that the owner was perhaps also from the Arados area, but Asklepiades' style is purely Greek. The circle in square composition (generally rare in Greek art) is unique here in developed tesserae mosaic but is found regularly in pebble and transitional floors from their beginning, *c.* 400 BC, to the late 3rd century BC.

See also GREECE, ANCIENT, §VII, 1(iii), and DELOS, §3.

BIBLIOGRAPHY

P. Bruneau: *Les Mosaïques* (1972), xxix of Explor. Archéol. Délos (Paris, 1909–), pp. 111–17, 235–9, figs 170–75, 210

MARTIN ROBERTSON

Asklepios, Sanctuary of. *See under* EPIDAUROS.

Askos. Ancient pottery form, used to contain oil (*see* HELLADIC, fig. 6c).

□

Asmar, Tell. *See under* DIYALA REGION.

Asmus, Dieter. *See under* ZEBRA.

Asmussen, Erik (*b* Copenhagen, 2 Nov 1913). Danish architect, active in Sweden. He did not complete his studies at the Kongelige Danske Kunstakademi in Copenhagen and moved to Sweden in 1939. His architectural training was mainly practical, therefore, first in the office of Ahrbom & Zimdahl and then, for almost two decades, with Nils Tesch (1907–74). In 1960 he established his own practice, which he moved to Järna in 1976. He is best-known as a representative of modern anthroposophic architecture. The Kristoffer School (1965–71) in Bromma, Stockholm, shows clearly the connections with the Expressionist, organic architectural principles derived from the philosophy of Rudolf Steiner. The central building of this school, with auditorium, eurythmics halls and classrooms, is a pale, rough-cast concrete volume; it is surrounded by smaller detached wooden pavilions in varying colours. The Rudolf Steiner School at Järna (begun 1968) is a complete environment with school buildings, students' homes, workshops, cultural facilities and a clinic. Close to this is a market garden and a flour mill and bakery. All these buildings are composed of highly sculptural volumes with irregular, softly modelled interiors, in a colour scheme based on Goethe's principles, each facility in its own hue. The predominant exterior colour is blue, applied in a semi-transparent painting technique that was developed in collaboration with the artist Arne Klingborg, the head of the school. The concrete and timber frames are clad mainly in wood. In his work he combined expressive, organic forms with simplicity and economy of detail, underlining the qualities of the materials used. Furniture, textiles and other fittings are also an integral part of the design.

WRITINGS

'Robygge jarna', *Arkitektur Dk*, lxxx/10 (1980), pp. 20–23 [Eng. summary, p. 36]

BIBLIOGRAPHY

Arkitektur Dk, lxxxiv/6 (1984) [issue devoted to Asmussen]

□

Asnova [Assotsiatsiya Novykh Arkhitektorov; Rus.: Association of New Architects]. Russian architectural group active in Moscow from 1923 to 1932. It was founded by NIKOLAY LADOVSKY, VLADIMIR KRINSKY and NIKOLAY DOKUCHAYEV and was the USSR's first avant-garde architectural association. Asnova intended to serve the new Soviet regime by establishing an architectural language based on economic and psychological efficiency. This Rationalist approach also attempted to secure an irrefutable, scientific foundation for the aesthetics of modern architecture.

Ladovsky, Dokuchayev and Krinsky had already associated in Zhivskulptarkh (Paintsculptarch; 1919–20), Obmas (United studios; 1920–23) and the 'First Working Group of Architects' in Inkhuk (Institute of Artistic Culture; 1921–3). Vasily Kandinsky, Kazimir Malevich and El Lissitzky, among others, contributed to these multidisciplinary groups, and their insights clarified the theoretical enquiries subsequently investigated by Asnova. From the early 1920s until its dissolution, Ladovsky, Dokuchayev and Krinsky taught at the Vkhutemas (Higher (state) artistic and technical workshops), Moscow. This academic context helped the trio to focus their ideas, create a coherent agenda and outline a methodological approach to architectural design. They restructured the curriculum of the 'Basic Division' (foundation course) to reflect Ladovsky's 'psycho-analytical' method and applied it in the studios and workshops devoted to three-dimensional arts. By setting the tone and the rationale of the obligatory introductory courses, the members of Asnova helped to catalyse the Vkhutemas's creative energies. There was also an attempt in 1926 to found a journal, *Izvestiya ASNOVA*, but only one issue was produced.

Asnova polemically opposed the Constructivist position of OSA, the competing wing of the Soviet architectural avant-garde during the 1920s. While the Constructivists argued that a building's programme, function and technical considerations sufficed to determine its architectural design, the members of Asnova encouraged designers to clarify architectural form for the public's mental, perceptual and psychological comfort, which was held to depend on the merging of a building's visual and conceptual realities. The architect was thus obliged to maximize optical stimuli, through the use of volume and structure, in order to minimize the discrepancies between perceived form and actual form. These ideas were reflected in such buildings as Krinsky's Vesenkha skyscraper (1922–3), Lubyanka Square, Moscow, and in such projects as Ladovsky's competition entry (1929) for the monument to *Christopher Columbus* in Santo Domingo, Dominican Republic. Functioning as a loose association of broadly like-minded architects, Asnova's fluid membership also included Konstantin Mel'nikov and El Lissitzky, some of whose designs reveal clear debts to Asnova precepts, for example the projects for the Lenin Podium (1924) and the Wolkenbügel (1924), Moscow, by El Lissitzky, and the Soviet pavilion at the Exposition Internationale des Arts Décoratifs et Industriels Modernes, Paris (1925), and Rusakov Club (1927), Moscow, by Mel'nikov.

WRITINGS

Izvestiya ASNOVA, i (1926)

Arkhitektura VKHUTEMAS: Raboty arkhitekturnogo fakulteta VKHUTEMASa, 1920–1927 [Architecture in the Vkhutemas: the work of the Architecture Department in the Vkhutemas, 1920–1927] (Moscow, 1927)

El Lissitzky: *Russland: Die Rekonstruktion der Architektur in der Sowjetunion* (Vienna, 1930; Eng. trans., 1970)

V. Krinsky: 'Voznikoveniye i zhizn' Assotsiatsii Novykh Arkhitektorov—ASNOVA [Emergence and life of the Association of New Architects—ASNOVA], *Sov. Arkhit.*, 18 (1969), pp. 20–28

V. Ye. Khazanova: *Iz istorii sovetskoy arkhitektury, 1926–1932: Dokumenty i materialy* [From the history of Soviet architecture, 1926–1932: documents and materials] (Moscow, 1970)

BIBLIOGRAPHY

A. Kopp: *Town and Revolution: Soviet Architecture and City Planning, 1917–1935* (New York, 1970)

M. Bliznakov: 'The Rationalist Movement in Soviet Architecture of the 1920s', *Russian Formalism*, ed. S. Bann and J. E. Bowlt (Edinburgh, 1973), pp. 147–61

S. O. Chan-Magomedov: 'Nikolaj Ladovskij—An Ideology of Rationalism', *Lotus Int.*, xx (1978), pp. 104–26

A. Senkevitch: 'Aspects of Spatial Form and Perceptual Psychology in the Doctrine of the Rationalist Movement in Soviet Architecture in the 1920s', *VIA*, vi (1983), pp. 78–115

S. O. Chan-Magomedov: *Pioniere der sowjetischen Architektur* (Dresden, 1983); Eng. trans. as S. O. Khan-Magomedov: *Pioneers of Soviet Architecture* (London, 1987)

K. PAUL ZYGAS

Asociación Arte Concreto Invención. Argentine group formed in November 1945 by Tomás Maldonado and other Constructivist artists and active until *c.* 1964. Its other original members were Lidy Prati (*b* 1921), Alfredo Hlito, Manuel Espinosa, Raúl Lozza (*b* 1911), Alberto Molenberg (*b* 1921), Ennio Iommi, Claudio Girola (*b* 1923), Jorge Souza (*b* 1919), Primaldo Mónaco (*b* 1921), Oscar Núñez (*b* 1919), Antonio Caraduje (*b* 1920) and the poet Edgar Bayley (*b* 1919). Maldonado and Prati were prominent among the artists involved in the publication of the single issue of the magazine *Arturo* in early 1944, in which the image-invention was proposed as an alternative to representational, naturalistic or symbolic imagery, but they did not take part in two exhibitions of associated artists in 1945 that led to the establishment of ARTE MADÍ. In fact their central role in setting up the Asociación Arte Concreto Invención was a way of declaring their independence from the other group.

The first exhibition of the Asociación opened on 18 March 1946. It was accompanied by the publication of the *Manifiesto invencionista*, which affirmed the values of concrete art over figurative art and stressed the importance of a social role for art. Works exhibited by group members later that year, together with the theories espoused by them in two issues of their magazine (the first, *Revista Arte concreto invención*, published in August 1946 and the second, *Boletín de la Asociación arte concreto invención*, following in December 1946), were concerned largely with investigating the shaped canvas in a variety of ways that anticipated the work of American painters in the 1960s. After exploring with great inventiveness the relationship between the painted surface and its shape or supporting wall, they concluded that these formal concerns were too limiting and returned to more conventional rectangular formats, leaving it to painters associated with Arte Madí and PERCEPTISMO to continue with these experiments. While the painters concerned themselves with clear and harmonious structures of form and colour, the group's sculptors used new materials in constructions that replaced solid mass with transparencies and intersecting planes. From 1952 to 1954 Maldonado and other members of the group banded together with four independent painters working in a semi-abstract style as ARTISTAS MODERNOS DE LA ARGENTINA. Although group members gradually went their own way, their common aesthetic remained influential not only on painting and sculpture but also on theories of architecture and design.

BIBLIOGRAPHY

N. Perazzo: *El arte concreto en la Argentina* (Buenos Aires, 1983), pp. 87–108

NELLY PERAZZO

Aspden, David (*b* Bolton, Lancs, 1 May 1935). Australian painter of English birth. He emigrated to Australia in 1950, settling in the coal and steel town Wollongong, where he worked as a painter and signwriter for 12 years, despite having no formal tuition. In 1964 he moved to Sydney and in 1965 exhibited simple colour studies inspired by the work of Washington Color Painters Kenneth Noland and Morris Louis, seen in both travelling exhibitions of American art and art magazine reproduction. Many young Australian artists adopted such mentors: they were interpreted, initially, through the framework of English perceptions of these artists, yet were soon seen more directly and adapted to local needs.

In 1969 Aspden broke with the stripes, circles, bands and grids ubiquitous in 1960s art, favouring 'torn' shapes of single colours, intensely hued and set against each other in flowing patchwork or in flashing horizontal runs across the canvas. In size, scale and surety, these paintings rivalled American work of the time. Their emphatically warm colours and vitality conveyed something of the energetic spirit of Sydney and of the eastern coastline of Australia.

They reached a climax in the *Brazil* series, which won a gold medal at the São Paulo Bienal of 1971. In the 1980s he began to apply slab-like strokes of earthy hues to a canvas, whose composition was divided into horizontal and vertical units; the scale and compositions of these works, for example *Big Red* (1980; Sydney, Rudy Komon A.G.), echoed the abstract symbolic narratives of tribal Aboriginal art, which interested Aspden at this time.

BIBLIOGRAPHY

T. Smith: 'The Painting of David Aspden', *A. Int.*, xiv/8 (1970), pp. 50–53, 79

N. Hutchinson: 'The Dynamiting of the Picture—David Aspden's Paintings', *A. & Australia*, ix (1971), pp. 224–33

David Aspden: Paintings, 1971–1975 (exh. cat., intro. P. McCaughey; Clayton, Victoria, Monash U. Exh. Gal., 1976)

TERRY SMITH

Aspendos [now Bilkis]. Site in southern Turkey of a Greek and Roman city that flourished *c.* 100 BC–AD 300. It is eight miles from the mouth of the River Köprüçay (anc. Eurymedon) in the region once known as Pamphylia. It was a Greek colony that claimed to have been founded by Argos, but was incorporated with all Pamphylia into the Lydian empire of Croesus (*c.* 560 BC), and was then lost by Croesus to Cyrus of Persia in 546 BC. Despite the Athenian general Kimon's double victory over the Persians at the mouth of the Eurymedon (*c.* 468 BC), and its subsequent membership of the Athenian-dominated Delian League, Aspendos remained voluntarily under Persian control until taken by Alexander the Great (334/333 BC). Thereafter it changed hands several times, being held successively by Antigonos, the Ptolemies and the Seleucids until it was ceded to Rome in 188 BC. Most of Pamphylia, with Lycia, was annexed into the new Roman province of Asia in 133 BC, but in 102 BC it became part of the province of Cilicia. Despite these and other changes, Aspendos prospered under the Roman peace, not least because the Eurymedon was navigable as far as the city; its principal monuments date from this period. The city was surveyed by Niemann and Petersen in the 1880s.

The flat-topped acropolis, which rises steeply to a height of some 30 m above the plain, consists of a main plateau and a small hill of similar height at its south-eastern corner. Recessed into the eastern flank of this hill stands the most completely preserved of all Roman theatres (late 2nd century AD; see fig.), built, according to an inscription at its south entrance, by Curtius Crispinus and Curtius Auspicatus in honour of the local gods and the family of Antoninus Pius (*reg* AD 138–61). Its remarkable state of preservation is partly due to its conversion into a palace by the Saljuq Turks (13th century). The *cavea* (auditorium), which could seat 7500 people, is divided into two levels, the lower with nine *cunei* ('wedges' of seats), the upper with twenty, surmounted by an arcaded gallery. The stage itself is lost, but the front wall of the stage-building (*scaenae frons*; 110×25 m) still bears much of its decorative detail and gives a clear impression of its architectural treatment. The 40 marble columns and corresponding pilasters, the projecting entablatures and pediments, and the statuary are almost all missing; only the central pediment above the Porta Regia survives, with a sculpted panel depicting *Dionysus*. The theatre was restored in the late 20th century.

Aspendos, *scaenae frons* of the theatre, late 2nd century AD

The remains on the main plateau of the acropolis date from the 2nd and 3rd centuries AD and include an exceptionally long Byzantine basilica, an agora with shops and an odeion (possibly the bouleuterion), although none has been fully excavated. A ruined nymphaeum (late 2nd century AD) marks the end of an aqueduct that brought in water from the mountains *c.* 1 km to the north. An inscription records that it was given to the city by Tiberius Claudius Italicus. Although comparatively short in length, the aqueduct was an impressive feat of hydraulic engineering. The main part is 15 m high and constituted the *venter* ('belly') of an inverted siphon (*see* ROME, ANCIENT, §III, 3). At each end a tower (h. 30 m) maintained sufficient head to raise the water to the acropolis. The water was conveyed under pressure through limestone pipes 860 mm long, with 280-mm bores.

BIBLIOGRAPHY

K. Lanckoroński, G. Niemann and E. Petersen: *Städte Pamphyliens und Pisidiens*, 2 vols (Vienna, 1890–92)

J. B. Ward-Perkins: 'The Aqueduct at Aspendos', *Pap. Brit. Sch. Rome*, xxiii (1955), pp. 115–23

G. E. Bean: *Turkey's Southern Shore* (London, 1968, 2/1979)

IAIN BROWNING

Asper, Hans (*b* Zurich, *c.* 1499; *d* Zurich, 21 March 1571). Swiss painter and draughtsman. He may have been the son of Heinrich Asper, from an old family of Zurich councillors. As there is no surviving evidence relating to his life until 1526, and no sign of his artistic activity until 1531, when it suddenly appears fully developed, it has been suggested that he was originally active in another profession. There is a plausible case (Wüthrich) for identifying him with Hans von Zürich, a member of a Zurich goldsmith family depicted in a portrait by Hans Holbein (ii) (1532; untraced) and in an etching by Wenceslaus Hollar (1647). According to this theory, Hans Asper was active in Basle following another profession but was inspired by Holbein to turn to portraiture. In 1526 he married the daughter of the master carpenter and Zurich councillor Ludwig Nöggi. Their 11 children included the painters Hans Rudolf Asper (*b* 1531) and Rudolf Asper (1552–1611). Hans Konrad Asper (*c.* 1588–?1666), son of Hans Rudolf, was an architect and sculptor in Vienna, Konstanz, Salzburg and Munich. Hans Asper was highly regarded in Zurich—in 1545 he was elected to the Great Council—but despite his unremitting industry as an artist, he was never able to derive an adequate income from his work.

Of Asper's work between 1531 and 1568 about 30 portraits, some heraldic panel paintings and murals, and woodcuts for book illustrations following his drawings have survived. His early portraits included those of the married couples *Rahn* and *Holzhalb* (1536, 1538) and that of *Hans Ulrich Stampfer I* (1540; all Zurich, Ksthaus). It was probably in reciprocation for the latter that Hans Ulrich's son Hans Jakob Stampfer produced a portrait medallion of Asper in 1540. In 1531–2 Asper executed a posthumous but probably authentic portrait (Winterthur, Kstmus.) of *Huldrych Zwingli* (1484–1531), the Zurich Reformer, but better known is that of 1549–50 (over 100 copies), with an accompanying double portrait of the Reformer's daughter and granddaughter, *Regula and Anna Gwalther-Zwingli* (Zurich, Zentbib.). He also produced two portraits of the early 16th-century Basle reformer Johannes Hüssgen or Hausschein, known as *Oecolampadius* (Basle, Kstmus.; priv. col.), and one of *Wilhelm Frölich* (1549; Zurich, Schweiz. Landesmus.), one of the first full-figure portraits in Swiss painting. His final surviving work is the three-piece '*Standestafel*' or picture of the social ranks (1567; Zurich, Rathaus), which he presented to the council of Zurich and which earned him a life annuity paid by the council for the support of his family.

Asper's style of painting is dry, almost brittle, and indebted to Late Gothic portraiture. Consequently he did not progress beyond a regionally limited mediocrity, although in his lifetime he was the most important representative of Zurich painting and was later mentioned by Joachim von Sandrart. His portraits are of special value as documents of the burgher's self-image and of the Reformation spirit in Zurich. In this light the constant monochrome, empty background to his figures should be related to the Protestant doctrine that human spirituality cannot be directly depicted. Accompanying the faithful picture of the living but transitory person, it shows the abstract but eternal image of his spirit and epitomizes the Christian's religious life.

BIBLIOGRAPHY

NDB; *SKL*; Thieme–Becker

M. Fischer and others: *Zürcher Bildnisse aus fünf Jahrhunderten* (Zurich, 1953), pp. 14–19

L. Wüthrich: *Die Zürcher Malerei im 16. Jahrhundert* (Zurich, 1981), pp. 9–14

Zürcher Kunst nach der Reformation. Hans Asper und seine Zeit (exh. cat., Zurich, Helmhaus, 1981)

MICHAEL EISSENHAUER

Asperg. *See* KLEINASPERGLE.

Aspertini, Amico (*b* Bologna, 1474–5; *d* Bologna, 19 Nov 1552). Italian painter, sculptor, illuminator and draughtsman. He was born into a family of painters, and his youthful facility reportedly astonished his contemporaries. His work developed in the Emilian-Ferrarese tradition of Ercole de' Roberti, Lorenzo Costa the elder and, above all, Francesco Francia. Until the re-evaluation by Longhi, critical assessment of Amico's oeuvre was over-reliant on literary sources, especially Vasari's unsympathetic account of an eccentric, half-insane master working so rapidly with both hands (the 'chiaro' in one, the 'scuro' in the other) that he was able to finish decorating an entire house façade in one day. Longhi presented Amico as a creative master whose expressive intensity and sensitive use of colour rescued Bolognese painting of the early 16th century from sterile echoes of Raphael. Today Aspertini is viewed as an influential precursor of Mannerism, and his highly individual study of antiquity has been brought to the fore by the publication of his sketchbooks. Amico was not a mere imitator of ancient artists, but their imaginative rival, whether in his grotesques derived from the decorations of Nero's Domus Aurea in Rome (e.g. the borders of his *Adoration of the Shepherds* in the Albani Hours, 1492–1503; London, BL, Yates Thompson MS. 29, fol. 15*v*), the pilasters for his fresco cycle (1506–8/9) in the chapel of S Agostino, Lucca, his monochrome reliefs *all'antica* (e.g. in *St Sebastian*, 1504–5; Washington, DC, N.G.A.) or in narrative works such as his major surviving fresco cycles (e.g. that of 1505–6 in the oratory of S Cecilia in S Giacomo Maggiore, Bologna, and the cycle of 1506–8/9 in S Frediano, Lucca).

There is general agreement on the main features of Amico's career, although questions remain about attributions and chronology. Most scholars accept his presence in Rome in 1500–03 and the attribution to those years of his earliest sketchbook after the Antique (Wolfegg Codex, Schloss Wolfegg, Fürstl. Samml.). Some scholars extend his service in and around Rome during the papacy of Alexander VI to activity in Bernardino Pinturicchio's workshop. Amico's return to Bologna is documented in 1504. Two signed, though undated, altarpieces, the *Adoration of the Shepherds* (Berlin, Gemäldegal.) and a *Nativity* (Bologna, Pin. N.), are generally placed at this stage of his career. Under the patronage of the Bentivoglio family, in 1505–6 he joined Costa, Francia and assistants in carrying out the fresco cycle for the newly restored oratory of S Cecilia. Universally attributed to Amico are the *Martyrdom of SS Valerian and Tiburtius* and their *Burial* (see fig.). In these frescoes Amico's calculated opposition of certain postures antedated counterpoised figures in Michelangelo's Sistine Chapel ceiling (Rome, Vatican), and elements of his colour harmony and composition anticipated Raphael's Vatican frescoes. Acknowledged influences from Perugino, however, explain the latter, while the former derives from ancient art. There are other Rome-inspired details in the *Burial*: a view of the Castel Sant'Angelo in the background and a direct quotation from painted decorations in the Domus Aurea. Amico's next major commission, the frescoes of the chapel of S Agostino in S Frediano, Lucca, includes 'historical' events, notably *St Frediano Changing the Course of the River Serchio*, based on a comparable representation on Trajan's Column in Rome. All display the value of Amico's antiquarian studies. He devoted most of the following two decades to sculpture, although he also produced paintings, including a *Pietà* (1519; Bologna, S Petronio) and the sides of the organ (1531) in S Petronio (discovered hidden beneath its Baroque enclosure and restored in the late 1970s). His work for the façade of S Petronio, documented from 1510 to 1530, includes a bust of a prophet for the main portal

Amico Aspertini: *Burial of SS Valerian and Tiburtius* (1505–6), fresco, oratory of S Cecilia, S Giacomo Maggiore, Bologna

(identified as the relief half-figure of *Moses* in the archivolt) and the *Dead Christ in the Arms of Nicodemus* in the lunette of the right portal.

Some indication of Aspertini's contemporary reputation may be gained from his selection in 1529 with another artist to decorate a triumphal arch for the entry into Bologna of Pope Clement VII and Emperor Charles V. The few surviving examples are not sufficient for appreciation of Amico's fame as a monochrome painter of architectural embellishments in which he had free rein to indulge his antiquarian lore. In the pictorial freedom and melting colour of his last works, such as the altarpiece of the *Holy Family* (Paris, St Nicolas-des-Champs), however, it is possible to comprehend Malvasia's likening of Amico to Giorgione.

BIBLIOGRAPHY

DBI; Thieme–Becker

G. Vasari; *Vite* (1550, rev. 2/1568); ed. G. Milanesi (1878–85), v, pp. 77, 179–82

C. C. Malvasia: *Felsina pittrice* (1678); ed. M. Brascaglia (1971), pp. 105–11

R. Longhi: *L'opera completa* (Florence, 1956/*R* 1975), pp. 81–5, 181–8, 238–9

P. P. Bober: *Drawings after the Antique by Amico Aspertini: Sketchbooks in the British Museum*, Stud. Warb. Inst., xxi (London, 1957)

M. Calvesi: *Gli affreschi di Santa Cecilia in Bologna* (Bologna, 1960)

P. Venturoli: 'Amico Aspertini a Gradara', *Stor. A.*, 1–4 (1969), pp. 417–32 [bibliog. on youthful works]

Ric. Stor. A., xvii (1982) [articles by G. Romano, M. Tazartes, P. Venturoli]

G. Schweikhart: *Der Codex Wolfegg: Zeichnungen nach der Antike von Amico Aspertini*, Stud. Warb. Inst., xxxviii (London, 1986)

M. Faetti: 'New Drawing by Amico Aspertini', *Master Drgs*, xxix (1991), pp. 145–72

PHYLLIS PRAY BOBER

Aspetti, Tiziano (*b* Padua, *c.* 1559; *d* Pisa, between 27 July and 3 Nov 1606). Italian sculptor. After Girolamo Campagna, he was the leading sculptor in Venice at the end of the 16th century and was particularly gifted in working bronze.

1. Life and work. 2. Critical reception.

1. LIFE AND WORK. Aspetti came from an artistic family: his grandfather Guido Minio (*fl* 1511–16), called Lazzaro, was a founder, while his uncle TIZIANO MINIO was a stuccoist and sculptor. Aspetti probably received his earliest training in the family workshop and may also have collaborated with Campagna. Doubtless through family connections, in 1577 in Venice Aspetti entered the service of Giovanni Grimani, Patriarch of Aquileia. Grimani was a distinguished patron of contemporary art, and his palazzo housed the finest and most extensive collection of antiquities outside Rome. Aspetti worked for the Patriarch for 16 years and hence, unlike any other Venetian artist of his day, began his career as a kind of court artist serving one particular patron. The Grimani were partisans of central Italian Mannerist art, and the family palazzo at S Maria Formosa in Venice contained stuccos and frescoes by Giovanni da Udine, Federico Zuccaro and Francesco Salviati. Because of its collection of antiquities, the palazzo was one of the principal sights for any 16th-century tourist; Aspetti was the house sculptor and restorer of the collection (a project in 1587 to restore ten antique sculptures is known). He thus passed his earliest career in one of the most splendid centres of Venetian private, as opposed to state, patronage, and the elegant panache of his mature works reflects something of this milieu.

(i) Reliefs and monumental statues.

(a) Veneto, before mid-1604. Aspetti's earliest works, the stolid reliefs in *pietra viva* of *St Mark* and *St Theodore* for the new Rialto Bridge (1589–90) and the gauche marble *Giant* (h. *c.* 3.2 m, without base; 1591) in what is now the entrance vestibule of the Libreria Marciana, have none of the elegance of his later work. A signed marble relief over the fireplace in the Sala dell'Anticollegio in the Doge's Palace dates to *c.* 1589; the atlantids (*c.* 1587) supporting this chimney, formerly given to Aspetti, are by Campagna. The over life-size figures of *Justice* and *Temperance* in the Grimani Chapel in S Francesco della Vigna—Aspetti's first attempts in bronze—were begun before 28 November 1592, when, in a codicil to his will, Patriarch Grimani ordered that Aspetti finish them. (Grimani also ordered that Aspetti make the statues of *Moses* and *St Paul* for the façade of the church; see below.)

Aspetti found his distinctive voice and medium in his first commission for Il Santo in Padua, two bronze reliefs that depict *St Daniel Dragged by a Horse* and the *Martyrdom of St Daniel*, delivered on 11 February 1593. (There are two sets of casts of the reliefs: one still in Padua, Mus. Dioc. A. Sacra; and one in New York, Met.) Raggio suggested that the latter originally decorated the altar of St Daniel in the crypt and that they were replaced by the casts in Padua sometime in the 19th century. In these multi-figured compositions, Aspetti manifested his profoundly pictorial talents and showed his true calling to be relief sculpture. Like his uncle, he was one of the few Venetian sculptors interested in the Florentine technique of low-relief sculpture, and the figures run from very light relief to being practically in the round. (This was entirely the artist's doing—the commission was for low relief, but the canons of Il Santo were so pleased at Aspetti's efforts that they almost doubled his pay.) In these scenes, the spatial richness is matched by a variety of emotions, poses and textures. The latter run from the brick and stone of the architectural background to armour, leather and naked flesh. The emotions range, in the *Martyrdom*, from the stolid executioner hammering nails into St Daniel's pathetic, nude body to the indifferent soldiers on the right and the rising crescendo of grief of the men on the left. Even aural effects are suggested, as in the *St Daniel Dragged by a Horse*, where, on the left, a man sounds a hunting horn adjacent to a neighing, rearing horse and barking dog. Both scenes are highly dynamic. The elongated, svelte figures with their generalized, classical facial features reveal Aspetti's knowledge both of Hellenistic art and of the contemporary Mannerist style. His love for painterly, colouristic effects is shown by the extensive stippling, engraving, tooling and other patterning all over the surface. With the exception of Alessandro Vittoria's *Annunciation*, known as the Pala Fugger (early 1580s; Chicago, IL, A. Inst.), they are the first worthy successors to Jacopo Sansovino's bronze reliefs for S Marco.

Because these reliefs were such a success, on 6 November 1593 Aspetti received a highly prestigious and lucrative commission to design a new marble altar in the chapel of

St Anthony in Il Santo and to adorn it with 11 bronze statues: three saints, *St Anthony*, *St Bonaventure* and *St Louis of Toulouse*; four Virtues, *Faith*, *Charity*, *Temperance* and *Fortitude* (or *Hope*); and four angels holding candelabra. (The *Virtues* were set in the choir in 1597 and are on the balustrade of the high altar.) This was the third and last great ensemble commissioned by Il Santo, after Donatello's high altar (completed 1450) with its bronze statues and the marble reliefs adorning the walls of the chapel of St Anthony. As has been observed, the statues of the three Franciscan saints are uncharacteristic of Aspetti, being emulations of Donatello. The half life-size *Virtues*, however, with their small heads, elongated figures and elegant draperies, sum up Aspetti's then-current figural style.

Aspetti had finished this project by 30 December 1595, when he was commissioned to make a marble *Christ* for Giovanni d'Antonio Minelli de' Bardi's holy water stoup in the front left nave, which was completed by 8 May 1599. The bronze busts of *Sebastiano Venier*, *Agostino Barbarigo* (victors at Lepanto, 1571) and *Marcantonio Bragadin* (the martyred defender of Famagusta; all Venice, Doge's Pal.) were apparently modelled and cast in the years 1596–9, as were the *St Paul* and *Moses* for S Francesco della Vigna, Venice (*in situ*). There are few finished church façades in Venice and even fewer façade sculptures (especially prior to 1600). Aspetti's *Moses* and *St Paul*, which fill the niches on the Palladian façade of S Francesco della Vigna, are among the first bronzes ever placed on a Venetian façade and also some of the finest. Their dark bronze contrasts strongly with the white marble background, and, well over life-size, with their animated poses, they project powerfully in their architectural setting. After completing these projects, Aspetti made his first known trip outside the Veneto. He is recorded in Carrara in October 1599 but had returned to Venice by 1602.

(b) Tuscany, mid-1604 and after. Aspetti left Venice forever sometime after 3 July 1604 to accompany to Pisa the great-nephew of Giovanni Grimani, Antonio Grimani, Bishop of Torcello, who had been named Papal Nuncio to Tuscany. That the Bishop was a great-nephew of Patriarch Grimani is evidence of Aspetti's lifelong ties to the family. The last two years of Aspetti's life, when he lived in Pisa in the house of Count Camillo Berzighelli, were highly productive. In this period he made two bronze crucifixes, a bronze relief of Berzighelli's second wife, *Luisa Paganelli*, eight bronze reliefs of mythological subjects, a silver *Christ at the Column with Two Flagellators* (bequeathed in Aspetti's will to Il Santo; last recorded in 1753), a marble *Hercules and Antaeus*, a marble *Adonis* and a marble *Sleeping Leda*. In his will Aspetti also mentioned several unfinished works. All of the above are untraced.

The lone surviving sculpture from Aspetti's Tuscan years is the bronze relief of the *Martyrdom of St Lawrence* commissioned by Senator Lorenzo Usimbardi (1547–1636), Berzighelli's uncle. Although throughout its history this relief has been the dossal of the altar in the Usimbardi Chapel (first to the left of the choir) in Santa Trinita,

1. Tiziano Aspetti: *Martyrdom of St Lawrence*, bronze, 1604–6 (Florence, Santa Trinità)

2. Tiziano Aspetti: *Mars*, bronze, h. 536 mm, 1590s (New York, Metropolitan Museum of Art)

Florence, a 17th-century source states that Usimbardi commissioned it 'for another place'. As the chapel is dedicated to St Peter, and Aspetti's relief is the sole subject not related to Peter in the decoration, this may be true. Since, however, Aspetti's disciple Felice Palma carried out the rest of the sculptural decoration of the chapel, it can be assumed that had he lived Aspetti would have done the work; Palma's bronze Crucifix over the altar may well reflect a design by Aspetti.

Aspetti's *Martyrdom of St Lawrence* in Santa Trìnita (see fig. 1) shows a more profound sensibility than the reliefs in Il Santo. It is less theatrical and even more pictorial; light flickers over its whole surface, which seems to vibrate dynamically. At the centre of the composition is the appropriately Counter-Reformatory steadfastness of the martyr: as he is being laid on the grill, Lawrence looks up diagonally to heaven, where angels appear to award him the martyr's palm. Aspetti's figural style and types are much more muscular and robust than in earlier work, as is especially apparent in the superbly modelled crouching figures in the front. The artist's greater mastery of the nude is also obvious. Lodovico Cigoli designed the pictorial decoration of the Usimbardi Chapel (from 1605), and, whether it was originally meant for that site or not, Aspetti's relief fits in well as an example of the early Baroque in Florence.

Aspetti added a codicil to his will on 27 July 1606 (1607 by the Pisan calendar, which is why 1607 is often given as his year of death). At his request, and Berzighelli's expense, he was buried in the cloister (now Mus. N. S Matteo) of the convent of the Carmine in Pisa, where an epitaph to him still exists, as well as a portrait bust by Felice Palma (1606). He apparently never married nor fathered any children, naming a niece as his heir in his will.

(ii) Statuettes. As with Vittoria, Campagna and Nicolò Roccatagliata, the bronze statuettes attributed to Aspetti vary widely in style and quality. No signed statuette exists; nonetheless most scholars rightly accept as by Aspetti a clothed *Mars* (New York, Met.; see fig. 2) and a nude *Mars* (New York, Frick). In terms of facial and figural type they closely resemble the *St Daniel* reliefs, and the extensive stippling and faceting on the armour and accoutrements of the clothed *Mars* also closely parallel the Padua reliefs. Silver figures of *St Peter* and *St Paul* (both Rotterdam, Mus. Boymans–van Beuningen) may well be, as suggested by Raggio, the pieces referred to by the artist in a letter of 1602 to Laura Gonzaga, Duchess of Mantua.

2. Critical reception. When Aspetti began his public career in Venice in the 1590s, Vittoria had virtually stopped working, and Campagna monopolized the major sculptural commissions. Although Aspetti beat Campagna in the competition for the altar of St Anthony in Padua, he did not have such success in Venice. Indeed, he never made a three-dimensional sculpture as powerful as Campagna's high altar (1590–93) in S Giorgio Maggiore or Vittoria's altar (*c.* 1590) in S Salvatore. As a relief artist, however, his only rivals were in Florence—Giovanni Battista Caccini and the by then aging Giambologna, and perhaps this is why he left Venice for Tuscany. He apparently flourished there, and until there is some knowledge of his untraced work (especially the eight bronze reliefs of mythological subjects) a true assessment of his stature as an artist is impossible.

BIBLIOGRAPHY

M. Benacchio: 'Vita e opere di Tiziano Aspetti', *Boll. Mus. Civ. Padova*, vi (1930), pp. 189–207; vii (1931), pp. 101–52; viii (1932), pp. 67–103; x–xi (1934–9), pp. 91–138

R. Gallo: 'Le donazioni alla Serenissima di Domenico e Giovanni Grimani', *Archv Ven.*, l–li (1952), pp. 34–77 [part of MS. in Venice, Archv Stato, Senato Terza, filza 137, 12 Sept 1594]

M. Perry: 'Cardinal Domenico Grimani's Legacy of Ancient Art to Venice', *J. Warb. & Court. Inst.*, xxxxi (1978), pp. 229–30 [part of MS. in Venice, Archv Stato, Senato Terza, filza 137, 12 Sept 1594]

O. Raggio: 'Tiziano Aspetti's Reliefs with Scenes of the *Martyrdom of St Daniel of Padua*', *Met. Mus. J.*, xvi (1981), pp. 131–46

S. Wilk: 'La decorazione cinquecentesca della cappella dell'arca di S Antonio', *Le sculture del Santo*, iv of *Fonti e studi per la storia del Santo a Padova*, ed. G. Lorenzoni (Vicenza, 1984), pp. 166–9

THOMAS MARTIN

Asplund, (Erik) Gunnar (*b* Stockholm, 22 Sept 1885; *d* Stockholm, 20 Oct 1940). Swedish architect and designer. He led the development of Swedish architecture from the classicism characteristic of the period of World War I to the Functionalism of the 1930s. His modern classical style was influential in Nordic countries, but his international reputation was founded on his Modernist work for the Stockholm Exhibition of 1930 and on his posthumous publications.

1. EDUCATION AND EARLY WORK, TO 1930. Asplund studied at the Royal Institute of Technology in Stockholm (1905–9), but he rejected the conventional continuation of training at the Academy of Arts. Instead he joined the Klara School, an alternative studio school which came into existence in 1910–11, where Ivar Tengbom, Carl Bergsten and Ragnar Östberg were among his teachers. Östberg inspired him to travel to Italy in 1913–14, and the lasting impression that Italy made on him was reinforced by the photographs he took there. He was especially interested in vernacular Italian architecture, and the interplay between buildings, landscape and light. He was also stimulated by visits to Denmark, where there was a growing interest in the architecture of the 18th century and early 19th.

Asplund's early work vacillated between classicism and a National Romanticism influenced by Östberg. A decisive success was the winning competition entry (1914–15) for the South (Woodland) Cemetery in Stockholm, on which he collaborated with his fellow student SIGURD LEWERENTZ. This project marked the beginning of each architect's association with cemetery architecture. Asplund's domestic architecture at this time showed the combined influence of Östberg and Italian vernacular architecture: for example the Villa Snellman (1917), Djursholm, near Stockholm, displays sophisticated handling of plan and elevation in which classical simplicity is combined with the irregularity characteristic of vernacular building. Inside, the ground-floor corridor is skewed, giving space for storage, and a rotunda hall in the form of an irregular polygon dominates the first floor (see fig.). A slight displacement of the windows adds interest to the garden façade, which is discreetly ornamented with classical festoons.

During World War I Asplund was active as a designer of storehouses, schools, emergency housing and tramsheds, but he also worked on such monumental projects as the competition plans for Götaplatsen and Gustav Adolfs Torg, two central squares in Göteborg (1913–17). A direct result was the rebuilding and extension of the Göteborg Law Courts. His earliest design for this project was in the National Romantic style; various adaptations moved through neo-classical idioms. The final result left the façade of the original building as it was but with a Functionalist annexe (1934–7) reflecting its colours and proportions.

Gunnar Asplund: interior of the Villa Snellman, Djursholm, near Stockholm, 1917

The design of interiors and furniture always formed an essential part of Asplund's work. A kitchen and living-room inspired by the writings of Heinrich Tessenow, which Asplund designed for the *Home Exhibition of the Swedish Society of Arts and Crafts* (1917) in Stockholm, received critical approval; as an assistant to Östberg on the Stockholm City Hall (1913–24), Asplund designed neo-classical furniture of which simplified versions were presented at the Exposition Internationale des Arts Décoratifs et Industriels Modernes, Paris (1925). His detailing often used symbolic elements, but its very elaboration lent an air of fragility in striking contrast to the massive shapes it adorned. His most important work as a designer of interiors was the Skandia Cinema (1923–4), Stockholm. Here his use of classical motifs was partly symbolic, partly in a more light-hearted spirit of pastiche. A miniature Pantheon adjoined the vestibule, with a false night sky above its oculus for pictures of film stars. In the auditorium he similarly created the illusion of night in a piazza surrounded by decorated 'buildings': the cinema's boxes and balconies. The vaulted ceiling, painted bluish-black, arched like a dark sky over dim pendant lamps (later removed). Gilt mouldings and pilasters reinforced the opulent classical effect, in part indebted to the neo-classical tradition of Gustavian theatre (*see* GUSTAVIAN STYLE) and garden architecture.

French Neo-classicism, especially as represented by the abstract, geometric designs of Louis-Jean Desprez and Claude-Nicolas Ledoux, was also an important source of inspiration for Asplund during this period. This is evident in the Lister District Law Courts (1917–21) at Sölvesborg and the Forest Chapel (1918–20) at the Woodland Cemetery, a consecrated burial chapel for smaller funerals. The chapel, built of wood on a concrete foundation, has a steeply pitched roof whose wide eaves are supported by unfluted Doric columns. The exterior walls are rendered.

The effect is immediately reminiscent of the later 18th-century garden pavilions of Denmark and Sweden, which, following contemporary French theory, were intended to recapitulate the origins of Classical Greek architecture in timber construction. The City Library (1920–28), Stockholm (*see* SWEDEN, fig. 6), is on a more monumental scale. It occupies a site on Observatory Hill, at the crossing of two main streets. After detailed study of the entire area, Asplund chose to set a detached, extremely self-contained and symmetrical building at a very slight angle to the street grid. The library's main hall, a clerestory-lit cylinder, rises out of a cubic block of reading rooms. The composition is reminiscent of Ledoux's Barrière de la Villette (1784–9) in Paris, but there are also Scandinavian references, such as the doorways, which resemble those painted on the façades of Gottlieb Bindesbøll's Thorvaldsens Museum in Copenhagen. Most of the detail and ornament, more sparse than on earlier projects, is based on Greek motifs.

2. THE STOCKHOLM EXHIBITION, 1930 AND AFTER. Asplund's designs for the Stockholm Exhibition of 1930, of which he was chief architect, represent an abrupt stylistic break with the cinema's sophisticated, symbol-laden classicism. His new approach was Constructivist, with exposed structural steel, laminated wood, glass and white surfaces of asbestos cement or plywood. A tall, open-work mast carrying neon advertising signs was the focal point for the exhibition buildings. The effect was not crude but light and airy, with a poetic spirit enhanced by colourful flags and canopies. Although these exhibition buildings marked the emergence of Modernism in Scandinavia, Asplund employed a strictly Functionalist vocabulary in only a few works, such as the Bredenberg Department Store (1933–5), Stockholm. He generally preferred to combine rational, unornamented designs with traditional materials such as brick, stone, copper and wood: an example is the State Bacteriological Laboratory outside Stockholm (1933–7).

Cemetery architecture played a major part in Asplund's work. The Oxelösund Cemetery and some refined granite mausoleums in the Stockholm Northern Cemetery belong to his classicist period of the 1920s, and his major work after the exhibition was the crematorium of the Woodland Cemetery (1935–40). This consists of a terrace of semi-underground technical facilities and, on the ground-level, the large chapel of the Holy Cross and two smaller chapels, of Faith and of Hope. A grand detached portico guards the entrance to the chapel of the Holy Cross. The façades of the chapels are reminiscent of the exhibition buildings' slabs but have marble cladding. Kviberg Crematorium outside Göteborg, and Skövde Crematorium, both completed posthumously, have a more robust character. The latter project (designed 1938), with its softly rounded limestone rubble walls and high open-work wooden roof, is a beautiful precursor of post-World War II religious architecture.

Asplund participated in architectural debate as Editor of *Arkitektur*, the Swedish architectural journal, in 1917–20, and he was Professor of Architecture at the Royal Institute of Technology in Stockholm from 1931. During his lifetime his influence on architecture outside Sweden was especially evident in the work of Alvar Aalto in Finland and the young Arne Jacobsen in Denmark. The Architecture Museum in Stockholm formerly held a nearly complete collection of Asplund's drawings, but parts are now in various American collections.

BIBLIOGRAPHY

H. Ahlberg and others: *Gunnar Asplund, arkitekt* (Stockholm, 1943; Eng. trans., Stockholm, 1950)
B. Zevi: *E. Gunnar Asplund* (Milan, 1948)
E. de Maré: *Gunnar Asplund: A Great Modern Architect* (London, 1955)
E. Nagy: *Erik Gunnar Asplund* (Budapest, 1974)
S. Wrede: *The Architecture of Erik Gunnar Asplund* (Cambridge, MA, 1980)
'Swedish Grace: Modern Classicism in Stockholm', *Int. Archit.*, i/8 (1982) [whole issue]
Nordisk Classicism/Nordic Classicism, 1910–1930 (exh. cat., ed. S. Paavilainen; Helsinki, Mus. Fin. Archit., 1982)
C. Caldenby and O. Hultin, eds: *Asplund* (Stockholm, 1985)
H. O. Andersson and F. Bedoire: *Swedish Architecture: Drawings, 1640–1970* (Stockholm, 1986)

□

Asprucci, Antonio (*b* Rome, 20 May 1723; *d* Rome, 14 Feb 1808). Italian architect. He trained first with his father, the architect Mario Asprucci *il vecchio*, and then with Nicola Salvi, for whom he later worked as an assistant, often supervising such works as the construction of S Maria in Gradi (1737), Viterbo, and the extension of the palace of the Duca di Bracciano on Piazza dei SS Apostoli in Rome. His early projects included the restoration of the monastery of S Francesca Romana in Rome and the construction of a monastic building for S Stefano in Cacco. In 1756 Asprucci was made architect to Francis, Grand Duke of Tuscany, for his Roman buildings, directing restorations at the Villa Medici from 1757 to 1762. In the same year he also became architect to Marcantonio IV Borghese, a wealthy, powerful nobleman and patron of the arts (*see* BORGHESE, (3)). He built a house at Pratica da Mare and remodelled the gallery of the Palazzo Borghese in Rome. His major undertaking for Marcantonio IV, also in Rome, was the reworking of the casino and gardens of the Villa Borghese into a Neo-classical 'display-case' for the Borghese art collection.

During the extensive remodelling of the Villa Borghese, carried out from the 1770s to the 1790s, Asprucci was both architect and administrator, directing a large group of Rome's leading artists, including such painters as Mariano Rossi and Gavin Hamilton and such sculptors as Vincenzo Pacetti, as well as stuccoists and masons. Painted and marble ornament covered the floors, walls and vaults of the casino. The decorative programme was designed to complement the sculpture and paintings assembled in each room; for example the Egyptian Room was decorated with hieroglyph panels and red and grey marble wall cladding, and housed Egyptian and Roman statues in porphyry and granite. The hall, which Asprucci believed to be his most successful design, reflected the contemporary trend for displaying Egyptian works in a separate room within a collection of antique sculpture. Current Roman taste was also manifested in the combination of Rococo and Neo-classical motifs in the decorative scheme for the casino. In the Hall of the Emperors, where antique busts of Roman emperors and Bernini's *Pluto and Persephone* were displayed, Asprucci inserted such Rococo elements as garland-bearing putti over the doors and grotesques in the vault painting into a classicizing articulation of vertical and horizontal elements. Every detail of the remodelling and reorganization of the art collection attracted Asprucci's attention, including designing the fireplaces and furniture to harmonize with the decorative programme.

Asprucci and his son Mario Asprucci (1764–1804) worked on the surrounding gardens throughout the 1780s and 1790s, dismantling the walls that divided the three sections of the villa, together with some 17th-century structures, to make way for new constructions within a large park setting. The two architects established the new garden structures as focal points within a grid pattern of avenues. The circular Temple of Diana, the oval circus of the Piazza di Siena on which they sited a chapel fronted by a porch of Doric columns, the false ruins of the Temple of Faustina and the Temple of Aesculapius, picturesquely situated on an island in a manmade lake, form a catalogue of Neo-classical garden architecture. In the Giardino del Lago around the Temple of Aesculapius, the Asprucci created the first example of the 'English' landscape garden in Rome. The Villa Borghese was Asprucci's most important work, and the decorative campaign, combining latent Rococo motifs with elegant Neo-classical ornamentation, was the most extensive and significant of the late 18th century in Rome. In 1790 Asprucci remodelled the seat of the Accademia di S Luca in Rome, of which he became president (1790–92), and in 1792 he designed the high altar of S Salvatore in Lauro. He served the government of Rome as Sotto Maestro delle Strade for the Trevi area (1795) and the Campo Marzio region (1796).

BIBLIOGRAPHY

G. Guattani: *Memorie enciclopediche romane sulle belle arti, antichità*, iv (Rome, 1809), pp. 86–9

L. Ferrara: 'La stanza di Elena e Paride nella Galleria Borghese', *Riv. Ist. N. Archeol. & Stor. A.*, n. s., iii (1954), pp. 242–56

E. Lavagnino: *L'arte moderna dai neoclassici ai contemporanei*, i (Turin, 1961), pp. 54–6

P. Della Pergola: *Villa Borghese* (Rome, 1962)

P. Arizzoli-Clémentel: 'Charles Percier et la salle égyptienne de la Villa Borghèse', *Piranèse et les Français*, ed. G. Brunel (Rome, 1978), pp. 1–24

B. di Gaddo: *Villa Borghese: Il giardino e la architettura* (Rome, 1985), pp. 111–52

A. Gonzáles-Palacios: 'Two Rediscovered Commodes from the Villa Borghese', *Apollo*, cxxvi (1987), pp. 105–9

A. Anselmi: 'Antonio Asprucci', *In urbe architectus: Modelli, disegni, misure, la professione dell'architetto, Roma, 1680–1750*, eds B. Contardi and G. Curcio (Rome, 1991), pp. 316–17

CHRISTINE CHALLINGSWORTH

Aspruck [Asbrugg], **Franz** [Franciscus] (*b* Brussels, ?*c*. 1570–80). Flemish goldsmith, draughtsman, sculptor, copper engraver and embosser. As a skilled goldsmith from Brussels, he is documented at Augsburg between 1598 and 1604, and from 1603 as a tax-paying citizen; before this he was probably living in Friedberg near by. After he is recorded as paying taxes three years in advance, traces of Aspruck fade away in 1604. Since he was not accepted as a master craftsman by the Augsburg goldsmiths' trade, he worked with them as a 'free artist'. His skills included draughtsmanship, modelling and casting as well as copper engraving, which he also taught to goldsmith apprentices and journeymen. Aspruck's drawings from 1597 to 1601 show an individual style influenced by Hendrick Goltzius and Bartholomäus Spranger, for example *Venus and Amor* (1598; Hamburg, Ksthalle). He also sketched for other engravers, as is known, first of all, from the surviving publishing production of the Antwerp engraver Dominicus Custos in Augsburg. In 1601 he used a new variation of engraving, furthering the art of mezzotint. A commission for Archduke Matthias in 1603 testifies to Aspruck's artistic significance in producing small-scale sculptures, of which a few survive (in bronze or wax) or are documented in silver.

BIBLIOGRAPHY

Meissner

A. Haemmerle: 'Franciscus Aspruck', *Schwäb. Mus.*, i (1925), pp. 46–55, figs 1, 3 and 4

MARION HAGENMANN

Assche, Auguste van. *See* VAN ASSCHE, AUGUSTE.

Assche, Henri [Henry] **van** (*b* Brussels, 30 Aug 1774; *d* Brussels, 11 April 1841). Flemish painter. He was taught by his father, an amateur painter, and then by Jean-Baptiste de Roy (1759–1839). He painted his first pictures in the countryside around Brussels (e.g. *View of Watermael*, 1806; untraced) and exhibited at the Ghent Salon from 1804. He painted the first of many landscapes of the Ardennes in 1808, and his subject-matter rarely strayed from this familiar ground. He was principally attracted to picturesque and hilly countryside and was keen to capture nature at its most forceful; he sought in particular settings that were in some way unusual, such as streams, mountains and closely observed rock formations (e.g. *River in the Ardennes*, 1821; Amsterdam, Rijksmus.). His concern for objectivity sometimes led to an emphasis on mere description of his subject at the expense of conveying its further evocative or symbolic value. In 1811 van Assche exhibited an Italian view, *Landscape near Tivoli* (untraced), in which he acknowledged contemporary Neo-classical taste. He did not visit Italy until 1815, however, and chose to remain in the north where the mountain scenery appealed to his Romantic sensibility. This two-year journey also included Switzerland, Germany and the Low Countries, and the work he showed on his return at various Salons across the country was well-received. Much of his later life was taken up with teaching responsibilities and, after 1823, the administration of the Musée de Bruxelles alongside François-Joseph Navez and Joseph-Denis Odevaere. He also continued to paint landscapes based on drawings from his travels, primarily of waterfalls (e.g. *Waterfall at la Toccia*, 1836; Brussels, Mus. A. Anc.).

BIBLIOGRAPHY

Thieme–Becker

1770–1830: Autour du néo-classicisme en Belgique (exh. cat. by D. Coekelberghs and others, Brussels, Mus. Ixelles, 1985–6), pp. 306–7

DOMINIQUE VAUTIER

Asse, (Louis-)Auguste (*b* Paris, 19 Nov 1799; *d* 1869). French colourman, stationer, dealer and collector. During the 1830s in Paris he was one of a small number of dealers in artists' supplies who turned to dealing in pictures as a side-line. He was also a stationer, and this brought him into contact with a number of young writers, including Alphonse de Lamartine, and Balzac, of whose talent he was an early admirer. At first Asse began to buy paintings for private enjoyment. In 1845 he moved premises from the Rue de Bellechasse to the Rue du Bac. His picture gallery there, decorated in the Renaissance Revival style popular in the reign of Louis-Philippe, was separated from the shop by an anteroom hung with green wool damask and displaying a painting of the *Virgin* by Pierre Mignard I. His tastes may have predisposed him to collecting paintings dealing with literary themes, a genre he admired. He bought Franz Xaver Winterhalter's first successful Salon painting, *Il dolce farniente* (1835; sold London, Christie's, 17 June 1994, lot 87), and would have bought Jean-Léon Gérôme's *The Cockfight* (1846; Paris, Louvre) after the Salon of 1847 had he not been too late in his bid. However, he was successful in purchasing Charles Gleyre's *Evening*, or *Lost Illusions* (Paris, Louvre; for illustration *see* GLEYRE, CHARLES), the success of the 1843 Salon, although he later sold it to the State for the collection of the Musée du Luxembourg. At times he was obliged to sell off parts of his stock, for the most part small pictures he kept for hire, as was then the practice. Among these were works by S. W. Reynolds, Charles Renoux (1795–1846) and Alexandre Evariste Fragonard and genre subjects by Asse's friend Paul-Emile Destouches (1794–1874)—all the stock-in-trade of the small-scale dealer. On his death, his collection passed to his son Eugène Asse (*b* Paris, 25 March 1830; *d* Paris, 1 Feb 1901), who left the residue, together with his father's books, to the Bibliothèque Municipale, Versailles.

BIBLIOGRAPHY

Catalogue de tableaux et dessins de l'école moderne pour vente et location . . . Galerie de Asse, rue de Belle-Chasse 14 (sale cat., Paris, Gal. Asse, 1836)
E. Asse: *Souvenirs et portraits de famille* (Paris, 1902)

LINDA WHITELEY

Asselijn [Asselein; Asselin; Asselyn], **Jan** [Janus; Jean] (*b* Dieppe, after 1610; *d* Amsterdam, 1652). Dutch painter and draughtsman, of French descent. With Jan Both and Jan Baptist Weenix, he was one of the most important artists of the second generation of DUTCH ITALIANATES. The Asselin family moved from Dieppe to Amsterdam *c.* 1621 and adopted the Dutch spelling of their surname after 1650. Of Jan's three brothers, Abraham Asselijn (1609–97) became a goldwire-maker. In Amsterdam Jan studied with Jan Martszen the younger (*c.* 1609–after 1647), Esaias van de Velde's nephew and follower, a specialist in depicting battle scenes with cavalry. Asselijn's early works, such as *Battle Scene* (1634; Brunswick, Herzog Anton Ulrich-Mus., see Steland-Stief, 1971, pl. VIII), show this influence.

Shortly after November 1635 Asselijn travelled, probably via France, to Rome, where he became a member of the SCHILDERSBENT, the association of northern artists in Rome (a counterproof of his drawing of some of the members, the *Bentvueghels*, is in Berlin, Kupferstichkab.). According to Houbraken, his bent-name was 'Krabbetje' (Little Crab) on account of his crippled left hand. He was in Rome for about seven years, where his principal influences up to *c.* 1641 were the paintings of Pieter van Laer, Jan Both and Andries Both. He drew and painted copies and variants of their compositions, depicting everyday life in Rome, either outdoors or in rocky grottoes. He went on to select his own subject-matter, chiefly landscapes with ruins, herdsmen and animals, broad panoramas, river views with bridges and quays, and picturesque seaports. Coarsely realistic figures, whose prototypes occur in his earlier cavalry scenes, animate these landscapes; whereas initially they are small and wildly gesticulating, later, better modelling gives them a degree of authority. His sensitive evocation of idyllic southern sunlight, as in *Landscape with the Ruins of an Aqueduct* (1646; Rome, Accad. N. S Luca; for illustration *see* DUTCH ITALIANATES), has much in common with Jan Both's manner. Yet although his works are apparently related stylistically to those of Claude Lorrain and Herman van Swanevelt, he did not adhere to their invented Arcadian imagery, preferring the actual Campagna for his naturalistic presentations of ruins, figures and the countryside.

On Asselijn's journey back to the northern Netherlands, he stayed *c.* 1644–5 in Lyon, where he married Antoinette Huaart [Houwaart], and in 1646 in Paris, where he provided three paintings (Paris, Louvre) for the decoration of the Cabinet d'Amour in the Hôtel Lambert. Shortly after his return to Amsterdam, aged between 35 and 40, his portrait was etched by Rembrandt (*c.* 1648; B. 277). He continued to produce Italianate works, such as *Panoramic Landscape* (*c.* 1649; Vienna, Akad. Bld. Kst.; see fig.), with characteristically warm colours and careful attention to naturalistic detail. In addition, between 1647 and 1652 he painted Dutch subjects, such as the *Collapse of the St Anthonis Dike, 1651* (Schwerin, Staatl. Mus.), *Repair of the St Anthonis Dike, 1652* (Berlin, Gemäldegal.) and the *Frozen Moat outside City Walls* (Worcester, MA, A. Mus.). In his earlier works Asselijn tended to apply the paint thickly; around 1650 his palette became lighter and clearer and he painted more smoothly, creating broader, occasionally summary effects. This change, perhaps prompted by Weenix, clearly acknowledged the market's taste for a more decorative style. (His paintings on copper, however, have an enamel-like quality.)

Asselijn was also a prolific draughtsman. His sketches, done both from nature and in the studio, include Roman ruins, buildings and landscapes. The 11 surviving preparatory drawings of ruins (e.g. *Aqueduct at Frascati*, New York, Pierpont Morgan Lib.) for the series of 18 engravings by Gabriel Perelle (Hollstein, nos 15–32) repeat subjects found in a Roman sketchbook (dispersed, e.g. *Temple of the Sibyl at Tivoli*, Darmstadt, Hess. Landesmus.). Eight pages of a second sketchbook are also preserved (London, BM). His architectural drawings display an unassuming naturalism and painstaking observation and representation of space, form, surface and atmosphere. He applied grey washes over pencil or chalk on white paper, sometimes adding white highlights, covering most of the surface of the paper. He also made compositional studies in either black and white chalk on blue paper, grey or brown wash, opaque white or sometimes pen and ink. The earlier studies, based on van Laer and Andries Both, add elements from his cavalry subjects (e.g. *Departure for the Hunt*, Brussels, Mus. Royaux A. & Hist.). Later, he developed his own rapid ideas, with energetic outlines on blue paper (e.g. Amsterdam, Rijksmus.; Hamburg, Ksthalle; Dresden, Kupferstichkab.; Leiden, Rijksuniv., Prentenkab.). In addition, he drew highly detailed preparatory sketches for

Jan Asselijn: *Panoramic Landscape*, oil on panel, 430×670 mm, *c.* 1649 (Vienna, Akademie der Bildenden Künste)

paintings, both types probably inspired by Claude's drawings on blue and white paper in the *Liber veritatis* (1636; London, BM).

During his lifetime, Asselijn's closest follower was Willem Schellinks, and, according to Houbraken, Frederick de Moucheron was his pupil. Others who were influenced by him include Adam Pijnacker, Nicolaes Berchem, Karel Dujardin and Thomas Wijck, who adopted architectural motifs from the Roman studies, as well as Allaert van Ererdingen, who adopted the waterfall subjects.

BIBLIOGRAPHY

Hollstein: *Dut. & Flem.*
J. von Sandrart: *Teutsche Academie* (1675–9); ed. A. R. Pelzer (1925), p. 182
A. Houbraken: *De groote schouburgh* (1718–21), ii, p. 327; iii, p. 64
A. von Bartsch: *Le Peintre-graveur* (1803–21) [B.]
J. Kusnetsow: 'Tableau de la jeunesse de Jan Asselijn au Musée de l'Hermitage', *Bull. Mus. Ermitage*, xiv (1958), pp. 34–7
A. C. Steland-Stief: 'Jan Asselijn und Willem Schellinks', *Oud-Holland*, lxxix (1964), pp. 99–110
Nederlandse 17e eeuwse Italiaanisierende landschapschilders (exh. cat., ed. A. Blankert; Utrecht, Cent. Mus., 1965); rev. and trans. as *Dutch 17th-century Italianate Painters* (Soest, 1978), pp. 129–44
A. C. Steland-Stief: 'Jan Asselijn und Karel Dujardin', *Raggi*, vii (1967), pp. 99–107
E. Knab: 'De genio loci', *Miscellanea J. Q. van Regteren Altena* (Amsterdam, 1969)
A. C. Steland-Stief: Drei Winterlandschaften des Italianisten Jan Asselijn und ihre Auswirkungen', *Kst. Hessen & Mittelrhein*, x (1970), pp. 59–65
——: *Jan Asselijn: Nach 1610 bis 1652* (Amsterdam, 1971)
——: 'Zum zeichnerischen Werk des Jan Asselijn', *Oud-Holland*, xciv (1980), pp. 213–58
——: 'Zu Willem Schellinks' Entwicklung als Zeichner: Frühe Zeichnungen der Frankreichreise um 1646 und die Ausbildung zum Italianisten in der Nachfolge des Jan Asselijn', *Niederdt. Beitr. Kstgesch.*, xxv (1986), pp. 79–108
——: 'Beobachtungen zur frühen Zeichnungen des Jan Both und zum Verhältnis zwischen Jan Both und Jan Asselijn in Rom vor 1641', *Niederdt. Beitr. Kstgesch.*, xxvii (1988), pp. 115–38
——: *Die Zeichnungen des Jan Asselijn* (Fridingen, 1989)

ANNE CHARLOTTE STELAND

Asselin, Maurice (*b* Orléans, 24 June 1882; *d* Neuilly-sur-Seine, nr Paris, 30 Oct 1947). French painter and printmaker. He studied design and painting at the Collège Sainte-Croix in Orléans and from 1903 at the Ecole des Beaux-Arts in Paris, where he was a pupil of Fernand Cormon. Although he greatly admired Cézanne and was friendly with the Fauves, he sought to develop a personal style characterized by subdued colours, sensitive brushwork and a strong sense of composition and design. As an oil painter, watercolourist and lithographer he produced landscapes (e.g. *Landscape at Neuilly*, 1924; Algiers, Mus. N. B.-A.), portraits and genre scenes such as *Coffee in the Garden* (1922; Paris, Mus. A. Mod. Ville Paris). He also worked as a book illustrator, particularly in the 1920s; among his works in this medium were editions of Francis Carco's *Rien qu'une femme* and *Mort de quelqu'un* by Jules Romains.

BIBLIOGRAPHY

F. Carco: *Maurice Asselin* (Paris, 1924)
J. Alazard: 'Maurice Asselin', *Amour A.*, xi (1928), pp. 433–6
R. Jean: *Maurice Asselin*, Collections des Cahiers d'Aujourd'hui (Paris, 1928) [illus.]

ALBERTO CERNUSCHI

Assemblage. Art form in which natural and manufactured, traditionally non-artistic, materials and *objets trouvés* are assembled into three-dimensional structures. As such it is closely related to COLLAGE, and like collage it is associated with Cubism, although its origins can be traced back beyond this. As much as by the materials used, it can be characterized by the way in which they are treated. In an assemblage the banal, often tawdry materials retain their individual physical and functional identity, despite artistic manipulation. The term was coined by Jean Dubuffet in 1953 to refer to his series of butterfly-wing collages and series of lithographs based on paper collages, which date from that year. Although these were in fact collages, he felt that that term ought to be reserved for the collage works of Braque, Picasso and the Dadaists of the period between 1910 and 1920. By 1954 Dubuffet had extended the term to cover a series of three-dimensional works made from primarily natural materials and objects. The concept of assemblage was given wide public currency by the exhibition *The Art of Assemblage* at MOMA, New York, in 1961. This included works by nearly 140 international artists, including Braque, Joseph Cornell, Dubuffet, Marcel Duchamp, Picasso, Robert Rauschenberg, Man Ray and Kurt Schwitters. Several of the works shown were in fact collages, but the breadth of styles and artists included reflects the wide application of the term and the sometimes fine distinction between assemblage and collage. The 'combine paintings' of Rauschenberg, for example, fall awkwardly between the two, being essentially planar but with often extensive protrusions of objects. The inclusion of real objects and materials both expanded the range of artistic possibilities and attempted to bridge the gap between art and life.

The ancestry of the assemblage can be traced back to the artistic and literary environment of late 19th-century France. In his later poetry, especially *Un Coup de dés jamais n'abolira le hasard* (1897), Stéphane Mallarmé adopted a technique in which poetic fragments were pieced together in unusual semantic and typographic arrangements. Guillaume Apollinaire later extended this method in his *Calligrammes* (1918). By emphasizing the visual appearance of words their traditional role of signification was both enhanced and expanded. In the same manner assemblage emphasizes the visual or tactile qualities of formerly utilitarian objects while nevertheless exploiting the perception of the banality of such objects. In the visual arts, one of the most notable early attempts to use non-artistic materials can be found in Edgar Degas's *Little Dancer Aged 14* (1880–81; bronze version, London, Tate). In an attempt to achieve greater realism, Degas included a real muslin skirt and hair ribbon in the bronze version, and the original clay and wax version also included a horse-hair wig.

The assemblages that emerged from Cubism include such pieces as Picasso's *Still-life* (1914; London, Tate), composed of carved wood elements and an upholstery fringe, and intended to be hung on the wall. His painted bronze *Glass of Absinthe* (1914; version, New York, MOMA) includes a real spoon and is free-standing. This development expressed a dissatisfaction with the deceptive illusionism of painting and sculpture that was overcome by the use of real objects. Another equally important pioneer of assemblage was Kurt Schwitters, who used the technique in his *Merz* works. *Merz Construction* (1921; Philadelphia, PA, Mus. A.), for example, was made from

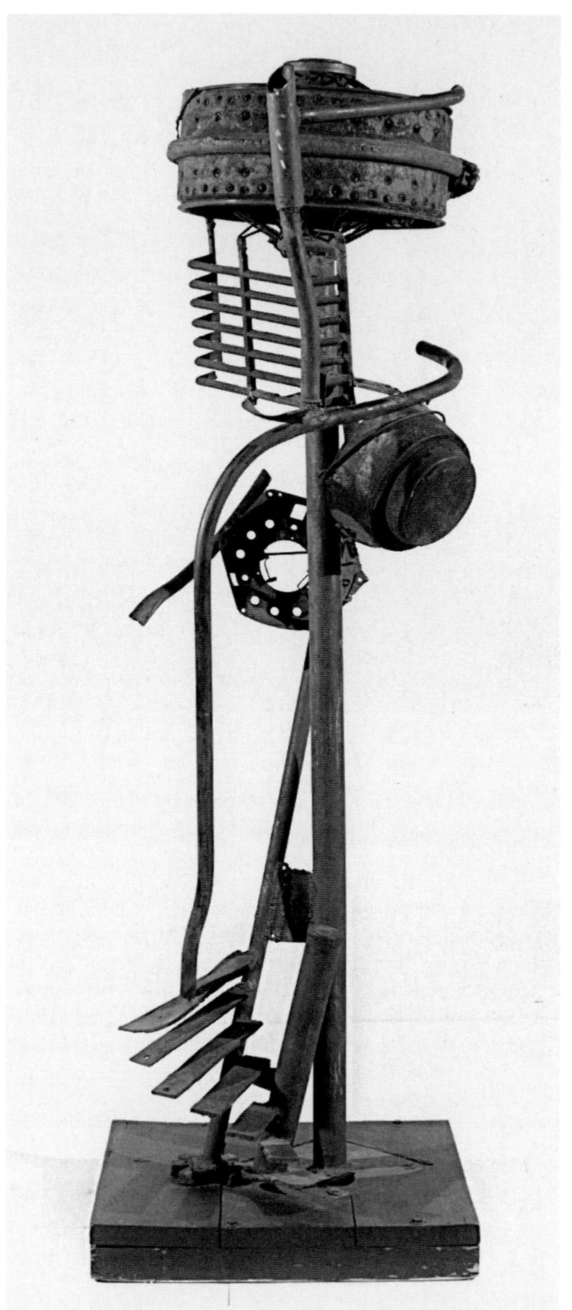

Assemblage by Richard Stankiewicz: *Kabuki Dancer*, iron and steel, 2.13×0.61×0.66 m, 1954 (New York, Whitney Museum of American Art)

pieces of wood, wire mesh, paper and cardboard to create a deliberately ugly, shabby work characteristic of Schwitters's Dadaist aesthetic. The ready-mades of Marcel Duchamp showed a similar anti-artistic intent, and little if any actual assembly was required for their production. The works of the Russian Constructivists also occasionally embodied the aesthetic of the assemblage but were better described as constructions, the materials used being more aesthetically pleasing in themselves and more malleable, and the separate elements being transformed and absorbed into a unified work.

The facility with which objects could be juxtaposed in assemblage made the medium ideally suited to the Surrealists in their quest for the marvellous. The Surrealist object thus became an important part of the movement's output, allowing a material equivalent to the juxtaposition of distant entities embodied in the Surrealist image, as in Meret Oppenheim's fur-lined cup and saucer, *Object* (1936; New York, MOMA). From the 1950s worthless or discarded materials were used in assemblage to various effect by Robert Rauschenberg and other American artists. Richard Stankiewicz used junk metal in such welded assemblages as *Kabuki Dancer* (1954; New York, Whitney; see fig.), in which the parts assume a menacing quality that can be seen as a comment on technological society. The exponents of Nouveau Réalisme also produced a range of assemblage works. For example Daniel Spoerri's *tableaux pièges*, such as *Table City Galerie* (1965; Amsterdam, Stedel. Mus.), were often made from the refuse of meals, illustrating human consumption and, more broadly, the consumer society (*see also* SWITZERLAND, fig. 12). This theme was developed more consistently in Pop art, which emphasized the synthetic, brash nature of mass-produced consumer products. The assemblage proved an effective way of realizing this aim, as shown, for example, by Tom Wesselmann's *Still Life #40* (1964; Saint-Etienne, Mus. A. & Indust.), which used brightly coloured synthetic materials. The environmental works of Edward Kienholz, such as *The Beanery* (1965; Amsterdam, Stedel. Mus.), used assemblage on a much larger scale and broke radically with the residual sculptural connotations of assemblage by literally surrounding the viewer and recreating reality in a distorted form. The continued use of the assemblage into the 1990s showed it to be a medium almost as flexible and important in modern art as painting or the traditional technique of sculpture.

BIBLIOGRAPHY

The Art of Assemblage (exh. cat. by W. Seitz, New York, MOMA; Dallas Mus. A.; San Francisco, Mus. A.; 1961–2)

A. Kaprow: *Assemblage, Environments and Happenings* (New York, 1966)

Lost and Found in California: Four Decades of Assemblage Art (exh. cat. by S. Leonard Starr, Santa Monica, CA, James Corcoran Gal.; Santa Monica, CA, Shoshana Wayne Gal.; Santa Monica, CA, Pence Gal.; 1988)

The Poetic Object (exh. cat. by P. Clothier and J. Edwards, San Antonio, TX, Mus. A.; and elsewhere; 1988–9)

Forty Years of California Assemblage (exh. cat. by A. Ayres and others, Los Angeles, UCLA, Wight A.G.; and elsewhere; 1989–90)

PHILIP COOPER

Assembly rooms. As applied to British buildings of the 18th century and the early 19th, a complex of rooms intended primarily for social gatherings. Chambers (1728) defined the assembly as 'a stated and general meeting of the polite persons of both sexes, for the sake of conversation, gallantry, news and play'. Assembly rooms developed from the social intermingling of the nobility with the gentry, who required a public place for entertainment when attending races, the Assizes and parties in a town not far removed from their country seats. Other factors contributing to the development of assembly rooms included the increasingly important role of women in social gatherings outside the home and the growing popularity of spas.

In the early 18th century assembly rooms were modest buildings intended for small gatherings, such as the Lower Rooms in Bath (1708). In smaller towns, however, they were commonly combined with another public building, as at John Carr's Newark Town Hall (1773–6), Notts; with a theatre, as at Waterford (*c.* 1780), Co. Waterford; or with a library, as at Wareham (*c.* 1799; destr.), Dorset. As new and more elaborate forms of entertainment were introduced, such as balls, masquerades and musical parties, a large building containing several rooms for different functions was required.

Situated in the centre of town, as most assembly rooms were to be, and classical in style, the York Assembly Rooms (1731–2), designed by Richard Boyle, 3rd Earl of Burlington, were among the earliest examples and set the standard (*see* BOYLE, (2), fig. 4). The only requirement that Burlington had to meet was that his design include a large dancing-room, another large room for cards and play, another for coffee and refreshments, a kitchen or place in which to make tea, a retiring-room for the ladies and a footman's room with a chimney near the entrance. Basing his design on Roman architecture as presented by Andrea Palladio in *Quattro libri dell'architettura* (Venice, 1570) and his drawings (*see* PALLADIANISM), Burlington created a series of free-flowing, interconnected rooms (see fig.). The vestibule is a rectangle with apses linking it to reception rooms with vaulted apses, a small rotunda, defined by four round-headed niches, and the Great Assembly Room, a long, rectangular Corinthian peristyle, lit by clerestory windows. The severe tripartite façade (destr. 1828) was based on Palladio's reconstruction of Roman baths and had a circular portico flanked by wings with the same arched opening followed by a broken pediment.

New assembly rooms proliferated in such provincial towns as Exeter, Norwich (1754, by Thomas Ivory) and Shrewsbury throughout the 18th century and into the early 19th. Many were designed by leading architects, the prevailing style being classical, either Roman or Greek Revival. The most elegant of all spa assembly rooms is the New or Upper Assembly Rooms, Bath (1769–71, by John Wood the younger). The restrained Neo-classical exterior with a Roman Doric portico leads into a tripartite complex of rooms, including an octagonal, domed card-room that links the large two-storey ballroom and tea-room, both of which have engaged columns lining the walls.

Another popular form for assembly rooms is the rotunda, exemplified by Dublin's Rotunda Assembly Rooms (1751, by Richard Castle), which were intended to be a source of income for the Lying-in Hospital; the rotunda was attached to the hospital by a card-room. In 1784 a ballroom and tea-room were added, and James Gandon, working in a severely Neo-classical style, added an entrance block to the rotunda as well as raising and decorating the rotunda's drum.

The prevailing style of Scottish assembly rooms in Aberdeen, Leith and Edinburgh was classical. The Edinburgh Assembly Rooms (1784–7) by John Henderson (*d* 1786), although greatly altered, are typical. The Roman Doric façade is restrained, with a first floor of seven

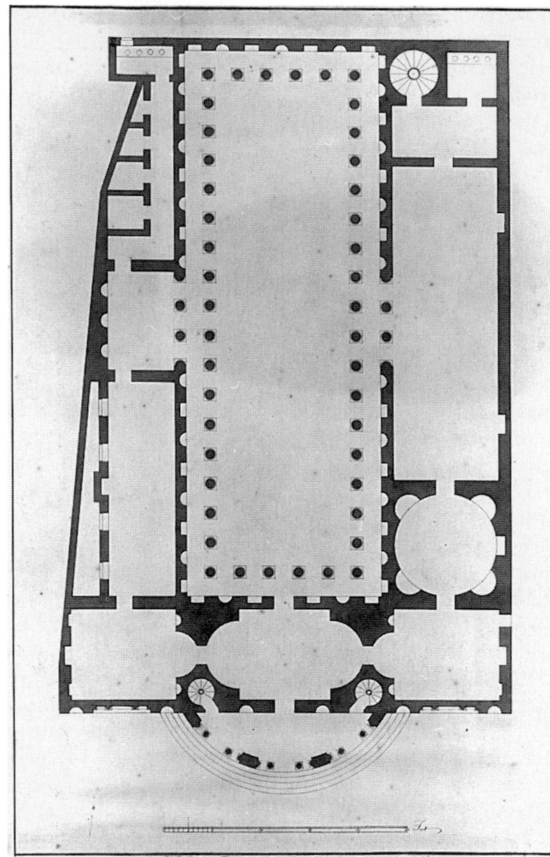

York Assembly Rooms, by Richard Boyle, 1731–2; ground-plan attributed to Henry Flitcroft, pen, ink and wash drawing, *c.* 1730 (London, British Architectural Library, Royal Institute of British Architects)

windows and a pair of giant pilasters at the ends; a portico was added in 1817–18 by William Burn. The interiors are dominated by a square, domed saloon lined with Doric columns and a majestic ballroom with a concave ceiling spanning the width of the building.

By the 1840s changing tastes and social habits signalled the demise of assembly rooms. Many were demolished, but some were first put to other uses: in 1812 the Prince Street Assembly Rooms in Bristol, for example, were converted into a theatre (destr.). Burlington's York Assembly Rooms, like others, underwent numerous alterations and suffered from years of misuse and neglect until re-emerging in 1951 as a restored, functional building that continues to serve the community's needs.

Following cultural and social traditions in Britain, assembly rooms proliferated in the British colonies, notably in India and the USA. Typical of assembly rooms in India was the 18th-century Madras Assembly Rooms. Located near the race-course, this was a two-storey building with an arcaded ground floor, a steep staircase leading to the first-floor terrace, and a balustraded roof, serving as a viewing platform. In the USA there were assembly houses as well as assembly rooms in taverns, inns and other public buildings. By 1750 there was an elegant assembly house in Portsmouth, NH, while residents of Alexandria, VA, had their assembly room in the City Tavern, now preserved in the American Wing of the Metropolitan Museum of Art, New York. The Assembly House in Salem, MA, built in 1782, exemplifies the austere, functional nature of the American assembly house. Consisting of a two-storey ballroom, extending the width of the house with rows of benches lining its walls, and two drawing-rooms with chambers above them, the Assembly House was a place for concerts, dancing, card-playing, polite conversation and the entertainment of dignitaries. In 1805–7 Samuel McIntire converted the Salem Assembly House into the residential Hamilton Hall. Assembly rooms in Britain and elsewhere have similarly yielded to other uses.

UNPUBLISHED SOURCES

York, City Lib. [Assembly Rooms Directors' Minute Book, 1729–58]

BIBLIOGRAPHY

Colvin

E. Chambers: *Cyclopedia: Or, an Universal Dictionary of Arts and Sciences* (London, 1728), i, p. 152

W. Ison: *The Georgian Buildings of Bristol* (London, 1952)

G. W. R. Ward: *The Assembly House* (Salem, MA, 1976)

M. Girouard: *Life in the English Country House* (New Haven and London, 1978/*R* 1980)

W. Ison: *The Georgian Buildings of Bath, from 1700 to 1830* (Bath, 1980)

The Central Area (1981), v of *City of York*, Royal Comm. Anc. & Hist. Mnmts & Constr. England (London, 1962–)

J. Gifford and others: *Edinburgh*, Bldgs Scotland (Harmondsworth, 1984, rev. 1988)

D. Cruickshank: *A Guide to the Georgian Buildings of Britain and Ireland* (London, 1985)

P. Davies: *Splendours of the Raj: British Architecture in India, 1660 to 1947* (London, 1985)

J. Morris and S. Winchester: *Stones of Empire: The Buildings of the Raj* (Oxford and New York, 1985)

PAMELA D. KINGSBURY

Asser, Eduard (Isaac) (*b* Amsterdam, 19 Oct 1809; *d* Amsterdam, 21 Sept 1894). Dutch photographer and lawyer. He made the earliest photographs to be found in the Netherlands, daguerreotypes of his daughters and other members of his family. In the 1840s a number of daguerreotypists, mostly foreign, settled in Dutch towns as professional portrait photographers. Asser, however, remained an amateur and experimented with a variety of photographic techniques and genres. He took self-portraits, pictures of his daughters, his son, his wife and of his friend E. Bour, also a photographer, using the calotype process (*see* PHOTOGRAPHY, §I). There are also studies of streets, buildings and canals in Amsterdam in his albums (Amsterdam, Rijksmus.). In his studio he made photographic still-lifes of vases, small sculptures and of the instruments from his physics cabinet. His compositions reveal a knowledge of the fine arts: in his youth the painter Jan Adam Kruseman had given him drawing and painting lessons.

In 1855, with Bour, Asser entered the first Dutch photographic exhibition, organized by the Vereeniging van Volksvlijt in Amsterdam and The Hague. This exhibition, which introduced photography for the first time to some people, included works by Louis-Désiré Blanquart-Evrard, André Adolphe Eugène Disdéri, Charles Nègre, Charles Marville, Bisson frères, Hermann Krone and others. In the same year Asser put himself forward for membership of the Société Française de Photographie.

Asser's work was shown at the *Tentoonstelling van Nijverheid en Kunst*, held at the Paleis voor Volksvlijt in Amsterdam, the Dutch Crystal Palace, in 1859. Towards the end of the 1860s he won international fame for the development of a photolithographic process, which was similar to the one developed by Alphonse Louis Poitevin. Debates about who was the first to develop photolithography, Asser or Henry James (1803–77), unleashed a fierce discussion in the English journal *Photographic News*. From 1864 Asser contributed regularly to *Tijdschrift voor Photographie* and was also a member of the editorial staff. His albums, with over 200 photographs, and a small number of daguerreotypes are now in the Photography Collection of the Rijksprentenkabinet, Amsterdam, Rijksmuseum.

BIBLIOGRAPHY

H. Gernsheim and A. Gernsheim: *The History of Photography* (London, 1969), p. 546

J. Coppens: 'Mr. Eduard I. Asser, portretfotograaf in de 19e eeuw', *Foto*, xxvii/8 (1972), pp. 30–34

I. T. Leijerzapf, ed.: *Fotografie in Nederland, 1839–1920* (The Hague, 1978)

M. Boom and J. Coppens: 'Eduard Isaac Asser', *Geschiedenis van de Nederlandse fotografie*, ed. I. T. Leijerzapf (Alphen aan den Rijn, 1984–) [entries in alphabetical order]

M. Boom: 'Keuze uit de aanwinsten. Schenking foto's van E. J. Asser' [A selection from the acquisition. Donation of photographs by E. J. Asser], *Bull. Rijksmus.*, xlii/3 (1994)

MATTIE BOOM

Assereto, Gioacchino (*b* Genoa, 1600; *d* Genoa, 28 June 1649). Italian painter. At the age of 12 he studied with Luciano Borzone and *c.* 1614 entered the Genoese studio of Andrea Ansaldo. Among a number of lost early paintings was a large *Temptation of St Anthony* done at the age of 16 (Soprani, p. 273). Several complex compositions with small figures, including the *Apotheosis of St Thomas Aquinas* (Lille, Mus. B.-A.), the *Last Supper* (Genoa, Mus. Accad. Ligustica B.A.), the *Stoning of St Stephen* (Lucca, Mus. & Pin. N.) and the *Crowning of the Virgin* (Taggia, Dominican Convent; see Pesenti, fig. 342), perhaps date from 1616–26. These are close in style to works such as Bernardo Strozzi's *bozzetto* (*c.* 1620; Genoa, Mus. Accad. Ligustica B.A.) for an altarpiece of *Paradise* (destr.) and to other contemporary works by Ansaldo, Giulio Benso and Giovanni Andrea de' Ferrari, which also derive their figure style from Mannerism. Assereto's earliest dated painting, *SS John the Baptist, Bernard, Catherine, Lucy and George* (1626; Recco, S Giovanni Battista), is distinguished by its silvery colour and dramatic contrasts of light and dark, and by the powerful realism and vitality of the individual saints. Here he absorbed Borzone's *sfumato* technique and skill as a portrait painter, while the crisp contours of the drapery suggest Ansaldo. Assereto's work from *c.* 1626–36 sparkles with rich colour and detail, as in the strikingly naturalistic and intense *Ecstasy of St Francis* (163(?6); Genoa, Cassa di Risparmio, see Pesenti, fig. 354). The work of the Lombard Mannerist painters Cerano, Morazzone and Giulio Cesare Procaccini that had influenced Strozzi and Ansaldo before 1620 also had an effect on Assereto's early work. This is apparent in the elongated figures and high-keyed colours of his two octagonal vault frescoes, *David and Abimelech* and *SS John and Peter Healing the Lame Man*, in SS Annunziata del Vastato, Genoa. The frescoes were dated after 1639 by Soprani, but a date of *c.* 1630 seems stylistically more convincing. Sharp-edged draperies, meticulous ornamental detail and jewel-like colours ranging from lime to pink and orange characterize Assereto's vivid narrative painting *Alexander and Diogenes* (*c.* 1630; Berlin, Gemäldegal.) and his altarpiece *SS Cosmas and Damian Curing the Sick* (Genoa, SS Cosma e Damiano), in which some of the figures resemble those by Orazio de' Ferrari, who may have worked with Assereto in Ansaldo's studio.

In 1639 Assereto went briefly to Rome where, according to Soprani, he visited the studios of many painters. However, what he saw disappointed him and only confirmed his belief in his own art. He must have met Genoese artists working in Rome, such as Domenico Fiasella's student Luca Salterello (1610–?1655), Giovanni Maria Bottalla, Benedetto Giovanni Castiglione and Giovanni Andrea Podesta. The influence of Caravaggio may have confirmed his interest in realism and encouraged him to continue with his detailed description of heads and hands. It may also have revealed to him the possibilities of compositions that depend on chiaroscuro rather than on colour. In the *Death of Cato* (Genoa, Gal. Pal. Bianco), Assereto moved away from the refinement of his early, vividly coloured narratives to a bolder, more powerful style where violent emotions are heightened by theatrical effects of flaming torches and candlelight. The picture suggests the influence of the works of northern Caravaggesque painters such as Gerrit van Honthorst and Matthias Stom.

In the 1640s Assereto was active as a fresco painter. Works of the period included frescoes for the Palazzo Granello: the *Virtues* and a *Sacrifice of Isaac* for the principal *salone* (1643; destr.) and *Virtues* and a *Coronation of the Virgin* for the façade (1647; destr.). Few frescoes remain from this time, however. Sole survivors are some fragments in S Agostino (see Gavazza, figs 311–12) and the frescoes Assereto was commissioned *c.* 1644 to execute for a decorative scheme in the Palazzo Airoli–Negrone that had been left unfinished on the death of Giovanni

Gioacchino Assereto: *Esau Selling his Birthright*, oil on canvas, 0.98×1.24 m, *c.* 1645 (Genoa, Galleria di Palazzo Bianco)

Maria Bottalla. There he painted a large vault medallion with *Apollo Flaying Marsyas* and completed Bottalla's lunettes and architectural wall decorations (see Pesenti, figs 362–73). These are characterized by muffled contrasts of light and dark, furrowed facial features and angular draperies. The figure style is robust and muscular, suggesting the influence of Rubens, and recurs in many dark canvases of the 1640s, such as *Cain and Abel* (Brunswick, Herzog Anton Ulrich-Mus.) and *Christ and the Woman Taken in Adultery* (Corsham Court, Wilts). Many of Assereto's late works show three-quarter-length figures, and such works as *Esau Selling his Birthright* (*c.* 1645; Genoa, Gal. Pal. Bianco; see fig.) are distinguished by their sober realism, the delicacy of the psychological tensions between the figures and the grave beauty of the still-lifes. They have been compared to works by Velázquez and Murillo. Assereto also painted compositions with figures softly modelled in broad brushstrokes of brown colour, which suggest a renewed influence from the *sfumato* of Borzone, and in works such as the *Supper at Emmaus* (ex-Mowinckel priv. col., see Pesenti, fig. 339) he approached the poetic expressiveness of Rembrandt. Soprani believed Assereto's work to be incomparable, an opinion shared by the artist, and in his last years many copies of his paintings were produced, some possibly by his son, Giuseppe Assereto, and others possibly by Giovanni Solaro (*d* ?1657).

BIBLIOGRAPHY

Enc. It.

R. Soprani: *Vite* (1674), pp. 167–73; ed. C. G. Ratti (1768–9), i, pp. 271–8

R. Longhi: 'L'Assereto', *Dedalo*, vii/2 (1926–7), pp. 355–77

——: 'E ancora dell'Assereto', *Pinacotheca*, i (1928–9), pp. 221–5

C. Marcenaro: 'Per il catalogo dell'Assereto', *Emporium*, cv (1947), pp. 138–44

J. Guerrero Lovillo: 'Murillo y Assereto', *Archv Esp. A.*, xxiii (1950), pp. 133–44

G. V. Castelnovi: 'Intorno al Assereto', *Emporium*, cx (1954), pp. 17–35

Mostra dei pittori genovesi a Genova nel '600 e nel '700 (exh. cat., ed. C. Marcenaro; Genoa, Gal. Pal. Bianco, 1969), pp. 45–55

G. V. Castelnovi: 'La pittura nella prima metà del seicento: Dall'Ansaldo a Orazio de Ferrari', *La pittura a Genova e in Liguria*, ed. E. Poleggi, ii (Genoa, 1971), pp. 59–151

V. Belloni: *Pittura genovese del seicento*, ii (Genoa, 1974), pp. 41–51

E. Gavazza: *La grande decorazione a Genova*, i (Genoa, 1974)

M. Newcome: 'An Unknown Early Painting and some Other Works by Assereto', *Jb. Berlin. Mus.*, xxvii (1985), pp. 61–75

F. R. Pesenti: *La pittura in Liguria: Artisti del primo seicento* (Genoa, 1986)

Kunst in der Republik Genua (exh. cat. by M. Newcome, Frankfurt am Main, Schirn Ksthalle, 1992), nos 19–25 [incl. bibliog.]

M. NEWCOME

Assisi. Pilgrimage town in Umbria, Italy, on the slopes of Mt Subiaso, south-east of Perugia, and the birthplace of St Francis (1181/2–1226), founder of the FRANCISCAN ORDER of Friars Minor. The church of S Francesco (*see* §II below), an example of early Italian Gothic architecture, was raised in honour of St Francis shortly after his death. The main focal points of pilgrims are the church's late 13th- to early 14th-century fresco cycles, which include the *Legend of St Francis* and lives of other saints.

I. History and urban development. II. S Francesco.

I. History and urban development.

Populated first by the Umbrians, the town later became the flourishing Roman settlement of Asisium. There are surviving remains of the Roman walls, forum, theatre, amphitheatre and the Temple of Minerva (now the church of S Maria) dating from the reign of Augustus. Most of the town was destroyed in AD 545. Assisi emerged as a free, Ghibelline commune in the late 12th century, having previously been in the power of the Duchy of Spoleto. The town developed considerably during the 13th century, a period during which it was under papal jurisdiction. In the early 14th century Assisi fell to Perugia and subsequently succumbed to a number of despots, including Gian Galeazzo Visconti and the Montefeltro. Despite continuing disputes between local families, however, Assisi returned to papal possession under Pope Pius II.

The town is crowned by the Rocca Maggiore, the old citadel of the feudal period. Ransacked by the townspeople in the early 12th century, the Rocca was rebuilt in 1367 on the orders of Cardinal Albornoz (1353–1367), official papal delegate for the establishment of orthodoxy. The Rocca assumed strategic and political significance in later periods of seigneurial rule. The medieval and early Renaissance buildings of the town, arranged on narrow terraces and joined by equally narrow streets and stairways, are built mostly in the characteristic pink and white local stone. The Romanesque churches of S Maria Maggiore and S Pietro, the cathedral of S Rufino and government buildings in the Piazza del Comune testify to the prosperity of medieval Assisi, while the 14th-century gate of S Francesco, the oratory of S Bernardino of Siena (*d* 1444) and the 17th-century palaces of the Bernabei and Giacobetti flanking the Via S Francesco are evidence of the continuing urban development during the early Renaissance and later centuries.

After St Francis was declared the patron saint of Italy in 1939 the town, which had slumbered peacefully during the preceding five centuries, became a major pilgrimage and tourist centre. Protected by its high, narrow position, the old town has been contained within the original city walls, while the new town has developed on the plain below, around the church of S Maria degli Angeli (1569–1684; rest. 1840), which covers the Porziuncola, the original centre of the Franciscan Order.

BIBLIOGRAPHY

F. Rodolico: *Le pietre delle città d'Italia* (Florence, 1965)

Atti del V convegno della società internazionale di studi francescani: Assisi al tempo di San Francesco: Assisi, 1977

ANABEL THOMAS

II. S Francesco.

Founded in 1228 following the canonization ceremony for St Francis, it is the mother church of the Franciscan Order. The building established many of the characteristics of Italian Gothic architecture, and it occupied a leading position in Italy at the beginning of this period.

1. Architecture. 2. Painting. 3. Stained glass. 4. Treasury.

1. ARCHITECTURE. The foundation-stone of the occidented double church was laid by Pope Gregory IX (*reg* 1227–41) in 1228, although the building may already have been begun. By 25 May 1230 the Lower Church was sufficiently advanced for the remains of St Francis to be translated there; both churches were consecrated in 1253

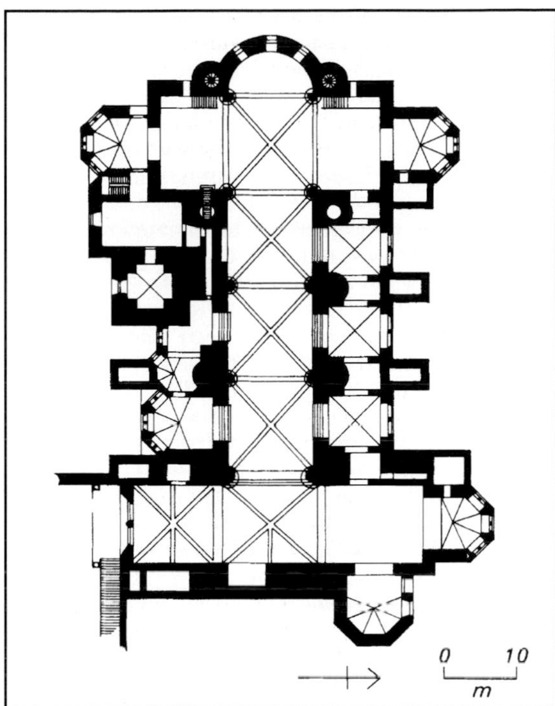

1. Assisi, S Francesco, founded 1228, plan of Lower Church

by Pope Innocent IV (*reg* 1243–54), who declared that for the next 25 years all alms collected there were to be used for its further development. The fact that the building had to fulfil two functions, as a conventual church for a mendicant order and as a great centre of pilgrimage, may have dictated its double form, supported by retaining walls. The Upper Church is bright and spacious, with a single-aisled, four-bay nave, a transept and polygonal apse; the Lower, with side chapels, narthex and crypt (containing the remains of St Francis), seems smaller and darker, a fit goal for pilgrimage (see fig. 1). Its ultimate appearance may also have been influenced by the fact that when Jerome of Ascoli, Master-General of the Order, became Pope Nicholas IV in 1288, the building became a papal church. Its character was determined by the harmonious relationship between the architecture and its fresco decoration (*see* §2 below). The architect was familiar with French Gothic: its influence, although unexplained, can be seen in the rose window of the façade, the clustered wall shafts and quadripartite vault of the nave and the traceried windows, the large expanse of glass in the choir contrasting with that in the rest of the building. White suggests that the prototype may have been the late 12th-century cathedral of Angers. At Assisi, however, a few strong, simple forms are repeated throughout the building both to unify and to articulate the space, with so powerful an effect that the architectural members are echoed in the painted framework to the frescoes.

BIBLIOGRAPHY

Fra L. de Pietralunga: *Descrizione della Basilica di S Francesco e di altri santuari di Assisi* (1568–80; Assisi, Bib. Comunale, Fond. Moderno, MS. 148); ed. P. Scarpellini (Treviso, 1982) [good summary of arguments]

B. Kleinschmidt: *Die Basilika San Francesco in Assisi*, 3 vols (Berlin, 1915)

E. Hertlein: *Die Basilika San Francesco in Assisi* (Florence, 1964)

J. White: *Art and Architecture in Italy*, Pelican Hist. A. (Harmondsworth, 1966, rev. 1987)

JACQUELINE COLLISS HARVEY

2. PAINTING. The double church of S Francesco contains the most important and extensive late medieval painted decoration in central Italy. Between *c.* 1260 and 1320 notable Roman, Umbrian and Tuscan painters created a standard Franciscan iconography and pattern of church decoration, the increasingly sophisticated imagery of which influenced later 14th-century artists and was of unparalleled importance in the evolution of Italian art. The decoration of the Upper and Lower churches reflects their different functions. The paintings of the Lower Church, with their juxtaposition of images from the *Passion* and *Infancy* cycles above the tomb of St Francis, are designed to accentuate the parallels that the Franciscans wished to stress between Christ and the Saint: the *passio* of one and the *compassio* of the other. On the other hand, those in the Upper Church, the great church of the Franciscan Order, concentrate on the life of St Francis with scenes taken from the *Legenda maior* of St Bonaventure, which from 1266 was the canonical biography of the Saint. Once completed, the cycle provided the orthodox hagiography for St Francis throughout Italy and further expanded the analogies between Christ and St Francis found in the Lower Church, elevating Assisi's importance to equal that of Rome. Both Upper and Lower churches have suffered from the effects of damp and decay. Major programmes of restoration have been undertaken from the 1950s onwards, particularly in 1956–8, 1968, 1974 and 1981–4.

(i) The Master of St Francis, the Northern and Roman Masters. (ii) Cimabue and his workshop. (iii) The biblical scenes of the Upper Church. (iv) The 'Legend of St Francis'. (v) Giotto's circle and followers in the Lower Church. (vi) Pietro Lorenzetti and Simone Martini. (vii) Andrea de' Bartoli.

(i) The Master of St Francis, the Northern and Roman Masters. The elaborate geometric and floral patterns surrounding the three quadripartite vaults of the Lower Church are among the earliest frescoes. Two cycles beginning in the easternmost bay of the nave are also part of the early campaign: a *Passion* cycle of five episodes emphasizing the *Crucifixion* (*c.* 1260–63; see fig. 2) lines the upper section of the north wall; five scenes from the *Life of St Francis* occupy the corresponding area of the south wall. Most images lower on the nave walls have been effaced, but a fragmentary *Virgin and Child with an Angel* survives beside the crossing on the north wall. Originally a triptych, this probably had a commemorative function since it was placed on the site of the entombment of Cardinal Pietro di Barro (*d* 1252). Fragments in the entrance hall indicate that these cycles may once have included more episodes, but these were partially destroyed by lateral chapels added *c.* 1270–1350. High humidity aggravated the severe deterioration of what remained, causing white lead used in the paintings to oxidize and turn black and azurite blue to change to malachite green. When the nave and vault paintings were cleaned in 1974 their bright colours were found to have been mainly executed in tempera on dry plaster. Another dramatic

2. Master of St Francis: *Crucifixion* (detail), tempera on plaster, from the *Passion* fresco cycle (*c.* 1260–63), north wall of the nave, Lower Church, S Francesco, Assisi

discovery was the use of convex mirrors for the gold stars that bedeck the blue-painted vaults.

Thode reconstructed the work of the MASTER OF ST FRANCIS (*see* MASTERS, ANONYMOUS, AND MONOGRAMMISTS, §I) on the *St Francis* cycle, refuting previous attributions to Cimabue or Giunta Pisano. Yet he retained Vasari's attribution of the *Passion* cycle to Cimabue. Subsequently, the stylistic similarities of the two cycles, painted in an expressive, drier manner influenced by Giunta Pisano and Byzantine art, were recognized, and they are unequivocally accepted as the work of the Master of St Francis. The work was probably completed *c.* 1260–63; this date is supported by the fact that features of the *Stigmatization of St Francis* and the *Dream of Innocent III* depend on the account in Thomas da Celano's *Vita secunda* (1246–7) rather than St Bonaventure's *Legenda maior* (1260–63). The juxtaposition of this, the earliest surviving monumental cycle illustrating the *Life of St Francis* opposite a *Passion* cycle, represents the Franciscans' desire to promote their founder as a second Christ. This intention is augmented by the location of the cycles on the approach to the Saint's tomb beneath the high altar in the crossing of the Lower Church. Typological parallels between Christ and St Francis reflecting St Bonaventure's ideology govern the programmes throughout both the Upper and Lower churches.

Extensive decoration continued in the Upper Church, at the highest level of the north transept. The *Transfiguration* in the east lunette faces a *Christ in Glory* in the west; beneath each in the triforium there are six *Apostles* under arcades and five busts of *Angels* in roundels. The stained-glass window in the north wall is flanked by *David* and *Isaiah*. The damp climate caused considerable decomposition here, often down to the brickwork. During 1978 the conservators of the Istituto del Restauro discovered that preliminary drawings and true fresco had again been eschewed in favour of the direct application of tempera on dry plaster. Cleaning revealed their brilliant primary hues and that the eastern *Apostles* were painted from the bottom up, contrary to standard practice. These north transept paintings were by at least two distinct artists. One, whose background must have been north European, possibly even English, executed the two lunettes and the *Apostles* and *Angel* roundels of the west wall. In contrast with these calligraphic, strongly coloured images, the Roman Master (*fl c.* 1260–80) painted the more classically influenced *David* and *Isaiah* and the rest of the wall under the eastern lunette. Comparisons between the *Apostles* of the east triforium and fresco fragments from the portico of Old St Peter's, Rome, painted between the pontificates of Urban IV (*reg* 1261–4) and Nicholas III (*reg* 1277–80), confirm the dating of the upper north transept frescoes to *c.* 1265–80. Technical evidence confirms that the Northern Master (*fl c.* 1260–80) began the painting. After the completion of this section, Cimabue's workshop took over the decoration of the lower level of the north transept. The Northern Master also executed the frescoes in the upper part of the choir before Cimabue commenced work on the subsequent decoration of the west end.

(ii) Cimabue and his workshop. The decoration of the west end comprises the *Four Evangelists* in the vault over the crossing and the eight scenes from the *Life of the Virgin* arranged south to north over the five faces of the apse. The end wall of the apse has two roundels with busts of *Popes*, and *Angels* and *Saints* painted in the arcade beneath the windows. Next to the choir on the west wall of the south transept, below a *St Michael and the Dragon* in the lunette and the *Archangels* under the arcade, there are the first two of five scenes of the *Apocalypse*, which continue on to the end wall of the transept. A great *Crucifixion* (early 1280s; see fig. 3) dominates the lower east wall, to some extent overshadowing the loss of the lunette fresco above. In the north transept, five apostolic episodes, four from the *Lives of SS Peter and Paul*, are similarly ordered, and a *Crucifixion* likewise adorns the lower part of the east wall.

These frescoes were already in poor condition when Vasari saw them in 1563. While the figures were outlined in yellow or red ochre on damp plaster, they were painted when the plaster was no longer fresh enough to bind the colours firmly. Damp and chemical changes to the lead white have made the frescoes resemble worn photographic negatives. Humidity had so swollen the south-west triforium *Angels* that in 1953 they were detached, revealing preparatory drawings directly on the masonry. Since their reinstallation other choir and transept frescoes have been removed and transferred to canvas before being replaced.

3. Cimabue: *Crucifixion* (early 1280s), fresco, east wall of the south transept, Upper Church, S Francesco, Assisi

After their analysis, made during the 1979 conservation campaign, White and Zanardi suggested that the entire project had been visualized as a single decorative entity. One large scaffold may have enabled the work to be undertaken simultaneously throughout the upper levels of the choir and south transept. Along the lower walls sizeable areas were executed in one work-stage, probably beginning with the south transept *Crucifixion*. Work then continued around the apse to the *Crucifixion* in the north transept. Except for the *Apocalypse* episodes, this left to right horizontal movement followed the narrative sequence.

Cimabue's activity in the Upper Church has been acknowledged from Vasari onwards. This Florentine artist and his workshop are credited with the frescoes of the west end except for the highest level of the north transept and choir (*see* CIMABUE, §1(ii)(a)). The inferior quality of the three apostolic episodes and accompanying *Crucifixion* in the north transept denotes shop work, but their poor condition prohibits the identification of specific assistants. The Orsini insignia on the Roman Senator's Palace in the *St Mark* vault (*see* CIMABUE, fig. 1) presumably allude to the senatorship offered to the Orsini pope, Nicholas III, but other factors indicate that work began *c.* 1280, although the dating remains controversial. The apostolic episodes modelled on the lost atrium frescoes of Old St Peter's and the numerous classicizing details throughout the west end reflect the time Cimabue spent in Rome from 1272 to 1273. Further cross-fertilization appears in an altarpiece of 1280 (Perugia, G.N. Umbria) by Vigoroso da Siena (*fl* 1276–92). Cimabue devised a symmetrical design previously unknown in Italian art. The programme celebrates the Virgin and the Apostles Peter and Paul in conjunction with the Apocalypse. The cycles lead to the depiction of St Francis genuflecting at the foot of the Cross in each of the *Crucifixion* scenes, demonstrating the Saint's veneration of Christ's Passion. Pietralunga, writing *c.* 1570, also attributed the *Virgin and Child with Angels and St Francis* on the east wall of the north transept in the Lower Church to Cimabue. Compositional and stylistic affinities with the Santa Trinita *Madonna* (Florence, Uffizi) confirm this attribution and suggest a date during the early 1280s. This damaged fresco was once either part of a cycle or an altarpiece; later Giottesque borders crop the left side and may obscure another saint. Considerable overpaint was removed in 1973.

(iii) The biblical scenes of the Upper Church. In the Upper Church subsequent fresco cycles resumed the thematic and decorative synthesis begun by Cimabue. Work seems to have begun on the vaults: the vault nearest the crossing was painted blue with gold stars bordered by foliate patterns and Classically inspired nudes. Roundels with busts of *Christ*, the *Virgin*, *St Francis* and *St John the Baptist* embellish the second vault. The third repeats the star-dappled sky motif, and the *Four Latin Doctors of the Church* are depicted in the entrance vault. Sixteen *Old Testament* scenes arranged from left to right in two registers

4. Jacopo Torriti: *Creation of the World* (detail; early 1280s), fresco, north wall of the nave, Upper Church, S Francesco, Assisi

decorate the upper part of the north wall of the nave, from the *Creation of the World* (see fig. 4), in the bay nearest the crossing, to *Joseph before his Brothers*. Sixteen corresponding *New Testament* episodes from the *Annunciation* to the *Resurrection* cover the south wall of the nave, while the *Ascension* and *Pentecost* occupy the upper register of the entrance wall. Eight pairs of *Saints* in arcades line the entrance arch intrados. The well-preserved vaults and *Saints* contrast markedly with the ruinous condition of the nave walls. Between 1956 and 1958 the Istituto del Restauro conservators detached several impressive red chalk studies from beneath frescoes of the first two bays, and further consolidation during 1980 showed that the painting was executed from the top down, progressing eastward to the entrance. The sole irregularity occurs on the second bay of the south wall, where a graffito dated 1345 implies this area was originally overlooked.

White observed how the attribution of these frescoes is complicated because the working season may have lasted only six months: sufficient time to paint just one bay. Consequently developmental changes within a workshop might be interpreted as the introduction of another master. Among the clearly distinguishable hands, the Roman JACOPO TORRITI painted the vault with *Christ*, the *Virgin* and *Saints* and three *Genesis* bays beginning with the *Creation*. The lower register of *Old Testament* episodes in the first two bays and most of the *New Testament* episodes are by followers of Cimabue. The controversial Roman-trained ISAAC MASTER (named after the scenes of the *Isaac* story; *see* MASTERS, ANONYMOUS, AND MONOGRAMMISTS, §I) completed the cycles and the vault with the *Four Doctors of the Church* (for discussion of alternative attributions *see* DUCCIO, §1; GIOTTO, §I, 3). Technical evidence supports the dating of the biblical cycles to the late 13th century, after the west end frescoes. This may have coincided with the call to complete the decoration of the church in the Papal Bull of 14 May 1288 by the first Franciscan Pope, Nicholas IV. A comparison with the advanced naturalism of Torriti's *Coronation of the Virgin* mosaic (1295–6) in S Maria Maggiore, Rome, suggests that the painting of the first Assisi biblical episodes began *c.* 1290, although some have suggested the 1280s. Interruption of the project at one point required the Isaac Master partially to repaint the *Presentation in the Temple*, and he may have continued working on the cycles during the mid-1290s.

(iv) The 'Legend of St Francis'. Twenty-eight scenes from the *Legend of St Francis* are painted immediately below the *Old Testament* and *New Testament* scenes. There are three scenes in each bay, two under the east galleries, and two along the entrance wall. Beneath the scenes are fragmentary inscriptions from St Bonaventure's *Legenda maior*. The cycle begins with *St Francis and the Madman of Assisi* on the north wall nearest the crossing and continues around the nave, ending with the *Liberation of Peter the Heretic* on the south wall, opposite the first scene. Over the entrance in the middle of the cycle two roundels with busts of *Angels* flank a *Virgin and Child*. In 1962 Tintori and Meiss established that this moderately well-preserved cycle was executed sequentially, apart from the first episode, *St Francis and the Madman of Assisi*, which had been left until last to enable the installation of the rood beam. Cleaning of the frescoes began in 1981 and, despite the appearance of cracks in several episodes after the October 1982 earthquake, the repair and conservation of the entire cycle was completed by 1984.

The unresolved question of Giotto's authorship of this cycle (*see* GIOTTO, §I, 3 and fig. 9) originated with the simple statement 'Giotto painted works in the Minorite church at Assisi' in Riccobaldo Ferrarese's *Compilatio chronologica* (*c.* 1312–18). The ambiguous phrase 'almost all the lower part' added in Lorenzo Ghiberti's *I commentarii*, ii (*c.* 1447–55) was eventually interpreted by Vasari and others to mean the *St Francis* cycle. Although many Italian scholars support the attribution to Giotto and his workshop, others have acknowledged the work of at least three separate artists: the Roman-trained Master of the Legend of St Francis, who probably planned and supervised the execution of the cycle and painted the episodes from *St Francis Donating his Cloak to a Beggar* (scene II; for illustration *see* MASTERS, ANONYMOUS, AND MONOGRAMMISTS, §I: MASTER OF THE LEGEND OF ST FRANCIS) to the *Stigmatization of St Francis* (scene XIX); the Master of the Obsequies of St Francis (*fl* 1290s), who painted the scenes from the *Death of St Francis* (scene XX) to the *Dream of Gregory IX* (scene XXV); and the Florentine ST CECILIA MASTER (*see* MASTERS, ANONYMOUS, AND MONOGRAMMISTS, §I), who was responsible for *St Francis and the Madman of Assisi* (scene I) and the last three episodes. The *St Francis Legend* was the final cycle painted in the Upper Church. Despite the doubts cast on Vasari's attribution of the work, his dating of 1296–1304, encompassing Giovanni da Murrovalle's minister generalship, remains the most likely, while Stubblebine's date of the early 1340s for the activity of the St Cecilia Master cannot be sustained. The number of painters at Assisi implied rapid completion of the *St Francis* cycle, presumably begun during the later 1290s and finished around 1300.

(v) Giotto's circle and followers in the Lower Church. The next campaign of painting appears to have been the decoration of the subsidiary chapels of S Nicola and S Giovanni Battista in the Lower Church. The chapels, off the north and south transepts respectively, were probably commissioned by Cardinal Napoleone Orsini while he was Papal Legate to Umbria (1300–05) and were among the first of several private mortuary or commemorative chapels in the Lower Church. By 6 March 1306 the S Nicola Chapel housed ten episodes of an unfinished cycle highlighting St Nicholas's charity and miracles. The narrative descends from the summit of the right vault around the side walls and ends at the lower left. Other principal images include the dedication across the inside of the entrance wall, which faces the frescoed altarpiece over the wall tomb of the Cardinal's brother, Giangaetano Orsini (*d* 1292–4). Saints and Orsini insignia cover subsidiary areas. These frescoes are well preserved: only two episodes, midway down the vault, have been damaged by humidity. During the 1913 cleaning, Brizi uncovered the six genuflecting cardinals on the dedication accompanying the scene of *Orsini before Christ, SS Francis and Nicholas.* In 1974 additional radical revisions were found: the figures of Cardinal Orsini and Deacon Giangaetano had been painted on dry plaster over the original fresco. Hueck (1984) suggested that these early 14th-century alterations replaced the figures of eight participants at the 1292–4 Perugia conclave with the explicit aggrandizement of the Orsini. The cycle, derived from Jacopo da Voragine's *Golden Legend*, may honour popes Nicholas III and IV and forms part of an interrelated, primarily Franciscan scheme amid the lateral chapels.

Vasari's confusion with the nearby chapel of S Stanislao prompted the assignment of the S Nicola Chapel frescoes to 'Giottino'. The paintings have subsequently been attributed to the Master of the S Nicola Chapel (*fl* 1295–1305). The influence of the *St Francis* cycle in the Upper Church on this Giottesque painter and his collaborators has been recognized. Despite Stubblebine's revival of a mid-1330s dating for many of the S Nicola Chapel frescoes, the *terminus ante quem* furnished by iconographic reflections in Giuliano da Rimini's *Virgin and Saints* altarpiece (Boston, MA, Isabella Stewart Gardner Mus.) of 1307, noted by Meiss (1962), remains valid. The Master of the S Nicola Chapel then painted the *Annunciation* across the entrance wall of the chapel, thereby introducing eight episodes from the *Infancy of Christ* arranged left to right in two horizontal tiers at the top of the barrel vault in the north transept. Below this, on the east wall, a *Crucifixion* and Cimabue's *Enthroned Virgin and Child* face *St Francis and Death.* One of the posthumous miracles of St Francis is alongside the latter image; another embellishes the façade of the S Nicola Chapel.

Of the north transept frescoes Vasari attributed only the *Miracle of the Child from Suessa* to Giotto, although they have all subsequently been attributed to him at various times. The incorporation of ancillary details that modify Giotto's volumetric and spatially innovative style, however, suggest that they were painted by his followers at a date after the Arena Chapel frescoes (1304–5) at Padua. Examination of the plaster revealed that the *Infancy* cycle was painted after the *Annunciation* as work advanced southwards *c.* 1315–20. Like their counterparts in the Upper Church, the north transept frescoes comprise part of an encyclopedic programme. The scenes of St Francis's *Miracles*, illustrating St Bonaventure's *De miraculis* II, 4 and 6, suitably complement the *Infancy* cycle and continue the supernatural events in the *St Francis* cycle, while the *Crucifixion* echoes that in the church above it.

Giotto's influence also dominates the frescoes of the adjacent chapel of the Maddalena. According to John XXII's Bull of 9 January 1330, Teobaldo Pontano, Bishop of Assisi (*reg* 1296–1329), had this chapel built and painted. Simon noted masonry evidence suggesting that it was built before the S Nicola Chapel. Each lateral wall has two scenes from the *Life of Mary Magdalene*, which read from left to right, above a donor portrait. The cycle terminates in three lunettes beneath roundels with busts of *Christ*, the *Virgin*, *Mary Magdalene* and *Lazarus* in the vault. Saints resembling those in the S Nicola Chapel and Pontano insignia cover subsidiary surfaces. Vasari attributed these frescoes to Puccio Capanna, and they were later thought to be by Buffalmacco, but they are now attributed to the school of Giotto. The local painter Palmerino di Guido (*fl* 1301–48) is recorded as having repaid Iolo Giuntarelli of Assisi 50 Cortonese lire on 4 January 1309 in Giotto's name, substantiating the idea that Giotto had recently been in Assisi, although it is uncertain whether he painted sections of the Maddalena Chapel. The stylistic similarities between the *Raising of Lazarus* and the *Noli me tangere* and the frescoes of the same subjects in the Arena Chapel suggest a date for the Maddalena Chapel decoration after that for the work at Padua and contemporary with the north transept frescoes. In 1319–20 Pontano was blamed for the theft of the Papal Treasure stored at Assisi by the Ghibellines, and John XXII placed Assisi under interdict from 1321 to 1359. The ensuing political strife sharply curtailed any possible artistic patronage. Although planned as a burial site, the Maddalena Chapel no longer contains traces of a tomb. The cycle, which is taken from the *Golden Legend*, the Gospels and an epistle of St Jerome, displays an unusual upward organization. High above the portraits of *Teobaldo Pontano*, the two scenes of the *Last Communion and Ecstasy of St Mary Magdalene* create an illusion of heavenly ascension suitable for a commemorative mortuary function.

The *Allegories of the Franciscan Virtues* on the crossing vault over St Francis's tomb constitute the Lower Church's supreme memorial. Long inscriptions under each scene identify the *Apotheosis of St Francis* accompanied by *Poverty*, *Chastity* and *Obedience.* Ornamental borders composed of *Saints*, *Angels* and *Apocalyptic* images spring from the central roundel showing the *Apocalyptic Christ.* This well-preserved vault was cleaned in 1968 during the conservation of the west end. The *Franciscan Allegories* celebrate the fundamental virtues of the Order; the *Apocalyptic* imagery is modelled on Dante and the tenets expounded by St Bonaventure. Vasari attributed these frescoes to Giotto, but this was amended by Venturi to the Master of the Assisi Vaults (*fl* 1330). Nonetheless, the *Franciscan Allegories* contain the vivid full-bodied figures typical of Giotto's circle. Technical investigation has confirmed that the crossing vault was executed after the *Infancy* cycle of the north transept. In the apse below the

5. Pietro Lorenzetti: *Crucifixion* (*c.* 1319), fresco with tempera, east wall of the south transept, Lower Church, S Francesco, Assisi

Apotheosis of St Francis, a *Redemption* allegory was described by Ghiberti: the *Celestial Glory* exemplified Bonaventure's *Itinerarium mentis in Deum* (1259). Attributed to Giotto's disciple Stefano Fiorentino, this fresco was destroyed in 1622 to make way for a *Last Judgement* by Cesare Sermei (*fl* 1609–68).

The composition of the chapel of S Stanislao, within the cantoria on the south side of the nave near the crossing, was inspired by early 14th-century Tuscan painting. The Soldani of Assisi, whose insignia embellish the arch, presumably commissioned the chapel's decoration. Present consensus favours Pietralunga's attribution of the frescoes to the local artist PUCCIO CAPANNA rather than to the Giottino mentioned by Vasari (but *see also* MASO DI BANCO). The unfinished *Coronation of the Virgin* lunette and the three episodes in the arch above display typically Giottesque figures inhabiting a three-dimensional space, whereas their colouring imitates Sienese painting. The frescoes were restored to a fair condition in 1974. The three scenes, *St Stanislas Resuscitating a Man* and the *Martyrdom of St Stanislas* over a *Crucifixion*, are appropriate to the burial chapel where on 17 August 1253 Innocent IV canonized the Bishop of Kraków. The turbulent events of the 1320s perhaps interrupted work on the chapel and eventually forced its abandonment.

(vi) Pietro Lorenzetti and Simone Martini. The chapel of S Giovanni Battista off the south transept was intended as a mortuary chapel for Cardinal Napoleone Orsini but was never realized as such. Dedicated to St Francis's patron saint, it houses a frescoed fictive altarpiece of the *Virgin and Child with SS John the Baptist and Francis* by PIETRO LORENZETTI. The good condition of this fresco is marred by losses throughout the borders and gilt background. It is Lorenzetti's most Ducciesque and, therefore, earliest Assisi fresco, dated by comparison some years before his *Virgin and Child* altarpiece for the pieve of S Maria, Arezzo, which was commissioned in 1320. There are other frescoes by Lorenzetti in the south transept: six scenes from the *Passion*, proceeding from left to right along the barrel vault, and on the east wall a magnificent *Crucifixion* (see fig. 5), beneath which is a frescoed altarpiece inside a fictive niche, with a small *Crucifixion with Donor and Liturgical Utensils*. A fictive bench and four half-length *Saints* cover the adjacent transept. Diagonally opposite are the *Suicide of Judas* and *Stigmatization of St Francis*. Four *Passion* episodes continue up into the transept where the *Resurrection* closes the narrative. The erection of an altarpiece in 1604–5 (removed between 1870 and 1871) permanently injured the *Crucifixion* and frescoes below, but

the paint surfaces, both tempera on dry plaster and true fresco, remain in good condition. The examination by Maginnis and Tintori in 1973 revealed 330 work-stages executed during one campaign.

The attribution to Pietro Lorenzetti was first made by Cavalcaselle in 1864, thus discrediting Vasari's previous attributions to Giotto, Puccio Capanna and Pietro Cavallini. The frescoes exhibit characteristically Sienese sensitive, linear figures, incandescent colours and gold ornament, but the last figures on the lower walls show the influence of the neighbouring Giottesque works. Among the cycle's important contributions are the earliest surviving representations of cast shadows since antiquity. The considerable number of work-stages, implying extensive shop assistance over several years, does not solve the chronology of these undocumented cycles. Maginnis (1984) supported an early date, *c*. 1319, not long after Pietro's presumed arrival in Assisi *c*. 1315, which is plausible on stylistic grounds.

Another elaborate scheme by a Sienese painter is found in Cardinal da Montefiore's chapel of S Martino, off the south side of the nave, adjoining the entrance hall (*see* GENTILE DA MONTEFIORE). The *Life of St Martin* is set out in ten episodes, spiralling upwards from the lower left to the top left wall of the vault. Beneath a ciborium drawn on the inner wall of the façade the Cardinal genuflects before St Martin. Montefiore insignia and half-length saints adorn the window embrasures opposite the dedication. Eight *Saints*, three of whom had Angevin connections, cover the entrance arch intrados. In 1957 the excessive humidity in the chapel forced the Istituto del Restauro conservators to detach the painting of *St Martin Dividing his Cloak*, revealing a full-scale preliminary red-chalk drawing. Moisture continued to impair the cycle's otherwise good condition, and in 1974 conservators reconstructed blistered true fresco surfaces, which had been frequently overpainted with tempera. During that campaign pentiments and areas of gilded tin and lead white were detected. Here, as elsewhere, the use of lead white accounts for some incongruous dark passages. Fehm and Tintori's examination of the plaster plotted over 120 work-stages; those on the entrance arch intrados being painted last. The generally accepted attribution to Simone Martini was first made by Ranghiasci in 1798 (Fea, 1820; *see* MARTINI, SIMONE and fig. 1). The discovery by Hoch (1985) of the record of payment, dated 30 March 1312, from Cardinal da Montefiore allocating 600 florins 'to make a chapel in S Francesco, Assisi' probably refers to the construction and future decoration of the S Martino Chapel. The stylistic similarities between the frescoes and Simone's *Maestà* (completed 1315–16; Siena, Pal. Pub.), combined with the strictures on Assisi after 1321 (*see* §(v) above), suggest a date for the execution of the *St Martin* cycle between *c*. 1317 and *c*. 1319.

6. Simone Martini: *Investiture of St Martin as a Knight* (*c*. 1317–19), fresco with tempera, S Martino Chapel, Lower Church, S Francesco, Assisi

The Cardinal's unexpected burial in the chapel of S Lodovico opposite modified the original sepulchral function of the S Martino Chapel. The cycle, organized after the Maddalena Chapel, ascends so that the scenes of the *Death and Obsequies of St Martin* beside the dedication commemorate, by extension, the donor. One exceptional episode, omitted from Sulpicius Severus's *Vita Sancti Martini* (393–6) but found in the *Golden Legend*, is the *Investiture of St Martin as a Knight* (see fig. 6). This contemporary-type ceremony, in which St Martin is transformed into the chivalric Franciscan ideal, also reflects the dynastic ambitions of the Angevin family, secured in 1307–11, when Cardinal da Montefiore was Papal Legate to Hungary. In his biography of Simone Martini, Vasari mentioned a frescoed altarpiece to St Elizabeth. This comprises the *Virgin and Child with Two Royal Saints* below the north transept *Crucifixion*; *Five Saints* on the adjoining wall complete the ensemble. In 1968 the Istituto del Restauro stabilized their moisture-damaged condition, but the conservators could not restore the effaced inscriptions beneath the three-quarter-length saints; only *St Francis* and *St Louis of Toulouse* are readily identifiable. The altar must have honoured St Elizabeth of Hungary, thereby connecting the figures of these saints to the S Martino Chapel frescoes executed immediately before. The nearby fresco of the *Five Franciscan Blessed*, beneath Cimabue's *Virgin and Child Enthroned*, is contemporary and painted in the manner of Pietro Lorenzetti. First described by Pietralunga, it was cleaned in 1968 during the conservation campaign on the north transept. These well-preserved, three-quarter-length praying figures, with their now illegible inscriptions, marked friars' graves.

(vii) Andrea de' Bartoli. The repeal of the interdict in 1359 inaugurated the last substantial period of fresco decoration, of which only two cycles are extant. The chapel of S Caterina at the north end of the entrance hall, the first burial site of Cardinal Egidio Albornoz (*reg* 1350–67),

emulates earlier 14th-century chapel designs in S Francesco. The 12 episodes illustrating the *Life of St Catherine* ascend the vault from the lower right wall. On the façade Cardinal Albornoz kneels before his titular saint, St Clement, who is standing near five further saints. Albornoz insignia and seated saints fill the window embrasures. Documents found by Filippini (1911) disprove the date of 1302 and the attribution to Buffalmacco given to them by Vasari. On 18 December 1367 Matteo di Giovanello di Maffeo, known as Gattapone, received 500 florins for work on the chapel; 450 florins had also been issued that year to the painter 'Andrea da Bologna', probably to be identified with Andrea de' Bartoli, whose expressionistic, stridently coloured style is evident throughout the frescoes that were completed in 1368. Andrea de' Bartoli was also paid to decorate the provisional tomb for Cardinal Albornoz. The Umbrian artist Pace di Bartolo (*fl* 1344–68) painted the tomb's inscription. St Catherine of Alexandria was particularly venerated in Bologna, the seat of Cardinal Albornoz's titular church. The frescoes emphasize the theme of conversion leading to martyrdom. The *Death and Ascension of St Catherine* at the top of the vault is in a similar position to the identical episode in the S Martino Chapel.

During the 1360s Andrea de' Bartoli also executed the fresco cycle in the small chapel of S Lorenzo between those of S Ludovico and S Antonio di Padova. Despite uncertainty about the circumstances of this commission, it seems likely that the *Martyrdom of St Lawrence* and the two scenes from the *Passion* were intended to refer to the Lower Church's funerary purpose.

BIBLIOGRAPHY

EARLY SOURCES

R. Ferrarese: *Compilatio chronologica* (MS.; *c.* 1312–18); ed. L. A. Muratori in *Rerum italicarum scriptores*, ix (Milan, 1726); Eng. trans., ed. J. H. Stubblebine, in *Giotto: The Arena Chapel Frescoes* (New York, 1969), p. 110

A. Billi: *Il libro di Antonio Billi* (MS.; 1516–35); ed. C. Frey (Berlin, 1892)

L'anonimo magliabechiano (*c.* 1542–8; Florence, Bib. N. Cent., MS. Magl. XVII, 17); ed. A. Ficarra (Naples, 1968)

G. Vasari: *Vite* (1550, rev. 2/1568); ed. G. Milanesi (1878–85)

Fra L. da Pietralunga: *Descrizione della Basilica di S. Francesco e di altri santuari di Assisi* (1568–80; Assisi, Bib. Com., Fond. Moderno, MS. 148); ed. P. Scarpellini (Treviso, 1982) [excellent commentary and bibliog.]

F. M. Angeli: *Collis paradisi amoenitas seu sacri conventus Assisiensis historiae libri II* (Montefalco, 1704)

P. Bini: *La verità scoperta ne' tre santuari della città di Assisi, la Basilica di San Francesco, la Porziuncola e Rivortorto* (Florence, 1721)

C. Fea: *Descrizione ragionata della Sagrosanta Patriarcale Basilica e Cappella Papale di S Francesco d'Assisi* (Rome, 1820)

L. Ghiberti: *Commentarii* (1912)

GENERAL

Italian 14th-century painting

DBI; Thieme–Becker

J. White: *The Birth and Rebirth of Pictorial Space* (London, 1957, 2/1967, rev. 3/1987)

E. Borsook: *The Mural Painters of Tuscany from Cimabue to Andrea del Sarto* (London, 1960, rev. Oxford, 2/1980)

J. White: *Art and Architecture in Italy, 1250–1400*, Pelican Hist. A. (Harmondsworth, 1966, rev. New Haven, 3/1993)

B. Cole: *Sienese Painting from its Origins to the Fifteenth Century* (New York, 1980)

E. Carli: *La pittura senese del trecento* (Milan, 1981)

E. Castelnuovo, ed.: *La pittura in Italia: Il duecento e il trecento*, 2 vols (Milan, 1986)

M. A. Lavin: *The Place of Narrative: Mural Decoration in Italian Churches, 431–1600* (Chicago, 1990)

S Francesco

N. Papini: *Storia di San Francesco di Assisi* (Foligno, 1825)

L. Carattoli, M. Guardabassi and G. B. Rossi-Scotti: *Descrizione del santuario di San Francesco d'Assisi* (Perugia, 1863); also in *Boll. Reale Deput. Stor. Patria Umbria*, xxviii (1928), pp. 91–227

G. Fratini and A. Cristofani: *Storia della Basilica e del Convento di San Francesco in Assisi* (Prato, 1882)

H. Thode: *Franz von Assisi und die Anfänge der Kunst der Renaissance in Italien* (Berlin, 1885, 2/1904); rev., ed. L. Bellosi (Rome, 1993)

A. Venturi: *La Basilica di Assisi* (Rome, 1908)

B. Kleinschmidt: *Die Basilika S. Francesco in Assisi*, 3 vols (Berlin, 1915–28)

I. B. Supino: *La Basilica di San Francesco d'Assisi* (Bologna, 1924)

G. Cristofani: 'Due preziose descrizioni della Basilica di San Francesco in Assisi', *Boll. Reale Deput. Stor. Patria Umbria*, xxviii (1928), pp. iii–xiii

B. Marinangeli: 'Note alle descrizioni di Fr. Ludovico da Città di Castello', *Boll. Reale Deput. Stor. Patria Umbria*, xxviii (1928), pp. 233–55

L. Coletti: *Gli affreschi della Basilica di Assisi* (Bergamo, 1949)

W. Schöne: 'Studien zur Oberkirche von Assisi', *Festschrift Kurt Bauch* (Munich, 1957), pp. 50–116

G. Zaccaria: 'Diario storico della Basilica e Sacro Convento di S. Francesco in Assisi, 1220–1927', *Misc. Francesc.*, i (1963), pp. 75–120; ii–iii (1963), pp. 290–361; iv (1963), pp. 495–536; v (1964), pp. 165–210; vi (1964), pp. 433–73

H. J. Ziemke: 'Ramboux und Assisi', *Städel-Jb.*, n. s., iii (1971), pp. 167–212

H. Belting: *Die Oberkirche von San Francesco in Assisi: Ihre Dekoration als Aufgabe die Genese einer neuen Wandmalerei* (Berlin, 1977)

A. Tantillo Mignosi: 'Restauri alla Basilica Inferiore di Assisi', *Boll. A.*, n. s., iii–iv (1977, dated 1975), pp. 217–31

I. Hueck: 'La Basilica Francescana di Assisi nell'ottocento: Alcuni documenti su restauri ed interventi eseguiti', *Boll. A.*, n. s., lxvi (1981), pp. 143–57

G. Ruf: *Das Grab des heiligen Franziskus: Die Fresken der Unterkirchen von Assisi* (Freiburg im Breisgau, 1981)

S. Nessi: *La Basilica di S. Francesco in Assisi e la sua documentazione storica* (Assisi, 1982)

M. Boskovits: 'Celebrazioni dell'VIII centenario della nascita di San Francesco: Studi recenti sulla Basilica di Assisi', *A. Cristiana*, lxxi (1983), pp. 203–13

L. Bellosi: *La pecora di Giotto* (Turin, 1985)

G. Lobrichon: *Assise: Les Fresques de la Basilique Inférieure* (Paris, 1985)

J. Poeschke: *Die Kirche San Francesco in Assisi und ihre Wandmalereien* (Munich, 1985) [excellent pls]

J. H. Stubblebine: *Assisi and the Rise of Vernacular Art* (New York, 1985)

F. Todini: 'Pittura del duecento e del trecento in Umbria e il cantiere di Assisi', *La pittura in Italia: Il duecento e il trecento*, ed. E. Castelnuovo, ii (Milan, 1986), pp. 375–413

M. V. Schwarz: 'Zerstört und wiederhergestellt: Die Ausmalung der Unterkirche von S. Francesco in Assisi', *Mitt. Ksthist. Inst. Florenz*, xxxvii (1993), pp. 1–28

THE MASTER OF ST FRANCIS

R. van Marle: 'Il Maestro di San Francesco', *Rass. A.*, xix (1919), pp. 9–21

W. B. Miller: *The Franciscan Legend in Italian Painting in the Thirteenth Century* (diss., New York, Columbia U., 1961), pp. 136–56

J. Schultze: 'Zur Kunst des "Franziskusmeister"', *Wallraf-Richartz Jb.*, xxv (1963), pp. 109–50

——: 'Die Fresken in der Unterkirche San Francesco in Assisi und andere Werke des "Franziskusmeister"', *Raggi*, vii (1967), pp. 44–58

S. Tsuji, K. Mogi and Y. Nagatsuka: *Assisi no San Francesco Seido koryu shoki no geijtsu* [Basilica of San Francesco in Assisi: art of the early period. History of the architecture and frescoes in the central nave of the Lower Church] (Tokyo, 1978), pp. 47–98

B. Brenk: 'Das Datum der Franzlegende der Unterkirche zu Assisi', *Roma anno 1300. Atti della IV settimana di studi di storia dell'arte medievale dell'Università di Roma 'La Sapienza': Roma, 1980*, pp. 229–37

S. Esser: *Die Ausmalung der Unterkirche von San Francesco in Assisi durch den Franziskusmeister* (diss., Bonn, Rhein. Friedrich-Wilhelms-U., 1981, rev. 1983)

J. Cannon: 'Dating the Frescoes by the Maestro di San Francesco at Assisi', *Burl. Mag.*, cxxiv (1982), pp. 65–9

S. Romano: 'Le storie parallele di Assisi: Il Maestro di S. Francesco', *Stor. A.*, xliv (1982), pp. 63–82

D. Blume: *Wandmalerei als Ordenspropaganda Bildprogramme im Chorbereich Franziskanischer Konvente Italiens bis zur Mitte des 14. Jahrhunderts* (Worms, 1983), pp. 29–32

J. Poeschke: 'Der "Franziskusmeister" und die Anfänge der Ausmalung von S Francesco in Assisi', *Mitt. Ksthist. Inst. Florenz*, xxvii (1983), pp. 125–70
E. Lunghi: 'Maestro di San Francesco', *La pittura in Italia: Il duecento e il trecento*, ed. E. Castelnuovo, ii (Milan, 1986), pp. 624–5

THE NORTHERN AND ROMAN MASTERS

E. Hertlein: *Die Basilika San Francesco in Assisi* (Florence, 1964), pp. 189–94
I. Hueck: 'Der Maler der Apostelszenen im Atrium von Alt-St. Peter', *Mitt. Ksthist. Inst. Florenz*, xiv (1969), pp. 115–44
C. Volpe: 'La formazione di Giotto nella cultura di Assisi', *Giotto e i Giotteschi in Assisi*, ed. G. Palumbo (Rome, 1969, rev. Assisi, 2/1979), pp. 15–59
J. T. Wollesen: *Die Fresken von San Piero a Grado bei Pisa* (diss., U. Heidelberg, 1975, rev. Bad Oeynhausen, 1977), pp. 107–12
A. Cadei: 'Assisi, S. Francesco: L'architettura e la prima fase della decorazione', *Roma anno 1300. Atti della IV settimana di studi di storia dell'arte medievale dell'Università di Roma 'La Sapienza': Roma, 1980*, pp. 141–74
V. Pace: 'Presenze Oltremontane ad Assisi: Realtà e mito', *Roma anno 1300. Atti della IV settimana di studi di storia dell'arte medievale dell'Università di Roma 'La Sapienza': Roma, 1980*, pp. 239–51
C. Fratini: 'Maestro Oltremontano di Assisi', *La pittura in Italia: Il duecento e il trecento*, ed. E. Castelnuovo, ii (Milan, 1986), pp. 264–5

CIMABUE

J. Strzygowski: *Cimabue und Rom* (Vienna, 1888), pp. 65–130
A. Aubert: *Die malerische Dekoration der S. Francesco Kirche in Assisi: Ein Beitrag zur Lösung der Cimabue Frage* (Leipzig, 1907), pp. 29–38, 79–125
G. Vitzthum: 'Zur Datierung der Chorfresken in der Oberkirche zu Assisi', *Repert. Kstwissen.*, xxx (1907), pp. 383–5
A. Nicholson: *Cimabue: A Critical Study* (Princeton, 1932), pp. 2–20
R. Salvini: *Cimabue* (Rome, 1946), pp. 16–23
——: 'Postilla a Cimabue', *Riv. A.*, xxvi (1950), pp. 43–60
G. Urbani: 'Restoration of Frescoes in Rome and Assisi', *Connoisseur*, cxxxvi (1955), pp. 155–60
E. Battisti: *Cimabue* (Milan, 1963; Eng. trans., 1966), pp. 27–55
A. Monferini: 'L'Apocalisse di Cimabue', *Commentari*, xvii (1966), pp. 25–55
C. Mitchell: 'The Imagery of the Upper Church at Assisi', *Giotto e il suo tempo. Atti del congresso internazionale per la celebrazione del VII centenario della nascita di Giotto: Roma, 1967*, pp. 113–34
J. H. Stubblebine: 'Cimabue's Frescoes of the Virgin at Assisi', *A. Bull.*, xlix (1967), pp. 330–33
E. Sindona: *Cimabue e il momento figurativo pregiottesco* (Milan, 1975), pp. 89–109
L. Tintori: 'Il bianco di piombo nelle pitture murali della Basilica di San Francesco ad Assisi', *Studies in Late Medieval and Renaissance Painting in Honor of Millard Meiss*, 2 vols (New York, 1977), pp. 437–44
M. Cordaro: 'L'abside della Basilica Superiore di Assisi, restauro e ricostruzione critica del testo figurativo', *Roma anno 1300. Atti della IV settimana di studi di storia dell'arte medievale dell'Università di Roma 'La Sapienza': Roma, 1980*, pp. 119–24
J. White and B. Zanardi: 'Cimabue and the Decorative Sequence in the Upper Church of S. Francesco, Assisi', *Roma anno 1300. Atti della IV settimana di studi di storia dell'arte medievale dell'Università di Roma 'La Sapienza': Roma, 1980*, pp. 103–17; also in *Studies in Late Medieval Italian Art* (London, 1984), pp. 110–34
Y. Christe: 'L'Apocalypse de Cimabue à Assise', *Cah. Archéol.*, xxix (1980–81), pp. 157–74
I. Hueck: 'Cimabue und das Bildprogramm der Oberkirche von S. Francesco in Assisi', *Mitt. Ksthist. Inst. Florenz*, xxv (1981), pp. 279–324
J. White: 'Cimabue and Assisi: Working Methods and Art Historical Consequences', *A. Hist.*, iv (1981), pp. 355–83; also in J. White: *Studies in Late Medieval Italian Art* (London, 1984), pp. 135–65

THE BIBLICAL SCENES OF THE UPPER CHURCH

M. Zimmerman: *Giotto und die Kunst Italiens im Mittelalter*, i (Leipzig, 1899), pp. 265–84
L. Lochoff: 'Gli affreschi dell'Antico e Nuovo Testamento nella Basilica Superiore di Assisi', *Riv. A.*, xix (1937), pp. 240–70
P. Toesca: *Gli affreschi del Vecchio e del Nuovo Testamento nella Chiesa Superiore del santuario di Assisi* (Florence, 1948)
P. Mora and R. Carita: 'Supporti per gli affreschi rimossi scheda n. 3', *Boll. Ist. Cent. Rest.*, ix (1958), pp. 171–9
C. Volpe: 'La formazione di Giotto nella cultura di Assisi', *Giotto e i Giotteschi in Assisi*, ed. G. Palumbo (Rome, 1969, rev. Assisi, 2/1979), pp. 15–59
M. Boskovits: 'Nuovi studi su Giotto ed Assisi', *Paragone*, ccii (1971), pp. 34–56
G. Ruf: *San Francesco e S. Bonaventura: Un interpretazione storico-salvifica degli affreschi della navata nella Chiesa Superiore di San Francesco in Assisi alla luce teologia di San Bonaventura* (Assisi, 1974)
L. Bellosi: 'La decorazione della Basilica Superiore di Assisi e la pittura romana di fine duecento', *Roma anno 1300. Atti della IV settimana di studi di storia dell'arte medievale dell'Università di Roma 'La Sapienza': Roma, 1980*, pp. 127–39
H. Belting: 'Assisi e Roma: Risultati, problemi, prospettive', *Roma anno 1300. Atti della IV settimana di studi di storia dell'arte medievale dell'Università di Roma 'La Sapienza': Roma, 1980*, pp. 93–101
J. R. Benton: *The Influences of Ancient Roman Wall Painting on Late Thirteenth Century Italian Painting: A New Interpretation of the Upper Church of S. Francesco in Assisi* (diss., Providence, RI, Brown U., 1981)
M. Boskovits: 'Gli affreschi della Sala dei Notari a Perugia e la pittura in Umbria alla fine del XIII secolo', *Boll. A.*, n. s., lxvi (1981), pp. 1–41
S. Tsuji: 'The Origins of Buon Fresco', *Z. Kstgesch.*, xlvi (1983), pp. 215–22
E. Lunghi: 'Maestro della Cattura', *La pittura in Italia: Il duecento e il trecento*, ed. E. Castelnuovo, ii (Milan, 1986), pp. 604–5
——: 'Maestro della Crocifissione di Assisi', *La pittura in Italia: Il duecento e il trecento*, ed. E. Castelnuovo, ii (Milan, 1986), p. 606
V. Terraroli: 'Jacopo Torriti', *La pittura in Italia: Il duecento e il trecento*, ed. E. Castelnuovo, ii (Milan, 1986), p. 665

THE 'LEGEND OF ST FRANCIS'

The Giotto problem

B. Marinangeli: 'La serie di affreschi giotteschi rappresentanti la vita di S. Francesco nella Chiesa Superiore di Assisi', *Misc. Francesc.*, xiii (1911), pp. 97–112
'Cappella di S. Nicolò', *Misc. Francesc.*, xv (1914), p. 32
G. Giovannoni: 'Gli affreschi della Chiesa Superiore di Assisi: Quesiti di restauro di monumenti', *Palladio*, i (1937), pp. 182–3
——: 'I restauri nella Basilica Superiore di Assisi', *Arti: Rass. Bimest. A. Ant. Mod.*, iv (1941–2), pp. 216–22
——: 'I restauri degli affreschi di Giotto nella Basilica Superiore di Assisi', *Arti: Rass. Bimest. A. Ant. Mod.*, v (1942), pp. 88–9
J. Bouret: *Giotto gli affreschi nella Chiesa Superiore di Assisi* (Milan, 1953)
J. D. Rey: *Giotto Frescoes in the Upper Church Assisi* (New York, 1954)
M. R. Fisher: 'Assisi, Padua and the Boy in the Tree', *A. Bull.*, xxxiii (1956), pp. 47–52
C. Gnudi: 'Il passo di Riccobaldo Ferrarese relativo a Giotto e il problema della sua autenticità', *Studies in the History of Art Dedicated to W. E. Suida* (London, 1959), pp. 26–30
P. Toesca: 'Una postilla alla *vita di S. Francesco* nella Chiesa Superiore di Assisi', *Studies in the History of Art Dedicated to W. E. Suida* (London, 1959), pp. 21–5
M. Sperlich: *Die Stellung der Fresken der Franzlegende in der Oberkirche von San Francesco in Assisi in der Geschichte der Perspektive* (Hamburg, 1960)
A. Smart: 'Ghiberti's "quasi tutta la parte di sotto" and Vasari's Attributions to Giotto at Assisi', *Ren. & Mod. Stud.*, viii (1963), pp. 5–24; also in *Giotto e il suo tempo. Atti del congresso internazionale per la celebrazione del VII centenario della nascita di Giotto: Roma, 1967* (Rome, 1971), pp. 79–91
G. Previtali: *Gli affreschi di Giotto ad Assisi* (Milan, 1965)
——: *Giotto e la sua bottega* (Milan, 1967, 2/1974); rev., ed. A. Conti (Milan, 3/1993), pp. 46–70
V. Mariani: 'Giotto nel ciclo della vita di San Francesco', *Giotto e i Giotteschi in Assisi*, ed. G. Palumbo (Rome, 1969, rev. Assisi, 2/1979), pp. 61–92
M. Gabrielli: *Il ciclo Francesco di Assisi* (Florence, 1970)
A. Smart: *The Assisi Problem and the Art of Giotto: A Study of the Legend of St. Francis in the Upper Church of San Francesco, Assisi* (London, 1971, rev. New York, 2/1983)
H. Herzmann and W. R. Cook: 'Bonaventure's Life of St. Francis and the Frescoes in the Church of San Francesco: A Study in Medieval Aesthetics', *Franziskanischer Stud.*, xlix (1972), pp. 29–37
M. Thomas: 'Zur Ikonographie der Franziskuslegende besonders der Fresken Giotto in der Oberkirche der Basilika San Francesco in Assisi', *Z. Religions und Geistesgeschichte*, xxvii (1975), pp. 245–55

L. Bellosi: 'La Sala dei Notai, Marino da Perugia e un ante quem per il problema di Assisi', *Per Maria Cionini Visani, scritti di amici* (Turin, 1977), pp. 22–5

E. Battisti: 'Body Language nel ciclo San Francesco ad Assisi: Una introduzione al problema', *Roma anno 1300. Atti della IV settimana di studi di storia dell'arte medievale dell'Università di Roma 'La Sapienza': Roma, 1980*, pp. 675–88

L. Bellosi: 'La barba di San Francesco: Nuove proposte per il "problema di Assisi"', *Prospettiva*, xxii (1980), pp. 11–34; also in L. Bellosi: *La pecora di Giotto* (Turin, 1985), pp. 3–40

B. Brenk: 'Zu den Gewolbefresken der Oberkirche in Assisi', *Roma anno 1300. Atti della IV settimana di studi di storia dell'arte medievale dell'Università di Roma 'La Sapienza': Roma, 1980*, pp. 221–8

The St Cecilia Master

L. Bracaloni: 'Assisi medioevale: Studio storico-topografico', *Archv Franciscanum Hist.*, vii (1909), pp. 3–19

R. Offner and K. Steinweg: *Corpus*, III/i (1931), pp. 18–23; rev. M. Boskovits and M. Gregori (1986), pp. 9, 21–3, 55–6, 58, 60–93 [excellent commentary, bibliog. and pls]

A. Parronchi: 'Attività del Maestro della Santa Cecilia', *Riv. A.*, xxi (1939), pp. 193–228

A. Smart: 'The St. Cecilia Master and his School at Assisi, I–II', *Burl. Mag.*, cii (1960), pp. 405–13, 431–7

L. Tintori and M. Meiss: *The Painting of the Life of St. Francis in Assisi with Notes on the Arena Chapel* (New York, 1962), pp. 45–54, 56, 82–4, 147–56

A. Smart: 'Reflections on the Art of Giotto', *Apollo*, lxxxi (1965), pp. 257–63

C. De Benedictis: 'Nuove proposte per il Maestro della Santa Cecilia', *Ant. Viva*, xi (1972), pp. 3–9

M. Bietti Fava: 'Gaddo Gaddi: Un'ipotesi', *A. Cristiana*, lxxi (1983), pp. 49–52

J. H. Stubblebine: 'A New Chronology for the St. Cecilia Master', *Tribute to Lotte Brand Philip, Art Historian and Detective* (New York, 1985), pp. 205–16

E. Biagi: 'Maestro della Santa Cecilia', *La pittura in Italia: Il duecento e il trecento*, ed. E. Castelnuovo, ii (Milan, 1986), p. 610

GIOTTO'S CIRCLE AND FOLLOWERS IN THE LOWER CHURCH

M. Meiss: *Giotto and Assisi* (New York, 1960)

G. Previtali: *Giotto e la sua bottega* (Milan, 1967, 2/1974); rev., ed. A. Conti (Milan, 3/1993)

The S Nicola Chapel Master

I. B. Supino: 'La Cappella di Gian Gaetano Orsini nella Basilica di San Francesco in Assisi', *Boll. A.*, vi (1926), pp. 131–5

——: 'La tomba del Cardinale Mattero Orsini nella Chiesa della Minerva in Roma e gli affreschi della Cappella Orsini in San Francesco in Assisi', *Boll. A.*, vii (1927), pp. 84–90

M. Meiss: 'Reflections of Assisi: A Tabernacle and the Cesi Master', *Scritti di storia dell'arte in onore di Mario Salmi*, ii (Rome, 1962), pp. 75–111

G. Previtali: 'Le Cappelle di S. Nicola e di S. Maria Maddalena nella Chiesa Inferiore di San Francesco', *Giotto e i Giotteschi in Assisi*, ed. G. Palumbo (Rome, 1969, rev. Assisi 2/1979), pp. 93–127

H. B. J. Maginnis: 'Assisi Revisited: Notes on Recent Observations', *Burl. Mag.*, cxvii (1975), pp. 511–17

R. Simon: 'Towards a Relative Chronology of the Frescoes in the Lower Church of San Francesco at Assisi', *Burl. Mag.*, cxviii (1976), pp. 361–6

L. Bellosi: 'Moda e cronologia (A): Gli affreschi della Basilica Inferiore di Assisi', *Prospettiva*, x (1977), pp. 21–31

R. Goffen: '*Nostra conversatio in caelis est*: Observations on the Sacra Conversazione', *A. Bull.*, lxi (1979), pp. 198–221

G. Bonsanti: 'Giotto nella Cappella di S. Nicola', *Roma anno 1300. Atti della IV settimana di studi di storia dell'arte medievale dell'Università di Roma 'La Sapienza': Roma, 1980*, pp. 199–208

I. Hueck: 'Il Cardinale Napoleone Orsini e la Cappella di S. Nicola nella Basilica Francescana ad Assisi', *Roma anno 1300. Atti della IV settimana di studi di storia dell'arte medievale dell'Università di Roma 'La Sapienza': Roma, 1980*, pp. 187–97

——: 'Die Kapellen der Basilika San Francesco in Assisi: Die Auftraggeber und die Franziskaner', *Patronage and Public in the Trecento. Proceedings of the St Lambrecht Symposium: St Lambrecht Abbey, 1984*, pp. 81–104

E. Lunghi: 'Maestro della Cappella di San Nicola', *La pittura in Italia: Il duecento e il trecento*, ed. E. Castelnuovo, ii (Milan, 1986), p. 603

——: 'Maestro Espressionista di Santa Chiara', *La pittura in Italia: Il duecento e il trecento*, ed. E. Castelnuovo, ii (Milan, 1986), p. 632

The North Transept and Crossing

G. Mestica: 'San Francesco, Dante e Giotto', *Nuova Antol.*, ix (1881), pp. 3–39; xi (1881), pp. 403–43; xiii (1881), pp. 38–64

P. Schubring: 'Die Fresken im Querschiff der Unterkirche S. Francesco in Assisi', *Repert. Kstwiss.*, xxii (1899), pp. 1–12

A. Venturi: 'Le *Vele* d'Assisi', *L'Arte*, ix (1906), pp. 19–34

G. Salvadori: 'Le *Vele* di Assisi e la poesia di Dante', *Rass. Contemp.*, iv (1911), pp. 31–54

A. Venturi: 'Affreschi del pittore delle *Vele* di Assisi', *L'Arte*, xiv (1911), pp. 25–8

L. Bracaloni: 'La Gloria Francescana nel grande affresco absidale già in San Francesco d'Assisi', *Stud. Francescana*, xxxiii (1936), pp. 3–17

M. Gabrielli: 'La Gloria Celeste di Stefano Fiorentino', *Riv. A.*, xxxi (1956), pp. 3–23

M. Gosebruch: 'Giottos römischer Stefaneschi Altar und die Fresken des sog. "Maestro delle Vele" in der Unterkirche S. Franziskus zu Assisi', *Kunstchronik*, ii (1958), pp. 288–91

L. Bracaloni: 'Apoteosi Francescana già nella Basilica Inferiore di Assisi', *Frate Francesco*, xxiii (1959), pp. 116–23

M. Gosebruch: 'Gli affreschi di Giotto nel braccio destro del transetto e nelle *Vele* centrali della Chiesa Inferiore di San Francesco', *Giotto e i Giotteschi in Assisi*, ed. G. Palumbo (Rome, 1969, rev. Assisi, 2/1979), pp. 129–98

E. Pagliani: 'Note su restauri degli affreschi giotteschi nella Chiesa Inferiore di San Francesco', *Giotto e i Giotteschi in Assisi* (Rome, 1969, rev. Assisi, 2/1979), pp. 199–209

J. Raspi Serra: 'Nuove ipotesi per le *Vele* di Assisi', *Commentari*, xx (1969), pp. 20–36

A. Tantillo Mignosi: 'Osservazioni sul transetto della Basilica Inferiore di Assisi', *Boll. A.*, n. s., cx (1975), pp. 129–42

L. Tintori: 'Il bianco di piombo nelle pitture murali della Basilica di San Francesco ad Assisi', *Studies in Late Medieval and Renaissance Painting in Honor of Millard Meiss*, 2 vols (New York, 1977), pp. 437–44

A. Smart: *The Dawn of Italian Painting, 1250–1400* (Oxford, 1978), pp. 62–9, 84

B. Zanardi: 'Da Stefano Fiorentino a Puccio Capanna', *Stor. A.*, xxxiii (1978), pp. 115–27

J. P. Cottier: *'Le Vele' nella Basilica Inferiore di Assisi* (Florence, 1981)

M. Thomas: 'Giottos Ordensallegorien in der Basilika S. Francesco in Assisi zu religionsgeschichtlichem Zusammenhang und theologischer Quelle', *Z. Religions und Geistesgeschichte*, xxxv (1983), pp. 72–80

E. Biagi: 'Parente di Giotto', *La pittura in Italia: Il duecento e il trecento*, ed. E. Castelnuovo, ii (Milan, 1986), pp. 648–9

E. Lunghi: 'Maestro delle Vele', *La pittura in Italia: Il duecento e il trecento*, ed. E. Castelnuovo, ii (Milan, 1986), p. 613

——: 'Stefano Fiorentino', *La pittura in Italia: Il duecento e il trecento*, ed. E. Castelnuovo, ii (Milan, 1986), p. 662

The Maddalena Chapel

P. Rotondi: 'Giotto nella Cappella della Maddalena in Assisi', *L'Arte*, i (1968), pp. 75–97

V. Martinelli: 'Un documento per Giotto ad Assisi', *Stor. A.*, xix (1973), pp. 193–208

L. C. Schwartz: *The Fresco Decoration of the Magdalen Chapel in the Basilica of St. Francis at Assisi* (diss., Indiana U., Bloomington, IN, 1980)

I. Hueck: 'Ein Dokument zur Magdalenenkapelle der Franziskuskirche von Assisi', *Scritti di storia dell'arte in onore di Roberto Salvini* (Florence, 1984), pp. 191–6

E. Lunghi: 'Palmerino di Guido', *La pittura in Italia: Il duecento e il trecento*, ed. E. Castelnuovo, ii (Milan, 1986), p. 647

L. Schwartz: 'Patronage and Franciscan Iconography in the Magdalen Chapel at Assisi', *Burl. Mag.*, cxxxiii (1991), pp. 32–6

Puccio Capanna

L. Coletti: 'Il Maestro Colorista di Assisi', *Crit. A.*, vi (1950), pp. 443–54

P. Scarpellini: 'Di alcuni pittori giotteschi nella città e nel territorio di Assisi', *Giotto e i Giotteschi in Assisi*, ed. G. Palumbo (Rome, 1969, rev. Assisi, 2/1979), pp. 211–70

——: 'Un capolavoro del trecento umbro', *Paragone*, cclxxix (1973), pp. 3–31

C. L. Ragghianti: 'Puccio Capanna', *Crit. A.*, xlii (1977), pp. 229–32

F. Todini: 'Contributo alla pittura del trecento ad Assisi: Puccio Capanna e i suoi seguaci', *Esercizi*, ii (1979), pp. 33–42

E. Lunghi: 'Puccio Capanna', *La pittura in Italia: Il duecento e il trecento*, ed. E. Castelnuovo, ii (Milan, 1986), p. 561

Puccio Capanna (exh. cat., ed. P. Scarpellini; Assisi, 1989)

PIETRO LORENZETTI

J. A. Crowe and G. B. Cavalcaselle: *A History of Painting in Italy*, ii (London, 1864, rev. 2/1885), p. 195
C. Brandi: *Pietro Lorenzetti, affreschi della Basilica di Assisi* (Rome, 1958)
C. Volpe: *Pietro Lorenzetti ad Assisi* (Milan, 1965)
M. Meiss: *The Great Age of Fresco Discoveries, Recoveries and Survivals* (New York, 1970), pp. 68–71
H. B. J. Maginnis: 'Cast Shadow in the Passion Cycle at San Francesco, Assisi: A Note', *Gaz. B.-A.*, cxiii (1971), pp. 63–4
——: *Pietro Lorenzetti and Assisi* (diss., Princeton U., 1975)
——: 'The Passion Cycle in the Lower Church of San Francesco, Assisi', *Z. Kstgesch.*, xxxix (1976), pp. 193–208
M. Seidel: 'Das Frühwerk von Pietro Lorenzetti', *Städel-Jb.*, viii (1981), pp. 79–158
L. Bellosi: *Pietro Lorenzetti ad Assisi* (Assisi, 1982)
H. B. J. Maginnis: 'Pietro Lorenzetti: A Chronology', *A. Bull.*, lvi (1984), pp. 183–211
C. Volpe: *Pietro Lorenzetti* (Milan, 1989)

SIMONE MARTINI

G. Paccagnini: *Simone Martini* (Milan, 1955; Eng. trans., 1957), pp. 60–78, 129–59
C. Brandi: 'Una sinopia di Simone Martini', *A. Ant. & Mod.*, 13–16 (1961), pp. 17–20
F. Bologna: *Gli affreschi di Simone Martini ad Assisi* (Milan, 1965)
——: *I pittori alla corte angioina di Napoli, 1266–1414, e un riesame dell'arte nell'età fridericiana* (Rome, 1969), pp. 150–73
G. Francastel: 'Simone Martini interprète de la politique française en Italie', *L'Arte*, v (1969), pp. 41–54
G. Contini and M. C. Gozzoli: *L'opera completa di Simone Martini* (Milan, 1970), pp. 90–96
L. Tintori: 'Il bianco di piombo nelle pitture murali della Basilica di San Francesco ad Assisi', *Studies in Late Medieval and Renaissance Painting in Honor of Millard Meiss*, 2 vols (New York, 1977), pp. 437–44
L. Tintori and S. A. Fehm jr: 'Observations on Simone Martini's Frescoes in the Montefiore Chapel at Assisi', *La pittura nel XIV e XV secolo: Il contributo dell'analisi tecnica alla storia dell'arte. Atti del XIV congresso internazionale di storia dell'arte: Bologna, 1979*, pp. 175–87
S. M. Newton: 'Tomaso da Modena, Simone Martini, Hungarians and St. Martin in Fourteenth Century Italy', *J. Warb. & Court. Inst.*, xliii (1980), pp. 234–8
A. S. Hoch: *Simone Martini's St. Martin Chapel in the Lower Basilica of San Francesco, Assisi* (diss., Philadelphia, U. PA., 1983)
J. Polzer: 'Simone Martini's Two Frescoes in the Lower Right Transept of the Church of San Francesco in Assisi', *A. Cristiana*, lxxii (1984), pp. 353–68
J. Brink: 'Sts Martin and Francis: Sources and Meaning in Simone Martini's Montefiore Chapel', *Renaissance Studies in Honor of Craig Hugh Smyth*, 2 vols (Florence, 1985), pp. 79–92
A. S. Hoch: 'A New Document for Simone Martini's Chapel of St. Martin at Assisi', *Gesta*, xxiv (1985), pp. 141–6
——: 'The Identity of a Saint in the Chapel of St. Martin at Assisi', *A. Cristiana*, lxxiv (1986), pp. 103–5
L. Tintori: 'Segnalazioni su costante progresso tecnico nelle pitture murali di Simone Martini (1315–30?)', *Tecnica e stile: Esempi di pittura murale del rinascimento italiano*, ed. E. Borsook and F. S. Gioffredi, 2 vols (Florence, 1986), pp. 11–14
A. S. Hoch: 'St Martin of Tours: His Transformation into a Chivalric Hero and Franciscan Ideal', *Z. Kstgesch.*, l (1987), pp. 471–82
A. Martindale: *Simone Martini: Complete Edition* (Oxford, 1988)
P. Leone de Castris: *Simone Martini: Catalogo completo* (Florence, 1989)
A. S. Hoch: 'The Dedication of the St Elizabeth Altar at Assisi', *Burl. Mag.*, cxxxiii (1991), pp. 36–7
——: 'Beata Stirps, Royal Patronage and the Identification of the Sainted Rulers in the St Elizabeth Chapel at Assisi', *A. Hist.*, xv (1992), pp. 279–95

ANDREA DE' BARTOLI

F. Filippini: 'Andrea da Bologna: Miniatore e pittore del secolo XIV', *Boll. A.*, v (1911), pp. 50–62
——: *Il Cardinale Egidio Albornoz* (Bologna, 1933), p. 416
R. Longhi: 'La mostra del trecento bolognese', *Paragone*, v (1950), pp. 5–44; also in R. Longhi: *Mostra della pittura bolognese del '300* (Bologna, 1982), p. 15
C. Volpe: 'Per il problema di Andrea de' Bartoli pittore dell'Albornoz', *El Cardenal Albornoz y el Colegio de España*, ed. E. Verdera y Tuells, v (Saragossa, 1979), pp. 45–54
——: 'Andrea de' Bartoli e la svolta antigotica nella seconda metà del trecento', *Paragone*, ccclxxiii (1981), pp. 3–16
D. Benati: 'Andrea de' Bartoli', *La pittura in Italia: Il duecento e il trecento*, ed. E. Castelnuovo, ii (Milan, 1986), p. 551
E. Lunghi: 'Pace di Bartolo', *La pittura in Italia: Il duecento e il trecento*, ed. E. Castelnuovo, ii (Milan, 1986), p. 646
S. Innamorati: 'Di nuovo su Andrea De' Bartoli e sulle origini di Carlo da Camerino', *Ant. Viva*, xxxi (1992), pp. 23–30

ADRIAN S. HOCH

3. STAINED GLASS. The glass of the Upper Church is devoted thematically to the *Life of Christ* (Bible windows in three biforium lancets of the apse), and the *Apostles* with *St Francis* (eight windows of the nave). The Christological scenes at the right of each lancet are paired with *Old Testament* scenes at the left in each of the Bible windows (*Bibelfenstern*). The contrast of Old Testament and New Testament is extended in the transept windows with scenes from *Genesis* and of *Virgin Saints* at the south, and of the *Appearances of Angels and of Christ after his Resurrection*, including the *Ascension* (see fig. 7) at the north. The glass of the Lower Church is in seven separate chapels, which are unrelated thematically. Some of the windows depict the lives of the saints to whom the chapels are dedicated (SS Mary Magdalene, Anthony and John). In other chapels the glass shows the titular saint in different

7. Stained-glass window with scenes of the *Appearances of Christ*, north transept of the Upper Church, S Francesco, Assisi, third quarter of the 13th century

sacred and secular scenes (SS Martin and Louis), and elsewhere there are scenes of various saints and donors (including SS Nicholas and Catherine). The consecration date of 1253 has been suggested as a *terminus post quem* for the glass, although evidence that there were grisaille panels in the Upper Church from around a decade earlier has been found. The statutes promulgated by the General Chapter of the Franciscans at Narbonne in 1260 specifically forbidding stained-glass windows in Franciscan churches provide a *terminus ante quem* for the Bible windows, generally thought to be the only ones in place before the ban. Glazing was probably not resumed until after the death of St Bonaventure, who was responsible for the Narbonne statutes.

The first glass for the Upper Church was produced largely by northern craftsmen, probably because stained glass was hitherto unknown in Italy. The Bible windows were executed by a German workshop, and they may be the earliest example of the kind of typological window that appeared only later in Germany. They have been related stylistically to the earlier glazing at the Franciscan Barfüsserkirche in Erfurt and, in style and iconographic detail, with a series of manuscript miniatures attributed to the Rhine–Main region, some of which have been associated with the Franciscan archbishop of Mainz, Gerhard I, Wildgraf von Daun (*reg* 1253–9). The south transept glass and the large standing figures in the nave of *St James the Great*, *St Andrew*, *St John the Evangelist* and *St Thomas*, together with narrative scenes of their lives, were produced by the 'Gothic Workshop'. These glaziers rendered figures in an elegantly mannered 'court style', comparable with French and English work and especially close to the Westminster retable and Douce *Apocalypse*. The north transept glass and the rest of the nave windows have been attributed variously to a Roman studio and to the Master of St Francis, who was responsible for the *St Francis* cycles in the nave of the Lower Church (*see* §2 above). The stained glass of the nave and both transepts of the Upper Church have all been dated *c.* 1275.

The Lower Church was glazed in the early 14th century. On the basis of Cennino Cennini's description of stained-glass workshops, in which work was divided between the designer and the craftsman who executed the design, several designs have been attributed to painters better known for their works in fresco. Thus the glass of the S Martino Chapel has sometimes been attributed to Simone Martini, who also did the frescoes. The glass of the S Giovanni Battista and S Nicola chapels is also deeply influenced by the wall paintings in those chapels. The particularly beautiful windows of the S Antonio Chapel, and those also of the S Lodovico and S Caterina chapels, have been attributed to Giovanni di Bonino (*fl* 1325), who is documented as a glass painter at Orvieto Cathedral.

In 1477 the Bible windows were replaced with a depiction of the *Coronation of Pope Sixtus IV* (1471–84). In the 18th century windows from Perugia and Foligno were introduced, and in 1839–45 Bertini rearranged many of the windows. In 1926 eight scenes of the *Infancy of Christ* from the Bible windows were restored, and in 1928 an attempt was made to bring the entire glazing back to its original state.

BIBLIOGRAPHY

H. Wentzel: 'Die ältesten Farbfenster in der Oberkirche von S Francesco zu Assisi', *Wallraf-Richartz Jb.*, xiv (1952), pp. 45–72

G. Marchini: *Le vetrate dell'Umbria*, Corp. Vitrearum Med. Aevi: Italia, i (Rome, 1973)

R. Haussherr: 'Der typologische Zyklus der Chorfenster der Oberkirche von S Francesco zu Assisi', *Kunst als Bedeutungsträger: Gedenkschrift für Günter Bandmann* (Berlin, 1978), pp. 95–128

I. Hueck: 'Le vetrate nelle copie del Ramboux e notizie sul restauro di Giovanni Bertini', *Boll. A.*, n.s. 5, lxiv/4 (1979), pp. 75-90

V. Roehrig Kaufmann: *Iconographic Study of the Christological Cycle of the Miniatures of the Aschaffenburg Golden Gospels (Aschaffenburg, Hofbibliothek MS. 13)* (diss., New York, Columbia U., 1986)

F. Martin: *Die Apsisverglasung der Oberkirche von S Francesco in Assisi: Ihre Enstehung und Stellung innerhalb der Oberkirchenaustattung* (Worms, 1993)

VIRGINIA ROEHRIG KAUFMANN

4. TREASURY. From the time of its foundation, S Francesco was constantly presented with valuable liturgical articles, the free use of which the friars were officially granted by Pope Innocent IV in 1253. Among those who donated were such figures as the first Franciscan pope Nicholas IV, St Bonaventure, King Louis IX of France, and Robert, King of Naples. The treasury was once one of the richest in the western world, but it was looted on several occasions and its holdings have been substantially diminished. Despite this, it contains a great number of valuable art objects, including panel paintings, for example the mid-13th-century *St Francis and Four Miracles*, and richly illuminated manuscripts, among which the missal of St Louis of Toulouse (1255–6) is particularly important. The treasury holds numerous chalices, crucifixes and reliquaries in precious metalwork. The most famous is the silver-gilt chalice of Pope Nicholas IV, made *c.* 1290 by GUCCIO DE MANNAIA and decorated with translucent enamels (*see* GOTHIC, fig. 90). Ivories include an extremely fine French *Virgin and Child* (*c.* beginning of the 14th century) preserving traces of delicate polychromy. There is also a good collection of textiles, among which is the embroidered antependium (1476–8) of Pope Sixtus IV, made with silk, gold and silver thread, possibly produced to designs by Antonio Pollaiuolo and Francesco Botticini.

BIBLIOGRAPHY

B. Kleinschmidt: *Die Basilika von San Francesco in Assisi*, i (Berlin, 1915), pp. 262–304; ii (Berlin, 1926), pp. 304–13

L. Alessandri and F. Pennachi: *Inventari della sacristia del sacro convento di Assisi* (Quaracchi, 1920)

B. Farnetani: *Museo-Tesoro della Basilica di S. Francesco* (Assisi, 1978)

P. Scarpellini: 'Le Sculture', *Il tesoro della Basilica di San Francesco ad Assisi* (Assisi, 1980)

S. Nessi: *La Basilica di San Francesco in Assisi e la sua documentazione storica* (Assisi, 1982), pp. 299–320

RUTH WOLFF

Assisi, Angelo di Pietro d'. *See* ANGELO DI PIETRO D'ASSISI.

Assisi, Tiberio (Ranieri di Diotallevi) d' (*b* Assisi, ?1460–70; *d* Assisi, before Oct 1524). Italian painter. He possibly received his early training from L'Ingegno [Andrea Alovigi d'Assisi] (*c.* 1470–1516). It is very probable that Tiberio subsequently joined the shop of Pinturicchio and accompanied him to Rome to work in S Maria del Popolo (1485–9) and on the Borgia apartments in the Vatican Palace (1492–*c.* 1495). In 1492–3 Tiberio was paid by the Comune of Assisi for various works, and in 1495 he was employed in Perugia Cathedral.

At the beginning of the 16th century, Tiberio was active in Assisi and Perugia. In 1510 he painted the Augusti family chapel in S Francesco, Montefalco, and during the next few years he worked at the convent of S Martino, Trevi. Subsequent documents record his intensive activity in Umbria up to 1524, when he painted several coats of arms for the Comune of Assisi, a commission for which payment was made to his heirs in October of that year. Despite the apparently high regard in which he was held (a document of 1504 described him as a 'sublime and almost divine painter'), Tiberio d'Assisi is now considered to be an extremely weak artist. Lacking originality, he was satisfied, throughout his career, with reproducing models borrowed from the repertory of Perugino.

BIBLIOGRAPHY

Thieme-Becker

U. Gnoli: 'Documenti inediti sui pittori perugini', *Boll. A.*, ix (1915), p. 312

——: *Pittori e miniatori nell'Umbria* (Spoleto, 1923/*R* Foligno, 1980), pp. 328–31

P. Scarpellini and F. F. Mancini, eds: *Pittura in Umbria tra il 1480 e il 1540* (Milan, 1984), p. 206

G. Briganti, ed.: *La pittura in Italia: Il cinquecento*, ii (Milan, 1988), pp. 851 2

GENNARO TOSCANO

Assiut. *See* ASYUT.

Association of American Painters and Sculptors. Group of artists founded in New York in 1911 with the aim of finding suitable exhibition space for young American artists. After preliminary meetings between the painters Jerome Myers (1867–1940), Elmer MacRae (1875–1955), Walt Kuhn (1877–1949) and others, a meeting was held at the Madison Gallery on 16 December 1911 for the purpose of founding a new artists' organization. At a subsequent meeting on 2 January 1912 they elected officers and began to discuss exhibition plans. The president, Julian Alden Weir, who had been elected *in absentia*, resigned, however, and the leadership passed to Arthur B. Davies.

Davies, Walt Kuhn and Walter Pach soon took the lead and developed the plan for a major international exhibition, much to the disapproval of the American Realists associated with Robert Henri; the latter group was interested in gaining broader exposure to a public that knew only of the major figures associated with the National Academy of Design and saw no reason to include foreign modernists. Davies and his allies, contemptuous of their provincialism, ignored their wishes. The result of the Association of American Painters and Sculptors' plans was the International Exhibition of Modern Art, known as the ARMORY SHOW (1913), which introduced European modernism to the art-viewing public, and which in the eyes of both the public and the artists stripped the National Academy of Design of its importance. The Association disbanded shortly afterwards.

BIBLIOGRAPHY

M. Brown: *American Painting from the Armory Show to the Depression* (Princeton, 1955)

——: *The Story of the Armory Show* (New York, 1963, rev. 1988)

DAVID M. SOKOL

Association of Artists of Revolutionary Russia [AKhRR; Rus. Assotsiatsiya Khudozhnikov Revolyutsionnoy Rossii]. Soviet group of artists active in Moscow and Leningrad (now St Petersburg) in 1922–32. It was established in January 1922 by a group of artists, including Aleksandr Grigor'yev (1891–1961), Yevgeny Katsman (1890–1976), Sergey Malyutin and Pavel Radimov (1887–1967), who were inspired by the 47th exhibition of the Peredvizhniki (the Wanderers). It was first called the Association of Artists Studying Revolutionary Life (Assotsiatsiya Khudozhnikov Izuchayushchikh Revolyutsionnyy Byt), then the Society of Artists of Revolutionary Russia (Obshchestvo Khudozhnikov Revolyutsionnoy Rossii) and finally, after the first group exhibition in Moscow in May 1922, the Association of Artists of Revolutionary Russia.

The primary goal of the artists of the Association, outlined in the first manifesto in 1922, was to depict post-revolutionary Russia—the everyday life of the proletariat, the peasantry and the Red Army—in a direct, accessible manner. Believing artists were 'the spokesmen of the people's spiritual life', they turned to the traditions of Russian 19th-century Critical Realism, concentrated on the didactic mission of art and voiced their opposition to the avant-garde. In addition to older Realists such as Abram Arkhipov, Nikolay Kasatkin and Konstantin Yuon, the Association immediately attracted many younger artists such as Isaak Brodsky, Aleksandr Gerasimov and Boris Ioganson, and, in order to acquaint themselves with the new Socialist reality, the members visited factories, railway workshops, shipyards etc, often using their experiences as the subject-matter of their paintings. The results of the desire expressed in the manifesto, 'to set down artistically and documentarily, the revolutionary impulse of this great moment of history' and to 'provide a true picture of events and not abstract concoctions discrediting our Revolution in the face of the international proletariat', showed a range of styles and treatments, including Boris Kustodiyev's dramatic *Bolshevik* (1920; Moscow, Tret'yakov Gal.), Malyutin's restrained portrait of *Dmitry Furmanov* (1922; Moscow, Tret'yakov Gal.) and Mitrofan Grekov's battle paintings (e.g. *Gun Carriage*, 1925; Moscow, Tret'yakov Gal.). Brodsky's almost photographic compositions (e.g. *V. I. Lenin in the Smolny*, 1930; Moscow, Tret'yakov Gal.) were offset by Aleksandr Gerasimov's rhetorical depictions of Lenin, such as *V. I. Lenin on the Tribune* (1929–30; Moscow, Cent. Lenin Mus.), and Yevgeny Katsman's use of Neue Sachlichkeit (e.g. *Kaliazin Lace-makers*, 1928; Moscow, Tret'yakov Gal.).

By the mid-1920s the Association was the most influential single body of artists in Soviet Russia, with affiliates throughout the country. It opened a special young artists' section, the Association of AKhRR Youth (OMAKhRR; Obedineniye Molodyozhi AKhRR), established its own publishing house and enjoyed direct governmental support. In 1928 the name was again changed, to the Association of Artists of the Revolution (AKhR; Assotsiatsiya Khudozhnikov Revolyutsii), and in 1929 it founded its own periodical *Iskusstvo v massy* ('Art to the masses'). In other words, the Association became a powerful and vociferous arbiter of official taste and took every opportunity to condemn 'formalist experimentation', not only among the radical members of the old avant-garde, such as Malevich, but also among the younger generation of artists belonging to the Society of Easel Painters (OST), such as Yury Pimenov and David Shterenberg. The Association was abolished along with all other formal art and literary groups by the state decree in 1932, *On the Reconstruction of Literary and Artistic Organizations*, but its legacy was enduring, for its emphasis on the simple and didactic illustration of contemporary reality contributed much to the development of Socialist Realism in the 1930s and 1940s.

BIBLIOGRAPHY

V. Kniazeva: *AKhRR* (Leningrad, 1967)

I. Gronsky and V. Perelman, eds: *AKhRR: Sbornik vospominaniy, statey dokumentov* [AKhRR: a collection of memoirs, articles and documents] (Moscow, 1973)

JOHN E. BOWLT

Association of Ottoman Painters [Association of Turkish Painters; Turkish Fine Arts Society; Turk. Osmanli ressamlar cemiyeti; Türk ressamlar cemiyeti; Türk sanayi-i nefise birliği; Güzel sanatlar birliği]. Turkish group of painters founded in 1908 by students from the Fine Arts Academy in Istanbul. They had their first exhibition in Istanbul in 1910 and also published the monthly journal *Naşir-i efkâr* ('Promoter of ideas'), which was supported financially by Crown Prince Abdülmecid (1868–1944), himself a painter and calligrapher and honorary president of the Association. The members included Ibrahim Çallı, who was recognized as the most prominent in the group, Ruhi Arel (1880–1931), Feyhaman Duran (1886–1970), Nazmi Ziya Güran, Namık Ismail (1890–1935), Avni Lifij (1889–1927), Hikmet Onat (1886–1977) and Sami Yetik (1876–1945). It was not very active from 1910, when some of its painters left Istanbul to study art in Europe, but their return at the outbreak of World War I brought renewed activity. Some members were responsible for bringing Impressionism and other European movements to Turkey, and they acquainted the Turkish public with figurative and narrative compositions, as well as portraiture. The Association organized annual exhibitions at the Galatasaray High School in Istanbul, and some of the artists were given workshops and taken to the Front during World War I. Many of the painters also became influential teachers at the Fine Arts Academy: Çallı from 1914, Onat from 1915, Güran from 1918, Duran from 1919, Ismail from 1927.

In 1921 the Association of Ottoman Painters was renamed the Association of Turkish Painters, and when the Turkish Republic was proclaimed in 1923 its members were responsible for the first painting exhibition in Ankara. Although challenged in the late 1920s by new ideas brought from Europe by younger Turkish artists, the members of the Association remained influential figures in Turkish art. The Association of Turkish Painters was renamed the Turkish Fine Arts Society in 1926, and was known as the Fine Arts Society from 1929.

BIBLIOGRAPHY

S. Tansuğ: *Çağdaş Türk sanatı* [Contemporary Turkish art] (Istanbul, 1986)

G. Renda and others: *A History of Turkish Painting* (Geneva, Seattle and London, 1988)

□

Association of Revolutionary Art of Ukraine [ARMU; Ukrain. Asotsiiatsiya Revolyutsiynoho Mystetstva Ukraïny]. Ukrainian group of artists active from 1925 to 1930. The association was founded by statute on 25 August 1925 in Kiev, with branches formed subsequently in other Ukrainian cities such as Kharokov (Kharkiv), Odessa, Dnepropetrovs'k (Dnipropetrivs'k) and Uman'. Members also lived in Moscow, Leningrad (now St Petersburg) and Paris. Artists of various artistic backgrounds and different training belonged to the association, but it was best represented by the avant-garde artists OLEKSANDR BOHOMAZOV, Nina Genke-Meller (1893–1954), Vasyl' Yermilov (1894–1967), Oleksandr Khvostov (1895–1968), Vadym Meller (1884–1962), Viktor Pal'mov (1888–1929) and VLADIMIR TATLIN. Its theoretical platform, formulated by Ivan Vrona (1887–1970), rector of the progressive Kiev State Art Institute, was based on Marxist principles, recognizing the era as a transitional stage towards a more cohesive national proletarian reality. The association's objective was to develop the strengths of Ukrainian artists and to be flexible enough to be able to consolidate a variety of formalist leanings without sacrificing high technical quality. Together with the Association of Artists of Red Ukraine (AKhChU: Asotsiiatsiya Khudozhnykiv Chervonoï Ukraïny), it succeeded in organizing one of the first exhibitions devoted to Ukrainian art of the 1920s. By 1927 ARMU was the single most influential body of artists in the country. It came to be dominated by painters who were attracted to the monumental art of MYKHAYLO BOYCHUK, which was inspired by the Byzantine period. Among those who followed Boychuk's style were Sofiya A. Nalepins'ka-Boychuk (1884–1939), Ivan I. Padalka (1897–1938), Oksana Pavlenko (1895–1991), Mykola Rokyts'ky (1901–44), and Vasyl' F. Sedlyar (1889–1937). In debating the means whereby ARMU's aim to revitalize the artistic culture of Ukraine could be realized, Sedlyar (1926) laid equal emphasis on the importance of concepts such as artistic industry and material culture, as well as on the visual arts. He defended the association against its rival, the ASSOCIATION OF ARTISTS OF REVOLUTIONARY RUSSIA (AKhRR), a group that turned to 19th-century Realism and by doing so stood in opposition to the left wing and to Productivist art as a whole. By June 1930, internal differences with ARMU had caused its leaders to dissolve it and to organize the group October (Ukrain. Zhovten') in its place.

BIBLIOGRAPHY

V. Sedlyar: *AKhRR ta ARMU* [AKhRR and ARMU] (Kiev, 1926)

I. Vrona: *Mystetstvo Revoliutsiï i ARMU* [Art of the Revolution and ARMU] (Kiev, 1926)

MYROSLAVA M. MUDRAK

Assos [now Behramkale]. City on the Aegean coast of Turkey, rising from the sea to the summit of the coastal ridge opposite the island of Lesbos. Ancient testimony and archaeological evidence indicate that Assos was founded in the 7th century BC by colonists from Methymna on Lesbos, and its strategic location and protected harbour assured its importance from the 6th century BC to the 4th century AD; Aristotle lived there from 348 to 345 BC. The site was first excavated by Americans in 1881–3; work resumed in 1981 under Turkish direction. Finds, including reliefs from the temple, are now in Paris (Louvre), Boston, MA (Mus. F.A.), Istanbul (Archaeol. Mus.), Çanakkale (Archaeol. Mus.) and at the site.

The plan of Assos followed the steep contours of the area; the buildings were constructed of local volcanic andesite. The Archaic temple on the summit (see fig. (a)), probably dedicated to Athena Polias and built in the second half of the 6th century BC, is the most significant Doric building in Asia Minor. The use of the Doric order and some iconographic motifs indicate outside influence, probably Athenian, but the design of the temple and the style of the sculpture reflect local craftsmanship. The peristyle (6 by 13 columns) surrounded a long, narrow cella, which had a distyle *in antis* pronaos; there was no opisthodomos or adyton. The columns had 16 flutes with arrises set on the cardinal points and capitals with a boldly flaring echinus. The most unusual feature of the temple was its continuously sculpted architrave, an invention partly inspired by the sculptural frieze in Ionic architecture and the decorated terracotta revetments of north-eastern

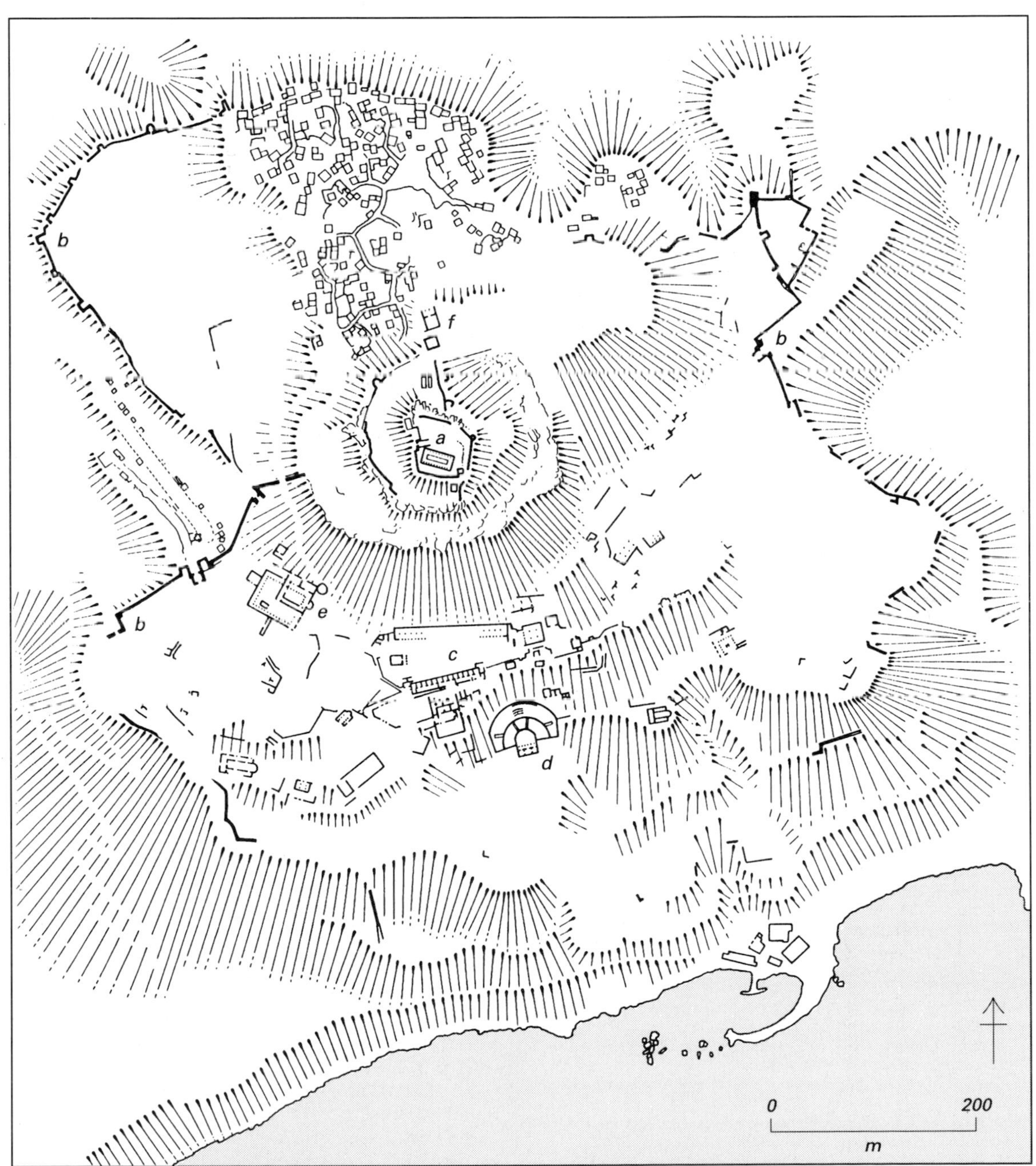

Assos, plan: (a) Temple of Athena; (b) city walls; (c) agora; (d) theatre; (e) gymnasium; (f) Hüdavendigar Camii

Greece and western Asia Minor. The 15 surviving relief blocks filled both façades and extended along part of the flanks. The iconography followed other Archaic programmes in combining animal and mythological scenes, including Herakles and Centaurs, Herakles wrestling with Triton, a symposium (?with Herakles), lions savaging prey, confronted sphinxes and butting bulls. In addition, the Doric frieze course had sculpted metopes at each end of the temple; the nine surviving scenes depict animals, *Europa on the Bull* and several figural scenes that may be mythological. There was no pedimental sculpture.

The city walls (b), built around the acropolis in the 4th century BC, and the northern extension with salient round and square towers added in the Hellenistic period (323–31 BC) are of excellent construction and have remarkably well-preserved main and lesser gates. Graves of the Archaic period (*c.* 750–*c.* 475 BC) have been unearthed in the western necropolis, and elaborate Hellenistic and Roman funerary monuments and sarcophagi later lined the paved streets leading from the principal eastern and western city gates.

The civic monuments constructed in the Hellenistic period (agora, theatre, gymnasium; c–e) occupied a series of partially excavated terraces cut into the sea-facing, southern side of the ridge below the temple. A long trapezoidal agora, which had a prostyle temple at the west end and a bouleuterion (council chamber) at the east, was framed on the south by a stoa with one storey facing the agora and two additional storeys reaching to a lower terrace; a two-storey northern stoa was built directly into the scarp of the acropolis.

Assos remained a small but important fortified settlement during the Middle Ages, taking on the name Behram after the Ottoman Conquest. On a dramatically projecting escarpment above the modern village, which occupies the northern, landward slope of the ridge, stands the Hüdavendigar Camii (f), a mosque traditionally associated with the Ottoman Sultan Murat I (*reg* 1362–89), as is the 14th-century bridge over the Tuzla Çayı to the north of the village. The mosque may have been converted from a ruined Byzantine church; it is clearly built with reused materials. The square prayer hall, covered by a dome 11 m across and containing a fine moulded plaster mihrab, was entered through a porch with three bays.

BIBLIOGRAPHY

J. T. Clarke: 'Report on the Investigations at Assos, 1881', *Pap. Archaeol. Inst. Amer.*, i (Boston, 1882)

——: 'Report on the Investigations at Assos, 1882, 1883', *Pap. Archaeol. Inst. Amer.*, ii (New York, 1898)

J. T. Clark, F. Bacon and R. Koldewey: *Investigations at Assos: Drawings and Photographs of the Buildings and Objects Discovered during the Excavations of 1881–1883* (Cambridge, MA, 1902–21)

F. Sartiaux: *Les Sculptures et la restauration du temple d'Assos en Troade* (Paris, 1915)

A. Kuran: *The Mosque in Early Ottoman Architecture* (Chicago, 1968), pp. 38–9

Y. Demiriz: *Osmanlı mimarisinde süsleme* [Decoration in Ottoman architecture], i (Istanbul, 1979), pp. 228–31

U. Finster-Hotz: *Der Bauschmuck des Athenatempels von Assos* (Rome, 1984)

B. D. Wescoat: 'Designing the Temple of Athena at Assos: Some Evidence from the Capitals', *Amer. J. Archaeol.*, xci (1987), pp. 553–68

Ü. Serdaroglu and others: *Ausgrabungen in Assos* (Munster, 1990)

BONNA D. WESCOAT

Assur [Ashur; now Qal'at ash-Sherqat]. Site in northern Iraq, *c.* 100 km south of Mosul and Nineveh, on a bluff on the right bank of the River Tigris. It was an important Assyrian city, at a natural crossroads for trade connecting Anatolia, Babylonia and Iran, and from the 3rd millennium BC until 614 BC, just before the fall of the Assyrian empire, it was the cult city of the god Assur. Throughout the 2nd millennium BC it was also the political capital of the land of Assur (*see also* ASSYRIAN). It was rediscovered in the mid-19th century, and AUSTEN HENRY LAYARD, Hormuzd Rassam and George Smith worked briefly there (*see also* ANCIENT NEAR EAST, §III, 1). From 1903 to 1914 the Deutsche Orient-Gesellschaft carried out systematic excavations, concentrating on the northern third of the city where the temples and palaces were located. From 1978 to 1986 the Iraq Department of Antiquities and Heritage conducted excavations and preservation work, and German excavations resumed in 1988. Finds are in the Pergamonmuseum in Berlin and the Iraq Museum in Baghdad, with a few in the British Museum, London, and the Museum of the Ancient Orient, Istanbul. (For a plan of Assur in the Neo-Assyrian period, see fig.)

1. Before 883 BC. 2. Neo-Assyrian period (883–612 BC) and after.

1. BEFORE 883 BC. The earliest known structure in Assur was the original Ishtar Temple, five levels of which were found superimposed. Temple G was built on the wall stumps of the earliest, H, and their plans were similar. Both had a courtyard, entered from the west, on the east side of which was a rectangular cella with a shallow cult chamber at its north end. In the debris of G were statues (Berlin, Pergamonmus.) resembling examples from Mari of the Early Dynastic IIIB period (*c.* 2400 BC) and suggesting a similar date. The scanty remains from the earliest levels of the temple dedicated to Assur (fig. a) at the north corner of the city were also of the 3rd millennium BC. Level E of the Assur Temple had two or more phases, at least one having the temple's characteristic later plan of a central court at the north and large outer court at the south-east. Ishtar Temple G was apparently destroyed in the Akkadian period (*c.* 2300 BC) and replaced by private houses. The earliest version of the palace (b), south-west of the later Assur ziggurat (c), had stone foundations apparently of Ur III date (*c.* 2050 BC) or Old Assyrian date. The line of the city wall in the 3rd millennium BC is unknown.

Ilushuma (*reg c.* 1950 BC) built a new city wall, probably roughly along the line of the Neo-Assyrian inner wall, enclosing *c.* 40 ha. Two of its western gates were the People's Gate and the Sheep Gate. Ilushuma probably built Ishtar Temple E, raised on a platform with its entrance marked by gate-towers and a stairway. Its cella and cult chamber were similar to levels G and H but larger. The next level, D, which may date to Sargon I (*reg c.* 1875 BC), although larger than E, was poorly preserved. The Assur Temple was rebuilt by Erishum I (*reg* 1939–1900 BC). Its plan, although fragmentary, seems to follow level E. The earliest version of the double Temple of Anu and Adad (d), west of the palace, was built by Erishum I and Ikunum (*reg c.* 1890 BC); no trace of it was recovered.

Shamshi-Adad I (*reg* 1813–1781 BC) rebuilt the Assur Temple in the form it retained until the fall of Assyria. The main part was rectangular with an entrance at the south-west end: then followed a forecourt, a large central court, an antechamber and the cella. On the south-east side was a large trapezoidal outer court. The Assur ziggurat (c) had two building phases, the first of which Andrae (1955) attributed to Shamshi-Adad I. The double Temple of Sin and Shamash (e), north-east of the Ishtar Temple, had three levels. The earliest, attributed to Shamshi-Adad I, had an entrance façade that stepped outwards from the ends towards a towered gate in the centre. The interior was planned around a courtyard with two identical shrines opening off its two shorter side walls. Shamshi-Adad I also rebuilt the Anu-Adad Temple, but only a small section of its stone foundation survived. Only the foundation walls of the Old Palace, attributed to Shamshi-Adad I, were recovered, directly over the remains of the 3rd-millennium BC palace (b): it was nearly square and comprised 172 rooms and 10 courtyards.

According to texts of later kings, Puzur-Assur III (*reg c.* 1500 BC) built the wall surrounding the New Town (f), adding some 15 ha to the south-east corner of the city. Later in the Middle Assyrian period Assur apparently had six city gates. The Assur Gate was in the north wall below the Assur Temple. The Shamash Gate should be on the east side of the city, but its location is unknown. The Tigris Gate was at the southern end of the New Town, where the wall joined the river. The Tisari Gate, near the south-east corner of the inner wall, connected the inner town with the New Town. The Sherûa Gate is probably the West Gate on the south-west side of the city wall. The Metalsmiths' Gate was at the west corner of the city.

The Ishtar Temple was rebuilt on stone foundations by Adad-nirari I (*reg* 1305–1274 BC) and Shalmaneser I (*reg* 1273–1244 BC). Reade (1970) identified this phase with some stone foundations built directly on the wall stumps of Ishtar Temple D that were identical to D in plan. Tukulti-Ninurta I (*reg* 1243–1207 BC) demolished the Ishtar Temple and rebuilt it to the north. He altered the orientation of the cella, before which he added an antechamber with a towered gate. At the south-west corner was a shrine dedicated to the goddess Dinitu. Assur-resh-ishi I (*reg* 1132–1115 BC) built a new, smaller Ishtar Temple (g) some 30 m north-east of Tukulti-Ninurta's.

The Assur Temple was rebuilt by Shalmaneser I, who followed the former plan, but added a courtyard to the south-west end. He also initiated the second phase of the Assur ziggurat. Tukulti-Ninurta I rebuilt the Sin-Shamash Temple, closely following the plan of the earlier building. The remains of his New Palace (h), on the north side of Assur between the Adad ziggurat and the Metalsmiths' Gate, were badly disturbed. A group of ivory inlays (Berlin, Pergamonmus.), including a water god, trees and a winged bull, were found at the foot of its terrace. The Anu-Adad Temple (d) was rebuilt by Assur-resh-ishi I and Tiglath-pileser I (*reg* 1114–1076 BC). Its entrance was in the long wall of a rectangular courtyard, opposite which were two identical shrines, side by side, flanked by two ziggurats.

The Old Palace (b) was rebuilt by Assur-nirari I (*reg c.* 1525 BC) and repaired by several of his successors.

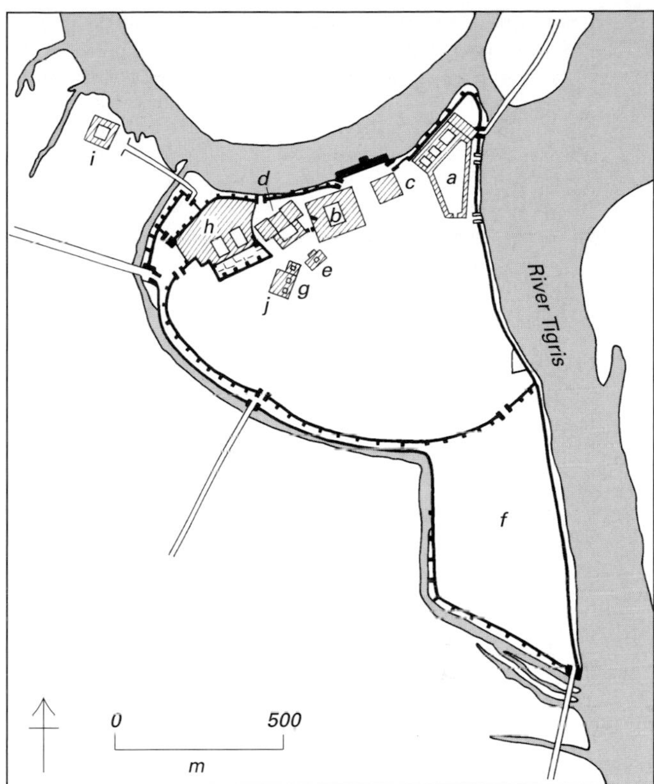

Assur, plan of the city, 9th–7th centuries BC: (a) Assur Temple; (b) Old Palace; (c) Assur ziggurat; (d) Anu-Adad Temple; (e) Sin-Shamash Temple; (f) New Town; (g) Ishtar Temple; (h) New Palace; (i) New *akītu*-festival Temple; (j) Nabu Temple

Tiglath-pileser I restored its gatehouse and decorated it with statues that may have represented a whale and a yak, to which Assur-bel-kala (*reg* 1073–1056 BC) added four lions and what may have been two whales and four yaks, all of basalt, two human-headed bull colossi of alabaster, and two limestone figures, possibly yaks; none survives. Assur-bel-kala was the first of several kings to build tombs on the south-east side of the palace. The plan of the Middle Assyrian Old Palace is fragmentary, but it is clear that it was roughly the same size as its Old Assyrian predecessor, although its layout was different and its rooms were larger.

2. NEO-ASSYRIAN PERIOD (883–612 BC) AND AFTER. The Neo-Assyrian period was characterized by extensive royal building projects (*see also* MESOPOTAMIA, §§II, 6(i) and III, 6(i)). Shalmaneser III (*reg* 858–824 BC) built a new outer city wall, which enclosed the New Town and ran just beyond the old wall at the south and west. He also planned an inner wall, but may not have completed it. A text of the time of Sennacherib (*reg* 704–681 BC) lists 13 city gates. To the six Middle Assyrian gates the Neo-Assyrian text adds a Royal Step Gate leading to the Old Palace, a Gate of the Ziggurats leading either to the Anu

and Adad ziggurats or the Assur ziggurat, and the Kakmû Gate, probably at the north end of the quay wall. Of the remaining four gates, the Mountain Gate should be at the north-east corner and may be part of the Kakmû Gate; the Sheep Gate and People's Gate may be those in the inner wall corresponding to the West Gate and Metalsmiths' Gate in the outer, with the Gate of Destiny at the north-west corner of the wall, opposite the Temple of the New Year's Festival (*akītu*).

The Old Palace (b) was rebuilt in the Neo-Assyrian period, apparently by Assurnasirpal II (*reg* 883–859 BC). The plan of the preserved part (*c.* 60 m square), at most only about a third of its original area, is typically Neo-Assyrian, with double ranks of rooms opening on to courtyards in the large apartments in the western section, and small service rooms surrounding a courtyard in the east wing. Assurnasirpal II, Shamshi-Adad V (*reg* 823–811 BC), and perhaps Sennacherib and Esharhamat, the wife of Esarhaddon (*reg* 680–669 BC), built tombs next to Assur-bel-kala's. Assurnasirpal II also rebuilt the Sin-Shamash Temple. Although its remains were fragmentary, the main lines of the plan, markedly different from the earlier phases, have been reconstructed (Haller and Andrae). The entrance hall, which ran through the building's centre to a courtyard at the far end, was flanked by two shrines entered from both the courtyard and the entrance hall. The Anu-Adad Temple (d) was rebuilt by Shalmaneser III (*reg* 858–824 BC) on the same general plan as its predecessor, but narrower and with smaller ziggurats. Finds (Istanbul, Mus. Anc. Orient) included an embossed strip of bronze that originally decorated a door, and a gold thunderbolt, the emblem of Adad.

Before the entrances of the Assur Temple (a), Tiglath-pileser III (*reg* 744–727 BC) and Sargon II (*reg* 721–705 BC) added podia faced with glazed bricks depicting subjects similar to those of the Assyrian wall reliefs. Sennacherib constructed a new court and entrance to the Assur Temple at the north end of the south-east wall, opposite the end of the cella, thereby moving the entrance on to the cella's main axis. Sennacherib also built a new *akītu*-festival temple outside the wall, *c.* 200 m north-west of the city. He claimed that it was entirely of limestone, a highly unusual building practice in Assyria. He later rebuilt it after a fire. Both phases were constructed around a large central court with the entrance at one end and a wide cella opening off the other; the side walls seem to have been screened by shallow porticos, or perhaps these 'pillars' were pedestals for statues. One text describes a bronze door for the temple, now untraced, decorated with the battle between the gods, led by Assur, and the hordes of Tiamat. Sin-shar-ishkun (*reg* ?–612 BC) built the Nabu Temple (k) abutting the south side of the Ishtar Temple of Assur-resh-ishi I. It was planned around two courts, from one of which opened the twin shrines of Nabu and Tashmetum, and from the other a single shrine, perhaps a bedroom for the divine couple.

After the fall of Assyria in 612 BC, two small temples, designated A and N, were built on top of the ruins of the south-west corner of the Assur Temple's outer court. The plan of their cult rooms is typically Neo-Babylonian, but they lack the courtyard and subsidiary rooms of Babylonian temples. It is not known to whom they were dedicated. In the 1st century AD Assur became an important Parthian settlement and remained so probably until the early 3rd century AD. The Parthians rebuilt some Assyrian structures and added new buildings. Their restoration of the outer city wall is particularly evident at the Metalsmiths' Gate. They built a temple dedicated to Assur and Sherua on the site of the sanctuary of the Assyrian Assur Temple. It had two phases: the earlier had two iwans (vaulted halls) opening off a court, while the later was similar but added a third iwan. Between the old Assur Temple and the Assur ziggurat were two new buildings: an iwan with a broad free-standing stairway in front and a single room to either side, and an iwan with an antecella and cella behind it and a peristyle on the sides and back. The post-Assyrian Temple A was rebuilt without altering its plan. Where the Assyrian inner wall had divided the old city from the new was a palace that included four iwans opening off the sides of a central courtyard, a large room with its ceiling supported by four piers and a peristyle courtyard. Outside the city wall the Parthians rebuilt the central part of Sennacherib's *akītu* temple (i).

BIBLIOGRAPHY

RLA [article by E. Unger]

W. Andrae: *Der Anu-Adad-Tempel in Assur*, Wiss. Veröff. Dt. Orient-Ges. (Leipzig, 1909)

——: *Die Festungswerke von Assur*, Wiss. Veröff. Dt. Orient-Ges., 2 vols (Leipzig, 1913)

——: *Die archaischen Ischtar-Tempel in Assur*, Wiss. Veröff. Dt. Orient-Ges. (Leipzig, 1922)

——: *Coloured Ceramics from Ashur* (London, 1925)

W. Andrae and H. Lenzen: *Die Partherstadt Assur*, Wiss. Veröff. Dt. Orient-Ges. (Leipzig, 1933)

W. Andrae: *Die jüngeren Ischtar-Tempel in Assur*, Wiss. Veröff. Dt. Orient-Ges. (Leipzig, 1935)

——: *Das wiedererstandene Assur* (Leipzig, 1938; rev. B. Hrouda, Munich, 1977)

A. Haller, W. Andrae and B. Hrouda: *Die Gräber und Grüfte von Assur*, Wiss. Veröff. Dt. Orient-Ges. (W. Berlin, 1954)

C. Preusser: *Die Wohnhäuser in Assur*, Wiss. Veröff. Dt. Orient-Ges. (W. Berlin, 1954)

A. Haller and W. Andrae: *Die Heiligtümer des Gottes Assur und der Sin-šamaš-Tempel in Assur*, Wiss. Veröff. Dt. Orient-Ges. (W. Berlin, 1955)

C. Preusser: *Die Paläste in Assur*, Wiss. Veroff. Dt. Orient-Ges. (W. Berlin, 1955)

D. Oates: *Studies in the Ancient History of Northern Iraq* (London, 1968)

G. van Driel: *The Cult of Assur* (Assen, 1969)

J. E. Reade: *The Design and Decoration of Neo-Assyrian Public Buildings* (diss., U. Cambridge, 1970)

M. T. Larsen: *The Old Assyrian City-state and its Colonies* (1976), iv of *Mesopotamia* (Copenhagen, 1972–)

Sumer, xxxv (1979) [14 articles on Assur]

E. Heinrich: *Die Tempel und Heiligtümer im alten Mesopotamien*, Dt. Archäol. Inst., Dkml. Ant. Archit., 2 vols (W. Berlin, 1982)

J. Margueron: *Recherches sur les palais mésopotamiens de l'Age du Bronze*, 2 vols (Paris, 1982)

E. Heinrich: *Die Paläste im alten Mesopotamien*, Dt. Archäol. Inst., Dkml. Ant. Archit. (W. Berlin, 1984)

Sumer, xlii (1986) [12 articles on Assur]

P. Miglus: 'Untersuchungen zum Alten Palast in Assur', *Mitt. Dt. Orient-Ges. Berlin*, cxxi (1989), pp. 93–133

B. Hrouda and others: 'Vorläufige Berichte über die neuen Ausgrabungen in Assur: Frühjahr 1990', *Mitt. Dt. Orient-Ges. Berlin*, cxxiii (1991), pp. 95–131

R. Dittman: 'Assur and Kār-Tukultī-Ninurta', *Amer. J. Archaeol.*, xcvi (1992), pp. 307–12

Assyrian Origins: Discoveries at Ashur on the Tigris; Antiques in the Vorderasiatisches Museum, Berlin (exh. cat., New York, Met., 1995)

Assyrian. Name given to people of the ancient land of Assur (Assyria) in northern Mesopotamia (now Iraq), named after their state god. The Assyrian heartland is bounded on the north and east by the Zagros Mountains and on the south and west by arid plains that receive insufficient rainfall to support agriculture (*see* MESOPOTAMIA, fig. 1). The area is well watered by the Tigris, Greater and Lesser Zab rivers and their tributaries, some stretches of which are suitable for irrigation, and also by rainfall, which allows most of the region to grow one crop of wheat annually. The Assyrians, a Semitic people speaking a dialect of Akkadian, appear in the historical record as traders at the beginning of the 2nd millennium BC and developed into an important power in Mesopotamia and then throughout the Ancient Near East until the fall of their empire in 612 BC. The most important Assyrian cities in the 2nd millennium BC were ASSUR and NINEVEH, joined in the 1st millennium BC by NIMRUD and KHORSABAD.

1. Before *c.* 2000 BC. 2. Old and Middle Assyrian periods (*c.* 2000–*c.* 1000 BC). 3. Neo-Assyrian period (883–612 BC).

1. BEFORE *c.* 2000 BC. Long before the Assyrians themselves were recorded in texts, the area that was to become their heartland was important for the rise of civilization (*see* MESOPOTAMIA, §I, 2(i)(a)–(c)). Some of the earliest villages in the world are here, such as Qermez Dere, M'lefaat, Nemrick and Maghzaliyah (9th–7th millennia BC). Hassuna, the type site of the proto-Hassuna (*c.* 6500–6000 BC) and Hassuna cultures (*c.* 6000–5000 BC), is also here, as are the important sites of Arpachiyah and Tepe Gawra, from the Halaf (*c.* 5500–5000 BC) and northern Ubaid (*c.* 5000–4000 BC) periods. The diversity of the area in the 4th millennium BC is apparent from the contrast between the 'Uruk-type' remains from Nineveh and the contemporary but different 'Gawra-type' remains from nearby Tepe Gawra (*c.* 4000–3000 BC). In the first half of the 3rd millennium BC the Ninevite 5 culture, contemporary with but distinct from the Early Dynastic culture of southern Mesopotamia, flourished at Nineveh and across northern Mesopotamia. The indigenous culture of the succeeding period, contemporary with Early Dynastic IIIB in the south (*c.* 2500–*c.* 2350 BC), is exemplified by the large town of TELL TAYA. Sculpture in the Early Dynastic IIIB style from the Ishtar Temple at Assur suggests that during this same period Assur was in the cultural sphere of southern Mesopotamia or of Mari on the middle Euphrates. Textual evidence indicates that during parts of the Akkadian (*c.* 2340–2150 BC) and Ur III (*c.* 2112–2004 BC) periods, both Assur and Nineveh were controlled by the south. Architectural remains and artefacts of these periods have been found at both sites; indeed, the finest example of Akkadian copper sculpture, a head of a king, comes from Nineveh (Baghdad, Iraq Mus.; *see* AKKADIAN, fig. 2).

2. OLD AND MIDDLE ASSYRIAN PERIODS (*c.* 2000–*c.* 1000 BC). The Assyrians as an independent group entered the historical record with the Old Assyrian kings, who ruled at Assur from the beginning of the 2nd millennium BC until the accession of Shamshi-Adad I (*reg* 1813–1781 BC). During this period Assur was a flourishing commercial centre with trading colonies in Anatolia, at one of which, KÜLTEPE (anc. Kanesh), excavations have recovered extensive documentation of this trade (*see also* ANATOLIA, ANCIENT, §I, 2(ii)(a)). Assur already had a palace and temples dedicated to Assur, Ishtar and Adad, and at this time it also received a new city wall. The most active builders at Assur were Ilushuma (*reg c.* 1950 BC) and his son Erishum I (*reg* 1939–1900 BC).

In 1813 BC the West Semitic usurper Shamshi-Adad I became king of Assyria and made Assur one of the capitals of his extensive north Mesopotamian kingdom. He seems to have rebuilt a number of its public buildings, including the palace, the Temple of Assur and the double Temple of Anu and Adad. He also may have built the Assur ziggurat and the double Temple of Sin and Shamash. Nineveh is less well documented than Assur in the Old Assyrian period, but texts say that Shamshi-Adad I rebuilt the ziggurat and Temple of Ishtar there. The palace and temple at Tell el Rimah were probably also built during or just after the reign of Shamshi-Adad I. The period following the fall of Shamshi-Adad's dynasty, about 1700 BC, is a 'dark age' in Assyria, at least in terms of the archaeological and textual records.

During the Middle Assyrian period (roughly the second half of the 2nd millennium BC) Assyria's varying fortunes are reflected in (and to some degree defined by) four peaks of building activity in the capital Assur. The first occurred in the reigns of Assur-nirari I (*reg c.* 1525 BC) and his son Puzur-Assur III (*reg c.* 1500 BC), around which time the wall, palace and all the major sanctuaries of the city were restored. The second, less pronounced than the first, was the period from 1417 BC to 1306 BC, when seven consecutive monarchs, most notably Assur-nadin-ahhe II (*reg* 1400–1391 BC) and his uncle Eriba-Adad I (*reg* 1390–1364 BC), carried out almost continuous maintenance work on Assur's major structures. At Nineveh, Assur-uballit I (*reg* 1363–1328 BC) restored the Ishtar Temple. The third peak was in the reigns of Adad-nirari I (*reg* 1305–1274 BC) and his successors Shalmaneser I (*reg* 1273–1244 BC) and Tukulti-Ninurta I (*reg* 1243–1207 BC): the city wall and Old Palace at Assur were restored, and the Assur Temple and ziggurat, the double Temple of Sin and Shamash, and the Temple of Ishtar of Nineveh were completely rebuilt. The Temple of Ishtar of Assur was completely rebuilt twice, and Tukulti-Ninurta I built the New Palace. At Nineveh, Shalmaneser I and Tukulti-Ninurta I restored the Ishtar Temple. In addition, Shalmaneser I founded or rebuilt the provincial capital city of Calah (*see* NIMRUD) and Tukulti-Ninurta I built a new, much larger national capital at KAR TUKULTI NINURTA, a few km north of Assur. The new city included inner and outer city walls, a temple dedicated to Assur and several other gods, and a palace decorated with wall paintings. The city ceased to be the Assyrian capital after Tukulti-Ninurta's death but was inhabited throughout the Neo-Assyrian period. The final peak of building activity was in the reigns of Assur-resh-ishi I (*reg* 1132–1115 BC), Tiglath-pileser I (*reg* 1114–1076 BC) and Assur-bel-kala (*reg* 1073–1056 BC). In Assur at this time the city wall, the Assur Temple and the New Palace were restored, the Old Palace was restored and embellished with sculpture, and a new Temple of Ishtar of Assur and a double Temple of Anu and Adad were constructed. At Nineveh, these kings restored the Ishtar Temple, built two palaces on Kuyunjik, and restored the 'back palace'. Their successor Assurnasirpal I (*reg* 1049–1031 BC) built a Temple of Adad.

3. NEO-ASSYRIAN PERIOD (883–612 BC). From the 9th century BC until the late 7th Assyria expanded into an empire larger than any previously known. The process was begun in the late 10th century BC by Assur-dan II (*reg* 934–912 BC) and continued by his successors Adad-nirari II (*reg* 911–891 BC) and Tukulti-Ninurta II (*reg* 890–884 BC). This new expansion was accompanied by a resumed building activity in Assur, with restoration work on the city wall, palaces and the Assur Temple.

Assurnasirpal II (*reg* 883–859 BC) continued his predecessors' policies of territorial expansion and construction in the capital. At Assur he made further repairs to the city wall and Assur Temple and rebuilt the Old Palace and double Temple of Sin and Shamash. At Nineveh he rebuilt the Ishtar Temple and worked on a palace. His primary architectural and artistic activity, however, was lavished on his new capital city at Nimrud. It is not clear why he considered a new capital necessary, but around the fifth year of his reign he moved the chief royal residence and administrative centre from Assur to the Middle Assyrian provincial capital of Kalhu (Heb. Calah) and began rebuilding on a massive scale; it is not known if any earlier buildings were standing when work began. His new constructions included a city wall and a large palace decorated with human-headed bull and lion colossi in its main doors and wall reliefs in its state apartments, possibly inspired by the portal figures and orthostats he had seen during his Syrian campaigns (*see* MESOPOTAMIA, §II, 6(i)). Of nine temples he built, four or five have been located.

Shalmaneser III (*reg* 858–824 BC), Assurnasirpal II's son, divided his attentions between Nimrud and Assur. His largest building at Nimrud was the arsenal, a huge new palace at the south-east corner of the city wall, which apparently served as a storehouse for military equipment and booty and as the assembly point for the army. Its decoration included the most complete Assyrian glazed-brick mosaic panel yet recovered and a stone throne-base carved with reliefs (both Baghdad, Iraq Mus.). Shalmaneser's other projects at Nimrud included the main ziggurat, which he built or rebuilt, a temple or palace at the centre of the citadel and three small 'palaces': the South-east Palace, the Governor's Palace and the '1950 Building'. At Assur, he restored the Assur Temple and rebuilt the double Temple of Anu and Adad. His greatest project at the old capital, however, was the rebuilding of the city walls, giving them the form they would retain until the fall of the city in 614 BC. One of Shalmaneser's political priorities was to dominate the rich trade with the west: he captured the major Euphrates ford at Til Barsip in 856 BC and made it the Assyrian city of Kar-Shalmaneser (*see* TIL BARSIP, §2), thus bypassing the powerful and troublesome competing ford city of Carchemish to the north. His palace beside the Euphrates in Til Barsip is important for its fine wall paintings (8th–7th centuries BC; e.g. Aleppo, N. Mus.; Paris, Louvre; *see* MESOPOTAMIA, fig. 21).

After the death of Shalmaneser III, Assyrian influence declined for some 80 years. The only relatively powerful monarch during this period was Adad-nirari III (*reg* 810–783 BC), who ruled from Nimrud, where he built the Nabu Temple, the neighbouring Burnt Palace and an addition to the south side of Assurnasirpal II's palace. At Nineveh, Adad-nirari III built or rebuilt the Nabu Temple and finished a palace, and at Assur he reinforced a stretch of the quay wall. Shamshi-ilu (?780–752 BC), the Assyrian governor of Til Barsip towards the end of this period of weakness, was sufficiently autonomous to set up monumental stone lions at Til Barsip (*in situ*) and, perhaps, at ARSLAN TASH, inscribed in his own name without any mention of his nominal overlord.

Assyria's expansionist policy was renewed by Tiglath-pileser III (*reg* 744–727 BC), with a change in emphasis from control of trade to political domination of foreign lands and peoples. This policy was so successful that by the time of Esarhaddon (*reg* 680–669 BC) the empire included all of modern Iraq, Syria, the Levant and Egypt, as well as large parts of Turkey and Iran. Tiglath-pileser III ruled from Nimrud, where he built a new royal palace decorated with wall reliefs (*see* MANUSCRIPT, fig. 1) in the manner of Assurnasirpal II's palace. At Assur he erected podiums faced with glazed bricks in front of the Assur Temple; he intended doing the same in front of the Adad Temple but died before the work was completed. He built or restored the west gate, the palace and the Ishtar Temple at the Assyrian outpost of Arslan Tash. Some of the wall paintings in the palace at Til Barsip may date to this period.

Sargon II (*reg* 721–705 BC) embellished the Assur Temple at Assur, built a New Year's Festival (*akītu*) temple and restored the Nabu and possibly the Ishtar temples at Nineveh, and restored Assurnasirpal II's palace at Nimrud, where he lived at the beginning of his reign. In his fifth year, however, Sargon founded a new capital city called Dur-Sharrukin (*see* KHORSABAD), *c.* 60 km north of Nimrud, where no city had been before. The site appears to have little to recommend it except for its scenic beauty and rich farmland, and Sargon's reasons for abandoning Nimrud in its favour remain a mystery, although a factor may have been the need to accommodate the tremendous influx of subject-foreigners deported to the Assyrian heartland by Tiglath-pileser III and himself. He built a city wall with seven gates, an arsenal and a fortified citadel, which contained a royal palace, four smaller palaces, a major temple dedicated to Nabu, and a group of six smaller temples with a ziggurat. His palace, the largest and most complete yet excavated, had human-headed bull colossi in the major entrances and wall reliefs in the state apartments. The smaller palaces and temples were decorated with glazed bricks and wall paintings. It is not clear how densely settled was the area inside the city walls, but three large residences and a temple have been located. The city was apparently abandoned after Sargon's death.

At the beginning of his reign Sennacherib (*reg* 704–681 BC) moved his capital to Nineveh, which he made the largest city in the known world, building a new city wall with 18 major gates, a huge new palace, an arsenal, temples, roads, bridges and canals. His palace, according to his texts the largest built by the Assyrians, was decorated with the traditional gateway colossi and wall reliefs, though on an unprecedented scale. The courses of his canals were also sometimes marked with reliefs, for example at BAVIAN, Faida and, perhaps, MALTAI, and by monumental feats of engineering, such as an aqueduct at Jerwan.

Assyrian wall relief of Assurbanipal and his queen relaxing in a garden (the 'Garden Party' relief), alabaster, w. 1.39 m, from the North Palace, Nineveh, *c.* 640 BC (London, British Museum)

Sennacherib was also active at Assur, particularly after his destruction of Babylon and the concomitant elevation of the god Assur in place of the Babylonian Marduk as king of the gods. His major works at Assur were the Assur Temple, which he rebuilt and enlarged, and the Temple of the New Year's Festival, a new building that replaced the one he destroyed at Babylon.

Esarhaddon (*reg* 681–669 BC) also ruled from Nineveh, at least at the beginning of his reign. He continued his father's work on the Nineveh arsenal and embellished or restored three temples. Later he may have intended to move the capital back to Nimrud, where he restored the arsenal and began a new palace, which was to have been decorated with wall reliefs. Slabs for this purpose were removed from the nearby palaces of Assurnasirpal II and Tiglath-pileser III, but the project was abandoned (presumably on the King's death) before any slabs were recarved. At Assur, Esarhaddon embellished the Assur Temple and enlarged the terrace and approach to the Old Palace.

Assurbanipal (*reg* 668–627 BC) ruled from Nineveh, living for a time in Sennacherib's palace, which he refurbished. At least one set of wall reliefs there, and perhaps others, date to this period. The new palace he built later at Nineveh had no colossi in its doorways, but its major rooms were decorated with wall reliefs, including the 'Garden Party' relief showing the King and Queen in a garden (*c.* 640 BC; London, BM; see fig.), that are among the finest surviving examples of Assyrian sculpture. He also worked on three temples at Nineveh and further embellished the Assur Temple at Assur.

Sin-shar-ishkun (*reg* ?–612 BC), the last king to rule from Nineveh, may have recarved the reliefs in a few rooms in Sennacherib's palace. His greatest project, however, seems to have been at Assur, where he built the Nabu Temple. He also repaired the Nabu Temple at Nimrud and possibly the double Temple of Anu and Adad at Assur. The Medes captured Assur in 614 BC, and Nineveh and Nimrud followed two years later. The three capitals were sacked and burnt, their populace of foreign deportees went home, and the remnant of the Assyrian court and army fled to Harran, being finally defeated in 609 BC. Everything the world had come to admire and fear as Assyrian vanished almost without trace.

BIBLIOGRAPHY

D. D. Luckenbill: *Ancient Records of Assyria and Babylonia*, 2 vols (Chicago, 1926–7)

C. J. Gadd: *The Stones of Assyria* (London, 1936)

W. Andrae: *Das wiedererstandene Assur* (Leipzig, 1938; rev. B. Hrouda, Munich, 1977)

J. Bottéro, ed.: *The Near East: The Early Civilizations* (New York, 1967)

D. Oates: *Studies in the Ancient History of Northern Iraq* (London, 1968)

G. van Driel: *The Cult of Assur* (Assen, 1969)

J. E. Reade: *The Design and Decoration of Neo-Assyrian Public Buildings* (diss., U. Cambridge, 1970)

M. T. Larsen: *The Old Assyrian City-state and its Colonies* (1976), iv of *Mesopotamia* (Copenhagen, 1972–)

J. E. Reade: 'Neo-Assyrian Monuments in their Historical Context', *Assyrian Royal Inscriptions: New Horizons in Literary, Ideological, and Historical Analysis*, ed. F. M. Fales (Rome, 1981), pp. 144–67

J. Börker-Klähn: *Altvorderasiatische Bildstelen und vergleichbare Felsreliefs*, Baghdad. Forsch., 2 vols (Mainz, 1982)

J. Curtis, ed.: *Fifty Years of Mesopotamian Discovery* (Hertford, 1982)

E. Heinrich: *Die Tempel und Heiligtümer im alten Mesopotamien*, Dt. Archäol. Inst., Dkml. Ant. Archit., 2 vols (Berlin, 1982)

S. Lackenbacher: *Le Roi bâtisseur: Les Récits de construction assyriens des origines à Teglatphalasar III* (Paris, 1982)

J. Margueron: *Recherches sur les palais mésopotamiens de l'Age du Bronze*, 2 vols (Paris, 1982)

J. E. Reade: *Assyrian Sculpture* (Cambridge, MA, 1983)

E. Heinrich: *Die Paläste im alten Mesopotamien*, Dt. Archäol. Inst., Dkml. Ant. Archit. (Berlin, 1984)

A. K. Grayson: *Assyrian Rulers of the Third and Second Millennia* BC (1987), i of *Royal Inscriptions of Mesopotamia: Assyrian Periods* (Toronto, 1987–)

M. Roaf: *Cultural Atlas of Mesopotamia and the Ancient Near East* (New York, 1990)

A. K. Grayson: *Assyrian Rulers of the Early First Millennium* BC (1991), ii of *Royal Inscriptions of Mesopotamia: Assyrian Periods* (Toronto, 1987–)

J. M. Russell: *Sennacherib's 'Palace without Rival' at Nineveh* (Chicago, 1991)

E. Porada and others: 'The Chronology of Mesopotamia, ca. 7000–1600 BC', *Chronologies in Old World Archaeology*, ed. R. W. Ehrich (Chicago, rev. 3/1992)

For further bibliography *see* ASSUR; KHORSABAD; MESOPOTAMIA, §§II, 6(i) and III, 6(i); NIMRUD; NINEVEH.

JOHN M. RUSSELL

Ford Madox Brown: *The Dream of Sardanapalus*, watercolour, 482×582 mm, 1871 (Wilmington, DE, Delaware Art Museum)

Assyrian Revival. Style of the second half of the 19th century and the early 20th, inspired by Assyrian artefacts of the 9th to 7th centuries BC. These were first brought to public attention through the excavations by Paul-Emile Botta (1802–70) at Khorsabad and AUSTEN HENRY LAYARD at Nimrud in the 1840s. By 1847 both the Louvre in Paris and the British Museum in London had begun to display these objects, the size and popularity of which were such that the Louvre created a separate Musée des Antiquités Orientales, while the British Museum opened its separate Nineveh Gallery in 1853. The same popularity, fuelled by Layard's best-selling *Nineveh and its Remains* (London, 1849) and Botta's elaborate *Monument de Ninive* (Paris, 1849–50), led to further explorations elsewhere in Mesopotamia.

1. AREAS OF INFLUENCE. Assyrian revivalism first appeared in England rather than France, which was then in political turmoil. The earliest forms of emulation can be found in the decorative arts, such as the 'Assyrian style' jewellery that was produced in England from as early as 1851 and flourished until at least the late 1870s. The 1853 revival of *The Death of Sardanapalus* by Lord Byron (1788–1824), produced by Charles Kean (1811–68) at the Princess's Theatre (destr.), London, took as its main claim to authenticity (and selling-point) the use of actual casts of Assyrian reliefs as part of the stage design, as well as costumes 'verified by the bas reliefs'. This representational strategy, in which exact attention to detail was intended to authenticate the whole, remained the prevalent scheme for visual representations of Assyria. Assyrianism in architecture was established most notably through James Fergusson's 'Nineveh Court' in the Sydenham Crystal Palace of 1854.

Commentators from Eugène Delacroix to Walter Crane praised Assyrian art especially for its representation of animals. By the late 19th century Assyrian art had clearly gained some currency in French animal sculpture: in 1889 Rodin said of Antoine-Louis Barye, who had specialized in images of wild beasts such as lions and tigers, 'One thinks of him and the Assyrians together, though it is not known that he knew anything about them.' There is no overtly Assyrian object in Barye's work, and it was only with his student Charles Valton (1851–1918), who continued and extended the tradition, that Assyrian imagery was introduced. Among Valton's many images of lions and tigers was a large-scale bronze based on the 'Wounded Lioness' relief from Nineveh, in the British Museum, London. This was placed prominently outside the City of Paris pavilion at the 1889 Exposition Universelle, and the sculpture jury, which included Rodin, awarded the artist a first-class medal.

Assyrian art may have influenced the stylistic canon of American Art Deco sculpture, particularly that of Paul Manship, yet there is little that can be described as directly Assyrian apart from a few animal groups. Indeed, within Manship's work Assyria was absorbed among several other stylistic influences, including Etruscan, Indian and Archaic Greek. A magazine cover design (*Der Bildermann*, iv, 20 May 1916) by August Gaul, perhaps the most prominent German animal sculptor of the early 20th century, demonstrates much stronger Assyrian influence in a detailed rendering of the dying lioness relief as the emblem of the German victory at Kut el-Amara in the Mesopotamian campaign of World War I. In English art there is evidence on a more monumental scale. The tomb of Oscar Wilde (1909–12; Paris, Père-Lachaise Cemetery) by JACOB EPSTEIN was modelled after an Assyrian winged bull, as letters and early drawings confirm, and carved on a comparable scale from a 20-ton block of stone.

2. WORKS AND MOTIFS. The most numerous and varied Assyrian Revival works are two dimensional and approach the theme in much the same fashion as did the theatrical presentations. A watercolour by Ford Madox Brown, *The Dream of Sardanapalus* (1871; Wilmington, DE, A. Mus.; see fig.), is a typical evocation of Assyria and one of a series of paintings and drawings, many now untraced. A number of costume details, such as the jewellery, helmet and dress of the Assyrian monarch, are taken directly from the reliefs. Sardanapalus wears a short, jutting 'Assyrian' beard, a style then current (its most famous wearer being Gustave Courbet) and derived from an idiosyncratic viewing of the reliefs.

Assyrian artefacts or elements can be found in many different contexts in late 19th- and early 20th-century art. Visual references were sometimes strictly limited to certain geographical and historical contexts, a mode prevalent among late 19th-century French salon painters; for example, the *Assyrian Marriage Market* (1896; Attigny, Hôtel de Ville) by Louis Marie Doyen (*b* 1864) localizes in ancient Assyria the common Orientalist theme of the market of women; nearly every aspect of the setting and costume is derived from Assyrian artefacts. The master of this genre was Georges Rochegrosse, whose range of subjects encompassed prehistory, pagan antiquity, the Middle Ages and the Orient. His most famous Assyrian (and not at all Babylonian) work was the enormous, violent, recondite and popular *Fall of Babylon* (1891; ex-New York, Murray's Restaurant). The sources for his panoply of interior details included reliefs (such as the Gilgamesh Relief in the Louvre), a zoomorphic weight discovered by Botta (Paris, Louvre) and the Black Obelisk of Shalmaneser III (*reg* 858–824 BC) excavated by Layard (London, BM).

Assyria also had a certain symbolic standing as the exemplar of a historical civilization, and as such its remains (almost invariably the great winged bulls and lions; e.g. London, BM) appeared in images of universal history, such as those of Paul Chenavard. Biblical imagery, however, accounts for the widest promulgation of Assyrian artefacts and the greatest range of artistic production. Specific details of Assyrian artefacts were used in biblical illustrations from as early as Gustave Doré's *La Sainte Bible selon la Vulgate* (1866). In G. F. Watts's *Jonah* (1894–5; London, Tate) and Gustav Klimt's *Judith I* (1901; Vienna, Belvedere), settings derived from specific Assyrian reliefs are represented on a shallow field behind the biblical figure and serve to establish the character.

A certain Assyrian presence also developed in architecture. Fergusson's work and the Assyrian house in Charles Garnier's series of buildings depicting the history of housing at the 1889 Paris Exposition Universelle introduced the concepts of Assyrian buildings to a wide public, including other architects. The massive building styles of the early 20th century, with their low-relief decorations, may be compared with widespread theories of ancient Mesopotamian architecture (Künzl). Perhaps the most direct connections are manifest in American Art Deco architecture. The elaborate brass entrance of the Fred French Building (1927, by T. Robinson), New York City, actually features Assyrian bulls. In Los Angeles the façade of the vast Samson Tire Company building (1929, by Morgan, Walls & Clements) is entirely based on Assyrian forms, featuring a crenellated roof-line with embossed mouldings, towers and corner pavilions, some with Assyrian relief figures (and pseudo-cuneiform inscriptions), and an elaborate entrance flanked by bulls and capped by a tower resembling a ziggurat.

The Assyrian Revival style cannot be compared in size and influence to the Gothic or Greek revivals. It was a limited but persistent thread in late 19th- and early 20th-century art, being absorbed into the period's depiction of antiquity. The contemporary view of Assyrian artefacts as embodying one of a series of newly found traditions and the use of the great winged bulls as a universal emblem are summed up in John Ruskin's remark in *The Stones of Venice* (1851–3), 'I hardly know whether most to admire the winged bulls of Nineveh, or the winged dragons of Verona' (E. T. Cook and A. Wedderburn, eds: *The Works of John Ruskin*, London, 1903–12, xi, p. 188).

BIBLIOGRAPHY

C. Kean: *Sardanapalus, King of Assyria: A Tragedy . . . by Lord Byron, Adapted for Representation by Charles Kean* (New York, n.d.) [intro.]
A. H. Layard: *The Nineveh Court in the Crystal Palace* (London, 1854)
W. Crane: *William Morris to Whistler* (London, 1911), pp. 185–204
E. Porada: 'The Assyrians in the Last Hundred Years', *Bull. Met.*, n. s., iv/1 (1945), pp. 38–48
R. Alexander: 'Courbet and Assyrian Sculpture', *A. Bull.*, xlvii (1965), pp. 447–52
H. Künzl: *Der Einfluss des alten Orients auf die europäische Kunst besonders im 19. und 20. Jh.* (Cologne, 1973)
I. Krengel-Strudthoff: 'Archäologie auf der Bühne: Das wiedererstandene Ninive: Charles Keans Ausstattung zu "Sardanapalus" von Lord Byron', *Kleine Schr. Ges. Theatgesch.*, xxxi (1981), pp. 3–24
H. Tate and others, eds: *The Art of the Jeweller: A Catalogue of the Hull Grundy Gift to the British Museum: Jewellery, Engraved Gems and Goldsmiths' Works*, 2 vols (London, 1984), nos 950–51
The Jeweler's Eye (exh. cat., ed. D. C. Pack; Yonkers, NY, Hudson River Mus., 1986), nos 111–14
F. N. Bohrer: 'Assyria as Art: A Perspective on the Early Reception of Ancient Near East Artifacts', *Culture and History*, 4 (1989), pp. 7–33
——: 'The Times and Spaces of History: Representation, Assyria, and the British Museum', *Museum Culture: Histories, Discourses, Spectacles*, ed. D. Sherman and I. Rogoff (Minneapolis, 1994), pp. 197–222
——: 'Les Antiquités assyriennes au XIXe siècle: Emulation et inspiration', *De Khorsabad à Paris: La Découverte des Assyriens* (exh. cat., Paris, Louvre, 1994), pp. 248–59

FREDERICK N. BOHRER

Ast, Balthasar van der (*b* Middelburg, ?1593–4; *d* Delft, *bur* 19 Dec 1657). Dutch painter. He was the brother-in-law of Ambrosius Bosschaert (i), whose household he entered in 1609, after the death of his father. He remained as Bosschaert's pupil, until he was 21. In 1615 van der Ast moved with the Bosschaert family to Bergen-op-Zoom. However, a year later the Bosschaerts were living in Utrecht, but van der Ast is not recorded there until 1619, when he was entered as a master in the Guild of St Luke. He remained in Utrecht until 1632, then lived in Delft, where he enrolled in the painters' guild on 22 June 1632. On 26 February 1633 he married Margrieta Jans van Bueren in Delft, where he spent the rest of his career; the marriage produced two children.

Van der Ast belonged to what Bol has called the Bosschaert dynasty: like his brother-in-law, he painted predominantly flower and fruit still-lifes, but as a new element he also painted shell still-lifes, which probably reflected the fashion for collecting exotic rarities. His oeuvre of *c.* 200 paintings is considerably larger than that of his teacher Bosschaert. However, the chronology of van der Ast's work is more difficult to establish: there are dated works only from 1620–28. Moreover, his compositions are more diverse, with fewer exact repetitions, and were carried out in a wider variety of formats, ranging from small copper paintings of *c.* 500 mm to canvases of 2 m.

Van der Ast's earliest works are clearly influenced by the flower still-lifes of his nephew Ambrosius Bosschaert (ii): usually they show a rich, vertically composed, symmetrical bouquet, the longitudinal axis being emphasized by a large leading flower, such as a tulip or an iris, and the lower arrangement filled with roses, peonies, carnations or asters. The bouquet, in an elegant vase of porcelain or glass before an open or closed background, is composed of flowers from different seasons, based on individual studies from nature (e.g. *Vase with Flowers and Shells*, 1628; Madrid, Mus. Thyssen-Bornemisza). What is also new in his work is the importance attached to realistically depicted animals, lizards, grasshoppers, toads or flies, used as accessories flanking the flowers and probably inspired by the work of Roelandt Savery (e.g. *Bouquet before a Landscape*, 1624; priv. col., see 1984 exh. cat., no. 13). Also novel, and clearly distinguishable from the work of his teacher, are van der Ast's depictions of individual flowers shown in a vase (e.g. *Tulip in a Glass Vase*, ex-art market, Solingen, 1980; see 1984 exh. cat., no. 15) and the

Balthasar van der Ast: *Still-life with Shells, Fruit and Red Currant Branch*, oil on panel, 290×375 mm (Dresden, Gemäldegalerie Alte Meister)

'still-lifes' of single flowers lying on a board or table (e.g. *Tulip and Forget-me-not*, priv. col., see 1984 exh. cat., no. 16). In composition and conception, these paintings anticipate the work of such artists as Jan van Kessel and Adriaen Coorte. Van der Ast's fruit still-lifes are often shown together with such non-European rarities as Chinese porcelain or parrots (e.g. *Flowers and Fruits with a Parrot*, Amersfoort, Mus. Flehite). His shell still-lifes are painted in a monochrome manner, which creates a unified composition and palette, despite the diversity of the objects depicted (e.g. *Still-life with Shells, Fruit and Red Currant Branch*, Dresden, Gemäldegal. Alte Meister; see fig.). His brother Johannes van der Ast was also a flower painter and probably a pupil of Ambrosius Bosschaert the elder.

BIBLIOGRAPHY

L. J. Bol: 'Bartholomaeus Assteijn', *Oud-Holland*, lxviii (1953), pp. 136–48

——: 'Een Middelburgse Breughel-Groep, Teil III', *Oud-Holland*, lxx (1955), pp. 138–54

——: *The Bosschaert Dynasty* (Leigh-on-Sea, 1960), pp. 36–40

P. Mitchell: *European Flower Painters* (London, 1973)

I. Bergström: 'Baskets with Flowers by Ambrosius Bosschaert the Elder and their Repercussions on the Art of Balthasar van der Ast', *Tableau*, vi (1983), pp. 721ff

Masters of Middelburg (exh. cat., Amsterdam, Waterman Gal., 1984), pp. 45–62

M.-L. Hairs: *Les Peintres flamands de fleurs au XVIIe siècle* (Brussels, 1985), pp. 130–31

IRENE HABERLAND

Astana. Site of an ancient cemetery for KHOCHO, 40 km south-east of Turfan in the Xinjiang Uygur Autonomous Region, China. The burial ground, which contains over 400 tombs, covers a large area and is divided into three sections: a north-western group with the earliest graves, a north-eastern group consisting of later, commoners' graves, and a later northern group intended for the nobility. A wooden document found at the site indicates that it was in use before AD 273. From other unearthed written evidence it is thought that Astana ceased to be used in the late 8th century. It appears that most of those buried here were Chinese.

Many tombs contained a couple, or in some cases a man and several wives. A few single burials have also been found. In several cases the exact dating of a tomb is possible owing to memorial inscriptions on clay slates placed next to the bodies. The early tombs were made by digging a vertical entry shaft into the ground with chambers on the sides, while the later tombs have an access ramp sloping down to the burial chamber, sometimes with side rooms and antechambers. The tombs made for the nobility are usually decorated with wall paintings depicting such motifs as birds and flowers, stylized landscapes and figures; many are in the style of the early Tang period (AD 618–907) and show Persian elements.

Burial goods include figures (100–400 mm)—horsemen, officials, retainers, palace ladies, guardians and hybrid monsters—resembling those known from tombs in China during the Tang period. Although some are of fired clay, many are a mixture of straw, clay and wooden sticks coated with plaster, which is then painted in bright colours. The figures are sometimes dressed in silk brocade or hemp. Several banner paintings on silk (New Delhi, N. Mus.; Seoul, N. Mus.; Tenri, Nara Prefect., Sankōkan Mus.) showing the entwined Fuxi and Nuwa—mythical beings who, according to the Chinese creation myth, were responsible for the creation of the universe—were among the burial goods. Wooden models of buildings were also found, as were large quantities of silk, wool and other textiles.

The tombs at Astana were visited by the expeditions led by Count Kozui Otani in 1902 and 1910, and by Aurel Stein in 1914. Although some tombs had been robbed, the Japanese expeditions and Stein were able to recover large numbers of important artefacts, including tomb figures of clay and wood, paintings, many fragments of silk and written materials. Systematic excavations were begun by the Chinese in 1959 and still continue. So far the Chinese archaeological teams have opened up more than 400 tombs. The artefacts recovered are said to number *c.* 10,000 pieces, which are now in the Museum of the Xinjiang Uygur Autonomous Region in Urumqi.

BIBLIOGRAPHY

Sizhou zhi lu [The Silk Route] (Beijing, 1973)

A. E. Dien, J. K. Riegel and N. T. Price: *Chinese Archaeological Abstracts*, Monumenta Archaeologica 11, iv [Post-Han] (Los Angeles, 1985), pp. 1802–12

R. Whitfield: *Textiles, Sculpture and Other Arts* (1985), iii of *The Art of Central Asia: The Stein Collection in the British Museum* (Tokyo, 1982–5), pp. 323–8, pls 86–94

Xinjiang gudai mingzu wenwu [Cultural relics of the people in ancient Xinjiang] (Beijing, 1985), pls 275–7

Ueno Aki: 'Darstellungen von Fu Hsi und Nü Kua aus Astana', *Japanische Studien zur Kunst der Seidenstrasse*, ed. H.-J. Klimheit, Studies in Oriental Religions, 16 (Wiesbaden, 1988), pp. 132–96

HENRIK H. SØRENSEN

Astbury, John (*b* Shelton, Staffs, 1688; *d* Shelton, Staffs, 3 March 1743). English potter. He worked mainly in earthenware and furthered the development of white, salt-glazed wares, which replaced the earlier, drab, salt-glazed stoneware and the brittle, yellow-brown slipwares. He was interested in the nature of clays and carried out experiments with combinations of different types; he is often credited (along with Thomas Heath) with the introduction of calcined flint into the clay body to enable the production of finer, crisper work. His output included teapots and other red earthenwares—some with applied, white relief decoration—including cow creamers and a variety of animal figures. He is perhaps best known, however, for his charming figures of soldiers (e.g. *Grenadier*; London, BM), musicians and horsemen modelled in brown-and-white clay with transparent lead glazes. Although these figures were cheaply produced from moulds they required a great deal of hand finishing. Similar but later figures, stained with underglaze metallic oxides, are referred to as 'Astbury Whieldon'. Astbury's rolled, pipeclay figures possess a cheerful, enthusiastic quality and he is also sometimes credited with modelling the naive and humorous 'Pew Groups' of seated men and women in finely detailed contemporary dress. From *c.* 1735 he is also reputed to have made figure jugs, precursors of the popular 'Toby' jugs. His work was not signed; where the name does appear it belongs to a later member of his family, after *c.* 1760. His name is used to classify the work of many other potters by type and of the period 1730 to 1740.

BIBLIOGRAPHY

R. K. Price: *Astbury, Whieldon and Ralph Wood Figures and Toby Jugs* (London, 1928)

H. A. B. Turner: *A Collector's Guide to Staffordshire Pottery Figures* (London, 1971)

JOHN MAWER

Astete y Concha, Luis (*b* Lima, 1866; *d* Lima, 12 Jan 1914). Peruvian painter. He studied at the Academia de S Fernando in Madrid, where he lived from 1883 to 1893; his friends there included Joaquín Sorolla y Bastida, a fellow student. On his return to Lima in 1893 he painted portraits and for 14 years taught drawing at the Academia Concha. He also worked as an illustrator for the review *Prisma*. In 1897 he was awarded first prize at the Exposición de Lima and was commissioned to execute a series of portraits of Peruvian personalities; these were later destroyed in a fire at the Biblioteca Nacional in Lima. In addition to landscapes and portraits he executed genre scenes and allegorical paintings.

BIBLIOGRAPHY

T. Núñez Ureta: *Pintura contemporánea: Primera parte, 1820–1920* (Lima, 1975)

C. Milla Batres, ed.: *Diccionario histórico y biográfico del Perú: Siglos XV–XX*, i (Lima, 1986)

LUIS ENRIQUE TORD

Astor, Diego de, the elder (*b* Mechelen, Flanders, *c.* 1585–90; *d* ?Madrid, *c.* 1650). Spanish engraver and medallist of Flemish birth. From the beginning of the 17th century until 1609 he lived in Toledo, where, under the supervision of El Greco, he worked as an engraver and printed (1605–6) such works of his master as *SS Peter and Paul* (1603–7; Stockholm, Nmus.) and *St Francis and Brother Leo* (*c.* 1600–05; Ottawa, N.G.). Other engravings from this period include frontispieces for *Historia de . . . Nuestra Señora de Valvanera* (Ávila, 1607) by Francisco de Ariz and the *Index librorum prohibitorum* (Madrid, 1612) by Bernardo de Sandoval y Rojas, the Archbishop of Toledo. From 1609 to 1636 he was engraver at the Casa de Moneda in Segovia, where he created designs for currency and made the printing plates. He also executed engravings for *Obras espirituales* (Alcalá de Henares, 1618) by St John of the Cross and the frontispiece for *Historia . . . de Segovia* (Segovia, 1637) by Diego de Colmenares. In 1636 he moved to Madrid as an employee of the Imprenta del Sello Real. Although his exact date of death is uncertain, he made his will in September 1650; it shows that he was owed a significant amount of money by Philip IV. His general style, as well as his working method, is similar to that of Flemish engravers, although his early prints after El Greco show an influence from the painter. His son Diego de Astor the younger (*fl* *c.* 1630–60) was also an engraver and in 1636 took over his father's position at the Casa de la Moneda, Segovia.

BIBLIOGRAPHY

A. M. Roteta de la Maza: *La ilustración del libro en la España de la Contrarreforma: Grabados de Pedro Angel y Diego de Astor, 1588–1637* (Toledo, 1985)

ISMAEL GUTIÉRREZ PASTOR

Astor, William Waldorf, 1st Viscount (*b* New York, 31 March 1848; *d* Hever Castle, Kent, 18 Oct 1919). British collector of American birth. He was a member of a wealthy family whose fortune came from fur trading; he became interested in art and antiquity during his appointment as American Minister in Rome (1882–5), rapidly acquiring a fine collection of ancient and Renaissance sculpture. He transferred the collection to England when his term as minister ended, dividing it between his country houses at Cliveden, Bucks, and Hever Castle, Kent. His eclectic, Neo-classical displays were in keeping with the nostalgic grandeur of Edwardian England. At Cliveden, eight Roman sarcophagi in the forecourt were matched on the rear terraces by Renaissance fountains and balustrades exported from the Villa Borghese in Rome. Hever Castle, the childhood home of Anne Boleyn, was restored and enlarged by Astor far beyond its medieval extent, and a Renaissance atmosphere was achieved by means of the placement of numerous Roman sculptures, including further fine sarcophagi (sold in 1983), among the lawns and herbaceous borders of the Italian gardens. Astor, who became a British subject in 1899 and a viscount in 1917, was the last of the great English collectors of ancient Roman sculpture, selfconsciously following and developing the traditions of acquisition and display inherited from Renaissance Italy and the Grand Tourists of the 18th century.

BIBLIOGRAPHY

L. Robert: 'A Collection of Roman Sarcophagi at Cliveden', *J. Hell. Stud.*, xx (1900), pp. 81–98

D. E. Strong: 'Some Unknown Classical Sculpture', *Connoisseur* (April 1965), pp. 215–25

G. Astor: *Statuary and Sculpture at Hever* (Ipswich, 1969)

V. Cowles: *The Astors* (New York, 1979)

H. Oehler: *Foto und Skulptur* (Cologne, 1980)

C. Aslett: *The Last Country Houses* (New Haven, 1982)

D. Wilson: *The Astors: The Life and Times of the Astor Dynasty, 1763–1992* (London, 1993)

GEOFFREY WAYWELL

Astorga, Marqueses de. *See* ALTAMIRA, Condes de.

Astragal. *See under* BEAD AND REEL.

Astrapas (*fl c.* 1290–1311). Byzantine painter active in Macedonia. 'Astrapas' (Gr.: 'lightning') is a pseudonym, and some scholars doubt that it refers to a particular artist. Although the name Astrapas appears together with the name Michael on the wall painting (1295) in the church of the Mother of God Peribleptos in OHRID, it is not clear whether the two names belong to one and the same artist or two different people. It is also not possible to distinguish the style of Astrapas from that of Michael and Eutychios who also painted frescoes there. The signature of 'Astrapas' as painter appears in the exonarthex of the church of the Mother of God (Sveta Bogorodica) Ljeviška (1307–9) in PRIZREN, where his work has been associated with that of the so-called 'Master of the Prophets'. Astrapas has also been credited with the frescoes (*c.* 1311) in the church of the Ascension in the monastery of Žića, in Serbia. His style of painting is characterized by dramatic composition and lively, lifelike figures achieved through the use of classicizing three-dimensional techniques and a palette of warm colours against dark blue backgrounds. His nationality has been disputed, some scholars believing him to be an itinerant Greek artist recruited from Thessaloniki into the service of the Serbian king Stephen Uroš II Milutin (*reg* 1282–1301), and others a Serb who was well versed in the Byzantine style.

BIBLIOGRAPHY

D. T. Rice: *Byzantine Painting: The Last Phase* (New York, 1968)

S. Radojčić: *Geschichte der serbischen Kunst* (Berlin, 1969)

A. DEAN MCKENZIE

Astrolabe. Principal instrument of the pre-modern astronomer for taking readings of the altitudes of stars and planets. The astrolabe was invented by the Greeks; together with Greek science it was passed to the Islamic world in the 8th and 9th centuries AD, and thence to western Europe. The earliest extant astrolabe (see fig. 1) was made in 927–8 by an Arab named Nastalus or Bastalus, and at least eight 10th-century astrolabes are known.

Astrolabes are of several types. The most familiar is the flat or planispheric (Arab. *sathī* or *musattah*) astrolabe employing a stereographic projection of the heavens. Spherical (*kūrī*) astrolabes were invented in antiquity, and a linear (*khattī*) astrolabe was invented by the Persian astronomer al-Muzaffar ibn Muzaffar al-Tusi (*d c.* 1213), but no examples of these types are known to have survived. Celestial globes (e.g. 1085–6; Florence, Mus. Stor. Sci.) and armillary spheres were made in the Islamic world, but as these models of the heavens have no provision for the solution of problems of spherical astronomy or for the calculation of trigonometric functions, they are not true astrolabes. Flat astrolabes employing non-stereographic projections are described in astronomical texts, but none seems to have been built.

Islamic planispheric astrolabes are made entirely of a copper alloy and range from 100 to 200 mm in diameter. This variety of astrolabe consists of a circular body with a crescent-shaped top or 'throne' (*kursī*), to the top of which is attached a handle (*'urwa* or *habs*) that may be moved from one side to another in the plane of the *kursī*; a ring (*halqa*) attached to the handle allows for suspension of the instrument by a cord (*'ilāqa*). The body has a front (*wajh*) and a back (*zahr*). On the front is a recess (*umm*), surrounded by a rim (*hajra*, *tawq* or *kuffa*), marked off in 360 degrees. In the recess, the back of which may contain inscribed information, are set a number of double-sided discs (*safā'ih*) engraved with stereographic projections of the northern celestial hemisphere, each disc adjusted for a different latitude. Additional discs may be constructed for the solution of particular astronomical and astrological problems. The discs are interchangeable but do not rotate, as each disc has a small notch at its bottom and the rim has a projecting detent (*mumsika*) to hold the discs in place. A pivot pin (*qutb*, *watad* or *mihwar*) passes through the centre of the astrolabe and the discs, from back to front. This pin is secured by a wedge or 'horse' (*faras*) inserted through an opening in one end of the pin outside a washer (*fals*) that protects the rete, a circular openwork 'spider' (*'ankabūt*) covering the discs; the rete fits into the recess that holds the discs and turns on the pin. On the back of the astrolabe an alidade (*al-'idāda*), a sort of ruler, also pivots on the pin. The design of the rete includes the circle of the zodiac or the ecliptic, which is smaller than the diameter of the rete and corresponds to the vault of the heavens as it rotates around the earth; it is marked off in 12 divisions corresponding to the houses (*burūj*) of the zodiac. The rete usually also has one or more knobs (*mudīr* or *muhrik*) to facilitate its rotation. Pointers set into the design of the rete indicate on the exposed disc the locations of selected fixed stars. By using the appropriate disc and turning the rete to the appropriate point the astronomer can model the position of the stars at a given latitude at any hour.

The backs of most astrolabes contain information and scales used in conjunction with the alidade. The user suspends the instrument, sights on a star, the sun or the top of some object which it is desired to measure, and reads the result from the markings on one of the four quadrants into which the space on the back of the instrument is customarily divided. The upper left quadrant is inscribed with horizontal (and on occasion vertical) lines used for calculating sines and cosines, and the upper right quadrant is inscribed with lines representing the altitude of the sun under various conditions. Near the centre, the lower two quadrants contain shadow squares, first introduced by the 11th-century Spanish astronomer al-Zarqali, relating to the tangents and cotangents of altitudes measured with the alidade. Around the shadow squares is inscribed calendrical, astrological and religious information.

The astrolabe is an instrument for the measurement of the heavens but also for the solution of geometrical problems, including terrestrial ones. The Islamic interest in astrolabes stems from religious, astrological and mathematical concerns. For religious purposes it was necessary to determine the qibla, the direction of Mecca prescribed for prayer, from any location. It was also necessary to calculate the times of the five conventional daily prayers, which are fixed in relation to the rising and setting of the sun and thus vary from one day to the next. Both of these problems are amenable to solution by the application of trigonometry, which was greatly developed in the first centuries of Islam, and in the solution it is necessary to measure the angle of the sun at particular times, as with the alidade. For example, to tell the time with an astrolabe one measures the angle of the sun with the alidade and then models the position of the sun by turning the rete to the appropriate position in relation to the underlying disc; the time is read from the markings on the rim of the front of the instrument. Another aspect of the same religious interest in chronographic science was the invention of mechanisms for keeping time. Timepieces, such as sundials and clepsydrae, were part of the equipment of a major mosque and were sometimes constructed by geometers who also made astrolabes. Astrology, which has no relationship to Islam, has nevertheless always been popular in the Islamic world, as in the West, and the astrolabe was

1. Astrolabe by Nastalus or Bastalus, cast and engraved bronze, diam. 175 mm, from Iraq, AD 927–8 (Kuwait City, Museum of Islamic Art, Al Sabah collection)

useful for astrological calculations as well as for astronomical ones. Finally, the astrolabe and astronomy were inherited from the Greeks along with algebra, geometry and other natural sciences, such as medicine, and these ancient sciences remained of interest to a portion of the educated population aside from their religious applications. Astronomers in the Islamic world made great improvements on Greek learning, and the astrolabe was indispensable to their efforts. The makers of astrolabes were generally geometers and engineers rather than professional brassworkers.

Astrolabes are composed according to extremely rigid conventions. Not only did the function of the device determine the shape of its moving parts, but the location of inscriptions and even the lobed outline of the *kursī* at the top of the instrument were fixed by custom. The *kursī* offers the largest non-functional area and is consequently the location of most of the decoration on artistically designed astrolabes, especially on Persian models, as their *kursīs* are larger than those of instruments made in the Islamic West. The rete may also be designed in decorative forms.

Greek scientific texts, including Ptolemy's *Syntaxis* (*Almagest*), were first translated into Arabic in 9th-century Baghdad, under the patronage of the Abbasid caliph al-Ma'mun (*reg* 813–33), and the earliest known Arabic treatise concerning astrolabes was written at his court. But astronomy and the making of astrolabes were never solely the province of Arabs or Muslims, and both were pursued

2. Astrolabe, cast and engraved bronze, diam. 402 mm, from Iran, 1712 (London, British Museum)

from an early date at all major Islamic courts, from Spain to Central Asia and India. The oldest surviving astrolabes are all well crafted as instruments, but few are notable for artistic decoration. One exception is an astrolabe (London, BM) made by ʿAbd al-Karim in Cairo in 1236: the *kursī* is inlaid front and back with silver and the pointers of the rete are remarkably formed by plants, animals, birds and a human figure. Some of the most beautifully decorated astrolabes were made in Safavid Iran. One of the finest was made for Husayn I in 1712 (see fig. 2): it has a large *kursī* inscribed on the front and decorated with an elegant arabesque on the back, a rete figured as a somewhat deformed arabesque of stems with palmette leaves, both stems and leaves engraved with small leaves as infill, and the body is thoroughly inscribed on front and back with fine calligraphy.

Interest in Islamic astronomical instruments has continued in the Islamic world, and Islamic astrolabes have been popular among Western collectors since the 18th century. As a result, working astrolabes, some of which are inscribed with false historical information, continue to be produced, as well as fine but non-functional fakes.

For further illustration *see* SCIENTIFIC INSTRUMENTS, fig. 2.

BIBLIOGRAPHY

Enc. Islam./2: 'Asṭurlāb'

W. H. Morley: *Description of a Planispheric Astrolabe, Constructed for Shah Sultan Husain Safawi* (London, 1856); also in R. T. Gunther: *Astrolabes of the World* (Oxford, 1932), i, pp. 1–49

D. J. Price: 'An International Checklist of Astrolabes (Part II)', *Archvs Int. Hist. Sci.*, xxxii (1955), pp. 363–81

L. A. Mayer: *Islamic Astrolabists and their Works* (Geneva, 1956)

W. Hartner: 'The Principle and Use of the Astrolabe', *Survey of Persian Art*, ed. A. U. Pope and P. Ackerman (2/1964–7), pp. 2530–54

O. Gingerich, D. King and G. Saliba: 'The ʿAbd al'A'imma Astrolabe Forgeries', *J. Hist. Astron.*, iii (1972), pp. 188–98

J. D. North: 'The Astrolabe', *Sci. Amer.* (Jan 1974), pp. 96–106

D. A. King: 'The Astronomy of the Mamluks: A Brief Overview', *Muqarnas*, ii (1984), pp. 73–94

O. Gingerich: 'Islamic Astronomy', *Sci. Amer.* (April 1986), pp. 74–83

D. A. King: *Islamic Astronomical Instruments* (London, 1987)

□

Astrological and astronomical manuscripts. Manuscripts describing the layout of the heavens, as prescribed by Classical astronomical theory, and its perceived effect on terrestrial events. This article is concerned primarily with the Western tradition; for information on other manuscript traditions, *see under* the relevant geographical and cultural articles.

1. ZODIACAL AND CONSTELLATIONAL IMAGERY. Astrological and astronomical configurations appear in several different types of manuscripts. The most common formula is that of the 12 zodiacal constellations in medieval and Renaissance calendars, where each zodiacal sign is used as the symbol for a particular month (*see* CALENDAR). The zodiacal signs are often paired with scenes depicting the related Labour of the Month, a tradition that may be traced back to Late Antiquity. Webster has argued that an early form appears in a Hellenistic frieze (Athens, Panagia Gorgoepikos), in which a row of standing figures representing the Greek months are interspersed at irregular intervals with zodiacal constellations. This kind of image must have been the impetus for such later manuscript illuminations as the zodiacal roundel in the Vatican Astronomical Tables (9th century; Rome, Vatican, Bib. Apostolica, MS. Vat. gr. 1291, fol. 9*r*), which shows a central figure of Apollo surrounded by half-length figures representing the hours and months, and is ringed by a circle of zodiacal signs. A similar design also appears in the planetary rota in two *Aratea* manuscripts (9th century; Leiden, Bib. Rijksuniv., MS. Voss. lat. Q. 79, fol. 93*v*; 11th century; Boulogne, Bib. Mun., MS. 188, fol. 20*r*; see below).

The tradition of illustrating Labours of the Months with zodiacal signs was most enduring in sculpture, as demonstrated by the architraves and jambs of countless church portals. Their influence on manuscript illumination is most obvious in such examples as the calendar illustrations to the 9th-century martyrological poem of Wandalbert, Abbot of Prüm (Rome, Vatican, Bib. Apostolica, MS. Reg. lat. 438), where the architectural frame is included in the composition. During the late Middle Ages, the illumination of the zodiacal figures in manuscript calendars became highly decorative and often quite fantastic, for example the zodiacal constellations in the calendar of the Rohan Hours (*c.* 1430–33; Paris, Bib. N., MS. lat. 9471, fols 1*r*–17*v*). Perhaps the most interesting series of zodiacal illustrations are those of the TRÈS RICHES HEURES (*c.* 1411/13–16; Chantilly, Mus. Condé, MS. 65, fols 1*v*–12*v*) of Jean, Duc de Berry. Each calendar page is surmounted by a lunette showing the Sun riding on his solar chariot through the appropriate signs of the zodiac. The span of the month itself is correctly depicted as split between two signs, since the natural break between them usually occurs during the third week of the calendar month (for illustration *see* VALOIS, (3)).

Manuscript illustrations of the extra-zodiacal constellations generally appear in two formats only. The first, and more rare, is as an illustrative testament to astronomical references in poetry. The best example is the Riccardiana Virgil, where the constellations populate the night sky during the sack of Troy in the *Aeneid* (15th century; Florence, Bib. Riccardiana, MS. 492, fols 81*r* and 101*r*). The second format for constellational iconography is as illustrations to astronomical texts, the history of which is long and complex. The impetus behind the inclusion of pictures in these texts was, presumably, to serve as aides-mémoires. The figures were supposed to provide a reminder of the mythological shape of the constellation and the location of the stars within it. Unfortunately, what may have originated as a mnemonic device for the Classical scholar interested in astronomy, and well acquainted with the configurations of the stars, became misunderstood as the continuity of Classical learning faltered during the Middle Ages.

1. Astronomical constellation, *Cepheus*; miniature from Germanicus: *Aratea*, 9th century (Leiden, Bibliotheek der Rijksuniversiteit Leiden, MS. Voss. lat. Q. 79, fol. 26*v*)

2. ILLUSTRATED ASTRONOMICAL TEXTS. There are essentially two traditions of the illustrated astronomical text: the poetic and the scientific. Both traditions seem to have originated in the common source of the astronomical poem of the Greek writer Aratus of Soli (*fl c.* 315–240 BC), who in turn based his description of the heavens on an earlier scientific work by the Greek astronomer Eudoxos of Knidos (*fl c.* 390–340 BC). Aratus' *Phaenomena* has approximately 1150 lines, its first half is devoted to a detailed description of the constellations, their forms and relative placements in the heavens. The poem was well known in the Latin West through numerous sources: the Latin translations, known as *Aratea*, of Cicero, Germanicus (15 BC–AD 19) and Rufus Avienus (4th century AD); two anonymous medieval versions of the *Aratus latinus*; the so-called 'Compilation of 810'; the excerpts ascribed to Bede (673–735); and the various citations of the poem in such early Roman encyclopedic authors as Pliny, Varro of Atax (*b* 82 BC) and Vitruvius. There are also numerous medieval *scholia* to the Latin translations. Furthermore, the four books of the *Astronomica* by the Roman mythographer Hyginus (2nd century AD), are virtually an expanded version of the *scholia* to the Germanicus translation of the *Phaenomena*.

In the widest sense, all of the manuscripts belonging to the Aratean poetic tradition share certain resemblances. Many have one or more celestial maps as prefaces, and many share roughly the same order of the constellations. The archetypal model for the constellation illustrations themselves is found in the marble bas-relief of the celestial globe held by the 2nd-century AD Roman copy of a much earlier Greek statue, the Farnese *Atlas* (Naples, Mus. Archeol. N.). Thiele demonstrated a direct link between the constellations depicted on the globe and those found in the earliest surviving Aratean manuscripts, for instance the 9th-century Germanicus translation in the Leiden manuscript (see fig. 1), and the two early 9th-century *Aratus latinus recensio interpolata* manuscripts (Cologne, Erzbischöf. Diöz.- & Dombib., MS. 83. II; Paris, Bib. N., MS. lat. 12957). Despite the early date of these manuscripts, there is still a gap of nearly 700 years between the Farnese *Atlas* globe and the earliest extant illustrated astronomical text; and during that time, a number of the pictorial traditions had become garbled and distorted. By the 15th century the resemblance of illuminated Germanicus manuscripts to their Classical models is all but lost and their 'astronomical' content virtually non-existent. Nevertheless, the convention for illustrated astronomical literature was sufficiently strong to generate a series of Renaissance imitations, including the *Astronomica*, an astronomical poem by Basinio de' Basini (1425–57), of which at least ten illustrated manuscripts are known (e.g. Parma, Bib. Palatina, MS. Parm. 27).

The second, scientific tradition for illustrated astronomical manuscripts is no less complex, but more exotic. During the 2nd century AD, Ptolemy composed a star catalogue of the 1032 visible stars in the 48 major constellations (*Syntaxis mathematica* VII and VIII, known through the Arabic as the *Almagest*). Later manuscript evidence of, for example, the 9th and 15th centuries suggests that a version of this text may have been illustrated (both Rome, Vatican, Bib. Apostolica, MSS Vat. gr. 1291 and 1087, respectively), but the main source for illustrated versions of the Ptolemaic stellar tables comes from the Arabic translations of the text by such scholars as Thabit ibn Qurra [Thabit] (AD 836–901), Zakariyya' ibn Muhammad al-Qazwini [Kazwini] (*c.* 1203–83), and most notably, ʿAbd al-Rahman al-Sufi [Sufi] (AD 903–86). In the Arabic tradition, each of Ptolemy's 48 constellations is purportedly seen from both an earthly and a heavenly perspective. Whereas the former view represents the constellation as seen in the night sky, the latter is claimed to illustrate the constellation as depicted on a celestial globe. Ptolemy describes the constellations from an earthly perspective: all the figures face the viewer. The figures depicted on a globe, on the other hand, are illustrated from a heavenly perspective and thus shown from behind. The Arabic illustrations thus show two mirror images of the constellation. Furthermore, because most Arabic scholars had lost contact with the iconography of the Hellenistic myths, the identity of many constellations became arabized. The constellation Cepheus, for example, is called *al-multahib* ('the one who burns') after the bright star in the headdress of the figure. Boötes is called *al-ṣayyāḥ* ('the Shouter'), and Orion is referred to as *al-jawzā'*, ('the Violent One'). Each is depicted in Arabic or Persian dress holding local tools and weapons as attributes. The mythology of the skies did not primarily interest the Arabs; what fuelled the translations was a fascination with the science of astronomy. The advantage of the Arabic astronomical manuscripts is that even though the images of the constellations and their identities became distorted, the astronomical positions of the stars remained surprisingly accurate for centuries (*see also* ISLAMIC ART, §III, 4(ii)(a)).

Sufi's version of Ptolemy's star catalogue became available to the Latin West through the translations of Gerard of Cremona (*c.* 1114–87) and Alfonso X, King of Castile-Leon (*reg* 1252–84). In the earliest extant manuscripts of these translations, for instance the 13th-century Sicilian version (Paris, Bib. Arsenal, MS. lat. 1036; see fig. 2) or the late 14th-century manuscript from Murano (Berlin, Kupferstichkab., MS. 78. D. 12), the Arabic flavour of the illustrations is unmistakable. Furthermore, the names of the constellations remain close to their Arabic models: Cepheus is called 'Inflammatus', Boötes is 'Vociferans' and Orion is 'Sublimator' and 'Audax'. The influence of this iconographic tradition was widespread and long-lived. More than 60 medieval and Renaissance manuscripts contain what might be called 'Arabic elements' in their illustrations. As the Aratean tradition influenced later writers, so the Latin Sufi tradition spawned a number of related works: the *Liber introductorius* of Michael Scot (*c.* 1175–*c.* 1234), the *Liber astronomicus* (*c.* 1270) of Guido Bonatti, the *Dittamondo* (*c.* 1350) of Fazio degli Uberti (*c.* 1310–*c.* 1370) and the *Fons memorabilia* (final version 1402–18) of Domenico d'Arezzo.

Astronomical illustrations also often appear in astrological and magical texts. One particularly popular tradition during the late Middle Ages was the illustration of the abbreviated version of the Latin translation, the *Introductorium in astronomiam*, of the treatise by Abu Maʿshar [Albumasar] (*d* 886), describing the figures that identified the constellations according to the Greek, Arabic and Indian traditions. The Greek and Arabic descriptions are

2. Astronomical constellation, *Orion*; miniature from an anonymous Latin translation of al-Sufi: *Liber de locis stellarum fixarum*, 13th century (Paris, Bibliothèque de l'Arsenal, MS. lat. 1036, fol. 36*r*)

recognizable as portions of the familiar Ptolemaic constellations (often referred to with the slight misnomer of *paranatellonta*). The Indian descriptions, however, are based on the astrological concept of the decan or decan-god, a quasi-mythological figure distantly related to early Egyptian chronometrical hieroglyphs. Illustrated versions of the *Introductorium* appear in several guises: in the *Liber astrologiae* of Hermannus Dalmata [Georgius Zotori Zapari Fenduli] (written between 1143 and 1200); the *Introductorium in iudiciis astrologiae* (1293), the Latin translation made by Pietro d'Abano (1250–*c.* 1315) from a French version (1273) of the Hebrew original by Abraham ibn Ezra (*c.* 1089–1164); the *De figura seu imagine mundi* (*c.* 1450) of Ludovico d'Angulo; and the *Astrolabium planum* (Augsburg, 1488) of Johannes Angelus based on Pietro d'Abano's *De imaginibus*. A number of the decan figures also appear in such magical texts as the Alfonsine *Lapidario* and *Libro de las formas & ymagenes*, the *Picatrix latinus*, and the *De imaginibus caelestibus* of Guglielmo Raimondo de Moncada [Flavius Mithridates]. As Pingree has pointed out, the iconographic tradition for these figures was tenuous at best. The large-scale versions of this type of illustration, as seen in the frescoes of the *salone* of the Palazzo della Ragione, Padua (*c.* 1430), or in the Salone dei Mesi of the Palazzo Schifanoia, Ferrara (completed before 1470), highlight the ambivalent status of the imagery (*see* FERRARA, fig. 3). Decans and *paranatellonta* seem to have been sufficiently important to warrant citation, but each version of a decan-god or *paranatellon* is strangely unique, never quite allowing its history to be traced directly back to earlier sources.

Numerous manuscripts contain astronomical diagrams that illustrate the relative motions of the planets, the structure of the cosmos, the phases of the moon, the phenomenon of solar and lunar eclipses or the apparent variation in planetary orbits. One kind of diagram worth noting is the so-called 'melothesia man', which depicts a human figure upon which the zodiacal constellations or their glyphs have been placed in order, starting with Aries at his head and ending with Pisces at his feet. The purpose of this diagram is to show the astrological 'rulers' of each part of the body. It was most often consulted for medical purposes, especially as a guideline for the times considered most auspicious for bleeding a patient (*see* MEDICAL ILLUSTRATED BOOKS, §1). The intellectual premise behind the diagram was the belief that the body of man was a reduced replica of the heavens, and that man was the microcosmos reflecting the macrocosmos of the spheres. The most convenient textual source for the illustration is the popular astrological work by Ptolemy, the *Tetrabiblos*, but his text was so widely diffused through secondary sources that much of it was probably 'common knowledge' for the medieval scholar and medical doctor.

BIBLIOGRAPHY

G. Thiele: *Antike Himmelsbilder: Mit Forschungen zu Hipparchos, Aratos und seinen Fortsetzern, und Beiträge zur Kunstgeschichte der Sternhimmels* (Berlin, 1898)

F. Saxl: *Verzeichnis astrologischer und mythologischer illustrierter Handschriften des lateinischen Mittelalters*, i: *Römische Bibliotheken* (Heidelberg, 1915); ii: *Die Handschriften der National-Bibliothek in Wien* (Heidelberg, 1927); iii, with H. Meier, ed. H. Bober: *Handschriften in englischen Bibliotheken* (London, 1953); iv, by P. McGurk: *Astrological Manuscripts in Italian Libraries (other than Rome)* (London, 1966)

A. Warburg: *Gesammelte Schriften*, ed. G. Bing (Leipzig and Berlin, 1932), ii, pp. 631–9 [contrib. on decan figs in the Palazzo Schifanoia in Ferrara by E. Jaffé]

E. Panofsky and F. Saxl: 'Classical Mythology in Mediaeval Art', *Met. Mus. Stud.*, iv/2 (1933), pp. 228–80

J. C. Webster: *The Labors of the Months in Antique and Mediaeval Art to the End of the Twelfth Century* (Evanston and Chicago, 1938)

J. Seznec: *La Survivance des dieux antiques: Essai sur le rôle de la tradition mythologique dans l'humanisme et dans l'art de la Renaissance* (London, 1940; Eng. trans., Princeton, 1953)

P. Kunitzsch: *Arabische Sternnamen in Europa* (Wiesbaden, 1959)

——: *Untersuchungen zur Sternnomenklatur der Araber* (Wiesbaden, 1961)

D. Pingree: 'The Indian Iconography of the Decans and Horâs', *J. Warb. & Court. Inst.*, xxvi (1963), pp. 223–54

V. A. Clark: *The Illustrated 'Abridged Astrological Treatise of Albumasar': Medieval Astrological Imagery in the West* (diss., Ann Arbor, U. MI, 1979)

K. Lippincott: 'The Astrological Vault of the *Camera di Griselda* from Roccabianca', *J. Warb. & Court. Inst.*, xlviii (1985), pp. 43–70

——: *The Frescoes of the 'Salone dei Mesi' in the Palazzo Schifanoia in Ferrara: Style, Iconography and Cultural Context* (diss., U. Chicago, 1987)

K. Lippincott and D. Pingree: 'Ibn al-Hatim on the Talismans of the Lunar Mansions', *J. Warb. & Court. Inst.*, l (1987), pp. 57–81

KRISTEN LIPPINCOTT

Astruc, Jules(-Godefroy) (*b* Avignon, 1862; *d* Paris, 1935). French architect. He entered the Ecole Nationale des Beaux-Arts in Paris in 1881. He studied there under Drouillard and Victor Laloux (the architect of the Gare d'Orsay). Astruc received his diploma in architecture in January 1889, submitting a collection of designs for a railway station 'following German principles'—a plan that he had presented to the Salon de la Société des Artistes Français in the previous year. He went on to design a large number of private buildings, but he is chiefly known for the church of Notre-Dame du Travail (1899–1901), 59, Rue Vercingétorix, 14e, Paris. Like Victor Baltard's church of St Augustin (1860–67) and Louis-Auguste Boileau's St Eugène (1854–5), Notre-Dame du Travail is built of stone and metal, but unlike them it uses industrial T-section and I-section iron girders, which are riveted and welded together. Its spacious, relatively empty surface at ground level, the openings high up that diffuse an even light throughout the building, and the use of brick and buhrstone make the church seem more closely related to contemporaneous factories than to other Parisian churches built with metal frameworks in various revival styles. The resemblance is intentional as the curate of the parish, Soulange-Bodin, required that the building should reflect, in its structure and materials, the factories in which the parishioners of this working-class suburb worked—hence also the dedication to Notre-Dame du Travail. He launched a nation wide appeal to raise money by popular subscription so that this universal church could be consecrated on the occasion of the Exposition Universelle (1900). The metal structure of the building, particularly the use of iron arches and iron columns to articulate the elevation of the nave, is incorporated into the design from a largely functional point of view, with a minimum of decorative features. As in the case of St Eugène, two lateral galleries cover the length of the nave and overhang the side chapels, a feature probably inspired by churches of the curate's native Basque region. The church is built on a conventional basilica plan, with masonry reserved for the choir and the solid structures of the façade. The decorative details include a neo-Palladian Venetian window on the end wall of the choir, Roman arches in the organ loft, and the trilobate windows and neo-Roman decorations of the façade. Astruc was also responsible for the design of a chapel at 18, Rue Lhomond, Paris, the schools of Notre-Dame in the Rue des Ursulines, Paris, and at the château of Presles, Val d'Oise. As assistant Architecte Voyer to the sixth arrondissement of Paris, he had an extensive practice in the southern districts of the city.

BIBLIOGRAPHY

'Eglise Notre-Dame de Plaisance', *Constr. Mod.*, xix (1903), pp. 77–8, 91, 100–01

'Eglise Notre-Dame du Travail à Plaisance', *Archit. Aujourd'hui*, 9 (1935), p. 13

L. Hautecoeur: *Architecture classique*, vii (1957)

M. Emery: *Un Siècle d'architecture moderne, 1850–1950* (Paris, 1971)

C. Callais and T. Jeanmonod: *Les Eglises parisiennes au XIXe siècle* (diss., U. Paris III, 1979)

JEAN-FRANÇOIS PINCHON

Astruc, Zacharie (*b* Angers, 20 Feb 1833; *d* Paris, 24 May 1907). French writer and artist. He was primarily known as an art critic in Paris from 1859 to 1872. His first major publication was *Les 14 Stations du Salon*, a compilation of his reviews of the Paris Salon of 1859, with an addendum devoted to Courbet. In 1863 Astruc edited *Le Salon*, a liberal newspaper that appeared daily during the annual Salon until it was suppressed by the government.

He devoted its last issue to a defence of the avant-garde artists, notably Manet, then exhibiting at the Salon des Refusés. During the 1860s he often served as a spokesman for the avant-garde circle that gathered at the cafés de Bade and Guerbois in Paris. Astruc also wrote for many major Parisian newspapers, including *Le Pays*, the *Nain jaune* and the *Dix Décembre*. In 1866 he began his three most influential years as a critic, writing for the Parisian daily, *L'Etendard*. There he published the first articles to describe the Japonisme movement. In 1865 he wrote the first Japanese-inspired play in France, *L'Ile de la demoiselle*.

After 1870 Astruc devoted himself increasingly to his career as a watercolourist and sculptor, exhibiting regularly at the Salons and showing a watercolour including Oriental *objets d'art*, the *Chinese Gifts* (New York, priv. col.), at the first Impressionist exhibition of 1874. He was decorated with the Légion d'honneur in 1898 and received a bronze medal for sculpture at the Paris Exposition Universelle of 1900.

Astruc is best remembered for his friendship with Manet. In articles of 1863, 1868–70 and 1872, Astruc defended Manet to a hostile public. He also sustained him in personal letters, most notably after the disastrous showing of *Olympia* (1863; Paris, Mus. d'Orsay) at the Salon of 1865. Manet included a poem by Astruc, *Olympia, la fille des îles*, in the Salon catalogue entry for *Olympia*. Astruc, who did much to promote renewed interest in Spanish art in France, suggested the itinerary for Manet's only trip to Spain in 1865 and introduced Manet to Monet in 1866. In the same year Manet painted Astruc's portrait (Bremen, Ksthalle). Manet also included Astruc in his *Music Lesson* (1870; Boston, MA, Mus. F.A.). In turn Astruc sculpted a head of Manet in 1881. Many other artists painted Astruc's portrait, including Carolus-Duran (1860, Paris, Mus. d'Orsay; 1884, Angers, Mus. B.-A.), Bazille (*c*. 1869; Montpellier, F. Bazille priv. col.) and Whistler (etching, 1859). Astruc also figures prominently in Henri Fantin-Latour's *Studio in Les Batignolles* (1870; Paris, Mus. d'Orsay), where he is shown seated, having his portrait painted by Manet.

1. Oviedo, S Julián de los Prados, nave interior looking east, begun before 842

UNPUBLISHED SOURCES

Paris, Louvre, Bib., C. Reiss donation [letters, sketchbooks, articles and notebooks]

WRITINGS

Les 14 Stations du Salon (Paris, 1859)
Le Salon intime: Exposition au Boulevard des Italiens (Paris, 1860)
'Salon des Refusés', *Le Salon* (20 May 1863)
'L'Empire du soleil levant', *L'Etendard* (27 Feb, 23 March 1867)
'Le Japon chez nous', *L'Etendard* (26 May 1868)
Regular contributions to *Le Salon* (1863), *L'Etendard* (1866–8) and *Echo B.-A.* (May–July 1870)

BIBLIOGRAPHY

S. Flescher: 'Manet's *Portrait of Zacharie Astruc*: A Study of a Friendship and New Light on a Problematic Painting', *A. Mag.* (June 1978), pp. 98–105
——: *Zacharie Astruc: Critic, Artist, and Japoniste (1833–1907)* (New York, 1978)

SHARON FLESCHER

Asturian architecture. The architecture of the 8th- to 9th-century kingdom of the Asturias, north-west Spain. European scholars discovered Asturian buildings at the beginning of the 20th century and at first regarded their style as rural and backward, a late survival of Roman architectural styles. Descriptions in contemporary chronicles, however, which correspond closely to the appearance of surviving buildings, make it clear that the survival of Roman architectural techniques enabled the Asturians to construct buildings in a style that anticipated Romanesque architecture in the rest of Europe by almost two centuries.

After the defeat of the Visigothic kingdom by the Muslims at the Battle of Janda (711), the Visigothic people took refuge in mountainous regions, and members of the defeated aristocracy organized resistance to the new rulers. The first and most important of these centres of Christian resistance was organized in the Asturias. By the end of the 8th century a kingdom had been established under the guidance of a small group of clerics who advised the warrior chief, converting him into an authentic king. This ruler was considered the direct heir of the kings of Toledo, the capital of the ancient Spanish Visigothic monarchy. The continuity of the monarchy from Toledo to the Asturias led ultimately to the Reconquest by the Christians in the north of the territory occupied by the Muslims.

The Asturian kings constructed beautiful buildings, fully in the late Roman Hispanic tradition. Asturian architecture is markedly different from contemporary Carolingian architecture, which, although also Roman in origin, was the product of a different culture that developed a different architectural iconography. Although documents refer to Asturian buildings of the 8th century, the earliest to survive date from the reign of Alfonso II (791–842), considered the creator of the true 'state' of Asturias. The most famous buildings were raised by his successors, Ramiro I and Alfonso III (*see* ASTURIAS).

According to the chronicles, Alfonso II's buildings in Oviedo, which were to form the nucleus of his capital, reproduced churches and palaces in the old city of Toledo. These buildings have walls of *petit appareil* with squared ashlar quoins and slightly stilted arches of brick. The main spaces were timber roofed, with small barrel vaults over the apses. The churches, like some Spanish Visigothic models, were characterized by a tripartite sanctuary divided by solid walls and an aisled nave with rectangular piers. Characteristic examples are the churches of S Pedro de

2. Oviedo, S María de Naranco, *c.* 842–50

Nora (destr. 1936; rest.) and, probably, S Tirso in Oviedo, although only parts of its walls survive. S Julián de los Prados or 'Santullano' was built by Alfonso II on the outskirts of Oviedo as a monastic church; here, however, a large transept and beautiful painted decoration of a late Roman type were added to the established scheme (see fig. 1). S María de Bendones, near Oviedo, is a simplified version of this church. Apart from some archaeological remains, the only surviving part of the royal palace built on the 'acropolis' of Oviedo is the two-storey palatine chapel, known as the Cámara Santa, partly altered during the Romanesque period. It follows the model of early Spanish *martyria*, with a lower storey intended for use as a shrine and an upper storey for an oratory.

Ramiro I (842–50) built a palace complex in Naranco, near Oviedo. It is described by chroniclers as having palaces, baths, triclinia and churches etc. Only the church of S Miguel de Lillo (or Liño) survives, with what is presumed to have been the palace hall, which has been converted into a chapel, S María de Naranco (see fig. 2; for an illustration of the entrance façade *see* SPAIN, fig. 2). Both buildings are completely vaulted, with reinforced walls and buttresses. The sculptures were executed specifically for the monuments, but their iconography has not been deciphered. Materials from an earlier building were used for the construction of S Miguel de Lillo, which has columnar arcades, a continuous barrel vault over the central vessel and transverse and longitudinal barrel vaults over the side bays. Only the west end of the church survives, including a porch with a tribune for the king. S María has two vaulted storeys with barrel vaults built over transverse arches of ashlar. The ground storey was divided into three, while above there was a large room with a belvedere at each end. Its function is unclear, but the traditional theory is that it would have served as a palace hall, although it lacks the characteristic domed apse, an architectural indication of such a use. Similar construction techniques were employed in the small church of S Cristina de Lena, which is accordingly dated to this period or to the rather retardataire period that followed.

Under Alfonso III (866–910) the Kingdom of Asturias stretched to the Duero Valley. The range of architectural elements was extended particularly by the introduction of horseshoe arches, features characteristic of the Visigothic monuments of the central plateau, which were now being restored by the conquerors. Alfonso's two best-known building works are the extension of the basilica in Santiago de Compostela (of which something is known from excavations) and the so-called palace chapel of S Salvador de Valdedios. S Salvador is a basilica, with square piers and longitudinal barrel vaults over each aisle. There is a tripartite porch at the west end, derived from Asturian models, which in turn reflect Spanish Visigothic buildings, and above it a royal tribune. A side portal, also vaulted, was built on the south façade.

See also TIODA.

BIBLIOGRAPHY

F. Selgas: *Monumentos ovetenses del siglo X* (Madrid, 1908)
H. Schlunk: *El arte visigodo, el arte asturiano*, A. Hisp., ii (Madrid, 1947)
Estudios sobre la monarquía asturiana (Oviedo, 1949)
E. Dyggve: 'Le Type architectural de la Cámara Santa d'Oviedo et l'architecture asturienne', *Cah. Archéol.*, vi (1952), pp. 125–33
J. Manzanares: *Arte prerrománico asturiano* (Oviedo, 1957)
H. Schlunk and M. Berenguer: *La pintura mural asturiana de los siglos IX y X* (Oviedo, 1957)
L. García Montoto: *Catálogo de las salas de arte asturiano prerrománico del Museo Arqueológico Provincial de Oviedo* (Oviedo, 1961)
Symposium sobre la cultura asturiana en la alta edad media: Oviedo, 1961–7
J. M. Pita Andrade: *Arte asturiano* (Madrid, 1963)
A. Bonet Correa: *Arte prerrománico asturiano* (Barcelona, 1967)
J. Fontaine: *L'Art préroman hispanique*, Nuit Temps (La Pierre-qui-Vire, 1973)
M. Nuñez Rodríguez: *La arquitectura prerrománica en Galicia* (Santiago de Compostela, 1977)
J. Yarza Luaces: *Arte y arquitectura en España, 500–1250* (Madrid, 1979)
H. Schlunk: 'El arte asturiano en torno al 800', *Simposio de Beato de Liébana: Madrid, 1980*, vol. ii
P. Lozinski: 'Tradition and Change in Asturias: The Royal Tribune and the Protorose Window', *Riforma religiosa e arti nell'epoca carolingia* (1983)
I. G. Bango: 'L'"ordo gotorum" et sa survivance dans l'Espagne du haut moyen âge', *Rev. A.*, lxx (1985), pp. 9–20
J. Yarza Luaces: *Arte asturiano, arte mozárabe* (Salamanca, 1985)
J. Dodd: 'Las pinturas de San Julian de los Prados', *Goya*, cxci (1986), pp. 258–63

For further bibliography, *see* ASTURIAS and OVIEDO, §1.

Asturias, House of. Spanish dynasty of rulers and patrons. The 8th- to 9th-century Asturian kingdom on the north-west coast of Spain was the nucleus of resistance to the Muslim invaders. It became organized into a genuine state, with proper ecclesiastical and court systems, in the reign of (1) Alfonso II. Following Alfonso's victories over the Muslims, the kingdom expanded and consolidated; it was maintained during the reign of (2) Ramiro I, while (3) Alfonso III took advantage of Muslim weakness and annexed the whole Duero Valley, repopulating the newly acquired lands with people from the north and Mozarabs

(Christians who had preserved their faith in areas under Muslim control). Alfonso's sons began a new dynasty with the capital in León.

(1) Alfonso II [Alfonso the Chaste], King of Asturias (*reg* 791–842). He had to overcome great difficulties in order to reach the throne, and his reign was marked by a number of conspiracies. From childhood he was under the protection of monastic communities, which influenced his whole life. He lived like a monk, surrounded by a monastic élite that was to be the inspiration for the whole administrative and political theory underlying the Asturian kingdom. There were numerous diplomatic contacts with the Carolingian empire. With the discovery of the tomb of St James the Great in Compostela, Alfonso began the construction of the first great basilica over the Apostle's grave. In OVIEDO, Alfonso's men established a hierarchical society, with a royal palace, a cathedral (S Salvador), a church dedicated to St Mary, in which the royal pantheon was later situated, and many other churches. The Cross of Angels in the cathedral treasury was a gift from Alfonso. Its form, a Greek cross, follows Visigothic models, but the techniques employed in the gold plating and the settings of stones and cameos are probably related to Carolingian work.

(2) Ramiro I, King of Asturias (*reg* 842–50). Half-nephew of (1) Alfonso II. His father was the son of Bermudo I, the Deacon. A chronicle from Albelda (Logroño) summarizes his reign: 'Ramiro reigned seven years. He was a staff of justice. He put out the eyes of thieves. He finished with witches by means of fire. He quickly accosted and exterminated those who tyrannically rebelled against him.' During his reign, Nepociano, Count palatine, claimed his throne and the Norsemen ravaged the coasts.

Although the chroniclers refer only in passing to Ramiro's work as a statesman, they greatly admired his architectural achievements. The Albelda chronicle records that he 'admirably built a church and palatial outbuildings covered by vaults' in the village of Liño while the chronicle of Alfonso III relates that 'he erected many buildings in marble without wood, with vaulted roofing, on the slopes of Mt Naranco at 2000 paces from Oviedo'. The references show that these buildings were considered exceptional works, without equal in either Christian or Muslim Spain (*cui si alicuis hedificium consimilare voluerit, in Spania non inveniet*). The Monte Naranco buildings (S Maria and S Miguel de Lillo) show the influence of earlier building traditions interpreted by an architect of genius who employed techniques that made them exceptional in Carolingian Europe.

(3) Alfonso III [Alfonso the Great], King of Asturias (*reg* 866–910). Grandson of (2) Ramiro I. Although his biographers awarded him the title Magno for his statesmanship, he also deserved it for his support of the arts. A cultured man and the possible author of a history of the Asturian kings, he was the first Spanish monarch whose library is known and still partly preserved: two copies of the works of St Isidore of Seville inscribed *Adefonso Principis liber* survive in the Escorial, Madrid.

He donated a silver-gilt reliquary casket to Astorga Cathedral, and the gold Victory Cross to Oviedo Cathedral. They are each plated over a wooden core, and the Victory Cross is set with enamels. Another cross given by Alfonso to Santiago Cathedral survived until the early 20th century. The small reliquary casket in Astorga has a complete iconographic programme: the Lamb and Evangelist symbols on the lid preside over what is possibly a vision of the Heavenly Jerusalem, represented by the angels and plants under arcading on the sides of the casket. These works show some similarity to those made by the goldsmiths and silversmiths who worked for Alfonso II; this workshop was in Gozón Castle.

Besides the palace, Alfonso's architectural works in Oviedo included adornments to the city, of which the fountain known as the Foncalada survives. He also enlarged the basilica at Santiago. The church of S Salvador de Valdedios, possibly his palace chapel, was long influential in Spanish art: the court chapel of Ferdinand I was still to adopt the same form in the 11th century.

See also ASTURIAN ARCHITECTURE.

BIBLIOGRAPHY

M. Gómez Moreno: *Iglesias mozárabes* (Madrid, 1919)

——: 'Las primeras crónicas de la Reconquista', *Bol. Real Acad. Hist.*, c (1932), pp. 600–23

A. Cotarelo: *Historica crítica de la vida de Alfonso III el Magno* (Madrid, 1933)

E. Camps Cazorla: 'Revisión de algunos problemas de los monumentos ramirenses', *Bol. Inst. Estud. Astur.*, v (1948)

M. Berenguer: 'Breves notas sobre San Salvador de Valdedios', *Bol. Inst. Estud. Astur.* (1955)

——: 'Puntualizaciones sobre los edificios ramirenses de Naranco', *Anu. Estud. Med.*, ix (1972–3), pp. 395–403

C. Sánchez Albornoz: *Orígenes de la nación española: El reino de Asturias*, 3 vols (Oviedo, 1972–5)

V. González García: *San Miguel de Lillo* (Oviedo, 1974)

H. Schlunk: *Las cruces de Oviedo: El culto de la Vera Cruz en el reino asturiano* (Oviedo, 1985)

For further bibliography *see* ASTURIAN ARCHITECTURE.

I. G. BANGO TORVISO

Astvatsatsin. *See under* ASHTARAK.

Asuka–Hakuhō period. Period in early Japanese history (*see* JAPAN, §I, 2). It is variously defined and dated, depending on the criteria under consideration, but conventional dates are from AD 552 (traditionally the year of the introduction of Buddhism into Japan) to 710, when the imperial capital was moved to Nara. In some contexts, for example ceramics or tomb-building, this century and a half is usually considered part of the KOFUN PERIOD, while in others it is either termed Asuka (as in discussion of some forms of religious and secular architecture) or subdivided (as for large-scale sculpture) into the Asuka (552–645) and Hakuhō (645–710) periods (the last is also referred to as 'Early Nara').

The most far-reaching development in Japan during this period was the formal introduction of Buddhism. When, in 552, the king of Paekche in Korea (Jap. Kudara) presented Emperor Kinmei (*reg* 531 or 539–71) in Japan with a bronze image of the Buddha, some canopies, banners and copies of Buddhist *sutras*, he was introducing a religion that had a millennium of growth and expansion behind it and was replete with sophisticated rituals, texts, architectural styles and iconographic images (*see* BUDDHISM). Its official acceptance into Japan from 584 was of epochal importance to the formal development of the arts in the country.

Asuka, a village situated on the Yamato Plain south-west of NARA, was the capital during the reign of Empress Suiko (*reg* 593–628) and her nephew, the prince regent SHŌTOKU. The noble character and innovative policies of Shōtoku permeated the history of this period. In 604 he introduced into the Japanese clan system moral principles of government based on Buddhist and Confucian teaching, expressed in his Seventeen Articles of government. Backed by the powerful Soga clan, he opened formal missions to China in 607. A sincere student of Buddhism, Shōtoku commissioned the construction of the three earliest Buddhist temples in Japan. One extant temple complex, the HŌRYŪJI, built in 607 and rebuilt between 670 and 711, is a rich repository of art of the period.

The arts of the Asuka–Hakuhō period represent a significant break from the pictorial and plastic images of Japan's prehistoric and protohistoric periods. The simple geometric lines and natural materials used in pillar-and-plank constructions, as seen, for example, in the ISE SHRINE, were surpassed by the imported architectural plans of temple compounds placed on stone foundations and laid out along strict north–south axes (*see* JAPAN, §III, 3). The skills of the various craftsmen who had served to outfit the horse-riders in earlier centuries—the bronze casters, dyers, wood-carvers and workers in clay—were now placed in the service of Buddhism. In the second half of the 7th century new influences were evident in sculpture, as for example in the temple of Yakushiji (*see* NARA, §III, 5), reflecting the more fleshly contours found in examples from the Northern Qi (550–77) and Sui (581–618) periods in China, and prefiguring, in style and scale, the classical Tempyō sculptures made at the height of Buddhist and cultural development in the following NARA PERIOD.

BIBLIOGRAPHY

R. T. Paine and A. Soper: *The Art and Architecture of Japan* (New York, 1955, rev. 3/1981)

S. Mizuno: *Asuka Buddhist Art: Hōryū-ji* (Tokyo, 1974)

Hōryū-ji: The Temple of the Exalted Law: Early Buddhist Art from Japan (exh. cat., ed. B. Kurata; New York, Japan Soc., 1981)

BONNIE ABIKO

Asum. *See* ASAM.

Asúnsolo, Ignacio (*b* Hacienda de San Juan Bautista, Durango, 15 March 1890; *d* Mexico City, 21 Dec 1965). Mexican sculptor. He served in the Mexican Revolution before enrolling in the Academia de S Carlos, continuing his studies from 1919 at the Ecole des Beaux-Arts in Paris. On his return to Mexico in 1921, he began a fruitful career as teacher and artist, applying an academic naturalism to official public monuments of nationalist inspiration such as monument to the *Fatherland* (1924; Mexico City, Mus. N. Hist.). His most ambitious works relating to the revolution are monument to *Obregón* (1933; Mexico City, Avenida Insurgentes), *Proletarian Family* (1934; Mexico City, Inst. Poli. N.) and monument to *Francisco Villa* (1957; Chihuahua, Avenida División del Norte). He also treated other subjects, such as female nudes and portraits, sometimes in wood or cast bronze, which contain reference to Pre-Columbian art. Essentially he was an artist resistant to change, a staunch and honourable traditionalist.

BIBLIOGRAPHY

M. Nelken: *Ignacio Asúnsolo* (Mexico City, 1957)

Ignacio Asúnsolo, escultor (exh. cat. by R. Tibol, Mexico City, Mus. N. A., 1985)

XAVIER MOYSSÉN

Aswan [anc. Egyp. Abu, Swenet; Copt. Sawan; Gr. Syene]. Egyptian city at the northern end of the first Nile cataract, *c*. 900 km south of Cairo. The modern town chiefly stretches along the eastern bank of a sandstone valley, which also contains numerous islands formed by the granite outcrops of the cataract; its ancient monuments are found on both the east and west banks and on some of the islands.

1. INTRODUCTION. In ancient times Aswan was a garrison town marking the traditional boundary between Egypt and Nubia; as such it served as the capital of the first nome (province) of Egypt and the seat of its governors. The town's wealth was generated by its position on an important trade route between the Nile Valley and the African lands to the south and by its granite quarries, which provided the material for countless ancient monuments. The islands of the cataract enjoyed religious status as the mythological source of the annual Nile inundation, while the Temple of Isis at PHILAE, south of the town, became an important pilgrimage centre, particularly in the Greco-Roman period (332 BC–AD 395). Although Christianity did not take hold in the area until the 5th century AD, the local Christian population subsequently resisted the Arab invasion of the 7th century, until finally subdued by the Ayyubids in the 12th century. In the Islamic period Aswan retained its status as a provincial administrative centre and also became an important entrepôt for African and Egyptian pilgrims, who crossed there on their way from the Nile Valley to the Red Sea, whence they embarked for Mecca.

When Egypt became an unofficial British protectorate in the late 19th century, it was decided to construct a dam at Aswan to control the inundation and to create a reserve of water for irrigation. However, the Aswan Dam, completed in 1902, proved inadequate and was replaced by the Aswan High Dam, built with Russian assistance in the 1960s. The consequent creation of Lake Nasser threatened the destruction of numerous ancient monuments, the most important of which were saved by a relocation programme carried out under UNESCO auspices. Relocated temples in the vicinity of Aswan include the Philae temples on Agilqiyya Island and the temples of Kalabsha and Beit el-Wali at New Kalabsha on the lake shore (*see* NUBIA, §§III and V). The construction of the High Dam and the consequent displacement of many Nubian villages also led to a rapid increase in the population of Aswan and the subsequent southward expansion of the city; projects undertaken in the 1980s and 1990s have included housing, schools, factories, hotels and the Africa University.

2. EAST BANK. Many areas now occupied by urban development were in antiquity granite quarries, and evidence of quarrying activities survives in the form of rock

inscriptions of various dates on granite outcrops around the town; these include a stele of Akhenaten (*reg c.* 1353–*c.* 1336 BC). Two groups of ancient quarries survive, respectively known as the Northern and Southern quarries; the former contains a huge, partially cut obelisk, probably of 18th Dynasty date (*c.* 1540–*c.* 1292 BC; *see* STONE (i), §I). However, the most important ancient monument on the east bank is the well-preserved Temple of Isis, erected by Ptolemy III (*reg* 246–221 BC) in honour of the goddess's warlike aspect as protectress of the city. The temple comprises a pillared hall and three shrines. Among the reliefs and hieroglyphic texts decorating the central door of the façade are scenes of Ptolemy III sacrificing to Isis, the local deities Khnum, Satis and Anukis and other Egyptian deities. The decoration also includes hymns in praise of Isis made by Ptolemy III and Ptolemy IV (*reg* 221–205 BC). The door on the south side and the sanctuary entrance are adorned with scenes of Ptolemy IV sacrificing to Isis, Osiris, Harpokrates and Hathor, and further sacrificial scenes of Ptolemy III and of Ptolemy VIII (*reg* 145–116 BC) are found in the sanctuary itself. The reliefs are typically Ptolemaic in style (*see* EGYPT, ANCIENT, §IX, 3(xii)(b)) and of good quality, although the decoration in the sanctuary shows signs of hurried execution. The walls of the large hall are not carved, but there is an interesting wall painting, showing a king offering wine to Isis, that can be dated to the end of the Ptolemaic period (*c.* 1st century BC). From the 6th century AD the temple was used as a church, perhaps dedicated to the cult of the Virgin. Coptic paintings including a Virgin seated on a jewelled throne and standing figures of bearded saints are found on the pillars in the hall.

No trace has been found of the temples of foreign deities that are known to have been worshipped at Aswan during the Persian period (6th–5th century BC). However, a necropolis for the Semites stationed at the Aswan garrison during the Persian period that was discovered during excavations by the local inspectorate, the Egyptian Antiquities Organisation, to the east of the Temple of Isis in 1963 contained stone sarcophagi decorated with Egyptian-style funerary scenes and Aramaic texts (Aswan, Aswan Museum). The remains of a small temple erected by Domitian (*reg* AD 81–96) lie behind the Grand Hotel.

Near the Northern Quarries is a large Muslim cemetery containing some 60 tombs of the 11th–12th century (*see* ISLAMIC ART, §II, 5(ii)(c)). These range from small domed cubes to more elaborate structures, such as the mausoleum of the Sabʿa wa Sabʿin Wali ('77 governors'; destr. 1901), which had nine domes and a minaret. The tombs are remarkable for the variety of squinches and pendentives used in the zone of transition and show the development of vernacular traditions in provincial Egypt. The tombs contained some 600 dated funerary stelae (Cairo, Mus. Islam. A.), which provide evidence for the development of Arabic epigraphy from the 8th to the 12th century; however, since they were hastily removed after a heavy rainstorm in 1887, they can no longer provide dates for the structures in which they were found. The Tabiya Minaret (11th century) has a square base and cylindrical brick shaft with an illegible inscription but is missing the upper lantern, found on two contemporary minarets at nearby Shellal. Notable 20th-century buildings include the colonial-style Cataract Hotel (1902) and the High Dam Monument (1971), a tall, lotiform tower bearing commemorative inscriptions in Arabic and Russian.

3. WEST BANK. The principal ancient site on the west bank is a sandstone escarpment known as Qubbet el-Hawa (Arab.: 'Dome of the wind') after the tomb of a Muslim saint on its summit. It contains the Old and Middle Kingdom rock-cut tombs of provincial governors, local princes, commanders of military and commercial expeditions to Nubia and New Kingdom officials. The cemetery remained in use until the Roman period (30 BC–AD 395). The Old Kingdom tomb of Harkhuf (A8) is a simple, undecorated room with four pillars; on the façade are important historical and autobiographical inscriptions referring to Harkhuf's three expeditions to various regions of Africa on behalf of the 6th Dynasty kings Merenre (*reg c.* 2256–*c.* 2246 BC) and Pepy II (*reg c.* 2246–*c.* 2150 BC). The tomb of Pepynakhte/Heqaib (A9) (for whose shrine *see* §4 below) consists of a courtyard with two conical pillars framing the entrance to a small room decorated with a few engraved scenes of mediocre quality. Associated tombs belonging to relatives of Heqaib include the adjacent tomb of his son Sabni, which is decorated with painted reliefs of accomplished workmanship. Another important Old Kingdom tomb is that of Mekhu and Sabni (A1), which has a large pillared hall and steep causeways descending to the river.

Aswan, tomb of Sebekhotpe, painted relief of offering scene, Middle Kingdom, 12th Dynasty, *c.* 1900 BC

The decoration of the Middle Kingdom tombs, such as that of Sebekhotpe (see fig.), is unusual in that the natural striations of the rock have been emphasized by painting the walls and pillars with horizontal black, grey, yellow and red lines. The most notable example, that of Sarenput II (A3), has a complex structure consisting of an entrance hall with six pillars and an inner chamber with four. The two rooms are connected by a narrow corridor with three niches on either side, each containing a mummiform statue of the deceased. On the left side of a large decorated niche at the rear of the inner room the painting has not been finished, and the preparatory grid for the drafting of a female figure remains visible.

In the desert west of the tombs is the monastery of St Simeon, a 7th-century AD foundation rebuilt in the 10th century but destroyed by Ayyubid forces in 1173. The walled enclosure contains a church, monastic cells, a refectory, a bathhouse, stables, stores and workshops. The church contains a well-preserved painting of *Christ Pantocrator* flanked by angels. To the south, the massive granite mausoleum of the third Aga Khan (1877–1957) overlooks the river. A square, single-domed structure in the Fatimid style, it contains a tomb of solid Carrara marble.

4. ISLANDS. The most important of Aswan's islands is Elephantine, known to the ancient Egyptians as Abu: '[the country of] the elephant', or 'the ivory'. In the southern half of the island was the Old Kingdom walled city (*see* EGYPT, ANCIENT, §VIII, 4). The principal temple in this area was dedicated to the ram-god Khnum as 'lord of the cataract region', with whom were associated the goddesses Satis and Anukis. The main visible remains of the temple are a granite naos of Nectanebo II (*reg* 360–343 BC), a gateway of Alexander IV (*reg* 316–304 BC) and the huge Roman quay. To the north is a group of Late Period vaulted mud-brick tombs that contained the mummified remains of sacred rams. To the north-east is the Temple of Satis, built in the Ptolemaic period, using blocks from the Temple of Khnum; a well-preserved Nilometer belonging to the temple survives on the east shore of the island. Two New Kingdom temples (destr. 1822) were respectively dedicated to Amenophis III (*reg c.* 1390–*c.* 1353 BC) and Ramesses II (*reg c.* 1279–*c.* 1213 BC). There is documentary evidence of a Temple of Yahweh that was built by Judaean military colonists some time after the end of the 26th Dynasty (*c.* 525 BC) and destroyed in 410 BC, but its location has not been identified.

The most interesting monument on Elephantine is the shrine of the Heqaib cult discovered by Labib Habachi in 1946. Heqaib was the familiar name of Pepynakhte, an official of Pepy II who was renowned for organizing expeditions to Nubia. By the 12th Dynasty (*c.* 1938–*c.* 1756 BC) Heqaib had been deified and was venerated with various dedications and inscriptions at his tomb in the necropolis of Qubbet el-Hawa. During the reign of Sesostris I (*reg c.* 1918–*c.* 1875 BC), Sarenput I, a nomarch (provincial governor), built a shrine on Elephantine consisting of a chapel for his own statue and one for that of Heqaib. His grandson, Sarenput II, added a shrine for his father Khema during the reign of Ammenemes II (*reg c.* 1876–*c.* 1842 BC). Other chapels with statues were added until the end of the 13th Dynasty (*c.* 1630 BC), when the cult of Heqaib became less important. The statues, more than 40 of which have been found, are an important source for the study of styles of private statuary in an ancient Egyptian provincial centre. Several examples are displayed in the nearby Aswan Museum, which also contains varied collections of archaeological material from the area, including pottery, mummies and coffins.

A number of the other islands are of importance for their rock inscriptions and graffiti: most notably, Sehel Island is known for the 'Famine Stele', a Ptolemaic account of an Old Kingdom famine.

BIBLIOGRAPHY

LÄ: 'Elephantine'; 'Heqaib'; *PM*, v, pp. 221–44
A. Mariette: *Monuments divers recueillis en Egypte et en Nubie* (Paris, 1872)
J. de Morgan: *Catalogue des monuments et inscriptions de l'Egypte antique*, i (Vienna, 1894)
U. Monneret de Villard: *La necropoli musulmana di Aswan* (Cairo, 1930)
K. A. C. Cresswell: *The Muslim Architecture of Egypt*, i (Oxford, 1952)
E. Edel: *Die Felsengräber der Qubbet el Hawa bei Assuan* (Wiesbaden, 1967–)
W. Kornfield: 'Aramäische Sarkophage in Assuan', *Wien. Z. Kunde Morgenlandes*, lxi (1967), pp. 9–16
H. Jaritz: 'Untersuchungen zum Tempel des Domitian in Assuan', *Mitt. Dt. Archäol. Inst.: Abt. Kairo*, xxxi (1975), pp. 237–57
'A. M. 'Abd al-Tawab: *Stèles islamiques de la nécropole d'Assouan*, 3 vols (Cairo, 1977–86)
E. Bresciani and S. Pernigotti: *Assuan: Il tempio tolemaico di Isi* (Pisa, 1978)
J. M. Bloom: 'Five Fatimid Minarets in Upper Egypt', *J. Soc. Archit. Hist.*, xliii (1984), pp. 162–7
L. Habachi: *Elephantine I: The Sanctuary of Heqaib*, 2 vols (Mainz, 1985)
J. Kamil: *Coptic Egypt: History and Guide* (Cairo, 1987)

EDDA BRESCIANI

Asylum. Obsolescent term for an institution for the care of the insane. The word originally denoted a place of refuge for debtors and others fleeing prosecution, but between the 17th century and the 19th it took on its more particular meaning, reflecting a perceived need to protect the insane from society and vice versa. In modern times, however, the belief that many mental disorders are treatable has largely led to the replacement of the asylum by specialized forms of HOSPITAL. In Renaissance Europe a broad distinction was made between the two main types of insane patient, the peaceable and the violent. The former remained at liberty, but the latter were imprisoned like criminals, and the first need was for the asylum as prison. In 16th-century Germany, for example, the violent were locked in round towers of old city walls. The distinction continued to be recognized in the 17th century, for example in Caius Gabriel Cibber's statues of *Melancholy* and *Raving Madness* (1680) for the Royal Bethlem Hospital, London. Later, both categories of insane were sequestered together under often unspeakable conditions, for example in the Salpêtrière Hospital for women, which had 7800 'patients' by the mid-18th century, and Bicêtre for men, both in Paris. Other countries followed suit in treating the two categories of patient together, the emphasis, however, continuing to be on restraining the violent. The *Narrenturm* (1789) in Vienna, for example, was a circular, five-storey fortress, with twenty-eight cells to a floor, each for two patients, who were chained to the reinforced side wall. In every oak cell door was a barred inspection window. Supervision was essential: the panoptic principle that Jeremy Bentham proposed for asylums

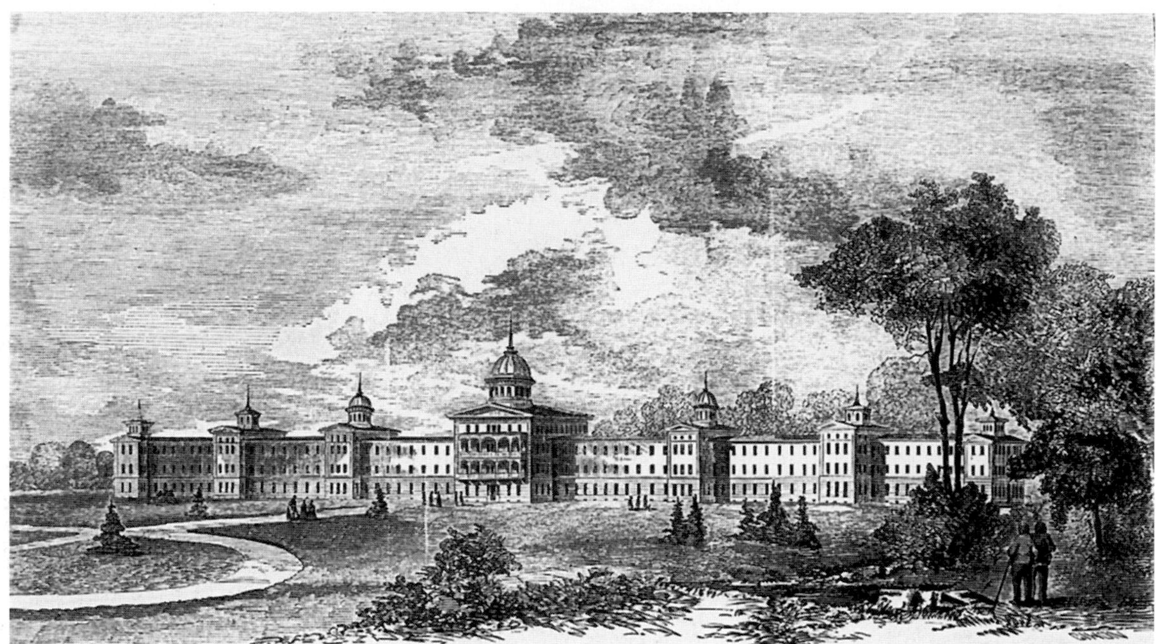

State Asylum for the Insane, Tuscaloosa, Alabama, 1860; engraving from T. Kirkbride: *Construction, Organization and General Arrangements of Hospitals for the Insane* (Philadelphia, 1880)

and prisons in his *Panopticon* (London, 1791) involved a central viewing space at the intersection of two long corridors or of four to eight radiating wings; in the latter cases the wedge-shaped spaces between ward wings formed exercise grounds, as at Glasgow Lunatic Asylum (1807). The two-winged, twenty-four-room Lunatic House (1797) at Guy's Hospital, London, designed on a panoptic plan, was a great improvement on the basement cells provided at this time in such institutions as the Pennsylvania Hospital for the Insane (1755) in Philadelphia.

Although decoration was not a priority in early asylums, there are instances of palatial designs intended to advertise the munificence of the patron. In Granada, the Hospital Real de Dementes (completed 1536; now part of the university), founded by Ferdinand and Isabella of Spain in 1504, was designed by Enrique Egas on a cross-shaped ground-plan. A rich Plateresque portal (added 1632) and two elegant front courts with the founders' monograms distract attention from two rough-walled and never completed rear courts. Another hospital on a cross-shaped plan was the Nuncio (1790–93) in Toledo, designed by Ignacio de Haám, where as recently as 1968 unruly patients were crowded into fortress-walled basement dormitories. Others of palatial design included the Royal Bethlem Hospital ('Bedlam', 1674–6; destr. 1815) at Moorfields, London, designed by Robert Hooke and modelled on the Tuileries Palace in Paris. It had a central administration pavilion, long patient wings and square end pavilions. For a penny, members of the public could stroll the corridors, as at a zoo. St Luke's Hospital (1786), London, which was designed by George Dance (ii) with the aim of correcting the faults of the Royal Bethlem Hospital, had fantastically high cell doors and tall narrow windows.

From the late 18th century changes in the treatment of the mentally ill, prompted by instances of abuse and pioneered in France by Jean-Baptiste Pussin (1746–1811) and Philippe Pinel (1745–1826) and in England by William Tuke (1732–1822), led to reforms in asylum design. A system of 'humane treatment' was introduced, based on reward and punishment, backed by awe of the physician and enforced by a number of firm, kind, dedicated, well-paid attendants. Charles-François Viel designed new small *loges* (1789), connected by internal corridors and aggressively ventilated, for the Salpêtrière, while in 1822 heating was added at Bicêtre, and elevated floorboards replaced cold flagstones. Tuke's Retreat (1813) at York, for 64 patients, resembled a large brick farmhouse and was set on a hill among gardens. It had no visible window bars (the dividers between the small panes were iron painted as wood), and the requisite 8-foot wall was hidden by the slope of the ground. Gradually in the first half of the 19th century it came to be believed that insanity was curable if caught early, and if the patient was well treated. At Hanwell Asylum (1842), London, John Connolly abolished all mechanical restraints, relying instead on supervision by committed attendants. Vastly encouraged, the American psychiatrist Thomas Kirkbride (1809–83), superintendent of the Pennsylvania Hospital, devised a 'linear plan' (1860), with a central administration block and a series of set-back wings, the unmanageable patients being housed still behind bars in single cells at the far ends. Between 1841 and 1877 variants of the plan were used in 32 American state mental hospitals (see fig.). Optimism grew, until it was realized that some forms of mental illness were not curable, with many discharged patients returning. As overcrowding ensued, conditions deteriorated and abuses reappeared, until the 1950s when, with the introduction of drugs to control schizophrenia, many patients were released to outpatient centres. In the USA in particular, however, elegant private mental hospitals continued to serve the rich, and there continued to be state institutions for the violent.

BIBLIOGRAPHY

J. Bentham: *Panopticon: Or the Inspection House* (London, 1791)
P. Pinel: *A Treatise on Insanity* (Sheffield, 1806/*R* New York, 1962)
S. Tuke: *Description of the Retreat* (York, 1813, rev. ed. R. Hunter and I. Macalpine, London, 1964)
J. Connolly: *The Construction and Government of Lunatic Asylums* (1847, rev. ed. R. Hunter and I. Macalpine, London, 1968)
S. Kirkbride: *On the Construction, Organization, and General Arrangements of Hospitals for the Insane* (Philadelphia, 1880)
H. C. Burdett: *Hospitals and Asylums of the World*, ii (London, 1891) [plans and bibliog.]
A. Deutsch: *The Shame of the States* (New York, 1948)
R. Hunter and I. Macalpine: *Three Hundred Years of Psychiatry, 1535–1860* (London, 1963) [collected readings]
D. B. Weiner: 'The Apprenticeship of Philippe Pinel: A New Document', *Amer. J. Psych.*, cxxxvi (1979), pp. 1128–34
D. Jetter: *Grundzüge der Geschichte des Irrenhauses* (Darmstadt, 1981) [the foremost modern authority]
S. Sheehan: *Is There No Place on Earth for Me?* (New York, 1982)
L. Thomas: 'On the Need for Asylums', *Late Night Thoughts on Listening to Maler's Ninth Symphony* (New York, 1984) pp. 95–100

GRACE GOLDIN

Asyut [Assiut; anc. Djauty, Gr. Lycopolis, Arab. Siūt]. Capital city of the 13th Upper Egyptian nome (administrative province), situated on the west bank of the Nile at the end of the caravan route from the el-Kharga oasis. The ancient town, with its temple dedicated to Wepwawet, the local canine deity, probably lies under the modern one. The necropolis was excavated by Emile Chassinat in 1903. The most important periods at Asyut were the Herakleopolitan (*c.* 2130–*c.* 1970 BC), when Asyut supported the northern kings against Thebes, and the Middle Kingdom (*c.* 2008–*c.* 1630 BC), although two Ramesside tombs have also been found.

The rock-cut tombs of the Herakleopolitan nomarchs are single-chambered, containing biographical inscriptions describing campaigns against the south. The Middle Kingdom tomb of Hepdjefa I, famous for its texts of contracts with funerary priests, introduced a new type: a series of chambers leading to a central shrine at the rear. The scanty remains of the reliefs indicate that a school of fine craftsmen was established in the Herakleopolitan period, producing good, formal work at a time when other provincial art was eccentric. A scene of soldiers in the tomb of Khety II is neatly carved in sunk relief with well-proportioned figures. The well-cut figure of Hepdjefa before the cartouches of Sesostris I shows that these standards were maintained into the 12th Dynasty. A life-size granite statue of his wife, Sennuwy (Boston, MA, Mus. F.A., 14.720), with its finely cut face, is exceptional for private statues of the period. Numerous wooden statues come from other tombs (see fig.). The number of large ones, some over life-size, is unusual for these periods. As representations of tomb owners, they stand in formal poses; the best are skilfully carved.

BIBLIOGRAPHY

LÄ: 'Assiut'
F. Ll. Griffith: *The Inscriptions of Siût and Dêr Rîfeh* (London, 1889)
E. Chassinat and C. Palanque: 'Une Campagne de fouilles dans la nécropole d'Assiout', *Mém. Inst. Fr. Archéol. Orientale*, xxiv (1911)

DIANA MAGEE

Asyut, wooden statue of the Chancellor Nakhti, h. 1.62 m, early Middle Kingdom, *c.* 2000 BC (Paris, Musée du Louvre)

Ataíde [Athaide], **Manoel da Costa** (*b* Mariana, Minas Gerais, *bapt* 18 Oct 1762; *d* Mariana, 2 Feb 1830). Brazilian painter. He was the most important painter active in the province of Minas Gerais during the Colonial period. He learnt his craft in the workshop with other artists and from such theoretical treatises as Andrea Pozzo's *Perspectivae pictorum atque architectorum* (1693–1700) and such technical manuals as the *Segredos necessarios para os officios, artes e manufaturas* (Lisbon, 1794), which was recorded in the inventory of his possessions. He was also strongly influenced by engravings of religious subjects in bibles and missals. He had a great influence on the development of religious painting in the region especially through his numerous pupils and followers, who until the middle of the 19th century continued to make use of his compositional methods, particularly in the perspective ceilings of churches. Often referred to in documents as 'professor de pintura', in 1818 he unsuccessfully petitioned for official permission to found an art school in his native city. He left an extensive body of work, which includes decorative painting of architecture, single pictures and the painting of religious statues (gilding and flesh-colouring). Especially famous are the vast perspective paintings such as the *Glorification of the Virgin* (1801–10; *see* BRAZIL, fig. 8) on the vaulted ceilings of the church of São Francisco de Assis da Penitência in Ouro Prêto and similar compositions for the parish churches of Sta Bárbara and Itaverava, in which he transforms the overweight Baroque schemes derived from Andrea Pozzo into light and graceful compositions of the purest Rococo, giving rise to an important regional tradition that has no equal elsewhere in colonial Brazil.

BIBLIOGRAPHY

S. de Vasconcellos: *Ataíde: Pintor mineiro do século XVIII* (Belo Horizonte, 1941)

C. del Negro: *Contribuição ao estudo da pintura mineira* (Rio de Janeiro, 1958)

I. Porto de Menezes: *Manoel da Costa Athaide* (Belo Horizonte, 1965)

J. Martins: *Dicionário de artistas e artífices dos séculos XVIII e XIX em Minas Gerais*, i (Rio de Janeiro, 1974), pp. 79–87

L. C. Frota: *Ataíde: Vida e obra de Manoel da Costa Ataíde* (Rio de Janeiro, 1982)

MYRIAM A. RIBEIRO DE OLIVEIRA

ATBAT [Fr. Atelier des Bâtisseurs]. Multi-disciplinary organization of architects, engineers, technicians, site managers and administrators based in Paris and active from 1947 to 1966. It was formed under the leadership of VLADIMIR BODIANSKY on the initiative of Le Corbusier, originally to carry out the detailed engineering design and construction of Le Corbusier's Unité d'Habitation (1945–52) in Marseille. The creation of ATBAT responded to a need for closer association between architects and engineers from the inception of a project; it was derived from Le Corbusier's research collective ASCORAL (Assemblée des Constructeurs pour une Rénovation Architecturale), formed in Paris (1943) to provide the basis for reconstruction after World War II (*see* LE CORBUSIER, §I, 1(iv)), and was also stimulated by Bodiansky's experience working with Marcel Lods and Eugène Beaudouin on large housing developments in France (e.g. Cité de la Muette, 1932–4; destr; Drancy). While it facilitated the optimization of architectural concepts, the work of ATBAT also resulted in simpler and faster execution, thus economizing on materials and labour and lowering project costs.

Organized like a family tree, ATBAT had four sections: architecture and urban planning, headed by André Wogensky (*b* 1916); technical studies, headed by Bodiansky; site management, headed by Marcel Py; and administration and policy direction, headed by Jacques Lefèbvre. In 1949 ATBAT separated from Le Corbusier's studio and began to participate in various projects around the world. A subsidiary, ATBAT-Afrique, was established in Morocco in 1951 by Georges Candilis, Shadrach Woods and Henri Piot, their main concern being to find housing solutions for the rapidly growing shanty towns of the region. Their approach was to integrate some of the traditional features and residential patterns of the North African city with low-cost industrialized building techniques. With Michel Ecochard they developed experimental housing units, the Beehive (1952) and the Semiramis (1953; *see* CANDILIS-JOSIC-WOODS), which were presented at CIAM IX (1953) at Aix-en-Provence and proved highly influential in consolidating the ideas of TEAM TEN. Other proposals from ATBAT-Afrique included 'Housing for the Greatest Number', a United Nations project for technical assistance (unexecuted); and the town hall (1950–52), Agadir, by Bodiansky and Lods, one of the few buildings to withstand the earthquake of 1960. After Moroccan independence in 1956, ATBAT-Afrique continued its work in Algeria until 1960.

ATBAT's capacity for technical innovation in all latitudes was clearly expressed in its plans (1954–9) for polar stations in Antarctica and Greenland: the building designed for Paul-Emil Victor's expedition in Adélieland, for example, was entirely prefabricated in plastic. Less spectacular but equally successful were such buildings as the monastery of La Clarté Dieu (1949; with the Arsène-Henry brothers); the Cité Ronsard (1953–9), Oran; the master plan for Accra (1954; with Dalidet, Devillard and Gaubert), Ghana; and schools in Niger and Beirut. ATBAT attracted many young professionals from all over the world to work in its Paris office, including Nicolas Charzidakis, Alexis Josic, André Maissonier, André Roux and Iannis Xenakis (*b* 1922). In 1952 Candilis, Josic, Woods and Piot left to form their own practice, and many other younger members also left in due course to practise independently. The successive deaths of Lefèbvre, the administrative 'cement' of the group, and Bodiansky, its driving force, in 1966 put an end to the organization, which had operated as a unique experiment in France.

BIBLIOGRAPHY

'Qu'est-ce que l'ATBAT?', *Homme & Archit.*, 11–12 (1947), p. 9 [special issue ded. to the Unité d'Habitation, Marseille]

M. T. Branly: 'History of ATBAT and its Influence on French Architecture', *Archit. Des.*, xxxv (1965), pp. 20–23

P. Saddy: 'Vladimir Bodiansky', *Le Corbusier: Une Encyclopédie* (Paris, 1987), pp. 76–7

GILLES RAGOT

Atchana, Tell [Açana; anc. Alalakh]. Site in the AMUK REGION, on the River Orontes in south-eastern Turkey, which is crucial for the study of Syrian history and art in the 2nd millennium BC. The low mound was excavated by Leonard Woolley from 1936 to 1939 and from 1946 to 1949. Finds are mostly in Antakya (Hatay Mus.), London (BM) and Oxford (Ashmolean). A deep sounding produced material dated by Woolley to the early 3rd millennium BC, but it is now acknowledged that the site was probably first occupied *c.* 2000 BC. It was destroyed by the Sea Peoples just after 1200 BC.

In level VII a palace was excavated, which was in use from *c.* 1725 BC for about a century; the plan underwent several alterations. The main reception-room had a columned entrance and a stairway to one side. A range of administrative rooms and another staircase lay to the south of a courtyard and here elephant tusks and the palace archive were found. From the clay tablets, written in Akkadian in the cuneiform script of Mesopotamia, it is known that this was the palace of the rulers of Alalakh, who were related to the kings of Iamhad (Aleppo). The fragmentary clay envelopes of the tablets bore the impressions of the seals of several generations of kings and governors and of high officials at Alalakh and Iamhad. The royal seals were modelled on Babylonian iconography, with the king accompanied by a goddess in Babylonian dress and facing another goddess, who wore Syrian dress with a tall horned headdress resembling a top-hat; the king wore a tall, round-topped headdress and a Syrian mantle with fringed ends and thick borders (*see* ANCIENT NEAR EAST, fig. 34f). From the inscriptions the royal seals may be arranged into a sequence in which the figures become progressively thinner, the borders narrower and the relief flatter, a tendency also found in the seals of private individuals. Egyptian figures and motifs appear on many impressions. Aegean influence is also manifest, and one impression shows two athletes doing a handstand on the back of a bull; this is earlier than any Cretan example of bull-leaping. Traces of wall paintings depicting naturalistic plants also recall those of Crete. A red marble Cretan lamp was found in a later level. In the adjacent temple was a finely carved head of a man with inlaid eyes, a short beard, small moustache and elaborate hairstyle (see fig.). The palace was destroyed by the Hittites, probably in the second half of the 17th century BC.

After an interval when the palace site was largely abandoned and occupation sparse, there was a second period of prosperity in level IV. A palace, fortress, temple, a large area of private housing and part of the city wall were excavated. Another archive of cuneiform tablets was found in the palace, which Woolley attributed to King Niqmepa. Several of the rooms had columned entrances and parts of the palace were several storeys high. From the tablets, which date to the 15th century BC, it is known that the city was, at this time, part of the empire of the Mitannians (*see* MITANNIAN) and half the population were Hurrians (*see* HURRIAN). Among the seal impressions on the tablets are those of the kings of Alalakh. There is a greater variety of styles than in level VII but the quality is less good and there is much reuse of earlier seals. The palace was destroyed by fire *c.* 1400 BC.

Tell Atchana, head belonging to the statue of a king, diorite, h. 612 mm, from the palace temple, 18th century BC (Antakya, Hatay Museum)

The later history of Alalakh is best seen in the private houses and temples. In the level I temple a basalt relief of a Hittite ruler, probably Tudhaliya IV (*reg c.* 1260–1230 BC), had been reused as a step. Somewhat crude basalt statues of lions were probably also reused from an earlier level. The very ugly but appealing statue in white stone (London, BM) of a seated, chinless man with staring, inlaid eyes, dressed like one of the level VII kings, is covered with an inscription which purports to be the autobiography of King Idrimi (*c.* 1500 BC). Woolley therefore dated it to level IV, but convincing arguments have been put forward for a dating in the 13th century BC.

Much of the pottery from Tell Atchana was painted with birds and animals, and it included Cypriot, Egyptian and Mycenaean imports. Particularly remarkable in the later levels is the local version of Nuzi ware with elaborate floral motifs in white paint on a dark ground. The excavations produced a range of figurines and objects of terracotta, bone, ivory and glass, together with many metal objects, weapons and vessels, gold jewellery, beads and a large number of seals, particularly cylinder seals.

See also SYRIA-PALESTINE, §I, 2(iv)(b).

BIBLIOGRAPHY

S. Smith: *The Statue of Idri-mi* (London, 1949)
C. L. Woolley: *A Forgotten Kingdom* (Harmondsworth, 1953)
——: *Alalakh: An Account of the Excavations at Tell Atchana in the Hatay, 1937–1949* (Oxford, 1955); review by M. J. Mellink in *Amer. J. Archaeol.*, lxi (1957), pp. 394–400
D. Collon: *The Seal Impressions from Tell Atchana/Alalakh*, Alter Orient und altes Testament 27 (Neukirchen-Vluyn, 1975)
M.-H. Carre Gates: *Alalakh Levels VI and V: A Chronological Reassessment*, Syro-Mesopotamian Studies 4/2 (Malibu, CA, 1981)
J. M. Sassaon: 'On Idrimi and Šarruwa, the Scribe', *Studies on the Civilization and Culture of Nuzi and the Hurrians, in Honour of Ernest R. Leichman* (Winona Lake, AR, 1981), pp. 309–24
D. Collon: *The Alalakh Cylinder Seals*, Brit. Archaeol. Rep. Int. Ser., 132 (Oxford, 1982)

DOMINIQUE COLLON

Atelier. *See under* ACADEMY, §5.

Atelier de Montrouge. *See under* RENAUDIE, JEAN.

Atelier des Bâtisseurs. *See* ATBAT.

Atelier d'Urbanisme et d'Architecture. *See* AUA.

Atelier 5. Swiss architectural partnership founded in 1955 in Berne by Erwin Fritz, Samuel Gerber, Rolf Hesterberg (*b* 1927), Hans Hostettler (*b* 1925) and Alfredo Pino (*b* 1932), four of whom had previously worked in the office of the Swiss architect Hans Brechbühler. There they had become familiar with the ideas of Le Corbusier. In their enthusiasm for Le Corbusier's *béton brut* (Fr.: raw concrete) and his idiom, the partnership ostensibly differed little from his other disciples of the time. Yet in their first work, the Halen Siedlung (1955–61) near Berne, they remodelled Le Corbusier's vertical residential block, the Unité d'Habitation, into a horizontal concept. The design of this self-contained structure of 81 terraced houses, of 150 sq. m floor space on average, with small front gardens, communal kindergarten, swimming-pool, restaurant, shops, underground garage and central heating plant made possible the combination of a high quality of life with a high density of residents. Yet for a long time this highly admired estate had little influence except, to a limited extent, on the Swiss terraced estate.

About the same time as the Halen estate, Atelier 5 produced smaller buildings, such as the pictorially conceived Haus Alder (1957–8), Rothrist; the terraced houses, Flamatt I (1957–8) and Flamatt II (1960–61), both near Berne; and the abstract architecture of the Haus Merz (1958–9), Motier, with its columns and frames. All of these acknowledge their model in the organization of space and the expressive qualities of the façades. In the 1960s the partnership's architectural idiom was tightened into a more severe, sober use of concrete, as in the Brunnadern residential block (1968–70), Berne. In the students' hostel (1966–72), Stuttgart-Vaihingen, consisting of a concrete grid with prefabricated façade elements, the partnership's study of structuralist principles, following Herman Hertzberger, is discernible in the ground-plan, with its cells and courtyard-type structure. Among competition entries in Germany and Great Britain in the 1970s, the design for the students' restaurant (1970–76) of the university at Stuttgart-Vaihingen, designed from the inside outwards, marked their first use of a square grid system and exposed service installations, moving towards an idiom influenced by High Tech. At the same time there was an attempt to meet human requirements through a small-scale approach and an abandonment of exposed concrete.

From 1974 competition entries in Berne gave rise to further important public commissions, which allowed Atelier 5 to explore the problems of building within a historic environment. In the extension (1976–81) of the Amtshaus, Berne, they used a light, elegant, transparent structure of glass and steel inserted in the courtyard of the existing neo-Baroque building. The Spar- und Leihkasse, Berne, was extended (1976–81) by a concrete skeleton with glass-filled spaces. The extension (1976–83) to the Kunstmuseum, Berne, looks from the outside like a High Tech museum machine, while providing a respectfully subdued environment for the displays. These three buildings showed a respect for the architectural ensemble and helped establish the partnership's reputation. Their most important activity, however, continued to be the design of estates, houses and hospitals, in which they drew increasing inspiration from Holland and English High Tech, as in the new administrative building (1986–7) of the psychiatric clinic, Münsingen. In the 1990s, augmented to 19 members, the partnership continued to focus on housing estate innovation, as in the Flamatt III estate (completed 1990), Berne, which took account of technical advances and current social ideas.

BIBLIOGRAPHY

G. Kidder Smith: *The New Architecture in Europe* (London and New York, 1961)
H. Schmalscheidt: *Entwurf und Planung Studentenheime* (Munich, 1973)
R. Zaugg: *Für das Kunstwerk: Kunstmuseum Bern, Atelier 5* (Zurich, 1983)
Atelier 5 (Zurich, 1986)

ROMAN HOLLENSTEIN

Atelier 66. *See under* ANTONAKAKIS.

Ateni. Village on the River Tana, 12 km from Gori in Georgia. It is known for Sioni Cathedral (7th century AD), dedicated to the Assumption of the Virgin, which, together with one other small church, is all that remains of the monastery founded there at the beginning of the 7th century. The small domed tetraconch church was built of undressed stone during the reign of King Stephanos II (*reg c.* 640–50) and rebuilt in the 10th century. In size and plan Sioni Cathedral is very similar to the Jvari Church at MTSKHETA. The core of the spatial conception is the dome (diam. *c.* 10 m), which, together with the church's other architectural elements, forms a spatial hierarchy corresponding to the descent from heaven to earth. Like the Jvari and the more provincial Dzveli Shuamta in Kakheti, Sioni Cathedral is an example of the pilgrims' churches that were to become, in the period following the Iconoclastic Controversy (726–843), the basic spatial design for monastic churches. On the east façade the founders, one of them holding a model of the church, are depicted in relief. Symbolic carvings, including representations of stag hunting, a dragon and Samson, decorate the other façades; a pair of stags are shown on the tympanum of the southern portal.

The wall paintings inside were executed in 1080 and probably replace earlier work: they also reflect the tripartite composition of a pilgrims' church. The uppermost, or heavenly, tier comprises the dome, sanctuary arch, squinches and apse. Contrary to contemporary Byzantine custom, the first is dominated by the relief of the Cross in the centre of the vault, reflecting the particular importance attached to its veneration in Georgia, while the *Christ Pantokrator*, which normally occupies this position in a Byzantine church, here appears on the sanctuary arch. Similarly, instead of carrying the traditional figures of the Evangelists, the squinches are occupied by the cosmic symbol of the four biblical rivers. The *Virgin Enthroned between the Archangels Gabriel and Michael* is depicted in the apse. The middle register is supplied by the remaining three apses and corresponds to the Holy Land. In the south apse is shown the *Life of the Virgin*; in the north, the *Twelve Great Feasts*; and in the west, the *Last Judgement*. The lower walls represent the earthly level of the composition and are occupied by saints, biblical characters and noble patrons. This arrangement reflects a relatively archaizing scheme of Christian church decoration.

BIBLIOGRAPHY

G. N. Chubinashvili: *Pamyatniki tipa Dzhvari* [Monuments of the Jvari type] (Tbilisi, 1948)
I. Ya. Amiranashvili: *Istoriya gruzinskoy monumental'noy zhivopisi* [History of Georgian monumental painting], i (Tbilisi, 1957), pp. 77–98
V. Beridze: *Dzveli Kartuli Khurotmodzgureba* [Old Georgian architecture] (Tbilisi, 1974)

OXANA CLEMINSON

Atget, (Jean-)Eugène(-Auguste) (*b* Libourne, nr Bordeaux, 12 Feb 1857; *d* Paris, 4 Aug 1927). French photographer. An only child of working-class parents, he was orphaned at an early age and went to sea. Determined to be an actor, he managed to study at the Conservatoire d'Art Dramatique in Paris for a year but was dismissed to finish his military service. Thereafter he acted for several seasons in the provinces but failed to distinguish himself and left the stage. An interest in painting but lack of facility led him to take up photography in the late 1880s. At this time photography was experiencing unprecedented expansion in both commercial and amateur fields. Atget entered the commercial arena. Equipped with a standard box camera on a tripod and 180×240 mm glass negatives, he gradually made some 10,000 photographs of France that describe its cultural legacy and its popular culture. He printed his negatives on ordinary albumen-silver paper and sold his prints to make a living. Despite the prevailing taste for soft-focus, painterly photography from *c.* 1890 to 1914, Atget remained constant in his straightforward record-making technique. It suited the notion he held of his calling, which was to make not art but documents.

By 1891 Atget had found a niche in the Parisian artistic community selling to painters photographs of animals, flowers, landscapes, monuments and urban views. In 1898 he began also to specialize in documents of Old Paris, to satisfy the popular interest in preserving the historic art and architecture of the capital. Working alone, Atget accumulated a vast stock of photographs of old houses, churches, streets, courtyards, doors, stairs, mantelpieces and other decorative motifs. He marketed these images not only to artists but also to architects, artisans, decorators, publishing houses, libraries and museums. While Atget made his name doing this work, much of his production was routine; his artistic fame came from his pursuit of this approach.

The oeuvre demonstrates this variance throughout; while Old Paris was Atget's main theme, as he worked he occasionally made photographs that seem more picturesque, imaginative or formally inventive than others. Besides these individual, idiosyncratic pictures, Atget also made some series of related images that denote a more vivid artistic presence. These include street scenes and the *petits métiers* series (1898–1900); vehicles, bars, markets, boutiques, gypsies, the quais and 'zone' (1910–14); prostitutes, shop displays and street circuses (1921–7); and the churches, châteaux and gardens of the Parisian environs, especially Versailles (from 1901), Saint-Cloud (from 1904) and Sceaux (1925; e.g. *Parc de Sceaux, March, 8 a.m.*, New York, MOMA, see fig.).

The tendency towards personal autonomy and free expression grew more marked as Atget's career progressed. Around 1910 he made seven carefully composed albums that he sold to the Bibliothèque Nationale (see Nesbit), and in 1912 he broke off a continuing assignment to survey the topography of the central wards of the old city for the Bibliothèque Historique de la Ville de Paris. His pictorial production continued to fall during World War I, when he photographed hardly at all.

In 1920 Atget sold most of his negatives of Old Paris to the government; he had completed that section of his work. While he retained an interest in the same genres of subject-matter thereafter, he increasingly chose different aspects to depict. Whereas his energies had been channelled into the relatively methodical production of good, serviceable documents from 1898 to 1914, from 1922 until his death Atget more often made pictures whose usefulness as reports to architects or decorators was questionable. The metaphorical power, suggestive mood and pictorial innovation in the late work appealed rather to an audience of poets and painters such as Man Ray, Jean Cocteau, Robert Desnos (1900–45) and other Surrealists, who hailed the photographer as a 'naive' whose straight yet sentient attitude had analogies with their own.

Eugène Atget: *Parc de Sceaux, March, 8 a.m.*, toned gelatin silverprint, 1925 (New York, Abbott Levy Collection, Museum of Modern Art)

In fact Atget's art has little to do with Surrealism, it expresses his acutely intelligent assessment of what he valued through the medium of photography. The early morning light on a Parisian street, the palpable atmosphere enveloping a pool at Saint-Cloud and the disarming gesture of a mannequin reflected as if in the street on a shop-window, were as directly and unselfconsciously apprehended and with the same seriousness, humility and humanity as the door-knockers and apple trees photographed early on. If the late works reveal the artist's own sensibility as much as the ostensible motif, it was not Atget's idea of his function that had changed but his vision of what was worth photographing.

Atget's best work is a poetic transformation of the ordinary by a subtle and knowing eye well served by photography's reportorial fidelity. His transcendent, haunting works transposed photography's function from the arena of 19th-century commercial documentation into the realm of art. This legacy, posthumously heralded as paralleling the rejection by 'art' photographers of Pictorialism and the return to the straight, unmanipulated approach, passed into the tradition of modern photographic history through the efforts of the American photographer Berenice Abbott, who met Atget in 1925 and who acquired his estate at his death. It is now owned by the Museum of Modern Art in New York.

BIBLIOGRAPHY

B. Abbott: *The World of Atget* (New York, 1964/*R* 1975)

J. Szarkowski and M. M. Hambourg: *The Work of Atget*, 4 vols (New York, 1981–5)

Eugène Atget: 1857–1927 (exh. cat. by J. Borcoman, Ottawa, N.G., 1984)
M. Nesbit: *Atget's Seven Albums* (New Haven, CT, 1992)

MARIA MORRIS HAMBOURG

Athaide, Manoel da Costa. *See* ATAÍDE, MANOEL DA COSTA.

Athelstan, King of Wessex. *See* WESSEX, (2).

Athena Painter. *See* VASE PAINTERS, §II.

Athenion (*fl* later 4th century BC–early 3rd). Greek painter from Maroneia in Thrace, none of whose work survives. The only account of Athenion is given by Pliny (*Natural History* XXXV.134), who said he was a pupil of Glaukion of Corinth. Some thought his work more pleasing than that of Nikias, who was thus probably a contemporary. Yet Athenion used a more severe colour scheme, an austerity that reflected the intellectual principles by which he painted. His work included *Odysseus Discovering Achilles Disguised as a Girl*, an *Assembly of Relatives* (at Athens) and, his most famous painting, a *Groom with a Horse.* He also painted a portrait of the cavalry commander *Phylarchus* for the temple at Eleusis, which seems to link him to the period of Athens' wars against Kassander, King of Macedon (*reg* 310–297 BC; cf. Pausanias: *Guide to Greece* I.xxvi.3). Athenion died young.

BIBLIOGRAPHY

K. Jex-Blake and E. Sellers: *The Elder Pliny's Chapters on the History of Art* (London, 1896/*R* Chicago, 1976)

C. HOBEY-HAMSHER

Athenis. *See under* BUPALOS AND ATHENIS.

Athenodoros. *See* HAGESANDROS, POLYDOROS AND ATHENODOROS.

Athens [Gr. Athinai]. Capital city of the Republic of Greece, occupying the greater part of the Attic plain, enclosed by the Imettos, Pentelikon and Parnis mountains to the east, north and west, and open to the Saronik Gulf to the south. On this side, about 10 km from the centre of Athens, is the city's port of Piraeus (anc. PEIRAEUS). Several lesser hills also form part of the city, including Lykabettos and a group of five hills to the south-west namely the Acropolis, the Areopagos, the Pnyx, and the hills of the Muses and of the Nymphs. From ancient times until the later 20th century the city was dominated by the rocky outcrop of the Acropolis, rising *c.* 155 m above sea level in the middle of the Attic plain (see fig. 1). Difficult to access on all sides except the west, it was a natural site for a fortified settlement that later became the centre of the city's cult of Athena and the location of some of the most celebrated buildings in world history.

I. History and urban development. II. Buildings and sculpture.

I. History and urban development.

The prehistory of Athens is known mainly from a wealth of myth and legend; however, the archaeological evidence suggests that the settlement began to flourish in the Mycenaean period (*c.* 1600–*c.* 1050 BC). Athens became one of the greatest centres of Classical civilization from the 6th century BC, only ceasing to be the seat of Greek education in AD 529 when the Christian Emperor Justinian I (*reg* AD 527–65) closed the philosophical schools. Athens continued as the capital of an eparchy in the Byzantine empire until 1204, when it was captured by the French Crusaders. In 1456 the city fell to the Ottoman Turks and remained under their control until 1821. In 1834, after many bitter struggles between the Greeks and Turks, Otto of Wittelsbach (*reg* 1832–62) proclaimed Athens the capital of a new Greek kingdom. In 1863 the Bavarian Wittelsbach line was ousted by the Danish Glücksburgs in the person of George I (*reg* 1863–1913). Despite numerous changes of government in Greece in the 20th century, Athens has continued to increase in importance as the country's

1. Athens, view of the Acropolis from the north-west; from a photograph of *c.* 1870

capital. Renowned as the cradle of European civilization, its main areas of archaeological and artistic interest are the Acropolis, initially a citadel, later the religious focus of the city (*see* §II, 1(i) below); the Agora, the commercial and civic centre (*see* §II, 2(i) below); and the Kerameikos, or potters' quarter, which includes a major cemetery near two important gates (*see* §II, 3(i) below).

1. Before 6th century BC. 2. 6th–1st century BC. 3. 1st century BC–*c.* AD 529. 4. *c.* AD 529–1204. 5. 1205–1834. 6. 1834 and after.

□

1. Before the 6th century BC. The continuous history of urban occupation and increasingly large-scale construction in the centre of Athens since at least the 6th century BC has effaced most traces of earlier settlements. The clearest evidence for the distribution and nature of these is provided by subterranean structures such as tombs and wells. The wells generally occur close to the Acropolis, presumably because of its high water-table, but the tombs, which occur mainly in small groups, are scattered on both sides of it, some to the south being at least 500 m distant. This pattern seems to imply the existence of satellite communities spread around a small central nucleus, and the occurrence of Mycenaean tombs in the Agora (the later civic centre) certainly suggests that Athens was not very urbanized even at the height of its importance as a prehistoric settlement.

Although substantial remains of Late Neolithic date have been discovered, including many wells and the oldest Agora grave, it is not certain that the site was continuously occupied from then on. The few Early Helladic (*c.* 3600/3000–*c.* 2050 BC) objects that have been found come from a wide area. The next substantial remains consist of wells, traces of levelling operations in the Agora and a developing pattern of pathways, dating to the Middle Helladic period (*c.* 2050–1600 BC), from when occupation was almost certainly continuous. Although imported Cycladic and Minoan vases imply the existence of a significant community, early Mycenaean remains are rare, and the first indications of real prosperity come from rich early 14th-century BC tombs in several cemeteries around the Acropolis, which contained luxury goods of types well known from contemporary burials at Knossos and Dendra, as well as Syro-Palestinian amphorae. The earliest significant architectural remains on the Acropolis, however, only date to the 13th century BC. They include a terrace system that may have supported a palace complex, but the clearest signs that Athens had become a major centre, able to expend considerable resources, are the fortifications and carefully engineered water supply system.

Evidence for most of the post-palatial Late Helladic (LH) IIIC period (no later than ?*c.* 1180–*c.* 1050 BC) is scanty, but includes Octopus stirrup jars, indicating that Athens retained contacts with the Aegean and, presumably, some of its earlier importance. Near the end of the period the first of the wide scatter of cemeteries that form a strongly marked feature of the Submycenaean phase (*c.* 1050–*c.* 1000 BC) were established. This suggests that numerous, mainly small, communities had become established around the Acropolis by the later 11th century BC; at least some of these may have been the precursors of the Classical demes (political districts). The LH IIIC and Submycenean finds from Athens are in the Agora Museum, the Kerameikos Museum and the National Archaeological Museum.

BIBLIOGRAPHY

S. A. Immerwahr: *The Neolithic and Bronze Ages* (1971), xiii of *The Athenian Agora* (Princeton, 1953–)
R. Hope Simpson and O. T. P. K. Dickinson: *The Mainland and Islands* (1979), i of *A Gazetteer of Aegean Civilisation in the Bronze Age* (Göteborg, 1979–), pp. 198–200
S. A. Immerwahr: 'The Oldest Athenian Grave', *Studies in Athenian Architecture, Sculpture and Topography* (Princeton, 1982), pp. 54–62
S. Iakovidis: *Late Helladic Citadels on Mainland Greece* (Leiden, 1983), pp. 73–90
P. S. Mountjoy: 'LH IIIC Late versus Submycenaean: The Kerameikos Pompeion Cemetery Reviewed', *Jb. Dt. Archäol. Inst.*, ciii (1988), pp. 1–33
J. Whitley: *Style and Society in Dark Age Greece* (Cambridge, 1991), pp. 87–97 [on Submycenaean cemeteries]

O. T. P. K. DICKINSON

2. 6th–1st century BC. As an independent city state in southern Greece, with substantial natural resources, including clay-beds, marble quarries on mounts Pentelikon and Imettos and silver mines at Laureion, Athens was a major regional power and artistic centre under different political regimes from the 6th to the 4th century BC. In the 6th century BC, under oligarchs and, later, tyrants, workshops in the city produced fine marble sculpture, while the unrivalled Athenian Black-figure and Red-figure pottery (*see* Greece, ancient, §V, 5(ii) and 6(i)) was exported throughout the Mediterranean. In the 5th century, under an energetic democracy, Athens levied heavy taxes from a league that included most Greek cities in the Aegean to finance a period of unparalleled cultural achievement. In addition to native talents, Athens attracted the best minds and artisans from all over the Greek world. Under one of the most active democracies ever formed, the finest architects, sculptors and painters flourished alongside outstanding philosophers, playwrights and orators. Most works of art and literature termed 'Classical Greek' were in fact produced in Athens during the 5th and 4th centuries BC.

(i) Archaic period (*c.* 600–480 BC). (ii) Classical period (480–323 BC). (iii) Hellenistic period (323–31 BC).

(i) Archaic period (c. *600–480* BC). The Acropolis had been fortified as early as the 13th century BC (*see* §1 above), but the development of the city that grew up around its lower slopes cannot be charted in any detail before the 6th century BC. Around this time the Acropolis, hitherto a place of refuge and perhaps a royal residence, assumed a purely religious function as a sanctuary of Athena, the patron goddess of the city, and many temples, treasuries and votive sculptures were erected there (*see* §II, 1(ii) below). The laying out of Athens' civic centre, the Agora (*see* §II, 2(i) below), also dates to this time. Lying on gently sloping ground north-west of the Acropolis, this vast square served a wide variety of public functions and, from the early 6th century BC onwards, became the location of the principal civic buildings. To the south-east, the area between the Acropolis and the Ilissos River contains traces of sanctuaries of Dionysos (see fig. 2a), Olympian Zeus (Olympieion; 2b) and Pythian Apollo (2c), also dating to the 6th century BC. Literary references suggest that the

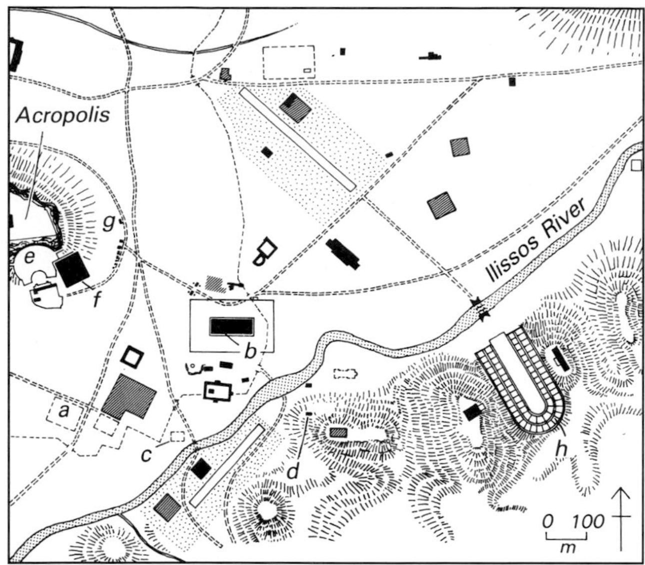

2. Athens, plan of lower city, 5th–4th centuries BC: (a) Sanctuary of Dionysos; (b) Sanctuary of Olympian Zeus; (c) Sanctuary of Pythian Apollo; (d) Temple of ?Artemis; (e) Theatre of Dionysos; (f) Odeion of Pericles; (g) Monument of Lysikrates; (h) Panathenaic Stadium

lower city was surrounded by a defensive wall, but no remains have been identified.

(ii) Classical period (480–323 BC). An abrupt break divides Archaic from Classical Athens. In 480/479 BC the Persian army under Xerxes I (*reg* 485–465 BC) took the city and destroyed it completely before withdrawing, also carrying off major works of art. Thucydides (I.lxxxix.3) and Herodotus (IX.13) attest the scale of the destruction, which has been confirmed by archaeological investigations. The returning Athenians hastily refortified their city with a large circuit wall incorporating many magnificently sculpted funerary monuments smashed by the Persians. Thereafter, the Athenians rebuilt civic buildings, such as the tholos (*c.* 470 BC) and the Royal Stoa (6th century and late 5th century BC), and added new ones, such as the Painted Stoa (*c.* 460 BC).

(a) Periclean building programme. To begin with, Athens' sanctuaries do not seem to have been repaired, apparently as the result of an oath taken at the time of the Battle of Plataia (479 BC) to leave the ruins as a permanent reminder of Persian barbarism. When peace was negotiated with Persia in the mid-5th century BC, however, the statesman PERICLES diverted funds collected from Athens' allies, hitherto used for the war, to finance the rebuilding of temples. Despite local and allied opposition, this plan was put into effect; thus, throughout the third quarter of the 4th century BC, magnificent marble temples were built in Athens and elsewhere in Attica (Plutarch: *Pericles* 12–13) as part of the 'Periclean building programme'. These monuments, constructed by the richest state in Greece at the height of its power, represent the acme of Classical Greek architecture (*see* GREECE, ANCIENT, §II, 2(iii); for explanation of Greek architectural terms in context *see* GREECE, ANCIENT, §II). Reflecting recent contacts with the Persians, the stone-built Odeion of Pericles (*c.* 440 BC; 2f) was modelled on the tent of Xerxes seized by the Athenians after the Battle of Plataia; it was erected, like the original, in the precinct of Dionysos, south of the Acropolis. This huge square hypostyle hall (l. *c.* 60 m, with 10×9 internal columns) served as a concert hall for rehearsals, a law court and a distribution point for grain in times of famine. In addition to temples on the Acropolis and in the Agora (*see* §II, 1(i) and 2(i) below), a small Ionic amphiprostyle temple (2d), similar in plan to the Temple of Athena Nike (*see* ORDERS, ARCHITECTURAL, fig. 3) on the Acropolis, was built near the Ilissos. Perhaps dedicated to Artemis Agrotera, it was drawn by JAMES STUART and NICHOLAS REVETT in the 1750s, but was subsequently dismantled to provide building material for fortifications.

(b) Period of Peloponnesian War to Lykourgos. From 431 to 404 BC Athens was engaged in the debilitating Peloponnesian War against Sparta and its allies. Work ceased on the temples but continued on less costly civic buildings in the Agora. In the 420s BC a plague led to the foundation of a sanctuary of the healing god Asklepios on the south slopes of the Acropolis, though its remains—a Doric two-storey stoa and the foundations of a temple and altar—seem to date largely to the 4th century BC.

Following their defeat in the Peloponnesian War, the Athenians undertook virtually no public building during the first half of the 4th century BC. Around 350 BC, however, intensive silver mining at Laureion improved their fortunes and stimulated a spate of building activity during the second half of the 4th century BC under the successive administrations of Euboulos (*c.* 405–335 BC) and Lykourgos (*c.* 390–325 BC). In addition to buildings in the Agora and Kerameikos (*see* §II, 3(i) below), the great Theatre of Dionysos (2e) was constructed on the south slopes of the Acropolis. Theatrical contests had been held in that place since the early 5th century BC, and there are traces of a modest earlier theatre. The existing monumental version, capable of accommodating an estimated 15,000 spectators, with marble seats for dignitaries, a limestone auditorium and conglomerate retaining walls, was built *c.* 330 BC, according to literary sources and inscriptions. The rest of the Sanctuary of Dionysos was refurbished at the same time with the addition of a Doric stoa (l. 62 m) and a new, tetrastyle prostyle, Doric temple of Dionysos.

Three choregic monuments (*choragos*: 'leader or organizer of a choir'), all of different architectural type, commemorate victories in the dramatic contests and originally displayed the bronze tripods given as prizes. The monument built by Thrasyllos and the Monument of Nikias date from 320/319 BC (*see* §(iii) below). The well-preserved Monument of Lysikrates (335/334 BC; 2g; *see* GREEK REVIVAL, fig. 1) stands in the 'Street of the Tripods' (Pausanias: *Guide to Greece* I.xx.1), which led round the Acropolis east of the theatre. It is a small, circular-plan building of Pentelic and Hymettian marble, set on a high podium and decorated with a carved frieze showing *Dionysos and the Pirates*. Its six Corinthian columns represent the earliest external use of this order (*see* ORDERS, ARCHITECTURAL, §I, 1(iii)).

Another great building of the second half of the 4th century BC was the Panathenaic Stadium (2h), set in a natural hollow between two hills on the south bank of the Ilissos. Carried out under Lykourgos (*Inscr. Gr./2,* II/i, 457), construction is attested in an inscription of 330/329 BC (*Inscr. Gr./2,* II/i, 351) stating that a thousand pairs of oxen were used. Its original form, however, is obscured by a reconstruction dating to the 2nd century AD. A final project, also probably of Lykourgan date, is the third phase of the Pnyx, the assembly place on the ridge west of the Acropolis. Its original auditorium (late 6th century or early 5th BC) sloped down to the north, overlooking the Agora. At the end of the 5th century BC, however, its orientation was reversed, necessitating the construction of an earth bank and a stepped retaining wall. Then, in the 4th century BC, the auditorium was enlarged by the construction of a massive new retaining wall of local limestone, made of the largest blocks ever used in Athens. Also associated with the Pnyx are foundations on the top of the ridge to the south-west, probably belonging to unfinished stoas.

(iii) Hellenistic period (323–31 BC). From the late 4th century BC are known two choregic monuments. One, directly above the Theatre of Dionysos, comprised an ornamental façade to a natural cave. Built by Thrasyllos in 320/319 BC, it consisted of three Doric piers surmounted by a frieze of wreaths. It was described and drawn by Stuart and Revett, and another early traveller, E. Dodwell, but was destroyed in the Turkish siege of the Acropolis in 1826–7 (*see* §5 below). West of the theatre stood the Monument of Nikias (320/319 BC), which took the form of a hexastyle, prostyle Doric temple. Pieces of its superstructure were built into a gate to the Acropolis in the 3rd century AD.

Throughout most of the 3rd century BC Athens was controlled by the Macedonian successors of Alexander the Great, and there are slight remains of a fort for the garrison installed on the Mouseion hill, just west of the Acropolis, in the 290s BC. Virtually no other 3rd-century BC structures date from before the re-establishment of Athenian independence in 228 BC. After this date Athens again became a centre of learning and culture, attracting students from all over the Mediterranean. Its admirers included Hellenistic kings in Pergamon, Egypt, Syria and Cappadocia, who often financed the construction of major public buildings, particularly in the 2nd century BC. On the south slopes of the Acropolis, Eumenes II of Pergamon (*d c.* 160 BC) built a great stoa (l. *c.* 160 m), extending westwards from the theatre. Described by Vitruvius (V.ix.1), it had two storeys, each with two aisles. The ground floor had Doric external columns and Ionic internal ones, while the first floor had double Ionic half-columns outside and columns with Pergamene palm-leaf capitals inside. Eumenes' involvement was not confined to funding: much of the marble used was Pergamene, while the masons' marks are also of Pergamene type. This building almost certainly influenced the stoa constructed in the Agora by Eumenes' younger brother, Attalos II (*reg* 160–139 BC). Other Hellenistic benefactions include work on the Temple of Olympian

3. Athens, Tower of the Winds (detail), 2nd century BC

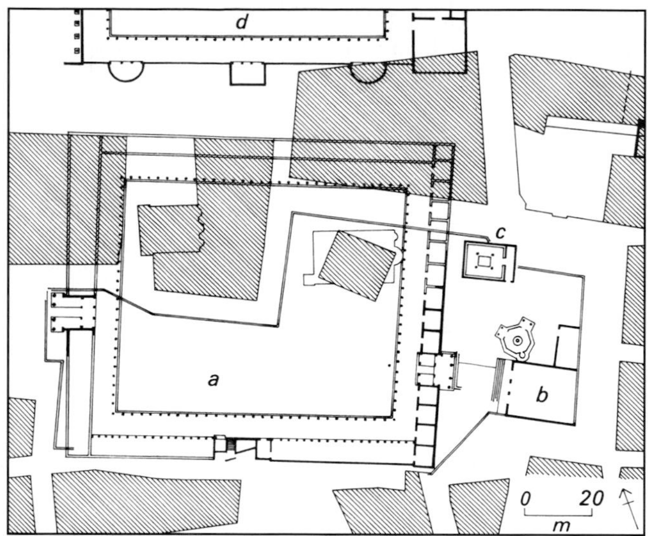

4. Athens, plan of Roman Agora and surroundings, 1st century BC–6th century AD: (a) Agora; (b) ?Agoranomion; (c) latrine; (d) Library of Hadrian

Zeus (*see* §II, 4 below), sponsored by Antiochos IV Epiphanes (*reg* 175–163 BC), and a gymnasium (unexcavated) donated by one of the Ptolemies of Egypt.

Though long-known, the famous 'Tower of the Winds' or 'Horologion of Andronikos', an octagonal marble structure described by Varro (*Res Rusticae* III.v.17) and Vitruvius (I.vi.4), which stands just east of the Roman Agora, has only recently been dated to the 2nd century BC (see fig. 3). Each of its sides was decorated with a sculpted figure representing the wind that blew from that direction. Its roof, which is one of the few ancient examples to have survived intact, supported a bronze triton serving as a weather-vane. The building's sides were also marked to serve as sundials, while inside stood a large water-clock, of which only the water tank built against the south wall and a few incisions in the floor now remain.

With the fall of Corinth and the Achaian League in 146 BC Athens came under Roman domination. Its architectural and cultural tradition, however, apparently persisted unabated. Roman influence became decisively marked only after Athens' revolt and the subsequent siege and capture of the city by the Roman general Sulla in 86 BC.

BIBLIOGRAPHY

Herodotus: *Histories*
Thucydides: *History of the Peloponnesian War*
Vitruvius: *On Architecture*
J. Stuart and N. Revett: *Antiquities of Athens*, 4 vols (Athens, 1762–1816)
E. Dodwell: *Classical and Topographical Tour through Greece*, 2 vols (London, 1819)
W. Judeich: *Topographie von Athen* (Munich, 1905, rev. 2/1931)
J. Travlos: *Poleodomiki exelixis ton Athinon* [The urban development of Athens] (Athens, 1960)
——: *Pictorial Dictionary of Athens* (London, 1971)
M. Pantelidou: *Ai proistorikai Athinai* [Prehistoric Athens] (Athens, 1975)
R. E. Wycherley: *The Stones of Athens* (Princeton, 1978)

3. 1ST CENTURY BC–*c.* AD 529. In the 1st century BC Athens made three successive political miscalculations involving Rome: siding with Mithradates of Pontus in his revolt of 88 BC, then backing first Brutus and later Antony in the Civil Wars (43–34 BC). Even so, Athens continued to flourish under the Roman Empire, largely because its position as a cultural and educational centre in the Mediterranean remained supreme. Following the example of the Hellenistic rulers of Asia Minor, the Roman emperors adorned Athens with a series of splendid public buildings.

(i) Roman Athens before Hadrian, 1st century BC*–early 2nd century* AD. The last known dedication by a Hellenistic king was the rebuilding of the Odeion of Pericles by Ariobarzanes of Cappadocia (*reg* 65–52 BC), and among the earliest benefactions by a Roman was a gift (?*c.* 50 BC) of money by Julius Caesar, which the Athenians used to start construction of a new market east of the Greek Agora (see figs 4a and 5a). When money ran out an embassy was sent to Augustus, who provided the funds necessary for the project's completion (11–9 BC). The new 'Roman Agora' was a large peristyle court with Ionic marble colonnades. Its main propylon (gateway) faced westwards, towards the old Agora, and consisted of four Doric columns with a pediment, carrying a dedicatory inscription to Athena Archegetis ('the founder'). An Ionic propylon provided access to the building from the east. Along the court's east side was a row of shops; along the south side, a double colonnade and fountains. The arrangement of the north and west sides is uncertain, and the building's long and complicated later history is not yet fully understood. Its marble paving, for instance, must be late, since some of the slabs were sawn from a stele inscribed with a letter from Marcus Aurelius to the Athenians (second half of the 2nd century AD). East of the market stood a building with a handsome façade of arches (4b). Its identity is uncertain, though inscriptions indicate that the Agoranomion (office of the market police) was somewhere in this vicinity. Near by is one of the largest extant Roman latrines (4c) with 68 marble seats over a water channel surrounding a small marble-paved impluvium (1st century AD). Other Augustan buildings in Athens include the Odeion (concert hall) built by Augustus' son-in-law Agrippa (late 1st century BC; 5b; for illustration *see* ODEION) in the middle of the Greek Agora, and a round temple dedicated to Rome and Augustus erected on the Acropolis some time after 27 BC (5c). This temple was a MONOPTEROS with nine Ionic columns, strongly influenced by the Erechtheion (*see* §II, 1(i) below).

The great period of Athenian prosperity and public works was the 2nd century AD, when both local benefactors and Roman emperors were actively involved in building projects. Around AD 100 a library was built in the Greek Agora at the expense of Flavius Pantainos (5d). Its dedicatory inscription refers to stoas, a peristyle and the library itself, all dedicated to Athena, the people of Athens, and the Emperor Trajan, early in his reign. Of the same period is one of the most conspicuous monuments of Roman Athens, the marble tomb of Antiochos Philopappos (*d c.* AD 114–16), who was a Roman consul, a descendant of the royal house of Commagene, and an Athenian citizen and benefactor of the city. The tomb (5e) stands on the Mouseion hill, west of the Acropolis, and thus contravenes the usual Athenian practice of extramural burial. The façade is a hemicycle, one and a half storeys high. The lower part was decorated with a frieze showing

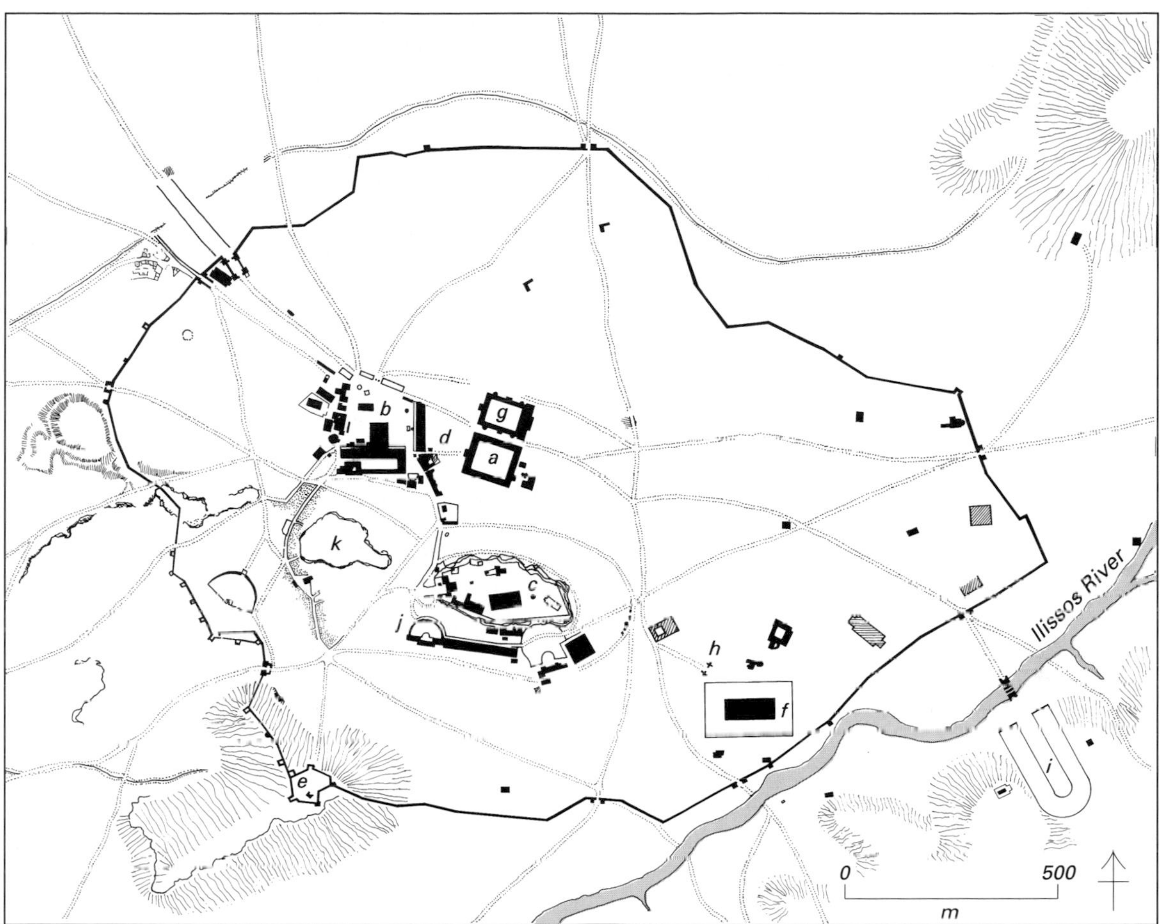

5. Athens, plan of city, 1st century BC–6th century AD: (a) Roman Agora; (b) Odeion of Agrippa; (c) Temple of Rome and Augustus; (d) Library of Flavius Pantainos; (e) tomb of Philopappos; (f) Temple of Olympian Zeus; (g) Library of Hadrian; (h) Arch of Hadrian; (i) Panathenaic Stadium; (j) Odeion of Herodes Atticus; (k) Areopagos

Philopappos in his Chariot. The upper part was decorated with Corinthian pilasters, niches, sculptures, and inscriptions recording Philopappos' royal ancestry and career at Rome.

(ii) Under Hadrian, AD *117–38.* The major Roman phase of Athenian building dates from the reign of HADRIAN, who was a notable philhellene and visited Athens no fewer than three times. Pausanias (*Guide to Greece,* I.xviii.6, 9) ascribed the following projects to him: the completion of the Temple of Olympian Zeus (5f; *see also* §II, 4 below); a temple of Hera and Zeus Panhellenios; a Pantheon; a library, and a gymnasium. The Library of Hadrian (4d and 5g; *see also* ROME, ANCIENT, fig. 43) has been identified and partially excavated. It lies just north of the Roman Agora and measures 125 m east–west by 87 m north–south. Its only entrance was a propylon of four Corinthian columns on its west side, and its western façade, largely of Pentelic marble, was decorated with 14 free-standing Corinthian columns with monolithic shafts of green-veined Karystian marble. The north half of the façade remains largely intact, standing *c.* 12 m high. Inside, the building took the form of a large peristyle court (22×30 columns), though none of its original colonnades, described by Pausanias as being of Phrygian marble, survives. In the middle of the court was a pool, and the long north and south walls behind the colonnades were punctuated with three large niches. The north, east and south walls are all of limestone, but were presumably revetted in marble. The principal rooms lay behind the eastern colonnade, the large one at the centre probably housing the library collection. Its east wall is preserved to a height of three storeys and has three rows of niches, which presumably held the wooden cabinets containing the scrolls. On either side were rooms of indeterminate function, while the corner rooms seem to have been lecture halls, with banked seating. The building's plan closely resembles the Imperial Fora at Rome (*see* ROME, §V, 2), particularly the Temple of Peace (AD 71–5). It was probably erected during Hadrian's third visit to Athens in AD 132. Other Hadrianic buildings have been excavated; some are identified with edifices listed by Pausanias, such as the Pantheon and Panhellenion. Just south of the Olympieion is a peristyle court surrounding a small temple, and just east of the Roman Agora is a huge (42×85 m) basilica-like building

with a large porch at its east end. There is also a smaller basilica at the north-east corner of the Greek Agora. According to a dedicatory inscription (once on the Lykabettos hill, now in the National Gardens), Hadrian was also responsible for the great aqueduct that brought water to Athens from the Kephalari springs on the slopes of Mt Pendelikon. A final monument associated with him is the two-storey Arch of Hadrian (5h), which lies north-west of the Olympieion. The lower part consists of an arch set in a wall and framed originally with free-standing columns. Above this, small engaged columns and pilasters form three open bays once filled with statues. Made of Pentelic marble, the arch carries two Greek inscriptions: one delimits the city of Theseus and the other that of Hadrian (*Inscr. Gr./2*, II/ii, 5185). Though it spans a street, the position and orientation of the arch are unusual, as are the inscriptions, which omit Hadrian's official titles. It may well have been erected for the dedication of the Olympieion to Hadrian, as well as Zeus, during the emperor's visit in AD 132.

(iii) Herodes Atticus to the later Empire, AD *138–529.* Soon after Hadrian's death the Athenians received the benefactions of a local magnate, HERODES ATTICUS. He rebuilt the Panathenaic Stadium (5i) entirely in marble (AD 139–44), thereby exhausting the quarries of Pentelikon, according to Pausanias (*Guide to Greece* I.xix.6), and constructed the great Odeion (5j) at the south-west foot of the Acropolis (AD 160–74). The façade of the Odeion, pierced by a series of large arches, still stands three storeys high in places, while the marble seating of the auditorium has been restored and accommodates *c.* 5000 people. Philostratos (*Lives of the Sophists* 551) remarked particularly on the building's cedarwood roof, and excavations in the 19th century uncovered a deep layer of ash on the orchestra floor along with roof-tiles, though it is unclear how the span of *c.* 50 m was bridged, in the apparent absence of internal supports.

After the 2nd century AD few public buildings were erected at Athens. Northern invaders reached Eleusis by the late 2nd century AD, and troubles during the reign of Valerian (*reg* AD 253–60) in the mid-3rd century AD led to a programme of fortification. In AD 267 the Heruli arrived in ships from the Black Sea and destroyed the city. Thereafter, the Athenians largely abandoned the circuit wall of the Classical city and constructed new walls around an area immediately north of the Acropolis. These begin at a large gate below the Propylaia, flanked by towers and known as the Beulé Gate, after its 19th-century discoverer, ERNEST-CHARLES-AUGUSTE BEULÉ. They continue down the east side of the Panathenaic Way, incorporating the ruins of the Library of Pantainos and the Stoa of Attalos, then turn due east to include the south wall of the Library of Hadrian. A bit further east they turn south and disappear under modern buildings. The stretch of wall in the Agora provides vivid testimony of the Herulian sack, for virtually every block is reused from a building destroyed by the invaders. Coins from the wall-fill indicate a construction date during the reign of Probus (*reg* AD 280–82).

Despite the Herulian sack, the Athenian philosophical school soon recovered, drawing students from all over the Mediterranean and making Athens a major cultural centre during the later Roman Empire. In AD 395 the city was attacked by the Visigoths under Alaric, though the literary sources disagree over the amount of damage done, and archaeological evidence from within the late circuit wall is inadequate. Whatever the case, Athens was clearly thriving again by the early 5th century AD, when several large buildings were erected in and around the Greek Agora. An impressive new building with three apses (each side 40 m long) was also constructed in the middle of the courtyard of the Library of Hadrian, which was refurbished with new colonnades. Some of the walls of this building were of rubble and mortar, but good marble blocks were also used and several floors were paved with mosaics. The building's function is uncertain, but it probably served as a church. Excavations on the north slopes of the Areopagos (5k) and the south slopes of the Acropolis have also uncovered several large villas inhabited from the 4th to the 6th century AD. Their great size and subsequent abandonment or rearrangement in the first half of the 6th century AD may imply that some belonged to pagan philosophers and doubled as schools, since in 529 AD the Christian emperor Justinian I (*reg* AD 527–65) forbade any pagan to teach philosophy at Athens.

BIBLIOGRAPHY

W. Judeich: *Topographie von Athen* (Munich, 1931)
I. T. Hill: *The Ancient City of Athens* (Cambridge, 1953)
J. Travlos: *Poleodomike exelixis ton Athenon* [The urban development of Athens] (Athens, 1960)
——: Pictorial Dictionary of Athens (London, 1971)
R. E. Wycherley: *The Stones of Athens* (Princeton, 1978)
D. J. Geagan: 'Roman Athens', *Aufstieg und Niedergang der römischen Welt*, II/vii, 1 (Berlin, 1979), pp. 371–437
A. Frantz: *Late Antiquity: AD 267–700* (1988), xxiv of *The Athenian Agora* (Princeton, 1988)

JOHN CAMP

4. *c.* AD 529–1204. The closing of the philosophical schools marked the demise of Athens as a cultural and educational centre, while its physical destruction occurred soon afterwards with the attacks of the Slavs (between 580 and 585). Other changes within the city during the 6th and 7th centuries were the conversion of several pagan temples and shrines into Christian churches. The first of these was the Parthenon (see fig. 6a; see also Korres, 1994), which became the city's cathedral dedicated to the Theotokos Atheniotissa (the Athenian Mother of God). Some time in the 3rd or 4th centuries (possibly in the Heruli attack of AD 267) the Parthenon had been damaged by a serious fire that consumed the gigantic timber roof beams and rafters and caused almost all of the marble roof to collapse. Many other marble surfaces were cracked while the two colossal doors disappeared. The temple was slowly repaired and the double inner colonnade was reconstructed, using columns and other members from nearby buildings. The new roof, made of baked clay tiles, covered only the cella. The area between the cella and the peristyle was left roofless. The east end was closed off by an apse. A main entrance on the west side and two lesser entrances on the north and south sides were opened, all leading into the west chamber which served as the narthex; three doors connected the narthex with the cella. The apse was fitted with marble seats for the clergy and a throne at the axis and the highest point. A free-standing, circular

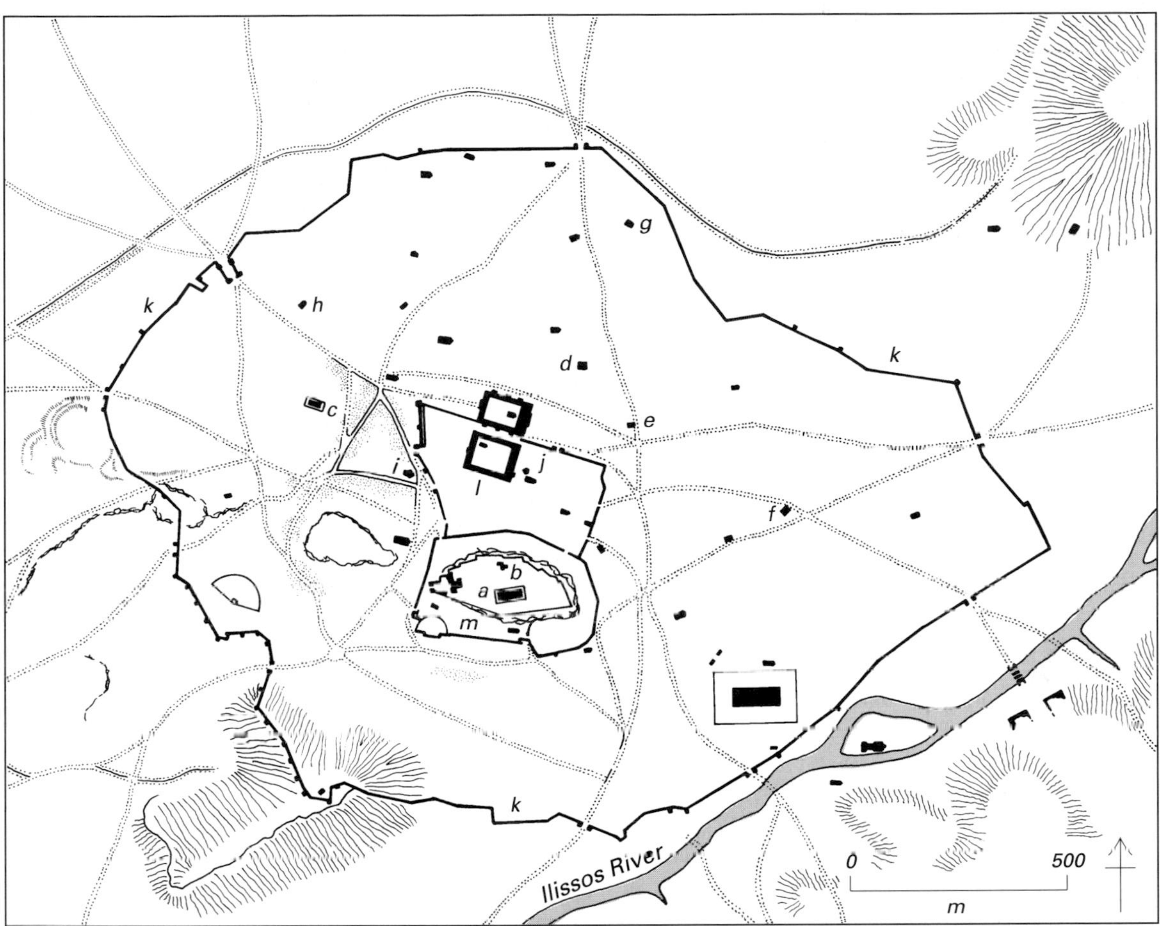

6. Athens, plan, *c.* AD 529–1204, from a reconstruction by J. Travlos, 1959: (a) Cathedral of the Theotokos Atheniotissa, 6th century (Parthenon); (b) church, 7th century (Erechtheion); (c) St George, 7th century (Hephaisteion); (d) Kapnikarea church, 1050; (e) Panagia Gorgeopikoos, late 12th century; (f) Soteira Lykodemou, before 1031; (g) Hagioi Theodoroi, 1065; (h) Hagioi Asomatoi, second half of the 11th century; (i) Hagioi Apostoloi, *c.* 1000; (j) late Roman walls; (k) Classical walls; (l) Agora district; (m) Rizokastron

marble ambon stood in the middle of the nave. In the 12th century the walls of the church were covered with paintings, while accounts from 1395 (Niccolò da Martoni) mention a mosaic of *Our Lady with the Holy Infant* in the apse of the sanctuary.

The Erechtheion (see figs 6b and 12 below; *see also* §II, 1(i)(c) below and CARYATID, fig. 1) and the Temple of Hephaistos (Hephaisteion; 6c) were also converted to churches, probably in the 7th century, the latter becoming the church of St George in the Kerameikos. Before 1834 foreign visitors, such as James Stuart and Nicholas Revett, could still see the ancient temple as it had been adapted to a church.

Much less is known about the development of Athens between the 8th and 10th centuries. In 797 Empress Eirene (*reg* 797–802) chose it as a suitable place for the exile of her brothers-in-law. Archaeological evidence from the Agora points to some building activity in the area, including the foundation in 871 of a church of St John Mangoutis (destr. early 19th century) at the foot of the Acropolis' north-east side. By *c.* 1000, however, it seems Athens' position had begun to improve. This may partly be explained by a general growth in prosperity in the regions of the Mediterranean following the Byzantine capture of Crete from the Arabs (961) and partly by the special relationship that had developed between Athens and the Byzantine MACEDONIAN DYNASTY (867–1056). In 1018 Basil II (*reg* 976–1025) even visited the city and donated money to the cathedral of the Theotokos on the Parthenon in thanksgiving for his subjugation of the Bulgarian kingdom and the Byzantine occupation of the whole Balkan peninsula. Further evidence of Athens' improved fortunes is suggested by the number of churches built between the 10th century and the 12th, which together with the converted temples and early Christian churches numbered an estimated 40 (Travlos). These were small parish churches that served several local neighbourhoods; for, unlike the ancient city centred on the Agora, Byzantine Athens lacked a political and cultural centre. The dominant architectural type was the domed, cross-in-square church (*see* EARLY CHRISTIAN AND BYZANTINE ART, §II, 2(iii)(b)), limited in size by virtue of its form. Basilican churches were also modest in size, reflecting the city's provincial status. Spolia from earlier buildings were incorporated into the new churches in a decorative manner, as in the churches of Kapnikarea (1050; 6d) and Panagia Gorgeopikoos (6e; *see also* §II, 6 below). Another feature of some of these churches is the use of kufic brick ornament, as in Soteira Lykodemou (before 1031; 6f) and Kapnikarea. It has been suggested that this kind of decoration resulted from Arabic settlement in Athens *c.* 900–1100. Considering, however, the general tendency of Byzantine art to incorporate eastern influences, it is more probable that these inscriptions were imitations of Arabic writing, disseminated in Greece through textiles, ceramics and manuscripts.

Of the 40 parish churches, 18 no longer survive, 14 are partially extant and 8 stand virtually unaltered. In addition to those already mentioned, the better-known examples include Hagioi Theodoroi (1065; 6g); Hagioi Asomatoi (second half of 11th century; 6h) and Hagioi Apostoloi (6i; *see also* §II, 5 below). Most of these churches were built outside the late Roman walls (6j), but within the Classical walls (6k). In the 11th century a community was established in the ancient Athenian Agora district (6l), which had remained largely uninhabited since the late 6th century or the 7th. Despite the raising of the ground level due to several deposits of silt, the street pattern was preserved, though the streets became narrower. At the same time a new set of walls, known as the Rizokastron (6m) was built around the Acropolis to protect the city from Saracen attacks.

In 1182 Michael Choniates (*c.* 1160–1220) became the archbishop of Athens. In his writings he lamented the political, cultural, and economic decline of the city. Unable to resist the forces of the Fourth Crusade, he finally surrendered the city to Boniface of Mont Ferrat in 1204.

BIBLIOGRAPHY

F. Gregorovius: *Geschichte der Stadt Athen im Mittelalter: Von der Zeit Justinians bis zur fränkischen Eroberung* (Stuttgart, 1870, 3/1889)
K. Setton: 'Athens in the later 12th Century', *Speculum*, xix/2 (1944)
J. Travlos: *Poleodomiki exelixis ton Athinon* [Urban development of Athens] (Athens, 1960)
A. Frantz: 'From Paganism to Christianity in the Temples of Athens', *Dumbarton Oaks Pap.*, xix, 1965
——: *Pictorial Dictionary of Ancient Athens* (London, 1971)
M. Korres: 'The Parthenon from Antiquity to the 19th century', *The Parthenon and its Impact in Modern Times*, ed. P. Tournikiotis (Athens, 1994)

5. 1205–1834. Most of the building activity undertaken by a succession of French, Catalan and Italian rulers during this period focused on Athens' defensive system. An observation tower known as the Frankish Tower (destr. 1875) was erected on the Acropolis in the 13th century, while the Propylaia became the palace of the Florentine dukes after they captured the city in 1387. Most of the city receded once again inside the late Roman walls (6j), numbering, according to Niccolò da Martoni only 1000 residences in 1395 (Travlos, p. 172).

In 1456 Athens surrendered peacefully to the Ottoman Turks. Respecting its ancient monuments and history, Mehmed II (*reg* 1444–81 with interruption), who visited Athens in 1458, awarded it special administrative privileges. The city's cathedral (the converted Parthenon: *see* §4 above), was transformed into a mosque and a minaret

7. Athens, mosque of the Parthenon; engraving, *c.* 300×550 mm, from Stuart and Revett: *The Antiquities of Athens* (London, 1762–1816)

was built next to it, as can be seen in 17th-century representations. The Ottoman rulers preserved the existing urban fabric, punctuating it with the addition of mosques, markets, baths, inns and poorhouses, which stamped the presence of the new government on to the ancient city. Some growth in prosperity resulted in the city's expansion beyond the late Roman walls; these and the Classical walls had been allowed to deteriorate. The Ottoman garrison occupied and built houses on the Acropolis hill. According to an account of 1671 by Charles Olier, Marquis de Nointel (*c.* 1630–85; see Stuart and Revett, vol. 4), the city had 2053 residences, 1300 of which belonged to Greeks, 600 to Turks, 150 to Albanians and 3 to other foreigners. Of the four major mosques dating before 1678, only the Fethiye ('Victory') Mosque survives. Other smaller mosques and places of prayer and several churches and monasteries were built throughout the city between 1456 and 1687.

The antiquities on the Acropolis survived mostly intact until the siege of the Acropolis by the Venetian army in 1687, when a Venetian shell falling on the Parthenon caused the explosion of the dynamite stored there by the Turks. After a brief but disastrous Venetian occupation of the city (Oct 1687–April 1688), the Ottomans returned to Athens, strengthened its defensive system and undertook several public works in the 18th century. The Ottoman garrison returned to the Acropolis, where there were nearly 200 houses. At the beginning of the 18th century a smaller mosque replaced the original mosque of the Parthenon, which had been destroyed. The later mosque, of which there are several 18th-century representations (see fig. 7), was taken down in 1842 during the archaeological restorations of the Acropolis. Although other mosques and places of prayer were erected after the Venetians departed, most have since disappeared.

The administrative, commercial and religious centre of late Ottoman Athens was in the market, which occupied the area of the Roman Agora and the Library of Hadrian (see figs 5a and 5g above); other public and religious buildings were dispersed throughout the city. In 1822, there were still 1235 stone houses, each occupying irregular plots, delineated by the city's ancient street pattern. During the War of Independence (1821–8), however, most houses were destroyed, and most Athenians fled to the countryside. In May 1827 the Acropolis was captured by the Turks and held until 1833. The following year Athens became the capital of liberated Greece. By the early 1830s, however, the city was in a poor state, with a population of *c.* 4000. Attempts to revitalize Athens had included a proposal for a new urban plan produced in 1832 by the architects Stamatis Kleanthis (1802–62) and Eduard Schaubert (1804-68). It comprised wide thoroughfares, large squares and public buildings, as well as suggestions for the preservation of ancient monuments. Despite the enthusiasm with which it was initially received, it soon became apparent that it conflicted with landowners' interests and was too costly to implement.

BIBLIOGRAPHY

J. Stuart and N. Revett: *Antiquities of Athens*, 4 vols (London, 1762–1816)
J. Travlos: *Poleodomiki exelixis ton Athinon* [Urban development of Athens] (Athens, 1960)
K. M. Setton: *Athens in the Middle Ages* (London, 1975)
D. Karydis: *Poleodomika ton Athinon tis Tourkokratias* [Urban issues of Athens under Turkish rule] (diss., N. Tech U. Athens, 1981)

ELENI BASTÉA

6. 1834 AND AFTER. The choice of Athens for the capital of the new Greek state was due primarily to its historical heritage. With the ensuing influx of new inhabitants including government officials, members of the royal court, army personnel, diplomats and ordinary Greek citizens, the need for a new urban plan became urgent. In 1834 LEO VON KLENZE submitted a modified version of the earlier plan by Stamatis Kleanthis and Edward Schaubert (*see* §5 above). The main roads and public plots were considerably reduced in size, while the city centre remained located at a short distance from the already densely inhabited foothills of the Acropolis. The construction of new streets and buildings began immediately. Considerable efforts were made to revive the city's Classical past, although these were sometimes taken to extremes, as, for example, in the scheme suggested by KARL FRIEDRICH SCHINKEL to build the Royal Palace on the Acropolis, or the zealous attempts of contemporary archaeologists to preserve exclusively Classical monuments, which resulted in the destruction of many later buildings, including numerous Byzantine churches. The Temple of Hephaistos was dismantled as a church and established as a museum for the city's antiquities.

By 1836 the population of Athens had doubled, and, although new houses were constantly being built, the development of the necessary infrastructure, such as the supply of water and sewage networks, was limited. In this year construction of the palace designed by Friedrich von Gärtner (*see* GARTNER, (2)) began. Gärtner rejected Schinkel's site and built the palace (now the Parliament; see fig. 8) in GREEK REVIVAL style on Syntagma Square in the eastern part of the city. Although the surrounding area was designated the official city centre, the old market in Plaka at the north-east foot of the Acropolis continued as the centre of city life for some time. In addition to the palace (completed 1841), the government commissioned several other public buildings, such as the Military Hospital (1837), the National Capodistrian University (1837–49), the Observatory (1843) and the Cathedral (1842–62), while wealthy Greeks of the Diaspora donated substantial funds for the construction of the Arsakeion (1857; destr.), the Polytechneion (1862), the Zappeion (1874), the Academy (1859–87), and the National Library (1851–91). Although most smaller private houses were built in a simple traditional style, Greek aristocrats commissioned prominent Greek or western European architects working in Athens to build imposing private mansions, mainly in the Neo-classical style.

By the end of the 19th century records indicate that, as the population grew substantially and construction spread in various directions, an effective municipal administration became established in order to deal with the city's requirements. In the 20th century, however, various changes occurred that were detrimental to Athens' urban development. The use of concrete in construction had disastrous consequences on the overall appearance of the city. The arrival of large numbers of Greek refugees from Asia Minor after 1922 and the severe housing shortage after

8. Athens, Royal Palace (now Parliament) by Friedrich von Gärtner, west façade, 1836–41

World War II were among the causes for the uncoordinated construction undertaken to resolve immediate practical needs.

During the 1950s and 1960s social and economic factors resulted in the further growth of Athens' population. Government policies, while encouraging private sector construction, failed to lay down any urban planning regulations or any environmental and stylistic guidelines. As a consequence, high-rise concrete residential blocks filled the crowded city centre and an increasing number of suburbs developed in a random manner with limited planning for green, public areas or for transport. Exceptions to this trend were mostly confined to areas of historical importance, as in the landscaping of the Acropolis and Philopappou hills by DIMITRIS PIKIONIS in which elements of Greek folk art and architecture were integrated with the Classical remains.

Since the 1970s legislation relating to environmental considerations, urban planning and the conservation of listed buildings (both public and private) has become increasingly important and effective. Several streets in the city centre have been made into pedestrian zones, while Plaka, the oldest part of the capital, has undergone major restoration work whereby it has regained most of its traditional character.

See also GREECE, §II.

BIBLIOGRAPHY

J. Travlos: *Poleodomiki exelixis ton Athinon* [The urban development of Athens] (Athens, 1960)

J. Travlos and A. Kokkou: 'Poleodomia kei architectoniki, 1833–1881' [Urban planning and architecture, 1883–1881], *Istoria ton Ellinikou Ethnous* [History of the Greek nation] (Athens, 1956–60), xiii, pp. 515–20

C. Biris: *Ai Athinai apo tou 19ou eis tou 20ou aiona* [Athens from the 19th to the 20th century] (Athens, 1966)

Athènes: Affaire européenne (exh. cat. by V. Tsiomis, Athens, Záppeion, 1985)

EVITA ARAPOGLOU

II. Buildings and sculpture.

1. Acropolis. 2. Agora. 3. Kerameikos. 4. Temple of Olympian Zeus. 5. Hagioi Apostoloi. 6. Panagia Gorgoepikoos.

1. ACROPOLIS. In ancient Greek the term *acropolis* means simply the 'upper or higher city' or 'citadel', although in general usage it has become firmly associated with the unparalleled architectural and sculptural ensemble of the Classical Athenian Acropolis.

(i) Architecture. (ii) Sculpture.

(i) Architecture. First inhabited and fortified in the Bronze Age (*c.* 1550–*c.* 1050 BC, the Acropolis was by the Archaic period (*c.* 700–480 BC) given over largely to cult activity, primarily the worship of Athena. The earliest remains of cult buildings may date to the 8th and the 7th century BC, but it was not until the 6th century BC that the Acropolis was adorned with monumental architecture.

(a) *c.* 600–*c.* 450 BC. (b) *c.* 450–*c.* 400 BC.

(a) c. *600*–c. *450* BC. The impetus for the first major building phase on the Acropolis seems to have been the Peisistratid family, who ruled Athens as tyrants (absolute, but not necessarily despotic, rulers; *see* PEISISTRATOS), and was apparently connected with their reorganization of the Panathenaic festival in honour of Athena around 566 BC. Sometime between 600 and 550 BC access to the citadel was made easy by means of a large straight ramp leading up to an entrance, now completely obscured by later structures. To the right of this ramp, outside the gate, a Sanctuary of Athena Nike ('Victory') was founded (see fig. 9a), and its 6th-century BC phase is represented by a statue base and an inscribed altar. On the Acropolis proper the exact disposition of the 6th-century BC buildings is uncertain. Numerous fragments survive from two monumental Doric temples, but the foundations for only one Archaic temple remain *in situ*. The hundreds of small

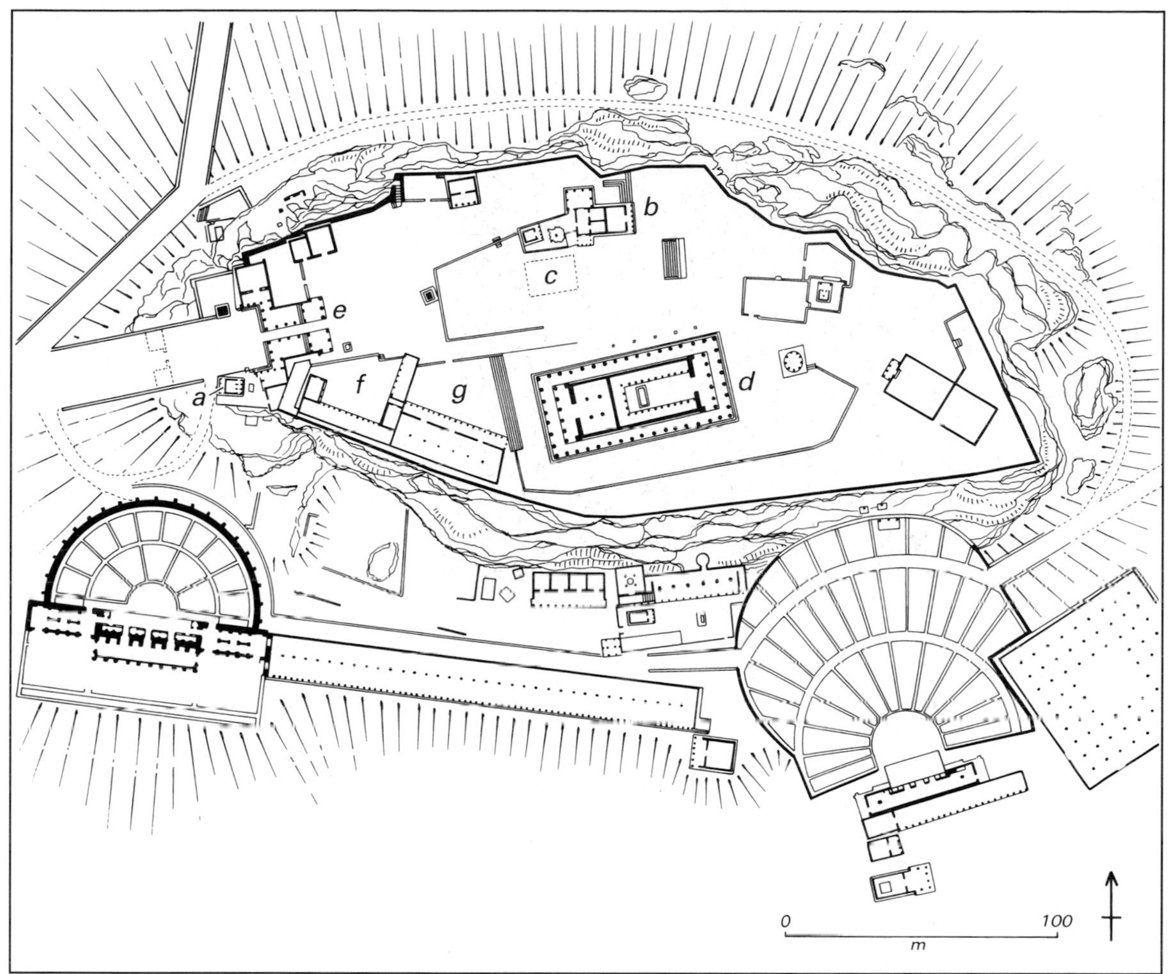

9. Athens, plan of Acropolis: (a) Sanctuary, later Temple, of Athena Nike, *c.* 427–424 BC; (b) Erechtheion, ?421–405 BC; (c) Old Temple of Athena, *c.* 530–500 BC; (d) Parthenon, 447–432 BC; (e) Propylaia, 437–432 BC; (f) Sanctuary of Artemis Brauronia; (g) Chalkotheke, *c.* 450 BC

fragments from the earlier temple, often referred to as the Hekatompedon ('100 footer') or the 'H' architecture, suggest that it was a peripteral building *c.* 20 m wide (length unknown) made largely of local grey limestone, but with marble metopes and a handsomely incised marble gutter. Its pediments were decorated with large, brightly painted limestone figures (Athens, Acropolis. Mus.), and the temple is dated stylistically to *c.* 570–550 BC. It was situated either partly beneath the north-east corner of the Parthenon, or on the same limestone foundations, just south of the Erechtheion (9b), used for the second 6th-century BC temple, known as the Old Temple of Athena or 'Dörpfeld's Temple' (9c). These foundations (22.0×43.5 m) supported a peripteral building of 6×12 columns. Numerous fragments of its columns and entablature survive, showing that it was of limestone, with marble decorative elements and marble pedimental sculpture. It is generally dated stylistically to *c.* 530–500 BC. In addition to these large temples, there were several treasuries, small simple chambers with a Doric porch at one end. Only fragments survive, belonging to at least five and perhaps as many as seven buildings; between three and five were adorned with pedimental sculpture. The locations and plans of the buildings are uncertain, but they may well have stood to the west of the later Parthenon.

In the 480s BC the Athenians began to build a third temple of Athena (the 'Older Parthenon'; see fig. 10a), perhaps in celebration of their victory over the Persians at Marathon (490 BC). This was apparently to have been a Doric peripteral building (6×16 columns) with foundations and steps of limestone, but with a colonnade and superstructure of Pentelic marble. The Persian destruction of the Acropolis in 480/479 BC, however, prevented its completion. The temple platform stands on the south side of the Acropolis, where the ground slopes down steeply to the south, so that its north side rests on bedrock, while its south side is supported on 20 courses of foundations. It was later reused as a base for the Classical Parthenon (9d).

Once the Persians had been driven out, the Athenians did not immediately rebuild what had been destroyed (*see* §I, 2(ii) above). Instead, many pieces of sculpture and

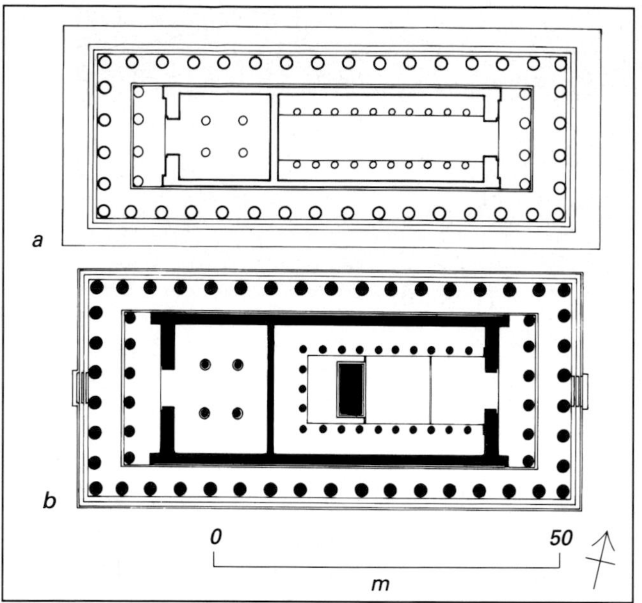

10. Athens, plans of temples on Acropolis: (a) 'Older Parthenon', 488–480 BC; (b) Parthenon, 447–432 BC

architecture were buried, while much of the superstructure of the Old Temple of Athena and the column drums of the 'Older Parthenon' were reused conspicuously in a new north wall for the Acropolis. The date of this is uncertain, and estimates range from 479 BC to the mid-5th century BC. The south wall was apparently built by the Athenian statesman Kimon (before 489 BC–after 450 BC) in the 460s BC, with spoils from the Battle of the Eurymedon (the whole circuit was heavily restored in medieval times). A new marble and limestone gateway to the Acropolis was also started after the Persian Wars. Its south-west anta and part of the south wall survive just south of the central hall of the Propylaia (9e), which obscures the rest of the structure.

(b) c. *450*–c. *400* BC. During the second half of the 5th century BC the Acropolis became the focal point of the great building programme initiated by PERICLES and was adorned with a group of magnificent marble buildings in honour of Athena (*see* GREECE, ANCIENT, fig. 6).

Parthenon. This temple dedicated to Athena Parthenos ('maiden') was the first and by far most impressive of the new structures. Inscriptions recording its building accounts show that it was started in 447 BC and that construction was sufficiently advanced by 438 BC for the cult statue of Athena to be installed. Further work on the architectural sculpture continued until 432 BC. Made entirely of Pentelic marble, the Parthenon is generally regarded as the most outstanding building in the Doric order (see fig. 11). While large (30.88×69.51 m), it is far smaller than the gigantic temples of Asia Minor and Sicily, and there are several other temples entirely of marble; even so, the Parthenon is set apart by the grandeur of its plan, its architectural refinements and the lavishness of its mouldings and sculptural decoration (*see* POLYCHROMY, colour pl. I, fig. 1). Its unusually wide interior, designed to house both the colossal chryselephantine cult statue of *Athena* by PHEIDIAS and an elaborate internal colonnade, required a grand outer peristyle: the façades received eight columns, rather than the canonical six, giving the flanks seventeen rather than the usual thirteen. The building had two chambers, back-to-back, each approached through a prostyle porch of six Doric columns. The larger, eastern chamber, referred to in the temple inventories as the Hekatompedon, was the cella proper, housing the cult statue. Its two storeys of internal Doric columns ran around three sides of the room; this innovative arrangement was designed as a frame and setting for the statue. The smaller, western chamber, which, according to the official inventories, was the Parthenon proper, had a ceiling supported by four Ionic columns and housed both sacred funds and the state treasury.

Though some of its architectural refinements are too subtle to be perceived consciously, the Parthenon hardly incorporates a single truly horizontal or vertical line (*see* GREECE, ANCIENT, figs 23 and 34). The exact function of the refinements is not fully understood, and some involve such precise workmanship that they are detectable only by careful measurement. The stylobate (platform) on which the columns stand rises slightly from the corners towards the centre, and the entablature exhibits a similar curve. Similarly, the taper of the columns themselves includes a slight swelling or ENTASIS halfway up. The corner columns, which were defined against the sky rather than the building, are slightly thicker than the others, and measurement of the columns' flutes reveals even subtler refinements. In addition, all the peristyle columns tilt in towards the centre of the building. Other Greek temples have some of these refinements, though none has as many as the Parthenon. Furthermore, some of the Parthenon's refinements are so striking that they free it from the static quality typical of the Doric order, with its emphasis on vertical and horizontal lines.

Literary sources agree in naming IKTINOS as one of the Parthenon architects, but, while Plutarch (*Pericles* XIII.4) names his associate as Kallikrates, Vitruvius (*On Architecture* VII. Preface. 12) names him as Karpion. It is unclear what role Pheidias played in its design, but, as sculptor of the cult statue and general overseer of the Periclean building programme, he must have had some influence. The building was not merely a temple but possibly also a belated monument to the Greek victory in the Persian Wars and a symbol of Athenian wealth and power. There is no evidence for cult activity (i.e. no priesthood and no altar), and, in common with Greek temples generally, the Parthenon functioned partly as a state treasury. A severe fire damaged the building at some unascertained date in antiquity (2nd century BC, 2nd or 3rd century AD), and its internal colonnades were rebuilt using material from a Hellenistic stoa. In the 6th century AD the Parthenon was converted for use as the city's cathedral and then, in the later 15th century, into a mosque, surviving virtually intact until 1687, when it was blown up during a Venetian siege of the Acropolis. A small mosque built in its ruins (see fig. 7 above) was removed in 1842, and restoration work was carried out early in the 20th century. A major new programme of repair has since been undertaken.

11. Athens, Parthenon, view from the Propylaia

Propylaia. This was the second building (9e) on the Acropolis constructed as part of the Periclean programme. According to building accounts and Plutarch's *Pericles* (XIII.7), the Propylaia or great gateway (*see* PROPYLON) was begun in 437 BC, and work apparently stopped in 432 BC. The architect was MNESIKLES. As constructed, the building consists of a large central hall flanked by wings to the south-west and north-west. Two additional wings were planned at the north-east and south-east, but these were curtailed during the course of construction. Even as built, the Propylaia was never entirely finished: lifting bosses were left on wall blocks and matrices of unworked marble protected the stylobates and steps.

The central hall had Doric hexastyle façades facing east and west, with their central intercolumniations widened by one metope to facilitate access. The door-wall between the façades was set well to the east, and the ceiling of the deeper western porch was supported on two rows of three Ionic columns. The ceilings of both porches were of marble, with deeply cut and ornately painted coffers. The door-wall itself was pierced with five doors, each centred on a façade intercolumniation. The central door was the largest, followed by the two doors to either side of it. The north-west wing faced south, with an unusual façade of three columns *in antis*; behind was a square room with an off-centre door and two windows. When Pausanias visited Athens (2nd century AD), this wing was used as a picture gallery (*Guide to Greece* I.xxii.6). Its original function is unknown, but it may have been a dining-hall. Balancing the north-west wing was a similar three-columned façade at the south-west, facing north. It had no chamber behind, however, but simply gave access to the Sanctuary of Athena Nike to the south-west, and it was merely designed to give a symmetrical effect to the Propylaia as seen from the long straight ramp that led to the building.

The Propylaia in many ways matches or surpasses the Parthenon in detailed subtlety of design and construction. It was clearly planned with the Parthenon in mind, and the two buildings share the same orientation. The intended width of the Propylaia, north to south, is almost equal to the length of the Parthenon, and the ratio of 3:7 governing the spacing and heights of various elements in the Propylaia is close to the Parthenon ratio of 4:9 (*see also* GREECE, ANCIENT, §II, 3(v)). Mnesikles' meticulous planning is apparent in his treatment of the building's steps. In the west façade, the four marble steps create a platform in correct proportional relation to the height and diameter of the columns which they support. The tristyle wings, however, have much smaller columns, though for structural reasons the steps are of the same height. Mnesikles' solution to this was to make the bottom step of grey Eleusinian limestone, so that only the three white marble steps above it stood out, in correct proportion to the columns above. The Propylaia was later altered to form part of the medieval defences of the Acropolis, and parts were used as the Frankish palace.

Erechtheion. The third great 5th-century BC marble building on the Acropolis is known as the Erechtheion

12. Athens, Erechtheion (*c.* ?421–405 BC) and foundations of Old Temple of Athena (*c.* 530–500 BC); view from the Parthenon

(see figs 9b and 12), though this name (Erechtheos was a mythical king of Athens) has been challenged. It housed the venerable wooden statue of *Athena Polias* ('guardian of the city'), so old that it was said to have fallen from heaven, and so formed the focus of the cult of Athena. Since the Parthenon stands immediately to the south, the architect of the Erechtheion did not attempt to make the building compete directly with this outstanding example of the Doric order, and instead chose the more ornate and delicate Ionic order. The building has an unusually complex plan. Pausanias' account of the 2nd century AD (*Guide to Greece* I.xxvi.5–xxvii.3), moreover, shows that it was required either to house or be adapted to numerous sacred relics, including a well of salt water, an olive tree, the marks of a thunderbolt or Poseidon's trident, the tomb of Kekrops and the sanctuary of Pandrosos. Its steeply sloping site also created drastic variations in building levels.

The original plan was apparently for an amphiprostyle temple with six columns at either end. The west porch was, however, replaced by an enclosed chamber with four Ionic columns engaged in its west façade. To compensate, a large prostyle porch with six Ionic columns was added to the west end of the building's north side, and, to balance this, a smaller prostyle porch with six caryatids was added to the west end of its south side (*see* CARYATID, fig. 1). The building is of Pentelic marble, except for its frieze, which is of grey Eleusinian stone with figures in white marble attached by pins. Its various architectural mouldings, column capitals (e.g. *see* GREECE, ANCIENT, fig. 17) and upper shafts are elaborately carved. Building work may have begun in either the 430s or 420s BC, and was certainly suspended for a while: a large inscription from the year 409/408 BC (*Inscr. Gr./2*, 372–4) preserves a detailed record of the state of the building, finished almost to its roof, prepared by the board of commissioners responsible for its completion. The accounts which follow record the prices paid for completing the upper parts of the building, producing the sculpture and the finishing touches, such as fluting the columns. Athenian citizens, resident aliens and slaves worked side by side on the temple. Architects are named, but it is unclear who designed the building as a whole.

Temple of Athena Nike. The final temple to be built on the Acropolis was a marble structure dedicated to Athena Nike (9a; *see also* ORDERS, ARCHITECTURAL, fig. 3). As noted above, the bastion immediately south-west of the gateway to the Acropolis had accommodated the cult of Athena Nike since the first half of the 6th century BC. At some time, perhaps as late as the mid-5th century BC, a small naiskos (shrine) of poros limestone had been built to enclose an early base, and a new monolithic limestone altar with mouldings had been erected to its east, replacing an earlier altar. The naiskos in turn was replaced by the Ionic amphiprostyle temple, reconstructed on the site today. Its small scale counteracts the bulky proportions of its columns, which have capitals almost identical to those of the Propylaia, though half their size. Work on the temple probably began *c.* 435–425 BC. While later than the Propylaia, it was clearly already planned before the Propylaia had progressed far. The architect is unknown. Towards the end of the 5th century BC a sculpted parapet was added around the edge of the bastion (*see* §(ii) below).

Other structures. With the Nike temple the major building activity on the Acropolis ceased. Numerous lesser sanctuaries and buildings, however, are known from inscriptions, Pausanias' account or scanty remains. These include a sanctuary of Artemis Brauronia (9f), at the south-west corner of the citadel, and the Chalkotheke (storeroom for bronzes; 9g), perhaps just to its east. Foundations for other buildings lie under the modern museum at the east end of the Acropolis, and along the north wall of the citadel, west of the Erechtheion. In the late 4th century BC the great Theatre of Dionysos was constructed on the south slope of the Acropolis hill (*see* GREECE, ANCIENT, §II, 1(i)(e)).

BIBLIOGRAPHY

O. Jahn and A. Michaelis: *Arx Athenarum a Pausania descripta* [The Acropolis as described by Pausanias] (Bonn, 1901)
T. Wiegand: *Die archaische Poros-Architektur der Akropolis zu Athen* (Kassel, 1904)
P. Kavvadias and G. Kawerau: *Die Ausgrabung der Akropolis, 1885–1890* (Athens, 1907)
R. Heberdey: *Altattische Porosskulptur* (Vienna, 1919)
H. Payne: *Archaic Marble Sculpture from the Acropolis* (London, 1936)
A. E. Raubitschek: *Dedications from the Athenian Acropolis* (Cambridge, 1949)
M. Brouskari: *The Acropolis Museum* (Athens, 1974)
J. A. Bundgaard, ed.: *The Excavations of the Athenian Acropolis, 1882–1890: The Original Drawings* (Copenhagen, 1974) [ed. from unpubd writings by G. Kawerau]
——: *Parthenon and the Mycenaean City on the Heights* (Copenhagen, 1976)

JOHN CAMP

(ii) Sculpture. The sculpture associated with the shrine of Athena and other cult places on the Acropolis unquestionably represents one of the most important collections of Greek sculpture. It comprises votive and architectural sculpture, with a middle category of cult statues. In formal terms, sculpture in the round and reliefs often occur alongside one another in temples and in statue bases bearing reliefs. As free-standing votive statues belonged to the shrine of the divinity to whom they were dedicated, they were associated with its architecture, and were even conceived partly with this in mind.

13. Athens, pedimental group from the Acropolis, showing the *Introduction of Herakles to Olympus*, limestone, h. 940 mm, early 6th century BC (Athens, Acropolis Museum)

(a) Architectural. (b) Non-architectural.

(a) Architectural.

Archaic period (c. *700–c. 500/480* BC*)*. A series of poros relief pediments dating from the end of the 7th century BC to the mid-6th are noteworthy. One largish pediment (late 7th century BC–early 6th; Athens, Acropolis Mus.), probably from the early Temple of Athena, represents two lionesses facing one another and tearing calves to pieces. A large Gorgoneion (Athens, Acropolis Mus.) in the style of the Dipylon Head (Athens, N. Archaeol. Mus.) seems to come from the adjoining acroterion. A little later, in the early 6th century BC, two pediments, probably from a reconstruction of the Temple of Athena, repeat the motif of the fighting lions in the middle, but in the angles they have snakes (east), and Herakles fighting Nereus opposite a three-bodied mythical creature (west). It was here (later in the Erechtheion) that the venerable cult statue of Athena that had 'fallen from the sky' was kept; in the late Archaic period drapery was added by Endoios (*fl c.* ?530–500 BC).

After the Persian destruction fragments of a series of small, experimental relief pediments of poros limestone were deposited, concentrated particularly to the south of the Parthenon, most still dating from before the mid-6th century BC. Some probably came from treasuries; others from smaller shrines. As well as the usual animal fights, they depict such mythological scenes as Herakles fighting the Hydra, lions and Triton, Herakles' introduction to Olympus, and a scene in a well-house. Extremely naive formation, combined with high-quality workmanship and particularly clearly preserved traces of polychrome painting heighten the impact of these pieces.

It was not until later in the 6th century BC that marble was first used in architectural sculpture. Possibly further in connection with the government reforms of Kleisthenes and the subsequent victory over the Boiotians and Khalkidians, the Temple of Athena was replaced by a new building with marble pediments featuring sculpture in the round. On the east pediment there was a rather static assembly of the gods with Zeus in the centre (see fig. 13), on the west the very much livelier gigantomachy. A large-scale mannered frieze of a procession of the gods with chariots dating from the late 6th century BC (Athens, Acropolis Mus.) was probably part of a balustrade.

Classical period (c. *500/480–323* BC*)*. Remains of inscriptions on buildings provide information about the dating and cost of architectural projects with sculptural decoration in the second half of the 5th century BC. The new Parthenon building was obviously inspired by Pericles; it was started soon after the mid-5th century BC and completed before the Peloponnesian War. It is the most important example of several High Classical temples designed by the Athenian architect IKTINOS that mix elements of the Ionic and Doric orders (*see* GREECE, ANCIENT, §II, 2(iii)); notable is the use of the Ionic picture

14. Athens, part of south frieze from the Temple of Athena Nike on the Acropolis, slab g, h. 490 mm, l. 1.85 m, *c.* 420–410 BC (London, British Museum)

frieze alongside the alternating metopes and triglyphs of the Doric frieze. In the Parthenon the Ionic frieze was used on the cella, the Doric on the peristyle (*see* FRIEZE, fig. 1).

The designs for the Parthenon's architectural sculpture are often attributed to PHEIDIAS, who played a leading role in the building, though it is unclear from the sources exactly what the sculpture was. The constantly recurring use of the celestial deities to frame pictorial sequences seems to be Pheidias' trademark. Thanks to a hasty sketch made by Jacques Carrey in the mid-17th century, shortly before the Parthenon was blown up during the siege by Morosini, and to Lord Elgin's removal of some pieces and making casts of others before the War of Greek Independence (*see* BRUCE, THOMAS), further information about the original sculptural scheme of the Parthenon has been preserved.

The metopes were obviously tackled first; they could be worked on, indeed completely finished, in the workshop. Each side of the Doric frieze is devoted to one of the various exemplary struggles against the enemies of the world of Civilization: on the east a Gigantomachy; on the south a Centauromachy; on the west an Amazonomachy; and on the north the Trojan War (*see* GREECE, ANCIENT, fig. 40). Next came the Ionic frieze round the cella. The treatment of the grooves between the blocks in carving the figural composition in the western section shows that these parts of the frieze were completed in the workshop, while those further to the east were not sculpted in detail until they had been put in place (the carving disregards the boundaries between adjacent blocks). Starting from the south-east corner, the Panathenaic procession travels along both sides of the frieze; before the horsemen of the ten phyles (artificial tribal units formed by Kleisthenes half a century earlier in his new constitution) and the *apobates* (armed soldiers jumping from and into careering chariots), the other representatives of the citizenry move towards a central cult scene at the east end, and the Olympian gods flanking them are awaiting the procession. The political significance of this positively revolutionary composition becomes clear only with the identification of the ten men deep in conversation. Shown in two groups, mediating between the gods and the Athenians, these are the fictional heroic ancestors of Kleisthenes' ten phyles.

Because of damage in early medieval times in the east and Morosini's attack in the west, it is impossible to reconstruct the compositions of the pediments completely. The contrast in composition between the more static birth of Athena in the presence of all the gods in the east pediment and the dramatic struggle between Athena and Poseidon to take possession of Attica in the west was in the old tradition of pedimental sculpture. In the Parthenon, however, its potential was considerably developed.

The sculptural programme of the temple interior matches that of Pheidias' colossal chryselephantine statue of *Athena Parthenos* (*see* §(b) below).

New buildings on the Acropolis were embarked on only when there was a break in the Peloponnesian War, and they were constructed on a smaller scale, in the more graceful Ionic order. It is uncertain whether the small amphiprostyle Ionic Temple of Athena Nike on the south-west bastion of the Acropolis (*see* ORDERS, ARCHITECTURAL, fig. 3) was built after earlier designs by the architect Kallikrates, dating from the mid-5th century BC, as inscriptional evidence suggests; its architectural sculpture unequivocally dates it at least 25 years later in the time of the Peloponnesian War. Scenes on friezes running round three sides of the building represent the struggle between the Athenians and hostile Greeks and Persians (see fig. 14), to which an assembly of the gods above the entrance on the east side referred. The pedimental sculpture is largely lost. Inside there was a wooden cult statue of a wingless *Nike*, obviously earlier in date, and several golden figures of Nike, which represented part of the city treasure. These were melted down during the Peloponnesian War and only replaced a century later by Lykourgos. Shortly afterwards the south-west bastion was surrounded with the Nike Balustrade, which was decorated with reliefs. The theme of the Nikes decorating trophies and sacrificing bulls for victory is widely and grandly varied here, with Athena watching over events on all three sides. This is a fine example of the Rich Style of sculpture of the last years before the defeat of Athens, and it may well have been the conception of the sculptor KALLIMACHOS.

Kallimachos' golden lamp adorned with acanthus burnt continuously inside the Erechtheion. This building, with its varied and inventive sculptural decoration, was erected in the same period beside the remains of and as successor to the Old Temple to Athena. The Ionic frieze of dark Eleusinian marble with white marble appliqués was highly innovative. Because of the technique used, it is almost impossible to reconstruct the exact sequence of the figures, though obviously the event depicted referred to the cults practised in the Erechtheion. The 'Porch of the Maidens', which still arouses controversy both architecturally and as regards its cult function, is also exceptional and pioneering. Its canopy roof is supported by six caryatids, suggesting a reinterpretation of a Late Archaic type of Ionic treasury. These maidens probably represent servants in the cult of Athena (*see* CARYATID, fig. 1).

The altar to Athena and Poseidon retained its position on the east side of the Old Temple of Athena, even after the temple itself had been destroyed. It has relief frieze panels, which were presumably constantly renovated, and the use of ornament on them indicates a new concept of sculpture in the later 4th century BC. The slope of the Acropolis was encircled by small cult sites, some extremely old. Some of these were restored at the same time, probably at the instigation of Lykourgos when he was financial administrator, and decorated with reliefs. A procession of archaizing erotes with sacred implements decorated a balustrade frieze in the Sanctuary of Eros and Aphrodite to the north; and a series of doves holding a woollen ribbon (taenia) decorated the frieze on the naiskos to Aphrodite Pandemos at the south-west end. Here, too, it was mainly dedicatory reliefs that increased in the 4th century BC, particularly in the Sanctuary of Asklepios, first established lower down on the south slope around the beginning of the 4th century BC.

Hellenistic period (323–31 BC*) and later.* In this period, right up until Imperial Roman times, there were few changes overall on the Acropolis, and little new building. Because of awareness of both the cultural and political significance for Athens of this monumental complex, efforts were evidently concentrated on conserving it. Furthermore, important statues and even reliefs were copied and reproduced, thus spreading knowledge of Classical Attic sculpture and its fame through the Mediterranean world and indirectly ensuring its continuing legacy.

(b) Non-architectural.

*Geometric and Archaic periods (*c. *900–*c. *500/480* BC*).* In both these periods, most dedications on the Acropolis were small statuettes or implements decorated with figures (the costly bronze tripods with ring handles supported by figures or feet decorated with reliefs are particularly lavish). Later 7th-century BC stone sculpture from the Acropolis includes marble lamps with women's heads. Terracotta votive offerings from this period and later included figures of standing or seated women, representing the goddess receiving the gift or the woman actually dedicating it.

Life-size marble statues began to be dedicated in the 7th century BC. These originally resembled small-scale statues and were dedicated either to deities (particularly Athena herself) or to Nike (personification of Victory) as thanksgiving for a victory, for example the *Nike* (Athens, Acropolis Mus., 690) promised by the Polemarch Kallimachos for victory in the battle of Marathon, in which he fell in 490 BC. Daemonic figures such as sphinxes were also popular. In the 6th century BC the nobility, soon followed by rich middle-class citizens, began dedicating free-standing statues representing themselves, preferably in the image of a youthful figure (*see* KORE and KOUROS). Girls from rich backgrounds served in the cult of Athena, and many korai (statues of maidens with elaborately draped clothes and rich jewellery) survive. This fashion reached its height in the later 6th century BC. Figures of young men are rarer, and are mostly in the standard form of the naked kouros; the transition from Archaic to Classical at the beginning of the 5th century BC is particularly clearly recognizable in these statues (*see also* GREECE, ANCIENT, §IV, 2(ii)(c) and (iii)(a)). Equestrian statues are confined to the Archaic period; they were a form of aristocratic self-depiction, which the democracy of the 5th century BC no longer tolerated. One horseman wears Scythian garb, which has been painted on (Athens, Acropolis Mus.).

Such statues were symbols of rank and dignity. They occasionally provide indications of the subject's age (e.g. the beard in the Rampin Horseman; Paris, Louvre) or have a dignified enthroned pose or, towards the end of the 6th century BC, adopt the prestigious form of the seated scribe. They also include such works as the *Calf Bearer* (*see* GREECE, ANCIENT, fig. 52) or even the statue of a man riding a hippalectryon (a hybrid creature combining a horse and a cock; both Athens, Acropolis Mus.). These Archaic statues are vital in establishing a chronology, since many were found in the Persian debris of 480/479 BC. Late in the Archaic period the motif of a round dance occurs in the first of a series of marble dedicatory reliefs (e.g. Athens, Acropolis Mus., 702). In these, too, the donor could consecrate himself in the image itself. There follow mannered sub-Archaic reliefs, showing people sacrificing before Athena (e.g. Athens, Acropolis Mus., 581), and small terracotta plaques depicting Athena.

*Classical period (*c. *500/480–323* BC*).* As soon as Athens had been liberated, dedications recommenced. Few original works survive, but inscriptions on stone bases for bronze statues can be correlated with Pausanias' account. A selection of the best-known statues, most of 5th-century BC date, mentioned in topographical sequence in his mid-2nd-century AD description of the Acropolis (*Guide to Greece* I.xxii.4–xxviii, 3) provides a rough idea of their position. When the Persians devastated the Acropolis only a few statues of Athena survived, including the seated *Athena* by Endoios (Athens, Acropolis Mus., 625) and the venerable cult images, no longer extant, of *Athena* and the wooden *Hermes*, which reputedly fell from the sky and were housed in the Erechtheion, as well as an older seated image of *Artemis Brauronia* in the Brauroneion. Bronze statues mentioned by Pausanias (e.g. the *Lioness* made by Amphikrates for Leaina, the woman friend of the Tyrannicides; Pliny *Natural History* XXXIV.72) could not have been made until after the Persian withdrawal, replacing what had been lost. The Chalkotheke was later used as a repository for all types of dedicatory gifts made of bronze.

The foremost sculptors of the Early Classical period (*c.* 480–*c.* 450 BC), KRITIOS AND NESIOTES, were responsible for the new *Tyrannicides* group in the Agora. There were increasing numbers of dedicatory reliefs from private donors; these include the 'Mourning Athena' (Athens, Acropolis Mus., 695) and the dedicatory relief of the

Graces by Sokrates of Thebes (*fl c.* 470–460 BC), which is known through Neo-Attic copies.

From the High Classical period Pausanias named works by KALAMIS, MYRON OF ELEUTHERAI, Myron's son Lykios (*fl?c.* 450–420 BC), Pheidias, ALKAMENES and KRESILAS. Kalamis is credited with an *Aphrodite* dedicated by Kallias, perhaps identical with his *Sosandra* (both untraced); Myron with *Perseus* and the group of *Athena and Marsyas* (copy of *Athena*, Frankfurt am Main, Städel. Kstinst. & Städt. Gal.; copy of *Marsyas*, Rome, Vatican, Mus. Gregoriano Profano); and Lykios with a bronze boy bearing a vessel for consecrated water and two equestrian statues.

Inside the Parthenon itself stood Pheidias' colossal chryselephantine cult statue of *Athena Parthenos* (h. *c.* 10 m; destr.). Winged horses and sphinxes adorned her helmet, Nike stood on her hand, and the snake of the citadel curled beneath her shield. The gold used for the statue represented part of Athens' gold reserves in a removable form. The subjects depicted on this huge work echoed those of the architectural sculpture (*see* §(a) above). On the outside of the shield was a relief of an Amazonomachy, while there was a painting of a Gigantomachy inside. Round the soles of her sandals was a Centauromachy. The relief on the plinth with the birth of Pandora complemented the birth of Athena in the east pediment. The varied attempts to produce smaller-scale versions of *Athena Parthenos* are far more numerous than in the case of any other ancient Greek statue.

In addition to his *Athena Parthenos* in the Parthenon, Pheidias is associated by Pausanias with the soaring bronze *Athena Promachos*, dedicated from the tithe levied on the spoils of Marathon, with reliefs on the shield by the metalworker Mys after a drawing by PARRHASIOS, remains of the base and foundations of which have been preserved on the Acropolis; with *Athena Lemnia*, a dedication from the Attic chleruchs (settlers) on Lemnos (*c.* 450–440 BC; copies Dresden, Gemäldegal. Neue Meister); and the *Apollo Parnopios*, possibly identical with the Kassel *Apollo* (*c.* 450 BC; copy, Kassel, Hess. Landesmus.). Pausanias mentioned Alkamenes in connection with the archaizing *Hermes Propylaios* (copy on a herm, Istanbul, Archaeol. Mus.) and *Prokne with Itys* (*c.* 430–20 BC; Athens, Acropolis Mus.), and Kresilas in connection with *Dieitrephes Pierced by Arrows* and *Pericles* (copy on a herm, London, BM). Furtwängler suggested that Pericles himself may have dedicated the statues of his father *Xanthippos* and of Xanthippos' friend, the poet *Anakreon in his Cups* (copy e.g. Copenhagen, Ny Carlsberg Glyp.), attributed to Pheidias. There was a bronze statue of *Athena Hygieia* by Pyrrhos, and Themistokles' sons dedicated a bronze image of *Artemis Leukophryne.* As well as the bronze *Trojan Horse* by STRONGYLION, the Peloponnesian War gave rise to statues of the generals Phormion, Tolmides and his seer, and Oinobios.

Pausanias also mentioned works by two pupils of Polykleitos from the Late Classical period (*c.* 375–*c.* 323 BC): *Phrixos Offering a Ram* by NAUKYDES, and *Io* and *Kallisto* by Deinomenes (from *c.* beginning of the 4th century BC). According to an inscription, the huge figure of *Syeris*, an old serving-woman attending Lysimache, the priestess of Athena, was by Nikomachos, while *Lysimache* herself was portrayed by the realistic portrait sculptor DEMETRIOS OF ALOPEKE (Pliny: *Natural History* XXXIV.76). In the Brauroneion there was a cult image of *Artemis* by PRAXITELES, while a statue of *Zeus* by LEOCHARES stood beside *Zeus Polieus.* Among original works on the Acropolis of late 5th- and 4th-century BC date, there was a preponderance of pedestals with reliefs commemorating victories, initially including military successes in the Peloponnesian War, then mainly victories at the Panathenaic games. Among the many dedicatory reliefs were distinctive record reliefs: these clearly dated monuments illustrate decisions made by the people of Athens and were publicly displayed on the Acropolis (*see* GREECE, ANCIENT, §IV, 1(i)(c)).

Most of the remaining statues mentioned by Pausanias not on account of the artists who made them but because of their significance or mythical subject-matter (e.g. the bronze bull on the Areopagus) probably also dated from the Classical period. This category included local myths, such as groups echoing the themes of the Parthenon pediment (*see* §(a) above): the contest between Athena (with the olive tree) and Poseidon (with the spring) for possession of Attica, or Athena's birth from the head of Zeus. Three sculptural groups represent the deeds of Theseus: his confrontations with the Minotaur and with the Marathonian bull (dedicated by the people of Marathon), and his legitimation by finding the tokens hidden by Aegeus under a rock. Herakles appeared only twice (strangling snakes as a child, and fighting Kyknos). A boar hunt (presumably the Kalydonian boar) must have been a group composed of several figures.

Hellenistic period (323–31 BC) and later. A quadriga with the statue of *Eumenes II of Pergamon* on a tall pedestal in front of the Propylaia dates from this period. His brother Attalos II (*reg* 160–139 BC) dedicated numerous programmatic statues depicting the foes of the civilized Greek world in their death throes, ranging from giants to Amazons and Persians to the Gauls whom the Pergamene kings had themselves conquered. Pausanias mentioned only this 'small' dedicatory gift from Attalos on the south wall of the Acropolis and the statue of the early Hellenistic general *Olympiodoros* beside it, and from the Imperial period only a statue of *Hadrian* inside the Parthenon.

BIBLIOGRAPHY

GENERAL

G. Dickins and S. Casson: *Catalogue of the Acropolis Museum*, i–ii (Cambridge, 1912–21)
M. Schede: *Die Burg von Athen* (Berlin, 1922)
O. Walter: *Beschreibung der Reliefs im kleinen Akropolismuseum in Athen* (Vienna, 1923)
A. E. Raubitschek and L. H. Jeffery: *Dedications from the Athenian Acropolis* (Cambridge, MA, 1949)
J. Travlos: *Pictorial Dictionary of Ancient Athens* (London, 1971)
M. S. Brouskari: *Musée de l'Acropole* (Athens, 1974)
J. Boardman: *Greek Sculpture: The Archaic Period* (London, 1978)
M. S. Brouskari: *The Monuments of the Acropolis* (Athens, 1978)
S. Bancroft: *Problems Concerning the Archaic Acropolis at Athens* (diss., Princeton U., NJ, 1979)
N. Himmelmann: 'Zur Entlohnung künstlerischer Tätigkeit in klassischen Bauinschriften', *Jb. Dt. Archäol. Inst.*, xciv (1979), pp. 127–42
F. Felten: *Griechische tektonische Friese archaischer und klassischer Zeit* (Waldsassen, 1984)
J. Boardman: *Greek Sculpture: The Classical Period* (London, 1985)
J. Floren: *Die griechische Plastik* (Munich, 1987)
U. Muss and C. Schubert: *Die Akropolis von Athen* (Graz, 1988)

L. Schneider and C. Höcker: *Die Akropolis von Athen: Antikes Heiligtum und modernes Reiseziel* (Cologne, 1990)

ARCHITECTURAL

T. Wiegand: *Die archaische Poros-Architektur der Akropolis zu Athen* (Kassel, 1904)
A. H. Smith: *The Sculptures of the Parthenon* (London, 1910)
R. Heberdey: *Altattische Porosskulptur* (Vienna, 1919)
R. Carpenter: *The Sculpture of the Nike Temple Parapet* (Cambridge, MA, 1929)
W.-H. Schuchhardt: 'Die Entstehung des Parthenonfrieses', *Jb. Dt. Archäol. Inst.*, xlv (1930), pp. 218–80
——: 'Die Sima des alten Athenatempels der Akropolis', *Mitt. Dt. Archäol. Inst.: Athen. Abt.*, lx–lxi (1935–6), pp. 1–111
F. Brommer: *Die Metopen des Parthenon* (Mainz, 1959)
——: *Die Skulpturen der Parthenon-Giebel* (Mainz, 1963)
W.-H. Schuchhardt: 'Archaische Bauten auf der Akropolis zu Athen', *Archäol. Anz.* (1963), pp. 798–823
P. N. Boulter: 'The Frieze of the Erechtheion', *Ant. Plast.*, x (1970), pp. 7–30
K. Stähler: 'Zur Rekonstruktion und Deutung der Gigantomachiegiebel von der Akropolis', *Antike und Universalgeschichte: Festschrift H. E. Stier* (Münster, 1972), pp. 88–112
M. Robertson: *The Parthenon Frieze* (London, 1975)
H. Lauter: 'Die Koren des Erechtheion', *Ant. Plast.*, xvi (1976), pp. 7–52
F. Brommer: *Der Parthenonfries* (Mainz, 1977)
K. Stähler: 'Der Zeus aus dem Gigantomachiegiebel der Akropolis', *Boreas*, i (1978), pp. 28–31
E. Berger, ed.: *Parthenon-Kongress: Basel, 1982*
J. Boardman: *The Parthenon and its Sculptures* (London, 1985)
R. Osborne: 'The Viewing and Obscuring of the Parthenon Frieze', *J. Hell. Stud.* (1987), pp. 98–105
M. Brouskari: 'Aus dem Giebelschmuck des Athena-Nike-Tempels', *Bonn. Jb. Rhein. Landesmus. Bonn. & Ver. Altertfreund. Rheinlande*, suppl. xlvii (1989), pp. 115–18 [Festschrift for N. Himmelmann]
W. Erhardt: 'Der Torso Wien I 328 und der Westgiebel des Athena-Nike-Tempels auf der Akropolis in Athen', *Bonn. Jb. Rhein. Landesmus. Bonn. & Ver. Altertfreund. Rheinlande*, suppl. xlvii (1989), pp. 119–27 [Festschrift for N. Himmelmann]
O. Palagia: *The Pediments of the Parthenon*, vii of *Monumenta graeca et romana* (Leiden, New York and Cologne, 1993)

NON-ARCHITECTURAL

A. Furtwängler: *Meisterwerke der griechischen Plastik* (Leipzig, 1893)
H. Payne and G. M. Young: *Archaic Marble Sculpture from the Acropolis* (London, 1936)
H. Schrader, W.-H. Schuchhardt and E. Langlotz: *Die archaischen Marmorbildwerke der Akropolis* (Frankfurt am Main, 1939)
E. Langlotz and W.-H. Schuchhardt: *Archaische Plastik auf der Akropolis* (Frankfurt am Main, 1943)
W. Fuchs: 'Die Vorbilder der neuattischen Reliefs', *Jb. Dt. Archäol. Inst.*, suppl. xx (1959) [whole issue]
G. M. A. Richter: *Korai: Archaic Greek Maidens* (London, 1966)
N. Leipen: *Athena Parthenos: A Reconstruction* (Toronto, 1971)
L. Schneider: 'Zur sozialen Bedeutung der archaischen Korenstatuen', *Hamburg. Beitr. Archäol.*, suppl. ii (1975) [whole issue]
H. Knell: 'Die Gruppe von Prokne und Itys', *Ant. Plast.*, xvii (1978), pp. 9–19
E. Voutiras: *Studien zu Interpretation und Stil griechischer Porträt des 5. und frühen 4. Jh* (diss., University of Bonn, 1980)
E. B. Harrison: 'Motifs of the City-siege on the Shield of Athena Parthenos', *Amer. J. Archaeol.*, lxxxv (1981), pp. 281–317
G. Daltrop and P. C. Bol: *Athena des Myron* (Frankfurt am Main, 1983)
O. Palagia: 'In Defense of Furtwängler's Athena Lemnia', *Amer. J. Archaeol.*, lxxxvii (1983), pp. 81–4
D. Mauruschat: 'Ein neuer Vorschlag zur Rekonstruktion der Schildamazonomachie der Athena Parthenos', *Boreas*, x (1987), pp. 32–58

REINHARD STUPPERICH

2. AGORA. The Agora was the large open square northwest of the Acropolis that constituted the civic and commercial centre of Classical Athens. It was reserved for public functions, meetings, theatrical events, festivals, markets, elections and the like. During the Bronze Age and Iron Age it had been used for habitation and as a burial-ground, and its use as the civic centre seems to date from the mid-6th century BC, when the first public buildings were erected along its west side. By the end of the 6th century BC its limits were clearly defined by boundary stones, and a great street, known as the Panathenaic Way, ran diagonally through the square, leading from the city gate in the west to the Acropolis (see figs 15 and 16). The ancient site has been excavated under the direction of the American School of Classical Studies at Athens since 1931.

(i) Architecture. (ii) Sculpture.

(i) Architecture.

(a) Greek.

Religious. Though few structures were set up within the square itself, one exception was the Altar of the Twelve Gods, erected by the younger Peisistratos in 522/521 BC. Though the altar itself has disappeared under the modern subway, part of its enclosure wall survives and was apparently rebuilt on several occasions. The altar's prominent location at the centre of the ancient city caused it to be regarded as the principal milestone, from which all distances were measured.

The main sacred structures in the Classical Agora were the Stoa of Zeus Eleutherios (15b and 16b) along the west side and the Temple of Hephaistos (Hephaisteion), which crowns the hill to the west (15c and 16c). The Stoa of Zeus, built around 430–420 BC to commemorate the Greek victory over the Persians in 479 BC, had a façade of Pentelic and Hymettian marble and limestone walls. Its outer columns were Doric, its inner ones Ionic, and it was

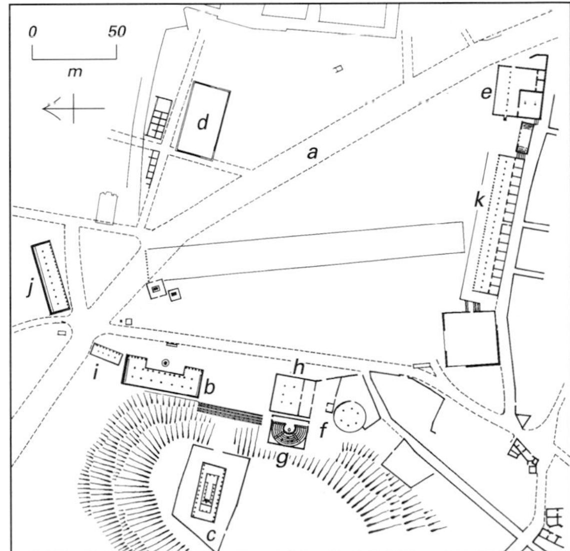

15. Athens, plan of the Agora, *c.* 400 BC; (a) Panathenaic Way; (b) Stoa of Zeus Eleutherios; (c) Temple of Hephaistos (Hephaisteion); (d) law courts; (e) mint; (f) tholos; (g) New Bouleuterion; (h) Metroon; (i) Royal Stoa; (j) Stoa Poikile; (k) South Stoa I

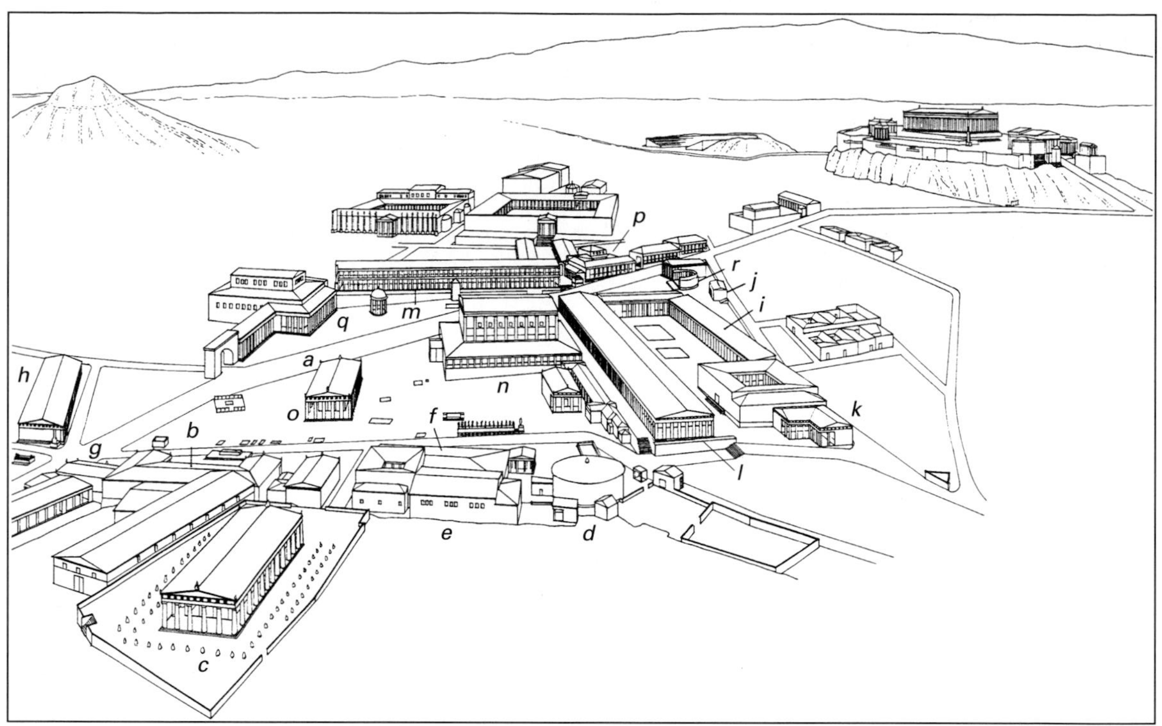

16. Athens, aerial reconstruction of Agora, *c.* AD 150: (a) Panathenaic Way; (b) Stoa of Zeus Eleutherios; (c) Temple of Hephaistos (Hephaisteion); (d) tholos; (e) New Bouleuterion; (f) Metroon; (g) Royal Stoa; (h) Stoa Poikile; (i) South Stoa I; (j) fountain-house, 6th century BC; (k) fountain-house, 4th century BC; (l) Middle Stoa; (m) Stoa of Attalos; (n) Odeion of Agrippa; (o) Temple of Ares; (p) Library of Flavius Pantainos; (q) Basilica of Hadrian; (r) nymphaeum

among the earliest stoas with projecting wings. The Hephaisteion, popularly though incorrectly known as the 'Theseion', remains the best preserved of all Doric temples. All the columns and the full entablature of its canonical peristyle (6×13 columns; for plan *see* GREECE, ANCIENT, fig. 8e) survive, as do the walls of the cella up to ceiling level, though the present roof is of later date. The temple is largely of Pentelic marble and dates from the mid-5th century BC, though it may have taken a generation or more to complete. It carries more sculptural decoration than any other Classical temple except for the Parthenon. Excavations around the building uncovered planting pits (*see* GREECE, ANCIENT, fig. 36), indicating that the sanctuary was landscaped with rows of shrubs and bushes. The Hephaisteion was converted into the Christian church of St George in the Kerameikos, probably in the 7th century AD, resulting in the addition of an apse at the east end and the removal of its pronaos columns and doorwall. This conversion also contributed to its unusually fine state of preservation (for illustration *see* TRABEATED CONSTRUCTION).

Civic. Around all four sides of the Agora square stood many of the buildings used in the administration of the city, of which the magistrates' offices, the senate house, the senate dining-room, the archives, the law courts (15d) and the mint (15e) have been identified. The complex along the west side served as the centre of government: Archaic buildings, destroyed by the Persians in 480 BC, were rebuilt and served with modifications for several centuries. The bouleuterion was the chamber for the 500 councillors selected annually from all qualified citizens, and the tholos (15f and 16d) served as dining-hall and dormitory for members of its executive committee (*prytaneis*). The Old Bouleuterion (early 5th century BC) was replaced around 415–406 BC by the New Bouleuterion (15g and 16e), recessed into the hillside behind it. This consisted essentially of an auditorium, but it received a porch on its south side and a propylon to its east in the later 4th century BC. The Old Bouleuterion, known as the Metroon (15h and 16f) because it had replaced a small Archaic temple as the focus for the worship of the Mother of the Gods, housed a cult statue by Pheidias or Agorakritos. However, it continued to serve as state archive, while more ephemeral notices were displayed on the long base carrying statues of the Eponymous Heroes. Though their poor state of preservation makes their internal arrangements uncertain, most of the public buildings of the Athenian democracy are surprisingly modest in their scale and building materials: there was only just room for 500 senators in the bouleuterion, the Royal Stoa (Stoa Basileios; 15i and 16g) is surprisingly small (17.72×7.18 m), and dining in the tholos must have been decidedly crowded. The superstructures of several public buildings seem to have been merely of mud-brick. Pausanias described paintings he saw in the bouleuterion (*Guide to Greece* I.iii.5), but lavish decoration was generally confined to religious buildings.

Other Archaic and Classical public buildings in the Agora that were not built to serve a single civic function include stoas, which provided shelter from both sun and rain. The several stoas in the Doric order illustrate the development of the type over a considerable period, from the Royal Stoa (*c.* 500 BC; *see* GREECE, ANCIENT, fig. 25) to the Stoa Poikile (*c.* 470–460 BC; 15j and 16h) to South Stoa I (*c.* 430–420 BC; 15k and 16i). Though all were generally modest in construction, they increased in size and became progressively more sophisticated in their interior design. In addition, two fountain-houses, one of the 6th century BC (16j) and another of the 4th (16k), provided water for the crowds that frequented the square (*see* GREECE, ANCIENT, §II, 1(i)(b)).

Major alterations to the Agora took place in late Hellenistic times after Athens had recovered its independence (228 BC) from the Macedonian successors of Alexander the Great. Several great stoas were built around the square, giving it a more regular layout similar to those of the planned agoras of the Hellenistic East. The southern part of the square was separated from the rest by the great Middle Stoa (l. *c.* 150 m, early 2nd century BC; 16l) built largely of limestone in the Doric order. A more lavish stoa was erected by King Attalos of Pergamon (*reg* 159–138 BC) along the east side of the square (16m; for illustration *see* STOA, §1). Rebuilt by the American School of Classical Studies in 1952–6, it was a two-storey structure of marble and limestone, with a double colonnade and 20 shops on each floor. Its columns were of both the Doric and Ionic orders, with a Pergamene adaptation of the Egyptian palm-leaf capital on the internal columns of the upper floor. To match the great colonnades to the south and east of the square, the old Metroon was rebuilt in the 2nd century BC and provided with a marble façade including 14 Ionic columns.

Early in the 1st century BC Athens unwisely sided with Mithradates of Pontus in his revolt against Rome, and in 86 BC the city was sacked by the Roman general Sulla. Several buildings in the Agora were damaged, especially those in the south part of the square. When Athens recovered its prosperity in Augustan times the Agora was transformed by the addition of new Roman buildings.

(b) Roman. Much of the central square was taken up by the Odeion of Agrippa (*c.* 15 BC; 16n; for illustration *see also* ODEION), built largely of marble and donated by M. Vipsanius Agrippa. This could seat about 1000 people, and its upper storey above the auditorium was surrounded on both the inside and outside by Corinthian columns and pilasters. However, little remains, except for one seat and part of the polychrome paving of the *orchestra* (the place where the chorus danced). The edifice was rebuilt in Antonine times. The open square was further diminished by the re-erection in the Agora of a 5th-century BC Doric temple, which seems from Pausanias' account (*Guide to Greece* I.viii.5) to have been dedicated to Ares (16o). Pieces of several other Classical buildings from Attica (Sounion, Thorikos) were also reused in 1st-century AD temples presumed to have housed imperial cults. Thereafter, buildings were added only gradually. In around AD 100 a library was donated by T. Flavius Pantainos (16p). It included a peristyle court and three stoas and stood alongside the Panathenaic Way, just south of the Stoa of Attalos. In Hadrianic times a great basilica was erected (16q); it is now extremely ruinous and largely concealed under modern buildings. It was sited at the north-east corner of the square. In Antonine times a large semicircular nymphaeum (16r) provided a new source of water at the south-east corner. By the mid-2nd century AD the Agora had reached the fullest limits of its architectural development.

The invasion of the Heruli in AD 267 struck a blow from which the Agora never really recovered. Many buildings were utterly destroyed and the rest severely damaged. When Athens was refortified, as late as AD 280, the western section of the city wall was built almost entirely with reused fragments from the Agora, and the old square was not even included within the defences of the late Roman city. The area lay in ruins for almost a century and a half, until building activity resumed in the early 5th century AD with the construction of a huge gymnasium complex comprising many rooms, large courtyards and bathing facilities. Reconstruction work also took place in the eastern part of the Library of Pantainos, and stoas were built to line the street leading across the north part of the square. Large villas on the slopes above may have housed the famous sophists and philosophers of the late Roman city. The closure of the Athenian philosophical schools by Justinian in AD 529 started the city's decline, and the buildings of the Agora were finally destroyed by the Slavs in AD 582/3.

BIBLIOGRAPHY

R. E. Wycherley: *Literary and Epigraphical Testimonia* (1957), iii of *The Athenian Agora* (Princeton, 1953–)

H. A. Thompson and R. E. Wycherley: *The Agora of Athens* (1972), xiv of *The Athenian Agora* (Princeton, 1953–)

J. M. Camp: *The Athenian Agora* (London, 1986)

——: *The Athenian Agora Guide* (Athens, 1990)

JOHN CAMP

(ii) Sculpture. The original contexts of only a few excavated sculptures from the Agora are known. Archaic groups depicting *Herakles and the Nemean Lion* (*c.* 530–520 BC; Athens, Agora Mus., S. 1449) and a *Lion Savaging a Bull* (*c.* 500–490 BC; Athens, Agora Mus., S. 1972) come from small unlocated buildings of poros limestone. The Webb Head (London, BM) is a Roman copy of Harmodias from the *Tyrannicides* group by ANTENOR, while fragments of plaster casts (Báia, Parco Archeol.) and Roman copies (e.g. Naples, Mus. Archeol. N.) of the later *Tyrannicides* by KRITIOS AND NESIOTES also survive. Herms were set up at the north-west corner of the Agora from the 6th century BC onwards.

Attempts have been made to identify copies of the ten bronze statues of the Eponymous Heroes mentioned by Pausanias (*Guide to Greece* I.v.1–5). The *Hero* in the Boboli Gardens, Florence, has been identified on stylistic grounds (Dörig, 1967) as a copy of the *Erechtheus* (*c.* 450–440 BC) by MYRON OF ELEUTHERAI referred to by Pausanias (*Guide to Greece* IX.xxx.1), though whether it stood on the base found in the Agora is uncertain. The statue of the *Enthroned Mother of the Gods* by AGORAKRITOS from the Metroon was the model for a copy (Chaironria, Archaeol. Mus.) now linked to a female crowned bronze head probably of the Augustan period (Paris, Bib. N., Cab. Médailles, 614) based on an original from *c.* 430 BC. Fragments from the Temple of Ares (5th century BC) by

17. Athens, Agora, cult statue of *Apollo Patroos* by Euphranor, mid-4th century BC (Athens, Agora Museum)

the workshop of ALKAMENES have not yet been interpreted. The Borghese *Ares* (Paris, Louvre), once mistakenly thought to be modelled on the cult image, originally formed part of a group of statues at Olympia (Pausanias: *Guide to Greece* V.xxii.2–3).

The metopes on the east façade of the Hephaisteion (mid-5th century BC) depict the *Labours of Herakles*, while four metopes on the north flank and four on the south show the *Deeds of Theseus.* The east frieze depicts *Erechtheus and the Athenians Fighting the Thracians*, while the west frieze bears a *Centauromachy.* The cult statue of *Athena* has survived as copies of the Cherchel type (e.g. Paris, Louvre), while the *Hephaistos* by Alkamenes is depicted on a Roman lamp (Athens, N. Archaeol. Mus.), and is copied by the Pharaklas Torso (Athens, N. Archaeol. Mus.) and a head (Rome, Vatican, Mus. Chiaramonti, 1211). The torso of the colossal *Apollo Patroos* (see fig. 17) by EUPHRANOR was discovered near its temple, and its appearance is also attested by the *Apollo Kitharoidos* (*c.* 2nd century AD; Rome, Vatican, Sala a Croce Greca).

BIBLIOGRAPHY

E. Harrison: *Archaic and Archaistic Sculpture* (1965), xi of *The Athenian Agora* (Princeton, 1953–)
J. Dörig: 'Myron's Erechtheus', *Ant. Plast.*, vi (1967), pp. 21–7
——: *La Frise est de l'Héphaisteion* (Mainz, 1985)
J. M. Camp: *The Athenian Agora* (London, 1986)

JOSÉ DÖRIG

3. KERAMEIKOS. The Kerameikos, or potters' quarter, was a large area demarcated as early as the 4th century BC with inscribed boundary stones, some of which have been found *in situ.* Its precise extent, origin and relation to the Agora nevertheless remain uncertain. The boundary stones and literary sources indicate that it covered an area both inside and outside the Themistoklean wall (479 BC), while in the 2nd century AD (Pausanias: *Guide to Greece* I.iii.1–xiv.6) it even included the Agora. The Kerameikos is now confined to a smaller district around the Dipylon ('double gate'; see fig. 18a), which lies to the north-west of the Library of Hadrian (see fig. 4d above) and has been excavated since the early 20th century by the German Archaeological Institute. This area was used for burials continuously from the 11th century BC until late Roman times, providing an excellent sequence of funerary sculpture and Attic pottery, as well as an insight into changing Athenian burial customs.

(i) Architecture. From the early 5th century BC onwards the Kerameikos was traversed by a section of the city wall. This was originally built in great haste at the instigation of

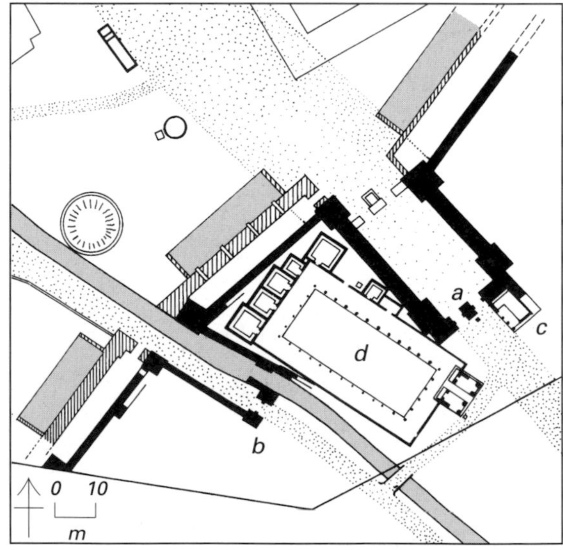

18. Athens, plan of the Kerameikos, late 4th century BC: (a) Dipylon; (b) Sacred Gate; (c) fountain-house; (d) Pompeion

Themistokles, and many tombstones overturned during the Persian invasion (480/479 BC) were incorporated in it. Despite repairs and rebuilding, in both the early and late 4th century BC and in Roman times, its structure remained largely unaltered, consisting of a stone socle with a mud-brick superstructure. In the 4th century BC a moat and outer wall were added in front of it, but the moat and much of the wall itself fell into disuse after the siege of Athens by Sulla in 86 BC. Included in this section of wall are two major city gates: the Sacred Gate (18b) and the larger Dipylon, a little to its north-east. However, only the gates' lower courses remain. Both were set back behind the face of the wall to form an open courtyard in which an enemy would be exposed to attack from three sides. The Sacred Gate gave access to the Sacred Way leading to Eleusis, while the Dipylon served a broad street stretching north-west as far as the Academy. Just inside the Dipylon was a small marble fountain-house (second half of the 4th century BC; 18c), comprising an L-shaped basin and porch of three Ionic columns with unusual bases.

A large building known as the Pompeion (18d) was crammed into the irregular area between the two gates. It had a peristyle courtyard with dining-rooms opening off its north-west and north-east sides and a far more lavish marble propylon set off-centre in its south-east side and leading to the Panathenaic Way. The building was apparently employed for marshalling the Panathenaic procession in honour of Athena and for storing equipment used in the parade, while the dining-rooms catered for the public feasts of priests and magistrates. The modest materials used in the main structure reflected Athens' straitened economic condition at the end of the 5th century BC. The building was destroyed by Sulla in 86 BC and was replaced by a basilica-like structure in the 2nd century AD. A little to the south of the Sacred Gate is another large building, 'Bau Z', still in the course of excavation.

BIBLIOGRAPHY

A. Brueckner: *Der Friedhof am Eridanos* (Berlin, 1909)

Kerameikos: Ergebnisse der Ausgrabungen (Berlin, 1939–)

U. Knigge: *Der Kerameikos von Athen: Führung durch Ausgraben und Geschichte* (Athens, 1988, Eng. trans. 1991)

JOHN CAMP

(ii) Sculpture. The tombs in the Kerameikos are among the most lavish in Athens and in the Geometric period (*c*. 900–*c*. 725 BC) were marked with large painted vases, such as those by the Dipylon Master (*see* GREECE, ANCIENT, fig. 85). In the Archaic period (*c*. 700–480 BC) these were replaced by sculpted stelai, which continued to be used in the Classical period (480–323 BC), except when prohibited by sumptuary laws. In addition to numerous private burials, there were public monuments for outstanding individuals and groups of warriors. The excavations have uncovered an official grave for a group of Spartans killed in the civil war of 403 BC, while the burial-ground for Athenian soldiers must have stood near by.

Most stone sculpture in the Kerameikos comes from grave monuments of various types. Among the earliest Archaic works is a relief on the shaft of a slender limestone stele (*c*. 580–570 BC; Athens, Kerameikos Mus., P 1132), which depicts the deceased in strict profile, as a naked warrior. Similar marble stelai depict male athletes (e.g. youthful discus thrower; *c*. 560 BC; Athens N. Archaeol. Mus., 38, 83; and a bearded boxer, *c*. 540–530 BC; Athens, Kerameikos Mus., P 1054). These stelai were surmounted by a crouching sphinx serving as a guardian of the tomb (example dated *c*. 570–560 BC; Athens, Kerameikos Mus., P 1050). During the Archaic period kouroi were also used to adorn the tombs of young aristocratic males (*see* KOUROS), and their remains include the colossal head and right arm of the Dipylon Kouros (*c*. 615–600 BC; Athens, N. Archaeol. Mus., 3372, 3965). A possibly helmeted head (shortly before 480 BC; Athens, Kerameikos Mus., P 1455) may belong to the statue of a soldier killed in the Persian Wars.

Three rectangular bases for funerary kouroi bear reliefs depicting cavalcades and chariot processions and scenes of youths exercising and playing games, which either allude to the heroization of the deceased or simply to their lifetime activities. Two bear identical scenes of naked ballplayers in various poses in a two-dimensional style (*c*. 520–510 BC; Athens, Kerameikos Mus., P 1002; Athens, N. Archaeol. Mus., 3476). When horsemen occur, they may be heroic symbols but more probably allude to the high social status of the deceased: examples include the body of a free-standing rider swathed in a cloak (*c*. 550 BC; Athens, Kerameikos Mus., P 1051-P 1051a). In contrast to those who had died while still relatively young, the elderly were commemorated by dignified seated statues (example dated *c*. 560 BC; Athens, Kerameikos Mus., P 1052).

During the Classical period the repertory of funerary sculpture changed, with the abandonment of symbols representing Archaic aristocratic ideals (kouros, sphinx, horseman) and the appearance of new ones. Sirens in the guise of musicians and mourners appeared from *c*. 370–360 BC as stelai finials or as independent statuettes, as in the two early examples connected with the workshop of KEPHISODOTOS (Athens, N. Archaeol. Mus., 774; Kerameikos Mus., P 761). Lions, which had also occurred on Archaic monuments, persisted; notable examples from the peribolus of Dionysios of Kollytos were depicted seizing the heads of calves, emphasizing the ferocity with which they would protect the tomb (*c*. 345–338 BC; Athens, N. Archaeol. Mus., 803, 804). A bull surmounting a pillar from the same peribolus *in situ* may allude to the name of the deceased or imply membership of a Dionysiac cult, while other monuments include two statues of Scythian archers (second half 4th century BC; Athens, N. Archaeol. Mus., 823, 824).

In the late 5th century BC marble vases—loutrophoroi and lekythoi—appeared as grave markers. Some were free-standing, with relief or painted decoration, but some stelai also bore depictions of loutrophoroi standing between lekythoi, imitating the emplacement of real vases on the peribolus tombs (e.g. the stele of a man from Skambonidai with lekythoi supported by sphinxes, *c*. 420–400 BC; Athens, Kerameikos Mus., P 280). Figural reliefs reappeared in Attica at the time of the building of the Parthenon (447–432 BC) and were carved on broad stelai, almost invariably featuring figures, as on the famous Hegeso Stele (*c*. 410 BC; Athens, N. Archaeol. Mus., 3624; *see* CHAIR, fig. 1 and GREECE, ANCIENT, fig. 42), showing a seated woman accompanied by the standing figure of her young maid. On the Ampharete Stele (*c*. 420 BC; Athens, Kerameikos

Mus., P 695) a dead grandmother is represented holding her dead grandchild, continuing to do in death what she had done in life; the 20-year-old Dexileos, who perished in the battle of Corinth, is depicted on his stele (*c.* 394/3 BC; Athens, Kerameikos Mus., P1130; *see* GREECE, ANCIENT, fig. 62) as a victorious mounted warrior in the iconographical tradition of cavalry battle scenes on state monuments for war dead. The Aristonautes Stele (*c.* 330–320 BC; Athens, N. Archaeol. Mus., 738) exemplifies several features of the latest monuments in the series. The figure of the deceased is almost free-standing and is housed in a deep naiskos (shrine-like stele); he is depicted alone, in the tradition of Archaic grave stelae, and his frontal pose hints at heroic status.

BIBLIOGRAPHY

H. Riemann: *Die Skulpturen vom 5. Jahrhundert bis in römische Zeit* (1940), ii of *Kerameikos: Ergebnisse der Ausgrabungen* (Berlin, 1939-)

K. F. Johansen: *The Attic Grave-reliefs of the Classical Period* (Copenhagen, 1951)

G. M. A. Richter: *The Archaic Gravestones of Attica* (London, 1961)

L. H. Jeffery: 'The Inscribed Gravestones of Archaic Attica', *Annu. Brit. Sch. Athens*, lvii (1962), pp. 123–6

C. W. Clairmont: *Gravestone and Epigram: Greek Memorials from the Archaic and Classical Period* (Mainz, 1970)

C. Dehl: 'Eine Gruppe früher Lutrophorenstelen aus dem Kerameikos', *Mitt. Dt. Archäol. Inst.: Athen. Abt.*, xcvi (1981), pp. 163–78

U. Knigge: 'Ein Jünglingskopf vom Heiligen Tor in Athen', *Mitt. Dt. Archäol. Inst.: Athen. Abt.*, xcviii (1983), pp. 45–56

U. Vedder: *Untersuchungen zur plastischen Ausstattung attischer Grabanlagen des 4. Jhs. v. Chr.* (Frankfurt am Main, 1985)

S. Ensoli: *L'Heróon di Dexileos nel ceramico di Atene: Problematica architettonica e artistica attica degli inizi del iv secolo a-C* (Rome, 1987)

C. W. Clairmont: *Classical Attic Tombstones*, 8 vols (Switzerland, 1993)

I. LEVENTI

4. TEMPLE OF OLYMPIAN ZEUS. This is the most conspicuous monument in the south-east part of ancient Athens (see figs 2b and 5f above). A massive temple (see fig. 19) originally laid out in the late 6th century BC by the Peisistratid tyrants (*see* PEISISTRATOS) on the remains of an earlier monumental structure, the building was in the Doric order and was planned on the scale of the great temples of Sicily and Asia Minor. All construction ceased with the downfall of the tyrants and the temple's massive limestone column drums were built into the Themistoklean fortification wall (479 BC). Building only resumed under Antiochos IV Epiphanes of Syria (175–163 BC), who identified himself with Zeus. He employed the Roman architect COSSUTIUS, and the new building was a giant octastyle dipteral Corinthian temple (110×43 m) with triple colonnades on its east and west fronts, making a total of 104 Pentelic marble columns. Work was carried out during Antiochos' reign, and in places had proceeded as high as the architrave by the time he died. It was left unfinished and only finally completed 300 years later by the Emperor Hadrian (*reg* AD 117–38), who took the epithet Olympios and shared the temple with Zeus. At this time a chryselephantine cult statue of *Zeus* was erected in the cella (Pausanias: *Guide to Greece* I.xviii.6), and a great marble-paved enclosure was built around the temple. Distinguishing between Roman and Hellenistic architectural phases is extremely difficult, however, especially since the column capitals of both eras are of canonical Corinthian type. Fragments from the roof of the building were found built into a nearby basilica of the 5th or 6th century AD, and the process of dilapidation has continued ever since. Only 15 of the original 104 columns remain standing, with a sixteenth stretched out on the ground where it fell during a storm in the 19th century.

19. Athens, Temple of Olympian Zeus, begun late 6th century BC, completed first half of 2nd century AD

BIBLIOGRAPHY

R. E. Wycherley: 'The Olympieion at Athens', *Gr., Roman & Byz. Stud.*, v (1964), pp. 161–79

H. Abramson: 'The Olympieion in Athens and its Connections with Rome', *CA Stud. Class. Ant.*, vii (1974), pp. 1–25

JOHN CAMP

5. HAGIOI APOSTOLOI. This Middle Byzantine church (see fig. 6i above) stands in the south-east corner of the Greek Agora. It closely resembles the churches of the Theotokos (*c.* AD 1000) at HOSIOS LOUKAS and Moni Petraki (?11th century AD) in Athens, combining the cross-in-square with a circular plan expanded by eight niches. It has no intermediate vault between the niches and main vaults, and, as in Moni Petraki, four free-standing columns support the central drum and dome. The drum is octagonal, with eight windows, each framed by a semicircular arch resting on slender colonettes and forming the characteristic rippling eaves line of Middle Byzantine Greek churches. Later additions to the church include the western narthex and interior tombs. Extensive remodelling and embellishment continued into the 19th century. The exterior of the church is richly patterned and colourful. The walls of poros limestone alternating with brick layers incorporate cloisonné masonry in the lower courses and ornamental dogtooth friezes, geometric patterns, and Kufic motifs higher up. The lower courses also contain large re-used stone blocks.

The dating of the church to the early 11th century is based on stylistic and structural comparisons with other churches. One of the main indicators for such a date is the Kufic brick ornament, which, according to the general trend of decreasing complexity in masonry patterns during their use in Greece, suggests that Hagioi Apostoloi was probably built after the Theotokos and Moni Petraki. The church was restored in 1954–7 by the American School of

Classical Studies during their excavation of the site. Additions mostly made in the 19th century were removed, and elements from other Agora buildings were added to the interior, for example the 17th-century wall paintings from the church of St Spyridon and some wall painting fragments from the 7th-century church of St George in the Temple of Hephaistos. Three colonnettes were restored to the dome drum, and the altar and altar screen were reconstructed on the basis of partial remains.

BIBLIOGRAPHY

A. Frantz: *The Church of the Holy Apostles* (1971), xx of *The Athenian Agora* (Princeton, 1953–)

R. Krautheimer: *Early Christian and Byzantine Architecture*, Pelican Hist. A. (Harmondsworth, 1965, rev. 4/1986)

ANNE McCLANAN

6. PANAGIA GORGOEPIKOOS. Middle Byzantine church situated to the south of Athens Cathedral. It is also known as St Eleutherios and the Small Metropolis. It is a cross-in-square church (12.2×7.6 m) with an eight-sided Athenian dome originally supported on four columns, which were replaced by piers during the restoration of 1833. The walls are built with blocks of Pentelic marble from ancient buildings and rest on a base with two steps as in ancient temples. The upper walls are decorated with a frieze of carved marble slabs from the ancient and Byzantine periods. Of special note is the architrave on the west façade with reliefs variously dated between 3rd century BC and 3rd century AD representing a calendar of Attic state festivals. Its decoration and evident classicism date the building to the end of the 12th century. At that time Michael Choniates (*c.* 1140–1220) was Metropolitan of Athens; he was a well-known classicist, with a background in the prominent intellectual circles of Constantinople, and the construction of this distinctively Athenian monument may be linked with his patronage. In the Turkish period the church served as a chapel to the Metropolitan House, and in 1839, when it housed the National Library, it still had wall paintings. In 1863, however, the interior was whitewashed, and the paintings were later destroyed.

BIBLIOGRAPHY

M. Chatzidakis: *Byzantini Athina: Keimena Manoli Chatzidaki* [Byzantine Athens: text by Manolis Chatzidakis] (Athens, n.d.)

A. Couchaud: *Choix d'églises byzantines en Grèce* (Paris, 1842)

D. Kampouroglou: *Ai palaiai Athenai* [Ancient Athens] (Athens, 1922)

A. Xyngopoulos: *Ta byzantina kai tourkika mnimeia ton Athinon: Euretirion ton mesaionikon mnimeion* [Byzantine and Turkish monuments of Athens: index of medieval monuments] (Athens, 1929)

A. Grabar: *Byzance: L'Art byzantin du moyen âge* (Paris, 1963)

A. Grabar: *Sculptures byzantines du moyen âge*, ii (Paris, 1976)

M. Chatzidakis: *Mesobyzantini techni* [Middle Byzantine art] (1979), viii of *Istoria Ellenikou ethnous* [History of the Greek nation] (Athens, 1901–79)

STAMATIA KALANTZOPOULOU

Athens Charter. *See under* CIAM.

Athfield, Ian (Charles) (*b* Christchurch, 15 July 1940). New Zealand architect. He studied at the University of Auckland School of Architecture (1961–3) and joined Structon Group Architects, Wellington, in 1963, becoming a partner in 1965. In 1968 he formed Athfield Architects with Ian Dickson (*b* 1949) and Graeme John Boucher (*b* 1944). An innovative designer who has continually questioned the orthodoxy of Modernism, Athfield established his reputation with small-scale domestic buildings during the 1970s. Additive plans, fragmented forms and allusions to the traditions of New Zealand colonial architecture characterize designs such as Athfield house, Wellington (begun 1968), and Cox house, Wellington (1975). Often clinging to precarious sites, his houses respond directly to the landscape. Athfield works closely with clients, often involving them in the construction process. In 1976 he won first prize in the International Competition for the Urban Environment of Developing Countries, Manila, Philippines, with a community-based project for rehousing Manila slum dwellers.

From 1980 the hand-crafted finishes and organic forms of Athfield's earlier works were replaced by greater refinement of detail and precision of forms (e.g. Custance house, Havelock North, 1982). His work ranged from sophisticated office towers (e.g. Hewlett-Packard building, Wellington, 1986, and Telecom building, Wellington, 1988), to highly individual, emotionally charged designs (e.g. Christian Science Church, Wellington, 1982) in which the iconoclasm and irreverence of his earlier works still prevailed. The Wellington Public Library (1987–91), part of a larger civic development, is Athfield's most significant public building to date, the classical restraint of its principal façade subverted by exuberant columns derived from indigenous nikau palms. Through his commitment to the social role of architecture and his success in creating a distinctive style from a diverse amalgam of historical and modern sources he played a major part in defining the individual qualities of contemporary New Zealand architecture.

BIBLIOGRAPHY

G. Melling: *Joyful Architecture: The Genius of New Zealand's Ian Athfield* (Dunedin, 1980)

R. Walden: 'New Zealand Rebel', *Archit. Rev.*, clxxi (1982), pp. 48–52

C. Aasen, ed.: 'Athfield Architects and Aasen-Athfield and Co., 1968–1993', *World Architecture Review*, iv (1993) [whole issue]

IAN J. LOCHHEAD

Athos. *See* MT ATHOS.

Athribis [anc. Egyp. Hwt-hery-ib; now Tell Atrib]. Site in Egypt, just north-west of Benha in the Nile Delta. The capital of the 10th nome administrative province of Lower Egypt, the town's religious name, Kemwer (the 'Great Black One'), was applied to the original local god (personified as a bull), the nome and the city itself. Subsequently the major deity was Khentekhtai, at first represented as a crocodile and additionally, from the 12th Dynasty (*c.* 1938–*c.* 1756 BC), as a falcon; mummified falcons dating from the Late Period (*c.*750–332 BC) have been found. The heart of Osiris was believed to be buried at Athribis, and Isis, Hathor, Sekhmet and Khwit, the major goddess after the New Kingdom (*c.* 1540–*c.* 1075 BC), also had cults there. It was also the birthplace of Amenhotpe, son of Hapu, royal architect to Amenophis III (*reg c.* 1390–*c.* 1353 BC). Apart from partial soundings and occasional discoveries by the Napoleonic expedition (1798), the Institute of Archaeology, Liverpool, under Sir Robert Mond and Emir Habib Lotfallah (1938) and others, the site was intermittently excavated by archaeologists from the University of Warsaw under Kazimierz Michałowski from 1957 to 1962.

Egyptian texts mention the existence of the town in the 4th Dynasty (*c.* 2575–*c.* 2465 BC), but no Old Kingdom monuments have yet been identified. The earliest known monuments date from the 12th Dynasty; thereafter, material exists for most periods until the 4th century AD. Among the New Kingdom monuments are a jamb of Tuthmosis III (*reg c.* 1479–*c.* 1426 BC; Cairo, Egyp. Mus.), a block with cartouches of Amenophis III (untraced), a stele (Cairo, Egyp. Mus., 46095), a pair of obelisks (one in Berlin, Ägyp. Mus., 12800), triad statues (badly damaged; *in situ*) and a figure of a lion (London, BM, 857) dating to the reign of Ramesses II (*c.* 1279–*c.* 1213 BC). Material from the Third Intermediate Period (*c.* 1075–*c.* 750 BC) includes reliefs of Shoshenq I (*reg c.* 950–*c.* 929 BC), a head from a royal statue (London, BM, 633), and a stele of Prince Meryre (London, BM, 1346). The earliest known temple remains are the foundation deposits of the 26th Dynasty king Amasis (*reg* 570–526 BC), who also dedicated a naos to Kemwer. Excavations in the northern part of the site yielded the sarcophagus of Queen Takhut, the wife of Psammetichus II (*reg* 595–589 BC) and the tombs of Tadubaste and Pefteuawiamun Tjaiemhorimu. In 1924 local people digging in the area discovered a cache of silver objects (Cairo, Egyp. Mus., 48859) weighing 50 kg and dating from the 26th Dynasty to the Ptolemaic period (664–30 BC), which contained ingots, jewellery and amulets. Ptolemy I (*reg* 304–284 BC) built a temple to Horus south of the main temple. Numerous Roman remains include a white marble stele with a Greek inscription of AD 374 from a triumphal archway bearing the name of the Emperor Valens (*reg* AD 364–78).

BIBLIOGRAPHY

LÄ

M. G. Daressy: 'Bas-reliefs d'Athribis', *An. Service Ant. Egypte*, xvii (1917), pp. 185–93

——: 'Statue de Zedher le Sauveur', *An. Service Ant. Egypte*, xviii (1919), pp. 114–58

M. H. Gauthier: 'Triade du Tell Atrib', *An. Service Ant. Egypte*, xxi (1921), pp. 211–13

R. Engelbach: 'The Treasure of Athribis (Benha)', *An. Service Ant. Egypte*, xxiv (1924), pp. 178–85

B. Porter and R. L. B. Moss, eds: *Topographical Bibliography*, iv (1934)

A. Rowe: 'A Short Report on Excavations of the Institute of Archaeology, Liverpool, at Athribis (Tell Atrib)', *An. Service Ant. Egypte*, xxxviii (1938), pp. 523–32

——: 'Preliminary Report on Excavations of the Institute of Archaeology, Liverpool, at Athribis', *An. Archaeol. & Anthropol.*, xxv (1938), pp. 123–37

P. Vernus: *Athribis* (Cairo, 1978)

J. Lecant: 'Fouilles et travaux en Egypte et au Soudan', *Orientalia*, lii (1983), p. 468; liii (1984), p. 354; liv (1985), pp. 342–3; lvi (1987), pp. 300–01; lvii (1988), p. 314

K. Myśliwiec: 'Polish Archaeological Work at Tell Atrib and Saqqara', *Proceedings of the Fifth International Congress of Egyptologists: Munich, 1989*, pp. 458–72

ANN BOMANN

Atkins [née Children]**, Anna** (*b* Tonbridge, Kent, 16 March 1799; *d* Halstead Place, Kent, 9 June 1871). English photographer and scientist. The only daughter of the scientist John George Children (1777–1852), she was a pioneering photographer and the first person to publish a photographically printed and illustrated book. Her privately published *British Algae*, issued in parts from 1843 to 1853, pre-dated William Henry Fox Talbot's *Pencil of Nature* (London, 1844) and stood for some time as the only sustained effort to apply photography to scientific illustration. Her plates of seaweed specimens were photograms, contact printed in the cyanotype, or blueprint, photographic process, invented in 1842 by her friend Sir JOHN HERSCHEL. In the early 1850s, collaborating with Anne Dixon (1799–1864), Atkins turned to creative expression with cyanotype photograms. Her visual approach, initially shaped by the requirements of scientific illustration rather than the conventions of Victorian art, was bold and direct and strongly anticipated the later photograms of Man Ray and others.

PHOTOGRAPHIC PUBLICATIONS

British Algae: Cyanotype Impressions, 3 vols (Sevenoaks, England, 1843–53)

BIBLIOGRAPHY

L. J. Schaaf: *Sun Gardens: Victorian Photograms by Anna Atkins* (New York, 1985)

J. Wilson: 'The Cyanotype', *Technology and Art: The Birth and Early Years of Photography*, ed. M. Pritchard (Bath, 1990), pp. 19–25

L. J. SCHAAF

Atkins, Roy. *See* ROY, NAMBA.

Atkinson, Fello. *See under* CUBITT, JAMES.

Atkinson, Isaac. *See* ANDERSON, JAMES.

Atkinson, John Augustus (*b* London, 1775; *d* ?London, ?1831–3). English painter and printmaker. At the age of nine he was taken to live in St Petersburg by his uncle, James Walker, who was an engraver in the service of Catherine II, Empress of Russia. Atkinson subsequently gained the patronage of the Empress and her son, Paul I (*reg* 1796–1801), executing a series of paintings on Russian history (e.g. *Victory of the Cossacks of the Don over the Tartars*) for them. He returned to England in 1801 and by 1808 was exhibiting as an Associate at the Royal Society of Painters in Water-Colours, showing such literary and patriotic pictures as *Shakespeare's 'Seven Ages'*. A series of his soft-ground etchings, *The Miseries of Human Life, by One of the Wretched* (London, BM), was published in London in 1807. He also produced sets of engravings of military costumes, such as *A Picturesque Representation of the Naval, Military and Miscellaneous Costumes of Great Britain* (London, 1812) and painted numerous watercolours (e.g. *HRH The Prince Regent, the Emperor of Russia and the King of Prussia Attended by Marshal Blücher at the Review in Hyde Park, 20 June 1814*, *c.* 1814; London, N. Army Mus.). In 1815 Josiah Boydell (1752–1817) sent him to the site of the Battle of Waterloo to collaborate with Arthur William Devis on a painting of the event (watercolour study, London, BM). In 1819 the painting was engraved by John Burnet. Atkinson aspired towards recognition as a painter of historical subjects and competed unsuccessfully in a competition sponsored by the British Institution for a military painting to hang in the Royal Military Hospital in Chelsea, London.

BIBLIOGRAPHY

Füssli; Redgrave

G. K. Nagler: *Neues allgemeines Künstler-Lexicon*, 22 vols (Munich, 1835–52, rev. Vienna, 2/1924)

T. Smith: *Recollections of the British Institution and Biographical Notices of the Artists Who There Received Premiums, 1805–1859* (London, 1860)

R. L. Binyon: *Catalogue of Drawings by British Artists and Artists of Foreign Origin Working in Great Britain, Preserved in the Department of Prints & Drawings in the British Museum*, i (London, 1898), p. 160

JOAN HICHBERGER

Atkinson, Lawrence [Laurence] (*b* Manchester, 17 Jan 1873; *d* Paris, 21 Sept 1931). English painter, sculptor and draughtsman. He studied singing and music in Berlin and Paris. At first he earned his living by establishing himself as a singing teacher in Liverpool and London. By July 1913, when he exhibited in the Allied Artists' Association in London, he was devoting an increasing amount of his energies to painting. His early work was Fauvist in affiliation, reflecting perhaps the teaching he had received at La Palette in Paris. Contact with Wyndham Lewis and the Vorticists led him to pursue a more abstract path. In the spring of 1914 he joined the REBEL ART CENTRE with Wyndham Lewis and other artists who appeared in *Blast* magazine later that year.

Little is known about the development of Atkinson's work at this crucial stage in his career. His signature was on the manifesto in the first issue of *Blast*, but his work was not reproduced in the magazine; his continuing involvement with other forms of art was demonstrated when his book of poems, *Aura*, was published in 1915. Atkinson seems to have remained on the margin of the Vorticist movement, agreeing to display three works, simply titled *Painting*, in the Vorticist Exhibition in London (June 1915), not as a group member but as one of the artists in a special 'Invited to show' section. The generality of the titles and reviews of the exhibition suggest that these pictures were abstract, even when they had a figurative basis. *Painting* (AC England), an elongated and austere work that suggests an interaction between a figure and its surroundings, may be one of them. The critic Horace Shipp, who knew Atkinson well and published a book about his art in 1922, wrote:

> Atkinson realizes that an object does not exist to itself alone, but that it is affected by its environment and in turn reacts towards it. Environment is thus given emotional as well as structural value. This element of what he has called 'spatial accordancy' is one which is of profound importance in his work.

Atkinson's finest surviving drawing is *Abstract Composition* (New York, MOMA), a large pyramidal design that displays a clear interest in the mechanistic forms explored by the other Vorticists. The image of an archetypal modern city is evoked in this monumental picture, but it lacks the explosive violence of Lewis's vision. Atkinson's work was fundamentally pacific in character, and after World War I his 'mystical temperament' (Shipp) led him towards a degree of abstraction more uncompromising than that of his recent allies. While the others gradually abandoned their former interest in machine forms and explored more representational alternatives, Atkinson started making sculpture in a pared-down idiom directly related to his Vorticist work. 'Atkinson has deliberately chosen to express himself in the graphic and plastic arts because he realizes the danger of the sensuous appeal of music as a power which holds the mind as he would say "to earth"' (Shipp); in his carvings of the 1920s Atkinson explored an interest in the subconscious which derived from 'the teachings and theories of Goethe and of his disciple Rudolf Steiner'.

Atkinson's sculpture has failed to survive in any quantity, but the reproductions in Shipp's book clearly reveal their simplified and geometric organization. His carving *L'Oiseau* (see Shipp: *The New Art*, p. 72) won him the Grand Prix at an exhibition in Milan (1921), and as a sculptor he exerted a profound influence on the early work of Merlyn Evans. Atkinson remained an isolated figure, however, out of step with the revival of interest in figurative art during the 1920s. By the time of his death his work was virtually forgotten, and only in retrospect can he be seen as an elusive yet single-minded pioneer of abstraction in 20th-century British art.

WRITINGS

Aura (London, 1915)

BIBLIOGRAPHY

Laurence Atkinson: Abstract Sculpture and Painting (exh. cat. by P. G. Konody and H. Leigh, London, Eldar Gal., 1921)

H. Shipp: *The New Art: A Study of the Principles of Non-representational Art and their Application in the Work of Lawrence Atkinson* (London, 1922)

——: *The Sculpture of Laurence Atkinson: A Brochure of Preferences* (London, 1922) [booklet]

R. Cork: *Vorticism and Abstract Art in the First Machine Age*, 2 vols (London, 1975–6)

RICHARD CORK

Atkinson, Robert (*b* Wigton, Cumbria, 1 Aug 1883; *d* London, 26 Dec 1952). English architect. A builder's son, he was articled in Newcastle upon Tyne and studied at University College and School of Art, Nottingham, before working in the London offices of John Belcher and Charles Edward Mallows (1864–1915) and R. Frank Atkinson (1871–1923), for whom in 1907 he designed a competition entry for County Hall (see *The Builder*, xciv, 1908, opp. p. 606), London. After returning from travel in Italy in 1904 Atkinson was in demand as a draughtsman and perspectivist; he 'ghosted' work for the landscape architect Thomas Hayton Mawson (1861–1933) and assisted R. Frank Atkinson in designing the Midland Adelphi Hotel (1912), Liverpool. As Headmaster of the Architectural Association School (1913–20), London, and Director of Education (1920–29), Atkinson helped to spread the Beaux-Arts style. His own work encompassed a simple Arts and Crafts style, neo-Georgian and even a Modernist style. His decorative skill was seen in the eclectic Regent Cinema (1922–4; destr.; see Ison), Brighton, with its vivid colouring. St Catharine's Church (1923; destr.; see exh. cat., pp. 28–9), Hammersmith, London, was a simple but effective arcaded structure. Other works include the Gresham Hotel (1927), O'Connell Street, Dublin, the Art Deco foyer of the Daily Express building (1932), London, Beddington and Wallington Town Hall (1935), Surrey, and the Barber Institute of Fine Arts (1939), Birmingham. Atkinson was influential both in the development of architectural education and as an assessor for several major competitions of the 1930s, including the RIBA building in London and Norwich City Hall.

WRITINGS

with H. Bagenal: *Theory and Elements of Architecture* (London, 1926), i/1

BIBLIOGRAPHY

'Review of the Architectural Work of Messrs R. Atkinson and G. L. Alexander, Architects', *Acad. Archit. & Archit. Rev.*, xlvii (1915), pp. 32–88 [special issue]

C. H. Reilly: *Representative British Architects of the Present Day* (London, 1931)
W. Ison: 'The Regent, Brighton: Europe's Wonder House of Entertainment', *J. Dec. A. Soc.*, vi (1981)
Robert Atkinson (exh. cat. by A. Powers, P. Spencer-Longhurst and G. Stamp, U. Birmingham, Barber Inst.; London, Archit. Assoc.; 1988)

ALAN POWERS

Atkinson, Thomas Lewis (*b* Salisbury, 4 April 1817; *d* 1889 or 1890). English engraver. He was active mainly in London, where he was apprenticed for seven years to the eminent engraver Samuel Cousins. Like his teacher, he engraved many plates after the works of John Everett Millais (e.g. the *Black Brunswicker*, 1860, Port Sunlight, Lady Lever A.G.; declared for publication on 16 June 1864 jointly by Henry Graves & Co. and Moore, McQueen & Co.) and Edwin Landseer (e.g. *In Time of War* and *In Time of Peace*, ex-Tate, London, destr.; published in 1864 by Henry Graves & Co. and Thomas Agnew). Francis Grant, William Powell Frith and Franz Xavier Winterhalter are among the other artists whose work he reproduced, but perhaps his best-known plate (untraced), published in 1877 by Thomas McLean, is that after *Flora* by Valentine W. Bromley (1848–72). One of his last plates was engraved in collaboration with Cousins: a reproduction in mezzotint of Millais's *Perfect Bliss* (untraced), declared by Thomas McLean on 30 March 1886.

BIBLIOGRAPHY

Victorian Engravings (exh. cat. by H. Beck, London, V&A, 1973)
R. K. Engen: *Dictionary of Victorian Engravers* (Cambridge, 1979)

ANTHONY DYSON

Atkinson, William (*b* Bishop Auckland, Durham, *c.* 1773; *d* Cobham, Surrey, 22 May 1839). English architect. He began his working life as a carpenter, but through the patronage of Dr Shute Barrington (1734–1826), Bishop of Durham, he became a pupil of James Wyatt. In 1796 he entered the Royal Academy Schools, London, where he gained a gold medal in 1797, and in 1805 he published a slim volume entitled *Picturesque Views of Cottages.* He is chiefly remembered as a country house architect and enjoyed an extensive practice in northern England and Scotland. His first major commissions were rebuilding works at Scone Palace (1803–6), Tayside, for the 3rd Earl of Mansfield and at Mulgrave Castle (1804), N. Yorks; a significant later commission was to extend Edward Blore's Abbotsford House (1822–3; for illustration *see* SCOTT, WALTER), Borders, for Sir Walter Scott; all these were early examples of the Gothic Revival style. His classical work at Broughton Hall (1809–11), N. Yorks, shows he was by no means bound to this style, and further proof of his adaptability can be found in his collaborations with the connoisseur Thomas Hope; they reconstructed The Deepdene (1818–19 and 1823), Surrey, in a picturesque Italianate manner and added a picture gallery to Hope's house (1819–20; destr. 1851) in Duchess Street, Portland Place, London. Through his interest in chemistry and geology, Atkinson invented a new form of cement that was widely used for both internal and external stucco work. His interest in botany led him to experiment in the 1820s with a system of hot water central heating for greenhouses (*see* GREENHOUSE), which he developed for domestic use with his kinsman and assistant, Thomas Tredgold (*fl* 1813–24); it apparently was widely employed in the 1830s, well in advance of other hot water systems.

PRINTS

Picturesque Views of Cottages (London, 1805)

BIBLIOGRAPHY

Colvin; Papworth
Gdnrs Mag., iii (1828)
A. Rowan: *The Castle Style* (diss., U. Cambridge, 1964)

NEIL BURTON

Atl, Dr [Murillo, Gerardo] (*b* Guadalajara, 3 Oct 1875; *d* Mexico City, 14 Aug 1964). Mexican painter, printmaker, writer, theorist, vulcanologist and politician. Better known by his pseudonym, which signifies 'Doctor Water' in Náhuatl and which he adopted in 1902, Murillo first studied art in Guadalajara and from 1890 to 1896 at the Academia de San Carlos in Mexico City, where his vocation became clear. In 1899 he travelled to Europe, settling in Rome, where the work of Michelangelo had a profound impact on him. He travelled to other countries to study and to learn about avant-garde painting. He returned to Mexico in 1904 and seven years later returned to Europe, only to rush back when the Revolution broke out in Mexico. He joined the revolutionary movement, taking an active role in its various activities, including the muralist movement, through which he was associated with Diego Rivera, José Clemente Orozco and David Alfaro Siqueiros. Although he practised portrait painting, his passion was for landscape in a variety of techniques and materials, some of them invented by him; for example he used 'atlcolours', which were simply crayons made of wax, resins and pigment with which he could obtain textures not obtainable with oil paint. His favoured supports were rigid surfaces such as wood or hardboard.

The different formative influences that set the parameters for Dr Atl's mature style are visible in his early works. *Seated Woman* (pastel, 1903; Mexico City, Fomento Cult. Banamex) is Impressionist in treatment, while the Post-Impressionism of Giovanni Segantini served as the model for his *Bathers* (Guadalajara, Mus. Reg. Antropol. & Hist.). Another Italian source, the Futurist work of Luigi Russolo, lay behind the style of paintings such as *Lightning on the Waves* (Guadalajara, Mus. Reg. Antropol. & Hist.). Japanese woodcuts left an unmistakable mark on his work as a printmaker, particularly on his experiments with stencils, for example *Landscape with Volcano* (Mexico City, Luis Felipe del Valle Prieto priv. col.).

Dr Atl's first landscapes fluctuate between bad academic habits and modernist techniques. The Valley of Mexico and its volcanoes soon made an appearance and became a frequent theme in his extensive production. As he was a mountaineer he chose his sites in the high mountain ranges, thus emphasizing the monumentality of the Mexican landscape. The vision he gained from the heights was not that of man but of the birds, space being one of his constant preoccupations. Until 1933 he used conventional perspective and a straight line to represent the horizon. After that date, inspired by the theories of the Mexican painter Luis G. Serrano (1894–1972), he made use of a curvilinear horizon in the large landscapes that form the most significant part of his work, such as the *Valley of Mexico* (Mexico City, A. Luna Arroyo priv. col.). In *Clouds over the Valley* (1933; Mexico City, Mus. N.A.) he took the theory to extremes, with the movement of the clouds obeying the guiding line of the earthly horizon.

An enthusiasm for innovation led Atl around 1957 to the practice of 'aerolandscape', which consisted in taking the essential sketches for a picture from the cockpit of a plane or helicopter. He concentrated on the peaks of the volcanoes, for example *Popocatepetl Seen from an Aeroplane* (1948; Mexico City, Octavio Barocio priv. col.). A natural event, the eruption of the volcano Paricutín in 1942, gave a new dimension to his art. He made a meticulous record of the volcano's development in a long series of drawings in charcoal and in works such as *Volcano in the Starry Night* (Mexico City, Mus. N.A.) also painted the impressive eruptions by day and night.

WRITINGS

El paisaje. Un ensayo (Mexico City, 1933)

BIBLIOGRAPHY

A. Luna Arroyo: *El Dr Atl: Sinopsis de su vida y su pintura* (Mexico City, 1952)
C. Pellicer: *Dr Atl: Pinturas y dibujos* (Mexico City, 1954)
A. Casado Navarro: *Gerardo Murillo, el Dr Atl* (Mexico City, 1984)

XAVIER MOYSSÉN

Atlan, Jean-Michel (*b* Constantine, Algeria, 23 Jan 1913; *d* Paris, 12 Feb 1960). French painter, lithographer and writer. The Jewish intellectual milieu in which he grew up led to his interest in philosophy and religion, and from 1930 to 1934 he studied philosophy at the Sorbonne. While in Paris, however, he was confronted with modern painting for the first time, and his interest in poetry was awakened. Recognizing a means of expressing his interest in magical phenomena, in 1941 he began to paint and write poetry. His activity in the Résistance and his Jewish ancestry led to his arrest in 1942; by pleading insanity he was able to save himself but was confined to the Sainte Anne asylum, where he wrote poetry and painted. In the autumn of 1944, shortly after leaving the asylum, his first and only collection of poems, *Le Sang profond*, was published, and he exhibited drawings at the Galerie Arc en Ciel.

During the immediate post-war years Atlan's work was well received in Paris. He had a one-man show in 1946 at the Galerie Denise René, and in 1947 at Galerie Maeght; he exhibited in 1948 in Copenhagen and Vienna. In 1945 Gertrude Stein bought some of his works and he was commissioned to produce lithographic illustrations for *Description d'un combat* (Paris, 1946), the French translation of a story of Franz Kafka. The violent expressionism of his work from 1941, in which masks were a recurring element, moved in 1944–5 towards an abstraction that evoked a swamp-like, fermenting universe. By 1946 increasingly strong elements of mythical plant, animal or human figures could be seen, for example in *Untitled* (1947; Alborg, Nordjylands Kstmus.).

During this period Atlan's studio in Montparnasse, where he and his wife held open house every Saturday, was a crossroads for many artists. He became involved with the Belgian/French movement Le Surréalisme Révolutionnaire, founded in 1947, and came into contact with the international COBRA movement (1948–51), in which he took an active role from 1949. Atlan's work, dominated by strange figures and creatures, became easily associated with Cobra. His abstract work from *c.* 1945 could also be seen as part of the *Art brut* developments in Paris at this time, for example *Untitled* (1945; Paris, priv. col., see 1983 exh. cat., p. 116).

Between 1949 and 1955 Atlan's initial success waned. In this period the mysterious mythical beings in his paintings became magical incantatory signs, which took on strongly ornamental forms. Black, ochre and deep red were characteristic colours for strongly rhythmical works in which Atlan wanted to portray 'battle or war, or the erotic struggle, or the dance', such as *Warrior of Baal* (1953; London, Tate). The ritual dances which formed part of various religions were an important source of inspiration for him. He felt a kinship in his style of expression with African and Assyrian art. Atlan received renewed attention from 1955 and he was presented at international exhibitions as an important member of the young Ecole de Paris. He also had numerous one-man shows in France and abroad.

WRITINGS

Le Sang profond (Paris, 1944)

BIBLIOGRAPHY

M. Ragon: *Atlan*, Bibliothèque de Cobra (Copenhagen, 1950) [Dan. and French]
A. Verdet: *Atlan* (Paris, 1957)
M. Ragon and A. Verdet: *Jean Atlan* (Geneva, 1960)
B. Dorival: *Atlan: Essai de biographie artistique* (Paris, 1962) [extensive bibliog.]
M. Ragon: *Atlan* (Paris, 1962)
Atlan (exh. cat., Paris, Mus. A. Mod. Ville Paris, 1963)
Atlan: Oeuvres des collections publiques françaises (exh. cat., Paris, Pompidou, 1980)
Cobra, 1948–1951 (exh. cat., Paris, Mus. A. Mod. Ville Paris; Chalon-sur-Saône, Maison Cult.; Rennes, Mus. B.-A. & Archéol.; 1983)

WILLEMIJN STOKVIS

Atlanta. North American city and capital of the state of Georgia. Situated in the north-western part of the state in the foothills of the Blue Ridge Mountains, the city (population of metropolitan area 2,233,229 at 1990 census) has been an important transportation centre from its foundation in 1837. Originally named Terminus, it was established as part of the construction of the Western and Atlantic Railroad, planned to link the Midwest, from the Tennessee state line to the north, with the Atlantic coast at Savannah, *c.* 570 km to the south-east. As a rail centre Atlanta was critical to the Southern Confederacy during the American Civil War (1860–65). The city was burnt by General William T. Sherman in 1864 but was rapidly rebuilt, marking the start of a period of extraordinary development and growth that made Atlanta more the leading city of the new south than a representative city of the rural old south. Its historic architecture is Victorian and eclectic, with academic classical and Tudor Revival styles predominating.

The late 19th-century city was characterized by the government district near the Italian Renaissance-style State Capitol (1885–9; by W. J. Edbrooke and Franklin P. Burnham) and by the business district developed south of Central City Park. Suburbs grew in West End and, especially after 1889, Inman Park, where some of the city's best Victorian Queen Anne Revival houses are found, for example Edward C. Peters's house (1883; now Mansion Restaurant), designed by Gottfried L. Norrman. Another tramline extended north to the Peters Estate, where

Atlanta, High Museum of Art by Richard Meier, 1980–83

substantial residential development is reflected by the few surviving mansions lining Piedmont Avenue in the Midtown Historic District, as well as by later middle-class houses and bungalows on parallel streets. Along the railway line connecting Atlanta to the nearby town of Decatur two small communities developed: Edgewood (now Candler Park) and Kirkwood, both annexed by Atlanta in 1908. They maintain the architectural character of their early years, with large, late Victorian residences and, in Kirkwood, some timber-framed houses from *c.* 1900; the character of Edgewood, however, is best defined by the popular, simple 'Craftsman' bungalows, of which there are hundreds; indeed, this style typifies pre-World War I housing throughout the city.

In Druid Hills, an area designed in the 1890s by Frederick Law Olmsted, larger houses were built from 1908 in the eclectic historicist styles of the American academic tradition: Tudor Revival manor houses, Mediterranean-style villas, Georgian Revival houses based on 18th-century colonial mansions and various Federal, Colonial Revival and Neo-classical buildings, all with ample plots of land. With its system of parks and landscaping, Druid Hills represents one of Olmsted's finest and most complete designs. In the early 20th century many wealthy families also established manorial country houses in the Buckhead area, encouraging the continuing northward growth of the city, and such buildings as Swan House (1926–8) by PHILIP TRAMMELL SHUTZE, with its elaborate Baroque-style details, introduced a new scale of elegance and new historicist dimensions. Smaller-scale suburbs designed around the motor-car were also developed from the late 1920s, for example in Garden Hills and Morningside.

In the late 1920s and 1930s the first phase of Modernism in Atlanta was seen in the Art Deco skyscrapers built by P. Thornton Marye and Pringle & Smith (e.g. the Southern Bell Telephone Company Building (1929) designed by Marye), but the modern image of the city was essentially formed in the 1960s and after, particularly in the work of JOHN PORTMAN. He developed and designed the Peachtree Center, a multi-purpose complex built between the 1960s and 1992 comprising high-rise office buildings and three major hotels: the Hyatt Regency (1966–7), designed around a pioneering 22-storey atrium conceived as a festival space, which established Portman's and Atlanta's international reputations in architecture; the Westin Peachtree Plaza (1976), then the world's tallest hotel building at 70 storeys; and the Marriott Marquis (1985), with a 45-storey atrium (*see* HOTEL, fig. 2). These and other developments of conference and trade facilities made Atlanta one of the USA's leading convention centres. The art life of Atlanta is enhanced by the presence of a number of museums, including the Emory University Museum of Art and Archaeology and the High Museum of Art (1980–83; see fig.), designed by Richard Meier.

BIBLIOGRAPHY

Atlanta: A City of the Modern South (New York, 1942)

Atlanta Architecture: The Victorian Heritage (exh. cat. by E. A. M. Lyon, Atlanta, GA, Hist. Soc. Mus., 1976)

E. Stanfield and others: *From Plantation to Peachtree: A Century and a Half of Classic Atlanta Houses* (Atlanta, 1987)

E. Dowling: *American Classicist: The Architecture of Philip Trammell Shutze* (New York, 1989)

P. Riani, P. Goldberger and J. Portman: *John Portman* (Milan, 1990)

W. Mitchell jr: *Classic Atlanta: Landmarks of the Atlanta Spirit* (New Orleans, 1991)

R. M. Craig: *Atlanta Architecture: Art Deco to Modern Classic, 1929–1959* (Gretna, LA, 1995)

ROBERT M. CRAIG

Atlantids from the Small Theatre, Pompeii, 1st century BC

Atlantid. Male figure (sometimes known as telamon, and equivalent to the female caryatid) used to replace a column. It is usually represented standing with its hands behind its bowed head, as if supporting a heavy weight on its shoulders, and is probably modelled on the mythical Atlas, who was said to hold up the sky. Unlike caryatids, surviving examples from the Greco-Roman world are scarce. The earliest and most famous, in the huge temple of Zeus Olympios at Akragas (begun *c.* 480 BC), are 7.65 m high and composed of 12 or 13 courses of stone. Several have been reconstructed on site from excavated fragments. Evidence from coins suggests that atlantids adorned other temples and sacred buildings. They are found in Roman secular architecture from the 1st century BC, for example at Pompeii in the *tepidarium* of the Forum Baths, where specimens in hairy loincloths are ranged around the upper part of the walls, and in the Small Theatre, where two kneeling figures support decorative brackets (see fig.). Later examples, such as those on the 2nd-century AD sarcophagus from Velletri (Rome, Mus. N. Romano) and variants on furniture and small artefacts, tended to have an entirely decorative function.

Atlantids formed part of the repertoire of Classical architecture from the Renaissance onwards. They were particularly popular during the Baroque period (for example decorating the *Sala terrena* by Johann Lukas von Hildebrandt at the Upper Belvedere, Vienna, of 1721–3; for illustration *see* SALA TERRENA) and into the Neo-classical period (e.g. Leo von Klenze's New Hermitage Museum, 1842–51, in St Petersburg).

BIBLIOGRAPHY

Vitruvius: *On Architecture* VI.vii.6
P. Marconi: *Agrigento: Topografia ed arte* (Florence, 1929)

G. LLOYD-MORGAN

Atlas. Term used to refer to a collection of maps, printed in a set order: world map, maps of the continents, each followed by maps of the several regions within that continent, and with an alphabetical gazetteer, or list of place-names, giving coordinates for the various names of places, rivers, regions etc. The first use of the term 'atlas' dates from 1595, with the publication in Duisburg of the *Atlas sive cosmographicae meditationes de fabrica mundi et fabricati figura* (see fig.) by Gerard Mercator (1512–94). Mercator's prestige as the premier cartographer of his time made the term part of general usage.

The prototype of modern atlases is the set of maps included with medieval editions of Claudius Ptolemy's *Geographia* (2nd century AD). There is no definite evidence

Frontispiece to *Atlas sive cosmographicae meditationes de fabrica mundi et fabricati figura* by Gerard Mercator (Duisburg, 1595) (London, British Library)

showing that the original of the *Geographia* was accompanied by maps, but there is consensus that the maps accompanying manuscript versions of the work that reached Italy in the early 1400s were designed in the later Middle Ages. Ptolemy's maps were first printed in 1477, to be followed by numerous editions during the 16th and 17th centuries. Italian mapmakers of the 16th century, including Giacomo Gastaldi (*c.* 1500–*c.* 1565, sometimes known as Jacopo) and Antoine Lafréry, began publishing maps of the world and regional maps, without a definite, set order, in the mid-1500s.

The first modern atlas was published in Antwerp in 1560, by Abraham Ortelius, mapmaker and dealer, with the title *Theatrum orbis terrarum*, a truly successful venture that remained popular for decades. Ortelius followed the 'Ptolemaic' model, but his maps lacked decorative features: the title, scale and other information were enclosed in simple, severe cartouches of the strapwork type. A more decorative set of maps was published by Ortelius's contemporary Gerard de Jode, *Speculum orbis terrarum* (Antwerp, 1573). The *Civitates orbis terrarum* (Cologne, 1572–1617) of Georg Braun and Franz Hogenberg (*see* HOGENBERG, (2)), with topographical views of European cities, many by Joris Hoefnagel, also dates from this early period. The 'Golden Age' of atlas publishing is associated with Dutch mapmakers and publishers, located mostly in Amsterdam. The Dutch atlases of the 17th century were sumptuous works, designed for the libraries, offices and counting-houses of merchants, statesmen and collectors. The title-page of the first volume of sets, engraved by the leading craftsmen employed by their publisher, and elegantly hand-coloured, was usually allegoric in character. As a rule each map in the atlas had its share of decorative elements: complex cartouches of title, scale and dedication, illustrating local costumes, farming, fishing, sailing; allegorical figures, often putti, handling surveyors' instruments and/or globes; coats of arms of the dedicatees. Beginning with the revised and enlarged editions of Mercator's atlas, published by Jodocus Hondius (*see* HONDIUS (i), (1)) from 1605, two map publishers vied for the worldwide market of their products: the families of Blaeu and Jansson. The Blaeu atlas series started with the *Atlas novus* (1634–5), the Jansson series with the *Novus atlas* (1638). From one- and two-volume sets, these works grew in size, culminating in the Blaeu *Atlas maior* (1662–6) in eleven volumes and the Jansson set in six (1658). Among the most handsome of the Blaeu maps were those of the English counties of Cambridgeshire and Oxfordshire, with dons in academic dress and the coats of arms of the several colleges of the two great universities.

The successors of Blaeu and Jansson, Danckerts, Allard, de Wit and van der Aa, continued the decorative tradition, with ever more elaborate cartouches and designs. At the turn of the 18th century the culmination of the atlasmakers' art took place, brought to its most elaborate form by two major works. The first of these, known as the 'Secret Atlas of the East India Company', featured elegantly decorated maps and watercolours of the principal centres of that great trading corporation. This set was incorporated into what is known as the *Atlas van der Hem* (Vienna, Österreich. Nbib.), a unique work in 50 volumes, later owned by one of the greatest of bibliophiles, Prince Eugene of Savoy, by whose name it is also known (*see* HEM, LAURENS VAN DER). In addition to the greatest number of maps available from the house of Blaeu, this set contains drawings, mostly hand-coloured, and watercolours of major cities and noteworthy places from around the world by such artists as Roelandt Savery, Lambert Doomer and Willem Schellincks. Another special work of that period is known as the 'Atlas of the Great Elector' (of Brandenburg), commissioned by Prince Johan Maurits of Nassau for presentation to Frederick William. In the format of wall maps, 1.7×1.1 m, it consists of 35 maps designed specifically for this monumental work (Berlin, Staatsbib.). Map publishers of the first half of the 18th century continued to cater for the tastes of collectors. The maps in their atlases contain elaborate cartouches, many amounting to sizeable pictures of cities, battles and the like. In the second half of the 18th century, as a result of the great surveys of the century, atlas maps gradually assumed a much more sober aspect as mapping became more of a scientific and accurate enterprise.

A special type of atlas is first referred to in the literature of the subject as a 'portolan atlas', and a 'sea atlas' later on. Portolan atlases were sets of manuscript maps designed for navigation, made when the chartmakers in many instances were master miniaturists as well; their maps are magnificently decorated with compass roses, types of sailing vessels, sea monsters and, in a few maps, birds' eye views of great seaports, for example Venice and Genoa. The later sea atlases were printed sets of navigation charts, and their decorative elements were displayed primarily on elaborate and elegant title-pages.

See also MAP.

BIBLIOGRAPHY

A. Ortelius: *Theatrum orbis terrarum* (Antwerp, 1560/*R* Amsterdam, 1964) [facs. ed. with intro. by R. A. Skelton)

G. Mercator: *Atlas sive cosmographicae meditationes de fabrica mundi et fabricati figura* (Duisburg, 1595/*R* Brussels, 1963)

A. E. Nordenskiöld: *Facsimile Atlas to the Early History of Cartography* (Stockholm, 1889/*R* 1973)

G. Kish: *La Carte: Images des civilisations* (Paris, 1980)

M. M. du Jourdin and M. de la Roncière: *Seacharts of the Early Explorers, 13th to 17th Century* (New York, 1984)

R. W. Shirley: *The Mapping of the World: Early Printed World Maps, 1472–1700* (London, 1984)

I. Kretschmer, J. Dörflinger and F. Wavrik, eds: *Lexikon zur Geschichte der Kartographie*, 2 vols (Vienna, 1986)

D. Woodward, ed.: *Art and Cartography: Six Historical Essays* (Chicago, 1987)

GEORGE KISH

Atmospheric perspective. *See under* PERSPECTIVE, §III.

Atri, Andrea Matteo III, Duca d'. *See* ACQUAVIVA D'ARAGONA, ANDREA MATTEO III.

Atrib, Tell. *See* ATHRIBIS.

Atrium (i). Main open central space of a Roman house (*see* ROME, ANCIENT, fig. 8).

Atrium (ii). Forecourt of a church or basilica.

Atrium (iii). Large and grand entrance space in a hotel or public building. □

Attalids. *See under* PERGAMON, §1.

Attavanti, Attavante [Vante di Gabriello di Vante Attavanti] (*b* Castelfiorentino, 1452; *d* Florence, 1520–25). Italian illuminator. He has been praised by art historians since his own times, although many of his autograph works were incorrectly assigned to his workshop. New attributions, supported by archival material, have made it possible to reconstruct his oeuvre and life more accurately. He worked for celebrated patrons and collaborated with the most important illuminators and painters of Florence: Francesco di Antonio del Chierico, the Master of the Hamilton Xenophon, the brothers Gherardo and Monte di Giovanni di Miniato del Foro and Domenico Ghirlandaio, and documents indicate contacts also with Leonardo da Vinci. Attavanti probably trained with del Chierico in 1471–2, while working on the Antiphonary for Florence Cathedral (Florence, Bib. Medicea-Laurenziana, MS. Edili 148). Among the work of late 15th-century illuminators, that of Attavanti is distinguished by his citations from the Antique, his ideas derived from Netherlandish and Florentine panel painting and his illustration of philosophical themes. Recurrent motifs include frontispieces with entablatures on columns, copies of sarcophagi as altar frontals, cameos, allegorical figures within medals and richly dressed figures isolated in framed medallions or symmetrically grouped.

Attavanti's individual style emerged as early as 1473 in his work on a manuscript in collaboration with Ghirlandaio, who signed the work (Rome, Vatican, Bib. Apostolica, MS. Ross. 1193). The latter's influence on Attavanti can be seen clearly in the scenic illustrations and in some of the initials in the Bible made for the Duke of Urbino, Federigo II da Montefeltro (1477–8; Rome, Vatican, Bib. Apostolica, MSS Urb. lat. 1–2), for example the miniatures of *Pentecost* (fol. 283*r*) and the *Martyrdom of the Seven Maccabee Brothers* (fol. 174*v*) in the second volume, which contain landscape backgrounds and views of contemporary Florentine palazzi. In the borders the inclusion of jewels among naturalistic floral motifs and the figures depicted beside a window opening on to a landscape are reminiscent of Ghirlandaio's work. In 1483 Attavanti signed and dated a Missal made for Thomas James, Bishop of Dol (Lyon, Bib. Mun.; detached *Crucifixion*, Le Havre, Mus. B.-A.). This work especially shows Attavanti's attention to antique objects, often represented with a precision that shows his consummate skill in copying from life: for example the della Valle–Medici Sarcophagus (Florence, Uffizi) and topographical depictions of the Castel Sant'Angelo, the Pantheon and St Peter's, Rome.

For Matthias Corvinus, King of Hungary, Attavanti produced a considerable number of signed works, including numerous non-liturgical books (all Modena, Bib. Estense) and a Missal (Brussels, Bib. Royale Albert 1er, MS. 9008), dated 1485 on the frontispiece (fol. 8*v*; see fig.) and 1487 on the miniature of the *Last Judgement* (fol. 206*r*). In these works there are clear references to the works of Ghirlandaio, Botticelli, Verrocchio and Leonardo, as in the representations of the *Baptism* and *Last Supper* in the Brussels Missal (fol. 205*v*) and the single leaf of the Missal of the Bishop of Dol. After the King's death, most of the codices were acquired by the Medici. A

Attavante Attavanti: frontispiece miniature to a Missal, 1485 (Brussels, Bibliothèque Royale Albert ler, MS. 9008, fol. 8*v*)

Breviary of 1487, still in progress in 1492 (Rome, Vatican, Bib. Apostolica, MS. Urb. lat. 112), includes archaeological references (e.g. *Neptune*, fol. 7*r*). This was followed by a copy of the work of Nicholas of Lyra, illuminated between 1494 and 1497 for Manuel I, King of Portugal (Lisbon, Arquiv. N.), to which Gherardo and Monte del Foro also contributed. In this work Attavanti integrated archaeological motifs into images of monastic life: in the incipit to the First Epistle of St Paul to the Corinthians there are compositions of arms, shield and helmet in Classical style and sequences of pairs of *Amazons*. In a series of incipits with scenes of *St Jerome in his Study*, Attavanti provided variations on the theme, which are sometimes directly inspired by Netherlandish models (e.g. Jan van Eyck) and Florentine (e.g. Ghirlandaio) art. They present a vast repertory of private Florentine *studioli* of the period, with acute observation of daily life. In his works for the Medici, Attavanti sometimes aimed at economy in his settings, taking great care with the representation of interiors. Particularly noteworthy are the pages of the Hours of Laudomia de' Medici (1502; London, BL, Yates Thompson MS. 30), on which Giovanni Boccardi, Mariano del Buono di Jacopo and Stefano Lunetti (a pupil of del Monte) also collaborated. In the *Ginesio* translated from the Latin of Marsilio Ficino (Florence, Bib. Medicea-Laurenziana, MS. 82.15) there are portraits from life with lighting effects reminiscent of Leonardo. From 1505 to

1514 Attavanti collaborated on the antiphonaries for Florence Cathedral (all Florence, Bib. Medicea-Laurenziana and Mus. Opera Duomo). Later documentation is scarce. The recognition of his hand in a *Cerimoniale dei Vescovi* (ex-Spitzer col.), which is dated 1520, has caused the presumed date of his death to be changed from 1517 to between 1520 and 1525, when he is mentioned as deceased.

BIBLIOGRAPHY

G. Milanesi: *Nuove indagini con documenti inediti per servire alla storia della miniatura italiana* (Florence, 1850), pp. 161–352
M. Levi D'Ancona: *Miniatura e miniatori a Firenze dal XIV al XVI secolo* (Florence, 1962), pp. 88, 254–9, 296, 350–52
A. Garzelli: *La bibbia di Federico da Montefeltro* (Rome, 1977)
——: *Miniatura fiorentina del rinascimento, 1440–1525: Un primo censimento*, 2 vols (Florence, 1985), pp. 217–45
The Painted Page: Italian Renaissance Book Illumination, 1450–1550 (exh. cat., ed. J. J. G. Alexander; London, RA, 1994)

PATRIZIA FERRETTI

Atterbury, Grosvenor (*b* Detroit, MI, 7 July 1869; *d* Southampton, NY, 18 Oct 1956). American architect, urban planner and writer. He studied at Yale University, New Haven, CT, and travelled in Europe. He studied architecture at Columbia University, New York and worked in the office of McKim, Mead & White before completing his architecture studies at the Ecole des Beaux-Arts in Paris. Atterbury's early work consisted of suburban and weekend houses for wealthy industrialists, such as the Henry W. de Forest House (1898) in Cold Springs Harbor on Long Island, NY. De Forest was a leader in the philanthropic movement to improve workers' housing, an interest that Atterbury shared; through him Atterbury was given the commission for the model housing community of Forest Hills Gardens, NY, begun in 1909 under the sponsorship of the Russell Sage Foundation; the co-planners and landscape designers were the brothers John Charles Olmsted (1852–1920) and Frederick Law Olmsted jr (1870–1957), the sons of Frederick Law Olmsted. Atterbury developed a system of precast concrete panels to build a varied group of multiple units and town houses suggesting an English country hamlet. He continued his research into prefabrication largely at his own expense throughout his life.

An active writer on planning, housing, and industrialized methods of construction, Atterbury put his views into practice on two other projects: Indian Hill (1915–16), a community of 58 single-family houses for employees of the Norton Company, Worcester, MA, and the new railway town of Erwin, TN, planned for an eventual population of 40,000 and begun in 1916. In his work for these and other housing groups, Atterbury used a traditional architectural idiom and a level of craftsmanship that matched that of his residences for the wealthy.

WRITINGS

The Economic Production of Workingmen's Homes (New York, 1930)

BIBLIOGRAPHY

DAB Suppl.
'The Work of Grosvenor Atterbury', *Amer. Architect*, xliv (Aug/Sept 1908), pp. 68–72, 76–80

LELAND M. ROTH

Attersee, Christian Ludwig (*b* Pressburg, 28 Aug 1940). Austrian painter, writer, film maker and musician. While still at school he wrote short novels and songs, drew comic strips, composed pieces for ocarina and piano and was three times Austrian junior national yachting champion. From 1957 to 1963 he was a student at the Hochschule für Angewandte Kunst in Vienna. His sensual pictures, which express a totally egocentric personality, sparkle with lively imagination. They incorporate the idea of metamorphosis as a consistent leitmotif and are therefore always undergoing a process of transformation. The idea of beauty, as part of a wide-ranging aesthetic view of the world, often forms the core of his artistic statements and is the basis of his numerous actions.

Attersee's invented words and objects, for example *Food-ball* or *Prosthesis-alphabet*, are the result of an intellectual exploration of ordinary objects in everyday reality, as well as of current linguistic patterns. From 1967 to 1968 he produced his *Attersee-Photo-cycles* and *Attersee-Photo-posters*, whose themes are the interchangeability of our notions of beauty in female and male sexuality. He also revealed his highly independent artistic character in his publications, including his book on Austria, published in 1965: *Komm mit nach Österreich*, a guide through the country for extra-terrestrial creatures; and in his film productions, such as a garden film made in 1966 in conjunction with the Actions-Concerts for Al Hansen, his film about the island of Lanzarote (1970–71), and the film about the 50th action of the Orgien-Mysterien-Theater (1975), presented by Hermann Nitsch in Schloss Prinzendorf.

BIBLIOGRAPHY

Attersee (exh. cat., Vienna, Mus. Mod. Kst, 1982)
Attersee: Bilder, 1975–1985 (exh. cat. by C. Haenlein, Hannover, Kestner-Ges., 1985)
Attersee: Brautweiss (exh. cat., Linz, Neue Gal., 1986)

ULRIKE GAISBAUER

Attic (i). Term used in Classical architecture for a small order placed above the main entablature of the building. The space so occupied, internally and on the façade, is called the 'attic storey'. Its front wall may be blank, as in the great panel above the cornice of a triumphal arch, or pierced by windows; in ancient Greek and Roman architecture it was sometimes decorated with relief sculpture or carried an inscription. An open parapet is not correctly described as an attic.

Attic (ii). Architectural term used in the English-speaking world, since the early 18th century, for the highest storey in a house; a garret.

□

Attiret, Claude-François (*b* Dôle, Jura, 14 Dec 1728; *d* Dôle, 15 July 1804). French sculptor. He was the son of a joiner, who sent him to Paris to train with Jean-Baptiste Pigalle. In 1757 Attiret was in Rome, where he received a prize from the Accademia di S Luca; returning to Paris, he was accepted as a member of the Académie de St Luc in 1760, and was a professor there. He exhibited several times at the Salon of the Académie de St Luc: among the works that he showed was *Roman Charity* (terracotta, 1726; Dijon, Mus. B.-A.); *Hannibal Preparing to Take Poison* (terracotta, 1764); and the *Chercheuse d'esprit* (terracotta, 1774; Dijon, Mus. B.-A.; marble version, Paris,

David-Weill col.). This idealized portrait bust of a young woman, graceful in concept and mischievous in expression, is his best-known work.

By 1776 Attiret had settled in Dijon and had executed two stone statues for St Bénigne, *St Andrew* and *St John the Evangelist*, and a bronze low relief of the *Apostles at the Tomb of the Virgin* (1773). Portraits dating from this period are: *Benigne Legouz de Gerland* (Beaune, Mus. Marey); bust of a *Young Girl* (terracotta; Dijon, Mus. B.-A.); bust of a *Woman* (marble; Paris, Louvre); and bust of *François Devosges* (Besançon, Bib. Mun.). Commissions from the local aristocracy gave scope to his talents as a decorative sculptor. He executed statues of the *Four Seasons* for the staircase of the château of Choisy-le-Roi; *Jupiter Hurling a Thunderbolt* and *Cybele* for the château of Bussy-Rabutin; and for the bishop's palace in Plombières-les-Dijon, four Tonnerre stone low reliefs of putti (*Spring*, *Summer*, *Autumn*, *Winter*; Dijon, Mus. B.-A.). The naturalism of Attiret's style is tempered by an increasingly distinct tendency to Neo-classicism, evident in the décor of the Salle des Antiques in the Palais des Etats de Bourgogne, now the Musée des Beaux-Arts in Dijon. Attiret retired to Dôle, where he executed a statue of *Louis XVI* (destr. 1793); two allegorical figures representing the *Arts* and the *Sciences* survive.

Attiret's uncle, the Jesuit Jean-Denis Attiret (*b* Dôle, 1702; *d* Beijing, 1768), was a painter who, after spending some time in Rome, travelled in 1737 to China. He became a favourite of the Emperor Qian Long. The famous series of engravings, the *Conquests of the Emperor of China* (1767–73) by Charles-Nicolas Cochin (1), was based on drawings by Attiret.

BIBLIOGRAPHY

Lami
E. Kyot: 'C. F. Attiret: Statuaire', *Rev. Bourgogne* (1923), pp. 5–39
P. Quarré: 'Un Buste d'Attiret', *Bull. Mus. Dijon* (1955–7), p. 83

CATHERINE LEGRAND

Atwood, Charles B(owler) (*b* Charlestown, MA, 18 May 1849; *d* Chicago, IL, 19 Dec 1895). American architect. He received his architectural training in the offices of Eldridge Boyden (1819–96) in Worcester, MA, and Ware & Van Brunt in Boston, with a year's study (1869–70) in the Lawrence Scientific School at Harvard University, Cambridge, MA. In 1872 he set up on his own, designing the State Mutual Assurance Building (1872) in Worcester, MA, and the Holyoke City Hall (1874–5), MA. In 1875 he settled in New York, working for Christian Herter's firm of decorators, Herter Brothers, and perhaps also for McKim, Mead & White. Between 1879 and 1881 he assembled a small team of draughtsmen to execute the design of the William Henry Vanderbilt house on Fifth Avenue (destr.), in collaboration with Herter Brothers and the architect John Butler Snook. After the death of John Wellborn Root in January 1891, Root's partner Daniel H. Burnham engaged Atwood as chief architect of the World's Columbian Exposition in Chicago, which opened on 1 May 1893, then made him a 27% partner in his firm, D. H. Burnham & Co. In these capacities he produced his most admired designs: the Fine Arts Building at the Exposition (rebuilt as the Museum of Science and Industry), the annexe of the Marshall Field Store (1892–3; interior altered) in Chicago, the Reliance Building (1891–5), Chicago (*see* SKYSCRAPER, fig. 1) and the Ellicott Square Building (1894–5), Buffalo, NY. His designs were not particularly original but, rather, in whatever style was practical or popular at the time; a crude Neo-Grec for the Vanderbilt houses, Beaux-Arts classical for the Fine Arts Building, Gothic Revival for the Reliance Building, Renaissance Revival for the Field annexe and Ellicott Square Building. His use of drugs caused him to be dismissed from Burnham's on 10 December 1895 and to commit suicide nine days later.

BIBLIOGRAPHY

D. H. Burnham: 'Charles Bowler Atwood', *Inland Architect & News Rec.*, xxvi (1906), pp. 56–7
A. L. Van Zanten: 'The Marshall Field Annex and the New Urban Order of Daniel Burnham's Chicago', *Chicago Hist.*, xi/3 (1982), pp. 130–41

DAVID VAN ZANTEN

AUA [Atelier d'Urbanisme et d'Architecture]. French multi-disciplinary architectural cooperative founded in Paris in 1960. Initial members, among whom were urban planners, architects, engineers and designers, included Jacques Allegret (*b* 1930), Jacques Berce (*b* 1929), Valentin Fabre (*b* 1927), Georges Loiseau (*b* 1928), Jean Perrottet (*b* 1925), Michel Steinebach (*b* 1928), Jean Tribel (*b* 1929), Paul Chemetov, Jean Deroche (*b* 1931), Annie Tribel (*b* 1933), Jacques Kalisz (*b* 1928), Michel Corajoud (*b* 1937), Jean-François Parent (*b* 1930), Henri Ciriani, Borja Huidobro (*b* 1936), Maria Deroche (*b* 1938) and Christian Devillers (*b* 1946). A total of about 200 architects and technicians collaborated at AUA between 1960 and 1986, when it was dissolved.

AUA was created in response to the situation prevailing in the building industry in France at the end of the 1950s, when much was being built, but badly, and when urban planning was little developed. It was thus considered necessary to bring together the different skills required for the proper planning of space, from the social sciences and urban planning to landscape and industrial design, and to enable architects and engineers to work together. This multi-disciplinary approach countered the corporatism of the architectural profession; members of AUA were also left-wing political activists and intellectuals, publishing the review *Forum* from 1962 to 1966. They built in the suburbs with relatively small commissions for that time, and these minority positions brought them close to the best French architects of their generation including the Atelier de Montrouge and Roland Simounet.

The work of AUA took two principal directions: urban planning and a critical consideration of construction. This was revealed by their industrialized buildings, such as the steel and glass swimming-pool (1969) at Aubervilliers; the experimental industrialized living module Tétrodon (1971); Roche et Bobois stores (1971); and the school complex (1972) at Pantin, but especially by the Brutalist style influenced by Le Corbusier that was seen in the brick and concrete residential units (1962) at Vigneux; a senior citizens' centre (1964) at La Courneuve; an open-air theatre (1964) in Hammamet, Tunisia; holiday villages (1967) at Gassin and Grasse, with Corbusian concrete vaults; and housing units and offices (1968) at Bagnolet, where AUA was located after 1968. Its most important urban planning project was Villeneuve de Grenoble (1968–77), a new town comprising 7000 housing units, 2000 of them on the Galerie de l'Arlequin, a covered street provided with shops and public amenities, on the edge of a park of 20 ha. This example of vertical urban integration with interior streets in the tradition of Le Corbusier's *unités d'habitation* was also the principle behind AUA's competition entry (1972; unexecuted) for the centre of the new town of Evry. This was planned along a 500 m by 50 m monumental spine, which linked a series of towers, bridges and terraced buildings.

At about this time, AUA began to adapt to contextual changes. Urban planning became the concern of government, and technical solutions were imposed by large contracts and planning departments. The engineers left AUA, which then transformed itself into a federation of architectural practices that became more and more autonomous. These included the offices of Chemetov and of Ciriani; the office of Perrottet and Fabre, who built the Théâtre de la Ville (1967), Paris, the Théâtre de Chaillot (1979), Paris, and the Théâtre de la Colline (1987), Paris; the office of Loiseau and Tribel, whose work included urban planning and several housing and commercial projects in Grenoble and Villeneuve d'Ascq; the office of Jean and Maria Deroche, who built numerous projects at Orly; that of Borja Huidobro, who built housing at Drancy (1980) and Montreuil (1985) and collaborated with Chemetov on other major projects; and the office of Christian Devillers (1979–84; with Chemetov), who undertook urban restructuring and housing at Saint-Etienne and the Parking des Chaumettes at Saint-Denis. AUA played an important role in French architecture. Its members were teachers and advisers to the civil service; it was responsible for a renaissance of landscape architecture in France, seen for example in the work of Corajoud in his parks in Grenoble (1973) and Maurepas-Elancourt (1974); and above all it was a reference point for professional standards and a place of apprenticeship for many young architects in the 1970s.

BIBLIOGRAPHY

Paul Chemetov et Borja Huidobro: Cinq projets, 1979–1982 (Paris, 1983)
Henri Ciriani (Paris, 1984)
'30 ans d'architecture française, 1950–1980', *Archit., Movt, Cont.*, ii (1986) [special issue]
P. Blin: *L'AUA: Mythe et réalités* (Paris, 1988)

CHRISTIAN DEVILLERS

Aubé, Jean-Paul (*b* Longwy, Meurthe et Moselle, 3 July 1837; *d* Capbreton, Landes, 23 Aug 1916). French sculptor. In 1851 he entered the Ecole Gratuite de Dessin, Paris, also studying with Antoine-Laurent Dantan, and in 1854 moved to the Ecole des Beaux-Arts. A grant from his native *département* enabled him to travel to Italy in 1866–7, though he was evidently little influenced by antique or Renaissance works of art. Apart from his bronze monument to *Dante Alighieri* (1879–80; Paris, Square Monge), his work is in a neo-Rococo style, as exemplified in his terracotta bust of his daughter *Marcelle Aubé* (1910; Paris, Mus. d'Orsay). Besides many portrait busts he also executed public monuments to notable Frenchmen, several of which were destroyed on the orders of the Vichy government in 1941. The most important, and most controversial, was that to *Léon Gambetta* (bronze, 1884–8), built in collaboration with the architect Louis-Charles Boileau in the courtyard of the Louvre in Paris; it was damaged during World War II and dismantled from 1954 onwards (model, Paris, Mus. d'Orsay). Aubé also supplied decorative sculpture for public buildings as well as private mansions in Paris such as the Hôtel de la Païva on the Champs-Elysées and the Palais Rose (destr. 1969), which belonged to Comte Boni de Castellane.

Aubé had a consistent interest in the decorative arts. Between 1876 and 1882 he supplied models for the Haviland atelier in Paris, and then for that of the ceramicist Ernest Chaplet, as well as for the national Sèvres porcelain manufactory. One of his table centrepieces (silver and rock crystal; Paris, Mus. d'Orsay) was exhibited at the Exposition Universelle (Paris, 1910). He was one of the first members of the Société Nationale des Beaux-Arts. In 1883 he was appointed professor of sculpture and later director of the Ecole Municipale Bernard Palissy, a school intended to promote the application of the fine arts to industry.

BIBLIOGRAPHY

La Sculpture française au XIXe siècle (exh. cat., ed. A. Pingeot; Paris, Grand Pal., 1986)

LAURE DE MARGERIE

Auberjonois, René (*b* Lausanne, 18 Aug 1872; *d* Lausanne, 11 Oct 1957). Swiss draughtsman, painter and illustrator. He began his career as an apprentice banker but abandoned this to study music and languages in Dresden, and then painting at the South Kensington School of Art, London (1895). In 1896 he went to Paris where he took courses in anatomy and became the pupil of Luc Olivier Merson and possibly of Whistler. In 1897 he entered the Ecole des Beaux-Arts but continued to frequent Merson's studio. At the end of 1899, after a short stay in Bavaria, Auberjonois went to Florence, where he passed several months studying and copying the paintings of the Old Masters and painting the Tuscan landscape. Returning to Paris in 1901, he began to work independently, exhibiting for the first time at the Salon in Paris and at the Exposition Nationale Suisse des Beaux-Arts in Vevey. From 1901 to World War I he lived alternately in Paris and in Switzerland.

Between 1903 and 1912 Auberjonois was strongly influenced by the works of the Neo-Impressionists, the Nabis, Toulouse-Lautrec, Maurice Denis, Charles Guérin and Cuno Amiet. In 1905 he met Charles Ferdinand Ramuz (1870–1947), a French-speaking Swiss writer, with whom he formed a deep and abiding friendship, illustrating several of Ramuz's books. In 1911 he returned to Paris, where he opened a new studio, and from 1913 the influence of Cézanne became apparent in his work; his colours became more subtle and at the same time more distinct. In 1914 he was one of twelve contributors to the first issue of the *Cahiers vaudois*, a review created by a group of French-Swiss artists.

Between 1915 and 1919 Auberjonois made prolonged stays in the Swiss canton Valais, which became one of the painter's important subjects, as for example the *Penal Settlement, Sion* (oil on canvas, 350×385 mm, 1929; Glaris, Ksthaus). In 1916, with Alexandre Blanchet (1882–1961) and Jean-Louis Gampert (1884–1924), he painted three backdrops for Ferdinand Chavannes's play *Guillaume le Fou*. It was probably in that same year that he met the composer Igor Stravinsky, who became his friend and whose portrait he painted in 1917. The circus theme appeared in his work for the first time in 1918 (e.g. *Menagerie: Lion, Antelope, Monkey and Ostrich*, oil on canvas, 3.0×3.5 m, 1927; Basle, Kstmus.). In the same year he painted the scenery, curtain and costumes for the *Histoire du soldat* by Ramuz, with music by Stravinsky. At the beginning of the 1920s the shapes of his figures, under Picasso's influence, became more solid. In 1922 the Musée des Beaux-Arts in Lausanne commissioned him to paint the portrait of *C. F. Ramuz* (oil on canvas, 345×315 mm, 1923; Lausanne, Pal. Rumine). He also worked on lithographs intended for the *Sept morceaux par C. F. Ramuz et sept dessins par René Auberjonois* (Lausanne, 1927), and in 1928–9 he concentrated on glass painting. In 1931 he exhibited his picture *Italian Lady* (Basle, Ksthalle), which in its expressiveness and in the abstract dimension of the individual represented was a key work in his development. He produced a wall painting for the Musée de minéralogie in Lausanne in 1933 and another in 1935 for the reception room of the abbey of Le Dézaley. In 1942 an important exhibition of his work was mounted at the Kunstmuseum in Winterthur and in 1948 he was invited by the Swiss Département Fédéral to take part in the Venice Biennale. From this time his works were characterized by the use of gold and a dark palette.

BIBLIOGRAPHY

H. Graber: *René Auberjonois* (Basle, 1925)
C. F. Ramuz: *René Auberjonois* (Lausanne, 1943)
E. Stadler: 'René Auberjonois und die Geschichte vom Soldaten', *Theater, Bühne, Bild* (exh. cat., Köniz, Kunstwoche, 1983), pp. 75–7
F. Auberjonois: *René Auberjonois peintre vaudois* (Lausanne, 1985)
H. Wagner: *René Auberjonois—l'oeuvre peint: Catalogue des huiles, pastels et peintures sous verre* (Zurich, 1987)

ANNE PASTORI ZUMBACH

Aubert, Jean (*fl* 1702; *d* 13 Oct 1741). French architect and designer. The son of a master carpenter employed by the Service des Bâtiments du Roi at various French royal residences, from 1702 to 1708 Aubert worked as a draughtsman under Jules Hardouin Mansart. He became the favourite architect of the princely Bourbon-Condé family with the remodelling of the château of Saint-Maur-des-Fossés (1709–10), near Paris. For Louis-Henri de Bourbon, Prince de Condé (1692–1740), the grandson of Louis XIV, Aubert carried out several projects at the château of Chantilly (Oise). The magnificent stables (designed 1719, built 1721–35; *see* STABLES, fig. 1) show the influence of Hardouin Mansart in Aubert's extensive use of arcades, the discreet presence of the classical orders, and the rich sculptural decoration, all elements drawn from the Grandes et Petites Ecuries of the Palace of Versailles. Aubert's most distinctive stylistic trait, emphatic horizontal channelling of rusticated wall surfaces, made its first appearance on the one-storey elevation of the stable wing facing the meadow.

By 1722 Louise-Françoise, dowager Duchesse de Bourbon, daughter of Louis XIV and Madame de Montespan, had engaged the services of several architects for the plan of the Palais Bourbon, Paris, including Robert de Cotte, Giovanni Giardini (*d* 1722) and Pierre Lassurance I, although the design was executed principally by Aubert (1724–6; rebuilt from 1795). He ingeniously divided the ground-floor into two parts, with the right wing housing the large formal rooms of the *appartement de parade* and the left sheltering the more intimate *appartements de commodité*. A similar situation prevailed at the neighbouring Hôtel de Lassay (1724–6; extensively modified 1845–8). Lassurance I drew up the initial design but Aubert was responsible for the definitive plan and the one-storey elevations, again featuring horizontal channelling. Jacques Gabriel V assisted in an advisory capacity.

From 1728 to 1730 Aubert built the Hôtel Peyrenc de Moras, one of the great Parisian houses of the 18th century, for the wealthy Abraham Peyrenc de Moras, chief adviser to the Duchess of Bourbon (this was erroneously attributed by Jacques-François Blondel to Gabriel). The service wings bordering the forecourt are independent from the free-standing block of the *corps-de-logis*, so that the building resembles a suburban villa (*maison de plaisance*). The extreme simplicity of the astylar court elevation reflects the style of de Cotte, while the curved end pavilions of the garden façade, with their striated channelling, derive from château architecture by way of the town houses of Germain Boffrand.

Aubert was also active as an interior designer. He worked at the Petit Château (1718–22), Chantilly; Palais Bourbon (1727–8; destr.), in collaboration with Gabriel; the Hôtel de Lassay (1727–8), with Gabriel and the sculptors Jules Du Goulon (*fl* 1698–1730s), Pierre Taupin (1662–1734) and Mathieu and André Legoupil (*d* 1733); and the Hôtel Peyrenc de Moras (completed by 1732, where Aubert supervised several workshops of craftsmen; most of the *boiseries* were dispersed in the 19th century). Aubert maintained a symmetrical disposition and geometric subdivision characteristic of earlier wooden panelling, but his use of abundant curvilinear elements, such as arched door frames and mirrors, floral swags and lacy fields of netlike mosaic, was Rococo in style. In 1736, towards the end of his career, he designed the Cistercian abbey of Chaâlis (Oise) for Louis de Bourbon-Condé, Comte de Clermont, who was commendatory abbot of the foundation. However, only half of the intended four-wing structure surrounding a cloister was completed.

BIBLIOGRAPHY

F. Souchal: 'Jean Aubert, architecte des Bourbon-Condé', *Rev. A.*, vi (1969), pp. 29–38
W. Kalnein and M. Levey: *Art and Architecture of the Eighteenth Century in France*, Pelican Hist. A. (Harmondsworth, 1972)
La Rue de Varenne (exh. cat., Paris, Mus. Rodin, 1981)
M. Gallet and Y. Bottineau, eds: *Les Gabriel* (Paris, 1982)
B. Pons: *De Paris à Versailles, 1699–1736* (Strasbourg, 1986)

ROBERT NEUMAN

Aubert, Marcel (*b* Paris, 9 April 1884; *d* Paris, 28 Dec 1962). French art historian. The son of an architect, he graduated from the Ecole des Chartes in Paris in 1907 and became a DLitt in 1921. He was a curator at the Bibliothèque Nationale, then in the department of sculpture at the Louvre, of which he became chief curator in 1940. He taught at the Ecole des Chartes, the Ecole du Louvre and at the universities of Harvard and Yale in the USA. He presided over the Société Française d'Archéologie for 25 years and was a member of the Académie des Inscriptions et Belles-Lettres from 1934. A specialist in the Middle Ages, Aubert particularly studied the cathedrals of Senlis and Notre-Dame, Paris, Cistercian architecture, and French sculpture and stained glass. He trained a generation of medievalists and above all influenced the study of medieval architecture, especially in his precise analysis of the details of a building in order to establish its chronology. His work on sculpture was of less value, however, because he was interested only in the development of style, not in sources or iconography. Aubert was editor of the *Répertoire d'art et d'archéologie*, the *Revue de l'art chrétien*, the *Bulletin monumental*, the *Congrès archéologique de France* and *Monuments Piot*.

WRITINGS

La Cathédrale de Senlis (Paris, 1909)
Notre-Dame de Paris et sa place dans l'architecture du XIIe au XIVe siècle (Paris, 1921)
with G. de Maillé: *L'Architecture cistercienne en France*, 2 vols (Paris, 1934)
La Sculpture française au Moyen Age (Paris, 1947)
Le Vitrail français (Paris, 1958)
Les Vitraux de Notre-Dame et de la Sainte-Chapelle de Paris (Paris, 1959)

ANNE PRACHE

Aubry, Charles(-Hippolyte) (*b* Paris, 3 June 1811; *d* Paris, 23 March 1877). French photographer. For more than 30 years Aubry worked as an industrial designer. In January 1864 he formed a Parisian company to manufacture plaster casts and photographs of plants and flowers. Although unsuccessful (he filed for bankruptcy in 1865), he continued to sell photographs to drawing schools throughout the 1870s. His albumen prints are often striking close-ups of natural forms taken with a flat perspective and symmetrical arrangement that was inspired by the lithographic plates traditionally used by industrial design students. The failure of Aubry's ideas on the use of photographs in the industrial design process can be attributed to both the French government's reluctance to introduce photography into art schools and the shift in French taste towards more abstract, simplified decorations for manufactured goods. His work is included in the collections of the Bibliothèque Nationale, the Bibliothèque des Arts Décoratifs and Musée d'Orsay, Paris, and the J. Paul Getty Museum, Malibu, CA.

BIBLIOGRAPHY

A. McCauley: 'Photographs for Industry: The Career of Charles Aubry', *Getty Mus. J.*, xiv (1986), pp. 157–72

ELIZABETH ANNE McCAULEY

Aubry, Etienne (*b* Versailles, 10 Jan 1745; *d* Versailles, 24 July 1781). French painter. He trained under Jacques-Augustin Silvestre (1719–1809) and Joseph Marie Vien, exhibiting portraits at the Salon from 1771 and becoming a member of the Académie Royale as a portrait painter in 1775. His portraits of such eminent contemporaries as the composer *Christoph Willibald Gluck* (Paris, Louvre) are characterized by a quiet, understated elegance. In 1775, ambitious to improve his status as an artist within the hierarchy of genres, he began to exhibit scenes of domestic life. *Paternal Love* (U. Birmingham, Barber Inst.) is indebted to the paintings of Jean-Baptiste Greuze, but the sentimental subject is depicted with a compositional clarity and restrained naturalism that make Aubry the most original and appealing of Greuze's imitators. The *Nurse's Farewell* (exh. Salon, 1777; Williamstown, MA, Clark A. Inst.) departs from prototypes by Greuze in its representation of a fashionable urban family in a landscape setting. In the late 1770s Aubry also painted melodramatic scenes, which demonstrate his desire to rival the success of Greuze's *Paternal Curse* (Paris, Louvre). Aubry's genre paintings were praised by contemporary critics, including Denis Diderot, and were bought by such notable collectors as the Comte d'Angiviller, Directeur des Bâtiments du Roi. In 1777, under the auspices of d'Angiviller, he went to Rome in order to study to become a history painter, but his progress disappointed the hopes of his patrons. Aubry's later paintings are untraced; his posthumously exhibited *Coriolanus' Farewell to his Wife* (exh. Salon, 1781; untraced) inspired many critics to express regret for his early death.

BIBLIOGRAPHY

F. Ingersoll-Smouse: 'Quelques tableaux de genre inédits par Etienne Aubry', *Gaz. B.-A.*, n.s. 5, xi (1925), pp. 77–86
P. Grigaut: 'Marmontel's Shepherdess of the Alps in Eighteenth Century Art', *A. Q.* [Detroit], xii (1949), pp. 30–47

EMMA BARKER

Aubry-Lecomte, Hyacinthe(-Louis-Victor-Jean-Baptiste) (*b* Nice, 31 Oct 1787; *d* Paris, 2 May 1858). French draughtsman and lithographer. The artist's family name was Aubry, but after his marriage he added his wife's maiden name to his own. Aubry-Lecomte was originally employed at the Ministry of Finance in Paris, but his interest in drawing led him to enrol at Girodet's atelier at the Ecole des Beaux-Arts. Aubry-Lecomte proved to be a proficient draughtsman and rapidly mastered the new technique of lithography, encouraged by Girodet, becoming one of its leading practitioners. He was also one of Girodet's most valued pupils, making lithographic reproductions of the master's paintings to be copied in the atelier. Among the most important of these are the suite of 16 prints (1822) showing the heads of the main figures from *Ossian and the French Generals* (1802; Malmaison, Château N.), a print (1824) of *Danaë* (1797) and another of an *Amazon* painted for the Duchesse de Berry (both untraced). With other pupils of Girodet he contributed lithographs based on the master's illustrations for two publications, *Les Amours des dieux* (1826) and the *Enéide* (1827). Aubry-Lecomte also made prints after Pierre-Paul Prud'hon, François Gérard, Horace Vernet, Louis Hersent and others. His original works consist mainly of landscape and genre subjects and portraits of his family and friends (e.g. *Mlle Aubry-Lecomte*, lithograph, 1834; Paris, Bib. N.). He exhibited regularly from 1819, won several medals and was popularly known as the 'prince of lithographers'. He did much to raise the status of printmaking and in 1849 was decorated with the Légion d'honneur.

BIBLIOGRAPHY

Auguste Gallimard: *Aubry-Lecomte* (Paris, 1860)
J. Adhémar: 'L'Enseignement académique en 1820: Girodet et son atelier', *Bull. Soc. Hist. A. Fr.* (1934), pp. 270–83
S. Nevison Brown: *Girodet: A Contradictory Career* (diss., U. London, 1980)

STEPHANIE NEVISON BROWN

Aubusson. Town situated on the River Creuse in the Creuse département (formerly La Marche) in central-southern France. Tapestries have been produced at Aubusson and the nearby town of Felletin since the 16th century, and carpet manufacture was established in Aubusson in 1743.

1. Tapestry. 2. Carpets.

1. TAPESTRY. It seems likely that the first looms in Aubusson were set up in the 14th century by Flemish refugees, although tapestry production did not begin until the 16th century. The tapestry industry in Felletin seems to have been established earlier than that of Aubusson: an inventory of 1514 written after the death of Charlotte D'Albret records tapestry pieces originating from Felletin. It was not until 1560 that Errard D'Ahun recorded the weavers of both towns, in *Histoire de l'antique ville d'Ahun en la province de Marche* (Clermont, 1857). The Aubusson and Felletin weavers wove many types of tapestries, using subject-matter similar to that favoured by their Flemish contemporaries. The quality of the work was, however, considerably less accomplished. The fact that La Marche was so far from Paris meant that the tapestry market was weak, as access to the richest clients was limited. Weavers often had to travel in search of profitable commissions or sell to local buyers who were unable to afford expensive, high-quality tapestries. Consequently the Aubusson weavers specialized in the cheaper, low-warp weaving technique. The cartoons from which the weavers worked were also of rather poor quality; they were often taken from contemporary engravings, which were simplified when copied.

With the end of the Wars of Religion (1559–93) Henry IV was keen to restore France's economic health and he took a great interest in the textile industry, consolidating the workshops in Paris and encouraging the weavers at Aubusson. In 1601 an edict was published forbidding the import of Flemish tapestries in an attempt to reduce foreign competition. In 1620 the weavers of La Marche were exempted from payment of customs duties on tapestries sent to Paris. This measure helped the growth of prosperity at Aubusson, and by 1637 2000 weavers were recorded as working there.

In 1625 a set of tapestries was commissioned from the weaver Lambert for the chapter house of the cathedral of Notre-Dame, Reims, and in 1649 a three-piece set was woven for the collegiate church of St Mainboeuf d'Angers. Subjects were taken from contemporary works: the painter Claude Vignon made copies of engravings by Abraham Bosse, which were used at Aubusson, and subjects from other workshops were copied with equal lack of respect. The *Loves of Gombault and Macée* (Guéret, Mus. Guéret), a tapestry modernized some time after 1650 by Laurent Goyot for the Paris workshops, was woven at Aubusson. As in the 16th century, the cartoons were mainly of inferior quality, and the wools and dyes were unrefined.

The low standard of the tapestry production at Aubusson was highlighted in 1664. Jean-Baptiste Colbert (*see* COLBERT, (1)), Louis XIV's Surintendant des Bâtiments, Arts et Manufactures, was eager to encourage the tapestry industry and bring all the concerns in France under his power. As part of this consolidation he ordered an inquiry into the weavers in La Marche and their needs. The main

Aubusson tapestry of 'Vintage', from the series *Daphnis and Chloe*, designed by Etienne Jeurat at the Gobelins, Paris, wool, 2.1×3.2 m, mid-18th century (London, Victoria and Albert Museum)

request from the weavers was for a painter and a dyer to be sent to Aubusson. Colbert responded in 1665 by issuing letters patent organizing the industry and giving it an official royal charter and the title of Manufacture Royale; the corporative nature and freedom of administration of the workshops were, however, maintained. Each tapestry was to have MRD or MRDB (Manufacture Royale Daubisson/Da Bission) woven into the fabric, and all tapestries were to have blue selvages. Felletin received its royal charter in 1689 and to differentiate its work from that of Aubusson it had to produce tapestries with brown borders. Despite the new charter, Aubusson was not very prosperous during the second half of the 17th century. The important request for a painter and a dyer had been ignored, and the revocation of the Edict of Nantes (1685) hit the industry badly: at least 200 Huguenot weavers fled and settled in more tolerant countries, especially Germany. The later wars of Louis XIV left France weakened financially, and this too hit the luxury industries heavily.

It was not until 1732 that the industry in Aubusson received a new impetus. New letters patent were issued, and the painter Jean-Joseph Dumons (1687–1779) was sent to Aubusson. He was expected to stay at Aubusson for three months in every two years, direct the overseers, teach drawing, correct models and supply the weavers with new cartoons. Firmazeau, a dyer from the Gobelins, was also sent *c.* 1730 to Aubusson. The position of the director was changed to that of inspector and was held mainly by members of the local Laboray family. In 1742 a school of design was established under the direction of the King's painter and attached to the factory. In 1748 an official was appointed with responsibility for the selection and matching of wools and silks in an effort to maintain high standards.

The reorganization during the 1730s and 1740s marked the beginning of a successful period for the workshops in La Marche. Many small workshops expanded, and several merchants bought shops in Paris as well as Aubusson as production increased. The tapestries of this period mainly depict pastoral landscapes (see fig.) or chinoiseries, reflecting the change in taste from the heavy *verdures* of the Baroque to lighter Rococo subjects and designs. The work of Jean-Baptiste Atria was frequently copied, especially his *Fables of La Fontaine.* In 1761 Aubusson was given cartoons by Atria of the *Metamorphoses* by the Beauvais factory. These were very popular, and the weaver François Picqueaux wove a total of seven sets. The paintings of Boucher were popular, and many chinoiserie tapestries woven at Aubusson were inspired by his designs; Jean Pillement's designs were also influential. The weavers, however, also continued to copy engravings (e.g. after Nicolas Lancret). Large quantities of furnishing fabrics for upholstery, often with oval vignettes of a pastoral scene framed by wreaths of flowers, were also produced at Aubusson during this period.

The French Revolution forced some of the workshops in La Marche to close, as the weavers lost many of their richest clients. Napoleon, however, took great interest in the textile industry and by commissioning several carpets from Aubusson helped revive it. During this period very few wall hangings were woven; carpets and furnishing textiles were almost exclusively produced. The fashion for patterned wallpapers had made wall hangings less popular for interiors. The factories at Aubusson, however, continued to prosper throughout the 19th century, mostly reproducing old designs. In 1869 a school of industrial art was founded at Aubusson, which became the Ecole Nationale des Arts Décoratifs in 1884.

During the 1920s and 1930s tapestries were produced at Aubusson after designs by such famous contemporary painters as Picasso, Matisse, Léger and Braque. In 1938 Jean Lurçat designed for Aubusson a set of upholstery covers to accompany his series of hangings the *Illusions of Icarus* (The Hague, Kon. Huisarchf), which had been made at the Gobelins. In 1939 Lurçat was appointed permanent designer at Aubusson. His ten-panel series called *Song of the World* (1957–64; Angers, Mus. Lurçat; for illustration *see* LURÇAT, (1)), made at the workshop of François Tabard (1902–69) in Aubusson, was directly inspired by the 14th-century Angers *Apocalypse* tapestry series (1373–82; Angers, Château, Col. Tap.). His work is full of natural forms, animals and fish, and his palette limited to a series of strong colours. Lurçat's involvement in the art and promotion of tapestry helped ensure its revival in France in the late 20th century. (For reference to 20th-century tapestry manufacture at Felletin *see* SUTHERLAND, GRAHAM, and TAPESTRY, colour pl. VIII, fig. 1.)

BIBLIOGRAPHY

H. Göbel: *Wandteppiche*, 3 vols (Leipzig, 1923–34; Eng. trans. of vol. i, New York, 1924)

Cinq siècles de tapisseries d'Aubusson (exh. cat., Paris, Mus. Gobelins, 1935)

A. Lejard: *French Tapestry* (London, 1946)

G. F. W. Digby: *French Tapestries from the 14th Century to 18th Century* (London, 1951)

R. A. Weitgert: *French Tapestry* (London, 1962)

A. S. Cavallo: *Tapestries of Europe and Colonial Peru in the Museum of Fine Arts* (Boston, 1967)

P. F. Bertrand, D. Chevalier and P. Chevalier: *Les Tapisseries d'Aubusson et de Felletin, 1457–1791* (Paris, 1988)

DIANA FOWLE

2. CARPETS. The production of carpets began at Aubusson in 1743. As the products of the SAVONNERIE in Paris were reserved for the exclusive use of the king, and as the best imported Turkish carpets were both expensive and difficult to obtain, Jean-Henri-Louis Orry de Fulvy (*d* 1751), Louis XV's Intendant des Finances, decided that Aubusson should also produce carpets to meet the growing demand. Samples of Turkish carpets together with looms and detailed instructions on how the work should be done were sent from Paris. For the first three years the venture was financed by the Crown, until the Paris merchants Pierre Mage and Jacques Dessarteaux took over the workshops as a private enterprise in 1746 and employed the tapestry designer Jean-Joseph Dumons (1687–1779) to produce cartoons. For several years his designs were almost direct copies of Turkish carpets, but by 1750 it became apparent that the clientele wanted something that was more French in style. In 1751 Pierre-Josse Perrot, a painter at the Gobelins who had designed carpets for the Savonnerie, was consulted, and Louis XV also sent three Savonnerie carpets to Aubusson to be used as models. In 1753 the painter Louis-Joseph Le Lorrain created a new style of carpet design called *à grande mosaïque*, which referred to a central medallion of flowers

of a completely French style (e.g. carpet, *c.* 1770; Paris, Mus. Nissim de Camondo). The new carpet designs were completely French in character, although they were much simpler than the complex arrangements of those of the Savonnerie. Two types of carpet were made at Aubusson: knotted-pile carpets woven on vertical looms, and from *c.* 1767 tapestry-woven carpets produced on horizontal looms. Aubusson carpets were cheaper than those of the Savonnerie and were not exclusive, which enabled the workshops to flourish; inventories show that several carpets were used in the smaller rooms at the château of Versailles. Many Aubusson carpets were sold abroad, especially in northern Europe, and some even reached the USA.

During the French Revolution the factory had only four workshops in operation. However, the advent of the First Empire in 1804 gave the town a new lease of life, and many orders were received from the Imperial household and associated nobility. Production was not seriously affected by the fall of Napoleon (1815) and the restoration of the monarchy, but as the 19th century progressed competition from England increased. By 1843 the number of orders for hand-woven carpets had decreased significantly, and many weavers were made redundant. Competition also came from factories in Tourcoing, Amiens, Abbeville and Lille, and in desperation workmen were brought over from Kidderminster in England to instruct the weavers in the production of carpets made using the Brussels technique (looped pile). The designs woven followed popular fashions. After 1880 the crisis became more acute: orders for carpets were few, sales were poor, and the workshops were sustained only by the weaving of tapestry wall hangings. In the 20th century well-designed carpets once again began to play an important role in interior design. By the mid-1920s contemporary artists gave a new impetus to the production of hand-knotted carpets, with Aubusson workshops leading the way. In the late 20th century craftsmen at Aubusson were engaged in the production of carpets for the refurbishment of the Grand Trianon at Versailles based on the original designs.

BIBLIOGRAPHY

M. Jarry: *Carpets of Aubusson* (Leigh-on-Sea, 1969)

——: 'Design in Aubusson Carpets', *Antiques*, xcv (1969), pp. 702–7

JENNIFER WEARDEN

Auckland. City in New Zealand. It is situated on a narrow isthmus between the Tasman Sea and the Pacific Ocean in the north of the country's North Island. The city is an important port, with harbours on both sides of the isthmus. It is New Zealand's largest centre of commerce and industry, with a metropolitan population of *c.* 900,000. European settlement began in 1840, when the British Lieutenant-Governor William Hobson chose the isthmus as the site for the capital of the new colony of New Zealand. In 1841 the Surveyor General drew up an elaborate town plan, but the unfavourable topography and early economic conditions meant that little of it was executed, although considerable foresight was shown then and subsequently in setting aside areas of parkland. The most significant surviving buildings of the early colonial period are the Old Government House (1855–7) by WILLIAM MASON (ii) and Hulme Court (1843), both in the Georgian tradition, and the Gothic Revival church buildings in the Early English style associated with Bishop George Augustus Selwyn, such as St John's College Chapel (1847), Kinder House (1858) and Bishopscourt (now Selwyn Court, 1863–5), designed by FREDERICK THATCHER. After 1865, when the seat of government was transferred to Wellington, Auckland began to develop as a leading commercial centre. Financial institutions such as the Bank of New Zealand and the New Zealand Insurance Company were founded and set new architectural standards for commercial premises. The Gothic Revival Supreme Court House (1865–7), designed by Edward Rumsey (1824–1909), was the result of an architectural competition, but the directors of the Bank of New Zealand commissioned LEONARD TERRY in Melbourne to design their handsome bank building, with its classical front (1865; extended 1880s). Fine houses such as Highwic and Alberton (both 1862) were built in the surrounding countryside, which was soon overtaken by suburban streets. A brief period of prosperity from gold-mining in the 1870s and early 1880s led to many new buildings being erected in a variety of styles, ranging from Venetian Gothic to Greek Revival (spectacularly, the later War Memorial Museum, 1925–9, by Grierson, Amier & Draffin) and French Renaissance, the latter being used, for example, in the Auckland City Art Gallery (1888) by the Melbourne firm of Grainger & D'Ebro. Another notable building from the same year is the Custom House by Thomas Mahoney (1854–1923). Built, like the City Art Gallery, on a corner site, the Custom House is notable for the ornamental treatment of its façade.

In the early 20th century the influence of the Arts and Crafts Movement is visible in some of the large houses built by such architects as R. K. Binney, W. H. Gummer and Gerald Jones. Binney's own house, for example, built *c.* 1916 in 1922 in Remuera Road, shows the influence of Edwin Lutyens, while Jones's work is closer to that of C. F. A. Voysey. Gummer, in partnership with C. R. Ford, also designed many fine public and commercial buildings in Auckland and elsewhere. Other architectural styles introduced around this time include the Spanish mission style, the influence of which is evident in Auckland Grammar School (1916) by R. Atkinson Abbot, whose private houses also have affinities with Californian bungalows. ROY LIPPINCOTT, meanwhile, who was influenced by Walter Burley Griffin and Frank Lloyd Wright, introduced the style of the Prairie school in his domestic architecture, while his design for the Arts Building (with Edward Billson, 1921–6; see fig.) at the University of Auckland draws heavily on elements of Gothic architecture. In the 1930s and 1940s, as a result of economic depression and World War II, there was a period of architectural mediocrity, but in the 1950s W. D. Wilson formed 'the Group', who sought to recreate the functional simplicity of early colonial domestic architecture. By contrast, the commercial architecture of the 1960s and after was dominated by the International Style, used to express urbanity and opulence, for example in the ANZ Bank in Auckland. Substantial commercial construction in the 1980s meant the loss of many smaller 19th-century buildings. Lavish office towers at this time were sometimes the work of international practices.

Auckland, Arts Building, University of Auckland, by Roy Lippincott and Edward Billson, 1921–5

Early painters in Auckland were chiefly watercolourists capturing the unfamiliar landscape, most notably JOHN KINDER and J. B. C. HOYTE. Albin Martin (1813–88), who had been a pupil of John Linnell (ii) and a friend of Samuel Palmer, was among the founders of the Society of Artists, which held its first exhibition in 1871 and was reformed as the Auckland Society of Arts ten years later. While several Auckland schools provided a limited art training under such instructors as Hoyte and Kennett Watkins (1847–1933), the foundation of the Elam School of Art in 1889 contributed greatly to the development of the fine arts in Auckland. Also important was the work of Louis John Steele (1843–1918), who had exhibited at the Royal Academy and the Paris Salon, and C. F. GOLDIE, who spent six years in Europe but returned to Auckland to paint a long series of Maori portraits. JOHN WEEKS was influential in the early 20th century.

From the 1950s, influenced by the pre-eminence of the City Art Gallery and the spread of commercial galleries, Auckland became the principal centre of art activity in New Zealand, with COLIN MCCAHON and PATRICK HANLY most prominent among the painters. Molly Macalister was a notable sculptor.

See also NEW ZEALAND, especially §§II, III, XI and XII.

BIBLIOGRAPHY

U. Platts: *The Lively Capital* (Christchurch, 1971)
C. R. Knight: *The Selwyn Churches of Auckland* (Wellington, 1972)
J. Fields and J. Stacpoole: *Victorian Auckland* (Dunedin, 1973)
J. Stacpoole: *Colonial Architecture in New Zealand* (Wellington, 1976)
Historic Buildings of New Zealand: North Island (Auckland, 1979)
B. Gamble and P. Shaw: *Auckland City Art Gallery: A Centennial History* (Auckland, 1988)

JOHN STACPOOLE

Auction. Public sale in which items are sold to the highest bidder. Until the 20th century the major trade in works of art was carried out primarily through dealing, with the dealer and the MARCHANDS-MERCIER acting as middlemen between the vendor and buyer. However, the sale in October 1958 at Sotheby's auction house, London, of seven Impressionist paintings from the collection of Erwin Goldschmidt (1882–1954) for £681,000 shifted the balance of power. After this sale the auction houses, particularly SOTHEBY'S and CHRISTIE'S, managed, through their large marketing and promotional machines, their ability to offer financial deals to both prospective sellers and buyers, and their development of international networks, to cream off much of the trade that had traditionally passed through dealers. Dealers are still, however, the biggest customers of the auction houses, both as sellers and as buyers.

1. EARLY HISTORY. Auctions have existed for at least 2500 years. Herodotus (?484–*c.* 427 BC) wrote of auctions of nubile women held annually in Babylon, and the Romans had a well-organized auctioneering system, which included works of art, for instance when legionaries sold off loot *sub hasta* (lit. beneath the spear; *asta* remains the Italian for auction). The roots of modern fine art auctions, however, can be traced to the Netherlands, where, in the late 16th century and throughout the 17th, paintings and prints were sold by 'Dutch' auction in which the price of a lot is set high and then lowered until a bid is accepted (*see* ART MARKET). General auctions were being held in London by the late 17th century, encouraged by the arrival of William III from the Netherlands in 1688. Any works of art on offer might well be the former possessions of bankrupts and be included alongside more homely objects. By the end of the 18th century Sotheby's and Christie's, who between them account for around two-thirds by value of all works of art sold at auction throughout the world, were well established in London, as were Phillips (est. 1796) and Bonhams (est. 1793), the other two leading British auction houses.

2. ORGANIZATION. The organization of an auction has changed very little over the years. The auctioneer has total discretion during the sale. Every lot usually has a reserve price, fixed in consultation with the vendor, which is the minimum for which the work of art can be sold. Most catalogues contain estimates to guide potential buyers, and the reserve price is often at the level of the low estimate, although in weak trading conditions vendors will have been persuaded by the auctioneer to accept bids below the low estimate. The auctioneer will also carry a list of commission bids from potential buyers who cannot be present at the auction. The auctioneer raises bids by fixed price bands and can turn away a bid that does not reach the next increment level. An auctioneer may take bids 'off the chandelier', forcing the prices up when there is no competitive bidding in the room, thus pushing the bids of a single buyer up to the vendor's reserve, or registering commission bids from absent participants.

Although there is still relatively little law relating to auctions, they now come under the scrutiny of local authorities and consumer bodies. In the past, auctioneers were reluctant to admit that an object was unsold as it could suggest that the market was weak, so deterring buyers. Instead, they would make up the name of a fictitious buyer, but they are now required to make unsold lots public. Although the auctioneer works for the vendor, most of his income can derive from the buyer. This situation arose following the introduction in 1975 by Sotheby's and Christie's in London of a buyer's premium of 10% on top of the hammer price, subsequently raised to 15% for most lots by 1993. This extra revenue dramatically changed the way auctions operate: the major auction houses will sometimes compete to secure large collections by reducing their charge to the seller to a figure approaching zero. Buyers might contribute most to the turnover of the auction houses, but the drive to secure goods to sell makes the vendor supreme. The introduction of the buyer's premium was greatly opposed by the dealers, the main customers of the auction houses, but they have accepted it and enjoy certain benefits over private buyers at auction in terms of credit facilities. Dealers have been known to form 'rings' at auctions where, having agreed beforehand on the top price that should be paid for various lots, they buy the best items very cheaply and then share the extra profit later. Rings usually operate either at regional salerooms or in certain specialist markets, in particular rugs and carpets, silver and jewellery.

Different auction houses tend to have different terms and conditions of sale; there are also vast variations in the tax burden of art auction houses in the industrialized world and the free movement of works of art (*see* ART LEGISLATION). The relative absence of government legislation enabled auction houses in London to enjoy a long period of international supremacy. In France, entrenched legislation has given the limited number of *commissaires-priseurs* a monopoly over the holding of auctions. The single European market should enable such British houses as Sotheby's and Christie's to hold auctions in France, which should greatly increase the prestige of French auction sales. In Germany, the autonomy of the various Länder and major cities has prevented the development of one international auction centre. The purchase of Sotheby's by the American businessman Alfred Taubman (*b* 1925) in 1983 led to a period of great expansion for the company. In the latter part of the 20th century New York was the main auction centre in terms of turnover, while London remained the centre for sales of Old Masters, antiquities and books. Sotheby's, and later Christie's, held important auctions in Hong Kong, and there were a few tentative sales in Tokyo. In 1990 both Christie's and Sotheby's set record prices for the sale of works of art at auction, respectively selling van Gogh's portrait of *Dr Gachet* for £82.5 million and Renoir's *Au Moulin de la Galette* for £78.1 million to a Japanese businessman. The economic recession of the 1990s soon precipitated a collapse in the art market, and by 1992 Sotheby's and Christie's were struggling to make a profit on turnovers that had halved.

See also INVESTMENT.

BIBLIOGRAPHY

W. Roberts: *Memorials of Christie's*, 2 vols (London, 1897)
G. Reitlinger: *The Economics of Taste*, 3 vols (London, 1961–70)
G. Keen: *The Sale of Works of Art: A Study Based on the Times-Sotheby Index* (London, 1971)
F. Herrmann: *Sotheby's: Portrait of an Auction House* (London, 1972)

ANTONY THORNCROFT

Audenarde. *See* OUDENAARDE.

Audio art. *See under* SOUND AND ART.

Audivert, Eduardo (*b* Buenos Aires, 2 Aug 1931). Argentine draughtsman and printmaker. He studied under the Argentine painter Demetrio Urruchúa (1902–78) and later at the Instituto Superior de Artes of the Universidad Nacional in Tucumán, under his father, Pompeyo Audivert (1900–77), and Lino Eneas Spilimbergo, who encouraged him to take up printmaking. After working in a realist style from 1954 to 1960 and in a linear style from 1960 to 1965 he began to produce technically accomplished drawings and prints in an idiom strongly influenced by Surrealism. Architectural supports such as plinths, pedestals, staircases and doors were among his favoured images, dominated by an atmosphere of anguish.

BIBLIOGRAPHY

J. Glusberg: *Del Pop-art a la Nueva Imagen* (Buenos Aires, 1985), pp. 235–40

JORGE GLUSBERG

Audran. French family of artists. Its history (see fig.) began with two engravers: Charles [Karl] Audran (*b* Paris, *c.* 1594; *d* Paris, 1674), who is thought to have trained in Italy with Matthäus Greuter (1564/6–1638) and produced much work of inconsistent quality, and his brother Claude Audran I (*b* Paris, *c.* 1592 or 1597; *d* Lyon, 18 Nov 1677), who made undistinguished book illustrations and portraits. Claude's eldest son, Germain (*b* Lyon, 6 Dec 1631; *bur* Lyon, 4 May 1710), was also an engraver of book illustrations and portraits and taught at the Académie des Sciences, Belles-Lettres et Arts in Lyon. The family's most prominent members were Claude I's two younger sons: (1) Claude Audran II, a painter, and particularly (2) Girard Audran, an engraver. The next generation produced artists of some distinction in three of Germain's sons: (3) Claude Audran III, a painter, and (4) Benoît Audran I and (5) Jean Audran, both engravers; the latter's son Benoît Audran II (*b* Paris, 17 Feb 1698; *d* Paris, 8 Jan 1772) was an engraver of minor importance.

(1) Claude Audran II (*b* Lyon, 27 March 1639; *d* Paris, 4 Jan 1684). Painter. He learnt the rudiments of painting in Lyon from Guillaume Perrier I (*d* 1656) and Guillaume Perrier II (1625–59), the brother and nephew of François Perrier. Around 1657 he moved to Paris, where he was employed by Noël Coypel and Charles Errard *le fils* on work in Versailles, the Louvre and the Tuileries. Charles Le Brun used him to make sketches for his *Battles of Alexander the Great* and for various works at the Louvre, Saint-Germain-en-Laye, Sceaux and Versailles; at Versailles, Audran collaborated with Charles de La Fosse and Gabriel Blanchard on the restoration of paintings in the Salon de Diane, and also provided some of his own compositions; he executed several easel paintings on religious subjects, including *St Denis*, *St Louis* and

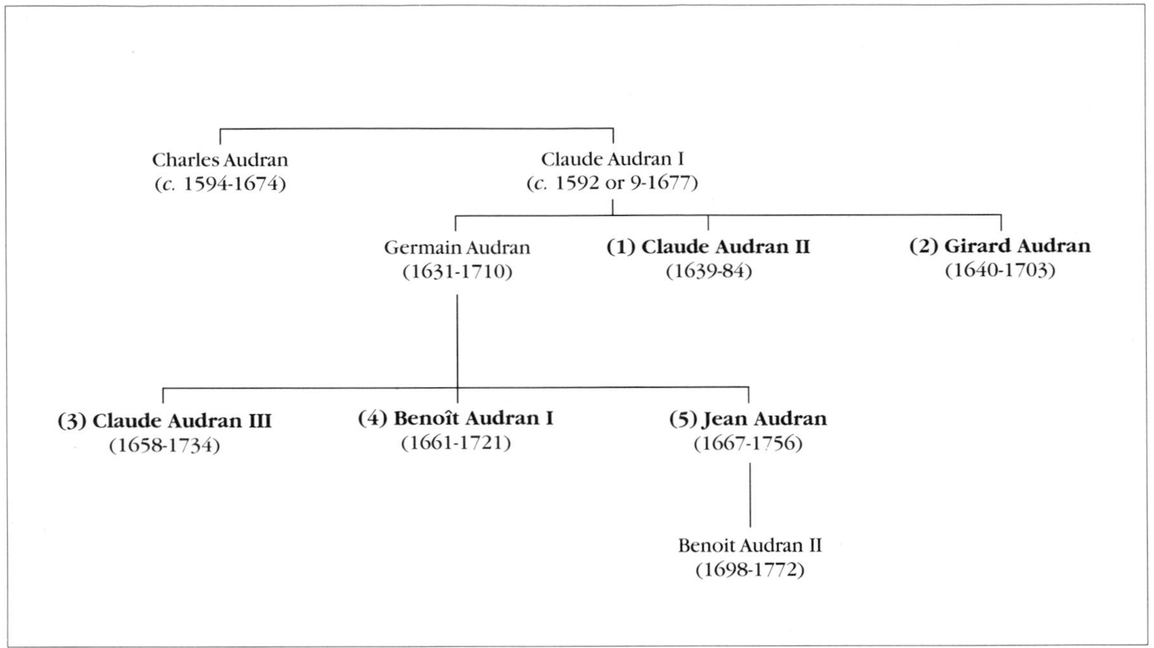

Family tree of the Audran family of artists

the *Miracle of the Loaves and Fishes* (Paris, Notre-Dame-des-Blancs-Manteaux). He was admitted (*reçu*) by the Académie Royale de Peinture et de Sculpture in 1657, with a painting of the *Last Supper*, and in 1669 he was appointed Peintre Ordinaire du Roi. In 1681 he was appointed professor at the Académie.

(2) Girard Audran (*b* Lyon, 2 Aug 1640; *d* Paris, 25 July 1703). Engraver, brother of (1) Claude Audran II. He was deservedly the most celebrated member of the family. Even though he first trained with his father, a mediocre artist, he made remarkably rapid progress: thus, in 1666 he engraved, in a very large format, the *Triumph of Constantine* and the *Battle of Constantine against Maxentius* after Charles Le Brun. As a consequence, he was sent that same year to Italy, where he perfected his skills, chiefly in Carlo Maratti's studio. Most particularly, he executed there (1668) prints after Pietro da Cortona's suites of *David and Goliath* and the *Story of Aeneas*, as well as prints after Raphael and Domenichino. On returning to France, Audran was welcomed by Le Brun, who obtained lodgings for him in the Gobelins and set him to reproduce his *Battles of Alexander the Great* in a large format. Audran carried out this enormous task, which earned him more than 10,000 francs, between 1672 and 1678; it remains his masterpiece. In 1674, when he had only just completed the first two compositions, he was admitted (*reçu*) to the Académie Royale, becoming a 'conseiller' in 1681. He settled *c.* 1677 in the Rue St Jacques, Paris, where he opened a print-selling and print-publishing business at the sign of *Les Deux Piliers d'or*. He published not only his own engravings but also those of the best of his contemporaries. After his death in 1703 his widow, sister of the painter Louis Licherie (1629–87), carried on his business, but in 1718 François Chéreau acquired the sign.

Girard Audran was an outstanding engraver, whose technique, combining etching with a free and vigorous use of the burin, was innovative. Although his engraved work numbers only *c.* 200 pieces, it is considerable because of the dimensions of the works, many of which were executed with two, three or four plates. The suite of 30 prints that he published in 1683, *Les Proportions du corps humain mesurées sur les plus belles figures de l'antiquité*, with a preface extolling the artists of antiquity, continued to be republished until 1855 and remained a standard manual for artists and students.

(3) Claude Audran III (*b* Lyon, 25 Aug 1658; *d* Paris, 28 May 1734). Painter, nephew of (1) Claude Audran. He trained with his uncles. He was solely a decorative artist, specializing in painted panelling, harpsichord cases and so on; he was, however, able to renew the genre with his arabesques, grotesques and *singeries* (see fig.). He worked at Versailles, Anet, Marly, Sceaux, Meudon and La Muette. He also made many tapestry cartoons for the Gobelins, including the *Douze mois grotesques* (1699) and the *Portières des dieux*. His decorations are now known mainly through his many drawings, a large collection of which is in the Nationalmuseum, Stockholm. His style influenced the decorators of the Régence. Watteau was one of his pupils.

(4) Benoît Audran I (*b* Lyon, 22 Nov 1661; *d* Louzouer, Loiret, 2 Oct 1721). Engraver, brother of (3) Claude Audran III. He was the pupil of his uncle (2) Girard Audran, as his style showed. His oeuvre, numbering more than 200 prints, included not only reproductions of paintings by such artists as Le Brun, François Verdier, Eustache Le Sueur and Pierre Mignard, but also numerous

Claude Audran III: decorative drawing, pen and ink and ink wash, 271×193 mm, *c.* 1704 (Stockholm, Nationalmuseum)

vignettes for books, among them a famous series (1718) for the Greek myth *Daphnis et Chloé* after compositions by the Regent, Philippe II, Duc d'Orléans. Audran was admitted (*reçu*) to the Académie Royale in 1709, with a portrait of *Jean-Baptiste Colbert* after Claude Lefèbvre and a *Raising of the Cross* after Le Brun.

(5) Jean Audran (*b* Lyon, 28 April 1667; *d* Paris, 17 June 1756). Engraver, brother of (3) Claude Audran III. He studied engraving in Paris with his uncle (2) Girard Audran, whose collaborator he became, most notably on the reproductive engravings of Charles Le Brun's *Battles of Alexander the Great.* Jean Audran made engravings after Italian masters, such as Pietro da Cortona, Francesco Albani and the Carracci family, and after 17th-century French masters, including Nicolas Poussin, Jean Jouvenet, Antoine Dieu, Antoine Coypel and Hyacinthe Rigaud. Later he reproduced works by more modern painters, such as Claude Gillot or Watteau, making 110 etchings for the latter's *Figures de différents caractères* (*c.* 1735). Jean's numerous works, like those of his uncle, often harmoniously combine etching and line engraving. In 1707 he was appointed Graveur Ordinaire du Roi; having been approved (*agréé*) by the Académie Royale in 1704, he was admitted (*reçu*) in 1708, with engravings of a portrait of *Antoine Coyzevox* after Rigaud and of a *Self-portrait* after Noël Coypel.

BIBLIOGRAPHY

Thieme–Becker
G. Duplessis: *Les Audran* (Paris, 1892)
M. Roux: *Inventaire du fonds français: Graveurs du dix-huitième siècle*, Paris, Bib. N., Cab. Est. cat., i (1930), pp. 217–68
R.-A. Weigert: *Inventaire du fonds français: Graveurs du dix-septième siècle*, Paris, Bib. N., Cab. Est. cat., i (1939), pp. 104–222

MAXIME PRÉAUD

Audsley, George Ashdown (*b* Elgin, 1838; *d* New York, 1925). Scottish architect, designer and writer. Trained as an architect, he moved to Liverpool, Lancs, in 1856 and set up an architectural practice with his brother William James Audsley (*b* 1833) in 1863. With him he wrote *Handbook of Christian Symbolism* (1865), and together they designed a number of buildings in and around Liverpool, among them the Welsh Presbyterian Church, Prince's Road, Toxteth (1865–7), Christ Church, Kensington (1870), and the church of St Margaret, Belmont Road, Anfield (1873). For the merchant William Preston they designed the church of St Mary (1873) in the grounds of his house, Ellel Grange, Lancs. Other commissions were for a synagogue and a tennis club. He was among the earliest publishers to exploit the graphic potential of chromolithography, and, contrary to other major books on ornament, he made a case for classifying designs by their basic motif rather than by nationality. He was an expert on Japanese art, lecturing on the subject and between 1870 and 1884 producing several books that proved influential as sources for japonaiserie, among them *Keramic Art of Japan* and *The Ornamental Arts of Japan.* In the 1890s he produced with Maurice Ashdown Audsley an ambitious guide entitled *The Practical Decorator and Ornamentalist.* In 1892 he moved to New York, where he continued to produce handbooks on applied ornament, turning and stencilling with his son Berthold Audsley.

WRITINGS

with W. Audsley: *Handbook of Christian Symbolism* (London, 1865)
Keramic Art of Japan (Liverpool, 1875)
with W. Audsley: *Outlines of Ornament in the Leading Styles* (London, 1881/*R* New York, 1882); as *Designs and Patterns from Historic Ornament* (New York, 1968)
The Ornamental Arts of Japan (London, 1882–4)
with M. A. Audsley: *The Practical Decorator and Ornamentalist* (Glasgow and Paris, 1892/*R* Stuttgart, 1893)

BIBLIOGRAPHY

Bldgs England
S. Jervis: *The Penguin Dictionary of Design and Designers* (London, 1984)

□

Audubon, John James (Laforest) [Fougère, Jean-Jacques] (*b* Les Cayes, Santo Domingo [now Haiti], 26 April 1785; *d* New York state, 27 Jan 1851). American naturalist, painter and draughtsman of French–Creole descent. Brought up in a French village near Nantes, he developed an interest in art and natural science, encouraged by his father and the naturalist Alcide Dessaline d'Orbigny. He is thought to have moved to Paris by 1802 to pursue formal art training; although the evidence is inconclusive, Audubon claimed to have studied in the studio of Jacques-Louis David.

In 1803 Audubon travelled to the USA to oversee Mill Grove, an estate owned by his father on the outskirts of Philadelphia, PA. Uninterested in practical affairs, he spent his time hunting and drawing birds. His drawings (many in Cambridge, MA, Harvard U., Houghton Lib.) from this period are executed primarily in pencil and pastel. They are conventional specimen drawings that define individual

John James Audubon: *Golden Eagle (Aquila chrysaetos)*, watercolour, 887×587 mm, 1833 (New York, New-York Historical Society)

birds in stiff profile with little or no background. A number of these works, however, bear notations from Mark Catesby's *Natural History of Carolina, Florida, and the Bahama Islands* (1731–47). Catesby's etchings, which were some of the first natural history illustrations to stress the interaction between organisms and their habitats, clearly impressed Audubon, and soon his work began to address the complex relations that exist between birds and their environments. He also began to use watercolour, the medium he employed most regularly as a mature artist.

In 1807 Audubon moved to Louisville, KY, where his passion for the study and depiction of birds accounted, at least in part, for the failure of a series of business ventures. In 1810 he was visited by the Philadelphia naturalist–artist Alexander Wilson, who was looking for subscribers for his illustrated *American Ornithology* (1808–14). Audubon, who believed himself the better artist, did not subscribe, but Wilson's work undoubtedly inspired him to begin his own large-scale publication on American birds.

Having been declared bankrupt in 1819, Audubon moved to Shippingsport, KY, where he began to draw portraits in chalk. The following year he briefly ran a drawing school in Cincinnati, OH, and also worked for the Western Museum at Cincinnati College (now the Museum of Natural History), where he stuffed animal specimens and drew landscape backgrounds for museum displays. It was during this time that he dedicated himself to the publication of his own watercolours of American birds. In October 1820, accompanied by his student, Joseph Mason (1807–83), Audubon left for a three-month collecting and drawing expedition down the Ohio and Mississippi rivers. At the end of this trip, in 1821 he explored the Louisiana bayous in search of birds; he painted each new species, and Mason supplied detailed backgrounds for over 50 of the watercolours. In 1824 Audubon attempted to publish his pictures in Philadelphia, but he met with a disappointing reception from the scientific community there, due partly to his own arrogance and partly to the community's loyalty to Wilson. For the next two years he continued to observe and paint the birds of the southern states.

In May 1826 Audubon left for England, where he exhibited his watercolours at the Liverpool Royal Institution to great acclaim. In order to increase his income, he sold a number of copies of his works in oil. He also exhibited at the Royal Society of British Artists, London, the Royal Scottish Academy and the Royal Institution of Edinburgh. In November 1826 Audubon entered into an agreement with the engraver William Home Lizars to publish his watercolours as handcoloured engravings. After several months, however, with only ten plates completed, the contract was terminated, and Audubon was compelled to find a new publisher. The engraver Robert Havell jr undertook the project, and by the autumn *The Birds of America* was under way.

While overseeing the production of the plates for *The Birds of America*, Audubon worked on his accompanying text, the *Ornithological Biography* (1831–8). He also commissioned Joseph Bartholomew Kidd (1808–89) to copy his watercolours in oil. From 1831 to 1833 Audubon received from Kidd at least 94 copies of watercolours for the first and second volumes of *The Birds of America*. These, however, were unsigned, and have consequently been difficult to distinguish from copies painted by Audubon himself, and by his sons Victor Gifford Audubon (1809–62) and John Woodhouse Audubon (1812–60), both accomplished artists.

Audubon returned to America to seek new subjects, in 1829–30 in New Jersey and Pennsylvania, and in 1831 in the Florida Keys, accompanied by the artist George Lehman (*d* 1870). In Charleston, SC, he befriended the Rev. John Bachman (1790–1874), a naturalist whose sister, Maria Martin (*d* 1863), provided watercolours of plants and insects for the backgrounds of approximately 35 plates. Audubon continued his explorations in Labrador, Newfoundland, with his son John, returning to England in 1834.

The Birds of America was completed in early 1839 as a double elephant folio. Issued by subscription in 87 parts, the set contains 435 handcoloured prints of 1065 life-sized birds representing 489 species. Havell produced these prints by a complex process of engraving, etching and aquatint. The original watercolours for the set belong to the New-York Historical Society, New York. The watercolours and the prints reflect the growing interest of naturalists to define species not only according to anatomical traits but also according to characteristic behavioural patterns. Audubon's works generally present several birds from the same species engaged in such typical group activities as hunting, feeding, courting or caring for their young (see fig.). Foreshadowing Darwinism, many of Audubon's most dramatic images openly challenge the traditional conception of a benevolent Creation by pitting predators against prey, and even showing members of the same species confronting one another in a violent struggle for survival.

Between 1840 and 1844 a seven-volume octavo version of *The Birds of America* was produced by the Philadelphia firm of J. T. Bowen. This publication, overseen by John Woodhouse Audubon, contains 500 lithographs of the original prints, as well as prints of several new birds. In 1842 Audubon settled on the Hudson River, at an estate called Minnie's Land, and began work on *The Viviparous Quadrupeds of North America* (150 plates, 1845–8). His sons assisted, with John Woodhouse Audubon producing more than half the studies for the 150 handcoloured lithographs. Seeking new specimens for this publication, Audubon made his last extended expedition along the upper Missouri and Yellowstone rivers in 1843, accompanied by John Bachman and the young naturalist Isaac Sprague (1811–95). Bachman wrote all of the text which accompanied the plates for *The Viviparous Quadrupeds* in the volumes that appeared between 1846 and 1854.

WRITINGS AND PRINTS

The Birds of America, from Original Drawings Made during a Residence of 25 Years in the United States, 4 vols (London, 1827–39); rev. in 7 vols (Philadelphia and New York, 1840–44/*R* 1967)

My Style of Drawing Birds (MS.; 1831); intro. M. Zinman (New York, 1979)

Ornithological Biography, 5 vols (Edinburgh, 1831–8) [text to accompany *The Birds of America*]

with J. Bachman: *The Viviparous Quadrupeds of North America* (New York, 1845–8 [pls], 1846–54 [text], rev. 3/1856)

L. Audubon, ed.: *The Life of John James Audubon, the Naturalist* (New York, 1869)

H. Corning, ed.: *Letters of John James Audubon, 1826–1840* (Boston, 1930)

BIBLIOGRAPHY

M. Audubon: *Audubon and his Journals*, 2 vols (New York, 1897/*R* 1972)

W. Fries: 'Joseph Bartholomew Kidd and the Oil Paintings of Audubon's *Birds of America*', *A. Q.* [Detroit], xxvi (1963), pp. 339–49

A. Ford: *John James Audubon* (Norman, OK, 1964)

A. Coffin: 'Audubon's Friend: Maria Martin', *NY Hist. Soc. Q.*, xlix (1965), pp. 29–51

A. Adams: *John James Audubon: A Biography* (New York, 1966)

W. Fries: *The Double Elephant Folio: The Story of Audubon's 'Birds of America'* (Chicago, 1973)

J. Chancellor: *Audubon: A Biography* (New York, 1978)

John James Audubon and his Sons (exh. cat., ed. G. Reynolds; New York U., Grey A.G., 1982)

R. Tyler: *Nature's Classics: John James Audubon's Birds and Animals* (Orange, TX, 1992)

A. Blaugrund and T. Stebbins: *John James Audubon: The Watercolours for 'The Birds of America'* (New York, 1993)

AMY MEYERS

Auer, Hans Wilhelm (*b* Wädenswil, 16 April 1847; *d* Konstanz, 30 Aug 1906). Swiss architect, teacher and writer. In Zurich he was trained (1863–4) by a master carpenter called Brunner and he then studied (1865–8) under Gottfried Semper at the Polytechnikum. He moved to Vienna to study (1869–70) at the Akademie der Bildenden Künste with Theophilus Hansen. From 1870 to 1884 he was Hansen's pupil and later chief collaborator. He was a professor at the Staatsgewerbeschule, Vienna (1884–8), and at Berne University (from 1890), from which time he was a member of almost every competition jury in Switzerland. In Vienna, Auer made major contributions to Hansen's buildings, including the Börse (1871–7) and the Reichsrat (1873–88). In his architecture as well as in his teaching he was centrally concerned with the Renaissance, two examples in this style being Dr Eder's Sanatorium (1886–7), Vienna, which has a domed vestibule, and the post office (1892) in Liestal, which is a symmetrical block in the style of a Renaissance palazzo. Auer's main work was the enlargement of the Bundeshaus in Berne (*see* BERNE, §3). In 1888–92 he worked on the east wing of the building, the plan and main structure of which matched the west wing (1852–7) by Friedrich Studer. The central section of the symmetrical complex, containing the parliament, was constructed in 1894–1902 and was influenced by the work of Semper. The façades are entirely rusticated and the north façade is given added importance by the depth of the projecting central section with its attached Corinthian portico and pediment. Both north and south façades are enriched with allegorical statues and ornament symbolic of Switzerland. Auer wrote a large number of historical studies on the architecture of antiquity and the Renaissance. His two most important works were on Palladio (1882) and the Bernese building style (1896).

BIBLIOGRAPHY

SKL

Obituary, *Schweiz. Bauztg*, xlviii (1906), pp. 112–13

CORNELIA BAUER

Auer, Jakob (*b* Heimingberg-Hopperg, Tyrol, 1645; *d* Grins, Tyrol, 7 May 1706). Austrian sculptor. From 1666 to 1671 he was an apprentice in the workshop of Michael Lechleitner (*c.* 1611–69), whose daughter he married. From 1671 to 1673 he probably worked in Otztal, Tyrol: the high altar in the church at Zwieselstein may be an early work of his. In 1673 he took over Lechleitner's workshop. The first certain work by Auer is an ivory relief of the *Fall of Man* (signed and dated 1677; Weimar, Schlossmus.). The almost transparent relief ground, the smooth, soft full figures and the highly detailed, naturalistic delineation of the accessories are typical of Auer's small sculptural work. The ceremonial goblet of rhinoceros horn carved with mythological scenes (signed I.A., *c.* 1680–90; Munich, Residenz) is probably also by Auer, as the small, lively figures are common in his work.

It is not easy to trace a stylistic development in Auer's art; thus, lacking documentation, it is not possible to establish the chronology of his small sculptural work, his work for the royal art collection or his devotional images. He may have travelled to Vienna *c.* 1685, possibly contributing to the work on the Trinity Column (also called the Plague Column, 1685–93). He chiefly worked, on both a large and a small scale, for rich religious foundations in Upper Austria: Lambach (1681–93), St Florian (*c.* 1685–*c.* 1704/5) and Kremsmünster (1681/2–1697/9). His most important large-scale sculptural work is the marble portal for the Benedictine monastery at Lambach. It is a High Baroque narrative composition, with *St Adalbert*, *St Kilian* and the *Virgin and Child* set above four columns, and below this a cartouche with the coats of arms of the abbot and the foundation. The heavy drapery with hems as if swinging is characteristic of Auer's work. He was influenced by the art of Italy (Gianlorenzo Bernini and the followers of Giambologna) and Flanders (Rubens and the circle of Anthony van Dyck). He learnt about the work of these artists through the sculpture of Michael Zürn the younger (*fl* 1617–51), Peter Strudel, the circle of Matthias Rauchmiller in Vienna and perhaps also Matthias Steinl.

BIBLIOGRAPHY

Barock im Oberland (exh. cat., Innsbruck, Tirol. Landesmus., 1973), pp. 44–6

E. V. Phillipowich: *Elfenbein* (Brunswick, 1961, rev. Munich, 2/1982), pp. 100, 208, 260

C. Theuerkauff: 'Jakob Auer: Bildhauer in Grins', *Pantheon*, xli (1983), pp. 194–208

A. GERHARDT

Auerbach, Frank (*b* Berlin, 29 April 1931). British painter and printmaker of German birth. He was sent to England in 1939 and moved from school in Kent to London in 1947, where he began attending art classes at Hampstead Garden Suburb Institute and acting in fringe theatre. From 1947 to 1948 he studied at Borough Polytechnic under David Bomberg, whose teaching was especially valuable in its emphasis on risk and on seeking an organic, unified form. Auerbach continued in Bomberg's evening life classes while at St Martin's School of Art (1948–52). He considered his first original achievement to have been *Summer Building Site* (1952; Mrs P. Hill priv. col., see 1986 exh. cat., p. 8), of a scene at Earls Court; this was rather geometric and painted in formal, prismatic colour, but much of his early work was thickly and laboriously impastoed in earth colours, as in *Head of E. O. W.* (1955; U. Cincinnati, OH). He studied from 1952 to 1955 at the Royal College of Art and had his first exhibition at the Beaux Arts Gallery, London, in 1956.

The subjects and intentions of Auerbach's paintings remained consistent. When he moved in 1954 to his studio in Camden Town, he began recording such locations as Primrose Hill, which were close enough to observe and draw each morning before returning to paint indoors. For his portraits he always found it most challenging to take as his subject a person he knew well. At first he laid brushstrokes on top of one another, whereas from the late 1960s he scraped down the impasto after each session; as a final step he allowed the relatively soft paint to form spontaneously a geography of peaks, channels and merged colours, corresponding to facts and feelings about the subject. This can be seen in *Head of Laurie Owen* (1972; U. Manchester, Whitworth A.G.).

After returning to large portrait drawings in charcoal in the mid-1970s, Auerbach found a way of simulating living, solid subjects and translucent spaces by drawing in oil. The inventive conjunctions of mixed neutral tones and decisive primary marks became more plastic and resonant than before, and more responsive to random incidents. Articulate about his own art and his responses to other painters, Auerbach claimed to work from inside his pictures. He stated (interview in *Metropolis-M*, 2, 1986, pp. 30–34):

> 'My motives are among the most common: the wish to retrieve a shameful life by making something and the wish to defeat the passing of time by preserving an experience. However, whatever the impulse, whatever the critical decision and consideration, at the moment of making, the work must arise as a living thing, with its own imperatives, under the artist's hand.'

From *c.* 1954 Auerbach also made prints: drypoints, etchings and screen prints. Their subject-matter has included nudes, reclining and seated figures, heads (e.g. *Head of Lucian Freud*, etching, 1980; see Podro, p. 296) and trees. Throughout his career Auerbach's art was highly regarded in Britain in the context of such painters as Francis Bacon, Lucian Freud and Leon Kossoff, who also document the physical by extreme measures. His international reputation grew during the 1980s; an example of his portraits from this period is *J. Y. M. Seated* (1980–81; Huddersfield, A.G.; see fig.). Auerbach represented Britain at the Venice Biennale in 1986, where he won joint first prize.

WRITINGS

'Fragments from a Conversation', *X: Q. Rev.*, i (1959), pp. 31–4

BIBLIOGRAPHY

C. Lampert: 'A Conversation with Frank Auerbach', *Frank Auerbach* (exh. cat., foreword L. Kossoff; ACGB, 1978)

Eight Figurative Painters (exh. cat. by A. Forge, intro. L. Gowing; New Haven, CT, Yale Cent. Brit. A.; Santa Barbara, Mus. A.; 1981)

M. Podro: 'Auerbach as Printmaker', *Print Q.*, ii (1985), pp. 283–98

Frank Auerbach: Paintings and Drawings, 1977–85 (exh. cat. by C. Lampert, Brit. Council Col., 1986) [rev. for Hamburg, Kstver., Essen, Mus. Flkwang and Madrid, Cent. Reina Sofía]

Frank Auerbach (exh. cat. by M. Gooding, Amsterdam, Rijksmus. van Gogh, 1989)

R. Hughes: *Frank Auerbach* (London, 1990)

CATHERINE LAMPERT

Frank Auerbach: *J. Y. M. Seated*, oil on board, 711×610 mm, 1980–81 (Huddersfield, Art Gallery)

Augbergh, Antonis van. *See* OBBERGHEN, ANTONIS VAN.

Augsburg. Capital since 1817 of Swabia, Bavaria, Germany, on the confluence of the rivers Lech and Wertach, with a population of *c.* 263,699 (1993).

1. History and urban development. 2. Art life and organization. 3. Centre of production. 4. Cathedral.

1. HISTORY AND URBAN DEVELOPMENT. The city is built on the site of a Roman settlement, Augusta Vindelicorum (founded 15 BC), which became the capital of the province of Raetia (est. *c.* AD 50). In AD 121 it was officially designated as a borough (*municipium*). In the 8th and 9th centuries the town's development centred around both the cathedral and the pilgrimage church of St Afra (7th century) south of the Roman town wall, on the site of the old Roman cemetery. After the defeat of the Hungarian army (955) at the battle of Lechfeld, with the support of Bishop Ulrich (*reg* 923–73), the city was granted the imperial privileges of a market and a mint. There followed rapid growth and the foundation of the convent of St Stephan (968); the adoption (1012) by the Benedictine order of the monastery of St Afra (in 1187 rededicated to SS Ulrich and Afra); and the foundations of St Peter (1067), St Martin (before 1077), St Gertrud (1071) and, north of the cathedral, St Georg (end of 11th century). The main part of the cathedral was consecrated in 1065 (*see* §4 below). From the 8th century to the two charters of 1156 and 1168 Augsburg was ruled by the bishop; from 1156/68 to 1276 power was divided between the bishop and the king. The codification of the municipal laws (1276) by Rudolf of Habsburg (1218–91) ended the episcopal domination of the town, which became an Imperial Free City. The increase in civic rights was reflected in the prominent extension (1365–1449) to the Gothic town hall (begun before 1260; replaced 1615–20). The oldest known view of Augsburg is that of 1457 (see fig. 1), which shows the city dominated by its numerous towers. From 1467 SS Ulrich and Afra was extended and then rebuilt after being destroyed in a storm in 1475. The development of other ecclesiastical buildings was made possible by funds from charitable foundations. Between 1487 and 1497 the Carmelite monastery church of St Anna was rebuilt and later became the centre of the Reformation in Swabia. The new church of St Georg for the Augustinian canons was built in 1494–1505/6, and the collegiate church of St Moritz was also completed in the 15th century. (*See also* ENGELBERG, BURKHARD.)

The cultural and economic rise of Augsburg, which peaked during the reign of Emperor Maximilian I, corresponded to the boom in silver and copper mining in the Tyrol, in which the Fugger and Welser merchant families played a major role. Both families had prestigious town residences built, and Jakob Fugger II financed the construction of the Fuggerei or alms houses (1517–23; *see* FUGGER, (1), (2) and (3) and ZWITZEL, (1)). Renaissance-style buildings constructed for other businessmen and patricians, for example the Böckenstein house (1544–6; now the Maximilianmuseum), incorporated a house with portico, inner courtyards with arcades, and side buildings.

1. View of Augsburg by Hektor Mülich, miniature, 270×195 mm, from Mülich's copy (1457) of Sigismund Meisterlin's town chronicle (Augsburg, Staats- und Stadtbibliothek)

Some houses had painted façades (*see* FAÇADE DECORATION, fig. 2).

During the Reformation, Augsburg supported the Protestant cause, and the Confession of Augsburg, a statement of the Lutheran faith, was presented to Emperor Charles V at the Imperial Diet held in the city in 1530. In 1534–7 the city council took vigorous action against the Catholic faith. Many monastic foundations and churches were closed, and many works of art were destroyed by Zwinglian iconoclasts (*see* §2 below). This unrest caused the bishop's residence to be transferred to neighbouring Catholic Dillingen. At the 'armed' Diet of 1548/9 Charles established a patrician government with two governors, which only from 1552 admitted tradesmen, and to a lesser extent craftsmen, as members. At this 1548/9 Diet a settlement between Protestants and Catholics was made, but it was only in 1555, at the Peace of Augsburg, that religious toleration was formally restored.

During the Counter-Reformation, which found support in Augsburg, the Jesuit college of St Salvator (1579/80–84; destr. 1773 except for the church (destr. 1872) and assembly hall) was founded with the support of the Fugger family (*see* FUGGER, (4)). While one of the Fuggers, Octavian Secundus Fugger, was superintendent of buildings, three bronze fountains, the Augustus Fountain

(1589–94) by HUBERT GERHARD and the Mercury (completed 1599) and Hercules (1597–1602) fountains by Adriaen de Vries, were set up, fed by a newly constructed large-scale water system. At the end of the 16th century and the beginning of the 17th the council effected lasting changes to the city by commissioning Elias Holl (*see* HOLL (i), (2)), the city architect, to design a number of buildings, among them the new central Renaissance-style Rathaus (1615–20; see fig. 2; *see also* WELSER), the new Zeughaus (1602–6; *see* REICHLE, HANS, fig. 2), the Stadtmetzg (1609), the Barfüsserbrücke and shops (from 1611), the St Anna Gymnasium (1612–16), the rebuilding of the Perlachturm (1614–16) and the Heilig-Geist-Spital (1625–30). The town's fortifications were also rebuilt, with new corner bastions on the Rotes Tor, Oblatterwall and Jakoberwall and on the Lueg-ins-Land. Building activity came to an end, however, during the Thirty Years War (1618–48), when the population fell from *c*. 48,000 to *c*. 16,000.

During the Baroque and Rococo periods a number of buildings were refashioned; these included the priory churches of St Georg (1681–1700), St Moritz (1714–15), Heilig Kreuz and St Magdalena (1716–24). The powerful weavers' guild commissioned a painted, barrel-vaulted hall (now Munich, Bayer. Nmus.) in the guildhall. The innovation of calico printing had a great impact on textile production in Augsburg. While calico factories looking like castles were built for the Gignoux family (1764–5) and for Johann Heinrich Schüle (1720–1811; built 1770–72), many weavers were impoverished as a result of competition from mechanized cloth production. Augsburg also became a centre of trade and banking, and such distinguished bankers as Baron Benedikt Adam Liebert von Liebenhofen (1730–1810) built palaces in the centre of the town. Liebert's impressive Schaezlerpalais (1765–7), built under Carl Albert von Lespilliez (1723–96), has a mirrored hall (1770) based on that at Versailles, decorated by GREGORIO GUGLIELMI.

As a result of secularization in 1802–3 property was seized from most of the religious institutions in the city (which had been overwhelmingly Catholic since the 18th century). After the Pressburg peace agreement (1805) Augsburg ceased to be an Imperial Free City and became part of Bavaria. The city's continued importance in financial matters is reflected in the Börse, built 1828–30 to plans by Johann Nepomuk Pertsch (1780–1835). The pattern of municipal building changed drastically in the wake of industrialization (from the 1830s and 1840s) and a consequent growth in population. In 1843 the railway station was built in late Neo-classical style. With the cooperation of the banking firm Schaezler, one of the first large textile factories in southern Germany was built. In the 1860s the fortifications were removed and the moat and walls levelled. Of the four inner and ten outer gates only the Rotes Tor and the Fischer, Jakober, Vogel and Wertachbrucker gates survived. Upper middle-class suburbs subsequently developed to the west and working-class ones to the north and east of the city. On the north–south axis the city walls were replaced by grand, landscaped boulevards: the present-day Konrad Adenauer Allee, the

2. Augsburg, Perlachplatz, showing (right) the Rathaus by Elias Holl (i), 1615–20, (centre) the Perlachturm and Peterskirche, and, in the square, the Augustus Fountain; engraving by Heinrich Jonas Ostertag, 1711 (Augsburg, Staats- und Stadtbibliothek)

Schiessgrabenstrasse and the Fuggerstrasse, which gave a new character to the west of the old town. In this area a new theatre, a library, archival and judicial buildings, schools and splendid hotels were constructed.

Between 1910 and 1916 the town continued to expand, absorbing several of the surrounding villages (a further expansion followed the Bavarian regional reform of 1972). The destruction caused by World War II, combined with post-war planning policies, greatly reduced the number of historic buildings in the city. Among the important buildings of the 20th century are the Catholic parish church of Herz Jesu (1907–10) in Pfersee, built in the *Jugendstil* by Michael Kurz (*b* 1876), and the Stadttheater (1956) in neo-Renaissance style.

BIBLIOGRAPHY

N. Lieb, ed.: *Fugger und Welser* (Augsburg, 1950)

N. Lieb: 'Augsburgs bauliche Entwicklung als Ausdruck des städtischen Kulturschicksals seit 1800', *Z. Hist. Ver. Schwaben*, viii (1951), pp. 1–112

Augsburger Renaissance (exh. cat., ed. N. Lieb; Augsburg, Schaezlerpal., 1955)

Augsburger Rokoko (Augsburg, 1956)

T. Breuer: *Die Stadt Augsburg*, Bayerische Kunstdenkmäler, i (Munich, 1958)

Augsburger Barock (exh. cat., ed. C. Thon; Augsburg, Rathaus; Augsburg, Holbeinhaus; 1968)

R. Pfaud: *Das Bürgerhaus in Augsburg* (Tübingen, 1976)

Architektur des 19. Jahrhunderts in Augsburg (exh. cat., ed. M. Arnold; Augsburg, Städt. Kstsammlungen, 1979)

Welt im Umbruch: Augsburg zwischen Renaissance und Barock, 3 vols (exh. cat., Augsburg, Rathaus; Augsburg, Zeughaus; 1980–81)

W. Liebhart: 'Die Reichsabtei Sankt Ulrich und Afra zu Augsburg (1006–1803): Studien zur Klostergeschichte mit besonderer Berücksichtigung von Besitz und Herrschaft', *Historischer Atlas von Bayern*, ii/2 (Munich, 1982)

J. Wilhelm: 'Augsburger Wandmalerei 1368 bis 1530: Künstler, Handwerker und Zunft', *Abh. Gesch. Stadt Augsburg*, xxix (1983) [whole issue]

B. Bushart: 'Beiträge zu Kunst und Stadtbild', *Geschichte der Stadt Augsburg von der Römerzeit bis zur Gegenwart*, ed. G. Gottlieb and others (Stuttgart, 1984), pp. 225–33, 363–85, 490–504, 674–81

B. Roeck: 'Kollektiv und Individuum beim Entstehungsprozess der Augsburger Architektur im ersten Drittel des 17. Jahrhunderts', *Elias Holl und das Augsburger Rathaus* (exh. cat., ed. W. Baer, H.-W. Kruft and B. Roeck; Augsburg, Stadtarchv, 1985), pp. 37–54

W. Wüst: 'Die fürstbischöfliche Residenz zu Augsburg: Ein Beitrag zum hochstiftischen Hof- und Verwaltungswesen im 17. und 18. Jahrhundert', *Z. Bayer. Landesgesch.*, xlviii (1985), pp. 352–67

WOLFGANG WÜST

2. ART LIFE AND ORGANIZATION. Under Bishop Ulrich, who had been educated at St Gall Abbey, the town reached its first highpoint in artistic activity with such works as the Ulrich chalice. Its individual parts were probably imported, but it was completed by an anonymous goldsmith in Augsburg before 1200. In the later 11th century stained-glass workshops were set up by monks from Tegernsee Abbey, and in the 12th century SS Ulrich and Afra was a flourishing centre for the arts, particularly book illumination (which continued to flourish, reaching a peak *c.* 1500). Outside such ecclesiastical establishments, artists active in the Middle Ages formed an artisan class, and there is known to have been some degree of guild organization as early as 1276. From 1368, when they rebelled and laid claim to a stake in the government, to 1548 the guilds made a major contribution to Augsburg's unique economic and cultural rise to become one of Europe's leading cities, aided also by individual guild families (e.g. Fugger, Hörbrot, Hoechstetter). The construction of the town's fortifications, the Perlachturm and the arsenal (Zeughaus) of the imperial city, made out of the granary (1548–85), stand as proof of their defence of their newly won civic rights. Increasing division of labour, affecting the quantity and quality of work, was accompanied by greater cooperation between crafts. A family-based workshop system is traceable from the beginning of the 15th century in the case of painters (e.g. the Kron/Zan, Giltlinger/Knoder (*see* GILTLINGER, (1)), Mauermüller, Apt, Breu, Burgkmair, Holbein and Furtenagel workshops), the numbers of journeymen being controlled by the guilds. The most important craft was that of the goldsmith (*see* §3(i) below; *see also* SELD, JÖRG); the goldsmiths' chapel (later the church of St Anna) was constructed from 1485. The principal sculptors of the early 16th century were Adolf Daucher and Hans Daucher (*see* DAUCHER, (2) and (3)).

Tanning and textile production are known to have been developed for export from the 13th century. Linen, and later fustian (sold from 1395), were made, the latter being central to the city's economic development in the 15th century. Textile waste was a necessary raw material for paper production and its availability, together with international connections through trade and humanism, led to Augsburg's rise in the 15th century as a centre of book production and of the book trade, areas in which the city achieved European status by the 18th century. Two-colour printing was introduced in 1468, and the first illustrated book was printed in 1471 (*see* §3(ii) below). The printing of music with movable type was introduced in 1507, and the first printed newspaper appeared in 1508/9.

Augsburg's cultural development reached its height during the reign of Emperor Maximilian I (*reg* 1493–1519), called the 'mayor of Augsburg' on account of his frequent visits there. The crafts of the goldsmiths, armourers, locksmiths and printers increased considerably. The most important masters in the field of painting and sculpture were Hans Holbein the elder, Hans Burgkmair the elder and the sculptor Gregor Erhart. However, the second generation of artists, such as Hans Holbein the younger, often left their home towns as the princely courts of the large European dynasties offered increasing competition to the imperial city. Hans Holbein the younger left Augsburg finally in 1514/15 to become court painter to Henry VIII. This had a detrimental effect on building initiatives, which was countered only in the 18th century, when more court and residential building was undertaken, largely by the imperial master builders, such as Johann Martin Pentenrieder.

The Reformation in Augsburg (1518–37), supported by humanism, contributed to losses among its art treasures through social and religious upheaval. The 'Bilderstürm' (destruction of pictures), for example, was the work of the followers of Zwingli, who also organized the destruction of altarpieces, such as the high altarpieces in the cathedral by Hans Holbein the elder, wood sculptures, stone figures in the inner rooms of churches and many epitaphs. The production of carved altars and panel paintings by, for example, Ulrich Apt the elder (*fl* before 1486; *d* 1532), Hans Burgkmair I (*see* BURGKMAIR, (2)), Leonhard Beck (*see* BECK (i), (2)), Jörg Breu the elder (*see*

BREU, (1)) and the artist known by the monogram LF (*fl* 1502) was also brought to an end. Numerous monasteries and foundations such as St Nikolaus, St Margareth, St Anna and the Barfusserkloster were secularized, and the practice of the Catholic religion was stopped for a whole decade. Finally, the Evangelical town authorities left open only St Anna's, the Barfusserkirche with the adjoining church of St Jakob, and the Predigthäuser (preaching houses) of St Ulrich, St Georg and the Hl. Kreuz.

On the other hand, the art of portrait painting flourished in the first half of the 15th century under Burgkmair, Holbein, Apt, Breu, Beck, Laux Furtenagel (*b* 1505; *d* after 1546) and CHRISTOPH AMBERGER and the art of façade painting also continued to flourish. Augsburg's centrality within the empire was also significant. The Imperial Diets of the 16th century caused Albrecht Dürer, Jakob Seisenegger, Matthes Gebel, Jan Cornelisz. Vermeyen, Sebald Beham, Titian, Lambert Sustris, Paulus Mor (*fl* 1548/9 or 1550/51), Lucas Cranach the elder and Leone Leoni to visit Augsburg and Amberger, Lorenz Stoer (*fl* 1557; *d* 1620 or later), Abraham del Hel (1534–98) and Giulio Licinio to settle there. The empire also promoted the growth of crafts, in terms of both productivity and employment. The imperial court employed such artists as Lorenz Helmschmied (1450/55–1532), Hans Schönsperger (*fl* 1481–1520) and Gregor Erhart and granted ennoblement to Holbein, Burgkmair and Daniel Hopfer I (*see* HOPFER, (1)).

An important role was played by the Fuggers, who not only arranged and financed art commissions for the emperor but also employed Jacopo Bellini and other important artists. The Fugger wedding in 1540/41 attended by Seisenegger and perhaps Paris Bordone and Georg Pencz exerted an attraction for artists comparable to that of the Imperial Diets. The emergence of the middle classes gave rise to private collections, such as those of the humanist CONRAD PEUTINGER and members of the Fugger family. Imperial patronage led to the development of international court art from *c.* 1550, and from 1590

3. Anton Mozart: *Presentation of the 'Pomeranian Cabinet of Art' to Philip, Duke of Pomerania-Stettin*, oil on panel, *c.* 1617 (Berlin, Tiergarten, Kunstgewerbemuseum); the panel, once part of the cabinet (destr. 1945), includes portraits of the artists who collaborated on the project from 1611 to 1617

artists were settling in Augsburg in contravention of guild regulations.

The Thirty Years War greatly reduced the number of craftsmen in the city and caused a temporary drop in quality through the lack of qualified specialist workers. Nevertheless, the city's central position and the market-orientated guild system, which by the 17th and 18th centuries operated in a proto-industrial manner in some cases, ensured employment for a large number of craftsmen working in many and various specialized fields both before and after the war. After the peace of Westphalia (1648) there was a rise in trade; weaving was now among the most important crafts and the powerful weavers guild commissioned a painted, barrel-vaulted room (now Munich, Bayer. Nmus.) in the guildhall. The innovation of calico printing had a great impact on textile production in Augsburg. While calico factories like castles were built (1770–72) for the Gignoux family and by Johann Heinrich von Schule, many craftsmen were impoverished as a result of competition from mechanized cloth production. The reconstruction of the empire that took place in the post-war years entailed the appointment of painters (e.g. Karl Wilhelm de Hamilton (1668–1754), Franz Maria Joseph Anton Maichelbeck (1702–50) and Johann Georg Bergmüller), chamber painters (e.g. Jonas Umbach) and court sculptors (including Placidus Verhelst (1727–?1778)) at the episcopal court, as well as the creation of a church hierarchy that awarded commissions.

The art academy, the second oldest in Germany, was founded by Joachim von Sandrart before 1674. Another academy with classicist, anti-Baroque aims was later established with imperial support in 1753, but it closed in 1790. Of importance throughout the 17th and 18th centuries was the production of ornamental clocks, scientific instruments, musical instruments, musical boxes, display weapons, cast fountains and luxury furniture (such as the 'Pomeranian Cabinet of Art' on which almost 30 artists from Augsburg collaborated; see fig. 3). Calico printing was introduced in 1689, coloured paper production *c.* 1690 and porcelain before 1728. Short-lived faience factories were founded by Johann Caspar Schaur (1735), the prince-bishop of Augsburg (1748–52) and Christian von Köpf (1752).

From 1648 artists had been settling in Augsburg despite guild restrictions; from 1730 they did so with the council's support. The restrictions were abolished for textile factory workers in 1737 and for silver and bronze factories during the 18th and 19th centuries. The Imperial Free City established an art and craft tribunal in 1721 that lasted until 1806. Various trades cooperated in an international sales network (e.g. musical instruments), leading to increasingly international styles, such as the Rococo 'Augsburg style' of printed products. Later developments contributing to the success of the printing industry included the introduction of lithography (1799), high-speed steam printing (1824) and rotary press printing (1873).

Augsburg lost its artistic centrality from *c.* 1770 although the calico, gold- and silversmiths' products and the copperplate engravings are among the most outstanding of their time. All monastic and some church patrons were lost in the secularization of 1802/3. In the 19th and 20th centuries a trade school (1856) and several art galleries were opened, including the Staatsgalerie für Altdeutsche Gemälde (opened in the Rathaus in 1810 as the first national collection of paintings in Bavaria), the Maximilianmuseum (1855), the Schaezlerpalais (1946), the Römisches Museum (opened in 1966 in the secularized Dominican church) and the Staatsgalerie für Moderne Kunst (1985).

BIBLIOGRAPHY

H. Rinn, ed.: *Augusta, 955–1955: Forschungen und Studien zur Kultur- und Wirtschaftsgeschichte Augsburgs* (Augsburg, 1955)

E. Steingräber: 'Die kirchliche Buchmalerei Augsburgs um 1500', *Abh. Gesch. Stadt Augsburg*, viii (1956)

B. Bushart: 'Augsburg und die Wende der deutschen Kunst um 1750', *Amici Amico. Festschrift Werner Gross*, ed. K. Badt and M. Gosebruch (Munich, 1968), pp. 261–304

R. Bettger: 'Das Handwerk in Augsburg beim Übergang der Stadt an das Königreich Bayern: Städtischen Gewerbe unter dem Einfluss politischer Veränderungen', *Abh. Gesch. Stadt Augsburg*, xxv (1979)

J. Wilhelm: 'Augsburger Wandmalerei, 1368–1530', *Abh. Gesch. Stadt Augsburg*, xxix (1983)

W. Baer and others, eds: *Augsburger Stadtlexikon: Geschichte, Gesellschaft, Kultur, Recht, Wirtschaft* (Augsburg, 1985)

M. Rauch: *Handwerk in Augsburg* (Augsburg, 1985)

P. Fassl: 'Konfession, Wirtschaft und Politik: Von der Reichstadt zur Industriestadt, Augsburg, 1750–1850', *Abh. Gesch. Stadt Augsburg*, xxxii (1988)

R. Reith: *Arbeits- und Lebensweise im städtischen Handwerk: Zur Sozialgeschichte Augsburger Handwerksgesellen im 18. Jahrhundert (1700–1806)*, Göttinger Beitr. Wirtschafts- & Sozgesch., xiv (Göttingen, 1988)

B. Bushart: 'Die Augsburger Akademien', *Academies of Art between Renaissance and Romanticism*, ed. A. W. A. Boschloo, Leids Ksthist. Jb., v–vi (The Hague, 1989), pp. 332–47

Festschrift Augsburg—Kunst und Architektur nach 1945: 85 Jahre Künstlervereinigung 'Die Ecke' (Augsburg, 1992)

3. Centre of production.

(i) Metalwork. Augsburg's mining industry and trade in metals gave the city a leading position in finance and as a supplier of credit. Goldsmiths were first documented in 1276: they had their own association from 1368, a meeting-room from 1447 and a funerary chapel, the 'Goldschmiedekapelle', St Anne's, from 1485, which was founded by the goldsmith Konrad Hirn. By 1420 the association had a system of control and the inspection mark of a pine-cone. The goldsmiths' trade, which was an important aspect of the economy of the city from the 16th to the 18th century, played a significant part in the prosperity of Augsburg after the Thirty Years War (1618–48). The city's rise as a specialized centre in the production of gold artefacts began *c.* 1470; by 1580 a local style had evolved and after 1650 Augsburg held a leading position as a centre of production in Germany. The art of the goldsmith flourished in the 16th century and particularly in the 18th: in 1546 there were *c.* 60 independent masters, in 1740 there were 275. Trading in silver bullion led to the emergence of specialized silversmiths by *c.* 1550. In the 16th century there were 30 silversmiths; by 1677 there were only 9. The silver trade profited by extensive mining of silver in the Tyrol from 1470 and by the import via Spain of silver from the New World. This ensured a plentiful supply of commissions for several workshops, which were capable of executing large, high-quality work in a short period. Silver artefacts were exported throughout Germany, and to Scandinavia, Poland, Russia, Bohemia, Austria, Hungary, Switzerland and Italy. The earliest

4. Silver-gilt dish with scenes from the *Story of Europa* by Christoph Lencker, late 16th century (Vienna, Kunsthistorisches Museum)

products characteristic of Augsburg were regalia, ambassadorial gifts, display items, drinking vessels in the form of human figures (*see* GERMANY, fig. 65) or animals that were used as table decoration, writing cabinets, jewel boxes or cabinets with silver ornament and figures (e.g. cabinet, 1580–90; Vienna, Ksthist. Mus.), private altars and reliquaries. Important ecclesiastical pieces produced in the Middle Ages include the monstrance of the 'Wunderbarliches Gut' (*c.* 1205, by Konrad of Lindau). The rise of Augsburg as a major centre of goldsmiths' work began with, above all, JÖRG SELD as its main representative. The outstanding masters of the 16th century and early 17th included CHRISTOPH LENCKER (see fig. 4), David Altenstetter (*c.* 1547–1617; *see* GILDING, colour pl. III, fig. 2), MATTHIAS WALBAUM and Abraham Lotter (1535–1612). Balduin DRENTWETT was the founder of a family of goldsmiths that continued to work up to the 18th century. Between 1600 and 1800, 27 members of the Drentwett family were practising goldsmiths. Numerous other goldsmith families included BILLER, Hoesslin (Bartholomäus, or Balthasar, 1669–1704; Philipp, 1690–1750), Manlich (Heinrich I, *c.* 1625–98; Johann Heinrich, 1660–1718) and Rad (Christoph I, 1628–1710; Christoph II, 1676–1730). JOHANN ANDREAS THELOTT was unquestionably one of the most important masters of his time.

Goldsmiths in Augsburg collaborated with watch- and clock-makers, makers of scientific instruments, armourers and gunsmiths. During the second half of the 17th century Augsburg took the lead from Nuremberg in the production of domestic plate, producing large numbers of fashionable services (e.g. tea service, agate and silver gilt, 1695–1706; Kassel, Hess. Landesmus.), travel and toilet sets, and, from *c.* 1680 to 1730, silver furniture (table, mirror and candlestands, *c.* 1700; Dutch Royal Col., on loan to Apeldoorn, Pal. Het Loo).

Augsburg gained a considerable reputation in the 16th century in the field of medal-making. While the leading medallists, for example Hans Schwarz, Friedrich Hagenauer, Christoph Weiditz, Hans Daucher and Balduin Drentwett, created mainly cast portrait medals, at the beginning of the 17th century the subject-matter changed to that of historical events, townscapes and religious subjects, while the process of medal-making changed to that of die-stamping. The most highly regarded figures in the 17th century included the goldsmith and die-cutter Philipp Heinrich Müller, and in the 18th century Jonas Thiébaud (1695–1770). Two private mints were still in existence in the 19th century.

BIBLIOGRAPHY

ADB; Forrer; Thieme–Becker

G. Habich: 'Studien zur Augsburger Medaillenkunst am Ende des XVI. Jahrhunderts', *Archv Medaillen- & Plakettenknd.*, iv (1913–14), pp. 175–99

M. Bernhart: 'Augsburgs Medailleure und Bildnisse Augsburger Kunsthandwerker auf Schaumünzen des 16. Jahrhunderts', *Mitt. Bayer. Numi. Ges.*, lv (1937)

D. Steinhilber: 'Geld- und Münzgeschichte Augsburgs im Mittelalter', *Jb. Numi. Geldgesch.*, v/6 (1954–5), pp. 5–142

H. Rinn, ed.: *Augusta, 955–1955: Forschungen und Studien zur Kultur- und Wirtschaftsgeschichte Augsburgs* (Augsburg, 1955), pp. 256–72, 323–32, 363–70

A. von Reitzenstein: 'Augsburger Plattner um die Mitte des 16. Jahrhunderts', *Münchn. Jb. Bild. Kst.*, n. s. 2, iii/13 (1962), pp. 163–78

S. Rathke-Köhl: *Geschichte des Augsburger Goldschmiedegewerbes vom Ende des 17. bis zum Ende des 18. Jahrhunderts* (Augsburg, 1964)

H. Müller: 'Augsburger Goldschmiedekunst der Zeit Hans Holbeins des Älteren', *Hans Holbein der Ältere und die Kunst der Spätgotik* (exh. cat., Augsburg, Rathaus, 1965), pp. 17–51

M. Bobinger: *Alt-Augsburger Kompassmacher* (Augsburg, 1966)

——: *Kunstuhrmacher in Alt-Augsburg* (Augsburg, 1969)

K. Maurice: *Die deutsche Räderuhr* (Munich, 1976)

C. Hernmarck: *Die Kunst der europäischen Gold- und Silberschmiede von 1450 bis 1830* (Munich, 1980)

H. Seling: *Die Kunst der Augsburger Goldschmiede, 1529–1868: Meister, Marken, Werke* (Munich, 1980)

R. Baumstark and H. Seling: *Silber und Gold: Augsburger Goldschmiedekunst für die Höfe Europas* (Munich, 1994)

(ii) Prints. From the 16th to the 18th century printmaking was the most important field of artistic work in Augsburg apart from the goldsmiths' trade, and at times it attained European importance. The first book with woodcut illustrations in Augsburg was printed in 1471 by Günther Zainer (*d* after 1478). The main producers of woodcuts were Hans Burgkmair I (*see* BURGKMAIR, (2)), JOST DE NEGKER, Jörg Breu the elder and Jörg Breu the younger (*see* BREU, (1) and (2)), Leonhard Beck (*see* BECK (i), (2)), Hans Schäufelein the elder (*see* SCHÄUFELEIN, (1)) and Hans Weiditz (ii) (who may have been the Master of Petrarch; see fig. 5; *see also* MASTERS, ANONYMOUS, AND MONOGRAMMISTS, §I: MASTER OF PETRARCH). Gold and coloured woodcuts were produced after 1510. The woodcut industry, aided by painters and woodblock carvers, spread from Augsburg after 1490 and continued to flourish until the book-printing crisis of 1550–90, which was caused by economic, political, religious and educational factors.

Engraving was first documented in Augsburg *c.* 1570. A resurgence in the production of single-leaf prints and in book illustration was brought about by the reintroduction of Catholicism and by the skill of such engravers as Domenicus Custos (1550–1612), his son-in-law Lucas Kilian and the latter's brother Wolfgang Kilian (*see* KILIAN, (1) and (2)) and by Melchior Küsel I (*see* KÜSEL, (1)) and his son-in-law Johann Ulrich Kraus (1655–1719), who inherited the publishing firm. The French engraver Etienne

5. Master of Petrarch: frontispiece of the first German edition of Francesco Petrarch's *De remediis utriusque fortunae*, printed in Augsburg, woodcut, 300×210 mm, 1532 (Augsburg, Staats- und Stadtbibliothek, 2° Phil. 57)

Delaune, who visited Augsburg in 1576, had a considerable impact on the goldsmiths' art; he produced *c.* 450 small format copperplates, of which most were ornamental pattern plates for goldsmiths.

The crisis of 1550–90 was succeeded by a brief period of productivity (1590–1620) and a renewed decline during the Thirty Years War before the production of prints became re-established from 1650. The foundation of the art academy contributed significantly to this revival. In the 17th century the most original and important engravers included Hans Ulrich Franck (*fl* 1659–90), Johann Heinrich Schönfeld (*see* SCHÖNFELD, JOHANN HEINRICH, §2) and JONAS UMBACH. Augsburg became an important German centre for the production of devotional prints (*see* DEVOTIONAL PRINTS, §2) and by the 18th century was a European centre for this trade. Outstanding producers of engraved reproductions in the 17th and 18th centuries were members of the Kilian (*see* KILIAN, (3) and (4)), Küsel, Wolfgang, Bodenehr, KLAUBER, Eichler (*see* EICHLER, GOTTFRIED, I) and HAINZELMANN families, and the mezzotint portrait painter Elias Christoph Heiss (1660–1731).

Printmaking again rose in importance during the 18th century, Augsburg regaining its position as a south German centre for the production of high-quality graphics. In 1730, 61 engravers and 23 publishers of engravings were documented. The leading engravers were Johann Georg Bergmüller (*see* BERGMÜLLER, JOHANN GEORG, §1), GOTTFRIED BERNHARD GÖZ, JOHANN EVANGELIST HOLZER, JOHANN ESAIAS NILSON, JOHANN ELIAS RIDINGER and GEORG PHILIPP RUGENDAS I. Outstanding in the field of the ornamental engraving were Jeremias Wachsmuth (1711–71) and FRANZ XAVER HABERMANN, while the Seutter family (Matthäus Seutter, 1678–1757; Albrecht Carl Seutter, 1722–62; and Matthäus's son-in-law Tobias Conrad Lotter Seutter, 1717–77) achieved special eminence among cartographers. In the 19th century, with the introduction of commercial lithography by the music printer and publisher Johann Carl Gombart in 1799 and as a result of the demise of the Imperial Free City, Augsburg lost its influence outside the region as a centre for printmaking.

BIBLIOGRAPHY

M. Gräfin Lanckoronska: 'Die Augsburger Druckgraphik des 17. und 18. Jahrhunderts', *Augusta, 955–1955: Forschungen und Studien zur Kultur- und Wirtschaftsgeschichte Augsburgs*, ed. H. Rinn (Augsburg, 1955), pp. 347–62

H. H. Schmid: *Augsburger Einzelformschnitt und Buchillustration im 15. Jahrhundert* (Baden-Baden, 1958)

J. Bellot: 'Augsburg: Porträt einer Druckerstadt', *Z. Bibwsn Bibliog.*, xvii (1970), pp. 257–64

W. Seitz: 'The Engraving Trade in Seventeenth- and Eighteenth-century Augsburg: A Checklist', *Prt Q.*, iii/2 (June 1986), pp. 116–27

H. Gier, ed.: *Katalog 450 Jahre Staats- und Stadtbibliothek Augsburg: Kostbare Handschriften und alte Drucke* (Augsburg, 1987)

JOSEF MANČAL

4. CATHEDRAL. An episcopal church probably existed as early as the late Roman period, and possible evidence of this was a 6th-century baptismal chapel dedicated to St John the Baptist, which survived until 1808. The Carolingian cathedral had its roots in a structure begun in the late 7th century, which was remodelled *c.* 700 and *c.* 800 and again, under Bishop Ulrich, in the 10th century. Later, under Bishop Henry II (*reg* 1047–63), a Romanesque aisled basilica (consecrated 1065) with a double choir, western transept, crypt and side towers (completed later) evolved. The Romanesque bronze door of the south aisle portal dates from around the time of consecration or later. It comprises two wings that are inlaid with formerly gilded relief metal plates. Models for this can be seen in Italian doors at Amalfi, Atrani, Salerno and Venice. Modern research indicates that the door was not imported, but rather reveals the style and knowledge of Ottonian painting and art. An iconographic peculiarity lies in the fact that allegories from antiquity are linked with biblical figures. Gothic alterations were carried out from 1326, including the vaulting of the west choir, transept and nave (1331–9), the addition of two extra aisles and the construction of the eastern hall choir (designed 1343; consecrated 1431) with an ambulatory and radiating chapels. The south and north towers were built in the late 15th century and the 16th. Baroque alterations took place from 1655, although the Gothic character was restored in the mid-19th century. □

(i) Sculpture. The most important sculpture of the cathedral is that which decorates the north and south portals of the eastern choir. These portals mark the original course of the Reichsstrasse and are akin to city gates. Both of them,

the south portal in particular, were seen by the citizens as the attributes of the bishop and the city, and viewed as proof of their right of way through the cathedral. The south portal facing the town is more elaborate than the northern one, which leads into the cathedral from the bishop's side. Both, however, are among the most elaborate entrance buildings in south Germany. The north portal had been begun as early as 1343 and its figural decoration points to an earlier formal repertory, related to that of the west portal of Strasbourg Cathedral and that of the Kapellenturm in Rottweil. The south portal, understood to have been underway only from 1356, suggests the style of the Parler family, which first evolved on the choir portal of the collegiate church of the Holy Cross in Schwäbisch Gmünd. Both portals have a programme based on the life of the Virgin and thereby make reference to the dedication of the cathedral. The arms of burghers under the statues of the south portal are prominent, again ensuring that the citizens' claim on the cathedral was unmistakably stated. Both portals have been extensively remodelled in restorations of the 19th and 20th centuries.

BIBLIOGRAPHY

G. Himmelheber: *Der Ostchor des Augsburger Doms* (Augsburg, 1963)
U. Mende: *Die Bronzetüren des Mittelalters* (Munich, 1983), p. 137
Das Südportal des Augsburger Domes: Geschichte und Konservierung (Munich, 1984) [23rd rep. of the Bayerisches Landesamt für Denkmalpflege]

HANS-JOACHIM KUNST

(ii) Stained glass. The 'Prophet' windows of Augsburg Cathedral are thought to be the earliest known stained-glass windows still in position. The five precursors of Christ, *Hosea*, *David*, *Daniel* (see fig. 6), *Jonah* and *Moses*, in the south nave clerestory are all that survive from a scheme of Old and New Testament figures on the north and south sides of the nave. The panels are each over 2 m high, made of glass between 3 and 7 mm thick. The main colours are white, green, brown and purple. The prophets are frontally posed, with solemn faces, the features painted with the minimum of detail. Each holds a scroll inscribed in Latin. The bodies are elongated and the feet turned out, with a foliage pattern at the bottom. Each figure has a different headdress and robe; the garments reach almost to the ankles and have jewelled hems made of small pieces of coloured glass, used also as decoration over the body. The name of each prophet is inscribed in a curve around the head. Although no earlier examples of such work survive, the windows are in a mature style. The techniques of painting and shading are assured, the glass is skilfully cut and the leads contribute to the design. The simplicity of outline and the large scale give a restrained yet monumental quality that is extremely sophisticated.

The figures probably date from the beginning of the 12th century. They have been compared with late 11th-century Ottonian painting, but the closest parallels are with early 12th-century manuscripts from Hirsau Abbey, such as the Stuttgart Passional (Stuttgart, Württemberg. Landesbib., bibl. fols 56–8), showing standing figures under arches in a Romanesque manner. The Augsburg windows, however, are not mere copies of manuscripts or wall paintings: the style has been developed for glass. Stained-glass workshops were established in Augsburg in the later 11th century by monks from Tegernsee Abbey, already an influential centre, and the windows are the

6. Augsburg Cathedral, south nave clerestory, stained-glass window of the Prophet *Daniel*, 2300×675 mm, beginning of the 12th century

products of this school. Although designed for the nave clerestory, the figures are probably not in their original positions and appear to have lost their backgrounds. They were modified when taken out in 1330, and restorations were made in the 15th and 16th centuries due to storm damage. The figure of *Moses* is almost entirely 16th-century, although a convincing copy of the Romanesque manner. In the 17th century much old glass was removed to provide more light, with only five figures surviving of the original twenty-two. The last major restoration of the stained glass was in 1972.

Other glass in the cathedral (*see also* GOTHIC, §VIII, 5) includes the easternmost window of the choir ambulatory, which has three lancets with circular medallions showing the *Flagellation*, *Crowning with Thorns* and *Christ Carrying the Cross* (all *c.* 1400); tracery lights show the *Wise and Foolish Virgins*. On the north nave aisle there are two lancets of the *Annunciation* and *Nativity* (second half of the 15th century) by the Strasbourg glazier PETER HEMMEL VON ANDLAU. The style is marked by facial modelling, rich colours and silvery pinnacles.

BIBLIOGRAPHY

C. H. Sherrill: *Stained Glass Tours in Germany, Austria and the Rhine Lands* (London, 1927)

A. Boeckler: 'Die romanischen Fenster des Augsburger Domes und die Stilwende vom 11. zum 12. Jahrhundert', *Z. Dt. Ver. Kstwiss.*, x (1943), pp. 153–82

L. Lee, G. Seddon and F. Stephens: *Stained Glass* (London, 1976)

L. Grodecki: *Le Vitrail roman* (Fribourg, 1977)

C. Brisac: *A Thousand Years of Stained Glass* (London, 1986)

CAROLA HICKS

Augst [anc. Augusta Raurica]. Swiss town on the Rhine, formerly a Roman colony. The well-preserved and extensively excavated Roman town is important for the study of urban planning and civic architecture. It was founded by a close colleague of Julius Caesar, L. Munatius Plancus, *c.* 44 BC in order to establish a bastion of Romanization in the region. The earliest surviving remains date from the Augustan period, and there was much building activity throughout the 1st and 2nd centuries AD, a period that marks the *floruit* of the colony. The centre of Augst was dominated by its forum–basilica–capitolium complex, laid out in the format typical of Gallic towns and one of the best examples of its type (*see* ROME, ANCIENT, §III, 2). Considerable rebuilding during the 2nd century included the addition of a circular curia. The axis of the complex was the same as that of the surrounding street grid. At the temple end of the forum, however, the axis changed orientation and led to a second major group of monuments, including a theatre, which faced a second large Classical temple (am Schönbühl). The theatre originated in the early 1st century but was transformed into an amphitheatre in the later 1st century and then back into a theatre in the mid-2nd century. The Schönbühl temple (2nd century), positioned on a low hill and aligned with the theatre, would have been a major backdrop to theatrical performances. It succeeded a group of much smaller Romano-Celtic temples. The town as a whole is notable for its religious remains.

By the mid-3rd century AD the town was in decline, especially after the Germanic invasions of 259–60, when the Imperial frontier was pulled back to the Rhine. At the end of the 3rd century the fort of Castrum Rauracense (now Kaiseraugst) was built within the town in order to defend the bridge across the river. Here the important Kaiseraugst Treasure was found, probably deposited *c.* 352–3 by a senior army officer (*see* ROME, ANCIENT, §IX, 1(iv)). The later history of the site is obscure, but Kaiseraugst became the new nucleus of the much-diminished town and was an Early Christian bishopric until its transfer, probably in the 7th century, to the newly ascendant town of Basle.

BIBLIOGRAPHY

R. Laur-Belart and L. Berger: *Führer durch Augusta Raurica* (Basle, 1937, 5/1991) [full site guidebook]

Augst. Mushft. (1976–)

Forsch. Augst (1977–)

A. Kaufmann-Heinimann: *Augst und das Gebiet der Colonia Augusta Raurica* (1977), i of *Die römischen Bronzen der Schweiz* (Mainz, 1976–80)

Jber. Augst & Kaiseraugst (1980–)

H. A. Cahn and A. Kaufmann-Heinimann: *Der spätrömische Silberschatz von Kaiseraugst*, 2 vols (Derendingen, 1984)

ANTHONY KING

Augur, Hezekiah (*b* New Haven, CT, 21 Feb 1791; *d* New Haven, CT, 10 Jan 1858). American sculptor. Although as a youth he showed talent for handling tools, his father, a joiner and carpenter, discouraged him from becoming a wood-carver. After opening a fruit shop in New Haven, he began carving musical instruments and furniture legs for a local cabinetmaker. With his invention of a lace-making machine, he was able to settle his business debts and devote himself entirely to sculpture.

About 1825 Samuel F. B. Morse encouraged Augur to try working in marble. Among his earliest attempts in this medium was a bust of *Professor Alexander Metcalf Fisher* (*c.* 1825–7; New Haven, CT, Yale U. A.G.), which was exhibited in 1827 at the National Academy of Design in New York. The impact of the Neo-classical style is clearly evident in his most ambitious work, *Jephthah and his Daughter* (*c.* 1828–30; New Haven, CT, Yale U. A.G.), a pair of free-standing half life-size marble figures. The treatment of the heads shows Roman influence, which Augur must have absorbed from engravings; this is borne out by the detailed work on Jephthah's armour. The bold handling of the hair and drapery reveals his experience as a wood-carver. In 1834 Augur received a commission to execute a marble bust of *Chief Justice Oliver Ellsworth* (completed 1837) for the Supreme Court Room in the US Capitol, Washington, DC. Four years later he was commissioned to design bronze medals for the bicentennial of New Haven's settlement; this is his last-known work.

BIBLIOGRAPHY

H. W. French: *Art and Artists in Connecticut* (New York, 1879), pp. 47–9

G. Heard Hamilton: *Hezekiah Augur: An American Sculptor, 1791–1854* (MA thesis, New Haven, CT, Yale U., 1934)

O. Larkin: 'Early American Sculpture: A Craft Becomes an Art', *Antiques*, lvi (1949), pp. 178–9

W. Craven: *Sculpture in America* (Newark, 1968, rev. New York, 1984), pp. 92–4

DONNA J. HASSLER

Augusta, Queen of Prussia and Empress of Germany. *See* HOHENZOLLERN, (13).

Augusta Emerita [now Mérida]. Roman town in southwest Spain, *c.* 56 km east of Badajoz, at the confluence of the Guadiana and Albarregas rivers. It was founded in 25 BC as a colony for army veterans and was the chief city of the Roman province of Lusitania. Its Roman remains are the most substantial in Spain. Roman bridges remain across both the rivers, that over the Guadiana being the larger (nearly 800 m long; early 2nd century AD), with 57 arches, although many of them have been rebuilt since

Roman times. The city had three aqueduct systems. The best preserved is Los Milagros, probably of Hadrianic date (AD 117–38), with three tiers of arches surviving up to 25 m high and piers with courses of small squared stones alternating with brick. The extant public buildings include the theatre, amphitheatre and circus. Inscriptions over the main entrances to the theatre record its original construction by Agrippa, Augustus' chief administrator, in 16 BC. The *scaenae frons*, probably of Hadrianic date, is remarkably complete, with two tiers of coloured marble columns re-erected from the material found in excavation. The large amphitheatre (ded. 8 BC) seated 15,000 and is like some early Italian amphitheatres in having only the upper part of the seating built on vaulting. The arena, which was sunk below ground level, has a rectangular pit in the centre with passages leading to it. The circus (probably 1st century AD, but substantially reconstructed AD 337–40), less well preserved, was modelled on the Circus Maximus in Rome (*see* CIRCUS, ROMAN): part of the seating and the starting boxes at the curved end remain. The decoration of the forum portico has striking parallels with that of the Forum Augustum in Rome (*see* ROME, §V, 2) in its caryatids and *clipei* (medallion relief portraits) with heads of Jupiter Ammon and Medusa. The so-called Temple of Diana (of Augustan date) near by and the Temple of Mars (mid-2nd century AD) still have several columns standing, with parts of the entablature. There was also a sanctuary of Oriental deities (2nd–3rd centuries), including Mithras, and several luxurious houses with atria, peristyle courtyards and mosaic floors; these include the House of the Mithraeum, with an outstanding 2nd-century AD mosaic depicting Nature and the Cosmos personified, and the House of the Amphitheatre, with geometric and figured mosaics of the 3rd and 4th centuries AD. A large brick-built bath building near the theatre has been restored and now houses the Museo Nacional de Arte Romano, which displays architectural and decorative fragments from the forum and floor mosaics from the houses.

BIBLIOGRAPHY

J. R. Mélida: *Monumentos romanos de España: Noticia descriptiva* (Madrid, 1925)

E. García Sandoval: *Informe sobre las casas de Mérida y excavaciones en la 'Casa del Anfiteatro'*, Excavaciones arqueológicas en España, 49 (Madrid, 1966)

Augusta Emerita: Actas del bimilenario de Mérida (Madrid, 1976)

A. Blanco Freijeiro: *Mosaicos romanos de Mérida* (Madrid, 1978)

J. H. Humphrey: *Roman Circuses: Arenas for Chariot Racing* (London, 1986), pp. 362–76

T. F. C. BLAGG

Augusta Suessionem. *See* SOISSONS.

Augusta Treverorum. *See* TRIER, §1(i).

Auguste. French family of gold- and silversmiths. Robert-Joseph Auguste (*b* 1723; *d* ?1805) became a master in 1757 after an apprenticeship that included work for Louis XV. His repertoire was unusual in that it embraced both silver tableware and gold objects of vertu; the latter includes four gold boxes made between 1762 and 1763, and 1769 and 1771 (Paris, Louvre; New York, Met.; London, V&A; Althorp House, Northants). In 1775 he received payment for the royal crown and other regalia (destr.) made for the coronation of Louis XVI in 1774. The majority of his work in silver is tableware and includes partial or complete services for the courts of Denmark (Copenhagen, Kon. Saml.) and Russia (St Petersburg, Hermitage) and for Gustav Filip Creutz of Sweden (1775–6; Stockholm, Kun. Slottet). He also made a service for George III of England (1776–85; Paris, Louvre). Auguste's style is characterized by a light and graceful Neo-classicism, in which festoons and figures of children as handles or finials are prominent.

Robert-Joseph's son Henri Auguste (*b* 1759; *d* 1816) became a master in 1785. He was *Orfèvre du Roi*, like his father, and produced plate for the French royal family between 1784 and 1786. William Beckford was among his clients during the French Revolution (e.g. teapot stand, 1788; Brodick Castle). Henri Auguste subsequently executed commissions for Napoleon and for the City of Paris, which commissioned a large table service (1804; Malmaison, Château N.) on the occasion of Napoleon's coronation. Henri Auguste was awarded a gold medal in the third Exposition de l'Industrie in Paris of 1802, but by 1809 he was bankrupt and had fled the country. A large collection of designs for his work, some by Jean-Guillaume Moitte, who worked for Robert-Joseph in the 1770s, was purchased by JEAN BAPTISTE CLAUDE ODIOT (examples in New York, Met.). The streamlined profiles of Henri Auguste's pieces, which are sparingly decorated with relief ornament, defined the transition from the late Neo-classical to the Empire style.

BIBLIOGRAPHY

H. Bouilhet: *L'Orfèvrerie française aux XVIIIe et XIXe siècles* (Paris, 1908–12), ii, pp. 45–59

H. Honour: *Goldsmiths & Silversmiths* (New York, 1971), pp. 222–5

Versailles et les tables royales en Europe (exh. cat., Versailles, Château, 1993), nos 266–72 [entry by Y. Carlier]

CLARE LE CORBEILLER

Augustin, Jean-Baptiste(-Jacques) (*b* Saint-Die, Vosges, 1759; *d* Paris, 1832). French painter. After receiving instruction in art from Jean Girardet (1709–78) and Jean-Baptiste-Charles Claudot (1733–1805), he went to Paris in 1781, where he won recognition as a miniature painter. The miniatures he painted in the 1790s, for example his portrait of *Mme Vanhée, née Dewinck* (1792; Paris, Louvre), are among his most animated works; often portraying figures in a landscape setting, they develop the exuberant style of Niclas Lafrensen and Peter Adolf Hall. He also admired the work of Jean-Baptiste Greuze, whose *Bacchante* (Waddesdon Manor, Bucks, NT) in his own collection he copied in miniature (London, Wallace) and in enamel (Paris, Louvre).

By the end of the century the influence of David's Neo-classicism had brought a new austerity to Augustin's style. He painted some presentation miniatures of Napoleon I. On the restoration of the monarchy in 1815 he was appointed Peintre-en-ordinaire to Louis XVIII. He remained a versatile artist: his large, rectangular portrait of the cornet-player *Frédéric Duvernois* (1817; Meilen, Holzscheiter priv. col., see Schidlof no. 48, pl. 26) is a penetrating theatrical portrait in the tradition of François Dumont (1751–1831). Following Dumont, it shows a clarity and freshness, and accents are highlighted in strong vivid colours. In smaller miniatures of the same period

Augustin shows an understanding of the British use of transparent washes on ivory. He had many English sitters and travelled to England in 1820. Among his pupils were Pauline Ducruet [Du Cruet] (1781–1865) whom he married in 1800, Alexandre Delatour (1780–1858) and Mme de Mirbel [née Rue] (1796–1849). Augustin's collection of works of art was auctioned in 1839. There is a representative collection of his miniatures in the Louvre, Paris.

BIBLIOGRAPHY

G. C. Williamson: *Catalogue of the Collection of Miniatures the Property of J. Pierpont Morgan*, iv (privately printed, 1908), pp. 112–69 [based on family papers; incl. biog. notes, lists of sitters and a facs. of 1839 sale cat.]

L. R. Schidlof: *The Miniature in Europe in the 16th, 17th, 18th and 19th Centuries* (Graz, 1964)

GRAHAM REYNOLDS

Augustinian [Austin] **Canons** [Canons Regular]. Religious order that developed in western Europe from the mid-11th century, when groups of priests began to live a communal life devoted to poverty, celibacy and obedience, following the Rule of St Augustine. Independent congregations that followed the Rule included the PREMONSTRATENSIAN CANONS and the VICTORINE CANONS.

1. THE RULE OF ST AUGUSTINE. The Rule on which the life of canons regular was based consists of two texts associated with St Augustine, Bishop of Hippo (AD 354–430), although they may not have been directly written by him. They draw on a third text, Letter 211, the so-called *Regula sororum*, which Augustine certainly did write *c.* 423 for the guidance of a religious community of women founded by him. It was not a complete guide to religious life but emphasized the importance of the common life as the necessary condition for religious perfection. The *Regula Sancti Augustini* comprises two parts: the *Regula secunda*, a practical guide of about 400 words, outlining daily offices, hours of reading and labour, discipline and obedience, and the longer and more detailed *Regula tertia*, an amplified masculine version of the *Regula sororum*. The two had been combined into a single text by the early 6th century, the date of the earliest manuscript.

In the Middle Ages the *Regula Sancti Augustini* seemed to provide a closer way to the *vita apostolica* than the Rule of St Benedict, and it was seen by founders as a useful combination of practical common sense and vagueness. As it was derived from the works of one of the most venerated Catholic theologians, the Rule did not require other official sanction, although the value of communal clerical life was affirmed by a Lateran Council of 1059 and reaffirmed by subsequent popes. It was only in the first half of the 12th century that the Rule of St Augustine came to hold the same place among the canons that the Rule of St Benedict held among monks.

2. GROWTH OF THE ORDER. The communal clerical life of canons regular was revitalized by the 11th-century reform movements that sought a return to the ideals of the primitive Church with an emphasis on the *vita apostolica*. Early houses of canons regular were largely inspired by the wish of churchmen to reform old churches or collegiate foundations. Secularized lands were restored, unworthy clergy banished, adequate endowments provided to prevent non-residence and a full communal life was introduced.

Canons were in the forefront of the spiritual movements of the age. One initial centre of the movement was the priory of S Frediano at Lucca, encouraged by Pope Alexander II (*reg* 1061–73), but it was in France that the canons regular principally flourished in the half-century after the 1060s. St Ruf on the outskirts of Avignon was founded *c.* 1039; later in the century it became the mother house of communities following the Rule of St Augustine and the customs of St Ruf. Another influential foundation was St Quentin in Beauvais, founded before 1079; its first abbot was St Ivo of Chartres (*d* 1115), and it came to be regarded as a model house of canons. Its observances were introduced into a number of houses, including the first English foundation (by 1106) at St Botolph's, Colchester. Other important early houses were St Aubert (1066), Cambrai; St Denis (1067), Reims; St Vincent (*c.* 1069), Senlis; Mont-Saint-Eloi (1068), near Arras; and St Nicolas d'Arroux (1090), near Autun, Burgundy. In Bavaria and Austria the movement was inspired by St Altmann, Bishop of Passau (*reg* 1061–91). Early houses here included St Nikola in Passau (1073), Rottenbuch (*c.* 1074) and Reichersberg (1084). Elsewhere in Germany canons regular did not make any real progress until the early 12th century.

Many of the early foundations were in urban centres where the canons were involved in pastoral care, but in the 12th century a contemplative tradition grew within the Order, especially to be seen in groups such as the Premonstratensians; their houses were founded on rural sites where there were no parochial commitments, and the life had more monastic characteristics. By the end of the Middle Ages there were 4500 houses all over Europe.

The Rule of St Augustine did not impose a strict constitutional organization on the houses; it contained general instructions about a way of life on which individual houses could build. Augustinian foundations were independent of each other and subject to the local diocesan. Exceptions to this were the autonomous congregations of Augustinians, such as the Victorines, Arroasians, Gilbertines and Premonstratensians, whose additional customs, often additionally influenced by the Cistercians, enjoined on them a system of mother and daughter houses and general chapters. The immense flexibility of the Rule is demonstrated by the number of orders that adopted it as their basis, from the intellectual Victorines to the military order of the Knights Hospitaller. In the 13th century St Dominic (1170–1221) drew on the Rule of St Augustine as the basis for the Dominican order.

The 15th century was a period of decline, and reform congregations of observants sprang up in response to this. In the 16th and 17th centuries many Augustinian houses in France were united in congregations (e.g. Grands Augustines, Petits Pères, Genofevains) in which individual communities retained their independence. In the 17th century a number of new congregations of men and women were founded, especially nursing and teaching orders, whose way of life was based on the Augustinian Rule. Most important among the female orders were the

Sisters of Charity and the Ursulines. An important contemplative order was that of the Visitation, founded in 1610. By the 17th century the Augustinian Order aggregated more than 1000 monasteries and they were active in the mission apostolate in the New World.

3. PATRONAGE AND ICONOGRAPHY. The wide variety of houses that followed the Rule makes it difficult to establish a simple iconography for the Order. Augustinian spirituality was based on the writings of St Augustine and insisted on the importance of prayer, ascetical practices and the common life, emphasizing the centrality of Christ in the order of salvation. Biblical studies were prominent, as were the teachings of Augustinian theologians, especially Giles of Rome (*d* 1316).

Representations of St Augustine and of incidents in his life, such as his baptism by St Ambrose, are common. (The earliest known cycle, in stained glass and dating from *c.* 1316, is in the Church of the Canons Regular in Erfurt.) He is depicted in various guises, as one of the four Latin Doctors, in episcopal vestments or as a member of the Order wearing over his habit a leather belt. He is sometimes portrayed with a flaming heart, the symbol of charity, or illustrated handing over a copy of his Rule. In the choir of Notre-Dame-des-Victoires, Paris, are scenes of his life painted in the 1750s by Carle Vanloo and Louis Galloche. His mother, St Monica, and SS Anthony, Paul the Hermit and John the Baptist were also regarded as particular patrons. The Counter-Reformation stimulated further interest in both early and contemporary saints and martyrs and their portrayal in Augustinian buildings. These occurred in wall paintings, in panel paintings and in statues: a figure of St Augustine was carved by Jean-Baptiste Pigalle for a chapel in Notre-Dame-des-Victoires, while in the 1640s a canon of the Augustinian house in Toulouse, who had been a pupil of Simon Vouet, filled the lesser cloister with stucco figures of the principal Augustinian saints. Branches of the Order owed devotion to their specific founders; the Premonstratensians, for example, frequently represented incidents in the life of St Norbert.

The Augustinians displayed a particular devotion to the Virgin; many of their houses were dedicated to her, and representations of her appear before and after the Reformation. Since the 15th century Mary has been especially honoured as the Virgin of Consolation. In the 18th century Abbé Jean-Louis de Cordemoy, canon of St-Jean-des-Vignes at Soissons, in his *Nouveau traité de toute l'architecture* (Paris, 1706), criticized contemporary monastic painting, in particular the representation of the Virgin in the habit of an order.

Augustinian buildings were varied, and there is no single Augustinian style. Early Augustinian customs say little of buildings except that there was a need for a common refectory and dormitory. With their emphasis on the communal life of the Apostles, they drew inspiration for their refectories from the Cenaculum in Jerusalem, where the Last Supper had traditionally taken place. Early foundations in urban areas testify to the parochial commitments of the canons. The priory of S Frediano in Lucca, which has a large nave for the people and an enormous elaborately decorated font for baptisms, is perhaps typical of the early urban canonical foundations. Many English and Welsh houses in particular, however, were rural, without urban

Augustinian college at Saint-Cyr, France, by Jules Hardouin Mansart, 1685

building constraints. Great variety can be seen, from the rich noble foundations such as St Mary de Pré at Leicester to small cells founded by poorer individuals.

Medieval Augustinian houses contained many works of art given by patrons, who adorned the church interiors. This continued after the Reformation, as did lavish architectural patronage. On occasion splendid buildings might be designed by the leading architects of the period, for example Jules Hardouin Mansart's building at Saint-Cyr (1685; see fig.), founded as a school following the Augustinian Rule, and St Marie de la Visitation in Paris, erected in 1632–4. Smaller houses were erected also, such as the Genofevain house of François Mansart's St Martin-des-Aires outside Troyes. The finest Augustinian buildings of the mid-18th century are those of St Vincent at Senlis and Notre-Dame-des-Victoires.

See also AUGUSTINIAN HERMITS.

BIBLIOGRAPHY

M. J. Heimbucher: *Die Orden und Kongregationen der katholischen Kirche*, i (Paderborn, 1896–7, rev. 3/1933–4)

C. Dereine: 'Vie commune, règle de Saint Augustin et chanoines réguliers au XIe siècle', *Rev. Hist. Ecclés.*, xli (1946), pp. 365–406

J. C. Dickinson: *The Origins of the Austin Canons and their Introduction into England* (London, 1950)

J. Evans: *Monastic Architecture in France from the Renaissance to the Revolution* (Cambridge, 1964)

L. Verheijen: *La Règle de S. Augustin*, 2 vols (Paris, 1967)

J. Evans: *Monastic Iconography in France from the Renaissance to the Revolution* (Cambridge, 1970)

J. A. Franklin: 'Bridlington Priory: An Augustinian Church and Cloister in the Twelfth Century', *British Archaeological Association Conference Transactions: Medieval Art and Architecture in the East Riding of Yorkshire: Hull, 1983*, pp. 44–61

P. Fergusson: 'The Refectory at Easby Abbey: Form and Iconography', *A. Bull.*, lxxi (1989), pp. 334–51

VIRGINIA DAVIS

Augustinian hermits. A religious order of mendicants brought together under the Rule of St Augustine (*see* AUGUSTINIAN CANONS) by the papal bull *Licet Ecclesiae* of 1256. The Order spread throughout urbanized western Europe, and included lay people in addition to priests and nuns. Its primary goals remain the ministry of souls, the pursuit of learning and the formulation of church policy. The growth of Observant reform congregations from the mid-14th century and during the Reformation (Martin Luther was an Augustinian hermit) threatened the original unity of the Order.

The Order's rapid and widespread expansion and its exclusive cultivation of the Augustinian way of life, particularly from the 14th century, favoured an emphasis on the life and cult of St Augustine of Hippo (AD 354–430). The saint's *Confessions*, life and teachings inspired numerous cycles and individual episodes. Three episodes within the 14th-century cycles are specific to the Order: Augustine's baptism and the donning of his monastic robes, Augustine visiting the hermits of Tuscany before returning to Africa, and the saint asking Simplician for 12 hermits to accompany him to Africa. The Order's artistically inventive interpretations should not, however, be considered in isolation from works connected to other Augustinian groups, such as the earliest known cycle, in stained glass, in the church of the Canons Regular, Erfurt (*c.* 1316). The selection and emphasis of the iconography are varied: at S Pietro in Ciel d'Oro, Pavia, for example, they are related

Founding of the Augustinian Order and the Parable of the Trinity (1463–5), fresco by Benozzo Gozzoli (San Gimignano, S Agostino)

to a dispute that took place there between the Canons Regular and the Order in the 14th century, and at S Agostino, San Gimignano, they explore the theme of faith reconciled with learning in the context of Observant reform. As a Doctor of the Latin Church, St Augustine also appears as a single figure (Padua, Eremitani) depicted as a hermit, dressed in black and with a crown or holding his burning, pierced heart.

The Order's convents commissioned works depicting St Augustine's life, appropriating the saint as its official founder. At S Pietro in Ciel d'Oro, Pavia, the saint's remains are housed in a shrine representing a unique sculptured cycle (*c.* 1362) of his life, including scenes from his posthumous miracles. Other cycles include frescoes (1338) by Guariento in the choir of the Eremitani, Padua, and the frescoes of Ottaviano Nelli and his workshop in the choir of S Agostino at Gubbio, explicitly glorifying the Order and in many ways heralding Benozzo Gozzoli's innovative fresco cycle (1463–5) in the choir of S Agostino, San Gimignano (see fig.), which projected the Order's image of the saint as theologian in the context of the Observant movement. These cycles have to be considered in relation to numerous manuscript interpretations (e.g. *Vita Sancti Augustini*, Boston, MA, Pub. Lib., MS. n. 1483), including those not directly connected to the Order. Later, more ecstatic, visionary series include the influential engravings (1624) produced by Schelte à Bolswert for the Order at Mechelen and the paintings gathered for St Augustinus, Antwerp (*c.* 1650; *in situ*), where, perhaps for the first time, Continence is depicted in the *Conversion of St Augustine.* The latter collection includes works by Peter Paul Rubens (*Madonna Adored by Saints*; 1628), by Jacob Jordaens and by Anthony van Dyck (*Ecstasy of St Augustine*; 1628). Other cycles include those by Miguel de Santiago (1625?–1706) in the monastery of S Agustin, Quito, Ecuador; by Erasmus Quellinus (ii) at Bruges Cathedral (*c.* 1667); and by Bartolomé Esteban Murillo in the Augustinian church (1678) at Seville.

Owing to the international nature of the Order, there is little conformity among its works of art. Its numerous foundations, particularly following an economic revival in the 17th century and perhaps related to the adoption of a mitigated vow of poverty, form an outstanding body that includes many convents in Italy, Spain, northern Europe and Latin America. The diverse patronage of the Order's lay confraternities, particularly that of the *Cintura* (named after the distinctive belt given to the saint by the Virgin), is also significant.

BIBLIOGRAPHY

Vita Sancti Augustini imaginibus adornata [15th century]; ed. P. Courcelle and J. Courcelle (Paris, 1964)
A. Höggmayr: *Monasteria ordinis fratrum eremitarum S. Augustini*, 2 vols (1731; *R* Heverlee-Leuven, 1974)
E. A. van Moé: 'Recherches sur les ermites de St-Augustin entre 1250 et 1350', *Rev. Questions Hist.*, ccxxxii (1932), pp. 274–316
Augustiniana, vi (1956) [whole issue]
D. Gutiérrez: 'Ermites de Saint-Augustin', *Dictionnaire de spiritualité*, ed. M. Viller, F. Cavallera and J. de Guibert, iv/2 (Paris, 1960), cols 983–1018
P. Courcelle and J. Courcelle: 'Scènes anciennes de l'iconographie augustinienne', *Rev. Etud. Augustin.*, x (1964), pp. 51–71
——: *Iconographie de Saint Augustin*, 4 vols (Paris, 1965–80)
G. Pelliccia and G. Rocca, eds: *Dizionario degli Istituti di Perfezione* (Rome, 1974) i, cols 155–415
D. Gutiérrez: *Die Augustiner von Beginn der Reformation bis zur katholischen Restauration 1518–1646* (Rome, 1975)
K. Walsh: 'Päpstliche Kurie und Reformideologie am Beispiel von Santa Maria del Popolo in Rom: Die Augustiner-Observanten im Spannungsfeld zwischen Borgia und Della Rovere', *Archv Hist. Pont.*, xx (1982), pp. 129–61
D. Cole Ahl: 'Benozzo Gozzoli's Frescoes of the Life of Saint Augustine in San Gimignano: Their Meaning in Context', *Artibus & Hist.*, vii/13 (1986), pp. 35–53
L. Dania and D. Funari: *S Agostino il Santo nella pittura dal XIV al XVIII secolo* (Milan, 1988)
Collectanea Augustinia IV, Augustine in Iconography: History and Legend, Augustinian Historical Institute (New York, 1995)

MEREDITH J. GILL

Augustus, Duke of Brunswick-Wolfenbüttel. *See* WELF, (3).

Augustus [Octavian; Gaius Octavius; Gaius Julius Caesar Octavianus Augustus] (*b* Rome, 23 Sept 63 BC; *reg* 27 BC–AD 14; *d* Nola, 19 Aug AD 14). Roman emperor and patron. When C. Octavius was named the heir of Julius Caesar (assassinated 44 BC), he was a politically unknown 18 year old. Early portrait types presented him bearded, as a sign of mourning for his adoptive father, thereby reinforcing his claim to be Caesar's rightful successor. Octavian's most important programme of artistic patronage, however, followed his assumption in 27 BC of the title 'Augustus' (Lat.: 'venerable') and with it effective monarchic power. Artistic patronage was a vehicle by which Augustus sought to legitimate his new position in terms of traditional Roman values. He rebuilt 82 temples in order to demonstrate his piety and to restore the *pax deorum* ('peace of the gods') disrupted by the civil wars of the late Republic (*see* ROME, ANCIENT, §II, 2(i)(b)). New building in the Forum Romanum (*see* ROME, §V, 1) allowed him to redefine civic space in order to display his exceptional power. A temple of his deified father, Julius Caesar, dominated the eastern end of the forum. Two triumphal arches celebrating Augustus' victories at Actium and against the Parthians flanked the temple and formed the entrance to the forum.

Such buildings provided the setting for an extensive programme of sculpture commissioned by Augustus. A series of some 70 portrait statues in the porticos of the Forum Augustum presented Augustus as the inevitable conclusion of two lines of succession: the first, *summi viri* ('great men') from Roman history stretching back to the founder of Rome, Romulus; the second, *summi viri* of the Julian family stretching back to Aeneas. Framed by these porticos was the Temple of Mars Ultor ('Mars the Avenger'), with cult statues of Mars, the father of Romulus, and Venus the mother of Aeneas, thus tying Augustus' succession to sole power into the divine order of things (*see also* ROME, ANCIENT, §IV, 2(ii)).

Augustus also sponsored innovations in iconography and style, again in order to legitimize the new political order. The cuirass of the statue of *Augustus* from the villa of Livia at Prima Porta (*c.* 19 BC; Rome, Vatican, Braccio Nuo.) developed a new iconography of victory. In the centre of the cuirass a Parthian returns a recaptured legionary standard to a figure in Roman military dress, perhaps the god Mars. Personifications of other conquered peoples or provinces (Gaul, Germany) and Augustus' patron gods, Apollo and Diana, frame the scene. Above, the sun god Sol and the moon goddess Luna give the scene a cosmic setting, whilst Aurora, the personified Dawn, sprinkles from an urn the morning dew which ushers in the Golden Age inaugurated by Augustus' Parthian victory. Below, the Earth reclines with a cornucopia and two infants symbolizing the prosperity of the new era. Both the pose of the statue and the classicizing features of the head of Augustus echo the 5th-century BC *Doryphoros* (*see* POLYKLEITOS, fig. 1). The Classical style, associated in ancient rhetorical and art-historical writing with holiness and grandeur, was adopted by Augustus in order to associate his rule with a return to traditional piety. The Ara Pacis (Altar of Peace; *see* ROME, §V, 4), dedicated in 9 BC to celebrate Augustus' successful conclusion of wars in Gaul and Spain, included two friezes showing Augustus and his family processing to sacrifice in a style that echoes the Parthenon frieze (*see* DRESS, fig. 4).

This politicization of aesthetic styles extended to Augustus' activity as a collector of art. He sought to undercut the prestige that other members of the élite could accumulate through their collections by suggesting that all Greek works of art should be displayed publicly. His supporter Agrippa, for example, set up Lysippos' *Apoxyomenos* in the gymnasium of a new bath complex. When Augustus displayed in his forum two portraits by the Classical Greek painter Apelles representing Alexander the Great as victor in battle and as the bringer of peace through victory, there was an obvious political metaphor, which ultimately undermined the aesthetic autonomy of these works of art: the emperor Claudius painted over Alexander's heads with portraits of Augustus.

Augustus' programme of artistic patronage gave a new shape to Roman art. The Classical style and Augustan iconography were adopted by private citizens for their own purposes. The figure of Mars Ultor, copied from the cult statue of the Forum Augustum, found its way on to gladiators' helmets. Representations of Victory and the *clipeus virtutis* ('shield of the emperor's virtues') decorated lamps exchanged as New Year's gifts. Augustan art laid the framework within which Roman art developed until the emperor Constantine's conversion to Christianity in the 4th century.

BIBLIOGRAPHY

S. Walker and A. Burnett: *The Image of Augustus* (London, 1981)
P. Zanker: *The Power of Images in the Age of Augustus* (Ann Arbor, 1988)

JEREMY J. TANNER

Augustus I, Elector of Saxony. *See* WETTIN, (5).

Augustus II, King of Poland. *See* WETTIN, (7).

Augustus III, King of Poland. *See* WETTIN, (8).

Augustusburg, Schloss. *See* BRÜHL, SCHLOSS.

Auldjo, John (*b* Montreal, 26 July 1805; *d* Geneva, 6 May 1886). British vulcanologist and collector. The son of Alexander Auldjo of Montreal, Auldjo matriculated at Trinity College, Cambridge, in 1822 and became a member of Lincoln's Inn, London, in 1827. In the early 1830s he settled in Naples, acting as one of the *ciceroni* of Sir Walter Scott there in 1832. Auldjo had ascended Mont Blanc in 1827 and his prolonged study of Vesuvius, published as *Sketches of Vesuvius* in 1832, led to his election to the Royal Society in 1840. While in Naples, Auldjo became a friend of the antiquary Sir William Gell and collected a large number of vases and other antiquities from Pompeii and other sites. He also acquired a considerable number of Neapolitan 17th- and 18th-century works, including substantial groups of oil sketches by Francesco Solimena and Francesco de Mura. His interest in Neapolitan Baroque painting, although paralleled by that of Edward Cheney in Tiepolo, placed Auldjo far from the mainstream of contemporary taste.

His literary friends included Bulwer Lytton, Thackeray and Macaulay. He was an accomplished amateur draughtsman and a friend of a number of artists, including George Cruickshank, who etched the illustrations to his *Journal of a Visit to Constantinople and the same of the Greek Islands* (1835). After his return to England he settled in London at Noel House, Kensington, where Waagen described his 'various works of art, of classical and of medieval character, and also of the period of the Renaissance'. The greater part of the collection, including the Old Master drawings of mostly indifferent quality and a large group of watercolours by William Leighton Leitch, was sold at Christie's, London, 14–16 July 1859. From 1873 until his death Auldjo was Consul at Geneva.

BIBLIOGRAPHY

G. A. Waagen: *Treasures of Art in Great Britain*, ii (London, 1854), pp. 340–41
Lugt: *Marques* (1921), no. 48
J. Venn and J. A. Venn: *Alumni Cantabrigienses*, 10 vols (Cambridge, 1922)
W. Gell: *Reminiscences of Sir Walter Scott's Residence in Italy, 1832*, ed. J. C. Corson (London, 1957), pp. 6, 9–10, 19
F. Russell: 'De Mura Sketches from the Auldjo Collection', *Burl. Mag.*, cxxv (1983), p. 78

FRANCIS RUSSELL

Aulenti, Gai (*b* Palazzolo della Stella, Udine, 4 Dec 1927). Italian architect, designer and teacher. After graduating in architecture from the Politecnico, Milan (1954), she began her own architectural practice in Milan. From 1954 to 1963 she was also art director for the avant-garde architectural journal *Casabella*. The influence of its editor, Ernesto Nathan Rogers, who fostered her interest in art, philosophy and literature as well as architecture, led her to believe that architecture is primarily an intellectual discipline and that specialization is wrong; her own work included, in addition to such buildings as houses, offices and museums, the design of exhibitions, stage sets, interiors, furniture and industrial products. In the 1960s she began associations with Olivetti Business Machines (from 1966) and Fiat Automobiles (from 1968), for whom she designed showrooms (e.g. Olivetti Shop, 1966, Paris; Fiat showrooms in Zurich, 1969–70, Brussels and Turin, 1970) as well as exhibitions and trade stands. Aulenti's general approach to design is akin to the modernism espoused by Frank Lloyd Wright, particularly in her expressive utilization of the sensuous qualities of materials, in her interest in the relationship of buildings to their site and function, and in an integration of classical concepts with industrial engineering. A harmonious juxtaposition of abstract modernist forms and recognizable historical elements is seen in small-scale works, such as Aulenti's own apartment and office (1974), Milan, and her country home (*c*. 1975) near Assisi, for which she designed a bed inspired by a fresco by Giotto. It is also apparent in one of her best-known works, the renovation and conversion (1980–86) of the 19th-century Gare d'Orsay, Paris, to form the Musée d'Orsay; in the sculpture hall, the severe, abstract stone slabs that frame and contain the sculpture also serve to enhance the steel-and-glass vault of the original building, which soars above the exhibition space. Aulenti began teaching at the University of Venice (1960–62) and the Politecnico, Milan (1964). She also designed furniture for such companies as Zanotta (1964–72) and Knoll International (1971–85); lamps for Artemide (1968–75); and a watch and pen-and-pencil set for Louis Vuitton (1988). Her work featured in several exhibitions and won a number of awards.

BIBLIOGRAPHY

Gae Aulenti (Milan, 1979)
B. Rose: 'Gai Aulenti: Renaissance Woman', *Vogue*, clxxv/5 (May 1985), pp. 320–25; 367
C. Vogel: 'The Aulenti Uproar: Europe's Most Controversial Architect', *NY Times Mag.*, cxxxvii (1987), pp. 26–32, 50–51
Gae Aulenti e il Museo d'Orsay (Milan, 1987)
C. Lorenz: *Women in Architecture: A Contemporary Perspective* (New York, 1990), pp. 16–19

WALTER SMITH

Aulnay, St Pierre. Church in Saintonge, western France, situated on the old pilgrimage road between Poitiers and Saintes. Towards the middle of the 11th century the church was in the possession of the Benedictine abbey of St Cyprien in Poitiers. It passed to the canons of Poitiers Cathedral between 1119 and 1122, when the decision to rebuild it was probably made. The church was restored in the 15th century (façade strengthened with buttresses) and in the 18th and 19th centuries (masonry repairs by Paul Abadie). Built of limestone, St Pierre has a five-bay aisled nave, a transept with apsidal chapels and a deep

Aulnay, St Pierre, west façade, detail of portal, *c.* 1130–*c.* 1150

apsidal choir. It has slightly pointed barrel vaults. There is no clerestory, the nave and aisles being united under a single roof, which, with the raised aisle walls, results in a triangular west façade. The crossing is surmounted by a beautiful bell-tower.

St Pierre houses Romanesque sculpture of great interest, synthesizing the characteristics of Poitou and Saintonge. Inside, sculptured capitals are confined to the nave and crossing. Carved in deep relief, capitals decorated with masks, animals and monsters alternate with a variety of foliate compositions; there seems to be no clear limit between the real and the fantastic world. One capital carries the inscription *hi sunt elephantes* and is carved with elephants with tiny ears. Also recognizable are *Adam and Eve*, *Cain Killing his Brother Abel*, *Delilah Cutting the Hair of the Sleeping Samson* and the story of *St George and the Dragon*.

On the exterior, sculptural ornament along the walls and around the chevet is concentrated at window level. This sobriety contrasts with the richness of the west and south façades of the church. On the west façade a programme common in Poitou and Saintonge is set out on the archivolts of the portal, employing allegory to illustrate the *Path to Salvation*. From the inner archivolt to the outer are represented the *Lamb and Angels*, *Virtues Triumphing over Vices*, the *Parable of the Wise and Foolish Virgins* with *Christ the Bridegroom* at the apex, and finally the *Signs of the Zodiac* and the *Labours of the Months*. Stylized foliate motifs are carved on the soffits. The style of these sculptures and the carved capitals and abaci supporting them is lively, especially in the elegant silhouettes of the Virtues, Virgins and angels, which are built up from long triangles and stand out from the concave grounds. The graphic surface carving is treated with finesse. The portal is flanked by blind, pointed arches framed by radial voussoirs carved with deeply undercut foliage, birds and monsters (see fig.). On the left tympanum is the *Crucifixion of St Peter*; on the right, *Christ between SS Peter and Paul*, the patron saints of the locality and of Poitiers Cathedral. The sculpture is softly modelled, but the style is powerful, especially of Christ and the two saints. Some traces of polychromy are discernible.

The combat of Virtues and Vices, treated more crudely, is found again on the archivolt on the upper part of the south transept façade. The programme of the small doorway below is distributed on the archivolts, which bear some of the most curious images in Romanesque art. The inner archivolt has a fine composition of griffins and centaurs. Placed radially on the second and third are saints caught up in a dancing movement and *31 Elders of the Apocalypse* supported by atlantids on the soffits; these Elect form a celestial court, inspired by the Apocalypse. As in the nave, the outer archivolt has recognizable animals and monsters (griffins, centaurs, sirens) mingling with strange creations. The world is turned inside out, as taught in the fables (ass musician), or held up to ridicule (ass saying mass). There are many animal battle scenes on the capitals of the exterior, some of which must have a decorative function, as must the numerous carved corbels that appear throughout the church.

The dates proposed for these sculptures lie between 1100 and 1170/80, of which the decades 1130 to 1150 are the most likely. Numerous artists from different backgrounds worked at Aulnay; several then left for other sites. The different styles at Aulnay are found in several country churches in western France for the next 10 or 15 years at least (e.g. Marestay, Fenioux and Pont-l'Abbé-d'Arnoult).

BIBLIOGRAPHY

J. Chagnolleau: *L'Eglise d'Aulnay-de-Saintonge* (Grenoble, 1938)
R. Crozet: *L'Art roman en Poitou* (Paris, 1948)
M. Aubert: 'Eglise d'Aulnay', *Congr. Archéol. France*, cxiv (1956), pp. 318–27
Y. Labande-Mailfert: *Poitou roman*, Nuits Temps (Pierre-qui-vire, 1957), pp. 108–238
R. Crozet: *L'Art roman en Saintonge* (Paris, 1971)
F. Werner: *Aulnay-de-Saintonge und die romanische Skulptur in Westfrankreich* (Worms, 1979)
L. Seidel: *Songs of Glory: The Romanesque Façades of Aquitaine* (Chicago and London, 1981)
M. T. Camus: 'Aulnay', *Charente-Maritime* (Paris, 1994)

M. T. CAMUS

Aulps, Pierre-Louis-Jean-Casimir Blacas d'. *See* BLACAS D'AULPS, PIERRE-LOUIS-JEAN-CASIMIR.

Aumale, Duc **d'.** *See* ORLÉANS, (10).

Aumonier, Frederic. *See under* WOOLLAMS & CO.

Aurangabad [Auraṅgābād]. Buddhist monastic and pilgrimage site—*fl c.* 100 BC–AD 600—and later city in Maharashtra, India. Together with AJANTA and ELLORA, it represents the culmination of Buddhist rock-cut art along the trade routes of western India. The Buddhist site, located in the hills north-west of the city, contains a dozen excavations, an aniconic prayer-hall (Skt *caityagṛha*) of the 1st century BC, two possibly Mahayana Buddhist designs that resemble examples at Ajanta closely enough to be by the same artists, a series of profusely decorated Vajrayana Buddhist *maṇḍala* shrines and a unique syncretic temple combining Brahmanical and Buddhist deities within a single sanctum. The richness and sensuousness of both the architecture and the sculpture is exceptional.

The earliest structure at the site is an aniconic *caitya* (Cave 4) of the 1st century BC. This prayer-hall was followed in the 5th century AD by two caves in the manner of later Ajanta: Cave 1, a *vihāra* after completion of its façade, and Cave 3, a shrine-*vihāra* with only four cells, the dormitory function of which seems to have been suppressed in favour of a ritual setting. The front aisle of the exceedingly ornate Cave 3 (*see* INDIAN SUBCONTINENT, fig. 32) carries the only narrative imagery surviving at the site. A dozen life-sized worshippers attending the seated Buddha of its shrine create a superbly affecting devotional setting. Caves 2 and 5, excavated in the early 6th century, are purely shrines for worship, without any habitation cells. Each contains a seated Buddha in a cell surrounded by a circumambulatory path (*pradakṣiṇāpatha*). The shrine of Cave 3 preserves the conception fully, with giant *bodhisattvas* flanking its column-screened entrance.

A second series of excavations, begun 2 km east in the mid- to late 6th century, continued this exploration of ritual space. In Cave 6 the shrine is preceded by two colonnades, and the Buddha of the sanctum is flanked by *bodhisattva* groups inside and outside. The inner temple is surrounded by cells: the two at the rear contain Buddhas and attendant *bodhisattvas*; those on the sides could have been inhabited but are just as likely to have been used for meditation, i.e. as stages in the devotee's progression through the temple *maṇḍala*. Temple 7 is a complex variation on this form and includes female imagery associated with Vajrayana worship. The walls carry *bodhisattva* panels, one including the Eight Great Perils. In the shrine a large Buddha is seated among six smaller ones in a paradise flanked by musicians, dancers, *bodhisattvas* and Taras. Outside are sensuously powerful sculpted panels of Taras. The unfinished Cave 9 is similarly complex and totally lacking in habitation cells. Three other caves were begun but then abandoned. Perhaps the most interesting temple at the site is the syncretic shrine uncovered by a rock-slide in 1962 that comprises an undecorated sanctum focused upon the Brahmanical deity Ganesha with the Seven Mothers on his right and a pair of Buddhas on his (ritually inferior) left. Interpreting the iconography of this modest chamber assumes greater importance in view of the disappearance of Buddhist art and patronage from western India in the early 7th century.

The subsequent history of Aurangabad is unclear until the early 17th century, when a nearby village known as Khirki was selected as the site for a new capital of the NIZAM SHAHI dynasty (*reg* 1490–1636) of Ahmadnagar. A palace, mosque and military buildings were erected; parts of these survived the devastation that followed the conquest by the Mughal army of Jahangir (*reg* 1605–27; *see also* INDIAN SUBCONTINENT, §III, 7(i)(c)). When Aurangzeb (*reg* 1658–1707) was sent as viceroy to the Deccan in 1657, he chose to reside in the city and changed its name to Aurangabad. Together with his nobles Aurangzeb was responsible for the present fortifications, the repair of the Naukonda Palace and the additions to the Jami' Masjid. Other mosques and tombs for Mughal notables were also built, the most important being the Bibi-ka Maqbara, a mausoleum for Aurangzeb's wife Rabi 'a Daurani. The architect, 'Atn Allah, was the son of Ustad Ahmad Lahauri, architect of the Taj Mahal at Agra upon which it is modelled. With the decline of Mughal power in the 18th century Aurangabad passed to the nizam of Hyderabad. Asaf Jah I (*reg* 1724–48) made additions to the palace and may also have been responsible for the Shah Ganj Mosque. In the colonial period churches and a cantonment were added to the western suburbs.

See also INDIAN SUBCONTINENT, §§III, 4(ii)(b) and 5(i)(d) and IV, 6(iii)(c).

BIBLIOGRAPHY

J. Burgess: *Report on the Antiquities in the Bidar and Aurangabad Districts*, iii of Archaeol. Surv. W. India, Rep. (London, 1878)
J. Fergusson and J. Burgess: *The Cave Temples of India* (London, 1880), pp. 280–349
J. Burgess: *Report on the Buddhist Cave Temples and their Inscriptions*, iv of Archaeol. Surv. W. India, Rep. (London, 1883)
R. S. Gupte: 'A Note on the First Brahmanical Cave of the Aurangabad Group', *Marathwada U. J.*, ii (1960–61), pp. 173–6
R. S. Gupte and B. D. Mahajan: *Ajanta, Ellora and Aurangabad Caves* (Bombay, 1962)
D. B. Levine: 'Aurangabad: A Stylistic Analysis', *Artibus Asiae*, xxviii (1966), pp. 175–88
A. Ray: *Aurangabad Sculptures* (Calcutta, 1966)
W. Spink: *Ajanta to Ellora* (Bombay, 1967) [chronological comparison]
V. Dehejia: *Early Buddhist Rock Temples* (Ithaca, 1972)
P. Stern: *Colonnes indiennes d'Ajanta et d'Ellora* (Paris, 1972)
D. C. Bhattacharyya: *Tantric Buddhist Iconographic Sources* (New Delhi, 1974)
J. C. Huntington: 'Cave Six at Aurangabad: A Tantrayāna Monument?', *Kalādarśana*, ed. J. G. Williams (New Delhi, 1981), pp. 47–55
K. V. Soundara Rajan: *Cave Temples of the Deccan*, iii of Archaeol. Surv. Temples (New Delhi, 1981), pp. 154–7
W. Spink: 'The Great Cave at Elephanta: A Study of Sources', *Essays on Gupta Culture*, ed. B. L. Smith (Delhi, 1983), pp. 235–82
C. Berkson: *The Caves at Aurangabad: Early Buddhist Tantric Art in India* (Ahmadabad, 1986) [excellent photographs]
C. B. Asher: *Architecture of Mughal India*, i/4 of *The New Cambridge History of India* (London, 1992)

GARY MICHAEL TARTAKOV

Aurangzeb. *See under* MUGHAL.

Aurelius, Marcus [before adoption, Marcus Annius Verus; as emperor, Marcus Aurelius Antoninus] (*b* Rome, 26 April AD 121; *reg* AD 161–80; *d* Vienna, 17 March AD 180). Roman emperor and patron who, in contrast to the long and pacific reign of his predecessor Antoninus Pius, had to deal with natural disasters, rebellions and attacks by the subject peoples of the Empire. One of the few surviving monuments from his reign is the base of the Column of Antoninus Pius near the Ustrinum in the Campus Martius, which was discovered in 1703 (*c.* AD 161; Rome, Vatican, Cortile Pigna; *see* ROME, ANCIENT, §IV, 2(vii) and fig. 71). A fragment of the column containing an inscription also survives. On the base is represented the apotheosis of the emperor Antoninus Pius, transported to heaven along with his wife Faustina by a winged Genius, while the goddess Roma and the Genius of the Campus Martius look on; the opposite side depicts a *decursio* (military parade). A triumphal arch dedicated to Marcus Aurelius was built by the senate; this structure may originally have contained both the reliefs that were later reused in the Arch of Constantine (*see* ROME, §V, 12), and those now in the Museo dei Conservatori, Rome. Between AD 176 and 193 the great column with spiral reliefs commemorating his wars against the Germans and the Sarmatians was erected in his honour. This column, obviously modelled on that of Trajan, was not as tall as the present one in the Palazzo Colonna, Rome; it was set on a base which in turn stood 3 m above the nearby Via Flaminia, from which it was reached by a stairway (*see also* ROME, ANCIENT, §IV, 2(vii) and fig. 79).

BIBLIOGRAPHY

C. Caprino and others: *La Colonna di Marco Aurelio* (Rome, 1955)
L. Vogel: *The Column of Antoninus Pius* (Cambridge, MA, 1973)
G. A. Mansuelli: *Roma e il mondo romano*, ii (Turin, 1981), pp. 43–57

LUCA LEONCINI

Aureller. Swedish family of painters. Working principally in Västergötland, (1) Johan Aureller (i) brought a more opulent and sophisticated European style to the restrained and formal art of provincial Sweden in the 17th century. In this he was followed, although with less talent, by his son (2) Johan Aureller (ii).

(1) Johan (Johansson) Aureller (i) (*b* Stockholm, 4 Feb 1626; *d* Medelplana, Västergötland, 21 April 1696). He was the son of Queen Maria Eleanora's secretary, Johan Mattsson Aurelius, himself the son of a goldsmith from Nuremberg. In 1653 Aureller was recorded as town painter in Gävle, where his first documented works were the portraits of *Barbara Cassiopea Aurivillius* (1654) and her husband *Olof Aurivillius* (1661; both priv. col., see *SVKL*), which are acutely characterized but sombrely coloured. The interval between the two portraits is accounted for by Aureller's presence in 1654 at the church in Delsbo, where he executed the decoration and a *Crucifixion with the Virgin, St John the Baptist and St Mary Magdalene*, with small portraits of the donors, *Marcus Wilhelmsson Björkman and his Wife* (all destr.). Aureller may also have painted another portrait (1654) in that church, of the same couple. In 1658 he was once more in Gävle, where he painted a magnificent large portrait group of the merchant *Henrik Marhein and his Wife Margareta Olofsdotter Gammal with their Children* (1659; Grensholm house), which represents his most assured portrait style. The couple are depicted with their four surviving children and two deceased babies, shown in their cradles, as though asleep. The formal style of 16th-century Swedish portraiture is here combined with a sumptuous attention to texture and colour that belies Aureller's provincial training.

In 1661 Aureller moved to Göteborg and executed a portrait of *Pontus De la Gardie* in antique costume (1663; Borrestad, Skåne, priv. col.). This marks his development of a more flamboyant portrait style, and his acquisition of more important patrons, further demonstrated by his pompous equestrian portrait of the governor of Halmstad, *Bengt Christofferson Lilliehöök* (*c.* 1660; priv. col.), in which the prancing horse and the subject's fluttering drapery and extravagant helmet plumage suggest familiarity with Ehrenstrahl's portrait of *Karl Gustaf Wrangel* (1652; Bålsta, Skoklosters Slott). In Aureller's portrait of *Three Members of the Gyllenkrona Family* (1666; Regnaholm house) the subjects are similarly depicted in antique costume, in an idyllic landscape. In 1668 he carried out work (destr.) for Gustaf Posse (1626–76) at his estate Hällekis in Medelplana; around this date he executed the decorative *Self-portrait with Wife* (1670–71; Skara, Skaraborgs Länsmus.), in which the figures are framed by auricular ovals set into simulated architectural niches, flanked by gods and allegories and hung with garlands and drapery.

Aureller worked for Chancellor Magnus Gabriel De la Gardie in 1672 at Karlberg Castle, Solna, and in 1680 at Läckö Castle, Lidköping, where he executed De la Gardie's portrait and probably supervised a group of painters decorating the castle. In 1680 he worked on the rich altarpiece donated by the Chancellor to the church at Lidköping, for which he also executed (1687) the epitaph of the minister *Jonas Rudberus*, his last documented work, which illustrates his failing artistic powers. Although Aureller's career is closely linked to the culturally remote province of Västergötland, his paintings were also influenced by Ehrenstrahl's classicizing style and also show that he was familiar with European trends, possibly through engravings.

(2) Johan Aureller (ii) (*b* Gävle, 1657; *d* Medelplana, Västergötland, 1733). Son of (1) Johan Aureller (i). He trained *c.* 1680 with his father at Läckö Castle; the rest of his career is largely undated. He was active as a portrait painter and his portrait of *Friherre Lars Hierta* (Dåderö; see *Svenska män och kvinnor*) illustrates his stylistic dependence on Ehrenstrahl's official portraits. He also executed the altarpiece (1706) depicting the *Crucifixion* and the *Deposition* in a Baroque frame. Between 1702 and 1732 Aureller produced a number of epitaphs and sacred works for churches in Västergötland, the most renowned of which is that of 1732 in the church of Medelplana; within a richly carved frame, around an image of *Christ as the Man of Sorrows with Angels*, are oval portraits of the artist's family. Although a mediocre painter, he introduced his father's style into church decoration in the Skara region, establishing a school that perpetuated this style throughout the 18th century.

BIBLIOGRAPHY

SVKL
A. Hahr: *Konst och konstnärer vid Magnus Gabriel De la Gardies hof* [Art and artists at the court of Magnus De la Gardie] (Uppsala, 1905), pp. 114, 116, 117, 128
Svenska män och kvinnor: Biografisk uppslagbok [Swedish men and women: a biographical record], iii (Stockholm, 1946) [portrait of *Lars Hierta*]
B. von Malmborg: *Svensk porträttskonst genom fem århundraden* [Five hundred years of Swedish portraiture] (Malmö, 1978), pp. 74, 95, 118, 120

ANTONIA BOSTRÖM

Aureole. Light encircling the head or body of a sacred figure. □

Auria, d'. Italian family of sculptors.

(1) Giovan Domenico d'Auria (*fl* Naples, 1541; *d* before March 1573). He trained with Annibale Caccavello in the workshop of Giovanni Marigliano and, with Caccavello, became Marigliano's assistant. After leaving the workshop, the two embarked on a lifelong partnership that was a model of cooperation for later sculptors. In

1541 d'Auria was paid for work on the Fontana dell'Olmo (destr.), Naples, commissioned from Marigliano by the Viceroy of Naples, Pedro de Toledo, and between 1544 and 1545 he is mentioned in connection with payments made to Marigliano for the tombs of members of the Sanseverino di Saponara family in SS Severino e Sossio, Naples. In 1547, with Caccavello, he worked on the tomb of *Nicola Antonio Caracciolo*, Marchese di Vico, in S Giovanni a Carbonara, Naples, probably executing the statue of the deceased.

The first independent work of d'Auria and Caccavello is the bas-relief with the *Virgin and Child in Glory with Souls in Purgatory* (Capua, Mus. Prov. Campano), commissioned in June 1550 by Bishop Luca Rinaldo for S Caterina, Capua. Mainly executed by d'Auria, the serenity and solemn classicism of the work derive from Marigliano. In addition to independent works, such as the bas-relief depicting the *Conversion of St Paul* (sometimes attributed to Caccavello) for the Poderico Chapel, S Maria delle Grazie a Caponapoli, Naples, d'Auria collaborated with his partner between 1553 and 1557 on a bas-relief (untraced) depicting the *Deposition*, for the Carlino Chapel in S Maria la Nova, Naples, and, from 1557, on the prestigious sculptural group for the di Somma Chapel, S Giovanni a Carbonara, Naples. In 1557, working mainly on his own, he executed the tomb of *Hans Walter von Hiernheim* in S Giacomo degli Spagnoli, Naples. Between 1560 and 1562, again with Caccavello, he worked on the Fontana Quattro al Molo (named after the four figures of rivers that adorned the fountain) formerly on the wharf at Naples (removed to Spain, 1670). From 1563, payments made to the two sculptors by the poet Bernardino Rota are documented. In 1569 d'Auria began work on his most important commission, the poet's tomb in the Rota family chapel at S Domenico Maggiore, Naples. In the same year he received payment for the tomb of *Traiano Spinelli*, Prince of Scalea, in S Caterina a Formiello, a work that was probably later completed by Salvatore Caccavello and Giovan Domenico's son, (3) Geronimo d'Auria. On 16 March 1573 a payment is recorded from Fabrizio Brancaccio to the heirs of the sculptor.

(2) Giovan Tomasso d'Auria (*fl* Naples, *c.* 1550–1600). His exact relationship to (1) Giovan Domenico d'Auria is unknown. He probably trained in the workshop of Giovanni Marigliano since he appears as a witness in the contracts for the Sanseverino di Saponara tombs in SS Severino e Sossio, Naples, and he is also recorded in payments registered in the *Diario* of Annibale Caccavello. In 1566 he collaborated with Giovan Domenico on the restoration of the Fontana della Selleria, Naples, while in 1573 he created a number of decorative elements for the Santini Altar in S Domenico Maggiore, Naples, and a white marble door for the palazzo of Marino Caracciolo. In the same year he carved the base of the statue of *Marcello Caracciolo*, Conte di Biccari, in the Carraciolo di Vico Chapel, S Giovanni a Carbonara.

(3) Geronimo d'Auria (*fl* Naples, 1573–1619). Son of (1) Giovan Domenico d'Auria. After the death of his father, in 1573 he worked on the completion of the tomb of *Fabrizio Brancaccio* in S Maria delle Grazie a Caponapoli, Naples. In June of that year he received payment for a statue of *Marcello Caracciolo*, Conte di Biccari, for the Caracciolo di Vico Chapel, S Giovanni a Carbonara, Naples, and in September he received further payment, from Bernardino Rota, for works carried out by his father in the Rota Chapel, S Domenico Maggiore, Naples. From 1576 Geronimo received a series of important commissions for the church of the Annunziata, Naples. Apart from the lavabo in the sacristy, based on the designs of the Neapolitan painter Giovan Bernardo Lama and executed in collaboration with Salvatore Caccavello, other surviving works by Geronimo include the wooden panels with scenes from the Old and New Testaments on the sacristy benches, again executed in collaboration with Caccavello and, in the decorative sections, with the Neapolitan carver Nunzio Ferraro. The work, one of the greatest achievements of Neapolitan sculptural art from the second half of the 16th century, reveals considerable variations in both style and quality. The scenes created by Geronimo often contain echoes of the classicizing academicism of his father and rarely achieve the extraordinarily dramatic quality of his more gifted colleague Salvatore Caccavello, to whom several figures of *Prophets* have been attributed. After this early phase Geronimo developed a style that was markedly influenced by the Counter-Reformation and by the presence in Naples of the Florentine sculptors Michelangelo Naccherino and Pietro Bernini, who dominated Neapolitan sculpture during the 16th and 17th centuries. This dry, academic style gained widespread popularity among members of the Neapolitan nobility, who commissioned numerous funerary monuments and sculptures from Geronimo for their private chapels. In 1583 he executed the large funerary structure for the Mastrogiudice family in the parish church of Monteoliveto and between 1586 and 1590 the funerary monument of *Giovanbattista Minutolo* in Naples Cathedral. Before 1590 he completed, in collaboration with Francesco Cassano, the sculptures for the Turbolo Chapel, S Maria la Nova, Naples. Again in collaboration with Cassano, he began work in 1590 on the sculptures, funerary monuments and epitaphs for the Barone Chapel, Nola Cathedral. In 1592 he received payment for a statue of the *Virgin and Child* for the Montalto Chapel, S Maria del Popolo agli Incurabili, Naples. In 1593–4 he executed a statue of *St John the Baptist*, universally acknowledged as his greatest work, for the Rota Chapel, S Domenico Maggiore.

BIBLIOGRAPHY

DBI

B. de Dominici: *Vite* (1742–5), ii, pp. 166–76

G. B. D'Addosio: *Origine, vicende storiche e progresso della R. S. Casa dell'Annunziata di Napoli* (Naples, 1883)

G. Filangieri di Satriano: *Documenti per la storia, le arti e le industrie delle provincie napoletane* (Naples, 1883–91), iv, pp. 355–62

G. Ceci: 'Per la biografia degli artisti del XVI e XVII secolo: Nuovi documenti II scultori', *Napoli Nob.*, xv (1906), pp. 133–9

G. B. D'Addosio: 'Documenti inediti di artisti napoletani dei secoli XVI e XVII dalle polizze dei banchi', *Archv Stor. Prov. Napoletane*, xxxviii (1913), pp. 585–90

O. Morisani: *Saggi sulla scultura napoletana del cinquecento* (Naples, 1941)

Sculture lignee nella Campania (exh. cat., ed. F. Bologna and R. Causa; Naples, Pal. Reale, 1950)

M. Rotili: *L'arte del cinquecento nel regno di Napoli* (Naples, 1972)

F. Abbate: 'Il sodalizio tra Annibale Caccavello e Gian Domenico d'Auria e un'ipotesi per Salvatore Caccavello', *An. Scu. Norm. Sup. Pisa*, n. s. 2, vi (1976), pp. 129–45

G. Toscano: 'La bottega di Benvenuto Tortelli e l'arte del legno a Napoli nella seconda metà del cinquecento', *An. Fac. Lett. & Filos. U. Napoli*, n. s., xiv (1983–4), pp. 229–69

For further bibliography *see* CACCAVELLO, ANNIBALE.

GENNARO TOSCANO

Auricular style [Dut. *Kwabornament*; Ger. *Knorpelwerk*, *Ohrmuschelstil*]. Term used to describe a type of ornament popular in the 17th century, characterized by smooth, curved and rippling forms resembling the human ear. This highly plastic style evolved during the first two decades of the 17th century in Utrecht, and in its fully developed form is found only in metalwork. The style in this medium is characterized by the use of amorphous, lobate scrolls and embossed, relief ornament that emphasize the malleable nature of the metal. At its most extreme, it exaggerates this quality by suggesting that objects were modelled in a semi-molten state. The goldsmiths Adam van Vianen and Paulus van Vianen (*see* VIANEN, VAN, (1) and (2)) of Utrecht are credited with the invention of the style, although its origins seem to lie in the graphic designs of such 16th-century Italian Mannerist artists as Giulio Romano (e.g. drawing for a fish-shaped ewer; Oxford, Christ Church) and Enea Vico. The latter's designs for plate were published in the mid-16th century and may have been known in Utrecht.

The earliest intimations of the style appear on a tazza (1607; Amsterdam, Rijksmus.) by Paulus van Vianen, probably made under the patronage of Emperor Rudolf II in Prague. In this work the basic form of a late 16th-century vessel has been retained, but the strapwork of conventional Mannerism has been replaced by a pattern of scrolls that are much more fluid in conception. The embossed scenes on the underside of the bowl are separated by a novel kind of ornament resembling bones. Similarly, a ewer and dish (1613; Amsterdam, Rijksmus.; for illustration *see* VIANEN, VAN, (2)) are decorated with relief scenes of the story of *Diana and Acteon*, which are contained within cartouches formed of fleshy scrolls and residual masks. The most dramatic and fully plastic of all the early works in the style is undoubtedly the silver-gilt ewer (1614; Amsterdam, Rijksmus.) made by Adam van Vianen in Utrecht in memory of his brother for the goldsmiths' guild of Amsterdam. The ewer was celebrated in its own time as a work of brilliant originality and technique: the entire body, which is modelled as a crouching monkey on a rippling base supporting a fleshy shell-like form, was raised from a single sheet of silver.

The Auricular style continued to enjoy some popularity during the second quarter of the 17th century, when it was promoted by such goldsmiths and designers as Christiaen van Vianen (*see* VIANEN, VAN, (3)), Johannes Lutma (*see* LUTMA, (1)) and Gerbrand van den Eeckhout. Lutma published two series of Auricular ornament, *Veelderhande nieuwe compartmente* (1653) and *Verscheide snakeryen* (1654); his most notable works in the style are a silver ewer (1647; Amsterdam, Rijksmus.) and the brass choir-screen in the Nieuwe Kerk, Amsterdam. It also became a popular style for carved picture-frames and ornament on furniture until the mid-17th century, and designs for Auricular ornament for woodwork appear in Friedrich Unteutsch's *Neues Zieratenbuch* (*c.* 1650). Thereafter, the style was integrated with the developing mainstream Baroque style.

BIBLIOGRAPHY

W. K. Zülch: *Entstehung des Ohrmuschelstils* (Heidelberg, 1932)

TIMOTHY SCHRODER

Aurier, (Georges-)Albert (*b* Châteauroux, 5 May 1865; *d* Paris, 5 Oct 1892). French writer and critic. He was educated at the lycée in Châteauroux where his father was a notary. After receiving his baccalauréat, in 1883 Aurier was encouraged to take up law and travel to Paris to begin his studies. Although he obtained his degree from the Faculté de Droit de Paris in 1888, he never practised law, since during 1886–8 he was drawn into a circle of Left Bank intellectuals. His career as an art critic began with his participation in Symbolist literary activities, and in 1886 he contributed poems and satirical short stories to A. Baju's 'petit-revue', *Le Décadent.* Like contemporary decadents, Aurier was deeply influenced by Baudelaire, whose anti-naturalism and cult of the 'dandy' formed the basis of their outlook on life. Aurier's first critical article, 'Sensationnisme', published in *Le Décadent* in November 1886, demonstrated his developing interest in subjectivist philosophy, in particular that of Arthur Schopenhauer, and contained the germ of his later views on art. He attacked the naturalists' fidelity to objective truth and called for a more acute literature and art, which extracted the essence from life following the dictates of an individual temperament.

From 1888 to 1892 Aurier's interests became focused on events in the art world, although he continued to write plays and novels, notably *Vieux*, published by Savine in 1891. During a holiday in St Briac, Brittany, in 1887 he met the painter Emile Bernard and through him gained entry into artistic circles. Bernard introduced Aurier to van Gogh, Gauguin, Guillaumin and the Nabi group, and was also involved in the creation of Aurier's own 'petit-revue', *Moderniste Illustré* (April–Sept 1889). This included articles by Gauguin and drawings by the Pont-Aven group, as well as Aurier's first writings on art: a review of the 1889 Groupe Impressionniste et Synthétiste exhibition at the Café Volpini and a Symbolist interpretation of the Salon artist Jean-Jacques Henner.

During the period 1890–92 Aurier wrote his most substantial art criticism, which appeared in *La Revue Indépendante* and *Mercure de France.* He produced the first critical article on van Gogh in January 1890, drawing attention to his vigorous technique, which he saw as the consequence of the painter's creative ability, heightened as a result of nervous disorders. In March 1891 Aurier's now well-known essay on 'Gauguin: Le Symbolisme en peinture' appeared in *Mercure de France.* Gauguin was described as the leader of a new 'idea-ist' art through his ability to communicate symbols in a subjective, synthetic and, above all, decorative form. Aurier expanded this category to include the Nabis in his last article, 'Les Peintres symbolistes' (1892). He saw the new 'idea-ist' art as countering the mediocrity of most official art where artists' ability to communicate images in symbolic form was prevented by their attachment to academic procedure.

Aurier also wrote short pieces on Pissarro, Monet, Renoir, Eugène Carrière and the Belgian artist Henri de

Groux. A plan to hold a conference of Symbolist artists including the Nabis and Odilon Redon with the writer and theatre director Paul Fort, as well as to compile a series of monographs for *Mercure de France*, was abandoned due to Aurier's sudden death. The December 1892 issue of *Mercure de France* constituted a posthumous tribute to the critic.

WRITINGS

Oeuvres posthumes, ed. with intro. by R. de Gourmont (Paris, 1893) [collected crit. essays, poetry and fiction]

Regular contributions to *Rev. Indép.* and *Mercure France* (1888–92); trans. excerpts in H. B. Chipp: *Theories of Modern Art* (Berkeley, 1968)

BIBLIOGRAPHY

A. Aurier: 'Le Symbolisme en peinture: Paul Gauguin', *Mercure France*, ii (1891), pp. 155–65

L. Dumur: 'G. Albert Aurier et l'évolution idéaliste', *Mercure France*, viii (1893), pp. 289–97

A. Rette: 'Albert Aurier', *Souvenirs de symbolisme* (Paris, 1903), pp. 55–66

M. Coulon: 'Une Minute de l'heure symboliste: Albert Aurier', *Mercure France*, cxlv (1921), pp. 599–640

S. Lövgren: *The Genesis of Modernism* (Stockholm, 1959; rev. Bloomington, 2/1971) [chap. on Aurier]

Doss. Acénonètes du Coll. Pataphys., 15 (1961) [issue on Aurier]

P. T. Mathews: *Aurier's Symbolist Art Criticism and Theory* (diss.; microfilm, Ann Arbor, 1986)

For further bibliography see J. Rewald: *The History of Post-Impressionism* (London, 1956, rev. 3/1978), p. 522

JULIET SIMPSON

Auriol, (Jean) George [Georges] **(Hulot)** (*b* Beauvais, 26 April 1863; *d* Paris, 6 Feb 1938). French illustrator, typographical designer, writer and printmaker. He went to Paris in 1883 to pursue a literary career. His first humorous essays were published that year in the *Chat Noir* journal. He was introduced to the many avant-garde artists and writers who frequented the Chat Noir cabaret in Montmartre and contributed to the journal. Of these Henri Rivière and Eugène Grasset were especially important to his artistic development, Rivière coaching Auriol in drawing while Grasset introduced him to typographical design. Auriol's close association with Rivière culminated in the latter's album of lithographs, *Les Trente-six Vues de la Tour Eiffel* (1902; for illustration *see* JAPONISME), for which Auriol designed the decorative cover, end-papers and typography.

Auriol served as writer, illustrator and editor of the *Chat Noir* for ten years (1883–93). He produced book covers for the *Chat-Noir Guide* (1888) and the two-volume *Les Contes du Chat Noir* (1889–91) as well as 15 programmes for the Chat Noir shadow theatre. From the end of the 1880s the bold colours and flat patterning of his illustrations and typographical designs show the influence of Japanese art. In 1888 he created his first monograms for Rivière and himself in the style of Japanese seals, and during the next decade he produced hundreds of such monograms for artists, writers and publishers, including Rivière, Théophile-Alexandre Steinlen, Toulouse-Lautrec, Paul Verlaine, Anatole France, Ernest Flammarion and others. In 1901 Henri Floury published the first collection of Auriol's *Cachets, marques et monogrammes*, followed by two more volumes in 1908 and 1924.

Auriol's contribution to printmaking at the turn of the century was limited to a few distinctive colour woodcuts and colour lithographs; among his most notable colour lithographs are *Bois frissonnants* for the first album of André Marty's *L'Estampe originale* (1893) and *Jeune femme assise* and *Tête d'enfant* for Ambroise Vollard's *Album des peintres-graveurs* (1896–7). More importantly, Auriol's assimilation of Japanese aesthetics resulted in highly decorative and often abstract floral designs for hundreds of book and sheet-music covers by the avant-garde writers and composers for the publishers Enoch, Flammarion and Ollendorff as well as ornamental typography for Larousse's encyclopedias (1895–1930). *Combinaisons ornamentales* (1901) illustrates numerous examples of ornamental designs by Maurice Pillard Verneuil (*b* 1869), Alphonse Mucha and Auriol, summing up the work of the principal Art Nouveau ornamental designers.

Auriol's collaboration with the G. Peignot & Frères type-face foundry (1901–5) resulted in the creation of Auriol type styles such as Française Legère and Auriol Labeur. He remained active as an influential illustrator, designer of type and ornament and teacher until the 1930s.

BIBLIOGRAPHY

A. Alexandre: 'George Auriol', *A. & Déc.*, v (June 1899), pp. 161–70

'George Auriol', *ABC*, 162 (July 1938), pp. 73–84

Japonisme: Japanese Influence on French Art, 1854–1910 (exh. cat., Cleveland, OH, Mus. A.; New Brunswick, NJ, Rutgers U., Zimmerli A. Mus.; Baltimore, MD, Walters A.G.; 1975–6), pp. 96–7

The Colour Revolution: Colour Lithography in France, 1890–1900 (exh. cat. by P. D. Cate and S. H. Hitchings, New Brunswick, NJ, Rutgers U., Zimmerli A. Mus.; Baltimore, MD, Mus. A.; Boston, MA, Pub. Lib.; 1978–9), pp. 6, 18, 27, 55, 88

A. Fields: *George Auriol* (Salt Lake City, 1985)

PHILLIP DENNIS CATE

Auriti, Giacinto (*b* Rome, 24 June 1883; *d* after 1958). Italian diplomat and collector. In 1907 he embarked upon a highly successful career in the Italian diplomatic service. His first foreign posting to Berne was followed by periods in Madrid, Bucharest (1913) and Vienna (1921–33), where in 1926 he was promoted to the post of Minister Plenipotentiary and Ambassador Extraordinary. In July 1933 Auriti was transferred from Vienna to Tokyo, where he served as ambassador until 1940. In this capacity he contributed to the development of Italo-Japanese political and cultural relations, including the signing by Italy in 1937 of the Anti-Comintern Pact, formed by Germany and Japan in 1936, and the foundation of such bodies as the Società degli Amici del Giappone, formed in 1938.

According to a lecture that Auriti gave to the Society for International Cultural Relations (Kokusai bunka shinkokai) in Tokyo on 27 May 1936, he had not at first intended to devote any time to the art of the country, having already spent 15 years learning to appreciate European art, but within four months of his arrival he had become a devotee of East Asian art in general and Japanese art in particular. Auriti began to collect at a time when the market was well stocked and competition limited, and he profited from the advice of Yukio Yashiro, Director of the Institute of Art Research (founded 1930; now National Research Institute of Cultural Properties) in Tokyo. As a result Auriti amassed a fine collection of Chinese, Korean and Japanese bronzes (both Buddhist sculptures and mirrors), which he was later able to transfer to Rome. The collection was donated during Auriti's lifetime to the Istituto Italiano per il Medio ed Estremo Oriente

(IsMEO), formed in 1958. In 1961 it went on display in a room of the Museo Nazionale d'Arte Orientale in Rome.

WRITINGS

On Japanese Art: Comparative Observations on Far-Eastern and Western Art (Tokyo, 1937)

Compendio di storia della cultura giapponese dalla età arcaica alla restaurazione dei Meigi (Florence, 1954)

BIBLIOGRAPHY

E. Savino: *La nazione operante* (Novara, 1937), p. 123 [with portrait]

A. C. Soper: *Chinese, Korean and Japanese Bronzes: A Catalogue of the Auriti Collection Donated to IsMEO and Preserved in the Museo Nazionale d'Arte Orientale in Rome*, Rome, Ist. Medio & Estremo Oriente cat. (Rome, 1966)

JANET SOUTHORN

Aust, Gottfried (*b* Heidersdorf, 5 April 1722; *d* Lititz, PA, 28 Oct 1788). American potter of German birth. Although originally trained as a weaver, he was apprenticed to a potter in Herrnhut, Germany, where the Moravian Brethren were centred. In 1754 he arrived in Bethlehem, PA, the Brethren's first colonial outpost. After ten months' work at the pottery there under master Michael Odenwald, Aust went to the new settlement in Bethabara, NC, where he established its first pottery. In 1768 the pottery was moved to another new settlement at Salem, NC. All the wares necessary for daily life were made in Aust's potteries including large stoves. Aust's most distinctive work is found on decorative plates embellished with floral or geometric ornament delineated in green, red, brown, white and dark brown slips (e.g. earthenware dish used by Aust as a trade sign, diam. 555 mm, 1773; Winston-Salem, NC, Old Salem; see Bivins, p. 224). He trained a number of apprentices who worked in the Piedmont region, thereby creating a 'school' of his style that is associated with the area.

BIBLIOGRAPHY

J. Bivins, jr: *The Moravian Potters in North Carolina* (Chapel Hill, NC, 1972)

ELLEN PAUL DENKER

Austalis. *See* AOSTALLI.

Austen, (Elizabeth) Alice (*b* Rose Bank, Staten Island, NY, 17 March 1866; *d* New York, 9 June 1952). American photographer. She was introduced to photography by a friend, Oswall Muller, sometime around 1876, and quickly learnt the complexities of working with a variety of cumbersome cameras, dry-plate negatives and contact printing. As an avid amateur photographer, she documented a social history of a bygone era. Her work, dating between the 1880s and 1930s, recorded a charming portrait of the genteel activities of upper middle-class society on Staten Island. Although her photographs primarily documented the everyday life of the wealthy inhabitants and friends of her home, Cold Comfort, which overlooked New York's Upper Bay, she also produced a challenging series of images of New York's Lower East Side. These 'street types' were published as a portfolio by the Albertype Company in 1896.

Unlike those of Jacob A. Riis and Lewis W. Hine, Austen's images of immigrants revealed no concern for social reform, but evidenced a hesitancy and curiosity experienced by both photographer and subject. Her life of stability was abruptly ended by the Stock Market Crash of 1929. She was eventually forced to sell all her possessions and ended up living in the City Farm Colony, a local poorhouse. With the aid of the Staten Island Historical Society, which had preserved her negatives and prints, and researcher Oliver Jensen, her photographs were sold to several publications, particularly *Life* and *Holiday*, bringing her fame at the age of 85.

BIBLIOGRAPHY

'The Newly Discovered Picture World of Alice Austen: Great Woman Photographer Steps Out of the Past', *Life* (24 Sept 1951), pp. 137–44

H. Humphries and R. Benedict: 'The Friends of Alice Austen: With a Portfolio of Historical Photographs', *Infinity* (July 1967), pp. 4–31

A. Novotny: *Alice's World: The Life and Photography of an American Original: Alice Austen, 1866–1952* (Old Greenwich, CT, 1976)

FIONA DEJARDIN

Austerlitz. *See* SLAVKOV U BRNA.

Austin, Henry (*b* Hamden, CT, 12 April 1804; *d* New Haven, 12 Nov 1891). American architect. He was based in New Haven, from where his work and influence spread over much of Connecticut, with two major forays out-of-state: a speculative development (*c.* 1840) in Trenton, NJ, and the lavish Morse–Libby house (1859) in Portland, ME. After neglect in the Colonial Revival period, he was later recognized as Connecticut's foremost 19th-century architect. His work is mainly associated with the Villa style of the 1840s and 1850s in its many variations, Grecian, Italian, Tuscan, Renaissance, Oriental, but continuing, with less intensity, through the Victorian Gothic and French Empire styles of the 1860s and 1870s (*see* UNITED STATES OF AMERICA, §II, 2–5). To these popular fashions of his day, Austin brought a personal interpretation and a sometimes startling imagination, distorting and exaggerating familiar proportions with long, dripping brackets and excessively broad, flat eaves, modelling surfaces with the deep shadows of strangely jutting pediments and short, square columns, and breaking the skyline with roof structures topped by exotic little finials from the Orient.

Austin trained as a carpenter in the environs of New Haven and moved to the city in the 1820s where he acted as agent for the New York firm of Ithiel Town and Alexander Jackson Davis while trying to start a practice of his own. Davis had a strong influence on his first attributed building, a Grecian villa of *c.* 1840 (destr.), and on his first major commission, a Gothic library (1842; now Dwight Chapel, Yale University, New Haven) for Yale College. The library was followed in 1845 by another major commission, the monumental Egyptian Revival style gate for the Grove Street Cemetery, New Haven. With these two projects, both highly visible and both in the vanguard of fashion, Austin's reputation was established. Over the next 20 years his output was enormous. Outstanding works include villas for the old New Haven gentry on Hillhouse Avenue and for the new manufacturing class around Wooster Square; three brownstone banks in the 1850s (all destr.); the Moses Beach house in Wallingford, CT (1850; destr.), and New Haven City Hall (1861), a precocious High Victorian Gothic design praised by critics then and since (destr. 1977 except for façade and tower). The Willis Bristol house (1845) is a rare example of an Oriental villa, while the Dana house (1848), New Haven, uses such exotic decorations as Indian plant columns and fringed cornices to embellish the basic cube of the Italian villa style, a formula that became an Austin trademark. The climactic building of this period is the New Haven Railroad Station (1848–9, destr. 1894), considered one of the most fanciful buildings ever erected in New England—a long, slim structure suggesting the proportions of a train, set directly over the tracks and topped with bizarre stupa-like forms.

After the American Civil War, patronage declined and Austin's work became tamer. However he retained his old verve in two late projects: Trinity Home (1868; mostly destr.), New Haven, an urban compound consisting of town houses framing the entrance to a tree-planted court containing chapel, school and home; and his swansong, the J. W. Clark seaside cottage at Stony Creek, Branford, CT (1879), with a high red-roofed tower that is one of the landmarks on the Connecticut shore.

Austin was among the first architects in Connecticut to establish a home-grown professional practice employing numerous draughtsmen, which affected the next generation of architects, including David R. Brown, Rufus G. Russell (1823–96) and Leon Robinson (1852–1923). His office exemplifies the transition from the builder–architects at the start of the 19th century to the local professional firms at the end.

BIBLIOGRAPHY

MEA

E. M. Brown: *New Haven: A Guide to Architecture and Urban Design* (New Haven, 1976)

ELIZABETH MILLS BROWN

Austin Canons. *See* AUGUSTINIAN CANONS.

Australia. Country and island continent. It is the world's smallest continent (area *c.* 8.5 million sq. km), located between the Indian and Pacific oceans south of South-east Asia, in latitudes parallel to those of the Sahara Desert (see fig. 1). With an average elevation of only 300 m, Australia is also the lowest continent, its ancient landforms being heavily eroded. The most prominent feature is the Great Dividing Range, the highlands of which run the full length of eastern Australia and recur in the island of Tasmania; in the western half of the continent are extensive plateaux and ridges, with vast desert areas in the centre. The extreme north is tropical, lying within the monsoon belt north of the Tropic of Capricorn; off the north-eastern coast is the Great Barrier Reef, the world's largest coral reef. Australia has extensive coastal plains and tablelands, those along the east coast being the most heavily populated parts of the country; the vegetation is typically dry, open woodland dominated by eucalypts. The Australian Aboriginal peoples arrived *c.* 40,000 years ago and developed a highly stable society with complex cultural traditions, aspects of which survived colonization. Australia was settled by the British from the late 18th century. In 1901 its separate colonies were joined in a federation of states as the Commonwealth of Australia, which became a dominion within the British empire and subsequently a member of the Commonwealth of Nations; it is the only continent to comprise a single nation-state (population *c.* 17 million).

For the history and art of Australia before colonization *see* ABORIGINAL AUSTRALIA.

I. Introduction.

The concept of *Terra australis* existed for centuries in the European imagination as the antipodean counterweight to the known world. The first authenticated landfalls by Europeans were those in the mid-17th century of Dutch explorers and merchants, who charted much of the north and west coast but found the land harsh and inhospitable. They were followed by French and British explorers, notably James Cook in the later 18th century, when the more fertile east coast was explored and the continent finally mapped (*see* §III, 1 below). British settlement began in 1788 when a convict colony was established at Sydney Cove, Port Jackson (*see* SYDNEY), to relieve over-crowding in British prisons. The colony of New South Wales accepted many thousands of transportees in the following decades, especially after the Napoleonic Wars in 1815, and other convict settlements were established in Tasmania (formerly Van Diemen's Land) in 1803 and in Queensland in 1824–5 (*see* BRISBANE). As free settlers became more numerous in the early 19th century, agricultural and urban development increased: British colonies were established at PERTH (1829), Western Australia; MELBOURNE (1835–6), Victoria (originally part of New South Wales); and ADELAIDE (1836), South Australia. A new period of exploration of the inland areas also began, which led to the discovery of a striking landscape with unique flora and fauna resulting from the long isolation of the continent; this fact, together with the crucial significance of land use to white settlement, accounts for the overwhelming predominance of landscape as an artistic genre in Australian art.

In 1851 the convict population of 27,000 comprised nearly half the population of Australia, but transportation was much reduced in the 1850s. At this time the discovery of gold in New South Wales and Victoria brought large numbers of immigrants from all over the world, including China, many of whom stayed to become settlers in the burgeoning pastoral industries. Most of the colonies received self-government in the 1850s; combined with the wealth flowing from primary industry, this resulted in the development of the cities with many fine public buildings. Despite the predominance of pastoral and mining industries over manufacturing, Australia experienced extraordinary urban concentration: by 1881 more than half the population lived in the cities, increasing to three-quarters by 1947. A deep recession marked the end of the 19th century, however, except in Western Australia, where gold was discovered in 1892.

After the federation of the states in 1901 the Northern Territory was separated from South Australia (1911) and the Australian Capital Territory was formed as an enclave within New South Wales to become the site of the new federal capital, CANBERRA. The Australian contribution to World War I was a turning-point in the emergence of a continuing ideology of national independence. It became a popular subject for art during the 1920s, although its

1. Map of Australia; those sites with separate entries in this dictionary are distinguished by CROSS-REFERENCE TYPE

most convincing representation remained in the diversification of landscape painting. After World War II Australia became increasingly industrialized, while important new mineral resources, including iron, bauxite, nickel, copper and oil, were developed. North American economic and cultural influences overtook those of Britain, but Australian cultural traditions were also greatly enriched and developed by European migrants in the 1950s and 1960s; in the last decades of the century the influence of Asian migrants became important, as did the increasing recognition of the distinctiveness of Aboriginal art and culture.

BIBLIOGRAPHY

W. Moore: *The Story of Australian Art*, 2 vols (Sydney, 1934, rev. 1980)

B. Smith: *Place, Taste and Tradition: A Study of Australian Art since 1788* (Sydney, 1945, rev. Melbourne, 2/1979)

N. Macgeorge: *The Arts in Australia* (Melbourne, 1948)

R. Hughes: *The Art of Australia* (Ringwood, Victoria, 1961, rev. 1971)

A. McCulloch: *Encyclopedia of Australian Art* (Melbourne, 1968, rev. 2/1994)

A. Galbally and M. Plant, eds: *Studies in Australian Art* (Melbourne, 1978)

A. Bradley and T. Smith: *Australian Art and Architecture: Essays Presented to Bernard Smith* (Melbourne, 1980)

TERRY SMITH

II. Architecture.

1. Before *c.* 1900. 2. After *c.* 1900.

1. Before *c.* 1900.

(i) Settlement and colonial architecture. (ii) Growth and boom styles.

(i) Settlement and colonial architecture. The first permanent European buildings erected in Sydney Cove after the landing of the first fleet were simple, single-cell structures

2. James Bloodworth (attrib.): Old Government House, Parramatta, New South Wales, Australia, *c.* 1800; porch (*c.* 1816) by Francis Greenway; wings (1820) by John Watts; engraving from L. C. de Freycinet: *Voyage autour du monde . . . 1817, 1818, 1819 et 1820* (Paris, 1825)

built with readily available local materials—initially wattle and daub with reed thatching. More effective shelter was provided by slab huts, with broad, vertical slabs of timber split from logs used for walls, and bark covering or shingles for the roof; slab huts subsequently became the most common form of pioneer's dwelling. By the end of April 1788, three months after arrival, the manufacture had begun of sandstock bricks and simple burnt-clay roof-tiles, which were directed to the construction of Sydney's first official buildings: the Governor's residence, a dry-store, military barracks and houses for the officers and their families. The buildings were crude, yet in their basic form and proportions they echoed the elegant architecture of Georgian England, sprung naturally from the culture of the settlers' former homeland. Government House (completed 1789; later extended; destr.), the first work with architectural pretensions, was a small, two-storey building with stone dressings, a hipped roof, glazed sash windows and a projecting gabled frontispiece; it was designed by JAMES BLOODWORTH, Australia's first official Superintendent of Works.

The exigencies of climate—hot summer sun and occasional torrential rain—soon led to the modification of the simple Georgian hipped-roof box by the addition of verandahs to protect walls and windows; several early examples (e.g. Elizabeth Farm, 1794; Experiment Farm Cottage, *c.* 1800) can be seen at Parramatta (formerly Rose Hill), *c.* 22 km up-river from Sydney Cove, where better farmland had been found. Encircling verandahs subsequently came to characterize the mainly single-storey Australian rural domestic vernacular, particularly in New South Wales (*see* VERNACULAR ARCHITECTURE, §II, 6); they were less common in Tasmania, where the cooler climate reduced the need for sun-shading, while in subtropical Brisbane and Queensland a distinct regional variation later developed, with houses raised on wooden stumps with wide verandahs shaded by timber lattice.

Around 1800 a new Government House (eventually known as Old Government House; see fig. 2) was built at Parramatta, probably by Bloodworth, and after the arrival of Governor Lachlan Macquarie (1810) other public buildings were erected in the simple colonial Georgian style; examples include the General, or 'Rum', Hospital (1810–15; surviving blocks now part of the NSW Parliament and Mint), Macquarie Street, Sydney, which has a two-storey galleried verandah; and the Lancer Barracks (1816–22), Parramatta, and other buildings by JOHN WATTS, who, with Francis Greenway, was among the first experienced architects in the colony (both arrived in 1814). The arrival of trained architects marked the development of a more sophisticated classicism for public buildings, with porches, pediments and mouldings detailed with the local Sydney sandstone—albeit simplified to suit available craftsmanship. Greenway, who became Civil Architect in 1816, produced the finest buildings of the period in New South Wales, his abilities coinciding with Macquarie's ambition to transform the colony from the ruinous convict settlement he found. Such buildings as St Matthew's (1817), Windsor, Hyde Park Barracks (1817; for illustration *see* GREENWAY, FRANCIS) and adjacent St James (1819), Queens Square, Sydney, were designed in brick with stone details in a simple yet original classical mode strongly suggestive of the work of John Soane. The design of St James was later echoed in one of the first churches built in Melbourne, St James Old Cathedral (begun 1839) by Robert Russell.

Macquarie's ambitious programme of works was officially censured, and after his departure in 1821 public building virtually ceased until the mid-1830s, apart from some utilitarian works. Domestic construction continued, however, stimulated by the development of the pastoral industry and increasing migration of free settlers, and the period 1821–40 marked the flowering of colonial architecture in New South Wales and Tasmania, marked by fine detailing, for example in doorways, fanlights, staircases and mouldings. Many beautiful houses were built in and around Sydney, notably those by JOHN VERGE, who worked in a stuccoed Regency style (e.g. Camden Park House, Camden, 1831). Government House (1839), Adelaide, by GEORGE KINGSTON was also built as a Regency villa, while in Tasmania such houses as Panshanger (1831), near Longford, and Clarendon (1838), Nile, reflect a more severe Neo-classicism, the latter having a giant two-storey Ionic portico. Public building continued in Tasmania under JOHN LEE ARCHER, Civil Engineer from 1827 to 1838, whose many buildings include the Customs House (1835; now Parliament House), Hobart, and St George (1836), Battery Point, Hobart, which has a Doric portico and stepped octagonal tower (added 1846 by James Blackburn).

In 1829 Governor Darling issued regulations for the planning of new towns, stipulating a rectilinear street pattern with no allowance for public open space. These regulations affected the initial design of most of the new settlements planned in the 1830s, including Perth (1829), Melbourne (1836) and Brisbane (opened to free settlement in 1842), as well as many smaller towns all over Australia. Adelaide was the striking exception: there a remarkable urban plan was designed by Surveyor-General Colonel William Light (1786–1839) in 1837 (for illustration *see* ADELAIDE), in which public squares and surrounding parkland featured prominently. The growth of migration during this period brought architects trained in the latest fashions in Britain. Greek Revival was introduced in such buildings as Darlinghurst Court House (1836), Sydney, by colonial architect MORTIMER LEWIS, and the Lady Franklin Museum (1842–3), Lenah Valley, Hobart, built as a miniature Greek temple by JAMES BLACKBURN. A picturesque medievalism had already appeared in Greenway's Government Stables (1817; now NSW Conservatorium of Music), Sydney. Castellated Tudor Gothic was employed for nearby Government House, begun by Lewis in 1837 to a design by the English architect Edward Blore; it also appeared in other grand houses (e.g. Carthona, Darling Point, Sydney (1844), built by Surveyor-General Thomas Mitchell), while many versions of 'rustic' and 'carpenter's' Gothic subsequently appeared in smaller houses.

(ii) Growth and boom styles. The gold rush of the 1850s brought an influx of new settlers to Australia, including such architects as W. C. VAHLAND, who practised in the Victorian goldfields area, and ANDREA GIOVANNI STOMBUCO, who worked mostly in Goulburn and Brisbane. The demand for housing was initially met by the import of prefabricated buildings: timber-framed from the USA and cast-iron from Britain. A notable example of the latter is the ornate Corio Villa (1856), Eastern Beach, Geelong, with classical columns and filigreed arches and bargeboards. Cast-iron elements and galvanized-iron corrugated sheeting had been introduced from England in the 1840s and were manufactured locally from the late 1850s; they subsequently became ubiquitous in domestic design, being cheap, easily transportable and quickly erected. Filigree cast-iron ornament ('lace') was particularly suited to the detailing of verandahs, and it came to characterize Italianate villas and whole suburbs of terraced housing in the 1860s and 1870s, particularly in Melbourne and Sydney, where it was lavishly applied. Increased suburban development was stimulated by the advent of the railways in the 1850s, aided by the ready availability of land. Subdivisions began in earnest in the 1860s, ultimately leading to the extensive suburban sprawl that characterizes all Australian cities.

The growth in population was accompanied by the emergence of a plethora of religious sects in Australia, and in the 1850s–1870s there was a wave of church-building throughout the country, supported by the Church Building Act (1836), which provided assistance for the construction of churches. Religious buildings formed a large part of the practices of the three most important architects of the period, EDMUND BLACKET, WILLIAM WILKINSON WARDELL and JOSEPH REED. Blacket used a traditional English Gothic Revival in stone for his ecclesiastical work, including country churches, St Andrew's Cathedral (1837–74; begun by James Hume), Sydney, and cathedrals in Bathurst, Goulburn and Perth, as well as for his main building and Great Hall (1854–*c.* 1860) at the University of Sydney, considered Australia's finest example of collegiate Gothic. Wardell's cathedrals include Roman Catholic St Patrick (from 1858), Melbourne, built in local bluestone with sandstone details (for illustration *see* WARDELL, WILLIAM WILKINSON), and St Mary's (begun 1865), Sydney. Reed, who practised with Frederick Barnes (1824–84) after 1862, introduced a freer Gothic Revival in his Wesley Church (1858) and a colourful brick Sienese Romanesque style for his Independent Church (1866; now Uniting Church), Collins Street. Polychrome brickwork was also used by PERCY OAKDEN for his Wesleyan Church (1872), Brunswick, Victoria, reflecting a renewed interest in brick that accompanied improved manufacturing techniques.

The granting of self-government to the colonies of Victoria, South Australia and Queensland in the 1850s combined with the enormous wealth flowing from the goldfields to produce a great wave of public building—particularly in Melbourne—in a variety of classical styles. New parliament buildings were erected in Melbourne (1856), Adelaide (1850s; rebuilt 1883–1939) and Brisbane (1865–8, 1878–80); Melbourne Public Library (1854; now the State Library of Victoria) by Joseph Reed has a Corinthian portico, and Wardell's Government House (1873), St Kilda, is a fine Italianate mansion. Renaissance Revival styles predominated, however, as in Melbourne's Treasury Building (1862) by J. J. Clark and the Melbourne Club (1858) by LEONARD TERRY, South Brisbane's florid Town Hall (1862) by John Hall, several of Adelaide's public buildings, including the Town Hall (1863–6) and

General Post Office (1867–72) by EDMUND WRIGHT and his partners, and Sydney's General Post Office (1866–86) and other buildings by JAMES BARNET, who was responsible for more than a thousand public buildings in New South Wales erected during his term as Colonial Architect (1860–90). Barnet also introduced a version of Italian Mannerism, for example in the entrance building (1886) of Bathurst Gaol.

Commercial prosperity, improved transport links and a financial boom in the 1880s led to an increase in the construction of banks, hotels and theatres in opulent classical styles that were increasingly eclectic and often richly ornamented with sculpture (*see* §IV below) and stucco decoration, as were the grand houses of the period (*see* BOOM STYLE). Fashions were inspired partly by the international exhibitions in Sydney (1879) and in Melbourne (1880), for which Reed and Barnes designed a vast, ornate timber-and-plaster structure (see fig. 3). Examples include the grandiose, colonnaded Queensland National Bank (1887), Queen Street, Brisbane, by F. D. G. Stanley (1835–1900; Government Architect 1862–81), which was claimed to be the finest bank in Australia; ANZ Bank (1875–8), King William Street, Adelaide, by Wright and Lloyd Tayler, loaded with columns, pilasters and ornament; and buildings in Sydney, Melbourne and Brisbane by John Sulman and J. P. Power. Variations appeared, for example in Melbourne in the work of JOHN A. B. KOCH and WILLIAM PITT: the latter used French Second Empire style in the Princess Theatre (1886) and a rich, polychrome free Gothic style in the Olderfleet and Rialto buildings (1889, 1890–91), Collins Street. Several public buildings were also erected in Sydney and Brisbane at this time to match those built earlier in Melbourne. In Sydney they include the Ionic-porticoed Art Gallery of New South Wales (1885–1909) by W. L. VERNON—who became the first NEW SOUTH WALES GOVERNMENT ARCHITECT in 1890—and the second stage of Sydney Town Hall (1866–88) by J. H. Wilson (1828–1908) and others, built in a 'wedding-cake' design that had Australia's first pressed-metal ceiling; in Brisbane the huge Treasury Building (1889–1922) was built by J. J. Clark in Greco-Roman style, while the Queensland Museum (1891) by G. H. M. Addison (*d* 1922) adopted a polychrome Byzantine style reminiscent of Westminster Cathedral, London.

3. Joseph Reed and Frederick Barnes: Exhibition Building, Melbourne, Australia, 1879

The recession of the 1890s, which was exacerbated by the artificial land boom of the preceding decade, severely affected construction: public and commercial building ceased virtually everywhere until the end of the century except in Western Australia, where gold was discovered in 1892. Development in the west had previously been slow, but in the next few years a concentration of late Victorian buildings was erected in Perth, Fremantle, Kalgoorlie and Coolgardie by such architects as JOSEPH JOHN TALBOT HOBBS and George Temple Poole (1856–1934), representing the final fling of the ornate eclecticism that had dominated Australian architecture in the last quarter of the 19th century. The end of the century was marked by the introduction of new influences from the USA: the American Romanesque Revival was employed in such commercial buildings as the massive Queen Victoria Markets Building (1893–8), Sydney, by George McRae, and also influenced the development of a simplified 'Warehouse style' (*see* §2 below). The American Shingle style appeared in domestic architecture, particularly in houses by JOHN HORBURY HUNT (e.g. Highlands, Waitara, Sydney, 1891). Together with the spreading influence of the English Arts and Crafts Movement and Queen Anne Revival, this marked a new approach towards a simpler architecture of brick and timber that suited the depressed economic conditions.

BIBLIOGRAPHY

W. H. Wilson: *Old Colonial Architecture in New South Wales and Tasmania* (Sydney, 1924)

M. Herman: *The Early Australian Architects and their Work* (Sydney, 1954, rev. 1970)

E. G. Robertson: *Victorian Heritage* (Melbourne, 1960)

J. M. Freeland: *Architecture in Australia: A History* (Melbourne, 1968, rev. Harmondsworth, 1972)

P. Cox, J. M. Freeland and W. Stacey: *Rude Timber Buildings in Australia* (London, 1969, rev. Sydney, 1980)

P. Cox and W. Stacey: *The Australian Homestead* (Melbourne, 1972, rev. 2/1978)

R. Roxburgh: *Early Colonial Houses of New South Wales* (Sydney, 1974, rev. 3/1980)

P. Cox, C. Lucas and W. Stacey: *Australian Colonial Architecture* (Melbourne, 1978)

E. Jensen and R. Jensen: *Colonial Architecture in South Australia* (Adelaide, 1980)

H. Tanner, ed.: *Architects of Australia* (South Melbourne, 1981)

The Heritage of Australia: The Illustrated Register of the National Estate (South Melbourne, 1981)

B. Saini and R. Joyce: *The Australian House: Homes of the Tropical North* (Sydney, 1982)

E. G. Robertson: *Decorative Cast Iron in Australia* (South Yarra, 1984)

R. Irving, ed.: *The History and Design of the Australian House* (Melbourne, 1985)

R. Apperly, R. Irving and P. Reynolds: *A Pictorial Guide to Identifying Australian Architecture: Styles and Terms from 1788 to the Present* (Sydney, 1989)

2. AFTER *c.* 1900.

(i) Federation and the emergence of Modernism. (ii) International and regional developments.

(i) Federation and the emergence of Modernism. The development of Australian architecture in the century preceding the federation of the states (1901) reflected the direct link between a culture imported from Europe and the necessary technical skills available in the colonies at any given time. Federation intensified the sense of national identity and the search for an Australian style of architecture. Australian motifs had already been used in ornament, as in the Arts and Crafts churches of ALEXANDER NORTH, and in the 1880s an Australian architectural order had been suggested by Lucien Henry, with local flora on the capitals of the Greek orders. In the 1900s the discussion was revived, for example in *Australian Architecture* (1908) by ROBERT HADDON, who was one of the most skilful exponents of the new decorative idiom of Art Nouveau; it was also a concern of HAROLD DESBROWE ANNEAR, a proponent of Arts and Crafts ideals, while GEORGE SYDNEY JONES was interested in developing houses designed for the Australian climate, some of them flat-roofed (e.g. Barncleuth, Pennant Hills, Sydney, 1909–11). The most popular style, however, which dominated Australian architecture before World War I, was the Australian version of Queen Anne Revival—later known as FEDERATION STYLE—which included elements of Arts and Crafts, the Shingle style and Art Nouveau decoration. Suburban houses, typically single-storey, were built with red brickwork, irregularly gabled roofs, timber detailing instead of cast-iron, and orange-red terracotta roof-tiles, which proved to have far better heat-insulating properties than the hitherto ubiquitous corrugated-iron or slate roofs. Commercial buildings were detailed in stone or cream-coloured plaster, with simplified classical mouldings in brick, and often with large arches on the façade. Among many exponents of the style were USSHER & KEMP in Melbourne.

The first indications of a more rationalist approach to architecture had already appeared in the 1890s in the 'Warehouse style' derived from the American Romanesque. Its characteristics—plain brickwork and giant semicircular recessed brick arches—were later adopted for use in other building types, including office buildings, factories and churches, for example St Andrew's Presbyterian Church (1907; see fig. 4), Brisbane, by G. D. PAYNE. Warehouses in the 1900s adopted still more functional lines and also began to incorporate reinforced concrete (first used in engineering works in 1896); the Sniders & Abrahams Warehouse (1909–10), Melbourne, by H. R. Crawford, for example, was built with C. A. P. Turner's system of mushroom columns and flat slabs. Such technological developments culminated in the shallow reinforced-concrete dome (diam. *c.* 35 m)—then the largest in the world—constructed in 1912 over the main reading-room of Melbourne Public Library by Bates, Peebles & Smart (now Bates, Smart & McCutcheon), successors to the practice of Joseph Reed. Meanwhile the introduction of passenger lifts in the 1880s had led to the construction of several buildings of 10 to 12 storeys, although height limitations were quickly imposed in all cities. In 1910 the first fully steel-framed building, Nelson House, Sydney, was completed by Louis Spier Robertson (1840–1910), and mass production of steel began in Newcastle in 1915, but steel-framed buildings of the 1920s continued to be clad in tiles or masonry in a classical form.

Suburban expansion had led to attempts in the 1890s—particularly by JOHN SULMAN—to develop a new approach to urban planning, based on respect for natural land forms. Such ideas were clearly expressed in the plan (1912) for the new national capital CANBERRA by Walter Burley Griffin, an American architect associated with Frank Lloyd Wright; Griffin designed a radial scheme related to the

4. G. D. Payne: St Andrew's Presbyterian Church, Brisbane, Australia, 1907

topography of the site (for further discussion and illustration *see* GRIFFIN, WALTER BURLEY). At the same time attempts to define an architecture appropriate to Australia led to a revival of early colonial Georgian design, particularly by W. HARDY WILSON, who produced the first studies of the colonial period as well as influential houses in Sydney (e.g. Eryldene, Gordon, 1913–14). ROBIN DODS reinterpreted the Queensland timber vernacular in his work in Brisbane with massive roofs and verandahs, and EUSTACE GRESLEY COHEN adopted a similar approach in Perth. LESLIE WILKINSON—Australia's first professor of architecture (1918–47), at the University of Sydney—combined Australian colonial architecture with the loggias of a Mediterranean idiom, which he promoted as being most suited to Australia's climate; this approach was also adopted in the later Melbourne Building (1927), Canberra, by Sulman and J. H. Kirkpatrick. Spanish mission influences are seen in work by JOHN CYRIL HAWES in Western Australia, notably St Francis Xavier Cathedral (1916), Geraldton, as well as in buildings by other architects in the 1920s, for example by MARSHALL CLIFTON in Perth.

After the war, however, the most popular house type throughout Australia was the California bungalow, which was particularly suited to expanding suburban development. Typical features include low-pitched roofs and deep verandahs supported on heavy, tapering piers and with solid balustrades; strikingly modern variations were produced by ALEXANDER STEWART JOLLY (e.g. 7 Cranbrook Avenue, Cremorne, Sydney, 1919). In contrast, Griffin developed a rugged, cubic architecture for houses at Castlecrag, Sydney, where he designed a model bushland suburb in the 1920s; this approach also characterized his municipal incinerators of the early 1930s in Victoria, South Australia and New South Wales (see fig. 5).

Commercial and public buildings in the 1920s continued to be dominated by classicism (e.g. Brisbane's City Hall, by Hall & Prentice, and War Memorial Shrine, by Buchanan & Cowper, both 1930); stripped classicism also appeared, for example in early public buildings in Canberra. Construction was temporarily halted by the Depression, however, and during the early 1930s, stimulated by the creation of the Royal Australian Institute of Architects (1930), architects engaged in debate that challenged traditional Australian architecture. This coincided with an influx of European migrants and an increase in travel by Australian architects, stimulating the introduction of new ideas from Europe and the USA. After a world tour EDWARD BILLSON, for example, employed a brick style reminiscent of W. M. Dudok, seen in the award-winning Sanitarium Health Food Building (1936–7), Warburton, Melbourne. Art Deco was introduced by such architects as Emil Sodersten (1901–61) and BRUCE DELLIT, for example in the latter's Anzac War Memorial (1930–34; sculpture by Raynor Hoff) and several commercial buildings in Sydney with vertically emphasized façades; some fine Art Deco cinemas and theatres were also built, including several in Perth.

The most popular version of early Modernism, often known as 'streamline Moderne', which became widespread in the 1930s, features continuous horizontal bands of windows, rounded corners and flat roofs, usually with a contrasting, ornamented vertical element. A stricter version of Modernism appeared in the work of BEST

5. Walter Burley Griffin: municipal incinerator at Willoughby, New South Wales, Australia, 1934

OVEREND, NORMAN H. SEABROOK and ARTHUR STEPHENSON and his partners, particularly in Stephenson's hospitals (e.g. Mercy Hospital, East Melbourne, 1934), with horizontal bands of balconies reminiscent of Alvar Aalto's work in Finland. FREDERICK ROMBERG, who trained in Zurich, was perhaps most influential in the introduction of the International Style, seen in his crisp, white, staggered blocks of flats, Newburn (1939–41) and Stanhill (1942–50), South Melbourne.

(ii) International and regional developments. After World War II the International Style became fully established in Australia. It appeared in early houses in Sydney by SYDNEY ANCHER and in the revolutionary work of HARRY SEIDLER, who had studied with Walter Gropius and Marcel Breuer in the USA and moved to Australia in 1948; his houses of 1948–52 in Sydney (e.g. Seidler House, Turramurra, 1950) introduced the rational aesthetic of the Bauhaus. European Modernism also appeared in some early commercial buildings, for example Anzac House (1948–52), Sydney, by W. R. Bunning and C. A. Maddison, which was reminiscent of Italian Rationalism. Commercial construction was severely curtailed by economic constraints, however, and while an 'austerity' style of traditional forms reduced to minimum standards predominated in mass housing in the 1950s, residential buildings designed by architects provided the laboratory of styles, as they had in the early 20th century.

In Melbourne CHANCELLOR & PATRICK adopted a regional idiom influenced by Frank Lloyd Wright and Richard Neutra. ROY GROUNDS, whose early houses also reflected a regional approach, subsequently experimented with geometric plan forms, designing triangular and circular houses. Dramatic structural forms using new technology were introduced by Robin Boyd (*see* BOYD, (1)), an important architectural writer, who practised with Grounds and Romberg in the 1950s and 1960s. Structural expressionism is also apparent in the early houses of PETER MCINTYRE as well as in his joint design for the Olympic Swimming Pool, Melbourne (1952–6; with KEVIN BORLAND, John Murphy and Phyllis Murphy). ALISTAIR KNOX worked in the mud-brick tradition of Victoria in the 1950s and is regarded by many as the originator of the Australian environmental building movement. These architects established a tradition of experimental domestic architecture in the Melbourne area that was later reflected in the work of GREGORY BURGESS, COCKS & CARMICHAEL, PETER CORRIGAN and PETER CRONE, for example, in the 1970s. Meanwhile in Sydney a group of architects working in the 1950s and 1960s produced houses that were intimately related to their natural bushland sites (*see* SYDNEY SCHOOL). They included PETER MULLER, KEN WOOLLEY, RICHARD NORMAN JOHNSON and Bruce Rickard (*b* 1929), and their buildings contained influences from Japanese architecture, Frank Lloyd Wright's organic architecture and Brutalism; they remained popular models for housing for many years.

Post-war recovery and a surge of new migrants to Australia resulted in an enormous expansion in construction from the mid-1950s. Commercial building recommenced, and the first skyscrapers appeared after the relaxation of height restrictions in Sydney and Melbourne in 1957. These factors resulted in the introduction of the American corporate style by such firms as BATES, SMART & MCCUTCHEON, whose ICI House (1958) pioneered glass curtain-walling techniques in Melbourne; Skidmore, Owings & Merrill also directly transplanted the style in several buildings in Melbourne.

In most cities the climate was unsuited to glass curtain-walls, and attempts were made to incorporate sun-shading: in the IBM Building (1964), Sydney, by Stephenson & Turner, precast concrete hoods were added to each level to protect the bands of glazing. Other architects recessed the glass curtain-wall behind the structural frame or eliminated it altogether, incorporating sun-shading devices as an integral part of a more solid structure; this can be seen in McConnel, Smith & Johnson's Water Board headquarters (1965), Sydney (see JOHNSON, RICHARD NORMAN), and in Seidler's high-rise commercial work of the 1960s and after, mostly in reinforced concrete, for example the MLC Centre (1972–5), Sydney (for illustration *see* SEIDLER, HARRY).

A new phase of public building also began in the late 1950s. The international competition for Sydney Opera House (1957) resulted in the construction of one of Australia's best-known buildings, with a remarkable sculptural composition of white shell roofs (completed 1973; for illustration *see* UTZON, JØRN). In Melbourne the Victorian Arts Centre (1959–84) by Roy Grounds features three geometric structures surmounted by a soaring, conical spire (for illustration *see* MELBOURNE). Canberra became a particular focus for Australian public and institutional building in the decades after its development recommenced in 1958. Notable early buildings include the circular Academy of Science Building (1957–9), Bruce, by

6. Edwards Madigan Torzillo & Briggs: High Court of Australia, Canberra, 1972–80

Grounds, Romberg & Boyd, entirely covered by a shallow, arcaded dome. In the late 1960s and 1970s work began in the Parliamentary Triangle on the robust, monumental High Court of Australia (1972–80; see fig. 6) and the Australian National Gallery (1973–82), both by Edwards Madigan Torzillo & Briggs (*see* MADIGAN, COLIN), followed by the new Parliament House of Australia (1980–88) by Mitchell/Giurgola & Thorp (for illustration *see* CANBERRA).

In the 1970s there was a surge of interest in Australia's historic buildings and their conservation, accompanied by a renewed interest in regionalism. John Dalton was influential in developing an architecture attuned to the Queensland environment, initially inspired by the work of the Sydney school. The Queensland timber vernacular was reinterpreted in such buildings as the Dunk Island Resort (1978) by Donald Gazzard & Associates, while a revival of the Australian rural vernacular, with its extensive use of corrugated galvanized metal sheeting, was seen especially in the work of GLENN MURCUTT (e.g. Marie I. Short Farmhouse, Crescent Head, NSW, 1974–5) and JOHN ANDREWS (e.g. Andrews Farmhouse, Eugowra, NSW, 1980). Both timber and corrugated-metal models were widely used in the 1980s and 1990s in innovative designs attempting to reflect an Australian tradition. In an urban context, medium- and high-density housing schemes began to echo the 19th-century verandahed terrace-house vernacular (e.g. Forbes Street Housing, Woolloomooloo, Sydney, 1980, by Allen Jack & Cottier).

Another tendency of the 1970s was High Tech, seen especially in the steel-masted sports structures of PHILIP COX in Canberra; a sophisticated version, reminiscent of the work of Norman Foster, appeared in his Sydney Exhibition Centre (1984–8), while Yulara Tourist Village (1982), Ayers Rock, features tent structures. Meanwhile an extraordinary commercial construction boom took place throughout Australia in the 1980s, combined with several Bicentennial projects planned for 1988, including the hosting of Expo 88 in Brisbane; further developments were planned for the hosting of the Olympic Games in Sydney in 2000. Together they completed the transformation of Australian cities begun in the 1960s. Such rundown waterfront areas as Darling Harbour, Sydney, were redeveloped, while all city centres received a new generation of sophisticated skyscrapers, many of striking late Modern design and often clad with mirror-glass and aluminium (for illustrations *see* BRISBANE and SYDNEY). Post-modern tendencies appeared in high-rise office buildings (e.g. No. 1 Collins Street, 1984, by Denton Corker Marshall, and 120 Collins Street, 1992, by DARYL JACKSON, both in Melbourne) as well as in housing: in Sydney, Alexander Tzannes and Espie Dods, for example, produced houses based on classical design. By the mid-1990s it was clear that no single national style had developed; nevertheless, a distinctive design philosophy, incorporating the functional tenets of Modernism, high technology and a respect for indigenous forms and materials, ensured that a regional identity continued to characterize much Australian architecture.

BIBLIOGRAPHY

R. Haddon: *Australian Architecture: A Technical Manual* (Melbourne, 1908)

S. U. Smith and B. Stevens, eds: 'Domestic Architecture in Australia', *A. Australia* (1919) [special issue]

R. Boyd: *Australia's Home* (Melbourne, 1952, rev. Ringwood, Victoria, 1968)

——: *The Australian Ugliness* (Melbourne, 1960, rev. 1968)

J. M. Freeland: *Architecture in Australia: A History* (Melbourne, 1968, rev. Harmondsworth, 1972)

H. Sowden: *Towards an Australian Architecture* (Sydney, 1968)

A. Knox: *Living in the Environment* (Mullaya, 1975)

H. Tanner: *Australian Housing in the Seventies* (Sydney, 1976)

D. L. Johnson: *Australian Architecture, 1901–51: Sources of Modernism* (Sydney, 1980)

H. Tanner, ed.: *Architects of Australia* (South Melbourne, 1981)

L. Paroissien and M. Griggs, eds: *Old Continent, New Building: Contemporary Australian Architecture* (Sydney, 1983)

J. Taylor: *Australian Architecture since 1960* (Sydney, 1986, rev. 1990)

R. Apperly, R. Irving and P. Reynolds: *A Pictorial Guide to Identifying Australian Architecture: Styles and Terms from 1788 to the Present* (Sydney, 1989)

R. Freestone: *Model Communities: The Garden City Movement in Australia* (Melbourne, 1989)

T. Howells and M. Nicholson: *Towards the Dawn: Federation Architecture in Australia, 1890–1915* (Sydney, 1989)

G. Jahn: *Contemporary Australian Architecture* (Sydney, 1994)

MICHAEL SPENS

III. Painting and graphic arts.

1. Before *c.* 1900. 2. After *c.* 1900.

1. BEFORE *c.* 1900. Despite the rich artistic traditions of its Aboriginal peoples (*see* ABORIGINAL AUSTRALIA, esp. §II), for most of the century after colonization Australia was a subject of European, primarily British art, as the cultural perceptions of the artists visiting or settling there remained essentially European. Although there were many instances throughout the 19th century of art based on direct observation of local phenomena, the beginnings of a widespread nationalist tendency emerged only during the lead-up to the federation of the colonies in 1901, when Australian landscape and life became the chief subject for self-consciously Australian artists.

(i) Speculation and signs of settlement. (ii) Visions of landscape and nationality.

(i) Speculation and signs of settlement. Images of the Australian land mass, albeit initially conjectural, had appeared in many maps of the 16th and 17th centuries, but only in the 18th century did the first scientific observations, measurements and drawings appear. Capt. James Cook's three voyages between 1768 and 1779 revolutionized, in turn, botany, meteorology and enthnography. On his first voyage (1768–71) he 'completed' the configuration of the Australian continent by charting its east coast, while Sir JOSEPH BANKS collected extraordinary specimens and draughtsman SYDNEY PARKINSON carefully recorded them. On his second voyage (1772–5) Cook proved the absence of any other vast continent in the Pacific, while remarkable sights in the volcanic islands of the region provoked travel artist William Hodges to paint with a Romantic sublimity that went beyond the work of his master, Richard Wilson (i). Of the two artists on Capt. Matthew Flinders's circumnavigation of Australia (1801–4), William Westall also turned topography into inspired landscape painting, while Ferdinand Bauer (1760–1858) raised natural science illustration to new heights. French

artists Charles-Alexandre Lesueur (1778–1846) and Nicholas-Martin Petit (1777–1804), on Nicholas Baudin's expedition to the region (1800–04), made finely detailed studies of marine specimens and of Aborigines.

The first two known delineations of the settlement established in 1788 at Sydney Cove predict much about the contradictory perspectives that have informed art in Australia ever since. In July 1788 Capt. John Hunter carefully rendered the shoreline, the depths of water and the positions of both the rudimentary buildings and the boats at anchor in the harbour in an engraving published in 1789. A sketch (Sydney, Mitchell Lib.) of the same place produced in April 1788 by the convict Francis Fowkes (*fl* 1786–1805) shows it quite differently, noting sites of work, living and control, as well as food sources. It has no larger vision, implies nothing beyond its vague borders, and its only aesthetic interest is in the detailing and finish supplied by the engraver in London. Both are instrumental images, aides to survival. They are evidence of different degrees and kinds of power.

While much of the imagery of first settlement recorded the exotic flora and fauna and the peculiarities of the indigenous peoples, the main themes of the drawings, watercolours and occasional oil paintings sent back to Britain were the gradual domestication of the colony of New South Wales and the steady development of Sydney Cove as a commercially viable port. This visual processing is evident in the first landscape in oils, a *Direct North General View of Sydney Cove. . . As it Appeared in 1794* (1794; Sydney, Mitchell Lib.) by THOMAS WATLING. The artist, who was sentenced to 14 years' transportation for forgery, transfigured his pencil sketches of a barren place denuded of trees and people into the pleasant prospect of a village in the Home Counties. Two soldiers converse, as if they were gentleman farmers casually met. Watling abhorred the 'little-varied' plainness of the countryside, complaining of its lack of 'happy-opposed off-scapes' (*Letters from an Exile at Botany Bay, to his Aunt in Dumfries*, Penrith, Scotland, 1794). To both sides of this painting he imported rainforest trees; an Aborigine encampment glows darkly from beneath them, and rows of convict huts can be discerned—by those able to read them as such—on the gently sloping hills in the distance.

Travelling artists such as Augustus Earle and resident amateur artists such as Sophia Campbell (1777–1833) were the major chroniclers of everyday life in the colony. The use of convicts for cheap labour, the degradation of the Aborigines by alcohol and the ubiquity of local militia are evident in their sketchbooks and in some cheap circulated prints (see fig. 7). More typical, however, were the topographic landscapes of Sydney town in the form of watercolours turned into engravings for publication in London, often in books. Outstanding among these is *A Panoramic View of Sydney* by Major James Taylor (1785–1829),

7. *Real Life in Sydney*, lithograph, 225×280 mm, *c.* 1835 (Sydney, Mitchell Library)

8. Eugene von Guérard: *Yalla-y-Poora Homestead*, oil on canvas, 699×1219 mm, 1864 (Melbourne, Joseph Brown Gallery)

engraved by Robert Havell & Sons, London, in 1823, in which classical motifs and white picket fences combine to create an ideal Georgian order. Taken together, these books from the first decades of the 1800s provide a record of steady progress in transforming convicts into civilized beings, and free settlers into successful small businessmen. The panorama was a favourite device, as was the sequential journey through streets, then countryside, to the next town. Both forms remained popular when photography was introduced to the colonies in the mid-1850s.

By the mid-19th century all the colonies had small but thriving artistic communities and had begun to build modest cultural institutions such as libraries, galleries and museums to match their new parliament buildings. The peculiarities of place began to be valued and regional perceptions started to grow. The hills around Launceston in northern Tasmania attracted the painter John Glover, who saw the area as a Claudian arcadia (e.g. pictures in Hobart, Tasman. Mus. & A.G., and Launceston, Queen Victoria Mus. & A.G.), while BENJAMIN DUTERRAU depicted the Aborigines of Tasmania. George French Angas (1822–86) recorded the growth of Edward Gibbon Wakefield's model town, Adelaide. CONRAD MARTENS depicted Sydney and its harbour as a stirring battle between natural and human elements (e.g. *Mosman's Bay*, 1842–3; Sydney, State Lib. NSW), with increasing confidence in the outcome. In contrast, when white explorers of the interior took artists with them, surviving watercolours show scenes of barren desolation instead of the hoped-for luxuriant hinterlands and inland seas. The drawings and watercolours of naturalist LUDWIG PHILIPP HENRICH BECKER are almost hallucinatory, especially those made on the ill-fated expedition of Robert O'Hara Burke and William John Wills (e.g. *Native from the Darling*, 1861; Melbourne, State Lib. Victoria, La Trobe Col.), which led to his own death in 1861.

The land itself became the victim of the human thirst for riches during the 1850s and thereafter. Images of the goldfields, particularly in Victoria, show a drastic clearing and turning over of the soil. S. T. GILL sketched everyday life on the diggings as well as in the newly prosperous cities. The new and popular medium of photography quickly became the primary recorder, with shops in every shanty town and photographers' wagons constantly mobile. Outstanding examples include the album *Australia* (1858) by Antoine Julien Fauchery (1823–61) and RICHARD DAINTREE, which was subsequently known as *Sun Pictures of Victoria*, and the detailed records of mines and towns of Hill End and Gulgong made in 1872 by the American and Australasian Photography Company (i.e. Beaufoy Merlin and Charles Bayliss under the direction of successful digger and entrepreneur Bernard Otto Holtermann). But the land was also the source of pastoral wealth, vast holdings having been secured by the 1860s, as well as many small settlements. Such fine landscape painters as EUGENE VON GUÉRARD produced many carefully observed portraits of these properties (see fig. 8).

(ii) Visions of landscape and nationality. In view of the power of the Australian landmass, only recently inhabited by Europeans, who clung to its edges and saw their whole future by looking inwards, that is, inland, it is little wonder that landscape became the chief subject of Australian art. Von Guérard was the major celebrant of Victoria's geological history, while others, including NICHOLAS CHEVALIER, inserted rustic farmhouses into their grand scenes. Farming, too, became a kind of harmonizing with nature in the landscapes of ABRAM-LOUIS BUVELOT (e.g. *Goodman's Creek, Bacchus Marsh*, 1876; Sydney, A.G. NSW).

Due largely to the example of such artists, together with JULIAN ROSSI ASHTON and WILLIAM CHARLES PIGUENIT, Northern Romantic landscape conventions, enlivened by the fresh perceptions of the Barbizon school, seemed best to represent the rapidly changing usages of the land in Australia during the 1860s and 1870s. Pleasing prospects, set in broadly sweeping vistas, became the preferred format. In his smaller watercolours Buvelot added another dimension: the intimate bush scene painted *en plein air* from direct observation.

All these elements fuelled the artistic flowering of the 1880s and 1890s, the moment of Australian painting's first maturity. The cultural groundwork of mid-century bore fruit in a generation of young artists, graduates from the state gallery schools, who joined to form the first artists' associations, to show in the increasing number of exhibitions and to sell work mainly from their studios. The state galleries and some local collectors began tentative purchasing of local art (*see* §XI below). A few critics devoted columns in the ubiquitous newspapers and magazines to important new paintings. During the 1880s 'marvellous Melbourne' was the key site for such developments, but after the depression of the early 1890s the centre of cultural activity shifted to Sydney.

TOM ROBERTS was the most active promoter of models of professional practice for artists, based on those of London and Paris. He also insisted that local standards match those of the Royal Academy and the Salon. Just as important, however, was the preferred subject-matter: Australian life and work. This overall approach, he believed, would lead to an art with universal value. During the later 1880s Roberts, ARTHUR STREETON, FREDERICK MCCUBBIN, CHARLES CONDER and others painted in camps on the outskirts of Melbourne, becoming known as the HEIDELBERG SCHOOL, after a town in the valley in which they frequently worked. These artists were responsible for the first intentionally avant-garde event in the colonies, the *9 by 5 Impression Exhibition* held in Buxton's Rooms, Melbourne, during August 1889. It consisted mainly of impressions of bush and city life swiftly sketched on cigar-box lids. The intense, often playful energy of such small works translated readily into large vistas across the Yarra River valley and into sweeping views of the main streets of Melbourne and of Sydney and its harbour. A similarly bold inventiveness activated the genre paintings of these artists, their scenes of bush life and work.

Streeton painted the 'slow soft movement' of evening light across the farmlands of the Heidelberg valley as if William Wordsworth were walking to an imaginary meeting with Claude Lorrain on the gentle slopes of the Dandenong Ranges. In such paintings as '*Still glides the stream and shall forever glide*' (1889; Sydney, A.G. NSW) and *Near Heidelberg* (1890; Melbourne, N.G. Victoria; for illustration *see* STREETON, ARTHUR) he joyously fused natural and social phenomena, the pastoral lyric and the pastoral industry, Romantic vision and Australian place. The opposite mood, one of struggle between Man and Nature, is captured in his long vertical panel '*Fire's on*', *Lapstone Tunnel* (see fig. 9), in which crumbling sandstone cliffs parallel bare earth cleared for a railway, and a dead worker is carried away on a stretcher.

9. Arthur Streeton: '*Fire's on*', *Lapstone Tunnel*, oil on canvas, 1.83×1.22 m, 1891 (Sydney, Art Gallery of New South Wales)

Shearers, swagmen, drovers and settlers: Roberts and McCubbin celebrated the dynamism of contemporary bush work, then went on to construct its history, painting ordinary working men and women as the pioneers of the country. In Roberts's *Shearing the Rams* (1890; Melbourne, N.G. Victoria; for illustration *see* ROBERTS, TOM), a row of strong men strip wool from huge sheep; in his painting entitled *A Breakaway* (1891; Adelaide, A.G. S. Australia) a drover vainly tries to halt a flock of sheep stampeding from drought to a painful death at the waterhole. In 1895 Roberts painted *Bailed Up* (Sydney, A.G. NSW), evoking a roadside robbery that took place 30 years earlier, using such restraint that all the participants seem to share the struggle against adversity. The despair of McCubbin's *Bush Burial* (1890; Geelong, A.G.; for illustration *see* MCCUBBIN, FREDERICK) is banished in the artist's three-part panel *The Pioneer* (1904; Melbourne, N.G. Victoria), a narrative of arriving in the dense bush, clearing it for farming and finally seeing through the trees the splendid vision of a glowing city rising.

It seems no accident that the studies of intimate bush scenes of the mid-1880s were succeeded by grand statements that emphasized the unique beauties of the local landscape and the peculiarities of living and working in the Australian colonies. Nor was it by chance that a sense of history entered many of these paintings, as it did the thoughts and writings of these artists. The centenary in

1888 of European settlement was celebrated as the successful introduction of British culture and European technological progress to a distant, alien land. It also marked a step towards the relative independence of the federation of the colonies, achieved in 1901. The painting of the Heidelberg school consciously participated in these social currents. It is scarcely surprising, then, that much of its imagery came to be regarded as symbolic of national identity.

In the 1880s and 1890s, however, it was the graphic arts that gave visual immediacy to the fast-emerging imagery of nationality. Since the 1850s Australian colonists had been avid readers of newspapers, especially such weeklies as the Melbourne and Sydney versions of *Punch*, the *Sydney Mail*, *Illustrated Australian News* and the *Australasian Sketcher*, all extensively illustrated by line engravings (themselves increasingly based on photographs). Such popular media culminated in the self-proclaimed 'bushman's bible', *The Bulletin*, based in Sydney, a weekly magazine of gossip, satire and republicanism, featuring the cartoons of 'Hop' (Livingston Hopkins; 1846–1927), Phil May and a dozen others, as well as the poetry of A. B. ('Banjo') Paterson and the stories of Henry Lawson. High-quality engravings were available in subscription publications, most notably *The Picturesque Atlas of Australasia* (1886–8), illustrated by a team of American, British and local artists.

By the end of the century, painting in Australia had become a thriving profession, newly aware of its recent history, stirred by the still-fresh achievements of Roberts, Streeton and their circle, and confident that it would soon match the most accomplished art being made anywhere. While the artists' standards were international, their focus was on the uniqueness of life around them, especially the bush and the outback imagined from the bustling centres of the east-coast cities. This they shared with the producers of the most vital visual imagery of the period, the black-and-white cartoonists of the illustrated mass media. The gap between city and country was, however, more and more traversed by the most modern image-maker, the photographer.

BIBLIOGRAPHY

A. Garran, ed.: *The Picturesque Atlas of Australasia*, 3 vols (Sydney, 1886–8)

B. Smith: *European Vision and the South Pacific* (Melbourne, 1959, rev. Sydney, 1984)

——: *Australian Painting, 1788–1960* (Melbourne, 1960, rev. 1971); rev. by T. Smith as *Australian Painting, 1788–1990* (Melbourne, 1991)

M. Mahood: *The Loaded Line: Australian Political Caricature, 1788–1901* (Melbourne, 1973)

R. White: *Inventing Australia: Images and Identity, 1688–1980* (Sydney, 1981)

L. Astbury: *City Bushmen: The Heidelberg School and the Rural Mythology* (Melbourne, 1985)

T. Bonyhady: *Images in Opposition: Australian Landscape Painting, 1801–1890* (Melbourne, 1985)

T. McCormick and others: *First Views of Australia, 1788–1825* (Sydney, 1987)

G. Newton: *Shades of Light: Photography and Australia, 1839–1988* (Canberra, 1987)

W. Eisler and B. Smith: *Terra Australis: The Furthest Shore* (Sydney, 1988)

D. Thomas, ed.: *Creating Australia: 200 Years of Art, 1788–1988* (Sydney, 1988)

A.-M. Willis: *Picturing Australia: A History of Photography* (Sydney, 1988)

J. Kerr, ed.: *Dictionary of Australian Artists: Painters, Sketchers, Photographers and Engravers, to 1870* (Melbourne, 1992)

2. AFTER *c.* 1900. From colonial dependence to national independence within a volatile international framework: this was the outstanding change in Australian art after Federation in 1901. By the last decade of the 20th century, the mature art world dreamt of by Tom Roberts—one led by professional practitioners, sustained by a lively market and supported by informed critics, theorists, curators, educators and administrators—had come into being. It was not a simple, smooth or in any sense natural transition. Nor did it occur in isolation: the much-delayed yet quite distinct growth in appreciation and development of Aboriginal art happened in tandem, and developments in art elsewhere, especially the European and American modernist avant-garde, had a powerful impact. Neither would have been imaginable to the artists of the Heidelberg school in the late 1880s.

(i) Edwardian landscape, modernism and war. (ii) Realism, abstraction and post-modern developments.

(i) Edwardian landscape, modernism and war. Until the late 1930s art in Australia was dominated by paintings of the local landscape. Key members of the Heidelberg school, such as Roberts and Streeton, spent the years around and after 1900 in England, seeking official recognition for their art and modifying it accordingly. That their English landscapes were so modest, their portraits so stiff, says as much for the inspiration of the places of their artistic youth as do their nostalgic letters recalling the delights of the camps around Melbourne in the late 1880s. To the further detriment of their art they imbibed some of the conservative social and cultural values of Edwardian England: the ideology of a privileged, hierarchic order consisting of strong yet flexible rulers presiding over an energetic and industrious people and a far-flung empire. When they and other expatriates returned to Australia in the 1920s they saw it, for all its much-vaunted differences, as an outpost of British civilization, as part of that system of values.

In the years after 1900, exhibitions of the Society of Artists in Melbourne and Sydney and their equivalents elsewhere were filled with studies of the local landscape, while in Sydney HAROLD CAZNEAUX developed a style of photography that was specifically Australian in its use of light. Gradually artists ventured beyond the fringes of the cities and country towns to find striking scenes on the slopes of the Great Dividing Range, the mountains that run the length of the eastern seaboard. Audiences appreciated likenesses of their localities and began to recognize regional differences. Streeton became the master of this genre, especially of broad vistas taken from mountain ranges across vast valleys populated with great herds of sheep or cattle, or glowing with fields of yellow wheat, set against the blue–greys of the eucalyptus bush. He gave his paintings such titles as *Australia Felix* (1907; Adelaide, A.G. S. Australia) or *Melba's Country* (1936; Sydney, priv. col.; see Burn, 1990, pp. 204–5), fully conscious of their symbolic power. In this way, through constant repetition of the genre itself, pictures of a particular place came to stand for the country as a whole.

These images might have been less potent, however, had not the Edwardian age been so threatened during World War I. In the years before the war, the Heidelberg school's romantic mix of breathtaking vista and intimate view had been gradually modified by successive artistic fashions, such as the Aesthetic Movement. In the mystic evocations of SYDNEY LONG, dark yet gentle 'spirits of the bush' were drawn with an Art Nouveau sinuousness. From similar beginnings HANS HEYSEN rendered gum trees in and around the Adelaide Hills with such intensity of observation and rhetorical effectiveness that they became quasi-humanoid forms, twisting mightily out of harsh yet pastoral land, great shapes attesting to the productivity of this ancient continent (see fig. 10). After ignorant questions as to his loyalty during the war, Heysen's vision grew less optimistic, and he turned to sombre, featureless studies of the primeval Flinders Ranges.

Although fought entirely outside Australia, World War I was as important for art as it was in the formation of a national consciousness. Cartoonists such as WILL DYSON recorded the living hell of trench warfare in Flanders, while leading painters such as Streeton became official war artists. Outstanding among these was GEORGE W. LAMBERT, known for his quasi-allegorical figure groups, in which ordinary people were heroized in the manner of a royal portrait by Velázquez. He accompanied Australian troops through the Middle East in the last years of the war and made the sketches that led to sensitive portraits of reluctant fighting men and formed the basis of mural-scale paintings of fierce battle scenes, showing much loss of life amid terrain very like that of Central Australia. Images of sacrifice, such as *Menin Gate at Midnight* (1927) by Will Longstaff (1879–1953), proved extraordinarily popular. They became the core of the collection of the Australian War Memorial, Canberra, which uniquely combined the functions of national mausoleum and gallery of war art. The ubiquitous imagery of gum-laden landscapes came to seem even more valuable when threatened by the disorder abroad.

To some artists of the landscape school and their many supporters among critics and gallery directors, this disorder was a cancerous insanity infecting European art. The distorted forms, wild colours and apparently trivial subject-matter of modernism in the 1920s represented cultural revolution. The art establishment in Australia resisted it with considerable success for nearly two decades. They were less disturbed, however, by 'the latest' in design and fashion and ignored the interest it aroused among women artists and craftworkers. Modernism entered Australian art through these largely unattended doors.

Roger Fry's interpretation in 1910 of the art of Cézanne, Seurat, Gauguin and van Gogh as 'Post-Impressionism' had a considerable impact on young Australian women studying in London, including Norah Simpson (1895–1974), and, through them, on students in Sydney, most notably GRACE COSSINGTON SMITH. Others went to Paris to study with the new masters: Grace Crowley (1890–

10. Hans Heysen: *Red Gold*, oil on canvas, 1.29×1.74 m, 1913 (Adelaide, Art Gallery of South Australia)

1979) studied there with André Lhote, for example. Magazines and early survey books began to circulate, precipitating brief experiments, such as the exhibition of colour–music paintings ('synchromies') held by ROLAND WAKELIN and ROY DE MAISTRE in Sydney in 1919. The latter travelled between Sydney and London in the 1920s, settling in London and later becoming a considerable neo-Cubist artist, addressing primarily religious themes, as in the *Stations of the Cross* (1956; London, Westminster Cathedral). JOHN JOSEPH WARDELL POWER—best known for his bequest that led to the establishment of the Power Institute of Fine Arts at the University of Sydney in 1967 (*see* §XII below)—worked between Paris and Bournemouth during the inter-war years, evolving a jazzy synthetic Cubism, then blending in Surrealism with a measured, ironic elegance. The broadest impact of the modern movement in Australia itself occurred when such prominent local landscape painters as ELIOTH GRUNER began to simplify their colours, flatten their spaces and tone down their compositions. The painter and teacher MAX MELDRUM, who had considerable influence between the two world wars, emphasized the importance of tonal quality above all else.

Of greater long-term significance was the vibrant marriage of abstraction with uniquely Australian motifs in the work of many women painters and printmakers, notably MARGARET PRESTON. She saw close parallels between Cubist and Aboriginal approaches to space, structure and the painted mark (see fig. 11). However, her call for a national art based on this fusion went unheeded. Just as important was the persistent Post-Impressionism of Cossington Smith: for more than seven decades she developed a picture-language that encompassed suburban streets, bush landscapes, daily news events and the intimacies of her own room with a quiet yet resilient intensity. In Australia, modernism worked best when it served to show the worlds of women, or the larger world as seen by these determinedly independent women.

11. Margaret Preston: *The Aeroplane*, woodblock print, 240×190 mm, *c.* 1925; reworked 1936 (Canberra, National Gallery of Australia)

Seen as a deadly struggle for civilization against the evil of Fascism, World War II in Europe profoundly affected an entire generation of Australian artists. German Expressionist artists seemed to have predicted it and offered many models, as did Surrealism's imagery of insanity. The loose group of painters associated in 1941–6 with the magazine *Angry Penguins* (a title at once absurdly improbable, mockingly combative and defiantly trivializing) pictured this mood in extraordinarily inventive ways. In *Images of Modern Evil* (e.g. No. 1, 1943; Canberra, N.G.), a series by ALBERT TUCKER, female creatures consisting of bloated erogenous zones, with teeth bared through scarlet lips, haunt the night city; Arthur Boyd (*see* BOYD, (2)) fused legendary gods and everyday soldiers and prostitutes in the Bruegel-like landscapes of people gone crazy in godlessness; and JOHN PERCEVAL evoked the endangerment of innocent children. Involvement in the war exposed artists such as the photographer MAX DUPAIN to non-Australian influences, while refugee artists vividly recalled European experiences: YOSL BERGNER, for example, who came from Poland, painted a series (*c.* 1943) on the Warsaw Ghetto (e.g. the *Pumpkin Eaters*, *c.* 1940; Canberra, National Collection). He also saw parallels to the immigrant and Jewish condition in the local treatment of Aborigines. To such social realists as NOEL COUNIHAN the war created a world of emotional turmoil and material deprivation for working-class people as devastating as the Depression of the 1930s. The war in the Pacific had little impact until the bombing of Darwin in December 1942. War artists, among whom DONALD FRIEND and Ivor Hele (*b* 1912) were outstanding, worked with the troops in Papua New Guinea. While the artists associated with the *Angry Penguins* and social realist artists were mostly based in Melbourne, Surrealist painters JAMES GLEESON in Sydney and Ivor Francis (*b* 1906), James Cant (1911–82) and Douglas Roberts (1919–76) in Adelaide also made striking images of the universal horror.

Both during the war and in its aftermath, it seemed to many that it was local uniqueness and personal experience that had been most threatened. The *Ned Kelly* series (26 in Canberra, N.G.) by SIDNEY NOLAN traced the adventures of the famous 19th-century bushranger as a set of strange, elusive memories. Beginning in 1945, Nolan returned often to this theme, doing further series in the 1950s and 1970s as if he were remembering for the community at large. Like Streeton's landscapes—and, indeed, his own of Central Australia—Nolan's image of Kelly's helmet, a simple shape yet so suggestively ambiguous, became a national icon. In Nolan's depiction of Kelly's last stand *Ned Kelly Glenrowan* (1946–7; see fig. 12), the outlaw's legend is being born—as both historical memory and media event—before our eyes.

12. Sidney Nolan: *Ned Kelly Glenrowan*, enamel on position board, 909×1212 mm, 1946 (Canberra, National Gallery of Australia)

(ii) Realism, abstraction and post-modern developments. Personal experience triggered much Australian art during the 1950s, often as an imagery of alienation from a relentlessly conventional society. JOY HESTER hauntingly conjured up women victimized by their emotions, often their subjugation to men, in black-and-white ink sketches. CHARLES BLACKMAN became one of the few male artists capable of picturing the private domains of women's feelings, as in his *Schoolgirl* (1953–4) and *Alice in Wonderland* series (1957; artist's col., see Hughes, p. 244). The stylized portraits of WILLIAM DOBELL caused great controversy, while life in the fast-spreading suburbs of the capital cities, particularly Melbourne, was acidulously chronicled by JOHN BRACK. In stark contrast, the sketches and paintings of RUSSELL DRYSDALE reveal the bleak emptiness of the far outback, as well as its many 'characters'. Drysdale began to paint the original inhabitants of the interior more and more frequently, as did Arthur Boyd in a powerful series, the *Love, Marriage and Death of Half-caste*, also known as the *Bride* series (1955–8; e.g. Melbourne, N.G. Victoria), and Noel Counihan in his paintings around 1960. Yet the most popular Australian painter at this time was the Aboriginal artist ALBERT NAMATJIRA, creator of attractive watercolours of his region near Alice Springs in Central Australia in a manner that fitted the framework of the dominant landscape school but also expressed aspects of his personal and tribal relationship to the land. LLOYD REES developed a variety of techniques to express the distinct qualities of different regions.

In the later 1950s it seemed to some artists and writers that Australian painters had developed an imagery of contemporary experience that was both unique and compelling. This was profoundly threatened by the accelerating spread of abstract painting, led by the artists of the New York school (*see* ABSTRACT EXPRESSIONISM). In response, a group of Melbourne artists, the ANTIPODEAN GROUP, including Boyd, Perceval, Blackman and Brack, joined the art historian Bernard Smith (*b* 1916) to mount an exhibition and to write a statement, the *Antipodean Manifesto*, in support of figurative art. The exhibition was held in Melbourne in August 1959. The artists stressed their commitment to modern art, to their social obligations and, above all, to 'the defence of the image'.

The international tide of abstract painting proved irresistible for nearly a decade after 1960. Yet it was rarely a matter of stylistic imitation. The leading abstract painter JOHN OLSEN, for example, owed as much to Paul Klee, the Cobra group and Aboriginal sandpainting as he did to the gestural art of Jackson Pollock and Willem de Kooning. His enthusiastic accumulations of graffiti, meandering lines, children's scrawlings and notations for trees, animals and people, all set in spaces that flipped from above or below, or from one side or the other, amounted to a new vision of landscape in Australia (see fig. 13). In a parallel way FRED WILLIAMS read back the flattened spaces and gestural flourishes of American abstraction into the vistas and close-ups of the landscape school, creating an equally powerful alternative path for landscape painting.

In the mid-1960s a younger generation of painters and sculptors rejected romantic images of the artist, expressive approaches to art-making and any obligation to national content. Cool, impersonal internationalism ruled for a few years in the colour paintings of the artists connected with Gallery A and the Central Street Gallery, Sydney, including Michael Johnson (*b* 1938) and DAVID ASPDEN. American art had its greatest impact: hard-edge and colour-field painters were most admired, formalist art criticism most imitated. Avant-garde modernism seemed to have arrived, ready to kick-start Australian art into internationalism. But the Melbourne artists most attracted to this style, such as DALE HICKEY and ROBERT ROONEY, soon treated it ironically: the configurations of their repeated sharp colour separations might also suggest a picket fence, knitting patterns or dog-biscuits. Allusions to popular imagery occur occasionally in Australian art, yet never to the extent of constituting a Pop art tendency. BRETT WHITELEY achieved early fame for painting in London a brilliant and shocking series (1964–5) of works about the common murderer John Christie. The constructions and installations of members of the short-lived group ANNANDALE IMITATION REALISTS—COLIN LANCELEY, Ross Crothall (*b* 1934) and MIKE BROWN—were wild assemblages of advertisements, children's sketches, magazine photographs, industrial junk and 'primitive' art. The group exhibited only twice, in Melbourne early in 1962 and in Sydney a few months later, then dissolved. Its art parallels the happenings and environmental art of the early 1960s rather than Pop art's bland enthusiasm for and calculated obsession with consumer culture.

The crisis of painting in the years around 1970 affected Australian painters profoundly. They reacted to the same precipitating factors as did artists elsewhere—the reductive, near-terminal extremities of Minimalism, the apparent culmination of modernism in the colour-field painting of Kenneth Noland, Jules Olitski's clouds of colour and the shaped canvases of Frank Stella—as well as to the challenge of conceptual art and the political critiques of the dissident movements. Artists of Boyd's and Nolan's generation saw the crisis as that of art itself and responded by painting strong series reworking earlier themes. Colour painters absorbed the brunt of the crisis, most taking more than a decade to reshape their art. The political activism of the 1970s inspired a few easel painters, such as Robert Boynes (*b* 1942), RICHARD LARTER and Peter Kennedy (*b* 1945). It was more apparent in mural painting, which quickly became a normality in the inner suburbs of the capital cities, addressing both international and neighbourhood issues. Political commitment led to a revival of banners for trade unions, of intricate images of allegory and work bordered with silk. It also provoked a renaissance in Australian printmaking, particularly in brightly coloured silkscreen posters noisily proclaiming issues of the moment, highlighting the misdeeds of political leaders and calling viewers to marches, demonstrations and actions. Community-orientated, self-help poster-making groups appeared all over the country, notably the Earthworks Poster Collective of Sydney and Redback Graffix of Wollongong.

13. John Olsen: *Man Absorbed in Landscape*, oil on board, 1.22×1.26 m, 1966 (Melbourne, Joseph Brown Gallery)

Another initiative of the 1970s that continued to shape Australian painting and graphic art was the women's art movement. First glimpsed in Vivienne Binn's (*b* 1940) defiant paintings of genitalia (1966), it grew rapidly in the later 1970s with the emergence of such artists as LESLEY DUMBRELL and took many forms, from support groups to the publication of the feminist multi-arts magazine *Lip* in 1976. A community artist, Binns led many projects that encouraged the creativity of women of all generations, frequently using graphic arts, including photo-stencilling on enamel, to enable the reproduction of images from family albums or their transfer from one medium to another.

The worldwide revival of expressionistic painting in the early 1980s had little presence in Australia, although it brought some comfort to abstract artists, whose assumptions had been devastated during the previous decade. The major development, post-conceptual painting, used painted imagery as its medium but was equally open to photography or performance. It drew inspiration from conceptual art's interrogation of art's objects, spatiality and relations to the spectator, and from contemporary philosophy, particularly semiotics and post-structuralism. Post-conceptual painting took unique forms in Australia. IMANTS TILLERS conflated images reproduced from international and local art, including Aboriginal visual cultures, to question the stability of conceptions of national identity. MIKE PARR staged obsessive repetitions of his self-portrait as mural-sized drawings, as painful performances or as haunting installations. JUAN DAVILA challenged conventional notions of obscenity in his elaborate narratives of explicit sexuality. Richard Dunn (*b* 1944) questioned aspects of historical memory and of the all-pervasiveness of power in modern societies.

A number of younger women artists pursued similar concerns. Jenny Watson (*b* 1951) evoked dreams of girlhood and adolescence in sketch-like notations. The dramatic struggles between shapes in the busy canvases of Susan Norrie (*b* 1953) were often war games between the sexes, while later they elegantly recorded shifts in sensibility between cultures—European, Australian and Asian. Mandy Martin (*b* 1952) likewise moved from reconceiving the landscape as a sexual battleground to noting the paradoxical beauties of heavily mined deserts and mountains. In all, these and other artists used Post-modernist devices, such as appropriation and quotation, not in a superficial, 'anything goes' manner, but to interrogate, critically and suggestively, aspects of a recurrent human phenomenon: the ceaseless reaching for identity—personal, social and national—through visual imagery.

During the last decades of the 20th century the traditional, media-based boundaries of painting and the graphic arts were transgressed so frequently that they remained relevant mainly to the art market. The brushmark or wash can be a painted sign, while a reproduced painting can be a sign for 'painting': for example Lindy Lee (*b* 1954) photocopied and erased an illustrated Rembrandt six times, Mike Parr etched a photocopied self-portrait and constructed a forbiddingly spare room from a charcoal drawing, while John Brack peopled his paintings with ideological battles between columns of marching pencils. Australian artists of all generations pursued questions of content and the dilemmas of representation with equal tenacity.

After 1970 white artists, writers and art lovers in Australia became increasingly aware of the phenomenal outpouring of painting by Aboriginal artists (*see* ABORIGINAL AUSTRALIA, §IV). There is no doubt that this constituted an artistic achievement eclipsing in scope and depth other Australian art of the period. Many white artists strongly supported this development; indeed some, such as Tim Johnson (*b* 1947), sought to base their own art substantially within it. Few artists recognized Australia's location in the Asian region, but more began to do so in the 1980s and 1990s. This, along with the fact that artists of immigrant background became prominent innovators, contributed to the diversity of outlook that typified late 20th-century practice. The days of dependence were over.

BIBLIOGRAPHY

B. Smith: *Australian Painting, 1788–1970* (Melbourne, 1960, rev. 1971); rev. by T. Smith as *Australian Painting, 1788–1990* (Melbourne, 1991)

R. Hughes: *The Art of Australia* (Ringwood, Victoria, 1961, rev. 1971)

N. Draffin: *Australian Woodcuts and Linocuts of the 1920s and 1930s* (Melbourne, 1976)

B. Smith: *The Antipodean Manifesto: Essays in Art and History* (Melbourne, 1976)

R. Haese: *Rebels and Precursors: The Revolutionary Years in Australian Art* (Ringwood, Victoria, 1981)

R. Butler: *Australian Prints in the Australian National Gallery* (Canberra, 1985)

I. Burn and others: *The Necessity of Australian Art* (Sydney, 1988)

A. Sayers: *Drawing in Australia: Drawings, Watercolours, Pastels and Collages from the 1770s to the 1980s* (Canberra, 1988)

D. Thomas, ed.: *Creating Australia: 200 Years of Art, 1788–1988* (Sydney, 1988)

I. Burn: *Landscape and National Life: Australian Painting 1900–1940* (Sydney, 1990)

TERRY SMITH

IV. Sculpture.

1. BEFORE *c.* 1900. In the first half of the 19th century few examples of sculpture of more than historical interest were produced. Benjamin Law (1807–90) modelled a fine portrait bust of *Truganini*, the last surviving pure-blooded Tasmanian Aborigine; Teresa Snell-Walker (1807–76) was the first woman sculptor in the country and in 1845 Charles Abrahams (1816–85) produced the country's first exhibition of sculpture: portrait busts of colonial worthies. The great wealth produced by the extensive gold discoveries of 1851 soon transformed muddy villages into fine, modern cities. Among the many thousands of eager prospectors who flooded into the country was the Pre-Raphaelite THOMAS WOOLNER. When he failed as a gold-miner, he turned to making bronze portrait medallions. John Simpson Mackennal (1832–1901), a young Scottish sculptor, also came in search of gold but soon abandoned the diggings in favour of becoming chief architectural modeller for Melbourne's new Parliament House (1856, by Kerr & Knight).

Apart from rare commissions for portrait statuary, architectural decoration was one of the few areas in which a sculptor could earn a living. The land boom of the 1880s stimulated the construction of many large buildings, which in turn meant more work for sculptors. One of these was the Italian Tommaso Sani (1839–1915), whose major work is a set of low-relief stone carvings for Sydney's General Post Office (1866–86, by James Barnet) depicting ordinary people engaged in their everyday affairs. Public expectation demanded of sculpture a high-minded Neo-classicism, and Sani's descent from the ideal to the ordinary provoked such outrage that efforts were made to have his work destroyed. The first large-scale bronze to be cast in Australia was made in Melbourne by CHARLES SUMMERS, an established English sculptor who had come to Australia in 1853 for his health. In 1864 he was commissioned to produce a memorial to the explorers *Robert O'Hara Burke and William John Wills* (Melbourne, Flagstaff Gdns). He looked to Michelangelo for inspiration and in 1865 unveiled a work that embodied the qualities of courage and fortitude attributed to the explorers, who had died on expedition in 1861.

For the first 100 years sculpture in Australia was dominated by artists who had arrived already trained in their profession. For the aspiring young, born or raised in Australia, the only chance to train as a sculptor was to go to London and the Royal Academy Schools. Both BERTRAM MACKENNAL and Charles Douglas Richardson (1853–1932) achieved this goal, establishing a pattern that continued in a modified form at the end of the 20th century. Mackennal arrived in London in 1882, to be influenced by British New Sculpture and by the work he later saw in Paris. He came to public notice in 1894 when a scandal was caused at the Royal Academy by the frank sexuality of the plaster version of his bronze *Circe* (1893; Melbourne, N.G. Victoria; see fig. 14). He went on to become a fashionable sculptor, producing, for example, the monuments to *Edward VII* and *Queen Alexandra*

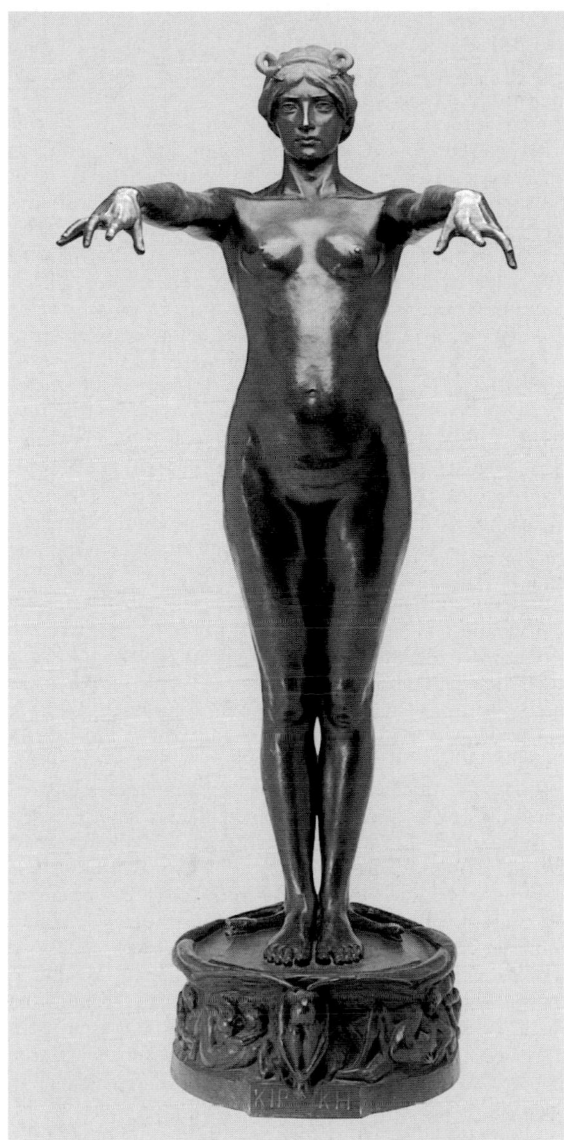

14. Bertram Mackennal: *Circe*, bronze, h. 2.8 m, 1893 (Melbourne, National Gallery of Victoria)

(both 1919) in St George's Chapel, Windsor. Knighted in 1922, Mackennal remains one of the best-known Australian-born sculptors, overshadowing his contemporaries Harold Parker (1873–1962), Paul Montford (1868–1938) and WEB GILBERT. For all his skill and high style, however, Mackennal was essentially a conservative who made little contribution to the development of sculpture.

2. AFTER *c.* 1900. Australian art in the 1890s had been dominated by the painter, who was more readily able to give expression to the growing nationalism that led in 1901 to the federation of the states. The new century gave prominence to two sculptors of great ability, Daphne Mayo (1897–1982) and GEORGE W. LAMBERT, whose work, despite their familiarity with overseas developments, showed a long-outmoded academic naturalism. Until well after World War I, sculpture in Australia remained backward-looking and impervious to any modernist influence. The first challenge to established attitudes came from RAYNER HOFF, a brilliant graduate of the Royal College of Art, London, who in 1923 was appointed head of sculpture at the East Sydney Technical College. Hoff's own work was strongly influenced by the Art Deco movement, and his elegant stylizations, used in the decoration of the Anzac War Memorial (1930–34, by Bruce Dellit) in Hyde Park, Sydney, surreptitiously imported quasi-modernist ideas under the cloak of an official commission.

In late 1930 Ola Cohn (1892–1964) returned to Melbourne after studying under Henry Moore at the Royal College of Art in London. While there she had developed a robust style indebted to various European sculptors, including Jacob Epstein, but the negative response to her work from the Melbourne public soon slowed her momentum and she retreated into a sentimental modernism. Her major contribution was made through her unflagging enthusiasm for sculpture and her continuing efforts to promote its cause.

The second phase of modernism in Australian sculpture was led by a small group of artists that included Gerald Lewers (1905–62) and his wife Margo Lewers (1908–78), Margel Hinder (*b* 1906) and LYNDON DADSWELL. All had worked overseas and had returned to Australia in the mid 1930s, eager to promote a modernist approach. In 1939 they combined with a group of like-minded painters to stage *Exhibition I*, a show that gave public exposure to the modernist aesthetic. Innovative as their work was in the conservative local context, from a wider perspective it could be seen to be strongly influenced by European ideas, in particular the organicism of Henry Moore. Lyndon Dadswell was at once the most eclectic and the most influential of this group. His own work was vigorous and varied—too varied, since he failed to establish a coherent stylistic position. As head of sculpture at East Sydney Technical College for more than 30 years Dadswell impressed generations of students with the need to question past solutions to sculptural problems and with the value of constant experimentation. One of the most extraordinary artists to settle in Australia in the 1930s was the Russian-born painter and sculptor DANILA VASSILIEFF. He was largely self-taught and his work owed stylistic allegiance to none; despite being figurative, it demonstrated the basic modernist tenet that the important aspect of sculpture was the plastic relationships, not the narrative content.

In the period around World War II a new wave of European artists arrived in Australia, some fleeing Nazi persecution, some as refugees. Among them was a surprising number of sculptors, including Julius Kane (1921–62). Keen to promote modern sculpture, he set about organizing a group of sculptors to lobby possible sources of commissions, especially architects. Eventually the group Centre 5 was formed; the members were Kane himself, INGE KING, Clifford Last (*b* 1918), LENTON PARR and Norma Redpath (*b* 1928). In 1956 their modernist approach was given official recognition when an exhibition of their work, plus that of the immigrant artists Vincas

15. Tony Coleing: *To Do with Blue*, painted steel, h. 7.32 m, 1975, Lake Burley Griffen, Canberra

Jomantas (*b* 1912) and Teisutis Zikaras (*b* 1922), was shown at the National Gallery of Victoria in Melbourne.

The most important single event in contemporary Australian sculpture was the staging in 1961 of the first Sculpture Triennial at the Victorian country town of Mildura. This large display of new sculpture brought together the best and most innovative work, and it soon became established as the foremost sculpture exhibition in the country. For over 25 years it attracted sculptors, curators and collectors from across the country and played a decisive role in giving exposure to both established sculptors and the aspiring young, in revealing new directions and in raising community awareness of sculpture. In 1962 the sculptor ROBERT KLIPPEL returned to Sydney after five years in the USA, where he had established a reputation for his metal junk sculpture. In his drawings Klippel had been pursuing the idea of sculpture as a collage of *objets trouvés* from as early as 1948, but he began to include fragments of discarded machinery in his work in 1961. Always independent in his approach, Klippel sought no disciples and inspired no followers. Quietly over the years he amassed a significant body of original work that united the mechanistic and the organic in a new and unexpected synthesis.

By the mid-1960s Australian sculptors had turned away from the organic, truth-to-materials dicta of Henry Moore and were investigating the possibilities of such new materials as welded steel and such new approaches as assembled sculpture and variations on geometric minimalism. In 1968 Ron Robertson-Swann (*b* 1941) returned from London eager to pass on the ideas developed by Anthony Caro and explored at St Martin's School of Art, where both Robertson-Swann and Caro had been lecturers. Through his work and his teaching Robertson-Swann did much to promote this formalist aesthetic in Australia.

The passion for the reductive, the anonymous and the stylistically homogeneous, strong aspects of sculpture in the late 1960s, was soon followed by a move to do away with sculpture entirely. The argument that only concept was of significance, and that the expression of that concept through painting or sculpture was of no importance, gained its supporters. This point of view was greeted with considerable scepticism by most sculptors, who held to the belief that giving tangible form to concept was still the sculptor's role. Despite the attention given to arcane experiments in conceptual art, most local sculptors continued to make object sculpture, although many did so in untraditional ways. Tony Coleing (*b* 1942), John Davis (*b* 1936), Ti Parks (*b* 1939) and Peter Cole (*b* 1946) all produced highly individual work that relied on a personal and perhaps regional response, rather than being a provincial paraphrase of metropolitan ideas (see fig. 15).

In the 1980s there were several important developments, often as a result of greater opportunities in training and in exhibiting and selling contemporary sculpture. In stylistic terms there was a move away from formal abstraction and a renewed interest in the figurative in the work of Bruce Armstrong (*b* 1957), Paul Juraszek (*b* 1953) and Michael Snape (*b* 1951). There was also a return to such traditional materials as wood (Tom Risely, *b* 1947; Hilary Mais, *b* 1952; Stephen Killick, *b* 1947) and bronze (Rodney Broad, *b* 1947; Les Kossatz, *b* 1943; Jock Clutterbuck, *b* 1945). Even such unlikely material as corrugated iron (Victor Meertens, *b* 1955) and papier mâché (Andrew Wright-Smith, *b* 1956; Akio Makigawa, *b* 1948; Bronwyn Oliver, *b* 1959) were used. In all of this activity the dominant attitude was one of freedom to do whatever seemed appropriate to the individual; no one style, medium or philosophical position was dominant.

Historically Australia was part of the European cultural tradition, and Australian sculptors looked to London, Paris or New York for direction. In the 1980s and after, with the growing acceptance that the country's economic future lay with Asia, its artists turned increasingly to the ancient cultures of this area for inspiration, providing a rich combination of influences for new sculptural possibilities.

BIBLIOGRAPHY

A. Australia (1916–42)
A. & Australia (1963–)
L. Parr: *Sculpture in Australia since 1945* (Melbourne, 1963)
C. B. Christesen, ed.: *The Gallery on Eastern Hill: The Victorian Artists' Society Centenary* (Melbourne, 1970)
R. Free: 'Late Victorian, Edwardian and French Sculpture', *A.G. NSW Q.*, xiii/2 (Jan 1972)
G. Sturgeon: *The Development of Australian Sculpture, 1788–1975* (London, 1978)
K. Scarlett: *Australian Sculptors* (Melbourne, 1980)
G. Sturgeon: *Sculpture at Mildura* (Mildura, 1985)

GRAEME STURGEON

V. Interior decoration.

Given Australia's origins in 1788 as a penal outpost of Britain and the ensuing prominence of British culture, it is not surprising that the predominant model for interior decoration has generally been British. For the wealthy in the early days of settlement the task of setting up house in the British manner was largely a matter of time—waiting for the furniture, furnishings and other components of an interior to arrive in the colony. Early records, together with a few surviving houses and documented pieces of furniture, indicate that the first Australian interiors were cast in the mould of the late Georgian style. In the second and third decades of the 19th century there is tangible evidence of the Greek Revival style in architecture and interior design, and of the Regency style in furniture and appointments. As in Britain, the classically inspired styles became more robust and pungent during the second quarter of the century and began to be seriously challenged by the other revival styles, particularly the persistent Gothic and the more novel 'Louis XIV' or Rococo Revival. Strict rules regulated the furnishing of the principal rooms of the early and mid-Victorian house: matched suites were *de rigueur*, and the furniture was arranged around two focal points—the fireplace and the centrally placed (usually under the gasolier) salon table or ottoman (see fig. 16).

Complete households of furniture and decorations were imported from Britain at this time. In 1859 William Smee & Son of London and a host of other English suppliers provided John Moffatt of Hopkins Hill, in Victoria's Western District, with a well-appointed house in the latest London style, and in 1863–4 John Gregory Crace of London furnished Government House, Perth, with designs made by A. W. N. Pugin some 15 years earlier. The needs of such wealthy Scottish settlers as Thomas Chirnside of Werribee Park, Victoria, and Peter Waite of Urrbrae, South Australia, were just as efficiently attended to by the Edinburgh cabinetmakers John Taylor & Son in the mid-1870s. For others there were the sumptuous emporia of W. H. Rocke & Co. in Melbourne and Farmer & Co. in Sydney, with their showrooms full of the latest elegancies from Paris and the other fashion capitals of the world. A flourishing native industry provided local imitations of imported designs.

The remarkable consistency of interiors of the third quarter of the century was blasted apart by the Aesthetic Movement in the late 1870s and early 1880s. Coinciding with a time of prosperity following the gold rush in Australia, particularly in Melbourne, the Aesthetic Movement and 'artistic' decoration became the rage in the 1880s. Contemporary commentators dated its first appearance to the Melbourne International Exhibition of 1880, but there had, in fact, been a few earlier manifestations of the style. By 1873 Daniel Cottier (1838–91), an important figure in the Aesthetic Movement in Britain and the USA, had opened a branch of his firm in Sydney with John Lamb Lyon, and in 1878 the English firm of Gillow & Co. had created a suite of consummately Aesthetic and very influential rooms for Joseph Clarke at Mandeville Hall, Toorak, Melbourne. During the 1880s and 1890s all the components of the Aesthetic interior were available in Australia: Doulton and Bretby art pottery, Liberty art silks,

16. *Sitting-room at Doogallook Station* by John Cotton, pen and ink, 173×249 mm, 1844 (Sydney, State Library of New South Wales)

copies of E. W. Godwin's furniture designs and a wide range of other art furniture. Such importers as Mr McIntyre in Sydney offered for sale vast quantities of Oriental furniture and *objets d'art.* Fitted carpets were superseded by Persian rugs; formal suites and symmetrical arrangements of furniture by 'harlequin' suites and odd chairs in informal groupings; doors by *portières*; and conventional floral arrangements by masses of reeds and pampas grass. Highly skilled local decorators, such as Lyon, Cottier & Co. in Sydney and the Paterson Bros in Melbourne, provided stylish backdrops for the rich. Those with the money and inclination continued to shop overseas: James Fairfax commissioned the London architect Maurice B. Adams to design the hall of his Sydney house, and the Barr Smith family of Adelaide became major customers of Morris & Co. Newspapers and journals published articles on interior decoration to guide the tentative in matters of taste, and style followed style in rapid succession: after the long affair with Anglo-Japanese, there were flirtations with the Adams, Chippendale and Queen Anne revival styles. In 1885 the Cairene was the latest novelty, and it was predicted that Sheraton, Louis XVI and Empire would dislodge Chippendale and Louis XV.

The economic depression of the early 1890s and the growing influence of the Rational and health movements had a purifying effect on interiors, which tended to become simpler and less cluttered. The principles of this new style were elucidated by the Melbourne architect Robert Haddon in his book *Australian Architecture* (Melbourne, 1908) as 'moderation', 'trained taste . . . with a careful consideration for the fitness of things', 'colour values', 'honesty of constructive purpose', and—for this was the golden age of nationalism—'the great value and beauty of our Australian finishing woods'.

Non-British cultures also influenced Australian interior decoration, paramount among these being that of the USA. The *Philadelphia* in 1792 had been the first foreign trading vessel to visit the colony, and throughout the 19th century American goods had flowed into Australia in increasing volume. The first import to have more than an incidental presence in Australian interiors was the American Romanesque style. Transmitted from about 1890 via journals and travelling architects, both American and Australian, it featured bespindled screens and rounded arches. It was followed before World War I by a vogue for rectilinear Craftsman or American Arts and Crafts furniture and by the open-plan interiors of the California bungalow style. The American architect Walter Burley Griffin, an associate of Frank Lloyd Wright, transplanted elements of the Chicago school style to Australia, particularly in his domestic work of the 1920s.

France, too, had a presence in Australian interiors, particularly from the 1870s when French goods were imported in quantity for the first time. In the 1880s and 1890s a brilliant French designer, Lucien Henry, worked in Sydney and championed the use of Australian motifs in the decorative arts and interior decoration. About 1900 the essentially French Art Nouveau style was belatedly introduced to Australia. Caught up with Australian nationalism and the Arts and Crafts Movement, it survived World War I. The most modish decorating style of the inter-war period was Art Deco, derived by a circuitous route from the Exposition Internationale des Arts Décoratifs et Industriels Modernes in Paris in 1925. Notable pioneers were the Sydney artists Roy de Maistre, Thea Proctor, Hera Roberts, Adrian Feint and Leon Gellert, who designed interiors and furniture in the late 1920s. In the mid-1930s the Melbourne decorator Cynthia Reed offered an alternative to the showy geometrics of the popular Art Deco style; her simple, functional and plainly painted Modernist interiors included wax-polished hardwood furniture by two of her designers, Frederick Ward and Sam Atyeo, and hand-printed textiles by the Englishman Michael O'Connell.

In the immediate post-World War II period the Festival of Britain, held in London in 1951, and utility furniture had an impact on Australian interiors, as did the industrial design revolution that was taking place in the USA and elsewhere. Such furniture designers as Douglas Snelling, Grant Featherston and Clement Meadmore and the textile designer Frances Burke rose to prominence at this time, as did the migrant cabinetmaker Schulim Krimper, who injected a dose of central European modernism into selected Australian homes. Another major influence at the time was that of Scandinavian design, with its streamlined teak furniture and emphasis on natural materials and textures. After 1960 there was a widespread vogue for interiors in the International Style, championed by such architects as Harry Seidler and Robin Boyd, featuring reproductions of classic furniture designs by Marcel Breuer, Le Corbusier, Ludwig Mies van der Rohe and others. Among the diversity of styles that characterized the interior decoration of the late 20th century, the international Post-modernist style emerged about 1980 as one of the most influential.

In the light of this very strong and all-pervading overseas influence, evident in even the most primitive of interiors, one might ask whether there is anything distinctive about Australian interiors. Many commentators, particularly during the second half of the 19th century, remarked on a certain brashness, provincialism and want of individuality in Australian houses, and there are only a few instances of overseas styles being transplanted in an absolutely pure form and of interiors being put together with the panache that might be found in the best London or New York houses of the day. Overseas styles often underwent a major adaptation in the process of importation. They were frequently misunderstood and misinterpreted, their philosophical bases rarely comprehended or even suspected.

The desire to reproduce European and American ways of life has been so strong that Australians have generally been guilty of disregarding the realities of climate and of reproducing styles that are patently inappropriate to their situations. From the mid-19th century critics have drawn attention to this anomaly, and architects, designers and craftspeople since the 1880s have called for a national style in architecture, the decorative arts and interior design. Many, like Lucien Henry, mistakenly thought that the solution was to substitute Australian motifs for overseas ones. A few others, for example the Melbourne weavers Eclarté (1940–62), in the 1940s and 1950s significantly advanced the cause by drawing inspiration from the colours and textures of the Australian bush. But ease of travel and the plethora of imported interior design journals seemed to perpetuate and reinforce Australia's dependence on foreign modes and deter the emergence of a popularly based national style.

BIBLIOGRAPHY

S. Forge: *Victorian Splendour: Australian Interior Decoration, 1837–1901* (Melbourne, 1981)

T. Lane and J. Serle: *Australians at Home: A Documentary History of Australian Domestic Interiors from 1788 to 1914* (Melbourne, 1990)

TERENCE LANE

VI. Furniture.

The principal characteristic of Australian furniture is its use of indigenous timbers, particularly red cedar. This timber found a ready acceptance with the early settlers because of its pronounced figure and similarity to the mahogany of the West Indies and Central America, which had been used in British furniture from the early 18th century. Botanically different from cedars of the northern hemisphere, this timber was found in Australia only in the coastal rainforests of New South Wales and Queensland. Its commercial exploitation by the end of the 19th century resulted in its near extinction. Other indigenous timbers used in Australian furniture manufacture include blackwood, regarded as similar to walnut, and varieties of she-oak, which were even exported to Britain, where they found a limited use with cabinetmakers. Tasmania's Huon pine, likened to bird's-eye maple, and Western Australian jarrah, also known as Swan River mahogany, were popular with colonial cabinetmakers. Several of these timbers were named for their superficial resemblance to northern hemisphere timbers by the settlers who first cut them, with little regard for correct botanical terminology. Early in the 19th century other timbers were imported from New Zealand and the Pacific Islands and later in the century from Britain, Europe, North America, India and South Africa. Their use in local furniture manufacture makes it often difficult to distinguish Australian-made furniture from its overseas prototypes.

The transmission of British furniture styles and methods of construction provided the basis of Australian furniture design. From the 1840s a limited but direct continental European influence was also evident in the German settlements of South Australia, which developed separately from that colony's English-speaking community, and to a lesser extent in New South Wales, Victoria and Queensland. Following the gold-rushes, from the 1850s a large number of Chinese cabinetmakers, whose work was little different in style from other colonial furniture-makers, were active in the larger Australian cities. By the early 20th century their importance had rapidly declined in the face of widespread anti-Chinese legislation and competition from better mechanized Australian manufactories.

1. Before *c.* 1880. Early Australian settlements faced an initial period of hardship, and little attention was devoted to matters of domestic furnishings beyond the essential. Apart from what was brought with them, most early settlers, living in pitched tents and huts, were little able to boast of furniture other than chests for storage and simple improvisations. 'Chairs grow abundantly in the New South Wales forests as any moderately sized tree cut into two foot lengths will testify', reported G. B. Earp. He also wrote of a bed made from saplings and crossed sticks: 'The bushman, like the Londoner, always rests on a four-post bedstead, the difference being that the posts are usually under instead of over him—he will sleep on one just as soundly as the other.' This utilization of whatever materials were to hand proceeded from immediate need rather than the poverty of pioneer settlers throughout Australia during the 19th century and early 20th. Once established, many settlers were soon able to replace their first crude shelters with more permanent and substantial structures, in which they installed more appropriate and formal furniture, whether imported or of local origin. The arrival in Australia of skilled tradesmen, including cabinetmakers, joiners, chairmakers and upholsterers, both convict and free, provided a ready alternative to the ever-dominant imported furniture in terms of convenience and cost.

Prior to 1840 local furniture manufacture centred on the principal towns of New South Wales and Tasmania. Documentary evidence (for examples see Bladen) indicates that an amount of furniture for public buildings and individual officials was produced in government workshops by convict labour in Sydney before 1800. It was not until 1804 that the first commercial advertisement by a cabinetmaker appeared in the *Sydney Gazette*, inviting public patronage for 'all kinds of folding desks, tea chests and caddies, writing, card, Pembroke, and oblong dining tables, sea and cloaths chests, quadrant cases richly ornamented with the native woods'.

The first important cabinetmaker in Australia was the Irish convict Lawrence Butler, who worked in Sydney between 1802 and 1820. Like other furniture workshops established in Sydney and Hobart during the early 19th century, Butler's was organized along the lines of those found in Britain, with a master, journeymen and apprentices. While no example of Butler's work has been authenticated, he is known to have produced furniture for government offices, and in 1815 he advertised for sale 'Chairs, tables and sofas, drawer and clothes presses, patent dining tables on pillars, on the newest construction, dressing and shaving boxes with glasses, card tables, an elegant cabinet and escritoire, bedsteads and mattresses, &c. made under his immediate supervision and warranted of the best materials'. A she-oak veneered cabinet on a stand (1815; Parramatta, Old Govt House) by one of his apprentices and Governor Macquarie's Gothic Revival-style armchair (1821; Sydney, Mus. Applied A. & Sci.; see fig. 17) of native timbers attributed to two convict craftsmen in Sydney employed in the government workshops, John Webster (1798–1842) and William Temple (1776–1836), are further indication of the repertory of forms, timbers used and the quality of furniture produced in Australia at this time.

Australian furniture styles during the first half of the 19th century parallel those current in Britain (*see* England, §VI, 5 and 6). Lighter Neo-classical designs were slowly replaced by those featuring a heavier treatment of classical form and decoration, accompanied by a coarsening of detail. Apart from the popular Greek Revival style, others including the Gothic, Elizabethan and Louis XIV revivals were in evidence. It has been suggested that there

17. Governor Macquarie's armchair, attributed to John Webster and William Temple, rose mahogany, she-oak and red cedar, with kangaroo skin upholstery, h. 1.31 m, 1821 (Sydney, Museum of Applied Arts and Sciences)

was a pronounced time-lag in the transmission of fashionable English furniture designs to Australia, but contemporary colonial newspaper advertisements indicate otherwise, although, as in provincial Britain, a number of furniture styles lingered long after they had ceased as a London fashion.

Early Australian furniture displays a subtle difference from English prototypes. It drew on memories of British urban and country traditions and imported furniture, as well as designs from a number of British furniture pattern books and trade catalogues. One of the most influential was John Claudius Loudon's *Encyclopaedia of Cottage, Farm and Villa Architecture and Furniture* (London, 1833), which found considerable circulation in Australia. Another was the trade catalogue *Designs for Furniture* issued *c.* 1850 by the London furniture manufacturers William Smee & Son. Both works and their later editions are known to have been used by colonial cabinetmakers as a source for furniture designs, as well as by furniture retailers for importing furniture into Australia. It was the modification of such furniture designs by Australian cabinetmakers that gives colonial furniture its individual quality. The Australian furniture industry was marked by a lesser degree of specialization and mechanization than that found in larger British establishments. Operators were also affected by the unfamiliar local conditions and the different and often intractable properties of the richly figured local timbers with which they worked. By the 1840s the use of trade labels and punch and stencil marks became more common with cabinetmakers and furniture retailers. While they can provide important evidence as to maker, date and place of origin or sale, they can also be found on furniture made at other premises or imported from abroad.

The rapid growth in population and wealth following the gold-rushes of the 1850s resulted in an increased demand for both locally produced and imported furniture. The older centres of government and commerce were overtaken by the development of Melbourne and newer towns on the Victorian goldfields. Large-scale furniture factories and furniture retailers emerged to replace the cabinetmaker's workshop as the prime source of furniture for the general public. In the second half of the 19th century eclectic historical revival and period furniture designs continued to appear, featuring in a number of trade catalogues issued by British furniture retailers or wholesalers and later by a few of their Australian equivalents. These were enthusiastically copied by the increasingly mechanized colonial furniture manufactories. The lighter commercial expressions of the Aesthetic Movement and the appearance of hand-crafted art furniture from the 1880s were to remain overshadowed by a wide variety of mass-produced decorative styles and often imaginary interpretations of 18th-century English period furniture.

High-quality documented work from this period can be found in Government House, Sydney, where in 1857 ANDREW LENEHAN provided £2204-worth of furnishings for the dining-, drawing- and bedrooms. In 1876 Thwaites & Son and James McEwan & Co. supplied furniture to the value of £11,585 for the state apartments and private rooms of the new Government House, Melbourne. International exhibitions held in Europe and North America during the second half of the 19th century included the work of a number of Australian furniture-makers: Lenehan, W. Jones & Son, Wallach Brothers and Verdich & Co. of Sydney; Peter Maclean (*d* 1904), Thwaites & Son, W. H. Rocke & Co., James McEwan & Co. and Moubray, Rowan & Hicks of Melbourne; and J. W. Woolley (1797–1880), William Hamilton (*c.* 1796–1885) and John Brown (*fl* 1840–54) of Tasmania. Similar international and intercolonial exhibitions held in the principal Australian cities at this time served as important showcases for the work of an increasing number of colonial furniture manufacturers.

2. AFTER *c.* 1880. At the end of the 19th century a number of artist-craftsmen began working in several Australian cities; their work was influenced by the Arts and Crafts Movement. Several became teachers in technical schools and colleges, where they had some impact on professional and amateur furniture-makers. They stressed the use of native timbers, a simplicity of construction and the qualities of hand-carved decoration. The Frenchman LUCIEN HENRY, for example, became the first

lecturer in art at the Sydney Technical College and actively promoted the use of native flora and fauna as appropriate furniture decoration (although they had featured spasmodically in Australian furniture decoration from as early as the 1850s). In 1888 Prussian-born Robert Prenzel (1866–1941) arrived in Melbourne, where he later established himself as a wood-carver and furniture-maker. Utilizing a number of previously neglected indigenous timbers, he combined the native flora and fauna with the sinuous lines of Art Nouveau. His work, along with that of Lewis J. Harvey (1871–1949) in Queensland and J. W. R. LINTON in Western Australia, was a fitting decorative complement to the new-found nationalism that followed the federation of the Australian colonies in 1901.

In the early decades of the 20th century debased period reproduction styles continued to be popular; these made use of imported timbers as well as such local timbers as Queensland maple, stained to look like mahogany. Custom-made furniture in a variety of contemporary styles in native timbers, marked by a high degree of craftsmanship, was also produced in Australia at this time by such firms as the Goldman Manufacturing Co. of Melbourne, which achieved recognition at the Panama–Pacific International Exposition of 1915 in San Francisco.

The American architect Walter Burley GRIFFIN, who from 1914 spent 21 years in Australia, designed some furniture for his architectural commissions based on simple, clearly defined lines in lightly stained imported oak. His work was in marked contrast to commercial attempts at mass-produced *art moderne* and exaggerated Art Deco furniture. In Sydney, Roy de Maistre, Adrian Feint, Leon Gellert, Thea Proctor and Hera Roberts designed furniture for an exhibition in 1929 that included painted chairs, tables, desks and cabinets of simple contemporary geometric shapes and forms. However, it was the locally produced tubular steel chairs and chromium-plated furniture that achieved more success with the Australian public at this time. By the early 1930s a number of young designers in Melbourne, including Frederick Ward (1900–90), introduced contemporary foreign styles to a small but increasingly aware public; their work features Australian timbers, detailed construction and texture.

The austerity imposed by World War II continued during the immediate post-war years. From the late 1940s the emergence of several designers, architects and decorators who introduced contemporary innovations made a considerable impact. Such designers as Douglas Snelling (1915–85), Roger McLay (*b* 1922) and Gordon Andrews (*b* 1914) in Sydney and Grant Featherston (*b* 1922) in Melbourne created well-designed and mass-produced furniture in contemporary European and American styles, which were marketed by a number of furniture manufacturers. SCHULIM KRIMPER in Melbourne and Paul Ernest Kafka (1907–72) in Sydney produced high-quality custom-made furniture, in selectively chosen indigenous and imported timbers and in contemporary styles.

In the 1950s and 1960s the influence of contemporary American and Scandinavian design, stressing natural surfaces and wood technology, inspired a number of local variants. The influence of contemporary British furniture-makers, with their refined sensibility to material and construction, was also in evidence. Media other than wood, including plastic, glass and metal, became more popular. In the late 20th century, apart from the International Style and one-off designs by artist-craftsmen, the most distinctly Australian development is the bush or folk style, based on the earlier tradition of utilizing irregularly shaped wood fragments. Together with the successful promotion by the Industrial Design Council of Australia, training programmes in wood crafts at tertiary institutions and exhibitions by both amateur and professional furniture-makers articulated a vitality and maturity in contemporary Australian furniture design and manufacture.

BIBLIOGRAPHY

G. B. Earp: *The Gold Colonies of Australia* (London, 1852), p. 108

F. M. Bladen, ed.: *Historical Records of New South Wales* (Sydney, 1895–6), iii, pp. 336, 750; iv, p. 280

C. Craig, K. Fahy and E. G. Robertson: *Early Colonial Furniture in New South Wales and Van Diemen's Land* (Melbourne, 1972/*R* 1981)

One Hundred Modern Chairs (exh. cat., ed. T. Lane; Melbourne, N.G. Victoria, 1974)

Australian Furniture from Early Colonial Times to the Present Day: Formed in Wood (exh. cat., ed. T. Lane; Melbourne, Banyule Extn Gal., 1982)

J. Hawkins: 'The Art of the Cabinet-maker: From the First Settlement, 1788–1820', *Austral. Ant. Colr*, xxv (1983), pp. 52–5; xxvi (1983), pp. 50–54; xxvii (1984), pp. 56–63

K. Fahy, C. Simpson and A. Simpson: *Nineteenth Century Australian Furniture* (Sydney, 1985) [includes over 800 illustrations]

M. Bogle: 'Australian Furniture', *Craft Australia Yb.* (1986), pp. 54–69

T. Hooper and J. Hooper: *Australian Country Furniture* (Ringwood, Victoria, 1988)

M. Bogle and P. Landman: *Modern Australian Furniture* (Sydney, 1989)

G. Cornall: *Memories: A Survey of Early Australian Furniture in the Collection of the Lord McAlpine of West Green* (Perth, 1990)

G. Cochrane: *The Craft Movement in Australia: A History* (Kensington, NSW, 1992)

KEVIN FAHY

VII. Ceramics.

1. Before *c.* 1900. 2. *c.* 1900–*c.* 1944. 3. After *c.* 1944.

1. BEFORE *c.* 1900. In 1788 samples of Australian clay from Sydney Cove were sent to Josiah Wedgwood in Staffordshire, and the following year he had them made into medallions showing Hope encouraging Art and Labour under the influence of Peace (e.g. of 1789; London, BM); the hoped-for trade in clay, however, did not follow. Australia at this time had no indigenous ceramic industry. Although bricks were fired in the first year of settlement (1788), the first record of domestic earthenwares is indicated by an advertisement placed by Samuel Skinner (*d* 1808) in the *Sydney Gazette* (2 Oct 1803). The Staffordshire potters John Moreton and Jonathon Leak (1777–after 1839) arrived as convicts in 1819 and made wares for the government. The earliest surviving dated item is a crude Staffordshire-style bust of George Washington bearing the name of Moreton's son Anson Moreton (1811–after 1847) and dated July 1822. The *Sydney Herald* (4 July 1831) reported the appearance of 'yellow Colonial manufactured glazed earthenware . . . made by a man residing on the Brickfields, . . . the first of the description manufactured in the Colony', and suitable for 'culinary work'. In the same year James Sherwin (*fl* 1831) established a pottery near Hobart in Van Dieman's Land. The Scottish entrepreneur James King (1797–1857) established a pottery at Irrawang, New South Wales (*c.* 1834–51), which produced lead- and salt-glazed wares and wares decorated with relief

figures. He brought potters and moulds from Staffordshire. In the course of the 19th century further potteries were established around Melbourne, Brisbane, Launceston and Adelaide. The wares generally reflected the influence of British ceramics, but J. G. Samuel Hoffman (*fl c.* 1850–80) and others, mostly in South Australia, worked in the tradition of German folk pottery. Imported goods from Britain dominated the tableware market, while local potters produced storage jars, water filters, ant-proof safe-stands and butter coolers to meet immediate needs.

Factories making decorated wares in addition to utilitarian ceramics in the 1880s and 1890s included the Lithgow Pottery (1879–1973), New South Wales, and the Bendigo Pottery (est. 1857), Victoria, the principal potter of which was the Scotsman George Guthrie (1828–1910). Typical products were bread plates and cheese dishes with majolica glazes and decorated in relief, glazed garden urns and Bristol, Rockingham and salt-glazed wares. A Belleek-style covered vase (1880s; Melbourne, N.G. Victoria) made in a porcellaneous body at Bendigo is unusually ambitious.

Although pottery classes were introduced in 1886 at the School of Design in Adelaide, there were few facilities available in the art schools, and Australia did not produce an art pottery movement as such in the 19th century. Isolated efforts included wares decorated with eucalyptus leaves made *c.* 1896 at the Mashman Bros Pottery in Sydney by Thomas Stevens, who had trained at the Doulton Ceramic Factory in England, and the 'grotesques' derived from wares made by the English Martin brothers, which William Ferry (*fl* 1898–1912) showed in 1898 with the Yarra Sculptors' Society in Melbourne.

2. *c.* 1900–*c.* 1944. Painting on imported blanks was the most common medium of ceramic expression in Australia from the late 19th century until the 1930s. Australian and European motifs were treated in styles reflecting Japonisme, art pottery from the Doulton Ceramic Factory and the restrained Art Nouveau of the Glasgow school. Work was exhibited with the arts and crafts societies formed in various states, starting with Tasmania in 1903. Notable painters were Ethel Atkinson (1887–1991), Lawrence H. Howie (1876–1963) and Mildred Lovett (1880–1955); examples of their work are in the Art Gallery of New South Wales and the Museum of Applied Arts and Sciences, both in Sydney. Martin Moroney (*fl c.* 1904–*c.* 1915) was unusual in using commercial blanks made to order as the base for underglaze floral decoration.

Among the first to exhibit studio pottery were Alan Finlay (*fl* 1908–25) and Harold F. Swanson (*fl* 1908–1920s), who showed with the Arts and Crafts Society of Victoria in 1908. Finlay also worked with his brother Ernest Finlay (*fl* 1913–*c.* 1930), making vases with landscape decoration and experimenting with Chinese-style transmutation glazes as early as 1914 (e.g. vase with gum trees and kangaroo, 1913; Sydney, A.G. NSW). The major figure from the first period of studio pottery was William Merric Boyd (1888–1959), who was active at Murrumbeena on the outskirts of Melbourne. His highly original style blended the organic forms of Art Nouveau with the hand-made aesthetic of the Arts and Crafts Movement (e.g. lamp in the form of a clump of trees, 1930; Melbourne, N.G. Victoria). Australian landscape and relief decoration, including koalas and kookaburras, was a special feature of his earthenwares. Boyd's wife, Doris Boyd (*c.* 1893–1960), often executed the painted decoration. Some porcelain was also made using commercial facilities. Boyd was influential in increasing public awareness of studio pottery.

Margaret MacPherson and Gladys Reynell (1881–1956) exhibited together in Adelaide in 1919 after studying pottery at the Camberwell School of Art in London (1916–17). Their work incorporated slip decoration and *sgraffito* techniques derived from English folk pottery (e.g. teapot by MacPherson with a design of boiling billies, *c.* 1918; Sydney, A.G. NSW). The spontaneity of their work also suggests the pottery of the Omega Workshops (e.g. plate by MacPherson, 1917; Canberra, N.G.). MacPherson was a strong advocate of abstract decoration based on the art of Australian Aborigines and she published on the subject after she gave up pottery to paint; such Aboriginal elements also appear in the work of Reynell, who continued to work as a potter at Reynella, South Australia, and at the Osrey Pottery in Ballarat, Victoria, until 1926. Other notable potters active before 1930 included the Tasmanian Maude Poynter (1869–1945), who studied pottery at the Kingston upon Thames School of Art (1913), Vi Eyre (1870–1956) in Sydney and the Adelaide potter Doreen Goodchild (*b* 1900), who trained at the Central School of Arts and Crafts in London (1926–9). L. J. Harvey (1871–1949) was the dominant figure at a school of pottery in Brisbane, which favoured carved decoration in an Arts and Crafts style.

The studio pottery movement expanded significantly during the 1930s with the emergence of the mostly Melbourne-based potters John Castle Harris (1893–1967), F. E. Cox (*d* 1965), who worked at the Jolliff Studio, Una Deerbon (1882–1972), John Barnard Knight (*b* 1910), Allan Lowe (*b* 1907), Klytie Pate (*b* 1912), Marguerite Mahood (1900–89) and William Ricketts (*b* 1899). Earthenware was still the main medium for these potters. There was continued interest in glaze effects inspired by Chinese wares and also in Australian motifs. Some connections with commercially based British art pottery is also apparent, as is an interest in English studio pottery; the influence of Bernard Leach and Michael Cardew, however, was not evident in Australia until the 1940s. Ricketts took an independent approach to Art Nouveau, while radical, Cubist-inspired works were sent back from Moly-Sabata in France by the expatriate Ann Dangar (e.g. jug, *c.* 1935; Canberra, N.G.). Commercial potteries of the 1930s also produced art wares: 'Melrose' ware (*c.* 1932–40) was made by the Hoffman Brick Co. (est. 1870) in Brunswick, Victoria, and was slip-cast with possums and relief eucalyptus. Wares marked REMUED from the Premier Pottery in Preston, Victoria (*c.* 1930–50), were decorated with applied gumnuts and streaky, variegated glazes.

3. AFTER *c.* 1944. After World War II several painters made major contributions to Australian studio ceramics: Merric Boyd's son Arthur Boyd (*see* BOYD, (2)), JOHN PERCEVAL and the New Zealander Neil Douglas (*b* 1911) established the Arthur Merric Boyd Pottery Workshop at

18. Earthenware tea set by Arthur Boyd and John Perceval, teapot h. 232 mm, Arthur Merric Boyd Pottery Workshop, Murrumbeena, 1948 (Melbourne, National Gallery of Victoria)

Murrumbeena (1944–58). Intended simply to provide a livelihood, it soon developed into a major phenomenon of the Australian studio pottery movement. Earthenwares with generous forms reminiscent of European folk pottery were freely painted with underglaze colours (see fig. 18). Boyd and Perceval worked in a figurative idiom based in Expressionism (e.g. 'Angel and Beast' platter by Boyd, 1948; Melbourne, N.G. Victoria). Douglas contributed delicate paintings of the bush and its characteristic fauna and flora. By 1954 Boyd also produced a series of ceramic sculptures and tile paintings. Perceval went on to make ceramic sculptures of charming but sometimes disturbing angels (e.g. *Angel Holding Child*, 1958; Melbourne, N.G. Victoria). Equally expressive earthenwares were made by another of Merric Boyd's sons, the painter David Boyd (*b* 1924), and his wife Hermia Lloyd-Jones (*b* 1931), including *sgraffito*-decorated wares with figurative imagery and sculptural works (e.g. tureen, 1956; Melbourne, N.G. Victoria). The couple also worked in England and France during the 1950s and 1960s. Similarly the Polish potter Stanislaw Halpern (*b* 1919) brought a painter's vision to his decoration of earthenwares derived from Polish peasant pottery, which he made between 1947 and 1950 and again in the 1960s.

In 1944 the potter Harold Hughan (1893–1987) built a kiln in Melbourne to fire stonewares. He was the first Australian potter to implement the ideas of Leach and Cardew, which were based on East Asian traditions and English folk pottery and were promoted through Leach's *A Potter's Book* (London, 1940/*R* 1956). Hughan is regarded as the pioneer of the modern craft movement in Australian ceramics. Typical works include cut-sided jars, large thrown platters and other vessels with celadon or temmoku glazes and calligraphic brush decoration. Peter Rushforth (*b* 1920) began making stoneware in 1951; with Mollie Douglas (*b* 1920) he promoted the ideas of Leach at art schools in Sydney during the 1950s. Ivan McMeekin (*b* 1919), who had worked with Cardew in England, established the Sturt Pottery in Mittagong, New South Wales, in 1953, where, during the 1950s, several important potters, including the English potter Les Blakebrough (*b* 1930), Ivan Englund (*b* 1915), Col Levy (*b* 1933) and Gwyn Hanssen Pigott (*b* 1935), worked. Such potters as Janet Mansfield (*b* 1934) and the Japanese potter Shigeo Shiga (*b* 1928) also worked there during the 1960s. The leaders of the new-style works included the American Carl McConnell (*b* 1926) and Milton Moon (*b* 1926) in Brisbane, the New Zealander Eileen Keys (*b* 1903) in Perth and the Scottish potter Alex Leckie (*b* 1932) in Adelaide. Through these artists the Leach aesthetic formed the basis for the craft revival of the 1960s and 1970s (see fig. 19). It was shaped, however, by a conscious assimilation of elements of the Australian landscape and the character of local materials. In addition, increasing contact with Japan played a decisive role from 1963, when Rushforth and Blakebrough visited the country. The treatment of form and decoration in the work of Milton Moon and in the raku ceramics made *c.* 1970 by Joan Campbell (*b* 1925) show an interpretation of the Japanese aesthetic that is closer to that of the American Abstract Expressionist potters Peter Voulkos (*b* 1924) and Paul Soldner than to the Leach tradition of functional ceramics. The example of such potters as Hans Coper, Ruth Duckworth (*b* 1919) and Lucie Rie encouraged experiment with new forms,

19. Stoneware pot with shino glaze by Col Levy, h. 503 mm, 1971 (Melbourne, National Gallery of Victoria)

both organic and geometric; Marea Gazzard (*b* 1928) made sculptural, hand-built vessels, and the English potter Derek Smith (*b* 1931) favoured geometric precision.

The position of ceramic art in relation to both the fine arts and the functional and technical basis of craft became an increasingly important issue from the early 1970s. It was brought into focus by Gazzard's treatment of the vessel as sculpture in the exhibition *Clay and Fibre* at the National Gallery of Victoria, Melbourne, in 1973. 'Funk' ceramics directly challenged the craft tradition: Margaret Dodd (*b* 1941) returned from California *c.* 1970 having studied and exhibited with Robert Arneson and David Gilhooly; she used the Australian Holden car as her central image in a series of works satirizing suburban life and the 'surfie' cult. 'Funk' ceramics developed in Adelaide with the anti-Vietnam war satire of Olive Bishop (*b* 1941) and the irreverent wit of Mark Thompson (*b* 1949). Low-fired earthenware, porcelain and the use of bright colours and lustres were all exploited. The humour of Lorraine Jenyns (*b* 1945) and the social satire of Sandra Taylor (*b* 1942) sprang from similar sentiments.

The broader stream of craft practice remained vessel-based through the 1970s and 1980s, enriched by a great variety of forms and techniques (e.g. the use of dry glazes, raku and bone china). Prominent figures included Greg Daly (*b* 1954), John Dermer (*b* 1949), Victoria Howlett (*b* 1945), Jeff Mincham (*b* 1950), Jenny Orchard (*b* 1951) and the English potter Alan Peascod (*b* 1943). The vitality of the crafts in the early 1970s encouraged such major painters as John Olsen, Brett Whitely and Fred Williams to decorate ceramic vessels.

Among the younger generation of ceramic artists of the 1980s, intensely personal styles emerged within the vessel format in the work of Stephen Benwell (*b* 1953), Deborah Halpern (*b* 1957), Fiona Murphy (*b* 1958) and David Potter (*b* 1955). The Post-modernist ceramics of the 1980s were inspired by many cultures, which evoked some resonance in the artist, whether as stimulus to nostalgia, as formal device or as a comment on the human condition and/or environmental concerns. Primitivism and archaeological references also played an important role.

A wide variety of non-functional ceramics claimed attention from the early 1980s, and many ceramic artists chose a sculptural format. Although typically they showed the characteristic sensitivity to material and process that distinguished traditional ceramics, the techniques of using mixed media and unfired clay were sometimes controversial. Of particular interest in this field are the works of Rod Bamford (*b* 1958), the English potter John Johnson (*b* 1939), the Polish potter Maria Kuczinska (*b* 1948), the Japanese potter Mitsuo Shoji (*b* 1946), John Teschendorff (*b* 1942), Alan Watt (*b* 1941) and Toni Warburton (*b* 1951).

BIBLIOGRAPHY

K. Hood and W. Garnsey: *Australian Pottery* (Melbourne, 1972)
M. Graham: *Australian Pottery of the 19th & Early 20th Century* (Sydney, 1979)
J. McPhee: *Australian Decorative Arts in the Australian National Gallery* (Canberra, 1982)
Contemporary Australian Ceramics (exh. cat. by K. Hood, Melbourne, N.G. Victoria, 1982)
The Painter as Potter: Decorated Ceramics of the Murrumbeena Circle (exh. cat. by G. Edwards, Melbourne, N.G. Victoria, 1982)
N. Ioannou: *Ceramics in South Australia, 1836–1986* (Netley, 1986)
P. Timms: *Australian Studio Pottery & China Painting* (Oxford, 1986)
Skangaroovian Funk: Peculiar Adelaide Ceramics, 1968–1978 (exh. cat. by J. Thompson, Adelaide, A.G. S. Australia, 1986)
V. Hammond, ed.: *Australian Ceramics: Shepparton Art Gallery* (Shepparton, 1987)
Beautiful & Useful: The Arts & Crafts Movement in Tasmania (exh. cat. by C. Miley, Launceston, Queen Victoria Mus. & A.G., 1987)
J. Mansfield: *A Collector's Guide to Modern Australian Ceramics* (Seaforth, NSW, 1988)
Bendigo Pottery: Selected Wares from 1857 to the Present Day (exh. cat. by D. O'Hoy, Bendigo, A.G., 1989)
D. Edwards: *Australian Decorative Arts at the Art Gallery of New South Wales* (Sydney, 1991)

MARGARET LEGGE

VIII. Glass.

Although modest efforts were made from 1812 to produce hand-blown glass in Australia, it was not until the period between the gold-rushes of the 1850s and the failure of the country's economy in the early 1890s that any notable achievement occurred in the local manufacture of glass. During this period the sophistication and quality of glass displayed at the international exhibitions held in Sydney (1879) and Melbourne (1880) provided both example and incentive for local producers of stained, etched and leaded glass to compete for a portion of the burgeoning domestic market for window cycles bearing decorative, commemorative or historical themes. Installed in churches, civic buildings and private residences, these windows served as symbols of social pride and new-found prosperity. In general, however, it remained common practice until the end of the 19th century to award ambitious commissions for window cycles to prominent firms in Britain or Germany. Nevertheless, from World War I important commissions for stained-glass windows were secured by a growing number of Australian artists; most conspicuous among them were Mervyn Napier Waller (1894–1972), who completed (1941) three major groups of towering windows for the Hall of Memory at the Australian War Memorial in Canberra, and Alan Sumner (*b* 1911), whose numerous ecclesiastical and secular commissions reveal a simple stylization of image informed by the artist's background as a painter and printmaker and, in particular, by his abiding interest in Cubism and Expressionism.

Such established painters as LEONARD FRENCH, WILLIAM GLEESON and Les Kossatz (*b* 1943) all undertook architectural commissions, which are notable for their use of experimental techniques and the artists' endeavours to extend the orthodox imagery of the flat-glass idiom into the realm of modernist abstraction. The most widely celebrated commissions included French's vast *dalle de verre* (chipped and faceted slab glass) ceiling (1962–8; see fig. 20), featuring the themes of birth and creation, for the Great Hall in the National Gallery of Victoria, Melbourne, which comprised densely pigmented glass slabs supported within a heavy framework of wood and aluminium.

Les Kossatz's most prestigious glass commissions included a cycle of 20 windows of leaded and laminated 'antique' glass (1968) for the Inter-denominational Chapel at Monash University and a massive pair of ceremonial doors (1978–80) for the High Court of Australia, Canberra.

20. Leonard French: *dalle de verre* ceiling (1962–8), Great Hall, National Gallery of Victoria, Melbourne, Australia

Unlike French's ceiling, Kossatz's ceremonial doors relinquish the visual drama provided by a traditional high-key palette and instead employ a tactile relief grid of translucent shield-shaped panels of colourless, laminated plate glass. These panels are sandblasted with an interconnecting, serpentine motif that is repeated by silver-plated bronze handles and in the deeply sandblasted glass sidelights.

William Gleeson is credited with having introduced a vital spirit of innovation and experiment to architectural and sculptural glass in Australia. His window commissions as well as his free-standing 'assemblages' reveal an assimilation of the trade skills acquired during his ten-year apprenticeship at the commercial glass firm of Brooks, Robinson & Co., Melbourne, and a sculptor's concern for modernist principles of design. In 1961 Gleeson established a course in flat-glass studies within the Art Department of the Melbourne Institute of Technology. Through this course Gleeson introduced students, including Les Kossatz, DAVID WRIGHT and KLAUS ZIMMER, to a fundamentally sculptural approach to the medium of glass. Wright's largest commission, *Regeneration and Growth* (1976), a glass wall in the Reception Centre at the Victorian Zoological Gardens, Melbourne, makes dynamic use of the muted palette and interlinked organic emblems that typify his large-scale public works.

An alternative direction was pursued by Zimmer, who was born in Germany. Among his most prominent public commissions is a cycle of 19 windows (1988–9) for the Uniting (formerly Independent) Church, Melbourne; this is a deeply symbolic cycle incorporating passages of biblical script with stylized devices representing traditional Christian emblems. Zimmer's lucid palette and fluid, graphic motifs indicate his admiration for early Chinese painting and provide evidence of his training as a printmaker.

The period 1960 to 1980 represents the great watershed in the contemporary Australian craft movement. Young Australian potters were quick to build on the foundations of an earlier, indigenous tradition of highly decorated studio pottery in the establishment of a new, robust and progressive identity for their work. By contrast, the studio glass movement cannot be considered as a truly coherent force until 1978, when a group of artists that included Nicholas Mount (*b* 1952), Warren Langley, Cedar Prest (*b* 1940), Cornelis Rhee (*b* 1941), Stephen Skillitzi (*b* 1947) and Gerry King (*b* 1945) resolved to form the Australian Association of Glass Artists (Ausglass). This professional organization promotes the achievements of its national membership and fosters within the community an appreciation of the fundamental issues and challenges inherent in the use of glass as a medium of expression in contemporary art.

In line with the poineering seminars held in the early 1960s at the Toledo Museum of Art in Toledo, OH, by the artist-technicians Harvey K. Littleton and Dominick Labino (*b* 1910), the first significant experiments with studio glass-blowing in Australia focused on a demonstration given in Sydney in February 1972 by the English-born artist Stephen Skillitzi. The small but enthusiastic group of Australian artists working in 'hot' glass was given a more substantial lead in 1973 and again in 1974, when Bill Boysen from the USA and Sam Herman from England were invited to Australia to develop facilities and training programmes for local glass artists. The considerable benefit of these endeavours was consolidated through subsequent tours by the American artist Richard Marquis and by the foundation in 1973 of the Jam Factory Craft Workshops in Adelaide, a crucial training and production facility for young artists interested in a diversity of art and craft disciplines.

Throughout the 1980s the most significant direction to emerge in Australian studio glass was kiln-worked glass, whereby sculptural objects and functional vessels were made by fusing sheets of clear or coloured glass in a kiln. From 1983 the German artist KLAUS MOJE was head of the glass workshop at the Canberra School of Art and was an important influence on the development and direction of Australian glass. He promoted kiln-working techniques, and his vividly patterned mosaic forms provided a valuable point of departure for such artists as Judi Elliott (*b* 1934) and Mezza Rijsdijk (*b* 1955), whose work is notable for a lyrical interpretation of mosaics. During the same period the Sydney artist WARREN LANGLEY established an international reputation for his frosted icons of fused and moulded sheet glass applied with miniature mosaic motifs, supported within angular structures of anodized aluminium tubing.

In the field of blown glass, Nicholas Mount from Norwood, South Australia, and Brian Hirst (*b* 1956) from Sydney produced ambitious vessel forms with innovative decorative treatments. Tony Hanning (*b* 1950) from Gippsland, Victoria, spearheaded a new appreciation of cameo decoration based on Surrealist or romantic landscape imagery, and Richard Clements (*b* 1950), who worked in Tasmania, is credited with having brought the process of lampworking to a new pitch of aesthetic potential in his continuing series of 'feathered', dappled and fluidly manipulated scent bottles, which were conceived as fanciful specimens of a mythical genus of decorated molluscs.

BIBLIOGRAPHY

I. Bell: 'Warren Langley', *Craft Australia*, iii (Spring 1979), p. 24

A. Hersey: 'Con Rhee', *Craft Australia*, iii (Spring 1979), p. 25

C. Prest: 'Glass and its Development', *Craft Australia*, iii (Spring 1979), pp. 13–16

J. Zimmer: 'A Bitter Suite: Collaborative Exhibition by Warren Langley and Nick Mount, Distelfink Gallery, Melbourne', *Craft Australia*, iii (Spring 1979), p. 55

Contemporary Australian Glass, Wagga Wagga: First National Contemporary Australian Glass Exhibition (exh. cat. by J. LeLievre, Wagga Wagga, C.A.G., 1981)

J. Zimmer: 'Glass', *Craft Australia Yb.* (1984), pp. 47–75

——: *Stained Glass in Australia* (Melbourne, 1984)

Glass from Australia and New Zealand (exh. cat., ed. J. Zimmer; Darmstadt, Hess. Landesmus., 1984)

GEOFFREY R. EDWARDS

IX. Metalwork and objects of vertu.

1. To 1850. 2. 1851–1900. 3. After 1900.

1. TO 1850. The first recorded silversmith in Australia was William Hogg, who arrived as a convict with the First Fleet in 1788. It is not known whether he produced any silverware before his death in 1795, but within another eight years gold- and silversmiths in Sydney were advertising their services. The earliest record of a silver item manufactured in Australia is a report in the *Sydney Gazette* of 14 August 1803 that describes a stolen silver spoon 'made in the colony'. As gold was not discovered in Australia until 1851, and silver was not mined in large quantities until the 1880s, the precious metals used in the manufacture of early colonial wares were imported, and old plate and coins were frequently melted down and refashioned. The oldest surviving example of Australian silver (or silver engraved in Australia) is a circular button mounted on the lid of a snuff mull (Sydney, Mitchell Lib.) engraved with a crest and inscribed *The Gift of Captn Woodriff R. N. Jan 13 1804.* A plain silver caster (priv. col., see Hawkins, ii, p. 252, pl. 86), in the late 18th-century style, inscribed *The First Piece Of Plate made in V. D. Land A. D. 1805 and used on the Anniversary of the Birthday of H. M. George III*, is the earliest extant item of hollow-ware. Neither work is marked, but both have been attributed to the convict James Grove (1769–1810), a die-sinker and engraver from Birmingham, who was transported in 1803. The oldest surviving example of the use of local motifs in Australian metalwork is a gold and shell snuff-box (*c.* 1808; Sydney, Mus. Applied A. & Sci.) attributed to Ferdinand Meurant (1765–1844), a jeweller, and John Austin (?1760–1837), a seal and copperplate engraver, both convicts from Dublin who arrived in the colony in 1800. The snuff-box is engraved with a depiction of a kangaroo from one of the many prints after a painting of the *Kongouro from New Holland* (exh. 1773; Parham House, W. Sussex) by George Stubbs.

The earliest extant marked wares date from the 1820s. A number of large gold- and silversmithing businesses were operating in Sydney by this period, notably those of Samuel Clayton (*d* 1853), James Robertson (1781–1868) and Jacob Josephson (1774–1845). One of the most important was that established by ALEXANDER DICK around 1825. His workshop, which employed a number of assigned convicts, produced smallwork and flatware, as well as relatively large items of hollow-ware, for example his Sydney Subscription Cup (1834; destr.), which was described as 15 inches (*c.* 350 mm) high and 84 ounces (*c.* 2.4 kg) in weight. Other surviving examples of Dick's plate are generally plain in design, some exhibiting Neo-classical features, although a rare example of his more elaborate work and another early example of local imagery in Australian metalwork is a silver snuff-box (1835; Sydney, Mus. Applied A. & Sci.) made for presentation to a T. B. Daniel. The lid is chased with a view of Sydney harbour, showing an Aborigine reclining in the foreground between an emu and a kangaroo. Newspaper advertisements and trade directories reveal that there were gold- and silversmiths operating in other colonial centres during the 1830s and 1840s, but there is relatively little record of their work. From those articles of marked plate that survive, the most important makers can be identified as David Barclay (?1804–84) of Hobart, Charles Brentani (?1817–53) of Melbourne and John Henry Pace (?1814–59) of Adelaide.

2. 1851–1900. In 1851 gold was discovered near Bathurst in New South Wales and at Ballarat and Bendigo in Victoria. The first of many gold-rushes followed, precipitating a rapid increase in prosperity and in the population. The local gold- and silversmithing trade also expanded. During the second half of the 19th century

many new businesses were established by immigrants, supplying both locally made and imported plate and jewellery. Some of the most important gold- and silversmiths operating in Sydney at this time were Christian Ludwig Qwist (1818–77) from Denmark, William Kerr (1839–96) and Evan Jones (1846–1917), and in Victoria William Edwards (*fl* 1857–92) of Melbourne, the Austrian Edward Francis Gunter Fischer (1828–1911) of Geelong and the Hungarian ERNEST LEVINY of Castlemaine. The most prominent makers in South Australia were the Germans Charles Firnhaber (1806–80) and Henry Steiner (1835–1914), and JOCHIM MATTHIAS WENDT from Denmark. Specialist craftsmen were employed in the workshops of the larger firms; some, however, for example the repoussé worker James Holt (1835–1921) of Melbourne, operated independently and had work subcontracted to them.

In contrast to most of the craftsmen active before 1851, many of these immigrant gold- and silversmiths had neither British nationality nor training, and consequently a stylistic heterogeneity appeared in Australian metalwork, although it generally accorded with the forms and styles of contemporary British and European silver and jewellery. Antipodean motifs were easily accommodated within this idiom. Although there are some early 19th-century pieces using such motifs, this type of decoration was more common from the mid-19th century. Depictions of Aborigines and native flora and fauna, as well as symbols of the local mining and farming industries, were used to decorate plate and jewellery of otherwise European design. This overlaying of Australian motifs is splendidly illustrated by the standing cup (*c.* 1860; Melbourne, N.G. Victoria; see fig. 21) made by Ernest Leviny of Castlemaine, which is elaborately decorated with symbols of the Old World and New World, combined in an allegory of colonial prosperity. Gold nuggets also feature prominently in the design. These are a common form of decoration in metalwork of the period, particularly in a popular type of souvenir jewellery from the goldfields, incorporating placenames and miniature mining implements. The prevalence of such solid gold presentation pieces as the Geelong Gold Cup (1880; Melbourne, N.G. Victoria) by E. F. G. Fischer during this period also reflects the importance of the gold-mining industry to colonial society.

An extremely popular and characteristically Australian item made in the 19th century and early 20th was the mounted emu egg, the production of which was an extension of the European tradition of mounting rare and precious objects. These items were particularly favoured in Australia for a wide variety of presentation pieces that ranged from centrepieces to toilet accessories (e.g. Horne Presentation Casket, *c.* 1869; Melbourne, N.G. Victoria). The quality of the mounts varies considerably, from finely executed castings to mass-produced confections in electroplate. Many of the better-quality mounts feature freestanding figures of Aborigines, kangaroos and emus arranged in charming vignettes of bush life, and the egg is often carved, inlaid, painted or dyed. Mounted emu eggs by such makers as Julius Schomburgk (*d* 1893), Henry Steiner and Jochim Matthias Wendt were displayed at various international exhibitions, including those held in London in 1862 and 1872 and in Paris in 1878.

21. Standing cup by Ernest Leviny, silver, h. 483 mm, *c.* 1860 (Melbourne, National Gallery of Victoria)

3. AFTER 1900. Such 19th-century firms as Wendts, Drummonds of Melbourne and Hardy Brothers of Sydney, Melbourne and Brisbane continued to operate in the 20th century but did not maintain their own gold- and silversmithing workshops. While the general trend of the larger firms during the 20th century was towards retailing, some successful enterprises incorporating manufacturing workshops were established before World War I, for example those of F. J. Mole of Brisbane (established 1911) and W. J. Sanders of Sydney (established 1913). One of the most important influences on Australian silversmiths during the early 20th century, however, was the work of the English Arts and Crafts Movement. While it had some impact on

design within the manufacturing trade, its purest expression is found in the work of independent craftworkers. The Arts and Crafts societies that were established in most Australian states by 1912 followed the general tenets of the English movement, while actively promoting the development of a distinctly Australian style through the use of local materials and motifs. Some goldsmiths utilized stones of local origin, for example opals, both as decoration and as jewellery settings. These can be seen in the work of Elizabeth Soderberg (*d* 1938) and Rhoda Wager (1878–1953), both from Sydney, J. W. R. LINTON of Perth, James Fawcett (1863–1934) of Melbourne and Alan C. Walker (1864–1931) of Hobart. Fawcett and Walker were among a number of practising architects associated with the movement in Australia. The most accomplished exponent of the Arts and Crafts style in metalwork, however, was WILLIAM MARK of Melbourne, who specialized in the use of enamel and worked in England from about 1900 to 1920, mainly in association with C. R. Ashbee and the Guild of Handicraft. In 1924 Mark was commissioned to produce a set of ecclesiastical plate (*in situ*) for the Warrior's Chapel in Christ Church Cathedral, Newcastle, NSW. Caroline Francis (1860–1953) of Melbourne was also skilled in enamelwork, although she spent most of her working life in Britain.

In the 1920s and 1930s the manufacturing workshops flourished. The firm of G. & E. Rodd, which was established in Melbourne in 1919, expanded from a modest jewellery-making business to a firm designing and mass-producing flatware in both sterling silver and electroplate. Other manufacturing workshops supplied a wide range of hollow-ware and smallwork to retailers both locally and in other Australian states, while also producing ecclesiastical wares. From this period to the 1960s the most innovative designs were produced outside the manufacturing trade by a few independent craftsmen. From the late 1930s David Grieve (1886–1951) of Melbourne made hollow-ware and jewellery that exhibits sophisticated and stylized decorative features influenced by contemporary American trends (e.g. gold and turquoise necklace, *c.* 1940; Melbourne, N.G. Victoria). Dan Flynn (1909–78) of Kyneton, Matcham Skipper (*b* 1921) of Eltham and Emily Hope (1940–79) of Melbourne pursued a figurative and expressionistic style that was related to certain contemporary developments in Australian painting and sculpture. Some fine jewellery was also produced by artists trained in other media, for example the sculptors Inge King (*b* 1918) and Emmanuel Raft (*b* 1938; e.g. silver brooch, 1963; Melbourne, N.G. Victoria).

From about 1960 most of the large silver manufacturing firms closed, amalgamated or considerably scaled down their operations. A number of their trained craftsmen established workshops of their own, the most celebrated being STUART DEVLIN, who trained at the firm of T. Gaunt & Co. of Melbourne during the late 1940s and who later worked in England. There was, however, a great resurgence of interest in craft production from the 1960s. The influence of modern Scandinavian and German design was largely transmitted through the work of such immigrant makers as Helge Larsen and his Australian-born wife Darani Lewers (*see* LARSEN AND LEWERS), Ernest Fries (*b* 1934) and Wolf Wennrich (*b* 1922). This influence was strengthened by the arrival of silversmiths from Scandinavia and Germany during the 1970s and early 1980s, notably Ragnar Hansen (*b* 1945; e.g. silver and ebony teaset, 1982; Canberra N.G.), Frank Bauer (*b* 1942), Hendrik Forster (*b* 1947) and Johannes Kuhnen (*b* 1952; e.g. aluminium, gold and stainless steel tray, 1985; Canberra, N.G.). Along with the jewellers David Walker (*b* 1941) from England and Jeanne Keefer (*b* 1951) from the USA, all these craftsmen held teaching positions in the gold- and silversmithing departments of such institutions as Sydney College of Arts, Canberra School of Art and the Royal Melbourne Institute of Technology. Some of the most innovative jewellers in the 1980s, including MARGARET WEST, Robert Baines (*b* 1949) and Carlier Makigawa (*b* 1952), were graduates of these institutions.

In the late 20th century many jewellers worked almost exclusively with non-metallic materials, including local stones, twigs, feathers, rubber, glass, paper and ceramics. This approach also extended to hollow-ware, with such makers as Johannes Kuhnen and Susan Cohn (*b* 1952) using anodized aluminium. The extent of Cohn's production, which included brief-cases (e.g. of 1987; Canberra, N.G.), as well as hollow-ware and jewellery, is indicative of the many new directions that gold- and silversmiths trained in craft techniques were pursuing. The great diversity of styles in late 20th-century Australian metalwork reflects the broad spectrum of international trends, although incorporating aspects peculiar to the Australian culture.

There has never been an officially regulated system for marking gold and silver articles made in Australia. The type and number of marks used, if any, has been left to the discretion of the maker. Imitation British hallmarks are common, although marks depicting such local wildlife as the kangaroo and emu have also been popular from the early 19th century. The British sterling standard is usually indicated either by a lion passant, the inscription STERLING SILVER or an abbreviation thereof.

BIBLIOGRAPHY

K. Albrecht: *Nineteenth Century Australian Gold and Silver Smiths* (Richmond, Victoria, 1969)

J. B. Hawkins: *Australian Silver, 1800–1900*, National Trust of Australia, 2 vols (Sydney, 1973)

Treasures from Australian Churches (exh. cat. by J. O'Callaghan, Melbourne, N.G. Victoria, 1985)

Australian Jewellers: Kate Durham, Rowena Gough, Carlier Makigawa, Margaret West (exh. cat. by J. O'Callaghan, Melbourne, N.G. Victoria, 1988)

J. B. Hawkins: *Nineteenth Century Australian Silver*, 2 vols (Woodbridge, 1990)

A. Schofield and K. Fahy: *Australian Jewellery: 19th and Early 20th Century* (Woodbridge, 1991)

JUDITH O'CALLAGHAN

X. Textiles.

The Australian textile tradition has developed from being a direct European transplant to a state in which its scope and richness are a reflection of the country's cultural diversity, unique Aboriginal culture, native flora and fauna, and self-assurance as a nation.

1. TO 1900. In the early period of the colony the scarcity of professional needlewomen meant that amateur needlework skills were a necessity. Even the wealthiest

women were obliged to carry out plain sewing, in addition to the more genteel fancywork, in order to maintain wardrobes, furnishings and household goods. A range of techniques was used, including whitework, netting, lacemaking, tatting, crochet, patchwork and embroidery. The fabrics, tools and thread were all imported.

By the mid-19th century women had more money to buy labour-saving devices, including sewing-machines, and to hire servants. Growth in trade and local manufacturing meant that household linen, furnishings and clothing could be more readily purchased, and with increased leisure time the fancywork fashionable in Victorian England was eagerly taken up. Imported women's journals and newspapers provided the latest ideas, and instructions, materials and patterns were sold locally. A diverse range of work is recorded and has survived, much of it Berlin woolwork. Not all of this work was based on European patterns: with the developing sense of national identity women began to look to the indigenous flora for inspiration. In the mid-19th century a number of Tasmanian women were embroidering native wildflowers in silk, chenille and wool. By the end of the century Australian publications were giving embroidery instructions for a variety of native flora, fauna, birds and insects, mainly on such household furnishings as hangings, screens and curtains.

Patchwork, appliqué and embroidered quilts had been made since the earliest days of the colony, though never in large numbers. Some of the first quilts were those made by convict women on the transport ships, but only one, dated 1841, is known to survive. The majority of the 19th-century quilts were made by wealthier women and followed the English styles. By the end of the century quilt making was quite popular, and the designs, which included crazy patchwork, central medallions and all-over repeating patterns, reflected the influence of North American prototypes.

Exhibitions were vital to the development of textiles in Australia, as they provided a forum for recognizing achievement and effort, for comparison and for showing the work of the leading designers and makers. Several art and industrial exhibitions were held from the 1840s, but none could compare with the 1879 Sydney International Exhibition, in which a separate Ladies Court displayed a range of crochet, knitting, embroidery and patchwork.

2. 1900–1960. By the beginning of the 20th century textiles were recognized in Australia as a specific area of achievement and endeavour. Education ensured most women had basic needlework skills, and the many journals and pattern books offered further training and ideas. Embroidery of all types was by far the most popular craft, though lacemaking and its variants, as well as quilting, were relatively well established.

The influence of the Arts and Crafts Movement, and the strong desire among leading makers and designers to establish a national style, led to the formation of arts and crafts societies in several states. Tasmania was the first in 1903. These societies aimed to raise standards and to encourage the use of Australian flora and fauna in design. They were the foundation of the studio craft tradition and a vital catalyst in the development of professional practice.

Hitherto there had been little weaving, largely because of the availability of imported cloth, but under the influence of Suzanne Gether (*fl* 1890–1913) from Denmark and Jessica Booth (*d* 1969) from Scotland it became a well-established craft by the 1920s. Other textile techniques also emerged in the early decades of the 20th century, including batik, hand-stencilling, painting and printing.

The period between the world wars was marked by several new developments. Despite the Depression and the relatively small market, a number of individuals began to design and produce textiles in commercial quantities. A few screenprinting studios were established, notably Frances Burke Fabrics (Melbourne, est. 1937 as Burway Prints) and Annan (Sydney, 1941–54). These two produced distinctive, bold textiles inspired by native flora and Aboriginal art. Another important initiative was that of the Silk and Textile Printers (Sydney and Hobart, 1939–69), which in 1946 produced the Modernage range designed by such leading contemporary Australian artists as William Dobell, Russell Drysdale, Margaret Preston and Donald Friend. Weaving became more firmly established with the foundation of the first Handweavers and Spinners Guild (1947) and a number of professional enterprises. Eclarté (1940–62) in Melbourne produced handwoven tweeds in the colours of the Australian landscape for clothing and furnishing. At Sturt Workshops, New South Wales, the weaving studio (est. 1951) was run by professional weavers from Germany, who brought new techniques based on the Bauhaus tradition.

3. After 1960. By the 1960s there was a resurgence in textile crafts, influenced and aided by immigrant craftspeople, the crafts revival in Great Britain and North America, increased government support and improved training. Such weavers as Mona Hessing (*b* 1933) were inspired by the international Fibre Art movement and by the 1970s were producing monumental sculptural pieces that explored the textural and technical qualities of fibre and broke away from the utilitarian tradition.

In the 1970s the emphasis among weavers was on natural fibres and dyes and off-loom techniques. In the following decade there was a shift to new technologies, including computer-aided design and the creation of new synthetic materials, to produce limited runs of furnishing and clothing fabric. One-off works were still made, but usually on a smaller scale and with a decided trend towards figurative and embellished work, often combining several textile techniques.

In 1976 the Victorian Tapestry Workshop was established to provide training and facilities to make world-class tapestries. It continues to produce high-quality work, mainly for architectural commissions, using both specific tapestry designs and the work of contemporary Australian painters as a source. A major commission was the 20-m-wide landscape tapestry designed by Arthur Boyd for the Parliament House, Canberra.

By the 1980s training in embroidery was offered as part of textile courses. This encouraged much freer use of embroidery techniques, including machine embroidery, as part of the overall trend to more painterly surfaces. There was also a renewed interest in quilting, which led to a range of novel techniques, including airbrushing and resist-dyeing. The repertory of traditional designs was expanded to incorporate personal statements and Australian themes, sometimes of a political nature.

The re-evaluation of the country's textile heritage led to an upsurge in contemporary lacemaking arising out of the tradition of domestic lacemaking. Like the practitioners of such related fibre techniques as macramé, off-loom weaving and embroidery, lacemakers began to explore the expressive and narrative possibilities of the medium, using Australian motifs, variants of traditional patterns and imagery from personal experience. At the same period knitting became an innovative industry, using both hand- and machine-production to make garments with increasingly inventive construction as well as distinctive colour and imagery.

The development of knitting was closely related to the emergence in the 1970s of art clothing. The making of limited-edition garments encompassed the full range of textile techniques and encouraged a disregard of traditional boundaries of practice. One of the leading figures was Linda Jackson (*b* 1950), who worked initially in partnership with Jenny Kee. Jackson's tailoring expertise provided a sound basis for her use of appliqué and screenprinted, resist-dyed and painted fabrics to make original garments that defined an avant-garde Australian fashion. Like others, she used the unique imagery offered by the Australian environment.

Textile printing had a slow start, largely due to the dominance of imported fabrics, but in the 1970s it began to flourish. One of the most fruitful initiatives was the introduction of batik to the Aboriginal communities at Ernabella (South Australia) and Utopia (Northern Territory). The simplicity and expressiveness of the technique proved well suited to these communities, who have developed a unique style drawing directly from their artistic traditions. At the same time, screenprinting was introduced to the Tiwi Aboriginal community (Northern Territory) with equal success, followed in 1987 by batik.

As training in textile printing developed and the boundaries between art and craft became increasingly blurred, many with art training turned to textiles as a medium for expression. Throughout the 1980s there was increasing variety in methods of dyeing and printing, making possible a new painterly expressiveness in surface design. Furnishing and fashion textiles were made with multi-layered designs and deep, vibrant colours. Mambo (est. 1985) uses popular motifs that appeal to the youth culture (see fig. 22).

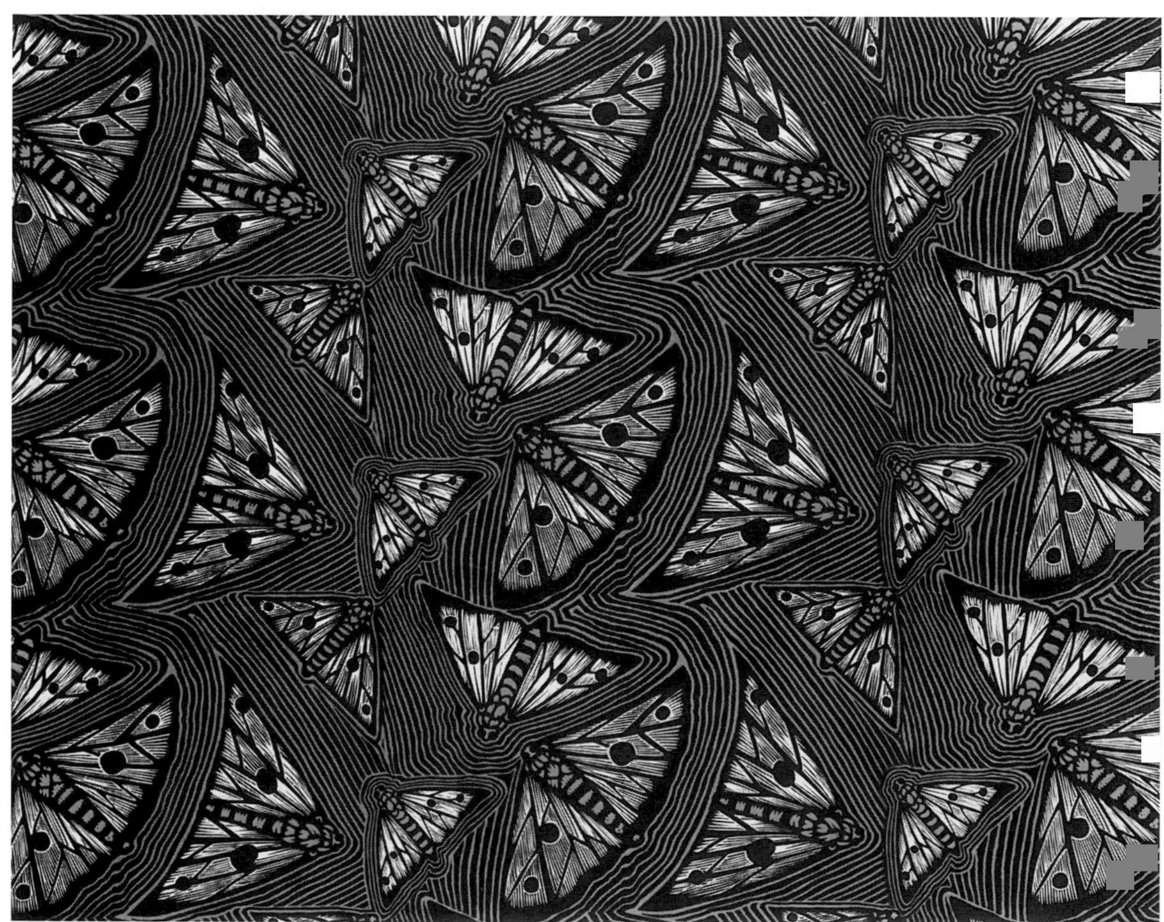

22. Textile length, *Bogong Moth* (detail), designed by Bruce Goold, screenprinted cotton, 1.50×4.14 m, made by Mambo Screenprinters for Mambo Graphics, 1990–91 (Sydney, Powerhouse Museum)

Australian textiles of the 1990s are distinguished by their strong colour and imagery inspired by the Australian environment and influenced by the cultural diversity of Australian society. Textiles are an acknowledged medium for expressing individual and community concerns, and a growing number of makers have succeeded in establishing viable small businesses.

BIBLIOGRAPHY

A New Approach to Textile Designing by a Group of Australian Artists, intro. by J. T. Burke (Sydney, 1947) [Modernage fabrics]

M. Betteridge: *Australian Flora in Art from the Museum of Applied Arts and Sciences* (Melbourne, 1979)

J. McPhee: *Australian Decorative Arts* (Canberra, 1982)

J. Isaacs: *The Gentle Arts: 200 Years of Australian Women's Domestic and Decorative Arts* (Sydney, 1987)

M. Rolfe: *Patchwork Quilts in Australia* (Richmond, Victoria, 1987)

Hearth & Home: Women's Decorative Arts & Crafts, 1800–1930, Historic Houses Trust of New South Wales (South Australia, 1988)

M. Fletcher: *Needlework in Australia: A History of the Development of Embroidery* (Melbourne, 1989)

Australian Fashion: The Contemporary Art (Sydney, 1989)

Decorative Arts and Design from the Powerhouse Museum (Sydney, 1991)

G. Cochrane: *The Crafts Movement in Australia: A History* (Sydney, 1992)

J. Sanders: 'Dress and Textiles', *The Age of Macquarie*, ed. J. Broadbent and J. Hughes (Melbourne, 1992)

JENNIFER SANDERS

XI. Patronage, collecting and dealing.

Patronage of the visual arts in Australia after European colonization was influenced by four principal factors: cultural life tended to favour literature and music over the visual arts; cultural institutions, almost without exception, resulted from legislation, not private patronage; Europe, and Britain in particular, provided the models for most art practice, theory and institutional organization; and most private patronage involved indirect assistance rather than the specific collection of art objects. The visual arts were first employed in Australia in the service of science and foreign markets; the botanical and zoological curiosities of Australia, for example, were recorded for such patrons as the Royal Society or rich subscribers. As a penal colony, Australia initially possessed neither the objects nor the class structure necessary for public or private support of the visual arts. Few early settlers had fine belongings, and the conspicuous consumption of luxuries did not become widespread until the gold-rushes of the 1850s. Only Tasmania, especially under the governorship (1836–43) of Sir John Franklin, developed a lively cultural centre that reflected contemporary cultured life in Britain. John Glover, the first migrant artist with an established British reputation, chose to settle in Tasmania in 1831. Some of his pictures sold in Australia, but they were primarily directed at the London 'view' market.

Early colonial work, including that done by European rather than British artists, usually conformed to the academic pictorial hierarchy, with the picturesque landscape becoming a vehicle for national identity. This conflicted with the intentions of Sir Redmond Barry, a judge of the Supreme Court of Victoria, who helped to establish Melbourne Public Library in 1854 and its art museum (later the National Gallery of Victoria) in 1861, based on the belief that art should be collected for the training of local artists and the improvement of public morals and education. The library bought everything mentioned in Edward Gibbon's *Decline and Fall of the Roman Empire* (1776–88), including plaster casts and samples of inferior academic genres. The label 'industrial baronial' fits much of the bric-à-brac and high art that private patrons purchased, either overseas from international exhibitions or from visiting dealers: Melbourne, despite its cultured European community, attempted to imitate a provincial city in Victorian Britain. In contrast, the principal gallery in Sydney, the Art Gallery of New South Wales (founded 1874), became known for its support of Australian art, due largely to the efforts of artist and teacher Julian Ashton. This reputation continued, especially as the National Gallery of Victoria began to concentrate on the acquisition of foreign art after 1904, when it received a large bequest from ALFRED FELTON that made it one of the richest galleries in the British Empire.

By the 1890s an institutional network of artist-run art societies offered sufficient exposure and credibility for Australian art to be widely collected. Federation of the states in 1901 and World War I fostered a sense of Australian identity, which remained a major force in collecting. Two groups, the Heidelberg school, active in Melbourne in the 1880s, and the graphic artists employed by the jingoistic magazine *The Bulletin* in Sydney in the 1880s–1920s, became popular Australian icons (*see* §III, 1 above). Nationalism also became an issue, fostered by the factions both for and against modernism in the 1930s and 1940s, and the Heidelberg school became central to the development of Australian art history. The artists George W. Lambert and Hans Heysen became cult figures cast in the Heidelberg tradition, which was continued in the late work of Arthur Streeton, and so they dominated the growing art market of the 1930s and 1940s.

Influential private collectors of the late 19th and early 20th centuries included the botanist and anthropologist Sir Baldwin Spencer and the shipping magnate Howard Hinton. Hinton was especially important because he was one of the few who donated works to public collections, notably the Art Gallery of New South Wales and Armidale City Art Gallery. Other major patrons were not primarily art collectors. J. F. Archibald (1856–1919), for example, who founded *The Bulletin*, donated the Archibald Fountain (1927, by François Sicard), Sydney, and endowed the Archibald Prize for portraits, which became a focus for fashionable artistic controversy. In 1939 the newspaper-owner Sir Keith Murdoch sponsored the Herald Show in Melbourne, then the most important survey of modern European art held in Australia, and in 1947 he funded the country's first chair of fine arts at the University of Melbourne. At Heide, near Melbourne, John Reed and Sunday Reed, who espoused figurative modernism, supported such artists as Sidney Nolan, the polemical magazine *Angry Penguins* (1941–6) and the Contemporary Art Society. Australia's most influential and versatile patron of the visual arts at this time, however, was the publisher Sydney Ure Smith (1887–1949). From 1916 to 1949 he published more material on Australian art than all other publishers combined, and he pioneered colour reproduction of art, for example in the periodical *Art in Australia* (1916–42) and in Bernard Smith's provocative book *Place, Taste and Tradition* (Sydney, 1945). Ure Smith's commercial art business, Smith & Julius, employed numerous painters, and in his role as President of the Society of Artists and a trustee of the Art Gallery of New South Wales, he championed moderately progressive local and foreign art, including photography and the graphic arts.

Between 1930 and 1950 the Australian art world experienced great upheavals that altered the nature of art patronage. Authority shifted from the artist to the art critic, historian, administrator, dealer and the interested public. Art was increasingly judged according to its style rather than its content. Artist-run societies were supplanted by private dealer galleries, for example the Macquarie Gallery in Sydney, so that by the 1960s such dealers as Rudy Komon, Brian Johnstone, JOSEPH BROWN (ii) and George Mora virtually controlled the art market. By underwriting artists' work, these dealers freed artists to paint full time. Art became an important financial commodity and carried more social cachet. While such individuals as Joseph Brown built important collections, few made them public; two exceptions were Mary Turner and Chandler Coventry, who gave collections to important regional galleries.

In the late 20th century patronage continued to be indirect and, in the private sector, to favour European culture and tertiary education, but the state galleries of South Australia and New South Wales showed growing interest in Asian art, and Aboriginal art became increasingly popular with serious collectors, particularly in the 1980s and after. The University of Sydney used its bequest (1962) from JOHN JOSEPH WARDELL POWER to build a department, library and important collection specializing in international contemporary art, and a foundation established with a legacy (1970) from the artist William Dobell endowed a chair of art history (1982) at the Australian National University, Canberra. It was Gough Whitlam's Federal Labor Government (1972–5), however, that instigated a remarkable cultural upsurge in Australia. The Australia Council was reconstructed, with boards for crafts, community and Aboriginal art as well as the traditional fine arts, and with a policy that ensured both direct and indirect funding. In 1973 work began on the new Australian National Gallery in Canberra, and during the 1970s tax incentives were introduced that encouraged corporations to collect for investment and public-image purposes—an approach adopted enthusiastically in the 1980s by such businessmen as Robert Holmes a'Court and Alan Bond. Federal government involvement in the arts continued in the 1980s, with the Parliament House Authority becoming Australia's largest and most diverse patron during construction of the new Parliament House (completed 1988) in Canberra. From adverse beginnings 200 years before, the arts had become one of Australia's largest and most widely based industries, and perhaps the principal vehicle for its national identity.

See also §XII below.

BIBLIOGRAPHY

E. Lindsay, ed.: *The Felton Bequest: An Historical Record, 1904–1959* (Melbourne, 1963)

D. Thomas: *Outlines of Australian Art: The Joseph Brown Collection* (Melbourne, 1973, rev. 2/1989)

B. Smith, ed.: *Documents on Art and Taste in Australia, 1788–1914* (Melbourne, 1975)

C. Lloyd and P. Sekuless: *Australia's National Collections* (Sydney, 1980)

U. Hoff: *The Felton Bequest* (Melbourne, 1983)

B. Murphy: 'The Whitlam Years', *Studio Int.*, cxcvi/1002 (1983), pp. 18–19

NANCY UNDERHILL

XII. Museums.

More than half a century passed after the beginning of Australian colonization in 1788 before any institutions functioning as a repository of art were established. The first seems to have been the Lady Franklin Museum, built in Hobart in 1842–3 at the instigation and personal expense of the wife of Sir John Franklin, Governor of Tasmania (1836–43), with the philanthropic aim of improving the cultural and intellectual life of the community; its holdings included a library and portraits of worthy individuals. These altruistic and didactic motives were typical of the foundation of art museums in the Australian colonies and help to explain their frequent association with libraries and scientific museums—a relationship subsequently relinquished in most regions.

Australia's first public museum specifically devoted to art (later the National Gallery of Victoria) was established in 1861 and its collection, initially of sculptural casts, occupied a room in Melbourne's Public Library (now the State Library of Victoria). Over the following decades, expanded by the acquisition of other, mainly British works, including paintings, it was progressively installed in newly built extensions; it was separated from the library in 1944 and ultimately moved in 1968 to a new building (by Roy Grounds) in the Victorian Arts Centre, Melbourne. Subsequent private endowments and bequests, especially that by Alfred Felton (*see* §XI above), helped to make the gallery pre-eminent in Australia; as the only art museum in Australia with its own art school, which was founded in 1870 and performed a vital role in art education (*see* §XIII below), it contributed greatly to the development of the Australian art profession.

The other colonies, partly spurred by inter-colonial rivalry, successively established art museums in their capital cities as well as in regional centres. The Art Gallery of New South Wales was founded in 1874, the Art Gallery of South Australia in 1881, and the Queensland Art Gallery and the Art Gallery of Western Australia in 1895. The first autonomous museum buildings were almost invariably in Neo-classical styles, such as the simple Doric temple (by James Barnet) commissioned by Lady Franklin for her museum in Hobart, and the porticoed Art Gallery of New South Wales (1885–1909, by W. L. Vernon), Sydney, which also has a modern extension. Other museums, according to political and economic considerations, have either prestigious new buildings, such as that (1982, by Robin Gibson) occupied by the Queensland Art Gallery in Brisbane, or more utilitarian structures, such as the building completed in Perth (1979, by Geoffrey Summerhayes) for the Art Gallery of Western Australia. The public buildings department of the Art Gallery of South Australia (1900) has been extended several times; from 1994 it has doubled in size in a major project (by Peddle Thorpe).

A national collection, initially of portraits, was begun in 1911 by the Commonwealth Government and developed from 1912 to 1972 under the supervision of the Commonwealth Art Advisory Board. This became the nucleus of holdings for the Australian National Gallery, which in

1982 moved into a monumental new building (by Edwards Madigan Torzillo & Briggs) in Canberra (now the National Gallery of Australia). Other art museums comprise buildings and their contents bequeathed as art museums by artists or patrons, for example the Norman Lindsay Gallery and Museum at Springwood, New South Wales, and Carrick Hill, Adelaide, comprising the estate and collection of Sir Edward Hayward (1903–83) and the first Lady Hayward (1907–70), eminent collectors. In some cases such museums are operated by the National Trust of Australia, in others by a separate trust or statutory body.

Among libraries holding collections of art works, the National Library of Australia in Canberra and the State Library of New South Wales in Sydney preserve and exhibit significant holdings of Australian works in independent divisions that are virtually autonomous art collections. Those in Sydney retain their separate identities as the Mitchell Library, the Dixson Library and the Dixson Gallery, named after their respective benefactors, David Scott Mitchell (1836–1907) and Sir William Dixson (1870–1952). The Australian War Memorial in Canberra also houses a large and important collection of Australian art, including major works dating from the 1880s. Although the collection was begun to commemorate the dead of World War I, its artistic scope was later extended to encompass all wars in which Australians participated and their social ramifications, latterly including anti-war campaigns. The War Memorial building was designed by Emil Sodersten in 1926–7 and opened in 1941, with extensions added in 1968–70.

In the 1960s and after, many art galleries were established by universities. The first such gallery had been founded at the University of Sydney with a collection of contemporary art bequeathed by JOHN JOSEPH WARDELL POWER in 1943. A further large monetary bequest received after the death of Power's wife (1962) enabled the university to establish the Power Institute of Fine Arts and the Power Gallery of Contemporary Art; the latter was incorporated into the autonomous Museum of Contemporary Art in 1989 and moved in 1992 to the former Maritime Services Building at Circular Quay, Sydney, made available by the state government. University art museums that function in conjunction with art-historical studies were inaugurated in Adelaide in 1966 with the foundation of what subsequently became the Art Museum at Flinders University of South Australia. The aim was to base teaching and research as much as possible on actual art works. This purpose was later emulated in other Australian universities, but most of these museums operate primarily as cultural amenities for the university community.

State and national art museums are directly or indirectly controlled and funded mainly by governments. In contrast, regional institutions, which began to be established in the 1880s and proliferated in the 1970s and 1980s, were usually inaugurated by private benefactors (e.g. Newcastle, NSW, Reg. A.G., 1956) or organized by bodies of public-spirited citizens (e.g. Ballarat, F.A. Gal., 1884). Some are private foundations administered by independent associations, while others are operated by local-government bodies. Non-profit-making private museums (e.g. Melbourne, Heide Park A.G., 1981) are generally assisted financially by grants from government sources. There is a growing tendency for governments to require museums to secure private-sector sponsorship for special projects, which is reflected in a corresponding increase in corporate patronage. The Australian government also supports the visual arts through its funding body, the Australia Council for the Arts, and through tax incentives to encourage private gifts to public collections, as well as by indemnifying the International Cultural Corporation of Australia to manage major touring exhibitions.

Display methods in Australian art museums tend to conform to European conventions, with contemporary developments being the result of fashion rather than a response to functional need. During the 1970s and 1980s there was a questionable antiquarian propensity for reviving 19th-century decorative schemes and display methods, including those earlier deprecated by artists and others. The result may have been to put art back into the archaic milieu of the museum, but attempts to present art in terms of its original historical context are few and rudimentary.

BIBLIOGRAPHY

L. B. Cox: *The National Gallery of Victoria, 1861 to 1968: A Search for a Collection* (Melbourne, [1970])

R. Smith: 'Australian Art Museums: A Historical View', *Proceedings of the Art Association of Australia Seminar on the Role and Constitution of Australian Art Museums: Adelaide, 1975*, pp. 33–9; also in *On Trusteeship*, ed. I. North (Adelaide, 1979)

C. Lloyd and P. Sekuless: *Australia's National Collections* (Sydney, 1980)

Australian National Gallery: An Introduction, Australian National Gallery (Canberra, 1982)

Australian Art Museums and Public Galleries Directory (Melbourne, 1994)

ROBERT SMITH

XIII. Art education.

After European settlement, art education in Australia was organized in three principal streams: private, professional and public. While varying greatly in size and in public impact, each has shared in the uneven but sustained growth of community interest in the visual arts that has been a feature of Australian cultural life for more than 200 years. Private instruction of amateur pupils has been conducted by artists since early colonial times. During the gold-rushes of the 1850s many artists, including S. T. Gill in Adelaide and William Strutt in Melbourne, found new pupils among the influx of migrants to the colonies. Such popular portrait painters as J. S. Watkins and J. Lawson Balfour taught in Sydney during the following decades, as did L. J. Harvey in Queensland, J. B. Mather in Adelaide, Lucien Dechaineux in Tasmania and J. R. Linton in Perth.

Professional training on the model of the French, German and especially British academies soon eclipsed private tuition when it was introduced at the National Gallery of Victoria Art School in 1870. For the next 50 years this school, led by Eugene von Guérard and then Bernard Hall (1859–1935), was challenged only by the atelier-style Académie Julian, established in Sydney in 1892 by the *plein air* painter JULIAN ROSSI ASHTON, who later founded the Sydney Art School (now Sydney College of the Arts). From 1916 the Melbourne tonal painter Max Meldrum created a school of followers unrivalled by any Australian artist. The introduction of modernist styles was heavily dependent on the influence of various artist-teachers, including Dattilo Rubbo, Roland Wakelin, Rah Fizelle (1891–1964), Dorrit Black and Grace Crowley

(1890–1979) in Sydney, and George Bell, Arnold Shore (1897–1963) and Jock Frater in Melbourne.

Sculpture was professionally taught by Rayner Hoff in the 1920s and 1930s at East Sydney Technical College, as it was by Vincas Jomantas (*b* 1912), Kevin Mortensen and others at the Royal Melbourne Institute of Technology in the 1960s. In 1947 the University of Melbourne established the country's first chair of fine arts, and art history and theory schools proliferated in universities in the 1960s. During that decade state governments incorporated professional training into colleges of advanced education, leading to the constant relocation of art schools as the national education system underwent successive reforms, culminating in their amalgamation into universities during the 1980s. This led to an increase in the availability of professional training and to a general uniformity of standards. It also provoked much unrest among staff and students, as well as experimental modes of learning, such as the mix of studio and theoretical studies at Sydney College of the Arts, created in 1975.

Before the establishment of an official state education system, public education in art formed part of the general education initiatives taken by the colonial authorities. The first of these was the founding of the Van Dieman's Land Mechanics School of Art (1826) in Hobart, where, for 63 years, working men were instructed in reading, writing and drawing; Benjamin Duterrau delivered the first public lecture on art there in 1833. The Sydney Mechanics School of Art was set up in 1843 and the School of Arts, Adelaide, in 1856. State education in art evolved through three broad phases. In the 1840s, in Sydney, Joseph Fowles introduced the South Kensington Department of Science and Art model of advancing the design skills of the artisan and clerical classes by sustained copying of basic shapes and simple natural forms. This 'art as technical drawing' system was introduced to all schools in the 1890s by Frederick Woodhouse, and it remained dominant in most states for 100 years, despite the growing knowledge of such alternative systems as Franz Cižek's child-centred art and Herbert Read's 'education through art'. Leading experimental teachers in Australia included Frances Derham in Victoria and May Marsden in Sydney. From the 1950s the concept of creativity entered the school syllabus and began to predominate in primary and secondary schooling, although augmented by the persistence of discipline-based learning and a greater stress on the social context of art. Exceptions to these trends are important. The Tin Sheds Art Workshop at the University of Sydney, for example, was a centre for critical and experimental art education in popular media for students from all over the city after 1968, and the Flying Art School, set up in 1971 by painter Mervyn Moriarty, conducted classes in various centres in the remote outback of Queensland and the Northern Territory.

Architectural education in the 19th century was dominated by outstanding individuals who taught by example but created few successors. Technical drawing was taught from 1865 at the Sydney Mechanics School of Art, and the first professional course was taught there in 1878, becoming the country's first four-year diploma course in 1890. Professional associations were established in the colonies—the first being the Victorian Institute of Architects in 1871—partly to regulate and oversee architectural training, and this role continued after their affiliation into the Royal Australian Institute of Architects in 1930. After 1900 architectural education was dominated by universities. Melbourne offered a diploma in 1906, Sydney appointed Leslie Wilkinson as Australia's first professor of architecture in 1918, and Adelaide introduced a degree in architectural engineering in 1919 following the initiative of Louis Laybourne Smith at the Adelaide School of Mines. After World War II, when the demand for architects increased, the University of Queensland began courses (1949), and the New South Wales Institute (now University) of Technology took over the courses of the Sydney Technical College. Leading architects continued to teach by example, in their offices and as visitors to tertiary schools. Others taught through public debate, most notably Robin Boyd, who produced several popular and influential books.

BIBLIOGRAPHY

B. Smith, ed.: *Education through Art in Australia* (Melbourne, 1958)

M. B. Lewis: *The Development of Architectural Teaching in the University of Melbourne* (Melbourne, 1970)

J. M. Freeland: *The Making of a Profession* (Sydney, 1971)

National Seminar on Art Education and Art Teacher Education. Visual Arts Board of the Australia Council: Sydney, 1974

G. Parr: *Tertiary Visual Arts Education in Australia: A Report to the Visual Arts Board of the Australia Council* (Sydney, 1980)

P. Johnson: 'Leslie Wilkinson at Sydney University', *Leslie Wilkinson: A Practical Idealist*, ed. M. Dupain (Sydney, 1982)

L. Mandelson: 'From Drawing to Art in Australian State Primary Schools', *J. Inst. A. Educ.*, ix/1 (1985), pp. 35–45

L. Broughton, G. Burrows and E. Lada: *A Place for Art: A Century of Art, Craft, Design and Industrial Arts Education in Hobart* (exh. cat., Hobart, U. Tasmania, Cent. A., Gal., 1988)

D. Boughton: 'The Changing Face of Australian Art Education: New Horizons or Sub-cultural Politics?', *Stud. A. Educ.*, xxx/4 (1989), pp. 197–211 [special issue, ed. G. Sullivan: 'Australian Art Education']

G. Hammond, ed.: 'Historical Research in Art Education', *Austral. A. Educ.*, xv/1 (1991)

N. Weston: *The Professional Education of Artists, 1863–1963, with Special Reference to the South Australian Model* (diss., U. Adelaide, 1992)

TERRY SMITH

XIV. Art libraries and photographic collections.

Australian art libraries had their beginnings in the 1820s–1840s with small collections attached to mechanics' institutes and the first schools of art, as well as in the state libraries founded in the 1850s and state galleries founded before 1900 (*see* §§XII and XIII above). The first survey of subject strengths (see Tauber) found no great research collections. The main collections in the fine arts, particularly Oriental art, are in the State Library of Victoria, the first to staff full-time a separately housed arts collection; this also served the National Gallery of Victoria and its art school, which shared the same building until 1968. Other important collections for research into Australian art are held in the Mitchell Library, Sydney, and the National Library of Australia, Canberra. The Queensland State Library, Brisbane, has among its holdings an Australian art library donated by James Hardy Pty Ltd. From the 1960s significant library resources were developed in universities as more art history courses were established, and the University of Sydney developed an art library with part of its bequest (1962) from John Joseph Wardell

Power. At the same time library resources were extended into new colleges of art, and staffing of state gallery libraries increased. The Australia Council's library (founded 1975) provided considerable support to arts organizations, including the Art Libraries Society, Australia and New Zealand Branch (ARLIS/ANZ), formed in Victoria in 1975. Of galleries that opened in the 1980s, the Australian National Gallery in Canberra and the Museum of Contemporary Art in Sydney both have fast-growing specialist libraries. There is no outstanding photographic archive for the study of world art in Australia, but the national and state libraries collect Australian primary sources, including historical paintings, prints and photographs. New electronic technology is providing wider access.

UNPUBLISHED SOURCES

Canberra, N. Lib. [M. Tauber: *Resources in Australian Libraries* (1962), iv, pp. 75–9]

Canberra, Churchill House Lib. [J. McGrath: *Report on a Tour of Art and Music Libraries* (1968), pp. 10–14]

BIBLIOGRAPHY

C. Downer: 'The Role of ARLIS in the Growth of Art Library Networks in the United Kingdom, the United States and Australia', *ARLIS/ANZ News*, 4 (1978), pp. 17–28

J. Viaux: *IFLA Directory of Art Libraries* (New York, 1985)

J. Volker: 'In the Twinkling of an Eye: Managing Change in Visual Arts Libraries', *ARLIS/ANZ News*, 39 (1994)

JOYCE MCGRATH

Australian Aboriginal art. *See* ABORIGINAL AUSTRALIA.

Australian Impressionism. *See* HEIDELBERG SCHOOL.

Austral Islands [Tubuai Islands]. Archipelago, including the islands of Rurutu and Raivavaé, in the south-west Pacific (*see also* RAPA). The Austral Islands are part of French Polynesia, of which the capital is Papeete on Tahiti in the Society Islands. Although colonization did not begin until the London Missionary Society established a hold in the 1820s, conversion to Christianity was fast and much of the traditional culture, including material culture, was destroyed. At the same time diseases and epidemics brought by the colonists caused population numbers to plummet. Thus little survives today of what was evidently once an exceptionally rich and highly skilled artistic culture. Indeed, it has become increasingly apparent that many of the finest art objects from central Polynesia originated in the Austral Islands. This makes the lack of a continuing tradition and of significant historical documentation even more unfortunate. Some archaeological research has been carried out especially at the *marae*, or religious centres, on Ra'vavaé (see Skjölsvold). The traditional art forms of the Austral Islands include bark cloth, wood-carving, stone sculpture and objects for personal adornment. Substantial collections are held by the Peabody Museum, Salem, MA, and the British Museum, London, while many other collections with Polynesian material include pieces from the Austral Islands.

As on other Polynesian islands, bark cloth (*tapa*) was used for clothing, death shrouds, blankets and bedding. The Peabody Museum has well-documented pieces collected by Martin Brunor in the 1960s. From the 1930s most of the mallets or beaters used to make *tapa* were destroyed as firewood or used as handles for tools, but many of those that survived were collected by Brunor for the Peabody Museum. In interviews with the last of those who made bark cloth Brunor was able to record the methods used.

Shell jewellery and necklaces were produced on the islands, but it has been difficult to establish the provenance of many pieces both because of their similarity to those

Austral Islands figure of A'a, wood, h. 1.17 m, from Rurutu, before 1821 (London, British Museum)

from other Polynesian islands and because of the lack of documentation made at the time of collection. Necklaces and breast ornaments were made from pearl shells combined with string fashioned from human hair and strings of shell ornament. Shells were also used in Rurutu to decorate grass skirts and as earrings. Because of their thin texture, giant clam (Pahua) shells were used for ornamentation, as were the tiny shells of the white-, black-, yellow- and red-striped Pupu or Hawaiian Pikaki land snails, which can be strung like pearls. In the late 20th century necklaces are made with plastic imitation shells for sale to tourists. Shell was also used as decoration on fish-hooks.

The wooden paddles of the Austral Islands bear distinctive carved ornamentation. The shapes of the staffs are usually based on the human form, with head-like protrusions, hair styles and limbs. It is thought that the paddles were used only on ceremonial occasions, as they are too fragile for practical use. Until the arrival of the missionaries in the 1820s, ceremonial drums were also intricately carved. Wooden bowls and ladles show evidence of the same skill in carving. A few wooden weapons and spearheads have survived, featuring decorative carvings similar to those on the paddles.

The imagery of Austral Islands carving and sculpture is little understood. A highly crafted wooden figure of the god A'a from Rurutu, taken by missionaries in 1821 as a trophy (London, BM), is a case in point. The main part is covered with small human figures in relief (see fig.), and a central cavity at the back once contained small figures, but the figure's use and significance remain matters of speculation. Of the few stone images that have survived, the Pitt Rivers Museum has a female figure of a god from Raivavaé well documented.

For general discussion of the art and architecture of the region *see also* PACIFIC ISLANDS.

BIBLIOGRAPHY

J. M. Brown: 'Raivvavaé and its Statues', *J. Polynes. Soc.*, xxvii/106 (1918), pp. 72–7

H. U. Hall: 'Wood Carvings of the Austral Islands', *Mus. J.*, xii (1921), pp. 179–99

K. Scoresby Routledge and W. Scoresby Routledge: 'Notes on Some Archaeological Remains in the Society and Austral Islands', *J. Royal Anthropol. Inst. GB & Ireland*, li (1921), pp. 438–55

R. T. Aitken: *Ethnology of Tubai*, Bishop Mus. Bull., 70 (Honolulu, 1930/*R* 1971)

E. S. Dodge: 'Austral Islands Tapa', *J. Polynes. Soc.*, l (1941), pp. 107–13

M. Urbain: 'Note sur les pagaies sculptées des îles Tubai', *J. Soc. Océanistes*, iii (1947), pp. 113–18

A. Skjölsvold: 'The Ceremonial Enclosure of Te Rae Rae with Brief Notes on Additional Marae (Raivavae Island, Report 7)', *Miscellaneous Papers*, Monographs of the School of American Research and the Kon-Tiki Museum, xxiv/2 (Stockholm, 1965), ii of *Reports of the Norwegian Archaeological Expedition to Easter Island and the East Pacific*, ed. T. Heyerdahl and E. N. Ferdon, jr (London, then Stockholm, 1961–5), pp. 97–107, pls. 25–34

Arts and Crafts of the Austral Islands (exh. cat. by M. A. Brunor; Salem, MA, Peabody Essex Mus., 1968–9)

P. Vérin: *L'Ancienne Civilisation de Rurutu (Iles australes, Polynésie française): La Période classique* (Paris, 1969)

S. Phelps: *Art and Artefacts of the Pacific, Africa and the Americas: The James Hooper Collection* (London, 1976), pp. 143–53

T. Barrow: *The Art of Tahiti and the Neighbouring Society, Austral and Cook Islands*, Tribal A. (London, 1979)

The Art of the Pacific Islands (exh. cat. by D. Newton, A. L. Kaeppler and P. Gathercole, Washington, DC, N.G.A., 1979), pp. 90, 155–62

L. Hanson and F. A. Hanson: *The Art of Oceania: A Bibliography*, Ref. Pubns A. Hist. (Boston, MA, 1984)

TAMARA LUCAS, JEREMY COOTE

Austria, Federal Republic of [Österreich]. Central European country, bordered by Germany, the Czech Republic, Hungary, Slovenia, Italy, Liechtenstein and Switzerland. It is divided into nine provinces: Styria, Tyrol, Salzburg, Vorarlberg, Upper Austria, Lower Austria, Vienna, Burgenland and Carinthia. The country is landlocked and is characterized geographically by its mountainous landscape. Its population is concentrated mainly in the river valleys, especially along the River Danube and its surrounding plains, with the most important centres developing at the junctions of major north–south routes with those running from east to west, for example at Salzburg, Innsbruck, Linz, Graz and the capital, Vienna (see fig. 1). There is evidence of human activity from Paleolithic and Neolithic times (*see* PREHISTORIC EUROPE, §§II and IV) and of Celtic settlements at DÜRRNBERG, Salzburg and HALLSTATT in the last centuries BC (*see also* PREHISTORIC EUROPE, §§V and VI), before the area was colonized by the Romans in the first century AD. This article concentrates on art in Austria from the Early Christian period to the present.

I. Introduction. II. Architecture. III. Painting and graphic arts. IV. Sculpture. V. Interior decoration. VI. Furniture. VII. Ceramics. VIII. Glass. IX. Metalwork. X. Gold boxes. XI. Textiles. XII. Patronage. XIII. Collecting and dealing. XIV. Museums. XV. Art education. XVI. Art libraries and photographic collections. XVII. Historiography.

DETAILED TABLE OF CONTENTS

I. Introduction.

Because of its geographical position at the heart of Europe, Austria has acted for much of its history as a mediator not only between the classical Italian world and the Romantic Germanic culture but also between the Latin countries, especially France, and the eastern Slavic, Hungarian and Turkish cultures. Because of the common language of the two countries, however, it was Germany that exerted the most significant influence. Many of the most important artists active in Austria came from other countries, including not only Germany but also Italy and elsewhere, and many of these gradually adopted an Austrian identity.

In the 4th century, successive waves of Germanic and Hunnish invaders overran the region, bringing Roman control to an end. Further invasions by Slavs, Avars and Magyars followed in the next centuries (*see* MIGRATION PERIOD), although there was enough stability for some important centres to be established. In the 8th century there was a brief period of Frankish rule under Charlemagne, and there was a significant church-building programme instigated by St Boniface, who established bishoprics in the region (*see* CAROLINGIAN ART), most notably at Salzburg. Magyar incursions from the east continued, however, until the Battle of Lechfeld in 955, when Otto I (*reg* 936–73; later Holy Roman Emperor) established the region as a dependency of the dukes of Bavaria (*see* OTTONIAN ART).

This laid the foundation for the first Austrian dynasty, the House of Babenberg, which ruled from 976 to 1246 and whose important position within the Holy Roman Empire allowed it to play an important role in the development of art in Austria. During this period Salzburg in particular was an important centre for High and Late Romanesque art (*see* ROMANESQUE, §§II, 2 and III, 1(ix)(e)) and was also distinguished for its own local school of painting. The Babenberg dukes also promoted development of the eastern parts of the country and patronized the expansion of the monastic orders, most notably the Cistercians and Benedictines.

After 30 years of rule by Ottakar II of Bohemia, in 1276 control of the region fell to the Habsburg family when Ottakar was defeated at the Battle of Marchfeld. The Habsburgs ruled Austria until 1918, making it the centre of a vast empire that included, from the 16th century, Istria (now in Croatia), Bohemia (now in the Czech Republic) and Hungary. The Habsburgs continued the tendency of the Babenbergs to encourage a diversity of artistic influences, with the bishoprics, the court, the monastic orders and urban culture all stimulating development in the arts in different ways.

In the 15th and 16th centuries the authority of the ruling Habsburgs was threatened on numerous occasions; one notable instance came in 1529, when the Turks laid siege to Vienna before being repulsed. Such political uncertainties during these centuries led paradoxically to a strengthening of the dynasty's artistic ambitions, with Frederick III (*reg* 1440–93) and Rudolf II (*reg* 1576–1612) supporting both contemporary artistic currents and, for ideological reasons, antiquarian or traditionalist interests. In the 16th and 17th centuries some parts of Austria embraced Protestantism, leading to the Thirty Years War (1618–48), after which the Roman Catholic ascendancy was reasserted in the wake of the Counter-Reformation. This prompted a period of intense building activity, especially in Vienna, and the rise of the Baroque in Austria is closely linked to the Counter-Reformation, although continued Turkish threats in the east of the country impeded its progress there; the new style only reached its full flowering—principally in court and monastic art—after the relief of the second siege of Vienna in 1683.

In the late 18th century, under the Holy Roman emperors Joseph II (*reg* 1780–90) and Leopold II (*reg* 1790–92), Vienna became the focus for Austrian cultural life (*see* VIENNA, §II, 2 and 3). After the demise in 1806 of the Holy Roman Empire, Francis I became Emperor of Austria. In 1805 and 1809 Vienna was

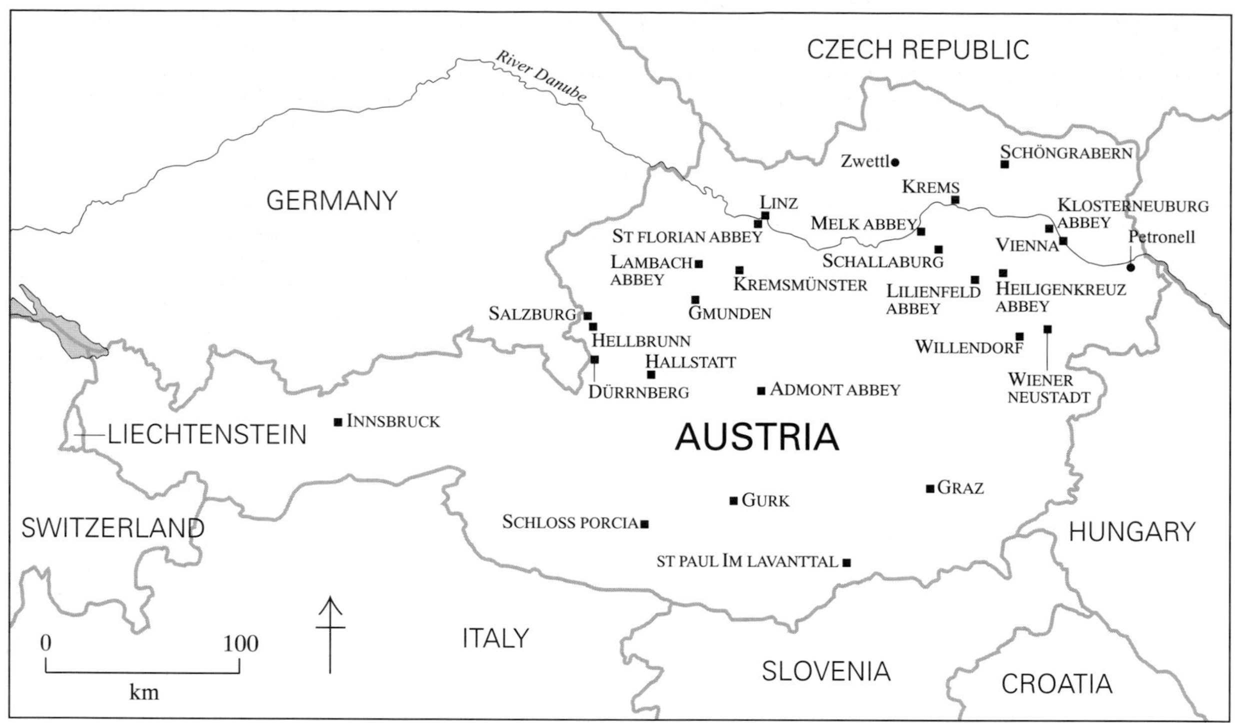

1. Map of Austria; those sites with separate entries in this dictionary are distinguished by CROSS-REFERENCE TYPE

occupied by Napoleon, but, although the Austrians helped towards his overthrow, successive political crises weakened Habsburg power. Nevertheless, the early 19th century was a particularly important period for the development of painting in Austria. In 1867 the Austrian empire was converted into the dual monarchy of Austro-Hungary. Such projects as the development of the Ringstrasse in Vienna constituted not only a brief attempt to create for the first time a national (rather than an imperial) style through the revival of earlier characteristic forms but also the last important union of imperial and bourgeois artistic influences. In the last decade of the 19th century, the development of the *Jugendstil*, a Viennese response to Art Nouveau, led to the founding of the Secession movement in 1897. The artists associated with the early years of the Vienna Secession, such as the painters Gustav Klimt and Egon Schiele and the architects Joseph Maria Olbrich, Adolf Loos and Josef Hoffmann, were highly innovative and influential. Later, however, the Secession became associated with a conservative version of modernism, for which it was criticized. After World War I and the demise of the Habsburg dynasty, Austria was proclaimed an independent republic. In 1938 the country was annexed by Germany, but after World War II it was again declared independent.

BIBLIOGRAPHY

Österreichische Kunsttopographie (Vienna, 1907–)

Reclams Kunstführer: Österreich, 2 vols (Stuttgart, 1961, rev. 1981)

R. Feuchtmüller: *Kunst in Österreich*, 2 vols (Vienna, 1972–3)

R. Wagner-Rieger: *Deutschland und Österreich: Bildende Kunst* (Vienna and Munich, 1980)

I. Robertson: *Austria*, Blue Guide (London, 1985)

Vienna, 1900: Art, Architecture and Design (exh. cat., ed. K. Varnedoe; New York, MOMA, 1986)

WALTER KRAUSE

II. Architecture.

1. Before *c.* 1500: Early Christian and medieval. 2. *c.* 1500–*c.* 1600: Renaissance. 3. *c.* 1600–*c.* 1750: The rise of the Baroque. 4. *c.* 1750–*c.* 1890: From Baroque classicism to Historicism. 5. After *c.* 1890: Modernism and beyond.

1. BEFORE *c.* 1500: EARLY CHRISTIAN AND MEDIEVAL. The first references to Christianity in the Austrian Danube region occur in the *Vita Sancti Severini* (Life of St Severinus), written by Eugrippius in the late 5th century. Religious buildings from this period have been excavated in Lorch and Mautern and take the form of simple apsidal halls or rectangular churches with a semicircular priest's bench. Early Christian churches in the Alpine region had a more intricate structure, for example the cruciform cemetery church at Teurnia (Carinthia), which is decorated with mosaics, or the cathedrals at Aguntum (East Tyrol) and Saeben (South Tyrol). A typical 5th-century group of churches, consisting of four religious buildings, was established on the Hemmaberg in Carinthia.

Of the Bavarian bishoprics created by St Boniface in 739, Salzburg soon achieved great prestige. The Abbot, Bishop Virgil, built a cathedral (destr.) of monumental proportions, which was dedicated in 774: the aisled church had no transepts, but an atrium and baptistery were built in front of the west end. The monastery (destr.) at Mondsee was founded between 739 and 748 by Otilo, Duke of Bavaria (*reg* 737–48); late 20th-century excavations have revealed that it was constructed among Roman buildings that had probably been assigned by the Duke to the foundation's estate. At LINZ excavations on the castle hill revealed a centrally planned church with a square core, a rounded ambulatory and three apses; this is the Carolingian Martinskirche, first mentioned in 799, which was probably founded during the campaign against the Avars. Reconstruction of the ransacked 8th-century churches in the east of Austria did not begin until the invading Magyars had been defeated at the Battle of Lechfeld (955), when the border was restored; an example of such a church is the cruciform St Ulrichskirche in Wieselburg, founded by St Wolfgang in 979. Austrian parish churches were built mainly of timber until the late 11th century, when Bishop Altmann of Passau instigated the building of a large number of stone churches. Monastic buildings from this period, such as the new Benedictine abbey church (ded. 1082) at Kremsmünster with an aisled nave, a tower flanking the choir and a Galilee (*see* KREMSMÜNSTER, §1), were influenced by the reform movements at Cluny and Gorze.

From the 12th century ecclesiastical politics led to considerable rivalry among the secular rulers in the Danube area (the margraves, later dukes, of Austria), the ecclesiastical metropolis of Salzburg and the bishopric of Passau (which extended along the Danube). This resulted in fierce competition in building ostentatious churches. In 1114 Leopold III, Margrave of Austria (*reg* 1096–1136), founded Klosterneuburg Abbey, near Vienna. The abbey church (consecrated 1136) was built of ashlar masonry with a crossing tower, transepts and a prince's gallery. In 1135 Leopold invited the first Cistercians to Austria and founded HEILIGENKREUZ ABBEY (consecrated 1187), which included a basilica with transverse rib-vaulting in the nave vaults and groin vaulting in the aisles. At Salzburg, Cardinal Archbishop Konrad II replaced Bishop Virgil's 8th-century cathedral with a Late Romanesque building that was important both for its size (122×48 m) and architectural quality; the building was destroyed by fire in 1598, and only the foundations and remnants of the exquisite sculptural works have survived. The archbishopric of Salzburg also extended its possessions in the Alps: Gurk became a bishopric in its own right, and the Late Romanesque cathedral there, which included a hall-crypt with 96 columns, was dedicated in 1174 (*see* GURK, §1(i) and fig.). The archbishops of Salzburg also built themselves an imposing residence in Friesach. The bishops of Passau were responsible for the rebuilding in 1150 and 1228 of St Pölten Abbey Church, using Late Romanesque and Early Gothic building forms. Kremsmünster Abbey Church was also reconstructed from 1232 to include a polygonal apse that resembled the one at Bamberg Cathedral. The Stephanskirche (from 1469 the Stephansdom) in Vienna also came under the bishopric of Passau, and *c.* 1237 it was enlarged in a Late Romanesque style, with Romanesque ornamentation that may have been influenced personally by Frederick II, Holy Roman Emperor (*see* VIENNA, §II, 1).

In the 13th century the ducal residence at Klosterneuburg attained the height of its cultural importance in the reign of Leopold VI, Duke of Austria (*reg* 1198–1230). A palace was built there with a lavishly furnished *capella speciosa* in accordance with contemporary French Gothic forms. At the Cistercian church at Lilienfeld, endowed by Leopold VI, the experimental use of new types of spatial arrangements is evident in the hall choir (*see* LILIENFELD ABBEY). The short reign in Austria of Ottakar II, King of Bohemia, in the second half of the 13th century, was marked by more organized urban planning, an increase in building by the mendicant orders and the development of specialized spatial forms, such as hall churches with two and three aisles or longer choirs. New architectural ideas developed more fully, however, from 1276 under the patronage of the Habsburgs; examples include the hall choir at Heiligenkreuz (ded. 1295), the hall church at Neuberg (begun 1327) and the hall choir with radiating chapels at the Cistercian monastery of Zwettl (begun 1342; see fig. 2). In addition, the Stephanskirche in Vienna was given a tiered hall choir (1304–40). Rudolf IV, Duke of Austria, wanted to set up a bishopric of his own in Vienna, independent of Passau, and he therefore had the Stephanskirche magnificently extended, competing with the cathedral building undertaken by his father-in-law, the Holy Roman Emperor Charles IV, in Prague. Of the overall plan, however, only the nave and the south tower were fully realized.

Around 1400 Late Gothic was introduced into Austrian architecture, characterized by lavish towers with ornate sculpture, and by chapels built as shrines with rich tracery decoration and stained-glass windows. In the 15th century a Late Gothic style specific to court architecture developed in the residences of the Habsburg Emperor Frederick III

2. Church of the Cistercian monastery at Zwettl, Austria, begun 1159, showing east end with radiating chapels (begun 1342)

at Graz, WIENER NEUSTADT and Vienna; its most prominent exponent was PETER VON PUSICA. This style refers to earlier forms, such as Early Gothic vaulting and the rounded arch. In the 15th century there was a rich, late flowering of imaginative net and stellar rib-vaulting in the architecture of country churches; as in Bohemia, curvilinear lierne patterns for vaults (e.g. Königswiesen, Göss) and branch-like forms for tracery (e.g. Eisenerz) were used in the Austrian Danube and Alpine regions. In the early 16th century individual architects began to develop personal styles, as can be seen in the work of ANTON PILGRAM, who was in charge of the masons' lodge at the Stephansdom (e.g. the ornate pulpit of the Stephansdom, *c.* 1510).

BIBLIOGRAPHY

D. Frey: *Die Denkmale des Stiftes Heiligenkreuz*, Österreichische Kunsttopographie, xix (Vienna, 1926)

R. K. Donin: *Die Bettelordenskirchen in Österreich*, Zur Entwicklungsgeschichte der österreichischen Gotik (Baden, 1935)

P. Buberl: *Die Kunstdenkmäler des Zisterzienserklosters Zwettl*, Ostmärkische Kunsttopographie, xxix (Baden, 1940)

W. Buchowiecki: *Die gotischen Kirchen Österreichs* (Vienna, 1952)

S. Hartwagner: *Der Dom zu Gurk* (Klagenfurt, Vienna and Frankfurt am Main, 1963)

R. Wagner-Rieger: 'Die Bautätigkeit Kaiser Friedrichs III.', *Wien. Jb. Kstgesch.*, xxv (1972), p. 128

H. Vetters: 'Die mittelalterlichen Dome in archäologischer Sicht', *1200 Jahre Dom zu Salzburg, 774–1974* (Salzburg, 1974), pp. 73–82

M. Schwarz: *Studien zur Klosterbaukunst in Österreich unter den letzten Babenbergern* (diss., U. Vienna, 1981)

H. Ubl: 'Frühchristliches Österreich', *Severin zwischen Römerzeit und Völkerwanderung* (exh. cat., ed. K. Pömer and D. Straub; Enns, Mus. Lauriacum, 1982), pp. 295–336

M. Schwarz: 'Die Architektur der mittelalterlichen Klosterkirche', *Dom und Stift St Pölten und ihre Kunstschätze* (St Pölten and Vienna, 1985), pp. 50–70

B. Rittinger: 'Die karolingische Martinskirche von Linz', *Kstjb. Stadt Linz* (1986), pp. 26–37

R. Wagner-Rieger: *Mittelalterliche Architektur in Österreich* (St Pölten and Vienna, 1988)

MARIO SCHWARZ

2. *c.* 1500–*c.* 1600: RENAISSANCE.

(i) Secular. Although the Late Gothic style persisted until *c.* 1520, at the end of the 15th century a humanist tendency began to develop with Renaissance influences being introduced from Italy, for example in the design of a portal (1495–7) of the Grosser Federlhof and the Hasenhaus (begun 1508; destr.), both in Vienna, in which the decorative Renaissance style from Lombardy and Venice was adopted and transformed. These influences took hold from the second quarter of the 16th century through the activities of the imperial Habsburg court. In 1521 the Holy Roman Emperor Charles V handed control of the eastern Austrian regions to his brother Ferdinand (later Emperor Ferdinand I), who had been educated in Spain. Ferdinand's Spanish chancellor and treasurer, Gabriel of Salamanca, and the widely educated court antiquary Jacopo Strada from Mantua not only passed on their knowledge of Italian architectural treatises, particularly those of Sebastiano Serlio and Andrea Palladio, but also introduced into Austria a large number of master masons chiefly from northern Italy. With their greater knowledge and direct experience of the new architecture, they soon displaced the indigenous masons, who clung to the Gothic style. Among the first imperial projects to display the new influences was the armoury in Wiener Neustadt, of which a portal (1524) survives, in a delicate, decorative early Renaissance style. More radically innovative, however, was the extensive rebuilding (1533–68) of the medieval Hofburg in Vienna, which reveals an increasing use of forms inspired by Italian architectural treatises, although modified to create a building that was strikingly sober, cubic and compact (*see* VIENNA, §V, 5(i)). The initial work of this style at the Hofburg is the Schweizertrakt with the Schweizertor (1552–3; see fig. 3): its classical appearance with massive rusticated forms derives from Serlio's treatises, which it interprets for the first time in central Europe. Such classicism later exerted a formative influence on the architecture of central Europe in the 17th century.

From 1558 Ferdinand had the Stallburg (stables) built at the Hofburg for his son Maximilian (later Emperor Maximilian II). These take the form of a massive cube articulated by horizontal bands, with an arcaded three-storey courtyard, and they constitute the first use north of the Alps of the modern form of the columnar arcade, while retaining the sobriety typical of imperial buildings in Vienna. This approach is still more evident in the Amalienburg (1575–7), built by Archduke Rudolf (later Emperor Rudolf II), with its rusticated façade and imposing central tower. From 1569 Emperor Maximilian II had a large pleasure palace, the Schloss Neugebäude (now altered; see fig. 4), built outside the gates of Vienna. This imposing structure, with terraces, towers, gardens, pools and fountains, was not intended as a residence but to accommodate the emperor's extensive collections of art and natural objects (*see* HABSBURG, §I(8)). The scheme was unique north of the Alps in terms both of its use and size, and it was much admired by contemporaries. It

3. Schweizertor, Hofburg, Vienna, 1552–3

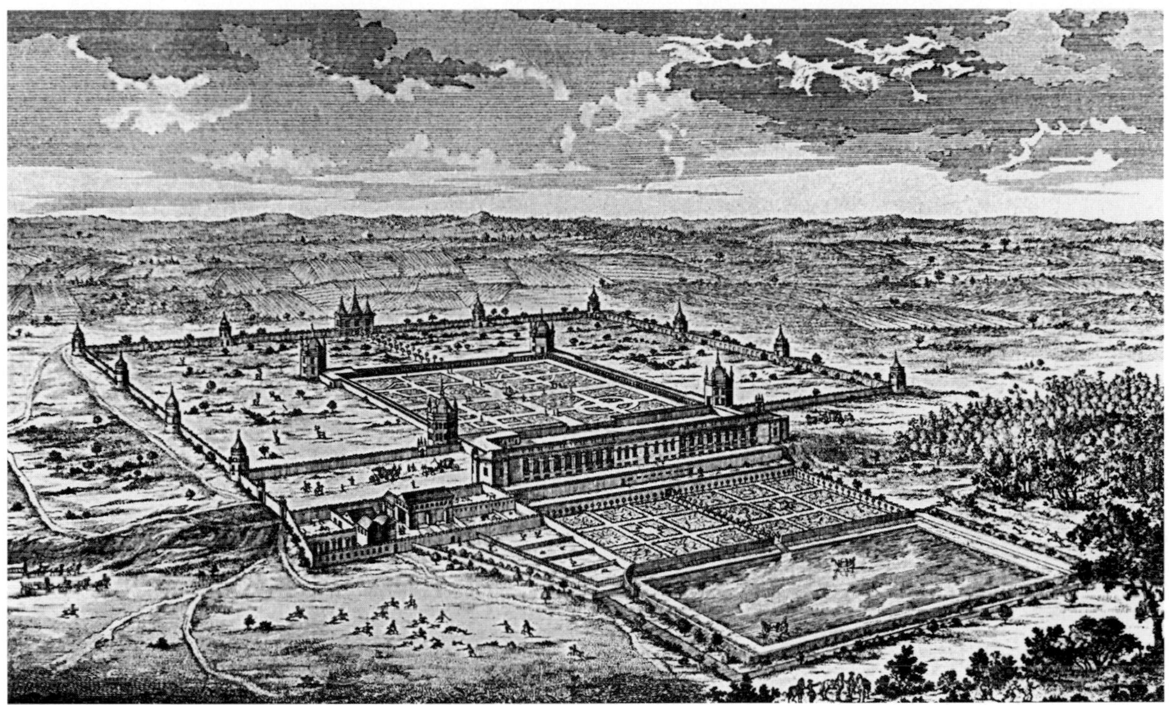

4. Schloss Neugebäude, Vienna, 1569–76; engraving by Joseph Emanuel Fischer von Erlach, *c.* 1715

incorporated influences from the circles of Andrea Palladio and Giulio Romano (such as the Palazzo del Tè, Mantua) in an individual manner that influenced later buildings in Austria.

Outside Vienna, little has survived of the alterations made to the Hofburg (1534–82) in Innsbruck and the Burg (16th century) in Graz. During the regency of Archduke Ferdinand of Tyrol (*reg* 1564–95), however, the Schloss Ambras, Innsbruck, was converted into a Renaissance palace, in which the Spanischer Saal (*c.* 1570; see fig. 24 below) is particularly outstanding in terms of its size and its rich coffered ceiling (*see* INNSBRUCK, §3(ii) and fig. 3). The rebuilding (1599–1607) of the palace at Linz, carried out under Emperor Rudolf II, with its rusticated portal (1604), makes use of the same severe monumentality as in the Schweizertrakt of the Hofburg, Vienna.

In the development of 16th-century Renaissance architecture in Austria, the buildings of the nobility undoubtedly also played an important part. Predominantly Protestant, the aristocracy tried to compete with the Catholic court, with the result that a large number of medieval castles were enlarged and turned into stately Renaissance palaces, with alterations and additions in the new style. The changes generally involved a regular façade with towers at the gate or angles and large inner courtyards with arcades. The interiors, too, were frequently restructured according to symmetrical Renaissance concepts. Of the many buildings of this type, the most important included Schloss Porcia (begun 1533) at Spittal an der Drau, built for Gabriel of Salamanca (*see* SPITTAL AN DER DRAU, SCHLOSS PORCIA). In addition to the façade of the cubic building, articulated by arched and coupled windows with balconies and by diagonal corner towers, the complex arcaded courtyard is outstanding, as is the courtyard of Schloss Schallaburg (1572–1600), Lower Austria, the elevations of which are covered in *all'antica* terracotta ornamentation. Schloss Hochosterwitz (1570–86), Carinthia, built by Georg Freiherr von Khevenhüller, is an imposing structure with mighty fortifications extending over the entire castle hill, and with numerous towers and gates. Subsequent derivatives of the symmetrical layout of four blocks with towers and an arcaded courtyard include the palaces at Aistersheim (*c.* 1600) and Greinburg (begun 1621), both in Upper Austria, and at Deutschkranz (begun 1621) in Burgenland.

The provincial diets (Landstände), representing the nobility, also competed with the court, erecting palatial residences (Landhäuser) in the capital of each province. Particularly sumptuous in the treatment of its façades and especially of its richly articulated courtyard is the Styrian Landhaus in Graz (1557–65), built by Domenico Allio I. The Landhaus in Linz (1568–77) by Christoph Canevale (*fl* 1568–95), with its splendid portal, and the Landhaus in Klagenfurt (1574–80) also feature massive towers as signs of sovereignty, while the Landhaus in Vienna (1562–86) is characterized mainly by its sumptuous interior decoration, including doors and timber ceilings, by Johann Savoye.

(ii) Ecclesiastical. Although the portal (*c.* 1515) of the Salvatorkirche in Vienna shows the influence of the Italian Renaissance in Austrian ecclesiastical architecture, this influence was not as evident in this field as in the secular architecture of the period. Few religious buildings were constructed in Austria in the 16th century, not only because

of the religious wars but also because the Protestants usually took over Catholic churches, which were subsequently returned during the Counter-Reformation. The few new churches of the Reformation, later heavily altered, follow the pattern of the barrel-vaulted hall with chapels and galleries between buttresses projecting into the body of the church, for example the cathedral (1582–91) in Klagenfurt (Carinthia), the parish church (1587–8) at Loosdorf and the Georgskirche (1593) at Horn (both in Lower Austria). Catholic churches also generally followed the pattern of the simple, barrel-vaulted hall church, for example in the abbey church (*c.* 1566–90) in Hall (Tyrol) by Giovanni Luchese and the church (1582–3) of the convent of the Order of St Clare, Vienna, by Jakob Vivian (*fl* 1582–94), although the latter was in fact built with transepts. A further example is the Franciscan church (1603–11) in Vienna, although its façade displays a curious reintroduction of Gothic elements, in the form of pointed-arch windows, alongside German Mannerist forms.

Such Gothic elements also characterize the most important church building of the 16th century in Austria, the Hofkapelle in Innsbruck (*see* INNSBRUCK, §3(i)). Built in 1553–63 by Andrea Crivelli (*fl* 1528–57) and Nikolaus Türing (*fl* 1549–58) at the instigation of Ferdinand, Archduke of Austria, it was intended to house the monumental tomb of Emperor Maximilian I. Conceived internally as a Gothic hall church with a nave and aisles of equal height, it uses the Renaissance idiom only in the vestibule and the portal of the otherwise unornamented façade.

(iii) Fortifications and urban planning. A highly important aspect of building in Austria in the 16th century, of which almost all trace has disappeared, was the fortification of Vienna following the failure of the Turkish attack of 1529. The obsolete fortifications were rebuilt from 1532 in keeping with the latest ideas, and in the course of the 16th century Vienna became one of the largest and most resilient fortresses in Europe. A leading role in this work was played by the Italian masters, who also worked for the emperor on other projects, and who included Domenico Allio I, Francesco Giuseppe Pozzo (1501/2–62), Pietro Ferabosco and Francesco Thebaldi; in addition, such local architects as Benedikt Kölbl, Johann Savoye, Bonifaz Wolmut, Hermes Schallautzer and Hans Tscherte were also involved. These specialists in fortifications subsequently produced similar structures in other strategically important towns including Graz, their mighty bastions dominating the appearance of these towns until the 19th century (*see* VIENNA, fig. 3).

The large towns in Austria retained their medieval structure during the 16th century, with narrow streets and tall, narrow gabled houses, although new forms were gradually introduced in the course of the century. This usually affected small groups of houses, giving rise to more imposing buildings with façades sparsely decorated with Renaissance elements such as windows and balconies, or with *sgraffito* paintings, and surmounted by gables or crenellations. The cloistered courtyards, common in the Middle Ages, were replaced by Renaissance arcades. Many examples of these rather simple, traditional burgher houses have survived in almost all Austrian towns, testifying to the ability of local building usage to assimilate new ideas.

The only example of the new Italian type of Renaissance town plan to appear in Austria was the remodelling of Klagenfurt. After a devastating fire, Domenico Allio I planned the new town (from 1535) on a grid pattern with large squares, surrounded by fortifications with bastions. This scheme did not go beyond the planning stage, however, and it was not until the re-organization of the archbishopric of Salzburg by MARCUS SITTICUS VON HOHENEMS, Prince-Archbishop of Salzburg, that the monumentality of Italian civic architecture was paralleled in Austrian planning.

BIBLIOGRAPHY

R. Wagner-Rieger: 'Die Baukunst des 16. und 17. Jahrhunderts in Österreich: Ein Forschungsbericht', *Wien. Jb. Kstgesch.*, xx (1965) p. 175

P. Baldass, R. Feuchtmüller and W. Mrazek: *Renaissance in Österreich* (Vienna and Hannover, 1966)

R. Feuchtmüller: *Kunst in Österreich*, i (Vienna, Hannover and Basle, 1972), p. 187

——: 'Die Architektur der Renaissance in Österreich', *Renaissance in Österreich* (exh. cat., Schallaburg, Schloss, 1974), p. 444

ECKART VANCSA

3. *c.* 1600–*c.* 1750: THE RISE OF THE BAROQUE. The development of Baroque architecture in Austria in the 17th century was fostered by the renewed confidence of the Catholic Church after the Counter-Reformation and the new prosperity of the nobility after the upheavals and deprivations of the Thirty Years War. Vienna and, especially at the beginning and towards the end of the century, Salzburg continued to be the dominant centres, but Lower Austria and Upper Austria also contributed to the development of the Baroque, which was heavily influenced by Italian examples and the settlement of Italian artists in Austria. There were also a few outstanding buildings in the Burgenland, while the Tyrol was more influenced by stylistic developments in southern Germany.

(i) Early Baroque, c. *1600–*c. *1690.*

(a) Ecclesiastical. The beginning of Baroque architecture north of the Alps was marked by the building of Salzburg Cathedral (see fig. 5). In 1604 WOLF DIETRICH VON RAITENAU, Archbishop of Salzburg, appointed Vincenzo Scamozzi, a pupil of Andrea Palladio, as architect, but Scamozzi's monumental plan for the cathedral (1606–7; Salzburg, Mus. Carolino Augusteum, no. 1870/49) was superseded by that of SANTINO SOLARI (begun 1614; dome and façade 1628). The building is derived ultimately from Il Gesù in Rome but exceeds the latter in its sculptural quality and the vertical emphasis of its structure. Its two four-storey towers (1652–5) constitute the prototype of the post-medieval twin-tower façade, and their contrast with the cubic main building reveals a firm architectural tone that became highly influential. The cathedral's basic design, comprising a hall structure with chapels, galleries and a dominant dome above the crossing, is repeated, for example, in the Jesuit church (1627–40), Innsbruck, by Karl Fontaner and in Cipriano Biasino's church (begun 1631) for the Benedictine abbey of Göttweig.

In Vienna the most important early Baroque buildings include the Jesuit church built in 1627–31 and the Dominican church (1631–4), the façade of which (completed after 1666) follows the early Baroque Roman type and has

5. Santino Solari: Salzburg Cathedral, façade 1628, towers 1652–5

no towers. In the three-storey structure of the city's Carmelite church (1623), also without towers, a Flemish influence is apparent. Contrastingly, the Servite church (1651–70) by Carlo Carnevale has two towers, although in other respects it has all the elements of the centralized structure with which Johann Bernhard Fischer von Erlach and Johann Lukas von Hildebrandt later introduced the High Baroque around the turn of the century: in producing this combination of the centralized and the nave-and-aisles structures, with a longitudinal oval space beneath the dome, rectangular transepts and side chapels, a revolutionary solution was introduced.

In the large towns it was the new religious orders therefore who emerged as the most significant architectural patrons. Most prominent among these were the Jesuits, who, in addition to their churches at Innsbruck and Vienna, were further responsible for the development of Baroque longitudinal churches at the Universitätskirche (1627–31) in Graz, a church (1660–65) in Leoben, attributed to Peter Franz Carlone (ii), and Carlone's Jesuit church of St Ignatius (1669–78) in Linz. Outside the urban centres, however, the most notable patrons were the monastic orders. Many abbeys had their older buildings transformed by Baroque decoration, including Kremsmünster (from 1601; for further discussion *see* KREMSMÜNSTER, §1), ADMONT ABBEY (*c.* 1615), Klosterneuburg (from 1616), Heiligenkreuz (*c.* 1643), Zwettl (from *c.* 1650) and St Peter in Salzburg (*c.* 1680). Large new buildings constructed in the 17th century included Ranshofen (after 1620), Reichersberg (begun 1629), Vorau (begun 1635), St Lambrecht (1639) by Domenico Sciassia, Lambach (begun 1652) by Philiberto Luchese, Garsten (begun 1677) by Peter Franz Carlone (ii), Carlo Antonio Carlone and Giovanni Battista Carlone the younger, and Schlierbach (begun 1680) by Peter Franz and Carlo Antonio Carlone.

Although many Italian architects, engineers and stuccoists were active in Austria, their work also shows some evidence of Austrian tradition. Carlo Antonio Carlone (ii) and his family developed, for example, a hall-like version of the wall-pillar church, without transepts or dome. A series of such churches began with Carlone's Jesuit church (1631–77) and his design for the Dominican church (1642–7), both in Steyr. These were followed by the former abbey church (1650–93) at Waldhausen, by Carlone and Christoph Colomba, Carlone's Jesuit church in Linz and the abbey churches at Garsten, Schlierbach and St Florian. The church at St Florian, begun *c.* 1685 by Carlone, is especially significant because, along with the Theatine church (1691–1711) and the Erhardskirche (1689; both in Salzburg and both built by Giovanni Gaspare Zuccalli), it reveals the first trace of the influence of the Italian High Baroque (for illustration *see* CARLONE (ii), (3); *see also* ST FLORIAN ABBEY, §1). Whereas in most early Baroque architecture in Austria the wall remains a uniformly planar element and is decorated in relief rather than being more three-dimensionally modelled, at St Florian and in Zucalli's churches there is an attempt to enliven and increase the sense of space through the sculptural power of the wall reliefs. It was only in the 18th century, however, that the wall structure itself underwent a major transformation.

A number of mausoleums were built during this period, and these also gave the opportunity to experiment with new forms, in particular a centralized version of the hall plan introduced in the mausoleum built (1597–1603) by Elia Castello for Archbishop Wolf Dietrich von Raitenau at the cemetery of St Sebastian in Salzburg, which consisted of a circular domed structure with a rectangular apse. The mausoleum of Ruprecht von Eggenburg in Ehrenhausen was begun in 1609 by Pietro de Pomis, and Pietro Valnegro, after the death of de Domis in 1633, completed the mausoleum of Ferdinand II (later decorated by Johann Bernhard Fischer von Erlach) at Graz Cathedral, built on a Latin cross-plan surmounted by a dome with an adjoining oval burial chapel. One area relatively unaffected by the new Italianate influences was the Tyrol. In North Tyrol, in particular, architecture was more influenced by developments in Bavaria and Swabia, evident for example in the Karl-Borromäuskirche (1620–54) in Volders, a centralized structure with triple apse by Hyppolytus Guarinoni, and in the Mariahilfkirche (1647–9) in Innsbruck, commissioned by the provincial diet and built by Christoph Gumpp (*see* GUMPP, (1)). The abbey church (begun 1651) at Wilten, also by Gumpp, is an important example of a longitudinal structure in the same stylistic vein.

(b) Secular. In the early 17th century the appearance of many cities was transformed in accordance with developments in Italian urban planning. Broad squares and huge blocks of buildings created new axes in the townscape, and the Baroque city arose from the Gothic. Even in the realm of secular architecture, however, it was the archbishops who were the most important patrons. In Salzburg, Archbishop Wolf Dietrich von Raitenau remodelled the Residenz in 1588, but following the cathedral fire of 1598

6. Johann Bernhard Fischer von Erlach: Karlskirche, Vienna, 1716–37

an entirely new scheme was planned, providing the palace with a broad symmetrical façade and a portal on the main axis. In 1606 von Raitenau had Schloss Altenau completed (now Schloss Mirabell; remodelled in 1721–7 to plans by JOHANN LUKAS VON HILDEBRANDT). MARCUS SITTICUS VON HOHENEMS, who succeeded von Raitenau as Archbishop of Salzburg, pursued his predecessor's architectural aims and completed the SCHLOSS HELLBRUNN (1614–19), designed by SANTINO SOLARI in the manner of an Italian villa suburbana.

In Graz, Schloss Eggenberg (*c.* 1623–55) by de Pomis continued the tradition of the 'country' house (Landhaus). It was commissioned by Hans Ulrich von Eggenberg, an adviser to Ferdinand II, as a modern palace built for show. In Eisenstadt, Carlo Martino Carlone enclosed Paul Esterházy's medieval palace in a Baroque shell (1663–72) to adapt it to the new stylistic requirements.

The large palaces built for the nobility in Vienna from 1660 to 1680 were later mostly destroyed, but their appearance is recorded in Wilhelm Praemer's *Architekturischer Schauplatz* (1672). The most extensive of them was the imperial Hofburg, parts of which from the late 16th century have survived in the Stallburg and the Amalienburg. The Leopoldinischer Trakt (*see* VIENNA, §V, 5(i)) was built (1660–67) by Philiberto Luchese and restored by Giovanni Pietro Tencalla from 1672, following a fire. Here Tencalla made use of the preferred type of early Baroque palace façade with a long, shallowly articulated wall without projections and with a central doorway, and with a continuous series of bays marked by colossal pilasters. The Palais Dietrichstein Lobkowitz (1685–7; now the Palais) by Tencalla was the first to complete the development of the façade from a planar division of panels to an organically centralized unity.

(ii) High Baroque, c. *1690–*c. *1750.* At the end of the 17th century architecture in Austria was dominated by Italian influences, represented by Domenico Egidio Rossi, Enrico Zuccalli and Domenico Martinelli. They were soon displaced, however, by such Austrian architects as Jakob Prandtauer, Johann Lukas von Hildebrandt and Johann Bernhard Fischer von Erlach (*see* FISCHER VON ERLACH, (1)), who ushered in the architecture of the Austrian High Baroque. Fischer von Erlach's success lay in his ability to assimilate a wealth of architectural forms, including motifs from late Hellenistic and Roman architecture, into the unique richness of a personal idiom. After training in Rome, he moved to Vienna, where the destruction wrought by the Turkish sieges of 1667 and 1683, and the mood of confidence after their repulsion, opened up new opportunities for architects. In 1690 Fischer von Erlach beat his Italian rivals in a competition for the triumphal gates for the entry of the future emperor Joseph I (*reg* 1705–11) into Vienna, following his coronation as King of Rome, a triumph that was celebrated by contemporaries as a victory for Germanic art. His subsequent patrons included Eugene, Prince of Savoy (winter palace; 1695–7), and families of the high nobility, including the Strattmans (town palace; 1692), Batthyánys (palace; 1699) and Starhembergs (garden palace; before 1706). In these works, Fischer von Erlach succeeded in breaking away from the traditional Viennese palace façade of the 17th century.

Fischer von Erlach's aesthetic principles in church architecture were first realized in the Dreifaltigkeitskirche (begun 1694) in Salzburg, which comprised a longitudinal oval plan with transepts and a receding concave façade, and in the Kollegienkirche (begun 1696), also in Salzburg. The centralized plan and the oval are basic to Fischer von Erlach's handling of space, attaining their most monumental grandeur in the Karlskirche (1716–37), the festive architecture of which produces an almost secular effect (see fig. 6; *see also* VIENNA, §V, 2). A three-dimensional animation of free-standing architectural forms was achieved at the Hofbibliothek (1722–36; now the Österreichische Nationalbibliothek; *see* VIENNA, §V, 5(i) and fig. 16), where two long wings adjoin a longitudinal oval domed hall on the transverse axis.

The work of JOHANN LUKAS VON HILDEBRANDT represents a rather more classicizing tendency. He arrived in Vienna in 1696 and in the following year was awarded the commission for the Gartenpalais Mansfeld-Fondi (Palais Schwarzenberg); this already shows an idiom diametrically opposed to that of Fischer von Erlach. As later in the Upper Belvedere, Vienna, two blocks of different heights and depths meet at the heart of the building. The Piarist church (1698), Vienna, a centralized domed structure attributed to Hildebrandt, adopts Guarino Guarini's principle of the interpenetration of space and built form, while St Peter's (1702–33) in Vienna is characterized by a longitudinal oval plan interrupted by transepts, and by canted façade towers. In 1702 Hildebrandt entered the service of Prince Eugene; he built the summer palaces of the Belvedere (Lower Belvedere, 1714–16; Upper Belvedere, 1721–3) and Schlosshof im Marchfeld (1725–9). In 1719, in competition with Prandtauer, Hildebrandt began remodelling Göttweig Abbey, which had been destroyed by fire; his plan is based on the Escorial in Spain. In the projected scheme, which was changed in execution, the domed church, surrounded by five courts, forms the architectural and spiritual centre of the complex. At Göttweig, as in the Palais Daun-Kinsky, Schloss Mirabell (*see* §3(i)(b) above) or the Belvedere, Hildebrandt's staircase hall (*Treppenhaus*) designs are particularly noteworthy.

JAKOB PRANDTAUER, who was influenced by Carlo Antonio Carlone, was responsible particularly for the development of abbey architecture in Austria. His first building, completed by Joseph Munggenast, was MELK ABBEY (1702–14), the south front of which represents a particularly successful synthesis of landscape and architecture. From Carlone, Prandtauer took over the building of St Florian (south wing of the courtyard, including the marble hall, 1717–24), Garsten and Kremsmünster. Prandtauer also planned and directed the building of the new Augustinian foundation (begun 1714; east wing and Kaisersaal to plans by Fischer von Erlach) at Herzogenburg, which was also completed (1726–40) by Joseph Munggenast and Franz Munggenast (1724–48). At Klosterneuburg, proposed designs by Prandtauer, who was involved with the abbey buildings at Dürnstein, Seitenstetten and St Pölten, were not executed; instead the plans of Donato Felice Allio (ii) were used (from 1730), which also owed much to the plan of the Escorial. After Charles VI's death in 1740, however, building work ceased.

Further developments in Austrian architecture in the 18th century are represented by the single-tower façades by Matthias Steinl and Joseph Munggenast in Zwettl (added to the Gothic church; 1722) and Dürnstein (1733). Munggenast's most imposing work, however, is probably the library (1730–43) at Altenburg Abbey (*see* MUNGGENAST, JOSEPH), articulated by canted columns grained in blue and white marbling. Here the translation of architecture into colour by rich gradations of different-coloured materials is a remarkable innovation.

JOHANN MICHAEL PRUNNER built in Upper Austria as well as in Passau and Regensburg. His two main works, the Dreifaltigkeitskirche in Stadl-Paura and the abbey church at Spital am Pyhrn, the last of a series of wall-pillar churches, were both begun in 1714. In Stadl-Paura, the circular plan of the dome inscribed within an equilateral triangle and the three identical façades framed by canted towers symbolize the Trinity. Baroque building in the Tyrol was largely influenced by the GUMPP family, who worked primarily at Innsbruck, Stams and Wilten. Such architects as Franz de Paula Penz and Franz Singer were also active mainly in the upper Inn valley, and Andrä Hueber and Wolfgang Hagenauer (1726–1801) from Salzburg also made important contributions to architecture in the Tyrol.

The development of a late Baroque style in Vienna was hampered by the reign of Empress Maria-Theresa (1745–80), during which conversions and extensions took precedence over new building. With the exception of the abbey church of Herzogenburg (1743–50) in Lower Austria, by Franz Munggenast, the main development of the late Baroque therefore took place mainly in Upper Austria and Styria. In Upper Austria, the late Baroque style, closely related to the Bavarian Rococo, is evident in the Cistercian abbey church (1701–41) at Wilhering by Johann Haslinger (*d* 1741) and the observatory (1748–59) at Kremsmünster Abbey (*see* KREMSMÜNSTER, §1 and fig.) by Anselm Desing. In Styria, perhaps the most important area for late Baroque architecture, notable examples include the church façade (1701–12) at St Veit, Pöllau, by Johann Joachim Carlone (ii), the pilgrimage church (1714) at Mariatrost by Andreas Stengg (*d* 1741) and his son Johann Georg Stengg (*d* 1753) and the latter's Barmherzigenkirche (1735–40) in Graz, a wall-pillar church, the façade of which, with its concave bays, resembles that by the same architect at Rein Abbey (1738–49). With the deaths of its main exponents, however, Baroque architecture went into decline, a fact symbolized by renewed engagement of foreign architects.

BIBLIOGRAPHY

H. Sedlmayr: *Österreichische Barockarchitektur, 1690–1740* (Vienna, 1930)

R. Wagner-Rieger: *Das Wiener Bürgerhaus des Barock und Klassizismus* (Vienna, 1957)

B. Grimschitz, R. Feuchtmüller and W. Mrazek: *Barock in Österreich* (Vienna, Hannover and Berne, 3/1962)

R. Wagner-Rieger: 'Barockarchitektur in Österreich: Literaturbericht', *Z. Kstgesch.*, xxvii (1964), pp. 264–71

——: 'Die Bedeutung und die Wandlung der Fassade im österreichischen Kirchenbau des Barocks', *Christ. Kstbl.*, cii/4 (1964), pp. 111–14

E. Hempel: *Baroque Art and Architecture in Central Europe*, Pelican Hist. A. (Harmondsworth, 1965)

R. Feuchtmüller: *Kunst in Österreich: Vom frühen Mittelalter bis zur Gegenwart*, ii (Vienna, Munich and Basle, 1973)

W. Braunfels: *Abendländische Klosterbaukunst* (Cologne, 2/1976)

C. Ressmann: *Das Benediktinerstift Göttweig und seine Voraussetzungen in der Klosterbaukunst des 17. und 18. Jahrhunderts* (diss., U. Vienna, 1976)

W. Hansmann: *Baukunst des Barock: Form, Funktion, Sinngehalt* (Cologne, 1978)

F. Matsche: *Die Kunst im Dienst der Staatsidee Kaiser Karls VI.*, 2 vols (Berlin and New York, 1981)

R. Wagner-Rieger: 'Die Kunst zur Zeit Maria Theresias und Josephs II.', *Wien. Jb. Kstgesch.*, xxxiv (1981), pp. 7–22

G. Brucher: *Barocke Architektur in Österreich* (Cologne, 1983)

K. Gutkas: *Prinz Eugen und das Barocke Österreich* (Salzburg and Vienna, 1985)

R. Feuchtmüller and E. Kovács, eds: *Welt des Barock* (Vienna, Freiburg and Basle, 1986)

Prinz Eugen und das Barocke Österreich (exh. cat., Marchfeld, Marchfeldschlösser Schlosshof & Niederweiden, 1986)

Welt des Barock (exh. cat., Stift St Florian, 1986)

A. Kreul: *Die Barockbaumeister Fischer von Erlach: Bibliographie zu Leben und Werk* (Wiesbaden, 1988)

H. Lorenz: *Domenico Martinelli und die österreichische Barockarchitektur* (Vienna, 1991)

Lust und Leid: Barocke Kunst, Barocker Alltag (exh. cat., Schloss Trautenfels, 1992)

L. G. Brucher, ed.: *Die Kunst des Barock in Österreich* (Salzburg, 1994)

INGONDA HANNESSCHLÄGER

4. *c.* 1750–*c.* 1890: FROM BAROQUE CLASSICISM TO HISTORICISM. The indivisibility and inseparability of the Habsburg states, established by the Pragmatic Sanction of 1713, formed the basis for an emerging national art in Austria, supported by the ruling dynasty and by the state. This national art, in contrast to the respective artistic traditions of the independently evolved states and in its capacity as the official representative medium, could make claim to the status of an all-Austrian art. Vienna, the dynastic centre, came to occupy a central position in the architectural activity of this period.

(i) *c.* 1750–1790. (ii) 1790–1848. (iii) 1848–*c.* 1890.

(i) c. *1750–1790.* Around 1750 a new generation of architects began to emerge, whose work was characterized by a shift towards a Baroque classicism derived from French models. Emperor Francis I (*reg* 1745–65), consort of Empress Maria-Theresa from 1736, was the first to introduce a French architect to Vienna, in the person of Jean-Nicolas Jadot de Ville-Issey, who was appointed chief court architect in 1750. His major work, the assembly hall (1753–7) of the old university (now the Österreichische Akademie der Wissenschaften), Vienna, was influenced by similar early 18th-century French schemes and contrasts the angularity of the exterior with the curvilinear nature of the vaulted ceiling bays within. The functional and severe articulation of the exterior of the Gardekirche (1755–63), Vienna, by Nikolaus Pacassi conceals a domed central space that is similarly surprising in the magnificence of its decoration; its cool white-and-gold ornamentation is typical of the restrained variety of Viennese Rococo, as also exemplified at his galleries (1743–9) at Schloss Schönbrunn (*see* PACASSI, NIKOLAUS; *see also* VIENNA, §V, 7(i)). Pacassi's façades (1767–73) on the Josephsplatz, Vienna, completed the integration—begun by Joseph Emanuel Fischer von Erlach—of the originally free-standing imperial library into the layout of the Hofburg (*see* VIENNA, §V, 5(i)), setting the grid-like articulation of the wings against the library range, while adopting Fischer von Erlach's colossal order on the projecting bays.

Under Emperor Joseph II (*reg* 1765–90; co-Regent with his mother, Empress Maria-Theresa, 1765–80), a new social order developed in Austria, the consequences of which were reflected in a shift of building activity to the public and functional. Accordingly, from *c.* 1770, imperial Baroque classicism began to give way to a stylistic pluralism. Local traditions remained important, but a trend influenced by French revolutionary classicism also emerged, characterized chiefly by interpreting the *corps de logis* as a stereometric object and by displaying function through form. A third stylistic strand comprised elements derived from the Gothic and the Antique.

In religious architecture this pluralism was evident in the construction of a large number of new churches built as a result of the Emperor's division of parishes in 1783–4. A great number of new parishes were founded, and payment of the parish priests brought an influx of church functionaries to work on behalf of the state and to administer the funds from dismantled monasteries and convents. Most of those new churches have two bays, with domed or sail-vaulted interiors, or have centralized plans, and they are distinguished by a crisp, restrained classicizing articulation. Further ecclesiastical buildings were constructed as a result of the tolerance acts of 1781 and 1782, which allowed non-Catholics and Jews to build their own places of worship. In the absence of traditional models for such buildings, contemporary building types were adapted instead, for example the Protestant church (1783–4), Vienna, by Gottlieb Nigelli (1744–1812) and the Greek Orthodox church (1782–7), Vienna, by Peter Mollner (1732–1801). (The most independent design was to be formulated a generation later by Joseph Kornhäusel, with his elliptical synagogue (1824–6) in the Seitenstettengasse, Vienna.) Medieval churches that were re-Gothicized form a distinct group and include the Michaelerkirche (1782), Vienna, by Jean-Baptiste d'Avrange (1728–89) and

7. Isidore Canevale: Josephinum, Vienna, 1783–5

the Augustinian and Minorite churches in Vienna, renovated by Johann Ferdinand von Hohenberg in 1784. Such works, probably inspired by the Gothicization (1720–25) of the church of the Teutonic Knights in Vienna, by the work of Giovanni Santini(-Aichel) in Bohemia and by examples of the vigorous survival of the Gothic tradition in France, have been interpreted as an act of politico-religious withdrawal by the Emperor from Rome.

In the field of public building, Joseph II favoured ISIDORE CANEVALE, who was appointed court architect in 1776 along with Hohenberg; Canevale's preoccupation with cubic forms and functionalism were apparently the first to accord with the Emperor's own ideas. His Allgemeines Krankenhaus (1783–4), Vienna, with its many courtyards, was modelled on barracks and monasteries, adopting their layout around a well-defined system of communications. In the final courtyard, the Narrenturm, a cylindrical building for the mentally ill surrounding a circular courtyard, may be seen as the realization of a design tending towards radical revolutionary classicism. Related by its imposing design to the Baroque, Canevale's Josephinum (1783–5; see fig. 7), a medical school in Vienna, is an example of the way imperial grandeur might be conferred on a public, functional building. The work of Hohenberg is particularly characteristic of the architecture in the reign of Joseph II, drawing as it did on a wide range of sources. The reorganization of the park at Schloss Schönbrunn (*see* VIENNA, §V, 7(ii)) derived its severe axial layout from mid-18th-century Italian models, but it is also remarkable for quoting antique formulae of grandeur, romantically interpreted in the manner of Piranesi (e.g. the obelisks (1777) and the Roman ruin (1778)). The Gloriette (completed 1775) at Schönbrunn (*see* HOHENBERG, JOHANN FERDINAND VON), the wings of which are linked to the central pavilion by an airy arcade, demonstrates the fundamentally different approach of Hohenberg from that of Canevale. Whereas Canevale's Augarten-Portal (1775) in Vienna, for example, is a succession of individual cubes, Hohenberg's design for the Gloriette recalls the villas of Palladio and pays homage to the magisterial use of columns in mid-18th-century French architecture. Hohenberg's Palais Fries-Pallavicini (1783–4), Vienna, on the other hand, combines ideas derived from High Renaissance palaces in Rome with an emphasis on the cubic mass of the building. In the similarly expanding field of residential building in this period, the plain *Plattenstil* ornamentation of the second quarter of the 18th century was once again taken up and combined with the *Zopfstil* of early Neo-classical ornamentation.

(ii) 1790–1848. The period after the death in 1790 of Joseph II was marked by a reaction to his reforms and by the revival of absolutism under emperors Leopold II (*reg* 1790–92) and Francis II (*reg* 1792–1835). Architecturally, this absolutism was expressed through a persistent classicism, most notably in the administrative buildings that were the embodiment of the state. A prominent exponent of this style was Johann Aman (1765–1834), who was involved in developing the Hofburg and rebuilding Schloss Schönbrunn (1817–19). In addition, a Romantic Gothic Revival trend developed, the most significant achievement of which was the Franzensburg (1798–1801) at Laxenburg by Franz Jäger (1743–1809), compiled from elements of medieval architecture from different parts of Austria. There was also a renewed interest in Italian models, ranging from the Antique via Palladio, to contemporary Milanese Neo-classicism, as in the work of Luigi Pichl (1782–1856), for example the palace he designed for the Archduchess Maria Beatris von Madena-Este in the Herrengasse, Vienna (now the Innenministerium). At the same time there arose alongside the BIEDERMEIER style (which combined the block-like character of revolutionary classicism with a more understated, bourgeois approach), a local version of classicism that assimilated and adapted contemporary ideas, evident, for example, in the arcaded façade of the National Bank (1819–23) in the Herrengasse, Vienna, by Karl Moreau. The most important exponent of this trend and its application to civic design was JOSEPH KORNHÄUSEL, responsible for the Schottenhof housing developments (1826–32) in Vienna. An example of the official classicism of the imperial court is Louis Montoyer's Zeremoniensaal (1802–6) in the Hofburg, Vienna. Other examples of this more retrospective classicism include Montoyer's Palais Rasumofsky (1805–11), Vienna, the layout of which owes much to Palladian as well as to English models, and the Lichtenstein Benefiziatshaus (1787–92; destr.) in Vienna, by Joseph Hardtmuth (1752–1816), which adopted themes from earlier imperial architecture with its references to the Michaelerplatz elevation of the Hofburg.

This period of architectural pomp was followed by a return to the more practical, rationalist architecture prefigured during the reign of Joseph II. Functional building, which was also becoming a feature of the major regional towns, typically had a restrained, block-like appearance that nevertheless did not dispense with the traditional grand motifs, such as colonnades, pediments and porticos (e.g. the Polytechnikum (1816–18; now the Technische Universität), Vienna, by Schemerl von Leytenbach (1752–1837), and the Veterinary Institute (1821–3; now the Veterinary College), Vienna, by Johann Aman). A prestigious project in the immediate vicinity of the Hofburg, Vienna, was begun in 1815 with the planning of the Burgtor. Although the eventual demolition (1858) of the outdated city fortifications had already been made necessary by the destruction of its bastions by Napoleon's troops in 1809, the ring of walls was in fact closed up by the Burgtor, a fortified gate built by PETER VON NOBILE in the style of Michele Sanmicheli (see fig. 8).

The second quarter of the 19th century was also marked by the clear beginnings of an early Romantic form of Historicism, for example in the work of KARL RÖSNER (e.g. St John Nepomuk (1841–6), Praterstrasse, Vienna, and the Redemptorist church (1834–6; now the church of the Comforters of Gethsemane), Rennweg, Vienna). Rösner combined the reduction to blocks of his built masses with the graphic flatness of 15th-century decoration. The works of PAUL EDUARD SPRENGER, the most prominent court architect of the second quarter of the 19th century, embraced a similar version of Historicism by closely bonding a sharp-edged flat decoration to the block (e.g. headquarters of the Mint (1835–8), the Customs Office

8. The Burgtor by Peter von Nobile, 1821–4, Heldenplatz, Vienna, and, beyond, the Naturhistorisches Museum by Karl Hasenauer and Gottfried Semper, 1872–81

(1840–44) and the Revenue Office (1844–7); all in Vienna). As a result of such developments, during the 1840s classicism was no longer regarded as the mandatory style for public buildings. During the same period the Gothic Revival style was more widely adopted, although at first it was used primarily for private buildings, where it relied less on Austrian than on English models, as in the renovation (1838–48) of Schloss Anif, Salzburg, by Heinrich Schönauer.

*(iii) 1848–*c. *1890.* The revolutions of 1848 brought not just a return to earlier national styles but also an increased readiness to engage critically with the past and a rejection of the doctrinaire form of classicism that symbolized the traditional apparatus of the state. An earlier debate about appropriate styles was revived by LUDWIG FÖRSTER and Theophilus Hansen (*see* HANSEN, (2)), and a free synthesis of themes from the architecture of earlier periods and from other cultures became possible. Hansen introduced Byzantine elements, for example at the Gustav-Adolf-Kirche (1846–9; in collaboration with Förster) and the Matzleinsdorf Friedhofskirche (1857–8), both in Vienna. Typical of this potential pluralism is the parish church at Altlerchenfeld in Vienna, plans for which were begun in 1845 by Paul Sprenger; completed in 1860 under the direction of Eduard Van der Nüll (*see* VAN DER NÜLL & SICCARDSBURG) to designs by JOHANN GEORG MÜLLER, it is one of Vienna's most important examples of a historicist *Gesamtkunstwerk*. The idea of a Romantic historicist church architecture remained influential until *c*. 1900.

The suppression of revolutionary forces by imperial troops in 1848 found political expression in the construction of several barracks and a new Arsenal, reflecting a new absolutism under the Emperor Francis Joseph I. The Arsenal, a military 'ideal city' in a strategically advantageous position, was built between 1849 and 1856 by Förster, Hansen, Van der Nüll, Rösner and August Sicard von Siccardsburg. The fortified nature of the barracks and gateways contrasts with the lavish flamboyance of the *Gesamtkunstwerk* of the Heeresgeschichtliches Museum, which serves as the army's hall of fame. Notable monumental civil buildings of early Historicism include the Bank- and Börsengebäude (1856–60) in Vienna by HEINRICH VON FERSTEL, a dynamically organized edifice composed in an additive manner and laid out around an iron and glass passageway, its decorative themes taken from the Florentine Quattrocento; and the Handelsakademie (1860–62), a commercial college on the Karlsplatz, Vienna, by Ferdinand Fellner, the plan of which is based on a rhythmical grid system. Residential and apartment building of the mid-19th century followed the grid system already established by Kornhäusel's apartment buildings, although the uniformity of the Biedermeier style was replaced by a lightly rhythmic articulation of bays and storeys, the façades being enriched with small-scale relief ornamentation. The project for the Court Opera House (now the State Opera) in Vienna from 1861 marks the pinnacle of early Historicism. Here a more modern approach to Historicism was rejected in favour of a design by Van der Nüll & Siccardsburg. The rich yet sharp-edged and graphic décor in 14th-century forms and the grid-like articulation already appeared outdated when the building opened in 1869, by which time the shift to a stricter Historicism had long since taken place.

Around 1860 a tendency towards a new, élitist monumental classicism began, replacing the cumulative, progressive system of early Historicism by concentrating the building units on a tautly designed, symmetrically planned block. The grid-like articulation of the early historicist façades also gave way to a layout of the bays and storeys that emphasizes the horizontal, thus taking up the classical zoning of High Renaissance palace façades. At the same time, High Renaissance forms of decoration were used to a degree unknown during the preceding, more pluralist decade. The reduction in the number of storeys, combined with a revival of 16th-century palace design, led not just to a strictly historicist decorative style but also to a revival of earlier forms. The palace, albeit briefly, became once again a subject for commissions, for example alongside the Ringstrasse at Schwarzenbergsplatz in Vienna, but also in the suburbs. Here they took the form not only of palaces for the nobility and members of the imperial household (e.g. Palais Erzherzog Wilhelm (1864–86) and Palais Epstein (1868–71)), but also of large palatial blocks of flats. With Hansen's Heinrichshof (1861–3; destr.), in a prominent position facing the State Opera, Vienna, a prototype emerged, the plan and elevation of which demonstrated the dominance of large-scale form over individual detail.

In 1856 Heinrich von Ferstel began the Votivkirche, the first large building to be erected in a Gothic Revival style (completed 1879; for illustration *see* FERSTEL, HEINRICH VON) in the Ringstrasse in Vienna, constructed to commemorate the army and its thwarting of an assassination attempt on Francis Joseph I. Another important figure in the introduction into Vienna of the Gothic Revival style was FRIEDRICH VON SCHMIDT, who had been involved in the restoration of Cologne Cathedral and the attempt there to resurrect the practices of the medieval masons' guilds. Schmidt's work had a lasting influence in Vienna through his designs for churches, such as Maria vom Siege (1867–9), and through his secular buildings, such as the Akademisches Gymnasium (1863–6). Linz Cathedral, begun in 1859 to designs by VINCENZ STATZ and completed in 1924, was based on similar principles to those introduced by Schmidt (*see* LINZ).

The Votivkirche was also important as the first element in the great urban planning project of the period, the Ringstrasse (for further discussion *see* VIENNA, §II, 3). Emperor Francis Joseph granted permission for the project in 1857, but although it began as an implicit expression of imperial absolutism, financed by the state fund for the expansion of the city, the Ringstrasse development was reinterpreted during the political backlash at the beginning of the liberal era of the 1860s. In 1862 Vienna acquired its own autonomous constitution, after which three large-scale, clearly delineated and tautly articulated building complexes were constructed on the site of the former Paradeplatz: the Rathaus (1872–83) by Schmidt, the Parlament (1873–83) by Hansen, with its treatment of Palladian and Classical Greek forms (for illustration *see* HANSEN, (2)) and the Universität (1873–84) by Ferstel (*see* VIENNA, fig. 6). The pinnacles of strict Historicism are the Kunsthistorisches Museum and the Naturhistorisches Museum (from 1872; see fig. 8) by KARL HASENAUER and GOTTFRIED SEMPER. These were to constitute a magnificent imperial forum, with the Burgtor and with the partly completed exedra of the Neue Burg (original plan 1871; completed 1913) by Hasenauer, Emil von Förster (1838–1909), FRIEDRICH OHMANN and Ludwig Baumann (1853–1936) (*see* VIENNA, §V, 5(i)).

The powerful three-dimensional quality of Semper's articulation already prefigured the stylistic change that led to the dissolution of the planar wall in favour of a more plastic handling of the surface. This change itself took place in the 1880s and was characterized by a renewed acceptance of stylistic pluralism, which had been evident in the early period of Historicism but which had been proscribed during the stricter 'élitist' period of classicist Historicism. The *Altdeutsch* style, a form of ornamentation that appeared around 1870 (e.g. extension (1873) to the National Bank, Vienna, by Schmidt), exhibited similarities in its neo-Romantic conception with the *Burgenstil* of early Historicism, used for castles and barracks. Sculptural façades, enhancing the effect of light and shadow with projections, oriels, balconies and loggias, were further enlivened by the use of towers, cupolas, gables and finials to break up the roofline (e.g. Dapontegasse, Vienna). With the abandonment of the planar wall façade, the appearance of a building when viewed from an angle also became important, for example in numerous villas built during the last quarter of the 19th century in the traditional holiday resorts on the Semmering (Lower Austria), in the Salzkammergut (Upper Austria, Salzburg and Styria) and on the Wörther See (Carinthia), as well as around Vienna. Medieval forms were also increasingly adopted in the church architecture of the late 19th century, as a consequence of Schmidt's influences, with Romanesque elements also becoming evident, for example in the Jubiläumskirche (1898–1913), Vienna, by Viktor Luntz (1840–1903). A specifically Austrian version of the Baroque Revival, inspired by the work of Johann Lukas von Hildebrandt, was widely used in secular building but was not used in religious architecture.

In the complex picture of Austrian late Historicism, we find the tendency that considered a building as a sculpturesque entity, as represented by Friedrich Ohmann (Wienflussverbauung, 1903–6; municipal park, Vienna) and Ludwig Baumann (former Ministry of War, 1909–13; Ringstrasse, Vienna). Opposed to this is a second tendency, geared to the cubic tradition of the buildings of Nobile, Sprenger and Hansen, and characterized by a Palladian and Graecizing component represented by Otto Wagner. His municipal railway buildings of 1894–1900 in Vienna bridge the gap between the cubic-classicist tradition and the simplified surface architecture of the late Secession. The school of OTTO WAGNER, of outstanding importance for Austrian architecture in the 20th century, as well as for architecture in the succession states of the Austro-Hungarian monarchy, had already effected the transition, shortly after the turn of the century, from proto-cubism to the Neo-classicism of the years around 1910.

BIBLIOGRAPHY

P. Kortz: *Wien am Anfang des 20. Jahrhunderts*, 2 vols (Vienna, 1906)
R. Wagner-Rieger: *Das Wiener Bürgerhaus des Barock und Klassizismus* (Vienna, 1957)
R. Feuchtmüller and W. Mrazek: *Biedermeier in Österreich* (Vienna, 1963)
H. Bobek and E. Lichtenberger: *Wien: Bauliche Gestalt und Entwicklung seit der Mitte des 19. Jahrhunderts* (Graz and Cologne, 1966)
O. A. Graf: *Die vergessene Wagnerschule* (Vienna, 1969)
R. Wagner-Rieger, ed.: *Die Wiener Ringstrasse: Bild einer Epoche*, 11 vols (Graz, 1969–79)
——: *Wiens Architektur im 19. Jahrhundert* (Vienna, 1970)
——: *Vom Klassizismus bis zur Secession*, Geschichte der bildenden Kunst in Wien, vii/3 (Vienna, 1973), pp. 81–244
Klassizismus in Wien: Architektur und Plastik (exh. cat., ed. R. Kassal; Vienna, Hist. Mus., 1978)
Vor 100 Jahren: Wien, 1879 (exh. cat., ed. R. Waissenberger; Vienna, Hist. Mus., 1979)
G. Hájos and E. Vancsa: *Die Kunstdenkmäler Wiens: Die Profanbauten des III., IV. und V. Bezirks*, Österreichische Kunsttopographie, xliv (Vienna, 1980)
Maria Theresa und ihre Zeit (exh. cat., Vienna, Schloss Schönbrunn, 1980)
Österreich zur Zeit Kaiser Josephs II (exh. cat., ed. K. Gutkas, Melk, Stiftsmus., 1980)
K. Eggert and others: *Landhaus und Villa in Niederösterreich* (Vienna and Graz, 1982)
Das Zeitalter Kaiser Franz Josephs (exh. cat., ed. H. Kühnel; Grafenegg, 1984), 2 vols
Traum und Wirklichkeit: Wien, 1870–1930 (exh. cat., Vienna, Kstlerhaus, 1985)
Bürgersinn und Aufbegehren: Biedermeier und Vormärz in Wien, 1815–1848 (exh. cat., ed. G. Düriegl; Vienna, Kstlerhaus, 1987)
Das Zeitalter Kaiser Franz Josephs, II (exh. cat., ed. R. Waissenberger; Grafenegg, 1987), 2 vols
G. Hájos: *Romantische Gärten der Aufklärung* (Vienna and Cologne, 1989)
W. Czerny and others: *Die Kunstdenkmäler Wiens*, ii–ix, xx (Vienna, 1993)

INGE PODBRECKY

5. AFTER *c.* 1890: MODERNISM AND BEYOND. The birth of Modernism in Austria came with the development of the infrastructure of Vienna at the end of the 19th century, made necessary by the rapid growth of the city. After building a number of speculative apartments (begun 1860s) in a classical style derived from the Florentine High Renaissance, Otto Wagner successfully combined classical motifs with a strong formal accentuation of constructional and functional elements in his buildings (1894–8) on the Danube Canal and his railway stations and bridges (1894–1901) for the Stadtbahn, Vienna. This rationalism culminated in the Am Steinhof Hospital and Church (1903–7) in Vienna and the headquarters of the Postsparkasse (1903–12; *see* WAGNER, OTTO, fig. 2 and ART NOUVEAU, §6), also in Vienna, in which the visible relationship between structure and cladding, and the aesthetic treatment of technical details are the most striking features. As a professor (1894–1912) at the Akademie der Bildenden Künste, Vienna, Wagner founded an influential school of Modernism that not only produced such figures as JOSEF HOFFMANN and RUDOLPH SCHINDLER but also trained architects who took on important projects after 1918 in Vienna and in Czechoslovakia, Hungary and Slovenia. Also at this time a Romantic tendency derived from the *Jugendstil* and the Baroque, which was opposed to Wagner's rationalist elements, was represented by FRIEDRICH OHMANN, especially in the Palmenhaus (1899–1906) in the Burggarten, the river authority buildings (1903–9) and the monument to *Empress Elizabeth* (1904–6) in the Volksgarten, all in Vienna.

9. Joseph Maria Olbrich: Secession Building, Vienna, 1898 (restored)

Further impetus was given to the development of Modernism by the adoption of English and Belgian models by Hoffmann and another of Wagner's followers, JOSEPH MARIA OLBRICH. The assimilation into the exquisite new decorative art of the Viennese *Jugendstil* of elements from the Arts and Crafts Movement and from painting was institutionalized by the founding of the Vienna Secession (1897; *see* SECESSION, §3), the exhibition building of which was constructed by Olbrich in 1898 (see fig. 9). Adolf Loos, however, countered this decorative trend with American influences derived from a stay in Philadelphia and Chicago between 1893 and 1896. Opposing the tenets of Secessionism, Loos's numerous writings advocated functional simplicity and the use of materials chosen for the appropriateness of their natural properties rather than artificial ornamentation. The 'eloquence' of buildings was thus reduced to a minimum. Loos's rejection of inappropriate ornamentation was manifested in the Goldmann and Salatsch residential and commercial building (1910; now the Looshaus; *see* LOOS, ADOLF, fig. 1) near the Hofburg, Vienna, which caused a sensation. His pursuit of economy subsequently led him to evolve his *Raumplan*, whereby the spaces in a house were integrated horizontally and vertically within a given volume according to functional criteria, for example at Haus Rufer (1922), Vienna. (For further discussion, *see* §V, 4 below.)

After 1918 the various strands of Viennese Modernism had to adjust to a radically changed economy. The primary need was for mass low-cost housing, but there were also developments in the provinces in relating architecture to landscape. In Vienna, OSKAR STRNAD, who had worked in Ohmann's office, and JOSEF FRANK applied themselves particularly to social questions. Even before 1918, they had formulated ideas on the psychological and spiritual functions of house design, manifested, for example, at the Villa Hock (1910) and the Villa Wassermann (1914), both in Vienna; these ideas were applied to the new situation in Vienna after 1918. The endeavours of Frank and Loos to create communal housing estates were unable, however, to prevail against the apartment-block style enforced by the city authorities (1924–33), and generally the economic situation between 1918 and 1938 fostered the growth of an 'objective' aesthetic parallel to the efforts of Le Corbusier, the Bauhaus and De Stijl. This was evident particularly in the work of such younger architects as ERNST PLISCHKE, for example at Haus Gamerith (1933–4), Attersee. In the model housing estate (1929–32), Vienna, of the Österreichischer Werkbund, a scheme initiated by Frank (the only Austrian member of CIAM), Austrian and international architects of different generations (including Hoffmann, Loos, Frank, Strnad, Gerrit Rietveld, CLEMENS HOLZMEISTER, Oswald Haerdtl and Richard Neutra) addressed the theme of the low-cost small dwelling. This brick manifesto of the objectives of the 1920s was also influenced by the teaching of Behrens and Holzmeister at the Akademie der Bildenden Künste, Vienna, and of Strnad, Haerdtl and Hoffmann at the Kunstgewerbeschule, Vienna. Holzmeister was also notable for making, with LOIS WELZENBACHER, the most significant contribution to the architecture of Austria's western provinces.

After the emigration and expulsion from Austria of the leading exponents of Modernism from 1933 to 1945, the international standard of building reached between the World Wars could not quickly be restored. The period from 1945 to 1960 was dominated by architects committed to a more moderate Modernism who had studied between the wars under Holzmeister, Behrens, Strnad or Hoffmann, and who, under the economic pressure of reconstruction, applied the traditions of the 1930s to housing and to prestigious public buildings (e.g. the reconstruction (completed 1955) of the Vienna State Opera House by Erich Boltenstern (1896–1991), Otto Prossinger (*b* 1906) and Ceno Kosak (1904–85)). More ambitious structures were generally produced only for special projects, for example the Gänsehäufel Lido (1948–50), Vienna, by Max Fellerer and Eugen Wörle (*b* 1909), and for churches, evident in works by pupils of Holzmeister, who also taught at the Akademie der Bildenden Künste from 1945. The first of Holzmeister's pupils to make an impact were WILHELM HOLZBAUER, Friedrich Kurrent (*b* 1931) and Johannes Spalt (*b* 1920), who, as ARBEITSGRUPPE 4, designed the parish church (1953–6) at Parsch, near Salzburg (see fig. 10): originally a secular building, it was transformed by the simplest means into a bright centralized space with the altar at the centre. Also significant was ROLAND RAINER, particularly for his single-storey houses, which strove for complete privacy (e.g. the Veitingergasse Estate (1953), Vienna, and the Puchenau Estate (1964–7), nr Linz), and for his town hall designs, which included the Stadthalle (1952–8), Vienna.

In the 1960s the development of architecture was concentrated on religious buildings, for example the theological college of St Joseph (1961–4) at Aigen, Salzburg, by Arbeitsgruppe 4, and the church of St Theresia (1957–62), Linz, by RUDOLF SCHWARZ. The main themes of the debate on church building were the exposure of structural features and the spatial involvement of the congregation. In the 1970s the teaching of Spalt and Plischke, who had returned to Austria from New Zealand, led to a revival of classical Modernism, evident, for example, in the Haus Gadenstätter (1972–3), Zell am See, by Luigi Blau (*b* 1945), and the Kleines Café (1973–4), Vienna, by HERMAN CZECH.

10. Arbeitsgruppe 4: parish church, Parsch, near Salzburg, 1953–6

The exhibition *Hollein-Pichler-Architektur* (1963) in Vienna introduced a new fashion for combining High-Tech and classical elements, and this was influential in the subsequent development of Post-modernism. HANS HOLLEIN, after producing designs for a number of shop buildings (e.g. Kerzenladen Retti, 1964–5), worked primarily outside Austria (e.g. Städtisches Museum Abteiberg (1972–82), Mönchengladbach; *see* MUSEUM, fig. 9) before being awarded major commissions in Vienna (e.g. the Volksschule Köhlergasse (1977–91) and Haas-Haus (1991)). The monumental style of Holzbauer initially also brought him commissions from abroad (e.g. Amsterdam, City Hall and Opera; 1967–86), but he too later executed major projects in Salzburg (University, 1978–82) and Vienna (office complex (begun 1978), Lasallestrasse; *see* HOLZBAUER, WILHELM). GUSTAV PEICHL first used a High-Tech style in his design for the studio of the Österreichischer Rundfunk (1970–81), Vienna, the first large-scale example of corporate design in Austria, before turning to projects in Germany. Towards the end of the 20th century the architects who had been part of the experimental avant-garde in the 1960s became established figures, including the CO-OP HIMMELBLAU (e.g. Kanzlei S. (1987–8), Vienna), Adolf Krischanitz (*b* 1946; e.g. Pilotengasse Estate (1987–91), Vienna) and Helmuth Richter (*b* 1941; e.g. house in Brunnerstrasse (1986–90), Vienna).

BIBLIOGRAPHY

K. Schwanzer, ed.: *Wiener Bauten: 1900 bis heute* (Vienna, 1964)
O. Uhl: *Moderne Architektur in Wien: Von Otto Wagner bis heute* (Vienna and Munich, 1966)

P. M. Bode and G. Peichl: *Architektur aus Österreich seit 1960* (Salzburg, 1980)
M. Potetto: *Die Schule Otto Wagners* (Vienna, 1980)
F. Achleitner: *Österreichische Architektur im 20. Jahrhundert*, 4 vols (Vienna and Salzburg, 1980–)
T. Franke and G. Langthaler, eds: *Building in Austria* (Vienna, 1983)
O. Kapfinger and A. Krischamitz: *Die Wiener Werkbundsiedlung* (Vienna, 1985)
H. Weihsmann: *Das rote Wien: Sozialdemokratische Architektur und Sozialpolitik, 1919–1934* (Vienna, 1985)
O. Kapfinger and F. Kneissl: *Dichte Packung, Architektur aus Wien* (Salzburg, 1989)
H. Hollein, ed.: *13 Austrian Positions* (exh. cat., Venice, Biennale, 1991)

MATTHIAS BOECKL

III. Painting and graphic arts.

1. Before *c.* 1530: Romanesque and Gothic. 2. *c.* 1530–*c.* 1600: Renaissance. 3. *c.* 1600–*c.* 1800: Baroque. 4. After *c.* 1800.

1. Before *c.* 1530: Romanesque and Gothic.

(i) Romanesque. (ii) Gothic.

(i) Romanesque.

(a) Wall paintings. The transition from Early Christian to Romanesque painting was undoubtedly a continuous process of evolution. However, few paintings have survived from before the late 11th century. There are some fragmentary wall paintings from the first half of the 11th century in the St Ulrichskirche in Wieselburg in Lower Austria, but it is difficult to assign these to any particular style, although they could be described as Byzantine–Ottonian. They have few stylistic links with other surviving works of the period. Wall paintings have also survived in the former west choir of the Benedictine abbey church of Lambach in Upper Austria, built between 1056 and 1089. The paintings, including scenes from the Old and New Testaments, can be compared with paintings and mosaics in northern Italy, in particular in their illusionism.

The majority of surviving Romanesque wall paintings date from the 12th century: those in the Winterkirche at Maria Wörth, Carinthia, from the early part of the century, have a two-dimensional figure style, indicating provincial workmanship, and also show the influence of late 11th-century Bavarian book illuminations. The greatest cycle of wall paintings after Lambach, and one that is relatively complete, is in the small Johanneskapelle at Pürgg in Styria, presumably once the chapel of the vanished palace of the Traungauer family, dukes of Styria. The subjects include biblical scenes and the famous war of the cats and mice, rooted in Byzantine legend. The paintings' style is linked with that of Salzburg book illumination, which also influenced the half-length pictures of the Fathers of the Church and saints (mid-12th century) in the church of the Benedictine abbey at Nonnberg in Salzburg. The most important cycle of wall paintings in Lower Austria is in the chapel of Burg Ottenstein, near Zwettl: *The Passion* (*c.* 1170–80) indicates the influence not only of Salzburg but also of Frauenchiemsee in Bavaria and of Pürgg. Although there was a sharp decline in quality in the early 13th century, wall paintings in Berg in Carinthia, Nauders in the Tyrol and Mariapfarr in the province of Salzburg developed Romanesque pictorial principles, while anticipating the Gothic use of line.

(b) Manuscript illumination. In the early Romanesque period monasteries in Austria gradually developed scriptoria, which were continually influenced by British and Mediterranean illumination, imported as early as the 8th century. Early examples of local work may include the Codex Millenarius Maior (late 8th century; Kremsmünster, Stiftsbib., Cim. 1). However, the place of production has not yet been conclusively established: both Mondsee Abbey (since dissolved) and a Bavarian monastery have been suggested. From the late 11th century important scriptoria were active, particularly in the area of Salzburg, from where considerable material has survived. This is mainly the work of the scriptoria of four monasteries: the St Peter's Monastery with the house associated with the cathedral of St Rupert and Nonnberg Abbey in Salzburg, and the nearby abbeys at Mondsee and Kremsmünster. Among the best-known works by early Salzburg illuminators is the Nonnberg Gospel (Munich, Bayer. Staatsbib., Cim. 15904), which has many stylistic features characteristic of Ottonian art but also foreshadows later developments. Other centres of illumination also appeared at Admont and Lambach, and Millstatt in Carinthia: two Gospels survive, one from Admont and the other from Millstatt (now Admont, Stiftsbib., Cod. 511; and Graz, Ubib., Cod. 805), associated with the first illuminator known by name, Kustos Perhtold (*fl* *c.* 1060–90). In the 12th century huge bibles, imported from Italy, began to

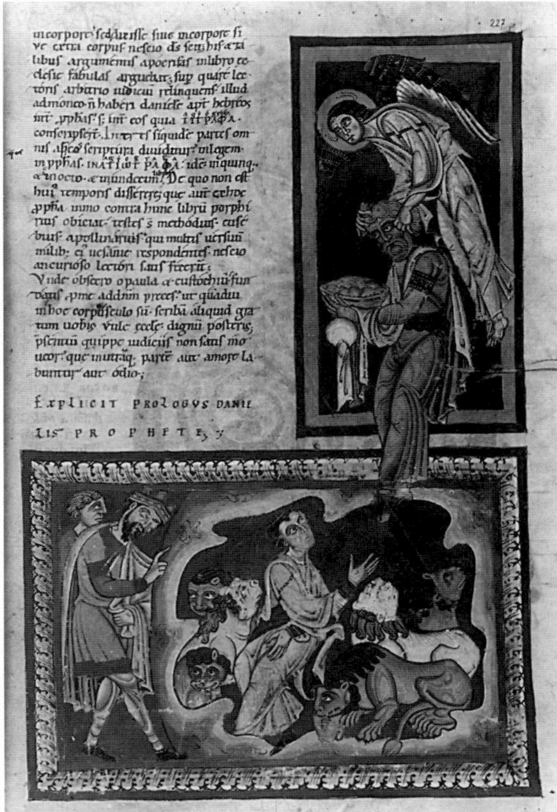

11. *Daniel in the Lions' Den* and *Habakkuk Delivering Food to Daniel*, miniatures from the Admont Bible, *c.* 1130–40 (Vienna, Österreichische Nationalbibliothek, Cods s.n. 2701–2)

12. Austrian school: *Throne of Solomon* (1260–70), wall painting on the east wall of the west gallery, Gurk Cathedral

attract local imitators (e.g. the Admont Bible, *c.* 1130–40, Vienna, Österreich. Nbib., Cods. s.n. 2701–2; see fig. 11). The illuminator 'Liutoldus monachus', active at Mondsee Monastery in the mid-12th century, was influenced by the Byzantine style, as well as by the Italian bibles, but he developed an influential personal style. Other high-quality workers were associated with the wall paintings in Pürgg.

In the later 12th century significant workshops were established in nearly all monasteries belonging to the Benedictines, the Augustinian canons and the Cistercians, and in most Carthusian houses. Monastic orders also exchanged manuscripts and scribes internationally: it can be demonstrated, for example, that there were links between Heiligenkreuz and Morimond in France, between Viktring, near Klagenfurt, and Lorraine, and between Admont and Bamberg. Manuscripts that have survived from the late 12th century and after are notable for their distinctive style of draughtsmanship, with little emphasis on line. The use of pictures was restricted to the initial letters and comprised purely ornamental leaf and tendril work, in a manner characteristic of the Cistercians (e.g. the Musterbuch, early 13th century; Vienna, Österreich. Nbib., Cod. 507).

(ii) Gothic.

(a) Wall paintings. From *c.* 1250 the transition to the Gothic style occurred, with the jagged ZACKENSTIL. This had become established in German book illumination by *c.* 1220 but appeared later in Austria, for example in the wall paintings of the 1260s (see fig. 12) in Gurk Cathedral in Carinthia. These highly influential works are the product of at least two masters. Krems in Lower Austria was another centre of outstanding Early Gothic wall painting: a *Coronation of the Virgin* and a *Crucifixion* from *c.* 1285 have been preserved in the former Dominican church (now the Historisches Museum). The *Zackenstil* reached its zenith at this point, although it lingered on in provincial works.

Around 1300 a new style of portraying figures appeared, as can be seen in the youthful faces, flowing lines and delicate colours at the Göttweiger Hof Chapel in Stein in Lower Austria. Stylistic parallels exist between wall paintings and the manuscripts produced at the abbey of St Florian in Upper Austria. During the 14th century Bohemian and Italian influences became stronger, indicating international travel among artists. Italian influences were strongest in the Tyrol and Carinthia, although also present elsewhere. An Italian artist was working *c.* 1350, for example, in the former Minorite church at Stein, where the paintings show links with Veronese works. The style of the ducal workshop in Vienna also was apparent in all fields of painting by *c.* 1400. From this period noteworthy examples of secular wall paintings have survived, for example scenes from a *Jealousy* cycle (*c.* 1400) in the house at Tuchlauben 19 in Vienna. They depict dancing figures and a sleigh ride among other activities, and their style indicates close links with Bohemian art.

In the Late Gothic period THOMAS ARTULA VON VILLACH was one of the greatest Austrian painters, both of wall and panel paintings: his interior painting (*c.* 1475) at Thörl, near Villach in Carinthia, includes a superbly conceived programme depicting the celestial hierarchy. Very Late Gothic wall painting shows a highly characteristic approach to decoration with leaves and flowers, particularly in the vaulting of churches. This is linked with the work of the DANUBE SCHOOL, led by Albrecht Altdorfer (*see* ALTDORFER, (1)) and active in various parts of central Europe, including Austria: it developed an innovative style of representing nature and landscape in the early part of the 16th century. Around this time Renaissance elements began to appear in the work of various painters, although they were still basically Gothic in style, for example Urban Görtschacher (*c.* 1485–*c.* 1530), who worked mainly in Carinthia.

(b) Panel paintings. The inception of panel painting can be traced back to before 1300, although such early examples are exceptional: the first evidence of an Austrian studio of panel painting, under Bohemian and Italian influence, is provided by the painting (*c.* 1331; *see* GOTHIC, fig. 82) on the reverse of an altar at Klosterneuburg Abbey, which also incorporates enamel plaques (completed 1181) by Nicholas of Verdun. The development of panel painting is associated with centres of production dating from the first half of the 14th century at St Florian, Vienna and Klosterneuburg, which inspired all forms of painting. The principal centre was undoubtedly Vienna, where the court developed into the intellectual centre of the Habsburg empire under Rudolf IV (*reg* 1358–65), depicted in a possibly posthumous portrait (*c.* 1365; Vienna, Dom- & Diözmus.).

The production of altar retables started to flourish only in the 15th century, although the retable from Schloss Tirol (Innsbruck, Tirol. Landesmus.) dates from as early as *c.* 1370: it has a strong sense of space and shows a clear Italian influence. Between *c.* 1380 and *c.* 1430 the soft graceful *Weicher Stil* developed, in particular in Salzburg, Vienna and Styria. The artists included the Master of the Vienna Adoration; the Master of the St Lambert Votive Altarpiece; and the Master of the London Throne of Mercy (or of the Madonna in the Nimbus), named after the *Throne of Mercy* (*c.* 1420) now in the National Gallery, London. The MASTER OF THE ALBRECHT ALTAR (*see* MASTERS, ANONYMOUS, AND MONOGRAMMISTS, §I) was active in the transition from the *Weicher Stil* to a greater realism and worked mainly in the area of Vienna and Klosterneuburg. He is notable mainly for the rounded style of his figures but is probably not the same person as JAKOB KASCHAUER, despite similarities in their work. A more definite exponent of realism was CONRAD LAIB, who was influenced by the art of Bavaria, Swabia, the Netherlands and northern Italy (e.g. the *Crucifixion*, 1457, Graz, Diözmus.; the *Crucifixion*, 1449; Vienna, Belvedere). In general the early 15th century was marked more strongly than before by realism, particularly with the increasing influence of Netherlandish art and the diffusion of prints.

Quattrocento Italian ideas of perspective were imported into Austria via the Tyrol by MICHAEL PACHER, whose pupils included MARX REICHLICH in Salzburg. In the late 15th century Rueland Frueauf (i) and the Master of Grossgmain also adopted the prevailing realism. The use of gold ground was gradually abandoned from the 1480s. However, despite stylistic influences from such Netherlandish artists as Dieric Bouts (i) and Rogier van der Weyden, a certain rigidification of forms took place, until the advent *c.* 1520 of the Danube school, which was particularly concerned with depicting the landscape of the Alps. Its principal artists were WOLFGANG HUBER and, in particular, Altdorfer, whose work included highly atmospheric landscapes, sometimes completely without figures. Lucas Cranach (i) also belonged to this group for a brief period.

(c) Manuscript illumination and graphic art. From the 14th century Gothic book illumination was commissioned by private individuals: Breviaries and Books of Hours were produced for private use by secular workshops, while liturgical books continued to be made by monastic centres. St Florian Abbey, whose work was influenced by imported French examples, was pre-eminent in the 14th century (*see* ST FLORIAN ABBEY, §2), while the abbey at Klosterneuburg also played an important role. Finally, from the late 14th century the ducal workshop in Vienna took over the leading role: there was also a productive workshop in Salzburg in the 15th century, as well as some travelling illuminators. In the reign of Duke Ernest (*reg* 1386–1424), scriptoria were set up in Wiener Neustadt and in Styrian monasteries, and probably also in the Duke's residence at Graz. Heinrich Aurhaym (*fl* 1410–20), who had trained in Bohemia and Vienna, was one of the best known of the illuminators in Graz. In the late 15th century ULRICH SCHREIER was active both in Salzburg and in Vienna, working for the imperial court, as were MARTINUS 'OPIFEX' and Jörg Kölderer (*d* 1540).

The principal role of graphic art was as a preparatory medium: prints that are unrelated to existing panel paintings are rare. The first notable drawings date from the period of the *Weicher Stil.* Although few have survived, significant works can be ascribed to the Master of Laufen and the Master of the St Lambert Votive Altarpiece. Around 1400 woodcuts, produced in the studios of painters and possibly monastery scriptoria, developed into an independent artistic category, gaining popularity because of their almost unlimited reproduction potential: they were frequently stuck into manuscripts. Important series of woodcuts were later made by such members of the Danube school as Altdorfer and Huber, both obviously influenced by Dürer.

BIBLIOGRAPHY

G. Swarzenski: *Die Salzburger Malerei von den ersten Anfängen bis zur Blütezeit des romanischen Stils*, 2 vols (Berlin, 1908–13)

P. Buberl: *Die illuminierten Handschriften in Steiermark: Die Stiftsbibliotheken zu Admont und Vorau* (Leipzig, 1911)

R. Noll: *Frühes Christentum in Österreich* (Vienna, 1954)

L. Baldass and others: *Gotik in Österreich* (Vienna, 1961)

——: *Romanische Kunst in Österreich* (Vienna, 1962)

G. Schmidt: *Die Malerschule von St Florian: Beiträge zur süddeutschen Malerei zu Ende des 13. und im 14. Jahrhundert* (Linz, 1962)

Romanische Kunst in Österreich (exh. cat., Krems, Hist. Mus., 1964)

Gotik in Österreich (exh. cat., Krems, Hist. Mus., 1967)

O. Demus: *Romanische Wandmalerei* (Munich, 1968)

E. Weiss: 'Der Freskenzyklus der Johanneskapelle in Pürgg', *Wien. Jb. Kstgesch.*, xxii (1969), pp. 7–43

E. Baum: *Katalog des Museums mittelalterlicher österreichischer Kunst* (Vienna, 1971)

Spätgotik in Salzburg: Die Malerei, 1400–1530 (exh. cat., Salzburg, Mus. Carolino Augusteum, 1972)

1000 Jahre Babenberger in Österreich (exh. cat. by E. Zollner, K. Gutkas, G. Stangler and G. Winkler, Lilienfeld, Cisterc. Abbey, 1976)

O. Mazal: *Buchkunst der Romanik* (Graz, 1978)

Die Zeit der frühen Habsburger—Dome und Klöster, 1279–1379 (exh. cat. by K. Bugmann and others, Wiener Neustadt, Stadtmus., 1979)

F. Röhrig, ed.: *Der Albrechtsaltar und sein Meister* (Vienna, 1981)

Die Kuenringer: Das Werden des Landes Niederösterreich (exh. cat. by H. Wolfram, K. Brunner, W. Kitlitschka and A. Rosenauer, Zwettl, Cisterc. Abbey, 1981)

G. Biedermann: *Katalog der mittelalterlichen Kunst in der Alten Galerie am Landesmuseum Joanneum* (Graz, 1982)

E. Lanc: *Die mittelalterlichen Wandmalereien in Wien und Niederösterreich*, Corpus der mittelalterlichen Wandmalerei Österreichs (Vienna, 1983)

J. Höfler: *Die Tafelmalerei der Gotik in Kärnten, 1420–1500* (Klagenfurt, 1987)

A. Saliger and W. Kuba-Hauk, eds: *Katalog der Bestände des Erzbischöflichen Dom- und Diözesanmuseums* (Vienna, 1987)

G. Biedermann and K. Roth: *Schatzkammer Steiermark* (Graz, 1992)

2. *c*. 1530–*c*. 1600: RENAISSANCE. The first stirrings of the Renaissance appeared tentatively, mainly in the decorative arts. However, a change from Gothic to Renaissance shapes *c*. 1530 is apparent even in the external form of winged painted and sculpted retables, although in general only scattered remains of altarpieces have survived from the 16th century. Wall paintings were more significant, for example outstanding tempera works (1536) in the Rittersaal at Schloss Goldegg, near St Johann im Pongau (Salzburg). An unidentified painter (possibly Hans Bocksberger I) created an extensive programme revealing a humanist interest in Antiquity. The allegorical and mythological pictures and the hunting and social scenes also reflect the taste of the castle's owner, a friend of the Archbishop of Salzburg.

The wall paintings of 1539 in the small parish church of Pölling, near Wolfsberg, depict Reformation themes of law and mercy, in their juxtaposition of the *Brazen Serpent* and the *Crucifixion*. As the churches in which these and other related subjects were depicted were not all Protestant, these paintings appear to indicate a remarkable tolerance towards Reformation ideas. In contrast, traditional medieval biblical themes appear in the wall paintings (1554–8) in the former Spitalkirche at Bad Aussee, Styria, with a style close to that of the Bocksbergers and their circle. At the castle of Freisaal on the edge of Salzburg, large grisaille wall paintings (1555–8) have survived, illustrating among other things the glorification of the newly elected Archbishop Michael Kuenburg. Again, Hans Bocksberger I has been associated with this work (*see* BOCKSBERGER, (1)) and also with the painting of the chapel (from 1579) at Burg Strechau, near Liezen in Styria, where the Protestant theologian David Chytraeus worked out the iconographic programme.

The princely courts at Vienna, Ambras in the Tyrol and Graz were important art centres, for example commissioning portraits from JAKOB SEISENEGGER. However, little remains of the grand decorations that were executed, except for pictures of *c*. 1570 at Schloss Ambras. In the late 16th century important work was produced in Carinthia by Anton Plumenthal (*d* 1604), whose paintings (begun 1598) in the choir and apse of Gurk Cathedral reveal close associations with the art of Tintoretto. From *c*. 1600 a remarkable example of exterior wall painting, depicting mythological, astrological and biblical themes, has survived on the façade of the castle of Parz, near Grieskirchen, Upper Austria. Rich townspeople, including the urban aristocracy, also commissioned paintings for the courtyards, façades and interiors of their homes.

Generally, 16th-century art in Austria was dominated by Italians, with the court at Graz attracting many artists—including Giulio Licinio, Teodoro Ghisi, Martino Rota and Ottaviano Zanuoli (*d* 1607)—during the reign of Archduke Charles II (*reg* 1564–90). Ghisi's main achievement was his role in painting the interior (see fig. 13) of the mausoleum of Archduke Charles in the church at Seckau Abbey, with themes clearly inspired by the Counter Reformation. Another prominent Italian was Donato Arsenio Mascagni (1579–1636), employed by the Archbishop of Salzburg, Marcus Sitticus von Hohenems. Mascagni created both ceiling paintings and altarpieces. Among Netherlandish artists active in Austria, Lucas van Valckenborch I was court painter to Archduke Matthias (subsequently emperor; *reg* 1608–19) and lived in Linz from 1582 to 1592–3.

In the graphic arts, important prints were made during the 16th century by several generations of the Bocksberger

13. Teodoro Ghisi and others: ceiling painting of the mausoleum of Archduke Charles (1587–90), Seckau Abbey

family: for example, Hans Bocksberger I produced a series of widely circulated Dürer-inspired woodcuts of the *Triumphal Procession* at the coronation of Maximilian II (*reg* 1564–76), now in the Albertina, Vienna. Drawings were not treated as an independent art form, mainly being used in the process of making paintings and prints by, for example, various of the Bocksbergers. A pupil of the Bocksbergers, Georg Peham (*c.* 1568–1604), produced both drawings and etchings for the archdukes of Inner Austria at Graz. Following the Danube school, HANNS LAUTENSACK and Augustin Hirschvogel (*see* HIRSCHVOGEL, (2)) became known as engravers of landscapes. Of the Italians in Austria, Rota made drawings and portrait engravings of the Habsburgs.

BIBLIOGRAPHY

E. Guldan and U. Rittinger: 'Die protestantischen Deckenmalereien der Burgkapelle auf Strechau', *Wien. Jb. Kstgesch.* (1960), pp. 28–86

G. Heinz: 'Studien zur Porträtmalerei an den Höfen der österreichischen Erblande', *Jb. Ksthist. Samml. Wien* (1963), pp. 99–224

R. Milesi: *Manierismus in Kärnten: Zur Kunst des späten 16. Jahrhunderts* (Klagenfurt, 1973)

R. Feuchtmüller: *Renaissance in Österreich* (Vienna, 1974)

B. Euler-Rolle: 'Entdeckung und Erhaltung der Renaissancefresken am Landschloss Parz', *Österreich. Z. Kst & Dkmlpf.*, xli/3–4 (1987), pp. 155–65

3. *c.* 1600–*c.* 1800: BAROQUE.

(i) Large-scale decorative programmes. In the early 17th century a few young artists introduced new forms, heralding the first stages in the development of Baroque art in Austria. Many of these artists were engaged in the decoration of imperial and aristocratic residences (the painting of the façades of town houses was also common as an indication of social status) and in the decoration of churches and monasteries, inspired by the Counter-Reformation zeal of Archduke Ferdinand II (*reg* 1619–37). Before moving to Vienna in 1619, Ferdinand had lived in Graz, where he employed almost exclusively Italian or Italian-influenced artists, including PIETRO DE POMIS, whose work was more inspired by Venetian Mannerism than the Baroque. Gradually an almost official artistic language evolved, with walls and ceilings being decorated with paintings depicting themes from Classical literature and mythology, executed often by Dutch or Italian artists, such as Carpoforo Tencala.

14. Johann Wenzel Bergl: *Exotic Scene* (1763), wall painting, garden pavilion, Melk Abbey, Lower Austria

For most of the 17th century, however, the wars against the Turks and other social factors militated against any continuous artistic development. Innovation was rare, and the influence of late Mannerism, rather than the Italian Baroque, was still evident in the works of the few artists with any claim to originality, such as Tobias Pock or Joachim von Sandrart. Sandrart, originally from Frankfurt am Main, was influenced by Rubens and worked in Vienna and in monasteries in Upper Austria, such as Mondsee and Lambach. The work of Johann Spillenberger I is characterized on the other hand by an academic dryness, reflecting the influence of late Renaissance artists such as Tintoretto.

The early Italian Baroque style was eventually introduced by Johann Carl Loth (*see* LOTH, (2)), who was later appointed court painter to the Emperor in 1692. Loth's pupils included Hans Adam Weissenkircher, who was active mostly in Styria. Important illusionistic painting was executed by the Tyrolean Egid Schor, the most famous member of an important artistic family (*see* SCHOR), who heavily influenced such artists as Kaspar Waldmann in Innsbruck. The famous Italian ANDREA POZZO himself made *trompe l'oeil* ceiling paintings in Vienna (for example in the Jesuit church, 1703–9).

Another important factor in the development of Baroque painting was the victory over the Turks outside Vienna in 1683, after which aristocratic patrons emerged with new confidence. ANTONIO BEDUZZI, whose work can be seen in Vienna and the Austrian monasteries along the Danube (such as Melk Abbey), best exemplifies the new monumental expression of Austrian greatness, known as the *Reichsstil.* In Vienna there were new opportunities for painting such buildings as the Belvedere and the Schönbrunn Palace (*see* VIENNA, §V, 6 and 7(i)). For the first time painting covered large interlinking surfaces, without the formal limitations imposed by stucco. An indigenous style was created, although influences were still felt from Italian art, and in 1692 an art school, the Kaiserliche Akademie, was publicly instituted in Vienna. In the early 18th century one of the most accomplished painters was JOHANN MICHAEL ROTTMAYR, whose work, inspired by Pozzo and Rubens (for example the frescoes (from 1725) in the Karlskirche, Vienna), illustrates the principle that painting and architecture should form a unity. Neapolitan art was the main influence on Martino Altomonte: born in Naples, he moved to Vienna sometime between 1699 and 1702, creating his masterpiece, the ceiling painting of the *Apotheosis of Prince Eugene of Savoy* (1716), for the Marmorsaal of the Lower Belvedere.

The outstanding artist of the following generation was PAUL TROGER, responsible for the dome fresco and altarpiece (from 1728) of the Kajetanerkirche in Salzburg. Troger's rivalry with his fellow Tyrolean Michael Angelo

Unterberger, who was also influenced by Venetian art, stimulated Austrian painting as a whole. Troger's pupils included Peter Anton Lorenzoni, Kaspar Franz Sambach, MARTIN KNOLLER and JOHANN WENZEL BERGL (see fig. 14). Daniel Gran, whose work was described by Winckelmann as sublime, was, like Troger, initially influenced by Venetian and Neapolitan art (in particular the work of Francesco Solimena). He was particularly skilful as a *trompe l'oeil* painter of Baroque frescoes (for illustration *see* GRAN, DANIEL). In 1755, in the Festsaal of Schloss Friedau, near St Pölten, he introduced classical elements, which ultimately led to a rigid academicism. Gran's work influenced Bartolomeo Altomonte, whose work is also reminiscent of his father, Martino Altomonte, and of the altar designs of the architect Johann Bernhard Fischer von Erlach. Of the many Italian artists in Austria in the Baroque period, Sebastiano Ricci painted an *Apotheosis of King Joseph I* (1701–2) at Schloss Schönbrunn, while Andrea Lanzani and Antonio Bellucci worked for noble families in Vienna. Other distinguished artists from Italian backgrounds included Carlo Carlone (ii) (for illustration *see* CARLONE (ii), (8)) and Gregorio Guglielmi, whose rivalry with FRANZ ANTON MAULBERTSCH marked the beginning of the development of late Baroque.

Maulbertsch's work was the climax of Austrian Baroque painting. Having trained at the Kaiserliche Akademie in Vienna (1739–45 and 1749–50), he produced altarpieces and wall and ceiling paintings, for example in the Piarist church (1752–3) in Vienna and in the parish church of Heiligenkreuz-Gutenbrunn (1757; see fig. 15). Maulbertsch was a master of illusionism, and his late work is particularly remarkable for its treatment of colour and light. Towards the end of his career, his compositions became redolent of classicism. Maulbertsch's pupils included Andreas Nesseltaler (1748–1821), Johann Caspar Fibich (*fl c.* 1760–90) and Franz Sigrist. The main legacy of MARTIN JOHANN SCHMIDT, the last great Baroque painter, is a large number of oil paintings and Baroque sketches, as well as a small number of frescoes. He produced work for almost all the important monasteries along the Danube (e.g. Melk Abbey) and for numerous parish and pilgrimage churches. His use of colour developed primarily from the Dutch and native Austrian traditions: the background of the pictures generally is in shades of brown, while objects and figures often have highly contrasted touches of blue and red.

15. Franz Anton Maulbertsch: *St Longinus* (1757), ceiling painting, parish church of Heiligenkreuz-Gutenbrunn, Lower Austria

(ii) Specialist subjects and graphic arts. During the Baroque period both aristocratic and middle-class patrons commissioned works from a large number of artists who specialized in particular subjects. For example, Franz Werner von Tamm, from Hamburg, produced fine still-lifes and flower paintings in Vienna, while landscapes and genre scenes were produced by Johann Jakob Hartmann (*c.* 1680–after 1728) and Franz de Paula Ferg. The tradition of Austrian landscape painting was strengthened by a special class at the Kaiserliche Akademie in Vienna. Such artists as Christian Hilfgott Brand produced smaller landscapes for middle-class clients. Brand was one of the 'Hollandists', influenced by 17th-century Dutch prototypes, although with Rococo elements. His son JOHANN CHRISTIAN BRAND depicted subjects that later became associated with Biedermeier landscape. He was influenced by such painters of *vedute* as Bernardo Bellotto, who stayed in Vienna from 1758 to 1761. The work of Salvator Rosa and 17th-century Dutch painters inspired the Tyrolean landscape painter Anton Faistenberger, who in turn influenced Maximilian Josef Schinnagl (1697–1762). Schinnagl's collaborator, Franz Christoph Janneck, also painted cabinet pictures with conversation scenes and other themes, as did his friend Johann Georg Platzer. Among portrait painters, Jan Kupecký and Jacob van Schuppen (1660–1751) showed the influence of such French artists as Hyacinthe Rigaud and Nicolas de Largillierre. MARTIN VAN MYTENS II painted superb idealized portraits of the imperial family (for illustration *see* VIENNA, fig. 9). CHRISTIAN SEYBOLD, on the other hand, far more directly conveyed the personality of his sitter. The work of Johann Baptist Lampi (i) developed this tendency, approaching the style of Biedermeier portraiture (*see* LAMPI (i), (1)).

Many painters also showed great drawing talent, for example Egid Schor and Johann Spillenberger II. The painterly style of Johann Carl Loth is reflected in various examples of his drawing, and his influence on the draughtsmanship of such artists as Rottmayr and Weissenkircher is unmistakable. Drawing also played a large role as a preparatory medium for the paintings of both Rottmayr and Weissenkircher, whose wash drawings rival those of Loth. The work of Peter Strudel appears very closely allied to that of Rottmayr and Weissenkircher, and the painterly style also influenced the superb drawings of Troger, who favoured pen drawing as a spontaneous form of expression. Troger also made etchings and engravings, particularly in the early part of his career. Excellent work was also produced by Franz Xaver Palko (1724–67), who drew character studies, as well as drawings for engravings, and by Martin Johann Schmidt, a highly versatile draughtsman and fine etcher. However, the highest quality as a draughtsman, watercolourist and etcher was undoubtedly achieved by Maulbertsch, who created colourful, painterly effects with skilful use of chiaroscuro.

BIBLIOGRAPHY

K. Garzarolli-Thurnlackh: *Die barocke Handzeichnung in Österreich* (Zurich, 1928)
K. Ginhart, ed.: *Die bildende Kunst in Österreich*, iii (Baden, 1939)
W. Mrazek: 'Ikonologie der barocken Deckenmalerei', *Anz. Österreich. Akad. Wiss. Philos.-Hist. Kl. Sber*, ccxxviii/3 (1953)
G. Aurenhammer: *Die Handzeichnung des 17. Jahrhunderts in Österreich* (Vienna, 1958)
B. Grimschitz and others: *Barock in Österreich* (Vienna, 1962)
C. Pack: *Graphik in Österreich* (Vienna, 1968)
G. Brucher: *Die barocke Deckenmalerei in der Steiermark* (Graz, 1973)
J. Ringler: *Die barocke Tafelmalerei in Tirol*, 2 vols (Innsbruck, 1973)
E. Baum: *Katalog des Österreichischen Barockmuseums im unteren Belvedere in Wien*, 2 vols (Vienna, 1980)
K. Garas: *Deutsche und österreichische Zeichnungen des 18. Jahrhunderts* (Budapest, 1980)
Barock in Innsbruck (exh. cat. by E. Egg and G. Ammann, Innsbruck, Tirol. Landesmus., 1980)
Österreich zur Zeit Kaiser Josephs II (exh. cat. by K. Gutkas, Melk, Stiftsmus., 1980)
Welt des Barock (exh. cat., St Florian Abbey, 1986)
Die Botschaft der Graphik (exh. cat. by R. Feuchtmüller and F. Kováks, Lambach, Benedictine Abbey, 1989)
Lust und Leid: Barocker Kunst, Barocker Alltag (exh. cat., Graz, Schloss Trautenfels, 1992)

4. AFTER *c.* 1800. 19th-century art was characterized by the presence of a number of styles and movements that overlapped chronologically. The first decades of the century were dominated by Neo-classicism and by the work of the Nazarenes. Notable exponents of Neo-classicism included HEINRICH FRIEDRICH FÜGER and Joseph Anton Koch, who spent most of his life in Rome and depicted historical subjects in a style that also incorporated some elements of Romanticism. The nucleus of the NAZARENES, a group who imitated early Italian painting and particularly the work of Raphael, lay in the Lukasbund, an association of six artists formed in Vienna in 1809. Active in both Rome and northern Europe, the Nazarenes also executed decorative interiors. In Austria the group's members included Julius Schnorr von Carolsfeld, Ferdinand Olivier and JOHANN SCHEFFER VON LEONHARDSHOFF.

In the second quarter of the century the BIEDERMEIER style was particularly important in extending the possibilities of landscape painting and establishing it as an independent genre, transcending the simple *vedute* produced in the early years of the century by such artists as JOSEF REBELL. Landscape became a vehicle for transmitting atmospheric values, with the area around Vienna affording appropriate subject-matter and the landscape classes at the Kaiserliche Akademie helping to train the artists. Outstanding among the Biedermeier landscape painters were Franz Steinfeld (1787–1868), THOMAS ENDER (one of the finest watercolourists), RUDOLF ALT and FRIEDRICH GAUERMANN, who painted atmospheric storm scenes. Ferdinand Georg Waldmüller's work has some affinities with the Biedermeier style but is also highly realistic in its detail (for illustration *see* WALDMÜLLER, FERDINAND GEORG; *see also* VIENNA, fig. 10). Many of these landscape painters produced small-scale works, and many also favoured watercolour and lithography, the relatively low cost of which allowed them to appeal to a middle-class market. The Biedermeier style was not, however, restricted to landscapes. Portraiture was practised by FRIEDRICH VON AMERLING, Josef Franz Danhauser and PETER FENDI, while flower paintings were executed by Johann Knapp (1778–1833) and MORITZ MICHAEL DAFFINGER, who worked in a more scientific or botanical style. Michael Neder (1807–82), like Waldmüller, was a master of genre painting, while Jakob Gauermann (1773–1843), Matthäus Loder (1781–1828) and Johann Kniep (1779–1809) were among the official court painters associated with Archduke John (1782–1859) who were commissioned to depict the unspoilt environment and everyday life of Styria.

The revolutionary period in mid-century led to the introduction of new artistic influences and approaches. Dominant among these, in an era preoccupied with the

16. Hans Makart: *Cleopatra's Nile Journey*, oil on canvas, 0.50×1.89 m, 1875 (Stuttgart, Staatsgalerie)

past, was a version of Historicism. The numerous opportunities for the development of history painting attracted not just native painters but also such foreign artists as Anselm Feuerbach, who created the mural of the *Fall of the Titans* (1874–80; installed 1892, *in situ*) for the Great Hall of the Akademie der Bildenden Künste in Vienna. The main representative of Historicism was undoubtedly Hans Makart (for illustration *see* MAKART, HANS), who achieved virtually neo-Baroque theatrical effects and attempted to emulate Rubens. Another important history painter, although a somewhat isolated figure, was Anton Romako (for illustration *see* ROMAKO, ANTON). Around the same time some artists, including Makart and Leopold Carl Müller (1834–92), developed a version of ORIENTALISM, based on English and French examples (see fig. 16).

Another artistic strand was formed by a group of Austrian painters who responded to contemporary developments in French painting. Some, inspired by the Barbizon school, formed a loose association with Hungarian artists, based in Szolnok in eastern Hungary (*see* SZOLNOK COLONY). These included AUGUST VON PETTENKOFEN, Johann Gualbert Raffalt (1835–65), Tina Blau (1845–1916) and Eugen Jettel (1845–1901), who painted and drew from nature *en plein air*. Emil Jakob Schindler (1842–92) was one of the first generation of Austrians to pursue intensive studies in France and also became an accomplished *plein-air* painter. Carl Schuch created still-lifes inspired by Impressionism. Schindler influenced other important painters, including Olga Wisinger-Florian (1844–1926) and Marie Egner (1850–1940), some of whom had already become familiar with European stylistic movements through travel in Hungary and France.

The turn of the 19th century was marked by the rise of *Jugendstil* (*see* ART NOUVEAU, §5): the outstanding figure was GUSTAV KLIMT, who significantly did not train at the Akademie, but at the less academic Kunstgewerbeschule. Klimt was notable for his erotic art (see fig. 17) and for his landscapes, influenced by Impressionism, but he also undertook large programmes of wall paintings, taking Makart as his main model. These included scenes from the Classical theatre, painted in 1886–8 for the Burgtheater in Vienna (*in situ*). In 1897 he was one of the founders of the Vienna Secession (*see* SECESSION, §3), which included such artists as Carl Moll. Although striving for a common goal, the group's members also sought to preserve their individual identities. Around this time drawing also began to establish a new importance in its own right, especially within the work of such artists as Kolo Moser, who produced designs for posters, textiles, tiles and stained glass.

In the early 20th century a distinctive version of Expressionism emerged from the Viennese exhibiting group known as the HAGENBUND (1900–30), which comprised a diverse range of artists. Albin Egger-Lienz, for example, concentrated on such subjects as war and death, while EGON SCHIELE, on the other hand, produced erotic works but also depicted landscapes devoid of people and isolated, at times highly distorted, figures. Another leading Expressionist was OSKAR KOKOSCHKA: influenced by Klimt and devastated by the suffering of World War I, he expressed his perception of the human condition in both his art and writings. RICHARD GERSTL concentrated on spiritual subjects in his work, which has some affinity to the poetry of Georg Trakl. Significant Expressionist work was also produced by the Nötsch school, centred on Anton Kolig and Franz Wiegele.

17. Gustav Klimt: *The Kiss*, oil on canvas, 1.8×1.8 m, 1907–8 (Vienna, Belvedere, Österreichische Galerie)

Anton Faistauer, who had exhibited with the Hagenbund in 1911, created wall and ceiling paintings in Salzburg from 1922. In Styria, Wilhelm Thöny and Alfred Wickenburg (1885–1978) created notable work, while in Carinthia Werner Berg (1904–81) revealed a lasting interest in the forms of Expressionism in his country scenes and landscapes. In Upper Austria the most significant representative of Expressionism was Alfred Kubin, who won international recognition, in particular for his graphic work, with such subjects as death, hunger and the nature of human existence (for illustration *see* KUBIN, ALFRED). Other significant graphic artists were Ludwig Heinrich Jungnickel, Oskar Laske (1874–1951) and the Tyrolean Paul Flora (*b* 1922), whose work is characterized by witty and somewhat macabre subject-matter.

Shortly after World War II the work of ALBERT PARIS VON GÜTERSLOH inspired the development in Vienna of PHANTASTISCHER REALISMUS, a style embraced by such artists as Ernst Fuchs, Anton Lehmden (*b* 1929), Rudolf Hausner, Wolfgang Hutter (*b* 1928) and Arik Brauer. The group also stimulated a new interest in printmaking, while around the same time HERBERT BOECKL, who was influenced by Kolig and Wiegele, showed a continued interest in mural decoration (see fig. 18). Abstract paintings influenced by *Art informel* were also produced by such artists as Max Weiler (*b* 1910), Wolfgang Hollegha (*b* 1929) and Josef Mikl (*b* 1929). Some of the most important post-war artists, such as Adolf Frohner (*b* 1934), Arnulf Rainer, Oswald Oberhuber and FRIEDENSREICH HUNDERTWASSER, remained independent of any collective groups or movements. Rainer's work progressed through several

18. Herbert Boeckl: *Apocalyptic Vision* (1952–60), from the mural cycle in the Engelskapelle, Seckau Abbey, Styria

stages of development and included such techniques as overpainting photographs and earlier paintings to produce almost monochrome effects (for illustration *see* RAINER, ARNULF). Hundertwasser's works were characterized by highly ornamental patterns and rich colours. Those who experimented with new—and sometimes shocking—forms include HERMANN NITSCH, Günter Brus and other artists associated with AKTIONISMUS, who early in their career produced a form of action painting before turning to performance art (for illustration *see* BRUS, GÜNTER). The international recognition that these artists achieved contributed to the high standing of Austrian art in the late 20th century.

BIBLIOGRAPHY

L. Hevesi: *Österreichische Kunst im 19. Jahrhundert* (Leipzig, 1903)

B. Grimschitz: *Österreichische Maler vom Biedermeier zur Moderne* (Vienna, 1963)

O. Breicha: *Aufforderung zum Misstrauen* (Salzburg, 1967)

Romantik und Realismus in Österreich (exh. cat. by R. Feuchtmüller, Laxenburg, Altes Schloss, 1968)

P. Vergo: *Art in Vienna, 1898–1918: Klimt, Kokoschka, Schiele and their Contemporaries* (London, 1975)

P. Pötschner: *Wien und die Wiener Landschaft: Spätbarocke und biedermeierliche Landschaftskunst in Wien* (Salzburg, 1978)

Nazarener in Österreich, 1809–1939: Zeichnungen und Druckgrafik (exh. cat. by C. Steinle and W. Skreiner, Graz, Steiermärk. Landesmus., 1979)

Österreichische Malerei nach 1945 (exh. cat. by K. Gutkas, St Pölten, Stadtmus., 1979)

Vor hundert Jahren Wien 1879, als Beispiel für die Zeit des Historismus (exh. cat. by G. Düriegl and others, Vienna, Hist. Mus., 1979)

C. E. Schorske: *Fin-de-siècle Vienna* (New York, 1980)

Wien, 1870–1930: Traum und Wirklichkeit (exh. cat., Vienna, Kstlerhaus, 1985)

Vienne, 1880–1938: L'Apocalypse joyeuse (exh. cat., ed. J. Clair; Paris, Pompidou, 1986)

GOTTFRIED BIEDERMANN

IV. Sculpture.

1. Before *c.* 1400: Romanesque and Gothic. 2. *c.* 1400–*c.* 1600: Late Gothic and Renaissance. 3. *c.* 1600–*c.* 1750: Baroque. 4. *c.* 1750–*c.* 1900: Neo-classicism to Historicism. 5. After *c.* 1900: Modern developments.

1. BEFORE *c.* 1400: ROMANESQUE AND GOTHIC. A considerable quantity of ornamental interlace survives from the 8th century (examples in Millstatt, Stiftsmus.), for the most part abstract, although a human figure survives (Molzbichl, St Tiburtius). Sculpture became gradually more independent of architecture. Among the earliest ecclesiastical wood figural sculptures in Austria was probably a small relief of the *Crucifixion* (360×575 mm; Linz, Oberösterreich. Landesmus.), produced in the region around Kremsmünster Abbey. Its expressive group of plain figures in wood corresponds in form to the relief of the doors of St Maria im Kapitol, Cologne, dating it to around the mid-11th century; other features refer to the 12th century. The sculpture produced in the period that followed was simple and symbolic (*see also* ROMANESQUE, §III, 1(ix)(e)) and is exemplified by the former Benedictine monastery of Millstatt in Carinthia. The west portal (*c.* 1170) at Millstatt is particularly notable for the richness of its decorative designs, showing the influence of Lombard tradition, while the cloister, dating from the same period, also contains richly detailed and resourceful sculpture (*see* ROMANESQUE, fig. 43). The slightly later sequence of relief sculptures (*c.* 1220) on the outer wall of the apse of the parish church of Mariae Geburt, Schöngrabern (Lower Austria), constitutes a Bible in stone. Staring masks and wild beasts are interspersed in scenes illustrating events from the *Fall* to the *Life of Christ* and the *Last Judgement.* The earliest preserved medieval monumental sculpture in Austria is in the Benedictine abbey at Seckau (Styria). It depicts a monumental lime-wood *Crucifixion* group (second half of the 12th century); the central figure of Christ was replaced in the early 13th century (original now in Innsbruck, Tirol. Landesmus.). The group has stylistic links with work produced in south Bavaria. The tall, slender figures appear withdrawn, their forms depicted in a linear manner. The purity of line, remote abstraction and solemn tranquillity are typically Romanesque, and in the frontal viewpoint the two-dimensional aspect of earlier work is continued.

Only a few works have survived from the early Gothic period in Austria, which began in the late 13th century. The first extant attempts to represent the figure in a new way and to show an emotional depth are found on various tympana depicting the *Virgin and Child.* The sandstone relief on the west portal (*c.* 1260) of Seckau Abbey shows the *Virgin and Child* on the lion's throne. This theme was first used in the Romanesque period, but the vivid and more human loveliness of the figures at Seckau is new. The tympanum relief (1283–93) on the west portal of the Early Gothic Leechkirche, Graz, shows the same stylistic development: the sandstone *Virgin and Child,* sitting on two interlaced dragons, has a poignant immediacy. The Klosterneuburg *Virgin,* in the lapidarium of the convent, is an over life-size figure in sandstone (early 14th century) with a natural structure and shape. The wood Admont *Virgin and Child* (*c.* 1310; Graz, Alte Gal.) and the sandstone 'Dienstbotenmadonna' (first quarter of the 14th century; Vienna, Stephansdom) are early examples of a number of Gothic sculptures of the high quality found in western Europe. The Admont *Virgin and Child* is particularly notable for its flowing, courtly elegance. The Virgin is representative of a rare type; her outer robe hangs open, and she carries the Child on her right arm. Similar Virgins are a French ivory sculpture (1320/30; The Hague, Bochstiz) and one depicted in the window of Wiener Neustadt (first quarter of the 14th century; Nuremberg,

19. *Pietà*, limestone, h. 890 mm, Admont I, Austria, *c.* 1400 (Graz, Alte Galerie)

Ger. Nmus.). Later examples of this type include the wood *Virgin and Child* from Erlach in Lower Austria and the stone *Virgin and Child* from Thernberg in Lower Austria (both Vienna, Dom- & Diözmus.). In the early 14th century some remarkable mystic crucifixes were produced in Austria. The wooden Y-shaped Crucifix (*c.* 1300) of the Dominican church in Friesach juxtaposes an intensely suffering Christ with a green cross symbolizing hope and eternal life. The arms of the figure of Christ on the Y-shaped Crucifix (*c.* 1350) in the parish church of Lassnitz, Styria, were made to be detachable, so that at Easter the body could be placed in the Holy Sepulchre.

In the second half of the 14th century a variety of European trends combined to form a characteristically Austrian style in the ducal workshop of the Stephanskirche (now Stephansdom; *see* VIENNA, §V, 1(ii)). Here important sculptural sequences were produced for the cathedral during alterations under Rudolf IV (*reg* 1358–65). The workshop is noted for its dramatic presentation and naturalism, and its series of statues of princes (1360–65; Vienna, Hist. Mus.) are among the first European portrait sculptures. The *St Catherine* (Vienna, Michaelerkirche) and the Sonntagberg *Virgin and Child* (Vienna, Belvedere, Österreich. Gal.), both by the Michaelermeister (*fl* 1365–70) of Vienna, anticipate the north European Renaissance. The master's figures are serene and natural, covered by classicizing drapery. He was possibly trained in Florence.

At the end of the 14th century there were two dominant themes in Austrian sculpture. The first of these was the *Schöne Madonna.* The scholastic interpretation of the Hohe Lied and the poetry of the 14th century influenced Madonnas of this type, which are notable for their bodily and spiritual beauty in the Gothic ideal. The limestone *Virgin and Child* (Altenmarkt in Pongau, Unsere Liebe Frau), for example, can be dated to before 1393 (*see* GOTHIC, §III, 1(iii)(c) and fig. 36). It is stylistically related to the Krumauer *Virgin and Child* (before 1400; Vienna, Ksthist. Mus.). The *Virgin and Child* (*c.* 1410–15) in the Franciscan monastery in Salzburg is conventional but unsentimental and is typical of that area. The second dominant theme was the Pietà. Important examples include those from Klosterneuburg Abbey (1385–90; Klosterneuburg, Mus. Chorherrenstiftes) and from Kreuzenstein Castle (*c.* 1395–1400). The *Pietà* of Admont I (*c.* 1400; Graz, Alte Gal.; see fig. 19) shows the grieving Virgin's left hand supporting her dead son's lifeless hands, which bear the stigmata. In the *Pietà* of Admont II (1420–25; Graz, Alte Gal.) the Virgin uses her veil to dry her tears.

In Styria the works attributed to the MASTER OF GROSSLOBMING (*see* MASTERS, ANONYMOUS, AND MONOGRAMMISTS, §I) and his workshop continue the elegant, vivid style of the ducal workshop in Vienna. The sandstone *Martha* (1380; Vienna, Belvedere) from Thann, near Grosslobming, represents the new *Schöner Stil.*

BIBLIOGRAPHY

E. Baum: *Katalog des Museums Mittelalterlicher Österreichischer Kunst* (Vienna, 1971)

U. Laubert: *Studien zur mittelalterlichen Plastik im Bereich der Südostalpen* (diss., U. Munich, 1974)

G. Schmidt: 'Vesperbilder um 1400 und der "Meister der Schönen Madonnen"', *Österreich. Z. Kst & Dkmlpf.*, xxxi (1977), pp. 94–114

Gotik in der Steiermark (exh. cat., Graz, Kultreferat Steiermark. Landesregierung (1978), pp. 25–42

G. Biedermann: *Katalog Alte Galerie am Landesmuseum Joanneum Mittelalterliche Kunst* (Graz, 1982)

L. Schultes: *Der Anteil Österreichs an der Entwicklung der Plastik des schönen Stils* (diss., U. Vienna, 1982)

G. Biedermann: *Romanik in Österreich* (Graz, 1990)

Der Meister von Grosslobming (exh. cat., Vienna, Belvedere, 1994)

MARGIT STADLOBER

2. *c.* 1400–*c.* 1600: LATE GOTHIC AND RENAISSANCE. In the Late Gothic period, which continued into the early 16th century, one of the most important sculptural forms was the retable. Several notable artists, including HANS VON JUDENBURG, JAKOB KASCHAUER, Michael Pacher, HANS KLOCKER and the KRIECHBAUM family, contributed to the development of the form, helping to introduce new stylistic elements that gradually ushered in the Renaissance. The Master of the Znaim Altar (*c.* 1435–45; Vienna, Belvedere, Österreich. Gal.), who may have worked in Kaschauer's studio in Vienna, introduced a new and radical realism influenced by Netherlandish art and a style of relief that paralleled the Italian early Renaissance. In the Tyrol, Hans Multscher's altarpiece (1456–8/9; dismantled 1779; fragments in Basle, priv. col.; Innsbruck, Tirol. Landesmus.; Munich, Bayer. Nmus.; Vipiteno, Mus. Muellscher, and Parrocchio) for the church of Unsere Liebe Frau, Sterzing (now Vipiteno, Italy) was particularly important in the development of the retable; for example, the figures leaning out of windows in the background of the shrine are repeated in Klocker's altars (Munich, Bayer. Nmus.; and Bolzano, Franciscan church).

While Klocker and Hans Harder (*d* 1491) accentuated Multscher's dry realism, MICHAEL PACHER, influenced by the Italian Renaissance, achieved an almost classical synthesis of Gothic and Renaissance styles, particularly in such early works as the *Virgin and Child* in the parish church of St Lorenzen (1462–3; now Pusteria, Italian Tyrol). His altars in the old parish church of Gries near

20. Gregor Erhart, Gilg Sesselschreiber, Stefan Godl, Jörg Muscat, Alexander Colin, Florian Abel and others: monument to *Maximilian I*, bronze, 1508–85 (Innsbruck, Hofkapelle)

Bolzano and in the pilgrimage church of St Wolfgang am Abersee, commissioned in 1471, reveal familiarity with the Upper Rhine circle centred on Nicolaus Gerhaert.

Although Gerhaert's only documented work in Vienna was the lid of the tomb of *Frederick III* (*d* 1493) in the Stephansdom, his impact on south German and Austrian sculpture was so great that it is possible to talk of him as introducing the *Reichsstil* ('imperial style') in sculpture. The monumental cycle of the *Apostles* in the cathedral at Wiener Neustadt, for example, was the work of an important follower of Gerhaert's from Strasbourg, who is tentatively identified with LORENZ LUCHSPERGER. One of Gerhaert's pupils, possibly Martin Kriechbaum, executed a figure of the *Virgin* (Vienna, Niederösterreich. Landesmus.) with the features of the Empress Eleanor. Kriechbaum, whose workshop in Passau delivered work as far afield as Wachau and the Waldviertel, was also influenced by the Erhart workshop in Ulm and, above all, by Veit Stoss, as in the lime-wood Kefermarkt Altar (1476–97).

In the early 16th century, Viennese sculpture was dominated by the works of ANTON PILGRAM. These demonstrate an unsparing realism, as in the busts of the Church Fathers and self-portraits on the pulpit (*c.* 1513–15) and organ base (1513) in the Stephansdom. While Pilgram's work was still essentially Late Gothic in character, however, the formal repertory of the south German Renaissance was being introduced into Austria probably by Martin Kriechbaum's sons Stefan and Sebastian, who had trained in Augsburg with Hans Holbein the elder and Gregor Erhart respectively. The altars at the pilgrimage church of Mauer near Melk (*c.* 1509–15) in Lower Austria (*see* MASTERS, ANONYMOUS, AND MONOGRAMMISTS, §I: MASTER OF THE MAUER ALTAR) and Altmünster (1518) in Upper Austria, the *Annenaltar* (1512; Vienna, Archbishop's Palace, Andreaskapelle) and the furnishings of the chapel at Schloss Sierndorf (1516–18) in Lower Austria are the most important examples of this Austrian Renaissance, combining 'modern' ornamentation with a style of figure that was still decidedly Late Gothic. The master of the Late Gothic former high altar of Zwettl Abbey (1516–25; now in parish church, Adamov, Czech Republic), for example, was simultaneously creating such Renaissance-style works as the sculptures on the doorway of the Salvatorkapelle (*c.* 1516–25) in Vienna.

The dominance of the influence of Augsburg on sculpture in Vienna in the early 16th century reflected the taste of Emperor Maximilian I (*see* HABSBURG, §I(3)). The imperial sculptor Gregor Erhart created the enthroned *Virgin of Mercy* (for illustration *see* ERHART, (2)) in the Wallfahrtskirche at Frauenstein (Upper Austria) and may also have been involved in beginning work in 1508 on the monument to *Maximilian I* (Innsbruck, Hofkapelle); Albrecht Dürer, Veit Stoss, Hans Leinberger and Conrat Meit also produced designs and models for its monumental bronze figures, which were cast by GILG SESSELSCHREIBER, STEFAN GODL and the Vischer workshop in Nuremberg. Around the same time the Danube school of sculpture was also important, however, producing the Heiligblutkirche altar at Pulkau in Lower Austria and the Irrsdorf reliefs (*c.* 1520; Salzburg, Mus. Carolino Augusteum). It also made KUNSTKAMMER pieces, including reliefs and articulated dolls from the workshop of MASTER I. P. (*see* MASTERS, ANONYMOUS, AND MONOGRAMMISTS, §III). The middle third of the 16th century was a period of crisis. Even the monument to *Maximilian I* was not resumed until 1561; it was completed in a much altered form in 1585 (see fig. 20) by Florian Abel, ALEXANDER COLIN and others and was eventually modelled on the marble tomb (*c.* 1530) by Loy Hering and his workshop of *Count Niclas Salm* in the Dorotheerkirche (destr.; now in the Votivkirche), Vienna.

Austrian sculpture finally regained international acclaim through the work of Hubert Gerhard and CASPAR GRAS, who made the bronze tomb of *Maximilian III* (1615–19; Innsbruck, St Jakob) and the Leopold Fountain (1623–30) in the Rennweg, Innsbruck. Contemporary with this courtly Mannerism, marked by early Baroque features, is a group of indigenous, mostly anonymous, works that nevertheless still reveal some Late Gothic tendencies, for example the high altar (*c.* 1581) of the Karl-Borromäuskirche in Hohenems (Vorarlberg) by Esaias Gruber (*fl* 1581–1604). The use of stucco decoration, a field dominated by Italian artists, was another characteristic of the late 16th century. Examples include the decoration by Elia Castello (*d c.* 1602) of the Gabrielskapelle at St Sebastian's Cemetery, Salzburg. The furnishings for the mausoleum of Archduke Charles II (begun 1587) in the basilica of Maria Himmelfahrt at Seckau meanwhile anticipate the Austrian early Baroque.

BIBLIOGRAPHY

K. Oettinger: *Altdeutsche Bildschnitzer der Ostmark* (Vienna, 1939)

——: *Anton Pilgram und die Bildhauer von St Stephan* (Vienna, 1951)

A. Feulner and T. Müller: *Geschichte der deutschen Plastik* (Munich, 1953)

W. Pinder: *Vom Wesen und Werden deutscher Formen*, ii and iii (Frankfurt am Main, 1956–7)
A. Schädler: *Deutsche Plastik der Spätgotik* (Königstein, 1962)
W. Paatz: *Süddeutsche Schnitzaltäre der Spätgotik* (Heidelberg, 1963)
P. Baldass, R. Feuchtmüller and W. Mrazek: *Renaissance in Österreich* (Vienna and Hannover, 1966)
Gotik in Österreich (exh. cat., Krems, 1967)
K. Ginhart: *Die gotische Bildnerei*, Gesch. Stadt Wien, vii/1 (Vienna, 1970), pp. 33–81
A. Jaenike and A. Legner: *Deutsche Bildwerke*, 2 vols (Krefeld, 1972, 1979)
Renaissance in Österreich (exh. cat., Schallaburg, Schloss, 1974)
H. Schindler: *Der Schnitzaltar* (Regensburg, 1978)
M. Baxandall: *The Limewood Sculpture of Renaissance Germany* (New Haven and London, 1980)
H. Schindler: *Meisterwerke der Spätgotik* (Regensburg, 1989)

LOTHAR SCHULTES

3. *c.* 1600–*c.* 1750: BAROQUE. There is an important distinction in Austrian Baroque sculpture between work produced in the Alpine region (especially Upper Austria and Salzburg) and court art, centred on Vienna. In the early 17th century, sculpture in the Alpine region was influenced by artists who migrated from southern Germany. Hans Waldburger (1571/3–1630), for example, worked in Salzburg, where he made the former high altar of Nonnberg Convent Church (1629), now in the parish church in Scheffau, Salzburg. He also executed the high altar (1626) of the former monastery church (now the parish church) of Mondsee in Upper Austria. In the second half of the 17th century Baroque sculpture flourished in Upper Austria; many carved altars richly decked with figures survive. Typically black and gold with turned columns, a heavy, moulded, curving entablature, gnarled, gilded work and acanthus ornamentation, in their composition they are the Baroque version of the Gothic shrine altar. This characteristically Alpine blend of local, traditional wood-carving and south German and north Italian influences is visible in the altars of such artists as Thomas Schwanthaler (*see* SCHWANTHALER, (1)).

Other important provincial sculptors in the late 17th century include the ZÜRN family in Upper Austria and MEINRAD GUGGENBICHLER and his workshop in Mondsee, where the pulpit and several side altars (1679–86) for the former monastery church at Mondsee were made. The influence of contemporary Venetian sculpture on Michael Zürn the younger (1626–91) is evident in the 16 monumental marble angels (1682–6) in the monastery church of Kremsmünster Abbey. In Salzburg, BERNHARD MÄNDL worked from *c.* 1690, making the monumental marble figures of *St Peter* and *St Paul* (1697) that flank the doorway of the cathedral. The leading exponent of High Baroque sculpture in Styria was JOSEF STAMMEL, who principally worked at Admont Abbey.

In Vienna and the surrounding area, there was lavish building activity after the second Turkish siege of Vienna in 1683. Architects were usually also responsible for the programmes of sculptural decoration for palaces, monasteries and churches, either as sculptors in their own right, or in collaboration with other sculptors. The *Trinity Column* (founded 1679) in the Graben in Vienna was originally designed by MATHIAS RAUCHMILLER; Johann Bernhard Fischer von Erlach inspired its design when it was rebuilt after the siege by Lodovico Ottavio Burnacini, who executed it with Paul Strudel (completed 1692; for illustration *see* BURNACINI, LODOVICO OTTAVIO). Strudel's work, influenced by Josse de Corte, the leading sculptor in Venice in the second half of the 17th century, includes portrait busts (*see* VIENNA, fig. 8) and a series of marble life-size standing figures depicting the *Habsburg Ancestors* (1696; Vienna, Österreich. Nbib., Prunksaal; and Laxenburg, Altes Schloss; *see also* STRUDEL, (1)). The important relationship between Vienna and Venice was sustained by GIOVANNI GIULIANI, who settled in Vienna in 1690 and undertook sculptural work for buildings and gardens for the aristocracy in Vienna, as well as executing a variety of sculpture (from 1694) for Heiligenkreuz Monastery. A more classically inspired style was introduced in Vienna by MATTHIAS STEINL (see fig. 21), a versatile artist who worked as an architect, engineer and sculptor. Steinl produced numerous designs for altars and church furnishings: the *Pietà* altar (*c.* 1705) in the Capuchin church in Vienna is attributed to him. His contemporary, Johann Stanetti (1665–1726), a sculptor close to Fischer von Erlach, was responsible for the gable relief and the kneeling figure of *St Carlo Borromeo* (1725) on the façade of the Karlskirche in Vienna.

21. Matthias Steinl: *Joseph I*, ivory, h. 708 mm including base, 1693 (Vienna, Kunsthistorisches Museum)

One of the most popular sculptors with the court and the aristocracy during the reign of Emperor Charles VI was Lorenzo Mattielli (1682/8–1748) from Vicenza, who had trained with Orazio Marinali. Mattielli created fine garden sculpture (1719–24) for the Schwarzenberg Palace in Vienna and also received numerous ecclesiastical commissions, including the main parts of the sculptural decoration (1725–6) of the front façade of the Karlskirche in Vienna. He also designed the statues (1731) on the high altar of the church of Melk Abbey, which were executed by the Tirolean sculptor Peter Widerin (1684–1760). Widerin was also responsible for the remaining artistically important sculptural decoration at Melk. Georg Raphael Donner was trained by Giovanni Giuliani, whose influence is evident in such works as the marble statues (1726) on the staircase at Schloss Mirabell in Salzburg. Donner turned to sculpture in lead and was inspired by Classical and 16th-century examples. His major works include the Providentia fountain (1739) in Neuer Markt (replica *in situ*; original in Vienna, Belvedere; for illustration *see* DONNER, (1)) and a *Pietà* (1741) in Gurk Cathedral. In turn Donner influenced Johann Nikolaus Moll (1709–43) in such works as the latter's sarcophagus for *Charles VI* (1742) in the crypt of the Capuchin church in Vienna. Moll's brother Balthasar Ferdinand Moll (*see* MOLL, (1)), who also worked mainly in metal, was commissioned by the Empress Maria-Theresa to make a number of sarcophagi for the same crypt.

BIBLIOGRAPHY

E. Tietze-Conrat: *Österreichische Barockplastik* (Vienna, 1920)

H. Decker: *Barockplastik in den Alpenländern* (Vienna, 1943)

G. Coudenhove: *Die Wiener Pestsäule* (Vienna and Munich, 1958)

B. Grimschitz, R. Feuchtmüller and W. Mrazek: *Barock in Österreich* (Vienna, 1962)

H. Busch and B. Lohse, eds: *Barock-Plastik in Europa: Monumente des Abendlandes* (Frankfurt am Main, 1964)

G. Schikola: 'Wiener Plastik der Renaissance und des Barocks', *Geschichte der bildende Kunst in Wien: Plastik in Wien*, Gesch. Stadt Wien, vii/1 (Vienna, 1970), pp. 85–162

E. Baum: *Katalog des Österreichischen Barockmuseums im Unteren Belvedere in Wien*, 2 vols (Vienna and Munich, 1980)

I. Schemper-Sparholz: 'Skulptur und dekorative Plastik zur Zeit des Prinzen Eugen', *Prinz Eugen und das barocke Österreich*, ed. K. Gutkas (Salzburg and Vienna, 1985), pp. 339–48

PETER KÖNIG

4. *c.* 1750–*c.* 1900: NEO-CLASSICISM TO HISTORICISM. In the second half of the 18th century there was a slow transition to Neo-classicism, although the influence of broader international developments was hampered by the strong local tradition established by George Raphael Donner (*see* §3 above). Students at the Akademie der Bildenden Künste in Vienna were still being taught by Donner's former pupils and collaborators at the beginning of the 1770s. This legacy lingered in the work of JOHANN MARTIN FISCHER even at the beginning of the 19th century. A belated blossoming of Rococo in the 1750s and 1760s, to which sculptors responded with varying intensity, also impeded the development of Neo-classicism. Although several Austrian artists sculpted significant works, for example Franz Xaver Messerschmidt's classically inspired portraits from the start of the 1770s (*see* MESSERSCHMIDT, FRANZ XAVER), the most influential early Neo-classical sculptor was the German CHRISTIAN FRIEDRICH WILHELM BEYER, who directed the sculptural decoration (1773–80) of the park at Schloss Schönbrunn, Vienna.

In 1772 the Akademie der Bildenden Künste in Vienna was reorganized, and the government's decision to send such gifted students as FRANZ ANTON ZAUNER to study in Rome significantly affected the development of Austrian Neo-classicism. Zauner's equestrian monument to *Emperor Joseph II* (1807; Vienna, Josefsplatz) was the first monumental bronze statue in Austria. Antonio Canova influenced several Austrian sculptors in Rome as well as executing commissions for the court and aristocracy in Vienna, notably the tomb of *Archduchess Maria Christina* (1798–1805; *see* CANOVA, ANTONIO, fig. 3) in the Augustinerkirche in Vienna. Canova's influence is also discernible in the work of artists who had not been sent to Rome, for example JOSEF KLIEBER, whose wide-ranging work approaches the Austrian Biedermeier style. The work of the Nazarenes meanwhile influenced Klieber's contemporary Johann Nepomuk Schaller (1777–1842).

With the onset of Neo-classicism, Vienna dominated Austrian sculpture, attracting artists from other regions. Vienna supplied smaller towns with works of art throughout the 19th century, such as Schaller's monument (1831–3) to *Andreas Hofer* in front of the Hofkirche, Innsbruck. By the 1840s, however, much Austrian sculpture had become somewhat rigid, and it was only rejuvenated by new influences from Munich. Ludwig von Schwanthaler, the leading sculptor of the Munich school, executed several commissions in Austria, including the marble *Nymph* (1841–8; Schloss Anif, nr Salzburg). HANS GASSER and Anton Dominik Fernkorn, who studied in Munich and were influenced by Schwanthaler, subsequently became prominent Romantic historicist sculptors. Fernkorn also acquired a sound knowledge of bronze-casting in Munich and founded the K. K. Kunst-Erzgiesserei (Imperial bronze foundry) in Vienna; the monument to *Archduke Charles* (1859; Vienna, Heldenplatz; for illustration *see* FERNKORN, ANTON DOMINIK) was the first public monument cast there. In the 1850s and 1860s a mood of patriotism and heroism was reflected in the Heldenberg, near Kleinwetzdorf (Lower Austria), intended as an 'Austrian Valhalla' and mainly designed by Adam Rammelmayer (*d* 1850). Another essentially Romantic trend was the fashion for reconstructing both old and new religious buildings in a Gothic Revival style, which continued for much of the 19th century (*see* §II, 4 above). This stimulated a partial revival of local wood-carving workshops, especially in the Tyrol. Josef Gasser (1816–1900), for instance, made statues for Heinrich von Ferstel's Votivkirche (1856–79), Vienna.

After the mid-19th century there was greater contact with the Dresden school of sculpture; the Akademie began to send its scholarship holders to Dresden rather than Rome, and prestigious commissions in Vienna were given to such Dresden sculptors as Ernst Julius Hähnel (bronze equestrian monument to *Feldmarschall Carl Schwarzenberg*, 1864–7; Schwarzenbergplatz). It was also around this time that the project to develop the Ringstrasse was begun, leading to a revival in the fine arts as distinguished artists from Vienna and elsewhere decorated the new buildings and created the many new monuments (*see* §II, 4, above; *see also* VIENNA, §§II, 3 and III, 3).

In 1868 KASPAR CLEMENS ZUMBUSCH came from Munich to Vienna, introducing a stricter historicist style in his bronze memorial to *Ludwig van Beethoven* (1873–80; Vienna, Beethovenplatz; see fig. 22). Zumbusch was also put in charge of the school for sculpture at the Akademie der Bildenden Künste. A second master class was also established under CARL KUNDMANN, another influential teacher and practitioner of Historicism, as in the marble memorial to *Franz Schubert* (1888; with Theophilus Hansen; Vienna, Cent. Cemetery).

Another, late, form of Historicism began in the 1870s, when VICTOR TILGNER and RUDOLF WEYR, friends of the influential painter Hans Makart, espoused the Rococo Revival. This was modelled on contemporary French art but was tempered by artistic developments in Munich, together with indigenous Baroque and Rococo art. These sculptors participated in the decoration of the Ringstrasse

22. Kaspar Clemens Zumbusch: *Ludwig van Beethoven*, bronze, 1873–80, Beethovenplatz, Vienna

buildings, notably the museums and the Burgtheater, as well as executing other commissions. Tilgner, for example, created a marble monument to *Wolfgang Amadeus Mozart* (1896; Vienna, Burggarten). Only at the end of the 19th century was there an attempt to break away from Historicism, inspired by several large international exhibitions that were held in Vienna in 1882 (featuring works by Rodin) and 1894 (with significant works by Italian exponents of *verismo*). These works influenced a variety of portraits and monuments in and outside Vienna, for example the bronze monument to *Johann Wolfgang von Goethe* (1890–1900; Vienna, Ringstrasse) by EDMUND HELLMER.

BIBLIOGRAPHY

W. Wagner: *Die Geschichte der Akademie der bildenden Künste in Wien* (Vienna, 1967)
G. Kapner: *Freiplastik in Wien* (Vienna and Munich, 1970)
M. Poch-Kalous: 'Wiener Plastik im 19. Jahrhundert', *Geschichte der bildende Kunst in Wien: Plastik in Wien*, Gesch. Stadt Wien, vii/1 (Vienna, 1970), pp. 165–250
R. Feuchtmüller: *Kunst in Österreich*, ii (Vienna, Munich and Basle, 1973)
M. Pötzl-Malikova: *Die Plastik der Ringstrasse: Künstlerische Entwicklung, 1890–1918* (1976), ix/2 of *Die Wiener Ringstrasse*, ed. R. Wagner-Rieger (Wiesbaden, 1972–)
Klassizismus in Wien: Architektur und Plastik (exh. cat. by S. Krasa-Florian, Vienna, Hist. Mus., 1978), pp. 73–83, 142–72
W. Krause: *Die Plastik der Wiener Ringstrasse: Von der Spätromantik bis zur Wende um 1900* (1980), ix/3 of *Die Wiener Ringstrasse*, ed. R. Wagner-Rieger (Wiesbaden, 1972–)

MARIA PÖTZL-MALIKOVA

5. AFTER *c.* 1900: MODERN DEVELOPMENTS. In the early 20th century, sculpture in Austria remained essentially traditional, with stylistic developments from other countries having only a limited influence and figurative works continuing to dominate. The naturalistic, academic style of the monuments associated with the development of the Ringstrasse in Vienna in the late 19th century (*see* §4 above) continued into the 1930s, with many of the leading 19th-century sculptors of monuments and portraits, such as Kaspar Clemens Zumbusch and Edmund Hellmer, continuing to work on into the 20th. The Secession (*see* SECESSION, §3) and Viennese *Jugendstil* (*see* ART NOUVEAU, §6) did, however, provide some new stylistic influences that could be adapted to the predominantly monumental approach. The statue of *Marcus Aurelius* (Vienna, Sezession) by Arthur Strasser (1834–1927) and the Mozart Fountain in Vienna by Carl Wollek (1862–1936) achieved a definite classicism characterized by a simplicity that avoided the merely decorative. Othmar Schimkowitz (1864–1946), Richard Luksch (1872–1936) and Ferdinand Andri (1871–1956) also rejected naturalism. Strictness of form and serenity were the main objectives of Wilhelm Frass (1886–1968) and Josef Müllner (1879–1968), who made the monument to *Lueger* (1926; Vienna, Luegerplatz), the last monumental project to be planned under the monarchy; its style could well have been influenced by that of Franz Metzner, who worked in Vienna from 1903 to 1906. Although Metzner's architectural style was influential in Vienna, generally naturalism and the Secession still dominated. A notable characteristic of Secessionist sculpture was its close relationship with architecture. Its subordinate role in this relationship meant that independently conceived sculpture was rare, and this reinforced the Arts and Crafts approach endemic in the work produced by the WIENER WERKSTÄTTE and the Österreichischer Werkbund. Nevertheless, Franz Barwig (1868–1931), who concentrated on animal subjects, and Franz Zelezny (1866–1932) did create individual sculptural ideas.

ANTON HANAK fulfilled the aims of his teacher, Edmund Hellmer, of truth to materials and a personal sculptural response. Hanak preferred large forms and, especially in his early public commissions, smooth surfaces, but his works in bronze are stirring and vital, with shimmering, tensely treated surfaces. His work contains allusions to ancient Egyptian and Greek art, as well as to Michelangelo and Rodin, and his subjects include symbolic expressions of universal human nature (e.g. *Burning Man*; 1922) and portraits (*Margaret Stonborough-Wittgenstein*, 1930; both in Langenzersdorf, Anton Hanak-Freilichtmus.). Hanak's sculpture and his teaching were both immensely influential on subsequent generations of Austrian sculptors. Among those who took Expressionism as their starting-point were Siegfried Charoux (*b* 1896), Gustinus Ambrosi (1893–1975) and GEORG EHRLICH. Ehrlich was also influenced by Wilhelm Lehmbruck, and his work is characterized by its humanity, amiability and sensitive clarity. By emphasizing volume and tectonics Franz Friedrich Blum (1914–42) achieved a unified, monumental form, while Josef Humplik (1888–1958) succeeded in conveying fleeting facial expression and contemplativeness in his portraits using rhythm and form.

The first sculptures of FRITZ WOTRUBA date from the 1930s; through his work and his followers he made an impact on Austrian sculpture that lasted for decades. In his early work Wotruba was influenced by Maillol as well as by Lehmbruck, and he concentrated on the human figure, which he broke down into cubic primary forms, evident in the figures created from 1948 to 1950 (see fig. 23). The application of architectonic principles to the construction of figures, the transformation of cubic and cylindrical shapes and the underlying reference to the figure are common stylistic features in an informal school of sculptors influenced by Wotruba, all of whom were nevertheless able to produce highly individual work in the period after World War II. They include Josef Pillhofer (*b* 1921), Franz Fischer (*b* 1920), Alfred Hrdlicka and JOANNIS AVRAMIDIS. Other artists who developed Wotruba's ideas include Otto Eder (*b* 1924), Erwin Reiter (*b* 1933) and Nausika Pastra (*b* 1932).

In the 1950s Wotruba's dominance was challenged by new influences derived from international modernism. Alongside Wotruba and his followers, various artists associated with the Art-Club (an association in Vienna of which Albert Paris von Gütersloh was president) became prominent, including Heinz Leinfellner (*b* 1911), Maria Biljan-Bilger (*b* 1912) and Wander Bertoni (*b* 1925). Leinfellner was inspired by the work of Henry Moore and Wotruba to develop a Cubist vocabulary of form, linking the theme of humanity with strict formal shaping. Biljan-Bilger's influences include Styrian and Slovenian folk art, visible in her early works in terracotta and later in her monumental painted reliefs. Bertoni, who moved to Vienna in 1943 and was taught by Wotruba, was concerned with pure form and was one of Austria's first non-figurative artists, as in his *Imaginary Alphabet: 'C'* (Vienna, Mus. 20. Jhts). RUDOLF HOFLEHNER is another artist who turned to abstract art after 1950, producing works in wood and iron based on a geometric simplification of the human form. Other artists of this generation to create abstract works or works based on archetypal symbolism include Walter Ritter (*b* 1904), Oskar Bottoli (*b* 1920) and Fritz Hartlauer (*b* 1919). Their near-contemporary, Karl Prantl (*b* 1923), who was self-taught as an artist, meanwhile concentrated on a few basic forms and on harmony with nature through contemplation. Prantl initiated the International Sculptors' Symposia in the quarry of St Margarethen; sculptures made there remain *in situ*. Roland Göschl (*b* 1932) also used basic shapes as the starting-point of his sculptures, which he then painted over in primary colours to create a form of optical illusion.

23. Fritz Wotruba: *Seated Figure*, limestone, h. 1.45 m, 1949 (Vienna, Belvedere, Österreichische Galerie)

Austrian sculpture in the second half of the 20th century was characterized by a wide variety of approaches. The abstract sculpture of Oswald Oberhuber (*b* 1931) represented a rebellion against theory and dogma, while Bruno Gironcoli (*b* 1936) created object-based assemblages in metal and wire, and also installations. They form a self-contained environment inspired by the fears of the commercial world. An architectural dimension also characterizes the work of Walter Pichler; his precisely prepared sculptures are housed in specially erected buildings derived from the vernacular architecture of Burgenland. Franz Xaver Ölzant and Cornelius Kolig (*b* 1942) created images by combining individual elements. Late 20th-century sculptural work ranges from reflexive intellectualization to subjective statements. Many sculptors were influenced by the experimental art of the 1960s, for example the members of AKTIONISMUS (*see also* §III, 4 above), who were inspired by action painting, or Peter Weibel (*b* 1945), whose work mirrored the increasing dependence of society on the media. By contrast, the miniature models of Thomas Stimm (*b* 1948) convey a sense of idyllic isolation experienced in an information-governed society. Franz West (*b* 1946) produced fetish-like sculptures in which the creative 'action' is again an integral part of the work. The different approaches of Heimo Zobernig (*b* 1958), Willi Kopf (*b* 1949), Hans Kupelwieser (*b* 1948) and Manfred Walkolbinger (*b* 1952) indicate the wide range of late 20th-century Austrian sculpture, from an overriding concern for context and setting in Zobernig's works to Walkolbinger's concrete solids. The figural stone sculptors Franz Rosei (*b* 1947) and Christian Frank (*b* 1956) are both principally interested in materials and a direct method of working, resulting in subjective and expressive works.

BIBLIOGRAPHY

W. Hofmann: *Die Plastik des 20. Jahrhunderts* (Frankfurt am Main, 1958)
G. Feuerstein and others: *Moderne Kunst in Österreich* (Vienna, Hannover and Berne, 1965)
Österreichische Bildhauer (exh. cat., Liberec, Reg. Gal., 1965)
J. Muschik: *Österreichische Plastik seit 1945* (Vienna, 1966)
O. Breicha and R. Urbach, eds: *Österreich zum Beispiel* (Salzburg and Vienna, 1982)
Kunst in Österreich, 1918–38 (exh. cat., Vienna, Ambrosi Mus., Schloss Halbturn, 1984)

Raum annehmen: Aspekte österreichischer Skulptur, 1950–1985 (Vienna, Gal. Grita Insam, 1985)
Ausstellungskatalog österreichische Skulptur Wien: Sezession, 1990 (exh. cat., Vienna, Mus. 20. Jhts, 1990)

WOLFGANG HUBER

V. Interior decoration.

1. Before 1600. 2. 1600–1780. 3. 1781–1897. 4. After 1897.

1. BEFORE 1600. There are no surviving remains of the simple wooden houses and living accommodation of the Romanesque and Gothic periods. It was not until 1450 to 1500 that individual rooms used for residential or ceremonial purposes were magnificently decorated, examples of which have been preserved mainly in the Tyrol and Styria. The Goldene Stube at the fortress of Hohensalzburg, Salzburg, dates from 1501 and is lavishly furnished with wainscoted walls and a ceiling painted in gold and carved with rosettes, animals and plants. Seating is provided by benches carved with Gothic ornamentation and tracery round the walls, while the showpiece is a Late Gothic tiled stove.

From the mid-16th century, after the division of the Habsburg empire and during the reign of Ferdinand, Innsbruck became the centre of the court, and of new building; superb rooms decorated in the Renaissance style were created especially in the area near Innsbruck. The coffered ceiling (1566–7; *in situ*) in the Fürstenchor of the Hofkirche, Innsbruck, was the first of many significant feats of joinery by HANS WALDNER. The walls, doors, seats, ceiling and floor are decorated with inlay work of many different woods including Hungarian ash and black ebony. Patterns for such intarsia work were published in 1563 as copper engravings by the court joiner GEORG HAAS. The ceilings depicted in the engravings were composed mainly of individual rectangular or cruciform coffers with raised frames and often a rosette or a cone emphasizing the centre. Such articulated ceilings dominated the architectonic expanse and perspective of the large ceremonial rooms of the Renaissance. The Renaissance interiors of Schloss Tratzberg, near Jenbach, have the best-preserved room furnishings of the pre-1600 period: the Königinnenzimmer (1568–9), with a coffered ceiling, wall panelling and biblical texts in inlay work running round the cornice, is attributed to Waldner. The Spanischer Saal at Schloss Ambras, near Innsbruck, which measures 43×10 m and was the largest secular ceremonial room in the Empire when it was created *c.* 1570, has survived unaltered (see fig. 24). The walls are decorated with frescoes portraying the princes of Tyrol, but the room is dominated by a gilt wooden coffered ceiling and by two magnificent doors decorated with intarsia on the two shorter walls. These doors are made of various exotic woods and decorated with strapwork and arabesques arranged to create a sense of perspective. The ceiling was the work of Conrad Gottlieb, who completed and signed it in 1571.

In Styria, the Rittersaal in Schloss Frondsberg, near Weiz, has coffered ceilings and walls incorporating doorways; the State Room (now in Graz, Steiermärk. Landesmus.) from Schloss Rabensdorf, also near Weiz, has coffered ceilings, wainscoting with small built-in wall cupboards and doors decorated with inlay walnut, yew, pear and alder on a maple background. A richly decorated Rittersaal also survives in the fortress at Riegersburg, Styria.

24. Spanischer Saal, *c.* 1570, Schloss Ambras, near Innsbruck

The only surviving interior furnishings and decoration in the Mannerist style are in the Landhaus buildings in Graz, Linz, Klagenfurt and Vienna. In the Vienna Landhaus only the ceiling and portal, completed by Haas in 1572, remain. A wooden coffered ceiling, originally installed at Burg Rapottenstein, Lower Austria, but now in the Franzensburg at Laxenburg near Vienna, was probably made by Haas (*c.* 1600). The ceiling is decorated throughout with intarsia, which uses complicated wood strutting to give an illusory perspective that foreshadows the Baroque interior.

BIBLIOGRAPHY

L. von Baldass, R. Feuchtmüller and W. Mrazek: *Renaissance in Österreich* (Vienna, 1966)

E. Egg: *Kunst in Tirol: Malerei und Kunsthandwerk* (Innsbruck, 1972)

2. 1600–1780. The 17th century was a period of continual wars against the Turks, and the spread of the Baroque building style was restricted by political circumstances. The prolonged period of peace in the early 18th century gave rise to a cultural blossoming in the reigns of Charles VI and his daughter Maria-Theresa. The former developed Vienna as a true capital for his court and set out to attract a first-rate workforce, guaranteeing certain privileges to journeymen and master craftsmen. The increased activity in the architectural field was reflected in the design of interiors: panelling (often gilded) was constructed by joiners who received their orders from such interior architects as Claude Le Fort du Plessy and Nikolaus Paccassi. The joiners working under their instructions made not only the panelling and furniture but floors, stairs, pulpits, altars and choirs for churches, bedsteads, cradles, coffins, tools and household equipment, as well as decorative wood-carving and intarsia. In Vienna the Upper Belvedere, the Kaiserliche Bibliothek (now the Nationalbibliothek), the Karlskirche and Schloss Schönbrunn were all outstanding architectural projects that included the creation of interiors. The many town houses for the nobility that were built, furnished and decorated in Vienna were smaller in scale but more numerous.

In the 18th century there was substantial building activity not only in Vienna but also in the provinces, where such great convent and monastery buildings as MELK ABBEY and ST FLORIAN ABBEY were constructed. The interior furnishings were created by master joiners who worked on the choir-stalls and altars as well as on furniture for the living quarters and state rooms. Most monasteries had a specially designed and furnished suite known as the Kaiserzimmer, which provided accommodation for the monarch and his entourage on their travels. St Florian is one of the few monastic foundations in Austria where the furniture and interiors remain to a large extent as they were originally conceived. A magnificent ceremonial staircase leads to the Kaiserzimmer, which is decorated with ceiling frescoes that illustrate the apotheosis of the Emperor, and then into the Kaisersaal or Marmorsaal, with a ceiling fresco glorifying Austrian and Hungarian victories against the Turks. The hall has marble or stucco pillars and is decorated with equestrian portraits of *Charles VI* and *Prince Eugene of Savoy* in richly carved frames (1731) by LEONHARD SATTLER, whose family, together with that

25. Millionenzimmer, *c.* 1750–60, Schönbrunn Palace, Vienna

26. Private salon of Joseph II (*c.* 1765), in the Hofburg, Vienna; in use as the office of the Austrian president

of STEPHAN JEGG, was responsible for fitting out the whole interior as well as for making the furniture and other related items, such as the three pairs of candle stands shaped like Moors or heyducks.

In general, however, Baroque interiors contained little furniture, and decoration concentrated on the more architectonic fashioning of walls and ceiling. There was an attempt to create a Baroque GESAMTKUNSTWERK by harmonizing colour and the elements used to form the décor: the sparse furnishing was made to conform with the wall decoration to create a unified effect. A degree of comfort in living areas was neither known nor sought until the Rococo period in Maria-Theresa's reign, when rooms were equipped with a greater variety of furniture, vases, clocks, sculptures, mirrors (made in Bohemian glassworks) and pictures.

Some of the state apartments created in the Schönbrunn Palace (*see* VIENNA, §V, 7(i)) from 1745 for Maria-Theresa are good examples of the court style of interior decoration: the Chinesisches Kabinett has lacquer panels from East Asia and Chinese vases, bottles and boxes, along with Viennese enamel chandeliers; the Vieux-Laque-Zimmer has a mixture of East Asian lacquer panels, Viennese Rococo and an intarsia floor composed of a variety of woods; the Millionenzimmer is the most magnificent example of an Austrian Rococo interior from the 1750 to 1760 period (see fig. 25). The panelling is made of a rare type of rosewood found in Guyana and the Antilles, into which 60 gilt cartouches have been inserted as frames for 260 Indian miniatures on parchment depicting Oriental genre scenes, which Maria-Theresa had acquired from Constantinople. Two mirrors arranged opposite one another seem to break up the wall surface and enlarge the room, turning it into a hall of mirrors. The Millionenzimmer illustrates stylistic elements of Austrian Rococo that are typical of many other rooms: ROCAILLE and foliage motifs predominate, and, as at the French court, the decorative is considered more important than the architectonic. The predominant colours used in interiors during Maria-Theresa's reign were brown and gold, giving way to white and gold with the onset of Classicism. Wall decorations and furnishings formed an indivisible unity, as shown by the console table—the most important piece of furniture of the period—which must have a wall behind it and may even be said to be a three-dimensional extension of the wall.

The shift from Rococo to Classicism is linked with Joseph II (1741–90), son of Maria-Theresa and from 1765 her co-regent. The 'Josephian' style—straight, functional, with classical overtones—evolved in Austria in the second half of the 18th century alongside the Rococo, which was still at its height. This new, more refined style was largely disseminated through the specialist sample and pattern books that were being produced in ever greater numbers and through such periodicals as the *Journal des Luxus und der Moden* or the *Magazin für Freunde des guten Geschmacks*, published from the late 18th century for a wider audience.

Joseph II inclined towards economy and simplicity in interior decoration, making use of existing furniture in preference to having new pieces made. He eliminated superfluous objects in his room arrangements and chose white furniture in preference to white and gold. The rooms he used in the Hofburg, Vienna, have economical white and gold wall panelling that is still basically Rococo in concept (see fig. 26). The general emphasis at court was on economy: activity centred on internal reforms and the machinery of government, so existing buildings were altered rather than new ones being constructed. The main building activity concentrated on public buildings and town housing. Among the few larger building projects were the alterations (1773–5) at Schloss Schlosshof on the Marchfeld, Vienna , where the walls were decorated in the French Neo-classical style. An elevation drawing of the room decoration shows motifs associated with the new style: medallions with trophies, laurel wreaths and meanders (see Leisching, p. 536), almost none of which has survived. After Maria-Theresa's death in 1780 the sober reforming style of Joseph II came fully into its own.

BIBLIOGRAPHY

E. Leisching: 'Theresianischer und Josephinischer Stil', *Kst & Kstgew.*, xv (1912), pp. 493–563

B. Grimschitz, R. Feuchtmüller and W. Mrazek: *Barock in Österreich* (Vienna, 1960)

F. Windisch-Graetz: 'Möbel und Raumkunst der Renaissance in Österreich', *Renaissance in Österreich: Geschichte, Wissensschaft, Kunst* (exh. cat., ed. R. Feuchtmüller; Schallaburg, Schloss, 1974), pp. 280–97

R. Goebl: 'Innenraumgestaltung', *Klassizismus in Wien: Architektur und Plastik* (exh. cat., Vienna, Hist. Mus., 1978), pp. 43–54

C. Witt-Döring: 'Die Farbgebung der Möbel am Wiener Hof während der Regierungszeit Maria Theresias', *Alte & Mod. Kst*, 158 (1978), pp. 8–12

P. Parenzan: 'Zum Josephinischen Möbelstil', *Österreich zur Zeit Kaiser Josephs II* (exh. cat., Melk, Stiftsmus, 1980), pp. 211–13

RENATE WONISCH-LANGENFELDER

3. 1781–1897. At the end of the 18th century and beginning of the 19th no significant Austrian designer influenced the style of contemporary interior decoration. In 1784–5 JOHANN FERDINAND VON HOHENBERG designed neo-Gothic furniture for the interiors of the Augustinerkirche and Minoritenkirche in Vienna. He built the Haus der Laune (*c.* 1801) in the park of the imperial country seat at Laxenburg, where contemporary taste for the bizarre can be seen in the sheet music painted on the walls of the music-room and the bales of straw painted on the walls of the 'straw-room'. Around 1800 a 'Pompeii room' was created in the Palais Caprara-Geymüller in Wallnerstrasse, Vienna (now in Vienna, Hist. Mus.), in which the walls were covered with silk and painted with floating female figures taken from classical models. At the same time Louis Montoyer designed the Neo-classical banqueting halls of the Palais Rasumofsky and the Hofburg in Vienna, incorporating monumental free-standing columns and decorative reliefs. In 1812 Innocenzo Chiesa (1744–1821) presented his designs for the apartment of the Empress Maria Ludovica (1787–1816) in the so-called Harrach Codices of the Hofburg, in which he included an Oriental *stanza cinese* and an Egyptian cabinet. The brothers Johann Heinrich Geymüller (1754–1824) and Johann Jacob Geymüller also built the Geymüller-Schlossl (1808). There Gothic and Oriental styles appear side by side in both the architecture and interior decoration. In 1818 Raphael Rigel (*b* 1787) published *Modebilder*, a collection of interior designs made up entirely of drapery that was clearly influenced by Percier and Fontaine.

The BIEDERMEIER interior was an ensemble of different elements rather than a *Gesamtkunstwerk* and has been documented by abundant descriptions of interiors and numerous amateur drawings. Living-rooms served several purposes: the light, low furniture was often placed in *Wohninseln* (sitting areas) and could be moved about as necessary. The soft furnishings—drapes on the windows, walls and furniture—were particularly important in creating a harmony of colour. In the first half of the 19th century plants were important, either displayed in vases, on trellises or in pots or as motifs on carpets or upholstery. In the late 1830s Josef Danhauser (*see* DANHAUSER, (2)) published *Wiener Möbelbilder*, which contains descriptions of standard neo-Gothic interiors and of the Rococo Revival style; surviving examples include the state rooms of the Stadt Palais Liechtenstein (see fig. 27), Vienna, decorated and furnished between 1843 and 1846 by Carl Leistler and Michael Thonet from the designs of the English architect Peter Hubert Desvignes (1804–83). On the occasion of the marriage of Francis Joseph I to Elizabeth (1837–98) in 1854, the Hofburg and the apartments of the Schönbrunn Palace in Vienna were also furnished in the Rococo Revival style, which remained dominant in Vienna until the 1860s.

At the same time, for prestigious non-domestic interiors, there was a preference for Oriental and medieval stylistic elements, for example the many Byzantine elements of the Vienna Arsenal (1849–56) by August Siccardsburg, Eduard Van der Nüll and Karl Rösner and the Greek Orthodox Church (1858–61) in Vienna by THEOPHILUS HANSEN. The Votivkirche, which HEINRICH VON FERSTEL began in 1856 (finished 1879), was furnished inside like a *Gesamtkunstwerk* of a French Gothic cathedral. In the secular field, the interior for the meeting-place of the Dürer Society, designed in 1858–9 by Leopold Ernst (1808–62), was pure Gothic. However, Ferstel's Bank- und Börsengebäude (1856–60) showed a penchant for the equally detailed elements of the Florentine early Renaissance. The Renaissance example became even more important in the 1860s as a result of the Vienna Kunstgewerbereform, as can be seen in the interior of the Vienna Staatsoper by Siccardsburg and Van der Nüll, the Arkadenhof, in the rooms in the Österreichisches Museums für Kunst und Industrie, Vienna, planned by Ferstel, and in the rooms in the Kaiserpavillon at the Vienna Weltausstellung of 1873 by Josef von Storck. The Palais Todesco (1861–4) and Palais Epstein (1868–72), both by Theophilus Hansen, illustrate the architect's intention to create a *Gesamtkunstwerk* by planning a house down to the smallest detail of the furnishings.

The dominance of the Renaissance Revival style was challenged by the Baroque and Rococo in the later 1870s and 1880s, as can be seen in Vienna, for example, in the formal interiors of the interval foyers of the Burgtheater (1874–86) by Gottfried Semper and Carl Hasenauer, in the interior of the Deutsches Volkstheater (1887–8) by Hermann Helmer (1849–1919) and Ferdinand Fellner and in the stairs and exhibition rooms of the Kunsthistorisches Museum, completed in 1891. A canon of multiple styles had developed in domestic interior decoration: a dining-room could now be furnished in a Renaissance Revival style while the sitting-room was Rococo Revival, as was shown by the exponents of the Elektrischen Ausstellung,

27. Interior of the Stadt Palais Liechtenstein, Vienna, decorated and furnished by Carl Leistler and Michael Thonet, 1837–46

Vienna, in 1883. The first modern interior was the Lefler-Zimmer, a collaboration by the painter Heinrich Lefler, the architect Joseph Urban and the sculptor and cabinet-maker Franz Schönthaler, which clearly revealed the influence of the English Reform movement and was installed at the Österreichisches Museum für Kunst und Industrie in 1897.

BIBLIOGRAPHY

J. Folnesics: *Alte Innenräume österreichischer Schlösser, Paläste und Wohnhäuser* (Vienna, n.d.)

M. Zweig: *Das zweite Rokoko* (Vienna, 1924)

R. Wagner-Rieger: *Wiens Architektur im 19. Jahrhundert* (Vienna, 1970)

R. Goebl: 'Innenraumgestaltung', *Klassizismus in Wien: Architektur und Plastik* (exh. cat., Vienna, Hist. Mus., 1978), pp. 43–54

C. Witt-Dörring: 'Die Wohnraumgestaltung des Biedermeier: Das Wiener Interieur, 1815–1848', *Alte & Mod. Kst*, 165 (1979), pp. 1–7

4. AFTER 1897. Around 1900 interior design became an even more important field for architects. The transition from furnishings and decoration based on Historicism to early Viennese Modernism was strongly influenced by the interiors designed by OTTO WAGNER. Although his designs from the 1880s and 1890s juxtaposed rooms decorated in a variety of styles, the walls of the apartments on the Köstlergasse/Linke Wienzeile site (1898–9) and of the Karlsplatz metropolitan railway station (1898), both in Vienna, used predominantly floral motifs, as did the hunting-lodge at Bergerhöhe, decorated and furnished by Josef Hoffmann (1899), and the exhibition area of J. & J. Kohn at the Exposition Universelle of 1900 in Paris, designed by Gustav Siegel (1880–1970). At the Beethoven Exhibition, created by Josef Hoffmann for the Vienna Secession (*see* SECESSION, §3) in 1902, a spare geometric style predominated. Structural, functional tendencies were expressed in such interiors by Wagner as those in the Postsparkasse (1904–6, 1910–12), especially the glass-roofed Kassensaal, which was fitted with aluminium components and bentwood furniture, and the Steinhofkirche (1904–7), Vienna, with its deliberately hygienic marble cladding. Inside the Wittgenstein hunting-lodge (1906), Hochreith, Hoffmann used valuable materials to turn these geometric shapes into a mannered, composite work of art. However, the interiors for the Kunstschau in Vienna (1908) showed a return to more ornamental decoration, which was even more noticeable in the Austrian contributions to the Werkbundausstellung in Cologne (1914; destr.) and was further illustrated by the Wiener Werkstätte's domestic interiors at the Palais Stoclet, Brussels (1905–11; *see* HOFFMANN, JOSEF, fig. 2), the Skywa-Primavesi House, Glorietgasse (1913–15), and the Knips House (1919–24; both in Vienna).

28. Living-room designed by Josef Frank and Oskar Wlach, Haus L. R. S., Vienna-Hietzing, *c.* 1933

From *c.* 1900 ADOLF LOOS was the leading exponent of the opposing theory that neither interiors nor household objects should be regarded as works of art, as demonstrated by his design for the Café Museum (1899), Vienna, with its simple bentwood chairs and non-architectonic décor. The many domestic interiors and shop premises he designed from 1909 (e.g. Salon Knize, Vienna) show his primary concern with functionalism, in the sense of a practical interior specifically designed to meet the requirements of the user. The form of his work was determined by three-dimensional thinking and was based on the English style of interior decoration, with inglenooks or such classical motifs as marble cladding and friezes. However, movable items were selected from current commercial ranges and varied accordingly.

The ideas elaborated by Loos were developed further by Josef Frank, Oskar Strnad and Oskar Wlach (1881–1963), both in the interiors of their domestic houses and in the furniture they designed, which was sold in the Haus und Garten furniture store founded in 1925 (see fig. 28). The work of these artists reflected the move from an interior totally designed by the architect to one that could be adapted to the changing needs of its users: furniture was light, movable and raised on slender legs so that the outer edges of the room remained visible; walls were white and undecorated to act as a neutral background; colour was introduced through such textiles as carpets and curtains. Architects also had to express the ever-widening difference between domestic and public workplace interiors, as exemplified in the Wenzgasse house (1932), the interiors of the Werkbundsiedlung (1929–32), both in Vienna, and Erich Boltenstern's *Die Wohnung für Jedermann* (1933).

After World War II an effort was made to use these principles to work out inexpensive ways to reconstruct public and private interiors: such books as Otto Niedermoser's *Schöner Wohnen, Schöner Leben* or Oskar Payer's *Praktische Wohnkunde* record these attempts. The interiors for shops and business premises designed by Oswald Haerdtl, who worked with Josef Hoffmann, show a thorough understanding of the inter-war traditions combined with a feeling for the forms typical of the 1950s. Good examples of public interiors in post-war Austrian architecture are the Vienna Stadthalle (1952–8) by Roland Rainer, a multipurpose space for sporting and other events, and what was called the '20iger Haus', created by Karl Schwanzer as the Austrian pavilion at the Exposition Universelle et Internationale of 1958 in Brussels and adapted in 1960–62 as the Museum des 20. Jahrhunderts, Vienna. In the 1970s a perceptible revival of interest in interior design coincided with a move away from classic Modernism, as can be seen in the business premises in Vienna designed by Hans Hollein, the work of the Co-op Himmelblau (founded 1968), the restaurants and cafés designed by Hermann Czech, and the work of Alessandro Alvera (*b* 1940), Luigi Blau (*b* 1945) and Boris Podrecca (*b* 1940), among others.

BIBLIOGRAPHY

E. Boltenstern: *Die Wohnung für Jedermann* (Stuttgart, 1933)
O. Niedermoser: *Schöner Wohnen, Schöner Leben* (Vienna, 1954)
O. Payer: *Praktische Wohnkunde* (Vienna, 1967)
F. Achleitner: *Österreichische Architektur des 20. Jahrhunderts* (Salzburg and Vienna, 1980)
Neues Wohnen: Wiener Innenraumgestaltung, 1918–1938 (exh. cat., Vienna, Mus. Angewandte Kst, 1980)
Versuche zur Baukunst (exh. cat., Vienna, Kstlerhaus, 1982)
P. Asenbaum and others: *Otto Wagner: Möbel und Innenräume* (Salzburg and Vienna, 1984)

EVA B. OTTILLINGER

VI. Furniture.

1. Before 1600. 2. 1600–1780. 3. 1781–1897. 4. After 1897.

1. Before 1600. The most important and widely available pieces of furniture in Austria in the Middle Ages were such storage items as the chest and the cupboard, followed by the bed, table and chair, with the washstand with a container for water and a bowl as a special form. Early forms of chests were crude round-topped (*Stollentruhen*) or gable-topped (*Satteldachtruhen*), named after the shape of the lid. Some Gothic tracery chests, richly carved with lily motifs and decorated with inlay work, were made *c.* 1490–1500 in Salzburg (Salzburg, Burgmus. and Mus. Carolino Augusteum). However, the most impressive Gothic and early Renaissance pieces of furniture were cupboards. The oldest is a sacristy cupboard with inlay work from Tamsweg, made by Peter Stampfer (Meister Pistator) in 1455 (now in Kreuzenstein, Schloss-Mus.). When intended for secular use, cupboards were often built in two separate stages with handles at the ends so that they could be moved more easily. This was the origin of the two-tiered chest cupboard; when fitted with drawers it could be used for storing linen, household goods and crockery. Enclosed chests of this kind were first made about the mid-15th century in South Germany and spread gradually throughout the Alpine area. A good example is the *Tugendenkasten* ('Chest of the Virtues'; *c.* 1600; Salzburg, Mus. Carolino Augusteum; see fig. 29). It has two tiers, with a base, drawers and a moulding round the top. The front is decorated with four intarsia panels illustrating in allegorical form the concepts that give the chest its name: Faith, Justice, Hospitality and Charity. There are also hunting scenes.

29. *Tugendenkasten*, carved ash inlaid with various woods, h. 2.6 m, south German, *c.* 1600 (Salzburg, Salzburger Museum Carolino Augusteum)

BIBLIOGRAPHY

L. von Baldass, W. Buchowiecki, R. Feuchtmüller and W. Mrazek: *Gotik in Österreich* (Vienna, 1961)

H. Kreisel: *Die Kunst des deutschen Möbels*, i (Munich, 1968)

N. Watteck: 'Salzburger Masswerktruhen', *Alte & Mod. Kst*, 105 (1969), pp. 25–30

2. 1600–1780. It is difficult to give an account of the development of Austrian furniture in this period because very few names of cabinetmakers are known, and few individual pieces of furniture are in their original location or indeed have survived at all. However, the history of chairs, tables, cupboards and beds can be traced, based on the pieces of furniture formerly owned by the imperial family, which are now kept either in various large houses or castles or in what was the court furniture depository (now the Bundesmobiliendepot, Vienna). Another rich source is the furniture collection at St Florian Abbey, near Linz. The archives establish that the furniture was made by the families of Leonhard Sattler and Stephan Jegg, who worked as cabinetmakers or sculptors at St Florian between 1710 and 1750, and that it has mainly been kept in its original location. A typical feature of Austrian furniture-making in the Baroque period is the close collaboration between cabinetmakers and sculptors. Furniture was regarded as an integral part of the interiors, and the sculptural elements made a vital contribution to the overall composition of individual pieces. As guild regulations prohibited cabinetmakers from doing sculptural work, it was essential for the two crafts to work together.

The state apartments at court had hardly any seating, as in general nobody was allowed to sit in the presence of the monarch. A sedan chair made *c.* 1740 for Maria-Theresa (Vienna, Schloss Schönbrunn) still adheres to the forms current in the reign of Charles VI, with elaborate gilded carving on the armrests and legs. The upholstered chairs of the period from 1740 have a Rococo lightness in their ornamentation, tapestry or woollen fabric seats and backs, the frames mainly painted white and gold; they appear almost bourgeois. On the whole no individual style characterizes Austrian seat furniture, which differed little from that made at the same time in south Germany. There was a preference for figures as supports for the seat and back, and at the beginning of the period chairs were still unupholstered and narrow with a high back; from the mid-17th century chairs became more comfortable with armrests and sometimes with upholstered seats and backs. The few surviving chairs and armchairs that were probably made in Austrian workshops of the time tend to follow Italian models, with ornate carving and gilding.

One of the most important pieces of furniture in the Baroque period was the console table, set against a wall and representing an extension of the architecture into the room. In the early 18th century there was a preference for ornate acanthus and floral carvings on the curvilinear legs, the form of the table being completely overwhelmed by exaggerated carvings. The elaborate modelling is reminiscent of shapes found in Italian Baroque art, and Italian architects and decorators were frequently commissioned to work for private patrons in Vienna. The penchant for over-ornate, non-structural table shapes is evident not only in Vienna, but throughout what was then the Austrian empire, including Bohemia. At the beginning of the 18th century veneers of the type used in boullework were popular; the oldest surviving piece was made in Vienna *c.* 1700 and consists of a table-top incorporating a portrait of *Leopold I* (Vienna, Hofburg, Präsidentschaftskanzlei). Magnificent writing-desks were also made in boullework in Viennese or Moravian workshops, including one for Tsar Peter I (*c.* 1720; now in St Petersburg, Hermitage); its base is a chest-of-drawers, with the sloping writing-top fixed above two drawers, and the desk is veneered with burr walnut and has brass mounts. Its ascription to a Viennese workshop is based on archival evidence only, as in style and execution it resembles furniture then being made in south Germany, as do most pieces of furniture coming from Austrian workshops or in Austrian ownership. The only features that pieces of furniture made in Austria have in common are the early use of strapwork decoration on veneered surfaces, together with marquetry representations of figures. Games-tables form a special sub-category, their function being readily recognized from the marquetry patterns, for example the games surface inlaid with a chessboard or a backgammon game, as in an example at St Florian, or 'strewn' with playing cards.

The most important type of furniture made *c.* 1600 was a rectangular chest-shaped cupboard on legs with many small drawers and compartments, often decorated with inlay work. Such a cupboard could either be designed to contain art treasures, in which case it was a sort of small-scale *Kunst- und Wunderkammer*, or as an escritoire. These cupboards were mainly produced in Augsburg, but the ebony pieces known as Eger cabinets (after the city) with marquetry or pietre dure inlay were also made in Bohemia. In the Alpine regions the themes of the inlay were mainly *Maikrüge* (handled vases decorated with flowers, especially lilies) and birds, together with strapwork and typically Austrian interwoven bands of marquetry. The cabinet retained its popularity as a piece of furniture for gentlemen in Austria and Bohemia throughout the whole of the 17th and 18th centuries: as late as 1723 a splendid example was made for Charles VI in black (Vienna, Mus. Angewandte Kst), the colour and style of its marquetry redolent of the 17th century, while the curving ornamentation looks towards later 18th-century design.

From about 1730 the cabinet conceived as an escritoire developed into the 'tabernacle' cabinet, so called because of the tabernacle-like arrangement of the middle section of the cabinet; it rested on a base like a chest-of-drawers, and the two stages were generally linked by a sloping hinged writing flap (see fig. 30). A large number of drawers, often including secret compartments, were provided for storing documents and letters, and a variety of locking devices and concealed cavities meant they could even be used to keep private papers. The tabernacle cabinet was an extremely popular item of gentlemen's furniture both among the upper and middle classes. The cabinetmaker could display his full veneering skill on the doors and drawers of escritoires and wardrobes; in Austria cupboards and cabinets were mainly decorated with strapwork intarsia made of burr walnut, often with inlays of tortoiseshell, mother-of-pearl or pewter.

The famous St Florian 'clock-cabinet' (1722; Markt St Florian, St Florian Abbey) is a supreme example of Austrian Baroque furniture. Lavishly enriched with ornamentation and gilding, it was created jointly by Stephan Jegg (cabinetmaker), Leonhard Sattler (sculptor), Marcus Müller (gilder and painter) and Philipp Gratzl (clockmaker). The cabinet is made from walnut and ebony; in the lower part gilded atlantids support the writing-desk section; above, near the tabernacle, are allegorical figures of Faith, Hope, Charity and Patience, and in the upper part there is a clock as a *memento mori* with putti and herms on either side, surmounted by the figure of Time swinging his scythe. The cabinet is also richly adorned with gilded rocaille decorations and strapwork.

30. 'Tabernacle' cabinet with writing-flap, painted wood, by Georg Henner, 1788 (Orth, Schloss, Donau-Museum)

In the 17th century and the early 18th, Austrian beds were Baroque showpieces lavishly decorated with carved acanthus leaves and sometimes gilded figures; however, they lacked a canopy. The most magnificent example is Prince Eugene's bed (*c.* 1711; Markt St Florian, St Florian Abbey; see fig. 31). At the four corners there are demi-figures of lancers or imprisoned Turks; on the headboard putti strike cymbals or drums, while a putto in front of the Turks' tent on the footboard is blindfolded as an allegory of sleep. The rails are decorated with coats of arms and trophies. This bed, which was made for the imperial apartments at the monastery, represents the apotheosis of Charles VI, in whose reign the Turks, who had constantly been invading Austria from the east, were finally driven out. This form of richly carved bedstead continued to be popular in Austria for a long time, even while four-poster beds from France with a canopy and a (largely concealed) wooden construction were becoming fashionable.

Towards the end of the 18th century the distinction between court furniture and everyday middle-class furniture became less marked. Furniture from the reign of Joseph II is noted for its simplicity, pure forms and classical ornament. The former furnishings of Schloss Schlosshof near Vienna (now in the Bundesmobiliendepot, Vienna) illustrate the dualism of the old and new, the Rococo and Neo-classical stylistic elements. Whereas Rococo-style tables still strove to mask the relationship between the supporting members and the load they were bearing, the Neo-classical stressed the structural design. The scrolls and rocaille decorations of the Rococo vied with such Neo-classical ornamental motifs as laurel wreaths, dentils, rosettes etc. Increasingly, white and gold or white with grey replaced brown and gold as the colouring for furniture, especially of seating. Nevertheless, restrained 'English' elements also started to become common, as expressed by a walnut settee (*c.* 1780; Vienna, Hofmobiliendepot), which has a clear, simple outline and sparing linear decoration on the back. When Joseph II, always more interested in political reform than ostentatious display, had economy forced upon him, he insisted on using available 'second-hand' pieces of furniture in the court apartments. His ideal was Classicism, inspired by the linear forms of antiquity, rather than the over-intricate, ornate Rococo.

BIBLIOGRAPHY

M. Zweig: *Das Wiener Hofmobiliendepot* (Vienna, n.d.)

——: *Wiener Bürgermöbel aus Theresianischer und Josephinischer Zeit (1740–1790)* (Vienna, 1922)

H. Kriesel: *Die Kunst des deutschen Möbels*, i–ii (Munich, 1968–70)

F. Windisch-Graetz: 'Barocke Möbelkunst in Österreich, Überblick und Forschungslage: Die Möbel des Stiftes St Florian', *St Florian: Erbe und Vermächtnis; Festschrift zur 900-Jahr-Feier*, Mitteilungen des oberösterreichischen Landesarchivs, 10 (Vienna, 1971), pp. 346–96

——: 'Möbel und Raumkunst der Renaissance in Österreich', *Renaissance in Österreich: Geschichte, Wissenschaft, Kunst* (exh. cat., ed. R. Feuchtmüller; Schallaburg, Schloss, 1974), pp. 280–97

C. Witt-Döring: 'Die Farbgebung der Möbel am Wiener Hof während der Regierungszeit Maria Theresias', *Alte & Mod. Kst*, 158 (1978), pp. 8–12

A. Feulner: *Kunstgeschichte des Möbels*, Propyläen-Kunstgeschichte, ii (Frankfurt am Main, 1980), pp. 211–13

P. Parenzan: 'Zum Josephinischen Möbelstil', *Österreich zur Zeit Kaiser Josephs II.* (exh. cat., Vienna, Niederösterreich. Landesmus., 1980)

RENATE WONISCH-LANGENFELDER

3. 1781–1897. The Viennese court of Maria-Theresa and Joseph II did not greatly appreciate interior decoration; as a result there was no vigorous tradition of cabinetmaking in Austria in the 18th century comparable to that of England or France. Josephian furniture, like a heavy version of the Louis XVI style with fluted tapered legs, remained fashionable into the 1790s. Even the Gothic Revival relief carving of furniture in the Franzensburg at Laxenburg, near Vienna, dating from *c.* 1800, betrays underlying classical shapes and decorative patterns. The pieces executed by Benedikt Holl (?1753/5–1833) between 1800 and 1810 to 1815 illustrate the transition from the

31. Prince Eugene's bed, carved wood, partly gilded, 2.05×2.65×2.70 m, made (1711) by Meinrad Guggenbichler and painted (1712) by Matthias Müller (Markt St Florian, St Florian Abbey)

use of 18th-century English and French furniture as models to the development of the Viennese Biedermeier style with its curved forms and predominantly smooth finishes. There was by and large no equivalent in Austria to the splendid designs inspired by Classical antiquity found in Empire or Regency furniture. Around 1815 to 1820 lighter, shapely forms were developed. The most important producer of such furniture was Josef Ulrich Danhauser (*see* DANHAUSER, (1)), who, in 1804, founded the Etablissment für alle Gegenstände des Ameublements, which supplied lamps, clocks and decorative items as well as furniture for the Albertina in Vienna and the Weilburg near Baden for Archduke Charles. During the 1820s rather squat furniture was fashionable (see fig. 32); in the 1830s there was a tendency towards the fragile and bold as exemplified in the chairs made *c.* 1835 to 1839 by Nepomuk Geyers (1807–74) for the Hofburg in Innsbruck.

In the late 1830s patrons became interested in Historicism, and the reproductions of Alexander Popp and the *Wiener Möbel Journal* by Ferdinand List, which appeared from 1841, promoted furniture in the neo-Gothic and Rococo Revival styles. Between 1843 and 1846 CARL LEISTLER and MICHAEL THONET furnished the Stadt Palais Liechtenstein (see fig. 27 above) in Vienna with imaginative Rococo Revival furniture designed by the English architect Peter Hubert Desvignes (1804–83); Thonet was already experimenting with the technique of bentwood construction for chairs, for which he later became well known. Their firms, together with that of the metal furniture manufacturer August Kitschelt, represented Austria at the Great Exhibition of 1851 in London, where their luxurious furniture in 17th- and 18th-century styles was a great success. This furniture remained fashionable in the 1850s, while at the same time Carl Leistler equipped the country seat of Prince Alois II (1796–1858)

32. Sofa by Josef Ulrich Danhauser, 0.99×1.92×0.82 m, *c.* 1820 (Vienna, Bundesmobiliensammlung)

at Eisgrub (now Lednice) with neo-Gothic furniture, a style encouraged by the guild in Lower Austria. The foundation of the Österreichisches Museum für Kunst und Industrie in 1864 led to the Kunstgewerbereform, which promoted Renaissance Revival furniture. The firms of Franz Schönthaler, Friedrich Otto Schmidt (1824–94) and Bernhard Ludwig (1834–97), and the architects Valentin Teirich (1844–76), Theophilus Hansen and in particular JOSEF VON STORCK all shared this objective. In the late 1870s and 1880s 17th- and 18th-century models again came to the fore, and many homes contained a series of rooms decorated in different period styles. The publication *Elegante Haus Möbel* by Ferdinand Gabriel and Storck's *Alte Mobel für moderne Bedürfnisse* (both Vienna, 1896) describe and illustrate all the different styles available to cabinetmakers.

BIBLIOGRAPHY

M. Zweig: *Zweites Rokoko* (Vienna, 1924)
100 Jahre österreichisches Museum für angewandte Kunst (exh. cat., Vienna, Österreich. Mus. Angewandte Kst, 1964)
G. Himmelheber: *Die Kunst des deutschen Möbels: Klassizismus, Historismus, Jugendstil* (Munich, 1973)
Vienna in the Age of Schubert (exh. cat., London, V&A, 1979)
E. B. Ottillinger: *Das Wiener Möbel des Historismus: Formgebungstheorie und Stil-Tendenzen* (diss., U. Vienna, 1986)
P. Parenzan: 'Auf dem Weg zur Wohnkultur', *Wien, 1815–1848: Bürgersinn und Aufbegehren; Die Zeit des Biedermeier und des Vormärz*, ed. R. Waissenberger (Vienna, 1986), pp. 109–138

4. AFTER 1897. It was an established principle among those advocating a shift in taste around 1900 that the distinction between the fine and applied arts should disappear. Members of such groups as the WIENER WERKSTÄTTE wanted to produce aesthetically pleasing utilitarian objects for all aspects of everyday living; thus furniture design became an important field for young Viennese architects. It was not only specially commissioned pieces that were to be designed on these principles, but also bentwood furniture by the Gebrüder Thonet and J. & J. KOHN, and wickerwork furniture by the Prag-Rudniker Co. (*see* WICKER, fig. 1), which had previously been anonymous mass-produced goods. Before 1900 the *Brettlstil* was dominant, exploiting shapes formed by wooden boards, as in the studio furniture designed by Josef Hoffmann for Kolo Moser in 1898. About 1900 this movement was succeeded by a floral phase, influenced by Belgian and French Art Nouveau, which can be seen in designs by Gustav Siegel (1880–1970) for J. & J. Kohn's furniture for the Exposition Universelle in Paris in 1900 and in the work of JOSEPH MARIA OLBRICH. From 1903 rectangular, rectilinear furniture shapes typical of the specifically Viennese *Jugendstil* developed, which can be seen in the furniture designed by Otto Wagner for the *Die Zeit* telegraph office and the Postsparkasse building. Other designers who worked in this style include Marcel Kammerer (1878–1959), Kolo Moser, Robert Oerley and Otto Prutscher. The Vienna Kunstschau in 1908 illustrated a perceptible change in style towards decorative furniture shapes marked to some extent with Biedermeier verve and classical heaviness. This trend was even more noticeable in the Viennese contributions to the Cologne Werkbund-ausstellung in 1914.

In the 1920s and 1930s the luxury furniture made by the Wiener Werkstätte and by Josef Hoffmann was indelibly influenced by the bizarre designs of Dagobert Peche, which anticipated the Art Deco movement. During the same period Adolf Loos advocated that furniture should be functional rather than a work of art and put this theory into practice by using commercially available furniture in his interiors. His ideas influenced Josef Frank, Oskar Strnad and Oskar Wlach (1881–1963). In 1921 they took part in the *Einfacher Hausrat* exhibition, and in 1925 founded the Haus und Garten furniture store, which stocked pieces that were light, easy to move and produced as single items rather than as suites (see fig. 28 above). In 1935 their designs were published by Erich Boltenstern in *Wiener Möbel.* Josef Frank carried on the tradition in Sweden, working for the Svenkst Tenn department store. The unit assembly furniture designed by Franz Schuster was a contribution to the international Modern Movement; he published his designs in *Ein Möbelbuch* (Stuttgart, 1927). Furniture designs by Rudolf M. Schindler in California or Ernst Plischke in Vienna demonstrated that the Viennese furniture world was thoroughly conversant with international Modernism.

In post-war Vienna Oswald Haerdtl, Otto Niedermoser (*b* 1903), Peter Payer (*b* 1932), Max Fellerer, Eugen Wörle (*b* 1909) and others attempted to redevelop an Austrian style of domestic furnishing appropriate to the period and in line with the requirements of 'social living' both in articles and in their designs. They adhered to the qualities of the Viennese furniture of the inter-war years, as did Anna Praun (*b* 1906) and Johannes Spalt (*b* 1920). More recently, such architects and designers as Hans Hollein, Hermann Czech, Luigi Blau (*b* 1945), Robert M. Stieg (1946–84) and Mateo Thun (*b* 1953) have provided evidence of a renewed interest in furniture design.

See also VIENNA, §IV, 1.

BIBLIOGRAPHY

E. Boltenstern: *Wiener Möbel* (Stuttgart, 1935)
Moderne Tischlersessel und ihre Werkzeichnungen (exh. cat., Vienna, Österreich. Mus. Angewandte Kst, 1969)
D. Müller: *Klassiker des modernen Möbel-designs* (Munich, 1980)
Neues Wohnen: Wiener Innenraumgestaltung, 1918–1938 (exh. cat., Vienna, Österreich. Mus. Angewandte Kst, 1980)
V. J. Behal: *Möbel des Jugendstils: Sammlung des österreichischen Museums für angewandte Kunst* (Munich, 1982)
A. Gmeiner and G. Pirhofer: *Der österreichische Werkbund* (Vienna and Salzburg, 1984)

EVA B. OTTILLINGER

VII. Ceramics.

1. Pottery. 2. Porcelain.

1. POTTERY. The oldest significant pottery wares made in Austria are tiles for stoves, which were produced in the Tyrol from the 15th century and which are *in situ* in castles and country dwellings in the South Tyrol (e.g. end 15th century; Burg Meran). Faience was first introduced from Italy in the 16th century and replaced pewterware for everyday wares. The two most important centres of faience production were Gmunden and Salzburg, but there is also evidence of isolated workshops in such towns as Wels, Upper Austria, where blue-painted pottery was produced, and Leobersdorf, Lower Austria, where red-painted pottery was made. Itinerant journeymen assisted in the exchange of technical knowledge and subject-matter.

In GMUNDEN a potter's workshop is mentioned as early as 1492, and the first potters' regulations were established there in 1625. From the 17th century artists

33. Faience workshop jug, h. 245 mm, from the Obermillner workshop, Salzburg, 1680 (Salzburg, Salzburger Museum Carolino Augusteum)

produced vessels with brightly coloured lead and tin glazes. The range of wares included jugs, dishes with handles, boxes with lids, christening-bowls, holy-water stoups, tiles, clock-cases and round fan-tiles, which served as wall decoration. In the mid-18th century ceramic artists preferred to paint dense blue decoration, copying wares from Delft; wares from the late 18th century depict such genre scenes as craftsmen and huntsmen.

In Salzburg (*see* SALZBURG, §3) the first potters' guild was established in 1578. The first important workshop was run by THOMAS OBERMILLNER. A workshop jug (1680; Salzburg, Mus. Carolino Augusteum; see fig. 33) depicts the activities of the workshop, including the preparation of clays and glazes. The workshop produced tiled stoves and tablewares—mostly jugs with double handles—which were probably painted by Martha Obermillner in four high-fired colours. A characteristic feature is the blue, undulating bands between the painted subjects, which were probably copied from Chinese wares. The subjects include groups of figures, landscapes, animals, saints and the theme of the 'world upside-down'. The workshop ceased production in 1733.

In 1736 another faience factory was established by Johann Michael Moser (*fl* 1736–76), who applied for permission to establish a workshop in the Riedenburg, outside the gates of Salzburg. Within a short period the new workshop was very successful, producing pear-shaped and cylindrical jugs, tiles, plates, coffee services, boxes and christening-bowls painted in such high-fired colours as blue and purple. Three principal types were produced by Moser: wares with a white ground painted in bright colours; wares with a blue ground over-painted with dark blue; and stoneware cylindrical jugs called *Leberkrüge*. After Moser's death, his son-in-law, Jakob Pisotti the elder (*fl* 1777–1820), took over the business; the execution and decoration of the pieces, however, remained the same. Some typical decorative motifs used during the Pisotti era include the trefoil with stems on either side; long, straight branches with attenuated leaves; and the five-petalled 'Pisotti' carnation. From 1800 jugs at the Riedenburg were decorated with representations of saints. In 1820 Jakob Pisotti the younger (1792–1869) took over his father's workshop; because of the growing competition from mass-produced earthenware, however, handmade pottery became less and less profitable to produce. In 1848 the factory ceased production owing to economic failure.

At the end of the 19th century Vienna became the centre of ceramic production in Austria. In 1885 FRIEDRICH GOLDSCHEIDER established the Goldscheiderische Porzellan-Manufaktur und Majolika-Fabrik in Vienna, which was continued by various family members until 1954. The concern manufactured 'majolica' decorative wares (heavily modelled earthenware, covered with thick lead glazes, imitating 16th-century Italian maiolica and the wares of Bernard Palissy), including vases, figures, busts and utilitarian items. Viennese *Jugendstil* was particularly represented at the Kunstgewerbeschule (now the Hochschule für Angewandte Kunst) in Vienna by Josef Hoffmann and Kolo Moser. As well as the floral form of Austrian *Jugendstil*, which was clearly influenced by Art Nouveau in France and Belgium, artists cultivated a more simplified and rectilinear form in ceramics. In 1906 MICHAEL POWOLNY founded the Wiener Keramik together with BERTOLD LÖFFLER; a specialization of Powolny was black-and-white faience figures. The studio was merged in 1913 with the Künstlerische Werkstätte Franz und Emilie Schleiss in Gmunden to become the Vereinigte Wiener und Gmundener Keramik. GUDRUN BAUDISCH was an associate at the Wiener Werkstätte from 1926 to 1930 under Josef Hoffmann. Her early works in Vienna include mainly women's heads and female figures. In 1937 Baudisch bought a house in Hallstatt, Upper Austria, which later became the centre of the Keramik Hallstatt (1947). This continued in production in the late 20th century; of the Gruppe H (Hallstatt/ Baudische-Werkstätte and Hohenberg/Gmundener Keramik) the latter are substantial producers of everyday and of ornamental pottery. Arno Lehmann (1905–73), who lived and worked in Salzburg, was a notable potter in the post-war years.

2. PORCELAIN. In 1718 the Wiener Porzellanmanufaktur was established in Vienna by Claudius Innocentius du Paquier (*d* 1751) from Trier; it was the second factory in Europe, after Meissen, to produce hard-paste porcelain, and from the beginning the factory rivalled the production at Meissen. The first dated object from the factory is a delicately fluted chocolate cup (Hamburg, Kst- & Gewsch.) inscribed with *3 May 1719* and a verse of thanks, *Gott allein die Ehr und sonst keinem mehr*. Initially the china clay (kaolin) came from Saxony, but soon indigenous Austrian clays were used. By 1720 the factory was producing chocolate beakers, coffee-cups, pipes, walking-stick handles, cutlery-handles, terrines, candelabra, holy-water stoups, clock-cases and mirror-frames. The production process was divided between the modellers and the painters, including such artists who signed their names as Franz Josef Klinger, Anton Lacher and Jakob Helchis. The factory supplied the porcelain for the creation of *Porzellankabinette*, for example the Dubsky Zimmer (1720–25; Vienna, Österreich. Mus. Angewandte Kst), which was originally in the palace of Graf Dubsky in Brno. The room contained 1450 pieces of porcelain decorated with chinoiseries and birds. Early vessel forms followed East-Asian models or copied European silverware. Decoration was taken from engravings and executed in *Schwarzlot* (painting in black) or in soft shades of purple, blue, iron-red, green and yellow. Decorative schemes included copies of Japanese Imari ware, flowers, gilded birds and sprigged prunus blossom (e.g. teapot, *c.* 1725; Budapest, Mus. Applied A.).

Under the Empress Maria-Theresa, the factory was converted to state ownership (1744) and became the Kaiserliche Porzellanmanufaktur. From 1740 the factory's 'sculptural period' had begun; previously figures had been produced only as seated figures that served as stoppers or knops (e.g. tureen, 1730–35; Budapest, Mus. Applied A.). From 1747, under the direction of the chief modeller Johann Joseph Niedermayer (*d* 1784) Rococo-style single figures and groups were produced. Porcelain table centrepieces were typical of this period (e.g. of *c.* 1767–8; Vienna, Österreich. Mus. Angewandte Kst; see fig. 34). The factory produced polychrome figures inspired by the dwarf-like figures of Jacques Callot, characters from the *commedia dell'arte* (e.g. of *c.* 1740; Frankfurt am Main, Mus. Ksthandwk), shepherds, musicians and mythological figures. Many of these figures were copied or adapted from Meissen models. About 1780 the factory completed its first experiments with biscuit porcelain.

The finest phase of the factory's production began in 1784 under Conrad Sörgel von Sorgenthal, who was director until his death in 1805. Sorgenthal led the factory out of financial crisis by auctioning off surplus stock and carried out social reforms among the workforce by establishing a pension fund and benefits for widows. The Rococo style was completely abandoned, and shapes became more Neo-classical. New colours were developed and wares, including urn-shaped vases and dinner- and tea-services were finely painted with landscapes and classical subjects, which were extensively embellished with raised gilding (e.g. gilded cup-and-saucer, 1799; Nuremberg, Ger. Nmus.). Several important commissions were received, including those from the Sicilian and Russian courts.

34. Porcelain centrepiece, h. 335 mm, from the Kaiserliche Porzellanmanufactur, Vienna, *c.* 1767–8 (Vienna, Österreichisches Museum für Angewandte Kunst)

After the death of the dynamic Sorgenthal the factory suffered severe setbacks, including the effects of the Napoleonic Wars and the establishment of a factory in Engelhartszell, Bavaria (1809). The Bohemian porcelain factories of Schlaggenwald (1792–1840), Klösterle (est. 1793), Pirkenhammer (1803–53) in Brezova and Dallwitz (1804–75), near Karlsbad, also rivalled the production at Vienna. In the early 19th century porcelain painting was central to the Viennese production. One of the best-known painters of the period was Josef Nigg (*fl* 1800–43), some of whose signed works are extant (e.g. *Blumenbild*, 1818; Vienna, Mus. Angewandte Kst). From 1830 popular subjects included floral still-lifes and copies of such famous paintings as Raphael's *Madonna della Sedia.* The introduction of transfer-printing on porcelain facilitated mass production. Etruscan-style gilded vases were also made. Despite its international recognition, the factory closed in 1864 due to the competition from the privately owned factories of Schlaggenwald and Pirkenhammer. Much of the undecorated stock was sold and painted in *Hausmaler* studios.

It was not until *c.* 1900 that Austrian porcelain manufacturers produced important independent creations once again. At this time Vienna experienced an artistic heyday, and the Secession movement stimulated production in the decorative arts. In porcelain design the floral form of *Jugendstil* did not predominate, as more rectilinear and geometric forms were preferred. The most important and influential artistic personality was Josef Hoffmann, who produced designs for porcelain dinner and coffee services using the principles of utility and form appropriate to the material. The Wiener Kunstgewerbeschule (now the Hochschule für Angewandte Kunst), where the designs were produced, worked with the porcelain firm of Josef Böckh (1879–1933), who produced services after designs by Hoffmann, Kolo Moser and Jutta Sika, which used simple architectural forms without decoration. Eventually the factory produced only coffee-, tea- and table services and wash-jugs and bowls. The Wiener Werkstätte, founded in 1903, could produce its own porcelain only from 1917 because until then it had no ceramic department of its own. The workshop of Hugo F. Kirsch, established in 1905, produced mainly Biedermeier-style figures and animals, but also vases painted with abstract decoration. The work produced by the Wiener Keramik, which was established in 1906 by MICHAEL POWOLNY and BERTOLD LÖFFLER, was influenced by wares from the Wiener Werkstätte and was often decorated with geometric patterns (e.g. black-and-white figure of a boy riding a snail, *c.* 1910; London, V&A). The Wiener Keramik was dissolved in 1913 when it merged with the Kunstlerische Werkstätte Franz und Emilie Schleiss in Gmunden to become the Vereinigte Wiener und Gmundener Keramik.

The Wiener Porzellanfabrik Augarten was established in 1922 and was linked to the tenets of traditional Viennese porcelain manufacture. The factory reproduced porcelain from the repertory of the original Viennese porcelain factory, including floral dinner services, figures of animals and Rococo style figures. Modern designs by contemporary artists were also produced.

See also VIENNA, §IV, 3.

BIBLIOGRAPHY

A. Walcher von Molthein: 'Die Gmundener Bauernfayencen', *Kst & Ksthandwk*, x (1907), pp. 407–81

J. Ringler: *Tiroler Hafnerkunst* (Innsbruck, 1965)

W. Neuwirth: *Österreichische Keramik des Jugendstils: Sammlung des Österreichischen Museums für angewandte Kunst in Wien* (Vienna and Munich, 1974)

——: *Porzellan aus Wien: Von du Paquier zur Manufaktur im Augarten* (Vienna and Munich, 1974)

——: *Wiener Keramik: Historismus—Jugendstil—Art Déco* (Brunswick, 1974)

F. H. Hofmann: *Das Porzellan der europäischen Manufakturen*, Propyläen-Kstgesch. (Frankfurt am Main, 1980)

O. Wutzel: *Gudrun Baudisch Keramik: Von der Wiener Werkstätte zur Keramik Hallstatt* (Linz, 1980)

Goldscheider Keramik: Historismus—Jugendstil—Art Déco (exh. cat., ed. S. Walther; Vienna, Hist. Mus., 1985–6)

W. Mrazek: 'Das Wiener Porzellan der Biedermeierzeit', *Bürgersinn und Aufbegehren: Biedermeier und Vormärz in Wien, 1815–1848* (exh. cat., ed. S. Krasa; Vienna, Hist. Mus., 1987), pp. 218–25

H. Langer: *Österreichische Fayencen* (Munich, 1988)

RENATE WONISCH-LANGENFELDER

VIII. Glass.

The first mention of a glassworks founded in Vienna by Onossorius de Blondi, a glass dealer and manufacturer of mirror-glass, was in 1428, and Niclas Walch offered in 1486 to establish a glassworks in Vienna to produce Venetian glass. In 1552 a Viennese glassworks was granted permission to manufacture glassware for Lower Austria. Further glassworks were founded in Henriettental (Carinthia) and Graz, probably for the production of window-glass and *Waldglas*. Drinking vessels, for example the *Krautstrunk* (a cylindrical beaker) and the *Maigelein* (a small, flat cup resting on a base), were the most common *Waldglas* wares, decorated with prunts and trailing. In many cases these vessels were adapted for use as reliquaries, which accounts for the numerous fine examples from the 14th and 15th centuries that survive.

In 1534, under the patronage of Ferdinand I, Wolfgang Vitl of Augsburg established a glassworks in Hall-in-Tirol. He employed numerous Italian glassblowers, and the products from Hall are characterized by their combination of Venetian and German taste. The production was mainly of vessels, generally decorated with diamond-point engraving and enamel painting in cold colours (gold, green and red). Following his move in 1567 to Innsbruck, Archduke Ferdinand of Austria, Count of Tyrol (*reg* 1564–95), established the rival Hofglashütte there in 1570. He had a personal interest in glass production and, through good connections with Venice, he was able to employ Venetian glassblowers. The main function of the glassworks was to supply the demands of the court, but permission was granted to sell products on the open market. Window-glass and various kinds of goblets were produced, the latter decorated with diamond-point engraving, unfired gilding and painting in cold colours. As at Hall, Venetian and German formal patterns were combined; the decoration, however, was softer and more opulent than at Hall.

In the 16th and 17th centuries glass production was threatened by increasingly strong competition from Bohemian and Silesian glassworks, with the result that Austrian glassworks could scarcely survive, and their products could achieve only local importance. It was not until the 18th century that the glass industry flourished again. The making of cut glass and the use of gold engraving became widespread; in this technique, a design in gold leaf was applied to the glass, and an additional protective layer of glass fused over it. Johann Joseph Mildner (1765–1808), a glasscutter at the Guttenbrunn Glassworks, revived the technique and achieved excellent results (e.g. medallion beaker, 1792; Hamburg, Mus. Kst & Gew.).

In the Biedermeier period glass production was dominated by the use of transparent enamelling, which Samuel Mohn (1762–1815), a porcelain painter and glass decorator active in Dresden, had rediscovered and popularized. In 1811 his son Gottlob Samuel Mohn (1789–1825) settled in Vienna, where his style of transparent enamel painting achieved much recognition. He worked principally on glass tumblers, often decorating them with either *vedute* or floral ornament. Initially these paintings were carried out on simple tumblers, but from *c.* 1815 the new *Ranftbecher* was preferred because of its larger size, the greater stability provided by its protruding base and its extended upper section, which made it more suitable as a surface for pictorial decoration. Anton Kothgasser adopted this technique and from 1815 to 1830 was a leader in the enamel decoration of glasses. The subjects depicted on his glasses encompass a wide range of *vedute* (see fig. 35), portraits, allegories etc; they differ from Mohn's glasses by virtue of their more picturesque presentation.

35. Glass *Ranftbecher* with transparent enamel painting depicting the Josefsplatz and the Hofbibliothek, Vienna, by Anton Kothgasser, h. 100 mm, *c.* 1830 (Vienna, Österreichisches Museum für Angewandte Kunst)

In 1823 Josef Lobmeyr (1792–1855) opened a glassworks in Vienna, which in 1855 was taken over by his sons Josef Lobmeyr jr (1828–64) and Ludwig Lobmeyr (1829–1917), under the name J. & L. LOBMEYR. The forms of Lobmeyr glasses often followed traditional 17th- and 18th-century models. The LÖTZ WITWE firm, founded in 1836 in Klostermühle, Bohemia, was the main rival to Lobmeyr. Through its development of a new iridizing process (from 1888), the firm became the main exponent of *Jugendstil* art glass in Austria and an important counterpart to the classical styles favoured by Lobmeyr. The glass retailer E. Bakalowits & Söhne, established in Vienna in 1845, worked in close liaison with Lötz Witwe. Inspired by Louis Comfort Tiffany, Bakalowits designed iridescent glass, which was manufactured by Lötz.

In the early 20th century Bakalowits convinced such Wiener Werkstätte members as Josef Hoffmann and Kolo Moser to design glass for Lötz. Hoffmann also designed for Lobmeyr and became the firm's artistic director in 1910. The Stölzle firm (est. 1843) in Waldviertel continues to produce household glass imitative of designs by Hoffmann and Adolf Loos. Austrian glass production was severely curtailed by the loss of concerns located in Bohemia when it formed part of the new Czechoslovakia in 1918 and by the turmoil of World Wars I and II. After World War II the Salzburger Cristallglas firm and the

Riedel Glassworks, under Carl Josef Riedel (*b* 1925), were established at Kufstein. In the late 20th century, apart from the production of household glassware, the main trend was the revival of glass painting for ecclesiastical buildings.

BIBLIOGRAPHY

E. Egg: *Die Glashütten zu Hall und Innsbruck im 16. Jahrhundert* (Innsbruck, 1965)

I. Schlosser: *Das alte Glas: Ein Handbuch für Sammler und Liebhaber* (Brunswick, 1965)

W. Neuwirth: *Das Glas des Jugendstils*, Vienna, Österreich. Mus. Angewandte Kst cat. (Vienna, 1973)

G. E. Pazurek and W. Spiegl: *Glas des 20. Jahrhunderts: Jugendstil—Art Deco* (Munich, 1983)

V. Arwas: *Glas vom Jugendstil zu Art Deco* (Stuttgart, 1987)

GABRIELE RAMSAUER

IX. Metalwork.

1. Gold and silver. 2. Base metals.

1. Gold and silver.

(i) Before 1700. The stock of gold- and silverwork in Austria has been severely depleted by war and the refashioning of objects as a result of changes in style, and consequently few medieval works have survived. The ecclesiastical goldwork made during the Middle Ages in Austria was often designed in accordance with the interior decoration of churches and in some cases is related thematically to religious services. Some extant monstrances and censers from this period represent the 'Heavenly Jerusalem' or the 'Temple of Solomon'. These pieces are, therefore, often representations in silver or gold of small buildings.

Goldsmithing in Austria in the Middle Ages was heavily influenced by extensive imports of products from the Meuse region, Lorraine and Lower Saxony. In Salzburg, however, gold- and silversmiths produced works of high quality, due to the status of the city as the seat of the most senior German prince-bishop and its importance as a cultural centre. The influence of Italian gold- and silverwork was also important. One of the few surviving Romanesque pieces made in Salzburg is the communion chalice from the priory of St Peter (1160–80; Vienna, Ksthist. Mus.). Examples of Gothic gold- and silverwork include the monstrance in the church of St Leonhard in Tamsweg and reliquaries in the treasury of Salzburg Cathedral. In the 13th and 14th centuries many simple gold and silver artefacts, primarily for liturgical use, were also produced. These are usually inexpensive copies of imported objects.

Even before the foundation of a goldsmiths' guild in Vienna in 1366, the work of Viennese craftsmen must have been of considerable quality, as they were responsible for the sumptuous decoration of the court of the Babenburg margraves, which was highly praised in contemporary songs. Unfortunately no examples of this work have survived. In 1330 the gold and enamel altarpiece made by Nicholas of Verdun *c.* 1181 for Klosterneuburg Abbey was damaged in a fire. This was used as an opportunity to convert the panels, originally a facing for an ambo, into an altar in 1331 (*in situ*). The goldsmith responsible for the restoration was thought to have been a resident of Vienna, but new research has indicated that this craftsman came from the Upper Rhine. At that time there was probably no goldsmith in Vienna who had mastered the difficult technique of *champlevé* needed to produce this work.

The few liturgical pieces of Viennese provenance surviving from the 14th century include the so-called Melk Cross, a reliquary cross from Melk Abbey, produced in 1363 (*in situ*). It is an outstanding work with figural and abstract ornament. The Corvinus Goblet (Wiener Neustadt, Stadtmus.; see fig. 36) is one of the major Viennese works from the late 15th century. It was probably produced between 1470 and 1490 by Wolfgang Zirlinger and represents the transitional style in late 15th-century gold and silver, in which architectonic features were replaced by a picturesque treatment with organic forms. Zirlinger was familiar with Hungarian goldsmiths' work, and the ornament of this goblet follows that of Hungarian models.

The Tyrol gradually became an important area of goldsmithing in the 15th century, as is shown by a series of monumental monstrances in Tyrolese towns, for example Hall-in-Tirol, a town that enjoyed great prosperity as a result of its trade in salt. In the 16th century there was a great flowering of art in the Tyrol, mainly due to the patronage of Ferdinand II, Archduke of Austria. He installed a *Kunstkammer*, in which all types of gold- and silverwork were included, in his residence of Schloss Ambras near Innsbruck (*see* INNSBRUCK, §3(ii)).

There were few important commissions for goldsmiths in Vienna in the 16th century, as the city was neither the permanent imperial residence nor a bishopric at this time. In consequence goldsmiths in Vienna were unable to produce works of equal quality to those made in the major European centres of goldsmithing, for example Paris, Antwerp and later Nuremberg and Augsburg. Production of gold- and silverwork in Vienna was also hindered by imports of high-quality goldwork from Italy and Spain, due to the links between the Austrian and Spanish branches of the ruling Habsburg dynasty. An example of the dominance of south German goldsmiths is the silver tableware (Florence, Pitti) made for Wolf Dietrich von Raitenau, Archbishop of Salzburg. It comprises about 100 silver-gilt objects produced in Augsburg around 1600. Although architecture, sculpture and painting flourished in Austria after the victories over the Turks in the 17th century, the demand for ecclesiastical silverware continued to be met predominantly by craftsmen in south German centres, especially in Augsburg, and Austrian goldsmiths slavishly copied the structure, ornamentation and iconography of works made in Augsburg.

(ii) 1700 and after. With the emergence of Johann Baptist Känischbauer (1668–1739), the Court Goldsmith of Emperor Charles VI, goldsmithing in Vienna improved dramatically. Känischbauer collaborated with the outstanding exponents of the Austrian High Baroque style: the architect Johann Bernhard Fischer von Erlach, the architect and sculptor Matthias Steinl and the sculptor Lorenzo Mattielli (*d* 1748). Känischbauer's best-known work, the jewelled monstrance in the Loreto Church, Prague, was produced *c.* 1700 and was probably designed by Fischer von Erlach. The figure of the Virgin forms the shaft, while the base represents the globe ruled by a

37. Gold (18 carat) breakfast service of the Empress Maria-Theresa by Anton Matthias Domanek, Vienna, 1755 (Vienna, Kunsthistorisches Museum)

dragon. The aureole surrounding the Virgin is also the nimbus of the monstrance. In its three-dimensional construction it differs from the traditional 'sun' type of monstrance of the early 18th century and is one of the outstanding examples of Austrian Baroque sculptural silver. Another masterpiece, made by Känischbauer in 1714 and in Klosterneuburg Abbey, is a tree-shaped monstrance that represents the legend of the foundation of the Abbey. Its most notable features are the sculptural decorative treatment and its monumental form, which is enriched by many narrative scenes.

Under Känischbauer's influence Viennese goldsmiths developed a style that differed markedly from south German production, and the pre-eminence of products from Augsburg was then diminished in Austria. While goldsmiths in Augsburg adapted more hesitantly to the rapid change of styles during the 18th century, Viennese goldsmiths were able to adapt current trends to their own idiom relatively quickly, because of the influx of engravings and pattern books of ornament, mainly from Paris. Despite the growing French influence in Austrian silver, the Italian culture established in Vienna in the late 17th century by immigrant Italian craftsmen and the training of Austrian craftsmen in Italy was preserved throughout the 18th century. This is expressed in an emphasis on solid forms and symmetrical, architectonic features.

Joseph Moser was the most important goldsmith in Vienna during the reign of the Empress Maria-Theresa (*reg* 1740–80). One of his important works is the Colman Monstrance (1752) in Melk Abbey, which develops Känischbauer's idea of pictorial representation in the form of a monstrance adorned with genre scenes. The martyrdom of the Irish prince Colman and the related legend of the foundation of the Abbey are represented in a free sculptural treatment. In this work, as in many of his ecclesiastical objects, for example chalices and reliquaries, Moser strove to depict the main theme of the work as naturalistically as possible, so that his works are often small-scale sculptures.

One of the few sets of secular objects produced in Austria during the 18th century is the 18-carat-gold breakfast service (1755; Vienna, Ksthist. Mus.; see fig. 37) of Maria-Theresa by Anton Matthias Domanek (1713–79), which is one of only three surviving pure gold services from this period. The simple shapes reflect the elegant but plain style favoured by the Viennese imperial court. The reform of the Church under Emperor Joseph II resulted

36. Corvinus Goblet, silver gilt and enamel, by Wolfgang Zirlinger, h. 810 mm, Vienna, *c.* 1470–90 (Wiener Neustadt, Stadtmuseum)

in the removal of superfluous ornament and the use of purely functional liturgical vessels. The simultaneous emergence of the Neo-classical style and the so-called *Zopfstil* in Vienna led to the production of plain silverware. A number of splendid silver objects from this period have survived; in their simple elegance they provided a model for later Biedermeier silver.

At the beginning of the 19th century there were great losses of goldsmiths' work in Austria: in 1806 and 1809 vast quantities of gold and silver items were confiscated and melted down to finance the war against Napoleon, and precious objects could only be saved by the payment of extremely high taxes in gold and silver coinage. In particular, the monasteries, which had already suffered under the reforms of Joseph II, had to sacrifice a major part of their treasuries. The improved economic situation in the 1820s favoured the prosperity of the middle classes. The increasing demand for functional silverware led to the extensive production of such domestic objects as candlesticks, dishes, small baskets, sugar bowls and tea and coffee wares in the Biedermeier style (e.g. coffee urn, 1825; Vienna, Österreich. Mus. Angewandte Kst; see fig. 38). Silver from this period is distinguished by the elegant forms and high technical quality that won it a reputation throughout Europe. The mechanically produced silverware that was manufactured from the 1830s, however, lowered the artistic quality of Viennese silver. The firm of Mayerhofer & Klinkosch of Vienna specialized in the production of Rococo Revival and Gothic Revival pieces during the 19th century; by 1873, when its work was shown at the Weltausstellung, it was said to be the largest silversmithing firm in Vienna with 250 employees, including French chasers and modellers.

At the end of the 19th century Josef Hoffmann and Kolo Moser, who were among the exponents of the Secession movement and founders of the Wiener Werkstätte, revived early Biedermeier forms in silverware. The functional elegance of their work can also be seen in many Art Nouveau designs. Hoffmann's early designs for silverware are characterized by pure, geometric forms (e.g. fruit basket, *c.* 1904; London, V&A); with the arrival of Dagobert Peche, the works produced by the Wiener Werkstätte from *c.* 1915 incorporate naturalistic floral motifs and scrolls.

2. Base metals. Few medieval base-metal objects of Austrian origin have survived. The extensive production of high-quality works, however, is evident from documentary sources and surviving pieces. Fifteen pewterers active in Salzburg in the Middle Ages have been recorded. They supplied functional domestic objects, which were usually copies of more expensive silver items, to the less wealthy classes. In the larger cities, however, the artistic standard of pewtermaking was high, as shown by a number of outstanding extant tankards and plates, as well as small sculptures. In many cases the rich decoration finely engraved on the body of the vessel is derived from printed ornament patterns.

Before *c.* 1500 bronze was used primarily for the manufacture of bells and mortars that was later replaced by the extensive production of cannon. The Tirol was the main area of bronze-casting, and during the reign of

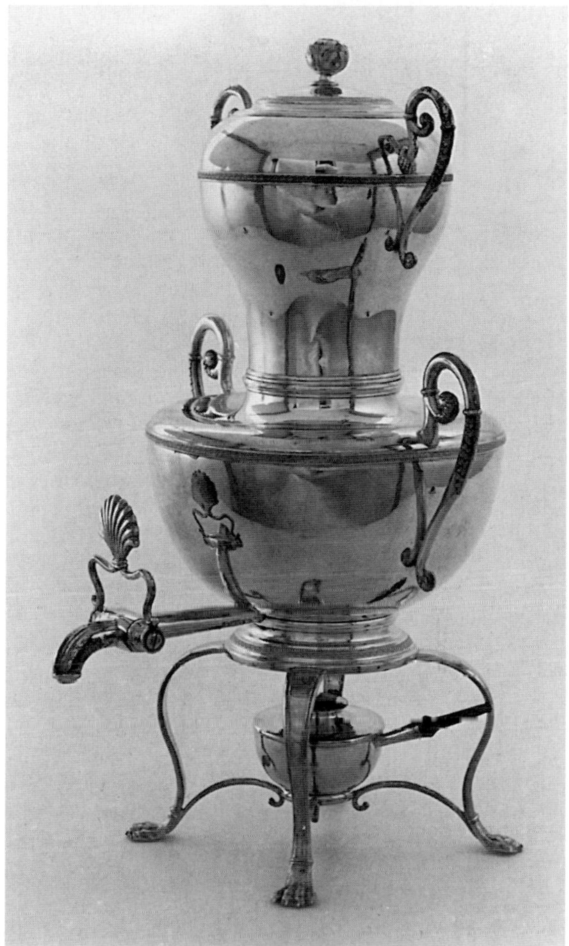

38. Silver coffee urn, h. 430 mm, 1825 (Vienna, Österreichisches Museum für Angewandte Kunst)

Emperor Maximilian I (*reg* 1493–1519) Innsbruck became the main centre of production for guns of all types. Two large foundries in Innsbruck and a number of smaller ones were involved in executing the monument (1508–85) to *Maximilian I* in the Innsbruck Hofkirche (see fig. 20 above). The high standard of the work of Tirolean metalworkers is shown by the large screen around the tomb, which incorporates complex ornament formed of interwoven loops (*see* Innsbruck, §3(i)).

Innsbruck was also the main centre of armour production, and in the 16th century craftsmen specialized in the manufacture of fine ceremonial armour. One of the most important Renaissance works is the 'Eagle' suit of armour (1547; Vienna, Ksthistmus.) decorated with golden eagles made by Jörg Seusenhofer (1516–80) for Ferdinand II, Archduke of Austria. In the 16th century clock-cases were also produced by Austrian bronze-founders, together with all kinds of small bronze objects. Many have been preserved in the *Kunstkammer* of Archduke Ferdinand II at Schloss Ambras, near Innsbruck (*see* Innsbruck, §3(ii)). In Graz two foundries were responsible for producing bells, mortars and guns. The bronze arbour of the fountain in the courtyard of the Landhaus, Graz, shows the artistic capabilities of these craftsmen.

The mining and smelting of iron was traditionally performed in Styria, where ironworkers specialized in the production of wrought-iron grilles, window baskets, signs, arbours and horseshoes. Some splendid examples of Styrian ironwork are the grille on the mausoleum of Archduke Charles II in the priory of Seckau and the wrought-iron arbour of the fountain in the Hauptplatz in Bruck an der Mur. Craftsmen in Steyr and Sterzing (now Vipiteno, Italy) produced cutlery. Cast-iron objects were produced at Werfen, near Salzburg. The high-quality products include the fine stove tiles produced in 1550 for Schloss Ambras, which depict pagan and Christian heroes. Woodcuts and engravings were probably used as patterns for the decoration.

In the late 17th century and the early 18th the main area of production of Baroque wrought ironwork was Upper Austria. There is a large number of wrought-iron railings in the abbeys of Kremsmünster, St Florian, Lambach and Spital am Phyrn. The most important metalworker of the first half of the 18th century was Andreas Ferdinand Lindemayr, whose work is characterized by the use of calligraphic ornament. The nine garden railings of Schloss Belvedere, produced about 1725, probably by Johann Georg Oegg (1703–80), are the most important examples of early 18th century ironwork in Vienna (see fig. 39). The decorative upper parts of these railings are notably different from the somewhat conservative contemporary Viennese style of wrought ironwork, for example in the symmetrically arranged Meidlinger Tor (1740) of the Schönbrunn Palace. The influence of French ornamental engravings is evident in ornamental ironwork from the second half of the 18th century. Such French-style examples as the open grille (1768) in St Peter's, Salzburg, are not, however, found in Vienna.

At the beginning of the 19th century cast iron became fashionable for such luxury articles as delicate jewellery, writing implements, clock-cases and small busts. At the same time the bronze industry was revived in Vienna. The peak period of production was the mid-19th century, when bronzework was used as a decorative feature for numerous buildings on the Ringstrasse. Luxury articles and architectural features were produced in such quantities that 233 bronzeworking factories were operating in Vienna at the end of the 19th century. The international exhibitions, which promoted industrial manufacture, stimulated the production of bronzework in Vienna. At the beginning of the 20th century, however, the craftsmen of the Secession movement and the Wiener Werkstätte revived the production of high-quality handmade articles in base metal (e.g. brass vase by Kolo Moser, 1903–4; Vienna, Mus. Angewandte Kst; for illustration *see* WIENER WERKSTÄTTE).

BIBLIOGRAPHY

M. Poch-Kalous: 'Das Kunstgewerbe', *Geschichte der Stadt Wien*, VII/ii (Vienna, 1955), pp. 236–41

H. Fillitz: 'Das kirchliche Kunstgewerbe der Barockzeit', *Jakob Prandtauer und sein Kreis* (exh. cat., ed. R. Feuchtmüller; Melk, Stiftsmus., 1960), pp. 264–8

P. Baldass, W. Buchowiecki, R. Feuchtmüller and W. Mrazek: *Gotik in Österreich* (Vienna, Hannover and Berne, 1961), p. 110

B. Grimschitz, R. Feuchtmüller and W. Mrazek: *Barock in Österreich* (Vienna, 1962), p. 83

R. Feuchtmüller and W. Mrazek: *Biedermeier in Österreich* (Vienna, Hannover and Berne, 1963), p. 236

39. Wrought-iron entrance gates, Schloss Belvedere, Vienna, probably by Johann Georg Oegg, *c.* 1725

H. Fillitz: 'Das Kunstgewerbe', *Romanische Kunst in Österreich* (exh. cat., Krems-Stein, Minoritenkirche, 1964), pp. 165–70
P. Baldass, R. Feuchtmüller and W. Mrazek: *Renaissance in Österreich* (Vienna and Hannover, 1966), p. 97
H. Krätzel, ed.: *Erzbischöfliches Dom- und Diözesanmuseum* (Vienna, 1973)
B. Wild: *Joseph Moser und die Wiener Goldschmiedekunst im 18. Jahrhundert* (diss., U. Vienna, 1982)
——: 'Das goldene Nachtzeug der Kaiserin Maria Theresia', *Gold und Silber aus Wien in Kopenhagen* (exh. cat., ed. B. Heitmann; Copenhagen, Christiansborg Slot, 1985), pp. 77–84
H. Fillitz: *Die Schatzkammer in Wien: Symbole abendländischen Kaisertums* (Salzburg, 1986)
900 Jahre Benediktiner in Melk (exh. cat., ed. E. Burckmüller; Melk, Stiftsmus., 1989)

BARBARA WILD

X. Gold boxes.

The makers and decorators of gold boxes in 18th-century Vienna were mainly influenced by Parisian designs. Philipp Ernst Schindler II (1723–93) was the most celebrated enameller of snuff-boxes in Vienna during the mid-18th century. His miniature paintings are generally signed *Schindler*, and the boxes inscribed *Schindler Wienn*. His style was formed by his training at the Meissen porcelain factory. He was probably not a maker of boxes, but it is more than likely that he prepared designs for the goldsmith or indicated the shape and extent of the areas on the box to be reserved for his enamel paintings. The maker with whom he worked is generally considered to be Pierre Michel Colas, who is known to have been active in Vienna *c.* 1775. The other possibilities are Franz Mackh (1730–1805) and the unidentified goldsmiths with the initials I. S. or S. I. and I. S. P. Johann Paul Kolbe (*fl* 1776), a member of a large family of goldsmiths scattered throughout Europe in the second half of the 18th century, worked in Vienna and made splendid drawings for snuff-boxes. During the late 18th century the mosaic technique of Johann Christian Neuber (1735–1808; *see* GERMANY, §X, 3) spread to Vienna, and the Empire-style box (*see* FRANCE, §X, 2) also appeared. The four-colour goldwork on these boxes was sometimes carried out in a particularly lavish and exaggerated manner, and it is this excess that distinguishes them from their French models.

BIBLIOGRAPHY

C. Le Corbeiller: *European and American Snuff-boxes, 1730–1830* (London, 1966)
A. K. Snowman: *18th Century Gold Boxes of Europe* (London, 1990)

A. KENNETH SNOWMAN

XI. Textiles.

The development of textiles in Austria was principally determined by its geographical position and by political circumstances. Situated on the northern slopes of the Alps, the Austrian dominions were unable to grow a textile raw material as important as silk and were dependent on deliveries from the south. Strong links with countries that had established textile production made it often more attractive to import textiles than to manufacture them locally. Tapestries, for example, though an important textile craft, were not widely made in Austria; they were obtained initially from southern Germany and Switzerland and later from the Netherlands, which had dynastic connections with Austria. Moreover, important branches of textile manufacture were the speciality of other regions of the Habsburg empire. These included linen-weaving in Silesia and the manufacture of linen damask and lace in the countries belonging to the Bohemian crown.

Within Austria itself plain linen was produced and woven domestically with the help of itinerant weavers—a tradition that survived into the 20th century. In some areas, for example the Mühl district of Upper Austria, domestic weavers produced more than they themselves needed and sold the surplus. The wool industry, for which evidence dates back to the Hallstatt period (*c.* 1220 BC–*c.* 450 BC), still exists, and for centuries its most important product has been loden. Its raised nap forms a wind and rain resistant surface, which is ideal for clothing in Alpine areas.

1. Before 1800.

(i) Embroidery. Since patterned textiles were not produced until the 18th century, embroidery was the main means of decoration. Initially the work was done in convents, and an early example can be seen in the large set of vestments produced at Göss, near Leoben (*c.* 1250; Vienna, Mus. Angewandte Kst). This is a rare survival of a complete set, consisting of a cope, chasuble, dalmatic and tunicle plus an antependium. It is worked with silk in stepped Gobelins stitch, which entirely covers the linen ground, and features majestic figures of Christ (in blessing and in judgement) with angels, animals, birds and geometric ornament. In the Gothic period as cities became more powerful and guilds emerged, master craftsmen also became involved in the manufacture of precious embroideries. Seidlin von Pettau (from the Steiermark) for example, is known to be

40. Antependium with *Scenes from the Passion*, from the convent of Königsfelden, Aargau, *c.* 1340 (Berne, Historisches Museum)

41. Chasuble, red satin embroidered with gold couchwork and metal threads over cords and paillettes, 1.02×0.70 m, *c.* 1630 (Kremsmünster, Benedictine Abbey)

the embroiderer of the antependium from Salzburg Cathedral (*c.* 1320–30; Vienna, Mus. Angewandte Kst). Vienna became prominent as a centre for embroidery, producing very fine work in silk and gold. The most important surviving example is the antependium of *c.* 1340 from the convent of Königsfelden (see fig. 40). In their design the embroideries of this period formed a direct parallel with contemporary painting, so towards the end of the 14th century the influence of Bohemia also became apparent in embroidery (e.g. mitre, 1375–1400, Admont Abbey; embroidered trimming of Georg von Liechtenstein, *c.* 1410, Trent, Mus. Dioc.).

In the 15th century and the early 16th embroidery underwent extensive development, especially in the Alpine regions. Highly qualified professional embroiderers were operating in such cities as Salzburg, but the very varied quality of surviving work suggests some of it was carried out by provincial craftsmen. Previously the silk embroidery had concealed the linen ground; now plain and patterned silks were being imported from Italy, and the embroidery was largely restricted to borders, apparels and orphreys, but it was often enriched with pearls and gems. Particularly rich examples were made in Tyrol, especially during the reign of Maximilian I, but the great value of the materials often led to the destruction of these embroideries. As early as the second half of the 16th century, the pearls, diamonds, rubies and other gems had been stolen and sold, and the fabrics burnt to retrieve the precious metal. This was true not only of magnificent imperial robes (e.g. the vestments ordered by Frederick III for his coronation in Rome in 1452, and the cloak made in Innsbruck in 1508 for Maximilian I by Master Leonhard von Strassburg), but equally of the finest liturgical vestments and the sumptuous articles of clothing—birettas, collars, etc with their trimmings of gold, pearls and gems—which are documented in contemporary portraits.

The introduction of rich materials coincided with the desire to create three-dimensional effects. Initially relief had been used only sparingly for framing architecture, but in the second half of the 15th century it was also employed for figures. In the most highly developed pieces the figures were modelled in fully three-dimensional manner beneath a baldacchino that projected right out of the surface. These effects were directly related to contemporary sculpture, and the designs were no longer composed of pictorial scenes but of individual figures in separately framed areas. Orphrey crosses, for example, generally incorporated the *Crucifixion* (e.g. *c.* 1500; Salzburg, St Peter) or the *Virgin and Child* (e.g. Mariazell, Wallfahrtskirche, Schatzkam.).

This style continued until the second half of the 16th century: the Late Gothic tradition clearly had enormous strength, and Renaissance influences were confined to details in ornament and dress. In the second half of the century the presence of new artistic concepts can be found only in the few surviving pieces that were made for the court (e.g. frieze with the coat of arms of Ferdinand II, Count of Tyrol, second half of the 16th century; Vienna, Mus. Angewandte Kst) and in those commissioned by the archbishops of Salzburg (e.g. chasuble, 1578; Salzburg, Dommus.).

The Counter-Reformation, however, stimulated a reawakening of art in Austria, and in the 17th century embroidery experienced a new heyday. The most important pieces were worked in gold on monochrome silk grounds. The rich and vigorous patterns composed of flowers enclosed by leafy stems were executed in a range of techniques from flat laid work to high relief and in a variety of metal threads, cords, purl and spangles (see fig. 41). This work, which could be exquisitely delicate in its details, was carried out not only in professional workshops but also in convents. There is no discernible difference in the quality and method of execution (e.g. Pentecostal vestments, 1636, Linz, Mariä Himmelfahrt; vestments for Bishop Breuner, 1649, Vienna, Stephansdom; Christmas vestments for the Niedernburg Convent, 1672, Kremsmünster, Benedictine Abbey; and vestments by Brother Benno Haan, Admont Abbey). In the last quarter of the century coloured silk embroidery was also produced. Its striking naturalism, achieved by needle-painting, relates directly to contemporary painting (e.g. vestments with naturalistic roses from the former Ursulinenkloster, Vienna, 1680–1710, Vienna, Österreich. Mus. Angewandte Kst; and vestments for Eleanor of Wittelsbach, Holy Roman Empress, 1697, Vienna, Stephansdom).

In the 18th century Vienna once again became an important centre of a thriving embroidery industry. Supremely accomplished works were produced, mainly in gold, and some of the craftsmen are known by name. Johann Jakob Edlmannsperger was first active in his native area of Melk, where in 1712 he made the Bertholdi vestments (Melk, Stiftsmus.). He then moved to Vienna, where in 1729 he made the Leopold vestments (Klosterneuburg Abbey). There were also two women embroiderers in Vienna: Maria Susanna Lindtner, who made a set of gold and silver vestments in 1742–3 (Seitenstetten, Benedictine Abbey) and Maria Susanna Hohensünderin, who made vestments for Abbot Bessel in 1744–5 (Göttweig, Benedictine Abbey). Finally, there was Wilhelm Jakob Seberth, a lay priest from Würzburg who worked in Vienna in the 1750s and 1760s. He made a large number of pictorial panels for vestments (e.g. Passiontide chasuble, 1763, Seitenstetten, Benedictine Abbey; Christmas chasuble, 1765, Vienna, Schottenkirche; and two chasubles, 1762 and 1765, Würzburg, Ursuline Convent).

Folk art remained rooted to its own traditions and was virtually untouched by artistic change. This was true not only of domestic weaving, which remained indistinguishable from late medieval work, but also of embroidery. Domestic textiles of wool or linen were decorated with counted-thread designs in cross or Holbein stitch influenced by printed pattern books. Some larger items, including linen-based chasubles, were worked with floral patterns in soft floss silks and spangles that reflect the influence of the professional gold and silk embroideries. By the late 18th century peasant dress had become formalized. Women's caps were elaborately embroidered with gold thread in dense floral patterns, and in the Tyrol belts and other leather accessories for both men and women were decorated with simple patterns worked with dyed peacock and turkey quills.

(ii) Other. Textile printing, which was directly related to the production of woodcuts, had taken place in the Gothic period. In the 15th and 16th centuries it was used to reproduce the effect of more expensive fabrics, especially velvet. The design was printed with a sticky substance on to which wool powder (flock) was immediately blown. This created patterned areas similar to those in relief velvet. These textiles were intended mainly for use as wall hangings, and Italian pomegranate designs were much copied. In folk textiles woodblocks distributed by peddlars, were used well into the 19th century.

The industrial manufacture of textiles also became important in Austria. In 1672 Christian Sindt established a factory in Linz for the production of woollen fabrics, and, after several changes of ownership, the State took over in 1754. Over the following decades the K. K. Linzer Wollenzeug- und Tuchfabrik developed into the largest textile concern in the Habsburg empire, and it survived until 1850. Its objective was to introduce new lines of production to make the country independent of imports and to create employment for the local population. As well as blankets and woollens with a simple pattern, from 1795 it produced machine-made carpets that won the factory a considerable reputation (*see* §2 below).

At the end of the 17th century the ideas of Johann Joachim Becher (1635–82) stimulated an attempt to cultivate silk in Austria. Although it yielded little in practical terms, this was important in establishing silk-weaving in Vienna. The leading weavers were emigrants from Northern Italy: in the first fraternity (est. 1710) ten masters out of twelve were of Italian extraction. The craft underwent rapid expansion, and from the mid-18th century received intensive State support. As early as 1749 the government put an embargo on silk imports, and in 1751 it passed the first legislation for quality control. The Manufakturzeichenschule which was established in Vienna in 1758 and modelled on the School of Design founded in Lyon two years earlier, gave weavers a better grounding in design. Manufacturers were encouraged to specialize in particular objects or types of silk, for which they were awarded certain privileges including tax concessions, and in the second half of the century heavy import duties were imposed on foreign goods.

Other areas of textile production, principally the processing and printing of cotton, went through a similar development during this period. The first cotton factory was established in 1726 in Schwechat, near Vienna, and many others followed in the second half of the century, so that Vienna and the south-eastern area of Lower Austria became the centre of Austrian textile production.

DORA HEINZ

2. 1800 AND AFTER. By the first half of the 19th century Austrian textile manufacture had three main lines of production: silks, shawls and Linz carpets. The centre of the textile industry was Vienna, where some 30,000 textile workers were employed *c.* 1800. In 1822 there were 600 silk-weaving manufacturers, Christian Georg Hornbostel and Paul and Vitalis Mestrozzi being among the most famous. While Hornbostel's firm had a long and chequered history (from 1768 to 1890), the Mestrozzi were in business only from 1798 to 1822. The factory-made textiles that are on display in the Kaiser Franz I Room at the Österreichisches Museum für Angewandte Kunst in Vienna provide a vivid illustration of the output between 1800 and 1835. They demonstrate the variety of fabrics used for clothing and interior decoration, and the development from simple, often brightly coloured and highly contrasted patterns to darker colours and ever more extravagant designs. After 1835 the Baroque Revival, with its luxuriant, naturalistic plant patterns, got under way, and with it Historicism.

Wiener shawls were first made *c.* 1820. They had oriental patterns and were modelled on the Indian shawls from Kashmir and their derivatives produced in England and France. Their production was facilitated by the Jacquard loom, which had been used in Vienna from 1816. From 1834 Rudolf Arthaber and Joseph Burde owned the largest shawl-weaving factory in Vienna.

Between 1795 and 1850 the K. K. Linzer Wollenzeug- und Tuchfabrik in Linz wove carpeting in the English and Dutch manner. The metre-wide strips could be sewn together to form loose carpets or used as wall-to-wall carpeting; borders were worked separately. Linz carpets are characterized by their floral and ornamental patterns: oriental models were used only in isolated cases. Striped, flat-woven mats were made for the cheaper end of the market.

About the middle of the 19th century further industrialization required the foundation of larger factories in Austria, as elsewhere. These were set up in the provinces, in Lower Austria, Bohemia and Moravia; Vienna continued to be the centre of trade. The eclectic mixture of revival styles was succeeded by the 'truth-to-materials' patterns promoted by Gottfried Semper: medieval and Renaissance fabrics and oriental ones, including those from East Asia, were used as sources of inspiration. The Österreichisches Museum für Kunst und Industrie (est. 1864), Vienna, gave manufacturers access to these textiles, and its Kunstgewerbeschule (est. 1867), as well as specialist technical colleges, provided training for pattern-drawers. Such firms as Philipp Haas & Söhne (est. 1810) or Carl Giani made use of the museum's collections, at the same time adding to them with generous gifts from their current lines of production. Giani's Kunstanstalt für Stückerei und Weberei specialized in ecclesiastical furnishings, which had been a speciality in Austria since the 1830s. Haas & Söhne produced furnishing fabrics, and their copies of oriental carpets became renowned.

At the end of the century the arts and crafts revival led artists to explore textile design. From 1898 Johann Backhausen & Söhne of Vienna produced furnishing fabrics from designs by such Secession artists as Josef Maria Olbrich, Josef Hoffmann and Kolo Moser (see fig. 42).

42. Tubular cotton fabric, 'Flowers Awakening', designed by Kolo Moser, 1.23×0.90 m, manufactured by Johann Backhausen & Söhne, Vienna, 1900 (Vienna, Österreichisches Museum für Angewandte Kunst)

Stylized natural forms, abstract linear patterns and, in particular, severe Japanese motifs formed the basis of their work. There was now a desire for a fundamental break with Historicism, and the copying of styles was vehemently rejected.

When the Wiener Werkstätte established a fabric division in 1910 popular primitive art and Expressionist and abstract painting provided further inspiration. Strong colours and forceful juxtapositions of colour, along with an incredible diversity of forms, were the outstanding characteristics of the fabrics produced by the Wiener Werkstätte. Josef Hoffmann and Carl Otto Czeschka had a decisive influence on the style of the early period, and Maria Likarz and Max Snischek on that of the 1920s. The fashion section of the Wiener Werkstätte, which was opened officially in 1911, tried to create a synthesis between artistic and haute couture clothing. Eduard Josef Wimmer-Wisgrill (1882–1961) was its director until 1922, when Snischek took over. Both these divisions of the Wiener Werkstätte, after a short, innovative, avant-garde phase, were swept along with more general, fashionable trends.

In the inter-war years fabrics based on current artistic notions were manufactured in the Werkstätten Haus und Garten founded in 1925 by the architects Josef Frank and Oskar Wiach, as well as in the Wiener Werkstätte. Frank's designs for printed linen and cotton fabrics, which were mostly based on stylized plant forms, are notable for their originality and a certain timeless quality, which meant that they were still in production in the late 20th century.

In 1920 the Wiener Gobelin Manufaktur was founded for the production of wall tapestries woven in the traditional manner but based on the work of contemporary Austrian artists. Albert Paris von Gütersloh and Oskar Kokoschka, for example, provided designs, and their paintings were also recreated in tapestry. The factory lost its raison d'être after World War II, when textile artists began to weave their own designs. Mention should be made of Friedensreich Hundertwasser and particularly of Fritz Riedl, later a professor at the Linz Hochschule für Gestaltung. Participation in the 7th Biennale of Art at São Paulo in 1963 was a triumph for Austrian textile design: the country was represented solely by textile art, and the Grand Prix was awarded to Fritz Riedl.

After World War II the centre of Austrian textile manufacture shifted increasingly to Vorarlberg. Firms such as Backhausen & Söhne, however, remained faithful to Vienna and the surrounding area. In the 1970s Backhausen began to reproduce their Art Nouveau textiles of *c.* 1900, an enterprise for which they received international acclaim.

ANGELA VÖLKER

BIBLIOGRAPHY

M. Dreger: 'Der Gösser Ornat im K. K. Österreichischen Museum für Kunst und Industrie', *Kst & Ksthandwk*, xi (1908), pp. 613–53

H. Deutsch: *Die Entwicklung der Seidenindustrie in Österreich* (Vienna, 1909)

M. Dreger: 'Beginn und Blüte der Wiener Seidenweberei', *Kst & Ksthandwk*, xviii (1915), pp. 325–99

——: 'Über die ältere Zeugdruck-Industrie in Österreich', *Kst & Ksthandwk*, xix (1916), pp. 1–68

——: 'Zu den Anfängen der Seidenbandweberei in Wien', *Kst & Ksthandwk*, xix (1916), pp. 397–494

——: 'Die Linzer Wollenzeug- und Teppichfabrik', *Kst & Ksthandwk*, xx (1917), pp. 289–369

V. Hofmann: 'Beiträge zur neueren österreichischen Wirtschaftsgeschichte: Die Wollenzeugfabrik zu Linz an der Donau', *Archv Österreich. Gesch.*, cviii (1920), pp. 347–782
——: 'Beiträge zur neueren österreichischen Wirtschaftsgeschichte: Die Anfänge der österreichischen Baumwollwarenindustrie in den österreichischen Alpenländern im 18. Jhdt', *Archv Österreich. Gesch.*, cx (1926), pp. 417–741 [whole issue]
D. Heinz: *Linzer Teppiche: Zur Geschichte einer österreichischen Teppichfabrik der Biedermeierzeit* (Vienna and Munich, 1955)
G. Otruba: 'Die Quellenlage zur Frühgeschichte der Industrialisierung in Niederösterreich', *Jb. Landesknd. Niederösterreich*, xxxiii (1957), pp. 82–9
——: 'Zur Geschichte der Frauen- und Kinderarbeit im Gewerbe und den Manufakturen Niederösterreichs', *Jb. Landesknd. Niederösterreich*, xxxiv (1958–60), pp. 143–79
E. Egg: 'Die Kunst der Seidensticker im Umkreis des Innsbrucker Hofes', *Schlern Schr.*, ccxxviii (1962), pp. 1–47 [whole issue]
M. Schuette and S. Müller-Christensen: *Das Stickereiwerk* (Tübingen, 1963)
D. Heinz: 'Textilien', *Gotik in Österreich* (exh. cat., Krems an der Donau, Minoritenkirche, 1967), pp. 243–61
M. Bucek: *Geschichte der Seidenfabrikanten Wiens im 18. Jhdt* (diss., U. Vienna, 1968)
Meisterwerke barocker Textilkunst (exh. cat. by D. Heinz, Vienna, Österreich. Mus. Angewandte Kst, 1972)
F. Wagner: 'Seidenstickerei', *Spätgotik in Salzburg: Die Malerei* (exh. cat., Salzburg, Mus. Carolino Augusteum, 1972), pp. 204–12
D. Heinz: 'Austria', *Needlework: An Illustrated History*, ed. H. Bridgeman and E. Drury (London, 1978), pp. 218–26
Textilkunst in Österreich, 1900–1979 (exh. cat. by A. Völker, Halbturn, Schloss, 1979)
A. Völker: 'Die Produktion der "Wiener Shawls" in der ersten Hälfte des 19. Jahrhunderts', *Documenta Textilia: Festschrift für Sigrid Müller-Christensen* (Munich, 1980), pp. 409–22
Art Nouveau: Textil-Dekor um 1900 (exh. cat. by R. Grönwoldt, Stuttgart, Württemberg. Landesmus., 1980)
A. Völker: 'Textilien', *Neues Wohnen: Wiener Innenraumgestaltung, 1918–1938* (exh. cat., Vienna, Österreich. Mus. Angewandte Kst, 1980)
D. Heinz: 'Wilhelm Jakob Saberth in Wien', *Documenta Textilia: Festschrift für Sigrid Müller-Christensen* (Munich, 1981), pp. 328–39
A. Völker: *Wiener Mode und Modephotographie: Die Modeabteilung der Wiener Werkstätte, 1911–1932* (Munich, 1983)
——: *Die Stoffe der Wiener Werkstätte* (Vienna, 1990)

DORA HEINZ, ANGELA VÖLKER

XII. Patronage.

1. BEFORE 1600. For several centuries art patronage in Austria was dominated by members of the HABSBURG dynasty, who ruled Austria from 1278 and, with one brief interruption, held the crown of the Holy Roman Empire from 1453. From the time of Rudolf IV, Duke of Austria (*see* HABSBURG §I(1)) in the 14th century, artistic patronage was one of many means used by the Habsburgs to assert their privileged destiny. Humanist theory, moreover, provided them with programmes based on Antique models that exploited art as an emanation of the ruler's virtues. The visual representation of claims to sovereignty and legitimization reached a peak in the reign of Holy Roman Emperor Maximilian I (*reg* 1493–1519; *see* HABSBURG §I(3)), who worked out complex artistic programmes with his carefully chosen staff of scholarly and artistic collaborators. The focus of activity during this period moved from Vienna, however, to such towns as Innsbruck. The Emperor's ideas are documented in his autobiographical writings, in the plans for his tomb and the graphic enterprises on a colossal scale undertaken by him. Maximilian saw his own genius as the source of artistic inspiration. In the art that was produced, there are obvious references to Burgundian models and to those from Antiquity, but the crucial factor was the great personal contribution made by the Emperor himself to the inception of these works. Holy Roman Emperor Charles V (*reg* 1530–56; *see* HABSBURG §I(5)) regarded art as a valuable medium for conveying status and moral worth. This is demonstrated in the portraits he commissioned of himself: they show a ruler of might and dignity. In a reference to Virgil's *Aeneid* he was celebrated in a bronze statue by Leone Leoni as Caesar and the prince of peace (1551; Madrid, Prado). In painting, only Titian's grandeur could fully meet the Emperor's exalted expectations.

Artists also worked specifically to provide items for the Habsburgs' encyclopedic KUNSTKAMMER. Products of the goldsmith's art, engraved gems, musical instruments, scientific instruments, mechanical devices, clocks, pieces made of glass, *objets d'art* produced by wood-turning or ivory-turning, items made of iron, wax and maiolica were juxtaposed on equal terms with paintings, sculptures and curiosities. While for Ferdinand of Austria, Count of Tyrol (*reg* 1564–95), as for his great-grandfather Maximilian, the genius of the prince was the central source of inspiration, his nephew Rudolf II, Holy Roman Emperor from 1576 to 1612 (*see* HABSBURG §I(10)) was more practical in his approach to the arts. He set about attaching the finest artists to the court, showing a predilection for engraved gems, clocks and mechanical devices, although his court workshop was not based on any one school.

2. 1600 AND AFTER. In the 17th century a fundamentally new attitude towards the arts arose. To Holy Roman Emperor Ferdinand II (*reg* 1619–37; *see* HABSBURG §I(16)) the arts were an instrument of propaganda for the Roman Catholic faith. As far as means permitted—his predecessor Matthias had already had to economize—he valued and promoted architecture, the decorative arts and music. The Habsburg fondness for architecture became even more marked in the reign of Holy Roman Emperor Leopold I (*reg* 1658–1705) while the minor arts became less popular. However, there were a number of painters, such as Franz Werner von Tamm and Andrea Pozzo, engravers and several sculptors including Mathias Rauchmiller and Matthias Steinl—the latter an ivory-carver—among the officially appointed court artists. During the 17th century and the early 18th, the Austrian branch of the Habsburgs began increasingly to identify itself with the idea of empire. This feeling, linked with the imperial armies' victories over the Turks, was given expression in the monumental architecture of Johann Bernhard Fischer von Erlach (*see* §II, 3 above) and in the recording of history in the form of monuments. In both form and content, analogies with Ancient Rome were sought, the Austrian Habsburgs representing themselves as the heirs of Ancient Rome. The Karlskirche (1716–37; see fig. 6 above), Vienna, with its two great flanking columns inspired by Trajan's column in Rome, was commissioned by Holy Roman Emperor Charles VI (*reg* 1711–40) and must be regarded as the masterpiece of the period.

During the Baroque period art was also promoted by the aristocracy in imitation of the court, but never on such an ambitious scale. Fortified castles and country houses were altered to make them more imposing, in line with the royal example. The holding of diplomatic or ecclesiastical office in the service of a Habsburg prince or of the

Emperor encouraged this tendency. For example MARCUS SITTICUS VON HOHENEMS, Prince-Archbishop of Salzburg, commissioned Santano Solari to build him a summer villa (Hellbrunn, 1614–19) with fountains and grottoes. Charles Eusebius, Prince of Liechtenstein (*see* LIECHTENSTEIN (ii), (2)), was the greatest patron of the arts in his family. As well as commissioning architecture, he wrote a book on the subject, *Das Werk von der Architektur*, which some scholars suggest may have influenced Fischer von Erlach in his unusual choice of location for the stairs at the Schönbrunn Palace (1695–1749), Vienna. He continued to promulgate the Renaissance concept of patronage, which he saw as creating monuments with a view to achieving immortal fame.

During the 17th and 18th centuries the Church was also notable for its patronage, particularly in the area of architecture. Many large-scale Baroque buildings were erected, and celebrated artists and architects were given commissions at a number of monastic foundations. Jakob Prandtauer was engaged as the architect at MELK ABBEY, where Johann Michael Rottmayr frescoed the ceiling. Johan Lukas von Hildebrandt served as the architect on the rebuilding of Gottweig Abbey, while Daniel Gran painted the high altarpiece and frescoed the choir at the Augustinian abbey at Herzogenburg, which was planned by Prandtauer (*see also* §II, 3(ii) above). Following the example set by the Emperor, the aristocracy commissioned buildings and works of art on a scale of luxury hitherto unknown. The most distinguished noble patron—in addition to his activities as a builder, collector and founder of a famous library—was undoubtedly Eugene, Prince of Savoy (*see* SAVOY, (10)), who won renown as a general in the imperial army and held high office at court. Prince Eugene commissioned Hildebrandt to design, and Martino Altomonte and Francesco Solimena to fresco the Lower Belvedere (*see* §III, 3 above), while his enormous winter palace in Vienna was built by Fischer von Erlach (1695–7) and extended by Hildebrandt. By building country houses and extending or rebuilding monastic churches and monasteries, the nobility and the religious orders also emphasized their place in the political hierarchy as divinely ordained.

The Akademie der Bildenden Künste in Vienna became established largely owing to the efforts of Emperor Charles VI. First set up in 1688 by Peter Strudel (*see* STRUDEL, (2)) as a private school, it became the Akademie in 1692 and was then turned into a state institution by Charles in 1725, under the direction of a Kammermaler (officially honoured court painter) on a fixed annual salary. The role of a prince as patron of the arts was henceforth defined, not by his personal association with the artist, but by his office of governor and administrator. This was particularly true in the case of Charles and, more than 100 years later, in that of Francis-Joseph, Emperor of Austria (*reg* 1848–1916). In the 18th century, the Habsburgs also promoted interest in the fine arts through reorganizing the imperial art collections and allowing limited public access. Aspiring artists were also allowed to copy works in the collections.

In 1857, when the expansion of Vienna was decided on, with the aim of turning it into a modern European city to rival Paris (*see* VIENNA, §II, 3), all branches of the fine arts were assigned enormous tasks. The image of Vienna was decisively shaped by buildings put up at that time, particularly those erected between the 1860s and the 1880s in the Ringstrasse: the Neue Hofburg, the Naturhistorisches Museum, the Kunsthistorisches Museum, the Parliament, the Burgtheater and the State Opera. The aim of some of the museums founded at this time was largely educational: the Österreichisches Museum für Kunst und Industrie, for example, established in 1864 (now the Museum für Angewandte Kunst), was intended to help new industries by providing models and encouraging good taste.

After centuries of dominance by the patronage of the Habsburgs, art in Austria in the 19th century began to show the influence of middle-class taste. This was most notable in the growth of artistic activity in the salons as the bourgeoisie began to support the arts. After World War I, however, patronage of art was almost completely taken over by public bodies. As a result of the urgent problems of reconstruction after World War II, expenditure on the arts and culture in the immediate post-war years was relatively low. Even when the economy began to improve, the share of the budget devoted to the arts continued to be meagre, leaving Austria far behind the majority of western and northern European countries in this respect. This state of affairs was still substantially unaltered in the 1990s, with officially appointed patrons having relatively slender means at their disposal and being duty-bound to distribute funds widely, rather than concentrating on specific areas.

BIBLIOGRAPHY

G. Handler: 'Fürstliche Mäzene und Sammler in Deutschland von 1500–1620', *Stud. Dt. Kstgesch.*, 297 (1933), pp. 1–112

G. Heinz: 'Die Galerie Harrach', *Alte & Mod. Kst*, v (1960), pp. 2–9

L. Popelka: 'Schlösser des Marchfeldes, II', *Alte & Mod. Kst*, vi (1961), pp. 6–9

P. Hirschfeld: *Mäzene: Die Rolle des Auftraggebers in der Kunst* (Berlin, 1968)

H. Kühnel: 'Die österreichische Adelskultur des 16. und 17. Jahrhunderts im Spiegel der Kunst- und Wunderkammer', *Österreich Gesch. & Lit.*, ix (1969), pp. 433–45

H. Wiesflecker: *Kaiser Maximilian I*, 5 vols (Vienna, 1971–)

F. Matsche: *Die Kunst im Dienst der Staatsidee Kaiser Karls VI: Ikonographie, Ikologie und Programmatik des Kaiserstils* (Berlin, 1981)

K. Vocelka: *Die politische Propaganda Kaiser Rudolfs II, 1576–1612*, Komm. Gesch. Österreichs, ix (Vienna, 1981)

M. Warnke: *Hofkünstler: Zur Vorgeschichte des modernen Künstlers* (Cologne, 1985)

G. Klupacek: 'Zur Museumspolitik zwischen 1945–1965', *Mitt. Österreich. Gal.*, 75 (1987), pp. 80–98

Fürsterzbischof Wolf Dietrich von Raitenau: Gründer des barocken Salzburg (exh. cat., Salzburg, Residenz, Neugebäude and Dommus., 1987)

ALFRED AUER

XIII. Collecting and dealing.

During its long period as the capital and residency of the Habsburg empire, Vienna was one of the European cities most richly endowed with art collections. The collections of the Habsburgs themselves were of course the most remarkable and evolved from the *Kunst- und Wunderkammer* (*see* KUNSTKAMMER), the art cabinets of the 16th century containing curious and wonderful objects. The Holy Roman Emperor Rudolf II (*reg* 1576–1612) shifted the emphasis of the collection to works of art, reflecting his craving to own the finest paintings in Europe (*see* HABSBURG, §I(10)). Rudolf's collection was plundered after the Thirty Years War, but Archduke Leopold William (*see* HABSBURG, §I(18)) also built up a large private collection, which was considerably expanded through the purchase of the collections of the English king Charles I (put on sale in London after the King's execution in 1649) and of the murdered George Villiers, 1st Duke of Buckingham (auctioned in 1648 in Antwerp). In the 17th century, and especially in the 18th, many large collections began to be formed by members of the nobility. Among the earliest such collections were the Kunstkammer of WOLF DIETRICH VON RAITENAU, which contained prints and battle paintings, and that formed by Joachim Enzelmillner at Windhaag, near Perg (Upper Austria), after his ennoblement in 1630. Another important collection was that of Eugene, Prince of Savoy, whose preference for Italian works was evident in the selection of works by Titian and Guido Reni that Cardinal Alessandro Albani acquired for him. Perhaps the outstanding collection of this era, however, was that of Ferdinand Bonaventura von HARRACH, who undertook several missions on behalf of Emperor Leopold I to Madrid, where he acquired some important Spanish works. The collection was subsequently added to in the early 18th century by other members of the family, who assembled some fine examples of Neapolitan Baroque painting. In the 20th century, however, the collection was depleted by sales, including that in 1991 of Pompeo Batoni's *Susanna and the Elders*, which had been acquired directly from the artist. The powerful chancellor of Maria-Theresa (*reg* 1740–80), Prince WENZEL ANTON KAUNITZ-RIETBERG, was another important 18th century collector. His paintings were eventually auctioned in Vienna in 1820, when they passed into the collection of the Esterházy princes; they were in turn sold later in the 19th century to the Hungarian state. The art treasures of the sovereign dynasty of the princes of Liechtenstein (*see* LIECHTENSTEIN (ii)), which remained in Vienna until the end of World War II when they were transferred to Vaduz, were also gradually reduced by sales. In addition to these aristocratic collections, the art cabinets of the large Baroque monasteries, such as Klosterneuburg, Seitenstetten and Kremsmünster, contained important collections, of which many are still *in situ*. In the 18th century noble and ecclesiastical collectors generally used agents and intermediaries to seek out appropriate purchases. Aristocrats, on the other hand, often acquired works while undertaking a Grand Tour of Europe.

Important collectors in the late 18th century and the 19th included Count ANTON FRANZ DE PAULA LAMBERG-SPRINZENSTEIN, Albrecht, Duke of Saxe-Teschen (*see* WETTIN, (9) and §XIV below), and Count Jan Rudolf Czernin (*see* CZERNIN, (2)). During this period a new wealthy class, comprising mainly Jewish merchants and bankers eager in the pursuit of prestige, also provided an enormous stimulus to the art trade. The names Fries, Arnstein, Pereira and Rothschild all rose to prominence in the art world at this time, although some returned to obscurity almost as quickly, such as Count MORITZ FRIES, whose newly acquired art collection had to be auctioned as early as the 1820s. It was also at the end of the 18th century that the first auction houses appeared, such as the Artaria'sche Kunsthandlung, traceable since 1770 (*see* ARTARIA). Among the most important figures in the art trade in the 19th century was Georg Plach, who was active from 1847 as adviser to such collectors as Rothschild and Gsell. Another important 19th-century Austrian dealer, Charles Sedelmeyer, moved to Paris in 1866 and tried, in addition to selling works by French artists to collectors in Vienna, to launch the careers of central European artists in Paris.

In the late 19th century—around the time of the Ringstrasse development in Vienna—art dealing, which had relatively little tradition compared to that of England, Italy or France, began to flourish. This broadening of interest in the arts continued through the period of the *Jugendstil* and of the Vienna Secession. H. O. Miethke and his artistic director, the important *Jugendstil* painter Carl Moll, dedicated themselves, among other things, to promoting Secessionist painters, who regularly exhibited at the Galerie Miethke from 1904. In 1901 the State auction house, the Dorotheum, which had been founded in 1707 as a pawnbroker's shop, joined the ranks of the Vienna auction houses. After the demise of the Galerie Miethke and other prestigious dealers, the Dorotheum acquired an almost monopolistic position in this sector. There were also many new collections being formed at the beginning of the 20th century. In 1900 there were approximately 40 documented collections in Vienna, and 50 years later their number had risen to 60. The new additions included, above all, the CZARTORYSKI, KAROL LANCKORONSKI, Gsell, Wertheimstein, Dumba, Miller von Aichholz and F. X. Meyer collections. While some collectors continued to favour the Old Masters, there was also a lively interest in contemporary Austrian painting at this time. It is notable in this context that the nobility and upper middle class were guided by the increasingly conservative taste of the imperial house, while the wealthy Jewish community significantly promoted progressive tendencies. For this reason it was such Jewish patrons as August Lederer and Bloch-Bauer who supported the Vienna Secession.

In the period after World War I many important collections were dispersed. The last great events on the Austrian art market were the dubious auctions of the collections of Camillo Castiglione and ALBERT FIGDOR in Vienna and Berlin in 1930. Only a few of the traditional firms of art dealers, including Nebehay, St Lukas, Gilhofer and Artaria, survived this era of decline. At the same time, however, two new galleries were opened with the aim of presenting Austrian and international modernist art. These were the Galerie Würthle and the Neue Galerie, opened in 1923 by Otto Nirenstein-Kallir, who moved to New York in 1933 and introduced the work of Klimt, Schiele, Kokoschka and others to the American public. Among modern collections in Austria, the best known is that of the Viennese optician Rudolf Leopold, who began collecting in the 1950s and assembled the world's largest collection of paintings by Schiele, as well as countless other important works of Austrian art.

BIBLIOGRAPHY

T. von Frimmel: *Geschichte der Wiener Gemäldesammlungen* (Leipzig, 1899)

——: *Lexicon der Wiener Gemäldesammlungen* (Munich, 1913–14)

E. Scheicher: *Die Kunst- und Wunderkammern der Habsburger* (Vienna, 1979)

C. M. Nebehay: *Antiquar und Kunsthändler in Leipzig, Wien und Berlin* (Vienna, 1983)

BARBARA WILD

XIV. Museums.

1. Federal museums. The history of federal museums in Austria again reflects the dominance of the Habsburg dynasty over the culture of central Europe in the Renaissance and Baroque periods. Indeed the *Kunstkammern* and *Wunderkammern* of Ferdinand, Count of Tyrol (*reg* 1564–95), at Schloss Ambras, near Innsbruck, and Holy Roman Emperor Rudolf II (*reg* 1576–1612) in Prague played an important part in the development of the museum as an institution generally (*see* Museum, §I). These collections, which were conceived as show collections with an instructive function, were eventually brought together in the castles and palaces of Vienna, when that city became the permanent residence of the emperor. Among the other art treasures owned by the Austrian line of the Habsburg family and kept in Vienna were the collections of Archduke Leopold William and Emperor Leopold I (*reg* 1658–1705). The collections were looked after by scholars and housed in appropriate galleries or cabinets. While being gradually augmented through the efforts of Emperor Charles VI (*reg* 1711–40), Maria-Theresa and others, in the 18th century the imperial collections were rearranged as a teaching vehicle, catalogued and made accessible to the public, in accordance with the Enlightenment emphasis on education.

In the late 19th century the collections of the Habsburgs were gathered together in a single building that was intended to form part of a great imperial forum in Vienna. This was the Kunsthistorisches Museum, built (1871–89) to the designs of Gottfied Semper and Karl Hasenauer and opened in 1889. The Museum's collection of sculpture and decorative arts is based on the Renaissance and Baroque *Kunstkammern* of the Habsburg princes, into which the collection of the Austrian Este family and a tapestry collection were incorporated after 1918. It was further supplemented in 1938 by a bequest from Gustav Benda, including masterpieces from the early Renaissance in Florence. The Museum's painting gallery is again based on the Habsburg collections of the Baroque period, with 16th- and 17th-century Venetian and Flemish painting being particularly well represented. Among other important departments of the Museum is its Egyptian and Oriental collection, begun in the 18th century but greatly expanded after 1821 by purchases made in Egypt. In 1880 the Miramare collection, which had belonged to Archduke Maximilian, Emperor of Mexico (*reg* 1864–7), was incorporated into the collection, and there are items from excavations in Egypt from 1912 to 1924. The oriental items in the collection are based on those provided by the traveller and explorer Eduard Glaser (*d* 1908). The Kunsthistorisches Museum also has significant collections of antiquities, early musical instruments, weapons, and secular and religious insignia and jewellery.

In the late 19th century many other important museum buildings were erected in Vienna (*see* Vienna, §II, 3). The Naturhistorisches Museum, built from 1872, was designed as a scientific counterpart to the Kunsthistorisches Museum. It too was based on the collections of the Habsburg family; Holy Roman Emperor Francis I (*reg* 1745–65) had created a systematic natural history collection by buying up the contents of complete cabinets on the death of their owners. The Museum für Völkerkunde was similarly based on Habsburg collections; it was established in 1876 as an ethnographic collection within the Naturhistorisches Museum and in 1928 moved to the Hofburg; the oldest items in the collection come from Schloss Ambras, near Innsbruck. The Graphische Sammlung Albertina is based on the collection of Albert, Duke of Saxe-Teschen (*see* Wettin, (9)), and the library built by Charles VI. It is one of the largest collections of its kind, with approximately 44,000 drawings, and 1.5 million prints arranged according to national schools, and within these in chronological order. The Gemäldegalerie der Akademie der Bildenden Künste, founded in 1822, is now housed in a building erected in 1872–6. Its collection, which is based on works submitted to the Akademie by members, bequests, gifts and purchases, is particularly strong in 17th-century painting, Gothic architectural drawings, Renaissance and Baroque drawings and early 19th-century German drawings.

In 1864 the Museum für Kunst und Industrie (now the Museum für Angewandte Kunst) was founded under the auspices of the Austrian state. It was modelled on the Victoria and Albert Museum in London (founded in 1853 as the South Kensington Museum) and was intended to provide models and artistic guidelines for the design of products for the new manufacturing industries, but it also sought to stimulate an awareness of design considerations among the public at large. The museum is housed in a building (1866–71) by Heinrich von Ferstel to which an extension was added in 1906–9 by Ludwig Baumann. It comprises a collection of East Asian art covering the period from 2000 BC to the 18th century AD; a section on Islamic art from the 7th century to the present; a library and a collection of art prints from the late 15th century to the present; a collection of glass and ceramics covering the same period; one of metals, furniture and woodwork; the Wiener Werkstätte and its legacies in the 20th century; textiles and carpets from late Antiquity to the present.

The Schloss Belvedere, which was commissioned by Eugene, Prince of Savoy, and built between 1714 and 1723, houses the Österreichische Galerie, established in the lower castle in 1903. The whole of the Belvedere became a museum in 1918 and since then has housed the Galerie des XIX. und XX. Jahrhunderts. The Österreichisches Barockmuseum was transferred to the Lower Belvedere in 1923, and in 1953 the Museum Mittelalterlicher Kunst was likewise installed in the Orangerie there. The collections embrace all periods of Austrian fine art from the late 12th century to the present day. The Museum Moderner Kunst was founded in 1962. Housed in the pavilion built for the Exposition Universelle et Internationale held in Brussels in 1958, and from 1979 in the Palais Liechtenstein, it aims to exhibit international art from 1900 to the present.

2. Provincial state museums. In the 19th century the middle classes and the nobility, inspired by the ideas of the Enlightenment, set out to found museums in the constituent states of the Kingdom of Austria, with the aim of recording and displaying the culture and history of each region. The first such museum was the Steiermärkische Landesmuseum Joanneum, founded in 1811 by Archduke John in the Styrian capital of Graz. This was followed in

1823 by the Tiroler Landesmuseum Ferdinandeum, Innsbruck. The Oberösterreichisches Landesmuseum in Linz was formed by the Verein des Vaterländischen Museums für Österreich ob der Enns in 1833; this was followed by the establishment of similar museums in Klagenfurt (Carinthia; 1844), Bregenz (Vorarlberg; 1857) and Vienna (also one of the federal states of Austria; 1877). Further provincial museums were established in Lower Austria (1902) and in Eisenstadt (Burgenland; 1926). All of these museums control a large number of smaller institutions with special collecting and research functions. As well as its collection of works of Styrian origin dating from the Romanesque to the late Baroque period, the Steiermärkische Landesmuseum Joanneum, for example, also has a collection of Baroque works from the whole region comprising modern Austria and southern Germany, as well as works of Dutch and Italian origin dating from the 16th to 18th centuries. In Klagenfurt, the Landesmuseum für Kärnten also has a remarkable collection of Late Gothic items and works from the Italian Renaissance. The Tiroler Landesmuseum Ferdinandeum has a major collection of Gothic sculpture, works by artists from the Danube school (*c.* 1500) and 16th- and 17th-century Dutch paintings.

BIBLIOGRAPHY

J. D. Köhler: *Anweisung für reisende Gelehrte, Bibliotheken, Münzkabinette, Antiquitätenzimmer, Bildersäle, Naturalien- und Kunstkammern* (Frankfurt am Main and Leipzig, 1762)

G. Klemm: *Zur Geschichte der Sammlungen für Wissenschaft und Kunst in Deutschland* (Zerbst, 1838)

J. Schlosser: *Die Kunst- und Wunderkammern der Spätrenaissance* (Leipzig, 1908; Brunswick, 2/1978)

R. Berliner: 'Zur älteren Geschichte der allgemeinen Museumslehre in Deutschland', *Münchn. Jb. Bild. Kst*, n. s. 1, i/5 (1928), pp. 327–52

A. Lhotsky: 'Festschrift des Kunsthistorischen Museums in Wien, 1891–1941', *Gesch. Samml.*, 2 (1941–5)

100 Jahre: Österreichisches Museum für Angewandte Kunst (exh. cat., Vienna, Österreich. Mus. Angewandte Kst, 1964)

C. Zoege von Manteuffel: 'Die Museumsbauten Gottfried Sempers: Altona, Dresden, Wien', *Museumskunde*, 30 (1967)

W. Koschatzky and A. Strobl: *Die Albertina in Wien* (Salzburg, 1969)

G. Hamann: *Die Geschichte der Wiener naturhistorischen Sammlungen bis zum Ende der Monarchie* (Vienna, 1976)

B. Deneke and R. Kahsnitz: 'Die kunst- und kulturgeschichtlichen Museen im 19. Jahrhundert: Vorträge des Symposiums im Germanischen Nationalmuseum Nürnberg', *Stud. Kst 19. Jhts*, 39 (1977)

J. G. Kugler: 'Die Geschichte der habsburgischen Kunstsammlungen', *Das Kunsthistorische Museum in Wien* (Salzburg, 1978)

E. Scheicher: *Die Kunst- und Wunderkammern der Habsburger* (Vienna, 1979)

M. Dawid and E. Egg: *Der österreichische Museumsführer* (Innsbruck and Frankfurt am Main, 1985, 2/1986)

G. Klupacek: 'Zur Museumspolitik zwischen 1945–1965', *Mitt. Österreich. Gal.*, 75 (1987)

ALFRED AUER

XV. Art education.

1. INTRODUCTION. The oldest higher institute of art in Austria, and in all central Europe, is the Kaiserliche Akademie, Vienna, founded in 1692 by Peter Strudel (*see* STRUDEL, (2)). It closed in 1714 but was revived in 1725 as the Akademie der Maler, Bildhauer und Baukünstler. In 1772 it joined with the Graveurakademie and the Kupferstichakademie to become the Akademie der Bildenden Künste, which since 1872 has had the status of a university. In the 19th century, important artists who taught there included the painter Ferdinand Georg Waldmüller and the architect Otto Wagner. 20th-century teachers included the sculptors Anton Hanak and Fritz Wotruba, the architects Clemens Holzmeister, Roland Rainer and Gustav Peichl, and the painters Herbert Boeckl, Rudolf Hausner, Friedensreich Hundertwasser and Arnulf Rainer. The Akademie holds master classes in painting, sculpture, stage design, medal-engraving and small-scale sculpture, graphic art, life study, architecture, restoration and conservation. One unique feature of the Akademie is its painting gallery, founded for teaching purposes and containing works by Bosch, Rembrandt, Rubens, Titian, Murillo and Guardi, and the Kupferstichkabinett with works by such artists as Dürer and Rembrandt.

In 1862 the Austrian government sent the art historian and university professor Rudolf Eitelberger von Edelberg (1817–85) on a study visit to the International Exhibition in London. At the Victoria and Albert Museum he was introduced to the English model of having an art school as part of a museum. In 1864, at his instigation, the Österreichisches Museum für Kunst und Industrie was founded in Vienna, with the aim of helping to cultivate taste through the provision of examples. Since 1970 the Museum's school of arts and crafts has been known as the Hochschule für Angewandte Kunst, a state institution equivalent in status to the universities. Its aims include the practical development of the arts (including architecture and design), the training of art teachers and academic research.

In 1947, the Künstlerische Volkshochschule was established within the Akademie der Bildenden Künste in Vienna. Its founder was Professor Gerda Matejka-Felden (1901–84), who for many years continued to run it. The Wiener Kunstschule (founded 1959), an adult education institution, offers a wide range of courses and awards a final diploma. Outside Vienna, other significant institutions include the Internationale Sommerakademie für Bildende Kunst at Salzburg, established in 1953 by Oskar Kokoschka, who ran the academy until 1963 and who taught a course entitled 'Die Schule des Sehens'. Internationally renowned artists continue to teach at its premises in Schloss Hohensalzburg. The 'Mozarteum' in Salzburg was founded in 1841, and from 1970 has been a university for music and the performing arts. Since 1975 it has also run courses in art education and product and textile design. In Linz, the Hochschule für Künstlerische und Industrielle Gestaltung, founded in 1973, offers training in painting and graphic arts, sculpture, industrial design, interior design, architecture, ceramics and textiles. Like the 'Mozarteum', it has tertiary level courses in art education and product and textile design at a higher level.

2. THEORETICAL DEVELOPMENTS. Drawing has always been an important part of the curriculum of art education in Austria. The first efforts to introduce the subject into schools began in 1772 under Maria-Theresa. In 1783, under Joseph II (*reg* 1765–90), drawing instruction became entirely functional, playing an important part in the qualification for craftsmen and industrial workers. The drawing of ornamentation and geometric figures and the sketching of plans and elevations were considered more useful than copying heads, animals or landscapes. By the 1850s, drawing was compulsory in secondary schools,

where it was intended to prepare pupils for technical universities. In the 1880s JOSEF STRZYGOWSKI introduced to higher education a method of learning to draw by studying other works of art; this concept was developed and adapted for schools by Strzygowski's pupil Luise Potpeschnigg. Research into child psychology gained ground after World War I and brought about a switch to child-centred methods of teaching, as exemplified in *Naturgemässer Zeichen- und Kunstunterricht* (Vienna, 1912–16) by Alois Kunzfeld (1858–1929) and Oskar Rainer (1880–1941). Rainer's idea of 'musical graphics' (drawing and painting to music) became internationally known and the art educationist Richard Rothe's (1885–1955) writings on drawing for the Austrian education ministry were of considerable influence. Another important figure was FRANZ CIŽEK, who arranged art classes for young people at the School of Arts and Crafts of the Österreichisches Museum für Kunst und Industrie (now the Hochschule für Angewandte Kunst; *see* §1 above).

After World War II Austrian art education tended to be orientated more towards the fine arts. One of the advocates of this new approach was Ludwig Praehauser (1877–1961), who advanced the principle of holistic education through a combination of physical movement and visual, musical and linguistic expression. Another was Wilhelm Pierzl (1911–81), who wished to counteract the 'self-alienation of people in our time' by a holistic experience of art. The journal *Bund Österreichischer Kunsterzieher*, founded in 1956, became the mouthpiece of Praehauser's and Pierzl's ideas. In the 1960s, ideas taken from the fine arts and from theories of developmental psychology, as well as the influence of the Bauhaus, provided the theoretical basis for developments in art education. By the 1970s Austrian art educators were responding to new approaches to the teaching of art taking place in West Germany: for example the theories propounded by Reinhard Pfennig (*b* 1914). Precepts for teaching purposes were elicited from the analysis of form called *bildernischer Denken* ('pictorial thinking'), originated by Paul Klee at the Bauhaus.

However, the scientific basis on which this type of art education was founded and its neglect of related social, political and ideological questions gave rise to student protest movements, which occurred somewhat later in Austria than in other Western countries. The protests did not lead to a transformation of the system, but they did succeed in enabling art education to be seen for the first time as a possible means of a larger emancipatory educational process. The conventional study of art and form was seen as too narrow and remote to serve as the sole focus of art education. The study of such new cultural forms as photography, film, video, posters, comics, advertising, kitsch, fashion and the aesthetics of everday objects seemed more relevant to the needs and experiences of most people.

BIBLIOGRAPHY

A. Prix: *Grundzüge der Geschichte des Zeichenunterrichtes* (Vienna, 1889)
A. Kunzfeld and O. Rainer: *Naturgemässer Zeichen- und Kunstunterricht*, 6 vols (Vienna, 1912–15)
A. Kunzfeld: *50 Jahre Zeichnenunterricht und Kunsterziehung* (Vienna, 1922)
O. Rainer: *Musikalische Graphik* (Vienna, 1924)
L. Praehauser: *Erfassen und Gestalten: Die Kunsterziehung als Pflege formender Kräfte* (Salzburg, 1950)
R. Rothe: *Kindertümliches Zeichnen—gesetzhafte Formen* (Vienna, 1952)
W. Pierzl: *Kunstbetrachtung als wesentliches Mittel der Menschenbildung* (Leoben, 1957)
H. Stumbauer: *Grundlagen der bildnerischen Erziehung* (Linz, 1967)
R. Pierzl: *Österreichische Kunsterziehung im 20. Jh.* (diss., U. Vienna, 1973)
G. Königstein, A. Malina and O. Seber: *Perspektiven 1–2* (Vienna, 1978) [1st/2nd years in primary school]
H. Sündermann and B. Ernst: *Klang-Farbe-Gebärde: Musikalische Graphik* (Vienna, 1981)
O. Seber: 'Franz Cižek: Wegbereiter österreichischer Kunstpädagogik', *Bildner. Erz./Werkerziehung/Textiles Gestalt.*, 1 (1986), pp. 9–15
R. Felzmann, O. Seber and W. Stach: *Bilder machen: Anregungen für Bildnerische Erziehung* (Vienna, 1987)
O. Seber: 'Vom Stigmenzeichnen zur bildnerischen Erziehung', *Orientierung und Aufbruch: Festschrift PÄDAK* (Vienna, 1991), pp. 90–109

OSKAR SEBER

XVI. Art libraries and photographic collections.

Many of the most important art libraries in Austria are housed within museums (*see* §XIV above). The library of the Kunsthistorisches Museum, for example, has a collection of 150,000 volumes. In its acquisitions it concentrates on publications on art history and cultural history, and on museums that share its special interests. For its Egyptian and oriental collection standard works are sought that deal with Egyptian archaeology and philology. The library of the Österreichisches Museum für Angewandte Kunst aims to promote a synthesis of science, technology, industry and art, and it has a collection covering art history, prints and crafts; there are 110,000 volumes, 25,000 hand drawings, 70,000 prints, 34 icons and 2500 photographic slides. The Museum des 20. Jahrhunderts, founded in 1962, has a library that was originally formed from the collection in the Ministry of Information. The library soon began to acquire items in the areas of architecture, painting and sculpture, mainly of the 20th century. It also houses the library of the Museum Moderner Kunst since the latter's move in 1979 to the Palais Liechtenstein. The library of the Österreichische Galerie in Schloss Belvedere has a collection of photographs of Austrian art from the Middle Ages to the present day, a collection of artists' biographies relating to art *c.* 1900, and publications on Austrian art. Libraries on art history are also attached to the provincial state museums.

Other notable libraries are within larger cultural institutions. The library in the Bundesdenkmalamt, Vienna, has publications on the care of monuments, restoration, Austrian art history and medieval glass and wall painting. It houses a central card index of art in Austria and has a collection of 4000 old views of Austria. There are 26,000 volumes in the collection, and the institution is also a collaborator in the International Council of Monuments and Sites in Paris. The Österreichische Nationalbibliothek has many special collections, one being the manuscript and incunabula collection, which possesses a large academic reference library on the arts of the book. The portrait collection and picture archive have *c.* 1.6 million objects of different types from prints to photographs. One outstanding collection is that of the Swiss physiognomist Johann Kaspar Lavater, bought in 1828. The books and periodicals acquired by the Nationalbibliothek that deal with graphic art, art history, crafts, painting, sculpture and topography are housed in the Graphische Sammlung

Albertina. Of particular importance in this collection are the monographs on individual artists, exhibition catalogues and auction catalogues. At the Stadt- und Landesbibliothek in Vienna documents are kept relating to art exhibitions in Vienna and exhibitions by Viennese artists in Austria and abroad.

A third significant group of art libraries consists of those housed in educational institutions. A good example is the library of the Hochschule für Künstlerische und Industrielle Gestaltung in Linz, which was installed as a college library in 1974 with the collection of the former Kunstschule in Linz. It has 15,848 volumes, covering art history, architecture, painting, sculpture, graphic art, and artistic and vocational education. The library of the Akademie der Bildenden Künste in Vienna is the oldest art and architecture library in Austria and has a collection of 80,000 volumes including valuable items from the 18th and 19th centuries. The Kupferstichkabinett affiliated to the library concentrates on the art and architecture of the 19th and 20th centuries, art history, art education, artistic methods and restoration. Since 1960 the central catalogue for art and architecture in all Austrian art libraries has been kept here. The library of the Hochschule für Angewandte Kunst was constructed in 1900 after the school separated from the Österreiches Museum für Angewandte Kunst. The collection specializes in the work of the Wiener Werkstätte. Corresponding to the subjects taught in the school, the library covers architecture, painting, sculpture, ceramics, film, photography, graphic art, theatre, fashion, costume design and restoration. The library of the Graphische Lehr- und Versuchsanstalt in Vienna was founded in 1888, at the same time as the institute itself. It has more than 30,000 volumes, including early photographic literature and more recent literature on reproduction methods, commercial art and advertising as well as original prints. It also houses another collection not open to the public, which has several thousand international photographs, 6000 original prints and 2500 posters. The library of the Institut für Kunstgeschichte at the Universität in Vienna includes literature on all areas of art history, including methodology and theory.

BIBLIOGRAPHY

H. Aurenhammer: *Die Österreichische Galerie im Belvedere in Wien* (Vienna, 1967)

W. Koschatzky and A. Strobl: *Die Albertina in Wien* (Salzburg, 1969)

Akademie der Bildenden Künste in Wien, 1872–1972 (Vienna, 1972)

Die Österreichische Galerie Wien: Schloss Belvedere: Ein Führer vom Mittelalter bis zur Gegenwart (Munich and Vienna, 1976)

Festschrift zur 90. Jahr-Feier der Höheren Graphischen Bundes-Lehr- und Versuchsanstalt: Wien, 1978

O. Mazal: 'Schatzkammer der Buchkunst, Pflegestätte der Wissenschaft', *Die Handschriften- und Inkunabelsammlung der Österreichischen Nationalbibliothek* (Graz, 1980)

Das Österreichische Museum für Angewandte Kunst, Kunsthistorisches Museum, Museum des 20. Jahrhunderts (Vienna, 1983)

SIEGLINDE FRAUNLOB

XVII. Historiography.

The historiography of art in Austria dates back at least to 1721, when Johann Bernhard Fischer von Erlach published his *Entwurf einer historischen Architektur*. The most important contribution to the subject, however, is probably that of the Viennese school, which sought to establish a method for the objective study of the fine arts through a synthesis of inter-disciplinary approaches. Although the school was highly informal and only identified by Julius von Schlosser as late as 1934, its origins can be traced back to the work of Moritz Thausing (1838–84) and Rudolf Eitelberger von Edelberg (1817–85). The two most notable pupils of Thausing and Eitelberger were FRANZ WICKHOFF, who was also strongly influenced by the quasi-scientific method of the Italian art historian Giovanni Morelli, and ALOIS RIEGL, whose special areas of interest included late Roman art and group portraiture in the Netherlands.

Both Wickhoff and Riegl were professors at the university in Vienna, and on their retirement both were succeeded by figures of similar importance, establishing two distinct lineages. Wickhoff's successor, appointed in 1909, was JOSEF STRZYGOWSKI, who was interested in the art of the Eastern Orthodox Church and wrote essays on the history of art in Armenia, Ravenna and the Middle East, as well as on aspects of northern European art. Strzygowski's work encouraged Wladimir Sas-Zaloziecky (1896–1959) in Graz and OTTO DEMUS in Vienna to study the history of Byzantine art. In the field of East Asian art it also helped inspire such scholars as DAGOBERT FREY in Wrocław and Heinrich Gerhard Franz (*b* 1916) in Graz. Frey's philosophical approach stands out; in his writings on style and African and Eurasian cultures the influence of Konrad Lange (1855–1921) is also evident. Riegl's successor, Max Dvořák, stressed the continuity of historical epochs. He had particular theories on the care of monuments, and his history of art derives from the broader intellectual history of a given period. JULIUS VON SCHLOSSER succeeded Dvořák in 1922, and with his emphasis on the autonomous character of the discipline of art history remained as counterpart to Strzygowski. HANS SEDLMAYR, who was taught by Dvořák and Schlosser, was the first to use the idea of *Kunstwollen*, perceived as the metaphysical driving force behind the laws of style. He also produced some important studies on architectural history and urban planning. Other important members of the school included Hermann Egger (1873–1949) and Christian Huelsen, while the research of Wilhelm Suida (1877–1959) on Titian and Dürer (1901) as well as his posthumously published *Kunst und Geschichte* (Cologne, 1960) were of fundamental significance. Otto Pächt (1902–88) continued the sceptical, reflective attitude of the Viennese school, applying it in particular to the study of iconography. He also, however, advocated a tendency to be less reliant on documentary sources and to place a much greater emphasis on stylistic criticism and structural analysis. Pächt's colleagues and followers accordingly came to be known as the New Viennese school.

Another important figure in redefining the aims and methods of the Viennese school was Karl Maria Swoboda (1889–1967), who in his teaching at the university in Vienna (1946–60) and in his 9-volume *Geschichte der Bildenden Kunst* (1976–84) aimed to achieve a synthesis of the various doctrines of the Viennese school, using a highly systematic approach exemplified in his early thesis on Roman and Romanesque palaces (1923). Swoboda's contemporaries included Bruno Grimschitz (1892–1964), who specialized in Baroque monastic and aristocratic architecture, and Wilhelm Mrazek (1913–89), who published the first fundamental appreciation of the iconology of Baroque ceiling painting (1953). Ludwig von Baldass (1887–1963) collaborated with Günther Heinz (1927–92) on studies of Giorgione (1964) and Hieronymus Bosch (1968), while Fritz Novotny (1903–83) was principally interested in modern art, and particularly the work of Van Gogh and Cézanne, which he discussed in *Über das 'Elementare' in der Kunstgeschichte* (Vienna, 1945).

The ideas of the Viennese school and the New Viennese school spread to art history departments in other Austrian universities, mainly through art historians who had trained in Vienna. Wladimir Sas-Zaloziecky, for example, taught in Graz from 1892, and Hans Semper (1845–1920) taught from 1879 in Innsbruck, where he was succeeded by Moritz Dreger (1868–1939), another former student of Franz Wickhoff and Alois Riegl. Dreger too, as a member of the Istituto Austriaco di Studi Storici in Rome, was influenced by the science of history. He remained in Innsbruck until 1926, when he transferred to the Institut für Kunstgeschichte of the Technische Hochschule in Vienna. Under Otto von Lutterotti (1909–91), however, whose teachers had included Schlosser and Strzygowski, developments of the New Viennese school were also influential in Innsbruck. Hans Sedlmayr was a professor in Munich (1951–64) before founding the Institute of Art History at Salzburg University, where he served as president from 1964 to 1969. Hermann Bauer (*b* 1929), Wilhelm Messerer (1920–89) and Friedrich Piel (*b* 1931), who had studied with Sedlmayr in Munich, followed him to Salzburg.

The influence and reputation of the Viennese school were disseminated more widely, however, through the emigration of young art historians fleeing from the Nazi regime, despite the justified criticism of Meyer Schapiro in the *Art Bulletin* (1936). These included Otto Kurz (1908–75), Otto Pächt (*b* 1902), Otto Demus, Ernst Kris and Ernst Gombrich. As director of the Warburg Institute in London, Gombrich was able to introduce iconology as a resource in art history, while in the USA Kris devoted himself to psychoanalysis. The work of leading art historians in Princeton, New York and London testifies to the enduring influence of the Viennese school.

The Austrian contribution to the historiography of art is not confined, however, to the work of the Viennese school and their successors. In 1969 Renate Wagner-Rieger (1921–80) published *Das Kunstwerk im Bild* (Vienna, 1969), the first of 16 volumes on the art of the period of the Ringstrasse development. In this series she drew on a long tradition of architectural writings, including those of Hans Semper, Adolf Loos, Otto Wagner and Camillo Sitte. Another notable work of architectural history is the *Bildwörterbuch der Architektur* (1968) by Hans Koepf (*b* 1916), a compendium of plans for Gothic buildings from collections in Vienna and Ulm that illuminates the working practices of Masonic lodges during the Gothic period.

BIBLIOGRAPHY

D. Frey: 'Max Dvořáks Stellung in der Kunstgeschichte', *Wien. Jb. Kstgesch.*, I (xv) (1923), pp. 1–21

A. Karasek-Langer: *Verzeichnis der Schriften von Josef Strzygowski* (Klagenfurt, 1933)

J. von Schlosser: 'Die Wiener Schule der Kunstgeschichte', *Mitt. Österreich. Inst. Geschforsch.*, xiii/2 (1934), pp. 145–226

M. Schapiro: 'The New Viennese School', *A. Bull.*, xviii (1936), pp. 258–66

H. Sedlmayr: 'Die Quintessenz der Lehren Riegls', *Kunst und Wahrheit* (Hamburg, 1958)

J. Bakos: 'The Vienna School's Views of the Structure of the Art Historical Process', *Akten des XXV. internationalen Kongress für Kunstgeschichte: Vienna, 1983*, i, pp. 117–22

J. Białostocki: 'Museum Work and History in the Development of the Vienna School', *Akten des XXV. internationalen Kongress für Kunstgeschichte: Vienna, 1983*, i, pp. 9–15

J. Hart: 'Some Reflections on Wölfflin and the Vienna School', *Akten des XXV. internationalen Kongress für Kunstgeschichte: Vienna, 1983*, i, pp. 53–64

Die ungarische Kunstgeschichte und die Wiener Schule, 1846–1930 (exh. cat., ed. E. Marosi; Vienna, Coll. Hung.; pubd Budapest, 1983)

W. Höflechner and G. Pochat, eds: '100 Jahre Kunstgeschichte an der Universität Graz, Kunstgeschichte an österreichischen Universitäten bis 1938' (1992), xxvi of *Publikationen aus dem Archiv der Universität Graz* (Graz, 1973–)

G. Kauffmann: *Die Entstehung der Kunstgeschichte im 19. Jahrhundert* (Opladen, 1993)

GREGOR M. LECHNER

Authenticity. Value is often placed on an aesthetic object being 'genuine', 'authentic' and so on, but nothing is 'authentic' *per se.* If we are asked whether what is before us is authentic, our response could justifiably be: 'Authentic *what*?' It might be an authentic oil painting, an authentic Italian painting, an authentic Renaissance painting, yet not an authentic Leonardo da Vinci painting, not the authentic *Mona Lisa.* Authenticity is always authenticity under one or another description. The question 'Is it authentic?' must be replaced by, or understood as, a question of the form 'Is it an (or the) authentic so-and-so?'

When the question at hand is thus clarified, the term 'authentic' tends to become superfluous. An authentic Leonardo painting is just a Leonardo painting, the authentic *Mona Lisa* is just the *Mona Lisa*, and a non-authentic Leonardo is just not a Leonardo. Everything is authentically what it is and not authentically what it is not. The terms 'authentic Leonardo' and 'not authentic Leonardo' dichotomize not the class of Leonardo paintings but some class of supposed or claimed, or hoped-to-be, Leonardo paintings.

This discussion is confined to painting and other autographic, one-stage, singular arts. Problems of identity and authenticity of works are somewhat different in the case of such arts as printmaking (autographic, two-stage, multiple), music (allographic, two-stage, multiple) and literature (allographic, one-stage, multiple) (see Goodman, pp. 99–123).

Questions of authenticity—of when, where and by whom a picture was painted—are in some cases settled by a complete and dependable record of the work since it left the artist's hands (*see* PROVENANCE). When no such record is available, the primary means of seeking to determine whether a picture was painted during a given period or in a given region or by a given artist is expert visual comparison with works already accepted and works already rejected as of the same period or region or by the same artist (*see* CONNOISSEURSHIP). The expert eye is, however, fallible, subject to countless perturbations and constantly in a process of learning—of becoming more perceptive and acute through training and study. Furthermore, the corpus of works taken as standards for comparison may itself be revised over time. The drastic changes proposed by the Rembrandt Research Project in the late 20th century to the list of works accepted as Rembrandt's could affect the judgement of every new case. Seeking answers to questions of authenticity, like seeking answers to most important questions, is a difficult process often yielding only tentative results.

In the critical comparisons of paintings, the naked eye may be aided or supplemented by a variety of devices and tests (*see* TECHNICAL EXAMINATION). Vision may be enhanced by optical instruments ranging from ordinary spectacles to magnifying lenses to powerful microscopes, each magnification sometimes revealing important features not perceptible by means of others. Some aspects may first become evident under light of different colours and intensities, polarized light or strong raking light from one angle or another. Radiography may disclose earlier painting beneath the surface, and infra-red light may reveal an artist's underlying pen drawing. Ultraviolet light can bring out recent retouching and restoration. Chemical analysis of paint sometimes proves that a picture was not painted before a given date: for example, the *St Catherine of Alexandria* in the Cleveland Museum of Art, Ohio, supposedly by the 16th century painter Matthias Grünewald, was found to contain materials not available until the 20th century. Thermoluminescent examination of a terracotta sculpture may fix its time of production within a few hundred years.

Nevertheless, the main responsibility usually lies with hard looking—attentive, inquisitive, sensitive, informed, practised, intelligent looking. Some of the most significant characteristics of a work are visible only by means of the skilled seeing gained through intensive and extensive experience in comparing works. Even simple, but subtle, differences in colours or shape may come to be discerned only after practice. Moreover, those complex features that may loosely be called stylistic have to be learnt or constructed before they can be seen. Intelligent seeing, like intelligent cognition of any sort, requires development and mastery of an intricate set of distinctions or concepts. Thus the expert eye—fallible and variable as it is—may perceive virtually indescribable stylistic qualities, and often in terms of these make discriminations far finer than those determined by scientific tests. When a laboratory examination of materials places a work within a century or two, a specialist's sharply tuned vision may sometimes place it within a decade or less.

The historical and commercial importance of authenticity, that is, of the right classification of works, is evident. Those that are copies (*see* COPY) or forgeries (*see* FORGERY) raise the question of aesthetic importance. Is a painting any better if chemical analysis shows that it was done, as claimed, in the 16th rather than the 20th century? If a copy can be told from the original only by means of a document, can there be any difference between the two as art? Doesn't aesthetic difference depend solely on what is seen in the pictures?

Discussion tends to be confused, since the notion of the aesthetic is hardly crystal clear. One thing is plain, however: authenticity is neither a necessary nor a sufficient condition for aesthetic merit. A copy of a Leonardo by Rembrandt is not an inferior work. A Michelangelo marble purporting to be Roman may equal in quality a great ancient work. And we have all seen many a painting such that almost any copy by a competent artist would be vastly superior to the original.

Yet although authenticity and aesthetic merit are thus independent of each other, aesthetics is more than a matter of merit. Works of different artists, schools, periods and styles are distinguished primarily not by degrees of excellence but by idiosyncratic characteristics of drawing, colour, design, modelling, brushwork, feeling-tones and so on. These features—frequently major factors in the determination of authenticity—are aesthetic if anything is. And their perception, discrimination, integration and interpretation are central functions of aesthetic understanding.

Can authenticity matter aesthetically, however, when determined only by such obviously non-aesthetic means as documents and the results of scientific tests? If a copy cannot be told from the original or a painting distinguished as of the 16th rather than the 20th century by visual examination, does authenticity make any aesthetic difference? It does, indeed, for authenticity, however determined, provides the classification of a picture as, for example, by or not by a given artist or as of or not of a given period. Such classification is the basis for comparison in making further judgements, and changes in it can even affect our vision. When the van Meegeren paintings were rejected as Vermeers on the confession of the forger (*see* MEEGEREN, HAN VAN), the class of accepted Vermeers taken as standards for comparison of a questioned painting became narrower, and the difference between Vermeers and van Meegerens, so long invisible to most experts, became evident even to the perceptive layman. So also the difference between the Cleveland forgery and genuine Grünewalds, indiscernible for some time to nearly all experts, became visible to most others once the laboratory proved that the Cleveland picture was not by Grünewald.

Even if we cannot see any difference between an original painting and a forgery or between an edible mushroom and a poisonous one, that difference matters in the bearing it has on our behaviour. We can either look harder for a difference or avoid paintings and mushrooms entirely.

BIBLIOGRAPHY

N. Goodman: *Languages of Art* (Indianapolis, 1968, 2/1976)
D. Dutton, ed.: *The Art of Forgery* (Berkeley, CA, 1983)

NELSON GOODMAN

Author portrait. The representation of an author in a volume of his or her writings, usually at the front of the book. Such portraits were made throughout the history of European manuscript illumination, from antiquity to the early Renaissance, and the custom continued, with decreasing artistic significance, into the era of printed books. Compositions similar to those of author portraits were also used to represent translators, especially St Jerome, and scribes. Except for certain works from later periods, manuscript illuminators were seldom aware of the actual appearance of the authors and the term 'portrait' is merely a convention.

There is evidence that author portraits were included in ancient literary rolls, although no examples have survived. The first extant portraits are in Late Antique codices, as in the 6th-century AD Byzantine copy of the writings of the physician Dioskurides (Vienna, Österreich. Nbib., MS. med. gr. 1), in which the author is shown in two paintings (see Weitzmann, 1977, p. 65). In Christian manuscripts there is a particularly large number of portraits of the Evangelists (*see* MANUSCRIPT, colour pl. I), since their images are regularly found before their respective Gospels in both Byzantine and Western Gospel books. Typically, the Evangelist is shown seated with pen, ink and writing desk, and in Western manuscripts he is accompanied by his symbol: the angel of Matthew, the lion of Mark (see fig.), the ox of Luke or the eagle of John. In many Byzantine Gospel books, however, the Evangelists are seen in isolated, standing poses, simply holding a bound book. Another frequently repeated type is that of David, supposed author of the psalms, placed at the front of Psalters or, in full Bibles, preceding the Book of Psalms. He is usually shown with a harp or other musical instrument and is sometimes accompanied by other musicians or dancers. In Bibles, each book of Old Testament prophecy can begin with a picture of the prophet in a historiated initial. Any Christian writer could be honoured with an author portrait, as, for example, the painting of St Augustine presiding over a group of disciples in a 12th-century English manuscript of his *City of God* (Florence, Bib. Medicea-Laurenziana, MS. Plut. XII.17), or the portrait of St Hildegard of Bingen in an early 13th-century German copy of her visionary writings (Lucca, Bib. Stat., MS. 1942). Occasionally an author is represented dictating to an amanuensis, as in certain Byzantine miniatures of the Evangelist John. In some instances the author is shown addressing a colleague or in disputation with an antagonist; there are several examples of this in a manuscript of St Ildefonsus's *De virginitate* (*c.* 1100; Parma, Bib. Palatina, MS. 1650), probably from Cluny. Alternatively, the author may be shown dedicating his book to a holy person; in many Carolingian and later manuscripts of Rabanus Maurus's book of Carmina figurata, *De laudibus sanctae crucis* (*see* CARMINA FIGURATA), the author is shown offering his book to Pope Gregory the Great or, in other images, being introduced by his teacher Alcuin into the presence of St Martin. The author can also serve as an intercessor himself, as in the elaborate frontispiece to an 11th-century Mosan manuscript of the *Homilies* of St Gregory of Naziansus (Brussels, Bib. Royale Albert 1er, MS. II. 2570), in which Gregory intercedes before Christ on behalf of the book's scribe.

Author portrait of St Mark, miniature from the Ebbo Gospels, before 835 (Epernay, Bibliothèque Municipale, MS. 1, fol. 60*v*)

In representations of Christian authors, a divine source of inspiration is frequently indicated, recalling the ancient concept of the author's muse. One of the earliest extant Christian author portraits, in the 6th-century Rossano Gospels (Rossano, Mus. Dioc.), shows St Mark accompanied by a female personification in a role clearly similar to that of a muse. In some portraits of the Evangelists the Evangelist's symbol is shown bringing the sacred word from on high (see fig.). A dove, symbol of the Holy Spirit, may be shown approaching the author's ear, as in many representations of David or of Pope Gregory the Great, and Old Testament prophets may be shown being spoken to by the Lord emerging from a cloud. All such images designate God as the primary author of the text and the writer as merely an inspired channel of transmission.

In the later medieval period there was an increase in the portraiture of secular authors. A remarkable example is a 14th-century collection of love poetry, the Manasse Codex (Heidelberg, Ubib., MS. Pal. germ. 848), probably made in Zurich, which has 137 full-page paintings of the troubadour-authors, each identified by a heraldic device. Various 14th- and 15th-century Italian manuscripts of the *Divine Comedy* open with a picture of Dante Alighieri writing. A late 14th-century Parisian manuscript of the poems of Guillaume Machaut (Paris, Bib. N., MS. fr. 1584) shows the author accompanied by such allegorical figures as Love and Pleasure. An early 15th-century English manuscript of Chaucer's *Troilus and Criseyde* (Cambridge, Corpus Christi Coll. Lib., MS. 61) contains a charming painting of the author reading his work to a large gathering of ladies and gentlemen. Late medieval portraits of earlier secular authors usually represent them as if they were of the artist's own time: for example, in a Flemish translation of Boethius's *De consolatione philosophiae*, produced at Ghent at the end of the 15th century (Paris, Bib. N., MS. néer. 1), the author is seen in discussion with Philosophy, Music and Rhetoric in a miniature in which costumes and furnishings have, like the text, been set forth in a contemporary Flemish idiom.

BIBLIOGRAPHY

LCI: 'Autorenbild'; *LM*: 'Bildnis II'; *RDK*: 'Autorenbild', 'Evangelisten, I–III'

A. M. Friend: 'The Portraits of Evangelists in Greek and Latin Manuscripts', *A. Stud.*, v (1927), pp. 115–47; vii (1929), pp. 3–29
J. Prochno: *Das Schreiber- und Dedikationbild in der deutschen Buchmalerei* (Leipzig, 1929)
K. Weitzmann: *Ancient Book Illustration* (Cambridge, MA, 1959), pp. 116–27
H. Stegner: *David Rex et Propheta* (Nuremberg, 1961)
K. Weitzmann: *Late Antique and Early Christian Book Illumination* (London, 1977)

DON DENNY

Autochrome. *See under* PHOTOGRAPHY, §I.

Auto-destructive art. Term applied to works of art in a variety of media, with the capacity to destroy themselves after a finite existence, ranging from a few moments to 20 years. This self-destruction may result from natural processes such as collisions, decomposition and dematerialization, or from mechanisms requiring collaboration between artists, scientists and engineers, and may be either random and unpredictable or strictly controlled. The term, which is also sometimes used more loosely to describe any works with the capacity to transform themselves, was first used by Gustav Metzger in a manifesto (November 1959). Metzger elaborated on what he saw as an inherently political art theory and practice in five manifestos, in public lectures and demonstrations and in his own innovative techniques, including 'painting' in acid on nylon (1960–62).

No formal, international movement grew out of Metzger's experiments, but various isolated and independent artists used destruction as a central element in their works in the early 1960s, including JEAN TINGUELY, whose *Homage to New York* burst into flames in March 1960. In 1961 KENNETH KEMBLE and the Arte Destructivo group organized the exhibition *Arte destructivo* in Buenos Aires, and in 1962 Rafael (Ralph) Montanez Ortiz (*b* 1934) wrote *Destruction Art*, a manifesto describing his destruction sculptures. These developments, and the performances of the Viennese AKTIONISMUS group *c.* 1962–70, often involving self-mutilation and ritual, were seen by some as manifestations of a common tendency. Recognizing this, Metzger organized the international Destruction in Art Symposium (DIAS) in London in 1966, in which artists, poets, musicians and psychologists met to create and discuss the social implications of Auto-destructive art.

WRITINGS

G. Metzger: *Auto-destructive Art* (London, 1959)
——: *Manifesto Auto-destructive Art* (London, 1960)
——: *Auto-destructive Art, Machine Art, Auto-creative Art* (London, 1961)
——: *Manifesto World* (London, 1962)
——: *On Random Activity in Material/Transforming Works of Art* (London, 1964)
——: *Auto-destructive Art* (London, 1965)

BIBLIOGRAPHY

Destruction to Art: Destroy to Create (exh. cat., intro. E. H. Varian; New York, Finch Coll. Mus. A., 1968)
K. Stiles: 'Synopsis of the Destruction in Art Symposium (DIAS)', *The Act* (1987), no. 1
——: *The Destruction in Art Symposium: The Radical Cultural Project of Event-structured Art* (diss., Berkeley, U. CA, 1987)
For further bibliography, *see* METZGER, GUSTAV.

KRISTINE STILES

Autograph etching [Fr. *autographie photographique*]. *See* CLICHÉ-VERRE.

Automata. Mechanical contrivances that once set in motion can continue to operate independently. Depending on the mechanism, the term is also sometimes used as a synonym for androids (machines that resemble human beings) and robots (devices designed to accomplish a task). Automata were often intended to be aesthetic as well as mechanical accomplishments, and they can be remarkable for the extent to which an inanimate object can convey convincingly the appearance of a living organism.

While the practice of inventing automata originated in antiquity, the only surviving mechanisms are from the 16th century or later. Knowledge of early examples is based on incidental accounts (some undoubtedly apocryphal) and several treatises, including the *Pneumatica* by Heron of Alexandria (1st century AD), *Shui shi tu jing* ('Book of hydraulic elegancies'), a 7th-century Chinese manual, and al-Jazari's *Kitāb fī ma'rifat al-ḥilal al-handasiyya* ('Book of knowledge of ingenious mechanical devices'), an Islamic manuscript of 1204 or 1206 (*see* ISLAMIC ART, §III, 4(v)(c)). Throughout antiquity, in Chinese, Greek, Indian and Islamic literature, there are accounts of mechanical snails, hissing snakes, flying doves, whistling birds that fluttered their wings, performing monkeys, squirting elephants and parrots that gave out articulate cries.

In the Middle Ages the Strasbourg Cock (Strasbourg, Mus. A. Déc; see fig.) was among the most famous automata; it was installed in 1352 as part of the astronomical clock of Strasbourg Cathedral (*see* STRASBOURG, §III,1) and was operative until 1789. With each chime the mechanical rooster marched out of the clock (accompanied by 12 other automata), flapped its wings, cocked its head and crowed three times. In the Renaissance artists were involved in the design of automata. Filippo Brunelleschi designed mechanical stage scenery, an imitation of Paradise (*c.* 1435–40; destr.), for S Felice, Florence. Leonardo da Vinci created a mechanical lion (*c.* 1509; sketches, Milan, Bib. Ambrosiana) that walked up to Louis XII and opened a compartment in its chest, unbosoming a model of the royal coat of arms, the fleur-de-lis.

The translation into French, German and Latin of the *Pneumatica* in the Renaissance influenced subsequent designs of gardens and grottoes. The gardens at PRATOLINO (1569), designed by Bernardo Buontalenti, included mechanical artifices based on the *Pneumatica.* In 1615 Salomon de Caus (*see* CAUS, DE, (1)) published *Les Raisons des forces mouvantes*, a collection of garden designs and plans for automata. At SCHLOSS HELLBRUNN there is a grotto with a mechanical theatre containing 113 automata. Around this time automata were fashionable as amusing table ornaments (*see* NEF; e.g. the 'Ship of Charles V'; Paris, Mus. Cluny).

The production of automata flourished in Europe in the 18th and 19th centuries, in large part because of the influence of René Descartes, who referred to living forms as 'organic machines', and who, in an effort to demonstrate his doctrine, constructed an android (*c.* 1640) called 'ma fille Francine', which performed somersaults on a tightrope and which was later thrown into the sea by a frightened ship-captain who believed it to be a satanic device. Among those influenced by Descartes was Jacques de Vaucanson (1709–82), who constructed three automata (all destr.) of

Crowing cock automaton, from Strasbourg Cathedral, 1352 (Strasbourg, Musée des Arts Décoratifs)

unprecedented complexity. In 1738 he invented a life-size flute player, which functioned by way of an air pump that enabled its lips to blow into the flute and its fingers to move, precisely closing and opening stops to create a repertory of 12 melodies.

The following year Vaucanson constructed a drummer (which also played a shepherd's pipe) and an amazingly intricate duck (each wing contained 400 moving parts), which imitated all the sounds and movements of an actual duck, including preening and flapping its wings, quacking, picking up grain, swallowing, digesting its food and defecating. He was later appointed to the post of Inspector of Silk Manufactures, in which capacity he made important contributions to the automation of the textile industry, including the invention of an automated loom (1745) which wove in accordance with patterns contained on perforated cards, and which was later restored and improved by Joseph-Marie Jacquard. Later, this system of punched cards was deliberately employed by Charles Babbage (1792–1871) in an 'analytical engine' (*c.* 1833–71), the first digital computer.

There are two automata from the late 18th century that are of particular relevance to the visual arts because they were attempts to make artistic androids. The first is a complex mechanical boy (Neuchâtel, Mus. A. & Hist.), which produces drawings while seated at a classroom desk. Invented in 1773 by Pierre Jaquet-Droz (1721–90), a Swiss watchmaker, his son Henri-Louis Jaquet-Droz (1752–91) and their collaborator Jean-Frédéric Leschot (1746–1824), the android's actions are controlled by 40 revolving discs. Also in 1773 a comparable draughtsman (Philadelphia, PA, Franklin Inst.) was produced by the Maillardet family: Henri Maillardet (*b* 1745); Jean-David Maillardet (*b* 1748); Julien-Auguste Maillardet (1779–1852); and Jacques-Rodolphe Maillardet. Initially a boy artist, through modification it was transformed into a girl which kneels at a desk as it writes in two languages (English and French) and makes tiny landscape drawings.

Some automata were not genuine mechanisms, but fraudulent imitations, of which the most noted example is a life-size Turkish chess player (destr.) which sat behind a wooden chest and challenged members of the audience (usually successfully) to chess matches. Devised by Baron Wolfgang von Kempelen (1734–1804) in 1769, the android is generally thought to have been operated by a human chess master, concealed inside the wooden chest.

In the 20th century the distinction between automata and art became less clear because of an increase in interest in KINETIC ART. Among its early practitioners were Naum Gabo, Marcel Duchamp and László Moholy-Nagy. Among some artists this interest in movement was partially stirred by the research in photography of ETIENNE-JULES MAREY and of EADWEARD MUYBRIDGE. In 1932 Duchamp coined the term MOBILE to describe the kinetic sculpture of Alexander Calder (*see* CALDER, (3)). Calder anticipated later developments in automatous art in that his gadgets were sometimes designed to malfunction or to accomplish preposterous tasks (e.g. his 'wife-tickling machine', see Trevelyan, 1957). These may have provided a precedent for the 'useless machines' of Bruno Munari and the auto-destructive contrivances (*see* AUTO-DESTRUCTIVE ART) of Jean Tinguely.

See also CLOCKS AND WATCHES; TOYS AND GAMES.

BIBLIOGRAPHY

J. Trevelyan: *Indigo Days* (London, 1957), p. 30
A. Chapuis and E. Droz: *Les Automates: Figures artificielles d'hommes et d'animaux. Histoire et technique* (Neuchâtel, 1949; Eng. trans., New York, 1958)
S. Giedion: *Mechanization Takes Command: A Contribution to Anonymous History* (New York, 1969)
A. W. J. G. Ord-Hume: *Clockwork Music* (New York, 1973)
F. Malina, ed.: *Kinetic Art: Theory and Practice* (New York, 1974)
M. Hillier: *Automata and Mechanical Toys* (London, 1976)
J. Reichardt: *Robots: Fact, Fiction and Prediction* (London, 1978)
Automata (exh. cat., Southampton, Hansard Gal., 1992)

ROY R. BEHRENS

Automatism. Term appropriated by the Surrealists from physiology and psychiatry and later applied to techniques of spontaneous writing, drawing and painting. In physiology, automatism denotes automatic actions and involuntary processes that are not under conscious control, such as breathing; the term also refers to the performance of an act without conscious thought, a reflex. Psychological automatism is the result of a dissociation between behaviour and consciousness. Familiarity and long usage allow actions to become automatic so that they are performed with a minimum of thought and deliberation. Pathological automatism, also the consequence of dissociative states, ensues from psychological conflict, drugs or trance states; automatism may also be manifested in sensory hallucinations.

During the late 19th century Pierre Janet, a French psychiatrist, treated mental disorders with hypnosis, as did other practitioners of dynamic psychiatry. In particular, he studied the automatic behaviour of mediums to determine the degree to which the subconscious interacts with the conscious during a trance. A medium, while in a self-induced trance, performs spontaneous physical acts with no conscious control. Psychiatry suggests that their apparent messages from a spirit world may actually be subliminal thoughts or feelings, released and given free expression.

While psychiatry considers automatism reflexive and constricting, the Surrealists believed it was a higher form of behaviour. For them, automatism could express the creative force of what they believed was the unconscious in art. Automatism was the cornerstone of Surrealism. André Breton defined Surrealism in his *Manifeste du surréalisme* (1924) as 'psychic automatism in its pure state'. This automatism was 'dictated by thought, in the absence of any control exercised by reason, exempt from any aesthetic or moral concern'. Breton's formulation of automatism borrowed ideas from the practices of mediums and from dynamic psychiatry, which emphasized the interplay among conscious and unconscious forces in directing behaviour. Although related to Freud's free association, the automatism of the Surrealists required only one person and was written rather than spoken. Automatic writing served as the Surrealists' first technique for tapping what they believed to be the unconscious; subsequently, hypnotic trances and dream narration provided other routes to the unknown.

Automatism in the visual arts can arise from manual techniques that involve chance in the creation of the work (*frottage*, *grattage*, decalcomania) or from psychological experiences (hallucination, intoxication, hypnotic trance, dream narration). André Masson's automatic drawings, such as *Furious Suns* (1925; New York, MOMA; see fig.), Joan Miró's paintings from the mid-1920s and Max Ernst's *frottages* are examples.

By the mid-1940s the American painters known as the Abstract Expressionists (in particular 'Action Painters'; *see* ACTION PAINTING) had adopted automatic methods in their work. Influenced by Surrealism, these artists introduced the appearance of automatism even when their pictures were deeply deliberated. They included Arshile Gorky, Jackson Pollock, Franz Kline and Willem de Kooning. Between 1946 and 1951 LES AUTOMATISTES, a group of Canadian Surrealist painters, painted in a technique based on automatic writing. In post-war Europe, the artists grouped under the label TACHISM produced paintings with swiftly registered, calligraphic signs and broad brushstrokes, which had the spontaneity associated with automatism.

BIBLIOGRAPHY

H. Ellenberger: *The Discovery of the Unconscious* (New York, 1970)

J. Gibson: 'Surrealism before Freud; Dynamic Psychiatry's "Simple Recording Instrument"', *A. J.* [New York], xlvi/1 (1987), pp. 56–60

For further bibliography *see* SURREALISM.

JENNIFER GIBSON

Automatic drawing by André Masson, *Furious Suns*, pen and ink, 422×317 mm, 1925 (New York, Museum of Modern Art)

Automatistes, Les. Canadian group of artists active during the 1940s and the early 1950s, led by PAUL-EMILE BORDUAS. They were named by Tancrède Marcil jr in a review of their second Montreal exhibition, published in February 1947 in *Le Quartier latin*, the student journal for the University of Montreal, Quebec. The earliest characteristic example of the group's work was Borduas's *Green Abstraction* (1941; Montreal, Mus. F.A.), a small oil painting intended as an equivalent to the automatic writing of the Surrealist poet André Breton; it was succeeded by a series of 45 gouaches exhibited by Borduas in the foyer of the Théâtre Ermitage in Montreal from 25 April to 2 May 1942 and by other works painted before he moved to New York in 1953 (*see* MONTREAL, fig. 2).

The group began to form around Borduas in the 1940s when students came to his studio to discuss Marxism, Surrealism and psychoanalysis, virtually forbidden subjects in Quebec at this time. Among these younger artists were Marcel Barbeau (*b* 1925), Jean-Paul Riopelle and Roger Fauteux, who studied under Borduas at the Ecole du Meuble, two students from the Ecole des Beaux-Arts, Pierre Gauvreau (*b* 1922) and Fernand Leduc, and Jean-Paul Mousseau (*b* 1927) from the Collège Notre-Dame. Although inspired by Surrealism and particularly by the concept of automatism, Les Automatistes extricated themselves from the illusionistic bias of the mainstream of that movement and applied its principles to an abstract idiom. Among the others associated with the group were Pierre Gauvreau's brother, the writer Claude Gauvreau (1925–71), the photographer and editor Maurice Perron, the ballet dancer Françoise Sullivan (*b* 1927), the future psychiatrist Bruno Cormier and the painter Marcelle Ferron (*b* 1924). The group exhibited in the studio of Franziska Boas in New York in January 1946 and twice in Montreal, in April 1946 and in February 1947, in improvised locations. In Paris Les Automatistes held an exhibition from June to July 1947 at the tiny Galerie du Luxembourg, where they were noticed by the French painter Georges Mathieu.

On 9 August 1948 Les Automatistes published their manifesto REFUS GLOBAL, which was regarded as anarchic and controversial, resulting in the ostracization of Borduas and the demoralization of the group. To help keep the group alive Claude Gauvreau organized two further exhibitions—*Les Etapes du vivant* in rue Ontario, Montreal, in May 1951 and *La Matière chante* at Galerie Antoine, Montreal, in April–May 1954—but by then two of the main exponents of Automatisme, Riopelle and Leduc, were living in Europe and other members of the group were keen to exhibit independently.

BIBLIOGRAPHY

G. Mathieu: *Au-delà du tachisme* (Paris, 1963)
Borduas et les Automatistes, 1942–1955 (exh. cat., ed. B. Teyssèdre; Paris, Grand Pal.; Montreal, Mus. A. Contemp., 1971)

FRANÇOIS-MARC GAGNON

Autun [Lat. Augustodunum]. City overlooking the Arroux valley below the Morvan granite massif in Saône-et-Loire, France. Its most important buildings are Roman and medieval. Two arcaded Roman gates, the Porte d'Arroux and Porte St André, were built soon after the city's foundation in the late 1st century BC (*see* §1 below). The large theatre illustrates the prosperity of the Roman city, which was famous as a scholastic centre. It became an episcopal see in the 3rd century. Medieval Autun was important for its pilgrimage cult of St Lazarus, to whom the 12th-century cathedral is dedicated (*see* §2 below); its flamboyant 15th-century exterior decoration was added by Cardinal Jean II Rolin. Relatively obscure since the Renaissance, Autun has retained its historic character with good examples of fortification towers (e.g. that of the Ursulines) and houses dating from the 12th to the 15th centuries, alongside later buildings such as Daniel Gittard's Ecole Militaire, built in the 17th century. The 15th-century Hôtel Rolin, the Cardinal's birthplace, now houses the municipal museum, the contents of which include Gallo-Roman exhibits, Gislebertus's masterly relief of the *Temptation of Eve*, the painting of the *Nativity with the Donor, Cardinal Rolin*, attributed to the Master of Moulins (*c.* 1480), and 19th-century paintings. The *Martyrdom of St Symphorien* (which took place in Autun in AD 179) by Ingres is in the cathedral. The Bibliothèque Municipale contains a rich collection of illuminated manuscripts (7th to 16th centuries).

1. Augustodunum. 2. Cathedral.

1. AUGUSTODUNUM. It was founded as a Roman city in the late 1st century BC, replacing Bibracte (20 km west) as the capital of the Gaulish tribe of the Aedui. Unusually at the time for a city that was not a Roman colony, it was walled. Two of its four original gates remain well preserved, the Porte d'Arroux to the north and Porte St André to the east (both Augustan, 27 BC–AD 14). Each has a pair of carriageways with narrower passageways for pedestrians at the sides. Above these barrel-vaulted passages was an open gallery with arched windows. Each gate had projecting semicircular towers at the sides: one remains by the Porte St André. The pedestrian passageways on its outer façade are in slightly projecting wings and, unlike those of the Porte d'Arroux, the lower storey has no decorated cornice. The gallery, restored in 1847, was a later Roman rebuilding in sandstone. That of the Porte d'Arroux, in finely cut limestone, has a cornice with acanthus and palmette decoration, and fluted pilasters with Corinthian capitals between the windows. This Augustan ornament seems to have influenced that of the 12th-century cathedral. The theatre, one of the largest in the empire (diam. 147.8 m), was still being constructed in Vespasian's reign (AD 69–79): the lower tiers of seats and supporting vaulting remain. Outside the city, two walls of the 'Temple of Janus' (2nd century AD) stand 24 m high. It was a temple of Romano-Celtic type, having a square central cella of *petit appareil* (a facing of courses of small squared blocks of stone) with three windows on each side and a surrounding ambulatory. Aerial photography in 1976 detected adjacent buildings of the rural sanctuary, including a theatre.

BIBLIOGRAPHY

H. de Fontenay: *Autun et ses monuments* (Autun, 1899)
A. Grenier: *Manuel d'archéologie gallo-romaine*, i (Paris, 1931), pp. 337–45; iii/2 (Paris, 1958), pp. 799–803
P. M. Duval and P. Quoniam: 'Relevés inédits des monuments antiques d'Autun', *Gallia*, xxi (1963), pp. 155–89

T. F. C. BLAGG

2. CATHEDRAL. The church of St Lazare was built from *c.* 1120 by Bishop Etienne de Bâgé (*reg* 1112–36) and the chapter of the existing cathedral, St Nazaire, on a nearby site donated by Hugh II, Duke of Burgundy (*reg* 1102–43). The motive for building a new church seems to have been the need to accommodate leprous pilgrims attracted by the cathedral's relics of St Lazarus, a saint often confused with poor Lazarus of the parable. The new church, as yet unfinished, was consecrated on 28 December 1130 by Pope Innocent II (*reg* 1130–43); the relics of the saint were translated there from St Nazaire only in 1146. St Lazare achieved cathedral status in 1195.

(i) Architecture. The church is 66.91 m long internally and comprises a seven-bay aisled nave (*see* FRANCE, fig. 3), projecting transepts and a two-bay aisled choir terminating in three apses. Lateral chapels, flying buttresses and other later accretions have altered its external appearance, but the interior is well preserved. The original dado and the two lower rows of windows, divided into seven bays by fluted pilasters, were left intact when the upper storey of the apse was reconstructed in the 15th century. A change of design, most apparent in decorative details, occurred between the two lit storeys: this involved differing fluted pilasters and the introduction of cusped jambs inspired by the third abbey church at Cluny (Cluny III); it also coincided with the arrival of Gislebertus (*see* §(ii) below). Work on the fabric progressed from east to west without interruption. The elevation has three storeys throughout, with a pointed arcade that is higher than the triforium and

clerestory combined. The main vessels have pointed barrel vaults (h. 23.38 m) with transverse arches carried to the ground by fluted pilasters. Such pilasters are similarly addorsed to the sides and backs of the cruciform piers, where they receive the main arcade arches and the transverse pointed arches of the groin-vaulted aisles; they also flank the triforium arches. Fluted pilasters had already been employed at Cluny Abbey and enjoyed a considerable vogue in 12th-century Burgundy: that this was inspired by Antique monuments surviving in the vicinity is attested by the Porte d'Arroux in Autun itself. The triforium consists of three arches per bay: in the choir and transept they are blind, but in the nave the central arch opens on to a passage over the aisle vaults. Each clerestory bay has a single round-headed window. The crossing is surmounted by a cupola on squinches; the crossing piers were restored by Eugène-Emmanuel Viollet-le-Duc in 1860. The crossing tower above the cupola was struck by lightning in 1469 and rebuilt by Cardinal Jean II Rolin. In 1178 the open west porch (three bays wide and two deep) was altered to encompass all three western entrances; at one time its aisles were blocked to form two small chapels, but these were removed in 1855.

(ii) Sculpture. The architectural sculpture is remarkably homogeneous in style and the inscription on the west portal tympanum, GISLEBERTUS HOC FECIT, is generally taken to reveal the name of its sculptor or at least the head of the sculptural workshop. The sculpture was probably carved following the progress of the building from east to west. The capitals of the main apse and the tympanum are carved from a whitish limestone quarried in the Tournus region, but most of the other capitals are of oolitic limestone, perhaps transported from the Charolais.

(a) Choir. The nook-shaft capitals of the side apses and the lower storey of the central apse, belonging to the first campaign (see §(i) above), are of the 'Brionnais' type found in numerous Burgundian churches of the late 11th century and the early 12th (e.g. Anzy-le-Duc Priory and Charlieu Abbey). At Autun these capitals frequently incorporate a Classical form of abacus. The baskets are generally carved with stiff, upright foliage, sometimes supporting an upper tier of addorsed or confronted beasts (*see* ROMANESQUE, §III, 1(ii)(f)). Two capitals are notable: one, carved with a nude figure of Anger piercing his body with a sword, is similar to a fragment from Cluny Abbey; another bears an owl. The eight pilaster capitals of the upper storey of the apse were badly damaged when the choir received a marble revetment in the 18th century, but one of them depicting a centrally enthroned figure, probably Christ, is recognizably in the style of GISLEBERTUS.

A number of choir capitals have been restored with stucco, including the *Four Rivers of Paradise*, the *Journey to Emmaus*, the *First Temptation of Christ* and *Luxuria.* Another capital depicting the Rivers of Paradise appears in this location at Cluny, but its form and composition are quite different. Others include 'Constantine', an equestrian figure found frequently in western France (e.g. Parthenay-le-Vieux, St Pierre) but rarely in Burgundy, and a three-headed bird. At Cluny, Perrecy-les-Forges Priory, Ste Madeleine and Vézelay similar birds confront a faun, but

1. Autun Cathedral, capital from the north east crossing pier depicting the *Dream of the Magi*, limestone, h. 730 mm, *c.* 1125–30 (Autun Cathedral, Salle Capitulaire)

at Autun the latter is carved on a separate capital, now opposing a siren. Viollet-le-Duc removed the crossing pier capitals in 1860, replacing some with copies. The originals in the chapter house include four carved with scenes from the *Infancy of Christ*, among them the *Dream of the Magi* (see fig. 1). The *Presentation of the Church* capital, on the south side of the crossing, may represent Hugh II presenting St Lazare, still lacking a nave, to Bishop Etienne de Bâgé in the presence of the patron saint.

(b) Nave. Most of the figured nave capitals are located on the main arcades and have biblical sources, but there is no unifying programme. There are twelve Old Testament scenes and nine from the New, as well as capitals depicting such subjects as *Virtues* and *Vices*, a cockfight, the *Fourth Tone of Music* and the *Ascent and Fall of Simon Magus.* Not all are attributed to Gislebertus: according to Grivot and Zarnecki the capitals showing *Christ Washing the Apostles' Feet* and *Samson and the Lion* were carved by an assistant, the Master of Moutiers-Saint-Jean. There are also some purely foliate capitals, both on the pilasters and on the nook shafts of the clerestory, that reflect the influence of Cluny III. A band of rosettes runs along the top of the main arcade.

(c) North transept portal. The north transept formerly contained the main entrance to the church, but it was remodelled in 1766, and only the foliate outer archivolt, figured capitals and decorative jambs were left in place. Early descriptions and surviving fragments give some idea of its original appearance. On the tympanum was the *Raising of Lazarus*, on the trumeau a small figure of *St Lazarus as Bishop of Marseille* and on the lintel *Adam and Eve.* The reclining figure of *Eve* (Autun, Mus. Rolin) is

one of the few large-scale nudes produced in the 12th century and displays sensitive modelling. Other fragments assigned to this portal include an angel (New York, Met.) and the *Assumption of the Virgin* (Autun, Mus. Rolin); the capitals still *in situ* depict *Dives and Lazarus*, the *Prodigal Son* and the *Widow of Nain*.

(d) West portal. The west doorway is dominated by the huge tympanum (4.62×6.53 m; see fig. 2), composed of 29 separate blocks and carved with the *Last Judgement*. In 1766 it was considered offensive and concealed with plaster. The projecting head of Christ, which was then broken off to achieve a level surface, was rediscovered and restored to its position in 1948. The figure of Christ, much larger than the others, is enthroned in a mandorla with a diapered border, as on the west portal of Cluny Abbey (destr.), and stretches his hands to right and left. The inscription around the mandorla, which is borne by four angels, reads: 'I alone dispose of all things and crown the just; those who follow crime I judge and punish'; above it are medallions containing the sun and moon. The scenes to either side are divided into two horizontal registers by narrow arcading: below to the right are a figure holding a book, perhaps St John, and the *Weighing of Souls* with cheating demons, and to the left are St Peter and eight Apostles, who turn towards Christ in adoration. Above to the right are two enthroned figures, possibly Enoch and Elijah, and a trumpeting angel, and to the left are the enthroned Virgin and a second trumpeting angel. The extremities of the tympanum are filled by scenes of Heaven and Hell, with two further trumpeting angels in the angles. Below, on the lintel, is the *Resurrection of the Dead*: the long procession of souls is separated by an angel wielding a sword. An inscription above contrasts the joy of the Blessed: 'Thus shall rise again everyone who does not lead an impious life, and endless light of day shall shine for him', with the despair of the Damned that reads: 'Let fear strike those whom earthly error binds, for their fate is shown by the horror of these figures.' One of the most powerful images is the figure whose head is grasped by two gigantic hands. This is perhaps the most expressive representation of the Last Judgement in 12th-century sculpture, surpassing in dramatic terms those on the tympana of Ste Foy, Conques and Beaulieu-sur-Dordogne Abbey.

2. Autun Cathedral, west portal, tympanum depicting the *Last Judgement*, limestone, 4.62×6.53 m, *c.* 1130–35

The outer archivolt of the doorway is carved with medallions containing the *Labours of the Months* and the *Signs of the Zodiac*, as at Ste Madeleine, Vézelay, while the middle arch comprises a deeply undercut foliate roll, similar to that on the doorway of Anzy-le-Duc Priory. The sculptures of the inner arch were destroyed in 1766, but there is evidence that they represented the Elders of the Apocalypse, like the inner archivolt of Anzy-le-Duc, and six Elders are carved on one of the supporting capitals. The trumeau capital sports two atlantids, and the two doorpost capitals, carved with Balaam and a figure perhaps representing an Ethiopian, have been replaced by copies; the remaining embrasure capitals represent the *Wolf and the Crane*, *Abraham Dismissing Hagar and Ishmael*, the *Presentation of the Virgin* and scenes from the lives of SS Eustace and Jerome. The trumeau, with St Lazarus and his sisters, was carved in 1863: no fragments of the original survive, but a document of 1482 justifies the choice of subject.

It has been estimated that Gislebertus, surely aided by assistants, completed his work at Autun within ten years (*c.* 1125–35); the west portal, the culmination of his achievement there, would therefore date from *c.* 1130–35. While there is evidence that he worked at Vézelay in the early 1120s, the relationship of the Autun sculpture to Cluny is enigmatic. The drapery carving at Cluny differs from Autun, but other details are closely related and there are stylistic parallels between heads from the west portal of Cluny (Cluny, Mus. Ochier; Paris, Louvre; and Providence, RI Sch. Des., Mus. A.) and those at Autun.

(e) Shrine of St Lazarus. The elaborate mausoleum of St Lazarus, which stood in the choir until its refurbishment in 1766, took the form of a miniature apsidal church, its west façade carrying a *Crucifixion*, rising above and behind the main altar. It was composed of coloured marbles and stone, enriched by polychrome inlay and incised plaques. Inside the 'church', which was entered through wooden doors, the enshrouded figure of Lazarus lay on a sarcophagus, its lid raised by four men; around him stood his sisters Mary and Martha, Christ and SS Peter and Andrew, carved in the round. Numerous pilaster and capital fragments survive, with the figures of *Mary*, *Martha* and *St Andrew* (each h. *c.* 1.25 m; Autun, Mus. Rolin) and the head of *St Peter* (Paris, Louvre). An inscription attributes this work to 'Martinus monachus', although evidently more than one artist was involved, and places it in the time of 'Stephanus magnus', a reference to either Bishop Etienne de Bâgé (*reg* 1112–36) or Bishop Etienne II (*reg* 1170–89); the stylistic affiliations, however, mostly with the Rhône Valley and St Lazare, Avallon, suggest a date in the mid-12th century. Martin and Gislebertus, both exceptionally skilful sculptors, were artistically quite independent, but their joint effort ensured Autun a prime place in the development of 12th-century sculpture.

BIBLIOGRAPHY

V. Terret: *La Sculpture bourguignonne aux XIIe et XIIIe siècles: Autun*, 2 vols (Autun, 1925)

D. Jalabert: 'L'Eve de la cathédrale d'Autun: Sa Place dans l'histoire de la sculpture romane', *Gaz. B.-A.*, xxx (1949), pp. 247–74

D. Grivot and G. Zarnecki: *Gislebertus, Sculptor of Autun* (London, 1961, rev. 1965)
P. Quarré: 'Les Sculptures du tombeau de Saint-Lazare à Autun et leur place dans l'art roman', *Cah. Civilis. Méd.*, v (1962), pp. 169–74
Le Tombeau de Saint-Lazare et la sculpture romane à Autun après Gislebertus (exh. cat., Autun, Mus. Rolin, 1985)

KATHRYN MORRISON

Auvera. *See* AUWERA.

Auvray, Louis (*b* Valenciennes, 7 April 1810; *d* Paris, ? 1890). French sculptor and writer. At an early age he showed a talent for drawing and enrolled at the Académie in Valenciennes under the sculptor Léonce de Fieuzal (1768–1844). In 1830 he received a scholarship from the city of Valenciennes to study in Paris at the Ecole des Beaux-Arts in the atelier of David d'Angers. In 1835 he first exhibited at the Salon and continued to show there regularly until 1884 without, however, receiving many awards. He mainly exhibited portrait busts of figures from various historical periods (e.g. *Antoine Watteau*, 1846; Paris, Louvre) and he received important official commissions for the decoration of public buildings in Paris. Portrait busts by him are found in the foyer of the Opéra (*Jean-François Le Sueur*, 1852), the Institution des Sourds-Muets (*Abbé Sicard*, 1852) and the vestibule of the library of the Institut de France (*Etienne de Condillac*, 1868). He executed the large statue of *Henry IV* on the Esplanade des Invalides, the figure of *Jean de la Vacquerie* (1863) for the façade of the Hôtel de Ville and of *Astronomy* for the Cour Napoléon of the Musée du Louvre. In 1868 he sculpted the monument to *Abbé de l'Epée* for the Cour d'Honneur of the Institution des Sourds-Muets. For his native city of Valenciennes he produced the large allegory in stone of *Commerce and Abundance* (1842), in the Place du Marché, as well as a stone *St Cecilia* for the church of St Nicolas and a marble *Christ* (1867) for the Cathedral. In 1869 he participated with Jean-Baptiste Carpeaux in the decoration of the façade of the new Hôtel de Ville in Valenciennes, sculpting five stone caryatids. In addition to being a sculptor, he was President of the Comité Central des Artistes, Vice-President of the Société Libre des Beaux-Arts and President of the Union Artistique, Scientifique et Littéraire Valenciennoise à Paris. He had an active career as an official art critic and wrote reviews of 18 annual Salons during the years 1834 to 1869. In 1860 he founded the *Revue littéraire et artistique*. His most important undertaking was to complete the *Dictionnaire général des artistes de l'école française* that had been begun by Emile Bellier de La Chavignerie.

WRITINGS

E. Bellier de La Chavignerie and L. Auvray: *Dictionnaire général des artistes de l'école française depuis l'origine des arts du dessin jusqu'à nos jours*, 2 vols (Paris, 1882–5), suppl. (Paris, 1887)
Regular contributions to *Rev. Litt. & A.* and *Rev. B.-A.* [Paris]

BIBLIOGRAPHY

Lami
Poinsignon: *Dictionnaire des sculpteurs valenciennois* (in preparation)

ANNIE SCOTTEZ-DE WAMBRECHIES

Auwera [Auvera]. German family of sculptors, of Flemish origin. Its two outstanding members, (1) Jakob von der Auwera and his eldest son, (2) Johann Wolfgang von der Auwera, carried out much sculptural work in the Franconian region. The latter's brilliantly complex Rococo church decorations had paramount influence in the development of that style in Würzburg. The second son, Lukas von der Auwera (1710–66), took over the family workshop after their deaths and ran it in partnership with Johann Peter Wagner (*see* WAGNER, (1)). The youngest son, Johann Michael Josef von der Auwera (1711–58), was also a sculptor, employed in the family workshop.

(1) Jakob von der Auwera (*b* Mechelen, 17 Feb 1672; *d* Würzburg, 1760). Around 1700 he arrived in Würzburg, where he entered the service of the Prince-Bishop, Johann Philipp von Greiffenklau, and became court sculptor. In 1706–8 he executed a fountain with a group of four river gods for the gardens of the Juliusspital. In 1715–19 he decorated the portal of the Jesuit college and in 1716–17 the façade of the Neumünster, both in Würzburg. The statues flanking the portal of St Peter, Würzburg, are also ascribed to him. Commissions from other parts of Franconia included the *Virgin* (*c.* 1720) over the high altar of the parish church of Hammelburg and the Trinity Column (1728) in the market-place of Lengfurt. In 1728–9 he produced the altar figures and the side altars for the parish church of St Mauritius, Wiesenheid. In 1749 he carved the choir-stalls for St Kilian Cathedral in Würzburg. In the same year he produced the huge fountain with a group of *Hercules Wrestling with Antaeus* in the garden of the former Cistercian monastery at Ebrach, a work showing the influence of Bernini.

(2) Johann Wolfgang von der Auwera (*b* Würzburg, 24 Oct 1708; *d* Würzburg, 27 March 1756). Son of (1) Jakob von der Auwera. He trained under his father and also with another court sculptor, Claude Curé (*d* 1745), before travelling to Vienna in 1730 to complete his artistic education at the Akademie. Returning to Würzburg in 1736, Johann Wolfgang took over his father's workshop. He worked for the Prince-Bishop, Friedrich Karl von Schönborn, producing a small-scale alabaster group of *Gladiators* (1736–8; Würzburg, Residenz), and in 1738 he was appointed court sculptor. In 1740 Auwera and the architect Balthasar Neumann spent some months together on a study tour through the Rhineland and the Netherlands. On his return, Johann Wolfgang married Curé's daughter, Maria Cordula Curé (*d* 1764). In 1743 he was granted citizenship of Würzburg.

Auwera's work for the churches in Würzburg included the high altar of the church of the Burgerspital zum Heiligen Geist (1742); the high altar of the parish church of St Caecilia (1744); and the high altar, designed by Neumann, of the Franciscan conventual church, now Heilige Maria zu den Engeln (1745). Between 1749 and 1752 he worked on the chancel of the Benedictine abbey church at Amorbach. At the same time he also executed façade decorations, including the Prince-Bishop's arms on the gable of the Residenz in Würzburg. Around 1750 he made garden statues for the park of Veitshöchheim Schloss for the Prince-Bishop (who by this time was Karl Philipp von Greiffenklau). Between 1751 and 1755 he produced an ornate high altar for the Carthusian monastery church (now the parish church) of St Georg at Tückelhausen (*in situ*). It is a splendid example of the Franconian art of altar construction.

Around 1745 Auwera also made marble epitaphs for the Schönborn family, commemorating *Lothar Franz von Schönborn*, Elector-Archbishop of Mainz and Bishop of Bamberg, and his nephew, *Friedrich Karl von Schönborn*, Prince-Bishop of Würzburg and Bamberg (both Mainz Cathedral). He repeated these epitaphs (1746–8), with some alterations, for Bamberg Cathedral; they were removed in 1837. That for *Friedrich Karl von Schönborn* (h. 5.52 m; Würzburg, Mainfränk. Mus.) is a wall sculpture in several colours of marble. It is constructed in three tiers crowned by an *Annunciation*, the figures of which are of Carrara marble. In the middle section of the epitaph, two lions hold the Bishop's insignia, the cartouche with the Schönborn arms being centrally placed. Flanking this are figures representing *Wisdom* and *Counsel*. Below this, the inscription appears on a spread lion's skin, surmounting a winged head of *Time*. Also part of this epitaph, but now exhibited separately, was a cartouche with a view of the Residenz and the signature: J : W AUWERA FEC:.

For each of his works Auwera, an accomplished draughtsman, made careful preliminary drawings and a terracotta *bozzetto*. The Mainfränkisches Museum, Würzburg, and the Martin Wagner Museum of the University of Würzburg hold a number of these drawings and *bozzetti*, including that of the *Lothar Franz von Schönborn* epitaph, and one of an allegorical figure of *Faith*, which has clearly been marked for scaled transfer. A life-size wooden carving of an angel was originally in the Marienkapelle, Würzburg (destr. 1945), probably as part of a side altar.

BIBLIOGRAPHY

M. Kranzbühler: 'Johann Wolfgang von der Auwera: Ein fränkisches Bildhauer des 18. Jahrhunderts', *Städel-Jb.*, vii–viii (1932), pp. 182–219

R. Sedlmaier: 'Wolfgang von der Auweras Schönborn-Grabmäler in Mainfränkischen Museum und die Grabmalkunst des Schönborn-Bischöfe', *Mainfränk. Hft.*, xxiii (1955)

M. Huth: *Johann Wolfgang von der Auwera* (Würzburg, 1970)

M. von Freeden: *Aus den Schätzen des Mainfränkisches Museums, Würzburg* (Würzburg, 1972)

H. P. Trenschel: 'Zur Rolle der Vorstudien bei Johann Wolfgang von der Auwera und Johann Peter Wagner', *Entwurf und Ausführung in der europäischen Barockplastik: Beiträge zum internationalen Kolloquium des Bayerischen Nationalmuseums und des Zentralinstituts für Kunstgeschichte: München, 1985*

HANNELORE HÄGELE

Auxerre. French city in Burgundy, préfecture of the Yonne département, with a population of *c.* 41,000. It lies in a wine-producing area overlooking the River Yonne. The Roman town of Autricus or Autissiodurum adopted Christianity in the 3rd century AD, and had its own bishop from early on until the French Revolution (1789–93), when it was combined with the diocese of Sens. St Germanus, second bishop of Auxerre (*reg* 418–48), founded the Abbey of St Germain, which became an important scholastic centre in the 9th century. Apart from the church of St Germain (*see* §2 below), the 12th-century dormitory is the earliest of the abbey buildings to survive. The present cathedral was begun in the early 13th century, replacing a series of earlier buildings (*see* §1 below). The nearby Romanesque Bishop's Palace (now the Préfecture) also dates from the 13th century, with subsequent additions. The city walls are now mostly destroyed, although several Renaissance gateways still stand.

1. Cathedral. 2. St Germain.

1. Cathedral.

(i) Architecture. (ii) Sculpture. (iii) Stained glass. (iv) Treasury.

(i) Architecture. The present building, dedicated to St Etienne, stands on the site of several predecessors going back to a group of churches mentioned in the 6th century. In the 9th century a western block was added to the church of St Etienne, which had already been extended and restored several times. A new Romanesque building replaced the early medieval conglomeration in 1023–57. The three-aisled crypt with ambulatory and axial chapel (originally apsidal) are all that remain of this building: they were retained as the foundations of the new choir when the Gothic Cathedral was erected in the early 13th century. The chapel was given a rectangular cladding, and, as at Chartres Cathedral (from 1194), the earlier church dictated the ground-plan of its successor, which also has an ambulatory (now polygonal) and a single axial chapel, the Lady Chapel.

The Gothic cathedral was begun in 1215 with the choir, which has five straight bays and was finished by 1234 at the latest. In elevation the choir follows the classic High Gothic three-storey scheme, with an arcade, a triforium and a clerestory that is almost the same height as the arcade (see fig.). The triforium is relatively high; each bay

Auxerre Cathedral, begun 1215; interior looking east

has a quadripartite arcade (tripartite in the apse) resting on very slender colonnettes. The clerestory has a passage; the windows consist of two simple lancets and a traceried oculus. There is another, rémois, passage in the aisle windows. The unusual elegance of this building was mentioned in a chronicle written in 1278. In an attempt to convey visually the structural framework of Gothic architecture the supports were made especially slender and the shell of the building was divided into two thin skins of wall of different heights, the outer one pierced by vast windows. The architect of Auxerre Cathedral consistently applied the Anglo-Norman THICK-WALL STRUCTURE to the type of three-storey elevation created at Chartres and Soissons; in so doing he created a style, so-called Burgundian Gothic, that was followed in a large surrounding area.

After the choir had been completed building progressed slowly in many short phases with long intervening periods of inactivity. The west façade was begun *c.* 1260; by 1300 only the south door and the inner west wall up to the height of the triforium had been completed, with the exterior of the other two doors standing only as high as the socles. The transepts and nave were begun in the first quarter of the 14th century. In spite of the protracted building campaign, the overall design was adhered to almost to the end, so that the western half of the cathedral gives an effect of unity. Formally, it represents a typically Parisian type of Rayonnant, with Flamboyant appearing only in the latest parts (the north transept façade and upper parts of the west front).

All the 14th- and 15th-century parts of the building follow the divisions and proportions of the choir. The completed building, 100 m long and 30 m high, has generous proportions. The ground storey of the nave with its aisles and chapels was completed *c.* 1350, and by *c.* 1400 the triforium and the clerestory of the east bays of the nave had been finished. The north transept was built between 1415 and 1513. Work was not resumed on the west façade and the corresponding upper sections of the nave until the last third of the 15th century. In spite of every effort only the nave, the middle section of the façade and the north tower (68 m high) not finished until 1547 were completed. The south tower never rose beyond the second storey.

BIBLIOGRAPHY

C. Porée: *La Cathédrale d'Auxerre* (Paris, 1926)

J. Vallery-Radot: 'Auxerre, la cathédrale Saint-Etienne: Les Principaux Textes de l'histoire de la construction', *Congr. Archéol. France*, cxvi (1958), pp. 40–50

R. Branner: *Burgundian Gothic Architecture* (London, 1960/*R* 1985), pp. 38–47

PETER KURMANN

(ii) Sculpture. Documentation is sparse concerning the sculpture of the west front. The portal sculptures were achieved over a long period, beginning some time after the mid-13th century and completed only towards the end of the 14th. Despite the chronological and stylistic differences that separate the earliest from the latest sections of the façade, there is remarkably little evidence of change in the iconographic programme. Typological and symbolic images are consistently rejected in favour of narrative scenes, which present sacred persons and events taking place in a contemporary courtly setting, a focus that is seen in other Burgundian monuments (e.g. Notre-Dame, Semur-en-Auxois; Saint-Thibault-en-Auxois). Although the emphasis on narrative cycles is also characteristic of sculpture executed during the second half of the 13th century in Paris and Reims, the stress on less familiar biblical and hagiographical stories that is a distinctive feature of Burgundian programmes, as well as the richly decorated wall surfaces found at Auxerre, set this sculpture somewhat apart from developments in the Ile-de-France, probably reflecting the tastes of local patrons, both secular and ecclesiastic.

The central portal of the façade depicts the *Last Judgement*, with *Christ and the Intercessors* on the tympanum, and the *Resurrection* and *Division of Souls* on the lintel and inner archivolt. The jamb niches once held figures of the Apostles, and scenes from their lives fill the corresponding archivolts. The *Wise and Foolish Virgins* are represented on the doorposts, and extensive cycles of *Joseph* and the *Parable of the Prodigal Son* are carved in low relief across the socle zone. The north portal is dedicated to the Virgin, with the *Coronation* on the tympanum and scenes from her life on the archivolts; a *Genesis* cycle is depicted on the socle. The south portal bears scenes from the lives of *St John the Baptist* and *Christ* on the tympanum and archivolts, while the socle reliefs recount the story of *David and Bathsheba.* Apart from a theological interpretation, the iconography of these cycles is often thought to mirror strictly local concerns, including even references to the lives of individual patrons.

Many characteristic features of the Auxerre sculpture appear at other sites. The depiction of the nude, for example, which has been connected with a renewed interest in antiquity, is a general phenomenon of the 1260s, to be observed both at Reims Cathedral and at Notre-Dame, Paris, where the figure of Adam from the south transept seems to be the model for the 'Hercules' figure at Auxerre. Similarly, the emphatic gestures and sharply characterized physiognomies at Auxerre are characteristic of the naturalistic tendency found in much northern French sculpture following the transept portals of Notre-Dame and the lintels at Reims.

The style of the reliefs has been compared to work at both Paris and Reims. The composition of the *Circumcision of St John the Baptist* from the south portal at Auxerre is identical to that of a group of figures listening to St Stephen preaching from the south transept portal at Notre-Dame, Paris (1260s), and drapery patterns and head types are also very similar. The figure of David spying on Bathsheba has been compared to Joachim in the *Meeting at the Golden Gate* from the reverse façade wall at Reims Cathedral. Both David and Joachim appear to derive from figures on the altarpiece of St Germer (now Paris, Mus. Cluny) and from the altarpieces of St Peregrinus and St Benoît at Saint-Denis, which have been convincingly dated to the 1260s, but at Reims the draperies are more mannered and the figure is less substantial, while at Auxerre the Parisian model is followed more closely.

These comparisons suggest that the workshop could have been installed at Auxerre by the mid-1260s, during the episcopate of Gui de Mello (*d* 1269); the Baptist portal would then have been begun in the late 1260s and most of its sculpture and that of the central portal completed in the 1270s and 1280s. The *Genesis* reliefs of the north

(Virgin) portal appear to be somewhat later, carved well after the sculpture on the west façade of Sens Cathedral, which post-dates the collapse of the south-west tower in 1278. The extremely attenuated figures and the simplified drapery patterns of the *Genesis* reliefs recall the style of Parisian works executed *c.* 1300, such as the choir enclosure at Notre-Dame and figures from St Louis, Poissy (now located in the church of Notre-Dame at Poissy). The archivolts of the Virgin portal follow the lower reliefs, and the sculpture of the south transept portal, its iconography reflecting both Paris and Sens, probably belongs to the same early 14th-century campaign. Other parts of the façade are still later, the archivolts of the central portal perhaps not being carved until *c.* 1380.

BIBLIOGRAPHY

J. Lebeuf: *Mémoires concernant l'histoire civile et ecclésiastique d'Auxerre et de son ancien diocèse*, ed. A. Challe and M. Quantin, 4 vols (Auxerre, 1848–55)

Gesta pontificum Autissiodorensium, ed. L.-M. Duru, Bibliothèque Historique de l'Yonne, i (Auxerre and Paris, 1850), pp. 309–509

C. Enlart: 'La Sculpture des portails de la cathédrale d'Auxerre du XIIe à la fin du XIVe siècle', *Congr. Archéol. France*, lxxiv (1907), pp. 599–626

C. Porée: *La Sculpture d'Auxerre* (Paris, 1926)

M. Aubert: 'Les Sculptures de la cathédrale d'Auxerre', *Congr. Archéol. France*, cxvi (1958), pp. 51–8

W. Sauerlander: *Gotische Skulptur in Frankreich, 1140–1270* (Munich, 1970; Eng. trans., London, 1972), pp. 499–501

F. Nordstrom: *The Auxerre Reliefs: A Harbinger of the Renaissance in France during the Reign of Philip le Bel* (Uppsala, 1974)

W. Craven: 'The Iconography of the David and Bathsheba Cycle at the Cathedral of Auxerre', *J. Soc. Archit. Hist.*, xxxiv (1975), pp. 226–37

D. Denny: 'Some Narrative Subjects in the Portal Sculpture of Auxerre Cathedral', *Speculum*, li (1976), pp. 23–34

U. Quednau: *Die Westportale der Kathedrale von Auxerre* (Wiesbaden, 1979)

DOROTHY GILLERMAN

(iii) Stained glass. References in the *Gesta pontificum Autissiodorensium* show that there was stained glass in the cathedral as early as the Carolingian period. The existing glass, however, dates from the building of the Gothic church after 1215. The glazing seems to have been financed by the canons, who commissioned glass workshops from the Ile-de-France *c.* 1235. The most productive workshop, that of the Genesis Master and a follower, was responsible for the windows depicting subjects from the Old Testament and New Testament and lives of various saints: the *Creation and Fall*, *Noah*, *Abraham and Lot*, *David*, *Exodus*, *Samson*, *Joseph*, the *Tree of Jesse*, the *Prodigal Son*, and lives of *St Mammes*, *St Margaret*, *St Andrew*, *St James*, *St Mary the Egyptian* and *St Mary Magdalene.* Distinctive of the Genesis workshop are the oval-pattern or 'plantain leaf' drapery folds, elongated faces, elegant gestures and open, spatially ambitious compositions.

A more dramatic, energetic style, comparable to that of the *Good Samaritan* window at Chartres Cathedral, is that of the Eustace workshop, found in the representations of *St Eustace*, *St Catherine*, *St Germanus* and *St Lawrence* (*see* STAINED GLASS, fig. 9), and the *Miracles of St Nicholas.* Here the style is calligraphic, with exaggeratedly elongated figures. Two additional windows of scenes from the *Life of St Nicholas* and the *Relics of St Stephen* were made by artists who worked at St Germain-lès-Corbeil and Troyes, and whose figure style and rich decorative borders can be related to those of the 13th-century *Bibles moralisées* (e.g. Vienna, N. Bib., MSS 1179 and 2554).

One workshop, associated with the Parisian manuscript traditions exemplified by the Sainte-Chapelle Evangeliary (Paris, Bib. N., MS. lat. 8892), enjoyed a long, productive existence at Auxerre, depicting short bodies with round heads and generously massed drapery in deep, hollow folds with heavy grisaille modelling. The style seems to mature from the *Apocalypse* and *Eligius* windows of *c.* 1238, to later work in the ambulatory and the large-scale figures of the axial chapel and the clerestory. The axial lancets of the clerestory, showing two versions of the glorified *Christ*, were relocated in western bays with the arrival of the Isaiah Master from the Sainte-Chapelle (*c.* 1248; *see* PARIS, §V, 2(iii)). The decision of Bishop Gui de Mello, an intimate of King Louis IX, to install new axial lancets on a *Passion* theme by the workshop of the royal chapel indicates his sensitivity to the political significance of the glazing programme. The glass was restored from 1866 under Louis-Charles-Auguste Steinheil.

BIBLIOGRAPHY

V. Raguin: *Stained Glass in 13th-century Burgundy* (Princeton, 1982)

VIRGINIA CHIEFFO RAGUIN

(iv) Treasury. Auxerre Cathedral treasury deserves to be known more for its resilience than for the antiquity of its present collection. A remarkable series of inventories dating from 1420 to 1892 reflect changing religious and political priorities over five centuries. The first full inventory, from 1531, reveals a rich storehouse of medieval devotion. Of the 70 items, 20 are valuable reliquaries in the form of statuettes and aediculae. The most notable of these was the *Joyau*, a construction of several gilt figures and emeralds used to display the sacrament in processions.

The next inventory of the collection was made in 1567, and its title carries the grim information that the entire treasury was removed by the Huguenots when they despoiled the cathedral in that year. Charles IX (*reg* 1560–74), under the pretext of offering to safeguard the treasure, removed a valuable crucifix covered in emeralds and replaced it with an inferior cross, whereupon the cathedral took up a lawsuit against him. The Huguenots removed 13 wagons of silver-gilt reliquaries and shrines, which were melted down, relics were thrown in the gutter, and a brass foundry for making cannon was set up in the cathedral nave, using church plate and chandeliers as raw materials. The pathetic inventory of 1569 shows that the cathedral's treasure was reduced to vessels of tin and pewter. During the 18th century treasures began to accumulate again: inventories of 1726 and 1733 show many donations of plate and textiles for private chapels. In 1790 the cathedral chapter was dissolved and the treasure was again removed, this time by revolutionaries. The present substantial treasury is based on a private collection donated by M. Duru in 1868 and is mainly from the 17th to 19th centuries.

BIBLIOGRAPHY

L. Courajod: 'Le Trésor de la cathédrale d'Auxerre en 1567', *Rev. Archéol.*, 2nd ser., xix (1869), pp. 328–40

M. Quantin: 'Inventaire du trésor de la cathédrale d'Auxerre en 1531', *Bull. Soc. Sci. Hist. & Nat. Yonne* (1887), pp. 113–27

F. Molard: 'Histoire de l'ancien trésor de la cathédrale d'Auxerre', *Bull. Soc. Sci. Hist. & Nat. Yonne*, xlvi (1892), pp. 103–93

H. Monceau, G. Bonneau and F. Molard: 'Inventaire du trésor actuel de la cathédrale d'Auxerre', *Bull. Soc. Sci. Hist. & Nat. Yonne*, xlvi (1892), pp. 194–285

P. Corberon: *Auxerre: Sa Cathédrale, ses monuments* (Auxerre, 1906)

JANE GEDDES

2. ST GERMAIN. The former Benedictine abbey church of St Germain now comprises the remains of a Carolingian crypt, a Gothic choir and transepts, and the four eastern bays of the nave; the western nave bays and the Carolingian westwork were destroyed in the early 19th century. A detached 12th-century bell-tower also survives. The medieval history of the abbey is dominated by the cult of St Germanus, the second bishop of Auxerre (*reg* 418–48), who was born in the town and was an important figure in the Church's campaign against the Pelagian heresy.

St Germanus's tomb lay below the level of the main apse of the Merovingian church built *c.* 493–533 by Queen Clotilde, wife of Clovis I (*reg* 481–511). Between 841 and 859 Conrad, Comte d'Auxerre, the uncle of Emperor Charles the Bald, decided to enhance the structure, and a contemporary description mentions the 'admirable unit of crypts' organized around the semi-subterranean confessio containing Germanus's remains. In this form of 'outer crypt' the confessio formed the nucleus of a small aisled, vaulted chamber surrounded by a corridor leading to small chapels in echelon. Attached to the crypt at the east was a circular oratory that was part of the same building programme. This elaborate arrangement, which provided access to the tomb on important feast days, reflects the growing importance of the cult of relics in the Carolingian period.

At the same time an oratory (destr.) dedicated to St John the Baptist was constructed to the west of the Merovingian nave. Eighteenth-century plans and elevations indicate that it was an imposing structure, similar to a westwork, comprising a central bay of three storeys flanked by two towers. The fire that consumed much of the abbey in 1064 also destroyed part of this western addition, but the extent of its subsequent reconstruction is debated; as a result there is confusion over the date of the patterned stonework and relief sculpture that appear in 18th-century drawings of the south wall, some scholars maintaining that the decoration, which is similar to that found in the middle stretches of the Loire Valley, dates to the 9th century, others claiming a date in the second half of the 11th. The Merovingian nave was, however, rebuilt after the fire.

In the western part of the crypt Carolingian wall paintings, a rare survival, depict three episodes from the *Martyrdom of St Stephen*: his trial, his preaching to the Sanhedrin and his martyrdom by stoning. In the last Stephen is depicted with arms outstretched towards the Hand of God. The style of the paintings is similar to works associated with the putative court school of Charles the Bald; Charles himself was present at the consecration and translation of the relics of St Germanus in 865.

The Rayonnant choir, begun in 1277, partly follows the lines of the Carolingian work and includes a five-sided apse and ambulatory leading through a vestibule to a decagonal axial chapel. The last is built over a substructure of two superimposed chapels on the site of the Carolingian rotunda, which was demolished to accommodate it. The elegant vestibule is bounded on east and west by a triple arcade of tall, thin columns and vaulted by eight ribs springing from a central boss. The choir has a three-storey elevation and is especially notable for its use of continuous orders. The eastern bays of the nave (i.e. the old monks' choir) were rebuilt between 1366 and 1398, partly with the aid of Pope Urban V (*reg* 1362–70), a former abbot of St Germain. The remaining nave bays were demolished in 1811, and in 1817 a new façade was built against the Gothic work; the old western block was destroyed shortly afterwards. Restorations were carried out in 1924, 1929 and 1948.

BIBLIOGRAPHY

Labbe: *Novae bibliothecae manuscriptorum librorum*, i (1657) [incl. early sources relating to the construction of St Germain]

E. King: 'The Carolingian Frescoes of the Abbey of St.-Germain d'Auxerre', *A. Bull.*, xi (1929), pp. 359–75

P. Deschamps: 'Peintures murales de l'époque carolingienne et du XIe siècle en France', *Rev. Acad. Inscr. & B.-Lett.* (1951), pp. 98–106

J. Hubert: 'L'Avant-nef carolingienne de St.-Germain, Auxerre', *Cah. Archéol.*, v (1951), pp. 151–62

——: '*Cryptae inferiores* et *cryptae superiores* dans l'architecture religieuse à l'époque carolingienne', *Mélanges d'histoire du moyen âge dédiés à la mémoire de L. Halphen* (Paris, 1951), pp. 351–7

J. Vallery-Radot: 'Saint-Germain d'Auxerre: L'Eglise haute', *Congr. Archéol. France*, cxvi (1958), pp. 26–39

R. Louis: 'Un Monument contemporain de Charles le Chauve: Les Cryptes carolingiennes de Saint-Germain d'Auxerre', *Archéologia*, lxvii (1974), pp. 20–36

J. Ottaway: 'Traditions architecturales dans le nord de la France pendant le premier millénaire', *Cah. Civilis. Méd.*, xxiii (1980), pp. 169–72

BARBARA A. WATKINSON

aux trois crayons [Fr.: 'with three chalks']. Term applied to a drawing in black, red and white chalks, often carried out on tinted paper; the technique was particularly employed by Antoine Watteau, among others, in the early part of the 18th century. The variant terms *aux deux crayons* (black and red chalks) and *aux quatre crayons* (black, white and two shades of red chalk) are occasionally also used (*see* DRAWING, colour pl. I, fig. 2).

□

Auzou [née Desmarquet(s)], **Pauline** (*b* Paris, 24 March 1775; *d* Paris, 15 May 1835). French painter. After studying in Jacques-Louis David's studio, at the age of 18 Auzou exhibited a *Bacchante* and a *Study of a Head* in the Salon of 1793. She exhibited regularly at the Salon until 1817. She was awarded a Prix d'Encouragement for *Departure for a Duel* in 1806 and a medal for *Agnès de Méranie* (untraced) in 1808. In 1810 Vivant Denon drew the Emperor Napoleon's attention to the 'genre anecdotique', which he maintained was unique to the French school. Denon cited Auzou as well as Pierre-Nolasque Bergeret, Jean-Antoine Laurent, Fleury-François Richard and Adolphe-Eugène-Gabriel Roehn (1780–1867) among the practitioners of this distinctive genre.

Auzou's oeuvre consists of portraits (e.g. *Portrait of a Musician*; Manchester, NH, Currier Gal. A.) and genre scenes, a great many of which still belong to the artist's descendants. In the early genre scenes she took her inspiration from history and Greek mythology or used playfully erotic subjects in the style of Louis-Philibert Debucourt. Later she sought inspiration in the history of the French kings (e.g. *Agnès de Méranie*, exh. Salon 1808;

untraced) or in contemporary history, as in the *Arrival of the Empress Marie-Louise at Compiègne* (exh. Salon 1810; Versailles, Château) and *Marie-Louise Taking Leave of her Family* (exh. Salon 1812; Versailles, Château). Avoiding the customary pompous rhetoric of such historical scenes, she depicted them in an intimate, sentimental manner. Auzou's genre scenes, which were exhibited from 1800 onwards, reveal her as one of the best representatives of 'anecdotal genre' or the TROUBADOR STYLE, as much in her choice of subjects—moralizing and emotive—as in her debts to 17th-century Dutch painters, particularly the smooth technique and the effects of light and composition found in the work of Pieter de Hooch and Gerrit Dou.

BIBLIOGRAPHY

P. Marmottan: *L'Ecole française de peinture (1789–1830)* (Paris, 1886), pp. 280–81
F. Benoit: *L'Art français sous la Révolution et l'Empire* (Paris, 1897), pp. 335–6
V. Cameron: 'Portrait of a Woman by Pauline Auzou', *Currier Gal. A. Bull.*, ii (1974), pp. 1–17
Women Artists, 1550–1950 (exh. cat. by A. B. Sutherland Harris and L. Nochlin, Los Angeles, Co. Mus. A., 1977)

MARIE-CLAUDE CHAUDONNERET

Ava [anc. Ratnapura]. City in Upper Burma at the confluence of the Irrawaddy and Myitnge rivers. It was founded *c.* 1365 as the third capital of the Shan rulers previously established at Pinya and Sagaing. In 1635 it became the capital of the Burman Toungoo dynasty. It was not finally abandoned as a royal capital until 1841 in favour of Amarapura. In contrast to the usual plan of Burmese cities (*see* BURMA, §III), Ava was built with its citadel, the plan of which was a rectangle with the two longer sides curving slightly outwards, at the north-east corner of an irregular, redented city wall. The wooden royal palace in the centre of the citadel and most of the other structures were either destroyed by the catastrophic earthquake of 1838 or dismantled three years later when the capital was definitively moved to Amarapura, 10 km to the north-east. The ruined Baga-ya-kyaung was, with its 267 teak posts, one of the largest wooden monasteries built.

One monument that survived and was repaired after the earthquake is the early 19th-century Maha-aung-myebonzan Monastery, which is built of brick following wooden models. The *pyatthat* (Burm.: 'tiered pavilion on a square plan') and the main building are aligned on a common axis on the platform, but instead of the large halls inside, there are two narrow rooms surrounded by two concentric corridors. This was probably done because the builder did not dare to construct a brick vault with such a wide span, even though this had previously been achieved in Pagan.

BIBLIOGRAPHY

H. Yule: *A Narrative of the Mission Sent by the Governor-General of India to the Court of Ava in 1855* (London, 1858/*R* Kuala Lumpur, 1968)
V. C. Scott O'Connor: *Mandalay and Other Cities of the Past in Burma* (London, 1907/*R* Bangkok, 1987)
U Myo Myint Sein and others: 'Kon-baung hkit hnaung phon-gyi kyaung-mya' [Monasteries of the later Konbaung period], *Tekkathou pyinnya padetha sa Shei Myan-ma ein-myà zaung* [University lectures in general education], v/3 (1970), pp. 269–92
U Aung Thaw: *Historical Sites in Burma* (Rangoon, 1972/*R* 1978)
U Kan Hla [S. Ozhegov]: 'Traditional Town Planning in Burma', *J. Soc. Archit. Hist.*, xxxvii/2 (1978), pp. 92–104

PIERRE PICHARD

Avantipura [Avantipur]. Temple site 28 km south-east of Srinagar in Kashmir, India. It was established, possibly as a secondary or ceremonial capital, by Avantivarman (*reg* AD 855–83), founder of the Utpala dynasty. The two major monuments attributed to him are the Avantisvamin Temple, dedicated to Vishnu and thought to be the earlier, and the Avantishvara Temple, dedicated to Shiva (*see* INDIAN SUBCONTINENT, §III, 5(i)(b)).

Only foundations and sections of walls survive at the Avantisvamin Temple, which was constructed on the five-shrined (Skt *pañcayātana*) plan comprising a sanctum, fronted by a stairway and centred in a spacious courtyard with four smaller shrines at the corners; two additional shrines on the eastern side of the enclosure are perhaps later additions. A square pavement before the stairway of the central shrine indicates a no longer extant forehall aligned to a well-preserved monumental gateway on the west side of the elaborately sculptured enclosure wall. The inner side of the wall contains a series of 69 cells fronted by a colonnade. Architectural forms are in the hellenizing style seen throughout Kashmir. Several images excavated from this temple (Srinagar, Sri Pratap Singh Mus.) show Vishnu in his four-faced (*caturvyūha*) form. The Avantishvara Temple had an enclosed five-shrined plan similar to that of the Avantisvamin Temple but is less well preserved and was left unfinished. Among its surviving relief sculptures are an image of Lakulisha and one of a royal couple, probably Avantivarman and his queen.

The 12th-century *Rājataraṅgiṇī* ('River of kings') of Kalhana mentions Avantipura in connection with kings of the 11th and 12th centuries, and finds of coins and references in later chronicles indicate that Avantipura retained some importance into the 15th century. However, no architectural remains from this period survive aside from expanses of stone walls and rubble.

BIBLIOGRAPHY

A. Cunningham: 'An Essay on the Arian Order of Architecture, as Exhibited in the Temples of Kashmir', *J. Asiat. Soc. Bengal*, xvii/2 (1848), pp. 241–327
M. A. Stein: *Kalhaṇa's Rājataraṅgiṇī: A Chronicle of the Kings of Kashmir*, 2 vols (London, 1900)
P. N. K. Bamzai: *A History of Kashmir* (Delhi, 1962)
H. Goetz: *Studies in the History and Art of Kashmir and the Indian Himalaya* (Wiesbaden, 1969)
D. Mitra: *Pandrethan, Avantipur, and Martand* (New Delhi, 1977)

WALTER SMITH

Avanzi, Jacopo [Jacopo d'Avanzi] (*fl* 1363–84). Italian painter. At least two painters of this name were recorded in Bologna: a Jacopo di Pietro Avanzi, who was dead by 1378, and one who was paid for a small commission on 13 April 1384. This has led to much confusion. The earliest reference is to a *Iacobus Avancini depintor*, resident in 1363 in the parish of S Cecilia in the Porta Piera quarter of Bologna. On 28 February 1375 a Jacopo Avanzi witnessed a notarial act and on 23 June 1377 a Jacopo Avanzi was one of several craftsmen paid for a bishop's pallium.

A panel of *Christ on the Cross between the Virgin and St John* (Rome, Gal. Colonna), which may have been the centre of an altarpiece, is signed *Jacobus de avanciis de bononia f.* and bears the arms of the Malatesta. The figures are monumental and sharply contoured, and the strong colours betray the painter's Bolognese origin. The emotional portrayal of the figures is direct and convincing.

Works attributed to the same artist on the basis of stylistic affinities with the Colonna panel include a fresco of the *Battle of San Ruffillo* (Bologna, S Francesco; destr.), a fresco of the *Massacre of the Jews* and the design, but not the execution, of the adjacent two scenes from the *Life of Moses*, all from the church of S Apollonia at Mezzaratta, Bologna (Bologna, Pin. N.). In the *Massacre of the Jews*, the square-jawed figures recall St John in the Colonna panel, and the sense of movement and the foreshortened postures are remarkable. The same qualities are also present in 12 monochrome illustrations to a manuscript of Statius's heroic poem *The Thebaid* (Dublin, Chester Beatty Lib.).

By the 16th century a tradition had grown up that a Jacopo Avanzi had collaborated with ALTICHIERO on two fresco cycles in Padua: Marcantonio Michiel's report that Avanzi and Altichiero had worked on the oratory of S Giorgio was based on an unreliable source and cannot be substantiated either by documents or by stylistic evidence. Michele Savonarola reported that Jacopo Avanzi painted the Cappella di S Giacomo (now S Felice) in the Santo in Padua; Michiel said that Altichiero painted it with a Jacopo Avanzi (from Padua, Verona or Bologna). Certainly there are stylistic reasons to attribute most of the lunettes of the Cappella di S Giacomo to a hand other than Altichiero's. In these the modelling of the figures is drier and less painterly, the colours less muted and naturalistic, while the expressions and gestures are more strident. The frescoes have stylistic similarities to the Colonna panel. Although Jacopo's oeuvre is fragmentary and confusingly documented, it forms one of the highest points of achievement in Bolognese painting of the late 14th century.

BIBLIOGRAPHY

M. Savonarola: *Libellus de magnificis ornamentis regiae civitatis Padue* (*c.* 1445–7); ed. A. Segarizzi (Città di Castello, 1902)

M. Michiel: *Notizie d'opere di disegno* (*c.* 1520–40); ed. G. Frizzoni (Bologna, 1884)

F. Filippini and G. Zucchini: *Miniatori e pittori a Bologna: Documenti dei secoli XIII e XIV* (Florence, 1947), p. 131

G. L. Mellini: *Altichiero e Jacopo Avanzi* (Milan, 1965) [good illus.]

H.-W. Kruft: *Altichiero und Avanzo: Untersuchungen zur oberitalienischen Malerei des ausgehenden Trecento* (diss., Bonn, Rhein. Friedrich-Wilhelms U., 1966)

R. Simon: 'Altichiero versus Avanzo', *Pap. Brit. Sch. Rome*, n. s. 32, xlv (1977), pp. 252–71

A. I. Pini: 'Miniatori, pittori e scrittori nelle "venticinquine" bolognesi del due e trecento', *Il Carrobbio*, vii (1981), pp. 347–65

D. Benati: 'Pittura del trecento in Emilia Romagna', *La pittura in Italia: Il duecento e il trecento*, ed. E. Castelnuovo (Milan, 1986), vol. i, pp. 193–232

——: *Jacopo Avanzi* (Bologna, 1992), pp. 120–29

S. Skerl Del Conte: *Vitale e la sua bottega nella chiesa di Sant'Apollonia Mezzaratta* (Bologna, 1993), pp. 144–53

ELIOT W. ROWLANDS

Avanzini, Bartolomeo [Aloisio] (*b* Rome, 1608; *d* Modena, 1658). Italian architect. He was the son of Sante Avanzini (1581–?1632). He worked as a painter in the papal court in 1644 and may have been trained in the Roman workshops of Carlo Maderno and Girolamo Rainaldi. In 1634 he was called to Modena to work as an architect for the ducal court of the Este family, an appointment possibly obtained through Rainaldi's influence. He was immediately engaged on the building programme begun by Francesco I d'Este, Duke of Modena, and submitted one of the many drawings for remodelling the old ducal residence in Modena, which had previously undergone a series of gradual and uncoordinated alterations. The first work to be completed by Avanzini in the Este duchy was the sanctuary of Fiorano (1634; now greatly altered). In the same year he was commissioned to begin the remodelling of the old fortress of Sassuolo, which had been enlarged in the 16th century to create a summer residence for the Este court. His scheme, which involved the whole of the little town of Sassuolo in an integrated civic design, shows affinities with Giovanni Battista Aleotti's treatment of the Palazzo Bentivoglio at Rocca Gualtieri. Avanzini's decision to distance the palace from the straight street by a piazza, in order to achieve an imposing effect, was a tribute to the urban layouts of Sixtus V in Rome. Baroque scenographic effects are evident on the exterior of the palace, in the horizontal development of the façade and the transformation of the bastions into terraces (destr.), and in the interior, in the arrangement of the reception rooms: a great salon, a long gallery and a grand staircase. The effect is enhanced by the illusionistic perspective decorations by Angelo Michele Colonna and Agostino Stanzani Mitelli (i). The original plans for the garden and fountains, with sculptural groups suggested by Gianlorenzo Bernini, are also attributed to Avanzini.

The models to which Avanzini refers show that he was aware of the most advanced works by Bernini, Francesco Borromini and Pietro da Cortona, having studied them during journeys to Rome in 1642 and 1650. In 1651 he presented the definitive scheme for the ducal palace in Modena (drawings held in Modena, Gal. & Mus. Estense) and may have contributed ideas for the design of the façade. This was inspired by the great royal palaces of Europe but differed from them in the omission of the high plinth (thus creating a more direct and immediate relationship with the urban environment) and the absence of a large central chapel. With its clear, classical lines the main three-dimensional interest of the scheme is concentrated on the large central keep, a feature contrary to Roman taste at that time. The great *cour d'honneur* became a focal point where the two principal axes meet: that of the three-aisled main atrium and the rear façade (with its double exedra and windows with a Serlian motif), and that on which the enfilade of rooms is located. The great stairway, built later, was designed to integrate the loggia, where the horizontal rhythm of the colonnades and balustrades intersects with the vertical lines.

In 1649 Avanzini had furnished the plan for the dome of the Theatine church of S Vincenzo in Modena. (The supervision of its building is the first architectural assignment recorded of Guarino Guarini.) Avanzini may have designed the articulated tabernacle there, which is in a decidedly northern style. He is also attributed with the plan for the main altar of the Benedictine abbey of S Giovanni Evangelista in Parma and with the church of S Carlo in Modena, which is typical of Avanzini in its centralized organization of the space with a longitudinal emphasis.

BIBLIOGRAPHY
I. Vedriani: *Storia di Modena* (Modena, 1666)
N. Carboneri: 'Guarino a Modena', *Guarino Guarini e l'internazionalità del barocco: Torino, 1970*, i, pp. 47–70
C. Roli Guidetti: 'I palazzi ducali di Modena e Sassuolo', *Residenze Estensi* (Modena, 1973), pp. 89–126
B. Adorni: *L'Abbazia benedettina di S Giovanni Evangelista a Parma* (Milan, 1979)
M. Pirondini, ed.: *Ducale Palazzo di Sassuolo* (Genoa, 1982)
A. Biondi, ed.: *Palazzo Ducale di Modena* (Modena, 1987)
G. Martinelli Braglia: 'Il tabernacolo a tempietto di Bartolomeo Avanzini ... Documenti inediti', *Atti & Mem. Reale Deput. Stor. Patria Prov. Moden.*, n. s. 11, xii (1990), pp. 107–18

ALESSANDRA FRABETTI

Avaricum. *See* BOURGES.

Avaris [now Tell el-Dab'a, eastern Delta, Egypt]. Ancient capital of Egypt that flourished during the Hyksos period (*c.* 1630–*c.* 1540 BC). The Greek name 'Avaris' derives from an ancient Egyptian name meaning 'royal fortified settlement of the district'. The northern part of Tell el-Dab'a was at first occupied by the town of Rowaty in the Middle Kingdom (*c.* 2008–*c.* 1630 BC). Avaris itself was founded *c.* 1720 BC as the capital of a local Delta kingdom independent of the ruling 13th Dynasty. The community was at that time largely of Syrian origin, employed originally by the Egyptian navy and treasury. A local Asiatic dynasty took control of Avaris and continued the existing cult of the god Seth. During the subsequent Hyksos rule (15th Dynasty, *c.* 1630–*c.* 1532 BC) Egypt was governed by monarchs of Asiatic origin. According to a late tradition of Flavius Josephus, Avaris was strongly fortified, and Egyptian sources suggest that it served as the Hyksos capital. Excavations at the site of Tell el-Dab'a revealed a huge town, covering 2.5 sq. km, which incorporated Canaanite cults and temples and evidently served as a powerful trading centre for the Eastern Mediterranean. Although Avaris seems to have been a centre of scarab production, the craftsmen produced few original works of art under the Hyksos, who preferred to usurp Middle Kingdom statues. The discovery of a temple of Seth, in southern Avaris, conforms with the statement in Papyrus Anastasi II (London, BM, 10243) that the 'house of Seth' lay in the south. This temple was restored by Horemheb (*reg c.* 1319–*c.* 1292 BC) and Sethos I (*reg c.* 1290–*c.* 1279 BC). Avaris continued in existence, as the harbour quarter of PIRAMESSE, until the 20th Dynasty (*c.* 1190–*c.* 1075 BC).

BIBLIOGRAPHY
LÄ: 'Avaris', 'Tell el-Dab'a'
M. Bietak: *Avaris and Piramesse* (Oxford, 1981, rev. 2/1986)

M. BIETAK

Avebury. Village in Wiltshire, south-west England, the site of a Late Neolithic ceremonial complex, including a massive HENGE and stone circle (see fig.; *see also* PREHISTORIC EUROPE, §IV, 2(iv)(a); MEGALITHIC ARCHITECTURE, 2). The Avebury monuments are close to the contemporary earthwork at Silbury Hill, the earlier causewayed camp at Windmill Hill and the megalithic tomb at West Kennet. Alexander Keiller excavated and partially restored Avebury in the 1930s.

At the centre of the complex is the great henge, consisting of a ditch (originally 9 m deep) and an outer bank. Sherds of Windmill Hill ware, Peterborough ware and Grooved ware pottery were excavated from the bottom of the ditch. No material from Avebury has yet been dated by radiocarbon analysis, but finds of these pottery types and comparison with other large henges in the locality (such as Durrington Walls) suggest that construction began after *c.* 2500 BC. The ditch may have

Avebury, aerial view of the henge and stone circle, Late Neolithic period, *c.* 2500 BC

been dug in sections allotted to gangs of workers, which would explain irregularities in the shape of the earthworks, as well as the barely circular layout of the stone ring (diam. *c.* 330 m) erected along the inner edge of the ditch. Inside this great ring are the remains of two precisely laid-out stone circles, each *c.* 100 m in diameter. Although the construction sequence at Avebury is not well understood, it seems possible that these circles predate the outer ring. The northern inner circle contained a smaller concentric circle, in the centre of which stood a few large stones, originally forming a simple open-ended enclosure (the Cove); the centre of the southern ring was marked by a very large stone (the Obelisk) and an enigmatic, roughly triangular arrangement of smaller stones. The main henge has four entrances, two of which were originally approached by way of processional avenues of standing stones. One of these avenues has been largely destroyed, while the other was partially excavated and restored by Keiller. The restored avenue follows a mysteriously curving route to a terminal ritual site, known as the Sanctuary, where excavation has revealed three successive circular arrangements of posts. Whether these posts supported roofs or formed free-standing timber circles is unclear, but they were eventually replaced by two small concentric rings of stones.

Avebury is often compared to the contemporary monument of STONEHENGE, but the differences between the two are illuminating. The sarsen blocks used at both sites occur naturally near Avebury; at Stonehenge they were augmented by bluestones imported from Wales. More significantly, the Avebury sarsens are entirely unshaped and free-standing, while those at Stonehenge are dressed and used in a formal construction. Therefore, although Stonehenge is a brilliant creation, Avebury represents the true climax of the megalithic tradition.

BIBLIOGRAPHY

A. Burl: *Prehistoric Avebury* (London, 1979)
C. Malone: *Avebury* (London, 1989)

ROB JAMESON

Aved, Jacques(-André-Joseph) [Camelot] (*b* Douai, 12 Jan 1702; *d* Paris, 4 March 1766). French painter and collector. His father, Jean-Baptiste Havet, a doctor of Armenian origin, died when Aved was a child. He was brought up in Amsterdam by his step-father, a captain in the Dutch Guards. At 16 he is said to have become a pedlar or 'camelot' (hence the nickname given to him by his French acquaintances) travelling through the Netherlands, drawing portraits at fairs. In 1721, after spending short periods in the Amsterdam studios of the French engraver Bernard Picart and of the draughtsman François Boitard (1652–1722), he left the Netherlands to work in the Paris studio of the fashionable portrait painter Alexis-Simon Belle. At this time he met other notable painters including Carle Vanloo and the portrait painters Maurice-Quentin de La Tour, Jean-Baptiste Perroneau and Jean-Etienne Liotard. He also formed a deep and lasting friendship with Jean-Siméon Chardin, with whom he may have collaborated on occasion; they used similar techniques, and he may have encouraged Chardin to turn from still-life painting to figure painting in the 1730s.

Aved was approved (*agréé*) by the Académie Royale in 1731 and was received (*reçu*) as a full member in 1734, on presentation of portraits of the painters *Pierre-Jacques Cazes* and *Jean-François de Troy* (both Versailles, Château). From 1737, when the Paris Salon reopened after a long closure, until 1759 he was a regular and much praised exhibitor of portraits. In rivalry with such artists of the older generation as Jean-Marc Nattier, Aved drew his clients from the nobility and upper bourgeoisie. Among his male portraits are those of *Jean-Gabriel de la Porte du Thiel* (exh. Salon, 1740; Cleveland, OH, Mus. A.), *Carl Gustav, Count Tessin* (exh. Salon, 1740; Stockholm, Nmus.; for illustration *see* TESSIN, (3)) and *Victor Riquetti, Marquis de Mirabeau* (exh. Salon, 1743; Paris, Louvre). Inspired by his full-length portrait of *Saïd Pasha*, Turkish ambassador to the court of Louis XV (exh. Salon, 1742; Versailles, Château), he painted a number of sitters in fashionable Turkish costume. These include the *Marquise de Sainte Maure* (exh. Salon, 1743; St Maurice de Montcalm, priv. col., see Wildenstein, 1922, no. 96), who is depicted as a sultana in the gardens of the Seraglio. Aved's official full-length portrait of the distinguished soldier *Gaspard de Clermont-Tonnerre* (exh. Salon, 1759; Ancy-le-Franc, Château) is a good example of his work in the Grand Manner.

At a time when French portrait painting was beginning to move away from the florid, mythologizing style of Nicolas Largillierre and his followers, however, Aved's most characteristic works combine discretion with a concern for veracity and psychological penetration, stemming perhaps from his Dutch background and his close

Jacques Aved: *Mme Crozat*, oil on canvas, 1.37×1.00 m, exhibited at the Salon of 1741 (Montpellier, Musée Fabre)

association with Chardin. His acknowledged masterpiece in this vein is the half-length portrait of *Mme Crozat* (exh. Salon, 1741; Montpellier, Mus. Fabre; see fig.), the elderly wife of the immensely rich banker Antoine Crozat. She is depicted, spectacles in hand, seated at her needlework. This work, like others by Aved, was attributed to Chardin throughout the 19th century. Although he worked mainly in oils, Aved also made a number of pastels and red chalk drawings, although these are mostly untraced.

Aved formed a remarkable art collection (see Wildenstein, 1922, i, pp. 104–7, 136–61). This consisted of ceramics, Oriental bronzes and sculpture and, most notably, Old Master and modern paintings, with a preference for the Dutch and Flemish schools. He bought at sales in the Netherlands as well as in Paris and acquired a reputation as one of the foremost connoisseurs of his day. He seems to have acted as a dealer as well, since many of the pictures he is known to have bought at sales, such as those of Count Wassenaer d'Obdam (The Hague, 1750) and of Edme Gersaint (Paris, 1750), do not appear in the catalogue of his own sale (reprinted in Wildenstein, 1922, i, pp. 141–59) organized by Pierre Rémy in 1766. From this catalogue and other sources it is known that he owned paintings by or attributed to Rembrandt, Gerrit Dou, Adrien van Ostade, Nicolaes Berchem, Philips Wouwerman, Anthony van Dyck, Domenichino, Tintoretto, Guercino, Claude Lorrain, Nicolas Poussin and many others. Among the highest priced pictures in the 1766 sale were a *Deposition* by van Dyck (probably the work now in Munich, Alte Pin.), a *Susanna and the Elders* by Rembrandt (probably that now in Berlin, Gemäldegal.) and two paintings by Poussin, one of which may be the *Tancred and Erminia* in the Hermitage, St Petersburg. He is also known to have commissioned allegories of *Painting*, *Lyric Poetry* and *Heroic Poetry* from Louis Lagrenée. His fine collection of Rembrandt prints was sold some time before 1755.

BIBLIOGRAPHY

Mariette
E. Goncourt and J. Goncourt: *Les Portraits intimes du XVIIIe siècle* (Paris, 1857)
G. Wildenstein: *Le Peintre Aved, sa vie, son oeuvre*, 2 vols (Paris, 1922)
——: 'Premier supplément à la biographie et au catalogue d'Aved', *Gaz. B.-A.*, n. s. 5, xiii (1935), pp. 159–72
Chardin, 1699–1779 (exh. cat., ed. P. Rosenberg; Paris, Grand Pal.; Cleveland, OH, Mus. A.; Boston, MA, Mus. F.A.; 1979)
M. Lespes: 'Catalogue des oeuvres du peintre Jacques Aved' (diss., U. Montpellier, 1985)
——: *Jacques Aved et le portrait parisien au XVIIIe siècle* (diss., U. Paris; in preparation)

MICHELLE LESPES

Avedon, Richard (*b* New York, 15 May 1923). American photographer. He studied philosophy at Columbia University, New York (1941–2), and from 1942 to 1944 served in the photography department of the US Merchant Marine, taking identity photographs of servicemen. He then studied photography under Alexey Brodovitch at the New School for Social Research, New York, from 1944 to 1950; from 1945 to 1965 he worked under Brodovitch and Carmel Snow for *Harper's Bazaar*, contributing fashion photographs. As a young boy he had seen various fashion magazines and had been particularly impressed by the photographs of Martin Munkacsi. This influence remained in evidence in his own fashion work for *Harper's Bazaar*, since he, too, photographed the models outside and in motion in order to arrive at dramatic, sometimes blurred, images. From 1950 he also contributed photographs to *Life*, *Look* and *Graphis* and in 1952 became Staff Editor and photographer for *Theatre Arts*. Towards the end of the 1950s he became dissatisfied with daylight photography and open air locations and so turned to studio photography, using strobe lighting. In 1965 he left *Harper's Bazaar* to work for *Vogue* under Diana Vreeland and Alexander Liberman. Avedon presented fashion photography as theatre, and his innovative style greatly influenced other photographers; his work of the 1960s hinted at the energy and sexual explicitness of the period.

Concurrent with his commercial assignments, Avedon produced portrait photographs of both celebrities and ordinary Americans. In his book *Nothing Personal* (1964), which includes portraits of figures such as the philosopher Bertrand Russell together with images of prisoners, the mentally ill and the poor, he created a disturbingly contrasting picture of society. In 1976 he photographed American businessmen and political leaders for a portfolio in *Rolling Stone*. His portraits, made with a view camera and often printed larger than life, are stark images with plain white backdrops, with the sitter generally looking directly at the camera. The unflinching quality of such works is especially evident in a series of portraits of his dying father exhibited in 1974 at the Museum of Modern Art in New York. He adapted this style for *In the American West*, a series of portraits produced from 1979 to 1984 for the Amon Carter Museum in Fort Worth, TX. The harsh realism of these portraits of miners, oil workers and slaughter house workers provides a powerful, if bleak, record of working life in the region. A major retrospective exhibition of Avedon's photographs was mounted in 1994 at the Whitney Museum of American Art in New York.

PHOTOGRAPHIC PUBLICATIONS

Nothing Personal, text J. Baldwin (New York, 1964)
Portraits, text H. Rosenberg (New York, 1976)
'The Family', text R. Adler, *Rolling Stone*, 224 (21 Oct 1976), pp. 50–97
Photographs, 1947–1977, text H. Brodkey (New York and Toronto, 1978)
In the American West: 1979–1984, text L. Wilson (New York, 1985)
An Autobiography: Richard Avedon (New York, 1993)
Evidence, 1944–1994: Richard Avedon, text by J. Livingston and A. Gopnik (New York, 1994)

BIBLIOGRAPHY

Avedon (exh. cat. by A. Clarke and C. Hartwell, Minneapolis, MN, Inst. A., 1970)
C. Beaton and G. Buckland: *The Magic Image: The Genius of Photography from 1839 to the Present Day* (London and Boston, 1975)
Avedon: Retrospective, 1946–1980 (exh. cat. by D. Ross, Berkeley, U. CA, A. Mus., 1980)

MARTHA A. SANDWEISS

Avelar, Francisco Gomes do. *See* GOMES DO AVELAR, FRANCISCO.

Avelar Rebelo, José de (*fl* 1634; *d* 1657). Portuguese painter. He was trained with a new generation of artists whose work shows naturalistic and tenebrist tendencies. He was a personal friend of the Duque de Bragança, the future John IV, who became king at the restoration of the Crown in 1640 and who made Avelar Rebelo a Knight of Aviz and his court painter (*pintor régio*). He was in favour in cultural circles at court and painted the frescoes of the *Triumph of Music* and the *Song of Songs* in the music-room (*c.* 1635; *in situ*) in the palace at Vila Viçosa, and three good portraits of *King John IV*, one of which (Vila Viçosa, Ducal Pal.) is signed and dated 1643 and shows his skill in depicting the state image. From 1639 to 1648, the years when he was considered the outstanding painter in Lisbon, he worked on 72 canvases for the ceiling of the church of the Mártires there (destr. 1755). He painted the excellent and strongly naturalistic *St Jerome* (*c.* 1640) for the library (now refectory) of the Jerónimos Monastery, Belém, a painting with warm colours and free modelling that is notable for the splendid still-life detail of such items as shelves, half-open books and a skull, all seen against the light. The altarpiece *Christ among the Doctors* (*c.* 1635; Lisbon, Mus. S Roque), influenced by Vicente Carducho and other naturalistic painters in Madrid, was praised by the critic Conde Athanasius Raczyńsky (1846). About 1650 Rebelo painted the retable in the chapel of Nossa Senhora dos Mártires in the parish church of Pias (Ferreira do Zêzere), commissioned in 1650 by Captain Manuel Ferreira, a former member of the conspiracy that had brought about the restoration of the Portuguese monarchy and independence from Spain. In addition to a warm and vigorous *Coronation of the Virgin*, this includes an interesting historical work, the *Conquest of Lisbon by Dom Afonso Henriques*, which is explicitly anti-Castilian and thus something of a polemical and nationalist work. A late painting is the *Rest on the Flight into Egypt* (Lisbon, Dr F. Castelo-Branco priv. col.), signed and dated 1643. In spite of the admiration and friendship he enjoyed both at court and in erudite circles, as well as in the Dominican community, Rebelo died in poverty, in lodgings near the Dominican convent at Benfica.

BIBLIOGRAPHY

Félix da Costa Meesen: *Antiguidade da arte da pintura* (MS; 1696); ed. G. Kubler (New Haven and London, 1967)

A. Raczyński: *Les Arts en Portugal* (Lisbon, 1846), p. 289

F. M. de Sousa Viterbo: *Notícia de alguns pintores portugueses*, iii (Coimbra, 1911), pp. 44–59

G. de Matos Sequeira: 'Um quadro da conquista de Lisboa aos Mouros', *Rev. Mun.*, xlii (1948), pp. 61–3

V. Serrão: 'Contributos para o estudo da pintura proto-barroca em Portugal', *Actas do IV simpósio luso-espanhol de história de arte: Coimbra, 1987*

VITOR SERRÃO

Aveline. French family of draughtsmen and engravers.

(1) Pierre Aveline (i) (*b* Paris, *c.* 1656; *d* Paris, 23 May 1722). He was also a print-publisher and print-seller. He probably trained with Adam Pérelle and, like him, specialized in topographical representations. He engraved in suites many views of Paris and of provincial, European and African cities, mixing etching and burin work in a style that was often rather unpolished. In 1685 he obtained a royal licence for ten years, authorizing him to reproduce 'le profil des maisons royales'; he then published views of *Versailles* (Weigert, nos 198–293). He also engraved and published some fashionable images, such as *Child of Good Family Walking with his Governess* (W 388). Among the 412 items that comprise his oeuvre, there are only two portraits and two prints of historical subjects. Also attributed to him are some engravings of designs for theatre and ballet scenery after Giacomo Torelli, Niccolò Enea Bartolini and C. Carpoli; they are signed *Aveline fecit.*

BIBLIOGRAPHY

R.-A. Weigert: *Inventaire du fonds français: Graveurs du dix-septième siècle*, Paris, Bib. N., Cab. Est. cat., i (Paris, 1939), pp. 241–59 [W]

M. Préaud, P. Casselle, N. Grivel and C. Le Bitouzé: *Dictionnaire des éditeurs d'estampes à Paris sous l'Ancien Régime* (Paris, 1987), pp. 37–8

(2) Pierre(-Alexandre) Aveline (ii) (*b* Paris, 1702; *d* 1760). Son of (1) Pierre Aveline (i). He was a student of Jean-Baptiste de Poilly. His oeuvre consists of 123 prints, most of them published by Gabriel Huquier. He worked with the burin on a previously etched base; usually he signed himself P. AVELINE, but he used the monogram P.A. on small-scale works. He was well known but, according to Michael Huber's *Notices des graveurs divisés par nations . . .* (Dresden and Leipzig, 1787), could have enjoyed a greater reputation if he had not 'spent part of his life in engraving merely sketches, and if he had been more discerning in his choice of subjects'. In 1737 he was approved (*agréé*) by the Académie Royale but was struck off in 1742, not having finished the portraits of *Louis Galloche* and *Jean-François De Troy* that had been set as his *morceaux de réception.* In 1753 he was once more approved but was never received (*reçu*) as an academician. He engraved many compositions after François Boucher, such as the *Bird-snare* (Roux, no. 35), the *Good Fortune* (R 34) and *Venus and Cupid* (R 90), and he finished the *Andromeda* that Boucher had begun. He also reproduced some of Charles-Joseph Natoire's paintings, including the *Four Elements* (R 61–5), and engraved the *Anatomies* and a *Livre d'enfants* (R 40–45) after Edme Bouchardon. He is best known for his reproductions of works by Antoine Watteau, including *L'Amante inquiète* (R 5), the *Récréation italienne* (R 16), the *Rape of Europa* (R 8) and especially *L'Enseigne de Gersaint* (R 14). He also supplied portraits, illustrations and many ornaments for books. He participated in two great printmaking enterprises: the engraving of Charles Le Brun's *Galerie de Versailles* (R 98–101) after designs by Jean-Baptiste Massé, and the *Fables* of Jean de La Fontaine (1755–9) after Jean-Baptiste Oudry.

BIBLIOGRAPHY

M. Roux: *Inventaire du fonds français: Graveurs du dix-huitième siècle*, Paris, Bib. N., Cab. Est. cat., i (Paris, 1931), pp. 309–38 [R]

VÉRONIQUE MEYER

Avellaneda y Haro. *See* CARPIO, Marqueses del.

Avelli, Francesco Xanto (*b* Rovigo, ?1486–7; *d* ?1542). Italian maiolica painter. More is known about Avelli than any other maiolica painter because of his many signed works and the autobiographical details included in his sonnets in honour of Francesco Maria I della Rovere, Duke of Urbino. Avelli considered himself to be not only an artist but also a poet and courtier. His intellectual abilities set him apart from his colleagues, even if as a painter he was not the most talented. He seems never to have directed his own workshop, but he is known to have worked in Urbino from 1530, the year of his first unequivocally signed and dated plate; some pieces from the 1520s signed F.R. and F.L.R. may also be ascribed to him. His familiarity with Classical and contemporary literature is evident in his choice of secular and religious subjects, taken from such authors as Virgil and Ovid, Ariosto and Petrarch (e.g. plate, 1531; London, BM). He also depicted contemporary events, sometimes in allegorical form, for example the Sack of Rome (1527). His style is characterized by a strong sense of line, an interest in anatomy and architecture and the use of a broad and usually harmonious palette that sometimes included iridescent lustres. His imaginative compositions frequently relied on a montage technique in which he juxtaposed figures drawn from prints, occasionally borrowing an entire scene from one graphic source. Several of his commissions were for important services, among them one for a member of the Pucci family of Florence.

BIBLIOGRAPHY

Atti del convegno internazionale di studi, Francesco Xanto Avelli da Rovigo: Rovigo, 1980
F. Cioci: *Xanto e il Duca di Urbino* (Milan, 1987)
T. Wilson: *Ceramic Art of the Italian Renaissance* (London, 1987)

WENDY M. WATSON

Aventicum [now Avenches, Switzerland]. Roman site, 17 km south-west of Berne, which flourished in the 2nd century AD. The town was founded *c.* 8 BC as the administrative centre of the *civitas Helvetiorum* and was elevated to the status of *colonia* during the Civil War of AD 69–70. It had suffered near total abandonment by the late 3rd century, although occupation may have continued in the vicinity of the existing medieval and modern town. The layout of the town—a good example of urban planning of the early Imperial period—is on a grid plan on a module of 75×110 m, with a central forum and baths, and a religious complex on the south side of the gridded area. The surrounding walls are 5.7 km in length, enclosing an area twice the size of the town. The reason for the disparity is not known: perhaps it represents an over-ambitious allowance for expansion, or perhaps the length of the walls was a symbol of civic pride. The most notable architectural feature is the temple building that includes the well-known standing column called Le Cigognier. The column forms one of the sides of the temple's pronaos, which was probably of Classical, not Romano-Celtic, form, to judge from the excavated plan. The temple faces the town's theatre across an expansive temenos, in a single ensemble dated to the 2nd century AD. Near the temple is a smaller shrine called La Grange du Dîme. Its exact nature is disputed, with some commentators interpreting it as a Classical-style temple to Jupiter Ammon, while others prefer a Romano-Celtic cult and temple layout. The decorative sculpture suggests the former and the plan the latter explanation. Adjacent to these two religious buildings is the amphitheatre, of typical size and form, with an additional courtyard of semi-elliptical shape focusing on the entrance to the arena on the east side.

Notable among the objects found in the town is the gold bust (Lausanne, Pal. Rumine), presumed to be of Marcus Aurelius, but possibly of Julian the Apostate. It depicts a bearded, cuirassed emperor, with hair and details in the style of the mid- to late 2nd century AD. It is 335 mm high and weighs 1.59 kg, a remarkable testimony to the wealth that a provincial Gallo-Roman town could amass.

BIBLIOGRAPHY

Bull. Aventico, i (194?–) [journal devoted to the site]
M. Verzàr: *Aventicum II: Un temple du culte impérial*, Cahiers d'Archéologie Romande, xii (Lausanne, 1977)
J. Balty: 'Le Prétendu Marc Aurèle d'Avenches', *Eikones, Festschrift H. Jucker* (Berne, 1980), pp. 57–63 [see reply by H. Jucker in *Bull. Aventico*, xxvi (1981), pp. 5–36]
P. Bridel: *Aventicum III: Le Sanctuaire du Cigognier*, 2 vols, Cahiers d'Archéologie Romande, xxii (Lausanne, 1982)
H. Bögli: *Aventicum: La Ville romaine et le musée* (Avenches, 1984) [site guidebook]
R. Etienne: 'Un Complexe monumental du culte impérial à Avenches', *Bull. Assoc. Pro Aventico*, xxix (1989), pp. 5–26
M. Bossert and M. Fuchs: 'De l'ancien sur le forum d'Avenches', *Bull. Assoc. Pro Aventico*, xxxi (1989), pp. 12–105

ANTHONY KING

Avercamp. Dutch family of painters and draughtsmen.

(1) Hendrick (Barentsz.) Avercamp [de Stomme van Kampen] (*bapt* Amsterdam, 27 Jan 1585; *bur* Kampen, 15 May 1634). He was the first artist in the northern Netherlands to paint winter landscapes. Before him only a few Flemish artists, among them Pieter Bruegel I and his sons, and Jacob Grimmer, had made winter scenery the main subject of their work. Avercamp created a new genre of Dutch painting by combining the panoramic scope, bright colours and high vantage point of these Flemish models with an emphasis on anecdotal detail.

1. LIFE AND WORK.

(i) Paintings. In 1586 the Avercamp family moved to Kampen, where Hendrick's father had been appointed a pharmacist. Hendrick was deaf-mute from birth, and throughout his life was commonly known by his nickname 'de Stom', or 'de Stomme' (Dut.: 'the mute'). It is generally assumed that he was a pupil of the history and portrait painter Pieter Isaacsz., in whose house in Amsterdam he was presumably living in 1607. This is inferred from a reference to 'the mute [who lives] at Pieter Isacqs's', documented as one of the buyers at a sale on 3 March 1607. During this period of training in Amsterdam Avercamp must have come across the work of Flemish landscape painters, including Hans Bol, Gillis van Coninxloo and David Vinckboons, who had fled to Amsterdam when Antwerp once again fell to the Spanish in 1585. He may have seen some of their drawings and paintings, but in any case was familiar with engravings made after their work. The high horizon and the use of trees and houses as devices to balance the composition in early works, for example the *Winter Landscape* of 1608 (Bergen, Billedgal.), clearly reveal their influence. In the *Winter Landscape* of 1609 (ex-Col. Thyssen-Bornemisza, Lugano) the horizon is much lower, and the composition is simpler with fewer details. Although the interval between the two pictures was only a year, the difference between them is considerable, leading some scholars (e.g. Blankert) to assert that Avercamp underwent a very rapid development in this period, while others (e.g. Stechow) have used these two works as evidence of the difficulty of establishing a chronology within Avercamp's oeuvre.

There are only a few reliably dated pictures after 1609, but it seems clear that in the later works the Flemish influence becomes less noticeable; the horizon tends to be lower, the perspective is suggested in a more natural way and the figures are grouped together more coherently. A good late example is the multi-figured *Winter Landscape with a Brewery* (*c.* 1615; London, N.G.; see fig. 1). In this work the horizon is low, and the colours suggest the

1. Hendrick Avercamp: *Winter Landscape with a Brewery*, oil on panel, 580×898 mm, *c.* 1615 (London, National Gallery)

wintry atmosphere remarkably well. A characteristic of Hendrick Avercamp's paintings is that the figures are the centre of attention; although usually numerous, they are skilfully arranged. Hendrick was a sharp observer of people, capturing their pose, dress, status and occupation. Once he had determined the details of a particular figure, or group of figures, they entered his repertory and were repeated often in both his paintings and his drawings. Although Hendrick is best known for his winter scenes, he also painted a number of summer landscapes, such as *River Landscape* (Enschede, Mrs van Heek-van Hoorn priv. col.), which has a fortress at the left and various boats on the river, but remarkably few figures. According to Kampen's city records, Hendrick Avercamp was paid in 1622 for painting two horses in the municipal stables, one of the few occasions on which he is mentioned in official documents. He probably lived in retreat because of his disability.

(ii) Drawings. Hendrick Avercamp was a prolific draughtsman. Some of his drawings are figure studies for paintings, such as the *Standing Gentleman in a High-crowned Hat* (see fig. 2), one of the many examples of Avercamp's work at the Royal Library, Windsor Castle, Berks. Others, for example *Winter Landscape* (Haarlem, Teylers Mus.), are as fully worked out and richly detailed as his paintings and were probably intended for sale. Most of these drawings were executed in Hendrick's preferred technique of pen and watercolour.

In contrast to the paintings, there is a considerable number of extant drawings dating from after 1609. In 1612 Claes Jansz. Visscher I made six engravings after drawings by Hendrick Avercamp showing summer landscapes strongly reminiscent of the Flemish countryside, but with Classical ruins. The drawings for these engravings may have been made before 1612 (Blankert). It seems that Hendrick Avercamp returned to Kampen no later than 1613, as can be deduced from an inscription on his *Oval River Landscape with Old Buildings* (Paris, Fond. Custodia, Inst. Néer.). Written in an old hand, probably that of the purchaser at the time, it states that the drawing was bought on 28 January 1613 from Hendrick Avercamp in Kampen. The drawing, showing a summer landscape, is very close to the engravings by Visscher and was possibly made in 1612 or earlier. Later drawings include a sheet that has always been thought to represent *The IJ in Winter* but is probably actually a view of Kampen (1620; Amsterdam, Rijksmus.) and *Water Landscape* (1624; Amsterdam, Rijksmus.).

It is generally assumed that Hendrick passed most of his life in Kampen, although he was long thought to have undertaken a journey to the Mediterranean. This assumption was based on a number of drawings, formerly attributed to him, of southern landscapes, resembling his early drawings of Flemish landscapes with Classical ruins. Welcker convincingly reattributed these to Gerrit van der Horst (1581/2–1629), a wine merchant who lived in Kampen from 1609. In 1610 Claes Jansz. Visscher made an engraving after one of these drawings.

2. Critical reception and posthumous reputation. During his life Hendrick Avercamp's paintings

2. Hendrick Avercamp: *Standing Gentleman in a High-crowned Hat*, pen and black ink with watercolours on brownish paper, 115×50 mm (Windsor, Windsor Castle, Royal Library)

were already much sought after and commanded high prices. Before Welcker's archival research, which established when Hendrick was buried, he was believed to have died at a much later date, and such paintings as the *View of Kampen* (1663) were thought to be by him. The weaker quality of this work and a small number of others was credited to Avercamp's increasing age and inability to keep up the high standards of the earlier work. As Hendrick signed his work with the monogram HA, Welcker concluded that the paintings bearing the signature 'Avercamp' or 'B. Avercamp' and/or those dated after 1634 should be attributed to his nephew (2) Barent Avercamp. Paintings by artists such as Arent Arentsz. (nicknamed 'Cabel'; 1585–before Oct 1635), Adam van Breen (*fl* 1611–29) and Anthonie Verstralen (1593/4–1641) all resemble, to a greater or lesser extent, the works of Hendrick Avercamp. Little is known about these painters, their oeuvre and their relationship with Hendrick Avercamp, and undoubtedly there are still paintings by them, as well as by Barent, among the works presently ascribed to him.

(2) Barent Avercamp (*b* Kampen, 1612/13; *bur* Kampen, 24 Oct 1679). Nephew of (1) Hendrick Avercamp. Barent Avercamp lived in Kampen for most of his life but spent extended periods in Zwolle (?1615–26) and Zutphen (?1640–50). He probably learnt how to paint from his uncle. He held many public positions, notably one in the Guild of St Luke, Kampen, and worked in various other capacities, including as a lumber merchant. For a long time, though his artistic activities were known from archival documents, his paintings were generally attributed to his uncle. A small group was ascribed to Barent Avercamp in the early 1920s by Welcker, who proposed that paintings dated after 1634 or signed 'Avercamp' or 'B. Avercamp' should be attributed to Barent instead of to Hendrick Avercamp.

Barent was less talented than his uncle. His figures, on occasion borrowed from his uncle's paintings, are sometimes wooden and often rather arbitrarily arranged. The transition from foreground to background is more abrupt and effected by rather obvious devices (e.g. a bank in the foreground). Another characteristic of his work is that some of the figures wear clothes that came into fashion *c.* 1650. His paintings frequently show people playing an outdoor game called 'kolf' wearing big hats, flat collars (usually tasselled) and boots with large flaps, for example *Fun on the Ice near Kampen* (1654; Atlanta, GA, High Mus. A.). One of his best-known paintings is the large *Winter Landscape near Kampen* (1663; Kampen, Stadhuis). There are only two drawings that can be attributed to Barent Avercamp with certainty, *Fishermen Pulling in Nets* (1654; Hamburg, Ksthalle) and *Two Married Couples* (1650; sold London, Sotheby's, 27 June 1974, lot 120).

BIBLIOGRAPHY

C. J. Welcker: *Hendrick Avercamp, 1585–1634, bijgenaamd 'de Stomme van Campen' en Barent Avercamp, 1612–1679: 'Schilders tot Kampen'* [Hendrick Avercamp, 1585–1634, nicknamed 'the mute from Kampen' and Barent Avercamp, 1612–1679: 'Painters in Kampen'] (Zwolle, 1933, rev. 1979)

W. Stechow: *Dutch Landscape Painting of the Seventeenth Century* (London, 1966), pp. 5, 82–7

A. Blankert: 'Hendrick Avercamp', *Frozen Silence* (exh. cat., Amsterdam, Waterman Gal., 1982), pp. 15–36

D. B. Hensbroek-van der Poel: 'Barent Avercamp (1612–79)', *Frozen Silence* (exh. cat., Amsterdam, Waterman Gal., 1982), pp. 57–62

D. B. HENSBROEK-VAN DER POEL

Averlino, Antonio di Pietro. *See* FILARETE.

Avery, Milton (*b* Altmar, NY, 7 March 1893; *d* New York, 3 Jan 1965). American painter and printmaker. He spent his childhood in Hartford, CT, where he remained until 1925, attending art school from 1911 to 1919 and thereafter painting in the surrounding countryside. His

Milton Avery: *Dunes and Sea No. 2*, oil on canvas, 1.32×1.82 m, 1960 (New York, Whitney Museum of American Art)

works from this period are characterized by shiny, enamel-like surfaces, created by applying colours with brushes and a palette knife and blending them with his fingers. After moving to New York in 1925 and his marriage, he replaced the light-drenched palette of his Hartford paintings with sombre tones. He also stopped using an impastoed, palette-knife technique and began to brush pigment on to his canvases in thin layers. His figurative and genre subjects resembled those of the realists, but his technique of dispensing with illusionistically modelled shapes in favour of simplified forms and flat colours derived from European artists such as Matisse and Picasso (e.g. *Harbour at Night*, 1932; Washington, DC, Phillips Col.). During the 1930s, this simplification of form, coupled with Avery's luminous colour harmonies, provided a model for a group of younger artists including Adolph Gottlieb and Mark Rothko. He also had the support of the Valentine Gallery from 1935 to 1943 and of the Paul Rosenberg Gallery from 1943 to 1950.

In 1944 Avery precipitously abandoned the anecdotal detailing and brushy paint application of his earlier endeavours for dense, more evenly modulated areas of flattened colour contained within crisply delineated forms (e.g. *Pink Tablecloth*, 1944; Utica, NY, Munson–Williams–Proctor Inst.). This mature style was heralded by a one-man exhibition at the Phillips Memorial Gallery in Washington, DC, in 1944. In June 1949 he suffered a major heart attack. While recuperating in Florida in autumn 1950 he began making monotypes, for example *Leaves* (1951; see Johnson, no. 41). Over the next two years he produced nearly 200 prints.

Avery's paintings underwent a subtle shift following his heart attack: quieter, more muted colour harmonies replaced the vibrant hues of earlier work, while thin washes of paint, applied one over another, created veiled, slightly mottled fields of colour. A further reduction of compositional elements and heightened colour effects occurred when Avery enlarged his paintings in summer 1957 while in Provincetown on Cape Cod. By mottling his colour and tinting his paint with white pigment, he created shimmering rhythms of colour that were simultaneously opulent and pastel. In paintings such as *Dunes and Sea No. 2* (1960; New York, Whitney; see fig.) he pushed towards the farthest limits of pure abstraction without abandoning his commitment to working from nature. Serenity and harmony had prevailed in all of Avery's work. Yet this work, more than ever, exuded a world of low-key emotions from which anger and anxiety were absent. These large canvases, perhaps because of their greater parity between abstract and recognizable shapes, elicited an enthusiastic critical response. As Avery's reputation began to grow, however, his physical condition worsened to the extent that he could not attend the opening of his retrospective at the Whitney Museum of American Art, New York, in 1960. In autumn 1961 he had a second heart attack from which he never fully recovered.

BIBLIOGRAPHY

Milton Avery (exh. cat., New York, Whitney, 1960)
U. E. Johnson: *Milton Avery: Prints and Drawings, 1930–1964*, essay by M. Rothko (New York, 1966)
Milton Avery (exh. cat., Washington, DC, Smithsonian Inst.; New York, Brooklyn Mus.; Columbus, OH, U. Gal. F.A.; 1970)
B. L. Grad: *Milton Avery*, foreword by S. Michel Avery (Strathcona, 1981)
M. Price: *Milton Avery* (in preparation)

BARBARA HASKELL

Avery, Samuel P(utnam) (*b* New York, 17 March 1822; *d* New York, 11 Aug 1904). American wood-engraver, art dealer, collector and philanthropist. His career as a wood-engraver and his involvement with the New York publishing trade began in the early 1840s. He worked for, among others, *Appleton's*, the *New York Herald* and *Harper's* and produced illustrations for trade cards, religious tracts, adventure stories and children's books. By the early 1850s Avery had begun compiling humorous books and commissioning drawings from such artist-illustrators as Felix Octavius Carr Darley, John Whetten Ehninger, Augustus Hoppin (1827–96), Tompkins Harrison Matteson and John McLenan (1827–66). His business contacts led to close relationships with such artists as Frederick Church, John F. Kensett and William Trost Richards.

By the late 1850s Avery had begun to collect drawings and small cabinet pictures by local artists. Other art collectors, notably William T. Walters, asked Avery's advice when commissioning works of art. In 1864 he turned his engraving practice over to Isaac Pesoa, his former apprentice, and became one of the first art dealers in the USA (*see* UNITED STATES OF AMERICA, §XIII). In 1867 Avery was appointed commissioner for the American section at the Exposition Universelle in Paris. Before leaving New York he liquidated his collection in order to buy works of art abroad. With the assistance of GEORGE A. LUCAS, Avery commissioned paintings from such artists as William-Adolphe Bouguereau, Jules Breton, Jean-Léon Gérome and Ernest Meissonier. He made annual buying trips to Europe during the 1870s; his diaries provide insight into the European art market and record information about contemporary Dutch, English, French and German artists. Avery auctioned his acquisitions in New York, although some works were selected for specific collectors, such as William Henry Vanderbilt. Avery's opinions were central in forming the Metropolitan Museum of Art in New York, of which he was a founder in 1872 and a lifelong trustee, and to which he donated some of his American pictures.

Avery bought books with exceptional bindings, and he encouraged contemporary designers by commissioning examples of their craftsmanship. He was instrumental in establishing a separate print room at the New York Public Library in December 1899, presenting it in 1900 with a gift of over 19,000 prints.

Avery remained active in numerous art societies. His son, Samuel P. Avery jr (1847–1920), assisted in his gallery, resumed the business in 1888 and left his collections mainly to the Brooklyn Museum, New York, and the Wadsworth Atheneum, Hartford, CT, where the Avery Wing was opened in 1934. Another son, Henry Ogden Avery (1852–90), studied at the Ecole des Beaux-Arts in Paris (1872–9) and worked as an architect. In 1887 he designed some exhibition rooms and a gallery in New York for his brother. Avery sr endowed the Avery Architectural Library at Columbia University, New York, in memory of Henry, bequeathing it part of his book collection.

WRITINGS

The Diaries 1871–1882 of Samuel P. Avery, Art Dealer, ed. M. Fidell-Beaufort, H. L. Kleinfield and J. K. Welcher (New York, 1979)

BIBLIOGRAPHY

R. Sieben-Morgan: *Samuel Putnam Avery (1822–1904), Engraver on Wood: A Bio-bibliographical Study* (MLS diss., New York, Columbia U., 1940, additions 1942)
M. Fidell-Beaufort: 'Whistling at one's Ruskins', *Confrontation* (Spring–Summer, 1979), pp. 58–63
——: 'Jules Breton in America: Collecting in the 19th Century', *Jules Breton and the French Rural Tradition* (exh. cat., Omaha, Joslyn A. Mus., 1982), pp. 51–61
M. Fidell-Beaufort and J. K. Welcher: 'Some Views of Art Buying in New York in the 1870s and 1880s', *Oxford A. J.*, v/1 (1982), pp. 48–55

MADELEINE FIDELL-BEAUFORT

Avetisyan, Minas (*b* Djadjur, Akhuryan district, 20 July 1928; *d* Erevan, 24 Feb 1975). Armenian painter and stage designer. He studied at the Institute of Theatre and Art in Erevan (1952–4), as well as at the Repin Institute of Painting, Sculpture and Architecture in Leningrad (now St Petersburg) from 1954 to 1960. He benefited from the advice of the Armenian painter, Martiros Saryan, but developed a style of his own, with an intense use of colour similar to that of Fauvism. The influence of Armenian medieval art is strongly apparent in his landscapes, self-portraits and scenes of peasant life, for example *Baking Lavash* (1972; Erevan, Pict. Gal. Armenia). His work combines an uncommon and expressive richness of colour with a dramatic monumentality of composition. He had a one-man show in Erevan in 1962 and another in Moscow in 1969. In 1972 his studio was burnt down and a large number of his canvases destroyed. He was also a stage designer, producing designs, for example, for sets for Aram Khachaturian's ballet *Gayane* at the A. Spendiarov Academic Theatre of Opera and Ballet in Erevan (1974; Erevan, Pict. Gal. Armenia), and a monumental painter (e.g. the painting for the vestibule of the Erevan Mechanical Engineering Technical School, 1974). A museum devoted to Avetisyan was established in Djadjur, after his death in a car accident.

BIBLIOGRAPHY

G. Igityan: *Minas Avetisyan* (Leningrad, 1975) [Eng. and Rus. text]
S. Kaplanova: *Minas Avetisyan: Grafika* [Minas Avetisyan: graphic works] (Moscow, 1987)

M. N. SOKOLOV

Aviano, Girolamo di Bartolomeo Strazzarolo da. *See under* GIROLAMO DA TREVISO (i).

Avignon. Capital city of the Vaucluse département, France. It was the seat of the papacy from 1309 to 1378.

1. History and urban development. 2. Art life and organization. 3. Buildings.

1. HISTORY AND URBAN DEVELOPMENT. Avignon is an ancient city situated on a cliff, the Rocher-des-Doms, on the east bank of the River Rhône overlooking the delta. The site first attracted settlers about 4000 BC. It became an important village for the Gallic tribe of Cavares, and

1. Avignon and the Palais des Papes; from a drawing by Father Martellange, early 17th century (Paris, Bibliothèque Nationale)

by the 1st century BC it was named Avennio, meaning either 'river city' or 'violent wind' (from the frequent mistral winds). At this time it was taken by the Romans, and by Hadrian's reign (AD 117–38) 'Avenionsis' had earned the title *Civitas Romana.* In the 3rd century a priest named Rufus founded the first Christian community just outside the city walls; the first Jewish community was established at about the same time. During the early Middle Ages Avignon's strategic position made it the target of invasions by Visigoths, Muslims and others; the resulting Spanish and Arab influences have played a formative role in the literary and artistic culture of Provence. By the 10th century Avignon was part of the Holy Roman Empire; after the era of invasions ended, Avignon (and Provence in general) flourished as a major trade centre, especially during the 12th century. After the commune was established in 1129, Avignon flourished as an autonomous republic nominally under the Counts of Toulouse.

There are few traces of pre-Romanesque Avignon. The Roman settlement has left only a few fragments of sculpture (Avignon, Mus. Lapidaire), and reminders of the city's early Christian and Carolingian history are almost non-existent. Surviving monuments date from the late 12th century onwards. The most famous is probably the Saint-Bénézet bridge, commemorated in the song, *Sous le Pont d'Avignon* (not *Sur le pont* as is often thought: the bridge was too narrow for dancing on in a ring—'tous en rond'—and the dancing therefore took place on the island in midstream). The legendary shepherd boy Bénézet led the construction of the first bridge over the Rhône from 1177 to 1185, with the St Nicolas chapel (now 16th century) placed midway across. Although the bridge was damaged many times and finally abandoned in the late 17th century, four of the original 22 arches survive. An almost contemporary monument is the cathedral, Notre-Dame-des-Doms (*see* §3(i) below), standing at the summit of the Rocher-des-Doms. In the 13th century, during the crusade against the Cathar (or Albigensian) heretics, Avignon withstood a long siege by Louis VIII (*reg* 1223–6); it surrendered in 1226 and its walls were destroyed. In 1251 Avignon was subjected to the Kingdom of Sicily and Naples.

Avignon reached the apogee of its history when it became the seat of the papacy in the 14th century. The quarrel between Pope Boniface VIII (*reg* 1294–1303) and Philip IV of France culminated in a brutal attack on the Pope and his subsequent death. In 1309 the French Pope Clement V, fearing the political turmoil and family wars in Rome, transferred the papal court to the Dominican friary in Avignon, a friendly neighbour of the Papal States. His successors remained in Avignon until 1378, and it became the cultural capital of western Christendom. The neighbouring town of VILLENEUVE-LÈS-AVIGNON, founded (1293) by Philip IV on the west bank of the River Rhône, also flourished during this period. In Avignon Benedict XII and Clement VI built and decorated the enormous Palais des Papes (*see* §3(ii) below), which dominates the city to this day (see fig. 1). In 1348 Clement VI purchased the city from Queen Joanna of Naples (*reg* 1343–82), and Innocent VI (*reg* 1352–62) rebuilt the city walls and erected many churches, convents and residences. Both secular and ecclesiastical architecture flourished in the city during the 14th century. Many cardinals built impressive palaces, which were opulently furnished and decorated. Churches built during this period include St Agricol (begun 1320), St Didier (1325) and St Pierre (1358).

Although Gregory IX (*reg* 1370–78) returned to Rome in 1377 the election of a new pope in 1378 induced a papal schism, and the anti-pope, Clement VII (*reg* 1378–94), who had been strongly supported by French cardinals, returned to Avignon, which was the residence of claimants to the papal see for the next 30 years. Even after the Great Schism was resolved in 1415, Avignon remained a papal city, directly governed by papal legates. Although much of the patronage of cardinals and pilgrims went to Rome when the papacy officially returned there, Avignon contains some important commissions from the late 14th century. The church of St Martial, with the tomb of *Cardinal Jean de La Grange* (destr. Revolution; fragments, Avignon, Mus. Lapidaire), was built from 1396 to 1402. It may be the product of the workshop of Pierre Morel (*see* MOREL, (1)), who was responsible for the Celestine Church (1395–1402). In fully Flamboyant style, with interior sculpture, fine mouldings and vaulting and curvilinear tracery patterns, the church is in contrast to the earlier style of buildings in Avignon, characterized by large areas of plain wall and tall, narrow windows.

Avignon's role as an artistic centre faded after the 15th century, but as a papal city it continued to attract architectural patrons. During the pontificate of Julius II, who had been a governing vice-legate, the Palais des Papes was renovated, and a new façade was built for the archbishop's palace (now the Musée du Petit Palais). Several aristocratic residences dating from the Baroque era have survived and have been turned into public institutions: the Musée Calvet and the Médiathèque Ceccano (municipal library) were once palatial homes, and the Musée Lapidaire occupies the 17th-century Jesuit College chapel. Other early 17th-century buildings include the former Mint and the Hôtel de Berton de Crillon.

Although Avignon was incorporated into the Papal States it maintained close relations with France from the 16th century to the 18th, and was even temporarily annexed three times during the reigns of Louis XIV and Louis XV. Its social and political development followed closely that of France; the French Revolution was greeted enthusiastically by many citizens but with notably less ardour by the Church. On 14 September 1791 the French Assembly voted to annex the city permanently, and the papal representatives were forcibly removed from the palace.

In the 19th century the Avignonese became aware of their special history. The *Félibrigistes*, led by the poet Frédéric Mistral (1830–1914), attempted to revive the Provençal language and draw attention to the richness of Provençal history. Travellers such as Stendhal, Prosper Mérimée (1803–70) and Charles Dickens visited the city and decried the deterioration of its monuments. This led to extensive renovation of the main buildings. Modern Avignon retains much of its medieval atmosphere: the 14th-century walls still surround the old city, and many old buildings have been preserved along the narrow, winding streets. Avignon is now a major French tourist and commercial centre, and it has pursued an energetic policy of conserving its medieval heritage.

2. ART LIFE AND ORGANIZATION. Painting in particular thrived in Avignon, but after the establishment there of the papal court in 1309, patrons such as Cardinal Giacomo Gaetani Stefaneschi brought goldsmiths, tapestry weavers and sculptors as well as painters from Italy. The most celebrated painter was SIMONE MARTINI, who spent his last years in Avignon. In addition to his work in Notre-Dame-des-Doms (*see* §3(i) below), he painted several small panels, such as the *Holy Family* (1342; Liverpool, Walker A.G.). Another was the MASTER OF THE CODEX OF ST GEORGE (*see* MASTERS, ANONYMOUS, AND MONOGRAMMISTS, §I), known for his manuscript illuminations and a diptych of the *Crucifixion* and *Lamentation* (New York, Cloisters). While much of the sculpture produced while the papacy was in Avignon has disappeared, in Notre-Dame-des-Doms there are fragments of an effigy, which has been said to be that of Benedict XII and with which the name of Jean Lavenier has been associated in documents (Paris, Archvs N., Collection Monteil, KK 393, f 94).

Italian tastes were still favoured in the 15th century by the Cardinal-Bishop Alain DE COËTIVY, who also ordered decorative work to be executed on the bishop's palace; but at the same time several works were created that are considered to be among the outstanding achievements of French painting. New Netherlandish influences enriched the earlier Italian trends to produce a school of painting that was at once dramatic and richly detailed. The altarpiece of the *Coronation of the Virgin by the Holy Trinity* (1453–4; Villeneuve-lès-Avignon, Mus. Mun.) by ENGUERRAND QUARTON recalls Dante's *Divine Comedy*: it combines the worldly landscape of Provence with a medieval cosmology of the universe as Paradise, Earth, Purgatory and Hell. The artist's finest work, it was commissioned by Jean de Montagnac, canon of St Agricol, Avignon. Quarton and a collaborator also painted a *Virgin of Mercy* (1452; Chantilly, Mus. Condé). NICOLAS FROMENT settled in Provence in 1462–5 and was in Avignon in 1468. Among his works for patrons in Avignon is the window of the *Annunciation* for the choir of St Pierre. The most celebrated work of the school is the poignant and intense *Pietà of Villeneuve-lès-Avignon* (*c.* 1450; Paris, Louvre), whose painter has not been identified with certainty: Sterling favoured Quarton, while others have associated the Moorish details with the Portuguese artist Nuno Gonçalves.

Avignon was also home to several Baroque painters, the most celebrated of whom were the brothers Nicolas Mignard and Pierre Mignard I. The latter was a well-known portrait painter who conducted a lengthy feud with the Académie Royale and Charles Le Brun. In the late 18th century Joseph Vernet, a native of Avignon, became famous for his proto-Romantic landscapes, several of which are in the Musée Calvet. There are important collections of French and Italian paintings in the Musée du Petit Palais (many from the collection of GIAMPIETRO CAMPANA), as well as the holdings of the Musée Calvet and the Roman and medieval sculpture in the Musée Lapidaire.

BIBLIOGRAPHY

R. André-Michel: *Avignon au temps des premiers papes* (Paris, 1915)

R. Brun: *Avignon au temps des papes: Les Monuments, les artistes, la société* (Paris, 1928)

J. B.Ford and G. S. Vickers: 'The Relation of Nuno Gonçalves to the *Pietà* from Avignon', *A. Bull.*, xxi/1 (1939), pp. 5–43

C. Sterling: *Les Peintres primitifs* (Paris, 1942)

G. Ring: *A Century of French Painting, 1400–1500* (London, 1949)

H. Becriaux: *Avignon: Son histoire, ses monuments* (Paris, 2/1971)

A. M. Morganstern: 'Pierre Morel: Master of Works in Avignon', *A. Bull.*, lviii/3 (1976), pp. 323–49

Avignon, 1360–1410: Art et histoire (exh. cat. by M.-C. Leonelli, Avignon, Petit Pal., 1978)

M. Laclotte and D. Thiebaut: *L'Ecole d'Avignon* (Paris, 1983)

PAULA HUTTON

3. Buildings.

(i) Notre-Dame-des-Doms. (ii) Palais des Papes.

(i) Notre-Dame-des-Doms. In its late 12th-century state the building was the result of several construction campaigns. Probably it was essentially completed at the time of its consecration in 1101. The unaisled nave has five bays covered by a broken barrel-vault, with the exception of the easternmost bay, which carries a cupola and an octagonal lantern. A comparison between the lantern capitals and the capitals (*c.* 1120) in the nave of St Trophîme, Arles, implies that the lantern was added around 1130. The west entrance porch was built in the late 12th century and leads into a barrel-vaulted narthex bay surmounted by a tall bell-tower, which was rebuilt in the 17th and 19th centuries. Cardinal Giacomo Gaetani Stefaneschi commissioned Simone Martini to paint frescoes (mostly destr. 1828) in the porch, of which a badly deteriorated *Madonna of Humility* (*c.* 1340; Avignon, Pal. Papes & Mus.) survives. In the 14th and the 16th centuries a series of lateral chapels was added to the nave. The Baroque tribune dates from 1671–2, when the east end was enlarged and the original apse east of the cupola bay was replaced by a choir bay opening on to a polygonal apse.

On the exterior, the porch decoration is a remarkably accurate reproduction of Classical forms. Only the south side of the nave, facing the sun, is decorated with blind arcading. The north side remains unadorned, a feature frequently found on Provençal buildings. The interior decoration of the nave consists of colonnettes and capitals inserted into the imposts of the piers that carry the transverse arches. Despite the use of such Classical elements as acanthus, these capitals are in form and treatment deliberately opposed to Classical principals (Borg). They differ not only from the orthodox porch capitals but also from the Corinthian capitals that decorate the cupola of the lantern. The west porch was built in the late 12th century.

In its simplicity of plan and elevation, Notre-Dame-des-Doms is typical of Provençal Romanesque architecture. However, the existence of a west tower and a lantern-tower, as well as the anti-Classical treatment of the nave capitals, single it out among other buildings of the region. Its anti-Classicism heavily influenced the nave capitals of the cathedrals of Aix-en-Provence and Cavaillon.

Avignon Cathedral houses a Romanesque episcopal throne and altar, both made of white marble. The cloister, originally situated to the east of the church, was destroyed in the 17th and 18th centuries. The cathedral contains the sculptured tomb of *John XXII* (*d* 1334; rest.).

BIBLIOGRAPHY

G. Barroul: 'Eglise Notre-Dame-des-Doms d'Avignon au XIIe siècle', *Congr. Archéol. France*, cxxi (1963), pp. 44–58

A. Borg: *Architectural Sculpture in Romanesque Provence* (Oxford, 1972)

J. Gardner: *The Tomb and the Tiara: Curial Tomb Sculpture in Rome and Avignon in the Later Middle Ages* (Oxford, 1992)

ALEXANDRA KENNEDY

(ii) Palais des Papes.

(a) Architecture. The massive Palais des Papes, the powerful walls and eight high towers of which still dominate the city, is both an outstanding achievement of Late Gothic architecture and a highly visible emblem of the most glorious period of Avignon's history. Its sprawling and dissonant appearance expresses the turbulent period in which it was erected and the diverse characters of the men responsible for its construction. It is, in fact, two distinct palaces: the Palais Vieux built by Benedict XII and the Palais Neuf undertaken by Clement VI. Both palaces were renovated by later popes and by the papal legates who continued to use the building after the Papacy's return to Rome in 1378.

When Clement V first moved to Avignon in 1309 he lived in the city's Dominican priory or in nearby castles. His successor, John XXII, who had been Archbishop of Avignon, resided in the old Archbishop's Palace next to the cathedral. John enlarged and refurbished this building as the papal court expanded, but by the election of Benedict XII (*reg* 1334–42) the episcopal palace was inadequate for the scope and majesty expected of the head of Christendom. Benedict immediately undertook the construction of an immense new palace; he bought John's episcopal palace (and much of the surrounding land) and gradually demolished it to make way for his own. He hired Pierre Poisson of Mirepoix (*d* 1338) as Master of the Works, and work began in 1335. The structure now known as the Tour des Papes served as the focal point for the new palace–fortress. It rises about 46.5 m from the solid rock, with walls about 3 m thick, and served as a defensive stronghold and as a well-protected home for the Pope, his library and part of his treasury.

In 1336 construction began on the series of towers that form the core of the Palais Vieux. They are based on the old episcopal palace and are arranged in a rectangle around an enclosed cloister with, on the east, the Consistoire wing, where both solemn rituals and festivities took place; on the west, the Aile des Familiers (the staff wing); on the south, the Conclave Wing (where guests were housed); and on the north, the Pope's chapel. Private 'apartments' (the equivalent of modern offices, rather than residences) were added to facilitate the business of the Church. A bell-tower was built in 1339, burnt down and quickly rebuilt. Two more towers were built on the north-east corner of the compound: the Latrine Tower and the tallest part of the palace, the Tour de Trouillas, in which the popular leader Cola di Rienzo (1313–54) was imprisoned in 1352–3. The Palais Vieux was a fairly self-sufficient compound,

2. Avignon, Palais des Papes, interior of the Great Chapel, 1342–52

much on the model of a monastic community, including not only living-quarters and business facilities but kitchens, gardens, fishponds, a wine cellar, pantry, and a large and a small dining hall. It takes the form of the castle–fortress (*château-fort*) commonly found in the Mediterranean area. Its heavy walls and proud towers clearly declare its defensive capacity. The Palais Vieux also bears the imprint of Benedict's past as a Cistercian monk: it follows the simplicity associated with that order's abbeys, austere and unadorned by exterior or interior sculpture. Most of the ceilings in the Palais Vieux were timber and the floors were covered with glazed tiles.

Such starkness was not to the taste of Benedict's successor, Clement VI (*reg* 1342–52), a former Benedictine abbot and a close colleague of the French king, Philip VI (*reg* 1328–56). Clement hired a new architect, Jean de Loubières (*d* ?1357), who expanded parts of the Palais Vieux, adding a kitchen tower with a huge chimney and renovating the study tower. Clement also commissioned the Palais Nouveau, an entirely new series of towers around a new courtyard at the south-west corner of Benedict's palace, doubling the size of the compound. The most important of his additions was the south wing, which contains both the Salle de la Grande Audience, used for sermons and legal hearings, and the Great (Clementine) Chapel (see fig. 2). These huge rooms (52×16 m) are barrel-vaulted with intersecting ribs, an important characteristic of Clement's palace. He also added a new gateway and façade, resulting in an exterior that is notably lighter and more distinctly Gothic than its predecessors, and marked by gables and turrets; the outer walls are punctuated by occasional gargoyles.

The Avignon popes continually renovated the palace. Innocent VI (*reg* 1352–62) added a new wing of apartments (known as 'Rome'; destr.). Further building was undertaken by the anti-popes Clement VII (*reg* 1378–94) and Benedict XIII (*reg* 1394–1423) after the schism. After the end of the 14th century, however, the palace was doomed to a long period of ruin. During Benedict XIII's strife-torn reign the palace was attacked twice, and many of the frescoes were destroyed by fire in 1413. The papal legates occupied it only occasionally until 1791, and it gradually deteriorated, partly owing to several assaults by French troops and anti-clerical revolutionaries. The palace was used as a barracks from 1822 to 1906 (and again in World War I); great damage was done to both the building and its paintings. In the mid-19th century a reawakened interest in France's medieval history led to the restoration of the palace from 1860, which has continued ever since.

BIBLIOGRAPHY

G. Mollat: *Les Papes d'Avignon, 1305–1378* (Paris, 1912, 9/1949)
G. Colombe: *Au Palais des Papes d'Avignon* (Paris, 1921, 3/1939)
L.-H. Labande: *Le Palais des Papes et les monuments d'Avignon au XIVe siècle*, 2 vols (Marseille, 1925)
Y. Renouard: *La Papauté à Avignon* (Paris, 1954)
B. Guillemain: *La Cour pontificale d'Avignon, 1309–1376* (Paris, 1962)
S. Gagnière: *Le Palais des Papes d'Avignon* (Avignon, 1983)

(b) Painting. The wall paintings of the palace have encountered numerous disasters: attacks during the Great Schism and the French Revolution, use for target practice under Napoleon and other French military leaders, and centuries of disinterest and neglect. Many of the paintings that once adorned the towers have disappeared either partially or entirely, and most of those remaining have been heavily restored. Nevertheless, the work that remains stands as a testimony to the vitality and imaginative power of the Italian and French artists employed on the decorations.

It was only to be expected that the new palace would be lavishly decorated with wall paintings; such frescoes existed in the papal enclave in Rome and in the various papal residences in such Italian cities as Anagni and Orvieto. There is some documentation that Pope Benedict XII requested the services of Giotto for his new palace, but the master died (1337) before setting out for Avignon. Simone Martini did come to Provence and may have left traces of *sinopie* (underdrawing) on the palace walls, but he, too, died before doing any extensive painting. Most of the painting in the palace took place under Pope Clement VI, and there is documentary evidence to show that they were executed by MATTEO GIOVANETTI and his workshop. From 1343 to at least 1355, Matteo and his assistants executed the frescoes in the Chapelle de St Jean outside the Consistoire and in the Chapelle de St Martial above (for illustration *see* GIOVANETTI, MATTEO); the prophets in the Salle de la Grande Audience; and scenes of saints' lives in the Tour St Michel, of which only traces remain. Several of Matteo's other paintings have been destroyed: a *Last Judgement* and a *Crucifixion* in the Salle de la Grande Audience, with portraits of four (unidentified) popes; almost all the painting in the Consistoire except for remnants of a starry sky motif on the ceiling; a *Crucifixion*; and murals for the Appartement de Rome of Innocent VI (1352–62). The most charming of Clement's frescoes, however, have been associated with an anonymous French painter: the scenes of hunting, fishing, falconry and other aristocratic pleasures in the Garde-robe, now known as the Chambre du Cerf (see fig. 3). Although partially damaged, several of these scenes are well preserved and evoke the images found in contemporary tapestries (*see* GOTHIC, §IV, 5(vii)). The contrast between these vivacious landscapes and the solemn religious images in the

3. Avignon, Palais des Papes, fresco (*c.* 1343–55) of a falconry scene in the Chambre du Cerf

more public areas of the palace has provoked much discussion (Roques).

Many other rooms in the palace are more simply painted. The Chambre du Pape, for example, is adorned with intertwined grapevines on a blue background and with lively depictions of birds, animals and flowers. It was once thought that these were painted for the quiet monastic tastes of Benedict XII, but there is now evidence that these naturalistic motifs were undertaken under Urban V (*reg* 1362–70; see Gagnière). It is recorded that Benedict hired several French and Italian painters (Roques), who may have been responsible for the floral and geometric patterns that embellish his study rooms, as well as the painted tiles on the palace floors.

BIBLIOGRAPHY

R. André-Michel: *Avignon: Les Fresques du Palais des Papes: Le Procès des Visconti* (Paris, 1920, 2/1926)

L.-H. Labande: *Le Palais des Papes et les monuments d'Avignon au XIVe siècle*, 2 vols (Marseille, 1925)

M. Roques: *Les Peintures murales du Sud-Est de la France (XIII–XVIe siècle)* (Paris, 1961)

E. Castelnuovo: *Un pittore italiano alla corte di Avignon* (Turin, 1962)

P. E. Burnham jr: 'The Patronage of Clement VI', *Hist. Today* (June 1978), pp. 372–81

S. Gagnière: *Le Palais des Papes d'Avignon* (Avignon, 1983)

PAULA HUTTON

Ávila. Capital city of Ávila province in Old Castile, Spain. Situated on a spur above the River Adaja at a height of *c.* 1130 m, it has a population of *c.* 40,000. It is surrounded by the most complete circuit of medieval walls in Spain and is also notable for its Gothic cathedral (*see* §2(i)) as well as many fine Romanesque churches, including S Vicente (*see* §2(ii)).

1. History and urban development. 2. Buildings.

1. History and urban development. Once occupied by the Romans, Ávila was repopulated by Count Raymond II of Burgundy (*reg* 1087–1107) in the 1090s under King Alfonso VI of León (*reg* 1065–1109), after centuries of abandonment in a no-man's-land between Christian and Muslim territories. This was succeeded by a century of important construction work, including Romanesque churches in a local style and the cathedral, one of the earliest Gothic buildings in Spain (*see* §2(i)(a) below). Defence was the most urgent concern, however, and walls were soon raised on the exposed eastern side of the spur with squared granite blocks from Roman structures, rough sandstone blocks and thick rubble. Construction continued throughout the 12th century along the north and west sides, where decorative brickwork below the battlements of the towers indicates Moorish workmanship. On the south wall, completed last, smaller blocks and fewer towers are evidence of fading interest and faltering resources. The battlemented ramparts, enclosing a roughly rectangular area, are punctuated by 88 semicircular towers and several gates, with the apse of the cathedral forming a bastion on the eastern side. The walls, approximately 12 m high and 3 m thick, form a circuit of *c.* 2.5 km.

The numerous Romanesque churches, many outside the walls, have simple basilican plans with single-cell or aisled naves, short presbyteries with semicircular apses and portals without tympana. The transept of S Vicente, the most ambitious church (*see* §2(ii) below), was imitated at S Pedro. Lively figured capitals on the apses of S Andrés and S Segundo were carved by Cantabrian sculptors influenced by S Martín, Frómista. Capitals and corbels at S Vicente, the nave of S Andrés and the apses of S Pedro bear a more limited repertory of animal and foliate motifs derived from Santiago de Compostela Cathedral and the western bays of S Isidoro, León. In the late 12th century sculptors from Burgundy worked at S Vicente, the cathedral and S Pedro, where they introduced rich acanthus capitals in the transepts, a rib-vaulted nave and an ornate rose window in the west façade (rest. 1967). The Romanesque features were blended with Mudéjar decoration at S Nicolas (ded. 1198), and brick was mixed with stone in the former parish church of S Bartolomé (ded. 1210) and the tower of S Martín. The golden sandstone of 12th-century churches gave way to coarser sandstone mottled with red in the cathedral choir, but after the early 13th century local granite dominated the architectural landscape of the city.

In the mid-15th century Ávila entered a second period of artistic splendour, attracting artists from court circles at Toledo and other Castilian towns, among them Juan Guas, who directed the Cathedral Works, and Martín de Solórzano, who in 1482 began the Dominican church of S Tomás. This soon attracted royal patronage, and in 1513 the tomb of Prince John (*d* 1497), son of the Catholic monarchs Ferdinand and Isabella, was installed there after being prepared in Genoa by DOMENICO FANCELLI. S Francisco, founded in the late 13th century and housing tombs of the local nobility, has an elegant star-vaulted nave and apse, while the cruciform chapel of Mosén Rubí de Bracamonte, founded in 1516, is one of the last manifestations of Gothic architecture in Ávila. A number of Gothic houses survive in the town, including the Casas de los Dávilas, a group of four medieval houses.

Italianate architectural ornament of Lombard origin was introduced by Vasco de la Zarza in the cathedral cloister, begun in 1508. His exuberant Plateresque style yielded in the 1550s to the restrained classicism of Pedro del Valle and Pedro de Tolosa (*d* 1583), inspired by Alonso de Covarrubias's work on the Alcázar and Tavera Hospital at Toledo. Among this group are the vestibule and lateral nave façade of the chapel of Mosén Rubin and the portals of Sta Catalina and the convent of las Gordillas. Secular buildings of this period show a severe local version of Plateresque architecture, constrained by the hard granite: the most notable example, the Palacio de Polentinos, has a galleried courtyard and machicolated façade sculptured with motifs of Zarza's school. The portal of the Casa de los Aguila is more sober, with slender columns, small shields and massive granite lintels.

By 1600 the classicizing style of Juan de Herrera appeared under Francisco de Mora (*see* MORA (i), (1)) in the chapel of S Segundo in the cathedral and the convent of S José, founded by St Teresa (1515–82) in 1562 and redesigned in 1608 with a galleried loggia sheltered by projecting nave walls. In the 17th century Ávila's artistic importance waned, despite work at sites associated with St Teresa. Nonetheless, Pedro de Ribera's hexagonal chapel of the Virgen de la Portería with a turreted dome, completed in 1731 at S Antonio and richly furnished in the 18th century, stands as a noteworthy example of the Churrigueresque style. At the end of the 18th century the Neo-classical architect Juan Antonio Cuerbo, disciple of Ventura Rodríguez, completed the chapel of Las Veladas in the cathedral and redesigned the principal square, the Plaza del Mercado Chico.

BIBLIOGRAPHY

L. Ariz: *Historia de las grandezas de la ciudad de Ávila* (Alcalá de Henares, 1607/*R* Ávila, 1978)

M. Gómez Moreno: *Catálogo monumental de la provincia de Ávila*, 3 vols [prepared 1901–2]; rev. by A. de la Morena and T. Pérez de Higuera (Madrid, 1983)

L. Cervera Vera: 'La iglesia del monasterio de San José en Ávila', *Bol. Soc. Esp. Excurs.*, liv (1950), pp. 5–155

S. Alcolea: *Ávila monumental* (Madrid, 1952)

A. Hernández Segura, ed.: *La crónica de la población de Ávila* (Valencia, 1966)

F. Hernández Martín: *Ávila* (León, 1967, rev. 5/1977)

M. Aumente Rivas: 'Notas sobre los Churriguera en Ávila', *Archv Esp. A.*, xlviii (1975), pp. 139–42

——: 'Juan Antonio Cuerbo: Sus obras en Ávila', *Archv Esp. A.*, xlix (1976), pp. 121–43

J. J. Martín González: 'El convento de Sta Teresa de Ávila y la arquitectura carmelitana', *Bol. Semin. Estud. A. & Arqueol. Valladolid*, xlii (1976), pp. 305–24

——: 'El convento de San José de Ávila (patronos y obras de arte)', *Bol. Semin. Estud. A. & Arqueol. Valladolid*, xlv (1979), pp. 349–76

J. M. Parrado del Olmo: 'La capilla de Mosén Rubi de Bracamonte', *Bol. Semin. Estud. A. & Arqueol. Valladolid*, xlvii (1981), pp. 285–306

L. Cervera Vera: *Complejo arquitectónico del monasterio de San José en Ávila* (Madrid, 1982)

J. L. Gutiérrez Robledo: *Las iglesias románicas de la ciudad de Ávila* (Ávila, 1982)

J. L. Gutiérrez Robledo, Carmelo L. López and others: *Guía del románico de Ávila y primer mudéjar de la Moraña* (Ávila, 1982)

A. Barrios García: *Estructuras agrarias y de poder en Castilla: El ejemplo de Ávila (1085–1320)* (Salamanca, 1983)

J. M. Parrado del Olmo: 'Sobre escultura abulense del siglo XVI', *Bol. Semin. Estud. A. & Arqueol. Valladolid*, l (1984), pp. 273–99

M. Vila da Vila: *La escultura románica en Ávila: Talleres de formación hispano-languedociana* (diss., U. Santiago de Compostela, 1990)

2. BUILDINGS.

(i) Cathedral. (ii) S Vicente.

(i) Cathedral.

(a) Architecture. No trace remains of the cathedral reportedly built under Raymond of Burgundy during the repopulation. Alfonso VIII's gifts to Bishop Sancho in 1175 may mark the start of the present structure, dedicated to S Salvador. Sancho died in 1181 and was buried in the easternmost chapel, while a charter of 1192 concerns lands bequeathed to Alfonso VIII by Fruchel, Master of the Works. Gómez Moreno cited a document of 1211, now lost, which named a chapel of St Michael in the north tower of the west façade, suggesting considerable work on the west end.

Building began with the five ambulatory chapels enclosed by the semicircular wall that formed part of the city ramparts. They are covered with ribbed semidomes (see fig. 1) and lit by deeply splayed slit windows. In the presbytery, four chapels with true rib vaults line the rib-vaulted double ambulatory, two on either side. Columns on high moulded plinths divide its two aisles, cylindrical

1. Ávila Cathedral, ambulatory, *c.* 1180

piers with applied shafts ring the hemicycle, and cruciform piers with responds mark the tall, narrow presbytery and crossing. Above, there was a high gallery with two two-light windows in each bay, and a small clerestory with windows framed by doubled wall ribs on colonnettes and salients. In the transepts and short, aisled nave, granite replaced the coarse, mottled sandstone of the east end. The early design, however, governed the use of cruciform piers, as in the choir. Corbels were set above the keystones of the nave arcade for sexpartite vaults, and a west porch flanked by towers was envisaged.

The design draws on Burgundian sources, but it also shows a wider awareness of Early Gothic experiments in northern France. The mouldings, corbelled supports and other details are found at Burgundian buildings (e.g. La Madeleine, Vézelay; Pontigny Abbey; and the cathedrals of Langres and Sens). As at Vézelay, the principal ribs of the sexpartite choir vault spring from intermediate supports; at Ávila, these are merely corbelled responds above the keystones of the arcade. The tall gallery and small clerestory, however, recall the proportions of four-storey elevations, such as that at Notre-Dame, Paris. The double ambulatory with slender columns is derived from Saint Denis Abbey and other Ile-de-France buildings, incorporating deep, independent chapels like those at Noyon Cathedral. There are parallels for the ambulatory chapels enclosed by a continuous wall at Pontigny, other Cistercian churches and Thérouanne Cathedral (destr.), and the difficult site may have recommended this plan at Ávila.

Although the evolution of rib vaults in the ambulatory chapels and choir suggests continuing contacts with the north, the unhappy organization of the choir vaults and awkward meeting of the ambulatory, aisles and transepts seem to be the makeshift solutions of architects working in isolation, perhaps relying on plans sent from France. In the emphasis on the wall and the use of thickly proportioned supports, the atelier adhered to Romanesque traditions, while the fortified ambulatory and small clerestory enabled only a little light to be admitted.

In the 13th century a sacristy with a complex rib vault, a chapter house with eight-part vault and squinches and a cloister were added, but construction slowed in the nave, where the arcades show evidence of sloppier workmanship. In 1319 Bishop Sancho Dávila sought funding to repair the cathedral, reportedly in danger of collapse. During his episcopate (1312–53) the clerestory with elaborately traceried windows and the quadripartite vaults over the nave were built, and the cloister was completed. To reinforce the structure, doubled flying buttresses replaced the choir gallery; and on the interior, stone struts were inserted to strengthen the outer ambulatory aisle, and arches were thrown across the transepts.

Subsequent work was centred on the chapels. Juan Guas was commissioned for one in the cloister in 1471, and Martín de Solórzano designed the library (Capilla del Cardenal) in 1495. Vasco de la Zarza introduced Italianate forms in the cresting of the cloister, begun in 1508, and *c.* 1559 two Renaissance chapels, the Capilla de la Concepción and the Capilla de la Piedad, were added to the north transept. South-east of the ambulatory stands the square, domed chapel of S Segundo, designed by Francisco de Mora in 1598. On the north side of the ambulatory, the Capilla de los Veladas was begun in 1603, but completed only in the 1790s to a Neo-classical design.

The cathedral was richly furnished in the late 15th century and the early 16th. Late 15th-century tombs, from the circle of Juan Guas, bear wild men and a restrained vocabulary of Hispano-Flemish decoration. Vasco de la Zarza employed Italianate forms in the woodwork of the main retable, the alabaster tomb of Bishop Alonso de Madrigal (el Tostado), the sacristy altar and other works. His followers, Juan Rodríguez (*d* 1544) and Lucas Giraldo (*fl* 1529–44), carved the *trascoro* (screen; 1531–6) with the *Infancy of Christ* and rich Plateresque decoration, and in 1534 they began the wooden choir-stalls with the Dutch artist Cornielis de Holanda. Isidoro Villoldo and Juan de Frias carved the alabaster altar of S Segundo (1547–8), and Juan Bautista Vázquez's copy of Michelangelo's *Pietà* (Rome, St Peter's) was installed by 1561. Pedro Berruguete was commissioned to paint the retable, largely completed after his death (1499) by Santa Cruz (*d c.* 1508) and Juan de Borgoña. The remaining stained glass dates mostly from this period.

(b) Sculpture. Architectural sculpture in the cathedral is limited, although the earliest work was lavishly decorated. The ribs of the axial bay of the outer ambulatory aisle are studded with rosettes, and the capitals of the eastern chapels bear acanthus, foliate scrolls, fantastic animals and a few historiated compositions, including an *Annunciation* with the Virgin crowned by angels. Sculptors from S Vicente (*see* §(ii) below) executed the decoration: one capital shows a soul punished in Hell and another lifted to Heaven by angels, quoting the tale of *Dives and Lazarus* from the tympanum there, a theme repeated in one of several tympanum reliefs in the choir and transept galleries. Elsewhere in the choir, the capitals have simple foliage, and those of the nave are plain.

The late 13th-century figures of the north portal may be compared with the tomb of *Bishop Blasco of Siguenza* (*d c.* 1291). Figures of the Apostles line the jambs, the voussoirs include scenes of Hell, and the tympanum is organized in four registers showing the *Coronation of the Virgin*, the *Last Judgement* and scenes from the *Life of Christ.* The sculpture was moved from the west façade and reset above a flattened arch by Juan Guas, who came from Toledo in 1459, early in his career, to execute a new west portal, of which the huge wild men now flanking the doorway formed part. The façade was redesigned by Ceferino Enríquez de la Serna (1779–86).

BIBLIOGRAPHY

E. Lambert: 'L'Architecture bourguignonne et la cathédrale d'Ávila', *Bull. Mnmtl*, lxxxiii (1924), pp. 263–92

L. Cervera Vera: 'La capilla de San Segundo en la catedral de Ávila', *Bol. Soc. Esp. Excurs.*, lvi (1952), pp. 181–232

A. Dimier: 'Origine des déambulatoires à chapelles rayonnantes non saillantes', *Bull. Mnmtl*, cxv (1957), pp. 23–33

P. Heliot: 'Les Déambulatoires dotés de niches rayonnantes', *Cah. Civilis. Méd.*, iv (1961), pp. 303–22

F. de las Heras Hernández: *La catedral de Ávila* (Ávila, 1967)

A. Barrios García: *La catedral de Ávila en la edad media: Estructura socio-jurídica y económica* (Ávila, 1973)

E. Rodríguez Almeida: *Ensayo sobre la evolución arquitectónica de la catedral de Ávila* (Ávila, 1974)

A. Barrios García: *Documentación medieval de la catedral de Ávila* (Salamanca, 1981)

M. J. Ruíz-Ayúcar: 'El sepulcro y la laude de "el Tostado"', *Archv Esp. A.*, liv (1981), pp. 93–100

(ii) S Vicente. Built of golden sandstone, S Vicente is distinguished by the elaborately carved shrine of St Vincent and his sisters, SS Sabina and Christeta, and rich architectural sculpture, mainly of limestone.

(a) Architecture. The only early reference to the fabric is connected with the Muslim raid of 1109, and must denote an earlier church that perhaps suffered damage, necessitating reconstruction. In the first building campaign a wide transept and three parallel apses with short presbyteries were built over a crypt on steeply sloping terrain, and the nave arcade and aisle walls were completed in four of the six bays. The strongly projecting transept imitates S Isidoro, León. In the western nave bays, the capitals of the León workshop are accompanied by those of a new atelier, suggesting that construction work was still continuing when the Burgundian craftsmen arrived *c.* 1170 to complete the nave, build the triforium and brick vaults, and add a west porch between two towers. The vault ribs spring from capitals set diagonally over salients of the cruciform piers, as in the nave at Pontigny Abbey, Burgundy. Inside the towers, the cusped arches recall the exterior decoration of towers at Notre-Dame, La Charité-sur-Loire.

The royal gifts of 1252, 1280, 1290 and 1292 probably financed the low crossing tower and granite south porch, while the north-west tower received a third storey in the 1440s. After 1849 the building was extensively restored by Andrés Hernández Callejo, who reconstructed the second storey of the south-west tower and perhaps replaced sculpture on the south cornice of the nave. Restoration resumed in 1882 and was supervised by Enrique Repullés y Vargas (1845–1922) after 1885.

(b) Sculpture. The interior arcades, shafted windows and engaged columns of the apses are decorated by carved capitals, imposts and string courses. Capitals and corbels bear bulky animals, and cusped leaves of a type found at Santiago de Compostela Cathedral, while flowers, palmettes and foliate scrolls adorn the imposts. The lateral portals have alternately moulded and decorated arches, a standard formula at Ávila. Two large figures from the first campaign were later set on the right jambs of the south portal. The sculpture derives from that of the second quarter of the 12th century in the western bays of S Isidoro, León, with close parallels at S Pedro, Ávila, and S Millán, Segovia.

The second atelier carved the *Annunciation* on the left jamb of the south portal and decorated the two western bays of the nave, the west porch and towers, the triforium, the arched corbel table of the nave and the martyrs' shrine. The rich decorative vocabulary is composed of luxuriant acanthus, spiralling foliage, deeply undercut rosettes, ball-flowers, inhabited foliate scrolls and beaded and drilled ornament, and stems from that of two Burgundian ateliers active between 1140 and 1175 (*see* ROMANESQUE, §III, 1(ii)(f)). One of these carved sculpture at St Lazare, Avallon, a tomb in Sainte-Magnance (Yonne) and, at Vézelay, the church of Ste Croix and the narthex tribunes and chapter house of La Madeleine. The other is associated with the abbeys of La Charité-sur-Loire, Donzy-le-Pré, Souvigny, the lateral portals of Bourges Cathedral and the fragments of the shrine at Saint-Menoux (Allier). The acanthus capitals and imposts of S Vicente resemble those at Avallon and on the upper storey of the narthex of La Madeleine, Vézelay, while the lavishly decorated archivolts on the west portal (see fig. 2) resemble those at Avallon and Bourges. The archivolts of the west portal frame a tympanum with broad proportions like the portals of Avallon and St Bénigne (destr.), Dijon. Within it, two small tympana bear the parable of *Dives and Lazarus.* The column statues, usually interpreted as Apostles, interact with one another in pairs and recall the jamb figures of the central portal at La Madeleine, Vézelay.

The style of the large figures, with their thinly sliced sheets of stone, deeply undercut draperies, marked chiaroscuro effects and excited, rippling hems, derives from baroque currents in Burgundian sculpture found at Donzy-le-Pré, Jonzy and Charlieu. In Spain, the immediate antecedents include a frieze at the church of Santiago, Carrión de los Condes, and fragmentary figures at Santiago de Compostela Cathedral, probably from the west crypt. At Ávila itself, both the large and small figures have similar facial types and channelled drapery, confirming that they are attributable to the same sculptors.

South of the crossing stands the martyrs' shrine (see fig. 3), a miniature aisled basilica under a baldacchino of 1465. The design is attributable to the Burgundian artists whose experience included the carving of shrines at Saint-Menoux and Sainte-Magnance. A caryatid and decorated columns with foliate capitals carry cusped arches crowned with a foliate string course. Above, sloping sides rise to

2. Ávila, S Vicente, west portal, *c.* 1175

3. Ávila, S Vicente, shrine of SS Vincent, Sabina and Christeta, *c.* 1175

the gabled sarcophagus where scenes on the long sides recount the saints' martyrdom in sophisticated narrative compositions. Six small reliefs of single figures under arches are set between the cusped arches, while larger panels with paired Apostles under canopies crown the corner capitals. *Christ in Majesty* and two Evangelist symbols on the west face and three reliefs of the *Magi* on the east complete the decoration. The apostles, small figures and panels on the short sides, however, were designed for different locations. Several conceal painted carving, while the west face offers no plausible setting for the two missing Evangelist symbols. The *Christ in Majesty* and *Dream of the Magi* were evidently recut during the 15th-century renovations, when they may have been mounted. Three figures of saints under arches also survive in the church and, with the awkwardly set *Annunciation* on the south portal, suggest that the plans for sculptural decoration were modified, perhaps after skilled sculptors abandoned the isolated town, leaving their work to be set by masons.

S Vicente contains the most extensive sculptural decoration by the artists who worked at Carrión de los Condes and the west crypt at Santiago de Compostela, providing the fullest picture of their relationship to mid- 12th-century Burgundy. In the sparsely settled areas around Ávila, where granite and brick were discouraging materials for sculpture, the style left no heirs, exhausting itself in the ambulatory chapels of the cathedral and the church of S Pedro. The best sculpture is probably the work of two or three artists active in Ávila between 1170 and 1185.

BIBLIOGRAPHY

A. Hernández Callejo: *Memoria histórico-descriptiva sobre la basilica de los santos mártires Vicente, Sabina y Cristeta en la ciudad de Ávila* (Madrid, 1849)

E. Repullés y Vargas: *La basilica de los santos mártires Vicente, Sabina y Cristeta en Ávila* (Madrid, 1894)

W. Goldschmidt: 'El pórtico de San Vicente, en Ávila', *Archv Esp. A. & Arqueol.*, xi (1935), pp. 259–73

——: 'El sepulcro de San Vicente, en Ávila', *Archv Esp. A. & Arqueol.*, xii (1936), pp. 161–70

——: 'The West Portal of San Vicente in Ávila', *Burl. Mag.*, lxxi (1937), pp. 110–23

J. M. Pita Andrade: *Escultura románica en Castilla: Los maestros de Oviedo y Ávila* (Madrid, 1955)

F. de las Heras Hernández: *La iglesia de San Vicente de Ávila: Memorias de un templo cristiano* (Ávila, 1971)

JAMES D'EMILIO

Ávila, Hernando de (*b* ?Toledo; *d* 1595). Spanish painter, miniaturist, sculptor, architect and writer. He belongs to the Toledan school of the second half of the 16th century. The son of the painter Lorenzo de Ávila, he developed a Mannerist style that is smooth and delicate and derives from his father's and from that of Juan Correa de Vivar and of Francisco Comontes (*d* 1565). He worked as painter to Toledo Cathedral from 1565 to 1581 and was painter (Pintor del Rey) to Philip II from 1583. He acted frequently as a valuer for the work of other artists.

Between 1563 and 1564, in collaboration with LUIS DE VELASCO, Hernando de Ávila painted the retable of the church of Miraflores (Madrid Province) with the *Life of Christ* and the *Life of the Virgin* (untraced); these are probably among his earliest works. He was commissioned to paint the retables of *St John the Baptist* and the *Adoration of the Magi* for the Capilla de la Torre, Toledo Cathedral (Toledo, Semin.), in 1565. In the same year he also painted the principal retable (untraced) for the parish church of S Nicolás, S Martín de Tours, Toledo. In 1566, in collaboration with Rodrigo de Vivar and Jerónimo Rodríguez, he was commissioned to paint the retable of the church of Colmenar Viejo (Madrid Province); also by Hernando de Ávila are the *Presentation in the Temple* and *Christ among the Doctors* (*in situ*). In 1569 he received payment from the chapter of Toledo for his painting of the *History of the Kings* for the Capilla de la Torre, Toledo Cathedral (*in situ*). In collaboration with the sculptor Nicolás de Vergara (*see* VERGARA, (1)), he worked between 1573 and 1576 on the retable of Don Juan Nuñez in the Capilla de la Encarnación, parish of S Tomé, Toledo. In 1574 he and Velasco de Ávila worked on the retable of the church at Santaolalla (Toledo Province), and he collaborated with Diego de Aguillar on the retable of Villalengua (Toledo Province), both altars with scenes from the *Life of Christ* and the *Life of the Virgin*.

In 1574 Hernando de Ávila painted the retable of the Castros, designed by the architect JUAN BAUTISTA MONEGRO, in the church of the convent of the Trinity, Toledo, with *St Jerome Penitent* (untraced) and *Bestowing of the Chasuble on St Ildefonso* (*in situ*). He made designs for the principal retable of S Domingo el Antiguo, Toledo, in 1575, but this commission was given to El Greco in 1576. The architectural decoration of the chapel of Don Pedro de Villaseca in the parish church of Arcicollar was given to him as a commission in 1576, and later he went to live in Madrid, where also in 1576 his daughter Ana was born, her baptism being witnessed by Alonso Sánchez Coelho. Between 1580 and 1583 Hernando de Ávila worked at the Escorial, painting choir-books and valuing works by Nicolás Granello and Diego de Romulo Cincinato. His connection with the Escorial continued until 1592. In 1586 he was in Toledo, where he valued the *Burial of Count Orgaz* by El Greco (1586–8; Toledo, S Tomé), and in 1587 Luis de Carvajal valued some tondos that Hernando de Ávila had carved on the arch of the Puerta del Perdón, Toledo Cathedral. In 1591 he worked on the decoration of the Sala de Reyes and Cuarto del Cierzo (Segovia, Alcázar). He competed in 1593 for the commission for the principal retable of Burgos Cathedral, and at his death in 1595 he left drawings for this project, which may have been used by Martín de Haya.

Hernando de Ávila made the pen-and-wash illuminations for *Retratos, letreros e insignias reales de los Reyes de Oviedo, Leon y Castilla de la Sala Real de los Alcacares de Segovia* (1594; MSS; first portrait book, untraced; a second, Madrid, Prado, on dep. Segovia, Alcázar). This commission from Philip II shows his great skill as a miniature painter. Hernando de Ávila was a versatile artist, who, in addition to his painting, sculpture and architecture, wrote an important treatise (untraced) on the *Arte de la pintura*, recorded by Diego de Villalta (1590; MS., London, BL).

BIBLIOGRAPHY

D. Angulo Iñiguez: *Pintura del siglo XVI*, A. Hisp., xii (Madrid, 1954), p. 295

C. Post: *A History of Spanish Painting*, xiv (Cambridge, 1966)

Camón Aznar: *Pintura española del renacimiento*, Summa A., xxii (Madrid, 1970), pp. 456–7

F. Marias: 'Maestros de la catedral, artistas y artesanos: Datos sobre la pintura de la segunda mitad del siglo XVI', *Archv Esp. A.*, liv (1981), pp. 321–8

F. Collar de Caceres: 'En torno al libro de retratos de los reyes de Hernando de Ávila', *Bol. Mus. Prado*, iv/10 (1983), pp. 7–35

M. I. Rodríguez Quintana: 'Hernando de Ávila y Luis de Velasco: El retablo de Casar de Escalona y otras noticias', *Archv Esp. A.*, lii (1989), pp. 15–33

ISABEL MATEO GOMEL

Ávila, Pedro de (*b* Valladolid; *d* after 1739). Spanish sculptor. He was the son of the sculptor Juan de Ávila (*fl* 1678–*c*. 1700) and a collaborator of Juan Antonio de la Peña (*fl* 1674–96), whose daughter he married in 1700. In his early works, such as *Pietà* (Valladolid, Colegio de los Ingleses), the folds are smoothly carved, like those of his father, but he subsequently developed towards a more Baroque style of great masses and sharply cut folds. In 1720 he undertook to make five sculptures for S Felipe Neri, Valladolid: in the *Immaculate Conception* the folds spread out from the centre of the figure; the contemplative *Mary Magdalene* continues the tradition of the 17th-century ascetic type. His *St Michael* (Palencia, Castil de Vela) is a heroic and courtly figure.

Ávila carved a series of statues for the high altar (the architecture of the retable probably being by Alonso de Manzano) of the parish church of Fuentes de Valdepero, Palencia (1711), and in this way the influence of the Valladolid school spread throughout the province of Palencia. In the heads of the *Ecce homo* and the *Dolorosa* (1730s; Valladolid, Convent of las Brígidas) he gave Baroque emphasis to a type created by Pedro de Mena. For the processional figure of the *Resurrected Christ* (Palencia, Colegiata de Ampudia) he abandoned the use of sumptuous polychrome in favour of plainer colouring and obtained a pictorial effect through deep concave folds. There is an *Immaculate Conception* by Ávila in S Francisco, Orense. Attributions to Ávila include the *St Peter Rejoicing* and *St Peter Weeping* (Valladolid, Iglesia del Salvador) and stone-carvings on the façade of the church of the Comendadores de Santa Cruz, Valladolid.

BIBLIOGRAPHY

E. García Chico: *Documentos para el estudio del arte en Castilla: II Escultores* (Valladolid, 1941)

J. J. Martín González: *Escultura barroca castellana* (Madrid, 1959)

J. J. MARTÍN GONZÁLEZ

Aviler [Daviler; Davillier]**, Augustin-Charles d'** (*b* Paris, 1653; *d* Montpellier, 23 June 1701). French architect, theorist and writer. He trained at the new Académie Royale d'Architecture, Paris, and in 1674 was appointed royal pensionary of the Académie Française in Rome. While travelling by sea from Marseille to Genoa, however, his boat was seized by corsairs and he was detained in Tunis, where he is said to have provided the design for the Sidi Mahrez Mosque. In 1676 he was released from captivity and arrived in Rome, where he studied ancient and modern architecture for nearly four years. On returning to France in 1680, he continued his studies, and in 1684 he entered the office of Jules Hardouin Mansart, with whom he was involved in work on the château of Versailles for almost eight years.

During this period d'Aviler published a translation (1685) of the sixth book of Vincenzo Scamozzi's treatise on architecture, followed by his *Cours complet d'architecture* (1691). This included a commentary on the life and work of Jacopo Vignola but was also a practical manual with plates illustrating various types of buildings, with a wealth of structural and decorative details. It concludes with an extensive glossary of architectural terms, which was later published separately as a dictionary. The book was a resounding success and was reprinted throughout the 18th century; a simplified version was published in 1825–6.

In 1691 d'Aviler accepted an invitation to supervise the construction of the Porte du Peyrou, Montpellier, a triumphal arch designed by his friend François d'Orbay; he completed the task with such success that the local authorities procured him the warrant Architecte du Roi and in 1693 appointed him Architecte de la Province for Languedoc. In the 1690s he became a focal-point for important building patrons and young architects in the province, and he took part in schemes at Sète, Saint-Pons, Alès, Carcassonne and Le Vigan. He also built barracks at Nîmes, Béziers, Lunel and Mèze; restored the fountains of Lattes, Le Pila St Gély, La Saunerie and La Putanelle, all at Montpellier, the Porte Ste Catherine at Narbonne, the great courtyards of Montpellier and the Hôtel de Ville, Nîmes; and he rebuilt the Archbishop's Palace, Toulouse, for Mgr de Colbert and the episcopal palace at Béziers. D'Aviler also worked on the restoration (1699) of the Pont du Gard. In MONTPELLIER he provided numerous plans for various town houses (hôtels), including the Hôtel Philippe de Moynier de Fourques and the Hôtel Tissier (1697), in which he revealed the full extent of his capabilities, abandoning the open staircase and adopting a Parisian-style layout. His resolutely classical style is distinguished by splendid carved portals and by doors and windows topped by a curve consisting of a single, depressed arch with mascarons on the keystone, a feature that became known as the Daviler arch. Despite his prolific activity as an architect, however, his reputation largely rests on his work as a theorist and writer. His son, Claude-Louis d'Aviler (*d* 1764), was also an architect and won the Grand Prix in architecture in 1730.

WRITINGS

Les Cinq Ordres d'architecture de Vincent Scamozzi tirés du VIe livre de l'idée générale d'architecture (Paris, 1685)

Cours complet d'architecture avec une ample explication de tous les termes de l'architecture civile et hydraulique: Cours d'architecture qui comprend les ordres de Vignole (Paris, 1693)

BIBLIOGRAPHY

Bauchal

P.-J. Mariette: 'Notice biographique', *Cours d'architecture par le sieur A.-C. d'Aviler* (Paris, 1738), pp. xxxv–xxxviii

Abbé C.-F. Lambert: *Histoire littéraire du règne de Louis XIV* (Paris, 1751), iii, pp. 104–7

P.-J. Mariette: *Archives de l'art français* (Paris, 1853–4), iv, pp. 65–7

L. de La Roque: *Biographie montpelliéraine: Peintres, sculpteurs et architectes* (Montpellier, 1877), pp. 113–8

R. Blomfield: *A History of French Architecture from 1661 to 1774*, ii (London, 1921)

L. Hautecoeur: *Architecture classique*, ii (1948), pp. 214–6

ALEXANDRA SKLIAR-PIGUET

Avisseau, Charles-Jean (*b* Tours, 25 Dec 1796; *d* Tours, 6 Feb 1861). French potter. He was the son of a stone-cutter and at a young age was apprenticed in a faience factory at Saint Pierre-des-Corps. In 1825 he entered the ceramic factory of Baron de Bezeval at Beaumont-les-Autels where he saw a dish made by the Renaissance potter Bernard Palissy, which was to inspire his work. In 1843 Avisseau established an independent factory on the Rue Saint-Maurice in Tours, where individual ceramics inspired by and in the style of Palissy's 'rustic' wares were produced (e.g. lead-glazed dish, 1857; Bagnères-de-Bigorre, Mus. A.). Although critics complained that his works merely imitated the Renaissance master, he never directly copied Palissy's pieces. During the 1840s and 1850s he received a number of major commissions, including a large dish for Frederick William IV, King of Prussia, by the Princesse de Talleyrand and a perfume burner for the Turkish Ambassador Prince Kallimaki. Avisseau exhibited his ceramics in Paris at the 1849 Exposition de l'Industrie, where he was listed as a 'fabricant de poterie genre Palissy', and again at the Exposition Universelle of 1855, where he received a second-class medal for the technical distinction of his work.

BIBLIOGRAPHY

E. Giraudet: *Les Artistes tourangeaux* (Tours, 1885)

R. Maury: 'Faïences en relief: Les figulines rustiques', *abc décor*, lxvi (1970), pp. 56–82

H.-J. Heuser: *Französische Keramik zwischen 1850 und 1910* (Munich, 1974)

DONNA CORBIN

Aviz, House of. Portuguese dynasty of rulers and patrons (see fig.). After the death of Ferdinand I, King of Portugal (*reg* 1367–83), the succession was contested by John I, King of Castile (*reg* 1379–90). The Castilian forces were defeated at the Battle of Aljubarrota (1385) by Ferdinand's illegitimate half-brother, the Grand Master of the religious military Order of Aviz, who succeeded as (1) John I. He was followed by his son (2) Edward and grandson (3) Alfonso V, under whom Edward's brother Henry the Navigator (1394–1460) sponsored Portuguese maritime expeditions that were to lead to a golden age of exploration and wealth through trade. Alfonso's son (4) John II continued the attempts to control the spice trade through the discovery of the sea route to the East. In 1471 John married his first cousin, (5) Eleanor of Viseu. After the death of their son Alfonso (1475–91), however, the succession passed to her brother (6) Manuel I, under whom the Portuguese finally reached India in 1498 and Brazil in 1500.

The wealth of the spice trade financed elaborate displays of royal patronage in architecture and the decorative arts, and enabled the introduction and collection of exotic goods, such as Chinese porcelain and Indian furniture. Manuel's children were important patrons and collectors: (7) John III built a series of forts from Lisbon to Goa to protect the empire's trading posts, (8) Luís and (10) Ferdinand collected Netherlandish tapestries and sponsored painters, while (12) Maria encouraged scholarship and was an active patron of religious art. John's wife, (9) Catherine of Austria, amassed collections for the royal palaces at Lisbon, Sintra and Almeirim. John III was succeeded by his grandson (13) Sebastian, who died in battle in 1578. The crown passed to John's brother (11) Henry, the Archbishop of Lisbon. On his death two years later, Luís's illegitimate son António, Prior of Crato (1531–95), claimed the throne, but the Portuguese forces were

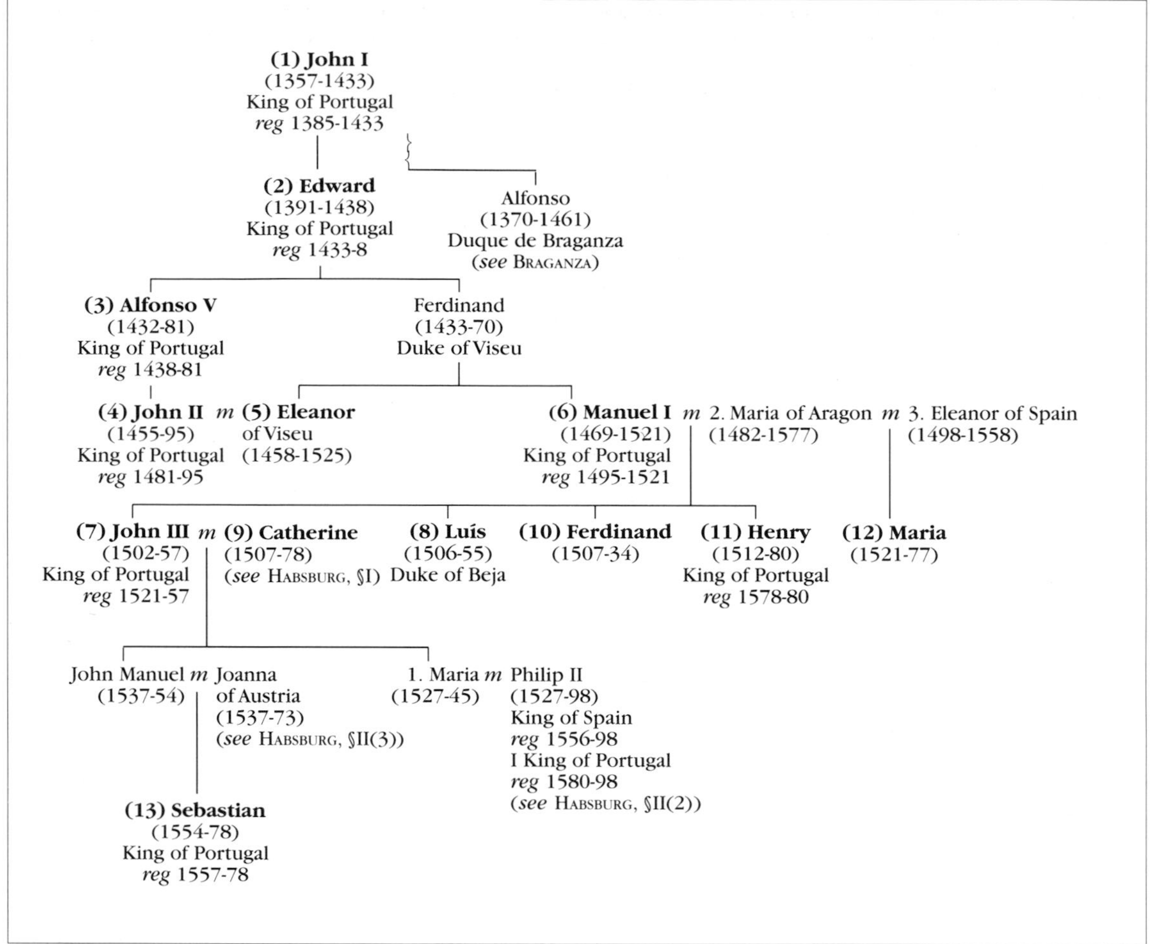

Family tree of the Aviz dynasty of rulers and patrons

defeated at the Battle of Alcântara (1580) and Philip II, King of Spain, was declared King in the following year.

BIBLIOGRAPHY

R. Smith: *The Art of Portugal, 1500–1800* (London, 1968)

G. Kubler: *Portuguese Plain Architecture: Between Spices and Diamonds, 1521–1706* (Middletown, CT, 1972)

A. M. Alves: *Iconologia do poder real no período manuelino: A procura de uma linguagem perdida* [Iconology of royal power in the Manueline period: the search for a lost language] (Lisbon, 1985)

S. Davidson: *African Ivories from Portuguese Domains: Symbols of Imperial Rule in European Courts, 1462–1650* (diss., Washington, DC, George Washington U., 1985)

A. Jordan: *Portuguese Royal Collections: A Bibliographic and Documentary Survey, 1505–1580* (diss., Washington, DC, George Washington U., 1985)

R. Moreira: *A arquitectura do renascimento no sul de Portugal: A encomenda régia entre o moderno e o romano* [Renaissance architecture in southern Portugal: royal patronage between the modern and the Roman] (diss., Lisbon, U. Nova, 1991)

ANNEMARIE JORDAN

(1) John [João] **I**, King of Portugal (*b* ?Lisbon, 14 Aug 1357; *reg* 1385–1433; *d* Lisbon, 14 Aug 1433). He was the illegitimate son of Peter I, King of Portugal (*reg* 1357–67), and half-brother of Ferdinand I, King of Portugal (*reg* 1367–83). John founded the Aviz dynasty, named after the military Order of Aviz, of which he was Master, in April 1385. On the eve of the Battle of Aljubarrota he vowed to build a monastery near the site if victorious. The convent of S Maria da Vitória, commonly known as the priory of BATALHA and which he presented to the Dominicans in 1388, is Portugal's most distinctive and influential Gothic monument, and constituted a reaffirmation of royal power and the new dynasty's legitimacy. In 1387 he married Philippa of Lancaster (1360–1415), daughter of John of Gaunt, Duke of Lancaster (1340–99), and the influence of the English Perpendicular style, as well as French Flamboyant, is evident at Batalha, for example in the Founder's Chapel, which was designed by Huguet as the royal pantheon (*see* GOTHIC, §II, 2(viii)). Two Italian painters, António Florentim and Master Jacome, the latter mentioned by Francisco de Holanda, were employed by the King. In 1428 Jan van Eyck visited Lisbon on a diplomatic mission to paint two portraits (1429; both untraced) of the King's daughter, Isabel (1397–1472), before her marriage to Philip the Good, Duke of Burgundy.

(2) Edward [Duarte], King of Portugal (*b* Viseu, 31 Oct 1391; *reg* 1433–8; *d* Tomar, 13 Sept 1438). Son of (1) John I. His most important patronage was at Batalha, where work continued on his predecessor's projects and he commissioned Huguet to start construction of the Capelas Imperfeitas (begun *c.* 1435) as his mausoleum (for illustration *see* BATALHA). The Hours of Edward I of Portugal (1433–8; Lisbon, Arquiv. N., MS. 140), which is attributed to a member of the Gold Scrolls Group, was probably a gift from his sister Isabel, Duchess of Burgundy.

(3) Alfonso [Afonso] **V**, King of Portugal (*b* Sintra, 15 Jan 1432; *reg* 1438–81; *d* Sintra, 28 Aug 1481). Son of (2) Edward. Under Alfonso work continued at Batalha on the Capelas Imperfeitas and the tombs of his four uncles were placed in the Founder's Chapel. The cloister of Alfonso V (1448–77), north of the Claustro Real, was altered in the 16th century. After his victories at Arzila and Tangiers in 1471, Alfonso ordered at least four tapestries (Pastrana, Colegiata) to celebrate the event; these were carried off, probably during the Spanish occupation (1580–1640), and were rediscovered in 1915 at Pastrana, near Guadalajara. They have been attributed to the workshop of Pasquier Grenier in Tournai, although the design of the cartoons has sometimes been attributed to NUNO GONÇALVES, who was appointed court painter in 1450, alongside João Eanes (*fl* 1350–71). The only work that may be securely identified with Gonçalves is the *St Vincent* retable (completed *c.* 1472; Lisbon, Mus. N. A. Ant.; *see* GONÇALVES, NUNO, fig. 1), in which the King and other members of the royal family are depicted.

SYLVIE DESWARTE-ROSA

(4) John [João] **II** [John the Perfect], King of Portugal (*b* 3 March 1455; *reg* 1481–95; *d* Alvor, 25 Oct 1495). Son of (3) Alfonso V. He was renowned for his statesmanship. His reign was also notable for the absorption of northern European and North African influences in art and architecture. In addition, the King ordered tapestries and silver- and gold-plated items from Flanders, Germany and Spain and brought in artisans from all these countries, as well as from Ireland. The fusion of the well-established south Netherlandish elements in painting with the new perception of colour and light associated with the Italian Renaissance, which began to emerge from the 1480s, is evident in the *Ecce homo* and *Supper at Emmaus* (both Lisbon, Mus. N. A. Ant.), both originally from the convent of S António, Varatojo. The introduction of *Mudéjar* elements in Late Gothic architecture was most apparent in the Alentejo region, notably at Évora in S João Evangelista (1485) and the hermitage of S Brâs (1482), where buttresses are replaced by conical-topped turrets. The most important achievement in this period, however, was the construction of the church of S Francisco (1491), which is situated in Évora next to the Palácio Real. Prefiguring a Manueline style, the church was worked on by the architect Mantims Lourenço, the painter Francisco Henriques and such Flemish artists as Olivier of Ghent. The principal examples of secular architecture during his reign include the moulded brick horseshoe arches of the Paço de Alvito (1491) and a series of houses built for the nobility, with conical chimneys and turrets, and elegant rooms divided by stilted arches (*see* PORTUGAL, §II, 1). In 1490, to celebrate the marriage of his only son, Prince Afonso, to the Princess Isabel, the King had the Palácio Real renovated and several large rooms added. A contract of employment dated 9 December 1492 substantiates Vasari's assertion that Andrea Sansovino worked at John II's court, but no work in Portugal has been attributed to him conclusively.

BIBLIOGRAPHY

E. Lavagnino: *L'opera del genio italiano all'estero, gli artisti italiani in Portugallo* (Rome, 1940)

M. T. Chico and others: *História da arte em Portugal*, ii (Oporto, 1948), pp. 17–135, 182–205

J. Höfler: 'New Light on Andrea Sansovino's Journey to Portugal', *Burl. Mag.*, cxxxiv (1992), pp. 234–7

A. N. de Gusmaõ: 'La Capitale de la Renaissance: Évora', *Mnmts Hist.*, clxxxxiv (1994), pp. 86–9

(5) Eleanor [Leonor] of Viseu, Queen of Portugal (*b* Beja, 2 April, 1458; *d* Lisbon, 17 Nov 1525). Granddaughter of (2) Edward. Her father was Ferdinand, Duke of Viseu (1433–70). In 1471 she married her cousin, the future (4) John II. She was a discriminating patron, notably of Gil Vicente, who was formally appointed her goldsmith in 1509. She also owned a fine Breviary of Hours (*c.* 1500; New York, Pierpont Morgan Lib., MS. M. 52), attributed to Sanders Bening and Gerard Horenbout. She founded the hospital (begun 1485; rebuilt) at the thermal spa of Caldas da Rainha, with its fine pre-Manueline church of Nossa Senhora del Pópulo (*c.* 1485–1500). After her husband's death in 1495, she became a Franciscan Tertiary and founded the charitable confraternity of Misericórdia (1498). She also founded the Madre de Deus convent, Lisbon, which was well advanced by 1509 and for which she commissioned many fine paintings, including the *St Auta* altarpiece (Lisbon, Mus. N. A. Ant.), attributed to Cristóvão de Figueiredo: the Queen is depicted on the panel of the *Arrival in Lisbon of the Relics of St Auta*, which had been given to her *c.* 1517 by the Emperor Maximilian I, together with books and liturgical objects. The *View of Jerusalem* (*c.* 1510; Lisbon, Mus. N. A. Ant.) of the Flemish school, formerly in the Madre de Deus convent, was probably another gift from the Emperor. She also imported relief tondi and other terracotta pieces (now Lisbon, Mus. N. A. Ant.) from Florence for the church and cloister. The extensive decoration that she commissioned *c.* 1509 at the Capelas Imperfeitas in Batalha Priory is a notable display of the Manueline style.

BIBLIOGRAPHY

M. T. Chico and others: *História da arte em Portugal*, ii (Oporto, 1948), pp. 225–321, 345–96

R. Moreira: 'O gosto italiano da Rainha D. Leonor: Nossa Senhora do Pópulo e S Marco del Popolo', *A Rainha D. Leonor* (exh. cat., Lisbon, Fund. Gulbenkian, 1958)

A Rainha D. Leonor (Lisbon, 1974)

J. C. Vigira da Silva: *A igrejo de Nossa Senhora do Pópulo* (Caldas da Rainha, 1993), pp. 79–86

LUCÍLIA VERDELHO DA COSTA

(6) Manuel I, King of Portugal (*b* Alcochete, 31 May 1469; *reg* 1495–1521; *d* Lisbon, Dec 1521). Cousin and brother-in-law of (4) John II. He was the son of Ferdinand, Duke of Viseu, and inherited the throne in accordance with the wishes of John II, who had shown him great affection and had given him as his device the mathematical and maritime armillary sphere, which has subsequently been interpreted as a symbol of predestination.

Manuel benefited from the centralization of power achieved by his predecessor and extended this policy by declaring himself absolute monarch. One of his concerns was to unify the kingdom, in fiscal, monetary and legislative terms, and this had a bearing on the arts, which flourished under the centralized monarchy. The role of the King was apparent in the array of symbols displayed on projects he initiated, among them the *Leitura nova* (1504–52; Lisbon, Arquiv. N.), a collection of legal documents gathered together with richly illuminated frontispieces by various artists, including Alvaro Pires (*fl* 1510–39; *see* PORTUGAL, §III, 1), the cycle of *Forais novos* (New charters) and the *Livro do armeiro-môr* (1509; Lisbon, Arquiv. N.), an armorial of the Portuguese nobility by Jean du Cros. The art of illumination was highly developed in the Manueline period; it was dependent on Netherlandish influences both directly, through the presence of such foreign artists as Antonio de Holanda (*see* HOLANDA, (1)), and indirectly. The recurrent use of the armillary sphere and the Cross (the symbol of the Order of Christ, of which Manuel had become Governor in 1492) on royal documents and on buildings erected through his patronage served as a unifying element in Portuguese art (*see* MANUELINE STYLE).

The most far-reaching events of Manuel's reign were the voyage of Vasco da Gama (*c*. 1460–1524) that opened up the sea route to India in 1497–8 and the 'official' discovery of Brazil in 1500 by Pedro Alvares Cabral (*c*. 1467–1519), both part of a policy of colonial expansion promoted by the King that confirmed Portugal as a leading power (*see also* VICENTE, GIL), with an empire based on a worldwide network of trading stations. The most important of these were set up at Calicut (1502), Cochin (1503), GOA (1510) and Malacca (1511) on the Malay peninsula, the latter two of which were captured by Alfonso de Albuquerque (1453–1515). By 1513 the Portuguese had reached China. The payment of tribute from the overseas territories enriched the kingdom, and porcelain and textiles from China and ivory-inlaid furniture and embroidered quilts from India were introduced in Portugal. The most sought-after spices and wares were traded through the southern Netherlands, with which Portugal maintained a special relationship and through which it had access to the European financial markets, necessary for maintaining its intense trading activity.

Manuel's campaigns in North Africa included the taking of Mogador (now Essaouira; 1506), Safim (now Safi; 1508) and Azamor (now Azemmour; 1513) in Morocco. He financed the construction of fortresses in his overseas possessions, sometimes using prefabricated materials transported by sea from Portugal. DIOGO BOITAC worked at Arzila (now Asilah; 1510–15) and extended the programme of fortifications to Tangiers, Alcácer-Seguer and Ceuta. Diogo de Arruda (*see* ARRUDA, (1)) was active in Safim (1512), Azamor (1516), where he built the remarkable bastion of S Cristovão and the imposing bastion of Raio, and Mazagão (now El Jadida; 1513). He was assisted on some projects by his brother Francisco de Arruda (*see* ARRUDA, (2)), who was in Ceuta in 1514.

Egidio de Viterbo (1469–1532), in a petition to the court of Pope Julius II, gave an account of Manuel I's activities, hailing them as marking the birth of a 'new Golden Age'. A personal mythology grew up around the King, which found expression in the arts: he was seen as 'Emmanuel' (Isaiah 7:14), or variously as King David, Solomon, Julius Caesar, the emperor Constantine and the emperor of Dante. This image was also projected in such festivities as the embassy of Tristão da Cunha (*c*. 1460–1540), who was sent to Pope Leo X in 1514, and in ephemeral architecture for court and public celebrations. The King fostered nationalism with works that included the monumental tombs by NICOLAU CHANTERENE of the two first kings of Portugal, *Alfonso I* and *Sancho I* (1518; Coimbra, Santa Cruz), and by minting new coinage commemorating the vision of Alfonso I (*reg* 1139–85) before his victory at Ourique (1139). Manuel commissioned many buildings, including the Franciscan Convento de Jesus (*c*. 1494–8) at Setúbal (for illustration *see* BOITAC, DIOGO) embodying the architectural style that bears his name. Ribs, corbels, doorjambs and other structural elements are decorated with highly realistic ropes, sea vegetation and tree trunks. The Hieronymite monastery built by Boitac from 1502 to 1516 and João de Castilho from 1517 to *c*. 1530 (*see* CASTILHO, (1)) at Belém (*see* BELÉM (i)) has a church of grand proportions and a cloister decorated with Manueline symbols (*see* PORTUGAL, fig. 3). The Tower of Belém (1515–20) by Francisco de Arruda bears several royal symbols, including the Cross of the Order of Christ, appropriate to a building the function of which was both defensive and representative of the absolute power of the monarch (for illustration *see* BELÉM (i)). The royal palace (destr.) built at Évora was in the courtly and exotic Luso-Morisco style of architecture, which Manuel cultivated in the centres of Lisbon, Évora and Beja: the most complete surviving example is the Palácio Nacional at SINTRA. Work was begun on the completion of the Capelas Imperfeitas at Batalha Priory. This, however, was to remain unfinished, although the entrance portal (completed 1509) by MATEUS FERNANDES I provides an indication of what was intended. As Governor of the Order of Christ, Manuel commissioned Diogo de Arruda to add the choir (1510–13) at Tomar, the celebrated west window of which is the most complete expression of Manueline style, and of the theological and political programme that informed the King's activities (for illustration *see* ARRUDA, (1)).

In painting, although the Gothic tradition persisted in regional styles into the 16th century, there was a marked preference for works by German and Netherlandish artists, such as Quinten Metsys. Foreign artists set up studios and settled in Portugal, among them FRANCISCO HENRIQUES, who painted altarpieces for the side chapels of the church of S Francesco, Évora, including *SS Thomas, Cosmas and Damian* (1509–11; Lisbon, Mus. N. A. Ant.), and FREI CARLOS, who was commissioned by Manuel to execute altarpieces (untraced) for the monastery of Espinheiro, Évora. Both artists were probably of Netherlandish origin and took part in the collective system known as '*parcerias*', by which commissions were shared between several masters and their assistants, both Netherlandish and Portuguese. JORGE AFONSO was appointed court painter in 1508; attributed to him is a group of paintings (*c*. 1515; Lisbon, Mus. N. A. Ant.) for the Madre de Deus convent, Lisbon.

BIBLIOGRAPHY

J. du Cros: *O livro do armeiro-môr* (MS.; 1509; Lisbon, Arquiv. N.); ed. A. Machado de Faria (Lisbon, 1956)

G. de Resende: *Miscellanea e variedade de histórias, costumes, casos e cousas que em seu tempo aconteceram* (MS.; 1554); ed. M. dos Remédios (Coimbra, 1917)
D. de Góis: *Crónica do felicíssimo rei D. Manuel*, 4 vols (Lisbon, 1566); ed. D. Lopes, 4 vols (Coimbra, 1949–55)
J. Osório: *De rebus Emmanuelis regis Lusitaniae* (Lisbon, 1571); Port. trans. as *Da vida e feitos de el-rei D. Manuel* (Rio de Janeiro, 1944)
J. de Vasconcelos: *Da architectura manuelina* (Coimbra, 1885)
R. dos Santos: *O Manuelino* (Lisbon, 1952)
M. C. M. Atanázio: *A arte do Manuelino* (Lisbon, 1984)
A. M. Alves: *Iconologia do poder real no periodo manuelino* (Lisbon, 1985)
P. Dias: *O Manuelino* (1987), v of *História da arte em Portugal* (Lisbon, 1987)
F. A. B. Pereira and D. Markl: *O renascimento* (1987), vi of *História de arte em Portugal* (Lisbon, 1987)
J. C. Vieria da Silva: *O tardo gótico em Portugal* (Lisbon, 1989)
P. Pereira: *A obra silvestre e a esfera do rei* (Coimbra, 1990)

PAULO PEREIRA

(7) John [João] **III**, King of Portugal (*b* Lisbon, 6 June 1502; *reg* 1521–57; *d* Lisbon, 11 June 1557). Son of (6) Manuel I. In 1525 he married (9) Catherine of Austria, sister of Charles V, Holy Roman Emperor. Portugal was then at the height of its political and commercial power, with colonies in Africa, India, China and South America, trading links with the Low Countries, and the court was one of the most extravagant in Europe. In him was combined a curious mixture of enlightenment and piety: he received a humanist education but submitted to clerical power, supporting the introduction of the Jesuits and establishing the Inquisition. John III presided over the final flourishing of the MANUELINE STYLE in architecture and the beginning of the Plain style (Kubler), the rather austere interpretation of Renaissance architecture in Portugal. An ardent amateur of architecture, he commissioned a large model (1547; untraced) of the Colosseum, Rome. During his reign work continued at Belém, Batalha and Tomar, where Diogo de Torralva was commissioned to build the Serlian main cloister (construction begun 1558; *see* TORRALVA, DIOGO DE, fig. 1). The King commissioned three new cathedrals at Miranda do Douro (1548, by Miguel de Arruda), Leiria (1550–74, by Afonso Alvares) and Portalegre (begun 1556, by Alvares), which incorporated Renaissance motifs. He also promoted urban improvements, including the reconstruction at Évora of the Agua de Prata aqueduct (inaugurated 1537, by Francisco de Arruda).

Painting and sculpture flourished during John III's reign. He established a college of arts at Coimbra in 1547 and provided scholarships for many of the artists who achieved later prominence, including Francisco de Holanda, who studied in Rome (1538–40) and introduced Renaissance artistic theory into Portugal. Royal patronage extended to members of the Viseu school under Vasco Fernandes (e.g. *Pentecost*; 1535; Coimbra, Santa Cruz, Sacristy) and the Lisbon school, who included Cristovão de Figueiredo (e.g. *Entombment*; 1529–30; Lisbon, Mus. N.A. Ant.; *see also* LOPES, (2)), Gregório Lopes and Garcia Fernandes. Other arts prospered, including cartography. Renaissance motifs appeared on *azulejos* and in religious sculpture, notably by Nicolau Chanterene (e.g. pulpit, 1521; Coimbra, Santa Cruz). Although John ruled over a culturally self-confident and expanding world, the extravagance of the court, the decline of agriculture and commercial competition, as well as growing religious fanaticism, contributed to the decline of Portugal in the second half of the 16th century.

BIBLIOGRAPHY

A. Pimenta: *D. John III* (Oporto, 1936)
H. V. Livermore: *A New History of Portugal* (Oxford, 1966, rev. Cambridge, 2/1976)
R. C. Smith: *The Art of Portugal, 1500–1800* (London, 1968)
G. Kubler: *Portuguese Plain Architecture: Between Spices and Diamonds, 1521–1706* (Middletown, CT, 1972)

□

(8) Luís, Duque de Beja (*b* Abrantes, 3 March 1506; *d* Lisbon, 27 Nov 1555). Son of (6) Manuel I. In 1535 he accompanied his cousin, Emperor Charles V, on the Tunis expedition and encountered the work of the finest Italian military engineers. As military adviser to his brother, (7) John III, Luís played a major role in the introduction of bastions and other Italian innovations to the design of fortifications in Portugal and its overseas possessions (*see* MILITARY ARCHITECTURE AND FORTIFICATION, §III, 2(v)(a) and fig. 17). These often returned to a design drawn up at Ceuta in 1541 by Benedetto da Ravenna (*d* 1556) and Miguel de Arruda (*see* ARRUDA, (3)).

Luís's patronage ranged widely from cosmography and cartography to literature and the arts. He was a poet and also wrote a number of mathematical treatises (untraced), including one on modes, proportions and measures. Among the artists under his patronage was Francisco de Holanda, who was paid an allowance and offered the Duke the Desenhos das Antigualhas (1538–40; Madrid, Escorial, Bib. Monasterio S Lorenzo, Inv. 28 I. 20; *see* HOLANDA, (2), fig. 1). Luís owned an extensive library, including the Hours of Edward I of Portugal (*see* (2) above) and the Genealogy of the Infante Dom Ferdinand (*see* (10) below), which he inherited after 1540 from his younger brother's collection.

As Grand Prior of the Order of Malta in Portugal, Luís resumed work on the monastery of S Maria de Flor da Rosa, near Crato, in the new Renaissance style, which was also used for the Prior's palace in Crato; of the latter only a balcony, adorned with wide rosettes, survives. He also commissioned the decoration of the convent of S João da Penitência (now the Misericórdia) in Estremoz. His vast construction programmes on his own estates included the foundation of the Franciscan convent of Jenicó of the Provincia de Nossa Senhora de Arrabida (1542), near Salvaterra de Magos, and a palace (begun 1542; most destr.) at Salvaterra, including the surviving chapel (1555) attributed to Miguel de Arruda. The covered market in the central square at Beja, probably based by Diogo de Torralva on Italian models provided by Holanda, was converted into the church of the Misericórdia on completion in 1550. The extensive plans made by Luís and John III for improvements in Lisbon remained unexecuted.

BIBLIOGRAPHY

R. Ricard: 'Pour une monographie de l'enfant D. Luis de Portugal', *Charles Quint et son temps: Colloques internationaux du Centre national de la recherche scientifique: Paris, 1958*, pp. 167–75
A. Betâmio de Almeida: 'O Infante D. Luís, fundador do convento de Jenicó', *Palestra*, v (1959), pp. 38–57
R. Moreira: 'A arquitectura militar', *O Maneirismo*, ed. V. Serrão (1987), vii of *História da arte em Portugal* (Lisbon, 1986), pp. 137–51
J. Rodrigues and P. Perreira: *Santa Maria de Flor da Rosa: Um estudo de história da arte* (Crato, 1986), pp. 98–100

S. Deswarte: 'Espoirs et désespoir de l'infant D. Luís', *Mare Liberum*, iii (1991), pp. 243–98

SYLVIE DESWARTE-ROSA

(9) Catherine [Catarina] of Austria, Queen of Portugal (*b* Torquemada, Spain, 14 Jan 1507; *d* Lisbon, 19 Jan 1578). Wife of (7) John III. She was the daughter of Philip I, King of Castile (*reg* 1504–6), and Joanna, Queen of Castile. Her art collection, which was the largest in Renaissance Portugal and was housed in the palace in Lisbon, included a library, examples of the decorative arts, reliquaries, tapestries, gems, jewellery and imported exotic wares. It reflected her status and bridged the collecting traditions of the late medieval treasury (*Schatzkammer*) and the early curiosity cabinet (*Kunstkammer* or *Wunderkammer*). After 1552 an extensive series of portraits was commissioned from Antonis Mor, Alonso Sánchez Coello and Cristóvão de Morais. Her patronage included the sanctuary (1563–72) of the Hieronymite monastery at Belém, which was designed by Jerónimo de Ruão as a new royal pantheon and in which she was buried. Its altarpiece, depicting the *Adoration of the Magi* and the *Passion* (five of six panels *in situ*) was painted by Lourenço de Salzedo (*d* 1577), who also executed for her the *Judgement of St Catherine*, *St Jerome*, the *Immaculate Conception* and the *Profession of St Paula* (all *c*. 1571; Lourinhã, Misericórdia) for the Hieronymite monastery at Valbemfeito, near Obidos.

BIBLIOGRAPHY

A. Jordan Gschwend: 'A capela-mor: Um panteão real para a dinastia de Avis' [The sanctuary: a royal mausoleum for the Aviz dynasty], *Jerónimos: Quatro séculos de pintura* (exh. cat., ed. A. Franco; Lisbon, Hieronymite Monastery, 1992), pp. 70–90

A. Jordan: *The Development of Catherine of Austria's Collection in the Queen's Household: Its Character and Cost* (diss., Providence, RI, Brown U., 1993)

——: *Retrato de corte em Portugal: O legado de Antonio Moro, 1552–1572* (Lisbon, 1994)

ANNEMARIE JORDAN

(10) Ferdinand [Fernando], Duque de Guarda (*b* Abrantes, 5 June 1507; *d* Abrantes, 7 Nov 1534). Son of (6) Manuel I. Among his large household was Francisco de Holanda, who may have received his earliest training there. Ferdinand was a man of letters with a special interest in history and he employed Damião de Góis (1502–74) in Antwerp to acquire manuscript and printed chronicles. Góis also arranged for the commissioning of tapestries showing the *Months of the Year* (1530; untraced). The most important commission was for the unfinished Genealogy of the Infante Dom Ferdinand (London, BL, Add. MS. 12534), which traces the Duke's ancestry from Noah through 13 illuminated vellum folios (*see* HOLANDA, (1)). This was a collaboration between António de Holanda, who drew the whole genealogy in Portugal and illuminated some of the marginal scenes, including views of Lisbon and other Portuguese cities, and Simon Bening in Bruges, who illuminated most of the folios. Ferdinand had several other chronicles illuminated, also probably by António de Holanda, including a copy of the *Chronicle of King John I* (Madrid, Bib. N., Vitrina 25–8) by Fernão Lopes (*c*. 1380–*c*. 1460), in which the Duke's coat of arms and motto appear on the frontispiece. He also commissioned altarpieces for churches on his estates, notably those ordered from Cristovão de Figueiredo in 1532 for the Franciscan convent at Ferreirim, near Lamego, and executed (1533–4; eight *in situ*) in collaboration with Garcia Fernandes and Gregório Lopes.

BIBLIOGRAPHY

L. Keil: 'Les Tapisseries de Flandres au Portugal pendant les XVe et XVIe siècles', *Miscellanea Leo van Puyvelde* (Brussels, 1949), p. 310

A. de Aguiar: *A genealogia iluminada do Infante Dom Fernando por António de Holanda e Simão Bening: Estudo histórico e crítico* (Lisbon, 1962)

M. de Albuquerque and J. P. de Abreu e Lima: *A genealogia do Infante Dom Fernando de Portugal* (Oporto and Lisbon, 1984)

SYLVIE DESWARTE-ROSA

(11) Cardinal Infante **Henry** [Henrique], King of Portugal, Archbishop of Lisbon (*b* Lisbon, 31 Jan 1512; *reg* 1578–80; *d* Almeirim, 31 Jan 1580). Son of (6) Manuel I. He was a patron of humanist writers, including Damião de Góis, as well as a strong supporter of the Jesuit movement in Portugal. He was appointed Archbishop of Braga (1532), General Inquisitor of the Holy Inquisition (1539), Archbishop of Évora (1540) and Archbishop of Lisbon (1564). From 1562 to 1568 he was regent during the minority of his great-nephew, (13) Sebastian, King of Portugal. After the latter's death, Henry sought papal dispensation to renounce his vows and marry.

In 1544 the Cardinal founded a Capuchin monastery near Évora at the country estate of Quinta da Mitra (or Quinta de Valverde). The designs of its church of Bom Jesus and the conventual buildings (1550–60) are attributed to Manuel Pires, his private architect, and show close collaboration between patron and architect in the realization of an advanced plan, based on geometric formulae. The Cardinal's patronage of the Jesuits resulted in new designs in the Plain style. At Évora he founded a Jesuit college in 1551, which became a university in 1559, and the church of S Antão (1557–63, by Pires). In 1570 Afonso Alvares, a member of his household, was sent to Évora to remove a Roman arch from in front of S Antão and build a fountain. Pero Gomes (*fl* from 1559) was Master of the Works at S Maria do Castelo (1557–63), Estremoz.

BIBLIOGRAPHY

V. Ribeira: *A fundadora da egreja do colegio de Santo Antão (da Companhia de Jesus) e a sua sepultura: Notícia documental* (Coimbra, 1911)

J. M. Queioz Velloso: *O reinado do Cardeal D. Henrique* (Lisbon, 1946)

M. Bataillon: *Etudes sur le Portugal au temps de l'humanisme* (Coimbra, 1952)

M. Domingues: *O Cardeal D. Henrique: O homen e o monarca* (Lisbon, 1964)

ANNEMARIE JORDAN

(12) Dona **Maria** (*b* 8 June 1521; *d* 10 Oct 1577). Daughter of (6) Manuel I. Her mother was the King's third wife, Eleanor (1498–1558), sister of Emperor Charles V. Dona Maria was educated by humanists, had a good knowledge of Latin and Greek and received the best instruction in philosophy, theology and music. From the age of 16 she had her own household at various palaces in Lisbon, first at Alcáçova Velha and then at S Clara, where were held the celebrated 'soirées of the Infanta', which were remarkable for the attention given to the arts and were known by her contemporaries as the 'feminine university'. She lived finally at the sumptuous palace of Santos-o-Novo.

Dona Maria's patronage was first directed to letters and education with her encouragement of humanists, many of whom were followers of Erasmus, such as André de Resende (1498–1573), João de Barros (1496–1570) and

Jerónimo Osório (1506–80), who, like many court poets, including Luis de Camões (1524–80), dedicated their works to her. Later she was interested in the work of theologians and ecclesiastical reformers, such as Fray Luís de Granada (1504–88) and St Francis Borgia (1510–72). She supported the publication of religious texts and bequeathed money for the foundation of university colleges for the Franciscans (at Coimbra) and impoverished gentlemen (at Évora).

Dona Maria, described as 'the wealthiest princess in Christendom' in 1571 by Michele Bonelli (later Cardinal Alessandrino; 1541–98), was given a dowry so large that the Portuguese monarchy and Charles V would never consent to her marriage; her fortune was further increased in 1558 by her inheritance from her mother. During her final years she became an active and devout patron of religious art. She was responsible for the commission to Afonso Alvares of S Engrácia (destr. 1630), Lisbon. Other commissions included the church and convent, which she founded herself, of the Encarnação, Lisbon; the convent of S Bento (1571; now the Military Hospital), Lisbon, also by Alvares, for the Order of St Benedict of Aviz; the convent of Cristo dos Milagros (destr.), Santarém; the convent of Barros (partially preserved) for the Arrábida Order in Torres Vedras; and the convent of S Helena do Monte Calávrio (1569–74, by Alvares), Évora. At Carnide she built the hospital and the important church of Nossa Senhora da Luz (1575–97; part destr. 1755), which she commissioned from Jeronimo de Ruão, and where she is buried.

Dona Maria's executors dispersed her jewels and works of art and delayed the execution of many of her commissions, with the result that these buildings do not always correspond to her original intentions. There are several portraits of the 'most beautiful Maria', as Camões called her, including those attributed to Gregório Lopes (*c.* 1541; Chantilly, Mus. Condé) and Antonis Mor (1552; Madrid, Convent of the Descalzas Reales). She appears alongside other members of the royal family in the *Veneration of the Virgin of Belém* (1553; Lisbon, Mus. N. A. Ant.), attributed to Francisco de Holanda, in *St Benedict Bestowing the Rule on his Order* (Lisbon, Nossa Senhora da Luz), perhaps by Diogo Teixeira, and on a reliquary in the church of S Engrácia, Lisbon.

BIBLIOGRAPHY

J. de Barros: *Panegyrico* (Lisbon, 1555/*R* 1791)

Frei M. Pacheco: *Vida de la serenissima Infanta Dona Maria* (Lisbon, 1675)

C. M. Vasconcelos: *A Infanta Dona Maria de Portugal, 1521–77, e as suas damas* (Oporto, 1902, rev. Lisbon, 1983)

A. Temudo: 'Um retrato da Infanta Dona Maria no Museu das Janelas Verdes', *Bol. Mus. Nac. A. Antiga*, i/2 (1939)

ANA MARIA ALVES

(13) Sebastian [Sebastião], King of Portugal (*b* Lisbon, 20 Jan 1554; *reg* 1557–78; *d* Alcazar Quivir (now al-Qasr al-Kabir), Morocco, 4 Aug 1578). Grandson of (7) John III. He was the son of the Infante John (1537–54) and Joanna of Austria (*see* HABSBURG, §II(3)). From 1554 to 1562 he was under the tutelage and regency of (9) Catherine of Austria, who was succeeded by (11) Henry, Cardinal Archbishop of Lisbon. Sebastian's reign coincided with Portugal's political, economic and artistic decline in the second half of the 16th century. His principal interests were military and civic architecture, disciplines that were taught by the royal architect, ANTÓNIO RODRIGUES (appointed 1568), along with mathematics and cosmography, in a court school that was established in 1562 at the Paço da Ribeira, Lisbon. The superb maps of the Portuguese empire produced during the reign by Fernão Vaz Dourado incorporated the latest cosmographical and navigational information.

In 1569 Sebastian appointed the court architect Afonso Alvares (*see* ALVARES, (1)) to design the basilican church of S Sebastião (begun 1570; unfinished; destr. 1755), Lisbon, beside the River Tagus near the royal palace. FILIPPO TERZI was invited to Lisbon in 1576 as a military engineer; he accompanied the King to Morocco, where he was captured. Sebastian did not commission any new royal residences in Lisbon: the palace of Xabregas (1556–9, by Miguel de Arruda; destr. 1755) remained unfinished and the medieval palace of Alcáçova (destr. 1755) was renovated.

BIBLIOGRAPHY

F. de Holanda: *Da fabrica que falece à cidade de Lisboa* (MS.; 1571); ed. J. de Vasconcellos (Oporto, 1879), fol. 27

D. B. Machado: *Memórias para a história de Portugal, que comprehendem o governo dol rey D. Sebastião*, 4 vols (Lisbon, 1736–51)

A. Danvila y Burguero: *Felipe II e el rey don Sebastián de Portugal* (Madrid, 1945)

J. M. Queiroz Velloso: *D. Sebastiao, 1554–78* (Lisbon, 1945)

R. Moreira: 'A escola de arquitectura do Paço da Ribeira e a Academia de Matemáticas de Madrid', *As relações artísticas entre Portugal e Espanha na época dos Descobrimentos: 2d Simpósio Luso-Espanhol de História da Arte: Coimbra, 1983*, pp. 65–77

F. A. Baptista Pereira: 'O retrato de D. Sebastião do Museu Nacional de Arte Antiga: Uma leitura iconológica', *Prelo*, xi (1986), pp. 53–66

ANNEMARIE JORDAN

Avnatamov. *See* HOVNAT'ANIAN.

Avont, Pieter van (*bapt* Mechelen, 14 Jan 1600; *d* Deurne, Antwerp, 1 Nov 1652). Flemish painter, draughtsman and printmaker. In 1622–3 he became a master in the Guild of St Luke, Antwerp. In 1625–6 he took on Peter van de Cruys (*fl* 1625–44) as his pupil, who was followed by Frans Wouters in 1629 and Wouters's brother, Pieter Wouters (1617–after 1632), in 1631–2. In 1631 van Avont became a citizen of Antwerp.

A recurring motif in van Avont's work is a group of figures dominated by children and putti; these appear in a variety of forms—the Infant Christ, John the Baptist, angels—in van Avont's many pictures of the Holy Family. The figure groups in these pieces are often of the same type: angels paying tribute to the Virgin and Child. The grouping is identical in several paintings. Van Avont also used figures of children in his bacchanals and in such allegorical scenes as the *Four Elements* (Basle, Kstmus.) and *War and Peace* (Brussels, Baron Coppée priv. col.). In all these works his style is characterized by a soft modelling of the figures using *sfumato* and warm colours. The scenes with children are often set in a landscape. Although van Avont signed many of these paintings, he did not always paint the landscapes himself. He himself added figures to landscapes by various other artists, such as David Vinckboons, Jan Breughel I and Jan Breughel II, Jacques d'Arthois, Lucas Achtschellinckx, Lodewijk de Vadder and Frans Wouters. Van Avont's collaboration with Jan Breughel II can usually be recognized at once in paintings with floral wreaths, for example *Garland with the Holy Family, St John the Baptist and Putti* (Antwerp, Kon. Mus. S. Kst.). Sometimes these garlands form a broad decorative border around a figure group painted by van Avont, who signed some of these works. The collaboration between the two artists is also alluded to by Jan Breughel in his diary. It seems possible that van Avont received commissions from the Archduke Leopold William, Governor of the Netherlands, who owned a landscape with the *Virgin and Child with Angels* by van Avont.

Apart from these most characteristic works there are a few examples of monumental history paintings by van Avont. In these pictures the figures—mostly saints—are represented life-size; they are, however, modelled in the same gentle way as van Avont's other figures. These paintings show van Avont's debt to Rubens, whose work he is known to have copied. A number of smaller works by van Avont have plump children and facial types reminiscent of Rubens's work. The elegant figures and the brownish tone of the chiaroscuro in some of van Avont's paintings also reveal the influence of van Dyck, whose work he also copied.

There are a number of drawings by van Avont. Several of these were published as prints, some made by the artist himself although most were made by others, including his friend Wenzel Hollar. Van Avont was also active as a print publisher. His drawings and prints often have the same themes and motifs as his paintings, although he seems sometimes to have experimented with other themes (e.g. *Portrait of a Man* and a study of *Brass Instruments*, both Hamburg, Ksthalle).

BIBLIOGRAPHY

Bénézit; Hollstein: *Dut. & Flem.*; Thieme–Becker

De eeuw van Rubens (exh. cat., ed. E. de Wilde; Brussels, Mus. A. Anc., 1965), p. 324

M.-L. Hairs: 'Jean Breughel le Jeune, peintre de fleurs', *Rev. Belge Archéol. & Hist. A.*, xxvi (1967), pp. 57–74

E. Valdivieso: 'Dos pinturas ineditas de Pieter van Avont', *Bol. Semin. Estud. A. & Arqueol.*, xxxviii (1972), pp. 530–34

JETTY E. VAN DER STERRE

Avostali. *See* AOSTALLI.

Avramidis, Joannis (*b* Batum, USSR [now Batumi, Georgia], 26 Sept 1922). Austrian sculptor of Greek descent. He was the son of Greek parents and grew up in Batum, where he studied at the Staatliche Kunstschule (1937–9). From 1939 to 1943 he was in Athens and in 1943 settled in Vienna. From 1945 to 1949 he studied painting at the Akademie der Bildenden Künste in Vienna with Robin Andersen. From 1953 to 1956 he studied sculpture with Fritz Wotruba. The starting-point of all Avramidis's sculptures was the human body, reduced to the simplest possible elements of a column and sphere. The archaic character, influenced principally by ancient Greek sculpture, merged with the notion of absolute beauty, which manifests itself in forms of perfect rotundity, for example *Head II* (bronze, h. 270 mm, 1965; Hamburg, Gal. Elke Dröscher). Whilst dispensing with individual details, he created bodies of immaculately tranquil harmony, their shape characterized by the interaction between individual parts and an imposingly dominant monumental whole. These often took the form of clusters of columnar forms suggesting intimate crowds of figures. From 1965 Avramidis held posts at the Akademie der Bildenden Künste. In the 1980s the figural elements of his work became more pronounced, being marked by segmentary lines (e.g. *Sitting Figure 1*, bronze, h. 1.22 m, 1983; see 1988 exh. cat.). Apart from numerous one-man exhibitions, Avramidis participated in major international exhibitions.

BIBLIOGRAPHY

Trigonpersonale 5: Joannis Avramidis—Plastik—Grafik (exh. cat., Graz, Neue Gal., 1974)

Joannis Avramidis: Skulpturen und Handzeichnungen (exh. cat., Bremen, Ksthalle, 1980)

Joannis Avramidis: Zeichnungen (exh. cat., Stuttgart, Staatsgal., 1986)

Joannis Avramidis: Skulpturen u. Zeichnungen (exh. cat., Ludwigsburg, Schloss, 1988)

ULRIKE GAISBAUER

Aw [Ow], **(Andreas) Meinrad von** (*b* Sigmaringen, 28 Nov 1712; *d* 3 Jan 1792). German painter. He probably trained with his stepfather, the painter Johann Joseph Veseer, and later with Franz Joseph Spiegler. In 1735 he went to Vienna, where he matriculated from the Akademie der Bildenden Künste. He possibly studied under Paul Troger and then spent some time in Augsburg. After qualifying as a master painter, von Aw settled *c.* 1740 in Sigmaringen, where he also held public office, being twice elected burgomaster; later he ran an inn.

Von Aw's early frescoes and altarpieces with their gentle, bright colours and their lively compositions belong to the tradition of south German Rococo painting. He often borrowed either single figures or even whole groups of figures from other artists; thus when he painted the interior of the castle church of the Holy Trinity at Haigerloch (1748–51) he used engravings after Carlo Carlone, Johann Georg Bergmüller and Matthäus Günther; for the ceiling frescoes (1758–60) in St Johann Evangelist in Sigmaringen he copied Paul Troger's frescoes from the cathedral at Brixen (now Bressanone). From the late 1750s a different approach to landscape became apparent in his work: in his paintings (1770–74) in St Martin, Messkirch, his increasing adoption of classicizing trends is evident. His colours became darker and heavier, the individual frescoes are no longer subordinate to a unified overall composition, the picture construction and the figures are less agitated, and there is greater use of classical ornament. In his late work, such as the choir frescoes (1780) in SS Maria and Verena, Rot an der Rot, there is a perceptible decline in creativity.

BIBLIOGRAPHY

A. Wagner-Würz: *Meinrad von Aw: Leben und Werk eines süddeutschen Rokokomalers* (Hechingen, 1936)

Meinrad von Aw, 1712–1792 (exh. cat., ed. E. Buri and I. M. Buck; Sigmaringen, 1992)

JOSEF STRASSER

Awatovi. Site in North America, in north-eastern Arizona. A Hopi village was established there by *c.* AD 1250 and destroyed in 1700. During excavations (1935–9) by the Peabody Museum, Harvard University, almost 150 wall paintings were discovered in 11 *kiva*s (subterranean ceremonial structures; *see* KIVA). The wall paintings were first executed *c.* 1375 using the *fresco secco* technique and continued up to Spanish contact in the early 17th century. Except for the black, inorganic pigments were used, including red, yellow, blue, green, pink, orange, brown, grey and white. Plant, animal and anthropomorphic forms are portrayed, as well as clouds, lightning, water symbols and geometric designs. The subject-matter is religious, depicting parts of ceremonies, events and creatures of Hopi oral history, and altars used to perform ceremonies. Later compositions convey a feeling of movement, many showing symbolic combat between two figures. The sudden appearance of elaborate *kiva* wall paintings seems to coincide with the development of *kachina* religion, and *kachina* figures (spirits of the benevolent dead) can be identified in the paintings. The construction of a Spanish mission at Awatovi in 1630 ended the painting of *kiva* murals; the mission was destroyed during the Pueblo Revolt of 1680; the pueblo was destroyed in 1700 through actions of other Hopi villages.

BIBLIOGRAPHY

R. Montgomery, W. Smith and J. O. Brew: *Franciscan Awatovi: The Excavations and Conjectural Reconstruction of a 17th-century Spanish Mission Establishment at a Hopi Indian Town in Northeastern Arizona*, Pap. Peabody Mus. Amer. Archaeol. & Ethnol., xxxvi (Cambridge, MA, 1949)

W. Smith: *Kiva Mural Decorations at Awatovi and Kawaika-a, with a Survey of Other Wall Paintings in the Pueblo Southwest*, Pap. Peabody Mus. Amer. Archaeol. & Ethnol., xxxvii (Cambridge, MA, 1952)

E. CHARLES ADAMS

Awazu, Kiyoshi (*b* Tokyo, 19 Feb 1929). Japanese graphic designer. He graduated from Hosei University (Tokyo). In 1955 he received an award from the Japan Advertising Artists Club for his poster *Give back the Sea*, establishing himself as a socially committed designer. He was initially influenced by the American designer BEN SHAHN. In 1962 he designed the iron gate for the government office building at the Izumo Grand Shrine (Shimane Prefect.). In 1965, along with many of Japan's leading designers, he was chosen to take part in the Persona Exhibition, which stressed the personal identities of individual designers. In 1975 Awazu was art director on Shūji Terayama's film *Den'en ni shinu* ('To die in the country'). During the 1960s and 1970s Awazu's work was influenced by the vernacular design that challenged Japanese modernism. He has designed for many national and international exhibitions, including Expo '70 (Osaka). Since the late 1980s much of Awazu's work has been commissioned by national and local government bodies.

BIBLIOGRAPHY

Posters: Japan, 1800–1980s (Nagoya, 1989)

The Work of Awazu Kiyoshi (Tokyo, 1989)

HIROSHI KASHIWAGI

Awliya Ata. *See* ZHAMBYL.

Axminster. English town in Devon, situated on the River Axe, known as a centre of carpet production from the mid-18th century to the mid-19th. In 1755 Thomas Whitty (*d* 1792), a weaver from Axminster, visited Pierre Parisot's carpet workshop in Fulham, London. An apprentice showed him the workshop, and on his return to Axminster Whitty built a large vertical loom, taught his daughters to tie the symmetrical or Ghiordes knot (*see* CARPET, §I, 1 and fig. 1) and began to produce carpets. In 1757 he submitted a carpet measuring 4.9×3.8 m to the Royal Society of Arts and was awarded a joint prize with Thomas Moore (*c.* 1700–1788; *see* CARPET, §II, 2(iii)) of Chiswell Street, London. Whitty valued his carpet at £15 and the Society ruled it the best carpet in proportion to its price. In 1758 he was asked to submit three carpets and shared the prize with Claude Passavant of Exeter (*see* EXETER, §2). In 1759 Whitty had to submit six carpets and was the sole winner. By now he had earned a considerable reputation, which increased over the years as his competitors ceased production: Passavant in 1761 and Moore *c.* 1793. Even as the sole producer of hand-knotted carpets in Britain, Whitty's carpets were always reasonably priced. After his death his son Thomas Whitty (1740–99) and later his grandsons Thomas Whitty (1775–1810) and Samuel Rampson Whitty (1784–1855) took over the factory and continued production until a disastrous fire in 1828 destroyed most of the workshops. The firm never fully recovered, as both workmen and orders were lost during the period of rebuilding. The company was declared bankrupt in 1835 and was purchased in 1836 by a Mr Blackmore, who moved the workshops and weavers to Wilton (*see* WILTON, §2), where fine hand-knotted carpets in the Axminster tradition were woven until the 1950s.

BIBLIOGRAPHY

A. F. Kendrick and C. E. C. Tattersall: *Handwoven Carpets: Oriental and European* (London, 1926)

C. E. C. Tattersall and S. Reed: *British Carpets* (London, 1966)

B. Jacobs: *Axminster Carpets* (Leigh on Sea, 1969)

C. Gilbert, J. Lomax and A. Wells-Cole: 'Country House Floors', *Temple Newsam Country House Stud.*, iii (1987)

JENNIFER WEARDEN

Axoum. *See* AKSUM.

'Ay. *See* AI.

Ayala [Aiala] **(e Cabrera), Josefa de** [Óbidos, Josefa d'] (*b* Seville, *c.* 1630; *d* Óbidos, 22 July 1684). Portuguese painter and engraver. She was the daughter of the Portuguese painter Baltazar Gomes Figueira (1597–1674) and a Spanish lady, Doña Catarina de Ayala y Cabrera. After the restoration of the Portuguese monarchy in 1640 the family moved to Coimbra. Here Josefa began her apprenticeship under her father, a painter of landscapes, still-lifes and religious works, who in 1644 painted the retable of Nossa Senhora da Graça, Coimbra, in the naturalist-tenebrist style he had learnt in Seville in the circles of Juan del Castillo, Juan de Roelas and Francisco de Zurbarán.

Josefa's first known work is an engraving of *St Catharine* (1646; Lisbon, Mateus José de Arriaga Xavier da Costa priv. col., see 1984 exh. cat., pl. 1). In 1647 she painted on copper the *Mystic Marriage of St Catharine* (Lisbon, Mus. N.A. Ant.), which, despite the artificial lighting, dainty figures and the almost obsessive piety, shows her promise as a painter in oils. The fine painting on copper of *St Mary Magdalene* (*c.* 1653; Coimbra, Mus. N. Machado de Castro), in its freshness of drawing, handling of light and transparency of colour, recalls the work of such Flemish painters as Daniel Seghers. Her work as an engraver includes the allegorical figure of *Knowledge* for the frontispiece to the *Estatutos da Universidade de Coimbra* (1653).

Some time after 1653 Josefa settled with her family in Óbidos. The greater refinement of her technique as a religious painter is seen in the precision and warmth of the brushwork in *Pentecost* (*c.* 1660; Coimbra, Mus. N. Machado de Castro). It is also apparent in the delicate paintings on copper of the *Virgin and Child* (1657; see fig.) and *St Joseph* (1661; both Lisbon, Mus. N.A. Ant.). The retable (1661) in the chapel of St Catharine, in the church of S Maria, Óbidos, is one of the few examples of her work that remains *in situ* and, as intended, is framed by carved and gilded wood surrounded by polychrome tiles. It consists of five canvases notable for their larger modelling, warm colouring and careful tenebrist style, particularly evident in the central *Mystic Marriage of St Catharine*. The *Adoration of the Shepherds* (1669; Lisbon, Mus. N.A. Ant.) was painted for the monastery of S Maria Madalena, Alcobaça. In 1673 she painted a series of the *Life of St Teresa* for the Discalced Carmelite convent, Cascais (Cascais, Nossa Senhora da Assunção).

The formal qualities and ideology of many of Josefa's works can be related to contemporary Spanish painting. This is seen especially in her still-lifes, largely influenced by Zurbarán though enlivened by the inclusion of scattered flowers, ribbons or elaborate containers. Her minute descriptive detail and vibrant sense of colour are exemplified in *Still-life with Fruit and Flowers* (1676; Santarém, Bib. Braamcamp Freire), which shows a Baroque bowl with a scalloped form typical of Portuguese silver of the late 17th century. Her works often combine sacred and profane subjects in an atmosphere full of sensuality and mysticism. The *Christ Child as Saviour of the World* (1673; Cascais, Nossa Senhora da Assunção), depicting the figure as a dressed statue with a wreath of flowers, is reminiscent of Juan de Arellano. The influence of Zurbarán is again marked and suggests that Josefa knew his paintings; several of his panel paintings were included in inventories of her father's property and in those of her uncle Bernabé Ayala, a little-known Spanish painter, and her sister Basilia Gomes Figueira.

Josefa de Ayala: *Virgin and Child*, oil on copper, 165×127 mm, 1657 (Lisbon, Museu Nacional de Arte Antiga)

An appreciation of the work of Zurbarán is also apparent in Josefa's later religious paintings, especially in the modelling, the luminosity of the whites and creams and in the types of faces and textiles. Notable examples include the *Veil of St Veronica* (1679), *Calvary* (1679) and the *Visitation* (all Peniche, Misericórdia), which express her pious temperament and deep sense of mysticism. She made several versions of the *Agnus Dei* theme, of which *Paschal Lamb* (*c.* 1670–80; Évora, Mus. Évora) derives directly from one of many versions of a composition by Zurbarán, *Agnus Dei* (e.g. San Diego, CA, Mus. A.). Of Josefa's portraits, which were highly praised by her contemporaries, only one survives, the fine psychological study of *Faustino das Neves* (1670–80; Óbidos, Mus. Mun.).

BIBLIOGRAPHY

F. da Costa Meesen: *Antiguidade da arte da pintura* (MS.; 1696); ed. G. Kubler (New Haven and London, 1967), pp. 270–71
L. X. da Costa: *Una aguafortista do século XVII (Josefa d'Ayala)* (Coimbra, 1931)
Josefa d'Óbidos (exh. cat. by J. Conto, Lisbon, Mus. N.A. Ant., 1949)
L. Reis-Santos: *Josefa d'Óbidos* (Lisbon, 1956)
J. H. Díaz: *Josefa de Ayala: Pintora ibérica del siglo XVII* (Seville, 1967)
E. J. Sullivan: 'Josefa de Ayala: A Woman Painter of the Portuguese Baroque', *J. Walters A.G.*, xxxvii (1978), pp. 22–35
——: 'Obras de Josefa de Ayala, pintora ibérica', *Archv Esp. A.*, liv (1981), pp. 87–93
L. de Moura Sobral: 'Três "bodegones" do Museu de Évora', *Colóq. A.*, 55 (1982), pp. 5–13
Josefa d'Óbidos (exh. cat. by V. Serrão, Óbidos, S Maria, 1984)
V. Serrão: *O essencial sobre Josefa d'Óbidos* (Lisbon, 1985)

VITOR SERRÃO

Ayck, Barthélemy de. *See* EYCK, BARTHÉLEMY D'.

Aycock, Alice (*b* Harrisburg, PA, 20 Nov 1946). American sculptor, draughtswoman, installation and environmental artist. She studied liberal arts at Rutgers University, New Brunswick, NJ (1964–8), and obtained an MA in studio art at the City University of New York (1968–71), where she worked under Robert Morris and became familiar with systems theory. From the 1960s Aycock developed phenomenologically site-orientated works to include metaphor and simile, referring to machinery and construction sites, archaeological sites, models, children's play areas and funfairs and other public or social settings. For example in a *Simple Network of Underground Wells and Tunnels* (1975) six concrete wells (1.62 sq. m) with connecting tunnels were sunk into an area of ground *c.* 6.1×12.2 m at Merriewold West, Far Hills, NJ (destr.). The curious sense of authority within her sophisticated, well-made structures is simultaneously articulated and undermined by a nonsensical, non-functional and fantastical element. Her works are often a synthesis of diverse elements. The imagery of the *Game of Flyers* (wood, steel, fire, water, birds, 1979–80; Washington, DC, Project A.) derives equally from tantric drawings, the problem of designing and constructing a machine for human flight and thoughts about World War II. By the 1990s Aycock produced both elaborate site-specific and gallery installation works. Examples of her work are housed in the Australian National Gallery, Canberra, the Museum Ludwig, Cologne, and the Whitney Museum of American Art, New York.

BIBLIOGRAPHY

Alice Aycock Projects (exh. cat., essay by E. F. Fry, Tampa, U. S. FL, 1979–81)

J. Fineberg and others: *Alice Aycock: Retrospective of Projects and Ideas (1972–1983)* (Stuttgart, 1983) [in Ger. and Eng.]

□

Aydhab. *See under* NUBIA, §VII.

Ayia Irini. *See under* KEA.

Ayia Kyriaki. *See under* LESBOS.

Ayia Paraskevi. *See under* LESBOS.

Ayia Triada. Minoan site, possibly Palatial, on a ridge at the west end of the Mesara plain in southern Crete, inhabited from *c.* 3800 to *c.* 1100 BC. The relationship between this important centre and PHAISTOS, only 3 km away, during the Neo-Palatial period (from Middle Minoan (MM) III to Late Minoan (LM) I, *c.* 1675–*c.* 1425 BC) is uncertain. Ayia Triada may have been a summer palace, or a wealthy dependent estate, and was perhaps the 'da-wo' referred to in the Linear B tablets. Excavation was begun by FREDERICO HALBHERR (1902–14) and has been continued most recently by Vincenzo La Rosa (1977 onwards). For the most part, finds are in the Archaeological Museum, Herakleion.

Neolithic material is known, but is haphazardly distributed. The Pre-Palatial period (from Early Minoan I to MM IA, *c.* 3500/3000–*c.* 1900 BC) is represented by localized deposits, wall traces and two tholoi with later, external annexes, most of which are to the north-east of the main site. MM IB-IIIA (*c.* 1900–*c.* 1635 BC) structures are also recorded on the site itself. Major redevelopment seems to have occurred in the Neo-Palatial period, permitting the construction of a radically different palace-like building, which was destroyed by fire at the end of LM IB (*c.* 1425 BC).

The main 'palace' has two wings, north and west, flanking a south-east court. It was a two-storey building containing the usual Minoan architectural components: pier-and-door halls, light wells, stairs, stores with pithoi and smaller service units. The more imposing rooms lay at either end of the north wing, and the building was clearly well furnished; in particular, a series of stone vessels decorated in low relief are justly famous for the quality of their execution and for the insight they provide into aspects of Minoan life (*see* MINOAN, fig. 28). Among the subjects depicted are boxing and bull-leaping, an agricultural festival and another, more serious ritual, perhaps military or the receiving of tribute. Other items include a shell-shaped stone vase (*see* MINOAN, fig. 27) and objects of ivory, bone and faience (*see* MINOAN, §§VI, 2, and VII). There are also notable frescoes, portraying, for example, cats stalking birds, and deer moving amid rocks and flowers (*see* MINOAN, §IV, 2(ii)). More prosaic finds show that the building served as an administrative and production centre; these include Linear A tablets, sealings, copper

Ayia Triada, sarcophagus with a ritual scene, painted plaster on limestone, l. 1.37 m, Late Minoan IIIA, *c.* 1390 BC (Herakleion, Archaeological Museum)

'ox-hide' ingots, potters' wheels and a kiln. In addition, Linear A graffiti occur on walls and on pottery. Also of this period were substantial town houses to the east and north-east of the 'palace' and an open area with a short colonnade to the north of it. Lower down the hillside to the north-east was a considerable spread of smaller, tightly packed units, with an occasional larger structure (such as the Cyclopaean Building) interspersed among them.

Little is known of the period (LM II, *c.* 1425–*c.* 1390 BC) following the site's destruction: pottery fragments alone remain. LM IIIA (*c.* 1390–*c.* 1335 BC) was an era of increasing and ultimately great architectural reorganization, however, during which Ayia Triada perhaps became an independent settlement. A megaron and ancillary building were constructed over the north range of the 'palace', the south-east court was expanded and the lower 'town' was relaid on a more unified plan, incorporating a large stoa fronting two-storey units interpreted as shops. The sacred character of the south-east area was intensified by the erection of a simple shrine, equipped with snake-tubes (clay tubular 'stands', with loops down the sides suggesting the snakes), its plaster floor (known as the Marine Floor) decorated with paintings of octopus and dolphins. Substantial deposits of figurines (humans, bulls and horses) accumulated in the yard to its west. A destruction in LM IIIB (*c.* 1335–*c.* 1190 BC) grievously affected the settlement, but some open-air religious activity persisted into Sub-Minoan Proto-Geometric times (*c.* 1050–*c.* 900 BC).

Contemporary with the LM IIIA refurbishments of the residential quarter are some chamber tombs in the area of the earlier tholoi, one of which yielded the famous limestone sarcophagus decorated in fresco technique (see fig.). The main sides of the sarcophagus portray scenes of worship (before double axes), presumably veneration of the dead, and the sacrifice of a bull to the accompaniment of music. The ends show female figures driving chariots drawn by goats and griffins. An Egyptian seal and a Hittite sphinx from the same cemetery indicate overseas contacts.

BIBLIOGRAPHY

F. Halbherr: 'Scoperti ad Haghia Triada presso Phaestos', *Mnmt. Ant.: Lincei*, xiii (1903), pp. 5–74

——: 'Rapporto sugli scavi ... ad Haghia Triada ed a Festo ... 1904', *Mem. Reale Ist. Lombardo Sci. Lett. & A.*, xxi (1905), pp. 235–54
S. G. Spanakis: *Kentriki-anatoliki* (1964), i of *I Kriti* (Herakleion, 1964–), pp. 111–19
F. Halbherr, E. Stefani and L. Banti: 'Haghia Triada nel Periodo Tardo Palaziale', *Annu. Scu. Archeol. Atene & Miss. It. Oriente*, lv (1977) [whole issue]
A. Di Vita and others: *Creta antica: Cento anni di archeologia italiana (1884–1984)* (Rome, 1984)
V. La Rosa: 'Ayia Triada', *The Aerial Atlas of Ancient Crete*, ed. J. M. Myers, E. E. Myers and G. Cadogan (Berkeley, 1992), pp. 70–77

D. EVELY

Ayin-Dara. *See* AIN DARA.

Ayioi Anargyroi. *See under* NAXOS, §1.

Ayios Dhimitrios. *See under* KALAVASOS.

Ayios Vasilios. *See* ZYGOURIES.

Ay-Khanum. *See* AI KHANUM.

Aylesford, 4th Earl of. *See* FINCH, HENEAGE.

Aymonino, Carlo (*b* Rome, 18 July 1926). Italian architect and urban planner. After training with Marcello Piacentini, he attended the University of Rome, from which he graduated in 1950, setting up practice in Rome in 1951. His first professional experience was with Mario Ridolfi and Ludovico Quaroni on the INA-Casa housing (1949–54) on Via Tiburtina, Rome, a notable example of Italian neo-realism, where he acquired the practical skills seen in later housing such as Spine Bianche (1955–7) at Matera, or the Tratturo dei Preti housing (1957–9) at Foggia. Aymonino was active on the editorial board of *Il contemporaneo* from 1954 and was a contributor to *Casabella* from 1957 to 1965, and thus participated in the architectural debates of the late 1950s. In 1957 he was a founder-member of the Società di Architettura e Urbanistica (S.A.U.). In 1960 he founded Studio AYDE with Maurizio Aymonino, his brother, and the brothers Baldo and Alessandro De Rossi. In urban planning he developed the idea of directional centres, linking cities with their environs in terms of recognizable urban typologies, and demonstrated it formally in his competition proposals for the city centres of Turin and Bologna (with others), both of 1962.

One of Aymonino's most significant works is the Gallaratese 2 housing development (1967–72; with AYDE and others) in the Monte Amiata suburb of Milan, where he was the director of the project, participants in which included Aldo Rossi. Seven-storey blocks are grouped around a centre to create an urban character through a synthesis of formal typologies. The new Rationalism also informs later buildings: the Liceo Scientifico G. Marconi (1970–73), Pesaro, a number of university proposals in the early 1970s and the law courts (1977–86) in Ferrara, as well as other directional city centre schemes such as Florence (1978; with Aldo Rossi), Pesaro (1979–83) and the IACP district (1985) on the Giudecca, Venice. He taught at the faculty of architecture in Rome, at the Istituto Universitario di Architettura in Venice (from 1963; Dean, 1973–9). From 1987 he was Assessor to Rome City Council where his projects included the restructuring of the archeological site of the Roman fora.

WRITINGS

Origine e sviluppo della città moderna (Padua, 1965)
Il significato della città (Bari, 1975, 2/1976)

BIBLIOGRAPHY

C. Conforti: *Carlo Aymonino: L'architettura non è un mito* (Rome, 1980) [good bibliography]
——: *Il Gallaratese di Aymonino e Rossi, 1967–1972* (Rome, 1981) [good bibliography]

MERCEDES DAGUERRE

ʿAyn al-Jarr. *See* ANJAR.

Aynalov, Dmitry (Vlas'yevich) (*b* Mariupol', 20 Feb 1862; *d* Leningrad [now St Petersburg], 12 Dec 1939). Russian art historian of Ukrainian birth. He studied first in Odessa at the Novorossiysky University under Professor N. P. Kondakov and in 1888 followed Kondakov to St Petersburg, where he completed his education. During his university years, together with his fellow student E. Redin Aynalov, he researched the mosaics and mural paintings of St Sophia in Kiev, where his main interest was devoted to their iconography. He received his master's degree in 1901. In 1903 Aynalov was appointed to a chair at Kazan' University.

In one of his first works, *Mosaics of the Fourth and Fifth Centuries* (1895), Aynalov not only gave a very complete survey of the material, but replaced the prevailing theory held by Western scholars concerning a Roman school that was said to have determined the initial history of Byzantine art. Aynalov considered that it was not the West but the East that had been responsible for its stylistic development. He dealt with another of the most fundamental problems of Byzantine art in his monograph *The Hellenistic Origins of Byzantine Art* (1900). By Hellenistic origins Aynalov understood not so much the art of mainland Greece as the art of Alexandria, Syria, Palestine and Asia Minor, where the traditions of antiquity had merged with the art of the East, thereby creating the Byzantine style. Aynalov went beyond the iconographic method in his work, devoting much attention to stylistic analysis and the artistic quality of a given school or work of art. Among the major works of his later years are his *Geschichte der russischen Monumentalkunst der vormoskowitischen Zeit* (1932) and *Geschichte der russischen Monumentalkunst zur Zeit des Grossfürstentums Moskau* (1933).

WRITINGS

Mozaiki IV, V vekov [Mosaics of the fourth and fifth centuries] (St Petersburg, 1895)
Ellinisticheskie osnovy vizantiyskogo iskusstva [The Hellenistic origins of Byzantine art] (St Petersburg, 1901); Eng. trans., ed. C. Mango (New Brunswick, 1961)
Geschichte der russischen Monumentalkunst der vormoskowitischen Zeit (Berlin, 1932)
Geschichte der russischen Monumentalkunst zur Zeit des Grossfürstentums Moskau (Berlin, 1933)

BIBLIOGRAPHY

N. Brunov: 'Pamyati D. V. Aynalova' [In memory of D. V. Aynalov], *Arkhit. SSSR*, 3 (1940), pp. 66–7
G. Vzdornov: *Istoriya otkrytiya i izucheniya russkoy srednevekovoy zhivopisi* [History of the discovery and study of medieval Russian art] (Moscow, 1986)

OXANA CLEMINSON

Aynard, Edouard (*b* Lyon, 1 Jan 1837; *d* Paris, 25 June 1913). French collector. He was the son of a banker and was educated at the Institution d'Oullins in Lyon and at the Jesuit Ecole de Brugelette in Belgium; in 1859–60 he lived in England. He was apprenticed to a silk weaver at the Croix-Rousse in Lyon and visited America in 1861. After his father's death he became a banker; he married in 1862 and had 12 children. In 1870 he established the Assistance Mutuelle Lyonnaise, which later became an institution issuing loans to working people. In 1871 he founded *Le Journal de Lyon*, which closed for lack of capital in 1874. In 1882 Aynard became a member of the Chamber of Commerce, of the Board of the Ecole des Beaux-Arts and of the Museum Council. In the latter capacity, he arranged for the great staircase of the museum to be decorated by Puvis de Chavannes. In 1889 he organized Lyon's contribution to the Universal Exhibition. He became a member of the fine arts' department of the Académie de Lyon in 1897 and a member of the Académie des Beaux-Arts in 1902. Aynard assembled an important collection of 15th-century paintings but had a special interest in Italian early Renaissance art. He owned some fine 17th- and 18th-century works by Dutch and French masters as well as paintings by Delacroix and Puvis de Chavannes. He collected ivories, furniture, tapestries and sculpture and also helped to organize the restoration of the Cistercian abbey of Fontenay, then in a ruinous condition. His collection was sold in 1913 at the Galerie Georges Petit in Paris.

BIBLIOGRAPHY

DBF

J. Buche: *Essai sur la vie et l'oeuvre d'Edouard Aynard* (Lyon, 1921)

L. de Vaucelles: *Le Nouvelliste de Lyon et la pensée religieuse* (Paris, 1971)

J.-P. Gutton, ed.: *Les Lyonnais dans l'histoire* (Toulouse, 1985)

MADELEINE ROCHER-JANNEAU

Ayn Ghazal. *See* AIN GHAZAL.

Ayodhya [Ayodhyā]. City in Faizabad District, Uttar Pradesh, India. Located on the right bank of the River Sarayu, it was the capital of the ancient Kosala kingdom, one of whose kings, Rama, is regarded by Hindus as an incarnation of Vishnu.

Excavations in 17 different parts of the ancient mounds have revealed that the first occupation at Ayodhya commenced *c.* 700 BC, as is indicated by the occurrence of the earliest variety of Northern Black Polished Ware (NBPW) and a few sherds assignable to a late stage in the production of Painted Grey Ware (PGW). The NBPW is very well fired, thin-sectioned, with a shining surface and showing a variety of colours: steel grey, coal black, indigo, silver, even gold. In the earliest levels the houses were of wattle and daub, but later they began to be constructed of kiln-fired bricks. Terracotta ringwells were used for disposing of sullage water. Concomitantly, systems of coinage (punch-marked and uninscribed cast coins) and weights (cylindrical pieces of jasper, chert etc) also came into being, laying the foundation of urbanization in the Ganga Valley around the middle of the 1st millennium BC. Occupation continued into the SHUNGA, KUSHANA and GUPTA periods. Of particular interest is the occurrence of a few sherds of Rouletted Ware in levels ascribable to *c.* 1st–2nd century AD, which is indicative of riverine trade with eastern India, where this ware has been found at a number of sites. Fine terracottas of the Gupta period, now in several museums in Uttar Pradesh, were also recovered at Ayodhya.

In some trenches evidence was found of occupation after the 6th century AD. In the Janma Bhumi area, in a trench that lay immediately south of the Babri Masjid (see below), parallel rows of square brick bases that evidently carried pillar-shafts on them were discovered 250–300 mm below the surface. The mosque incorporates 14 stone pillars, which have Hindu sculptures and motifs assignable to about the same time as the brick bases found in the excavation, i.e. 11th century. In all probability, therefore, these brick bases and stone pillars belong to some sort of complex that stood at the site immediately prior to the construction of the mosque. Other indications of art activity after the 6th century are provided by sculptural fragments enshrined in modern temples. About 1 km south of the town there is an artificial mound, Mani Parbat, possibly the site of a Buddhist stupa.

A building at Ayodhya, which had become very widely known because of a controversy surrounding it, was the so-called Babri Masjid (destr. 1992). Commonly attributed to the Mughal emperor Babar (*reg* 1526–30), it was built by a Mughal nobleman, Mir Baqi, whose inscription on the mosque dated to AH 935 (AD 1529). The mosque had three bays, each with an arched entrance, and three domes. The central entry was flanked by two columns of black stone dating to about the 12th century. From the debris of the demolished Babri Masjid have been recovered a large number of sculptural and architectural components of a temple, besides three inscriptions on stone slabs. One of the inscriptions, in Sanskrit verse and Nagri script of the 11–12th century, refers to the erection of a temple dedicated to an incarnation of Vishnu, who killed the ten-headed Ravana (Skt. *Daśānana*).

Ayodhya's status as a major pilgrimage site was established at least by the early 17th century. Numerous temples are found within the city and along with bathing *ghats* on the bank of the River Sarayu. The oldest buildings date only to the 18th century. Several are important for Hindu pilgrims. The Hanuman Garhi (Hanuman's Fort), the most popular shrine, is thought by many local Muslims to be built on the ruins of a mosque, though there is no evidence to support it. The Treta-ke-Thakur is associated with a horse-sacrifice made by Rama; an earlier structure was restored by the Holkar queen Ahalya Bai in 1784. Among Ayodhya's Islamic monuments are the ruins of several 18th-century mosques, as well as the graves and tombs of Muslim saints and several modern mosques. Various Jaina temples date from the late 18th century to the mid-20th. Guru Nanak (1469–1539), the founder of Sikhism, visited Ayodhya; a modern shrine (*gurudvārā*) marks the spot where he is believed to have preached.

BIBLIOGRAPHY

E. B. Joshi: *Faizabad*, Uttar Pradesh District Gazetteers (Allahabad, 1960)

H. Bakker: *Ayodhya* (Groningen, 1986)

S. Gopal, ed.: *Anatomy of a Confrontation: The Babri Masjid-Ramjanmabhumi Issue* (New Delhi, 1990)

S. Srivastava: *The Disputed Mosque: A Historical Inquiry* (New Delhi, 1991)

S. Pollock: 'Rāmāyana and Political Imagination in India', *J. Asian Stud.*, lii (1993), pp. 261–97

A. M. Shastri: article in *Puratattva*, xxiii (1993)

B. B. LAL

Ayres, Gillian (*b* London, 3 Feb 1930). English painter. She studied at Camberwell School of Art, London (1946–50), where she detested the influence then prevalent of the EUSTON ROAD SCHOOL, and she worked at the AIA Gallery in London (1951–9) and the Bath Academy, Corsham, Wilts (1959–65). Painters such as Henry Mundy (*b* 1919), Roger Hilton, Robyn Denny (*b* 1931) and Howard Hodgkin were close friends. In 1960 she took part in the *Situation* exhibition at the RBA Galleries in London but, unlike most of her colleagues, who worked in a cool hard-edge style, she painted in a free tachist manner inspired in part by photographs of Jackson Pollock working on the floor. From 1964 to 1976 she worked in acrylic, producing powdery, close-toned canvases that were similar in their textures to the contemporary work of the Americans Jules Olitski and Larry Poons.

In 1977 Ayres changed over to oil paint, manipulating it like strands of clay to build up thick iridescent surfaces where colours seem to merge into each other or waft outwards, as in *Orlando furioso* (1977–9; AC England). While such painting may evoke the shimmering floral confusion of late Monets, the directness of the handling—often the paint is pressed into place by hand—ensures a strong physical presence. From the late 1970s, Ayres's consistently lyrical abstract paintings began to emphasize the decorative role of the internal forms within simple formats, often square or circular in shape. She taught at St Martin's School of Art for 12 years before becoming Head of Painting at Winchester School of Art in 1978; in 1981 she resigned, leaving London to live in Wales. She became well known with her large, sumptuous oil paintings of the 1980s, which combine the broad gestural improvisation of Abstract Expressionism and the rich colouring of Venetian painting.

BIBLIOGRAPHY

G. Williams: 'Notes on Gillian Ayres', *A. Int.*, xxiv/7–8 (1981), pp. 98–104, 160

Gillian Ayres: Paintings (exh. cat., ed. D. Elliott, text T. Hilton; Oxford, MOMA, 1981)

Gillian Ayres (exh. cat., text T. Hilton; London, ACGB, 1983)

JAMES FAURE WALKER

Ayrtam [Aïrtam]. Site in Uzbekistan, on the right bank of the Amu River, 18 km east of Termez. In 1932 the accidental discovery of a stone relief with the busts of three musicians against a background of acanthus leaves (*see* CENTRAL ASIA, §I, 3(ii)(a) and fig. 22) led the following year to the excavation by M. Ye. Masson of a further seven reliefs of the same type. In the 1960s–70s excavations by G. A. Pugachenkova and B. A. Turgunov revealed a settlement that dated from shortly before the time of Christ and flourished during the Kushana period (1st–4th century AD), when it formed an oasis extending 2.5–3.0 km along the river bank without planned layout or defensive wall. Several archaeological sites have been uncovered in the area of the settlement. The largest mound, which occupied the western part of the site, was enclosed by a wall and was probably a fortified citadel or acropolis. Excavations in 1964–6 of the base of the mound revealed the remains of about ten rooms of the mud-brick fort that guarded the crossing point on the river. A tomb *c.* 2 km further north was approximately contemporary with the fort. During the Kushana period the remains of the fort were covered by a Buddhist complex *c.* 600 sq. m in extent. A mud-brick platform (16×9 m) in the centre was probably the base of the main stupa. To the east was a shrine (7×7 m) containing a reliquary (shaped like a votive stupa) and a stucco statue of the Buddha. Two pylons flanking the entrance to the shrine were faced with stone slabs and crowned with capitals, each comprising four of the relief slabs found in 1932–3. A stone relief fragment with the legs of two standing figures and a six-line Bactrian inscription also seem to belong to this complex. Excavation of a second Buddhist complex further to the east revealed a small mud-brick stupa on a square foundation (9.20×8.85 m) and a mud-brick building with the remains of stone capitals and other architectural fragments.

BIBLIOGRAPHY

M. Ye. Masson: *Nakhodka fragmenta skul'pturnogo karniza pervykh vekov n.e.* [The discovery of a fragment of sculpted cornice from the first centuries AD] (Tashkent, 1933)

K. V. Trever: *Pamyatniki greko-baktriiskogo iskusstva* [Monuments of Greco-Bactrian art] (Moscow and Leningrad, 1940), pp. 149–58

G. A. Pugachenkova: 'Novyye dannyye o khudozhestvennoy kul'ture Baktrii' [New facts about the artistic culture of Bactria], *Iz istorii antichnoy kul'tury Uzbekistana* [From the history of the ancient culture of Uzbekistan] (Tashkent, 1973), pp. 81–90, 93–5, 99–100, 102–3.

M. Ye. Masson: *Iz vospominaniy sredneaziatskogo arkheologa* [Memoirs of a Central Asian archaeologist] (Tashkent, 1976)

B. Ya. Stavisky: *Kushanskaya Baktriya: Probelmy istorii i kultury* (Moscow, 1977); Fr. trans. as *La Bactriane sous les Kushans: Problèmes d'histoire et de culture* (Paris, 1986), pp. 185–7, 261–2, fig. 23, pls XI–XII

B. A. Turgunov, V. A. Livshits and Ye. V. Rtveladze: 'Otkrytiye baktriiskoy monumental'noy nadpisi v Ayrtame' [The discovery of a Bactrian monumental inscription in Ayrtam], *Obshchestvennyye nauki v Uzbekistane*, iii (1981), pp. 38–48

B. YA. STAVISKY

Ayrton, Michael (*b* London, 20 Feb 1921; *d* London, 16 Nov 1975). English sculptor, painter, printmaker and writer. He left school at 14 to begin his painting career. After spending time in France, Ayrton returned to England in 1939, finding success in stage design and art criticism. His writings in *The Spectator* (1946–8) were important in the acceptance of NEO-ROMANTICISM. From 1946 he travelled widely in Italy, admiring the Quattrocento painters, especially Piero della Francesca. At Cumae he began the preoccupation with Greek mythology that continued throughout his life; he visited Greece regularly from 1957. After 1955 sculptures became his preferred medium, although drawing remained essential and he produced etchings and lithographs. However, his many bronzes of the Minotaur, Daedalus and Icarus (e.g. *Icarus III*, 1960; London, Old Change Court) remain his best-known images. The *Arkville Maze* (1968), built of brick and masonry, contains two lifesize bronze sculptures and still stands in the estate of Armand Erpf in the Catskill Mountains, New York (see Hopkins, p. 402).

Ayrton worked in broadcasting and film-making; his book illustrations were widely admired. He published novels, essay collections and a scholarly monograph, and his illustrated edition of Archilochos's poems, *Archilochus Introduced, Translated and Illustrated by Michael Ayrton*, appeared posthumously (London, 1977). His reinvention of the achievements and techniques of antiquity and his experiments using perspex in reflective sculpture place him among the most original sculptors of his time, although determination to follow personal obsessions in defiance of accepted trends left him isolated from the mainstream. Troubled all his life by ill-health, he died before the ideas he was still exploring could be fully developed.

WRITINGS

Drawings and Sculpture (London, 1966)

BIBLIOGRAPHY

J. Matthews, ed.: *Labrys 3: Michael Ayrton* (London, 1978)
M. Yorke: *The Spirit of the Place* (London, 1988)
J. Hopkins: *Michael Ayrton: A Biography* (London, 1994)

JUSTINE HOPKINS

Aytaç, Hamid [Azmi, Musa; al-Amidi, Hamid] (*b* Diyarbakir, 1891; *d* Istanbul, 10 May 1982). Turkish calligrapher. Originally called Musa Azmi, he was the grandson of Seyyid Adem, a famous calligrapher of Diyarbakir. He practised writing in Diyarbakir with his school teacher Mustafa Akif Tütenk and others, and in 1908 went to Istanbul to continue his education, first at the School of Law and then at the Fine Arts Academy. However, he was soon forced to give up his studies to earn a living. In 1910 he became a writing teacher at the Gülşen school in Istanbul, where he taught the calligrapher Halim Özyazıcı. He went on to direct the Rusumat press and then worked at the press of the Military Academy in Istanbul. During World War I he worked for one year in Germany, where he prepared military maps. After the war he resigned his job and began to work independently. He changed his name to Hamid Aytaç, and in the early years of the Turkish republic made labels and calling cards. As a calligrapher he practised the *jali-thuluth* (Turk. *celi-sülüs*) style with Mehmed Nazif (1846–1913), the *naskh* and *thuluth* styles with Kamil Akdic (1862–1941) and the *ta'līq* style with Mehmed Hulusi (1869–1940). He worked on a number of magnificent manuscripts, including Korans. He also worked at the Şişli Mosque in Istanbul and on other buildings in Istanbul and Ankara.

BIBLIOGRAPHY

S. Rado, ed.: *Türk hattatlari* [Turkish calligraphers] (Istanbul, n.d.), pp. 267–8 [Turk. text]
M. Ülker: *The Art of Turkish Calligraphy from the Beginning up to the Present* (n.p., 1987), pp. 90–91 [Eng. and Turk. texts]

□

Ayuso, Emilio Rodríguez. *See* RODRÍGUEZ AYUSO, EMILIO.

Ayutthaya [Ayudhya; Ayuthia; Ayuthaya]. Thai city 77 km north of Bangkok, founded in 1350 by a prince of U Thong, later named King Ramathibodi I (*reg* 1351–69). It was the capital of the kingdom, also known as Ayutthaya, that succeeded Sukhothai as the most powerful Thai state in the region and, at its height, exercised varying degrees of hegemony over a large area from the north of Thailand to the Malaysian Peninsula in the south, and from Burma in the west to Cambodia in the east. The city of Ayutthaya

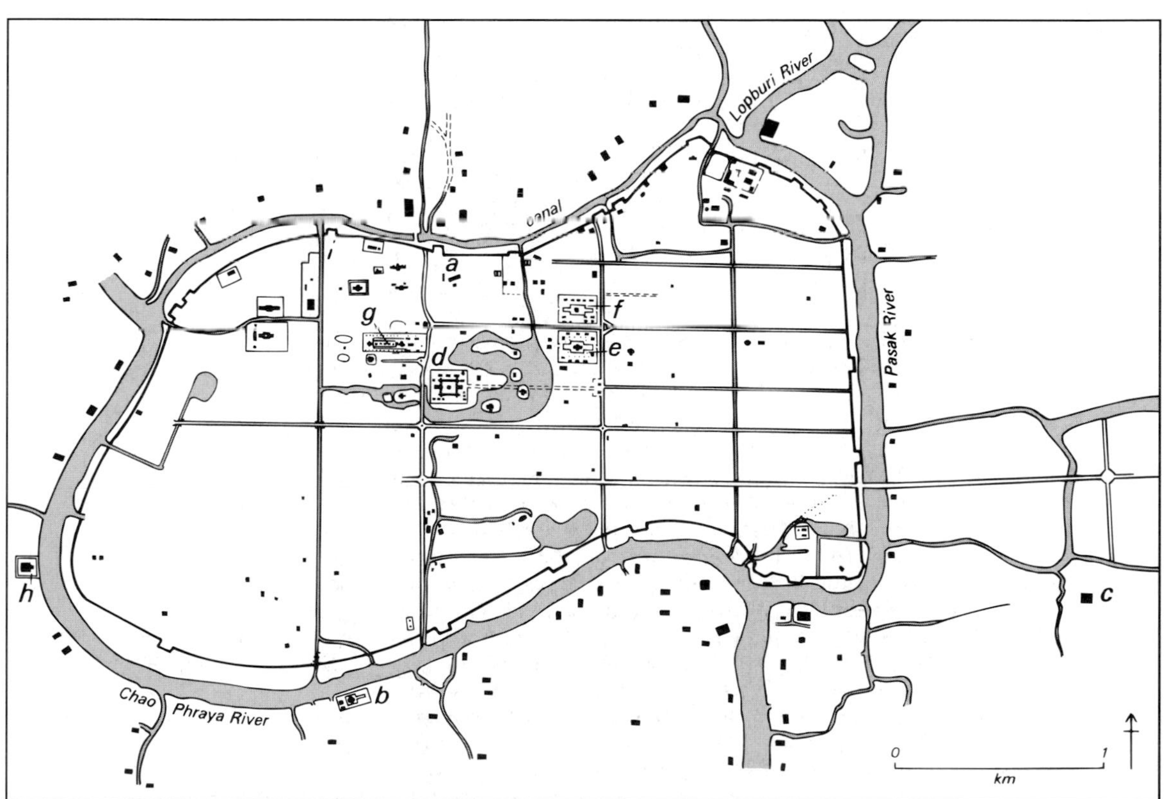

1. Plan of Ayutthaya: (a) Wat Thanmikarat; (b) Wat Phutthaisawan; (c) Wat Yai Chaimongkhol; (d) Wat Phra Ram; (e) Wat Mahathat; (f) Wat Ratchaburana; (g) Wat Phra Si Sanphet (site of the former Royal Palace); (h) Wat Chai Wathanaram; (i) site of the 15th-century Royal Palace

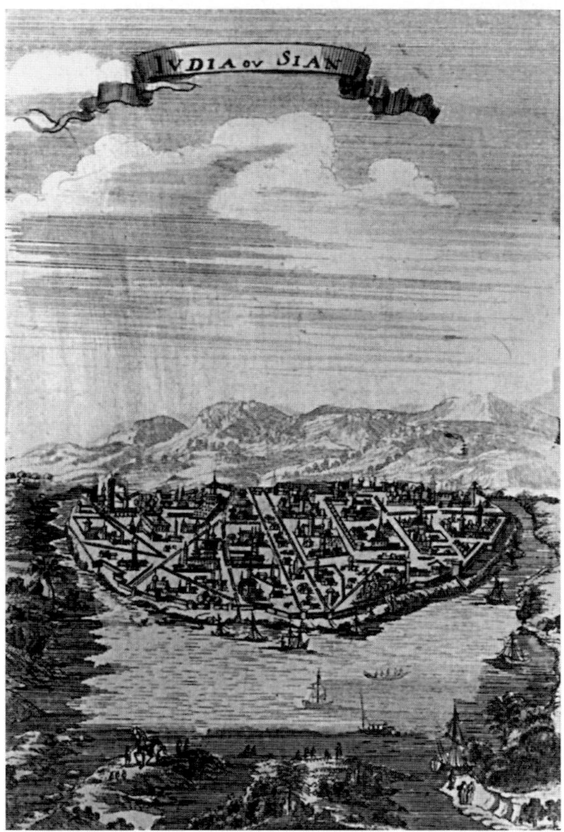

2. Map of Ayutthaya by the French cartographer Alain Manesson Mallet (1630–1706), *c.* 1685

(see fig. 1) is strategically situated on a peninsula at the confluence of the Pasak, Lopburi and Chao Phraya rivers; it was made into an artificial island by the digging of a canal on the eastern side. The Chao Phraya is navigable for large vessels as far as this point, so that from the outset Ayutthaya was an important commercial centre attracting traders from many countries, including Europe (see fig. 2). The city flourished until 1767, when it was destroyed by the Burmese.

1. Building styles and materials. 2. Principal monuments.

1. BUILDING STYLES AND MATERIALS. The architecture of Ayutthaya may be divided into four phases. The first lasted from 1350 to about 1450 and was marked by strong Khmer influence. The central sanctuary of the *wat* (Thai: Buddhist monastery) was always in the form of a many-tiered, ogival *prang* (tower-sanctuary) derived from Khmer models. From about 1450 to 1650 influences from Sukhothai increasingly replaced this Khmer influence and the Khmer *prang* was replaced by the bell-shaped stupa or *chedi* as the principal structure in the temple complex. The *chedi* of Ayutthaya, however, unlike those of Sukhothai, generally have a colonnade of short pillars on the square box-like structure between the top of the dome and the base of the spire (Skt *harmikā*). It seems that between about 1650 and 1700 the Thais regained hegemony over Cambodia and consequently Khmer influences were revived. Many *wat* were built during this period in imitation of Khmer models and with a Khmer *prang* as the main sanctuary. However, although many of the Buddha images in this period were made of stone, brick was the principal building material. During the first half of the 18th century many earlier *wat* were meticulously restored, but few new ones were built.

Remains of large brick *wihan* (Thai: assembly halls containing Buddha images) and *ubosot* (ordination halls) have been found. The *ubosot* and *wihan* of the late Ayutthaya period usually have curved bases and roofs (*see* THAILAND, fig. 8) and round or octagonal brick columns supporting the roof, with capitals in the form of lotus-buds, probably derived from Sukhothai models. Some late Ayutthaya capitals, however, are in the form of a stylized flowering lotus, a motif that was also popular during the subsequent Ratanakosin period. The piercing of brick walls by narrow rectangular slits instead of large windows is also a feature of the Ayutthaya style. The eaves of Ayutthaya buildings are usually shorter than those of Bangkok buildings. These religious structures were probably at first roofed with unglazed terracotta tiles; glazed tiles seem not to have come into use until the reign of King Phra Phetratcha (*reg* 1688–1703), who built Wat Borom Phuttharam on the site of his former residence and had the *ubosot* roofed with glazed tiles.

The brick bases of important domestic buildings have also been unearthed in the enclosure of the royal palace at Ayutthaya. The upper parts were probably built of wood or brick and the roofs of timber covered with terracotta tiles or tin. The roof decorations were probably gilt and displayed stylized *garuḍa* figures (Skt: mythical creatures, half-human, half-bird) holding *nāga*s (serpents) as the frame of the pediment. This is a Khmer motif, which is still in use and is believed to have the power of chasing away evil spirits. The gables were also of carved wood and usually represented Vishnu on his mount, Garuda, among floral and vegetal motifs. During the reign of King Narai (*reg* 1656–88), who employed many Europeans in his service, domestic buildings began to be constructed in brick both at Ayutthaya and at Lopburi. Formerly, brick or stone had been reserved for religious architecture. A number of buildings were constructed for the European merchant communities: for example, the Roman Catholic cathedral of St Joseph, on the south bank of the Chao Phraya River, near Wat Phutthaisawan, was built by Mgr de Bérythe in classical style in the late 17th century.

2. PRINCIPAL MONUMENTS. The ancient city of Ayutthaya is said to have had some 400 *wat*. Eight of these of particular interest and the royal palace complex are discussed below. The *wat* are presented roughly in chronological order according to the date of their foundation, though precise dating of each monument is impossible owing to later renovations and additions.

Five important *wat* probably date from the 14th century. Situated in the north of the city, Wat Thanmikarat (see fig. 1a), one of the earliest temples in Ayutthaya, may have been built even before the foundation of the city in 1350. It was burnt down in the sack of 1767 and was excavated and restored by the Thai Fine Arts Department in 1991.

It has a remarkable round *chedi* (diam. 14 m) on a square base (each side 23 m) with a staircase decorated with a *nāga* balustrade at each cardinal point and seated stucco lions in Khmer style round the base. To the west is a *wihan* surrounded by a low wall enclosing an area measuring 33×80 m. The *wihan* originally had 20 brick columns in two rows of which only nine remain. The *ubosot* (8.5×24.5 m) stands to the south of the *wihan* and is also surrounded by a low wall. It has *bai sema* (Thai: sacred boundary stones) made of slate. As Wat Thanmikarat is near the royal palace, it is thought to have been where the king came to listen to sermons on Buddhist feast days.

Wat Phutthaisawan (1b), on the outskirts of Ayutthaya on the south bank of the Chao Phraya River, was constructed by Ramathibodi I three years after he had founded the city. The main structure of the *wat* is a *prang* in Khmer style surrounded by galleries (54×74 m) housing rows of seated stucco Buddha images. The *prang* itself faces east with a long porch on that side. There is, however, access to the *prang* on both the east and the west. On the north and south sides are *mondop* (halls) each with a staircase on the east and housing a Buddha image. In the porch of the main *prang* stands a crowned Buddha image dedicated to King Ramathibodi. In front of the *prang* is a *wihan* (16×48 m), behind which are two staircases that give access to the galleries. Behind the *prang* to the west stands a well-preserved *ubosot* (32×14 m). To the north of the main *prang* is a group of five *chedi*. In the centre is a redented *chedi* of the late Ayutthaya period flanked on the west by two round *chedi* and on the east by two others of the same form but with octagonal bases. On the west, outside the rectangular wall surrounding the *prang*, the *wihan* and the *ubosot*, is a structure built of brick as a residence of the abbot of this monastery, probably in the reign of King Phra Phetratcha. It contains a rare example of Ayutthaya wall painting depicting Buddhist scenes (*see* THAILAND, §VI, 1(iii))

Wat Yai Chaimongkhol (1c), which is to the east outside the city and island of Ayutthaya, was also probably founded in the reign of Ramathibodi, for a community of orthodox Theravada Buddhist monks who wished to live outside the city. Later, King Naresuan (*reg* 1590–1605) constructed a large round brick *chedi* there to commemorate his victory over the Burmese in 1592, hence the name of Wat Yai Chaimongkhol ('Great Monastery of Victory'). The *chedi* is about 60 m high and rests on an octagonal base above a square pedestal 32.4 m on each side. There is a smaller *chedi* on each corner of this square base. Access to the base is provided by a long staircase on the east. In front of the *chedi* stand two *wihan*, each containing a Dvaravati-period Buddha image. The whole complex is surrounded by rectangular galleries (59.0×47.4 m) containing rows of seated Buddha images. On the east is a large *ubosot* (15.9×44.0 m) and on the west a *wihan* (15.3×39.0 m) with a porch on the western side. This latter building has no base for a Buddha image inside and seems to have been used only for ceremonies. There are also many other round brick *chedi* outside the galleries on the north, east and south. A *wihan* (12.5×24.0 m) built to accommodate a large reclining Buddha image lies in the north-eastern corner of the *wat*. The whole monastery is surrounded by brick walls, measuring 130.8×183.7 m. The monks' quarters were built of wood and have therefore all disappeared.

According to the Royal Chronicles of Ayutthaya, Wat Phra Ram (1d), which is near the royal palace, was built by King Ramesuan, the second king of Ayutthaya (*reg* 1369–70 and 1388–95), on the cremation site of his father, Ramathibodi I, but it seems to have been either extensively restored or only finally completed in the reign of King Borom Trailokanat (*reg* 1448–88). Despite further later renovations, it retains features of the early Ayutthaya period when Khmer influence was strong. Facing east, it consists of a central *prang* on a square base, with a large porch on the east and the west, and two smaller *prang* on the north and south of the main one, sharing the same base. The whole complex is square and is surrounded by galleries housing stone Buddha images. There is a large *wihan* on the east and the west. The *ubosot* lies to the north and is quite a small building, which may indicate that at the time of its construction there was only a small community of monks attached to the *wat*. Within the precinct are many large and small *chedi* of various sizes and *wihan* containing Buddha images. There is an artificial pool in the north-eastern corner, and the whole monastery is surrounded by brick walls, pierced by a gate at each cardinal point.

The construction of Wat Mahathat (1e), which was the residence of the supreme patriarchs of Ayutthaya (the head of the Buddhist *saṅgha*), was probably begun in the reign of King Borom Ratchathirat I (*reg* 1370–88), the third king of Ayutthaya, but finished during King Ramesuan's second reign. The central sanctuary originally consisted of five laterite *prang* in quincunx. The central one, which was originally taller than the other four, contained relics of the Buddha, discovered during excavations carried out *c.* 1950. The base of each of the five *prang* is about 4 m high and has a large staircase decorated with two *nāga* balustrades and stucco *garuda* figures as well as the four guardians of the earth, demons and other mythical creatures. Surrounding the five *prang* are galleries housing stone Buddha images. The *ubosot* is on the west and is lit by slits in the two lateral brick walls. The *wihan*, which measures 60×20 m, is on the east and is decorated with mural paintings. There are also many small *wihan* and *chedi* of various forms in the precincts of the *wat*. The front section on the east is surrounded by brick walls and behind it were the residence of the supreme patriarch and other monastic buildings, but, since these were built of wood and were burnt down in 1767, all traces of them have disappeared. Behind the monks' quarters is a canal that flows into the river in the north of the city. This monastery used to house Khmer bronze images that King Borom Ratchathirat II (*reg* 1424–48) brought from Cambodia after he captured Angkor in 1431.

Wat Mahathat has on several occasions been extensively restored. The five *prang* were restored in brick by King Prasat Thong (*reg* 1629–56) and the height of the central one increased to 50 m. Since it was the residence of the supreme patriarch, it was probably always well maintained and new *wihan* as well as new *chedi* of different forms were added to it. Although it was almost totally destroyed by the Burmese in 1767, the main *prang* survived until 1911, when it collapsed. It is now only 20 m high.

Two important *wat* probably date from the 15th century. Wat Ratchaburana (1f), situated to the north of Wat Mahathat and parallel to it, dates from 1424 and is among the finest examples of the first Khmerizing period of Ayutthaya architecture (see fig. 3). According to the Royal Chronicles of Ayutthaya, King Nakhon In or Inthararatcha died in that year and his two elder sons, Prince Ai and Prince Yi Phraya, contested the throne by fighting a duel on elephant-back; during this they were both killed. The third brother, Prince Sam Phraya, thus became king and took the regnal name of Borom Ratchathirat II. He cremated the remains of his two elder brothers and built Wat Ratchaburana on the cremation site.

The central edifice of this *wat* is a single laterite *prang* on a square base of 48 m on each side. Like most temples of this type and date, it is oriented and it therefore has a long porch on the eastern side with steps leading up to it. At each corner of the base of the *prang* is a brick *chedi* and there are 12 more *chedi* surrounding it. There are also short flights of steps leading up to the main *prang* on the north, the south and the west, but the walls on these three sides are solid and contain a standing stucco Buddha image on their outer faces. The lower section of the roof of the *prang* is decorated with stucco figures of *garuḍa*s and demons and at the top of the upper section under a niche at the four cardinal points is a seated Buddha image. Stone antefixes decorate each section of the roof.

To the east of the *prang* is a large *wihan* (63×20 m) with three staircases, one in front and one on each side, and three doors in front. Near the base of the main Buddha image inside the *wihan* are two further doors, one on the north and one on the south, and there are also two doors behind the base. The back part of the *wihan* projects into the walls round the main *prang*. Outside the wall to the west of the *prang* lies the *ubosot* (47.5×17.5 m), facing west. To the north and the south there are numerous remains of *chedi* and *wihan*. Some of the *chedi* may contain the ashes of princes of Ayutthaya.

Wat Phra Si Sanphet (1g) was founded in 1448 by Borom Trailokanat on the site of the former royal palace after he had built his new palace (see below) in the north of Ayutthaya. As it was in the precinct of the royal palace, it had no quarters for monks and, like Wat Phra Kaeo (the Temple of the Emerald Buddha) in Bangkok, it was used only for ceremonies such as taking the oath of allegiance to the king. Wat Phra Si Sanphet consists of three large round *chedi* built to enshrine the ashes of the founder and his two sons, Borom Ratchathirat III (*reg* 1488–91) and Ramathibodi II (*reg* 1491–1529). The form of these round *chedi* probably derives from a type found in Sukhothai that

3. Ayutthaya, Wat Ratchaburana, east front of *wihan* and main *prang*, 1424

was in turn influenced by Sri Lanka (*see* THAILAND, fig. 7). Many important Buddha images were kept in the principal *wihan* of Wat Phra Si Sanphet, and there are many ruined subsidiary *chedi* and *wihan*, some of which may date back to the reign of King Narai, as they have arched windows in the 'Saracenic' style introduced by European architects during his reign. The numerous *chedi* were probably constructed to enshrine the ashes of kings and princes of Ayutthaya. Relics of the Buddha have also been brought to light in some of them, as it was the custom to enshrine relics of the Buddha above the human ashes.

Between the three principal *chedi* there were originally three *mondop*. The one in front of the eastern *chedi* formerly contained the Buddha's footprint. The *ubosot* on the south side is much smaller than the grand *wihan* near by. During the late Ayutthaya period, a *wihan* was constructed on the west of Wat Phra Si Sanphet behind the three principal *chedi*, with four porches, each containing a Buddha image in the Sukhothai style in one of the four postures: seated, reclining, standing and walking. In the middle stands a *chedi* with many small cavities on all four sides to enshrine royal ashes.

Representative of the last period of Ayutthaya art, when Khmer styles were revived, is Wat Chai Wathanaram (1h), situated to the west of Ayutthaya. It was built in 1630 by King Prasat Thong (*reg* 1629–56) on the site where his mother lived before he became king. The principal monument of this *wat* is a large brick *prang* of Khmer type about 35 m high on a square base (33.6 m on each side). At each corner of the base stands a smaller *prang* 12 m high. The main *prang* faces east, but there are staircases 2 m wide on each side leading to a platform for circumambulation round the *prang*. There are also four staircases in the centre of each side of the square base. The *prang* is surrounded by four brick galleries housing seated stucco Buddha images in the gesture of subduing Mara (Skt *Marāvijaya mudrā*) and pierced by two doors on the eastern and western sides. These galleries are intersected at the eight points of the compass by eight brick edifices built in a more authentically Thai form resembling a mountain. Each one is 18 m high, with a seven-tiered roof surmounted by a tower. Inside is a chamber about 5.6 m wide decorated with pilasters supporting foliated capitals. The ceilings are coffered and made of wood, painted and decorated with glass, and there are mural paintings on the walls. In each of the edifices at the four cardinal points is a seated crowned Buddha image in stucco in the gesture of subduing Mara, and the edifices at the four intermediate points each contain two crowned Buddha images. Behind these edifices are niches housing low reliefs representing scenes of the life of the Buddha in stucco. The whole complex is surrounded by four brick walls. To the east of the main *prang*, attached to the eastern wall, lies an *ubosot* (52.75×20.00 m) containing three stone Buddha images. The *bai sema* round the *ubosot* are carved stone slabs. In front of the *ubosot* stand two brick *chedi* (h. 12 m), with the characteristic redentation of the late Ayutthaya period. The outer walls of the monastery are in brick and measure 143×180 m. In 1991 Wat Chai Wathanaram was excavated and restored by the Thai Fine Arts Department.

Most of the buildings of the royal palace (1i), called Wang Luang, of which only the brick bases remain, date from the beginning of the second period of Ayutthaya architecture, when the influence of Sukhothai, which had recently come under the hegemony of Ayutthaya, was paramount. The original palace was built by Ramathibodi I on a site south of the present royal palace, where Wat Phra Si Sanphet now stands. The Ayutthaya chronicle states that until 1448 there were five buildings in the old royal palace. They were probably built of wood, with roofs covered with tin and much gilt ornamentation. King Borom Trailokanat converted this palace into a Buddhist temple without quarters for monks and built a new palace to the north against the city wall. This new palace was divided into three sections like the later royal palace in Bangkok. The outer section on the east had a parade-ground as well as various ministries and other official buildings, most of them built of wood. King Prasat Thong had a large hall constructed at the southern corner of this outer section, from which he could watch military parades. The middle section of the palace is composed of three halls, as in Bangkok. It is on the northern side of the middle section of the royal palace. The three halls are built on a north–south axis. The northernmost, which is near the Lopburi River, was used as living-quarters by several kings and was also the place from where they watched processions of boats. This part of the river later became a canal. The central hall was used for coronations and for the reception of foreign ambassadors. The white stables for elephants were in this section. The southernmost building was also used for ceremonial purposes. The inner section, where the queens, concubines and court ladies had their apartments, occupied the western part of the palace complex. There is one building entirely of brick in this section where the king himself lived. It stands in the middle of a pond, and other ponds are also to be found in the vicinity. There were many wooden structures in this inner section, but all of them have disappeared. Later kings used the back part of this section as an audience hall, in the same way as the middle section.

See also THAILAND, §§I, 2; II, 1(vi); IV, 6; and VI, 1(iii).

BIBLIOGRAPHY

R. LeMay: *A Concise History of Buddhist Art in Siam* (Cambridge, 1938, rev. Rutland, VT, and Tokyo, 2/1963/*R* 1971)

M. C. Subhadradis Diskul: *Ayudhya Art* (Bangkok, 1956)

T. Bowie, ed.: *The Arts of Thailand* (Bloomington, IN, 1960)

HRH Prince Damrong Rajanubhab: *A History of Buddhist Monuments in Siam* (Bangkok, 1962); rev. as *Monuments of the Buddha in Siam* (Bangkok, 1973)

M. C. Subhadradis Diskul: *Art in Thailand: A Brief History* (Bangkok, 1970, 6/1986)

H. W. Woodward jr: *The Art and Architecture of the Ayudhya Period* (Bangkok, 1971)

Pisit Charoenwongsa and M. C. Subhadradis Diskul: *Thaïlande* (Geneva, 1976; Eng. trans., London, 1978)

Promsak Jermsawatdi: *Thai Art with Indian Influences* (New Delhi, 1979)

S. Van Beek and L. Invernizzi Tettoni: *The Arts of Thailand* (Hong Kong, 1985, rev. 1991)

M. C. SUBHADRADIS DISKUL

Ayvan. *See* IWAN.

Ayvazovsky, Ivan (Konstantinovich) (*b* Feodosiya [now Kaffa], 29 July 1817; *d* Feodosiya, 2 June 1900). Russian painter of Armenian descent. The son of an Armenian merchant, throughout his life he kept his links with the ancient traditions of Armenian Christian culture.

He studied at the Academy of Arts, St Petersburg, in 1833–7 under Maksim Vorob'yov (1787–1855), a prominent Russian landscape painter of the Romantic period. From 1845 Ayvazovsky worked predominantly in Feodosiya, an ancient city in the Eastern Crimea. He travelled widely in Russia and Europe, the Near East, Africa and America. Ayvazovsky's first significant paintings testify to his attentive assimilation of the canons of Romantic seascape painting, going back to Claude Lorrain, as well as the influence of Vorob'yov and the late works of Sil'vestr Shchedrin. In Ayvazovsky's early works the accurate rendering of views is combined with a classicist rationality of composition, as in *View of the Seashore in the Environs of St Petersburg* (1835; Moscow, Tret'yakov Gal.).

A purely Romantic view of the world and exaltation in the face of the boundless, eternally changing sea find mature expression in the works of the 1840s, when Ayvazovsky gained renown throughout Europe. A number of foreign academies made him an honorary member, and J. M. W. Turner wrote an enthusiastic ode in honour of one of his pictures. The best-known work of this period is the *Ninth Wave* (1850; St Petersburg, Rus. Mus.), which is imbued with a spirit of lofty heroicism: the theme of shipwreck and the struggle of man against the elements, typical of Romantic iconography, is presented in a setting of strong chiaroscuro effects which intensify the overall impression of the boundlessness of the raging expanse. An uncommonly prolific painter, Ayvazovsky frequently fell back on melodramatic clichés, making repeated variations on them. However, in his finest pictures, such as the well-known masterpiece the *Black Sea* (1881; Moscow, Tret'yakov Gal.), the best features of his talent emerge: a highly poetic generalization of images and an impressive mastery of tonal painting, sensitively reproducing the movement of water and light.

Ayvazovsky also executed a large number of landscapes, among which the series of pictures inspired by his journeys in Ukraine and the Caucasus (1850s–1860s) stand out. He extended the thematic limits of his painting more than once, drawing on the biblical subjects of the Creation and the Flood and on motifs from the Gospels; as with Turner or John Martin, the cosmic element in these pictures completely dominates the staffage. In his late period Ayvazovsky turned repeatedly to the image of Aleksandr Pushkin, in whose verse he found a poetic expression of his understanding of the sea. Battle painting also forms an important aspect of his legacy. From 1844 he was painter to the Main Staff of the Russian Navy, painting many important pictures on historical naval subjects (e.g. the *Battle of Chesme*, 1848; Feodosiya, Ayvazovsky Pict. Gal.). The work of Ayvazovsky, the most important Russian marine artist, is most fully represented in the Ayvazovsky Picture Gallery, Feodosiya (now Kaffa), which he founded.

BIBLIOGRAPHY

N. S. Barsamov: *I. K. Ayvazovsky* (Moscow, 1967)

L. A. Vagner and N. S. Grigorovich: *I. K. Ayvazovsky* (Moscow, 1970)

V. N. Pilipenko: *I. K. Ayvazovsky* (Leningrad, 1983) [with Eng. summary]

M. N. SOKOLOV

Ayyubid. Islamic dynasty that ruled 1169–1252 in Egypt, 1180s–1260 in Syria and south-east Anatolia, and 1174–1229 in the Yemen, with minor branches continuing until the end of the 15th century. The Ayyubids were the Kurdish clan brought to power in 1169 by Salah al-Din (Saladin; *reg* 1169–93) and his nephew Shirkuh when they occupied Egypt on behalf of the ZANGID ruler of Damascus, Nur al-Din. Shirkuh soon died, and Salah al-Din became master of Egypt. He ended the Shi'ite FATIMID dynasty of Egypt in 1171 and brought Aleppo and Damascus under his control in 1183 and 1186. Salah al-Din is best known in both East and West as a tireless foe of the crusaders, and for his liberation of Jerusalem in 1187. The Ayyubid lands were governed by leading members of his family. The sultan ruling in Cairo was paramount, and Damascus was the second capital, but Ayyubid possessions extended to the Yemen and into Anatolia. The counter-crusade continued throughout the Ayyubid period; notable is the failed treaty between al-Malik al-Kamil (*reg* 1218–38) with Frederick II in 1229, ceding Jerusalem for ten years; the city was retaken in 1244. In 1250 Turkish troops overthrew al-Malik al-Ashraf (*reg* 1249–50) and founded the Mamluk dynasty in Egypt (*see* MAMLUK, §II). All major branches of the Ayyubid dynasty in the Levant were liquidated in the Mongol invasion of 1260; after the Mongols were defeated by the Mamluks they fell heir to most of the former Ayyubid empire.

The Ayyubids, with their multiple courts, were great builders. The dozens of extant Ayyubid buildings include many madrasas in such cities as Cairo, Damascus and Aleppo; these religious colleges reflect the resolute Sunnism of the dynasty (*see* MADRASA). Most Ayyubid buildings are austere stone constructions, but under the Ayyubids Syrian architects brought the MUQARNAS vault into common use and invented the most popular form of striped masonry (Arab. *ablaq*), setting the stage for Mamluk developments (*see* ISLAMIC ART, §II, 5(ii)(c) and (e)). The constant crusader threat made fortifications important (*see* MILITARY ARCHITECTURE AND FORTIFICATION, §IV, 2). Salah al-Din founded the citadel of Cairo, which was expanded by al-Malik al-ʿAdil I (*reg* in Damascus from 1196, in Egypt 1200–18), who also built other castles and the citadel of Damascus. It is notable for its east gate with *muqarnas* decoration. Al-Malik al-Zahir (*reg* 1186–1216) and his son al-Malik al-ʿAziz (*reg* 1216–37) built much of the citadel of Aleppo and two of the city's finest madrasas, the Zahiriyya (1215) and the Sultaniyya (1223). Al-Malik al-Salih Najm al-Din Ayyub (*reg* in Damascus from 1239, in Egypt 1240–49) is represented by his madrasa in Cairo (1243; with tomb added by his wife Shajarat al-Durr, 1249–50). The women of the Ayyubid house were unusually active patrons of architecture: among their finest works are the Madrasa al-Sahiba in Damascus (1233), built by Salah al-Din's sister Rabiʿa Khatun, and the Madrasa al-Firdaws (1237) in Aleppo, built by al-Malik al-Zahir's wife Dayfa Khatun.

The Ayyubids were also major patrons of the decorative arts, including brass inlaid with silver, enamelled glass and intricately carved wood, sometimes inlaid with ivory or bone. Artisans' signatures show that some of the best inlaid brasses were produced by artisans from Mosul who fled west to escape the Mongol conquest (beginning in 1219; *see* ISLAMIC ART, §IV, 3(ii)). A group of at least 15 brasses are decorated with Christian scenes, including a charger (Paris, Mus. A. Déc.) and a large basin (Washington, DC, Freer), with the names of Ayyubid princes. An enamelled glass bottle (h. 320 mm; Cairo, Mus. Islam. A., 4261) is inscribed with the name of the last Ayyubid ruler of Aleppo, Salah al-Din Yusuf (*reg* 1237–60; *see* ISLAMIC ART, §VIII, 5(ii)). Ayyubid woodwork continued the traditions established under the Zangids and Fatimids and is exemplified by the splendid carved cenotaph in the mausoleum of Imam al-Shafi'i in Cairo. Ceramics, including *sgraffito* splashware, lustreware and an underglaze-painted version of enamelled ware, were produced in Syria and were inspired by techniques in Saljuq Iran (*see* ISLAMIC ART, §V, 3(ii)). Many of these techniques formed the basis for artistic achievements in the Mamluk period.

BIBLIOGRAPHY

Enc. Islam/2
J. Sauvaget: *Les Monuments ayyoubides de Damas*, 4 vols (Paris, 1938–50)
K. A. C. Creswell: *The Muslim Architecture of Egypt*, 2 vols (Oxford, 1952–9/*R* New York, 1978)
H. L. Gottschalk: *Al-Malik al-Kāmil von Egypten und seine Zeit* (Wiesbaden, 1958)
K. M. Setton, ed.: *History of the Crusades*, 3 vols (Madison, 1969–74)
R. S. Humphreys: *From Saladin to the Mongols: The Ayyubids of Damascus, 1193–1260* (Albany, 1977)
M. C. Lyons and D. E. P. Jackson: *Saladin: The Politics of the Holy War* (Cambridge, 1982)
M. Wenzel: 'Towards an Assessment of Ayyubid Glass Style', *The Art of Syria and the Jazira, 1100–1250*, ed. J. Raby (Oxford, 1985), pp. 99–112
E. Baer: *Ayyubid Metalwork with Christian Images* (Leiden, 1989)
N. D. MacKenzie: *Ayyubid Cairo: A Topographical Study* (Cairo, 1992)

□

Azande. *See* ZANDE.

Azara, José Nicolás de (*b* Barbuñales, 1730; *d* Paris, 26 Jan 1804). Spanish diplomat, writer and patron. He studied at the University of Salamanca and entered the Ministerio de Estado at an early age. His political career included service in the Spanish Embassy in Rome as Agente de Preces from 1766, and he rose to be Ambassador there from 1784 to 1798, when he was appointed Ambassador to Paris; a second appointment to this post lasting until shortly before his death.

Azara was a typical figure of the Age of Enlightened Despotism—a Royalist and convinced anti-Jesuit. He cultivated the 18th-century literary genre of letter-writing, corresponding with leading figures such as the statesman and general Don Pedro Pablo Conde de Aranda, the printer Giambattista Bodoni, Manuel de Roda and Bernardo de Iriarte. He was in touch with intellectual circles, and among his friends were the Spaniards E. Llaguno (*d* 1799) and E. de Arteaga (1747–99), Italians such as Carlo Fea (1753–1834) and Ennio Quirino Visconti, Germans such as Johann Joachim Winckelmann and Anton Raphael Mengs and Frenchmen such as Cardinal de Bernis; and even Napoleon publicly showed his esteem for Azara.

Azara promoted and subscribed to publications, translations and re-editions, some of which he prepared himself, including poetry by Garcilaso de la Vega (1503–36) and the English clergyman William Lisle Bowles (1762–1850), writings about art by Mengs and Francesco Milizia (1725–98), and works by Classical writers such as Horace, Virgil and Cicero. In the plastic arts he admired the art of Classical antiquity, patronizing archaeological excavations and collecting medals, cameos and busts on a large scale; he bequeathed much of his collection of these to the Bourbon Charles IV. He was a friend and patron of Mengs (in Spain 1761–9), who painted his portrait (Saragossa, Mus. Prov. B.A.), and owned a fine collection of his works which passed to the crown when he died. He also possessed a magnificent library, which was later destroyed.

BIBLIOGRAPHY

C. E. Corona Baratech: *José Nicolás de Azara: Un embajador español en Roma* (Saragossa, 1948)
S. Nicolás Gomez: 'José Nicolás de Azara, representante en Italia del pensamiento ilustrado español', *Academia*, 54 (1982), pp. 241–76
R. Olaechea: 'José Nicolás de Azara: Literato y mecenas', *Actas del seminario de ilustración aragonesa: Saragossa, 1987*, pp. 241–75

MERCEDES AGUEDA

Azay-le-Rideau. French château near Tours, Indre-et-Loire. It was built in 1518–28 by an unknown architect for Gilles Berthelot (*d* 1529), a financier from Tours in the service of Francis I. The stone château, surrounded on three sides by the River Indre, has an L-shaped plan under steep slate roofs. The medieval château of Azay, belonging to the Ridel family, had been destroyed by fire in 1418, although its original keep survived. The château subsequently passed to the Berthelot family, and in 1518 Gilles Berthelot put his wife, Philippe Lesbahy, assisted by the curé of St-Cyr, Guillaume Artault, in charge of supervising its reconstruction. Berthelot, however, was implicated in the prosecution of Jacques, Baron de Semblançay (*c*. 1457–1527), Minister of Finance to Francis I, and in 1528 the château was confiscated by the King. This effectively put an end to the building programme, leaving unfinished two of the four wings. In 1845 the medieval keep was rebuilt as a circular tower in Renaissance style, terminating the east wing, and a corbelled circular corner turret was added at the end of the south wing over the moat, to balance the turret built in the 16th century.

Each three storey wing consists of five bays marked out by mullioned windows, united vertically by pilasters and ending with elaborately decorated gables above the third-storey dormer windows. These interrupt a false walkway with battlements and machicolations. The main decorative feature is the *escalier d'honneur* in the centre of the south wing. This is signalled externally by a virtuosic four-storey frontispiece with alternating pairs of superimposed round-headed and basket arches forming the entrance (*see* FRANCE, fig. 6) and the lighting to the landings. The frontispiece is articulated with pilasters, half columns, carved relief panels and niches for statues; it terminates in a carved gable with *all'antica* candelabra and other Renaissance ornaments, reaching to the level of the roof ridge. Within, the straight flights of the Italianate staircase are covered with a coffered vault decorated with profile medallions *all'antica*, rosettes and other motifs.

BIBLIOGRAPHY

J. Guillaume: *Azay-le-Rideau et l'architecture française de la Renaissance* (Paris, 1976)

JEAN MARTIN-DEMÉZIL

Ažbe, Anton (*b* Dolenčice, nr Škofja Loka, 30 May 1862; *d* Munich, 5 Aug 1905). Slovenian painter and teacher, active in Germany. He trained in Ljubljana with the Slovenian painter Janez Wolf (1825–84), who taught him in a style derived from Anselm Feuerbach and the work of the Nazarenes and emphasized the ethical ideals and role of art. Ažbe studied at the Akademie der Bildenden Künste, Vienna (1882–4), and at the Akademie der Bildenden Künste, Munich (1884–91), where he became an excellent draughtsman, especially with nudes and portrait heads. In the spring of 1891 he opened his own private school, the Ažbè-Schule, which established a reputation. From 1898 to 1901 Igor' Grabar' joined him as a teacher there. Its students included the Slovenian Impressionists Matija Jama (*b* 1872), Rihard Jakopič and Matej Sternen (*b* 1870), the Serbian Nadežda Petrović, the Croatian Josip Račić (1885–1909) and the Czech Ludvík Kuba, as well as Vasily Kandinsky and Alexei Jawlenski. He was looked on as an infallible and tolerant teacher, but his own painting was restricted by his teaching duties and his bohemian way of life, much of it spent in the Dichtelei and Simplicissimus cafés in the Schwabing district of Munich. In his own works and in his teaching he promoted the use of unmixed colours, applied directly on to the canvas. His drawings (e.g. *Portrait of a Bavarian*, 1890; Ljubljana, N.G.) and such paintings as *Negro Woman* (1895; Ljubljana, N.G.) adhere to his Realist doctrine, while *In the Harem* (after 1900; Ljubljana, N.G.) shows greater ease, using strong, colourful brushstrokes. Ažbe was greatly influenced by the emphasis within the artistic circle in Munich on Realism in portraits and genre paintings and by an interest in representational problems that also stimulated the artists of the Secession.

BIBLIOGRAPHY

Anton Ažbè in njegova šola [Anton Ažbe and his school] (exh. cat., ed. K. Dobida; Ljubljana, N.G., 1962)

Wege zur Moderne und die Ažbe Schule in München (exh. cat., ed. K. Ambrožić and others; Wiesbaden, Mus. Wiesbaden; Ljubljana, N.G.; 1988)

H. Wilhelm: *Die Münchner Bohème: Von der Jahrhundertwende bis zum Ersten Weltkrieg* (Munich, 1993), pp. 133–8

KSENIJA ROZMAN

Azerbaijan [anc. Athropatena, Azarbaijan]. Transcaucasian republic on the west side of the Caspian Sea, bounded by the Dagestan republic of the Russian Federation to the north, the Republic of Georgia and the Republic of Armenia to the west, and Caucasus Mountains to the north and west (see fig. 1). Armenian territories separate the region of NAKHCHYVAN from the rest of Azerbaijan. To the south, the Araks River (anc. Araxes) forms the border with Iran. The capital, Baku, is a natural port on the Absheron Peninsula of the Caspian coast. Other major towns are Gandja, Shamakhy, Quba, Shaki, Qazakh, Lankaran, Nakhchyvan, in the centre of Nakhchyvan region, and Khankandi, in the centre of Daghly Qarabagh (Nagorno-Karabakh) district.

1. Map of Azerbaijan; those sites with separate entries in this dictionary are distinguished by CROSS-REFERENCE TYPE

I. Introduction. II. Architecture. III. Sculpture. IV. Painting. V. Other arts.

I. Introduction.

Azerbaijan is located on the principal route from Europe to Asia along the Caspian Sea. Its origins date from the 5th century BC, when it was the 11th district of a Persian empire dominated by Caspian tribes (Herodotus III.93). At the beginning of the Christian era, the kingdom known as Albania by the Greeks was formed by tribes that were probably of Indo-European origin, to judge from the white skin indicated by the name 'Albanian'. They lived along the Kura and Arax rivers (Strabo: *Geography* XII.4). From the 3rd to the 7th century, Albania was a district known as Arran within the Sasanian empire. The Sasanians defended the Albanians, who were Zoroastrians, from the inroads of Christianity as it spread into Azerbaijan during the 4th century. Arab armies invaded Azerbaijan in 642, and in the 9th and 10th centuries it was divided into provinces that were nominal vassals of the caliphate: Arran (south of the Kura River) belonged to the Sadjids and Salarids; Gandja belonged to the Shadids; Shirvan (north of the Kura River), which formed the Shirvan kingdom, belonged to the Azeri dynasty of Shirvanshahs Kesranids (*reg* 1073–1382). Until the 10th century, the population was partly Muslim and partly Christian. Christianity was especially strong in the Artsakh-Khachen principality (Daghly Qarabagh and Qazakh regions), ruled by the Djalalid dynasty from the 11th to the 13th century, where an autocephalous Albanian church was established in the 12th century.

At the end of the 11th century, the Great Saljuqs invaded Azerbaijan and brought pronounced Turkish elements into the culture and language. The subsequent arrival of Turkish peoples and rulers, who established states primarily in the region of Tabriz, led to the formation of a specifically Azeri people. The Atabegs Ildegizid dynasty (*reg* 1136–1225) ruled an area from Tabriz to Arran and Shirvan. In the 13th century, the Mongols invaded the region and established a capital at Tabriz, and, until the 14th century, a large portion of Azerbaijan was part of the Timurid empire (1370–1506). The Timurids were followed by the Qaraqoyunlu (*reg* 1410–68) and the Aqqoyunlu (*reg* 1468–1501), Turkoman dynasties that controlled the south of Azerbaijan. However, the Shirvan kingdom kept its independence until the end of the 14th century, and the Derbent Shirvanshahs (*reg* 1382–1583) retained the northern part of the country until the end of the 16th century.

In the early 16th century, the Azeri dynasty of the Safavids (*reg* 1501–1736) took power in Tabriz and developed a culture that influenced the development of all Caucasian peoples. In the middle of the 16th century, the Ottoman empire made repeated attempts to take control of Azerbaijan. Shah Abbas I Safavi (1587–1628) defeated the Ottoman armies in Transcaucasia, and in the early 16th century Azerbaijan became part of the Safavid empire and was ruled by governors. In order to oppose the Ottoman expansion into the Caucasus, Shah Abbas attempted to form a union with Russia, offering Tsar Theodore I (*reg* 1584–98) both Derbent and Baku. In the 18th and 19th centuries, during the reign of the Kadjar Shahs, Persia and Russia struggled for control over Azerbaijan, a dispute that ended in 1813 with the Treaty of Gulistan, under which Gandja, Baku, Quba, Derbent, Georgia and Dagestan were ruled by military commandants. The Treaty of Turkmanchai was signed in 1828, and the border between the two states was established along the Arax River, with Azerbaijan entering the Russian empire.

After the Russian Revolution of 1917, the Bolsheviks delegated the Baku commissars, headed by S. Shaumian, to establish Soviet rule in Azerbaijan. On 28th May 1918, the Azerbaijan Democratic Republic was founded in Gandja by the prime minister Khan Khoisky. The Ottoman empire sent troops under Nuri Pasha, and Allied troops also tried to oppose the Bolsheviks' plan to bring Azerbaijan into the Soviet Union. In April 1920, the Red Army occupied Azerbaijan, and by the summer had defeated the forces of the Democratic Republic. Azerbaijan became a part of the Soviet Union, and the Nakhchyvan region was separated from Azerbaijan and made into an autonomous republic. Daghly Qarabagh, with its considerable Armenian population, was given the status of an autonomous district. In 1992, as a result of the growing democratic movement, Soviet power collapsed and a national government, headed by A. Elchibay, proclaimed independence. Since 1992, western Azerbaijan, including Daghly Qarabagh and Nakhchyvan, has been occupied by Armenia. In 1993, Azerbaijan became a member of the Commonwealth of Independent States.

BIBLIOGRAPHY

Enc. Islam/2: 'Adharbaydjan'

Istoriya Azerbaydzhana [History of Azerbaijan], Academy of Sciences of Azerbaijan SSR (Baku, 1958)

Istoriya iskussty narodov SSSR [History of the arts of the peoples of the USSR], i–iii (Moscow, 1971–4)

R. N. Frye: *The Golden Age of Persia* (London, 1975)

K. V. Trever: *Ocherki po istorii i kul'ture Kavkazskoy Albanii* [Studies in history and culture of Caucasian Albania] (Moscow and Leningrad, 1958)

T. Swietochowsky: *Russian Azerbaijan, 1905–1920* (Cambridge, 1985)

A. L. Altstadt: *The Azerbaijani Turks: Power and Identity under Russian Rule* (Stanford, 1992)

II. Architecture.

1. 5th–6th centuries. 2. 17th century–early 20th. 3. After 1917.

1. 5TH–16TH CENTURIES. The oldest surviving buildings in Azerbaijan date from the 5th–6th century AD. These include the basilica at Kum, which is tetraconch in plan with four semicircular vaults resting on square columns; the centrical, three-tiered church at Lekit, which has horseshoe arches incorporated into the first tier; and the foundations of the Maiden's Tower, the core structure in the centre of Baku.

Following the conquest of Azerbaijan by the Arabs in the 7th century, there was a hiatus in the construction of large buildings. The first 8th-century religious buildings, the mosque in Akhsu and the Djuma Mosque in Shamakhy, provide evidence of the adaption or reworking of the earlier three-aisled temple plan, with each aisle or nave having its own mihrab. An example of a new architectural scheme, built by Muhammad ibn Abu Bakr in Baku in 1078–9, was the square Muhammad Mosque (destr.). The adjacent stone minaret, a substantial structure known as the Synyk-kala ('Demolished fortress'), had a balcony decorated with large *muqarnas*.

The construction of a strong citadel, encircled by a rough oval of massive fortification walls, was begun at Baku in the 11th century and completed during the reign of the Shirvanshah ruler Manuchihr II (*reg* 1120–49) of the Kesranid dynasty. The Maiden's Tower (h. 28 m; diam. 16 m; see fig. 2), a great donjon, was also completed in the 12th century. The inner city (Icheri-sheher) developed radially around the Maiden's Tower and contained a whole complex of public, religious and residential structures of different periods, including the Muhammad Mosque and Synyk-kala (11th century), the castle (14th century), the Bukhara caravanserai (14th century), the Djuma Mosque (15th century), the Multani or Indian caravanserai (17th century) and the Shamakhy gates (17th century). The palace complex of the Shirvanshahs (13th–16th century) was built on a small raised area of the inner city and included an official area (Pers. *dīvan-khānā*) for ceremonies and archival records, the Kay Qubad Mosque (13th century), the Chin Mosque (14th century), the burial vault of the Shirvanshahs, built by the architect ʿAli in 1435–6, the mosque and minaret of the Shirvanshahs (1441–4), the palace itself (15th–16th century), the palace baths and the mausoleum of Seyyid Yahya Bakuvi (16th century).

Other examples of defensive architecture include the square fortification built by the architect ʿAbd al-Majid ibn Masʿud at MARDAKAN in 1232. It has semicircular buttresses reinforcing the external walls and a small, round defensive tower in the centre. Fortress towers of the 14th century were square in plan, like the one at Ramana, which has, in addition, round buttresses and is surrounded by a high wall. Perhaps the best example of fortifications of this type on the Apsheron Peninsula is the much larger fortress (h. 22 m) that was built at Mardakan at the end of the 14th century.

2. Maiden's Tower, Baku, Azerbaijan, 12th century

Other fortified structures were the pilgrims' rest houses (*khānaqah*) that were built from the 13th century onwards. These contained cells for travellers and a mosque with a minaret, all protected by walls with defensive towers. The fort built on an island in Baku Bay by Zayn al-Din ibn Abi-Rashid in 1234–5 has two-roomed cells opening on to a large courtyard (180×40 m), enclosed by massive walls with 15 round towers.

Another architectural school developed during the 12th century in the city of NAKHCHYVAN in south-western Azerbaijan, where the architect ʿAjami ibn Abu Bakr was active. The articulation of the integrated architectural mass through the use of relief ceramics, glazed or large fancy-shaped bricks and carved plaster was a particular characteristic of the Nakhchyvan school, best seen in the mausoleum of Yusuf ibn Kusayr, built by ʿAjami in 1162–3. The mausoleum of Mo'mina Khatun (1186), again the work of ʿAjami, employs more developed forms of architectural decoration. The decagonal tower has a diorite base and, on each of the sides, a shallow iwan with a *muqarnas* arch.

The development of tomb towers can be traced in an example in BARDA built by Ahmad ibn Ayyub al-Hafiz al-Nakhchyvani in 1322. Here the round drum of the tower stands on a stone base and is crowned with a conical roof. The low portal is decorated with glazed relief ceramic. The unusual 14th-century mausoleum in Qarabaghlar has a round brick body comprising a series of linked half-columns that seem to echo the powerful pillars of the two nearby tall minarets, the only extant remains of a 12th-century mosque.

In the Artsakh-Khachen principality (mod. Nagorno-Karabakh and Kalbadjar region of Azerbaijan) there was an upsurge in religious architecture during the 11th–13th century. Churches remained tetraconch in plan, as in the earlier Kum basilica, with a central dome as already seen in the church at Lekit. The monastery at Khashavank, the spiritual centre of the principality from the 10th to the 15th century, consisted of a complex of diverse religious and secular buildings. The oldest structure was the cathedral, built by Hovanes Khachen in the 11th century, which had an asymmetrical plan. The hall-like interior was vaulted and had a lateral porch with an arched colonnade. During the reign of Prince Hasan (*reg* 1142–82) a domed church was built within the monastic complex, followed by a pilgrims' rest house, a refectory, a library and the small domed church of Arzu-Khatun, the wife of Hasan's son Prince Vakhtang. The complex also included a palace chamber erected in 1211 by Grigory, another of Hasan's sons. This was a square hall (8.4×9.0 m), with the arches of the tent-shaped roof resting on four round columns and eight semicircular pilasters.

The further development of architecture in these regions is evident in the complex of the Gandzasar Monastery, the residence of the head of the Albanian church, which contained the family burial vault of the

Djalalid Albanian princes. The architectural scheme of the church at Gandzasar is based on the plan of a Greek cross, in which two short crossed transepts are covered by a dome. The eastern transept forms a semicircular apse, while the western one is elongated to form an unusual pronaos.

2. 17TH CENTURY–EARLY 20TH. Among the religious buildings of Azerbaijan, the fire temple (Pers. *atash-gāh*) stands apart. This 18th-century religious complex stands on the site of an ancient fire sanctuary in the village of Surakhany on the Apsheron Peninsula, where there are abundant natural gas outlets. In plan the complex recalls a caravanserai, with cells arranged around an irregularly pentagonal courtyard and a perimeter wall with merlons and gates fortified with towers. The fire temple in the centre of the courtyard is a four-sided pavilion with semicircular arches crowned by a low faceted cupola.

As a result of political complexities and unceasing wars in the 17th and 18th centuries there was a sharp decrease in the construction of public buildings, and most development was confined to domestic architecture. In the southern regions a type of two-storey, L-shaped or trapezoidal building was widespread, with enfilades of rooms leading off a six- or eight-sided vestibule. These buildings were constructed of mud-brick on a framework of unfinished tree trunks and had flat roofs. Around Gandja the typical building had a semi-basement vaulted lower floor that was used for domestic purposes, and a domed room above. In the northern regions there was a widespread use of a type of two-storey building, with a tiled, pitched roof; the first storey had an open arched gallery, the second a glazed verandah. The summer palace of the Shaki khans (1797) is a two-storey construction. On both floors the central room or hall is flanked by smaller rooms and has windows, many screened. The main façade is pierced by deep openings with two arrow-shaped arches. The rich decoration of coloured windows, mosaics, wall paintings and mirror *muqarnas* gave this simple architectural construction an impressive appearance.

The growth of towns in the 18th century led not only to the development of standard building types but also to radical changes in town planning, including a transition from radial building around the fortress within the confines of the town walls to an open European system with a grid of straight, intersecting streets. BAKU, however, did not expand beyond the limits of its fortified walls until the early 1860s, when an oil boom resulted in the rapid growth of the city.

At the end of the 19th century and beginning of the 20th, the architecture of Baku was dominated by the Eclectic style, which combined neo-Renaissance and Neo-classical motifs with forms imitative of the architecture of the Maghrib, Cairo and other countries in the Near East. Architects of this period working in Baku include I. K. Ploshko (*c.* 1866–1930), who designed the Venetian Gothic building of the Ismailiya charitable society (1908–13) and the French Gothic Mukhtarov House (1911–12). G. M. Termikelov (1873–1949) was author of the Public Assembly building (1910–12) in the Governor's Garden, which uses Neo-classical forms, while his residence for the Sadykhov brothers was an example of the 'Mauritanian style'. In building the grandiose Taza-Pir Mosque (1905–14), A. Akhmedbekov (1873–1925), an Azerbaijani architect educated in Europe, was influenced by the style of Cairo mosques and completely ignored the local traditional forms of religious buildings. In the town Duma (1900–04), the architect I. V. Zaslavsky (1865–1904) made skilful use of Italian Baroque motifs in creating a picturesque façade, precisely articulated by superb tiers of windows and a sculpturally moulded tower in the centre. The civil engineer N. G. Bayev (1878–1949) built the Theatre of the Mailov Brothers (1910–11) using the artistic forms of the mature Art Nouveau style to give the façade a unique appearance, pierced by arches with moulded decoration, wide windows and crowned with two small towers.

Several indigenous architects and engineers, such figures as M. G. Gadzhinsky (1875–1931), K. Ismaylov and K. S. Garabagi, gave architecture a certain national and romantic appearance at the turn of the 20th century. This trend is particularly noticeable in the work of Garabagi, who designed many buildings in Aghdam, Fizuli and SHUSHA. His designs, such as those for mosques in Aghdam and Barda, employ simple devices wholly based on Azerbaijani architectural traditions. The large scale of construction in this period gave rise to numerous workshops, employing not only masons, such as the master builder Hadzhi-Abbas, master Kerbalai Mirza (*d* 1965) and Kerbalai Ahmed of Amiradjan, but also architects.

3. AFTER 1917. After the 1917 October Revolution a new stage in the development of architecture in Azerbaijan began, which reached a high-point at the end of the 1920s. Between 1925 and 1928, new housing for workers, equipped with all modern conveniences, was built in the villages of Razin, Binagadi, Bibi-Eybat, Surakhany, Shuvelyan and Zabrat. A large contribution to residential construction in Baku was made by the Soviet architects, the VESNIN brothers: L. A. Vesnin, V. A. Vesnin and A. A. Vesnin.

Constructivism brought new materials and devices to Azerbaijani building techniques: the use of reinforced concrete, bands of continuous glass and open construction. The Palace of Culture (1928–31) in Bailov was built by the Vesnin brothers with reinforced-concrete panels in the form of a simple rectangular mass, its façade articulated only by projecting rectangular windows and vertical buttresses under balconies and awnings. Constructivism found its greatest stylistic expression in the Azerneshr Palace of Printing (1931), designed by the architect S. Pen, who gave the façades the appearance of a ship, with the walls of the printing house pierced by porthole windows, while the conning-tower administrative block has bands of windows, bridge-balconies and mast-antennae.

In 1929 the first Azerbaijani architects graduated from the architecture and construction faculty of the Polytechnical Institute, among them S. A. Dadashev and Mikael' Useynov, who both later achieved renown (*see* USEYNOV & DADASHEV). The creative union of Useynov and Dadashev produced positive results in the design of a number of large public buildings in Baku. The Nizami Cinema (1934) and the Ministry of the Food Industry (1937–9) combined elements of Constructivism with forms from ancient Greece and the Renaissance. The

3. U. Revazov and P. Yarinovsky: Oriental Bazaar trading centre, Baku, Azerbaijan, 1983

architectural design of the Nizami Museum of Literature (1940), comprising an open loggia and arcades, ceramic mosaics and carved plaster, marked a true renaissance in Azerbaijani architecture.

After 1945 architects turned to the planning and construction of the new industrial towns of Sumgait, Dashkasan and Mingachevir and to the reconstruction and replanning of the old towns of Nakhchyvan, Gandja, Kankandi and Shusha, where new public buildings were erected (the Musical Dramatic Theatre in Nakhchyvan by E. Ismailov and G. Medzhidov; the Administrative Building in Gandja by Ismailov and F. Leont'yev; and the Gor'ky Dramatic Theatre in Kankandi by I. Vartanesov). In Baku, as a result of the reconstruction of the town centre, various oil companies from 1951 onwards built residential blocks to individual designs, such as Buzonyneft', designed by Dadashev and Useynov, Azneft'zavody, designed by Useynov, and Azenergo, designed by Ismailov. The main squares of the city were also completed at this time: Nizami, Fizuli and Petrov squares, as well as the main Lenin Square (now Azadlyg Square), with the new Government House (1952) in the centre, the work of architects LEV RUDNEV, V. Munts and I. Tkachenko' and sculptor Dj. Karyagdy (*b* 1915). This had a U-shaped plan incorporating an internal courtyard. The colonnades in the reception area of the Shirvanshah palace complex provided the prototype for three tiers of arcades resting on clustered piers of multiple columns.

Architecture of the 1960s and 1970s in Baku is distinguished by the construction of high-rise blocks of flats in reinforced concrete with glazed façades. Among the buildings of this period are the Hotel Azerbaijan (1969), the Hotel Baku (1970; architect G. Medjidov), the Republic Statistical Administration Building (1971; architects T. Khanlarov and S. Markaryan), the Lenin Palace of Culture (1972; architects B. Ginzburg, V. Shul'gin and E. Mel'khisedekov; engineer K. Kerimov) and the Hotel Moscow (1978; architect M. Useynov). The strict rigorism of the façades of these buildings was determined by the minimal use of architectural devices. In the early 1980s a spatial approach to form developed, using modern interpretations of traditional architectural elements, as seen in the Gyulistan Palace of Ceremonies (1982; architects N. Hadjibekov and A. Amirkhanov), which has the appearance of a multi-faceted prism, with façades of complex faceted arches. The most successful embodiment of this tendency, the Oriental Bazaar trading centre (1983; architects U. Revazov and P. Yarinovsky, see fig. 3), comprises several trading halls linked by small courtyards, arcades and passages on different levels, covered by a system of domes in the style of a traditional Oriental bazaar.

BIBLIOGRAPHY

V. A. Krachkovskaya: *Izraztsy mavzoleya Pir-Khuseyna* [Tiles of the Pir-Khuseyn Mausoleum] (Tbilisi, 1946)

Pamyatniki arkhitektury Azerbaydzhana [Monuments of Azerbaijan architecture], 2 vols (Moscow and Baku, 1946–50)

Arkhitektura Azerbaydzhana epokhi Nizami (Moscow and Baku, 1947)

L. Bretanitsky: 'Shirvanshah Palace in Baku', *Archaeology* (1948)

S. A. Dadashev and M. A. Useynov: *Arkhitektura sovetskogo Azerbaydzhana* (Moscow, 1950)

Arkhitektura Azerbaydzhana: Ocherki [The architecture of Azerbaijan: outlines] (Baku, 1952)

S. A. Dadashev and M. A. Useynov: *Ansambl' dvortsa Shirvanshakhov* [The ensemble of the Shirvanshahs' palace] (Moscow, 1956)

L. A. Mayer: *Islamic Architects and their Works* (Geneva, 1956)

N. S. Askerova: *Arkhitekturnyy ornament Azerbaydzhana* (Baku, 1960)

L. S. Bretanitsky and A. V. Salamzade: *Kirovabad* (Moscow, 1961)

M. A. Useynov, L. S. Bretanitsky and A. V. Salamzade: *Istoriya arkhitektury Azerbaydzhana* (Moscow, 1963)

A. V. Salamzade: *Arkhitektura Azerbaydzhana, XVI–XIX vv.* (Baku, 1964)

L. S. Bretanitsky: *Baku* (Leningrad, 1965)

——: *Zodchestvo Azerbaydzhana XII–XV vv. i yego mesto v arkhitekture Perednego Vostoka* [The architecture of Azerbaijan in the 12th–15th century and its place in the architecture of the Near East] (Moscow, 1966)

S. R. Scherr-Thoss and H. C. Scherr-Thoss: *Design and Color in Islamic Architecture* (Washington, 1968)

Vseobshchaya istoriya arkhitektury [General history of architecture], viii and xii (Moscow, 1969–75)

D. A. Akhundov: *Arkhitektura drevnego i rannesrednevekovogo Azerbaydzhana* [The architecture of ancient and early medieval Azerbaijan] (Baku, 1986)

Sh. S. Fatullayev: *Gradostroitel'stvo i arkhitektura Azerbaydzhana XIX–nachala XX vekov* [The town planning and architecture of Azerbaijan in the 19th and early 20th centuries] (Leningrad, 1986)

III. Sculpture.

In medieval Azerbaijan three-dimensional stone figures of ancestors (known as *baba* (in Azeri, 'forefather')) marked the territory of different tribal settlements. Stone images of rams (symbols of wealth) and saddled horses with weapons are found everywhere in the valleys, forests and mountains of Azerbaijan. Tombstones and walls were often decorated with ornamental reliefs. Relief carving reached its height in the decoration of architectural monuments in the Apsheron Peninsula. The 13th-century Bailov stone reliefs (Baku, Shirvanshah Pal. Mus.) are decorated with an Arabic inscription in which the letters are embellished with humans and animals. The sculptural decoration of contemporary churches consists of complex relief compositions that reveal great skill in the treatment of forms. The donor figures of Prince Hasan and his sons carrying a model of a church, which are depicted on the walls of the church of Arzu-khatun (1214), are evidence of an attempt by the sculptor to create generalized portraits of princely rulers. The most complex system of reliefs decorates Gandzasar Cathedral (1316–41); these comprise carefully worked, somewhat generalized forms of the Virgin and Child, kneeling female figures and the head and other members of the Hasan Jalal family. From the 16th century onwards tombstones were decorated with genre scenes of sacrifice, feasting and hunting, as well as depictions of riders, weavers or blacksmiths bearing attributes of the craft of the deceased.

The 15th–16th century portal reliefs of the palace of the Shirvanshahs in Baku combine *muqarnas* and arabesque ornament with inscriptions and calligrams. These reliefs were carved *in situ* on the façade of closely fitted stone blocks. There was a great revival of stone-carving traditions during the rapid expansion of Baku in the second half of the 19th century, when numerous new buildings, designed in various 'historical' styles, all needed sculptural decoration.

From 1920 Baku was home to several Russian sculptors and to the republic's first sculptural workshop, organized by S. Gorodetsky. In 1923 the sculptor Ye. Tripol'skaya produced a monument to the 26 commissars of Baku, which depicts a muscular worker resting on a stele inscribed with the number 26. In the 1920s and 1930s S. P. Sabsai (1893–1980) was prominent in the design of sculptural monuments that can be associated with the architectural developments of the period. The monument to *M. F. Akhundov* (1812–78), erected in 1930 in the square bearing his name, depicts the great philosopher deep in thought over a book and is marked by a pronounced intimacy and some spiritual force.

After 1945 the development of sculpture was dominated by monumental compositions. The work of such sculptors of the 1930s as F. G. Abdurakhmanov (1915–71) and D. M. Karyagdy (*b* 1914) influenced the style of the monuments to various historical figures in the centres of numerous reconstructed and new squares. The monument to *Nizami* (1141–1209) (1949; Nizami Square, Baku) by Abdurakhmanov is a generalized portrait of the great humanist: the inspired poet has a scroll in his hand and is draped in a robe that falls to the ground. The portrait of *Lenin* (1954), the nucleus of the architectural design of the Government House in Baku, is a central work of the sculptor D. M. Karyagdy. The ideological and artistic form of the monument is determined by the architecture. The covered courtyard is enclosed on three sides and has a tower-like pedestal in the centre for the sculpture, which is designed so that the silhouette of the figure is easily visible against the background of the huge building. The monuments designed by the sculptor O. G. Eldarov (*b* 1927) are marked by intimacy and lyricism. The statue of the 19th-century poetess *Khurshud-banu Natavan* (1960) in Baku has the appearance of an intimate portrait, the sitter captured in momentary thought as she rests on a chair.

Small sculptures in the round appeared as an independent genre in the 1950s and 1960s. Initially these were portraits of heroes of labour or of culture (e.g. that of *Shepherd* by F. Abdurakhmanov and the portrait of *S. Rustamov* by P. Sabsay) and historical figures (e.g. *Nizami* by T. Mamedov and *Natavan* by Eldarov). In portrait sculpture there was a tendency towards the generalization of the sitter that concentrated on the main features of a contemporary figure; but at the same time some sculptors attempted a more psychological portrait of the sitter (e.g. *Bakhlul-zade* by Eldarov, 1965). In the 1970s sculptors tried their hand at complex compositions in thematic sculpture, using such materials as wood, marble and granite. In the sculptural group *Lovers* (1962; wood) by G. G. Abdullayev (*b* 1912) the world of contemporary feelings is expressed through the use of restrained plastic form. The *Female Torso* (1972) by F. E. Salayev (*b* 1943) reveals a superb mastery of the canons of Classical sculpture.

BIBLIOGRAPHY

N. D. Gabibov and M. N. Nadzhafov: *Iskusstvo sovetskogo Azerbaydzhana: Zhivopis', skul'ptura, grafika: Ocherki* [The art of Soviet Azerbaijan: painting, sculpture, graphic art: outlines] (Moscow, 1960)

Iskusstvo sovetskogo Azerbaydzhana: Zhivopis', grafika, skul'ptura [The art of Soviet Azerbaijan: painting, graphic art, sculpture] (Moscow, 1970)

D. G. Novruzova: *Scul'ptura sovetskogo Azerbayzhana* (Baku, 1979)

IV. Painting.

In the late 13th century Tabriz in southern Azerbaijan developed as a centre of book illustration (*see* ISLAMIC ART, §III, 4(v)(b)). In the north, artists concentrated mainly on copying books and calligraphy. The only illustration in a manuscript of Nizami's poem *Iskandarnāma* (1418; Baku, Azerbaijan Acad. Sci., MS. Fund) shows a scene of the destruction, on the orders of Alexander the Great, of the temples of fire-worshippers, who according to tradition originally came from Azerbaijan. Traditions of book illustration remained unbroken in succeeding centuries, as can be seen in the illustrations (see fig. 4) to the collection of animal fables *Kalila and Dimna* (18th century) in the Azerbaijani language; these comprise a series of marvellous, expressive drawings executed with a reed pen and ink and touches of watercolour.

In the 19th century painters turned to portraiture, seeking to combine stylized drawing and decorative colour with European devices of spatial composition and modelling to create a sense of volume. Such works as *Portrait of a Young Man*, a *Seated Woman* and *Portrait of a Young Woman* by Mirza Kadym Irevani (1825–75) combined a highly finished drawing technique and rich colour with soft and lyrical execution. A true synthesis of classical book painting and European watercolour is demonstrated by the works of Bekhruz Kengerli (1892–1922), who created numerous portraits of his contemporaries as well

4. Illustration from the animal fables *Kalila and Dimna*, pen and ink with watercolour, 18th century (Baku, Azerbaijan Academy of Sciences, Manuscript Fund)

as painting the landscapes and monuments of the Nakhchyvan region. His miniature the *Water Carrier* succeeds through its folk character and fine watercolour hues.

Many Azerbaijani artists during the 17th to the 19th century used oil paints on residential buildings, palaces and bathhouses, thereby creating an unusual school of wall painting that depicted not only decorative motifs but also historical portraits and scenes of hunts and battles. The wall-painting tradition was rooted in the frescoes of the 12th-century Oren-kala settlement and also of the church of Arzu-khatun in Khashavank (1312), where fragments of complex monumental religious compositions have been found, including depictions of the stoning of archdeacon Stephanos and Nicholas the Miracle-Worker being given a mitre by Christ and an omophorian by the Virgin. In the 18th and 19th centuries, affluent house-owners began to commission artists to paint their reception rooms with historical subjects. Examples of work from this period include the palace of Husein Guli khan in Baku, the palace of the Sardars in Erivan executed by M. M. Navvab (1829–1918), the house of Haji Baba decorated by Ashraf and the palace of the Shaki khans painted by Gambar. The most comprehensive series of wall paintings is found in the palace of the Shaki khans. These paintings were executed by various artists over the course of the 19th century and at the beginning of the 20th.

The founder of contemporary oil painting on canvas in Azerbaijan was Alibek Huseinzade (1864–1940). His *Mosque in Bibi-Eybat*, the portrait of *Sheykh-ul' Islam* and an *Azerbaijani Family* show him to be a versatile artist, able to produce landscapes, portraits and genre pictures.

Books in the Azerbaijani language began to be printed in the early 20th century, and graphic art appeared in magazines and books. The leading representative of this trend was the talented self-taught artist Azim Azimzade (1880–1943), who illustrated M. A. Sabir's (1862–1911) satirical poem *Hop-Hop-name* and created numerous drawings on everyday, anti-religious and political themes for the periodicals *Molla Nasreddin* and *Mazali* ('Humour'). Another superb draughtsman was the 19th-century poetess Khurshud-banu Natavan (1830–96), the first Azerbaijani woman artist, whose pencil drawings of landscapes illustrating her diaries are filled with lyrical natural charm.

After the establishment of Soviet power in Azerbaijan in 1920, the Azerbaijan State Artistic Studio (1920–21) concentrated on teaching students European artistic forms. Painting of the 1920s and 1930s was dominated by devices borrowed from European modernism: extremely simplified and geometricized forms and the use of generalized local colour built up on the combination of pure colours. An exhibition devoted to ten years of Soviet power in Azerbaijan revealed an interest in the new social themes (e.g. *Thread-spinning Factory* and *Opening of the Machine Tractor Station*, 1930, both by S. Salamzade; *Gathering Cotton* by Sh. Mangasarov; *Women's Section* by G. Khalykov (1898–1981)). These decades were marked by the appearance of the first Azerbaijani woman painters, among them B. Dashdamirova, E. Shakhtakhtinskaya (*b* 1930), U. Useynova and S. Karasharly, whose works were marked by abstract schematism and ornamental forms.

In the second half of the 1930s there was a break in painting themes and techniques. New subjects included historical revolutionary themes (e.g. *V. I. Lenin in the Kremlin* by T. Tagiyev), contemporary portraits (e.g. the portrait of the artist A. Azimzade by G. Akhverdiyev) and thematic pictures (e.g. *Gathering Grapes* by S. Sharifzade), all painted in a realistic style that sought to solve complex problems of colour. In the work of the graphic artists Azimzade, I. Akhundov, E. Hadjiyev, K. Kazymzade and M. Rahmanzade there was an interest, on the one hand, in new social themes and, on the other, in the historic past of Azerbaijan. Azimzade, the oldest of the Azerbaijani graphic artists, produced *Figures of Old Baku*, a series of pen drawings washed with watercolour on the theme of Azerbaijan's past.

In the late 1940s and early 1950s the tendency towards superficial impressiveness and standard compositions was overcome and artists tried to find a fresh painting style. The work of Mikhail G. Abdullayev (*b* 1921) was devoted to the depiction of his contemporaries through psychological characterization (e.g. the portrait of the writer *G. Seidbeyli* and that of *Farkhad Badalbeyli*). *Masally Suite*, a series of genre pictures of life in an Azerbaijani village, and *Indian Suite*, for which he won the Jawaharlal Nehru Prize, are marked by a unity of colour and a direct perception of everyday life. The works of Tahir Salakhov are among the most outstanding examples of Soviet portraiture (e.g. portraits of the poet *Rasul Rza* and the composers *Kara Karayev*, *Dmitry Shostakovich* and *Fikret Amirov*; see fig. 5). The cycle of landscapes of the Apsheron Peninsula, produced by the artist in the 1970s in strong, contrasting colour combinations, conveys the extraordinary beauty of his native countryside. Nadir G. Abdurakhmanov (*b* 1926) devoted himself to historical and religious subjects (e.g. the *Arrest of the Baku Commissars* and *Lenin's Word*) and to depictions of rural labourers. His landscapes and scenes of Azerbaijani village life use strong, frank colours (e.g. *Sowing Rice*, *Mountain Girl* and *Talysh Girl*).

In the 1960s a trend developed that combined simplified forms of borrowed folkloric motifs and images with the characteristically contrasting intense colours of Azerbaijani folk art. R. G. Babayev (*b* 1927), a gifted and versatile artist, created a series of pictures filled with images from Azerbaijani folklore (*Div*, 1980). The resonant colour, at times imitative of the colour schemes of traditional carpets, the free construction of form and the decorative nature of the images in the work of the painter Togrul F. Narimanbekov (*b* 1930) all recall folk art. Folkloric motifs are most strongly seen in the paintings of M. Mirdjavadov (*b* 1922), whose gallery of fairytale heroes and beautiful girls and fantastic scenes full of ancient symbols combine images of good and evil forces that have relevance in contemporary life (e.g. *Mafiosi*, 1984). The work of the talented Ashraf Muradogly (1925–79) stands apart. He took pictorial form to the level of an abstract symbol while preserving a clearly readable meaning, and he used pure colour as a means of expressing feelings. His series of *Bathing Women* and *Sportswomen* (1970s), which include the first depictions of the naked body in Azerbaijani painting, show expressive, vibrant figures of girls moving across a dark blue-black sea. In his light-filled landscape paintings of the 1960s and 1970s S. Bakhlulzade (1909–74) revealed himself as a master of lyrical pictures of nature (e.g. *In the Gardens of Novkhany*, 1965).

Theatrical design reached a high point in the 1960s with the work of R. Mustafayev (1910–40), I. Seydov, B. Afganly, I. G. Akhundov (1906–69), N. Fatullayev (*b* 1913) and others, who were responsible for productions by Azerbaijani, Russian and foreign playwrights. In designs for plays by national authors there was wide use of traditional devices from the decorative and applied art of Azerbaijan. T. F. Narimanbekov's designs for the ballet *A Thousand and One Nights* (composer F. Amirov (*b* 1922), Akhundov Theatre of Opera and Ballet, Baku, 1979) are a successful example of the artist's painterly style expressed through contemporary set design.

After 1945 printmaking utilized new developments in linocut and etching. Using the linocut technique A. A. Rzaguliyev (1903–74) depicted humorous scenes from everyday life in old Baku (e.g. *Taking Presents to the Bride*, 1965). The main themes of M. Yu. Rahmanzade's (*b* 1916) linocuts are different aspects of the lives of women labourers, while motherhood and childhood are represented in the lithographs of the woman artist B. Hadyiyeva (*b* 1927). Watercolour was another popular medium, particularly with Rahmanzade (e.g. landscapes of Nakhchyvan and Khynalyk) and E. G. Shakhtakhtinskaya (*b* 1930).

In book illustration there were two trends. The first was founded on the principles of manuscript painting (e.g. illustrations, 1958, by K. Kazymzade (*b* 1913) to Nizami's poem *Khusraw and Shirin*; illustrations, 1957, by M. Abdullayev to the epic *Kitabi Dede Gorgud*); the second used a black-and-white, graphic style (e.g. Rahmanzade's illustrations for the poems of Heiram Khanym, 1962).

The different branches of decorative and applied art in Azerbaijan shared a common ornamental system based on multi-ray stars derived from various combinations of polygons (*djafari*) and vegetal designs formed by regular spirals crowned with petals (*islimi*). There were also numerous other classical motifs: an irregular free form of vegetal ornament (*khatay*), a trellis of rhombuses (*benderumi*), combinations of stylized depictions of whirling clouds (*abr*), and vegetal ornament with branches crowned with human heads or real and fantastical beasts (*vag*). These designs were widely used in festooned cartouches of *ketebe* and in the ornamentation of calligraphic inscriptions.

5. Tahir Salakhov: *Fikret Amirov*, oil on canvas, 1967 (Baku, Mustafayev Azerbaijani Museum of Arts)

BIBLIOGRAPHY

L. Rempel': *Iskusstvo narodov SSSR: Azerbaydzhan, Armeniya, Gruziya* [The art of the peoples of the USSR: Azerbaijan, Armenia, Georgia] (Moscow, 1932)

Iskusstvo Azerbaydzhana [The art of Azerbaijan], 12 vols (Baku, 1949–68)

Yu. A. Kaziyev: 'Ob Azerbaydzhanskom isskusstve nachala XX veka: Ob izobrazitel'nom iskusstve, 1900–1920' [On Azerbaijani art of the beginning of the 20th century: on fine art, 1900–1920], *Isk. Azerbaydzhana*, iv (1954), pp. 109–210

R. S. Efendi: *Sattar Bakhlul-zade* (Moscow, 1959)

Vseobshchaya istoriya iskusstv [General history of arts], ii/2 (Moscow, 1961)

Khudozhniki sovetskogo Azerbaydzhana [Artists of Soviet Azerbaijan] (Moscow, 1962)

M. N. Nadzhafov: *Azim Azimzade* (Baku, 1965)

N. D. Gabibov: *Mikhail Abdullayev* (Moscow, 1969)

M. N. Nadzhafov: *Iskusstvo Azerbaydzhanskoy SSR* [The art of the Azerbaijani SSR] (Leningrad, 1972) [Azerbaij., Rus. and Eng. text]

L. I. Akimova: *Nadir Abdurakhmanov* (Moscow, 1973)

N. M. Miklashevskaya: *Stanovleniye i razvitiye iskusstva sotsialisticheskogo realizma v Azerbaydzhane* [The establishment and development of the art of Socialist Realism in Azerbaijan] (Baku, 1974)

L. S. Bretanitsky and B. V. Veymarn: *Iskusstvo Azerbaydzhana, IV–XVIII vv.* [The art of Azerbaijan of the 4th–18th century] (Moscow, 1976)

K. D. Kerimov: *Stennaya rospis'* [Wall painting] (Baku, 1983)

A. A. Dekhtyar': *Togrul Narimanbekov: Zhivopis'* [Togrul Narimanbekov: painting] (Moscow, 1984)

A. M. Kolyadenko, ed.: *Tair Salakhov* (Moscow, 1986) [Eng. summary]

V. Other arts.

1. Ceramics and glass. 2. Interior decoration. 3. Metalwork. 4. Textiles and embroidery. 5. Woodwork.

1. Ceramics and glass. In the medieval period mastery of the potter's wheel and hand-modelling and the complex technology of firing and of different glazes and types of glass had already led to the production of glazed ceramic pieces of intricate design and ornament covered with polychrome painting. Sherds from Baku and Mingachevir of the early 11th century provide evidence of a type of hemispherical bowl on a tall base, decorated predominantly with geometric or simplified vegetal designs in yellow, violet and green on white or red engobe and covered with a transparent lead glaze. Initially in the 11th century occasional elements of the decoration were incised, but by the end of the century the whole design was formed in this way. *Sgraffito* was also used in Baylakan as a means of utilizing the natural clay body beneath a layer of slip as an additional colour.

In the 12th century the two main centres of production were Baylakan, which produced high-quality vessels, and Nakhchyvan, which produced tiles. Other secondary centres were the towns of Shamakhy, Baku and, in particular, a large settlement between the Kura estuary and the Bandovan promontory, which disappeared at the turn of the 13th century. Baylakan ceramics of the 12th and 13th centuries can be divided stylistically into several types. The first includes a platter and bowl decorated with freely drawn rosettes within a network of wavy lines forming medallions. The design was incised into the damp clay with a sharp instrument, then painted green, yellow and a range of hues from red to violet. A second group, datable to the 13th century, is decorated with small detailed vegetal designs, while a third type has complex geometrical elements in the form of symmetrically drawn plaits, bands and knots, verses in cursive script and the potter's name. The platters have a deeper, more spherical shape, with a round foot and sometimes also the potter's mark in relief. The rim has a wide border, painted with plaited or interwoven bands. Sherds provide the names of many craftsmen, such as Sayyid ʿAli, Nas'r, ʿAli, Hasan, Ahmad, Yusuf and Ibrahim, the most common being the name Khattab. The inscriptions sometimes include not only the *nisba* (the potter's place of origin or residence), as in 'the work of Ahmad, son of Abu Bakr from Gandja', but also direct references to the place where the object was produced, such as 'made by Fadlun in al-Baylakan'.

In Nakhchyvan, bricks with turquoise glazes were used in the geometrical ornament of façades, combined with ceramic mosaic mainly in turquoise, dark blue and white. Tile mosaic was also used for inscriptions in cursive script on the portals of mausolea, for example the 14th-century mausoleum in the village of Qarabaghlar.

In the 15th century in Baku, Nakhchyvan and Shabran the production of polychrome ceramics declined following the expansion of the export of faience and developments in the production of copper vessels, which were more expensive but more durable than ceramics. However, various pottery forms for everyday purposes continued to be produced.

The development of ceramics in the first half of the 20th century was linked with L. G. Kerimov, a versatile artist who in 1939 designed a porcelain vase decorated with cotton flowers and stems and the republic's coat of arms in a scalloped medallion. The decoration of the Nizami Museum (1940; architects S. Dadashev and M. Useynov) in Baku once again used the technique of polychrome glazed-tile mosaic. New vessel forms appeared, such as the coffee set designed in 1962 by G. U. Huseinov (*b* 1920). There were also new interpretations of traditional ewer forms, such as the vessels produced in 1961 by L. Agamalova and T. Agababayeva, while miniature painting techniques began to be used in the decoration of ceramic pieces, for example the 'Farhad and Shirin' vase (1958) by O. Yu. Shikhaliyev (*b* 1931). A totally new genre, the painted ceramic statuette, also appeared. In 1955 G. A. Abdullayeva created a group of painted porcelain statuettes of girls standing around the seated Shah Bahram, a subject taken from Nizami's poem *Haft paykar* ('Seven beauties'). A humorous approach to folklore can be seen in the realistic statuette by R. G. Khalafov (*b* 1928) of *Molla and the Ass* (1959), one in a series of compositions entitled the *Anecdotes of Molla Nasreddin.*

Artists in the 20th century turned their attention to glass after the opening of a glass factory in Baku in 1950. Initially forms and ornament were dominated by traditional vegetal motifs, as can be seen in the glass tumbler (1956) by S. Yu. Shakhsuvarova (*b* 1927), which is decorated with a faceted vegetal design, while the saucer has an eight-petalled rosette. The coloured glass sherbet service (1959) by L. Agamalova, although based on traditional vessel forms, nevertheless has a contemporary appearance. In the crystal service (1959), T. Agababov simplified form to the utmost, so that the play of the crystal facets of the glass predominates.

BIBLIOGRAPHY

N. N. Nadzhafova: *Khudozhestvennaya keramika Azerbaydzhana, XII–XV vv.* [Artistic ceramics of Azerbaijan of the 12th–15th century] (Baku, 1964)

2. Interior decoration. The interior of the traditional Azerbaijani house was always a simple, open arrangement of space, with divisions into living and reception rooms. In both types of room there were few partitions and low furniture, for people usually sat on the floor. Carpets and rugs were the main elements, as denoted by the word *besat* (carpet), which was also used when referring to the overall interior. The undecorated wall surfaces were pierced by arched windows or niches for utensils and everyday objects. Some crockery or small objects were kept on shelves in the upper part of the wall or on consoles. Niches and openings that linked the inner rooms were hung with embroidered curtains or flat-woven rugs with decorative panel designs. The simple, wooden-frame furniture consisted of a wooden sofa for sleeping or sitting, with cushions, a large chest for clothes and shoes and small chests or boxes for smaller items and valuables (*mudzhru*). Bedding was kept in a carpet chest, a large rectangular bag with a top that could be thrown back. Various objects, including food, could be kept in a sectioned wooden cupboard.

Ornamental stuccowork was used in the artistic decoration of the interior, surrounding niches, cornices and *muqarnas*. In the houses of the wealthy and the palaces of the khans the walls were covered with paintings on plaster and canvas or decorative panels with scenes of hunts and feasts. Decorative painting was also used on architectural details made of papier-mâché. In houses with verandahs and large window openings, partitions were built of coloured glass mosaic reinforced in a wooden frame. The wooden columns, open struts, roofs and doors were all decorated with carving. The interiors of the palaces of the Shaki khans (19th–20th century) employed a wide range of techniques, including mirror-glass *muqarnas* and friezes painted with historical and literary subjects.

After 1920 the traditional principles of interior decoration were also applied to the design of public buildings. In the Azerbaijani SSR pavilion at the All-Russian Agricultural Exhibition in Moscow in 1937, the architects S. Dadashev and M. Useynov and the artist L. G. Kerimov (*b* 1906) created a hall with complex decoration. Motifs carved on the plaster friezes and panels included five-pointed stars, hammers and sickles, flowers, fruit, vines and cotton bolls. From the 1960s onwards the use of stucco relief was largely replaced by decorative painting, mosaic and chased techniques. In conjunction with the traditional glasswork, forms for making glass were introduced, as were epoxy resins to attach the pieces.

BIBLIOGRAPHY

M. A. Tarlanov: *Dekorativno-prikladnoye iskusstvo sovetskogo Azerbaydzhana* [Decorative and applied art of Soviet Azerbaijan] (Baku, 1968)

R. S. Efendi: *Dekorativno-prikladnoye iskusstvo Azerbaydzhana: Sredniye veka* [Decorative and applied art of Azerbaijan: Middle Ages] (Baku, 1976) [Rus., Azerbaij. and Eng. text]

N. S. Askerova: *Mastera dekorativno-prikladnogo iskusstva Azerbaydzhana, XII–XIX vv.* [Masters of the decorative and applied art of Azerbaijan of the 12th–19th century] (Baku, 1983)

3. METALWORK.

(i) Vessels. Different types of vessel, in a variety of metals, dating from the 12th century onwards, have survived. One such is a pear-shaped bronze ewer commissioned in 1190 by ʿUthman ibn Sulayman al-Nakhichivani (Paris, Louvre, 6314). The vessel has a broad base, a neck decorated with an elongated head and a body with fine bands of ornament and medallions inlaid in copper and silver. There are silver jugs, plates and chalices from the same period and later. A bronze cauldron of the 13th–14th century, found near the ruins of the fortress of Kale-i-bogurt, is notable not only for its size and geometric ornament but also for its form of flanges with a spout and rings, which allows the cauldron to stand or be suspended over the fire. A 15th–16th-century bowl (Baku, Hist. Mus. Acad. Sci. Azerbaijan) provides a rare example of the decoration of copper objects using the cloisonné enamel technique. The bird seated on a branch of a flowering almond tree and the quatrefoil cartouche have been embossed from the inside of the bowl to form the divisions that are infilled with dark blue, white, green and pink enamel. A copper bowl of the 17th century (Baku, Hist. Mus. Acad. Sci. Azerbaijan) is decorated with incised bands of floral designs (see fig. 6). On drinking vessels artists used fine engraved ornament, including inscribed wishes for well-being and verses from well-known poems. An 18th-century sherbet bowl (Baku, Hist. Mus. Acad. Sci. Azerbaijan) has numerous images of animals, trees and plants set in a honeycomb pattern comprising three rows of medallions. The traditional ways of producing complex forms survived until the modern period. Evidence of this can be seen in a copper jug by Akhad Keble Kerbalai Huseinoghly, from the village of Laghych, which received a prize at the Vienna Universal Exhibition in 1873. Until the 20th century Laghych remained the primary centre of quality copper production. Several generations of famed masters had their workshops in the village, including Ali (17th century), Akhad Keble Kerbalai Husein (19th century), the Mammadov family (19th–20th century) and Sarkhan and Nagi Aliyev (20th century). The technique of embossing copper is still widely used by contemporary artists to produce reliefs for the interiors of public buildings.

6. Bowl, incised copper, from Azerbaijan, 17th century (Baku, Historical Museum of the Academy of Sciences of Azerbaijan)

At the end of the 19th century and in the early 20th new types of object appeared to cater for the demands of the local bourgeoisie who had grown rich during the oil boom. These objects included small boxes, address files, covers for anniversary albums, and ewers and trays commemorating particular events. In the 1950s new forms of crockery and tableware appeared, with figural decoration. A silver nielloed wine-set, designed by D. M. Mammadova (*b* 1929), comprises a tray, a ewer bearing a portrait of the poet Nizami and seven glasses decorated with the figures of seven girls from Nizami's poem *Haft paykar* ('Seven Beauties').

(ii) Jewellery. Casting, embossing, engraving, stamping and niello were used from ancient times for making jewellery in Azerbaijan. Filigree and enamel were introduced in the medieval period. From the 12th century onwards rubies, emeralds, turquoise, coral, pearls and different kinds of chalcedony were inset in the form of cabochons. During this period the principal types of jewellery developed, with different pieces often being grouped together in sets. The work of medieval Azerbaijani jewellers was highly regarded in the Orient and was named according to its place of

origin: *Shamakhy* (after the town Shamakhy) or *Arran* (after the Arabic name for the region). These pieces were very carefully finished and had unusual decoration. Surviving examples date mainly from the 19th and early 20th centuries but repeat traditional forms. Since jewellers did not sign their works, precise attributions to particular craftsmen or places of production are difficult, although the names of many masters who worked in Gandja, Baku, Shaki, Shusha, Nakhchyvan and Barda are known. The most prevalent forms are pointed oval medallions, a pear-shaped motif with a curved tip, crescents and five-pointed stars, arrow-shaped arches, an elongated rhombus, multi-petalled flowers and geometrical and stylized zoomorphic elements in the form of fish, birds and animals. The pieces are further enlivened by additional details attached with hooks and hinges and the unusual combination of such techniques as filigree and beading, sharply projecting deep settings, which emphasize the colour of inset gems or hardstones, and bright red, green and blue enamelling, either overlaid with a fine, semi-transparent layer on a beaded ground or poured into a deep form, for instance a precious stone. Vegetal ornament painted in enamel on a white ground was also used.

The demand for jewellery increased during the second half of the 19th century and at the beginning of the 20th as a result of the oil boom in Baku and the appearance of rich clients among the local bourgeoisie. The traditional centres for jewellery production, Gandja, Shamakhy and Shaki, were joined by Baku, where there were many famous craftsmen. The city's most renowned jeweller was Mirdadash Mirahmadov, who was master of all the different techniques, particularly enamelling, which he combined with casting, stamping, niello and filigree. In 1903 he received a Gold Medal from the Shah of Iran, Muzaffar al-Din Qajar (*reg* 1896–1907), for a set of jewellery. In the 1920s, following the Russian Revolution, individual craftsmen formed communal workshops. In 1936 all craftsmen were invited to work in a new jewellery factory in Baku. Work from this period includes the imitation of traditional jewellery forms as well as new designs using emblems such as stars, hammers and sickles, oil rigs and cotton bolls on a background of traditional ornament. From the 1950s onwards the range of jewellery widened to include modern forms and designs.

(iii) Arms and armour. During the medieval period armourers in Azerbaijan produced superb examples of the curved sabre, short dagger, defensive cuirasse, gloves, helmets and shields. Battle weapons were made from a particular type of hard but flexible damascened steel developed in Azerbaijan, which had a surface pattern of projections that gave the metal an aesthetic quality. Sword blades were decorated with engraving and gold inlay, usually giving the names of the armoury master and the owner, or excerpts from the Koran set in a cartouche near the hilt. Occasionally there was also a verse praising weapons. The hilt was made of horn dyed black or green. The best battle swords of damascened steel were noted for their very economic use of ornament. The blades were made by famed masters in all the metalwork centres, including the village of Laghych where the armoury master Abdulrahim worked in the 18th century.

From the 17th century onwards the decoration of guns and pistols was concentrated on the flintlock, which had a cartouche bearing the name of the craftsman set against a background of vegetal ornament. Gold inlay also covered the breech of the barrel and the abutment of the gunstock. By the mid-19th century the spread of more modern types of gun had signalled the end of the production of traditional flintlock pistols and shotguns. During the Soviet period, however, highly decorated guns and swords were still produced for awards and presents to important military figures. These high-quality weapons had butts and scabbards of gold and silver, decorated with engraving and niello or silver and enamel.

BIBLIOGRAPHY

I. A.Orbeli: 'Albanskiye rel'yefy i bronzovyye kotly, XII–XV vv.' [Albanian reliefs and bronze cauldrons of the 12th–15th centuries], *Pamyatniki epokhi Rustaveli* [Monuments of the era of Rustaveli] (Leningrad, 1938)

R. S. Efendi: *Yuvelirnoye iskusstvo Azerbaydzhana* [Jewellery of Azerbaijan]

S. D. Asadova and N. A. Abdullayeva: *Khudozhestvennaya obrabotka metalla* [Artistic metalwork] (Baku, 1983)

M. I. Atakishiyeva: *Yuvelirnyye izdeliya* [Jewellery] (Baku, 1987) [Rus., Eng. and Fr. text]

S. Dzhangirova: *Vostochnoye oruzhiye* [Oriental weaponry] (Baku, 1987) [Rus., Eng. and Fr. text]

A. Radzhabli: *Drevniye i srednevekovyye monety* [Ancient and medieval coins] (Baku, 1987) [Rus., Eng. and Fr. text]

4. Textiles and embroidery.

(i) Fabrics. From ancient times diverse panel and roll fabrics of wool, cotton and silk were produced on horizontal looms in Azerbaijan. The oldest and most common decoration was a repeat design of coloured weft stripes. From the 10th century block printing also began to be widely used. Simple silk or wool fabrics, usually dyed black, cheap linen or sateen were used for everyday wear. More expensive silk fabrics were largely produced from the 12th century onwards in Gandja, Barda and Shaki. The main types of silk were clearly developed at this time: a type of brocade, moire, satin, taffeta and striped silk. Fabrics of the 12th or 13th century found in the tomb of the poet Nizami bear traces of four-petalled rosette ornament and provide evidence of the use of repeat motifs to decorate fabrics in this period. In the 14th and 15th centuries Chinese motifs such as the cloud-band, dragon and phoenix (a symbol of prosperity) were used to decorate fabrics. At the end of the 16th century figural motifs and more complicated techniques were introduced, including multi-weft weaving of coloured threads and gold-thread silk. From the end of the 17th century onwards designs were built up of a repeat of small elements such as bouquets of flowers, rosettes and the Paisley pattern motif (*buta*).

In the 19th century fabrics were produced in Shamakhy, Gandja, Shusha and Baku but with simplified decoration. Block-printing again became widespread. During the second half of the 19th century a silk-winding factory was opened in Nukha. Fabrics began to be imported from Russia, which had a negative influence on hand-weaving. Small weaving shops continued to produce rolls of cloth of the kilim type and individual silk panels; the latter were used for large head-scarves of two types: a kerchief with a border and a large central medallion surrounded by stamped yellow and brown *buta* motifs; and a kerchief covered with small flowers on a white, red, dark-lilac or ochre ground, with a broad, richly ornamented border. The best-quality head-scarves of the medallion type are those by master Aga Alesker Safaroghly, which have a complex composition consisting of a central medallion surrounded by *buta* elements and a border printed with blocks in four colours. Until the late 1940s some workshops still produced fabric woven from bands of coloured silk crossed by fine lines in a contrasting colour.

In the 1960s a group of artists began work at the Shaki Silk Combine, seeking to introduce new designs for block-printed fabrics. Repeated figures of cotton-gatherers among large bundles of cotton are depicted on the fabric design *Cotton* (1960) by S. M. Shykhly (*b* 1927), which in colour and composition recalls fabrics of the 17th and 18th centuries. *Djeyran* (1961) by A. Bilalova has echoes of folk art with its simple graphic silhouette of an animal standing among trees. Constructivist graphics of the 1920s and 1930s were also reflected in such fabrics as the voiles (1950–60) by G. Voronova.

(ii) Embroidery. In the 18th century the art of embroidery is reputed to have reached its height in the towns of Shamakhy, Shaki and Shusha, but only 19th-century examples have survived, mainly on clothes and everyday objects. Embroidery was used to adorn bed and cushion covers, tablecloths, prayer mats, small shoulder bags, covers for smaller items such as mirrors, combs and the Koran, curtains, screens, horse- and saddle-cloths, pistol holsters, moustache protectors, stems for hookahs and tobacco pouches.

The principal motifs used in embroidery were flowers and fruit (rose, narcissus, carnation, poppy, almond and quince blossom, and pomegranate) and birds (nightingale, peacock, turtle-dove, pheasant and partridge). An ornamental composition usually comprised a large flower or decorative branch and a pair of birds facing one another (symbol of the meeting of lovers) or addorsed (symbol of parting and sorrow). The main technique was chain stitch, in deep red, black, dark blue or green tones on coarse cloth or velvet, which was used for bedspreads, cushion covers, tablecloths and small items. Satin stitch, either single or double-sided, using untwisted silk, was preferred for embroidering clothes, veils and curtains. Golden embroidery was used on cloth, brocade, satin and fine leather. During the second half of the 19th century numerous workshops flourished in Shamakhy, Shaki and Shusha. Embroidery from Shaki was exported to Russia and other parts of Transcaucasia. The major Azerbaijani artists Mirza Kadym Irevani (1825–75) and M. M. Navvab (1829–1918) produced embroidery designs, while the poetess Khurshud-banu Natavan (1830–96) was famed as an excellent needlewoman, having mastered the various stitches and techniques of beaded embroidery, including the use of sequins and gold or silver spangles.

In the 1920s a number of small embroidery workshops in Baku and Shaki produced tablecloths, bedspreads, panels and traditional hats. Chain stitch was used exclusively for vegetal motifs combined with newly introduced Soviet iconographical designs that included coats of arms, orders, badges and even portraits.

In 1930 the setting up of the Strochevyshivka workshop in Baku produced a revival of traditional techniques and types of embroidery. A follower of the traditional style was Abuzar Latifov from Shaki, who embroidered cushion covers, bedspreads and tablecloths. The artists sought to create sets of embroidered objects. A series created in 1939 by the Shaki master Rza Taghyzade comprised a small rug, a tablecloth and covers for a divan and cushions, all with densely embroidered geometric and vegetal designs in chain stitch.

(iii) Carpets. In terms of style, Azerbaijani carpets can be divided into three groups: Quba–Shirvan (carpets woven in Quba, Baku and the Shirvan region), Gandja–Qazakh (carpets from the Gandja and Qazakh regions) and Qarabagh (carpets from the Qarabagh, Shusha and Djabrail regions). Carpets from the Quba–Shirvan group have a border comprising several bands of repeat design and a central field in white or a saturated tone, either containing one or more large geometrical medallions or a number of small geometrical or stylized ornamental flower elements. The key design elements of the Gandja–Qazakh group are a chain of three polygonal medallions or one large medallion surrounded by stylized trees or small stars and S-shaped volutes symbolizing a dragon. The S-shaped volute or dragon design is also a principal element in flat-woven rugs (*see* KILIM). The border consists of three bands of rhomboids and wavy lines or simplified figures of birds.

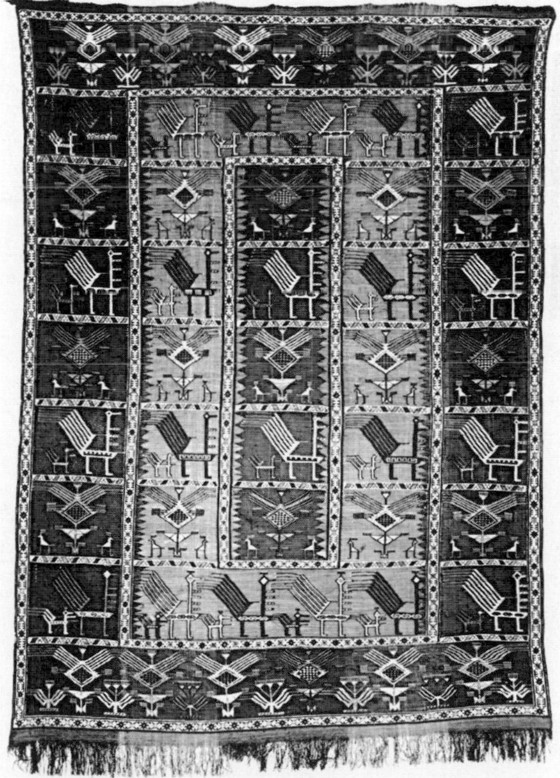

7. Woollen kilim, 2.00×1.48 m, from Khizi village, Azerbaijan, 19th century (Baku, Museum of Carpets and Applied Art)

Repeated squares of stylized birds are also found in a 19th-century kilim from the village of Khizi (Baku, Mus. Carpets & Applied A.; see fig. 7). In carpets of the Qarabagh group the central medallion and surrounding elements derive from vegetal, floral, bird or animal forms. In some instances the central field is completely filled with large rosettes linked by geometrical designs. There are no precise stylistic borders and often variations of the same motif, such as the *buta*, are incorporated into the ornamental schemes of carpets in all three carpet groups.

The carpet-weaving technique was used in the making of many other objects: carpet chests for bed linen and blankets, saddle bags, small shoulder bags, sacks for grain or stores, horsecloths and saddle cloths. There was also a trade in knitting wool and cotton socks. Technically Azerbaijani carpets are of high quality, averaging 1600 knots per sq. decimetre in flat-woven rugs and 4900 knots per sq. decimetre in pile carpets. This factor and the ornamental compositions ensured that Azerbaijani carpets became greatly sought after on the international carpet market when an export route via Russia developed in the late 19th to early 20th century. During this period the carpets of Shirvan and Qarabagh began to include multi-figure designs imitating Western tapestries (*see also* ISLAMIC ART, §VI, 4(iv)(b)).

In 1940 an artists' collective consisting of K. Kazimzade (1913–92), G. Khalykov (1898–1981), A. G. Mosesyan (*b* 1917), E. Hadjiyev and M. Shirinov worked with L. Kerimov (1906–92) to create five monumental carpets on the subject of Nizami's *Khamsa* ('Five poems'). These were the first figural carpets in which the central field, surrounded by traditional motifs, included realistic thematic scenes in a somewhat stylized form imitative of miniature painting. After 1945 the export of traditional carpets greatly increased. At the same time new motifs appeared in the repertory, including elements based on such diverse designs as oil rigs, stars, the hammer and sickle, spikes and cotton bolls. There was also a trend towards using the carpet as another pictorial form, with the creation of portrait carpets (e.g. *A. M. Gor'ky*, 1942, by R. Teymurova; *S. M. Kirov*, 1941, by A. Mammadova; *Indira Gandhi*, 1983, by K. Aliyev).

BIBLIOGRAPHY

R. S. Efendi: *Azerbaydzhanskiy kostyum* [Azerbaijani costume] (Baku, 1963)

N. A. Abdullayeva: *Kovrovoye iskusstvo Azerbaydzhana* [The art of carpets in Azerbaijan] (Baku, 1971)

M. I. Atakishiyeva, M. A. Dzhebrailova and V. M. Islamova: *Azerbaydzhanskiye vyshivki* [Azerbaijani embroidery] (Moscow, 1971)

I. Bennett, ed.: *Rugs and Carpets of the World* (London, 1977/*R* 1981), pp. 138–57

L. Kerimov: *Azerbaydzhanskiy kovyor* [Azerbaijani carpets] (Baku, 1985)

M. Dzhebrailova: *Azerbaydzhanskiye vyshivki* [Azerbaijani embroidery] (Baku, 1987) [Rus., Eng. and Fr. text]

——: *Azerbaydzhanskaya natsional'naya odezhda* [Azerbaijani national dress] (Baku, 1987) [Rus., Eng. and Fr. text]

M. Kuliyeva: *Kovry i kovrovyye izdeliya* [Carpets and woven objects] (Baku, 1987) [Rus., Eng. and Fr. text]

5. WOODWORK. There are three categories of woodwork in Azerbaijan: carving, ornamental grilles and inlay. It was standard practice for all carpenters in Azerbaijan to carve the wooden internal columns, beams and awnings of houses. Khaqani Shirvani, a 12th-century poet, called his father, ʿAli, from the village of Melkham, the most elegant carpenter. Specialists in wood-carving worked on the decoration of doors, tables, stools, bookstands and wooden vessels. The technique of wood-carving was similar to plaster-carving: fine relief with vegetal ornament of even height, with lightly modelled details. Geometric ornament in the form of paired squares, eight- and sixteen-pointed stars and a combination of angles formed the main elements in the carving of grilles. The grilles were made up of wooden modules that were either blind, openwork or glazed with coloured glass. One particular group used the inlay technique in which the geometrical ornament combined different species of coloured wood, ivory, mother-of-pearl and copper or silver wires.

After 1917 there was a decline in wood craftsmanship until the 1930s, when national motifs carved in wood were incorporated into the design of an increasing number of large public buildings. Abdulhusein Babayev (1877–1961) was one of the most talented master carvers and familiar with all the different techniques. His bookstand (1937) is made from a single piece of wood that opens to form a lectern for one, two or three books and is a marvel of contemporary design.

After World War II the brothers Ali and Husein Pariab (*b* 1928) and Ali Minai revived the inlay technique. A box depicting the hero of the national epic *Koroghly*, by the Pariab brothers, is a mosaic of tiny inlays of ivory, mother-of-pearl, silver, brass and different woods. The brothers also used the inlay technique for portraits of Azerbaijani notables such as Nariman Narimanov (1870–1925), Samed Burgun (1906–56), M. A. Sabir (1862–1911), M. F. Akhundov (1812–78) and M. Fizuli. Ali Minai used the filigree technique for the frames and panels of his pieces. In the 1970s the master Ashraf Rasulov used the openwork grille technique in the restoration of old buildings as well as in the decoration of modern interiors.

BIBLIOGRAPHY

A. S. Aliyeva: *Khudozhestvennaya obrabotka dereva* [Artistic woodwork] (Baku, 1983)

EMILE R. SALMANOV

Azevedo, Fernando de (*b* Vila Nova de Gaia, 17 Jan 1923). Portuguese painter, graphic artist, critic and art administrator. In 1947 he was a founder-member of the Grupo Surrealista de Lisboa, with which he exhibited in 1949. By 1952 he was one of the few remaining members of the original group still involved in Surrealism. That year he held a large exhibition with two other artists, showing *Occultations*, photographs in which parts of the images were masked by overpainting. At the time he was more interested in the process of image-making, in the unconscious genesis of images and their internal rhythms, than in the result as an aesthetic object. From the mid-1950s, Azevedo's paintings were almost entirely abstract and gestural, with greater overt affinities to lyrical abstraction than to automatism, for example *Painting* (1961; Lisbon, Mus. Gulbenkian). While in smaller works he often returned to the Surrealist use of collaged photographs introducing an element of shock or surprise, in his paintings there is an overriding interest in morphological dissolution and mutation, which remains lyrical rather than violent.

Azevedo illustrated various publications and designed stage sets for, among others, António Pedro's Experimental Theatre in Oporto and the Gulbenkian Ballet Group in Lisbon. He was an influential art critic from the 1950s. For a while he was the artistic director of the magazine *Colóquio artes*, started in 1971. As an art administrator, he played an important role in Portugal. Having been president of Gravura, the Portuguese cooperative of graphic artists, he was later one of the administrators of the fine arts section of the Calouste Gulbenkian Foundation in Lisbon as well as President of the National Society of Fine Arts. He was also vice-president of the Association Internationale des Critiques d'Art (AICA).

BIBLIOGRAPHY

J.-A. França: *Da pintura portuguesa* (Lisbon, 1960)
——: *Da pintura surrealista em Portugal* (Lisbon, 1966)

RUTH ROSENGARTEN

Azevedo, Francisco de Paula Ramos de (*b* São Paulo, 8 Dec 1851; *d* Guarujá, 13 June 1928). Brazilian architect. He studied at the Escola Militar in Rio de Janeiro (1869–72) and then trained as an engineer architect, graduating in 1878 from the University of Ghent, Belgium, under the patronage of the Visconde de Parnaíba, who subsequently provided him with his first commissions in Rio. His architectural education was based on the classicism of the Beaux-Arts tradition, and one of his designs represented his school at the Exposition Internationale (1878) in Paris. He began his career in Campinas, where his family had originated, in 1883 when he completed some unfinished work on the 18th-century parish church; this project became well known for his use of the *taipa de pilão* (Port.: 'pounded gravel wall') construction techniques of the earlier builders, a considerable engineering feat.

In 1886 Azevedo began to work in São Paulo and designed for the government two neo-Renaissance buildings, the Tesouraria da Fazenda Nacional (1891) and the Secretaria da Agricultura (1896); these were the first scholarly works in what was then a provincial city, but one expanding rapidly in size and wealth owing to its coffee-producing industry and large-scale immigration, mainly from Italy. These two factors stimulated a revival of eclecticism in architecture, and Azevedo's academically correct buildings received great acclaim and marked the beginning of a prosperous career; he subsequently became the leading architect and builder in Brazil, employing the best practitioners in his profession. He also established companies concerned with the production of building materials of all kinds, including a comprehensive import business, and after the closure of the Banco União he became president of a substantial property development company. A founder-member of the Escola Politécnica, São Paulo, at the turn of the century, he combined business activities with the role of professor of architecture there, becoming director from 1917 to 1928. He strongly encouraged the expansion of the Liceu de Artes e Ofícios, the craft and trade school at which joiners, ironworkers, sculptors, artists and other craftsmen connected with the building trade received a rigorous training.

Azevedo continued to design in the classical style, for example the Secretaria da Justiça, the new wing of the Palacio do Governo, the Escola Normal (1894) and several primary schools. Impressed by the ornate Second Empire architecture of Paris after its replanning in the 1860s, having seen the folios of buildings in Paris published by César-Denis Daly, he found the Paris Opéra (1861–75) the obvious model for the Municipal Theatre (1911), São Paulo, his most important work. It was based on a project devised by the Italian scenographer Claudio Rossi (*b* 1850), for which the Italian architect Domiziano Rossi (1865–1920) made the plans and drawings; Azevedo directed the building work and determined the final design. In 1907 Azevedo was joined by the Portuguese engineer Ricardo Severo (1869–1940), who through his lectures launched the neo-colonial style in Brazil, a nationalist style based on the Baroque ornament of 18th-century buildings. From 1915 the Escritório Técnico F. P. Ramos de Azevedo, by then a large organization of architects, draughtsmen, engineers and artists, was responsible for the diffusion of this new style, which became very popular in the 1920s, through the design of many houses, including one for Numa de Oliveira (1916–17), Avenida Paulista, São Paulo. Azevedo was an important architect in São Paulo at a time when it was said to be the fastest-growing city in the world. His office remained active until the 1960s.

BIBLIOGRAPHY

J. F. da Silveira: *Ramos de Azevedo e sua atividade* (São Paulo, 1941)
A. Salmoni and E. Debenedetti: *Arquitectura italiana em São Paulo* (São Paulo, 1981), pp. 75–95
C. A. C. Lemos: *Alvenaria burguesa* (São Paulo, 1985)
A. Fabris, ed.: *O ecletismo na arquitectura brasileira* (São Paulo, 1987), pp. 79–96
C. A. C. Lemos: *História da casa brasileira* (São Paulo, 1989), pp. 48–53

CARLOS A. C. LEMOS

Azhur, Zair [Azgar, Zair Isaakovich] (*b* Maŭŭany, Viciebsk [Vitebsk] region, 15 Jan 1908). Belarusian sculptor. He studied in Belarus' under Yury Pen and M. Kerzin during the early 1920s and then learnt from contemporaries such as Matvey Manizer as well as from the Hermitage collection in St Petersburg. In 1929, after visiting Ukraine and Georgia, he returned to Belarus' and was commissioned to decorate the art museum, the opera house and the government building in Minsk. These Socialist Realist projects were made of non-durable plaster and have not survived. During World War II he sculpted a series of Neo-classical monuments to heroes of the war. In 1948–51 he created a series of sculptures of women collective farmworkers, for example *Ye. P. Lesnichaya* (bronze, 1949; Minsk, Belarus' A. Mus.), that portray the idealized citizen of the USSR towering above her surroundings and reforming the world. Emulating Russian Neo-classical sculptors, he executed monuments to *Pyotr Bagration* and *Mikhail Barclay de Tolly* (bronze and granite, 1946–9; Borodino, Mus.-Reserve Mil. Hist.). He contributed to the creation of numerous expressionless monuments to *Lenin* in various regions of the USSR during the 1950s and 1960s. Among his later works is the multi-figured monument to *Yakub Kolas* in Minsk (1972) and the statue of *Yevgeny Vuchetin* (1981) in Moscow.

WRITINGS

To, chto pomnitsay . . . Rasskaz obo vremeni, ob iskusstve i o lyudyakh [What I remember . . . a story about time, art and people], 4 vols (Minsk, 1977–92)

BIBLIOGRAPHY
F. S. Roginskaya: *Zair Isaakovich Azgur* (Moscow, 1961)
B. A. Krepak, ed.: *Zair Isaakovich Azgur* (Moscow, 1989)

SERGEY KUZNETSOV

Azincourt, Barthélémy-Augustin Blondel d' [Dazaincourt] (*b* Paris, 6 June 1719; *d* Paris, 31 May 1794). French patron, collector, amateur engraver and soldier. He was the only son of the collector AUGUSTIN BLONDEL DE GAGNY and joined the army at 15, being awarded the Croix de St Louis in 1745. He retired from the army in 1753, having married a great heiress, Catherine Edmée de la Haye des Fosses; they divided their time between hôtels particuliers in the Rue de Vendôme and the Rue Nazareth, Paris, and an elegant château at Bonneuil. Azincourt was an honorary member of the Académie Royale in Paris and the academy of Marseille. In 1776 he helped to arrange the acquisition by the Maison du Roi of the Cabinet de l'Amour from the Hôtel Lambert, Paris. In *La Première Idée de la curiosité* (1749), he described the principles of collecting and offered advice on display. His eclectic collection ranged from Italian, Northern European and French works to curiosities of natural history. After 1760 it was distinguished by paintings and drawings by contemporary French artists, which included *Diana after the Bath* (1742; Paris, Louvre; *see* BOUCHER, FRANÇOIS, fig. 3). Azincourt owned over 500 drawings by Boucher and works by Jean-Baptiste Oudry, Jean-Honoré Fragonard, Jean-Baptiste Le Prince, Hubert Robert, François Lemoyne and Joseph Vernet; he acquired a number of works at the sale of his father's collection in 1776. He was a patron of the painter and engraver Jean-Pierre-Louis-Laurent Hoüel and was himself one of the pioneers of engraving in the crayon manner; he made a number of plates after some of his Boucher drawings.

Azincourt held two sales of his collections; the first (Paris, Pierre Remy, 18 April 1770) was of miniatures, drawings, prints, *objets d'art* and curiosities; the second (Paris, Alexandre-Joseph Paillet, 10–27 Feb 1783) was of paintings, drawings, prints, ceramics, sculpture and furniture. Following his death in Paris during the French Revolution, an inventory of his collection was made in 1794.

UNPUBLISHED SOURCES
Paris, Archvs N., Minutier Central, LV/146 [Inventaire après décès (1 Brumaire an III/22 Oct 1794)]

WRITINGS
B.-A. Blondel d'Azincourt: *La Première Idée de la curiosité* (Paris, 1749)

BIBLIOGRAPHY
C. Blanc: *Le Trésor de la curiosité* (Paris, 1857), i, pp. 172–4; ii, pp. 68–76
M. Roux: *Inventaire du fonds français: Graveurs du dix-huitième siècle*, Paris, Bib. N., Cab Est. cat., vi (Paris, 1949), pp. 1580–60
P. Jean-Richard: *L'Oeuvre gravé de François Boucher dans la collection Edmond de Rothschild* (Paris, 1978), pp. 104–5
C. B. Bailey: 'Conventions of the Eighteenth-century "cabinet de tableaux": Blondel d'Azincourt's "La Première Idée de la curiosité"', *A. Bull.*, lxix (1987), pp. 431–47

□

Azmi, Musa. *See* AYTAÇ, HAMID.

Aznavurtepe. *See under* PATNOS.

Aztatlán. Pre-Columbian culture of north-west Mexico. It belongs to the area between the Sinaloa River in the north and the Río Grande de Santiago in the south, probably extending as far south-east of this area as the Chapala Basin of Jalisco–Michoacán, and it flourished *c.* AD 880–*c.* 1400. Major sites are Culiacán, Chametla, Guasave (all in Sinaloa) and AMAPA (Nayarit). Aztatlán sites have been explored by Carl Sauer and Donald Brand (1932), Gordon Ekholm (1942), Clement W. Meighan (1976) and more recently by Joseph B. Mountjoy (1990), although in general the archaeology of this vast area is still little known.

By *c.* AD 500 the area was occupied by many complex sites with elaborate architecture and large populations. The Aztatlán archaeological complex is characterized by some of the most elaborate prehistoric pottery in the New World, including four-, five- and six-colour polychrome wares, engraved wares, negative painting and some moulded ceramics, as well as abundant metal artefacts, primarily copper, but also bronze, silver and gold (*see* MESOAMERICA, PRE-COLUMBIAN, §IX, 5). Metallurgy appeared on the west coast of Mexico by *c.* AD 800, and many techniques and processes seem to have been introduced directly from north-west South and Central America, probably by sea routes. Ornamental objects such as bells, tweezers, rings and other small items predominate over such functional artefacts as axes, adzes, needles and chisels. The decoration of Aztatlán pottery has numerous elements that are specifically Central Highland or Mexican, including motifs found in Aztec art or in the Mixteca–Puebla style. These similarities (i.e. codex-like designs, plumbate pottery and Mazapa mould-made figurines; *see* MESOAMERICA, PRE-COLUMBIAN, §VII, 2) are convincing evidence that Sinaloa, Nayarit and Jalisco, despite their distance from the heartland of Mesoamerica, were fully involved in the central Mexican civilization of the period immediately before the Spanish Conquest.

Other archaeological remains attributed to the Aztatlán complex include slab-like figurines, spindle whorls decorated with incised designs, ceramic pipes, cylindrical seals, prismatic obsidian blades, stone axes, *metates* (grinding stones) without supports, stone bowls, petroglyphs and stone 'idols', burials in ceramic urns and mounds constructed to support domestic or ceremonial buildings. In architecture civic–ceremonial centres became more complex, with groups of monumental pyramid-platforms arranged around plazas.

Aztatlán was the most widespread archaeological culture in West Mexico, as well as the most typically Mesoamerican development in this area in Pre-Columbian times, amid cultures that otherwise had closer links with areas of north-western South America until the Post-Classic period (*c.* AD 900–1521). During the Post-Classic period a wave of influences extended the cultures of the Central Highlands (*see* MESOAMERICA, PRE-COLUMBIAN, §II, 4(ii)) to Amapa and far to the north into Sinaloa. The changes that appear, beginning *c.* AD 900, are so extensive and striking that a military–religious invasion is probable, paralleling similar events taking place towards the Maya region in the south (*see* MESOAMERICA, PRE-COLUMBIAN, §II, 4(iv)). During the Post-Classic period Aztatlán sites were involved in a complex trade network linking all cultures and areas of Mesoamerica. One of the most precious resources was turquoise, traded from the south-west USA to central

Mexico and beyond, by way of Guasave and other Aztatlán sites.

BIBLIOGRAPHY

C. Sauer and D. Brand: *Aztatlán: Prehistoric Mexican Frontier on the Pacific Coast*, Ibero Americana, i (Berkeley, 1932)

G. Ekholm: 'Excavations at Guasave, Sinaloa, Mexico', *Anthropol. Pap. Amer. Mus. Nat. Hist.*, xxxviii/2 (1942) [whole issue]

B. Bell, ed.: *The Archaeology of West Mexico* (Ajijíc, 1974)

C. W. Meighan: *The Archaeology of Amapa, Nayarit* (Los Angeles, 1976)

M. Foster and P. Weigand, eds: *The Archaeology of West and Northwest Mesoamerica* (New York, 1985)

EDUARDO WILLIAMS

Aztec. Term applied to the culture of the Nahuatl-speaking peoples of late Pre-Columbian central Mexico that flourished *c.* AD 1400–1520.

1. INTRODUCTION. At the time of the Spanish arrival in 1519 most central Mexican city states were tributary to a powerful Triple Alliance headed by Tenochtitlán (*see* MEXICO CITY, §1) in confederation with Tetzcoco (*see* TETZCOTZINGO) and Tlacopan. Although each city state exhibited some distinctive features, a similar cultural pattern prevailed throughout the region in the century before the arrival of the Spaniards. Azteca was originally a gentilitial designation borne by the migrating ancestors of the people (also known as Mexica) who, early in the 14th century, established the twin cities of Tenochtitlán and TLATELOLCO in the Basin of Mexico. In the 19th century the term Aztec was popularized by Alexander von Humboldt and William Prescott as a useful generic label for the final period of Pre-Columbian central Mexican cultural history. Aztec is also the standard term for the concurrent stylistic and iconographic synthesis, with Tenochtitlán as its type site, that flourished throughout central Mexico and beyond following the Triple Alliance conquests. The Aztecs inherited many earlier Central Highland Mesoamerican traditions, including those of Olmec–TLATILCO, TEOTIHUACÁN, XOCHICALCO and TOLTEC, and blended them into a distinctive style that differed from these predecessors, as well as those elsewhere in Mesoamerica. They also absorbed significant influences from further afield, especially from the MIXTECA-PUEBLA heartland in southern Puebla, western Oaxaca and the Gulf Coast, and perhaps from western Mexico.

The major immediate predecessor of Aztec culture was Toltec, a somewhat eclectic tradition that flourished *c.* AD 900–1200 at Tollen (*see* TULA) in central Mexico, north of the Basin of Mexico. The period between the collapse of Tollan in the 13th century and the emergence of the Triple Alliance (1433–4) was marked by considerable political upheaval in central Mexico, sometimes known as the 'Chichimec Interregnum'. Barbaric peoples from the north and west, collectively referred to as Chichimeca, moved into the area, overrunning the old centres of power and establishing new states. Of these the Azteca/Mexica, the Acolhuaque and the Tepaneca eventually emerged as the allied masters of central Mexico, with their capitals at Tenochtitlán, Tetzcoco and Tlacopan.

The cultural course of the Chichimec Interregnum is poorly known. Its first phase, *c.* 1250–1350, seems to have been dominated by the city-state of Colhuacán in the southern Basin of Mexico, ruled by an epigonal Toltec dynasty. Between *c.* 1350 and 1428 Tepanec Azcapotzalco, in the western Basin, carved out a sizeable dominion until overthrown by a coalition that developed into the Triple Alliance. Many Toltec traditions certainly survived in some form, although there was probably a considerable decline from such impressive achievements as Toltec monumental sculpture. In later tradition the Toltecs were credited with outstanding artistic skills, such that 'Tolteca' was synonymous with master artisan. There is also evidence that the final phase of the sophisticated Mixteca–Puebla tradition influenced artistic movements within the Basin of Mexico.

The overall Aztec achievement must be ranked very high when compared to the art of various earlier civilizations that flourished and faded in Pre-Columbian Mesoamerica. In its final years the Aztec tradition constituted a well-integrated stylistic and iconographic synthesis that successfully met the artistic and religious needs of a dynamic, imperialistic society. Its distinctive style, related to, but distinguishable from, all other major Mesoamerican stylistic traditions was displayed in many forms, though most powerfully in monumental sculpture. (For further discussion *see* MESOAMERICA, PRE-COLUMBIAN.)

2. ARCHITECTURE. Aztec architecture is not usually highly regarded by Mesoamerican scholars, particularly when compared with the achievements of, for example, the Lowland MAYA. Nevertheless, the larger palaces of the principal rulers, complex multi-roomed structures arranged around patios and constructed mainly of plastered adobe, sometimes with stone foundations, must have been impressive (*see also* PALACE, §XV, 1). Although limited to certain traditional patterns, the religious architecture featured structures, particularly the staged pyramid-temple, that, when fully embellished with monumental stone sculpture and polychrome paintings, must have created a powerfully effective religious atmosphere appropriate to the theatrical Aztec ritual of blood sacrifice.

3. SCULPTURE. Much Aztec sculpture has survived. Evidence of the earlier developments in monumental sculpture that led to the mature Aztec synthesis has been provided by the Proyecto Templo Mayor, the excavation between 1978 and 1982 of the principal pyramid-temple of Tenochtitlán, dedicated to Tlaloc, the god of rain, and Huitzilopochtli, the Aztec patron god of war. Of the structures superimposed on the site, Stage II (?*c.* 1400) features a well-preserved painted *chacmool* (reclining figure) in front of the Tlaloc shrine, as well as relief carvings of two year-dates, one possibly the year 2 Tochtli (?1390), and a stone mask set into the top of the steps leading up to the Huitzilopochtli shrine. At the base of the Stage III (?*c.* 1430) stairway nine anthropomorphic stone images were found; these may have been brought down from the top platform and buried at the time of the Stage IV (?*c.* 1450) enlargement. Compared with Aztec sculptures that can be dated to *c.* 1500, these are cruder and more archaic in style. Accepting the tentative dating of Stage II

to the final years of the Tepanec empire, when Tenochtitlán was tributary to Azcapotzalco, and Stage III to shortly after the city gained its independence, this indicates the rapid development of a more sophisticated and complex sculptural style in official religious art, corresponding to Tenochtitlán's spectacular rise to power during the 15th century.

Aztec sculpture includes many large monuments, most of which come from Tenochtitlán. A generalized developmental sequence is evident, but opinions differ concerning the precise chronological placement of particular pieces. A few monuments bear year-dates, but their correlations with the Christian calendar are often ambiguous. The earliest might be the putative 2 Tochtli inscription from the Templo Mayor, but most appear to cluster between *c.* 1450 and *c.* 1519. A few bear the name signs of the Tenochtitlán rulers, but none is apparently earlier than Tizoc (*reg* 1481–6). It appears likely that the final sculptural style of the capital and most of the other main centres in the Basin of Mexico and adjoining territory had crystallized by the mid-15th century, coinciding with the long reign of the greatest ruler of Tenochtitlán, Motecuhzuma I (*reg* 1440–69).

It is three-dimensional stone sculpture that represents the outstanding Aztec artistic achievement. Most examples have been discovered accidentally, often in colonial building foundations, and many are exceptionally fine, especially those representing a wide range of animals. No earlier Mesoamerican tradition produced nearly as many three-dimensional carvings of zoomorphs (see fig. 1), which often show remarkable realism, especially rattlesnakes and jaguars. Plant forms, such as the organ cactus and squash, were also accurately replicated in stone. Three-dimensional anthropomorphic images are also typical of Aztec sculpture, again occurring much more frequently than in any earlier tradition. Most represent identifiable deities (see fig. 2).

No example has been discovered in its original location, as all those functioning as sacred images were destroyed or removed during the Spanish Conquest. It is known from ethnohistorical sources that they were typically located in temples or household shrines, and propitiatory rituals were performed before them. The most common type is the standing figure, feet firmly planted on a quadrangular pedestal, in a stiff frontal pose. Male figures were sometimes portrayed in a seated posture with knees drawn up, while females were sometimes depicted kneeling. The carved figures frequently bear ornaments, costume and distinguishing iconographic features, but many are virtually nude, unadorned male figures; appropriate ornaments and attire composed of perishable materials were originally added to these figures. Aztec anthropo-

1. Aztec zoomorphic *cuauhxicalli* (vessel for the heart of a human victim), stone, carved in the form of an eagle, h. 720 mm, from the Great Temple of Huitzilopochtli, Tenochtitlán, 15th century (Mexico City, Museo del Templo Mayor)

2. Colossal stone image of Coatlicue, an aspect of the earth/fertility goddess, mother of the Mexica patron deity, Huitzilopochtli, h. 2.56 m, 15th century (Mexico City, Museo Nacional de Antropología)

morphic images are generally more static and stylized, particularly in their facial features, than the more realistic zoomorphic sculptures, with heads characteristically exaggerated in size relative to bodies.

In style and iconography Aztec relief-carving is close to that of the painted ritual–divinatory and historical manuscripts (see §4 below). The major relief-decorated monuments of Tenochtitlán and related centres show a steady development towards increasing sophistication and iconographic complexity. Some of the later pieces, such as the Calendar Stone and the Teocalli de la Guerra Sagrada (both Mexico City, Mus. N. Antropol.) and the Stone of the Five Suns (Chicago, IL, A. Inst.), are particularly impressive.

Most Aztec stone sculptures, both reliefs and three-dimensional works, were painted in bright colours that had symbolic meanings. The disappearance of most of this colour has led to Aztec sculptures appearing rather drab and grey, a very different sight from that which must have greeted the conquistadors when they saw them *in situ* (*see also* MESOAMERICA, PRE-COLUMBIAN, §IV, 4(ii)(b)).

Aztec wood sculpture, both in relief and in the round, was also richly developed. Judging from the few pieces that have survived—including anthropomorphic deity figures, vertical and horizontal cylindrical drums, masks and *atlatls* (spear-throwers)—the style and iconography were identical to those of stone sculpture; and were also used in shellwork and in bone-carving.

4. PAINTING. Aztec wall paintings include those on the pilasters and inner walls of the Templo Mayor Stage II Tlaloc shrine. One appears to depict a high-ranking personage or deity, in a style and iconography somewhat simpler and less evolved than that prevailing at the time of the Conquest, as exemplified by manuscripts such as the Codex Borbonicus (Paris, Bib. Assemblé N., Y. 120). Aztec painting reached its highest achievements, however, in pictorial manuscripts on paper, skin and cloth. The most sophisticated examples occur in the ritual or divinatory screenfolds, especially the *tonalamatl* ('books of day signs'), that served as manuals for diviners. The only surviving example in pure Aztec style and format is the *tonalamatl* of the Codex Borbonicus, perhaps produced not far south of Tenochtitlán. Its skilful layout, draughtsmanship and application of colour compares favourably with the larger surviving body of ritual–divinatory screenfolds from the Mixteca–Puebla heartland to the south-east. From this perspective, Aztec pictographic writing may be considered a major substyle of a broader Mixteca–Puebla style. The historical pictorials, judging from a few surviving early colonial examples, generally employed a less complex style and iconography, as did the tribute lists and maps. (*See also* MESOAMERICA, PRE-COLUMBIAN, §VI.)

5. POTTERY. Aztec pottery was more varied than is often recognized and frequently of high quality. The commonest type of late Aztec pottery was a mass-produced black-on-orange ware, mostly with abstract and symbolic decorative motifs, and frequently combined with sets of parallel black lines. From the early 16th century, and continuing into the colonial period, various naturalistic motifs, both floral and zoological, were often featured. Other ceramic types were also produced and used in central Mexico, alongside many imported wares from all over the empire of the Triple Alliance. The most striking were various painted wares that can be assigned to the Mixteca–Puebla tradition, particularly those featuring complex iconographic motifs almost identical to those of the ritual–divinatory manuscripts. Although not usually considered Aztec in the narrower sense, this elaborate painted pottery, of which the best known is called Cholulteca, circulated widely throughout the empire.

Large ceramic anthropomorphic sculptures, comparing favourably with those of the Gulf Coast region, were also significant in Aztec pottery. They are perhaps best exemplified by the two life-sized eagle warriors discovered at Tenochtitlan during the Templo Mayor project. Small ceramic images of various deities are common, particularly fertility goddesses, which probably served as votive offerings or household gods. These were mass-produced in moulds and are not normally distinguished, but some of the more carefully designed and crafted examples may be compared favourably to the stone images of the same deities.

6. OTHER ARTS.

(i) Featherwork. The Spaniards were particularly impressed with the beauty of Aztec featherwork, which employed the brilliantly coloured plumage of tropical birds, and the art persisted well into the colonial period. A few Pre-Columbian examples survive, notably a large quetzal feather headdress and a shield with a gold-trimmed coyote motif (Vienna, Mus. Vlkerknd.; see MESOAMERICA, PRE-COLUMBIAN, fig. 37) and two shields with stepped fret motifs (Stuttgart, Württemberg. Landesmus.). These superb specimens are the tiny remnant of a genre that embraced a wide range of productions, especially élite military costumes and accoutrements (*see also* MESOAMERICA, PRE-COLUMBIAN, §IX, 3).

(ii) Lapidary arts. Aztec lapidaries skilfully crafted a wide array of jewellery for the élite, employing various hard, lustrous stones, including jade, turquoise, obsidian, rock crystal, serpentine, amethyst, opal and agate, as well as jet and amber. Nearly all of the personal adornments produced by the metalsmiths were also made in stone. Some ornaments, especially pectorals, were finely carved with religious images and symbolic motifs.

(iii) Mosaic. Hardstone mosaic, using tesserae of turquoise, other coloured stones, shell, coral and gold, was also outstanding. Objects decorated with this technique included masks, anthropomorphic and zoomorphic images, shields, *atlatls*, sceptres, pectorals, nose and ear ornaments, armlets, bracelets and anklets. Fewer than 30 major specimens survive, mostly in Europe, where they were taken after the Spanish Conquest. Judging from their stylistic and iconographic features, some of these probably originated in the Gulf Coast region and in Oaxaca, though it is likely that at least some of the others were produced in central Mexico, where the art also thrived. (*See also* MESOAMERICA, PRE-COLUMBIAN, §IX, 4, 6 and 9.)

(iv) Ornamental metalwork. Ornamental metalwork was highly developed, with the use of gold, copper and, to a lesser extent, silver. In addition to human and animal effigies, masks and bells, characteristic products included jewels for a variety of items for personal adornment, such as pectorals and ear- and nose-plugs, labrets, necklaces, armlets, bracelets, anklets and finger rings. Several techniques were employed, the two most important being the lost-wax method of casting and sheet hammering. The former capital of the Tepanec empire, Azcapotzalco, was a major metalworking centre before the Spanish Conquest. Unfortunately, few central Mexican specimens of the goldsmith's art escaped the melting pot. (*See also* MESOAMERICA, PRE-COLUMBIAN, §IX, 3.)

BIBLIOGRAPHY

G. Kubler: 'The Cycle of Life and Death in Metropolitan Aztec Sculpture', *Gaz. B.-A.*, xxiii (1943), pp. 257–68

F. Anders: 'Las artes menores/Minor Arts', *A. México*, cxxxvii (1970), pp. 4–69

H. B. Nicholson: 'Major Sculpture in Pre-Hispanic Central Mexico', *Hb. Mid. Amer. Ind.*, x (1971), pp. 92–134

——: 'The Late Pre-Hispanic Central Mexican (Aztec) Iconographic System', *The Iconography of Middle American Sculpture* (New York, 1973), pp. 72–97

F. R. Solís Olguín: 'The Formal Pattern of Anthropomorphic Sculpture and the Ideology of the Aztec State', *The Art and Iconography of Late Post-classic Central Mexico: Dumbarton Oaks, 1977*, pp. 73–110

C. Aguilera: *El arte oficial Tenochca: Su significación social* (Mexico City, 1978)

D. Robertson: *Mexican Manuscript Painting of the Early Colonial Period: The Metropolitan Schools* (New Haven, 1979)

R. F. Townsend: *State and Cosmos in the Art of Tenochtitlán*, Studies in Pre-Columbian Art and Archaeology, xx (Washington, DC, 1979)

N. Gutiérrez Solana Rickards: *Objetos ceremoniales en piedra de la cultura Mexica* (Mexico City, 1983)

H. B. Nicholson and E. Quiñones Keber: *Art of Aztec Mexico: Treasures of Tenochtitlán* (Washington, DC, 1983)

E. Pasztory: *Aztec Art* (New York, 1983)

Glanz und Untergang des alten Mexiko: Die Azteken und ihre Vorläufer, 2 vols (exh. cat., Hildesheim, Roemer-Mus., 1986)

E. Boone, ed.: *The Aztec Templo Mayor* (Washington, DC, 1987)

E. M. Moctezuma: *The Great Temple of the Aztecs: Treasures of Tenochtitlán* (London, 1988)

F. R. S. Olís Olguín: *Gloria y fama Mexica/Fame and Glory of the Mexica* (Mexico City, 1991) [bilingual text]

Circa 1492: Art in the Age of Exploration (exh cat., ed. J. A. Levenson, Washington, DC, N.G.A., 1991)

R. F. Townsend: *The Aztecs* (London, 1992)

The Ancient Americas (exh. cat., ed. R. Townsend; Chicago, IL, Art Inst.) (Munich, 1992)

The Art of Ancient Mexico (exh. cat., ed. M. Ryan; London, Hayward Gal., 1992)

H. B. NICHOLSON

Azuchi Castle. Japanese castle in Azuchi-chō, Shiga Prefecture. It was the prototype of the sumptuous residential castles of the Momoyama period (1568–1600) of Japanese history (often called the Azuchi–Momoyama period, taking its name from the castle). This palatial citadel was built as the visible sign of the new order imposed on Japan by ODA NOBUNAGA, chief unifier of the country after a century of military conflict and political disorder. Begun in February 1576 and inaugurated as Nobunaga's official residence on 5 June 1579, Azuchi Castle was burnt down by marauding soldiery on 4 July 1582, 13 days after Nobunaga was assassinated in Kyoto. Apart from the tiles, fragments of ceramic vessels and metal fittings uncovered in the course of archaeological surveys, stoneworks are all that remain.

The citadel was composed of the lord's main castle, which was divided into three enceintes, and a number of separately enclosed outbuildings, the residences of Nobunaga's principal vassals. Its grounds occupied *c.* 15 ha on a hill that rose 105 m above the level of Lake Biwa, which in the 16th century bordered the site on three sides. At the castle's centre, and forming the symbolic focal point of the realm (*tenka*) of strict allegiances ruled by Nobunaga, stood a seven-storey donjon (*tenshukaku*), an early example of the great tower that became one of the chief features of Japanese castle architecture (*see* JAPAN, §III, 4(ii)(c)). The donjon, said to have been some 32.5 m tall, was the work of the master builder Okabe Mataemon (*d* 1582) and 'the best craftsmen to be found in all of Japan … for Nobunaga utterly discountenanced any imperfection', as the Jesuit eye-witness P. Giovanni Francesco Stephanoni noted. The gilded surfaces of its top storey and the lavish use of gilt on its roof tiles were singled out for mention in the accounts of Jesuit missionaries, which agree on the dazzling effect produced by the tower's exterior. Beyond that the architectural details are obscure, as contemporary descriptions are fragmentary, contradictory and fanciful.

In 1976 the architectural historian Akira Naitō published an elaborate reconstruction, on the basis of what is ostensibly an 18th-century copy of the original builder's plans. This work contained some ingenious but improbable notions, such as that of a vast unceilinged space at the centre of the edifice. The builder's plans to which he referred were probably a theoretical exercise based on an inspection of the site and some of the same written sources that were available to Naitō. The most reliable written source is *Azuchi nikki* ('An Azuchi diary') by Ōta Gyūichi (1527–after 1610), a noted chronicler of Oda Nobunaga's deeds. This account includes a storey-by-storey description of the donjon's general layout, specifying the subject-matter of the wall paintings (*shōhekiga*) in many of its chambers. The interior's pictorial decoration, which Nobunaga entrusted to Kanō Eitoku (*see* KANŌ, (5)) and his atelier, can therefore be reconstructed fairly accurately. Eitoku deployed an impressive repertory of talents in this sumptuous decorative scheme, which represented culture as an adornment to the sublime authority to which Nobunaga aspired.

Nobunaga's residential suite, on the donjon's second storey, was apparently decorated with paintings, probably monochrome, on various bird-and-flower themes, the topic of Chinese scholars (*see* CHINA, §V, 3(v)), and a standard landscape subject, *Evening Bell from a Distant Temple*. The reception rooms on the floor above were resplendent with paintings done in strong colours on gold ground (*kinpeki*), the style that made Eitoku famous; in addition to birds and flowers and *Horses in Pasture*, the themes in the several chambers on this floor included Daoist immortals and the civet cat, an exotic creature to Japanese eyes. On the fourth storey some rooms were decorated with aggressive subjects that evoked the image of imperative power, including *Combat between Dragon and Tiger*, while other chambers also featured metaphors for virtuous rule (e.g. *Phoenix in Paulownia Tree*) and nourishing largesse (e.g. *Young Falcons in their Bamboo Coop*). There were no wall paintings in the two rooms for the tea ceremony that occupied the fifth level. The sixth storey was an octagonal Buddhist chapel with paintings of the *Ten Great Disciples of Buddha* and *Buddha Establishing the Way and Preaching the Law*. In the square room on the donjon's seventh storey, which *Azuchi nikki* described as 'all gold' on the inside, Eitoku evidently painted the 'Three Emperors and the Five Sovereigns, the Four Wise Men of Mt Shang and the Seven Sages of the Bamboo Grove', thus creating at the apex of the tower a representation of the Mandate of Heaven, a concept derived from the loftiest Chinese classical sources.

BIBLIOGRAPHY

A. Naitō: 'Azuchijō no kenkyū' [A study of Azuchi Castle], *Kokka*, 987 and 988 (1976)

S. Miyakami: 'Azuchijō tenshu no fukugen to sono shiryō ni tsuite: Naitō Akira-shi "Azuchijō no kenkyū" ni taisuru gimon' [On the reconstruction of the donjon of Azuchi Castle and its sources: doubts about 'A study of Azuchi Castle' by Mr Akira Naitō], *Kokka*, 998 and 999 (1977) [998 includes the text of *Azuchi nikki*]

C. Wheelwright: 'A Visualization of Eitoku's Lost Paintings at Azuchi Castle', *Warlords, Artists and Commoners: Japan in the Sixteenth Century*, ed. G. Elison and B. L. Smith (Honolulu, 1981), pp. 87–111

H. Akita: *Oda Nobunaga to Azuchijō* [Oda Nobunaga and Azuchi Castle] (Osaka, 1990)

JURGIS ELISONAS

Azuchi–Momoyama period. *See under* MOMOYAMA PERIOD.

Azuma, Takamitsu (*b* Osaka, 20 Sept 1933). Japanese architect and writer. After graduating in 1957 from the School of Architecture, Osaka University, he worked for three years as a designer for the Ministry of Postal Services in Tokyo and Osaka and then joined Junzō Sakakura Architect & Associates (1960–67). He established his own office in Tokyo in 1967. Azuma's architecture is characterized by the expression of opposing elements such as individuality and collectivity, enclosure and openness, inside and outside etc. For example, his own house, Tower House (1967), Tokyo, expresses the idea of defensive living in the modern urban setting. Standing on a tiny plot of land in the heart of the city, it has a closed concrete exterior with no windows on the street elevation; this, however, is extended outwards to the city by a slanting parapet and overhanging roof-terrace acting as transitional elements between inside and out. Inside is an ingenious sequence of spaces expressing individuality in an area of traditionally designed houses. A prolific architect, Azuma produced designs with simple and clear-cut images: for instance, in the Seijin Nursery School (1974), Kyoto, he created an open central space hidden behind walls blank except for geometric cut-outs to the street. In the 1980s he developed the theory of 'polyphony' in architecture, the layering of different qualities of space and the juxtaposition of different materials and details. By allowing contradictory elements to co-exist he believed that the user could have maximum freedom to determine his own environment. An example of this work is the Biblical Church (1982), Tokyo, where Azuma has layered three elements in the façade, including a steel-frame screen, producing different effects from different viewpoints. Azuma was one of the five architects who formed the avant-garde group ARCHITEXT in 1971, but they worked independently, with no common design philosophy. He taught in several universities and was appointed Professor in the Department of Environmental Engineering at Osaka University in 1986.

WRITINGS

'Cognizance and Method', *Japan Architect*, 232 (1976), pp. 41–8

'Slit—Heterogeneous Forms, Spaces, and Actions Side by Side', *Japan Architect*, 294 (1981), pp. 36–42

'Polyphony in Architecture', *Japan Architect*, 310 (1983), pp. 38–47

BIBLIOGRAPHY

Azuma Takamitsu, Nihon gendai kenchikuka shirīzu [Modern Japanese architects series], iv (Tokyo, 1982)

U. Kultermann: 'Coincidentia Oppositorum', *Japan Architect*, 310 (1983), pp. 48–50

TOSHIAKI NAGAYA

Azzolini [Azzolino]**, Decio** (*b* Fermo, 11 April 1623; *d* Rome, 8 June 1689). Italian cardinal, diplomat and patron. A member of a noble family from the Marches, he was made Cardinal Deacon of S Adriano by Pope Innocent X on 2 March 1654 and was entrusted with diplomatic missions by Pope Alexander VII. Azzolini was an intermediary between the papacy and Queen Christina of Sweden (*see* VASA, (5)) when she settled in Rome in 1655, having converted to Catholicism and abdicated. They shared an interest in literature and art and both admired Bernini, in particular, among several artists they employed. Christina delegated to him the management of her court and business affairs. In her will, dated 1673 and confirmed early in 1689 (she died 19 April 1689), she named Azzolini as her sole heir. He thus inherited one of the finest private collections of Baroque art, but he survived her by only two months. His heir was his nephew, Pompeo Azzolino, who in turn sold a large part of his important inheritance to Prince Livio Odescalchi in 1692. Cardinal Azzolini was buried in S Maria in Vallicella, Rome. There is a portrait bust of him from the school of Bernini in the Nationalmuseum at Stockholm.

BIBLIOGRAPHY

DBI

J. Bignami Odier and G. Morelli, eds: *Istoria degli intrighi galanti della regina Cristina di Svezia e della sua corte durante il di lei soggiorno a Roma* (Rome, 1979)

URSULA VERENA FISCHER PACE

Azzolino, Giovanni [Giovan] **Bernardino** (*b* Cefalù, Sicily, *c.* 1572; *d* Naples, 12 Dec 1645). Sicilian painter and sculptor. He was probably trained in Sicily, yet he is recorded in Naples from 1594, and his artistic roots are Neapolitan. The painting of the *Presentation in the Temple* (1599; Naples, S Maria la Nova) is his earliest datable work. It demonstrates that Azzolino was already aware of trends in late 16th-century Neapolitan painting and that he knew the art of Belisario Corenzio, Fabrizio Santafede and Luigi Rodriguez (*fl* 1594–1606). He took his lead at first from Corenzio and was, like him, an expert fresco painter. In 1599 Azzolino was commissioned to execute the decoration (untraced) for the church of the Spirito Santo, Naples. In the canvases and frescoes that he painted between 1606 and 1610 for the church of Gesù e Maria, Naples, and in the earlier *Pentecost* for the church of S Francesco at Caiazzo (*in situ*; his only signed work) it is possible to discern the influences of both Corenzio and Santafede. An awareness of the new clarity and naturalism of the Florentine reformers Lodovico Cigoli, Agostino Ciampelli and Domenico Passignano had spread in Naples through Santafede, whose role in the development of Azzolino's style was fundamental. Both artists subsequently remained faithful to the devotional art of the Counter-Reformation, although they later demonstrated an awareness of the innovative work of Caravaggio. Azzolino countered both the excessive intellectual subtleties of Mannerism and the experimental naturalism of Caravaggio with serene and familiar renderings of sacred stories such as the *Circumcision* (1607; Naples, Capodimonte); these works, like the art of the Florentine reformers, retain a classical sense of design.

Despite his lack of understanding of Caravaggio's revolutionary ideas, Azzolino nevertheless had close contact with his circle in Naples: the Genoese prince Marcantonio Doria, a patron of Caravaggio, was his friend, and he worked alongside Neapolitan Caravaggesque painters such as Giovanni Battista Caracciolo and Jusepe de Ribera, who married his daughter. Some of his paintings rework aspects of works by Caravaggio. The *Virgin of the Rosary* (1609; Naples, Gesù e Maria) is indebted to Caravaggio's painting of that title (1607; Vienna, Ksthist. Mus.), using the same pyramidal composition and imitating certain passages, while freely translating others. Azzolino's *Martyrdom of St Apollonia* (*c.* 1610; Genoa, S Giuseppe) similarly refers to Caravaggio's *Flagellation* (1607; Naples, Capodimonte), placing the saint, rather than Christ, in a central position between the executioners. Yet the picture has none of Caravaggio's powerful naturalism and remains a devotional image, exalting and glorifying the saint, the ray of light falling on the girl being of no more than supernatural significance and creating none of Caravaggio's optical effects.

It is possible that Azzolino went to Genoa in 1610, in the service of Marcantonio Doria, to execute portraits of the Doria family and to make some wax sculptures. The *Martyrdom of St Ursula* (priv. col.) is a little later than Caravaggio's painting for Doria of the same theme (1610; Naples, Banca Commerc. It.), and Azzolino, using Caravaggio's iconography, again reinterpreted his work. He did not depict the violence of Ursula's murder, as did Caravaggio, but rather the moment after death. Light again has a symbolic significance, but here, although it does not derive from a specific source, it does follow Caravaggio's practice in creating rounded volumes and areas of light and shade.

Azzolino's output is documented until the end of his life; examples of his later work include the *Virgin of the Rosary with Saints* (1612–14; Naples, S Maria della Sanità), the *Miracle of St Bernardino* (Naples, Eremo dei Camaldoli), which presents the miracle simply and directly, *St Carlo Borromeo* (1620; Naples, S Carlo Borromeo) and *St Paulinus Freeing the Slave* (1630; Naples, Pio Monte della Misericordia), a clear narrative, which sets the two main figures against a crowded background and conveys meaning through expression and gesture.

BIBLIOGRAPHY

F. Ferrante: 'Aggiunte all'Azzolino', *Prospettiva* [Florence], xvii (1979), pp. 16–30

——: 'Giovan Bernardino Azzolino tra tardomanierismo e protocaravaggismo', *Scritti in onore di Raffaello Causa* (Naples, 1989)

FLAVIA FERRANTE

Illustration Acknowledgements

We are grateful to those listed below for permission to reproduce copyright illustrative material and to those contributors who supplied photographs or helped us to obtain them. The word 'Photo:' precedes the names of large commercial or archival sources who have provided us with photographs, as well as the names of individual photographers (where known). It has generally not been used before the names of owners of works of art, such as museums and civic bodies. Every effort has been made to contact copyright holders and to credit them appropriately; we apologize to anyone who may have been omitted from the acknowledgements or cited incorrectly. Any error brought to our attention will be corrected in subsequent editions. Where illustrations have been taken from books, publication details are provided in the acknowledgements below.

Line drawings, maps, plans, chronological tables and family trees commissioned by the *Dictionary of Art* are not included in the list below. All of the maps in the dictionary were produced by Oxford Illustrators Ltd, who were also responsible for some of the line drawings. Most of the line drawings and plans, however, were drawn by the following artists: Diane Fortenberry, Lorraine Hodghton, Chris Miners, Amanda Patton, Mike Pringle, Jo Richards, Miranda Schofield, John Tiernan, John Wilson and Philip Winton. The chronological tables and family trees were prepared initially by Kate Boatfield and finalized by John Johnson.

Ancona Photo: Archivi Alinari, Florence
Andachtsbild Hermitage Museum, St Petersburg/Photo: AKG Ltd, London
Andō, Tadao Architectural Association, London/Photo: Bruno Murawiec
Andō Hiroshige Board of Trustees of the Victoria and Albert Museum, London
André, Carl Photo: © Carl André/DACS, London/VAGA, New York, 1996
Andrea da Firenze (i) Photo: Archivi Alinari, Florence
Anet Trustees of the British Museum, London
Angelico, Fra *1* Kimbell Art Museum, Fort Worth, TX; *2, 5–6* Photo: Archivi Alinari, Florence; *3* Photo: Archivi Alinari, Florence; *4* Photo: Scala, Florence
Angermair, Christoph *1* Trustees of the British Museum, London; *2* Bayerisches Nationalmuseum, Munich
Angers *1, 3* Photo: Anthony Kersting, London; *2* Photo: James Austin, Cambridge; *4* Photo: Arch. Phot. Paris/© DACS, 1996
Angkor *2* Photo: Guy Nafilyan; *3* Photo: Henri Stierlin, Geneva; *4* Photo: Madeleine Giteau
Anglo-Saxon art *2* Photo: B.T. Batsford Ltd, London; *3* Photo: Anthony Kersting, London; *4–6* Photo: Conway Library, Courtauld Institute of Art, London; *7* Dean and Chapter of Winchester Cathedral/© Winchester Excavations Committee; *8* © Martin Biddle/Photo: Richard C. Anderson; *9* British Library, London (Add. MS. 49598, fol. 90*v*); *10* British Library, London (Harley MS. 603, fol. 25); *11* Bibliothèque Municipale, Rouen; *12–13* Trustees of the British Museum, London; *14* Board of Trustees of the National Museums and Galleries on Merseyside; *15* Dean and Chapter of Durham Cathedral
Angola *1* Diamang Archives; *2* Glasgow Museums (Art Gallery and Museum, Kelvingrove)
Anguier: (1) François Anguier Photo: Arch. Phot. Paris/© DACS, 1996
Anguissola: (1) Sofonisba Anguissola By kind permission of the Earl Spencer/Photo: Courtauld Institute of Art, London
Anhui school Photo: © Collection of C.C. Wang, New York
Ani Conway Library, Courtauld Institute of Art, London/Photo: Judith Herrin
Animalier sculpture Board of Trustees of the Victoria and Albert Museum, London
Animal style *1–2* Hermitage Museum, St Petersburg
Animal subjects *1* Trustees of the British Museum, London; *2* Hermitage Museum, St Petersburg; *3* Museum of Fine Arts, Boston, MA (S.A. Denio Collection)
Anjou, §II: (1) Louis I Photo: © RMN, Paris
Anjou, §II: (4) René I Bildarchiv, Österreichische Nationalbibliothek, Vienna
Annaberg Photo: Klaus G. Beyer
Annapolis Maryland Historical Society, Baltimore, MD
Ansaldo, Andrea Board of Trustees of the Victoria and Albert Museum, London
Anselmi, Michelangelo Soprintendenza per i Beni Artistici e Storici di Modena e Reggio Emilia
Antefix Photo: Nancy Winter
Antelami, Benedetto Photo: Studio Fotografico Tosi, Parma
Anthemion Museum of Fine Arts, Boston, MA (Catharine Page Perkins Collection)
Anthonisz., Cornelis Rijksmuseum, Amsterdam
Antico *1* Photo: Ursula Edelmann; *2* Kunsthistorisches Museum, Vienna
Antigna, Alexandre Musée des Beaux-Arts, Orléans
Antigua (i) Consejo Nacional para la Protección de la Antigua Guatemala, Guatemala City/Photo: Julio Taracena
Antilles, Lesser *1* Trustees of the British Museum, London; *2* Photo: Larsen Collinge International, Bath; *3* Photo: Robert Harding Picture Library, London; *4* Photo: Yellow Poui Art Gallery, St Georges, Grenada; *5* Photo: Alissandra Cummins
Antioch (i) *1* Vatican Museums, Vatican City, Rome; *2* Art Museum, Princeton University, Princeton, NJ (Gift of the Committee for the Excavation of Antioch); *3* Hatay Museum, Antakya
Antique, the *1* Bibliothèque Nationale de France, Paris; *2* British Library, London (no. 679K5, pl. III); *3* Photo: Archivi Alinari, Florence; *4* Trustees of the British Museum, London
Antoine, Jacques-Denis Photo: James Austin, Cambridge
Antonelli, Alessandro Photo: Archivi Alinari, Florence
Antonello da Messina *1, 4* Trustees of the National Gallery, London; *2* Kunsthistorisches Museum, Vienna; *3* Photo: © RMN, Paris
Antonio Veneziano Photo: Archivi Alinari, Florence
Antunes, João Photo: Arquivo Nacional de Fotografia, Lisbon
Antwerp *1* Stedelijk Prentenkabinet, Antwerp; *2* Photo: Anthony Kersting, London; *3* Rubenshuis, Antwerp; *4* Museo del Prado, Madrid; *5* College van Burgemeester en Schepenen, Antwerp; *6* Bayerische Verwaltung der Staatlichen Schlösser, Gärten und Seen, Munich; *7* Royal Collections, Stockholm; *8–9* Photo: © ACL Brussels
Antwerp Mannerism Staatliche Museen zu Berlin, Preussischer Kulturbesitz
Anyang Photo: Robert W. Bagley
Aoki Mokubei Tokyo National Museum, Tokyo
Aphrodisias *2* Photo: Prof. Kenan Erim
Apocalypse *1* Stadtbibliothek, Trier; *2* Bodleian Library, Oxford (MS. Douce 180, fols 33 and 51); *3* National Gallery of Art, Washington, DC
Apollonio di Giovanni Art Institute of Chicago, IL/© 1996
Appel, Karel Stedelijk Museum, Amsterdam/© DACS, 1996
Appiani, Andrea Museo d'Arte Antica, Castello Sforzesco, Milan

Aqar Quf © Department of Antiquities and Heritage, Baghdad
Aquamanile Metropolitan Museum of Art, New York (Robert Lehman Collection, 1975; no. 1975.1.1416)
Aquatint *1–2* Syndics of the Fitzwilliam Museum, Cambridge
Aquileia Photo: Brisighelli, Udine
Arabesque Photo: Dr Christian Ewert
Arabia, Pre-Islamic *2* Department of Antiquities and Museums, Riyadh/Photo: Julian Bowsher; *4, 14* Department of Antiquities and Museums, Riyadh; *5* British Library, London (no. PP.1925.dff); *6, 10–11, 13* Photo: D.T. Potts; *7* Discovered, 1952, American Foundation for the Study of Man, Wendell Phillips, Leader/Property of Yemen National Museum, San'a; *8* Yemen National Museum, San'a; *15* French Mission in Kuwait, Kuwait City; *16* Prof. Dr Abdul Rahman Al Ansary, King Saud University, Riyadh
Aragon: (6) Isabella Photo: Ampliaciones y Reproducciones MAS, Barcelona
Arakan *2* British Library, London (no. 7701.c.1[2])
Aranjuez Palace Photo: Paisajes Españoles, Madrid
Arausio Photo: Anthony Kersting, London
Arcangelo di Cola da Camerino Frick Art Museum (Frick Art and Historical Center), Pittsburgh, PA
Archaeology *1, 3* Photo: RCHME/© Crown Copyright; *4* © Sutton Hoo Research Trust/Photo: Nigel Macbeth
Archer, Thomas Photo: RCHME/© Crown Copyright
Archigram Photo: Ron Herron/Archigram Archive
Archipenko, Alexander Solomon R. Guggenheim Museum, New York (no. FN 56.1445)/Photo: Robert E. Mates
Architect *1* Bildarchiv, Österreichische Nationalbibliothek, Vienna; *2* Devonshire Collection, Chatsworth, Derbys. By permission of the Duke of Devonshire and the Chatsworth Settlement Trustees/Photo: Courtauld Institute of Art, London; *3* Photo: AKG Ltd, London
Architectural conservation and restoration *1* British Architectural Library, RIBA, London; *2* Photo: H.A. Meek; *3* Photo: Anthony Kersting, London; *4* Photo: Richard Bryant/Arcaid
Architectural drawing *1* Musées de la Ville de Strasbourg; *2* Rheinische Bildarchiv, Cologne; *3* Gemäldegalerie der Akademie der Bildenden Künste, Vienna; *4* Biblioteca Medicea Laurenziana, Florence; *5* Photo: Archivio Fotografico Vasari, Rome; *6* Photo: British Architectural Library, RIBA, London; *7* Trustees of Sir John Soane's Museum, London; *8* Ecole Nationale Supérieure des Beaux-Arts, Paris; *9* Mies van der Rohe Archive, Museum of Modern Art, New York (Gift of the architect)
Architectural model Trustees of Sir John Soane's Museum, London
Architectural pictures *1* Sacro Convento di San Francesco, Assisi/Photo: Scala, Florence/Photo: P. Gerhard Ruf; *2* Royal Collection, Windsor Castle/© Her Majesty Queen Elizabeth II; *3* Trustees of the National Gallery, London; *4* Photo: Archivi Alinari, Florence
Architectural proportion *5* British Library, London (no. 2261.f.14); *6* British Library, London; *7* British Library, London (no. 60.g.10); *8* Fondation Le Corbusier, Paris/© DACS, 1996
Arcimboldo, Giuseppe *1* National Gallery, Prague; *2* Archive, Skokloster Slott, Bålsta
Ardagh Treasure National Museum of Ireland, Dublin
Arequipa Photo: Robert Harding Picture Library, London
Arezzo Photo: Tim Benton, Cambridge
Argentina *2–3* South American Pictures, Woodbridge, Suffolk/Photo: Tony Morrison; *4* Bibliográfica Omeba, Buenos Aires; *5* Museo Nacional de Bellas Artes, Buenos Aires; *6* Arts Council Collection, London/© Gyula Kosice, Buenos Aires; *7* Museo de Motivos Populares Argentinos, Buenos Aires
Argunov, Ivan Photo: NOVOSTI Photo Library, London
Arles Fototeca Unione, American Academy in Rome
Arman Musée National d'Art Moderne, Paris/© ADAGP, Paris, and DACS, London, 1996
Armant British Library, London (no. 1899.k.1)
Armenia *2–3* Photo: Prof. A. Zarian; *4* Photo: Centro Studie Documentazione della Cultura Armenia, Milan; *5* Matenadaran Institute of Ancient Armenian Manuscripts, Erevan; *6* State Picture Gallery of Armenia, Erevan; *7* Photo: CEDACO/N. Thierry, Etampes; *8–9* Photo: Lucy Der Manuelian; *10* Photo: Dickram Kouymjian
Arms and armour *1* Münsterschatzmuseum, Essen; *2* Bayerische Verwaltung der Staatlichen Schlösser, Gärten und Seen, Munich; *3, 15* Kunsthistorisches Museum, Vienna; *4–5* Board of Trustees of the Victoria and Albert Museum, London; *6* Metropolitan Museum of Art, New York (Gift of William H. Riggs, 1913; no. 14.25.1425); *7* Hermitage Museum, St Petersburg; *8* Livrustkammaren, Stockholm; *9* Photo: James D. Lavin; *10* Board of Trustees of the Royal Armouries; *11* Metropolitan Museum of Art, New York (Gift of Stephen V. Grancsay, 1942; no. 42.50.2); *12* Kunsthistorisches Museum, Vienna; *13* Metropolitan Museum of Art, New York (Gift of William H. Riggs and Rogers Fund, 1919; no. 19.131.1-2); *14* Metropolitan Museum of Art, New York (Gift of J. Pierpont Morgan, 1917; no. 17.190.1720)
Arnolfo di Cambio *1–4* Photo: Archivi Alinari, Florence
Arp, Hans *1–2* Photo: © ADAGP, Paris, and DACS, London, 1996
Arpino, Cavaliere d' Archivio Fotografico dei Musei Capitolini, Rome
Arras Photo: Arch. Phot. Paris/© DACS, 1996
Arruda: (1) Diogo de Arruda Photo: Conway Library, Courtauld Institute of Art, London
Arslantepe Missione Archeologica Italiana nell'Anatolia Orientale, Rome/Photo: Roberto Ceccacci
Artaud, Antonin Musée National d'Art Moderne, Paris
Art brut Collection de l'Art Brut, Lausanne
Art Deco *1–2* Musée des Arts Décoratifs, Paris/Photo: Laurent Sully Jaulmes, Paris
Arte Povera Staatsgalerie, Stuttgart/© DACS, 1996
Artesonado Photo: Ampliaciones y Reproducciones MAS, Barcelona
Artificial stone Photo: National Trust Photo Library, London
Artigas, João B. Vilanova Photo: Julio Roberto Katinsky
Art informel Solomon R. Guggenheim Foundation, New York (Gift of Thomas and Remi Messer, 1974; no. FN 74.2082)/© ADAGP, Paris, and DACS, London, 1996/Photo: Robert E. Mates
Artist's house *1, 4–5* Photo: Hans Peter Schwarz; *2* Photo: Werner Moller; *3, 7* Photo: Bildarchiv Foto Marburg; *6* Drawing by Hugh Ferriss
Art Nouveau *1* Christie's Images, London/Photo: Bridgeman Art Library, London; *2* Museum of Decorative Art, Copenhagen/© DACS, 1996/Photo: Ole Woldbye, Copenhagen; *3* Art Archive of the Calouste Gulbenkian Foundation, Lisbon; *4* Photo: Bildarchiv Foto Marburg
Arts and Crafts Movement *1* Board of Trustees of the Victoria and Albert Museum, London; *2* Photo: Morley Baer
Arup, Ove Photo: British Architectural Library, RIBA, London
Asam: (1) Hans Georg Asam Photo: Bildarchiv Foto Marburg
Asam: (2) Cosmas Damian Asam Photo: Bildarchiv Foto Marburg
Asam: (3) Egid Quirin Asam *1–2* Photo: Bildarchiv Foto Marburg
Asante and related peoples *1, 4–6* Photo: Dr Doran Ross; *2* Ministry of Information, Accra; *3* Trustees of the Wallace Collection, London
Ascoli Piceno Photo: Conway Library, Courtauld Institute of Art, London
Ashbee, C. R. Board of Trustees of the Victoria and Albert Museum, London
Ashcan school Wadsworth Atheneum, Hartford, CT/© DACS, 1996
Aspendos Photo: R.J.A. Wilson
Aspertini, Amico Photo: Archivi Alinari, Florence
Aspetti, Tiziano *1* Photo: Conway Library, Courtauld Institute of Art, London; *2* Metropolitan Museum of Art, New York (Gift of Irwin Untermyer, 1970; no. 1970.314)
Asplund, Gunnar Photo: Stadsmuseum, Stockholm
Asselijn, Jan Gemäldegalerie der Akademie der Bildenden Künste, Vienna
Assemblage Whitney Museum of American Art, New York/Photo: Geoffrey Clements
Assembly rooms Photo: British Architectural Library, RIBA, London
Assereto, Gioacchino Archivio Fotografico del Servizio Beni Culturali, Genoa
Assisi *2* Sacro Convento di San Francesco, Assisi/Photo: P. Gerhard Ruf; *3–6* Photo: Archivi Alinari, Florence; *7* Photo: Gabinetto Fotografico Nazionale, Istituto Centrale per il Catalogo e la Documentazione, Rome
Assyrian Trustees of the British Museum, London
Assyrian Revival Delaware Art Museum, Wilmington, DE (Samuel and Mary R. Bancroft Collection)
Ast, Balthasar van der Gemäldegalerie, Dresden/Photo: AKG Ltd, London
Astrolabe *1* Al-Sabah Collection, Dar al-Athar al-Islamiyya, Kuwait City; *2* Trustees of the British Museum, London
Astrological and astronomical manuscripts *1* Leiden University Library (MS. Voss. Lat. Q. 79, fol. 26*v*); *2* Bibliothèque Nationale de France, Paris
Asturian architecture *1–2* Photo: Prof. I.G. Bango Torviso
Aswan Photo: Prof. Edda Bresciani
Asylum Wellcome Institute Library, London
Asyut Photo: © RMN, Paris
Atchana, Tell Turkish Ministry of Culture and Tourism
Atget, Eugène Museum of Modern Art, New York (Abbott-Levy Collection, partial gift of Shirley C. Burden)

Athens *1* Photo: AKG Ltd, London; *3* Photo: Ancient Art and Architecture Collection, London; *7* British Library, London (no. 745.E.9, vol. 2); *8* Photo: Conway Library, Courtauld Institute of Art, London; *11, 19* Photo: James Austin, Cambridge; *12* American School of Classical Studies at Athens: Agora Excavations/Photo: Alison Frantz; *13* Acropolis Museum, Athens (Archaeological Receipts Fund); *14* Trustees of the British Museum, London; *17* American School of Classical Studies at Athens: Agora Excavations

Atlanta Architectural Association, London/Photo: René Davids

Atlantid Photo: R.J.A. Wilson

Atlas British Library, London (no. Maps C.3.c3)

Attavanti, Attavante Bibliothèque Royale Albert 1er, Brussels

Aubusson Board of Trustees of the Victoria and Albert Museum, London

Auckland Photo: John Stacpoole

Audran: (3) Claude Audran III Statens Konstmuseer, Stockholm

Audubon, John James New-York Historical Society, New York

Auerbach, Frank Kirklees Library and Art Gallery, Huddersfield

Augsburg *1–2, 4–6* Städtische Kunstsammlungen Augsburg; *3* Staatliche Museen zu Berlin, Preussischer Kulturbesitz; *4* Kunsthistorisches Museum, Vienna

Augustinian Canons Bibliothèque Nationale de France, Paris

Augustinian hermits Photo: Archivi Alinari, Florence

Aulnay, St Pierre Photo: Zodiaque, St-Léger-Vauban

Australia *2, 4–5, 7, 16* Photo: Image Library, State Library of New South Wales, Sydney; *3* Photo: Conway Library, Courtauld Institute of Art, London; *6* Photo: Image Library, State Library of New South Wales, Sydney/Edwards Madigan Torzillo Briggs; *8, 13* Joseph Brown Collection, Melbourne, Australia; *9* Art Gallery of New South Wales, Sydney; *10* Art Gallery of South Australia, Adelaide (Gift of the Rt Hon. Sir Charles Booth, 1913); *11–12* National Gallery of Australia, Canberra; *14, 21* National Gallery of Victoria, Melbourne (Felton Bequest, 1910); *15* Photo: Sheridan Brown, East Hawthorn; *17* Powerhouse Museum, Sydney; *18–20* National Gallery of Victoria, Melbourne; *22* Trustees of the Museum of Applied Arts and Sciences, Sydney

Austral Islands Trustees of the British Museum, London

Austria *2, 5–6, 20* Photo: Bildarchiv Foto Marburg; *3–4, 12–15, 18, 26, 41* Photo: Bundesdenkmalamt, Vienna; *7–8, 10–11, 27, 36* Bildarchiv, Österreichische Nationalbibliothek, Vienna; *9* Photo: Overseas Agenzia Fotografica, Milan; *16* Staatsgalerie, Stuttgart; *17, 23* Österreichische Galerie im Belvedere, Vienna; *19* Steiermärkisches Landesmuseum Joanneum, Graz; *21, 24, 37* Kunsthistorisches Museum, Vienna; *22* Austrian National Tourist Office; *25* Schlosshauptmannschaft Schönbrunn, Vienna; *28* Photo: British Architectural Library, RIBA, London; *29, 33* Salzburger Museum Carolino Augusteum, Salzburg; *30, 34–35, 38, 42* Österreichisches Museum für Angewandte Kunst, Vienna; *31* Oberösterreichisches Landesmuseum, Linz; *32* Bundesmobiliensammlung, Vienna; *39* Photo: Anthony Kersting, London; *40* Historisches Museum, Berne

Author portrait Bibliothèque Nationale de France, Paris

Automata Musées de la Ville de Strasbourg

Automatism Museum of Modern Art, New York (Purchase)/ © ADAGP, Paris, and DACS, London, 1996

Autun *1–2* Photo: James Austin, Cambridge

Auxerre Photo: Anthony Kersting, London

Avebury Photo: RCHME/© Crown Copyright

Aved, Jacques Musée Fabre, Montpellier

Avercamp: (1) Hendrick Avercamp *1* Trustees of the National Gallery, London; *2* Royal Collection, Windsor Castle/© Her Majesty Queen Elizabeth II

Avery, Milton Whitney Museum of American Art, New York/© ARS, New York, and DACS, London, 1996/Photo: Geoffrey Clements

Avignon *1* Bibliothèque Nationale de France, Paris; *2* Photo: Arch. Phot. Paris/© DACS, 1996; *3* Photo: Giraudon, Paris

Ávila *1* Photo: Prof. James D'Emilio; *2* Photo: Hirmer Fotoarchiv, Munich; *3* Photo: Ampliaciones y Reproducciones MAS, Barcelona

Ayala, Josefa de Photo: Arquivo Nacional de Fotografia, Lisbon

Ayia Triada National Archaeological Museum, Athens (Archaeological Receipts Fund)

Ayutthaya *2* Photo: John Villiers; *3* Photo: © Tettoni, Cassio and Associates Pte Ltd, Singapore

Azerbaijan *2–7* Photo: VAAP, Moscow

Aztec *1–2* Museo Nacional de Antropología, Mexico City/Coordinador Nacional de Asuntos Juridos del Instituto Nacional de Antropologia e Historia, Mexico City